RELATED PRODUCTS FROM WEST

COURTROOM HANDBOOK ON FEDERAL EVIDENCE
Steven Goode and Olin Guy Wellborn III

MODERN SCIENTIFIC EVIDENCE
David L. Faigman, David H. Kaye, Michael J. Saks and Joseph Sanders

FEDERAL JURY PRACTICE AND INSTRUCTIONS
Kevin F. O'Malley, Jay E. Grenig and William C. Lee
[Instructions available in CD-ROM]

FEDERAL TRIAL OBJECTIONS
Charles B. Gibbons

FEDERAL PRACTICE AND PROCEDURE
Charles Alan Wright, Arthur R. Miller, Mary Kay Kane,
Edward H. Cooper, Richard L. Marcus, Kenneth W. Graham,
Victor James Gold, Richard D. Freer, Vikram David Amar,
Joan E. Steinman, Nancy J. King, Susan R. Klein,
Andrew D. Leipold, Peter J. Henning, Sarah N. Welling,
Charles H. Koch, Jr. , Catherine T. Struve and Michael H. Graham
[Also available in CD-ROM]

MULTIDISTRICT LITIGATION MANUAL
David F. Herr

LEGAL ETHICS: THE LAWYER'S DESKBOOK
ON PROFESSIONAL RESPONSIBILITY
Ronald D. Rotunda and John S. Dzienkowski
[In joint venture with the American Bar Association]

WEST'S FEDERAL ADMINISTRATIVE PRACTICE
Federal Practice Experts

WEST'S FEDERAL FORMS
Federal Practice Experts
[Also available in CD-ROM]

FEDERAL COURT OF APPEALS MANUAL
David G. Knibb

FEDERAL PRACTICE DESKBOOK
Charles Alan Wright and Mary Kay Kane

HANDBOOK OF FEDERAL EVIDENCE
Michael H. Graham

TREATISE ON CONSTITUTIONAL LAW
Ronald D. Rotunda and John E. Nowak

HANDBOOK OF FEDERAL CIVIL DISCOVERY AND DISCLOSURE
Jay E. Grenig and Jeffrey S. Kinsler
[Includes Forms on Disk]

ANNOTATED MANUAL FOR COMPLEX LITIGATION
David F. Herr

RELATED PRODUCTS FROM WEST

THE JUDGE'S EVIDENCE BENCH BOOK
Leo H. Whinery

ADMINISTRATIVE LAW AND PRACTICE
Charles H. Koch, Jr.

Federal Case News

Federal Civil Judicial Procedure and Rules

Federal Sentencing Guidelines Manual

Manual for Complex Litigation

Reference Manual on Scientific Evidence

USCA

US Code Congressional and Administrative News

Westlaw®

West Books, CD–ROM Libraries, Disk Products and Westlaw
The Ultimate Research System

To order any of these Federal practice tools, call your West Representative or 1–800–328–4880.

NEED REFERENCE HELP?

If you have research questions concerning Westlaw or West books, call West's Reference Attorneys at 1–800–733–2889.

FEDERAL CIVIL RULES HANDBOOK

2008

By

STEVEN BAICKER-McKEE
Babst, Calland, Clements & Zomnir, P.C.

WILLIAM M. JANSSEN
Assistant Professor of Law
Charleston School of Law

JOHN B. CORR
Professor of Law, American University
Washington College of Law

THOMSON
WEST

Mat #40521255

© 2007 Thomson/West

ISBN: 978-0-314-97257-6

TEXT IS PRINTED ON 10% POST CONSUMER RECYCLED PAPER

PREFACE TO THE 2007 HANDBOOK

It was 1938. Franklin Delano Roosevelt was President, the New York Yankees had just won their third-in-a-row World Series (it was also a mere two years before Bob Feller led the Indians ... almost ... to the A.L. Pennant), the National Football League was adolescent, and the Nation's economy was still recovering from the crash of 1929.

It was also the year lawyers across the country came to terms with a new set of Rules of Procedure for federal civil cases. At least in that sense, history repeats itself in December 2007, when the "restyled" Federal Rules of Civil Procedure become effective to govern civil practice in the burgeoning world of modern federal practice. Coupled with important "non-style" changes to the Federal Civil Rules, the new E-Government Act privacy protection rule (Rule 5.2), a complete re-drafting of all federal civil forms, the consuming debate over the scope and effect of the Supreme Court's May 2007 decision in *Bell Atlantic Corp. v. Twombly*, and the typically unrelenting wave of new case law interpreting and applying the Rules, one could make the case that 1938 had nothing on 2007.

Each year we take this opportunity to thank you for adding this newest edition of *The Federal Civil Rules Handbook* to your desk or law library. We are very pleased to include special orienting explanations and guidance as you navigate through the new Rules and interpretive case law, and we hope that the special features of this 2008 *Handbook* serve your needs for quick and thoughtful information. Our mission with the *Handbook*, begun with our first edition in 1993, has been to provide practitioners with a roadmap to the Federal Rules of Civil Procedure that is user-friendly, sharply (and annually) updated, affordable, and contained in one, soft-bound volume. The *Handbook* not only reprints the Rules themselves, but offers an extensive national survey of their practical applications as well. In this format, we intend the *Handbook* to bridge the gap between the cost and benefits of larger, more comprehensive multi-volume treatises and the mere text of the Rules themselves.

__What's New In The 2008 Edition:__ This Edition of the *Handbook* is peculiarly designed to help you recognize the changes to each Rule, understand them, and be alerted to changes that are likely to have substantive ramifications, beyond mere stylistic improvement:

New "Part III-A": This is your roadmap to the federal "Style Project". It offers a summary view of the objectives and mechanics of the Style Project, and highlights major themes and "conventions" of the restyling effort.

New Rules: The Handbook now contains the text of the new Rules (*__Part III__*), each in the form effective on December 1, 2007.

New Forms: The *Handbook* also contains the all-new federal forms (***Part IV***), adopted for use on the same date.

The 2007 "Roadmaps": Immediately below each Rule in Part III, we have included a new descriptive "feature" that summarizes both the "Restyling" and substantive changes to that Rule. This "roadmap" is your quick-reference tool for a rule-by-rule re-orientation to the Federal Rules of Civil Procedure.

Pleading and Practice after *Bell Atlantic v. Twombly*: The Supreme Court's May 2007 decision in *Twombly* expressly overruled the familiar pleading standard that had forbidden dismissals unless the pleader could prove "no set of facts" that would authorize relief. We discuss what effect this overruling decision is likely to have on pleading practice under Rule 8 and motion practice under Rule 12(b).

E-Government Act Privacy Rule: To implement the E-Government Act of 2002, the Rules now contain a new "privacy" rule (***Rule 5.2***), designed to facilitate the protection of key "personal data identifiers".

More Than 1,000 New Citations: Even without this mammoth "restyling" effort, the cascade of new case interpretations continues. We have added more than **1,000 new citations** to interpretative decisions from the Nation's federal courts, most of which were decided between Fall 2006 and late Summer 2007.

Navigating practitioners through these vast changes to the Federal Rules of Civil Procedure, our *Handbook's* familiar format remains the same. We reprint the text of each Federal Rule (as amended), followed immediately by our *Authors' Commentary* to the Rule and its subparts. Our Commentary first distills the Rule's "Purpose and Scope", summarizes the "Core Concept" of each Rule's subsections, and then follows with an extended textual discussion of the Rule in application, including citations to case authorities from the Supreme Court, the national Courts of Appeals, and District Courts. Each Rule treatment ends with references to other research authorities and finding aids. As further resources for litigators, the *Handbook* includes a complete set of all of the Advisory Committee Notes to the Rules, beginning with the first Notes to the original 1937 Rules through the Notes accompanying the most recent Rule revisions. Our introduction to the Advisory Committee Notes explains the legal authority of this quasi "legislative history".

The *Handbook*'s Rule-by-Rule commentary is preceded by an introduction to general concepts in federal practice (federal jurisdiction, venue, removal and remand, the *Erie* doctrine, and res judicata and collateral estoppel). We've also included an introduction to federal multidistrict litigation (MDL) and federal appellate practice, along with a full reprint of the MDL, appeals, and evidence rules. Full-text reprints of many frequently consulted sections of the Judicial Code are also included. Other

PREFACE

handy tools, including Civil Rule and Appellate Rule forms, addresses and telephone numbers for all the federal courts, a schedule of all federal judges, a Circuit map, and a perpetual calendar, also appear in this Handbook.

This is a year for all those engaged in federal practice to take a deep breath, and dive in. We hope that you find our Handbook an important resource as you leap from the dock. Thank you, again, for your kind patronage. We warmly encourage suggestions, observations, and criticisms from our readers. Please continue to send them to us by email, fax, regular mail, or telephone call. Each year, we endeavor to incorporate your many helpful recommendations in our annual revisions to the Handbook to implement ideas, address new practice questions, or sharpen our commentary in response to your suggestions. Your annual comments help us keep the Handbook a current and useful practice resource. We appreciate your many contributions!

THE AUTHORS

November 2007

THE AUTHORS

STEVEN BAICKER–MCKEE is a litigation shareholder and member of the Board of Directors at Babst, Calland, Clements and Zomnir, a Professional Corporation, in Pittsburgh, Pennsylvania. His practice includes a wide variety of commercial litigation, with and emphasis on environmental and toxic torts, and complex commercial disputes. He has been recognized as one of the Outstanding Lawyers of America.

Mr. Baicker-McKee received his B.A. from Yale University, then spent the next several years building fine furniture and custom cabinets in Charlottesville, Virginia before attending law school. Mr. Baicker-McKee received his J.D. from Marshall–Wythe School of Law, College of William and Mary, where he was on the Board of Editors of the *William and Mary Law Review*. He served a two-year clerkship with the Honorable Glenn E. Mencer of the United States District Court for the Western District of Pennsylvania, to whom he is forever indebted. Mr. Baicker-McKee's tenure as Judge Mencer's law clerk provided the inspiration for this book.

Mr. Baicker-McKee resides in Pittsburgh, Pennsylvania with his wife, Carol, and their three children, Kyle, Eric, and Sara. Their love and support were instrumental in the development of this book. Mr. Baicker-McKee is also grateful for the support of his parents, Joe and Macky Baicker.

JOHN B. CORR is a Professor of Law at the American University, Washington College of Law, in Washington, D.C. As a specialist in civil procedure, conflict of laws, and bankruptcy, he has advised and consulted with private practitioners in a variety of litigation matters. The author of articles dealing with civil procedure and/or conflicts in a number of journals, Mr. Corr has also received numerous "outstanding professor" awards, based on student ballots.

As a member of the New York and District of Columbia Bars, Mr. Corr practiced in the litigation department of the Washington office of Fried, Frank, Harris, Shriver & Kampelman before he began a career in legal education.

Mr. Corr graduated from the Georgetown University Law Center, where he was an editor of the *Georgetown Law Journal*. Before receiving his J.D. degree, Mr. Corr earned M.A. and Ph.D. degrees in history. He also served for two years in the U.S. Army as a captain in military intelligence.

WILLIAM M. JANSSEN is an Assistant Professor of Law at the Charleston School of Law in Charleston, South Carolina. Mr. Janssen teaches courses in civil procedure, products liability, and first amendment law. Before his appointment to the faculty in Charleston, Mr. Janssen was a litigation partner, the Chair of the Life Sciences Practices, and a member of the Executive Committee at the Midatlantic law firm of Saul Ewing LLP, with whom he practiced for almost seventeen years. Mr. Janssen helped design and implement Saul Ewing's nationally recognized "We're All In!" *pro bono* initiative. He focused his private practice in pharmaceutical and medical device risk management and litigation. Mr. Janssen is a member of the *International Association of Defense Counsel* and its Drug, Device, & Biotech committee, the Defense Research Institute, and the American and Pennsylvania Bar Associations. He is admitted to practice law in the federal and State courts of Pennsylvania, the Federal Circuit, and the United States Supreme Court, and has practiced *pro hac vice* in various other jurisdictions. For five academic terms, from 1991 to 1996, Mr. Janssen served as an Adjunct Instructor at the Temple University School of Law.

Mr. Janssen graduated from Saint Joseph's University in Philadelphia and The American University, Washington College of Law, in Washington, D.C. He served as Executive Editor of the *American University Law Review* and as a member of the Moot Court Board. After law school, Mr. Janssen clerked for the Honorable James McGirr Kelly, on the United States District Court for the Eastern District of Pennsylvania, and for the Honorable Joseph F. Weis, Jr., on the United States Court of Appeals for the Third Circuit.

Mr. Janssen thanks his family and friends for teaching him that you have not truly lived until you've answered, for the thousandth time: "No, we're still not done with that book yet." Mr. Janssen dedicates this effort to his parents, Bill and Catherine, and to TMcP.

The authors welcome any comments, suggestions, or constructive criticisms of this book. Their telephone and telefax numbers and email addresses are provided below.

Steven Baicker-McKee
(412) 394–5499
(412) 394–6576 (fax)
sbaicker@bccz.com (email)

John B. Corr
(202) 274–4208
(202) 274–4130 (fax)
jbcorr@cox.net (email)

William M. Janssen
(843) 329–1000 x2442
(843) 853–2519 (fax)
wjanssen@charlestonlaw.org (email)

TABLE OF CONTENTS

FEDERAL CIVIL RULES HANDBOOK

2008

PART I

JUDICIAL RULEMAKING

A. THE FEDERAL RULES OF PRACTICE AND PROCEDURE *

The federal rules govern procedure, practice, and evidence in the federal courts. They set forth the procedures for the conduct of court proceedings and serve as a pattern for the procedural rules adopted by many state court systems.

Authority

The Congress has authorized the federal judiciary to prescribe the rules of practice, procedure, and evidence for the federal courts, subject to the ultimate legislative right of the Congress to reject, modify, or defer any of the rules. The authority and procedures for promulgating rules are set forth in the Rules Enabling Act. 28 U.S.C. §§ 2071–2077.

The Judicial Conference of the United States is also required by statute to "carry on a continuous study of the operation and effect of the general rules of practice and procedure." 28 U.S.C. § 331. As part of this continuing obligation, the Conference is authorized to recommend amendments and additions to the rules to promote

- simplicity in procedure,
- fairness in administration,
- the just determination of litigation, and
- the elimination of unjustifiable expense and delay.

The Rules Committees

The Judicial Conference's responsibilities as to rules are coordinated by its Committee on Rules of Practice and Procedure, commonly referred to as the "Standing Committee." 28 U.S.C. § 2073(b). The Standing Committee has five advisory committees, dealing respectively with the appellate, bankruptcy, civil, criminal, and evidence rules. 28 U.S.C. § 2073(a)(2). The Standing Committee reviews and coordinates the recommendations of the five advisory committees, and it recommends to the Judicial Conference proposed rules changes "as may be necessary to maintain consistency and otherwise promote the interests of justice." 28 U.S.C. § 2073(b).

The Standing Committee and the advisory committees are composed of federal judges, practicing lawyers, law professors, state chief justices,

* This description of current procedures for federal judicial rulemaking is a summary prepared for the bench and bar by the Administrative Office of the U.S. Courts.

and representatives of the Department of Justice. Each committee has a reporter, a prominent law professor, who is responsible for coordinating the committee's agenda and drafting appropriate amendments to the rules and explanatory committee notes.

The Assistant Director for Judges Programs of the Administrative Office of the United States Courts currently serves as secretary to the Standing Committee, coordinates the operational aspects of the rules process, and maintains the records of the committees. The Rules Committee Support Office of the Administrative Office provides the day to day administrative and legal support for the secretary and the committees.

Open Meetings and Records

Meetings of the rules committees are open to the public and are widely announced. All records of the committees, including minutes of committee meetings, suggestions and comments submitted by the public, statements of witnesses, transcripts of public hearings, and memoranda prepared by the reporters, are public and are maintained by the secretary. Copies of the rules and proposed amendments are available from the Rules Committee Support Office. The proposed amendments are also published on the Judiciary's website <http:\\www.uscourts.gov>.

B. HOW THE RULES ARE AMENDED

The pervasive and substantial impact of the rules on the practice of law in the federal courts demands exacting and meticulous care in drafting rule changes. The rulemaking process is time-consuming and involves a minimum of seven stages of formal comment and review. From beginning to end, it usually takes two to three years for a suggestion to be enacted as a rule.

The process, however, may be expedited when there is an urgent need to enact an amendment to the rules.

All interested individuals and organizations are provided an opportunity to comment on proposed rules amendments and to recommend alternative proposals. The comments received from this extensive and thorough public examination are studied very carefully by the committees and generally improve the amendments. The committees actively encourage the submission of comments, both positive and negative, to ensure that proposed amendments have been considered by a broad segment of the bench and bar.

STEP 1. INITIAL CONSIDERATION BY THE ADVISORY COMMITTEE

Making suggestions for changes

Proposed changes in the rules are suggested by judges, clerks of court, lawyers, professors, government agencies, or other individuals and organizations. They are considered in the first instance by the appropriate advisory committees (appellate, bankruptcy, civil, criminal, or evidence). Suggestions for changes, additions, or deletions must be submitted in writing to the secretary, who acknowledges each letter and distributes it to the chair of the Standing Committee and the chair and reporter of the advisory committee.

The reporter normally analyzes the suggestions and makes appropriate recommendations to the advisory committee. The suggestions from the public and the recommendations of the reporter are placed on the advisory committee's agenda and are normally discussed at its next meeting. The advisory committees usually meet twice a year, and they also conduct business by telephone and correspondence.

Consideration of suggestions

In considering a suggestion for a change in the rules, the advisory committee may take several courses of action, including:

1. Accepting the suggestion, either completely or with modifications or limitations:

2. Deferring action on the suggestion or seeking additional information regarding its operation and impact;

3. Rejecting a suggestion because it does not have merit or would be inconsistent with other rules or a statute; or

4. Rejecting a suggestion because, although it may be meritorious, it simply is not necessary or important enough to warrant the significant step of an amendment to the federal rules.

The secretary is required, to the extent feasible, to advise the person making a suggestion of the action taken on it by the advisory committee.

Drafting Rules Changes

When an advisory committee decides initially that a particular change in the rules would be appropriate, it normally asks its reporter to prepare a draft amendment to the rules and an explanatory committee note. The draft amendment and committee note are discussed and voted upon at a committee meeting.

The Standing Committee has a style subcommittee that works with the respective advisory committees in reviewing proposed amendments to ensure that the rules are written in clear and consistent language. In addition, the reporter of the Standing Committee and the reporters of the five advisory committees are encouraged to work together to promote clarity and consistency among the various sets of federal rules.

STEP 2. PUBLICATION AND PUBLIC COMMENT

Once an advisory committee votes initially to recommend an amendment to the rules, it must obtain the approval of the Standing Committee, or its chair, to publish the proposed amendment for public comment. In seeking publication, the advisory committee must explain to the Standing Committee the reasons for its proposal, including any minority or separate views.

After publication is approved, the secretary arranges for printing and distribution of the proposed amendment to the bench and bar, to publishers, and to the general public. More than 10,000 persons and organizations are on the mailing list, including

- federal judges and other federal court officers,
- United States attorneys,
- other federal government agencies and officials,
- state chief justices,
- state attorneys general,
- legal publications,
- law schools,
- bar associations, and
- interested lawyers, individuals, and organizations requesting distribution.

In order to promote public comment, the proposed amendments are sent to points of contact that have been established with 53 state bar associations.

The public is normally given 6 months to comment in writing to the secretary regarding the proposed amendment.

In an emergency, a shorter time period may be authorized by the Standing Committee.

During the 6–month comment period, the advisory committee schedules one or more public hearings on the proposed amendments. Persons who wish to appear and testify at the hearings are required to contact the secretary at least 30 days before the hearings.

STEP 3. CONSIDERATION OF THE PUBLIC COMMENTS AND FINAL APPROVAL BY THE ADVISORY COMMITTEE

At the conclusion of the public comment period, the reporter is required to prepare a summary of the written comments received from the public and the testimony presented at the hearings. The advisory committee then takes a fresh look at the proposed rule changes in light of the written comments and testimony.

If the advisory committee decides to make a substantial change in its proposal, it will provide a period for additional public notice and comment.

Once the advisory committee decides to proceed in final form, it submits the proposed amendment to the Standing Committee for approval. Each proposed amendment must be accompanied by a separate report summarizing the comments received from the public and explaining any changes made by the advisory committee following the original publication. The advisory committee's report must also include minority views of any members who wish to have their separate views recorded.

STEP 4. APPROVAL BY THE STANDING COMMITTEE

The Standing Committee considers the final recommendations of the advisory committee and may accept, reject, or modify them. If the Standing Committee approves a proposed rule change, it will transmit it to the Judicial Conference with a recommendation for approval, accompanied by the advisory committee's reports and the Standing Committee's own report explaining any modifications it made. If the Standing Committee makes a modification that constitutes a substantial change from the recommendation of the advisory committee, the proposal will normally be returned to the advisory committee with appropriate instructions.

STEP 5. JUDICIAL CONFERENCE APPROVAL

The Judicial Conference normally considers proposed amendments to the rules at its September session each year. If approved by the Conference, the amendments are transmitted promptly to the Supreme Court.

STEP 6. SUPREME COURT APPROVAL

The Supreme Court has the authority to prescribe the federal rules, subject to a statutory waiting period. 28 U.S.C. § 2072, 2075. The Court normally transmits proposed rules amendments to the Congress by May 1 of each year. 28 U.S.C. §§ 2074, 2075.

STEP 7. CONGRESSIONAL REVIEW

The Congress has a statutory period of at least 7 months to act on any rules prescribed by the Supreme Court. If the Congress does not enact legislation to reject, modify, or defer the rules, they take effect as a matter of law on December 1. 28 U.S.C. §§ 2074, 2075.

C. SUMMARY OF PROCEDURES

Action	Date
STEP 1	
• Suggestion for a change in the rules. *(Submitted in writing to the secretary.)*	At any time.
• Referred by the secretary to the appropriate advisory committee.	Promptly after receipt.
• Considered by the advisory committee.	Normally at the next committee meeting.
• If approved, the advisory committee seeks authority from the Standing Committee to circulate to bench and bar for comment.	Normally at the same meeting or the next committee meeting.
STEP 2	
• Public comment period.	6 months.
• Public hearings.	During the public comment period.
STEP 3	
• Advisory committee considers the amendment afresh in light of public comments and testimony at the hearings.	About one or two months after the close of the comment period.
• Advisory committee approves amendment in final form and transmits to the Standing Committee.	About one or two months after the close of the comment period.

Action	Date
STEP 4	
• Standing Committee approves amendment, with or without revisions, and recommends approval by the Judicial Conference.	Normally at its June meeting.
STEP 5	
• Judicial Conference approves amendment and transmits to the Supreme Court.	Normally at its September session.
STEP 6	
• The Supreme Court prescribes the amendment.	By May 1.
STEP 7	
• Congress has statutory time period in which to enact legislation to reject, modify, or defer the amendment.	By December 1.
• Absent Congressional action, the amendment becomes law.	December 1.

D. 2008 CIVIL RULE DEVELOPMENTS

Under the usual schedule, amendments to the Bankruptcy Rules, the Criminal Rules and Evidence Rules will become effective on December 1, 2008 if they are approved by the Supreme Court and if they are not altered by Congress. No new amendments are contemplated for the Civil Rules in this time frame.

Just as well. Throughout 2008 the extraordinary effect, since December 1, 2007, of the longstanding Civil Rules Style Project will continue to work itself out in practical application in law offices, chambers and courtrooms across the country. The new plain-English style is intended to simplify, clarify, and eliminate ambiguities without changing substance, "to translate present text into clear language that does not change the meaning" [Edward H. Cooper, *Restyling the Civil Rules: Clarity without Change*, 79 Notre Dame L. Rev. 1761 (2004)]; even as some have wondered whether the benefits of restyling outweigh the cost of implementing and assimilating the new Rules into practice, arguing that "the goal of preserving existing meaning is at war with the goal of clarity and simplicity." Edward A. Hartnett, *Against (Mere) Restyling*, 82 Notre Dame L. Rev. 15 (2006). In any case, *alea iacta est*, the Rubicon is crossed. 2008 and beyond will be a period of great adjustment as the restyled Rules are digested, even without any further Civil Rule amendments.

PART II

GENERAL CONCEPTS IN FEDERAL PRACTICE—
Personal Jurisdiction, Notice Requirements, Federal Subject Matter Jurisdiction, Venue, Forum Non Conveniens, Removal, *Erie*, Res Judicata and Collateral Estoppel

Table of Sections

A. FEDERAL JURISDICTION, VENUE AND *ERIE*

B. RES JUDICATA AND COLLATERAL ESTOPPEL

A. FEDERAL JURISDICTION, VENUE AND *ERIE*

§ 2.1   Introduction

Although the Federal Rules of Civil Procedure control many aspects of a civil suit in a district court, the Rules do not contain all the elements that must be satisfied before the suit can be prosecuted successfully. Of particular importance at the onset of litigation are the concepts of jurisdiction and venue. For the most part, these elements are not discussed in the Rules. In fact, Rule 82 provides that the Rules neither increase nor limit a district court's power and obligations in the areas of jurisdiction and venue. A claimant's failure to satisfy requirements of subject matter jurisdiction and venue, however, will usually assure failure in the suit.

Before a federal district court may hear a plaintiff's claim, it must satisfy three prerequisites. These are: (1) jurisdiction over persons or things (*i.e.,* the court's ability to drag an individual into its district); (2) subject matter jurisdiction (*i.e.,* the court's ability to hear a particular kind of claim);[1] and (3) venue.

Every cause of action sued upon in a case, irrespective of whether it is a count brought by the plaintiff, a counterclaim, crossclaim, or impleader, must satisfy one of the kinds of jurisdiction over persons or things, *as well as* some kind of subject matter jurisdiction.[2] However, requirements of venue, discussed below, apply only to the claims brought by a plaintiff. If, upon appropriate notice to the court, it is found that any of these requirements are lacking, the court will not hear the case.

§ 2.2   Jurisdiction Over Persons or Things—Introduction

There are three kinds of jurisdiction over persons or things: personal jurisdiction (the normal form of action against an individual, company, or other entity, also known as *in personam* jurisdiction); quasi in rem jurisdiction (actions in the nature of attachment); and in rem jurisdiction (where an object or piece of land is the subject of the lawsuit). Every count in a case must satisfy one or another of these jurisdictional standards.[1] There is no requirement that a count satisfy more than one. However, in cases where one kind of jurisdiction over persons or things

---

1. *Ruhrgas AG v. Marathon Oil Co.,* 526 U.S. 574, 119 S.Ct. 1563, 143 L.Ed.2d 760 (1999) (while jurisdictional issues should generally be resolved before court addresses merits of a case, there is no rigid rule directing court to decide questions of subject matter jurisdiction before deciding questions of personal jurisdiction).

2. *Insurance Corp. of Ireland, Ltd. v. Compagnie des Bauxites de Guinee,* 456 U.S. 694, 701, 102 S.Ct. 2099, 2103, 72 L.Ed.2d 492 (1982) ("The validity of an order of a federal court depends upon that court's having jurisdiction over both the subject matter and the parties.").

1. *See, e.g., Youn v. Track, Inc.,* 324 F.3d 409, 417 (6th Cir.2003) ("The party seeking to assert personal jurisdiction bears the burden of demonstrating that such jurisdiction exists;" standard of proof is preponderance of evidence).

is uncertain, it would be a wise tactic to try to satisfy another kind as well. In certain factual settings there may also be advantages if one particular kind or other is achieved.

Important: In the area of jurisdiction over persons or things, it should be kept in mind that in many circumstances the power of a federal court to hear cases is closely analogous to the power of a state court in the state where the federal court sits. Thus, jurisdiction over persons or things should not pose many new problems for practicing attorneys already familiar with similar jurisdictional concepts in state courts.

Important: If jurisdiction over persons or things is absent, and the court also has no quasi in rem jurisdiction or in rem jurisdiction, the typical remedy is to dismiss the claim.[2]

ADDITIONAL RESEARCH REFERENCES

C.J.S. Federal Courts §§ 4(1)–6.

West's Key No. Digests, Federal Courts ⚷3–5.

§ 2.3 Jurisdiction Over Persons or Things—Requirements for Personal Jurisdiction

Two elements play important roles in determining the requirements for personal jurisdiction. These are notions of fair play, as developed under Due Process provisions of the Constitution, and state limitations on the authority of the state courts to exercise personal jurisdiction. Fair play, or due process, divides into two components: an evaluation of the contacts that exist between the defendant and the state where the court sits; and an evaluation of the quality of notice of the suit that the defendant received.

§ 2.4 Jurisdiction Over Persons or Things—Requirements for Personal Jurisdiction—Due Process: Consent, In–State Service, or Minimum Contacts

CORE CONCEPT

Before a federal trial court may exert personal jurisdiction over a defendant, it must satisfy the due process standard of the 5th and 14th Amendments of the Constitution. This requirement must be met for each defendant.[1]

---

2. *See* Rule 12(b)(2)(authorizing dismissal for lack of personal jurisdiction); *See, e.g., Swaim v. Moltan Co.,* 73 F.3d 711, 718 (7th Cir.1996) ("If the district court finds itself without [personal] jurisdiction ... then it is obligated to dismiss the case because it has no authority over the defendant.").

1. *Cf., Rush v. Savchuk,* 444 U.S. 320, 332, 100 S.Ct. 571, 572, 62 L.Ed.2d 516 (1980) ("The requirements of *International Shoe* ... must be met as to each defendant over whom a ... court exercises jurisdiction." Acknowledging, however, that parties' relationships among themselves may be relevant to their relationships to the forum). *See also Patin v. Thoroughbred*

This requirement has meant primarily that the exercise of personal jurisdiction must not be fundamentally unfair to the defendant. The most common means of satisfying this fairness requirement are: (1) the defendant's consent to jurisdiction; (2) service of process on the defendant within the territorial confines of a state in which the district court sits; or (3) service of process on a non-consenting defendant not within a state, when such service is fair because the defendant has sufficient "contacts" with the state.

APPLICATIONS

Consent to Jurisdiction

If a party consents to jurisdiction, the Due Process requirement of fairness is satisfied. Consent may occur in a variety of ways. The following examples are typical of circumstances where persons may have consented to personal jurisdiction:

(1) *By Contract:* If the parties, through a contract or agreement prior to the initiation of litigation, consent to the jurisdiction of a court, such agreements will generally be enforced even if the chosen court might not otherwise have been able to sustain its jurisdiction.[2] Exceptions arise when there was substantially unequal bargaining power between the parties that gave one side an unfair advantage in choosing the jurisdiction, or there was the absence of *any* rational link between the court chosen and the parties or cause of action.[3]

A related question that arises about forum selection clauses in contracts is whether such clauses may properly *exclude* the use of judicial fora not chosen in the clause (even if such courts could, in the absence of the clause, have exercised personal jurisdiction under, e.g., principles of minimum contacts, discussed elsewhere in this text), or whether forum selection clauses may only provide the potential to *expand* the available fora to include courts that might otherwise have not enjoyed jurisdiction over the parties. It is now settled that such clauses are to be construed according to standard principles of contract law, which may result–depending on the wording of specific clauses in individual cases–in either restriction or expansion of the available fora.[4]

Power Boats, Inc., 294 F.3d 640, 653 (5th Cir.2002) (*Rush* "does not preclude us from imputing the jurisdictional contacts of a predecessor corporation to its successor corporation or individual alter ego.").

2. *National Equipment Rental v. Szukhent,* 375 U.S. 311, 315-16, 84 S.Ct. 411, 414, 11 L.Ed.2d 354 (1964). ("[I]t is settled.... that parties to a contract may agree in advance to submit to the jurisdiction of a given court."). *See also Burger King Corp. v. Rudzewicz,* 471 U.S. 462, 473 n. 14, 105 S.Ct. 2174, 2182 n. 14, 85 L.Ed.2d 528 (1985) ("[P]articularly in the commercial context, parties frequently stipulate in advance to submit their controver-

sies for resolution within a particular jurisdiction.").

3. *See, e.g., Shell v. R.W. Sturge, Ltd.,* 55 F.3d 1227 (6th Cir.1995)(holding that forum selection clause is presumptively enforceable in the absence of fraud, overreaching, grave inconvenience, or violation of forum's public policy).

4. *See, e.g., Dunne v. Libbra,* 330 F.3d 1062, 1063 (8th Cir.2003) (applying general principles of contract construction). *But cf., M.B. Restaurants, Inc. v. CKE Restaurants, Inc.,* 183 F.3d 750, 752 n. 4 (8th Cir.1999) (noting split among circuits as to whether forum selection clauses in diversity cases

(2) *Waiver:* A party who does not object to personal jurisdiction in a timely manner waives objections, and thereby consents.[5] In the federal courts, timely objections to personal jurisdiction are controlled by Rule 12(b)(2), (g), and (h)(1), and must be raised in the answer or before the answer is filed.

(3) *Counterclaims:* A plaintiff sued on a counterclaim may consent to personal jurisdiction on the counterclaim by filing the original complaint.[6] It is unclear if this consent to jurisdiction over the counterclaim is limited to countersuits closely related to plaintiff's original claims, or whether consent extends to unrelated counterclaims.[7]

On the other hand, most courts agree that if a defendant files *both* an objection to jurisdiction and a claim that is either a counterclaim, cross-claim, or third party impleader, the objection to jurisdiction is not waived[8]—provided that the new claim does not involve the joinder of new parties.[9] The conclusion is that an objection to jurisdiction may be preserved if it is filed with a claim asserted against someone who is already a party.

It is unsettled whether filing an in rem action constitutes consent to personal jurisdiction to a counterclaim.[10]

should be construed pursuant to federal or state law; not reaching a conclusion in instant case); *Excell, Inc. v. Sterling Boiler & Mechanical, Inc.,* 106 F.3d 318, 320–21 (10th Cir.1997) (also not deciding issue).

5. *See, e.g., Preferred RX, Inc. v. American Prescription Plan, Inc.,* 46 F.3d 535 (6th Cir.1995)(defendants objected to personal jurisdiction in their original answer; but when plaintiff filed amended complaint containing new count, defendants answered but did not challenge jurisdiction as to new count; held, as to new count, defendants waived defense of lack of personal jurisdiction).

6. *Adam v. Saenger,* 303 U.S. 59, 58 S.Ct. 454, 82 L.Ed. 649 (1938). (By suing, a plaintiff submits to the court's jurisdiction over counterclaims). *Cf., General Contracting & Trading Co. v. Interpole, Inc.,* 940 F.2d 20, 22 (1st Cir.1991) (third-party defendant in first suit filed second, related suit against original defendant in same court; held, by filing second suit, third-party defendant submitted to personal jurisdiction in first suit).

7. *But see, Threlkeld v. Tucker,* 496 F.2d 1101, 1103 (9th Cir.1974) (action to enforce state court judgment; held, state court had jurisdiction to hear counterclaim because filing complaint meant plaintiff had submitted to jurisdiction as to *any* counterclaim). *See also Frank's Casing Crew & Rental Tools, Inc. v. PMR Technologies, Ltd.,* 292

F.3d 1363, 1372 (Fed.Cir.2002) ("Where ... a defendant seeks to bring into the same action new claims against new parties, not arising out of the same transaction or occurrence, such action is not authorized by the joinder rules, and we think that such an attempted joinder constitutes a waiver as to the claims then pending in the action against the party seeking to add the additional claims.").

8. *Bayou Steel Corp. v. M/V Amstelvoorn,* 809 F.2d 1147, 1149 (5th Cir.1987) (not distinguishing between compulsory and permissive counterclaims; holding that view is majority position).

9. *See, e.g., Frank's Casing Crew & Rental Tools, Inc. v. PMR Technologies, Ltd.,* 292 F.3d 1363, 1372 (Fed.Cir.2002) (counterclaims, cross-claims and impleader actions against persons already parties do not, by themselves, constitute a waiver of properly raised objections to jurisdiction; different result if claims do not arise from original transaction or occurrence and are brought against new parties).

10. *Compare, United States v. One Lear Jet Aircraft,* 836 F.2d 1571, 1576–77 (11th Cir.1988) (en banc) (filing an in rem action does not usually equal consent to personal jurisdiction), *with United States v. 51 Pieces of Real Property, Roswell, New Mexico,* 17 F.3d 1306, 1313 (10th Cir.1994) (rejecting *One Lear Jet Aircraft;* concluding that gov-

(4) *Consent to Determine Jurisdiction:* Perhaps the most subtle form of consent occurs when a defendant objects to personal jurisdiction, claiming that sufficient links between the defendant and the court do not exist. In that circumstance, the defendant, though preserving the objection to jurisdiction, has consented for the limited purpose of allowing the court to determine whether personal jurisdiction exists.[11]

Transient Jurisdiction ("Tag" Jurisdiction)

A defendant served with process while physically present within a state is normally subject to the personal jurisdiction of the trial courts within that state. It is irrelevant whether the defendant lives within the state or was just passing through; personal jurisdiction is present in such cases simply because the defendant was properly served within the state.[12] One important exception to exercise of "tag" jurisdiction occurs when a defendant was either forced into a jurisdiction, or induced there by fraud. Enticing a defendant to come to a state for bogus reasons will vitiate personal jurisdiction.[13]

Minimum Contacts

A defendant served with process outside the territorial confines of the state where a court sits may nonetheless be subject to the personal jurisdiction of courts within that state. Personal jurisdiction may be sustained even if the defendant does not consent to jurisdiction. For such jurisdiction to be constitutional, the defendant has to have "contacts" with the state in which the court sits of such a quality and nature that exercise of personal jurisdiction would not offend "traditional notions of fair play and substantial justice." [14] It should be noted, however, that the "contacts" neces-

---

ernment submits to personal jurisdiction upon filing forfeiture action).

11. *Insurance Corp. of Ireland v. Compagnie des Bauxites de Guinee,* 456 U.S. 694, 102 S.Ct. 2099, 72 L.Ed.2d 492 (1982). *See also Transaero, Inc. v. La Fuerza Aerea Boliviana,* 162 F.3d 724, 729 (2d Cir.1998) ("[W]hen a defendant appears and challenges jurisdiction, it agrees to be bound by the court's determination on the jurisdictional issue.").

12. *Burnham v. Superior Court,* 495 U.S. 604, 110 S.Ct. 2105, 109 L.Ed.2d 631 (1990) (plurality opinion). *See generally* Fed. R. Civ. P. 4(e)(2). *See also, Edelman v. Taittinger,* 295 F.3d 171 (2d Cir.2002) (tag jurisdiction that is constitutional under *Burnham,* supra, is *a fortiori* applicable to personal service of a discovery subpoena on a non-party); *First American Corp. v. Price Waterhouse LLP,* 154 F.3d 16, 20 (2d Cir. 1998) (subpoena served on non-party witness; "We are satisfied that in light of *Burnham* ... the assertion of personal ju-

risdiction ... based upon service [within a state] satisfies due process."); *Kadic v. Karadzic,* 70 F.3d 232, 247 (2d Cir.1995) ("Fed. R. Civ. P. 4(e)(2) specifically authorizes personal service of a summons and complaint upon an individual physically present within a judicial district of the United States, and such personal service comports with the requirements of due process for the assertion of personal jurisdiction." Citing *Burnham,* supra).

13. *See, e.g., Wyman v. Newhouse,* 93 F.2d 313 (2d Cir.1937). *See also, Amusement Equipment, Inc. v. Mordelt,* 779 F.2d 264, 271 (5th Cir.1985)(where defendant's presence is obtained by fraud, service can be quashed).

14. *International Shoe Co. v. Washington,* 326 U.S. 310, 66 S.Ct. 154, 90 L.Ed. 95 (1945). *Cf., ALS Scan, Inc. v. Digital Service Consultants, Inc.,* 293 F.3d 707, 711 (4th Cir.2002) ("However minimal the burden of defending in a foreign tribunal, a

sary to sustain personal jurisdiction need not always be physical contacts. In appropriate circumstances an intentional relationship with residents of a state can be a basis for sustaining personal jurisdiction.[15]

Once such minimum contacts have been identified, the court will then typically evaluate the reasonableness of an assertion of personal jurisdiction over the defendant. The following factors are often considered when a court is determining whether a defendant's contacts with a state are sufficient to sustain personal jurisdiction. There is no requirement that all these factors be satisfied before personal jurisdiction attaches.[16] Moreover, other considerations, not yet identified, may arise and be more significant in the factual settings of other cases.[17]

(1) *Magnitude of Defendant's Contacts:* The greater the defendant's contacts with a state, the more likely it is that a court within that state will sustain personal jurisdiction.[18] Means of measuring magnitude may include the dollar value of defendant's activity or the nature and size of the wrong that defendant is alleged to have committed.

(2) *Purposefulness of Defendant's Contacts:* If a defendant has deliberately engaged in activity within a state, then such purposeful-

defendant may not be called upon to do so unless he has had the 'minimal contacts' with that State that are a prerequisite to its exercise of power over him."); *IMO Industries, Inc. v. Kiekert AG,* 155 F.3d 254, 259 (3d Cir.1998) (where plaintiff has not met burden of demonstrating defendant's minimum contacts with forum, court need not reach question of whether exercise of jurisdiction would satisfy fair play and substantial justice). *See also Shaffer v. Heitner,* 433 U.S. 186, 204, 97 S.Ct. 2569, 2579, 53 L.Ed.2d 683 (1977) ("[T]he relationship among the defendant, the forum, and the litigation ... [is] the central concern of the inquiry into personal jurisdiction.").

15. *Burger King v. Rudzewicz,* 471 U.S. 462, 476, 105 S.Ct. 2174, 2184, 85 L.Ed.2d 528 (1985) ("So long as a commercial actor's efforts are 'purposefully directed' toward residents of another State, we have consistently rejected the notion that an absence of physical contacts can defeat personal jurisdiction there."). *See also, e.g., Oriental Trading Co. v. Firetti,* 236 F.3d 938, 943 (8th Cir.2001) (in fraud case, "numerous" telephone calls, faxes and invoices sent to forum state should have caused defendants to understand that injury from fraud would be felt in forum–held, absence of physical contacts with forum may not necessarily defeat personal jurisdiction). *But see Truserv Corp. v. Flegles, Inc.,* 419

F.3d 584, 589 (7th Cir.2005) ("[S]imply contracting with a party based in [a state] is not enough to establish the required minimum contacts.").

16. *Cf., e.g., Northern Laminate Sales, Inc. v. Davis,* 403 F.3d 14, 25 (1st Cir.2005) ("This circuit divides [the] minimum contacts analysis into three inquiries: relatedness, purposeful availment, and reasonableness.").

17. *International Shoe Co. v. Washington,* 326 U.S. 310, 66 S.Ct. 154, 90 L.Ed. 95 (1945). *See also Asahi Metal Industry Co. v. Superior Court,* 480 U.S. 102, 113, 107 S.Ct. 1026, 1032, 94 L.Ed.2d 92 (1987) (plurality opinion) (to determine reasonableness, "[a] court must consider the burden on the defendant, the interests of the forum State, and the plaintiff's interest in obtaining relief. It must also weigh in its determination 'the interstate judicial system's interest in obtaining the most efficient resolution of controversies; and the shared interest of the several States in furthering fundamental substantive social policies.' ").

18. *See, e.g., Omeluk v. Langsten Slip & Batbyggeri A/S,* 52 F.3d 267, 270 (9th Cir. 1995)(if defendant's activities had been substantial, then jurisdiction would have been good even if activities had been unrelated to cause of action).

ness may support a finding of jurisdiction.[19]   Often facts exist where a defendant had no deliberate contact with a state, but could reasonably have foreseen that activities outside a state might have consequences within the state.   Thus, selling products into an interstate "stream of commerce," with only an expectation that they will go to a particular state, may nevertheless cause the defendant reasonably to foresee that the products might enter the state and thereby give rise to a cause of action.[20] However, when the facts of a particular case will only support "specific jurisdiction" (if any jurisdiction at all), courts may require that the defendant's contacts with the forum state be more purposeful.[21]

(3) *Systematic and Continuous Nature of Defendant's Contacts:* The longer a defendant's contacts with a state endure, the greater the possibility that such contacts may be used to sustain personal

---

19. *Burger King v. Rudzewicz,* 471 U.S. 462, 474, 105 S.Ct. 2174, 2183, 85 L.Ed.2d 528 (1985)("the constitutional touchstone remains whether the defendant purposefully established minimum contacts in the forum state."). *Keeton v. Hustler Magazine, Inc.,* 465 U.S. 770, 774, 104 S.Ct. 1473, 1478, 79 L.Ed.2d 790 (1984) (purposeful contact with forum will satisfy requirement that defendant has fair warning of vulnerability to jurisdiction in forum). *But see Alperin v. Vatican Bank,* 410 F.3d 532, 538 n. 1 (9th Cir.2005) ("bare-bones assertion that [defendant] has been 'active' within the United States at some point and at least a few members have ties to this country are insufficient ... to conclude that the exercise of jurisdiction [is constitutional]").

20. *World–Wide Volkswagen Corp. v. Woodson,* 444 U.S. 286, 296, 100 S.Ct. 559, 567, 62 L.Ed.2d 490 (1980)(good jurisdiction over corporation that injects products into stream of commerce with expectation of sales in forum). *See also, e.g., Bell Helicopter Textron, Inc. v. Heliqwest International, Ltd.,* 385 F.3d 1291, 1295 (10th Cir.2004) ("In the context of products liability the minimum contacts requirement turns, in some measure, on foreseeability."). *Clune v. Alimak AB,* 233 F.3d 538, 542 (8th Cir. 2000) (noting that in *Asahi Metal Industry Co. v. Superior Court,* 480 U.S. 102, 107 S.Ct. 1026, 94 L.Ed.2d 92 (1987), five justices of Supreme Court rejected ruling that jurisdiction based on stream of commerce also requires purposeful contact).

21. *Quill Corp. v. North Dakota,* 504 U.S. 298, 112 S.Ct. 1904, 119 L.Ed.2d 91 (1992) (as long as "commercial actor's efforts are 'purposefully directed' toward residents of another State," mail and wire communications can satisfy requirements of personal jurisdiction, notwithstanding absence of physical contacts with State). *See, e.g., Inamed Corp. v. Kuzmak,* 249 F.3d 1356, 1360–61 (Fed.Cir.2001) (discussing three-part test: "(1) whether the defendant 'purposefully directed' its activities at residents of the forum; (2) whether the claim 'arises out of or relates to' the defendant's activities with the forum; and (3) whether assertion of personal jurisdiction is 'reasonable and fair;' " letter sent by defendant to plaintiff's lawyer in New York held to be purposeful contact with California forum because defendant intended plaintiff to receive letter, and plaintiff was in California; held, letter alone did not satisfy personal jurisdiction over defendant in California; but where defendant also negotiated license agreements with plaintiff, and received royalty payments from plaintiff (who remained in California), jurisdiction is satisfied; held irrelevant that defendant remained in New Jersey while conducting most negotiations); *Chew v. Dietrich,* 143 F.3d 24 (2d Cir.1998) (purposeful availment required for specific jurisdiction). *See also, Asahi Metal Industry Co. v. Superior Court,* 480 U.S. 102, 111, 107 S.Ct. 1026, 1032, 94 L.Ed.2d 92 (1987) (plurality opinion) (to satisfy due process, defendant's substantial connection with state must have been purposefully directed toward state; mere foreseeability of contact following injection of defendant's product into stream of commerce, without more, does not establish personal jurisdiction). *But see Kernan v. Kurz–Hastings, Inc.,* 175 F.3d 236 (2d Cir.1999) (expressing doubt, but not deciding, whether finding of purposeful availment is prerequisite to assertion of specific jurisdiction).

jurisdiction.[22] Thus, a corporation doing substantial business within a state for a prolonged period of time will be more vulnerable to personal jurisdiction within that state.[23] Similarly, a defendant domiciled in a state is very likely to be vulnerable to suit in that state (even if process is served outside the state), because domicile usually connotes a longstanding relationship with a state. Note, however, that a single contact for a short period of time may not be systematic or continuous, but could still sustain personal jurisdiction because the contact is large enough, purposeful enough, and sufficiently related to a cause of action so that the exercise of jurisdiction is not unfair.

(4) *Relation Between Defendant's Contacts and the Cause of Action:* If a defendant's contacts with a state have nothing to do with a cause of action, the burden of establishing personal jurisdiction based on such contacts will be more difficult to achieve.[24] If the contacts are closely related to the cause of action, it is more likely that jurisdiction based on such contacts will be upheld.[25]

(5) *Availability of Witnesses and Evidence:* If the plaintiff's choice of forum will make it burdensome or impossible for the defendant to produce relevant testimony and other evidence, personal jurisdiction will be more difficult to sustain.[26]

(6) *Forum Interest in a Suit:* Although not strictly a contact between a defendant and a state, the presence of a special state interest in a suit might help sustain personal jurisdiction.[27] A state's interest in title to land within its boundaries is such an interest.[28] In practice, however, special state interests are rarely identified, and even when identified, are not often significant in the weighing of factors of fairness.[29]

22. *See, e.g., Omeluk v. Langsten Slip & Batbyggeri A/S,* 52 F.3d 267 (9th Cir. 1995)("systematic and continuous" contacts usually equals good jurisdiction). *Cf., Streber v. Hunter,* 221 F.3d 701, 718 (5th Cir.2000) (where defendant's contact with forum is not continuous, personal jurisdiction is satisfied only when defendant purposefully avails himself of protection of forum law through minimum contacts and where exercise of jurisdiction does not offend fair play and substantial justice).

23. *See also, e.g., Doe v. Unocal Corp.,* 248 F.3d 915, 925–28 (9th Cir.2001) (existence of parent-subsidiary relationship, by itself, does not establish personal jurisdiction over parent based on subsidiary's contacts with forum; instead, to be subject to jurisdiction based on subsidiary's contacts, subsidiary must be either alter ego of parent or agent of parent).

24. *See, e.g., Glater v. Eli Lilly & Co.,* 744 F.2d 213, 216 (1st Cir.1984)(if suit is unrelated to defendant's instate activities, the standard for satisfying jurisdiction is "considerably more stringent").

25. *Cf., Inamed Corp. v. Kuzmak,* 249 F.3d 1356, 1362 (Fed.Cir.2001) ("arise out of or related to" standard "has not been clearly delineated by the Supreme Court").

26. *See, e.g., Terracom v. Valley National Bank,* 49 F.3d 555, 561 (9th Cir. 1995)(availability of witnesses and evidence should be weighed).

27. *Keeton v. Hustler Magazine, Inc.,* 465 U.S. 770, 776, 104 S.Ct. 1473, 1479, 79 L.Ed.2d 790 (1984) (fairness of jurisdiction depends partially on whether state has "legitimate interest" in requiring defendant to answer claim related to defendant's activities).

28. *Shaffer v. Heitner,* 433 U.S. 186, 206, 97 S.Ct. 2569, 2581, 53 L.Ed.2d 683 (1977)(state has interest in marketability of property within its borders that may help support some form of jurisdiction).

29. *See, e.g., Kulko v. Superior Court,* 436 U.S. 84, 98–101, 98 S.Ct. 1690, 1700–01, 56 L.Ed.2d 132 (1978)(state's "substantial interests" in care of children do not

Jurisdictional Discovery

Sometimes a plaintiff will allege that the defendant has possession of facts demonstrating that the defendant has contacts with the state sufficient to support personal jurisdiction. In such circumstances a court may grant limited discovery to determine such jurisdictional facts. If such discovery is allowed, it will take place within the rules of discovery discussed elsewhere in this text and within any limits the court may impose.

Before authorizing such discovery, courts normally require that the plaintiff make a good faith showing that discovery might lead to facts demonstrating existence of personal jurisdiction over the defendant.[30]

Specific Jurisdiction v. General Jurisdiction

Frequently courts use the terms "specific jurisdiction" and "general jurisdiction." These terms may appear daunting, but in fact they are merely explanations for the application of personal jurisdiction to different sets of facts.[31] "Specific jurisdiction" is generally used to indicate that a defendant's contacts with a state may not be large or systematic and continuous. However, the contact may still satisfy jurisdictional requirements if the contacts are related to the cause of action and purposeful, and jurisdiction based on the contacts is otherwise reasonable.[32] By contrast, "gen-

---

sustain jurisdiction; interest can be vindicated through existing interstate means of cooperation).

30. *Cf., e.g., Caribbean Broadcasting System, Ltd. v. Cable & Wireless PLC,* 148 F.3d 1080, 1089–90 (D.C.Cir.1998) (plaintiff's failure to make good faith showing justifies refusal to grant jurisdictional discovery). *See also Phoenix Consulting, Inc. v. Republic of Angola,* 216 F.3d 36, 40 (D.C.Cir.2000) (jurisdictional discovery should not be permitted if defendant has raised other procedural defenses, such as forum non conveniens or other jurisdictional issues).

31. *See generally, Helicopteros Nacionales de Colombia, S.A. v. Hall,* 466 U.S. 408, 414–15, 104 S.Ct. 1868, 1872, 80 L.Ed.2d 404 nn. 8–9 (1984)(identifying "specific" and "general" jurisdiction, and distinguishing them). *See also, e.g., ALS Scan, Inc. v. Digital Service Consultants, Inc.* 293 F.3d 707, 711 (4th Cir.2002) (two approaches exist for *International Shoe*–"by finding specific jurisdiction based on conduct connected to the suit or by finding general jurisdiction"); *Alpine View Co. v. Atlas Copco, A.B.,* 205 F.3d 208, 215 (5th Cir.2000) (" 'Minimum contacts' can be established either through contacts sufficient

to assert specific jurisdiction, or contacts sufficient to assert general jurisdiction.").

32. *See, e.g., Harris Rutsky & Co. Insurance Services v. Bell & Clements, Ltd.,* 328 F.3d 1122, 1129 (9th Cir.2003) (specific jurisdiction requires: purposeful contact; related to cause of action; and exercise of jurisdiction must be consistent with fair play and substantial justice); *Phillips Exeter Academy v. Howard Phillips Fund, Inc.,* 196 F.3d 284, 288 (1st Cir.1999) ("Short of general jurisdiction, a court may still hear a particular case if that case relates sufficiently to, or arises from, a significant subset of contacts between the defendant and the forum." Specific jurisdiction requires that court find that plaintiff has satisfied three elements: (1) "direct relationship" between cause of action and defendant's contacts; (2) contacts constitute "purposeful availment" of laws and benefits of forum state; and (3) overall fairness, on facts of particular case, of exercise of personal jurisdiction; however, while all three elements must be met, "the relative strength or weakness of the plaintiff's showing on the first two elements bears upon the third element"); *Mink v. AAAA Development, LLC,* 190 F.3d 333, 336 (5th Cir.1999) (same definition of specific jurisdiction). *Cf., Pennzoil Products Co. v. Colelli & Associ-*

eral jurisdiction" may be found where the defendant's contacts with the state are unrelated to the cause of action, but are substantial, systematic and continuous.[33] However, it should be emphasized that when a plaintiff seeks to sustain a suit based on unrelated contacts, the contacts should indeed be substantial.[34]

ADDITIONAL RESEARCH REFERENCES

C.J.S. Constitutional Law §§ 1150, 1153; Federal Courts §§ 165(1)–190 et seq.

West's Key No. Digests, Constitutional Law ⟩305(4); Federal Courts ⟩76–76.35.

ates, Inc., 149 F.3d 197 (3d Cir.1998) (so holding; also explaining that two standards exist for specific jurisdiction, "the first mandatory and the second discretionary;" first standard looks at whether defendant had minimum contacts that should make defendant reasonably anticipate being forced to litigate in forum; second standard asks whether assertion of personal jurisdiction satisfies fair play and substantial justice).

33. *See, e.g., LSI Industries, Inc. v. Hubbell Lighting, Inc.,* 232 F.3d 1369, 1375 (Fed.Cir.2000) (patent dispute; defendant is subject to jurisdiction where defendant nets several million dollars in annual sales within forum; general jurisdiction exists, notwithstanding fact that disputed product itself was not sold within forum); *Phillips Exeter Academy v. Howard Phillips Fund, Inc.,* 196 F.3d 284, 288 (1st Cir.1999) ("[A] defendant who has maintained a continuous and systematic linkage with the forum state brings himself within the general jurisdiction of that state's courts in respect to all matters, even those that are unrelated to the defendant's contacts with the forum."); *Mink v. AAAA Development, LLC,* 190 F.3d 333, 336 (5th Cir.1999) (similar definition of general jurisdiction). *But cf., Bancroft & Masters, Inc. v. Augusta National, Inc.,* 223 F.3d 1082, 1086 (9th Cir.2000) (for general jurisdiction, factors to consider include "whether the defendant makes sales, solicits or engages in business in the state, serves the state's markets, designates an

agent for service of process, holds a license, or is incorporated there;" defendant who is registered or licensed to do business, does not pay forum taxes or maintain forum bank accounts, does not advertise in forum, and whose website cannot be used to make purchases, is not subject to general jurisdiction; occasional unsolicited sales do not alter results, nor do license agreements with forum television networks and "a handful of [forum] vendors. These agreements constitute doing business with [the forum] but do not constitute doing business in [the forum].").

34. *See, e.g., Epps v. Stewart Information Services Corp.,* 327 F.3d 642, 648 (8th Cir.2003) (general jurisdiction requires systematic and continuous contacts, plus other enumerated factors of fairness); *ALS Scan, Inc. v. Digital Service Consultants, Inc.,* 293 F.3d 707, 712 (4th Cir.2002) ("To establish general jurisdiction over the defendant, the defendant's activities in the State must have been 'continuous and systematic,' a more demanding standard than is necessary for establishing specific jurisdiction."); *Chaiken v. VV Publishing Corp.,* 119 F.3d 1018, 1028 (2d Cir.1997) (circulation of 183 copies of publication in state, creating annual gross revenues of $21,000, does not of itself satisfy general jurisdiction); *Nichols v. G.D. Searle & Co.,* 991 F.2d 1195, 1200 (4th Cir.1993)(held, unrelated advertising and solicitation insufficient for general jurisdiction; "broad constructions of general jurisdiction should be generally disfavored").

§ 2.5 Jurisdiction Over Persons or Things—Requirements for Personal Jurisdiction—State Limitations: Long–Arm Statutes

CORE CONCEPT

Before a federal trial court may exert its personal jurisdiction over an out-of-state, non-consenting defendant, the court must usually satisfy requirements laid down by the legislature of the state in which it sits. These requirements are found in the so-called "long-arm" statutes, which every state has enacted. Satisfying the long-arm requirements is a burden additional to the obligations of fairness imposed by the Constitution.[1]

The long-arm powers may not exceed the constitutional limits of due process, discussed above. In fact, some state long-arm statutes are drafted to allow trial courts to reach as far as due process will allow. However, it is possible that a state will choose not to permit an exercise of personal jurisdiction to the fullest extent permitted by the Constitution. In that circumstance, the court's ability to reach defendants outside the territory of the state may be constrained by the long-arm statute.[2] These distinctions between the long-arm statutes of particular states require attorneys to consult, and become familiar with, the long-arm statutes of individual states relevant to their practices.

APPLICATIONS

Consent

Where a defendant has already consented to the personal jurisdiction of the court, the need for application of a long-arm statute is eliminated.[3]

Service Within a State

Long-arm statutes authorize exercise of personal jurisdiction beyond the boundaries of the state in which a court sits. Thus if a defendant is properly served with process within a state, the long-arm statute of that state will have no application.

---

1. *See, e.g., GTE New Media Services, Inc. v. BellSouth Corp.,* 199 F.3d 1343, 1347 (D.C.Cir.2000), *rejected,* 2002 WL 31261330 (E.D.Pa.2002) (even if long-arm statute is satisfied, requirement of due process must still be met); *Wenz v. Memery Crystal,* 55 F.3d 1503 (10th Cir.1995)(for jurisdiction over nonresident defendant, court must examine both the state long-arm statute and issues of due process).

2. *See, e.g., Talbot v. Johnson Newspaper Corp.,* 71 N.Y.2d 827, 829–30, 522 N.E.2d 1027, 1028–29, 527 N.Y.S.2d 729 (1988) ("[T]he New York long-arm statute ... does not provide for in personam juris-

diction in every case in which due process would permit it.").

3. *See, e.g., General Contracting & Trading Co. v. Interpole, Inc.,* 940 F.2d 20, 22 (1st Cir.1991) (long-arm analysis is unnecessary if defendant has submitted to personal jurisdiction); *Knowlton v. Allied Van Lines, Inc.,* 900 F.2d 1196, 1197–99 (8th Cir.1990) (existence of consent to jurisdiction, whether expressly or by waiver, eliminates need to satisfy state long-arm statute; appointment of agent to receive service of process is "[o]ne of the most solidly established ways of giving ... consent").

Overlap With Due Process

The long-arm statutes of some states permit their courts to exercise personal jurisdiction over out-of-state defendants to the full extent of Due Process limitations of the Constitution.[4] In such states there is thus no need to make separate analyses to determine if both the constitutional requirements of fairness and long-arm requirements are satisfied: if due process is satisfied, so is the long-arm statute.[5] However, in states that do not permit exercise of personal jurisdiction to the fullest constitutional extent, it is necessary to make two different analyses. Jurisdiction must satisfy due process, and it must also fit within the statutory scheme of the long-arm statute.[6]

Example

The New York long-arm statute permits exercise of personal jurisdiction in New York courts over many out-of-state defendants who commit tortious acts outside the state which create injury within the state.[7] However, that authority explicitly excludes cases where defendants are accused of defamatory acts outside New York that cause injury within the state. Thus a federal court in New York could not use the New York long-arm statute to exercise personal jurisdiction over a defendant who was accused of defamation outside New York that caused injury within the state. This would be true even if the due process requirements for personal jurisdiction, discussed above, were satisfied.

---

4. *See, e.g.,* Rhode Island General Laws Annotated § 9–5–33(a). *See also, e.g., Pennzoil Products Co. v. Colelli & Associates, Inc.,* 149 F.3d 197, 200 (3d Cir.1998) ("We have acknowledged that the [long-arm] statute permits Pennsylvania courts to exercise personal jurisdiction over nonresident defendants 'to the constitutional limits of the Due Process Clause of the Fourteenth Amendment' ").

5. *See, e.g., Fielding v. Hubert Burda Media, Inc.,* 415 F.3d 419, 424 (5th Cir. 2005) ("Texas's jurisdictional statute is a "long-arm" statute, extending the personal jurisdiction of Texas courts to the extent allowed by the Due Process Clause."); *Chan v. Society Expeditions, Inc.,* 39 F.3d 1398, 1405 (9th Cir.1994) (when long-arm statute is "coextensive" with due process, court needs only to examine the due process requirement).

6. *Cf., e.g., Best Van Lines, Inc. v. Walker,* 490 F.3d 239 (2d Cir. 2007) (district court properly looked first to New York law to determine if personal jurisdiction was satisfied; no need to look to 14th Amendment due process consideration unless court could determine that it had jurisdiction under New York law); *Mwani v. bin Laden,* 417 F.3d 1, 9 (D.C.Cir.2005) (noting that some portions of District of Columbia long-arm statute reach as far as due process permits, but others do not; for application of the latter provisions court must be satisfied that more stringent requirements are met); *New Wellington Financial Corp. v. Flagship Resort Development Corp.,* 416 F.3d 290, 294 n.6 (4th Cir.2005) ("It is nonetheless still possible for the contacts of a non-resident defendant to satisfy due process but not meet the specific grasp of a Virginia long-arm statute provision.").

7. New York Civil Practice Law and Rules 302(a)(3).

ADDITIONAL RESEARCH REFERENCES

C.J.S. Constitutional Law §§ 1150, 1153; Federal Courts §§ 165(1)–190 et seq.

West's Key No. Digests, Constitutional Law ⬤⇒305(4); Federal Courts ⬤⇒76–76.35.

§ 2.6   Jurisdiction Over Persons or Things—Requirements for Personal Jurisdiction—Notice

CORE CONCEPT

The notice requirement for personal jurisdiction overlaps substantially with the fairness requirements. Both "notice" and "minimum contacts" are requirements derived from the Due Process clauses of the Constitution. Even so, there are a few distinctions to be made between notice and minimum contacts. For example, if a defendant had elaborate contacts with a state, but was never notified of the pendency of a lawsuit, the defendant would never have a fair opportunity to present a defense. Thus, personal jurisdiction would be lacking—even though minimum contacts were present—because requirements of notice were not satisfied.[1]

APPLICATIONS

Due Process Standard

To satisfy Due Process requirements, notice to the defendant must be of a quality that is reasonably likely, in all the circumstances of the case, to apprise the defendant of the pending action and afford an opportunity to make a defense.[2] This standard is very fact-dependent.[3] Normally, notice by first-class mail is satisfactory

---

1. *Murphy Bros., Inc. v. Michetti Pipe Stringing, Inc.*, 526 U.S. 344, 350, 119 S.Ct. 1322, 1327, 143 L.Ed.2d 448 (1999) ("In the absence of service of process (or waiver of service by the defendant), a court ordinarily may not exercise power over a party the complaint names as a defendant."). *See, e.g., Peay v. BellSouth Medical Assistance Plan*, 205 F.3d 1206, 1209 (10th Cir.2000) ("While service of process and personal jurisdiction both must be satisfied before a suit can proceed, they are distinct concepts that require separate inquiries.").

2. *Nelson v. Adams, USA, Inc.*, 529 U.S. 460, 467, 120 S.Ct. 1579, 1585, 146 L.Ed.2d 530 (2000) (amended complaint joining new party; held, where newly joined defendant is "adjudged liable the very first moment his personal liability was legally at issue" he is denied an opportunity to prepare a defense and is thereby denied due process).

3. *Mennonite Board of Missions v. Adams*, 462 U.S. 791, 799, 103 S.Ct. 2706, 2711, 77 L.Ed.2d 180 (1983) (heightened duty to provide notice where state knows of opponent's inexperience or incompetence). *See, e.g., Folger Adam Security, Inc. v. DeMatteis/MacGregor, JV*, 209 F.3d 252, 265 (3d Cir.2000) (notice of bankruptcy auction that provides sale of assets will be free and clear of "interests" is not adequate notice that affirmative defenses and contract defenses will be extinguished); *Petrovic v. Amoco Oil Co.*, 200 F.3d 1140, 1153 (8th Cir.1999) (notice of proposed settlement of class action under Rule 23(e) must have sufficient detail to permit estimate of potential costs and benefits "or at least whether additional investigation into the matter would be an efficient use of ... time"); *Lakeshore Broadcasting, Inc. v. FCC*, 199 F.3d 468, 474 (D.C.Cir.1999) (publication

for Due Process purposes[4] (*but see* Rule 4 for acceptable methods of service of original pleadings.) However, where the names or addresses of defendants are not known and cannot reasonably be known, little in the way of notice is required.[5]

Statutory Notice

In addition to satisfying constitutional requirements for notice, a party must also serve process in accordance with the statute or rule of procedure governing service in a particular court. For federal courts, Rule 4 (discussed elsewhere in this text) governs service of process at the beginning of a suit. Rule 4 cannot establish standards for service that do not meet the constitutional requirements for notice. However, Rule 4 could prescribe requirements for service more rigorous than those required by the Constitution.

ADDITIONAL RESEARCH REFERENCES

C.J.S. Constitutional Law § 1154; Federal Courts §§ 165(1)–190 et seq.

West's Key No. Digests, Constitutional Law ⋘309; Federal Courts ⋘76–76.35.

notice of regulations gave party that had initiated administrative process sufficient notice; distinguishing *Mullane v. Central Hanover Bank & Trust* as applying to parties who had no reason to know a judicial proceeding was pending).

4. *Robinson v. Hanrahan*, 409 U.S. 38, 93 S.Ct. 30, 34 L.Ed.2d 47 (1972) (mail service of notice of forfeiture to home address of party government knows to be incarcerated does not meet constitutional requirement). *See, e.g., United States v. One Toshiba Color Television*, 213 F.3d 147 (3d Cir.2000) (forfeiture case involving incarcerated party; held, while mailing is usually adequate notice, mailing is not "per se satisfaction of notice requirements"; noting differences among circuits, but holding that in providing mail service on prisoner held in state confinement, using proper address of jail, federal government need not prove actual notice; instead, government must demonstrate that methods of service used are reasonably calculated to result in actual notice). *But cf., United States v. Five Thousand Dollars in United States Currency*, 184 F.3d 958, 960 (8th Cir.1999) ("[I]f the government is incarcerating the property owner when it institutes forfeiture proceedings, we have consistently held that fundamental fairness requires that the property owner or his or her counsel receive actual notice of the forfeiture in time to decide whether to compel the government to proceed by judicial condemnation.").

5. *Dusenbery v. United States*, 534 U.S. 161, 170, 122 S.Ct. 694, 701, 151 L.Ed.2d 597 (2002) (Due process "does not say that the State *must provide* actual notice, but that it *must attempt to provide* actual notice"; and attempt need not involve "heroic efforts" by government); *Mullane v. Central Hanover Bank & Trust Co.*, 339 U.S. 306, 314, 70 S.Ct. 652, 94 L.Ed. 865 (1950). *But cf., Jones v. Flowers*, ___ U.S. ___, ___, 126 S.Ct. 1708, 1713–14, 164 L.Ed.2d 415 (2006) (notice of tax sale sent by certified mail was returned unclaimed; held, state "must take additional reasonable steps to attempt to provide notice to the property owner before selling his property, if it is practicable to do so;" but still acknowledging that actual notice is not required; distinguishing earlier cases as circumstances where government was unaware that attempt at service had failed).

§ 2.7   Jurisdiction Over Persons or Things—Requirements for Personal Jurisdiction—Special Considerations in Federal Court

CORE CONCEPT

In matters of jurisdiction over persons and things, federal courts generally behave in much the same way as state courts sitting in the same state:[1] the jurisdictional authority is much the same in the two systems.   Rule 4(k), which generally governs the territorial limit of service of process from a federal court, makes that point explicitly. However, there are a few circumstances where a federal court may have a somewhat greater jurisdictional reach than its state counterpart.   Rule 4(k) contains some of these exceptions.   Others are creatures of Congressional legislation.

APPLICATIONS

Nationwide Personal Jurisdiction

For several federal causes of action, including suits under federal antitrust laws and the federal securities laws, Congress has authorized federal courts to exercise their personal jurisdiction throughout the United States.   Thus, in hearing an antitrust claim filed in Baltimore, a federal court in Maryland has personal jurisdiction over a defendant in Hawaii, Puerto Rico, Alaska, or some other distant jurisdiction, even if it could not otherwise reach that defendant under the considerations mentioned earlier in this section on personal jurisdiction.[2]   These statutes, while not rare, are generally the exceptions to the normal practice. When such statutes come into play, it is possible that the court will make a minimum contacts analysis that may differ somewhat from the concept developed for domestic defendants. In the first place, a court evaluating personal

---

1.   *See, e.g., Ruiz de Molina v. Merritt & Furman Insurance Agency, Inc.,* 207 F.3d 1351, 1355 (11th Cir.2000) ("A federal court sitting in diversity may exercise jurisdiction over a nonresident defendant to the same extent as a court of that state."); *Access Telecom, Inc. v. MCI Telecommunications, Inc.,* 197 F.3d 694, 716 (5th Cir. 1999) (same holding). *Cf., Deprenyl Animal Health, Inc. v. University of Toronto Innovations Foundation,* 297 F.3d 1343, 1350 (Fed.Cir.2002) (*International Shoe* applies to federal courts through Fifth Amendment as it applies to state courts through Fourteenth Amendment).

2.   *See, e.g.,* 15 U.S.C.A. § 22. *See also In re Federal Fountain, Inc.,* 165 F.3d 600, 601–02 (8th Cir.1999) (en banc) (where Congress has authorized personal jurisdiction nationwide and defendant is found within territory of United States, federal courts may exercise personal jurisdiction over defendant; concluding that "virtually every ... court" has reached same conclusion). *Accord, Board of Trustees v. Elite Erectors, Inc.,* 212 F.3d 1031, 1035 (7th Cir.2000) (agreeing with *Federal Fountain;* rejecting *Peay;* "we have concluded that nationwide service under [certain] statutes is proper, as long as the defendants have adequate contacts [within] the United States as a whole"). *But see Peay v. Bell-South Medical Assistance Plan,* 205 F.3d 1206, 1210 (10th Cir.2000) (acknowledging disagreement with *Federal Fountain;* citing other cases in conflict; concluding that even where Congress has authorized nationwide service, plaintiff's choice of forum must still be "fair and reasonable"). *See also Republic of Panama v. BCCI Holdings (Luxembourg), S.A.,* 119 F.3d 935, 943–44 (11th Cir.1997) (concluding that fairness and convenience are still relevant to analysis).

jurisdiction in a case involving a federal cause of action that authorized nationwide jurisdiction will be less concerned with issues of state/federal relationships and more concerned about the federal policies underlying the federal right that has been asserted by the plaintiff.[3] Secondly, it is uncertain whether, in making a minimum contact analysis in the context of nationwide personal jurisdiction, the court should examine only whether minimum contacts exist[4] or whether the court should also look to whether an exercise of jurisdiction reasonable in a particular district.[5]

For many other federal causes of action, such as civil rights claims or truth-in-lending cases, the more conventional forms of obtaining personal jurisdiction must be followed.

Important: Nationwide personal jurisdiction should not be equated with personal jurisdiction throughout the world. If the defendant in the antitrust action filed in Baltimore was in Brazil, the Congressional grant of nationwide jurisdiction would not be effective to reach the Brazilian defendant. In such a circumstance the federal court would still have resort to the considerations of minimum contacts and either state long-arm statutes or the special provision of Rule 4(k)(2), discussed immediately below. But if those tools were insufficient then personal jurisdiction could not be sustained.

Special Considerations of Rule 4(k)

As is discussed elsewhere in this study, Rule 4(k) authorizes federal courts in certain circumstances to exercise personal jurisdiction over certain designated persons who may be served within 100 miles, measured in a straight line in any direction, from the federal courthouse. This Rule applies irrespective of how many state boundaries may intervene. Such designated persons include those who may be joined under the applicable state long-arm law, parties impleaded under Rule 14, parties joined under Rule 19, parties who can be served under federal statutory interpleader legislation, 28 U.S.C.A. § 1335, and parties subject to service authorized by any other applicable federal legislation. Note that Rule 4(k) does not provide the 100 mile bulge to plaintiffs seeking to initiate an action by serving a defendant.

This 100 mile rule applies only within the United States. A federal court in Detroit, Michigan, for example, could not use Rule 4(k) to serve a person in Windsor, Ontario, even though Windsor is much less than 100 miles from Detroit. If a federal court is located

---

3. *See, e.g., Pinker v. Roche Holdings, Ltd.,* 292 F.3d 361 (3d Cir.2002).

4. *See, e.g., Securities Investor Protection Corp. v. Vigman,* 764 F.2d 1309, 1316 (9th Cir.1985) (looking only to whether defendant has minimum contacts with United States as a whole; not concerned with any potential absence of contacts with particular federal district).

5. *See, e.g., Republic of Panama v. BCCI Holdings (Luxembourg), S.A.,* 119 F.3d 935, 945–46 (11th Cir.1997) (district court should weigh fairness to defendant in particular district against "federal interest involved in the litigation;" asserting that other circuits follow this approach).

in the center of a state, more than 100 miles from its borders, Rule 4(k)'s 100–mile bulge has little utility. If, however, a federal court is located in a part of a state immediately adjacent to a neighboring state, Rule 4(k) may provide advantages not available in a state court.

Finally, Rule 4(k)(2) explicitly permits exercise of personal jurisdiction in federal causes of action where the defendant has sufficient contacts with the United States as a whole, but not with any particular state.[6]

ADDITIONAL RESEARCH REFERENCES

C.J.S. Constitutional Law § 1154; Federal Civil Procedure §§ 204–221 et seq., 486 et seq.; Federal Courts § 16 et seq.

West's Key No. Digests, Constitutional Law ⟊305; Federal Civil Procedure ⟊461–505; Federal Courts ⟊71.

§ 2.8   Jurisdiction Over Persons or Things—Special Requirements for Quasi in Rem Jurisdiction

CORE CONCEPT

Quasi in rem jurisdiction is an alternative to personal jurisdiction. It is employed most commonly as a means of obtaining the presence of a defendant in a court by judicial attachment (i.e., seizure) of property belonging to the defendant. In order for the court to attach such property, the property must be located within the state in which the court sits.

APPLICATIONS

Prerequisites

A court may exercise quasi in rem jurisdiction when six elements are present: 1) thing of value; 2) territorial limit; 3) defendant's asset; 4) seizure or attachment; 5) notice; and 6) minimum contacts are satisfied. *All six* elements must be satisfied.[1]

(1) *Thing of Value:* Quasi in rem jurisdiction presupposes that the thing seized has value. Because a judgment in favor of a

---

6. *See also, e.g., Medical Mutual of Ohio v. deSoto,* 245 F.3d 561, 566–67 (6th Cir. 2001) (in case brought under Employee Retirement Income and Security Act, 29 U.S.C.A. § 1132 provided nationwide personal jurisdiction; court, therefore, could look to defendant's contacts with entire country, rather than only forum state; rejecting contrary approach of requiring plaintiff to demonstrate that defendant had sufficient contacts with both United States as a whole and forum state). *But see Peay v. BellSouth Medical Assistance Plan,* 205 F.3d 1206, 1210–12 (10th Cir.2000) (29

U.S.C.A. § 1132 authorizes nationwide service of process, but requirement of personal jurisdiction requires separate due process analysis to determine whether plaintiff's choice of forum is fair and reasonable).

1. *See, e.g., Winter Storm Shipping v. TPI,* 310 F.3d 263, 269 (2d Cir.2002) (due process requirements for quasi in rem jurisdiction similar to those for personal jurisdiction). For a fuller discussion of the requirements for quasi in rem jurisdiction, *see Shaffer v. Heitner,* 433 U.S. 186, 97 S.Ct. 2569, 53 L.Ed.2d 683 (1977).

plaintiff will often be enforced through forced sale or forfeiture of the thing seized, quasi in rem jurisdiction would have little meaning if the asset had no value. Moreover, the value of the asset seized determines the monetary limit of the court's jurisdiction in quasi in rem cases.[2]

> **Example:** If a plaintiff's claim had a maximum value of one million dollars, that would normally be the amount for which the plaintiff would like to sue. If the court had personal jurisdiction over the defendant, normally the defendant would have potential liability (assuming a judgment for the plaintiff) up to the full amount of the claim. However, if the court's jurisdiction was based on quasi in rem jurisdiction, and the thing seized was a bank account with a value of $400,000, the limit of the court's quasi in rem jurisdiction would be $400,-000—the value of the asset.[3] The plaintiff would retain a claim for $600,000, but normally could not prosecute it in that same court, unless additional assets could be seized, or jurisdiction could be established on the basis of personal jurisdiction.

Important: Although quasi in rem jurisdiction may sometimes be less advantageous from a plaintiff's point of view, historically it has also posed dilemmas for defendants. Consider again the example mentioned above. If the plaintiff cannot obtain personal jurisdiction, the limit of the court's jurisdiction will be $400,000. An out-of-state defendant will have the choice of appearing in court to defend on the merits, or staying outside the state and defaulting. A decision to default obviously forfeits defenses on the merits. If the defendant appears, however, the plaintiff may be able to serve process in-state that will satisfy personal jurisdiction. The court could then hear plaintiff's claim for the full amount of $1,000,000. Thus defendant would be faced with the hard choice of defaulting on $400,000, or appearing and risking exposure for an additional $600,000. Some courts—but by no means all—resolved this dilemma by allowing defendant to make a "limited appearance," in which defendant could contest the merits of the quasi in rem claim ($400,000), but remain immune from service of process for personal jurisdiction while the $400,000 claim was litigated.[4] Nowadays the sixth requirement for quasi in rem jurisdiction, minimum contacts, has substantially eased this problem.

2. *Shaffer v. Heitner,* 433 U.S. 186, 207 n. 23, 97 S.Ct. 2569, 2581, n. 23, 53 L.Ed.2d 683 (1977) (liability in an in rem action is limited to the value of the property).

3. *Shaffer v. Heitner,* 433 U.S. 186, 209 n. 32, 97 S.Ct. 2569, 2582 n. 32, 53 L.Ed.2d 683 (1977)("the value of the property seized [serves] to limit the extent of possible liability."). *Cf., Teyseer Cement Co. v. Halla Maritime Corp.,* 794 F.2d 472, 477 (9th Cir.1986)(certain kinds of maritime jurisdic-

tion are actually quasi in rem, "because any judgment rendered is limited to the value of the attached property").

4. *See, e.g., United States v. First Nat'l City Bank,* 379 U.S. 378, 390 n. 8, 85 S.Ct. 528, 535 n. 8, 13 L.Ed.2d 365 (1965)(noting split of authority on availability of limited appearance). *See also Shaffer v. Heitner,* 433 U.S. 186, 196 n. 12, 97 S.Ct. 2569, 2575 n. 12, 53 L.Ed.2d 683 (1977)(Delaware does not permit a limited appearance).

(2) *Territorial Requirement:* Courts exercising quasi in rem jurisdiction have a definite territorial limit to their jurisdiction. For quasi in rem jurisdiction to be sustained, the asset must be seized while it is within the territorial confines of the state in which the court sits.[5] Where the asset is something as tangible and immoveable as realty, the territorial requirement is not a substantial hurdle—if the land is within the state, the land is not going to change its location. More mobile assets, such as automobiles, present somewhat more significant problems because there is some risk that they will be moved before attachment can occur. The biggest questions of territoriality, however, arise when the asset is an intangible item. Things such as accounts receivable or stock ownership in a corporation certainly have value, but they have no definite situs comparable to that of land or automobiles. Courts have resolved these problems with rules arbitrary in their nature, but generally followed for lack of a better solution. Depending on the law of the state where a corporation is incorporated, for example, shares in a corporation are generally held to be located either where the certificate evidencing ownership is found, or in the state where the entity is incorporated.[6]

Important: Quasi in rem jurisdiction is always territorial in nature. Thus, there is no need to address long-arm statutes, because such statutes are applicable only when the court is attempting to reach outside its own state's territory.[7]

(3) *Defendant's Asset:* Because the purpose of quasi in rem jurisdiction is to sue a particular defendant or group of defendants, it would make little sense if a suit against one person was sustained by seizure of the asset of another person, who was not a party and had no connection to the case. Certainly, in that case, the true defendant would have no incentive to appear in court, and the person whose property was seized would be entitled to retain the asset. Thus, the third requirement for quasi in rem jurisdiction is that the asset seized must at least arguably belong to the defendant. The defendant's title need not be absolutely clear, however. If the purpose of the plaintiff's suit is to resolve a dispute between the parties as to title in the asset that was seized, this requirement of quasi in rem jurisdiction is satisfied if the defendant merely claims the property or will claim the property.

5. *See, e.g., Koken v. Viad Corp.,* 307 F.Supp.2d 650, 655 (E.D. Pa. 2004) ("If jurisdiction is based on the court's power over property within its territory, the action is in rem or quasi in rem."). *See also Glencore Grain Rotterdam B.V. v. Shivnath Rai Harnarain Co.,* 284 F.3d 1114, 1127 (9th Cir.2002) ("[T]he sine qua non of basing jurisdiction on a defendant's assets in the forum is the identification of [such an] asset.").

6. *See, e.g., Shaffer v. Heitner,* 433 U.S. 186, 191, 97 S.Ct. 2569, 2573, 53 L.Ed.2d 683 (1977)(Delaware law makes Delaware the situs of stock ownership in Delaware corporations).

7. *See, e.g., Newhard, Cook & Co. v. Inspired Life Ctrs., Inc.,* 895 F.2d 1226, 1228 n. 3 (8th Cir.1990)(if case is based on quasi in rem jurisdiction, long-arm requirements generally need not be satisfied).

(4) *Seizure or Attachment:* The court's quasi in rem jurisdiction cannot begin until the court has effective control of the asset. The nature of the seizure depends heavily on the nature of the property seized, but generally it is enough that the court has effectively interfered with the defendant's control, even if the court does not have actual possession. With land, for example, the court can simply order that title be frozen in the local records office pending the outcome of the suit. With stock shares, the same can be accomplished by ordering the appropriate authority to halt trading in the particular shares at issue. By contrast, if the asset was a rare diamond, or an automobile, the court might take physical custody of the property.

(5) *Notice:* As with personal jurisdiction, quasi in rem jurisdiction requires notice to the defendant that will satisfy both constitutional due process and the service of process requirements of Rule 4. Application of the due process requirement is similar to that imposed on personal jurisdiction, with allowance for the fact that quasi in rem cases may sometimes require less notice to the defendant. This may occur because sometimes the act of seizing a defendant's property may reasonably be assumed to notify a defendant of the pendency of the case.

(6) *Requirements of Fair Play: Minimum Contacts:* The due process requirement of "traditional notions of fair play and substantial justice" applies to quasi in rem jurisdiction. In practice, this means quasi in rem jurisdiction is likely to be sustained only in circumstances where the assets seized bear a substantial relation to the cause of action on which plaintiff is suing, or in circumstances where other facts suggest that exercise of quasi in rem jurisdiction would not be fundamentally unfair to defendant.[8] Both of those standards are highly fact-specific. An attorney uncertain whether, under due process, quasi in rem jurisdiction can be sustained, should research carefully the developing case law in this area.

Relation to Rule 4

Rule 4(n) limits the circumstances in which a federal court may assert quasi in rem or in rem jurisdiction, even if an assertion of such jurisdiction is constitutionally sound. Basically, there are two circumstances where a federal court may employ such jurisdiction. First, Rule 4(n) permits jurisdiction if a federal statute authorizes it. In that situation, notice to affected parties is governed by other applicable provisions of Rule 4, presumably including nationwide service when it is appropriate. Second, Rule 4(n) permits such jurisdiction even in the absence of a federal statute authorizing it, if the court is unable to obtain personal jurisdiction over the defendant(s). In that circumstance, Rule 4(n) provides that jurisdiction

---

8. *See, e.g., Louring v. Kuwait Boulder Shipping Co.,* 455 F.Supp. 630 (D.Conn. 1977)(permitting quasi in rem jurisdiction over assets of foreign defendant unrelated to cause of action; reasoning that United States plaintiffs should not be required to litigate their claims in foreign courts).

will be obtained according to the process of the state in which the district court sits.

Enforcing Judgments

It should be noted that the "minimum contacts" requirement for quasi in rem jurisdiction is applicable only in cases in which the plaintiff has brought a cause of action that will be litigated (assuming good jurisdiction) on the merits. By contrast, if the plaintiff has already won a judgment and seeks only to enforce the judgment against a defendant's assets, the requirement that the asset must have some relationship to the underlying litigation does not apply.[9] All the other elements, however, must still be met.

ADDITIONAL RESEARCH REFERENCES

C.J.S. Constitutional Law § 1139; Courts §§ 54–60; Federal Courts § 25(1, 2).

West's Key No. Digests, Constitutional Law ☞305; Courts ☞21; Federal Courts ☞93.

§ 2.9 Jurisdiction Over Persons or Things—Requirements for in Rem Jurisdiction

CORE CONCEPT

As its name suggests, in rem jurisdiction is closely related to quasi in rem jurisdiction—so much so, in fact, that courts occasionally use the two terms interchangeably. The most important difference is that in rem jurisdiction usually involves trying title to property and, in theory, determining the rights of all people throughout the world in that property. Quasi in rem jurisdiction, by contrast, usually involves a much more discrete group of defendants, whose claims are usually far less theoretical. In practice, federal courts use in rem jurisdiction infrequently. Those areas in which in rem jurisdiction may most often be employed are actions in admiralty, involving shipping on navigable waters where the vessel is seized as the basis of jurisdiction;[1] bankruptcy cases;[2] and condemnation of property that was the instrumentality of a crime, which the government now seeks to keep as its own.[3]

---

9. *Shaffer v. Heitner,* 433 U.S. 186, 210 n. 36, 97 S.Ct. 2569, 2583, n. 36, 53 L.Ed.2d 683 (1977) ("Once it has been determined by a court of competent jurisdiction that the defendant is a debtor of the plaintiff, there would seem to be no unfairness in allowing an action to realize on that debt in a State where the defendant has property, whether or not that State would have jurisdiction to determine the existence of the debt as an original matter.").

1. *See, e.g., The Belgenland,* 114 U.S. 355, 5 S.Ct. 860, 29 L.Ed. 152 (1885).

2. *Central Virginia Community College v. Katz,* ___ U.S. ___, ___, 126 S.Ct. 990, 1000, 163 L.Ed.2d 945 (2006) ("Bankruptcy jurisdiction, as understood today and at the time of the framing, is principally in rem jurisdiction.").

3. *See, e.g., United States v. United States Coin & Currency,* 401 U.S. 715, 91 S.Ct. 1041, 28 L.Ed.2d 434 (1971). *See also, United States v. One Parcel of Real Estate at 10380 SW 28th Street,* 214 F.3d 1291, 1294 (11th Cir.2000). ("The focus of an in rem narcotics forfeiture is not the guilt of any person or the attempt to punish a per-

Important: If in rem jurisdiction is lacking, and the court also lacks personal jurisdiction and quasi in rem jurisdiction, the typical remedy is to dismiss the claim.

APPLICATIONS

Prerequisites: There are five prerequisites for a court to exercise in rem jurisdiction.

(1) *Thing of Value:* If the property whose title is at issue had no value, there would be little point to the litigation itself. As might be expected, this element of in rem jurisdiction is usually not difficult to satisfy.

(2) *Territorial Requirement:* Like quasi in rem jurisdiction, in rem jurisdiction is territorial in nature. The property must be located within the state in which the court sits at the onset of the action.

(3) *Seizure by the Court:* The court's in rem jurisdiction cannot begin until the court has effective control of the asset. The nature of the seizure depends heavily on the nature of the property seized, but generally it is enough that the court has effectively interfered with the defendant's control, even if the court does not have actual possession. With land, for example, the court can simply order that title be frozen in the local records office pending the outcome of the suit. With stock shares, the same can be accomplished by ordering the appropriate authority to halt trading in the particular shares at issue. By contrast, if the asset was a rare diamond, or an automobile, the marshal might take physical custody of the property.

(4) *Notice Requirement:* As with personal jurisdiction and quasi in rem jurisdiction, in rem jurisdiction requires notice to the defendant that will satisfy both due process and the service of process requirements of Rule 4. Otherwise, this is an area where in rem jurisdiction differs somewhat from quasi in rem jurisdiction. Because the nature of an in rem case—trying title as to potential claimants throughout the world—is much more diffuse than that of a typical quasi in rem case, notice that will satisfy constitutional requirements of due process will often be by publication in newspapers, etc., rather than some form of personal service on a defendant. In this area in rem requirements are probably substantially more relaxed than those of personal or quasi in rem jurisdiction. It is important to note, however, that if the identity and location of a particular claimant is known to the defendant, then the requirement of better notice, such as mail service, probably applies. Additionally, courts must satisfy their own rules on service, in addition to constitutional requirements. Under Rule 4(e)(2), governing in rem attachments, federal courts are authorized to use the service of process rules of the state in which they sit.

son, but the 'guilt' of the property, *i.e.,* whether the property had been used in connection with illicit drug activity."). *United* States v. $506,231 in United States Currency,* 125 F.3d 442, 447 (7th Cir.1997) ("Civil forfeiture actions are in rem proceedings.").

(5) *Requirements of Fair Play:* As with cases grounded upon personal jurisdiction or quasi in rem jurisdiction, cases founded on in rem jurisdiction must also satisfy requirements of due process.[4] Because in rem actions always involve suits closely related to the property seized, however, the fairness requirements of due process are usually met without difficulty.[5]

No Competing Assertions of In Rem Jurisdiction

At least for federal courts, it is settled that if one court has established in rem jurisdiction over an asset, "a second court will not assume *in rem* jurisdiction over the same *res.*"[6]

Relation to Rule 4

Rule 4(n) limits the circumstances in which a federal court may assert quasi in rem or in rem jurisdiction, even if an assertion of such jurisdiction is constitutionally sound. Basically, there are two circumstances where a federal court may employ such jurisdiction. First, Rule 4(n) permits jurisdiction if a federal statute authorizes it. In that situation, notice to affected parties is governed by other applicable provisions of Rule 4, presumably including nationwide service when it is appropriate. Second, Rule 4(n) permits such jurisdiction even in the absence of a federal statute authorizing it, if the court is unable to obtain personal jurisdiction over the defendant(s). In that circumstance, Rule 4(n) provides that jurisdiction will be obtained according to the process of the state in which the district court sits.

ADDITIONAL RESEARCH REFERENCES

C.J.S. Constitutional Law § 1139; Courts §§ 54–60; Federal Courts § 25(1, 2).

West's Key No. Digests, Constitutional Law ⟜305; Courts ⟜21; Federal Courts ⟜93.

§ 2.10 Subject Matter Jurisdiction in Federal District Courts—Introduction

Attorneys unfamiliar with federal trial courts often have substantial difficulty with two points about federal subject matter jurisdiction. First, federal courts are courts of *limited* subject matter jurisdiction, and thus will be unable to hear certain types of cases that could be brought routinely in a state trial court, which often enjoys a broader scope of subject matter jurisdiction. Second, the need to meet standards of

4. *See, e.g., Harrods Ltd. v. Sixty Internet Domain Names,* 302 F.3d 214, 224 (4th Cir.2002) (minimum contacts analysis of *International Shoe* also apply to in rem actions).

5. *See, e.g., Porsche Cars North America, Inc. v. Porsche.net,* 302 F.3d 248, 260 (4th Cir.2002) (in case based upon in rem jurisdiction, where property itself is cause of action, jurisdiction is good in state where property is located).

6. *Marshall v. Marshall,* ___ U.S. ___, ___, 126 S.Ct. 1735, 1748, 164 L.Ed.2d 480 (2006).

federal subject matter jurisdiction is an *additional* requirement, separate from jurisdiction over persons and things, that must be satisfied before a federal trial court will hear a case.[1] *Both* subject matter jurisdiction and jurisdiction over persons and things must be satisfied *as to each count in a case* before a federal court will hear a count.[2] Failure to satisfy either requirement as to any count creates a substantial risk that the count will be dismissed, even if other counts may proceed. These requirements apply irrespective of whether the count arises in plaintiff's complaint, a counterclaim, a crossclaim, an impleader, or under any other relevant rule.

Distinctions between jurisdiction over persons or things and subject matter jurisdiction are best understood by considering the limitations each kind of jurisdiction places on a federal court. Jurisdiction over persons or things defines the limits of a court's reach to take control of litigation affecting a specific person or piece of property. Subject matter jurisdiction, by contrast, limits the kind of cases a court may hear, irrespective of where the affected persons or pieces of property may be found. Thus, if a person is served with process within a state where a court sits, the personal jurisdiction of the court is probably satisfied. But if the cause of action is of a kind that a federal court cannot hear, the court would still lack subject matter jurisdiction and the case should be dismissed.

> *Example:* Subject to exceptions discussed below under supplemental jurisdiction, federal courts may not hear causes of action based on state law if the plaintiff and defendant are citizens of the same state. This particular difference between subject matter jurisdiction and jurisdiction over persons and things may be explained by the following case. If plaintiff and defendant are both citizens of New York, and if the cause of action is a tort under state law, personal jurisdiction will be satisfied if the defendant is served with process within New York. However, the federal court will not have subject matter jurisdiction because suits based on state law, where the parties are citizens of the same state, do not fall within any of the categories of suits a federal court can hear. Thus the case should be dismissed, even though personal jurisdiction is satisfactory.

Affirmative Duty to Plead Jurisdiction: The burden of demonstrating that the requirements of federal subject matter jurisdiction

---

1. *Bell v. Hood*, 327 U.S. 678, 682, 66 S.Ct. 773, 776, 90 L.Ed. 939 (1946) (issue of whether complaint states cause of action should be decided after court determines that it has jurisdiction). *See, e.g., Glencore Grain Rotterdam B.V. v. Shivnath Rai Harnarain Co.*, 284 F.3d 1114, 1128 (9th Cir. 2002) (existence of subject matter jurisdiction, but not also personal jurisdiction, requires dismissal of case); *Southern Cross Overseas Agencies, Inc. v. Wah Kwong Shipping Group*, 181 F.3d 410, 414 (3d Cir.

1999) (courts should decide jurisdiction first "and then address other issues only if there is jurisdiction").

2. *But cf., Goetzke v. Ferro Corp.*, 280 F.3d 766, 778–79 (7th Cir.2002) (state statute providing that claim may be heard only by administrative board may operate to strip state courts of jurisdiction, but not federal courts; if jurisdiction meets standards set by Congress, state law cannot bar federal district court's jurisdiction).

are met rests on the party asserting the claim.[3]

Dismissal if Subject Matter Jurisdiction Absent: As the foregoing example suggests, the standard remedy for failure to satisfy subject matter jurisdiction is dismissal of the claim.[4]

Consent: Unlike personal jurisdiction, subject matter jurisdiction cannot be obtained through consent of the parties.[5] The rationale is that limits on a federal district court's subject matter jurisdiction are grounded in a proper balance of federal and state judicial power, and it is not the prerogative of the parties to enter into agreements that have the effect of upsetting that balance. Moreover, because the parties cannot by consent confer subject matter jurisdiction on the court,[6] Rule 12(h) provides no time limit on objections to subject matter jurisdiction. Instead, Rule 12(h)(3) stipulates that objections to subject matter jurisdiction can be raised "[w]henever" they appear, and that the court can act on motion of either party or on its own motion.[7]

Comparison with Quasi in Rem Jurisdiction: Quasi in rem jurisdiction and subject matter jurisdiction are separate and distinct concepts. Quasi in rem jurisdiction permits a court to exercise

3. *Merrell Dow Pharmaceuticals, Inc. v. Thompson,* 478 U.S. 804, 810 n. 6, 106 S.Ct. 3229, 3233 n. 6, 92 L.Ed.2d 650 (1986) ("[J]urisdiction may not be sustained on a theory that the plaintiff has not advanced."). *See Leipzig v. AIG Life Insurance Co.,* 362 F.3d 406, 410 (7th Cir.2004). *See also* Fed.R.Civ.P. Form 2 (indicating that subject matter jurisdiction should be alleged in complaint).

4. *Arbaugh v. Y&H Corp.,* __ U.S. __, __, 126 S.Ct. 1235, 1237, 163 L.Ed.2d 1097 (2006) ("[W]hen a federal court concludes that it lacks subject-matter jurisdiction, the complaint must be dismissed in its entirety."); *Steel Co. v. Citizens for a Better Environment,* 523 U.S. 83, 118 S.Ct. 1003, 140 L.Ed.2d 210 (1998) (first responsibility of court is to determine jurisdiction; if jurisdiction is lacking, court should dismiss without addressing merits); *Louisville & Nashville R.R. Co. v. Mottley,* 211 U.S. 149, 29 S.Ct. 42, 53 L.Ed. 126 (1908). *But cf., McCready v. eBay, Inc.,* 453 F.3d 882 (7th Cir.2006) (if practicable, prior to dismissal, plaintiff will typically be allowed to amend complaint to correct defect in allegation of jurisdiction).

5. *Insurance Corp. of Ireland, Ltd. v. Compagnie des Bauxites de Guinee,* 456 U.S. 694, 702, 102 S.Ct. 2099, 2104, 72 L.Ed.2d 492 (1982) ("[N]o action of the parties can confer subject-matter jurisdiction upon a federal court. Thus, the consent

of the parties is irrelevant."); *Capron v. Van Noorden,* 6 U.S. (2 Cranch) 126, 126, 2 L.Ed. 229 (1804). *See also, Days Inns Worldwide, Inc. v. Patel,* 445 F.3d 899, 904 (6th Cir.2006) ("[T]he parties cannot confer subject matter jurisdiction where it does not otherwise exist."); *Smith v. Ashland, Inc.,* 250 F.3d 1167 (8th Cir.2001) (subject matter jurisdiction cannot be conferred on court by consent of parties; however, parties may stipulate to fact of diversity based on citizenship of party).

6. *See, e.g., Tamiami Partners, Ltd. v. Miccosukee Tribe of Indians,* 177 F.3d 1212, 1222 (11th Cir.1999) ("It is well-settled that parties cannot create subject matter jurisdiction by agreement.").

7. *Bender v. Williamsport Area School District,* 475 U.S. 534, 541, 106 S.Ct. 1326, 1331, 89 L.Ed.2d 501 (1986) ("[E]very federal appellate court has a special obligation 'to satisfy itself not only of its own jurisdiction, but also that of the lower courts in a case under review,' even though the parties are prepared to concede it."). *See, e.g., Fax Telecommunicaciones, Inc. v. AT & T,* 138 F.3d 479, 485 (2d Cir.1998) ("[W]e have an obligation to determine *sua sponte* whether the district court had jurisdiction to hear the case."); *State Farm Mutual Automobile Ins. Co. v. Powell,* 87 F.3d 93 (3d Cir. 1996)(permitting challenge to diversity jurisdiction, notwithstanding that issue was raised only in appellate court).

power over a defendant, because the court has control of property belonging to the defendant. Subject matter jurisdiction defines the kind of cases the court may hear. In a case where the plaintiff and defendant were both New York citizens, for example, a federal court in California might have quasi in rem jurisdiction if it attached property in California belonging to defendant. If the cause of action was based on state law, however, subject matter jurisdiction would be lacking because the parties were not of diverse citizenship.

The three kinds of federal subject matter jurisdiction most frequently encountered are: (1) federal question jurisdiction; (2) jurisdiction based on diversity of citizenship; and (3) supplemental jurisdiction.

§ 2.11 Subject Matter Jurisdiction in Federal District Courts—Federal Question Jurisdiction

CORE CONCEPT

Congress authorized jurisdiction in federal district courts "of all civil actions arising under the Constitution, laws, or treaties of the United States." 28 U.S.C.A. § 1331.[1] In addition, Congress has enacted specific statutes authorizing federal district courts to hear causes of action relating to certain areas of federal law. For example, 28 U.S.C.A. § 1337 authorizes federal courts to hear civil actions arising under federal laws regulating commerce. In the same fashion, 28 U.S.C.A. § 1338 provides subject matter jurisdiction over claims arising under federal patent law, and 28 U.S.C.A. § 1343 authorizes a federal court to hear claims alleging violations of federally guaranteed civil rights.

APPLICATIONS

28 U.S.C.A. § 1331 and Specific Jurisdictional Statutes

The substantial overlap between the broad jurisdictional grant of § 1331 and the more discrete grants mentioned above does not necessarily make the specific jurisdictional statutes superfluous. For example, 28 U.S.C.A. § 1333, conferring subject matter jurisdiction over admiralty claims, preempts § 1331 when the case arises in admiralty. Thus the plaintiff must sue under § 1333, not § 1331,[2] and that has several important consequences.

1. *See also Up State Federal Credit Union v. Walker,* 198 F.3d 372, 375 n. 4 (2d Cir.1999) (contract disputes with federal government are controlled by federal common law and are thus federal questions within meaning of § 1331); *Sam L. Majors Jewelers v. ABX, Inc.,* 117 F.3d 922, 926 (5th Cir.1997) (§ 1331 also provides jurisdictional foundation for cases arising under federal common law).

2. *See, e.g., New York State Waterways Ass'n v. Diamond,* 469 F.2d 419 (2d Cir. 1972). *See also Shalala v. Illinois Council on Long Term Care, Inc.,* 529 U.S. 1, 4, 120 S.Ct. 1084, 1089, 146 L.Ed.2d 1 (2000) (most claims under Medicare Act cannot invoke federal question jurisdiction under § 1331; such claims are usually consigned by statute to a special administrative review process); *International Science and Technology Institute, Inc. v. Inacom Communications, Inc.,* 106 F.3d 1146, 1154 (4th Cir. 1997) ("It is clear ... that § 1331 is a general federal-question statute, which gives the district courts original jurisdiction

(1) *Exclusive Subject Matter Jurisdiction:* Under § 1333, the jurisdiction of the federal district court is *exclusive,* i.e., the claim cannot be brought in a state court. Exclusive subject matter jurisdiction is characteristic of many of the specific jurisdictional statutes like § 1333. Federal jurisdiction under § 1331, by contrast, is usually concurrent with that of state courts, which means the claims could have been filed *either* in federal court *or* in state court.[3] It is settled that if a federal cause of action is silent as to whether it lies within exclusive federal jurisdiction, or instead is subject to the concurrent jurisdiction of federal and state trial courts, the jurisdiction is concurrent—not exclusive.[4]

(2) *Limitations in Specific Statute:* If a cause of action must be filed under a specific jurisdictional statute like § 1333, the limitations associated with that cause of action attach to the filing. In admiralty cases, for example, there is no right to a jury trial. Under § 1331, jury trials are available as they would be under the more general constraints of the Seventh Amendment to the Constitution.[5]

Additionally, if other federal law precludes a court's use of § 1331 to obtain jurisdiction over a case, § 1331 is simply not available as a source of jurisdiction.[6]

(3) *Absence of Specific Statute:* For many federal causes of action, the only statute authorizing enforcement in a federal court is 28 U.S.C.A. § 1331.[7] That is, many federal causes of action do not enjoy their own specific grant of jurisdiction, equivalent to those of §§ 1333, 1337, 1338, and 1343.

(4) *Suits Based on Treaties:* 28 U.S.C.A. § 1331 is the only provision authorizing subject matter jurisdiction in a federal district court to enforce a cause of action arising under "treaties of the United States."

unless a specific statute assigns jurisdiction elsewhere.").

3. *Grubb v. Public Utilities Comm'n of Ohio,* 281 U.S. 470, 50 S.Ct. 374, 74 L.Ed. 972 (1930).

4. *Tafflin v. Levitt,* 493 U.S. 455, 458–59, 110 S.Ct. 792, 794–95, 107 L.Ed.2d 887 (1990) (presumption is in favor of concurrent jurisdiction, not exclusive jurisdiction).

5. *See also, e.g., McCarthy v. Apfel,* 221 F.3d 1119, 1123 (9th Cir.2000) (jurisdiction based on 42 U.S.C.A. § 405(g) of Social Security Act, rather than on 28 U.S.C.A. § 1331, would alter, *inter alia,* standard of proof from preponderance of evidence (§ 1331) to substantial evidence (§ 405(g))).

6. *Your Home Visiting Nurse Servs., Inc. v. Shalala,* 525 U.S. 449, 456, 119 S.Ct. 930, 933, 142 L.Ed.2d 919 (1999) (citing 42 U.S.C.A. § 405(h), providing that "no action against ... the [Secretary] or any offi-

cer or employee thereof shall be brought under section 1331 ... of title 28 to recover on any claim under" the Medicare Act). *See also, e.g., GTE North, Inc. v. Strand,* 209 F.3d 909, 916 (6th Cir.2000) (subject matter jurisdiction under § 1331 requires showing that cause of action arose under federal law *and* that § 1331 is not preempted by a more specific statute that strips district courts of subject matter jurisdiction).

7. *Cf., Verizon Maryland, Inc. v. Global Naps, Inc.,* 377 F.3d 355, 369 (4th Cir.2004) ("When a 'case's resolution depends on resolution of a federal question sufficiently substantial to arise under federal law within the meaning of 28 U.S.C. § 1331,' there is § 1331 jurisdiction even though the relevant statute does not explicitly or implicitly provide for a cause of action.").

Well–Pleaded Complaint Rule

In general, subject matter jurisdiction based on a federal question requires that the federal question must appear on a fair reading of a well-pleaded complaint.[8] Federal questions raised in the answer do not create jurisdiction. The significance of the rule is to restrict substantially federal question jurisdiction. It is always possible, and often happens, that important federal questions will arise on the defendant's side of the case, *i.e.,* as a federal defense to a state cause of action. Such defenses, though otherwise appropriate, and perhaps even central to the merits of a case, will not typically confer federal question jurisdiction on a federal district court[9]—not because there is no federal question, but because the federal question arises only in a defense and not in a well-pleaded complaint.[10]

8. *Cf., Duke Power Co. v. Carolina Environmental Study Group, Inc.,* 438 U.S. 59, 98 S.Ct. 2620, 57 L.Ed.2d 595 (1978) (test is not whether plaintiff can actually recover on cause of action; test is whether allegation of federal cause of action is patently without merit and thereby deserves dismissal); *Perpetual Securities, Inc. v. Tang,* 290 F.3d 132, 136–37 (2d Cir.2002) (allegation of federal question must be colorable; mere allegation of federal question, without more, "will not automatically confer federal question jurisdiction"); *Harris v. Owens,* 264 F.3d 1282, 1289 (10th Cir.2001) ("If the federal claim is not wholly frivolous, it suffices to establish federal jurisdiction even if it ultimately is rejected on the merits.").

9. *See, e.g., Penobscot Nation v. Georgia–Pacific Corp.,* 254 F.3d 317 (1st Cir. 2001) (fact that case involves federal issue does not, of itself, satisfy § 1331; Supreme Court "has, for some time, required that it be apparent from the fact of the plaintiff's complaint either that a cause of action arise under federal law ... or at least (in some cases) that a traditional state-law cause of action (e.g., a tort or contract claim) present an important federal issue;" also noting that second alternative is very narrow exception); *Gritchen v. Collier,* 254 F.3d 807 (9th Cir.2001) ("Simply raising a constitutional argument in defense of an action that is brought in state court does not open the federal forum."); *Iowa Management & Consultants, Inc. v. Sac & Fox Tribe,* 207 F.3d 488, 489 (8th Cir.2000) (plaintiff's anticipation that defendant will raise federal law as defense in contract litigation does not create federal question jurisdiction). *Cf., Transit Express, Inc. v. Ettinger,* 246 F.3d 1018, 1024 (7th Cir.2001) ("[T]he mere existence

of a federal regulatory framework does not convey federal jurisdiction over contractual disputes between private parties that are ancillary to the governmental interest.").

10. *See, e.g., Metropolitan Life Ins. Co. v. Taylor,* 481 U.S. 58, 63, 107 S.Ct. 1542, 1546, 95 L.Ed.2d 55 (1987)("It is long settled law that a cause of action arises under federal law only when the plaintiff's well-pleaded complaint raises issues of federal law."). *See also Holmes Group, Inc. v. Vornado Air Circulation Systems, Inc.,* 535 U.S. 826, 122 S.Ct. 1889, 153 L.Ed.2d 13 (2002) (subject matter jurisdiction of Federal Circuit cannot be invoked when sole basis of such jurisdiction is a counterclaim, not a count in complaint; citing close analogy to well-pleaded complaint requirement of § 1331; *Louisville & Nashville R.R. Co. v. Mottley,* 211 U.S. 149, 29 S.Ct. 42, 53 L.Ed. 126 (1908); *Butero v. Royal Maccabees Life Ins. Co.,* 174 F.3d 1207, 1212 (11th Cir. 1999) ("As an affirmative defense, [federal] preemption does not furnish federal subject-matter jurisdiction under 28 U.S.C. § 1331."). *Cf., Club Comanche, Inc. v. Government of Virgin Islands,* 278 F.3d 250, 260 (3d Cir.2002) (action to quiet title to land where defendant's claim to land is based on federal law does not satisfy federal question jurisdiction; noting, however, authority reaching opposite result if action is to remove cloud on title, not to quiet title); *McClelland v. Gronwaldt,* 155 F.3d 507, 512 (5th Cir.1998) (accepting general rule that federal preemption does not, of itself, create jurisdiction under § 1331; noting, however, that when federal law completely preempts an area, so that any "state" claim is actually a mislabeled federal claim, claim is a federal cause of action under § 1331; ac-

It should be noted that the term "well pleaded complaint" is a term of art and does not require the plaintiff to plead with any particular special skill. For purposes of federal question jurisdiction under § 1331 it is only necessary that the facts alleged in the complaint establish a cause of action arising under the Constitution, law or treaties of the United States.[11]

Congressionally Chartered Corporations

Most companies incorporated in the United States are created and organized under the law of a particular state. However, a small number of corporations are created through Congressional enactment. Such federally created corporations may sue or be sued under § 1331 without regard to whether claims at issue arise under federal or state law.[12]

Constitutional Torts

In a few unusual circumstances the Supreme Court has recognized a right to a private suit for a constitutional violation, notwithstanding that neither the relevant constitutional provision nor federal statutory law expressly recognizes such a right.[13] The authority to file such an implied constitutional tort in federal district court is derived from 28 U.S.C.A. § 1331.[14]

Refusing to Plead a Federal Claim: Complete Preemption

Ordinarily, the plaintiff has control of the counts in his complaint and may therefore avoid federal question jurisdiction simply by foregoing claims based on federal law.[15] However, in areas where federal law has completely preempted state law, a plaintiff cannot

knowledging that this principle of complete preemption has limited application).

11. *Franchise Tax Board of California v. Construction Laborers Vacation Trust for Southern California,* 463 U.S. 1, 27–28, 103 S.Ct. 2841, 2855–56, 77 L.Ed.2d 420 (1983) (case arises under § 1331 if "a well-pleaded complaint establishes either that federal law creates the cause of action or that the plaintiff's right to relief necessarily depends on resolution of a substantial question of federal law"). *See, e.g., Radici v. Associated Insurance Companies, Blue Cross Blue Shield of Indiana,* 217 F.3d 737 (9th Cir. 2000) (complaint erroneously asserted diversity jurisdiction; where court could clearly find federal question jurisdiction, error was insignificant). *See also Flowers v. First Hawaiian Bank,* 295 F.3d 966 (9th Cir. 2002) ("An appropriate allegation that a claim arises 'under the Constitution, laws, or treaties of the United States,' 28 U.S.C. § 1331, is sufficient to vest a federal district court with jurisdiction to determine whether or not the claim actually does so arise, and if it does, to decide the issue the claim presents.").

12. *Pacific Railroad Removal Cases,* 115 U.S. 1, 5 S.Ct. 1113, 29 L.Ed. 319 (1885). *See also, e.g., Aliotta v. National R.R. Passenger Corp.,* 315 F.3d 756, 758 n. 1 (7th Cir.2003) ("Federal question jurisdiction exists for congressionally incorporated corporations under 28 U.S.C.A. § 1331.").

13. *See, e.g., Bivens v. Six Unknown Federal Narcotics Agents,* 403 U.S. 388, 91 S.Ct. 1999, 29 L.Ed.2d 619 (1971) (federal officers' alleged violation of Fourth Amendment gives rise to private cause of action).

14. *Correctional Services Corp. v. Malesko,* 534 U.S. 61, 122 S.Ct. 515, 151 L.Ed.2d 456 (2001) (also citing Supreme Court cases creating private rights of action under Fifth and Eighth Amendments, as well as cases refusing to recognize additional rights; refusing to extend *Bivens* principles to permit suit for damages by halfway-house inmate against private defendants).

15. *Caterpillar, Inc. v. Williams,* 482 U.S. 386, 389, 107 S.Ct. 2425, 2427, 96 L.Ed.2d 318 (1987) (normally, non-diverse plaintiff who has federal cause of action but who prefers to avoid federal district court "may avoid federal jurisdiction by exclusive

avoid the federal question by pleading only state law.[16] It should be noted, however, that assertion of federal question jurisdiction under this corollary to the well-pleaded complaint rule applies only where federal law has completely preempted an area.[17]

Preemption as a Cause of Action

As is discussed immediately above, preemption is normally a defense available when a plaintiff has pleaded only state law claims and thereby tried to avoid applicable federal law. However, it is settled that the doctrine also permits a cause of action on grounds of preemption when the plaintiff seeks "to enjoin state officials from interfering with federal rights." [18]

State Claims That Depend on Federal Law

There is another narrow exception to the general rule that jurisdiction under § 1331 may be based only upon an allegation of a federal question in a well-pleaded complaint. Where the plaintiff's cause of action arises from state law, but depends for its resolution on "a substantial question of federal law," it is possible that a district court will have federal question jurisdiction under § 1331.[19] However, attorneys are cautioned that this is indeed a narrow

reliance on state law"); *The Fair v. Kohler Die & Specialty Co.,* 228 U.S. 22, 25, 33 S.Ct. 410, 411, 57 L.Ed. 716 (1913) ("[T]he party who brings a suit is master to decide what law he will rely upon.").

16. *Beneficial National Bank v. Anderson,* 539 U.S. 1, 8, 123 S.Ct. 2058, 2063, 156 L.Ed.2d 1 (2003) ("When the federal statute completely pre-empts the state-law cause of action, a claim which comes within the scope of that cause of action, even if pleaded in terms of state law, is in reality based on federal law."); *Avco Corp. v. Aero Lodge No. 735,* 390 U.S. 557, 88 S.Ct. 1235, 20 L.Ed.2d 126 (1968) (plaintiff sued union for breach of no-strike clause in contract; plaintiff did not assert applicable federal labor law; held, union could remove case to district court, because case was controlled by federal law notwithstanding plaintiff's plea of state law). *See also, Franchise Tax Bd. v. Construction Laborers Vacation Trust,* 463 U.S. 1, 103 S.Ct. 2841, 77 L.Ed.2d 420 (1983) ("[O]riginal federal jurisdiction is unavailable unless it appears that some substantial, disputed question of federal law is a necessary element of one of the well-pleaded state claims, or that one or the other claim is 'really' one of federal law.").

17. *Beneficial National Bank v. Anderson,* 539 U.S. 1, 7, 123 S.Ct. 2058, 2063, 156 L.Ed.2d 1 (2003) (test of complete preemption is whether federal statute "wholly displaces" otherwise relevant state

claims). *See, e.g., Plumbing Industry Bd. v. E.W. Howell Co.,* 126 F.3d 61, 66 (2d Cir. 1997) ("Ordinarily, a claim of preemption is a defense to be raised in the defendant's answer, and thus cannot support jurisdiction ... because it would not appear on the face of a well-pleaded complaint;" different result only when Congress completely preempts an area, so that "any civil complaint raising a state law claim in that area is of necessity so federal in character that it arises under federal law for purposes of 28 U.S.C. § 1331"). *See also, e.g.,* 42 U.S.C.A. § 2014(hh) (federal courts have exclusive jurisdiction over torts arising from nuclear accidents).

18. *Shaw v. Delta Air Lines, Inc.,* 463 U.S. 85, 96 n. 14, 103 S.Ct. 2890, 2899 n. 14, 77 L.Ed.2d 490 (1983).

19. *Grable & Sons Metal Products, Inc. v. Darue Engineering & Manufacturing, Inc.,* 545 U.S. 308, 125 S.Ct. 2363, 2367, 162 L.Ed.2d 257 (2005) (but doctrine requires that state-law claim "really and substantially involves a dispute or controversy respecting the validity, construction, or effect of [federal] law"). *See also Verizon Maryland, Inc. v. Global Naps, Inc.,* 377 F.3d 355(4th Cir.2004) ("When a 'case's resolution depends on resolution of a federal question sufficiently substantial to arise under federal law within the meaning of 28 U.S.C. § 1331,' there is § 1331 jurisdiction even though the relevant statute does not

exception to the general rule, extending the scope of jurisdiction under § 1331 only modestly.[20]

Declaratory Judgments

The well-pleaded complaint rule applies to declaratory judgments in the following fashion. For a declaratory judgment action to rest on federal question jurisdiction, the federal question must be found on the defendant's side of the case. In other words, federal question jurisdiction exists if, had the suit been brought as a conventional case, the pleading of the declaratory judgment defendant, as a conventional plaintiff, would have stated a federal question.[21]

Weak Federal Claims: "Insubstantiality"

It is settled that the probability of defeat on the merits does not, by itself, strip a plaintiff's claim of federal question jurisdiction.[22] However, where a plaintiff files a claim that superficially appears to

explicitly or implicitly provide for a cause of action.").

20. *Empire Healthchoice Assurance, Inc. v. McVeigh,* ___ U.S. ___, 126 S.Ct. 2121, 165 L.Ed.2d 131 (2006) (no subject matter jurisdiction where insurance carrier sought reimbursement for payment of federal government's health insurance costs for third parties; held, claim was based on state law contract rights, not federal law; existence of great interest of federal government in health and welfare of federal workforce is insufficient to convert contract cause of action into federal cause of action; noting that category of exceptions is "special and small"); *Merrell Dow Pharmaceuticals, Inc. v. Thompson,* 478 U.S. 804, 813–14, 106 S.Ct. 3229, 3234, 92 L.Ed.2d 650 (1986) ("[T]he mere presence of a federal issue in a state cause of action does not automatically confer federal-question jurisdiction." Congressional determination that no federal remedy exists for violation of federal statute means that claimed violation of federal statute as element of state claim "is insufficiently 'substantial' to confer federal-question jurisdiction"). *But cf., Downey v. State Farm Fire & Casualty Co.,* 266 F.3d 675, 682 (7th Cir.2001) (insurance contract between private parties fell within § 1331 for two reasons: first, on particular facts of case it implicated provisions of federal flood control program; second, if private insurer did not pay, federal funds were at risk).

21. *Skelly Oil Co. v. Phillips Petroleum Co.,* 339 U.S. 667, 70 S.Ct. 876, 94 L.Ed. 1194 (1950) *See also, e.g., Heydon v. MediaOne of Southeast Michigan, Inc.,* 327 F.3d 466, 470 (6th Cir.2003) ("The Declara-

tory Judgment Act does not create an independent basis for federal subject matter jurisdiction."); *Columbia Gas Transmission Corp. v. Drain,* 237 F.3d 366, 370 (4th Cir. 2001) ("One does need to understand ... that in a declaratory judgment action, the federal right litigated may belong to the declaratory judgment defendant rather than the declaratory judgment plaintiff."); *Northeast Illinois Regional Commuter Railroad Corp. v. Hoey Farina & Downes,* 212 F.3d 1010, 1014 (7th Cir.2000) ("[I]f the plaintiff cannot get into federal court by anticipating what amounts to a federal defense to a state-law cause of action, he also should not be able to use the Declaratory Judgment Act to do so by asserting what is really a preemptive federal defense as the basis of his complaint."); *State of Missouri ex rel. Missouri Highway & Transp. Comm'n v. Cuffley,* 112 F.3d 1332, 1335 (8th Cir.1997) (In a declaratory judgment suit, "we must consider whether a well-pleaded complaint in ... a traditional action would present a federal issue."). *But cf., Textron Lycoming Reciprocating Engine Division, Avco Corp. v. United Automobile, Aerospace and Agricultural Implement Workers of America,* 523 U.S. 653, 659–60, 118 S.Ct. 1626, 1630, 140 L.Ed.2d 863 (1998) ("No decision of this Court has squarely confronted and explicitly upheld federal-question jurisdiction on the basis of the anticipated claim against which the declaratory-judgment plaintiff presents a non-federal defense;" suggesting application of *Skelly Oil* to such facts is unclear, but declining to decide issue).

22. *Bell v. Hood,* 327 U.S. 678, 66 S.Ct. 773, 90 L.Ed. 939 (1946).

be a federal question but is actually only a "dressed up" state claim offered to satisfy federal question jurisdiction, the court may dismiss the claim. This "insubstantiality doctrine" is only employed rarely.[23]

No Jurisdiction to Review State Court Decisions

Even in circumstances where a federal question may be found in a well-pleaded complaint, it is settled that district courts have no authority under § 1331 to hear challenges to existing state court judgments based on the presence of that federal question. Parties who wish to challenge such a judgment may ultimately seek relief from the United States Supreme Court, but the original jurisdiction vested in federal district courts by § 1331 does not extend to appellate jurisdiction over state judgments.[24]

Post-Filing Events

In general, jurisdiction is evaluated on the basis of facts as they existed at the time the complaint was filed. Events that occur subsequent to filing of the complaint normally have no bearing on the court's jurisdictional decision.[25]

Amount in Controversy

Unlike diversity jurisdiction, there is usually no requirement that federal question cases satisfy any specific dollar amount.[26] Thus, if a case arose under the federal civil rights laws, and the amount at issue was only ten dollars, the case would still qualify for federal subject matter jurisdiction.

Citizenship

Unlike diversity jurisdiction, the citizenship of parties in federal question cases has no relevance to subject matter jurisdiction. It is irrelevant, for example, if both the plaintiff and the defendant are citizens of the same foreign country, or if both the plaintiff and the defendant are citizens of the same American state.

ADDITIONAL RESEARCH REFERENCES

C.J.S. Federal Courts §§ 27–43 et seq.

West's Key No. Digests, Federal Courts ⟐161–247.

23. See, e.g., Dixon v. Coburg Dairy, Inc., 330 F.3d 250, 255–56 (4th Cir.2003) (noting that pretextual motive for miscast claim or patently insubstantial and frivolous claim is ground for invocation of rarely used doctrine).

24. District of Columbia Court of Appeals v. Feldman, 460 U.S. 462, 476, 103 S.Ct. 1308, 1311, 75 L.Ed.2d 206 (1983); Rooker v. Fidelity Trust Co., 263 U.S. 413, 416, 44 S.Ct. 149, 150, 68 L.Ed.2d 362 (1923). See also Verizon Maryland, Inc. v. Public Service Commission of Maryland, 535 U.S. 635, 644 n.3, 122 S.Ct. 1753, 1759 n.3, 152 L.Ed.2d 871 (2002) ("The Rooker–Feldman doctrine ... recognizes that

[§ 1331] is a grant of original jurisdiction, and does not authorize district courts to exercise appellate jurisdiction over state-court judgments, which Congress has reserved to this Court.").

25. See, e.g., Sallen v. Corinthians Licenciamentos LTDA, 273 F.3d 14, 23 (1st Cir.2001) (noting only very narrow exceptions to general rule).

26. Arbaugh v. Y&H Corp., ___ U.S. ___, ___, 126 S.Ct. 1235, 1239, 163 L.Ed.2d 1097 (2006) ("Congress amended 28 U.S.C. § 1331 ... to eliminate the amount-in-controversy threshold.").

§ 2.12 Subject Matter Jurisdiction in Federal District Courts—Requirements for Diversity Jurisdiction

CORE CONCEPT

Subject matter jurisdiction based on diversity of citizenship permits a federal district court to hear state causes of action if two basic requirements are fulfilled: the plaintiff must be a citizen of a state or jurisdiction other than that in which the defendant is a citizen; and the amount in controversy must exceed $75,000, exclusive of interest and costs.[1] Such claims are within the concurrent jurisdiction of federal courts, which means that they can be filed in either state court or federal court. Between twenty and twenty-five percent of the cases in federal court are founded on diversity jurisdiction, but a larger percentage of jurisdictional difficulties arise in this area.

APPLICATIONS

Diverse Citizenship

28 U.S.C.A. § 1332 describes four different circumstances that satisfy diversity of citizenship:

(1) when the plaintiff is a citizen of an American state other than that of which the defendant is a citizen;

(2) when the parties on one side are citizens of American states, and the opposing parties are citizens or subjects of foreign states;[2]

(3) when the parties are citizens of different American states, and additional parties are citizens or subjects of foreign states;[3] and

(4) when a foreign state is a plaintiff suing citizens of American states.

Citizenship of an Individual

For purposes of diversity jurisdiction, 28 U.S.C.A. § 1332(a) defines citizenship for an individual in an American state as domicile in the state.[4] Domicile normally requires that the individual has both a physical presence in the state and an intent to reside in the state indefinitely.[5] 28 U.S.C.A. § 1332(a) also provides specifi-

---

1. 28 U.S.C.A. § 1332.

2. *Cf., Iraola & CIA, S.A. v. Kimberly–Clark Corp.*, 232 F.3d 854, 859 (11th Cir. 2000) (citizens of American states on one side of case may themselves be citizens of various American states; rejecting argument that § 1332(a)(2) requires American citizens to be citizens of only one American state).

3. Under this provision it appears settled that citizens or subjects of foreign states may be "additional parties" on both sides of a case. *See, e.g., Dresser Indus., Inc. v. Underwriters at Lloyd's of London*, 106 F.3d 494, 497-98 (3d Cir.1997) (so holding; citing other authority).

4. *See, e.g., Denlinger v. Brennan*, 87 F.3d 214, 216 (7th Cir.1996)(" 'Citizenship' for purposes of § 1332 means domicile rather than residence."). *Cf., Tylka v. Gerber Products Co.*, 211 F.3d 445, 447 (7th Cir. 2000) (reference to parties' "residence," not citizenship, is "obvious shortcoming" that does not satisfy § 1332).

5. *See, e.g., Kanter v. Warner–Lambert Co.*, 265 F.3d 853, 857 (9th Cir.2001) (state citizenship is domicile, not mere residence; residence is only physical presence, while domicile is residence plus intention to make permanent abode); *Palazzo v. Corio*, 232 F.3d 38, 41 (2d Cir.2000) ("An individual's citizenship . . . is determined by his domi-

cally that an alien permanently residing in the United States is, for diversity purposes, a "citizen" of the American state where the alien is domiciled.[6]

Corporate Citizenship

28 U.S.C.A. § 1332(c) provides that for diversity purposes a corporation is a citizen both of the state where it is incorporated and the state in which it has its principal place of business.[7] If a corporation is incorporated in more than one state, then it is a citizen of every state where incorporated.[8] However, a corporation will have only one principal place of business.[9] Thus, depending on the particular facts of incorporation and location of business operations, a corporation may be a citizen of one, two, or even more jurisdictions for diversity purposes.[10] The lower federal courts have developed two distinct approaches to defining "principal place of business": the location of the corporation's headquarters (i.e., its

---

cile;" a natural person "has but one domicile"); *Mas v. Perry*, 489 F.2d 1396, 1399 (5th Cir.1974) (noting twin requirements of physical presence and intent). *See also Wachovia Bank, N.A. v. Schmidt*, 546 U.S. 303, 318, 126 S.Ct. 941, 951, 163 L.Ed.2d 797 (2006) (an individual with multiple residences is nevertheless a citizen of only one state); *Preston v. Tenet Healthsystem Memorial Medical Center, Inc.*, 485 F.3d 793, 797–98 (5th Cir. 2007) ("A person's state of domicile presumptively continues unless rebutted with sufficient evidence of change."); *Mitchell v. Brown & Williamson Tobacco Corp.*, 294 F.3d 1309, 1314 (11th Cir.2002) (incarcerated party is citizen of state in which he was domiciled at time of imprisonment, not state in which he is held); *McCormick v. Aderholt*, 293 F.3d 1254, 1257–58 (11th Cir.2002) (change of domicile requires, concurrently, physical presence at new domicile and intention to reside there indefinitely).

6. *See, e.g., Saadeh v. Farouki*, 107 F.3d 52, 58 (D.C.Cir.1997).

7. *See, e.g., MacGinnitie v. Hobbs Group, LLC*, 420 F.3d 1234, 1239 (11th Cir.2005) ("For diversity purposes a corporation is a citizen of both the state where it is incorporated and the state where it has its principal place of business.").

8. *See, e.g., Freeman v. Northwest Acceptance Corp.*, 754 F.2d 553, 558 (5th Cir. 1985)(if parent and subsidiary are treated as a single corporation, then all states of incorporation are states in which the corporation is a citizen). *Cf., Wild v. Subscription Plus, Inc.*, 292 F.3d 526, 528–29 (7th Cir. 2002) (held, where corporate charter is revoked at time of filing but was later re-

stored, revocation does not affect corporation's status for diversity purposes; noting that state law permitted corporation to sue and be sued in its own name until corporation was actually dissolved). *But see Universal Licensing Corp. v. Paola del Lungo, S.p.A.*, 293 F.3d 579, 581 (2d Cir.2002) (corporation "could not be considered to be incorporated in a state that had revoked its corporate charter").

9. *Wachovia Bank, N.A. v. Schmidt*, ____ U.S. ____, ____, 126 S.Ct. 941, 951, 163 L.Ed.2d 797 (2006) (ordinarily a corporation is a citizen "of at most 2 States;" "[A] corporation surely is not deemed a citizen of every State in which it maintains a business establishment."); *Cf., Cincinnati Insurance Co. v. Eastern Atlantic Insurance Co.*, 260 F.3d 742, 747 (7th Cir.2001) (noting with some irritation that doing business is not the same as the rule that corporate citizenship may rest upon corporation's principal place of business).

10. *See, e.g., Union Pacific Railroad Co. v. 174 Acres of Land Located in Crittenden County*, 193 F.3d 944, 946 (8th Cir.1999) (for purposes of diversity it is "long recognized that a corporation can be incorporated in more than one State"). *Cf., Wachovia Bank, N.A. v. Schmidt*, ____ U.S. ____, ____, 126 S.Ct. 941, 945, 163 L.Ed.2d 797 (2006) (for purposes of diversity, nationally chartered bank is "located," pursuant to 28 U.S.C.A. § 1348, only in state where main office is located); *Lincoln Property Co. v. Roche*, ____ U.S. ____, ____, 126 S.Ct. 606, 614–16, 163 L.Ed.2d 415 (2005) (for purpose of diversity, corporation that is a real party in interest does not acquire citizenship of its affiliates).

corporate nerve center) [11] or the place where the bulk of the corporation's assets may be found.[12] More recently courts have sometimes combined both tests into a "total activity" test to find the principal place of business.[13]

Important: If a corporation has citizenship in more than one jurisdiction, the opposing party must be diverse from *all* the citizenships, or diversity is not established.[14]

Corporations No Longer Doing Business

In unusual cases it may occur that a corporation has *no* place of business at the time a lawsuit is filed. This situation can occur when a corporation remains incorporated but is simply not presently doing any business. Two differing approaches have been developed to deal with that situation. The first looks to the corporation's most recent place of business to help determine citizenship.[15] The second approach concludes that because a corporation ceased operations before the lawsuit was filed, it has no place of business for purposes of diversity jurisdiction.[16]

There is also some uncertainty as to the threshold issue of the kinds of facts necessary to establish whether a corporation has actually ceased business operations.[17] This entire area obviously requires that attorneys consult the local practice.

11. *See, e.g., Metropolitan Life Ins. Co. v. Estate of Cammon,* 929 F.2d 1220, 1222 (7th Cir.1991). (applying "nerve center" approach).

12. *See, e.g., Kelly v. United States Steel Corp.,* 284 F.2d 850 (3d Cir.1960) (looking to center of production or service activities). *Cf., Gadlin v. Sybron International Corp.,* 222 F.3d 797, 800 (10th Cir.2000) (affirming Colorado as principal place of business where president of corporation lived in California, but 36 of 46 employees worked in Colorado and manufacturing, production, and distribution facilities were in Colorado).

13. *See, e.g., United Computer Systems, Inc. v. AT & T Corp.,* 298 F.3d 756 (9th Cir.2002) (principal place of business "is determined by the following two-part inquiry: (1) in what state does a 'substantial predominance' of corporate activity take place? or (2) if the corporation's activities are not predominant in a single state, then the principal place of business is where the majority of its executives and administrative functions are performed"); *Harris v. Black Clawson Co.,* 961 F.2d 547, 549 (5th Cir.1992)(balancing both earlier tests to determine principal place of business). *See also Peterson v. Cooley,* 142 F.3d 181, 184 (4th Cir.1998) (noting approval of both tests in Fourth Circuit and endorsing "neither to the exclusion of the other"). It

should be noted that when an American corporation's principal place of business is found in a foreign country, there is authority holding that the corporation is a citizen of its (American) state of incorporation only, and that the "place of business" standard therefore does not apply at all. *See, e.g., Torres v. Southern Peru Copper Corp.,* 113 F.3d 540 (5th Cir.1997).

14. *See, e.g., Hall v. Rental Assocs., Inc.,* 833 F.2d 370 (D.C.Cir.1987)(plaintiff must be diverse from both corporate citizenships).

15. *See, e.g., Harris v. Black Clawson Co.,* 961 F.2d 547, 551 (5th Cir.1992) (state where corporation last conducted business is relevant to inquiry); *William Passalacqua Builders, Inc. v. Resnick Developers South, Inc.,* 933 F.2d 131, 141 (2d Cir.1991) (diversity includes state where party "last transacted business").

16. *See, e.g., Midlantic National Bank v. Hansen,* 48 F.3d 693, 696 (3d Cir.1995) (inactive corporation has no principal place of business and therefore is citizen of state of incorporation).

17. *See, e.g., Grand Union Supermarkets of the Virgin Islands v. H.E. Lockhart Management,* 316 F.3d 408, 409–11 (3d Cir. 2003) ("corporate trappings," such as paying franchise taxes, filing corporate reports,

Unincorporated Associations

For diversity purposes, unincorporated associations such as partnerships, joint ventures, and labor unions are treated as citizens of every state in which one or more of their members is a citizen.[18] Thus, for very large unincorporated entities, such as national labor unions with members in every state, diversity of citizenship is unlikely to exist between the labor union and its opponent in a lawsuit.[19]

Exception: When the case involves class litigation, a recent amendment to 28 U.S.C.A. § 1332 may produce a different result than was available under established case law. In the future, for class actions, the citizenship of an unincorporated association shall be both the state where it has its principal place of business and the state under whose laws it is organized.[20]

"Stateless" Foreign Persons and Corporations

Section 1332(a)(2) confers diversity jurisdiction in suits between citizens of an American state and citizens or subjects of foreign states (assuming that the amount-in-controversy requirement is also satisfied). However, some parties, who are clearly not citizens of any American state, also may not enjoy the status of citizens of foreign states because they are citizens of some sort of governmental unit that does not possess the elements of sovereignty. Until recently there was substantial disagreement as to whether corporations who are not citizens of American states and do not enjoy full citizen status under a foreign sovereign could nevertheless be citizens or subjects of a foreign state for purposes of § 1332(a)(2). The disagreement is now resolved. Such a corporation is now treated as a citizen or subject of a foreign sovereign for purposes of diversity.[21]

---

or the qualifications required to potentially conduct business in the future are not enough if company is not entering contracts, hiring employees, making sales, maintaining an address, possessing office equipment or owning property; "[A] corporation must actually conduct business for it to have a principal place of business.").

18. *Carden v. Arkoma Associates,* 494 U.S. 185, 195–96, 110 S.Ct. 1015, 1021, 108 L.Ed.2d 157 (1990) (in diversity cases a limited partnership has the citizenship of every general partner and limited partner). *See, e.g., American Vantage Companies, Inc. v. Table Mountain Rancheria,* 292 F.3d 1091, 1093 (9th Cir.2002) ("[A]n unincorporated Indian tribe ... is not a 'citizen' of a state within the meaning of the federal diversity statute ... and thus cannot sue or be sued in diversity."); *Riley v. Merrill Lynch, Pierce, Fenner & Smith, Inc.,* 292 F.3d 1334 (11th Cir.2002) (business trust has citizenship of all its shareholders); *Ninigret Development Corp. v. Narragansett*

Indian Wetuomuck Housing Authority, 207 F.3d 21, 27 (1st Cir.2000) (Indian tribes are not citizens of any state; for diversity purposes they are "analogous to a stateless person;" presence of Indian tribe destroys diversity, "notwithstanding the joinder of other diverse parties"). *Cantor Fitzgerald, L.P. v. Peaslee,* 88 F.3d 152, 154 n. 1 (2d Cir.1996)(Partnerships "take the citizenship of each of their respective partners.").

19. *See, e.g., Belle View Apartments v. Realty Refund Trust,* 602 F.2d 668 (4th Cir.1979) (diversity fails because citizenships of unincorporated associations' memberships overlap).

20. 28 U.S.C.A. § 1332(d)(10).

21. *JPMorgan Chase Bank v. Traffic Stream (BVI) Infrastructure Limited,* 536 U.S. 88, 122 S.Ct. 2054, 153 L.Ed.2d 95 (2002) (British Virgin Islands corporation may appropriately be a citizen of United Kingdom for diversity purposes; issue is governed by construction of § 1332, not

Foreign Citizens Suing One Another

28 U.S.C.A. § 1332 contains no provision authorizing citizens or subjects of one foreign state to sue citizens or subjects of another foreign state in diversity. Thus if a subject of Great Britain sought to use a federal district court to sue a citizen of Brazil on a state cause of action, diversity jurisdiction would not exist, unless an additional party was a citizen of an American state.[22]

District of Columbia, Puerto Rico, and U.S. Territories

For purposes of diversity jurisdiction, 28 U.S.C.A. § 1332(e) treats jurisdictions such as the District of Columbia, Puerto Rico, the Virgin Islands, Guam, etc., as American states. Thus, persons domiciled in those jurisdictions will typically be treated as citizens of those "states" for diversity purposes.[23]

U.S. Citizens Domiciled in Foreign Countries

Americans domiciled abroad are obviously not domiciled in an American state. Thus, they cannot be citizens of an American state for diversity purposes. At the same time, American citizens domiciled abroad are not citizens or subjects of the foreign countries in which they reside. Thus they do not qualify for diversity jurisdiction as citizens or subjects of foreign states. The result, anomalous as it may seem, is that American citizens domiciled abroad do not qualify for diversity jurisdiction under any of the four categories of 28 U.S.C.A. § 1332, and thus may not sue or be sued in a federal district court on the basis of diversity jurisdiction.[24]

foreign law (although in instant case foreign law and § 1332 are harmonious); held, corporation may be a citizen of United Kingdom notwithstanding that it is organized under law of British Overseas Territory, not law of Britain itself).

22. *See, e.g., MCC-Marble Ceramic Ctr., Inc. v. Ceramica Nuova d'Agostino, S.p.A.,* 144 F.3d 1384, 1385 n. 15 (11th Cir.1998) (Section 1332 provides "no statutory grant for suits between aliens unless a citizen of a State is present."). *See also, Franceskin v. Credit Suisse,* 214 F.3d 253, 258 (2d Cir. 2000) (if plaintiff is citizen of a foreign country and defendant is incorporated in a different foreign country but maintains principal place of business in United States, diversity is still lacking). *Cf. Dresser Indus., Inc. v. Underwriters at Lloyd's of London,* 106 F.3d 494, 497–98 (3d Cir.1997) (if foreign subjects are only additional parties to suit between citizens of different American states, diversity jurisdiction may be satisfied). *But see Universal Licensing Corp. v. Paola del Lungo, S.p.A.,* 293 F.3d 579, 581 (2d Cir.2002) ("[D]iversity is lacking … where the only parties are foreign entities, or where on one side there are citizens and

aliens and on the opposite side there are only aliens.").

23. Until recently, the relevant provision was § 1332(d). However, that provision is now re-designated as § 1332(e). *See, e.g., United States v. Cirino,* 419 F.3d 1001, 1004 (9th Cir.2005) ("Congress … has determined that Puerto Rico is to be treated as a 'state' for purposes of diversity jurisdiction."); *Brown v. Francis,* 75 F.3d 860, 865 (3d Cir.1996)(for purposes of diversity jurisdiction, Virgin Islands is a state). *But cf., Barwood, Inc. v. District of Columbia,* 202 F.3d 290, 292 (D.C.Cir.2000) (District of Columbia is treated as a state under § 1332, but it is "not a citizen of a state (or of itself)"; thus, where District of Columbia is a defendant, there is no diversity).

24. *See, e.g., Coury v. Prot,* 85 F.3d 244, 248 (5th Cir.1996) ("An American national, living abroad, cannot sue or be sued in federal court under diversity jurisdiction … unless that party is a citizen, *i.e.* domiciled, in a particular state of the United States."); *Cresswell v. Sullivan & Cromwell,* 922 F.2d 60, 68–69 (2d Cir.1990) (noting failure of diversity where some plaintiffs and several partners of defendant law

Note, however, that such persons may qualify for federal court if the cause of action rests on a federal question, discussed above. It is also possible that such persons may sue or be sued in federal court if they fit within the description of supplemental jurisdiction, discussed below.

Timing of Citizenship

The parties must be diverse at the time the suit is filed.[25] It is irrelevant that the parties may not have been diverse at the time the cause of action arose,[26] or that a party diverse at the time of filing acquires a non-diverse citizenship in the course of the lawsuit.[27] Thus, if a citizen of New York seeks to sue another New York citizen in federal district court over a state cause of action, the plaintiff could create diversity of citizenship by making a genuine change of domicile from New York to another jurisdiction prior to filing suit. Conversely, if the parties are diverse when the suit is filed, a subsequent change of domicile will not *defeat* diversity, either.[28]

It should be noted that recent Congressional amendments to 28 U.S.C.A. § 1332, governing diversity jurisdiction, have tended to adopt the existing case law approach to the timing of diversity

firm were United States citizens domiciled abroad); *Sadat v. Mertes,* 615 F.2d 1176, 1183 (7th Cir.1980)(An American citizen's domicile abroad does not thereby make him a citizen of a foreign state.).

25. *Grupo Dataflux v. Atlas Global Group, L.P.,* 541 U.S. 567, 124 S.Ct. 1920, 158 L.Ed.2d 866 (2004) (party's post-filing change in citizenship cannot cure lack of subject matter jurisdiction that existed at time of filing); *Dole Food Co. v. Patrickson,* 538 U.S. 468, 477, 123 S.Ct. 1655, 1662, 155 L.Ed.2d 643 (2003) ("It is well settled ... that federal-diversity jurisdiction depends on the citizenship of the parties at the time suit is filed."). *But see Wild v. Subscription Plus, Inc.,* 292 F.3d 526, 528 (7th Cir.2002) (held, where corporate charter is revoked at time of filing but was later restored, revocation does not affect corporation's status for diversity purpose; noting that state law permitted corporation to sue and be sued in its own name until corporation was actually dissolved; citing this circumstances as exception to general rule); *Soberay Machine & Equipment Co. v. MRF Ltd.,* 181 F.3d 759, 763 (6th Cir.1999) ("Although we agree that a party may not create diversity by dropping a nondiverse and indispensable party, we note that it is appropriate to drop a nondiverse and dispensable party from litigation in order to achieve diversity.").

26. *See, e.g., Associated Ins. Management Corp. v. Arkansas General Agency,*

Inc., 149 F.3d 794 (8th Cir.1998) ("[W]e determine diversity of citizenship at the time an action is filed; ... the district court cannot retroactively create diversity jurisdiction if it did not exist when the complaint was filed."). *Rodriguez–Diaz v. Sierra–Martinez,* 853 F.2d 1027, 1029 (1st Cir. 1988)("It is the domicile at the time suit is filed which controls, and the fact that the plaintiff has changed his domicile with the purpose of bringing a diversity action in federal court is irrelevant."). *See also Hartford Insurance Group v. Lou–Con, Inc.,* 293 F.3d 908 (5th Cir.2002) (facts underlying jurisdictional amount are judged as of filing complaint).

27. *See, e.g., Bank One, Texas, N.A. v. Montle,* 964 F.2d 48, 49 (1st Cir. 1992)("Domicile is determined as of the time the suit is filed, and once diversity jurisdiction is established, it is not lost by a later change in domicile."). *But cf., Dominium Austin Partners, L.L.C. v. Emerson,* 248 F.3d 720, 725 (8th Cir.2001) (subject matter jurisdiction is usually evaluated at commencement of action; exception exists where nondiverse but indispensable party is later joined under Rule 19).

28. *Cf., Meridian Security Insurance Co. v. Sadowski,* 441 F.3d 536, 538 (7th Cir. 2006) (if amount in controversy was met at outset, subsequent award of less than that amount does not terminate diversity jurisdiction).

jurisdiction.[29]

Complete Diversity

To satisfy diversity jurisdiction, *all* plaintiffs must have citizenship different from that of *all* defendants.[30] There is no requirement that plaintiffs have citizenships different from one another, or that defendants have citizenships different from each other. Thus if a plaintiff was a citizen of Ohio, diversity jurisdiction would fail if any defendant was also a citizen of Ohio. However, if five plaintiffs were citizens of Ohio, diversity jurisdiction could still exist if all defendants were citizens of states other than Ohio.

Diversity Jurisdiction in Class Actions

Congress recently enacted[31] major changes in the requirements for diversity jurisdiction in most cases involving class actions governed by Rule 23.[32] These changes are fairly complex, but their net effect will sometimes be to ease substantially the requirements for diversity jurisdiction in class actions from what had been the established requirements for such jurisdiction in class lawsuits. The changes, incorporated as an amendment to 28 U.S.C.A. § 1332,[33] provide that diversity jurisdiction shall be satisfied when the following new requirements are met. First, diversity jurisdiction for class actions will be satisfied when the amount in controversy exceeds $5,000,000, exclusive of interest and costs. This amount in controversy need not be satisfied by every single individual member of the class. Instead, the individual claims of the class members will be

---

29. 28 U.S.C.A. § 1332(d)(7) (citizenship in most class actions to be determined as of date of filing original or amended complaint, or, if case did not originally qualify for federal subject matter jurisdiction, as of date federal subject matter jurisdiction might have existed).

30. *Exxon Mobil Corp. v. Allapattah Services, Inc.,* 545 U.S. 546, ___, 125 S.Ct. 2611, 2617, 162 L.Ed.2d 502 (2005) (acknowledging that complete diversity is not a constitutional mandate, but "we have consistently interpreted § 1332 as requiring complete diversity: In a case with multiple plaintiffs and multiple defendants, the presence of a single defendant deprives the district court of original diversity jurisdiction over the entire action;" citing *Strawbridge, supra*); *Strawbridge v. Curtiss,* 7 U.S. (3 Cranch) 267, 267, 2 L.Ed. 435 (1806).

31. *See, e.g., Plubell v. Merck & Co., Inc.,* 434 F.3d 1070, 1074 (8th Cir.2006) (original complaint pre-dated effective date of legislation, but amended complaint post-dated effective date of legislation; held, where amended complaint relates back to date of original pleading, applicable law on jurisdiction is law as of date original complaint was filed); *Bush v. Cheaptickets, Inc.,* 425 F.3d 683, 686 (9th Cir.2005) (by its

terms, new legislation applied to all class actions "commenced on or after" February 18, 2005; for purpose of this law, action commences when it commenced in state court as defined by state law; date of removal is *not* date that action commenced); *Pritchett v. Office Depot, Inc.,* 420 F.3d 1090, 1094 (10th Cir.2005) (same). *But cf., Knudsen v. Liberty Mutual Insurance Co.,* 435 F.3d 755, 758 (7th Cir.2006) (original complaint filed in state court prior to effective date of legislation; amended complaint, involving new claims, was filed after effective date of new legislation; held, amended complaint did not relate back, and defendant was therefore entitled to benefit of new legislation's broader definition of subject matter jurisdiction; "[A] novel claim tacked on to an existing case commences new litigation for purposes of the Class Action Fairness Act.").

32. *See* Fed.R.Civ.P. 23.

33. As amended, the provision that is currently designated as § 1332(d) is renamed § 1332(e). A new provision, governing jurisdiction in class actions, is inserted as 28 U.S.C.A. § 1332(d).

aggregated to determine if the amount in controversy has been satisfied.[34] Second, diversity jurisdiction in most class actions now requires that one of three other requirements is met. Diversity is satisfied if, in addition to meeting the amount in controversy requirement: (a) any member of a class of plaintiffs is a citizen of an American state different from the American state of citizenship of any defendant; (b) any member of a class of plaintiffs is a foreign state or a citizen or subject of a foreign state and any defendant is a citizen of an American state; or (c) any member of a class of plaintiffs is a citizen of an American state and any defendant is a foreign state or a citizen or subject of a foreign state.[35] It is worth noting that *all* class actions based on diversity must satisfy the amount in controversy requirement. However, the additional requirement for diverse citizenship can be met by satisfying *any* of the three foregoing descriptions of diverse citizenship.[36]

It should be noted that recent legislation affecting jurisdiction in class actions did not, for the most part, change one settled rule. It remains true that, even in class actions, the party asserting federal jurisdiction through removal or an original filing bears the burden of establishing such jurisdiction.[37] However, the enactment creates an exception to that general rule in one circumstance. When, in a case removed to federal court in which the removing defendants have already met their jurisdictional burdens, plaintiffs who seek remand to state court under the newly created "local controversy" exception[38] must bear the burden of proving that the "local controversy" exception applies.[39] The "local controversy" exception is discussed in greater detail in the pages immediately following.

Declining Diversity Jurisdiction in Class Actions

Notwithstanding the possibility that a class action has met the requirements for diversity jurisdiction discussed immediately above, the recent amendments to § 1332 also provide federal district courts

---

34. 28 U.S.C.A. § 1332(d)(6). *See, e.g., Pastor v. State Farm Mutual Automobile Insurance Co.,* 487 F.3d 1042, 1044 (7th Cir. 2007) ("Although the class members' claims are small the Class Action Fairness Act authorized the aggregation of class members' claims to satisfy the minimum amount in controversy required in a diversity suit, which in the case of a suit governed by the Act is $5 million."); *Frazier v. Pioneer Americas, L.L.C.,* 455 F.3d 542 n. 10 (5th Cir.2006) (new legislation "explicitly allows aggregation of each class member's claim"). *But cf., DiTolla v. Doral Dental IPA of New York, L.L.C.,* 469 F.3d 271, 276–77 (2d Cir. 2006) (where total pool of funds is not in dispute, only that part of fund which is in controversy may be used to satisfy amount in controversy requirement; acknowledging that on instant facts calculation of amount in controversy is difficult).

35. *See, e.g., Blockbuster, Inc. v. Galeno,* 472 F.3d 53, 56 (2d Cir. 2006) (noting minimal diversity requirement).

36. 28 U.S.C.A. § 1332(d)(2).

37. *See, e.g., Blockbuster, Inc. v. Galeno, Inc.,* 472 F.3d 53, 57 (2d Cir. 2006) (identifying settled rule); *Morgan v. Gay,* 471 F.3d 469, 473 (3d Cir. 2006) ("[T]he party seeking to remove the case to federal court bears the burden to establish that the amount in controversy requirement is satisfied.").

38. 28 U.S.C.A. § 1332(d)(4).

39. *See, e.g., Hart v. FedEx Ground Package System, Inc.,* 457 F.3d 675, 680 (7th Cir. 2006); *Evans v. Walter Industries, Inc.,* 449 F.3d 1159, 1165 (11th Cir. 2006).

with some substantial opportunities to refrain from hearing such a class lawsuit. The first of these, governed by new § 1332(d)(3), provides the court with discretion to decline to exercise diversity jurisdiction when two requirements are met[40] and some other prudential considerations are weighed. The first of the two requirements is that more than one-third and less than two-thirds of the total membership of a plaintiff class is comprised of citizens of the state in which the action was originally filed. The second requirement is that the "primary" defendants are citizens of the state in which the action was originally filed.[41] In addition to the existence of those two requirements the court must also weigh the following factors.

(a) whether the claims in question involve matters of national or interstate interest;

(b) whether the claims will be controlled by the law of the state where the case was originally filed or by the law of another state or states;

(c) whether the plaintiffs have, through artful pleading, sought to avoid federal subject matter jurisdiction;

(d) whether the action was filed in a court with a clear relationship with the plaintiffs, the underlying events, or the defendants;

(e) whether the number of class plaintiffs who are citizens of the state in which the case was filed is substantially larger than the number of plaintiffs from any other state, and the citizenship of other plaintiffs is dispersed among a significant variety of other states; and

(f) whether during the three years prior to filing the instant action, some other class action has been filed asserting similar claims, without regard to whether the claims were asserted on behalf of the identical plaintiffs.[42]

"Local Controversy" Exception

While § 1332(d)(3) provides the court with discretion to refuse to exercise diversity jurisdiction in class actions, § 1332(d)(4) identifies factual situations in which the court must decline to exercise jurisdiction. Specifically, § 1332(d)(4) directs the court to decline jurisdiction when three requirements are met. First, more than two-thirds of the class members of a plaintiff class are citizens of the state in which the case was originally filed.[43] Second, one or more

---

40. *See, e.g., Frazier v. Pioneer Americas, L.L.C.,* 455 F.3d 542 (5th Cir.2006) (plaintiffs have burden of showing applicability of exceptions under § 1332(d)(3)); *Evans v. Walter Industries, Inc.,* 449 F.3d 1159, 1164 (11th Cir.2006) (burden of showing jurisdictional basis of removal falls on defendant/opponent of class; but burden of showing applicability of exceptions to removal under new legislation falls on class members). *But see Miedema v. Maytag*

Corp., 450 F.3d 1322, 1327–28 (11th Cir. 2006) (placing burden on removing party); *Abrego v. Dow Chemical Co.,* 443 F.3d 676, 685 (9th Cir.2006) (same as *Miedema*).

41. 28 U.S.C.A. § 1332(d)(3).

42. 28 U.S.C.A. § 1332(d)(3).

43. *But cf., Preston v. Tenet Healthsystem Memorial Medical Center, Inc.,* 485 F.3d 793, 801 (5th Cir. 2007) (acknowledging "that marshaling evidence of citizen-

defendants from whom the class seeks substantial relief and whose conduct allegedly forms a significant basis for the class claims is a citizen of the state in which the case was originally filed. Third, the principal injuries pleaded by the class or any related conduct were incurred in the state in which the action was originally filed, and either of two other elements are met: in the preceding three years prior to the instant action, no similar allegations have been filed against any of the same defendants by the same or other plaintiffs; or, both two-thirds or more of the class plaintiffs and the primary defendants are citizens of the state in which the action was originally filed.[44]

Unlike the provisions of the recent legislation that leave unchanged the pre-existing burdens of proof regarding subject matter jurisdiction, § 1332(d)(4) has been construed in removal cases to place the burden of proving the applicability of the "local controversy" exception on the plaintiffs. Thus, if the defendants have met their burden of proving the existence of diversity jurisdiction, the burden shifts to the plaintiffs to show that the "local controversy" exception should be invoked to block the exercise of federal subject matter jurisdiction.[45]

Class Actions Unaffected by Amendments

Notwithstanding the broad scope of the recent amendment to § 1332, certain fairly narrow categories of class actions are expressly excluded from the scope of the new provisions. Specifically, amended § 1332 does not apply to any class action in which the primary defendants are "States, State officials, or other governmental entities against whom the district court may be foreclosed from ordering relief."[46] Thus, for example, a suit against a state that was barred by the Eleventh Amendment of the Constitution[47] if it had been brought by an individual plaintiff does not somehow acquire subject matter jurisdiction because it has been brought by a class of plaintiffs pursuant to new § 1332. Additionally, the amendments to § 1332 may not be used to satisfy diversity jurisdiction when the aggregate number of class plaintiffs is less than 100.[48] It may, however, be possible to satisfy subject matter jurisdiction over classes that are comprised of less than 100 plaintiffs through appli-

ship for the unnamed class members may be a formidable task", but still noting obligation to prove elements of citizenship).

44. 28 U.S.C.A. § 1332(d)(4).

45. *See, e.g., Hart v. FedEx Ground Package System, Inc.,* 457 F.3d 675, 680 (7th Cir. 2006); *Evans v. Walter Industries, Inc.,* 449 F.3d 1159, 1165 (11th Cir. 2006).

46. 28 U.S.C.A. § 1332(d)(5)(A). *See also Frazier v. Pioneer Americas, L.L.C.,* 455 F.3d 542 (5th Cir.2006) (plaintiffs have burden of showing applicability of exceptions under § 1332(d)(5)); *Evans v. Walter Industries, Inc.,* 449 F.3d 1159, 1164 (11th

Cir.2006) (burden of showing jurisdictional basis of removal falls on defendant/opponent of class; but burden of showing applicability of exceptions to removal under new legislation falls on class members). *But see Miedema v. Maytag Corp.,* 450 F.3d 1322, 1327–28 (11th Cir.2006) (placing burden on removing party).

47. U.S. Const., Amend. 11.

48. 28 U.S.C.A. § 1332(d)(5)(B). *See, e.g., Blockbuster, Inc. v. Galeno,* 472 F.3d 53, 56 (2d Cir. 2006) (applying requirement of at least 100 class members).

cation of the Supreme Court's recent holding on the use of supplemental jurisdiction[49] in certain class actions. This possibility is discussed at greater length in the treatment of both supplemental jurisdiction and Federal Rule of Civil Procedure 23 elsewhere in this book.

Finally, the new version of § 1332 does not apply to class actions that rest "solely" upon a claim arising under certain federal securities laws, the laws of a state involving the internal affairs of corporations or other business entities (provided that the corporation or entity is incorporated or organized in that state), or laws that relate to rights and duties, including fiduciary duties, created by any security or the federal Securities Act of 1933.[50] Where parties may seek to file such cases on the basis of diversity jurisdiction, case law requirements for subject matter jurisdiction will presumably be the applicable standard.[51]

Mass Actions

As amended by the Class Action Fairness Act of 2005, § 1332(d) treats many mass actions as the equivalent of class actions for purposes of diversity jurisdiction or removal from state court. The definition of a mass action, as provided in § 1332(d)(11)(B)(i), is a civil action in which one hundred or more persons each seek monetary relief and a joint trial because their claims involve common questions of law or fact.[52] Section 1132(d)(11)(B)(i) also provides that mass actions which meet that definition are deemed eligible for treatment as class actions only if they meet the additional requirement that each plaintiff's individual claim meets the amount in controversy requirement established in § 1332(a),[53] governing more conventional non-class diversity actions. Because § 1332(a) requires an amount in controversy in excess of $75,000 for each plaintiff's claims, it establishes a more rigorous standard that must be met before all of § 1332(d) can apply to a case. By contrast, class action plaintiffs entitled to the full range of benefits of § 1332(d)(2)–(10) need meet only the often more modest requirement that the aggregate claim of the entire class exceeds $5,000,000.[54]

49. *Exxon Mobil Corp. v. Allapattah Services, Inc.,* 545 U.S. 546, 125 S.Ct. 2611, 162 L.Ed.2d 502 (2005) (overruling existing precedent; holding that in some circumstances district court's supplemental jurisdiction may extend to cases in which class members would not satisfy amount-in-controversy requirement for diversity jurisdiction).

50. 28 U.S.C.A. § 1332(d)(9).

51. *See, e.g., Exxon Mobil Corp. v. Allapattah Services, Inc.,* 545 U.S. 546, 125 S.Ct. 2611, 162 L.Ed.2d 502 (2005) (in some circumstances district court's supplemental jurisdiction may extend to cases in which class members would not satisfy amount-in-

controversy requirement for diversity jurisdiction); *Supreme Tribe of Ben Hur v. Cauble,* 255 U.S. 356, 41 S.Ct. 338, 65 L.Ed. 673 (1921) (in class actions based on diversity jurisdiction, citizenship of class representatives (not all members of class) should be compared to citizenship of opponents of class).

52. 28 U.S.C.A. § 1332(d)(11)(B)(i).

53. 28 U.S.C.A. § 1332(d)(11)(B).

54. 28 U.S.C.A. § 1332(d)(2). *But see Lowery v. Alabama Power Co.,* 483 F.3d 1184, 1201 (11th Cir. 2007) (suggesting that mass actions may only have to meet the aggregate amount in controversy require-

If a mass action falls within the scope of § 1332(d)(11), and is not excepted by provisions of § 1332(d)(11)(B)(ii), it will be treated like most class actions for purposes of diversity jurisdiction and removal.[55] Section 1332(d)(11)(B)(ii) is discussed immediately below.

Exceptions: Mass Actions Not Within the Scope of § 1332(d)

Section 1332(d)(11)(B)(ii) expressly provides that certain civil actions containing elements of mass actions shall nevertheless not be treated as mass actions for purposes of 1332(d) if those civil actions fall into any of several categories. The four enumerated exceptions are:

Local Events: A lawsuit is not a mass action for purposes of § 1332(d) if the claims involved arise from events that occurred in the state where the lawsuit was filed and the injuries from the event are found in that state or contiguous states.[56]

Joinder by Defendant: A lawsuit is not a mass action for purposes of § 1332(d) if the claims in question were joined by a motion of a defendant.[57]

Public Interest Claims/Private Attorneys General: Some state laws authorize some lawsuits by private plaintiffs on behalf of the general public. These lawsuits are distinguishable from cases brought to assert rights belonging to individuals or classes of claimants. When such public interest claims form the entire basis of a lawsuit, the case cannot be a mass action for purposes of § 1332(d).[58]

Consolidation for Pretrial Proceedings Only: If the claims at issue have been consolidated for pretrial purposes only, the lawsuit cannot be a mass action within the meaning of § 1332(d).[59]

An additional exception to the treatment of mass claims as mass actions for purposes of § 1332(d) is implicit in the requirement that mass actions must involve individual claims for monetary relief in

---

ment of $5,000,000). It is respectfully suggested that the 11th Circuit has made an error on this point, for it appears clear that for mass actions (as opposed to class actions), § 1332(d)(11)(B)(i) expressly provides that the amount in controversy is defined by § 1332(a), which requires more than $75,000 for each claim, making the $5,000,000 standard of § 1332(d)(2) inapplicable to mass actions. The error may only be an administrative error, for *Lowery* later quotes accurately the applicability of § 1332(a). 483 F.3d at 1202 (quoting without comment about earlier statement). See *also Pastor v. State Farm Mutual Automobile Insurance Co.,* 487 F.3d 1042, 1044 (7th Cir. 2007) ("Although the class members' claims are small, the Class Action Fairness Act authorized the aggregation of

class members' claims to satisfy the amount in controversy required in a diversity suit, which in the case of a suit governed by the Act is $5 million."); *Frazier v. Pioneer Americas, L.L.C.,* 455 F.3d 542 n. 10 (5th Cir. 2006) (new legislation "explicitly allows aggregation of each class member's claim").

55. *See, e.g., Lowery v. Alabama Power Co.,* 483 F.3d 1184, 1195 (11th Cir. 2007) (any lawsuit qualifying as a mass action is generally a class action for purposes of diversity jurisdiction and removal).

56. 28 U.S.C.A. § 1332(d)(11)(B)(ii)(I).

57. 28 U.S.C.A. § 1332(d)(11)(B)(ii)(II).

58. 28 U.S.C.A. § 1332(d)(11)(B)(ii)(III).

59. 28 U.S.C.A. § 1332(d)(11)(B)(ii)(IV).

amounts greater than $75,000.[60] The requirement that claims for monetary relief be an element of a mass action necessarily means that cases involving claims only for non-monetary equitable relief cannot be treated as mass actions under § 1332(d).

Restrictions on Transfers of Mass Actions

In many cases 28 U.S.C.A. § 1407 authorizes transfer of cases involving common questions of fact so that they may be consolidated in a particular district.[61] One unusual feature of § 1332(d) is a provision prohibiting transfer under § 1407 unless a majority of the plaintiffs in an action request such transfer.[62] Thus, in mass actions, it may be possible to remove a case from state court to a federal district court that sits in the same state, but transfer to another federal district court will normally be unavailable to a defendant. An exception to this exceptional provision provides, however, that § 1332(d)(11)(C) does not apply to cases certified, or proposed to be certified, as class actions pursuant to Rule 23 of the Federal Rules of Civil Procedure.[63]

Mass Actions: Statutes of Limitations

Section 1332(d)(11)(D) tolls statutes of limitations for claims included in a mass action for the period that the action is in a federal court.[64]

State Constraints on Diversity Jurisdiction

It is settled that where the requirements of § 1332 are met, a state has no authority to deprive a district court of diversity jurisdiction.[65]

Exceptions for Domestic Relations and Probate Cases

Although § 1332 is silent on the issue, federal courts routinely do not exercise diversity jurisdiction over cases in which divorce, child custody or matters of probate are at issue.[66] However, these

---

60. 28 U.S.C.A. § 1332(d)(11)(B)(i).

61. 28 U.S.C.A. § 1407(a).

62. 28 U.S.C.A. § 1332(d)(11)(C).

63. 28 U.S.C.A. § 1332(d)(11)(C)(ii).

64. 28 U.S.C.A. § 1332(d)(11)(D).

65. *See, e.g., Superior Beverage Co. v. Schieffelin & Co.,* 448 F.3d 910, 917 (6th Cir.2006) ("[A] state may not deprive a federal court of jurisdiction merely by declaring in a statute that it holds exclusive jurisdiction."); *Dunlap v. Nestle USA, Inc.,* 431 F.3d 1015, 1017 (7th Cir.2005) ("[S]tate law may not enlarge or contract federal jurisdiction. ... The exclusivity provisions of Illinois' workers' compensation statute do not (indeed, may not) affect the scope of the jurisdictional authority granted to the federal courts by Congress."). *See also Railway Co. v. Whitton's Administrator,* 80 U.S. (13 Wall.) 270, 286, 20 L.Ed.

571 (1871) ("In all cases, where a general right is thus conferred, it can be enforced in any Federal court within the State having jurisdiction of the parties.").

66. *Markham v. Allen,* 326 U.S. 490, 494, 66 S.Ct. 296, 298, 90 L.Ed. 256 (1946) ("[A] federal court has no jurisdiction to probate a will or administer an estate;" but the district court may hear a suit against an estate, provided it is only to establish the claim against the estate and does not interfere with the probate court's jurisdiction or proceedings). *See also Moser v. Pollin,* 294 F.3d 335, 338 (2d Cir.2002) (probate matter is outside scope of diversity jurisdiction in either of two circumstances: when district court is asked "to directly probate a will or administer an estate;" or when hearing the action would cause district court to interfere with probate proceedings, disrupt state jurisdiction of probate court, or take control

exceptions to the application of diversity jurisdiction are construed narrowly. Thus, if a case involved a dispute over property arising out of a divorce decree previously granted, the federal court might hear the case if the requirements of diversity jurisdiction were otherwise satisfied.[67]

Insurance Companies and Direct Action Suits

A few states permit plaintiffs in tort actions to sue the defendant's insurance company directly, rather than proceeding first against the alleged tortfeasor. 28 U.S.C.A. § 1332(c)(1) takes account of that circumstance, providing that in such cases insurance companies will be treated as citizens of the state where the alleged tortfeasors have citizenship, in addition to the states where the insurance company has citizenship. When applicable, the practical effect of this provision is to reduce somewhat a plaintiff's possibilities for obtaining diversity jurisdiction.

It should be noted that attribution of an insured's citizenship to the insured's own insuror applies only to circumstances where a plaintiff has a claim against the insured that may also properly be asserted against the insuror without necessarily first joining or suing the insured.[68] If the suit is a dispute between the insuror and the insured, conventional standards of diversity jurisdiction apply.[69]

Decedents, Infants, and Incompetents

28 U.S.C.A. § 1332(c)(2) provides that, for diversity purposes, parties acting as representatives of decedents' estates, infants, or incompetent persons shall be deemed to take the citizenship of the estate or persons whom they represent.[70] 28 U.S.C.A. § 1332(c)(2) was enacted to preclude creation of diversity in such cases simply by appointing a representative of different citizenship than the party the representative opposes.

Diversity Jurisdiction and Federal Causes of Action

In the ordinary course of events it would seem unnecessary to decide whether, if the requirements for diversity jurisdiction are met, such jurisdiction could attach to a federally created cause of action. Such causes of action would, after all, normally be tested

---

of property that was controlled by probate court).

67. *Ankenbrandt v. Richards,* 504 U.S. 689, 112 S.Ct. 2206, 119 L.Ed.2d 468 (1992) (domestic relations exception only prevents issuing divorce, alimony, or child custody decrees). *See, e.g., Rash v. Rash,* 173 F.3d 1376 (11th Cir.1999) (rule of refusing jurisdiction is not absolute and is narrowly confined; court will not adjudicate parties' "domestic affairs," but will resolve dispute over assets).

68. *See, e.g., Searles v. Cincinnati Ins. Co.,* 998 F.2d 728, 729 (9th Cir.1993) (so holding).

69. *See, e.g., Clark v. Chubb Group of Insurance Cos.,* 337 F.3d 687 (6th Cir.2003) (Ohio insured sued insurer that was citizen of state other than Ohio; held, standard requirements for diversity apply because suit was not direct action suit governed by § 1332(c)(1)).

70. *See, e.g., PaineWebber, Inc. v. Cohen,* 276 F.3d 197, 201 (6th Cir.2001) (for diversity purposes § 1332(c)(2) makes representatives of decedent's estate citizen of same state as decedent); *Long v. Sasser,* 91 F.3d 645, 647 (4th Cir.1996) (same).

against the requirements for federal question jurisdiction.[71] However, in unusual circumstances where Congress has created a federal cause of action but has withheld federal question jurisdiction, there is some authority permitting district courts to use diversity jurisdiction if the requirements for diversity are met.[72]

Citizenship of Persons not Joined as Parties

It is now settled that the citizenship of a person not joined as a party cannot destroy diversity jurisdiction, notwithstanding that the absent person has an interest in the lawsuit.[73] Thus, if a plaintiff has a state claim against one potential defendant who is diverse and another potential defendant who is not diverse, and the non-diverse defendant is not an indispensable party under Rule 19,[74] the plaintiff may choose to sue only the diverse defendant and thereby satisfy diversity jurisdiction.

Collusive Invocation of Diversity Jurisdiction

The diversity provisions of 28 U.S.C.A. § 1332 are modified by 28 U.S.C.A. § 1359, governing collusive invocation of jurisdiction. Section 1359 provides that if a party, "by assignment or otherwise," has been "improperly or collusively . . . joined" to invoke jurisdiction, the federal district court will not have jurisdiction. Section 1359 prohibits invocation of diversity jurisdiction where a corporation, not diverse from the defendant, assigned its cause of action to another person for the primary purpose of creating diversity. This rule applies even if the assignment itself is lawful and valid under state law.[75] However, it is still reasonable to assume that an assignment lawful under state law, and made primarily for purposes other than to create diversity, may surmount this obstacle.[76]

Fraudulent Joinder and Removal

Fraudulent joinder occurs when a plaintiff who has sued in state court joins a nondiverse defendant against whom the plaintiff obviously has no cause of action under settled law. The purpose of such joinder, of course, is to prevent removal of the real case, against a diverse defendant, to federal district court. When the true

---

71. 28 U.S.C.A. § 1331.

72. *See, e.g., Gottlieb v. Carnival Corp.,* 436 F.3d 335, 340 (2d Cir.2006) (permitting use of § 1332 in case arising under Telephone Consumer Protection Act, 47 U.S.C.A. § 227 *et seq.*; "Nothing in § 1332 limits its application to state-law causes of action.").

73. *Lincoln Property Co. v. Roche,* ___ U.S. ___, ___, 126 S.Ct. 606, 615, 163 L.Ed.2d 415 (2005) (noting that lower court "had no warrant . . . to inquire whether some other person might have been joined as an additional or substitute defendant").

74. In some circumstances, Rule 19 may direct the joinder of a party not previously sued. If that provision of Rule 19 is applica-

ble to a case, and such a joinder destroys diversity, the district court may be obligated to dismiss the action for failure of subject matter jurisdiction. *See* Author's Commentary on Rule 19.

75. *Kramer v. Caribbean Mills, Inc.,* 394 U.S. 823, 827, 89 S.Ct. 1487, 1490, 23 L.Ed.2d 9 (1969). (legality of assignment under state law does not necessarily equate to validity for purposes of federal jurisdiction).

76. *Cf. Yokeno v. Mafnas,* 973 F.2d 803, 811 (9th Cir.1992)(even if jurisdictional motive is apparent, assignment may create jurisdiction if independent business motive is "sufficiently compelling").

defendant nevertheless files a removal petition, the court, upon identifying a fraudulent joinder of the nondiverse defendant, will deny a motion to remand and retain jurisdiction over the removed case.[77]

Amount in Controversy

Diversity jurisdiction requires not only that the parties be citizens of different states or countries, but also that the matter in controversy exceed $75,000, exclusive of interest and costs.[78] The time at which the amount in controversy is measured is the date that the suit is filed. Later events that may reduce the amount recoverable do not nullify diversity jurisdiction that was proper at the time of filing.[79]

"Legal Certainty" Test

In the ordinary case, determination of the amount in controversy is made by reference to plaintiff's prayer for relief. Unliquidated claims for more than $75,000 will normally be taken at face value as satisfying the amount in controversy requirement.[80] Only in the

---

77. *Morris v. Princess Cruises, Inc.,* 236 F.3d 1061, 1067–68 (9th Cir.2001).

78. *See, e.g., Colavito v. New York Organ Donor Network, Inc.,* 438 F.3d 214, 221 (2d Cir.2006) (plea for punitive damages may satisfy amount in controversy requirement even if plaintiff would only be entitled to compensatory damages that are nominal). *But cf., State Farm Mutual Automobile Ins. Co. v. Powell,* 87 F.3d 93 (3d Cir. 1996)(amount in controversy not satisfied by pleading exact amount identified in § 1332; amount pleaded must *exceed* amount identified in § 1332). *Cf., Missouri State Life Insurance Co. v. Jones,* 290 U.S. 199, 202, 54 S.Ct. 133, 134, 78 L.Ed. 267, 269 (1933) (attorney's fees may be counted toward amount in controversy when prevailing party may collect them as part of damages per, e.g., state statute; held, state characterization of such fees as "costs" is irrelevant to diversity jurisdiction). *See, e.g., Manguno v. Prudential Property & Casualty Insurance Co.,* 276 F.3d 720, 723 (5th Cir.2002) ("If a state statute provides for attorney's fees, such fees are included as part of the amount in controversy."). *But see Martin v. Franklin National Corp.,* 251 F.3d 1284, 1292 (10th Cir.2001) ("[A]ttorneys fees cannot be aggregated for purposes of diversity jurisdiction."); *Spielman v. Genzyme Corp.,* 251 F.3d 1 (1st Cir.2001) (denying aggregation of attorney's fees even where state statute authorizes such fees).

79. *See, e.g., Hart v. Schering–Plough Corp.,* 253 F.3d 272 (7th Cir.2001) ("The amount in controversy is whatever is re-

quired to satisfy the plaintiff's demand in full, on the date suit began;" issue of $90,000 annual salary does not satisfy amount in controversy because defendant had paid plaintiff more than $17,000 in severance payments prior to suit); *Wolde–Meskel v. Vocational Instruction Project Community Servs., Inc.,* 166 F.3d 59, 62 (2d Cir.1999) (defendant obtained summary judgment on one count, resulting in decline in amount in controversy; held, trial court retained jurisdiction over other counts because once jurisdiction is obtained, a change in domicile or amount in controversy does not oust court's jurisdiction; summarizing cases and citing contrary minority view).

80. *See, e.g., Meridian Security Insurance Co. v. Sadowski,* 441 F.3d 536, 538 (7th Cir.2006) (if amount in controversy was met at outset, subsequent award of less than that amount does not terminate diversity jurisdiction); *Kroske v. U.S. Bank Corp.,* 432 F.3d 976, 980 (9th Cir.2005) (where the amount sought is not clear in complaint, court may require "summary-judgment-type evidence" as to amount in controversy); *Zunamon v. Brown,* 418 F.2d 883, 885 (8th Cir.1969)(Plaintiff's claim ordinarily decides amount in controversy.). *See also, Mitchell v. Brown & Williamson Tobacco Corp.,* 294 F.3d 1309, 1315 (11th Cir.2002) (where plaintiff filed in state court and defendant removed, plaintiff's allegation of damages in state court that satisfy amount in controversy requirement should have "strong presumption" that pleading does not allege large amount sim-

unusual case, where it is certain—based on the liquidated nature of the claim, the manifestly frivolous nature of the prayer for relief, or an existing statutory limitation on damages recoverable—that the plaintiff cannot possibly recover the jurisdictional amount, will the court disregard the plaintiff's prayer.[81]

If the amount in controversy is at issue, it is normally the plaintiff's burden to demonstrate that the requirement is met. An exception arises when a plaintiff originally files suit in state court and the defendant successfully removes the case to federal court. In that circumstance, if it is unclear whether the plaintiff's state claim met the amount in controversy requirement, the burden of proving the existence of the jurisdictional amount is shifted to the defendant who removed.[82]

Recovery of Less than $75,000

If a plaintiff initially seeks more than $75,000, but ultimately recovers less than that amount, 28 U.S.C.A. § 1332(b) provides that the court may deny recovery of costs to the plaintiff, and may assess costs against the plaintiff. However, jurisdiction that was proper at the outset is unaffected.[83] The calculation of the plaintiff's recovery

ply to satisfy diversity); *Cohn v. Petsmart, Inc.,* 281 F.3d 837, 840 (9th Cir.2002) ("A settlement letter is relevant evidence of the amount in controversy if that appears to reflect a reasonable estimate of the plaintiff's claim."); *Neuma, Inc. v. AMP, Inc.,* 259 F.3d 864, 881 (7th Cir.2001) (amount in controversy satisfied by "good faith, minimally reasonable" assertion of requisite amount or more); *United States Fire Insurance Co. v. Villegas,* 242 F.3d 279, 284 (5th Cir.2001) (if applicable law permits recovery of punitive damages, good-faith pleading of such damages may be included in determination of amount in controversy, notwithstanding that jury ultimately did not award such damages); *Massachusetts Casualty Ins. Co. v. Harmon,* 88 F.3d 415 (6th Cir.1996)(where validity of disability insurance policy is at issue, assessment of amount in controversy may include future potential benefits). *But cf., Middleton v. City of Blue Springs,* 145 F.3d 993 (8th Cir.1998) (if amount in controversy is challenged by opponent or court, claimant must prove amount by preponderance of evidence; court must dismiss if it concludes to legal certainty that claimant cannot recover required amount); *Larkin v. Brown,* 41 F.3d 387, 388 (8th Cir.1994)(if claim for punitive damages is necessary to satisfy amount in controversy requirement, the claim should get closer scrutiny than claim for compensatory damages.).

81. *See, e.g., Chase Manhattan Bank, N.A. v. American Nat'l Bank & Trust Co. of*

Chicago, 93 F.3d 1064, 1070 (2d Cir.1996) (where plaintiff suffered no damages, there is "a legal certainty" that jurisdictional amount is not satisfied); *Burns v. Anderson,* 502 F.2d 970, 972 (5th Cir.1974)(broken thumb with no lingering pain or disability; only modest lost wages; held, jurisdictional amount not satisfied).

82. *See, e.g., Smith v. American General Life & Accident Insurance Co.,* 337 F.3d 888 (7th Cir.2003) (explaining general rule, but noting exception applies in removal cases because plaintiff is unlikely to have fabricated an amount in controversy when plaintiff originally filed in state court). *See generally Kokkonen v. Guardian Life Insurance Co. of America,* 511 U.S. 375, 377, 114 S.Ct. 1673, 1675, 128 L.Ed.2d 391 (1994) ("[T]he burden of establishing [subject matter jurisdiction] rests upon the party asserting jurisdiction."). *See also TIG Insurance Co. v. Reliable Research Co.,* 334 F.3d 630 (7th Cir.2003) (intervening plaintiff bears burden of establishing subject matter jurisdiction).

83. *See, e.g., Meridian Security Insurance Co. v. Sadowski,* 441 F.3d 536, 538 (7th Cir.2006) (if amount in controversy was met at outset, subsequent award of less than that amount does not terminate subject matter jurisdiction). *Pratt Central Park Ltd. Partnership v. Dames & Moore, Inc.,* 60 F.3d 350, 351 (7th Cir.1995)("The penalty for recovering less than [the jurisdiction-

under § 1332(b) is made solely on the basis of awards to plaintiff, and does not include deductions for the defendant's successful claims against the plaintiff. The court's authority under § 1332(b) is discretionary.[84] Moreover, "costs" do not include recovery of attorney fees.

Jurisdictional Amount in Equity Cases

Because suits seeking equitable relief are grounded in an allegation that traditional money damages are an inadequate remedy, federal courts have had to adjust the more-than $75,000 requirement to the peculiarities of such cases. Perhaps the most common approach is to try to measure the amount in controversy in equity cases by the value of the right the plaintiff seeks to enforce.[85] A similar approach is to measure the amount in controversy by the value of vindication to the plaintiff.[86] A less favored approach is to measure the amount in controversy by the costs of compliance a defendant will face.[87] As these constructions suggest, there are a variety of techniques for attempting the evaluation, and lower courts enjoy substantial discretion in how they make their determinations.

> ***Example:*** Assume a plaintiff owns a small plot of land worth less than $75,000 immediately below a large dam owned by the defendant. If the defendant intends to release water held by the dam, it may not do damage worth more than $75,000 to the plaintiff's property. Measuring the amount in controversy by the value to the plaintiff of an injunction preventing the release would therefore not satisfy the amount in controversy. However, the cost to the defendant of not releas-

al amount] is the denial of costs ... not the loss of the whole judgment."). *Cf. Herremans v. Carrera Designs, Inc.,* 157 F.3d 1118, 1121 (7th Cir.1998) (no dismissal for failure to win more than amount in controversy; "The test for whether a case satisfies the amount in controversy requirement is whether the complaint makes a good-faith claim for the amount, ... not whether the plaintiff is actually entitled to such an amount. Otherwise every diversity case that a plaintiff lost on the merits would be dismissed for lack of federal jurisdiction, allowing the plaintiff to start over in state court.").

84. *See, e.g., Coventry Sewage Assocs. v. Dworkin Realty Co.,* 71 F.3d 1, 8 n. 6 (1st Cir.1995)("The determination of whether or not to impose such cost sanctions is, of course, within the sound discretion of the district court.").

85. *Glenwood Light & Water Co. v. Mutual Light, Heat & Power Co.,* 239 U.S. 121, 36 S.Ct. 30, 60 L.Ed. 174 (1915). *See also Hartford Insurance Group v. Lou–Con Inc.,* 293 F.3d 908, 911 (5th Cir.2002) (in declar-

atory judgment action over validity of insurance policy, amount in controversy is usually measured by limits of policy; however, if issue is applicability of policy to particular occurrence, amount in controversy is usually not policy limit, but value of claim underlying the particular dispute).

86. *See, e.g., Cohen v. Office Depot, Inc.,* 204 F.3d 1069, 1077 (11th Cir.2000) ("When a plaintiff seeks injunctive or declaratory relief, the amount in controversy is the monetary value of the object of the litigation from the plaintiff's perspective.").

87. *See, e.g., Justice v. Atchison, Topeka & Santa Fe Ry. Co.,* 927 F.2d 503, 505 (10th Cir.1991)(looking to defendant's cost of compliance; noting authority for looking either to cost to defendant or value to plaintiff). *But see McCauley v. Ford Motor Co.,* 264 F.3d 952, 960–61 (9th Cir.2001), *cert. granted in part,* 534 U.S. 1126, 122 S.Ct. 1063, 151 L.Ed.2d 966 (2002) (refusing to measure jurisdictional amount by cost to defendant of complying with injunction).

ing the water might be considerably more than $75,000. If so, measuring the amount in controversy by the cost to defendant of complying with the injunction would satisfy the jurisdictional requirement.

Aggregation of Claims

If a plaintiff has more than one claim against a defendant, but no single claim exceeds $75,000 in value, questions arise as to whether the plaintiff may add the value of the claims together to satisfy the amount in controversy requirement. Case law indicates that a single plaintiff may aggregate claims against a single defendant, no matter how dissimilar the claims may be.[88] However, if each claim is merely an alternative theory for which only one recovery would be permitted, only the amount of that potential recovery may be considered when calculating the amount in controversy.

When multiple parties are involved, the case law is less liberal. It appears that two or more plaintiffs can add their claims together to satisfy the jurisdictional amount only if the claims are truly joint.[89] For example, if two plaintiffs each owned, as joint tenants, half of an automobile worth $80,000, and the suit alleged that the defendant had destroyed the automobile completely, the plaintiffs could probably add their individual $40,000 claims to satisfy the jurisdictional amount. But if the allegations were that the two plaintiffs each suffered $40,000 in personal injuries at the hands of the defendant, aggregation would not be permitted because the claims would be seen as distinct—even if the injuries occurred in the same accident.[90]

---

88. *See, e.g., Werwinski v. Ford Motor Co.,* 286 F.3d 661, 666 (3d Cir.2002) ("Only claims, whether related or unrelated, of a single plaintiff against a single defendant may be aggregated."); *Galt G/S v. JSS Scandinavia,* 142 F.3d 1150 (9th Cir.1998) (upholding aggregation of statutorily authorized attorneys' fees with principal claim); *Klepper v. First American Bank,* 916 F.2d 337, 341 (6th Cir.1990) ("It is well established that claims [brought by a single plaintiff against a single defendant] can be aggregated to satisfy the jurisdictional amount requirement."); *But see In re Abbott Laboratories,* 51 F.3d 524, 529 (5th Cir.1995) (Congressional enactment of supplemental jurisdiction, 28 U.S.C.A. § 1367, obviated need for each plaintiff to satisfy independently the requisite amount in controversy in class actions).

89. *See, e.g., Snyder v. Harris,* 394 U.S. 332, 334, 89 S.Ct. 1053, 1056, 22 L.Ed.2d 319 (1969)(allowing multiple plaintiffs to aggregate where they have "common and undivided interest"). *But cf. Ard v. Trans-continental Gas Pipe Line Corp.,* 138 F.3d 596 (5th Cir.1998) (acknowledging differences among appellate courts; holding that, generally, several plaintiffs may not aggregate their individual claims for punitive damages).

90. *See also Spielman v. Genzyme Corp.,* 251 F.3d 1 (1st Cir.2001) (denying aggregation of attorney's fees even where state statute authorizes such fees). *Cf., e.g., Mehlenbacher v. Akzo Nobel Salt, Inc.,* 216 F.3d 291 (2d Cir.2000) (claims are separate and distinct where plaintiffs "seek recovery for their losses as individuals only, and not collectively"; thus no aggregation permitted in instant case); *Meritcare, Inc. v. St. Paul Mercury Ins. Co.,* 166 F.3d 214, 218 (3d Cir.1999) (plaintiffs claimed losses on similar insurance policies covering a single event; denying aggregation when "the plaintiffs have a community of interest, but fall short of establishing a single title or right in which they have a common and undivided interest").

The precedent in cases where a single plaintiff seeks to sue more than one defendant follows a similar pattern. Aggregation is permitted only if the claims against the defendants involve joint liability.[91]

ADDITIONAL RESEARCH REFERENCES

C.J.S. Federal Courts §§ 44–73 et seq.

West's Key No. Digests, Federal Courts ⊕261–319.

§ 2.13 Subject Matter Jurisdiction in Federal District Courts—Requirements for Supplemental Jurisdiction

CORE CONCEPT

Supplemental jurisdiction, authorized by Congress at 28 U.S.C.A. § 1367, is the means by which parties may add state law counts in a federal court case, even though the state law counts could not have been brought by themselves because they cannot satisfy the requirements of either federal question or diversity jurisdiction.

> *Example:* Suppose that a New York plaintiff had two causes of action against a New York defendant: one arising under federal antitrust law, the other under state law. Federal antitrust claims are within the exclusive subject matter jurisdiction of federal district courts. The state claim, by contrast, does not qualify for diversity jurisdiction because both parties are New York citizens. Thus the plaintiff in a situation such as this might theoretically have to prosecute two separate suits, one in federal court and the other in state court, and incur all the extra expenditures in time and money such suits would entail for both the parties and the taxpayers. Supplemental jurisdiction is intended to reduce such diseconomies, and at the same time limit damage to federalism by limiting the circumstances in which nondiverse state claims may be prosecuted in federal district courts.

NOTE: 28 U.S.C.A. § 1367, governing supplemental jurisdiction only became effective in December 1990. Prior to that date the area was governed by two closely related doctrines of case law: pendent jurisdiction and ancillary jurisdiction. In creating supplemental jurisdiction, Congress combined much of those two doctrines.[1] However, Congress also overruled some previously existing features of the case law, so that judicial precedent prior to December 1990 should be approached with care.

---

91. *See, e.g., Jewell v. Grain Dealers Mutual Ins. Co.,* 290 F.2d 11, 13 (5th Cir. 1961)(Permitting aggregation against multiple defendants only where they are jointly liable to plaintiff).

1. *Peacock v. Thomas,* 516 U.S. 349, 355 n. 5, 116 S.Ct. 862, 867 n. 5, 133 L.Ed.2d 817 (1996). *See, e.g., IFC Interconsult, A.G. v. Safeguard International Partners, L.L.C.,* 438 F.3d 298, 309 (3d Cir.2006) ("We do not see the relevant inquiries for ancillary and supplemental jurisdiction as separate.").

APPLICATIONS

Prerequisite for Supplemental Jurisdiction

As its name suggests, supplemental jurisdiction is not an independent basis for satisfying requirements of federal subject matter jurisdiction in the same way as federal question jurisdiction or diversity jurisdiction. Instead, counts based on supplemental jurisdiction must be able to attach themselves to some other count already properly present in the lawsuit. Thus, before supplemental jurisdiction can be invoked, there must already exist at least one count that can satisfy federal subject matter jurisdiction through either, e.g., federal question jurisdiction, diversity jurisdiction, or a suit where the United States is a party.[2]

Prohibitions Contained in Other Federal Statutes

By its terms, § 1367(a) provides that the exercise of supplemental jurisdiction pursuant to § 1367 may be prohibited if another federal statute expressly creates that prohibition.[3]

Same Case or Controversy

28 U.S.C.A. § 1367(a) establishes that supplemental jurisdiction will be effective, if at all, only over non-diverse state claims that "form part of the same case or controversy" as another count or counts in the action. This requirement confirms the need for at least one count in the case that can independently satisfy one of the kinds of federal subject matter jurisdiction discussed above.[4] It goes further than that, however, in requiring some relationship between the supplemental count and the counts that already satisfy jurisdiction.[5] The pre–1990 case law concentrated on how much similarity existed between the witnesses and evidence relevant to the respective counts. Where substantial similarity existed, the court's power

---

2. 28 U.S.C.A. § 1367(a). *See also, e.g., Herman Family Revocable Trust v. Teddy Bear,* 254 F.3d 802, 805 (9th Cir.2001) ("[W]here there is no underlying original federal subject matter jurisdiction, the court has no authority to adjudicate supplemental claims under § 1367."); *Nowak v. Ironworkers Local 6 Pension Fund,* 81 F.3d 1182, 1187 (2d Cir.1996)(A court "cannot exercise supplemental jurisdiction unless there is first a proper basis for original federal jurisdiction.").

3. 28 U.S.C.A. § 1367(a). *See also* 42 U.S.C.A. § 13981(e)(4) (prohibiting use of § 1367 to establish jurisdiction over state law claims seeking divorce, alimony, equitable distribution of marital property, or child custody). *See, e.g., Handberry v. Thompson,* 446 F.3d 335, 345–46 (2d Cir.2006) (18 U.S.C.A. § 3626(a)(1)(A), governing civil suits for prospective relief regarding prison conditions, restricts use of § 1367; where legislative intent is clear, restriction on § 1367 applies notwithstanding that ex-

press language of prohibition is absent from statute). *But cf., Lindsay v. Government Employees Insurance Co.,* 448 F.3d 416, 424 n. 10 (D.C. Cir.2006) ("Rule 23 does not fit section 1367(a)'s '[f]ederal statute' exception.").

4. *See, e.g., Lindsay v. Government Employees Insurance Co.,* 448 F.3d 416, 423 (D.C. Cir.2006) (§ 1367(a) "encompasses both diversity jurisdiction and federal question jurisdiction").

5. *See, e.g., Ammerman v. Sween,* 54 F.3d 423, 424 (7th Cir.1995) ("A loose factual connection between the claims" may satisfy the requirements of same case or controversy.). *But see Serrano–Moran v. Grau–Gaztambide,* 195 F.3d 68, 69 (1st Cir. 1999) (civil rights claim against police officers accused of beating deceased does not share common nucleus of facts with supplemental claim of malpractice against medical defendants).

to hear non-diverse state claims could probably be established. Cases applying the "same case or controversy" standard of § 1367 are likely to employ much the same approach to determining whether the non-diverse state counts are sufficiently related to the other counts to satisfy supplemental jurisdiction.[6]

Joined or Intervening Parties

28 U.S.C.A. § 1367(a) specifically provides that in appropriate circumstances supplemental jurisdiction may be extended to include counts involving joined or intervening parties.[7] This provision overrides prior case law holding that courts could not extend their ancillary jurisdiction to persons not already parties to the case.[8] However, this provision is limited somewhat by § 1367(b), discussed below.

Nondiverse Pendent Parties and Claims

Closely related to some of the issues addressed by § 1367(b) is the question of nondiverse pendent parties. Prior to enactment of § 1367, it was fairly well settled that simply because one plaintiff could assert diversity jurisdiction, a nondiverse plaintiff could not attach a state claim to the first plaintiff's diverse count. That result applied even if the two claims were closely related.

Now, however, a different result may apply. The settled rule now is that where all the other requirements of supplemental jurisdiction are satisfied, and at least one plaintiff already named in the action satisfies the amount in controversy requirement, claims by other plaintiffs that fall short of the jurisdictional amount may be

6. *See, e.g., Tamiami Partners, Ltd. v. Miccosukee Tribe of Indians of Florida*, 177 F.3d 1212 (11th Cir.1999) (all claims arose from defendant's actions relating to underlying agreement; holding requirement for commonality satisfied even though success of federal claims did not depend on success of state claims); *see also 3D Systems, Inc. v. Aarotech Laboratories, Inc.*, 160 F.3d 1373, 1377 (Fed.Cir.1998) (state claims of trade libel and unfair competition are "hand-in-hand" with federal claims of patent infringement when all claims arise out of defendant's sales activity for certain products in California); *Itar-Tass Russian News Agency v. Russian Kurier, Inc.*, 140 F.3d 442, 445–48 (2d Cir.1998) (state law motion for fees for plaintiff's attorney and expert witness are supplemental to underlying federal copyright claims). *Cf., Southwestern Bell Telephone Co. v. Brooks Fiber Communications of Oklahoma, Inc.*, 235 F.3d 493, 498 (10th Cir.2000) (in addition to review for compliance with federal law, district court may use § 1367(a) to review state administrative agency's decision for compliance with state law). *See also Achtman v. Kirby, McInerney & Squire, L.L.P.*, 464

F.3d 328, 335 (2d Cir. 2006) (rejecting contrary authority in some district courts holding that supplemental jurisdiction can be applied, if at all, to claims being heard in same action; concluding that supplemental jurisdiction can be applied to claims in a related, but separate, lawsuit).

7. *See, e.g., Ciambriello v. County of Nassau*, 292 F.3d 307, 325 (2d Cir.2002) (federal claims against one defendant (but not others) dismissed; but state claims against defendant who obtained dismissal of federal claim remain in federal court under § 1367(a)); *Tamiami Partners, Ltd. v. Miccosukee Tribe of Indians of Florida*, 177 F.3d 1212, 1223–24 (11th Cir.1999) ("[T]he parties to the federal and supplemental claims need not be identical in order for supplemental jurisdiction to lie.").

8. *See, e.g., Abbott Laboratories, Inc. v. CVS Pharmacy, Inc.*, 290 F.3d 854, 858 (7th Cir.2002) ("Ever since 28 U.S.C. § 1367(a) overturned [prior case law], the supplemental jurisdiction has been capacious enough to include claims by or against third parties.").

treated as supplemental to the claim that satisfies original jurisdiction.

Claims under Foreign Law

If a cause of action arising under foreign law could be heard by a state court, it appears that such a claim could be a supplemental claim under § 1367.[9]

Sua Sponte Application

It is settled that federal courts may dismiss a case for lack of subject matter jurisdiction even when the parties have not raised the issue.[10] However, when a party asserting a nondiverse claim has not attempted to invoke supplemental jurisdiction, there is uncertainty as to whether courts should invoke such jurisdiction *sua sponte*.[11] Attorneys are encouraged to investigate the local practice.

Restrictions on Supplemental Jurisdiction

28 U.S.C.A. § 1367(b) eliminates the use of supplemental jurisdiction when certain facts are present. Thus, even if a non-diverse state count meets the "same case or controversy" requirement of § 1367(a), it may still not qualify for supplemental jurisdiction. This possibility occurs when the counts already satisfying federal subject matter jurisdiction are based solely on diversity jurisdiction under § 1332 and either of two other elements are present:

(1) the non-diverse counts are claims by plaintiffs[12] in the original action against persons made parties under Rule 14 (impleader), Rule 19 (joinder), Rule 20 (permissive joinder), or Rule 24 (intervention);[13] *or*

---

9. *See, e.g., Voda v. Cordis Corp.,* 476 F.3d 887, 894 (Fed. Cir. 2007) (this result assumes that all requirements for supplemental jurisdiction are met).

10. *See, e.g., Pennsylvania Nurses Ass'n v. Pennsylvania State Education Ass'n,* 90 F.3d 797, 801 (3d Cir.1996) ("[W]e must consider the jurisdictional question even where the parties are prepared to concede it.").

11. *Compare, e.g., United States ex rel. Ramseyer v. Century Healthcare Corp.,* 90 F.3d 1514 n. 8 (10th Cir.1996)(declining to invoke supplemental jurisdiction where plaintiff failed to assert it in complaint), *with Rodriguez v. Doral Mortgage Corp.,* 57 F.3d 1168 (1st Cir.1995)(holding that federal court, with proper notice to parties, may invoke supplemental jurisdiction on its own initiative over previously unpleaded nondiverse state claim that court identified for parties).

12. *But cf., Kemper/Prime Industrial Partners v. Montgomery Watson Americas, Inc.,* 487 F.3d 1061, 1063 (7th Cir. 2007)

("[A] defendant's impleader under Fed. R. Civ. P. 14 of a party that is not diverse from the plaintiff does not destroy jurisdiction."). *United Capitol Ins. Co. v. Kapiloff,* 155 F.3d 488 (4th Cir.1998) (defendants in declaratory judgment action sought to use supplemental jurisdiction to join nondiverse parties on counterclaim; held, § 1367(b) does not bar such joinder).

13. *See, e.g., Ryan ex rel. Ryan v. Schneider National Carriers, Inc.,* 263 F.3d 816, 820 (8th Cir.2001) (per curiam) (diversity claims by several plaintiffs; cross-claim by some plaintiffs against another plaintiff, who was not diverse from them; held, § 1367(b) does not prevent use of supplemental jurisdiction over cross-claim because original plaintiff sued on cross-claim was not made party by other plaintiffs under any of Rules 14, 19, 20 or 24); *Burka v. Aetna Life Ins. Co.,* 87 F.3d 478 n. 4 (D.C.Cir.1996)(noting that § 1367(b) does not prevent use of supplemental jurisdiction over claims against parties added pursuant to Rule 25(c)).

(2) the non-diverse counts are claims by persons who entered the case as plaintiffs under either Rule 19 (joinder) or Rule 24 (intervention).

The exceptions in 28 U.S.C.A. § 1367(b) are a legislative adoption of existing case law. An example may demonstrate their operation.

> ***Example:*** If a plaintiff wanted to sue two defendants on a tort claim, but only one of the defendants was of citizenship diverse from that of the plaintiff, a claim against both defendants could not be filed in federal court. Instead, the plaintiff might sue only the diverse defendant, in which case (assuming other requirements of jurisdiction are satisfied), the federal court could hear the claim. In those circumstances it would often be predictable that the diverse defendant would use Rule 14 to implead the non-diverse defendant. Now that the non-diverse defendant is in the case, the plaintiff might seek to bring a new count against the non-diverse defendant. Requirements of § 1367(a) would be satisfied, because the count against the non-diverse defendant certainly forms part of the same case or controversy as the original count against the diverse defendant. Notice, however, what the effective result is, if this "supplemental" count against the non-diverse defendant is allowed. The plaintiff, by anticipating the impleader, will have achieved suit in federal district court against both defendants— even though diversity jurisdiction would have failed if plaintiff had sought to sue them both directly. However, § 1367(b) prohibits the plaintiff from using supplemental jurisdiction to sue a party joined under Rule 14. In fact, § 1367(b) usually precludes use of supplemental jurisdiction by a plaintiff if the original basis of federal subject matter jurisdiction is diversity jurisdiction under § 1332.

NOTE: Note that 28 U.S.C.A. § 1367(b) restricts a plaintiff's use of supplemental jurisdiction only when the original cause of action is based upon diversity jurisdiction under § 1332 and the exercise of supplemental jurisdiction would contradict the requirements of § 1332.[14] Thus, where the underlying facts do not conflict with the requirements of § 1332, the prohibition contained in § 1367(b) is inapplicable.[15] If the original basis for federal jurisdiction is a federal question, under § 1331, the restrictions imposed by

---

14. 28 U.S.C.A. § 1367(b).

15. *See, e.g., Mattel, Inc. v. Bryant,* 446 F.3d 1011, 1014 (9th Cir.2006) ("Neither § 1332 nor § 1367 upset the long-established judge-made rule that the presence of a nondiverse and not indispensable defendant intervenor does not destroy complete diversity."); *Aurora Loan Services, Inc. v. Craddieth,* 442 F.3d 1018, 1025 (7th Cir. 2006) ("Section 1367(b)'s purpose of preventing plaintiffs who would have destroyed federal jurisdiction had they joined a suit at its outset from using Rule 24 to circumvent the requirement of complete diversity has no application to a party forced to intervene to protect an interest that arose during the course of a federal litigation in which he had no stake at the outset. Such a party has no say in deciding where the suit is brought and so cannot be gaming the system;" also noting that federal jurisdiction is usually determined as of date complaint is filed).

§ 1367(b) on the use of supplemental jurisdiction simply do not apply.

Sovereign Immunity

It is settled that § 1367 does not create a waiver of the sovereign immunity of the United States.[16]

Criminal Cases

It appears settled that § 1367 has no applicability to the jurisdiction of federal courts when they exercise ancillary jurisdiction in criminal cases.[17]

Court's Discretion

Even if supplemental jurisdiction exists under 28 U.S.C.A. § 1367(a) and (b), § 1367(c) provides the court with substantial discretion to refuse to hear the supplemental counts.[18] When a district court dismisses state counts under any provision of § 1367(c), it will typically do so without prejudice to any re-filing of those counts in state court.[19]

The four circumstances in which a federal court might choose to dismiss a count that otherwise qualifies for supplemental jurisdiction are:

(1) *Difficult Questions of State Law:* This provision of 28 U.S.C.A. § 1367(c)(1) codifies the common sense precedent permit-

16. *See, e.g., Dunn & Black, P.S. v. United States,* ___ F.3d ___ n.3, 2007 WL 2693088 (9th Cir. 2007) ("§ 1367 merely grants federal court supplemental jurisdiction over state claims related to certain federal claims in any civil action of which the district court has original jurisdiction ... and that section cannot 'operate as a waiver of the United States sovereign immunity.'").

17. *See, e.g., Garcia v. Teitler,* 443 F.3d 202, 207 (2d Cir.2006) (noting that § 1367, by its terms, relates to "civil action").

18. *See, e.g., Saglioccolo v. Eagle Ins. Co.,* 112 F.3d 226, 233 (6th Cir.1997) ("[T]he presence of supplemental jurisdiction does not mean that the district court must entertain this claim."). *Cf., International Association of Firefighters of St. Louis, Local 2665 v. City of Ferguson,* 283 F.3d 969, 976 (8th Cir.2002) ("The District Court would always be free, of course, to proceed to the merits of the state claim, in its discretion, even if one of the conditions in 28 U.S.C. § 1367(c) for dismissal of the state claim had been satisfied."); *Acri v. Varian Associates, Inc.,* 114 F.3d 999, 1000 (9th Cir.1997) (en banc) (when district court has jurisdiction under § 1367(a), there is no obligation on the court to make a sua sponte analysis under § 1367(c) when no party sought such an analysis). *But cf. Southern Council of Industrial Workers v. Ford,* 83 F.3d 966, 969 (8th Cir. 1996)("Where original jurisdiction exists, exercise of supplemental jurisdiction over all adequately related claims is mandatory, absent certain exceptions."). *See also, Seabrook v. Jacobson,* 153 F.3d 70 (2d Cir.1998) (nondiverse state claims satisfied requirements of § 1367(a); nevertheless, where federal claims were dismissed, district court abused discretion by exercising supplemental jurisdiction to retain state claims).

19. *See, e.g., Scott v. Clay County,* 205 F.3d 867, 880 (6th Cir.2000) (district court has discretion to dismiss without prejudice or to hear the claims); *Horton v. Board of County Commissioners of Flagler County,* 202 F.3d 1297, 1300 n. 3 (11th Cir.2000) (if district court dismisses under § 1367(c) plaintiff can refile in state court); *Bass v. Parkwood Hospital,* 180 F.3d 234, 236 (5th Cir.1999) ("When a court dismisses all federal claims before trial, the general rule is to dismiss any pendent claims. ... However, the dismissal of the pendent claims should expressly be without prejudice so that the plaintiff may refile his claims in the appropriate state court.").

ting district courts to dismiss a non-diverse state count if it is clear state courts would be better able to untangle the uncertain questions of state law. However, it is likely that federal courts will employ § 1367(c)(1) only in unusual cases involving the greatest difficulty in applying state law.[20]

(2) *Non–Diverse State Claim Predominates:* The court may decline to exercise supplemental jurisdiction when the non-diverse state claim predominates over the claims which formed the original basis of the court's subject matter jurisdiction.[21] Such cases are probably fairly unusual.

(3) *Original Counts Dismissed:* Sometimes the court may decline to exercise supplemental jurisdiction when it has already dismissed the claims over which it has federal question or diversity jurisdiction.[22] Whether the court "may" dismiss, or "must" dismiss, the supplemental claims depends heavily on the reasoning that underlies the dismissal of the claims that asserted original subject matter jurisdiction. If the basis for dismissal of those claims is a finding that the court lacked original jurisdiction, the supplemental claims must be dismissed.[23] If, on the other hand, the basis for

---

20. *See, e.g., D.D. v. New York City Board of Education,* 480 F.3d 138 (2d Cir. 2007) (supplemental jurisdiction inappropriate because "State and City regulatory schemes are intricate and difficulty to interpret"); *Houlton Citizens' Coalition v. Town of Houlton,* 175 F.3d 178 (1st Cir.1999) (federal claims resolved before trial; state claim was both difficult and novel question; held, district court should dismiss state claim without prejudice); *Edmondson & Gallagher v. Alban Towers Tenants Ass'n,* 48 F.3d 1260 (D.C.Cir.1995)(justifying refusal to hear state claims because the applicable law has been the subject of conflicting decisions). *Cf., Parker v. Scrap Metal Processors, Inc.,* 468 F.3d 733, 743–44 (11th Cir. 2006) ("Generally, state tort claims are not considered novel or complex. ... Moreover, negligence, nuisance, and property damage claims have been held as not raising novel or complex issues of state law.").

21. *See, e.g., Diven v. Amalgamated Transit Union Int'l,* 38 F.3d 598, 602 (D.C.Cir.1994)(apparent primacy of state claim indicated by weakness of federal claim—"even before discovery"). *Cf., San Pedro Hotel Co. v. City of Los Angeles,* 159 F.3d 470, 478 (9th Cir.1998) (if court dismisses under § 1367(c)(2), failure to state reasons for doing so is not abuse of discretion; nevertheless, suggesting that courts should provide explanation, and noting that statement of reasons is required for dismissal under § 1367(c)(4)).

22. *See, e.g., Roche v. John Hancock Mutual Life Ins. Co.,* 81 F.3d 249, 256-57 (1st Cir.1996) (identifying factors of "comity, judicial economy, convenience, fairness, and the like" in deciding whether to dismiss under § 1367(c)(3)). *But cf., Goodson v. City of Corpus Christi,* 202 F.3d 730, 741 (5th Cir.2000) (if district court erroneously dismisses claims that enjoyed original jurisdiction, it is abuse of discretion to dismiss state claims on ground that original jurisdiction is lacking).

23. *Arbaugh v. Y&H Corp.,* ___ U.S. ___, ___, 126 S.Ct. 1235, 1244, 163 L.Ed.2d 1097 (2006) ("[W]hen a federal court concludes that it lacks subject-matter jurisdiction, the court must dismiss the complaint in its entirety."). *See, e.g., Ward v. Alternative Health Delivery Systems, Inc.,* 261 F.3d 624, 626 (6th Cir.2001) ("If [the district court] dismisses the claims within its original jurisdiction for lack of subject matter jurisdiction ... it *must* remand the remaining claims." [italics in original]); *Pinney Dock & Transport Co. v. Penn Central Corp.,* 196 F.3d 617, 621 (6th Cir.1999) (if dismissal of counts alleging original jurisdiction occurs under Rule 12(b)(1) (failure of subject matter jurisdiction), dismissal of supplemental claim "must occur;" if dismissal of original jurisdiction counts occurs under Rule 12(b)(6) (failure to state a claim for which relief may be granted), a " 'strong presumption' " favors dismissal of supplemental claim); *Scarfo v. Ginsberg,* 175 F.3d

dismissal of the supplemental claims relates to the merits, the district court may have discretion to retain the supplemental claims under § 1367(c).[24]

Courts applying § 1367(c) also give substantial weight to the point in the case at which dismissal on the merits occurred. If the federal court was able to dismiss the federal question or diversity claims at the outset of the case, it would probably be appropriate to dismiss the supplemental claims immediately (or remand to state court if the case reached federal court through the process of removal).[25] If, however, the federal court proceeded through much of the litigation and had informed itself of the merits of the supplemental claims, then dismissal of the other claims would probably not justify dismissing the supplemental claims.[26]

957 (11th Cir.1999) ("The federal courts of appeals ... have uniformly held that once the district court determines that subject matter jurisdiction over a plaintiff's federal claims does not exist, courts must dismiss a plaintiff's [nondiverse] state law claims."). *But see Eastman v. Marine Mechanical Corp.,* 438 F.3d 544, 551 (6th Cir.2006) (subject matter jurisdiction is evaluated as of date of removal of case from state court; "but if an amendment eliminates all the federal claims, remand becomes a discretionary decision.").

24. *Arbaugh v. Y&H Corp.,* ___ U.S. ___, ___, 126 S.Ct. 1235, 1244–45, 163 L.Ed.2d 1097 (2006) ("[W]hen a court grants a motion to dismiss for failure to state a federal claim, the court generally retains discretion to exercise supplemental jurisdiction, pursuant to 28 U.S.C. § 1367, over pendent state-law claims."). *See, e.g., Herman Family Revocable Trust v. Teddy Bear,* 254 F.3d 802 (9th Cir.2001) ("A dismissal on the merits is different from a dismissal on jurisdictional grounds. If the district court dismisses all federal claims on the merits, it has discretion under § 1367(c) to adjudicate the remaining claims; if the court dismisses for lack of subject matter jurisdiction, it has no discretion and must dismiss all claims.")

25. *Carnegie-Mellon University v. Cohill,* 484 U.S. 343, 350 n. 7, 108 S.Ct. 614, 614 n. 7, 98 L.Ed.2d 720 (1988) (noting absence of inflexible or mandatory rule, but "[i]n the usual case in which all federal-law claims are eliminated before trial, the balance of the factors to be considered under [supplemental jurisdiction]–judicial economy, convenience, fairness, and comity–will point toward declining to exercise jurisdiction over the remaining state-law claims"). *See, e.g., O'Connor v. Commonwealth Gas*

Co., 251 F.3d 262 (1st Cir.2001) ("Courts generally decline to exercise supplemental jurisdiction over state claims if the federal predicate is dismissed early in the litigation."); *Hedges v. Musco,* 204 F.3d 109, 123 (3d Cir.2000) (where claim that was basis for original jurisdiction is dismissed before trial, district court " 'must decline to decide [supplemental claims] unless consideration of judicial economy, convenience, and fairness to the parties provide an affirmative justification for doing so' "); *Annulli v. Panikkar,* 200 F.3d 189, 202–03 (3d Cir.1999) (no abuse of discretion to dismiss state claims even though federal claims were on "eve of trial" when defendant filed motion for summary judgment; although federal court was site of two years of litigation, fifteen pages of court docket, 1,800 pages of depositions, and 2,800 pages of discovery documents, plaintiff could still use evidence in state court; moreover, plaintiff assumed risk of dismissal of state claims when plaintiff filed in federal court and invoked § 1367). *But cf., Blakely v. United States,* 276 F.3d 853, 863 (6th Cir.2002) (pretrial dismissal of claims supporting original jurisdiction should generally result in remand, but "that rule is not absolute").

26. *See, e.g., Tomaiolo v. Mallinoff,* 281 F.3d 1, 11 (1st Cir.2002) (retention of state claims was not abuse of discretion when "[t]he litigation was far advanced, the court had before it cross-motions for summary judgment, discovery had closed, [the plaintiff] had filed her sixth amended complaint, and all claims arose from the same core of facts"); *Miller Aviation v. Milwaukee County Board of Supervisors,* 273 F.3d 722, 731–32 (7th Cir.2001) (abuse of discretion to dismiss state count when previous disposition of federal claim left nothing of state

(4) *Other Exceptional Circumstances:* This provision of 28 U.S.C.A. § 1367(c) obviously provides the court with discretion in circumstances not anticipated by Congress.[27]

Important: It is important to note that if a non-diverse state claim fails to qualify for supplemental jurisdiction and is dismissed (or remanded to state court) by the court, the dismissal has no consequence for claims that qualify for the court's jurisdiction. Those latter claims may continue to be prosecuted.[28] It is possible, however, that for reasons of economy a claimant may choose to dismiss the qualifying claims and prosecute those claims, along with the dismissed claims, in state court.

Statutes of Limitations

28 U.S.C.A. § 1367(d) provides that actions filed in federal court under § 1367(a), and subsequently dismissed, will usually not be barred by a statute of limitations because of time lost in federal court.[29] Section 1367(d) accomplishes this end by tolling statutes of limitations while the claim is pending, and by providing a period of at least 30 days after dismissal in which the claim may be refiled in state court. Moreover, § 1367(d) provides that if state law will allow more than 30 days in which to refile, the claimant will enjoy

claim for state court to decide, or when substantial investment of judicial resources have already been expended and dismissal would therefore produce judicial efficiency). *Mizuna, Ltd. v. Crossland Fed. Savings Bank,* 90 F.3d 650 (2d Cir.1996)(claim supporting original jurisdiction voluntarily dismissed; held, because court had properly acquired original jurisdiction, it enjoyed discretion to retain supplemental jurisdiction over related nondiverse claims; discretion to retain supplemental counts properly exercised where "three judicial officers had already expended substantial resources . . . over a year's time"); *Metropolitan Wholesale Supply, Inc. v. M/V Royal Rainbow,* 12 F.3d 58, 61 (5th Cir.1994)(federal counts already resolved; but court, having before it all facts as to non-diverse state claim, may decide that count).

27. *See, e.g., Gregory v. Shelby County,* 220 F.3d 433, 446 (6th Cir.2000) (where state law provides that cause of action against state officer in his official capacity is within "exclusive original jurisdiction" of state trial court, state legislature's "clear preference" to have such claims tried in state court is exceptional circumstance within scope of § 1367(c)(4)); *Birchem v. Knights of Columbus,* 116 F.3d 310 n. 3 (8th Cir.1997) (if plaintiff, who is entitled to jury trial, seeks to join federal claims with state claims, but state cause of action places

burden of proof on defendant, trial court should consider dismissing state claim under § 1367(c)(4)); *Hays County Guardian v. Supple,* 969 F.2d 111 (5th Cir.1992) (finding exceptional circumstances and compelling reasons where adjudicating state claims in federal court would parallel adjudication of identical claims in state court). *Cf., Treglia v. Town of Manlius,* 313 F.3d 713, 723 (2d Cir.2002) (court has discretion to decline supplemental jurisdiction only if reason is based on at least one of four enumerated categories in § 1367(c)); *Executive Software North America, Inc. v. U.S. District Court,* 24 F.3d 1545, 1557 (9th Cir.1994) (if court dismisses under § 1367(c)(4), it must identify the circumstances the court found "exceptional").

28. *See, e.g., In re City of Mobile,* 75 F.3d 605, 607–08 (11th Cir.1996)(although properly remanding nondiverse counts to state court, district court has no authority under § 1367(c) to remand counts within its original subject matter jurisdiction).

29. *But cf., Raygor v. Regents of the University of Minnesota,* 534 U.S. 533, 122 S.Ct. 999, 152 L.Ed.2d 27 (2002) (when state claims asserted under § 1367 are dismissed on Eleventh Amendment grounds, § 1367(d) does not toll statute of limitations for such claims against non-consenting defendants).

the benefit of the longer period.[30] Section 1367(d) is a most unusual provision, in that it is a circumstance where federal law extends a state statute of limitations for a claim that arises under state law. However, it is now settled that the provision is constitutional.[31]

Tolling Other Claims

If a claim filed under 28 U.S.C.A. § 1367(a) is dismissed by the federal court, it is possible the claimant will want to dismiss other claims that qualify for federal subject matter jurisdiction, so that the entire case may be refiled in state court. To permit such a possibility free of the bar of statutes of limitations, § 1367(d)'s tolling provisions also extend to claims voluntarily dismissed in the aftermath of a denial of supplemental jurisdiction to one claim.

"State" Defined

28 U.S.C.A. § 1367(e) provides that whenever the term "State" is used in § 1367, it shall also include the District of Columbia, Puerto Rico, and United States Territories.

ADDITIONAL RESEARCH REFERENCES

C.J.S. Federal Courts §§ 11–26 et seq.

West's Key No. Digests, Federal Courts ⚲14–25.

§ 2.14 Venue

CORE CONCEPT

The requirement of venue sets the appropriate federal districts in which a particular case should be heard. Requirements to satisfy venue are additional to the jurisdictional prerequisites. Thus, even if a plaintiff satisfied both kinds of jurisdiction, the case might still be dismissed if venue was lacking.[1] State courts are also subject to the venue requirements established by their respective legislatures, and such requirements may differ significantly from the federal venue statutes. For federal courts, however, the only venue requirements that must be met are those enacted by Congress.

For certain specific causes of action, Congress has enacted special venue statutes. For example, venue in civil suits arising under the federal copyright laws is controlled by 28 U.S.C.A. § 1400. Similarly, venue in a stockholder's derivative suit is controlled by 28 U.S.C.A.

---

30. *Myers v. County of Lake,* 30 F.3d 847, 848 (7th Cir.1994) (§ 1367(d) "removes the principal reason for retaining a case in federal court when the federal claim belatedly disappears.").

31. *Jinks v. Richland County,* 538 U.S. 456, 123 S.Ct. 1667, 155 L.Ed.2d 631 (2003). *But cf., Raygor v. Regents of University of Minnesota,* 534 U.S. 533, 122 S.Ct. 999, 152 L.Ed.2d 27 (2002) (§ 1367(d) does not toll limitations period when suit is dis-

missed because a State, as defendant, has asserted 11th Amendment immunity to suit against federal court).

1. *Cf., e.g., United States ex rel. Rudick v. Laird,* 412 F.2d 16, 20 (2d Cir.1969) ("[J]urisdiction must first be found over the subject matter and the persons involved in the cause before the question of venue can be properly reached.").

§ 1401. When a cause of action arises within those particular areas of law, the case law indicates that the ability of a plaintiff to choose between general venue provisions and more specific provisions depends on whether Congress intended to make the more specific provision the exclusive source of venue.[2] In the absence of a special venue provision, venue for diversity suits and federal questions is controlled by § 1391.

APPLICATIONS

Venue Generally

Section 1391 restricts the choice of federal district court in which a plaintiff may sue to those districts that Congress deems fair. This assessment of fairness is sometimes quite distinct from the concepts of constitutional fairness discussed under jurisdiction over persons or things. Thus, it is possible that a federal district court might have satisfactory personal jurisdiction over a defendant, but the action could still be dismissed for failure to meet venue requirements. For example, a defendant might be served with process within the state where the federal court sits, which would normally satisfy personal jurisdiction, but requirements of § 1391 might still not be met. In that sense, venue can be an additional trap for the unwary plaintiff.

Considerations of the relative merits of venue requirements aside, § 1391 can influence significantly the suitability of the particular federal district court a plaintiff has chosen. For that reason alone, the technical elements of venue are also important to successful prosecutions and defenses of civil claims in federal court.

NOTE: 28 U.S.C.A. §§ 1391(a) and (b) were substantially rewritten in December 1990. Section 1391(c) was also substantially rewritten shortly before that. These and other changes in § 1391 make some, but not all, of the older case law on venue unreliable.

Federal Judicial Districts

State borders matter significantly in questions of jurisdiction. For venue questions, however, the important boundary is that which exists between federal judicial districts. In smaller states, the entire state may be a single district. In Rhode Island, for example, the United States District Court for the District of Rhode Island is the only federal district court within the state. Larger states may have as many as four federal judicial districts within them. New York, for example has four judicial districts: the Eastern, Western, Southern, and Northern Districts.

---

2. See, e.g., Textile Unlimited v. A .. BMH & Co., 240 F.3d 781 (9th Cir.2001) (where venue provision of Federal Arbitration Act, 9 U.S.C.A. § 1 et seq., are permissive, they supplement § 1391 and do not supplant it); Delong Equip. Co. v. Washington Mills Abrasive Co., 840 F.2d 843, 855 (11th Cir.1988) (when venue is satisfied under general venue statute, no need to look at venue under Clayton Act (i.e., antitrust law)). But see Garus v. Rose Acre Farms, Inc., 839 F.Supp. 563, 566 (N.D.Ind. 1993)(Title VII civil rights claims have their own venue provisions, which displace general venue statute).

NOTE: It is also possible that a federal judicial district will break itself down into still smaller components. For example, the United States District Court for the Eastern District of Virginia is one of two federal district courts within Virginia. The Eastern District, in turn, is subdivided into four divisions: the Alexandria Division; the Norfolk Division; the Richmond Division; and the Newport News Division. Local rules of a federal district court might supplement venue statutes by requiring that a case be filed not only within the proper judicial district, but also within the appropriate division within that district.[3]

Residence Requirements

Reference is frequently made throughout 28 U.S.C.A. § 1391 to judicial districts in which a defendant resides. Although the case law is not unanimous, it appears that "residence," when applied to venue requirements, is similar to the jurisdictional concepts of "citizenship" and "domicile". Though natural persons may have several houses scattered around the country, only one is a domicile, which confers state citizenship for diversity purposes. Probably only one is a residence, for venue purposes.[4]

Counterclaims and Crossclaims

Generally speaking, only plaintiffs have the burden of satisfying requirements of venue. Counterclaims, crossclaims, and similar actions normally do not raise venue questions.[5] This distinction is a significant departure from jurisdictional requirements, discussed above, for which every count in a case must satisfy some form of both jurisdiction over persons or things and subject matter jurisdiction.

Consent to Venue

If parties consent to personal jurisdiction in a particular district or state, it appears settled that they also consent to venue there.[6] Moreover, if the plaintiff files suit in a federal judicial district where venue is improper, the court may still hear that case if the defendant does not object to venue.[7] Rule 12(g) and (h), governing timing

---

3. *See, e.g., Garus v. Rose Acre Farms, Inc.*, 839 F.Supp. 563, 566 n. 2 (N.D.Ind. 1993)(noting that local rule divides division into subdivision for venue purposes).

4. *See, e.g., Manley v. Engram*, 755 F.2d 1463, 1466 (11th Cir.1985)("mere residence" in a state does not equal venue; "rather, it is the individual's 'permanent' residence—*i.e.*, his domicile that is the benchmark for determining proper venue.").

5. *See, e.g., Bredberg v. Long*, 778 F.2d 1285, 1288 (8th Cir.1985)(where venue is proper as to plaintiff's claims, it is improbable that an objection to venue will be heard as to counterclaims or cross-claims).

6. *See, e.g., Doctor's Assocs., Inc. v. Stuart*, 85 F.3d 975 (2d Cir.1996)(party may consent to venue by consenting to personal jurisdiction).

7. *See, e.g., Leroy v. Great Western United Corp.*, 443 U.S. 173, 99 S.Ct. 2710, 61 L.Ed.2d 464 (1979)(both personal jurisdiction and venue may be waived). *See also Tri-State Employment Services, Inc. v. Mountbatten Surety Co.*, 295 F.3d 256, 260 n. 2 (2d Cir.2002) (defendant's failure to raise venue means defendant has waived issue); *King v. Russell*, 963 F.2d 1301 (9th Cir.1992) (per curiam) (improper venue waived if defendant does not object to venue while raising other Rule 12 issues). *Cf., Algodonera De Las Cabezas, S.A. v. Ameri-*

and waiver of certain motions to dismiss, identify the time frame in which a defendant must either raise objections to venue or forego them.[8]

Venue and Removal

If a claim is removed from a state court to a federal district court, § 1391 does not apply. Thus, a removed claim is treated somewhat differently than a case originally filed in federal court.[9] However, a party who sought removal of a claim does not thereby waive a challenge to the state court's venue. That challenge is preserved and may be raised in federal court.[10] Another way of understanding the interplay of these two points is to recognize that for a removed claim the applicable venue standard is that which governed the state court in which the claim was originally filed.

Remedy

If the court, on timely objection of a party, finds venue to be deficient, the court may dismiss the action, allowing plaintiff to refile the claim elsewhere if the action is not otherwise barred.[11] This can raise significant statutes of limitations problems for a plaintiff. With limitations periods in mind, Congress enacted 28 U.S.C.A. § 1406, which allows a federal district court, on finding venue to be faulty, to *transfer* a cause of action to a judicial district or division where venue is proper. The court's discretion to employ this remedy is broad, constrained only by "the interest of justice." The practical consequence of transfer is that the court need not dismiss the action—which means the plaintiff will not run afoul of statutes of limitations.[12]

Venue in Diversity Cases

28 U.S.C.A. § 1391(a) provides three opportunities for venue in cases where subject matter jurisdiction is based solely on diversity of citizenship. Subject to some qualifications on the third option discussed below, the plaintiff may file in any of the following districts,[13] as tactics in a particular suit may require:

---

can Suisse Capital, Inc., 432 F.3d 1343, 1345 (courts may dismiss sua sponte for lack of venue, but only after giving defendant a chance to waive venue requirement).

8. *But see Costlow v. Weeks,* 790 F.2d 1486, 1488 (9th Cir.1986)(where defendant has made no appearance whatever, court may dismiss for lack of venue *sua sponte*).

9. *See, e.g., PT United Can Co. v. Crown Cork & Seal Co.,* 138 F.3d 65, 72 (2d Cir. 1998) (In a removed case "one may not challenge venue in the district court as of right, according to that court's venue rules, as if the case had been originally brought there."). *See generally Polizzi v. Cowles Magazines, Inc.,* 345 U.S. 663, 665, 73 S.Ct. 900, 902, 97 L.Ed. 1331 (1953) ("[T]he ven-

ue of removed actions is governed by ... § 1441(a) [the federal removal statute].").

10. *See, e.g., PT United Can Co. v. Crown Cork & Seal Co.,* 138 F.3d 65, 73 (2d Cir.1998) (so holding; citing *Polizzi, supra*).

11. *Polizzi v. Cowles Magazines,* 345 U.S. 663, 73 S.Ct. 900, 97 L.Ed. 1331 (1953).

12. *See, e.g., Smith v. Thompson,* 685 F.Supp. 177 (N.D.Ill.1988) (where pro se inmate files in an improper venue, this court usually transfers in preference to a dismissal).

13. *See, e.g., Willis v. Caterpillar, Inc.,* 199 F.3d 902, 905 (7th Cir.1999) (venue proper either in district where defendant resides or where allegedly defective forklift was manufactured).

(1) *Where Defendants Reside:* in any judicial district where a single defendant resides, provided that all defendants reside in the same state;[14]

(2) *Where Substantial Events or Omissions Occurred:* in any judicial district where a substantial part of the relevant events occurred,[15] or where a substantial part of the property that gave rise to the action is found, such as a district in which damage occurred in a tort case, or where performance was to have occurred in a contract action.[16] It should be noted that in making this assessment, courts generally consider acts of both the plaintiff and the defendant.[17] It should also be noted that, depending on the facts of individual cases, venue under § 1391(a)(2) may be possible in more than one juridical district.[18] Section 1391(a)(2)'s provision for venue where property is located is a reference to attachments of property in quasi in rem actions as well as the location of property disputed in a case of personal jurisdiction;[19] or

(3) *Where Any Defendant is Subject to Personal Jurisdiction:* in any judicial district in which any defendant is subject to personal jurisdiction at the time a suit is filed. Note that for purposes of § 1391(a)(3), personal jurisdiction is measured by the boundaries of a federal judicial district. Thus, in states which have more than one federal judicial district, § 1391(a)(3) may be used to satisfy venue

---

14. *See, e.g., Algodonera De Las Cabezas, S.A. v. American Suisse Capital, Inc.,* 432 F.3d 1343, 1345 (11th Cir.2005) (corporations that conduct business, receive correspondence, and are subject to service of process in a district are "residents" in that district under § 1391(c); if such corporations are the only defendants, § 1391(a)(1) is satisfied); *Willis v. Caterpillar, Inc.,* 199 F.3d 902, 905 (7th Cir.1999) (principle place of business of sole defendant, a corporation, satisfies § 1391).

15. *See, e.g., Uffner v. La Reunion Francaise, S.A.,* 244 F.3d 38, 42 (1st Cir.2001) (when events underlying claim occurred in different places, "venue may be proper in any number of districts;" but when single event supports allegation of venue in particular district, event must be substantial); *Setco Enters. Corp. v. Robbins,* 19 F.3d 1278 (8th Cir.1994)(issue is not whether other judicial districts had more significant contacts; issue is only whether district chosen by plaintiff had "a substantial connection" to the cause of action).

16. *See, e.g., Voest-Alpine Trading USA Corp. v. Bank of China,* 288 F.3d 262, 265 (5th Cir.2002) (dispute over validity of letter of credit that was issued in China; held, good venue in Houston (Southern District of Texas) where: letter was partially negoti-

ated in Houston; letter was accepted in Houston; letter was presented to correspondent bank in Houston; and payment was to be made to correspondent bank in Houston); *Ciena Corp. v. Jarrard,* 203 F.3d 312, 318 (4th Cir.2000) (trade secrets case; venue appropriate in district where defendant was trained and employed by plaintiff and where alleged damage to plaintiff might occur).

17. *See, e.g., Uffner v. La Reunion Francaise, S.A.,* 244 F.3d 38, 43 n. 6 (1st Cir. 2001) (collecting cases and adopting majority view). *But see Woodke v. Dahm,* 70 F.3d 983, 985 (8th Cir.1995) (only location of defendant's activities is relevant; location of plaintiff's contacts held irrelevant).

18. *See, e.g., Reliance Insurance Co. v. PolyVision Corp.,* 474 F.3d 54, 59 (2d Cir. 2007) ("[C]ourts are not, in general, required to determine the 'best venue,' but merely a logical one with a substantial connection to the litigation."); *Jenkins Brick Co. v. Bremer,* 321 F.3d 1366, 1371 (11th Cir.2003) ("The ... language [of § 1391(a)(2)] thus contemplates some cases in which venue will be proper in two or more districts.").

19. *See, Cottman Transmission Sys., Inc. v. Martino,* 36 F.3d 291 (3d Cir. 1994)(contacts must be "substantial").

requirements only when a defendant is subject to personal jurisdiction in that portion of the state which comprises the federal judicial district. It should be noted that § 1391(a)(3) may only be employed if a party is unable to satisfy venue requirements under either § 1391(a)(1) or (a)(2). If either of those options are available, the party may not employ § 1391(a)(3).[20]

28 U.S.C.A. § 1391(a) and Other Venue Statutes

Section 1391(a) controls venue for cases whose subject matter jurisdiction is based solely on diversity jurisdiction "except as otherwise provided by law." Thus, it defers explicitly to the provisions of other, more specific, venue statutes such as 28 U.S.C.A. § 1401, governing shareholder's derivative actions. In theory, that deference may afford a plaintiff greater venue opportunities under the provisions of the more specific venue statute. Generally, however, the current version of § 1391(a) provides the broadest opportunities for venue selection, and the more specific venue provisions, such as § 1401, tend to be more restrictive. Whether a litigant may employ the venue opportunities of § 1391 depends on whether Congress enacted a special venue provision and provided for its exclusive use.[21]

Cases Not Based Solely on Diversity

28 U.S.C.A. § 1391(b) controls when subject matter jurisdiction is not based solely on diversity of citizenship. Like § 1391(a), § 1391(b) provides three opportunities for venue. The first two of these are identical to their counterparts in § 1391(a). Until recently, the third contained several subtle differences, whose significance was unclear. However, all but one of these differences have now been eliminated. Thus, § 1391(a)(3) is now identical to § 1391(b)(3), with one exception. Where § 1391(a)(3) refers to "a judicial district in which any defendant is subject to personal jurisdiction at the time the action is commenced," § 1391(b)(3) refers to "a judicial district in which any defendant may be found." It appears that the legislative drafters intended no significant distinction between these two phrases, but obviously some uncertainty remains. The provisions of § 1391(b) are as follows:

(1) *Where Defendants Reside:* in any judicial district where a single defendant resides, provided that all defendants reside within the same state;[22]

---

20. *See, e.g., Algodonera De Las Cabezas, S.A. v. American Suisse Capital, Inc.,* 432 F.3d 1343, 1345 (11th Cir.2005) ("[V]enue may be predicated on § 1391(a)(3) only when neither § 1391(a)(1) or (2) are satisfied.").

21. *Compare, e.g., Garus v. Rose Acre Farms, Inc.,* 839 F.Supp. 563, 566 (N.D.Ind. 1993)(Title VII civil rights claims have their own venue provisions, which displace general venue statute) *with, e.g., Urrutia v. Harrisburg County Police Department,* 91 F.3d 451, 462 (3d Cir.1996) ("[42 U.S.C. §] 1983 contains no special venue provision. ... Therefore, the general venue provisions of 28 U.S.C. § 1391 apply.").

22. *See, e.g., Manley v. Engram,* 755 F.2d 1463, 1466 (11th Cir.1985)(for purposes of venue, "residence" for natural persons means "domicile.").

(2) *Where Substantial Events or Omissions Occurred:* in any judicial district where a substantial part of the relevant events occurred, or where a substantial part of the property that gave rise to the action is found, such as a district in which damage occurred in a tort case,[23] or where performance was to have occurred in a contract action. The requirement that the events in question be "substantial" is important, for it seems clear that venue will not be appropriate in a district that has only a casual relationship with the underlying cause of action.[24] At the same time, however, it is settled that under § 1391(b)(2), venue may be possible in more than one judicial district, provided that each district was the site of a "substantial" part of the event in question.[25] Section 1391(b)(2)'s provision for venue where property is located is a reference to attachments of property in quasi in rem actions as well as the location of property disputed in a case of personal jurisdiction; or

(3) *Where Any Defendant May Be Found:* in any judicial district in which a single defendant may be found, "if there is no district in which the action may otherwise be brought." The liberal reach of § 1391(b)(3) can be deceptive, for this third option can only be employed "if there is no district in which the action may otherwise be brought." This means § 1391(b)(3) cannot be used as a first resort. Instead, a plaintiff seeking venue in cases not founded solely on diversity must use either § 1391(b)(1) or (b)(2) if they are available. Only if venue *fails* under *both* those provisions may plaintiff seek the benefit of § 1391(b)(3). Thus the practical utility of (b)(3), while potentially significant as a device for saving venue, is still substantially less than might appear at first glance.

28 U.S.C.A. § 1391(b) and Other Venue Statutes

Section 1391(b), like its counterpart in Section 1391(a), also permits use of more specific venue statutes if they are available to the plaintiff for a given cause of action. Given the fairly broad provisions of § 1391(b), however, there may be little benefit from using other, more specific venue statutes. Whether special venue statutes displace § 1391 depends on whether Congress made the

23. *See, e.g., Friedman v. Revenue Management of New York, Inc.,* 38 F.3d 668, 671 (2d Cir.1994)(defendant is New York corporation, servicing New York hospitals, collecting from New York debtors, employs New York law firm, and sues in New York; but no good venue where alleged acts of commingling, mismanagement and fraud related to assets, books and records that are in Illinois).

24. *See, e.g., Gulf Insurance Co. v. Glasbrenner,* 417 F.3d 353 (2d Cir.2005) ("[W]e caution district courts to take seriously the adjective 'substantial.' . . . It would be error . . . to treat the venue statute's 'substantial part' test as mirroring the minimum con-

tacts test employed in personal jurisdiction inquiries.").

25. *See, e.g., Daniel v. American Board of Emergency Medicine,* 428 F.3d 408, 432 (2d Cir.2005) ("Section 1391(b)(2) does not restrict venue to the district in which the 'most substantial' events or omissions giving rise to a claim occurred;" but events that occurred in chosen district must be a "substantial part" of the case). *Cf., Jenkins Brick Co. v. Bremer,* 321 F.3d 1366, 1371 (11th Cir.2003) ("The . . . language [of § 1391(a)(2)] thus contemplates some cases in which venue will be proper in two or more districts.").

particular venue statute at issue the exclusive source of venue for that particular cause of action.[26]

Residence for Corporations

28 U.S.C.A. § 1391(c) establishes the standards of residence for corporations for purposes of venue. This is a complicated provision, but if properly understood it can substantially expand opportunities for satisfying venue when a corporation is a defendant. To understand § 1391(c), it is best to break this provision into three component parts.

(1) *Corporate Venue Based on Personal Jurisdiction:* Corporations are deemed to be residents of any judicial district in which they would be subject to personal jurisdiction at the time an action is commenced.[27]

(2) *Multi–District States:* If a state has more than one judicial district, corporations are residents only of the judicial districts within the state in which they would be subject to personal jurisdiction, if the judicial district was a separate state.[28] Thus, while a corporation's contacts in one judicial district of a multi-district state might create personal jurisdiction over the corporation in all judicial districts in that state, the corporation's activity might satisfy venue only in the judicial district in which its contacts occurred.

(3) *Corporate Activities Dispersed Throughout a Multi–District State:* The third layer of § 1391(c) arises from the possibility that in a state with multiple federal districts, a corporation might have sufficient contacts with the state as a whole to satisfy personal jurisdiction; but the contacts could be sufficiently dispersed among the judicial districts so that, if each of the districts was a "state," personal jurisdiction could not be achieved in any of them. In that case neither the first nor second provisions within § 1391(c) would give the corporation residence in any of the judicial districts of that state. Section 1391(c) deals with this possibility by providing that if it arises, a corporation is deemed to reside in the judicial district with which the corporation has "the most significant contacts."

NOTE: The complexities of venue should not be allowed to obscure the fact that for purposes of venue, as it relates to corporations, the important element is "residence," not domicile or citizenship. This is an important difference from venue for natural persons, where residence usually arises from domicile.[29] Thus, while 28 U.S.C.A. § 1391(c) bears some facial similarity to the

26. *See, e.g., Garus v. Rose Acre Farms, Inc.,* 839 F.Supp. 563, 566 (N.D.Ind.1993) (Title VII civil rights claims have their own venue provisions, which displace § 1391).

27. *See, e.g., Waeltz v. Delta Pilots Retirement Plan,* 301 F.3d 804, 809 (7th Cir. 2002) (for purposes of § 1391(c), residence is tested by amenability to personal jurisdiction); *Jumara v. State Farm Ins. Co.,* 55 F.3d 873 (3d Cir.1995)(venue proper in judi-

cial district where corporate defendant transacts business, signed contract, and where cause of action arose).

28. *See, e.g., id.*

29. *See Manley v. Engram,* 755 F.2d 1463, 1466 (11th Cir.1985)(for purposes of venue, "residence" for natural persons means "domicile.").

statute governing diversity citizenship for corporations, the results of these two rules can be quite different. For example, assume that General Motors, a large company, is for diversity purposes a citizen of Delaware (place of incorporation) and of Michigan (principal place of business). This would mean that for a party to sue General Motors on a state claim in federal court on the basis of diversity of citizenship, the plaintiff would have to be a citizen of some state (or foreign country) other than Delaware and Michigan. For venue, however, the fact that General Motors is a large company doing business in many judicial districts means, first, that General Motors is probably subject to personal jurisdiction in all of those districts. That means, in turn, that General Motors has residence in many judicial districts, and venue may be appropriate in all of them. Thus the company's widespread business activity makes it subject to personal jurisdiction, as well as venue, in many places. But for purposes of diversity jurisdiction, it is a citizen of only two states, affording plaintiffs from other states and foreign countries substantial opportunities to sue in federal court on state claims involving more than $75,000. As these examples indicate, the interplay of venue, subject matter jurisdiction, and jurisdiction over persons or things can create major complexities for plaintiffs, as well as important opportunities for defendants to oppose plaintiff's initial choice of forum.

Unincorporated Associations

For venue purposes, the case law treats partnerships, sole proprietorships, and other unincorporated associations in much the same manner as corporations, so that unincorporated associations are probably deemed to reside in every judicial district where they are subject to personal jurisdiction, according to the same threefold analysis of 28 U.S.C.A. § 1391(c).[30]

Aliens

Section 1391(d) provides that aliens may be sued in any judicial district. Case law suggests that this provision applies equally to alien corporations as well as alien natural persons,[31] so venue requirements for most alien defendants are not difficult to satisfy. It is uncertain whether a non–U.S. citizen domiciled in an American state (and therefore a citizen of that state for diversity purposes, under 28 U.S.C.A. § 1332(a)), is an "alien" for purposes of § 1391(d). Assuming such a person is not an alien, § 1391(d) would have no application in a suit where that person was the defendant. Thus ordinary requirements for venue, found in § 1391(a) and (b), would have to be satisfied.

---

30. *Denver & Rio Grande Western R.R. Co. v. Brotherhood of Railroad Trainmen,* 387 U.S. 556, 87 S.Ct. 1746, 18 L.Ed.2d 954 (1967)(multi-state unincorporated association has residence, for venue purposes, wherever it does business).

31. *See, e.g., Go–Video, Inc. v. Akai Elec. Co., Ltd.,* 885 F.2d 1406, 1413 (9th Cir.1989)(permitting use of § 1391(d) to establish venue in suit against foreign corporations).

The United States

Section 1391(e) expands venue possibilities if the United States, a federal agency, or a federal officer acting in an official capacity is a defendant. These provisions apply to the governmental defendant only, and only to governmental defendants who are part of the executive branch of the federal government.[32] A separate basis for venue must be found as to other defendants. The three venue possibilities available under § 1391(e) are:

(1) *A Single Defendant's Residence:* in a judicial district where a single defendant in the action resides. It is important to note that the United States, its agencies or officers can thereby be sued in a judicial district where some other defendant resides.[33] That would be true even if the federal officer, for example, did not reside in that district and did no business there; or

(2) *Location of Events or Property:* in a judicial district where "a substantial part of the events or omissions giving rise to the claim occurred, or a substantial part of property that is the subject of the action is situated;"[34] or

(3) *Plaintiff's Residence:* in a judicial district where a single plaintiff resides,[35] provided that the cause of action does not involve real property.[36] Section 1391(e)(3), in particular, is a major expansion of venue opportunities for suits against the United States and its agents.

It is important to note that a plaintiff may obtain the benefit of 28 U.S.C.A. § 1391(e) even if the suit also contains additional, non-federal defendants. In fact, the presence of non-federal defendants, and the use of their residences, creates the foundation for using § 1391(e)(1) to satisfy venue as to the United States, its agencies, and officers in judicial districts where venue as to the governmental defendant would not otherwise be possible.

NOTE: The additional venue possibilities of § 1391(e) are available *only against federal defendants in a case.*[37] Section 1391(e) specifically provides that if non-federal parties are also

32. *See, e.g., Trackwell v. United States Government,* 472 F.3d 1242, 1246 (10th Cir. 2007) (suggesting that venue under § 1391(e) cannot be applied to legislative or judicial branches or their officers).

33. *See also Bartman v. Cheney,* 827 F.Supp. 1, 3 (D.D.C.1993)(residence for federal officer or agency exists in any district where defendant performs "significant amount" of official duties).

34. *See, e.g., Andrean v. Secretary of United States Army,* 840 F.Supp. 1414, 1422 (D.Kan.1993)(for purposes of § 1391(e)(2), court is not restricted to only events or activities involving named defendant; court may examine "all" events that gave rise to claim).

35. *See, e.g., Sidney Coal Co. v. Social Security Administration,* 427 F.3d 336, 344–45 (6th Cir.2005) ("§ 1391(e)(3) contains no requirement that all plaintiffs must reside in the same district;" noting unanimity of federal courts on this view of § 1391(e)(3)).

36. *See, e.g., Immigrant Assistance Project of the Los Angeles County Federation of Labor v. Immigration & Naturalization Service,* 306 F.3d 842, 868 (9th Cir.2002).

37. *See, e.g., King v. Russell,* 963 F.2d 1301, 1303 (9th Cir.1992) (§ 1391(e) "only applies to suits against officers of the executive branch").

defendants, venue as to them must be satisfied under § 1391(a) or (b), or some other specific venue statute. Thus, § 1391(e) may permit a plaintiff to satisfy venue as to a federal officer in a judicial district where venue would not be available as to the federal defendant under § 1391(a) or (b), but as to non-federal defendants the normal requirements of other venue provisions would apply.

Nationwide Personal Jurisdiction Over Federal Agencies and Officers

To ensure that the broad venue authority of § 1391(e) is not nullified by problems of personal jurisdiction, § 1391(e) also provides that the federal district court shall be able, by certified mail, to obtain personal jurisdiction over federal agencies and officers not found within the state in which the court sits.

Personal Suits Against Federal Officers

The venue opportunities provided by 28 U.S.C.A. § 1391(e) as to federal officers are available only when the officers are sued in their official capacities. If they are sued personally for money damages, § 1391(e) is not applicable.[38] In such circumstances the provisions of § 1391(a) or (b), or some other more specific venue statute, would control.

Suits Against Foreign Countries

Section 1391(f) prescribes the venue when foreign countries, or their agencies, are defendants. Four possibilities for venue exist, depending on whether suit is against the foreign sovereign itself, its agency, or its shipping or cargo. These possibilities are:

(1) *Location of Events or Property:* in a judicial district where a substantial portion of the events giving rise to the claim occurred,[39] or where a substantial part of property that is the subject of the claim is located.

(2) *Location of Vessel or Cargo:* in any judicial district where a vessel or cargo belonging to a foreign state is located. This venue possibility is available only if the claim arose under 28 U.S.C.A. § 1605(b), governing suits in admiralty against foreign states; or

(3) *Location of Agency That is Doing Business:* if the defendant is an agency or instrumentality of the foreign state, as described in 28 U.S.C.A. § 1603(b), in any judicial district in which the agency is licensed to do business or doing business. It is important to note that privately owned non-American corporations do not fit within the description of a foreign state's instrumentality as defined by § 1603(b). For § 1603(b) to apply, the foreign state itself, not

---

38. *Stafford v. Briggs,* 444 U.S. 527, 100 S.Ct. 774, 63 L.Ed.2d 1 (1980)(§ 1391(e) unavailable where suit is for money damages against federal employees individually).

39. *See, e.g., U.S. Titan, Inc. v. Guangzhou Zhen Hua Shipping Co.,* 241 F.3d 135, 153–54 (2d Cir.2001) (noting parallel language of § 1391(b)(2) and (f)(1); requirement of substantial events satisfied by fact that defendant directed relevant communications to plaintiff in form district).

merely its citizens, must be the majority owner of an instrumentality;[40] or

(4) *Venue in the District of Columbia:* if the defendant is a foreign state itself, or a political subdivision of a foreign state, venue may be satisfied in the United States District Court for the District of Columbia.[41]

Sovereign Immunity

Nothing in § 1391(f) waives whatever immunity a foreign state, or its agencies or instrumentalities, may have. Instead, § 1391(f) provides venue possibilities only on the assumption that the suit is otherwise permitted by law, and that immunities either do not apply or have been waived for the purposes of the suit.

ADDITIONAL RESEARCH REFERENCES

C.J.S. Federal Courts §§ 16–21 et seq., 165–190 et seq.

West's Key No. Digests, Federal Courts ⚷71–157.

§ 2.15 Forum Non Conveniens

CORE CONCEPT

The forum non conveniens doctrine provides that a court selected by the claimant will not hear a cause of action if the court is an "inappropriate" forum. A trial court enjoys substantial discretion to determine whether it is an appropriate forum for a case, but that discretion is qualified by some important requirements, discussed below, that must be satisfied before a court's determination receives such deference.

APPLICATIONS

Relationship to Jurisdiction and Venue

Forum non conveniens shares some characteristics with jurisdiction and venue, but operates independently of those requirements. Thus, even if a plaintiff has chosen a court that enjoys: personal jurisdiction or quasi in rem jurisdiction over the defendant; subject matter jurisdiction over the kind of case at issue; and satisfactory venue, the court may refuse to hear the case if it determines that the court is an inappropriate forum.[1] At the same

40. *See, e.g., Transaero, Inc. v. La Fuerza Aerea Boliviana,* 30 F.3d 148, 152 (D.C.Cir.1994) (limiting venue under § 1391(f)(3) to commercial enterprise that is agent or instrumentality of foreign state).

41. *See, e.g., Telcordia Tech, Inc. v. Telkom SA, Ltd.,* 458 F.3d 172, 176 n. 4 (3d Cir. 2006) (where majority owner of company is foreign country, district court in District of Columbia is an additional option for venue).

1. *Sinochem International Co. v. Malaysia International Shipping Corp.,* ___ U.S. ___, 127 S.Ct. 1184, 167 L.Ed.2d 15 (2007) ("A district court ... may dispose of an action by a forum non conveniens dismissal, bypassing questions of subject-matter and personal jurisdiction, when considerations of convenience, fairness, and judicial economy so warrant."); *American Dredging Co. v. Miller,* 510 U.S. 443, 453, 114 S.Ct. 981, 127 L.Ed.2d 285 (1994) (Forum non conve-

time, the court will typically not address the question of forum non conveniens until it first determines whether requirements of jurisdiction and venue are satisfied.[2]

Timing

In the ordinary course of events a motion to dismiss under the doctrine of forum non conveniens or a motion to transfer a case under 28 U.S.C.A. § 1404 (discussed below) will normally be made early in the litigation. A motion made after judgment will not be granted.[3]

Moreover, even a motion made earlier in a case is substantially less likely to prevail on appeal once the case has proceeded through trial to judgment.[4]

Forum Selection Clauses

In circumstances where the parties have agreed in advance to a forum selection clause, that choice of forum will normally be resistant an attack on grounds of forum non conveniens.[5] Other factors of public and private interest may still be examined, but they will normally not prevail over an otherwise valid forum selection clause.[6]

niens is "a supervening venue provision, permitting displacement of the ordinary rules of venue when, in light of certain conditions, the trial court thinks that jurisdiction ought to be declined."). *See, e.g., Wiwa v. Royal Dutch Petroleum Co.,* 226 F.3d 88, 100 (2d Cir.2000) (forum non conveniens is "a discretionary device permitting a court in rare instances to dismiss claims even if the court is a permissible venue with proper jurisdiction over the claim.").

2. *Gulf Oil Corp. v. Gilbert,* 330 U.S. 501, 504, 67 S.Ct. 839, 840, 91 L.Ed. 1055 (1947) ("[T]he doctrine of forum non conveniens can never apply if there is absence of jurisdiction or venue."); *Baris v. Sulpicio Lines, Inc.,* 932 F.2d 1540, 1542 (5th Cir. 1991) (court should typically address issue of forum non conveniens only after determining that jurisdiction exists). *See also Albion v. YMCA Camp Letts,* 171 F.3d 1, 2 (1st Cir.1999) (transfer under 28 U.S.C.A. § 1404 also inappropriate where court lacked personal jurisdiction over defendant). *But see Monegasque de Reassurances, S.A.M. v. Nak Naftogaz of Ukraine,* 311 F.3d 488, 498 (2d Cir.2002) (sometimes acceptable for district court to decide forum non conveniens prior to addressing jurisdiction); *In re Papandreou,* 139 F.3d 247 (D.C.Cir.1998) (in some cases dismissal on grounds of forum non conveniens may not require court to address issues of jurisdiction first).

3. *See, e.g., Ortiz v. Gaston County Dyeing Machine Co.,* 277 F.3d 594, 597–98 (1st Cir.2002) ("Once the court entered judgment . . . it was too late to request a transfer.").

4. *See, e.g., Zelinski v. Columbia 300, Inc.,* 335 F.3d 63 (7th Cir.2003) (once trial was finished, public interest in favor of not moving case may arise from policy of not wasting judicial resources already expended on case); *McLennan v. American Eurocopter Corp., Inc.,* 245 F.3d 403, 423–24 (5th Cir. 2001) (when case is tried to conclusion, denial of motion is strengthened; to prevail on appeal, moving party must show "great prejudice").

5. *Stewart Organization, Inc. v. Ricoh Corp.,* 487 U.S. 22, 29, 108 S.Ct. 2239, 2243, 101 L.Ed.2d 22 (1988) ("The presence of a forum-selection clause . . . will be a significant factor that figures centrally in the district court's calculus."). *See, e.g., P & S Business Machines, Inc. v. Canon USA, Inc.,* 331 F.3d 804, 807–08 (11th Cir.2003) (choice made in forum selection clause will rarely be disturbed).

6. *See, e.g., Bonny v. Society of Lloyd's,* 3 F.3d 156, 160 n. 11 (7th Cir.1993) ("[A] party's financial status at any given time in the course of litigation cannot be the basis for enforcing or not enforcing a valid forum selection clause."); *Moses v. Business Card Express, Inc.,* 929 F.2d 1131, 1138–39 (6th Cir.1991), *cert. denied,* 502 U.S. 821, 112

Requirement of an Adequate Alternative Forum

An important limit on a trial court's discretion to dismiss a case on forum non conveniens grounds arises from the requirement that, before the court employs its discretion in the matter, it must first determine that an adequate alternative forum exists.[7] The defendant has the burden of demonstrating the availability of such a forum.[8] Even if the plaintiff's choice of forum seems strained, that choice will not be overruled (assuming no problems with jurisdiction and venue) until the trial court makes that determination.[9] If there is no other such forum, the court will retain the case.

Evaluating the adequacy of an alternative forum requires a determination as to whether the defendants are subject to service of process in the alternative forum, and whether the alternative forum will hear the case. For other American jurisdictions this analysis tends to focus on the question of jurisdiction over the defendant.[10] If there is some question about jurisdiction in the proposed alternative forum, a defendant can usually eliminate the issue by stipulating to jurisdiction in that forum.[11]

S.Ct. 81, 116 L.Ed.2d 54 (1991) (economic disparity between parties and one party's claim of financial hardship cannot overcome valid forum selection clause).

7. *Gulf Oil Corp. v. Gilbert,* 330 U.S. 501, 506–07, 67 S.Ct. 839, 91 L.Ed. 1055 (1947) ("[F]orum non conveniens ... presupposes at least two forums in which the defendant is amenable to process."). *See, e.g., DiRienzo v. Philip Services Corp.,* 294 F.3d 21, 28 (2d Cir.2002) ("A forum non conveniens motion cannot be granted absent an adequate alternative forum."); *Iragorri v. International Elevator, Inc.,* 203 F.3d 8, 13 (1st Cir.2000) (district court should determine adequacy of alternative forum before weighing factors of private and public interest).

8. *See, e.g., Duha v. Agrium, Inc.,* 448 F.3d 867, 873 (6th Cir.2006) (first requirement is that defendant show "available and adequate alternative forum"); *Jones v. GNC Franchising, Inc.,* 211 F.3d 495, 499 n. 22 (9th Cir.2000) (defendant has burden of proving existence of "adequate alternative forum"); *Gschwind v. Cessna Aircraft Co.,* 161 F.3d 602, 606 (10th Cir.1998) ("Plaintiff correctly notes that the defendant bears the burden of proving that an adequate alternative forum exists.").

9. *Piper Aircraft Co. v. Reyno,* 454 U.S. 235, 255 n. 22, 102 S.Ct. 252, 265, 70 L.Ed.2d 419 (1981) ("At the outset of any forum non conveniens inquiry, the court must determine whether there exists an alternative forum."). *See also Norex Petro-*

leum, Ltd. v. Access Industries, Inc., 416 F.3d 146 (2d Cir.2005) (if movant fails to identify adequate alternative forum, "the forum non conveniens motion must be denied regardless of the degree of deference accorded plaintiff's forum choice"); *Alpine View Co. v. Atlas Copco AB,* 205 F.3d 208, 221 (5th Cir.2000) ("A court facing a motion to dismiss for forum non conveniens must first assess whether an alternative forum is both available and adequate."); *Boosey & Hawkes Music Publishers, Ltd. v. Walt Disney Co.,* 145 F.3d 481 (2d Cir.1998) (failure to consider whether issues are justiciable in at least one alternative forum mandates reversal of dismissal).

10. *Piper Aircraft Co. v. Reyno,* 454 U.S. 235, 255 n. 22, 102 S.Ct. 252, 265, 70 L.Ed.2d 419 (1981) ("Ordinarily, this requirement [of an adequate alternative forum] will be satisfied when the defendant is 'amenable to process' in the other jurisdiction.").

11. *See, e.g., Monegro v. Rosa,* 211 F.3d 509, 514 (9th Cir.2000) (abuse of discretion where, *inter alia,* district court did not condition dismissal on defendant's participation in judicial proceedings in Dominican Republic; case also had significant relation with plaintiff's chosen forum and evidence was at least as likely to be available in United States); *Gschwind v. Cessna Aircraft Co.,* 161 F.3d 602, 606 (10th Cir.1998) ("Defendants agreed to be subject to suit in France. That concession is generally enough to make the alternative forum available.").

However, if the proposed alternative forum is found in another country, the trial court hearing the forum non conveniens motion will, in addition to questions of jurisdiction and service of process, also examine whether the foreign court has the capacity to provide an adequate remedy.[12] In extreme cases, there may also be questions about the integrity of a particular foreign court.[13] When the court believes that another forum would be more appropriate but still retains some concern over whether a case will actually be heard in

Cf., Jota v. Texaco, Inc., 157 F.3d 153, 159 (2d Cir.1998) ("[D]ismissal for forum non conveniens is not appropriate, at least absent a commitment by [defendant] to submit to the jurisdiction of the Ecuadoran courts for purposes of this action"). *See also Alpine View Co. v. Atlas Copco, AB,* 205 F.3d 208, 221 (5th Cir.2000) (foreign court is available if " 'entire case and all parties' " are subject to its jurisdiction); *Reid–Walen v. Hansen,* 933 F.2d 1390, 1393 n. 2 (8th Cir.1991) (case involved more than one defendant; "An alternative forum is available if **all** parties are amenable to process and come within the jurisdiction of the forum." [emphasis added]). *But cf., Wild v. Subscription Plus, Inc.,* 292 F.3d 526, 531 (7th Cir.2002) ("[T]here is no absolute bar to the transfer of a multidefendant suit to a district in which one of the defendants cannot be served." Treating § 1404 as closely analogous to § 1406 for this purpose); *In re Papandreou,* 139 F.3d 247, 256 n. 6 (D.C.Cir.1998) (dicta; if district court dismisses case, involving possible foreign sovereign immunity issues, on grounds of forum non conveniens, dismissal should not "be subject to conditions, *e.g.,* a condition that defendants promise to submit to the jurisdiction of another court, for exaction of such a condition would appear inescapably to constitute an exercise of jurisdiction").

12. *See, e.g., Nemariam v. Federal Democratic Republic of Ethiopia,* 315 F.3d 390, 394 (D.C.Cir.2003) (alleged alternative forum is inadequate where foreign tribunal cannot make award directly to plaintiff, and government that would be claimant in place of plaintiff has no duty to send any award to her); *Gonzalez v. Chrysler Corp.,* 301 F.3d 377, 382 (5th Cir.2002) (Mexico's low cap on tort damages does not make Mexico an inappropriate forum); *Leon v. Million Air, Inc.,* 251 F.3d 1305, 1311 (11th Cir. 2001) ("Courts have been strict about requiring that defendants demonstrate that the alternative forum offers at least some relief."); *Satz v. McDonnell Douglas Corp.,* 244 F.3d 1279, 1283 (11th Cir.2001) ("An adequate forum need not be a perfect fo-

rum;" concerns about filing fees, lack of discovery, and delay do not automatically render foreign forum inadequate; noting that, in instant case, defendant agreed to use of discovery rules of American federal courts); *DiRienzo v. Philip Services Corp.,* 232 F.3d 49, 58 (2d Cir.2000) (procedural differences, such as possibility that foreign court will not certify a class action, do not make foreign forum inadequate); *Alpine View Co. v. Atlas Copco AB,* 205 F.3d 208, 221 (5th Cir.2000) (foreign court is available when " 'entire case and all parties' " are subject to its jurisdiction; it is adequate where parties " 'will not be deprived of all remedies or treated unfairly' "; availability of United States procedure in foreign court is not dispositive); *El–Fadl v. Central Bank of Jordan,* 75 F.3d 668, 678 (D.C.Cir.1996) (Jordanian courts unsuitable in part because recently enacted Jordanian law immunized defendants from liability for actions in question).

13. *See, e.g., BP Chemicals, Ltd. v. Jiangsu Sopo Corp.,* 285 F.3d 677, 688 (8th Cir.2002) ("[P]roper resolution of the forum non conveniens argument will depend heavily upon whether [plaintiff] could receive a fair hearing in the Chinese courts."). *Cf., Monegasque de Reassurances S.A.M. v. Nak Naftogaz of Ukraine,* 311 F.3d 488, 499 (2d Cir.2002) ("We have been reluctant to find foreign courts 'corrupt' or 'biased.' "); *Leon v. Million Air, Inc.,* 251 F.3d 1305 (11th Cir.2001) (plaintiff's assertion that foreign court is too corrupt to be fair usually does not prevail; significant evidence of severe problems of partiality or years of delay needed to upset presumption that foreign forum is adequate); *Iragorri v. International Elevator, Inc.,* 203 F.3d 8, 13 (1st Cir.2000) (notwithstanding State Department advisory on danger of traveling in Columbia, native Columbians who are naturalized United States citizens face less danger and are more familiar with culture and language of Columbia than other Americans).

the foreign court, the appropriate practice is to include a clause in the dismissal order providing that parties may return to the dismissing court to resume their case.[14]

The probability that a foreign court will not apply American substantive law is usually not weighed heavily in determining the adequacy of an alternative forum.[15] However, the result may be different in cases where distinctions in procedural law preclude a reasonable opportunity for the plaintiff to present a case.[16]

Deference to Plaintiff's Choice of Forum: Exceptions and Modification

Normally, the court will give substantial deference to a plaintiff's choice of forum.[17] Thus, for a defendant to prevail on a forum

14. *See, e.g., Vasquez v. Bridgestone/Firestone, Inc.,* 325 F.3d 665, 675 (5th Cir.2003) (if foreign forum may not be open or defendant may not submit to jurisdiction there, it is abuse of discretion to fail to include "return jurisdiction" clause in dismissal order; remedy for such abuse of discretion is to remand to insert clause); *Ford v. Brown,* 319 F.3d 1302, 1311 (11th Cir. 2003) (approving dismissal that is conditioned on defendant's waiver of jurisdiction and limitations defenses in foreign forum and willingness of foreign court to hear case).

15. *Piper Aircraft Co. v. Reyno,* 454 U.S. 235, 247, 102 S.Ct. 252, 261, 70 L.Ed.2d 419 (1981) ("The possibility of a change in substantive law should ordinarily not be given conclusive or even substantial weight in the forum non conveniens inquiry."). *See, e.g., Dickson Marine, Inc. v. Panalpina, Inc.,* 179 F.3d 331, 342 (5th Cir.1999) ("[D]ifferences in substantive law should not be given conclusive weight in a forum non conveniens inquiry."). *Cf., Boosey & Hawkes Music Publishers, Ltd. v. Walt Disney Co.,* 145 F.3d 481, 492 (2d Cir.1998) (noting that refusal to dismiss case on grounds of forum non conveniens will require trial court to apply foreign law, but also noting that "[w]hile reluctance to apply foreign law is a valid factor favoring dismissal, . . . standing alone it does not justify dismissal.").*But cf., Gschwind v. Cessna Aircraft Co.,* 161 F.3d 602, 606 (10th Cir. 1998) (in 10th Cir. There is an additional threshold requirement beyond existence of alternative forum; court should also determine whether foreign law applies; only if both thresholds are met should court weigh public and private interests).

16. *See, e.g., Lacey v. Cessna Aircraft Co.,* 932 F.2d 170, 185 n. 12 (3d Cir.1991)

(Canadian forum inadequate because plaintiff would face "serious impediments" to obtaining sources of proof). *But see Alpha Therapeutic Corp. v. Nippon Hoso Kyokai,* 199 F.3d 1078, 1090 (9th Cir.1999) (fact that Japan's civil procedure rules "are not friendly to plaintiffs" did not by itself make erroneous district court's finding that Japan was adequate alternative forum); *Alfadda v. Fenn,* 159 F.3d 41, 48 (2d Cir.1998) (inability of plaintiff to use materials obtained through U.S. discovery in a French court is a relevant factor, but not necessarily dispositive).

17. *Koster v. (American) Lumbermens Mutual Casualty Co.,* 330 U.S. 518, 524, 67 S.Ct. 828, 831, 91 L.Ed. 1067 (1947) (plaintiff's choice of forum gets great deference when suit is in plaintiff's home forum); *Gulf Oil Corp. v. Gilbert,* 330 U.S. 501, 508, 67 S.Ct. 839, 843, 91 L.Ed. 1055 (1947) ("[U]nless the balance is strongly in favor of the defendant, the plaintiff's choice of forum should rarely be disturbed."). *See also Iragorri v. United Technologies Corp.,* 274 F.3d 65, 71–72 (2d Cir.2001) (noting sliding scale of deference involving several factors, but beginning with high deference for plaintiff's choice of home forum and sliding to less deference for foreign plaintiff; "the more it appear that a domestic or foreign plaintiff's choice of forum has been dictated by reasons that the law recognizes as valid, the greater the deference that will be given to the plaintiff's forum choice"); *Nowak v. Tak How Investments, Ltd.,* 94 F.3d 708, 719 (1st Cir.1996), ("We have emphasized that the doctrine of forum non conveniens is used to avoid 'serious unfairness' and that a plaintiff's choice of a forum will be disturbed only rarely."). Moreover, in a case where the plaintiff is a United States citizen and one or more defendants

non conveniens motion, the defendant must demonstrate that the plaintiff's choice of forum was significantly inappropriate, notwithstanding the existence of satisfactory jurisdiction and venue. As applied to the facts of particular cases, this deference means that when the court is weighing the public and private interests discussed below, the plaintiff's choice of forum will not be defeated by a mere preponderance of interests favoring dismissal. In fact, in most cases the forum non conveniens motion will not be granted unless the weighing factors discussed below "weigh heavily in favor of trial in the alternative forum."[18] In all cases the trial court's discretion in weighing factors may not be used to nullify the deference to which a plaintiff's choice of forum is entitled.[19]

Additionally, it should be clear that the entire question of the amount of deference due to the plaintiff's choice of forum does not even arise until the defendant establishes the existence of an adequate alternative forum. If there is no such forum, the motion to dismiss will simply be denied.[20]

Exception: Non–American Plaintiffs: In federal courts it is settled that American plaintiffs receive substantially more deference in their choices of fora than do non-American plaintiffs.[21] However, "less deference" is not the same as no deference at all, and a foreign plaintiff's choice of forum is still entitled to some respect.[22]

Exception: Certain Declaratory Judgment Plaintiffs: If the plaintiff who has chosen the forum has sought relief in the form of a

are non-Americans, the plaintiff's decision to sue in a judicial district other than the one in which the plaintiff resides does not nullify the deference to which the plaintiff's choice is entitled. *See, e.g., Wiwa v. Royal Dutch Petroleum Co.,* 226 F.3d 88, 103 (2d Cir.2000) ("The benefit for a U.S. resident plaintiff of suing in a U.S. forum is not limited to suits in the very district where the plaintiff resides, especially considering that the defendant may not be amenable to suit in the plaintiff's district of residence."); *Reid–Walen v. Hansen,* 933 F.2d 1390, 1394 (8th Cir.1991) (assuming plaintiff has not selected the forum to harass or vex the defendant, "the 'home' forum for the plaintiff is any federal district in the United States, not the particular district where the plaintiff lives").

18. *R. Maganlal & Co. v. M.G. Chemical Co.,* 942 F.2d 164, 167 (2d Cir.1991).

19. *See also DiRienzo v. Philip Services Corp.,* 232 F.3d 49, 60 (2d Cir.2000) (presumption in favor of home forum not weakened by fact that case is class action; acknowledging, however, that such weakening exists in shareholder's derivative suit, per *Koster v. (American) Lumbermens Mutual Casualty Co.,* 330 U.S. 518, 525, 67 S.Ct.

828, 832, 91 L.Ed. 1067 (1947)); *Wiwa v. Royal Dutch Petroleum Co.,* 226 F.3d 88, 101 (2d Cir.2000) (deference to plaintiff's choice of forum "increases as the plaintiff's ties to the forum increase"); *Guidi v. Inter–Continental Hotels Corp.,* 224 F.3d 142 (2d Cir.2000) (failure to give American plaintiffs choice of forum "significant deference" is "unsound").

20. *Norex Petroleum, Ltd. v. Access Industries, Inc.,* 416 F.3d 146 (2d Cir.2005).

21. *Piper Aircraft Co. v. Reyno,* 454 U.S. 235, 256, 102 S.Ct. 252, 266, 70 L.Ed.2d 419 (1981) ("Because the central purpose of any forum non conveniens inquiry is to ensure that the trial is convenient, a foreign plaintiff's choice deserves less deference.").

22. *See, e.g., Bigio v. Coca–Cola Co.,* 448 F.3d 176, 179 (2d Cir.2006) (even a foreign plaintiff's choice of forum is entitled to some deference; moreover, deference should increase if choice of forum has legitimate foundation); *Lacey v. Cessna Aircraft Co.,* 862 F.2d 38, 45–46 (3d Cir.1988) (Less deference for foreign plaintiffs "is 'not an invitation to accord a foreign plaintiff's selection of an American forum no deference.' ").

declaratory judgment, with a "bad faith" motive of taking advantage of the true plaintiff in a race to the forum, it appears that the declaratory judgment plaintiff's choice of forum is not entitled any deference.[23]

Modification: Corporate Plaintiffs in International Business: If the plaintiff is an American corporation with substantial experience in international business transactions and is suing on a cause of action that arose outside the United States, it appears that such a plaintiff will receive less deference than would, *e.g.,* an individual American plaintiff suing on a personal injury incurred while on vacation outside the United States.[24]

Weighing Factors: Judicial Discretion

Once a trial court has identified an adequate alternative forum in which the defendants will be subject to jurisdiction, it is authorized to weigh the important factors of public and private interest in determining whether to grant a defendant's forum non conveniens motion. In doing so, the court enjoys significant discretion that will not lightly be overturned on appeal, including the power to impose conditions on its decisions.[25] However, failure to weigh all the factors of public or private interest that arise in a particular case may be abuse of discretion.[26]

---

23. *See, e.g., Hyatt Inaternational Corp. v. Coco,* 302 F.3d 707, 718 (7th Cir.2002) (plaintiff's choice of forum normally gets deference, but "[w]e have wariness at the prospect of 'a suit for declaratory judgment aimed solely at wrestling the choice of forum from the natural plaintiff.'"); *NSI Corp. v. Showco, Inc.,* 843 F.Supp. 642, 645 (D.Ore.1994) (using declaratory judgment proceeding to obtain unfair advantage in choice of forum is ground for dismissal).

24. *See, e.g., Pollux Holding Ltd. v. Chase Manhattan Bank,* 329 F.3d 64, 70–71 (2d Cir.2003) (corporations with status of United States citizen residing abroad receives deference only to extent that corporations have significant connections with forum; otherwise, corporations get less deference); *Guidi v. Inter–Continental Hotels Corp.,* 224 F.3d 142 (2d Cir.2000) (because plaintiffs are "ordinary American citizens," they face significant inconvenience in litigating in Egypt; corporate defendant with principal place of business in forum faces no comparable hardship in defending in United States); *Kamel v. Hill–Rom Co., Inc.,* 108 F.3d 799, 804 (7th Cir.1997) (suggesting that sophisticated American corporate plaintiff suing on foreign cause of action receives "somewhat discounted" deference).

25. *See, e.g., Bank of Credit and Commerce International (Overseas) Ltd. v. State*

Bank of Pakistan, 273 F.3d 241, 244–48 (2d Cir.2001) (in granting motion, court has discretion to require party prevailing on motion to: waive statute of limitation defense; agree that if opponent obtains final judgment on in foreign court, it may be enforced elsewhere; and to waive forum non conveniens defense if foreign court refused to hear case on statute of limitations grounds).

26. *See, e.g.,EFCO Corp. v. Aluma Systems USA, Inc.,* 268 F.3d 601, 603 (8th Cir.2001) ("Abuse of discretion occurs when the district court does not hold the defendants to their burden of persuasion on all the elements of the forum non conveniens analysis, fails to consider the relevant public and private interest factors established in *Piper Aircraft* ... or clearly errs in weighing the *Piper Aircraft* factors."); *Dickson Marine, Inc. v. Panalpina, Inc.,* 179 F.3d 331, 341 (5th Cir.1999) ("[A] district court abuses its discretion when it grants a motion to dismiss without oral or written reasons or when it fails to address and balance the relevant principles and factors."); *Reid–Walen v. Hansen,* 933 F.2d 1390, 1393 (8th Cir.1991) ("An abuse of discretion may occur when the district court fails to consider one or more of the important private or public interest factors, does not hold the defendants to their bur-

Public Interest Factors

The public interest factors may differ somewhat from one case to another, but it is settled that they include: "(1) having local disputes settled locally; (2) avoiding problems of applying foreign law; and (3) avoiding burdening jurors with cases that have no impact on their community."[27] In some cases there may also be questions about the enforceability of a judgment that the court would render if it retained the case.

Local Disputes: The desire to settle local disputes locally (or, alternatively, the desire to avoid imposing distant disputes on a local court) takes into account questions such as local court congestion or burdens on jurors.[28]

Application of Foreign Law: Courts may be reluctant to take cases in which they will be obligated to apply the law of another jurisdiction. However, in a weighing of factors related to forum non conveniens, this consideration normally carries only limited weight.[29]

Burdening Jurors with Cases of No Local Interest: This factor contains two parts: whether local citizens should have to carry the burden of trying a case unrelated to their community; and whether the citizenry of another area has a greater interest in the outcome of a case.[30]

Enforceability of a Judgment: If enforcement of a prospective judgment could require further litigation outside the United States, the court may weigh that factor in determining whether the case should be heard in the United States in the first instance.[31] This consideration would carry particular weight if there was a significant possibility that the judgment would be unenforceable, thus potentially reducing the American judicial proceeding to a waste of time and judicial resources. However, this "enforceability" factor

den of persuasion on all elements of the forum non conveniens analysis, or has clearly erred in weighing the factors the court must consider.").

27. *Alfadda v. Fenn,* 159 F.3d 41, 46 (2d Cir.1998) (citing *Piper Aircraft* and *Gulf Oil). See also Zelinski v. Columbia 300, Inc.,* 335 F.3d 633 (7th Cir.2003) (once trial was finished, public interest in favor of not moving case may arise from policy of not wasting judicial resources already expended on case).

28. *Gulf Oil Corp. v. Gilbert,* 330 U.S. 501, 67 S.Ct. 839, 91 L.Ed. 1055 (1947). *But cf., Guidi v. Inter–Continental Hotels Corp.,* 224 F.3d 142 (2d Cir.2000) (district court's finding that it is " 'heavily overburdened' " is of "little or no significance" where all judicial vacancies have recently been filled; moreover, while the existence of related litigation in another forum may sometimes

justify dismissal so that judicial efficiency is served by permitting consolidation of cases, this consideration usually arises only when the parties in both lawsuits are substantially identical).

29. *See, e.g., Boosey & Hawkes Music Publishers, Ltd. v. Walt Disney Co.,* 145 F.3d 481, 492 (2d Cir.1998) (by itself, burden of applying foreign law does not justify dismissal).

30. *Gulf Oil Corp. v. Gilbert,* 330 U.S. 501, 67 S.Ct. 839, 91 L.Ed. 1055 (1947). *But cf., P & S Business Machines, Inc. v. Canon USA, Inc.,* 331 F.3d 804, 808 (11th Cir. 2003) (docket congestion is an appropriate consideration, but "case law does not suggest that docket congestion is, by itself, a dispositive factor").

31. *Gulf Oil Corp. v. Gilbert,* 330 U.S. 501, 67 S.Ct. 839, 91 L.Ed. 1055 (1947).

normally plays no role in forum non conveniens determinations if enforcement will occur in the United States, because the Full Faith and Credit clause of the Constitution generally requires an American court to enforce the final judgment of another American court.

Public Policy: In unusual cases, courts may retain a particular lawsuit because public policy favors an American forum for such a suit.[32]

Private Interest Factors

Private interest factors include: "(1) ease of access to evidence;[33] (2) the cost for witnesses to attend trial;[34] (3) the availability of compulsory process;[35] and (4) other factors that might shorten trial or make it less expensive."[36] For the most part, these factors revolve around the impact of forum selection on the ability of parties to prove their case. If a plaintiff's choice of forum—or the defendant's proposed alternative—substantially affects a party's ability to put forward witnesses and evidence, the court will be inclined to weigh that consideration heavily.[37]

---

32. *See, e.g., DiRienzo v. Philip Services Corp.,* 294 F.3d 21, 29–31 (2d Cir.2002) (private interest factors: documents in Canada, but no particular problems of transport; most witnesses in Canada, but all within a few hours of New York forum by automobile and air travel; some third-party witnesses in Canada cannot be forced to testify in New York, but videotaped depositions arranged through letters rogatory may be suitable substitute; public interest factors: most tend not to weigh heavily on instant facts, but United States has strong interest in hearing cases arising under federal securities laws, and this factor strongly supports plaintiff's choice of forum); *Wiwa v. Royal Dutch Petroleum Co.,* 226 F.3d 88, 105 (2d Cir.2000) (federal law reflects policy in favor of hearing claims of torture under color of foreign law).

33. *See, e.g., Duha v. Agrium, Inc.,* 448 F.3d 867, 876 (6th Cir.2006) (where courts are dealing with "cases involving foreign language documents," they "normally consider their impact and perhaps the cost of translation in the balance of convenience").

34. *See, e.g., Gates Learjet Corp. v. Jensen,* 743 F.2d 1325, 1335–36 (9th Cir.1984) (issue is not number of witnesses in each location, but access and convenience to forum and cost of travel).

35. *See, e.g., Duha v. Agrium, Inc.,* 448 F.3d 867, 877 (6th Cir.2006) (availability of compulsory process carries weight only where it appears that important witnesses would be unwilling to testify).

36. *Alfadda v. Fenn,* 159 F.3d 41, 46 (2d Cir.1998) (citing *Piper Aircraft* and *Gulf Oil*). *See also Leon v. Million Air, Inc.,* 251 F.3d 1305 (11th Cir.2001) (private interest factors generally considered more significant than public factors, but both kinds of facts should be weighed); *Guidi v. Inter–Continental Hotels Corp.,* 224 F.3d 142 (2d Cir.2000) (abuse of discretion for district court not to consider emotional burden of litigating in Egypt, where plaintiff's or their relatives were attacked by terrorists and where plaintiffs justifiably fear for their safety).

37. *Piper Aircraft Co. v. Reyno,* 454 U.S. 235, 102 S.Ct. 252, 70 L.Ed.2d 419 (1981) (large proportion of relevant evidence in foreign country is factor weighing in favor of dismissal). *See also, e.g., Alpine View Co. v. Atlas Copco AB,* 205 F.3d 208, 222 (5th Cir.2000) (upholding district court's assessment of private factors where no witness was identified in United States who would be needed for "general discovery" and documents existed mostly outside United States; private interest factors favor dismissal sufficiently so that circuit court need not address factors of public interest). *But see DiRienzo v. Philip Services Corp.,* 294 F.3d 21 (2d Cir.2002) (private interest factors: documents in Canada, but no particular problems of transport; most witnesses in Canada, but all within a few hours of New York forum by automobile and air travel; some third-party witnesses in Canada cannot be forced to testify in New York, but videotaped depositions arranged through

Application of Doctrine *Sua Sponte*

Normally, a forum non conveniens issue is raised by a party. At the same time, parties are free to waive the issue, and such waiver may occur in a variety of circumstances.[38] However, a party's decision to waive the issue is subject to the court's authority to raise the issue *sua sponte*.[39] For example, the court might do so if the convenience of non-party witnesses was an important issue.

Transfer

Congress has provided a special remedy for forum non conveniens cases originally filed in federal district courts. 28 U.S.C.A. § 1404 provides that a federal court that is an inappropriate forum may *transfer* the case to another federal district court in which the case "might have been brought."[40] Because a transferred case is not dismissed, transfer creates no statute of limitations problems.[41] Transfer is now the standard remedy in cases where it can be applied.[42]

Limits on Transfer

Federal district courts may use § 1404 only to transfer cases to other federal district courts. If a federal court recognizes that the appropriate forum for an action is outside the United States, the only remedy available is dismissal of the action, with permission to the plaintiff to file the cause of action elsewhere.[43] This remedy can

letters rogatory may be suitable substitute; public interest factors: most tend not to weigh heavily on instant facts, but United States has strong interest in hearing cases arising under federal securities laws, and this factor strongly supports plaintiff's choice of forum).

38. *See, e.g., Corporacion Mexicana de Servicios Maritimos, S.A. de C.V. v. M/T Respect,* 89 F.3d 650, 656 n. 1 (9th Cir. 1996)(by intervening, party waived forum non conveniens); *Heller Fin., Inc. v. Midwhey Powder Co.,* 883 F.2d 1286, 1293 (7th Cir.1989)(valid forum-selection clause waives defense of forum non conveniens).

39. *See, e.g., Corporacion Mexicana de Servicios Maritimos, S.A. de C.V. v. M/T Respect,* 89 F.3d 650, 656 n. 1 (9th Cir. 1996).

40. *But cf., Wild v. Subscription Plus, Inc.,* 292 F.3d 526, 531 (7th Cir.2002) ("[T]here is no absolute bar to the transfer of a multidefendant suit to a district in which one of the defendants cannot be served." Treating § 1404 as closely analogous to § 1406 for this purpose).

41. *Ferens v. John Deere Co.,* 494 U.S. 516, 110 S.Ct. 1274, 108 L.Ed.2d 443 (1990)(transfer to state where applicable statute of limitations will bar suit has no ill

consequence for suit, because statute of limitations of transferor jurisdiction remains in effect).

42. *Quackenbush v. Allstate Ins. Co.,* 517 U.S. 706, 116 S.Ct. 1712, 135 L.Ed.2d 1 (1996)(for federal courts, transfer pursuant to § 1404 is preferred remedy for problems arising from forum non conveniens; dismissal appropriate "only in 'cases where the alternative forum is abroad' "). *Sinochem International Co. v. Malaysia International Shipping Corp.,* ___ U.S. ___, 127 S.Ct. 1184, 167 L.Ed.2d 15 (2007) (also acknowledging use of common-law doctrine of forum non conveniens "in rare instances where a state or territorial court serves litigation convenience best"). *See, e.g., Monegro v. Rosa,* 211 F.3d 509, 512 (9th Cir. 2000) (§ 1404(a) applicable when alternative forum is within United States).

43. *See, e.g., Piper Aircraft Co. v. Reyno,* 454 U.S. 235, 102 S.Ct. 252, 70 L.Ed.2d 419 (1981). *See also Sinochem International Co. v. Malaysia International Shipping Corp.,* ___ U.S. ___, 127 S.Ct. 1184, 167 L.Ed.2d 15 (2007) ("For the federal court system Congress has codified the doctrine and has provided for transfer, rather than dismissal, when a sister federal court is the more convenient place for the trial of the action.").

create practical problems for plaintiffs, so courts often condition a grant of a defendant's motion to dismiss for forum non conveniens on understandings that the defendant will submit to jurisdiction in another country and will not challenge the suit on statute of limitations grounds.[44]

ADDITIONAL RESEARCH REFERENCES

C.J.S. Federal Courts §§ 10(1) et seq.

West's Key No. Digests, Federal Courts ⟿45.

§ 2.16 Removal

CORE CONCEPT

Removal permits a defendant to move a case from a state trial court to a federal district court. The process is controlled by federal law.

28 U.S.C.A. § 1441 identifies most of the kinds of lawsuits that may be removed from a state court to federal district court. These include most diversity suits, most federal question suits, non-diverse state claims which are joined with federal questions, and suits against foreign states.[1] Section 1441 also contains a provision permitting removal even in circumstances where a state court lacked jurisdiction over the case when it was originally filed.

APPLICATIONS

Removal Statutes

The most important removal provisions are 28 U.S.C.A. § 1441 (governing removal for diversity cases, most federal questions, and non-diverse claims joined with federal questions), 28 U.S.C.A. § 1446 (establishing the procedure for accomplishing removal), and § 1447 (governing procedure after removal). Specific statutes provide for removal in particular circumstances, such as suits against federal officers or agencies (28 U.S.C.A. §§ 1442, 1442a, and 1444), and suits where a defendant might not be able to assert a federal civil right in a state court (28 U.S.C.A. § 1443). Additionally, 28 U.S.C.A. § 1445 provides that certain kinds of cases (*e.g.,* suits against railroads under the Federal Employers' Liability Act and suits arising under state workers' compensation laws) may not be removed. If a case has been removed, 28 U.S.C.A. §§ 1447–49 establish the procedures a court will follow after a case has been

---

44. *See, e.g., Leon v. Million Air, Inc.,* 251 F.3d 1305 (11th Cir.2001) (affirming dismissal, subject to following conditions: (1) admission of liability for damage caused by plane crash; (2) acceptance of service of process and jurisdiction in appropriate foreign court; (3) waiver of statute of limitations; (4) payment of final judgments of foreign court; and (5) case may be reinstated if foreign court rejects jurisdiction).

1. *Cf. City of Chicago v. International College of Surgeons,* 522 U.S. 156, 163, 118 S.Ct. 523, 529, 139 L.Ed.2d 525 (1997) ("The propriety of removal ... depends on whether the case originally could have been filed in federal court.").

removed. Finally, Congress recently enacted 28 U.S.C.A. § 1453, which now governs removal of class actions.

Exceptions to § 1441(a)

Section 1441(a) provides that the general right of removal is subject to such exceptions as Congress may create.[2] Congress has preserved some exceptions in 28 U.S.C.A. § 1445, such as cases arising under state workers' compensation statutes.

Jurisdictional Requirement

Removal is permissible only when at least one claim filed by the plaintiff falls within the original subject matter jurisdiction of the federal district court.[3]

Removal from State Court Only

For removal to be effective under § 1441, the case must have been in state court at the time the removal petition was filed. Section 1441 provides no authority to remove a case from a state administrative agency to a federal district court.[4]

---

2. *Breuer v. Jim's Concrete of Brevard, Inc.,* 538 U.S. 691, 123 S.Ct. 1882, 155 L.Ed.2d 923 (2003) (if federal subject matter jurisdiction is satisfied, statutory prohibition against removal must be express). *Cf., e.g., Nevada v. Hicks,* 533 U.S. 353, 121 S.Ct. 2304, 150 L.Ed.2d 398 (2001) (federal civil rights claims governed by 42 U.S.C.A. § 1983 may not be filed in tribal courts, partly because § 1441 does not authorize removal of federal claims from such courts; only claims in state courts might qualify for removal under § 1441).

3. *Beneficial National Bank v. Anderson,* 539 U.S. 1, 8, 123 S.Ct. 2058, 2063, 156 L.Ed.2d 1 (2003) ("[A] state claim may be removed to federal court in only two circumstances–when Congress expressly so provides . . . or when a federal statute wholly displaces the state-law cause of action through complete pre-emption."); *Jefferson County, Alabama v. Acker,* 527 U.S. 423, 430, 119 S.Ct. 2069, 2074, 144 L.Ed.2d 408 (1999) ("It is the general rule that an action may be removed from state court to federal court only if a federal district court would have original jurisdiction over the claim in suit."). *See, e.g., Sikirica v. Nationwide Insurance Co.,* 416 F.3d 214 (3d Cir. 2005) (thus party seeking removal bears burden of satisfying subject matter jurisdiction, and § 1441 "must be strictly construed against removal"); *Carpenter v. Wichita Falls Indep't Sch. Dist.,* 44 F.3d 362, 365 (5th Cir.1995)(noting that propriety of removal depends on existence of original jurisdiction of federal courts). *Cf. Wis-*

consin Dept. of Corrections v. Schacht, 524 U.S. 381, 118 S.Ct. 2047, 141 L.Ed.2d 364 (1998) (presence of one claim that is barred by Eleventh Amendment immunity does not prevent removal of other claims that meet jurisdictional requirements). *See also Barbers, Hairstyling for Men & Women, Inc. v. Bishop,* 132 F.3d 1203, 1204 (7th Cir.1997) (noting that plaintiffs prevented removal of state claims by seeking relief in an amount that was $50 less than the jurisdictional requirement for diversity); *Duncan v. Stuetzle,* 76 F.3d 1480, 1485 (9th Cir.1996) (nondiverse plaintiff may defeat removal by foregoing federal claim and pleading only state claims). *Cf., Caterpillar, Inc. v. Lewis,* 519 U.S. 61, 117 S.Ct. 467, 136 L.Ed.2d 437 (1996) (removal occurred at a time when one defendant was not diverse from plaintiff; held, while removal was improper at time it occurred, defect was curable by dismissal of non-diverse defendant prior to trial; judgment was valid because diversity existed at time of judgment). *But cf., Marcus v. AT&T Corp.,* 138 F.3d 46, 52–53 (2d Cir.1998) (where federal law has completely preempted an area, plaintiff cannot defeat removal by pleading state claims, because those claims are really federal in nature). *See also Wellness Community-Nat'l v. Wellness House,* 70 F.3d 46, 50 (7th Cir.1995) (after case is removed, diversity jurisdiction cannot be defeated by amending claim to seek less than jurisdictional amount).

4. *See, e.g., Oregon Bureau of Labor & Industries ex rel. Richardson v. U.S. West*

Defendant's Right

Section 1441(a) restricts the right of removal to parties who are defendants to the plaintiff's case in chief. The majority view appears to be that defendants on counterclaims, crossclaims, or third-party impleaders have no right to remove cases from state court.[5] However, these defendants may find claims affecting them removed if a defendant on an original count files a notice of removal. This possibility is discussed below, under *Joinder of "Non–Removable" Claims.* Further, if the basis of removal is a third-party claim against a foreign state, § 1441(d) (governing removal of claims against foreign states) will permit removal, notwithstanding the different result reached in cases governed by § 1441(a) or (b).[6]

Unanimous Consent: Complications

Although nowhere stated in the removal statutes, case law has established that an action generally cannot be removed to federal district court unless *all* defendants join in the notice of removal.[7] Thus, if two defendants are sued on a single count that might qualify for removal, but only one seeks to remove, the case is not eligible for removal.

Communications, Inc., 288 F.3d 414, 415 (9th Cir.2002) ("§ 1441(a) authorizes removal only from a 'state court,'" not an administrative agency).

5. *See, e.g., First National Bank of Pulaski v. Curry,* 301 F.3d 456, 461 (6th Cir. 2002) ("[N]either § 1441(a) nor § 1441(c) provides third-party defendants with the right to remove a case to federal court."); *Lewis v. Windsor Door Co.,* 926 F.2d 729, 733 (8th Cir.1991)(removal cannot be based on third-party claim that may be within original jurisdiction of federal court); *Thomas v. Shelton,* 740 F.2d 478, 487–88 (7th Cir.1984) (third party defendants may not remove). *But see In re Wilson Indus., Inc.,* 886 F.2d 93, 96 (5th Cir.1989)(removal "can be based on a third-party claim where a separate and independent controversy is stated"; apparent minority view).

6. *See, e.g., Davis v. McCourt,* 226 F.3d 506 (6th Cir.2000) (collecting cases; also noting that entire lawsuit, not merely third-party complaint against foreign entity, is removed).

7. *Chicago, Rock Island and Pacific Railway Co. v. Martin,* 178 U.S. 245, 248, 20 S.Ct. 854, 855, 44 L.Ed. 1055 (1900) ("[I]t was well settled that a removal could not be effected unless all the parties on the same side of the controversy united in the petition."). *See, e.g., Durham v. Lockheed Martin Corp.,* 445 F.3d 1247, 1253 (9th Cir.2006) ("If the defendant can't convince

his co-defendants to remove, he's stuck in state court."); *McMahon v. Bunn–O–Matic Corp.,* 150 F.3d 651 (7th Cir.1998) (noting requirement that all defendants must sign removal notice); *Henry v. Independent American Savings Ass'n,* 857 F.2d 995, 999 (5th Cir.1988). ("Although failure of all defendants to join is usually a bar to removal, if one defendant's removal petition is premised on removable claims 'separate and independent' from the claims brought against other defendants, consent of the other defendants is not required."). *But cf., Vasquez v. North County Transit District,* 292 F.3d 1049 (9th Cir.2002) (removal is "procedurally defective" when some defendants do not join removal–but defect was waived by failure to make timely motion to remand); *Akin v. Ashland Chemical Co.,* 156 F.3d 1030, 1034 (10th Cir.1998) (under 28 U.S.C.A. § 1442(a), requirement for unanimous consent to removal does not apply to United States as a defendant or to federal officers sued for actions taken under color of federal office); *Lewis v. Rego Co.,* 757 F.2d 66, 68 (3d Cir.1985) (removing defendants file petition before non-resident defendants had been served with process; held, removal petition may still be effective, provided that petition explains that defendants who did not join petition were not yet served in state proceeding; when such defendants are finally served, 28 U.S.C.A. § 1448 may permit such defendants to challenge removal).

It should be noted that many district courts have extended the requirement for unanimous consent a step further. There is a substantial body of precedent in district courts holding that the petition for removal must not only reflect the unanimous agreement of the defendants, but that each individual defendant must personally, or through that defendant's own counsel, confirm to the court that the individual defendant has consented to the removal petition. In other words, an attorney for one defendant cannot speak on this matter for defendants the attorney does not represent. Any attempt to do so may result in rejection of the removal petition and remand to state court. District courts holding this view do not consider the obligations of an attorney under Rule 11 (governing representations to the court) to be controlling in this area, notwithstanding the express admonition of 28 U.S.C.A. § 1446(a) (governing removal procedure) that Rule 11 applies to removal petitions.[8] In this area attorneys must consult the local precedent to avoid a snare of potentially great significance.

It should also be noted that Congress recently enacted 28 U.S.C.A. § 1453, governing removal of class actions from state court to federal district court. One of the provisions of new § 1453 eliminates the case law requirement for unanimous consent among the defendants before removal is appropriate. Instead, § 1453 provides that in cases involving class actions eligible for removal, *any* defendant may seek removal "without consent of all defendants."[9] Thus, the requirement in some district courts that each defendant express individually a consent to removal, discussed immediately above, will presumably not be applicable to most class actions. Section 1453 is discussed in greater detail elsewhere in this text.

Geography of Removal

Cases removed from state court are removed to the federal court of the district (or division) that includes the location in which the

---

8. *See, e.g., Sansone v. Morton Machine Works, Inc.,* 188 F.Supp.2d 182, 185 (D. R.I. 2002) (calling this approach the "overwhelming weight of authority"); *Landman v. Borough of Bristol,* 896 F.Supp. 406, 408 (E.D. Pa. 1995) ("[O]ne defendant's attempt to speak on behalf of another defendant will not suffice."); *Creekmore v. Food Lion, Inc.,* 797 F.Supp. 505, 509 (E.D. Pa. 1992) (§ 1446 "requires all defendants, individually, or through their counsel, to voice their consent before the court, not through another party's attorney"); *Moody v. Commercial Insurance Co. v. Newark,* 753 F.Supp. 198, 200 n.6 (N.D. Tex. 1990) (each defendant must provide a written, timely statement of consent; Rule 11 is not a remedy for a misrepresentation by one lawyer of the agreement of another lawyer's client because, while sanctions may be appropriate under Rule 11, that Rule "does

not bind the allegedly consenting co-defendant to the removal action").

9. 28 U.S.C.A. § 1453(b). *See, e.g., Abrego v. Dow Chemical Co.,* 443 F.3d 676, 681 (9th Cir.2006) (noting that § 1453 "overrides the judge-created requirement that each defendant consent to removal"). The exceptions created by § 1453 for class actions are themselves subject to an exception. Specifically, § 1453(d) provides that § 1453 is inapplicable to any class action "solely" involving: (1) a claim concerning a covered security under certain federal securities laws; (2) a claim relating to the internal affairs or governance of a corporation or other business entity arising under the laws of the state that incorporated organized the enterprise; or (3) a claim relating to the rights and duties, including fiduciary duties, created by the Securities Act of 1933.

state court sits.[10]   Thus, a case removed from a Pennsylvania state trial court in Harrisburg, Pennsylvania would be sent to the United States District Court for the Middle District of Pennsylvania, the federal district court that includes Harrisburg.

Fictitious Names Disregarded

When determining whether the federal court has diversity jurisdiction over a removed case, § 1441(a) provides that if state procedure allows suits against defendants under fictitious names (*e.g.* General Motors v. John Doe, Mary Roe, and Jane Coe), the citizenship of such defendants will be disregarded.[11]

Federal Question Cases

Section 1441(b) authorizes a defendant to remove any cause of action based upon the Constitution, laws or treaties of the United States, if the federal court has original jurisdiction over the claim.[12] In general, this provision is treated as authorizing removal of cases that could have been filed originally in federal district court pursuant to 28 U.S.C.A. § 1331 (governing federal subject matter jurisdiction over federal questions).[13] 28 U.S.C.A. § 1445(a) creates an exception to this general right of removal by prohibiting removal of suits against railroads based upon the Federal Employers' Liability Act.

Diversity Cases

Section 1441(b) also authorizes removal of cases where the parties meet requirements of diversity jurisdiction, subject to one significant exception. If any defendant sued on a diversity count is a citizen of the state in which the claim was filed, that count is not eligible for removal to federal district court.[14]

---

10. 28 U.S.C.A. § 1441(a). *Global Satellite Communication Co. v. Starmill U.K., Ltd.,* 378 F.3d 1269, 1271 (11th Cir.2004) (in venue issues relating to removal, the controlling statute is § 1441(a), not the general venue statute, 28 U.S.C.A. § 1391); *See, e.g., Kerobo v. Southwestern Clean Fuels, Corp.,* 285 F.3d 531, 534 (6th Cir.2002) (removal from state court within area embraced by Eastern District of Michigan could only be to Eastern District of Michigan). *But cf. Peterson v. BMI Refractories,* 124 F.3d 1386, 1394 (11th Cir.1997) (removal to "wrong" district court is procedural error that is waivable; issue is not jurisdictional in nature).

11. *See, e.g., Howell v. Tribune Entertainment Co.,* 106 F.3d 215, 218 (7th Cir. 1997) ("[N]aming a John Doe defendant will not defeat the named defendants' right to remove a diversity case if their citizenship is diverse from that of the plaintiffs.").

12. *Rivet v. Regions Bank of Louisiana,* 522 U.S. 470, 118 S.Ct. 921, 139 L.Ed.2d 912 (1998) (basis for removal of federal question claim must appear on face of well-pleaded complaint; "a defendant cannot remove on the basis of a federal defense," *e.g.,* res judicata). *But cf., Romero v. International Terminal Operating Co.,* 358 U.S. 354, 368–69, 79 S.Ct. 468, 478, 3 L.Ed.2d 368 (1959) (admiralty case filed in state court may not be removed to federal court as federal question; thus, if removal was possible at all, it would have to rest on some other ground, e.g., diversity jurisdiction).

13. *See, e.g., Eastman v. Marine Mechanical Corp.,* 438 F.3d 544, 549 (6th Cir. 2006) (scope of § 1441(b) "is considered to be identical to the scope of federal question jurisdiction under § 1331.").

14. *Lincoln Property Co. v. Roche,* ___ U.S. ___, ___, 126 S.Ct. 606, 613, 163 L.Ed.2d 415 (2005); *See, e.g., Tillman v. R.J. Reynolds Tobacco,* 253 F.3d 1302 (11th Cir.2001) ("no defendant can be a citizen of the state in which the action was brought;"

Congress recently enacted § 1453, which eliminated the applicability of this exception to removal of cases that are class actions. For such class actions, the exception contained in § 1441(b) is replaced by an express provision making removal possible "without regard to whether any defendant is a citizen of the State in which the action is brought."[15] Section 1453 is discussed at greater length elsewhere in this text.

It should also be noted that removal cannot be defeated simply by joining defendants with no real interest in the claim. In such cases of "fraudulent joinder," the court will dismiss the unnecessary parties and uphold removal.[16]

Fraudulent Joinder

It is possible that a plaintiff will join a nondiverse defendant for the purpose of preventing removal of an otherwise diverse claim. Such a tactic is permissible if there is a legitimate basis for the joinder. It is not always easy to identify the standard for fraudulent joinder.[17] However, if there is no colorable basis for the claim against the nondiverse defendant, federal case law provides that the court will disregard the nondiverse defendant when ruling on a motion for remand to state court.[18] Where relevant, this doctrine is an important exception to the requirement of complete diversity. Fraudulent joinder may also be found when a plaintiff engages in

---

one narrow exception arises if a defendant is such a citizen but "there is no possibility that the plaintiff can establish any cause of action against that defendant;" in that circumstance, court may dismiss that defendant and retain diversity jurisdiction); *Coury v. Prot,* 85 F.3d 244 (5th Cir. 1996)("[A] defendant may not remove a state action to federal court if a defendant is a citizen of the state in which the action is filed."). *But cf. McCall v. Scott,* 239 F.3d 808, 813 n. 2 (6th Cir.2001) ("[T]he inclusion of an unserved resident defendant in the action does not defeat removal."); *Blackburn v. United Parcel Service, Inc.,* 179 F.3d 81 n. 3 (3d Cir.1999) (suit against defendant in defendant's home state court that would meet requirements for diversity jurisdiction is nevertheless not eligible for removal; however, defect is waivable under 28 U.S.C.A. § 1447(c) if not raised within 30 days of filing of notice of removal).

15. 28 U.S.C.A. § 1453(b). *See also Abrego v. Dow Chemical Co.,* 443 F.3d 676, 681 (9th Cir.2006) (noting that § 1453 "overrides the judge-created requirement that each defendant consent to removal"). It should be noted that the exceptions created by § 1453 for class actions are themselves subject to an exception. Specifically,

§ 1453(d) provides that § 1453 is inapplicable to any class action "solely" involving: (1) a claim concerning a covered security under certain federal securities laws; (2) a claim relating to the internal affairs or governance of a corporation or other business entity arising under the laws of the state that incorporated or organized the enterprise; or (3) a claim relating to the rights and duties, including fiduciary duties, created by the Securities Act of 1933.

16. *See e.g., Pampillonia v. RJR Nabisco, Inc.,* 138 F.3d 459, 461 (2d Cir.1998) (so holding; but noting that defendant bears heavy burden of proof on "fraudulent joinder").

17. *See, e.g., Travis v. Irby,* 326 F.3d 644, 647 (5th Cir.2003) ("Neither our circuit nor other circuits have been clear in describing the fraudulent joinder standard;" collecting cases). *But cf., In re Briscoe,* 448 F.3d 201, 218 (3d Cir.2006) ("Unless the claims against the non-diverse defendant could be deemed 'wholly insubstantial and frivolous,' ... the joinder could not be considered fraudulent.").

18. *See, e.g., Jerome–Duncan, Inc. v. Auto-By-Tel, L.L.C.,* 176 F.3d 904 (6th Cir. 1999).

"outright fraud" in pleading jurisdictional allegations.[19] A third type of fraudulent joinder may arise when the plaintiff joins a nondiverse defendant who has no joint, several or alternative liability with a diverse defendant, and there is no connection between the claims against the diverse and nondiverse defendants.[20]

Post-Removal Events Affecting Jurisdiction

It is unclear whether a case that was properly removed on the basis of diversity jurisdiction must or should be remanded to state court when events occurring after removal would have defeated removal had those events occurred prior to removal. The circuits are in conflict,[21] and attorneys must consult local precedent.

Forum Selection Clauses

If the parties have an enforceable agreement that any dispute between them is to be heard in state court, an otherwise removable claim will be remanded to state court.[22]

Joinder of "Non–Removable" Claims

Section 1441(c) governs circumstances in which many counts, including counts removable under § 1441(b) and counts that do not qualify for removal under that section, are filed in the same case. If at least one separate and independent count would qualify for federal question jurisdiction, then § 1441(c) provides that a notice of removal will cause *all* counts in the case to be removed to federal

---

19. *See, e.g., Triggs v. John Crump Toyota, Inc.,* 154 F.3d 1284, 1287 (11th Cir. 1998).

20. *See, e.g., Tapscott v. MS Dealer Service Corp.,* 77 F.3d 1353, 1360 (11th Cir. 1996).

21. *Compare, e.g., Spencer v. United States District Court,* 393 F.3d 867, 870–71 (9th Cir.2004) (in instant case, removal appropriate at time it occurred; after removal, defendant who was diverse but was also a local resident was joined; held, district court was not obligated to remand case to state court; refusing to decide whether district court had discretion to remand); *Poore v. American–Amicable Life Insurance Co.,* 218 F.3d 1287, 1290–91 (11th Cir.2000) (post-removal reduction in amount in controversy does not destroy district court's subject matter jurisdiction); *Van Meter v. State Farm Fire & Casualty Co.,* 1 F.3d 445, 450 (6th Cir.1993) (removal that was valid when it occurred need not be upset by post-removal events that would otherwise destroy subject matter jurisdiction); *In re Shell Oil Co.,* 966 F.2d 1130, 1133 (7th Cir.1992) (jurisdiction valid at time of removal "is unaffected by subsequent acts"); *with, e.g., Mayes v. Rapoport,* 198 F.3d 457, 461 (4th Cir.1999) (post-removal joinder of

non-diverse defendant requires remand to state court; only alternative would be to deny joinder, if that is appropriate); *Cobb v. Delta Exports, Inc.,* 186 F.3d 675, 677 (5th Cir.1999) ("[P]ost-removal joinder of non-diverse defendants pursuant to Fed.R.Civ.P. 19 destroys diversity for jurisdictional purposes and requires remand, even when the newly joined defendants are not indispensable."); *Casas Office Machines, Inc. v. Mita Copystar America, Inc.,* 42 F.3d 668, 673 (1st Cir.1994) (post-removal substitution of real parties in place of fictitious names destroyed diversity, and thereby also defeated subject matter jurisdiction); *In re Merrimack Mutual Fire Insurance Co.,* 587 F.2d 642, 646 (5th Cir.1978) (requiring remand upon post-removal joinder of indispensable parties).

22. *See, e.g., Florida Polk County v. Prison Health Servs., Inc.,* 170 F.3d 1081 (11th Cir.1999) (applying principles of contract law to determine whether to enforce forum selection clause). *But cf., Kerobo v. Southwestern Clean Fuels, Corp.,* 285 F.3d 531, 534–35 (6th Cir.2002) (suit in Michigan state court; parties had forum selection clause choosing California venue; held, such a clause could not prevent removal to Michigan federal court).

district court.[23]   Removal of the entire case includes removal of counterclaims, crossclaims, and claims against third parties.

By contrast, there is no authority in § 1441(c), or anywhere else in § 1441, to remove nondiverse state claims to federal court when the basis for removal is a diverse count. Little or no authority exists on the topic, but it appears that in such circumstances the diverse claim may be removed under § 1441(b), and the nondiverse claims must remain in state court.

A possible way around this situation in some circumstances might be for the defendant to remove the diverse claim to federal court. Then, with the case pending in federal court, the defendant might file a nondiverse counterclaim (nondiverse, e.g., because it does not meet the amount in controversy) and try to sustain the federal court's supplemental jurisdiction over the nondiverse claim under 28 U.S.C.A. § 1367.

Discretion to Retain/Remand Claims

Once a multi-count case has been removed to federal district court in the manner provided by § 1441(c), the court has discretion to retain jurisdiction over the "non-removable" counts.[24]   A court will retain those non-removable counts which form part of the same case or controversy as the count(s) which qualified for removal in their own right.[25]   If the court chooses not to retain the non-removable counts, the appropriate remedy is to remand those counts to the state court from which they were removed.[26]

Additionally, there is a modest trend in courts to permit remand under § 1441(c) of both federal and state claims if the state claims

23.   *See, e.g., Gaming Corp. of America v. Dorsey & Whitney*, 88 F.3d 536 (8th Cir.1996)("[T]he presence of even one federal claim gives the defendant the right to remove the entire case to federal court."). *But see Reed v. Heil Co.*, 206 F.3d 1055, 1058 (11th Cir.2000) (noting that some claims, such as those governed by § 1445(c) (barring removal of claims arising under workers' compensation laws), cannot be removed even if basis for removal is other claims falling within court's federal question jurisdiction); *In re City of Mobile*, 75 F.3d 605 (11th Cir.1996) (single accident, giving rise to both state and federal claims, does not create "separate and independent" claims within meaning of § 1441(c)).

24.   *See, e.g., Justice v. Atchison, Topeka and Santa Fe Railway Co.*, 927 F.2d 503, 504 (10th Cir.1991)(remand of non-diverse state claims is within court's discretion). *But cf., Ward v. Alternative Health Delivery Systems, Inc.*, 261 F.3d 624, 626 (6th Cir. 2001) (acknowledging that district court normally has discretion to remand; but "[i]f it dismisses the claim within its original jurisdiction for lack of subject matter juris-

diction ... it *must* remand the remaining claims" [italics in original]).

25.   *See, e.g., Smith v. Amedisys, Inc.*, 298 F.3d 434 (5th Cir.2002) (state and federal claims involved common allegations of sexual harassment, discrimination, and retaliation; held, district court had no discretion to remand); *Anderson v. Red River Waterway Commission*, 231 F.3d 211, 214 (5th Cir.2000) (where liability of third-party defendant is based on same operative facts as claim against defendant/third-party plaintiff, there is no separate and independent claim and district court must retain such claim). *Metro Ford Truck Sales, Inc. v. Ford Motor Co.*, 145 F.3d 320, 327 (5th Cir.1998) ("[F]or remand to be proper, the claim remanded must be (1) a separate and independent claim or cause of action; (2) joined with a federal question; (3) otherwise non-removable; and (4) a matter in which state law predominates.").

26.   *See, e.g., Ondis v. Barrows*, 538 F.2d 904, 908 (1st Cir.1976)(dismissal is inappropriate; remand is the appropriate remedy).

predominate.[27] Whether this view of a court's authority under § 1441(c) will prevail is currently uncertain.[28]

Suits Against Foreign States

Section 1441(d) authorizes removal of suits filed in state court[29] against foreign countries or their agents,[30] without regard to whether the suit was based on a federal question or state law.[31]

This right to remove applies without regard to the amount in controversy, and permits removal even after the time limits of § 1446(b) have expired–at least when the party seeking removal can show cause.[32]

Foreign States—Jury Trials

In any suit where removal was based upon § 1441(d), the court must try the case without a jury.

Time: Cases Involving Foreign Counties

If a defendant seeks removal because a suit is against a foreign country, § 1441(d) authorizes the court to extend the provisions in § 1446(b) that normally govern time limits for filing a removal notice. However, extensions are granted only "for cause shown."

State Court Jurisdiction

Section 1441(e) permits a federal district court to hear a removed case even if the state court in which the case was originally filed lacked jurisdiction.[33] Section 1441(e) was added in December

27. See, e.g., Wirtz Corp. v. United Distillers & Vintners North America, Inc., 224 F.3d 708, 713 (7th Cir.2000) (state interest in administration of alcoholic beverage program outweighs diversity jurisdiction; reversing denial of motion to remand); Eastus v. Blue Bell Creameries, L.P., 97 F.3d 100, 106 (5th Cir.1996) (collecting cases, so holding). See Metro Ford Truck Sales, Inc. v. Ford Motor Co., 145 F.3d 320 (5th Cir.1998) (permitting remand of federal claims within concurrent jurisdiction of federal and state courts; noting different result if federal court's jurisdiction is exclusive).

28. See generally Gaming Corp. of America v. Dorsey & Whitney, 88 F.3d 536, 542 (8th Cir.1996) ("A district court has no discretion to remand a claim that states a federal question.").

29. Cf., Attorney General of Guam v. Torres, 419 F.3d 1017, 1025 (9th Cir.2005) (for purposes of § 1441(d), territorial courts of Guam are state courts).

30. Dole Food Co. v. Patrickson, 538 U.S. 468, 477, 123 S.Ct. 1655, 1662, 155 L.Ed.2d 643 (2003) (for a corporation to remove on ground it is instrumentality of foreign state, the foreign state must own a majority of the corporation's shares; mere

control of corporation is not enough; such majority ownership must exist at time lawsuit is filed).

31. See, e.g., Hanil Bank v. PT. Bank Negara Indonesia, 148 F.3d 127 (2d Cir. 1998)(noting removal of breach of contract claim against bank owned by Indonesian government). See also Davis v. McCourt, 226 F.3d 506 (6th Cir.2000) (noting that § 1441(d) authorizes removal even where count against foreign entity is third-party complaint; further, where removal occurs under § 1441(d), entire lawsuit, not merely third-party complaint against foreign entity, is removed); Alonzi v. Budget Const. Co., 55 F.3d 331, 332–33 (7th Cir.1995)(noting that § 1441(d) allows removal by foreign states; also noting that under majority view, § 1441(d) permits removal of entire case, including otherwise non-removable claims against citizens of American states; but also citing contrary authority).

32. See, e.g., Suter v. Munich Reinsurance Co., 223 F.3d 150, 156 (3d Cir.2000) (removal outside time limits of § 1446(b) permitted "for cause shown").

33. See, e.g., In re Brand Name Prescription Drugs Antitrust Litig., 123 F.3d 599, 611 (7th Cir.1997) (case is removable

1990, and renders obsolete prior case law on the matter. However, nothing in § 1441(e) excuses a federal court from its own obligation to satisfy federal jurisdictional requirements, which generally means that at least one count in the removed case must satisfy requirements for federal question jurisdiction or diversity jurisdiction.[34]

Venue

Section 1441(e), governing the authority of a federal court to retain a case where a state court lacked jurisdiction, does not address the additional question of venue. However, case law indicates that while a removed claim does not have to satisfy the federal venue statute, 28 U.S.C.A. § 1391, it must have satisfied the venue rules governing the state court from which it was removed.[35]

ADDITIONAL RESEARCH REFERENCES

C.J.S. Removal of Causes §§ 1–46 et seq., 52–101 et seq., 126–171 et seq., 177–226 et seq., 235–275 et seq., 297–310 et seq.

West's Key No. Digests, Removal of Cases ⚫1–120.

§ 2.17   Removal Procedure

CORE CONCEPT

Defendants eligible for removal from state court to federal district court should file a notice of removal with the appropriate federal court[1] within 30 days of receipt of the plaintiff's original pleading. Filing the notice automatically removes the case from the jurisdiction of the state court, and the federal court will make decisions as to how the case will thereafter be processed. If the federal court determines that removal was erroneous, the remedy is remand to the state court from which the case was originally removed.

APPLICATIONS

Contents of Notice

The notice of removal should contain a concise statement of the

even where state court could not hear it because case is within exclusive federal jurisdiction).

34. *See, e.g., In re CSX Transp., Inc.,* 151 F.3d 164 (4th Cir.1998) ("While state court jurisdiction is not ordinarily a prerequisite for removability ... jurisdiction in the district court is.").

35. *See, e.g., PT United Can Co. v. Crown Cork & Seal Co.,* 138 F.3d 65, 72 (2d Cir.1998) (so holding; citing other cases). *But see Hollis v. Florida State University,* 259 F.3d 1295, 1296 (11th Cir.2001) ("We conclude that state-law venue deficiencies cannot be the basis for dismissal of a re-

moved action because 28 U.S.C. § 1441(e) ... abrogated the theory of derivative jurisdiction. Upon removal the question of venue is governed by federal law, not state law, and under § 1441(a) a properly removed action necessarily fixes venue in the district where the state court action was pending." Suggesting that if defendant dislikes federal venue, motion to transfer to another division or district is appropriate).

1. *See, e.g., Global Satellite Communication Co. v. Starmill U.K. Ltd.,* 378 F.3d 1269 (11th Cir.2004) (appropriate court is district court in district and division where case is pending).

grounds upon which removal is based.[2] The notice should be accompanied by copies of "all process, pleadings, and orders served upon" the defendant seeking removal.[3]

Filing Equals Removal

Removal occurs as soon as the defendant files an appropriate notice of removal with the federal district court.[4] The federal court may then make decisions on the sustainability of the removal.

Rule 11

Section 1446(a) explicitly provides that notices of removal are subject to the provisions of Rule 11, which permits the court to impose sanctions for inappropriate pleadings and motions. However, there is no rule prohibiting a party from filing more than one petition for removal, provided that each petition meets the requirements of Rule 11 and is timely.[5]

Time

In general, § 1446 provides that a defendant eligible for removal has thirty days in which to file a notice of removal.[6] That apparently innocuous time limit, however, has produced uncertainty as to its application in a variety of different circumstances. As a reader progresses through the tangles arising in this area, an effort to keep in mind a few considerations may help the reader understand the complexities of the issue and the need to apply the time limit to a number of different factual settings. Perhaps the most important consideration to grasp is that because the case at issue will have been filed originally in a state trial court, state rules governing service of initial pleadings in that court will have a significant impact on the determination of when the 30–day period begins to run. Second, because the presence or absence of federal question jurisdiction or diversity jurisdiction is a federal matter that

---

2. *But cf., Williams v. Costco Wholesale Corp.*, 471 F.3d 975, 976 n. 1 (9th Cir. 2006) ("The civil removal statute, unlike the removal statute for criminal cases, has no requirement that all grounds for removal be listed in the notice." Noting that if removal could be sustained on both diversity jurisdiction and federal question jurisdiction, defendant did not have to list both grounds in notice).

3. *See, e.g., L & O Partnership No. 2 v. Aetna Casualty & Surety Co.*, 761 F.Supp. 549 (N.D.Ill.1991). *Cf., Usatorres v. Marina Mercante Nicaraguenses, S.A.*, 768 F.2d 1285, 1286 (11th Cir.1985)(defendant filed motion to dismiss in state court, then filed removal petition; held, defendant had no duty to file copy of motion to dismiss with removal petition, because motion was not "served upon" defendant within meaning of § 1446(a)). *See also Asociacion Nacional de Pescadores a Pequena Escala O Artesa-*

nales de Colombia v. Dow Quimica de Colombia, S.A., 988 F.2d 559, 565 (5th Cir. 1993) (removal petitions are more persuasive when defendant has, *inter alia*, jurisdictional facts at hand.).

4. *See, e.g., Speiser, Krause & Madole P.C. v. Ortiz*, 271 F.3d 884, 887 (9th Cir. 2001) (removal is automatic upon proper filing and service of papers; thereafter, case is controlled by rules of federal district court); *Yarnevic v. Brink's, Inc.*, 102 F.3d 753, 754 (4th Cir.1996) ("A proper filing of a notice of removal immediately strips the state court of its jurisdiction.").

5. *See, e.g., Benson v. SI Handling Systems, Inc.*, 188 F.3d 780, 782 (7th Cir.1999) ("Nothing in § 1446 forecloses multiple petitions for removal." Rejecting per se rule that a party may seek removal only once).

6. 28 U.S.C.A. § 1446(b).

may often be of no importance to a state court, documents filed in state court or served on defendants while a case is in its early stages may make no reference whatsoever to such concepts as, e.g., the presence of a federal cause of action, the amount in controversy between the parties, or the citizenship of the parties. Thus, facts crucial to a determination of federal subject matter jurisdiction, and therefore to a determination of eligibility for removal, may simply be glossed over in state pleadings or not appear at all. Third, even in cases where, for some reason, it is apparent early on that a particular case filed in state court may qualify for removal to federal district court, it is nevertheless possible that service of process on all defendants may not occur simultaneously. Thus, if the case involves more than one defendant, it is possible that months will elapse between the date when the first defendant gets notice of the possibility of removal and the date when the last-served defendant obtains similar information. All of these issues carry great potential for confusing the question of when the thirty day period identified in § 1446(b) begins to run.

To avoid making the problem of determining when the thirty day period begins to run more difficult than it has to be, it is important to recognize that some issues, at least, are settled and may be addressed without undue difficulty by a diligent attorney. In cases where the initial documents filed or served in a case (summons and/or complaint) make clear that a case is eligible for removal, the rules are fairly clear as to the running of the time limit. In particular, it is now settled that in circumstances where any of four possible scenarios for service of process may be imposed by state rules, there are the following answers: (1) if state law provides for service of the summons and complaint simultaneously and that requirement is met, the thirty day limitation begins to run upon receipt of that service; (2) if, as permitted or required by state law, a summons is served on the defendant, but the complaint is not "furnished" until a later date, the thirty day period begins to run from the date the defendant received the complaint;[7] (3) if a defendant is served with a summons, but the complaint is filed in court under a state rule that does not mandate service of the complaint, the limitation on removal starts to run on the date that the complaint is available to the defendant through filing; and (4) if a complaint is filed in state court before any service on the defendant, the removal limitation period begins to run from the date of service of the summons on the defendant.[8]

7. *Murphy Brothers, Inc. v. Michetti Pipe Stringing, Inc.,* 526 U.S. 344, 354, 119 S.Ct. 1322, 1328, 143 L.Ed.2d 448 (1999) (apparently equating a "furnished" complaint with a served complaint).

8. *Murphy Brothers, Inc. v. Michetti Pipe Stringing, Inc.,* 526 U.S. 344, 354, 119 S.Ct. 1322, 1328, 143 L.Ed.2d 448 (1999). *See, e.g., Sikirica v. Nationwide Insurance*

Co., 416 F.3d 214 (3d Cir.2005) (in instant case plaintiff served summons but not complaint; "a writ of summons alone [cannot] be the 'initial pleading' that triggers the 30–day period for removal"). *Cf., Whitaker v. American Telecasting, Inc.,* 261 F.3d 196, 204–05 (2d Cir.2001) (defendant was served with copy of summons with notice; complaint was served more than two months

In all the scenarios laid out above, it is important to note that, subject to an exception discussed immediately below, the time limit in which a defendant must file a notice of removal does not begin to run until some form of formal service, as directed by state law, has been accomplished on the defendant.[9] The exception is that if a defendant has, pursuant to applicable state law, voluntarily waived the formal requirements of service of process, there is of course no formal service and therefore the thirty day limitation period will begin to run on the occurrence of some other event,[10] such as the date waiver of service becomes effective.

Unfortunately, as settled as those particular points may be, they do not comprise the universe of variables and problems an attorney is likely to encounter in this area of law. To aid in resolution of some of these other difficulties, § 1446(b) contains a second paragraph that attempts to address the date the thirty day limit begins to run when the original pleading does not disclose a basis for removal. In that circumstance the beginning of the limitation period is not tied to service of a summons and/or complaint (as is discussed above). Instead, the thirty day limitation begins to run when the defendant receives, "through service or otherwise,"[11] a copy of some document–amended pleading, motion, or other paper–giving notice that the case is removable. Thus, if the defendant learns for the first time from answers obtained in the discovery process that a case is removable, the thirty day period begins to run from the date of receipt of the answers.[12] Similarly, if the defendant learns for the first time from information contained in a post-filing settlement proposal sent by the plaintiff that a case is removable, the thirty day period apparently begins to run on the date of receipt of that proposal.[13]

In cases involving multiple defendants who are served at different times, the problem is different. When defendants are served on

---

later, at which time defendant sought removal; held, removal was untimely because "initial pleading" is not necessarily complaint; summons with notice could trigger running of time; noting that in New York, summons is broad document that includes statement of nature of action and relief sought).

9. *Murphy Brothers, Inc. v. Michetti Pipe Stringing, Inc.*, 526 U.S. 344, 356, 119 S.Ct. 1322, 1329, 143 L.Ed.2d 448 (1999) (rejecting informal service through fax delivery of a "courtesy copy" of complaint as starting the running of the thirty day limitation period).

10. *Murphy Brothers, Inc. v. Michetti Pipe Stringing, Inc.*, 526 U.S. 344, 350, 119 S.Ct. 1322, 1326, 143 L.Ed.2d 448 (1999) ("Unless a named defendant agrees to waive service, the summons continues to function as the *sine qua non* directing an individual or entity to participate in a civil action or forgo procedural or substantive rights.").

11. 28 U.S.C.A. § 1446(b).

12. *See, e.g., Peters v. Lincoln Electric Co.*, 285 F.3d 456, 466 (6th Cir.2002) (information obtained through plaintiff's response to deposition questions is "other paper" for purpose of § 1446(b)); *S.W.S. Erectors, Inc. v. Infax, Inc.*, 72 F.3d 489, 494 (5th Cir.1996) (if deposition testimony is first time defendant learned of eligibility for removal, testimony is "other paper" pursuant to § 1446(b))

13. *See, e.g., Addo v. Globe Life and Accident Insurance Co.*, 230 F.3d 759, 761 (5th Cir.2000) ("post-complaint letter concerning settlement terms may constitute an 'other paper' under § 1446(b)").

different days, it is possible that the thirty day limit could begin to run upon the occurrence of several different events: (1) service on the first defendant served;[14] (2) service on the last defendant served;[15] or (3) service on each defendant as that service takes place,[16] with each defendant having a different thirty day period in which to file a notice of removal that (with the consent of all defendants) could result in the successful removal of the entire case many months after the first defendant was served. This tangled area must also be consigned to a careful study of local practice to determine the applicable approach.

At least two other questions remain. First, when should the thirty day limit begin to run if a defendant is aware of the possibility of removal before a case has even been filed? If such a defendant files a notice of removal after the case is filed, but before formal service on the defendant, and then takes no further action on removal after being served, what is the result when more than thirty days elapses after service? This problem, which could be called an issue of premature removal, may be answered by distinguishing the solutions provided in the second paragraph of this discussion, above. Those solutions apply to situations in which some form service, or filing and service, occurred under state law, and a notice of removal was filed at a later date. The instant problem, involving filing of a notice of removal before service, has been treated as unrelated to those solutions. Instead, it appears that such a removal prior to service can be a timely removal.[17]

Second, it will be obvious to all attorneys that sometimes a pleading filed in state court may not fall within one of only two possibilities—removable or not. That is, while sometimes a state complaint will be clear on its face that removal is possible, or be totally unclear as to a removal possibility, a third contingency exists and may even be commonplace. It is entirely possible that a state pleading will hint at, but not confirm, the possibility of removal. In such a circumstance, the common practice is to relieve the defendant of guessing at removal eligibility or investigating the question further. Instead, the defendant's time limit for removal begins to run only where it is clear, from a reading of the state court document

14. *See, e.g., Getty Oil Corp. v. Insurance Co. of North America,* 841 F.2d 1254, 1262–63 (5th Cir.1988) (in case with multiple defendants, time limit begins to run from service of summons and complaint on first defendant served; if later-served defendant prefers state court forum, it may move to remand; only "exceptional circumstances" may alter this approach).

15. *See, e.g., Brierly v. Alusuisse Flexible Packaging, Inc.,* 184 F.3d 527, 533 (6th Cir.1999) (adopting "last-served" rule); *McKinney v. Board of Trustees of Mayland Community College,* 955 F.2d 924, 927 (4th Cir.1992) (same).

16. *See, e.g., Marano Enterprises of Kansas v. Z–Teca Restaurants,* 254 F.3d 753 (8th Cir.2001) (in case involving multiple defendants, each defendant is entitled to thirty days from service of that particular defendant).

17. *See, e.g., Delgado v. Shell Oil Co.,* 231 F.3d 165, 177 (5th Cir.2000) (formal service of process "is not an absolute prerequisite to removal;" requirement exists that suit be commenced before removal, but defendant need only have receipt of a document, through service or otherwise, that case is eligible for removal; distinguishing *Murphy Brothers*).

itself, that removal is possible. Thus, the defendant generally has no burden to make an independent investigation or to fear running of the limitation period when the state document's meaning for removal is ambiguous.[18]

"After–Acquired" Eligibility for Removal

If a case does not qualify for removal at the time of receipt of the original process on a defendant, the defendant will have 30 days to file a notice of removal from the time an amended pleading motion, order, or other paper giving notice of eligibility for removal is served.[19]　However, if the basis for removal is subject matter jurisdiction based on diversity of citizenship, the period of time for "after-acquired" eligibility will normally be no more than one year after the initiation of the lawsuit.[20] For purposes of the one-year

18. *See, e.g., Harris v. Bankers Life & Casualty Co.,* 425 F.3d 689, 695 (9th Cir. 2005) (where it is unclear from complaint whether case is removable, time limit does not begin to run against defendant; only where basis for removal is "revealed affirmatively" does time begin to run; further, defendant has no duty to investigate ambiguity).

19. *See, e.g., Durham v. Lockheed Martin Corp.,* 445 F.3d 1247, 1250 (9th Cir. 2006) (thirty-day time limit starts from receipt of original pleading that " 'affirmatively reveals on its face the facts necessary for federal court jurisdiction.' … Otherwise, the thirty-day clock doesn't begin ticking until a defendant receives 'a copy of an amended pleading, motion, order or other paper' from which it can be determined that the case is removable.' "); *Knudsen v. Liberty Mutual Insurance Co.,* 411 F.3d 805, 807 (7th Cir.2005) ("[A]n amendment to the pleadings that adds a claim under federal law (where only state law claims had been framed before) or adds a new defendant, opens a new window of removal."); *Peters v. Lincoln Electric Co.,* 285 F.3d 456, 466 (6th Cir.2002) (adapting majority rule that plaintiff's response to deposition questions may constitute an "other paper" for purposes of § 1446(b)); *Green v. R.J. Reynolds Tobacco Co.,* 274 F.3d 263, 266 (5th Cir.2001) (appellate decision in unrelated but similar case can be "order" for purposes of triggering application of second paragraph of § 1446(b); collecting cases, acknowledging that holding is minority view); *Huffman v. Saul Holdings Limited Partnership,* 194 F.3d 1072, 1078–79 (10th Cir. 1999) (adopting majority rule that for purpose of § 1446(b) a discovery deposition is treated as equivalent to receipt of "an actu-

al written document"; combination of "petition setting out the factual premise of plaintiff's lawsuit; financial documents produced in discovery; and, most importantly, the voluntary and unequivocal testimony of [one plaintiff] that plaintiffs were seeking $300,000 in damages" gave defendant notice–no later than date of plaintiff's deposition testimony–that jurisdictional amount was satisfied); *S.W.S. Erectors, Inc. v. Infax, Inc.,* 72 F.3d 489, 494 (5th Cir. 1996)(§ 1446(b) permits removal more than 30 days after service of process on defendant only in circumstances where plaintiff's "voluntary act" created right to removal; right to removal cannot be created by judicial act, such as issuance of order).

20. *Cf., e.g., In re Burns & Wilcox, Ltd.,* 54 F.3d 475, 476 n. 4 (8th Cir.1995)(noting that diversity case may not be removed if one year has elapsed since commencement of suit; but issue waived when claimant failed to raise it). *But cf. Braud v. Transport Service Co.,* 445 F.3d 801, 806 (5th Cir.2006) (where new defendant is added more than one year after initial filing, and case is now eligible for removal, removal clock starts to run again notwithstanding passage of more than one year); *Brierly v. Alusuisse Flexible Packaging, Inc.,* 184 F.3d 527 (6th Cir.1999) (plaintiff sued two defendants on state diversity claim; after lengthy delay, second defendant was finally served; thereupon both defendants sought removal; because of delay in service of second defendant, more than one year passed before both defendants sought removal together; held, one year time limit is inapplicable to cases that were removable from their inception; time limit "applies only to those [diversity cases] that were not initially removable").

limitation, courts usually measure "commencement" of the case under the rules governing commencement in the relevant state court.[21]

In unusual cases where it would be inequitable to apply the time limit strictly, it is apparently possible to obtain an extension of time in which to seek removal.[22] It should also be noted that the time limit for § 1446(b) can be enlarged for good cause shown in cases controlled by § 1441(d) (governing removal of suits against foreign states).[23]

Congress recently enacted § 1453, which eliminated the one year time limit for removal of cases based on "after-acquired" diversity jurisdiction if the case is a class action.[24] Thus, while it is still necessary for a defendant seeking removal to do so within 30 days of notice of eligibility of removal, there is no requirement in class action lawsuits for such a defendant to have sought removal within the one year period for seeking removal in non-class action suits that are based on diversity. Section 1453 is discussed in greater detail elsewhere in this text.

Criminal Matters

Removal is also available for a narrow range of criminal actions. Section 1446(c) governs procedure in such matters, but has no relevance to removal in civil cases.

Notification to State Court and Other Parties

Section 1446(d) requires that the defendants seeking removal "promptly" notify the state court and other parties, through filing and service of copies of the notice of removal.

State Court Jurisdiction

Section 1446(d) also directs the state court, upon receipt of notice of removal, to take no further action in a removed case. The

---

21. *See, e.g., Bush v. Cheaptickets, Inc.,* 425 F.3d 683, 688 (9th Cir.2005) (for purposes of one year limitation, "great majority" of federal courts look to state court rules controlling commencement of action; rejecting minority approach of invariably starting running of one year from date of service).

22. *See, e.g., Tedford v. Warner–Lambert Co.,* 327 F.3d 423, 428–29 (5th Cir. 2003) (plaintiff's inequitable forum manipulation justifies extension of time; but noting that equitable exception is subject of substantial disagreement among various district courts).

23. *See, e.g., EIE Guam Corp. v. Long Term Credit Bank of Japan, Ltd.,* 322 F.3d 635, 649 (9th Cir.2003).

24. 28 U.S.C.A. § 1453(b). *See, e.g., Miedema v. Maytag Corp.,* 450 F.3d 1322–

27 n.3 (11th Cir.2006) (§ 1453(b) eliminates the one-year limitation of § 1446(b)); *Abrego v. Dow Chemical Co.,* 443 F.3d 676, 681 (9th Cir.2006) (same). It should be noted that the exceptions created by § 1453 for class actions are themselves subject to an exception. Specifically, § 1453(d) provides that § 1453 is inapplicable to any class action "solely" involving: (1) a claim concerning a covered security under certain federal securities laws; (2) a claim relating to the internal affairs or governance of a corporation or other business entity arising under the laws of the state that incorporated or organized the enterprise; or (3) a claim relating to the rights and duties, including fiduciary duties, created by the Securities Act of 1933.

state court may only re-acquire jurisdiction if the federal court remands one or more counts.[25]

Bond, Rule 11 and Sanctions

Until 1991, § 1446 required that a defendant seeking removal post a bond to cover the plaintiff's costs if the federal court determined that removal was inappropriate. Congress amended the removal statutes in 1991 to remove that requirement, and case law addressing the issue of bonds is obsolete. However, there are still two provisions that may provide reimbursement to a plaintiff whose case has been wrongly removed. Section 1446(a) explicitly provides that notices of removal are subject to the provisions of Federal Rule of Civil Procedure 11, which permits the court to impose sanctions for inappropriate pleadings and motions. Additionally, 28 U.S.C.A. § 1447(c) authorizes a district court that has decided to remand a case to impose costs and actual expenses, "including attorney fees," as part of an order remanding a case to a state court.[26]

Remedy for Inappropriate Removal

If the federal court determines that removal was inappropriate, it may remand part or all of the case to the state court. Dismissal is *not* an appropriate remedy.[27]

ADDITIONAL RESEARCH REFERENCES

C.J.S. Removal of Causes §§ 8, 182–230 et seq., 235–275 et seq., 297–310 et seq.

West's Key No. Digests, Removal of Cases ☞77–120.

25. *See, e.g., California v. United States,* 215 F.3d 1005 (9th Cir.2000) ("The removal of an action to federal court necessarily divests state and local courts of their jurisdiction over a particular dispute."); *Kansas Public Employees Retirement Sys. v. Reimer & Koger Assocs., Inc.,* 77 F.3d 1063, 1069 (8th Cir.1996) (§ 1446(d) is "express authorization to stay state court proceedings"). *But see Lawrence v. Chancery Court of Tennessee,* 188 F.3d 687, 693 (6th Cir. 1999) (§ 1446(d) does not prohibit state court from taking "ministerial steps that do not affect the adjudication of the parties' dispute," such as collection of accrued costs from state-court party who signed cost bond).

26. *See, e.g., Maguire Oil Co. v. City of Houston,* 143 F.3d 205, 207 (5th Cir.1998).

27. *See, e.g., University of South Alabama v. American Tobacco Co.,* 168 F.3d 405, 411 (11th Cir.1999) ("[A] federal court must remand for lack of subject matter jurisdiction notwithstanding the presence of other motions pending before the court."); *Ondis v. Barrows,* 538 F.2d 904, 908 (1st Cir.1976) (dismissal is inappropriate; remand is appropriate remedy). *See also, Glover v. Midland Mortgage Co. of Oklahoma,* 228 B.R. 293, 294 n. 1 (N.D.Ala.1998) (comparing Federal Rule of Civil Procedure 12(h)(3) and 28 U.S.C.A. § 1447(c); noting that when jurisdiction is lacking in a case originally filed in federal district court, Rule 12 requires dismissal; however, in case removed to federal district court, failure of jurisdiction produces remand to state court where case was originally filed, as directed by 28 U.S.C.A. § 1447). *But cf. Caterpillar, Inc. v. Lewis,* 519 U.S. 61, 77, 117 S.Ct. 467, 477, 136 L.Ed.2d 437 (1996) (if district court denies motion to remand removed case, and denial of motion is subsequently found to be error on appeal, "the judgment must be vacated").

§ 2.17a   Procedure After Removal

CORE CONCEPT

Once a case has been removed to a federal district court, 28 U.S.C.A. §§ 1447–49 provide much of the direction for decisions that the court may be required to make in the initial processing of the removed case. The areas governed by these sections include: authority to issue orders and process; acquisition of the record of the case during the period that the case was in state court; timing of remand motions; appeals of remand decisions; and joinder after removal.

APPLICATIONS

Authority to Issue Orders and Process

Section 1447(a) supplies the district court with authority to issue orders and process necessary to bring parties within the jurisdiction of the court. This authority is supplemental to process that may already have been served under the authority of the state court before the case was removed. Section 1447(a) has been the source of very few reported decisions in the past two decades.

Obtaining Case Record

Section 1447(b) authorizes the district court to obtain all records of a removed case in either of two ways. The court may require the party who sought removal to provide such copies, or the court may, through writ of certiorari to the state court, obtain the records directly. If the district court chooses to impose the burden on the party who sought removal, a party's failure to comply may be a consideration in a decision to remand the case to state court.[1]

Timing of Motion to Remand

Section 1447(c) provides two different time limits on motions to remand cases to state court. If the ground for remand is any basis other than the federal court's lack of subject matter jurisdiction, a party seeking remand must file an appropriate motion within 30 days of the date of the petition to remove required by § 1446(a).[2] However, if the basis for seeking remand is an allegation that the federal court lacks subject matter jurisdiction over the case, § 1447(c) provides that the motion to remand may be made at any time prior to final judgment in the case.[3]

---

1. *See, e.g., Patel v. Moore,* 968 F.Supp. 587, 591 (D.Kan.1997) ("[C]ompliance with section 1446(a) does not satisfy the additional requirement authorized by section 1447(b).").

2. *See, e.g., Vasquez v. North County Transit District,* 292 F.3d 1049 (9th Cir. 2002) (failure to make timely objection to erroneously removed workers' compensation claim waives right to remand); *Handelsman v. Bedford Village Associates, L.P.,* 213 F.3d 48, 50 n. 2 (2d Cir.2000) (procedural defect—in case based on diversity ju-

risdiction, defendant was citizen of forum state—was waived when plaintiff failed to object within 30 days of removal).

3. *Wisconsin Dep't of Corrections v. Schacht,* 524 U.S. 381, 391, 118 S.Ct. 2047, 2054, 141 L.Ed.2d 364 (1998) ("[Section 1447(c)] differentiates between removals that are defective because of lack of subject matter jurisdiction and removals that are defective for some other reason, *e.g.,* because the removal took place after relevant time limits had expired. For the latter kind of case, there must be a motion to remand

Remand *Sua Sponte*

If the federal district court notices its own lack of subject matter jurisdiction, § 1447(c) provides that the court need not wait for a motion to remand from a party. Instead, the court can and must remand the case on its own initiative. Such action must be taken if the court notices its lack of subject matter jurisdiction at any time prior to final judgment.[4]

However, if the basis for remand is not a lack of subject matter jurisdiction but only a procedural defect, it is error for the district court to remand *sua sponte*.[5]

No Discretion to Dismiss

While § 1447(c) directs a district court to remand a case that was removed without a basis in subject matter jurisdiction, there is no authority to dismiss such a case.[6]

Section 1447(c) and Non–Jurisdictional Grounds for Remand

Although lack of subject matter jurisdiction is probably the most common reason alleged for seeking remand, a number of other possibilities exist. Because these other possible grounds for remand do not address the district court's subject matter jurisdiction, motions for remand on these grounds may fall within the 30 day time limit established by § 1447(c).[7]

An example of such a ground is failure to comply with the time limits of § 1446(b), which mandates that a petition for removal must be filed within 30 days of receipt of the "pleading, motion, order or other paper" which put the defendant on notice that the case is removable. Additionally, § 1446(b) requires that if the original basis for subject matter jurisdiction is diversity of citizenship under 28 U.S.C.A. § 1332, no petition for removal is allowable if it is filed more than one year after commencement of the action. If the party seeking removal did not comply with either of these time limits when they are applicable, there is authority that the opposing party's motion to remand must be filed within the 30 day limit imposed by § 1447(c).[8]

Less certain is whether an objection to removal because one of the defendants on a state claim was a citizen of the state in which

---

no later than 30 days after the filing of the removal notice. ...For the former kind of case, remand may take place without such a motion and at any time.").

4. *Id.* (Whenever the district court concludes that it lacks subject matter jurisdiction, "remand may take place without ... a motion and at any time.").

5. *See, e.g., In re FMC Corp. Packaging Systems Division,* 208 F.3d 445, 451 (3d Cir.2000) (citing other circuit courts).

6. *See, e.g., Hudson Savings Bank v. Austin,* 479 F.3d 102, 108–09 (1st Cir. 2007) ("This command [to remand] is obligatory

and does not affect district courts leeway to dismiss rather than remand.").

7. *Id.* (when removal is defective on grounds other than lack of subject matter jurisdiction, motion to remand must be made within 30 day time limit of § 1447(c)).

8. *See, e.g., Huffman v. Saul Holdings Limited Partnership,* 183 F.3d 1180, n. 3 (10th Cir.1999) (although time limits of § 1446 are mandatory, defect may be waived by failing to file motion to remand within time limit of § 1447(c)).

the case was filed falls within the time limit of § 1447(c). On the one hand, if the parties are diverse from one another and the amount in controversy was satisfied, the federal court would have had subject matter jurisdiction over any case originally filed in the district court. On the other hand, removal is prohibited notwithstanding the presence of diversity jurisdiction if a defendant is sued in the defendant's home state court (§ 1441(b)).[9]

It should also be noted that although § 1447(c) itself is held to specify only two grounds for remand (lack of subject matter jurisdiction and defects in removal procedure),[10] other grounds for remand may exist, such as an exercise of the district court's discretion to abstain from deciding a question.[11] Such grounds are certainly not jurisdictional and they also do not necessarily indicate a defect in removal procedure. In that sense, they are not specified by § 1447(c), and it is unclear whether they are subject to the 30 day time limit § 1447(c) provides for filing remand motions on grounds

9. *Compare, e.g., Handelsman v. Bedford Village Associates, L.P.,* 213 F.3d 48, 50 n. 2 (2d Cir.2000) (erroneous removal of case based on diversity jurisdiction where defendant was citizen of forum state; held, error was procedural defect, waived when plaintiff failed to object within 30 days of removal); *Blackburn v. United Parcel Serv., Inc.,* 179 F.3d 81 n. 3 (3d Cir.1999) (although complete diversity existed in case, removal was inappropriate because one defendant was a citizen of state in which case was filed; however, defect in removal waived when motion to remand was not made within 30 days, as provided in § 1447(c)) *with, e.g., Hurt v. Dow Chemical Co.,* 963 F.2d 1142, 1145 (8th Cir.1992) (original jurisdiction present if plaintiff has originally filed in federal court; however, removal authority was lacking under § 1441(b); held, plaintiff did not waive objection to removal by waiting more than 30 days to file motion to remand, because lack of removal authority under § 1441(b) should be treated as jurisdictional defect). *See also Williams v. AC Spark Plugs Division of General Motors Corp.,* 985 F.2d 783, 787 (5th Cir.1993) (removal of workers' compensation case in violation of 28 U.S.C.A. § 1445(c) is equivalent to "procedural defect" within meaning of § 1447(c) and is therefore not subject to 30 day time limit of § 1447(c)).

10. *Quackenbush v. Allstate Ins. Co.,* 517 U.S. 706, 712, 116 S.Ct. 1712, 1718, 135 L.Ed.2d 1 (1996) (section 1447(c) specifies only two grounds for remand; however, other grounds not specified in § 1447(c) may conceivably arise).

11. As an example, consider the effect of 28 U.S.C.A. § 1441(c). Section 1441(c) provides that if the basis for removal of a case is the presence of a separate and independent federal question, as defined in 28 U.S.C.A. § 1331, the entire case, including "otherwise non-removable claims" may be removed at the same time. Presumably these non-removable claims would typically be claims where diversity jurisdiction was lacking or, perhaps, situations in which the parties were diverse but the defendant had been sued in a state court of a state in which the defendant is a citizen. Section 1441(c) provides not only that such claims may be removed, but also that the district court shall decide whether to retain or remand such "non-removable" claims in which state law predominates. The meaning of § 1441(c), when considered in light of § 1447(c), is that certain claims may be remanded to state court even when there was no defect in removal procedure and the requirement of federal subject matter jurisdiction is satisfied (assuming, *e.g.,* that non-diverse state claims fall within the supplemental jurisdiction of the district court under 28 U.S.C.A. § 1367). A district court's decision to remand non-diverse supplemental claims is not subject to the ban on judicial review established by § 1447(d), *see, e.g., Eastus v. Blue Bell Creameries, L.P.,* 97 F.3d 100, 103 (5th Cir.1996) (§ 1447(d) does not bar review of remand based on district court's discretionary authority under § 1441(c)), but it is unclear whether the time limit of § 1447(c) is applicable to a motion to remand on such discretionary grounds.

other than jurisdiction. However, as is discussed further below, the fact that these grounds are not specified in § 1447(c) has an impact on the ability of a party to seek review of a district court's decision to remand on such grounds.

Discretion to Impose Costs and Fees

As is discussed above, § 1446(a) imposes the signature requirements of Federal Rule of Civil Procedure 11 to notices of removal. Additionally, § 1447(c) expressly authorizes the district court, when remanding a case, to impose costs and actual expenses, "including attorney fees," where such action would be appropriate.[12] The authority to consider a motion for costs and fees continues even if the underlying case has already been remanded to state court.[13]

Notice of Remand: Termination of Federal Jurisdiction

When the district court decides to remand a case to state court, § 1447(c) directs the clerk of court to send a certified copy of the notice of remand to the clerk of the relevant state court. This mailing has significance beyond its value as notification to the state court. In addition to fulfilling the purpose of notice, it is generally held that mailing of the notice of remand divests the federal district court of its jurisdiction over the case.[14] At that point, jurisdiction has been returned to the state court.

Appeal or Reconsideration of Remand Order

Section 1447(d) governs the circumstances in which a district court's decision to remand a case to state court may be reviewed, either by that court or upon appeal. It will probably come as a significant surprise to many attorneys to learn that, subject to fairly narrow exceptions, remand orders are not reviewable by any court whatsoever.[15] In fact, § 1447(d) provides that subject to an excep-

---

12. *Martin v. Franklin Capital Corp.,* ___ U.S. ___, ___, 126 S.Ct. 704, 711, 163 L.Ed.2d 547 (2005) ("Absent unusual circumstances, courts may award attorney's fees under § 1447(c) only where the removing party lacked an objectively reasonable basis for seeking removal. Conversely, when an objectively reasonable basis exists, fees should be denied."). *Cf., e.g., Wisconsin v. Hotline Industries, Inc.,* 236 F.3d 363, 364 (7th Cir.2000) (recovery for expenditures on salaried government attorneys is limited to "actual outlays," not prevailing market rates for private attorneys); *Maguire Oil Co. v. City of Houston,* 143 F.3d 205, 209 (5th Cir.1998) (discretion to impose sanctions under § 1447(c) for inappropriate removal should take into account any responsibility plaintiff may bear for case's period of time in district court). *But see Circle Industries, USA, Inc. v. Parke Construction Group, Inc.,* 183 F.3d 105, 109 (2d Cir.1999) (§ 1447(c) does not authorize award of fees if defendant successfully opposes remand;

fee award possible under § 1447(c) only if remand granted).

13. *Bryant v. Britt,* 420 F.3d 161 (2d Cir.2005).

14. *See, e.g., Bryan v. BellSouth Communications, Inc.,* 492 F.3d 231 (4th Cir. 2007) ("A remand is effective when the district court mails a certified copy of the remand order to the state court, ... or, if the remand is based on lack of subject-matter jurisdiction or a defect in the removal process, when the remand order is entered."). *See, e.g., Arnold v. Garlock, Inc.,* 278 F.3d 426, 438 (5th Cir.2001) ("Once the remand order is certified and mailed ... the matter remanded is removed from federal jurisdiction.").

15. *See, e.g., In re World Trade Center Disaster Site,* 414 F.3d 352 (2d Cir.2005) (neither appeal nor mandamus is available); *Smith v. American States Preferred Insurance Co.,* 249 F.3d 812, 813 (8th Cir.2001)

tion, once remand orders based on either procedural defects raised within thirty days of removal or lack of subject matter jurisdiction are certified to the appropriate state court, they "are not reviewable on appeal or otherwise." The "or otherwise" provision has been construed to mean that even the district court may not look again at a final remand order, because the effect of entering the order (as is discussed immediately above) divests the district court of jurisdiction.[16] Further, if this prohibition on review of a certified remand order is applicable, it usually acts as a bar to a second effort at removal by the same parties on similar grounds.[17]

Exceptions to § 1447(d)

The impact of the prohibition in § 1447(d) on review of a certified remand order is difficult to overstate. Moreover, the exceptions to the general rule of § 1447(d) are varied.[18] The most important of these exceptions are discussed immediately below.

(1) *Statutory Exception:* Section 1447(d) expressly provides that if the original ground for removal was found in § 1443

("The remand order must stand whether it is erroneous or not."); *Snodgrass v. Provident Life & Accident Ins. Co.,* 147 F.3d 1163, 1165 (9th Cir.1998) ("Ordinarily, a district court's order remanding a case to the state court in which it was originally filed is not reviewable."). *See also Horton v. Board of County Commissioners of Flagler County,* 202 F.3d 1297, 1302 (11th Cir. 2000) (believing that district court erred in remanding case to state court on ripeness or exhaustion grounds, but noting that § 1447(d) precludes review of remand; expressly acknowledging that appellate court's view is therefore dicta). *See also Kircher v. Putnam Funds Trust,* ___ U.S. ___, ___ n.10, 126 S.Ct. 2145, 2154 n.10, 165 L.Ed.2d 92 (2006) (Private Securities Litigation Reform Act, 15 U.S.C.A. § 77 et seq., does not create exception to the ban on appellate review imposed by 28 U.S.C.A. § 1447(d)); *Things Remembered, Inc. v. Petrarca,* 516 U.S. 124, 116 S.Ct. 494, 133 L.Ed.2d 461 (1995) (§ 1447(d)'s proscription on review also applies to bankruptcy cases; holding § 1447(d) applicable to 28 U.S.C.A. § 1452, governing remand of federal bankruptcy case to state court).

16. *See, e.g., Doe v. American Red Cross,* 14 F.3d 196, 199 (3d Cir.1993) ("Courts have construed Section 1447(d) as prohibiting appeals of remand orders as well as reviews by district courts of their own remands based on the same grounds as the initial removals."); *Seedman v. United States District Court for the Central District of California,* 837 F.2d 413, 414 (9th Cir.

1988) (per curiam) (Section 1447(d) "has been universally construed to preclude not only appellate review but also reconsideration by the district court. Once a district court certifies a remand order to state court it is divested of jurisdiction and can take no further action on the case."). This result still applies in the context of statutes of limitations. *Jinks v. Richland County,* 538 U.S. 456, 123 S.Ct. 1667, 155 L.Ed.2d 631 (2003) (dicta) ("For *Erie* purposes . . . statutes of limitation are treated as substantive;" citing *Guaranty Trust*). *But see Roe v. O'Donohue,* 38 F.3d 298, 301 (7th Cir.1994) (noting that Northern District of Illinois "automatically delays remands to afford time for reconsideration").

17. *See, e.g., Hunt v. Acromed Corp.,* 961 F.2d 1079, 1081 (3d Cir.1992) (court may not reconsider remand through device of second removal effort based on same reasoning as original removal effort). *But cf., Benson v. SI Handling Systems, Inc.,* 188 F.3d 780, 783 (7th Cir.1999) (second effort to remove not prohibited if allegations of jurisdictional facts had changed after initial remand).

18. *See generally Adkins v. Illinois Central Railroad Co.,* 326 F.3d 828, 831 (7th Cir.2003) ("The naïve reader might think that [§ 1447(d)] meant no appellate consideration by appeal, by writ of mandamus, or by any other device that lawyers might serve up, but that reader would be wrong.").

(removal of civil rights cases), the prohibition on review of the remand order found in § 1447(d) does not apply.[19]

(2) *Remand Not Based on § 1447(c):* Section 1447(c), discussed above, identifies two grounds for remanding removed cases: defects in removal procedure, and lack of federal subject matter jurisdiction.[20] It appears settled that when the district court has remanded a case based on either of these grounds, § 1447(d) almost always prohibits review of the decision.[21] However, when the ground for remand falls outside the scope of §§ 1443 and 1447(c), review of the remand decision is possible either in the district court that granted it or upon appellate review.[22] Examples of such grounds for

---

19. *See, e.g., Patel v. Del Taco, Inc.,* 446 F.3d 996, 998 (9th Cir.2006) (remand, based on lack of jurisdiction, of removal under § 1441 not reviewable; but where removal was based on § 1443, appellate review of remand is permissible); *First Union Mortgage Corp. v. Smith,* 229 F.3d 992, 994 (10th Cir.2000) (remand where removal was based on § 1443 does not fit within scope of § 1447(d) and may therefore be reviewed by circuit court).

20. *Quackenbush v. Allstate Ins. Co.,* 517 U.S. 706, 712, 116 S.Ct. 1712, 1718, 135 L.Ed.2d 1 (1996). *Cf., Carlson v. Arrowhead Concrete Works, Inc.,* 445 F.3d 1046, 1051 (8th Cir.2006) (scope of judicial review of remand order under § 1447(d) is limited to verification that lack of subject matter jurisdiction was "actual basis for remand").

21. *Powerex Corp. v. Reliant Energy Services, Inc.,* __ U.S. __, 127 S.Ct. 2411, 168 L.Ed.2d 112 (2007) ("[R]eview of the District Court's characterization of its remand as resting upon lack of subject-matter jurisdiction, to the extent that it is permissible at all, should be limited to confirming that characterization was colorable." Also holding that a district court's decision to remand a properly removed case because a subject matter jurisdiction problem arose is unreviewable under § 1447(d)). *See, e.g., Tmesys, Inc. v. Eufala Drugs, Inc.,* 462 F.3d 1317 (11th Cir. 2006) ("Under 28 U.S.C. § 1447(d) we are generally deprived of appellate jurisdiction over remand orders."); *Carlson v. Arrowhead Concrete Works, Inc.,* 445 F.3d 1046, 1053–54 (8th Cir.2006) (collateral order rule does not create exception to ban on reviews of remand orders under § 1447(c)); *Webb v. B.C. Rogers Poultry, Inc.,* 174 F.3d 697, 700 (5th Cir.1999) ("[I]n 28 U.S.C. § 1447(d), Congress denied us jurisdiction over remands pursuant to 28 U.S.C. § 1447(c), which requires a district

court to remand if it lacks subject matter jurisdiction or if the removal was defective."). *But see American Soda, L.L.P. v. U.S. Filter Wastewater Group, Inc.,* 428 F.3d 921, 924 (10th Cir.2005) (permitting review of remand based on forum selection clause; using collateral order doctrine as vehicle for review); *Heaton v. Monogram Credit Card Bank of Georgia,* 297 F.3d 416 (5th Cir.2002) (remand based on lack of jurisdiction is normally not appealable, but 12 U.S.C. § 1819(b)(2)(C) creates exception to § 1447(d) for Federal Deposit Insurance Corporation); *Poore v. American–Amicable Life Insurance Co.,* 218 F.3d 1287, 1291 (11th Cir.2000) (notwithstanding § 1447(d), finding of lack of subject matter jurisdiction was reviewable where district court exceeded its authority by erroneously relying on post-removal amendment to complaint); *Carr v. American Red Cross,* 17 F.3d 671, 680 (3d Cir.1994) (district court dismissed cross-claim against one defendant and remanded remainder of case on jurisdictional grounds; held, bar to appellate review of jurisdictionally motivated remand did not apply because district court's dismissal of cross-claim meant that cross-claim would not be heard in state court; thus, where that order triggered the removal, both the dismissal and the remand must be subject to appellate review).

22. *Quackenbush v. Allstate Ins. Co.,* 517 U.S. 706, 712, 116 S.Ct. 1712, 1718, 135 L.Ed.2d 1 (1996). *See also, e.g., City of Tucson v. U.S. West Communications, Inc.,* 284 F.3d 1128, 1131 (9th Cir.2002) ("[I]t is clear that non-jurisdictional, discretionary remands are not barred from appellate review."); *In re CSX Transp., Inc.,* 151 F.3d 164, 167 (4th Cir.1998) (citing Supreme Court holding that "§ 1447(d) only restricted appellate review of remand orders based

remand that have been subjected to review include: a remand order based on either a motion of a party or the court's own motion that asserts a procedural defect, but which does so more than thirty days after removal;[23] a district court's decision to abstain from deciding state questions;[24] a *sua sponte* remand by the district court based only on a procedural defect in removal (not a defect in subject matter jurisdiction);[25] a remand based on the discretionary jurisdiction of the Declaratory Judgment Act;[26] a magistrate judge's remand order;[27] a remand based on the district court's discretionary authority under § 1441(c);[28] a discretionary remand of claims within a district court's supplemental jurisdiction under 28 U.S.C.A. § 1367(c);[29] situations

on § 1447(c)–a provision addressing remands where a removal was improvident or the district court was without subject matter jurisdiction"); *Snodgrass v. Provident Life & Accident Ins. Co.,* 147 F.3d 1163, 1165 (9th Cir.1998) (" 'Exceptional' remand orders, entered pursuant to some doctrine or authority other than § 1447(c), are not subject to § 1447(d)'s prohibition."). *But see Stevens v. Brink's Home Security, Inc.,* 378 F.3d 944, 949 (9th Cir.2004) (appeal based on district court's obligation to remand under § 1447(e) after joinder of non-diverse parties is immunized from appellate review under § 1447(d)).

23. *See, e.g., Mitskovski v. Buffalo & Fort Erie Public Bridge Authority,* 435 F.3d 127, 131–32 (2d Cir.2006). *Cf., Horton v. Conklin,* 431 F.3d 602, 604–05 (8th Cir. 2005) (more than thirty days after removal, remand motion made that is based on defendant's citizenship in forum state in case originating under state law; held, such remand motion raises jurisdictional objection to removal and is therefore not reviewable, notwithstanding date of removal; rejecting contrary authority that treats issue as procedural defect (in which circumstance remand order would be reviewable because thirty day time limit for procedural objections had passed)).

24. *See, e.g., Carvel v. Thomas & Agnes Carvel Foundation,* 188 F.3d 83, 86 (2d Cir.1999) (remand on grounds of abstention based on comity among courts is reviewable, because issues are not jurisdictional); *Webb v. B.C. Rogers Poultry, Inc.,* 174 F.3d 697, 700 (5th Cir.1999) (§ 1447(d) has no impact on appellate court's authority to review district court's possible abuse of discretion in remanding on abstention grounds).

25. *See, e.g., Whole Health Chiropractic & Wellness, Inc. v. Humana Medical Plan, Inc.,* 254 F.3d 1317 (11th Cir.2001) (noting that all circuits addressing this issue agree).

26. *See, e.g., Snodgrass v. Provident Life & Accident Ins. Co.,* 147 F.3d 1163, 1165 (9th Cir.1998). *See also Long v. Bando Manufacturing of America, Inc.,* 201 F.3d 754, 758 (6th Cir.2000) (remand of claims within supplemental jurisdiction of district court was within discretion of court and was therefore not jurisdictional; thus, remand was reviewable); *Xiong v. Minnesota,* 195 F.3d 424, 426 (8th Cir.1999) (district court ignored clear circuit court precedent in remanding on ground of lack of jurisdiction; thus, "there was simply no jurisdictional question" to be resolved in district court, and circuit court could hear appeal of remand).

27. *See, e.g., Vogel v. U.S. Office Products Co.,* 258 F.3d 509, 517–18 (6th Cir. 2001) (remand order is dispositive matter, which magistrate judge cannot enter; instead, magistrate judge must submit findings and recommendations to district judge for review and approval; thus, § 1447(d)'s prohibition on appellate review of remand order does not apply to magistrate judge's attempted remand order, which itself is invalid and subject to review by both district court and appellate court; noting some disagreement, collecting cases).

28. *See, e.g., Niehaus v. Greyhound Lines, Inc.,* 173 F.3d 1207, 1210 (9th Cir.), *cert. denied,* 528 U.S. 986, 120 S.Ct. 445, 145 L.Ed.2d 362 (1999) (asserting authority to review district court's remand of pendent state claims); *Eastus v. Blue Bell Creameries, L.P.,* 97 F.3d 100, 103 (5th Cir.1996).

29. *See, e.g., Green v. Ameritrade, Inc.,* 279 F.3d 590, 595 (8th Cir.2002) (remand

where the Supreme Court has clarified a party's right to remove in the period between the original remand decision and a party's second attempt to remove;[30] circumstances in which, if a federal court did not review an order that determines a claim for attorney fees, no court would be able to review it because the state court would lack jurisdiction to do so;[31] a remand based on defendants' waiver of their arbitration rights;[32] an erroneous holding that multiple efforts to remove are barred even where changed allegations of fact demonstrate that subject matter jurisdiction is now satisfied;[33] a remand order issued after the district judge erroneously refused to recuse himself;[34] and a remand granted as enforcement of a valid forum selection clause.[35] Finally, the circuit court may properly look at the "objective merits" of the remand order to determine the appropriateness of an award of costs and fees under § 1447(c).[36] As

based on § 1367(c) is appealable); *In re U.S. Healthcare, Inc.,* 193 F.3d 151, 158–59 (3d Cir.1999) (remand of supplemental claims under discretionary provision of 28 U.S.C.A. § 1367(c)(3) is reviewable; contrary result if remand had been ordered under § 1447(c)). *But see Heaton v. Monogram Credit Card Bank of Georgia,* 231 F.3d 994, 997 (5th Cir.2000) (party's allegation that true basis for remand was § 1367(c)(3), not district court's stated reason that subject matter jurisdiction was lacking, is not reviewable).

30. *See, e.g., Baker v. Kingsley,* 387 F.3d 649, 654 (7th Cir.2004) (basis for remand was discretionary power to decline jurisdiction under § 1367, governing supplemental jurisdiction; held, § 1447(d) does not bar appellate review); *Doe v. American Red Cross,* 14 F.3d 196 (3d Cir.1993) (Red Cross had attempted to remove, but district court remanded; after Supreme Court upheld right of Red Cross to remove in unrelated case, appellate court approved second effort at removal in instant case).

31. *See, e.g., Hornbuckle v. State Farm Lloyds,* 385 F.3d 538, 541 (5th Cir.2004) ("Although this Court may not review a district court's remand for lack of subject matter jurisdiction, we may review the district court's award of attorney fees."); *Garbie v. DaimlerChrysler Corp.,* 211 F.3d 407, 409 (7th Cir.2000) (award of attorney's fees for wrongful removal is "independently appealable order").

32. *See, e.g., Restoration Preservation Masonry, Inc. v. Grove Europe, Ltd.,* 325 F.3d 54, 59 (1st Cir.2003) (appellate court is not engaging in prohibited review of jurisdictional issue where its review of waiver of

arbitration may be made separately from jurisdiction).

33. *See, e.g., Benson v. SI Handling Systems, Inc.,* 188 F.3d 780, 783 (7th Cir. 1999) (§ 1447(d) does not bar review of remand of second effort to remove—on second effort district court acknowledged that subject matter jurisdiction was now satisfied, but remanded on ground that multiple efforts to remove are not permitted).

34. *See, e.g., Republic of Panama v. American Tobacco Co., Inc.,* 217 F.3d 343, 345–46 (5th Cir.2000) (remand order that was issued after district judge denied recusal motion may technically be insulated from review by § 1447(d); however, when recusal was appropriate, erroneous failure to recuse means that all orders issued after that failure should be vacated; in such circumstances, vacating remand order is " 'ministerial task' unrelated to the remand itself, and thus not prohibited by § 1447(d)").

35. *See, e.g., American Soda, L.L.P. v. U.S. Filter Wastewater Group, Inc.,* 428 F.3d 921, 924 (10th Cir.2005) (permitting review, under collateral order doctrine, if remand based on forum selection clause); *Global Satellite Communication Co. v. Starmill U.K. Ltd.,* 378 F.3d 1269 (11th Cir. 2004) ("§ 1447(d) does not bar review of remand order based upon a forum selection clause").

36. *See, e.g., Dahl v. Rosenfeld,* 316 F.3d 1074, 1079 (9th Cir.2003) (although remand was error that cannot be reversed, award of attorneys' fees based on such error is reviewable and may be reversed);

these examples indicate, however, the exceptions to the general rule that remand orders are not reviewable are themselves fairly limited. In particular, remands on the grounds of defects in removal procedure or lack of subject matter jurisdiction remain almost entirely beyond the scope of any review, even if they are mixed with considerations that appear to fall outside the scope of the prohibition of § 1447(d).[37]

It should be noted that *denial* of remand does not implicate § 1447(d). Thus, such a denial is reviewable on appeal.[38]

New Exception: Appeal of Grant or Denial of Remand in Class Actions

Congress recently created an exception to the general rule that, pursuant to § 1447(d), remand of a case removed from state court is not appealable. Pursuant to 28 U.S.C.A. 1453(c), in a case involving class action litigation, district court decisions granting or denying remand may be appealed to the appropriate court of appeals. Such an appeal must be made within seven days of entry of the original order.[39]

The appellate court must decide such an appeal within 60 days of the filing of the appeal,[40] unless one of two circumstances arises. First, the time may be extended for any amount of time if all parties consent to the extension.[41] Alternatively, the time may be extended

Roxbury Condominium Assocation, Inc. v. Anthony S. Cupo Agency, 316 F.3d 224, 227 (3d Cir.2003) (when court examines attorney's fees, it may not reverse remand order but it may evaluate merits of order to help determine whether fee award is appropriate); *Stuart v. UNUM Life Insurance Co. of America,* 217 F.3d 1145, 1148 (9th Cir. 2000) (acknowledging, however, that remand order itself may not be reviewed with any view to reversing it).

37. *See, e.g., Yakama Indian Nation v. State of Washington Department of Revenue,* 176 F.3d 1241 (9th Cir.1999) (treating remand order based primarily, but not entirely, on jurisdictional issues as not reviewable). *But cf. In re U.S. Healthcare,* 159 F.3d 142, 146 (3d Cir.1998) (where magistrate judge issues remand order and lacks authority to do so under § 1447(c), prohibitions on review under § 1447(d) do not apply).

38. *See, e.g., City & County of San Francisco v. PG & E Corp.,* 433 F.3d 1115, 1121 (9th Cir.2006) (prohibition on appellate review inapplicable where district court denies remand motion); *Bracken v. Matgouranis,* 296 F.3d 160 (3d Cir.2002)

("[A]ppellate review of District Court orders denying remand is not prohibited.").

39. 28 U.S.C.A. § 1435(c)(1). *See, e.g., Miedema v. Maytag Corp.,* 450 F.3d 1322–26 (11th Cir.2006) (notwithstanding § 1447(d), § 1453(c)(1) provides that circuit court may review remand order if removal took place under 28 U.S.C.A. § 1332(d) (jurisdictional portion of Class Action Fairness Act)); *Prime Care of Northeast Kansas, L.L.C. v. Humana Insurance Co.,* 447 F.3d 1284, 1285 (10th Cir.2006) (same). It should be noted that the exceptions created by § 1453 are themselves subject to an exception. Specifically, § 1453(d) provides that § 1453 is inapplicable to any class action "solely" involving: (1) a claim concerning a covered security under certain federal securities laws; (2) a claim relating to the internal affairs or governance of a corporation or other business entity arising under the laws of the state that incorporated or organized the enterprise; or (3) a claim relating to the rights and duties, including fiduciary duties, created by the Securities Act of 1933.

40. 28 U.S.C.A. § 1453(c)(2).

41. 28 U.S.C.A. § 1453(c)(3).

for up to ten days, for good cause shown.[42] If the appellate court does not act within the specified time limits, including any applicable extensions, the appeal is automatically denied.[43] Section 1453 is discussed at greater length elsewhere in this text.

Joinder After Removal

If a district court retains jurisdiction of a removed case, § 1447(e) vests the court with considerable discretion to determine whether to permit joinder of additional parties. This discretion includes authority to join parties whose participation in the case destroys subject matter jurisdiction.[44] However, if such non-diverse parties are joined, the court must remand the case to state court. In other words, the district court has discretion to refuse to join parties whose presence destroys subject matter jurisdiction.[45] If, on the other hand, such parties are joined, the court may not retain the case, and must remand because it lacks jurisdiction.[46]

Appellate Review of Remand Pursuant to § 1447(e)

As has been discussed earlier, § 1447(d) often prevents appellate review of a district court's decision under § 1447(c) to remand a case to state court based on lack of subject matter jurisdiction. A question that remains is whether a remand order pursuant to § 1447(e) is subject to the same limitations on review. To this date it appears that a § 1447(e) decision to remand based on lack of subject matter jurisdiction is similarly non-reviewable.[47] It should be

42. 28 U.S.C.A. § 1453(c)(3)(B).

43. 28 U.S.C.A. § 1453(c)(4).

44. *Cf., Kabakjian v. United States,* 267 F.3d 208, 212 (3d Cir.2001) (§ 1447(e) is exception to general rule, particularly applicable to diversity cases, that jurisdiction is determined at time of filing); *Ryan ex rel. Ryan v. Schneider National Carriers, Inc.,* 263 F.3d 816, 819 (8th Cir.2001) ("In the case of a removed action diversity must exist both when the state petition is filed and when the petition for removal is filed.").

45. *See, e.g., Mayes v. Rapoport,* 198 F.3d 457, 462 (4th Cir.1999) (where plaintiff joined new non-diverse defendant without leave of court (using provision of Rule 15(a) permitting plaintiff one amended complaint as of right), district court still retains authority under § 1447(e) to reject joinder of new defendant; where purpose of joinder is to defeat diversity jurisdiction, decision to reject joinder is within court's discretion); *Newcombe v. Adolf Coors Co.,* 157 F.3d 686, 691 (9th Cir.1998) (affirming district court's decision not to join non-diverse party under § 1447(e)). *See also Casas Office Machines, Inc. v. Mita Copystar America, Inc.,* 42 F.3d 668, 674 (1st Cir. 1994) (§ 1447(e) also gives court discretion

to add or reject later-named fictitious parties, with similar results).

46. *See, e.g., Mayes v. Rapoport,* 198 F.3d 457, 461 (4th Cir.1999) ("[T]he statute does not allow a district court to retain jurisdiction once it permits a nondiverse defendant to be joined in the case."); *Ingram v. CSX Transp., Inc.,* 146 F.3d 858, 863 (11th Cir.1998) ("Because § 1447(e) was applicable here, the district court was left with only two options: (1) deny joinder; or (2) permit joinder and remand [the] case to state court. The district court chose to permit the diversity-destroying joinder and, as a result, it should have remanded this action to [state] court.").

47. *See, e.g., Stevens v. Brink's Home Security, Inc.,* 378 F.3d 944 (9th Cir.2004) (applying proscription of § 1447(d) to remand under § 1447(e)); *In re Florida Wire and Cable Co.,* 102 F.3d 866, 868–69 (7th Cir.1996) (no jurisdiction to review, by mandamus or otherwise); *Washington Suburban Sanitary Commission v. CRS/Sirrine, Inc.,* 917 F.2d 834, 836 n. 5 (4th Cir.1990) (remand under § 1447(e) should be treated similarly to remand under § 1447(c)—no appellate review of remand based on lack of subject matter jurisdiction).

noted, however, that when a district court decides to retain a case and *not* remand under § 1447(e), that decision is reviewable.[48]

Serving Defendants After Removal Has Occurred

It is possible that in a case involving several defendants, the first defendant served with process will be eligible to petition for removal. Such a defendant might promptly seek removal in order to avoid the time limit on removal petitions (30 days from service) established in § 1446. That might mean that some defendants remain unserved after removal. To correct that situation, 28 U.S.C.A. § 1448 addresses two points. First, § 1448 expressly authorizes the district court to permit completion of service initiated in the state proceeding or to issue its own service on unserved defendants.[49] Second, once such defendants have been served, § 1448 permits them to make a decision either to challenge the removal by seeking remand or to accept the removal that has already occurred.[50] In establishing this potential right for later-served defendants to seek remand or removal, § 1448 does not affect in any way whatever rights a plaintiff might have to file a motion to remand.[51]

Failure of State Court to Supply Record

In the unusual circumstance where a state court does not supply the federal court with the record of proceedings that occurred before the case was removed, 28 U.S.C.A. § 1449 provides the district court with authority to re-create the record "by affidavit or otherwise." Such authority under § 1449 exists only where the state court's failure to provide the record is inappropriate. If, for example, the party seeking use of the record failed to pay appropriate legal fees to the state court, a district court would not have authority

48. See, e.g., *Ingram v. CSX Transportation, Inc.,* 146 F.3d 858, 863 (11th Cir. 1998) ("Because § 1447(e) was applicable here, the district court was left with only two options: (1) deny joinder; or (2) permit joinder and remand [the] case to state court. The district court chose to permit the diversity-destroying joinder and, as a result, it should have remanded this action to [state] court."). Cf., *Roche v. Lincoln Property Co.,* 373 F.3d 610, 613 (4th Cir.2004), cert. granted, 543 U.S. 1186, 125 S. Ct. 1398, 161 L. Ed. 2d 189 (2005) and judgment rev'd, 546 U.S. 81, 126 S. Ct. 606, 163 L. Ed. 2d 415 (2005) (denial of remand is reviewed *de novo*).

49. *Murphy Bros., Inc. v. Michetti Pipe Stringing, Inc.,* 526 U.S. 344, 354, 119 S.Ct. 1322, 1329, 143 L.Ed.2d 448, n. 6 (1999) ("[Section 1448] allows the plaintiff to serve an unserved defendant or to perfect flawed service once the action has been removed.").

50. *Id.* (second paragraph of § 1448 "explicitly reserves the unserved defen-

dant's right to take action (move to remand) after service is perfected"). See also, e.g., *McKinney v. Board of Trustees of Mayland Community College,* 955 F.2d 924, 926 n. 3 (4th Cir.1992) (if second defendant is served more than 30 days after first defendant is served, the first defendant can file for, and obtain, removal, and the second defendant can use authority of § 1448 to seek remand); *Getty Oil Corp. v. Insurance Co. of North America,* 841 F.2d 1254, 1263 (5th Cir.1988) ("[I]f a removal petition is filed by a served defendant and another defendant is served after the case is thus removed, the latter defendant may still either accept the removal or exercise its right to choose the state forum by making a motion to remand.").

51. See, e.g., *Lewis v. Rego Co.,* 757 F.2d 66, 69 (3d Cir.1985) ("The right which the statute gives to such a defendant to move to remand the case confers no rights upon a plaintiff.").

under § 1449 to re-create the record. Section 1449 has not been the subject of significant reported precedent in the past two decades.

§ 2.17b Removal of Class Actions

CORE CONCEPT

In 2005 Congress enacted the Class Action Fairness Act, which has been encoded in 28 U.S.C.A. §§ 1332, 1453, and 1711–15. Section 1453 governs circumstances in which a class action that was filed in state court may be removed to a federal district court. The most important features of § 1453 are two: first, most class actions are now generally much less difficult to remove to district court than more conventional civil actions; and second, if a district court decides to remand to state court a class action that had been removed, § 1453 generally affords the defendant who removed the action significantly better access to an appeal of that district court decision. The most important exception to the two foregoing generalizations is also contained in § 1453.

APPLICATIONS

Definitions

Section 1453(a) defines four terms (class, class action, class certification order, and class member) by incorporating the definitions of these terms found in § 1332(d)(1), which is another portion of the newly enacted Class Action Fairness Act. Section 1332 is discussed at greater length elsewhere in this text.

Application of Standard Removal Requirements: Exceptions

Sections 1332, 1441 and 1446, discussed elsewhere in this text, govern many of the requirements applicable to removal of cases from state court to federal court, including class actions.[1] However, when a case falls within the scope of the Class Action Fairness Act, a number of provisions of §§ 1332, 1441, 1446, and case law are inapplicable to removal of a class action. Most of these exceptions to removal of class actions are identified in § 1453(b), but two of them are located in § 1332(d)(2). All of these exceptions are identified immediately below.

Exception: Diversity of Citizenship. In the ordinary course of events, a party seeking to establish subject matter jurisdiction in a federal district court based on diversity of citizenship must establish complete diversity between all plaintiffs and all defendants.[2] However, § 1332(d)(2) expressly provides that for purposes of class actions within the scope of the Class Action Fairness Act, diversity jurisdic-

---

1. *See, e.g., Progressive West Insurance Co. v. Preciado,* 479 F.3d 1014, 1017 (9th Cir. 2007) (§ 1453 does not change "longstanding rule that a plaintiff/cross-defendant cannot remove an action to federal court").

2. *Exxon Mobil Corp. v. Allapattah Services, Inc.,* 545 U.S. 546, ___, 125 S.Ct. 2611, 2617, 162 L.Ed.2d 502 (2005) ("[W]e have consistently interpreted § 1332 as requiring complete diversity.").

tion may be satisfied simply by establishing that a single class member is diverse from the class opponents.[3]

Exception: Amount in Controversy. In civil cases that do not involve class actions, diversity jurisdiction is not established unless the amount in controversy for each plaintiff exceeds $75,000, exclusive of interest and costs.[4] However, in cases controlled by the Class Action Fairness Act, the amount in controversy in most class actions must exceed $5,000,000, exclusive of interest and costs.[5] This figure is obviously larger than the more traditional monetary requirement for individual parties in cases not involving class actions, but it will often be easier to achieve in class actions because the total amount in dispute in many cases often exceeds $5,000,000, even where the claims of individual participants are for amounts that may be less than the $75,000 requirement.

Exception: One–Year Limitation on Removal of Diversity Cases. In cases not controlled by the Class Action Fairness Act, § 1446(b) permits removal on the basis of diversity jurisdiction only within the first year after commencement of the action in state court.[6] By contrast, § 1453(b) expressly provides that "the 1–year limitation under § 1446(b) shall not apply."[7]

Exception: Citizenship of Defendants. Section 1441 provides that in cases where a defendant is a citizen of the state where the case is filed, removal may not be based on diversity of citizenship—even if the diversity requirements themselves are satisfied.[8] However, in cases controlled by the Class Action Fairness Act, the citizenship of a defendant in the forum state is not an impediment to removal.[9]

Exception: Unanimous Consent. For more conventional cases, case law has long imposed a requirement that *all* defendants join in the removal petition.[10] However, cases controlled by the Class Action Fairness Act may be removed by a single defendant, without the need for unanimous consent among defendants.[11]

3. 28 U.S.C.A. § 1332(d)(2). *See also Miedema v. Maytag Corp.,* 450 F.3d 1322, 1327 (11th Cir.2006) (§ 1332(d) establishes requirement of only minimal diversity in Class Action Fairness Cases).

4. 28 U.S.C.A. § 1332(a).

5. 28 U.S.C.A. § 1332(d). *See also Miedema v. Maytag Corp.,* 450 F.3d 1322, 1327 (11th Cir.2006) (noting requirement of more than $5,000,000).

6. 28 U.S.C.A. § 1446(b).

7. 28 U.S.C.A. § 1446(b). *See, e.g., Lowery v. Alabama Power Co.,* 483 F.3d 1184, 1195 (11th Cir. 2007) (§ 1453 eliminates one-year limitation on removal of class action diversity suits); *Miedema v. Maytag Corp.,* 450 F.3d 1322, 1327 n. 3 (11th Cir. 2006) (also noting that § 1446(b)'s one year limitation is not applicable).

8. 28 U.S.C.A. § 1441(b). *Lincoln Property Co. v. Roche,* ___ U.S. ___, ___, 126 S.Ct. 606, 613, 163 L.Ed.2d 415 (2005).

9. 28 U.S.C.A. § 1453(b).

10. *Chicago, Rock Island, Corning & Pacific Railway Co. v. Martin,* 178 U.S. 245, 248, 20 S.Ct. 854, 855, 44 L.Ed. 1055 (1900) ("[I]t was well settled that a removal could not be effected unless all the parties on the same side of the controversy united in the petition.").

11. 28 U.S.C.A. § 1453(b). *See also Frazier v. Pioneer Americas, L.L.C.,* 455 F.3d 542 (5th Cir.2006) (§ 1453(b) eliminates requirement of unanimous consent to removal); *Miedema v. Maytag Corp.,* 450 F.3d 1322, 1329 (11th Cir.2006) (§ 1453(b) permits a single defendant to remove; normal unanimity requirement is discarded for Class Action Fairness Act cases).

Appellate Review

In conventional removal cases, § 1447(d) imposes a broad general prohibition on appellate review or reconsideration of remand orders based on procedural defects in the removal petition or lack of subject matter jurisdiction.[12] In cases controlled by the Class Action Fairness Act, however, § 1453(c)(1) provides that, while § 1447 itself generally applies to removal of class actions, the prohibition in § 1447(d) does not.[13]

Discretionary Appeal

There is no right to appeal a district court's order granting or denying remand of a class action to a state court. Instead, § 1453(c)(1) gives the circuit court discretion to hear such an appeal.[14]

Time Limit for Application to Appeal

Although the literal language of § 1453(c)(1) is a bit confused, courts are in accord in holding that parties seeking review of a decision on remand must apply to the circuit court within seven days of the order granting or denying the motion to remand.[15]

Time Limit for Circuit Court to Decide

If the court of appeals accepts an application to appeal, § 1453(c)(2) directs the appellate court to decide the issue within sixty days,[16] subject to extensions of that time (discussed immediate-

---

12. *See, e.g., In re World Trade Center Disaster Site,* 414 F.3d 352, 364 (2d Cir. 2005) (neither appeal nor mandamus is available). Section 1447(d), and its exceptions, are discussed in greater detail elsewhere in this text.

13. 28 U.S.C.A. § 1453(c)(1). *See, e.g., Lowery v. Alabama Power Co.,* 483 F.3d 1184, 1193 (11th Cir. 2007) (§ 1453(c) permits review de novo of district court's decision to remand case that was removed pursuant to Class Action Fairness Act); *Miedema v. Maytag Corp.,* 450 F.3d 1322, 1326 (11th Cir.2006) (notwithstanding § 1447(d), remand orders in cases that were removed pursuant to Class Action Fairness Act may be reviewed by appellate court). *But cf., Saab v. Home Depot U.S.A., Inc.,* 469 F.3d 758, 759 (8th Cir. 2006) (where removal of class action was based on "traditional diversity jurisdiction," § 1453(c) exception to non-appealibility of remand orders does not apply).

14. 28 U.S.C.A. § 1453(c)(1) ("[A] court of appeals *may* accept an appeal." (italics added)). *See also, e.g., Evans v. Walter Industries, Inc.,* 449 F.3d 1159, 1162 (11th Cir.2006) (§ 1453(c)(1) makes acceptance of petition discretionary); *Prime Care of*

Northeast Kansas, L.L.C. v. Humana Insurance Co., 447 F.3d 1284, 1285 (10th Cir. 2006) (same).

15. *See, e.g., Miedema v. Maytag Corp.,* 450 F.3d 1322 (11th Cir.2006) (appeal must be made within seven days of date of remand order; acknowledging that § 1453(c)(1) requires application within "not less than 7 days," but holding that literal application of that language would produce "absurd result;" noting agreement with other circuits); *Pritchett v. Office Depot, Inc.,* 420 F.3d 1090, 1093 n. 2 (10th Cir.2005) ("The statute should read that an appeal is permissible if filed 'not more than' seven days after entry of the remand order."). *See also Patterson v. Dean Morris, L.L.P.,* 444 F.3d 365, 368 n.1 (5th Cir.2006) (also excluding weekends and holidays from calculation of seven days); *Amalgamated Transit Union Local 1309, AFL–CIO v. Laidlaw Transit Services, Inc.,* 435 F.3d 1140, 1146 (9th Cir.2006) (same).

16. 28 U.S.C.A. § 1453(c)(2). *See, e.g., Braud v. Transport Service Co. of Illinois,* 445 F.3d 801, 803 n. 2 (5th Cir. 2006) (60 days begin to run "from the date on which [the court] granted application for leave to appeal").

ly below). The 60–day time limit begins to run from the date that the court of appeals granted the petition to appeal.[17]

Extension of Time Limit to Decide

Section 1453(c)(2) authorizes the circuit court to extend the sixty days in which it must decide an appeal in either of two circumstances.[18] First, if all parties consent to an extension, the court may extend the sixty days "for any period of time." [19] Second, without regard to the consent of parties, the court may extend the time "for good cause shown and in the interests of justice." [20] If an extension is granted for good cause and without the consent of all parties, § 1453(c)(3)(B) limits the extension to a maximum of ten days.[21]

Failure to Decide Appeal Within Time Limit

Section 1453(c)(4) governs the result if an appellate court does not decide an appeal within the time limit (including extensions, if any). If no decision is forthcoming, the appeal is denied.[22]

Cases Outside Scope of § 1453

Section 1453(d) establishes several categories of actions not within the scope of removal provisions of the Class Action Fairness Act, even if the cases in question are in fact potential class actions.* These exceptions are: (1) cases involving "solely" claims under federal securities laws; and (2) cases involving "solely" claims arising under state corporate laws governing the internal affairs or governance of state chartered corporations.[23]

§ 2.18   The *Erie* Doctrine

I. THE PROBLEM

Federal district courts are sometimes called upon to hear state law disputes—that is, disputes arising under a state's constitution, statutes, or common law, rather than under federal law. The two most frequent circumstances when federal courts hear state disputes arise when the

17. *See, e.g., Evans v. Walter Industries, Inc.,* 449 F.3d 1159, 1162–63 (11th Cir. 2006) (rejecting start of running of sixty days as of date petition to appeal is filed).

18. *See, e.g., Bush v. Cheaptickets, Inc.,* 425 F.3d 683, 686 n. 2 (9th Cir.2005) (noting alternative grounds for extension of time).

19. 28 U.S.C.A. § 1453(c)(3)(A). *See also, e.g., Prime Care of Northeast Kansas, L.L.C. v. Humana Insurance Co.,* 447 F.3d 1284, 1285 n. 1 (10th Cir.2006) (noting extension of sixty days by consent of parties).

20. 28 U.S.C.A. § 1453(c)(3)(B). *See also, e.g., Braud v. Transport Service Co. of Illinois,* 445 F.3d 801, 803 n. 2 (5th Cir.

2006) (noting standard for extension to which parties did not consent).

21. *See, e.g., Braud v. Transport Service Co. of Illinois,* 445 F.3d 801, 803 n. 2 (5th Cir.2006) (noting limit of ten days).

22. 28 U.S.C.A. § 1453(c)(4) (in such circumstances "the appeal shall be denied"). *See also, e.g., Miedema v. Maytag Corp.,* 450 F.3d 1322, 1327 n. 2 (11th Cir. 2006) (failure to decide is denial of petition).

23. *See, e.g., Brill v. Countrywide Home Loans, Inc.,* 427 F.3d 446, 450 (7th Cir. 2005) (citing 28 U.S.C.A. § 1453(d) for the "list of claims to which [the Class Action Fairness Act's] removal provisions are inapplicable").

court's jurisdiction is based on diversity of citizenship[1] or supplemental jurisdiction.[2] When a federal court is confronted with a state law dispute, what substantive law should it apply: federal law or state law? In adjudicating state law disputes, should federal or state procedural rules apply? Efforts to determine when federal or state substantive or procedural law applies have bewitched federal courts almost since the founding of the Republic.

Questions of the subject matter jurisdiction of federal district courts over state causes of action (that is, when federal courts are even entitled to hear state claims) are difficult enough in their own right. However, even after jurisdictional questions are resolved, a party's ability to file a state cause of action in a federal district court gives rise to another set of difficult questions, going to the law that the court should apply to the state claim. As will become evident below, the answers to such questions are still a source of some uncertainty. For that reason alone, it is important not to make the investigation of this problem more difficult than it needs to be.

With that consideration in mind, it should be clear at the outset that the question of identifying the appropriate law a federal district court should apply to a state cause of action is not a matter of jurisdiction. Generally, before a court reaches this question, usually it will have addressed and resolved jurisdictional issues in the case. In other words, if the court lacks jurisdiction to hear the case, normally it will dismiss the action. When that happens, the court need not concern itself with identifying the law that would apply if the court could hear the case. Therefore, the court usually will address questions of the appropriate law to apply to a case only after determining that the court has jurisdiction to hear the claims.[3]

II. *ERIE R.R. CO. v. TOMPKINS*[4]

The current approach to identifying the proper law to apply to a state cause of action in a federal court[5] is based on the *Erie* doctrine. *Erie* rests on two important premises: (1) a claimant should not be encouraged to shop for a federal forum because doing so might result in

---

1. 28 U.S.C.A. § 1332.

2. 28 U.S.C.A. § 1367.

3. It sometimes happens that a court may take an objection to its jurisdiction under advisement and render a decision only after hearing other portions of the case. This approach is an exception to the more typical practice. Moreover, it means that at least tentatively the court has assumed that it possesses jurisdiction to hear the case, subject to the possibility of a different decision later.

4. 304 U.S. 64, 58 S.Ct. 817, 82 L.Ed. 1188 (1938).

5. It should be noted that while the original *Erie* doctrine developed in the context of cases based on the diversity jurisdic-

tion of federal district courts, it appears now to be applied also to cases in which district courts have supplemental jurisdiction over non-diverse state claims. *Felder v. Casey,* 487 U.S. 131, 151, 108 S.Ct. 2302, 2313, 101 L.Ed.2d 123 (1988) (*Erie* also applies to claims based on predecessors to supplemental jurisdiction). *See, e.g., Lytle v. City of Haysville, Kansas,* 138 F.3d 857, 868 (10th Cir.1998) ("When examining jurisdiction over [supplemental] state claims, we must apply the substantive law of the forum state and reach the same decision we believe the state's highest court would, just as we would if our jurisdiction rested on diversity of citizenship.").

application of federal law that would affect the outcome of the case; and (2) federal courts hearing state claims lack Constitutional authority to create common law independent of the law that state courts would apply to those claims. Thus, the established approach prior to *Erie*, which permitted federal courts to create so-called "federal general common law" that might be at odds with state law, was unconstitutional.

The case arose out of an injury that Tompkins suffered while walking alongside a railroad track. When Tompkins sued, the possibility of recovery rested on a determination of his legal status while he was walking on what was clearly railroad property. Under state common law, Tompkins was a trespasser, to whom the railroad owed at most a minimal duty of care. If state law was applied, Tompkins was entitled to no damages. Federal general common law, developed prior to *Erie*, offered the plaintiff greater possibilities. By placing less emphasis on Tompkins' status as an individual not invited onto railroad property, and more emphasis on the railroad's duty of care to individuals who were on its property, federal general common law afforded Tompkins substantial possibilities for a sizeable award of damages.[6]

However, when the Supreme Court got the case, it abolished the body of law that existed prior to *Erie*. At one stroke the Court overruled older precedent and held that in the future there would be no federal general common law. Instead, federal trial courts hearing diversity cases were directed to apply the same state law that a state court hearing the same case would have used.[7]

Part of the impact was immediate and lasting. Federal courts would, in the future, defer to state common law as well as to state statutes. If this rule had been in effect at the time that Tompkins was injured, his lawyer would have known that state law, identifying Tompkins as a trespasser, would have given him little in the way of a claim against the railroad. That result—the federal court's use of state law to determine if the plaintiff has a cognizable cause of action, and to determine if any applicable substantive defenses block the suit—continues to be the law of *Erie* to the present day.

Abolition of federal general common law also meant that the Constitutional concern that the Court expressed in *Erie* was resolved. Recognition of the requirement to apply state substantive law meant that the Constitutionally questionable practice of creating a body of federal substantive law in competition with state law was at an end.

Finally, the temptation to engage in forum shopping was reduced, though not eliminated. Once federal general common law was no more, lawyers lost an important reason to file in federal district courts (*i.e.,* to get different substantive law than a state court would apply). The transformation was radical and, in some respects, complete.

But some new and knotty problems emerged in the wake of *Erie*. It is those problems which continue to cluster around the *Erie* doctrine to

6. *Id.* at 68, 79, 58 S.Ct. at 818, 823.   7. *Id.* at 79, 58 S.Ct. at 823.

the current day, and which are the subject of the remainder of this section.

III. SUBSTANCE v. PROCEDURE: *GUARANTY TRUST CO. v. YORK*[8]

A clue to the central problem arising in the aftermath of *Erie* can be found in a concurring opinion. One justice agreed with the central holding of *Erie, i.e.,* that federal general common law should be abolished and that federal district courts should apply state substantive law. At the same time, he also commented that it was obvious federal courts would remain free to apply their own procedural law—even in diversity cases.[9] But what seemed obvious at the time the Court decided *Erie* proved to be somewhat less clear as additional time passed.

Courts have long identified differences between substantive law and procedural law. Usually substantive law is described as the law that determines whether a party has a claim cognizable in a court, and whether the defendant has a legal defense that bars such a claim on the merits. For example, if a plaintiff sued on a claim of negligence, most states would permit recovery only if the plaintiff could demonstrate that: (1) the defendant owed the plaintiff a duty of care; (2) the defendant breached that duty; and (3) the breach proximately caused injury to the plaintiff or damage to the plaintiff's property. Those are the substantive elements of the tort of negligence.[10] In a state that recognized the defense of contributory negligence, a defendant could defeat the claim by demonstrating that the plaintiff had been contributorily negligent in the event that led to the plaintiff's injury. This assertion of contributory negligence is a substantive defense.

By contrast, procedural law does not address whether the plaintiff has a cause of action or whether the defendant necessarily has a defense. Instead, procedure governs the way in which both plaintiff and defendant must present their sides of the case to the court. At its simplest level, procedural law will control the length of paper on which pleadings must be filed (*e.g.,* letter size or legal size) or whether the complaint may be written out by hand. More complex problems arise over procedure regulating the joining of additional parties, the conduct of discovery, or the admissibility of evidence. These procedural rules help direct the course of a lawsuit and, pragmatically, can often determine the outcome of a case. At the same time, they do not directly address the substantive legal standard a plaintiff must meet in order to demonstrate negligence to the satisfaction of the court.

8.   326 U.S. 99, 65 S.Ct. 1464, 89 L.Ed. 2079 (1945).

9.   *Erie,* 304 U.S. at 90, 58 S.Ct. at 828 (Reed, J., concurring) ("No one doubts federal power over procedure."). The passage of time, however, has demonstrated that Justice Reed's optimism about the primacy of federal procedure should be approached with care. *See Jinks v. Richland County,* 538 U.S. 456, 123 S.Ct. 1667, 155 L.Ed.2d

631 (2003) (implying that courts cannot always easily untangle the relationship between substance and procedure, no matter what the purpose may be for trying to do so).

10.   These elements may be stated somewhat differently in different states, but the basic requirements are usually very similar.

In the context of the *Erie* doctrine, the ability of federal courts to apply their own procedure (or not) remains the central unresolved question that *Erie* produced. On the one hand, there is no serious question about the Constitutional authority of federal courts and Congress to create procedural law that governs federal courts. In that sense, the decision of a federal district court to apply its own procedure to a case involving a state cause of action does not raise the same Constitutional doubts that application of federal general common law had raised in the era prior to *Erie*.

At the same time, in many cases procedure can alter the outcome of a case as surely as substantive law. For example, a case can easily be lost when a party is unprepared to cross-examine effectively an opponent's expert. In some states, preparation to cross-examine an expert is impaired by rules of procedure limiting or prohibiting deposition of opposing experts. By contrast, Federal Rule of Civil Procedure 26 generally permits such depositions. Therefore, to the extent that a federal court's procedure might be different than that of a state court, lawyers might still choose to file cases in federal court (when, *e.g.*, diversity requirements are satisfied) in order to obtain the benefit of federal procedure. Potential problems of forum shopping thus remain when federal courts are able to apply their own procedure.

After *Erie*, the Supreme Court returned to the problem of determining when, if at all, federal courts may use their own procedure in diversity cases. One of the most important early decisions was *Guaranty Trust Co. v. York*,[11] in which the Court had to choose between application of a federal doctrine limiting the time in which a case had to be filed or a state statute of limitations that set a different time limit. Under the state statute, the plaintiff's claim was barred. Under the federal doctrine, the plaintiff's case could proceed.

In its own way, *Guaranty Trust* was more difficult than *Erie*. *Guaranty Trust* involved an arguably procedural issue, and there could be no question that federal courts are authorized to apply their own procedure in many of the cases they hear. For example, when a cause of action arises out of federal law, a federal court must have procedure with which to process the case. The federal court cannot be bound to the application of the procedure of the state in which the federal court sits, because that would mean the procedure applied to federal questions would differ from one state to another. The result would be an unacceptable lack of uniformity in the way federal claims were heard across the United States. Additionally, the Court could not simply order lower federal courts to apply federal procedure when hearing federal claims and state procedure when hearing state claims. In the first place, that approach would require federal judges to learn, and apply, two different bodies of procedure on a regular basis. Secondly, when cases appeared on the federal docket involving both federal and state claims, an attempt to apply federal procedure to federal claims and state procedure to state claims might often produce unacceptable confusion. Consider, for example, what would happen if federal rules of evidence treated a piece of

---

11.   326 U.S. 99, 65 S.Ct. 1464, 89 L.Ed.   2079 (1945).

testimony as inadmissible, while state rules of evidence would admit the testimony.

Guaranty Trust took a tentative step toward resolving the problem by directing federal courts to use state procedure whenever the choice of procedure would determine the outcome of the case. As applied to the facts of *Guaranty Trust,* this approach meant that the federal court should use the state statute of limitations.[12] The reasoning was that under the state rule, the plaintiff's claim was time barred. Application of the federal limitation period would permit the plaintiff to pursue the claim. While it was still possible that the plaintiff might lose the case on the merits, the difference between certain defeat for the plaintiff under the state law and a possibility of victory under the federal law is a sufficient difference in outcome to justify barring the use of federal procedure.

IV. CONTINUING DEVELOPMENT: SOURCES OF FEDERAL PROCEDURE

The underpinning of the decision in *Guaranty Trust* was a concern that a sufficiently large potential difference in outcome caused by the application of federal procedure would create unacceptable levels of forum shopping of the kind that *Erie* originally sought to prevent. This linkage between outcome determination and forum shopping was an important step in extending the *Erie* doctrine to procedural issues as well as matters of substantive law. However, at the same time, an emphasis on "outcome determination" as the basis for choosing between federal procedure and state procedure can easily be an overly broad assessment. In a given case, even the most modest differences in procedure, *e.g.,* page limitations in different courts on the length of briefs, can produce a significantly different outcome. For example, conforming to such page limitations might force an attorney to abandon arguments of potential value. Moreover, because sensible lawyers will litigate only issues that could have a bearing on the outcome of a case, a test that considered only outcome determination might require application of state procedure for almost every state claim filed in federal court— including claims filed in conjunction with federal causes of action.

For that reason, the continuing evolution of the *Erie* doctrine has included the identification of other factors to weigh in a determination as to the applicability of state or federal procedure. Perhaps the most significant factor identified in later cases is the importance of identifying the source of the federal procedure that is arguably applicable to a state cause of action. Over time, the Supreme Court has addressed the relationship of *Erie* to three different sources of federal procedure somewhat differently, as follows.

12. This result still applies in the context of statutes of limitations. *Jinks v. Richland County,* 538 U.S. 456, 123 S.Ct. 1667, 155 L.Ed.2d 631 (2003) (dicta) ("For *Erie* purposes ... statutes of limitation are treated as substantive;" citing *Guaranty* *Trust). But cf., Utica Lloyd's of Texas v. Mitchell,* 138 F.3d 208, 210 (5th Cir.1998) (refusing to apply attorney's fee provision of Texas Declaratory Judgment Act because "it functions solely as a procedural mechanism").

A. Federal Case Law Procedure.

In instances where the pertinent federal procedure develops through case law, and not through statutes or rules, the choice between federal and state procedure depends heavily on a weighing of interests. In *Byrd v. Blue Ridge Rural Electric Cooperative, Inc.,*[13] a worker's compensation case, one key issue was whether the injured plaintiff was an employee, for purposes of the worker's compensation statute, of the defendant. A second issue, and the one that raised the *Erie* question, was whether the jury or the judge should decide the plaintiff's employment relationship (if any) with the defendant. Under state procedure the judge was authorized to make that decision, while the established federal practice was to leave the question to the jury.

The Supreme Court acknowledged that if the only *Erie* measurement was outcome determination, identification of the proper role of judge and jury might well require application of state procedure. However, the Court concluded that other factors, in addition to outcome determination, were also relevant to the case. In particular, the Court extended the *Erie* analysis to include consideration of the competing state and federal interests in applying state and federal procedure, respectively. These considerations, along with an evaluation of the possibility that application of federal procedure might significantly affect the outcome of the case, were to be weighed to determine whether state or federal procedure should control.[14] In other words, a strong state interest in application of state procedure weighs in favor of applying state procedure, while a weak state interest reduces the argument for using state procedure. A strong federal interest in applying federal procedure supports use of federal procedure, while a weak federal interest reduces the argument for using federal procedure. And if the use of federal procedure might significantly affect the outcome of the case, such a prospect argues in favor of using state procedure.[15]

A major difficulty in applying *Byrd* arises when the court tries to identify state and federal interests and to weigh their relative importance in a particular case. Additionally, an assessment of the impact that application of federal procedure might have on the outcome of a case can also be uncertain.[16] The only way attorneys can approach this question is to research the policies behind the competing state and federal procedures and then see how those policies measure up against one another.[17]

---

13. 356 U.S. 525, 78 S.Ct. 893, 2 L.Ed.2d 953 (1958).

14. *Id.* at 533–539, 78 S.Ct. at 899–902.

15. *Id.* at 539, 78 S.Ct. at 902.

16. *Id.* (noting uncertainty of effect of difference between judge and jury on outcome of case). *See also, e.g., Esfeld v. Costa Crociere, S.P.A.,* 289 F.3d 1300, 1306–09 (11th Cir.2002) (noting that "vast majority" of federal appellate courts use federal law of forum non conveniens; holding that while forum non conveniens will often be outcome-determinative, federal interest in controlling its own process in a way that is uniform across the country outweighed the outcome-determinative factor; holding that federal law of forum non conveniens should control; citing other cases). It is probably worth noting that *Esfeld* used a modified version of *Byrd*, because the *Esfeld* court appeared not to have factored in the potential significance of the state's interest in application of state law on forum non conveniens.

17. This suggestion is not meant to indicate that thorough research alone will yield an answer upon which diligent attor-

For assessing prospects of outcome determination, the inquiry is more nearly a pragmatic evaluation of the way in which application of federal procedure might affect the course of the litigation.

The weighing analysis developed in *Byrd* is still used today for one category of procedural questions arising under *Erie*. When the federal procedure potentially applicable to a case is procedure developed by judicial practice (*i.e.*, case law procedure), courts typically weigh the three factors identifies in *Byrd*: (1) relative strength of state interests behind state procedure; (2) relative strength of federal interests behind federal procedure; and (3) likelihood that application of federal procedure will significantly alter the outcome of the case.[18]

B. Rules Enabling Act:[19] Federal Rules of Procedure.

Case law is not the only source of federal procedure. In fact, only a few years before the Supreme Court decided *Erie*, Congress enacted legislation creating a process by which federal rules of procedure could be enacted without necessarily involving direct participation in each rule by Congress. The Rules Enabling Act was the source of, *inter alia*, the current Federal Rules of Civil Procedure, which are so important to the processing of civil cases in federal courts.

Interplay between the *Erie* doctrine and federal rules developed under the authority of the Rules Enabling Act was inevitable. For example, in a case where state procedure required a plaintiff to post a bond before proceeding with a suit, but Federal Rule of Civil Procedure 23.1 required no bond, the Court had to decide whether the state bond requirement prevailed over a federal rule that otherwise appeared to be relevant to the case.[20] In another case, state procedure provided that an applicable statute of limitations continued to run after a case was filed with the court until the defendant was served. By contrast, Federal Rule of Civil Procedure 3 provides that a federal case is "commenced" by

---

neys may confidently rely. Indeed, continuing developments in the Supreme Court indicate that *Byrd* does not identify a single true path with the clarity and precision of a laser. In *Gasperini v. Center for Humanities, Inc.*, 518 U.S. 415, 116 S.Ct. 2211, 135 L.Ed.2d 659 (1996), a jury awarded a large verdict to the plaintiff. Under New York law, a state appellate court has authority to order a new trial when the jury's verdict "deviates materially" from reasonable compensation. Federal procedure differs from that standard in two important respects. First, a federal district judge normally has less discretion to modify a jury's verdict than the New York law allows. Second, New York vests this power in an appellate court. By contrast, the Seventh Amendment to the United States constitution normally imposes much stricter limits on the authority of federal appellate courts to modify jury verdicts.

The Supreme Court grappled with this cluster of problems in the following manner. First, in diversity cases federal district courts—not circuit courts—will apply the New York statute's standard for modifying jury verdicts. This practice, of course, is not directly consistent with the New York mandate to provide such review in appellate courts. Second, in a bow to the Seventh Amendment, federal circuit courts will review the district court's application of the New York law under the existing federal standard for circuit courts, *i.e.*, an abuse of discretion.

18. It should be noted that the *Byrd* analysis does not assess directly the possible impact that application of state procedure will have on the outcome of a case.

19. 28 U.S.C.A. § 2072.

20. *Cohen v. Beneficial Industrial Loan Corp.*, 337 U.S. 541, 69 S.Ct. 1221, 93 L.Ed. 1528 (1949).

filing a complaint with the federal district court. A possible construction of Rule 3 is that once the case is filed, the statute of limitations is tolled. The case before the Supreme Court was one in which the plaintiff had filed the complaint in federal district court before the statute of limitations had expired, but service of process on the defendant did not occur until after the statute of limitations would have expired.[21] Under state procedure, therefore, the plaintiff's suit was untimely. Under the apparent literal language of Federal Rule 3, the plaintiff's filing was timely, and the case could proceed.

In both cases, the Supreme Court concluded that the applicable procedure was state procedure, but the reasoning was insufficiently persuasive to lay to rest concerns about the impact of the *Erie* doctrine on cases involving rules of procedure developed under the authority of the Rules Enabling Act. Some, but by no means all, of this uneasiness was laid to rest when the Supreme Court decided *Hanna v. Plumer*.[22]

In *Hanna* a plaintiff served the defendant by leaving a copy of the summons and complaint with the defendant's spouse at the defendant's residence. This was lawful service under Federal Rule of Civil Procedure 4. However, under state procedure, service was not satisfactory unless the defendant was served personally. The Supreme Court re-examined its growing body of precedent under the *Erie* doctrine and concluded that service was satisfactory because Rule 4 applied, not the state procedure.[23]

The reasoning of the Court's majority was that the relation of *Erie* to the Rules Enabling Act required a two-step analysis of the possible application of a federal rule of civil procedure to a state cause of action. The first step was to determine if the rule at issue could lawfully be made. Because the Rules Enabling Act only permitted creation of federal rules which were purely procedural, and which did not alter substantive rights, the first inquiry was to determine if the rule in question in a particular case was procedural. In the case at bar Rule 4, governing the means of making service of process on a defendant, affected no substantive rights and clearly passed this "pure procedure" requirement.

The second step was to determine if the federal rule (such as Rule 4) could be harmonized with state procedure, or whether the federal and state procedures were locked in conflict. The Court explained that if the two could be harmonized because, *e.g.*, they did not address the same concerns, no choice between them was necessary. However, if they actually collided, then a federal rule of civil procedure lawfully created under the Rules Enabling Act should be applied over the state procedure.[24]

The literal rule of *Hanna* appears to be that if a federal rule of civil procedure is a lawful exercise of rule-making power under the Rules Enabling Act, and the rule conflicts directly with state procedure, the

21. *Ragan v. Merchants Transfer & Warehouse Co.,* 337 U.S. 530, 69 S.Ct. 1233, 93 L.Ed. 1520 (1949).

22. 380 U.S. 460, 85 S.Ct. 1136, 14 L.Ed.2d 8 (1965).

23. *Id.* at 462, 85 S.Ct. at 1140.

24. *Id.* at 468, 85 S.Ct. at 1143.

federal rule applies. That approach appears to leave little room for considerations of outcome determination, which had been so important to the Supreme Court in both *Erie* and *Guaranty Trust*. However, an important concurring opinion in *Hanna* helps explain the interplay between the federal rules of civil procedure and concerns about outcome determination under *Erie*.

While agreeing with the result in *Hanna* (application of Rule 4 over conflicting state procedure), Justice Harlan added that a determination of the applicability of a federal rule to a case arising under state law should also take into account whether the possible application of federal procedure would have influenced an attorney's decision to choose the federal court in order to avoid the application of state procedure.[25] Where such a decision might reasonably have been made, and where the application of federal procedure would impinge on a significant state policy, Justice Harlan believed the state procedure should apply—even if, under the majority's test, state procedure conflicted with a valid federal rule of procedure.[26] When applied, Justice Harlan's approach refined the "outcome-determinative" test for procedure that had been so important at least since *Guaranty Trust*. In essence, Justice Harlan avoided the possibility that a difference in procedure could always determine the outcome by concentrating his analysis on the estimated importance of procedure at the time an attorney was choosing the court in which the case would be heard. Put another way, if a reasonable attorney, upon noticing that federal procedure offered a significant advantage not available under state procedure, would choose the federal court in order to obtain the benefit of federal procedure, the federal procedure would be sufficiently outcome determinative to justify displacing it with state procedure. While Justice Harlan made these observations in the context of federal rules of procedure, they appear to have applicability also to the circumstances governed by *Byrd, i.e.,* situations in which federal procedure arising purely from case law may conflict with state procedure.

Understanding *Hanna* can be difficult enough. However, the difficulty is sometimes compounded when *Hanna* is applied in particular cases. In *Walker v. Armco Steel Corp.,*[27] for example, the Supreme Court returned to a question it had originally addressed a generation earlier. *Walker* involved a plaintiff who had sued on a state claim in federal district court. The claim was filed before the statute of limitations expired, but the complaint was not served on the defendant until after the statute would have expired. Applicable state law provided that the statute continued to run until service on the defendant. The plaintiff argued that Federal Rule of Civil Procedure 3, describing an action as "commenced" when filed with the district court, meant that the statute of limitations was tolled by the plaintiff's timely filing with the clerk's office.

25. *Id.* at 474, 85 S.Ct. at 1146 (Harlan, J., concurring).

26. *Id.*

27. 446 U.S. 740, 100 S.Ct. 1978, 64 L.Ed.2d 659 (1980).

Walker was a reprise of *Ragan v. Merchants Transfer & Warehouse Co.*,[28] in which the Court had held that state procedure controlled, and Rule 3 did not apply.[29] Many observers believed that the intervening decision in *Hanna* had nullified the result in *Ragan*. A unanimous Supreme Court, applying *Hanna*, concluded otherwise. The Court recognized that under the *Hanna* analysis, Rule 3 was a lawful rule of procedure, enacted within the authority of the Rules Enabling Act. However, the Court also concluded that Rule 3, at least in diversity cases, was not intended to toll state statutes of limitations. The Court was a bit vague as to the precise purpose of Rule 3 when state claims were before a federal district court.[30] However, its conclusion was that state procedure for tolling a statute of limitation (service on the defendant) controlled because there was "no direct conflict" between the state law and Rule 3.[31] Thus, the requirement of *Hanna* that, before a lawful federal rule can apply to a diversity case it must first be in direct conflict with state procedure was not met, and state law applied.

Walker suggests that there can be grave uncertainty as to the circumstances when a federal rule conflicts to a substantial degree with state procedure. To that extent, *Walker* casts doubt on the predictability of the *Hanna* test as it applies to cases concerning the applicability of federal rules of procedure enacted under the Rules Enabling Act. The Supreme Court appears to be sensitive to this problem, and in the aftermath of *Walker* the Court emphasized that the analysis enunciated in *Hanna* continues to govern in most circumstances.[32] Nevertheless, *Walker* serves as a caution to attorneys that, before assuming a federal rule of procedure displaces state procedure, one must first establish not only that the federal rule is authorized by the Rules Enabling Act, but also that the federal rule truly clashes with otherwise applicable state procedure.

C.   Procedure Enacted Directly by Congress.

Although Congress enacted the Rules Enabling Act to authorize a process for creating rules of procedure in which Congress itself did not have to be actively involved, Congress has also created other important procedural provisions independent of the Rules Enabling Act. These provisions are codified at Title 28 of the United States Code.

When one of these statutory procedures is arguably applicable in a diversity case, considerations related to *Erie* arise again. In this circumstance, as with case law controlled by *Byrd* or rules of procedure controlled by *Hanna*, the federal district court must decide whether federal statutory procedure may be applied, or whether it must defer to

28.   337 U.S. 530, 69 S.Ct. 1233, 93 L.Ed. 1520 (1949).

29.   *See supra,* notes 24–25 and accompanying text.

30.   *Walker,* 446 U.S. at 750, 100 S.Ct. at 1985 ("Rule 3 governs the date from which various timing requirements of the Federal Rules begin to run, but does not affect state statutes of limitations.").

31.   *Id.* at 751, 100 S.Ct. at 1986.

32.   *See, e.g., Burlington Northern Railway Co. v. Woods,* 480 U.S. 1, 107 S.Ct. 967, 94 L.Ed.2d 1 (1987) (applying *Hanna* test, finding Federal Rule of Appellate Procedure 38 applicable in place of state procedure).

state procedure. The Supreme Court addressed this question in *Stewart Organization, Inc. v. Ricoh Corp.*[33] *Stewart* addressed whether a motion to transfer a case pursuant to a contractual forum selection clause was enforceable under 28 U.S.C.A. § 1404(a) or unenforceable because state procedure disfavored such clauses.

The Supreme Court held that the standards for transfer of venue under the federal statute controlled. In a straightforward opinion the Court concluded that federal courts are bound to apply procedure enacted by Congress, provided only that Congress was within its Constitutional authority and that the statute was relevant to the issue before the district court.[34] *Stewart* may have left some modest room for questioning when an attorney can be certain that the federal statutory procedure controls. However, it appears that this question can be answered with somewhat more confidence than the question posed by *Hanna* when a federal rule is at issue, *i.e.*, does the rule conflict sufficiently with state procedure?

V. IDENTIFYING STATE LAW

In cases where a federal district court recognizes that it is obligated to apply state law on an issue, a question remains as to how to identify the state law. Of course, if the relevant state supreme court has addressed the matter clearly, its word on state law is normally final. The question becomes more difficult, however, if state law is not entirely clear.[35]

Federal judges hear many cases where state law is implicated. However, they still lack the experience with state law that state judges will typically have. Moreover, when a state judge decides a difficult question of state law, a party has the ability to seek review of that decision by state appellate judges, who presumably are also familiar with state law. By contrast, if a federal district judge applies state law in a potentially erroneous way, the challenge to that decision is heard by other federal judges. Those federal appellate judges, in turn, may not even be from the state whose law is at issue.

To address the problems raised by this situation, three distinct approaches have evolved. The first is simply to recognize that difficult questions of state law are best handled in the state court system, and to abstain from deciding the case. This approach has the advantage of ensuring that a decision will not be made by a federal court. However, it imposes on the parties all the delay and additional expense involved in re-starting the case in state court. For this reason and others, federal courts have not employed the abstention option frequently.[36]

---

33. 487 U.S. 22, 108 S.Ct. 2239, 101 L.Ed.2d 22 (1988).

34. *Id.* at 26, 108 S.Ct. at 2242.

35. *West v. AT & T Co.*, 311 U.S. 223, 236, 61 S.Ct. 179, 183, 85 L.Ed. 139 (1940) ("The highest court of the state is the final arbiter of what is state law." Citing *Erie.* Possible exception if state supreme court

has made clear its previous view has changed.).

36. *Meredith v. City of Winter Haven*, 320 U.S. 228, 234, 64 S.Ct. 7, 11, 88 L.Ed. 9 (1943) (abstention should be employed only in "exceptional circumstances"). *See also Minot v. Eckardt–Minot*, 13 F.3d 590, 593 (2d Cir.1994) (in some limited circumstances, abstention may be appropriate ba-

The second option is to certify the difficult question to the high court of the state whose law is at issue. In states whose legislatures have enacted certification legislation, federal courts may apply to state supreme courts for resolution of difficult questions of state law. Certification carries with it the prospect of a definitive answer to a hard question, but its promise has always been limited by some real-world obstacles. In the first place, certification is expensive for litigants, involving a possible need to brief and argue an issue before yet another court. Second, certification is almost certain to produce delay in obtaining a final judgment in the federal case, for the federal litigation must be held in abeyance pending the decision in the state supreme court.[37] Finally, a certification statute does not necessarily require a state supreme court to answer a question from a federal court. In circumstances where state high courts already feel themselves overburdened by their own dockets, it is sometimes possible that in the end no answer will be forthcoming. A more frustrating conclusion to a search for a solution to a hard question can hardly be imagined. Thus, while certification is used more frequently than abstention, it has been much less than a universal solution to the problem of getting a good answer to a hard question of state law.

The third option available to federal courts is the course followed most frequently. Federal courts simply address the difficult question directly, and try to resolve it themselves with the tools available.[38] To undertake this effort, federal courts look to a variety of sources, including: analogous decisions by the state high court; reported decisions from lower state courts;[39] trends in neighboring states; and even "scholarly treatises, the Restatement of Law, and germane law review articles."[40] This approach has the greatest potential for producing analyses of state law that are later established to be incorrect.[41] At the same time, it provides the best answer a federal court can achieve without forcing the

---

sis to remand case previously removed to federal court, but "courts should be wary of using judicially-crafted abstention doctrines to deny out-of-state litigants a federal forum that they prefer"). *Cf., Hawthorne Savings, F.S.B. v. Reliance Insurance Co.,* 421 F.3d 835 (9th Cir.2005) ("The reasons [for abstention] must be all the more compelling where it is the defendant—the party that removed the case—urging abstention.").

37. *See, e.g., West American Ins. Co. v. Bank of Isle of Wight,* 673 F.Supp. 760, 764 (E.D.Va.1987) (certification imposes on time and resources of both state supreme court and parties).

38. *But cf., David v. Tanksley,* 218 F.3d 928, 930 (8th Cir.2000) ("[O]ur duty is to 'ascertain and apply' Arkansas law, 'not to formulate the legal mind of the state.' ").

39. *See, e.g., Matheny v. Glen Falls Insurance Co.,* 152 F.3d 348, 354 (5th Cir. 1998) ("In making this prediction, the deci-

sions of the intermediate state courts provide guidance, but are not controlling."); *State Farm Mutual Automobile Insurance Co. v. Pate,* 275 F.3d 666, 669 (7th Cir. 2001) ("When the state Supreme Court has not decided the issue, the rulings of the state intermediate appellate courts must be accorded great weight, unless there are persuasive indications that the state's highest court would decide the case differently.").

40. *McKenna v. Ortho Pharmaceutical Corp.,* 622 F.2d 657, 662 (3d Cir.1980).

41. *See, e.g., Rotella v. Pederson,* 144 F.3d 892 (5th Cir.1998) (referring to this process as requiring the court to make an "*Erie* guess"). *See also Calbillo v. Cavender Oldsmobile, Inc.,* 288 F.3d 721, 729 (5th Cir.2002) (when making *Erie* guess, court may not decide as it thinks best; instead, court must do what it believes state supreme court would do).

parties into the delay and expense that may attend abstention or certification.

VI. THE JOB IS NOT DONE

As difficult as it may be to follow the evolution of the *Erie* doctrine on these pages, the reader should understand that *Erie* and some related issues have still other ramifications. Many of these questions are outside the scope of the current discussion, but their importance in cases where they arise cannot be overstated. Consider, for example, the following two issues.

A. Using the Law the State Court Would Use.

The heart of *Erie* is a rule directing federal district courts to apply the substantive law that a state court would use. In *Erie* itself, application of that rule meant that a federal district court sitting in New York would apply the same substantive law that a New York state trial court would use.

That application may seem straightforward enough, but it contains a subtle distinction. *Erie* does not direct a federal district court sitting in New York to use New York substantive law in every single case controlled by *Erie*. Instead, it directs the federal district court to defer to the state courts in two different ways: first, to use the same substantive law that the state court would use; and second, to use the same system for determining which state's substantive law the state court would actually apply. The second point is complicated, but can be seen more clearly using *Erie* itself as an example.

The injury to Tompkins that gave rise to the *Erie* case occurred in Pennsylvania. The lawsuit was heard in a federal district court in New York. If the case had been heard in a state court in New York, the state court would have had to decide whether to use New York substantive law (the law of the state where the case was heard), Pennsylvania substantive law (the law of the state where the incident took place), or the substantive law of some other state. On the facts of *Erie*, it was clear at the time the case was heard that a New York state court would have applied the substantive law of Pennsylvania on the ground that the accident giving rise to the suit occurred in Pennsylvania.[42] Because a New York court would have used Pennsylvania law, the duty of the federal district court in New York under the *Erie* doctrine—to apply the same law that a state court would use—was also to use Pennsylvania law.

An entire body of law (called either "conflict of laws" or "choice of law") is devoted to determining when a state trial court should use its own law or the law of another state. While the study of conflict of laws is

---

42. This point was so thoroughly settled at the time of *Erie* that the discussion of applicable law centered solely on whether federal general common law or Pennsylvania law controlled the case. There was, in short, no suggestion that a federal district court in New York would apply New York substantive law to the facts of *Erie*. That same result might not be quite as clear today, but it was eminently clear when *Erie* was decided.

not immediately within the scope of *Erie*, it is probably apparent how important conflict of laws can be for cases to which the *Erie* doctrine applies.

B. A Residue of Federal Common Law.

Although *Erie* abolished federal general common law, another form of federal common law continues to exist on the margin of *Erie*. The Supreme Court has held that such common law may apply to cases nominally involving state law, but in which the United States has such a strong interest in a uniform body of law applied across the country that *Erie* must defer to other considerations. It should be emphasized that the federal common law at issue is not the kind of federal general common law that the older rule of *Swift v. Tyson* imposed on most state causes of action in federal courts. At the same time, this surviving body of federal common law can be substantive law, notwithstanding *Erie*. For example, in *Clearfield Trust Co. v. United States*,[43] the Supreme Court concluded that federal law controlled whether the federal government was liable to an innocent party that had cashed a stolen federal payroll check. The need for uniform treatment of federal checks throughout the country was held to require the application of federal common law on this substantive issue.[44]

The number of circumstances in which federal common law may, notwithstanding *Erie*, displace state substantive law is uncertain but probably quite limited.[45] In any event, the question arises only infrequently, and is therefore not central to an understanding of the problems raised more frequently by *Erie*. However, in the occasional case where precedent like *Clearfield Trust* may displace *Erie*, an awareness of the continuing vitality of this pocket of surviving federal common law can be crucial.

VII. SUMMARY

The following summary addresses the central points of *Erie*. If a reader appreciates the reasoning underlying these summary points, the reader will probably have a working understanding of this challenging doctrine.

A. *Erie* resolved that federal courts hearing most state causes of action will apply state substantive law.

---

43. 318 U.S. 363, 63 S.Ct. 573, 87 L.Ed. 838 (1943).

44. *Id.* at 365, 63 S.Ct. at 575.

45. *See, e.g., Empire Healthchoice Assurance, Inc. v. McVeigh,* ___ U.S. ___, 126 S.Ct. 2121, 2131–32, 165 L.Ed.2d 131 (2006) (acknowledging *Clearfield* as "a pathmarking precedent on the authority of federal courts to fashion uniform federal common law on issues of national concern," but noting that such common law is still unusual); *Boyle v. United Technologies Corp.,* 487 U.S. 500, 507, 108 S.Ct. 2510, 2515, 101 L.Ed.2d 442 (1988) (noting that presence of "an area of uniquely federal interest ... establishes a necessary, not a sufficient, condition for the displacement of state law"); *Bank of America Nat'l Trust & Savings Ass'n v. Parnell,* 352 U.S. 29, 77 S.Ct. 119, 1 L.Ed.2d 93 (1956) (applying state law to determine who had burden of proof on issue of defendants' good faith; refusing to extend rule of *Clearfield Trust*). *See also United States v. City of Las Cruces,* 289 F.3d 1170, 1186 (10th Cir.2002) ("The reluctance to create common law is a core feature of federal court jurisprudence.").

B. *Erie's* impact on the possible application of federal procedure in diversity cases is more complicated. It is clear that *Guaranty Trust* was an important starting point for this matter, but over time more sophisticated approaches have developed. In particular, determining whether federal or state procedure applies depends heavily on the source from which federal procedure emanates.[46]

1. If the source of federal procedure is federal case law, *Byrd v. Blue Ridge Rural Electric Co-op., Inc.* provides the analytical framework. *Byrd* requires identification and weighing of the purpose behind the state's procedure, the purpose behind federal procedure, and the prospect that application of federal procedure might encourage litigants to shop for the federal forum in order to obtain a more favorable outcome.

2. If the source of federal procedure is one of the Federal Rules of Civil Procedure, or another rule promulgated under the Rules Enabling Act (or a case construing such a rule), *Hanna v. Plumer* provides the framework. First, it will be important to determine if the rule at issue is a lawful rule of procedure within the scope of the Rules Enabling Act. Second, if the rule is legitimately procedural, it will be necessary to determine if the rule conflicts with otherwise applicable state procedure, or if it is possible to harmonize the rule with state procedure. If federal and state procedure conflict, federal law will apply. However, there remains the question as to whether the federal law actually conflicts with state procedure. Additionally, there is uncertainty as to whether federal procedure will apply if a litigant chose the federal court in order to obtain a more favorable outcome in the case through application of the federal rule.

3. If the source of federal procedure is Title 28 of the United States Code, *Stewart Organization, Inc. v. Ricoh Corp.* directs the application of federal procedure if: (1) the federal statute is on point, and; (2) is a Constitutional exercise of power by Congress.

C. If the federal district court decides that it should apply state law (whether substantive or procedural), but the state law to be applied is uncertain, the court may have three options to consider: (1) abstain from deciding the issue; (2) certify the question to the state supreme court, if a certification statute is available; or (3) attempt, from available sources, to predict how the state supreme court would have decided the matter.

B. RES JUDICATA AND COLLATERAL ESTOPPEL

§ 2.19 Introduction

Generally

Res judicata and collateral estoppel are related doctrines that address the consequences of an entry of judgment in one lawsuit on subsequent cases that are related to the original case. Subject to some

---

46. The source of state procedure, it   should be noted, is not relevant.

important exceptions, these judicial doctrines establish the rule that once a case has reached a final judgment, many claims or issues related to that case should be treated as finally decided, once and for all. Thus, if res judicata applies to a case, a plaintiff who lost a lawsuit will often be precluded from raising claims which were raised (or perhaps, which could have been raised) in that lawsuit. In a roughly analogous way, collateral estoppel provides that once an issue has been decided in litigation, that issue may be treated as decided—without further proof—in any subsequent litigation in which the issue is relevant.

The policies behind these related doctrines are judicial economy and finality in litigation. At the same time, when these doctrines are potentially applicable to a case they can create the possibility of substantial risk or opportunity for opposing parties. For example, under the doctrine of res judicata, a plaintiff who has several related claims against the same defendant may often find it necessary to raise both claims in the same litigation, or risk foregoing any claims that are not asserted.

Case Law Doctrine

Res judicata and collateral estoppel owe their existence almost entirely to development in the courts. Legislative influence on these doctrines is limited, and constitutional considerations arise only in circumstances where res judicata or collateral estoppel might have the potential to limit the due process right of an interested party to a fair hearing. Thus, if res judicata was applied to preclude a claim by a party that had not yet had a fair opportunity to be heard in court, it is possible that res judicata would run afoul of due process and the claim would have to be heard.[1] The due process limitation on these doctrines is therefore important. However, as is discussed below, due process can sometimes be satisfied even in circumstances where an interested person was not, literally, a party to a case.

Because res judicata and collateral estoppel are not constitutional in nature, the influence of the Supreme Court on these doctrines is somewhat limited. The Court can and does establish the standards for these two doctrines when they are used in federal courts, but the states are free to accept or reject federal views of these doctrines. Supreme Court cases may therefore be an important source of influence on the application of res judicata or collateral estoppel in state courts, but such decisions are not necessarily the final word.[2]

1. *See, e.g., South Central Bell Tel. Co. v. Alabama,* 526 U.S. 160, 168, 119 S.Ct. 1180, 1185, 143 L.Ed.2d 258 (1999) (due process prevents application of res judicata to bar litigation by parties who did not participate in prior action, either personally, through concept of privity, or through membership in a class).

2. Because state courts often develop their own case law in this area, federal courts hearing diversity claims must sometimes determine whether to apply state pro-

cedure or federal procedure. In other words, federal courts must make an analysis under the rule of *Erie v. Tompkins,* discussed in Part II. As a general rule, federal courts have concluded that where state and federal views of res judicata differ, state views should be applied in a diversity case. See, e.g., *Xantech Corp. v. Ramco Indus., Inc.,* 159 F.3d 1089, 1092 (7th Cir.1998) ("[W]e look to the law of Indiana in this diversity action to determine whether the claims that

Basic Terminology

Two basic areas of terminology can produce some confusion in application of these doctrines, but the confusion can be clarified without difficulty. The first source of confusion arises from the fact that some older cases apply the term "res judicata" indiscriminately to circumstances involving either res judicata or collateral estoppel. The doctrines certainly share some common attributes, but they are also different enough to deserve the distinctive names that have come to be applied to them. Thus, when using an older case that describes what appears to be an application of collateral estoppel as "res judicata," a reader should simply be cautioned to remember the now generally discarded habit of using "res judicata" as an umbrella term covering both doctrines.[3]

The second source of confusion may arise from more recent efforts to replace the terms "res judicata" and "collateral estoppel" with labels that are more descriptive of what the underlying doctrines try to do. Thus, "res judicata" is sometimes described as "claim preclusion," and "collateral estoppel" may be called "issue preclusion."[4] Reception of these newer terms has been mixed over the past generation or so of judicial decisions,[5] but enough cases use the terms so that a reader must be familiar with them. However, for purposes of reducing confusion in this section, the terms "res judicata" and "collateral estoppel" will be used exclusively.

These two areas are not the only sources of difficulty with terms that attach to the two doctrines. Case law developments in collateral estoppel, especially, have produced a few terms that will be discussed in greater detail below.

§ 2.20   Res Judicata—Elements

Elements

Before a court will apply res judicata to a claim, ordinarily three elements must be satisfied. First, there must have been prior litigation in which "identical" claims were raised, or at least could have been raised. Second, the parties in the second litigation must be "identical" in some manner to the parties in the original litigation. Third, there must have been a final judgment on the merits in the original litigation.[1]

[the plaintiff] makes in this suit are barred on res judicata grounds.").

   3. *Migra v. Warren City Sch. Dist. Bd. of Educ.,* 465 U.S. 75, 77 n. 1, 104 S.Ct. 892, 894 n. 1, 79 L.Ed.2d 56 (1984) (noting older practice of using res judicata as term describing both res judicata and collateral estoppel; also noting Court's more recent tendency to apply label of res judicata only to matters of claim preclusion).

   4. *See, e.g., id.* (using *"claim preclusion"* in case addressing principals of res judicata, as means of distinguishing res judicata from collateral estoppel). *See also*

Baker v. General Motors Corp., 522 U.S. 222, 223 n. 5, 118 S.Ct. 657, 664, 139 L.Ed.2d 580 (1998).

   5. *Kircher v. Putnam Funds Trust,* ___ U.S. ___, ___ n. 14, 126 S.Ct. 2145, 2157 n. 14, 165 L.Ed.2d 92 (2006) ("Modern usage calls for the descriptive term, 'issue preclusion,' in place of 'collateral estoppel.' But we are backsliders out of pity for the tired reader; 'preclusion' by statutory fiat is enough preclusion for one opinion.").

   1. *Cromwell v. County of Sac,* 94 U.S. (4 Otto) 351, 352–53, 24 L.Ed. 195 (1876).

As may already be obvious, these three seemingly straightforward requirements contain within them some important ambiguities, which will be examined in turn. Immediately before doing so, however, it would be useful to keep in mind an underlying feature of res judicata that is also a useful means of spotting potential res judicata issues. Res judicata may potentially apply to a case only in circumstances where that case bears some relationship to a prior lawsuit that has already been decided. In the absence of previous litigation, a court in a pending case would have no prior decision to which to refer. Thus, while the existence of prior litigation does not necessarily establish the existence of res judicata questions, the absence of prior litigation means there is no possibility of res judicata problems in a pending case.

"Identical Claims"; Same Transaction or Occurrence

If the claims at issue in pending litigation bear no relationship to claims that were raised in prior litigation, the instant claims will not be barred by res judicata. For example, if a plaintiff now suing a defendant on a contract claim that arose six weeks ago had previously brought a lawsuit against the same defendant for an utterly unrelated claim that occurred a decade before the breach claim arose, the claims in the two cases would not be identical and res judicata would not be applied. However, if a plaintiff had two claims against a defendant arising out of the same event—and had previously sued on one claim, but not the other—there is a substantial possibility that the requirement for identical claims would be satisfied. Thus, if the defendant was a state police officer who allegedly beat and injured a citizen for motives arising from religious bias, the plaintiff might have at least two civil causes of actions against the police officer, such as: (1) a federal civil rights claim under 42 U.S.C.A. § 1983 (deprivation of a federal civil right by a person acting under color of state law); and (2) a state law claim of battery. If we assume that the plaintiff sued on the state battery claim in previous litigation, and then tried to sue on the federal claim in the pending litigation, it is likely that the requirement of "identical" claims between the two lawsuits would be satisfied.

It is important to note that the claims need not be literally identical to satisfy this requirement for res judicata. In the example above, the federal claim shares much in common with the state claim that was previously litigated, but to prevail on the merits of the federal claim the plaintiff would have to demonstrate additional evidence not necessary to win on the state lawsuit. For the state battery claim, the plaintiff would have to demonstrate only the elements of the common law tort of battery. However, for the federal cause of action, the plaintiff would also have to demonstrate that the defendant was acting under color of state law (*i.e.*, a police officer) and that there was some intent to violate the plaintiff's federal civil rights (religious discrimination). These elements would be additional to the requirements for common law battery, and in a particular case they might require proof that the plaintiff does not possess. In that sense, the two claims in the example are not literally "identical," because they rest on distinct theories of recovery.

Courts once struggled to develop rules to determine when two claims share enough in common to satisfy the requirement that the claims are "identical" for purposes of res judicata. However, many years ago most courts abandoned the notion that claims based on the same facts, but different theories of recovery, were insufficiently "identical" to satisfy this requirement. Today, most courts have accepted the proposition that two claims are "identical" if their "underlying facts are 'related in time, space, origin, or motivation, whether they form a convenient trial unit, and whether their treatment as a unit conforms to the parties' expectations or business understanding or usage.' "[2] Put another way, the claim in the second suit is sufficiently "identical" to the claim that was or could have been litigated in the first suit if both claims share a common "nucleus of operative fact."[3] This language shares much in common with judicial commentary about the requirement in supplemental jurisdiction, 28 U.S.C.A. § 1367(a), for the "same case or controversy."[4] It is also related to the idea in Federal Rule of Civil Procedure 13(a) that counterclaims may be compulsory if they arise out of the same "transaction or occurrence" as the opposing party's claim.[5]

Applying this transactional test to the claims in the case involving the alleged beating inflicted by the police officer, most courts would almost certainly conclude that the state battery claims and the federal civil rights claim share enough common features to satisfy this requirement of "identical" claims for res judicata. The primary reason courts would likely reach that conclusion is that the two claims, though based on somewhat differing legal theories, arose from the same occurrence, at the same time, and would require substantially overlapping items of proof.[6]

At the same time, the transactional test for "identical" claims should not be pushed too far. If the transactions or events at issue took place at significantly different points in time, claims arising from those

---

2. *Interoceanica Corp. v. Sound Pilots, Inc.,* 107 F.3d 86, 90 (2d Cir.1997) (quoting Restatement (Second) of Judgments § 24(b) (1982)).

3. *Apparel Art Int'l, Inc. v. Amertex Enters., Ltd.,* 48 F.3d 576, 583 (1st Cir.1995) ("Under this approach, a cause of action is defined as a set of facts which can be characterized as a single transaction or a series of related transactions."). *See also, e.g., Lane v. Peterson,* 899 F.2d 737, 742 (8th Cir.1990) (standard for measuring same cause of action is whether both claims derive from "same nucleus of operative facts").

4. *See, e.g., United Mine Workers of America v. Gibbs,* 383 U.S. 715, 86 S.Ct. 1130, 16 L.Ed.2d 218 (1966) (developing the concept of "common nucleus of operative fact" in the context of judicial predecessor of supplemental jurisdiction).

5. Fed.R.Civ.P. 13(a). *See also, e.g.,* Fed. R.Civ.P. 15(c)(2) (permitting relation back of amended pleading if, inter alia, "the claim or defense asserted in the amended pleading arose out of the conduct, transaction, or occurrence set forth or attempted to be set forth in the original pleading"); Fed. R.Civ.P. 20(a) (permitting joinder of parties as plaintiffs if, inter alia, their claims arise from "the same transaction, occurrence, or series of transactions or occurrences").

6. *See, e.g., National Labor Relations Bd. v. United Technologies Corp.,* 706 F.2d 1254, 1260 (2d Cir.1983) (for res judicata, test is whether "same evidence is needed to support both claims, and [whether] the facts essential to the second were present in the first").

different times will generally not be treated as "identical."[7] Thus, in a circumstance where ship pilots had sued to recover fees owed by a shipping company under a state statute, the judgment in that case would not preclude subsequent claims for fees arising from voyages that had not yet taken place at the time of the first litigation.[8]

"Identical" Parties; Privity

The second requirement for res judicata is that the parties in the second action must be identical to the parties in the first action, or in privity with parties in the first action. Thus, if two pedestrians walking along a sidewalk were injured by a motorist whose automobile went out of control and struck them, the outcome of a suit involving only the first pedestrian as a plaintiff would not be a bar to a second and independent suit by the second pedestrian. Even though the claims of both pedestrians arose from the same occurrence, the obvious difference between the parties would preclude application of res judicata.

For purposes of this second requirement for res judicata, parties who are literally the same persons or business entities are clearly "identical." The question that may arise, however, is whether persons who are different but who share a common interest may be treated as "identical." The issue raised here is a concept of privity of interest between two distinct individuals or business entities.

In general, there are several circumstances in which someone not literally a party to the first action may nevertheless be treated as in privity with a person or entity that was a party: (1) where the nonparty succeeded to the interest of a party, for example, by purchasing whatever interest the party may have had after completion of the first litigation; (2) where the nonparty, though technically not participating in the first suit, nevertheless controlled one party's litigation in that suit—where, for example, the nonparty is an insurance company for a party; (3) where the nonparty shares a property interest with the party;[9] (4) where the party and nonparty have an agent-principal relationship; or (5) where the party otherwise "adequately represented" the interest of the nonparty.[10]

These categories may superficially appear straightforward. However, it appears that privity is applied only after careful scrutiny of the

---

7. *See, e.g., Securities & Exchange Comm'n v. First Jersey Securities, Inc.,* 101 F.3d 1450, 1464 (2d Cir.1996) ("If the second litigation involved different transactions, and especially subsequent transactions, there generally is no claim preclusion;" presence of same parties or even overlapping facts need not be dispositive to prove "identical" claims).

8. *See, e.g., Interoceanica Corp. v. Sound Pilots, Inc.,* 107 F.3d 86, 91 (2d Cir.1997) ("While the subsequent voyages represent wrongs that are the 'same' in legal theory, they are not related in time, space, or origin to the wrongs litigated [earlier].").

9. *See, e.g., Hart v. Yamaha–Parts Distrib., Inc.,* 787 F.2d 1468, 1472 (11th Cir. 1986) (citing these examples). *See also, e.g., Nero v. Ferris,* 222 Va. 807, 813, 284 S.E.2d 828, 831 (1981) ("[P]rivity generally involves a party so identical in interest with another that he represents the same legal right [but making this determination requires] a careful examination into the circumstances of each case.").

10. *Howell Hydrocarbons, Inc. v. Adams,* 897 F.2d 183, 188 (5th Cir.1990).

nuances of particular cases, and perhaps not always with consistency. For example, where one entity holds a twenty percent interest in another entity's lawsuit, the two interests were deemed "completely identical" with one another and the entities were held to be in privity.[11] However, defendants sued individually may not be in privity with their employers.[12] A general rule is that while privity may in some circumstances substitute adequately for the requirement that the parties in both lawsuits be identical, there should be no assumption that a court will support an assertion of privity without a careful examination of the facts underlying the assertion.

It should be noted that in this requirement of identical parties (or privity), the doctrine of res judicata differs in an important respect from case law addressing the doctrine of collateral estoppel. As is discussed later in this analysis, courts do not invariably require that the parties be identical before applying collateral estoppel to issues in a case. However, this distinction comes with several important qualifications, which are addressed under the discussion of collateral estoppel.

Final Judgment "On the Merits"

The third and final prerequisite for application of res judicata is the requirement that the first litigation has proceeded to a final judgment on the merits of the case. When considering application of this prerequisite there are two points to keep in mind. First, not all judicial decisions are "final." Second, not all final judgments are based on the merits of the case.

It is generally well settled that when a trial judge enters judgment, so that the parties are now in a position to enforce or appeal the judgment, finality has been achieved and this element of res judicata has been satisfied.[13] By contrast, one apparently obvious example of litigation that does not constitute a final judgment arises when the parties settle their case. A settlement that does not involve action by the court does not constitute a judgment. The result may be different, however, if the parties seek to have their settlement entered by the court as a judgment or decree. Such action may convert a settlement into a final judgment, which therefore may qualify as res judicata for subsequent litigation.[14]

---

11. *Virginia Surety Co. v. Northrop Grumman Corp.,* 144 F.3d 1243, 1247 (9th Cir.1998).

12. *See, e.g., Willner v. Budig,* 848 F.2d 1032, 1034 (10th Cir.1988) ("Res judicata does not bar [plaintiff's] claims against the defendants in their individual capacities because the defendants are not in privity with the University."); *Headley v. Bacon,* 828 F.2d 1272, 1277–79 (8th Cir.1987) (distinguishing privity between principal and agent from privity between a governmental entity and officials sued in their individual capacities).

13. *Clay v. United States,* 537 U.S. 522, 526, 123 S.Ct. 1072, 1076, 155 L.Ed.2d 88 (2003) ("[A] federal judgment becomes final for appellate review and claim preclusion purposes when the district court disassociates itself from the case, leaving nothing to be done at the court of first instance save execution of the judgment.").

14. *See, e.g., Richardson v. Alabama State Bd. of Educ.,* 935 F.2d 1240, 1244 (11th Cir.1991) ("We specifically have held that res judicata applies to Title VII consent decrees."). *But cf. Keith v. Aldridge,* 900 F.2d 736, 740 (4th Cir.1990) (where parties consent to resolution of one portion of a

Res judicata also may not apply to situations in which a judge makes an important decision which is, nevertheless, less than a final judgment. For example, in a case in which plaintiffs seek certification of their lawsuit as a class action, denial of such certification may not necessarily be a final judgment, even though the reality of the situation is that denial of class status is often a punishing blow to the parties seeking certification.[15]

For res judicata to apply, a judgment must also be on the merits of a case. Litigation that goes through to a jury verdict obviously meets this requirement. However, the applicability of res judicata to litigation terminated under, for example, a subsection of Federal Rule of Civil Procedure 12(b) may depend on both the particular subsection employed as well as the facts of a particular case. In general, cases dismissed for failure to state a claim for which relief may be granted—e.g., Rule 12(b)(6)—are judgments on the merits for purposes of res judicata.[16] By contrast, cases dismissed on jurisdictional grounds, such as Rule 12(b)(1) (lack of subject matter jurisdiction) have res judicata effect only to the extent that the jurisdictional issue is foreclosed. If the claimant subsequently files a second suit alleging a different theory of recovery, or files in a different, appropriate forum, the original dismissal will normally not block the second suit because the jurisdictional dismissal was not on the merits of the case.[17]

§ 2.21   Res Judicata—Scope

When it is applicable to a case, res judicata bars re-litigation of claims which have previously been litigated—or which could have been litigated in a prior lawsuit. This scope of res judicata differs significantly from the requirement for collateral estoppel, because collateral estoppel applies only to claims which were actually litigated—not claims that could have been litigated but were not.

When applied to claims that were not actually raised, but which could have been raised, the scope of res judicata is rather broad. Thus,

case but expressly reserve right to continue litigating other claims, res judicata will not block continuation of unresolved litigation).

15. *See, e.g., In re General Motors Corp. Pick–Up Truck Fuel Tank Prods. Liability Litig.,* 134 F.3d 133, 146 (3d Cir. 1998) ("Denial of class certification is not a 'judgment' for the purposes of the Anti–Injunction Act while the underlying litigation remains pending."). *But cf. In re Varat Enters., Inc.,* 81 F.3d 1310, 1315 (4th Cir.1996) (bankruptcy court's order confirming debtor's plan of reorganization "is treated as a final judgment with res judicata effect").

16. *Federated Dep't Stores, Inc. v. Moitie,* 452 U.S. 394, 399 n. 3, 101 S.Ct. 2424, 2428 n. 3, 69 L.Ed.2d 103 (1981)(dismissal under Rule 12(b)(6) is final judgment for

purposes of res judicata). *Cf., Manufacturers Hanover Trust Co. v. United States,* 399 U.S. 392, 481, 90 S.Ct. 2054, 2104, 26 L.Ed.2d 691 (1970) (failure to appeal adverse decision makes that decision a matter of res judicata).

17. *Semtek International Inc. v. Lockheed Martin Corp.,* 531 U.S. 497, 121 S.Ct. 1021, 149 L.Ed.2d 32 (2001) (judgment "on the merits" does not always trigger application of claim preclusion in subsequent lawsuit). *See, e.g., Costner v. URS Consultants, Inc.,* 153 F.3d 667, 673 (8th Cir.1998) (distinguishing between application of res judicata for jurisdictional issue in first case and inapplicability of res judicata to different theory of recovery, even where second suit arises from same facts as first claim).

where a police officer allegedly attacked and beat a citizen in circumstances that give rise to both a state battery claim and a federal civil rights claim, a plaintiff's decision to sue only on the state claim may preclude assertion of the federal claim at a later date. Provided that the federal claim and the state claim could have been raised concurrently in the court in which the plaintiff filed and provided that the other elements of res judicata are satisfied, the claim not raised would be barred because it could have been raised.[1] This corollary of res judicata should strongly encourage attorneys to consider carefully all their potential theories of recovery in the first litigation.

By contrast, if a claim could not have been raised in the first lawsuit, assertion of that claim in later litigation is not barred by collateral estoppel. Thus, if the first court lacked jurisdiction to hear a particular kind of claim, that claim may be asserted later in a court of competent jurisdiction.[2] This circumstance may most commonly arise when a plaintiff has both a state cause of action and a federal claim which is within the exclusive subject matter jurisdiction of a federal court. If the plaintiff files first in a state court, the outcome of that case will not serve as a bar, under res judicata, to a subsequent filing on the federal claim in a federal court. However, if the plaintiff filed first in a federal district court which had jurisdiction (either diversity or supplemental jurisdiction) over the state claim, failure to file both claims at once would probably create a situation in which the unasserted claim will be barred in later litigation.

§ 2.22　Res Judicata—Counterclaims: Rule 13(a)

In the federal system, res judicata is not generally applied to potential counterclaims by defendants. Thus, when a defendant does not assert counterclaims, res judicata does not bar their assertion in subsequent litigation. However, the fact that the case law doctrine of res judicata is generally inapplicable to potential counterclaims in federal court does not mean defendants are free to raise or withhold all of their counterclaims. Instead, Federal Rule of Civil Procedure 13(a) provides that counterclaims deemed "compulsory" must be asserted.[1] Failure to do so usually results in judicial refusal to hear the claim in subsequent litigation.[2]

Some state court systems have no compulsory counterclaim rule comparable to Rule 13(a). In such states, the use of collateral estoppel to bar a claim that was not raised as a counterclaim in prior litigation may vary significantly from the federal practice.

---

1. *Cromwell v. County of Sac,* 94 U.S. (4 Otto) 351, 352–53, 24 L.Ed.195 (1876) (when applicable, res judicata bars claims actually raised and which might have been raised).

2. *Crossroads Cogeneration Corp. v. Orange & Rockland Utilities, Inc.,* 159 F.3d 129 (3d Cir.1998).

1. *See generally,* Fed.R.Civ.P. 13(a).

2. *See, e.g., New York Life Ins. Co. v. Deshotel,* 142 F.3d 873, 882 (5th Cir.1998) ("It is well settled that a failure to plead a compulsory counterclaim bars a party from bringing a later independent action on that claim.").

§ 2.23   Res Judicata—Affirmative Defense: Rule 8(c)

In the federal system, res judicata is specifically listed within Federal Rule of Civil Procedure 8(c) as an affirmative defense. That means a defendant seeking to use res judicata to preclude a plaintiff's claim must affirmatively raise the defense. Subject to some important exceptions, failure to raise the defense means that it is waived.[1]

§ 2.24   Res Judicata—Relationship to Full Faith and Credit

Full faith and credit is a constitutional provision[1] controlling the circumstances when courts of one state must enforce the judicial decisions of another state. This constitutional provision relies on res judicata in the following manner. If the res judicata doctrine of the state in which a judgment was rendered would require other courts in that same state to treat the judgment as final and preclusive, full faith and credit will generally require the courts of other states to give the same effect to the judgement as would be given in the state that rendered the judgment. Analogous rules usually require federal courts to give similar deference to the final judgments of state courts of competent jurisdiction.[2]

§ 2.25   Collateral Estoppel—Elements

As will be explained in greater detail below, the requirements for the application of collateral estoppel (or "issue preclusion")[1] vary more significantly among the jurisdictions than does the application of res judicata. Nevertheless, there are several requirements for collateral estoppel that are applied fairly consistently throughout the United States. First, there must have been a prior litigation in which the identical issue was before the court.[2] Second, the issue must have been actually litigated in the first judicial proceeding.[3] Third, the issue must

---

1. See, e.g., *McKinnon v. Kwong Wah Restaurant,* 83 F.3d 498, 505 (1st Cir.1996) ("To avoid waiver, a defendant must assert all affirmative defenses in the answer."). *But cf. Jakobsen v. Massachusetts Port Authority,* 520 F.2d 810, 813 (1st Cir.1975) (no waiver where failure to plead affirmative defense does not unfairly prejudice opposing party).

1. U.S. Const. Art. IV § 1.

2. *Durfee v. Duke,* 375 U.S. 106, 84 S.Ct. 242, 11 L.Ed.2d 186 (1963) (where Nebraska had considered, inter alia, jurisdictional issues and would treat the judgment as res judicata, federal district court in Missouri had duty under full faith and credit provisions to give the same effect to judgement as Nebraska would give it). *See also, e.g., Community Bank of Homestead v. Torcise,* 162 F.3d 1084 n. 5 (11th Cir.1998) ("Under the Full Faith and Credit Act, 28 U.S.C.

§ 1738 (1994), state court judgments are to be given the same preclusive effect in federal court that they would have in the state in which judgment was rendered.").

1. *See, e.g., Dodd v. Hood River County,* 136 F.3d 1219, 1224 (9th Cir.1998) (acknowledging that most courts still use "collateral estoppel" as appropriate term, but noting that the Ninth Circuit prefers to use "issue preclusion").

2. See, e.g., *United States v. Shanbaum,* 10 F.3d 305, 311 (5th Cir.1994) ("[T]he issue under consideration in a subsequent action must be identical to the issue litigated in a prior action.").

3. *Regions Hosp. v. Shalala,* 522 U.S. 448, 461, 118 S.Ct. 909, 918, 139 L.Ed.2d 895 (1998) ("Absent actual and adversarial litigation ... principles of issue preclusion do not hold fast.").

necessarily have been decided in a case in which a final judgment was entered.[4]

On the surface there is an apparent overlap between the requirements for collateral estoppel and the requirements, discussed earlier, for res judicata. However, while there is reason to recognize the two bodies of case law as related, the similarities can easily be overstated, with resulting unfavorable consequences. As is explained immediately below, some of the superficial similarities actually conceal differences between res judicata and collateral estoppel that can affect the outcome of a particular case.

Identical Issues

The standard for determining whether, for purposes of applying collateral estoppel, an issue in a prior lawsuit is the same as an issue in pending litigation is very different from the standard for identical claims in matters of res judicata. As discussed earlier, most courts conclude that two claims are identical for purposes of res judicata if they arise from the same transaction or occurrence. By contrast, in determining whether two issues are identical, most courts require that the issues track each other more closely than that. However, once such a substantial amount of similarity is identified, it is unimportant whether claims in one case bear any significant relationship to claims in another case.[5]

Actually, Vigorously Litigated

The requirement in collateral estoppel for actual litigation of an issue in a prior proceeding differs in at least two important respects from the possibility under res judicata that claims which were not litigated, but which could have been litigated, may be barred in later litigation. First, it is settled that collateral estoppel will not bar litigation of any issue that was not actually raised in a prior proceeding, regardless of whether the issue could have been raised. For example, in a breach of contract suit, it is possible that a defendant would make a tactical decision not to raise questions about whether the contract was unenforceable for a failure of consideration. If the plaintiff sued to enforce another obligation on the contract that only became due after the first suit was resolved, collateral estoppel would not prevent the defendant from raising the consideration simply because it could have been (but was not) raised in the first litigation. An even simpler example would arise if, in the first suit, the defendant chose to default and not enter any defense. The plaintiff would thereby win, but when the second cause of

---

4. *Cf., Arizona v. California,* 530 U.S. 392, 120 S.Ct. 2304, 147 L.Ed.2d 374 (2000) ("[S]ettlements ordinarily occasion no issue preclusion ... unless it is clear ... that the parties intend their agreement to have such an effect."). *See, e.g., Murdock v. Ute Indian Tribe of Uintah and Ouray Reservation,* 975 F.2d 683, 687 (10th Cir.1992) (to apply collateral estoppel, "the prior action [must have] finally adjudicated on the merits").

5. *United States v. Shanbaum,* 10 F.3d 305, 311 (5th Cir.1994) ("[U]nder issue preclusion, unlike claim preclusion, the subject matter of the later suit need not have any relationship to the subject matter of the prior suit.").

action arose all issues about consideration would still be available for the defendant to raise.[6]

Similarly, for collateral estoppel to apply an issue must have been litigated with some vigor. Thus, if an issue was raised in a passing way but did not engage the attention of the litigants significantly, the issue may not be estopped in later litigation because it was not litigated vigorously. To permit collateral estoppel to apply to issues raised in such a casual manner, perhaps because their importance to subsequent litigation was not yet foreseen, would produce unfair surprise for litigants.[7] It might also force needless complexity on the first litigation, as parties jockeyed to ensure that they would not be estopped collaterally in subsequent litigation.

Necessarily Decided on the Merits

This requirement has two parts, and courts sometimes treat them as distinct requirements. However, a decision to do so does not alter the analysis of this standard.

The first part of this requirement is that for collateral estoppel to apply, the issue decided in the first suit must have been decided in a way that is consistent with the judgment in the first suit. Thus, in the contract example used above, assume that the defendant was not found liable in the first suit because the plaintiff was found to have been in breach. If the jury also found that the consideration underlying the contract was good consideration, that finding would, in a literal sense, be unnecessary to the judgment that vindicated the defendant. Thus, if the same contract later gave rise to another cause of action not available at the time of the first lawsuit, the defendant would not be precluded from asserting lack of consideration as a defense. Keep in mind, of course, that permission to relitigate the issue does not mean the defendant will prevail on the consideration issue. Refusal to apply collateral estoppel does not, of itself, guarantee victory for anyone. Instead, it only provides that the issue will be fought over again.

Similarly, if a jury finds for a plaintiff without explaining which of two distinct grounds (or both) is the basis for the verdict, a defendant retains the right to challenge those same grounds if they arise as issues in subsequent litigation.[8] Conversely, if a jury expressly finds for a plaintiff on two distinct grounds, both of which were vigorously litigated

---

6. *Cromwell v. County of Sac,* 94 U.S. (4 Otto) 351, 356–57, 24 L.Ed. 195 (1876) (default judgments not eligible for collateral estoppel).

7. Id. at 356 ("Various considerations, other than the actual merits, may govern a party in bringing forward grounds of recovery or defence in one action, which may not exist in another action upon a different demand, such as the smallness of the amount or the value of the property in controversy, the difficulty of obtaining the necessary evidence, the expense of the liti-

gation, and his own situation at the time."). *But cf. Community Bank of Homestead v. Torcise,* 162 F.3d 1084 (11th Cir.1998) (observing that this requirement does not examine the quality or quantity of evidence or argument presented, only that fair opportunity to present the issue arose in a context where party understood potential adverse consequences).

8. *Cf., e.g., In re Caton,* 157 F.3d 1026, 1029 (5th Cir.1998) ("We only require that the record introduced have sufficient detail to allow the use of collateral estoppel.").

and which were decided in the plaintiff's favor, both may be treated as eligible for collateral estoppel in subsequent lawsuits.[9]

The second part of this requirement is that collateral estoppel applies only to issues resolved in cases decided on the merits.[10] Often, this will mean that cases which were dismissed on, for example, jurisdictional grounds will not develop issues in ways that qualify for collateral estoppel in subsequent cases. However, if the issues for which collateral estoppel treatment is sought are the procedural issues on which the original case was actually decided, then the requirement that the prior judgment "on the merits" is satisfied, at least for the procedural issues.[11]

§ 2.26 Collateral Estoppel—Mutuality v. Nonmutual Estoppel

As discussed previously under the law of res judicata, there is a requirement that the parties in the second suit must be identical to (or in privity with) parties in the first suit before any claims may be precluded. At one time, a similar requirement of identical parties also applied to situations involving collateral estoppel. In the context of collateral estoppel, this requirement has been referred to as the "mutuality requirement,"[1] meaning that estoppel could not apply unless it applied mutually to all parties in a lawsuit. However, that requirement has experienced substantial erosion over the past half century. Today most jurisdictions (but not all)[2] have substantially abandoned this requirement.

The replacement for the mutuality requirement—the requirement that parties in the second suit be identical to or in privity with parties in the first suit—is an assessment of fairness that, when satisfied, is ground for permitting application of nonmutual collateral estoppel.

---

9. *But cf., National Satellite Sports, Inc. v. Eliadis, Inc.,* 253 F.3d 900, 909–10 (6th Cir.2001) (if prior decision involved resolution of two issues, either of which could have supported prior decision, prior judgment is not conclusive as to either issue standing alone; collecting substantial authority on both sides of question).

10. *Arizona v. California,* 530 U.S. 392, 120 S.Ct. 2304, 147 L.Ed.2d 374 (2000) (noting that while settlement entered by court as judgment can have res judicata effect, such a settlement normally does not have collateral estoppel effect).

11. *See, e.g., Transaero, Inc. v. La Fuerza Aerea Boliviana,* 162 F.3d 724, 731 (2d Cir.1998) ("[T]he service of process and personal jurisdiction issues were necessary to support the D.C. Circuit's final judgment—indeed, these issues were the subject of that judgment.").

1. *See, e.g., Blonder–Tongue Laboratories, Inc. v. University of Illinois Foundation,* 402 U.S. 313, 91 S.Ct. 1434, 28 L.Ed.2d 788 (1971).

2. *See, e.g., State Farm Fire & Casualty Co. v. Mabry,* 255 Va. 286, 289, 497 S.E.2d 844, 846 (1998) (imposing requirement that parties in current litigation be identical with parties in prior litigation or in privity with such parties). It should also be noted that collateral estoppel may be invoked against the federal government when the United States is a party to litigation and the elements of collateral estoppel (including requirements of mutuality) are established. *United States v. Stauffer Chemical Co.,* 464 U.S. 165, 104 S.Ct. 575, 78 L.Ed.2d 388 (1984). However, it is also settled that nonmutual collateral estoppel may not be invoked against the federal government. *United States v. Mendoza,* 464 U.S. 154, 104 S.Ct. 568, 78 L.Ed.2d 379 (1984).

The terminology of this area of the law of collateral estoppel can be awkward and initially difficult to grasp. However, because courts tend to use the terms that have been created for this area, it is essential that they be understood before proceeding any further. First, to repeat, a "mutuality" requirement means merely that a court will not apply collateral estoppel unless the parties in the second action are identical to (or in privity with) the parties in the original case. Second, when a court says it follows an approach of "nonmutuality," the court merely means that it may not always impose a requirement that the parties in the second lawsuit be identical to the parties in the first suit. Thus, subject to the requirements discussed below, an application of "nonmutual" collateral estoppel means that the court found collateral estoppel appropriate even though the parties in both suits were not identical. Third, "defensive" nonmutual collateral estoppel means that the court is being asked to apply collateral estoppel in a circumstance where the defendant in the second lawsuit is trying to use nonmutual collateral estoppel defensively—as a shield—to ward off the plaintiff's attack. Fourth, "offensive" nonmutual collateral estoppel means that the court is being asked to apply collateral estoppel to prevent a defendant from raising an issue that was (allegedly) litigated in a prior lawsuit. Thus, the plaintiff is trying to use nonmutual collateral estoppel as a sword, to strike down a defense raised by a defendant. The distinction between defensive and offensive nonmutual collateral estoppel is important, because it is distinctly possible that the requirements for defensive nonmutual collateral estoppel might be less difficult to meet than the requirements for offensive nonmutual collateral estoppel.

Defensive Nonmutual Collateral Estoppel

Suppose a plaintiff sues a defendant for patent infringement. Suppose further that the essence of the defense is that the patent on which the plaintiff's claim is based is not a valid patent. If the defendant wins the case on that ground, the matter is obviously res judicata between the two parties. But if the plaintiff later files a second lawsuit, against a different defendant, asserting that the same patent was infringed, it is clear that the parties in the second suit are not identical with the parties in the first suit. Additionally, it will often be true that the defendant in the second suit will not be in privity with the defendant in the first suit. In those circumstances, if the mutuality requirement is imposed, the plaintiff will not be estopped from asserting (in the second suit) the validity of the patent that was found to be invalid in the first suit. This is inefficient for the courts, and also creates the possibility that a finding of a valid patent in the second suit will create an unacceptable situation for other parties trying to discern the validity of the patent. Thus, the majority of judicial systems facing such problems now permit a party in the position of the defendant in the second suit to assert the defense of collateral estoppel, provided only that the plaintiff had a full and fair opportunity to litigate the patent validity issue in the first lawsuit.[3]

---

3. *See, e.g., Blonder–Tongue Laboratories, Inc. v. University of Illinois Foundation,* 402 U.S. 313, 91 S.Ct. 1434, 28 L.Ed.2d 788 (1971).

Offensive Nonmutual Collateral Estoppel

A more problematic use of nonmutual collateral estoppel arises when a party seeks to use the rule as more than a defense to an action. In a well known case decided by the Supreme Court,[4] the defendants had previously been sued by the Securities and Exchange Commission for making false proxy statements. The Commission sought an injunction, and the defendants lost that lawsuit. Subsequently a class of shareholders sued the defendants on the same grounds and sought collateral estoppel for the previous court's finding that the proxy statements had been false and misleading. In contrast to defensive nonmutual collateral estoppel, where collateral estoppel is used as a shield to ward off a subsequent claim by a plaintiff who had lost a prior lawsuit, this case was an attempt to use the defendants' prior loss as a sword with which to produce a second unfavorable result for those defendants.

The Supreme Court concluded that, at least sometimes, nonmutual collateral estoppel could be used offensively as well as defensively. However, for collateral estoppel to be applied offensively, the Court directed lower federal courts to examine all the circumstances of a case to ensure that application of collateral estoppel is fair. Specifically, the Court suggested that lower courts examine: (1) whether the plaintiff seeking offensive nonmutual collateral estoppel could have participated in the previous suit; (2) whether the defendant had a fair chance to litigate the issue with knowledge of the fact that the same issue might arise in subsequent litigation; (3) whether the judgment in the litigation for which collateral estoppel is sought was inconsistent with results in any litigation which had taken place still earlier;[5] and (4) whether, in the previous suit, procedural limitations had prevented the defendant from offering some evidence or otherwise defending himself in ways now open in the later litigation.[6]

Nonmutuality and the United States

Although the United States is as vulnerable as any party to the application of collateral estoppel when the requirement of mutuality is

---

4. *Parklane Hosiery Co. v. Shore,* 439 U.S. 322, 99 S.Ct. 645, 58 L.Ed.2d 552 (1979).

5. An example of how this situation could occur arises if one posits a one-car automobile accident in which three passengers in the car are injured. If the first passenger sues the driver and alleges that the driver was intoxicated at the time of the accident, the driver might win by introducing into evidence a police report showing that the driver was free of intoxicants. That finding, of course, would not bind the two passengers who had not yet sued. If the second passenger then sued, making the same allegation about intoxication, that passenger might win by demonstrating that the police test for intoxicants in the driver's blood was administered improperly. Thus, if

the third passenger waited to sue until he/she was sufficiently healed to participate actively in a lawsuit, offensive nonmutual collateral estoppel might apply to the victory of the second passenger over the driver. Given the fact that the driver had both a prior victory and a prior defeat on the issue of intoxication, it might seem unfair to treat the issue as estopped against the driver in the third lawsuit. Thus, the Supreme Court's approach suggests that in such circumstances no party should be able to claim estoppel, and the parties in the third suit should relitigate the issue of intoxication again.

6. *Parklane Hosiery Co. v. Shore,* 439 U.S. 322, 99 S.Ct. 645, 58 L.Ed.2d 552 (1979).

satisfied, it is settled that nonmutual collateral estoppel (defensive or offensive) may not be applied against the United States.[7]

§ 2.27 Collateral Estoppel—Application to Issues of Law and Fact

Older cases expressed doubt that collateral estoppel was applicable to issues of law as well as fact. While some jurisdictions may still follow that rule, the clear trend in most circumstances is to apply collateral estoppel to issues of both law and fact.[1]

§ 2.28 Collateral Estoppel—Exceptions to Collateral Estoppel

Even in situations where all the requirements of collateral estoppel are satisfied, it is still possible that additional considerations may make application of estoppel unfair in a particular case. For example, as has already been discussed above, courts are reluctant to impose collateral estoppel in circumstances where the affected party might not reasonably have appreciated the risk of collateral estoppel in subsequent cases. Additionally, if the law or facts of a situation undergo material change between the first lawsuit and the second one, it might be unfair to impose collateral estoppel on issues decided in the first suit.[1] Finally, collateral estoppel will typically be inapplicable to situations where a district court judgment is not appealable.[2]

§ 2.29 Collateral Estoppel—Affirmative Defense: Rule 8(c)

Collateral estoppel, like res judicata, is listed as an affirmative defense under Federal Rule of Civil Procedure 8(c).[1] In theory, affirmative defenses must be raised or waived.[2] However, if a party is seeking to

---

7. *United States v. Mendoza,* 464 U.S. 154, 162, 104 S.Ct. 568, 573, 78 L.Ed.2d 379 (1984).

1. *Montana v. United States,* 440 U.S. 147, 162, 99 S.Ct. 970, 978, 59 L.Ed.2d 210 (1979) (normal rules of collateral estoppel apply to questions of law, provided that both lawsuits involve substantially related claims).

1. *Montana v. United States,* 440 U.S. 147, 159, 99 S.Ct. 970, 976, 59 L.Ed.2d 210 (1979) ("[C]hanges in facts essential to a judgment will render collateral estoppel inapplicable in a subsequent action raising the same issues."); *Commissioner v. Sunnen,* 333 U.S. 591, 601, 68 S.Ct. 715, 721, 92 L.Ed. 898 (1948) (collateral estoppel inapplicable where relevant law changed between first and second proceeding). *But cf. Hickerson v. City of New York,* 146 F.3d 99, 105 (2d Cir.1998) (failure to offer evidence

already available in first suit is not a defense to collateral estoppel in second suit).

2. *Kircher v. Putnam Funds Trust,* ___ U.S. ___, ___, 126 S.Ct. 2145, 2156–57, 165 L.Ed.2d 92 (2006) (28 U.S.C.A. § 1447(d) makes unreviewable, as a matter of law, many district court decisions to remand removed cases; in such cases there is no collateral estoppel result barring a state court from re-examining the reasoning underlying the decision of the district court–even though the state court should treat the remand decision itself as final).

1. *See also Blonder–Tongue Laboratories, Inc. v. University of Illinois Foundation,* 402 U.S. 313, 91 S.Ct. 1434, 28 L.Ed.2d 788 (1971).

2. *But cf., e.g., Petrocelli v. Daniel Woodhead Co.,* 993 F.2d 27, 29 n. 1 (3d Cir.1993) (affirmative defense not raised in original pleading is not waived if it can be

apply nonmutual collateral estoppel offensively, so as to preclude a defendant from relitigating an issue previously decided, such use of collateral estoppel is obviously not a "defense" to a claim and therefore raises no issues that would be governed by Rule 8(c).

§ 2.30   Collateral Estoppel—Relationship to Full Faith and Credit

The command that courts of one jurisdiction must give full faith and credit[1] to the judgments of another jurisdiction applies to matters of collateral estoppel. Thus, if the courts of a jurisdiction where a case was decided would treat an issue in that case as controlled by collateral estoppel, other courts have a duty to give the issue the same status of collateral estoppel as would be accorded by the court that decided the case.[2]

properly raised under Rule 15, governing amendments to pleadings).

1. U.S. Const. Art. IV § 1. See also, 28 U.S.C.A. § 1738.

2. *See, e.g., Community Bank of Homestead v. Torcise,* 162 F.3d 1084, 1087 n. 5 (11th Cir.1998) (noting obligation to use Florida standard for collateral estoppel because prior judgment was rendered in Florida).

PART III–A

AN INTRODUCTION TO THE 2007 AMENDMENTS AND THE FEDERAL RULES "STYLE" PROJECT

Effective December 1, 2007, the Federal Rules of Civil Procedure undergo their most comprehensive overhaul since they were first adopted in 1937. These revisions fall, effectively, into five categories:

- *Internal Rule Restyling:* Every Rule has been reworded (and, in some cases, reorganized) for added clarity and uniformity. This rewriting is *not* intended to have a substantive effect, and each revised Rule's Advisory Committee Note confirms as much (although the reality may not be quite so clear). [*Affecting: All Civil Rules.*]

- *Inter-Rule Restyling:* To achieve the added clarity the drafters sought, some content within the Rules has been relocated, some to new subparts of the same Rule and one to a new position within another Rule. These relocations are important to recognize because they will obviously complicate legal researching projects. [*Affecting: Rules 5, 6, 7, 8, 12, 16, 17, 22, 23.1, 25, 26, 30, 33, 37, 43, 50, 52, 53, 55, 56, 58, 60, 80, and 81.*]

- *New Forms:* The original, circa–1937 forms have been replaced with a new set of updated and re-styled forms. [*Affecting: All forms.*]

- *Substantively-Minor Restyling:* In a few instances, the restyling project included minor substantive changes to a few Rules. Although more than merely stylistic, these technical alterations were made because the restyling project presented the opportunity for this further Rule clean-up. [*Affecting: Rules 4(k), 9(h), 11(a), 14(b), 16(c), 26(g), 30(b), 31(c), 40, 71.1(d), and 78(a).*]

- *Truly Substantive Amendments:* As with nearly every year, several plainly substantive amendments and additions to the Rules have been made. [*Affecting: Rules 5.2 [new], 16, 26, 33, 34, 37, and 45.*]

The drafters are rightly proud of the restyling project. Earlier this year, the revised Civil Rules were acclaimed by the prestigious *Burton Awards for Legal Achievement* with their "2007 Reform in Law Award". Antiquated language, often using archaic words and legalese, has been largely removed. The newly-worded Rules are shorter, easier to read, more clearly articulated, more intuitively presented, and more uniformly assembled.

Once the concern caused by the project settles into familiarity, judges and practitioners both are likely to welcome the revisions and their concomitant benefit for federal civil practice.

How This Handbook Can Help You Re–Orient:

1. ***This Introduction:*** This brief survey of the restyling project offers the reader a bird's-eye view of the restyling–how it was designed and implemented, what it affects, and which language/structuring conventions the drafters used.

2. ***Stated Drafting Intention:*** Throughout the restyling revisions, the drafters continuously reiterate that their wording changes "are intended to be stylistic only", and "are intended to make no changes in substantive meaning". *See* Rule 1 Advisory Committee Note to 2007 amendments. Thus, while the new Rules text might be unnerving, the reader should take comfort in this prevailing reassurance from the drafters of their intention.

3. ***Unintended Drafting Effects:*** Nevertheless, though perhaps understandably, the drafters were not always able to avoid introducing changes that were more than merely stylistic. This year's edition of the *Handbook* was prepared to help readers highlight those changes that are potentially more substantive in effect than the drafters' references to their "restyling" intentions might suggest.

4. ***2007 Amendments "Roadmaps:"*** Just below the newly-worded text of each Rule, the reader will find a new feature in this *Handbook* edition that summarizes both the restyling and substantive revisions to that Rule. These "roadmaps" offer the reader a quick orientation to how that particular Rule was reassembled.

5. ***Sub-Rule Notations:*** When a Rule's content has been moved (either to a new position within the same Rule or to a new Rule entirely), the reader will find a notation identifying this move and providing the repositioning details. These notations remind the reader to take special care in researching pre–2007 amendment caselaw interpreting the Rule due to its repositioning.

6. ***Side-by-Side Comparisons:*** The drafters prepared helpful side-by-side tables that compare the pre–2007 version of each Rule with its new restyled version. Although the enormous space needed for these tables prevented this *Handbook* from reprinting them, the tables are easily accessible electronically at the website of the Administrative Office of the Federal Courts: http://www.uscourts.gov/rules/supct 1106/Excerpt_CV_Style.pdf

A Summary of the Restyling Conventions:

This Civil Rules Restyling Project took four years to complete, and it concludes a national Federal Rules restyling effort that has already rewritten the Federal Rules of Appellate Procedure (effective 1998) and the Federal Rules of Criminal Procedure (effective 2002).

The restyled Rules are graphically restructured. New internal subparts to Rules were added, and the Rules are now presented in a more visually-orienting fashion. Often, new labels were added to both former and new sub-parts to help the reader more quickly identify the content.

The restyled Rules use far more active voice phrasing than had their predecessors, and sentence placements within a Rule were reordered to make the content easier to follow. More direct, austere sentence structure was included throughout. Repeated content was, where possible, gathered and then re-grouped in one location.

The restyled Rules cure many of the earlier inconsistencies in language. Among the most significant, the confusing use of the word "shall" was omitted. The restyled Rules now use "must", "may", or "should", depending on context. Other confusing uses of synonyms to describe the same conduct were corrected. For example: "for good cause" now replaces "for cause shown", "for good cause shown", "shows good cause", "showing of good cause", and "for valid cause". Other examples are legion: courts now "issue" (rather than "make" or "enter") orders; "attorney" replaces "counsel"; "allege" replaces "aver"; "considered" replaces "deemed"; "attorney's fees" replaces "attorney fees" and "attorneys' fees"; and "crossclaim" replaces "cross-claim".

The restyled Rules eliminate misleading "intensifiers". For example, the redundant phrase "the court in its discretion may" was conflated to a simple "the court may". (This, incidentally, is one of those instances where the effect of the rephrasing may convey more than the drafters intended, a prediction this *Handbook* helps the reader flag.)

The restyled Rules deleted antiquated or unnecessary words and references. For example, "infant" and has been replaced by "minor", and references to "at law or in equity" and "suits of a civil nature" were reworked. Similarly, unnecessary repetition and cross-references were avoided. For example, reminders in some (but not all) Rules that certain conduct is subject to Rule 11 were omitted as unnecessary and vulnerable to an unintended negative inference where those references did not appear. Empty Rule subparts (which once held content long since stricken) were often filled with repositioned content.

PART III

FEDERAL RULES OF CIVIL PROCEDURE WITH COMMENTARY AND PRACTICE POINTERS

Rules Effective September 16, 1938

Including Amendments Effective December 1, 2007

Research Note

Rule requirements, case law applications, commentary, and references to treatises and law reviews are available in Wright, Miller, et al., Federal Practice and Procedure, Volumes 4 to 20.

Use WESTLAW ®to find cases citing or applying rules. WESTLAW may also be used to search for terms in court rules or to update court rules. See the US–RULES and US–ORDERS SCOPE screens for detailed descriptive information and search tips.

Table of Rules

APPENDIX OF FORMS

[The Appendix of Forms is reproduced in Part IV, below.]

I. SCOPE OF RULES—FORM OF ACTION

RULE 1

SCOPE AND PURPOSE

These rules govern the procedure in all civil actions and proceedings in the United States district courts, except as stated in Rule 81. They should be construed and administered to secure the just, speedy, and inexpensive determination of every action and proceeding.

[Amended December 29, 1948, effective October 20, 1949; February 28, 1966, effective July 1, 1966; April 22, 1993, effective December 1, 1993; April 30, 2007, effective December 1, 2007.]

──────────── **2007 AMENDMENTS ROADMAP** ────────────

STYLE PROJECT CHANGES: Historical reference to the federal courts' merger of law and equity was omitted, and the outdated "suits of a civil nature" phrase was updated to "civil actions and proceedings".

NON-STYLE CHANGES: None.

NOTE: The Federal Rules "Style Project" is explained in Part III-A.

AUTHORS' COMMENTARY ON RULE 1

──────────── **PURPOSE AND SCOPE** ────────────

The Federal Rules generally apply to all civil actions in the district courts of the United States. Federal courts, and the attorneys who appear before them, are required to construe and administer the Rules in a manner that achieves the just, speedy, and inexpensive determination of each civil action.

APPLICATIONS

Creation, Status, and Validity of the Federal Rules

Under the authority vested by the Rules Enabling Act of 1934,[1] the United States Supreme Court promulgated the original Federal Rules of Civil Procedure in December 1937. The original Rules

---

1. Act of June 19, 1934, ch. 651, 48 Stat. 1064, codified in current form at 28 U.S.C.A. §§ 2071–77.

became effective in September 1938, and have been amended on numerous occasions since. The Rules have the force and effect of law. They superseded inconsistent statutes enacted prior to their effective date.

With the exceptions noted below, the Rules define the procedures for all civil actions in the District Courts of the United States. Unless a Rule requires or permits the application of State procedure, the federal courts do not apply State procedural laws, procedural rules, or procedural decisions.[2]

The Federal Rules enjoy "presumptive validity".[3] Nevertheless, although promulgated by the United States Supreme Court, a Federal Rule may still be challenged as inconsistent with the rulemaking power delegated by Congress to the Supreme Court under the Rules Enabling Act.[4] To date, however, no Rule has been declared invalid.[5]

The Advisory Committee and Its Committee Notes

To help draft the original Federal Rules, the Supreme Court appointed an Advisory Committee on Rules comprising a panel of judges, attorneys, and law professors. This consultative tradition continues today, in the form of the Judicial Conference of the United States' Advisory Committee on Civil Rules, which investigates and recommends amendments to the Federal Rules. The members of the Advisory Committee have included federal and State judges, practicing attorneys, law professors, and Department of Justice representatives.[6]

Both the original Advisory Committee and its successors have published "Notes" as an aid in construing and interpreting the particular purpose and intent of each Rule and its amendments. The Committee Notes are only guides; the Notes neither are a part of the Rules nor have they been approved by the Supreme Court. However, in practice, the Notes have assumed the force of a veritable legislative history to the Rules and their amendments. The Notes can be cited as formidable (though non-binding) authority for construing the Rules.[7]

2. *See E.E.O.C. v. HBE Corp.*, 135 F.3d 543, 551 (8th Cir.1998) (federal rules apply to all civil actions tried in federal court, and control over conflicting State law).

3. *See Exxon Corp. v. Burglin*, 42 F.3d 948, 950 (5th Cir.1995).

4. *See Mississippi Publ'g Corp. v. Murphree*, 326 U.S. 438, 444, 66 S.Ct. 242, 246, 90 L.Ed. 185 (1946)("The fact that this Court promulgated the rules as formulated and recommended by the Advisory Committee does not foreclose consideration of their validity, meaning or consistency"). *See also Hanna v. Plumer*, 380 U.S. 460, 471, 85 S.Ct. 1136, 1143, 14 L.Ed.2d 8 (1965) (when situation is covered by Federal Rules, court

must apply them unless "the Rule in question transgresses [ ] the terms of the [Rules] Enabling Act [or the Constitution]").

5. *See Exxon Corp. v. Burglin*, 42 F.3d 948, 950 (5th Cir.1995).

6. The procedure for amending the Federal Rules is more specifically described in Part I of this text.

7. A discussion of the history behind and the legal effect of the Advisory Committee Notes, the collected case law discussing the interpretative value and weight of the Notes, and the full text of the original and amending Notes appears in Part VII of this text.

Where the Rules Apply

Rule 1 implements Article 3, Section 2 of the Constitution which extends the judicial power of the United States "to all Cases, in Law and Equity, arising under this Constitution, the Laws of the United States, and [its] Treaties ... [and] to all Cases of admiralty and maritime Jurisdiction."[8] The Rules apply to all "district courts" of the United States. By special congressional enactments, the Rules have been extended to the United States District Court for the District of Columbia,[9] and to the territorial and insular courts of Guam,[10] the Northern Mariana Islands,[11] Puerto Rico,[12] and the Virgin Islands.[13] Because it is not a "district court", the Rules do not apply to the United States Tax Court.[14]

Rules to be Harmonized Together

The Rules were designed to be "interdependent".[15] Thus, in interpreting them, courts seek to "harmonize" the Rules with one another, and will only allow one Rule to take precedence over another where truly irreconcilable conflicts arise.[16]

Civil Rules and the Courts of Appeals

By their terms the Federal Rules of Civil Procedure apply only to the federal District Courts. However, the policies that underlie the Rules may apply equally to the Courts of Appeals.[17]

Specialized Proceedings

The Rules set the procedure in district courts "in all civil

8. *See Vodusek v. Bayliner Marine Corp.*, 71 F.3d 148, 153 n. 2 (4th Cir.1995) (citing U.S. Const. art. 3, § 2).

9. *See* 28 U.S.C.A. § 88 (officially confirming that the District of Columbia is a judicial district of the United States). *See also* Rule 81(e) (applying law of District of Columbia, where appropriate, when word "state" is used).

10. *See* 48 U.S.C.A. § 1424 (creating district court of Guam and vesting it with the jurisdiction of a district court of the United States).

11. *See* 48 U.S.C.A. §§ 1821 & 1822 (creating district court of the Northern Mariana Islands and vesting it with the jurisdiction of a district court of the United States).

12. *See* 28 U.S.C.A. § 119 (creating Puerto Rico as a judicial district).

13. *See* 48 U.S.C.A. §§ 1611 & 1612 (creating district court of the Virgin Islands and vesting it with the jurisdiction of a district court of the United States).

14. *See Michaels v. Commissioner*, 144 F.3d 495, 497 (7th Cir.1998) (commenting that although the Rules are not binding on the Tax Court, they "provide a source of persuasive authority to that court in filling any gaps in its own rules of procedure"); *Smith v. Commissioner*, 926 F.2d 1470, 1478 (6th Cir.1991) (same); *Scherping v. Commissioner*, 747 F.2d 478, 480 (8th Cir. 1984) (noting that Tax Court operates under its own Rules of Practice and Procedure). *See generally* 26 U.S.C.A. § 7453 (authorizing promulgation of Tax Court Rules of Practice & Procedure); Tax Ct. R. 1(b) (providing that "These Rules shall be construed to secure the just, speedy, and inexpensive determination of every case").

15. *See Weiss v. Regal Collections*, 385 F.3d 337, 342 (3d Cir.2004).

16. *See Weiss v. Regal Collections*, 385 F.3d 337, 342 (3d Cir.2004).

17. *See Newman–Green, Inc. v. Alfonzo–Larrain*, 490 U.S. 826, 832, 109 S.Ct. 2218, 2223, 104 L.Ed.2d 893 (1989); *Wilson v. Maritime Overseas Corp.*, 150 F.3d 1 (1st Cir.1998); *Balgowan v. New Jersey*, 115 F.3d 214 (3d Cir.1997).

actions and proceedings".[18] Specialized proceedings are governed by the Rules,[19] unless they are expressly included in Rule 81's list of those to which the Rules do not apply.[20] Under Rule 81, for example, the Federal Rules apply in bankruptcy proceedings, but only to the extent prescribed by the Federal Rules of Bankruptcy Procedure.[21] Although the Rules apply generally to admiralty proceedings,[22] they do *not* apply to prize proceedings in admiralty.[23] In the absence of federal law providing otherwise, the Rules also apply to, among other proceedings: admission to citizenship proceedings,[24] habeas corpus and quo warranto proceedings,[25] and to federal arbitrations, proceedings to review orders by the Secretaries of Agriculture and Interior, proceedings to enforce National Labor Relations Board orders and Longshore and Harbor Workers' Compensation Act compensation orders, reviewing orders denying a certificate of clearance, and reviewing railway labor dispute arbitration awards.[26].

Likewise, the Rules also apply generally to de novo immigration proceedings,[27] civil contempt proceedings (when the original proceeding was governed by the Rules), civil actions for forfeiture and penalty actions by the United States,[28] patent cases, removed cases,[29] civil actions in which the United States or one of its officers or agencies is a party,[30] and proceedings to compel compliance with a subpoena to testify or to produce documents, as issued by an officer or agency of the United States pursuant to federal statute.[31]

"Just", "Speedy", and "Inexpensive" Mandate

Aside from defining when the Rules apply, Rule 1 also fixes the broad objectives of the Federal Rules: they are to be construed and administered so as to achieve the "just, speedy, and inexpensive determination of every action".[32] Often cited, these goals have been

---

18. *See* Rule 1.

19. *See S.J. v. Issaquah Sch. Dist. No. 411*, 470 F.3d 1288, 1292 (9th Cir. 2006) (citing Rule 1 to reject claim that IDEA actions, because of their "appellate flavor", are not controlled by the Rules).

20. Rule 81 was amended in 2001 to omit references that had formerly excluded the Rules from Copyright cases and from mental health proceedings in the United States District Court for the District of Columbia. With the abrogation of the separate Copyright Rules, the Rules now apply in copyright cases, and because Congress has now transferred such proceedings to local courts in the District of Columbia, the mental health proceedings provision was eliminated as superfluous.

21. *See* Rule 81(a)(2).

22. *See Blanchard v. Cortes–Molina*, 453 F.3d 40 (1st Cir.2006).

23. *See* Rule 81(a)(1).

24. *See* Rule 81(a)(3).

25. *See* Rule 81(a)(4).

26. *See* Rule 81(a)(6).

27. *See Alvear v. Kirk*, 87 F.Supp.2d 1241, 1243 (D.N.M.2000) (holding that Rules 12 and 56 governed de novo immigration proceedings pursuant to 8 U.S.C. § 1421(c)).

28. *Cf. United States v. Mosavi*, 138 F.3d 1365 (11th Cir.1998) (Federal Rules of Civil Procedure do not apply to criminal forfeitures).

29. *See* Rule 81(c)(i).

30. The Rules were not designed to extend the jurisdiction of the federal courts. Consequently, the Rules' references to procedures for suing or being sued by the United States does not constitute a waiver of sovereign immunity.

31. *See* Rule 81(a)(5).

32. *See Wood v. GCC Bend, LLC*, 422 F.3d 873, 882–83 (9th Cir.2005) (noting that the "first of the Federal Rules of Civil

heralded by the Supreme Court as "the touchstones of federal procedure".[33] The text of the Rule emphasizes the District Court's affirmative duty to exercise the procedural authority the Rules bestow so as to ensure that civil litigation in the federal courts is resolved fairly and without undue cost or delay.[34] This affirmative duty is shared by practicing attorneys, as officers of the court.[35] To realize Rule 1's goals of "just, speedy, and inexpensive" determinations of federal cases, the parties are expected to work diligently to follow the Rules and the courts are called upon to resolutely enforce the Rules, otherwise the Rules—and the laudable objectives they seek—will become illusory.[36]

The courts have quoted these touchstones, typically in combination with other Rules, as authority for their constructions and interpretations of many other Rules. Indeed, Rule 1 has been cited as authority for preventing a litigant from flouting the "spirit" of the Rules, even where the litigant's conduct might otherwise comport with the Rule's literal meaning.[37]

Examples of the courts' reliance on Rule 1 to achieve these objectives are legion. For instance, the Supreme Court cited Rule 1's mandate to justify a broadening of the long-cramped reach of the summary judgment rule.[38] The Supreme Court also mentioned the Rule 1 mandate in rejecting an overly technical interpretation of pleading procedure, noting that, led by Rule 1, the Rules "reject the approach that pleading is a game of skill in which one misstep by counsel may be decisive to the outcome and accept the principle that

Procedure mandates construing the rest" to achieve the Rule 1 touchstones).

33. *Brown Shoe Co. v. United States*, 370 U.S. 294, 306, 82 S.Ct. 1502, 1513, 8 L.Ed.2d 510 (1962). *See In re Bayer AG*, 146 F.3d 188, 189 (3d Cir.1998) (commenting that the Rules and Rule 1's touchstones "initiated a revolution in the litigation process in the federal courts in this country" and, ultimately, influenced foreign litigation as well).

34. *See* Rule 1 advisory committee notes 1993. *See also Johnson v. Board of County Comm'rs for County of Fremont*, 868 F.Supp. 1226 (D.Colo.1994)(commenting that public interest demands a seemly and efficient use of judicial resources to achieve Rule 1 goals, and courts are thus obligated to raise perceived dangers to these objectives even if parties do not).

35. *See Reebok Int'l v. Sebelen*, 959 F.Supp. 553, 558 n. 1 (D.P.R.1997) (citing Herman Melville's fable, *Bartleby the Scrivener*, as a valuable reminder that "the lawyer's role extends beyond filing motions and be an unquestioning mouthpiece for his client. His role is to engage in the adversarial process in good faith and in accordance with" the precepts of Rule 1); *Hill v.*

MacMillan McGraw–Hill Sch. Publ'g Co., No. C–93–20824, 1995 WL 317054 (N.D.Cal. 1995) (noting that litigants have obligation to court to refrain from conduct that frustrates the aims of Rule 1), *appeal dismissed*, 102 F.3d 422 (9th Cir.1996).

36. *See Mused v. United States Dep't of Agriculture Food & Nutrition Serv.*, 169 F.R.D. 28, 35 (W.D.N.Y.1996).

37. *See United States v. High Country Broad. Co.*, 3 F.3d 1244, 1245 (9th Cir. 1993). *But see Central States, Southeast & Southwest Areas Pension Fund v. Central Cartage Co.*, 69 F.3d 1312, 1314–15 (7th Cir.1995) (cautioning that "the need to consider the objectives in Fed.R.Civ.P. 1 when construing all of the rules does not justify disregarding limitations explicitly built into them").

38. *See Celotex Corp. v. Catrett*, 477 U.S. 317, 327, 106 S.Ct. 2548, 2555, 91 L.Ed.2d 265 (1986)(commenting how summary judgment constitutes an integral role in implementing the Federal Rules' task of a just, speedy, and inexpensive resolution of litigation).

the purpose of pleading is to facilitate a proper decision on the merits."[39]

Courts of Appeals have quoted the touchstones to guide the interpretations of other Federal Rules,[40] to eschew an "unduly rigid application" of local rules,[41] to reject overly technical gamesmanship pleading maneuvers,[42] to forbid parties from "ambushing" a trial court by ignoring conflict-of-law objections until after they learn whether they've won or lost at trial,[43] to deny a perceived "end-run" around the statutory prohibition against a *pro se* representation of a corporate party,[44] to criticize a trial court's delay in issuing its findings of fact and conclusions of law,[45] to approve a trial court's immediate, oral announcement of its findings of fact,[46] to approve the summary rejection of a belated dispositve motion seeking to assert immunity defenses,[47] to affirm a trial court's discretionary refusal to reconsider and vacate its earlier summary judgment ruling,[48] to justify the imposition of sanctions for discovery abuses,[49] to reject a trial court's decision to admit into evidence a previously undisclosed surveillance videotape,[50] to overrule a rigid, prior precedent commanding that the trial court always grant a plaintiff one chance to amend a dismissed complaint even where no such leave had ever been sought,[51] to excuse the failure to file a motion for

39. *See Conley v. Gibson*, 355 U.S. 41, 48, 78 S.Ct. 99, 103, 2 L.Ed.2d 80 (1957). *See also Foman v. Davis*, 371 U.S. 178, 181–82, 83 S.Ct. 227, 230 (1962) (same quotation).

40. *See Transamerica Occidental Life Ins. Co. v. Aviation Office of America, Inc.*, 292 F.3d 384, 389 (3d Cir.2002) (citing Rule 1 in concluding that policy underlying Rule 13(a) is "judicial economy"); *In re Grand Jury*, 286 F.3d 153, 159 (3d Cir.2002) (citing Rule 1 in explaining that Rule 26(c) protective orders are intended to "secure the just, speedy, and inexpensive determination" of civil trials by "encouraging full disclosure of all evidence that might conceivably be relevant").

41. *See Mitskovski v. Buffalo & Fort Erie Pub. Bridge Auth.*, 435 F.3d 127, 133 (2d Cir.2006).

42. *See Rodi v. Southern New England Sch. of Law*, 389 F.3d 5, 20 (1st Cir.2004) (finding it "antithetic" to spirit of Rules to hold that "pleading of cases is a game in which every miscue should be fatal").

43. *See Celle v. Filipino Reporter Enters. Inc.*, 209 F.3d 163, 175–76 (2d Cir. 2000) (such ruling "would permit a losing party to lead a trial court into error and then to profit on appeal from the misguidance").

44. *See United States v. High Country Broad. Co.*, 3 F.3d 1244, 1245 (9th Cir. 1993).

45. *See Ashelman v. Wawrzaszek*, 111 F.3d 674, 675 n. 3 (9th Cir.1997) (chastising trial court's five year delay in issuing findings and conclusions, noting that the just, speedy, and inexpensive resolution of every action is "the first principle of the Federal Rules of Civil Procedure" and "should not be forgotten, as it apparently was here").

46. *See Lansford-Coaldale Joint Water Auth. v. Tonolli Corp.*, 4 F.3d 1209, 1214–15 (3d Cir.1993).

47. *See Torres v. Puerto Rico*, 485 F.3d 5, 10 (1st Cir. 2007).

48. *See Calpetco 1981 v. Marshall Exploration, Inc.*, 989 F.2d 1408, 1415 (5th Cir.1993)(citing Rule 1 to hold that, on applications for reconsideration, trial court must have "considerable discretion in determining when enough is enough").

49. *See Malautea v. Suzuki Motor Co.*, 987 F.2d 1536, 1546 (11th Cir.1993).

50. *See Chiasson v. Zapata Gulf Marine Corp.*, 988 F.2d 513, 518 n. 10 (5th Cir. 1993)(noting that non-disclosure thwarted Rule 1's policies because it eliminated an opportunity for a pretrial settlement).

51. *See Wagner v. Daewoo Heavy Indus. America Corp.*, 314 F.3d 541, 542–43 (11th Cir.2002) (overruling prior rule).

judgment as a matter of law before submission to the jury where such a filing would have violated the law-of-the-case doctrine,[52] to credit the general public's interest in "prompt" resolution of civil cases,[53] and to affirm a judgment instead of remanding for a subsequent amendment to a party's complaint.[54] The Rule 1 mandates have also been cited as support for the conclusion that a federal district's local rules on proper forms for filed documents are not jurisdictional, and do not justify a prejudicial dismissal.[55]

Yet, the Rules' flexibility is certainly not unbounded. Rule 1's touchstones cannot be cited, for example, to distort a clearly pleaded claim into alleging something that it certainly does not under the banner of liberality.[56]

The District Courts, too, have cited Rule 1's touchstone mandate as support for various rulings. For example, federal trial judges have cited this mandate in regulating "Rambo"-style litigation tactics,[57] in decrying misbehavior by counsel,[58] in striking several legal papers and ordering a defendant's answer so as to advance an aging case to trial,[59] in permanently enjoining a plaintiff from filing frivolous complaints and seeking further *in forma pauperis* status,[60] in fining a non-appearing attorney for the monetary value of lost federal court trial time,[61] in refusing to assess against "impoverished" plaintiffs the fees charged by defendants' experts for appearing at a deposition taken by plaintiffs' counsel,[62] in issuing

---

52. *See Kerman v. City of New York*, 374 F.3d 93, 118–19 (2d Cir.2004) ("Such a motion would invite the trial court to commit error" and, if wrongly granted, "a new trial ... would be required—hardly a just, speedy, or inexpensive course").

53. *See Microfinancial, Inc. v. Premier Holidays Int'l*, 385 F.3d 72, 79 n.4 (1st Cir.2004).

54. *See Boston & Maine Corp. v. Town of Hampton*, 987 F.2d 855, 867 (1st Cir. 1993).

55. *See Ordonez v. Johnson*, 254 F.3d 814, 816 (9th Cir.2001) (treating such technical local rules as jurisdictional "would conflict with the mandate of Federal Rule of Civil Procedure 1 to provide a just and speedy determination of every action").

56. *See Lee v. MBNA Long Term Disability & Benefit Plan*, 2005 WL 705771, at *12 (6th Cir.2005) (commenting that, although Rule 1 directs liberal construction of pleadings, it will not justify finding a State claim in a complaint pleaded as an ERISA case).

57. *See In re Amezaga*, 195 B.R. 221 (Bkrtcy.D.P.R.1996) (noting that "Rambo Litigation" is not tolerated because, although it may project zealous advocacy, it

does not promote Rule 1's goals); *Applied Telematics, Inc. v. Sprint Corp.*, No. 94–CV–4603, 1995 WL 79237 (E.D.Pa. 1995)(decrying counsel's "Rambo Litigation" deposition defense tactics as failing to promote goals of Rule 1).

58. *See Nissan Motor Co. v. Nissan Computer Corp.*, 180 F.Supp.2d 1089, 1096 (C.D.Cal.2002) (holding that counsel's conduct in threatening to record, or actually recording, conversations with opposing counsel "interferes with the just and speedy determination of this action").

59. *See Hill v. Blue Cross & Blue Shield of Mich.*, 237 F.R.D. 613, 613–18 (E.D.Mich. 2006).

60. *See Hill v. Gates*, 940 F.Supp. 108 (M.D.Pa.1996) (filing of frivolous complaints containing offensive and derogatory material justified a permanent injunction against future such filings and a requirement that plaintiff pay filing fees).

61. *See Specialized Plating, Inc. v. Federal Envtl. Servs., Inc.*, 975 F.Supp. 397 (D.Mass.1997).

62. *See Reed v. Binder*, 165 F.R.D. 424, 427–28 (D.N.J.1996) (citing Rule 1, and concluding that "the imposing economic obstacle facing these plaintiffs seeking redress

discovery orders,[63] in permitting a defendant to file a "renewed" motion for summary judgment,[64] in denying a late intervention motion,[65] in excusing the need for a full *Daubert* evidentiary hearing on an expert's reliability,[66] in limiting the number of expert witnesses,[67] in embracing the videotaping of discovery depositions,[68] and in otherwise generally controlling pretrial conduct.[69] In the words of one court, this "simple" Rule is a reminder that form should not be exalted over substance.[70]

ADDITIONAL RESEARCH REFERENCES

Wright & Miller, *Federal Practice and Procedure* §§ 1011–1040.

C.J.S. Federal Civil Procedure §§ 5 et seq.; Federal Courts § 284.

West's Key No. Digests, Federal Civil Procedure ☞21, 31–44; Federal Courts ☞522.

for the death of their wife and mother ... requires that these costs be shifted to the defendants").

63. *See Jackson v. County of Sacramento,* 175 F.R.D. 653, 658 (E.D.Cal.1997) (citing Rule to limit scope of discovery); *Zapata v. IBP, Inc.,* 160 F.R.D. 625, 628 (D.Kan. 1995)(ruling that general, blanket protective order barring parties in one case from sharing discovery with litigants in another case (where that same discovery would have been allowed) "would hardly accord with the purpose of the rules set forth in Fed. R.Civ.P. 1"); *Johns Hopkins Univ. v. Cellpro,* 160 F.R.D. 30 (D.Del.1995)(citing Rule 1's goals as justification for refusing to stay certain discovery until after one component of trial was completed); *Agostino Ferrari, S.p.A. v. Antonacci,* 858 F.Supp. 478 (E.D.Pa.1994)(denying reopening of discovery and concomitant lengthening of litigation as injuring public's interest in Rule 1 goals).

64. *See Fleischer v. Resolution Trust Corp.,* 882 F.Supp. 1010 (D.Kan. 1995)(noting that "renewed" motion represented the most efficient vehicle for resolving certain issues).

65. *See Coburn v. DaimlerChrysler Servs. N.A., L.L.C.,* 218 F.R.D. 607, 610–11 (N.D. Ill.2003).

66. *See Lanni v. New Jersey,* 177 F.R.D. 295, 303 (D.N.J.1998).

67. *See Planned Parenthood of Central N.J. v. Verniero,* 22 F.Supp.2d 331, 339 (D.N.J.1998).

68. *See Fanelli v. Centenary Coll.,* 211 F.R.D. 268, 271 (D.N.J.2002) (because it may foster careful assessment of the strengths and weaknesses of trial testimony of witnesses (including how a jury might view that testimony), videotaped discovery depositions may lead to more prompt settlements).

69. *See Myers v. County of Orange,* 870 F.Supp. 555 (S.D.N.Y.1994) (in ruling on summary judgment motion, court refused to consider informal comments by counsel during off-the-record pretrial conferences because to consider such comments would have a chilling effect on the open discussions necessary to promote Rule 1 objectives).

70. *See Hall v. Sullivan,* 229 F.R.D. 501, 504 (D.Md.2005).

RULE 2

ONE FORM OF ACTION

There is one form of action—the civil action.

2007 AMENDMENTS ROADMAP

STYLE PROJECT CHANGES: Cumbersome wording was culled.

NON-STYLE CHANGES: None.

NOTE: The Federal Rules "Style Project" is explained in Part III-A.

AUTHORS' COMMENTARY ON RULE 2

PURPOSE AND SCOPE

The Rules have merged the law and equity sides of the federal courts, providing a single procedural framework for all claims and defenses. All relief may now be obtained in the same action, whether the case seeks legal remedies, equitable remedies, or both.

APPLICATIONS

Civil Action Defined

For civil claims, the Rules establish only one form of proceeding, known as a "civil action". This term refers to the entire civil proceeding, including all component "claims" and "cases" within that proceeding.[1] Thus, for example, a party may not remove to federal court only a portion of lawsuit filed in State court.[2]

1. *See Nolan v. Boeing Co.*, 919 F.2d 1058, 1066 (5th Cir.1990)(ruling that "case" and "action" refer to the same thing—the entirety of a civil proceeding, including third party claims). *See also Fogg v. Ashcroft*, 254 F.3d 103, 107 (D.C.Cir. 2001) (citing Rule 2 as support for holding that statutory cap on damages in "an action brought" under the Civil Rights of Act of 1964 applies to entire lawsuit, not just to individual claims within lawsuit); *Hudson v. Reno*, 130 F.3d 1193, 1199 (6th Cir.1997) (same); *United States v. NL Indus.*, 2005 WL 1267419, at *5 (S.D.Ill. May 4, 2005) (citing *Federal Civil Rules Handbook*, not-

ing that all component claims are encompassed in "civil action"); *In re Hinote*, 179 F.R.D. 335 (S.D.Ala.1998); (State court petition filed to obtain pre-commencement discovery in likely ERISA case was not removable because it was not commenced by the filing of a complaint and, thus, was not a "civil action" within the meaning of Rule 2).

2. *See, e.g., Clark Const. Group v. Hellmuth, Obata & Kassabaum, Inc.*, 286 F.Supp.2d 1348, 1348–52 (M.D.Fla.2003) (litigant's attempt to remove less than whole civil action, and "unilaterally sever ... claims and remove only part of the

Equity Principles Applicable

Although the Rules have fused law and equity into a single procedural framework, the federal courts still apply equity principles in appropriate cases.[3]

Determining Form of Action

Although the federal courts no longer recognize a distinction in procedure between cases on the "law-side" and cases in "equity",[4] this distinction still persists in some limited contexts in which the federal courts may yet be called upon to discern the substantive "form" of the litigation (*i.e.*, legal or equitable).[5] This inquiry may arise when the court has to decide whether a litigant enjoys a right to a trial by jury,[6] or when, in diversity cases, the controlling State law retains the law / equity distinction as to such substantive issues as the applicable statute of limitations.

Joinder of All Claims and Defenses

Without a separate law-side and equity-side to the federal courts, a party may now join all claims and defenses (legal and equitable) against all opposing parties in one action.[7] Note, however, that the Rules and certain judiciary title statutes may limit such joinder.[8]

Complete Relief

When granting final judgment, a court may grant all the relief to which a party is entitled (legal and equitable), regardless of the relief demanded in the pleadings.[9] Note, however, that many judi-

---

State Court Action", was foreclosed by Rules and deprived Court of subject matter jurisdiction).

3. *See Stainback v. Mo Hock Ke Lok Po*, 336 U.S. 368, 382 n. 26, 69 S.Ct. 606, 614 n. 26, 93 L.Ed. 741 (1949)(noting that Rules' merger of law and equity did not affect the substantive principles of equity); *In re U.S. Brass Corp.*, 110 F.3d 1261, 1267 (7th Cir. 1997) (commenting that since law and equity were merged in the federal courts, judges have freely imported equitable defenses into suits at law).

4. *See Cablevision of Midwest, Inc. v. City of Brunswick*, 117 F.Supp.2d 658, 661 (N.D. Ohio 2000) (noting that purpose of Rule 2 "was to abolish the distinction between actions at law and suits in equity, and thereby to simplify procedure in the federal courts").

5. *See Burlington N. R.R. v. Nebraska Pub. Power Dist.*, 931 F.Supp. 1470, 1479 (D.Neb.1996).

6. *See Wooddell v. Int'l Bhd. of Elec. Workers, Local 71*, 502 U.S. 93, 97, 112 S.Ct. 494, 497, 116 L.Ed.2d 419 (1991)(to

decide whether a particular lawsuit would resolve "legal" rights, and thus entitle the litigants to a trial by jury, the courts: (1) compare the action to 18th Century claims brought in English courts prior to the merger of law and equity; and (2) determine whether the remedy sought is legal or equitable in nature). *See also* Rule 38 (discussing effect of action "in equity" in assessing a party's Seventh Amendment right to a jury trial).

7. *See United States ex rel. Rahman v. Oncology Assocs., P.C.*, 198 F.3d 502, 508–09 (4th Cir.1999) (citing Rule 2 as support for the proposition that mandamus relief can be sought in same lawsuit that involved other, unrelated relief because "the modern trend in civil pleading has been to encourage that all claims for relief be brought in a single suit").

8. *See, e.g.,* 28 U.S.C.A. § 1367 (enumerating the federal court's supplemental jurisdiction over state law claims); Rule 18 (joinder of claims and remedies); Rule 19 (joinder of parties).

9. *See* Rule 54(c).

cial districts require parties to list in a pretrial memorandum the specific relief they intend to seek and, thereafter, to remain bound by that listing at trial.[10]

ADDITIONAL RESEARCH REFERENCES

Wright & Miller, *Federal Practice and Procedure* §§ 1041–1050.

C.J.S. Federal Civil Procedure §§ 4, 37 et seq.

West's Key No. Digests, Federal Civil Procedure ☞5–7, 71–73, 81–86.

---

10. *See, e.g.,* E.D. Pa. Loc. R. 16.1(c)(3) & (d)(2)(b)(3) (requiring party seeking relief to identify the precise monetary and non-monetary relief requested).

TITLE II. COMMENCING AN ACTION; SERVICE OF PROCESS, PLEADINGS, MOTIONS, AND ORDERS

RULE 3

COMMENCING AN ACTION

A civil action is commenced by filing a complaint with the court.

─────────── 2007 AMENDMENTS ROADMAP ───────────

STYLE PROJECT CHANGES: Rule title was changed to active voice.

NON-STYLE CHANGES: None.

NOTE: The Federal Rules "Style Project" is explained in Part III-A.

AUTHORS' COMMENTARY ON RULE 3

─────────── PURPOSE AND SCOPE ───────────

A civil action is commenced under Rule 3 on the date on which a complaint is filed, *not* the date of service. This dating function is important for many purposes, including the tolling of the statute of limitations in federal question cases. Note, however, that local effect of Rule 3 may be supplanted in diversity cases by State commencement statutes and, where they exist, by contrary federal statutes in other cases.

NOTE: Plaintiffs only receive the benefit of this Rule if they serve the summons and the complaint on the defendant within 120 days after commencement or have good cause for not doing so.[1]

APPLICATIONS

Action "Commences" When Complaint is Filed

An action becomes "pending" when the complaint is delivered for filing to a court officer authorized to receive it.[2] Prior to filing,

---

1. *See* Rule 4(m).

2. *See United States v. $8,221,877.16 in U.S. Currency*, 330 F.3d 141, 159 (3d Cir. 2003) (noting that the word "commence" is

term of art with only one unambiguous meaning–it does not "encompass broad concepts, but rather requires 'invocation of the judicial process' "). *See also Local Union*

the federal district court lacks authority to act in the dispute.[3]

Service Generally Not Required for Action to "Commence"

Service of process is generally not required for the lawsuit to "commence". So long as service is completed within 120 days after the complaint is filed with the court, the litigants become "plaintiff" and "defendant" when the complaint is filed, not when it is served.[4]

"Commencement" is Provisional—Action Dismissed in 120 Days Without Service

Although an action becomes "pending" when the complaint is delivered for filing, Rule 4(m) authorizes the district court to dismiss the action, without prejudice, if service of both the summons and the complaint is not made within 120 days of commencement (unless good cause is shown why service was not accomplished during that period).[5]

Uses of Rule 3's Dating Function

Rule 3's function of "dating" the commencement of a lawsuit as of the day the complaint is filed with the court is useful in many contexts. This dating function may be used to evaluate:

- The timeliness of the action, under the applicable statute of limitations and/or laches (see discussions below);

- Ripeness;

- Personal Jurisdiction, which generally vests at the time an action is commenced;[6]

- Diversity Jurisdiction, which also generally vests at the time an action is commenced;[7]

No. 38, Sheet Metal Workers' Int'l v. Pelella, 350 F.3d 73, 82 (2d Cir.2003) (an action is instituted in federal court "a plaintiff files a complaint as that constitutes the first step invoking the judicial process").

3. *See Powell v. Rios,* 2007 WL 2057001, at *4 n.4 (10th Cir. 2007) (intimating that filing a TRO, without a complaint, would not be sufficient to commence a federal action). *But see* Rule 27 (permitting depositions before complaint is filed).

4. *See Howell by Goerdt v. Tribune Entm't Co.,* 106 F.3d 215, 217 (7th Cir. 1997). *See also Clay v. United States,* 199 F.3d 876, 880 (6th Cir.1999) ("A person becomes 'a party' only by beginning a lawsuit, Fed. R. Civ. P. 3, or by being joined as a party after a suit has been instituted").

5. *See* Rule 4(m). Note, however, that Rule 4(m) does not apply to service within a foreign country, *see* Fed. R. Civ. P. 4(m)(referencing Rule 4(f)); or to service upon a foreign state and its political subdivisions, agencies, and instrumentalities, *see*

Fed. R. Civ. P. 4(m)(referencing Rule 4(j)(1)).

6. *See Burnham v. Superior Court of California,* 495 U.S. 604, 110 S.Ct. 2105, 109 L.Ed.2d 631 (1990) (holding that court had personal jurisdiction over nonresident defendant who was served with process while temporarily in forum State for purposes unrelated to lawsuit). *But see United States v. Certain Real & Personal Property Belonging to Hayes,* 943 F.2d 1292 (11th Cir.1991) (court's in rem jurisdiction depends upon court's continued control over property; if property is sold or removed from the court's jurisdiction, the forum is divested of jurisdiction).

7. *See Freeport–McMoRan, Inc. v. K N Energy, Inc.,* 498 U.S. 426, 428, 111 S.Ct. 858, 859, 112 L.Ed.2d 951 (1991) (if diversity jurisdiction exists at the time the lawsuit is filed, jurisdiction will not be divested by subsequent events). *Cf. Stevens v. Nichols,* 130 U.S. 230, 231–32, 9 S.Ct. 518, 518–19, 32 L.Ed. 914 (1889) (case may be removed

- Venue, which likewise is generally assessed as of the date the action is commenced;

- Procedural Timing Deadlines, such as the earliest moment for propounding discovery and filing summary judgment motions;

- Competing Jurisdiction Issues, when complaints involving the same parties and issues are filed in two different courts and the law provides that the first court to obtain jurisdiction should proceed and the second court should dismiss the case or abstain from exercising jurisdiction;

- Litigation of Claims Accruing After the Filing of the Complaint, where new claims usually cannot be litigated in the same case absent an amendment to the complaint;[8] and

- Compulsory Counterclaims, which must be filed or are deemed waived unless they are already the subject of another "pending" action.

"Commencement" in Federal Question Jurisdiction Cases

Ordinarily, in cases involving federal question jurisdiction, Rule 3 will govern when a lawsuit "commences" and will, typically, serve to toll the statute of limitations upon the filing of the complaint.[9] One exception exists–where the federal question is based on a statute that, itself, contains a separate "commencement" provision, the terms of that statute will control. In neither event will State law apply to the issue of "commencement". Even where the federal law lacks a specific statute of limitations, and the applicable limitations period is "borrowed" either from another federal law[10] or from State law,[11] Rule 3's commencement function will govern, and the filing of the complaint will generally toll the limitations period.

"Commencement" in Diversity Jurisdiction Cases

In diversity cases, Rule 3 will apply for the purposes of evaluating uniquely federal issues, such as the presence or absence of diverse citizenship and the computation of time under the Federal Rules.

to federal court only if diversity exists both at the time the action is commenced and at the time removal is sought).

8. *See* Rule 15. *See also Altseimer v. Bell Helicopter Textron Inc.*, 919 F.Supp. 340, 342–43 (E.D.Cal.1996) (citing Rule 3's "commencement" dating function in refusing to apply new federal statute to existing civil action, where new Act expressly did not apply to lawsuits "commenced" before the date of the Act's enactment).

9. *See Henderson v. United States*, 517 U.S. 654, 657 n.2, 116 S.Ct. 1638, 1641 n.2, 134 L.Ed.2d 880 (1996). *See also Iran Air v. Kugelman*, 996 F.2d 1253, 1257 (D.C.Cir. 1993) (applying Rule 3 to toll statute of limitations on federally-created right even

though service not accomplished until after period had expired).

10. *See West v. Conrail*, 481 U.S. 35, 107 S.Ct. 1538, 95 L.Ed.2d 32 (1987) (in action under Railway Labor Act, which lacked specific statute of limitations or commencement period, Rule 3 tolled the applicable statute of limitations upon filing).

11. *See Sain v. City of Bend*, 309 F.3d 1134, 1135–38 (9th Cir.2002) (joining other federal circuits in ruling that Rule 3 provides tolling function for limitations period borrowed from State law in Section 1983 case); *Moore v. Indiana*, 999 F.2d 1125, 1129–30 (7th Cir.1993) (same).

However, Rule 3 will not always toll the applicable State law statute of limitations upon the mere filing of a diversity complaint. The *Erie* doctrine [12] compels that, where State law provides a contrary tolling requirement or tolling limitation, Rule 3 cannot be permitted to give the State law cause of action a longer life in a federal court than it would otherwise have in the State courts.[13] Thus, if, for example, under State law, the limitations period would not be tolled until service is accomplished or the filing fee is paid,, Rule 3 will not act to toll the limitations period merely upon filing.[14] Similarly, where State law requires the issuance of a summons before the applicable statute of limitations is tolled, the federal courts will honor that requirement: until the summons is issued, the limitations period will continue to run.[15]

"Commencement" in Supplemental Jurisdiction Cases

Where a complaint, invoking the federal courts' supplemental jurisdiction, pleads both federal claims and State law claims, the courts will follow the same rules as they do in diversity cases. Rule 3 will not give a State law cause of action longer life in a federal forum than that same cause of action would enjoy in State court.[16]

12. *Erie R.R. Co. v. Tompkins,* 304 U.S. 64, 58 S.Ct. 817, 82 L.Ed. 1188 (1938). Generally, the *Erie* doctrine obligates the federal courts to apply State law as the substantive law of decision in diversity cases.

13. *See Walker v. Armco Steel Corp.,* 446 U.S. 740, 100 S.Ct. 1978, 64 L.Ed.2d 659 (1980)(holding that Oklahoma law, which tolls the statute of limitations only upon service, will supersede Rule 3's tolling effect); *Ragan v. Merchants Transfer & Warehouse Co.,* 337 U.S. 530, 69 S.Ct. 1233, 93 L.Ed. 1520 (1949)(same, under Kansas law).

14. *See Henderson v. United States,* 517 U.S. 654, 657 n. 2, 116 S.Ct. 1638, 1641 n. 2, 134 L.Ed.2d 880 (1996) (commenting that in a federal-court action upon a right created by State law, the plaintiff must serve process before the statute of limitations has expired, if the law of that State so requires); *Walker v. Armco Steel Corp.,* 446 U.S. 740, 100 S.Ct. 1978, 64 L.Ed.2d 659 (1980) (holding that Oklahoma law, which tolls the statute of limitations only upon service, supersedes Rule 3's tolling effect); *Ragan v. Merchants Transfer & Warehouse Co.,* 337 U.S. 530, 69 S.Ct. 1233, 93 L.Ed. 1520 (1949) (same conclusion under Kansas law); *Schorsch v. Hewlett–Packard Co.,* 417 F.3d 748 (7th Cir.2005) (noting potential variations among States); *Larsen v. Mayo*

Med. Ctr., 218 F.3d 863 (8th Cir.2000) (holding that Minnesota's commencement rule applies, which dates commencement by service); *Habermehl v. Potter,* 153 F.3d 1137, 1139 (10th Cir.1998) (ruling that case was time-barred under Wyoming law, where limitations periods are only tolled 60 days for service, and service was not completed until 107 days after filing); *Jenkins v. City of Topeka,* 136 F.3d 1274, 1275 (10th Cir.1998) (under Kansas law, plaintiff could rely on filing date as "commencement" only if service was complete within 90 days of filing, thereafter "commencement" would occur on date of actual service). *But cf. Hart v. Bates,* 897 F.Supp. 710 (E.D.N.Y. 1995) (applying federal, rather than Pennsylvania, time limitation for proper service of process where Pennsylvania did not condition the "commencement" of a civil action upon effective service, and did not deem service as integral to the tolling of its statute of limitations).

15. *See Eades v. Clark Distrib. Co.,* 70 F.3d 441 (6th Cir.1995).

16. *See Anderson v. Unisys Corp.,* 47 F.3d 302, 309 (8th Cir.1995) (affirming dismissal of State law claims where, under Minnesota law, an action is not "commenced" until the initial process is served); *Appletree Square I, Ltd. v. W.R. Grace & Co.,* 29 F.3d 1283, 1286 (8th Cir. 1994)(same).

Commencement and Removed Cases

Ordinarily, a case is not considered "re"-commenced if it is removed to federal court. Instead, the general federal approach holds that a lawsuit is deemed "commenced" at one, discrete moment in time–typically, when the original lawsuit is filed in a court of competent jurisdiction.[17] Nevertheless, if an applicable State law requires effective service in order for "commencement" to be complete, the time for removal might be postponed; in such cases, the lawsuit might not be considered "commenced" (and, thus, eligible for removal) until the defendants are actually served.[18]

Commencement and Amended Complaints

Because an amended complaint often cannot be filed until leave of court has first been granted,[19] many courts have ruled that the amended complaint is deemed filed, for "commencement" and statute of limitations purposes, as of the date that the motion for leave to amend is filed.[20] Practitioners should rely on this principle with great care, however. Whether this treatment applies to all cases (or just those where an earlier amendment was made impossible by circumstances), whether this treatment applies where the motion neither attaches the proposed amended complaint nor properly describes it, and whether this treatment has any effect where the leave is denied, are each unclear.

Unique Prerequisites for Commencement

Certain federal statutes contain special prerequisites for commencing a civil action, such as receiving a right-to-sue letter or exhausting administrative remedies.[21] Thus, merely filing a complaint pursuant to Rule 3 might not toll the statute of limitations if such prerequisites are not met. Particular statutes should be consulted carefully for such prerequisites.

Filing By Mail

The "mailbox" rule generally will not apply in Rule 3 circumstances. If original papers are mailed to the Clerk's Office for filing, filing is only complete—and the lawsuit only "commences"—upon the Clerk's receipt of the complaint.[22]

---

17. *See Pritchett v. Office Depot, Inc.,* 420 F.3d 1090, 1094 (10th Cir.2005).

18. *See, e.g., Dinkel v. General Motors Corp.,* 400 F.Supp.2d 289, 293 (D.Me.2005).

19. *See* Rule 15.

20. *See, e.g., Mayes v. AT & T Info. Sys.,* 867 F.2d 1172, 1173 (8th Cir.1989); *Koch v. Shell Oil Co.,* 8 F.Supp.2d 1264, 1267–68 (D.Kan.1998); *Massachusetts Pub. Interest Research Group v. ICI Americas Inc.,* 777 F.Supp. 1032, 1036 (D.Mass.1991); *Wallace v. Sherwin Williams Co.,* 720 F.Supp. 158, 158–60 (D.Kan.1988). *See also Nett v. Bellucci,* 437 Mass. 630, 630–47, 774

N.E.2d 130, 130–42 (2002) (on certified question from the First Circuit Court of Appeals, citing cases, and extensively discussing "commencement" effect of motion for leave to amend); *Children's Store v. Cody Enterps.,* 154 Vt. 634, 640–42, 580 A.2d 1206, 1209–11 (1990) (same effect).

21. *See, e.g., Truitt v. County of Wayne,* 148 F.3d 644 (6th Cir.1998) (discussing EEOC right-to-sue letter procedure).

22. *See McIntosh v. Antonino,* 71 F.3d 29, 36–37 (1st Cir.1995); *Cooper v. City of Ashland,* 871 F.2d 104, 105 (9th Cir.1989).

Filing After Business Hours

Rule 77 prescribes that the District Courts are "always open". Accordingly, a complaint will ordinarily be deemed to be filed as of the time it was delivered to the Clerk's Office, even if delivered after the Clerk's business hours.[23] Likewise, a complaint transmitted for electronic filing with the court will still be deemed filed, even if the receiving computer rejected it.[24]

Filing Fees

The federal courts are divided over whether the payment of filing fees is required prior to commencing an action (and tolling the limitations period).[25] To avoid any risk on this point, fees should be paid properly at the time the complaint is delivered to the court.

Pauper and Prisoner Plaintiffs

The federal courts have an *in forma pauperis* procedure for plaintiffs who lack the ability to pay filing fees. A plaintiff proposing to proceed *in forma pauperis* can toll the statute of limitations by filing a proper motion for leave to proceed *in forma pauperis*.[26] However, if the petition to proceed *in forma pauperis* is denied, the plaintiff must promptly pay the court filing fees or risk losing the limitations period tolling benefit of having "commenced" the lawsuit.[27]

In complaints prepared by *pro se* prisoner plaintiffs, the courts have generally followed a variation of the "mailbox" rule that deems a lawsuit as "commenced" upon delivery of the complaint to the prison officials.[28]

23. *See Turner v. City of Newport*, 887 F.Supp. 149 (E.D.Ky.1995) (holding that complaint was timely filed when delivered to the Clerk's post office box, after the office had closed, on last day before statute of limitations ran).

24. *See Farzana K. v. Indiana Dep't of Educ.*, 473 F.3d 703, 706–07 (7th Cir. 2007).

25. *Compare Robinson v. America's Best Contacts & Eyeglasses*, 876 F.2d 596 (7th Cir.1989)(in Rule 4 context, construing local court rule to require payment of fee as prerequisite for filing) *with McDowell v. Delaware State Police*, 88 F.3d 188, 191 (3d Cir.1996) (filing fee is not jurisdictional; although complaint is not deemed to be formally filed until fee is paid, it is constructively filed when the Clerk receives it, so long as the plaintiff ultimately pays the fee or is granted leave to proceed *in forma pauperis*); *Cintron v. Union Pac. R. Co.*, 813 F.2d 917, 920–21 (9th Cir.1987)(filing fee is not jurisdictional); *Rodgers on Behalf of Jones v. Bowen*, 790 F.2d 1550 (11th Cir.1986)(holding that dismissal was inappropriate sanction for non-payment of filing fees); *Wrenn v. American Cast Iron Pipe*

Co., 575 F.2d 544, 547 (5th Cir.1978)(timely payment of filing fee is not a jurisdictional prerequisite).

26. *See Powell v. Jacor Communications Corporate*, 320 F.3d 599, 602–03 (6th Cir. 2003) (ruling that complaint, which would have been timely filed under Kentucky law had the acceptance of the complaint not been delayed by the *in forma pauperis* petition, was deemed timely filed under Rule 3).

27. *See Truitt v. County of Wayne*, 148 F.3d 644 (6th Cir.1998) (pauper litigant must pay filing fee within applicable limitations period, as tolled during the pendency of the *in forma pauperis* application); *Williams-Guice v. Board of Educ. of Chicago*, 45 F.3d 161 (7th Cir.1995) (limitations period resumes running once *in forma pauperis* application is denied); *Jarrett v. U.S. Sprint Communications Co.*, 22 F.3d 256 (10th Cir.1994) (same).

28. *See Cooper v. Brookshire*, 70 F.3d 377 (5th Cir.1995); *Dory v. Ryan*, 999 F.2d 679 (2d Cir.1993); *Garvey v. Vaughn*, 993 F.2d 776 (11th Cir.1993); *Lewis v. Richmond City Police Dep't*, 947 F.2d 733 (4th

Plaintiff Must Prosecute Diligently After Commencement

Once a plaintiff files the complaint, the plaintiff must prosecute the action with due diligence. Rule 3 does not relieve plaintiffs of their obligation to prosecute the complaint after filing. The court may dismiss any action for lack of due diligence in proceeding with the lawsuit.[29]

ADDITIONAL RESEARCH REFERENCES

Wright & Miller, *Federal Practice and Procedure* §§ 1051–57.

C.J.S. Federal Civil Procedure § 3.

West's Key No. Digests, Federal Civil Procedure ☞4.

Cir.1991). *Cf. Houston v. Lack*, 487 U.S. 266, 108 S.Ct. 2379, 101 L.Ed.2d 245 (1988)(holding that notice of appeal is "filed" within the meaning of the Federal Rules of Appellate Procedure when delivered by a *pro se* prisoner to the prison authorities); Fed.R.App.P. 4(c)(same). *But see Jackson v. Nicoletti*, 875 F.Supp. 1107 (E.D.Pa.1994)(after recounting six reasons for refusing to extend the Supreme Court's *Houston v. Lack* appeal-period mailbox rule to assessing "commencement" of a *pro se* prisoner's lawsuit under Rule 3, the district court dismissed the lawsuit as time-barred where the complaint was not delivered to the clerk of court within two years after the prisoner's claim accrued).

29. *See* Rule 41(b).

RULE 4

SUMMONS

(a) Contents; Amendments.

    (1) *Contents.* A summons must:

        (A) name the court and the parties;

        (B) be directed to the defendant;

        (C) state the name and address of the plaintiff's attorney or—if unrepresented—of the plaintiff;

        (D) state the time within which the defendant must appear and defend;

        (E) notify the defendant that a failure to appear and defend will result in a default judgment against the defendant for the relief demanded in the complaint;

        (F) be signed by the clerk; and

        (G) bear the court's seal.

    (2) *Amendments.* The court may permit a summons to be amended.

(b) Issuance. On or after filing the complaint, the plaintiff may present a summons to the clerk for signature and seal. If the summons is properly completed, the clerk must sign, seal, and issue it to the plaintiff for service on the defendant. A summons—or a copy of a summons that is addressed to multiple defendants—must be issued for each defendant to be served.

(c) Service.

    (1) *In General.* A summons must be served with a copy of the complaint. The plaintiff is responsible for having the summons and complaint served within the time allowed by Rule 4(m) and must furnish the necessary copies to the person who makes service.

    (2) *By Whom.* Any person who is at least 18 years old and not a party may serve a summons and complaint.

    (3) *By a Marshal or Someone Specially Appointed.* At the plaintiff's request, the court may order that service be made by a United States marshal or

deputy marshal or by a person specially appointed by the court. The court must so order if the plaintiff is authorized to proceed in forma pauperis under 28 U.S.C. § 1915 or as a seaman under 28 U.S.C. § 1916.

(d) Waiving Service.

(1) *Requesting a Waiver.* An individual, corporation, or association that is subject to service under Rule 4(e), (f), or (h) has a duty to avoid unnecessary expenses of serving the summons. The plaintiff may notify such a defendant that an action has been commenced and request that the defendant waive service of a summons. The notice and request must:

   (A) be in writing and be addressed:

      (i) to the individual defendant; or

      (ii) for a defendant subject to service under Rule 4(h), to an officer, a managing or general agent, or any other agent authorized by appointment or by law to receive service of process;

   (B) name the court where the complaint was filed;

   (C) be accompanied by a copy of the complaint, two copies of a waiver form, and a prepaid means for returning the form;

   (D) inform the defendant, using text prescribed in Form 5, of the consequences of waiving and not waiving service;

   (E) state the date when the request is sent;

   (F) give the defendant a reasonable time of at least 30 days after the request was sent—or at least 60 days if sent to the defendant outside any judicial district of the United States—to return the waiver; and

   (G) be sent by first-class mail or other reliable means.

(2) *Failure to Waive.* If a defendant located within the United States fails, without good cause, to sign and return a waiver requested by a plaintiff located within the United States, the court must impose on the defendant:

      (A) the expenses later incurred in making service; and

      (B) the reasonable expenses, including attorney's fees, of any motion required to collect those service expenses.

    (3) *Time to Answer After a Waiver.* A defendant who, before being served with process, timely returns a waiver need not serve an answer to the complaint until 60 days after the request was sent—or until 90 days after it was sent to the defendant outside any judicial district of the United States.

    (4) *Results of Filing a Waiver.* When the plaintiff files a waiver, proof of service is not required and these rules apply as if a summons and complaint had been served at the time of filing the waiver.

    (5) *Jurisdiction and Venue Not Waived.* Waiving service of a summons does not waive any objection to personal jurisdiction or to venue.

(e) Serving an Individual Within a Judicial District of the United States. Unless federal law provides otherwise, an individual—other than a minor, an incompetent person, or a person whose waiver has been filed—may be served in a judicial district of the United States by:

    (1) following state law for serving a summons in an action brought in courts of general jurisdiction in the state where the district court is located or where service is made; or

    (2) doing any of the following:

      (A) delivering a copy of the summons and of the complaint to the individual personally;

      (B) leaving a copy of each at the individual's dwelling or usual place of abode with someone of suitable age and discretion who resides there; or

      (C) delivering a copy of each to an agent authorized by appointment or by law to receive service of process.

(f) Serving an Individual in a Foreign Country. Unless federal law provides otherwise, an individual—other than a minor, an incompetent person, or a person whose waiver has been filed—may be served at a place not within any judicial district of the United States:

(1) by any internationally agreed means of service that is reasonably calculated to give notice, such as those authorized by the Hague Convention on the Service Abroad of Judicial and Extrajudicial Documents;

(2) if there is no internationally agreed means, or if an international agreement allows but does not specify other means, by a method that is reasonably calculated to give notice:

    (A) as prescribed by the foreign country's law for service in that country in an action in its courts of general jurisdiction;

    (B) as the foreign authority directs in response to a letter rogatory or letter of request; or

    (C) unless prohibited by the foreign country's law, by:

        (i) delivering a copy of the summons and of the complaint to the individual personally; or

        (ii) using any form of mail that the clerk addresses and sends to the individual and that requires a signed receipt; or

(3) by other means not prohibited by international agreement, as the court orders.

(g) Serving a Minor or an Incompetent Person. A minor or an incompetent person in a judicial district of the United States must be served by following state law for serving a summons or like process on such a defendant in an action brought in the courts of general jurisdiction of the state where service is made. A minor or an incompetent person who is not within any judicial district of the United States must be served in the manner prescribed by Rule 4(f)(2)(A), (f)(2)(B), or (f)(3).

(h) Serving a Corporation, Partnership, or Association. Unless federal law provides otherwise or the defendant's waiver has been filed, a domestic or foreign corporation, or a partnership or other unincorporated association that is subject to suit under a common name, must be served:

(1) in a judicial district of the United States:

  (A) in the manner prescribed by Rule 4(e)(1) for serving an individual; or

  (B) by delivering a copy of the summons and of the complaint to an officer, a managing or general agent, or any other agent authorized by appointment or by law to receive service of process and—if the agent is one authorized by statute and the statute so requires—by also mailing a copy of each to the defendant; or

 (2) at a place not within any judicial district of the United States, in any manner prescribed by Rule 4(f) for serving an individual, except personal delivery under (f)(2)(C)(i).

(i) Serving the United States and Its Agencies, Corporations, Officers, or Employees.

 (1) *United States.* To serve the United States, a party must:

  (A)(i) deliver a copy of the summons and of the complaint to the United States attorney for the district where the action is brought—or to an assistant United States attorney or clerical employee whom the United States attorney designates in a writing filed with the court clerk—or

  (ii) send a copy of each by registered or certified mail to the civil-process clerk at the United States attorney's office;

  (B) send a copy of each by registered or certified mail to the Attorney General of the United States at Washington, D.C.; and

  (C) if the action challenges an order of a nonparty agency or officer of the United States, send a copy of each by registered or certified mail to the agency or officer.

 (2) *Agency; Corporation; Officer or Employee Sued in an Official Capacity.* To serve a United States agency or corporation, or a United States officer or employee sued only in an official capacity, a party must serve the United States and also send a copy of the summons and of the complaint by registered or certified mail to the agency, corporation, officer, or employee.

(3) *Officer or Employee Sued Individually.* To serve a United States officer or employee sued in an individual capacity for an act or omission occurring in connection with duties performed on the United States' behalf (whether or not the officer or employee is also sued in an official capacity), a party must serve the United States and also serve the officer or employee under Rule 4(e), (f), or (g).

(4) *Extending Time.* The court must allow a party a reasonable time to cure its failure to:

(A) serve a person required to be served under Rule 4(i)(2), if the party has served either the United States attorney or the Attorney General of the United States; or

(B) serve the United States under Rule 4(i)(3), if the party has served the United States officer or employee.

(j) Serving a Foreign, State, or Local Government.

(1) *Foreign State.* A foreign state or its political subdivision, agency, or instrumentality must be served in accordance with 28 U.S.C. § 1608.

(2) *State or Local Government.* A state, a municipal corporation, or any other state-created governmental organization that is subject to suit must be served by:

(A) delivering a copy of the summons and of the complaint to its chief executive officer; or

(B) serving a copy of each in the manner prescribed by that state's law for serving a summons or like process on such a defendant.

(k) Territorial Limits of Effective Service.

(1) *In General.* Serving a summons or filing a waiver of service establishes personal jurisdiction over a defendant:

(A) who is subject to the jurisdiction of a court of general jurisdiction in the state where the district court is located;

(B) who is a party joined under Rule 14 or 19 and is served within a judicial district of the United

States and not more than 100 miles from where the summons was issued;

(C) when authorized by a federal statute.

(2) *Federal Claim Outside State–Court Jurisdiction.* For a claim that arises under federal law, serving a summons or filing a waiver of service establishes personal jurisdiction over a defendant if:

(A) the defendant is not subject to jurisdiction in any state's courts of general jurisdiction; and

(B) exercising jurisdiction is consistent with the United States Constitution and laws.

(*l*) Proving Service.

(1) *Affidavit Required.* Unless service is waived, proof of service must be made to the court. Except for service by a United States marshal or deputy marshal, proof must be by the server's affidavit.

(2) *Service Outside the United States.* Service not within any judicial district of the United States must be proved as follows:

(A) if made under Rule 4(f)(1), as provided in the applicable treaty or convention; or

(B) if made under Rule 4(f)(2) or (f)(3), by a receipt signed by the addressee, or by other evidence satisfying the court that the summons and complaint were delivered to the addressee.

(3) *Validity of Service; Amending Proof.* Failure to prove service does not affect the validity of service. The court may permit proof of service to be amended.

(m) Time Limit for Service. If a defendant is not served within 120 days after the complaint is filed, the court— on motion or on its own after notice to the plaintiff— must dismiss the action without prejudice against that defendant or order that service be made within a specified time. But if the plaintiff shows good cause for the failure, the court must extend the time for service for an appropriate period. This subdivision (m) does not apply to service in a foreign country under Rule 4(f) or 4(j)(1).

(n) Asserting Jurisdiction over Property or Assets.

(1) *Federal Law.* The court may assert jurisdiction over property if authorized by a federal statute. Notice to claimants of the property must be given as provided in the statute or by serving a summons under this rule.

(2) *State Law.* On a showing that personal jurisdiction over a defendant cannot be obtained in the district where the action is brought by reasonable efforts to serve a summons under this rule, the court may assert jurisdiction over the defendant's assets found in the district. Jurisdiction is acquired by seizing the assets under the circumstances and in the manner provided by state law in that district.

[Amended January 21, 1963, effective July 1, 1963; February 28, 1966, effective July 1, 1966; April 29, 1980, effective August 1, 1980; amended by Pub.L. 97-462, § 2, January 12, 1983, 96 Stat. 2527, effective 45 days after January 12, 1983; amended March 2, 1987, effective August 1, 1987; April 22, 1993, effective December 1, 1993; April 17, 2000, effective December 1, 2000; April 30, 2007, effective December 1, 2007.]

──────────── **2007 AMENDMENTS ROADMAP** ────────────

STYLE PROJECT CHANGES: New orienting labels were added, and although all principal Rule parts retained their original numbering, most parts were further subsectioned. Within subsections, material was repositioned to group like topics together. Active voice generally replaced passive voice; "must" replaced "shall"; "minor" replaced "infant"; and "made by" replaced "effected by".

NON-STYLE CHANGES: Three changes: (1) an inadvertent Rule 4(d) waiver error was corrected (two copies of "waiver form", not notice form, must be sent); (2) a misleading reference to "plaintiff" in Rule 4(i) was corrected to "party"; and (3) a redundant reference to the federal interpleader statute in Rule 4(k)(1)(C) was deleted in view of Rule 4(k)(1)(D)'s already broad inclusion of all federal statutes (with that deletion, Rule 4(k)(1)(D) was renumbered to 4(k)(1)(C)).

NOTE: The Federal Rules "Style Project" is explained in Part III-A.

AUTHORS' COMMENTARY ON RULE 4

──────────── PURPOSE AND SCOPE ────────────

Rule 4 sets forth the procedure for notifying defendants that a federal civil lawsuit has been filed against them. This procedure requires that the defendants be served with "original process"—a copy of a summons and complaint. Rule 4 does *not* address whether a defendant is amenable to jurisdiction within the particular judicial district, or whether service on a defendant is consistent with the Due Process Clause of the United States Constitution. Instead, Rule 4 simply sets forth the procedure for serving the summons and complaint, *assuming* the defendant can be served properly and constitutionally.

GOAL OF RULE 4

The central function of service of process under Rule 4 is to provide notice that a legal action has been filed, and to provide this notice in such a manner and at such a time that the defending party will have a fair opportunity to answer the pleading and raise defenses and objections.[1] Service and the provisions of Rule 4 are distinct from the question of the court's jurisdiction either to entertain the subject matter of the dispute or to render a judgment against a particular person or entity.[2]

"Actual Notice" Alone Is *Not* Enough: Although one of the goals of service of process is to make the defendants aware that a lawsuit has been filed against them, simply demonstrating that the defendant has received actual notice of the lawsuit is not enough— Rule 4's formal requirements for proper service must also be satisfied.[3]

DISTINCTIONS BETWEEN SERVICE, JURISDICTION, AND VENUE

Rule 4 does not determine whether the district court enjoys subject matter jurisdiction. It also does not resolve whether a defendant has the requisite contacts with the forum to justify personal jurisdiction there. These questions must be addressed and resolved before the lawsuit is filed, and before Rule 4 is consulted in determining how to serve process. These topics are discussed in greater detail in Part II of this text (General Concepts In Federal Practice). A brief summary of these topics follows.

Subject Matter Jurisdiction. Federal courts are courts of limited jurisdiction. The district courts are authorized to hear disputes over "federal questions," such as those involving federal laws or the

---

1. *See Henderson v. United States*, 517 U.S. 654, 672, 116 S.Ct. 1638, 1648, 134 L.Ed.2d 880 (1996).

2. *See Henderson v. United States*, 517 U.S. 654, 670, 116 S.Ct. 1638, 1647, 134 L.Ed.2d 880 (1996).

3. *See Albra v. Advan, Inc.*, 490 F.3d 826, 828 (11th Cir. 2007); *Bridgeport Music, Inc. v. Rhyme Syndicate Music*, 376 F.3d 615, 623 (6th Cir.2004); *McMasters v. United States*, 260 F.3d 814, 817–18 (7th Cir. 2001); *Ayres v. Jacobs & Crumplar, P.A.*, 99 F.3d 565, 567–68 (3d Cir.1996). *See also Prewitt Enters. v. Organization of Petro-*

leum Exporting Countries, 353 F.3d 916, 924 n.14 (11th Cir.2003) (noting that although "receipt of actual notice is an important factor in considering whether service of process is adequate ... actual notice alone ... [is] not enough to allow the court personal jurisdiction over the defendant"). *But cf. Direct Mail Specialists, Inc. v. Eclat Computerized Techs.*, 840 F.2d 685, 688 (9th Cir.1988) (commenting that Rule 4 is "flexible" and "should be liberally construed" when plaintiff receives "sufficient notice" of the complaint).

United States Constitution, admiralty, bankruptcy, patents, copyrights, and postal matters. *See* 28 U.S.C.A. §§ 1331, 1333–67. The district courts may also hear "diversity jurisdiction" disputes: where the amount in controversy—exclusive of interest and costs—exceeds $75,000, and the dispute is between citizens of different States, or between American citizens and foreign nationals or a foreign country. *See* 28 U.S.C.A. § 1332. In those instances where a district court possesses federal subject matter jurisdiction over certain claims, the trial court is entitled to exercise its "supplemental jurisdiction" over other claims that, although not federal question or diversity claims, are nevertheless so related to the existing claims that they form part of the same Article III case or controversy. *See* 28 U.S.C. § 1367. The federal courts' subject matter jurisdiction is discussed in more detail in Part II of this text, §§ 2.10–2.13.

Personal Jurisdiction. Like all courts, federal courts may exercise personal (or "in personam") jurisdiction over a defendant only when the defendant is amenable to suit and when the Constitution's Due Process Clause permits the lawsuit to go forward. Amenability to suit is determined by State statute in diversity cases and by either federal or State statute in federal question cases. In addition, the constitutional Due Process limitations require that "traditional notions of fair play and substantial justice" not be offended by forcing the defendant to travel to the plaintiff's chosen forum and defend a lawsuit there.[4] Of necessity, this assessment is made on the basis of the particular facts in an individual case. The federal courts alternatively may exercise "in rem" or "quasi in rem" jurisdiction over a defendant's property when permitted by State law and the Due Process Clause. The federal courts' personal, in rem, and quasi in rem jurisdiction is discussed in more detail in Part II of this text, §§ 2.2–2.9.

Venue. Finally, a particular district court may hear a lawsuit only if "venue" is proper—where the judicial district is a logical, convenient site to decide the dispute. *See* 28 U.S.C.A. §§ 1391–1412. Federal statutes control what constitutes proper venue in a particular case. The proper venue in the federal courts is discussed in more detail in Part II of this text, § 2.14.

Summary. Each of these three characteristics—subject matter jurisdiction, personal jurisdiction, and venue—must be present before a defendant can be served properly with a summons and complaint. The practitioner must remember that Rule 4 does *not* address whether these three characteristics are present, but only guides the procedural means for serving process. Service (or waiver of service) is, however, a prerequisite to the district court's exercise of personal jurisdiction over any defendant.[5]

---

4. *See International Shoe Co. v. Washington,* 326 U.S. 310, 316, 66 S.Ct. 154, 158, 90 L.Ed. 95 (1945).

5. *See Omni Capital Int'l v. Rudolf Wolff & Co.,* 484 U.S. 97, 103, 108 S.Ct. 404, 409, 98 L.Ed.2d 415 (1987).

IMMUNITY FROM SERVICE OF PROCESS

In certain circumstances, a defendant who might otherwise be properly served with a summons and complaint may be deemed to be "immune" from service. Immunity from service is governed by federal case law, and exists where the due administration of justice demands it.[6] Whether to confer the immunity is vested in the discretion of the district court; the purpose of the immunity is *not* primarily to protect the defendant seeking to avoid service, but instead to aid the court in its judicial administration.[7] The courts have held that persons are generally immune from service when they are present in the jurisdiction to attend court, give a deposition, or conduct settlement discussions in connection with another, unrelated lawsuit, or when they enter the jurisdiction to participate in a legislative or administrative hearing process.[8] This immunity generally encompasses not only the time when the person is actually present in court or attending other formal proceedings, but also typically extends for a reasonable period before and after the proceedings to allow the person to enter and then freely leave the jurisdiction.[9]

Persons may also be immune from service when they are lured by fraud or trickery into the jurisdiction by the plaintiff who then attempts to serve them with a summons and complaint.[10] Indeed, some courts have even adopted a bright line rule for in-State negotiations: these courts hold that when a plaintiff invites a defendant to enter the foreign jurisdiction for settlement discussions, the plaintiff may not, during those discussions, serve the defendant with process unless the defendant is either cautioned that she may be served while present or, after having entered the jurisdiction, she is first given an opportunity to depart immediately after the discussions fail.[11]

This immunity, however, can be waived. A defendant who fails to timely assert immunity may be deemed to have waived it.[12] Likewise, a defendant who is immune for the purposes of attending court or a deposition may waive the immunity by arriving in the jurisdiction prematurely, by conducting other business while in the

---

6. *See Stewart v. Ramsay,* 242 U.S. 128, 37 S.Ct. 44, 61 L.Ed. 192 (1916). *See also ARW Exploration Corp. v. Aguirre,* 45 F.3d 1455 (10th Cir.1995)(noting that immunity from service is a procedural, not substantive, rule, and *Erie* concerns do not dictate that State law apply).

7. *See Northern Light Tech., Inc. v. Northern Lights Club,* 236 F.3d 57, 62 (1st Cir.2001); *Estate of Ungar v. Palestinian Auth.,* 396 F.Supp.2d 376, 381 (S.D.N.Y. 2005).

8. *See Lamb v. Schmitt,* 285 U.S. 222, 52 S.Ct. 317, 76 L.Ed. 720 (1932); *Page Co.*

v. Macdonald, 261 U.S. 446, 43 S.Ct. 416, 67 L.Ed. 737 (1923).

9. *See Cabiri v. Assasie–Gyimah,* 921 F.Supp. 1189, 1193 (S.D.N.Y.1996).

10. *See May Dep't Stores v. Wilansky,* 900 F.Supp. 1154, 1163–64 (E.D.Mo.1995); *Henkel Corp. v. Degremont, S.A.,* 136 F.R.D. 88, 91 (E.D.Pa.1991).

11. *See May Dep't Stores v. Wilansky,* 900 F.Supp. 1154, 1164–65 (E.D.Mo.1995) (collecting cases).

12. *See Republic Prods., Inc. v. American Fed'n of Musicians of U.S. & Canada,* 173 F.Supp. 330 (S.D.N.Y.1959).

jurisdiction, or by failing to leave the jurisdiction promptly.[13] One ruling has even suggested that a defendant–already named and served with process–might not enjoy immunity if he enters the forum to attend proceedings in his case as a "spectator" (and was not required to appear).[14] In addition, this service immunity may not apply where the defendant is served with process in conjunction with the same case, or a case arising out of or involving the same subject matter, as the one in which the defendant is present in the forum attending at the time of service.[15]

CASES REMOVED TO FEDERAL COURT

Once a case has been removed from State court to federal court, service of process can be completed (or, if defective, new process can issue) as though the lawsuit had been filed originally in federal court.[16] Prior to removal, the applicable State laws will typically govern the propriety of service and process; following removal, the federal Rules will govern.[17]

SERVICE "OTHERWISE PROVIDED BY FEDERAL LAW"

Congress has, on occasion, accompanied its lawmaking with specific service of process provisions. When such particular service means are, in that way, "otherwise provided by federal law", service of process on individuals, corporations, associations, and other non-governmental entities can ordinarily be accomplished by effecting service in accordance with the specific statutory directive.[18]

- *Multiparty, Multiforum Jurisdiction Statute:* Where federal jurisdiction is based, in whole or in part, upon the federal multiparty, multijurisdictional statute,[19] service can be made

13. *See Uniroyal, Inc. v. Sperberg*, 63 F.R.D. 55 (S.D.N.Y.1973) (applying the "dual purpose rule", which forfeits service immunity when a person, present in a foreign jurisdiction for the purpose of the administration of justice, engages in unrelated business dealings or social activity while present in the foreign jurisdiction). *Cf. Fun–Damental Too, Ltd. v. Hwung*, 1997 WL 289712, at *2–*3 (S.D.N.Y.1997) (immunity not waived where nonresident defendant traveled to the forum for a deposition and, on the night before his deposition, visited a showroom for one hour and had dinner; such activities were "trivial and insubstantial").

14. *See Northern Light Tech., Inc. v. Northern Lights Club*, 236 F.3d 57, 63 (1st Cir.2001)

15. *See ARW Exploration Corp. v. Aguirre*, 45 F.3d 1455 (10th Cir.1995); *Sullivan v. Sullivan*, 2003 WL 22218166, at *1 (D.Conn.2003); *Cabiri v. Assasie–Gyimah*,

921 F.Supp. 1189 (S.D.N.Y.1996); *In re Aluminum Phosphide Antitrust Litig.*, 160 F.R.D. 629 (D.Kan.1995).

16. *See* 28 U.S.C.A. § 1448.

17. *See Norsyn, Inc. v. Desai*, 351 F.3d 825, 829 n.4 (8th Cir.2003) (federal service rules apply only when attempted service is accomplished after removal; before that, State rules apply).

18. *See* Rule 4(e) (permitting service on individuals within the United States in accordance with means "otherwise provided by federal law"); Rule 4(f) (same, for individuals in a foreign country); Rule 4(h) (same, for corporations and associations). *But see* Rule 4(g) (service on infants and incompetents contains no such "otherwise provided by federal law" provision); Rule 4(i) (same, for United States, its agencies, corporations, officers, or employees); Rule 4(j) (same, for foreign, state, or local governments).

19. *See* 28 U.S.C.A. § 1369.

at any place within the United States or, if otherwise permitted by law, anywhere outside the United States.[20]

SERVING AMENDED COMPLAINTS

Generally, amended complaints are served under Rule 5, and the rigors of proper Rule 4 service are not implicated.[21] However, Rule 4 service could nevertheless still be required for the amended complaint if the claims contained there differ significantly from those in the original pleading, if circumstances persuade the court that Rule 5 service on the attorney is unlikely to ensure notice to the party, if extraterritorial service was made originally and the amendment contains claims unrelated to the original dispute, or if the precepts of Due Process otherwise require it.[22]

BURDEN OF PROOF

The party attempting service generally bears the burden of establishing that the service is proper.[23] This burden may shift, however, if the opposing party does not promptly move to challenge the purported service. If a default judgment is entered against such a party, that party may bear the burden of proving that the purported service was defective.[24]

RULE 4(a).   CONTENTS OF AND AMENDING SUMMONS

CORE CONCEPT

The form of a federal summons is the same in all federal cases. The earlier practice of permitting the use of State forms of summons has been abandoned. A standardized federal summons form has been approved by the United States Supreme Court.[25] The summons must:

- *Issue from the Clerk:* The summons must be issued by the clerk of court, and must bear the court's seal and the clerk's signature.

- *Identify the Case:* The summons must also identify the district court, name the parties to the lawsuit, and list the name and address of plaintiff or plaintiff's attorney.

- *Directed to the Defendant:* The summons must be directed specifically to the defendant.

---

20. See 28 U.S.C.A. § 1697.

21. See Employee Painters' Trust v. Ethan Enters., Inc., 480 F.3d 993, 999 (9th Cir. 2007); Mach v. Florida Casino Cruise, Inc., 187 F.R.D. 15, 17 (D.Mass.1999).

22. See Employee Painters' Trust v. Ethan Enters., Inc., 480 F.3d 993, 999 (9th Cir. 2007); Beckham v. Grand Affair of North Carolina, Inc., 671 F.Supp. 415, 418 (W.D.N.C.1987). See also Authors' Commentary to Rule 5(b) ("**New Claims Against Existing Parties**").

23. See Grand Entm't Group, Ltd. v. Star Media Sales, Inc., 988 F.2d 476, 488 (3d Cir.1993); Aetna Bus. Credit, Inc. v. Universal Decor & Interior Design, Inc., 635 F.2d 434, 435 (5th Cir.1981); Commer v. McEntee, 283 F.Supp.2d 993, 997 (S.D.N.Y. 2003).

24. See Burda Media, Inc. v. Viertel, 417 F.3d 292, 299 (2d Cir.2005).

25. See Form 1 ("Summons"), included with the Appendix of Forms as reprinted in this text.

- *Time to Appear:* The summons must state the time within which the defendant must appear and defend.

- *Warn Against Default:* The summons must caution the defendant that a failure to appear and defend will result in the entry of a default judgment for the relief requested in the complaint.

APPLICATIONS

Purpose of Summons

The purpose of the summons is to alert the defendant that a lawsuit is pending against him and that he has a limited time in which to respond. The summons is not required to advise the defendant of every conceivable response he could make to the lawsuit.[26]

Form of Summons Liberally Examined

If the summons omits one of the requirements for proper form, but otherwise generally complies with the Rule's requirements, the court may choose not to dismiss the lawsuit but instead may permit an amendment to the summons or grant some other cure. For example, a summons that is properly "directed" to the defendant, but prints a wrong address, will generally not prompt the court to dismiss the lawsuit for this mistake.[27] Similar inconsequential failings may be ignored as well.[28] Where the summons more fundamentally fails to comply with the Rule, the court may enter a dismissal.[29]

RULE 4(b). ISSUANCE OF SUMMONS

CORE CONCEPT

26. *See Frye v. Bowman, Heintz, Boscia, Vician, P.C.,* 193 F.Supp.2d 1070, 1080 (S.D.Ind.2002) (noting the "inherent difficulties in attempting to provide all potentially helpful information in a summons", the court wrote that it "would hardly seem practical to attach to a summons a copy of the Federal Rules of Civil Procedure and portions of the United States Code").

27. *See Spiess v. Meyers,* 483 F. Supp. 2d 1082, 1093 (D. Kan. 2007); *Sullivan v. Potter,* 2006 WL 785289, at *2 (D.D.C. 2006).

28. *Wortham v. American Family Ins. Co.,* 2002 WL 31128057, at *2–3 (N.D. Iowa 2002) (dismissal denied, and leave to amend summons granted, where only one defendant's name appeared on summons, although other defendants were clearly identified in caption of both summons and complaint); *George W. v. United States Dep't of Educ.,* 149 F.Supp.2d 1195, 1200–02 (E.D.Cal.2000) (noting that Rule 4 is "flexible" and "should be liberally con-

strued so long as a party receives sufficient notice of the complaint"); *GMAC Mortg. Corp. v. Weisman,* 1997 WL 83416, at *2 (S.D.N.Y.1997) (although summons failed to state the time for response, because defendant did not immediately object to the defect and even reached stipulation on time for response, court would not dismiss the complaint). *But see Sene v. MBNA America, Inc.,* 2005 WL 2304181 (D.Del.2005) (summons contained neither seal of court nor signature of clerk, and court dismissed lawsuit).

29. *See Wasson v. Riverside County,* 237 F.R.D. 423 (C.D.Cal.2006) (quashing service on party not named in complaint and for whom no summons was issued by the Clerk); *Schroeder v. Kochanowski,* 311 F.Supp.2d 1241, 1256 (D.Kan.2004) (dismissal granted where served summons was copy, lacking court seal, and omitted plaintiff's name and address).

191

Once the complaint is filed, the plaintiff is responsible for preparing the summons in an appropriate form, and submitting it to the clerk of court for signing and sealing. If the plaintiff's summons is proper, the clerk will sign and seal the form, and issue it to the plaintiff for service. Copies of the summons must be issued for each defendant.

APPLICATIONS

Form of Summons Liberally Examined

Courts liberally construe the issuance requirements of Rule 4(b). If the summons is sufficiently accurate to provide proper notice, and any alleged defect in form has not prejudiced the defendant, a defect in the form of summons as issued will be discounted as harmless and the plaintiff will be afforded an opportunity to amend the summons to cure the error.[30]

Photocopies of Summons in Multi–Defendant Cases

An original summons–containing a raised seal-of-the-court and a pen-signed signature of the clerk–may not be necessary in cases involving multiple defendants. In such cases, copies of the original summons (that bear the name of the served defendant) may be used.[31]

RULE 4(c).   SERVICE

CORE CONCEPT

A summons and complaint are served together. The plaintiff is responsible for effective service. A U.S. Marshal will serve process only if ordered to do so by the court.

APPLICATIONS

Both Summons and Complaint Must Be Served

In order for Rule 4 service to be proper, *both* the summons and complaint must be served. Neglecting either one entitles the defendant to a dismissal for improper service.[32]

Plaintiff Selects the Process Server

Except in certain cases, such as those involving pauper plaintiffs or seamen plaintiffs, the plaintiff generally is responsible for selecting an appropriate person to serve all defendants with copies of the summons and complaint. Typically, the plaintiff appoints a commercial process server who accomplishes the service task for a fee.[33]

---

30. *See Time Prods. v. J. Tiras Classic Handbags, Inc.*, 1994 WL 363930 (S.D.N.Y. 1994).

31. *See New York Transp., Inc. v. Naples Transp., Inc.*, 116 F.Supp.2d 382, 386 (E.D.N.Y.2000).

32. *See Albra v. Advan, Inc.*, 490 F.3d 826, 828 (11th Cir. 2007).

33. *See Byrd v. Stone*, 94 F.3d 217, 219 (6th Cir.1996).

Service by Adult Non–Party

Any person over the age of 18 who is not a party to the lawsuit may serve original process. Because they are "parties" to the lawsuit, plaintiffs may not serve process themselves.[34] This bar against permitting a party to serve original process applies to service by certified mail (in those instances where such service is permitted). If the party herself mails her own certified letter, the service is improper.[35] However, the attorneys for a party may serve process for their clients, although such service is not the "most preferable method".[36]

Service by Commercial Overnight Courier Service

It remains an unresolved question whether original process can be served "personally", at a dwelling house, or otherwise when delivered via a commercial overnight courier service (such as FedEx, UPS, DHL, or the like).[37]

Service by U.S. Marshal or Others Specially Appointed

The court, upon a plaintiff's request, may direct that the United States Marshal or some other specially-appointed person serve process. Such court-appointed service is required, however, in the cases of pauper plaintiffs[38] or seamen plaintiffs.[39] If such an appointment is made, and as long as the plaintiff was entitled to Marshal service in the first instance, and cooperated with the Marshal in accomplishing service, the plaintiff is permitted to rely on the Marshal to complete service.[40]

Service Must Occur *After* the Complaint is Filed

Service is not effective unless the complaint that is served has first been filed with the court. Thus, the practice of informally presenting an adversary with a copy of a complaint before it is filed

---

34. *See Walker v. University of Colorado Bd. of Regents*, 139 F.3d 913 (10th Cir. 1998) (Table; text available on Westlaw at 1998 WL 67321, at **1) (although disfavored, the Tenth Circuit permits this opinion to be cited if it has persuasive value on a material issue and copies are supplied to the court) (holding that plaintiff's attempt to effect service of process himself was not effective); *Boltes v. Entex*, 158 F.R.D. 110 (S.D.Tex.1994)(commenting that plaintiff, as a party, is expressly prohibited from serving process upon a defendant).

35. *See Stinecipher v. United States*, 239 F.R.D. 282, 283 (D.D.C. 2006); *Speelman v. United States*, 461 F.Supp.2d 71, 73–74 (D.D.C. 2006); *Smith v. United States*, 475 F.Supp.2d 1, 9 (D.D.C. 2006) (collecting cases).

36. *See Trustees of Local Union No. 727 Pension Fund v. Perfect Parking, Inc.*, 126 F.R.D. 48, 51–52 (N.D.Ill. 1989). *Accord C.F.T.C. v. American Metal Exchange Corp.*,

693 F.Supp. 168, 186 (D.N.J.1988); *Jugolinija v. Blue Heaven Mills*, 115 F.R.D. 13, 15 (S.D.Ga.1986).

37. *See Cambridge Holdings Group, Inc. v. Federal Ins. Co.*, 489 F.3d 1356, 1362 (D.C.Cir. 2007) (noting, but failing to rule upon this "novel and unlikely theory").

38. 28 U.S.C.A. § 1915(c). *See Lindsey v. United States R.R. Ret. Bd.*, 101 F.3d 444, 447–48 (5th Cir.1996); *Byrd v. Stone*, 94 F.3d 217, 219 (6th Cir.1996).

39. 28 U.S.C.A. § 1916.

40. *See Olsen v. Mapes*, 333 F.3d 1199, 1204–05 (10th Cir.2003) (finding that plaintiffs were not culpable for failing to comply with Rules or court orders when they relied on Marshal to complete service); *Thompson v. Maldonado*, 309 F.3d 107, 109 n.2 (2d Cir.2002) (noting that *in forma pauperis* plaintiffs may use Marshals to effect service).

with the clerk of court will not satisfy the requirements for service of process under Rule 4.[41]

RULE 4(d).   WAIVING SERVICE

CORE CONCEPT

A defendant is duty-bound to avoid the unnecessary costs of formal personal service of process, or risk being taxed with the costs of service and associated attorney's fees. The waiver-of-service procedure enforces this duty.

APPLICATIONS

Precaution In Citing Earlier Cases

Prior to 1993, Rule 4 permitted "service by mail" in limited circumstances. In 1993, this "service by mail" provision was replaced with the current waiver-of-service procedure of Rule 4(d). Case authority under the former service-by-mail procedure cautioned against construing the mail service Rule in so literal a manner that it could promote "sandbagging" or "blindsiding" an opponent into overlooking or misinterpreting the type of service of process that was being attempted.[42]   The current waiver-of-service provision, with its prerequisite of a formal and executed acknowledgment form, is designed to cure the risks inherent in practice under the former Rule.

Constitutionality

The constitutionality of the waiver-of-service rule has been addressed in only one case, and only cursorily. Due to the unique circumstances in that case, the Court there chose not to include a full discussion of its reasoning for rejecting the constitutional challenge.[43]

Certain Defendants Exempt From Rule

By its terms, the waiver-of-service procedure applies only to individuals, corporations, or associations served under Rule 4(e), (f), or (h). Accordingly, the procedure is not available for serving: (1) the United States as defendant;[44] (2) agencies, corporations, or

---

41. *See J.O. Alvarez, Inc. v. Rainbow Textiles, Inc.,* 168 F.R.D. 201 (S.D.Tex. 1996) (default judgment not proper against defendants who failed to answer a complaint that was served before it was filed; defendants' actual or constructive notice of lawsuit does not satisfy the Rule 4 service requirements).

42. *See Carimi v. Royal Carribean Cruise Line, Inc.,* 959 F.2d 1344,1348 (5th Cir.1992) (commenting that service-by-mail provisions were intended to provide a convenient way to eliminate the costly and time consuming traditional methods of ser-

vice, but "being a less dependable and less formal alternative to conventional service and citation, [the old service-by-mail Rule] must be construed strictly as must all rules in derogation of the norm.").

43. *See United States v. Hafner,* 421 F.Supp.2d 1220, 1224 (D.N.D.2006) (rejecting constitutional challenge in case where defendant signed waiver-of-service form, commenting that the challenge was rejected for "obvious reasons").

44. *See Robinson v. Turner,* 886 F.Supp. 1460, 1465 n. 5 (S.D.Ind.1995)(commenting that unreliability caused United States and

officers[45] of the United States as defendants; (3) other governments and government-related entities as defendants;[46] (4) minors as defendants; and (5) incompetent persons as defendants.[47] Note, however, that although federal workers are exempt from the waiver-of-service provisions when sued in their official capacities, they are *not* exempt when sued as individuals.[48]

Applies to Defendants Outside the United States, But Without Penalties

Although Rule 4 generally emphasizes a strong preference for proceeding under international service treaty agreements (such as the Hague Service Convention), the waiver-of-service procedure is intended to permit waiver of service by foreign (non-governmental) defendants because of the cost savings to both plaintiff and defendant.[49]

Note, however, that the penalties for refusing to waive formal service of process do *not* apply to foreign defendants.[50]

Venue and Jurisdiction Defenses Preserved

A defendant who waives formal service of process does not lose the right to contest venue and jurisdiction.[51] The defendant does, however, waive any objection to service and to the form of process.

Plaintiff's Option

A plaintiff is not required to seek a waiver of service. The plaintiff may choose to seek a waiver, or instead immediately pro-

its facilities to be exempted from Rule 4(d) waiver provisions).

45. *See Emuchay v. Catron*, 2000 WL 303223, at *2 (D.Conn.2000) (confirming that Rule does not authorize waiver of service in lawsuits against federal employees sued in their official capacities).

46. *See Lepone-Dempsey v. Carroll County Comm'rs*, 476 F.3d 1277, 1281 (11th Cir. 2007) (not applicable to local governments); *Chapman v. New York State Div. for Youth*, 227 F.R.D. 175, 180 (N.D.N.Y. 2005) (not applicable to State, State agency, or State official); *Mosley v. Douglas County Correctional Ctr.*, 192 F.R.D. 282, 283 (D.Neb.2000) (not applicable to municipal corporations, thus District of Columbia not subject to the procedure).

47. *See* Rule 4(d)(1).

48. *See Mosley v. Douglas County Correctional Ctr.*, 192 F.R.D. 282, 283 (D.Neb. 2000). *See also* Rule 4(i)(3) (noting that federal officers and employees sued in their individual capacity are served in the manners prescribed by Rule 4(e), (f), or (g)). *See also* Rule 4(i)(2) advisory committee notes to 2000 amendments ("Invocation of the

individual service provisions of subdivisions (e), (f), and (g) invokes also the waiver-of-service provisions of subdivision (d)").

49. *See* Rule 4(d) advisory committee rule (noting specifically the cost-saving nature of the waiver procedure for defendants who otherwise would be served under an international service of process convention, which costs might include "the sometimes substantial expense of translation that may be wholly unnecessary for defendants fluent in English").

50. *See* Rule 4(d)(2). *See also Quilling v. Shaw*, 2001 WL 611147, at *1 (N.D. Tex. 2001) (cost provisions of Rule 4(d) do not apply to defendants located outside United States). Note that at least one district court has rejected the argument that a foreign defendant should be considered "located" in the United States within the meaning of Rule 4(d) when that defendant has such significant contacts with the forum that it is susceptible to personal jurisdiction in the United States. *See Hoffman–La Roche, Inc. v. Invamed, Inc.*, 183 F.R.D. 157 (D.N.J. 1998).

51. *See* Rule 4(d)(5).

ceed to traditional formal service of process.[52]

Incentives for Waiving

By agreeing to waive formal service of process, a defendant's time for responding to the complaint is tripled—from 20 days (following personal service) to 60 days (following request for waiver).[53] For defendants who are addressed outside the United States, the extension is even longer: a defendant addressed outside the United States who agrees to waive formal service has 90 days to respond to the complaint.[54]

Consequences of Not Waiving

The Rule 4(d) waiver provision does *not* discharge a plaintiff's obligation to complete service of process. If a plaintiff requests waiver, but the defendant ignores the request or otherwise refuses to waive, the plaintiff must then proceed with formal service of process in accordance with Rule 4(e), (f), or (h).[55] However, if the defendant lacks "good cause" for refusing to waive service, the court must tax costs against the defendant.[56] These costs include the expenses incurred in formally serving process on the defendant, as well as a reasonable attorney's fee for any motion practice required to collect those service costs.[57] Before any costs and attorney's fees will be taxed, the prescribed time for the defendant to waive service must first have expired.[58]

> *"Good Cause" Defined:* The Advisory Committee comments that the necessary "good cause" for refusing to waive formal service of process should be rare. This "good cause" test is not satisfied by a belief that the claim is unjust[59] or that the court

---

52. *See Budget Rent A Car Sys. v. Miles,* 2005 WL 1106335, at *3 (S.D.Ohio May 9, 2005).

53. *See* Rule 4(d)(3). One district court extended the 60–day period to 63 days, citing the 3–day addition for mailed service under Rule 6(d), formerly Rule 6(e). *See Petrousky v. Civil Air Patrol, Inc.,* 1998 WL 213726, at *1 (N.D.N.Y.1998).

54. *See* Rule 4(d)(3).

55. *See Cambridge Holdings Group, Inc. v. Federal Ins. Co.,* 489 F.3d 1356 (D.C.Cir. 2007); *Lepone-Dempsey v. Carroll County Com'rs,* 476 F.3d 1277, 1281 (11th Cir. 2007); *O.J. Distrib., Inc. v. Hornell Brewing Co.,* 340 F.3d 345, 354 (6th Cir. 2003).

56. *See Marcello v. Maine,* 238 F.R.D. 113, 115 (D.Me. 2006) (absent good cause, imposition of costs is mandatory); *United States v. Butterfield,* 91 F.Supp.2d 704, 706 (D.Vt.2000) (granting federal government reimbursement of costs); *Mathon v. Marine Midland Bank, N.A.,* 875 F.Supp. 986 (E.D.N.Y.1995)(effect of Rule 4(d) is to shift

cost of service to defendant who refuses to agree to waive formal service).

57. *See* Rule 4(d)(2). *See Graves v. Church of Lord Jesus Christ of Apostalic Faith, Inc.,* 2003 WL 21659168, at *1 (E.D.Pa.2003) (awarding plaintiff costs for process server, courier, and photocopying, and expenses (including reasonable attorney's fee) to collect those costs from defendant); *United States v. First Midwest Bank,* 1995 WL 447762 (N.D.Ill.1995)(awarding service costs and motion preparation fee against defendant who knew of pending lawsuit, but refused to cooperate in facilitating service).

58. *See* Rule 4(d) advisory committee note.

59. *See Marcello v. Maine,* 238 F.R.D. 113, 115–16 (D.Me. 2006) (rejecting as good cause claim that lawsuit was frivolous, motion was premature, and pending motion to dismiss would require cost shift in the other direction); *Morales v. SI Diamond Tech., Inc.,* 1999 WL 144469, at *2 (S.D.N.Y.1999) (defendants' belief that the complaint lacks

lacks jurisdiction, or by counsel's claim that he or she was busy or otherwise preoccupied.[60] However, non-receipt of the waiver request,[61] a failure to otherwise comply with all the prerequisites of Rule 4(d),[62] a good faith belief that, as a matter of law, the waiver-of-service provisions would not apply,[63] an illiteracy in English, or defects in waiver form would likely satisfy the "good cause" test.[64]

Waiver Procedure

The waiver-of-service procedure is triggered when (but only when) a plaintiff formally requests a defendant to waive formal service of process. A failure to meet—literally—each of these prerequisites may result in defective service[65] and/or a refusal by the court to impose the penalties for a refusal to waive service.[66]

merit and desire to increase plaintiff's costs do not constitute "good cause").

60. See D'Agostine v. United Hosp. Supply Corp., 1996 WL 417266, at *5 (E.D.Pa. 1996) (rejecting as "good cause" defendants' counsel's assertion that "he was in the process of relocating his practice and was in the middle of various litigations . . . A busy schedule hardly constitutes good cause for failing to comply with the Federal Rules of Civil Procedure.").

61. See Hy Cite Corp. v. badbusinessbureau.com, L.L.C., 418 F.Supp.2d 1142, 1153–54 (D.Ariz.2005) (no expenses where defendant was never mailed a request for waiver–even if defendant informed plaintiff that the process was futile); Hausmann v. Roscher, 2001 WL 115462, at *2 (E.D.Pa. 2001) (physically absent from residence is "good cause"). But see Double S Truck Line, Inc. v. Frozen Food Exp., 171 F.R.D. 251, 253–54 (D.Minn.1997) (service costs taxed against defendant, notwithstanding defendant's claim that it did not receive sufficient time to respond to waiver form; form had been delivered to defendant's agent but was delayed in reaching defendant because agent lacked defendant's current, accurate address).

62. See McGann v. New York, 77 F.3d 672 (2d Cir.1996) (waiver-of-service procedure not effective where plaintiff failed to include acknowledgment form along with the mailed summons and complaint); Perez v. County of Westchester, 83 F.Supp.2d 435, 441 (S.D.N.Y.2000) (denying reimbursement, where notice and request were not addressed directly to the defendant, were not accompanied by a copy of the complaint, and lacked a prepaid means for compliance in writing); Steinberg v. Quintet Publ'g Ltd., 1999 WL 459809, at *2 (S.D.N.Y.1999)

(assessing no costs because waiver request form defectively failed to name an officer or managing agent of the defendant); Mason Tenders Dist. Council Pension Fund v. Messera, 1997 WL 221200, at *6 (S.D.N.Y. 1997) (no costs taxed where plaintiffs sent acknowledgment form with self-addressed return envelope, but did not stamp the return envelope); Spivey v. Board of Church Extension & Home Mission of Church of God, 160 F.R.D. 660 (M.D.Fla. 1995)(refusing to award costs where waiver form was sent errantly addressed to "Edwin Ross" rather than "R. Edward Ross", and was mailed to corporate defendant generally, rather than addressed to an officer or managing general agent of the corporation).

63. See Mosley v. Douglas County Correctional Ctr., 192 F.R.D. 282, 283 (D.Neb. 2000) (finding good cause for failure to waive service because no legal authority addressed whether employees of a municipal corporation were susceptible to this procedure).

64. See Rule 4(d) advisory committee note.

65. See Larsen v. Mayo Med. Ctr., 218 F.3d 863 (8th Cir.2000) (where Rule 4(d) provisions not complied with strictly, waiver-of-service procedure not complied with and personal service must be obtained); McGann v. New York, 77 F.3d 672 (2d Cir.1996) (waiver-of-service procedure not effective where plaintiff failed to include acknowledgment form along with the mailed summons and complaint).

66. See Green v. Benden, 2000 WL 1468764, at *6 (N.D.Ill.2000) (service costs denied where waiver request failed to con-

The waiver-of-service procedure follows:

(1) *Request For Waiver:* The plaintiff formally requests a defendant to waive formal service of process. The request must:

- Actually be sent (even if the defendant tells the plaintiff in advance that requesting a waiver is "futile");[67]

- Be in writing; [68]

- Conform to the federal "Notice Of A Lawsuit & Request For A Waiver" form, which will list: (a) the date on which the plaintiff's request was sent; (b) the date by which the defendant's waiver is due; (c) the identity of the court; and (d) the consequences of both waiver and a refusal to waive;[69]

- Contain two (2) copies of a waiver form and a prepaid means to return it to the plaintiff;[70]

  Note: Although Rule 4(d) does not compel the use of the officially-approved federal Notice form[71] and Waiver form,[72] prudent practitioners are wise to use both in order to ensure that all necessary information is correctly included.

- Contain a copy of the complaint; [73]

- Be sent by first-class mail or by "other reliable means", including private hand delivery and facsimile transmission;[74] and

tain copies of commencement notice, request for waiver, or prepaid means of compliance), *aff'd in part, vac'd in part on other grounds*, 281 F.3d 661 (7th Cir.2002); *Perez v. County of Westchester*, 83 F.Supp.2d 435, 441 (S.D.N.Y.2000) (denying reimbursement, where notice and request were not addressed directly to the defendant, were not accompanied by a copy of the complaint, and lacked a prepaid means for compliance in writing).

67. *See* Rule 4(d)(1)(G). *See also Hy Cite Corp. v. badbusinessbureau.com, L.L.C.*, 418 F.Supp.2d 1142, 1153–54 (D.Ariz.2005) (holding that defendant cannot be ordered to pay Rule 4(d) expenses if he was never mailed a request for waiver–even if defendant informed plaintiff that the process was futile).

68. *See* Rule 4(d)(1)(A).

69. *See* Rule 4(d)(1)(B), (D), (E), & (F). *Cf. Trevino v. D.H. Kim Enters.*, 168 F.R.D. 181, 182–83 (D.Md.1996) (service not defective where plaintiffs did not use the official Notice form, but did advise defendants of consequences of compliance and non-compliance); *Dymits v. American Brands, Inc.*, 1996 WL 751111, at *15 (N.D.Cal.1996) (finding that plaintiff "substantially com-

plied" with waiver procedures, even though plaintiff omitted a small portion of the official form warning).

70. *See* Rule 4(d)(1)(C). *See also McGann v. New York*, 77 F.3d 672 (2d Cir.1996) (waiver-of-service procedure not effective where plaintiff failed to include an acknowledgment form along with the mailed summons and complaint); *Mason Tenders Dist. Council Pension Fund v. Messera*, 1997 WL 221200, at *6 (S.D.N.Y. 1997) (waiver-of-service procedure found to be defective where plaintiffs sent to defendant the acknowledgment form with self-addressed return envelope, but failed to stamp the return envelope).

71. *See* Form 5 ("Notice of a Lawsuit and Request to Waive Service of a Summons"), included in Appendix of Forms, reprinted in this text at Part IV.

72. *See* Form 6 ("Waiver of the Service of Summons"), included in Appendix of Forms, reprinted in this text at Part IV.

73. *See* Rule 4(d)(1)(C).

74. *See* Rule 4(d)(1)(G). *See also* Rule 4(d) advisory committee note (describing availability of and procedure for electronic

Note: If electronic means are used for requesting a waiver, the plaintiff should maintain proof of transmission.

- Be addressed directly to the individual defendant or, if the defendant is a corporation or association, to the individual subject to, or authorized to accept, service.[75]

  Note: Merely mailing "blind" to a business address will not constitute proper delivery.

(2) *Response Time:* After the request is sent, the defendant must be given at least 30 days (60 days if outside the United States) to respond by returning the waiver.[76]

  120–Day Warning: Rule 4(m)'s 120–day period for completing service continues to run while the waiver-of-service request is outstanding. This 120–day period does *not* toll while the defendant considers whether to waive.[77] Either waiver of service or, alternatively, formal service must be accomplished within the 120–day period.[78] In addition, in some jurisdictions, the statutes of limitation are not tolled in diversity or supplemental jurisdiction cases until actual service is made. Thus, in such jurisdictions, this waiver-of-service procedure should not be used if the limitations period is close to expiring.

(3) *Date of Service:* If the defendant agrees to waive service by returning the waiver, the date of service is deemed to be the date the plaintiff files the waiver form with the court.[79]

Motion to Recover Service Expenses

Where a defendant refuses, without good cause, to waive formal service of process, a motion to collect the costs and expenses of actual service can be filed promptly after the actual service is completed. The plaintiff need not wait until the bill of costs is submitted at the end of the case to recover these expenses.[80] A defendant's obligation to reimburse these costs is *not* affected by who eventually becomes the prevailing party in the litigation; rather, this obligation remains even if the defendant is otherwise enti-

communications, such as facsimile transmission).

75. *See* Rule 4(d)(1)(A). *See also Spivey v. Board of Church Extension & Home Mission of Church of God*, 160 F.R.D. 660 (M.D.Fla.1995)(to comply with Rule 4(d) waiver procedure, waiver form must be accurately addressed to individual defendants and must be addressed to an authorized agent of corporate defendants).

76. *See* Rule 4(d)(1)(F).

77. *See* Rule 4(d) advisory committee note to 1993 amendment. *See also Weldon*

v. Electronic Data Sys. Corp., 138 Fed.Appx. 136 (11th Cir.2005) (per curiam) (refusing to apply equitable tolling to claim that plaintiff was "misled" by defendant's failure to timely respond to request for waiver of service) (unpublished decision).

78. *See Chicago Dist. Council & Carpenters Pension Fund v. Wright Erectors, Inc.*, 1994 WL 592068 (N.D.Ill.1994).

79. *See* Rule 4(d)(4).

80. *See Double S Truck Line, Inc. v. Frozen Food Exp.*, 171 F.R.D. 251, 253–54 (D.Minn.1997).

tled to its bill of costs at the end of the case.[81] These expenses may include a reasonable attorney's fee for prosecuting the motion to collect costs, but may *not* include any attorney's fee associated with arranging for formal service after the defendant's refusal to waive.[82] Attorney's fees might not be reimbursed when the plaintiff proceeds *pro se*.[83]

The reported practice under Rule 4(d) suggests that courts are scrutinizing carefully the requested fees and costs to ensure against overreaching by counsel in their requests for reimbursement.[84]

U.S. Marshal's Use of Waiver-of-Service Procedure

When the Rules authorize service by the U.S. Marshal, the Marshal may mail the waiver-of-service forms to the defendants, prior to attempting to serve process personally.[85]

RULE 4(e).   SERVING INDIVIDUALS WITHIN A JUDICIAL DISTRICT OF THE UNITED STATES

CORE CONCEPT

Original process may be served upon any competent, adult individual found within the United States in the following manners:

(1) ***Specific Federal Law***: In any manner specifically authorized by federal law for such service, where Congress has determined that a particular type of service is necessary or proper;[86] or

(2) ***Waiver***: Under the waiver-of-service provisions of Rule 4(d); or

(3) ***State Law***: In the manner authorized by the State in which the district court sits, or by the State in which the service is to be accomplished; or

81. *See Estate of Darulis v. Garate*, 401 F.3d 1060, 1063–64 (9th Cir.2005) (commenting that Rule 4(d)'s policy "would be undermined if a defendant who creates unnecessary costs can gamble that he or she will be able to sidestep Rule 4(d)(2) via Rule 54(d)(1)").

82. *See Graves v. Church of Lord Jesus Christ of Apostolic Faith, Inc.*, 2003 WL 21659168, at *1 (E.D.Pa.2003) (denying plaintiff's request for reimbursement for attorney's fees spent arranging formal service on defendant after waiver was refused).

83. *See Marcello v. Maine*, 238 F.R.D. 113, 117–18 (D.Me. 2006).

84. *See, e.g., Ahern v. Northern Tech. Int'l Corp.*, 206 F.Supp.2d 418, 422 (W.D.N.Y.2002) (finding request for $1,845 in attorney's fees "unreasonable", and granting a reduced fee award of $80 instead); *Donaghue v. CT Holdings, Inc.*, 2001 WL 1543816, at *1 (S.D.N.Y.2001)

(granting motion, and awarding plaintiff reasonably fee of $406.25 for the preparation, service, and filing of motion, and costs of $140.00 for effecting service).

85. *See Hairston v. Falano*, 1999 WL 412440, at *3 (N.D.Ill.1999); *Rose v. Garbs*, 1999 WL 299892, at *3 (N.D.Ill.1999).

86. *See, e.g., Commodity Futures Trading Com'n v. Worldwide Commodity Corp.*, 366 F.Supp.2d 276, 280 (E.D.Pa.2005) (noting that because Commodities Exchange Act has its own specific service provisions, statute governs proper execution of service of summons); *Green v. William Mason & Co.*, 996 F.Supp. 394, 395–96 (D.N.J.1998) (noting that ERISA contains just such a jurisdictional provision, permitting breach of fiduciary duty claims to be served in any district court where the defendants reside or may be found) (citing 29 U.S.C.A. § 1132(e)(2)).

(4) **Personal Service**: By personally delivering the summons and complaint to the individual being served; or

(5) **Left at Dwelling House**: By leaving the summons and complaint at the individual's dwelling house or usual place of abode with a person of suitable age and discretion residing there; or

(6) **Agent**: By delivering the summons and complaint to an agent appointed by the individual to receive service, or to an agent authorized by law to receive service.

APPLICATIONS

Service Upon Individuals, Generally

This Rule applies whenever service is made upon individual persons. Thus, the individual service Rule will apply when the served defendant is the unincorporated business trade name by which a natural individual conducts his or her business.[87]

Service by Personal Delivery

Personal delivery may not always require that the recipient walk away from the encounter holding the summons and complaint. The service documents must be "tendered" to the recipient. Thereafter, once the recipient is physically confronted with service, and refuses to take personal possession of the service documents, service by personal delivery may still, under certain circumstances, be accomplished by leaving the documents near the recipient (such as on a nearby table or on the floor near the person).[88]

Service on Non–Resident Individual's Agent

A non-resident person, not otherwise present in the forum, may be served properly with process by serving that individual's agent for service. The recipient "agent", however, must be authorized to accept service either by appointment or by operation of law.[89] Some

---

87. See, e.g., Bridgeport Music, Inc. v. Rhyme Syndicate Music, 376 F.3d 615, 624–25 (6th Cir.2004) ("Service on Carrumba Music, the d/b/a for Jorge Hinojosa, is governed by Fed.R.Civ.P. 4(e), the provision for service of process on individuals").

88. See Novak v. World Bank, 703 F.2d 1305, 1310 n.14 (D.C.Cir.1983) ("When a person refuses to accept service, service may be effected by leaving the papers at a location, such as on a table or on the floor, near that person"); Republic Credit Corp. I v. Rance, 172 F.Supp.2d 1178, 1181 (S.D. Iowa 2001) (service effected by leaving summons and complaint at front gate, when process server encountered defendant, advised defendant of service papers, and defendant turned and entered residence without speaking; "This Court has no interest in forcing process servers to chase down

defendants and jam court papers into their hands in order to effect personal service, as depicted on television").

89. See Rule 4(e)(2)(C). See also Silvious v. Pharaon, 54 F.3d 697, 701–02 (11th Cir.1995). Compare Nazareth Nat'l Bank & Trust Co. v. E.A. Int'l Trust, 1999 WL 549036, at *2 (W.D.Pa.1999) (holding service proper because return of service showed that summons and complaint "were left with a specified security guard at defendant's residence who was 'instructed by [defendant] to accept service' ") with Staudinger v. Hoelscher, Inc., 166 F.Supp.2d 1335, 1339 (D.Kan.2001) (holding service improper where no authority offered to establish that plant manager (on whom service was made) was authorized by virtue of that position to accept service for president and owner of plant).

States have provided, by statute, that service on non-residents (who are otherwise amenable to jurisdiction within the State) may be accomplished by serving the secretary of State or some similar State law official; in such States, service in this manner may be appropriate service under federal law as well.[90]

Service on Individual's Attorney

Service upon an individual is proper by serving the individual's attorney *only* when the attorney has been specifically authorized to accept service on the individual's behalf.[91]

Service on Implied-in-Fact Agents

The concept of implied-in-fact agents for service of process has been recognized by several courts.[92]

Service at Individual's Dwelling House

An individual can be served with process by delivering the summons and complaint to a "person of suitable age and discretion" residing at the defendant's dwelling house or usual place of abode. In such cases, the process need not be handed directly to the served defendant.[93] Moreover, the recipient need not necessarily be an adult, so long as the court reaches the case-by-case, fact-specific determination that the recipient was of "suitable age and discretion". Nevertheless, the recipient ordinarily must be "residing" at the home;[94] service upon a non-resident maid or landlady might be ineffective.[95]

> *Traveling Defendants:* A traveling defendant's "usual place of abode" is likely to include either the place where she is actually living at the time of service or the place she

90. *See, e.g., Goktepe v. Lawrence,* 220 F.R.D. 8, 8–12 (D.Conn.2004) (Connecticut statute).

91. *See Guess ?, Inc. v. Chang,* 163 F.R.D. 505, 507–08 (N.D.Ill.1995).

92. *See, e.g., United States v. Ziegler Bolt & Parts Co.,* 111 F.3d 878, 881 (Fed. Cir.1997); *United States v. Balanovski,* 236 F.2d 298, 303 (2d Cir.1956). *See also In re Focus Media Inc.,* 387 F.3d 1077, 1082–83 (9th Cir.2004) (recognizing implied authority to receive service in bankruptcy context).

93. *See Limon–Hernandez v. Lumbreras,* 171 F.R.D. 271 (D.Or.1997).

94. *See United States v. Rose,* 437 F.Supp.2d 1166 (S.D.Cal.2006) (dwelling-house service requires that address be defendant's usual place of abode *and* that papers be left with someone actually residing there); *Srein v. Silverman,* 2001 WL 366620, at *2 (E.D.Pa.2001) (dwelling-house service only complete when papers

left with person who actually resides at defendant's home, not merely present at the time of service).

95. *Compare Franklin America, Inc. v. Franklin Cast Prods., Inc.,* 94 F.R.D. 645 (E.D.Mich.1982)(service on part-time housekeeper deemed insufficient) *with Barclays Bank of New York v. Goldman,* 517 F.Supp. 403 (S.D.N.Y.1981)(service on resident maid deemed sufficient). *See also Jaffe & Asher v. Van Brunt,* 158 F.R.D. 278 (S.D.N.Y.1994)(although defendant was not staying at his parents' home when service was made there, service ruled proper where defendant resided at that address when in the area, maintained private bedroom, clothes, phone line, and fax there, received mail there (which mother forwarded to him), and represented to plaintiff that this was his residence); *TRW, Inc. v. Derbyshire,* 157 F.R.D. 59 (D.Colo.1994)(holding that service on defendant's mother, at address defendant represented to be his current forwarding address, was proper).

recognizes as her legal residence, even if business takes her away on a regular basis.[96]

Transient Defendants: Service at a "dwelling house" or "usual place of abode" may not always be an available option. In certain circumstances, there may be no acceptable "dwelling house" service location for transient defendants, such as those living aboard ships or those who are homeless, living on the streets or in shelters.[97]

Hotels and Motels: In certain circumstances, particularly during long, extended stays, service can be appropriate at a hotel or motel where the defendant is residing.[98]

Multiple "Usual Abodes": A person made have two or more "usual places of abode" (and may be properly served at any one of them), so long as each contains sufficient indicia of the permanence of the person's residence there.[99]

State Law Service Generally

The Rules permit service in any manner authorized by *either* the State in which the district court sits *or* the State in which the service is to be accomplished.[100] If service is accomplished in accordance with either of those State service laws, Rule 4(e) is satisfied.[101]

State Law Service–Serving at Place of Business

The Federal Rules do *not* specifically authorize serving individuals by leaving a copy of the summons and complaint at the individual's regular place of business.[102] This type of service is, never-

96. *See S.E.C. v. Marino,* 29 Fed.Appx. 538, 540–41 (10th Cir.2002) (citation restricted—not selected for publication in Federal Reporter) (finding service proper because, even though defendant's vocation took him on extended trips abroad, he maintained his home and family in service location).

97. *See Cox v. Quigley,* 141 F.R.D. 222 (D.Me.1992)(young college graduate, who left home and was serving on board a ship, had no "dwelling house" or "usual place of abode", other than his ship); *see id.* at 226 ("The last shelter at which a homeless person slept will often not furnish reasonable assurance that process will reach the defendant. For such defendants service at the dwelling house or place of abode is unavailable; personal service may be a plaintiff's only option then, no matter how difficult").

98. *See Howard Johnson Int'l, Inc. v. Wang,* 7 F.Supp.2d 336 (S.D.N.Y.1998) (finding hotel to be defendant's dwelling place or usual place of abode).

99. *See National Dev't Co. v. Triad Holding Corp.,* 930 F.2d 253, 257–58 (2d

Cir.1991); *United States v. Rose,* 437 F.Supp.2d 1166 (S.D.Cal.2006).

100. *See* Rule 4(e)(1).

101. *See Vax-D Medical Techs., LLC v. Texas Spine Med. Ctr.,* 485 F.3d 593, 596 (11th Cir. 2007) (service complied with Texas case law regarding individuals who conduct business under assumed name); *Estate of Klieman v. Palestinian Auth.,* 467 F.Supp.2d 107, 112–14 (D.D.C. 2006) (serving researcher employed by PLO was insufficient without proof that he was PLO's authorized agent for service of process); *Homer v. Jones–Bey,* 415 F.3d 748, 754 (7th Cir.2005) (noting that effectiveness of service in such circumstances turns on relevant provisions of State law); *Webster Indus., Inc. v. Northwood Doors, Inc.,* 244 F.Supp.2d 998, 1005–06 (N.D.Iowa 2003) (noting that if service is proper under the rules of one qualifying state, court need not consider law of other qualifying State, nor conduct any "choice of law" analysis).

102. *See Melkaz Int'l Inc. v. Flavor Innovation Inc.,* 167 F.R.D. 634 (E.D.N.Y. 1996). *See also Boateng v. Inter American*

theless, often still available to the plaintiff because many States authorize service at business addresses.[103]

RULE 4(f). SERVING INDIVIDUALS IN A FOREIGN COUNTRY

CORE CONCEPT

Original process may be served upon any competent, adult defendant outside the United States, who is both amenable to service and subject to the court's personal jurisdiction, as follows:

(1) ***Specific Federal Law***: In any manner specifically authorized by federal law for such service, where Congress has determined that a particular type of service is necessary or proper; or

(2) ***Waiver***: Under the waiver-of-service provisions of Rule 4(d), if not prohibited by the law of the foreign country of service;[104] or

(3) ***International Agreement***: Where Congress has not established otherwise, and where the waiver-of-service provisions either are prohibited by foreign law or are not honored by an executed acknowledgment of service, service may be completed in any internationally agreed upon manner that is reasonably calculated to give notice, such as the *Hague Convention on the Service Abroad of Judicial and Extrajudicial Documents in Civil or Commercial Matters*;[105] or

(4) ***Court Order***: In any other manner directed by the court, so long as the chosen method is not prohibited by international agreement.

If no international agreement exists, or if the agreement permits service by other means, then original process may be served upon any competent, adult defendant outside the United States, who is both amenable to service and subject to the court's personal jurisdiction, as follows:

(5) ***Foreign Law***: In the manner prescribed by the law of the foreign country; or

(6) ***Letters Rogatory***: In the manner directed in response to a letter rogatory or letter of request; or

(7) ***Personal Service / Mail Delivery***: Unless prohibited by the foreign country's law: (a) by personally delivering the

---

Univ. of P.R., 188 F.R.D. 26 (D.P.R.1999) (holding that place of employment is not "dwelling place" or "usual place of abode").

103. *See* Rule 4(e)(1).

104. *See R. Griggs Group Ltd. v. Filanto Spa*, 920 F.Supp. 1100, 1103 (D.Nev. 1996).

105. Nov. 15, 1965, 20 U.S.T. 361, T.I.A.S. No. 6638, 658 U.N.T.S. 163. The text of the Convention on the Service Abroad of Judicial and Extrajudicial Documents in Civil or Commercial Matters is reprinted in the Supplement to 28 U.S.C.A. following Rule 4 (WESTLAW: USCA database, **ci(frcp/2 4) & treaties**).

summons and complaint to the individual defendant, or (b) by the clerk of court mailing process in a manner requiring a signed receipt; or

(8) ***Court Order***: In any other manner directed by the court, so long as the chosen method is not prohibited by international agreement.

APPLICATIONS

Hague Service Is Required, If Available

The Supreme Court has ruled that service in accordance with the Hague Service Convention is mandatory, wherever that Convention applies.[106] Note, however, that a substantial number of foreign Nations are *not* signatories to the Hague Service Convention.[107] Note also, that there is a division among the courts as to whether the Hague Service Convention authorizes original service of process by mail.[108] Consequently, practitioners should take special care to research well the construction of the Hague Service Convention applicable to their litigation.

Internationally Agreed Upon Service

Process served pursuant to an international agreement must comport with all specific, peculiar requirements imposed by the host country, such as the translation of process into the local language.[109]

Applies to Foreign Service, Not to Foreign Citizens

The provisions of Rule 4(f) are not triggered merely because the defendant is a citizen of a foreign country. Foreign nationals living, traveling, or conducting business within the United States generally may be served with process domestically under Rule 4(e), just as any other individual may. Instead, Rule 4(f) is triggered only when the

---

106. *See Volkswagenwerk Aktiengesellschaft v. Schlunk*, 486 U.S. 694, 108 S.Ct. 2104, 100 L.Ed.2d 722 (1988). *See also Marcantonio v. Primorsk Shipping Corp.*, 206 F.Supp.2d 54, 57 (D.Mass.2002) (Rule 4(f) requires the use of the Hague Convention provisions when Convention is in effect); *In re CINAR Corp. Secs. Litig.*, 186 F.Supp.2d 279, 303–04 (E.D.N.Y.2002) (same); *Taft v. Moreau*, 177 F.R.D. 201, 203 (D.Vt.1997) (same). *Cf. Brown v. Bandai America, Inc.*, 2002 WL 1285265, at *3 (N.D.Tex.2002) (because Japan is signatory to Hague Convention, court must determine whether defendant was properly served in accordance with Convention requirements).

107. *See Mayoral–Amy v. BHI Corp.*, 180 F.R.D. 456, 459 n. 3 (S.D.Fla.1998).

108. *Compare Nuovo Pignone v. Storman Asia M/V*, 310 F.3d 374, 384 (5th Cir. 2002) (Federal Express service not permitted by Hague Convention) *and Bankston v.*

Toyota Motor Corp., 889 F.2d 172, 173–74 (8th Cir.1989) (mail service not permitted by Hague Convention) *with Brockmeyer v. May*, 383 F.3d 798, 801–03 (9th Cir.2004) (permitting mail service under Hague Convention) *and Ackermann v. Levine*, 788 F.2d 830, 838 (2d Cir.1986) (same).

109. *See Friedman v. Israel Labour Party*, 1997 WL 379181 (E.D.Pa.1997) (holding service improper on Israeli defendant where plaintiff failed to send complaint directly to Israeli Director of Courts, as Israel required in its adoption of the Hague Service Convention); *Pennsylvania Orthopedic Ass'n v. Mercedes–Benz A.G.*, 160 F.R.D. 58 (E.D.Pa. 1995)(ruling that service attempted under the Hague Convention on a German corporate defendant was ineffective because the complaint had not been translated into German).

defendant—whether an American national or a citizen of another country—is served outside the United States.[110]

Service on United States Agent

When formally serving an individual located in a foreign country, a plaintiff has two options. First, the individual may be served personally in the foreign country, pursuant to the various provisions of this Rule 4(f). Second, the individual may be served by serving process within the United States on the individual's authorized agent (if one exists), pursuant to Rule 4(e).[111]

Service Internationally through the Mails

The effectiveness of international postal service can vary widely depending on the forum court and the Nation where such service is attempted. *First*, many Nations are signatories to the Hague Convention, and some (but not all) Circuits hold that international mail service can be permitted by the Convention to non-objecting Nations.[112] *Second*, international mail service may be accomplished if the Nation of service does not forbid it *and* if it is dispatched by the American clerk of court with a signed receipt required *and* if there is no applicable international agreement in place (*e.g.*, the Nation of service is not a Hague signatory) or, if in place, any agreement permits such service.[113] *Third*, such service may be expressly ordered by the American court, provided, too, that it is not forbidden by the Nation of service *and* there in no applicable international agreement or the applicable agreement permits such service.[114] *Fourth*, the Rule broadly permitting service in a manner "prescribed by the law of the foreign country for service in that country" probably will not suffice to authorize international mail service.[115]

"Court–Ordered" Type of Service, Generally

So long as the method of service is not prohibited by "international agreement", the plaintiff can request and the district court can order a means of service specifically tailored to achieve service upon individuals in a foreign country.[116]

---

110. *See Stars' Desert Inn Hotel & Country Club, Inc. v. Hwang*, 105 F.3d 521, 524 (9th Cir.1997).

111. *See Silvious v. Pharaon*, 54 F.3d 697 (11th Cir.1995)(per curiam).

112. *Compare Nuovo Pignone v. Storman Asia M/V*, 310 F.3d 374, 384 (5th Cir. 2002) (Federal Express service not permitted by Hague Convention) *and Bankston v. Toyota Motor Corp.*, 889 F.2d 172, 173–74 (8th Cir.1989) (mail service not permitted by Hague Convention) *with Brockmeyer v. May*, 383 F.3d 798, 801–03 (9th Cir.2004) (permitting mail service under Hague Convention) *and Ackermann v. Levine*, 788 F.2d 830, 838 (2d Cir.1986) (same).

113. *See* Rule 4(f)(2)(C)(ii). *See also Brockmeyer v. May*, 383 F.3d 798, 806–08 (9th Cir.2004) (discussing such service).

114. *See* Rule 4(f)(3). *See also Brockmeyer v. May*, 383 F.3d 798, 806–08 (9th Cir.2004) (discussing such service).

115. *See* Rule 4(f)(2)(A). *See also Brockmeyer v. May*, 383 F.3d 798, 806–08 (9th Cir.2004) (rejecting mail service to United Kingdom under this provision); *Prewitt Enters. v. OPEC*, 353 F.3d 916, 925 (11th Cir.2003) (same, mail to Austria).

116. *See Forum Fin. Group, LLC v. President, Fellows of Harvard College*, 199 F.R.D. 22, 23–24 (D.Me.2001) (authorizing service upon foreign defendant by certified mail sent to his American attorney).

This type of "court-ordered" service has been particularly useful to the courts when encountering elusive international defendants, especially those striving to evade service of process.[117] Few restrictions restrain the district court's creativity in crafting an alternate means of service. So long as the alternative service is (1) ordered by the court, (2) not prohibited by applicable international agreement, and (3) reasonably calculated, under the circumstances, to apprise the defendant of the pendency of the action and afford an opportunity to respond, the courts enjoy wide discretion.[118] Indeed, at least one court has confirmed that this "court-ordered" service option may even be employed where service could otherwise be accomplished through the various options set forth in Rule 4(f)(2).[119] The "court-ordered" service option has been applied by the courts to authorize service by publication, ordinary mail, mail to a last known address, delivery to certain members of the defendant's family, delivery to the defendant's attorney, and telex.[120]

"Court–Ordered" Service by E–Mail

Recently, and cautiously, courts have, on occasion, ordered alternate service of process by electronic mail (e-mail) in cases involving international defendants with a known e-mail address, engaged in internet activities, and attempting to evade service by other means.[121] Noting the many complications with e-mail service

---

117. *See Rio Props., Inc. v. Rio Int'l Interlink*, 284 F.3d 1007, 1018 (9th Cir. 2002) (justifying alternate service because plaintiff was "faced with an international e-business scofflaw, playing hide-and-seek with the federal court"). *See also Smith v. Islamic Emirate of Afghanistan*, 2001 WL 1658211, at *3 (S.D.N.Y.2001) (permitting alternative service on Osama Bin Laden and Al Qaeda terrorist network).

118. *See Rio Props., Inc. v. Rio Int'l Interlink*, 284 F.3d 1007, 1014–18 (9th Cir. 2002) (discussing analysis for crafting alternative service under Rule 4(f)). *But see id.* at 1014 (briefly discussing controversy over whether court's discretion to craft alternative service includes methods in violation of foreign country's internal laws).

119. *See Rio Props., Inc. v. Rio Int'l Interlink*, 284 F.3d 1007, 1014–15 (9th Cir. 2002) (expressly rejecting argument that Rule creates "a hierarchy of preferred methods of service of process" that first requires failed service under each of the Rule 4(f)(2) options before resorting to court-ordered service). *But see FMAC Loan Receivables v. Dagra*, 228 F.R.D. 531, 534 (E.D.Va.2005) (although no express hierarchy exists, the trial judge may, in the exercise of its discretion, require plaintiffs to show that they have made reasonable attempts to serve the defendants without court intervention, but that court intervention is necessary to avoid unduly burdensome or likely-futile service methods).

120. *See Rio Props., Inc. v. Rio Int'l Interlink*, 284 F.3d 1007, 1016 (9th Cir. 2002) (listing alternate service authorizations by other courts, and granting alternative service on local affiliate, on American attorney consulted by defendant, and by e-mail). *See also United States v. Padilla*, 2002 WL 471838, at *1 (E.D.Cal.2002) (authorizing United States to serve defendant by personally delivering a copy of summons and complaint to both defendant's daughter and defendant's attorney, currently representing defendant in another matter, with letter requesting that recipients forward the summons and complaint to defendant, and offering to send copies directly to defendant's residence if the recipient provides the government with defendant's address); *Smith v. Islamic Emirate of Afghanistan*, 2001 WL 1658211, at *3 (S.D.N.Y.2001) (permitting alternative service on Osama Bin Laden and Al Qaeda terrorist network by publication in Afghani newspapers, Pakistani newspaper where Bin Laden published his Fatwahs, and broadcast advertising on local television networks).

121. *See Rio Props., Inc. v. Rio Int'l Interlink*, 284 F.3d 1007, 1017–18 (9th Cir. 2002) (listing alternate service authoriza-

(*e.g.*, an inability to confirm actual receipt of an e-mail message, system compatibility issues, possible failure of attachments (such as exhibits) to transmit, be received, or be "opened" in comprehensible form, etc.), courts have granted e-mail service only upon a proper balancing, on a case-by-case basis, of these limitations against the corresponding benefits of such service in particular circumstances.[122]

Return of Service

Once service abroad is complete, the proof of service can be made in the manner provided by Rule 4(*l*), by the law of the foreign country, or by order of court. If service was accomplished by mail, the proof of service shall include a signed return receipt.

Effect of Foreign Service

Foreign countries are not parties to the Constitution's Full Faith and Credit Clause, and thus the enforcement abroad of a judgment entered by an American federal court is dependent on comity and international treaties. Moreover, in certain foreign countries, failure to adhere to the host nation's service regulations could even subject the unwary process server to criminal penalties.[123]

RULE 4(g).   SERVING MINORS AND INCOMPETENT PERSONS

CORE CONCEPT

Original process may be served upon any minor or incompetent person in the following manners:

- *Service in the United States:* In any manner authorized for the service of process on minors or incompetent persons by the State in which service is to be made.

- *Service Outside the United States:* In any manner: (1) prescribed by the law of the foreign country, (2) directed in response to a letter rogatory or letter of request; or (3) by such other means as the court may direct.

APPLICATIONS

State Law Dictates Proper Service

For service of process to be effective upon a minor or incompetent person, the service must comply with the requirements for such

tions by other courts, and granting alternative service on local affiliate, on American attorney consulted by defendant, and by e-mail).

122. *See Rio Props., Inc. v. Rio Int'l Interlink*, 284 F.3d 1007, 1017–18 (9th Cir. 2002) (discussing e-mail option, and finding that e-mail service was perhaps most likely method to notify defendant of summons and complaint). *See also Popular Enters., LLC v. Webcom Media Group, Inc.*, 225 F.R.D. 560, 560–63 (E.D.Tenn.2004) (per-

mitting e-mail service, under the circumstances, as most likely to apprise defendant of lawsuit).

123. *See Volkswagenwerk Aktiengesellschaft v. Schlunk*, 486 U.S. 694, 108 S.Ct. 2104, 100 L.Ed.2d 722 (1988)(commenting on possible adverse consequences of failing to comply with applicable international treaties). *See generally* Joseph F. Weis, Jr., *The Federal Rules and the Hague Conventions: Concerns of Conformity and Comity*, 50 U. Pitt. L. Rev. 903 (1989).

service as promulgated by the State in which service is attempted.[124]

RULE 4(h).   SERVING CORPORATIONS, PARTNERSHIPS, AND ASSOCIATIONS

CORE CONCEPT

Original process may be served upon any domestic or foreign corporation, partnership, or unincorporated association subject to suit under a common name, in the following manners:

(1) *Specific Federal Law*: In any manner specifically authorized by federal law for such service, where Congress has determined that a particular type of service is necessary or proper; or

(2) *Waiver*: Under the waiver-of-service provisions of Rule 4(d); or

(3) *SERVICE IN THE UNITED STATES*:

    (a) *State Law*: In the manner authorized by the State in which the district court sits, or by the State in which the service is to be accomplished; or

    (b) *Officer, Managing Agent, or General Agent*: By delivering the summons and complaint to an officer, managing agent, or general agent;[125] or

    (c) *Agent*: By delivering the summons and complaint to an agent appointed to receive service or authorized by law to receive service;[126] and if required by statute, by also mailing the summons and complaint to the defendant; or

(4) *SERVICE OUTSIDE THE UNITED STATES*:

    In any manner provided for service upon individuals in a foreign country, except personal service.[127]

---

124. *See Seibels, Bruce & Co. v. Nicke,* 168 F.R.D. 542, 545 (M.D.N.C.1996) (mailing complaint to minor's last place of residence was defective service because Indiana law required service on both minor and the minor's custodial parent).

125. *Cf. Ayres v. Jacobs & Crumplar, P.A.,* 99 F.3d 565, 567–68 (3d Cir.1996) (service upon "office manager" was insufficient service under Rule 4(h)); *Adams v. AlliedSignal Gen. Aviation Avionics,* 74 F.3d 882, 885 (8th Cir.1996) (service upon officer of a subsidiary does not satisfy Rule 4(h) service on the parent corporation, absent probative evidence that the subsidiary and the parent are not independently operated); *Baade v. Price,* 175 F.R.D. 403, 405 (D.D.C.1997) (holding that generally person served must have "some measure of discretion in operating some phase of the defen-

dant's business or in the management of a given office", must have "such status that common sense would expect the recipient to see that the summons promptly gets into the hands of the appropriate personnel", and must be working for the company at the time of service); *Romand v. Zimmerman,* 881 F.Supp. 806 (N.D.N.Y. 1995)(holding that service on chairperson of board of trustees was insufficient service under Rule 4(h)).

126. *Cf. Schollenberger v. Sears, Roebuck & Co.,* 876 F.Supp. 153 (E.D.Mich. 1995)(ruling that delivery to defendant's insurance claims representative was not sufficient service).

127. *See* Rule 4(f); *but see* Rule 4(f)(2)(C)(i)(no personal service).

APPLICATIONS

Service on Domestic Corporation's Officer, Manager, or General Agent

To effectively serve a corporation through an officer, manager, or general agent, the summons and complaint must be served on that person. Simply addressing the mail to the corporation generally, or to its legal department, will generally not suffice.[128] Whether a particular person qualifies as an officer, managing agent, or general agent of a corporation or association is determined on the basis of the particular facts presented.[129] This service need not occur at the company's headquarters, however; proper service could be proper anywhere the officer, manager, general officer, or authorized agent may be found.[130] Plaintiff bears the burden of establishing the basis for an inference that the served person was duly authorized to accept process.[131]

Service at Domestic Corporate Headquarters

The Federal Rules do *not* specifically authorize service by leaving a copy of the summons and complaint with a person of suitable age and discretion at the corporation's headquarters.[132] This type of service, however, may still be permitted. Rule 4(h) authorizes service in the federal courts in any manner permitted by the forum's State law.[133] For example, some States permit service on corporations by certified mail,[134] and others forgive service on the wrong

---

128. *See Larsen v. Mayo Med. Ctr.*, 218 F.3d 863 (8th Cir.2000) (holding that papers mailed to "Medical/Legal Department, Mayo Clinic" was ineffective service under Rule 4(h)).

129. *See, e.g., Vax-D Medical Techs., LLC v. Texas Spine Med. Ctr.*, 485 F.3d 593, 596 (11th Cir. 2007) (service upon company's manager was sufficient); *Battie v. Freeman Decorating*, 2001 WL 1345927, at *1 (E.D.La.2001) (commenting the delivery of summons and complaint to corporation's receptionist is sufficient service); *Reed v. Weeks Marine, Inc.*, 166 F.Supp.2d 1052, 1056 (E.D.Pa.2001) (same); *Estates of Ungar ex rel. Strachman v. Palestinian Auth.*, 153 F.Supp.2d 76, 89–91 (D.R.I.2001) (service on general or managing agent accomplished when process was delivered to Chief PA and PLO Representative in United States and to PLO's Deputy Permanent Observer to United Nations).

130. *See Mommaerts v. Hartford Life & Acc. Ins. Co.*, 472 F.3d 967, 967–68 (7th Cir. 2007).

131. *See Nature's First Inc. v. Nature's First Law, Inc.*, 436 F.Supp.2d 368 (D.Conn.2006).

132. *See Melkaz Int'l Inc. v. Flavor Innovation Inc.*, 167 F.R.D. 634 (E.D.N.Y. 1996). *See also Dailey v. R & J Commercial Contracting*, 2002 WL 484988, at *3 (S.D.Ohio 2002) ("When a corporation holds itself out to the public as receiving mail at a particular address, it must take some minimal steps to insure that when certified mail service is directed to that address, it receives actual notice, and its failure to do so cannot be attributed to the plaintiff, who is entitled to rely upon the address in requesting certified mail service"); *Battie v. Freeman Decorating*, 2001 WL 1345927, at *1 (E.D.La.2001) (commenting the delivery of summons and complaint to corporation's receptionist is sufficient service); *Reed v. Weeks Marine, Inc.*, 166 F.Supp.2d 1052, 1056 (E.D.Pa.2001) (same).

133. *See* Rule 4(h)(1)(A) (incorporating Rule 4(e)(1)).

134. *See Alfa Corp. v. Alfagres, S.A.*, 385 F.Supp.2d 1230, 1238 (M.D.Ala.2005) (Alabama law).

corporate person, so long as service is made at the corporate offices following the instructions of corporate employees found there.[135]

Service on Foreign Corporation

Proper service on a foreign corporation or association is governed by the foreign service on individuals rule, Rule 4(f). Failure to comply with those provisions will render the service ineffective.[136]

RULE 4(i).   SERVING THE UNITED STATES, ITS AGENCIES, CORPORATIONS, AND OFFICERS

CORE CONCEPT

To properly serve the United States, its agencies, corporations, or officers with original process, the summons and complaint must be served at several different locations. This multiple service obligation is mandatory, not discretionary.

APPLICATIONS

The United States as Defendant

Original process must be served upon the United States as follows:

(1) *United States Attorney*: By *either* (a) personally delivering the summons and complaint to the United States Attorney for the judicial district in which the action is brought, or her designee, *or* (b) sending the summons and complaint by registered or certified mail to the civil process clerk at the office of the United States Attorney; *and*

(2) *Attorney General*: By *also* sending a copy of the summons and complaint by registered or certified mail to the United States Attorney General in Washington, D.C.; *and*

(3) *Federal Officer or Agency*: In lawsuits attacking the validity of an order of a non-party officer or agency of the United States, by *also* sending a copy of the summons and complaint by registered or certified mail to such officer or agency.

Federal Officers, Agencies, or Corporations as Defendants

Original process may be served upon an officer, agency, or corporation of the United States as follows:

(1) *United States*: By serving the United States (see above); *and*

---

135. *See M'Baye v. World Boxing Ass'n,* 429 F.Supp.2d 652, 656–57 (S.D.N.Y.2006) (New York law).

136. *See Emery v. Wood Indus., Inc.,* 2001 WL 274747, at 2–3 (D.N.H.2001)

(hand-delivery of complaint and summons to Assistant Manager for Public Relations in Taiwan failed to comply with procedures authorized by Rule 4).

(2) *Federal Officer, Agency, or Corporation*: By also sending a copy of the summons and complaint by registered or certified mail to the federal officer, agency, or corporation named as a defendant.[137]

Suing Federal Officers/Employees in their Individual Capacities

In certain instances, federal officers and employees may be sued in their individual—rather than official—capacities.[138] In such cases, the type of service required will depend on the allegations of the pleading:

- *On-the-Job Claims:* If the federal officers or employees are sued in their individual capacities for acts or omissions occurring in connection with the performance of their federal duties, then proper service requires (1) service upon the United States *and* (2) service upon the officer or employee under Rule 4(e), (f), or (g).[139]

- *Claims Unrelated to the Job:* If the federal officers or employees are sued in their individual capacities for any other acts or omissions (that is, for conduct unrelated to the performance of their federal duties), then proper service requires only service under Rule 4(e), (f), or (g). Service on the United States is not required.[140]

These procedures apply to former federal officers and employees, as well as current personnel.[141]

If the plaintiff intends to sue the federal officials in *both* their individual and official capacities, the plaintiff must: (1) individually serve the officials under Rule 4(e), (f), or (g); *and* (2) serve the United States as well under Rule 4(i).[142] The plaintiff generally does not need to serve the official twice personally, however (*i.e.*, one service for each capacity).[143]

---

137. *See* Rule 4(i)(2). *See also Cleveland v. Williams*, 874 F.Supp. 270 (E.D.Cal. 1994)(where United States was not also served in lawsuit against IRS agents sued in their official capacities, complaint was dismissed as to all defendants).

138. *See Bivens v. Six Unknown Named Agents of Fed. Bureau of Narcotics*, 403 U.S. 388, 91 S.Ct. 1999, 29 L.Ed.2d 619 (1971) (permitting action for money damages against federal officers acting under color of their official authority for injuries caused by the officers' unconstitutional conduct).

139. *See* Rule 4(i)(3).

140. *See* Rule 4(i)(2)(B) advisory committee note to 2000 amendments ("Many actions are brought against individual federal officers or employees of the United States for acts or omissions that have no connection whatever to their government

roles. There is no reason to require service on the United States in these actions").

141. *See* Rule 4(i)(2)(B) advisory committee notes to 2000 amendments (noting that an action against former federal personnel "is covered by paragraph (2)(B) in the same way as an action against a present officer or employee").

142. *See McCaslin v. Cornhusker State Indus.*, 952 F.Supp. 652, 658–59 (D.Neb. 1996) (construing Rule 4(j), holding that service delivered directly to government employees conferred jurisdiction over them only in their individual capacities; to sue the government itself, service on the chief executive officer or the State attorney general's office was required).

143. *See* Rule 4(i)(2) advisory committee notes to 2000 amendments (commenting that amendments are intended "to en-

Careful! Name the Correct Federal Defendant

Practitioners should take special care while consulting the applicable substantive law to ensure that the proper defendant is named. A lawsuit may be dismissed if the practitioner mistakenly names a federal officer or agency as a defendant when the proper defendant is the United States, or mistakenly names the United States as a defendant when the proper defendant is a federal agency or officer, or mistakenly names federal officers as defendants in their official rather than individual capacities.[144]

Curing Incomplete Service on Federal Defendants

In view of the complexity of these multiple service obligations, Rule 4(i) establishes a "cure" for incomplete service in cases requiring service on multiple officers, agencies, or federal corporations. So long as either the United States Attorney or the Attorney General has been properly served in such cases, the court must allow a plaintiff a reasonable period of time to fulfill the multiple service obligations at all other locations.[145]

"Cure" is Opportunity for Extension, Not an Excuse of Obligation: The "cure" provision in Rule 4(i) does not authorize the courts to excuse or forgive incomplete service on the United States. To the contrary, the "cure" provision only authorizes an extension of time to complete the plaintiff's obligations–the full, required service under Rule 4(i) must still be achieved.[146]

"Cure" in Federal Agency, Corporation, & Official Capacity Lawsuits: If the plaintiff succeeds in serving either the United States Attorney or the Attorney General in a lawsuit asserting Rule 4(i)(2) claims (claims against a federal agency or corporation, or official capacity claims against federal officers of employees), but the plaintiff neglects to serve other required parties, the courts will allow the plaintiff a "reasonable time" to perfect proper service.[147] Note, however, that this "cure" provision applies *only* when proper service has already been achieved on the United States Attorney or the Attorney General.[148]

sure that no one would read the seemingly independent provisions of paragraphs 2(A) and 2(B) to mean that service must be made twice both on the United States and on the United States employee when the employee is sued in both official and individual capacities"). *See also Buttler v. Keller,* 169 F.R.D. 9, 10 (N.D.N.Y.1996) (under applicable State law, a single service upon an individual, named in both his individual and representative capacities, suffices to confer jurisdiction).

144. *See, e.g.,* 28 U.S.C.A. § 2671 (under Federal Torts Claims Act, actions to recover for the torts of a federal agency must name the United States as a defendant).

145. Rule 4(i)(4).

146. *See McMasters v. United States,* 260 F.3d 814, 817–18 (7th Cir.2001).

147. *See* Rule 4(i)(4)(A).

148. *But see Gargano v. I.R.S.,* 207 F.R.D. 22, 23 (D.Mass.2002) (commenting that some courts, confronted by a failure to serve the U.S. Attorney or Attorney General, "see room for a grant of equitable relief where overly strict adherence to the literal wording of the Rule appears to elevate form over substance", and have applied a four-part analysis that could grant such relief where: (1) all necessary governmental parties have actual notice of the lawsuit; (2) the government has suffered no prejudice from the service defect; (3) the plaintiff had

"Cure" in On-the-Job Individual Capacity Lawsuits: In a lawsuit against federal officers or employees sued for Rule 4(i)(3) claims (individual capacity, "on-the-job" claims), a plaintiff who successfully serves the officer or employee will be granted a "reasonable time" to serve the United States as well.[149]

"Cure" Not General Extension of Time: The "cure" is not triggered unless effective service is first accomplished upon the United States Attorney or the Attorney General.[150] Similarly, the extension is not unlimited; the "cure" must be accomplished within a "reasonable time" after service is made on the United States Attorney or the Attorney General.[151]

RULE 4(j).   SERVING FOREIGN, STATE, OR LOCAL GOVERNMENTS

CORE CONCEPT

Original process may be served upon a foreign, State, or local government as follows:

- **On Foreign Governments, their political subdivisions, agencies, or instrumentalities:** Service must be accomplished in accordance with the federal Foreign Sovereign Immunities Act, 28 U.S.C.A. § 1608, which permits service in the following order of preference:

- **On Foreign Governments:**

    (1) **Agreed-Method:** In any manner arranged between the plaintiff and the foreign State, but if not then:

    (2) **International Agreement:** In accordance with an applicable international treaty or convention, such as the *Hague Convention on the Service Abroad of Judicial and Extrajudicial Documents in Civil or Commercial Matters*,[152] but if not then:

a justifiable excuse for the failure to make proper service; and (4) the plaintiff would be severely prejudiced by a dismissal).

149. *See* Rule 4(i)(4)(B).

150. *See Parham v. Lamar*, 1 F.Supp.2d 1457 (M.D.Fla.1998) (Court refuses cure period where plaintiff failed to properly serve either the United States Attorney General or the local United States Attorney); *T & S Rentals v. United States*, 164 F.R.D. 422, 425–26 (N.D.W.Va.1996) (same).

151. *See Tuke v. United States*, 76 F.3d 155, 158 (7th Cir.1996) (cure not reasonable where plaintiff failed to serve "for months" and, after being notified by the United States of the deficiency, failed to act promptly or properly); *Mused v. United*

States Dep't of Agric. Food & Nutrition Serv., 169 F.R.D. 28, 35–36 (W.D.N.Y.1996) (cure not reasonable where plaintiff waited nearly a year to cure service defect). *See also Mused v. United States Dep't of Agric. Food & Nutrition Serv.*, 169 F.R.D. 28, 36 n. 7 (W.D.N.Y.1996) (rejecting argument that duration of defect be marked from date defect was "discovered", rather than when defect actually occurred).

152. Nov. 15, 1965, 20 U.S.T. 361, T.I.A.S. No. 6638, 658 U.N.T.S. 163. The text of the Convention on the Service Abroad of Judicial and Extrajudicial Documents in Civil or Commercial Matters is reprinted in the Supplement to 28 U.S.C.A. following Fed.R.Civ.P. 4 (WESTLAW: USCA database, **ci(frcp/2 4) & treaties**).

(3) *Ministry of Foreign Affairs:* By the clerk of court mailing a copy of the summons and complaint and a notice of suit, along with translations thereof, in a manner requiring a signed receipt, to the head of the ministry of foreign affairs, but if such service is not available within 30 days, then:

(4) *Special Consular Services:* By the clerk of court mailing a copy of the summons and complaint and a notice of suit, along with translations thereof, in a manner requiring a signed receipt, to the United States Director of Special Consular Services, for transmittal to the foreign State through diplomatic channels.

- **On Foreign Agencies or Instrumentalities:**

    (1) *Agreed–Method:* By serving process in any manner arranged between the plaintiff and the foreign agency or instrumentality,[153] but if not then:

    (2) *Agent or International Agreement: Either* (a) by delivering process to an officer, managing agent, or general agent of the foreign agency or instrumentality, or to an agent appointed by the foreign agent or instrumentality to receive service of process or authorized by law to receive such service; *or* (b) by serving process in accordance with an applicable international treaty or convention, such as the *Hague Convention on the Service Abroad of Judicial and Extrajudicial Documents in Civil or Commercial Matters,*[154] but if not then:

    (3) *Letter Rogatory, Clerk Mailing, or Court Order:* In one of the following manners: (a) by delivering process (together with a translation thereof) as directed in response to a letter rogatory or letter of request; *or* (b) by the clerk of court mailing process (along with translations thereof) in a manner requiring a signed receipt, to the agency or instrumentality; *or* (c) by order of court consistent with the law of the place where service is to be accomplished.

- *On States, Municipal Corporations, and Other Governmental Organizations:* A State, municipal corporation, or other governmental organization may be served with process:

    (1) *Chief Executive Officer:* By personally delivering the summons and complaint to the chief executive officer of the State, municipal corporation, or governmental organization;[155] or

153. *See In re Arbitration Between Trans Chem. Ltd. & China Nat'l Mach. Import & Export Corp.,* 978 F.Supp. 266 (S.D.Tex.1997) (service upon foreign agency was proper because it was made in accordance with the terms of the contract between the agency and the plaintiff).

154. Nov. 15, 1965, 20 U.S.T. 361, T.I.A.S. No. 6638, 658 U.N.T.S. 163. The text of the Convention on the Service Abroad of Judicial and Extrajudicial Documents in Civil or Commercial Matters is reprinted in the Supplement to 28 U.S.C.A. following Fed.R.Civ.P. 4 (WESTLAW: USCA database, **ci(frcp/2 4) & treaties**).

155. *See Coleman v. Milwaukee Bd. of Sch. Dirs.,* 290 F.3d 932, 933–34 (7th Cir. 2002) (where school board had no "chief

(2) **State Law:** By serving the summons and complaint in the manner authorized by the State in which the service is to be accomplished (note, some States require service on *multiple* persons in order to be valid).[156]

Note: The Eleventh Amendment to the United States Constitution restricts the authority of the federal courts to hear lawsuits against States.[157] Additionally, individual State and municipal sovereign immunity laws limit the federal courts' ability to enter awards against States, municipalities, and governmental entities.

APPLICATIONS

Applicability of Waiver-of-Service Procedure

The waiver-of-service procedure of Rule 4(d) does not apply to service of foreign, State, or local governments,[158] but the courts are divided on whether the procedure may be used to serve employees of those governments who are sued in their official capacities.[159]

RULE 4(k). TERRITORIAL LIMITS OF EFFECTIVE SERVICE

CORE CONCEPT

Service of a summons and complaint is effective to confer personal, or *in personam*, jurisdiction over any defendant amenable to service under the forum State's long-arm statute, under the federal interpleader statute,[160] or under other federal long-arm statutes. Additionally, persons or entities joined to the lawsuit as third-parties, necessary parties, or indispensable parties may be served with original process anywhere in the "bulge" region—within 100 miles of the place from where the summons issued (whether within or outside the State). Finally, service

executive officer", only option for plaintiff was to serve as prescribed by State law); *McCaslin v. Cornhusker State Indus.*, 952 F.Supp. 652, 658–59 (D.Neb.1996) (holding that service delivered directly to government employees conferred jurisdiction over them only in their individual capacities; to sue the government itself, service on the chief executive officer or the State attorney general's office was required).

156. *See Peak v. District of Columbia*, 236 F.R.D. 13 (D.D.C.2006) (proper service upon the District of Columbia requires service on both the District's Attorney General and Mayor).

157. *See Pennhurst State Sch. & Hosp. v. Halderman,* 465 U.S. 89, 104 S.Ct. 900, 79 L.Ed.2d 67 (1984)(noting that Eleventh Amendment prevents federal courts from hearing suits for damages filed by citizens against States, unless the defending State

first consents). *See also Florida Dep't of State v. Treasure Salvors, Inc.,* 458 U.S. 670, 102 S.Ct. 3304, 73 L.Ed.2d 1057 (1982)(confirming that Eleventh Amendment extends to bar suits by citizens against their own State of residence, in the absence of that State's consent to suit).

158. *See Cupe v. Lantz*, 470 F. Supp. 2d 136, 138 (D.Conn. 2007).

159. *Compare Cupe v. Lantz*, 470 F. Supp. 2d 136, 138 (D.Conn. 2007) (Rule 4(d) inapplicable to state employees sued in their official capacities) *with Marcello v. Maine*, 238 F.R.D. 113, 115 (D.Me. 2006) (serving public employees in their official capacities is done through Rule 4(e) which, in turn, permits Rule 4(d) waiver-of-service procedure).

160. 28 U.S.C.A. § 1335.

may also confer personal jurisdiction over a defendant who is not subject to the jurisdiction of any particular State.

APPLICATIONS

Exercise of Federal Personal Jurisdiction

Absent a waiver of formal service, the federal courts may generally exercise personal jurisdiction over the following categories of parties who are served with process:

- *State Long–Arm Statutes:* Defendants who are amenable to suit in the State where the district court is sitting in accordance with the provisions of that State's long-arm statute; [161]

- *100 Mile "Bulge" Rule:* Defendants joined as third-parties, necessary parties, or indispensable parties and who are served within 100 miles of the place where the summons issues; [162] and

  > *Note:* The bulge rule does *not* apply to service on the original parties to the lawsuit, nor does it constrict the range for service when a State or federal statute authorizes broader (or unlimited) service of process.

- *Federal Long–Arm Statutes:* Defendants who are amenable to suit in the district court pursuant to a federal statute providing for national or worldwide service of process (such as, for example, the federal interpleader statute, 28 U.S.C. § 1335.)[163]

Jurisdiction Over No–State–Resident

The federal courts also have personal jurisdiction over defendants who are not residents of the United States, but who have sufficient contacts with the United States as a Nation to warrant the application of federal law, yet who lack sufficient contacts with any single, particular State to support personal jurisdiction under State law long-arm statutes.[164]

---

161. Rule 4(k)(1)(A). *See Sole Resort, S.A. de C.V. v. Allure Resorts Mgmt., LLC,* 450 F.3d 100, 102–03 (2d Cir.2006); *ePlus Tech., Inc. v. Aboud,* 313 F.3d 166, 176 (4th Cir.2002).

162. Rule 4(k)(1)(B).

163. Rule 4(k)(1)(C). *See SEC v. Carrillo,* 115 F.3d 1540 (11th Cir.1997) (where federal statute authorizes nationwide or worldwide service, the requisite "minimum contacts" analysis tests for contacts with the United States as a Nation).

164. *See* Rule 4(k)(2). *See also Omni Capital Int'l v. Rudolf Wolff & Co.,* 484 U.S. 97, 111, 108 S.Ct. 404, 413, 98 L.Ed.2d 415 (1987)(defendant had sufficient contacts to satisfy constitutional due process concerns, but insufficient contacts to fall within narrower State long-arm statute); *Eskofot A/S v. E.I. Du Pont De Nemours & Co.,* 872 F.Supp. 81 (S.D.N.Y.1995)(holding that federal courts may exercise this jurisdiction over non-State defendants only where the defendants have sufficient contacts with United States generally so that due process concerns are not offended, such as where the defendants transact business in the United States, perform an act within the United States, or have an effect in the United States by an act done elsewhere).

Prerequisites for Asserting No–State–Resident Jurisdiction

To qualify for this type of national-contacts service of process, three conditions are first required:[165]

(1) Federal Claims: Plaintiff's claims against the No–State–Resident defendant must arise under federal law;[166]

(2) No Conventional Jurisdiction Possible: The defendant is beyond the jurisdictional reach of any individual State court and no situation-specific federal statute applies to confer jurisdiction;[167]

(3) Exercise of Personal Jurisdiction is Constitutional: The exercise of personal jurisdiction over the defendant would not offend the Constitution or other federal law.[168] Ordinarily, this will require that the defendants' contacts with the Nation generally (1) must relate to the plaintiff's cause of action or have given rise to it, (2) must involve some act whereby the defendant purposefully avails itself of the privilege of conducting activities within the forum, and (3) must be such that defendant should reasonably have anticipated being haled into court there.[169] This third condition helps ensure that such defendants are afforded "fair warning" before being subjected to the coercive power of the federal courts.[170] In conducting this constitutional inquiry, courts may apply the familiar "general" and "specific" jurisdictional concepts used in the traditional due process analysis.[171]

165. *See Holland America Line Inc. v. Wartsila North America, Inc.*, 485 F.3d 450, 461 (9th Cir. 2007) (listing elements); *Mwani v. bin Laden*, 417 F.3d 1, 10 (D.C.Cir.2005) (same); *Base Metal Trading, Ltd. v. OJSC "Novokuznetsky Aluminum Factory"*, 283 F.3d 208, 215 (4th Cir.2002) (same).

166. *See Holland America Line Inc. v. Wartsila North America, Inc.*, 485 F.3d 450, 461 (9th Cir. 2007); *World Tanker Carriers Corp. v. M/V Ya Mawlaya*, 99 F.3d 717, 720–23 (5th Cir.1996); *United States v. Offshore Marine Ltd.*, 179 F.R.D. 156, 158–60 (D.V.I.1998) (Rule 4(k)(2) applies to admiralty cases).

167. *See Holland America Line Inc. v. Wartsila North America, Inc.*, 485 F.3d 450, 461 (9th Cir. 2007); *United States v. Swiss American Bank, Ltd.*, 191 F.3d 30, 38 (1st Cir.1999); *See World Tanker Carriers Corp. v. M/V Ya Mawlaya*, 99 F.3d 717, 720 (5th Cir.1996). *See also In re Telectronics Pacing Sys.*, 953 F.Supp. 909, 914 (S.D.Ohio 1997) (Rule unavailable where case arises under State law).

168. *See Holland America Line Inc. v. Wartsila North America, Inc.*, 485 F.3d 450, 461 (9th Cir. 2007); *Dardana Ltd. v. Yugan-*

skneftegaz, 317 F.3d 202, 207 (2d Cir.2003); *Associated Transport Line, Inc. v. Productos Fitosanitarios*, 197 F.3d 1070, 1074 (11th Cir.1999).

169. *See Associated Transport Line, Inc. v. Productos Fitosanitarios*, 197 F.3d 1070, 1074 (11th Cir.1999). *Cf. Consolidated Dev't Corp. v. Sherritt, Inc.*, 216 F.3d 1286 (11th Cir.2000) (holding that personal jurisdiction will not lie where foreign corporation, that does not engage in general business in the forum, simply negotiates a contract there or has a subsidiary that markets defendant's products).

170. *See Saudi v. Northrop Grumman Corp.*, 427 F.3d 271, 275 (4th Cir.2005).

171. *See Submersible Sys., Inc. v. Perforadora Central, S.A. de C.V.*, 249 F.3d 413, 420–21 (5th Cir.2001); *BP Chems. Ltd. v. Formosa Chem. & Fibre Corp.*, 229 F.3d 254, 258–63 (3d Cir.2000); *Consolidated Dev't Corp. v. Sherritt, Inc.*, 216 F.3d 1286, 1291–94 (11th Cir.2000). *See also Base Metal Trading, Ltd. v. OJSC "Novokuznetsky Aluminum Factory"*, 283 F.3d 208, 216 (4th Cir.2002) (rejecting Rule 4(k)(2) jurisdiction because alleged contacts with United States "appear sparse and limited to a few ship-

Burden of Proof in No–State–Resident Cases

The plaintiff bears the burden of establishing that the prerequisites exist for Rule 4(k)(2) national-contacts service.[172] To satisfy this burden, one court requires that the plaintiff make three prima facie showings and one certification: (1) that the claim arises under federal law, (2) that personal jurisdiction is not available under any situation-specific federal statute, (3) that the defendant's contacts with the Nation generally comport with the Constitution's requirements; and (4) that the plaintiff certify, based on information readily available to the plaintiff and counsel, that the defendant is not subject to the jurisdiction of any particular State's court.[173] The plaintiffs may be granted limited jurisdictional discovery to help them carry this burden.[174]

If the plaintiff makes these showings, the burden shifts to the defendant to come forward with evidence that, if credited, would show that jurisdiction would be proper in some State. If the defendant fails to carry this burden, the factfinder can infer that no State enjoys personal jurisdiction. If, however, the defendant carries this burden, the inference drops from the case. Thereafter, the plaintiff may (a) seek a transfer to a State where proper jurisdiction exists, (b) discontinue the lawsuit and re-file it, or (c) challenge the defendant's assertions.[175]

This burden-shifting technique invests the defendant with the ability to "knock out" Rule 4(k)(2) by actually consenting to personal jurisdiction in some other State. Conversely, failing to so consent will permit the federal courts to proceed with the Rule 4(k)(2) analysis without the accompanying burden of a 50–State constitutional analysis.[176]

Several other federal courts have now endorsed this burden-shifting approach to assessing jurisdiction under Rule 4(k)(2).[177]

ments of aluminum arriving in American ports", and refusing to commit "the limited resources of the federal courts ... [to] resolving disputes between two foreign corporations with little or no connection to our country").

172. *See United States v. Swiss American Bank, Ltd.*, 191 F.3d 30, 38 (1st Cir. 1999).

173. *See United States v. Swiss American Bank, Ltd.*, 191 F.3d 30, 38 (1st Cir. 1999).

174. *See Toys "R" Us, Inc. v. Step Two, S.A.*, 318 F.3d 446, 458 (3d Cir.2003) (allowing jurisdictional discovery on limited issue of defendant's business activities in United States, including business plans, marketing strategies, sales, and other commercial interactions); *Dardana Ltd. v. Yugansknefteqaz*, 317 F.3d 202, 208 (2d Cir. 2003) (remanding for discovery).

175. *See United States v. Swiss American Bank, Ltd.*, 191 F.3d 30, 38 (1st Cir. 1999). *See also ISI Int'l, Inc. v. Borden Ladner Gervais LLP*, 256 F.3d 548, 552 (7th Cir.2001).

176. *See ISI Int'l, Inc. v. Borden Ladner Gervais LLP*, 256 F.3d 548, 552 (7th Cir. 2001) ("This procedure makes it unnecessary to traipse through the 50 states, asking whether each could entertain the suit"); *Mwani v. bin Laden*, 417 F.3d 1, 12 (D.C.Cir.2005) (same); *Adams v. Unione Mediterranea Di Sicurta*, 364 F.3d 646, 651 (5th Cir.2004) (agreeing that "a piecemeal analysis of the existence vel non of jurisdiction in all fifty states is not necessary").

177. *See Holland America Line Inc. v. Wartsila North America, Inc.*, 485 F.3d 450, 461 (9th Cir. 2007); *Mwani v. bin Laden*, 417 F.3d 1, 12 (D.C.Cir.2005); *Adams v. Unione Mediterranea Di Sicurta*, 364 F.3d

Sufficient Contacts: Whether personal jurisdiction can be exercised in "no-State-resident" cases hinges on the nature of the defendant's contacts with the United States generally, and whether those contacts are constitutionally adequate to support the exercise of jurisdiction.[178] But *physical* contacts are not the only ones that qualify in this analysis. Where a defendant's contacts will foreseeably cause injury within the United States, those contacts may justify personal jurisdiction.[179]

RULE 4(*l*). PROVING SERVICE

CORE CONCEPT

Where formal service has not been waived, the process server must present proof of service to the court.

APPLICATIONS

Nature of Proof

The proof of service should contain sufficient facts to confirm that valid service has been accomplished (*e.g.*, the dwelling place where process was left, the name of the receiving agent or corporate officer). Where service was made by someone other than a United States Marshal, an affidavit of service is required.

Service Outside the United States

If service is made under treaty or other international agreement, proof of service must be in accordance with that treaty or agreement. If service is made in any other manner, proof of service must include a receipt signed by the addressee or other satisfactory evidence of delivery.

Failure to Present Proof of Service

So long as the plaintiff demonstrates that the defendant was properly served, the process server's technical failure to present proof of service will not affect the validity of the service.

Amendment to Proof of Service

Where an amendment would cure the defect in the proof of service, the courts generally will grant leave to so amend.[180]

646, 651 (5th Cir.2004); *ISI Int'l, Inc. v. Borden Ladner Gervais LLP*, 256 F.3d 548, 552 (7th Cir.2001).

178. *See Holland America Line Inc. v. Wartsila North America, Inc.*, 485 F.3d 450, 461–62 (9th Cir. 2007); *Mwani v. bin Laden*, 417 F.3d 1, 12 (D.C.Cir.2005).

179. *See Mwani v. bin Laden*, 417 F.3d 1, 13–14 (D.C.Cir.2005) (permitting exercise of jurisdiction over international terrorist who orchestrated bombing abroad that killed Americans, intended to "cause pain and sow terror" back in the United States, and participated in an ongoing conspiracy to attack the United States, with local overt acts).

180. *See Nolan v. City of Yonkers*, 168 F.R.D. 140, 143 (S.D.N.Y.1996) (noting that request to amend proof of service should rarely be refused, and then granting leave to do so).

RULE 4(m). TIME LIMIT FOR SERVICE

CORE CONCEPT

The summons and complaint must be served within 120 days after the complaint is filed. However, if the plaintiff is able to show "good cause" why process could not be served within those 120 days, the district court must extend the time for service. If "good cause" is not shown, the district court must either dismiss the lawsuit without prejudice or, in its discretion, direct that service be accomplished within a specified time.

APPLICATIONS

"Good Cause" Defined

The plaintiff bears the burden of proving that "good cause" exists to excuse a delay in service of process.[181] No fixed guidelines define "good cause".[182] Whether "good cause" exists is a matter committed to the sound discretion of the trial court.[183] Minimally, good cause requires a showing of good faith and a reasonable basis, beyond the plaintiff's control, for failing to comply with the Rules.[184] This standard is ordinarily applied narrowly to protect only those litigants who have exercised meticulous care in attempting to complete service.[185] As one court has aptly warned: "The lesson to the

181. *See Lepone-Dempsey v. Carroll County Comm'rs,* 476 F.3d 1277, 1281 (11th Cir. 2007); *Nafziger v. McDermott Int'l, Inc.,* 467 F.3d 514, 521 (6th Cir. 2006); *Habib v. General Motors Corp.,* 15 F.3d 72, 73 (6th Cir.1994).

182. *See Sidney v. Wilson,* 228 F.R.D. 517, 522 (S.D.N.Y.2005).

183. *See Byrd v. Stone,* 94 F.3d 217, 219 (6th Cir.1996).

184. *See Lepone-Dempsey v. Carroll County Comm'rs,* 476 F.3d 1277, 1281–82 (11th Cir. 2007). *See also Coleman v. Milwaukee Bd. of Sch. Dirs.,* 290 F.3d 932, 934 (7th Cir.2002) (good cause requires showing valid reason for delay, such as defendant attempting to evade service); *In re Sheehan,* 253 F.3d 507, 512 (9th Cir.2001) (to qualify for "good cause", plaintiff may be required to show that (a) defendant received actual notice of the lawsuit; (b) defendant would not suffer prejudice; and (c) plaintiff would be severely prejudiced if lawsuit were dismissed); *De Tie v. Orange County,* 152 F.3d 1109 (9th Cir.1998) (pending bankruptcy stay of service of process qualified as "good cause"); *Matasareanu v. Williams,* 183 F.R.D. 242, 246 (C.D.Cal.1998) (ill health may constitute "good cause", depending on the factual showing made); *Gambino v. Village of Oakbrook,* 164 F.R.D. 271, 274 (M.D.Fla.1995) (noting that, although good cause is not defined, courts look to circum-stances beyond plaintiff's control, "such as sudden illness, natural catastrophe, or eva-sion of service of process").

185. *See Despain v. Salt Lake Area Metro Gang Unit,* 13 F.3d 1436, 1438 (10th Cir.1994). *Accord Lepone-Dempsey v. Carroll County Comm'rs,* 476 F.3d 1277, 1281–82 (11th Cir. 2007) (noting that good cause exists when outside factors, other than inadvertence or negligence, defeated service); *Hamilton v. Endell,* 981 F.2d 1062, 1065 (9th Cir.1992) (inadvertent error or igno-rance of governing rules will not excuse a failure to timely serve process). *Compare Lepone-Dempsey v. Carroll County Comm'rs,* 476 F.3d 1277, 1282 (11th Cir. 2007) (relying on defendant's assertion that he would sign waiver form was not good faith) *and Despain v. Salt Lake Area Metro Gang Unit,* 13 F.3d 1436, 1438 (10th Cir. 1994)(neither mere absence of prejudice nor mistake of counsel constitutes "good cause") *and Powell v. Starwalt,* 866 F.2d 964 (7th Cir.1989)(attorney inadvertence will not constitute "good cause") *and Mata-sareanu v. Williams,* 183 F.R.D. 242, 246 (C.D.Cal.1998) (lack of legal training and attorney guidance does not constitute "good cause") *and Braithwaite v. Johns Hopkins Hosp.,* 160 F.R.D. 75 (D.Md.1995)(delay re-sulting from the psychological distress caused by the murder of plaintiff's only daughter during 120–day service period did

federal plaintiff's lawyer is not to take any chances. Treat the 120 days with the respect reserved for a time bomb.''[186]

"Good Cause" and U.S. Marshal Service Delays

Ordinarily, *pro se* litigants for whom the United States Marshal's Service may be directed to serve process will be granted a "good cause" extension of the 120–day period where a delay in service is attributable to the Marshal's Service.[187]

Effect of Showing "Good Cause"

Under old Rule 4 (prior to the 1993 Amendments),[188] unless the plaintiff could demonstrate "good cause" for failing to serve process within 120 days of filing, the district court had no alternative but to dismiss the lawsuit without prejudice. New Rule 4(m) changed this practice in 1993. Now, courts distinguished between justified delay ("good cause") and excusable neglect.[189] As to the former (justified delay), the district court *must* grant a plaintiff an extension for "an appropriate period" when good cause is shown.[190] When good cause is not shown, the district court has the option of either dismissing the lawsuit without prejudice or, in the exercise of its discretion, excusing the delay by issuing an order that directs that service be completed within a specified addition period of time.[191] In such a case, where the plaintiff is unable to show good cause, he essentially "throws himself on the mercy of the district court.''[192]

not constitute "good cause") *with Habib v. General Motors Corp.*, 15 F.3d 72, 73 (6th Cir.1994)(*pro se* litigant's medical conditions, combined with diligent efforts to complete service, satisfies "good cause" test).

186. *Braxton v. United States*, 817 F.2d 238, 241 (3d Cir.1987)(quoting *Siegel, Practice Commentary on Amendment of Federal Rule 4 (Eff. Feb. 26, 1983) with Special Statute of Limitations Precautions*, 96 F.R.D. 88, 103 (1983)).

187. *See Graham v. Satkoski*, 51 F.3d 710 (7th Cir.1995) (if Marshals Service should have been able to obtain new address for defendants with reasonable efforts, but failed to do so, "good cause" exists to extend time); *Dumaguin v. Secretary of Health & Human Servs.*, 28 F.3d 1218 (D.C.Cir.1994) (Marshal's failure to serve United States Attorney with *in forma pauperis* complaint was "good cause" to extend time); *Scott v. Reno*, 902 F.Supp. 1190, 1196 n. 4 (C.D.Cal.1995) (indigent plaintiffs cannot be penalized for the United States Marshals failure to serve process as ordered).

188. The prior practice, former Rule 4(j), provided: "If a service of the summons and complaint is not made upon a defendant within 120 days after the filing of the complaint and the party on whose behalf

such service was required cannot show good cause why such service was not made within that period, the action shall be dismissed as to that defendant without prejudice upon the court's own initiative with notice to such party or upon motion".

189. *See Coleman v. Milwaukee Bd. of Sch. Dirs.*, 290 F.3d 932, 934 (7th Cir.2002).

190. *See Efaw v. Williams*, 473 F.3d 1038, 1040 (9th Cir. 2007); *United States v. McLaughlin*, 470 F.3d 698, 700 (7th Cir. 2006). *Cf. Bogle–Assegai v. Connecticut*, 470 F.3d 498, 508–09 (2d Cir. 2006) (extension denied where no showing of good cause was made and extension would have spanned more than 600 days, a delay not consistent with "an appropriate period").

191. *See Lepone-Dempsey v. Carroll County Comm'rs*, 476 F.3d 1277, 1282 (11th Cir. 2007); *Efaw v. Williams*, 473 F.3d 1038, 1040 (9th Cir. 2007); *United States v. McLaughlin*, 470 F.3d 698, 700 (7th Cir. 2006). *But see Mendez v. Elliot*, 45 F.3d 75 (4th Cir.1995)(relying on former Rule 4(j), and without commenting on broadened language under 1993 Amendments, the court held that district court lacks discretion if "good cause" is not shown).

192. *See United States v. McLaughlin*, 470 F.3d 698, 700 (7th Cir. 2006).

Permissive Extensions

When "good cause" is not shown, the decision whether to dismiss or grant a further extension is committed to the district court's discretion.[193] Although Rule 4(m) lists no criteria for making this determination,[194] the district court is nevertheless still obligated to consider whether circumstances exist to warrant an extension of the 120–day service period.[195] In making this evaluation, the court may examine, among other factors, whether the applicable statute of limitations would bar a re-filing, whether the failure to timely serve was due to a difficulty in serving government officials, whether the offending party is proceeding *pro se*, whether the unserved defendant has been evading service or concealing a defect in service, and whether service was eventually accomplished and, if so, how far beyond the 120–day period actual, effective service occurred.[196] Moreover, a defendant's admission of liability will prove an important factor tilting in favor of granting a permissive extension.[197] The courts of appeals review such decisions under an abuse of discretion standard, and can be expected to most often affirm any reasoned and principled decision by the trial court.[198]

Note: Although the effect of the statute of limitations may be considered by the court in evaluating whether to grant a permissive extension,[199] this does not mean that a permissive extension is mandatory whenever a dismissal would result in a time-bar.[200] Instead, the district court must assess whether all

---

193. See *Lepone-Dempsey v. Carroll County Comm'rs*, 476 F.3d 1277, 1282 (11th Cir. 2007); *Efaw v. Williams*, 473 F.3d 1038, 1041 (9th Cir. 2007).

194. See *United States v. McLaughlin*, 470 F.3d 698, 700 (7th Cir. 2006).

195. See *Lepone–Dempsey v. Carroll County Comm'rs*, 476 F.3d 1277, 1282 (11th Cir. 2007); *Panaras v. Liquid Carbonic Indus. Corp.,* 94 F.3d 338, 341 (7th Cir.1996); *Thompson v. Brown*, 91 F.3d 20, 22 (5th Cir.1996); *Espinoza v. United States,* 52 F.3d 838, 841 (10th Cir.1995); *Petrucelli v. Bohringer & Ratzinger, GMHB,* 46 F.3d 1298, 1307–08 (3d Cir.1995).

196. See *Lepone-Dempsey v. Carroll County Comm'rs*, 476 F.3d 1277, 1282 (11th Cir. 2007) (listing certain factors); *Efaw v. Williams*, 473 F.3d 1038, 1041 (9th Cir. 2007) (same); *Espinoza v. United States*, 52 F.3d 838 (10th Cir.1995)(same); *Petrucelli v. Bohringer & Ratzinger*, 46 F.3d 1298 (3d Cir.1995)(same). *Cf. Bogle–Assegai v. Connecticut*, 470 F.3d 498, 508–09 (2d Cir. 2006) (more than 600–day extension not consistent with "an appropriate period").

197. See *United States v. McLaughlin*, 470 F.3d 698, 701 (7th Cir. 2006).

198. See *Coleman v. Milwaukee Bd. of Sch. Dirs.*, 290 F.3d 932, 934 (7th Cir.2002) (affirming denial of permissive extension under abuse of discretion standard, notwithstanding that "most district judges probably would exercise lenity and allow a late service" in similar cases where actual harm is not shown, where defendant likely received timely actual notice of the lawsuit, and where dismissal would bar a re-filing because the limitations period has expired). *See also United States v. McLaughlin*, 470 F.3d 698, 701 (7th Cir. 2006) (where service delay causes "zero prejudice" to any party or the court, granting permissive extension "cannot be an abuse of discretion").

199. See *Mann v. American Airlines*, 324 F.3d 1088, 1090–91 (9th Cir.2003) (district court has discretion to grant permissive extension, even where limitations period would otherwise bar a re-filing of the case).

200. See *Lepone-Dempsey v. Carroll County Comm'rs*, 476 F.3d 1277, 1282 (11th Cir. 2007); *Panaras v. Liquid Carbonic Indus. Corp.*, 94 F.3d 338, 340 (7th Cir. 1996). *See also Boley v. Kaymark*, 123 F.3d 756, 759 (3d Cir.1997) ("it is not a factor that

criteria, in addition to time-bar, warrant the permissive extension.

Dismissal Without Prejudice

Dismissals under this Rule for failure to timely serve process are made without prejudice.[201] If, however, a re-filed complaint would be beyond the applicable statute of limitations, the Rule 4(m) dismissal "without prejudice" will not act to defeat an affirmative defense asserting time-bar.[202]

Substantive State Law Rules Can Undercut The 120–Day Period

This 120–day period is simply a creation of federal procedural rules—it merely acts to preserve, from dismissal, a federal complaint for 120 days so as to facilitate service of process. Under the *Erie* doctrine, however, the federal courts are obligated to apply State substantive law to State causes of action that are pending in federal court under diversity or supplemental jurisdiction. The substantive laws of some States provide that merely filing a complaint does not toll the applicable statutes of limitations. In those instances, Rule 4(m) will not prevent a cause of action from becoming time-barred during the 120–day service period, if State law would so dictate.[203]

Defendants Can Waive 120–Day Service Period

Although Rule 4(m) contains mandatory-sounding dismissal language, defendants may still waive the 120–day period by filing an omnibus Rule 12 motion and omitting from that motion the claim that process was served beyond Rule 4(m)'s 120–day time period.[204]

Sua Sponte Dismissals

When service has not been effected within the 120–day period, the action may be dismissed upon motion, or upon the court's own initiative.[205] Such *sua sponte* dismissals under Rule 4(m) require prior "notice to the plaintiff".[206]

---

standing alone supports a finding of prejudice to the defendant").

201. *See Betty K Agencies, Ltd. v. M/V MONADA*, 432 F.3d 1333, 1342 n.5 (11th Cir.2005); *Bann v. Ingram Micro, Inc.*, 108 F.3d 625, 626 (5th Cir.1997).

202. *See Conover v. Lein*, 87 F.3d 905, 908–09 (7th Cir.1996) (commenting that dismissals "without prejudice" under Rule 4(m) are not necessarily dismissals "without consequence," if the pertinent statutes of limitations have run); *Hawkins v. McHugh*, 46 F.3d 10 (5th Cir. 1995)(applying Louisiana law and holding that dismissal under this Rule does not interrupt prescription or toll the prescription period).

203. *See Torre v. Brickey*, 278 F.3d 917, 919–20 (9th Cir.2002) (holding that Rule 4(m) did not preserve claims for 120–day

period where substantive law of forum State, Oregon, does not toll statute of limitations until service is effected); *Larsen v. Mayo Med. Ctr.*, 218 F.3d 863 (8th Cir.2000) (same, under Minnesota law); *Habermehl v. Potter*, 153 F.3d 1137, 1139 (10th Cir.1998) (same, under Wyoming law). *See also* Authors' Commentary to Rule 3 ("Diversity Jurisdiction Cases" and "Supplemental Jurisdiction Cases").

204. *See McCurdy v. American Bd. of Plastic Surgery*, 157 F.3d 191, 195 (3d Cir. 1998) (citing cases).

205. *See* Rule 4(m).

206. *See Thompson v. Maldonado*, 309 F.3d 107, 110 (2d Cir.2002) (vacating *sua sponte* dismissal because court had not given plaintiff prior notice of the intent to dismiss under Rule 4(m)). *Cf. TIG Ins. Co. v. 2200 M St., LLC.*, 216 F.R.D. 2, 3 (D.D.C.

Time Limitation Does Not Apply to Foreign Service

The 120–day service rule does not apply to service within a foreign country,[207] or to service upon a foreign state and its political subdivisions, agencies, and instrumentalities.[208] However, the time allowable for accomplishing foreign service is not unlimited, as district courts must retain the ability to control their dockets.[209] Some courts have conditioned this foreign service "exemption" upon a showing that good faith attempts were made to serve within the 120–day period; if no such attempts were made, these courts hold that the exemption will not apply and the passage of 120 days can justify a dismissal.[210]

New 120–Day Period For Newly Added Parties

When a complaint is amended to add new parties, the plaintiff is given 120 days from the date of amendment to serve the new defendants.[211] Note, however, that this new 120–day clock will apply only to the newly-added parties; amendments will ordinarily not extend the time for serving parties who were named earlier.[212]

In Forma Pauperis Motions and 120–Day Period

Because the statute of limitations is ordinarily tolled during the pendency of a motion for leave to proceed *in forma pauperis*, the Rule 4(m) 120–day period for service will not begin to run until the complaint is stamped "filed" (either when the *in forma pauperis* motion is granted without a fee or the filing fee is actually paid).[213]

2003) (dismissing action *sua sponte* under Rule 4(m) where plaintiff failed to respond to court's prior notice by "show-cause" order).

207. *See* Fed.R.Civ.P. 4(m)(referencing Fed. R. Civ. P. 4(f))(providing for service upon individuals in foreign countries). *See Goodstein v. Bombardier Capital, Inc.*, 167 F.R.D. 662, 665–66 (D.Vt.1996) (holding that Rule 4(m)'s timeliness requirement is only excused where service is attempted in a foreign country); *Sang Young Kim v. Frank Mohn A/S*, 909 F.Supp. 474, 479–80 (S.D.Tex.1995) (noting that exclusion of foreign service from the 120–day limit "helps to counterbalance the complex and time-consuming nature of foreign service of process"); *Pennsylvania Orthopedic Ass'n v. Mercedes–Benz A.G.*, 160 F.R.D. 58 (E.D.Pa. 1995)(commenting that, to compensate for the possibility of very complex and time-consuming service, Rule 4(m) acts to remove all deadlines for serving a complaint in a foreign country).

208. *See* Fed.R.Civ.P. 4(m)(referencing Fed.R.Civ.P. 4(j)(1)) (providing for service

upon foreign States and their political subdivisions, agencies, and instrumentalities).

209. *See Nylok Corp. v. Fastener World Inc.*, 396 F.3d 805, 807 (7th Cir.2005).

210. *See Thayer v. Dial Indus. Sales, Inc.*, 85 F.Supp.2d 263, 266 n. 1 (S.D.N.Y. 2000) (holding that because plaintiff never attempted to complete service and the 120–day period expired, the claims will be dismissed for failure to prosecute). *See also Montalbano v. Easco Hand Tools, Inc.*, 766 F.2d 737, 740 (2d Cir.1985) (same holding, construing former Rule 4(j) (predecessor to Rule 4(m))).

211. *See City of Merced v. Fields*, 997 F.Supp. 1326, 1338 (E.D.Cal.1998); *Del Raine v. Carlson*, 153 F.R.D. 622, 628 (S.D.Ill.1994), *rev'd in part on other grounds*, 77 F.3d 484 (7th Cir.1996) (Table).

212. *See Bolden v. City of Topeka*, 441 F.3d 1129, 1148–49 (10th Cir.2006).

213. *See Scary v. Philadelphia Gas Works*, 202 F.R.D. 148 (E.D.Pa.2001).

RULE 4(n). ASSERTING JURISDICTION OVER PROPERTY OR ASSETS

CORE CONCEPT

If authorized by federal statute, the district court may exercise jurisdiction over property. Moreover, if personal jurisdiction over a particular defendant is not possible, the district court may exercise jurisdiction over that defendant's property by seizing the property as permitted under State law.

APPLICATIONS

Effect

A judgment in a quasi-in-rem or in-rem lawsuit acts only upon the seized property; it has no *in personam* effect. Thus, a plaintiff cannot enforce a quasi-in-rem or in-rem judgment against property of the defendant located outside the forum State.[214]

Amount in Controversy

A quasi-in-rem or in-rem action only permits execution of the seized property; the courts, however, are divided on the proper method for computing the amount in controversy—either by the value of the seized property or the sum stated in the complaint's demand clause.[215]

Note: If the plaintiff's claim exceeds the value of seized property, the plaintiff is free to sue elsewhere for the remaining, unrecovered amount of the claim.

Due Process

Just as in the personal jurisdiction context, a federal court can hear a quasi-in-rem action only if the Due Process "traditional notions of fair play and substantial justice" test is satisfied.[216]

ADDITIONAL RESEARCH REFERENCES

Wright & Miller, *Federal Practice and Procedure* §§ 1061–1137.

C.J.S. Federal Civil Procedure §§ 187–223.

West's Key No. Digests, Federal Civil Procedure ☞403, 404, 411–427, 441–446, 461–505, 511–518, 531–540.

214. *See Sara Lee Corp. v. Gregg*, No. 1:02CV00195, 2002 WL 1925703, at *2 (M.D.N.C.2002) (noting that quasi in rem jurisdiction over defendant's property is limited to the property located within forum). The effect of quasi-in-rem and in-rem actions are discussed in greater depth in Part II of this text, §§ 2.8–2.9.

215. *See Great American Ins. Co. v. Louis Lesser Enters., Inc.*, 353 F.2d 997 (8th Cir.1965)(noting disagreement among courts).

216. *See Shaffer v. Heitner*, 433 U.S. 186, 97 S.Ct. 2569, 53 L.Ed.2d 683 (1977).

RULE 4.1

SERVING OTHER PROCESS

(a) In General. Process—other than a summons under Rule 4 or a subpoena under Rule 45—must be served by a United States marshal or deputy marshal or by a person specially appointed for that purpose. It may be served anywhere within the territorial limits of the state where the district court is located and, if authorized by a federal statute, beyond those limits. Proof of service must be made under Rule 4(l).

(b) Enforcing Orders: Committing for Civil Contempt. An order committing a person for civil contempt of a decree or injunction issued to enforce federal law may be served and enforced in any district. Any other order in a civil-contempt proceeding may be served only in the state where the issuing court is located or elsewhere in the United States within 100 miles from where the order was issued.

[Adopted April 22, 1993, effective December 1, 1993; April 30, 2007, effective December 1, 2007.]

───────────── **2007 AMENDMENTS ROADMAP** ─────────────

STYLE PROJECT CHANGES: Bulky word choice and sentence structure culled; active voice replaced passive voice.

NON-STYLE CHANGES: None.

NOTE: The Federal Rules "Style Project" is explained in Part III-A.

AUTHORS' COMMENTARY ON RULE 4.1

───────────── PURPOSE AND SCOPE ─────────────

Rule 4.1 sets the procedure for service of types of process other than a civil summons or a subpoena. Such process is served either by a United States Marshal or by an individual specially appointed by the court.

APPLICATIONS

What Is "Other Process"

The procedures for service of a civil summons and complaint or a subpoena are defined elsewhere in the Rules.[1] Similarly, once initial process is served, the service of all subsequent papers in that same case is prescribed by Rule 5. Rule 4.1 is intended to establish the procedure for service of process in all other cases, such as in the case of execution orders and orders of civil commitment,[2] as well as temporary restraining orders, injunctions, attachments, arrests, and judicial sales orders.[3]

This Rule does *not* apply to civil contempt orders intended to enforce non-federally created rights, such as contempt orders issued in a diversity proceeding where the substantive rights in dispute arise under State law.[4] The Rule also does *not* apply to orders of criminal commitment.

Process Server

"Other process" must be served either by the United States Marshal, a deputy Marshal, or some other person specially appointed for the purpose by the court. (Whether to appoint a Marshall is left to the court's discretion, unless the plaintiff is a pauper or seaman.[5]) Service performed by anyone else is defective.[6] To date, the only case law exception to this requirement appears in the context of process to enforce a judgment for the payment of money. Such enforcement proceedings are governed in the Federal Rules by Rule 69(a), which provides that the "procedure on execution" must follow State practice. At least one court has held that, notwithstanding the broad, general language of Rule 4.1, the provisions of Rule 69(a) compel that State practice govern the service of process in such execution proceedings.[7]

1. *See* Rule 4 (procedure for serving summons and complaint); Rule 45 (procedure for serving subpoena).

2. *See Schneider v. National R.R. Passenger Corp.*, 72 F.3d 17 (2d Cir.1995) (applying Rule 4.1 to execution orders); *Federal Trade Comm'n v. Verity Int'l, Ltd.*, 140 F.Supp.2d 313, 318 (S.D.N.Y.2001) (applying Rule 4.1 to civil commitment order which directed that defendants, who had willfully disobeyed court order, were to be arrested and detained if they enter the United States, until such time as they complied with court order), *order vacated,* 443 F.3d 48 (2d Cir.2006); *Spectacular Venture, L.P. v. World Star Int'l, Inc.*, 927 F.Supp. 683 (S.D.N.Y.1996) (applying Rule 4.1 to civil contempt orders).

3. *See JTH Tax Inc. v. Lee*, 2007 WL 1320505, at *2 n.2 (C.D.Ill. 2007).

4. *See Spectacular Venture, L.P. v. World Star Int'l, Inc.*, 927 F.Supp. 683 (S.D.N.Y.1996) (holding that, in a diversity case, contempt of federal orders issued under the Judicial Code and Rules of Civil Procedure is not contempt of "laws of the United States" and, thus, the provisions of Rule 4.1 would not apply).

5. *See JTH Tax Inc. v. Lee*, 2007 WL 1320505, at *2 (C.D.Ill. 2007).

6. *See Schneider v. National R.R. Passenger Corp.*, 72 F.3d 17 (2d Cir.1995) (State sheriff who had "seized" Amtrak locomotives in the course of executing upon a $1.8 million plaintiff's personal injury judgment was not a Marshal, deputy Marshal, or specially appointed process server, and thus process was defective under Rule 4.1 and the sheriff was not entitled to his service fee for executing upon the trains).

7. *See Apostolic Pentecostal Church v. Colbert*, 169 F.3d 409, 414 (6th Cir.1999).

Limits of Service

"Other process" may be served either within the State in which the district court is sitting or as otherwise provided by federal statute.[8] An order of civil commitment, however, may be served and enforced in any federal district. All other civil contempt orders may be served either within the State in which the district court is sitting or within 100 miles of the place where the order was issued.

Proof of Service

The process server—the Marshal, deputy Marshal, or specially appointed person—must file a proof of service with the court as provided in Rule 4(l).[9]

---

8. *See Hoult v. Hoult*, 373 F.3d 47, 53 (1st Cir.2004).

9. *See* Rule 4.1(a).

RULE 5

SERVING AND FILING PLEADINGS AND OTHER PAPERS

(a) Service: When Required.

(1) *In General.* Unless these rules provide otherwise, each of the following papers must be served on every party:

    (A) an order stating that service is required;

    (B) a pleading filed after the original complaint, unless the court orders otherwise under Rule 5(c) because there are numerous defendants;

    (C) a discovery paper required to be served on a party, unless the court orders otherwise;

    (D) a written motion, except one that may be heard ex parte; and

    (E) a written notice, appearance, demand, or offer of judgment, or any similar paper.

(2) *If a Party Fails to Appear.* No service is required on a party who is in default for failing to appear. But a pleading that asserts a new claim for relief against such a party must be served on that party under Rule 4.

(3) *Seizing Property.* If an action is begun by seizing property and no person is or need be named as a defendant, any service required before the filing of an appearance, answer, or claim must be made on the person who had custody or possession of the property when it was seized.

(b) Service: How Made.

(1) *Serving an Attorney.* If a party is represented by an attorney, service under this rule must be made on the attorney unless the court orders service on the party.

(2) *Service in General.* A paper is served under this rule by:

    (A) handing it to the person;

    (B) leaving it:

          (i) at the person's office with a clerk or other person in charge or, if no one is in charge, in a conspicuous place in the office; or

          (ii) if the person has no office or the office is closed, at the person's dwelling or usual place of abode with someone of suitable age and discretion who resides there;

    (C) mailing it to the person's last known address— in which event service is complete upon mailing;

    (D) leaving it with the court clerk if the person has no known address;

    (E) sending it by electronic means if the person consented in writing—in which event service is complete upon transmission, but is not effective if the serving party learns that it did not reach the person to be served; or

    (F) delivering it by any other means that the person consented to in writing—in which event service is complete when the person making service delivers it to the agency designated to make delivery.

  (3) *Using Court Facilities.* If a local rule so authorizes, a party may use the court's transmission facilities to make service under Rule 5(b)(2)(E).

(c) Serving Numerous Defendants.

  (1) *In General.* If an action involves an unusually large number of defendants, the court may, on motion or on its own, order that:

    (A) defendants' pleadings and replies to them need not be served on other defendants;

    (B) any crossclaim, counterclaim, avoidance, or affirmative defense in those pleadings and replies to them will be treated as denied or avoided by all other parties; and

    (C) filing any such pleading and serving it on the plaintiff constitutes notice of the pleading to all parties.

  (2) *Notifying Parties.* A copy of every such order must be served on the parties as the court directs.

(d) Filing.

(1) *Required Filings; Certificate of Service.* Any paper after the complaint that is required to be served—together with a certificate of service—must be filed within a reasonable time after service. But disclosures under Rule 26(a)(1) or (2) and the following discovery requests and responses must not be filed until they are used in the proceeding or the court orders filing: depositions, interrogatories, requests for documents or tangible things or to permit entry onto land, and requests for admission.

(2) *How Filing Is Made—In General.* A paper is filed by delivering it:

(A) to the clerk; or

(B) to a judge who agrees to accept it for filing, and who must then note the filing date on the paper and promptly send it to the clerk.

(3) *Electronic Filing, Signing, or Verification.* A court may, by local rule, allow papers to be filed, signed, or verified by electronic means that are consistent with any technical standards established by the Judicial Conference of the United States. A local rule may require electronic filing only if reasonable exceptions are allowed. A paper filed electronically in compliance with a local rule is a written paper for purposes of these rules.

(4) *Acceptance by the Clerk.* The clerk must not refuse to file a paper solely because it is not in the form prescribed by these rules or by a local rule or practice.

[Amended January 21, 1963, effective July 1, 1963; March 30, 1970, effective July 1, 1970; April 29, 1980, effective August 1, 1980; March 2, 1987, effective August 1, 1987; April 30, 1991, effective December 1, 1991; April 22, 1993, effective December 1, 1993; April 23, 1996, effective December 1, 1996; April 17, 2000, effective December 1, 2000; April 23, 2001, effective December 1, 2001; April 12, 2006, effective December 1, 2006; April 30, 2007, effective December 1, 2007.]

—————————————— **2007 AMENDMENTS ROADMAP** ——————————————

STYLE PROJECT CHANGES: New orienting labels were added, and some Rule parts were subsectioned. Rule 5(d) and Rule 5(e) were folded together (with all text retained) into an omnibus "Filing" subpart. Active voice generally replaced passive voice; "must" replaced "shall".

NON-STYLE CHANGES: Three changes: (1) a reference to service of the designation of the record on appeal was omitted in favor of reserving for the Appellate Rules all appellate procedures; (2) a confusing reference to court transmission facilities was corrected; and (3) "a judge" replaced "the judge" in light of the practice in some districts of not assigning a designated judge for the life of each case.

NOTE: The Federal Rules "Style Project" is explained in Part III-A.

AUTHORS' COMMENTARY ON RULE 5

PURPOSE AND SCOPE

Rule 5 sets forth the general filing requirements for all pleadings and other papers, and the general service requirements for all pleadings and other papers *except* the complaint (Rule 4 governs the service of the complaint). The provisions of Rule 5 are designed to achieve two objectives: to ensure that each party to a civil action obtains a copy of all documents formally used in prosecuting and defending the case, and to create a rationally-assembled record with the clerk of court.

This is a general service and filing rule. Other Rules establish separate requirements crafted for particular circumstances (*e.g.,* Rule 45(b), governing service of subpoenas). Likewise, many federal district courts have developed specific local service and filing requirements that supplement the provisions of Rule 5. Practitioners should *always* check the other Rules and the district's local rules to ensure that they understand how the requirements of Rule 5 may have been supplemented in their courts.

RULE 5(a). SERVICE REQUIRED

CORE CONCEPT

Unless specifically excused by the Court, every party who has entered an appearance must be served with a copy of the following:

- *All Orders required by their terms to be served (i.e.,* Rule 77(d) notices of entry of orders);

- *All Pleadings After the Original Complaint,* generally including amended complaints (the original complaint and summons must be served in accordance with Rule 4);

- *All Discovery Papers;*

- *All Written Motions* (except *ex parte* motions); and

● *All Other Appropriate Legal Papers* (such as written notices, appearances, demands, offers of judgment,[1] and similar papers).

APPLICATIONS

Broadly Construed

Rule 5 is interpreted expansively to apply to nearly all court papers (*e.g.*, affidavits in support of motions must be served under Rule 5). The Rule thus applies to amended complaints which, unless they assert new claims for relief,[2] need be served only under this Rule 5, and not through the more elaborate, formal procedures of Rule 4.[3]

Unserved Pleadings and Papers

Unserved pleadings and other papers may be found to lack any legal force and effect, until service is accomplished. For example, exhibits that have not been served may not be relied upon to support or oppose motions,[4] and amended complaints that are not served (even if they are filed with the clerk of court) may be deemed ineffective in superseding the original complaint.[5] However, when a party is not served, but receives actual notice of the document and is not prejudiced by the lack of service, the document may still be accepted as effective.[6]

Exceptions

Rule 5 does *not* apply to the service of:

● Original complaints (controlled by Rule 4);

● *Ex parte* motions;

● Pleadings between numerous defendants (when service is excused by court order under Rule 5(c)); or

● As provided otherwise in the Rules (*i.e.*, Rule 45(b) subpoena requirements).

1. *See Magnuson v. Video Yesteryear*, 85 F.3d 1424, 1429 (9th Cir.1996) (service of Rule 68 offers must comply with Rule 5).

2. *See infra* Authors' Commentary to Rule 5(b) ("**New Claims Against Existing Parties**") (noting instances in which amended complaints must be served under Rule 4).

3. *See Vax–D Med. Techs., LLC v. Texas Spine Med. Ctr,*, 485 F.3d 593, 597 (11th Cir. 2007); *Employee Painters' Trust v. Ethan Enters., Inc.*, 480 F.3d 993, 995–99 (9th Cir. 2007).

4. *See Thorne v. Steubenville Police Officer*, 463 F. Supp. 2d 760, 770 (S.D. Ohio 2006).

5. *See International Controls Corp. v. Vesco*, 556 F.2d 665, 669 (2d Cir. 1977)(amended complaint remains inchoate until served under Rule 5(a)).

6. *See McKinnie v. Roadway Express, Inc.*, 341 F.3d 554, 557–59 (6th Cir.2003) (holding that where party is not properly served with summary judgment motion, but has actual notice of the motion prior to disposition, a court's decision to grant the motion will not be reversed on appeal for this reason unless the affected party demonstrates a genuine issue of material fact that would defeat summary judgment).

Impact of an Appearance

Once proper service of original process is accomplished under Rule 4, it is expected that the served party will appear to defend the case. If that party, instead, defaults for failing to appear, no further service of papers needs to be made upon that party.[7] There is one exception. If a later pleading asserts a new claim for relief against the non-appearing party, that later pleading must be served upon the non-appearing party under Rule 4.[8]

Seizure Actions

Actions begun by the seizure of property (arrest, attachment, garnishment) are subject to Rule 5. In these cases, any paper required to be served before filing an answer, claim, or appearance must be served on the person with custody or possession of the property at the time of seizure.

RULE 5(b). METHOD OF SERVICE

CORE CONCEPT

Service is ordinarily made on each party's attorney, not on the party directly. Service may be accomplished in several ways:

SERVICE BY PERSONAL DELIVERY:

(1) *Hand Delivery*: The served document is handed either to the attorney or, if unrepresented or if the court orders otherwise, to the party; *or*

(2) *Office*: The served document is left at the recipient's office with the person "in charge" of the office or, if no one is "in charge" of the office, at the recipient's office in a conspicuous place; *or*

(3) *Home*: If hand delivery and office service are unavailable, the served document may be left at the recipient's residence with a person of suitable age and discretion residing there.

SERVICE BY MAIL:

Last Known Address: The served document is mailed to the recipient's last known address.

SERVICE BY OTHER AGREED MEANS:

Electronic Transmission or Otherwise: The served document is delivered or transmitted by "any other means" to which the person served has agreed, in writing.

SERVICE WHERE NO ADDRESS IS KNOWN:

7. *See* Rule 5(a)(2). *See also Trustees of St. Paul Elec. Const. Indus. Fringe Benefit Funds v. Martens Elec. Co.*, 485 F. Supp. 2d 1063, 1066 (D.Minn. 2007).

8. *See Trustees of St. Paul Elec. Const. Indus. Fringe Benefit Funds v. Martens Elec. Co.*, 485 F. Supp. 2d 1063, 1066 (D.Minn. 2007).

> ***Clerk of Court***: If the recipient's last known address is unavailable, the served document may be left with the clerk of court.

APPLICATIONS

Service on Attorney, Not Party

Pleadings and other papers generally must be served on the party's attorney, and not on the party directly. However, service may be made on the party directly if a specific Rule so requires, if the party is unrepresented, or if the court so requires.

Parties Represented by Multiple Attorneys

Service is complete upon serving one attorney for each represented party. If a party is represented by multiple counsel, multiple service is ordinarily not required.[9]

New Claims Against New Parties

Pleadings asserting claims against new parties (*e.g.*, third-party claims) must be served in accordance with Rule 4.

New Claims Against Existing Parties

Pleadings asserting new claims against existing parties must be served in accordance with Rule 4, if:

- The new claims differ significantly from those in the original pleading;[10]

- Circumstances persuade the court that service on the attorney is unlikely to ensure notice to the party;

- Extraterritorial service of process was used in the original pleading and a new claim is unrelated to the initial claim; or

- Due Process requires Rule 4 service (*i.e.*, federal jurisdiction was premised on a particular injury-causing event, and the complaint was amended to assert an unrelated claim which could not otherwise be brought in that district).

Service by Mail

Service by mail is complete at the moment a properly posted envelope is deposited with the Post Office.[11] The Post Office's failure to postmark the envelope on the day of deposit does not alter

---

9. *See Buchanan v. Sherrill*, 51 F.3d 227, 228 (10th Cir.1995); *Daniel Int'l Corp. v. Fischbach & Moore, Inc.*, 916 F.2d 1061, 1063 (5th Cir.1990); *United States v. Schooner Windspirit*, 161 F.R.D. 321, 323 (D.V.I.1995).

10. *See O'Callaghan v. Sifre*, 242 F.R.D. 69, 73 (S.D.N.Y. 2007). *See also Beckham v. Grand Affair of North Carolina, Inc.*, 671 F.Supp. 415, 418 (W.D.N.C.1987)(holding that amended complaint containing new theory of liability should be served on de-

fendant pursuant to Rule 4, rather than on the defendant's appearing attorney as per Rule 5).

11. *See* Rule 5(b)(2)(C). *See also United States v. Clingman*, 288 F.3d 1183, 1185 (10th Cir.2002); *United States v. Novaton*, 271 F.3d 968, 1015–16 (11th Cir.2001); *Greene v. WCI Holdings Corp.*, 136 F.3d 313, 315 (2d Cir.1998); *United States v. Kennedy*, 133 F.3d 53, 59 (D.C.Cir.1998).

this effect.[12] Non-receipt or non-acceptance usually does not affect the validity of service.[13]

- Notices of Removal can be served by mail.

- *Note:* Rule 6(e) gives the recipient of mailed service 3 extra days to respond. Accordingly, if a quick response is preferred, personal service will eliminate this additional 3 day response period.

Service By Electronic Transmission

Service by electronic transmission may be made, but only if the person served has expressly consented to such service.[14] The consent must be in writing; consent may not be implied from conduct (such as an e-mail address on a defendant's letterhead).[15] Thus, service by facsimile remains ineffective, absent this written consent.[16]

When consent has been obtained, service by electronic transmission (including both direct transmission of the document and transmission of a notice that the document is available through a certain electronic link) is deemed complete upon transmission.[17] (Each district may, by local rule, authorize the making of such transmissions from common court facilities.[18]) Parties are "encouraged" by the Advisory Committee to reach specific agreement on the specific scope of the written consent, including (1) the name of the person to whom service should be made, (2) the appropriate address (facsimile number, e-mail address, etc.) for such service, (3) the format to be used for attachments, and (4) the duration of the consent.[19]

> *Failed Transmission:* If the serving party learns, after the electronic transmission is attempted, that the transmission failed and did not reach the person to be served, the service is not considered effective.[20] Such a transmission failure can be a mechanical one (*e.g.*, an "incomplete" or "failed" fax message) or one relating to a change in the recipient's profile (*e.g.*, original counsel consents to the District's electronic filing service, but a change in counsel renders this consent ineffective).[21]

12. *See Larez v. Holcomb*, 16 F.3d 1513, 1515 n. 1 (9th Cir.1994)(noting that document placed in the mail on the last day for service was timely served, even though Post Office did not postmark the envelope until the next day).

13. *Dunlap v. Transamerica Occidental Life Ins. Co.*, 858 F.2d 629 (11th Cir.1988).

14. *See* Rule 5(b)(2)(E).

15. *See* Rule 5(b)(2)(E) advisory committee note to 2001 amendments. *See also RFR Indus., Inc. v. Century Steps, Inc.*, 477 F.3d 1348, 1352 (Fed.Cir. 2007) (rejecting argument that a showing of "exceptional good cause" could excuse noncompliance with the consent-in-writing requirement).

16. *See Magnuson v. Video Yesteryear*, 85 F.3d 1424, 1430 (9th Cir.1996); *United States v. Galiczynski*, 44 F.Supp.2d 707, 713 (E.D.Pa.1999).

17. *See* Rule 5(b)(2)(E). *See also* Rule 5(b)(2)(E) advisory committee note to 2001 amendments.

18. *See* Rule 5(b)(3).

19. *See* Rule 5(b)(2)(E) advisory committee note to 2001 amendments.

20. *See* Rule 5(b)(2)(E).

21. *See McKinnie v. Roadway Express, Inc.*, 341 F.3d 554, 557 (6th Cir.2003).

Service By "Other Means"

Service by some "other means" is also approved, provided that the recipient has consented, in writing, to the alternative method of service.[22] When permitted, such service by "other means" is deemed complete when the person making the service delivers the document to the entity engaged to make the delivery.[23]

Private Overnight Courier Services

Private overnight courier services (such as FedEx) are not the Post Office, and they do not provide "mail" service. Thus, handing legal papers to a private courier service might not constitute "service by mail" under Rule 5(b)(2)(C), and therefore might not entitle the sender to completed service upon mailing. Rather, service by a courier service is more likely to be deemed a type of personal service, complete only upon the courier's delivery of the document to the ultimate recipient.[24] If, however, service by private overnight courier has been consented to, it will qualify as effective service by "other means".[25]

Service At Home

Service can be accomplished at the recipient's home, if hand delivery or office service are unavailable.[26] Presumably, this Rule will be interpreted by the courts in the same manner as Rule 4. Thus, the recipient of service need not necessarily be an adult, so long as the court reaches the case-by-case factual determination that the recipient is of "suitable age and discretion". Generally, service

22. *See* Rule 5(b)(2)(F).

23. *See* Rule 5(b)(2)(F).

24. *See Transco Leasing Corp. v. United States*, 992 F.2d 552, 554 n. 2 (5th Cir. 1993)(commenting, without deciding, that service by overnight courier might not qualify as service by mail under Rule 5). *Compare Schudel v. General Elec. Co.*, 120 F.3d 991 (9th Cir.1997) (noting that personal delivery or delivery to U.S. Postal Service could have satisfied service requirement, delivery to Federal Express did not) *and Magnuson v. Video Yesteryear*, 85 F.3d 1424, 1430–31 (9th Cir.1996) (holding that delivery by Federal Express is not "mail", noting that drafters in 1937—working in an "era that predates modern overnight delivery services"—could not have intended to authorize service by private delivery services) *and Audio Enters. v. B & W Loudspeakers of America*, 957 F.2d 406, 409 (7th Cir.1992) (noting that Federal Express is not first class mail within the meaning of Rule 4) *and Prince v. Poulos*, 876 F.2d 30, 32 n. 1 (5th Cir.1989)(in construing Federal

Rule of Appellate Procedure 25, the court held that Federal Express is not a "public authority" and is not a form of "mail") and *Chudasama v. Mazda Motor Corp.*, 1995 WL 641984, at *16 n. 20 (M.D.Ga.1995) (holding that service by private courier is not complete under Rule until the paper is handed to counsel or delivered to counsel's office), *vacated on other grounds*, 123 F.3d 1353 (11th Cir.1997) *and Edmond v. United States Postal Serv.*, 727 F.Supp. 7 (D.D.C. 1989) (holding that service via Federal Express was effective when delivered to litigant's home); *aff'd in part and reversed in part on other grounds*, 949 F.2d 415 (D.C.Cir.1991) *with United States v. Certain Real Property & Premises Known as 63–29 Trimble Rd., Woodside, N.Y.*, 812 F.Supp. 332, 334 (E.D.N.Y.1992) (service via Federal Express "mail" is valid because Rule 5(b) does not require that "mailing" occur through the United States Postal Service).

25. *See* Rule 5(b)(2)(F).

26. *See* Rule 5(b)(2)(B).

must be made on a person "residing" at the home; service on a maid, a landlady, or some other non-resident might be ineffective.[27]

Prisoner Plaintiffs

For documents served by *pro se* prisoners, the courts generally recognize a "mailbox" rule that deems documents as served upon delivery of those documents to the prison officials.[28]

RULE 5(c).   SERVING NUMEROUS DEFENDANTS

CORE CONCEPT

Where an unusually large number of defendants are sued, the court may order that the defendants need not serve every other defendant with pleadings and responses, and that cross-claims, counterclaims, and affirmative defenses are deemed automatically denied or avoided as between the numerous defendants.

APPLICATIONS

Court Order

Rule 5(c) is seldom used, and is effective only upon court order. The court's enabling order must be served on all parties.

Plaintiff Must Be Served

Rule 5(c) does not excuse service on the plaintiff of all papers.

Court Filing Still Required

Rule 5(c) also does not excuse the pleader's obligation to *file* the pleading with the Court.[29]

Only Pleadings/Responses

This limitation applies only to pleadings and responses; all papers other than pleadings and responses must be served.

Defendants Only

If the action involves a large number of plaintiffs (*e.g.*, a mass tort case), service must still be made on each plaintiff.

RULE 5(d).   FILING WITH THE COURT

CORE CONCEPT

Any paper required to be served must also be filed with the court within a reasonable time after service. Along with any such paper, the party must also include a certificate of service. Papers are

---

27. *See supra* Authors' Commentary to Rule 4(e) ("**Service at Individual's Dwelling House**") (discussing service on maid and landlady).

28. *See Schroeder v. McDonald*, 55 F.3d 454 (9th Cir.1995)(noting that incarcerated *pro se* litigants effect service under Rule 5(b) by submitting their documents to pris-

on authorities); *cf.* Fed.R.App.P. 4(c)(document deemed "filed" by prisoner when deposited into prison's internal mail system).

29. *See United States v. Atlas Lederer Co.*, 282 F.Supp.2d 687, 701–03 (S.D.Ohio 2001).

to be filed with the clerk of court, unless the court permits filing with the judge personally. Where so provided by proper local rules (but *only* where so provided), papers may be filed by electronic means, including by facsimile transmission. The clerk of court may not refuse to accept a paper for filing simply because the paper does not conform to these Rules or the district's local rules.

APPLICATIONS

"Reasonable" Time Defined

Whether the time between service and filing is "reasonable" is a matter left to the discretion of the district court.[30] Consequently, practitioners should err on the side of caution and file their papers simultaneously with service, or as soon thereafter as possible. Moreover, this Rule only sets the ordinary procedure to be followed. Where, for example, the court fixes a specific time for filing a particular paper, that Order must be obeyed (not the more general "reasonable time" procedure of Rule 5(d)).[31]

Certificate of Service

A party's certificate of service should identify the document served, the date of service, and the manner of delivery.[32] Nevertheless, because the principal purpose of a certificate of service is to verify for the court that proper service has been accomplished, the court will likely not invalidate a legal filing that lacks a certificate of service, so long as proper service is not contested.[33]

Enforcing the Rule

Ordinary, in the absence of contumacious behavior, a failure to timely file a missed pleading will be remedied by an order compelling the filing, and not with a dismissal.[34] Practitioners should, however, be wary of relying on this informal liberality; the practice of merely compelling compliance, rather than dismissing, is not expressly guaranteed by the Rules.

30. *See Chesson v. Jaquez*, 986 F.2d 363, 365 (10th Cir.1993)(holding that filing within six days after service is "reasonable", particularly because a weekend fell within that period); *Biocore Med. Techs., Inc. v. Khosrowshahi*, 181 F.R.D. 660, 668 (D.Kan.1998) (noting that courts have decided that documents filed up to six days after service are filed within a "reasonable time" under Rule 5(d); holding that filing almost two months after service is not "reasonable"); *Ives v. Guilford Mills, Inc.*, 3 F.Supp.2d 191, 194 (N.D.N.Y.1998) (finding three weeks reasonable under the circumstances).

31. *See Raymond v. Ameritech Corp.*, 442 F.3d 600, 605–06 (7th Cir.2006).

32. *See Golden v. McCaughtry*, 915 F.Supp. 77, 79 (E.D.Wis.1995) (noting certificate of service filing obligation).

33. *See Russell v. City of Milwaukee*, 338 F.3d 662, 665–67 (7th Cir.2003) (finding that failure to include certificate of service with suggestion of death did not defeat court's finding that service had, in fact, been made); *Ives v. Guilford Mills, Inc.*, 3 F.Supp.2d 191 (N.D.N.Y.1998) (concluding that an invalidation under such circumstances "would seem to serve no purpose except to fruitlessly extend the length of this litigation").

34. *See Betty K Agencies, Ltd. v. M/V MONADA*, 432 F.3d 1333, 1340 (11th Cir. 2005).

Other Rules

Certain Rules and the district's local rules may prescribe specific service/filing guidelines. Consult the specific Rule and the applicable local rules.

Discovery Papers

The widespread proliferation of local rules establishing, on a district-by-district basis, whether discovery materials should be filed with the clerk's office is addressed in Rule 5(d). In order to conserve the physical resources of the clerk's office and federal courthouses, discovery requests and discovery responses are *not* to be filed with the court unless and until (a) they are actually "used" in court proceedings or (b) the trial court so orders.[35] This prohibition applies to depositions notices and objections, interrogatories and their objections and responses, requests for documents and their objections and responses, requests to permit entry upon land and their objections and responses, and request for admission and their objections and responses.[36] Local rules that prescribe different filing requirements are superseded and invalidated in favor of this uniform, national approach.[37]

The phrase "used in the proceeding" is to be interpreted broadly to include those discovery materials used in connection with motions, pretrial conferences, and otherwise.[38] However, a party who "uses" discovery materials while interrogating witnesses during depositions need not file those materials with the court.[39] Moreover, if a party "uses" only a portion of a voluminous discovery document, only the "used" portion need be filed with the court (although any other party would be free to file other relevant portions used).[40]

Document Itself Must Be Filed

A document will not be deemed "filed" unless it is separately and formally filed with the court. Thus, attaching a document as an exhibit to another paper will not constitute a "filing" of the attachment.[41]

Possession by Clerk

Documents are only filed when placed in the clerk's possession.[42] Thus, leaving a document lying against the clerk's office

---

35. *See* Rule 5(d)(1). *See also* Rule 5(d) advisory committee note to 2000 amendments (discussing resource conservation objective).

36. *See* Rule 5(d) advisory committee note to 2000 amendments.

37. *See* Rule 5(d) advisory committee note to 2000 amendments.

38. *See* Rule 5(d) advisory committee note to 2000 amendments.

39. *See* Rule 5(d) advisory committee note to 2000 amendments.

40. *See* Rule 5(d) advisory committee note to 2000 amendments.

41. *See Orsini v. Kugel*, 9 F.3d 1042, 1045 (2d Cir.1993)(holding that a stipulation had not been "filed" merely because it was attached as an exhibit to another court paper).

42. *See McIntosh v. Antonino*, 71 F.3d 29, 36–37 (1st Cir.1995); *Flying Cross Check, L.L.C. v. Central Hockey League, Inc.*, 153 F.Supp.2d 1253, 1257 (D.Kan. 2001); *Central States, S.E. & S.W. Areas Pension Fund v. Paramount Liquor Co.*, 34 F.Supp.2d 1092, 1094 (N.D.Ill.1999).

door or slipping a document underneath the clerk's office door will generally *not* be considered an effective filing until the day the clerk actually receives the document. However, placing a document in a box designated by the clerk as an after-hours depository should constitute effective filing as of the time of deposit.[43]

Filing by Mail

Because documents are only deemed to be filed when they come into the clerk's possession, a document will *not* be deemed "filed" when it is placed in the United States Mail, addressed to the clerk. Instead, mailed documents are "filed" on the date they are actually received by the clerk.[44]

Filing With the Judge

Where the judge so permits,[45] papers may be "filed" with the judge directly, after which the judge is required to transmit the papers "forthwith" to the clerk's office.[46]

Fees

It is unresolved whether filing is effective prior to the payment of any applicable filing fees. Thus, prudence dictates that all filing fees be paid at the time a document is filed with the court.

Filing by Electronic Means, Including Facsimile Transmission

Electronic filing is *not* permitted in every district, although the Rules permit each court, on a district-by-district basis, to provide for such filing in their local rules. Consequently, each district's local rules must be consulted. Attempting to file by facsimile or by other electronic means in a district that has not adopted such a procedure will not constitute effective, or timely, filing.[47]

---

43. *See* Rule 77(a) ("District Courts Always Open"). *See also Greenwood v. State of New York, Office of Mental Health,* 842 F.2d 636 (2d Cir.1988)(document placed in night depository box operated by Clerk's Office, and bearing date/time stamp imprinted on document by device also operated by Clerk's Office, was deemed to have been "filed" as of the date and time stamped on document); *Turner v. City of Newport,* 887 F.Supp. 149 (E.D.Ky.1995) (holding that complaint was timely filed when placed in the Clerk's post office box at 11:30 p.m. on the final day of the statute of limitations), *rev'd on other grounds,* 119 F.3d 425 (6th Cir.1997).

44. *See Raymond v. Ameritech Corp.,* 442 F.3d 600, 604–05 (7th Cir.2006); *McIntosh v. Antonino,* 71 F.3d 29, 36–37 (1st Cir.1995).

45. *See Tran v. Minnesota Dep't of Transp.,* 2006 WL 2917037, at *2 (D.Minn. 2006) (noting that no judge is under an obligation to permit a filing in this way).

46. *See Life Ins. Co. of North America v. Von Valtier,* 116 F.3d 279, 282–83 (7th Cir. 1997) (disapproving of trial judge's delay in transmitting motion to the clerk's office, noting that "the system will break down unless the judge scrupulously follows the directions to note the date and transmit the documents immediately to the clerk. Less than perfect adherence to these instructions will mean that actual filing dates will become as uncertain as the former dates of service were, and something as important as the jurisdictional time limit for taking an appeal will once again be subject to factual disputes").

47. *See McIntosh v. Antonino,* 71 F.3d 29, 34–35 (1st Cir.1995) (litigant's claim that a facsimile "filing" was effective, when such filing was not expressly authorized under the local rules, "is whistling past the graveyard"—without a local rule permitting such transmissions, "facsimile filings in a federal court are dead on arrival"); *In re Fisherman's Wharf Fillet, Inc.,* 83 F.Supp.2d 651, 657 (E.D.Va.1999) (absent

Rule 5(d)(3) also allows each judicial district to permit (or even require), under its local rules, the electronic filing, signing, or verifying of documents. A document properly filed electronically, in accordance with local rules, qualifies as a "written paper" within the meaning of the Rules. Any judicial district that *requires* electronic filing must allow reasonable exceptions in order to accommodate litigants for whom such filing would be a hardship.[48]

Prisoner Plaintiffs

As with service under Rule 5(b), a *pro se* prisoner's papers are usually deemed "filed" under Rule 5(d) upon delivery of those documents to the prison officials.[49]

Refusal to File

A paper is considered "filed" upon the completion of the act of delivering it to the clerk of court; procedural flaws in the paper will not impede the "filing".[50] Although neither the clerk of court (nor the clerk's computer system) may refuse to file a paper that does not conform to the Rules or to the district's local rules,[51] the clerk may advise the filing party or attorney of the paper's deficiencies. The task of enforcing rules concerning procedure and form are, therefore, reserved exclusively for the district judge.[52] However, a local rule may instruct the clerk to inform the judge of the paper's defect.

ADDITIONAL RESOURCE SOURCES

Wright & Miller, *Federal Practice and Procedure* §§ 1141–53.

C.J.S. Federal Civil Procedure §§ 261, 349.

West's Key No. Digests, Federal Civil Procedure ⚭664, 665.

local rule permitting such filings, facsimile transmission "filings" are "deemed null and of no legal effect"); *Johnson v. United Steel Workers of America*, 172 F.R.D. 185, 187 n. 5 (W.D.Va.1997) (refusing to consider faxed copy of affidavit because it was a facsimile copy, not an original, and no local rule permitted filing of facsimile papers in lieu of originals).

48. *See* Rule 5(d)(3). *See also* Rule 5(e) advisory committee note to 2006 amendments.

49. *See Cooper v. Brookshire*, 70 F.3d 377 (5th Cir.1995); *Dory v. Ryan*, 999 F.2d 679 (2d Cir.1993), *modified on other grounds* 25 F.3d 81 (2d Cir.1994); *Garvey v. Vaughn*, 993 F.2d 776 (11th Cir.1993). *Cf. Houston v. Lack*, 487 U.S. 266, 108 S.Ct. 2379, 101 L.Ed.2d 245 (1988)(holding that a *pro se* prisoner's notice of appeal was

"filed" within the meaning of the Federal Rules of Appellate Procedure when the notice was delivered to the prison authorities).

50. *See Castleberry v. Goldome Credit Corp.*, 408 F.3d 773, 784 (11th Cir.2005); *Wilson v. Lowe's Home Ctr.*, 401 F.Supp.2d 186, 189 (D.Conn.2005).

51. *See Farzana K. v. Indiana Dep't of Educ.*, 473 F.3d 703, 707–08 (7th Cir. 2007) (holding that court clerks "must take in whatever is tendered to them; a document may be rejected later if a judicial officer finds a problem, but the initial filing ensures that the process of vetting papers for compliance with the rules does not prevent satisfaction of time limits").

52. *See Jones v. Warden of Stateville Correctional Ctr.*, 918 F.Supp. 1142, 1151 (N.D.Ill.1995).

RULE 5.1

CONSTITUTIONAL CHALLENGE TO A STATUTE—NOTICE, CERTIFICATION, AND INTERVENTION

(a) Notice by a Party. A party that files a pleading, written motion, or other paper drawing into question the constitutionality of a federal or state statute must promptly:

(1) file a notice of constitutional question stating the question and identifying the paper that raises it, if:

(A) a federal statute is questioned and the parties do not include the United States, one of its agencies, or one of its officers or employees in an official capacity; or

(B) a state statute is questioned and the parties do not include the state, one of its agencies, or one of its officers or employees in an official capacity; and

(2) serve the notice and paper on the Attorney General of the United States if a federal statute is questioned—or on the state attorney general if a state statute is questioned—either by certified or registered mail or by sending it to an electronic address designated by the attorney general for this purpose.

(b) Certification by the Court. The court must, under 28 U.S.C. § 2403, certify to the appropriate attorney general that a statute has been questioned.

(c) Intervention; Final Decision on the Merits. Unless the court sets a later time, the attorney general may intervene within 60 days after the notice is filed or after the court certifies the challenge, whichever is earlier. Before the time to intervene expires, the court may reject the constitutional challenge, but may not enter a final judgment holding the statute unconstitutional.

(d) No Forfeiture. A party's failure to file and serve the notice, or the court's failure to certify, does not forfeit a constitutional claim or defense that is otherwise timely asserted.

[Added April 12, 2007, effective December 1, 2006.]

─────────────── **2007 AMENDMENTS ROADMAP** ───────────────

STYLE PROJECT CHANGES: Very modest syntax changes (likely due to the very recent promulgation of Rule 5.1 in 2006). The Rule remains unchanged in labels, structure, and substructure.

NON-STYLE CHANGES: None.

NOTE: The Federal Rules "Style Project" is explained in Part III-A.

AUTHORS' COMMENTARY ON RULE 5.1

─────────────── **PURPOSE AND SCOPE** ───────────────

Rule 5.1 was added in 2006, and is the repositioning of the former final three sentences of Rule 24(c). The Rule is designed to ensure that an affected federal or State official is given notice and the opportunity to intervene in a case that litigates the constitutionality of a federal or State statute. The Rule compels the party challenging constitutionality to promptly notify the appropriate attorney general, and directs the district court to make a certification of the challenge to the appropriate attorney general.

RULE 5.1(a).   NOTICE BY A PARTY

CORE CONCEPT

Any party who draws into question the constitutionality of a federal or State statute must ensure that the appropriate attorney general is informed of the pending litigation challenge.

APPLICATIONS

Prior Precedent

Because portions of Rule 5.1 track rather closely the purpose of the now abrogated last three sentences of Rule 24(c), it is likely that until a new body of judicial precedent develops that construes Rule 5.1, courts will look to existing precedent construing those sentences of old Rule 24(c) where such precedent does not contradict the slightly different language of Rule 5.1.

Notice and Service by a Party

With one exception (see below), Rule 5.1(a) requires a party who files a writing (whether a pleading, written motion, or other paper) that challenges the constitutionality of a federal or state statute to file a notice of the challenge with the district court. The contents of the notice must state the nature of the challenge and identify the document that contains the challenge. Both the notice and the challenge document must then be served on the affected attorney general (federal or State).[1]

Method of Service

Service of the notice on the affected federal or State attorney general must be made via certified or registered mail, or by electronic service through the electronic address established by the attorney general for this purpose.[2]

Exception to Notice and Service Requirement

Rule 5.1(a) contains one important exception to the notice and service requirement it normally mandates. If a federal or state statute is challenged, but the United States or the affected state is already a party itself or through agencies or officers sued in an official capacity, there is obviously no need for the special notice requirement of Rule 5.1(a). Such notice is therefore not required in those circumstances.[3]

Elimination of Requirement of "Affecting the Public Interest"

The former language of Rule 24(c) limited this notify-and-serve obligation to situations in which the constitutional challenge to a statute affected the public interest. Rule 5.1(a) intentionally omits this limiting language.[4]

No New Claim or Right

This Rule is not intended to create a new or independent cause of action or basis for relief; it is, instead, merely a vehicle to help ensure that notice to the affected federal or State attorney general will occur.[5]

RULE 5.1(b). CERTIFICATION BY THE COURT

CORE CONCEPT

The district court must, additionally, certify to the appropriate federal or State attorney general the presence of a constitutional challenge. This requirement supplements a party's duty as described in Rule 5.1(a).

APPLICATION

Court's Duty to Certify

The district court, independent of and in addition to the duties of notice and service imposed on parties by Rule 5.1(a), must certify

---

1. *See* Rule 5.1(a)(1).

2. *See* Rule 5.1(a)(2).

3. *See* Rule 5.1(a)(1)(A)–(1)(B). *See also* *Lee v. United States*, 2007 WL 1111250, at *2 n.1 (S.D.Fla. 2007).

4. *See* Rule 5.1 Advisory Committee Note to 2006 amendments ("It is better to assure, through notice, that the attorney general is able to determine whether to seek intervention on the ground that the act or statute affects a public interest.").

5. *See Lee v. United States*, 2007 WL 1111250, at *2 n.1 (S.D.Fla. 2007).

to the affected federal or State attorney general that a party has made a constitutional challenge to a federal or State statute.[6] This certification obligation is imposed on the court by 28 U.S.C.A. § 2403, and is important for two reasons. First, if the constitutional challenge was not raised by a party's pleading, written motion, or other paper, the court's certification is the only means of assuring that the interested federal or state attorney general will receive notice of the challenge.[7] Second, because Rule 5.1(d) prohibits a forfeiture of a properly asserted constitutional claim or defense for a party's failure to serve notice of a written challenge to the interested federal or State attorney general, or for the court's failure to certify[8] (and judicial precedent derived from old Rule 24(c) seems to hold that no lesser sanction exists),[9] the judicial certification requirement of Rule 5.1(b) is the only means of assuring that notice actually reaches the federal or State attorney general when the United States or a State is not a party to a case.

RULE 5.1(c). INTERVENTION; FINAL DECISION ON THE MERITS

CORE CONCEPT

Rule 5.1(c) creates a right of intervention for the federal or State attorney general potentially affected by a constitutional challenge. It also establishes the rather flexible time limits within which the affected attorney general must act. Rule 5.1(c) also provides that the court may continue to process the case while the attorney general is contemplating intervention, but the court may not enter a final judgment holding the statute unconstitutional.

APPLICATIONS

Time to Intervene

An attorney general may intervene of right within 60 days of filing of the notice of constitutional challenge or certification of the challenge, whichever is earlier. However, the court is authorized to extend the 60 day limit.[10] Such an extension may be obtained

---

6. See Rule 5.1(b).

7. See Rule 5.1 Advisory Committee Note to 2006 amendments ("The court's certification obligation remains, and is the only notice" when the challenge was not raised in a manner identified in Rule 5.1(a).).

8. See Rule 5.1(d).

9. See, e.g., Tonya K. v. Board of Educ. of Chicago, 847 F.2d 1243, 1247 (7th Cir. 1988) ("Failure to notify the Attorney General is not a jurisdictional defect."); Merrill v. Town of Addison, 763 F.2d 80, 83 (2d Cir.1985) ("Absent indication of harm, or

prejudice to the government's opportunity to fully present its views, belated certification, while not ideal, is sufficient to honor the purpose of section 2403."). Cf. United States v. Crystal Evangelical Free Church, 82 F.3d 1407, 1412 (8th Cir.1996) (temporarily removing case from argument calendar so that appellate court can certify constitutional question and give United States time to intervene; "Certification has occurred even after judgment at the appellate level.").

10. See Rule 5.1(c).

pursuant to a motion or the court's *sua sponte* act.[11]

Other Activity

While an attorney general is contemplating intervention, Rule 5.1 envisages that most of the routine activity of the court will continue in the case.[12] The important exception to that generalization is that the court may not enter a final judgment holding the statute in question unconstitutional while the period for potential intervention is still running.[13] However, Rule 5.1(c) expressly authorizes the court to reject the constitutional challenge, even if done before the attorney general decides to intervene.[14]

RULE 5.1(d). NO FORFEITURE

CORE CONCEPT

Failure by a party or a court to fulfill the requirements of Rule 5.1 does not work a forfeiture of any constitutional claim or defense that is asserted in a timely manner.[15]

APPLICATIONS

No Other Sanction

Beyond prohibiting forfeiture of a constitutional claim or defense, Rule 5.1(d) is silent as to whether some lesser sanction could be imposed on a party for failure to meet the requirements of Rule 5.1(a). However, existing judicial precedent derived from the similar language of old Rule 24(c) seems also to bar such a sanction.[16]

---

11. *See* Rule 5.1 Advisory Committee Note to 2006 amendments ("The court may extend the 60–day period on its own or on motion.").

12. *See* Rule 5.1 Advisory Committee Note to 2006 amendments ("Pretrial activities may continue without interruption during the intervention period, and the court retains authority to grant interlocutory relief.").

13. *See* Rule 5.1(c).

14. *See* Rule 5.1(c).

15. *See* Rule 5.1(d). *But see Citizens For A Better Lawnside, Inc. v. Bryant,* 2006 WL 3825145, at *8 (D.N.J. 2006) (finding that plaintiffs failed, pursuant to Rule 5.1, to file and serve written notice and, thus, their constitutional challenge was dismissed without prejudice).

16. *See, e.g., Tonya K. v. Board of Educ. of Chicago,* 847 F.2d 1243, 1247 (7th Cir. 1988) ("Failure to notify the Attorney General is not a jurisdictional defect."); *Merrill v. Town of Addison,* 763 F.2d 80, 83 (2d Cir.1985) ("Absent indication of harm, or prejudice to the government's opportunity to fully present its views, belated certification, while not ideal, is sufficient to honor the purpose of section 2403."). *Cf. United States v. Crystal Evangelical Free Church,* 82 F.3d 1407, 1412 (8th Cir.1996) (temporarily removing case from argument calendar so that appellate court can certify constitutional question and give United States time to intervene; "Certification has occurred even after judgment at the appellate level.").

RULE 5.2

PRIVACY PROTECTION FOR FILINGS MADE WITH THE COURT

(a) Redacted Filings. Unless the court orders otherwise, in an electronic or paper filing with the court that contains an individual's social-security number, taxpayer-identification number, or birth date, the name of an individual known to be a minor, or a financial-account number, a party or nonparty making the filing may include only:

(1) the last four digits of the social-security number and taxpayer-identification number;

(2) the year of the individual's birth;

(3) the minor's initials; and

(4) the last four digits of the financial-account number.

(b) Exemptions from the Redaction Requirement. The redaction requirement does not apply to the following:

(1) a financial-account number that identifies the property allegedly subject to forfeiture in a forfeiture proceeding;

(2) the record of an administrative or agency proceeding;

(3) the official record of a state-court proceeding;

(4) the record of a court or tribunal, if that record was not subject to the redaction requirement when originally filed;

(5) a filing covered by Rule 5.2(c) or (d); and

(6) a pro se filing in an action brought under 28 U.S.C. §§ 2241, 2254, or 2255.

(c) Limitations on Remote Access to Electronic Files; Social–Security Appeals and Immigration Cases. Unless the court orders otherwise, in an action for benefits under the Social Security Act, and in an action or proceeding relating to an order of removal, to relief from removal, or to immigration benefits or detention, access to an electronic file is authorized as follows:

(1) the parties and their attorneys may have remote electronic access to any part of the case file, including the administrative record;

(2) any other person may have electronic access to the full record at the courthouse, but may have remote electronic access only to:

(A) the docket maintained by the court; and

(B) an opinion, order, judgment, or other disposition of the court, but not any other part of the case file or the administrative record.

(d) Filings Made Under Seal. The court may order that a filing be made under seal without redaction. The court may later unseal the filing or order the person who made the filing to file a redacted version for the public record.

(e) Protective Orders. For good cause, the court may by order in a case:

(1) require redaction of additional information; or

(2) limit or prohibit a nonparty's remote electronic access to a document filed with the court.

(f) Option for Additional Unredacted Filing Under Seal. A person making a redacted filing may also file an unredacted copy under seal. The court must retain the unredacted copy as part of the record.

(g) Option for Filing a Reference List. A filing that contains redacted information may be filed together with a reference list that identifies each item of redacted information and specifies an appropriate identifier that uniquely corresponds to each item listed. The list must be filed under seal and may be amended as of right. Any reference in the case to a listed identifier will be construed to refer to the corresponding item of information.

(h) Waiver of Protection of Identifiers. A person waives the protection of Rule 5.2(a) as to the person's own information by filing it without redaction and not under seal.

[Added April 30, 2007, effective December 1, 2007.]

STYLE PROJECT CHANGES: None (this is a new Rule for 2007).

NON-STYLE CHANGES: None.

NOTE: The Federal Rules "Style Project" is explained in Part III-A.

AUTHORS' COMMENTARY ON RULE 5.2

———————— PURPOSE AND SCOPE ————————

The vulnerability of electronically-accessible court files to privacy and security mischief prompted the adoption in 2007 of Rule 5.2. The Rule allows for a heightened measure of protection for certain personal data identifiers, with additional protections in social security and immigration cases. Invoking these benefits is a burden placed on parties and their counsel.

CORE CONCEPT

From many categories of court filings, parties may redact or seal certain personal data identifiers. In social security and immigration cases (where such identifiers are likely to be both especially relevant and peculiarly vulnerable), the redaction right does not generally apply, but electronic access to those files will now be restricted. For good cause, parties may seek enhanced protections beyond those set forth in Rule 5.2. The right to claim these protections (and the duty of doing so) lies with parties and their counsel.

APPLICATIONS

Privacy and Security Objectives

Rule 5.2 is the federal courts' implementation of the E–Government Act of 2002.[1] It is intended to protect the privacy and security interests implicated by electronic filing of (and the consequent public access to) court papers.[2]

The Redaction Right

Both parties and nonparties who are making a filing with the court may redact, as of right, the following information from their court filings:

---

1. Pub.L. No. 107–347, § 205(c)(3), 116 Stat. 2899, 2914 (2002) (codified at 44 U.S.C. § 3501 note, as amended 2004).

2. *See* Rule 5.2 advisory committee note.

- *Social Security Number / Taxpayer ID Number:* In lieu thereof, the filer may include only the last four digits of those numbers;

- *Birth Year:* The filer may omit entirely;

- *Minor's Name:* In lieu thereof, the filer may include only the minor's initials; and

- *Financial Account Numbers:* In lieu thereof, the filer may include only the last four digits of those numbers.[3]

In order to facilitate the ready use of the redacted information, the filer may, if he or she wishes, choose among two supplementation alternatives. The filer may supplement the redacted version of the materials with an unredacted copy filed under seal.[4] Or the filer may supplement the redacted version by filing, under seal, a "reference list" that allows the redactions to be decoded.[5]

The Sealing Right

In addition to the sealing options to which a filer is entitled as a supplement to redacted filings, the court may withdraw the right of redaction, in favor of a filing under seal, which the court may later unseal or order a replacement redaction.[6]

Applies to Paper Filings (and Trial Exhibits), As Well As Electronic Filings

Although the E–Government Act was directed principally at electronically-filed materials, Rule 5.2 applies broadly to all filings, whether made electronically or in paper form. The drafters recognized that many judicial districts scan materials filed in paper format into their electronic case files, thus rendering those materials as electronically accessible to the public in much the same way as they would have been had they been filed electronically in the first instance.[7] Trial exhibits, if filed with the court, are likewise encompassed within the reach of Rule 5.2.[8]

Exceptions to the Redaction Right

The right of redaction does *not* apply in the following circumstances: (a) when the court orders otherwise,[9] (b) in a forfeiture proceeding, if the financial account number identifies property claimed to be subject to forfeiture,[10] (c) to the record of an administrative or agency proceeding,[11] (d) to the official record of a State court proceeding,[12] (e) to the record of a court or tribunal where the record was not subject to the redaction requirement when originally

3. *See* Rule 5.2(a).

4. *See* Rule 5.2(f).

5. *See* Rule 5.2(g).

6. *See* Rule 5.2(d).

7. *See* Rule 5.2 advisory committee note ("It is electronic availability, not the form of the initial filing, that raises the privacy and security concerns addressed in the E–Government Act.").

8. *See* Rule 5.2 advisory committee note.

9. *See* Rule 5.2(a).

10. *See* Rule 5.2(b)(1).

11. *See* Rule 5.2(b)(2).

12. *See* Rule 5.2(b)(3).

filed,[13] (f) to social security and immigration cases,[14] (g) to cases where the court orders that filings not be redacted but, instead, be filed under seal,[15] and (h) to *pro se* filings in actions brought under 28 U.S.C.A. §§ 2241, 2254, or 2255.[16]

The Burden of Redacting / Sealing

The drafters revised the proposed language of Rule 5.2, following the public comment period, to make unambiguous their intent that the burden of exercising this new right of redaction or sealing rests with the filer of the materials, and not with the courts or otherwise.[17] Consequently, if a party intends to take advantage of the privacy and security benefits of this right, either the party himself or his counsel must remember to perform the redaction or seek the sealing. The drafters urged counsel to remind their clients that personal data identifiers that could have been, but were not, protected will be publicly accessible over the internet.[18]

Intended (and Inadvertent) Waivers

Parties may, balancing costs against benefits, waive their entitlement to Rule 5.2's protection by filing their information without redaction and not under seal.[19] An inadvertent failure to redact or seal may be remedied upon motion to the court.[20]

Additional Privacy / Security Protections

The denomination in Rule 5.2 of certain categories of personal data identifiers is not intended to give rise to a negative presumption that *only* those categories of data are entitled to protection or that the abbreviated identifiers (*e.g.*, last four digits, minor's initials) are not themselves, in an appropriate case, entitled to be shielded entirely.[21] For "good cause", the court may grant protective orders allowing the redaction of additional information, or either limiting or barring remote electronic access by a nonparty to a filed document.[22]

13. *See* Rule 5.2(b)(4).

14. *See* Rule 5.2(b)(5).

15. *See* Rule 5.2(b)(5).

16. *See* Rule 5.2(b)(6).

17. *See* Rule 5.2(h). *See also* Rule 5.2 advisory committee note ("The clerk is not required to review documents filed with the court for compliance with this rule. The responsibility to redact filings rests with counsel and the party or nonparty making the filing.").

18. *See* Rule 5.2 advisory committee note ("Parties must remember that any personal information not otherwise protected by sealing or redaction will be made available over the internet. Counsel should notify clients of this fact so that an informed decision may be made on what information is to be included in a document filed with the court.").

19. *See* Rule 5.2(h). *See also* Rule 5.2 advisory committee note ("One may wish to waive the protection if it is determined that the costs of redaction outweigh the benefits to privacy.").

20. *See* Rule 5.2 advisory committee note ("If a person files an unredacted identifier by mistake, that person may seek relief from the court.").

21. *See* Rule 5.2 advisory committee note (noting that, in certain cases, all parts of an account number or social security number may need protection, or that protection should extend to other identifiers, like driver's license numbers and alien registration numbers).

22. *See* Rule 5.2(e).

Social Security and Immigration Cases

Citing the "prevalence of sensitive information and the volume of filings", the drafters singled out certain social security and immigration cases for special treatment.[23] These cases are *not* entitled to the automatic right of redaction.[24] Although parties and their counsel enjoy unrestricted access to such filings, nonparties are entitled to remote electronic access only to case docket numbers and court disposition documents; to gain full access to the files, nonparties must access them in-person at the courthouse (and may do so, at the courthouse, electronically).[25]

23. *See* Rule 5.2 advisory committee note. This Rule applies to actions for benefits under the Social Security Act, and actions or proceedings relating to orders of removal, relief from removal, or immigration benefits or detention. *See* Rule 5.2(c).

24. *See* Rule 5.2(b)(5).

25. *See* Rule 5.2(c).

RULE 6

COMPUTING AND EXTENDING TIME; TIME FOR MOTION PAPERS

(a) Computing Time. The following rules apply in computing any time period specified in these rules or in any local rule, court order, or statute:

(1) *Day of the Event Excluded.* Exclude the day of the act, event, or default that begins the period.

(2) *Exclusions from Brief Periods.* Exclude intermediate Saturdays, Sundays, and legal holidays when the period is less than 11 days.

(3) *Last Day.* Include the last day of the period unless it is a Saturday, Sunday, legal holiday, or—if the act to be done is filing a paper in court—a day on which weather or other conditions make the clerk's office inaccessible. When the last day is excluded, the period runs until the end of the next day that is not a Saturday, Sunday, legal holiday, or day when the clerk's office is inaccessible.

(4) *"Legal Holiday" Defined.* As used in these rules, "legal holiday" means:

(A) the day set aside by statute for observing New Year's Day, Martin Luther King Jr.'s Birthday, Washington's Birthday, Memorial Day, Independence Day, Labor Day, Columbus Day, Veterans' Day, Thanksgiving Day, or Christmas Day; and

(B) any other day declared a holiday by the President, Congress, or the state where the district court is located.

(b) Extending Time.

(1) *In General.* When an act may or must be done within a specified time, the court may, for good cause, extend the time:

(A) with or without motion or notice if the court acts, or if a request is made, before the original time or its extension expires; or

       (B) on motion made after the time has expired if the party failed to act because of excusable neglect.

    (2) *Exceptions.* A court must not extend the time to act under Rules 50(b) and (d), 52(b), 59(b), (d), and (e), and 60(b), except as those rules allow.

(c) Motions, Notices of Hearing, and Affidavits.

    (1) *In General.* A written motion and notice of the hearing must be served at least 5 days before the time specified for the hearing, with the following exceptions:

       (A) when the motion may be heard ex parte;

       (B) when these rules set a different time; or

       (C) when a court order—which a party may, for good cause, apply for ex parte—sets a different time.

    (2) *Supporting Affidavit.* Any affidavit supporting a motion must be served with the motion. Except as Rule 59(c) provides otherwise, any opposing affidavit must be served at least 1 day before the hearing, unless the court permits service at another time.

(d) Additional Time After Certain Kinds of Service.
When a party may or must act within a specified time after service and service is made under Rule 5(b)(2)(C), (D), (E), or (F), 3 days are added after the period would otherwise expire under Rule 6(a).

[Amended effective March 19, 1948; July 1, 1963; July 1, 1966; July 1, 1968; July 1, 1971; August 1, 1983; August 1, 1985; August 1, 1987; December 1, 1999; April 23, 2001, effective December 1, 2001; April 25, 2005, effective December 1, 2005; April 30, 2007, effective December 1, 2007.]

––––––––––––– 2007 AMENDMENTS ROADMAP –––––––––––––

   STYLE PROJECT CHANGES: Rescinded Rule 6(c) (empty since 1966) was deleted, and old Rules 6(d) and 6(e) were repositioned as new Rules 6(c) and 6(d). Extensive subsectioning and new orienting labeling was added. Cumbersome "enlargement" terms were replaced with "extension". The limiting preface to Rule 6(b) ("When by these rules or by a notice given thereunder or by order of court...") was omitted, although the drafters announce that changes are "stylistic only".

   NON-STYLE CHANGES: For accuracy, "legal holiday" was replaced by "day set aside for observing" those same holidays.

NOTE: The Federal Rules "Style Project" is explained in Part III-A.

AUTHORS' COMMENTARY ON RULE 6

PURPOSE AND SCOPE

Rule 6 sets the procedure for computing the passage of time under the Rules. Although other, substantive Rules define the length of allowable time for such acts as answering pleadings or filing motions, Rule 6 dictates how those defined time periods are to be calculated. Rule 6 also authorizes the district court to enlarge the time periods fixed in the Rules.

Note: A perpetual calendar can be found in Part XI of this text.

RULE 6(a). COMPUTING OF TIME

CORE CONCEPT

None of the time periods established in the Rules may end on a Saturday, Sunday, or legal holiday. In addition, if a Rule requires the filing of legal papers with the clerk of court, the applicable time period also may not end on a day when weather or other conditions make the clerk's office inaccessible. When a defined time period ends on such days, the time period is deemed extended until the end of the next day that is not a Saturday, Sunday, legal holiday, or inclement weather day.

Moreover, when a time period fixed in the Rules is less than 11 days, intermediate Saturdays, Sundays, and legal holidays are excluded when computing the passage of time.

APPLICATIONS

No Effect on Dates Certain

When the court sets a "date certain" for an act or a filing, Rule 6(a) will *not* extend that date if it falls on a Saturday, Sunday, or holiday.[1]

When Counting Begins

The computation of time periods set in the Rules begin on the day *after* the triggering act, event, or default occurs. For example,

---

1. *See Violette v. P.A. Days, Inc.,* 427 F.3d 1015, 1016–20 (6th Cir.2005) (Rule 6(a) does not apply to extend a date-certain, set by the court, which expired on a Saturday of a long, federal holiday weekend); *Fleischhauer v. Feltner,* 3 F.3d 148, 151 (6th Cir.1993). *But see Modaressi v. Vedadi,* 441 F.Supp.2d 51, 54 n. 2 (D.D.C. 2006)(rejecting as "frivolous" litigant's "unsupported contention that 'Rule 6 does not apply to *firm calendar dates* issued by the Court's orders and is only applicable to *numeric computations of time*'") (emphasis in original).

Rule 12(a) requires a defendant to serve an answer within 20 days of service of process. If the defendant is served with process on February 1, the 20-day answering period begins to run on February 2.

When Counting Ends

If the defined time period would expire on a Saturday, Sunday, or legal holiday, the time period is deemed extended to the next day that is not a Saturday, Sunday, or legal holiday. Thus, in the example above, if the 20th day after service (February 21) is a Saturday, February 22 is a Sunday, and February 23 is Washington's Birthday, the defendant's answering date would be deemed extended until February 24.

Designated Legal Holidays

The category "legal holiday" encompasses the days set aside by statute for observing the following holidays:

1. New Year's Day

2. Birthday of Dr. Martin Luther King, Jr.

3. Washington's Birthday

4. Memorial Day

5. Independence Day

6. Labor Day

7. Columbus Day

8. Veterans' Day

9. Thanksgiving

10. Christmas Day

"Any Other" Holiday

In addition to the Rule's delineated list of federal holidays, time periods are also extended on other days "declared a holiday" by the President, the Congress, or the State where the district court is located. From time to time, such federal holidays have been clearly designated.[2] Also, the federal courts recognize officially designated State holidays as well, even if the federal judiciary remains open on those days.[3] On occasion, however, whether a certain holiday qualifies under Rule 6(a) has been unclear. In making that determination, the courts recognize that the Rule provides "reasonable flexibility" in the measurement of time periods, and is intended to abate

---

2. *See, e.g., Reyes–Cardona v. J.C. Penney Co.,* 690 F.2d 1 (1st Cir.1982) (legal holiday in Puerto Rico honoring Eugenio Maria de Hostos was properly excluded from computation of time under Rule 6(a)).

3. *See Wright v. Trinity Catering, Inc.,* 2007 WL 2155728, at *1–*3 (E.D.La. 2007) (Louisiana officially recognizes Mardi Gras holiday (though done parish by parish),

which thus qualifies as State holiday); *Seacor v. Secretary of Dep't of Health & Human Servs.,* 34 Fed.Cl. 141, 143–44 (1995) (Massachusetts State holiday, "Patriot's Day", was excluded properly from computation of time even though federal court was open and filing could have been made on that date).

the "hardship" of permitting "days of rest to shorten already tight deadlines".[4] One court has adopted a "simplicity" rule, which holds that any day the President closes the federal government for celebratory or commemorative reasons, a snow emergency, a terrorist act, or some other *force majeure*, a rebuttable presumption is created that a federal holiday was declared.[5] Days when the clerk's office is declared closed by the Chief Judge might not, however, qualify for this extension.[6] By its terms, the Rule allows for extensions granted by the President, Congress, and the State; less formal, District-specific "holidays" are not encompassed in the Rule.

Extended Dates for Filing When Courthouse Inaccessible

When the defined time period sets the date for filing a paper in court, the time period is deemed extended past any day on which weather or other conditions make the office of the clerk inaccessible. The clerk's office has been deemed "inaccessible" when inclement weather forces it to close,[7] when local weather conditions near the courthouse make travelling to the clerk's office dangerous, difficult, or impossible,[8] or when other circumstances make the courthouse inaccessible as a practical matter.[9] An individual's own, personal weather-related difficulties, which do not also cause the clerk's office to close, close early, or be otherwise dangerous to reach, generally will not qualify for this extension.[10]

Time Periods Less than 11 Days

When the defined time period is less than 11 days, intermediate

4. *See Mashpee Wampanoag Tribal Council, Inc. v. Norton*, 336 F.3d 1094, 1098–99 (D.C.Cir.2003) (recognizing Christmas Eve 2001 as qualifying holiday for federal litigators, where President gave all Executive Branch employees that day off).

5. *See Hart v. Sheahan*, 396 F.3d 887, 891 (7th Cir.2005).

6. *See Garcia–Velazquez v. Frito Lay Snacks Caribbean*, 358 F.3d 6, 9–11 (1st Cir.2004) (New Year's Eve not excluded, even though Chief Judge declared clerk's office closed); *In re Cascade Oil Co.*, 848 F.2d 1062, 1064 (10th Cir.1988) (day after Thanksgiving not excluded, same reasoning); *Kirby v. General Elec. Co.*, 2000 WL 33917974, at *2 (W.D.N.C.2000) (Christmas Eve and New Year's Eve not excluded, same reasoning), *aff'd*, 20 Fed.Appx. 167 (4th Cir. 2001) (per curiam).

7. *See Telephone & Data Sys., Inc. v. Amcell F Atlantic City, Inc.*, 20 F.3d 501 (D.C.Cir.1994)(clerk's office is "inaccessible" within the meaning of Rule 6(a) when inclement weather forces office to close, notwithstanding that clerk's office's 24–hour "drop box" was still available).

8. The courthouse need not be physically closed in order for the clerk's office to be

deemed "inaccessible". *See U.S. Leather, Inc. v. H & W P'ship*, 60 F.3d 222 (5th Cir.1995)("An ice storm that temporarily knocks out an area's power and telephone service and makes travelling dangerous, difficult or impossible, thereby rendering the federal courthouse inaccessible to those in the area of the courthouse, is enough to come within Rule 6(a)'s weather exception").

9. *See Latham v. Dominick's Finer Foods*, 149 F.3d 673 (7th Cir.1998) (holding that district court was "inaccessible as a practical matter without heroic measures" on December 26, 1997 because chief judge ordered the court closed, in recognition of President's executive order closing executive branch of federal government on that day).

10. *See O'Malley v. Town of Egremont*, 453 F.Supp.2d 240, 246–47 (D.Mass. 2006). *See generally* William G. Phelps, *When is Office of Clerk of Court Inaccessible Due to Weather or Other Conditions for Purpose of Computing Time Period for Filing Papers under Rule 6(a) of Federal Rules of Civil Procedure*, 135 A.L.R. Fed. 259 (2006).

Saturdays, Sundays, and legal holidays are not counted.[11]   For example, if judgment in a lawsuit was entered on Friday, February 10, the parties would have 10 days under Rule 59 to move for a new trial.   This 10-day period would begin on Monday, February 13 and expire on Monday, February 27, since intermediate Saturdays (February 11, 18, 25), Sundays (February 12, 19, 26), and legal holidays (*e.g.*, Washington's Birthday—February 20) would not be counted.

Effect on Rule 23(f) Applications

Rule 23(f) permits a court of appeals to allow an appeal from a grant or denial of class action certification if an application is made for the appeal within ten days of the trial court's order. Rule 6 applies to such applications.[12]

Effect on Time Periods Set by Private Contracts

Ordinarily, the computation procedures embodied in Rule 6 do *not* apply to time periods set in private contracts.[13]

Effect on Federal Statutes of Limitation

The federal courts are divided on whether these time computation methods apply to federal statutes of limitation.[14]   Congress may, of course, fix a different method for time computation applicable to particular statutes.[15]

11.   *See Union Nat'l Bank v. Lamb*, 337 U.S. 38, 69 S.Ct. 911, 93 L.Ed. 1190 (1949)(observing that Rule 6(a) provides that an act which must, by statute, be performed within a prescribed period of time may be performed a day later when the time period ends on a Sunday).

12.   *See Beck v. Boeing Co.*, 320 F.3d 1021, 1021–23 (9th Cir.2003); *In re Veneman*, 309 F.3d 789, 793 (D.C.Cir.2002); *In re Sumitomo Copper Litig.*, 262 F.3d 134, 137 n.1 (2d Cir.2001).

13.   *See J. Aron & Co. v. S/S Olga Jacob*, 527 F.2d 416, 417 (5th Cir.1976).

14.   *See Bartlik v. United States Dep't of Labor, Tenn. Valley Auth.*, 62 F.3d 163 (6th Cir.1995) (en banc) (majority view: holding that computational extensions under Rule 6(a) do not enlarge a court's jurisdiction, and thus petition for review of agency decision due on Saturday, Sunday, federal holiday, or courthouse-inaccessible day is timely if filed on the next day courthouse is open for business). *Compare Westland Holdings, Inc. v. Lay*, 462 F.3d 1228, 1233–34 (10th Cir. 2006) (noting law applying Rule 6(a) to statute of limitations) *and Moore v. Campbell*, 344 F.3d 1313, 1319–20 (11th Cir.2003) (same) *and Sain v. City of Bend*, 309 F.3d 1134, 1136–38 (9th Cir. 2002) (same) *and Reid v. Universal Maritime Serv. Corp.*, 41 F.3d 200 (4th Cir.1994) (same) *and Newell v. Hanks*, 283 F.3d 827,

833 (7th Cir.2002) (same) *and Flanagan v. Johnson*, 154 F.3d 196, 201–02 (5th Cir. 1998) (same) *and Merriweather v. City of Memphis*, 107 F.3d 396, 398 n. 2 (6th Cir. 1997) (same) *and Frey v. Woodard*, 748 F.2d 173 (3d Cir.1984)(same) *with Scanio v. United States*, 37 F.3d 858, 860–61 (2d Cir. 1994) (minority view: rejecting argument that Rule 6(a) applies to expand time for filing habeas motion, and holding that final filing day is not extended when statutory last day is a Saturday, Sunday, holiday, or a day on which the clerk's office is inaccessible). *See also Union Nat'l Bank v. Lamb*, 337 U.S. 38, 40–41, 69 S.Ct. 911, 912–13, 93 L.Ed. 1190 (1949) (holding that a petition for review of State supreme court decision filed on Monday—the ninety-first day of the statutory ninety-day filing period, was timely filed: "[s]ince [Rule 6(a)] had the concurrence of Congress and since no contrary policy is expressed in the statute governing this review, we think that the considerations of liberality and leniency which find expression in Rule 6(a) are equally applicable").

15.   *See FDIC v. Enventure V*, 77 F.3d 123, 125–26 (5th Cir.1996) (Rule 6(a) counting procedure does not apply when Congress' statute of limitations expressly states otherwise).

Effect on Other Federal Statutes

Noting the broadly encompassing language of Rule 6(a),[16] at least one court has adopted as a general policy, guided by perceived legislative intent, to apply the Rule to every federal statute enacted or amended after the adoption of the Rule, unless the statute at issue itself conveys a contrary drafting intention.[17]

Effect on State Statutes of Limitation

In diversity cases, the federal courts typically apply the time computation methods set by State law.[18] If, however, the applicable State law is silent on the computation question, the courts may apply Rule 6.

RULE 6(b). EXTENDING TIME

CORE CONCEPT

The district courts may extend many of the time periods set by the Rules.

APPLICATIONS

No Stipulations

The parties cannot unilaterally extend the time periods set in the Rules by simply stipulating to the extension.[19] Court approval of the stipulated extension is required.[20]

Extensions Before the Time Period Expires

If the extension request is made *before*[21] the time period expires, the district court, in its discretion, may grant an extension "for cause shown".[22] Neither notice to the adversary nor a formal motion is required by the Rule, although applicable local rules may establish a more specific extension procedure. Pre-expiration extensions are granted routinely if they are sought in good faith and do not prejudice the adversary.

Extensions After the Time Period Expires

If the extension request is made *after* the time period expires, the district court's discretion is more restricted. The district court

---

16. *See* Rule 6(a) ("in computing *any* time period specified in *these rules, or in any local rule, court order, or statute...*") (emphasis added).

17. *See American Canoe Ass'n v. City of Attalla*, 363 F.3d 1085, 1086 (11th Cir. 2004).

18. *See Walker v. Armco Steel Corp.*, 446 U.S. 740, 100 S.Ct. 1978, 64 L.Ed.2d 659 (1980).

19. *See Orange Theatre Corp. v. Rayherstz Amusement Corp.*, 130 F.2d 185 (3d Cir.1942).

20. *See Gray v. Lewis & Clark Expeditions, Inc.*, 12 F.Supp.2d 993 (D.Neb.1998);

Allstate Ins. Co. v. Administratia Asigurarilor De Stat, 163 F.R.D. 196, 199 (S.D.N.Y. 1995).

21. *See Hetzel v. Bethlehem Steel Corp.*, 50 F.3d 360, 367 (5th Cir.1995)(observing that district courts are granted "broad discretion" under Rule 6(b) to expand filing deadlines).

22. *See Lujan v. National Wildlife Fed'n*, 497 U.S. 871, 896, 110 S.Ct. 3177, 3192, 111 L.Ed.2d 695 (1990) (noting that cause must be shown before an enlargement of time is granted).

may grant such post-expiration extensions if: (1) cause is shown, *and* (2) the failure to act was the result of excusable neglect. The courts have tested carefully a litigant's claim of excusable neglect; unfamiliarity with the Rules or a crowded professional schedule will not constitute excusable neglect.[23] Demonstrating excusable neglect is not easily done, and was not intended to be.[24] As one court aptly wrote: "When parties wait until the last minute to comply with a deadline, they are playing with fire."[25] Moreover, a formal request for an excusable neglect extension is required; trial courts abuse their discretion in granting such relief in the absence of a motion by the affected litigant.[26]

The Supreme Court has noted that excusable neglect is a "somewhat elastic concept", not limited exclusively to omissions caused by circumstances outside the moving party's control, but which must be assessed in view of all relevant circumstances surrounding the omission.[27] Negligent oversight (if that oversight is deemed excusable) is encompassed in this standard.[28] Yet, the Court considers this excusable neglect hurdle as the "greatest" substantive obstacle of all.[29] In testing whether the neglect was excusable, courts have considered some or all of the following factors:

1. The prejudice to the opponent;

2. The length of the delay and its potential impact on the course of the judicial proceedings;

3. The causes for the delay, and whether those causes were within the reasonable control of the moving party;

4. The moving party's good faith;

5. Whether the omission reflected professional incompetence, such as an ignorance of the procedural rules;

6. Whether the omission reflected an easily manufactured excuse that the court could not verify;

7. Whether the moving party had failed to provide for a consequence that was readily foreseeable; and

23. *See In re Veritas Software Corp. Secs. Litig.*, 496 F.3d 962, 973 (9th Cir. 2007); *Corwin v. Walt Disney Co.*, 475 F.3d 1239, 1255 (11th Cir. 2007); *Quigley v. Rosenthal*, 427 F.3d 1232, 1237–38 (10th Cir. 2005).

24. *See Thompson v. E.I. DuPont de Nemours & Co.*, 76 F.3d 530, 534 (4th Cir. 1996).

25. *Spears v. City of Indianapolis*, 74 F.3d 153, 157 (7th Cir.1996).

26. *See Smith v. District of Columbia*, 430 F.3d 450, 456–57 (D.C.Cir.2005); *IPXL Holdings, L.L.C. v. Amazon.com, Inc.*, 430 F.3d 1377, 1385–86 (Fed.Cir.2005).

27. *See Pioneer Inv. Servs. Co. v. Brunswick Assocs. Ltd. P'ship*, 507 U.S. 380, 390–95, 113 S.Ct. 1489, 1496–98, 123 L.Ed.2d 74 (1993)(construing excusable neglect in the context of Bankruptcy Rule 9006(b), which was patterned after Rule 6(b)).

28. *See Mommaerts v. Hartford Life & Acc. Ins. Co.*, 472 F.3d 967, 968 (7th Cir. 2007) (quoting *Pioneer Inv. Servs. Co. v. Brunswick Assocs. L.P.*, 507 U.S. 380, 395, 113 S.Ct. 1489, 123 L.Ed.2d 74 (1993)).

29. *Lujan v. National Wildlife Fed'n*, 497 U.S. 871, 897, 110 S.Ct. 3177, 3193, 111 L.Ed.2d 695 (1990).

8. Whether the omission constituted a complete lack of diligence.[30]

Significantly, the fact that the error lies with the attorney, and not with the attorney's client, is *not* dispositive on whether "excusable neglect" exists. Clients will be held responsible for the omissions of their attorneys, even if the clients are not otherwise culpable for the error.[31] Moreover, courts are reluctant to approve extensions of time after prior extensions have been granted and ignored.[32]

No Extensions

Rule 6(b)(2) prohibits the district court from extending the following time periods: [33]

(1) Time for seeking a judgment as a matter of law, under Rules 50(b) or 50(c)(2);

(2) Time for requesting an amendment or expansion of the court's findings in a non-jury case, under Rule 52(b);

(3) Time for granting a new trial or proposing to alter or amend the judgment, under Rule 59(b), (d), or (e); and

(4) Time for requesting relief from judgment, under Rule 60(b).

In these instances, a party's failure to act within the designated period deprives the district court of its power of extension.[34] There are two possible exceptions to his prohibition. First, it may be that the prohibition is a waivable affirmative defense that could be forfeited if not properly asserted.[35] Case law on this interpretation is still emerging. Second, a forty-year-old case law exemption from the Seventh Circuit Court of Appeals held that in "unique circumstances" these periods could be extended, provided there was a genuine ambiguity in the Rule language to begin with and the district court took action that gave the parties the specific assurance (albeit improperly) that an extension had been granted.[36] The validi-

30. *See Pioneer Inv. Servs. Co. v. Brunswick Assocs. Ltd. P'ship*, 507 U.S. 380, 390–95, 113 S.Ct. 1489, 1496–98, 123 L.Ed.2d 74 (1993); *In re Veritas Software Corp. Secs. Litig.*, 496 F.3d 962, ___, 2007 WL 2120274, at *8 (9th Cir. 2007); *Nafziger v. McDermott Int'l, Inc.*, 467 F.3d 514, 522 (6th Cir. 2006).

31. *See In re Veritas Software Corp. Secs. Litig.*, 496 F.3d 962, ___, 2007 WL 2120274, at *8—*9 (9th Cir. 2007); *Allen v. Murph*, 194 F.3d 722, 724 (6th Cir.1999).

32. *See Spears v. City of Indianapolis*, 74 F.3d 153 (7th Cir.1996) (finding no abuse of discretion where the district court refused to grant a 24–hour extension, after having previously granted several, earlier extensions); *McIntosh v. Antonino*, 71 F.3d 29 (1st Cir.1995) (finding no abuse of discretion in court's "exasperated denial" of a third extension).

33. Although not listed specifically as a non-extending Rule, the courts have construed Rule 71A as prohibiting the district court from enlarging the time to answer in a condemnation proceeding.

34. *See Browder v. Director, Dep't of Corrections*, 434 U.S. 257, 261–62 n. 5, 98 S.Ct. 556, 559–60 n. 5, 54 L.Ed.2d 521 (1978). *See also Rodick v. City of Schenectady*, 1 F.3d 1341, 1346 (2d Cir.1993) (noting jurisdictional nature of time periods).

35. *See National Ecological Found. v. Alexander*, 496 F.3d 466, 474–4754 (6th Cir. 2007).

36. *See Eady v. Foerder*, 381 F.2d 980 (7th Cir. 1967). *See also Varhol v. National R.R. Passenger Corp.*, 909 F.2d 1557 (7th Cir. 1990) (equally divided en banc court considered but refused to overrule *Eady*).

ty of this case law exemption has been often questioned, and always limited tightly,[37] and the Supreme Court has rejected its application in a closely related context.[38]

Other Enlargement Rules

Several other Rules authorize the district court to grant extensions of time in particular circumstances.[39] Both Rule 6 and the specifically applicable enlargement Rule should be consulted.

Time Periods Set by Statute

The court may only extend time periods set in the Rules or by court order. The court generally may not extend statutory time periods unless otherwise authorized to do so.[40]

Scope of Extension

The language of a party's proposed extension order should be chosen carefully. An order extending the time for a defendant to "answer" the complaint does not necessarily extend the time for "moving" to dismiss the complaint. Therefore, broad language is advised: *e.g.,* requesting an extension to "answer, move, or otherwise plead".

RULE 6(c).   MOTIONS, NOTICES OF HEARING, AFFIDAVITS

CORE CONCEPT

A written motion and notice of hearing must be served on the non-moving party not later than 5 days before a motion hearing date, unless the district court specifies otherwise.

APPLICATIONS

2007 Amendments

Beginning in 1937, former Rule 6(c) had provided that the computation of time under the Rules was not affected when formal

---

37. *See Robinson v. City of Harvey*, 489 F.3d 864, 870–71 (7th Cir. 2007).

38. *See Bowles v. Russell*, ___ U.S. ___, ___, 127 S.Ct. 2360, 2366, 168 L.Ed.2d 96 (2007) (denouncing doctrine as "illegitimate", overruling prior case law, and emphasizing "that the timely filing of a notice of appeal in a civil case is a jurisdictional requirement").

39. *See, e.g.,* Rule 4(m)(extensions to serve summons and complaint); Rule 30(d)(1)(extensions for oral depositions); Rule 31(a)(5)(extensions for depositions on written interrogatories); Rule 33(b)(2)(extensions to answer interrogatories); Rule 34(b)(2) (extensions to respond to production requests); Rule 36(a)(3) (extensions to answer requests for admission); Rule

39(b)(extensions to demand jury trial); Rule 59(c)(extensions to submit affidavits in opposition to new trial motion).

40. *See Kreutzer v. Bowersox*, 231 F.3d 460, 463 n.2 (8th Cir.2000) ("Rule 6(b), by its own terms, only applies to time limits set by the Federal Rules of Civil Procedure, or to limits set by the court. ... It cannot be used to extend a statutory limit."). *See supra* Authors' Commentary to Rule 6(a) (**"Effect on Federal Statutes of Limitation"** and **"Effect on State Statutes of Limitation"**) (discussion regarding application of Rule 6(a)'s time computation procedures to federal and State statutes of limitation).

court terms expired. In 1963, Congress ended court terms for the district courts, and in 1966, this language of Rule 6(c) was rescinded as unnecessary. Rule 6(c) remained an empty shell ever since. The 2007 Style Project deleted this shell, and moved up old Rules 6(d) and 6(e) as newly repositioned Rules 6(c) and 6(d) respectively. The text of the moved Rules remains substantively identical. Practitioners searching for pre–2007 interpretations of these Rules should bear this repositioning in mind in doing their research. Current Rule 6(c) was, from 1937 to 2007, old Rule 6(d).

Motion Days

This 5–day notice procedure applies to those district courts with "motion days" or the equivalent (where all motions are heard orally). The Rule provides that the non-moving party must be served with notice of all motions at least 5 days before the hearing day, unless the court directs otherwise.[41]

Saturdays/Sundays/Legal Holidays Excluded

The 5–day notice period is computed in accordance with Rule 6(a), with intermediate Saturdays, Sundays, and Legal Holidays excluded from the 5–day period.

Special Notice Rules

Some Rules contain specific notice requirements, such as Rule 56's provision that summary judgment motions be served within 10 days of a hearing or Rule 65(b)'s provision that motions to dissolve a temporary restraining order be served within 2 days of a hearing. In these unusual instances, the special notice requirements supplant Rule 6(c)'s notice period.

Special Timing When Court Directs Otherwise

The 5–day notice requirement is a rule of general application. It is subject to change by court order when circumstances warrant a different time period.[42]

Motion Affidavits

When a motion is supported with affidavits, the supporting affidavits must be served simultaneously with the motion. When an opposition to a motion is supported with affidavits, the opposing affidavits must be served not less than 1 day before the hearing. These service requirements do not apply to affidavits submitted in support of reply briefs;[43] but many courts will accept a reply affida-

---

41. *See Stewart Title Guar. Co. v. Cadle Co.*, 74 F.3d 835, 837 n. 1 (7th Cir.1996) (noting that judicial district adopted a different schedule by local rule, permitting written motions to be filed just two days before hearing).

42. *See Ciena Corp. v. Jarrard*, 203 F.3d 312, 319–20 (4th Cir.2000) (permitting different time periods in the context of interlocutory injunctions).

43. *See McGinnis v. Southeast Anesthesia Assocs., P.A.*, 161 F.R.D. 41 (W.D.N.C. 1995)(ruling that affidavits submitted with reply brief during a motion to dismiss briefing were not governed by Rule 6). Note, however, that such affidavits must still be filed simultaneously with the reply brief. *Id. See also Kershner v. Norton*, 2003 WL 21960605, at *1–2 (D.D.C.2003) (no error in relying on affidavit submitted simultaneously with reply to motion to transfer);

vit if filed simultaneously with the reply brief and addresses matters raised in the adversary's opposition brief.[44] The district court may modify these service requirements.[45]

> *Exception:* Affidavits opposing a motion for new trial must be served within 10 days after service of the motion, unless an additional period of time not to exceed 20 days is permitted by stipulation or court order.[46]

RULE 6(d). ADDITIONAL TIME AFTER CERTAIN KINDS OF SERVICE

CORE CONCEPT

A party is given 3 extra days in which to act, if that party is to act within a specified time after service of a document and that document was served by mail, by other pre-agreed means (such as electronically), or by leaving it with the clerk (if permitted).

APPLICATIONS

2007 Amendments

Beginning in 1937, former Rule 6(c) had provided that the computation of time under the Rules was not affected when formal court terms expired. In 1963, Congress ended court terms for the district courts, and in 1966, this language of Rule 6(c) was rescinded as unnecessary. Rule 6(c) remained an empty shell ever since. The 2007 Style Project deleted this shell, and moved up old Rules 6(d) and 6(e) as newly repositioned Rules 6(c) and 6(d) respectively. The text of the moved Rules remains substantively identical. Practitioners searching for pre–2007 interpretations of these Rules should bear this repositioning in mind in doing their research. Current Rule 6(d) was, from 1937 to 2007, old Rule 6(e).

Purpose

Rule 5(b)(2) permits service of papers, under certain circumstances, to be made by mail, by other pre-agreed means (such as electronically), and by leaving the papers with the court clerk.[47] Such service is generally considered complete at the time of mailing or other transmission; completed service does *not* await actual receipt. To compensate for time lapses caused by these special means of mailing, Rule 6(d) adds 3 extra days to certain time periods. Rule 6(b) thus assumes that postal deliveries will typically

---

Ironworkers Dist. Council of Pac. N.W. v. George Sollit Corp., 2002 WL 31545972, at *5 (W.D.Wash.2002) (court will not strike reply affidavits when filed simultaneously with reply and do not prejudice adversary).

44. *See Cardenas v. Dorel Juvenile Group, Inc.*, 230 F.R.D. 635, 636 (D.Kan. 2005).

45. *See Lovelace v. Lee*, 472 F.3d 174, 204 (4th Cir. 2006) (district court has dis-cretion to accept untimely affidavit); *Orsi v. Kirkwood*, 999 F.2d 86, 91–92 (4th Cir. 1993)(although district court may enlarge time period of this Rule, such enlargements should generally be granted only if cause or excusable neglect is shown).

46. *See* Rule 59.

47. *See* Rule 5(b)(2)(C), (D), (E), (F).

arrive at their destinations within 3 days of mailing.[48] Similarly, when service is made by electronic transmission or other means, this additional 3–day period is added to offset possible transmission or delivery delays.[49]

> *Exception:* Three days are not added in those instances when the defined time period begins to run only upon actual receipt.[50]

Applies to "Service" Deadlines Only

This 3–day extension applies only to responses due within a certain time after "service" of a preceding document.

No 3-Day Extension to "Filing" Deadlines

There is *no* 3–day extension when responses are due within a prescribed time after the "filing" of a document, even if that document is subsequently served through the mails (or through the special service means provided in Rules 5(b)(2)(C), (D), (E), and (F)).[51] Nor is a 3–day extension self-acquired by the act of mailing a document that must otherwise be filed by a particular date.[52]

No 3–Day Extension to "Receipt"–Based Deadlines

There generally is also *no* 3-day extension where responses are due within a prescribed period after actual "receipt" of a document, even though the received document was served through the mails (or through the special service means provided in Rules 5(b)(2)(C), (D), (E), and (F)).[53] However, a party may receive additional "mail" time when a party receives notice that the delivery of a letter was attempted, unsuccessfully, and is now ready to be picked up. In such cases, the courts may choose to extend the time period so as to allow that party a few extra days to retrieve the letter.[54]

No 3–Day Extension for Certain Rules

For Rule 6(b)'s list of jurisdictional time periods, the clerk's mailing of an order or filing will not activate Rule 6(d)'s 3–day extension provision.[55]

48. *See Sherlock v. Montefiore Med. Ctr.*, 84 F.3d 522, 525–26 (2d Cir.1996) (noting "assumption" that mailed documents are received 3 days after mailing).

49. *See* Rule 6(d). *See also* Rule 6(e) advisory committee note to 2001 amendments (noting that electronic transmission is not always instantaneous, and may not arrive in a readable format, causing further delays).

50. *See Mosel v. Hills Dep't Store, Inc.*, 789 F.2d 251 (3d Cir.1986).

51. *See Delta Airlines v. Butler*, 383 F.3d 1143, 1145 (10th Cir.2004); *Johnson v. McBride*, 381 F.3d 587, 589 (7th Cir.2004); *Jackson v. Crosby*, 375 F.3d 1291, 1293 n.5 (11th Cir.2004); *Rouse v. Lee*, 339 F.3d 238, 245–46 (4th Cir.2003).

52. *See Johnson v. McBride*, 381 F.3d 587 (7th Cir.2004).

53. *See Begay v. St. Joseph's Indian Sch.*, 922 F.Supp. 270, 272–73 (D.S.D.1996) (Rule 6(e) does not provide an additional 3-days for responses to mailed right-to-sue letter, where response period begins to run only from date of receipt of the letter).

54. *See Zillyette v. Capital One Fin. Corp.*, 179 F.3d 1337, 1341–42 (11th Cir. 1999); *Sousa v. N.L.R.B.*, 817 F.2d 10, 11 (2d Cir.1987).

55. *See Albright v. Virtue*, 273 F.3d 564, 570–71 (3d Cir.2001) (motions for reconsideration under Rule 59(e) cannot be enlarged by this Rule); *Parker v. Board of Pub. Utilities of Kansas City*, 77 F.3d 1289, 1291 (10th Cir.1996) (same).

No 3–Day Extension to Most Statutes of Limitation

The prevailing view among the courts is that the 3–day extension period does not apply to extend statutes of limitation.[56]

Applies to No–Known–Address Service

The 3–day extension also applies in those cases where, aware of a defendant's last known address, the serving party delivers the documents to the clerk of court.[57]

11 Day or Greater Time Periods

If an act required to be accomplished in 11 days or longer is performed by mail, (or through the special service-means provided in Rules 5(b)(2)(C), (D), (E), and (F)), 3 days are added to the end of the defined time period.

Less Than 11 Day Time Periods

If an act required to be accomplished in less than 11 days is performed by mail, (or through the special, service-by-consent means provided in Rules 5(b)(2)(C), (D), (E), and (F)), the method for including the added 3 days is unclear. (Time periods of less than 11 days are counted specially: these time periods exclude intervening Saturdays, Sundays, and legal holidays.[58])

The 2005 amendments to former Rule 6(e) (current Rule 6(d)) resolved an interpretational conflict regarding the addition of these 3 days). Under the revised Rule, the 3 days are added to the end of the specified period. Thus, if a party serves a legal document by mail to which the adversary must respond within 10 days, the 10–day period is counted off first (excluding Saturdays, Sundays, and legal holidays), and then the 3 extra days are added (with the due date extended further to the next business day, if the 3–day period expires on a Saturday, Sunday, or legal holiday).[59]

There appears to be general agreement in the case law that Rule 6(a) and Rule 6(d) should never be applied in such a way that a 10–day period (in which intervening Saturdays, Sundays, and legal holidays are excluded) is itself converted into an 11–day-or-more period (in which intervening Saturdays, Sundays, and legal holidays *are* counted) by virtue of the added 3 days. Such a reading would defeat the very objectives of Rule 6(d). The purpose of the 3–day added period is to attempt to ensure that the responding party is afforded the same amount of response time, whether service results in immediate receipt (through hand delivery) or is delayed a few days (by postal or electronic delivery).[60]

---

56. *See Donovan v. Maine*, 276 F.3d 87, 91 (1st Cir.2002) (noting prevailing view); *Berman v. United States*, 264 F.3d 16, 19 (1st Cir.2001) (same).

57. *See* Rule 6(d); *see also* Rule 5(b)(2)(D). *See also* Rule 6(e) advisory committee note to 2001 amendments.

58. *See* Rule 6(a).

59. *See* Rule 6(e) (as amended Dec. 1, 2005)(now Rule 6(d)).

60. *See Lerro v. Quaker Oats Co.*, 84 F.3d 239, 242 (7th Cir.1996).

Note: This 3–day period is not, itself, a "time period" subject to Rule 6(a). Consequently, the 3–day extension is not further expanded if the 3 days include intervening Saturdays, Sundays, holidays, or weather inaccessible days.[61]

Additional 3–Day Period Applies to Objections to Magistrate Judge Rulings

A district judge may direct a magistrate judge to consider and decide nondispositive pretrial matters, and to consider and submit a recommendation on dispositive motions.[62] The parties, thereafter, have 10 days from service to file objections to the magistrate judge's order or recommendation.[63] If the magistrate judge's order or recommendation is served upon the parties by mail, the additional 3–day period of Rule 6(d) applies to extend this 10–day objection period.[64]

ADDITIONAL RESEARCH REFERENCES

Wright & Miller, *Federal Practice and Procedure* §§ 1161–71.

C.J.S. Federal Civil Procedure §§ 194, 250, 302, 331, 354–369, 394–436, 569, 571, 701, 732, 764–789 et seq., 933–934; Time §§ 2–17 et seq.

West's Key No. Digests, Federal Civil Procedure ☞417, 624, 734–735, 824, 865, 868, 923, 956, 1033, 1051, 1143, 1342–1343, 1612, 1679–1680, 1701–1705, 1991–1998; Time ☞2–15.

61. *See CNPq–Conselho Nacional de Desenvolvimento Cientifico e Technologico v. Inter–Trade, Inc.,* 50 F.3d 56 (D.C.Cir. 1995). *See also Ramsdell v. Bowles,* 64 F.3d 5, 8 n. 1 (1st Cir.1995) (noting District of Maine's local rule which excludes intervening weekends and holidays from ten-day period, but not from three-day mailing period).

62. *See* 28 U.S.C. § 636(b)(1); Fed. R. Civ. P. 72(a)-(b).

63. *See* 28 U.S.C. § 636(b)(1); Fed. R. Civ. P. 72(a)-(b).

64. *See* Rule 72(b) advisory committee's note 1983 Addition; *Vanderberg v. Donaldson,* 259 F.3d 1321, 1325 (11th Cir.2001); *Lerro v. Quaker Oats Co.,* 84 F.3d 239, 241–42 (7th Cir.1996).

III. PLEADINGS AND MOTIONS

RULE 7

PLEADINGS ALLOWED; FORM OF MOTIONS AND OTHER PAPERS

(a) Pleadings. Only these pleadings are allowed:

(1) a complaint;

(2) an answer to a complaint;

(3) an answer to a counterclaim designated as a counterclaim;

(4) an answer to a crossclaim;

(5) a third-party complaint;

(6) an answer to a third-party complaint; and

(7) if the court orders one, a reply to an answer.

(b) Motions and Other Papers.

(1) *In General.* A request for a court order must be made by motion. The motion must:

(A) be in writing unless made during a hearing or trial;

(B) state with particularity the grounds for seeking the order; and

(C) state the relief sought.

(2) *Form.* The rules governing captions and other matters of form in pleadings apply to motions and other papers.

[Amended effective March 19, 1948; July 1, 1963; August 1, 1983; April 30, 2007, effective December 1, 2007.]

─────────── 2007 AMENDMENTS ROADMAP ───────────

STYLE PROJECT CHANGES: New subsectioning and labeling was added, and cumbersome language was culled and replaced for clarity. Redundant references to Rule 11 and to fulfilling the requirement by written notice of hearing were deleted. Former Rule 7(c), which noted the abolition of demurrers, pleas, and exceptions, was deleted as no longer necessary.

NON-STYLE CHANGES: Courts are now authorized to order replies to a counterclaim and crossclaim answer, in addition to replies to original answers and third-party answers.

NOTE: The Federal Rules "Style Project" is explained in Part III-A.

AUTHORS' COMMENTARY ON RULE 7

PURPOSE AND SCOPE

Rule 7 lists the pleadings permitted in federal court, and sets forth the general requirements for the form of motions. The provisions of this Rule are often supplemented extensively by local rules, which practitioners should consult carefully.

RULE 7(a). PLEADINGS PERMITTED AND REPLIES

CORE CONCEPT

Rule 7(a) lists the six types of pleadings that may be filed in federal court: (1) a complaint; (2) an answer to a complaint; (3) a reply to a counterclaim, if the counterclaim is so designated; (4) an answer to a crossclaim; (5) a third-party complaint; and (6) a third-party answer. In addition to these six pleadings, the court may, in its discretion, order a reply to an answer, a third-party answer, or a counterclaim answer.

APPLICATIONS

Not Pleadings

The list in Rule 7(a) is exhaustive.[1] Assuming no counterclaim or crossclaim is filed, the pleadings are considered closed once a complaint and answer have been filed.[2] Consequently, the following documents—which do not appear in the Rule 7(a) list—are *not* "pleadings": a writ, a motion to dismiss,[3] a motion for summary judgment,[4] a motion for sanctions,[5] a response to a motion, a "suggestion" under Rule 12(h)(3) of a lack of subject matter jurisdic-

1. *See Yuhasz v. Brush Wellman, Inc.,* 341 F.3d 559, 569 (6th Cir.2003) (Rule 7 provides exhaustive list of pleadings).

2. *See Doe v. United States,* 419 F.3d 1058, 1061 (9th Cir.2005); *Wedgewood Ltd. P'ship v. Township of Liberty,* 456 F.Supp.2d 904, 917 (S.D.Ohio 2006).

3. *See Tahoe–Sierra Pres. Council, Inc. v. Tahoe Reg'l Planning Agency,* 216 F.3d 764, 788 (9th Cir.2000); *Maldonado v. Dom-*

inguez, 137 F.3d 1, 11 n. 8 (1st Cir.1998); *Gupta v. Northrop Grumman Corp.,* 462 F.Supp.2d 56, 61 (D.D.C. 2006).

4. *See Principal Health Care of Louisiana, Inc. v. Lewer Agency, Inc.,* 38 F.3d 240, 244 (5th Cir.1994).

5. *See Phinney v. Paulshock,* 181 F.R.D. 185 (D.N.H.1998).

tion, a brief or memorandum,[6] a reply brief or memorandum,[7] discovery papers,[8] a notice of appeal,[9] affidavits,[10] declarations,[11] filings in a condemnation proceeding, and special pre-answer "reports" required of defendants in certain cases, such as prisoner civil rights lawsuits.[12]

Definitions

(1) *Complaint:* A complaint is the document that sets forth either the initial plaintiff's claim for relief or a third-party plaintiff's claim for relief.

(2) *Answer:* An answer is the document that sets forth a defendant's opposition to a complaint, a counterclaim, a crossclaim, or a third-party complaint.[13]

(3) *Counterclaim:* A counterclaim is the document that sets forth a defendant's or third-party defendant's claims against the original plaintiff or third-party plaintiff.

(4) *Crossclaim:* A crossclaim is the document that sets forth one defendant's claims against one or more co-defendants. In many cases, defendants crossclaim against one another for indemnification or contribution. Note that answers to crossclaims are "pleadings", but the crossclaims themselves (which ordinarily are contained in a defendant's answer to the original complaint) are not considered "pleadings".[14]

(5) *Reply:* A reply is the pleading by which a party responds to an answer, a counterclaim answer, a crossclaim answer, or a third-party answer.[15] Replies are permitted in only limited circumstances. They are only permitted if the court so directs.[16]

> *Note:* Practitioners may encounter answers that include an averment designated as a "counterclaim" but which, in reality, is actually only an affirmative defense. Although responses are only required to bona fide counterclaims,

6. *See Sunlight Saunas, Inc. v. Sundance Sauna, Inc.,* 427 F.Supp.2d 1022, 1029 (D.Kan.2006); *Bush v. Barnett Bank,* 916 F.Supp. 1244, 1249 (M.D.Fla.1996).

7. *See Nwachukwu v. Rooney,* 362 F.Supp.2d 183, 190 (D.D.C.2005).

8. *See Carlson v. Reed,* 249 F.3d 876, 878 n.1 (9th Cir.2001) (interrogatories are not pleadings).

9. *See Adkins v. Safeway, Inc.,* 985 F.2d 1101, 1102 (D.C.Cir.1993).

10. *See Aftergood v. Central Intelligence Agency,* 355 F.Supp.2d 557, 564 (D.D.C. 2005); *Int'l Longshoremen's Ass'n, S.S. Clerks Local 1624 v. Virginia Int'l Terminals, Inc.,* 904 F.Supp. 500, 504 (E.D.Va. 1995).

11. *See Finke v. Kirtland Cmty. Coll. Bd. of Trustees,* 359 F.Supp.2d 593, 596–97 (E.D.Mich.2005).

12. *See Burns v. Lawther,* 53 F.3d 1237 (11th Cir.1995) (in prisoner civil rights case, special, pre-answer reports filed by defendants as requested by magistrate judge did not constitute "pleadings" within the meaning of Rule 7(a)).

13. *See LeBoeuf, Lamb, Greene & MacRae, L.L.P. v. Worsham,* 185 F.3d 61, 66–67 (2d Cir.1999) (noting that responsive pleading (an answer) is required to a complaint).

14. *See In re Cessna Distributorship Antitrust Litig.,* 532 F.2d 64, 67 (8th Cir.1976).

15. *See* Rule 7(a)(7). *See also* Rule 7 advisory committee note from 2007.

16. *See, e.g., Mihos v. Swift,* 358 F.3d 91, 106 (1st Cir.2004); *United States v. Shanbaum,* 10 F.3d 305, 312 n. 4 (5th Cir. 1994); *Sevcik v. Unlimited Const. Servs., Inc.,* 462 F.Supp.2d 1140, 1143 n.1 (D.Hawaiʻi 2006).

practitioners should reply to all labeled "counterclaims"—whether they appear facially proper or not—to avoid any risk that the averments of the "counterclaim" might be deemed admitted.

Motion to Permit or Compel a Reply

Although otherwise not required, replies to an answer may be permitted or compelled by the court. To be granted leave to make such a filing, or to compel such a filing by another litigant, the moving party must make a clear and convincing showing that substantial reason or necessity or extraordinary circumstances require a reply.[17] Courts may permit or compel a reply to an answer for several reasons: when a type of new matter is pleaded in the answer that might affect the outcome of the trial or might otherwise greatly broaden the issues in the case, when the information sought through the reply cannot be acquired through discovery, when a misdesignated affirmative defense must be answered or clarified, or when the case otherwise should not proceed without a reply.

> *Note:* More recently, courts have required that plaintiffs in federal civil rights cases file specific and particularized replies when the defendants are public officials and assert qualified immunity as an affirmative defense.[18]

RULE 7(b).   MOTIONS AND OTHER PAPERS

CORE CONCEPT

Rule 7(b) sets the procedures for motion practice in the federal courts.

APPLICATIONS

Motion Defined

A motion is a request to the court, usually submitted in writing, that seeks an order.[19]

WARNING: Consult the Local Rules

Nearly every district has promulgated local rules governing motion practice before their courts and, in some instances, individual judges have issued "standing orders" for their Chambers or case-specific orders regulating such particulars as the time for and

17. *See Moviecolor Ltd. v. Eastman Kodak Co.,* 24 F.R.D. 325 (S.D.N.Y.1959).

18. *See Crawford–El v. Britton,* 523 U.S. 574, 118 S.Ct. 1584, 140 L.Ed.2d 759 (1998) (commenting that trial court may order a reply to an answer that asserts a public official's qualified immunity, to protect the substance of the defense by compelling the plaintiff to aver some "specific, nonconclusory factual allegations" that demonstrate improper motive); *Reyes v. Sa-*zan, 168 F.3d 158, 161 (5th Cir.1999) (commenting that trial courts, when faced with sparse details of claimed wrongdoing alleged against public officials, should routinely require plaintiffs to file a reply under Rule 7(a) to qualified immunity defenses).

19. *See United States ex el. Atkins v. McInteer,* 470 F.3d 1350, 1361 (11th Cir. 2006); *In re Vogel Van & Storage, Inc.,* 59 F.3d 9, 12 (2d Cir.1995).

method of responding to motions, page limitations for motions and responses, the proper form for such filings, the acceptability of "reply briefs", chambers' policies on courtesy copies for the judge, the number of motion copies that must be submitted, and the scheduling of oral arguments. Practitioners should always consult the local rules of court and chambers' standing orders to locate any unique procedures for motion practice within a specific district.

Rules Governing Pleading Forms Also Apply to Motions

The Rules that govern the styling of captions and the form of pleadings also apply to motions.[20]

Formal Requirements for Motions

All motions must be in writing, unless they are presented during a hearing or trial. A written "notice of hearing" on the motion will satisfy this requirement.

Form: Written motions must comply with the requirements of Rule 10—they must include a caption listing the name of the court, the title of the action, the docket number, and the title of the motion.

Contents: Written motions must set forth "with particularity" the grounds for the relief the motion requests. The purpose of this "particularity" requirement is to provide both the court and the adversary with ample notice of the grounds supporting the motion and the specific relief requested, so that the court may fully comprehend the request and the adversary can have a meaningful opportunity to respond.[21] Although "ritualistic detail" is not required,[22] and the Rule is often given a liberal application,[23] the courts look for "reasonable particularity" in assessing whether this requirement is satisfied,[24] and will examine a supporting brief or memoranda in making this evaluation.[25] Where an insufficiently particularized motion specifically

---

20. This directive is not a license for creative lawyering designed to evade either the requirements of other Rules or the express instructions of the court. *See Swanson v. United States Forest Serv.*, 87 F.3d 339, 345 (9th Cir.1996) (when court denied counsel the right to file an overlength motion brief, counsel could not escape this ruling by relying on Rule 7(b)(2) to justify the "incorporation by reference" under Rule 10(c) of an additional 69 pages of argument contained in earlier filings).

21. *See Feldberg v. Quechee Lakes Corp.*, 463 F.3d 195, 197 (2d Cir. 2006); *Fort James Corp. v. Solo Cup Co.*, 412 F.3d 1340, 1347 (Fed. Cir.2005); *Kelly v. Moore*, 376 F.3d 481, 484 (5th Cir.2004). *See also Goodman v. 1973 26 Foot Trojan Vessel, Arkansas Registration No. AR1439SN*, 859 F.2d 71, 74 (8th Cir.1988)(commenting that requirement protects district courts from

becoming subject to reversal on rulings where courts lacked benefit of argument from opposing counsel, and affords opposing parties notice of opponents' positions).

22. *See Kelly v. Moore*, 376 F.3d 481, 484 (5th Cir.2004).

23. *See Intera Corp. v. Henderson*, 428 F.3d 605, 612–14 (6th Cir.2005).

24. *See Fort James Corp. v. Solo Cup Co.*, 412 F.3d 1340, 1347 (Fed. Cir.2005); *Talano v. Northwestern Med. Faculty Found., Inc.*, 273 F.3d 757, 760 (7th Cir. 2001). *See also Allender v. Raytheon Aircraft Co.*, 439 F.3d 1236, 1240 (10th Cir. 2006) ("reasonable specification" required).

25. *See Lac Du Flambeau Band of Lake Superior Chippewa Indians v. Wisconsin*, 957 F.2d 515, 516 (7th Cir. 1992)(simultaneously filed brief satisfied Rule 7(b)'s particularity requirement).

references another filed document, the court may consult the referenced filing to assess whether the required specificity can be discerned.[26] The courts will decide challenges to a motion's particularity by evaluating whether any party is prejudiced by the motion's form and whether the court can discern the motion's basis and rule upon it fairly.[27] If the motion fails to satisfy the particularity requirement, it may be dismissed or denied.[28]

    Motions to Amend: When a party submits a motion to amend, the particularity requirement of Rule 7(b) may require the party to attach to the motion a copy of the proposed amended pleading, unless the motion sets forth the substance of or otherwise adequately describes the contemplated revision.[29] Informal amendment requests— unaccompanied by the proposed amended pleading itself or a summary of its substance—do not conform to Rule 7(b) and may be refused by the trial court for that reason.[30]

    Supporting Memorandum or Brief: Rule 7 does not expressly require a party to submit a supporting memorandum or brief along with motions or oppositions to motions. Note, however, that many districts have promulgated local rules requiring supporting memoranda, and providing that a motion lacking such support may be dismissed.

    Form of Order: Many districts also have local rules obligating the moving party to attach a form of order to the motion which, if signed and entered, would grant the relief requested in the motion. Similarly, the party opposing a motion may be required to attach a form of order which would deny the requested relief.

    Attaching Affidavits and Other Exhibits: A party may support a motion with affidavits or other materials. Practitioners are cautioned, however, that such attachments can have substantial procedural consequences.[31]

---

26. *See Fort James Corp. v. Solo Cup Co.,* 412 F.3d 1340, 1347 (Fed.Cir.2005).

27. *See Cambridge Plating Co. v. Napco, Inc.,* 85 F.3d 752, 760 (1st Cir.1996).

28. *See, e.g., Evans v. Pearson Enters., Inc.,* 434 F.3d 839, 853 (6th Cir.2006); *Butler v. Coral Volkswagen, Inc.,* 804 F.2d 612, 614–15 (11th Cir.1986). *Cf. Hopkins v. Bowen,* 850 F.2d 417, 420 (8th Cir.1988)(memorandum in support of summary judgment considered a "motion" for summary judgment where it described particular grounds for the motion, prayed for specific relief, provided the opponent sufficient opportunity to respond, and caused no prejudice).

29. *See Long v. Satz,* 181 F.3d 1275 (11th Cir.1999); *Moore v. Indiana,* 999 F.2d 1125, 1131 (7th Cir.1993); *Wolgin v. Simon,* 722 F.2d 389, 394 (8th Cir.1983).

30. *See PR Diamonds, Inc. v. Chandler,* 364 F.3d 671, 699–700 (6th Cir.2004); *Calderon v. Kansas Dep't of Social & Rehab. Servs.,* 181 F.3d 1180, 1186 (10th Cir.1999); *Posner v. Essex Ins. Co.,* 178 F.3d 1209, 1222 (11th Cir.1999).

31. *See, e.g.,* Rule 12(b)(if matters outside the pleadings are presented to, and considered by, the court on a Rule 12(b)(6) motion to dismiss, court must convert motion into Rule 56 motion for summary judgment); Rule 12(c)(same, in context of motion for judgment on the pleadings).

Signing: The written motion must be signed in accordance with Rule 11 by the party's counsel or, if unrepresented, by the party herself. If the motion is not signed after the omission is called to the attention of the party or her counsel, the court may strike the document.

Service: A signed copy of the motion or "notice of hearing" must be served upon counsel for represented parties or, if unrepresented, upon the party herself. Unless the court directs otherwise, service must be accomplished not later than 5 days prior to the hearing on the motion.[32]

Certificate of Service: The motion must contain a certificate of service verifying that the document was served.[33]

Filing: The written motion or "notice of hearing" must be filed within a reasonable time after service.[34] Note, however, that local rules may prescribe other, supplemental filing requirements.

Opposing Written Motions

Rule 7 contains no requirement that an opponent file an "answer" to any motion and, absent local rule requirements to the contrary, a motion can be opposed solely by filing a brief or memorandum. The form, signing, filing, and service requirements for motions are generally applicable to oppositions as well.

Withdrawing Written Motions

A written motion should ordinarily be withdrawn with the same formality with which it was filed. Consequently, written motions should be withdrawn in writing.[35]

Hearings and Arguments on Written Motions

The court may, in its discretion, schedule a motion for a hearing or oral argument. Neither is expressly required under the Rules, although local rule provisions may specify additional hearing and argument requirements. Hearings held *ex parte* (without notice to the opponent) are generally discouraged and are permitted only in exceptional circumstances, such as applications for temporary restraining orders.[36]

Oral Motions

Oral motions may be made, so long as they are raised in open court at a hearing or trial.[37] This presentation will satisfy the writing requirement of Rule 7 if the oral motion is transcribed or

---

32. *See* Rule 5 and Rule 6(c).

33. *See* Rule 5(d)(1).

34. *See* Rule 5(d)(1).

35. *See United Coin Meter Co. v. Seaboard Coastline RR.,* 705 F.2d 839, 843 (6th Cir.1983).

36. *See* Rule 65(b).

37. *See Meriwether v. Coughlin,* 879 F.2d 1037, 1042 (2d Cir.1989)(noting that, because oral motion was asserted in open court, written document not required). *See also Kerry Steel, Inc. v. Paragon Indus., Inc.,* 106 F.3d 147, 154 (6th Cir.1997) (noting that Rules allow motions at hearings, and refusing to hold as significant the attorney's omission of the utterance: "I move").

otherwise recorded.[38] This "writing" requirement for oral motions functions to ensure that the motion is accurately memorialized and that both the court and the opponent have sufficient opportunity to prepare for the motion.[39]

Amendments to Motions

A party may seek leave to amend a motion. Leave is generally granted if the amendment is sought before the opponent has filed the opposition memorandum or brief, before the court has entertained oral argument, and before a ruling has been issued. Motions are amended, rather than just refiled, where a new, replacement motion would be improper or out of time.[40]

ADDITIONAL RESEARCH REFERENCES

Wright & Miller, *Federal Practice and Procedure* §§ 1181–1200.

C.J.S. Federal Civil Procedure §§ 124, 247–280 et seq., 301–319 et seq., 363–375 et seq.

West's Key No. Digests, Federal Civil Procedure ⚷295, 621–665, 671–680, 731–745, 771–786, 903, 921–928.

38. *See Atchison, Topeka & Santa Fe Ry. Co. v. California State Bd. of Equalization*, 102 F.3d 425, 427 (9th Cir.1996); *People of Illinois ex rel. Hartigan v. Peters*, 871 F.2d 1336, 1341 (7th Cir.1989).

39. *See Taragan v. Eli Lilly & Co.*, 838 F.2d 1337, 1340–41 (D.C.Cir. 1988)(requirement of adequate opportunity to prepare and respond satisfied by oral motions if they are germane to hearing or trial).

40. *See, e.g.*, Rule 12(g) and 12(h)(providing that defenses of improper personal jurisdiction, lack of venue, insufficient process, or inadequate service of process are deemed waived if not asserted in original Rule 12(b) motion).

RULE 7.1

DISCLOSURE STATEMENT

(a) Who Must File; Contents. A nongovernmental corporate party must file two copies of a disclosure statement that:

(1) identifies any parent corporation and any publicly held corporation owning 10% or more of its stock; or

(2) states that there is no such corporation.

(b) Time to File; Supplemental Filing. A party must:

(1) file the disclosure statement with its first appearance, pleading, petition, motion, response, or other request addressed to the court; and

(2) promptly file a supplemental statement if any required information changes.

[Added April 29, 2002, effective December 1, 2002; April 30, 2007, effective December 1, 2007.]

──────────── **2007 AMENDMENTS ROADMAP** ────────────

STYLE PROJECT CHANGES: Subsectioning was added to first paragraph, but otherwise very few language changes to this relatively new Rule.

NON-STYLE CHANGES: None.

NOTE: The Federal Rules "Style Project" is explained in Part III-A.

AUTHORS' COMMENTARY ON RULE 7.1

──────────── **PURPOSE AND SCOPE** ────────────

Rule 7.1 was added to the Rules in 2002 to help assist district judges in making properly informed decisions on whether certain financial interests require their disqualification in particular cases.

CORE CONCEPT

Rule 7.1 is modeled after Rule 26.1 of the Federal Rules of Appellate

Procedure,[1] and requires specific financial disclosures by all non-governmental corporate parties to an action or proceeding in district court.[2] The Rule is intended to provide the appropriate level and volume of financial disclosures necessary to allow for properly informed disqualification decisions in those circumstances where automatic financial interest disqualification is compelled.[3]

APPLICATIONS

Automatic Financial Interest Disqualifications

Rule 7.1 was not designed to cover all circumstances that might call for a district judge's disqualification.[4] Instead, the information compelled by Rule 7.1 reflects the financial interest standard for automatic disqualification under the Code of Conduct for United States Judges.[5]

Disclosure Procedures

The disclosure obligation applies to non-governmental corporate litigants. Such parties must file with the court a written statement that either (1) identifies each parent corporation and publicly held corporation owning 10% or more of their stock, *or* (2) states that no such corporation exists.[6] Two copies of the statement must be filed.[7] The filing must be made when the party files its first appearance, pleading, petition, motion, response, or other request addressed to the court.[8]

Supplementing the Statement

Parties are also obligated under the Rule to "promptly" file a supplemental statement when any change in the required informa-

---

1. *See* Rule 7.1 advisory committee note to 2002 amendments. *See also* Fed. R. App. P. 26.1 (setting forth filing requirements for "Corporate Disclosure Statements").

2. Rule 7.1(a).

3. *See* Rule 7.1 advisory committee note to 2002 amendments (explaining that Rule strikes balance between requiring adequate amount of financial information and more detailed disclosures that "will be difficult", would unnecessarily "place a burden on the parties and on the courts", and "create a risk that a judge will overlook the one bit of information that might require disqualification, and also may create a risk that unnecessary disqualifications will be made rather than attempt to unravel a potentially difficult question"). *See also Ha v. Deutsche Bank New Jersey Servs., Inc.*, 2005 WL 589408, at *2 (S.D.N.Y.2005) (noting that "primary purpose of the Rule 7.1 Disclosure Statement is to place judges on notice of the financial affiliations of a nongovernmental corporate party that appears before them"); *Gebhart v. Raytheon Aircraft Co.*, 2004 WL 1212047, at *2 n.13 (D.Kan.2004) (State-

ment is required "so that the assigned judge can ascertain whether he or she has a financial interest in the party or associated entities, which would require recusal").

4. *See* Rule 7.1 advisory committee note to 2002 amendments.

5. *See* Rule 7.1 advisory committee note to 2002 amendments. *See also* Code of Conduct for United States Judges at Canon 3C(1)(c) ("A judge shall disqualify himself or herself in a proceeding in which the judge's impartiality might reasonably be questioned, including but not limited to instances in which ... (c) the judge knows that the judge, individually or as a fiduciary, or the judge's spouse or minor child residing in the judge's household, has a financial interest in the subject matter in controversy or in a party to the proceeding, or any other interest that could be affected substantially by the outcome of the proceeding").

6. *See* Rule 7.1(a).

7. *See* Rule 7.1(a).

8. *See* Rule 7.1(b)(1).

tion occurs.[9]

More Extensive Financial Disclosures Required by Local Rules

The drafters of Rule 7.1 expressly noted that local rules may require additional disclosures (and those regional experiences along with advances in electronic technology may one day justify additional National disclosures and an amendment to this Rule).[10]

Effect of Non–Filing

There is little caselaw discussing the consequence of a failure to file (or timely file) the Rule 7.1 disclosure statement. The modest emerging authority suggests that a failure to file, if remedied, may be excused.[11]

Collateral Effects of Statement

Although court decisions construing this newly promulgated Rule are few, early indications are that litigants and the courts have used (or considered using) these Statements for purposes other than those for which it was intended. For example, one court used a defendant's Statement to resolve a dispute concerning the parties' draft settlement agreement under which the plaintiff had agreed to refrain from seeking or accepting employment from defendant-affiliated entities,[12] and another court ordered that a plaintiff be judicially estopped from substituting another party-plaintiff due, in part, to confusion created by a delinquent Statement.[13] But another court ruled that the Statement could not be relied upon for a substitution of parties or an amendment to a complaint,[14] nor would a failure to file the Statement affect a litigant's pending motion to dismiss.[15]

---

9. *See* Rule 7.1(b)(2).

10. *See* Rule 7.1 advisory committee note to 2002 amendments.

11. *See Ferro Corp. v. Continental Cas. Co.*, 2007 WL 120761 (N.D.Ohio 2007) (belated, post-removal filing of disclosure statement did not defeat removal or compel remand).

12. *See Ha v. Deutsche Bank New Jersey Servs., Inc.*, 2005 WL 589408, at *2 (S.D.N.Y.2005).

13. *See Engines Southwest, Inc. v. Kohler Co.*, 2006 WL 1896071 (W.D.La.2006).

14. *See Gebhart v. Raytheon Aircraft Co.*, 2004 WL 1212047, at *2 (D.Kan.2004).

15. *See Smith v. Argent Mortg. Co.*, 2006 WL 581157, at *1 (D.Colo.2006).

RULE 8

GENERAL RULES OF PLEADING

(a) Claim for Relief. A pleading that states a claim for relief must contain:

(1) a short and plain statement of the grounds for the court's jurisdiction, unless the court already has jurisdiction and the claim needs no new jurisdictional support;

(2) a short and plain statement of the claim showing that the pleader is entitled to relief; and

(3) a demand for the relief sought, which may include relief in the alternative or different types of relief.

(b) Defenses; Admissions and Denials.

(1) *In General.* In responding to a pleading, a party must:

(A) state in short and plain terms its defenses to each claim asserted against it; and

(B) admit or deny the allegations asserted against it by an opposing party.

(2) *Denials—Responding to the Substance.* A denial must fairly respond to the substance of the allegation.

(3) *General and Specific Denials.* A party that intends in good faith to deny all the allegations of a pleading—including the jurisdictional grounds—may do so by a general denial. A party that does not intend to deny all the allegations must either specifically deny designated allegations or generally deny all except those specifically admitted.

(4) *Denying Part of an Allegation.* A party that intends in good faith to deny only part of an allegation must admit the part that is true and deny the rest.

(5) *Lacking Knowledge or Information.* A party that lacks knowledge or information sufficient to form a belief about the truth of an allegation must so state, and the statement has the effect of a denial.

281

(6) *Effect of Failing to Deny.* An allegation—other than one relating to the amount of damages—is admitted if a responsive pleading is required and the allegation is not denied. If a responsive pleading is not required, an allegation is considered denied or avoided.

(c) Affirmative Defenses.

(1) *In General.* In responding to a pleading, a party must affirmatively state any avoidance or affirmative defense, including:

- accord and satisfaction;
- arbitration and award;
- assumption of risk;
- contributory negligence;
- discharge in bankruptcy;
- duress;
- estoppel;
- failure of consideration;
- fraud;
- illegality;
- injury by fellow servant;
- laches;
- license;
- payment;
- release;
- res judicata;
- statute of frauds;
- statute of limitations; and
- waiver.

(2) *Mistaken Designation.* If a party mistakenly designates a defense as a counterclaim, or a counterclaim as a defense, the court must, if justice requires, treat the pleading as though it were correctly designated, and may impose terms for doing so.

(d) Pleading to Be Concise and Direct; Alternative Statements; Inconsistency.

(1) *In General.* Each allegation must be simple, concise, and direct. No technical form is required.

(2) *Alternative Statements of a Claim or Defense.* A party may set out two or more statements of a claim or defense alternatively or hypothetically, either in a single count or defense or in separate ones. If a party makes alternative statements, the pleading is sufficient if any one of them is sufficient.

(3) *Inconsistent Claims or Defenses.* A party may state as many separate claims or defenses as it has, regardless of consistency.

(e) Construing Pleadings. Pleadings must be construed so as to do justice.

[Amended effective July 1, 1966; August 1, 1987; April 30, 2007, effective December 1, 2007.]

——————— **2007 AMENDMENTS ROADMAP** ———————

STYLE PROJECT CHANGES: Rule 8(d), describing the effect of a failure to deny, was folded into a new comprehensive admissions-and-denials treatment in Rule 8(b). Rule 8(b) was restructured accordingly. Rules 8(e) and 8(f) have been repositioned to fill the gap, and are now Rules 8(d) and 8(e). Subsectioning and new labeling was added throughout. Redundant references to Rule 11, "substantial" justice, and the scope of the merger of law and equity were deleted.

NON-STYLE CHANGES: Rule 8(b)'s instruction that a responsive pleading need only specify what allegations are true "and material" was deleted, to avoid the inference that allegations may be denied on the mere subjective belief that they are not "material".

NOTE: The Federal Rules "Style Project" is explained in Part III-A.

AUTHORS' COMMENTARY ON RULE 8

——————— PURPOSE AND SCOPE ———————

Rule 8 establishes the "notice" pleading protocol for the federal courts. It sets the requirements for pleading claims and defenses, and outlines both the procedures for proper denials and the consequences for failing to deny. Rule 8 entitles pleaders to allege claims or defenses alternatively, hypothetically, or inconsistently—provided the pleading complies with the requirements of Rule 11. In federal court, pleadings are construed liberally so as to do justice.

RULE 8(a). CLAIMS FOR RELIEF

CORE CONCEPT

In a "short" and "plain" statement, a party asserting a claim must include: (1) the grounds for the court's jurisdiction; (2) a statement of a claim showing that the pleader is entitled to relief; and (3) a demand for relief.

APPLICATIONS

Element 1: Grounds for Jurisdiction

A party filing a claim in a complaint, counterclaim, crossclaim, or third-party complaint must state in short and plain terms the basis for the court's subject matter jurisdiction for each count.[1]

● *Diversity Jurisdiction:* When jurisdiction is based on diversity of citizenship,[2] the plaintiff must allege: (1) the citizenship of each party (for individuals, their State of citizenship; for corporations, their State of incorporation *and* their principal place of business); and (2) that the amount in controversy—exclusive of interest and costs—exceeds $75,000.

● *Federal Question Jurisdiction:* When jurisdiction is based on the presence of a federal question,[3] the claimant must identify the Constitutional provisions, laws, or treaties that create such jurisdiction.

● *Admiralty Jurisdiction:* A claim that has both an admiralty or maritime basis for jurisdiction and another basis for jurisdiction may be brought under either the federal court's specific admiralty jurisdiction or its ordinary jurisdiction. A party wishing to proceed under the rules governing admiralty or maritime claims must include a statement in the complaint that the action is an admiralty or maritime claim within the meaning of Rule 9(h).[4]

● *Supplemental Jurisdiction:* When diversity, federal question, or admiralty/maritime jurisdiction exists as to one or more claims in the complaint, the pleader may litigate other, non-federal claims in the same case so long as the non-federal claims are so related to the

---

1. For a discussion of jurisdiction in the federal courts, see §§ 2.1—2.13 of this text. *See McNutt v. General Motors Acceptance Corp.*, 298 U.S. 178, 189, 56 S.Ct. 780, 785, 80 L.Ed. 1135 (1936) (commenting that pleader "must allege in his pleading the facts essential to show jurisdiction"); *United States v. Bustillos*, 31 F.3d 931, 933 (10th Cir.1994) (noting that party seeking to invoke the jurisdiction of a federal court must affirmatively allege facts supporting jurisdiction and, if challenged, bear the burden of proving that).

2. 28 U.S.C.A. § 1332.

3. 28 U.S.C.A. § 1331.

4. 28 U.S.C.A. § 1333.

federal claims that they form part of the same "case or controversy".[5]

● *Personal ("In Personam") Jurisdiction:* Ordinarily, plaintiffs need not allege personal jurisdiction in their complaint; Rule 8(a) requires only that subject matter jurisdiction be alleged.[6]

Element 2: Short and Plain Statement of the Claim

The Rules impose a relatively lenient obligation upon pleaders in federal court.[7] Litigants are generally[8] required to satisfy only "notice" pleading obligations: they must provide their opponent with fair notice of their claim and the grounds upon which that claim rests.[9] A pleader meets this obligation by notifying the opponent of the claim and proposed relief to such a degree that the opponent is able to formulate a response.[10] In this respect, federal court practice differs from the more elaborate and demanding responsibilities imposed by many State courts in "fact" pleading jurisdictions.[11] A pleader does *not* have to set forth legal theories,[12] and pleading an incorrect legal theory is not necessarily fatal.[13] The simplified federal "notice" pleading standard counts on the discovery rules and summary judgment practice to further define the disputed facts in the case and remove unmeritorious claims.[14]

5. 28 U.S.C.A. § 1367.

6. *See Caribbean Broad. Sys., Ltd. v. Cable & Wireless P.L.C.,* 148 F.3d 1080, 1090 (D.C.Cir.1998) (commenting that, because lack of personal jurisdiction is an affirmative defense, pleader's complaint was not required to make specific personal jurisdiction allegations). *See also Purdue Research Found. v. Sanofi–Synthelabo, S.A.,* 338 F.3d 773, 781–82 (7th Cir.2003) (noting that federal complaints need not set forth facts alleging personal jurisdiction).

7. *See Dura Pharm., Inc. v. Broudo,* 544 U.S. 336, 347, 125 S.Ct. 1627, 1634, 161 L.Ed.2d 577 (2005) ("ordinary pleading rules are not meant to impose a great burden upon a plaintiff"); *Pelman ex rel. Pelman v. McDonald's Corp.,* 396 F.3d 508, 511 (2d Cir.2005) ("bare-bones" requirements).

8. Note, however, that this liberality is qualified in certain cases (see *Exceptions,* below).

9. *See Tellabs, Inc. v. Makor Issues & Rights, Ltd.,* ___ U.S. ___, 127 S.Ct. 2499, 2507, 168 L.Ed.2d 179 (2007); *Erickson v. Pardus,* ___ U.S. ___, 127 S.Ct. 2197, 2200, 167 L.Ed.2d 1081 (2007) (per curiam); *Bell Atlantic Corp. v. Twombly,* 550 U.S. ___, ___, 127 S.Ct. 1955, 1964, 167 L.Ed.2d 929 (2007); *Jones v. Bock,* ___ U.S. ___, ___, 127 S.Ct. 910, 919, 166 L.Ed.2d 798 (2007); *Swierkiewicz v. Sorema N. A.,* 534 U.S. 506, 512, 122 S.Ct. 992, 998, 152 L.Ed.2d 1

(2002); *Conley v. Gibson,* 355 U.S. 41, 47, 78 S.Ct. 99, 102, 2 L.Ed.2d 80 (1957).

10. *See, e.g., Dura Pharms., Inc. v. Broudo,* 544 U.S. 336, 346–47, 125 S.Ct. 1627, 161 L.Ed.2d 577 (2005) (noting that even a short and plain statement "must provide the defendant with 'fair notice' ", including the nature of the claim "plaintiff has in mind"); *Mann v. Boatright,* 477 F.3d 1140, 1148 (10th Cir. 2007) (plaintiffs required "to state their claims intelligibly so as to inform the defendants of the legal claims being asserted"); *Rodriguez v. Doral Mortg. Corp.,* 57 F.3d 1168, 1171 (1st Cir. 1995) (court must protect "defendant's inalienable right to know in advance the nature of the cause of action being asserted against him.").

11. *See Bell Atlantic Corp. v. Twombly,* 550 U.S. ___, ___ & ___ n.3, 127 S.Ct. 1955, 1964 & 1965 n.3, 167 L.Ed.2d 929 (2007) (noting that ordinary complaint "does not need detailed factual allegations", a "cumbersome requirement" eliminated by the Rules).

12. *See Crull v. GEM Ins. Co.,* 58 F.3d 1386 (9th Cir.1995).

13. *See Williams v. Seniff,* 342 F.3d 774 (7th Cir.2003).

14. *See Swierkiewicz v. Sorema N. A.,* 534 U.S. 506, 512, 122 S.Ct. 992, 998, 152 L.Ed.2d 1 (2002).

Yet, although liberal and encouraging of brevity, the federal pleading duty is far from trivial; the pleading must still contain "enough" to give defendants fair notice of complaint's claims and grounds for those claims.[15] This requires the pleader to do more than merely incant labels, conclusions, and the formulaic elements of a cause of action.[16] Rather, pleaders must show that their allegations "possess enough heft" to establish an entitlement to relief (and, thus, to permit the costly process of litigation to continue).[17] Thus, pleaders must allege enough facts to raise their claims beyond the level of speculation,[18] and must "nudge[] their claims across the line from conceivable to plausible".[19]

A Note on Bell Atlantic v. Twombly: In this antitrust decision released in May 2007, the Supreme Court (in a 7–2 opinion) expressly overruled its oft-quoted language from the 1957 decision in *Conley v. Gibson* that no complaint should be dismissed for failing to properly state a claim "unless it appears beyond doubt that the plaintiff can prove no set of facts in support of his claim which could entitle him to relief".[20] Because this famous, but "incomplete", phrase could allow any conclusory statement of claim that might theoretically find support from undisclosed facts, the *Conley* language had, wrote the Court, "earned its retirement".[21] In its place, the Court articulated the plausibility standard, outlined above. Courts are just beginning to digest the *Twombly* decision and assess its effect, whether limited to a smaller cluster of federal cases (*e.g.*, antitrust claims only, or only where the allegations are pleaded upon "information and belief" and require significant inferential

---

15. *See Tellabs, Inc. v. Makor Issues & Rights, Ltd.*, ___ U.S. ___, ___, 127 S.Ct. 2499, 2507, 168 L.Ed.2d 179 (2007) ("Although the rule encourages brevity, the complaint must say enough to give the defendant 'fair notice of what the plaintiff's claim is and the grounds upon which it rests' "); *Dura Pharms., Inc. v. Broudo*, 544 U.S. 336, 346–47, 125 S.Ct. 1627, 161 L.Ed.2d 577 (2005) ("We concede that ordinary pleading rules are not meant to impose a great burden upon a plaintiff", but allegations must still give fair notice); *Calvi v. Knox County*, 470 F.3d 422, 430 (1st Cir. 2006) ("Notice pleading rules do not relieve a plaintiff of responsibility for identifying the nature of her claim"); *Amron v. Morgan Stanley Inv. Advisors Inc.*, 464 F.3d 338, 343–44 (2d Cir. 2006) ("we stop well short of saying that Plaintiffs bear no burden at the pleading stage", because they must allege "those facts *necessary* to a finding of liability").

16. *See Bell Atlantic Corp. v. Twombly*, 550 U.S. ___, ___, 127 S.Ct. 1955, 1964–65, 167 L.Ed.2d 929 (2007).

17. *See Bell Atlantic Corp. v. Twombly*, 550 U.S. ___, ___, 127 S.Ct. 1955, 1966, 167 L.Ed.2d 929 (2007).

18. *See Bell Atlantic Corp. v. Twombly*, 550 U.S. ___, ___, 127 S.Ct. 1955, 1965, 167 L.Ed.2d 929 (2007).

19. *See Bell Atlantic Corp. v. Twombly*, 550 U.S. ___, ___, 127 S.Ct. 1955, 1974, 167 L.Ed.2d 929 (2007). The cross into "the realm of plausible liability", the allegations must be factual (not conclusory) and suggestive (not neutral). *See id.* at ___ n.5, 127 S.Ct. at 1966 n.5.

20. *See Bell Atlantic Corp. v. Twombly*, 550 U.S. ___, ___, 127 S.Ct. 1955, 1964–65, 167 L.Ed.2d 929 (2007) (abrogating language in *Conley v. Gibson*, 355 U.S. 41, 45–46, 78 S.Ct. 99, 2 L.Ed.2d 80 (1957)).

21. *See Bell Atlantic Corp. v. Twombly*, 550 U.S. ___, ___, 127 S.Ct. 1955, 1969, 167 L.Ed.2d 929 (2007).

leaps) or broadly applicable to all federal cases.[22] Practitioners should attentively follow these developments.

● *Pleading With Unnecessary Factual Detail:* Pleadings may sometimes contain a level of factual detail far beyond that required under "notice" pleading standards.[23] The wisdom of pleading in such detail is widely debated among practitioners. Some favor detailed pleadings as tactically wise because they may offer the trial judge a favorable early impression of the claim and incline the judge to belief in the pleader's ability to marshal a factual record to support it. Others disfavor detailed pleadings, satisfied that the "educating-the-judge" mission can be accomplished later in the case. In either event, detailed pleading is certainly a risky endeavor. It may offer an adversary too much detail too quickly, presenting the formidable danger that the very detail offered so gratuitously could be cited in a pre-answer Rule 12 challenge to the complaint to defeat the lawsuit.[24] Moreover, detail in a pleading harnesses the attorney by allowing less room to maneuver if other facts come to light through discovery or otherwise. In extreme circumstances, excessively verbose claims for relief may even be subject to dismissal.[25] Although more austere than fact-pleading jurisdictions, federal notice pleading still requires a comprehensible presentation, "so that judges and adverse parties need not try to fish a gold coin from a

22. *See, e.g., E.E.O.C. v. Concentra Health Servs., Inc.*, 496 F.3d 773, 776 (7th Cir. 2007) (commenting that *Twombly* "impose two easy-to-clear hurdles"–fair notice to defendants of claim and grounds, and plausible allegations); *Gregory v. Dillard's, Inc.*, 494 F.3d 694, ___ (8th Cir. 2007) (plaintiffs' racial discrimination allegations satisfied *Twombly* because they stated "how, when, and where they were discriminated against"); *Iqbal v. Hasty*, 490 F.3d 143, 155–58 (2d Cir. 2007) (generally analyzing impact of *Twombly*, and theorizing that *Twombly* does not create new heightened pleading standard, but a flexible approach requiring pleaders to amplify their claim only when needed for plausibility).

23. *See, e.g., Chaveriat v. Williams Pipe Line Co.*, 11 F.3d 1420, 1430 (7th Cir. 1993)(noting increasing trend toward greater specificity in complaints).

24. *See, e.g., Barry Aviation Inc. v. Land O'Lakes Municipal Airport Comm'n*, 377 F.3d 682 (7th Cir.2004) (noting that litigant "may plead itself out of court by alleging (and thus admitting) the ingredients of a defense") (citation omitted); *Sparrow v. United Air Lines, Inc.*, 216 F.3d 1111, 1116 (D.C.Cir.2000) ("In some cases, it is possible for a plaintiff to plead too

much: that is, to plead himself out of court by alleging facts that render success on the merits impossible"); *Jackson v. Marion County*, 66 F.3d 151, 153–54 (7th Cir.1995) (noting that plaintiffs can plead themselves out of court by alleging facts showing they have no claim, even though they were not required to allege those facts in first instance; "[w]e have expressed our puzzlement that lawyers insist on risking dismissal by filing prolix complaints").

25. *See, e.g., Mann v. Boatright*, 477 F.3d 1140, 1147–48 (10th Cir. 2007) (99-page, single-spaced pleading failed to meet "a short and plain statement" standard, justifying dismissal); *United States ex rel. Garst v. Lockheed–Martin Corp.*, 328 F.3d 374, 378 (7th Cir.2003) (finding no error when trial judge, after "wading through" four complaints and an ensuing statement, properly dismissed plaintiff's "distended" 400–paragraph, 155–page pleading accompanied by 99 attachments); *Magluta v. Samples*, 256 F.3d 1282, 1284 (11th Cir. 2001) (vacating judgment and directing that plaintiff replead because 58–page, group-pleaded "complaint is a quintessential 'shotgun' pleading of the kind we have condemned repeatedly" where "any allegations that are material are buried beneath innumerable pages of rambling irrelevancies").

bucket of mud".[26]

• *Relying On Federal Forms:* Rule 84 provides that the federal form models contained in the Appendix of Forms[27] are sufficient to meet the notice pleading requirements of Rule 8.[28]

• *Notice Pleading Exceptions:* More than mere notice pleading is required in three circumstances: (1) pleading fraud and mistake, under Rule 9(b); (2) pleading demand futility in a shareholder derivative action, under Rule 23.1; and (3) pleading scienter under the Private Securities Litigation Reform Act of 1995, 15 U.S.C.A. § 78U–4(b).[29] Moreover, where those special categories are inseparably intertwined with the essential allegations of other elements of a claim, those elements might be held to the "particularity" requirement as well.[30]

• *Rule 9(b) and RICO Case Statements:* Many Districts now require that pleaders alleging violations of the federal Racketeer Influenced and Corrupt Organizations Act ("RICO") submit "RICO Case Statements", using a template prepared by the District, to flesh out the factual predicates and legal theory underlying such claims.[31] Such Statements have been approved, unless they would obligate the pleader to allege more information than Rule 8(a) and Rule 9(b) would otherwise require.[32]

26. *See United States ex rel. Garst v. Lockheed–Martin Corp.*, 328 F.3d 374, 378 (7th Cir.2003). *See also Mann v. Boatright*, 477 F.3d 1140, 1148 (10th Cir. 2007) (not "district court's job to stitch together cognizable claims for relief from the wholly deficient pleading").

27. Fed.R.Civ.P. App. Forms 1–82. (reprinted in Part IV of this text).

28. *See* Rule 84 (noting that Appendix forms are "sufficient under the rules" and are "intended to indicate the simplicity and brevity of statement which the rules contemplate"). *See also Swierkiewicz v. Sorema N. A.*, 534 U.S. 506, 512 n.4, 122 S.Ct. 992, 998 n.4, 152 L.Ed.2d 1 (2002) (same); *General Elec. Capital Corp. v. Posey*, 415 F.3d 391, 396 (5th Cir.2005) (same).

29. *See Kanter v. Barella*, 489 F.3d 170, 175–76 (3d Cir. 2007) (listing exceptions). *See also Eternity Global Master Fund Ltd. v. Morgan Guar. Trust Co. of N.Y.*, 375 F.3d 168, 177 (2d Cir.2004) (liberal notice pleading provides standard for judging complaints, except in claims for fraud and mistake, which Rule 9(b) requires be pleaded with particularity); *In re Credit Suisse First Boston Corp.*, 431 F.3d 36, 46 (1st Cir.2005) (noting that PSLRA imposed pleading obligations beyond Rule 8(a)).

30. *See Lachmund v. ADM Investor Servs., Inc.*, 191 F.3d 777 (7th Cir.1999) (holding that general allegations of agency do not suffice where the substantive fraud allegations offered by plaintiff are necessary to establish the agency relationship).

31. *See Northland Ins. Co. v. Shell Oil Co.*, 930 F.Supp. 1069, 1074 (D.N.J.1996). Where claims are asserted under the federal Racketeer Influenced and Corrupt Organizations Act ("RICO"), 18 U.S.C.A. §§ 1961–68, many judicial districts now require, by Standing Order, chambers policy, or otherwise, that the pleader answer a series of questions that supplement the RICO allegations of the complaint. *See, e.g.*, S.D. Cal. Rule 11.1; W.D. N.Y. Rule 5.1; *National Org. for Women, Inc. v. Scheidler*, 510 U.S. 249, 249, 114 S.Ct. 798, 800, 127 L.Ed.2d 99 (1994)(noting local rule in force in Northern District of Illinois). This pleading obligation is especially important where the facts noted in the RICO Case Statement are deemed to be pleading averments, properly considered in ruling upon a motion to dismiss. *See Glessner v. Kenny*, 952 F.2d 702, 712 n. 9 (3d Cir.1991)(collecting cases so holding).

32. *See Wagh v. Metris Direct, Inc.*, 363 F.3d 821, 826–28 (9th Cir.2003).

● *Case Law Exceptions:* Although courts occasionally have tried to impose more elaborate pleading standards in certain categories of cases, it now appears settled that the only permissible exceptions to the "notice" pleading standard of Rule 8(a) are those contained in other Rules themselves.[33] (Note, however, that the recent *Twombly* decision (discussed above) impacts our understanding of what qualifies as proper "notice" pleading.)

● *Pleading in Anticipation of Defenses:* Ordinarily, a pleader need not anticipate defenses, nor preemptively include averments to "plead around" an expected defense.[34]

Element 3: Demand for Judgment

The claimant must make a demand for judgment that identifies the remedies desired and the parties against whom relief is sought.[35] A party is not required to plead a specific sum certain in the demand.

● *Diversity of Citizenship Cases:* In cases based upon diversity of citizenship jurisdiction, a claimant must demand an amount in excess of $75,000, exclusive of interest and costs.[36]

● *Federal Question Cases:* In cases where jurisdiction is based upon a federal question, a claimant is not required to demand a certain minimum amount to obtain federal jurisdiction as required in cases based upon diversity jurisdiction.

● *Pleading Damages Claim:* Although pleaders are not required to do more than state "the relief sought", the Rules *do* require pleaders to identify the type of relief they seek.[37] Thus, a pleading for equitable relief that does not include a demand for damages might not permit the pleader to later insist upon a damages award.[38]

33. *See, e.g., Swierkiewicz v. Sorema N. A.,* 534 U.S. 506, 512–15, 122 S.Ct. 992, 152 L.Ed.2d 1 (2002) (no enhanced "prima facie case of discrimination" standard required in employment discrimination cases); *Leatherman v. Tarrant County Narcotics Intelligence & Coordination Unit,* 507 U.S. 163, 113 S.Ct. 1160, 122 L.Ed.2d 517 (1993)(no "heightened pleading standard" in civil rights cases filed under 42 U.S.C.A. § 1983); *Pratt v. Tarr,* 464 F.3d 730, 731 (7th Cir. 2006) (noting that it is now "emphatically clear" that courts may not supplement Rule 9(b)'s list of claims that must be pleaded with particularity).

34. *See Barry Aviation Inc. v. Land O'Lakes Municipal Airport Comm'n,* 377 F.3d 682 (7th Cir.2004); *United States v. Northern Trust Co.,* 372 F.3d 886, 888 (7th Cir.2004).

35. *See, e.g., Goldsmith v. City of Atmore,* 996 F.2d 1155, 1161 (11th Cir. 1993)(requirement of demand for judgment easily met by identifying requested remedies and parties from whom remedies are sought).

36. *See St. Paul Mercury Indem. Co. v. Red Cab Co.,* 303 U.S. 283, 58 S.Ct. 586, 82 L.Ed. 845 (1938).

37. *See* Rule 8(a)(3). *See also Seven Words LLC v. Network Solutions,* 260 F.3d 1089, 1098 (9th Cir.2001) ("Surely a simple request 'for damages' would satisfy the notice requirement without imposing any undue burden on the drafter").

38. *See Seven Words LLC v. Network Solutions,* 260 F.3d 1089, 1098 (9th Cir. 2001) (where damages claim was made years into litigation, after various representations that only declaratory and injunctive relief was sought, after a motion to dismiss, and only days before oral argument on appeal, court joins other Courts of Appeals in declining to read a damages claim into complaint as improper under Rule 8(a)).

- *Pleading Unliquidated Damages:* By local rule, certain Districts expressly forbid a plaintiff to plead a specific sum of unliquidated damages; instead, the pleader in those jurisdictions is permitted only to demand unliquidated damages generally.[39] Practitioners should consult their own local rules on this point.

- *Equitable and Declaratory Relief:* A party seeking equitable relief must plead the specific act to be prohibited or compelled. A party seeking declaratory relief must plead the specific declaration sought.

- *Special Damages:* A claimant must plead special damages with specificity, as provided by Rule 9(g).

- *Default Judgment:* In cases of default judgment, a claimant is limited to the specific amount of the demand, as provided by Rule 54(c).

- *Jury Demand:* A jury demand may be part of the original pleading. Rule 38 controls the circumstances in which a party may request trial by jury.

- *Alternative, Hypothetical, and Cumulative Demands:* A party may assert all demands for legal or equitable relief alternatively, hypothetically, and/or cumulatively. Rule 8 protects a party's right to plead inconsistently; under this Rule, portions of a pleading cannot be offered as admissions against other portions containing inconsistent or alternative averments.[40]

Rule 8's Rules Supplant Inconsistent State Rules

Some States impose by statute specialized pleading obligations for the courts in their jurisdiction. Where such pleading provisions conflict with Rule 8, those inconsistent State requirements will not apply in the federal courts of that State.[41]

---

39. *See, e.g.,* D. Del. Loc. R. 9.4 ("A pleading which sets forth a claim for relief in the nature of unliquidated money damages shall state in the ad damnum clause a demand specifying the nature of the damages claimed, e.g., 'compensatory,' 'punitive,' or both, but shall not claim any specific sum"); D. N.J. Loc. R. 8.1 ("A pleading which sets forth a claim for relief in the nature of unliquidated money damages shall state in the ad damnum clause a demand for damages generally without specifying the amount"); E.D. Pa. Loc. R. 5.1.1 ("No pleading asserting a claim for unliquidated damages shall contain any allegation as to the specific dollar amount claimed"); M.D. Pa. Loc. R. 8.1 ("The demand for judgment ... shall not claim any specific sum where unliquidated damages are involved"); W.D. Pa. Loc. R. 8.1 ("any pleading demanding general damages unliquidated in amount shall, without claiming any

specific sum, set forth only that money damages are claimed").

40. *See Rodriguez-Suris v. Montesinos,* 123 F.3d 10, 20 (1st Cir.1997); *Independent Enters. Inc. v. Pittsburgh Water & Sewer Auth.,* 103 F.3d 1165, 1175 (3d Cir.1997); *Henry v. Daytop Village, Inc.,* 42 F.3d 89, 95 (2d Cir.1994).

41. *See Cohen v. Office Depot, Inc.,* 184 F.3d 1292 (11th Cir.1999) (finding that Florida statute, which requires plaintiffs to obtain leave from court before including punitive damages prayer, "conflicted" with Rule 8's requirement of concise statement identifying pleader's remedies; because federal rule occupied field in this regard, Florida statute could not apply to federal district court), *opinion vacated in part,* 204 F.3d 1069 (11th Cir.2000) (Rule 8(a) discussion expressly reaffirmed).

Pleadings from *Pro Se* Litigants

Pleadings filed by *pro se* litigants are held to a less stringent standard than those prepared by attorneys.[42] Nevertheless, although they will be construed liberally, *pro se* pleaders are not relieved of the obligation to allege sufficient facts to support a proper legal claim.[43]

RULE 8(b). DEFENSES; ADMISSIONS AND DENIALS

CORE CONCEPT

To respond to a pleading, parties must state their defenses (in short and plain terms) and admit or deny the allegations asserted against them. Denials must fairly respond to the substance of the allegations. If a responsive pleading is required, parties are deemed to have admitted all allegations they do not deny (except for allegations relating to the amount of damages).

APPLICATIONS

2007 Amendments

Former Rule 8(b) ("Defenses; Form of Denials") and former Rule 8(d) ("Effect of Failure to Deny") were combined and restructured in 2007. Current 8(b) now contains the substance of both former Rules, and has been reorganized to address in a more rational, omnibus fashion the federal practice for general defenses, admissions, and denials. Practitioners searching for pre–2007 interpretations of these Rules should bear this repositioning in mind in doing their research. Current Rule 8(b)(6) was, until the 2007 amendments, old Rule 8(d), and current Rule 8(d) contains new content (namely, the substance of former Rule 8(e)).

"Notice" Pleading of Defenses

Rule 8(b) contemplates that defenses, like claims for relief under Rule 8(a), must be short and concise.[44]

Responsive Pleading Options

When an allegations has been asserted against them, and a responsive pleading is required, pleaders have only three options: (1) admit, (2) deny, or (3) deemed deny, because the pleaders lack the knowledge or information necessary to respond.[45] The Rules do not appear to approve or permit other types of responses, and choosing to answer in other ways is a dangerous practice. An averment in a

---

42. *See Erickson v. Pardus,* __ U.S. __, __, 127 S.Ct. 2197, 2200, 167 L.Ed.2d 1081 (2007) (per curiam); *Estelle v. Gamble,* 429 U.S. 97, 106, 97 S.Ct. 285, 50 L.Ed.2d 251 (1976).

43. *See Taylor v. Books A Million, Inc.,* 296 F.3d 376, 378 (5th Cir. 2002); *Riddle v. Mondragon,* 83 F.3d 1197, 1202 (10th Cir. 1996).

44. *See* Rule 8(b)(1)(A). *See also Home Ins. Co. v. Matthews,* 998 F.2d 305, 309 (5th Cir.1993)(differentiating defenses under Rule 8(b) from the somewhat higher standard of pleading that may be required for affirmative defenses under Rule 8(c)).

45. *See In re TCW/Camil Holding L.L.C.,* 2004 WL 1151562, at *5 (D.Del. 2004).

pleading that is not properly denied is deemed to be admitted,[46] thus failing to properly counter-plead could be catastrophic. One court has gone to great lengths to caution responsive pleaders away from antiquated (and perhaps now meaningless) pleading practices, such as "denied as a conclusion of law",[47] no response is required because the written document "speaks for itself",[48] or neither admitted nor denied, but "strict proof" is demanded at trial.[49] Finding such pleading responses to be inconsistent with Rule 8(b), this court ordered a re-pleading with specific instructions to counsel *not* to bill the client for "correcting" the "counsel's errors"[50] and, in some instances, has even deemed paragraphs containing such responses to be admissions, binding the party throughout the trial.[51]

Failure to Deny Amount of Damages

Although a failure to deny generally causes the allegation to be deemed admitted, this result does not occur with allegations relating to the amount of damages.[52]

---

46. *See* Rule 8(b)(6).

47. *See Gracedale Sports & Entertainment, Inc. v. Ticket Inlet, LLC,* 1999 WL 618991 (N.D.Ill.1999) (refusing to answer "legal conclusions" "flies in the face of the established doctrine that legal conclusions are a proper part of federal pleading, to which Rule 8(b) also compels a response"); *Saldana v. Riddle,* 1998 WL 373413 (N.D.Ill.1998) (dismissing as "nonsense" the responsive pleader's claim that legal conclusions need not be admitted or denied); *Pessler v. CBS, Inc./WBBM–TV,* 1998 WL 246138 (N.D.Ill.1998) (commenting that "Rule 8(b) does not confer on any pleader a right of self-determination as to any allegation that the pleader believes does not require a response"); *Ponce v. Sheahan,* 1997 WL 798784 (N.D.Ill.1997) (Rule 8(b) "requires a defendant to respond to all allegations in a complaint" and "creates no exception for so-called 'legal conclusions' "). *See also Farrell v. Pike,* 342 F.Supp.2d 433, 440–41 (M.D.N.C.2004) (noting that Rules do not permit defendants to avoid responding to complaint's legal allegations). *See generally Neitzke v. Williams,* 490 U.S. 319, 324, 109 S.Ct. 1827, 1831, 104 L.Ed.2d 338 (1989) (observing that federal civil complaints "contain[] ... both factual allegations and legal conclusions").

48. *See Chicago Dist. Council of Carpenters Pension Fund v. Balmoral Racing Club, Inc.,* 2000 WL 876921, at *1 (N.D.Ill. 2000)(deriding "speaks for itself" responses, commenting that "[t]his Court has been attempting to listen to such written materials for years (in the forlorn hope that one will indeed give voice)—but until some such

writing does break its silence, this Court will continue to require pleaders to employ one of the three alternatives that are permitted by Rule 8(b)"); *Central States, Southeast & Southwest Areas Pension Fund v. Pilger Transp. Servs., L.L.C.,* 1997 WL 656209 (N.D.Ill.1997) (same holding). *But see Scott v. Harris,* ___ U.S. ___, ___ n.5, 127 S.Ct. 1769, 1775 n.5, 167 L.Ed.2d 686 (2007) (Supreme Court majority notes that they "are happy to allow the videotape to speak for itself").

49. *See Gracedale Sports & Entm't, Inc. v. Ticket Inlet, LLC,* 1999 WL 618991 (N.D.Ill.1999) (noting that demand for "strict proof" is meaningless); *King Vision Pay Per View, Ltd. v. J.C. Dimitri's Restaurant, Inc.,* 180 F.R.D. 332 (N.D.Ill.1998) (commenting that under Rule 8(d), defendant was not entitled to respond that averments where "[n]either admit[ted] nor den[ied]" but instead that "strict proof thereof" was demanded).

50. *See Bobbitt v. Freeman Cos.,* 2000 WL 1131948, at *1–*2 & *2 n. 2 (N.D.Ill. 2000); *Chicago Dist. Council of Carpenters Pension Fund v. Balmoral Racing Club, Inc.,* 2000 WL 876921 (N.D.Ill.2000) (same).

51. *See King Vision Pay Per View, Ltd. v. J.C. Dimitri's Restaurant, Inc.,* 180 F.R.D. 332 (N.D.Ill.1998) (deeming "strict proof" paragraphs to be admitted, and commenting that "this action will proceed on that basis") (Shadur, J.).

52. *See* Rule 8(b)(6). *See also Vevelstad v. Flynn,* 230 F.2d 695, 703 (9th Cir. 1956) (noting that "allegations as to amounts of

General Denial

A party makes a general denial by denying each and every averment of the pleading.

Qualified General Denial

A party may also assert a qualified general denial when the party wishes to deny all of the averments in the complaint except certain specific averments.

Specific Denial

A specific denial more narrowly denies a particular paragraph or portion of a claim. The most common denial is the specific denial.

Fairly Meeting the Substance of the Allegation

In a denial, the responding party must fairly meet the substance of the allegation.[53] Although the party may qualify the response (by, for example, admitting part and denying part[54]), the response may not improperly equivocate or confuse the issues.[55] The purpose of the answer is to assist the court and the opposing parties in clarifying the issues in dispute.[56]

Denials Based Upon Lack of Knowledge or Information

(1) *Substance of Denial:* A party may deny by pleading a lack of knowledge or information. But to do so, the party must plead *both* lack of knowledge *and* lack of information.[57] A party may assert lack of information when the information exists but is difficult to uncover, such as information that must be uncovered through an accounting. A party pleading lack of knowledge and information is also bound by the obligation of honesty in pleading; an allegation that is obviously within the responding party's knowledge or information cannot be avoided, and averring lack of knowledge or information in such circumstances may have the unintended effect of *admitting* the allegation.[58]

(2) *Duty of Investigation:* A party denying based upon a lack of knowledge or information has the duty to reasonably investigate whether the information exists and how difficult it would be to find.[59]

damages are never admitted through failure to deny").

53. *See* Rule 8(b)(2).

54. *See* Rule 8(b)(3)-(b)(4).

55. *See Reis Robotics USA, Inc. v. Concept Indus., Inc.*, 462 F.Supp.2d 897, 907–08 (N.D.Ill. 2006) (striking improperly qualified answer, and ordering repleading).

56. *See Hill v. Blue Cross & Blue Shield of Mich.*, 237 F.R.D. 613, 616 (E.D.Mich. 2006).

57. *See Bobbitt v. Freeman Cos.*, 2000 WL 1131948, at *1 (N.D.Ill.2000).

58. *See Djourabchi v. Self*, 240 F.R.D. 5, 12 (D.D.C. 2006) (citing lack of knowledge, pleader denied allegation that he lacked a license to perform general contracting work in the forum; court found that pleader should have known the answer and deemed the allegation admitted). *In re TCW/Camil Holding L.L.C.*, 2004 WL 1151562, at *5 (D.Del.2004).

59. *See Greenbaum v. United States*, 360 F.Supp. 784, 787 (E.D.Pa.1973).

(3) *Effect:* A pleading based upon a lack of knowledge or information is not an admission of the adverse party's averments, but a denial.

No Duty to Respond to Allegations Against Others

The 2007 amendments to Rule 8(b) make express what was long understood in practice, namely that a pleader need not responsively plead to allegations directed at someone else.[60]

Special Matters

Rule 9 requires that certain matters be denied specifically, such as the capacity of a party to sue or be sued, the legal existence of a party, the authority of a party to sue or be sued in a representative capacity, the occurrence or performance of conditions precedent, the issuance of a judgment, or the legality of a document or act.[61]

Affirmative Defenses

Affirmative defenses are automatically denied and do not need to be answered, unless required by court order.[62]

Fifth Amendment

Where an answer would subject a party to criminal charges or be used as evidence or a link in the evidence in a criminal proceeding, the pleader may refuse to answer by claiming the privilege to be free from self-incrimination, founded in the Fifth Amendment to the United States Constitution.[63]

RULE 8(c). AFFIRMATIVE DEFENSES

CORE CONCEPT

An affirmative defense is any *fact* asserted by the respondent that vitiates the opposing party's claim. Rule 8(c) provides for the pleading of affirmative defenses, and also provides that misdesignated counterclaims will be deemed affirmative defenses. A party must raise all affirmative defenses as affirmative defenses or they are waived. In practice, courts may excuse or liberally apply this rule in appropriate cases.

APPLICATIONS

Duty to Plead Affirmative Defenses

Affirmative defenses must be asserted in a party's response to a preceding pleading. The goal of this requirement, consistent with

60. *See* Rule 8(b)(1)(B) (in a counterpleading, party must "admit or deny the allegations asserted *against it* by an opposing party") (emphasis added).

61. *See* Rule 9(a), (c), (d), & (e).

62. *See* Rule 8(b)(6) ("If a responsive pleading is not required, an allegation is considered denied or avoided."); Rule 7(a) (absent court order, no counter-pleading to an answer (where affirmative defenses are ordinarily contained) is permitted).

63. *See, e.g., LaSalle Bank Lake View v. Seguban,* 54 F.3d 387, 389–91 (7th Cir. 1995)(complaint cannot be deemed admitted when defendant invokes Fifth Amendment; complainant must produce evidence to support allegations); *Industrial Indem. Co. v. Niebling,* 844 F.Supp. 1374, 1376 (D.Ariz.1994)(proper invocation of Fifth Amendment avoids invocation of Rule 8).

federal pleading practice generally, is to provide notice to the opponent, avoid surprise and undue prejudice, and afford the opponent a chance to argue, if able, why the defense is unfounded.[64] In pleading affirmative defenses, parties have the "short and plain" statement obligations of Rule 8(b)(1)(A) to provide reasonable notice of the defense to the opponent. Parties should plead affirmative defenses in separate paragraphs and label each as an affirmative defense.

But No Duty to Respond to Affirmative Defenses

Although the party asserting them must plead affirmative defenses, there is no general duty (absent court order) on the party opposing an affirmative defense to answer or otherwise counter-plead to them. Instead, the Rules deem any affirmative defenses automatically denied or avoided.[65]

Definition of Affirmative Defenses

An affirmative defense is an assertion by the defendant of new facts or arguments that, if true, would defeat plaintiff's claim, even if all plaintiff allegations were presumed correct.[66] A defense is an affirmative one if the defendant bears the burden of proving it or if it does not controvert the plaintiff's proofs.[67]

Enumerated Affirmative Defenses

Rule 8(c) contains a *non-exhaustive*[68] list of defenses that must be pleaded affirmatively: accord and satisfaction, arbitration and award, assumption of risk, contributory negligence, discharge in bankruptcy, duress, estoppel, failure of consideration, fraud, illegality, injury by fellow servant, laches, license, payment, release, res judicata, statute of frauds, statute of limitations, and waiver.

Unenumerated Affirmative Defenses

In addition to the matters enumerated as affirmative defenses, parties are generally required under Rule 8(c) to plead as affirmative defenses any new factual matter that would come as a surprise at trial.[69] To determine whether a defense qualifies as an unenumerat-

---

64. *See Blonder–Tongue Labs., Inc. v. Univ. of Illinois Found.*, 402 U.S. 313, 350, 91 S.Ct. 1434, 1453, 28 L.Ed.2d 788 (1971); *Mickowski v. Visi–Trak Worldwide, LLC*, 415 F.3d 501, 506 (6th Cir.2005).

65. *See* Rule 7(a) (absent court order, there is no duty to counter-plead to an answer, the place where affirmative defenses are typically contained); Rule 8(b)(6) ("If a responsive pleading is not required, an allegation is considered denied or avoided.").

66. *See Emergency One, Inc. v. American Fire Eagle Engine Co.*, 332 F.3d 264, 271 (4th Cir.2003); *Saks v. Franklin Covey Co.*, 316 F.3d 337, 350 (2d Cir.2003).

67. *See Brunswick Leasing Corp. v. Wisconsin Cent., Ltd.*, 136 F.3d 521, 530 (7th Cir.1998).

68. *See Jones v. Bock*, ___ U.S. ___, ___, 127 S.Ct. 910, 919, 166 L.Ed.2d 798 (2007) (noting that list is nonexhaustive).

69. *See, e.g., Frederick v. Kirby Tankships, Inc.*, 205 F.3d 1277, 1286–87 (11th Cir.2000) (failure to mitigate is affirmative defense); *Brinkley v. Harbour Recreation Club*, 180 F.3d 598, 612 (4th Cir.1999) ("factor-other-than-sex" defense to Equal Pay Act claims is affirmative defense); *Ringuette v. City of Fall River*, 146 F.3d 1 (1st Cir.1998) (qualified immunity is an affirmative defense);*Gray v. Bicknell*, 86 F.3d 1472, 1480 (8th Cir.1996) (merger is an affirmative defense); *Federal Deposit Ins. Corp. v. Calhoun*, 34 F.3d 1291, 1299 (5th Cir. 1994)("ratification" is an affirmative defense recognized by State law); *Union Mut. Life Ins. Co. v. Chrysler Corp.*, 793 F.2d 1,

ed "residual" affirmative defense, the courts check the logical relationship between the defense and the cause of action, and decide whether a failure to timely plead the defense could cause unfair surprise.[70] The courts may also consult the applicable State law to determine which party bears the burden of proving the defense and, thus, whether the defense is an "affirmative" one or not.[71]

Burden of Proof

The party raising an affirmative defense has the burden of proving it.[72]

Special Matters

When asserting an affirmative defense that contains special matters, such as the capacity of a party to sue or be sued, fraud or mistake, the performance of conditions precedent, the authority of a party to sue or be sued in a representative capacity, the legal existence of a party, the legality of an official document or act, or the issuance of a judgment, the party must plead with particularity, as provided in Rule 9.[73]

Misdesignated Affirmative Defenses

Misdesignated counterclaims will be deemed affirmative defenses.[74] Affirmative defenses labeled as denials will be treated as affirmative defenses and will not be deemed waived where their proper assertion will promote a disposition of the case on the merits and will not prejudice the adverse parties.[75]

Waiver

An affirmative defense that is not pleaded may be deemed waived.[76] But waiver does not follow inexorably.[77] Where "peculiar facts" and the "interests of judicial economy" counsel otherwise,

---

13 (1st Cir.1986) ("novation" is an affirmative defense); *Red Deer v. Cherokee County, Iowa*, 183 F.R.D. 642 (N.D.Iowa 1999) ("after-acquired evidence" is an affirmative defense).

70. *See National Market Share, Inc. v. Sterling Nat'l Bank*, 392 F.3d 520, 526–27 (2d Cir.2004); *Oden v. Oktibbeha County*, 246 F.3d 458, 467 (5th Cir.2001).

71. *See National Market Share, Inc. v. Sterling Nat'l Bank*, 392 F.3d 520, 526–27 (2d Cir.2004); *Brunswick Leasing Corp. v. Wisconsin Cent., Ltd.*, 136 F.3d 521, 530 (7th Cir.1998).

72. *See, e.g., Goodman v. Praxair, Inc.*, 494 F.3d 458, 464 (4th Cir. 2007); *Jakimas v. Hoffmann–La Roche, Inc.*, 485 F.3d 770, 782 (3d Cir. 2007); *Caban Hernandez v. Philip Morris USA, Inc.*, 486 F.3d 1, 8 (1st Cir. 2007).

73. *See Rule 9(a), (c), (d), & (e).*

74. *See Hatco Corp. v. W.R. Grace & Co.*, 59 F.3d 400, 411 n.8 (3d Cir.1995).

75. *See Reiter v. Cooper,* 507 U.S. 258, 113 S.Ct. 1213, 122 L.Ed.2d 604 (1993). *See also Giles v. General Elec. Co.*, 245 F.3d 474, 491–92 (5th Cir.2001) (affirmative defense not waived if asserted "at a pragmatically sufficient time" and did not prejudice the opponent).

76. *See, e.g., Day v. McDonough,* 547 U.S. 198, ___, 126 S.Ct. 1675, 1679, 164 L.Ed.2d 376 (2006); *Arismendez v. Nightingale Home Health Care, Inc.*, 493 F.3d 602, 610 (5th Cir. 2007); *McKithen v. Brown*, 481 F.3d 89, 104 (2d Cir. 2007); *First Union Nat'l Bank v. Pictet Overseas Trust Corp.*, 477 F.3d 616, 622 (8th Cir. 2007).

77. *See Old Line Life Ins. Co. of America v. Garcia*, 418 F.3d 546 (6th Cir.2005); *Rose v. AmSouth Bank of Florida*, 391 F.3d 63, 65 (2d Cir.2004).

such waiver may be excused.[78] Thus, waiver might not be found where the defense is later pleaded–without undue delay or prejudice to the opponent–or where a timely assertion is prevented because the predicates for the defense had not yet arisen by the time the answer was filed.[79] Moreover, where the plaintiff receives sufficient actual notice of the affirmative defense by some method other than a pleading *and* is not prejudiced in the process, a failure to plead the affirmative defense may be excused.[80] Thus, for example, in an appropriate case, an affirmative defense asserted for the first time by motion for summary judgment may be considered by the court a motion to amend the defendant's answer, which would prevent waiver.[81] Notwithstanding this possible liberality, the trial court enjoys broad discretion, and its decision will likely not be disturbed unless it is completely unreasonable.[82] In exercising their discretion, the courts remain vigilant to protect the plaintiff against being "ambushed" by an unpleaded affirmative defense–a naked "failure-to-state-a-claim" defense, therefore, is unlikely to be considered by the court a preservation of an otherwise unpleaded affirmative defense.[83]

Raising Affirmative Defenses *Sua Sponte*

Some courts have held that certain defenses–such as *res judicata* and collateral estoppel–may, in certain instances, be raised by the court *sua sponte*, even when they had not been properly pleaded, mindful of the strong public interest in conserving scarce judicial resources by avoiding improper relitigations.[84]

RULE 8(d).   PLEADING TO BE CONCISE AND DIRECT; ALTERNATIVE STATEMENTS; INCONSISTENCY

CORE CONCEPT

Parties must plead claims and defenses in a simple, direct, and concise manner consistent with the federal notice pleading standard.

78. *See Shell Rocky Mountain Prod., LLC v. Ultra Resources, Inc.*, 415 F.3d 1158, 1164 (10th Cir.2005).

79. *See Williams v. Lampe*, 399 F.3d 867, 870–71 (7th Cir.2005); *Rose v. Am-South Bank of Florida*, 391 F.3d 63, 65 (2d Cir.2004); *Davignon v. Clemmey*, 322 F.3d 1, 15 (1st Cir.2003).

80. *See Arismendez v. Nightingale Home Health Care, Inc.*, 493 F.3d 602, 610 (5th Cir. 2007); *First Union Nat'l Bank v. Pictet Overseas Trust Corp.*, 477 F.3d 616, 622 (8th Cir. 2007); *Huss v. King Co.*, 338 F.3d 647 (6th Cir.2003).

81. *See Anthony v. City of New York*, 339 F.3d 129, n.5 (2d Cir.2003).

82. *See Old Line Life Ins. Co. of America v. Garcia*, 418 F.3d 546 (6th Cir.2005);

Castro v. Chicago Housing Auth., 360 F.3d 721, 735 (7th Cir.2004). *See also Harris v. Secretary, U.S. Dep't of Veterans Affairs*, 126 F.3d 339, 344–45 (D.C.Cir.1997) (holding that affirmative defense may not be raised in post-answer motion for the first time, unless answer has first been amended).

83. *See Saks v. Franklin Covey Co.*, 316 F.3d 337, 350 (2d Cir.2003).

84. *See Curry v. City of Syracuse*, 316 F.3d 324, 330 (2d Cir.2003). *But cf. Arizona v. California*, 530 U.S. 392, 412–13, 120 S.Ct. 2304, 2317–18, 147 L.Ed.2d 374 (2000) (cautioning that *sua sponte* consideration of statute of limitations affirmative defenses should be allowed only sparingly).

They may do so alternatively, hypothetically, and inconsistently (subject, of course, to their Rule 11 duty of honest pleading). No technical pleading forms are necessary. Parties should set forth the averments in general terms and should omit evidentiary material.

APPLICATIONS

2007 Amendments

Former Rule 8(d) ("Effect of Failure to Deny") was combined with Rule 8(b) in 2007. The Rules that followed, Rules 8(e) and 8(f), were moved up and repositioned as new Rules 8(d) and 8(e) respectively. Practitioners searching for pre–2007 interpretations of these Rules should bear this repositioning in mind in doing their research. Current Rule 8(d) was, until the 2007 amendments, old Rule 8(e).

Improper Pleadings

Although liberally construed, when pleadings are not simple, concise, and direct, but instead are so convoluted and difficult to understand that it is impossible to assess whether the pleader has alleged a meritorious claim, the trial court may either grant a motion to dismiss for violating Rule 8 or, alternatively, grant a motion for a more definite statement.[85]

Incorporation by Reference

A party may adopt by reference paragraphs of previous counts rather than repleading each alternative or hypothetical claim or defense, as provided by Rule 10(c).

Alternative, Hypothetical, And Inconsistent Pleading Permitted

Statements of claims or defenses may be asserted in the alternative, hypothetically, and even inconsistently.[86] Thus, for example, a pleader may allege an unjustment enrichment claim as an alternative to an uncertain breach of contract claim.[87] Of course, the pleader cannot recover on both inconsistent theories.[88] Moreover,

85. *See Mann v. Boatright*, 477 F.3d 1140, 1147–48 (10th Cir. 2007) (99–page, single-spaced pleading failed to meet "a short and plain statement" standard, justifying dismissal); *Hassek v. Simmons*, 2003 WL 22416698, at *1 (N.D.Cal.2003). *See also Desardouin v. United Parcel Serv., Inc.*, 285 F.Supp.2d 153, 157 (D.Conn.2003) (noting that dismissal is permitted where complaint "is so confused, ambiguous, vague, or otherwise unintelligible that its true substance, if any, is well disguised").

86. *See* Rule 8(d)(2)–(d)(3). *See also Cleveland v. Policy Mgmt. Sys. Corp.*, 526 U.S. 795, 805, 119 S.Ct. 1597, 1603, 143 L.Ed.2d 966 (1999) ("Our ordinary Rules recognize that a person may not be sure in advance upon which legal theory she will succeed, and so permit parties to 'set forth two or more statements of a claim or defense alternately or hypothetically,' and to 'state as many separate claims or defenses as the party has regardless of consistency' ").

87. *See In re Wal–Mart Wage & Hour Employment Practices Litig.*, 490 F.Supp.2d 1091, 1117 (D.Nev. 2007). *But cf. CBS Broad. Inc. v. Jones*, 460 F.Supp.2d 500, 506 (S.D.N.Y. 2006) (granting judgment on the pleadings against unjust enrichment claim as improperly inconsistent, where there was no question but that a valid, enforceable contract exists).

88. *See also American Int'l Adjustment Co. v. Galvin*, 86 F.3d 1455, 1461 (7th Cir. 1996) (commenting that "a pleader may assert contradictory statements of fact only when legitimately in doubt about the facts in question").

the court must be able to readily identify claims or defenses that are pleaded alternatively, hypothetically, or inconsistently. Although no "magic words" are required, it must be reasonably obvious from the pleading itself that these types of claims or defenses are being asserted.[89] While separate inconsistent *claims* and *defenses* are permitted under the Rules, the factual allegations *within* each claim or defense cannot be inconsistent with the alleged right of recovery, or else the claim or defense could defeat itself.[90] Pleaders are also expressly reminded by Rule 8(d) that all pleaded statements–including alternative, hypothetical, and inconsistent ones–are still subject to the obligations of Rule 11.[91]

Inconsistent Pleadings As Admissions Against the Pleader

Because Rule 8(d) protects a party's right to plead inconsistent claims and defenses, statements made in claims or defenses cannot generally be offered as admissions against other claims or defenses within the same pleading that contain inconsistent or alternative averments.[92] However, unequivocal averments of fact, made *within* a particular claim or defense, may constitute judicial admissions that conclusively bind the pleader throughout the litigation.[93] Additionally, if the positions taken by the pleader are accepted by the court, the pleader may be foreclosed by judicial estoppel from taking an inconsistent, contrary position in later proceedings.[94]

RULE 8(e). CONSTRUING PLEADINGS

CORE CONCEPT

89. *See Holman v. Indiana*, 211 F.3d 399, 407 (7th Cir.2000) ("While the [pleaders] need not use particular words to plead in the alternative, they must use a formulation from which it can be reasonably inferred that this is what they were doing").

90. *See In re Livent, Inc. Noteholders Sec. Litig.*, 151 F.Supp.2d 371 (S.D.N.Y. 2001) (commenting that Rule 8(e) does not "grant[] plaintiffs license to plead inconsistent assertions of facts within the allegations that serve as the factual predicates for an independent, unitary claim. Internally conflicting factual assertions that constitute integral components of a claim must be distinguished from a permissible alternative statement embodying a theory of a whole sufficient claim") (citation omitted). *See also Aetna Cas. & Sur. Co. v. Aniero Concrete Co.*, 404 F.3d 566, 585–86 (2d Cir. 2005) (affirming on basis of district court's opinion, from which quotation comes) (noting that claim that is "at war with itself" cannot survive summary judgment).

91. *See American Int'l Adjustment Co. v. Galvin*, 86 F.3d 1455, 1461 (7th Cir.1996) (commenting that "a pleader may assert contradictory statements of fact only when

legitimately in doubt about the facts in question").

92. *See Aholelei v. Department of Public Safety*, 488 F.3d 1144, 1149 (9th Cir. 2007); *Rodriguez-Suris v. Montesinos*, 123 F.3d 10, 20 (1st Cir.1997); *Independent Enters. Inc. v. Pittsburgh Water & Sewer Auth.*, 103 F.3d 1165, 1175 (3d Cir.1997); *Henry v. Daytop Village, Inc.*, 42 F.3d 89, 95 (2d Cir.1994). *See also American Int'l Adjustment Co. v. Galvin*, 86 F.3d 1455, 1460 (7th Cir.1996) (noting that, in pleading context, Rules abolish doctrine of election of remedies).

93. *See Astroworks, Inc. v. Astroexhibit, Inc.*, 257 F.Supp.2d 609, 615 n.10 (S.D.N.Y. 2003); *Friedmann v. United States*, 107 F.Supp.2d 502, 510–11 (D.N.J.2000).

94. *Cf. Montrose Medical Group Participating Savings Plan v. Bulger*, 243 F.3d 773, 782 (3d Cir.2001) (judicial estoppel will not apply to the assertion of contrary positions in different proceedings when the initial claim was never accepted or adopted by the court).

Courts must construe pleadings "so as to do justice". Consequently, so long as the pleading provides the adverse party with proper notice of claims and defenses, it will not be construed hypertechnically.

APPLICATIONS

2007 Amendments

Former Rule 8(e) ("Pleading to be Concise and Direct") was moved up to new Rule 8(d) in 2007, with the combining together of former Rule 8(b) and former Rule 8(d). Practitioners searching for pre–2007 interpretations of these Rules should bear this repositioning in mind in doing their research. Current Rule 8(e) was, until the 2007 amendments, old Rule 8(f).

All Pleadings Construed Liberally

The "fundamental tenor of the Rules is one of liberality rather than technicality."[95] Because Rule 8(e) requires the courts to construe pleadings "as to do justice", all pleadings are construed liberally.[96] In federal practice, form is never exalted over substance.[97] Likewise, the familiar contract law tenet of construing documents against their drafter is not applied in reviewing federal pleadings.[98] Courts will not rely solely on the labels used by the pleader to describe claims or defenses, but may reach deeper and seek out the true substance of the allegations.[99] Where those allegations, so construed, would state a cognizable claim or defense, the requirements of Rule 8 are satisfied. This liberal constructing practice does not, however, obligate courts to invent for the pleader a claim she has not included in her pleading, and courts will not do so.[100]

Inferring Types of Relief Not Actually Demanded

Although liberally construed, a pleading will not be construed in a manner that would entitle the pleader to seek a type of relief not concisely demanded in the allegations, particularly where such a construction would prejudice an opponent.[101]

---

95. *See Minger v. Green*, 239 F.3d 793, 799 (6th Cir.2001).

96. *See, e.g., Rodriguez v. Doral Mortg. Corp.*, 57 F.3d 1168, 1171 (1st Cir.1995) (noting that while courts construe pleadings generously, defendants enjoy right to know in advance the nature of the claims asserted against them); *Brinson v. Linda Rose Joint Venture*, 53 F.3d 1044, 1049 (9th Cir. 1995)("Rule 8(f) ... requires a liberal reading of complaints.").

97. *See Phillips v. Girdich*, 408 F.3d 124, 128 (2d Cir.2005).

98. *See Miller v. Philadelphia Geriatric Ctr.*, 463 F.3d 266, 272 (3d Cir. 2006) ("Pleadings need not be construed most strongly against the pleader, rather we

should make a determined effort to understand what she is attempting to set forth.").

99. *See Mead Corp. v. ABB Power Generation, Inc.*, 319 F.3d 790, 795 (6th Cir. 2003) (noting that courts do "not rely solely on labels", but "probe deeper and examine the substance of the complaint"). *See also Minger v. Green*, 239 F.3d 793, 799 (6th Cir.2001) (construing claim labeled as "negligent misrepresentation" (which would have been barred by discretionary function doctrine) as one for intentional misrepresentation (which could go forward)).

100. *See Smith v. Aztec Well Servicing Co.*, 462 F.3d 1274, 1284 (10th Cir. 2006).

101. *See Seven Words LLC v. Network Solutions*, 260 F.3d 1089, 1098 (9th Cir.

Pleadings Drafted by Laypersons

Courts generally apply less stringent standards to pleadings drafted by laypersons, such as *pro se habeas corpus* petitions and social security applications.[102]

ADDITIONAL RESEARCH REFERENCES

Wright & Miller, *Federal Practice and Procedure* §§ 1201–1290.

C.J.S. Federal Civil Procedure §§ 252–280 et seq., 301–308.

West's Key No. Digests, Federal Civil Procedure ☞631–653, 654–657, 671–680, 731–745, 751–759.

2001) (where damages claim was made years into litigation, after various representations that only declaratory and injunctive relief was sought, after a motion to dismiss, and only days before oral argument on appeal, court joins other Courts of Appeals in declining to read a damages claim into complaint).

102. *See Erickson v. Pardus,* ___ U.S. ___, ___, 127 S.Ct. 2197, 2200, 167 L.Ed.2d 1081 (2007) (per curiam); *Hughes v. Rowe,* 449 U.S. 5, 101 S.Ct. 173, 66 L.Ed.2d 163 (1980); *Haines v. Kerner,* 404 U.S. 519, 92 S.Ct. 594, 30 L.Ed.2d 652 (1972) ; *Estelle v. Gamble,* 429 U.S. 97, 106, 97 S.Ct. 285, 50 L.Ed.2d 251 (1976).

RULE 9

PLEADING SPECIAL MATTERS

(a) Capacity or Authority to Sue; Legal Existence.

(1) *In General.* Except when required to show that the court has jurisdiction, a pleading need not allege:

(A) a party's capacity to sue or be sued;

(B) a party's authority to sue or be sued in a representative capacity; or

(C) the legal existence of an organized association of persons that is made a party.

(2) *Raising Those Issues.* To raise any of those issues, a party must do so by a specific denial, which must state any supporting facts that are peculiarly within the party's knowledge.

(b) Fraud or Mistake; Conditions of Mind. In alleging fraud or mistake, a party must state with particularity the circumstances constituting fraud or mistake. Malice, intent, knowledge, and other conditions of a person's mind may be alleged generally.

(c) Conditions Precedent. In pleading conditions precedent, it suffices to allege generally that all conditions precedent have occurred or been performed. But when denying that a condition precedent has occurred or been performed, a party must do so with particularity.

(d) Official Document or Act. In pleading an official document or official act, it suffices to allege that the document was legally issued or the act legally done.

(e) Judgment. In pleading a judgment or decision of a domestic or foreign court, a judicial or quasi-judicial tribunal, or a board or officer, it suffices to plead the judgment or decision without showing jurisdiction to render it.

(f) Time and Place. An allegation of time or place is material when testing the sufficiency of a pleading.

(g) Special Damages. If an item of special damage is claimed, it must be specifically stated.

(h) Admiralty or Maritime Claim.

(1) *How Designated.* If a claim for relief is within the admiralty or maritime jurisdiction and also within the court's subject-matter jurisdiction on some other ground, the pleading may designate the claim as an admiralty or maritime claim for purposes of Rules 14(c), 38(e), and 82 and the Supplemental Rules for Admiralty or Maritime Claims and Asset Forfeiture Actions. A claim cognizable only in the admiralty or maritime jurisdiction is an admiralty or maritime claim for those purposes, whether or not so designated.

(2) *Designation for Appeal.* A case that includes an admiralty or maritime claim within this subdivision (h) is an admiralty case within 28 U.S.C. § 1292(a)(3).

[Amended effective July 1, 1966; July 1, 1968; July 1, 1970; August 1, 1987, April 11, 1997, effective December 1, 1997; April 12, 2006, effective December 1, 2006; April 30, 2007, effective December 1, 2007.]

─────────── **2007 AMENDMENTS ROADMAP** ───────────

STYLE PROJECT CHANGES: Rules 9(a) and 9(h) were subsectioned, given labels, and reworded for clarity. Cumbersome language was culled and replaced throughout. Rule 9(a)'s "specific negative averment" was shortened to "specific denial". Active voice replaced passive voice; "must" replaced "shall".

NON-STYLE CHANGES: Rule 9(h)(2), containing a redundant reference to Rule 15 amendments, was deleted as unnecessary. Rule 9(h)(3) was moved up to Rule 9(h)(2).

NOTE: The Federal Rules "Style Project" is explained in Part III-A.

AUTHORS' COMMENTARY ON RULE 9

─────────── **PURPOSE AND SCOPE** ───────────

Special requirements apply for pleading capacity and authority, fraud, mistake, conditions of the mind, conditions precedent, official documents or acts, judgments, time and place, special damages, and admiralty and maritime claims.

RULE 9(a). CAPACITY OR AUTHORITY TO SUE; LEGAL EXISTENCE

CORE CONCEPT

Unless necessary to establish the court's subject matter jurisdiction over the dispute, a pleading need not aver capacity or authority to sue, or an association's legal existence. A defendant may challenge these issues, but must do so by specific denial in a responsive pleading or motion.

APPLICATIONS

Pleading Capacity When Jurisdictional

Unless it is necessary to establish the jurisdiction of the federal courts, a party's capacity or authority to sue, or an association's legal existence need not be pleaded. When necessary to establish jurisdiction, however, these defenses must be averred.[1]

Procedure For Challenging Capacity

Ordinarily, a litigant seeking to challenge (a) a party's legal existence, (b) a party's capacity to sue or be sued, or (c) a party's authority to sue or be sued in a representative capacity must raise the issue by specific denial in a responsive pleading or pre-answer motion.[2] This specific denial must, additionally, include all specific facts that are "peculiarly within the party's knowledge".[3]

> *Note:* Prior to the 2007 amendments, Rule 9(a) used the language "specific negative averment" in place of the current (and simpler) "specific denial". Practitioners researching Rule 9(a) should note this change.

Liberal Construction

Under appropriate circumstances, courts have given Rule 9(a)'s pleading duty a liberal interpretation. Thus, a pleader who mislabels a capacity defense as a challenge to standing may be excused the oversight.[4] Likewise, when warranted, Rule 9(a) defenses have been accepted even when asserted by a motion to dismiss under Rule 12(b)(6), a motion for judgment on the pleadings under Rule 12(c), a motion for summary judgment under Rule 56, and at trial by a motion to dismiss when appropriate evidence is presented.[5]

---

1. *See Moore v. City of Harriman*, 272 F.3d 769, 772–74 (6th Cir.2001) (noting division among appellate courts as to whether, given limitations of Eleventh Amendment, a Section 1983 defendant's "capacity" must be formally alleged in the complaint, and ruling that such capacity may be pleaded or, in certain circumstances, discerned under "course of proceedings" test).

2. *See* Rule 9(a)(1). *See also Federal Deposit Ins. Corp. v. Calhoun*, 34 F.3d 1291, 1299 (5th Cir.1994); *Brown v. Williamson*, 134 F.Supp.2d 1286, 1291 (M.D.Ala.2001).

3. *See* Rule 9(a)(2).

4. *See Masood v. Saleemi*, 2007 WL 2069853, at *4 (W.D.Wash. 2007).

5. *See e.g., Cooper v. Wal–Mart Stores, Inc.*, 959 F.Supp. 964, 966 n. 2 (C.D.Ill. 1997) (commenting that case law supports

Waiver By Failing To Raise Lack Of Capacity

The defense of lack of capacity or authority to sue, or an association's legal existence may be waived if it is not timely and specifically asserted by the party challenging it.[6] Waiver might not occur, however, where the defect in a party's capacity, authority, or legal existence is affirmatively apparent from the face of the complaint, and a specific denial is found to be unnecessary.[7] Similarly, when capacity, authority, or legal existence is jurisdictional (*i.e.,* such as when suing the United States or when relevant to a party's citizenship for diversity jurisdiction), a party may assert those defenses to vitiate subject matter jurisdiction *at any time*, as provided by Rule 12(h)(3), or the court may raise the issue *sua sponte*.[8]

RULE 9(b). FRAUD, MISTAKE, CONDITION OF MIND

CORE CONCEPT

A party must plead fraud and mistake with particularity, but may plead malice, intent, knowledge, and other conditions of a person's mind generally.

APPLICATIONS

Goal of Pleading With Particularity

Some claims—like fraud—may have an *in terrorem* or stigmatizing effect on defendants and their reputations.[9] The courts expect pleaders to perform a greater pre-complaint investigation in such cases, to ensure that any Rule 9(b) claim is "responsible and supported, rather than defamatory and extortionate".[10] This practice also allows an early and informed response from the party defending against such accusations.[11] Thus, requiring that such claims be pleaded with particularity (1) ensures that the defendants

notion that capacity issues under Rule 17(b) may be raised by motion to dismiss) *But cf. Srock v. United States,* 2006 WL 2460769, at *4—*5 (E.D.Mich. 2006) (collecting cases and scholarship on late assertion of Rule 9(a) defenses, and ruling that these defenses should be subject to an early waiver rule).

6. *See, e.g., BondPro Corp. v. Siemens Power Generation, Inc.,* 463 F.3d 702, 705 (7th Cir. 2006); *De Saracho v. Custom Food Machinery, Inc.,* 206 F.3d 874, 878 (9th Cir.2000).

7. *See Brown v. Williamson,* 134 F.Supp.2d 1286, 1291 (M.D.Ala.2001). *But cf. Srock v. United States,* 2006 WL 2460769, at *4—*5 (E.D.Mich. 2006) (collecting cases and scholarship on late assertion of Rule 9(a) defenses, and ruling that these defenses should be subject to an early waiver rule).

8. *See E.R. Squibb & Sons, Inc. v. Accident & Cas. Ins. Co.,* 160 F.3d 925, 935–36 (2d Cir.1998) (if party with capacity defense is strategically not asserting it in order to preserve federal jurisdiction, court may assess the capacity of the parties *sua sponte*).

9. *See United States ex rel. Fowler v. Caremark RX, L.L.C.,* 496 F.3d 730, 740 (7th Cir. 2007); *Vess v. Ciba–Geigy Corp. USA,* 317 F.3d 1097, 1104 (9th Cir.2003); *Schaller Tel. Co. v. Golden Sky Sys., Inc.,* 298 F.3d 736, 745 (8th Cir.2002).

10. *See Borsellino v. Goldman Sachs Group, Inc.,* 477 F.3d 502, 507 (7th Cir. 2007) (internal citation omitted).

11. *See BJC Health Sys. v. Columbia Cas. Co.,* 478 F.3d 908, 917 (8th Cir. 2007); *Swartz v. KPMG LLP,* 476 F.3d 756, 764 (9th Cir. 2007).

have fair notice of the plaintiff's claim, (2) helps safeguard the defendants against spurious accusations, and the resulting reputational harm, (3) reduces the possibility that a meritless fraud claim can remain in the case, by ensuring that the full and complete factual allegation is not postponed until discovery, and (4) protects defendants against "strike" suits.[12]

No Common Law Additions to Rule 9(b)'s List

Rule 9(b) requires that only fraud and mistake be pleaded with particularity.[13] It is now "emphatically clear" that courts are not permitted to add to this list and require, by common law, that other claims be pleaded with particularity.[14]

Fraud

A party must plead each of the elements of fraud with particularity.[15] When pleading fraud the claimant must allege more than mere conclusory allegations of fraud or the technical elements of fraud.[16] The added pleading burden varies somewhat from circuit to circuit, and allegation to allegation. The typical common law elements of fraud are: (1) false representation or omission of material fact; (2) knowledge of or belief in its falsity by person making it; (3) belief in its truth by receiver of statement; (4) intent that statement will be acted upon; and (5) detrimental reliance by the person who was deceived.[17]

● *Claims "Grounded" in Fraud:* The "particularity" requirement of Rule 9(b) applies not only to claims expressly denominated as "fraud" allegations, but also to claims that are "grounded" in fraud or that "sound" in fraud,[18] as well as other claims involving deceptive conduct.[19]

12. *See ATSI Commc'ns, Inc. v. Shaar Fund, Ltd.*, 493 F.3d 87, ___, 2007 WL 1989336, at *6 (2d Cir. 2007); *United States ex el. Atkins v. McInteer*, 470 F.3d 1350, 1359 (11th Cir. 2006); *In re Rockefeller Ctr. Props., Inc. Secs. Litig.*, 311 F.3d 198, 216 (3d Cir.2002). *Schaller Tel. Co. v. Golden Sky Sys., Inc.*, 298 F.3d 736, 745 (8th Cir. 2002); The term "strike suit" is "professional slang" to refer to litigation that is not brought to redress genuine wrongs, but to inflict a nuisance upon the defendant. *See Cohen v. Beneficial Indus. Loan Corp.*, 337 U.S. 541, 548, 69 S.Ct. 1221, 1226, 93 L.Ed. 1528 (1949).

13. Note, however, that other Rules and other federal statutes contain additional particularity requirements. *See supra* Authors' Commentary to Rule 8(a) (*"Notice Pleading Exceptions"*).

14. *See Pratt v. Tarr*, 464 F.3d 730, 731 (7th Cir. 2006). *See also Swierkiewicz v. Sorema N. A.*, 534 U.S. 506, 512–15, 122 S.Ct. 992, 152 L.Ed.2d 1 (2002); *Leather-*

man v. Tarrant County Narcotics Intelligence & Coordination Unit, 507 U.S. 163, 168, 113 S.Ct. 1160, 122 L.Ed.2d 517 (1993).

15. *See, e.g., Shushany v. Allwaste, Inc.*, 992 F.2d 517, 521 (5th Cir.1993).

16. *See BJC Health Sys. v. Columbia Cas. Co.*, 478 F.3d 908, 917 (8th Cir. 2007); *In re Burlington Coat Factory Sec. Litig.*, 114 F.3d 1410, 1418 (3d Cir.1997).

17. *See, e.g., In re Rockefeller Ctr. Props., Inc. Secs. Litig.*, 311 F.3d 198, 216 (3d Cir.2002); *In re Burlington Coat Factory Sec. Litig.*, 114 F.3d 1410, (3d Cir.1997); *Williams v. WMX Technologies, Inc.*, 112 F.3d 175, 177 (5th Cir.1997).

18. *See Borsellino v. Goldman Sachs Group, Inc.*, 477 F.3d 502, 507 (7th Cir. 2007); *Vess v. Ciba–Geigy Corp. USA*, 317 F.3d 1097, 1103–04 (9th Cir.2003).

19. *See Simpson v. AOL Time Warner Inc.*, 452 F.3d 1040, 1046 (9th Cir.2006).

- *Federal Statutory Fraud Claims:* Generally, the "particularity" requirement of Rule 9(b) also applies to federal statutory fraud claims as well as federal common law fraud claims.[20]

- *State Law Fraud Claims:* The "particularity" requirement applies to both federal and State-law fraud claims.[21]

Mistake

A party must also plead mistake with particularity. When pleading mistake with particularity, the pleader should state what the parties intended and identify the mistaken result.

Amount of Particularity Required

The amount of particularity or specificity required for pleading fraud or mistake will differ from case to case,[22] but generally depends upon the amount of access the pleader has to the specific facts,[23] considering the complexity of the claim, the relationship of the parties, the context in which the alleged fraud or mistake occurs,[24] and the amount of specificity necessary for the adverse party to prepare a responsive pleading.[25] The particularity requirement of Rule 9 is not, however, intended to abrogate or mute the Rule 8 "notice" pleading standard that applies in federal courts, and the two Rules must be read in harmony with one another.[26] Plaintiffs are still obligated to plead only "notice" of a fraud or mistake

20. *See, e.g., Abrams v. Baker Hughes Inc.,* 292 F.3d 424, 430 (5th Cir.2002) (applies in Private Securities Litigation Reform Act claims); *United States ex rel. Clausen v. Laboratory Corp. of America, Inc.,* 290 F.3d 1301, 1308–09 (11th Cir.2002) (applies in False Claims Act lawsuits); *Warden v. McLelland,* 288 F.3d 105, 114 (3d Cir.2002) (applies in mail/wire fraud RICO cases).

21. *See Vess v. Ciba–Geigy Corp. USA,* 317 F.3d 1097, 1102–03 (9th Cir.2003); *Williams v. WMX Techs., Inc.,* 112 F.3d 175, 177 (5th Cir.1997) (finding "no principled reason" why State law fraud claims should escape pleading requirements of federal rules).

22. *See BJC Health Sys. v. Columbia Cas. Co.,* 478 F.3d 908, 917 (8th Cir. 2007); *Benchmark Elec., Inc. v. J.M. Huber Corp.,* 343 F.3d 719, 724 (5th Cir.2003), *modified on other grounds,* 355 F.3d 356 (5th Cir. 2003).

23. *See, e.g., In re Rockefeller Ctr. Props., Inc. Secs. Litig.,* 311 F.3d 198, 216 (3d Cir.2002) (noting that rigidity of pleading requirements may be relaxed in situations where requisite factual information is peculiarly within defendant's knowledge or control); *Devaney v. Chester,* 813 F.2d 566, 569 (2d Cir.1987) ("[W]e recognize that the degree of particularity required should be

determined in light of such circumstances as whether the plaintiff has had an opportunity to take discovery of those who may possess knowledge of the pertinent facts.").

24. *See, e.g., In re Craftmatic Sec. Litig. v. Kraftsow,* 890 F.2d 628, 645 (3d Cir. 1989)("[I]n the case of corporate fraud, plaintiff cannot be expected to have personal knowledge of the details of corporate internal affairs."). *See also In re GlenFed, Inc. Sec. Litig.,* 60 F.3d 591 (9th Cir. 1995)("In cases of corporate fraud where the false and misleading information is conveyed in prospectuses, registration statements, annual reports, press releases, or other 'group-published information,' it is reasonable to presume that these are collective actions of the officers. [Thus,] a plaintiff fulfills the particularity requirement of Rule 9(b) by pleading the misrepresentations with particularity and where possible the roles of the individual defendants in the misrepresentations.").

25. *See Dudley v. Southeastern Factor & Finance Corp.,* 446 F.2d 303 (5th Cir.1971).

26. *See Saltire Indus., Inc. v. Waller, Lansden, Dortch & Davis, PLLC,* 491 F.3d 522, 526 (6th Cir. 2007); *BJC Health Sys. v. Columbia Cas. Co.,* 478 F.3d 908, 917 (8th Cir. 2007); *Ziemba v. Cascade Int'l, Inc.,* 256 F.3d 1194, 1202 (11th Cir.2001).

claim; Rule 9(b) simply compels a higher degree of that notice.[27] Thus, Rule 9(b) generally requires the pleader to fill-in "the first paragraph of any newspaper story"—the "who, what, when, where, and how" of the alleged scheme.[28] In the context of fraud claims, many courts require the pleader to allege (1) the time, place, and contents of the false representations or omissions, and explain how they were fraudulent, (2) the identity of the person making the misrepresentations, (3) how the misrepresentations misled the plaintiff, and (4) what the speaker gained from the fraud.[29] In the end, the pleaded facts must give rise to a "strong inference" of fraud to comport with Rule 9(b).[30]

Pleading on Information and Belief

The rigors of Rule 9(b) do not necessarily foreclose pleading upon information and belief, although such pleading is still subject to the Rule's particularity requirements and, further, the pleader generally must aver the facts upon which the information and belief rests.[31]

Exception to Particularity Requirement

If the facts necessary to plead fraud or mistake are peculiarly within the defendant's knowledge, some courts may relax the particularity requirement of Rule 9(b) in favor of permitting discovery to proceed.[32] Although the rigors of Rule 9(b) may be lightened a bit, they are not ignored altogether: the pleader must still plead an adequate factual premise for concluding that the fraud claim is a

---

27. *See Schaller Tel. Co. v. Golden Sky Sys., Inc.*, 298 F.3d 736, 746 (8th Cir.2002).

28. *See United States ex rel. Fowler v. Caremark RX, L.L.C.*, 496 F.3d 730, 740 (7th Cir. 2007); *BJC Health Sys. v. Columbia Cas. Co.*, 478 F.3d 908, 917 (8th Cir. 2007); *In re Alpharma Inc. Secs. Litig.*, 372 F.3d 137, 148 (3d Cir.2004); *Alternative Sys. Concepts, Inc. v. Synopsys, Inc.*, 374 F.3d 23, 29 (1st Cir.2004).

29. *See, e.g., Ambrosia Coal & Const. Co. v. Pages Morales*, 482 F.3d 1309, 1316–17 (11th Cir. 2007); *BJC Health Sys. v. Columbia Cas. Co.*, 478 F.3d 908, 917 (8th Cir. 2007); *Swartz v. KPMG LLP*, 476 F.3d 756, 764 (9th Cir. 2007); *Tal v. Hogan*, 453 F.3d 1244, 1263 (10th Cir.2006); *Power & Tel. Supply Co. v. SunTrust Banks, Inc.*, 447 F.3d 923, 931 (6th Cir.2006).

30. *See Lerner v. Fleet Bank, N.A.*, 459 F.3d 273 (2d Cir.2006).

31. *See United States ex rel. Karvelas v. Melrose–Wakefield Hosp.*, 360 F.3d 220, 226 (1st Cir.2004).

32. *See, e.g., In re Rockefeller Ctr. Props., Inc. Secs. Litig.*, 311 F.3d 198, 216 (3d Cir.2002) (rigidity of pleading require-

ments may be relaxed where requisite factual information is peculiarly within defendant's knowledge or control); *Corley v. Rosewood Care Ctr.*, 142 F.3d 1041, 1051 (7th Cir.1998) (particularity requirement "must be relaxed where the plaintiff lacks access to all facts necessary to detail his claim"); *In re Burlington Coat Factory Sec. Litig.*, 114 F.3d 1410, 1418 (3d Cir.1997) (courts should be sensitive to risk that strict application of particularity rule prior to discovery could permit sophisticated defrauders to conceal their fraud); *Tuchman v. DSC Communications Corp.*, 14 F.3d 1061, 1068 (5th Cir.1994)(accord, but noting that exception is not a "license to base claims of fraud on speculation and conclusory allegations"). *See also United States ex rel. Karvelas v. Melrose–Wakefield Hosp.*, 360 F.3d 220, 228–29 (1st Cir.2004) (noting "relaxation" as permitting a general pleading originally, which must later be amended, following discovery, with particulars); *Katz v. Household Int'l, Inc.*, 91 F.3d 1036 (7th Cir.1996)("We acknowledge that Rule 9(b) does not require plaintiffs to plead facts to which they lack access prior to discovery").

plausible one.[33] Other courts hold otherwise, refusing to relax the requirements of Rule 9(b) even where the facts lie exclusively within the defendant's knowledge.[34] Whether this relaxation is even permitted in the context of certain federal statutory fraud claims remains an unresolved question.

Malice, Intent, Knowledge, and Condition of Mind

A party may allege malice, intent, knowledge, and condition of mind generally, as with any ordinary allegation under Rule 8.[35]

Pleading Tensions Between Fraud and Intent

There is some internal tension between Rule 9(b)'s requirement that fraud—including the fraud element of intent—be pleaded with particularity, and Rule 9(b)'s provision that intent itself may be pleaded generally. Courts usually resolve this apparent inconsistency by requiring that when the claim is based upon allegations of fraud, the party has a duty to follow the requirement to plead fraud with particularity, and intent generally.[36] Nevertheless, many courts require that the pleaded facts must give rise to a "strong inference of fraudulent intent".[37]

Group Pleading

The particularized pleading requirement is designed to notify each defendant of his, her, or its purported role in the alleged

33. *See In re Rockefeller Ctr. Props., Inc. Secs. Litig.*, 311 F.3d 198, 216 (3d Cir.2002) (noting that even where defendant retains control over information flow, "boilerplate and conclusory allegations" are not sufficient, and the pleaders must still include "factual allegations that make their theoretically viable claim plausible").

34. *See, e.g., Koch v. Koch Indus., Inc.*, 203 F.3d 1202, 1237 (10th Cir.2000) (explaining that prior precedent did not relax Rule 9(b)'s particularity requirements when the fraud facts are within an opponent's knowledge and control; however, those facts can be premised on information and belief); *Greebel v. FTP Software, Inc.*, 194 F.3d 185, 193 (1st Cir.1999) (holding that even when allegations are premised on information and belief, the facts supporting that belief must be set forth in the complaint).

35. *See Wight v. Bankamerica Corp.*, 219 F.3d 79 (2d Cir.2000) (although actual fraud must be alleged with particularity, the intent of the perpetrator need not be alleged with specificity). *But see Johnson v. Waddell & Reed, Inc.*, 74 F.3d 147, 150 (7th Cir.1996)("At least some facts need to be pled under Rule 9(b) to show why this breach of contract is also a malicious tort.").

36. *See, e.g., Wight v. Bankamerica Corp.*, 219 F.3d 79 (2d Cir.2000) (although actual fraud must be alleged with particu-

larity, the intent of the perpetrator need not be alleged with specificity); *In re Glen-Fed, Inc., Sec. Litig.*, 42 F.3d 1541 (9th Cir.1994)(en banc)(same result; rejecting contrary precedent). *See also Chill v. General Elec. Co.*, 101 F.3d 263, 267 (2d Cir.1996) (commenting that speaker's intent need not be pleaded with specificity because plaintiff realistically cannot be held to allege a defendant's actual state of mind).

37. *See Campaniello Imports, Ltd. v. Saporiti Italia S.p.A.*, 117 F.3d 655 (2d Cir. 1997); *In re Burlington Coat Factory Sec. Litig.*, 114 F.3d 1410, 1418 (3d Cir.1997) (quoting authority, that requisite inference of fraud may be shown either (a) by alleging facts to show that defendants had both motive and opportunity to commit fraud, or (b) by alleging facts that constitute strong circumstantial evidence of conscious misbehavior or recklessness); *Suna v. Bailey Corp.*, 107 F.3d 64, 68 (1st Cir.1997); *Chill v. General Elec. Co.*, 101 F.3d 263, 267 (2d Cir.1996); *DiLeo v. Ernst & Young*, 901 F.2d 624, 629 (7th Cir.1990). *But see In re GlenFed, Inc. Sec. Litig.*, 42 F.3d 1541, 1545–47 (9th Cir.1994) (in banc) (rejecting such requirement, holding that plaintiff need not allege facts from which intent to commit fraud may be inferred).

misconduct. Lumping multiple defendants together in a group pleading (*e.g.*, "defendants misled the plaintiff by stating . . .") may
defeat this notice objective and, thus, may be found to be improper
under Rule 9(b).[38] Although the courts might not require a pleader
to parse each fact and attribute every false statement to a particular
defendant (especially in cases alleging conspiracy), the pleader will
be obligated, at the very least, to notify each defendant as to how he
or she is alleged to have participated in the fraud.[39]

Counterclaims and Affirmative Defenses

When asserting fraud or mistake in counterclaims or affirmative
defenses, the pleader must assert fraud or mistake there with
particularity.

Non-Party Fraud or Mistake

It has been held that where fraud or mistake was caused by
non-parties [40] or when alleging that non-parties were defrauded,[41] a
party may plead fraud or mistake more generally.

Opposing an Insufficiently Particular Pleading

A party may oppose a pleading that fails to plead fraud or
mistake with particularity by filing a Rule 12(e) motion for a more
definite statement,[42] a Rule 12(f) motion to strike, or a Rule 12(b)
motion to dismiss.[43]   Often, parties assert these motions in the
alternative.

Granting Leave to Amend

Where a complaint is dismissed for failing to allege with particularity, leave to amend should generally be granted freely.[44] Leave to

38. *See Brooks v. Blue Cross & Blue
Shield of Florida, Inc.*, 116 F.3d 1364, 1381
(11th Cir.1997); *Vicom, Inc. v. Harbridge
Merchant Servs., Inc.*, 20 F.3d 771, 777–78
(7th Cir.1994). *But see Phillips v. Scientific–Atlanta, Inc.*, 374 F.3d 1015, 1018–19
(11th Cir.2004) (noting permissive "group
pleading doctrine" in securities cases,
which allows presumption of group responsibility for statements and omissions).

39. *See Swartz v. KPMG LLP*, 476 F.3d
756, 764–65 (9th Cir. 2007).

40. *See, e.g., Uni*Quality, Inc. v. Info-
tronx, Inc.*, 974 F.2d 918, 923 (7th Cir.1992)
"([W]here a plaintiff is alleging fraud
against a third party, less detail may be
required.").

41. *See, e.g., Segal v. Gordon*, 467 F.2d
602, 607 (2d Cir.1972) ("when the pleader
is asserting that third persons have been
defrauded, he may be unable to detail the
claim and less specificity should be required.").

42. *See, e.g., Coffey v. Foamex L.P.*, 2
F.3d 157, 162 (6th Cir.1993)(approving use
of Rule 12(e) to force correction of complaint defective under Rule 9(b)).

43. *See, e.g., Kowal v. MCI Communications Corp.*, 16 F.3d 1271, 1279 (D.C.Cir.
1994)(affirming   dismissal   under   Rule
12(b)(6) for failure to meet requirements of
Rule 9(b)).

44. *See United States ex rel. Willard v.
Humana Health Plan of Texas Inc.*, 336
F.3d 375, 387 (5th Cir.2003); *Koehler v.
Bank of Bermuda (New York) Ltd.*, 209 F.3d
130, 138 (2d Cir.2000), *amended*, 229 F.3d
424 (2d Cir.2000). *See also United States ex
rel. Williams v. Bell Helicopter Textron Inc.*,
417 F.3d 450, 454–55 (5th Cir.2005) (reversing dismissal with prejudice as improperly
circumventing one purpose of Rule 9(b)–
avoiding unnecessary, preliminary litigation).

amend may be denied, however, where an amendment is "futile" and could never offer the particularity necessary under Rule 9.[45]

Constitutionality of Enhanced Pleading

Any enhanced pleading duty necessarily carries with it the unfortunate risk that, on occasion, it might cause the dismissal of a valid claim which, had the claim been permitted to reach discovery, could have found sound evidentiary support. The Supreme Court has considered this possibility and, citing the authority of Congress and the Rules' drafters to adopt special pleading procedures, found no Seventh Amendment (jury right) impediment.[46]

RULE 9(c). CONDITIONS PRECEDENT

CORE CONCEPT

Where applicable to the cause of action pleaded (such as in contract cases and in certain exhaustion contexts), a plaintiff may aver *generally* that all conditions precedent have been performed or have occurred. Conversely, a response alleging that a requisite condition precedent has *not* been performed or has not occurred must be set forth *specifically* and with particularity.

APPLICATION

Applies to Both Contractual And Statutory Conditions Precedent

The pleading practice set forth in Rule 9(c) for conditions precedent applies whether the conditions precedent are contractual or statutory in nature.[47]

Rule Sets Procedure Only

Rule 9(c) does *not* require that conditions precedent be alleged; rather, the Rule simply provides the procedure for doing so.[48]

General Allegations Sufficient To Plead Conditions Precedent

The complaint does not need to allege in detail how each condition was performed; the allegations are sufficient if they aver generally that all conditions precedent have been performed[49] and plead facts from which an inference arises that all conditions precedent have been met.[50]

45. *See Chill v. General Elec. Co.*, 101 F.3d 263, 271–72 (2d Cir.1996).

46. *See Tellabs, Inc. v. Makor Issues & Rights, Ltd.*, ___ U.S. ___, ___ n.9, 127 S.Ct. 2499, 2519 n.9, 168 L.Ed.2d 179 (2007).

47. *See Walton v. Nalco Chem. Co.*, 272 F.3d 13, 21 n.13 (1st Cir.2001).

48. *See Kiernan v. Zurich Cos.*, 150 F.3d 1120, 1123–24 (9th Cir.1998); *Bizmark, Inc. v. Industrial Gas & Supply Co.*, 358 F.Supp.2d 518, 522 (W.D.Va.2005).

49. *See, e.g., Wyatt v. Terhune*, 315 F.3d 1108, 1118 n.12 (9th Cir.2003); *Walton v. Nalco Chem. Co.*, 272 F.3d 13, 22 (1st Cir. 2001); *Anderson v. United Tele. Co.*, 933 F.2d 1500, 1505 (10th Cir.1991); *Peterson v. Brownlee*, 314 F.Supp.2d 1150, 1153 (D.Kan.2004).

50. *See Floorcoverings, Int'l, Ltd v. Swan*, 2000 WL 528480, at *4 (N.D.Ill. 2000).

Specific Allegations Necessary To Challenge Conditions Precedent

Where a defendant seeks to challenge a plaintiff's allegation that a condition precedent has been fulfilled, the denial must be pleaded with specificity and particularity. Once the issue is joined in this way, the burden returns to plaintiff to prove that the condition precedent contested by the defendant has been met.[51]

RULE 9(d).   OFFICIAL DOCUMENT OR ACT

CORE CONCEPT

A party asserting the existence or legality of an official document need only assert that the official document was issued legally or the official act was performed legally.   Conversely, a party opposing the official document or act must specifically assert the defect in the official document or the illegality of the official act.

RULE 9(e).   JUDGMENT

CORE CONCEPT

When pleading the issuance of a judgment, a party need not set forth matter showing the jurisdiction of the tribunal issuing the judgment.

APPLICATION

Pleading Issuance of Judgment

When pleading the issuance of a judgment or a decision of any court, judicial or quasi-judicial tribunal, board, or officer, a party should specifically identify the judicial body issuing the judgment, the date of the judgment, the parties participating in the proceeding, and the character or effect of the judgment.   A party challenging the judgment in the answer must specifically state the defect in the judgment, and cannot deny generally.

RULE 9(f).   TIME AND PLACE

CORE CONCEPT

Time and space averments are material allegations and can, if appropriate, support a dismissal of a claim or defense.

APPLICATION

Specificity *Not* Required, But If Made, Averments Are Material

Rule 9(f) does *not* require that averments of time and place be

---

51. *See Runnemede Owners, Inc. v. Crest Mortg. Corp.*, 861 F.2d 1053, 1057–58 (7th Cir. 1988); *Hill v. Citibank Corp.*, 312 F.Supp.2d 464, 473–74 (S.D.N.Y.2004); *Richey v. City of Lilburn*, 127 F.Supp.2d 1250, 1257 (N.D.Ga.1999).

pleaded specifically.[52] Instead, Rule 9(f) simply confirms that, if pleaded, averments of time and place are material and can be considered in testing the sufficiency of a pleading.[53] Thus, if the averments of time and place establish an obvious defense (such as time-bar), the inclusion of those averments can support a dismissal.[54]

RULE 9(g). SPECIAL DAMAGES

CORE CONCEPT

Special damages must be pleaded with particularity.

APPLICATIONS

Purpose

The obligation to plead special damages with specificity is designed to alert the defending parties to the nature of the claimed damages (and, thus, avoid surprise) and to advise the court of the existence of such a claim.[55]

Defined

Identifying special damages (which must be specially pleaded) is not always clear.[56] Generally, special damages are those damages that are proximately caused by the defendant's alleged wrongdoing, but which were unforeseeable or which might not come to the defendant's attention unless pleaded with specificity.[57] In other words, special damages are those that are usual for the particular type of claim pleaded.[58] Emotional distress damages,[59] attorney's fees,[60] punitive damages,[61] defamation damages,[62] and damages flow-

---

52. *See Matthew v. United States*, 452 F.Supp.2d 433, 446 (S.D.N.Y. 2006).

53. *See Rosen ex rel. Egghead.Com, Inc. v. Brookhaven Capital Mgmt. Co.*, 179 F.Supp.2d 330, 334 (S.D.N.Y. 2002).

54. *See Matthew v. United States*, 452 F.Supp.2d 433, 446 (S.D.N.Y. 2006); *Jairett v. First Montauk Secs. Corp.*, 203 F.R.D. 181 (E.D.Pa.2001).

55. *See Bowles v. Osmose Utilities Servs., Inc.*, 443 F.3d 671, 675 (8th Cir. 2006); *Great American Indem. Co. v. Brown*, 307 F.2d 306, 308 (5th Cir.1962).

56. *See 44 Liquormart, Inc. v. Rhode Island*, 940 F.Supp. 437, 438–39 (D.R.I. 1996).

57. *See, e.g., LINC Fin. Corp. v. Onwuteaka*, 129 F.3d 917, 922 (7th Cir.1997) (noting that special damages "are damages that are unusual for the type of claim in question—that are not the natural damages associated with such a claim"). *See also Figgins v. Advance America Cash Advance*

Centers of Michigan, Inc., 482 F.Supp.2d 861, 869 (E.D.Mich. Mar 27, 2007) (surveying definitions).

58. *See Figgins v. Advance America Cash Advance Centers of Michigan, Inc.*, 482 F.Supp.2d 861, 869 (E.D.Mich. Mar 27, 2007).

59. *See Botosan v. Fitzhugh*, 13 F.Supp.2d 1047, 1053 (S.D.Cal.1998).

60. *See, e.g., United Indus., Inc. v. Simon–Hartley, Ltd.*, 91 F.3d 762 (5th Cir. 1996); *Private One of N.Y., LLC v. JMRL Sales & Serv., Inc.*, 471 F.Supp.2d 216, 224–25 (E.D.N.Y. 2007); *United States v. All Meat & Poultry Prods. Stored at Lagrou Cold Storage*, 470 F.Supp.2d 823, 835 (N.D.Ill. 2007); *Botosan v. Fitzhugh*, 13 F.Supp.2d 1047, 1053 (S.D.Cal.1998); *44 Liquormart, Inc. v. Rhode Island*, 940 F.Supp. 437, 439 (D.R.I.1996).

61. *See Teel v. United Techs. Pratt & Whitney*, 953 F.Supp. 1534, 1537 (S.D.Fla. 1997). *But see Figgins v. Advance America*

ing from trade disparagement[63] are examples of special damages that must be pleaded with specificity. Whether prejudgment interest is an item of special damages is unclear.[64]

Specificity

A party should plead special damages by alleging the claimed actual damages with particularity and, then, by averring how those damages were the natural and direct result of the defendant's conduct.[65] A pleading is sufficiently specific if the opposing party can respond to the allegations of special damages.[66] This obligation is not "reducible to formula", and will depend on the nature of the claim at issue, the alleged injury, and the causal connection between the two.[67] An appropriate statement of special damages will generally include an estimate of the total damages, along with a listing of the specific items that comprise that sum.[68] Conversely, a conclusory declaration that a party was "damaged" and that "business" was "curtail[ed]" will generally be found inadequate.[69]

Consequences of Failing to Plead Special Damages

A party's failure to plead special damages with specificity may bar that party's recovery of special damages.[70] Vague, conclusory catch-all allegations (such as "including but not limited to") are likely to be insufficient under Rule 9(g).[71] However, because there is

Cash Advance Centers of Michigan, Inc., 482 F.Supp.2d 861, 869–70 (E.D.Mich. Mar 27, 2007) (ruling that punitive damages are not special damages).

62. *See Muzikowski v. Paramount Pictures Corp.*, 322 F.3d 918, 924–27 (7th Cir. 2003).

63. *See KBT Corp., Inc. v. Ceridian Corp.*, 966 F.Supp. 369 (E.D.Pa.1997).

64. *See United States v. All Meat & Poultry Prods. Stored at Lagrou Cold Storage*, 470 F.Supp.2d 823, 834–35 (N.D.Ill. 2007) (noting, but not resolving, question).

65. *See Browning v. Clinton*, 292 F.3d 235, 245–46 (D.C.Cir.2002).

66. *See, e.g., Matos v. Ashford Presbyterian Cmty. Hosp., Inc.*, 4 F.3d 47, 52 (1st Cir.1993)("We believe the purpose [of Rule 9(g)] is to give notice; the more natural are the damages, the less the pleading is needed."); *Morton Grove Pharms., Inc. v. National Pediculosis Ass'n, Inc.*, 494 F.Supp.2d 934, 941 (N.D.Ill. 2007) (allegation is sufficient when it notifies defendant of nature of claimed damages); *Italiano v. Jones Chems., Inc.*, 908 F.Supp. 904, 907 (M.D.Fla.1995) (commenting that Rule 9(g) requires nothing more than specific statement permitting defendants to prepare responsive pleading and begin their defense).

67. *See Marseilles Hydro Power, LLC. v. Marseilles Land & Water Co.*, 2003 WL 259142, at *6 (N.D.Ill.2003).

68. *See City & County of San Francisco v. Tutor–Saliba Corp.*, 2005 WL 645389, at *17 (N.D.Cal.2005). *But see Marseilles Hydro Power, LLC. v. Marseilles Land & Water Co.*, 2003 WL 259142, at *6 (N.D.Ill. 2003) (commenting that estimates of final lost dollar amounts may be unnecessary).

69. *See Artista Records, Inc. v. Flea World, Inc.*, 356 F.Supp.2d 411, 428 (D.N.J. 2005).

70. *See, e.g., United Indus., Inc. v. Simon–Hartley, Ltd.*, 91 F.3d 762, 764 (5th Cir.1996) (failure to plead attorney's fees waives the right to collect them); *44 Liquormart, Inc. v. Rhode Island*, 940 F.Supp. 437, 439 (D.R.I.1996) (noting that court properly bars items of special damages that were not pleaded specifically). *Woodmont Corp. v. Rockwood Ctr. P'ship*, 811 F.Supp. 1478, 1484 (D.Kan.1993)(if complaint is not amended to reflect special damages, court is free to dismiss the case).

71. *See Marseilles Hydro Power, LLC. v. Marseilles Land & Water Co.*, 2003 WL 259142, at *6 (N.D.Ill.2003) (holding that court would not require answer to such "including but not limited to" allegation, and would not permit an unpleaded damages item to reach trial).

no timing requirement in the Rule, a party can seek leave from the court to amend to include further items of special damages in the pleading.[72] Moreover, because the goal is to protect against unfair surprise, the court may even excuse a failure to particularly plead special damages where the adversary was not actually prejudiced.[73]

RULE 9(h). ADMIRALTY AND MARITIME CLAIMS

CORE CONCEPT

Special rules apply to admiralty and maritime claims.[74] When the plaintiff asserts an admiralty or maritime claim, the plaintiff[75] should identify in the complaint that the case is one in admiralty. When a party asserts a claim containing an admiralty claim and another basis of subject matter jurisdiction, the party may designate whether the claim is premised on admiralty jurisdiction or on another basis of subject matter jurisdiction.[76]

APPLICATIONS

Significance of Election: No Jury Trial in Admiralty

Ordinarily, choosing to proceed in admiralty means that the claims in the case are decided by the court, and not by a jury.[77]

Type of Designation Required

To invoke the federal courts' admiralty jurisdiction, a plaintiff must include an affirmative statement in the pleadings identifying the proceeding as an admiralty or maritime claim.[78] Failing to so identify the claim means that it is not one.[79] However, a plaintiff need not specifically incant a citation to Rule 9(h), although that is certainly the preferred practice; instead, a simple statement assert-

72. See Jones v. Krautheim, 208 F.Supp.2d 1173, 1178 (D.Colo.2002).

73. See Bowles v. Osmose Utilities Servs., Inc., 443 F.3d 671, 675 (8th Cir. 2006).

74. The full text of the Supplemental Rules For Certain Admiralty And Maritime Claims appears at the end of Part III of this text.

75. See, e.g., Lewis v. United States, 816 F.Supp. 1097, 1100–01 (E.D.Va.1993)(in appropriate cases, choice of invoking Rule 9(h) rests with plaintiff—who thereby may alter certain features of litigation, including availability of jury trial).

76. See, e.g., Murphy v. Florida Keys Elec. Co-op. Ass'n, 329 F.3d 1311, 1319 (11th Cir.2003) (when claim has multiple jurisdictional bases, pleading may contain statement identifying claim as one in admiralty or maritime law); Fedorczyk v. Caribbean Cruise Lines, Ltd., 82 F.3d 69, 73 (3d

Cir.1996)(so holding; additionally, noting that plaintiff invoking admiralty jurisdiction must affirmatively identify claim in pleading as "admiralty or maritime claim").

77. See Wingerter v. Chester Quarry Co., 185 F.3d 657 (7th Cir.1998); Concordia Co. v. Panek, 115 F.3d 67, 70–71 (1st Cir.1997); Canal Barge Co. v. Commonwealth Edison Co., 2002 WL 206054, at *4 (N.D.Ill.2002); Gaines v. Ampro Fisheries, Inc., 836 F.Supp. 347, 348–49 (E.D.Va.1993). But cf. Miles v. M/V HANSA CALEDONIA, 245 F.Supp.2d 1261, 1263 (S.D.Ga.2002) (noting that Circuits differ on question of whether jury trials are permitted where plaintiff asserts both admiralty and diversity jurisdiction).

78. See Fedorczyk v. Caribbean Cruise Lines, Ltd., 82 F.3d 69, 73 (3d Cir.1996).

79. See Murphy v. Florida Keys Elec. Co-op. Ass'n, 329 F.3d 1311, 1319 (11th Cir.2003).

ing claims in admiralty or maritime law is sufficient.[80] The absence of a jury demand is one indication that the party intends to proceed in admiralty.[81]

Appellate Review

Admiralty claims enjoy a right of immediate interlocutory appeal, including admiralty claims contained in cases having non-admiralty claims as well.[82]

ADDITIONAL RESEARCH REFERENCES

Wright & Miller, *Federal Practice and Procedure* §§ 1291–1320.

C.J.S. Federal Civil Procedure §§ 252–257 et seq.

West's Key No. Digests, Federal Civil Procedure ☞633–651.

80. *See Foulk v. Donjon Marine Co.*, 144 F.3d 252, 256 (3d Cir.1998) (noting that direct citation to Rule 9(h) is unambiguous and may be preferable, but it is not required); *Concordia Co. v. Panek*, 115 F.3d 67, 72 (1st Cir.1997) (although preferred technique is to expressly invoke Rule 9(h), including the phrase "In Admiralty" in the caption, with no accompanying demand for a jury trial, found sufficient); *Rosales v. Bouchard Coastwise Mgmt. Corp.*, 2004 WL 1146953, at *1 (E.D.La.2004) (same effect).

81. *See Concordia Co. v. Panek*, 115 F.3d 67, 72 (1st Cir.1997).

82. *See* 28 U.S.C.A. § 1292(a)(3).

RULE 10

FORM OF PLEADINGS

(a) Caption; Names of Parties. Every pleading must have a caption with the court's name, a title, a file number, and a Rule 7(a) designation. The title of the complaint must name all the parties; the title of other pleadings, after naming the first party on each side, may refer generally to other parties.

(b) Paragraphs; Separate Statements. A party must state its claims or defenses in numbered paragraphs, each limited as far as practicable to a single set of circumstances. A later pleading may refer by number to a paragraph in an earlier pleading. If doing so would promote clarity, each claim founded on a separate transaction or occurrence—and each defense other than a denial—must be stated in a separate count or defense.

(c) Adoption by Reference; Exhibits. A statement in a pleading may be adopted by reference elsewhere in the same pleading or in any other pleading or motion. A copy of a written instrument that is an exhibit to a pleading is a part of the pleading for all purposes.

[April 30, 2007, effective December 1, 2007.]

--------------- **2007 AMENDMENTS ROADMAP** ---------------

STYLE PROJECT CHANGES: Modest, general language simplification throughout. No new subsectioning, and no new labels. "Must" replaced "shall".

NON-STYLE CHANGES: None.

NOTE: The Federal Rules "Style Project" is explained in Part III-A.

AUTHORS' COMMENTARY ON RULE 10

--------------- PURPOSE AND SCOPE ---------------

Rule 10 establishes the form generally required for pleadings and motions. Pleadings and motions must contain a caption. Claims and defenses must be set forth in numbered paragraphs, with each paragraph limited to a single set of circumstances. Separate counts must be pleaded for each claim or defense premised on a separate transaction or occurrence. Earlier paragraphs may be adopted by reference to avoid repetition, and exhibits may be attached to pleadings.

RULE 10(a). CAPTION; NAMES OF PARTIES

CORE CONCEPT

Every pleading and motion must contain a caption. In the original complaint, the names of all parties must be listed in the caption. For later pleadings (except notices of appeal), listing the first named party on each side is sufficient.

APPLICATIONS

Contents of Caption

Captions must contain: (a) the name of the court; (b) the title of the action (including all party names); (c) the file or docket number; and (d) the document's designation (*e.g.*, complaint, answer, reply to counterclaim).

Party Names

The title of a lawsuit properly includes the names of all parties, and these names must be listed in the original complaint.[1] Ordinarily, persons and entities not listed in the original complaint's caption are not parties to the lawsuit.[2] In all pleadings subsequent to the complaint, however, the court and the parties may shorten the caption to include only the names of the first plaintiff, the first defendant, and (where necessary) an indication that others are parties to the case (*e.g.*, "et al.").[3]

> *Warning for Notices of Appeal:* The parties to an appeal must be individually named. Omitting party names with the use of "et al." or similar phrases may be fatally deficient. The courts of appeals may disregard these shortened phrases and may accept the appeal *only* as to those parties individually named in

---

1. *See Myles v. United States*, 416 F.3d 551, 551 (7th Cir.2005) ("to make someone a party the plaintiff must specify him in the caption and arrange for service of process"). *Cf. Ferdik v. Bonzelet*, 963 F.2d 1258, (9th Cir.1992)(striking original complaint that listed parties-defendant as "et al.").

2. *See Trackwell v. U.S. Gov't*, 472 F.3d 1242, 1243–44 (10th Cir. 2007) (even in *pro se* case, failure to name person in caption or even in text of complaint violates Rule); *W.N.J. v. Yocom*, 257 F.3d 1171, 1172 (10th Cir.2001) (federal courts lack jurisdiction over unnamed parties since a case has not been commenced with respect to them); *Ahmed v. Goldberg*, 2001 WL 1842398, at

*3 n.7 (D.N.Mar.I.2001) (because claimant not identified in complaint, and without class action status, court lacked jurisdiction to hear unnamed claimant's case). *But cf. Williams v. Bradshaw*, 459 F.3d 846 (8th Cir.2006) (holding that caption is not determinative as to who are parties to lawsuit, but is entitled to "considerable weight" on the question).

3. *See Spivey v. Board of Church Extension & Home Mission of Church of God*, 160 F.R.D. 660, 662 n. 3 (M.D.Fla. 1995)(requesting counsel to use short form captioning of case in all future court documents).

the notice of appeal or those parties who make their intent to appeal objectively clear.[4]

Actual Names: The caption must state the parties' actual names. Descriptive titles will only be deemed appropriate where they clearly identify the party.[5] False names (such as an alias) are not permitted, and pleading under a false name will justify a dismissal.[6]

Fictitious Name and Pseudonym Litigation

New Rule 5.2 grants parties a limited entitlement to a right of redaction of certain "personal data identifiers".[7] Minors, for example, are now permitted by right to litigate using only their initials, instead of their full names.[8] Rule 5.2 also allows parties to seek protective orders to grant the redaction of additional personally identifying information, when "good cause" exists.[9] Prior to the promulgation of Rule 5.2, there had been no specific provision in the Rules for parties who wished to litigate an anonymously.[10]

Nevertheless, in very unusual circumstances, the courts had permitted parties to identify themselves throughout the lawsuit by a fictitious name or pseudonym (*e.g.* "Jane Doe").[11] Such permission is extraordinary and conflicts with the public's right to open access to the judiciary,[12] a concern of constitutional dimension.[13] In fact,

4. *See* Fed.R.App.P. 3(c)(modifying *Torres v. Oakland Scavenger Co.*, 487 U.S. 312, 108 S.Ct. 2405, 101 L.Ed.2d 285 (1988)(holding that use of "et al." phrase did not constitute an effective appeal as to parties not specifically named)).

5. *See Mitchell v. Maynard*, 80 F.3d 1433, 1441 (10th Cir.1996) (commenting that a party not properly named in caption may still be deemed in the case if the allegations in the text of the complaint make plain that the party is intended as a defendant, although simply mentioning the party's name in a brief will not suffice). *Compare OTR Drivers at Topeka Frito–Lay, Inc.'s Distrib. Ctr. v. Frito–Lay, Inc.*, 988 F.2d 1059 (10th Cir.1993)("Over–The–Road Drivers" was insufficient identification of plaintiffs in the lawsuit) *with Dean v. Barber*, 951 F.2d 1210 (11th Cir.1992)(naming "Chief Deputy of County Jail" was sufficient identification of defendant) *and English v. Cowell*, 969 F.2d 465 (7th Cir. 1992)(use of alleged pseudonym permitted where party may have legally changed name to adopt pseudonym and where no claim of confusion or prejudice was asserted).

6. *See Zocaras v. Castro*, 465 F.3d 479, 481–84 (11th Cir. 2006) ("A trial is not a masquerade party nor is it a game of judicial hide-n-seek where the plaintiff may of-

fer the defendant the added challenge of uncovering his real name.").

7. *See* Rule 5.2, and Authors' Commentary to Rule 5.2.

8. *See* Rule 5.2(a)(3).

9. *See* Rule 5.2(e).

10. *See Rose v. Beaumont Indep. Sch. Dist.*, 240 F.R.D. 264, 265–66 (E.D.Tex. 2007) (pre-Rule 5.2 decision).

11. *See Roe v. Aware Woman Center for Choice, Inc.*, 253 F.3d 678, 684–85 (11th Cir.2001) (reversing trial court's refusal to permit pseudonym litigation in abortion case); *Doe No. 2 v. Kolko*, 242 F.R.D. 193, 196 (E.D.N.Y. 2006) (public has strong interest in protecting identities of sexual assault victims to incentivize others to report).

12. *See M.M. v. Zavaras*, 139 F.3d 798 (10th Cir.1998) (public has right to know full circumstances of the case); *Doe v. Frank*, 951 F.2d 320 (11th Cir. 1992)("[l]awsuits are public events"); *Rowe v. Burton*, 884 F.Supp. 1372 (D.Alaska 1994)(access to judicial proceedings is believed to improve the integrity and quality of justice). *See also Barth v. Kaye*, 178 F.R.D. 371, 376–77 (N.D.N.Y.1998) (denying request where plaintiff failed to make

some courts have written that a presumption exists against such pleading,[14] and others have emphasized that parties in civil cases, bringing lawsuits of their own volition to vindicate their own interests, must be prepared to stand publicly behind their allegations.[15] The practice is, therefore, often forbidden, even in cases involving issues of great intimacy and sensitivity.[16]

There are no "hard and fast" rules that the courts apply in judging whether to permit pseudonym litigation.[17] Instead, the courts consider many factors, including whether the anonymous plaintiffs are challenging governmental activity, whether pressing the lawsuit will compel the plaintiffs to reveal highly intimate information or disclose an intention or desire to engage in illegal activity, and whether a child plaintiff is involved.[18] The courts may also examine whether disclosure of identities would create a risk of retaliatory physical or mental harm.[19] To proceed by pseudonym, the party must petition the court for permission.[20] Permission, if granted, may be accompanied by a requirement that the true names of the parties be disclosed to the defendants and the court, although the names would remain sealed to the general public.[21] More narrowly, a party may temporarily identify an opponent with a fictional name so long as the identities of the opponents are clear and their actual names will be uncovered through discovery.[22]

Alterations to the Caption

As noted above, Rule 10(a) specifically encourages parties and the court to shorten the case caption in all documents subsequent to the complaint by listing only the first named plaintiff and defendant.

adequate showing of need, and citing public's right of access to the courts).

13. See Rose v. Beaumont Indep. Sch. Dist., 240 F.R.D. 264, 265–66 (E.D.Tex. 2007); Doe v. Del Rio, 241 F.R.D. 154, 156 (S.D.N.Y. 2006).

14. See Doe v. Del Rio, 241 F.R.D. 154, 156 (S.D.N.Y. 2006).

15. See Rose v. Beaumont Indep. Sch. Dist., 240 F.R.D. 264, 267–68 (E.D.Tex. 2007); Doe v. Bell Atlantic Bus. Sys. Servs., Inc., 162 F.R.D. 418 (D. Mass. 1995).

16. See Rose v. Beaumont Indep. Sch. Dist., 240 F.R.D. 264, 265–66 (E.D.Tex. 2007) (denying pseudonym status for young girl in case concerning her involvement in school sex club); Doe v. Bell Atlantic Bus. Sys. Servs., Inc., 162 F.R.D. 418 (D.Mass. 1995)(denying pseudonym status to alleged victim of sexual harassment who claimed her traditional Chinese family would react negatively if the allegations became public).

17. See Rose v. Beaumont Indep. Sch. Dist., 240 F.R.D. 264, 266 (E.D.Tex. 2007).

18. See Doe v. Porter, 370 F.3d 558, 560 (6th Cir.2004); W.N.J. v. Yocom, 257 F.3d 1171 (10th Cir.2001); Roe v. Aware Woman Center for Choice, Inc., 253 F.3d 678, 684–85 (11th Cir.2001); Does I thru XXIII v. Advanced Textile Corp., 214 F.3d 1058, 1068 (9th Cir.2000); Rose v. Beaumont Indep. Sch. Dist., 240 F.R.D. 264, 265–68 (E.D.Tex. 2007); Doe v. Del Rio, 241 F.R.D. 154, 156–57 (S.D.N.Y. 2006).

19. See Does I thru XXIII v. Advanced Textile Corp., 214 F.3d 1058, 1068 (9th Cir. 2000) (in retaliation-case petitions, district court should weigh (1) severity of threatened harm, (2) reasonableness of fear of harm, (3) plaintiff's vulnerability to harm, (4) prejudice, at each stage of the proceedings, to the defendants and how that prejudice could be mitigated, and (5) whether public's interest would be best served by requiring disclosure of identities).

20. See W.N.J. v. Yocom, 257 F.3d 1171 (10th Cir.2001).

21. See W.N.J. v. Yocom, 257 F.3d 1171 (10th Cir.2001).

22. See Dean v. Barber, 951 F.2d 1210 (11th Cir.1992).

Other immaterial alterations to the caption, such as changes in capitalization, fonts, or type faces, likewise are generally not improper and will not require remedy by the court.[23]

Pro Se Pleadings

In reviewing *pro se* pleadings, courts may scavenge the documents with greater vigor to discern whether the identities of parties are clear from the text of the allegations (if not so in the captions), but even in those instances, if the identities of the intended parties are not clear, the pleading is subject to dismissal.[24]

RULE 10(b). PARAGRAPHS; SEPARATE STATEMENTS

CORE CONCEPT

Pleadings should contain separately-numbered paragraphs, each of which, as far as practicable, should contain a single set of circumstances. Pleadings should contain separate counts for claims arising from different transactions or occurrences. Defenses (other than denials) should be set forth in separate counts as well. In all other instances, separate counts are permitted, though not required.

APPLICATIONS

Paragraphing a Pleading's Facts

As far as practicable, a party should set forth each distinct allegation of fact in a separate paragraph, and each paragraph should be numbered.[25] The purpose of Rule 10(b) is to require the drafting of a pleading that is easily understood by both the opponent and the court.[26]

"Group" Pleading

"Group" pleading allegations (*e.g.*, accusing the "defendants" generally of engaging in certain misconduct, without particularizing which defendant committed what act) are generally inappropriate in many cases. Such "group" pleading techniques may defeat the clarity objectives of the separate-paragraph requirement by failing to specify what each party is alleged to have done wrong.[27] This is

23. *See Jaeger v. Dubuque County*, 880 F.Supp. 640 (N.D.Iowa 1995) (finding no Rule 10 violation by capitalization of party names or other alterations of fonts, type faces, ink types, printer types, or printing methods).

24. *See Trackwell v. U.S. Gov't*, 472 F.3d 1242, 1243–44 (10th Cir. 2007).

25. *See Politico v. Promus Hotels, Inc.*, 184 F.R.D. 232, 234 (E.D.N.Y.1999) (as far as possible, complaint should avoid multiple allegations per paragraph); *Bieros v. Nicola*, 851 F.Supp. 683 (E.D.Pa.1994)(commenting that each factual allegation should be pleaded in a separate paragraph).

26. *See RTC v. Hess*, 820 F.Supp. 1359, 1371 (D.Utah 1993). *See also O'Donnell v. Elgin, J. & E. Ry.*, 338 U.S. 384, 392, 70 S.Ct. 200, 205, 94 L.Ed. 187 (1949)(chastising that "the unfortunately prolonged course" of trial was due, in part, to counsel's failure to separate issues in counsel's pleading, preparation, and thinking).

27. *See Veltmann v. Walpole Pharmacy, Inc.*, 928 F.Supp. 1161, 1164 (M.D.Fla.1996) (finding pleading insufficient where complaint made it impossible to determine which defendant committed which alleged act); *Gen-Probe, Inc. v. Amoco Corp.*, 926

particularly true with claims that must be alleged with particularity.[28]

Pleading in Separate Counts

A party may include in a single count all theories of recovery, so long as those theories are all premised on the same facts.[29] The better practice, however, is to plead distinct claims and theories in separate counts.[30] In any event, where the claims and theories rest on different facts [31] or where clarity otherwise requires it,[32] distinct claims and theories must be pleaded in separate counts.[33] In those circumstances, separate counts help to ensure that the pleadings achieve their goals of framing the issues and providing a platform for informed pretrial proceedings and the effective management of discovery.[34] The paragraphing and separate counts practice also enables a court to grant dispositive relief with respect to an entire count, and not just part of one.[35] Thus, the dictates of Rule 10 are not intended to be exceptions to the federal practice against technical forms of pleading, but instead provide the guidelines that help ensure that pleadings are "simple, concise, and direct".[36]

Violations and Remedy

Improper paragraph numbering or conciseness will not defeat a pleading, unless the violations interfere with the ability to understand the claims or otherwise cause prejudice.[37] However, when a

F.Supp. 948, 962 (S.D.Cal.1996) (counts must identify which averments relate to which claims and to which defendants). *See also Magluta v. Samples*, 256 F.3d 1282, 1284 (11th Cir.2001) (vacating judgment and directing that plaintiff replead because 58–page, group-pleaded "complaint is a quintessential 'shotgun' pleading of the kind we have condemned repeatedly"). *Cf. In re GlenFed, Inc. Sec. Litig.*, 60 F.3d 591, 592–93 (9th Cir.1995) (noting that "group" pleading might be appropriate if complaint alleged that outside directors either participated in day-to-day activities of business, or had special relationship with business, such as participating in preparing or communicating group information).

28. *See supra* Authors' Commentary to Rule 9(b) ("**Group Pleading**").

29. *See Lamar Adver. of Mobile, Inc. v. City of Lakeland*, 980 F.Supp. 1455, 1458 (M.D.Fla.1997) (holding that Rule 10(b) is inapplicable to multiple claims arising out of single transaction); *FDIC v. Miller*, 781 F.Supp. 1271 (N.D.Ill.1991).

30. *See Stone Mountain Game Ranch, Inc. v. Hunt*, 746 F.2d 761, 763 n. 1 (11th Cir.1984); *Selep v. City of Chicago*, 842 F.Supp. 1068 (N.D.Ill.1993).

31. *See RTC v. Hess*, 820 F.Supp. 1359 (D.Utah 1993)(granting motion for more

definite statement where multiple transactions were included within a single count).

32. *See Dodge v. Susquehanna Univ.*, 796 F.Supp. 829 (M.D.Pa.1992)(because failure to separate into distinct counts gave defendant the impression that no breach of contract claim was being pressed, the belatedly asserted breach of contract theory was dismissed from the complaint); *Gilbert v. Feld*, 788 F.Supp. 854 (E.D.Pa. 1992)(separate counts not required where such practice would not enhance the clarity of the presentation of an already clear pleading). *See also Pelletier v. Zweifel*, 921 F.2d 1465, 1479 n. 29 (11th Cir.1991) (claim of pendent State law cause of action discounted where no separate count was pleaded).

33. *See Bautista v. Los Angeles County*, 216 F.3d 837, 840–41 (9th Cir.2000).

34. *See Bautista v. Los Angeles County*, 216 F.3d 837, 840–41 (9th Cir.2000).

35. *See Savin v. Robinson*, 2001 WL 1191192, at *1 (N.D.Ill.2001).

36. *See Phillips v. Girdich*, 408 F.3d 124, 128 (2d Cir.2005).

37. *See Phillips v. Girdich*, 408 F.3d 124, 128 (2d Cir.2005).

party's pleading provides insufficient notice of the claims because of its confusing structure, the absence of numbered paragraphs, or the improper combination of multiple claims in a single count, the opposing party may move for a more definite statement or to strike the pleading.[38]   Such a motion must be made before filing a response. The typical remedy granted by the court is an order directing the party to replead, or a dismissal without prejudice and with leave to amend within a short period of time.[39]

RULE 10(c).   ADOPTION BY REFERENCE;   EXHIBITS

CORE CONCEPT

A party may adopt by reference statements from the same pleading, or from a different pleading or motion filed in the same case.   A party may also attach exhibits or writings to the pleading, thereby making the exhibits part of the pleading for all purposes.

APPLICATIONS

Adopting Paragraphs by Reference

By clearly identifying the adopted paragraphs, a party may incorporate by reference allegations made in an earlier portion of the same pleading.   Parties frequently adopt such allegations in order to avoid repeating the same factual allegations in each count.

Adopting Documents or Pleadings by Reference

A party may adopt documents or pleadings (in whole or in part) by reference so long as the adopted document or pleading is expressly named.   Generally, this practice is limited to documents and pleadings that are already before the court.   Documents or pleadings filed in another lawsuit usually cannot be adopted by reference.

Attaching Exhibits

A party may (but is not required to) attach copies of "written instruments" as exhibits to a pleading.   Generally, newspaper articles[40] and affidavits[41] do not qualify for attachment as exhibits. A videotape recording, however, may qualify.[42]

38.   *See Gonzales v. Wing*, 167 F.R.D. 352, 354–355 (N.D.N.Y.1996) (dismissing plaintiff's 287–page, numberless complaint because it presented a "far too . . . heavy burden" upon the defendants to frame a comprehensive defense and provided the court with no meaningful basis to assess the claims' sufficiency).

39.   *See, e.g., Phillips v. Girdich*, 408 F.3d 124, 128 (2d Cir.2005); *Nicolaysen v. BP Amoco Chem. Co.*, 2002 WL 1060587 (E.D.Pa.2002); *Perez v. Radioshack Corp.*, 2002 WL 1335158 (S.D.Fla.2002). *But cf. Frederiksen v. City of Lockport*, 384 F.3d 437, 439 (7th Cir.2004) (affirming dismissal

with prejudice for failure to comply with Rule 10(b) after four chances over more than two years).

40.   *See Perkins v. Silverstein*, 939 F.2d 463, 467 n. 2 (7th Cir.1991)(commenting that newspaper articles, commentaries, and editorial cartoons are not the type of documentary evidence or written instruments that Rule 10(c) contemplates).

41.   *See Rose v. Bartle*, 871 F.2d 331, 339 n. 3 (3d Cir.1989)(noting that affidavits are not Rule 10(c) materials).

42.   *See Howell by Goerdt v. Tribune Entm't Co.*, 106 F.3d 215, 218–19 (7th Cir. 1997) (citing Rule 10(c) in treating video-

Attachments by Opponent: If the pleader does *not* attach, but instead merely refers to, a written instrument in the pleading, the opponent may usually still attach that instrument to the responsive pleading, so long as the instrument is referred to in the first pleading, is indisputably authentic, and is "central" to the pleader's claim.[43]

Effect of Attaching Exhibits

Exhibits attached to a pleading are made a part of that pleading for all purposes.[44]

Possible Dismissal: In ruling on a motion to dismiss, the court may consider not only the textual averments of the pleading itself, but also the contents of all exhibits attached to the pleading.[45] Where an inconsistency exists between an attached document and any allegation in the pleading based on that document, the document controls.[46] Similarly, where an attached document reveals a "built-in" defense that precludes recovery as a matter of law, the court may recognize the defense and dismiss the action.[47]

"Vouching" Risk: By adopting by reference a portion of an attached document, the pleader does not necessarily "vouch" for the truth of all the contents of the document. The attached document will be read in conjunction with the pleading that adopts it. Thus, a defamation plaintiff may safely attach an allegedly libelous writing without being deemed to have admitted as true all the asserted libels contained in the writing, just as a commercial plaintiff, alleging the non-receipt of goods, may attach an allegedly forged receipt without admitting that the document truthfully recounts that the goods were received.[48] Likewise, an aggrieved litigant generally can safely attach a copy of an appealed-from opinion, order, or other ruling without

tape as "appended" to the complaint, where plaintiff's counsel urged the court to view it).

43. *See United States v. Ritchie,* 342 F.3d 903, 908 (9th Cir.2003); *Beddall v. State St. Bank & Trust Co.,* 137 F.3d 12, 17 (1st Cir.1998); *Weiner v. Klais & Co.,* 108 F.3d 86, 89 (6th Cir.1997).

44. *See Local 15, Int'l Bhd. of Elec. Workers, AFL–CIO v. Exelon Corp.,* 495 F.3d 779, 782 (7th Cir. 2007); *Park Univ. Enters., Inc. v. American Cas. Co. of Reading, PA,* 442 F.3d 1239, 1244 (10th Cir. 2006); *General Elec. Capital Corp. v. Posey,* 415 F.3d 391, 398 n.8 (5th Cir.2005).

45. *See Katun Corp. v. Clarke,* 484 F.3d 972, 975 (8th Cir. 2007); *Ferrer v. Chevron Corp.,* 484 F.3d 776, 780 (5th Cir. 2007);

Witzke v. Femal, 376 F.3d 744, 749 (7th Cir.2004); *E.E.O.C. v. Staten Island Savings Bank,* 207 F.3d 144, 148 (2d Cir.2000).

46. *See Chicago Dist. Council of Carpenters Welfare Fund v. Caremark, Inc.,* 474 F.3d 463, 466 (7th Cir. 2007); *General Elec. Capital Corp. v. Posey,* 415 F.3d 391, 398 n.8 (5th Cir.2005); *ALA, Inc. v. CCAIR, Inc.,* 29 F.3d 855 (3d Cir.1994); *Fayetteville Investors v. Commercial Builders, Inc.,* 936 F.2d 1462, 1465 (4th Cir.1991).

47. *See Hamilton v. O'Leary,* 976 F.2d 341 (7th Cir.1992).

48. *See Guzell v. Hiller,* 223 F.3d 518, 519 (7th Cir.2000) (giving examples); *Gant v. Wallingford Bd. of Educ.,* 69 F.3d 669, 674–75 (2d Cir.1995)(giving these examples).

being deemed to have thereby "vouched" for the very reasoning
or result she is in the process of challenging.[49]

ADDITIONAL RESEARCH REFERENCES

Wright & Miller, *Federal Practice and Procedure* §§ 1321–1330.

C.J.S. Federal Civil Procedure § 251.

West's Key No. Digests, Federal Civil Procedure ☞625–629.

49. In fact, one Court of Appeals harshly derided this sort of "vouching" argument as "beyond nonsensical" and "unworthy" of the attorneys who asserted it. *See Carroll v. Yates*, 362 F.3d 984, 986 (7th Cir.2004) ("The logic of the . . . argument is that an appellant, required by the appellate rules to append to his brief the decision of the district court or administrative agency that he is appealing, . . . by doing so kills the appeal because appending amounts to vouching for the truth of the propositions in the appended decision. The argument if accepted would do wonders for our workload, but is beyond nonsensical and unworthy of the office of the Attorney General of Illinois."). The Court, then, directed the filing attorneys to show cause why they should not be sanctioned for briefing "frivolous argumentation". *Id.*

RULE 11

SIGNING PLEADINGS, MOTIONS, AND OTHER PAPERS; REPRESENTATIONS TO THE COURT; SANCTIONS

(a) Signature. Every pleading, written motion, and other paper must be signed by at least one attorney of record in the attorney's name—or by a party personally if the party is unrepresented. The paper must state the signer's address, e-mail address, and telephone number. Unless a rule or statute specifically states otherwise, a pleading need not be verified or accompanied by an affidavit. The court must strike an unsigned paper unless the omission is promptly corrected after being called to the attorney's or party's attention.

(b) Representations to the Court. By presenting to the court a pleading, written motion, or other paper—whether by signing, filing, submitting, or later advocating it—an attorney or unrepresented party certifies that to the best of the person's knowledge, information, and belief, formed after an inquiry reasonable under the circumstances:

(1) it is not being presented for any improper purpose, such as to harass, cause unnecessary delay, or needlessly increase the cost of litigation;

(2) the claims, defenses, and other legal contentions are warranted by existing law or by a nonfrivolous argument for extending, modifying, or reversing existing law or for establishing new law;

(3) the factual contentions have evidentiary support or, if specifically so identified, will likely have evidentiary support after a reasonable opportunity for further investigation or discovery; and

(4) the denials of factual contentions are warranted on the evidence or, if specifically so identified, are reasonably based on belief or a lack of information.

(c) Sanctions.

(1) *In General.* If, after notice and a reasonable opportunity to respond, the court determines that Rule 11(b) has been violated, the court may impose an

appropriate sanction on any attorney, law firm, or
party that violated the rule or is responsible for the
violation. Absent exceptional circumstances, a law
firm must be held jointly responsible for a violation
committed by its partner, associate, or employee.

(2) *Motion for Sanctions.* A motion for sanctions must
be made separately from any other motion and must
describe the specific conduct that allegedly violates
Rule 11(b). The motion must be served under Rule
5, but it must not be filed or be presented to the
court if the challenged paper, claim, defense, contention, or denial is withdrawn or appropriately corrected within 21 days after service or within another
time the court sets. If warranted, the court may
award to the prevailing party the reasonable expenses, including attorney's fees, incurred for the
motion.

(3) *On the Court's Initiative.* On its own, the court may
order an attorney, law firm, or party to show cause
why conduct specifically described in the order has
not violated Rule 11(b).

(4) *Nature of a Sanction.* A sanction imposed under this
rule must be limited to what suffices to deter repetition of the conduct or comparable conduct by others
similarly situated. The sanction may include nonmonetary directives; an order to pay a penalty into
court; or, if imposed on motion and warranted for
effective deterrence, an order directing payment to
the movant of part or all of the reasonable attorney's fees and other expenses directly resulting from
the violation.

(5) *Limitations on Monetary Sanctions.* The court must
not impose a monetary sanction:

(A) against a represented party for violating Rule
11(b)(2); or

(B) on its own, unless it issued the show-cause
order under Rule 11(c)(3) before voluntary dismissal or settlement of the claims made by or
against the party that is, or whose attorneys
are, to be sanctioned.

(6) *Requirements for an Order.* An order imposing a sanction must describe the sanctioned conduct and explain the basis for the sanction.

(d) Inapplicability to Discovery. This rule does not apply to disclosures and discovery requests, responses, objections, and motions under Rules 26 through 37.

[Amended April 28, 1983, effective August 1, 1983; March 2, 1987, effective August 1, 1987; April 22, 1993, effective December 1, 1993; April 30, 2007, effective December 1, 2007.]

──────────── 2007 AMENDMENTS ROADMAP ────────────

STYLE PROJECT CHANGES: Minor changes were made in the title of the Rule and in the title of subsection (b). Minor language changes were also made in the text of the Rule to aid readability. Subsection (c) was previously organized into three subparts, two of which also contained further subparts. New Rule 11(c) is reorganized into six subparts, with new subtitles.

NON-STYLE CHANGES: Rule 11(a) now requires parties to provide e-mail addresses, if any.

NOTE: The Federal Rules "Style Project" is explained in Part III-A.

AUTHORS' COMMENTARY ON RULE 11

──────────── PURPOSE AND SCOPE ────────────

Rule 11 establishes the standards attorneys and parties must meet when filing pleadings, motions, or other documents in court. It also regulates the circumstances in which sanctions may be imposed if the standards of Rule 11 are not met.

RULE 11(a). SIGNATURE

CORE CONCEPT

Rule 11(a) requires that documents be signed by an attorney or (if there is no attorney) the party. It abolishes old verification requirements, unless they have been preserved by rule or statute.

APPLICATIONS

Scope

Rule 11 applies to every pleading, written motion, or other

paper filed or served[1] in the course of litigation, as well as to advocacy of documents previously filed.[2] Rule 11 does not apply to misconduct unrelated to signed motions, pleadings or other papers.[3] Rule 11 is also inapplicable to state-court filings.[4]

Rule 11 and Appellate Jurisdiction

In general, Rule 11 is applicable only to lawsuits in district courts. Federal Rule of Appellate Procedure 38 usually controls sanctions for groundless appeals to circuit courts.[5] However, an exception to that delineation of authority occurs when a party files a notice of appeal. In that circumstance it is Rule 11 that requires the appellant to sign the notice of appeal. Thus, a failure to sign the notice is an error, which may be correctable under Rule 11(a), and an appellate court does not lose jurisdiction of an appeal if the appellant corrects the original failure to sign.[6]

1. *See, e.g., Antonious v. Spalding & Evenflo Companies, Inc.,* 281 F.3d 1258, 1261 (Fed.Cir.2002) (court ordered filing of document; through apparent inadvertence document was served but not filed; held, party which served offending document falls within scope of Rule 11 notwithstanding that document was never actually filed with court; acknowledging general principle that Rule 11 does not apply to documents not filed with court).

2. *See, e.g., In re Highgate Equities, Ltd.,* 279 F.3d 148, 153–54, 154 (2d Cir. 2002) (bankruptcy case involving analogous Federal Rule of Bankruptcy Procedure 9011; Rule 11 generally applicable only to documents served or filed with court; letter sent to court but not filed is normally not within scope of Rule 11); *Legault v. Zambarano,* 105 F.3d 24, 27–28 (1st Cir.1997) (letter is within scope of Rule 11 only where letter was motion in disguise that was intended to affect judicial decision on such matter as whether to issue a preliminary injunction; acknowledging general rule that letter is outside scope of Rule 11); *O'Brien v. Alexander,* 101 F.3d 1479, 1489 (2d Cir. 1996) (oral advocacy flowing directly from documents filed with court fall within scope of Rule 11; other oral statements are not controlled by Rule 11).

3. *See, e.g., Christian v. Mattell,* 286 F.3d 1118, 1130–1131 (9th Cir.2002) (Rule 11 inapplicable to discovery abuses or oral misrepresentations unrelated to document filings); *Loggerhead Turtle v. County Council of Volusia County, Florida,* 148 F.3d 1231, 1256 (11th Cir.1998) (Rule 11 applies only to court filings. "Assuming the author acts in good faith, an investigation preceding an intent to sue letter need not be as

thorough as that leading up to the complaint."); *Milltex Industries Corp. v. Jacquard Lace Co., Ltd.,* 55 F.3d 34, 37 n. 5 (2d Cir.1995)(Rule 11 applicable only to circumstances involving pleadings, motions, or other papers; Rule 11 inapplicable to attorney's defiance of judicial order). *But see, Antonious v. Spalding & Evenflo Companies, Inc.,* 281 F.3d 1258, 1261 (Fed.Cir. 2002) (court ordered filing of document; through apparent inadvertence document was served but not filed; held, party which served offending document falls within scope of Rule 11 notwithstanding that document was never actually filed with court; however, acknowledging general principle that Rule 11 does not apply to documents not filed with court). *Turner v. Sungard Business Systems, Inc.,* 91 F.3d 1418, 1421 (11th Cir.1996) (attorney whose only written document was notice of appearance was nevertheless subject to sanctions for later oral advocacy).

4. *See, e.g., Edwards v. General Motors Corp.,* 153 F.3d 242, 245 (5th Cir.1998) (Rule 11 inapplicable to filing made in state court before case was removed to federal court; sanctions may be imposed on post-removal filings; noting general agreement among circuit courts); *Bisciglia v. Kenosha Unified School District No. 1,* 45 F.3d 223, 226 (7th Cir.1995)(filing in state court not sanctionable under Rule 11).

5. *See, e.g., In re 60 East 80th Street Equities, Inc.,* 218 F.3d 109, 118–19 n. 3 (2d Cir.2000) (Rule 11 inapplicable to appellate litigation).

6. *Becker v. Montgomery,* 532 U.S. 757, 121 S.Ct. 1801, 149 L.Ed.2d 983 (2001) (distinguishing Rule 11 from jurisdictional

Administrative Litigation

Normally Rule 11 is not applicable in proceedings before administrative agencies. Application of Rule 11 occurs in such cases only when the case becomes a lawsuit in a federal court.[7]

Documents Filed in State Court

If a document was filed when a case was pending in state court, Rule 11 cannot be used to sanction the signer of the document in federal district court. Thus, a failure to update or amend a state complaint, by itself, is not sanctionable in federal court.[8]

Party v. Attorney

Rule 11 does not authorize actions in favor of a party against the party's attorney.[9]

Pro se Litigants

Rule 11 applies to pro se litigants. Thus, a pro se litigant may be sanctioned for violating Rule 11. However, a party's pro se status is a factor that is weighed in determining whether the party's behavior was reasonable under the standard of Rule 11.[10]

Lack of Subject Matter Jurisdiction

Rule 11 applies even in cases where it is subsequently determined that the district court lacked subject matter jurisdiction.[11]

Voluntary Dismissal: Rule 41

It appears that a district court retains jurisdiction to impose Rule 11 sanctions even after a case has been voluntarily dismissed

---

requirements of Rules 3 and 4; also suggesting that appropriate means of adjusting signature requirement of Rule 11 "to keep pace with technological advances" is through process of rule amendment, not judicial decision).

7. *See, e.g., Santa Maria v. Pacific Bell,* 202 F.3d 1170, 1179 (9th Cir.2000) ("The obligations of Rule 11 extend only to suits filed in federal court, not to such administrative procedures as filing a charge with the EEOC. ... In fact, the very nature of an EEOC charge makes this clear: the charge serves as an allegation of wrongdoing which the EEOC investigates to determine if it has merit.").

8. *See, e.g., Bisciglia v. Kenosha Unified School District No. 1,* 45 F.3d 223, 226–27 (7th Cir.1995).

9. *See, e.g., Mark Industries, Ltd. v. Sea Captain's Choice, Inc.,* 50 F.3d 730 (9th Cir.1995)(purpose of Rule 11 is to deter abuses that harm the opponent, not the client).

10. *See, e.g., Kennedy v. National Juvenile Detention Association,* 187 F.3d 690, 696 (7th Cir.1999) (affirming conclusion

that claim was not frivolous, "especially considering the plaintiff's lack of legal representation"); *Moore v. Time, Inc.,* 180 F.3d 463, 463 (2d Cir.1999) (affirming district court's denial of Rule 11 sanctions on attorney who appeared pro se where district court had reasoned that attorney was "not sophisticated"; however, also imposing sanctions under Federal Rule of Appellate Procedure 38 for frivolous appeal; attorney had received "clear warning" from district court and had previously brought other frivolous appeals to appellate court).

11. *Willy v. Coastal Corp.,* 503 U.S. 131, 112 S.Ct. 1076, 117 L.Ed.2d 280 (1992). *See also, e.g., Tropf v. Fidelity National Title Insurance Co.,* 289 F.3d 929, 938 (6th Cir.2002) (citing *Willy,* supra; noting that sanctions in such circumstances do not violate Article III of Constitution); *Perpetual Securities, Inc. v. Tang,* 290 F.3d 132, 141 (2d Cir.2002) (same result); *Branson v. Nott,* 62 F.3d 287, 293 (9th Cir.1995) (absence of subject matter jurisdiction does not preclude application of Rule 11 sanctions).

without prejudice under Rule 41.[12]

Signature of Attorney

If a party has retained counsel, at least one attorney must sign the document and provide the attorney's address and telephone number.[13] Rule 11 requires that an individual attorney must sign the document. Under older law that is probably still good precedent, a signature that purports to be on behalf of an entire law firm does not satisfy the signature requirement of Rule 11.[14]

Signature of Party

A party must sign the document if the party is not represented by counsel.[15] The party must also provide an address, e-mail address, and telephone number, if any. Although courts may be more lenient with pro se litigants, it should not be assumed that they are immune from Rule 11 sanctions.[16]

Verification and Affidavits

Rule 11 abolishes requirements of verification and affidavits for documents filed or served in the course of litigation, except where such a requirement is expressly preserved by another rule or statute.[17] The signature of a party or counsel is the substitute for prior verification practices. Continuing requirements for verification are most commonly encountered in suits at state law. Occasionally, however, a federal rule or statute may also require verification. For example, Rule 23.1, governing derivative actions by shareholders, requires verification of a plaintiff-shareholder's complaint.[18]

Failure to Sign

If a document subject to Rule 11 is not signed, the court has power to strike the document unless the proponent signs it promptly upon notification of the missing signature.[19]

---

12. *See, e.g., Sequa Corp. v. Cooper,* 245 F.3d 1036, 1037 (8th Cir.2001) (also acknowledging some potentially contrary results in earlier cases).

13. *See, e.g., Duran v. Carris,* 238 F.3d 1268, 1271 (10th Cir.2001) (attorney's failure to disclose that brief submitted by allegedly pro se party was actually ghostwritten by attorney, who did not enter appearance, is violation of Rule 11(a)).

14. *Pavelic & LeFlore v. Marvel Entertainment Group,* 493 U.S. 120, 110 S.Ct. 456, 107 L.Ed.2d 438 (1989).

15. *Maxwell v. Snow,* 409 F.3d 354, 356 (D.C.Cir.2005) ("[A]ll pleadings by a *pro se* plaintiff must be signed by the party."). *Cf., Business Guides v. Chromatic Communications Enterprises,* 498 U.S. 533, 111 S.Ct. 922, 112 L.Ed.2d 1140 (1991).

16. *Maxwell v. Snow,* 409 F.3d 354, 356 (D.C.Cir.2005) (failure of pro se plaintiff to sign complaint must, upon notification of

defect, be corrected promptly or pleading must be stricken). *Warren v. Guelker,* 29 F.3d 1386, 1390 (9th Cir.1994)(Rule 11 "explicitly applies to parties not represented by attorneys.").

17. *See, e.g., Cobell v. Norton,* 391 F.3d 251, 255 (D.C.Cir.2004) (subject to exceptions, Rule 11 eliminates the need for verification).

18. *See also, e.g.,* 15 U.S.C.A. § 78u–4 (requiring sworn certification by proposed class representative in cases within scope of Private Securities Litigation Reform Act of 1995).

19. *See, e.g., De Aza–Paez v. United States,* 343 F.3d 552, 552 (1st Cir.2003) (per curiam) ("Rule 11(a) provides that an unsigned paper will not be stricken for lack of signature if it is corrected promptly"); *Kovilic Construction Co. v. Missbrenner,* 106 F.3d 768, 772 (7th Cir.1997) ("[D]ocuments

RULE 11(b). REPRESENTATIONS TO COURT

CORE CONCEPT

Rule 11(b) establishes the standards that documents which are regulated by Rule 11 must meet. It also specifically provides that the standards are applicable to later advocacy of such documents, as well as to the initial submission of the documents.

APPLICATIONS

Unsuccessful Pleadings and Motions

Under the previous version of Rule 11, a violation occurred only when a client or attorney engaged in improper behavior or failed to demonstrate due care. Thus, mere failure to prevail on a particular pleading or motion does not, of itself, establish a violation of Rule 11.[20] This standard will presumably carry over into the current version of Rule 11.

Claims Evaluated Individually

Although the literal language of Rule 11 might seem to address whether entire documents meet the Rule's requirements, it is settled that portions of a document might be in violation of Rule 11, notwithstanding that other portions of the same document are satisfactory.[21]

Improper Rule 11 Motions

Attorneys are cautioned that because Rule 11 violations may be raised by motions, such motions themselves are subject to review under Rule 11, and can be the subject of additional allegations of violations of Rule 11.[22]

---

should be struck only where the failure to sign severely prejudiced the opposing party.").

20. *Altran Corp. v. Ford Motor Co.,* 502 U.S. 939, 112 S.Ct. 373, 116 L.Ed.2d 324 (1991)(if party's position is reasonable, a loss on the merits does not trigger Rule 11 sanctions). *See, e.g., Morris v. Wachovia Securities, Inc.,* 448 F.3d 268, 278 (4th Cir. 2006) (Rule 11(b) violation triggers sanctions only when violation renders the entire complaint a "substantial failure."); *Obert v. Republican Western Insurance Co.,* 398 F.3d 138, 146 (1st Cir.2005) (objectively hopeless motion, filed in good faith, need not invariably be basis for sanctions; to impose sanctions in such cases on a routine basis "would tie courts and counsel in knots"); *Hartmarx Corp. v. Abboud,* 326 F.3d 862, 868 (7th Cir.2003) (reasonable position on close question under new rule is not sanctionable even if other position is superior). *But cf., Holgate v. Baldwin,* 425 F.3d 671,

677 (9th Cir.2005) (presence of one non-frivolous claim does not immunize entire complaint from Rule 11).

21. *See, e.g., Perez v. Posse Comitatus,* 373 F.3d 321 (2d Cir.2004) ("A complaint challenged under Rule 11(b) is not ordinarily analyzed as an individual unit. ... [T]he fact that a claim is properly asserted against one defendant does not mean that the same claim may properly be asserted against a different defendant."). *But cf., CUNA Mutual Insurance Society v. Office & Professional Employees Union, Local 39,* 443 F.3d 556, 561 (7th Cir.2006) (in Seventh Circuit, meritless challenges to arbitration awards are particularly vulnerable to Rule 11 sanctions).

22. *But see, Blue v. United States Department of the Army,* 914 F.2d 525, 548 (4th Cir.1990) ("Litigants should be able to defend themselves from the imposition of sanctions without incurring further sanctions.").

Reasonable Inquiry

Rule 11(b) provides that persons who sign, file, submit or later advocate documents are certifying to the court that the document or advocacy is based upon the person's best knowledge, information or belief, which is in turn based upon an inquiry that was reasonable in the circumstances of the particular case.[23] This is a change in language from the previous Rule 11 standard, and is intended to lower the burden on the proponent of a document.[24] However, an attorney operates under a "continuous obligation to make inquiries."[25] Moreover, although the matter is still uncertain, the unwillingness of a party's opponent to cooperate in a pre-litigation examination of facts might not justify a party's failure to undertake a reasonable inquiry.[26]

23. *See, e.g., Roger Edwards, L.L.C. v. Fiddes & Son, Ltd.,* 437 F.3d 140, 142 (1st Cir.2006) ("To support a finding of frivolousness, some degree of fault is required, but the fault need not be a wicked or subjectively reckless state of mind; rather an individual 'must, at the very least, be culpably careless to commit a violation.' "); *United States Bank National Association, N.D. v. Sullivan–Moore,* 406 F.3d 465, 470 (7th Cir.2005) (empty head but pure heart is no excuse); *Belleville Catering Co. v. Champaign Market Place, L.L.C.,* 350 F.3d 691, 692–93 (7th Cir.2003) (reliance on lease agreement's erroneous description of corporation as Missouri corporation does not meet requirement of reasonable inquiry; "counsel must secure jurisdictional details from original sources"); *Antonious v. Spalding & Evenflo Companies,* 275 F.3d 1066, 1072 (Fed.Cir.2002) ("Rule 11 requires that the attorney not rely solely on the client's claim interpretation, but instead perform an independent claim analysis."); *View Engineering, Inc. v. Robotic Vision Systems, Inc.,* 208 F.3d 981, 984–86 (Fed.Cir.2000) (upholding sanctions for patent infringement suit filed on basis of no facts; only basis for filing was belief of key person, which was in turn based on knowledge of company's own patents, opponent's advertising, and opponent's statements to customers; financial inability to purchase opponent's machine for inspection prior to lawsuit does not provide defense to sanctions; opponent's refusal to permit pre-litigation examination of its machine also irrelevant because opponent has no duty to permit such pre-litigation discovery); *Hernandez v. Joliet Police Department,* 197 F.3d 256, 264 (7th Cir.1999) (failure to perform basic legal research to learn that suit against state's attorney's office was barred by 11th Amendment to federal constitu-

tion). *But see Commercial Cleaning Services, L.L.C. v. Colin Service Systems, Inc.,* 271 F.3d 374, 386 (2d Cir.2001) (error for district court not to provide sanctioned plaintiff with opportunity to conduct discovery to fill deficiencies in information; Rule 11(b) does not require plaintiff "to know at the time of pleading all facts necessary to establish the claim"); *Dubois v. United States Department of Agriculture,* 270 F.3d 77, 82 (1st Cir.2001) (duty to investigate need not be pursued until absolute certainty is achieved); *Garr v. U.S. Healthcare, Inc.,* 22 F.3d 1274, 1278 (3d Cir.1994) (the "obligation personally to comply with the requirements of Rule 11 clearly does not preclude the signer from any reliance on information from other persons"). *See also Circuit City Stores, Inc. v. Najd,* 294 F.3d 1104 (9th Cir.2002) (abuse of discretion to impose sanctions on party who would have prevailed, but for Supreme Court's intervening contrary decision in unrelated case while instant appeal was pending).

24. *Hadges v. Yonkers Racing Corp.,* 48 F.3d 1320, 1329–30 (2d Cir.1995)(amended Rule 11 permits attorney to rely on objectively reasonable representation of client; thus, duty of attorney to make inquiry is relaxed).

25. *Battles v. City of Ft. Myers,* 127 F.3d 1298, 1300 (11th Cir.1997) (failure to do so may be sanctionable if attorney advocates position that has become untenable).

26. *Compare View Engineering, Inc. v. Robotic Vision Systems, Inc.,* 208 F.3d 981, 986 (Fed.Cir.2000) (an opponent "is not required to allow pre-litigation discovery" and lack of such an opportunity is not a defense to sanctions for failure to make

Bad Faith

Rule 11(b)(1) provides that by presenting a document or arguing on its behalf, a person certifies that the document has no improper purpose, such as harassment[27] or undue delay or expense. This language carries over from the previous version of Rule 11, and is intended to regulate bad faith filings.[28] It should already be clear, of course, that while bad faith may indeed trigger sanctions under Rule 11, conduct that does not involve bad faith may also be sanctionable.[29]

Standard for Attorney's Motion v. Judicial Show Cause Order

It is clear that the means by which a Rule 11 issue is raised differ, depending on whether an attorney or the court raises the issue. In particular, an attorney or party seeking a sanction under Rule 11 must first comply with the "safe harbor" requirement of Rule 11(c)(1)(A), while a judicially initiated "show cause" order need not. However, it is less clear whether the objective standard for imposition of a Rule 11 sanction also differs, depending on whether the issue arises from an attorney's motion or a judge's order.[30] Attorneys must consult local precedent on this point.

reasonable inquiry), *with Hoffmann–La Roche, Inc. v. Invamed, Inc.,* 213 F.3d 1359 (Fed.Cir.2000) (reasonable inquiry met where claimants sought information from opponent prior to litigation, but were rejected; opponent was bound by confidentiality agreement with third party, but had not sought any sort of release; opponent released samples of drug at issue, but claimants were unable to reverse engineer samples to determine if patent infringement had occurred).

27. *See, e.g., Whitehead v. Food Max of Mississippi, Inc.,* 332 F.3d 796 (5th Cir. 2003) (en banc) (even a nonfrivolous submission to court may be sanctionable when document was submitted for improper purpose; noting that excessive motions can constitute harassment, and even legitimate documents that also "use abusive language toward opposing counsel" can trigger sanction). *But see Building & Construction Trades Council of Buffalo v. Downtown Development, Inc.,* 448 F.3d 138 n. 6 (2d Cir.2006) (Rule 11(b) not triggered simply because otherwise proper lawsuit was motivated in substantial part by "interests unrelated to the subject matter of the action").

28. *See, e.g., CUNA Mutual Insurance Society v. Office & Professional Employees Union, Local 39,* 443 F.3d 556, 561 (7th Cir.2006) (in Seventh Circuit, meritless challenges to arbitration awards are particularly vulnerable to Rule 11 sanctions);

American International Adjustment Co. v. Galvin, 86 F.3d 1455 (7th Cir.1996)("[A] pleader may assert contradictory statements of fact only when legitimately in doubt about the facts in question;" citing Rule 11). *But cf., In re Pennie & Edmonds, L.L.P.,* 323 F.3d 86, 87 (2d Cir.2003) (where court decides to impose sanctions sua sponte, law firm did not have benefit of "safe harbor" provision; thus sanctions were only appropriate for subjective bad faith, not for unreasonable but genuine subjective good faith).

29. *See, e.g., Young v. City of Providence,* 404 F.3d 33 (1st Cir.2005) (no bad faith requirement for sanctions under Rule 11); *Anjelino v. New York Times Co.,* 200 F.3d 73, 100 (3d Cir.1999) (Rule 11 does not require finding of bad faith).

30. *Compare, e.g., Clark v. United Parcel Service, Inc.,* 460 F.3d 1004, 1010 (8th Cir.2006) (finding it unnecessary to revolve the issue of whether a finding of subjective bad faith was necessary to impose sanctions on a court's own initiative as such a finding had been made by the district court in that case); *Kaplan v. DaimlerChrysler, A.G.,* 331 F.3d 1251, 1255–56 (11th Cir.2003) (court-initiated sanction requires finding of more serious misconduct); *In re Pennie & Edmonds, L.L.P.,* 323 F.3d 86, 90–93 (2d Cir. 2003) (standard is analogous to contempt of court standard); *and United National Insurance Co. v. R & D Latex Corp.,* 242 F.3d

Advocating Changes in Law

Rule 11(b)(2) provides that by presenting a document or arguing on its behalf, a person certifies that the arguments in the document are either justified by existing law or are "nonfrivolous" arguments for alteration in existing law.[31] Rule 11(b)(2) is a change from the previous version of Rule 11, and is intended to be a lesser burden on an advocate than the former standard of "good faith" arguments.[32]

Foundation for Factual Allegations

Rule 11(b)(3) requires persons alleging facts to do so with "evidentiary support" or, when specifically stated, to believe they can develop evidentiary support through further investigation. Rule 11(b)(3) thus establishes a lesser standard than the former requirement that allegations be "well grounded" in fact.[33]

Foundation for Denials

Rule 11(b)(4) requires denials of factual allegations to be warranted by the evidence unless a person specifically states that the

1102, 1115 (9th Cir.2001) (higher standard required for judicially imposed sanctions) *with Young v. City of Providence,* 404 F.3d 33, 39 (1st Cir.2005) (specifically rejecting foregoing precedent; holding that standard is the same for sanctions sought by attorney or initiated by judge).

31. *See, e.g., Brunt v. Service Employees International Union,* 284 F.3d 715, 721 (7th Cir.2002) (although parties' claims "were barred by existing Supreme Court and Seventh Circuit case law," district court could still properly find that complaint was not frivolous under rule 11); *In re Sargent,* 136 F.3d 349, 352 (4th Cir.1998) (standard of Rule 11(b)(2) is "objective reasonableness. . . . [P]ut differently, a legal position violates Rule 11 if it 'has absolutely no chance of success under the existing precedent.' "). *Cf., Hartmarx Corp. v. Abboud,* 326 F.3d 862, 868 (7th Cir.2003) (reasonable position on close question under new rule is not sanctionable even if other position is superior).

32. *See, e.g., Independent Lift Truck Builders Union v. NACCO Materials Handling Group, Inc.,* 202 F.3d 965, 968 (7th Cir.2000) (no sanction for advocating position in conflict with two controlling decisions where position was " 'not totally baseless' " and " 'had some logical and practical appeal' "); *Protective Life Insurance Co. v. Dignity Viatical Settlement Partners, L.P.,* 171 F.3d 52, 57 (1st Cir.1999) (party's attempt "to squeeze too much from [prior case law] . . . though aggressive, did not justify the imposition of Rule 11 sanctions;" using analogous case law as "building block" may not be persuasive to court, but can still be good faith). *Cf., Holgate v. Baldwin,* 425 F.3d 671, 680 (9th Cir.2005) (failure to cite adverse authority does not by itself trigger Rule 11 sanctions). *But see, e.g., Margo v. Weiss,* 213 F.3d 55 (2d Cir.2000) (Rule 11(b)(2) "establishes an objective standard, intended to eliminate any 'empty-head pure-heart' justification for patently frivolous arguments").

33. *Rotella v. Wood,* 528 U.S. 549, 120 S.Ct. 1075, 145 L.Ed.2d 1047 (2000) (Rule 11(b)(3) provides flexibility by "allowing pleadings based on evidence reasonably anticipated after further investigation or discovery"). *See, e.g., Tennessee Valley Authority v. Whitman,* 336 F.3d 1236 n. 6 (11th Cir.2003) (when EPA files suit, it need not possess evidence sufficient for victory at trial; instead, it need only meet equivalent of "probable cause" standard of criminal law, and not even "more rigorous 'substantial evidence' " standard of administrative law); *O'Brien v. Alexander,* 101 F.3d 1479, 1489 (2d Cir.1996) ("[S]anctions may not be imposed unless a particular allegation is utterly lacking in support."). *But cf., Morris v. Wachovia Securities, Inc.,* 448 F.3d 268, 277 (4th Cir.2006) ("Factual allegations fail to satisfy Rule 11(b)(3) when they are 'unsupported by *any* information obtained prior to filing.' "); *Macken v. Jensen,* 333 F.3d 797 (7th Cir.2003) (Rule 11(b)(3) requires plaintiff "to establish evidentiary support [of amount in controversy], or at least a likelihood of obtaining that support, *before* filing suit in federal court.").

denial is reasonably based upon a lack of information or on belief. Like Rule 11(b)(3), this provision also establishes a lesser standard than the former version of Rule 11.[34]

RULE 11(c).   SANCTIONS

CORE CONCEPT

Rule 11(c) regulates who may be sanctioned for violations of Rule 11(b), as well as how the sanction process may be initiated.   Rule 11(c) also governs the extent and limitations of the court's sanctioning power.

APPLICATIONS

Applicability to Rule 11(a)

By its terms, Rule 11(c) applies only to violations of Rule 11(b), not Rule 11(a).   It is unnecessary to apply Rule 11(c) to Rule 11(a) because the last sentence of Rule 11(a) contains its own sanction.

Persons Sanctioned

Rule 11(c) provides that in appropriate circumstances the court may sanction attorneys, law firms, or parties.[35]   This is a change from the former provision, which was construed as not permitting sanctions against an entire law firm.

Sovereign Immunity

It appears that government attorneys and their clients are subject to sanctions, including monetary sanctions, notwithstanding considerations of sovereign immunity.[36]

Magistrate Judges

It appears that magistrate judges do not have independent authority to order sanctions under Rule 11.[37]   However, the issue is

---

34.   *But see, e.g., Attwood v. Singletary,* 105 F.3d 610, 613 (11th Cir.1997) (actions based on arguably good faith belief are sanctionable where party failed to make reasonable inquiry into accuracy of information).

35.   *See, e.g., Union Planters Bank v. L & J Development Co.,* 115 F.3d 378, 384 (6th Cir.1997) ("Rule 11 explicitly allows for the imposition of sanctions upon a party responsible for the rule's violation, provided that a represented party is not sanctioned for a violation of subsection (b)(2) involving unwarranted legal contentions."). *See also Holgate v. Baldwin,* 425 F.3d 671, 677 (9th Cir.2005) (even lawyer who withdraws from case due to conflict of interest is not immune from Rule 11 sanctions for conduct prior to withdrawal). *See generally In re Cardizem CD Antitrust Litigation,* 481 F.3d 355, 360 (6th Cir.2007) (court does not have power to impose costs on attorney absent

express power granted by statute such as Rule 11 or 28 U.S.C. § 1927); *Salkil v. Mount Sterling Township Police Dept., 458 F.3d 520, 530 (6th Cir.2006)* (court should avoid using hindsight in assessing whether counsel's conduct was reasonable under the circumstances).

36.   *See, e.g., Mattingly v. United States,* 939 F.2d 816, 817–18 (9th Cir. 1991)(affirming monetary sanctions; held, government is not immune from Rule 11); *Adamson v. Bowen,* 855 F.2d 668, 672 (10th Cir.1988)(sovereign immunity does not bar monetary sanctions awarded under Rule 11); *cf., King v. Cooke,* 26 F.3d 720, 722 (7th Cir.1994) (noting with approval imposition of Rule 11 sanctions on Indiana Office of the Attorney General; however, no discussion of sovereign immunity).

37.   *See, e.g., Rajaratnam v. Moyer,* 47 F.3d 922, 923 (7th Cir.1995)(Congress has restricted independent authority of magis-

sufficiently unsettled so that attorneys should investigate local practice.

Judicial Discretion

The denial of a motion for sanctions is reviewed under the abuse-of-discretion standard.[38] In close cases the district court should provide an explanation of its reasons for denying sanctions,[39] and a circuit may remand close questions regarding a motion for sanctions where a district court denies sanctions without explanation.[40] Congress, of course, retains authority to reduce judicial discretion, and has occasionally done so.[41]

(1) HOW INITIATED

(A) BY MOTION

Specificity

Motions for sanctions under Rule 11(c) must be made separately

trate judges to three areas, none of which includes Rule 11 matters); *Bennett v. General Caster Service of N. Gordon Company, Inc.,* 976 F.2d 995, 998 (6th Cir. 1992)(magistrate judge may not order sanctions pursuant to Rule 11). *But see, Maisonville v. F2 America, Inc.,* 902 F.2d 746 (9th Cir.1990) (permitting Rule 11 sanction by magistrate judge).

38. *Cooter & Gell v. Hartmarx Corp.,* 496 U.S. 384, 405, 110 S.Ct. 2447, 110 L.Ed.2d 359 (1990). *See also Reinhardt v. Gulf Ins. Co.,* 489 F.3d 405, 416 (1st Cir. 2007) ("A district court's decision to impose Rule 11 sanctions is reviewed for abuse of discretion, and any findings of fact supporting that decision are reviewed for clear error.").

39. *Willhite v. Collins,* 459 F.3d 866, 870 (8th Cir.2006) (district courts should state the authority for each sanction imposed "as different sources of authority require different standards of proof and permit different types of sanctions against different parties.").

40. *See, e.g., Fuqua Homes, Inc. v. Beattie,* 388 F.3d 618, 623 (8th Cir.2004) (remanding for failure to identify the source of authority for the sanctions imposed). *See also S. Bravo Systems Inc. v. Containment Techs. Corp.,* 96 F.3d 1372, 1375 (Fed.Cir. 1996) ("When the requesting party makes a strong showing that Rule 11 violations may have occurred, however, the district court should provide some explanation for disregarding the proffered showing."). *Compare Moross Ltd. Partnership v. Fleckenstein*

Capital, Inc., 466 F.3d 508, 520 (6th Cir. 2006) (finding that the issue of sanctions was not so close that the district court's lack of explanation constituted abuse of discretion); *Detabali v. St. Luke's Hosp.,* 482 F.3d 1199, 1204 (9th Cir.2007) (reversing district court's award of sanctions because "it would be perverse to uphold an award of sanctions against counsel for taking actions that ultimately preserved his client's right to proceed with her case.").

41. *See, e.g., Simon DeBartolo Group, L.P. v. Richard E. Jacobs Group, Inc.,* 186 F.3d 157, 166–67 (2d Cir.1999) ("Ordinarily, courts are under no particular obligation to make findings with regard to the compliance of litigants and their counsel with Rule 11 or to impose sanctions once a violation is found." However, the Private Securities Litigation Reform Act of 1995 requires courts, at the conclusion of all private lawsuits arising under the Securities Exchange Act of 1934 to make specific findings as to compliance with Rule 11. If a violation occurs in such cases, the court has no discretion and must impose sanctions, which are rebuttably presumed to be attorneys' fees and other expenses incurred in the lawsuit. The standard for determining whether a Rule 11 violation has occurred, however, remains unchanged by this legislation). *See also Rombach v. Chang,* 355 F.3d 164, 178 (2d Cir.2004) (PSLRA requires court to make findings as to each party's and attorney's compliance with every element of Rule 11(b); where violations are found, court must impose sanctions; no discretion, as is normally the case with Rule 11 issues).

from other motions [42] and must allege with specificity the alleged violation of Rule 11(b).[43]

Service and Due Process

Rule 11(c)(2) provides that motions for sanctions must be served as required under Rule 5. Of course, any entity who may be subjected to Rule 11 sanctions, whether on a party's motion or on the court's initiative, has a due process right to present a defense before any sanction is imposed.[44] In practice, the quality and nature of hearings is controlled by the specific factual circumstances in which the alleged Rule 11 violation occurs.[45]

"Safe Harbor"

Rule 11(c)(2) does not permit sanctions motions to be filed with the court until 21 days after service of the motion, or within any other time frame the court provides.[46] If the document challenged by the sanctions motion is withdrawn or corrected within that time

42. *See, e.g., Perpetual Securities, Inc. v. Tang*, 290 F.3d 132, 142 (2d Cir.2002) (abuse of discretion to grant party's motion for sanctions which was not made separately, and was only included in memorandum addressing other issues before court); *Johnson v. Waddell and Reed, Inc.*, 74 F.3d 147, 150 (7th Cir.1996)(current version of Rule 11 requires "that a motion for sanctions ... shall be made separately from other motions"). *But see Nisenbaum v. Milwaukee County*, 333 F.3d 804 (7th Cir.2003) (sending "letter" or "demand" to opposing party's lawyer instead of "motion" is nonetheless substantial compliance with Rule 11(c)(1)(A)).

43. *See, e.g., Johnson v. Cherry*, 422 F.3d 540, 551–52 (7th Cir.2005) ("A general notice that the court is contemplating sanctions is insufficient; rather, the offending party must be on notice of the specific conduct for which she is potentially subject to sanctions.").

44. *See, e.g., Perpetual Securities, Inc. v. Tang*, 290 F.3d 132, 141 n. 2 (2d Cir.2002) (whether on motion of party or on court's initiative, award of sanctions is inappropriate if party to be sanctioned has no opportunity to respond; when court initiates Rule 11 matter *sua sponte,* it must issue "show cause" order); *Vollmer v. Publishers Clearing House and Campus Subscriptions, Inc.*, 248 F.3d 698 (7th Cir.2001) (evidence of violation "must be stated with some specificity in the record" and there must be a full and fair opportunity to respond; also noting that court may consider past record of questionable conduct); *Tompkins v. Cyr*, 202 F.3d 770, 788 (5th Cir.2000) (where

motion is served after trial had concluded, opponents of motion had no opportunity to defend or correct complaint).

45. *See, e.g., Spiller v. Ella Smithers Geriatric Center*, 919 F.2d 339, 346 (5th Cir.1990)(in Rule 11 cases, Due Process is usually satisfied if the accused has a chance to respond with a brief); *Union Planters Bank v. L & J Development Co.*, 115 F.3d 378, 385 (6th Cir.1997) (evidentiary hearing not required where sanctioned parties had "ample" notice and "meaningful" opportunity to be heard).

46. *See, e.g., Roth v. Green*, 466 F.3d 1179, 1192 (10th Cir.2006) (warning letters sent by defendants months in advance of filing Rule 11 motion for sanction did not satisfy safe harbor requirement); *Moore v. LaFayette Life Ins. Co.*, 458 F.3d 416, 446 (6th Cir.2006) (sanctions under Rule 11 based on motion made after disposition of the case on summary judgment constituted abuse of discretion; however sanctions proper under 28 U.S.C.A. § 1927). *First Bank of Marietta v. Hartford Underwriters Insurance Co.*, 307 F.3d 501, 510–11 (6th Cir.2002) (Rule 11 sanction inapplicable where moving party did not comply with safe harbor provision); *Rector v. Approved Federal Savings Bank*, 265 F.3d 248, 252–53 (4th Cir.2001) (movant must serve Rule 11 motion at least 21 days before filing it with court; however, sanctioned party's failure to enter timely objection to movant's untimely service waives issue); *Hadges v. Yonkers Racing Corp.*, 48 F.3d 1320 (2d Cir.1995) (sanctions cannot be imposed on motion against party not afforded "safe harbor").

frame, the motion may not be filed with the court, and thus no sanctions will be imposed.[47]

Costs of Presenting or Opposing Sanctions Motion

Rule 11(c)(2) provides the court with discretion to award costs, including attorney's fees, associated with presenting or opposing a sanctions motion.[48]

It should be noted that if a party arguably entitled to attorneys' fees pursuant to Rule 11 asks for an exorbitant amount, such a request may itself be an abuse of process and therefore may be grounds for denial of an award.[49]

Law Firm's Liability: Presumptions

When a sanction is to be imposed, Rule 11(c)(2) creates a strong presumption in favor of imposing it upon an entire law firm, in addition to whatever sanction may be imposed upon an individual attorney. This provision changes the old rule, which was construed to apply only to individual attorneys, not to their firms.

Standing: Non–Parties

In general, persons who are not parties to litigation have no standing to bring a Rule 11 motion.[50] Exceptions to that general rule arise in narrow circumstances where a non-party is affected directly by otherwise sanctionable conduct.[51]

47. *See, e.g., Brickwood Contractors, Inc. v. Datanet Engineering, Inc.,* 369 F.3d 385, 389 (4th Cir.2004) (en banc) (safe harbor is mandatory condition precedent to sanctions); *Barber v. Miller,* 146 F.3d 707, 710–11 (9th Cir.1998) (motion served and filed after offending complaint was dismissed does not meet safe harbor requirement because no opportunity existed to withdraw complaint); *AeroTech, Inc. v. Estes,* 110 F.3d 1523 (10th Cir.1997) (where offending party dismissed its claim before Rule 11 motion was filed, sanctions were not possible because offending party had no opportunity to cure offense within time limit provided by safe harbor provision). *But see Truesdell v. Southern California Permanente Medical Group,* 293 F.3d 1146 (9th Cir.2002) (district court dismissed complaint, with leave to amend, on twentieth day after service of motion for sanctions; held, full 21–day period was provided because: (1) moving party had provided informal written notice of Rule 11 motion 27 days prior to actually filing motion; and (2) dismissal with leave to amend left offending party with additional time to withdraw complaint).

48. *See, e.g., Margolis v. Ryan,* 140 F.3d 850 (9th Cir.1998) (so noting; also observ-

ing that this provision alters earlier case law prohibiting award of fees and costs relating to filing sanctions motions).

49. *See, e.g., Budget Rent–A–Car System, Inc. v. Consolidated Equity, L.L.C.,* 428 F.3d 717, 718 (7th Cir.2005) (but to trigger this response, request must be exorbitant, not "merely excessive").

50. *See, e.g., New York News, Inc. v. Kheel,* 972 F.2d 482, 488–89 (2d Cir.1992) (person who had not met intervention requirements of Rule 24 lacked standing to seek sanctions; moreover, such a person may not intervene solely to seek sanctions).

51. *See, e.g., Nyer v. Winterthur International,* 290 F.3d 456 (1st Cir.2002) (person not made party because judge reserved judgment on motion to amend complaint nevertheless had standing to seek Rule 11 sanctions because he had to prepare possible defense against against pending amended complaint); *Greenberg v. Sala,* 822 F.2d 882 (9th Cir.1987) (individuals named in frivolous complaint, but not served, incurred costs and attorney fees and had Rule 11 standing); *Westmoreland v. CBS, Inc.,* 770 F.2d 1168 (D.C.Cir.1985) (non-party is entitled to Rule 11 after party's attorney commenced contempt proceedings against him).

(B) ON COURT'S INITIATIVE
Show Cause Orders

When the court believes there may have been a violation of Rule 11(b), it may initiate the sanction process without waiting for a party to make a motion.[52] This is done by issuing an order directing the attorney, law firm, or party to show cause why it has not violated a provision of Rule 11(b). Rule 11(c)(3) requires the court to identify the potentially offending conduct with reasonable specificity,[53] and guarantees an affected party both notice and an opportunity to defend against the proposed sanction.[54] Normally, a "show cause" order will be issued only in circumstances analogous to contempt of court.[55]

No Formal "Safe Harbor"

Rule 11(c)(3) contains no explicit "safe harbor" provision such as is found in Rule 11(c)(2), although the court in its discretion may afford an offending party substantial leeway.[56]

(2) NATURE OF SANCTION; LIMITATIONS
Policy of Deterrence

For the most part, sanctions for violations of Rule 11(b) are to be imposed primarily to deter similar violations by the offender or "others similarly situated." [57] This policy represents a substantial

52. *But cf., Perpetual Securities, Inc. v. Tang,* 290 F.3d 132, 141 n. 2 (2d Cir.2002) (when court initiates Rule 11 matter *sua sponte,* it must issue "show cause" order).

53. *See, e.g., Clark v. United Parcel Service, Inc.,* 460 F.3d 1004, 1007–1009 (8th Cir.2006) (court notified attorney of six specific paragraphs in 480–page pleading that the court viewed as exemplary of widespread flaws and imposed sanctions based on length of document, numerous misstatements and mischaracterizations of the record, which "had a cumulative effect which [the] Court found to be repugnant to the very concept of judicial economy."); *Thornton v. General Motors Corp.,* 136 F.3d 450, 455 (5th Cir.1998) (per curiam) (order that does not identify specific offending conduct does not afford adequate notice and constitutes abuse of district court's discretion).

54. *See, e.g., Nuwesra v. Merrill Lynch, Fenner & Smith, Inc.,* 174 F.3d 87 (2d Cir.1999) (abuse of discretion to impose sanctions *sua sponte* without prior notice and opportunity to be heard); *Johnson v. Waddell & Reed, Inc.,* 74 F.3d 147, 151 (7th Cir.1996) (noting court's duty, when considering Rule 11 sanctions *sua sponte,* to identify offending contact specifically, and to provide adequate notice). *See also Dailey v. Vought Aircraft Co.,* 141 F.3d 224 (5th Cir.

1998) (hearing on sanction that takes place after sanction has already been imposed violates due process).

55. *See, e.g., Kaplan v. DaimlerChrysler, Inc.,* 331 F.3d 1251, 1255 (11th Cir. 2003) (Because Rule 11(c)(1)(B) does not provide safe harbor, court must provide notice and opportunity to be heard and "a higher standard ('akin to contempt') than in the case of party-initiated sanctions.").

56. *See, e.g., Elliott v. Tilton,* 64 F.3d 213, 216 (5th Cir.1995) (noting contrast between "safe harbor" provision applicable when parties seek Rule 11 sanctions, and absence of "safe harbor" when court acts *sua sponte*). *See also In re Pennie & Edmonds, L.L.P.,* 323 F.3d 86, 87 (2d Cir. 2003) (where court decides to impose sanctions sua sponte, law firm did not have benefit of "safe harbor" provision; thus sanctions were only appropriate for subjective bad faith, not for unreasonable but genuine good faith).

57. *See, e.g., DiPaolo v. Moran,* 407 F.3d 140 (3d Cir.2005) ("Although monetary sanctions are not encouraged under Rule 11, they are not forbidden. ... We have emphasized that the main purpose of Rule 11 is to deter, not to compensate.").

change from previous versions of Rule 11, which included a substantially stronger interest in compensating parties who had been damaged by Rule 11 violations.[58]

Sanctions Available

Rule 11(c)(4) authorizes the court to issue nonmonetary orders,[59] to require payment of a penalty into court, to require payment of some or all of an opposing party's attorney's fees[60] and expenses, or any combination thereof.[61] Payment to an opposing party requires a motion by a party,[62] and is unlikely to occur unless the court believes such payment serves a deterrent purpose.[63] All of the monetary sanctions listed in Rule 11(c)(4) are subject to additional significant limitations, discussed below.

Attorney's Fees

If a sanction includes payment of an opposing party's attorney's fees or associated costs, courts generally use a "lodestar" method of

But cf., *Union Planters Bank v. L & J Development Co.* 115 F.3d 378 (6th Cir. 1997) (acknowledging general rule, but authorizing payment to injured party where sanctionable conduct was produced by bad motive).

58. *But see* 15 U.S.C.A. § 78u–4 (subject to some exceptions, when party or attorney violates Rule 11(b) in litigation controlled by Private Securities Litigation Reform Act of 1995, there is a rebuttable presumption that appropriate sanction is reasonable attorney's fees and expenses directly resulting from violation). *See also Gurary v. Nu–Tech Bio-Med, Inc.,* 303 F.3d 212, 221–22 (2d Cir.2002) (under P.S.L.R.A., substantial violation of Rule 11 requires sanction of repayment of full cost of violation to victim unless such a sanction would either be unreasonable burden or violation was de minimus; held, violation is not de minimus simply because offending complaint contains both frivolous and nonfrivolous allegations).

59. *See, e.g., Ortman v. Thomas,* 99 F.3d 807, 811 (6th Cir.1996) (rejecting permanent injunction on filing federal court lawsuit that arises out of claims alleged in, or underlying, case at bar; imposing, however, prefiling requirement mandating that, in future, sanctioned party would be required to satisfy magistrate judge that proposed claims were not frivolous or asserted for an improper purpose). *But see Tropf v. Fidelity National Title Insurance Co.,* 289 F.3d 929, 940–41 (6th Cir.2002) (approving permanent injunction against future lawsuit arising out of claims underlying instant case; applying injunction to federal and

state filings as well as administrative proceedings; distinguishing *Ortman,* supra); *Villar v. Crowley Maritime Corp.,* 990 F.2d 1489, 1498–99 (5th Cir.1993) (permanent injunction against similar lawsuits in both federal and state court).

60. *See, e.g., Claiborne v. Wisdom,* 414 F.3d 715 (7th Cir.2005) ("[S]anctions may include appropriate attorneys' fees incurred as a direct result of the violation."). *But cf., Massengale v. Ray,* 267 F.3d 1298, 1302 (11th Cir.2001) (per curiam) (pro se litigant who is also a lawyer is not entitled to attorney's fees because pro se parties, by definition, have no such fees).

61. *See, e.g., Riccard v. Prudential Life Insurance Co. of America,* 307 F.3d 1277, 1295 (11th Cir.2002) (order enjoining new actions without first obtaining leave of court was reasonable where monetary sanction would not prevent further harassment of opposing party or clogging of judicial machinery).

62. *See, e.g., Methode Electronics, Inc. v. Adam Technologies, Inc.,* 371 F.3d 923, 926 (7th Cir.2004) (if sanction is not imposed as result of motion by party but instead on court's initiative, attorney fees cannot be imposed); *Baffa v. Donaldson, Lufkin & Jenrette Securities Corp.,* 222 F.3d 52, 57 (2d Cir.2000) (attorneys' fees may be awarded only pursuant to motion; such fees may not be awarded by court on its own initiative).

63. *See, e.g., Barber v. Miller,* 146 F.3d 707 (9th Cir.1998) (if court initiates sanction, payment must be to court, not to party; payment to party appropriate only

calculating the appropriate amount. "The lodestar is determined by multiplying the number of hours reasonably expended by the reasonable hourly rate."[64] It should be noted, however, that the amount of fees recoverable from the offending party is limited to fees "incurred as a direct result of the [violation]."[65] Fees for government attorneys are calculated on the same basis as prevailing rates in the private sector.[66]

The court may not award attorney's fees under Rule 11 when sanctions are imposed sua sponte,[67] but may award attorney's fees under its inherent powers if the person being sanctioned has acted in bad faith.[68]

Nonmonetary Sanctions

Nonmonetary sanctions include dismissal unfavorable to the offender[69] or court-ordered pro bono service.[70] Under previous versions of Rule 11, nonmonetary sanctions included reprimands and suspension of an attorney.[71] Presumably these sanctions are available under the current version of Rule 11.

when sanction initiated by motion and only to serve deterrent purpose).

64. *View Engineering, Inc. v. Robotic Vision Systems, Inc.,* 208 F.3d 981, 987 n. 7 (Fed.Cir.2000). *Skidmore Energy, Inc. v. KPMG,* 455 F.3d 564, 568 (5th Cir.2006) (upheld lodestar analysis which multiplied the reasonable number of hours expended in defending the suit by the reasonable hourly rates; reasonableness of the hours expended was supported by the complexity of the litigation, the number of individual and foreign defendants, and the number of claims asserted).

65. *Divane v. Krull Electric Co.,* 200 F.3d 1020, 1030 (7th Cir.1999) (error to impose all fees incurred in litigation where at least some of such expenses are unrelated to violations of Rule 11).

66. *See, e.g., Napier v. Thirty or More Unidentified Federal Agents, Employees or Officers,* 855 F.2d 1080, 1092–93 (3d Cir. 1988) (assistant United States attorney should be billed at appropriate market rate in private sector, even in the absence of a regular billing rate for government lawyers).

67. *MHC Inv. Co.* v. *Racom Corp.,* 323 F.3d 620, 627 (8th Cir.2003).

68. *See, e.g., Willhite v. Collins,* 459 F.3d 866, 869–870 (8th Cir.2006) (upheld sanction of one half of plaintiff's attorney's fees, amounting to $66,698.30, when district court had said sanctions were under both Rule 11 and its inherent authority but did not state authority for each sanction imposed).

69. *Zocaras v. Castro,* 465 F.3d 479, 484 (11th Cir.2006).

70. *Reinhardt v. Gulf Ins. Co.,* 489 F.3d 405, 416 (1st Cir.2007) (court imposed 10 hours of pro bono service based on attorney's refusal to enter into negotiations).

71. *In the Matter of Dragoo,* 186 F.3d 614, 615–16 (5th Cir.1999) (husband and wife attorneys suspended from practice before bankruptcy court for four years; readmission conditioned upon (1) 15 hours of continuing legal education in consumer bankruptcy law, (2) submission of records of all grievance and malpractice claims brought against attorneys, and disposition of such claims, and (3) evidence of mental stability of husband, who had used depression as defense against Rule 11 sanctions; however, rejecting requirement that wife, who had indicated no mental instability, must also demonstrate mental stability). *But see, Hutchinson v. Pfeil,* 208 F.3d 1180, 1186 (10th Cir.2000) (sanctions should not be used to drive attorneys out of practice; when district court believes such remedies are appropriate, referral should be made to appropriate authorities who will ensure that attorneys receive due process); *Thornton v. General Motors Corp.,* 136 F.3d 450, 455 (5th Cir.1998) (suspension from practice before court is inappropriate sanction under Rule 11(c)(1)(B); "[W]hen a district court finds that a disciplinary sanction more severe than admonition, reprimand or censure under Rule 11 is warranted, it should refer the matter to the appropriate disciplinary authorities.").

Punitive Damages

The previous version of Rule 11 was construed to permit punitive damages when the court found that sanction appropriate.[72] It appears that under the current version of Rule 11, punitive damage payments to parties are inappropriate.

Financial Status of Offender

In assessing monetary sanctions, courts take into account the financial status of the offender. However, if the offender wants the court to know of the offender's limited ability to pay sanctions, the burden is on the offender to bring the relevant facts before the court.[73]

Alternative Remedies

Rule 11 is in addition to whatever remedies, such as censure or reprimand,[74] contempt, disciplinary complaints to a bar, Federal Rule of Appellate Procedure 38 (frivolous appeals), state claims such as abuse of process,[75] 28 U.S.C.A. § 1447(c) (expenses, including attorney's fees, for improper removal),[76] 28 U.S.C.A. § 1915(a) and (d)(frivolous filings *in forma pauperis*), and 28 U.S.C.A. § 1927 (unreasonable and vexatious multiplication of proceedings), the court or other persons may have.[77]

Duty to Mitigate

Under the previous version of Rule 11, a party seeking damages under Rule 11 must have made reasonable efforts to mitigate its losses.[78] Presumably that requirement carries over to the current

72. *See, e.g., Robeson Defense Committee v. Britt,* 132 F.R.D. 650 (E.D.N.C.1989), *affirmed in part, vacated in part on other grounds,* 914 F.2d 505 (4th Cir.1990).

73. *See, e.g., Silva v. Witschen,* 19 F.3d 725 (1st Cir.1994)(if the offender presents no such facts, the court has no duty to inquire into them).

74. *See, e.g., Thomas v. Tenneco Packaging Co.,* 293 F.3d 1306 (11th Cir.2002) (per curiam) (separate from Rule 11, district court has inherent power to sanction attorney for documents that were rude and demeaning, with no purpose except harassment and intimidation of opposing counsel). *See also Miller v. Cardinale,* 361 F.3d 539, 548 (9th Cir.2004) (noting that sanctions under court's inherent power require finding of bad faith, while imposition of Rule 11 sanctions "requires only a showing of objectively unreasonable conduct").

75. *See, e.g., U.S. Express Lines, Ltd. v. Higgins,* 281 F.3d 383, 393 (3d Cir.2002) (Federal Rules do not preempt abuse of process and similar state torts).

76. *See, e.g., Wisconsin v. Hotline Industries, Inc.,* 236 F.3d 363, 366 (7th Cir.

2000) (§ 1447(c) is alternative to Rule 11, which " 'can be used to impose a more severe sanction when appropriate.' ").

77. *Clinton v. Jones,* 520 U.S. 681, 709 n. 42, 117 S.Ct. 1636, 1652 n. 42, 137 L.Ed.2d 945 (1997) (court may apply broad array of authority, including Rule 11, 28 U.S.C.A. § 1927, and/or its inherent powers). *See also Xantech Corp. v. Ramco Industries, Inc.,* 159 F.3d 1089, 1094 (7th Cir.1998) ("[F]ee requests made under Rule 11 do not pose a res judicata bar to subsequent actions for claims akin to malicious prosecution.").

78. *See, e.g., Pollution Control Industries of America, Inc. v. Van Gundy,* 21 F.3d 152, 156 (7th Cir.1994)(aggrieved party has duty to mitigate its costs "by resolving frivolous issues quickly and efficiently"). *See also Andretti v. Borla Performance Industries, Inc.,* 426 F.3d 824, 834 (6th Cir.2005) (where both parties contributed to waste of judicial resources, no abuse of discretion to refuse to award sanctions).

Rule 11, at least as to those unusual circumstances where a party may be entitled to compensation for a violation.

(A)

Monetary Sanctions: Frivolous Arguments of Law

Rule 11(c)(5) explicitly prohibits application of monetary sanctions against a represented party for violations of Rule 11(b)(2), governing requirements that arguments for changes in law be non-frivolous.[79] Monetary sanctions obviously remain available against attorneys or non-represented parties who violate Rule 11(b)(2).

(B)

Court–Initiated Monetary Sanctions: Settlement

If the court seeks to impose monetary sanctions on its own initiative, it may not do so if its show cause order was not issued before the parties voluntarily dismissed or settled the claims. However, Rule 11(c)(5) provides no similar protection if the case goes to judgment.

Motions for Sanctions: Timing

Under the previous version of Rule 11, courts generally required that motions for sanctions be filed as soon as practicable after the alleged violation has occurred.[80] That principle carries over to the current version of Rule 11. However, courts using the previous version were divided as to whether motions may be filed after the case has ended. Under the current version of Rule 11, it appears settled that a movant's duty to offer the offending party a "safe harbor" means that an injured party may not move for sanctions after a case has ended or the court has rejected the offending contention.[81]

---

79. *See, e.g., Tropf v. Fidelity National Title Insurance Co.,* 289 F.3d 929, 939 (6th Cir.2002) ("[M]onetary sanctions may not be imposed on represented parties for the violation of subsection (b)(2) involving unwarranted legal contentions."); *Gurary v. Winehouse,* 235 F.3d 792, 797 (2d Cir.2000). *See also Baffa v. Donaldson, Lufkin & Jenrette Securities Corp.,* 222 F.3d 52, 57 (2d Cir.2000) (order to represented party to pay attorney's fees for Rule 11(b)(2) violation is abuse of discretion because it contravenes prohibition on monetary sanctions against represented parties under Rule 11(c)(2)).

80. *See, e.g., Hunter v. Earthgrains Co. Bakery,* 281 F.3d 144, 152 (4th Cir.2002) (delay of 14 months in moving for sanctions is unacceptable, even where opponent of sanctions has not alleged prejudice or lack of notice).

81. *See, e.g., Roth v. Green,* 466 F.3d 1179, 1193 (10th Cir.2006) (motion for sanctions filed after district court dismissed complaint should have been denied). *Tompkins v. Cyr,* 202 F.3d 770, 787–88 (5th Cir. 2000) (rejecting sanctions where Rule 11 motion was not filed until after conclusion of trial); *Ridder v. City of Springfield,* 109 F.3d 288 (6th Cir.1997). *But cf., Divane v. Krull Electric Co.,* 200 F.3d 1020, 1025–26 (7th Cir.1999) (initial Rule 11 motion was premature, but gave clear notice to offending party that appropriateness of motion could not be determined until, after trial, lack of evidentiary support for offending claims might be clear; result was that trial court extended period of safe harbor for duration of trial; additionally appellate court notes that "Rule 11(c)(1)(A) does not specify any time period when a motion for sanctions must be filed, and we see no need to establish one. . . . By themselves, the purposes of Rule 11(c)(1)(A) do not justify a broad rule that sanctions cannot be imposed as a result of a motion properly sub-

(3) ORDER

Order Imposing Sanctions

Rule 11(c)(6) provides that if the court imposes sanctions, it will describe the offending conduct and explain the basis for the sanction the court imposed.[82]

Rule 11(d). INAPPLICABILITY TO DISCOVERY

CORE CONCEPT

Rules 26 through 37, governing the discovery process, control the circumstances when sanctions may be imposed for inappropriate behavior in discovery. For that reason, Rule 11(d) provides that Rule 11(a), (b) and (c) have no applicability to discovery issues.[83]

ADDITIONAL RESEARCH REFERENCES

Wright & Miller, *Federal Practice and Procedure* §§ 1331–39.

C.J.S. Federal Civil Procedure §§ 260.

West's Key No. Digests, Federal Civil Procedure ⊛660–661, 2750–2848.

mitted to the court after a judgment."). By contrast, when a court initiates a sanctions process by issuing a show cause order before a plaintiff voluntarily dismisses a case, the court retains power to impose sanctions even after dismissal. *Cooter & Gell v. Hartmarx Corp.*, 496 U.S. 384, 110 S.Ct. 2447, 110 L.Ed.2d 359 (1990); *Red Carpet Studios Div. of Source Advantage, Ltd. v. Sater*, 465 F.3d 642, 645 (6th Cir.2006) (discussion of court's jurisdiction to issue sanctions under Rule 11 after judgment on the merits is dictum). *But cf., Woodard v. STP Corp.*, 170 F.3d 1043, 1045 (11th Cir.1999) (held, error for court to enter order retaining jurisdiction to impose sanctions under Rule 11 if plaintiff's attorneys bring a subsequent lawsuit in another forum; held, only court hearing subsequent lawsuit could impose such sanctions).

82. *See, e.g., Vollmer v. Publishers Clearing House*, 248 F.3d 698, 711 (7th Cir.2001) (failure to explain imposition of $50,000 sanction requires remand for explanation). *But cf., McLane, Graf, Raulerson & Middleton, P.A. v. Rechberger*, 280 F.3d 26, 44–45 (1st Cir.2002) (district court encouraged, but not required, to give rea-

sons for denying sanctions); *Anderson v. Boston School Committee*, 105 F.3d 762, 769 (1st Cir.1997) (no requirement for explicit findings explaining denial of sanctions "where the record itself, evidence or colloquy, clearly indicates one or more sufficient supporting reasons. The occasional statements referring to an inflexible requirement for explicit findings in every case do not reflect our present considered judgment.").

83. *See, e.g., Patelco Credit Union v. Sahni*, 262 F.3d 897, 913 n. 15 (9th Cir. 2001) ("Rule 11(d) specifically exempts discovery motions and objections from its procedural requirements."); *Baffa v. Donaldson, Lufkin & Jenrette Securities Corp.*, 222 F.3d 52, 57 (2d Cir.2000) (failure to answer interrogatories fully is not sanctionable under Rule 11). *But cf., Semien v. Life Insurance Co. of North America*, 436 F.3d 805, 814–15 (7th Cir.2006) (ERISA case; circuit court notes that in such cases discovery is "normally disfavored," but where it is appropriate "the district court should employ all available tools, including the imposition of Rule 11 sanctions against those who would abuse the discovery process").

RULE 12

DEFENSES AND OBJECTIONS: WHEN AND HOW PRESENTED; MOTION FOR JUDGMENT ON THE PLEADINGS; CONSOLIDATING MOTIONS; WAIVING DEFENSES; PRETRIAL HEARING

(a) Time to Serve a Responsive Pleading.

(1) *In General.* Unless another time is specified by this rule or a federal statute, the time for serving a responsive pleading is as follows:

(A) A defendant must serve an answer:

(i) within 20 days after being served with the summons and complaint; or

(ii) if it has timely waived service under Rule 4(d), within 60 days after the request for a waiver was sent, or within 90 days after it was sent to the defendant outside any judicial district of the United States.

(B) A party must serve an answer to a counterclaim or crossclaim within 20 days after being served with the pleading that states the counterclaim or crossclaim.

(C) A party must serve a reply to an answer within 20 days after being served with an order to reply, unless the order specifies a different time.

(2) *United States and Its Agencies, Officers, or Employees Sued in an Official Capacity.* The United States, a United States agency, or a United States officer or employee sued only in an official capacity must serve an answer to a complaint, counterclaim, or crossclaim within 60 days after service on the United States attorney.

(3) *United States Officers or Employees Sued in an Individual Capacity.* A United States officer or employee sued in an individual capacity for an act or omission occurring in connection with duties performed on the United States' behalf must serve an answer to a complaint, counterclaim, or crossclaim

within 60 days after service on the officer or employee or service on the United States attorney, whichever is later.

(4) *Effect of a Motion.* Unless the court sets a different time, serving a motion under this rule alters these periods as follows:

(A) if the court denies the motion or postpones its disposition until trial, the responsive pleading must be served within 10 days after notice of the court's action; or

(B) if the court grants a motion for a more definite statement, the responsive pleading must be served within 10 days after the more definite statement is served.

(b) How to Present Defenses. Every defense to a claim for relief in any pleading must be asserted in the responsive pleading if one is required. But a party may assert the following defenses by motion:

(1) lack of subject-matter jurisdiction;

(2) lack of personal jurisdiction;

(3) improper venue;

(4) insufficient process;

(5) insufficient service of process;

(6) failure to state a claim upon which relief can be granted; and

(7) failure to join a party under Rule 19.

A motion asserting any of these defenses must be made before pleading if a responsive pleading is allowed. If a pleading sets out a claim for relief that does not require a responsive pleading, an opposing party may assert at trial any defense to that claim. No defense or objection is waived by joining it with one or more other defenses or objections in a responsive pleading or in a motion.

(c) Motion for Judgment on the Pleadings. After the pleadings are closed—but early enough not to delay trial—a party may move for judgment on the pleadings.

(d) Result of Presenting Matters Outside the Pleadings. If, on a motion under Rule 12(b)(6) or 12(c), matters outside the pleadings are presented to and not excluded by the court, the motion must be treated as one for summary judgment under Rule 56. All parties must be given a reasonable opportunity to present all the material that is pertinent to the motion.

(e) Motion for a More Definite Statement. A party may move for a more definite statement of a pleading to which a responsive pleading is allowed but which is so vague or ambiguous that the party cannot reasonably prepare a response. The motion must be made before filing a responsive pleading and must point out the defects complained of and the details desired. If the court orders a more definite statement and the order is not obeyed within 10 days after notice of the order or within the time the court sets, the court may strike the pleading or issue any other appropriate order.

(f) Motion to Strike. The court may strike from a pleading an insufficient defense or any redundant, immaterial, impertinent, or scandalous matter. The court may act:

(1) on its own; or

(2) on motion made by a party either before responding to the pleading or, if a response is not allowed, within 20 days after being served with the pleading.

(g) Joining Motions.

(1) *Right to Join.* A motion under this rule may be joined with any other motion allowed by this rule.

(2) *Limitation on Further Motions.* Except as provided in Rule 12(h)(2) or (3), a party that makes a motion under this rule must not make another motion under this rule raising a defense or objection that was available to the party but omitted from its earlier motion.

(h) Waiving and Preserving Certain Defenses.

(1) *When Some Are Waived.* A party waives any defense listed in Rule 12(b)(2)–(5) by:

(A) omitting it from a motion in the circumstances described in Rule 12(g)(2); or

(B) failing to either:

(i) make it by motion under this rule; or

      (ii) include it in a responsive pleading or in an amendment allowed by Rule 15(a)(1) as a matter of course.

  (2) *When to Raise Others.* Failure to state a claim upon which relief can be granted, to join a person required by Rule 19(b), or to state a legal defense to a claim may be raised:

      (A) in any pleading allowed or ordered under Rule 7(a);

      (B) by a motion under Rule 12(c); or

      (C) at trial.

  (3) *Lack of Subject–Matter Jurisdiction.* If the court determines at any time that it lacks subject-matter jurisdiction, the court must dismiss the action.

(i) Hearing Before Trial. If a party so moves, any defense listed in Rule 12(b)(1)–(7)—whether made in a pleading or by motion—and a motion under Rule 12(c) must be heard and decided before trial unless the court orders a deferral until trial.

[Amended December 27, 1946, effective March 19, 1948; January 21, 1963, effective July 1, 1963; February 28, 1966, effective July 1, 1966; March 2, 1987, effective August 1, 1987; April 22, 1993, effective December 1, 1993; April 17, 2000, December 1, 2000; April 30, 2007, effective December 1, 2007.]

———————— **2007 AMENDMENTS ROADMAP** ————————

    STYLE PROJECT CHANGES: Some new subsectioning was added, and labels were added throughout. Timing for parties to answer counterclaims was included. The duties to convert Rule 12(b)(6) and Rule 12(c) motions to summary judgment motions when extrinsic materials are considered were consolidated into a single location, new Rule 12(d). The now-relocated language from Rules 12(b) and 12(c) was deleted. The text of old Rule 12(d), relating to pretrial hearings on defenses, was moved to new Rule 12(i). Often-confusing Rule 12(g) and Rule 12(h) were reworded for clarity. Active voice replaced passive voice; "must" replaced "shall"; "trial" replaced "trial on the merits".

    NON-STYLE CHANGES: None.

NOTE: The Federal Rules "Style Project" is explained in Part III-A.

AUTHORS' COMMENTARY ON RULE 12

──────────────── PURPOSE AND SCOPE ────────────────

Rule 12 sets the time and procedures for serving responsive pleadings, for asserting factual and legal defenses and objections, and for making preliminary motions and motions for judgment on the pleadings.

Answers to complaints generally must be served within 20 days after service of process. If a defendant waives formal service of process, the answer is due within 60 days. Answers to crossclaims and counterclaims must be served within 20 days of service. Longer periods apply to service made on the United States and federal employees or when service is made outside the country. These response periods may be modified by court-approved stipulation, by court order, or by the defendant's filing of a Rule 12 motion.

Parties generally must assert their defenses and objections in their first responsive pleadings. However, certain enumerated defenses and objections may, at the party's discretion, be raised earlier by motion. If the party chooses to file such a motion, the party must assert all enumerated defenses and objections in the same motion.

A failure to assert all defenses and objections in the responsive pleading, or alternatively, a failure to include all enumerated defenses and objections when making a Rule 12 motion, results in a waiver of certain unasserted defenses and objections.

RULE 12(a). TIME FOR SERVING RESPONSIVE PLEADINGS

CORE CONCEPT

Responsive pleadings generally must be filed within 20 days after service of the document to which they relate. If, however, the defendant waives formal service of process, the answer generally is due within 60 days after the plaintiff's request for waiver was sent.

APPLICATIONS

Answers and Replies

Unless a Rule 12 motion is filed, a party must serve an answer within 20 calendar days after being served with a summons and complaint, a counterclaim or a crossclaim. A party must serve a reply within 20 calendar days after being served with a court order directing a reply.

> *Note:* The time limitations set in this Rule run from the date of "service", not the date of "filing". Under Rule 5, a responsive pleading may be "filed" with the court within a reasonable time after service. The method for "counting" days during the Rule 12 time periods is set forth in Rule 6.

350

State Court Rules Do Not Apply

Unless, by a statute applicable to the particular lawsuit at issue, Congress has provided otherwise, the time for responding to a summons and complaint is set forth in Rule 12(a). The federal time periods apply even if the defendant is served pursuant to State law and the relevant State law would otherwise afford the defendant a longer time to reply.[1]

Exception When Formal Service of Process is Waived

The Rules encourage defendants to waive the requirement of formal service of process.[2] In return for waiving formal service, Rule 12(a)(1)(A)(ii) gives the defendant additional time to respond. If the request for waiver was mailed to a defendant within the United States, a defendant who waives formal service of process has 60 calendar days from the date the request for waiver was sent in which to serve an answer. If the request was mailed to a defendant outside the United States, a defendant who waives service has 90 calendar days from the date the request for waiver was sent in which to serve an answer. These provisions apply only to service of original process, and not to counterclaims or cross-claims.

Exception for United States and Federal Officers and Agencies

Responsive pleadings must be served within 60 calendar days by the United States, by its agencies, and by those federal officers and employees who are *either* sued in their "official" capacities or sued in their "individual" capacities for acts or omissions occurring in connection with the performance of their federal duties.[3] In "individual" capacity, "on-the-job" claim lawsuits against federal personnel, this 60–day period begins to run when the individual is served or when the United States Attorney is served, whichever is later.[4] In all other cases (lawsuits against the United States, a federal agency, or a federal officer or employee sued in an official capacity), the 60–day period begins to run when the United States Attorney is served.[5] This pleading timetable applies to both current and former federal officers and employees.[6]

> *Note:* When a pleading names as defendants both a governmental party and a non-governmental party, only the governmental party has 60 days in which to serve a responsive pleading. The non-governmental party's time for serving a responsive pleading remains 20 days.

Extension of Time by Court

The court may extend the time for serving responsive pleadings. Upon stipulation approved by the court, the parties can agree to an extension of time for serving responsive pleadings.

1. *See Beller & Keller v. Tyler*, 120 F.3d 21 (2d Cir.1997).

2. *See* Rule 4(d).

3. *See* Rule 12(a)(2).

4. *See* Rule 12(a)(3).

5. *See* Rule 12(a)(2)(A).

6. *See* Rule 12(a)(3) advisory committee notes to 2000 amendments.

Tolling Effect of Rule 12(b) Motion, Generally

Rule 12(b) motions must be filed before a responsive pleading (because, by their nature, the relief sought by such motions is a pre-answer dismissal of the claim).[7] The act of serving a Rule 12(b) motion ordinarily suspends the party's time for serving a responsive pleading,[8] and that tolling will usually continue to run until the court has ruled on the pending motion.[9] Thereafter, the time for the delayed responsive pleading is as follows:

- If the court's order on the motion denies relief or postpones resolving the motion until trial, the responsive pleading must be served within 10 days after "notice" of the court's action,[10]

- If the court's order resolves a motion for more definite statement (Rule 12(e)) by requiring a clearer claim, the responsive pleading to the more definite statement must be served within 10 days after service of the more definite statement.[11]

If service is made on a party by mail or by any of Rule 5's service-by-consent methods, these 10–day periods are extended further by 3 extra days.[12] The court may, however, deviate from these timing rules entirely by setting a different schedule of its own.[13]

Exceptions to Tolling Effect Rule

The tolling effect of a pending Rule 12(b) motion may be altered (or eliminated completely) in the following circumstances:

- *Motion by Other Defendant:* The tolling effect of a pending Rule 12(b) motion does not inure to the benefit of all defendants; only those defendants who file a Rule 12(b) motion receive the tolling.[14]

7. *See* 12(b) (noting that Rule 12(b) motions "must be made before pleading if a responsive pleading is allowed").

8. *See* Rule 12(a)(4).

9. *But cf. Hill v. Blue Cross & Blue Shield of Mich.,* 237 F.R.D. 613, 616–17 (E.D.Mich. 2006) (to resolve longstanding delays in case, court strikes motion to dismiss, without prejudice, and orders defendant to file its answer).

10. *See* Rule 12(a)(4)(A). Neither the Advisory Committee Notes nor published case law have expositively defined when a party is deemed to have received "notice" of such a court order within the meaning of Rule 12(a)(4)(A) (*e.g.,* when the order is docketed, when it arrives at counsel's office or the party's home, when counsel or the party actually sees it, etc.). The sparse case law references to this section either offer no substantive guidance at all or use language that appears directly inconsistent with the

plain terms of the Rule itself. *See, e.g., United States v. $57,960.00 in U.S. Currency,* 58 F.Supp.2d 660, 668 (D.S.C.1999) (citing Rule as requiring party to file an answer within 10 days "of being served" with the denial order); *Ziegler v. Ziegler,* 28 F.Supp.2d 601, 620 (E.D.Wash.1998) (citing Rules as requiring party to file an answer within 10 days "after receipt" of denial order); *United States v. Ware,* 172 F.R.D. 458, 459 (D.Kan.1997) (citing Rule as mandating that party file an answer within ten days "after the court's denial" of the motion); *Johnson-Medland v. Bethanna,* 1996 WL 612467, at *6 (E.D.Pa.1996) (citing Rule as requiring party to serve an answer within 10 days "of the date of this order").

11. *See* Rule 12(a)(4)(B).

12. *See* Rule 6(d).

13. *See* Rule 12(a)(4).

14. *See Hanley v. Volpe,* 48 F.R.D. 387, 387–88 (E.D.Wis.1970).

- *Motions Filed Against Amended Pleadings:* It is not clear whether a party who files a Rule 12(b) motion to an amended pleading is entitled to a new tolling period. One court has ruled that there may be no tolling under this situation, and the moving party may be obligated to file its responsive pleading even while its motion is pending.[15]

- *Motions Converted to Summary Judgment Motions:* When materials outside the pleadings are presented with a Rule 12(b) motion (and not excluded by the court), the Rule 12(b) motion generally must be converted to a Rule 56 motion for summary judgment.[16] Rule 12(b) motions receive the tolling effect; Rule 56 motions do not. One court has decided that when a Rule 12(b) motion converts under these circumstances, the tolling effect will still apply.[17]

- *Partial Motions:* It now seems fairly settled that a party who files a Rule 12(b) motion to a portion, but not all, of a pending pleading (*e.g.*, motion to dismiss counts I, III, and VI) will have a tolling of its entire responsive pleading obligation. The very substantial majority of the courts to have considered the question favor a complete tolling,[18] although a minority and some practitioner commentary favor the view that the responding party must serve an interim responsive pleading to all unchallenged portions.[19]

15. See *General Mills, Inc. v. Kraft Foods Global, Inc.*, 487 F.3d 1368, 1376–77 (Fed.Cir. 2007), *modified on reh'g*, 495 F.3d 1378 (Fed.Cir. 2007). The 2007 amendments to Rule 15(a) may have diminished the effect of this decision by replacing the party's duty to "plead in response" with the newly worded duty to supply "any required response". *See* Rule 15(a)(3).

16. *See* Rule 12(d).

17. *See Marquez v. Cable One, Inc.*, 463 F.3d 1118, 1120–21 (10th Cir. 2006).

18. *See Ideal Instruments, Inc. v. Rivard Instruments, Inc.*, 434 F.Supp.2d 598, 637–40 (N.D.Iowa 2006) (following majority approach, and holding that motion to dismiss suspends time for responding to all portions of complaint, even unchallenged ones). *Accord Godlewski v. Affiliated Computer Servs., Inc.*, 210 F.R.D. 571, 572–73 (E.D.Va.2002); *Rosa v. California Bd of Accountancy*, 2005 WL 1899515 (E.D.Cal. 2005); *Batdorf v. Trans Union*, 2000 WL 635455 (N.D.Cal.2000); *Finnegan v. University of Rochester Med. Ctr.*, 180 F.R.D. 247, 249–50 (W.D.N.Y.1998); *Schwartz v. Berry College, Inc.*, 1997 WL 579166 (N.D.Ga. 1997) (same); *Oil Express Nat'l, Inc. v. D'Alessandro*, 173 F.R.D. 219, 221 (N.D.Ill. 1997); *Alex. Brown & Sons Inc. v. Marine Midland Banks, Inc.*, 1997 WL 97837

(S.D.N.Y.1997); *Porter v. United States Dep't of Army*, 1995 WL 461898 (N.D.Ill. 1995), *aff'd*, 99 F.3d 1142 (7th Cir.1996) (Table); *Becker v. Fitzgerald*, 1995 WL 215143 (N.D.Ill.1995); *Circuit City Stores, Inc. v. Citgo Petroleum Corp.*, 1994 WL 483463 (E.D.Pa.1994); *Rawson v. Royal Maccabees Life Ins. Co.*, 1994 WL 9638 (N.D.Ill.1994); *Brocksopp Eng'g, Inc. v. Bach–Simpson, Ltd.*, 136 F.R.D. 485, 486–87 (E.D.Wis.1991); *Ricciuti v. New York City Transit Auth.*, 1991 WL 221110 (S.D.N.Y.1991); *Baker v. Universal Die Casting, Inc.*, 725 F.Supp. 416, 420–21 (W.D.Ark.1989); *Business Incentives Co. v. Sony Corp. of America*, 397 F.Supp. 63 (S.D.N.Y.1975).

19. *See Gerlach v. Michigan Bell Tel. Co.*, 448 F.Supp. 1168 (E.D.Mich. 1978)(holding that responsive pleading was required to unchallenged counts, refusing to enter default, but awarding plaintiffs attorney fees for filing for default). *See also Okaya (USA), Inc. v. United States*, 2003 WL 22284567, at *5 (CIT 2003) (noting that that motion to dismiss part of a complaint did not extend time to answer remainder). *See generally* Scott L. Cagan, *A "Partial" Motion to Dismiss Under Federal Rule of Civil Procedure 12: You Had Better Answer*, 39 Fed.B.J. 202 (1992)(advocating

- *Appellate Remands:* It is also not clear how much time a defendant has to responsively plead if an appellate court reverses a Rule 12(b) motion the trial court had granted. One court has held that, in the absence of any guidance in the Rules themselves, a defendant should receive a 20–day period.[20]

Manipulative Motions and Tolling Effect

Courts will not tolerate the use of this Rule 12 tolling feature in attempts to frivolously manipulate the time period for responsive pleading. Thus, for example, the tolling rule will not apply where a motion for summary judgment is deliberately mislabeled as a Rule 12 motion solely to avoid the obligation to file an answer.[21]

RULE 12(b). DEFENSES AND OBJECTIONS

CORE CONCEPT

All legal and factual defenses to a claim for relief must be asserted in the responsive pleading to the claim. However, seven enumerated defenses may alternatively be asserted by motion served before the responsive pleading is due (normally 20 days from service of the initial pleading or 60 days with waiver of service).

APPLICATIONS

Enumerated Defenses

As to the following seven defenses, a party may assert the defense either in the responsive pleading or by motion served before the responsive pleading is due:

- Lack of Subject Matter Jurisdiction, Rule 12(b)(1).

- Lack of Personal ("In Personam") Jurisdiction, Rule 12(b)(2).

- Improper Venue, Rule 12(b)(3).

- Insufficient Process, Rule 12(b)(4).

- Insufficient Service of Process, Rule 12(b)(5).

- Failure to State a Claim for which Relief Can Be Granted, Rule 12(b)(6).

---

same result). *But see Tingley Sys., Inc. v. CSC Consulting, Inc.*, 152 F.Supp.2d 95, 122 (D.Mass.2001) (noting that "no court has relied on [*Gerlach*'s] reasoning or followed its ruling" and that "one court explicitly rejected its reasoning").

20. *See Greenberg v. National Geographic Soc'y*, 488 F.3d 1331, 1340–41 & 1340 n.12 (11th Cir. 2007) (granting 20 days, although noting counsel had not argued to apply the 10–day period of Rule 12(a)(4)(A)).

21. *See Ricke v. Armco, Inc.*, 158 F.R.D. 149, 150 (D.Minn.1994)("Such an attempt to manipulate the Federal Rules of Civil Procedure should not be condoned or encouraged by the Court"). *See also RTC v. Ruggiero*, 994 F.2d 1221 (7th Cir. 1993)(holding that frivolous motion under Rule 12 buys the movant no additional time within which to serve a responsive pleading).

• Failure to Join a Party Under Rule 19 (persons needed for just adjudication), Rule 12(b)(7).

Waived Defenses and Objections

If a party chooses to assert a Rule 12 motion, the party must join all Rule 12 defenses and objections in that motion. If the party makes a Rule 12 motion but omits a potential Rule 12 objection to (2) personal jurisdiction, (3) venue, (4) process, or (5) service, that objection is waived and cannot be asserted later in the responsive pleading or in a subsequent motion or trial objection.[22]

Time for Making Motion

A party who intends to assert a Rule 12 defense or objection in a pre-answer motion must do so before the responsive pleading is due.[23] This requires Rule 12 motions to be served generally within 20 calendar days after service of the complaint, cross-claim, or counterclaim to which the motions are directed; defendant who waives formal service of process is given 60 calendar days in which to respond.[24] The parties can, upon court approval, stipulate to an extension of time. Moreover, although the time for filing a Rule 12 motion is logistically tied to the time for filing an answer, a delay in filing such a motion may, under certain circumstances, still be permitted.[25]

Note: Where a responsive pleading is not required, the responding party's defenses and objections can be asserted at trial.[26]

Amended Pleadings

When litigants amend their pleadings, the responding parties may withdraw their answers or replies, and replead. If an amendment adds new matter that gives rise to a new, previously inapplicable Rule 12 motion, the responding party may assert the new Rule 12 defense by motion or responsive pleading.[27]

Note: An amendment does not give the responding party an entirely new opportunity to assert Rule 12 defenses. A possible Rule 12 defense that was not asserted to the original pleading (and, thus, was waived) cannot be revived and asserted to the amended pleading unless it relates to new matter added by the amendment.[28]

Preliminary Motions Not Listed in Rule 12

Rule 12 does not provide an exhaustive list of all possible

---

22. *See* Rule 12(h).

23. *See* Rule 12(b).

24. *See* Rule 12(a).

25. *See Luv N' Care, Ltd. v. Babelito, S.A.*, 306 F.Supp.2d 468, 468–73 (S.D.N.Y. 2004) (ruling that motion was not waived where delay was explained by settlement discussions and certain service complications).

26. *See* Rule 12(b).

27. *But see supra* Authors' Commentary to Rule 12(a) ("**Exceptions to Tolling Effect Rule**") (such motions to amended pleadings might *not* entitle the moving party to tolling).

28. *See Sohns v. Dahl*, 392 F.Supp. 1208, 1220 n. 7 (W.D.Va.1975).

preliminary motions.[29] Motions for extensions of time, to amend a pleading, to intervene, to substitute parties, or for the entering of a stay or an order commanding the posting of security, may all be raised as preliminary motions. The court's broad discretion and the federal policy against unwarranted, dilatory motions are the principal limitations on such unenumerated motions.

Form of Motion

Rule 12 provides only sparse guidance on the form and procedure for federal motion practice.[30] The other Rules provide some additional detail. For example, Rule 7 requires that motions generally be in writing, include a caption, state with particularity the basis for the motion, and request specific relief.[31] Rule 5 requires that motions be served upon each party to the litigation and be filed within a reasonable time after service.[32] Rule 11 mandates that all motions be signed and be presented for only proper, legally-warranted, factually-warranted purposes.[33] Rule 78 provides for the hearing and disposition of motions, and provides that the district court, by rule or order, may permit motions to be submitted and determined on the papers only, without oral argument.[34]

Most of the other details of federal motion practice and procedure are governed by local court rules.[35] Practitioners are strongly cautioned: these details often vary greatly from one judicial district to another. For example:

> *Pre-Filing Consultation:* Some districts require that the moving party meet and confer with the adversary prior to filing any motion, and then certify—in a manner subjecting the movant to sanctions—that good faith attempts to resolve the motion before filing have failed.[36]

> *Form of Order Required:* Some districts require that the moving party include with the motion a blank form of order which, if signed by the judge, would grant the relief that the movant requests.[37]

---

29. *See Custom Vehicles, Inc. v. Forest River, Inc.,* 464 F.3d 725, 727 (7th Cir. 2006) ("Motions may be proper despite the lack of a specific rule"); *International Ass'n of Entrepreneurs of America v. Angoff,* 58 F.3d 1266, 1271 (8th Cir.1995)(commenting that although Rule 12(b) ostensibly enumerates available pre-answer motions, the district courts have discretion to permit other, unenumerated pre-answer motions).

30. *See, e.g.,* Rule 12(b) (enumerating types of pre-answer motions; requiring motion before answer; permitting extrinsic materials to be submitted on converted motions).

31. *See* Rule 7(b)(1).

32. *See* Rule 5(a)-(b) (duty to serve); Rule 5(d) (duty to file).

33. *See* Rule 11.

34. *See* Rule 78.

35. *See* Rule 83(a) (authorizing districts to establish local rules of practice).

36. *See, e.g.,* D. Colo. Loc. R. 7.1.A. (pre-filing meet and confer duty); E.D. Mich. Loc. R. 7.1(a) (duty to seek concurrence in motion); D. Or. Loc. R. 7.1(a) (good faith certification requirement); M.D. Pa. Loc. R. 7.1 (certification of concurrence / non-concurrence obligation).

37. *See, e.g.,* D. Idaho Loc. R. 7.1(a)(1) (requiring proposed order under certain circumstances); E.D. Pa. Loc. R. 7.1(a) (every motion must be accompanied by form of order); W.D. Pa. Loc. R. 7.1(B) (motion improper if proposed order is not included);

Legal Memorandum Required: Some districts require that a brief or legal memorandum accompany the motion.[38]

Page Limits: Many districts set formal page limits that must be followed strictly, unless leave of court is sought and granted for the filing of a longer document.[39]

Oral Argument: Some districts establish a formal procedure for seeking oral argument on a motion.[40]

Miscellaneous Requirements: Local rules provide a myriad of other requirements, varying from district to district. For example, some districts dictate the number of copies of each motion or memorandum that must be submitted. Some districts require that the motion or memorandum begin with a formal statement of the exact legal question presented for the court's decision.[41] Other districts require that, under the signature line, attorneys identify themselves by attorney registration or identification numbers.

Because these types of significant differences abound, practitioners must carefully consult their district's local rules before engaging in motion practice.

Time for / Form of Response to Motion

Likewise, the Federal Rules provide very little guidance on the practice and procedure for responding to motions. This detail is also almost always governed by the district's local rules of practice, which may establish requirements regarding:

Time for Responding: Many districts require non-moving parties to file their opposition papers within a certain number of days after *either* the filing of or service of the motion.[42]

Forms of Order: Some districts require that the non-moving party include a form of order which, if signed by the judge, would deny or modify the relief sought in the pending motion.[43]

Page Limits: Many districts establish page limits for opposition papers.[44]

W.D. Tenn. Loc. R. 7.2(a)(1)(A) (all motions must be accompanied by form of order).

38. *See, e.g.,* E.D. Pa. Loc. R. 7.1(c); D.R.I. Loc. R. 7(a); D.S.C. Loc. R. 7.04.

39. *See, e.g.,* M.D. Pa. Loc. R. 7.8(b) (requiring double-spaced briefs limited to 15 pages); D.S.C. Loc. R. 7.05(B)(1) (35 page limit for initial brief); E.D. Tenn. Loc. R. 7.1(b) (25 page limit for initial brief).

40. *See, e.g.,* D.Az. Loc. R. 7.2(f) (request made by notation directly on motion or response); D.S.D. Loc. R. 7.1 (request made either in conclusion of motion or by separate pleading); D. Utah Loc. R. 7.1(f) (oral argument only granted for "good cause shown").

41. *See, e.g.,* M.D. Pa. Loc. R. 7.8(a).

42. *See, e.g.,* Alaska Loc. R. 7.1(e) (opposition due within 15 days after service of motion); D.S.C. Loc. R. 7.06 (opposition due within 15 days after motion is filed); E.D. Tenn. Loc. R. 7.1(a) (opposition to dispositive motion due within 20 days of service); E.D. Va. Loc. R. 7(F)(1) (opposition due within 11 days of service).

43. *See, e.g.,* E.D. Pa. Loc. R. 7.1(a); W.D. Tenn. Loc. R. 7.2(a)(2).

44. *See, e.g.,* D. Az. Loc. R. 7.2(e) (opposition brief limited to 15 pages); M.D. Fla. Loc. R. 3.01(b) (opposition brief limited to 20 pages); D. Vt. Loc. R. 7.1(a)(4) (opposi-

Reply Briefs: Some districts permit the moving party to file a reply brief, so long as the reply is filed within a prescribed period after filing or service of the opposition papers.[45] Local rules may also set reply brief page limits.[46]

Because these response provisions vary so greatly from judicial district to judicial district, non-moving parties must also take care to consult the district's local rules before responding to a pending motion.

Liberal Reading of Motions

Liberality applies to motions to dismiss. A motion to dismiss will not generally be rejected merely because it fails to specify which particular Rule it invokes.[47] Nevertheless, careful practitioners will ensure that the court is accurately focused on the precise nature of the motion's attack.

RULE 12(b)(1). DISMISSAL FOR LACK OF SUBJECT MATTER JURISDICTION

CORE CONCEPT

A case will be dismissed under this provision if the court lacks the statutory authority to hear and decide the dispute (*e.g.,* if there is no federal question at issue, if the parties are not completely diverse, or if the amount in controversy does not exceed $75,000).

APPLICATIONS

Types of Challenges

A claim can be challenged under this provision both facially and substantively.[48] On a *facial* challenge, the defendant contests the adequacy of the language used in the pleading.[49] The pleader is required to formally aver the basis for jurisdiction in federal court; if

---

tion to dispositive motions limited to 25 pages); D. Wyo. Loc. R. 7.1(b)(2)(B) (same).

45. *See, e.g.,* D. Neb. Loc. R. 7.1(c) (reply briefs must be filed within 5 days after opposition brief is filed and served); D.S.C. Loc. R. 7.07 (reply briefs are "discouraged", but may be filed within 5 days after service of the opposition); N.D. Tex. Loc. R. 7.1(f) (reply briefs must be filed within 15 days after opposition is filed). *But see* M.D. Fla. Loc. R. 3.01(b) (no reply briefs permitted absent leave of court); D.N.H. Loc. R. 7.1(e) (no reply briefs to nondispositive motions).

46. *See, e.g.,* E.D. Mich. Loc. R. 7.1(c) (reply briefs limited to 5 pages); N.D. Tex. Loc. R. 7.2(c) (reply briefs limited to 10 pages); D. Utah Loc. R. 7.1(b)(3) (same).

47. *See Travel All Over the World, Inc. v. Kingdom of Saudi Arabia,* 73 F.3d 1423, 1429 (7th Cir.1996).

48. *See Gould Elecs. Inc. v. United States,* 220 F.3d 169 (3d Cir.2000) (discussing differences between facial and factual subject matter jurisdiction attacks). *See also Arbaugh v. Y&H Corp.,* 546 U.S. 500, 126 S.Ct. 1235, 1240, 163 L.Ed.2d 1097 (2006); *Petruska v. Gannon Univ.,* 462 F.3d 294, 302 (3d Cir. 2006).

49. *See United States ex rel. Atkinson v. PA. Shipbuilding Co.,* 473 F.3d 506, 514 (3d Cir. 2007); *Paper, Allied–Indus., Chem. & Energy Workers Int'l Union v. Continental Carbon Co.,* 428 F.3d 1285, 1292 (10th Cir. 2005); *Wolfe v. Strankman,* 392 F.3d 358, 362 (9th Cir.2004).

the pleader fails to do so, the pleading can be dismissed.[50] On a *substantive* challenge, the defendant objects to the factual merits of the asserted federal jurisdiction.[51] In such a challenge, the pleading itself may have adequately alleged the presence of federal subject matter jurisdiction, but the actual facts and allegations before the court may belie that averment, confirming that federal jurisdiction is absent and, thus, compelling the case's dismissal.[52]

Timing & Waiver

Verifying its subject matter jurisdiction is a federal court's "first duty" in every case.[53] Consequently, challenges to subject matter jurisdiction may be raised at any time, by any party, or by the court.[54] Such challenges can even be raised after final judgment is entered.[55] A party cannot waive or forfeit the requirement of subject matter jurisdiction,[56] nor can the parties consent to have a case heard in federal court where subject matter jurisdiction is absent.[57] A Rule 12(b) motion challenging subject matter jurisdiction questions the "very power" of the court to hear the case.[58]

Sua Sponte Dismissals

It is well established that dismissals for lack of subject matter jurisdiction may be ordered *sua sponte* by the trial court or even by a subsequent appeals court.[59] Indeed, courts have an independent obligation to confirm that subject matter jurisdiction is present, whether an objection on that ground is made or not.[60]

Burden of Proof

When a defendant challenges subject matter jurisdiction, the plaintiff (as the party asserting the existence of jurisdiction) must bear the burden of establishing jurisdiction.[61] The plaintiff must

50. *See Gibbs v. Buck,* 307 U.S. 66, 59 S.Ct. 725, 83 L.Ed. 1111 (1939). *See also Valentin v. Hospital Bella Vista,* 254 F.3d 358, 363–64 (1st Cir.2001).

51. *See Paper, Allied–Indus., Chem. & Energy Workers Int'l Union v. Continental Carbon Co.,* 428 F.3d 1285, 1292 (10th Cir. 2005); *Savage v. Glendale Union High Sch.,* 343 F.3d 1036, 1039 n.2 (9th Cir.2003).

52. *See Gibbs v. Buck,* 307 U.S. 66, 59 S.Ct. 725, 83 L.Ed. 1111 (1939); *Scarfo v. Ginsberg,* 175 F.3d 957, 960–61 (11th Cir. 1999); *United States v. North Carolina,* 180 F.3d 574, 580 (4th Cir.1999).

53. *See McCready v. White,* 417 F.3d 700, 702 (7th Cir.2005).

54. *See Sucampo Pharms., Inc. v. Astellas Pharma, Inc.,* 471 F.3d 544, 548–49 (4th Cir. 2006); *Taliaferro v. Darby Twp. Zoning Bd.,* 458 F.3d 181 (3d Cir.2006); *Paper, Allied–Indus., Chem. & Energy Workers Int'l Union v. Continental Carbon Co.,* 428 F.3d 1285, 1292 (10th Cir.2005).

55. *See Arbaugh v. Y&H Corp.,* 546 U.S. 500, ___, 126 S.Ct. 1235, 1240, 163 L.Ed.2d 1097 (2006). *See also* Rule 60(b)(4).

56. *See Arbaugh v. Y&H Corp.,* 546 U.S. 500, ___, 126 S.Ct. 1235, 1244, 163 L.Ed.2d 1097 (2006); *Sucampo Pharms., Inc. v. Astellas Pharma, Inc.,* 471 F.3d 544, 548–49 (4th Cir. 2006); *Nesbit v. Gears Unlimited, Inc.,* 347 F.3d 72, 76–77 (3d Cir.2003).

57. *See Neirbo Co. v. Bethlehem Shipbuilding Corp.,* 308 U.S. 165, 60 S.Ct. 153, 84 L.Ed. 167 (1939); *Laughlin v. Kmart Corp.,* 50 F.3d 871, 873 (10th Cir.1995).

58. *See Petruska v. Gannon Univ.,* 462 F.3d 294, 302 (3d Cir. 2006).

59. *See Arbaugh v. Y&H Corp.,* 546 U.S. 500, ___, 126 S.Ct. 1235, 1240, 163 L.Ed.2d 1097 (2006).

60. *See Arbaugh v. Y&H Corp.,* 546 U.S. 500, ___, 126 S.Ct. 1235, 1244, 163 L.Ed.2d 1097 (2006).

61. *See Thomson v. Gaskill,* 315 U.S. 442, 62 S.Ct. 673, 86 L.Ed. 951 (1942);

carry this burden by a preponderance of the evidence.[62] The burden, however, is generally not a heavy one.[63] In federal question cases, the party must demonstrate a non-frivolous claim based on federal law,[64] and must meet all other statutory prerequisites for litigating the federal claim (such as exhaustion of administrative remedies and compliance with all claims-filing limitations and requirements).[65] In diversity cases, the party must demonstrate complete diversity of citizenship[66] and a claim that in good faith exceeds $75,000, exclusive of interest and costs.[67] In all cases, the lawsuit must remain a live "case or controversy" subject to the federal courts' judicial power under Article III of the Constitution.[68]

Lujan v. Defenders of Wildlife, 504 U.S. 555, 561, 112 S.Ct. 2130, 2136, 119 L.Ed.2d 351 (1992); *Hamm v. United States*, 483 F.3d 135, 137 (2d Cir. 2007); *Merida Delgado v. Gonzales*, 428 F.3d 916, 919 (10th Cir.2005).

62. *See Hamm v. United States*, 483 F.3d 135, 137 (2d Cir. 2007); *Toxgon Corp. v. BNFL, Inc.*, 312 F.3d 1379, 1383 (Fed. Cir.2002).

63. *See Garcia v. Copenhaver, Bell & Assocs.*, 104 F.3d 1256, 1260–61 (11th Cir. 1997) ("extremely difficult" to dismiss claim for lacking subject matter jurisdiction); *Musson Theatrical, Inc. v. Federal Express Corp.*, 89 F.3d 1244, 1248 (6th Cir. 1996), *amended on denial of rehearing*, 1998 WL 117980 (6th Cir.1998) (plaintiff's burden not onerous). *See also Michigan So. R.R. v. Branch & St. Joseph Counties Rail Users Ass'n*, 287 F.3d 568, 573 (6th Cir. 2002) (commenting that claim will generally survive motion to dismiss if plaintiff shows "any arguable basis in law" for claims alleged).

64. *See Neitzke v. Williams*, 490 U.S. 319, 327 n. 6, 109 S.Ct. 1827, 1832 n. 6, 104 L.Ed.2d 338 (1989)(noting that a patently insubstantial complaint may be dismissed for want of subject matter jurisdiction); *Hagans v. Lavine*, 415 U.S. 528, 536–37, 94 S.Ct. 1372, 1378–79, 39 L.Ed.2d 577 (1974) (commenting that federal courts lack power to hear cases otherwise within their jurisdiction but which are "so attenuated and unsubstantial" as to be clearly devoid of merit); *Bell v. Hood*, 327 U.S. 678, 682–83, 66 S.Ct. 773, 776, 90 L.Ed. 939 (1946)(observing that actions may sometimes be dismissed for lack of jurisdiction where the federal claim "clearly appears to be immaterial and made solely for the purpose of obtaining jurisdiction or where such a claim is wholly insubstantial and frivolous"). *Cf. Boock v. Shalala*, 48 F.3d 348, 353 (8th Cir.1995)(holding that federal

claims, although "clearly meritless", were not so patently frivolous that they failed to confer subject matter jurisdiction); *Health Cost Controls v. Skinner*, 44 F.3d 535 (7th Cir.1995)(holding that subject matter dismissal is proper only where allegations are frivolous). Allegations that fail to meet the "frivolous" test warranting dismissal under Rule 12(b)(1) may nevertheless still be dismissed under Rule 12(b)(6) for failing to state a cognizable claim for relief.

65. *See Hart v. Department of Labor*, 116 F.3d 1338 (10th Cir.1997) (analyzing under Rule 12(b)(1) the defense that plaintiff failed to file timely claim with proper agency as required by the Federal Tort Claims Act). Whether the *Feres* doctrine applies (barring lawsuits against the United States where the alleged injury was incident to military service) is also tested under Rule 12(b)(1).

66. *See City of Indianapolis v. Chase Nat'l Bank*, 314 U.S. 63, 62 S.Ct. 15, 86 L.Ed. 47 (1941).

67. *See St. Paul Mercury Indem. Co. v. Red Cab Co.*, 303 U.S. 283, 58 S.Ct. 586, 82 L.Ed. 845 (1938)(ruling that dismissal only proper where it appears, to a "legal certainty", that claim is truly for less than the jurisdictional amount); *NLFC, Inc. v. Devcom Mid–America, Inc.*, 45 F.3d 231, 237 (7th Cir.1995) (noting that amount in controversy alleged, in good faith, by plaintiff is decisive as to jurisdictional amount, unless it appears to a legal certainty that the true claim falls below the [then-applicable] $50,000 threshold).

68. *See Bateman v. City of West Bountiful*, 89 F.3d 704, 706 (10th Cir. 1996)(ripeness challenges are examined under Rule 12(b)(1)); *Super Sack Mfg. Corp. v. Chase Packaging Corp.*, 57 F.3d 1054 (Fed.Cir.1995)(Rule 12(b)(1) motion granted where actual controversy had been re-

Legal Test

In evaluating technical (or facial) subject matter jurisdiction attacks, the court ordinarily construes the complaint liberally, accepts all uncontroverted, well-pleaded factual allegations as true, and views all reasonable inferences in plaintiff's favor.[69] The court views the allegations as a whole; if a conclusory averment of subject matter jurisdiction is contradicted by other allegations in the pleading, the case may be dismissed.[70] Whether subject matter jurisdiction exists is tested as of the date the lawsuit was filed.[71]

Conversely, in the case of factual (or substantive) subject matter jurisdiction attacks, the court will *not* presume that plaintiff's factual allegations are true,[72] and will not accept conclusory allegations as true[73] but may instead weigh the evidence before it and find the facts, so long as this factfinding does not involve the merits of the dispute.[74] In doing so, the court enjoys broad discretion. The court may receive and consider extrinsic evidence.[75] The court must permit the pleader to respond with supporting evidence and, where necessary, may convene an evidentiary hearing or plenary trial to find the facts.[76] Whether a hearing *must* be held or not depends on the circumstances, and whether the parties have otherwise received notice and a fair opportunity to be heard.[77] A central consideration in whether to convene such a hearing is whether any of the parties

moved and the remaining issues had been rendered moot).

69. *See Scheuer v. Rhodes,* 416 U.S. 232, 94 S.Ct. 1683, 40 L.Ed.2d 90 (1974); *Ballentine v. United States,* 486 F.3d 806, 810 (3d Cir. 2007); *Paper, Allied–Indus., Chem. & Energy Workers Int'l Union v. Continental Carbon Co.,* 428 F.3d 1285, 1292 (10th Cir.2005). *See also Valhal Corp. v. Sullivan Assocs., Inc.,* 48 F.3d 760 (3d Cir.1995)(observing that the threshold necessary to withstand Rule 12(b)(1) scrutiny is lower than that necessary to survive dismissal under Rule 12(b)(6)).

70. *See Gibbs v. Buck,* 307 U.S. 66, 59 S.Ct. 725, 83 L.Ed. 1111 (1939); *New Mexicans for Bill Richardson v. Gonzales,* 64 F.3d 1495, 1499 (10th Cir.1995).

71. *See Grupo Dataflux v. Atlas Global Group, L.P.,* 541 U.S. 567, 574, 124 S.Ct. 1920, 1925, 158 L.Ed.2d 866 (2004); *Conolly v. Taylor,* 27 U.S. (2 Pet.) 556, 7 L.Ed. 518 (1829) (Marshall, C.J.); *Rosa v. Resolution Trust Corp.,* 938 F.2d 383, 392 n. 12 (3d Cir.1991).

72. *See Nesbit v. Gears Unlimited, Inc.,* 347 F.3d 72, 77 (3d Cir.2003); *APWU v. Potter,* 343 F.3d 619, 623 (2d Cir.2003); *Sizova v. National Inst. of Standards & Tech.,* 282 F.3d 1320, 1324 (10th Cir.2002).

73. *See Zappia Middle East Const. Co. v. Emirate of Abu Dhabi,* 215 F.3d 247, 253 (2d Cir.2000).

74. *See McCann v. Newman Irrevocable Trust,* 458 F.3d 281 (3d Cir.2006); *See Hernandez-Santiago v. Ecolab, Inc.,* 397 F.3d 30, 33 (1st Cir.2005); *DLX, Inc. v. Kentucky,* 381 F.3d 511, 516 (6th Cir.2004); *Coalition for Underground Expansion v. Mineta,* 333 F.3d 193, 198 (D.C.Cir.2003).

75. *See Hamm v. United States,* 483 F.3d 135, 137 (2d Cir. 2007); *United States ex rel. Atkinson v. PA. Shipbuilding Co.,* 473 F.3d 506, 514 (3d Cir. 2007); *Hernandez-Santiago v. Ecolab, Inc.,* 397 F.3d 30, 33 (1st Cir.2005); *Savage v. Glendale Union High Sch.,* 343 F.3d 1036, 1039 n.2 (9th Cir.2003); *Coalition for Underground Expansion v. Mineta,* 333 F.3d 193, 198 (D.C.Cir.2003).

76. *See McCann v. Newman Irrevocable Trust,* 458 F.3d 281 (3d Cir.2006); *Skwira v. United States,* 344 F.3d 64, 71–72 (1st Cir.2003); *Turicentro, S.A. v. American Airlines Inc.,* 303 F.3d 293, 300 n.4 (3d Cir. 2002); *United Tribe of Shawnee Indians v. United States,* 253 F.3d 543, 546 (10th Cir. 2001).

77. *McCann v. Newman Irrevocable Trust,* 458 F.3d 281 (3d Cir.2006).

have requested it.[78] Moreover, if a material fact concerning jurisdiction is disputed, a plenary hearing may be necessary to resolve the contested issue.[79]

If the merits are implicated by the jurisdictional challenge, the court will treat the motion as any other substantive challenge to the merits of the dispute, constrained by the limitations of summary judgment practice and reserving the resolution of genuine issues of material fact for the ultimate factfinder.[80] Such a treatment is appropriate when the jurisdictional issue is so "intertwined" with the merits that the two cannot be separated.[81]

Allowing Jurisdictional Discovery

When a defendant moves to dismiss for lack of subject matter jurisdiction, discovery of the factual issues implicated by the motion may be permitted.[82] This is especially true where the discovery seeks information peculiarly within the knowledge of the adversary.[83] Although the trial judge enjoys broad discretion in resolving such motions, a refusal to grant jurisdictional discovery may constitute an abuse of discretion if it prejudices the plaintiff.[84]

Mislabeled Motions

Provided no prejudice is caused, courts often excuse a mislabeling of a Rule 12(b)(1) motion as a Rule 12(b)(6) failure to state a claim motion, and *vice versa*. In such an instance, the court will merely apply the appropriate legal standard and rule accordingly.[85]

Remedy

Generally, the court will permit a party to amend unless it is clear that subject matter jurisdiction cannot be truthfully averred.[86]

78. *McCann v. Newman Irrevocable Trust*, 458 F.3d 281 (3d Cir.2006).

79. *McCann v. Newman Irrevocable Trust*, 458 F.3d 281 (3d Cir.2006).

80. *See Paper, Allied–Indus., Chem. & Energy Workers Int'l Union v. Continental Carbon Co.*, 428 F.3d 1285, 1292 (10th Cir. 2005); *Autery v. United States*, 424 F.3d 944, 956 (9th Cir.2005); *Gonzalez v. United States*, 284 F.3d 281, 287 (1st Cir.2002).

81. *See Gonzalez v. United States*, 284 F.3d 281, 287 (1st Cir.2002) (noting that jurisdictional issue is intertwined with merits where court's subject matter jurisdiction depends upon statute that governs substantive claims). *See also Paper, Allied–Indus., Chem. & Energy Workers Int'l Union v. Continental Carbon Co.*, 428 F.3d 1285, 1292 (10th Cir.2005); *Autery v. United States*, 424 F.3d 944, 956 (9th Cir.2005); *Montez v. Department of Navy*, 392 F.3d 147, 150 (5th Cir.2004).

82. *See Skwira v. United States*, 344 F.3d 64, 71–72 (1st Cir.2003); *Sizova v.*

National Inst. of Standards & Tech., 282 F.3d 1320, 1326 (10th Cir.2002).

83. *See Gualandi v. Adams*, 385 F.3d 236, 244 (2d Cir.2004).

84. *See Sizova v. National Inst. of Standards & Tech.*, 282 F.3d 1320, 1326 (10th Cir.2002) (noting that such prejudice exists if "pertinent facts bearing on the question of jurisdiction are controverted … or where a more satisfactory showing of the facts is necessary").

85. *See Zimmerman v. Cambridge Credit Counseling Corp.*, 409 F.3d 473, 475 n.4 (1st Cir.2005) (discounting as "immaterial" dispute as to whether Rule 12(b)(1) or Rule 12(b)(6) was correct form for motion); *Jarrard v. CDI Telecomms., Inc.*, 408 F.3d 905, 909 n.3 (7th Cir.2005) (holding that trial judge "properly" construed Rule 12(b)(1) motion as Rule 12(b)(6) challenge).

86. *See Leaf v. Supreme Court of Wisconsin*, 979 F.2d 589, 595 (7th Cir.1992) (noting that leave to amend defective allegations of subject matter jurisdiction should be freely given).

If, however, the court lacks subject matter jurisdiction, it must dismiss the case in its entirety.[87]

Extrinsic Materials

In cases involving factual or substantive (rather than facial or technical) attacks to the court's subject matter jurisdiction, the parties may produce affidavits and other materials to support their positions on subject matter jurisdiction.[88] The court may also consider matters of public record.[89]

Ruling Deferred

Although the question of subject matter jurisdiction is resolved by the court, not the jury, the court may defer ruling on the challenge until after further materials are presented, after discovery is conducted, or after evidence is received at trial.[90] The court may *not*, however, defer ruling upon a subject matter jurisdictional challenge so as to rule instead upon a potentially simpler dispositive motion attacking the merits of the lawsuit.[91] Because the judicial power of the United States is limited, jurisdiction must be established as a threshold matter before any merits ruling is possible.

Prejudice on Dismissal

A dismissal for lack of subject matter jurisdiction is usually not a decision on the merits, and generally will not preclude the plaintiff from filing the claim in a court that may properly hear the dispute.[92]

Dismissal's Effect on Supplemental Jurisdiction Claims

If a lawsuit's federal claims are dismissed for lack of subject matter jurisdiction, then all supplemental jurisdiction claims must

87. *See Arbaugh v. Y&H Corp.*, 546 U.S. 500, ___, 126 S.Ct. 1235, 1244, 163 L.Ed.2d 1097 (2006).

88. *See Hamm v. United States*, 483 F.3d 135, 137 (2d Cir. 2007);*United States ex rel. Atkinson v. PA. Shipbuilding Co.*, 473 F.3d 506, 514 (3d Cir. 2007); *Paper, Allied–Indus., Chem. & Energy Workers Int'l Union v. Continental Carbon Co.*, 428 F.3d 1285, 1292 (10th Cir.2005); *Savage v. Glendale Union High Sch.*, 343 F.3d 1036, 1039 n.2 (9th Cir.2003).

89. *See White v. Lee*, 227 F.3d 1214, 1242 (9th Cir.2000).

90. *See Land v. Dollar*, 330 U.S. 731, 67 S.Ct. 1009, 91 L.Ed. 1209 (1947); *Valentin v. Hospital Bella Vista*, 254 F.3d 358, 364 n.3 (1st Cir.2001).

91. *See Steel Co. v. Citizens for a Better Env't*, 523 U.S. 83, 118 S.Ct. 1003, 140 L.Ed.2d 210 (1998) (rejecting the so-called doctrine of "hypothetical" or "assumed" jurisdiction). But the Supreme Court has confirmed that there is no "unyielding hier-

archy" *among* jurisdictional requirements, and courts are free to resolve *personal* jurisdiction challenges before reaching potentially more difficult questions of *subject* matter jurisdiction. *See also Ruhrgas AG v. Marathon Oil Co.*, 526 U.S. 574, 119 S.Ct. 1563, 143 L.Ed.2d 760 (1999); *Deniz v. Municipality of Guaynabo*, 285 F.3d 142, 149–50 (1st Cir.2002).

92. *See Mitchell v. Chapman*, 343 F.3d 811, 820 (6th Cir.2003); *Ramming v. United States*, 281 F.3d 158, 161 (5th Cir.2001); *Nowak v. Ironworkers Local 6 Pension Fund*, 81 F.3d 1182, 1188 (2d Cir.1996); *Leaf v. Supreme Ct. of Wis.*, 979 F.2d 589, 595 (7th Cir.1992). *But cf. Frigard v. United States*, 862 F.2d 201 (9th Cir. 1988)(noting that although Rule 12(b)(1) dismissals are ordinarily without prejudice to a re-filing in a court of competent jurisdiction, some dismissals (such as those premised on sovereign immunity) are absolute such that no court could hear the case and no re-drafting of the pleadings could cure the defect).

ordinarily be dismissed as well.[93]

Appealability

A dismissal premised upon a lack of subject matter jurisdiction is ordinarily considered a "final order", subject to immediate review by the court of appeals.[94] However, denying a motion to dismiss for lack of subject matter jurisdiction generally is interlocutory and not immediately appealable.[95]

RULE 12(b)(2). DISMISSAL FOR LACK OF PERSONAL JURISDICTION

CORE CONCEPT

A particular defendant may be dismissed from the lawsuit if that defendant or the dispute concerning that defendant lacks sufficient "contacts" with the forum for the court to exercise personal jurisdiction over the defendant and, thus, to require the defendant travel into the forum to defend the lawsuit.[96]

APPLICATIONS

Special Appearances

The Federal Rules have abandoned the concepts of "special" and "general" appearances.[97] Now, a defendant can assert jurisdictional defenses, venue defenses, and even substantive defenses under Rule 12 without impliedly consenting to the court's personal jurisdiction.

In Rem and Quasi in Rem Actions

A party may use this Rule to challenge the court's in rem and quasi in rem jurisdiction, as well as its personal jurisdiction.[98]

Timing and Waiver

Challenges to personal jurisdiction are waived, unless raised by

93. See Musson Theatrical, Inc. v. Federal Express Corp., 89 F.3d 1244, 1255 (6th Cir.1996), amended on denial of rehearing, 1998 WL 117980 (6th Cir.1998) (dismissal under Rule 12(b)(1) presumes that no valid federal claim ever existed, thus defeating any supplemental jurisdiction over non-federal claims).

94. See Carson Harbor Village Ltd. v. City of Carson, 37 F.3d 468, 471 n. 3 (9th Cir.1994). Similarly, a dismissal "without prejudice" and with the right to file an amended complaint may be immediately appealable if the plaintiff elects not to amend and to stand on the dismissed complaint. Id.

95. See Harrison v. Nissan Motor Corp., 111 F.3d 343, 347–48 (3d Cir.1997).

96. For a detailed discussion of personal jurisdiction, see Part II of this text, §§ 2.3–2.7.

97. See Chase v. Pan–Pacific Broad., Inc., 750 F.2d 131 (D.C.Cir.1984); Davenport v. Ralph N. Peters & Co., 386 F.2d 199, 204 (4th Cir.1967); DIRECTV, Inc. v. Meyers, 214 F.R.D. 504, 507 n.1 (N.D.Iowa 2003). See also Orange Theatre Corp. v. Rayherstz Amusement Corp., 139 F.2d 871, 874 (3d Cir.1944)(writing that a defendant "is no longer required at the door of the federal courthouse to intone that ancient abracadabra of the law, de bene esse, in order by its magic power himself to remain outside even while he steps within").

98. See Newhard, Cook & Co. v. Inspired Life Ctrs., Inc., 895 F.2d 1226, 1228 n. 2 (8th Cir.1990).

motion (if there is one) or in the responsive pleading.[99] This defense may still be deemed waived, even if properly preserved in the answer, if the defendant fails to timely bring the defense to the court for a ruling, and instead chooses to participate in the litigation as though jurisdiction existed.[100] But the defense is not deemed to be waived (at least under the approach followed by a majority of the Circuits) merely because a defendant's responsive pleading includes a claim for affirmative relief (*e.g.*, filing a counterclaim, cross-claim, or third-party claim), provided the defendant asserts a timely objection to jurisdiction.[101]

Sua Sponte Dismissals

In some Circuits, a trial court may dismiss on its own initiative for lack of personal jurisdiction but, if it does so, the court of appeals will generally permit the plaintiffs to raise their arguments supporting personal jurisdiction (and even proffer new supporting evidence) for the first time on appeal.[102] Other Circuits reject this approach, holding that personal jurisdiction is a defense that ordinarily must be raised by the affected parties or will be deemed waived. In those Circuits, the trial court may not raise this issue *sua sponte*.[103]

Burden of Proof

The burden lies with the party invoking the court's jurisdiction to establish the existence of that jurisdiction.[104]

Types of Challenges

A defendant can challenge personal jurisdiction theoretically or

---

99. *See Jaworowski v. Ciasulli*, 490 F.3d 331, 336 (3d Cir. 2007); *Preferred Capital, Inc. v. Associates in Urology*, 453 F.3d 718, 721 (6th Cir.2006); *Pakootas v. Teck Cominco Metals, Ltd.*, 452 F.3d 1066, 1076 (9th Cir.2006); *Stubbs v. Wyndham Nassau Resort & Crystal Palace Casino*, 447 F.3d 1357, 1364 (11th Cir.2006).

100. *See Rates Tech. Inc. v. Nortel Networks Corp.*, 399 F.3d 1302, 1308–09 (Fed. Cir.2005) (noting waiver authority, but finding defendant did not "dally" but moved to dismiss at its "earliest opportunity"). *Cf. Hamilton v. Atlas Turner, Inc.*, 197 F.3d 58, 62 (2d Cir.1999) (defense "forfeited" by failing to move to dismiss during four-year period following inclusion of defense in party's answer); *Trustees of Central Laborers' Welfare Fund v. Lowery*, 924 F.2d 731, 732–33 (7th Cir.1991) (same, six-year period).

101. *See Rates Tech. Inc. v. Nortel Networks Corp.*, 399 F.3d 1302, 1307–08 (Fed. Cir.2005) (adopting majority view); *Chase v. Pan–Pac. Broad., Inc.*, 750 F.2d 131, 132 (D.C.Cir.1984) (same); *Gates Learjet Corp. v. Jensen*, 743 F.2d 1325, 1330 (9th Cir. 1984) (same); *Neifeld v. Steinberg*, 438 F.2d

423, 428–29 (3d Cir.1971) (same). *See also Bayou Steel Corp. v. M/V Amstelvoorn*, 809 F.2d 1147 (5th Cir.1987)(discussing divergent views, and adopting majority approach).

102. *See Buchanan v. Manley*, 145 F.3d 386, 388–89 (D.C.Cir.1998). *Cf. Trujillo v. Williams*, 465 F.3d 1210, 1217 (10th Cir. 2006) (*sua sponte* rulings on personal jurisdiction are proper under 28 U.S.C.A. § 1915 where defense is obvious from complaint's face and no further factual record is necessary).

103. *See, e.g., Pakootas v. Teck Cominco Metals, Ltd.*, 452 F.3d 1066, 1076 (9th Cir. 2006); *Uffner v. La Reunion Francaise, S.A.*, 244 F.3d 38, 40 (1st Cir.2001).

104. *See Best Van Lines, Inc. v. Walker*, 490 F.3d 239, 242 (2d Cir. 2007); *Negron-Torres v. Verizon Commc'ns, Inc.*, 478 F.3d 19, 23–24 (1st Cir. 2007); *Snow v. DirecTV, Inc.*, 450 F.3d 1314, 1317 (11th Cir.2006); *Brunner v. Hampson*, 441 F.3d 457, 462 (6th Cir.2006); *Fielding v. Hubert Burda Media, Inc.*, 415 F.3d 419 (5th Cir.2005).

factually.[105] Theoretical challenges contest the plaintiff's theory of jurisdiction (*e.g.*, that the defendant subjected itself to jurisdiction in the forum by engaging in a particular set of actions). In testing theoretical challenges, the court will ordinarily (and provisionally) accept as true the plaintiff's rendition of the relevant disputed facts.[106] If the court determines that those facts, if proven to be true, would subject the defendant to personal jurisdiction in the forum, no hearing or factual resolution is required and the theoretical challenge fails.[107] Alternatively (or additionally), the defendant may challenge personal jurisdiction factually by disputing the facts the plaintiff has alleged. When jurisdiction is challenged factually, the court or the factfinder must resolve the factual dispute.[108]

Legal Test

The nature of the court's inquiry on a Rule 12(b)(2) challenge depends upon how the motion is supported.[109] If the motion rests upon the pleadings alone, or on affidavits and a cold record, the court will hold the plaintiff to merely a prima facie standard obligating the plaintiff to make a proffer which, if credited by the factfinder, would be sufficient to confer personal jurisdiction.[110] In this posture, the uncontroverted allegations in the complaint are accepted as true, and factual disputes are resolved in the pleader's favor.[111] Uncontradicted facts offered by the defendant are also considered.[112] Alternatively, in those instances where the court finds it unfair to require a defendant to attend and participate in the

---

105. See *Credit Lyonnais Secs. (USA), Inc. v. Alcantara*, 183 F.3d 151, 153–54 (2d Cir.1999).

106. See *Negron-Torres v. Verizon Commc'ns, Inc.*, 478 F.3d 19, 23 (1st Cir. 2007); *Preferred Capital, Inc. v. Associates in Urology*, 453 F.3d 718, 720 (6th Cir. 2006); *Snow v. DirecTV, Inc.*, 450 F.3d 1314, 1317 (11th Cir.2006); *Electronics For Imaging, Inc. v. Coyle*, 340 F.3d 1344, 1349 (Fed.Cir.2003).

107. See *In re Magnetic Audiotape Antitrust Litig.*, 334 F.3d 204, 206 (2d Cir.2003); *Doe v. Unocal Corp.*, 248 F.3d 915, 921 (9th Cir.2001).

108. See *Credit Lyonnais Secs. (USA), Inc. v. Alcantara*, 183 F.3d 151, 153 (2d Cir.1999).

109. See *Foster–Miller, Inc. v. Babcock & Wilcox Canada*, 46 F.3d 138 (1st Cir. 1995)(discussing three levels of inquiry under Rule 12(b)(2)).

110. See *Negron-Torres v. Verizon Commc'ns, Inc.*, 478 F.3d 19, 23 (1st Cir. 2007); *Preferred Capital, Inc. v. Associates in Urology*, 453 F.3d 718, 720 (6th Cir. 2006); *Snow v. DirecTV, Inc.*, 450 F.3d 1314, 1317 (11th Cir.2006); *Fielding v. Hu-*

bert *Burda Media, Inc.*, 415 F.3d 419 (5th Cir.2005); *Northern Laminate Sales, Inc. v. Davis*, 403 F.3d 14, 22 (1st Cir.2005); *Schwarzenegger v. Fred Martin Motor Co.*, 374 F.3d 797, 800 (9th Cir.2004). *Cf. Nationwide Mutual Ins. Co. v. Tryg Int'l Ins. Co.*, 91 F.3d 790 (6th Cir.1996) (surmising, but not conclusively ruling, that Circuit would apply the prima facie inquiry in cases where trial judge permits limited discovery into the jurisdictional issue but does not convene an evidentiary hearing).

111. See *Negron-Torres v. Verizon Commc'ns, Inc.*, 478 F.3d 19, 23 (1st Cir. 2007); *Preferred Capital, Inc. v. Associates in Urology*, 453 F.3d 718, 720 (6th Cir. 2006); *Snow v. DirecTV, Inc.*, 450 F.3d 1314, 1317 (11th Cir.2006); *Fielding v. Hubert Burda Media, Inc.*, 415 F.3d 419 (5th Cir.2005). *But cf. Massachusetts Sch. of Law at Andover, Inc. v. American Bar Ass'n*, 142 F.3d 26, 34 (1st Cir.1998) (cautioning that despite Rule 12(b)(2)'s liberal approach, "the law does not require us struthiously to 'credit conclusory allegations or draw farfetched inferences' ").

112. See *Negron–Torres v. Verizon Commc'ns, Inc.*, 478 F.3d 19, 23 (1st Cir. 2007).

trial prior to a conclusive ruling on personal jurisdiction, the court may convene an evidentiary hearing. In that case, the plaintiff will have to establish personal jurisdiction by a preponderance of the evidence.[113] Finally, the court might adopt a middle course, known as the "likelihood" standard, during which the court makes no conclusive ruling on personal jurisdiction, but requires the plaintiff to come forward with evidence showing a likelihood that personal jurisdiction exists.[114]

Extrinsic Materials

The parties may produce affidavits, interrogatories, depositions, oral testimony (if an evidentiary hearing is convened), and other materials to support their positions on personal jurisdiction.[115]

Ruling Deferred

The court may defer ruling on the challenge until after further materials are presented or after jurisdictional discovery is conducted.[116] But a court generally must resolve personal jurisdiction issues before reaching merits issues.[117]

Discretion to Permit Pre–Ruling Jurisdictional Discovery

Generally, discovery is available to aid the pleader in establishing the existence of personal jurisdiction.[118] Consequently, courts may grant limited jurisdictional discovery before ruling on a Rule

113. See Purdue Research Found. v. Sanofi–Synthelabo, S.A., 338 F.3d 773, 782–83 (7th Cir.2003); Epps v. Stewart Info. Servs. Corp., 327 F.3d 642, 646–47 (8th Cir.2003).

114. See Foster–Miller, Inc. v. Babcock & Wilcox Canada, 46 F.3d 138 (1st Cir. 1995). See also Purdue Research Found. v. Sanofi–Synthelabo, S.A., 338 F.3d 773, 782–83 (7th Cir.2003) (noting national precedent that once defendant submits affidavits or other evidence in opposition to jurisdiction, plaintiff must go beyond pleadings and submit affirmative evidence supporting jurisdiction).

115. See Negron-Torres v. Verizon Commc'ns, Inc., 478 F.3d 19, 23 (1st Cir. 2007); Schwarzenegger v. Fred Martin Motor Co., 374 F.3d 797, 800 (9th Cir.2004); Purdue Research Found. v. Sanofi–Synthelabo, S.A., 338 F.3d 773, 782–83 (7th Cir. 2003).

116. See Theunissen v. Matthews, 935 F.2d 1454 (6th Cir.1991); Data Disc, Inc. v. Systems Technology Assocs., Inc., 557 F.2d 1280 (9th Cir.1977); Klockner–Pentaplast of America, Inc. v. Roth Display Corp., 860 F.Supp. 1119, 1121–22 (W.D.Va. 1994)(holding that factually intensive inquiry into personal jurisdiction would be deferred until trial, because a jurisdictional ruling would translate into a ruling on the merits).

117. See OMI Holdings, Inc. v. Royal Ins. Co., 149 F.3d 1086 (10th Cir.1998); Republic of Panama v. BCCI Holdings (Luxembourg) S.A., 119 F.3d 935, 940 (11th Cir.1997). See also Chudasama v. Mazda Motor Corp., 123 F.3d 1353, 1367–68 (11th Cir.1997) (commenting that motions to dismiss should be resolved before full discovery is permitted). See generally Steel Co. v. Citizens for a Better Env't, 523 U.S. 83, 118 S.Ct. 1003, 140 L.Ed.2d 210 (1998) (rejecting so-called "hypothetical" or "assumed" jurisdiction theory, and prohibiting federal courts from postponing subject matter jurisdiction challenge in preference to an easier, and also potentially dispositive, merits challenge). But see Ruhrgas AG v. Marathon Oil Co., 526 U.S. 574, 119 S.Ct. 1563, 143 L.Ed.2d 760 (1999) (holding that there is no "unyielding hierarchy" among jurisdictional requirements, and courts are free to resolve simpler personal jurisdiction challenges before reaching potentially more difficult questions of subject matter jurisdiction).

118. See Oppenheimer Fund, Inc. v. Sanders, 437 U.S. 340, 351 n. 13, 98 S.Ct. 2380, 2389 n. 13, 57 L.Ed.2d 253 (1978) ("discovery is . . . available to ascertain the facts bearing on [jurisdictional] issues"). See generally Doe v. Unocal Corp., 248 F.3d 915, 921 (9th Cir.2001); Eaton v. Dorchester

12(b)(2) motion to dismiss for lack of personal jurisdiction.[119] Whether, and under what constraints, to permit jurisdictional discovery are matters typically reserved for the trial judge's discretion.[120] Jurisdictional discovery will generally be allowed where a "colorable" case for jurisdiction has been made, the material facts that bear on jurisdiction are controverted, where a more satisfactory development of those facts is necessary, and where plaintiff has demonstrated that discovery will permit a supplementation of the jurisdictional allegations.[121] Conversely, such discovery may be properly refused when it is untimely sought,[122] where the request is improperly supported,[123] where the claim is "attenuated",[124] where a colorable case for jurisdiction has not been made,[125] where the plaintiff's claim is "clearly frivolous",[126] or where the plaintiff lacks a good faith belief that such discovery could support the jurisdictional allegations.[127] Jurisdictional discovery is often dependent on the specific circumstances presented. Thus, jurisdictional discovery into

Dev't, Inc., 692 F.2d 727, 729 n. 7 (11th Cir.1982); Note, *The Use of Discovery to Obtain Jurisdictional Facts*, 59 Va. L. Rev. 533 (1973).

119. *See United States v. Swiss American Bank, Ltd.*, 274 F.3d 610, 625 (1st Cir.2001) (noting that a "timely and properly supported" motion for jurisdictional discovery "merits solicitous attention"). *See, e.g., GTE New Media Servs. Inc. v. BellSouth Corp.*, 199 F.3d 1343, 1351–52 (D.C.Cir.2000); *United States v. Swiss American Bank, Ltd.*, 191 F.3d 30, 45–46 (1st Cir.1999); *Massachusetts Sch. of Law at Andover, Inc. v. American Bar Ass'n*, 107 F.3d 1026, 1042 (3d Cir.1997).

120. *See Best Van Lines, Inc. v. Walker*, 490 F.3d 239, 255 (2d Cir. 2007); *Negron-Torres v. Verizon Commc'ns, Inc.*, 478 F.3d 19, 23 (1st Cir. 2007); *Laub v. United States Dep't of Interior*, 342 F.3d 1080, 1093 (9th Cir.2003).

121. *See Platten v. HG Bermuda Exempted Ltd.*, 437 F.3d 118, 139–40 (1st Cir. 2006); *Trintec Indus., Inc. v. Pedre Promotional Prods., Inc.*, 395 F.3d 1275, 1283 (Fed.Cir.2005); *Laub v. United States Dep't of Interior*, 342 F.3d 1080, 1093 (9th Cir. 2003).

122. *See Platten v. HG Bermuda Exempted Ltd.*, 437 F.3d 118, 139–40 (1st Cir. 2006). *See also Massachusetts Sch. of Law at Andover, Inc. v. American Bar Ass'n*, 142 F.3d 26, 37 (1st Cir.1998) (refusing to consider jurisdictional discovery challenge on appeal where not raised below).

123. *See Carefirst of Md., Inc. v. Carefirst Pregnancy Ctrs., Inc.*, 334 F.3d 390, 402–03 (4th Cir.2003) (denial of jurisdic-

tional discovery proper where plaintiff "offers only speculation or conclusory assertions about contacts with a forum state"); *Terracom v. Valley Nat'l Bank*, 49 F.3d 555 (9th Cir.1995) (affirming denial of jurisdictional discovery where plaintiff failed to demonstrate how further discovery could establish jurisdiction). *Cf. United States v. Swiss American Bank, Ltd.*, 191 F.3d 30, 45–46 (1st Cir.1999) (holding that timely, properly supported motion for jurisdictional discovery "merits solicitous attention").

124. *See Pebble Beach Co. v. Caddy*, 453 F.3d 1151, 1160 (9th Cir.2006).

125. *See Negron–Torres v. Verizon Commc'ns, Inc.*, 478 F.3d 19, 27 (1st Cir. 2007) (no colorable case). *See also Best Van Lines, Inc. v. Walker*, 490 F.3d 239, 255 (2d Cir. 2007) (no prima facie case).

126. *See Massachusetts Sch. of Law at Andover, Inc. v. American Bar Ass'n*, 107 F.3d 1026, 1042 (3d Cir.1997).

127. *See Caribbean Broad. Sys. v. Cable & Wireless P.L.C.*, 148 F.3d 1080, 1090 (D.C.Cir.1998) (discussing good faith belief requirement). *See also Kelly v. Syria Shell Petroleum Dev't B.V.*, 213 F.3d 841, 855–56 (5th Cir.2000) (holding that discovery may be denied where the discovery sought could not have added any significant facts); *Terracom v. Valley Nat'l Bank*, 49 F.3d 555 (9th Cir.1995) (affirming denial of jurisdictional discovery where plaintiff failed to demonstrate how further discovery could establish jurisdiction); *Poe v. Babcock Int'l*, 662 F.Supp. 4, 7 (M.D.Pa.1985) (jurisdictional discovery denied where plaintiff responded to motion with "mere specula-

whether a corporate defendant is adequately "doing business" within the forum may be granted more liberally[128] than such discovery of an individual[129] or a foreign sovereign.[130]

Foreign Discovery: Generally, a party may (but is not necessarily obligated to) pursue foreign discovery through the Hague Evidence Convention.[131] When personal jurisdiction over the foreign party is contested, the courts are divided as to whether discovery can proceed simply under the Rules or whether Convention discovery is required until the question of jurisdiction is resolved.[132]

Effect of Denial of Motion

If a party's Rule 12(b)(2) motion is denied, her active participation in the ensuing trial will not constitute a waiver of *either* her ability to renew the motion before the district judge at time *or* her right to contest personal jurisdiction on appeal.[133] When renewed before the district judge, the contesting party can rely on the actual evidence admitted during the trial itself, in which case the court will apply a preponderance of the evidence standard in assessing personal jurisdiction.[134] But the contesting party must request such an evidentiary re-examination to ensure receiving it. Although the trial court may, in its discretion, consider the trial evidence *sua sponte*, unless the contesting party actually requests the court to do so, the court is entitled to instead rule upon the motion under a reconsideration standard, considering only the original, pretrial jurisdictional presentation in doing so.[135]

Prejudice on Dismissal

A dismissal for lack of personal jurisdiction generally does not preclude the plaintiff from refiling the lawsuit against the defendant

---

tion"). Cf. *GTE New Media Servs. Inc. v. BellSouth Corp.*, 199 F.3d 1343, 1351–52 (D.C.Cir.2000) (jurisdictional discovery is justified if party demonstrates that discovery can supplement jurisdictional allegations).

128. See *Massachusetts Sch. of Law at Andover, Inc. v. American Bar Ass'n*, 107 F.3d 1026, 1042 (3d Cir.1997) (noting that jurisdictional discovery often relates to "doing business" inquiry).

129. See *Massachusetts Sch. of Law at Andover, Inc. v. American Bar Ass'n*, 107 F.3d 1026, 1042 (3d Cir.1997) (observing that presumption in favor of jurisdictional discovery is reduced when defendant is an individual).

130. See *Alpha Therapeutic Corp. v. Nippon Hoso Kyokai*, 199 F.3d 1078, 1087–88 (9th Cir.1999) (discussing the circumspection under which jurisdictional discovery from foreign sovereign should be ordered).

131. Hague Convention on the Taking of Evidence Abroad in Civil or Commercial Matters, opened for signature, Mar. 18, 1970, 23 U.S.T. 2555, T.I.A.S. No. 7444, *reprinted in* 28 U.S.C. § 1781 Note. See *Societe Nationale Industrielle Aerospatiale v. United States Dist. Ct.*, 482 U.S. 522, 533–36, 107 S.Ct. 2542, 2550–51, 96 L.Ed.2d 461 (1987) (first resort to Convention discovery is not required).

132. See *In re Automotive Refinishing Paint Antitrust Litig.*, 358 F.3d 288, 299–305 (3d Cir.2004) (ruling that Convention discovery is not required, but citing case law split).

133. See *Northern Laminate Sales, Inc. v. Davis*, 403 F.3d 14, 23 (1st Cir.2005).

134. See *Northern Laminate Sales, Inc. v. Davis*, 403 F.3d 14, 23 (1st Cir.2005).

135. See *Northern Laminate Sales, Inc. v. Davis*, 403 F.3d 14, 23 (1st Cir.2005).

in a forum where that defendant is amenable to jurisdiction.[136]

Appealability

A dismissal as to all defendants for lack of personal jurisdiction is generally considered an appealable "final order".[137] Conversely, a dismissal as to less than all defendants[138] or a denial of the motion to dismiss is not a final order and ordinarily cannot be immediately appealed.[139]

RULE 12(b)(3). DISMISSAL FOR IMPROPER VENUE

CORE CONCEPT

A case will be dismissed or transferred if venue is improper or inconvenient in the chosen forum.

APPLICATIONS

Transfer

A request for a *transfer* of venue (rather than a *dismissal* for improper or inconvenient venue) is made under federal statute, not under Rule 12(b)(3).[140] However, if the trial court grants a Rule 12(b)(3) motion for improper venue, it enjoys the discretion, in lieu of a dismissal, to transfer the matter to a forum where venue is proper.[141]

Dismissal; Forum Non Conveniens

Rule 12(b)(3) is the proper mechanism for asserting that the action should be dismissed either for lack of proper venue, or under the common law doctrine of forum non conveniens,[142] pursuant to a forum selection clause (generally) or otherwise.[143]

Timing and Waiver

Venue challenges are waived unless raised by motion (if there is

---

136. *See Kendall v. Overseas Dev't Corp.*, 700 F.2d 536 (9th Cir.1983).

137. *See Carteret Savings Bank, FA v. Shushan*, 919 F.2d 225, 230 (3d Cir. 1990)(noting that dismissal as to all defendants for lack of personal jurisdiction is appealable under the final order doctrine).

138. *See Morton Int'l, Inc. v. A.E. Staley Mfg. Co.*, 460 F.3d 470, 476 (3d Cir. 2006).

139. *See Northern Laminate Sales, Inc. v. Davis*, 403 F.3d 14, 23 (1st Cir.2005); *SEC v. Blazon Corp.*, 609 F.2d 960 (9th Cir.1979).

140. *See* 28 U.S.C.A. § 1404 (authorizing transfer to more convenient district); 28 U.S.C.A. § 1406 (authorizing transfer to proper district).

141. *See, e.g., Meteoro Amusement Corp. v. Six Flags*, 267 F.Supp.2d 263, 266

(N.D.N.Y.2003); *Audi AG & Volkswagen of America, Inc. v. Izumi*, 204 F.Supp.2d 1014, 1017 (E.D.Mich.2002).

142. *See Gulf Oil Corp. v. Gilbert*, 330 U.S. 501, 67 S.Ct. 839, 91 L.Ed. 1055 (1947).

143. *See Continental Cas. Co. v. American Nat. Ins. Co.*, 417 F.3d 727, 733 (7th Cir.2005); *Lim v. Offshore Specialty Fabricators, Inc.*, 404 F.3d 898, 902 (5th Cir. 2005). *But see Rainforest Cafe, Inc. v. Eklec-Co, L.L.C.*, 340 F.3d 544, 545 n.5 (8th Cir. 2003) (noting division among Circuits on question of whether motion to dismiss on grounds of forum selection clause is properly brought under Rule12(b)(3) or Rule 12(b)(6)).

one) or in the responsive pleading.[144]   Once the Rule 12 motion
period and the responsive pleading time have passed, an otherwise
"waived" venue defense cannot ordinarily be raised by the court on
its own initiative.[145] A defaulting defendant, thus, generally is
deemed to have waived any objections to venue.[146]

Burden of Proof

The case law is fractured as to who bears the burden of proof on
a Rule 12(b)(3) challenge.[147]   One approach (evidently the substantial majority view) vests the plaintiff with the burden of proving that
the chosen forum is proper;[148] the minority approach requires that
the defendant, as the party challenging venue, bear this burden.[149]

Legal Test

The procedure for resolving a Rule 12(b)(3) motion is the same
as the procedure used for testing challenges to personal jurisdiction.[150] Plaintiffs' well-pleaded factual allegations regarding venue
will be accepted as true, all reasonable inferences from those allegations will be drawn in plaintiffs' favor, and factual conflicts will be
resolved in plaintiffs' favor as well.[151] Legal conclusions need not be
accepted as true, however.[152] The court may resolve the motion on
the basis of the written submissions alone, or may convene an

---

144. *See* Rule 12(h)(1); *Wachovia Bank
v. Schmidt*, 546 U.S. 303, ___, 126 S.Ct.
941, 950, 163 L.Ed.2d 797 (2006); *Stjernholm v. Peterson*, 83 F.3d 347, 349 (10th
Cir.1996).

145. *See Stjernholm v. Peterson*, 83 F.3d
347, 349 (10th Cir.1996) (noting that until
defendants waive their venue defense, district courts may raise *sua sponte* defective
venue, although the case may not be dismissed without affording the parties an opportunity to present their views on the
question). *See also Buchanan v. Manley*,
145 F.3d 386, 388–89 (D.C.Cir.1998) (to allow plaintiff to raise arguments supporting
venue after a *sua sponte* dismissal by the
trial court, court of appeals will permit
plaintiffs to raise such arguments and proffer supporting evidence for the first time on
appeal).

146. *See Union Planters Bank, N.A. v.
EMC Mortg. Corp.*, 67 F.Supp.2d 915, 920
(W.D.Tenn.1999).

147. *See Beckley v. Auto Profit Masters,
L.L.C.*, 266 F.Supp.2d 1001, 1003 (S.D.Iowa
2003) (noting division among the courts on
burden in venue challenges); *McCaskey v.
Continental Airlines, Inc.*, 133 F.Supp.2d
514, 522 (S.D.Tex.2001) (same); *Bacik v.
Peek*, 888 F.Supp. 1405, 1412 (N.D.Ohio
1993) (same).

148. *See, e.g., Gulf Ins. Co. v. Glasbrenner*, 417 F.3d 353, 355 (2d Cir.2005); *Bar-
tholomew v. Virginia Chiropractors Ass'n,*

612 F.2d 812 (4th Cir.1979); *Cohen v. News-
week, Inc.*, 312 F.2d 76, 78 (8th Cir.1963);
Estate of Moore v. Dixon, 460 F.Supp.2d
931, 935 (E.D.Wis. 2006); *Country Home
Prods., Inc. v. Schiller–Pfeiffer, Inc.*, 350
F.Supp.2d 561, 568 (D.Vt.2004); *Multi-Me-
dia Int'l, LLC v. Promag Retail Servs.*, 343
F.Supp.2d 1024, 1033 (D.Kan.2004); *Wai v.
Rainbow Holdings*, 315 F.Supp.2d 1261,
1268 (S.D.Fla.2004).

149. *See Myers v. American Dental
Ass'n*, 695 F.2d 716 (3d Cir.1982); *International Truck & Engine Corp. v. Quintana*,
259 F.Supp.2d 553, 558 (N.D.Tex.2003).

150. *See Gulf Ins. Co. v. Glasbrenner*,
417 F.3d 353, 355 (2d Cir.2005); *Wai v.
Rainbow Holdings*, 315 F.Supp.2d 1261,
1268 (S.D.Fla.2004).

151. *See Murphy v. Schneider Nat'l,
Inc.*, 362 F.3d 1133, 1137 (9th Cir.2004);
Estate of Moore v. Dixon, 460 F.Supp.2d
931, 935 (E.D.Wis. 2006); *Zimmer Enters.,
Inc. v. Atlandia Imports, Inc.*, 478
F.Supp.2d 983, 986 (S.D.Ohio 2007); *Wai v.
Rainbow Holdings*, 315 F.Supp.2d 1261,
1268 (S.D.Fla.2004); *Langton v. Cbeyond
Commc'n, L.L.C.*, 282 F.Supp.2d 504, 508
(E.D.Tex.2003).

152. *See Quarles v. General Inv. &
Dev't Co.*, 260 F.Supp.2d 1, 8 (D.D.C.2003).

evidentiary hearing.[153] In the absence of an evidentiary hearing, a challenge to venue will be defeated if plaintiffs set forth sufficient facts which, if proven true, would confer venue.[154] However, if the court holds an evidentiary hearing, the allegations are not presumed true, and plaintiff must instead establish venue by a preponderance of the evidence.[155]

Cases Involving Multiple Defendants And Multiple Claims

Where a case involves more than one defendant, or more than one claim against a defendant, venue must be proper as to each defendant and as to each claim.[156]

Extrinsic Materials

The parties may submit affidavits and other materials to support their positions on improper venue.[157]

Pre-Ruling Discovery

The court may permit limited discovery to aid in resolving the motion.[158]

Ruling Deferred

The court may defer ruling on a venue challenge pending further factual development.[159]

Prejudice on Dismissal

A dismissal for improper venue generally does not preclude the plaintiff from re-filing the claim in a forum where venue is proper.[160]

Appealability

Ordinarily, a dismissal for improper venue or forum non conveniens is immediately appealable as a "final order".[161] Conversely, a

153. See Centerville ALF, Inc. v. Balanced Care Corp., 197 F.Supp.2d 1039, 1046 (S.D.Ohio 2002).

154. See Langton v. Cbeyond Commc'n, L.L.C., 282 F.Supp.2d 504, 508 (E.D.Tex. 2003); Darby v. United States Dep't of Energy, 231 F.Supp.2d 274, 276–77 (D.D.C. 2002).

155. See Gulf Ins. Co. v. Glasbrenner, 417 F.3d 353, 355 (2d Cir.2005).

156. See Multi-Media Int'l, LLC v. Promag Retail Servs., 343 F.Supp.2d 1024, 1033 (D.Kan.2004); Centerville ALF, Inc. v. Balanced Care Corp., 197 F.Supp.2d 1039, 1046 (S.D.Ohio 2002).

157. See Continental Cas. Co. v. American Nat. Ins. Co., 417 F.3d 727, 733 (7th Cir.2005); Kukje Hwajae Ins. Co., Ltd. v. M/V HYUNDAI LIBERTY, 408 F.3d 1250, 1254 (9th Cir.2005); Estate of Moore v. Dixon, 460 F.Supp.2d 931, 935 (E.D.Wis. 2006); Wai v. Rainbow Holdings, 315 F.Supp.2d 1261, 1268 (S.D.Fla.2004).

158. See Centerville ALF, Inc. v. Balanced Care Corp., 197 F.Supp.2d 1039, 1046 (S.D.Ohio 2002).

159. See Tenpenny v. United States, 285 F.2d 213 (6th Cir.1960).

160. See In re Hall, Bayoutree Assocs., Ltd., 939 F.2d 802, 804 (9th Cir. 1991)(holding that although district court had discretion to either dismiss or transfer for improper venue, court erred in dismissing the case with prejudice; "A determination of improper venue does not go to the merits of the case and therefore must be without prejudice").

161. See Young Props. Corp. v. United Equity Corp., 534 F.2d 847, 852 (9th Cir. 1976)(noting general rule that order dismissing for improper venue or under the doctrine of forum non conveniens is final and appealable).

denial of a motion to dismiss for lack of venue or forum non conveniens is interlocutory and not immediately appealable.[162]

RULES 12(b)(4)–(5).   DISMISSAL FOR (OR QUASHING OF) INSUFFICIENT PROCESS OR SERVICE

CORE CONCEPT

Process or service may be quashed or, in certain cases, the action dismissed if the process or the service is improper.[163]

APPLICATIONS

Insufficient Process—Rule 12(b)(4)

The process (summons and complaint) may be insufficient if the forms are technically deficient[164] (*e.g.*, wrong name[165]) or not sealed by the clerk.[166] Because dismissals for defects in the forms of summons are generally disfavored, courts often overlook minor technical defects (particularly where they can be cured), unless the complaining party is able to demonstrate actual prejudice.[167]

Insufficient Service—Rule 12(b)(5)

Service of the process may be insufficient if, for example, the mode of delivery is invalid, if service is made improperly on an incompetent, a minor, or a non-agent,[168] or if delivery is either never accomplished or not accomplished within 120 days after commencement.[169]

---

162. *See Hohn v. United States*, 524 U.S. 236, 248, 118 S.Ct. 1969, 1976, 141 L.Ed.2d 242 (1998); *Rux v. Republic of Sudan*, 461 F.3d 461, 476 (4th Cir. 2006); *Louisiana Ice Cream Distribs., Inc. v. Carvel Corp.*, 821 F.2d 1031, 1033 (5th Cir. 1987).

163. *See Davies v. Jobs & Adverts Online, Gmbh*, 94 F.Supp.2d 719, 721 n. 5 (E.D.Va.2000) (noting difference between Rule 12(b)(4) (insufficient process) and Rule 12(b)(5) (insufficient service)).

164. *See Wasson v. Riverside County*, 237 F.R.D. 423, 424 (C.D.Cal.2006).

165. *See Austin v. Spaulding*, 2001 WL 345602, at *2 (D.R.I.2001); *Ericson v. Pollack*, 110 F.Supp.2d 582, 584 (E.D.Mich. 2000); *Richardson v. Alliance Tire & Rubber Co.*, 158 F.R.D. 475, 477 (D.Kan.1994); *Crane v. Battelle*, 127 F.R.D. 174 (S.D.Cal. 1989).

166. *See Ayres v. Jacobs & Crumplar, P.A.*, 99 F.3d 565, 569 (3d Cir.1996).

167. *See U.S.A. Nutrasource, Inc. v. CNA Ins. Co.*, 140 F.Supp.2d 1049, 1052–53

(N.D.Cal.2001) (refusing to dismiss where summons used service mark / tradename, rather than formal corporate name, where technical error caused no prejudice and where complaint could be amended to insert "doing-business-as" designation for clarity); *Louisiana Acorn Fair Housing v. Quarter House*, 952 F.Supp. 352, 355 (E.D.La.1997) (refusing to dismiss for insufficient process where summons served on "Quarter House Owners' Association" incorrectly identified the party as "Quarter House Homeowners Association, Inc.", absent showing that defendant did not receive notice or had suffered any prejudice from the technical error).

168. *See Schaeffer v. Village of Ossining*, 58 F.3d 48 (2d Cir.1995)(service quashed where process served on clerk not authorized to accept service on municipality defendant's behalf).

169. *See Rzayeva v. United States*, 492 F.Supp.2d 60, ___ (D.Conn. 2007); *Smith v. United States*, 475 F.Supp.2d 1, 7 (D.D.C. 2006); *Wasson v. Riverside County*, 237 F.R.D. 423, 424 (C.D.Cal.2006).

Distinguishing Between Rules 12(b)(4) and 12(b)(5)

Courts have noted that, although academically distinct, the differences between motions under Rules 12(b)(4) and 12(b)(5) have not always been clear or observed in practice.[170] Practitioner confusion that results in a mislabeling of a Rule 12(b)(4) or 12(b)(5) motion, particularly if that confusion does not prejudice the non-moving party, may well be overlooked by the courts.[171]

Timing and Waiver

Service and process challenges are waived, unless raised by pre-answer motion (if there is one) or in the responsive pleading.[172] Thus, a defendant may not move for such a dismissal under these Rules *after* filing an answer that omits that defense[173] or *after* filing an earlier Rule 12 motion.[174] Such challenges also may not be raised by the court on its own. A defendant, of course, does *not* waive service and process objections by appearing in the case to object on those grounds.[175]

Waiting for Default to Raise Service Objections

Although defendants must raise their objections to process, service, and personal jurisdiction either in their omnibus Rule 12 motion or in their answer (if no Rule 12 motion is filed), these defenses are *not* waived where the failure of service is so complete that the defendants never even received actual notice of the unanswered pleading.[176] In such a case, the Constitutional protections of due process should permit the defendants to raise those objections in opposition to a motion for default.[177] But defendants act at their peril if, after receiving actual notice of a pleading, they choose to ignore the lawsuit in reliance on their own, untested belief that either the process or service was faulty. They must guess correctly.

---

170. *See Wasson v. Riverside County,* 237 F.R.D. 423, 424 (C.D.Cal.2006). *See also Richardson v. Alliance Tire & Rubber Co.,* 158 F.R.D. 475, 477 (D.Kan.1994) (discussing distinctions between these Rules).

171. *See Richardson v. Alliance Tire & Rubber Co.,* 158 F.R.D. 475, 477–78 (D.Kan. 1994).

172. *See Williams v. Jones,* 11 F.3d 247, 251 n. 4 (1st Cir.1993); *Hammann v. 1–800 Ideas.com, Inc.,* 455 F.Supp.2d 942, 959 (D.Minn. 2006).

173. *See* Rule 12(h)(1)(B). Practitioners should note that at least one court has interpreted the Rules to foreclose a litigant's right to contest objections to service or process if an answer is filed before the motion. *See Green v. City of Bessemer,* 202 F.Supp.2d 1272, 1273–74 (N.D.Ala.2002) (finding Rule 12(b)(5) motion untimely because it was filed three days after party answered the complaint).

174. *See Chute v. Walker,* 281 F.3d 314, 319 (1st Cir.2002) (because defendant omitted Rule 12(b)(5) insufficiency of service defense from Rule 12(b)(6) motion to dismiss, insufficiency of service of process defense was waived).

175. *See Cataldo v. United States Dep't of Justice,* 2000 WL 760960, at *7 (D.Me. 2000).

176. *See Corestates Leasing, Inc. v. Wright–Way Exp., Inc.,* 190 F.R.D. 356, 358 (E.D.Pa.2000).

177. *See Stinecipher v. United States,* 239 F.R.D. 282, 283 (D.D.C. 2006) (unless proper service is satisfied, court lacks power to assert personal jurisdiction). *See also Trustees of St. Paul Elec. Const. Indus. Fringe Benefit Funds v. Martens Elec. Co.,* 485 F.Supp.2d 1063, 1065 (D. Minn. 2007) (noting that defendants who are not properly served are protected against default).

There is case precedent and commentary for the conclusion that this conduct may constitute a waiver of these defenses.[178]

Burden of Proof

The burden lies with the plaintiff to demonstrate sufficient process and service; when process or service is challenged, the plaintiff must make a prima facie showing that the court's personal jurisdiction is properly exercised.[179] The process server's return is prima facie evidence—but not conclusive proof—of good service.[180] Likewise, a conclusory representation that the defendant was properly served will not overcome a defendant's sworn affidavit that she was not.[181]

Legal Test

A motion to dismiss under these Rules must be made with specificity, must describe any prejudice suffered by the defendant, and must specify the manner in which the process or service failed to meet the requirements of Rule 4.[182] The court will resolve

178. *See Corestates Leasing, Inc. v. Wright–Way Exp., Inc.*, 190 F.R.D. 356, 358 (E.D.Pa.2000). *See also In re Worldwide Web Sys., Inc.*, 328 F.3d 1291, 1300 (11th Cir.2003) (service objection waived if Rule 60(b) "voidness" challenge to default judgment is made but claim of improper service is not "squarely raised"); *O'Meara v. Waters*, 464 F.Supp.2d 474, 476 (D.Md. 2006) (if defendants receive actual notice, failure to comply strictly with Rule 4 might be excused and service deemed valid). *See also* 5A Charles Alan Wright & Arthur R. Miller, *Federal Practice & Procedure* § 1391, at 755–56 (1990) ("But when the party has received actual notice of the suit there is no due process problem in requiring him to object to the ineffective service within the period prescribed by Rule 12(h)(1) and the defense is one that he certainly can waive if he wishes to do so. This is because the defendant has failed to do what the rule says he must do if he is to avoid a waiver.").

179. *See Grand Entm't Group, Ltd. v. Star Media Sales, Inc.*, 988 F.2d 476, 488 (3d Cir.1993); *Rzayeva v. United States*, 492 F.Supp.2d 60 (D.Conn. 2007); *Koss Corp. v. Pilot Air Freight Corp.*, 242 F.R.D. 514 (E.D.Wis. 2007); *Stinecipher v. United States*, 239 F.R.D. 282, 283 (D.D.C. 2006); *O'Meara v. Waters*, 464 F.Supp.2d 474, 476 (D.Md. 2006); *Weston Funding, LLC v. Consorcio G Grupo Dina, S.A. de C.V.*, 451 F.Supp.2d 585, 589 (S.D.N.Y. 2006).

180. *See O'Brien v. R.J. O'Brien & Assocs., Inc.*, 998 F.2d 1394, 1398 (7th Cir.

1993)(holding that signed return of service constitutes prima facie evidence of valid service that can be overcome by only "strong and convincing evidence"); *Oltremari v. Kansas Social & Rehab. Serv.*, 871 F.Supp. 1331, 1350 (D.Kan.1994)(noting that once plaintiff files return of service, Rule 12(b)(5) dismissal requires strong and convincing evidence that service was improper); *Blue Ocean Lines v. Universal Process Equip., Inc.*, 1993 WL 403961 at *4 n. 2 (S.D.N.Y.1993)(discussing evidentiary effect of private process server's return of service, noting that the return is not conclusive proof of good service but either creates a rebuttal presumption of good service or shifts the burden to the defendant to come forward with "strong and convincing evidence" that service failed).

181. *See Cooper v. Connecticut Public Defender's Office*, 480 F.Supp.2d 536, 538 n.1 (D.Conn. 2007); *C3 Media & Mktg. Group, LLC v. Firstgate Internet, Inc.*, 419 F.Supp.2d 419, 427 (S.D.N.Y.2005).

182. *See O'Brien v. R.J. O'Brien & Assocs., Inc.*, 998 F.2d 1394, 1400 (7th Cir. 1993)(holding that objections to the sufficiency of process must be specific and must identify how plaintiff failed to satisfy service); *Photolab Corp. v. Simplex Specialty Co.*, 806 F.2d 807, 810 (8th Cir.1986)(same); *Berk v. City of New York*, 2001 WL 1029401, at *3 (S.D.N.Y.2001) (holding that motion must describe any prejudice to defendant, and set forth in detail manner in which service failed to satisfy Rule 4).

disputed questions of fact by considering affidavits, depositions, and oral testimony received in connection with the motion.[183]

Remedy

A party may request that the case be dismissed under this Rule or, alternatively, that service be quashed and re-attempted.[184] If service or process is found to be ineffective, the court has discretion to either dismiss or quash.[185] The courts will generally prefer to quash, rather than dismiss, where there is a reasonable prospect that the defendant can be properly served with sufficient process.[186] The courts will only dismiss when the failure of process or service prejudices the defendant or where proper service is unlikely to be accomplished.[187] Any dismissal is likely to be without prejudice.[188]

Extrinsic Materials

The parties may produce affidavits and other materials to support their positions on insufficient process or service.[189] The court may properly receive and consider such materials in deciding the motion,[190] and may do so without converting the motion to dismiss into a motion for summary judgment.[191]

---

183. *See Travelers Cas. & Sur. Co. of America v. Telstar Const. Co.*, 252 F.Supp.2d 917, 923 (D.Ariz.2003); *Mende v. Milestone Tech., Inc.*, 269 F.Supp.2d 246, 251 (S.D.N.Y.2003).

184. *See Boateng v. Inter American Univ. of P.R.*, 188 F.R.D. 26, 27 (D.P.R. 1999) (holding that Rules offer trial court option of quashing deficient service); *R. Griggs Group Ltd. v. Filanto Spa*, 920 F.Supp. 1100, 1102 (D.Nev.1996)(noting that federal courts possess the authority to quash improper service of process, rather than dismissing the complaint, even though the Rules technically do not provide for a "Motion to Quash").

185. *See Ramirez De Arellano v. Colloides Naturels Int'l*, 236 F.R.D. 83, 85 (D.P.R.2006); *Sampath v. Concurrent Techs. Corp*, 227 F.R.D. 399, 401 (W.D.Pa. 2005); *Dimensional Communications, Inc. v. OZ Optics Ltd.*, 218 F.Supp.2d 653, 655 (D.N.J.2002).

186. *See Umbenhauer v. Woog*, 969 F.2d 25, 30–31 (3d Cir.1992)(noting that dismissal, rather than quashing, is inappropriate where there is a reasonable prospect for effective service); *Pell v. Azar Nut Co.*, 711 F.2d 949, 950 n. 2 (10th Cir.1983) (although courts should generally quash insufficient service and permit pleader another opportunity to serve properly, trial judges have broad discretion to dismiss if it is not likely

that proper service can or will be accomplished). *See also Ramirez De Arellano v. Colloides Naturels Int'l*, 236 F.R.D. 83, 85 (D.P.R.2006) (same).

187. *See Gonzalez v. Ritz Carlton Hotel Co. of Puerto Rico*, 241 F.Supp.2d 142, 147–48 (D.P.R.2003); *Oltremari v. Kansas Social & Rehab. Serv.*, 871 F.Supp. 1331, 1349 (D.Kan.1994).

188. *See Speelman v. United States*, 461 F.Supp.2d 71, 72–73 (D.D.C. 2006).

189. *See Travelers Cas. & Sur. Co. of America v. Telstar Const. Co.*, 252 F.Supp.2d 917, 923 (D.Ariz.2003); *Mende v. Milestone Tech., Inc.*, 269 F.Supp.2d 246, 251 (S.D.N.Y.2003); *Bernard v. Husky Truck Stop*, 1994 WL 171732 (D.Kan.1994).

190. *See Fagan v. Deutsche Bundesbank*, 438 F.Supp.2d 376 (S.D.N.Y.2006); *Metropolitan Alloys Corp. v. State Metals Indus., Inc.*, 416 F.Supp.2d 561, 563 (E.D.Mich.2006).

191. *See BPA Int'l, Inc. v. Kingdom of Sweden*, 281 F.Supp.2d 73, 80 (D.D.C.2003); *Travelers Cas. & Sur. Co. of America v. Telstar Const. Co.*, 252 F.Supp.2d 917, 923 (D.Ariz.2003). *But see Cubero Valderama v. Delta Air Lines, Inc.*, 931 F.Supp. 119, 120 (D.P.R.1996) (because court considered documents filed by party challenging service of process, it applied summary judgment standards to motion).

Prejudice on Dismissal

A dismissal for insufficient process or service is generally without prejudice and will not preclude the plaintiff from attempting to re-serve properly.[192]

RULE 12(b)(6). DISMISSAL FOR FAILURE TO STATE A CLAIM UPON WHICH RELIEF CAN BE GRANTED

CORE CONCEPT

A motion to dismiss for failure to state a claim is the descendant of the common law demurrer.[193] It tests the legal sufficiency of a party's claim for relief. The Rule allows trial courts to terminate lawsuits "that are fatally flawed in their legal premises and destined to fail, and thus to spare litigants the burdens of unnecessary pretrial and trial activity."[194]

APPLICATIONS

Legal Test

Rule 12(b)(6) motions test the sufficiency of a pleading.[195] Consequently, they compel an examination of whether the pleader did what she was obligated to do under the federal pleading Rules, Rule 8 and Rule 9.[196] Under Rule 12(b)(6), a claim may be dismissed either because it asserts a legal theory that is not cognizable as a matter of law or because it fails to allege sufficient facts to support an otherwise cognizable legal claim.[197] When a claim is challenged under this Rule, the court construes the pleading liberally in the pleader's favor.[198] The court presumes that all well-pleaded allegations are true, resolves all doubts and inferences in the pleader's favor, and views the pleading in the light most favorable to the non-moving party.[199] No claim will be dismissed merely because the trial

---

192. *See Umbenhauer v. Woog,* 969 F.2d 25, 30 n. 6 (3d Cir.1992); *Savior v. McGuire,* 2002 WL 1906023, at *2 n.2 (D.Minn.2002); *Malone v. Dallas City Manager's Office,* 2001 WL 910396, at *2 (N.D.Tex.2001). *But cf. Coffin v. Ingersoll,* 1993 WL 208806 at *5 n. 15 (E.D.Pa. 1993)(noting general rule that dismissal is without prejudice, but observing that where statute of limitations has lapsed, dismissal effectively bars plaintiff from court).

193. *See De Sole v. United States,* 947 F.2d 1169, 1178 n. 13 (4th Cir.1991); *Podell v. Citicorp Diners Club, Inc.,* 859 F.Supp. 701, 704 (S.D.N.Y.1994).

194. *Advanced Cardiovascular Sys., Inc. v. Scimed Life Sys., Inc.,* 988 F.2d 1157, 1160 (Fed.Cir.1993). *See Port Auth. of N.Y. & N.J. v. Arcadian Corp.,* 189 F.3d 305 (3d Cir.1999) (noting that Rule is designed to "screen out cases" where no remedy exists for the wrong alleged or where no relief could possibly be granted).

195. *See Smith v. Frye,* 488 F.3d 263, 274 (4th Cir. 2007); *Christensen v. County of Boone,* 483 F.3d 454, 458 (7th Cir. 2007); *Petruska v. Gannon Univ.,* 462 F.3d 294, 302 (3d Cir. 2006).

196. *See Hefferman v. Bass,* 467 F.3d 596, 599–600 (7th Cir. 2006) (noting that Rule 12(b)(6) "does not stand alone", but implicates Rules 8 and 9).

197. *See SmileCare Dental Group v. Delta Dental Plan of Cal., Inc.,* 88 F.3d 780, 783 (9th Cir.1996).

198. *See Kaltenbach v. Richards,* 464 F.3d 524, 526–27 (5th Cir. 2006).

199. *See Tellabs, Inc. v. Makor Issues & Rights, Ltd.,* ___ U.S. ___, ___, 127 S.Ct. 2499, 2509, 168 L.Ed.2d 179 (2007); *Bell Atlantic Corp. v. Twombly,* ___ U.S. ___, ___, 127 S.Ct. 1955, 1965, 167 L.Ed.2d 929 (2007); *Jackson v. Birmingham Bd. of Educ.,* 544 U.S. 167, 170-71, 125 S.Ct. 1497,

judge disbelieves the allegations or feels that recovery is remote and unlikely.[200]

Yet, although liberal and encouraging of brevity, the federal pleading duty is far from trivial; to satisfy Rules 8 and 9, the pleading must still contain "enough" to give defendants fair notice of both the complaint's claims and the grounds for those claims.[201] Although "detailed factual allegations" need not be supplied, a "showing" by the pleader is nevertheless required.[202] A pleader must do more than merely incant labels, conclusions, and the formulaic elements of a cause of action.[203] Likewise, the court need not accept as true bald assertions and legal conclusions,[204] or legal conclusions "couched" or "masquerading" as facts.[205] Rather, a pleader must show that the allegations "possess enough heft" to establish an entitlement to relief (and, thus, to permit the costly process of litigation to continue).[206] Pleaders must allege enough facts to raise their claims beyond the level of speculation,[207] and must instead "nudge[] their claims across the line from conceivable to plausible".[208] The facts they plead must be sufficient to give rise to a

---

1502–03, 161 L.Ed.2d 361 (2005); *Albright v. Oliver*, 510 U.S. 266, 267, 114 S.Ct. 807, 810, 127 L.Ed.2d 114 (1994); *Scheuer v. Rhodes*, 416 U.S. 232, 94 S.Ct. 1683, 40 L.Ed.2d 90 (1974).

200. See *Bell Atlantic Corp. v. Twombly*, 550 U.S. ___, ___ , 127 S.Ct. 1955, 1965, 167 L.Ed.2d 929 (2007); *Swierkiewicz v. Sorema N. A.*, 534 U.S. 506, 508, n. 1, 122 S.Ct. 992, 152 L.Ed.2d 1 (2002); *Neitzke v. Williams*, 490 U.S. 319, 327, 109 S.Ct. 1827, 104 L.Ed.2d 338 (1989) *Scheuer v. Rhodes*, 416 U.S. 232, 236, 94 S.Ct. 1683, 40 L.Ed.2d 90 (1974).

201. See *Tellabs, Inc. v. Makor Issues & Rights, Ltd.*, ___ U.S. ___, ___, 127 S.Ct. 2499, 2507, 168 L.Ed.2d 179 (2007) ("Although the rule encourages brevity, the complaint must say enough to give the defendant 'fair notice of what the plaintiff's claim is and the grounds upon which it rests' "); *Dura Pharms., Inc. v. Broudo*, 544 U.S. 336, 346–47, 125 S.Ct. 1627, 161 L.Ed.2d 577 (2005) ("We concede that ordinary pleading rules are not meant to impose a great burden upon a plaintiff", but allegations must still give fair notice); *Calvi v. Knox County*, 470 F.3d 422, 430 (1st Cir. 2006) ("Notice pleading rules do not relieve a plaintiff of responsibility for identifying the nature of her claim"); *Amron v. Morgan Stanley Inv. Advisors Inc.*, 464 F.3d 338, 343–44 (2d Cir. 2006) ("we stop well short of saying that Plaintiffs bear no burden at the pleading stage", because they must allege "those facts *necessary* to a finding of liability").

202. See *Bell Atlantic Corp. v. Twombly*, 550 U.S. ___, ___ & ___ n.3, 127 S.Ct. 1955, 1964–65 & 1965 n.3, 167 L.Ed.2d 929 (2007).

203. See *Bell Atlantic Corp. v. Twombly*, 550 U.S. ___, ___ , 127 S.Ct. 1955, 1964–65, 167 L.Ed.2d 929 (2007).

204. See *Aulson v. Blanchard*, 83 F.3d 1, 3 (1st Cir.1996)(commenting that Rule's deferential standard does not obligate a court "to swallow the plaintiff's invective hook, line, and sinker; bald assertions, unsupportable conclusions, periphrastic circumlocutions, and the like need not be credited").

205. See *Bell Atlantic Corp. v. Twombly*, ___ U.S. ___, ___, 127 S.Ct. 1955, 1965, 167 L.Ed.2d 929 (2007) (quoting *Papasan v. Allain*, 478 U.S. 265, 286, 106 S.Ct. 2932, 92 L.Ed.2d 209 (1986)). See also *Mezibov v. Allen*, 411 F.3d 712, 716 (6th Cir.2005); *Ashley v. U.S. Dep't of Interior*, 408 F.3d 997, 1000 (8th Cir.2005); *Centro Medico del Turabo, Inc. v. Feliciano de Melecio*, 406 F.3d 1, 5–6 (1st Cir.2005).

206. See *Bell Atlantic Corp. v. Twombly*, 550 U.S. ___, ___ , 127 S.Ct. 1955, 1966, 167 L.Ed.2d 929 (2007).

207. See *Bell Atlantic Corp. v. Twombly*, 550 U.S. ___, ___ , 127 S.Ct. 1955, 1965, 167 L.Ed.2d 929 (2007).

208. See *Bell Atlantic Corp. v. Twombly*, 550 U.S. ___, ___ , 127 S.Ct. 1955, 1974, 167 L.Ed.2d 929 (2007). The cross into "the realm of plausible liability", the allegations

"reasonably founded hope that the discovery process will reveal relevant evidence" in support of their claims.[209] Pleaders must met their pleading burden for each element required for a recovery under some actionable theory. Thus, the inquiry under Rule 12(b)(6), while guided by the liberal federal pleading standard, is certainly not toothless.[210] Pleadings that are unable to "show" the requisite entitlement to relief are thereby exposed by Rule 12(b)(6) at an early stage in the litigation so as to minimize the costs of time and money by the litigants and the courts.[211]

A Note on *Bell Atlantic v. Twombly*:

In this May 2007 antitrust decision, the Supreme Court (in a 7–2 opinion) expressly overruled the oft-quoted language from its 1957 decision in *Conley v. Gibson* that no complaint should be dismissed for failing to properly state a claim "unless it appears beyond doubt that the plaintiff can prove no set of facts in support of his claim which could entitle him to relief".[212] Because this famous, but "incomplete", phrase could allow any conclusory statement of claim that might theoretically find support from undisclosed facts, the *Conley* language had, wrote the Court, "earned its retirement".[213] In its place, the Court articulated the plausibility standard, outlined above. Courts are just beginning to digest the *Twombly* decision and assess its effect, whether limited to a smaller cluster of federal cases (*e.g.*, antitrust claims only, or only where the allegations are pleaded upon "information and belief" and require significant inferential leaps) or broadly applicable to all federal cases.[214] Practitioners should attentively follow these developments.

must be factual (not conclusory) and suggestive (not neutral). *See id.* at ___ n.5, 127 S.Ct. at 1966 n.5.

209. *See Bell Atlantic Corp. v. Twombly*, 550 U.S. ___, ___, 127 S.Ct. 1955, 1967, 167 L.Ed.2d 929 (2007) (citations omitted).

210. *See Doyle v. Hasbro, Inc.*, 103 F.3d 186, 190 (1st Cir.1996) (pleading requirement, though low, "is real" and is "not entirely a toothless tiger"). *See also Platten v. HG Bermuda Exempted Ltd.*, 437 F.3d 118, 127 (1st Cir.2006) ("may be low, but it is real"); *Educadores Puertorriquenos en Accion v. Hernandez*, 367 F.3d 61, 67–68 (1st Cir.2004) ("minimal requirements are not tantamount to nonexistent requirements").

211. *See Bell Atlantic Corp. v. Twombly*, 550 U.S. ___, ___, 127 S.Ct. 1955, 1966, 167 L.Ed.2d 929 (2007) (citations omitted).

212. *See Bell Atlantic Corp. v. Twombly*, 550 U.S. ___, ___, 127 S.Ct. 1955, 1968–69, 167 L.Ed.2d 929 (2007) (abrogating language in *Conley v. Gibson*, 355 U.S. 41, 45–46, 78 S.Ct. 99, 2 L.Ed.2d 80 (1957)).

213. *See Bell Atlantic Corp. v. Twombly*, 550 U.S. ___, ___, 127 S.Ct. 1955, 1969, 167 L.Ed.2d 929 (2007). The Court explained the proper understanding of *Conley*'s message this way: "once a claim has been stated adequately, it may be supported by showing any set of facts consistent with the allegations in the complaint" *Id.* at ___, 127 S.Ct. at 1969.

214. *See, e.g., E.E.O.C. v. Concentra Health Servs., Inc.*, 496 F.3d 773, 776 (7th Cir. 2007) (commenting that *Twombly* "impose two easy-to-clear hurdles"–fair notice to defendants of claim and grounds, and plausible allegations); *Gregory v. Dillard's, Inc.*, 494 F.3d 694, 710 (8th Cir. 2007) (plaintiffs' racial discrimination allegations satisfied *Twombly* because they stated "how, when, and where they were discriminated against"); *Iqbal v. Hasty*, 490 F.3d 143, 155–58 (2d Cir. 2007) (generally analyzing impact of *Twombly*, and theorizing that *Twombly* does not create new heightened pleading standard, but a flexible approach requiring pleaders to amplify their claim only when needed for plausibility).

Time will tell how *Twombly* impacts the Rule 12(b)(6) case precedent that has developed in the federal courts over the many years since *Conley* was decided. Before *Twombly*, it was understood that the pleader's stated legal theory and specific requests for relief were not necessarily dispositive in ruling on a Rule 12(b)(6) motion.[215] In fact, the complaint might not need to identify a particular legal theory at all.[216] A claim generally would not be dismissed, even though the asserted legal theories were not cognizable or the relief sought were unavailable, so long as other tenable legal claims are evident from the facts averred on the face of the complaint[217] or the pleader was otherwise entitled to any type of relief under another possible legal theory.[218] The courts were especially hesitant to dismiss, at the pleading stage, claims pressing novel legal theories, if the claims could be better examined following development of the facts through discovery,[219] or if they were peculiarly fact-intensive cases[220] or involved significant state-of-mind issues.[221] Conversely, commentators had observed that the courts tended to judge claims more strictly when they involved "disfavored" causes of action, such as malicious prosecution or defamation.[222]

"Clarifying" the Complaint with Briefs and Oral Argument

Although the factual averments in the *pleading* are deemed true on a motion to dismiss, the court may refuse to accept as true the pleader's statements made for the first time in a legal memorandum or brief that forms no part of the official pleadings.[223] However, the

215. *See Williams v. Seniff,* 342 F.3d 774, 792 (7th Cir.2003); *Barrett v. Tallon,* 30 F.3d 1296, 1299 (10th Cir.1994).

216. *See Williams v. Seniff,* 342 F.3d 774, 792 (7th Cir.2003).

217. *See Glover v. Liggett Group, Inc.,* 459 F.3d 1304 (11th Cir.2006) (dismissal proper when, due to a dispositive issue of law, no construction of the plaintiff's facts would support a cause of action).

218. *See Bowers v. Hardwick,* 478 U.S. 186, 106 S.Ct. 2841, 92 L.Ed.2d 140 (1986); *Figueroa v. Rivera,* 147 F.3d 77 (1st Cir. 1998).

219. *See McGary v. City of Portland,* 386 F.3d 1259, 1270 (9th Cir.2004); *Baker v. Cuomo,* 58 F.3d 814, 818–19 (2d Cir. 1995).

220. *See Dickson v. Microsoft Corp.,* 309 F.3d 193, 212 (4th Cir.2002) (recognizing that dismissal and other "summary procedures" should be applied "sparingly" in complicated antitrust litigation "where motive and intent play leading roles", but antitrust litigation does not have an exemption from Rule 12(b)(6) and plaintiff must allege facts supportive of each element of antitrust claim). Note, however, that *Twombly* was an antitrust case (see *infra*).

221. *See Tello v. Dean Witter Reynolds, Inc.,* 410 F.3d 1275, 1283 (11th Cir.2005) (inquiry notice of securities fraud is "often inappropriate for resolution on a motion to dismiss"); *Pryor v. National Collegiate Athletic Ass'n,* 288 F.3d 548, 565 (3d Cir.2002) (noting that cases "involving state of mind (e.g., intent) are often unsuitable for a Rule 12(b)(6) motion to dismiss").

222. *See* 5A Charles A. Wright & Arthur R. Miller, *Federal Practice & Procedure* § 1357, at 359–60 (1990). In 1993, the Supreme Court rejected the practice of applying a "heightened pleading standard" to certain civil rights claims under 42 U.S.C.A. § 1983, holding that, with the exception of fraud, mistake, and certain conditions precedent governed expressly by Rule 9(b) and 9(c), the federal notice pleading standards apply universally. *See Leatherman v. Tarrant County Narcotics Intelligence & Coordination Unit,* 507 U.S. 163, 113 S.Ct. 1160, 122 L.Ed.2d 517 (1993). Consequently, courts may no longer have the ability to apply a stricter standard of review to malicious prosecution and defamation claims.

223. *See Henthorn v. Department of Navy,* 29 F.3d 682 (D.C.Cir.1994).

pleader's memorandum or brief can be used to "clarify" allegations of the pleading[224], as can statements made by the pleader during oral argument.[225]

Pleading in Anticipation of Affirmative Defenses

Ordinarily, plaintiffs need not anticipate the defendants' likely affirmative defenses, nor attempt to preemptively "plead around" them in the complaint.[226] Whether the complaint states a claim upon which relief can be granted is generally not dependent on whether the defendant has a defense.[227] Failure to "plead around" a likely affirmative defense is typically not a proper basis for dismissal.[228]

"Built–In" Defenses

The court will dismiss for failing to state a claim where the face of the complaint reveals obvious, "built-in" affirmative defenses, such as statute of limitations, assumption of risk, or statute of frauds.[229] Thus, plaintiffs can "plead themselves out of court" by averring facts that establish an affirmative defense[230] or that otherwise demonstrate that success on the merits is not possible.[231] Similarly, the court may also dismiss under Rule 12(b)(6) where extrinsic materials (such as the complaint's exhibits and other materials properly considered by the court) reveal the same type of obvious, "built-in" defenses.[232] To support such a dismissal, two prerequisites are necessary: the facts that establish the defense are readily ascertainable from the complaint, the public record, or other allowable sources of judicial notice, *and* those facts conclusively demonstrate the defense.[233]

Timing

The defense of failure to state a claim may be asserted at any

224. *See Pegram v. Herdrich*, 530 U.S. 211, 229, 120 S.Ct. 2143, 2155 n. 10, 147 L.Ed.2d 164 (2000).

225. *See Maio v. Aetna, Inc.*, 221 F.3d 472, 485 n. 12 (3d Cir.2000).

226. *See Hollander v. Brown*, 457 F.3d 688 (7th Cir.2006); *Memphis, Tenn. Area Local, American Postal Workers Union v. City of Memphis*, 361 F.3d 898, 902 (6th Cir.2004).

227. *See United States v. Northern Trust Co.*, 372 F.3d 886, 888 (7th Cir.2004).

228. *See Xechem, Inc. v. Bristol–Myers Squibb Co.*, 372 F.3d 899, 901 (7th Cir. 2004).

229. *See Goodman v. Praxair, Inc.*, 494 F.3d 458, 464 (4th Cir. 2007); *EPCO Carbon Dioxide Prods., Inc. v. JP Morgan Chase Bank, NA*, 467 F.3d 466, 470 (5th Cir. 2006); *Financial Sec. Assur., Inc. v. Stephens, Inc.*, 450 F.3d 1257, 1268 (11th Cir.2006); *Xechem, Inc. v. Bristol–Myers Squibb Co.*, 372 F.3d 899, 901 (7th Cir. 2004).

230. *See Hollander v. Brown*, 457 F.3d 688 (7th Cir.2006).

231. *See Trudeau v. Federal Trade Comm'n*, 456 F.3d 178 (D.C.Cir.2006).

232. *See Thompson v. Illinois Dep't of Professional Regulation*, 300 F.3d 750, 754 (7th Cir.2002) ("where a plaintiff attaches documents and relies upon the documents to form the basis for a claim or part of a claim, dismissal is appropriate if the document negates the claim"); *Jacobsen v. Deseret Book Co.*, 287 F.3d 936, 941–42 (10th Cir.2002) (in deciding Rule 12(b)(6) motion in copyright cases, "the legal effect of the works are determined by the works themselves rather than by allegations in the complaint" if the works are attached as exhibits). *See also infra* Authors' Commentary to Rule 12(b)(6) ("**Extrinsic Materials**").

233. *See Nisselson v. Lernout*, 469 F.3d 143, 150 (1st Cir. 2006).

time, even at trial,[234] but is waived if not asserted during trial.[235] Rule 12(b)(6) *motions* seeking dismissal of such claims, however, must ordinarily be filed before a responsive pleading is served. Once the pleadings are closed, the defense may be pressed on a Rule 12(c) motion for judgment on the pleadings or a Rule 56 motion for summary judgment.[236] A post-pleadings / pre-discovery motion that mistakenly asserts this defense under Rule 12(b)(6) will typically, absent prejudice to the nonmoving party, be treated as a Rule 12(c) motion.[237]

Waiver

A party generally does not waive the right to challenge a lawsuit for failing to state a claim,[238] provided the defense is asserted at some point before the conclusion of trial.[239]

Burden of Proof

The burden lies with the moving party.[240] In fact, even a failure by the non-moving party to oppose the motion will not necessarily justify an automatic dismissal (unless by local rule or court order a response is required on pain of dismissal).[241] The trial court must still determine whether a dismissal is appropriate.

Sua Sponte Motions

Provided it adopts a fair procedure for doing so, the trial court may, on its own initiative, and without an adversary's motion, dismiss a pleading for failing to state a claim upon which relief may be granted.[242] Such dismissals, however, are "strong medicine, and

234. *See* Rule 12(h)(2).

235. *See Arbaugh v. Y&H Corp.*, 546 U.S. 500, ___, 126 S.Ct. 1235, 1240, 163 L.Ed.2d 1097 (2006) (Rule 12(b)(6) objection "endures up to, but not beyond, trial on the merits").

236. *See Patel v. Contemporary Classics of Beverly Hills*, 259 F.3d 123, at 125–26 (2d Cir.2001); *Turbe v. Government of Virgin Islands*, 938 F.2d 427, 428 (3d Cir. 1991).

237. *See MacDonald v. Grace Church Seattle*, 457 F.3d 1079 (9th Cir.2006); *McMillan v. Collection Prof'ls Inc.*, 455 F.3d 754, 757 (7th Cir.2006).

238. *See* Rule 12(h)(2). *See also McIntosh v. Antonino*, 71 F.3d 29, 38 (1st Cir. 1995)(refusing to find waiver of statute of limitations defense, asserted as an affirmative defense, where defendant chose not to move for judgment earlier in the proceedings: "This assertion has no foothold in the law").

239. *See Arbaugh v. Y&H Corp.*, 546 U.S. 500, ___, 126 S.Ct. 1235, 1240, 163 L.Ed.2d 1097 (2006) (Rule 12(b)(6) objec-

tion "endures up to, but not beyond, trial on the merits").

240. *See Ragin v. New York Times Co.*, 923 F.2d 995, 999 (2d Cir.1991); *Yeksigian v. Nappi*, 900 F.2d 101, 104–05 (7th Cir. 1990); *Anyanwu v. Columbia Broad. Sys., Inc.*, 887 F.Supp. 690, 692 (S.D.N.Y. 1995)(observing that Rule 12(b)(6) imposes substantial proof burdens upon the movant). *See Brever v. Rockwell Int'l Corp.*, 40 F.3d 1119, 1125 (10th Cir.1994)(noting that Rules "erect a powerful presumption against rejecting pleadings for failure to state a claim")(citation omitted).

241. *See Pomerleau v. West Springfield Public Sch.*, 362 F.3d 143, 145 (1st Cir. 2004).

242. *See Martinez-Rivera v. Sanchez Ramos*, ___ F.3d ___, ___, 2007 WL 2254586, at *2–*3 (1st Cir. 2007); *Lee v. City of Los Angeles*, 250 F.3d 668, 683 (9th Cir.2001); *Ledford v. Sullivan*, 105 F.3d 354, 356 (7th Cir.1997); *Best v. Kelly*, 39 F.3d 328, 331 (D.C.Cir.1994). *But cf. Blue Cross & Blue Shield of Alabama v. Sanders*, 138 F.3d 1347, 1354 (11th Cir.1998) (holding that because "failure to state a claim"

should be dispensed sparingly.''[243] Generally, fair procedure requires that the trial court notify the pleader of its intention to grant a *sua sponte* dismissal and permit an opportunity to amend or otherwise respond.[244] One court forbids *sua sponte* dismissals (1) if no responsive pleading has been filed and an amendment as of right would still be timely, (2) if the complaint was filed in good faith, and (3) if the plaintiff has not been given notice of the *sua sponte* intent to dismiss coupled with a right to respond.[245] Nevertheless, a *sua sponte* dismissal entered without forewarning to the plaintiff may still be affirmed if the pleading's allegations are "patently meritless" and without any hope of cure.[246]. In such a case, the party defending the dismissal carries the burden of demonstrating that the allegations, drawn most favorably to the pleader, are beyond all hope.[247]

Postponing Discovery

Some courts permit a postponement of discovery after a Rule 12(b)(6) motion is filed, and then continuing for so long as it remains pending.[248]

Pro Se Litigants

Courts are particularly cautious while inspecting pleadings prepared by plaintiffs who lack counsel and are proceeding *pro se*. Often inartful, and rarely composed to the standards expected of practicing attorneys, *pro se* pleadings are viewed with considerable liberality and are held to less stringent standards than those expected of pleadings drafted by lawyers.[249] Notwithstanding this liberality, unrepresented plaintiffs are not relieved of their obligation to

is not a jurisdictional issue, court may not *sua sponte* decide the question unless plaintiff has preserved it); *Baker v. Cuomo*, 58 F.3d 814, 818 (2d Cir.1995) (commenting that *sua sponte* dismissals without service of process and a responsive filing by the opponent are disfavored).

243. *Chute v. Walker*, 281 F.3d 314, 319 (1st Cir.2002).

244. *See Martinez-Rivera v. Sanchez Ramos*, __ F.3d __, __, 2007 WL 2254586, at *2-*3 (1st Cir. 2007); *Lee v. City of Los Angeles*, 250 F.3d 668, 683 (9th Cir.2001).

245. *See American United Life Ins. Co. v. Martinez*, 480 F.3d 1043, 1057 (11th Cir. 2007).

246. *See Chute v. Walker*, 281 F.3d 314, 319 (1st Cir.2002) (commenting that *sua sponte* dismissal without notice may stand "[i]f it is crystal clear that the plaintiff cannot prevail and that amending the complaint would be futile").

247. *Martinez-Rivera v. Sanchez Ramos*, __ F.3d __, __, 2007 WL 2254586, at *2—*3 (1st Cir. 2007).

248. *See Mitchell v. McNeil*, 487 F.3d 374, 379 (6th Cir. 2007) (because plaintiffs failed to state a cognizable claim, there was no error in denying discovery); *Tucker v. Union of Needletrades, Industrial & Textile Employees*, 407 F.3d 784, 787–88 (6th Cir. 2005) (noting that "very purpose" of Rule 12(b)(6) is to permit challenge to legal sufficiency of complaints without subjecting party to discovery); *Rutman Wine Co. v. E. & J. Gallo Winery*, 829 F.2d 729, 738 (9th Cir.1987) (same, and noting that it is "sounder practice to determine whether there is any reasonable likelihood that plaintiffs can construct a claim before forcing the parties to undergo the expense of discovery").

249. *See Erickson v. Pardus*, __ U.S. __, __, 127 S.Ct. 2197, 2200, 167 L.Ed.2d 1081 (2007) (per curiam); *Estelle v. Gamble*, 429 U.S. 97, 106, 97 S.Ct. 285, 50 L.Ed.2d 251 (1976); *Haines v. Kerner*, 404 U.S. 519, 520–21, 92 S.Ct. 594, 595–96, 30 L.Ed.2d 652 (1972).

allege sufficient facts to support a cognizable legal claim.[250] The court will dismiss a claim filed *in forma pauperis* if the claim is legally frivolous.[251]

Extrinsic Materials

The parties may produce affidavits and other materials either in support of or in opposition to a motion for failure to state a claim.[252] However, if the court, in its discretion,[253] considers such extrinsic evidence, the motion must be converted into a request for summary judgment under Rule 56.[254] The process for this conversion (which once was set forth in the text of Rule 12(b)(6)) was relocated by the 2007 amendments to its new location in Rule 12(d).

Oral Argument

The trial judge may, but is not obligated to, convene oral argument on a Rule 12(b)(6) motion to dismiss.[255]

Ruling Deferred

Where circumstances persuade the court that claims should not be dismissed until further factual development is accomplished, the court may deny the Rule 12(b)(6) motion and revisit the merits of claims on a Rule 12(c) motion for judgment on the pleadings or a Rule 56 motion for summary judgment.[256]

250. *See Taylor v. Books A Million, Inc.,* 296 F.3d 376, 378 (5th Cir.2002); *Riddle v. Mondragon,* 83 F.3d 1197, 1202 (10th Cir. 1996).

251. *See* 28 U.S.C.A. § 1915(e)(2)(B); 28 U.S.C.A. § 1915A. *See also Neitzke v. Williams,* 490 U.S. 319, 109 S.Ct. 1827, 104 L.Ed.2d 338 (1989)(describing standards for dismissals of *in forma pauperis* pleadings as frivolous).

252. *See Ford Motor Co. v. Summit Motor Prods., Inc.,* 930 F.2d 277 (3d Cir.1991).

253. *See Pueschel v. United States,* 369 F.3d 345, 353 n.3 (4th Cir.2004); *Stahl v. United States Dep't of Agric.,* 327 F.3d 697, 701 (8th Cir.2003); *Lybrook v. Members of Farmington Mun. Schs. Bd. of Educ.,* 232 F.3d 1334, 1341–42 (10th Cir.2000).

254. *See R.J. Corman Derailment Servs., LLC v. International Union of Operating Eng'rs, Local Union 150, AFL–CIO,* 335 F.3d 643, 647 (7th Cir.2003); *Pryor v. National Collegiate Athletic Ass'n.,* 288 F.3d 548, 560 (3d Cir.2002); *Trustmark Ins. Co. v. ESLU, Inc.,* 299 F.3d 1265, 1265 (11th Cir.2002); *Country Club Estates, L.L.C. v. Town of Loma Linda,* 213 F.3d 1001, 1005 (8th Cir.2000). *But cf. Terracom v. Valley Nat'l Bank,* 49 F.3d 555 (9th Cir. 1995)(noting that because court made only "minor parenthetical observation" concern-

ing an affidavit submitted by the parties, conversion was not required).

255. *See* Rule 78 ("By rule or order, the court may provide for submitting and determining motions on briefs, without oral hearings."); *Greene v. WCI Holdings Corp.,* 136 F.3d 313, 316 (2d Cir.1998) ("Every circuit to consider the issue has determined that the 'hearing' requirements of Rule 12 ... do not mean that an oral hearing is necessary, but only require that a party be given the opportunity to present its views to the court"). *See also Pueschel v. United States,* 369 F.3d 345, 354 (4th Cir.2004); *Cline v. Rogers,* 87 F.3d 176, 184 (6th Cir. 1996); *Riddle v. Mondragon,* 83 F.3d 1197, 1208 (10th Cir.1996).

256. *See Keys Jet Ski, Inc. v. Kays,* 893 F.2d 1225, 1230 (11th Cir.1990)(refusing to affirm district court's dismissal ruling in the absence of further factual development to support the claims); *Flue–Cured Tobacco Co-op. Stabilization Corp. v. United States EPA,* 857 F.Supp. 1137, 1145 (M.D.N.C. 1994)(deferring determination of legal sufficiency of due process claim where adjudication on that issue can be more accurately accomplished after a factual record is developed); *Evello Invs., N.V. v. Printed Media Servs., Inc.,* 158 F.R.D. 172, 173 (D.Kan. 1994)(citing Rule 12(d), court elected to defer consideration of Rule 12(b)(6) motion in

Voluntary Dismissals While Motion is Pending

Plaintiffs may voluntarily dismiss a lawsuit at any time prior to the point where their adversaries serve an answer or a motion for summary judgment.[257] Consequently, plaintiffs are generally permitted to voluntarily dismiss their lawsuits during the pendency of a Rule 12(b)(6) motion to dismiss. This entitlement is *not* automatically lost when a defendant serves a motion to dismiss that is accompanied improperly by extrinsic materials (which could require that the motion be converted to a summary judgment proceeding); rather, until such a motion is formally converted by the court, the plaintiffs should still be permitted to voluntarily dismiss.[258]

Remedy and Amendments

The court will generally permit the pleader an opportunity to amend unless an amendment would be futile.[259] Even where the court doubts that the pleading defects can be overcome, the federal policy favoring decisions on the merits, rather than on technicalities, counsels in favor of permitting the plaintiff leave to amend and re-file the pleading at least once, prior to entry of judgment, unless the exercise is plainly futile.[260]

> *NOTE*: A plaintiff who is otherwise entitled to file an amended complaint following a Rule 12(b)(6) dismissal may choose instead to stand on the original complaint and appeal the dismissal.[261]

Prejudice on Dismissal

Unless the ruling is premised on mere technical pleading defects or the court directs otherwise (or permits an amended pleading), a dismissal for failing to state a claim is deemed to be a ruling on the merits, and, once final, is accorded full res judicata effect.[262]

"highly contentious and complicated case" where dismissal motion hinged on "complicated factual and legal questions"). *But see First Commercial Trust Co., N.A. v. Colt's Mfg. Co.,* 77 F.3d 1081, 1083 n. 4 (8th Cir.1996)(noting that litigants have no entitlement to discovery in the absence of a plausible legal theory).

257. *See* Rule 41(a)(1)(A)(i).

258. *See Swedberg v. Marotzke,* 339 F.3d 1139, 1142–45 (9th Cir.2003); *Finley Lines Joint Protective Bd. Unit 200 v. Norfolk So. Corp.,* 109 F.3d 993 (4th Cir.1997); *Aamot v. Kassel,* 1 F.3d 441 (6th Cir.1993).

259. *See E.E.O.C. v. Concentra Health Servs., Inc.,* 496 F.3d 773, 7870 (7th Cir. 2007); *Public Utility Dist. No. 1 v. IDA-CORP Inc.,* 379 F.3d 641 (9th Cir.2004); *Alston v. Parker,* 363 F.3d 229, 235 (3d Cir.2004).

260. *See Ostrzenski v. Seigel,* 177 F.3d 245, 252–53 (4th Cir.1999).

261. *See Alston v. Parker,* 363 F.3d 229, 235 (3d Cir.2004) ("If the plaintiff does not desire to amend, he may file an appropriate notice with the district court asserting his intent to stand on the complaint, at which time an order to dismiss the action would be appropriate"). *See also WMX Techs., Inc. v. Miller,* 104 F.3d 1133 (9th Cir.1997) (holding that plaintiff must obtain final judgment from district court before "standing" on original complaint and taking immediate appeal).

262. *See Federated Dep't Stores, Inc. v. Moitie,* 452 U.S. 394, 399 n. 3, 101 S.Ct. 2424, 2428 n. 3, 69 L.Ed.2d 103 (1981); *Davila v. Delta Air Lines, Inc.,* 326 F.3d 1183, 1189–90 (11th Cir.2003); *Stewart v. U.S. Bancorp,* 297 F.3d 953, 957 (9th Cir. 2002); *Criales v. American Airlines, Inc.,* 105 F.3d 93, 97 (2d Cir.1997). *Cf. Davis v. Davis,* 526 F.2d 1286 (5th Cir.1976) (conversely, commenting that denial of Rule 12(b)(6) dismissal is not forecast of likely

Appealability

Whether Rule 12(b)(6) rulings are immediately appealable presents complex issues that require careful study by practitioners. The general rule holds that a district court decision that grants a Rule 12(b)(6) motion is a "final order" within the meaning of 28 U.S.C. § 1291, from which an immediate appeal must be taken,[263] but a ruling that denies a Rule 12(b)(6) motion is interlocutory, and ordinarily is not immediately appealable.[264] Exceptions, however, are numerous. For example, denials of motions to dismiss that assert certain types of immunity issues have been deemed immediately appealable under the collateral order doctrine.[265] The question of appealability from Rule 12(b)(6) rulings, therefore, must be carefully researched within the context of the specific issues presented in the motion.

RULE 12(b)(7). DISMISSAL FOR FAILURE TO JOIN A RULE 19 PARTY

CORE CONCEPT

A case will be dismissed if there is an absent party under Rule 19, without whom complete relief cannot be granted or whose interest in the dispute is of such a nature that to proceed without that party could prejudice either that party or others.

APPLICATIONS

Legal Test

The courts are hesitant to dismiss for failure to join absent parties, and will not do so on a vague possibility that unjoined persons may have an interest in the litigation.[266] When a Rule

---

outcome of case). *But see Ostrzenski v. Seigel*, 177 F.3d 245, 252–53 (4th Cir.1999) (holding that dismissal under Rule 12(b)(6) generally is neither final nor a merits ruling).

263. *See ALA, Inc. v. CCAIR, Inc.*, 29 F.3d 855 (3d Cir.1994). *But see Eberhardt v. O'Malley*, 17 F.3d 1023, 1024 (7th Cir. 1994)(order dismissing complaint "is not in itself a final, appealable judgment, since the plaintiff may be entitled to replead or be given leave to replead").

264. *See Ridpath v. Board of Governors Marshall Univ.*, 447 F.3d 292, 304 (4th Cir.2006); *Hill v. City of New York*, 45 F.3d 653, 659 (2d Cir.1995); *Foster Wheeler Energy Corp. v. Metropolitan Knox Solid Waste Auth., Inc.*, 970 F.2d 199, 202 (6th Cir. 1992). *See also Bennett v. Pippin*, 74 F.3d 578, 585 (5th Cir.1996) (holding that Rule 12(b)(6) motions to dismiss become moot after plaintiff prevails following a full trial

on the merits; thereafter, any pleading defect may be cured by amendment).

265. *See, e.g., Puerto Rico Aqueduct & Sewer Auth. v. Metcalf & Eddy, Inc.*, 506 U.S. 139, 113 S.Ct. 684, 121 L.Ed.2d 605 (1993)(holding that denial of Eleventh Amendment immunity was immediately appealable collateral order); *Mitchell v. Forsyth*, 472 U.S. 511, 105 S.Ct. 2806, 86 L.Ed.2d 411 (1985)(holding that ruling denying qualified immunity was an immediately appealable collateral order); *Zamani v. Carnes*, 491 F.3d 990, 994 (9th Cir. 2007) (denial of anti-SLAPP motion immediately appealable under collateral order doctrine); *Goldstein v. City of Long Beach*, 481 F.3d 1170, 1172 (9th Cir. 2007) (denial of absolute immunity motion immediately appealable).

266. *See Sever v. Glickman*, 298 F.Supp.2d 267, 275 (D.Conn.2004); *Swartz*

12(b)(7) motion is filed, the court will apply the standards of Rule 19(a) to determine whether joinder is essential and, if so, whether the factors of Rule 19(b) make dismissal appropriate.[267] The court conducts this inquiry on the basis of the pleadings as they appear at the time the joinder is proposed.[268] The court will accept all of the pleader's well-pleaded factual allegations as true, and will draw all reasonable inferences in the pleader's favor.[269]

Timing and Waiver

An objection to the absence of a Rule 19 indispensable party may be asserted by motion filed before a responsive pleading, in the responsive pleading itself, by motion for judgment on the pleadings, or during the trial on the merits.[270] One court, however, has held that the trial judge enjoys the discretion to reject such a motion as untimely, if the motion is found to have been submitted belatedly and for a litigant's own defensive purposes, rather than to protect the interests of the absent party.[271]

Sua Sponte Motions

Although the absence of a Rule 19 party is *not* a jurisdictional defect, the court may, on its own initiative, raise the absence of a Rule 19 party.

Burden of Proof

The burden lies with the person seeking the dismissal to demonstrate the "indispensable" nature of the absent party.[272]

Remedy

The court will, if possible, order that the absent party be joined in the lawsuit. If joinder is not possible, the court will consider whether in equity and good conscience the lawsuit should continue without the absent party.[273] Dismissals are disfavored, however.[274]

---

v. Beach, 229 F.Supp.2d 1239, 1250–51 (D.Wyo.2002).

267. *See HS Resources, Inc. v. Wingate*, 327 F.3d 432, 439 (5th Cir.2003); *Boulevard Bank Nat'l Ass'n v. Philips Med. Sys. Int'l B.V.*, 15 F.3d 1419, 1422 (7th Cir.1994); *Alcoa Inc. v. ALcan Inc.*, 495 F.Supp.2d 459, ——, 2007 WL 2083813, at *4 (D.Del. 2007); *Register v. Cameron & Barkley Co.*, 467 F.Supp.2d 519, 530 (D.S.C. 2006); *Barrett v. Ambient Pressure Diving, Ltd.*, 235 F.R.D. 263, 268 (E.D.Pa.2006).

268. *See Register v. Cameron & Barkley Co.*, 467 F.Supp.2d 519, 530 (D.S.C. 2006).

269. *See Rotec Indus., Inc. v. Aecon Group, Inc.*, 436 F.Supp.2d 931, 933 (N.D.Ill.2006); *Trademark Retail, Inc. v. Apple Glen Investors, LP*, 196 F.R.D. 535, 536 n.2 (N.D.Ind.2000).

270. *See Legal Aid Society v. City of N.Y.*, 114 F.Supp.2d 204, 219 (S.D.N.Y.

2000) (noting that failure to join indispensable party is not a "threshold defense"; instead, defendant may raise this challenge through end of trial).

271. *See Fireman's Fund Ins. Co. v. National Bank of Cooperatives*, 103 F.3d 888, 896 (9th Cir.1996).

272. *See Citizen Band Potawatomi Indian Tribe v. Collier*, 17 F.3d 1292, 1293 (10th Cir.1994); *Ilan–Gat Eng'rs, Ltd. v. Antigua Int'l Bank*, 659 F.2d 234 (D.C.Cir. 1981); *Rotec Indus., Inc. v. Aecon Group, Inc.*, 436 F.Supp.2d 931, 933 (N.D.Ill.2006).

273. *See* Rule 19(b). *See also United States v. White*, 893 F.Supp. 1423 (C.D.Cal. 1995)(dismissal under Rule 12(b)(7) will be granted only where the unjoined party is "indispensable", and not just "necessary", and the party cannot otherwise be joined).

274. *See Gorsuch v. Fireman's Fund Ins. Co.*, 360 F.2d 23 (9th Cir.1966).

Extrinsic Materials

The parties may produce affidavits and other materials to support their positions on the absence of a Rule 19 party.[275] However, when matters outside the pleadings are submitted with the Rule 12(b)(7) motion to dismiss, some courts have held that the filing must be converted into a motion for summary judgment, affording all parties notice of the conversion and the opportunity to file summary judgment oppositions.[276]

Ruling Deferred

The court may defer ruling on the challenge until after discovery is conducted.[277]

Prejudice on Dismissal

A dismissal for lack of a Rule 19 party is proper only when the defect cannot be cured.[278] Moreover, such a dismissal generally does not preclude the plaintiff from re-instituting the claim in a court that can join the "indispensable" absent party.[279]

Appealability

The district court's denial of a Rule 12(b)(7) motion is usually interlocutory and not immediately appealable.[280]

RULE 12(c).   JUDGMENT ON THE PLEADINGS

CORE CONCEPT

After the pleadings are closed, a party may move for judgment on the pleadings if no material facts remain at issue and the parties' dispute can be resolved on both the pleadings and those facts of which the court can take judicial notice.

APPLICATIONS

Infrequently Used

Rule 12(c)'s usefulness has been displaced in many instances by the more prevalent use of pre-answer Rule 12(b) motions to dismiss and post-answer Rule 56 motions for summary judgment.

275. *See Davis Cos. v. Emerald Casino, Inc.,* 268 F.3d 477, 480 n.4 (7th Cir.2001); *Citizen Band Potawatomi Indian Tribe v. Collier,* 17 F.3d 1292, 1293 (10th Cir.1994); *Rotec Indus., Inc. v. Aecon Group, Inc.,* 436 F.Supp.2d 931, 933 (N.D.Ill.2006); *Picuris Pueblo v. Oglebay Norton Co.,* 228 F.R.D. 665, 666 (D.N.M.2005).

276. *See Raytheon Co. v. Continental Cas. Co.,* 123 F.Supp.2d 22, 32 (D.Mass. 2000); *Steward v. Gwaltney of Smithfield, Ltd.,* 954 F.Supp. 1118, 1121 (E.D.Va.1996), *aff'd,* 103 F.3d 120 (4th Cir.1996) (Table).

277. *See Raytheon Co. v. Continental Cas. Co.,* 123 F.Supp.2d 22, 32 (D.Mass. 2000); *Mije Assocs. v. Halliburton Servs.,* 552 F.Supp. 418 (S.D.N.Y.1982).

278. *See Sever v. Glickman,* 298 F.Supp.2d 267, 275 (D.Conn.2004).

279. *See Dredge Corp. v. Penny,* 338 F.2d 456 (9th Cir.1964); *Raytheon Co. v. Continental Cas. Co.,* 123 F.Supp.2d 22, 33 n.9 (D.Mass.2000). *See De Wit v. Firstar Corp.,* 879 F.Supp. 947, 992 (N.D.Iowa 1995)(dismissals with prejudice appropriate only where the court first orders joinder of the indispensable party and joinder is not accomplished).

280. *See PepsiCo. v. FTC,* 472 F.2d 179 (2d Cir.1972)(noting that general principle the denial of any motion to dismiss is not a "final order" is applicable to Rule 12(b)(7) rulings).

Purpose

A motion for judgment on the pleadings may be used either to press Rule 12(b) defenses to the pleading's procedural defects or to seek a substantive disposition of the case on the basis of its underlying merits.[281]

Timing

A motion for judgment on the pleadings can be made any time after the pleadings are closed.[282] Such a motion need *not* await discovery.[283] A Rule 12(c) motion is premature if made before an answer is filed.[284] An unlabeled or mislabeled (Rule 12(b)(6)) motion to dismiss submitted after an answer is filed will be treated as a Rule 12(c) motion.[285] However, a motion filed too long after the pleadings are closed may be refused as untimely.[286]

Waiver

A motion for judgment on the pleadings cannot assert defenses and objections that a party has waived by failing to timely assert in a preliminary Rule 12(b) motion or in the responsive pleading.

Legal Test

A motion under Rule 12(c) is generally treated in the same manner as a Rule 12(b)(6) motion to dismiss.[287] The pleadings are construed liberally,[288] and court does not resolve contested facts.[289]

---

281. *See Alexander v. City of Chicago*, 994 F.2d 333 (7th Cir.1993).

282. *See Hughes v. Tobacco Inst., Inc.*, 278 F.3d 417, 420 (5th Cir.2001); *Republic Steel Corp. v. Pennsylvania Eng'g Corp.*, 785 F.2d 174 (7th Cir.1986). *See also Warzon v. Drew*, 60 F.3d 1234, 1237 (7th Cir. 1995)(where answer had already been filed, district court converted defendants' Rule 12(b)(6) motion for dismissal into a Rule 12(c) motion for judgment on the pleadings).

283. *See Carlson v. Reed*, 249 F.3d 876, 878 n.1 (9th Cir.2001) (rejecting as "frivolous" an argument that a Rule 12(c) motion was granted prematurely where discovery had not yet been completed).

284. *See Doe v. United States,* 419 F.3d 1058 (9th Cir.2005) (premature and should have been denied); *Progressive Cas. Ins. Co. v. Estate of Crone,* 894 F.Supp. 383 (D.Kan. 1995). *But see Resolution Trust Corp. v. Woods*, 870 F.Supp. 797, 804 (W.D.Tenn. 1994)(ruling that, even where pleadings were not yet closed at the time the motions were filed, court would nevertheless consider the pleadings where plaintiff does not object to the motions as premature). However, the courts may agree to choose to treat premature, pre-answer Rule 12(c) motions as motions to dismiss under Rule

12(b)(6). *See also Warzon v. Drew*, 60 F.3d 1234 (7th Cir.1995); *Seber v. Unger*, 881 F.Supp. 323, 325 n. 2 (N.D.Ill.1995)(same).

285. *See Steele v. Federal Bureau of Prisons*, 355 F.3d 1204, 1212 n.4 (10th Cir. 2003).

286. *See* Rule 12(c) (motion must be made "[a]fter the pleadings are closed but within such time as not to delay the trial"). *See General Elec. Co. v. Sargent & Lundy*, 916 F.2d 1119, 1131 (6th Cir. 1990)(reversing "timeliness" denial of Rule 12(c) motion where no allegation of prejudice was pressed and where the basis for any alleged prejudice was not articulated).

287. *See Lindsay v. Yates*, ___ F.3d ___, ___, 2007 WL 2316626, at *2 (6th Cir. 2007); *Chauvin v. State Farm Fire & Cas. Co.*, 495 F.3d 232, ___ (5th Cir. 2007); *ITI Holdings, Inc. v. Odom*, 468 F.3d 17, 18–19 (1st Cir. 2006); *Cleveland v. Caplaw Enters.*, 448 F.3d 518, 521 (2d Cir.2006); *Park Univ. Enters., Inc. v. American Cas. Co.*, 442 F.3d 1239, 1244 (10th Cir.2006).

288. *See Brittan Commc'ns Int'l Corp. v. Southwestern Bell Tel. Co.*, 313 F.3d 899, 904 (5th Cir.2002).

289. *See Aponte–Torres v. University of Puerto Rico*, 445 F.3d 50, 54 (1st Cir.2006).

Instead, the court accepts all well-pleaded material allegations of the nonmoving party as true, and views all facts and inferences in a light most favorable to the pleader.[290] A pleading's legal conclusions, however, are not deemed admitted.[291] Likewise, unwarranted factual inferences will not be drawn to aid the plaintiff.[292] A Rule 12(c) judgment will be granted if the pleadings demonstrate that the moving party is entitled to judgment as a matter of law.[293] If a material issue of fact remains in dispute, the court must deny the Rule 12(c) motion.[294]

> *Note:* A party who, for the purposes of Rule 12(c), presumes all of an opponent's well-pleaded facts as true, is not bound by any "admission" of this kind at trial. The party is free at trial to disprove or contradict the opponent's facts if the Rule 12(c) motion is denied.[295]

A Note on Bell Atlantic v. Twombly:

Because the standard for testing a pleading under Rule 12(c) mirrors the Rule 12(b)(6) standard, the Supreme Court's recent Rule 12(b)(6) decision in *Twombly* is almost certain to impact Rule 12(c) motion practice.[296] As discussed more extensively above,[297] the Court in *Twombly* "retire[d]" the oft-quoted language from the 1957 *Conley v. Gibson* decision that no complaint should be dismissed for failing to properly state a claim "unless it appears beyond doubt that the plaintiff can prove no set of facts in support of his claim which could entitle him to relief".[298] Courts are just beginning to digest the *Twombly* decision and assess its effect on Rule 12(c).[299] Practitioners should attentively follow these developments.

---

290. *See Lindsay v. Yates*, __ F.3d __, __, 2007 WL 2316626, at *2 (6th Cir. 2007); *Chauvin v. State Farm Fire & Cas. Co.*, 495 F.3d 232, 237 (5th Cir. 2007); *Mongeau v. City of Marlborough*, 492 F.3d 14, 16 (1st Cir. 2007); *Ventress v. Japan Airlines*, 486 F.3d 1111, 1114 (9th Cir. 2007); *Cleveland v. Caplaw Enters.*, 448 F.3d 518, 521 (2d Cir.2006).

291. *See Kottmyer v. Maas*, 436 F.3d 684, 689 (6th Cir.2006); *Republic Steel Corp. v. Pennsylvania Eng'g Corp.*, 785 F.2d 174, 178 n. 2 (7th Cir.1986); *See also Northern Ind. Gun & Outdoor Shows, Inc. v. City of South Bend*, 163 F.3d 449, 452 (7th Cir.1998) (commenting that court is not required to ignore facts in complaint that undermine plaintiff's claim or to give weight to unsupported conclusions of law).

292. *See Mixon v. Ohio*, 193 F.3d 389, 400 (6th Cir.1999).

293. *Sikirica v. Nationwide Ins. Co.*, 416 F.3d 214 (3d Cir.2005); *United States v. Any & All Radio Station Transmission Equip.*, 207 F.3d 458, 462 (8th Cir.2000).

294. *See Brittan Communications Int'l Corp. v. Southwestern Bell Tel. Co.*, 313 F.3d 899, 904 (5th Cir.2002); *United States v. Any & All Radio Station Transmission Equip.*, 207 F.3d 458, 462 (8th Cir.2000); *Gustafson v. Jones*, 117 F.3d 1015 (7th Cir. 1997).

295. *See Wyman v. Wyman*, 109 F.2d 473 (9th Cir.1940).

296. *See Bell Atlantic Corp. v. Twombly*, 550 U.S. __, __ , 127 S.Ct. 1955, 167 L.Ed.2d 929 (2007).

297. *See supra* Authors' Commentary to Rule 12(b)(6) ("**Legal Test**" and "**A Note on Bell Atlantic v. Twombly**").

298. *See Bell Atlantic Corp. v. Twombly*, 550 U.S. __, __ , 127 S.Ct. 1955, 1968–69, 167 L.Ed.2d 929 (2007) (abrogating language in *Conley v. Gibson*, 355 U.S. 41, 45–46, 78 S.Ct. 99, 2 L.Ed.2d 80 (1957)).

299. *See, e.g., Lindsay v. Yates*, __ F.3d __, __, 2007 WL 2316626, at *2 (6th Cir. 2007) (post-*Twombly* decision, still citing the "no set of facts" language from *Conley*);

Civil Rights Cases

At least one court has held that the Rule 12(c) test is to be applied with "particular strictness" in cases involving federal civil rights claims.[300] In such cases, that court has characterized the pleading requirements as "very lenient, even de minimis".[301]

Extrinsic Materials

If the court, in its discretion, considers (or does not exclude[302]) extrinsic evidence presented by the parties on a Rule 12(c) motion, the court must convert the motion into a request for summary judgment under Rule 56.[303] The process for this conversion (which once was set forth in the closing sentences of Rule 12(c)) was relocated by the 2007 amendments to its new location in Rule 12(d).

New Factual Allegations Asserted on Appeal

In unusual instances, the pleader may be able to raise new factual allegations in support of her pleading for the first time on appeal, provided those new allegations are consistent with her complaint.[304]

Remedy

If the Rule 12(c) motion is granted, the prevailing parties obtain a final judgment in their favor.[305]

Appealability

For the same reasons noted in Rule 12(b)(6)'s discussion of appealability, practitioners must proceed with care in analyzing whether an immediate appeal will lie from Rule 12(c) motions for judgment on the pleadings.[306] Generally, a decision granting such a motion is considered a "final order", and is immediately appealable, but a decision denying such a motion is ordinarily deemed "interlocutory" and must await a final disposition on the merits.[307]

Chauvin v. State Farm Fire & Cas. Co., 495 F.3d 232, 237 (5th Cir. 2007) (same); *Mongeau v. City of Marlborough*, 492 F.3d 14, 16 (1st Cir. 2007) (same).

300. *See Cleveland v. Caplaw Enters.*, 448 F.3d 518, 521 (2d Cir.2006); *Irish Lesbian & Gay Org. v. Giuliani*, 143 F.3d 638, 644 (2d Cir.1998).

301. *See Deravin v. Kerik*, 335 F.3d 195, 200 (2d Cir.2003).

302. There is a division among the Circuits as to when the conversion obligation is triggered. There are three approaches. Some courts require conversion anytime extrinsic evidence is not expressly excluded, others require conversion only if the court "considers" the extrinsic evidence, and still others require conversion only if, after considering the extrinsic evidence, the court chooses to "rely" on it. *See Max Arnold & Sons, LLC v. W.L. Hailey & Co.*, 452 F.3d

494, 502–03 (6th Cir.2006) (collecting cases, and electing first approach).

303. *See* Rule 12(d). *See also Cleveland v. Caplaw Enters.*, 448 F.3d 518, 521 (2d Cir.2006); *McCord v. Horace Mann Ins. Co.*, 390 F.3d 138, 141–42 (1st Cir.2004); *Olsen v. Idaho State Bd. of Med.*, 363 F.3d 916, 921–22 (9th Cir.2004).

304. *See Guise v. BWM Mortg.*, 377 F.3d 795, 798 (7th Cir.2004).

305. *See Republic Steel Corp. v. Pennsylvania Eng'g Corp.*, 785 F.2d 174, 178 n. 2 (7th Cir.1986)(commenting that Rule 12(c) motions are directed towards obtaining final judgments on the merits).

306. *See supra* Authors' Commentary to Rule 12(b)(6) ("**Appealability**").

307. *See Paskvan v. City of Cleveland Civil Serv. Com'n*, 946 F.2d 1233 (6th Cir. 1991). *But see Estate of Drayton v. Nelson*,

RULE 12(d). PRESENTING MATTERS OUTSIDE THE PLEADINGS

CORE CONCEPT

Motions under Rule 12(b)(6) and Rule 12(c) are designed to test the pleadings. Consequently, with a few narrow exceptions, courts may not consider materials outside the pleadings when ruling on these motions. If, in deciding one of these motions, a court is presented with, and does not exclude, matters outside the pleadings, the court must often convert the motion to one for summary judgment under Rule 56, and allow the parties a reasonable opportunity to present all materials pertinent to such a motion.

APPLICATIONS

2007 Amendments

The current language of Rule 12(d) was formerly found in the closing sentences of both old Rule 12(b) (motions to dismiss) and old Rule 12(c) (motions for judgment on the pleadings). The 2007 amendments consolidated this language from both former Rules into this new omnibus location. The content from old Rule 12(d) ("Preliminary Hearings") has been moved to the bottom of Rule 12 and given a new number, Rule 12(i). Practitioners searching for pre–2007 interpretations of these Rules should bear this repositioning in mind in doing their research.

Extrinsic Materials in Rule 12(b)(6) Practice

To support or oppose a Rule 12(b)(6) motion for failure to state a claim, parties may submit affidavits and other materials to the court.[308] The court enjoys the discretion to consider or exclude such materials.[309] If the court chooses to consider the materials, it must generally convert the Rule 12(b)(6) motion into a motion for summary judgment under Rule 56.[310] This conversion requirement ensures that the distinct policies undergirding Rule 12(b)(6) (testing

---

53 F.3d 165, 166 (7th Cir.1994)(holding that order granting judgment on the pleadings was not final, appealable order because the lawsuit remained pending against other defendants).

308. *See Ford Motor Co. v. Summit Motor Prods., Inc.,* 930 F.2d 277 (3d Cir.1991).

309. *See Pueschel v. United States,* 369 F.3d 345, 353 n.3 (4th Cir.2004); *Stahl v. United States Dep't of Agric.,* 327 F.3d 697, 701 (8th Cir.2003); *Lybrook v. Members of Farmington Mun. Schs. Bd. of Educ.,* 232 F.3d 1334, 1341–42 (10th Cir.2000).

310. *See R.J. Corman Derailment Servs., LLC v. International Union of Operating Eng'rs, Local Union 150, AFL–CIO,* 335 F.3d 643, 647 (7th Cir.2003); *Pryor v.*

National Collegiate Athletic Ass'n., 288 F.3d 548, 560 (3d Cir.2002); *Trustmark Ins. Co. v. ESLU, Inc.,* 299 F.3d 1265, 1265 (11th Cir.2002); *Country Club Estates, L.L.C. v. Town of Loma Linda,* 213 F.3d 1001, 1005 (8th Cir.2000). *But cf. McNair v. Lend Lease Trucks, Inc.,* 62 F.3d 651, 656 (4th Cir.1995)(conversion not required where trial court considers specific extrinsic evidence to which opposing party had opportunity to, and actually did, respond); *Terracom v. Valley Nat'l Bank,* 49 F.3d 555 (9th Cir.1995)(noting that because court made only "minor parenthetical observation" concerning an affidavit submitted by the parties, conversion was not required).

the formal sufficiency of the pleading) and Rule 56 (testing the availability of facts to support the claim) are respected.[311] The court must give all parties notice of such a conversion, and provide them with an opportunity both to be heard and to present further materials in support of their positions on the motion.[312] This required notice may be actual or constructive; in some instances, a litigant's act of submitting extrinsic materials may be considered notice enough.[313] Following conversion, the court is likely to permit the parties to engage in appropriate discovery before ruling on the converted motion.

One important exception to this "conversion" requirement must be kept in mind, however. A court may consider allegations contained in the complaint, exhibits attached to or otherwise incorporated in the complaint,[314] matters of public record,[315] orders of record in the lawsuit,[316] and other materials subject to judicial notice,[317] all without converting the motion to one for summary

311. *See Global Network Commc'ns, Inc. v. City of New York*, 458 F.3d 150 (2d Cir.2006). *See also id.* ("The conversion requirement of Rule 12(b) thus furthers the policies of both Rules by directing a pretrial motion to the vehicle most appropriate for its resolution, ensuring that the motion is governed by the rule specifically designed for the fair resolution of the parties' competing interests at a particular stage of the litigation.").

312. *See R.J. Corman Derailment Servs., LLC v. International Union of Operating Eng'rs, Local Union 150, AFL–CIO*, 335 F.3d 643, 647 (7th Cir.2003); *Trustmark Ins. Co. v. ESLU, Inc.*, 299 F.3d 1265, 1265 (11th Cir.2002).

313. *See Trustmark Ins. Co. v. ESLU, Inc.*, 299 F.3d 1265, 1267–68 (11th Cir. 2002) (noting "limited exception" to notice rule where non-movant's knowledge is established by non-movant's own pleadings); *Country Club Estates, L.L.C. v. Town of Loma Linda*, 213 F.3d 1001, 1005 (8th Cir. 2000); *David v. City of Denver*, 101 F.3d 1344, 1352 (10th Cir.1996) (collecting cases).

314. *See Tellabs, Inc. v. Makor Issues & Rights, Ltd.*, ___ U.S. ___, ___, 127 S.Ct. 2499, 2509, 168 L.Ed.2d 179 (2007); *Local 15, Int'l Bhd. of Elec. Workers, AFL–CIO v. Exelon Corp.*, 495 F.3d 779, 782 (7th Cir. 2007); *Roth v. Jennings*, 489 F.3d 499, 509 (2d Cir. 2007); *Secretary of State For Defence v. Trimble Navigation Ltd.*, 484 F.3d 700, 705 (4th Cir. 2007); *Swartz v. KPMG LLP*, 476 F.3d 756, 763 (9th Cir. 2007); *Quinn v. Ocwen Federal Bank FSB*, 470 F.3d 1240, 1244 (8th Cir. 2006).

315. *See Roth v. Jennings*, 489 F.3d 499, 509 (2d Cir. 2007); *Secretary of State For Defence v. Trimble Navigation Ltd.*, 484 F.3d 700, 705 (4th Cir. 2007); *Levy v. Ohl*, 477 F.3d 988, 991 (8th Cir. 2007); *Financial Acquisition Partners LP v. Blackwell*, 440 F.3d 278, 286 (5th Cir.2006). *See also Financial Acquisition Partners LP v. Blackwell*, 440 F.3d 278, 286 (5th Cir.2006) (public disclosure documents filed with SEC and on which claims rely); *Blue Tree Hotels Inv. (Canada), Ltd. v. Starwood Hotels & Resorts Worldwide, Inc.*, 369 F.3d 212, 217 (2d Cir.2004) (complaints filed in State court); *Bryant v. Avado Brands, Inc.*, 187 F.3d 1271, 1280 (11th Cir.1999) (public documents required to be (and actually) filed with SEC); *Southern Cross Overseas Agencies, Inc. v. Wah Kwong Shipping Group*, 181 F.3d 410, 426 (3d Cir.1999) (public records, including judicial proceedings); *Shaw v. Hahn*, 56 F.3d 1128, 1129 n.1 (9th Cir. 1995) (public record including State administrative records used in collateral estoppel challenge); *Henson v. CSC Credit Servs.*, 29 F.3d 280, 284 (7th Cir.1994) (public court documents filed in earlier State court proceeding).

316. *See Oshiver v. Levin, Fishbein, Sedran & Berman*, 38 F.3d 1380, 1384 n.2 (3d Cir.1994).

317. *See Tellabs, Inc. v. Makor Issues & Rights, Ltd.*, ___ U.S. ___, ___, 127 S.Ct. 2499, 2509, 168 L.Ed.2d 179 (2007); *Swartz v. KPMG LLP*, 476 F.3d 756, 763 (9th Cir. 2007); *Wyser-Pratte Mgmt. Co. v. Telxon Corp.*, 413 F.3d 553, 560 (6th Cir.2005).

judgment. In some instances, the courts may even properly consider case-specific documents that are not attached as exhibits to the complaint. For example, where a portion of a document is attached as an exhibit to the complaint, the court may consider other portions, not attached as exhibits, in ruling on the motion.[318] Moreover, many courts also permit the Rule 12(b)(6) consideration of "undisputably authentic documents", even though the documents were *not* attached to the complaint, so long as the authenticity of the documents is not challenged, the documents are attached to the motion to dismiss, and plaintiff's claims are premised upon the documents.[319]

Furthermore, even when extrinsic materials are improperly attached to a Rule 12(b)(6) motion to dismiss, a conversion to a summary judgment proceeding does not occur automatically.[320] The motion still need not be converted into a summary judgment proceeding if the district court does not consider the materials in making its ruling[321] or if the materials are otherwise "irrelevant" to the court's resolution of the motion.[322]

Extrinsic Materials in Rule 12(c) Practice

The same conversion approach that governs Rule 12(b)(6) motions also applies to Rule 12(c) motions for judgments on the pleadings.[323] If the court, in its discretion, considers (or does not exclude[324]) extrinsic evidence presented by the parties on a Rule 12(c) motion, the court must generally convert the motion into a request for summary judgment under Rule 56.[325] The court must give all parties notice of such a conversion, and provide them with an opportunity to be heard and present further materials in support of their positions on the motion.[326] Constructive notice can suffice.[327]

---

318. *See Cooper v. Pickett*, 137 F.3d 616, 622–23 (9th Cir.1997); *In re Stac Elec. Sec. Litig.*, 89 F.3d 1399, 1405 n. 4 (9th Cir. 1996).

319. *See Alvarado v. KOB–TV, L.L.C.*, 493 F.3d 1210, 1213 (10th Cir. 2007); *Roth v. Jennings*, 489 F.3d 499, 509 (2d Cir. 2007); *Minch v. City of Chicago*, 486 F.3d 294, 300 n.3 (7th Cir. 2007); *Secretary of State For Defence v. Trimble Navigation Ltd.*, 484 F.3d 700, 705 (4th Cir. 2007); *Swartz v. KPMG LLP*, 476 F.3d 756, 763 (9th Cir. 2007).

320. *See Swedberg v. Marotzke*, 339 F.3d 1139, 1142–45 (9th Cir.2003); *Casazza v. Kiser*, 313 F.3d 414, 417–18 (8th Cir. 2002).

321. *See Pueschel v. United States*, 369 F.3d 345, 353 n.3 (4th Cir.2004); *Casazza v. Kiser*, 313 F.3d 414, 417–18 (8th Cir.2002).

322. *See Stahl v. United States Dep't of Agriculture*, 327 F.3d 697, 701 (8th Cir. 2003).

323. *See Rubert–Torres v. Hospital San Pablo, Inc.*, 205 F.3d 472, 475 (1st Cir. 2000).

324. There is a division among the Circuits as to when the conversion obligation is triggered. There are three approaches. Some courts require conversion anytime extrinsic evidence is not expressly excluded, others require conversion only if the court "considers" the extrinsic evidence, and still others require conversion only if, after considering the extrinsic evidence, the court chooses to "rely" on it. *See Max Arnold & Sons, LLC v. W.L. Hailey & Co.*, 452 F.3d 494, 502–03 (6th Cir.2006) (collecting cases, and electing first approach).

325. *See* Rule 12(d). *See also Cleveland v. Caplaw Enters.*, 448 F.3d 518, 521 (2d Cir.2006); *McCord v. Horace Mann Ins. Co.*, 390 F.3d 138, 141–42 (1st Cir.2004); *Olsen v. Idaho State Bd. of Med.*, 363 F.3d 916, 921–22 (9th Cir.2004).

326. *See R.J. Corman Derailment Servs., LLC v. International Union of Oper-*

Courts have held that constructive notice exists where the conversion mandate is obvious or the parties otherwise had sufficient opportunity to make their summary judgment record.[328] Thus, a movant cannot complain of a purportedly unnoticed conversion if his own motion is accompanied by clearly extrinsic materials.[329] Similarly, the non-moving party will not be permitted to complain about an allegedly unnoticed conversion if she opposes the motion with extrinsic materials of her own.[330]

A conversion is *not* required when the court considers documents attached as exhibits to pleadings, documents referred to in the complaint and central to plaintiff's claim, and documents of which the court may take judicial notice.[331] Although a "written instrument" attached to a pleading becomes "a part thereof for all purposes",[332] a litigant cannot avoid this summary judgment conversion provision merely by attaching any random document to her answer–the attached document still can only be relied upon by the court on a Rule 12(c) motion if that document is both central to the plaintiff's claim and indisputably authentic.[333]

RULE 12(e).   MOTION FOR MORE DEFINITE STATEMENT

CORE CONCEPT

If a pleading is so vague or ambiguous that a responsive pleading cannot be prepared, the responding party need not serve a response, but may instead move the court for an order directing the pleader to serve a more definite statement.

APPLICATIONS

Distinct from Rule 12(b)(6) Motions

Motions to dismiss and motions for more definite statements are not interchangeable. A motion to dismiss under Rule 12(b)(6)

ating Eng'rs, Local Union 150, AFL–CIO, 335 F.3d 643, 647 (7th Cir.2003); Rubert–Torres v. Hospital San Pablo, Inc., 205 F.3d 472, 475 (1st Cir.2000). *But see Gagliardi v. Village of Pawling*, 18 F.3d 188 (2d Cir. 1994)(notwithstanding introduction of extrinsic evidence, conversion rule not relevant where motion decided solely on a review of the complaint).

327. *See Rubert–Torres v. Hospital San Pablo, Inc.*, 205 F.3d 472, 475–76 (1st Cir. 2000).

328. *See Max Arnold & Sons, LLC v. W.L. Hailey & Co.*, 452 F.3d 494, 504 (6th Cir.2006).

329. *See Sira v. Morton*, 380 F.3d 57 (2d Cir.2004); *Olsen v. Idaho State Bd. of Med.*, 363 F.3d 916, 921–22 (9th Cir.2004).

330. *See McCord v. Horace Mann Ins. Co.*, 390 F.3d 138, 141–42 (1st Cir.2004).

331. *See R.G. Fin. Corp. v. Vergara–Nunez*, 446 F.3d 178, 182 (1st Cir.2006); *Park Univ. Enters., Inc. v. American Cas. Co.*, 442 F.3d 1239, 1244 (10th Cir.2006); *Sira v. Morton*, 380 F.3d 57 (2d Cir.2004).

332. *See Rule 10(c).*

333. *See Horsley v. Feldt*, 304 F.3d 1125, 1134–35 (11th Cir.2002) ("Otherwise, the conversion clause of Rule 12(c) would be too easily circumvented and disputed documents attached to an answer would have to be taken as true at the pleadings stage. The written instrument provision of Rule 10(c) does not require that.").

attacks a pleading for failing to allege a cognizable legal theory eligible for some type of relief. In contrast, a Rule 12(e) motion for more definite statements attacks pleadings that do, in fact, state cognizable legal claims, yet those pleadings are so unclear that drafting a response to them is impossible.[334] Where the defending party is unable to frame a fair response to a pleading because the pleading's meaning is unclear, the proper remedy is not a motion to dismiss but instead a motion for a more definite statement.[335]

> *Conversion:* A motion to dismiss under Rule 12(b)(6) that, more correctly, is a motion for a more definite statement may be so converted by the court in its discretion.[336]

> *Filing Both Motions:* A party may file a motion to dismiss and a motion for more definite statement at the same time. In an appropriate case, the court may consider the motion for more definite statement first and hold the motion to dismiss in abeyance.[337]

Disfavored Motion

The Rules require the pleader to serve only a short, plain statement showing an entitlement to relief.[338] Due to these liberal pleading requirements in federal court, motions for a more definite statement are disfavored and granted only sparingly.[339] They are not a substitute for discovery,[340] and ordinarily will not be granted where the information sought could be obtained in discovery.[341]

334. *See Humpherys v. Nager,* 962 F.Supp. 347, 352–53 (E.D.N.Y.1997).

335. *See American Nurses' Ass'n v. Illinois,* 783 F.2d 716, 725 (7th Cir.1986). *See also McClellon v. Lone Star Gas Co.,* 66 F.3d 98, 103 (5th Cir.1995)(vacating court's dismissal of deficient complaint, without first permitting the pleader an opportunity to replead).

336. *See Carter v. Newland,* 441 F.Supp.2d 208, 214 (D.Mass.2006); *Untracht v. Fikri,* 368 F.Supp.2d 409, 412 n.6 (W.D.Pa.2005); *Hall v. Tyco Int'l Ltd.,* 223 F.R.D. 219 (M.D.N.C.2004).

337. *See Thomas v. Independence Twp.,* 463 F.3d 285, 301 (3d Cir. 2006).

338. *See* Rule 8.

339. *See McQueen v. Woodstream Corp.,* ___ F.Supp.2d ___, ___, 2007 WL 2284747, at *7 (D.D.C. 2007); *Philip Morris USA, Inc. v. Lee,* 481 F.Supp.2d 742, 751 (W.D.Tex. 2006); *Vaden v. Lantz,* 459 F.Supp.2d 149, 151 (D.Conn. 2006); *Houlihan v. Sussex Technical Sch. Dist.,* 461 F.Supp.2d 252, 262 (D.Del. 2006); *Babcock*

& Wilcox Co. v. McGriff, Seibels & Williams, Inc., 235 F.R.D. 632, 633 (E.D.La. 2006).

340. *See McQueen v. Woodstream Corp.,* ___ F.Supp.2d ___, ___, 2007 WL 2284747, at *7 (D.D.C. 2007); *Vaden v. Lantz,* 459 F.Supp.2d 149, 151 (D.Conn. 2006); *Wood v. Apodaca,* 375 F.Supp.2d 942, 949 (N.D.Cal. 2005); *Doe v. Bayer Corp.,* 367 F.Supp.2d 904, 917 (M.D.N.C.2005).

341. *See McQueen v. Woodstream Corp.,* ___ F.Supp.2d ___, ___, 2007 WL 2284747, at *7 (D.D.C. 2007); *Flentye v. Kathrein,* 485 F.Supp.2d 903, 911 (N.D.Ill. 2007); *Babcock & Wilcox Co. v. McGriff, Seibels & Williams, Inc.,* 235 F.R.D. 632, 633 (E.D.La. 2006). *See also Cross Timbers Concerned Citizens v. Saginaw,* 991 F.Supp. 563, 572–73 (N.D.Tex.1997) (quoting Local Rule 12.1, which provides that "[e]xcept for motions complaining of failure to plead fraud or mistake with particularity pursuant to Fed. R.Civ.P. 9(b), a motion for more definite statement may only be filed where the information sought cannot be obtained by discovery").

Legal Test

As a disfavored remedy, motions for a more definite statement will ordinarily only be granted where the pleading is "unintelligible": so hopelessly vague and ambiguous that a defendant cannot fairly be expected to frame a response or denial, at least not without risking prejudice.[342] Such motions are particularly ill-suited to situations where the information sought is already within the defendant's knowledge, and the motion merely seeks a formal particularization of known facts.[343] Nevertheless, courts continue to grant these motions, even though disfavored, where the minimal federal "notice pleading" standards are not met.[344] Just as Rule 12(e) motions are not legitimate substitutes for discovery, discovery is not a fair substitute for proper notice pleading.[345] Both the court and the litigants are entitled to know, at the pleading stage, who is being sued, why, and for what.[346] The decision to grant or deny a motion for a more definite statement is committed to the district court's sound discretion.[347]

When proper and appropriate, Rule 12(e) motions can seek more definite statements concerning the pleader's claim for relief, the court's jurisdiction, or the pleader's capacity to press the lawsuit.

342. *See McQueen v. Woodstream Corp.*, ___ F.Supp.2d ___, ___, 2007 WL 2284747, at *8 (D.D.C. 2007); *Flentye v. Kathrein*, 485 F.Supp.2d 903, 911 (N.D.Ill. 2007); *Houlihan v. Sussex Technical Sch. Dist.*, 461 F.Supp.2d 252, 262 (D.Del. 2006); *Columbia Ins. Co. v. Brown Shoe Co.*, 233 F.R.D. 250, 251 (D.Conn.2005); *Hilchey v. City of Haverhill*, 233 F.R.D. 67, 69 (D.Mass.2005); *United States v. Sequel Contractors, Inc.*, 402 F.Supp.2d 1142, 1147 (C.D.Cal.2005); *Pelman ex rel. Pelman v. McDonald's Corp.*, 396 F.Supp.2d 439, 443 (S.D.N.Y.2005).

343. *See Babcock & Wilcox Co. v. McGriff, Seibels & Williams, Inc.*, 235 F.R.D. 632, 633 (E.D.La.2006).

344. *See Swierkiewicz v. Sorema N. A.*, 534 U.S. 506, 512, 122 S.Ct. 992, 998, 152 L.Ed.2d 1 (2002) (noting that if pleading "fails to specify the allegations in a manner that provides sufficient notice", defendant can move for more definite statement before responding).

345. *See Eisenach v. Miller–Dwan Med. Ctr.*, 162 F.R.D. 346, 348 (D.Minn. 1995)("any current view that the deficiencies in pleading may be cured through liberalized discovery is at increasingly mounting odds with the public's dissatisfaction with exorbitantly expansive discovery, and the impact that the public outcry has had upon our discovery Rules").

346. *See McHenry v. Renne*, 84 F.3d 1172, 1179–80 (9th Cir.1996) (writing that "[p]rolix, confusing complaints such as the ones plaintiffs filed in this case impose unfair burdens on litigants and judges. As a practical matter, the judge and opposing counsel, in order to perform their responsibilities, cannot use a complaint such as the one plaintiffs filed, and must prepare outlines to determine who is being sued for what. Defendants are then put at risk that their outline differs from the judge's, that plaintiffs will surprise them with something new at trial which they reasonably did not understand to be in the case at all, and that res judicata effects of settlement or judgment will be different from what they reasonably expected. ...The judge wastes half a day in chambers preparing the 'short and plain statement' which Rule 8 obligated plaintiffs to submit. He then must manage the litigation without knowing what claims are made against whom. This leads to discovery disputes and lengthy trials, prejudicing litigants in other case who follow the rules, as well as defendants in the case in which the prolix pleading is filed.").

347. *See Vaden v. Lantz*, 459 F.Supp.2d 149, 151 (D.Conn. 2006); *Sheffield v. Orius Corp.*, 211 F.R.D. 411, 414 (D.Or.2002); *DVI Business Credit Corp. v. Crowder*, 193 F.Supp.2d 1002, 1009 (S.D.Tex.2002).

- *Special Pleading Obligations:* The motion may be appropriate where the pleader fails to allege properly facts that must be specially pleaded, such as fraud, mistake, denial of performance or occurrence, and special damages.[348]

- *Threshold Defenses:* The motion may also be appropriate where the pleading fails to provide facts necessary to determine whether threshold defenses exist, such as statute of limitations (when claim arose) or statute of frauds (whether contract was written or oral, term for performance).[349]

- *RICO Case Statements*: Rule 12(e), among other Rules, has been cited as authority for compelling the filing of "RICO Case Statements", as now required in many judicial districts to flesh out the factual predicates and legal theory underlying federal civil racketeering claims.[350] Such Statements have been approved, unless they would obligate the pleader to allege more information than Rule 8(a) and Rule 9(b) would otherwise require.[351]

Burden of Proof

The burden lies with the moving party to demonstrate that the challenged pleading is too vague or ambiguous to permit a response. The moving party must identify the deficiencies in the pleading, list the details sought to be provided, and assert an inability to frame a response.[352]

Sua Sponte Motions

The district court may, on its own initiative, strike a deficient

---

348. *See* Rule 9. *See also Wagner v. First Horizon Pharm. Corp.*, 464 F.3d 1273, 1280 (11th Cir. 2006).

349. *See Thomas v. Independence Twp.*, 463 F.3d 285, 289 & 301 (3d Cir. 2006) (noting motion's usefulness in immunity cases); *Doe v. Bayer Corp.*, 367 F.Supp.2d 904, 917 (M.D.N.C.2005) (courts generally willing to demand more definite statement of dates where they are definite, but not where uncertain or where events occur over periods of time). *See also Rose v. Kinevan,* 115 F.R.D. 250 (D.Colo.1987).

350. *See Northland Ins. Co. v. Shell Oil Co.*, 930 F.Supp. 1069, 1074 (D.N.J.1996). Where claims are asserted under the federal Racketeer Influenced and Corrupt Organizations Act ("RICO"), 18 U.S.C.A. §§ 1961–68, many judicial districts now require, by Standing Order, chambers policy, or otherwise, that the pleader answer a series of questions that supplement the RICO allegations of the complaint. *See, e.g.,* S.D. Cal. Rule 11.1; W.D. N.Y. Rule 5.1; *National Org. for Women, Inc. v. Scheidler*, 510 U.S. 249, 249, 114 S.Ct. 798, 800, 127 L.Ed.2d 99

(1994)(noting local rule in force in Northern District of Illinois); *O'Ferral v. Trebol Motors Corp.*, 45 F.3d 561, 562 (1st Cir. 1995) (same, District of Puerto Rico); *Frank v. D'Ambrosi*, 4 F.3d 1378, 1381 (6th Cir.1993)(same, Northern District of Ohio); *Boogaerts v. Bank of Bradley*, 961 F.2d 765, 767 n. 3 (8th Cir.1992)(same, Western District of Arkansas). This pleading obligation is especially important where the facts noted in the RICO Case Statement are deemed to be pleading averments, properly considered in ruling upon a motion to dismiss. *See Glessner v. Kenny*, 952 F.2d 702, 712 n. 9 (3d Cir.1991)(collecting cases so holding).

351. *See Wagh v. Metris Direct, Inc.*, 363 F.3d 821, 826–28 (9th Cir.2003).

352. *See Philip Morris USA, Inc. v. Lee*, 481 F.Supp.2d 742, 751 (W.D.Tex. 2006); *Pelman ex rel. Pelman v. McDonald's Corp.*, 396 F.Supp.2d 439, 443 (S.D.N.Y.2005); *Osborne v. County of Riverside*, 385 F.Supp.2d 1048, 1052 (C.D.Cal.2005); *Davenport v. Rodriguez*, 147 F.Supp.2d 630, 639–40 (S.D.Tex.2001).

pleading and direct the pleader to file a more definite statement.[353] This *sua sponte* option is especially valuable to resolve "shotgun pleading" deficiencies,[354] or when a motion to dismiss is pending but the more appropriate relief is re-pleading with a more definite statement.[355]

Applies only to Pleadings

By its terms, Rule 12(e) is available to compel more definite statements only in pleadings. It cannot be used to require added detail in motions.[356]

Timing

Obviously, a motion for more definite statement must be filed before the party serves a response to the pleading claimed to be too vague or ambiguous.[357] Additionally, the moving party should appreciate the significance of moving for Rule 12(e) relief–once a Rule 12 motion is made, any waivable defense that could have been, but was not, joined in that Rule 12 motion may be lost.[358] To abate the harshness of this result, the court may permit the moving party to withdraw the Rule 12(e) motion for more definite statement so as to permit a larger Rule 12 filing.[359]

Tolling Effect

While the motion is pending, the party's time for serving a responsive pleading is tolled. Once the court rules on the motion, a new (but shortened) response time begins. If the motion is granted, the party must serve a responsive pleading within 10 days after the more definite statement is served or within such other time as the court may direct. If the motion is denied, the party must serve a responsive pleading within 10 days of the court's order.

Complying With Court's Order For More Definite Statement

To comply with a Rule 12(e) order for a more definite statement, the pleader must amend the pleading to add sufficient detail

---

353. *See Cesnik v. Edgewood Baptist Church*, 88 F.3d 902, 907 n. 13 (11th Cir. 1996); *Fikes v. City of Daphne*, 79 F.3d 1079, 1083 n. 6 (11th Cir.1996).

354. *See Wagner v. First Horizon Pharm. Corp.*, 464 F.3d 1273, 1275 & 1280 (11th Cir. 2006).

355. *See Thomas v. Independence Twp.*, 463 F.3d 285, 289 & 301 (3d Cir. 2006).

356. *See Marcello v. Maine*, 489 F.Supp.2d 82, 85 (D.Me. 2007).

357. *See Marx v. Gumbinner*, 855 F.2d 783, 792 (11th Cir.1988); *Santana Prods., Inc. v. Sylvester & Assocs., Ltd.*, 121 F.Supp.2d 729, 738 (E.D.N.Y.1999) (because Rule 12(e) motions must be presented before filing a responsive pleading, defen-

dants' decision to file an answer precluded relief under motion); *Clark v. Associates Commercial Corp.*, 149 F.R.D. 629, 633 (D.Kan.1993) (same).

358. *See* Rules 12(g) & 12(h). *See also Caldwell–Baker Co. v. Southern Illinois Railcar Co.*, 225 F.Supp.2d 1243, 1259, (D.Kan.2002) (noting substantial number of courts that had ruled that a party moving for more definite statement may not later assert by motion another Rule 12(b) defense that was then available).

359. *See Caldwell–Baker Co. v. Southern Illinois Railcar Co.*, 225 F.Supp.2d 1243, 1259 (D.Kan.2002) (holding that party's withdrawal of Rule 12(e) motion abated possible waiver of motion to dismiss for lack of personal jurisdiction).

to satisfy the court and to meet the adversary's objections.[360] If the pleader fails to serve the more definite statement, or fails to do so within the designated time period, the court may strike the pleading or make such other order as it deems just.[361]

RULE 12(f).   MOTION TO STRIKE

CORE CONCEPT

On its own initiative or upon motion, the court may strike from a pleading any insufficient defense or any redundant, immaterial, impertinent, or scandalous matter.

APPLICATIONS

Purpose

Both insufficient defenses and redundant, immaterial, impertinent, or scandalous matter are properly stricken from a pleading in order to avoid the time, effort, and expense necessary to litigate spurious issues.[362] Such motions may be granted when necessary to clean up the pleadings, streamline the litigation, or sidestep unnecessary efforts on immaterial issues.[363] They are not, consequently, available to generally cull pleadings of "inappropriately hyperbolic allegations, ill-conceived attempts at levity, and other similar manifestations of bad judgment in drafting".[364]

General Test

Motions to strike are disfavored by the courts.[365] In considering a motion to strike, courts will generally apply the same test used to determine a Rule 12(b)(6) motion[366]—the courts will deem as admitted all of the non-moving party's well-pleaded facts, draw all reasonable inferences in the pleader's favor, and resolve all doubts in favor of denying the motion to strike.[367] But the court will not accept as

360. See Sefton v. Jew, 204 F.R.D. 104, 106 (W.D.Tex.2000).

361. See Sefton v. Jew, 204 F.R.D. 104, 106 (W.D.Tex.2000); Iacampo v. Hasbro, Inc., 929 F.Supp. 562, 571 (D.R.I.1996).

362. See Fantasy, Inc. v. Fogerty, 984 F.2d 1524, 1527 (9th Cir.1993), rev'd on other grounds, 510 U.S. 517, 114 S.Ct. 1023, 127 L.Ed.2d 455 (1994); Taylor v. Quall, 471 F.Supp.2d 1053, 1058–59 (C.D.Cal. 2007); Wilkins v. Ramirez, 455 F.Supp.2d 1080, 1111–12 (S.D.Cal. 2006).

363. See Hoffman v. Sumner, 478 F.Supp.2d 1024, 1028 (N.D.Ill. 2007); McInerney v. Moyer Lumber & Hardware, Inc., 244 F.Supp.2d 393, 402 (E.D.Pa.2002).

364. See Saylavee LLC v. Hockler, 228 F.R.D. 425, 426 (D.Conn.2005).

365. See Boreri v. Fiat S.p.A., 763 F.2d 17, 23 (1st Cir.1985)(commenting that motions to strike "are narrow in scope, disfa-

vored in practice, and not calculated readily to invoke the court's discretion"). See also BJC Health Sys. v. Columbia Cas. Co., 478 F.3d 908, 917 (8th Cir. 2007); Hoffman v. Sumner, 478 F.Supp.2d 1024, 1028 (N.D.Ill. 2007); S.E.C. v. Durgarian, 477 F.Supp.2d 342, 360 (D.Mass. 2007); United States ex rel. Pogue v. Diabetes Treatment Ctrs. of America, 474 F.Supp.2d 75, 79 (D.D.C. 2007); Taylor v. Quall, 471 F.Supp.2d 1053, 1058–59 (C.D.Cal. 2007); Sobba v. Elmen, 462 F.Supp.2d 944, 946 (E.D.Ark. 2006).

366. See Breedlove v. Cabou, 296 F.Supp.2d 253, 274–75 (N.D.N.Y.2003); Solvent Chem. Co. ICC Indus., Inc. v. E.I. Dupont De Nemours & Co., 242 F.Supp.2d 196, 212 (W.D.N.Y.2002).

367. See Jankovic v. Int'l Crisis Group, 429 F.Supp.2d 165, 170 (D.D.C.2006); Montecino v. Spherion Corp., 427 F.Supp.2d 965, 966–67 (C.D.Cal.2006); Black v. Long

true the non-moving party's conclusions of law.[368] If disputed questions of fact or law remain as to the challenged material or defense, the motion to strike must be denied.[369] Likewise, if any doubt remains as to the potential later relevance of the contested allegations, the motion will be denied.[370]

Burden of Proof

The burden lies with the party moving to strike.[371] Given the disfavored nature of the relief, the burden on the moving party is "formidable".[372] The moving party must generally make at least two showings: first, the challenged allegations must be clearly unrelated to the pleader's claims,[373] *and*, second, the moving party must be prejudiced by permitting those allegations to remain in the pleading.[374] Prejudice exists when the contested allegation would confuse the issues or, by its length and complexity, would place an undue burden on the respondent, would confuse the issues, inject the possibility of unnecessarily extensive and burdensome discovery, improperly increase the time, expense, and complexity of the trial, or otherwise unduly burden the moving party.[375] The moving party must state the basis for the motion with particularity and identify specifically the relief sought.[376]

Test For Striking Defenses

A motion to strike is the pleader's parallel to a Rule 12(b)(6) motion to dismiss. The pleader can seek to use this Rule to strike an opponent's defense as legally insufficient.[377] The court may strike any defense that is legally insufficient under the controlling substan-

Term Disability Ins., 373 F.Supp.2d 897, 904 (E.D.Wis.2005); *Naegele v. Albers*, 355 F.Supp.2d 129, 142 (D.D.C.2005).

368. See *United States v. Rohm & Haas Co.*, 939 F.Supp. 1142, 1151 (D.N.J.1996).

369. See *Canadian St. Regis Band of Mohawk Indians v. New York*, 278 F.Supp.2d 313, 325 (N.D.N.Y.2003); *Graff v. Prime Retail, Inc.*, 172 F.Supp.2d 721, 731 (D.Md.2001). See also *Bristol–Myers Squibb Co. v. IVAX Corp.*, 77 F.Supp.2d 606, 619 (D.N.J.2000) (commenting that motion should not be used as vehicle to determine disputed and substantial questions of law or fact).

370. See *Beatie & Osborn LLP v. Patriot Scientific Corp.*, 431 F.Supp.2d 367, 398 (S.D.N.Y.2006); *Montecino v. Spherion Corp.*, 427 F.Supp.2d 965, 966–67 (C.D.Cal. 2006).

371. See *Haught v. The Louis Berkman, LLC*, 377 F.Supp.2d 543 (N.D.W.Va.2005); *Naegele v. Albers*, 355 F.Supp.2d 129, 142 (D.D.C.2005); *Canadian St. Regis Band of Mohawk Indians v. New York*, 278 F.Supp.2d 313, 325 (N.D.N.Y.2003).

372. See *United States ex rel. Pogue v. Diabetes Treatment Ctrs. of America*, 474 F.Supp.2d 75, 79 (D.D.C. 2007).

373. See *Poole v. Taylor*, 466 F.Supp.2d 578, 583 (D.Del. 2006); *Sobba v. Elmen*, 462 F.Supp.2d 944, 946 (E.D.Ark. 2006); *Montecino v. Spherion Corp.*, 427 F.Supp.2d 965, 966–67 (C.D.Cal.2006).

374. See *Hoffman v. Sumner*, 478 F.Supp.2d 1024, 1028 (N.D.Ill. 2007); *S.E.C. v. Durgarian*, 477 F.Supp.2d 342, 360 (D.Mass. 2007); *Poole v. Taylor*, 466 F.Supp.2d 578, 583 (D.Del. 2006); *Sobba v. Elmen*, 462 F.Supp.2d 944, 946 (E.D.Ark. 2006).

375. See *Canadian St. Regis Band of Mohawk Indians v. New York*, 278 F.Supp.2d 313, 325 (N.D.N.Y.2003); *Hart v. Baca*, 204 F.R.D. 456, 457 (C.D.Cal.2001).

376. See *Credit General Ins. Co. v. Midwest Indemnity Corp.*, 916 F.Supp. 766, 771 (N.D.Ill.1996).

377. See *United States v. Winnebago Tribe of Nebraska*, 542 F.2d 1002, 1007 (8th Cir.1976); *Environ Prods., Inc. v. Total Containment, Inc.*, 951 F.Supp. 57, 59 (E.D.Pa.1996).

tive law,[378] or that contains matters that would confuse the issues in the case.[379] An insufficient defense is one where no evidence in support of the allegation would be admissible.[380] The objective of such strikes is to eliminate irrelevant and frivolous defenses, the trial of which would otherwise unnecessarily waste time and money.[381] For example, a defense that is invalid under the facts alleged, and which would confuse the issues in the case, should be stricken.[382] Thus, to strike a defense, the moving party must show (a) there is no question of fact or law which might allow the challenged defense to succeed, (b) it appears to a certainty that the defense will fail regardless of what evidence is marshalled to support it, and (c) prejudice if the defense remains in the case.[383] In conducting this analysis, the court will construe the pleadings liberally in the favor of the defendant (the non-moving party).[384] Ordinarily, if the motion has merit, the court will strike the insufficient defense in its entirety, and will not attempt to carve the defense in portions.[385] Moreover, if the defense is stricken, the pleader will generally be granted leave to file an amended answer unless the amendment would be futile.[386]

- *Strikes Involving Inference–Drawing*: Defenses will not be stricken on a motion to strike if the court would be required to draw factual inferences or decided disputed questions of fact.[387]

- *Strikes Involving Substantial and Disputed Questions:* Motions to strike are generally not intended to resolve substantial and disputed questions of law–legal issues on which

378. *See Owens v. UNUM Life Ins. Co.,* 285 F.Supp.2d 778, 780 (E.D.Tex.2003) (whether defense is invalid, as a matter of law, depends on nature of claim and asserted defense).

379. *See Waste Mgmt. Holdings, Inc. v. Gilmore,* 252 F.3d 316, 347 (4th Cir.2001); *Kaiser Aluminum & Chem. Sales, Inc. v. Avondale Shipyards, Inc.,* 677 F.2d 1045 (5th Cir.1982).

380. *See Openshaw v. Cohen, Klingenstein & Marks, Inc.,* 320 F.Supp.2d 357, 364 (D.Md.2004); *Microsoft Corp. v. Jesse's Computers & Repair, Inc.,* 211 F.R.D. 681, 683 (M.D.Fla.2002).

381. *See E.E.O.C. v. Bay Ridge Toyota, Inc.,* 327 F.Supp.2d 167 (E.D.N.Y.2004); *In re Complaint of J.A.R. Barge Lines, L.P.,* 307 F.Supp.2d 668, 670 (W.D.Pa.2004);

382. *See Allapattah Servs., Inc. v. Exxon Corp.,* 372 F.Supp.2d 1344, 1371 (S.D.Fla. 2005).

383. *See Specialty Minerals, Inc. v. Pluess–Staufer AG,* 395 F.Supp.2d 109, 111 (S.D.N.Y.2005); *E.E.O.C. v. Bay Ridge Toyota, Inc.,* 327 F.Supp.2d 167 (E.D.N.Y.

2004); *Resolution Trust Corp. v. Massachusetts Mut. Life Ins. Co.,* 93 F.Supp.2d 300, 303 (W.D.N.Y.2000). *See also Chao v. Linder,* 421 F.Supp.2d 1129, 1133 (N.D.Ill. 2006) (to be sufficient, defense must (a) be properly pleaded, (b) comply with Rules 8 and 9, and (c) withstand a Rule 12(b)(6) analysis).

384. *See Employers Ins. Co. of Wausau v. Crouse–Cmty. Ctr., Inc.,* 489 F.Supp.2d 176, 179 (N.D.N.Y. 2007); *Taylor v. Quall,* 471 F.Supp.2d 1053, 1058–59 (C.D.Cal. 2007); *Estee Lauder, Inc. v. Fragrance Counter, Inc.,* 189 F.R.D. 269, 271 (S.D.N.Y. 1999).

385. *See Stowe Woodward, L.L.C. v. Sensor Prods., Inc.,* 230 F.R.D. 463, 468–69 (W.D.Va.2005).

386. *See United States v. Green,* 33 F.Supp.2d 203, 212 (W.D.N.Y.1998); *See United States v. 416.81 Acres of Land,* 514 F.2d 627 (7th Cir.1975).

387. *See Augustus v. Board of Public Instruction,* 306 F.2d 862 (5th Cir.1962); *Ammirati v. Bonati,* 1994 WL 34175 at *1 (M.D.Fla.1994).

courts are divided, confused or unsettled legal areas, or issues involving close or new questions of law.[388]

- *Strikes Before Discovery:* Although motions to strike must generally be filed before a responsive pleading is served, some courts have noted their reluctance to strike defenses where there has been "no significant discovery".[389]

Test For Striking Redundant, Immaterial, Impertinent, or Scandalous Matter

A motion to strike redundant, immaterial, impertinent, or scandalous matter is also viewed with disfavor as a time-waster.[390] The court will not strike such matter unless it bears no possible relation to the parties' dispute, or could confuse the issues.[391] Moreover, mere redundancy, immateriality, impertinence, or scandalousness is not sufficient to justify striking an allegation—the allegation must also be shown to be prejudicial to the moving party.[392] Thus, absent a "strong reason for so doing", courts will generally "not tamper with pleadings".[393] If any doubt exists whether the contested matter should be stricken, the motion should be denied.[394] The court will also be disinclined to strike matter where the case will be tried without a jury.

If granted, the court's order will typically describe in detail the precise matter that must be stricken.[395]

---

388. *See Canadian St. Regis Band of Mohawk Indians v. New York*, 278 F.Supp.2d 313, 324 (N.D.N.Y.2003) (noting that, otherwise, courts would risk "offering an advisory opinion on an abstract and hypothetical set of facts"); *Solvent Chem. Co. ICC Indus., Inc. v. E.I. Dupont De Nemours & Co.*, 242 F.Supp.2d 196, 212 (W.D.N.Y.2002) (noting that defense must not present disputed and substantial questions of law).

389. *See Canadian St. Regis Band of Mohawk Indians v. New York*, 278 F.Supp.2d 313, 324–25 (N.D.N.Y.2003).

390. *See Florance v. Buchmeyer*, 500 F.Supp.2d 618, ___, 2007 WL 2192635, at *19 (N.D.Tex. 2007); *Germaine Music v. Universal Songs of Polygram*, 275 F.Supp.2d 1288, 1299–1300 (D.Nev.2003); *Rosales v. Citibank, Federal Sav. Bank*, 133 F.Supp.2d 1177, 1180 (N.D.Cal.2001).

391. *See Salahuddin v. Cuomo*, 861 F.2d 40, 42 (2d Cir.1988)(commenting that dismissals under Rule 12(f) are reserved for instances where the pleading "is so confused, ambiguous, vague, or otherwise unintelligible that its true substance, if any, is well disguised"); *Lipsky v. Commonwealth United Corp.*, 551 F.2d 887 (2d Cir.1976); *Florance v. Buchmeyer*, 500 F.Supp.2d 618,

___, 2007 WL 2192635, at *19 (N.D.Tex. 2007); *Montecino v. Spherion Corp.*, 427 F.Supp.2d 965, 966–67 (C.D.Cal.2006). *Cf. Delaware Health Care, Inc. v. MCD Holding Co.*, 893 F.Supp. 1279, 1291–92 (D.Del. 1995)(allegations that might create better understanding of plaintiff's claims or perform some other useful purpose in the dispute's just disposition will not be stricken).

392. *See Southwestern Bell Tel., L.P. v. Missouri Pub. Serv. Comm'n*, 461 F.Supp.2d 1055, 1064 (E.D.Mo. 2006); *Black v. Long Term Disability Ins.*, 373 F.Supp.2d 897, 904 (E.D.Wis.2005); *Anderson v. Board of Ed. of Chicago*, 169 F.Supp.2d 864, 867–68 (N.D.Ill.2001).

393. *See Black v. Long Term Disability Ins.*, 373 F.Supp.2d 897, 904 (E.D.Wis. 2005); *Lazar v. Trans Union LLC*, 195 F.R.D. 665, 668 (C.D.Cal.2000); *Lennon v. Seaman*, 63 F.Supp.2d 428, 447 (S.D.N.Y. 1999).

394. *See Southwestern Bell Tel., L.P. v. Missouri Pub. Serv. Comm'n*, 461 F.Supp.2d 1055, 1064 (E.D.Mo. 2006).

395. *See Salahuddin v. Cuomo*, 861 F.2d 40, 43 (2d Cir.1988)(noting that court would strike only so much of pleading as is redundant or immaterial).

- *Redundant Matter:* A redundant allegation is a needless repetition of other averments.[396]

- *Immaterial Matter:* Immaterial allegations are those that either bear no essential or important relationship to the pleader's claim for relief or contain a statement of unnecessary particulars.[397] Allegations are immaterial if no evidence to support them would be admissible at trial.[398]

- *Impertinent Matter:* An impertinent allegation is an averment that does not pertain to, or is unnecessary to, the issues in dispute. If the pleader would not be permitted to offer evidence at trial in support of the allegation, the allegation is likely impertinent.[399]

- *Scandalous Matter:* Scandalous matter does not merely offend someone's sensibilities; it must improperly cast a person or entity in a derogatory light.[400] Moreover, such matter will not be stricken if it describes acts or events relevant to the parties' dispute, unless the descriptions contain unnecessary detail.[401]

---

396. *See Wilkerson v. Butler*, 229 F.R.D. 166, 170 (E.D.Cal.2005); *Germaine Music v. Universal Songs of Polygram*, 275 F.Supp.2d 1288, 1299 (D.Nev.2003). *See also Sorosky v. Burroughs Corp.*, 826 F.2d 794, 802 (9th Cir.1987) (where no arguments were presented in support of theory, it was vulnerable to dismissal as redundant). *But cf. Dethmers Mfg. Co. v. Automatic Equip. Mfg. Co.*, 23 F.Supp.2d 974, 1008–09 (N.D.Iowa 1998) (mere duplicative remedies do not necessarily make claims "redundant" if those claims require proof of different elements, but claim that simply recasts same elements under the guise of different theory may be stricken as redundant).

397. *See Fantasy, Inc. v. Fogerty*, 984 F.2d 1524, 1527 (9th Cir.1993), *rev'd on other grounds*, 510 U.S. 517, 114 S.Ct. 1023, 127 L.Ed.2d 455 (1994); *Wilkins v. Ramirez*, 455 F.Supp.2d 1080, 1112 (S.D.Cal. 2006); *Standfacts Credit Servs., Inc. v. Experian Info. Solutions, Inc.*, 405 F.Supp.2d 1141, 1154 (C.D.Cal.2005). *See also Bureerong v. Uvawas*, 922 F.Supp. 1450, 1478 (C.D.Cal. 1996)(striking Complaint's reference to "Slave Sweatshop").

398. *See Johnson v. M & M Commc'ns, Inc.*, 242 F.R.D. 187, ___ (D.Conn. 2007); *Lennon v. Seaman*, 63 F.Supp.2d 428, 446–47 (S.D.N.Y.1999).

399. *See Fantasy, Inc. v. Fogerty*, 984 F.2d 1524, 1527 (9th Cir.1993), *rev'd on other grounds*, 510 U.S. 517, 114 S.Ct. 1023,

127 L.Ed.2d 455 (1994); *Johnson v. M & M Commc'ns, Inc.*, 242 F.R.D. 187, ___ (D.Conn. 2007); *Wilkins v. Ramirez*, 455 F.Supp.2d 1080, 1112 (S.D.Cal. 2006); *Wilkerson v. Butler*, 229 F.R.D. 166, 170 (E.D.Cal.2005); *Judicial Watch, Inc. v. U.S. Dep't of Commerce*, 224 F.R.D. 261, 263 (D.D.C.2004).

400. *See Alvarado–Morales v. Digital Equip. Corp.*, 843 F.2d 613 (1st Cir. 1988)(striking as "scandalous" references to "concentration camp", "brainwash", and "torture" which impugned the characters of the defendant); *Florance v. Buchmeyer*, 500 F.Supp.2d 618, ___, 2007 WL 2192635, at *19 (N.D.Tex. 2007) (must "unnecessarily reflect[] on the moral character of an individual or state[] anything in repulsive language that detracts from the dignity of the court"); *Global View Ltd. Venture Capital v. Great Central Basin Exploration, L.L.C.*, 288 F.Supp.2d 473, 481 (S.D.N.Y. 2003) (striking reference to defendants as "unscrupulous, unprincipled con artists" since it "amounts to nothing more than name calling, and does not contribute to [the] ... substantive claims"); *Sierra Club v. Tri–State Generation & Transmission Ass'n*, 173 F.R.D. 275 (D.Colo.1997) (irrelevant allegations will be stricken as scandalous if they degrade the defendants' moral character, contain repulsive language, or detract from the court's dignity).

401. *See Talbot v. Robert Matthews Distrib. Co.*, 961 F.2d 654, 664–65 (7th Cir. 1992)(matter is "scandalous" only if it

Striking Prayers For Relief

The court may also use Rule 12(f) to strike prayers for relief where the damages or other relief sought are not recoverable as a matter of law.[402]

Striking Documents Other Than Pleadings

As defined in Rule 12(f), motions to strike are directed to "pleadings" only. Consequently, these motions are technically not available to strike material contained in motions, briefs, memoranda, or affidavits.[403] Some courts, however, have permitted Rule 12(f) motions to strike affidavits and other materials that support pleadings.[404] Such motions may be treated by the court as an invitation to adjudicate the admissibility of certain material.[405] Some courts, however, permit the "striking" of documents other than pleadings, reasoning that Rule 12(f) offers the "only viable method" for attacking the materiality and pertinence of such papers.[406]

Discretion of Trial Court

The decision to grant or deny a motion to strike is vested in the trial judge's sound discretion.[407]

bears no possible relation to the controversy before the court); *Javier H. v. Garcia–Botello*, 239 F.R.D. 342, 350 (W.D.N.Y. 2006) (inclusion of criminal pleas not stricken if factual basis for allegations); *Sierra Club v. Tri–State Generation & Transmission Ass'n*, 173 F.R.D. 275 (D.Colo.1997) (relevant allegations will be stricken as scandalous only if they meet the "scandalous" test and contain unnecessary detail); *Delaware Health Care, Inc. v. MCD Holding Co.*, 893 F.Supp. 1279 (D.Del.1995)(defining "scandalous" allegations as matter bearing no possible relation to the dispute and which may cause prejudice to the movant).

402. See *Arcilla v. Adidas Promotional Retail Operations, Inc.*, 488 F.Supp.2d 965, 968 (C.D.Cal. 2007); *Wells v. Board of Trs. of Cal. State Univ.*, 393 F.Supp.2d 990, 994–95 (N.D.Cal.2005).

403. See *Pilgrim v. Trustees of Tufts College*, 118 F.3d 864 (1st Cir.1997) (rules do not apply to motion papers or supporting affidavits); *Dragon v. I.C. Sys., Inc.*, 241 F.R.D. 424, 425–26 (D.Conn. 2007) (not to summary judgment statements); *Jeter v. Montgomery County*, 480 F.Supp.2d 1293, 1295–96 (M.D.Ala. 2007) (not to opposition papers to motion to dismiss); *United States ex rel. Pogue v. Diabetes Treatment Ctrs. of America*, 474 F.Supp.2d 75, 80 (D.D.C. 2007) (not to expert testimony); *Johnson v. Manitowoc Boom Trucks, Inc.*, 406 F.Supp.2d 852, 864 n.10 (M.D.Tenn.2005) (not to affidavits); *Milk Drivers, Dairy &*

Ice Cream Employees, Laundry & Dry Cleaning Drivers, Clerical & Allied Workers v. Roberts Dairy, 219 F.R.D. 151, 152–53 (S.D.Iowa 2003) (not to motion for summary judgment); *VanDanacker v. Main Motor Sales Co.*, 109 F.Supp.2d 1045, 1047 (D.Minn.2000) (not to legal memorandum); *Transamerica Leasing, Inc. v. La Republica de Venezuela*, 21 F.Supp.2d 47, 55–56 (D.D.C.1998) (not to declarations and exhibits); *Phinney v. Paulshock*, 181 F.R.D. 185 (D.N.H.1998) (not to motion for sanctions), aff'd, 199 F.3d 1 (1st Cir.1999); *International Longshoremen's Ass'n, S.S. Clerks Local 1624, AFL–CIO v. Virginia Int'l Terminals, Inc.*, 904 F.Supp. 500, 504 (E.D.Va.1995) (not to reply briefs).

404. See *Moret v. Geren*, 494 F.Supp.2d 329, ___, 2007 WL 1880735, at *5 (D.Md. 2007); *United States ex rel. Pogue v. Diabetes Treatment Ctrs. of America*, 474 F.Supp.2d 75, 79 n.4 (D.D.C. 2007).

405. See *United States v. Southern Cal. Edison Co.*, 300 F.Supp.2d 964, 973 (E.D.Cal.2004).

406. See *Judicial Watch, Inc. v. U.S. Dep't of Commerce*, 224 F.R.D. 261, 263 (D.D.C.2004).

407. See *Talbot v. Robert Matthews Distrib. Co.*, 961 F.2d 654, 665 (7th Cir.1992); *BJC Health Sys. v. Columbia Cas. Co.*, 478 F.3d 908, 917 (8th Cir. 2007); *S.E.C. v. Durgarian*, 477 F.Supp.2d 342, 360 (D.Mass. 2007); *United States ex rel. Pogue*

Timing

A motion to strike must be made before a responsive pleading is served or, if no responsive pleading is required, within 20 days after service of the preceding pleading.[408] In view of the court's authority to strike on its own initiative, (see "*Sua Sponte* Strikes" below), this 20–day period is often not applied strictly when the proposal to strike has merit.[409]

Sua Sponte Strikes

At any time, the court may, on its own initiative, strike matter from a pleading.[410] Thus, the court may properly consider a party's untimely motion or "suggestion" under Rule 12(f) to strike matter from the pleading.[411]

Extrinsic Materials

Generally, the court will not consider extrinsic materials on a motion to strike.[412] Instead, the grounds supporting the motion to strike must be readily apparent from the face of the pleadings themselves or from materials that may be judicially noticed.[413] If the court does consider extrinsic materials, the motion to strike must ordinarily be converted into a motion for summary judgment.[414]

v. Diabetes Treatment Ctrs. of America, 474 F.Supp.2d 75, 79 (D.D.C. 2007); *Poole v. Taylor*, 466 F.Supp.2d 578, 583 (D.Del. 2006); *Sobba v. Elmen*, 462 F.Supp.2d 944, 946 (E.D.Ark. 2006).

408. *See United States v. $38,000.00 Dollars in U.S. Currency*, 816 F.2d 1538, 1547 n. 20 (11th Cir.1987); *Culinary & Serv. Employees Union v. Hawaii Employee Benefit Admin., Inc.*, 688 F.2d 1228 (9th Cir.1982); *Taylor v. Quall*, 471 F.Supp.2d 1053, 1058–59 (C.D.Cal. 2007). *See also Circuit Sys., Inc. v. Mescalero Sales, Inc.*, 925 F.Supp. 546, 548 (N.D.Ill.1996)(motion made beyond 20–day period is untimely and subject to denial).

409. *See In re Complaint of Rationis Enters. of Panama*, 210 F.Supp.2d 421, 424–25 (S.D.N.Y.2002) (noting that while rule requires motion to strikes to be filed within 20 days after service, court's power to strike on its own initiative permits consideration of untimely motions to strike); *Wine Markets Int'l, Inc. v. Bass*, 177 F.R.D. 128, 133 (E.D.N.Y.1998) (holding that court's discretion "renders the twenty (20) day rule 'essentially unimportant' ").

410. *See Calcutti v. SBU, Inc.*, 224 F.Supp.2d 691, 701 (S.D.N.Y.2002); *Wine Markets Int'l, Inc. v. Bass*, 177 F.R.D. 128, 133 (E.D.N.Y.1998); *Owens v. Blue Tee Corp.*, 177 F.R.D. 673, 678 (M.D.Ala.1998).

411. *See United States v. Lot 65 Pine Meadow*, 976 F.2d 1155, 1157 (8th Cir. 1992); *In re Complaint of Rationis Enters. of Pananma*, 210 F.Supp.2d 421, 424–25 (S.D.N.Y.2002).

412. *See Employers Ins. Co. of Wausau v. Crouse–Cmty. Ctr., Inc.*, 489 F.Supp.2d 176, 179 (N.D.N.Y. 2007). *See also Diamond Scientific Co. v. Ambico, Inc.*, 848 F.2d 1220, 1226 (Fed.Cir.1988) (noting that although extrinsic materials are generally not considered on a motion to strike, they may be accepted by the court where they present uncontested factual matters); *Oneida Indian Nation of New York v. New York*, 194 F.Supp.2d 104, 117 (N.D.N.Y.2002). *But see Fantasy, Inc. v. Fogerty*, 984 F.2d 1524, 1528–29 (9th Cir.1993)(in ruling on Rule 12(f) motion to strike, district court did not act improperly in considering materials of which it could take judicial notice, nor was submission of affidavits improper where court did not consider them), *rev'd on other grounds*, 510 U.S. 517, 114 S.Ct. 1023, 127 L.Ed.2d 455 (1994).

413. *See Johnson v. Anhorn*, 334 F.Supp.2d 802, 809 (E.D.Pa.2004); *Wailua Assocs. v. Aetna Cas. & Sur. Co.*, 183 F.R.D. 550, 553–54 (D.Haw.1998).

414. *See Liberty Mut. Ins. Co. v. Precision Valve Corp.*, 402 F.Supp.2d 481, 484 (S.D.N.Y.2005).

Prejudice on Dismissal

Where an allegation or defense is stricken as technically deficient, the dismissal is generally without prejudice to refile with a
technically correct pleading.[415]

RULE 12(g). JOINING MOTION

CORE CONCEPT

If a party chooses to make a motion under Rule 12, the party must
include all Rule 12 defenses and objections then available in a single,
omnibus motion. Rule 12(g) must be read in conjunction with Rule
12(h), concerning waiver and preservation of certain defenses.

APPLICATIONS

Joining Rule 12 Motions: General Rule, and Consequences

Any Rule 12 motion may be joined with any other Rule 12
motion.[416] The consequences of making a Rule 12 motion are twofold. *First*, a party is generally permitted to make only one Rule 12
motion; thus, a party must consolidate all Rule 12 motion claims
together, or risk losing the right to have them decided by pre-answer
motion later.[417] *Second*, a party waives several Rule 12 defenses if
they are not asserted in the Rule 12 motion (if any such motion is
made on any ground).[418]

Successive Rule 12 Motions to Dismiss May Be Prohibited

The plain language of Rule 12(g) protects the defense of failure
to state a claim from this risk of waiver.[419] Some courts have
interpreted this language so as to permit multiple, successive pre-
answer Rule 12(b)(6) motions.[420] Other courts have taken the opposite approach, holding that a defendant is generally precluded from
filing successive pre-answer motions to dismiss to raise arguments
that the defendant could have raised, but did not, in the first
motion[421] (although this general prohibition is not absolute[422]). This

---

415. *See D.S. America (East), Inc. v.
Chromagrafx Imaging Sys., Inc.*, 873
F.Supp. 786, 798 (E.D.N.Y.1995).

416. *See* Rule 12(g)(1).

417. *See* Rule 12(g)(2). *See McCurdy v.
American Bd. of Plastic Surgery*, 157 F.3d
191, 194 (3d Cir.1998). *See also Skrtich v.
Thornton*, 280 F.3d 1295, 1306 (11th Cir.
2002) (affirming dismissal of untimely asserted qualified immunity defense because
Rule 12(g) prohibits party from filing a
second pre-answer motion to dismiss raising omitted defense that could have been
presented in earlier motion).

418. *See* Rule 12(h)(1).

419. *See* Rule 12(g)(2) (no successive
Rule 12 motions permitted "[e]xcept as provided in Rule 12(h)(2) or (3)"); Rule

12(h)(2) (defense of failure to state a claim
upon which relief can be granted may also
be made by pleading, by Rule 12(c) motion
for judgment on the pleadings, or at trial).

420. *See In re Parmalat Secs. Litig.*, 497
F.Supp.2d 526, 530 (S.D.N.Y. 2007); *Ong ex
rel. Ong v. Sears, Roebuck & Co.*, 459
F.Supp.2d 729, 740 n.10 (N.D.Ill. 2006);
Lindsey v. United States, 448 F. Supp. 2d
37, 55–57 (D.D.C. 2006); *Stoffels ex rel.,
SBC Concession Plan v. SBC Commc'ns,
Inc.*, 430 F. Supp. 2d 642, 646–50 (W.D.
Tex. 2006).

421. *See Candido v. District of Columbia*, 242 F.R.D. 151 (D.D.C. 2007); *766347
Ontario Ltd. v. Zurich Capital Mkts., Inc.*,
274 F.Supp.2d 926, 930 (N.D.Ill.2003); *Waf-
ra Leasing Corp. 1999–A–1 v. Prime Capital*

prohibition ordinarily applies even after an amended complaint is filed; if the basis for the motion to dismiss was available to the defendant at the time of the original complaint, the filing of an amended complaint will not trigger a new opportunity to assert the motion.[423] Although Rules 12(g) and 12(h)(2) specifically preserve a party's right to file a pre-answer motion to dismiss for failure to state a claim *and*, later, assert a failure to state a claim by motion for judgment on the pleadings[424] or at trial, this right might not be unrestricted. There is some authority for supposing that a defendant may not be permitted to file a Rule 12(b) motion to dismiss for failure to state a claim, lose on the motion, and then file a Rule 12(c) motion for judgment on the pleadings that makes the very same arguments the court had just rejected.[425]

Exception—Prohibition Applies Only to Defenses "Then Available"

A party is required to assert in an omnibus motion only those defenses and objections "then available" to that party.[426] Thus, if new defenses or objections are prompted by an amended pleading or a more definite statement, the responding party may generally file a new Rule 12 motion to assert defenses and objections to such newly introduced matter.[427] Similarly, parties may generally file a new Rule 12 motion if, while their case has been pending, a change in the law offers them a new legal defense or objection.[428] But parties must act promptly. An unnecessarily lengthy delay in asserting a latent Rule 12 objection may, itself, be deemed a waiver.[429]

Corp., 247 F.Supp.2d 987, 999 (N.D.Ill. 2002); *Federal Express Corp. v. United States Postal Serv.*, 40 F. Supp. 2d 943, 948 (W.D. Tenn. 1999).

422. See infra Authors' Commentary to Rule 12(g) ("**Exception—No Unnecessary Delay**").

423. *See Albany Ins. Co. v. Almacenadora Somex*, 5 F.3d 907, 909 (5th Cir.1993); *766347 Ontario Ltd. v. Zurich Capital Mkts., Inc.*, 274 F.Supp.2d 926, 930 (N.D.Ill. 2003).

424. *See Marrero–Gutierrez v. Molina*, 491 F.3d 1 (1st Cir. 2007).

425. *See Sprint Telephony PCS, L.P. v. County of San Diego*, 311 F.Supp.2d 898, 904–05 (S.D.Cal.2004), *clarified on other grounds*, 2004 WL 859333 (S.D.Cal.2004) (although permitting Rule 12(c) motion asserting same arguments raised in earlier Rule 12(b)(6) motion, court noted the "tension" between Rule 12(g)'s consolidation policy and this sort of practice).

426. *See Candido v. District of Columbia*, 242 F.R.D. 151 (D.D.C. 2007).

427. *See McCurdy v. American Bd. of Plastic Surgery*, 157 F.3d 191, 196 n. 1 (3d Cir.1998); *Glater v. Eli Lilly & Co.*, 712 F.2d 735, 738–39 (1st Cir.1983) *Chatman–Bey v. Thornburgh*, 864 F.2d 804 (D.C.Cir. 1988).

428. *See Holzsager v. Valley Hosp.*, 646 F.2d 792, 796 (2d Cir.1981) (courts will not demand clairvoyance from litigants; parties not deemed to have waived defenses or objections not then known to them); *Engel v. CBS, Inc.*, 886 F.Supp. 728, 728–730 (C.D.Cal.1995)(holding that Rule 12(g) will not fault defendants for failing to press a defense they did not then know was available to them).

429. *See Overseas Partners, Inc. v. PROGEN Musavirlik ve Yonetim Hizmetleri, Ltd. Sikerti*, 15 F.Supp.2d 47 (D.D.C. 1998) (holding that, although service objections were not "available" at the time a first motion to dismiss was filed, litigants delayed in raising the new defense and this failure to promptly amend the motion constituted a waiver of the defense).

Exception—Prior Motions to Stay/Dismiss on Abstention Principles

Some courts have ruled that this preclusion of successive Rule 12 motions to dismiss will not apply where the preceding motion to dismiss or to stay was based on an alleged lack of federal jurisdiction under some abstention principle.[430]

Exception—No Unnecessary Delay

Even where other exceptions do not apply, the prohibition on successive Rule 12 motions to dismiss is not absolute. Some courts have permitted such a practice where the second motion would not result in unnecessary delay, expense, or inconvenience, yet would allow a more expeditious resolution of the case.[431]

Exception—Objections to Subject Matter Jurisdiction

Objections to subject matter jurisdiction concern the court's authority to hear and decide the case. Consequently, such objections cannot generally be lost through waiver.[432]

"Amending" a Rule 12 Motion

To avoid waiving Rule 12 defenses that were omitted inadvertently from a Rule 12 motion, parties may seek leave of court to "amend" or supplement their Rule 12 motions to include the omitted defenses or objections.[433] In considering such amendments, the court may examine whether the amendment request was filed before the Rule 12 motion was heard, the time interval between the original Rule 12 motion and the attempted correction, the moving party's good faith, and the likelihood that the omission was intentional and tactical, or merely inadvertent.[434]

Applies Only to Rule 12 Motions

This omnibus "consolidation" provision applies only to Rule 12 motions and only to defenses that may be asserted under Rule 12 (*e.g.*, lack of personal jurisdiction, improper venue, improper service). Affirmative defenses generally are not waived if asserted in the responsive pleading filed after a Rule 12 motion.[435] This Rule

---

430. See *Aetna Life Ins. Co. v. Alla Med. Servs., Inc.*, 855 F.2d 1470, 1475 (9th Cir. 1988); *Bacardi, U.S.A., Inc. v. Premier Beverage, Inc.*, 352 F.Supp.2d 1188, 1194 (D.Kan.2005).

431. See *Lindsey v. United States*, 448 F.Supp.2d 37, 55–57 (D.D.C.2006); *Stoffels ex rel., SBC Concession Plan v. SBC Commc'ns, Inc.*, 430 F.Supp.2d 642, 646–50 (W.D.Tex.2006); *Muhammad v. Village of Bolingbrook*, 2004 WL 1557958, at *1 (N.D.Ill. July 8, 2004); *MCW, Inc. v. Badbusinessbureau.com, L.L.C.*, 2004 WL 833595, at *5–*6 (N.D.Tex. April 19, 2004).

432. See Rule 12(h)(3). See also *Williams v. Roche*, 2002 WL 1585568, at *4 (E.D.La.2002).

433. See *Chatman–Bey v. Thornburgh*, 864 F.2d 804 (D.C.Cir.1988); *Glater v. Eli Lilly & Co.*, 712 F.2d 735, 738 (1st Cir. 1983); *Gray v. Snow King Resort, Inc.*, 889 F.Supp. 1473 (D.Wyo.1995).

434. See *Nycal Corp. v. Inoco PLC*, 949 F.Supp. 1115, 1119–20 (S.D.N.Y.1997) (setting out considerations, and denying leave to supplement where the omission was found to be a deliberate intent to obtain a tactical advantage).

435. See *Parker v. United States*, 110 F.3d 678, 682 (9th Cir.1997). See also *Tahoe–Sierra Preservation Council, Inc. v. Tahoe Regional Planning Agency*, 992 F.Supp. 1218, 1225–26 (D.Nev.1998), *aff'd in part, rev'd in part*, 216 F.3d 764 (9th Cir.2000)

does not apply to motions allowed under other Rules.[436] Moreover, certain Rule 12 defenses and objections, even though not raised in the Rule 12 motion, are not deemed forever waived. Rule 12(h)(2) expressly preserves a pleader's right to assert in any pleading, in a Rule 12(c) motion, or at trial the defenses of (a) failure to state a claim upon which relief can be granted, (b) failure to join an indispensable party, and (c) failure to state a legal defense.[437]

Effect of Same Counsel for Multiple Defendants

Where the same attorney represents multiple defendants and files a consolidated Rule 12(b) motion jointly on their behalf, there is some uncertainty as to the effect of the attorney's decision to assert certain Rule 12(b) defenses by motion as to some, but not all, defendants. One view, emphasizing the goal of avoiding the dilatory effect of successive Rule 12(b) motions, would preclude a later Rule 12(b) filing by the other defendants.[438] An opposing, more recent, and more authoritative (and perhaps better reasoned) view rejects this result, citing the absence of any such consolidated defendant provision in Rule 12(g).[439]

RULE 12(h).   WAIVING AND PRESERVING CERTAIN DEFENSES

CORE CONCEPT

Rule 12(h) sets forth the defenses and objections that are waived if not timely asserted, and lists the defenses and objections that are not waivable.

APPLICATIONS

Waived Defenses and Objections

Defenses and objections to personal jurisdiction (Rule 12(b)(2)), improper venue (Rule 12(b)(3)), insufficient process (Rule 12(b)(4)), and insufficient service (Rule 12(b)(5)), are waived[440] unless they are:

(holding that omitting statute of limitations defense from pre-answer motion is not a waiver).

436. *See Aetna Life Ins. Co. v. Alla Med. Servs., Inc.,* 855 F.2d 1470 (9th Cir.1988). *See also Norwood v. Raytheon Co.,* 455 F.Supp.2d 597, 601 (W.D.Tex. 2006) (motion for transfer of venue does not trigger Rule 12(g) consolidation requirement); *Baranof Fisheries Ltd. P'ship v. Elsey,* 1996 WL 467323 (D.Or.1996)(nor does Rule 41 motion for voluntary dismissal).

437. *See* Rule 12(h)(2). *See also Vega v. State Univ. of New York Bd. of Trustees,* 2000 WL 381430, at *2 (S.D.N.Y.2000) (permitting successive Rule 12(b)(6) motions under circumstances); *United States ex rel. S. Prawer & Co. v. Verrill & Dana,* 962

F.Supp. 206, 209 n. 4 (D.Me.1997) (noting that Rule 12(b)(6) motions are not encompassed in Rule 12(g), and can be considered even after the Rule 12 motion is ruled upon). *But see Federal Express Corp. v. United States Postal Serv.,* 40 F.Supp.2d 943, 948 (W.D.Tenn.1999) (although failure-to-state-a-claim is not a waived defense, Rule 12(g) precludes successive, pre-answer Rule 12(b)(6) motions).

438. *See Church of Scientology v. Linberg,* 529 F.Supp. 945, 966–67 (C.D.Cal. 1981).

439. *See Schnabel v. Lui,* 302 F.3d 1023, 1034 (9th Cir.2002).

440. *See, e.g., Wachovia Bank v. Schmidt,* 546 U.S. 303, ___, 126 S.Ct. 941, 950, 163 L.Ed.2d 797 (2006) (venue waived

- *Asserted By Motion*: In an omnibus Rule 12(b) motion, but only if one is filed, *or*

- *Asserted By Responsive Pleading:* If such an omnibus Rule 12(b) motion is not filed.

Similarly, a defendant's denials to the pleader's factual allegations, as well as the defendants' affirmative defenses, are also waived if they are not asserted in the responsive pleading.[441]

Purpose

Judicial economy underlies this waiver provision. Automatic waiver is designed to prevent the delaying effect of the piecemeal assertion of Rule 12 objections and defenses through multiple motions, and to permit the early dismissal of inappropriate claims before the court devotes unnecessary time and resources to adjudication.[442]

Waiver is Mandatory, Not Discretionary

The waiver provision of Rule 12(h) imposes a mandatory, not discretionary, obligation upon the district court.[443]

Avoiding Waiver by Seeking Leave to Amend

A party's failure to assert a timely factual denial or defense can be cured if the court grants the party leave to amend the pleading or Rule 12 motion.[444] Before granting leave to amend or supplement a Rule 12 motion, the court may examine whether the amendment request was filed before the Rule 12 motion was heard, the time interval between the original Rule 12 motion and the attempted correction, the moving party's good faith, and the likelihood that the omission was intentional and tactical, or merely inadvertent.[445]

if not timely raised); *Rates Tech. Inc. v. Nortel Networks Corp.*, 399 F.3d 1302, 1307 (Fed.Cir.2005) (cautioning "great diligence" in challenging personal jurisdiction, venue, and service); *Taubman Co. v. Webfeats*, 319 F.3d 770, 773 (6th Cir.2003) (personal jurisdiction challenge waived if not raised in first responsive pleading); *Farm Credit Bank of Baltimore v. Ferrera–Goitia*, 316 F.3d 62, 68 (1st Cir.2003) (personal jurisdiction defense waived if not made by first-filed motion or included in initial responsive pleading); *Porsche Cars North America, Inc. v. Porsche.Net*, 302 F.3d 248, 256 (4th Cir.2002) (personal jurisdiction defense indubitably waived absent timely objection); *Posner v. Essex Ins. Co.*, 178 F.3d 1209, 1213 n. 4 (11th Cir.1999) (defendant waived personal jurisdiction challenge by omitting this defense from Rule 12(b) motion); *McCurdy v. American Bd. of Plastic Surgery*, 157 F.3d 191, 195 (3d Cir.1998) (untimely service waived if not raised timely);

Texas Mun. Power Agency v. EPA, 89 F.3d 858, 867 (D.C.Cir.1996)(improper venue waived for failure to object).

441. *See Pusey v. Dallas Corp.*, 938 F.2d 498 (4th Cir.1991).

442. *See Flory v. United States*, 79 F.3d 24, 25 (5th Cir.1996); *Schneider v. National R.R. Passenger Corp.*, 72 F.3d 17, 20 (2d Cir.1995).

443. *See Polaroid Corp. v. Feely*, 889 F.Supp. 21 (D.Mass.1995).

444. *See* Rule 15; *Gray v. Snow King Resort, Inc.*, 889 F.Supp. 1473 (D.Wyo. 1995).

445. *See Nycal Corp. v. Inoco PLC*, 949 F.Supp. 1115, 1119–20 (S.D.N.Y.1997) (setting out considerations, and denying leave to supplement where the omission was found to be a deliberate intent to obtain a tactical advantage).

Raising Defenses/Objections in Answer Only (Without Motion)

If the defendant elects *not* to file a Rule 12 motion, the waivable Rule 12 defenses and objections are preserved if included in the party's answer.[446] However, in certain circumstances, a waiver may be implied by conduct that is deemed inconsistent with an intention to preserve a defense.[447]

Implied Waiver

The courts may, under certain circumstances, find that a party has waived personal jurisdiction, venue, insufficient process, or insufficient service of process, even though those defenses were set forth in a timely motion to dismiss or in a responsive pleading. For example, a defendant who asserts a timely but waivable Rule 12(b) defense, but then interposes an affirmative claim for relief (*e.g.*, a permissive counterclaim), may be deemed to have abandoned the waivable Rule 12 defenses.[448] The court may consider the party's act of pressing such an affirmative claim as inconsistent with an objection to jurisdiction, venue, process, or service.

> *Note:* The case law is unclear on this issue. However, the developing trend seems to suggest that a party does *not* waive a properly, timely asserted objection to jurisdiction by pressing an affirmative claim for relief,[449] or by filing ancillary motions (*e.g.*, for stay or injunction pending appeal) premised on the asserted jurisdictional defense.[450] This trend construes such affirmative claims for relief as simply contingent on the court's denial of the party's jurisdictional objections.[451]

Similarly, a defendant who timely objects to personal jurisdiction, but then fails to timely bring the defense to the court for a ruling,

---

446. *See McIntosh v. Antonino*, 71 F.3d 29, 38 (1st Cir.1995)(statute of limitations defense is not waived even if no motion for judgment on that issue is filed, so long as the defense is preserved in the Answer).

447. *See infra* Authors' Commentary to Rule 12(h) ("**Implied Waiver**").

448. *See Frank's Casing Crew & Rental Tools, Inc. v. PMR Tech., Ltd.*, 292 F.3d 1363, 1372 (Fed.Cir.2002) (holding that non-resident defendant in patent noninfringement declaratory judgment action waived personal jurisdiction objection when it filed class action counterclaim asserting unrelated infringements of patent by others).

449. *See Rates Tech. Inc. v. Nortel Networks Corp.*, 399 F.3d 1302, 1307–08 (Fed. Cir.2005) (adopting majority view); *Paine-Webber Inc. v. Chase Manhattan Private Bank (Switzerland)*, 260 F.3d 453, 461 (5th Cir.2001) (same); *Kaplan v. First Options of Chicago, Inc.*, 19 F.3d 1503, 1520 (3d Cir. 1994) (same), *aff'd*, 514 U.S. 938, 115 S.Ct.

1920, 131 L.Ed.2d 985 (1995); *Chase v. Pan–Pac. Broad., Inc.*, 750 F.2d 131, 132 (D.C.Cir.1984) (same); *Gates Learjet Corp. v. Jensen*, 743 F.2d 1325, 1330 (9th Cir. 1984) (same). *See also Media Duplication Servs., Ltd. v. HDG Software, Inc.*, 928 F.2d 1228, 1233 & n. 2 (1st Cir.1991) (ineffective service of process defense was not waived where it was seasonably raised and consistently pressed, notwithstanding filing of counterclaim).

450. *See PaineWebber Inc. v. Chase Manhattan Private Bank (Switzerland)*, 260 F.3d 453, 461 (5th Cir.2001) (defendant who timely and properly asserted personal jurisdiction objection by motion, and engaged in no counterclaim or third-party practice, did not waive defense by filing motion for stay and injunction pending appeal premised on the jurisdictional defense).

451. *See Bayou Steel Corp. v. M/V Amstelvoorn*, 809 F.2d 1147, 1149 (5th Cir.1987) (discussing divergent views, and adopting majority approach).

choosing instead to participate actively in the litigation as though jurisdiction, venue, and proper service existed, may be deemed to have waived the jurisdictional objection.[452] This implied waiver effect is not limited only to defendants. A plaintiff, obviously, by the very act of suing, submits herself to the jurisdiction of the court for purposes of a defendant's counterclaims.[453]

Preserved Defenses and Objections

Defenses and objections to a failure to state a claim upon which relief can be granted (Rule 12(b)(6)), failure to join an indispensable party (Rule 12(b)(7)), and failure to state a legal defense (Rule 12(f)) are waived *only* if not asserted before the close of trial.[454] There is also authority for the proposition that the filing of a Rule 12(b)(6) motion on certain grounds will not be deemed a waiver of other grounds not asserted then, but raised later.[455] Thus, these defenses, though generally preserved throughout the lawsuit, may not be raised for the first time in post-trial motions or on appeal.[456]

- *Only One Pre-Answer Rule 12(b)(6) Motion May Be Permitted:* Although the Rule 12(b)(6) defense of failure to state a claim is generally not waived (so long as it is asserted before the time of trial), it ordinarily may not be asserted in multiple pre-answer motions. Some (but not all) courts have ruled that successive, pre-answer Rule 12(b)(6) motions are prohibited by Rule 12(g)'s requirement that all Rule 12 defenses (including failure to state a claim) be raised in a single, omnibus, pre-answer motion—if the party chooses to file a motion at all.[457]

- *Non-Waiver Applies to "Indispensable" Parties Only:* Rule 12(h) preserves only the defense of dismissal for failing to join an "indispensable" party. Where a party is necessary for proper adjudication under Rule 19, but can be joined as a party in the lawsuit, a motion for joinder may not be made if omitted from an omnibus Rule 12 motion or, alternatively,

452. *See Hamilton v. Atlas Turner, Inc.,* 197 F.3d 58, 62 (2d Cir.1999) (defense "forfeited" by failing to move to dismiss during four-year period following inclusion of defense in party's answer); *Trustees of Central Laborers' Welfare Fund v. Lowery,* 924 F.2d 731, 732–33 (7th Cir.1991) (same, six-year period). *See also White v. National Football League,* 41 F.3d 402, 407 (8th Cir.1994)*Cf. Rates Tech. Inc. v. Nortel Networks Corp.,* 399 F.3d 1302, 1308–09 (Fed.Cir.2005) (noting waiver authority, but finding defendant did not "dally" but moved to dismiss at its "earliest opportunity").

453. *See Adam v. Saenger,* 303 U.S. 59, 67–68, 58 S.Ct. 454, 458, 82 L.Ed. 649 (1938).

454. *See Arbaugh v. Y&H Corp.,* 546 U.S. 500, ___, 126 S.Ct. 1235, 1236, 163 L.Ed.2d 1097 (2006); *Sucampo Pharms., Inc. v. Astellas Pharma, Inc.,* 471 F.3d 544. 548–49 (4th Cir. 2006); *Eberhardt v. Integrated Design & Const., Inc.,* 167 F.3d 861, 870–71 (4th Cir.1999); *Romstadt v. Allstate Ins. Co.,* 59 F.3d 608, 610–11 (6th Cir.1995).

455. *See Peltz ex rel. Estate of Peltz v. Sears, Roebuck & Co.,* 367 F.Supp.2d 711, 721 (E.D.Pa.2005).

456. *Brown v. Trustees of Boston Univ.,* 891 F.2d 337 (1st Cir.1989).

457. *See infra* Authors' Commentary to Rule 12(g) ("**Successive Rule 12 Motions to Dismiss May Be Prohibited**").

from the responsive pleading.[458]

Objections to Subject Matter Jurisdiction

Because objections to the court's subject matter jurisdiction concern the court's authority to hear and decide the parties' dispute, no one can waive such an objection, be estopped from raising the objection, or cure such a problem by consenting to jurisdiction where none exists.[459]

- *Asserted At Any Time:* Objections to subject matter jurisdiction may be made in the omnibus Rule 12 motion, in the responsive pleading, in subsequent pretrial motions, in a motion for relief from final judgment, or on appeal.[460] The objection, however, must be made while the case is still pending (*e.g.*, before trial, at trial, or on appeal); it cannot be raised for the first time as a collateral attack on the earlier judgment.[461]

- *"Suggestions":* Although a motion to dismiss for lack of subject matter jurisdiction is technically untimely if filed after the pleadings are closed, the courts will typically treat such a belated motion as a "suggestion" to the court that it lacks subject matter jurisdiction, and will then proceed to consider it on its merits.[462]

- *Raised By Court:* The trial court or the court of appeals may raise an objection to subject matter jurisdiction on its own initiative.[463]

Waiting for Default to Raise Service Objections

Although defendants must raise their objections to process, service, and personal jurisdiction either in their omnibus Rule 12 motion or in their answer (if no Rule 12 motion is filed), these defenses are *not* waived where the failure of service is so complete

458. *See Citibank, N.A. v. Oxford Properties & Fin. Ltd.,* 688 F.2d 1259 (9th Cir. 1982).

459. *See Rule 12(b)(1); Wachovia Bank v. Schmidt,* 546 U.S. 303, ___, 126 S.Ct. 941, 950, 163 L.Ed.2d 797 (2006) (subject matter jurisdiction must be considered by court, even if parties do not raise it). *See also American Fiber & Finishing, Inc. v. Tyco Healthcare Group, LP,* 362 F.3d 136, 139 (1st Cir.2004); *Taubman Co. v. Webfeats,* 319 F.3d 770, 773 (6th Cir.2003); *In re Stock Exchanges Options Trading Antitrust Litig.,* 317 F.3d 134, 151 (2d Cir. 2003). *Cf. Moravian School Advisory Bd. v. Rawlins,* 70 F.3d 270 (3d Cir. 1995)(where district court lacked subject matter jurisdiction to hear the case, it also lacked jurisdiction to transfer it; the only remedy for lack of subject matter jurisdiction is dismissal).

460. *See Arbaugh v. Y&H Corp.,* 546 U.S. 500, ___, 126 S.Ct. 1235, 1236, 163 L.Ed.2d 1097 (2006); *Wachovia Bank v. Schmidt,* 546 U.S. 303, ___, 126 S.Ct. 941, 950, 163 L.Ed.2d 797 (2006).

461. *See City of South Pasadena v. Mineta,* 284 F.3d 1154, 1156–57 (9th Cir. 2002).

462. *See S.J. v. Hamilton County,* 374 F.3d 416, 418 n.1 (6th Cir.2004).

463. *See Insurance Corp. of Ireland, Ltd. v. Compagnie des Bauxites de Guinee,* 456 U.S. 694, 704, 102 S.Ct. 2099, 2105, 72 L.Ed.2d 492 (1982). *See also Ward v. Brown,* 22 F.3d 516 (2d Cir.1994)("it has been the rule since nearly the inception of our republic that subject matter jurisdiction may be raised any time").

that the defendants never even received actual notice of the unanswered pleading.[464] In such a case, the Constitutional protections of due process should permit the defendants to raise those objections in opposition to a motion for default.[465] But defendants act at their peril if, after receiving actual notice of a pleading, they choose to ignore the lawsuit in reliance on their own, untested belief that either the process or service was faulty. They must guess correctly. There is case law precedent and commentary for the conclusion that this conduct may constitute a waiver of these defenses[466] or otherwise materially compromise their assertion.[467]

RULE 12(i).   HEARING BEFORE TRIAL

CORE CONCEPT

Unless the court orders that such motions are deferred until trial, a party may request the court to schedule Rule 12(b) and Rule 12(c) motions for a pretrial hearing and resolution.

APPLICATIONS

2007 Amendments

The substance of Rule 12(i) was formerly Rule 12(d). That content was moved to this new positioning by the 2007 amendments. Practitioners searching for pre–2007 interpretations of this Rule should bear this repositioning in mind in doing their research. Current Rule 12(i) was, until 2007, old Rule 12(d).

Rule 12(b) Defenses Asserted by Motion

When a Rule 12(b) defense or objection is asserted on a Rule 12(b) or Rule 12(c) motion, the moving papers themselves should include a "notice of hearing" or similar references following the practice dictated by the specific judicial district's local rules. As a matter of usual practice, the court will ordinarily resolve Rule 12(b)

---

464. *See Corestates Leasing, Inc. v. Wright–Way Exp., Inc.*, 190 F.R.D. 356, 358 (E.D.Pa.2000).

465. *See Stinecipher v. United States*, 239 F.R.D. 282, 283 (D.D.C. 2006) (unless proper service is satisfied, court lacks power to assert personal jurisdiction). *See also Trustees of St. Paul Elec. Const. Indus. Fringe Benefit Funds v. Martens Elec. Co.*, 485 F.Supp.2d 1063, 1065 (D. Minn. 2007) (noting that defendants who are not properly served are protected against default).

466. *See Corestates Leasing, Inc. v. Wright–Way Exp., Inc.*, 190 F.R.D. 356, 358 (E.D.Pa.2000); *O'Meara v. Waters*, 464 F.Supp.2d 474, 476 (D.Md. 2006) (if defendants receive actual notice, failure to comply strictly with Rule 4 might be excused and service deemed valid). *See also* 5A Charles Alan Wright & Arthur R. Miller,

Federal Practice & Procedure § 1391, at 755–56 (1990) ("But when the party has received actual notice of the suit there is no due process problem in requiring him to object to the ineffective service within the period prescribed by Rule 12(h)(1) and the defense is one that he certainly can waive if he wishes to do so. This is because the defendant has failed to do what the rule says he must do if he is to avoid a waiver.").

467. *See Burda Media, Inc. v. Viertel*, 417 F.3d 292 (2d Cir.2005) (ruling that where defaulting defendant had actual knowledge of proceeding, but delayed challenging allegedly improper service of process, that defendant will, in subsequent motion to vacate default, bear burden of proving that contested service did *not* occur).

and Rule 12(c) motions by issuing a pretrial Memorandum and Order.

Rule 12(b) Defenses Asserted in Responsive Pleading Only

When a Rule 12(b) defense or objection is asserted only in the responsive pleading (*i.e.*, where no pre-answer Rule 12(b) motion for dismissal is filed), a Rule 12(d) application for preliminary hearing is necessary to obtain a pretrial determination from the court on those defenses and objections.[468]

When Pretrial Determinations are Appropriate

Notwithstanding the presence of a genuine factual dispute, the court may decide to make its own findings and resolve pretrial contests challenging (1) the litigants' domiciles for diversity jurisdiction purposes, (2) the court's exercise of personal jurisdiction over a defendant, (3) a litigant's standing to press a claim, (4) the propriety of venue as laid, or (5) the assertion of claim preclusion defenses.[469] In deciding whether these types of issues should be determined preliminarily (or should, instead, await resolution at trial), the courts weigh the need to test these defenses and the litigants' interest in having the objections resolved promptly, against the expense and delay of a preliminary hearing, the court's difficulty in deciding the issues preliminarily, and the likelihood that the issues will become so interconnected with the merits that deferring them until trial would be preferable.[470]

Resolving Personal Jurisdiction Challenges

When the Rule 12(b)(2) defense of lack of personal jurisdiction is raised, the court has three options for resolving the motion:

(1) The court may hear and resolve the motion before trial, by applying the preponderance-of-the-evidence standard;

(2) The court may defer the motion until time of trial, provided the plaintiff has offered a prima facie showing of jurisdiction; or

(3) The court may apply an intermediate scrutiny in circumstances where it would be unfair to require a defendant to incur the expenses and burden of a trial on the merits in view of a substantial jurisdictional question. In those instances, the court will defer the motion until trial only if the

---

468. *See Rivera–Gomez v. de Castro,* 900 F.2d 1, 2 (1st Cir.1990)(Rule 12(d) is "perhaps too infrequently invoked and too often overlooked"; it can, in appropriate instances, "be an excellent device for conserving time, expenses, and scarce judicial resources by targeting early resolution of threshold issues").

469. *See Cameron v. Children's Hosp. Med. Ctr.,* 131 F.3d 1167, 1170 (6th Cir. 1997).

470. *See Cameron v. Children's Hosp. Med. Ctr.,* 131 F.3d 1167, 1170–71 (6th Cir. 1997). *See also Cuoco v. United States Bureau of Prisons,* 2000 WL 347155, at *8 (S.D.N.Y.2000) (noting that Rule 12(d) request for the pretrial determination of a defense is not limited to only Rule 12(b) defenses, but is available for other types of defenses as well).

plaintiff first demonstrates a likelihood that personal jurisdiction exists over the defendant.[471]

Ruling Deferred

This Rule confirms that a district court's *pretrial* review and
disposition of Rule 12(b) defenses and Rule 12(c) motions is discretionary, not mandatory. In appropriate cases, involving peculiarly
complicated factual and legal issues, or where further factual development is necessary, the court may defer resolving Rule 12(b)
defenses until time of trial.[472]

Oral Argument and Hearing

The moving party is generally not *entitled* to oral argument or a
hearing on the motion; whether to permit such argument or hearing
is usually committed to the trial court's discretion.[473] Moreover, the
term "hearing" can mean, in an appropriate case, simply oral
argument on the motion.[474]

ADDITIONAL RESEARCH REFERENCES

C.J.S. Federal Civil Procedure §§ 302, 376–409 et seq., 413–440 et seq., 796 et
seq., 842 et seq.

West's Key No. Digests, Federal Civil Procedure ☞734–735, 941–1020, 1031–
1033, 1041–1068, 1101–1150, 1721–1842.

471. *See Foster–Miller, Inc. v. Babcock
& Wilcox Canada*, 46 F.3d 138 (1st Cir.
1995); *Boit v. Gar–Tec Prods., Inc.*, 967
F.2d 671 (1st Cir.1992).

472. *See Nissim Corp. v. ClearPlay,
Inc.*, 351 F.Supp.2d 1343, 1346 (S.D.Fla.
2004); *Evello Invs., N.V. v. Printed Media
Servs., Inc.*, 158 F.R.D. 172, 173 (D.Kan.
1994).

473. *See Greene v. WCI Holdings Corp.*,
136 F.3d 313, 316 (2d Cir.1998) ("Every

circuit to consider the issue has determined
that the 'hearing' requirements of Rule 12
... do not mean that an oral hearing is
necessary, but only require that a party be
given the opportunity to present its views
to the court"). *See also Pueschel v. United
States*, 369 F.3d 345, 354 (4th Cir.2004).

474. *See Obert v. Republic Western Ins.
Co.*, 398 F.3d 138, 143 (1st Cir.2005).

RULE 13

COUNTERCLAIM AND CROSSCLAIM

(a) Compulsory Counterclaim.

(1) *In General.* A pleading must state as a counterclaim any claim that—at the time of its service—the pleader has against an opposing party if the claim:

    (A) arises out of the transaction or occurrence that is the subject matter of the opposing party's claim; and

    (B) does not require adding another party over whom the court cannot acquire jurisdiction.

(2) *Exceptions.* The pleader need not state the claim if:

    (A) when the action was commenced, the claim was the subject of another pending action; or

    (B) the opposing party sued on its claim by attachment or other process that did not establish personal jurisdiction over the pleader on that claim, and the pleader does not assert any counterclaim under this rule.

(b) Permissive Counterclaim. A pleading may state as a counterclaim against an opposing party any claim that is not compulsory.

(c) Relief Sought in a Counterclaim. A counterclaim need not diminish or defeat the recovery sought by the opposing party. It may request relief that exceeds in amount or differs in kind from the relief sought by the opposing party.

(d) Counterclaim Against the United States. These rules do not expand the right to assert a counterclaim— or to claim a credit—against the United States or a United States officer or agency.

(e) Counterclaim Maturing or Acquired After Pleading. The court may permit a party to file a supplemental pleading asserting a counterclaim that matured or was acquired by the party after serving an earlier pleading.

(f) Omitted Counterclaim. The court may permit a party to amend a pleading to add a counterclaim if it was omitted through oversight, inadvertence, or excusable neglect or if justice so requires.

(g) Crossclaim Against a Coparty. A pleading may state as a crossclaim any claim by one party against a coparty if the claim arises out of the transaction or occurrence that is the subject matter of the original action or of a counterclaim, or if the claim relates to any property that is the subject matter of the original action. The crossclaim may include a claim that the coparty is or may be liable to the crossclaimant for all or part of a claim asserted in the action against the crossclaimant.

(h) Joining Additional Parties. Rules 19 and 20 govern the addition of a person as a party to a counterclaim or crossclaim.

(i) Separate Trials; Separate Judgments. If the court orders separate trials under Rule 42(b), it may enter judgment on a counterclaim or crossclaim under Rule 54(b) when it has jurisdiction to do so, even if the opposing party's claims have been dismissed or otherwise resolved.

[Amended effective March 19, 1948; July 1, 1963; July 1, 1966; August 1, 1987; April 30, 2007, effective December 1, 2007.]

2007 AMENDMENTS ROADMAP

STYLE PROJECT CHANGES: Minor changes were made in the title of the Rule and in the title of some subsections. Minor language changes were also made in the text of the Rule to aid readability. Subsection (a), previously organized as a single paragraph, has been partitioned into two subparts, which themselves contain subparagraphs.

NON-STYLE CHANGES: Previously subsection (b) identified the most common factual distinction between a compulsory counterclaim (governed by subsection (a)) and a permissive counterclaim (governed by subsection (b)) by expressly describing permissive counterclaims as inclusive of counterclaims that did not arise out of the same transaction or occurrence as the opposing party's claim. This old language apparently gave rise to an erroneous impression that *only* those counterclaims arising out of dissimilar transactions or occurrences may be treated as permissive. Because subsection (a), in addition to identifying compulsory counterclaims, also identifies some exceptional circumstances in which counterclaims arising out of the same transaction or occurrence may nonetheless be permissive in nature, the provision in old subsection (b) referring to claims not arising out of the same transaction or occurrence was deleted. The new language of subsection (b) is intended to eliminate any confusion by providing that any counterclaim that is not compulsory is, *ipso facto*, permissive.

NOTE: The Federal Rules "Style Project" is explained in Part III-A.

AUTHORS' COMMENTARY ON RULE 13

———————— PURPOSE AND SCOPE ————————

Rule 13 authorizes persons who are already parties to an action to assert counterclaims against an opposing party. The Rule distinguishes between counterclaims that must be raised in pending litigation, and counterclaims that may either be raised in the pending litigation or retained for subsequent litigation.[1] Rule 13 also controls the circumstances in which cross-claims against co-parties—*i.e.*, against persons who are aligned on the same side of the case as the cross-claimant—may be maintained in a pending action.

RULE 13(a). COMPULSORY COUNTERCLAIM

CORE CONCEPT

Subject to some exceptions discussed below, compulsory counterclaims are those counterclaims arising from the same transaction or occurrence that gave rise to the plaintiff's complaint. Such counterclaims are so closely related to claims already raised by a plaintiff that they can be adjudicated in the same action without creating confusion for a trier of fact or undue prejudice to the plaintiff. Consequently, Rule 13(a) generally requires that compulsory counterclaims must be asserted in the pending litigation or they are waived.

APPLICATIONS

Procedure

Compulsory counterclaims are asserted by pleading them in the answer to a complaint or a reply to a previously asserted counterclaim.[2]

Same Transaction or Occurrence

Courts generally agree that this standard for identifying compulsory counterclaims should be construed liberally, so as to further the goal of judicial economy.[3] However, courts differ in the way they

---

1. *Cf., Tank Insulation International, Inc. v. Insultherm, Inc.*, 104 F.3d 83, 88 (5th Cir.1997) ("[U]nder rule 13 a counterclaim is either compulsory or permissive—it cannot be both.").

2. *See, e.g., Shelter Mutual Insurance Co. v. Public Water Supply District No. 7 of Jefferson County, Missouri*, 747 F.2d 1195 (8th Cir.1984).

3. *See, e.g., Transamerica Occidental Life Insurance Co. v. Aviation Office of America, Inc.*, 292 F.3d 384, 390 (3d Cir. 2002) ("[T]he objective of Rule 13(a) is to promote judicial economy, so the term 'transaction or occurrence' is construed generously to further this purpose.").

actually apply the standard to specific facts. One application holds that the standard should be based on four inquiries: (1) whether the issues of law and fact in the various claims are essentially the same; (2) whether, in the absence of the compulsory counterclaim rule, res judicata would bar a subsequent suit on the counterclaim; (3) whether the same evidence could be used to support or refute the claim and counterclaim; and (4) whether a logical relationship exists between claim and counterclaim.[4] However, this approach does not require that all the questions be answered affirmatively before a counterclaim may be deemed compulsory.[5] Other courts are even more liberal in the way they apply the "same transaction or occurrence" standard, sometimes finding a compulsory counterclaim when there is any significant logical relationship between the plaintiff's claim and the counterclaim.[6] Thus, if a plaintiff sued on a contract, and the defendant had a counterclaim resting on an assertion that the contract was a violation of federal antitrust law, the "logical relationship" test would probably treat the counterclaim as compulsory.[7]

Other, less broad, applications of the standard may require substantial overlap in all elements of the claims before a counterclaim is deemed compulsory.[8]

4. *See, e.g., Q. International Courier, Inc. v. Smoak*, 441 F.3d 214, 219 (4th Cir. 2006) (citing line of cases using this approach).

5. *See, e.g., Painter v. Harvey*, 863 F.2d 329, 331 (4th Cir.1988) (inquiries are not a "litmus test"; better analogy is to a "guideline").

6. *See, e.g., Transamerica Occidental Life Insurance Co. v. Aviation Office of America, Inc.*, 292 F.3d 384, 389 (3d Cir. 2002) (using only "logical relationship" inquiry, noting that concept "has been viewed liberally to promote judicial economy."). *See also Ross ex rel. Ross v. Board of Educ. of Township High School Dist. 211*, 486 F.3d 279, 284 (7th Cir.2007) (there is no formalistic test for determining whether suits arise out of the same transaction or occurrence; courts should consider the totality of the claims). *But see, e.g., Consolidation Coal Co. v. United Mine Workers of America, District 12, Local Union 1545*, 213 F.3d 404, 408 (7th Cir.2000) (labor-management disputes all arose out of same disagreement over staffing; all disputes submitted to different arbitrators; union sought to bar management from seeking enforcement of management victories in later arbitrations, arguing that union suit to enforce union victory in earlier arbitration required management to assert its arbitration victories as compulsory counterclaims; held, "while the seven arbitrations all arose out of the

same transaction or occurrence, namely the staffing dispute, the two district court proceedings did not. They arose out of the arbitrations, which we deem to have been separate transactions or occurrences."); *Whigham v. Beneficial Finance Co. of Fayetteville*, 599 F.2d 1322, 1324 (4th Cir.1979) (held, insufficient "logical relationship" between complaint under Truth in Lending Act and lender's counterclaim on the loan).

7. *See, e.g., Great Lakes Rubber Corp. v. Herbert Cooper Co.*, 286 F.2d 631, 634 (3d Cir.1961) (using logical relationship standard to determine whether counterclaim is compulsory). *See also Berrey v. Asarco Inc.*, 439 F.3d 636, 645–46 (10th Cir.2006) (where Indian tribe sued mining company and others for environmental contamination of tribal lands, counterclaims for common law contribution and indemnity sounded in recoupment and were compulsory counterclaims under Rule 13 (a); using same four-part inquiry discussed in *Q. International Courier, supra*).

8. *See, e.g., In re Pegasus Gold Corp.*, 394 F.3d 1189, 1196 (9th Cir.2005) (claims shared similar facts, but bankruptcy claim was not barred as a compulsory counterclaim that should have been raised in original proceeding because bankruptcy claim arose subsequent to original proceeding).

Exceptions to "Same Transaction" Standard

As stated immediately above, a counterclaim is not compulsory unless it arises from the same transaction or occurrence as one of the claims filed by an opposing party. However, the converse—that counterclaims arising from the same transaction or occurrence are compulsory—is not always true. Listed below are the circumstances in which a counterclaim need not be asserted even though it shares the same transaction or occurrence as a claim filed by an opposing party.[9]

(1) *Exception: Immature Claims:* A counterclaim that does not mature until after the party has served a pleading is not a compulsory counterclaim, even if it arises from the same transaction or occurrence as a claim filed by an opposing party.[10] Rule 13(e) provides that such a claim may be asserted as a permissive counterclaim by filing a supplemental pleading, as provided by Rule 15(d), or it may be retained for future litigation, at the discretion of the party who holds the claim.

(2) *Exception: Rule 13(a) Inapplicable to Claims Until Service of Pleading:* Even if a counterclaim arises from the same transaction or occurrence as a plaintiff's claim, Rule 13(a) provides that it does not become a compulsory counterclaim until the time when the party holding the counterclaim is required to file a responsive pleading. Thus, if a defendant initially filed a motion to dismiss under Rule 12(b), that rule provides that no pleading need be filed until the court decides the Rule 12(b) motion. If the court granted the motion to dismiss, the defendant never had an obligation to file a responsive pleading. In that circumstance, any claim the defendant had against the plaintiff would not be deemed a compulsory counterclaim, and would be preserved for assertion in subsequent litigation. Similarly, if a plaintiff and defendant settle the plaintiff's claim before expiration of the time in which the defendant must answer, any counterclaim the defendant might have is not compulsory.[11]

---

9. *See, e.g., Kane v. Magna Mixer Co.,* 71 F.3d 555, 561–62 (6th Cir.1995) ("If the claim does arise out of the same transaction or occurrence, it is not a permissive counterclaim, although ... it may not be required to be asserted.").

10. *See, e.g., In re Kaiser Group Intern. Inc.,* 399 F.3d 558, 568 (3d Cir.2005) ("maturity" requirement of Rule 13(a) is a separate and additional requirement for compulsory counterclaims; it exists independently from "same transaction" requirement of Rule 13); *Harbor Insurance Co. v. Continental Bank Corp.,* 922 F.2d 357, 360 (7th Cir.1990)(counterclaim that did not exist when complaint was filed is not compulsory counterclaim).

11. *See, e.g., Bluegrass Hosiery, Inc. v. Speizman Industries, Inc.,* 214 F.3d 770 (6th Cir.2000) (permitting claims not raised as counterclaims in prior lawsuit in state court; claims not barred as compulsory counterclaims because prior suit was settled before party had a duty to file an answer; "Rule 13(a) ... only requires a compulsory counterclaim if the party who desires to assert a claim has served a pleading. ...In other words, Rule 13(a) does not apply unless there has been some form of pleading."); *Carteret Savings & Loan Association v. Jackson,* 812 F.2d 36, 38 (1st Cir. 1987)(Rule 13(a) does not apply "if a pleading had never been required, as for example, if 'the time of serving, had never been reached.' ").

(3) *Exception: Lack of Jurisdiction Over Third Parties:* If a counterclaim requires joinder of some additional person not subject to the court's jurisdiction, the counterclaim will not be deemed compulsory, irrespective of the amount of overlap it shares with the plaintiff's claim.[12]

(4) *Exception: Pending Lawsuits:* A counterclaim is not compulsory within the meaning of Rule 13(a) if it has already been sued upon in other litigation. Thus, if one person filed suit in a state court, and the opponent of that claim then sued in federal court, the original state claim would not be a compulsory counterclaim in federal court because it is already the subject of pending litigation.[13]

(5) *Exception: Quasi in Rem/In Rem Jurisdiction:* Where the plaintiff's complaint rests on the court's quasi in rem or in rem jurisdiction, a counterclaim will not be compulsory,[14] so long as the defendant refrains from raising any counterclaims under Rule 13. If, however, the defendant raises a Rule 13 counterclaim, then all other counterclaims that fall within the same transaction or occurrence as the plaintiff's claim—and not exempted by other exceptions, discussed above—are compulsory counterclaims and must be asserted.

(6) *Exception: Injunction/Declaratory Judgment Actions:* In some circumstances, defendants who have been sued only on equity claims may not be required to assert claims for money damages as counterclaims.[15]

"Opposing Party"

When a party seeks to use Rule 13(a) to bar a claim in a later lawsuit because the claim should have been raised as a compulsory counterclaim against the plaintiff in the original litigation, a question may arise as to the applicability of the Rule when the party seeking to bar the claim shares a close identity with the original plaintiff but is not literally identical to that plaintiff. Precedent on the issue is not plentiful, but in general it appears that the term

---

12. *See, e.g., Landmark Bank v. Machera,* 736 F.Supp. 375, 379 (D.Mass. 1990)("Rule 13(a) specifically precludes compulsory counterclaims that require for adjudication the presence of third parties over whom 'the court cannot acquire jurisdiction.' ").

13. *See, e.g., In re Piper Aircraft Corp.,* 244 F.3d 1289, 1296 n. 3 (11th Cir.2001) (for a counterclaim to fit within this exception to the compulsory counterclaim requirement "Rule 13(a) literally requires that the [counterclaim] be pending before the other action was commenced"). *See also, United States v. Dico, Inc.,* 136 F.3d 572, 577 (8th Cir.1998) (pending administrative claim is not a compulsory counterclaim; "[Rule 13] does not require that the action be pending before another court, to the exclusion of an administrative tribunal of competent jurisdiction.").

14. *Baker v. Gold Seal Liquors,* 417 U.S. 467, 469, 94 S.Ct. 2504, 2506 n. 1, 41 L.Ed.2d 243 (1974)("The claim is not compulsory ... if the opposing party brought his suit by attachment or other process not resulting in personal jurisdiction but only in rem or quasi in rem jurisdiction.").

15. *See, e.g., United States v. Snider,* 779 F.2d 1151, 1156 (6th Cir.1985)(plaintiff sought only declaratory and injunctive relief; then sought preliminary injunction; court, pursuant to Rule 65, held trial on merits simultaneously with preliminary injunction hearing; held, defendant was not obligated to file counterclaim for money damages).

"opposing party" is read rather broadly. Thus, a party who is sufficiently closely related to a plaintiff who should have been sued on a compulsory counterclaim in previous litigation is entitled to raise Rule 13(a) as a defense when that counterclaim is finally raised in a subsequent lawsuit.[16]

Of course, a party who sues in a representative capacity is not subject to counterclaims against him in his individual capacity.[17]

Subject Matter Jurisdiction

Compulsory counterclaims must satisfy subject matter jurisdiction. They do so by satisfying the requirements of either federal question jurisdiction or diversity jurisdiction, or by qualifying for supplemental jurisdiction. Because compulsory counterclaims must arise from the same transaction or occurrence as the plaintiff's claim, counterclaims that do not qualify for federal question jurisdiction or diversity jurisdiction nevertheless usually meet the requirements for supplemental jurisdiction.[18]

It should be noted that the party asserting a counterclaim must include an allegation of facts demonstrating that the requirement of subject matter jurisdiction is met.[19] Subject matter jurisdiction is discussed at Part II, §§ 2.10–2.13.

16. *See, e.g., Transamerica Occidental Life Insurance Co. v. Aviation Office of America, Inc.,* 292 F.3d 384, (3d Cir.2002) (successor in interest to party in prior litigation is "opposing party" under Rule 13(a) and therefore can raise bar to claim that should have been raised as counterclaim against predecessors in previously filed litigation); *Avemco Insurance Co. v. Cessna Aircraft Co.,* 11 F.3d 998, 1001 (10th Cir. 1993) (airplane crash; first suit brought by one passenger against plane owner and pilot, but not insurer-subrogee; first suit was settled; second injured passenger then sued plane owner and pilot, as well as airplane manufacturer; manufacturer filed third-party complaint against insured for negligence in operation of plane; insured plane owner and pilot filed no counterclaim for contribution or indemnification for money paid in settlement of first claim; later, in third lawsuit, insurer of owner and pilot sought such indemnification from manufacturer, but was barred by Rule 13(a); court noted that insurer controlled defense of owner and pilot in both previous lawsuits and should have raised issues of contribution and indemnification); *Banco Nacional de Cuba v. First National Bank of New York,* 478 F.2d 191, 193 n. 1 (2d Cir.1973) (counterclaim against Republic of Cuba is proper, notwithstanding that named plaintiff is Cuban national bank; held, bank and government are one and the same and thus government is proper "opposing party" within scope of Rule 13(a)).

17. *See Pioche Mines Consol., Inc. v. Fidelity-Philadelphia Trust Co.,* 206 F.2d 336, 337 (9th Cir.1953). *Cited in In re Adbox, Inc.,* 488 F.3d 836, 840 (9th Cir.2007). ("The question presented here, however, is whether the trustee is an 'opposing party' when he has brought a preference action that belongs to the bankruptcy estate and not to the debtor, but the counterclaim alleges causes of action that could have been brought against the debtor prior to its bankruptcy filing. We hold that he is not.")

18. *Baker v. Gold Seal Liquors,* 417 U.S. 467, 94 S.Ct. 2504, 41 L.Ed.2d 243 (1974). *See, e.g., St. Jude Medical, Inc. v. Lifecare International, Inc.,* 250 F.3d 587 (8th Cir.2001) ("Because [defendant's] claims were compulsory counterclaims, there was supplemental jurisdiction to hear them in federal court."). *See also Columbia Gas Transmission Corp. v. Drain,* 191 F.3d 552, 559 (4th Cir.1999) (where party raised counterclaims only to comply with Rule 13(a), and otherwise vigorously and successfully challenged district court's subject matter jurisdiction over original complaint, justice requires adherence to counterclaimant's request to dismiss counterclaim without prejudice).

19. *McNutt v. General Motors Acceptance Corp.,* 298 U.S. 178, 189, 56 S.Ct. 780,

Personal Jurisdiction Over Plaintiffs

Assertion of a compulsory counterclaim usually involves very few problems with personal jurisdiction over the plaintiff. By instituting an action, a plaintiff is held to have consented to the court's jurisdiction to adjudicate related claims,[20] and by definition, a compulsory counterclaim is closely related to the plaintiff's claim. Consent to personal jurisdiction is discussed at § 2.4.

Venue

Most courts hold that compulsory counterclaims need not satisfy venue requirements.[21]

Failure to Assert a Compulsory Counterclaim

Defendants who do not assert compulsory counterclaims are usually barred from raising the counterclaims in subsequent litigation.[22] The harshness of this result is mitigated by Rule 13(f), authorizing the court to permit amended pleadings that include counterclaims, when the court believes such permission serves the

---

785, 80 L.Ed. 1135 (1936) ("[P]rerequisites to the exercise of jurisdiction ... are conditions which must be met by the party who seeks the exercise of jurisdiction in his favor. He must allege in his pleading the facts essential to show jurisdiction."). *Cf., e.g., Martin v. Franklin Capital Corp.,* 251 F.3d 1284 (10th Cir.2001) (removal case; "As the parties invoking the federal court's jurisdiction in this case, defendants bear the burden of establishing that the requirements for the exercise of diversity jurisdiction are present.").

20. *Adam v. Saenger,* 303 U.S. 59, 58 S.Ct. 454, 82 L.Ed. 649 (1938). *See e.g., Schnabel v. Lui,* 302 F.3d 1023, 1037 (9th Cir.2002) ("[P]laintiffs who avail themselves of the district court consent to personal jurisdiction" over counterclaims.) *See also In re Charter Oak Associates,* 361 F.3d 760, 768 (2d Cir.2004) (most circuits agree that state's decision to file bankruptcy claim is waiver of immunity as to compulsory counterclaims).

21. *See, e.g., Schoot v. United States,* 664 F.Supp. 293, 295 (N.D.Ill.1987)("[I]n the case of compulsory counterclaims, the venue statutes have been construed to apply only to the original claim, and not to the compulsory counterclaims.").

22. *Baker v. Gold Seal Liquors, Inc.,* 417 U.S. 467, 469 n. 1, 94 S.Ct. 2504, 2506, 41 L.Ed.2d 243 (1974) ("A counterclaim which is compulsory but is not brought is thereafter barred."). *See, e.g., Polymer Industrial Products Co. v. Bridgestone/Fire-*

stone, Inc., 347 F.3d 935, 938 (Fed. Cir. 2003) ("Rule 13(a) makes [a patent] infringement counterclaim to a declaratory judgment action for noninfringement compulsory"); *New York Life Insurance Co. v. Deshotel,* 142 F.3d 873, 882 (5th Cir.1998) ("It is well settled that a failure to plead a compulsory counterclaim bars a party from bringing a later independent action on that claim."). *See also Q. International Courier Inc. v. Smoak,* 441 F.3d 214, 220 (4th Cir. 2006) (corporation's action against shareholders following district court judgment in favor of corporation reversed and remanded for district court to decide whether claims constituted compulsory counter-claims under Rule 13(a) in the first action). *But see Handy v. Shaw, Bransford, Veilleux & Roth,* 325 F.3d 346, 350–53 (D.C.Cir.2003) (practice of barring counterclaim in subsequent litigation "is usually applied in subsequent litigation on res judicata or collateral estoppel principles;" where district court has good subject matter jurisdiction, determination to proceed with claim not raised as counterclaim in previously filed lawsuit is matter of discretion which should take into account value of proceeding with related claims in one case and importance of exercising subject matter jurisdiction when it exists; held, where initial suit in state court had already been dismissed, no substantial proceedings had occurred in state court, and statute of limitations had in the meantime become a bar if instant litigation was dismissed, it is possible that district court should hear claim notwithstanding apparent mandate of Rule 13(a)).

interest of justice. Rule 13(a) is also limited by Rule 15(a), which permits a party to amend a pleading once as of right within certain designated time frames. Thus, a party who failed to include a compulsory counterclaim within an initial answer might be able to use Rule 15(a) to amend the answer of right or, if the time in which to amend of right has already passed, to seek leave of opposing counsel or leave of court to amend. However, once judgment is entered on a plaintiff's claim, compulsory counterclaims that were not raised are effectively barred, unless they can fit within the stricter standards of Rule 60(b), governing relief from judgments.

Exception: Class Actions

The normal requirement that a compulsory counterclaim must be timely raised is generally inapplicable to claims held by class action defendants.[23]

Mislabelled Counterclaims

Parties sometimes mistakenly identify counterclaims as cross-claims, and *vice versa*. They may also mislabel a counterclaim as a defense. Courts usually attach no significance to such errors, unless somehow they unfairly prejudice an opposing party.[24]

Statutes of Limitations

Courts are substantially divided as to the effect that a complaint has on statutes of limitations applicable to compulsory counterclaims. Most agree that if the counterclaim was still timely at the time the complaint was filed, the limitation period on the counterclaim is tolled by the filing of the complaint.[25]

RULE 13(b). PERMISSIVE COUNTERCLAIM

CORE CONCEPT

Permissive counterclaims include those counterclaims that do not arise out of the same transaction or occurrence as the opposing party's claim. Although not stated expressly in Rule 13(b), permissive counterclaims also include counterclaims arising out of the same transaction or occurrence as the opposing party's claims, but which fall within one or more of the exceptions to Rule 13(a) compulsory counterclaims, discussed above. Counterclaims denoted as permissive may be filed in the pending action, but they may also be asserted in a separate action.

---

23. *See, e.g., Allapattah Services, Inc. v. Exxon Corp.,* 333 F.3d 1248 n. 14 (11th Cir.2003) (normal practice is to wait until liability is established and individual class members file damage claims; at that point setoffs and counterclaims can properly be adjudicated on an individual basis).

24. *Reiter v. Cooper,* 507 U.S. 258, 262, 113 S.Ct. 1213, 1217, 122 L.Ed.2d 604 (1993)(holding that counterclaim mislabelled as defense should simply be treated as counterclaim).

25. *See, e.g., Kirkpatrick v. Lenoir County Board of Education,* 216 F.3d 380, 388 (4th Cir.2000) ("Because [plaintiffs] timely filed [their] actions, [defendant's] counterclaim relates back to the date of the original filing. Therefore, the counterclaim was timely regardless of whether the statute of limitations governing the matter was thirty days or three years.").

However, parties often encounter substantially greater difficulties with jurisdiction over permissive counterclaims than they normally encounter with compulsory counterclaims.

APPLICATIONS

Procedure

Permissive counterclaims are filed in answers to complaints or replies to counterclaims.[26]

Different Transaction or Occurrence

The standard for measuring whether a permissive counterclaim arises from a transaction or occurrence dissimilar from that underlying the complaint is the mirror image of the same transaction or occurrence test of compulsory counterclaims. For dissimilarity, courts usually look for the absence of a logical relationship between the complaint and counterclaim.[27] Thus, if a plaintiff sued on a contract, and the defendant had a counterclaim resting on a tort that had allegedly occurred at a different place and time, and had no relationship to the contract claim beyond the happenstance that the parties to both claims were identical, the counterclaim would probably be deemed permissive.

Subject Matter Jurisdiction

Permissive counterclaims must satisfy requirements for subject matter jurisdiction. Subject matter jurisdiction can be satisfied through any of three routes: federal question jurisdiction; diversity jurisdiction; or supplemental jurisdiction. However, as is discussed immediately below, it is uncertain whether supplemental jurisdiction is available in cases involving permissive counterclaims. Jurisdiction is discussed more elsewhere in this text.

(1) *Restrictions on Use of Supplemental Jurisdiction:* Generally, most permissive counterclaims do not arise from the same transaction or occurrence as the claim of the opposing party. Thus there is some question as to whether permissive counterclaims that do not meet the requirements for original subject matter jurisdiction (usually diversity or a federal question) and also do not arise from the same transaction or occurrence as the opponent's initial claims may either qualify for supplemental jurisdiction or may nevertheless be heard by a federal district court notwithstanding these deficiencies. The established view is that such permissive counterclaims cannot use supplemental jurisdiction. Therefore a lack of original subject matter jurisdiction would mandate dismissal of the claims.[28]

---

26. *See, e.g., Shelter Mutual Insurance Co. v. Public Water Supply District No. 7 of Jefferson County, Missouri,* 747 F.2d 1195 (8th Cir.1984).

27. *See, e.g., Warshawsky & Co. v. Arcata National Corp.,* 552 F.2d 1257, 1261 (7th Cir.1977)("[A] counterclaim that has its roots in a separate transaction or occurrence is permissive.").

28. *See, e.g., Oak Park Trust and Savings Bank v. Therkildsen,* 209 F.3d 648, 651 (7th Cir.2000) (counterclaim arose from events unrelated to plaintiff's claim; "a permissive counterclaim ... is outside the supplemental jurisdiction ... and requires an independent basis of federal jurisdiction"); *Unique Concepts v. Manuel,* 930 F.2d 573, 574 (7th Cir.1991) (compulsory counter-

A more recent view, however, is that the established view is either incorrect[29] or, if it was ever correct, enactment of 28 U.S.C.A. § 1367 (governing supplemental jurisdiction) renders it obsolete.[30] Resolution of this question will probably require a decision by the Supreme Court. In the meantime attorneys must consult local precedent. Section 1367 is discussed in greater detail elsewhere in this text.

(2) *Supplemental Jurisdiction: Exceptional Circumstances:* The foregoing discussion of uncertainty about the jurisdictional foundation of permissive counterclaims not arising from the same transaction or occurrence as the opponent's initial claims should not obscure one fact. Permissive counterclaims that arise from the same transaction or occurrence but which are not for some reason compulsory may nevertheless satisfy subject matter jurisdiction through the requirements of federal question jurisdiction, diversity jurisdiction, or supplemental jurisdiction.[31]

It should be noted that the party asserting a permissive counterclaim must include an allegation of facts demonstrating that the requirement of subject matter jurisdiction is met.[32]

Personal Jurisdiction: Waiver of Defense

The objection to personal jurisdiction is waived where a defendant seeks affirmative relief in the form of a permissive counterclaim. This may be true even where those defenses were set forth in a timely motion to dismiss or in a responsive pleading.[33]

claims are eligible for supplemental jurisdiction, but permissive counterclaims "require their own jurisdictional basis").

29. *See, e.g., Jones v. Ford Motor Credit Co.,* 358 F.3d 205, 212–13 (2d Cir.2004) ("[I]t is no longer sufficient for courts to assert, without any reason other than dicta or even holdings from the era of judge-created ancillary jurisdiction, that permissive counterclaims require independent jurisdiction.").

30. *See, e.g., Jones v. Ford Motor Credit Co.,* 358 F.3d 205, 213 (2d Cir.2004) ("We share the view that section 1367 has displaced, rather than codified, whatever validity inhered in the earlier view that a permissive counterclaim requires independent jurisdiction (in the sense of federal question or diversity jurisdiction)."); *Channell v. Citicorp National Services, Inc.,* 89 F.3d 379, 385 (7th Cir.1996) (holding that § 1367 broadened the power of courts to hear non-diverse permissive counterclaims that are based on state law).

31. *See, e.g., Leipzig v. AIG Life Insurance Co.,* 362 F.3d 406, 410 (7th Cir.2004) ("Even a permissive counterclaim, if part of

the same case or controversy, ... may be brought under the supplemental jurisdiction statute, 28 U.S.C. § 1367(a), without an independent basis of jurisdiction."); *Crosby Yacht Yard, Inc. v. Yacht "Chardonnay",* 164 F.R.D. 135 (D.Mass. 1996)(permissive counterclaim arising from same case or controversy—but not compulsory for unrelated reasons—may nevertheless satisfy requirements for supplemental jurisdiction).

32. *McNutt v. General Motors Acceptance Corp.,* 298 U.S. 178, 189, 56 S.Ct. 780, 785, 80 L.Ed. 1135 (1936) ("[P]rerequisites to the exercise of jurisdiction ... are conditions which must be met by the party who seeks the exercise of jurisdiction in his favor. He must allege in his pleading the facts essential to show jurisdiction."). *Cf., e.g., Martin v. Franklin Capital Corp.,* 251 F.3d 1284 (10th Cir.2001) (removal case; "As the parties invoking the federal court's jurisdiction in this case, defendants bear the burden of establishing that the requirements for the exercise of diversity jurisdiction are present.").

33. *See* **Author's Commentary** to Rule 12 (h), *supra,* "Implied Waiver."

Venue

It is unclear whether permissive counterclaims must satisfy venue requirements.[34]

Failure to Assert a Permissive Counterclaim

No sanction attaches if a party holding a permissive counterclaim chooses not to assert it in pending litigation. The claim is not treated as barred, and may be asserted at a later date.[35]

Mislabelled Counterclaims

Parties sometimes mistakenly identify counterclaims as cross-claims, and *vice versa*. They may also mislabel a counterclaim as a defense. Courts usually attach no significance to such errors, unless somehow they unfairly prejudice an opposing party.[36]

Statutes of Limitations

An opposing party's decision to file a claim does not toll the time in which a permissive counterclaim not arising from the same transaction or occurrence must be filed.[37]

Counterclaims Maturing After Pleading

Rule 13(b) should be read in conjunction with Rule 13(e), which provides that counterclaims maturing or acquired after pleading are permissive counterclaims that may be filed in the pending action, subject to the court's discretion.

Separate Trials

Permissive counterclaims not arising from the same transaction or occurrence as the opposing party's claim may contain substantial potential for confusing the trier of fact or delaying adjudication of the original claims. Thus, Rule 13(i) authorizes the court to order separate proceedings.

RULE 13(c).   RELIEF SOUGHT IN A COUNTERCLAIM

CORE CONCEPT

Rule 13(c) provides that: (1) counterclaims may be for any amount, irrespective of whether the amount sought in the counterclaim exceeds the amount sought in the other party's claim; and (2) counterclaims may seek kinds of relief not sought in the opposing party's claim. For example, if the opposing party's claim sought money damages only, the

34. *See, e.g., Hansen v. Shearson/American Express, Inc.,* 116 F.R.D. 246, 251 (E.D.Pa.1987)(suggesting that "in some circumstances" permissive counterclaims must satisfy venue requirements; but rejecting challenge to venue in instant case).

35. *See, e.g., U.S. Philips Corp. v. Sears Roebuck & Co.,* 55 F.3d 592, 599 (Fed.Cir. 1995) (permissive counterclaim not asserted is not thereby barred in subsequent litigation).

36. *Reiter v. Cooper,* 507 U.S. 258, 262, 113 S.Ct. 1213, 1217, 122 L.Ed.2d 604 (1993)(holding that counterclaim mislabelled as defense should simply be treated as counterclaim).

37. *See, e.g., Employers Insurance of Wausau v. United States,* 764 F.2d 1572, 1576 (Fed.Cir.1985)("[A] permissive counterclaim does not generate a ... tolling period.").

counterclaim could seek either money damages, equitable relief, or both money damages and equitable relief.

RULE 13(d). COUNTERCLAIM AGAINST THE UNITED STATES

CORE CONCEPT

As a general rule, the United States and its officers and agencies are immune from suits in federal courts, unless the United States waives that sovereign immunity. Rule 13(d) expressly provides that the counterclaim provisions of Rule 13(a) and (b) do not alter the current law of sovereign immunity.[38]

APPLICATIONS

Waiver of Immunity

A decision by the United States to sue on a claim generally does not constitute a waiver of sovereign immunity as to counterclaims for amounts above those sums for which the United States is suing. This result applies even if the counterclaims arise from the same transaction or occurrence as the complaint brought by the United States.[39]

Setoffs

Some courts have permitted counterclaims against the United States where: the claim and counterclaim arise from the same transaction or occurrence; and the money sought is a setoff against the government's claim that will only reduce the government's recovery.[40]

RULE 13(e). COUNTERCLAIM MATURING OR ACQUIRED AFTER PLEADING

CORE CONCEPT

Rule 13(e) provides that if counterclaims mature or are acquired after a party has pleaded, the party may choose to assert them in a supplemental pleading, subject to the court's discretion.

---

38. *See, e.g., In the Matter of Armstrong,* 206 F.3d 465, 473 (5th Cir.2000) ("[T]he law is clear that a compulsory counterclaim shall not be used to expand claims against the United States beyond their limits as already established by law. See Fed.R.Civ.P. 13(d)."); *United States ex rel. Fallon v. Accudyne Corp.,* 921 F.Supp. 611 (W.D.Wis. 1995)(limitations on waivers of sovereign immunity are enforceable against counterclaims; citing Rule 13(d)).

39. *See, e.g., United States v. Johnson,* 853 F.2d 619, 621 (8th Cir.1988)(so holding).

40. *See, e.g., United States v. Forma,* 42 F.3d 759, 765 (2d Cir.1994) (counterclaim permissible only to extent of reducing government's claim; barring affirmative relief). *Compare Berrey v. Asarco Inc.,* 439 F.3d 636, 643 (10th Cir.2006) (Indian tribal immunity which is deemed coextensive with the immunity of the United States did not preclude counterclaim sounding in recoupment).

APPLICATIONS

Procedure

A party seeking to assert a Rule 13(e) counterclaim must file a motion and supporting materials explaining the circumstances in which the counterclaim matured or was acquired.[41]

Party's Discretion

Rule 13(e) is permissive in nature, even if it arises from the same transaction or occurrence as the opposing party's claim. Thus, a party holding a counterclaim of the kind controlled by Rule 13(e) may assert it, subject to the court's permission, but is under no obligation to do so.[42]

Judicial Discretion

If a party seeks to raise a Rule 13(e) counterclaim, the court retains discretion to refuse to hear the counterclaim in the pending action.[43] Generally, courts permit Rule 13(e) counterclaims where they will not confuse the trier of fact or where they will not unfairly prejudice other parties, particularly through excessively delaying the litigation.[44] Additionally, Rule 13(e) counterclaims that arise out of the same transaction or occurrence as the opposing party's claim are more likely to be heard in the pending litigation, than are claims that arise out of dissimilar transactions or occurrences.

Regardless of whether a counterclaim is compulsory or permissive, a district court does not abuse its discretion in dismissing a counterclaim in deference to state court litigation which involves the same matters. The common-law doctrine of abstention is not subservient to Rule 13 and the compulsory-permissive distinction does not limit a district court's power to abstain in a given case.[45]

Jurisdiction

Rule 13(e) counterclaims must meet one of the bases of subject matter jurisdiction, such as federal question jurisdiction, diversity jurisdiction, or supplemental jurisdiction. If the Rule 13(e) counterclaim arises out of the same transaction or occurrence as the original claim, then it will likely satisfy supplemental jurisdiction. If not, the counterclaim will need an independent basis of jurisdiction. For a more detailed discussion of subject matter jurisdiction, see §§ 2.10–2.13.

---

41. *See, e.g., All West Pet Supply Co. v. Hill's Pet Products Division, Colgate–Palmolive Co.,* 152 F.R.D. 202, 204 (D.Kan. 1993)(court has discretion to permit or reject supplemental counterclaim).

42. *Stone v. Department of Aviation,* 453 F.3d 1271 (10th Cir.2006) (where plaintiff had not received his right-to-sue letter at time of initial filing, claim has not matured and was not barred as a compulsory counterclaim under Rule 13(e)).

43. *See, e.g., id.*

44. *See, e.g., id.* (noting that in absence of factors indicating unfair prejudice to opponent, policy of liberally granting leave to file supplemental claims also applies to Rule 13(e) counterclaims).

45. *See American Home Assur. Co. v. Pope,* 487 F.3d 590, 604 (8th Cir.2007).

Venue

There is no venue requirement for Rule 13(e) counterclaims.

RULE 13(f). OMITTED COUNTERCLAIM

CORE CONCEPT

Rule 13(f) permits assertion of counterclaims that were omitted through oversight, inadvertence, or excusable neglect, or that should be heard in the interest of justice. Rule 13(f) counterclaims are within the discretion of the court. Although counterclaims permitted under Rule 13(f) may be either permissive or compulsory, the most important effect of Rule 13(f) is to permit filing of compulsory counterclaims that might otherwise be barred.

APPLICATIONS

Procedure

A party seeking to file a counterclaim under Rule 13(f) should file a motion and supporting materials explaining the circumstances causing the delay as well as the reasons why it would now be just to permit the party to use Rule 13(f).[46]

Judicial Discretion

Courts generally permit assertion of counterclaims under Rule 13(f) in circumstances where the late filing does not unfairly prejudice an opposing party.[47]

Compulsory Counterclaims

Because they would be lost forever if not included, compulsory counterclaims are more likely to be permitted under Rule 13(f) than are permissive counterclaims. Permissive counterclaims may typically be sued upon in later suits, and are more likely to confuse the trier of fact if permitted in the pending litigation.[48]

46. *Pioneer Investment Services Co. v. Brunswick Associates Limited Partnership,* 507 U.S. 380, 392, n. 10, 113 S.Ct. 1489, 1497 n. 10, 123 L.Ed.2d 74 (1993)(noting that courts assess factors such as: good faith; extent of delay; and prejudice to opposing party).

47. *See, e.g., Fields v. Atchison, Topeka and Santa Fe Railway Co.,* 167 F.R.D. 462 (D.Kan.1996)(factors to weigh in interest of justice under Rule 13(f) are: type of counterclaim; prejudice to opposing party; and delay of trial for additional discovery); *but see, Lone Star Steakhouse & Saloon, Inc. v. Alpha of Virginia, Inc.,* 43 F.3d 922, 940–41 (4th Cir.1995)(leave to file omitted counterclaim is normally granted freely when such leave is in the interest of justice; however, leave should not be granted when defendant had early information as to counter-

claim, but waited nearly to the close of discovery to try to raise issue; delay and need for additional discovery would be unfair to opponent of proposed counterclaim). *See also, Triad Electric & Controls, Inc. v. Power Systems Engineering, Inc.,* 117 F.3d 180, 193–95 (5th Cir.1997) (Rule 13(f) affords court substantial discretion to add a counterclaim; but where counterclaim asserts fraud, particularity requirements of Rule 9(b) indicate that opponent of counterclaim cannot easily be assumed to have adequate notice of such a counterclaim unless Rule 9(b) is satisfied).

48. *See, e.g., Budd Co. v. Travelers Indemnity Co.,* 820 F.2d 787, 792 n. 3 (6th Cir.1987)(counterclaims that are compulsory are treated more liberally under Rule 13(f)).

RULE 13(g). CROSSCLAIM AGAINST CO–PARTY

CORE CONCEPT

Rule 13(g) permits persons who are already parties to a suit to bring related claims against persons on the same side of the litigation. An essential difference between a cross-claim and a counterclaim is that cross-claims are suits against persons who had not, until the cross-claim was filed, been opponents of the person asserting the cross-claim. Counterclaims, by contrast, are suits against persons who have already sued the person asserting the counterclaim.

APPLICATIONS

Procedure

Cross-claims are typically raised in a responsive pleading.

Cross–Claims Are Always Permissive

Unlike compulsory counterclaims under Rule 13(a), Rule 13(g) does not create a category of compulsory cross-claims. Instead, under Rule 13(g), all cross-claims are permissive, and may therefore be asserted in the pending litigation or in a separate action.[49]

Same Transaction or Occurrence

Cross-claims must arise out of the same transaction or occurrence as the original action, or relate to the same property that is in dispute in the original action.[50] In this important sense cross-claims, though permissive, are fundamentally different from permissive counterclaims, which often arise from a transaction or occurrence that is different than the original action. The standard of same transaction or occurrence varies from court to court. The most liberal interpretation requires a logical relation between the cross-claim and the original action.[51] Other courts look to the degree of overlap between the evidence to be used in the cross-claim and the evidence relevant to the original action.[52]

Cross–Claims Against Co–Parties; Other Parties

Rule 13(g) provides that cross-claims may be brought only if at least one cross-claim defendant is a person already party to an

---

49. *See, e.g., United States v. Confederate Acres Sanitary Sewage and Drainage System, Inc.,* 935 F.2d 796, 799 (6th Cir. 1991)(Rule 13(g) makes cross-claims permissive). *But cf., Paramount Aviation Corp. v. Gruppo Agusta,* 178 F.3d 132 (3d Cir. 1999) (observing that while cross-claims themselves are never compulsory, filing a cross-claim may make co-defendants into opposing parties, which might make a counterclaim on the cross-claim compulsory; not deciding, but suggesting that such counterclaims might never be compulsory if they

were responses to cross-claims that merely sought contribution or indemnity).

50. *See, e.g., Federal Land Bank of St. Louis v. Cupples Brother,* 116 F.R.D. 63, 65 (E.D.Ark.1987).

51. *See, e.g., Seattle Audubon Society v. Lyons,* 871 F.Supp. 1286, 1290 (W.D.Wash. 1994)(treating same transaction or occurrence as synonymous with "logical relationship" test).

52. *See, e.g., Danner v. Anskis,* 256 F.2d 123 (3d Cir.1958).

action.[53]   However, if a single cross-claim defendant is a party to the original action, additional persons may also be sued on the cross-claim, as provided by Rule 13(h)(discussed below).

Comparison With Impleader

A key difference between Rule 13(g) and Rule 14 impleader is that Rule 13(g) requires that at least one cross-claim defendant be a party.   Rule 14, by contrast, provides a means of joining persons who were not previously parties to a pending suit.[54]

Derivative Liability

A cross-claimant may seek either affirmative relief or compensation for any liability the cross-claimant may have as a result of claims already filed against the cross-claimant.

Subject Matter Jurisdiction

Cross-claims must meet the standards of either federal question jurisdiction, diversity jurisdiction, or supplemental jurisdiction. Moreover, the party asserting a counterclaim must include an allegation of facts demonstrating that the requirement of subject matter jurisdiction is met.[55]   However, subject matter jurisdiction is usually not a problem with cross-claims; because Rule 13(g) requires that cross-claims arise out of the same transaction or occurrence as the original action, cross-claims that cannot meet the standards of federal question jurisdiction or diversity jurisdiction usually will nevertheless satisfy the requirements of supplemental jurisdiction.[56]

Personal Jurisdiction

Cross-claims must meet the requirements of personal jurisdiction.   If the court in the original action has already acquired jurisdiction over the parties, it will normally also have jurisdiction over cross-claim defendants.   If, however, jurisdiction is defective in the original action, it is possible that the cross-claim will suffer from

---

53.   *See, e.g., In re Oil Spill by Amoco Cadiz off Coast of France on March 16, 1978,* 699 F.2d 909, 913 (7th Cir.1983) ("[A] Rule 13(g) cross-claim will lie only against an existing defendant."); *Mauney v. Imperial Delivery Services, Inc.,* 865 F.Supp. 142, 153 (S.D.N.Y.1994)(cross-claim cannot be filed against third-party defendant because cross-claims are filed between co-parties).

54.   *See, e.g., National Union Fire Insurance Co. of Pittsburgh v. Continental Illinois Corp.,* 658 F.Supp. 781, 794 (N.D.Ill. 1987).

55.   *McNutt v. General Motors Acceptance Corp.,* 298 U.S. 178, 189, 56 S.Ct. 780, 785, 80 L.Ed. 1135 (1936) ("[P]rerequisites to the exercise of jurisdiction ... are conditions which must be met by the party who seeks the exercise of jurisdiction in his fa-

vor. He must allege in his pleading the facts essential to show jurisdiction."). *Cf., e.g., Martin v. Franklin Capital corp.,* 251 F.3d 1284 (10th Cir.2001) (removal case; "As the parties invoking the federal court's jurisdiction in this case, defendants bear the burden of establishing that the requirements for the exercise of diversity jurisdiction are present.").

56.   *See, e.g., Ryan ex rel. Ryan v. Schneider National Carriers, Inc.,* 263 F.3d 816, 819, 820 (8th Cir.2001) (per curiam) (addition of cross-claim against co-plaintiff that satisfies requirements of Rule 13(g) satisfies supplemental jurisdiction); *Meritor Savings Bank v. Camelback Canyon Investors,* 783 F.Supp. 455, 457 (D.Ariz. 1991)(permitting supplemental jurisdiction over cross-claim).

similar jurisdictional defects. For a further discussion of jurisdiction over persons or things, see §§ 2.2–2.9.

Venue

Cross-claims need not satisfy venue requirements.[57]

Mislabelled Cross–Claims

Parties sometimes mistakenly identify cross-claims as counterclaims, and *vice versa*. Courts usually attach no significance to such errors, unless somehow they unfairly prejudice an opposing party.[58]

Statutes of Limitations: "Relation Back"

The precedent addressing whether statutes of limitations for cross-claims are tolled by the filing of the original action is unsettled, but some generalizations are possible. Cross-claims seeking "affirmative and independent relief" do not relate back to the original complaint. By contrast, cross-claims "in the nature of recoupment, indemnity, or contribution" will typically enjoy the benefit of relation back to the date of the filing of the original action.[59]

RULE 13(h). JOINING ADDITIONAL PARTIES

CORE CONCEPT

Many times a counterclaim or cross-claim will require, for the just adjudication of the case, the joinder of persons who are not yet parties. Rule 13(h) expressly authorizes the use of Rules 19 and 20, governing joinder of persons, to achieve that end.

APPLICATIONS

Procedure

Although the law is not entirely settled, it appears that when counterclaimants or cross-claimants seek to join additional parties under Rule 13(h), they may simply make appropriate service on the parties to be joined and provide notice to those already parties. There appears to be no need to file a motion requesting leave to join the parties.[60]

---

57. *See, e.g., Bredberg v. Long,* 778 F.2d 1285, 1288 (8th Cir.1985)(if venue is proper on original claims, there may be no venue objection to cross-claims).

58. *See, e.g., Schwab v. Erie Lackawanna Railroad Co.,* 438 F.2d 62, 64 (3d Cir. 1971)(mislabelling need not be fatal).

59. *See, e.g., Kansa Reinsurance Co. v. Congressional Mortgage Corp. of Texas,* 20 F.3d 1362, 1367–68 (5th Cir.1994) (making distinction between two categories of cross-claims; noting also that Rule 15(c), governing relation back of pleadings, does not automatically permit an untimely cross-

claim to relate back simply because the cross-claim arose from the same transaction or occurrence).

60. *See, e.g., Northfield Insurance Co. v. Bender Shipbuilding & Repair Co.,* 122 F.R.D. 30 (S.D.Ala.1988)(1966 amendment to Rule 13(h) eliminated requirement to obtain judicial approval for joinder); *but see, Mountain States Sports, Inc. v. Sharman,* 353 F.Supp. 613, 618 (D.Utah 1972), *reversed on other grounds,* 548 F.2d 905 (10th Cir.1977) (general practice is to seek an order joining additional parties).

Prerequisite of One Party

Rule 13(a), (b), and (g) provide that counterclaims and cross-claims cannot be sued upon unless at least one person being sued is already a party to the action. However, once one such person is sued on a counterclaim or cross-claim, Rule 13(h) permits joinder of other persons on that counterclaim or cross-claim, subject to the authority of Rules 19 and 20.[61]

Subject Matter Jurisdiction

Rule 13(h) claims must satisfy either federal question jurisdiction, diversity jurisdiction, or supplemental jurisdiction.[62] For a further discussion of subject matter jurisdiction, see §§ 2.10–2.13.

(1) *Claims by Original Plaintiff:* If the counterclaim or cross-claim is part of a case based solely on diversity of citizenship, and was filed by someone who was a plaintiff on the original claim, supplemental jurisdiction is not available as to new parties joined under either Rule 19 or Rule 20.[63]

(2) *Dissimilar Claims or Occurrences:* If a counterclaim does not arise from the same transaction or occurrence as the original action, Rule 13(h) may usually be employed only where the court has federal question jurisdiction or diversity jurisdiction over the counterclaim.[64] For a further discussion of subject matter jurisdiction, see §§ 2.10–2.13.

Personal Jurisdiction

Additional parties may be joined under Rule 13(h) only if they are subject to the jurisdiction of the court.[65] For a further discussion of personal jurisdiction, see §§ 2.3–2.7.

Venue

Venue requirements do not apply to counterclaims or cross-claims in which Rule 13(h) joinder is sought.[66]

RULE 13(i). SEPARATE TRIALS; SEPARATE JUDGMENTS

CORE CONCEPT

Because additional claims added to a case through Rule 13(a), (b), and (g) have substantial potential for confusing the trier of fact or

61. *See, e.g., Asset Allocation and Management Co. v. Western Employers Insurance Co.,* 892 F.2d 566, 574 (7th Cir. 1989)(noting interplay of Rules 13(h) and 20).

62. *But see, Rayman v. Peoples Savings Corp.,* 735 F.Supp. 842, 854 (N.D.Ill. 1990)(noting, however, that compulsory counterclaims or cross-claims will usually satisfy supplemental jurisdiction).

63. 28 U.S.C.A. § 1367(b).

64. *See, e.g., Federal Deposit Insurance Corp. v. La Rambla Shopping Center, Inc.,*

791 F.2d 215, 220 (1st Cir.1986)(noting that counterclaims arising from unrelated transactions do not usually qualify for supplemental jurisdiction, and must have independent basis for jurisdiction).

65. *See, e.g., Cordner v. Metropolitan Life Ins. Co.,* 234 F.Supp. 765, 769 (S.D.N.Y.1964)(Rule 13(h) requires jurisdiction over parties to be joined).

66. *See, e.g., Lesnik v. Public Industrials Corp.,* 144 F.2d 968, 977 (2d Cir. 1944)(so holding).

delaying adjudication of the original claims, Rule 13(i) authorizes the court to hold separate hearings, as provided by Rule 42(b), and/or enter separate judgments, as provided by Rule 54(b).

APPLICATIONS

Judicial Discretion

Courts have substantial discretion to order separate trials and enter separate judgments, and the decision to process claims separately is not normally disturbed on appeal.[67]

Jurisdiction

Rule 13(i) is subject to the prerequisite that the court have jurisdiction over the claims and parties before it.[68]

ADDITIONAL RESEARCH REFERENCES

Wright & Miller, *Federal Practice and Procedure* §§ 1401–37.

C.J.S. Federal Civil Procedure §§ 309–319 et seq.

West's Key No. Digests, Federal Civil Procedure ⟜771–786.

67. *See, e.g., McLaughlin v. State Farm Mutual Automobile Insurance Co.,* 30 F.3d 861, 870 (7th Cir.1994) (noting discretion of trial court in deciding whether to bifurcate trial).

68. *See, e.g., Chattanooga Corp. v. Klin-gler,* 621 F.Supp. 756 (E.D.Tenn.1985).

RULE 14

THIRD–PARTY PRACTICE

(a) When a Defending Party May Bring in a Third Party.

(1) *Timing of the Summons and Complaint.* A defending party may, as third-party plaintiff, serve a summons and complaint on a nonparty who is or may be liable to it for all or part of the claim against it. But the third-party plaintiff must, by motion, obtain the court's leave if it files the third-party complaint more than 10 days after serving its original answer.

(2) *Third-Party Defendant's Claims and Defenses.* The person served with the summons and third-party complaint—the "third-party defendant":

(A) must assert any defense against the third-party plaintiff's claim under Rule 12;

(B) must assert any counterclaim against the third-party plaintiff under Rule 13(a), and may assert any counterclaim against the third-party plaintiff under Rule 13(b) or any crossclaim against another third-party defendant under Rule 13(g);

(C) may assert against the plaintiff any defense that the third-party plaintiff has to the plaintiff's claim; and

(D) may also assert against the plaintiff any claim arising out of the transaction or occurrence that is the subject matter of the plaintiff's claim against the third-party plaintiff.

(3) *Plaintiff's Claims Against a Third–Party Defendant.* The plaintiff may assert against the third-party defendant any claim arising out of the transaction or occurrence that is the subject matter of the plaintiff's claim against the third-party plaintiff. The third-party defendant must then assert any defense under Rule 12 and any counterclaim under Rule 13(a), and may assert any counterclaim under Rule 13(b) or any crossclaim under Rule 13(g).

(4) *Motion to Strike, Sever, or Try Separately.* Any party may move to strike the third-party claim, to sever it, or to try it separately.

(5) *Third-Party Defendant's Claim Against a Nonparty.* A third-party defendant may proceed under this rule against a nonparty who is or may be liable to the third-party defendant for all or part of any claim against it.

(6) *Third-Party Complaint In Rem.* If it is within the admiralty or maritime jurisdiction, a third-party complaint may be in rem. In that event, a reference in this rule to the "summons" includes the warrant of arrest, and a reference to the defendant or third-party plaintiff includes, when appropriate, a person who asserts a right under Supplemental Rule C(6)(a)(i) in the property arrested.

(b) When a Plaintiff May Bring in a Third Party. When a claim is asserted against a plaintiff, the plaintiff may bring in a third party if this rule would allow a defendant to do so.

(c) Admiralty or Maritime Claim.

(1) *Scope of Impleader.* If a plaintiff asserts an admiralty or maritime claim under Rule 9(h), the defendant or a person who asserts a right under Supplemental Rule C(6)(a)(i) may, as a third-party plaintiff, bring in a third-party defendant who may be wholly or partly liable—either to the plaintiff or to the third-party plaintiff—for remedy over, contribution, or otherwise on account of the same transaction, occurrence, or series of transactions or occurrences.

(2) *Defending Against a Demand for Judgment for the Plaintiff.* The third-party plaintiff may demand judgment in the plaintiff's favor against the third-party defendant. In that event, the third-party defendant must defend under Rule 12 against the plaintiff's claim as well as the third-party plaintiff's claim; and the action proceeds as if the plaintiff had sued both the third-party defendant and the third-party plaintiff.

[Amended effective March 19, 1948; July 1, 1963; July 1, 1966; August 1, 1987; April 17, 2000, effective December 1, 2000; April 12, 2006, effective December 1, 2006; April 30, 2007, effective December 1, 2007.]

—————————— **2007 AMENDMENTS ROADMAP** ——————————

STYLE PROJECT CHANGES: Rule 14(a) and (c), previously treated as single paragraphs, have been divided into subparts, each with their own new subtitles. Minor language changes were made throughout the Rule to aid readability.

NON-STYLE CHANGES: Old Rule 14(a) authorized both the plaintiff and the third-party defendant to bring counterclaims and crossclaims against each other pursuant to Rule 13. New Rule 14(a) has been amended to highlight that such counterclaims and crossclaims are subject to the provisions of Rule 13 that distinguish between compulsory counterclaims, permissive counterclaims, and crossclaims (which are always permissive).

NOTE: The Federal Rules "Style Project" is explained in Part III-A.

AUTHORS' COMMENTARY ON RULE 14

—————————— PURPOSE AND SCOPE ——————————

Rule 14 permits parties who are defending against claims to join other persons, not yet parties, who may be obligated to reimburse the party defending the claim for some or all of that party's liability. The decision to seek joinder, or to hold the claim for assertion in later litigation, belongs to the party defending on the claim: Rule 14 contains no requirement similar to Rule 13(a), which makes compulsory the assertion of certain counterclaims. Typically, a person is joined because that person, as a guarantor of some transaction, has an obligation to indemnify a party if the party is forced to pay on a claim. Third-party practice is also commonly employed when an alleged tortfeasor seeks contribution from others who may also be liable but whom the plaintiff has not sued. The Rule also describes the rights of persons who are joined as third-party defendants to claim and defend against the original plaintiffs and defendants, as well as to join still other persons who may be liable to the third parties.

NOTE: The labels necessitated by Rule 14 are superficially complex, but follow a consistent pattern. A party who seeks to join another person under Rule 14 is called a third-party plaintiff. The person joined is called a third-party defendant. Thus, if a defendant in a pending action sought to join someone not yet a party under Rule 14, the defendant would carry the additional title of third-party plaintiff, and the person joined would be a third-party defendant. If the third-party defendant sought, in turn, to join someone else, the person joined would be a fourth-party defendant, and the third-party defendant would carry the additional title of fourth-party plaintiff.

RULE 14(a). A DEFENDING PARTY MAY BRING IN THIRD PARTY

CORE CONCEPT

Rule 14(a) describes the power of defendants to implead third parties. The Rule also describes the defenses available to third-party defendants, as well as the circumstances in which third-party defendants may claim against plaintiffs and defendants. Finally, Rule 14(a) authorizes third-party defendants to implead potential fourth-party defendants who may be liable for some or all of any claim the third-party defendants might have to pay.

APPLICATIONS

Third–Party Plaintiff's Discretion

Where applicable, a party's right to implead under Rule 14 is optional. There is no obligation to implead third parties.[1]

Who May Be Impleaded

Only persons not already parties may be impleaded.[2] This provision of Rule 14 stands in contrast to provisions of Rule 13, governing counterclaims and cross-claims, in which at least one of the persons sued on a counterclaim or cross-claim must already be a party to the case.

Procedure

A third-party defendant is joined upon service of a proper summons and third-party complaint.[3] For purposes of impleader under Rule 14, Rule 4(k) permits service on a third-party defendant found within 100 miles of the place from where the summons issued–without regard to whether such service takes place within another state.[4] This is a small but sometimes crucial expansion of personal jurisdiction in the context of Rule 14.

Time; Leave of Court

Rule 14(a) permits service of a third-party complaint "at any time." However, a party may file a third-party complaint without obtaining leave of court only in the ten-day period following that

---

1. See, e.g., Fernandez v. Corporacion Insular De Seguros, 79 F.3d 207 (1st Cir. 1996)(no obligation to implead; decision to forego impleader does not require instruction that jury is authorized to draw adverse inference).

2. See, e.g., Mauney v. Imperial Delivery Services, Inc., 865 F.Supp. 142, 153 (S.D.N.Y.1994)(under Rule 14, third-party suit cannot be filed against a third-party defendant who is already a party).

3. See, e.g., Jackson v. Southeastern Pennsylvania Transportation Authority, 727 F.Supp. 965, 966 (E.D.Pa.1990)(by its terms, Rule 14(a) authorizes service of third-party complaints).

4. Fed.R.Civ.P. 4(k).

party's service of an answer to a claim.[5]   Thereafter, a third-party complaint may be filed only upon motion, served on all parties, and after obtaining leave of court.[6]   Generally, courts permit assertion of impleader claims unless they are raised so late in a pending suit that they unreasonably prejudice persons who are already parties.[7]

Relationship to Pending Claims

Rule 14(a) explicitly provides that claims against third-party defendants must relate to claims pending against the third-party plaintiff and must depend in some degree on the outcome of the original action.   Rule 14(a) provides no authorization to assert claims against third-party plaintiffs that are unrelated to claims already pending.[8]

Affirmative Relief; Derivative Liability and Rule 18

Although Rule 14(a)'s literal language might seem to limit third-party practice to claims for reimbursement or compensation,[9] a minority of courts have used Rule 18(a), governing joinder of claims, to permit third-party claims even when the amount sought is greater than that for which the third-party plaintiff might be liable on the original claim.[10]   However, it appears settled that once a party is properly impleaded under Rule 14, that party may also be sued for affirmative relief under Rule 18.[11]

Defenses Available

Third-party defendants are entitled to raise their own defenses against the third-party plaintiff.   The explicit language of Rule 14(a) also authorizes third-party defendants to assert defenses that the

---

5.   *See, e.g., Smith v. Local 819 I.B.T. Pension Plan,* 291 F.3d 236 n. 2 (2d Cir. 2002) (defendant's third-party complaint filed within ten days of serving answer, so no need to obtain leave of court).

6.   *See, e.g., Raytheon Aircraft Credit Corp. v. Pal Air International, Inc.,* 923 F.Supp. 1408 (D.Kan.1996)(no obligation to obtain leave of court when impleader is brought within 10 days of answer).

7.   *See, e.g., New York v. Solvent Chemical Co.,* 875 F.Supp. 1015 (W.D.N.Y. 1995)(impleader allowed more than 10 years after original complaint was filed; case was still in discovery, and third-party defendant still had good opportunity to prepare case). *See also Marseilles Hydro Power, L.L.C. v. Marseilles Land and Water Co.,* 299 F.3d 643, 650 (7th Cir.2002) (suit filed in February; counterclaim and third-party complaint filed in June; held, "clearly wrong" for district court to assert that third-party plaintiff waited too long to file third-party complaint; "We cannot for the life of us see what procedural economy

could be gained by forcing [third-party plaintiff] to sue [third-party defendant] in a separate action or how the plaintiff could be prejudiced.").

8.   *See, e.g., United States v. Olavarrieta,* 812 F.2d 640, 643 (11th Cir.1987) (Rule 14 requires that outcome of impleader must at least partly depend on outcome of original suit; "Rule 14(a) does not allow the defendant to assert a separate and independent claim even though the claim arises out of the same general set of facts as the main claim.").

9.   *See, e.g., Federal Deposit Insurance Corp. v. Bathgate,* 27 F.3d 850, 872 (3d Cir.1994) (limiting Rule 14(a) to claims based on derivative liability).

10.   *See, e.g., King Fisher Marine Service, Inc. v. 21st Phoenix Corp.,* 893 F.2d 1155, 1158 (10th Cir.1990) (permitting joinder of unrelated third-party claims, provided that jurisdiction and Rule 14 are already satisfied).

11.   *Id.*

third-party plaintiff may have against the original claim.[12]

Counterclaims by Third–Party Defendants

Rule 14(a) authorizes third-party defendants to file claims against third-party plaintiffs,[13] consistent with the requirements of Rule 13. Applying Rule 13 to such claims means that, when the counterclaims satisfy the requirements of Rule 13(a), governing compulsory counterclaims, they must be filed in the pending action or they are waived.

Cross–Claims by Third–Party Defendants

If more than one third-party defendant has been impleaded, Rule 14(a) authorizes the third-party defendants to file claims against one another, subject to the requirements of Rule 13. Because Rule 13(g) is permissive, such claims may be filed or may be retained for subsequent litigation. Additionally, because Rule 13(g) only permits cross-claims that arise out of the same transaction or occurrence as the original claims, third-party claims must relate to the transaction or occurrence underlying the original claims by the third-party plaintiff.

Claims Against Plaintiffs

Rule 14(a) permits a third-party defendant to make claims against an original plaintiff that arise out of the same transaction or occurrence as the claims originally filed by the plaintiff. Such claims are permissive, in that they may either be raised or retained for subsequent litigation. Note, however, that if an original plaintiff has already sued the third-party defendant in the litigation, the third-party defendant's claims against the plaintiff may be compulsory counterclaims subject to Rule 13(a). In such a circumstance, a third-party defendant's claims against a plaintiff are not permissive. Counterclaims against plaintiffs are discussed below.

Plaintiffs' Claims Against Third–Party Defendants

Rule 14(a) also permits plaintiffs to sue persons joined as third-party defendants, provided that the claim arises out of the same transaction or occurrence as the original claims against the defendants.[14] The language of Rule 14(a) makes clear that assertion of such claims is discretionary, and a plaintiff may choose to retain the claims for subsequent litigation.[15]

---

12. Fed.R.Civ.P. 14(a).

13. *Cf., Thomas v. Barton Lodge II, Ltd.,* 174 F.3d 636 (5th Cir.1999) (observing that some courts prohibit third-party defendants' suits against original defendants who are not third-party plaintiffs; concluding that such prohibitions are erroneous, and permitting such claims).

14. *United States ex rel. S. Prawer & Co. v. Fleet Bank of Maine,* 24 F.3d 320, 328 (1st Cir.1994)(Rule 14(a) requires that plaintiff's claim against third-party defendant arose from same transaction or occur-

rence as claim against original defendant). *Cf., Project Hope v. M/V Ibn Sina,* 250 F.3d 67 (2d Cir.2001) (apparent dicta; if third-party defendant "is effectively on notice that it will be held liable on the plaintiff's claims and the two proceed against one another in an adverse manner," plaintiff need not formally amend complaint to include causes of action against impleaded party).

15. *See, e.g., Atchison, Topeka and Santa Fe Railway Co. v. Hercules, Inc.,* 146 F.3d 1071, 1073 (9th Cir.1998) ("Rule 14

Third–Party Defendants' Counterclaims Against Plaintiffs

If a plaintiff sues a third-party defendant, any counterclaims the third-party defendant may have are governed by Rule 13.

Third–Party Defendants' Cross–Claims Upon Suit by Plaintiffs

Just as Rule 14(a) permits third-party defendants to cross-claim against one another after being joined by a third-party plaintiff, the Rule also permits third-party defendants to cross-claim against one another if one or more third-party defendant is sued by a plaintiff. Rule 14(a) expressly provides that such cross-claims are regulated by Rule 13.

Severance; Separate Trials

Third-party practice has obvious potential for complexity and for confusing a trier of fact. Rule 14(a) therefore provides that *any* party to the litigation may move to strike or sever the claims. Courts have substantial discretion when deciding such motions.[16] Courts weigh numerous factors in determining whether third-party claims should be severed.[17]

Fourth–Party Practice

Rule 14(a) grants third-party defendants the same power to implead as is enjoyed by the defendants. Thus, third-party defendants may join persons not yet parties who may be liable to the third-party defendants for part or all of the liability the third-party defendants may have to the third-party plaintiffs.

Rights of Fourth–Party Defendants

Although not explicitly addressed in Rule 14(a), it seems settled that fourth-party defendants enjoy all the rights and authority the Rule provides to third-party defendants, including availability of defenses, counterclaims, cross-claims, and impleader of additional persons.[18]

Admiralty and Maritime Cases; In Rem Jurisdiction

Rule 14(a) provides that third-party complaints arising under the admiralty jurisdiction of the court may be in rem actions against maritime property. In such cases, the summons used in conventional litigation may be supplanted by admiralty process, and the termi-

---

makes claims by a plaintiff against a third-party defendant permissive, not compulsory.").

16. *See, e.g., First Nat. Bank of Nocona v. Duncan Savings & Loan Ass'n.,* 957 F.2d 775, 777 (10th Cir.1992) ("The granting of leave for a defendant to prosecute a third party proceeding under Rule 14 rests in the sound discretion of the trial court."). *Williams v. Ford Motor Credit Co.,* 627 F.2d 158 (8th Cir.1980)(noting that trial court has substantial, but not unlimited, discretion to dismiss a third-party complaint).

17. *See, e.g., Oklahoma ex rel. Edmondson v. Tyson Foods, Inc.* , 237 F.R.D. 679, 681 (N.D. Okla. 2006) (listing factors considered by courts in deciding whether to sever and granting plaintiff's motion to sever approximately 160 third-party defendants with a myriad of third-party claims).

18. *See, e.g., Garnay, Inc. v. M/V Lindo Maersk,* 816 F.Supp. 888 (S.D.N.Y. 1993)(processing fourth-party complaint under same jurisdictional standards as any third-party complaint).

nology for third-party plaintiffs and defendants may conform to admiralty practice.

Subject Matter Jurisdiction

Every third-party claim must fall within at least one of the forms of subject matter jurisdiction: *e.g.*, federal question jurisdiction; diversity jurisdiction; or supplemental jurisdiction. Because third-party claims of necessity are closely related to the original claims between the plaintiff and defendant, subject matter jurisdiction can usually be obtained under supplemental jurisdiction even in the absence of federal question jurisdiction or diversity jurisdiction.[19] However, an important exception to that generalization exists when the third-party claim is asserted by a plaintiff. 28 U.S.C.A. § 1367(b), governing restrictions on supplemental jurisdiction, expressly provides that when the original claims in the case are based solely on diversity jurisdiction, suits by plaintiffs against persons made parties under Rule 14 may not be founded on supplemental jurisdiction.[20] For a further discussion of subject matter jurisdiction, see §§ 2.10–2.13.

Personal Jurisdiction; Service of Process

Every third-party claim must also satisfy requirements of jurisdiction over persons and things.[21] For a further discussion of such jurisdiction, see §§ 2.2–2.9. For service of process on parties joined under Rule 14, a special provision in Rule 4(k)(1)(B) provides a sometimes useful extension of normal limits on service.[22] Rule 4 is discussed elsewhere in this text.

Venue

Requirements of venue do not apply to claims asserted under

---

19. *See, e.g., Grimes v. Mazda North American Operations,* 355 F.3d 566, 572 (6th Cir.2004) (third-party claim for contribution falls within scope of supplemental jurisdiction if "common nucleus" requirement is met); *LaSalle National Trust, N.A. v. Schaffner,* 818 F.Supp. 1161, 1164–65 (N.D.Ill.1993)(observing that when requirements of Rule 14(a) are met, requirements of § 1367 will also typically be satisfied). *See also Spring City Corp. v. American Buildings Co.,* 193 F.3d 165, 169 (3d Cir. 1999) ("[A] third-party defendant joined under [Rule 14] does not become a defendant as against the original plaintiff, so that federal jurisdiction is not destroyed where those parties are citizens of the same state.").

20. *See, e.g., State National Insurance Co. v. Yates,* 391 F.3d 577, 579 (5th Cir. 2004) ("Where ... the district court's original jurisdiction is based solely on diversity the district court does *not* have supplemental jurisdiction" over Rule 14 claims assert-

ed by a plaintiff); *Grimes v. Mazda North American Operations,* 355 F.3d 566, 572 (6th Cir.2004) (§ 1367(b) is intended to prevent original plaintiffs, "but not defendants or third parties – from circumventing the requirements of diversity"); *Herrick Co. v. SCS Communications, Inc.,* 251 F.3d 315 n. 7 (2d Cir.2001) (generally in diversity cases, there is "no supplemental jurisdiction over claims by plaintiffs against persons made parties under Fed. R. Civ. P. 14"). *But see Ryan ex rel. Ryan v. Schneider National Carriers, Inc.,* 263 F.3d 816, 820 (8th Cir. 2001) (permitting supplemental jurisdiction over third-party complaint brought by some plaintiffs against co-plaintiff; holding that co-plaintiff was not made party by other plaintiffs under, *inter alia,* Rule 20).

21. *See, e.g., Rodd v. Region Construction Co.,* 783 F.2d 89 (7th Cir.1986).

22. *See, e.g., ESAB Group v. Centricut, Inc.,* 126 F.3d 617, 622 (4th Cir.1997) (so noting).

Rule 14.[23]

RULE 14(b). WHEN A PLAINTIFF MAY BRING IN A THIRD PARTY

CORE CONCEPT

Rule 14(b) provides that if a plaintiff is the subject of a counterclaim, the plaintiff may join third parties who may be liable for part or all of that claim, in the same manner that Rule 14(a) authorizes defendants to join third parties.

APPLICATIONS

When Plaintiff is Sued

A plaintiff may not join persons under Rule 14 until the plaintiff has been sued, and then only on third-party claims related to the counterclaim. Thus, if a plaintiff sued a defendant on a single count, and the defendant counterclaimed on an unrelated count, the plaintiff would be entitled to employ Rule 14 to implead third-party defendants.[24]

Applicability of Rule 14(a) to Plaintiff's Third–Party Claims

Once a plaintiff has been served with a counterclaim, Rule 14(b) provides that the plaintiff may employ third-party practice as to that counterclaim in the same manner that Rule 14(a) makes third-party practice available to a defendant.[25]

Subject Matter Jurisdiction; Restraints on Supplemental Jurisdiction

If the original cause of action in the case is based solely on diversity of citizenship, a plaintiff's third-party claims must satisfy either federal question jurisdiction or diversity jurisdiction. Title 28 U.S.C.A. § 1367(b), governing restraints on the use of supplemental jurisdiction, expressly provides that the court has no supplemental jurisdiction over claims by plaintiffs against persons made parties under Rule 14.[26] For a further discussion of subject matter jurisdiction, see §§ 2.10–2.13.

Personal Jurisdiction

A plaintiff's third-party claims must satisfy requirements of jurisdiction over persons and things. For a further discussion of such jurisdiction, see §§ 2.2–2.9.

---

23. See, e.g., Gundle Lining Construction Corp. v. Adams County Asphalt, Inc., 85 F.3d 201 (5th Cir.1996)(Rule 14 claims are not subject to venue requirements).

24. See, e.g., Chase Manhattan Bank, N.A. v. Aldridge, 906 F.Supp. 866, 867 (S.D.N.Y.1995)(once plaintiff is sued on a counterclaim, Rule 14(b) affords plaintiff same impleader powers provided to defendant by Rule 14(a)).

25. See, e.g., Powell, Inc. v. Abney, 83 F.R.D. 482, 485 (S.D.Tex.1979)("Rule 14(b) ... places a plaintiff in the same position as a defendant under Rule 14(a) when a counterclaim is filed.").

26. See, e.g., Guaranteed Systems, Inc. v. American National Can Co., 842 F.Supp. 855 (M.D.N.C.1994)(clear language of § 1367(b) prohibits use of supplemental jurisdiction by plaintiff, where original suit is based on diversity).

RULE 14(c).   ADMIRALTY OR MARITIME CLAIM

CORE CONCEPT

Rule 14(c) provides that when the original cause of action arose under the court's admiralty jurisdiction, the defendant may join third persons by alleging either that: they are liable to reimburse the defendant for some or all of the defendant's liability, or that the third persons are liable directly to the plaintiff.   This expands the general practice of impleader under Rule 14(a), where a defendant may implead only to establish that the person joined is liable to the defendant, and may not implead by alleging that the person to be joined is liable directly to the plaintiff.[27]   The practical result of this feature of Rule 14(c) is that the third person becomes a co-defendant in the original action, rather than a third-party defendant.[28]

APPLICATIONS

Demand for Judgment

In order to designate an impleaded third-party defendant as a defendant to the plaintiff's original complaint, the literal language of Rule 14(c) appears to require that the third-party complaint "demand judgment against the third-party defendant in favor of the plaintiff." The precise meaning of this language is not entirely free from doubt. However, while there is some authority indicating that the third-party complaint must specifically demand judgment in that precise way, the greater weight of authority is that the requirement of Rule 14(c) should be liberally construed. Thus, clear language intending to implead third-party defendants as co-defendants to the original complaint satisfies the requirement of Rule 14(c).[29]

Applicability of Rule 14(a)

Beyond the special provision of Rule 14(c) that may make the third party a co-defendant, Rule 14(c) impleader actions generally proceed as though controlled by relevant provisions of Rule 14(a).[30]

---

27.   *See, e.g., Spring City Corp. v. American Buildings Co.,* 193 F.3d 165, 169 (3d Cir.1999) ("[A] third-party defendant joined under [Rule 14(a)] does not become a defendant as against the original plaintiff.").

28.   *See, e.g., LeBlanc v. Cleveland,* 198 F.3d 353, 355 (2d Cir.1999) ("Pursuant to Rule 14(c) ... third-party complaints allowed the case to proceed as if [plaintiffs] had sued [the impleaded third party] as well as [the original defendants]."); *Galt G/S v. Hapag–Lloyd AG,* 60 F.3d 1370, 1374 n. 2 (9th Cir.1995)(noting distinction between Rule 14(a) and (c)). *But see Texaco Exploration and Production Co. v. AmClyde Engineered Products Co.,* 243 F.3d 906, 910 (5th Cir.2001) (statutory right to enforce

contractual arbitration provision overrides liberal joinder provision of Rule 14(c) when the two provisions are in conflict).

29.   *See, e.g., Royal Insurance Co. of America v. Southwest Marine,* 194 F.3d 1009, 1018 (9th Cir.1999) (collecting cases; also noting that while third-party complaints in instant case did not specifically demand judgment against third parties in favor of plaintiff, both complaints made specific and repeated references to Rule 14(c) and to defendants' alleged liability to plaintiff).

30.   *See, e.g., Rosario v. American Export–Isbrandtsen Lines,* 531 F.2d 1227, 1231–32 (3d Cir.1976), *Rosario v. United States,* 429 U.S. 857, 97 S.Ct. 156, 50

Prerequisite of Rule 9(h)

By its terms, Rule 14(c) is available only when the plaintiff has asserted a claim "within the meaning of Rule 9(h)."[31]

Subject Matter Jurisdiction

Persons impleaded under the special provision of Rule 14(c) will generally be subject to the admiralty jurisdiction of the court.[32]

Personal Jurisdiction

Persons impleaded under Rule 14(c) must be within either the personal jurisdiction, quasi in rem jurisdiction, or in rem jurisdiction of the court. Because in rem jurisdiction is generally available in admiralty practice, however, jurisdictional requirements may usually be satisfied without difficulty.

Venue

Venue requirements do not generally apply to claims asserted under Rule 14.[33]

ADDITIONAL RESEARCH REFERENCES

Wright & Miller, *Federal Practice and Procedure* §§ 1441–65.

C.J.S. Federal Civil Procedure §§ 117–126 et seq., 318.

West's Key No. Digests, Federal Civil Procedure ☞281–293.

L.Ed.2d 135 (1976) (noting that apart from special provision, Rule 14(c) does not operate exclusive of Rule 14(a)). *See also Greenwell v. Aztar Indiana Gaming Corp.*, 268 F.3d 486, 493–94 (7th Cir.2001) (if plaintiff does not choose to notify opponent and court that plaintiff chooses to prosecute a claim as an admiralty claim that qualifies for both admiralty jurisdiction and ordinary civil jurisdiction, case will proceed under ordinary civil rules, and special admiralty provisions will not apply). *Royal Insurance Co. of America v. Southwest Marine*, 194 F.3d 1009, 1019 (9th Cir.1999) (once a direct relationship exists between plaintiff and third-party defendants pursuant to Rule 14(c), plaintiff must assert its claims directly against the third-party defendants

and they must answer the complaint; however, where third-party defendants have sufficient notice of lawsuit from original complaint, plaintiff had no duty to amend original complaint to assert claim against them).

31. *See, e.g., Foulk v. Donjon Marine Co.*, 144 F.3d 252 (3d Cir.1998).

32. *See, e.g., Harrison v. Glendel Drilling Co.*, 679 F.Supp. 1413, 1417 (W.D.La. 1988)(Rule 14(c) can be invoked only in admiralty cases).

33. *See, e.g., Gundle Lining Construction Corp. v. Adams County Asphalt, Inc.*, 85 F.3d 201 (5th Cir.1996)(Rule 14 claims are not subject to venue requirements).

RULE 15

AMENDED AND SUPPLEMENTAL PLEADINGS

(a) Amendments Before Trial.

(1) *Amending as a Matter of Course.* A party may amend its pleading once as a matter of course:

    (A) before being served with a responsive pleading; or

    (B) within 20 days after serving the pleading if a responsive pleading is not allowed and the action is not yet on the trial calendar.

(2) *Other Amendments.* In all other cases, a party may amend its pleading only with the opposing party's written consent or the court's leave. The court should freely give leave when justice so requires.

(3) *Time to Respond.* Unless the court orders otherwise, any required response to an amended pleading must be made within the time remaining to respond to the original pleading or within 10 days after service of the amended pleading, whichever is later.

(b) Amendments During and After Trial.

(1) *Based on an Objection at Trial.* If, at trial, a party objects that evidence is not within the issues raised in the pleadings, the court may permit the pleadings to be amended. The court should freely permit an amendment when doing so will aid in presenting the merits and the objecting party fails to satisfy the court that the evidence would prejudice that party's action or defense on the merits. The court may grant a continuance to enable the objecting party to meet the evidence.

(2) *For Issues Tried by Consent.* When an issue not raised by the pleadings is tried by the parties' express or implied consent, it must be treated in all respects as if raised in the pleadings. A party may move—at any time, even after judgment—to amend the pleadings to conform them to the evidence and to raise an unpleaded issue. But failure to amend does not affect the result of the trial of that issue.

449

(c) Relation Back of Amendments.

(1) *When an Amendment Relates Back.* An amendment to a pleading relates back to the date of the original pleading when:

(A) the law that provides the applicable statute of limitations allows relation back;

(B) the amendment asserts a claim or defense that arose out of the conduct, transaction, or occurrence set out—or attempted to be set out—in the original pleading; or

(C) the amendment changes the party or the naming of the party against whom a claim is asserted, if Rule 15(c)(1)(B) is satisfied and if, within the period provided by Rule 4(m) for serving the summons and complaint, the party to be brought in by amendment:

(i) received such notice of the action that it will not be prejudiced in defending on the merits; and

(ii) knew or should have known that the action would have been brought against it, but for a mistake concerning the proper party's identity.

(2) *Notice to the United States.* When the United States or a United States officer or agency is added as a defendant by amendment, the notice requirements of Rule 15(c)(1)(C)(i) and (ii) are satisfied if, during the stated period, process was delivered or mailed to the United States attorney or the United States attorney's designee, to the Attorney General of the United States, or to the officer or agency.

(d) Supplemental Pleadings. On motion and reasonable notice, the court may, on just terms, permit a party to serve a supplemental pleading setting out any transaction, occurrence, or event that happened after the date of the pleading to be supplemented. The court may permit supplementation even though the original pleading is defective in stating a claim or defense. The court may order that the opposing party plead to the supplemental pleading within a specified time.

[Amended January 21, 1963, effective July 1, 1963; February 28, 1966, effective July 1, 1966; March 2, 1987, effective August 1, 1987; April 30, 1991, effective December 1, 1991; amended by Pub.L. 102–198, § 11, December 9, 1991, 105 Stat. 1626; amended April 22, 1993, effective December 1, 1993; April 30, 2007, effective December 1, 2007.]

─────────── 2007 AMENDMENTS ROADMAP ───────────

STYLE PROJECT CHANGES: Rule 15(a), (b), and (c) has been further subdivided into additional subparts to aid readability. Minor changes have been made in some titles of subsections and in language with the Rule to aid readability.

NON-STYLE CHANGES: Old Rule 15(c)(3) required, as a condition of permitting an amendment changing a party or the name of a party to relate back to the date of the original pleading, that the affected party has timely notice of the "institution" of the action. New Rule 15(c)(3)(A) deletes the word "institution," concentrating instead on the adequacy of notice of the action that the party received.

NOTE: The Federal Rules "Style Project" is explained in Part III-A.

AUTHORS' COMMENTARY ON RULE 15

─────────── PURPOSE AND SCOPE ───────────

Rule 15 governs the circumstances in which parties who have already pleaded in a case will be permitted to amend such pleadings. The Rule also provides the circumstances in which parties will be allowed to file new pleadings describing events that have occurred since the original pleadings were filed.

RULE 15(a). AMENDMENTS BEFORE TRIAL

CORE CONCEPT

Rule 15(a) provides an automatic right to amend pleadings a single time before a response is filed or, if no response is required, within 20 days after the original pleading to be amended was served, provided that the case has not been placed on the court's trial calendar. Otherwise, a party must seek leave of court or permission of the opposing party to amend pleadings. The Rule also governs time limits in which a party served with an amended pleading must file a responsive pleading to the amendment.

NOTE: On some occasions an amended pleading may be feasible under Rule 15(a), but the effects of the pleading will be restricted by Rule 15(c). Rule 15(c) determines whether an amended pleading will be treated as though it was filed on the date of the original pleading or on the date of filing. When the timing of a pleading (particularly a claim for relief) is at issue, attorneys should consult both Rule 15(a) and Rule 15(c).

APPLICATIONS

2007 Amendments

The 2007 Style Project amended Rule 15(a) by subdividing it into three subparts, each with its own subtitle. This change should not present great difficulty for attorneys.

Amendment of Right

A party may amend a pleading without leave of court or consent of opposing parties *once,* under either of two circumstances. First, a pleading may be amended of right if the amendment is filed before receipt of a responsive pleading to the earlier, unamended version of the pleading.[1] Alternatively, if the pleading to be amended is one requiring no responsive pleading, and the action has not yet been placed on the court's trial calendar, Rule 15(a) expressly provides for an amendment of right if the amendment is filed within 20 days after service of the previous version of the pleading.

Motions and Rule 15(a)

Motions are not pleadings, as Rule 7(a) and (b) makes clear. A motion filed in opposition to a pleading is therefore not a responsive pleading within the meaning of Rule 15(a). Thus, if a plaintiff's complaint was opposed only by a Rule 12(b)(6) motion to dismiss for failure to state a claim for which relief may be granted, the plaintiff could amend the complaint as of right because the complaint had not yet evoked a responsive pleading.[2]

---

1. *Mayle v. Felix,* 545 U.S. 644, 125 S.Ct. 2562, 2569, 162 L.Ed.2d 582 (2005). *See, e.g., Thompson v. Carter,* 284 F.3d 411, 415 n. 2 (2d Cir.2002) (motion to dismiss is not a responsive pleading and therefore does not, in the absence of a responsive pleading, terminate a plaintiff's right to amend a complaint); *Washington v. New York City Board of Estimate,* 709 F.2d 792, 795 (2d Cir.1983) (when defendant has not yet answered complaint, plaintiff's first amendment of complaint is as of right). *But see, Duda v. Board of Education of Franklin Park Public School District No. 84,* 133 F.3d 1054, 1057 (7th Cir.1998) (court may reject even an amendment filed prior to receipt of responsive pleading if "examination of the proposed complaint makes clear that it does not cure the deficiencies of the original pleading and the amended complaint is doomed not to survive a motion to dismiss").

2. *See, e.g., Shaver v. Operating Engineers Local 428 Pension Trust Fund,* 332 F.3d 1198 (9th Cir.2003) (motion to dismiss not responsive pleading; thus plaintiff retained "absolute right" to amend complaint); *Bowden v. United States,* 176 F.3d 552 (D.C.Cir.1999) (alternative motions to dismiss and for summary judgment are not responsive pleadings and therefore do not nullify plaintiff's right to amend); *Domino Sugar Corp. v. Sugar Workers Local Union 392,* 10 F.3d 1064, 1068 n. 1 (4th Cir.1993) (motion to dismiss is not a responsive pleading; thus if defendant has not filed a responsive pleading, plaintiff may still amend once as of right). *See also Sorbo v. United Parcel Service,* 432 F.3d 1169, 1177 (10th Cir.2005) (Rule 15(a) cannot be used to permit an otherwise untimely motion under Rule 60(b)).

Right to Amend: Irrelevance of Futility

When a party has no right to amend and must obtain leave of court to do so, it is proper for a court to deny such leave if an amendment would be futile.[3] However, if a party still has a right to amend, the court cannot reject the amendment because it would be futile.[4] It is possible, of course, that such an amendment would fall within the scope of Rule 11, governing sanctions for certain acts related to, inter alia, pleading.[5]

Cases Removed from State Court: 28 U.S.C. § 1447(e)

Section 1447(e) of Title 28 of the United States Code provides that if, after a case is removed, a plaintiff seeks to join non-diverse defendants whose joinder would destroy diversity, the district may permit or deny joinder. If joinder is denied, the court continues to have jurisdiction over the case. However, if joinder is permitted, diversity jurisdiction no longer exists and (in the absence of some other basis for subject matter jurisdiction) the court must then remand the case to state court.

That situation gets more complicated if, after removal but before a responsive pleading has been filed, a plaintiff exercises the right to amend a pleading and join a non-diverse defendant under Rule 15(a) without needing leave of court. If Rule 15(a) could be used in that manner, it would undermine the district court's discretion under § 1447(e) to retain the removed case by denying joinder. Courts have resolved this conflict by concluding that they have authority to deny joinder under Rule 15(a), notwithstanding the plaintiff's apparent right under that Rule.[6]

Removal and § 1447(e) are discussed at greater length elsewhere in this text.

Rights of Joined Parties

If a party is served with an amended pleading permitted under Rule 15, that party normally enjoys a minimum of 10 days from the date of service of the amended pleading to respond to it.[7] Rule 15(a) expressly provides the district court with authority to modify that time limit.

---

3. *See* Authors' Commentary on Rule 15(a), "Futile Amendments."

4. *See, e.g., Williams v. Board of Regents,* 441 F.3d 1287, 1296 (11th Cir.2006) (In that circumstance "the plain language of Rule 15(a) shows that the court lacks the discretion to reject the amended complaint based on its alleged futility.").

5. *See* Authors' Commentary on Rule 11.

6. *See, e.g., Mayes v. Rapoport,* 198 F.3d 457, 461 n. 11 (4th Cir.1999) ("[A] district court has the authority to reject a post-removal joinder that implicates 28 U.S.C. § 1447(e), even if the joinder was without leave of court.").

7. *Nelson v. Adams, USA, Inc.,* 529 U.S. 460, 465, 120 S.Ct. 1579, 1584, 146 L.Ed.2d 530 (2000) ("This opportunity to respond, fundamental to due process, is the echo of the opportunity to respond to original pleadings secured by Rule 12." Held, where grant of leave to amend occurred simultaneously with entry of judgment against joined party, due process has been denied).

Termination of Right to Amend

Many courts hold that once the court has entered an order of final judgment, a party's ability to amend of right terminates.[8] Thus if the court grants a motion to dismiss, and enters judgment, the dismissed party's right to amend expires.[9]

Motions to Amend: Particularity and Rule 7(b)

When a party submits a motion to amend, the particularity requirement of Rule 7(b) may require the party to attach to the motion a copy of the proposed amended pleading, unless the motion adequately describes the contemplated revision.[10]

Multiple Opposing Parties

If some opposing parties have already filed responsive pleadings and others have not, courts generally hold that the original pleading may be amended as of right, at least as to those parties that have not yet pleaded.[11]

---

8. *Ahmed v. Dragovich,* 297 F.3d 201 (3d Cir.2002) (once final judgment is entered, Rule 15 is inapplicable unless a party obtains relief under Rule 59 or Rule 60; unless judgment is set aside, party cannot use Rule 15 to amend); *Dwares v. City of New York,* 985 F.2d 94, 101 (2d Cir. 1993)(right to amend "did not survive the entry of final judgment"). *Cf., Morse v. McWhorter,* 290 F.3d 795, 799 (6th Cir. 2002) ("Where a timely motion to amend judgment is filed under Rule 59(e), the Rule 15 and Rule 59 inquiries turn on the same factors."). *But cf., Camp v. Gregory,* 67 F.3d 1286 (7th Cir.1995) (if complaint is dismissed but judgment is not yet entered, Rule 15(a) may still be available); *see also, Whitaker v. City of Houston,* 963 F.2d 831, 835 (5th Cir.1992)(if complaint is dismissed but court has not indicated that dismissal is with prejudice, or that an amendment is futile, plaintiff loses right to amend, but may be permitted to amend with leave of court.); *Diersen v. Chicago Car Exchange,* 110 F.3d 481, 488 n. 6 (7th Cir.1997) (to obtain such leave, party should first move to have judgment set aside or vacated under Rule 59 or 60).

9. *See, e.g., Lewis v. Fresne,* 252 F.3d 352 (5th Cir.2001) (noting termination of right to amend; also noting that leave to amend may still be available, but court has substantial discretion to refuse leave). *But see generally Pure Country, Inc. v. Sigma Chi Fraternity,* 312 F.3d 952, 956 (8th Cir. 2002) ("[S]eeking leave to amend does not, by itself, invoke the district court's discretionary authority to deny leave if the amendment would otherwise fall within the

purview of the first sentence of rule 15(a) [governing a party's right to amend]").

10. *See, e.g., United States ex rel. Atkins v. McInteer,* 470 F.3d 1350, 1362 (11th Cir. 2006) (noting requirement that movant submit copy of proposed amendment "or set forth the substance thereof"). *Moore v. Indiana,* 999 F.2d 1125, 1131 (7th Cir.1993) (noting that courts may require submission of copy of proposed amended complaint, and commenting that motion alone might be adequate if it places adversary on proper notice of amendment's content); *Wolgin v. Simon,* 722 F.2d 389, 394 (8th Cir.1983) (commenting that Rule 7(b)'s particularity requirement is satisfied by accompanying motion for leave to amend with copy of proposed amendment). *See also Joblove v. Barr Laboratories, Inc.,* 429 F.3d 370, 404 (2d Cir.2005) ("It is within the court's discretion to deny leave to amend implicitly by not addressing the request when leave is requested informally in a brief filed in opposition to a motion to dismiss."); *Long v. Satz,* 181 F.3d 1275, 1279 (11th Cir.1999) (plaintiff did not file motion for leave to amend; request for leave to amend was found only in memorandum opposing defendant's motion to dismiss; held, district court could properly deny leave to amend for failure to request leave properly).

11. *See, e.g., Williams v. Board of Regents,* 441 F.3d 1287, 1296 (11th Cir.2006) ("If the case has more than one defendant, and not all have filed responsive pleadings, the plaintiff may amend the complaint as a matter of course with regard to those defendants that have yet to answer."); *Barksdale*

Relation to Joinder Rules

It should be noted that when a party seeks to amend a complaint under Rule 15(a) to join additional claims or parties, the joinder will not be permitted simply because the requirements of Rule 15 have been met. In addition, the applicable joinder rules must also be satisfied.[12]

Relation to Rule 41(a)

When a party moves to amend a complaint to dismiss one of its pending counts, it may appear that the motion may be made pursuant to either Rule 15(a) or Rule 41(a)(2). The appearance may often be reflective of reality, particularly if the complaint contains only a single count.[13] However, there is precedent for a clear distinction between the rules when a complaint contains more than one count and the plaintiff seeks dismissal of less than all the counts. In that circumstance the applicable rule is Rule 15(a), not Rule 41. By contrast, if all the counts are to be dismissed, the motion should be filed under Rule 41(a).[14]

In either case, however, dismissal is ordinarily granted without prejudice to a possible subsequent refilling of the dismissed counts.[15]

Relation With Rule 81(c)

If a case is removed from state court, it is possible that a party will be ordered under Rule 81(c) to file a repleading that conforms to federal practice. Generally, such a mandated repleading will not deprive a party of a one-time right to amend that may be available under Rule 15(a).[16]

Adverse Party's Consent

If a party's proposed amendment falls outside the time limits described above, it is often practical to ask the opposing party to consent to the amendment. When their duties to their own clients

---

v. King, 699 F.2d 744 (5th Cir. 1983)(plaintiff retains right to amend against defendant who filed motion to dismiss but not a responsive pleading; held, right to amend lost only as to codefendant who filed responsive pleading).

12. *See, e.g., Hinson v. Norwest Financial South Carolina, Inc.,* 239 F.3d 611, 618 (4th Cir.2001) (joinder of additional plaintiffs triggers application of Rule 20 requirements).

13. *See, e.g., Jet, Inc. v. Sewage Aeration Systems,* 223 F.3d 1360, 1364 (Fed. Cir.2000) (in case at bar the Rules are "functionally interchangeable," although Rule 15(a) is preferred).

14. *See, e.g., Hells Canyon Preservation Council v. United States Forest Service,* 403 F.3d 683, 687 (9th Cir.2005) (Rule 41 "does not allow for piecemeal dismissals;" Rule 15(a) is applicable to such circumstances);

Klay v. United Healthgroup, Inc., 376 F.3d 1092, 1106 (11th Cir.2004) (plaintiff who wishes to dispose of only part of a claim should normally cite Rule 15; Rule 41(a) should normally be used to dismiss an entire action).

15. *Klay v. United Healthgroup, Inc.,* 376 F.3d 1092, 1107 (11th Cir.2004) (under either Rule 15 or Rule 41, dismissal is normally without prejudice); *Jet, Inc. v. Sewage Aeration Systems,* 223 F.3d 1360, 1364 (Fed. Cir.2000) (dismissal under either rule is typically without prejudice).

16. *See, e.g., Kuehl v. Federal Deposit Insurance Corp.,* 8 F.3d 905, 907 (1st Cir. 1993) (but where party engages in dilatory conduct in meeting Rule 81(c) requirements, Rule 15(a) right to amend may be treated as exhausted).

are not at issue, attorneys often cooperate in such matters as a matter of professional courtesy, and/or because they recognize that withholding consent will only force the party trying to amend to seek leave of court. If the opposing party consents to an amendment, there is no need to obtain court approval.[17] Rule 15(a) requires that consent of other parties be in writing,[18] which is usually filed with the court in the form of a praecipe.

Leave of Court

If a proposed amendment cannot be filed as of right, and the opposing party will not consent, a motion may be filed with the court seeking leave to amend. In that circumstance, permission to amend rests within the discretion of the court. However, Rule 15(a) directs the court to grant leave to amend "when justice so requires," and in practice the burden is usually on the party opposing the amendment to demonstrate why the amendment should not be permitted.[19] Moreover, at least some courts hold that where a

---

17. *See, e.g., American States Insurance Co. v. Dastar Corp.,* 318 F.3d 881, 888 (9th Cir.2003) (parties who consent to amendment need not obtain court's approval).

18. *See, e.g., Minter v. Prime Equipment Co.,* 451 F.3d 1196, 1204 (10th Cir.2006) (noting writing requirement). *But cf., Mooney v. City of New York,* 219 F.3d 123 (2d Cir.2000) (plaintiff's response on merits to defense raised on motion rather than by responsive pleading is construed "as an implied grant of leave to amend the answer").

19. *Foman v. Davis,* 371 U.S. 178, 83 S.Ct. 227, 9 L.Ed.2d 222 (1962). *See, e.g., Lyn-Lea Travel Corp. v. American Airlines, Inc.,* 283 F.3d 282, 286 (5th Cir.2002) (no error to permit defendants' amended pleadings to raise affirmative defense of preemption when new issue is question of law based on undisputed facts in instant case; also noting that no new discovery was necessary in this case); *Laurie v. Alabama Court of Criminal Appeals,* 256 F.3d 1266, 1274 (11th Cir.2001) ("There must be a substantial reason to deny a motion to amend."); *Bryant v. DuPree,* 252 F.3d 1161 (11th Cir.2001) (plaintiffs' previous amendment, filed as of right under Rule 15(a), should not be counted as a prior opportunity to amend with leave of court when defendants later file a motion to dismiss); *Pangburn v. Culbertson,* 200 F.3d 65, 70 (2d Cir.1999) (liberal approach to leave to amend "applies with particular force to pro se litigants"); *Martin's Herend Imports, Inc. v. Diamond & Gem Trading United States of America Co.,* 195 F.3d 765, 770 (5th Cir.1999) (Rule 15(a) " 'evinces a bias in favor of granting leave to amend.' ").

See also Rose v. Hartford Underwriters Insurance Co., 203 F.3d 417, 420 (6th Cir. 2000) (marginal entry order denying leave to amend, without explanation, is abuse of discretion; but error is harmless if amendment would be futile; proposed amendment is futile if it cannot withstand motion to dismiss under Rule 12(b)(6)); *Firestone v. Firestone,* 76 F.3d 1205, 1209 (D.C.Cir. 1996)(per curiam)(criticizing district court's "complete failure" to explain grounds for denying leave to amend); *Viernow v. Euripides Development Corp.,* 157 F.3d 785, 799 (10th Cir.1998) (court is required to offer reason for denying leave to amend, but error is harmless if reason is obvious). *But see, Wentwood Woodside I.L.P. v. GMAC Commercial Mortgage Corp.,* 419 F.3d 310 (5th Cir.2005) (plaintiff could have pleaded claim in the alternative, but did not do so; held, no abuse of discretion to deny post-summary judgment leave to amend); *Duncan v. Manager, Department of Safety,* 397 F.3d 1300, 1315 (10th Cir.2005) ("no authority suggesting that Rule 15 requires court to accept a supplemental complaint based on evidence would not be admissible in court"); *Miller v. Champion Enterprises, Inc.,* 346 F.3d 660, 690 (6th Cir.2003) (in cases involving Private Securities Litigation Reform Act, 15 U.S.C.A. § 78u–4(b)(2) and (3), heightened pleading requirements of that law restrict liberal amendment standard of Rule 15(a); thus, failure to allege fraud with particularity may result in dismissal rather than leave to amend); *Lans v. Digital Equipment Corp.,* 252 F.3d 1320 (Fed.Cir.2001) (patent infringement case; no abuse of discretion in denying permis-

complaint's deficiency could be cured by an amendment, leave to amend must be given—and where a party has not sought such leave, district courts are expected to notify parties of the opportunity to amend within whatever time limits are appropriate.[20]

Requirement to Submit Proposed Amendment

A party seeking leave to amend must, inter alia, submit a proposed amendment to the court.[21]

Termination of Leave to Amend; Rule 59

Some courts hold that once a case has been dismissed—with or without prejudice—leave to file subsequent amendments to pleadings lapses. The situation may change if a plaintiff can meet the requirements of Rule 59(e) (governing motions to alter or amend judgments).[22] Otherwise, only if a district court dismisses without prejudice *and* expressly grants leave to amend will the possibility of amending a pleading still exist.[23] However, at least one circuit court

sion to amend when plaintiff/inventor had assigned patent to wholly owned company; original lack of standing in assignor meant there was no action to amend); *Lake v. Arnold,* 232 F.3d 360, 374 (3d Cir.2000) (failure to provide draft amended complaint to district court is ground for denying leave to amend even where court did not provide reasons for denial); *Doe v. Howe Military School,* 227 F.3d 981, 989 (7th Cir.2000) (proper exercise of discretion to deny motion to amend where plaintiffs did not state specifically what amended pleadings would allege; motion to amend or supplement complaint is held to higher standard of specificity than original complaint); *Glatt v. Chicago Park District,* 87 F.3d 190 (7th Cir.1996)(it is within court's discretion to require substantiation of proposed amended or supplemental complaint (unlike original complaint), to ensure that motive is not simply to harass opponent).

20. *Shane v. Fauver,* 213 F.3d 113 (3d Cir.2000). *Cf., Lopez v. Smith,* 203 F.3d 1122, 1130 (9th Cir.2000) (leave to amend should be granted—even if not requested— unless district court determines that amendment is futile). *But see Myles v. United States,* 416 F.3d 551 (7th Cir.2005) (no need for district judge to tell *pro se* plaintiff "he *ought* to amend; even *pro se* litigants are masters of their own complaints. . . . Fomenting litigation is not part of the judicial function.").

21. *See, e.g., Spadafore v. Gardner,* 330 F.3d 849, 853 (6th Cir.2003) (otherwise court is unable to determine whether to grant leave to amend); *Meehan v. United Consumers Club Franchising Corp.,* 312

F.3d 909, 913–14 (8th Cir.2002) (no abuse of discretion to deny leave to amend when party fails to make motion to amend and to submit proposed amended complaint). *Gilmour v. Gates, McDonald & Co.,* 382 F.3d 1312, 1315 (11th Cir.2004) ("A plaintiff may not amend her complaint through argument in a brief opposing summary judgment.").

22. *See, e.g., Crestview Village Apartments v. United States Department of Housing and Urban Development,* 383 F.3d 552, 557–58 (7th Cir.2004) (entry of final judgment terminates right to amend; plaintiff must then meet requirements of Rule 59 or Rule 60); *Ciralsky v. CIA,* 355 F.3d 661, 672 (D.C. Cir.2004) (once judgment is entered, ability to amend is terminated unless party can re-open judgment pursuant to Rule 59(e)).

23. *Mirpuri v. ACT Manufacturing, Inc.,* 212 F.3d 624 (1st Cir.2000). *See also Rodriguez v. United States,* 286 F.3d 972, 980 (7th Cir.2002) (after judgment is entered, presumption in favor of leave to amend is inapplicable, and party must pursue relief under Rule 59 or Rule 60); *Building Industry Association of Superior California v. Norton,* 247 F.3d 1241, 1245 (D.C.Cir.2001) ("Ordinarily post-judgment amendment of a complaint under Rule 15(a) requires reopening of the judgment pursuant to Rule 59(e) or 60(b)."); *Vielma v. Eureka Co.,* 218 F.3d 458, 468 (5th Cir. 2000) (after grant of summary judgment, leave to amend complaint "can only occur once the judgment itself is vacated under Fed. R. Civ. P. 59 or 60."). *See also The*

treats dismissal without prejudice, by itself, as an opportunity to amend a defective pleading.[24] Attorneys are advised to consult the local precedent.

Rule 16 and Case Management

While, as a general rule, leave to amend may be granted freely in the interest of justice, the likelihood of obtaining permission to amend diminishes drastically after the court enters a scheduling order (with deadlines for amendments).[25] The same is true when the court enters a pretrial order limiting trial issues.[26] The converse, however, is probably not true. That is, compliance with a court order's time limits for filing motions to amend does not thereby enhance the probability that the motion will be granted.

A pretrial order under Rule 16 also affects pleadings–amended or not amended–in another important way. When a final pretrial order is entered, it supersedes all prior pleadings.[27]

Tool Box, Inc. v. Ogden City Corp., 419 F.3d 1084, 1087 (10th Cir.2005) ("[E]ven though Rule 15(a) states that 'leave [to amend] shall be freely given when justice so requires,' this presumption is reversed in cases ... where a plaintiff seeks to amend a complaint after judgment has been entered and a case has been dismissed.").

24. *Borelli v. City of Reading,* 532 F.2d 950, 951 (3d Cir.1976) (per curiam) ("Although the district court did not mention amendment, an implicit invitation to amplify the complaint is found in the phrase 'without prejudice.' " Also encouraging district courts to state expressly whether party has leave to amend).

25. *See, e.g., O'Connell v. Hyatt Hotels of Puerto Rico,* 357 F.3d 152, 154–55 (1st Cir.2004) ("good cause" standard of Rule 16(b) is "more stringent" than standard of Rule 15(a); bad faith and unfair prejudice considerations of Rule 15 may still be considered, but Rule 16 emphasizes evaluation of a party's diligence in seeking the amendment); *Leary v. Daeschner,* 349 F.3d 888, 909 (6th Cir.2003) (once deadline for scheduling order has passed, requirement for good cause under Rule 16(b) must be satisfied; but district court must also evaluate potential of prejudice to opposing party); *Grochowski v. Phoenix Construction,* 318 F.3d 80, 86 (2d Cir.2003) (after entry of scheduling order, the lenient standard of Rule 15(a) must be balanced against more rigorous "good cause" requirement of rule 16(b)). *But cf., Clark v. Martinez,* 295 F.3d 809 (8th Cir.2002) ("[W]hen an issue is tried by consent [pursuant to Rule 15(b), discussed infra], it becomes of little moment whether it was encompassed in the pretrial

order."); *Papio Keno Club, Inc. v. City of Papillion,* 262 F.3d 725, 729 (8th Cir.2001) (noting that pretrial orders should be 'construed liberally' to include theories that might fit within order; also holding that notwithstanding pretrial order, issue tried with consent of parties may properly be heard).

26. *See, e.g., In re Milk Products Antitrust Litigation,* 195 F.3d 430, 437 (8th Cir.1999); *Rainy Lake One Stop, Inc. v. Marigold Foods, Inc.,* 529 U.S. 1038, 120 S.Ct. 1534, 146 L.Ed.2d 348 (2000) ("When the district court has filed a Rule 16 pretrial scheduling order, it may properly require that good cause be shown for leave to file an amended pleading that is substantially out of time under that order."). *Byrd v. Guess,* 137 F.3d 1126, 1131–32 (9th Cir. 1998) ("Once the district court enters a scheduling order setting forth a deadline for the amendment of pleadings, modifications are allowed only upon showing of 'good cause.' ... And once a pretrial order has been entered pursuant to rule 16(e) setting forth the parties and issues for trial, modifications are allowed 'only to prevent manifest injustice.' ").

27. *Rockwell International Corp. v. United States,* ___ U.S. ___, 127 S.Ct. 1397, 167 L.Ed.2d 190 (2007) ("[W]e look to the allegations as amended–here, the statement of claims in the final pretrial order.") *See, e.g., Wilson v. Muckala,* 303 F.3d 1207, 1215 (10th Cir. 2002) ("Claims, issues, defenses, or theories of damages not included in the pretrial order are waived even if they appeared in the complaint and, conversely, the inclusion of a claim in the pretrial order

Standard of Discretion

Generally, leave to amend is granted unless a weighing of several factors suggests that leave would be inappropriate.[28] In particular, if leave to amend is denied, it will often occur because an amendment would create unfair prejudice to another party.[29] Prejudice is most commonly found when there has been substantial unjustified delay in moving to amend that creates an unfair disadvantage for an opposing party.[30] By contrast, no unfair prejudice

is deemed to amend any previous pleadings which did not include that claim.'').

28. *See, e.g., Jackson v. Rockford Housing Authority,* 213 F.3d 389 (7th Cir.2000) ("The general rule that amendment is allowed absent undue surprise or prejudice to the plaintiff is widely adhered to by our sister courts of appeals.''); *Lowrey v. Texas A & M University System,* 117 F.3d 242 (5th Cir.1997) (Rule 15(a) creates "strong presumption" in favor of permitting amendment); *DCD Programs, Ltd. v. Leighton,* 833 F.2d 183, 186 (9th Cir.1987), *cert. granted, judgment vac'd,* 492 U.S. 914, 109 S.Ct. 3236, 106 L.Ed.2d 584 (1989)(weighing "bad faith, undue delay, prejudice to the opposing party, and futility of the amendment"). *Cf., United States ex rel. Lee v. SmithKline Beecham, Inc.,* 245 F.3d 1048, 1052 (9th Cir.2001) (citing same factors, but noting they do not get equal weight; futility of amendment, by itself, can be ground for denying leave to amend). *But cf., James Cape & Sons Co. v. PCC Construction Co.,* 453 F.3d 396, 401 (7th Cir. 2006) (no abuse of discretion in denying leave where party never sought leave).

29. *See, e.g., Eminence Capital, L.L.C. v. Aspeon, Inc.,* 316 F.3d 1048, 1052 (9th Cir. 2003) ("[I]t is the consideration of prejudice to the opposing party that carries the greatest weight.''). *See also Thornton v. McClatchy Newspapers, Inc.,* 261 F.3d 789, 799 (9th Cir.2001) (finding of bad faith in party's history of dilatory tactics and "doubtful value of proposed amendment" may also justify denial of leave to amend). *Cf., SCS Communications, Inc. v. Herrick Co.,* 360 F.3d 329, 345 (2d Cir.2004) (abuse of discretion to grant leave to amend without examining possible prejudice to opponent). *But see Kenda Corp. v. Pot O' Gold Money Leagues, Inc.,* 329 F.3d 216, 232 (1st Cir.2003) (absence of prejudice to nonmoving party is not always dispositive of issue; court may consider other factors and still deny motion to amend; failure to explain lengthy delay in making motion to amend can be fatal to proposed amendment).

30. *See, e.g., Jin v. Metropolitan Life Insurance Co.,* 295 F.3d 335 (2d Cir.2002) (no abuse of discretion to find undue delay in filing motion to amend over four years after original filing; more than three years after close of discovery; and nearly three months after ruling on summary judgment motions); *United States ex rel. Bernard v. Casino Magic Corp.,* 293 F.3d 419 (8th Cir. 2002) (no abuse of discretion to deny leave to amend "two and a half years into the litigation," especially when plaintiff can obtain desired information without joining company as party); *Campania Management Co. v. Rooks, Pitts & Poust,* 290 F.3d 843, 848 (7th Cir.2002) (proper denial of leave to amend when defendant failed to act with diligence and proposed amended answer "would have injected a new issue into the case on the eve of trial"); *Walton v. Nalco Chemical Co.,* 272 F.3d 13, 19–20 (1st Cir. 2001) (affirming denial of motion to amend that was made eight months after date in scheduling order; six months after close of discovery; and one week prior to scheduled start of trial); *Owens Corning v. National Union Fire Insurance Co.,* 257 F.3d 484, 496–97 (6th Cir.2001) (unfair prejudice when amendments "suddenly appear" as opponent "was preparing to litigate the remaining issues by motion for summary judgment"); *Monahan v. New York City Department of Corrections,* 214 F.3d 275 n. 3 (2d Cir.2000) (Prejudice may be found where a new claim or defense would " '(i) require the opponent to expend significant additional resources to conduct discovery and prepare for trial; (ii) significantly delay the resolution of the dispute; or (iii) prevent the plaintiff from bringing a timely action in another jurisdiction.' ''); *Rhodes v. Amarillo Hospital District,* 654 F.2d 1148, 1154 (5th Cir.1981) (undue delay where motion to amend was filed 30 months after filing original complaint and three weeks before trial, "where the only apparent reason for the delay was the plaintiff's retention of a new attorney"). *But compare Dennis v. Dillard Department Stores, Inc.,* 207 F.3d 523,

exists simply because a party has to defend against new or better pleaded claims.[31]   However, while Rule 15(a) imposes no time limits on motions for leave to amend pleadings, substantial unexplained and unjustified delays in seeking leave to amend generally reduce the prospects for obtaining leave to amend.[32]

Additionally, proposed amendments that contain a strong hint of sharp practice, unaccompanied by some justifying explanation, may also be rejected.[33]

Abuse of Discretion

Failure by the district court to explain its reasons for denying leave to amend may by itself be abuse of the court's discretion, unless the reason for the court's decision is apparent on the record.[34]

526 (8th Cir.2000) (discovery had closed, but no unfair prejudice to opposing party where three months remained before trial date which could be used to reopen limited discovery–and district court could impose costs of new discovery on party seeking amendment), *and Bowles v. Reade,* 198 F.3d 752, 758 (9th Cir.1999) ("Undue delay by itself . . . is insufficient to justify denying a motion to amend." Such delay justifies denial of leave to amend only when accompanied by unfair prejudice, bad faith, or futility), *with Jennings v. BIC Corp.* 181 F.3d 1250, 1258 (11th Cir.1999) ("The U.S. Supreme Court has held that undue delay is an adequate basis for denying leave to amend.").

31. *See, e.g., Popp Telcom, Inc. v. American Sharecom, Inc.,* 210 F.3d 928, 943 (8th Cir.2000) ("The inclusion of a claim based on facts already known or available to both sides does not prejudice the non-moving party."); *Busam Motor Sales v. Ford Motor Co.,* 203 F.2d 469, 472 (6th Cir.1953)(Rule 15 amendment is not barred simply because it raises new issue of law).

32. *Zenith Radio Corp. v. Hazeltine Research, Inc.,* 401 U.S. 321, 91 S.Ct. 795, 28 L.Ed.2d 77 (1971). *See also, Wade v. Knoxville Utilities Board,* 259 F.3d 452, 459 (6th Cir.2001) ("When amendment is sought at a late stage in the litigation, there is an increased burden to show justification for failing to move earlier."); *In re Burlington Coat Factory Securities Litigation,* 114 F.3d 1410, 1434 (3d Cir.1997) (also citing bad faith and "dilatory motive" as grounds for denying leave to amend). *See, e.g., Edwards v. City of Goldsboro,* 178 F.3d 231 (4th Cir.1999) ("Delay alone is an insufficient reason to deny leave to amend. . . . Rather, the delay must be accompanied by prejudice, bad faith, or futility."); *and Harrison*

v. Rubin, 174 F.3d 249 (D.C.Cir.1999) (undue delay where plaintiff sought to change factual allegations is ground for denying leave to amend; but where "amendment would do no more than clarify legal theories or make corrections" undue delay without prejudice to opposing party does not justify denial of leave to amend); *Viernow v. Euripides Development Corp.,* 157 F.3d 785, 799 (10th Cir.1998) (untimeliness alone is insufficient ground to deny leave to amend). *See also California Public Employees' Retirement System v. Chubb Corp.,* 394 F.3d 126 (3d Cir.2004) (failure to follow district court's instructions on meeting heightened pleading requirements of Rule 9 justifies denial of leave to amend). *See generally, Loggerhead Turtle v. County Council of Volusia County, Florida,* 148 F.3d 1231, 1257 (11th Cir.1998) (finding error in denial of leave to amend; "Any amendment to an original pleading necessarily involves some additional expense to the opposing party.").

33. *See, e.g., Hayes v. Whitman,* 264 F.3d 1017, 1027 (10th Cir.2001) (rejecting proposed amendment that attempted to "salvage a lost case by untimely suggestion of new theories of recovery"); *Viernow v. Euripides Development Corp.,* 157 F.3d 785, 800 (10th Cir.1998) (rejecting dubious effort to employ complaint as "moving target"); *Pallottino v. City of Rio Rancho,* 31 F.3d 1023, 1027 (10th Cir.1994) (rejecting offers of "theories seriatim" to try to fend off dismissal).

34. *Foman v. Davis,* 371 U.S. 178, 182, 83 S.Ct. 227, 230, 9 L.Ed.2d 222 (1962). *Cf., HDM Flugservice GmbH v. Parker Hannifin Co.,* 332 F.3d 1025 (6th Cir.2003) (abuse of discretion to fail to state basis for denial of leave to amend or to fail to consider competing interests of parties and likeli-

Futile Amendments

Amended pleadings that would clearly not prevail or improve the position of a party will be rejected.[35] For example, if the proposed amendment would not survive a motion to dismiss, it will be rejected.[36]

Imposition of Costs

Rule 15 does not address issues of costs arising from amended pleadings. However, it appears settled that, as a condition of granting leave to amend, a court may require an amending party to pay the opponent's costs caused by the amendment.[37]

Effect of Amendment

If an amendment is appropriate under Rule 15(a), it displaces the earlier pleading to which it is directed.[38] If a party filing an amendment wishes to preserve some portions of the original pleading, the party should incorporate those portions by specific reference in the amended pleading.

hood of prejudice to opponent); *Grayson v. Mayview State Hospital,* 293 F.3d 103 (3d Cir.2002) (moreover, when plaintiff does not seek leave to amend deficient complaint after defendant has moved to dismiss, court must inform plaintiff of leave to amend and provide time to do so; however, court has no such duty if amendment would be futile or inequitable).

35. *Foman v. Davis,* 371 U.S. 178, 83 S.Ct. 227, 9 L.Ed.2d 222 (1962); *Jefferson County School District No. R–1 v. Moody's Investor's Services, Inc.,* 175 F.3d 848 (10th Cir.1999) ("[T]he district court may deny leave to amend where amendment would be futile."); *Wisdom v. First Midwest Bank of Poplar Bluff,* 167 F.3d 402, 409 (8th Cir. 1999) ("[P]arties should not be allowed to amend their complaint without showing how the complaint could be amended to save the meritless claim."). *But see, Van Le v. Five Fathoms, Inc.,* 792 F.Supp. 372 (D.N.J.1992)(opponent of proposed amendment carries burden of clearly establishing futility).

36. *See, e.g., Rodriguez v. United States,* 286 F.3d 972, 980 (7th Cir.2002) ("A district court may properly deny a motion to amend as futile if the proposed amendment would be barred by the statute of limitations."); *Rose v. Hartford Underwriters Insurance Co.,* 203 F.3d 417, 420 (6th Cir. 2000) (proposed amendment is futile if it cannot withstand motion to dismiss under Rule 12(b)(6)); *Newland v. Dalton,* 81 F.3d 904, 907 (9th Cir.1996)("[D]istrict courts need not accommodate futile amendments."); *Bailey v. Sullivan,* 885 F.2d 52, 59 (3d Cir.1989)("No purpose would be served by allowing [an] amendment to the complaint to add a challenge which would be dismissed."). *Cf., Kropelnicki v. Siegel,* 290 F.3d 118, 130 (2d Cir.2002) (proper denial of leave to amend where proposed complaint added no new facts or allegations that would alter district court's earlier conclusion that plaintiff lacked standing to sue); *Roskam Baking Co., Inc. v. Lanham Machinery Co.,* 288 F.3d 895, 906 (6th Cir. 2002) (proper denial of leave to amend if party fails to provide court with substance of proposed amendment so that court could evaluate it); *Diesel "Repower," Inc. v. Islander Investments, Ltd.,* 271 F.3d 1318, 1322 (11th Cir.2001) (if amendment is futile, it is irrelevant that movant sought to amend in a timely manner and opposing party suffered no prejudice). *But cf., Wight v. Bankamerica Corp.,* 219 F.3d 79 (2d Cir. 2000) (amended fraud complaint not futile where plaintiff could plead circumstances of fraud with particularity; intent of defendant need be stated only generally).

37. *See, e.g., General Signal Corp. v. MCI Telecommunications Corp.,* 66 F.3d 1500, 1514 (9th Cir.1995) (so noting, and citing other authority).

38. *See, e.g., In re Wireless Telephone Federal Cost Recovery Fees Litigation,* 396 F.3d 922, 928 (8th Cir.2005) ("It is well-established that an amended complaint supercedes an original complaint and renders the original complaint without legal effect."); *King v. Dogan,* 31 F.3d 344, 346 (5th Cir.1994) (same, "unless the amended complaint specifically refers to and adopts or incorporates by reference the earlier pleading").

Responding to Amended Pleadings

Rule 15(a) provides that if the pleading amended is one to which a responsive pleading is appropriate, the opposing party will have either the time remaining before a response to the unamended version was due, or ten days—whichever is longer—in which to respond. However, the court has authority to alter those time limits as may be appropriate in the circumstances of the case.[39]

Relationship to Rule 15(b)

Technically, a motion for leave of court to amend a pleading may be made at any time under Rule 15(a). However, if a suit has advanced to trial or post-trial motions, Rule 15(b), pertaining to amendments to conform to the evidence, is probably a more appropriate vehicle for amendments to pleadings. However, the difference between Rule 15(a) and (b) is not a bright line, and generally courts are liberal in granting permission for substantive amendments under either provision provided that no unfair prejudice thereby accrues to other parties.[40]

RULE 15(b). AMENDMENTS DURING AND AFTER TRIAL

CORE CONCEPT

Rule 15(b) permits amendments to pleadings in two circumstances. The first situation arises when an issue not raised in the original pleadings is tried[41] by consent of the parties. The second occurs when an issue not raised in the pleadings is objected to, but the proposed amendment will either not create unfair prejudice, or such prejudice as may result can be cured by other judicial action.

APPLICATIONS

2007 Amendments

The 2007 Style Project amended Rule 15(b) by subdividing it into three subparts, each with its own subtitle. This change should not present great difficulty for attorneys.

Timing; Relationship to Rule 15(a)

Motions to amend under Rule 15(b) may theoretically be made at any time. The language of the Rule, however, speaks to matters raised at trial, suggesting that the Rule should not generally be used

---

39. *See also California Public Employees' Retirement System v. Chubb Corp.,* 394 F.3d 126 (3d Cir.2004) (failure to follow district court's instructions on meeting heightened pleading requirements of Rule 9 justifies denial of leave to amend).

40. *Compare Bank v. Pitt,* 928 F.2d 1108 (11th Cir.1991)(applying Rule 15(a) standards to amending dismissed complaint) *with United States for Use and Benefit of Seminole Sheet Metal Co. v. SCI, Inc.,*

828 F.2d 671 (11th Cir.1987)(applying Rule 15(b) standards to amending dismissed complaint).

41. *Cf., Marsh v. Butler County, Alabama,* 268 F.3d 1014, 1024 n. 4 (11th Cir. 2001) (although Rule 15(b) discusses cases that have been "tried" by consent, "we accept Rule 15(b) as a guide–by way of analogy, at the appellate level–for cases never tried, but litigated on motions").

at early stages of litigation.[42]   Instead, early in the litigation it is more appropriate to seek to amend a pleading under the authority of Rule 15(a). Generally speaking, motions to amend under Rule 15(b) are made at trial or in the immediate aftermath of a trial.[43]

Relationship to Rule 15(c)

If a new claim is asserted through a pleading amended pursuant to Rule 15(b), there may still be questions about the timeliness of the claim. While Rule 15(b) may permit the amended pleading, Rule 15(c) controls whether the amended pleading is deemed to have been filed on the date of the original pleading or the date of the amendment. The distinction is significant when questions of statutes of limitations are raised.

Claims for Relief

Rule 15(b) may be employed to assert claims for affirmative relief, even after a trial is ended. Thus, for example, a counterclaim may be asserted through a Rule 15(b) amendment where the evidence on the counterclaim was heard at trial.[44]

Failure to Object

Rule 15(b) provides that an opposing party's consent to an amendment may be express or implied.[45] Thus, the court may find that parties who fail to object to the litigation of matters not within the four corners of the original pleadings have impliedly consented to adjudication of those matters.[46] In those circumstances, the court

42. *See, e.g., Gold v. Local 7 United Food and Commercial Workers Union,* 159 F.3d 1307, 1309 n. 3 (10th Cir.1998) ("Rule 15(b) seems a totally inappropriate vehicle for a motion to amend prior to trial."). *But see Ahmad v. Furlong,* 435 F.3d 1196, 1203 n. 1 (10th Cir.2006) (noting extensive split of authority as to whether Rule 15(b) should be applied to issues raised in a motion for summary judgment on the eve of trial; collecting cites).

43. *See, e.g., Triple Five of Minnesota, Inc. v. Simon,* 404 F.3d 1088, 1095 (8th Cir.2005) (Rule 15(b) "motion may be made at any time, even after judgment.").

44. *See, e.g., In re Meyertech Corp.,* 831 F.2d 410, 421 (3d Cir.1987)(approving use of Rule 15(b) to raise a counterclaim).

45. *See, e.g., United States ex rel. Modern Electric, Inc. v. Ideal Electronic Security Co.,* 81 F.3d 240 (D.C.Cir.1996)(noting that express or implied consent is "a condition for treating unpled issues as though they were raised in the pleadings"); *Rodriguez v. Doral Mortgage Corp.,* 57 F.3d 1168, 1172 (1st Cir.1995) (implied consent may be found where claim not mentioned in complaint is addressed "by means of a sufficiently pointed interrogatory answer or in a

pretrial memorandum" to which opponent responds by engaging claim or by " 'silent acquiescence;' " alternatively, " 'consent to the trial of an issue may be implied if, during the trial, a party acquiesces in the introduction of evidence which is relevant only to that issue' "). *But see Koch v. Koch Industries, Inc.,* 203 F.3d 1202, 1217 (10th Cir.2000)) (no implied consent to new issue where testimony was relevant to issues already at trial.

46. *See, e.g., Eich v. Board of Regents for Central Missouri State University,* 350 F.3d 752, 762 (8th Cir.2003) (failure to object to jury instructions on economic damages means issue was tried by consent). *But see Sasse v. United States Department of Labor,* 409 F.3d 773, 781 (6th Cir.2005) (no implied consent if issue was tried inadvertently; evidence going to both pleaded issue and unpleaded issue is not notice of new unpleaded issue's presence in case; *Moncrief v. Williston Basin Interstate Pipeline Co.,* 174 F.3d 1150, 1162 (10th Cir.1999) ("Implied consent cannot be based upon the introduction of evidence that is relevant to an issue already in the case when there is no indication that the party presenting the case when there is no indication that the

will permit an amended pleading that reflects the issues actually litigated.

Failure to File an Amended Pleading; Motions to Amend

Rule 15(b) expressly provides that if parties are found to have consented to litigation of issues outside the original pleadings, there is no requirement that a formal amended pleading be filed. Instead, the result in the case will stand, irrespective of the presence or absence of amendments.[47]

However, if an opposing party makes a proper objection to evidence going to a new claim, the party seeking relief under Rule 15(b) must make an appropriate motion to amend.[48]

Amendments Over Objections to Evidence

If a party objects to the use of evidence on the ground that it does not address issues raised in the original pleadings, Rule 15(b) authorizes the court to allow amendments that encompass such evidence.[49] Such amendments may be permitted on either of two grounds: the absence of unfair prejudice to the objecting party,[50] or the ability of the court to cure such prejudice.[51]

---

party presenting the evidence intended to raise a new issue."); *Kenda Corp. v. Pot O' Gold Money Leagues, Inc.,* 329 F.3d 216, 232 (1st Cir.2003) (evidence directly relevant to pleaded issue cannot be used to imply consent to litigation of non-pleaded issue); *Kovacevich v. Kent State University,* 224 F.3d 806, 831 (6th Cir.2000) (" 'Implied consent' " requires considerable litigation of a matter—" 'it must appear that the parties understood the evidence to be aimed at the unpleaded issue.' "); *Moody v. FMC Corp.,* 995 F.2d 63, 66 (5th Cir.1993)(if evidence in support of amended pleading is also relevant to issues already pleaded in the case, opposing party could not reasonably have notice of new issue, and therefore could not have consented to amended pleading). *But cf., IES Industries, Inc. v. United States,* 349 F.3d 574, 579 (8th Cir.2003) ("It is axiomatic that evidence bearing on both claims and the defenses to those claims may well overlap in a given case. Such an inevitability does not foreclose amendment under Rule 15(b).").

47. *See, e.g., People for the Ethical Treatment of Animals v. Doughney,* 263 F.3d 359, 367 (4th Cir.2001) ("Even without a formal amendment, 'a district court may amend the pleadings merely by entering findings on the unpleaded issues.' "); *Southwestern Stationery and Bank Supply, Inc. v. Harris Corp.,* 624 F.2d 168, 171 (10th Cir.1980) ("When evidence is not objected to, a formal amendment to the pleadings is normally not necessary."). *See also, Creative Demos, Inc. v. Wal–Mart Stores,*

Inc., 142 F.3d 367, 371–72 (7th Cir.1998) (approving district court's amendment to conform to "what the parties were arguing about at trial, although they did not use the magic words"). *But see United States v. Davis,* 261 F.3d 1, 59 (1st Cir.2001) ("Where the party seeking amendment of the pleadings has shown no justification for its delay in doing so, we have affirmed the trial court's ruling to deny the amendment.").

48. *See, e.g., Green Country Food Market, Inc. v. Bottling Group, L.L.C.,* 371 F.3d 1275 , 1281 (10th Cir.2004) (where proper objection was made but advocate of amendment made no motion, "the lack of prejudice to a party does not provide a basis for amendment.").

49. *Cf., Moncrief v. Williston Basin Interstate Pipeline Co.,* 174 F.3d 1150 (10th Cir.1999) (after objection has been made and ruled on, party seeking amendment under Rule 15(b) must make motion to amend; court cannot make amendment *sua sponte*).

50. *See, e.g., New York State Electric & Gas Corp. v. Secretary of Labor,* 88 F.3d 98 (2d Cir.1996)("In assessing whether the pleadings should conform to the proof, the pivotal question is whether prejudice would result.").

51. *See, e.g., Green Country Food Market, Inc. v. Bottling Group, L.L.C.,* 371 F.3d 1275, 1280 (10th Cir.2004) ("The court may

Grounds for Denying Rule 15(b) Amendments

Courts deny Rule 15(b) amendments on any of four grounds: bad faith; undue delay; unfair prejudice to an opponent; or futility of a proposed amendment.[52]

Unfair Prejudice

Determinations of unfair prejudice are highly fact specific. The most likely circumstance in which such prejudice will be found occurs when the objecting party is surprised by the evidence and has no reasonable opportunity to meet it.[53]

Curing Unfair Prejudice

If the source of unfair prejudice is surprise, courts may attempt to cure the problem by using their authority under Rule 15(b) to grant a continuance, so that the objecting party can prepare for the new evidence.[54] Such an order may include re-opening opportunities for discovery.

Resisting Rule 15(b) Motions to Amend

An attorney seeking to resist introduction of new issues at trial that are outside the original pleadings is substantially handicapped by the liberal approach of Rule 15(b) to intra-trial and post-trial amendments. If no challenge to the new issues is made, the attorney will often be deemed to have consented to the insertion of the new issues at trial.[55] If an objection is made, the attorney may

grant a continuance to enable the objecting party to meet such evidence.").

52. *See, e.g., FilmTec Corp. v. Hydranautics,* 67 F.3d 931, 935 (Fed.Cir.1995), *cert. denied,* 519 U.S. 814, 117 S.Ct. 62, 136 L.Ed.2d 24 (1996)(listing grounds). *But cf., Kenda Corp. v. Pot O' Gold Money Leagues, Inc.,* 329 F.3d 216, 232 (1st Cir.2003) (absence of prejudice to nonmoving party is not always dispositive of issue; court may consider other factors and still deny motion to amend; failure to explain lengthy delay in making motion to amend can be fatal to proposed amendment).

53. *See, e.g., Walton v. Nalco Chemical Co.,* 272 F.3d 13, 20 (1st Cir.2001) (implied consent found only if there is acquiescence to introduction of evidence relevant only to proposed new issue; if evidence also addresses existing issues, there is no implied consent); *Deere & Co. v. Johnson,* 271 F.3d 613, 622 (5th Cir.2001) (same reasoning; also noting that jury's verdict form never mentioned new theory, which is something to which advocate of new theory would have objected if it believed both parties had implicitly accepted new theory); *Gussack Realty Co. v. Xerox Corp.,* 224 F.3d 85, 94 (2d Cir.2000) ("Generally, introducing new claims for liability on the last day of the

trial will prejudice the defendant;" prejudice found where plaintiffs moved to amend pleadings at close of their evidence after district court dismissed their nuisance claim); *United States v. Banks,* 115 F.3d 916, 918 (11th Cir.) (unfair prejudice can be lack of notice to opposing party or some other denial of a fair opportunity to defend). *But see IES Industries, Inc. v. United States,* 349 F.3d 574, 579 (8th Cir.2003) (rejecting view that overlap of evidence vitiates consent; "It is axiomatic that evidence bearing on both claims and the defenses to those claims may well overlap in a given case.").

54. *See, e.g., Menendez v. Perishable Distributors, Inc.,* 763 F.2d 1374, 1379 (11th Cir.1985)(approving amendment, but noting need to give opponent opportunity to collect evidence). *But cf., Kenda Corp. v. Pot O' Gold Money Leagues, Inc.,* 329 F.3d 216, 232 (1st Cir.2003) (absence of prejudice to nonmoving party is not always dispositive of issue; court may consider other factors and still deny motion to amend; failure to explain lengthy delay in making motion to amend can be fatal to proposed amendment).

55. *See, e.g., Winger v. Winger,* 82 F.3d 140 (7th Cir.1996)(failure to object, along

be granted only the limited relief of a continuance. It is an unusual circumstance when claims, issues, or evidence relevant to a case is precluded from the trial entirely because its admission, through an amended pleading, creates incurable, unfair prejudice.[56] Such cases occur most commonly where a party seeks to amend after judgment has been entered.[57]

Relation to Rule 16

Rule 16 governs pre-trial conferences, including, *inter alia,* determination of issues that will be omitted from the trial. However, if an issue omitted under Rule 16 is actually tried, and if the issue arose with the express or implied consent of the parties pursuant to Rule 15(b), then the issue is properly before the court. In other words, in that circumstance Rule 15(b) governs.[58]

Relation to Rule 56

Rule 15(b) questions usually arise in situations where a case has gone to trial and a dispute has arisen as to whether an issue or claim has been "tried by express or implied consent." Whether the principles underlying Rule 15(b) apply to cases decided on summary judgment, pursuant to Rule 56, appears to be an open question. Attorneys are advised to consult local precedent.[59]

with other factors, "demonstrates that the issue was tried by implied consent"); *Kirkland v. District of Columbia,* 70 F.3d 629, 633 (D.C.Cir.1995)("Trial of the issue without objection normally is enough to satisfy the Rule 15(b) requirement."). *Cf., Ale v. Tennessee Valley Authority,* 269 F.3d 680, 693 (6th Cir.2001) (acknowledging that opponent may not have impliedly consented to litigate new issue during liability phase of trial; holding nevertheless that no prejudice arose from amended complaint because court told opposing party it "would have ample opportunity to respond to this issue during the damages phase of the trial"); *Estate of Dietrich v. Burrows,* 167 F.3d 1007, 1013 (6th Cir.1999) (amended complaint never filed with court but nevertheless accepted because, *inter alia,* defendants "treated the amendment as filed by specifically asking the district court to grant ... summary judgment on the [amended] claim").

56. *But see Pinkley, Inc. v. City of Frederick, Maryland,* 191 F.3d 394, 401 (4th Cir.1999)(amendment improper under rule 15(b) "where the defendant never conceded implicitly or explicitly that a conversion claim was at issue").

57. *See, e.g., DCPB, Inc. v. City of Lebanon,* 957 F.2d 913, 917–18 (1st Cir. 1992)(where plaintiff, without good cause, did not raise claim until after judgment,

court should deny "injection of new and different theory of liability at the very stroke of midnight"); *but cf., Pulla v. Amoco Oil Co.,* 72 F.3d 648, 658 (8th Cir. 1995)(where evidence on new claim also related to original claim, amendment can be denied because defendant lacked notice).

58. *See, e.g., Clark v. Martinez,* 295 F.3d 809 (8th Cir.2002) ("[W]hen an issue is tried by consent [pursuant to Rule 15(b), discussed infra], it becomes of little moment whether it was encompassed in the pretrial order."); *Kirkland v. District of Columbia,* 70 F.3d 629, 633–34 (D.C.Cir.1995)(noting that if Rule 16 controlled, amendment by implied consent under Rule 15(b) would be "dead letter").

59. *See, e.g., Independent Petroleum Association of America v. Babbit,* 235 F.3d 588, 596 (D.C.Cir.2001) ("It is an open question whether the Federal Rules permit parties to impliedly consent to 'try' issues not raised in their pleadings through summary judgment motions;" citing cases). *See also Eddy v. Virgin Islands Water and Power Authority,* 256 F.3d 204, 209 (3d Cir. 2001) (suggesting disapproval of raising affirmative defense for first time in motion for summary judgment, but permitting such amendment if opponent is not prejudiced); *Whitaker v. T.J. Snow Co.,* 151 F.3d 661, 663 (7th Cir.1998) ("Because both parties squarely addressed the strict liability theory

RULE 15(c).   RELATION BACK OF AMENDMENTS

CORE CONCEPT

Assuming that an amended pleading will be permitted under the standards of either Rule 15(a) or (b), Rule 15(c) governs the circumstances in which the amendment will be treated as though it was filed on the date of the original pleading.   This determination is highly relevant to the applicability of statutes of limitations to claims raised or parties joined in amended pleadings.

NOTE: Rule 15(c) was changed in December 1991, making many previous decisions unreliable precedent.   In particular, new Rule 15(c) is an express rejection of *Schiavone v. Fortune,* 477 U.S. 21, 106 S.Ct. 2379, 91 L.Ed.2d 18 (1986).

APPLICATIONS

2007 Amendments

The 2007 Style Project amended Rule 15(c) by consolidating two existing subparts into three subparts. This change should not present great difficulty for attorneys.

Prerequisite of Right to Amend

Rule 15(c) deals only with whether an amendment will be treated as though it was filed at an earlier date rather than the actual date of filing—whether the amendment, in the words of Rule 15(c), ''relates back'' to the date the original pleading was filed. Before such relation back is contemplated, however, the proponent of the amended pleading must first persuade the court that an amended pleading should be permitted at all.[60]   The standards governing authority to file an amended pleading are discussed in Rule 15(a) and (b).[61]

Right to Amend Not Restricted to "Pleadings"

Although Rule 15(c) itself refers only to amendments of pleadings, it is also appropriately applied to amendments of some other documents filed in district court.[62]

Relation Back Permitted

Rule 15(c) permits an amended pleading to relate back to the date of the original pleading in any of three circumstances: (1) when

in their summary judgment briefs, the complaint was constructively amended to include that claim.'').

60.   *Cf., Williams v. Lampe,* 399 F.3d 867 (7th Cir.2005) (''In order to benefit from [Rule 15(c)'s] 'relation back' doctrine, the original complaint must have been timely filed.'').

61.   *See, e.g., Ellzey v. United States,* 324 F.3d 521, 527 (7th Cir.2003) (before relation back occurs, proposed ''amendment still must be appropriate under the criteria of Rule 15(a)''); *Caban–Wheeler v. Elsea,* 71

F.3d 837, 841 (11th Cir.1996)(noting difference in standards between permission to amend complaint and whether amended claim should relate back to original complaint). *See also Henderson v. Bolanda,* 253 F.3d 928 (7th Cir.2001) (''[I]n order to benefit from Rule 15(c)'s relation back doctrine, the original complaint must have been timely filed.'').

62.   *Scarborough v. Principi,* 541 U.S. 401, 416–18, 124 S.Ct. 1856, 1867–68, 158 L.Ed.2d 674 (2004) (applying Rule 15(c) to application for award of attorney fees; noting previous decisions to apply Rule 15 to

the statute of limitations governing the cause of action permits relation back; (2) when the claim or defense in the amended pleading arose from the same transaction or occurrence as that set forth in the original pleading; or (3) when a new party is joined and it is not unfair, as defined in Rule 15(c), for the claim against that party to be treated as if it was raised on the date the original pleading was filed. Each of these circumstances is discussed in greater detail below.

Statutes of Limitations

Rule 15(c)(1)(A) provides that if the statute of limitations governing a particular cause of action permits relation back of amended pleadings, relation back is permitted. The purpose of Rule 15(c)(1)(A) is to ensure that the Rule is not used to contravene statutes of limitations specifically permitting relation back, if a statute is more generous to the amended pleading. Rule 15(c)(1)(A) defers to a statute of limitations only if the statute is more generous on relation back. By its own terms, Rule 15(c)(1)(A) does not apply if the statute is more restrictive. In that circumstance the provisions of Rule 15(c)(1)(B) or (C) would determine whether an amended pleading would relate back.

Same Transaction or Occurrence

Rule 15(c)(1)(B) permits an amended pleading to relate back if the amended claim or defense arose out of the same transaction or occurrence as the original pleading.[63] The standard of "same transaction or occurrence" has heretofore varied substantially within the circuits, with the broadest description encompassing all events that bear a logical relationship to the original transaction.[64] Other courts have looked to the degree of overlap of evidence between the occurrences raised in the amended pleading and the original pleading.[65] However, the Supreme Court recently held that the somewhat

---

notice of appeal and EEOC discrimination charge).

63. *But cf., Slayton v. American Express Co.,* 460 F.3d 215, 227 (2d Cir. 2006) (no exercise of discretion when application of only Rule 15(c)(1)(B) is at issue; instead, if requirements of Rule 15(c)(2) are met, proposed amendments relate back; however, questions may remain under Rule 15(a), which would require use of judicial discretion). *See also Rasberry v. Garcia,* 448 F.3d 1150 (9th Cir.2006) (Rule 15(c)(1)(B) applies to habeas petitions; however, if original petition is dismissed, second petition cannot relate back to first).

64. *See, e.g., Wilson v. Fairchild Republic Co.,* 143 F.3d 733, 738 (2d Cir.1998) ("The pertinent inquiry ... is whether the original complaint gave the defendant fair notice of the newly alleged claims."); *Alpern v. UtiliCorp United, Inc.,* 84 F.3d 1525,

1543 (8th Cir.1996)("The basic inquiry is whether the amended complaint is related to the general fact situation alleged in the original pleading."). *See generally, Miller v. American Heavy Lift Shipping,* 231 F.3d 242, 249–50 (6th Cir.2000) (injury claims amended to include exposure to benzene in addition to original claim of exposure to asbestos arises from same transaction or occurrence where other allegations of employment and negligence remained unchanged); *Stevelman v. Alias Research, Inc.,* 174 F.3d 79 (2d Cir.1999) (new allegations added specificity but did not add new counts; held, "same transaction" requirement clearly satisfied; "Where no new cause of action is alleged, as here, this Court liberally grants relation back under Rule 15(c).").

65. *See, e.g., Martell v. Trilogy Limited,* 872 F.2d 322, 325 (9th Cir.1989)(noting more restrictive construction of the "same transaction or occurrence" standard previously applied by a majority of the circuit courts is now the applicable law.[66] Thus, the broadest description appears to be available no longer.

It should be noted that this standard is measured by the facts pleaded. It does not depend on the legal theory offered. Thus, an amendment may relate back notwithstanding that the proffered amendment offers a new legal theory.[67]

Amendments That Add a Party or Change a Party's Name

To obtain the benefits of relation back when a new party is named[68] or a party's name is changed, the amended pleading must satisfy the elements of Rule 15(c)(1)(C): (1) it must arise from the same transaction or occurrence as the original pleading, as provided by Rule 15(c)(1)(B); and (2) within the 120–day period after filing of the original pleading that Rule 4(m) provides for service of process, the party named in the amended pleading must have both received sufficient notice of the pendency of the action so as not to be prejudiced in preparing a defense, and have known or should have known that but for a mistake of identity the party would have been named in the original pleading. The first element—same transaction or occurrence—follows the discussion of Rule 15(c)(1)(B), above. The other element has two parts—fair notice and awareness of a mistake in identity—that are explained immediately below. In addition to the requirement of same transaction or occurrence, *both* fair notice and awareness of a mistake concerning identity, must be satisfied before an amended pleading may relate back under Rule 15(c)(1)(C).

(1) *Notice:* The kind of notice Rule 15(c)(1)(C) requires is that which, in the particular circumstances of a case, ensures that the party joined is not unfairly prejudiced by an amended pleading that relates back to an earlier date.[69] If a party to be joined in an

that original and amended pleadings share "a common nucleus of operative facts"). *But see Massachusetts Bay Transportation Authority v. United States,* 254 F.3d 1367, 1380 (Fed.Cir.2001) (original complaint for damage to property did not include allegation of damage to terazzo floor; thus clam for damage to terrazo floor did not arise from same occurrence as required by Rule 15(c)(1)(B); apparent dicta, however, because statute of limitations had not yet run and requirements of Rule 15(c)(1)(B) were therefore irrelevant).

66. *Mayle v. Felix,* ___ U.S. ___, 125 S.Ct. 2562, 2569–75, 162 L.Ed.2d 582 (2005).

67. *See, e.g., Maegdlin v. International Association of Machinists and Aerospace Workers,* 309 F.3d 1051, 1053 (8th Cir. 2002). *Cf., Johnson v. Crown Enterprises,*

Inc., 398 F.3d 339, 342 (5th Cir.2005) (focus is not on caption of count, but underlying facts).

68. *See, e.g., Gallas v. Supreme Court of Pennsylvania,* 211 F.3d 760, 777 (3d Cir. 2000) (replacing "John Doe" with real name of party changes a party within meaning of Rule 15(c)(3)). *See also Moore v. City of Harriman,* 272 F.3d 769, 774 (6th Cir.2001) (applying Rule 15(c)(1)(C), rather than Rule 15(c)(1)(B) to permit plaintiff to amend complaint to clarify that same defendants were being sued in their personal capacities).

69. *See, e.g., Garvin v. City of Philadelphia,* 354 F.3d 215, 222 (3d Cir.2003) (prejudice is that which might be caused, for lack of notice, by difficulty in gathering evidence and preparing defense in case that became stale).

amended complaint learned of a suit within the 120–day period provided by Rule 4(m) for service of the original complaint, and that party's opportunity to prepare a defense was not hindered by the time lag between the original pleading and the amended pleading, Rule 15(c)(1)(C)'s requirement of notice generally would be satisfied.[70] For example, corporations in a parent-subsidiary relationship with an entity sued in the original complaint would probably be held to have notice of the original action.[71] Similarly, if the proposed change merely corrects a "misnomer," the complaint may relate back.[72] However, where the original complaint cited only aliases of police officer defendants and not their actual names, the issue of notice is a more serious problem.[73] Finally, a person who had not been named as a defendant in the original complaint, but who was impleaded under Rule 14 by the original defendant, would probably be held to have had fair notice under Rule 15(c)(1)(C), if the impleader was served on that person within the 120–day period provided by Rule 4(m).

(2) *Knowledge of Mistaken Identity*: Before an amended pleading may relate back under Rule 15(c)(1)(C), the proponent of the pleading must also establish that within the 120–day period provided by Rule 4(m) the person to be joined knew, or should have known, that the person would have been sued under the original pleading but for some mistake in identity. Thus, if a subsidiary corporation was sued when the claim should have been against its parent, and was served within the period provided by Rule 4(m), the parent might be charged with timely knowledge of the fact that the proper defendant should have been the parent.[74] With natural

70. *See, e.g., Singletary v. Pennsylvania Department of Corrections,* 266 F.3d 186, 189 (3d Cir.2001) (in absence of actual notice to potential new party, identifying two means of imputing notice received by original defendants to party sought to be added: (1) through sharing same attorney; or (2) identity of interest between original parties and party sought to be added). *Cf., e.g., Atchinson v. District of Columbia,* 73 F.3d 418, 427 (D.C.Cir.1996)(noting, *inter alia,* prejudice because individual defendant would probably have adopted different discovery and defense tactics if he had received adequate notice of claim of his individual liability).

71. *See, e.g., Andrews v. Lakeshore Rehabilitation Hospital,* 140 F.3d 1405, 1408 n. 5 (11th Cir.1998) (if subsidiary had notice of suit, parent holding 100% of subsidiary "is deemed to have had notice"); *G.F. Co. v. Pan Ocean Shipping Co.,* 23 F.3d 1498, 1503 (9th Cir.1994)(original defendant was claims agent for new party and both parties shared the same attorney; held, good notice to new party).

72. *See, e.g., Datskow v. Teledyne, Inc.,* 899 F.2d 1298, 1301–02 (2d Cir.1990) (complaint properly served, but correct name of defendant was "Teledyne Industries, Inc.;" held, defendant had adequate notice of suit and thus "case may be categorized as one of mislabeling").

73. *See, e.g., Eison v. McCoy,* 146 F.3d 468 (7th Cir.1998) (complaint's listing of "T.C., Cronie, Pac Man, and Crater Face" does not provide notice where police department has more than 17,000 employees). *But cf., Moore v. City of Harriman,* 272 F.3d 769, 774 (6th Cir.2001) (police officers sued on state tort claims as well as federal civil rights claims have "clear notice" from state claims and federal claim under 42 U.S.C.A. § 1983 that "they faced individual liability of some sort").

74. *See, e.g., Peterson v. Sealed Air Corp.,* 902 F.2d 1232 (7th Cir.1990)(service was on agent of both parent and subsidiary).

persons, the requirement may be satisfied when the name of the proper defendant is similar to the name of the person originally designated as a defendant, *and* the proper defendant knew of the mistake within the time limit established by Rule 4(m).[75]

Rule 15(c)(3); Requirement of "Mistake"

Relation back under Rule 15(c)(3) is permitted only if the party joined by amendment knew or should have known that it would have been sued originally but for a mistake. It is unclear whether the mistake may be one of either fact or law,[76] but in other respects this requirement has been construed rather strictly. Thus if the party seeking to amend made no mistake, relation back is not permitted under Rule 15(c)(1)(C).[77]

Moreover, addition of a new defendant will generally not relate back if the new defendant is not being substituted for someone who is already a defendant.[78]

75. *See, e.g., Brown v. Shaner,* 172 F.3d 927, 933 (6th Cir.1999) (police officers sued in civil rights case; plaintiff's complaint identified individual wrongful acts but did not state whether defendants were sued in their official capacity or individually; held, failure to identify allegation of individual liability satisfies "mistake" requirement, and defendants should have known that but for mistake they were being sued individually).

76. *Compare, e.g., Woods v. Indiana University—Purdue University at Indianapolis,* 996 F.2d 880, 887 (7th Cir.1993) (indicating that mistake may be of fact or law), *with Rendall–Speranza v. Nassim,* 107 F.3d 913, 918 (D.C.Cir.1997) (amendment permitted, if at all, only for mistake of fact).

77. *See, e.g., Garrett v. Fleming,* 362 F.3d 692 (10th Cir.2004) (lack of knowledge of relationship between entities does not satisfy requirement of error as to identity of proper party); *Worthington v. Wilson,* 8 F.3d 1253, 1256–57 (7th Cir.1993)(lack of knowledge as to joined party's identity does not satisfy "mistake" requirement of Rule 15(c)(3)); *see also, Louisiana–Pacific Corp. v. ASARCO, Inc.,* 5 F.3d 431, 434 (9th Cir.1993)(mistake in choosing who is vulnerable to suit does not meet mistake of identity requirement of Rule 15(c)(1)(C)). *But see, Arthur v. Maersk, Inc.,* 434 F.3d 196, 208 (3d Cir.2006) (rejecting majority view that only a "misnomer or misidentification" may be a Rule 15(c)(3) mistake; "A mistake is no less a 'mistake' when it flows from lack of knowledge as opposed to an inaccurate description."); *G.F. Co. v. Pan Ocean Shipping Co.,* 23 F.3d 1498, 1503 (9th Cir.1994)(held, requirement of mistake satisfied where named defendant is agent of true defendant, and where plaintiff's attorney swears in affidavit that initial failure to sue proper plaintiff was inadvertent); *Brown v. Shaner,* 172 F.3d 927, 933 (6th Cir.1999) (police officers sued in civil rights case; plaintiff's complaint identified individual wrongful acts but did not state whether defendants were sued in their official capacity or individually; held, failure to identify allegation of individual liability satisfies "mistake" requirement). *See also, Alston v. Parker,* 363 F.3d 229, 236 (3d Cir.2004) (considering possibility that civil rights plaintiffs may have unusual problem of not knowing precisely who "relevant actors" were, and should therefore perhaps have access to "some initial discovery"); *Woods v. Indiana University—Purdue University at Indianapolis,* 996 F.2d 880, 887 (7th Cir.1993)(suit originally named police department rather than individual officers; held, police should have known that police department had sovereign immunity, and thus should have known of mistake; relation back permitted). *But cf., King v. One Unknown Federal Correction Officer,* 201 F.3d 910, 914 (7th Cir.2000) ("[T]he mistake requirement is independent from whether the purported substitute party knew that the action would be brought against him.").

78. *See, e.g., Braud v. Transport Service Co. of Illinois,* 445 F.3d 801, 807 (5th Cir. 2006) (distinguishing between misnomer that should be corrected and mere addition of party).

Undue Delay and Relation Back

Under Rule 15(a), a court may sometimes properly deny leave to amend a pleading when a party has delayed excessively and without good cause in seeking leave.[79] However, undue delay plays no role in an evaluation of relation back under Rule 15(a).[80]

Relation to Laches

Laches is a case law doctrine that may be raised by a defendant where the plaintiff unreasonably delays in bringing a lawsuit, and thereby unfairly harms the defendant. Rule 15(c) governs circumstances where application of the Rule might avoid unfairness arising from strict application of a statute of limitations. Because laches applies, if at all, only in the absence of a relevant statute of limitations, Rule 15 "has no controlling force where ... a defendant's remedy is provided by the equitable doctrine of laches." [81]

Rule 17: Amendments Changing or Adding Plaintiffs

Rule 15(c)(1)(C) discusses adding parties who are the subject of claims. Its applicability when the proposed amendment seeks to add a plaintiff is not entirely clear. On the one hand, there is precedent citing language in the Advisory Committee Notes to Rule 15(c) indicating that Rule 15(c) also governs that circumstance.[82] At the same time, Rule 17(a), governing requirements to prosecute a case in the name of the real party in interest, expressly provides that joinder or substitution of the real party in interest automatically relates back to the original filing date, apparently without regard to the requirements of Rule 15. Although the matter is not free of doubt, it appears that in such circumstances Rule 17(a), and not Rule 15, should control.[83]

Commencement and Amended Complaints

Because an amended complaint often cannot be filed until leave of court has first been granted,[84] many courts have ruled that the amended complaint is deemed filed, for "commencement" and stat-

79. *See* Authors' Commentary on Rule 15(a).

80. *See, e.g., Arthur v. Maersk, Inc.*, 434 F.3d 196, 203 (3d Cir.2006) ("There is no allowance in Rule 15(c) for inquiry into a party's delay in moving for leave to amend.").

81. *Brzozowski v. Correctional Physician Services, Inc.*, 360 F.3d 173, 182 (3d Cir.2004).

82. *See, e.g., McCabe v. Trombley*, 867 F.Supp. 120, 127 n. 7 (N.D.N.Y.1994)(citing Advisory Committee notes for application of Rule 15(c) to situations where a party seeks to add a plaintiff). *See also Immigrant Assistance Project of the L.A. County Federation of Labor v. Immigration and Naturalization Service*, 306 F.3d 842, 857 (9th Cir. 2002) (relation back should be measured by

whether: (1) defendant already had notice of claim of new plaintiff; (2) presence of new plaintiff creates unfair prejudice for defendant; and (3) new plaintiff shares identity of interest with original plaintiff); *Young v. LePone*, 305 F.3d 1, 14 (1st Cir. 2002) (Rule 15(c)(1)(C) "can be applied to amendments that change the identity of plaintiffs").

83. *See, e.g., Scheufler v. General Host Corp.*, 126 F.3d 1261, 1271 (10th Cir.1997) (noting uncertainty; applying relation-back provisions of Rule 17(a)). *But cf., Cliff v. Payco General American Credits, Inc.*, 363 F.3d 1113, 1132 (11th Cir.2004) (concluding that use of Rule 15(c)(1)(C) "rests on solid ground;" no discussion of Rule 17).

84. *See* Rule 15.

ute of limitations purposes, as of the date that the motion for leave to amend is filed.[85] Practitioners should rely on this principle with great care, however. Whether this treatment applies to all cases (or just those where an earlier amendment was made impossible by circumstances), whether this treatment applies where the motion neither attaches the proposed amended complaint nor properly describes it, and whether this treatment has any effect where the leave is denied, are each unclear.

Relation Back Against the United States

When the United States is a defendant, Rule 15(c)(3) provides that the requirements of timely notice of the action and knowledge of a mistake in identity, discussed immediately above, are satisfied if the original pleading was served on the United States Attorney (or designee), the Attorney General, or an agency or officer who would have been a proper defendant if named in the original complaint.[86] This express provision cuts through much of what might otherwise have been substantial technical obstacles to use of relation back against the United States under Rule 15(c)(1)(C).[87] However, even when the United States is a defendant, the amended pleading must still arise out of the same transaction or occurrence as the original pleading, and service of the original pleading upon the federal officers identified above must occur within the 120–day period provided by Rule 4(m).

RULE 15(d).   SUPPLEMENTAL PLEADINGS

CORE CONCEPT

Rule 15(d) governs circumstances in which parties are permitted to supplement previous pleadings to encompass events that have occurred since the earlier pleadings were filed.

APPLICATIONS

Leave of Court

There is no unqualified right to file a supplemental pleading.[88] Authority to file a supplemental pleading is obtained by filing a

---

85. *See, e.g., Mayes v. AT & T Information Sys.,* 867 F.2d 1172, 1173 (8th Cir. 1989).

86. *See, e.g., Roman v. Townsend,* 224 F.3d 24, 28 (1st Cir.2000).

87. *See, e.g., Delgado–Brunet v. Clark,* 93 F.3d 339, 344 (7th Cir.1996) (so noting; but also noting that notice to government officers who are sued personally cannot be inferred from service on another government officer).

88. *See, e.g., Zenith Radio Corp. v. Hazeltine Research, Inc.,* 401 U.S. 321, 91 S.Ct. 795, 28 L.Ed.2d 77 (1971). *See, e.g., Weeks v. New York,* 273 F.3d 76, 88 (2d Cir.2001)

(acknowledging that supplemental pleadings that have a relationship with originally pleading are normally freely permitted, but holding that denial of supplemental pleading motion is within district court's discretion—even when opposing counsel does not object—when motion was presented to court on Friday preceding beginning of Monday trial and "the granting of the motion would potentially have entailed an amended pre-trial order, additional documents and additional witnesses (with any associated evidentiary issues), additional briefing, an expanded jury charge, and a longer trial than anticipated"). *Cf., Burns v.*

motion.[89]   Courts grant such leave when the supplemental pleadings will not unfairly prejudice other parties.[90]

Party's Discretion

Supplemental pleadings are optional. Thus, if a party acquires a claim as a result of facts arising after the original pleading was filed, and the requirements of Rule 15(d) are satisfied, there is an opportunity but not a duty to file a supplemental claim.[91]

Same Transaction or Occurrence

If the issues addressed in a proposed supplemental pleading are related to the transaction or occurrence that gave rise to the original pleadings, and no other considerations of fairness weigh against hearing the supplemental pleading, courts generally permit the supplemental pleading.[92]   A supplemental pleading may be permitted even if it arises from a separate transaction, but totally unrelated supplemental pleadings are disfavored.[93]

Relation to Rule 15(a)

Judicial decisions to grant or deny Rule 15(d) motions to supplement pleadings are generally based on the same factors of fairness courts weigh when considering motions to amend pleadings under Rule 15(a).[94]

Time to File

Rule 15(d) contains no restriction on the time in which a supplemental pleading may be filed.   However, the court may con-

Exxon Corp., 158 F.3d 336, 343 (5th Cir. 1998) ("While the text of Rule 15(a) provides that leave should be freely granted, the text of Rule 15(d) does not similarly provide." Also noting that plaintiffs had failed to allege that an event had occurred since filing of complaint).

89.   *See, e.g., Bornholdt v. Brady,* 869 F.2d 57, 68 (2d Cir.1989) (noting that Rule 15(d) requires a motion). *But see Cabrera v. City of Huntington Park,* 159 F.3d 374, 382 (9th Cir.1998) (per curiam) (Plaintiff's "failure formally to plead a malicious prosecution claim either in an amended or supplemental pleading does not preclude the district court from considering the claim.").

90.   *See, e.g., Quaratino v. Tiffany & Co.,* 71 F.3d 58, 66 (2d Cir.1995)("Leave is normally granted, especially when the opposing party is not prejudiced."). *See also Glatt v. Chicago Park District,* 87 F.3d 190, 194 (7th Cir.1996) (motion to amend or supplement original complaint is held to higher standard of specificity than original complaint).

91.   *See, e.g., Lundquist v. Rice Memorial Hospital,* 238 F.3d 975, 977 (8th Cir. 2001) (decision not to file supplemental

claim does not prevent assertion of that claim in later separate proceeding; doctrine of res judicata does not apply).

92.   *See, e.g., Keith v. Volpe,* 858 F.2d 467, 473 (9th Cir.1988). *City of Hawthorne v. Wright,* 493 U.S. 813, 110 S.Ct. 61, 107 L.Ed.2d 28 (1989)(noting that use of Rule 15(d) is "favored"). *See also Weeks v. New York,* 273 F.3d 76, 88 (2d Cir.2001) (although other factors may be crucial, "[t]he threshhold consideration ... is whether 'the supplemental facts connect [the supplemental pleadings] to the original pleadings' ").

93.   *See, e.g., Id.* at 474 (noting that Rule 15(d) does not require "same transaction," but does require "some relationship").

94.   *See, e.g., Klos v. Haskell,* 835 F.Supp. 710, 715 (W.D.N.Y.1993), *affirmed,* 48 F.3d 81 (2d Cir.1995)(Rule 15(a) and (d) share same standard); *See also, Glatt v. Chicago Park District,* 87 F.3d 190 (7th Cir.1996)(under both Rule 15(a) and (d), court has authority to require substantiation of proposed amended or supplemental complaint, to ensure that motive is not simply to harass opponent).

sider inappropriate delay in attempting to assert supplemental claims as grounds for refusing to grant permission to file the supplemental pleading.[95] Additionally, a supplemental pleading is normally inappropriate if it attempts to introduce a new and distinct cause of action after the original case has gone to final judgment.[96]

Scope of Supplemental Pleadings

Supplemental pleadings should be restricted to events occurring since initiation of the suit. If the issues raised predate the original pleadings, supplemental pleadings are not the appropriate mechanism for raising them. Instead, a party should consider amending the original pleadings, pursuant to Rule 15(a) or (b).[97]

Intervening Judicial Decisions

It appears that intervening judicial decisions that change the applicable law are not the sort of "occurrences or events" that might implicate Rule 15(d).[98]

Additional Parties

In general, supplemental pleadings may join additional parties, subject to the normal requirements of jurisdiction. However, where such joinder might confuse the trier of fact or unduly distract attention from the original claims, proposals to add new parties may reduce the prospects for obtaining permission from the court to file a supplemental pleading.[99]

Relationship to Original Pleadings

Unlike amended pleadings, supplemental pleadings do not displace the original pleadings. Thus, there is no necessity to incorporate portions of the original pleadings in a supplemental pleading simply to preserve the original pleadings. However, it may often be convenient to incorporate portions of original pleadings and thereby avoid possible duplication.

95. *See, e.g., Quaratino v. Tiffany & Co.,* 71 F.3d 58, 66 (2d Cir.1995)(undue delay may be ground for denying supplemental pleading).

96. *See, e.g., Planned Parenthood of Southern Arizona v. Neely,* 130 F.3d 400, 402–03 (9th Cir.1997) (per curiam) (final judgment divested district court of jurisdiction; noting possible exception in circumstances where district court retained jurisdiction or where plaintiff's supplemental allegation is that defendant was attempting to thwart original judgment; held, normal remedy after judgment is entered is to bring the "supplemental" allegations in a separate lawsuit).

97. *See, e.g., Flaherty v. Lang,* 199 F.3d 607, 613 n. 3 (2d Cir.1999) (Rule 15(d) applies to events that arise subsequent to a

pleading; Rule 15(a) applies to efforts to replead facts that occurred prior to original pleadings.); *Federal Deposit Insurance Corp. v. Knostman,* 966 F.2d 1133, 1138 (7th Cir. 1992)(identifying distinction between subdivisions of Rule 15).

98. *See, e.g., United States v. Hicks,* 283 F.3d 380, 385 (D.C.Cir.2002) (Rule 15(d) is addressed to relevant new facts, not changes in law).

99. *See, e.g., Albrecht v. Long Island Railroad,* 134 F.R.D. 40, 41 (E.D.N.Y.1991) (rejecting Rule 15(d) motion because new assertions of unrelated claims may confuse trier of fact). *See also, Planned Parenthood of Southern Arizona v. Neely,* 130 F.3d 400, 402 (9th Cir.1997) (supplemental pleading cannot be used to introduce new and distinct claim).

Mislabelled Pleadings

If a party inadvertently mislabels a supplemental pleading as an amended pleading, the court will disregard the error if it does not unfairly prejudice an opposing party.[100]

Defective Original Pleadings

Rule 15(d) explicitly provides that defects in the original pleadings have no effect on a party's ability to file a supplemental pleading. Thus, even an uncorrectable defect in the original pleading, requiring dismissal of the counts that pleading contains, does not necessarily bar filing of a supplemental pleading, if the supplemental pleading itself is free from substantial defects.

Responses to Supplemental Pleadings

Rule 15(d) does not create either a right or duty to respond to a supplemental pleading. Instead, the Rule vests the court with authority to order a response when appropriate in the circumstances of a case. Typically, an opportunity to respond will be permitted when the supplemental pleading asserts a new cause of action.

Relation Back of Supplemental Pleadings

Because supplemental pleadings address only events that have occurred since the original pleadings were filed, no question normally arises as to whether supplemental pleadings relate back to the date the original pleadings were filed. However, where relation back is important to the supplemental pleadings, courts tend to apply the standards of Rule 15(c) to determine whether relation back should be permitted.[101]

ADDITIONAL RESEARCH REFERENCES

Wright & Miller, *Federal Practice and Procedure* §§ 1471–1510.

C.J.S. Federal Civil Procedure §§ 322–356 et seq.

West's Key No. Digests, Federal Civil Procedure ☞821–853, 861–871.

100. *See, e.g., Cabrera v. City of Huntington Park,* 159 F.3d 374, 382 (9th Cir. 1998) (per curiam) (erroneously characterizing supplemental pleading as amended pleading is immaterial).

101. *See, e.g., Federal Deposit Insurance Corp. v. Knostman,* 966 F.2d 1133, 1138 (7th Cir.1992)(using standards of Rule 15(c)).

RULE 16

PRETRIAL CONFERENCES; SCHEDULING; MANAGEMENT

(a) Purposes of a Pretrial Conference. In any action, the court may order the attorneys and any unrepresented parties to appear for one or more pretrial conferences for such purposes as:

(1) expediting disposition of the action;

(2) establishing early and continuing control so that the case will not be protracted because of lack of management;

(3) discouraging wasteful pretrial activities;

(4) improving the quality of the trial through more thorough preparation; and

(5) facilitating settlement.

(b) Scheduling.

(1) *Scheduling Order.* Except in categories of actions exempted by local rule, the district judge—or a magistrate judge when authorized by local rule—must issue a scheduling order:

(A) after receiving the parties' report under Rule 26(f); or

(B) after consulting with the parties' attorneys and any unrepresented parties at a scheduling conference or by telephone, mail, or other means.

(2) *Time to Issue.* The judge must issue the scheduling order as soon as practicable, but in any event within the earlier of 120 days after any defendant has been served with the complaint or 90 days after any defendant has appeared.

(3) *Contents of the Order.*

(A) *Required Contents.* The scheduling order must limit the time to join other parties, amend the pleadings, complete discovery, and file motions.

(B) *Permitted Contents.* The scheduling order may:

(i) modify the timing of disclosures under Rules 26(a) and 26(e)(1);

477

       (ii) modify the extent of discovery;

       (iii) provide for disclosure or discovery of electronically stored information;

       (iv) include any agreements the parties reach for asserting claims of privilege or of protection as trial-preparation material after information is produced;

       (v) set dates for pretrial conferences and for trial; and

       (vi) include other appropriate matters.

  (4) *Modifying a Schedule.* A schedule may be modified only for good cause and with the judge's consent.

(c) Attendance and Matters for Consideration at a Pretrial Conference.

  (1) *Attendance.* A represented party must authorize at least one of its attorneys to make stipulations and admissions about all matters that can reasonably be anticipated for discussion at a pretrial conference. If appropriate, the court may require that a party or its representative be present or reasonably available by other means to consider possible settlement.

  (2) *Matters for Consideration.* At any pretrial conference, the court may consider and take appropriate action on the following matters:

    (A) formulating and simplifying the issues, and eliminating frivolous claims or defenses;

    (B) amending the pleadings if necessary or desirable;

    (C) obtaining admissions and stipulations about facts and documents to avoid unnecessary proof, and ruling in advance on the admissibility of evidence;

    (D) avoiding unnecessary proof and cumulative evidence, and limiting the use of testimony under Federal Rule of Evidence 702;

    (E) determining the appropriateness and timing of summary adjudication under Rule 56;

(F) controlling and scheduling discovery, including orders affecting disclosures and discovery under Rule 26 and Rules 29 through 37;

(G) identifying witnesses and documents, scheduling the filing and exchange of any pretrial briefs, and setting dates for further conferences and for trial;

(H) referring matters to a magistrate judge or a master;

(I) settling the case and using special procedures to assist in resolving the dispute when authorized by statute or local rule;

(J) determining the form and content of the pretrial order;

(K) disposing of pending motions;

(L) adopting special procedures for managing potentially difficult or protracted actions that may involve complex issues, multiple parties, difficult legal questions, or unusual proof problems;

(M) ordering a separate trial under Rule 42(b) of a claim, counterclaim, crossclaim, third-party claim, or particular issue;

(N) ordering the presentation of evidence early in the trial on a manageable issue that might, on the evidence, be the basis for a judgment as a matter of law under Rule 50(a) or a judgment on partial findings under Rule 52(c);

(O) establishing a reasonable limit on the time allowed to present evidence; and

(P) facilitating in other ways the just, speedy, and inexpensive disposition of the action.

(d) Pretrial Orders. After any conference under this rule, the court should issue an order reciting the action taken. This order controls the course of the action unless the court modifies it.

(e) Final Pretrial Conference and Orders. The court may hold a final pretrial conference to formulate a trial plan, including a plan to facilitate the admission of evidence. The conference must be held as close to the start of trial as is reasonable, and must be attended by at least one attorney who will conduct the trial for each party and by any unrepresented party. The court may modify the order issued after a final pretrial conference only to prevent manifest injustice.

(f) Sanctions.

    (1) *In General.* On motion or on its own, the court may issue any just orders, including those authorized by Rule 37(b)(2)(A)(ii)–(vii), if a party or its attorney:

        (A) fails to appear at a scheduling or other pretrial conference;

        (B) is substantially unprepared to participate—or does not participate in good faith—in the conference; or

        (C) fails to obey a scheduling or other pretrial order.

    (2) *Imposing Fees and Costs.* Instead of or in addition to any other sanction, the court must order the party, its attorney, or both to pay the reasonable expenses—including attorney's fees—incurred because of any noncompliance with this rule, unless the noncompliance was substantially justified or other circumstances make an award of expenses unjust.

[Amended April 28, 1983, effective August 1, 1983; March 2, 1987, effective August 1, 1987; April 22, 1993, effective December 1, 1993; April 12, 2006, effective December 1, 2006; April 30, 2007, effective December 1, 2007.]

2007 AMENDMENTS ROADMAP

STYLE PROJECT CHANGES: Minor changes were made in the titles of some subsections. Non-substantive organizational changes were made in subsections (b), (c), and (f). Old subsections (d) and (e) were redesignated. Old subsection (d) is now, with minor language changes, new subsection (e). Similarly, old subsection (e) is now, with minor language changes, new subsection (d). Other minor language changes were made throughout Rule 16.

NON-STYLE CHANGES: None.

NOTE: The Federal Rules "Style Project" is explained in Part III-A.

AUTHORS' COMMENTARY ON RULE 16

——————————— PURPOSE AND SCOPE ———————————

Rule 16 authorizes the district court to convene pretrial conferences with the purpose of processing a case efficiently. While the court has discretion to hold such pretrial conferences, Rule 16 *requires* the court to issue a scheduling order setting procedures for discovery and trial, unless the case falls into a category which the court, by local rule, has exempted from the requirement for a scheduling order. Further, if a pretrial conference is held, Rule 16 also requires the court to issue a pretrial order after such a pretrial conference detailing the action at the conference and establishing the course of action to be followed. The order is binding unless subsequently modified by the court.

RULE 16(a). PRETRIAL CONFERENCES

CORE CONCEPT

Rule 16(a) outlines the parameters and objectives for the court's pretrial conferences with the parties. When preparing for a pretrial conference, the litigants should consult both Rule 16(c) and the local rules concerning the subjects to be discussed at a pretrial conference.

APPLICATIONS

Pretrial Conferences

(1) *Initial or First Conference:* The court may convene the first pretrial conference as soon as all of the parties have been served with the complaint. Typically, the court will delay the pretrial conference until after an answer is filed or preliminary motions to dismiss are resolved. The first pretrial conference permits the parties to familiarize the court with the issues in the case and to propose a discovery schedule. After the conference, the court will issue an order detailing the decisions reached and action taken. Typically, the initial conference will address issues of scope and timing of discovery, filing of parties' pretrial narrative statements, the timing for filing of motions, alternative dispute resolution, and possibly an anticipated date for trial.

(2) *Subsequent and Final Pretrial Conferences:* Ordinarily, the court holds a final pretrial conference after the close of discovery, after ruling on dispositive pretrial motions and after the filing of the pretrial narrative statements.[1] At this conference, the court sets a trial date, seeks to further clarify the issues, discusses any extraneous matters, sets a schedule for any remaining motions, and encourages settlement discussions.

---

1. *But see Mizwicki v. Helwig,* 196 F.3d 828, 833 (7th Cir.1999) (there is no require- ment that the court conduct a final pretrial conference).

(3) *Other Pretrial Conferences:* Local rule may require the court to hold one pretrial conference, but the court may hold as many pretrial conferences as it deems necessary to apprise the court of the progress of the case.

Pretrial Orders

The court is required to issue a pretrial order detailing the action taken at any pretrial conference conducted pursuant to Rule 16, as provided by Rule 16(e).

Who Must Attend

Rule 16(a) authorizes the court to order attorneys and unrepresented parties to attend pretrial conferences,[2] and makes no reference to represented parties. Courts have held that represented parties (in contrast to their attorneys) may also be directed to attend.[3] Additionally, at least one court has held that the judge must also attend, and cannot delegate that function to a law clerk.[4]

Motion for Pretrial Conference

Generally, the court will set the time for pretrial conferences. However, the parties may seek a pretrial conference either by informal request or by motion.[5] The court has discretion to order additional pretrial conferences.

RULE 16(b).   SCHEDULING

CORE CONCEPT

After receiving the discovery report required under Rule 26(f) or after conducting a scheduling conference under Rule 16(a), the court will issue a scheduling order setting timetables for pretrial matters. This scheduling order must be issued within 90 days after the appearance of a defendant and within 120 days of the service of the complaint.[6] The district judge may prepare the scheduling order or may refer this task to a magistrate judge.

APPLICATIONS

Mandatory Topics

Rule 16(b) requires the court's order to include time limits for: joining parties[7] and amending pleadings;[8] filing motions;[9] and completing discovery.[10]

2. *Royal Palace Hotel Associates, Inc. v. International Resort Classics, Inc.*, 178 F.R.D. 595, 597 (M.D.Fla.1998) (local rule requiring attendance of lead trial counsel is enforceable).

3. *See, e.g., In the Matter of Sargeant Farms, Inc.*, 224 B.R. 842, 845 (Bkrtcy. M.D.Fla.1998) (requiring party representative with settlement authority to attend Rule 16 conference); *G. Heileman Brewing Co. v. Joseph Oat Corp.*, 871 F.2d 648, 650–53 (7th Cir.1989)(en banc)("mere absence of language in the federal rules specifically authorizing or describing a particular judicial procedure should not, and does not, give rise to a negative implication of prohibition").

4. *Connolly v. National School Bus Service, Inc.*, 177 F.3d 593 (7th Cir.1999).

5. *See, e.g., DiDomenico v. New York Life Insurance Co.*, 837 F.Supp. 1203, 1206 (M.D.Fla.1993)(motion for a conference under Rule 16(a)).

6. *O'Connell v. Hyatt Hotels of Puerto Rico*, 357 F.3d 152, 154 (1st Cir.2004).

Optional Topics

At the court's discretion, the scheduling order may also include: modifications of time limits for disclosures under Rule 26(a) and (e)(1) and of the amount of discovery parties shall be permitted; the disclosure or discovery of electronic data;[11] provisions for recalling privileged documents after production;[12] dates for pretrial conferences and for trial; and other matters the court deems appropriate.[13]

Modification of Scheduling Order Deadlines

For good cause shown,[14] the court may grant a motion modifying or enlarging the deadlines in the scheduling order.[15] The Advisory Committee Notes provide that good cause is shown when the

7. Howell v. Standard Motor Products, Inc., 2001 WL 196969 (N.D.Tex.2001).

8. *See, e.g., Millennium Partners, L.P. v. Colmar Storage, L.L.C.,* 494 F.3d 1293 (11th Cir. 2007) (Rule 16(b) scheduling orders and their underlying "good cause" requirement would be meaningless if Rule 15(a) was applied without considering impact of Rule 16(b)); *AmerisourceBergen Corp. v. Dialysist West, Inc.,* 445 F.3d 1132, 1141 (9th Cir.2006) ("where a motion to amend the pleadings is made within the time established by the pretrial scheduling order for the making of such motions, the motion is presumptively timely"); *O'Connell v. Hyatt Hotels of Puerto Rico,* 357 F.3d 152, 154 (1st Cir.2004) (the purpose of limiting the period for amending the pleadings is to assure that at some point both the parties and the pleadings will be fixed).

9. *Rosario-Diaz v. Gonzalez,* 140 F.3d 312 (1st Cir.1998)(Rule 16 mandates that the court set a deadline for pretrial motions); *Lozada v. Dale Baker Oldsmobile, Inc.,* 145 F.Supp.2d 878 (W.D.Mich.2001).

10. *Suntrust Bank v. Blue Water Fiber, L.P.,* 210 F.R.D. 196, 199 (E.D.Mich.2002). *But see Dodson v. Runyon,* 86 F.3d 37, 41 (2d Cir.1996) (explaining that a judge's failure to enter a scheduling order does not relieve counsel of the duty to his client to move forward with litigation).

11. See the discussion in the commentary to Rule 26 for a discussion of the aspects of the discovery of electronic data that the parties may want to discuss in the Rule 16 conference and include in the Rule 26(f) report.

12. See the discussion in the commentary to Rule 26(b)(5) and the Advisory Committee Note to the 2006 Amendment to Rule 26(b)(5) for discussions of the method for recalling produced privileged information prescribed by Rule 26(b)(5) and for alternative procedures.

13. *Does I thru XXIII v. Advanced Textile Corp.,* 214 F.3d 1058, 1068 (9th Cir. 2000) (the court may use its powers under Rule 16 to address a party's need for anonymity).

14. *Hussain v. Nicholson,* 435 F.3d 359, 368 (D.C.Cir.2006) (attorney error generally does not constitute good cause, but may in extreme circumstances); *Andretti v. Borla Performance Industries, Inc.,* 426 F.3d 824, 830 (6th Cir.2005) (court should consider possible prejudice to party opposing a motion to amend the schedule); *Leary v. Daeschner,* 349 F.3d 888, 906 (6th Cir.2003) (a court choosing to modify the schedule upon a showing of good cause may do so only if the schedule cannot reasonably be met despite the diligence of the party seeking the extension); *Inge v. Rock Financial Corp.,* 388 F.3d 930, 934 (6th Cir.2004) (district court improperly denied motion to amend where good cause was present); *Zivkovic v. Southern California Edison Co.,* 302 F.3d 1080, (9th Cir.2002).

15. *See, e.g., O'Connell v. Hyatt Hotels of Puerto Rico,* 357 F.3d 152, 154 (1st Cir. 2004) (Rule 16(b)'s "good cause" standard, rather than Rule 15(a)'s "freely given" standard, governs motions to amend filed after scheduling order deadlines); *Parker v. Columbia Pictures Industries,* 204 F.3d 326, 339–40 (2d Cir.2000).

schedule cannot reasonably be met despite the diligence of the party seeking the extension.[16]

RULE 16(c). ATTENDANCE AND MATTERS FOR CONSIDERATION AT PRETRIAL CONFERENCES

CORE CONCEPT

Rule 16(c) contains a list of topics that the court may consider at Rule 16 conferences. Rule 16(c) also allows for the consideration of any other matters that may facilitate the "just, speedy, and inexpensive disposition of the action."

APPLICATIONS

Topics for Conferences

During a pretrial conference, the court may seek to define and simplify the contested facts, theories, and issues,[17] eliminate frivolous claims or defenses,[18] determine whether an amendment of the pleadings is necessary, address disclosure and discovery issues, seek the admission or denial of facts or documents, make advance rulings on the admissibility of evidence[19] and the appropriateness of expert witnesses, require parties to file lists identifying witnesses[20] and documents, entertain requests to limit witnesses,[21] govern the order of proof at trial,[22] and discuss pretrial narrative statements, pending motions, stipulations limiting the issues for trial,[23] and scheduling matters. The court may consider stays, consolidations, or separate

---

16. Advisory Committee Notes to Rule 16 (1983 amendments). *See also Hussain v. Nicholson*, 435 F.3d 359, 367 (D.C.Cir. 2006); *Leary v. Daeschner*, 349 F.3d 888, 906 (6th Cir.2003).

17. *See Kemin Foods, L.C. v. Pigmentos Vegetales del Centro S.A. de C.V.*, 384 F.Supp.2d 1334, 1352 (S.D.Iowa 2005) (Rule 16 imposes a duty on each party to assist the court in defining the issues for trial); *Castillo v. Norton*, 219 F.R.D. 155, 163 (D.Ariz.2003).

18. *Chavez v. Illinois State Police*, 251 F.3d 612 (7th Cir.2001); *Rogan v. Menino*, 175 F.3d 75 (1st Cir.1999) (the court cannot ignore the procedural safeguards of summary judgment under Rule 56 by dismissing defendants at the pretrial conference); *In re HealthSouth Corp.*, 308 F.Supp.2d 1253 (N.D.Ala.2004) (a groundless contention without support in the facts or the law need not be heard in the district court).

19. *Tucker v. Ohtsu Tire & Rubber Co. Ltd.*, 49 F.Supp.2d 456 (D.Md.1999) (motions in limine may be presented at pretrial conferences);

20. *Hollander v. Sandoz Pharmaceuticals Corp.*, 289 F.3d 1193 (10th Cir.2002), *cert. denied*, 537 U.S. 1088, 123 S.Ct. 697, 154 L.Ed.2d 632 (2002).

21. *Planned Parenthood of Central New Jersey v. Verniero*, 22 F.Supp.2d 331, 339 (D.N.J.1998).

22. *Dick v. Dep't of Veterans Affairs*, 290 F.3d 1356 (Fed.Cir.2002).

23. *In re Air Crash Over Taiwan Straits on May 25, 2002*, 331 F.Supp.2d 1176, 1194 (C.D.Cal.2004) (discussing the split in authority over whether a court can require a party to stipulate as to uncontested facts); *United States v. One 48 Ft. White Colored Sailboat Named "Libertine"*, 24 F.Supp.2d 174, 178 (D.Puerto Rico 1998) (stipulations at a Rule 16 conference are enforceable); *Briggs v. Dalkon Shield Claimants Trust*, 174 F.R.D. 369, 373 (D.Md.1997) (stating that the trial court may have "authority to order one party to accept a stipulation offered by the opposing party.").

trials.[24] The court may also require parties to schedule presentation of evidence so that, if judgment as a matter of law or judgment on partial findings is appropriate, the court may reach those questions early in the trial. The court will also likely pursue the potential for settlement.[25] At the pretrial conference in a non-jury case, the court may decide to refer certain matters to another district judge, a magistrate judge, or a master.

Authority of Representatives

At the appropriate pretrial conference, which is usually the final pretrial conference, an attorney or party representative with the authority to enter stipulations and make admissions (not settlement) must be present. Rule 16(c) also authorizes the court, if appropriate, to require that an attorney or party representative with authority to settle the case be present or available by telephone.

Memorializing Pretrial Conference

A court reporter generally will be present whenever the court expects to discuss and rule on issues at pretrial conference. In unusual circumstances, parties may bring their own stenographers if the court does not order a court reporter.

Settlement

It has been held that the court may order parties to attend a conference where settlement will be discussed[26] but may not coerce those parties into settlement.[27] However, a bankruptcy court may bar non-settling parties from bringing contribution claims against settling parties in an effort to facilitate a settlement.[28]

Rulings on Motions

At the pretrial conference, the court may rule on discovery motions, jurisdictional challenges, Rule 12(b) defenses preserved under Rule 12(g) and 12(h), other Rule 12 motions if those motions were not decided previously, motions for summary judgment,[29] or motions in limine.[30]

24. *Dick v. Dep't of Veterans Affairs,* 290 F.3d 1356 (Fed.Cir.2002).

25. *F.T.C. v. Freecom Communications, Inc.,* 401 F.3d 1192, 1208 (10th Cir.2005) (the court may require that a party or its representative be present or available by telephone in order to consider settlement); *Sloan v. State Farm Mut. Auto. Ins. Co.,* 360 F.3d 1220, 1227 (10th Cir.2004) (while settlement is an appropriate topic for a pretrial conference, some cases cannot be settled and the parties' desire for a trial must be respected); *In re Atlantic Pipe Corp.,* 304 F.3d 135, 143 (1st Cir.2002) (discussing the use of required mediation).

26. *In Re Patenaude,* 210 F.3d 135, 144 (3d Cir.2000).

27. *Goss Graphics Systems, Inc. v. DEV Industries, Inc.,* 267 F.3d 624, 627 (7th Cir. 2001).

28. *Matter of Munford, Inc.,* 97 F.3d 449, 455 (11th Cir.1996).

29. *Pine Ridge Coal Company v. Local 8377, United Mine Workers of America,* 187 F.3d 415, 419 (4th Cir.1999); *but see Rogan v. Menino,* 175 F.3d 75, 80 (1st Cir.1999) (court may not deprive a party of the procedural protections of Rule 56 by granting summary judgment under Rule 16).

30. *Tucker v. Ohtsu Tire & Rubber Co., Ltd.,* 49 F.Supp.2d 456, 462–63 (D.Md.1999) (motions in limine may be presented at pretrial conferences).

Binding Effect of Statements at Pretrial Conference

A party is held at trial to admissions and stipulations made at a pretrial conference. However, the court may permit a party in certain circumstances to withdraw its stipulations.

Pretrial Memorandum or Narrative Statement

(1) *Time:* At the first pretrial conference and in its scheduling order the court will usually provide a date on which the parties must file a pretrial memorandum or pretrial narrative statement. The court usually orders the plaintiff's pretrial narrative statement to be filed several weeks after the close of discovery and the defendant's pretrial narrative statement several weeks after the filing of the plaintiff's statement.

(2) *Contents:* Local rule or court order will define the information parties are required to include in their pretrial narrative statements. Ordinarily, the parties must state their legal theories or defenses, provide a list of witnesses and documents to be presented at trial, detail the intended use of expert witnesses, and describe any exceptional legal or evidentiary questions that will be asserted at trial.

(3) *Effect and Amendment of:* The pretrial narrative statements are generally binding on the parties at trial, and failure to raise a legal issue may constitute waiver of that issue.[31] However, the court may permit the amendment of a pretrial narrative statement to include evidence not available at the time of filing the statement or for other legitimate reasons.[32]

(4) *Failure to File:* When a party fails to file a pretrial narrative statement required by local rule or court order, the court may impose sanctions under Rule 16(f).

RULE 16(d). PRETRIAL ORDERS

CORE CONCEPT

Rule 16(d) requires the court to issue a pretrial order memorializing the action taken at any pretrial conference.[33] Once a pretrial order has been entered,[34] it supercedes all pleadings and controls the subsequent course of the case.[35] A pretrial order may include amendments to the pleadings,[36] stipulations, a statement of the issues for trial, the defenses

---

31. *See McLean Contracting Co. v. Waterman Steamship Corp.,* 277 F.3d 477 (4th Cir.2002); *Olsen v. American Steamship Co.,* 176 F.3d 891 (6th Cir.1999).

32. *Payne v. S.S. Nabob,* 302 F.2d 803, 807 (3d Cir.1962).

33. *Athridge v. Rivas,* 141 F.3d 357, 362 n. 3 (D.C.Cir.1998).

34. *Wall v. County of Orange,* 364 F.3d 1107, 1111 (9th Cir.2004) (a pretrial order that was lodged but not entered is not controlling).

35. *Rockwell International Corp. v. U.S.,* ___ U.S. ___, 127 S.Ct. 1397, 167 L.Ed.2d 190 (2007) (final pretrial order supercedes all prior pleadings).

36. *Deere v. Goodyear Tire and Rubber Co.,* 175 F.R.D. 157, 164–65 (N.D.N.Y. 1997); *but see Wilson v. Muckala,* 303 F.3d 1207, 1215 (10th Cir.2002) (amendment to pleading not necessary if issue is addressed in a pretrial order, because the pretrial order supersedes the pleadings).

available, the date for the filing of pretrial narrative statements, evidentiary or witness lists, and the date set for trial. The court may order a party to draft the order on the court's behalf.

APPLICATIONS

Pretrial Order Binding on Parties

All matters mentioned in the pretrial order are binding on the parties at trial.[37] Evidence or legal theories that are not at least implicitly raised in the pretrial order will be barred at trial unless admitted without objection.[38] Pretrial orders may not, however, be binding in retrials of the matter[39] or in subsequent litigation.[40] Because the purpose of Rule 16 is to clarify the real nature of the dispute,[41] a claim or theory not raised in the pretrial order should not be considered by the factfinder.[42] The court may impose sanctions under Rule 16(f) for a party's failure to comply with the order.

Objection to Pretrial Order and Preservation of Right to Appeal

In order to preserve a party's rights on appeal, a party should object to a pretrial order at the time it is issued or at the commencement of trial by asserting a motion to amend the order.

Modification of Pretrial Order

Where its modification will not unduly prejudice the opposing party, the court has discretion to modify a pretrial order to prevent manifest injustice.[43] The court may also modify a pretrial order when evidence not raised in the pretrial statement is discovered after the pretrial order has been issued,[44] or is introduced at trial.[45]

37. *Kay-Cee Enterprises, Inc. v. Amoco Oil Co.*, 45 F.Supp.2d 840 (D.Kan.1999) ("The pretrial order supersedes the pleadings and controls the subsequent course of the litigation.").

38. *Arsement v. Spinnaker Exploration Co., LLC*, 400 F.3d 238, 245 (5th Cir.2005); *DP Aviation v. Smiths Industries Aerospace and Defense Systems Ltd.*, 268 F.3d 829, 841 (9th Cir.2001).

39. *Johns Hopkins University v. Cellpro, Inc.*, 152 F.3d 1342, 1357 (Fed.Cir.1998) (rulings in pretrial order are controlling at trial, but may not control the scope of a retrial).

40. *Atchison, Topeka and Santa Fe Railway Co. v. Hercules Inc.*, 146 F.3d 1071, 1074 (9th Cir.1998) (pretrial order limiting joinder of additional parties did not preclude a separate action against such additional parties).

41. *See, e.g., Doe v. Tangipahoa Parish School Board*, 478 F.3d 679 (5th Cir. 2007) ("One purpose of the pretrial order is to put the parties on notice as to the evidence they must be prepared to present.").

42. *Kona Technology Corp. v. Southern Pacific Transp. Co.*, 225 F.3d 595, 604 (5th Cir.2000) (if a claim or issue is omitted from the pretrial order, it is waived, even if it appeared in the complaint); *Elvis Presley Enterprises, Inc. v. Capece*, 141 F.3d 188, 206 (5th Cir.1998).

43. *Galdamez v. Potter*, 415 F.3d 1015, 1020 (9th Cir.2005) (setting forth a four part test for determination of whether to modify a pretrial order); *In re Olshan*, 356 F.3d 1078, 1085 (9th Cir.2004); *In the Matter of: El Paso Refinery, L P*, 171 F.3d 249, 255 (5th Cir.1999) (trial court has broad discretion in determining whether a pretrial order should be modified).

44. *Ross v. Garner Printing Co.*, 285 F.3d 1106, 1114 (8th Cir.2002).

45. *See United Phosphorus, Ltd. v. Midland Fumigant, Inc.*, 205 F.3d 1219, 1236 (10th Cir.2000).

Appeal of Pretrial Order

Prior to the entry of judgment, a party has no right to a direct appeal from a pretrial order.[46]   Ultimately, the pretrial order will be reviewed for abuse of discretion.[47]

RULE 16(e).   FINAL PRETRIAL CONFERENCE AND ORDERS

CORE CONCEPT

The court will usually conduct the final pretrial conference after the pretrial narrative statements have been filed and as close to trial as possible.   At the final pretrial conference, the court will make a schedule for any remaining motions and set a trial date.   An attorney who will conduct the trial or an unrepresented party must attend the conference with the authority to enter stipulations and make admissions (not settlement).

RULE 16(f).   SANCTIONS

CORE CONCEPT

Upon motion or on the court's own initiative, the court will impose sanctions to force parties to comply with scheduling and pretrial orders and to compensate parties for expenses caused by an opposing party's noncompliance.[48]   Sanctions may also attach to incorrect or incomplete pretrial statements,[49] or the failure to participate in a settlement conference in good faith.[50]

APPLICATIONS

Procedural and Substantive Errors

When a party commits a procedural error, courts generally will not impose sanctions that compromise the merits of the case.[51] Instead the court should impose costs and fees.[52]   When a party

---

46. *Bradley v. Milliken,* 468 F.2d 902 (6th Cir.1972).

47. *Harper v. Albert,* 400 F.3d 1052, 1063 (7th Cir.2005); *Koch v. Koch Industries, Inc.,* 203 F.3d 1202, 1222 (10th Cir. 2000), *cert. denied,* 531 U.S. 926, 121 S.Ct. 302, 148 L.Ed.2d 242 (2000); *Gorlikowski v. Tolbert,* 52 F.3d 1439 (7th Cir.1995).

48. *Garlepied v. Main,* 2001 WL 305264 (E.D.La.2001).

49. *Bronk v. Ineichen,* 54 F.3d 425 (7th Cir.1995)(excluding testimony of witness not named in pretrial statement).

50. *Smith v. Northwest Financial Acceptance, Inc.,* 129 F.3d 1408, 1419 (10th Cir. 1997); *Landmark Legal Foundation v. E.P.A.,* 272 F.Supp.2d 70, 88 (D.D.C.2003)

(Rule 16(f) sanctions apply only to actions related to pretrial conferences and orders, not to other potential violations).

51. *Rice v. City of Chicago,* 333 F.3d 780, 786 (7th Cir.2003) (a judge should consider punishing the lawyer through sanctions rather than the plaintiff through dismissal of the suit); *John v. Louisiana,* 828 F.2d 1129 (5th Cir.1987).

52. *Sanders v. Union Pacific Railroad Co.,* 154 F.3d 1037, 1042 (9th Cir.1998) (imposing monetary sanctions on attorney can appropriately punish the one responsible for the harm), *rehearing granted, opinion withdrawn,* 179 F.3d 1244 (9th Cir. 1999).

commits a substantive error the court may impose sanctions which compromise the merits of a party's case.[53]

Sanctions Imposed on Party's Motion

A party may file a motion for sanctions when a party or a party's attorney does not obey a scheduling[54] or pretrial order, when a party does not appear at a pretrial conference,[55] when a party is unprepared at a pretrial conference, or when a party does not act in good faith at a pretrial conference. The motion should be asserted as soon as possible after the sanctionable activity. Unless made during a hearing or trial, a party must file a written motion stating the reasons for the sanctions with particularity and the relief or order sought.

Sanctions Imposed Sua Sponte

When the court seeks to impose sanctions on its own initiative, the court must first provide notice and an opportunity to be heard to the sanctionable party.[56]

Purposes of Sanctions

Sanctions may be assessed to punish for improper conduct,[57] for purposes of deterrence, or to compensate the party injured by the improper conduct.[58]

Finding of Sanctionable Activity

The court will examine the record and any materials submitted by the parties. The court must make a specific finding of sanctionable activity. When it finds that a party has committed sanctionable activities, the court has discretion to impose sanctions, even in the absence of bad faith.[59] The court will not impose sanctions when the party can substantially justify its violation[60] or where the award of expenses would be unjust.

---

53. *See, e.g., Lucien v. Breweur,* 9 F.3d 26, 29 (7th Cir.1993)(willful failure to attend final pretrial conference can be cause for dismissal with prejudice). *But see, Ball v. City of Chicago,* 2 F.3d 752, 758 (7th Cir.1993)(punishing a lawyer through monetary sanctions preferable to punishing plaintiff through dismissal when fault lies with lawyer).

54. *Lucas Automotive Engineering, Inc. v. Bridgestone/Firestone, Inc.,* 275 F.3d 762 (9th Cir.2001) (sanctioning a party for failing to appear for a scheduled mediation); *Engineered Products Co. v. Donaldson Co., Inc.,* 313 F.Supp.2d 951 (2004) (sanctions imposed for failure to meet deadline for expert reports).

55. *Templet v. HydroChem Inc.,* 367 F.3d 473, 481 (5th Cir.2004); *Lititz Mutual Ins. Co. v. Royal Ins. Co. Of America,* 58 F.Supp.2d 1287, 1292 (D.Kan.1999).

56. *Ford v. Alfaro,* 785 F.2d 835 (9th Cir.1986); *Newton v. A.C. & S., Inc.,* 918 F.2d 1121 (3d Cir.1990).

57. *United States v. Samaniego,* 345 F.3d 1280, 1284 (11th Cir.2003).

58. *See, e.g., Media Duplication Services, Ltd. v. HDG Software, Inc.,* 928 F.2d 1228, 1242 (1st Cir.1991) (court may consider deterrence when assessing sanctions under Rule 16(f)); *Royal Palace Hotel Assoc., Inc. v. International Resort Classics, Inc.,* 178 F.R.D. 588, 591 (M.D.Fla.1997).

59. *Rice v. Barnes,* 201 F.R.D. 549, 551 (M.D.Ala.2001) (the court does not need to find that the violation was willful); *Martin Family Trust v. Heco/Nostalgia Enterprises Co.,* 186 F.R.D. 601, 604 (E.D.Cal.1999).

60. *Firefighter's Institute for Racial Equality ex rel. Anderson v. City of St. Louis,* 220 F.3d 898, 902 (8th Cir.2000).

(1) *Against Whom:* The court may impose sanctions against the party and/or any attorney of the party.[61] Where a represented party has no knowledge of the sanctionable activity, the court may order sanctions against the attorney alone and preclude reimbursement from the client.

(2) *Notice and Hearing:* Before imposing sanctions, the court must provide the alleged sanctionable party with notice and an opportunity to be heard either orally or in writing.[62]

Nature of Sanctions

The court will design a sanction that appropriately matches the violation.[63] The court can impose any sanctions it deems appropriate,[64] including but not limited to the following:[65]

(1) *Discovery Sanctions:* Rule 16(f) incorporates the discovery sanctions found in Rule 37(b)(2)(B),[66] (C),[67] and (D), such as refusing to allow a party to support or oppose designated claims or defenses,[68] striking pleadings or parts thereof, precluding witnesses not properly disclosed,[69] or treating the conduct as contempt of court.[70]

(2) *Reasonable Expenses:* The court must require the sanctionable person to pay reasonable expenses,[71] including attorney fees caused by noncompliance with Rule 16, unless the court finds that the noncompliance was "substantially justified" or that an award of

61. *Nick v. Morgan's Foods, Inc.*, 270 F.3d 590, 597 (8th Cir.2001); *Republic of the Philippines v. Westinghouse Electric Corp.*, 43 F.3d 65 (3d Cir.1994).

62. *Ford v. Alfaro*, 785 F.2d 835 (9th Cir.1986).

63. *Republic of the Philippines v. Westinghouse Electric Corp.*, 43 F.3d 65 (3d Cir. 1994); *Smith v. Rowe*, 761 F.2d 360 (7th Cir.1985).

64. *Young v. Gordon*, 330 F.3d 76 (1st Cir.2003); *Arnold v. Krause, Inc.*, 233 F.R.D. 126, 129 (W.D.N.Y.2005) (Rule 16(f) allows the court to impose sanctions it deems just).

65. *Nick v. Morgan's Foods, Inc.*, 270 F.3d 590, 595–96 (8th Cir.2001).

66. *Velez v. Awning Windows, Inc.*, 375 F.3d 35, 44 (1st Cir.2004).

67. *Ray v. Eyster*, 132 F.3d 152, 154 n. 2 (3d Cir.1997).

68. *Velez v. Awning Windows, Inc.*, 375 F.3d 35, 42 (1st Cir.2004).

69. *Potomac Electric Power Co. v. Electric Motor Supply, Inc.*, 190 F.R.D. 372 (D.Md.1999) (setting forth factors for determining whether to exclude a witness); *Trost v. Trek Bicycle Corp.*, 162 F.3d 1004, 1008

(8th Cir.1998) (court may exclude untimely expert evidence because failure to disclose timely was neither harmless nor substantially justified); *but see Lory v. General Electric Co.*, 179 F.R.D. 86, 89 (N.D.N.Y.1998) (exclusion of expert witness too severe a sanction where late disclosure was sole transgression and did not prejudice the defendant).

70. *Trilogy Communications, Inc. v. Times Fiber Communications, Inc.*, 109 F.3d 739, 745 (Fed.Cir.1997) (striking expert's reports from record when submitted after due date); *Bronk v. Ineichen*, 54 F.3d 425 (7th Cir.1995)(excluding testimony of witness not named in pretrial statement); *Hathcock v. Navistar International Transportation Corp.*, 53 F.3d 36 (4th Cir. 1995)(default can be appropriate sanction for failure to obey a scheduling order).

71. *See O. Ahlborg & Sons, Inc. v. United States*, 233 F.R.D. 224, 226 (D.Mass. 2005); *Former Employees of Tyco Electronics, Fiber Optics Div. v. U.S. Dept. of Labor*, 259 F.Supp.2d 1246 (CIT 2003) (attorney fees can be reduced even if reasonable for the tasks at issue); *Lithuanian Commerce Corp. v. Sara Lee Hosiery*, 177 F.R.D. 205, 214–15 (D.N.J.1997) (reasonableness is to be determined outside of opposing party's actual expenses).

expenses would be "unjust."[72] These expenses may be the only sanctions ordered or in addition to another sanction.

(3) *Court Costs:* The court may impose court costs on a party who causes court expense by the sanctionable activities.

(4) *Fines and Disciplinary Action:* In lieu of or in addition to other sanctions, the court may impose a fine[73] upon or seek disciplinary action against the sanctionable party.[74]

(5) *Dismissal:* The court may even dismiss a case[75] or enter default judgment[76] for failure to obey pretrial orders.[77] However, a trial court must apply lesser sanctions than dismissal except in an extreme situation were there is a clear record of delay or disobedience.[78] Some pertinent factors considered by the courts are the severity of the violation, the legitimacy of the party's excuse, repetition of violations, the deliberateness of the misconduct, mitigating excuses, prejudice to the court or opponent, and the adequacy of lesser sanctions.[79]

Appeal

An order imposing sanctions for failing to obey a Rule 16 scheduling or pretrial order is appealable only after final judgment has been entered in the underlying action.[80] "A district court's imposition of sanctions will be upheld unless an abuse of discretion or clearly erroneous."[81]

ADDITIONAL RESEARCH REFERENCES

Wright & Miller, *Federal Practice and Procedure* §§ 1521–1540.

C.J.S. Federal Civil Procedure §§ 905–914.

West's Key No. Digests, Federal Civil Procedure ⊙═1921–1943.

72. *Richardson v. Nassau County,* 184 F.R.D. 497 (E.D.N.Y.1999).

73. *Nick v. Morgan's Foods, Inc.,* 270 F.3d 590, 595–96 (8th Cir.2001).

74. *See Legault v. Zambarano,* 105 F.3d 24, 28–29 (1st Cir.1997).

75. *Hernandez v. Conriv Realty Assoc.,* 182 F.3d 121 (2d Cir.1999) (court must have subject matter jurisdiction to enter dismissal).

76. *DIRECTV, Inc. v. Huynh,* 318 F.Supp.2d 1122 (M.D.Ala.2004)

77. *Bay Fireworks, Inc. v. Frenkel & Co., Inc.,* 359 F.Supp.2d 257, 262 (E.D.N.Y. 2005) (dismissal for failure to file a timely third party complaint deemed not on the merits).

78. *Tower Ventures, Inc. v. City of Westfield,* 296 F.3d 43, 45–46 (1st Cir. 2002) (court may impose dismissal of ac-

tion as a sanction for violation of court orders without consideration of lesser sanctions because disobedience of court orders constitutes extreme conduct); *Tunica–Biloxi Indians of Louisiana v. Pecot,* 227 F.R.D. 271, 278 (W.D.La.2005) (district court is bound to impose the least severe sanction available).

79. *Gripe v. City of Enid, Okl.,* 312 F.3d 1184, 1188 (10th Cir.2002); *Robson v. Hallenbeck,* 81 F.3d 1, 2 (1st Cir.1996).

80. *Cato v. Fresno City,* 220 F.3d 1073, 1074 (9th Cir.2000).

81. *United States v. Samaniego,* 345 F.3d 1280, 1284 (11th Cir.2003); *Young v. Gordon,* 330 F.3d 76 (1st Cir.2003); *Spain v. Board of Educ. of Meridian Community Unit School Dist. No. 101,* 214 F.3d 925 (7th Cir.2000); *Olcott v. Delaware Flood Company,* 76 F.3d 1538, 1556 (10th Cir. 1996).

IV. PARTIES

RULE 17

PLAINTIFF AND DEFENDANT; CAPACITY; PUBLIC OFFICERS

(a) Real Party in Interest.

(1) *Designation in General.* An action must be prosecuted in the name of the real party in interest. The following may sue in their own names without joining the person for whose benefit the action is brought:

(A) an executor;

(B) an administrator;

(C) a guardian;

(D) a bailee;

(E) a trustee of an express trust;

(F) a party with whom or in whose name a contract has been made for another's benefit; and

(G) a party authorized by statute.

(2) *Action in the Name of the United States for Another's Use or Benefit.* When a federal statute so provides, an action for another's use or benefit must be brought in the name of the United States.

(3) *Joinder of the Real Party in Interest.* The court may not dismiss an action for failure to prosecute in the name of the real party in interest until, after an objection, a reasonable time has been allowed for the real party in interest to ratify, join, or be substituted into the action. After ratification, joinder, or substitution, the action proceeds as if it had been originally commenced by the real party in interest.

(b) Capacity to Sue or Be Sued. Capacity to sue or be sued is determined as follows:

(1) for an individual who is not acting in a representative capacity, by the law of the individual's domicile;

(2) for a corporation, by the law under which it was organized; and

(3) for all other parties, by the law of the state where the court is located, except that:

 (A) a partnership or other unincorporated association with no such capacity under that state's law may sue or be sued in its common name to enforce a substantive right existing under the United States Constitution or laws; and

 (B) 28 U.S.C. §§ 754 and 959(a) govern the capacity of a receiver appointed by a United States court to sue or be sued in a United States court.

(c) Minor or Incompetent Person.

(1) *With a Representative.* The following representatives may sue or defend on behalf of a minor or an incompetent person:

 (A) a general guardian;

 (B) a committee;

 (C) a conservator; or

 (D) a like fiduciary.

(2) *Without a Representative.* A minor or an incompetent person who does not have a duly appointed representative may sue by a next friend or by a guardian ad litem. The court must appoint a guardian ad litem—or issue another appropriate order—to protect a minor or incompetent person who is unrepresented in an action.

(d) Public Officer's Title and Name. A public officer who sues or is sued in an official capacity may be designated by official title rather than by name, but the court may order that the officer's name be added.

[Amended effective March 19, 1948; October 20, 1949; July 1, 1966; August 1, 1987; August 1, 1988; November 18, 1988; April 30, 2007, effective December 1, 2007.]

─────────────── **2007 AMENDMENTS ROADMAP** ───────────────

 STYLE PROJECT CHANGES: Rule 17(a), (b), and (c) were previously treated as individual paragraphs. Those subsections are now subdivided into additional subparts, each with individual titles. Minor changes were made in the titles of subsections (a), (b), and (c), and minor language changes were made throughout the text of Rule 17.

NON-STYLE CHANGES: A new subsection, Rule 17(d), governs identification of a public officer who sues or is sued in an official capacity. This provision was previously located in old Rule 25(d)(2). Although this change involves more than matters of style, there is no change in the substance of the provision.

NOTE: The Federal Rules "Style Project" is explained in Part III-A.

AUTHORS' COMMENTARY ON RULE 17

PURPOSE AND SCOPE

Rule 17 controls the determination of who may prosecute an action, or defend against one, in federal court. The standards are mandatory, but they can usually be satisfied without fundamentally altering the litigation.

RULE 17(a).　REAL PARTY IN INTEREST

CORE CONCEPT

The only parties on whose behalf suits may be initiated are those persons whose interests will be materially affected by the outcome.[1] Such persons should be the named plaintiffs, except that Rule 17(a) permits certain exceptions. This requirement is imposed on plaintiffs so that defendants will only have to face one suit over the same interest.[2]

APPLICATIONS

2007 Amendments

The 2007 Style Project amended Rule 17(a) by subdividing it into three subparts (of which the first was further divided into six paragraph). This change should not present great difficulty for attorneys.

Naming the Interested Party

Subject to exceptions discussed below, the suit must be commenced not only on behalf of the real party in interest but also in the name of the real party in interest. Thus, the real party in interest generally must be named in the caption.[3]

---

1. *See, e.g., United HealthCare Corp. v. American Trade Insurance Co.,* 88 F.3d 563, 569 (8th Cir.1996)(Rule 17(a) "requires that the party who brings an action actually possess, under the substantive law, the right sought to be enforced.").

2. *See, e.g., Marina Management Services, Inc. v. Vessel My Girls,* 202 F.3d 315,

318 (D.C.Cir.2000) ("Rule 17(a) protects a defendant against a subsequent claim for the same debt underlying a previously entered judgment.").

3. *Lincoln Property Co. v. Roche,* 546 U.S. 81, 126 S.Ct. 606, 163 L.Ed.2d 415 (2005) (Rule 17(a) mandates joinder of parties who assert claims that are pending

Mandatory Joinder of All Plaintiffs: Rule 19

Rule 17(a) requires that the plaintiff (or claimant) must generally be a real party in interest. However, once the requirements of Rule 17(a) are satisfied, there is no need to join all other persons who are real parties in interest with similar claims.[4] It may still be true, of course, that a non-party's absence could trigger dismissal of the action pursuant to Rule 19.[5]

Rule 17(a) and Defendants

Rule 17(a) governs circumstances in which plaintiffs (or persons asserting claims) must be added. It does not address whether defendants must be joined.[6]

Standing v. Real Party in Interest

While the requirements of standing and Rule 17(a) may differ in some respects, it is clear that both share the requirement that the plaintiff has a personal interest in the case.[7]

Raising a Rule 17 Defense

The manner in which a party may invoke Rule 17(a) is not clear.[8] Some courts indicate that the appropriate way to raise Rule 17 is through a pleading,[9] while other authority indicates it might be

before the court). *See, e.g., Ross v. Marshall,* 426 F.3d 745, 757 (5th Cir.2005) (Rule 17(a) applicable only to those asserting claims, usually plaintiffs); *Green v. Daimler Benz, AG,* 157 F.R.D. 340, 344 (E.D.Pa.1994)(ordering change in caption after substituting party). *But cf., HB General Corp. v. Manchester Partners,* 95 F.3d 1185, 1196 (3d Cir.1996) ("[I]f the plaintiffs are real parties in interest, Rule 17(a) does not require the addition of other parties also fitting that description.").

4. *See, e.g., Excimer Associates, Inc. v. LCA Vision, Inc.,* 292 F.3d 134, 140 (2d Cir.2002) (If "plaintiff's injury is direct, the fact that another party may also have been injured and could assert its own claim does not preclude the plaintiff from asserting its claim directly."); *HB General Corp. v. Manchester Partners,* 95 F.3d 1185, 1196 (3d Cir.1996) ("[I]f the plaintiffs are real parties in interest, Rule 17(a) does not require the addition of other parties also fitting that description.").

5. *See, e.g., International Equity Investments, Inc. v. Opportunity Equity Partners, Ltd.,* 411 F.Supp.2d 458, 464 (S.D. N.Y. 2006). *See also* Authors' Commentary on Rule 19.

6. *Lincoln Property Co. v. Roche,* 546 U.S. 81, 90, 126 S.Ct. 606, 614, 163 L.Ed.2d 415 (2005) ("Rule 17(a) . . . as its text dis-

plays, speaks to joinder of *plaintiffs*, not defendants."). *See, e.g., Salazar v. Allstate Texas Lloyd's, Inc.,* 455 F.3d 571, 573 (5th Cir. 2006) ("By its terms . . . Rule 17(a) applies only to plaintiffs.").

7. *See, e.g., APCC Services, Inc. v. Sprint Communications Co.,* 418 F.3d 1238 (D.C. Cir.2005) (also noting that Rule 17(a) may be satisfied by valid assignment of interest). *But see Kent v. Northern California Regional Office of American Friends Service Committee,* 497 F.2d 1325, (9th Cir. 1974) (trustees of trusts containing funds arguably owed as federal tax were real parties in interest under Rule 17(a); but in challenge to constitutionality of tax, trustees had no standing; only taxpayers who arguably owed tax had such standing).

8. *See, e.g., Whelan v. Abell,* 953 F.2d 663, 672 n. 7 (D.C.Cir.1992) ("We note that the question of how a Rule 17(a) defense is raised (as a 12(b)(6) motion or as a Rule 8(c) affirmative defense) remains unsettled.").

9. *See, e.g., Weissman v. Weener,* 12 F.3d 84, 85 (7th Cir.1993) (citing older authority indicating that preferred method is by raising Rule 17 in a defendant's answer); *Howerton v. Designer Homes by Georges, Inc.,* 950 F.2d 281, 283 (5th Cir.1992) ("The issue of capacity is subject to waiver if not specifically raised by negative averment.").

the appropriate subject of a motion.[10] Attorneys are encouraged to examine carefully the local practice.

Invoking Rule 17(a) Sua Sponte

Most courts hold that the district court, as well as the parties, may raise a Rule 17(a) issue.[11]

Timing; Waiver

Rule 17(a) does not provide an express time limit within which an objection must be made. However, if the objection is not made with reasonable promptness, in the circumstances of a particular case, it is waived.[12]

Exceptions to Naming Interested Party

Rule 17(a) explicitly exempts certain categories of persons from the general principal that the named party be the real party in interest. The most important of these enumerated exceptions are executors, administrators, guardians, trustees,[13] persons who have made contracts on behalf of third parties,[14] and circumstances where a statute authorizes suit in the name of a representative party.[15]

10. *Cf., e.g., Lans v. Digital Equipment Corp.,* 252 F.3d 1320 (Fed.Cir.2001) (affirming grant of defendant's motion for summary judgment on ground of lack of Rule 17–related standing; affirming denial of plaintiff's motion to use Rules 15 and 17 to substitute a person who allegedly satisfied standing requirement).

11. *See, e.g., Weissman v. Weener,* 12 F.3d 84 (7th Cir.1993)(no recent decisions overrule district courts that invoke Rule 17(a) *sua sponte*).

12. *See, e.g., Rogers v. Samedan Oil Corp.,* 308 F.3d 477, 483 (5th Cir.2002) ("[T]he defense is waived when it is not timely asserted."); *International Meat Traders, Inc. v. H & M Food Systems,* 70 F.3d 836, 840 (5th Cir.1995) ("Raising this defense for the first time on a motion for judgment as a matter of law, at the close of all evidence, offends the Rule where it is not to be used as a trial-by-ambush tactic."); *Allegheny International, Inc. v. Allegheny Ludlum Steel Corp.,* 40 F.3d 1416, 1431 (3d Cir.1994) (approving denial of Rule 17 defense where party did not raise issue with reasonable promptness); *First Union Discount Brokerage Services, Inc. v. Milos,* 997 F.2d 835, 842 n. 12 (11th Cir. 1993) (collecting precedent in some circuits requiring timely assertion of Rule 17 issue).

13. *See, e.g., Lenon v. St. Paul Mercury Insurance Co.,* 136 F.3d 1365, 1370 n. 2 (10th Cir.1998) (per curiam) (noting that trustee of express trust is real party in interest for purposes of Rule 17(a)).

14. *See, e.g., Local 538 United Brotherhood of Carpenters and Joiners of America v. United States Fidelity and Guaranty Co.,* 70 F.3d 741, 743 (2d Cir.1995)(noting general principle that named party to contract may sue in own name without joining third-party beneficiary; but refusing to extend Rule 17(a) to permit labor union to sue employer on behalf of welfare fund without first joining the fund).

15. *See, e.g., United States ex rel. Long v. SCS Business & Technical Institute, Inc.,* 173 F.3d 870 (D.C.Cir.1999) (in *qui tam* action under False Claims Act, 31 U.S.C.A. § 3730(b) provides that both the United States and the relator are real parties in interest). *Cf., Femedeer v. Haun,* 227 F.3d 1244, 1246 (10th Cir.2000) (acknowledging possibility that some exceptional circumstances may require anonymity in unusual cases, but holding that previously convicted sex offender who is challenging state law requiring his registration as a sex offender must sue under his real name). *Marina Management Services, Inc. v. Vessel My Girls,* 202 F.3d 315, 318 (D.C.Cir.2000) (noting lack of judicial consensus as to whether "an agent authorized to sue based solely on a power of attorney is a real party in interest under Rule 17(a)").

Subject Matter Jurisdiction

Rule 17(a) has some similarity with the requirements for diversity jurisdiction found in 28 U.S.C.A. § 1332. However, the two requirements can also diverge significantly from one another, with important consequences.[16] For example, Rule 17(a) permits, *inter alia,* an executor of a decedent's estate to be a real party in interest. However, such a person's status as a real party in interest under Rule 17(a) does not mean that person's citizenship is used for purposes of establishing diversity jurisdiction under 28 U.S.C.A. § 1332. Instead, § 1332(c)(2) provides that for purposes of diversity jurisdiction in an action brought on behalf of a decedent, infant, or incompetent person, the relevant citizenship is that of the deceased, infant, or incompetent person. Thus, under Rule 17(a) the executor may initiate the suit, but diversity is dependent on the citizenship of the represented person.[17]

Suits in the Name of the United States

If a statute allows the United States to sue on behalf of a real party in interest, Rule 17(a) also permits the United States to be the named plaintiff.

Intervenors under Rule 24

If a person seeks to intervene in an action under Rule 24 in order to assert a claim, that potential party must meet the requirements of Rule 17(a).[18]

Relation to Rule 25(c)

Both Rules 17 and 25 govern who should be a party to a suit. However, Rule 17 applies to transfers of interest prior to initiation of the suit, while Rule 25(c) controls transfers occurring after the suit is filed.[19]

---

16. *Navarro Savings Association v. Lee,* 446 U.S. 458, 463 n. 9, 100 S.Ct. 1779, 1783 n. 9, 64 L.Ed.2d 425 (1980) ("There is a 'rough symmetry' between the 'real party in interest' standard of Rule 17(a) and the rule that diversity jurisdiction depends upon the citizenship of real parties to the controversy. But the two rules serve different purposes and need not produce identical outcomes in all cases. ... In appropriate circumstances, for example, a labor union may file suit in its own name as a real party in interest under Rule 17(a). To establish diversity, however, the union must rely upon the citizenship of each of its members.").

17. *See, e.g., Airlines Reporting Corp. v. S and N Travel, Inc.,* 58 F.3d 857, 862 n. 4 (2d Cir.1995). *See also St. Paul Fire & Marine Insurance Co. v. Universal Builders Supply,* 409 F.3d 73, 81 (2d Cir.2005) (acknowledging symmetry between Rule 17(a) and diversity jurisdiction, but noting that

outcomes can still be different); *Stichting Ter Be Hartiging van de Belangen van Oudaandeelhouders in Het Kapitaal van Saybolt International, B.V. v. Schreiber,* 407 F.3d 34, 37 (2d Cir.2005) (diversity case; where defect in real party in interest is created by noncompliance with state substantive law, Rule 17(a) is inapplicable).

18. *See, e.g., Ross v. Marshall,* 426 F.3d 745, 757 (5th Cir.2005) (Rule 17(a) applicable to intervenors who assert claims).

19. *See, e.g., FDIC v. Deglau,* 207 F.3d 153, 159 (3d Cir.2000) (Rule 17(a) governs who may bring a suit at time of filing; thus it considers transfers of interest that occur prior to filing; however, once case is filed, the impact of a post-filing transfer is governed by Rule 25(c)); *Barker v. Jackson National Life Insurance Co.,* 163 F.R.D. 364, 365 (N.D.Fla.1995)(explaining distinction between Rules).

Remedy

The preferred remedy is to allow the party an opportunity to amend so that the action can thereafter be prosecuted by the real party in interest.[20] Dismissal is a disfavored remedy for violation of the requirement to name the real party in interest as plaintiff.[21] Before a court grants a motion to dismiss, it must allow a real party in interest a reasonable opportunity to correct the defect by joining the action, or, if permitted as an exception to Rule 17(a), to ratify continuation of the action in the name of the original plaintiff. If the real party in interest takes such action, it is effective as if the joinder or ratification had occurred at the onset of the litigation.[22]

Relation to Rule 15

If an existing party must be replaced for failure to meet the requirements of rule 17, the real party in interest would normally join the litigation through the amendment process of rule 15.[23]

RULE 17(b).   CAPACITY TO SUE OR BE SUED

CORE CONCEPT

This provision chooses the law that will govern the capacity of a person to prosecute or defend a suit in federal court.

20. *See, e.g., Esposito v. United States,* 368 F.3d 1271, 1272 (10th Cir.2004) (party bringing action is entitled, after objections, to reasonable time to substitute real party in interest; such a right requires only that party's original mistake was "honest"); *Dunmore v. United States,* 358 F.3d 1107, 1112 (9th Cir.2004) (purpose behind allowing plaintiff to cure defect without dismissal is to prevent plaintiff from being time-barred for "understandable mistake").

21. *See, e.g., Wieburg v. GTE Southwest, Inc.,* 272 F.3d 302, 308–09 (5th Cir. 2001) (where plaintiff lacks standing because civil causes of action are property of plaintiff's bankruptcy estate, case should not be dismissed until bankruptcy trustee has opportunity to substitute himself for plaintiff); *Intown Properties Management, Inc. v. Wheaton Van Lines, Inc.,* 271 F.3d 164, 170 (4th Cir.2001) (Rule 17 expressly provides that case shall not be dismissed until real party in interest has reasonable opportunity to join litigation). *But see Consul General of Republic of Indonesia v. Bill's Rentals, Inc.,* 330 F.3d 1041, 1047–48 (8th Cir.2003) (dismissal with prejudice appropriate when Consul General did not act to cure defect within 18 months).

22. *See, e.g., O'Hara v. District No. 1– PCD, MEBA, AFL–CIO,* 56 F.3d 1514, 1519 (D.C.Cir.1995)("substitution of real party in interest for party prosecuting a suit has same effect as if action had been commenced in the name of real party in interest"). *See also, Scheufler v. General Host Corp.,* 126 F.3d 1261, 1270 (10th Cir.1997) (when parties are joined as real parties in interest under Rule 17(a), joinder falls under "mandatory relation-back" authority of rule 17(a) and is not governed by Rule 15(c); thus claims of such parties automatically relate back to commencement of litigation).

23. *See, e.g., Intown Properties Management, Inc. v. Wheaton Van Lines, Inc.,* 271 F.3d 164, 170 (4th Cir.2001) (Rule 17 expressly provides that case shall not be dismissed until real party in interest has reasonable opportunity to join litigation). *See also* Advisory Committee Note to Rule 15 (1966).

APPLICATIONS

2007 Amendments

The 2007 Style Project amended Rule 17(b) by subdividing it into three subparts. This change should not present great difficulty for attorneys.

Natural Persons

For individuals, the law which determines their capacity to sue or be sued is the law of their domicile.[24] Domicile is generally defined as the jurisdiction where a person has established a physical presence and has the intent to remain for an indefinite period.[25] Thus, a person's home is generally that person's domicile. For many persons, the state of domicile will not be the same state in which the case is heard. Particularly in diversity cases, at least one party will be domiciled outside the state where the case is heard.

Natural Persons as Representatives of Others

Natural persons suing on behalf of another, such as guardians or executors of estates, are governed by the law of the state in which the court sits.[26]

Pro Se Litigants

While a non-attorney parent may bring an action on behalf of a child, such a parent must be represented by an attorney.[27]

Corporations

The capacity of a corporation to sue or be sued is governed by the law of the jurisdiction in which the corporation is incorporated.[28]

Unincorporated Associations

If the cause of action is based on a federal question, Rule 17(b) provides that unincorporated associations have capacity to sue or be sued.[29]

---

24. *See, e.g., Johns v. County of San Diego,* 114 F.3d 874 (9th Cir.1997) (so holding).

25. *See, e.g., Stifel v. Hopkins,* 477 F.2d 1116, 1120 (6th Cir.1973) (using definition and discussing relationship to Rule 17(b)).

26. *See, e.g., Maroni v. Pemi–Baker Regional School District,* 346 F.3d 247, 249 n. 2 (1st Cir.2003) ("State law is used to determine the age of majority," citing Rule 17(b)); *Gibbs v. Carnival Cruise Lines,* 314 F.3d 125, 135 (3d Cir.2002) (state law controls whether representative has been duly appointed to litigate on behalf of infant); *Davis v. Piper Aircraft Corp.,* 615 F.2d 606, 609 (4th Cir.1980) (citing Rule 17(b); state law controls capacity to bring wrongful death suit).

27. *See, e.g., Cheung v. Youth Orchestra Foundation of Buffalo, Inc.,* 906 F.2d 59, 61 (2d Cir.1990) ("The choice to appear pro se is not a true choice for minors who under state law, see Fed.R.Civ.P. 17(b), cannot determine their own legal actions.").

28. *See, e.g., Citizens Electric Corp. v. Bituminous Fire & Marine Insurance Co.,* 68 F.3d 1016, 1019 (7th Cir. 1995)(approving application of state law under Rule 17(b)).

29. *See, e.g., Curley v. Brignoli, Curley & Roberts Associates,* 915 F.2d 81, 87 (2d Cir.1990) (observing that Rule 17(b) grants "association capacity in federal question cases".)

Receivers

Rule 17(b) provides that the capacity of receivers appointed by a federal court to litigate in a federal court is governed by 28 U.S.C.A. §§ 754 (appointment of receivers in different federal judicial districts) and 959(a)(suits against receivers).

Capacity in All Other Cases

Notwithstanding the numerous specific provisions for capacity in Rule 17(b), there are other circumstances not addressed by those provisions. For example, when a partnership or other unincorporated association sues, or is sued, on a state cause of action in federal court, the law governing capacity is that of the state in which the court sits.[30]

Capacity Distinguished From Real Party in Interest

There are two important differences between capacity (Rule 17(b)) and real parties in interest (Rule 17(a)) and the concerns they address. The first is that satisfying real party in interest requirements is the duty of those who file claims, most typically plaintiffs. Capacity, by contrast, measures the ability of both plaintiffs and defendants to participate in a suit, even if the defendant has not filed a counterclaim or a crossclaim. The second difference is in the concepts underlying the respective provisions of Rule 17. Individuals may, because they are individuals, have capacity to sue. Capacity alone, however, does not permit those individuals to initiate a suit or to defend one. Unless they also have a material interest in the outcome of a cause of action, they may not bring a suit (or defend against a suit) because they are not also the real parties in interest.[31] Thus, to bring a suit, a party must have both "capacity," under the applicable law chosen by Rule 17(b), as well as a real stake in the outcome, as defined by Rule 17(a). To be sued, a defendant need only satisfy the law of capacity selected by Rule 17(b).

RULE 17(c).   MINOR OR INCOMPETENT PERSONS

CORE CONCEPT

This portion of Rule 17 controls the manner in which infants and other persons unable to represent their own interests will be represented in suits in federal court. The provisions apply irrespective of whether the infant or incompetent person is participating in the suit as a plaintiff or defendant.

---

30. *See, e.g., Kauffman v. Anglo–American School of Sofia,* 28 F.3d 1223, 1225 (D.C.Cir.1994)(cause of action based on state law means capacity of unincorporated association is also based on state law). *See also Streit v. County of Los Angeles,* 236 F.3d 552, 565 (9th Cir.2001) (in federal civil rights suit against county sheriff's department, Rule 17(b) deferred to state law to determine capacity of defendant to be sued).

31. *See, e.g., Lans v. Digital Equipment Corp.,* 252 F.3d 1320 (Fed.Cir.2001) (no right to amend complaint to name proper plaintiff where currently named plaintiff lacked standing to sue; original misrepresentation was apparently intentional).

APPLICATIONS

2007 Amendments

The 2007 Style Project amended Rule 17(c) by subdividing it into two subparts. This change should not present great difficulty for attorneys.

Infants and Incompetents Already Represented

Where persons unable to care for their own interests already have others charged with the duty to care for them outside of litigation, such as guardians, Rule 17(c) grants such guardians authority to sue on behalf of the persons in their care.[32]

Infants and Incompetents Not Already Represented

Where persons unable to care for their own interests are not already within the legal authority of others, they may be represented in litigation by persons chosen to protect their interests. The court has power to appoint such guardians *ad litem* (persons who will represent the interest of others in litigation),[33] and to make other orders consistent with the best interests of infants and incompetents in litigation.[34]

In the absence of "actual documentation or testimony by a mental health professional, a court of record, or a relevant public agency," the district court has no duty to make a sua sponte inquiry into a pro se party's lack of mental capacity.[35]

However, if it is settled that an unrepresented party is an infant or an incompetent person, the district court has an affirmative duty to appoint a guardian ad litem or to take other appropriate action.[36]

---

32. *Cf., Gonzalez v. Reno,* 212 F.3d 1338 (11th Cir.2000) (where child-plaintiff is "ably represented" by next friend, court need not appoint guardian ad litem); *Neilson v. Colgate–Palmolive Co.,* 199 F.3d 642, 650 (2d Cir.1999) ("[O]nly one party may act in a representative capacity with respect to an infant or incompetent who comes before the court."); *In re Kjellsen,* 53 F.3d 944 (8th Cir.1995)(when incompetent person already has a guardian, Rule 17(c) does not authorize suit by another person). *See generally, In the Matter of Chicago, Rock Island and Pacific Railroad Co.,* 788 F.2d 1280, 1282 (7th Cir.1986) (in circumstances where an infant or incompetent person is only a potential party, or whose interest is already represented, court has no duty to appoint a guardian ad litem, but may do so at its discretion; but if interest is not represented adequately, court has duty to appoint a representative).

33. *See, e.g., Gibbs v. Carnival Cruise Lines,* 314 F.3d 125, 135–36 (3d Cir.2002) (where infant is unrepresented, Rule 17(c) authorizes court to appoint guardian ad litem; unlike Rule 17(b), Rule 17(c) does not

defer to state standards for appointment; instead Rule 17(c) directs court to look to best interests of infant); *T.W. v. Brophy,* 124 F.3d 893, 895 (7th Cir.1997) ("next friend" usually appointed for plaintiff, while guardian ad litem usually appointed for defendant; but terms are not controlling).

34. *See, e.g., Krain v. Smallwood,* 880 F.2d 1119, 1121 (9th Cir.1989) (if infant or incompetent is unrepresented, "the court should not enter ... a judgment on the merits without complying with Rule 17(c)"). *See also, Wenger v. Canastota Central School District,* 146 F.3d 123 (2d Cir.1998) (under Rule 17(c) court may act *sua sponte* to protect interests of infants and incompetent persons).

35. *See, e.g., Ferrelli v. River Manor Health Care Center,* 323 F.3d 196, 202 (2d Cir.2003) ("bizarre behavior" by itself does not require examination of competence).

36. *See, e.g., Buchanan County v. Blankenship,* 406 F.Supp.2d 642, 645 (W.D.Va.2005) (noting contrast with con-

Prior Determination of Incompetence

There is no prerequisite that a state authority determine incompetence before a district court appoints a guardian ad litem.[37]

Incompetence: Delay of Trial

A criminal defendant who suffers from significant mental impairment may be entitled to a delay in trial proceedings until the impairment eases. However, in civil litigation mental incompetence may not have the same result. Instead, the court may employ Rule 17(c) to appoint a guardian ad litem.[38]

Authority of Representative

When a representative is appointed under Rule 17(c), that person has most of the authority that a competent client would have. However, Rule 17(c) does not by itself give the appointed person the right to serve as legal counsel for the infant or incompetent person.[39]

Other Orders

Section 17(c) expressly authorizes the district court to issue other orders necessary to protect infants and incompetents. This authority includes the power to determine rates of compensation for guardians ad litem and to determine which party shall bear the cost of such expenses.[40]

RULE 17(d). PUBLIC OFFICER'S TITLE AND NAME

CORE CONCEPT

Rule 17(d) was added in 2007. It continues a provision previously found under Rule 25(d). It allows suit by or against a public officer under either that person's official title or personal name. The court, however, may add the individual's name in cases where the official title alone has been used. The primary advantage of suing a public officer by title, rather than individual name, is that departure of the person from office thereby does not require consideration of a substitution of names under Rule 25.

victed prisoners, to whom the court owes no equivalent duty).

37. *See, e.g., Fonner v. Fairfax County,* 415 F.3d 325 (4th Cir.2005) ("Nothing in the rule prohibits the district court from appointing a guardian ad litem to represent a person not previously adjudicated as incompetent through a state proceeding.").

38. *See, e.g., United States v. Mandycz,* 351 F.3d 222, 225 n. 1 (6th Cir.2003) (explaining application of Rule 17(c); "a civil defendant's mental incompetence does not trigger an abatement of trial as it does in the criminal context").

39. *See, e.g., Tindall v. Poultney High School District,* 414 F.3d 281 (2d Cir.2005) (right to proceed *pro se* does not apply to

non-attorney parents who are guardians ad litem of minor children); *Cavanaugh v. Cardinal Local School District,* 409 F.3d 753, 755 (6th Cir.2005) (Rule 17(c) does not authorize parents "to serve as legal counsel for their minor children's cause of action;" ordinary *pro se* rules do not apply); *Devine v. Indian River County School Board,* 121 F.3d 576, 581 (11th Cir.1997) (Rule 17(c) "permits authorized representatives, including parents, to sue on behalf of minors, but does not confer any right upon such representatives to serve as legal counsel.").

40. *Gaddis v. United States,* 381 F.3d 444, 453 (5th Cir.2004) (en banc)(court may apportion guardian ad litem fees as court costs).

ADDITIONAL RESEARCH REFERENCES

Wright & Miller, *Federal Practice and Procedure* §§ 1541–73.

C.J.S. Federal Civil Procedure §§ 46–62 et seq.

West's Key No. Digests, Federal Civil Procedure ⟳111–116, 131–149.

RULE 18

JOINDER OF CLAIMS

(a) In General. A party asserting a claim, counterclaim, crossclaim, or third-party claim may join, as independent or alternative claims, as many claims as it has against an opposing party.

(b) Joinder of Contingent Claims. A party may join two claims even though one of them is contingent on the disposition of the other; but the court may grant relief only in accordance with the parties' relative substantive rights. In particular, a plaintiff may state a claim for money and a claim to set aside a conveyance that is fraudulent as to that plaintiff, without first obtaining a judgment for the money.

[Amended effective July 1, 1966; August 1, 1987; April 30, 2007, effective December 1, 2007.]

--------------------- **2007 AMENDMENTS ROADMAP** ---------------------

STYLE PROJECT CHANGES: The Rule title was shortened. Cumbersome language was culled to aid readability. Outdated reference to "legal, equitable, or maritime claims" was eliminated.

NON-STYLE CHANGES: None.

NOTE: The Federal Rules "Style Project" is explained in Part III-A.

AUTHORS' COMMENTARY ON RULE 18

--------------------- **PURPOSE AND SCOPE** ---------------------

Rule 18 permits claimants to bring all claims they may have against persons already parties to a case, notwithstanding the fact that the claims may be unrelated to one another.[1]

---

1. *See, e.g., Deajess Medical Imaging, P.C. v. Allstate Insurance Co.,* 381 F.Supp.2d 307, 310 (S.D.N.Y.2005) (Rule 18 "does not require that the aggregated claims be factually related.").

RULE 18(a). IN GENERAL

CORE CONCEPT

Rule 18(a) abolishes prohibitions against bringing unrelated claims against the same defendant(s) in a single action. The origin of the claims, whether equitable, legal, or originating in admiralty, is irrelevant to the right to plead claims in a single action.[2]

APPLICATIONS

Parties Who May Join Claims

The right to join claims is available to any claimant who is a party to the case, irrespective of whether the claims filed will be counterclaims, crossclaims, third-party claims, or original claims filed by the plaintiff.[3]

Rule 18(a) is Permissive, Not Compulsory

A party choosing not to bring unrelated claims is free to file them in separate actions.[4] This assumes the claim is not otherwise barred by considerations such as a statute of limitations.

NOTE: Notwithstanding the permissive nature of Rule 18(a), there may be problems in subsequent litigation if the claims not filed in the initial litigation were related to the claims actually raised. In that circumstance, suits filed later may be subject to the bar of res judicata or collateral estoppel.

Separate Trials

Notwithstanding the liberal nature of this joinder provision, the trial court may still exercise its discretion to order separate trials on different claims pursuant to Rule 42(b).[5]

Relation to Rule 14

Rule 18 provides that a party properly asserting a third-party claim may join all claims that party has against a third-party defendant. However, it is still true that Rule 14, governing third-party practice, must first be applied to determine whether a third-party claim is permitted. If one of the claims does not meet the requirements of Rule 14, *e.g.*, if none of the asserted third-party claims relate to the claims against the third-party plaintiff, then impleader is not permissible. In that circumstance, there can be no joinder of third-party claims pursuant to Rule 18.[6]

2. *See, e.g., Dodoo v. Seagate Technology, Inc.,* 235 F.3d 522, 529 (10th Cir.2000) (joinder of claims is "common and preferred method"); *Vodusek v. Bayliner Marine Corp.,* 71 F.3d 148, 154 (4th Cir.1995)(Rule 18 permits "joinder of claims at law, in equity, and in admiralty").

3. *See, e.g., First National Bank of Cincinnati v. Pepper,* 454 F.2d 626, 635 (2d Cir.1972)(party asserting cross-claim that meets requirements of Rule 13(g) may also join unrelated claims pursuant to Rule 18(a)).

4. *See, e.g., Perkins v. Board of Trustees of the University of Illinois,* 116 F.3d 235 (7th Cir.1997) ("Rule 18(a) permits rather than compels the joinder of distinct claims against one adversary.")

5. *See, e.g., Parmer v. National Cash Register Co.,* 503 F.2d 275, 277 (6th Cir. 1974)(per curiam)(separation is within trial court's discretion).

6. *See, e.g., Lehman v. Revolution Portfolio, L.L.C.,* 166 F.3d 389, 394 (1st Cir. 1999) (once defendant, in role of third-party plaintiff, properly impleaded a third-party

Relation to Rule 15

Rule 18 identifies the circumstances in which a party may, in the party's original pleading, join more than one claim against other parties. However, if an additional claim is asserted after an original claim has been filed, the additional claim must also meet the requirements of Rule 15, governing amendments to pleadings.[7]

Jurisdiction and Venue

Joinder under Rule 18(a) is subject to requirements of jurisdiction and venue. Thus, Rule 18(a) permits joinder of claims only where the claims independently satisfy such requirements.[8] For a further discussion of jurisdiction and venue, see §§ 2.1–2.14.

Joinder of Parties

Rule 18(a) authorizes only joinder of claims, not the addition of parties.[9] If joining a particular claim also requires joining additional parties, such parties may be added only as permitted under other applicable Rules.[10]

RULE 18(b). JOINDER OF CONTINGENT CLAIMS

CORE CONCEPT

This portion of Rule 18 permits joining two claims in a single action, even if the situation is one in which the court must decide the first claim before the second claim can be determined. For example, a plaintiff may sue on a personal injury, and add a count accusing a defendant of fraudulently transferring assets to the defendant's spouse as a means of frustrating enforcement of a judgment the plaintiff might obtain.

APPLICATION

Timing

In the example cited above, a plaintiff can present evidence on both claims at the same time, even though recovery on the allegation of fraudulent conveyance would first require that the defendant be held liable on the personal injury claim.[11]

---

defendant, Rule 18(a) permits joinder of all claims that third-party plaintiff has against third-party defendant); *Tietz v. Blackner,* 157 F.R.D. 510, 512 (D.Utah 1994) ("Rule 18(a) would apply only after a suitable joinder under Rule 14 has been allowed.").

7. *See, e.g., Mackensworth v. S.S. American Merchant,* 28 F.3d 246, 251 (2d Cir. 1994)(adding claim to existing complaint requires compliance with Rule 15; Rule 18 "deals only with pleading requirements").

8. *See, e.g., King Fisher Marine Service, Inc. v. 21st Phoenix Corp.,* 893 F.2d 1155, 1158 n. 2 (10th Cir.1990) ("[A] court may decide claims joined under Rule 18(a) only if independent jurisdiction and venue re-

quirements are satisfied."). It should be noted that where two counts are sufficiently related, courts may use supplemental jurisdiction as an "independent" source of subject matter jurisdiction. *See, e.g., Kunkel v. Topmaster International, Inc.,* 906 F.2d 693, 697 n. 1 (Fed.Cir.1990)(so holding).

9. *See, e.g., Bradbury Co. v. Teissier-duCros,* 231 F.R.D. 413, 415 (D.Kan.2005) ("The text of this rule clearly relates to the joinder of claims not parties.").

10. *See* Rule 20, concerning joinder of parties.

11. *See, e.g., Huntress v. Huntress' Estate,* 235 F.2d 205, 207–08 (7th Cir.

NOTE: Rule 18(b) may afford a plaintiff substantial opportunity to gain advantage with a jury by using evidence of a fraudulent conveyance to color the jury's view of the personal injury claim. In theory, the court's authority under Rule 42(b) to separate the claims is a safeguard against the risk of such inappropriate prejudice to the defendant. In practice, the need to separate the claims may not be sufficiently obvious at the outset of the trial, when Rule 42(b) is most likely to be employed.

ADDITIONAL RESEARCH REFERENCES

Wright & Miller, *Federal Practice and Procedure* §§ 1581–94.

C.J.S. Federal Civil Procedure §§ 40–41, 301; Fraudulent Conveyances §§ 331, 494.

West's Key No. Digests, Federal Civil Procedure ⇔81–86, 733; Fraudulent Conveyances ⇔241(2).

1956)(noting that Rule 18(b) permits join-   der of such counts).

RULE 19

REQUIRED JOINDER OF PARTIES

(a) Persons Required to Be Joined if Feasible.

(1) *Required Party.* A person who is subject to service of process and whose joinder will not deprive the court of subject-matter jurisdiction must be joined as a party if:

(A) in that person's absence, the court cannot accord complete relief among existing parties; or

(B) that person claims an interest relating to the subject of the action and is so situated that disposing of the action in the person's absence may:

(i) as a practical matter impair or impede the person's ability to protect the interest; or

(ii) leave an existing party subject to a substantial risk of incurring double, multiple, or otherwise inconsistent obligations because of the interest.

(2) *Joinder by Court Order.* If a person has not been joined as required, the court must order that the person be made a party. A person who refuses to join as a plaintiff may be made either a defendant or, in a proper case, an involuntary plaintiff.

(3) *Venue.* If a joined party objects to venue and the joinder would make venue improper, the court must dismiss that party.

(b) When Joinder Is Not Feasible. If a person who is required to be joined if feasible cannot be joined, the court must determine whether, in equity and good conscience, the action should proceed among the existing parties or should be dismissed. The factors for the court to consider include:

(1) the extent to which a judgment rendered in the person's absence might prejudice that person or the existing parties;

(2) the extent to which any prejudice could be lessened or avoided by:

(A) protective provisions in the judgment;

508

(B) shaping the relief; or

(C) other measures;

(3) whether a judgment rendered in the person's absence would be adequate; and

(4) whether the plaintiff would have an adequate remedy if the action were dismissed for nonjoinder.

(c) Pleading the Reasons for Nonjoinder. When asserting a claim for relief, a party must state:

(1) the name, if known, of any person who is required to be joined if feasible but is not joined; and

(2) the reasons for not joining that person.

(d) Exception for Class Actions. This rule is subject to Rule 23.

[Amended effective July 1, 1966; August 1, 1987; April 30, 2007, effective December 1, 2007.]

─────────────── **2007 AMENDMENTS ROADMAP** ───────────────

STYLE PROJECT CHANGES: The Rule title was shortened. New orienting labels were added. Parts (a), (b), and (c) were further subsectioned to enhance clarity. Definite articles (e.g., "the" person) replaced indefinite articles (e.g., "a" person); "must" replaced "shall"; and active voice generally replaced passive voice.

NON-STYLE CHANGES: A person qualifying for joinder under Rule 19(a), but who cannot be joined (for reasons of, e.g., improper venue or lack of jurisdiction), is no longer described as an "indispensable" person in Rule 19(b). The term was eliminated as redundant.

NOTE: The Federal Rules "Style Project" is explained in Part III-A.

AUTHORS' COMMENTARY ON RULE 19

─────────────── PURPOSE AND SCOPE ───────────────

Rule 19 addresses distinct but related questions concerning joinder of parties. Rule 19(a) describes when a court should order the joinder of a person who is not yet a party to the case. If such a person should be joined, the court will then evaluate whether, under principles of jurisdiction and venue, the person can be joined.[1] If joinder is not feasible, Rule 19(b) addresses whether the court should dismiss the case or continue without that person. Application of Rule 19 typically arises when a defendant makes a motion to dismiss the action under Rule 12(b)(7), alleging that the plaintiff failed to join a person whose presence is "indispensable" to the action.

AMENDMENT OF RULE

This Rule was substantially rewritten in 1966. Judicial decisions that predate 1966 should be cited with great care, if at all.

NOTE: More than most Rules, the application of Rule 19 is highly fact specific.[2] Thus, when the court addresses questions of impairment of interest, the court will examine both legal and actual, real-world, impairment.

RULE 19(a). PERSONS REQUIRED TO BE JOINED IF FEASIBLE

CORE CONCEPT

When feasible, persons should be joined when their absence will either materially reduce the likelihood that the court can provide justice for those already parties or be detrimental to the non-parties themselves.[3]

APPLICATIONS

Joinder of Parties Necessary

The court may join necessary parties in the following cases:[4]

(1) The court may order joinder of a person in whose absence complete relief cannot be granted to those already parties to the

---

1. *See, e.g., Keweenaw Bay Indian Community v. State of Michigan,* 11 F.3d 1341, 1347 (6th Cir.1993)(describing Rule 19 as a "three-step" analysis, including the jurisdiction/venue analysis).

2. *See, e.g., Gonzalez v. Metropolitan Transportation Authority,* 174 F.3d 1016, 1019 (9th Cir.1999) ("Whether a party is necessary and indispensable is a pragmatic and equitable judgment, not a jurisdictional one."); *United States ex rel. Hall v. Tribal Development Corp.,* 100 F.3d 476, 481 (7th Cir.1996) (Rule 19 analysis is pragmatic and fact specific).

3. *See, e.g., Hammond v. Clayton,* 83 F.3d 191, 195 (7th Cir.1996) ("Rule 19 is designed to protect the interests of absent persons, as well as those already before the court, from duplicative litigation, inconsis-

tent judicial determinations, or other practical impairment of their legal interests.").

4. *Cf., Johnson v. Smithsonian Institution,* 189 F.3d 180, 188 (2d Cir.1999) (error to find party necessary under Rule 19(a) because in party's absence district court " 'could not begin to determine whether [that party] unlawfully retained pieces of ... art in 1946, or which pieces of the art were kept, or how [others] came to learn of this tortious act.' ... The question of whether or not an entity or individual should be a party to an action is something quite different from the questions and problems associated with obtaining evidence from such an entity or individual." The need to obtain evidence is not a factor under Rule 19(a)).

case.[5] For example, when an Indian group sues a state for exclusive fishing rights, and does not join other competing Indian groups, the state is denied complete relief.[6]

(2) The court may order joinder of a party whose interest[7] may be impaired either practically or legally.[8] For example, when a plaintiff seeks to recover from a limited fund controlled by the defendant, and a non-party has a claim against the fund, the court may join the non-party so as to protect that person's possibility of sharing in the fund before it is exhausted.[9]

5. *See, e.g., Disabled Rights Action Committee v. Las Vegas Events, Inc.,* 375 F.3d 861 (9th Cir.2004) (party is "necessary" if in its absence meaningful relief cannot be afforded to those who are already joined, thus risking multiple lawsuits on same issue).

6. *See, e.g., Citizen Potawatomi Nation v. Norton,* 248 F.3d 993, 998 (10th Cir. 2001), *opinion modified on reh'g,* 257 F.3d 1158 (10th Cir.2001) (Rule 19(a) does not require possession of "actual" interest, but only a claimed interest where the claim is not "patently frivolous"). *See also Dawavendewa v. Salt River Project Agriculture Improvement & Power District,* 276 F.3d 1150, 1153 (9th Cir.2002) (plaintiff cannot get complete relief by obtaining injunction barring enforcement of lease provision giving preferential hiring to Navajo tribe; suit against tribe was barred by tribal sovereign immunity, and in absence of tribe, result of suit would bind only plaintiff and defendant (which has lease with tribe), but not tribe); *Manybeads v. United States,* 209 F.3d 1164, 1165 (9th Cir.2000) (plaintiff cannot be provided complete relief without damage to prior settlement with rival Indian tribe; held, rival tribe is necessary party under Rule 19(a)(1)); *Keweenaw Bay Indian Community v. State of Michigan,* 11 F.3d 1341, 1345 (6th Cir.1993)(so holding). *But see, Angst v. Royal Maccabees Life Insurance Co.,* 77 F.3d 701, 705 (3d Cir.1996)(risk that successful party in instant lawsuit might face challenge to rights by receiver in later suit does not equal a lack of complete relief).

7. *Cf., National Union Fire Insurance Co. of Pittsburgh v. Rite Aid of South Carolina, Inc.,* 210 F.3d 246, 250–51 (4th Cir. 2000) ("A court should hesitate to conclude . . . that a litigant can serve as a proxy for an absent party unless the interests of the two are identical.").

8. *See, e.g., Davis v. United States,* 192 F.3d 951, 958 (10th Cir.1999) ("Rule 19 . . . does not require the absent party to actual-

ly possess an interest; it only requires the movant to show that the absent party 'claims an interest relating to the subject of the action.' "); *Laker Airways, Inc. v. British Airways, PLC,* 182 F.3d 843, 847–48 (11th Cir.1999) (outside entity has interest in case where court must pass on neutrality of its behavior, because finding of failure of neutrality might affect British government's view of entity's legal obligation to behave in a neutral manner). *International Paper Co. v. Denkmann Associates,* 116 F.3d 134, 137 (5th Cir.1997) (party held indispensable where it owned parcels of land "interspersed" among land parcels held by other party—adjudication of some parcels will be affected by other land). *But see, Rishell v. Jane Phillips Episcopal Memorial Medical Center,* 94 F.3d 1407, 1411 (10th Cir.1996) (non-party husband's loss of consortium dependent on outcome of wife's right to recover on injury claim; but husband's interest is adequately represented by wife's guardian).

9. *See, e.g., In re Torcise,* 116 F.3d 860, 865 (11th Cir.1997) ("It is well established under Rule 19 that all claimants to a fund must be joined to determine the disposition of that fund."); *Angst v. Royal Maccabees Life Insurance Co.,* 77 F.3d 701, 705 (3d Cir.1996)(where defendant insurance company is sued in both state and federal court and will have to pay into escrow account for same policy in two cases, plaintiff in state suit should be joined under Rule 19(a)(2)(ii)). *But see HS Resources, Inc. v. Wingate,* 327 F.3d 432, 439 (5th Cir.2003) (in dispute over landowner's right to royalty payments on natural gas well, case between instant landowner and gas company could be decided without joinder of other landowners whose leases were not affected); *State of Washington v. Daley,* 173 F.3d 1158 (9th Cir.1999) (held, absent party need not be joined as necessary party if current party will adequately represent absent party's interest; adequate representation found

(3) Where several persons have overlapping interests in a defendant's property, the court may order their joinder to preclude the possibility of inconsistent obligations. For example, if a tenant seeks an injunction to enforce a lease against a landlord, complications can arise if the property is also subject to a potentially conflicting lease held by another person. In that circumstance, joinder of the second tenant will prevent the risk that the landlord will be subject to inconsistent duties to the two tenants.[10]

(4) As a general rule, courts construing contracts require that parties to the contract be joined.[11] Additionally, a shareholder's

where: (1) absent party and current party share similar interests; (2) current party will raise all appropriate issues; and (3) absent party will not add any important element to litigation). *Cf., Dawavendewa v. Salt River Project Agriculture Improvement & Power District,* 276 F.3d 1150, 1156–57 (9th Cir.2002) (action to set aside lease or contract threatens non-party's interest in lease, thereby raising Rule 19(a)(2)); *National Union Fire Insurance Co. of Pittsburgh v. Rite Aid of South Carolina, Inc.,* 210 F.3d 246, 252 (4th Cir.2000) ("[A] contracting party is the paradigm of an indispensable party."). *See also United States v. Bowen,* 172 F.3d 682, 689 (9th Cir.1999) (if absent party knows of litigation and does not claim a legally protected interest, joinder is unnecessary).

10. *See, e.g., Helzberg's Diamond Shops, Inc. v. Valley West Des Moines Shopping Center, Inc.,* 564 F.2d 816 (8th Cir.1977). *See also, Dawavendewa v. Salt River Project Agriculture Improvement & Power District,* 276 F.3d 1150, 1157–58 (9th Cir.2002) (absence of Navajo tribe, due to tribal sovereign immunity, leaves defendant, who is contracting party with tribe on lease that is challenged by plaintiff, vulnerable to later suit by tribe to enforce agreement); *National Union Fire Insurance Co. of Pittsburgh v. Rite Aid of South Carolina, Inc.,* 210 F.3d 246, 252 (4th Cir.2000) ("[A] contracting party is the paradigm of an indispensable party."). *But cf., Bassett v. Mashantucket Pequot Tribe,* 204 F.3d 343, 358–60 (2d Cir. 2000) (in suit for copyright infringement and tort, plaintiff need not sue all defendants; thus, a defendant immune from suit is not indispensable; not deciding on indispensability of person who was party to contract action, but noting that such a person might be indispensable in action on contract); *Temple v. Synthes Corp., Ltd.,* 498 U.S. 5, 7, 111 S.Ct. 315, 316, 112 L.Ed.2d 263 (1990) (per curiam) ("It has long been the rule that it is not necessary for all joint

tortfeasors to be named as defendants in a single lawsuit."); *Delgado v. Plaza Las Americas, Inc.,* 139 F.3d 1 (1st Cir.1998) (per curiam) (defendant was sued in two different courts over liability relating to rape; parent of rape victim sued for parent's emotional anguish in instant case, while daughter sued as victim of rape herself in a different court; held, Rule 19(a)(2)(ii) does not make daughter a necessary party in parent's lawsuit; requirement of Rule 19(a)(2)(ii) is for finding of inconsistent obligations–*i.e.,* inability of defendant to comply with one court's order without breaching another court's order; inconsistent adjudications, where defendant wins one suit and loses another arising from the same incident, do not trigger applicability of Rule 19(a)(2)(ii)).

11. *See, e.g., Dawavendewa v. Salt River Project Agriculture Improvement & Power District,* 276 F.3d 1150, 1156–57 (9th Cir. 2002) (action to set aside lease or contract threatens non-party's interest in lease, thereby raising Rule 19(a)(2)); *Harris Trust and Savings Bank v. Energy Assets International Corp.,* 124 F.R.D. 115, 117 (E.D.La. 1989)("[W]here interpretation of a contract is involved, parties to that contract must be joined."). *But cf., Extra Equipamentos e Exportacao Ltda. v. Case Corp.,* 361 F.3d 359, 363–64 (7th Cir.2004) (litigation over settlement agreement may not require presence of corporate subsidiary whose parent is already a party and whose parent is sole owner of subsidiary; in such a circumstance the "complete identity" of interest between parent and subsidiary means absence of subsidiary may not be harmful to subsidiary); *Davis Companies v. Emerald Casino, Inc.,* 268 F.3d 477, 482–83 (7th Cir.2001) (if absent party has separate and independent contract with a party, which did not implicate issues raised in separate contract dispute between those already parties, there is no need to join absent party).

derivative suit against a corporation typically makes the corporation itself an indispensable party.[12]

Procedure

Only a party may make a Rule 19 motion.[13]   In the ordinary course of events, use of Rule 19 is triggered when a claimant has not joined everyone potentially affected by a claim.   The party claimed against may then file a motion to dismiss the claim under Rule 12(b)(7), governing dismissals for failure to join a person who should be a party.[14]   To determine whether the motion should be granted, the court will apply the standards of Rule 19.   Typically, the court will either: (1) order the person joined, and deny the motion to dismiss; (2) refuse to order joinder, and deny the motion to dismiss; or (3) acknowledge that the person crucial to the action cannot (for reasons of jurisdiction or venue) be joined, and grant the motion to dismiss.

Service on Non-parties

If the court determines that a person should be joined in pending litigation, it will direct that service be made upon that person.[15] It should be noted that such service may properly employ the "bulge" provision of Rule 4(k), permitting service within 100 miles of the place where the service issued without regard to normal limitations that may be imposed by state law.[16]

Prerequisite that Non–Party to be Joined as Defendant be Subject to Cause of Action

It is not clear whether the person whose joinder as a defendant is sought must, as a prerequisite to joinder, be subject to a cause of action. The judicial precedent appears to be in conflict.[17] Attorneys are therefore forced to consult local precedent and practice.

12. *Gabriel v. Preble,* 396 F.3d 10, 13 (1st Cir.2005).

13. *See, e.g., Arrow v. Gambler's Supply, Inc.,* 55 F.3d 407, 409 (8th Cir. 1995)(while non-parties may not make motions under Rule 19, "a court may sua sponte join a party for good cause"). *See also Sac and Fox Nation of Missouri v. Pierce,* 213 F.3d 566 n. 11 (10th Cir.2000) (raising joinder question sua sponte).

14. *See, e.g., HS Resources, Inc. v. Wingate,* 327 F.3d 432, 438–39 (5th Cir.2003) (describing relationship of rule 12(b)(7) to Rule 19).

15. *See, e.g., PaineWebber, Inc. v. Cohen,* 276 F.3d 197, 200 (6th Cir.2001) ("If the party is deemed necessary for the reasons enumerated in Rule 19(a), the court must next consider whether the party is subject to personal jurisdiction and can be joined without eliminating the basis for subject matter jurisdiction.").

16. Fed.R.Civ.P. 4(k). *See also Quinones v. Pennsylvania General Insurance Co.,* 804 F.2d 1167, 1173–74 (10th Cir.1986) (minimum contacts in bulge area made person amenable to service of process therein).

17. *Compare, e.g., Vieux Carre Property Owners v. Brown,* 875 F.2d 453, 457 (5th Cir.1989) ("[I]t is implicit in Rule 19(a) itself that before a party … will be joined as a defendant the plaintiff must have a cause of action against it."); *Davenport v. International Board of Teamsters, AFL–CIO,* 166 F.3d 356, 366 (D.C. Cir.1999) (same), *with EEOC v. Peabody Western Coal Co.,* 400 F.3d 774, 783 (9th Cir.2005) (permitting joinder notwithstanding lack of cause of action against third person where joinder will help effect complete relief between parties; citing, *inter alia, International Brotherhood of Teamsters v. United States,* 431 U.S. 324, 356 n. 43, 97 S.Ct. 1843, 1865 n. 43, 52 L.Ed.2d 396 (1977),

Time

Rule 19 contains no express time limit within which a party seeking joinder must file a motion. However, undue delay in filing can be grounds for denying a motion,[18] particularly if absent persons will not be prejudiced by nonjoinder.[19]

Joinder of Plaintiffs

When a person should join as a plaintiff but refuses to do so, the court may join the person as an involuntary plaintiff or even a defendant.[20]

Joinder in Diversity Cases

In diversity cases joining an additional party may adversely affect jurisdiction. Courts have limited ability to avoid the problem, depending on whether the person to be joined should be joined as a plaintiff or a defendant. If the person to be joined could be made either an involuntary plaintiff or a defendant, the court may preserve jurisdiction simply by aligning the joined person in a way that maintains diversity.[21] However, if the person can only be joined as a defendant, and that joinder would destroy diversity, the court has no room to maneuver. In this situation, the court must apply Rule 19(b) to determine whether to proceed without the non-joined party.[22]

Venue

Joined persons retain the right to object to venue within the time frame provided in Rule 12(h)(1), governing preservation of certain defenses. When venue is inappropriate, the court must deny the motion to join a party. In that circumstance the court must

and attempting to distinguish *Vieux* and *Davenport, supra*).

18. *See, e.g., Northeast Drilling, Inc. v. Inner Space Services, Inc.*, 243 F.3d 25, 36–37 (1st Cir.2001) (affirming denial of joinder when motion was made "well after" time limit set in scheduling order, with no explanation for delay); *Gil Enterprises, Inc. v. Delvy*, 79 F.3d 241, 247 (2d Cir. 1996)(citing excessive delay in raising Rule 19 issue as ground to deny motion).

19. *See, e.g., Sierra Club v. Hathaway*, 579 F.2d 1162, 1166 (9th Cir.1978)(because absent persons were not prejudiced by judgment, parties' failure to raise Rule 19 issue did not undermine judgment).

20. *Independent Wireless Telegraph Co. v. Radio Corp. of America*, 269 U.S. 459, 46 S.Ct. 166, 70 L.Ed. 357 (1926); *but see, Eikel v. States Marine Lines, Inc.*, 473 F.2d 959, 962 (5th Cir.1973)("involuntary" plaintiffs should not be joined freely; such joinder should occur only in unusual cases

where the person has an obligation to participate).

21. *Koster v. (American) Lumbermens Mutual Casualty Co.*, 330 U.S. 518, 67 S.Ct. 828, 91 L.Ed. 1067 (1947). *Cf., Mayes v. Rapoport*, 198 F.3d 457, 462 (4th Cir.1999) (in cases removed from state court, 28 U.S.C. § 1447(e) provides district courts with considerable discretion to permit or deny post-removal joinder; however, if court permits joinder of non-diverse party and thereby destroys diversity jurisdiction, § 1447(e) requires court to remand case to state court; in any event, decision to permit or deny joinder in such removed cases is not controlled by Rule 19).

22. *Cf., Cobb v. Delta Exports, Inc.*, 186 F.3d 675, 677 (5th Cir.1999) ("[P]ost-removal joinder of non-diverse defendants pursuant to [Rule 19] destroys diversity for jurisdictional purposes and requires remand, even when the newly joined defendants are not indispensable.").

consult Rule 19(b) to determine whether to proceed without the non-joined party. For a further discussion of venue, *see* § 2.14.

RULE 19(b). WHEN JOINDER IS NOT FEASIBLE

CORE CONCEPT

Rule 19(b) governs whether the court should proceed without persons who should be joined, but who cannot be joined because their joinder would defeat jurisdiction or venue. The court has substantial discretion to determine, under the considerations listed in Rule 19(b), whether to continue the litigation without the person or to dismiss the action because a party cannot be joined.[23]

NOTE: In most cases under Rule 19(b) the court attempts to continue the suit rather than dismiss it.[24] Thus a defendant who has filed a motion under Rule 12(b)(7) should contemplate ways to reach a compromise with the court and opposing counsel that continues the suit on terms more favorable to the defendant. Shaping appropriate remedies is one area that might offer particularly good prospects for such terms.

APPLICATIONS

Relation to Rule 19(a)

If joinder is not required under Rule 19(a), the court will proceed without joinder. In such cases, the court does not have to evaluate the applicability of Rule 19(b).[25]

Who May Raise Rule 19(b)

The parties may raise Rule 19 issues. Additionally, the court may raise Rule 19(b) issues *sua sponte*.[26]

Relative Weight of Factors in Rule 19(b)

The considerations listed in Rule 19(b) are factors to be weighed, so that in a given case one might be more important than others.[27] The list is not one where every consideration must be

---

23. *See, e.g., Soberay Machine & Equipment Co. v. MRF Limited, Inc.,* 181 F.3d 759, 765 (6th Cir.1999) (determination under Rule 19(b) should be made on case by case assessment; "there is no prescribed formula for determining whether a party is indispensable").

24. *See, e.g., Teamsters Local Union No. 171 v. Keal Driveway Co.,* 173 F.3d 915, 918 (4th Cir.1999) ("Dismissal of a case is a drastic remedy ... which should be employed only sparingly."). *Jaser v. New York Property Insurance Underwriting Association,* 815 F.2d 240, 242 (2d Cir. 1987)("[V]ery few cases should be terminated due to the absence of nondiverse parties unless there has been a reasoned determi-

nation that their nonjoinder makes just resolution of the action impossible.").

25. *See, e.g., Snap–On Tools Corp. v. Mason,* 18 F.3d 1261, 1267 (5th Cir. 1994)(no need to apply Rule 19(b) standards when joinder is not mandated under Rule 19(a)).

26. *See, e.g., Manning v. Energy Conversion Devices, Inc.,* 13 F.3d 606, 609 (2d Cir.1994)(even if parties make no Rule 19(a) objections, the court is "obliged" to raise Rule 19(b) issues if they are present).

27. *See, e.g., Delgado v. Plaza Las Americas, Inc.,* 139 F.3d 1 (1st Cir.1998) (referring to elements of Rule 19(b) as "gestalt factors").

satisfied before dismissal is ordered, or before the case may proceed.[28] Additionally, it is possible that in a particular case other factors not listed in Rule 19(b) could be important.[29]

Factors

(1) *Adverse Consequences of Proceeding Without a Person:* The court will examine whether adverse consequences such as legal or practical damage may result by proceeding without a party.[30] For example, persons already parties may be damaged if the suit creates the potential for inconsistent judgments discussed in Rule 19(a).[31] Similarly, a person not joined may be harmed if the suit proceeds to judgment and exhausts a fund from which compensation might otherwise have been anticipated.[32] Finally, if there is a risk of collateral estoppel for the absent person, that factor weighs in favor of dismissing the action.[33] By contrast, if a potential party shows no interest in a case, its interests probably are not significantly affected by the outcome of the case.[34]

If the interest at risk is that of the absent party, and that interest is adequately represented by someone already in the case, it is possible that a court will consider the risk of impairment to be

28. *See, e.g., Universal Reinsurance Co. v. St. Paul Fire & Marine Insurance Co.,* 312 F.3d 82, 88–89 (2d Cir.2002) ("Rule 19(b) . . . does not require that every factor support the district court's determination."); *Rhone-Poulenc, Inc. v. International Insurance Co.,* 71 F.3d 1299, 1301 (7th Cir. 1995)("Rule 19(b) sets forth a standard, not a rigid rule."); *Glenny v. American Metal Climax, Inc.,* 494 F.2d 651, 653 (10th Cir. 1974)(each factor should be evaluated for its significance in the particular case).

29. *See, e.g., Gardiner v. Virgin Islands Water & Power Authority,* 145 F.3d 635, 640 (3d Cir.1998) (listed factors "are not exhaustive, but they are the most important considerations"). *Cf., Davis v. United States,* 192 F.3d 951, 960 (10th Cir.1999) (inability of court to join Indian tribe shielded by sovereign immunity may also be weighed, but presence of this additional factor does not eliminate application of factors listed in Rule 19(b)).

30. *Cf., HB General Corp. v. Manchester Partners, L.P.,* 95 F.3d 1185, 1193 (3d Cir. 1996) (if all partners are parties, partnership itself may not be indispensable because its interests are represented adequately).

31. *See, e.g., Helzberg's Diamond Shops, Inc. v. Valley West Des Moines Shopping Center, Inc.,* 564 F.2d 816 (8th Cir.1977). *See also Estate of Alvarez v. Donaldson Co.,* 213 F.3d 993 (7th Cir.2000) (finding preju-

dice to plaintiff by proceeding in case without absent persons where, after potential favorable judgment, plaintiff would have to sue absent persons in state court); *National Union Fire Insurance Co. of Pittsburgh v. Rite Aid of South Carolina, Inc.,* 210 F.3d 246, 252 (4th Cir.2000) (first factor of Rule 19(b) "addresses many of the same concerns as Rule 19(a)(2)").

32. *See, e.g., In re Torcise,* 116 F.3d 860, 865 (11th Cir.1997) ("It is well established under Rule 19 that all claimants to a fund must be joined to determine the disposition of that fund.").

33. *See, e.g., Schulman v. J.P. Morgan Investment Management, Inc.,* 35 F.3d 799, 806 (3d Cir.1994)("Prejudice under Rule 19(b) . . . implicates principles of collateral estoppel.").

34. *See, e.g., Gardiner v. Virgin Islands Water & Power Authority,* 145 F.3d 635 (3d Cir.1998) (so holding; moreover, a party's right to contribution or indemnity from a person not joined "does not render that absentee indispensable"). *But cf., Tell v. Trustees of Dartmouth College,* 145 F.3d 417 (1st Cir.1998) (fact that potential party is silent does not mean it does not claim an interest; language of Rule 19 merely means potential party "appears to have such an interest;" however, it is a different situation where potential party disclaimed an interest).

nullified.[35] However, courts are cautious in reaching the conclusion that an interest is adequately represented by existing parties.[36]

(2) *Avoiding Adverse Consequences:* The second consideration directs the court to determine if means are available to the court for minimizing potential damage. When applying this factor, the court should make a fact-specific analysis. For example, as illustrated in the discussion of Rule 19(a), if a tenant sought injunctive relief against a landlord, and the tenant agreed to a damage remedy rather than an injunction, the risk to the landlord of mutually inconsistent injunctions is minimized, and the case may be allowed to proceed.[37]

(3) *Adequacy of a Judgment:* This consideration addresses "adequacy" primarily from the point of view of the public interest in efficient and final disposition of legal disputes. Thus a judgment in a person's absence that will leave related claims by or against that person undecided, may be deemed an "inadequate" judgment.[38]

35. *See, e.g., Hooper v. Wolfe,* 396 F.3d 744, 749 (6th Cir.2005) ("When assessing prejudice, the court must consider whether the interests of an absent party are adequately represented by those already a party to the litigation."); *Dainippon Screen Manufacturing Co. v. CFMT, Inc.,* 142 F.3d 1266 (Fed.Cir.1998) (presence of parent corporation in suit assures adequate representation of absent subsidiary).

36. *See, e.g., Tell v. Trustees of Dartmouth College,* 145 F.3d 417 (1st Cir.1998) ("[W]ithout a perfect identity of interests, a court must be very cautious in concluding that a litigant will serve as a proxy for an absent party."). *See also Citizen Potawatomi Nation v. Norton,* 248 F.3d 993, 999 (10th Cir.2001), *opinion modified on reh'g,* 257 F.3d 1158 (10th Cir.2001) (where some tribes will win and others will lose in litigation, federal government's presence in suit cannot adequately represent interests of all tribes). *But cf., Dixon v. Edwards,* 290 F.3d 699, 714 (4th Cir.2002) (plaintiff faces no substantial risk of inconsistent obligation because, *inter alia,* non-parties support plaintiff's case and have stated that plaintiff represents overlapping interests they share with plaintiff); *Kansas v. United States,* 249 F.3d 1213 (10th Cir.2001) (when interests of existing defendants are "substantially similar, if not identical," to absent party, potential for prejudice to absent party is "largely nonexistent").

37. *See also Jota v. Texaco, Inc.,* 157 F.3d 153, 162 (2d Cir.1998) (absent party asserted sovereign immunity; without absent party, some aspects of equitable relief, such as environmental cleanup of polluted area, would be impossible; but dismissal was error because current defendant could provide all of legal relief and some of equitable relief plaintiff demanded; thus, relief could be shaped to diminish prejudice caused by inability to join absent party). *But see Laker Airways, Inc. v. British Airways, PLC,* 182 F.3d 843, 849 (11th Cir. 1999) (although plaintiff no longer seeks injunctive relief, prejudice to absent entity would still be significant because finding in favor of plaintiff would still require court to find that absent entity acted improperly, which might damage that entity's relationship with British government).

38. *Provident Tradesmens Bank & Trust Co. v. Patterson,* 390 U.S. 102, 88 S.Ct. 733, 19 L.Ed.2d 936 (1968). *See, e.g., Estate of Alvarez v. Donaldson Co.,* 213 F.3d 993 (7th Cir.2000) (judgment is inadequate when plaintiff would have to relitigate in state court to recover against absent persons). *But see Universal Reinsurance Co. v. St. Paul Fire & Marine Insurance Co.,* 312 F.3d 82, 89–90 (2d Cir.2002) (party had already won on merits; thus judgment can be "adequate" because resolution of issue on merits means time and expense of trying issues has already been expended); *Sac and Fox Nation of Missouri v. Pierce,* 213 F.3d 566 n. 11 (10th Cir.2000) (where joinder is addressed for first time on appeal, "the preference for joinder ... on efficiency grounds has all but disappeared at this late date"; thus, possibility that judgment in case will not settle whole controversy is not compelling).

(4) *Availability of Another Forum:* The court will examine whether another forum is available in which the claimant may sue existing defendants as well as the person who cannot be joined.[39] When another forum is not available to the claimant, the court in most cases will proceed with the action.[40]

Public Interest Exception

In some cases where a public right is to be litigated, but some persons cannot be joined, courts have fashioned a "public interest exception" to Rule 19. When applicable, this exception means that such absent persons are not deemed crucial, without regard to whatever a Rule 19 analysis might have concluded. The scope of this exception seems unclear, and attorneys are advised to consult local precedent.[41]

Failure to Intervene

If a person who would practically be affected by a judgment nevertheless refuses to intervene, it might seem that a court would not weigh that person's interests as heavily. However, in some circumstances it appears that the interests of such a person may still be taken into account in determining whether to proceed in the person's absence.[42]

39. *Cf., City of Marietta v. CSX Transportation, Inc.,* 196 F.3d 1300, 1307 (11th Cir.1999) (where case has been pending for three years, and remand to state court would cause more delay, court may take such facts into account in determining whether plaintiff's possible alternative form is truly adequate); *Laker Airways, Inc. v. British Airways, PLC,* 182 F.3d 843, 849 (11th Cir.1999) (plaintiff has adequate remedy in right to file complaints with administrative agencies of United States or British governments).

40. *Cf., e.g., Estate of Alvarez v. Donaldson Co.,* 213 F.3d 993 (7th Cir.2000) (dismissal appropriate in part because plaintiff can sue all parties in state court); *Angst v. Royal Maccabees Life Insurance Co.,* 77 F.3d 701, 706 (3d Cir.1996)(because plaintiff may assert claims in pending state action, case should be dismissed). *Virginia Electric and Power Co. v. Westinghouse Electric Corp.,* 485 F.2d 78 (4th Cir.1973); *but compare, Manybeads v. United States,* 209 F.3d 1164, 1166 (9th Cir.2000) (where first three factors of Rule 19(b) weigh against continuing case, fact that plaintiff will have no other forum in which to pursue First Amendment claim does not prevent dismissal when continuation of case would cause "a sovereign, not a party to the case, [to] suffer substantially from [plaintiff's] vindication"); *Guerrero v. Clinton,* 157 F.3d 1190 (9th Cir.1998) (plaintiff's interest in

litigation outweighed by Indian tribe's interest in sovereign immunity; dismissal appropriate even where plaintiff has no other forum), *with Dawavendewa v. Salt River Project Agriculture Improvement & Power District,* 276 F.3d 1150, 1161 (9th Cir.2002) ("If no alternative forum exists, we should be 'extra cautious' before dismissing the suit." Concluding, however, that instant case should be dismissed).

41. *See, e.g., Kickapoo Tribe v. Babbitt,* 43 F.3d 1491, 1500 (D.C.Cir.1995) (explaining exception, collecting cases addressing it). *Cf., Kettle Range Conservation Group v. United States Bureau of Land Management,* 150 F.3d 1083, 1087 (9th Cir.1998) (exception applicable, if at all, where absent parties' private interests will not be destroyed by continuation of litigation).

42. *See, e.g., Kickapoo Tribe of Indians of the Kickapoo Reservation v. Babbitt,* 43 F.3d 1491, 1497 (D.C.Cir.1995)("Failure to intervene is not a component of the prejudice analysis where intervention would require the absent party to waive sovereign immunity."). *But see, Thunder Basin Coal Co. v. Southwestern Public Service Co.,* 104 F.3d 1205, 1208 (10th Cir.1997) ("We specifically hold that an entity or individual subject to impleader under Fed. R. Civ. P. 14 and entitled to intervene under Fed. R. Civ. P. 24 is never an indispensable party." But the court did not decide whether avail-

Effect of Dismissal: Relation to Rule 41(b)

Rule 41 governs the effects of dismissals. In cases that have been dismissed for failure to join a party under Rule 19, Rule 41(b) provides that the dismissal is without prejudice to re-filing unless the order of dismissal provides otherwise.[43]

RULE 19(c).   PLEADING THE REASONS FOR NONJOINDER

CORE CONCEPT

Rule 19(c) places an affirmative duty on parties seeking relief to identify in their pleadings potentially interested persons who have not been joined. A court may use such information to notify these persons, so that they may join on their own initiative.

APPLICATIONS

Motions to Dismiss

The defendant may use the names provided by the plaintiff as a basis for a motion to dismiss the action for failure to join necessary parties under Rule 12(b)(7). In addition, defendants may make similar use of any such knowledge they possess independently of the pleadings.

RULE 19(d).   EXCEPTION FOR CLASS ACTIONS

CORE CONCEPT

When Rule 19 and Rule 23, governing class actions, both apply to a case, and they are in conflict, Rule 23 controls.

ADDITIONAL RESEARCH REFERENCES

Wright & Miller, *Federal Practice and Procedure* §§ 1601–26.

C.J.S. Federal Civil Procedure §§ 95–112 et seq.

West's Key No. Digests, Federal Civil Procedure ⚯201–233.

ability of impleader or intervention, "standing alone," makes a party not indispensable.).

43. *O'Rourke Brothers, Inc. v. Nesbitt Burns, Inc.,* 201 F.3d 948, 950 (7th Cir. 2000).

RULE 20

PERMISSIVE JOINDER OF PARTIES

(a) Persons Who May Join or Be Joined.

(1) *Plaintiffs.* Persons may join in one action as plaintiffs if:

(A) they assert any right to relief jointly, severally, or in the alternative with respect to or arising out of the same transaction, occurrence, or series of transactions or occurrences; and

(B) any question of law or fact common to all plaintiffs will arise in the action.

(2) *Defendants.* Persons—as well as a vessel, cargo, or other property subject to admiralty process in rem—may be joined in one action as defendants if:

(A) any right to relief is asserted against them jointly, severally, or in the alternative with respect to or arising out of the same transaction, occurrence, or series of transactions or occurrences; and

(B) any question of law or fact common to all defendants will arise in the action.

(3) *Extent of Relief.* Neither a plaintiff nor a defendant need be interested in obtaining or defending against all the relief demanded. The court may grant judgment to one or more plaintiffs according to their rights, and against one or more defendants according to their liabilities.

(b) Protective Measures. The court may issue orders—including an order for separate trials—to protect a party against embarrassment, delay, expense, or other prejudice that arises from including a person against whom the party asserts no claim and who asserts no claim against the party.

[Amended effective July 1, 1966; August 1, 1987; April 30, 2007, effective December 1, 2007.]

STYLE PROJECT CHANGES: New orienting labels were added. Part (a) was further subdivided. Cumbersome wording was culled, and dashes were inserted in Rule 20(b) to aid readability.

NON-STYLE CHANGES: None.

NOTE: The Federal Rules "Style Project" is explained in Part III-A.

AUTHORS' COMMENTARY ON RULE 20

———————— PURPOSE AND SCOPE ————————

Rule 20 describes the circumstances in which a plaintiff may join with other plaintiffs against a single defendant, or join several defendants in a single action. It is permissive only, allowing joinder in many situations, but not requiring it.[1] However, if plaintiffs do not voluntarily join, the court retains discretion to consolidate actions that were brought separately under Rule 42(a). Rule 20 also gives the court authority to sever claims for separate trials against parties already joined. In addition, Rule 21 provides that a court may, in appropriate circumstances, dismiss parties joined under Rule 20.

RULE 20(a). PERSONS WHO MAY JOIN OR BE JOINED

CORE CONCEPT

Joinder of parties is generally encouraged in the interest of judicial economy, subject to fulfillment of two prerequisites: the persons who join as plaintiffs or who are joined as defendants must be interested in claims that arise out of the same transaction or occurrence, or series of transactions or occurrences; and all the parties joined must share in common at least one question of law or fact.[2]

APPLICATIONS

"Same Transaction or Occurrence" Test

The courts have adopted various standards for determining whether a claim arises out of the same transaction or occurrence. The assessment is very specific to the facts of the particular case, but in general this requirement is satisfied if there is a substantial logical relationship between the transactions or occurrences at issue.[3]

---

1. *See, e.g., Applewhite v. Reichhold Chemicals, Inc.,* 67 F.3d 571, 574 (5th Cir. 1995)(Rule 20(a) is a plaintiff's option, once requirements are met).

2. *See, e.g., A.M. Alexander v. Fulton County, Georgia,* 207 F.3d 1303, 1323 (11th Cir.2000) (identifying both requirements).

3. *See, e.g., Mosley v. General Motors Corp.,* 497 F.2d 1330, 1333 (8th Cir.1974);

Duty to Explain Analysis

Before the district court reaches a conclusion on the appropriateness of joinder under Rule 20(a), it is obligated to explain its analysis of the "same transaction or occurrence" test. Failure to do so is error.[4]

Common Question of Fact or Law

Rule 20(a) requires only that the joined parties share a single common question of fact or law. There is no requirement that the actions involving various parties overlap with one another to any greater degree.[5]

Denial of Joinder

Rule 20(a) is intended to afford broad opportunities for joinder of parties who have—or are the subject of—substantially related claims. However, the trial court retains substantial discretion to deny joinder in circumstances where joinder might produce jury confusion or undue delay in resolving a case.[6]

Improper Joinder v. Fraudulent Joinder

Rule 20(a) governs whether parties are properly joined. Presumably a fraudulent joinder will be improper joinder under Rule 20. However, for joinder to be improper, it is not necessary that it

("[A]ll reasonably related claims for relief by or against different parties [should] be tried in a single proceeding."). *See also A.M. Alexander v. Fulton County, Georgia,* 207 F.3d 1303, 1323 (11th Cir.2000) (noting that courts use precedent construing rule 13(a) to determine existence of "same transaction or occurrence" under Rule 20(a)); *Blesedell v. Mobil Oil Co.,* 708 F.Supp. 1408, 1422 (S.D.N.Y.1989) ("A company-wide policy purportedly designed to discriminate against females in employment arises out of the same series of transactions or occurrences."). *But see Coughlin v. Rogers,* 130 F.3d 1348, 1350 (9th Cir. 1997) (approving holding that transactions are dissimilar where plaintiffs sue alleging unreasonable delay in processing petitions relating to immigration status; noting that allegation of general delay does not of itself create common transaction or occurrence where delays are of different length, with different causes; "Moreover, Plaintiffs do not allege that their claims arise out of a systematic pattern of events and, therefore, arise from the same transaction or occurrence;" also, there is no allegation of a "common policy" at issue); *Saval v. BL Ltd.,* 710 F.2d 1027, 1031 (4th Cir. 1983)(joinder properly denied when plaintiffs suing on breach of warranty claims relating to defective automobiles each purchased individual cars separately; more-

over, cars had different driving records and service histories).

4. *Moore v. Rohm & Haas Co.,* 446 F.3d 643, 647 (6th Cir.2006).

5. *See, e.g., Dougherty v. Mieczkowski,* 661 F.Supp. 267, 278 (D.Del.1987)("By its terms, Rule 20(a) only requires a single basis for commonality, in either law or fact, for the joinder to be acceptable."). *But see, Coughlin v. Rogers,* 130 F.3d 1348, 1350–51 (9th Cir.1997) (approving holding that no common question exists simply because all claims arise under same general law; noting that each claim is discrete on facts, standards, and procedures).

6. *See, e.g., Chavez v. Illinois State Police,* 251 F.3d 612 (7th Cir.2001) (affirming denial of rule 20 joinder when discovery had already been terminated two years earlier and defendants would be unfairly prejudiced by need to reopen discovery); *Thompson v. Boggs,* 33 F.3d 847, 858 (7th Cir. 1994) (in civil rights case against police officer, joinder of second party properly denied where the following factors would create jury confusion: the two alleged incidents were separated by two years; the injury claims were separate and distinct; and the second complaint would require joinder of additional police officers as defendants).

always be fraudulent. Simple failure to meet the requirements of Rule 20(a) will render joinder improper without regard to whether it is also fraudulent.[7]

Admiralty Actions

Under Rule 20(a) a party may join parties, vessels, and other property subject to admiralty jurisdiction (typically, admiralty actions are not based on personal jurisdiction over a vessel's owner, but upon the court's jurisdiction over the vessel, which is normally exercised when the vessel is served within the territorial confines of the jurisdiction in which the court sits).

Prisoners' Lawsuits

When a prison inmate files a civil suit *in forma pauperis,* the Prison Litigation Reform Act requires, *inter alia,* the prisoner to pay the full filing fee.[8] The effect of this legislation when multiple inmates seek to join their claims under Rule 20 is to require each such plaintiff to file a separate complaint and to pay separately the full filing fee, rather than pro-rate a single filing fee among all the plaintiffs. To the extent that joinder of multiple plaintiffs is permitted under Rule 20, the question that arises in inmate cases is whether such plaintiffs may file together and pay only a single fee. The appellate courts have so far reached different results on this issue.[9]

Complete Relief Unnecessary

Joinder of parties is feasible even if the court may not grant complete relief to each plaintiff or defendant. Thus, it is possible that two plaintiffs would join in a suit, even if the court could anticipate at the time of joinder that the judgment, if favorable, will satisfy the claim of one plaintiff completely, but will leave the other plaintiff with only partial satisfaction.[10]

Right to Relief Still Judged Separately

Notwithstanding joinder, parties still receive judgment according to the respective merits of their individual cases. Though important, this concept means no more than this: the victory of one of the joined parties in a case does not necessarily guarantee victory (or defeat) to another joined party.[11]

---

7. *See, e.g.,Crockett v. R.J. Reynolds Tobacco Co.,* 436 F.3d 529, 533 (5th Cir.2006) ("If [Rule 20] requirements are not met, joinder is improper even if there is no fraud in the pleadings.").

8. 28 U.S.C.A. § 1915(b). *See, e.g., Abdul–Akbar v. McKelvie,* 239 F.3d 307, 331 (3d Cir.2001) (legislative intent was to deter frivolous prisoner litigation).

9. *See Hubbard v. Haley,* 262 F.3d 1194, 1198 (11th Cir.2001) (28 U.S.C.A. § 1915(b)(1) requires each inmate to pay a full filing fee and, if relevant, a full appellate filing fee). *But see Boriboune v. Berge,*

391 F.3d 852, 853–55 (7th Cir.2004) (permitting allocation of fees across all plaintiffs); *Talley–Bey v. Knebl,* 168 F.3d 884, 887 (6th Cir.1999) (permitting pro-rated assessment of fees).

10. *See, e.g., Triggs v. John Crump Toyota, Inc.,* 154 F.3d 1284, 1290 (11th Cir. 1998) ("[T]he express language of Rule 20 indicates that all plaintiffs need not seek relief against all defendants.").

11. *See, e.g., Id. at* 1288 ("[T]he fact that a great many members of the putative plaintiff class can seek no relief against one of the defendants ... would be no obstacle

Jurisdiction: Relation to 28 U.S.C. § 1367

The supplemental jurisdiction of district courts is governed by 28 U.S.C. § 1367. In general, § 1367(a) authorizes courts to exercise supplemental jurisdiction over non-diverse state claims that arise from the same case or controversy as other claims that satisfy the original subject matter jurisdiction of district courts. However, § 1367(b) and (c) create some exceptions to the application of § 1367(a). In particular, § 1367(b) prohibits exercise of supplemental jurisdiction when: (1) the basis for original jurisdiction is diversity; (2) the supplemental claim is asserted by a plaintiff; and (3) the person who is the target of the claim was joined under, *inter alia,* Rule 20. It is settled that in a case based on diversity jurisdiction, § 1367 and Rule 20 may not be used to join non-diverse defendants.[12] However, until recently it was unclear whether § 1367(b) also prohibited joinder of non-diverse plaintiffs. That question is now settled: § 1367(b) is not a barrier to joinder of most non-diverse plaintiffs.[13] Supplemental jurisdiction is discussed at greater length elsewhere in this text.

Relation to Rule 15

Rule 15 generally governs the circumstances when a party may amend a pleading, including amendments to add new parties. However, because Rule 20 also regulates whether parties may be joined, a proposed amended pleading to add a party must meet the requirements of both Rules 15 and 20.[14]

Compare With Rule 18

Though Rule 20(a) is quite liberal in permitting joinder of parties, it is still somewhat more restrictive than Rule 18, which governs joinder of *claims* by a single plaintiff against a single defendant. Rule 18 does not require that the claims arise from a common transaction or occurrence, and the claims need not share even a single question of law or fact in common.[15]

to the permissive joinder of [that defendant] under Rule 20."). Cf., *United States v. Real Property Known as 22249 Dolorosa St.,* 190 F.3d 977, 982 (9th Cir.1999) (claims in forfeiture proceeding joined under Rule 20; held, where government won most claims but lost others, government's liability for attorneys' fees in unsuccessful case cannot be shielded by fact that government prevailed on related claims; government liability for each forfeiture claim must be decided separately).

12. *See, e.g., Stromberg Metal Works, Inc. v. Press Mechanical, Inc.,* 77 F.3d 928, 932 (7th Cir.1996) ("Claims *against* persons made parties under Rule 20 are forbidden.").

13. *Exxon Mobil Corp. v. Allapattah Services, Inc.,* 545 U.S. 546, 125 S.Ct. 2611, 162 L.Ed.2d 502 (2005) (where other elements of diversity jurisdiction are met, plaintiffs permissively joined under Rule 20 with a plaintiff who meets amount in controversy requirement may enjoy supplemental jurisdiction under § 1367).

14. *See, e.g., Hinson v. Norwest Financial South Carolina, Inc.,* 239 F.3d 611, 618 (4th Cir.2001).

15. *See, e.g., Intercon Research Associates, Ltd. v. Dresser Industries, Inc.,* 696 F.2d 53, 57 (7th Cir.1982)("[J]oinder of claims under Rule 18 becomes relevant only after the requirements of Rule 20 ... has [sic] been met.").

RULE 20(b).   PROTECTIVE MEASURES

CORE CONCEPT

Although Rule 20(a) may permit plaintiffs to join together, or to join several defendants together, the court retains discretion to order separate trials or other proceedings if necessary in the interest of justice.

APPLICATIONS

Embarrassment, Expense, or Delay

Primary factors considered by the court in determining whether to order separate trials are unreasonable embarrassment, expense or delay. These broad standards afford the trial court significant discretion in determining whether to separate the parties.

Source of Embarrassment, Expense or Delay

Rule 20(b) appears to permit relief in the form of separate trials if the source of the embarrassment, expense, or delay is someone not adverse to the affected party. It does not apply to circumstances where a party's embarrassment is produced by addition of an adverse party. In actuality, this distinction is not a substantial impingement on a court's discretion to separate. The rule's language is construed to be broad enough to permit separation when injustice would occur.[16] Moreover, the court has discretion to order separate proceedings of any claim in the interest of justice or convenience under Rules 21 and 42(b).

ADDITIONAL RESEARCH REFERENCES

Wright & Miller, *Federal Practice and Procedure* §§ 1651–60.

C.J.S. Federal Civil Procedure §§ 94–116, 318, 917, 918.

West's Key No. Digests, Federal Civil Procedure ☞241–267, 1956.

16. *See, e.g., Coleman v. Quaker Oats Co.,* 232 F.3d 1271, 1296 (9th Cir.2000) (although joinder was proper under Rule 20(a), separate trials under Rule 20(b) were also appropriate where ten plaintiffs, alleging age discrimination, might have confused jury as to individual facts; defendant would also have faced risk of prejudice from having "all ten plaintiffs testify in one trial"); *Avitia v. Metropolitan Club of Chicago, Inc.,* 49 F.3d 1219, 1224 (7th Cir.1995)(Rule 20(b) permits court to weigh embarrassment to defendant from multiple claims of labor law violations, against cost to other parties and to courts of having more than one trial; denying motion for separate trials).

RULE 21

MISJOINDER AND NONJOINDER OF PARTIES

Misjoinder of parties is not a ground for dismissing an action. On motion or on its own, the court may at any time, on just terms, add or drop a party. The court may also sever any claim against a party.

[April 30, 2007, effective December 1, 2007.]

─────────────── 2007 AMENDMENTS ROADMAP ───────────────

STYLE PROJECT CHANGES: A dash was eliminated in the title. Cumbersome wording was culled. Active voice replaced passive voice in the text of the rule.

NON-STYLE CHANGES: None.

NOTE: The Federal Rules "Style Project" is explained in Part III-A.

AUTHORS' COMMENTARY ON RULE 21

─────────────── PURPOSE AND SCOPE ───────────────

Rule 21 contains the remedy for misjoinder or nonjoinder that violates other Rules governing multiparty litigation. It ensures that inappropriate joinder of a party, or failure to join a party that should have been joined, need not result in dismissal of the action. It also provides the court with discretion to sever claims against a party for separate trials, or to order separate trials for joined parties, even if the joinder was otherwise appropriate.

APPLICATIONS

What Constitutes Inappropriate Joinder

Joinder may be inappropriate for a variety of reasons, including situations in which joinder of parties produces defects in jurisdiction or venue.[1] Additionally, joinder that does not meet the require-

---

1. *See, e.g., Whitaker v. American Telecasting, Inc.,* 261 F.3d 196, 206–07 (2d Cir. 2001) (approving use of rule 21 to dismiss non-diverse defendant who had no real connection to litigation).

ments of Rule 20(a) is inappropriate, and may necessitate the use of Rule 21.[2]

Inappropriate Joinder: Consequences

The consequence of an inappropriate joinder need not be dismissal of the entire action. Instead, the court will order the inappropriately joined party dismissed, so that the remainder of the action may continue.[3]

Failure to Join

If a party should have been joined but was not, the court will simply order appropriate service of process.[4]

Relationship to Rule 15

If parties seek to add a party under Rule 21, courts use the standard of Rule 15, governing amendments to pleadings, to determine whether to allow the addition.[5]

Relation to Rule 19; Diversity Jurisdiction

The authority of a district court to protect its diversity jurisdiction by dismissing a party under Rule 21 is subject to the restriction of Rule 19, which requires the presence of parties deemed indispensable to the action. In practice, that relationship means that if an indispensable party is also not diverse, the court cannot simply

---

2. *Jonas v. Conrath*, 149 F.R.D. 520, 523 (S.D.W.Va.1993)("[P]arties are misjoined when they fail to satisfy either of the preconditions for permissive joinder . . . set forth in Rule 20(a).").

3. *Newman–Green, Inc. v. Alfonzo–Larrain*, 490 U.S. 826, 832, 109 S.Ct. 2218, 2222, 104 L.Ed.2d 893 (1989) ("[I]t is well settled that Rule 21 invests district courts with authority to allow a dispensable nondiverse party to be dropped at any time, even after judgment has been rendered;" suggesting that federal appellate courts have similar authority). *See, e.g., CGB Occupational Therapy, Inc. v. RHA Health Services, Inc.*, 357 F.3d 375, 382 (3d Cir.2004) ("[I]t is well settled that courts, both district and circuit alike, have the power under Fed.R.Civ.P. 21 to dismiss dispensable parties to the suit in order to preserve diversity"). *But cf., DirecTV, Inc. v. Leto*, 467 F.3d 842, 846 (3d Cir. 2006) ("Although a district court has discretion to choose either severance or dismissal in remedying misjoinder, it is permitted under Rule 21 to opt for the latter only if 'just' – that is, if doing so 'will not prejudice any substantial right.' "). *Elmore v. Henderson*, 227 F.3d 1009, 1012 (7th Cir.2000) (where party was inappropriately joined, Rule 21 permits district court to sever that party and hear that case separately rather than dismiss it, if

dismissal would produce harsh result under applicable statute of limitations). *See also McLaughlin v. Mississippi Power Co.*, 376 F.3d 344 (5th Cir.2004) (Rule 21 permits dismissal of misjoined parties, but not misjoined properties).

4. *See, e.g., Teamsters Local Union No. 116 v. Fargo–Moorhead Automobile Dealers Ass'n*, 620 F.2d 204 (8th Cir.1980).

5. *See, e.g., Frank v. U.S. West, Inc.*, 3 F.3d 1357, 1365 (10th Cir.1993)("A motion to add a party is governed by [Rule] 15(a)."); *see, also, United States ex rel. Precision Co. v. Koch Industries, Inc.*, 31 F.3d 1015, 1018 (10th Cir.1994)(citing *Frank* for applicability of Rule 15(a), rather than Rule 21, when a party seeks to add a party through an amendment as of right). *Cf., Soberay Machine & Equipment Co. v. MRF Ltd.*, 181 F.3d 759, 763 (6th Cir.1999) ("[I]t makes no difference whether Rule 15 or Rule 21 is used to retain federal diversity jurisdiction over a case."). *But see McIntyre–Handy v. APAC Customer Services, Inc.*, 422 F.Supp.2d 611, 617 n. 11 (E.D.Va. 2006) ("The specific provisions of Rule 21 control the general provisions of Rule 15, such that even if the time for amending once as a matter of course has not expired, an amendment dropping or adding parties requires leave of court.").

dismiss the party but must consider dismissing the action under Rule 19.[6]

Additionally, and notwithstanding the broad language of Rule 21, it appears settled that Rule 21 cannot be used to create diversity by substituting a diverse party for a non-diverse party.[7]

Relation to Rule 25

Rule 25 governs substitution of parties in any of the specific sections addressed by that Rule. By contrast, Rule 21 governs substitution "in the discretion of the court in situations not covered by Rule 25."[8]

Relation to Rule 42(b)

When a claim is severed under Rule 21, it ceases to be part of the same suit.[9] By contrast, if an issue is separated under Rule 42(b), it will be tried separately but remain part of the same lawsuit. The most important result of this distinction is that severed proceedings under Rule 21 become final as each proceeding goes to judgment, and may be appealed individually. Separate trials under Rule 42(b), by contrast, are typically *not* ready for appeal until all claims and issues are decided.[10]

Timing

The court may order dismissal or the addition of a party at any time in the action, subject only to the need to protect all parties from unfair prejudice.[11]

---

6. *See, e.g., Kirkland v. Legion Insurance Co.*, 343 F.3d 1135, 1142 (9th Cir. 2003).

7. *See, e.g., Salazar v. Allstate Texas Lloyd's, Inc.*, 455 F.3d 571 (5th Cir.2006) ("Rule 21 does not allow for substitution of parties to create jurisdiction."); *Northern Trust Co. v. Bunge Corp.*, 899 F.2d 591, 597 (7th Cir.1990) ("We have found no case in which Rule 21 has been used to add parties to cure a defect in statutory jurisdiction."); *Field v. Volkswagenwerk AG*, 626 F.2d 293, 306 (3d Cir.1980) (substituting diverse plaintiff for non-diverse plaintiff "is simply not within the scope of Rule 21, which is not a rule providing for the substitution of parties").

8. *Mathis v. Bess*, 761 F.Supp. 1023, 1026 (S.D.N.Y.1991), *opinion modified on denial of reargument*, 763 F.Supp. 58 (D.N.Y.1991).

9. *See, e.g., Rice v. Sunrise Express, Inc.*, 209 F.3d 1008, 1013 (7th Cir.2000), *cert. denied*, 531 U.S. 1012, 121 S.Ct. 567, 148 L.Ed.2d 486 (2000) ("Under Rule 21 ... severance creates two separate actions where previously there was but one.").

10. *See, e.g., Acevedo–Garcia v. Monroig*, 351 F.3d 547, 559–60 (1st Cir.2003) (observing that courts sometimes confuse the two rules; noting that important practical difference is that under Rule 21 a judgment entered is final and appealable without regard to whether other severed portions of original case have proceeded to judgment; under Rule 42(b), however, separate trials do not usually become appealable until all of the trials have been decided); *Rice v. Sunrise Express, Inc.*, 209 F.3d 1008, 1013 (7th Cir.) ("Under Rule 21 ... severance creates two separate actions where previously there was but one"); *White v. ABCO Engineering Corp.*, 199 F.3d 140, 145 n. 6 (3d Cir.1999) (same analysis).

11. *Newman-Green, Inc. v. Alfonzo–Larrain*, 490 U.S. 826, 832, 109 S.Ct. 2218, 2223, 104 L.Ed.2d 893 (1989) ("It is well-settled that Rule 21 invests district courts with authority to allow a dispensable nondiverse party to be dropped at any time [to preserve diversity jurisdiction], even after judgment has been rendered." However, while appellate courts also possess such authority, they should probably exercise it much more sparingly.). *See also, e.g., California Credit Union League v. City of Anaheim*, 190 F.3d 997, 999 (9th Cir.1999)

Motion

Adding or dropping a party may be done upon motion of someone already a party, or upon the court's own initiative.[12]

Preserving Diversity Jurisdiction

Even where a party is appropriately joined, circumstances can arise where the court can apply Rule 21 to drop a party. A notable example arises when a court dismisses a nondiverse party in order to obtain diversity jurisdiction over the remaining parties.[13]

Severance of Claims or Parties

Even if parties or claims have been appropriately joined, the court may nonetheless use this Rule to order separate trials in the interest of justice.[14]

ADDITIONAL RESEARCH REFERENCES

Wright & Miller, *Federal Practice and Procedure* §§ 1681–89.

C.J.S. Federal Civil Procedure §§ 117–126 et seq., 171–177 et seq., 318, 343, 803–809.

West's Key No. Digests, Federal Civil Procedure ⬤281–297, 384–386, 387–388, 1747–1750.

(Rule 21 may permit joinder on appeal "when the party seeking joinder requests the same remedy as the original party and offers the same reasons for that remedy, and earlier joinder would not have affected the course of the litigation."); *Galt G/S v. JSS Scandinavia,* 142 F.3d 1150, 1154 (9th Cir.1998) ("Rule 21 specifically allows for the dismissal of parties at any stage of the action. There is no requirement that diversity exist at the time of the filing of the complaint.").

12. *See, e.g., Delgado v. Plaza Las Americas, Inc.,* 139 F.3d 1 (1st Cir.1998) (court may raise nonjoinder *sua sponte*).

13. *See, e.g., Newman–Green, Inc. v. Alfonzo–Larrain,* 490 U.S. 826, 832–33, 109 S.Ct. 2218, 2222–23, 104 L.Ed.2d 893 (1989) (Rule 21 permits dismissal of "dispensable" non-diverse defendants to cure jurisdictional defects; such dismissal can occur "even after judgment" and even by appellate court). *See, e.g., Fielder v. Credit Acceptance Corp.,* 188 F.3d 1031, 1039 (8th Cir.1999) ("Rule 21 is often used to allow federal courts to escape a multi-party jurisdictional quandry."); *Tuck v. United Services Automobile Association,* 859 F.2d 842, 845 (10th Cir.1988) (so noting, provided that the party dismissed is not indispensable under Rule 19).

14. *See, e.g., Rice v. Sunrise Express, Inc.,* 209 F.3d 1008, 1016 (7th Cir.2000) (noting district courts' "broad discretion" under Rule 21; "[a]s long as there is a discrete and separate claim, the district court may exercise its discretion and sever it"); *Old Colony Ventures I, Inc. v. SMWNPF Holdings, Inc.,* 918 F.Supp. 343 (D.Kan.1996)(in employing Rule 21, court should consider convenience of parties, avoidance of prejudice, and judicial efficiency.). *See also In re High Fructose Corn Syrup Antitrust Litigation,* 361 F.3d 439, 441 (7th Cir.2004) (in the course of applying Rule 21, district court has authority to empanel separate juries in appropriate circumstances).

RULE 22

INTERPLEADER

(a) Grounds.

(1) *By a Plaintiff.* Persons with claims that may expose a plaintiff to double or multiple liability may be joined as defendants and required to interplead. Joinder for interpleader is proper even though:

(A) the claims of the several claimants, or the titles on which their claims depend, lack a common origin or are adverse and independent rather than identical; or

(B) the plaintiff denies liability in whole or in part to any or all of the claimants.

(2) *By a Defendant.* A defendant exposed to similar liability may seek interpleader through a crossclaim or counterclaim.

(b) Relation to Other Rules and Statutes. This rule supplements—and does not limit—the joinder of parties allowed by Rule 20. The remedy this rule provides is in addition to—and does not supersede or limit—the remedy provided by 28 U.S.C. §§ 1335, 1397, and 2361. An action under those statutes must be conducted under these rules.

[Amended effective October 20, 1949; August 1, 1987; April 30, 2007, effective December 1, 2007.]

2007 AMENDMENTS ROADMAP

STYLE PROJECT CHANGES: New orienting labels were added. Parts (1) and (2) were re-labeled as parts (a) and (b). Part (a) was furthered subsectioned. The reference to Rule 20 was re-written to add clarity and was transferred from former part (1) to re-labeled part (b). Cumbersome wording was culled, and active voice replaced passive voice.

NON-STYLE CHANGES: None.

NOTE: The Federal Rules "Style Project" is explained in Part III-A.

AUTHORS' COMMENTARY ON RULE 22

———————— PURPOSE AND SCOPE ————————

Rule 22 permits a person who may be subject to multiple liability by claimants with overlapping or inconsistent claims to interplead or join such claimants as defendants in a single action. In the ordinary procedure, once claimants are joined they will compete with one another to establish the validity and priority of their claims against the interpleader plaintiff.

RULE 22(a). GROUNDS

CORE CONCEPT

Interpleader complements liberal joinder of parties under Rule 20 by allowing a stakeholder to join multiple, mutually inconsistent claims of various parties, and thereby determine rights in the asset (the "stake") in a single proceeding.

NOTE: Rule 22 interpleader is not the only kind of federal interpleader available. Statutory interpleader, found at 28 U.S.C.A. §§ 1335, 1397, and 2361, discussed below, is at least as important a source of interpleader authority as Rule 22. Although the two kinds of interpleader may often be employed in the same action, the differing characteristics of the two interpleaders sometimes make one more desirable, or available when the other is unavailable.[1] Thus, both versions should be considered when contemplating an interpleader action.

APPLICATIONS

Stakeholder as Claimant

The interpleader plaintiff may also be a claimant, as for example where a limited insurance fund is subject to claims exceeding the value of the fund. The insurance company may in appropriate circumstances be permitted to initiate the interpleader action, and then to participate as a claimant, if it contends that the other claims against the insurance fund are without merit.[2]

Claims Against the Stake

The only requirement under Rule 22 is that the interpleader plaintiff plead that the competing claims are at least partly inconsistent with one another, e.g., where the claims against a fund exceed the value of the fund.[3] Interpleader actions need not be based on

1. *See, e.g., Federal Insurance Co. v. Tyco International, Ltd.,* 422 F.Supp.2d 357 (S.D.N.Y.2006) (explaining distinction between two kinds of interpleader).

2. *Cf., Nationwide Mutual Fire Insurance Co. v. Eason,* 736 F.2d 130, 133 (4th Cir.1984)(stakeholder is "not precluded" from making a claim on the asset).

3. *See, e.g., Rhoades v. Casey,* 196 F.3d 592, 600 n. 8 (5th Cir.1999) ("A prerequisite to filing an interpleader action is that there must be a single, identifiable, fund."). *Pan American Fire & Casualty Co. v. Re-*

identical competing claims, or claims with a common origin, nor must the claims be totally incompatible with one another. In establishing this standard, Rule 22 eases significantly the requirements previously imposed on common law interpleader actions.

Defendants May Employ Interpleader

Sometimes a stakeholder will already have been sued by a claimant, but other claimants are not parties to the action. In such circumstances the stakeholder is entitled to initiate the interpleader action through a counterclaim or cross-claim, and then join the other claimants in the action.[4]

Subject Matter Jurisdiction

This Rule does not create jurisdiction in interpleader actions. Instead, it only authorizes interpleader *if* jurisdictional requirements in the federal courts are met. Federal subject matter jurisdiction is still required.[5] If the underlying cause of action is a federal question, subject matter jurisdiction for an interpleader is usually satisfied without difficulty. More commonly, however, the interpleader will arise from a state cause of action, and then the standard requirements for diversity jurisdiction must also be satisfied. The citizenship of the stakeholder must be diverse from that of the claimants, and the amount in controversy must exceed $75,000. The claimants need not be diverse among themselves.[6]

vere, 188 F.Supp. 474 (E.D.La. 1960)(adversity requirement satisfied if claims against stake amount to more than stakeholder's maximum liability); *see also, Hussain v. Boston Old Colony Insurance Co.,* 311 F.3d 623, 634 n. 40 (5th Cir.2002) ("[I]t is well settle that claims to the stake need not be mutually exclusive. ... We and other courts have also found that adversity of claims is also satisfied when additional claims to a fund are derivative of one particular claimant's right to the fund."); *Hebel v. Ebersole,* 543 F.2d 14, 17 (7th Cir. 1976)(adversity requirement satisfied by "the risk of a double payment on single liability;" additional independent stakeholder liability does not defeat right to relief through interpleader).

4. *Grubbs v. General Electric Credit Corp.,* 405 U.S. 699, 92 S.Ct. 1344, 31 L.Ed.2d 612 (1972). *See, e.g., Forcier v. Forcier,* 406 F.Supp.2d 132, 140 n. 7 (D.Mass. 2005) (defendant insurer "faced with competing claims to the proceeds of a life insurance policy" has standing to assert interpleader). *See also Hussain v. Boston Old Colony Insurance Co.,* 311 F.3d 623, 633 n. 39 (5th Cir.2002) (substance of pleading and nexus to existing parties predominates over nominal label on pleading).

5. *See, e.g., Aetna Life Insurance Co. v. Bayona,* 223 F.3d 1030, 1033 (9th Cir.2000)

("Rule 22 interpleader is only a procedural device ... –the rule does not convey [sic] jurisdiction on the courts"); *Commercial National Bank of Chicago v. Demos,* 18 F.3d 485, 487 (7th Cir.1994)("Rule 22(1) provides a procedural framework for interpleader actions, but it does not confer subject matter jurisdiction.").

6. *See, e.g., Hussain v. Boston Old Colony Insurance Co.,* 311 F.3d 623, 635 n. 46 (5th Cir.2002) (diversity met when amount in controversy is satisfied and stakeholder is diverse from all claimants "even if citizenship of the claimants is not diverse"); *State Street Bank & Trust Co. v. Denman Tire Corp.,* 240 F.3d 83, 89 n. 4 (1st Cir. 2001) (statutory interpleader not available in diversity case "because the potential claimants are not diverse;" only Rule 22 is available); *Franceskin v. Credit Suisse,* 214 F.3d 253 (2d Cir.2000) (for Rule 22, diverse citizenship is satisfied if stakeholder is diverse from every claimant; thus, where stakeholder and claimants are all aliens, diversity requirement as defined by 28 U.S.C. § 1332 is not met; requirement of diversity for statutory interpleader is that two or more claimants must be diverse from one another; where all claimants are citizens of Argentina, this requirement is not met); *Commercial Union Insurance Co. v.*

Personal Jurisdiction

Interpleader actions are actions against individuals, not against the asset, and so must satisfy requirements of personal jurisdiction. This means that service of process on claimants must satisfy Rule 4 service requirements as well as constitutional Due Process protections discussed in the section on personal jurisdiction.[7]

Venue Requirements

Rule 22 interpleader actions are subject to the general venue requirements contained in 28 U.S.C.A. § 1391.[8] These requirements are discussed earlier in this text.

Disinterested Stakeholders: Attorney's Fees

It appears settled that a disinterested stakeholder is entitled to recover attorney's fees.[9]

Payment into Court: Relation to Rule 67

Rule 22 does not require that the stakeholder turn the asset in dispute over to the custody of the court.[10] However, in practice, payment into court occurs in many Rule 22 cases.[11] It should be noted that Rule 67 authorizes a party, with leave of court, to pay a sum of money in dispute into court pending the outcome of the case. Rule 67 is sometimes the mechanism cited for payment of the stake into court in Rule 22 cases.[12]

Inconsistent Actions

Rule 22 interpleader contains no authority for the court to enjoin individual actions brought by claimants against the stakeholder in state courts. This is one of the important disadvantages of Rule 22 interpleader,[13] as compared with statutory interpleader, discussed immediately below.

United States, 999 F.2d 581, 584 (D.C.Cir. 1993)(Rule 22 looks to diversity between stakeholder and claimants; in contrast, statutory interpleader looks to diversity between claimants).

7. *See, e.g., Metropolitan Life Insurance Co. v. Chase*, 294 F.2d 500, 502 (3d Cir. 1961)(interpleader under Rule 22 requires personal jurisdiction over the claimants).

8. *See, e.g., Leader National Insurance Co. v. Shaw*, 901 F.Supp. 316, 320 (W.D.Okl.1995)("In cases of 'Rule' interpleader, venue is determined by reference to ... § 1391.").

9. *See, e.g., Perkins State Bank v. Connolly*, 632 F.2d 1306, 1311 (5th Cir. 1980)("[C]osts and attorney's fees are generally awarded by federal courts to the plaintiff who initiates the interpleader as a mere stakeholder.").

10. *See, e.g., Central Bank of Tampa v. United States*, 838 F.Supp. 564, 566

(M.D.Fla.1993)(Rule 22 interpleaders do not require payment into court).

11. *See, e.g., In the Matter of Bohart*, 743 F.2d 313, 317 (5th Cir.1984)(in Rule 22 case, stakeholder turned fund over to court); *Kurland v. United States*, 919 F.Supp. 419 (M.D.Fla.1996)(noting that Rule 22 does not require payment into court, but ordering such payment with consent of all parties).

12. *See, e.g., Southtrust Bank of Florida, N.A. v. Wilson*, 971 F.Supp. 539, 542 (M.D.Fla.1997) (using Rule 67 in a Rule 22 interpleader case).

13. If the Rule 22 interpleader action has gone to judgment, a district court has authority to issue an injunction to protect the integrity of the judgment. *See, e.g., New York Life Insurance Co. v. Deshotel*, 142 F.3d 873 (5th Cir.1998) (if judgment has been entered in interpleader case, court may act under authority of All Writs Stat-

RULE 22(b). RELATION TO OTHER
RULES AND STATUTES

CORE CONCEPT

Rule 22 explicitly states that interpleader under the Rule exists alongside and complements, rather than supercedes, statutory interpleader, discussed below.

ADDITIONAL RESEARCH REFERENCES

Wright & Miller, *Federal Practice and Procedure* §§ 1701–21.

STATUTORY INTERPLEADER

—————————— **PURPOSE AND SCOPE** ——————————

The sections of 28 U.S.C.A. that together comprise the federal interpleader statute share much in common with Rule 22. Like the Rule, the interpleader statute permits a stakeholder plaintiff to file an action against two or more adverse claimants to a stake that the plaintiff holds.[14] Once joined, the statute also contemplates that the claimants will then litigate against one another to determine the best disposition of the stake. However, the federal statute differs significantly from Rule 22 in a number of important respects. Thus there may be circumstances where both sources of interpleader authority should be employed, or where only one source and not the other will suffice.

The three specific sections of 28 U.S.C.A. that govern statutory interpleader are §§ 1335, 1397, and 2361. Section 1335 establishes the elements of a statutory interpleader action. Section 1397 establishes the special venue provisions governing statutory interpleader. Section 2361 establishes the broad personal jurisdiction of a court hearing an interpleader action, and also authorizes the court to enjoin other federal or state judicial actions that may interfere with the interpleader.

---

ute, 28 U.S.C.A. § 1651, to prevent relitigation of issues precluded by res judicata or collateral estoppel; injunction applies to other federal proceedings). This authority, however, falls short of the authority federal courts enjoy in statutory interpleader cases to enjoin litigation that may compete with a pending interpleader action. This distinction is discussed again under statutory interpleader, below.

14. Cf., *Airborne Freight Corp. v. United States,* 195 F.3d 238, 240 (5th Cir.1999) ("central prerequisite" for interpleader is

that the "plaintiff-stakeholder runs the risk–but for determination in interpleader– of multiple liability when several claimants assert rights to a single stake"); *Minnesota Mutual Life Insurance Co. v. Ensley,* 174 F.3d 977 (9th Cir.1999) (held, it is not necessary, prior to initiation of the interpleader action, that more than one claimant has actually filed on the stake; "The court's jurisdiction under the interpleader statute extends to potential, as well as actual, claims.").

28 U.S.C.A. § 1335. INTERPLEADER

CORE CONCEPT

The interpleader statute allows a stakeholder to join multiple, mutually inconsistent claims of various parties, and thereby determine rights in the asset (the "stake") in a single proceeding.[15]

APPLICATIONS

Stakeholder as Claimant

The interpleader plaintiff may also be a claimant,[16] as is the case with Rule 22 interpleader.

Claims Need Not Be Identical

Like Rule 22, the federal interpleader statute requires that the interpleader plaintiff plead that the claims are independent of, and at least partly inconsistent with, one another, *e.g.*, where the claims against a fund exceed the value of the fund. Interpleader actions need not be based on identical competing claims, or claims with a common origin, nor must the claims be totally incompatible with one another.[17] These provisions are similar to those contained in Rule 22 interpleader.

Defendants May Employ Interpleader

Unlike Rule 22, the federal interpleader statute contains no *explicit* authority for defendants to initiate interpleader actions through a counterclaim or crossclaim. However, it appears settled that defendants may employ the interpleader statute in a manner parallel to that explicitly authorized by Rule 22.[18]

Subject Matter Jurisdiction

As with Rule 22, a federal court must have subject matter jurisdiction before it can hear interpleader claims. However, the requirements for subject matter jurisdiction in statutory interpleader are considerably more relaxed when compared to those which Rule 22 actions must satisfy. In diversity cases, statutory interpleader actions satisfy subject matter jurisdiction if the stake at issue is worth $500 or more,[19] and if the citizenship of only one of

15. *See, e.g., Rhoades v. Casey,* 196 F.3d 592, 600 n. 8 (5th Cir.1999) ("A prerequisite to filing an interpleader action is that there must be a single, identifiable, fund.").

16. *State Farm Fire & Casualty Co. v. Tashire,* 386 U.S. 523, 533, 87 S.Ct. 1199, 1205, 18 L.Ed.2d 270 n. 9 (1967)(stakeholder need not be a disinterested party).

17. *See, e.g., Metropolitan Property & Casualty Insurance Co. v. Shan Trac, Inc.,* 324 F.3d 20, 23 (1st Cir.2003) (state law duty of insurers to settle legitimate claims promptly in good faith creates potential obligation greater than value of stake; thus

there "may" be sufficiently adverse claims within the meaning of § 1335); *Abex Corp. v. ABC Rail Corp.,* 158 F.R.D. 75, 76 (W.D.Pa.1994) (citing requirement that conflicting claims need only be adverse to one another).

18. *See, e.g., Ellis National Bank of Jacksonville v. Irving Trust Co.,* 786 F.2d 466, 467 (2d Cir.1986)(noting without comment use of statutory interpleader as a counterclaim).

19. *See, e.g., NYLife Distributors, Inc. v. Adherence Group, Inc.,* 72 F.3d 371, 374 (3d Cir.1995) (noting $500 requirement).

the claimants is diverse from that of any other claimant (not including the stakeholder).[20] If federal subject matter jurisdiction is based upon the presence of a federal question, the requirements are the same as those for Rule 22 actions, or for any other federal question sued upon in a federal court.

Payment Into Court

The interpleader statute requires that the plaintiff deposit the asset at issue with the court.[21] This requirement is relaxed only if the plaintiff provides a bond in an amount subject to the court's discretion.[22] There is no similar explicit requirement for a bond in a Rule 22 action, but courts often require similar performance by plaintiffs in Rule 22 cases anyway.

28 U.S.C.A. § 1397.   INTERPLEADER

CORE CONCEPT

Section 1397 provides that venue in a statutory interpleader action may be found in any judicial district in which one of the claimants resides.[23] This requirement differs from the traditional federal court venue requirements for Rule 22 interpleader. *See* 28 U.S.C.A. § 1391.

20. *See, e.g., First Trust Corp. v. Bryant,* 410 F.3d 842, 852 (6th Cir.2005) ("[O]nly two or more claimants need to be of diverse citizenship."); *State Street Bank & Trust Co. v. Denman Tire Corp.,* 240 F.3d 83, 89 n. 4 (1st Cir.2001) (statutory interpleader not available in diversity case "because the potential claimants are not diverse;" only Rule 22 is available); *Franceskin v. Credit Suisse,* 214 F.3d 253 (2d Cir.2000) (requirement of diversity for statutory interpleader is that two or more claimants must be diverse from one another; where all claimants are citizens of Argentina, this requirement is not met; for Rule 22, diverse citizenship is satisfied if stakeholder is diverse from every claimant; thus, where stakeholder and claimants are all aliens, diversity requirement as defined by 28 U.S.C. § 1332 is not met); *Commercial Union Insurance v. United States,* 999 F.2d 581, 584 (D.C.Cir. 1993)(for diversity in statutory interpleader cases, the focus is on diversity of claimant-defendants; citizenship of stakeholder is irrelevant in statutory interpleader). *But cf., Forcier v. Metropolitan Life Insurance Co.,* 469 F.3d 178, 182 n. 2 (1st Cir. 2006) (where all claimants are citizens of same state, subject matter jurisdiction for statutory interpleader is unavailable; however, it is possible that the case will meet the differing requirements for subject matter jurisdiction that apply in Rule 22 cases).

21. *See, e.g., Federal Insurance Co. v. Tyco International, Ltd.,* 422 F.Supp.2d 357, 395 (S.D.N.Y.2006) ("The deposit of such funds is a jurisdictional requirement."); *Schneider v. Cate,* 405 F.Supp.2d 1254, 1267 (D.Colo.2005) ("The statute makes clear that 'the making of the deposit or the giving of the bond is a condition precedent to the acquisition of jurisdiction.' ").

22. *See e.g., United States Fire Insurance Co. v. Asbestospray, Inc.,* 182 F.3d 201, 210 (3d Cir.1999) ("A proper deposit or bond is a jurisdictional prerequisite to bringing an interpleader [under § 1335]. The stakeholder invoking interpleader must deposit the largest amount for which it may be liable in view of the subject matter of the controversy." However, the amount to be deposited or bonded is measured by the realistic scope of the interpleader, not an "uncritical" assessment of "the highest amount claimed by the adverse claimants."). *Cf., Gaines v. Sunray Oil Co.,* 539 F.2d 1136, 1141 (8th Cir.1976)("The subject matter of an interpleader action is defined by the fund deposited by the stakeholder."); *see also, Prudential Insurance Co. of America v. Bank of Commerce,* 857 F.Supp. 62, 64 (D.Kan.1994)(when plaintiff seeks to post bond "the bond ... should contain an obligor other than plaintiff as surety").

23. *See, e.g., First Trust Corp. v. Bryant,* 410 F.3d 842, 853 n.7 (6th Cir.2005).

28 U.S.C.A. § 2361. PROCESS AND PROCEDURE

CORE CONCEPT

Section 2361 provides substantially expanded personal jurisdiction over the claimants. These powers often provide the plaintiff with a major advantage over analogous provisions governing Rule 22 actions. Section 2361 also authorizes the district court to enter final judgment discharging the stakeholder from further liability, thereby making the injunction permanent.[24]

APPLICATIONS

Process and Personal Jurisdiction

Statutory interpleader provides for nationwide personal jurisdiction and service of process.[25] Rule 22 actions, by contrast, must satisfy standard requirements for personal jurisdiction and service of process.

Injunctive Powers

In statutory interpleader cases, the federal court has authority to enjoin other federal or state proceedings that may affect the assets that are the subject of the interpleader action.[26] No comparable authority exists in Rule 22 actions.[27]

---

24. *Advantage Title Agency, Inc. v. Rosen,* 297 F.Supp.2d 536, 539 (E.D.N.Y. 2003).

25. *See, e.g., Rhoades v. Casey,* 196 F.3d 592, 600 (5th Cir.1999) ("[T]he district court may also enter an order restraining the claimants from instituting any proceeding affective property until further order of the court."); *NYLife Distributors, Inc. v. Adherence Group, Inc.,* 72 F.3d 371, 375 (3d Cir.1995) (noting availability of nationwide service on all claimants); *Carolina Casualty Insurance Co. v. Mares,* 826 F.Supp. 149, 154 (E.D.Va.1993)(nationwide service of process under § 2361 available only in statutory interpleader actions).

26. *But cf., First Trust Corp. v. Bryant,* 410 F.3d 842, 856 n.11 (6th Cir.2005) (rejecting assertion that § 2361 could be statutory basis for award of attorney's fees in absence of more explicit authority); *United States Fire Insurance Co. v. Asbestospray, Inc.,* 182 F.3d 201, 211 (3d Cir.1999) (injunction extends only to portion of fund that is subject matter of interpleader action; injunction does not extend to portions beyond reach of interpleader dispute; moreover, district courts should ensure that parallel proceedings in state court that pre-

date interpleader action are treated with deference, especially if state actions have resulted in judgments "or settlements in principle"). *See, e.g., NYLife Distributors, Inc. v. Adherence Group, Inc.,* 72 F.3d 371, 375 (3d Cir.1995) (noting injunctive power under § 2361). *Estrella v. V & G Management Corp.,* 158 F.R.D. 575, 578 (D.N.J. 1994)(noting that 28 U.S.C.A. § 2361 provides an "automatic stay" on related state claims).

27. *Cf., New York Life Insurance Co. v. Deshotel,* 142 F.3d 873 (5th Cir.1998) (All Writs Statute, 28 U.S.C.A. § 1651, authorizes district court, after entry of judgment in Rule 22 action, to enter injunction against proceedings in other federal courts that would relitigate issues precluded by judgment). Note, however, that injunctive authority here applies only to cases decided, not to pending cases; to that extent the injunctive authority that a court enjoys under statutory interpleader is much broader, including both pre-judgment and post-judgment orders. *See, e.g., General Electric Capital Assurance v. Van Norman,* 209 F.Supp.2d 668, 670 (S.D.Tex.2002) (judicial authority under § 2361 includes power to enter appropriate orders to ensure that judgments can be enforced).

ADDITIONAL RESEARCH REFERENCES

Wright & Miller, *Federal Practice and Procedure* §§ 1701–21.

C.J.S. Interpleader §§ 2–52, 53–57.

West's Key No. Digests, Interpleader ⊖1–43.

RULE 23

CLASS ACTIONS

(a) Prerequisites. One or more members of a class may sue or be sued as representative parties on behalf of all members only if:

(1) the class is so numerous that joinder of all members is impracticable;

(2) there are questions of law or fact common to the class;

(3) the claims or defenses of the representative parties are typical of the claims or defenses of the class; and

(4) the representative parties will fairly and adequately protect the interests of the class.

(b) Types of Class Actions. A class action may be maintained if Rule 23(a) is satisfied and if:

(1) prosecuting separate actions by or against individual class members would create a risk of:

(A) inconsistent or varying adjudications with respect to individual class members that would establish incompatible standards of conduct for the party opposing the class; or

(B) adjudications with respect to individual class members that, as a practical matter, would be dispositive of the interests of the other members not parties to the individual adjudications or would substantially impair or impede their ability to protect their interests;

(2) the party opposing the class has acted or refused to act on grounds that apply generally to the class, so that final injunctive relief or corresponding declaratory relief is appropriate respecting the class as a whole; or

(3) the court finds that the questions of law or fact common to class members predominate over any questions affecting only individual members, and that a class action is superior to other available methods for fairly and efficiently adjudicating the

controversy. The matters pertinent to these findings include:

    (A) the class members' interests in individually controlling the prosecution or defense of separate actions;

    (B) the extent and nature of any litigation concerning the controversy already begun by or against class members;

    (C) the desirability or undesirability of concentrating the litigation of the claims in the particular forum; and

    (D) the likely difficulties in managing a class action.

(c) Certification Order; Notice to Class Members; Judgment; Issues Classes; Subclasses.

  (1) *Certification Order.*

    (A) *Time to Issue.* At an early practicable time after a person sues or is sued as a class representative, the court must determine by order whether to certify the action as a class action.

    (B) *Defining the Class; Appointing Class Counsel.* An order that certifies a class action must define the class and the class claims, issues, or defenses, and must appoint class counsel under Rule 23(g).

    (C) *Altering or Amending the Order.* An order that grants or denies class certification may be altered or amended before final judgment.

  (2) *Notice.*

    (A) *For (b)(1) or (b)(2) Classes.* For any class certified under Rule 23(b)(1) or (b)(2), the court may direct appropriate notice to the class.

    (B) *For (b)(3) Classes.* For any class certified under Rule 23(b)(3), the court must direct to class members the best notice that is practicable under the circumstances, including individual notice to all members who can be identified through reasonable effort. The notice must clearly and concisely state in plain, easily understood language:

(i) the nature of the action;

(ii) the definition of the class certified;

(iii) the class claims, issues, or defenses;

(iv) that a class member may enter an appearance through an attorney if the member so desires;

(v) that the court will exclude from the class any member who requests exclusion;

(vi) the time and manner for requesting exclusion; and

(vii) the binding effect of a class judgment on members under Rule 23(c)(3).

(3) *Judgment.* Whether or not favorable to the class, the judgment in a class action must:

(A) for any class certified under Rule 23(b)(1) or (b)(2), include and describe those whom the court finds to be class members; and

(B) for any class certified under Rule 23(b)(3), include and specify or describe those to whom the Rule 23(c)(2) notice was directed, who have not requested exclusion, and whom the court finds to be class members.

(4) *Particular Issues.* When appropriate, an action may be brought or maintained as a class action with respect to particular issues.

(5) *Subclasses.* When appropriate, a class may be divided into subclasses that are each treated as a class under this rule.

(d) Conducting the Action.

(1) *In General.* In conducting an action under this rule, the court may issue orders that:

(A) determine the course of proceedings or prescribe measures to prevent undue repetition or complication in presenting evidence or argument;

(B) require—to protect class members and fairly conduct the action—giving appropriate notice to some or all class members of:

(i) any step in the action;

(ii) the proposed extent of the judgment; or

(iii) the members' opportunity to signify whether they consider the representation fair and adequate, to intervene and present claims or defenses, or to otherwise come into the action;

(C) impose conditions on the representative parties or on intervenors;

(D) require that the pleadings be amended to eliminate allegations about representation of absent persons and that the action proceed accordingly; or

(E) deal with similar procedural matters.

(2) *Combining and Amending Orders.* An order under Rule 23(d)(1) may be altered or amended from time to time and may be combined with an order under Rule 16.

(e) Settlement, Voluntary Dismissal, or Compromise. The claims, issues, or defenses of a certified class may be settled, voluntarily dismissed, or compromised only with the court's approval. The following procedures apply to a proposed settlement, voluntary dismissal, or compromise:

(1) The court must direct notice in a reasonable manner to all class members who would be bound by the proposal.

(2) If the proposal would bind class members, the court may approve it only after a hearing and on finding that it is fair, reasonable, and adequate.

(3) The parties seeking approval must file a statement identifying any agreement made in connection with the proposal.

(4) If the class action was previously certified under Rule 23(b)(3), the court may refuse to approve a settlement unless it affords a new opportunity to request exclusion to individual class members who had an earlier opportunity to request exclusion but did not do so.

(5) Any class member may object to the proposal if it requires court approval under this subdivision (e); the objection may be withdrawn only with the court's approval.

(f) Appeals. A court of appeals may permit an appeal from an order granting or denying class-action certification under this rule if a petition for permission to appeal is filed with the circuit clerk within 10 days after the order is entered. An appeal does not stay proceedings in the district court unless the district judge or the court of appeals so orders.

(g) Class Counsel.

  (1) *Appointing Class Counsel.* Unless a statute provides otherwise, a court that certifies a class must appoint class counsel. In appointing class counsel, the court:

   (A) must consider:

     (i) the work counsel has done in identifying or investigating potential claims in the action;

     (ii) counsel's experience in handling class actions, other complex litigation, and the types of claims asserted in the action;

     (iii) counsel's knowledge of the applicable law; and

     (iv) the resources that counsel will commit to representing the class;

   (B) may consider any other matter pertinent to counsel's ability to fairly and adequately represent the interests of the class;

   (C) may order potential class counsel to provide information on any subject pertinent to the appointment and to propose terms for attorney's fees and nontaxable costs;

   (D) may include in the appointing order provisions about the award of attorney's fees or nontaxable costs under Rule 23(h); and

   (E) may make further orders in connection with the appointment.

  (2) *Standard for Appointing Class Counsel.* When one applicant seeks appointment as class counsel, the

543

court may appoint that applicant only if the applicant is adequate under Rule 23(g)(1) and (4). If more than one adequate applicant seeks appointment, the court must appoint the applicant best able to represent the interests of the class.

(3) *Interim Counsel.* The court may designate interim counsel to act on behalf of a putative class before determining whether to certify the action as a class action.

(4) *Duty of Class Counsel.* Class counsel must fairly and adequately represent the interests of the class.

(h) Attorney's Fees and Nontaxable Costs. In a certified class action, the court may award reasonable attorney's fees and nontaxable costs that are authorized by law or by the parties' agreement. The following procedures apply:

(1) A claim for an award must be made by motion under Rule 54(d)(2), subject to the provisions of this subdivision (h), at a time the court sets. Notice of the motion must be served on all parties and, for motions by class counsel, directed to class members in a reasonable manner.

(2) A class member, or a party from whom payment is sought, may object to the motion.

(3) The court may hold a hearing and must find the facts and state its legal conclusions under Rule 52(a).

(4) The court may refer issues related to the amount of the award to a special master or a magistrate judge, as provided in Rule 54(d)(2)(D).

[Amended effective July 1, 1966; August 1, 1987; April 24, 1998, effective December 1, 1998; March 27, 2003, effective December 1, 2003; April 30, 2007, effective December 1, 2007.]

──────────── **2007 AMENDMENTS ROADMAP** ────────────

STYLE PROJECT CHANGES: New labels were added, some subsections were re-titled. Within subsections, material was repositioned and restructured to make it more readable. Unnecessary language was culled or simplified. In Rule 23(f), governing appeals of orders granting or denying class-action certification, reference to a court of appeals' "discretion" in determining whether to hear such an appeal was eliminated as a redundant statement of the appellate court's power. In Rule 23(g), especially, considerable alterations were made in the location of individual provisions of that subsection, but the substance of the subsection was not altered.

NON-STYLE CHANGES: Rule 23(d) was altered to emphasize that while an order pursuant to Rule 23(d) (governing conduct of an action) may be combined with an order under Rule 16, the district court's authority to amend a Rule 23(d) order remains broader than the more stringent standard for amending a Rule 16 order.

NOTE: The Federal Rules "Style Project" is explained in Part III-A.

AUTHORS' COMMENTARY ON RULE 23

PURPOSE AND SCOPE

Rule 23 provides a means of joining parties in situations where the number of parties is sufficiently large so that it is impractical or inefficient for the parties to pursue their claims individually or through more conventional methods of joinder. Class actions are distinct from typical joinder situations in both the number of litigants involved and in the manner in which most class members participate in the case. Rule 23 contemplates that the class of litigants will be represented both by counsel and by "class representatives," *i.e.,* active members of the class who make many decisions for the entire class. Because there is potential for abusing the large number of class members who are not representatives and who therefore do not participate fully in many decisions, the court is charged with the obligation to monitor carefully important steps in the litigation process, such as approval of class litigation at the onset and potential settlements at the end. Class actions also present special problems of case management for the courts, so Rule 23 provides the trial judge with substantial additional authority to supervise progress in the case.

RULE 23(a).   PREREQUISITES

CORE CONCEPT

The specialized purpose of class actions—handling large numbers of litigants through class representatives—makes necessary a series of requirements intended to ensure that the opportunity to bring a class action is not misused or abused. Two of these requirements have developed in case law. Others are listed in Rule 23(a). *All* requirements, whether in Rule 23(a) or developed in case law, must be satisfied before the court will certify a case as a class action.[1]

---

1.   *See, e.g., Berger v. Compaq Computer Corp.,* 257 F.3d 475, 481 (5th Cir.2001)

NOTE: In addition to the requirements of case law and Rule 23(a), a class action will not be certified unless it fits within some provision of Rule 23(b) as well. Class actions must also meet the requirements of both personal jurisdiction and federal subject matter jurisdiction, and these requirements apply somewhat differently to class actions. Thus, while Rule 23(a) must be satisfied, meeting the requirements of Rule 23(a) alone will not produce a court-certified class action. With the exception of Rule 23(b), discussed separately, the additional prerequisites not mentioned in Rule 23(a), including case law requirements, venue and special questions of jurisdiction, are discussed immediately below. Additionally, it should be understood that even if a proposed class meets all the requirements mentioned above, the district court may still retain discretion not to certify the class action.

APPLICATIONS

Burden of Proof

It is settled that the party seeking certification has the burden of proving that the requirements for class certification are satisfied.[2]

Case Law Requirements for a Class

(1) *Class Must Be Logical:* Before a class is certified, the court must be satisfied that the litigants who are to be joined as a group actually comprise a class. The definition of a class is not entirely clear. It is clear, however, that the class must be sufficiently describable so that the court can contemplate with some confidence who is, and who is not, a member of the class.[3] Merely because the actual identities of the individuals are unknown does not prevent a class certification. However, the class' description must not be so vague as to make membership in the class meaningless. A class made up of "all females in the world," for example, would not be certified. A class of all American citizens who support national health insurance is also probably not certifiable, not because their identities are unknown, but because there is no way to ascertain with confidence what "support national health insurance" means, nor any reason to believe personal views on national health insur-

("[T]he party seeking certification bears the burden of establishing that *all* requirements of rule 23(a) have been satisfied.").

2. *See, e.g., Zinser v. Accufix Research Institute, Inc.,* 253 F.3d 1180 (9th Cir.2001), *opinion amended and superseded on denial of reh'g,* 273 F.3d 1266 (9th Cir.2001) (party seeking class certification bears burden of satisfying requirements of Rule 23(a) and (b)).

3. *See, e.g., Tefel v. Reno,* 180 F.3d 1286, 1304 (11th Cir.1999) (class that includes both aliens who had unsuccessfully applied for suspension of deportation and aliens who have never applied is "overly

broad"); *Berman v. Narragansett Racing Ass'n,* 414 F.2d 311, 317 (1st Cir.1969) ("amorphously defined" class should not be certified; but class of racing horse owners who win purses is adequately defined); *see also, Simer v. Rios,* 661 F.2d 655, 669 (7th Cir.1981) ("It is axiomatic that for a class action to be certified a 'class' must exist."). *Cf., Mullen v. Treasure Chest Casino, LLC,* 186 F.3d 620, 624 n. 1 (5th Cir.1999) (class of employees alleging illness caused by defective ventilation system is not deficient because allegation of defective system or injury from it has yet to be proven on merits).

ance will not change.[4] On the other hand, a class of all females who suffered, or may suffer, through past use of a defectively designed or manufactured birth control device is certifiable as a class action.

(2) *Representative Must Be a Member of the Class:* At least initially, the class representative must be a member of the class.[5] The purpose of this requirement is part of the courts' determination that class representatives will reflect the interests of the class. If a class representative was once a member but ceases to be a member of the class, the proper remedy is to select a new, suitable member of the class as a replacement representative.[6]

"Implicit" or "Implied" Classes

Rule 23 establishes a rigorous procedure to be followed before a case will be certified as a class action.[7] However, it is possible (though unusual) that in some circuits, classwide relief may be obtained notwithstanding the fact that the district court failed to follow the Rule 23 requirements for class certification.[8] Other courts

---

4. *See, e.g., Simmons v. Poe*, 47 F.3d 1370, 1381–82 (4th Cir.1995)(approving denial of class certification for "all African-American males residing in Virginia"). *But cf., Hilao v. Estate of Marcos*, 103 F.3d 767, 774 (9th Cir.1996) (affirming certification of all "Philippines citizens who were (or whose decedents were) tortured, summarily executed, or 'disappeared' while in military custody during a 14–year period;" class totalled approximately 10,000 people).

5. *See, e.g., Holmes v. Pension Plan of Bethlehem Steel Corp.*, 213 F.3d 124, 135 (3d Cir.2000) ("[A] plaintiff who lacks the personalized, redressable injury required for standing to assert claims on his own behalf would also lack standing to assert claims on behalf of a class."); *Great Rivers Cooperative of Southeastern Iowa v. Farmland Industries, Inc.*, 120 F.3d 893, 899 (8th Cir.1997) ("Inherent in Rule 23 is the requirement that the class representatives be members of the class."). *East Texas Motor Freight System, Inc. v. Rodriguez*, 431 U.S. 395, 403, 97 S.Ct. 1891, 1896, 52 L.Ed.2d 453 (1977)(error to certify class where named representatives are not members of class).

6. *See, e.g., Holmes v. Pension Plan of Bethlehem Steel Corp.*, 213 F.3d 124, 135–36 (3d Cir.2000) (if class representative has "live claim" at time of motion for class certification, "neither a pending motion nor a certified class action need be dismissed if his individual claim subsequently becomes moot"; but if claim became moot prior to motion for class certification, motion will be denied and case will be dismissed); *Hardy v. City Optical, Inc.*, 39 F.3d 765, 770 (7th

Cir.1994)(party dismissed "can no longer be the class representative"). *But see Kifer v. Ellsworth*, 346 F.3d 1155, 1156 (7th Cir. 2003) (initially, class representative was prison inmate who was subsequently released from jail; because class sought prospective relief through an injunction, class representative's personal claim had therefore become moot; "but the mooting of the class representative's personal claim does not bar him from continuing to represent the class, ... as otherwise defendants might delay the grant of relief in class actions indefinitely by buying off the class representatives in succession.").

7. *See, e.g., Garcia v. Johanns*, 444 F.3d 625, 631 (D.C. Cir.2006) (plaintiff seeking class certification must meet all requirements of Rule 23(a) and one requirement of Rule 23(b)).

8. *See, e.g., Doe v. Bush*, 261 F.3d 1037, 1050 (11th Cir.2001) (case was filed as class action and plaintiffs made timely motion for class certification; magistrate judge recommended certification; parties and district court all behaved as though classwide relief might be appropriate; failure to certify formally was court's error, not caused by plaintiffs; no administrative problems will arise by treating case as class action; held, implied class appropriate; also citing several older cases); *Navarro-Ayala v. Hernandez–Colon*, 951 F.2d 1325, 1334 (1st Cir.1991) (approving implied class "because this case was instituted by a complaint seeking class relief, implicitly granted class relief, and was conducted for years as a de facto class action").

have been generally reluctant to embrace this concept,[9] and to reject it where the de facto finding of class certification was not embraced (at least tacitly) by the actions of all parties and the court.[10] On this point attorneys must consult both the local precedent as well as the facts of individual cases.

Settlement Classes

It appears settled that a class may be certified for purposes of settlement only. However, it is also settled that certification of such classes must fully satisfy the relevant requirements of Rule 23.[11]

Relation to Rule 68

Rule 68 governs offers of judgment. Circuit courts have identified at least two points of overlap between Rule 23 and Rule 68.

The first problem can arise because a defendant has made an offer of judgment for the full amount that a plaintiff may lawfully collect if the plaintiff's claim prevailed on the merits. This situation may occur most commonly when there is a statutory cap on the plaintiff's claim. When such an offer of judgment is made, courts normally use Rule 68 to impose an end to the litigation, without regard to any preference the plaintiff may have.[12] Whatever the merit this approach may have in ordinary civil litigation, it can produce a complication in a case that has been or may be certified as a class action. For example, if a defendant made an offer of judg-

---

9. *See, e.g., Partington v. American International Specialty Lines Insurance Co.,* 443 F.3d 334, 341 (4th Cir.2006) ("the Fourth Circuit has never allowed the rigorous Rule 23 analysis to be accomplished implicitly;" noting that implicit certification has been approved "only in the context of contested actions where the parties and the court acted at all times as though a class existed").

10. *See, e.g., Davis v. Hutchins,* 321 F.3d 641, 649 (7th Cir.2003) (plaintiff had filed for class certification and defendant had not responded to complaint or motion; default was properly entered, but court had independent duty to address Rule 23 issues before it granted classwide relief; held, no default certification).

11. *Amchem Products, Inc. v. Windsor,* 521 U.S. 591, 117 S.Ct. 2231, 138 L.Ed.2d 689 (1997) (certification of settlement class requires "heightened attention" of trial court; affirming denial of certification for failure to satisfy Rule 23(a)(4) and (b)(3); but noting that consideration of trial management is irrelevant to settlement class; also holding that court's authority to approve settlement under Rule 23(e) does not authorize court to disregard requirements of Rule 23(a) and (b)). *See, e.g., Denney v.*

Deutsche Bank Securities, Inc., 443 F.3d 253, 270 (2d Cir.2006) ("Before certification is proper for any purpose—settlement, litigation, or otherwise—a court must ensure that the requirements of Rule 23(a) and (b) have been met. These requirements should not be watered down by virtue of the fact that the settlement is fair or equitable."). *See also, Ortiz v. Fibreboard Corp.,* 527 U.S. 815, 119 S.Ct. 2295, 144 L.Ed.2d 715 (1999) (holding that ruling of *Amchem* requiring settlement classes for which certification is sought under rule 23(b)(3) to meet requirements of Rule 23(a) applies equally to settlement classes for which certification is sought under Rule 23(b)(1)(B)). *But cf., Smith v. Sprint Communications Co., L.P.,* 387 F.3d 612, 614 (7th Cir.2004) (if settlement has been reached, "a district court need not inquire whether the case, if tried, would present intractable management problems, for the proposal is that there by no trial;" citing *Amchem, supra;* however, other elements of Rule 23 must still be met).

12. *See, e.g., McCauley v. Trans Union, L.L.P.,* 402 F.3d 340, 341–42 (2d Cir.2005) (where plaintiff rejects such offer, proper remedy is to enter default judgment for full dollar amount, plus costs).

ment to an individual litigant for a full statutory amount, a court's decision to use a default judgment to effectively force a settlement of the case could preclude litigation of issues that were appropriate for treatment as a class action. Courts recognize this potential problem, and have held that a Rule 68 offer of judgment to an individual plaintiff cannot be used to render a putative class action moot.[13]

The second problem arises because Rule 68 provides that if a proper offer of judgment is made, followed by a filing with the district court of the offer, notice of proper acceptance, and proof of service, the court has no discretion in the matter, and must enter judgment.[14] Rule 23, by contrast, affords the court substantial authority to review and approve (or veto) a proposed settlement of a class action. Courts have resolved this apparent conflict by treating the authority of a district court under Rule 23 as an exception to the general requirement of Rule 68, controlling most offers of judgment outside the context of class litigation.[15]

Rule 23(a) Requirements for a Class

(1) *Numerosity:* Rule 23(a)(1) requires that the class membership be sufficiently large to warrant a class action because the alternative of joinder is "impracticable".[16] There is no threshold number of class members guaranteed to satisfy the "numerosity" requirement of Rule 23(a).[17] A class comprised of many hundreds, or

---

13. *See, e.g., Carroll v. United Compucred Collections, Inc.,* 399 F.3d 620, 625 (6th Cir.2005) (in instant case motion for class certification was pending but not yet decided when offer of judgment was made; if complaint could be rendered moot by use of Rule 68, court could never reach class action even in cases where class certification would be appropriate); *Weiss v. Regal Collections,* 385 F.3d 337, 348 (3d Cir.2004) (same, but making exception for "undue delay" in filing motion for class certification).

14. Fed.R.Civ.P. 68. *See, e.g, Webb v. James,* 147 F.3d 617, 621 (7th Cir.1998) (noting that Rule 68 mandates entry of judgment on an offer that meets the requirements of Rule 68).

15. *See, e.g., Ramming v. Natural Gas Pipeline Co.,* 390 F.3d 366, 371 (5th Cir. 2004) (duty of court to review settlement of class action under Rule 23 provides exception to Rule 68; same result, slightly different reasoning, when case involves plea for injunctive relief).

16. *See, e.g., Mullen v. Treasure Chest Casino, LLC,* 186 F.3d 620, 624 (5th Cir. 1999) (class of 100 to 150 members sufficient; additional factors supporting finding of adequate numerosity are reluctance of current employees to sue individually for

fear of retaliation and possibility that transient nature of employment in gambling business would tend to make joinder difficult because members of potential class would tend to disperse geographically); *Robidoux v. Celani,* 987 F.2d 931, 935 (2d Cir.1993)(emphasizing that for certification, joinder need only be impracticable, not necessarily impossible).

17. *See, e.g., Trevizo v. Adams,* 455 F.3d 1155 (10th Cir.2006) (holding that there is no set formula or number for determining numerosity; concluding that 84 potential class members is insufficient where joinder is not difficult); *Bittinger v. Tecumseh Products Co.,* 123 F.3d 877, 884 n. 1 (6th Cir. 1997) (noting that Rule 23(a)(1) is not a "strict numerical test;" holding, however, that where class comprises over 1,100 persons, suggestion that joinder is not impractical is "frivolous"); *Robidoux v. Celani,* 987 F.2d 931, 935 (2d Cir.1993) (numerosity does not require exact estimate of class size, but only a reasonable estimate). *But see Consolidated Rail Corp. v. Town of Hyde Park,* 47 F.3d 473, 483 (2d Cir.1995) ("[N]umerosity is presumed at a level of 40 members."); *Polich v. Burlington Northern, Inc.,* 116 F.R.D. 258, 261 (D. Mont. 1987) (sixty members sufficient to support presumption that joinder was not practicable).

thousands, of members will almost surely meet this test.[18] Classes of ten litigants or less will almost certainly not meet this test,[19] and will instead be consigned to joinder of parties under Rule 20. When the number of members falls between, approximately, twenty-five and one hundred, the probability of meeting the numerosity requirement varies from one judicial district to another.[20]

While the numerosity requirement is very fact specific, the requirement of impracticability of joinder must be affirmatively and specifically addressed in the certification motion.[21]

(2) *Common Questions of Law or Fact:* Rule 23(a)(2) requires the existence of common questions of law or fact among the class members before the case will be certified as a class action. To satisfy the requirement of Rule 23(a)(2), the common questions need not predominate. Courts generally have a liberal attitude toward this requirement, and close questions as to the existence of sufficient commonality tend to be resolved in favor of finding common questions.[22] In class actions involving fraud, however, there can be some

---

18. *See, e.g., Bacon v. Honda of America Manufacturing, Inc.,* 370 F.3d 565, 570 (6th Cir.2004) ("There is no automatic cut-off point at which the number of plaintiffs makes joinder impracticable, [but] sheer number of potential litigants in a class, especially if it is more than several hundred, can be the only factor needed to satisfy Rule 23(a)(1).").

19. *General Telephone Co. of the Northwest, Inc. v. Equal Employment Opportunity Commission,* 446 U.S. 318, 330, 100 S.Ct. 1698, 1706, 64 L.Ed.2d 319 (1980) (classes of 15 members will often be too small). *See, e.g., National Association of Government Employees v. City Public Service Board of San Antonio,* 40 F.3d 698, 715 (5th Cir. 1994)(affirming that class of 11 members does not satisfy requirement of numerosity). *But cf., Grant v. Sullivan,* 131 F.R.D. 436, 446 (M.D.Pa.1990)(approving certification of class of 14 members).

20. *See, e.g., Stewart v. Abraham,* 275 F.3d 220, 226–27 (3d Cir.2001) (no minimum number required but more than 40 is generally sufficient). *But cf., Pruitt v. City of Chicago,* 472 F.3d 925, 926 (7th Cir. 2007) (if joinder is practicable "then the other criteria don't matter;" acknowledging that sometimes a class of 40 is unmanageable, but not in instant case).

21. *Golden v. City of Columbus,* 404 F.3d 950, 965 (6th Cir.2005).

22. *See, e.g., Stewart v. Abraham,* 275 F.3d 220, 227 (3d Cir.2001) (commonality can be satisfied if class representatives share a single question of fact or law with

class members); *Armstrong v. Davis,* 275 F.3d 849, 868 (9th Cir.2001) ("[I]n a civil–rights suit ... commonality is satisfied where the lawsuit challenges a system-wide practice or policy that affects all of the putative class members." Rejecting significance of such individual factors as, e.g., hearing disability and learning disability); *Mullen v. Treasure Chest Casino, LLC,* 186 F.3d 620, 625 (5th Cir.1999) ("The test of commonality is not demanding." Held, sufficient commonality in allegations of: protection by same federal law; negligence of defendant in ignoring safety hazards; and unseaworthiness of vessel; indeed, each allegation is sufficient to satisfy requirement. "It is therefore irrelevant whether the class members uniformly allege damages from second-hand smoke."); *Keele v. Wexler,* 149 F.3d 589, 594 (7th Cir.1998) (common nucleus of operative fact will satisfy requirement of Rule 23(a)(2); moreover, "factual variations among class members' grievances do not defeat a class action"); *Hanlon v. Chrysler Corp.,* 150 F.3d 1011 (9th Cir. 1998) (requirements of Rule 23(a)(2) are "minimal"); *Lightbourn v. County of El Paso,* 118 F.3d 421, 426 (5th Cir.1997) ("The commonality test is met when there is at least one issue, the resolution of which will affect all or a significant number of the putative class members."); *Baby Neal v. Casey,* 43 F.3d 48, 56 (3d Cir.1994) ("Commonality and typicality are broadly defined and tend to merge." Nevertheless, commonality addresses the suitability of a class action, and typicality goes to suitability of plaintiff.). *But see, Love v. Johanns,* 439

tension between this fairly generous approach to commonality for purposes of Rule 23(a)(2) and the more stringent requirements for pleading fraud with particularity under Rule 9(b). In securities cases it was settled until recently that the plaintiff could properly plead a generalized rebuttable presumption of fraud. However, in securities cases controlled by the Private Securities Litigation Reform Act of 1995,[23] it is now settled that a plaintiff seeking to serve as a class representative must plead with particularity sufficient to satisfy the requirements of Rule 9(b).[24] result is reached in cases where the plaintiff's degree of reliance on the alleged fraudulent statements varies significantly. In such cases, the particularity requirements of Rule 9(b) will probably be imposed and it will be difficult to establish that the requirement of Rule 23(a)(2) for commonality has been met.[25]

NOTE: Although Rule 23(a) may be satisfied even if the common questions of law or fact do not predominate in the case, a class seeking certification under Rule 23(b)(3) must nevertheless include common questions of law or fact that *do* predominate over other questions. The interplay between Rule 23(a) and Rule 23(b) is discussed further below.

(3) *Class Representatives' Claims Must Be Typical:* Rule 23(a)(3) requires that the claims of class representatives be typical of the class as a whole, not merely some portion thereof.[26] General-

F.3d 723, 728 (D.C. Cir.2006) (in racial discrimination case, commonality of disparate treatment of class requires showing of "(i) discrimination (ii) against a particular group (iii) of which the plaintiff is a member, *plus* (iv) some additional factor that 'permit[s] the court to infer that members of the class suffered from a common policy of discrimination.' "); *Reeb v. Ohio Department of Rehabilitation & Correction,* 435 F.3d 639, 644–45 (6th Cir.2006) (commonality not satisfied simply because issue of whether defendant violated federal civil rights law is common to class; "If this were the test, every plaintiff seeking to certify a class in a Title VII action would be entitled to that certification;" noting that "the same general policy of discrimination can affect many different aspects of employment, such as hiring, firing, promoting, giving benefits, providing vacation time, or delegating work assignments;" moreover, "a general policy of discrimination is not sufficient to allow a court to find commonality or typicality"); *Tefel v. Reno,* 180 F.3d 1286, 1304 (11th Cir.1999) (insufficient commonality where significant differences exist in laws applicable to various sub-groups of aliens who may be subject to deportation); *Simmons v. Poe,* 47 F.3d 1370 (4th Cir.1995)(no common questions of law or fact where class repre-

sentative—unlike most of class—fits within factual questions in case).

23. 15 U.S.C.A. § 78u.

24. *See, e.g., Berger v. Compaq Computer Corp.,* 257 F.3d 475, 478 n. 3 (5th Cir. 2001) (explaining statutory requirement to plead scienter with particularity).

25. *See, e.g., Broussard v. Meineke Discount Muffler Shops, Inc.,* 155 F.3d 331, 340–41 (4th Cir.1998) (where members of class claimed fraud based on both uniform documents and non-standard oral statements made to individual plaintiffs, requirement of commonality under rule 23(a)(2) is not met).

26. *See, e.g., Rector v. City & County of Denver,* 348 F.3d 935, 950 (10th Cir.2003) ("By definition, class representatives who do not have Article III standing to pursue the class claims fail to meet the typicality requirements of Rule 23."); *Schachner v. Blue Cross and Blue Shield of Ohio,* 77 F.3d 889, 896 n. 8 (6th Cir.1996) (representative holding federal claim does not adequately represent certain class members who hold only state claims). *See also Wooden v. Board of Regents,* 247 F.3d 1262, 1287 (11th Cir.2001) ("It should be obvious that there cannot be adequate typicality between

ly the class representatives need not have claims identical in all respects with those of other members of the class.[27] Substantial commonality appears to be sufficient, even if differences among the claims, *e.g.*, issues of damages, also exist.[28] This requirement is intended to ensure that class representatives will represent the best interests of class members who take a less active part in managing the litigation. It also overlaps considerably the case law requirement that class representatives be members of the class.[29]

a class and a named representative unless the named representative has individual standing to raise the legal claims of the class").

27. *See, e.g., Lightbourn v. County of El Paso,* 118 F.3d 421, 426 (5th Cir.1997) ("The test for typicality, like the test for commonality, is not demanding."); *Paxton v. Union National Bank,* 688 F.2d 552, 561 (8th Cir.1982) ("The Rule does not require that every question of law or fact be common to every member of the class."); *Appleyard v. Wallace,* 754 F.2d 955, 958 (11th Cir.1985) ("strong similarity of legal theories" may satisfy Rule 23(a)(2), even where substantial factual differences exist). *But cf., Cummings v. Connell,* 402 F.3d 936, 945 (9th Cir.2005) ("Awarding nominal damages to only the named class representatives results in a divergence of interests between the class representative and the absent class members. This is in direct contravention of Rule 23."); *Cornett v. Donovan,* 51 F.3d 894, 897 n. 2 (9th Cir.1995) (because claims of class representatives must be typical of class, class lacks standing if representatives lack standing).

28. *See, e.g., Ball v. Union Carbide Corp.,* 376 F.3d 554 (6th Cir.2004) (requirements of Rule 23(a)(2) and (3) "tend to merge"); *Mullen v. Treasure Chest Casino, LLC,* 186 F.3d 620, 625 (5th Cir.1999) ("Like commonality, the test for typicality is not demanding."); *Alpern v. UtiliCorp United, Inc.,* 84 F.3d 1525, 1540 (8th Cir. 1996)("Factual variations in the individual claims will not normally preclude class certification if the claim arises from the same event or course of conduct as the class claims, and gives rise to the same legal or remedial theory." Variations in damages do not necessarily undermine typicality.). *But see Stirman v. Exxon Corp.,* 280 F.3d 554, 562 (5th Cir.2002) (although typicality is not normally a demanding text, finding insufficient typicality where class is based on implied lease covenant, and leases vary between market-value leases and proceeds leases under one state's law, and other

states have even greater range of differences in law); *Piazza v. Ebsco Industries, Inc.,* 273 F.3d 1341, 1347 (11th Cir.2001) ("Without individual standing to raise a legal claim, a named representative does not have the requisite typicality to raise the same claim on behalf of a class. ...It is by now clear that a class representative whose claim is time-barred cannot assert the claim on behalf of the class."); *Armstrong v. Davis,* 275 F.3d 849, 868–69 (9th Cir.2001) (typicality satisfied by comparing type of injury alleged by named plaintiff with injuries of other class members; injuries must be similar but need not be identical; but class representatives should include parties who together have suffered the entire range of injuries alleged, from kidney disability to hearing impairment). *See also United States Parole Commission v. Geraghty,* 445 U.S. 388, 404, 100 S.Ct. 1202, 1212, 63 L.Ed.2d 479 (1980) (at time of class certification, class representatives must have standing; but subsequent mootness of individual claims of class representatives does not make class action moot—"even though class certification has been denied"); *Martens v. Thomann,* 273 F.3d 159, 173 (2d Cir.2001) (class representative still has fiduciary duty to class notwithstanding that class representative's individual claim subsequently became moot). *But see Reeb v. Ohio Department of Rehabilitation & Correction,* 435 F.3d 639, 644–45 (6th Cir.2006) (typicality not satisfied where proposed representatives are not "an adequate cross-section" of class). *Cf., Johnson v. Board of Regents, University of Georgia,* 263 F.3d 1234, 1268 (11th Cir.2001) (distinguishing case in which plaintiff lacked standing at time of complaint and time of class certification; in such cases, plaintiff cannot represent class).

29. *See, e.g., Robinson v. Sheriff of Cook County,* 167 F.3d 1155, 1157 (7th Cir.1999) (Rule 23(a)(3) "is really an aspect of [Rule 23(a)(2)]; if [the representative's] claim is atypical, he is not likely to be an adequate representative.").

(4) *Representatives Must Fairly Protect the Class:* Because class actions vest authority over the interests of passive members of the class in the hands of class activists, Rule 23(a)(4) requires the court to ensure that class representatives will be individuals who will meet those responsibilities fully. There is no "bright line" establishing when Rule 23(a)(4) is satisfied.[30] Nevertheless, courts tend to be particularly sensitive to this requirement.[31] Potential conflicts of interest may disqualify applicants,[32] as can a suggestion that the proposed class representative lacks integrity.[33] If in the course of litigation the trial court finds that class representatives previously approved have become inadequate, the court retains authority to order appointment of new representatives.[34]

(5) *Adequacy of Counsel:* Rule 23(a)(4) contains no express language addressing the issue of whether it authorizes the court to examine the ability of the class' legal counsel to represent the class.

30. *But cf., Denney v. Deutsche Bank Securities, Inc.,* 443 F.3d 253, 268 (2d Cir. 2006) ("Adequacy is twofold: the proposed class representative must have an interest in vigorously pursuing the claims of the class, and must have no interests antagonistic to the interests of other class members."); *Wolfert v. Transamerica Home First, Inc.,* 439 F.3d 165, 173 (2d Cir.2006) ("There is no litmus test for determining when interests of one or more absent class members are sufficiently distinct from those of the class representatives to render those representatives inadequate.").

31. *See, e.g., Stirman v. Exxon Corp.,* 280 F.3d 554, 563 (5th Cir.2002) (error not to examine adequacy of class representatives as well as counsel; questioning adequacy of class representatives where leases may be dissimilar to those of class; and where representative may have waived statute of limitations issue unimportant to her individually but potentially significant to others in class; noting, inter alia, that adequacy of class representative often overlaps typicality requirement). *Cf., Dechert v. Cadle Co.,* 333 F.3d 801 (7th Cir.2003) (bankruptcy trustee is not per se unsuitable as class representative, but trustee's duty to protect interest of bankruptcy creditors may often conflict with interest of class members).

32. *Ortiz v. Fibreboard Corp.,* 527 U.S. 815, 119 S.Ct. 2295, 144 L.Ed.2d 715 (1999) (class comprised of holders of both present and future tort claims should be divided into subclasses with different counsel for each subclass; failure to provide different counsel means requirements of Rule 23(a)(4) are not met). *See, e.g., London v. Wal–Mart Stores, Inc.,* 340 F.3d 1246, 1255–

56 (11th Cir.2003) (personal friendship between class representative and lawyer, plus fact that class representative had been lawyer's stockbroker and might resume that role in future, meant class representative "cannot fairly and adequately represent the class"); *Pickett v. Iowa Beef Processors,* 209 F.3d 1276, 1280–81 (11th Cir.2000) (acknowledging that requirements of rule 23(a)(4) can be satisfied unless conflict "is a fundamental one, going to the specific issues in controversy"; finding such conflict where plaintiffs are challenging contracts and marketing agreements that harmed some class members but benefited others). *Cf., Fymbo v. State Farm Fire and Casualty Co.,* 213 F.3d 1320 (10th Cir.2000) (where class members each have "a sufficiently large stake to be able to litigate" separately, that factor weighs against certifying class). *Mullen v. Treasure Chest Casino, LLC,* 186 F.3d 620, 625–26 (5th Cir.1999) (Rule 23(a)(4) satisfied where class representatives' interests are identical to class, leaving no basis for significant conflict of interest, and where attorneys have extensive experience in class actions and relevant federal law; variance in proof of causation and damages between class members who smoke and others who don't "does not affect the alignment of their interests").

33. *See, e.g., Savino v. Computer Credit, Inc.,* 164 F.3d 81, 87 (2d Cir.1998) ("To judge the adequacy of representation, courts may consider the honesty and trustworthiness of the named plaintiff.").

34. *See, e.g., Swanson v. Wabash,* 577 F.Supp. 1308, 1326 (N.D.Ill.1983)(citing cases).

Nevertheless, courts have heretofore routinely cited Rule 23(a)(4) for their authority to examine the ability of the class' legal counsel to represent the class. With the introduction of Rule 23(g) in 2003, however, it is no longer necessary for courts to rely on Rule 23(a)(4) for supervision of class counsel. Instead, Rule 23(g) expressly grants a district court the right and responsibility to appoint suitable counsel. Until enough time has elapsed to permit the courts to develop their authority and duties under Rule 23(g), it is likely that much of the case law originally developed under the authority of Rule 23(a)(4) will continue to guide courts in this work. Rule 23(g) is discussed at greater length elsewhere in this text.

(6) *The "Most Sophisticated" Investor:* When a class action also falls within the scope of the Private Securities Litigation Reform Act of 1995[35] the court is obligated to appoint as lead plaintiff the "most adequate plaintiff." Such a person is identified as that member of the class who is most capable of representing the class. This requirement, however, has been held not to require that the chosen person possess unique advantages of experience, expertise, wealth or intellect.[36]

General Considerations

(1) *Diversity Jurisdiction:* In most class actions, federal subject matter jurisdiction based on diversity of citizenship is now governed by a recent addition to 28 U.S.C.A. § 1332. In 2005 Congress amended § 1332 to include special provisions applicable only to class actions. These provisions are found in § 1332(d). Subject to a few exceptions, § 1332(d)(2) provides that the amount in controversy requirement for class actions is a sum that exceeds $5,000,000, exclusive of interest and costs.[37] This requirement is often easier to meet than the standard for non-class litigation of more than $75,000 for each plaintiff, exclusive of interest and costs.[38] The reason is that the figure of more than $5,000,000 may be met by adding all the claims of the class members together,[39] whereas the amount of more than $75,000 is normally a requirement that each plaintiff must meet individually.

Section 1332(d)(2) permits the requirement of diversity of citizenship in most class actions to be met in any of three ways: (A) a single member of the class may be a citizen of an American state that is different from the citizenship of any defendant; (B) a single

---

35. 15 U.S.C.A. § 78u–4(a)(3)(B).

36. *Berger v. Compaq Computer Corp.,* 279 F.3d 313 (5th Cir.2002). *See also Herrgott v. United States District Court for the Northern District of California,* 306 F.3d 726, 729 (9th Cir.2002) (party with largest financial stake in litigation presumptively is most adequate party and, assuming requirements of Rule 23 are met, will typically be lead plaintiff).

37. 28 U.S.C.A. § 1332(d)(2). *See also, e.g., Frazier v. Pioneer Americas, L.L.C.,*

455 F.3d 542 (5th Cir.2006) ("Unlike § 1332(a), [§ 1332(d)(6)] explicitly allows aggregation of each class member's claim.").

38. 28 U.S.C.A. § 1332(a).

39. 28 U.S.C.A. § 1332(d)(6). *See also, e.g., Frazier v. Pioneer Americas, L.L.C.,* 455 F.3d 542 (5th Cir.2006) ("Unlike § 1332(a), [§ 1332(d)(6)] explicitly allows aggregation of each class member's claim.").

member of the class may be a citizen or subject of a foreign state and any defendant is a citizen of an American state; or (C) a single member of a class may be a citizen of an American state and any defendant is either a foreign state or a citizen or subject of a foreign state.[40] It should be noted that this requirement permits the diversity of citizenship requirement to be satisfied even where some members of the class might not be of diverse citizenship from one or more defendants, which is a very different standard from the requirement for diverse citizenship in non-class litigation.[41]

Section 1332(d) also contains a number of exceptions to the special jurisdictional standards for class actions. Together, however, these exceptions probably constitute a relatively small proportion of the total number of class actions that are now otherwise jurisdictionally eligible to be filed in federal district court. The first potential exception arises when more than one-third, but less than two-thirds, of the class members as well as the primary defendants are citizens of the same state in which the action was originally filed. In that circumstance, § 1332(d) affords the district court discretion to decline to exercise its jurisdiction, after considering six factors: whether the claims involve matters of national or interstate interest; whether the claims will be subject to the law of the forum state or the laws of other states; whether the original pleading in the class action was pleaded in a manner intended to avoid federal jurisdiction; whether the action was filed in a forum with a "distinct" nexus with the class, the alleged wrong, or the defendants; whether the forum is the place of citizenship of a disproportionate number of class members, and the remaining class members are dispersed among a substantial number of other states; and whether, during the previous three years, other class actions asserting similar claims were filed on behalf of the same persons.[42]

Another exception, found in 28 U.S.C.A. § 1332(d)(4), requires the district court to decline jurisdiction if the following elements are met: more than two-thirds of the class members are citizens of the forum state; at least one significant defendant is a citizen of the forum state; principal injuries giving rise to the cause of action occurred in the forum state; and during the previous three years, no similar class action involving essentially the same parties has been filed.[43]

Additionally, the more generous jurisdictional standards of § 1332(d) do not apply if the primary defendants are states, state agencies, or state officials, or if the membership of the proposed class is less than one hundred.[44] Finally, these new jurisdictional standards do not apply to three distinct categories of class actions:

40.   28 U.S.C.A. § 1332(d)(2)(A)-(C).

41.   *See, e.g., Evans v. Walter Industries, Inc.,* 449 F.3d 1159, 1163 (11th Cir.2006) (noting that requirement is only minimal diversity); *Abrego v. Dow Chemical Co.,* 443 F.3d 676, 680 (9th Cir.2006) (§ 1332(d)

"abandons the complete diversity rule for covered class actions.").

42.   28 U.S.C.A. § 1332(d)(3).

43.   28 U.S.C.A. § 1332(d)(4).

44.   28 U.S.C.A. § 1332(d)(5).

lawsuits arising under designated federal securities laws; lawsuits relating to the internal affairs of corporations arising under the laws of the states where such corporations are incorporated; and lawsuits relating to the rights, duties, and obligations pursuant to a security as defined by federal law.[45]

Where the new § 1332(d) does not apply, it is probably safe to assume that pre-existing standards for determining diversity jurisdiction remain in place. In such circumstances, diversity of citizenship is probably satisfied if the class representatives are diverse from the party opposing the class.[46] Additionally, the amount in controversy requirement for class actions that do not fall within the more generous jurisdictional provisions of § 1332(d) is probably still controlled by the standard for non-class litigation. However, this standard has been loosened considerably, as is discussed under *Supplemental Jurisdiction*, immediately below.

For purposes of § 1332(d), an unincorporated association is deemed a citizen of the state in which its principal place of business is located as well as the state in which it was organized.[47] This new provision for affected class actions differs from the treatment of unincorporated associations in non-class litigation.[48]

It should be noted that § 1332(d)(11) provides that most mass actions will, for jurisdictional purposes, be treated in a manner similar to the way other provisions of § 1332(d) address most class actions.

2) *Supplemental Jurisdiction:* The Supreme Court recently resolved substantial uncertainty as to whether plaintiffs certified as members of a Rule 23 class had to satisfy the amount in controversy requirement individually. The Court held that when Congress enacted 28 U.S.C.A. § 1367 (governing supplemental jurisdiction), it effectively provided that if a single member of the class meets the amount in controversy requirement for diversity jurisdiction, all other members whose claims fall short of the requirement amount may nonetheless qualify for supplemental jurisdiction if the other elements of § 1367 are satisfied.[49] This holding is applicable to classes governed by Rule 23, but usually not to parties intervening in a class pursuant to Rule 24. Section 1367 is discussed in greater detail elsewhere in this text.

(3) *Federal Question Suits:* Federal courts have subject matter jurisdiction over class actions involving federal questions in the same manner as conventional litigation.

(4) *Personal Jurisdiction:* Jurisdiction over a defendant in a class action is obtained in the same manner, and subject to the same requirements, as jurisdiction over any defendant in conventional

---

45. 28 U.S.C.A. § 1332(d)(9).

46. *Supreme Tribe of Ben Hur v. Cauble,* 255 U.S. 356, 41 S.Ct. 338, 65 L.Ed. 673 (1921).

47. 28 U.S.C.A. § 1332(d)(10).

48. *See* § 2.12 of this text, "Unincorporated Associations."

49. *Exxon Mobil Corp. v. Allapattah Services, Inc.,* 545 U.S. 546, 125 S.Ct. 2611, 2621–25, 162 L.Ed.2d 502 (2005).

litigation. The same is true for personal jurisdiction over a class of defendants, *i.e.*, each individual must be subject to the jurisdiction of the court before that individual is subject to the judgment. For a class of plaintiffs, however, class members may be included in the suit even if they have no link with the state where the case is being heard. This holding applies only to cases where members of the plaintiff class were afforded an opportunity to drop out of the class early in the litigation, and chose not to do so.[50] The Supreme Court has not yet ruled on a circumstance where members of a plaintiff class have no contact with the state in which the case is being heard, *and* had no opportunity to drop out of the suit.

(5) *Venue:* Venue in class actions does not generally differ from venue in conventional litigation. One potential exception should be noted. If venue is based on the residence of the class, the residences of the class representatives are examined, not those of the entire class.[51]

(6) *Choice of Law:* In class actions based on state law, the court can only apply the law of a jurisdiction that has a sufficient relationship with an individual litigant. Thus individual litigants from states other than the forum may be entitled to have the law of some other state applied to their claims. In a class action, therefore, it is possible that the court may have to apply the laws of a variety of states to different class members.[52]

(7) *Defendant Classes:* Most class action cases are suits in which the class is the plaintiff. However, it is possible that a class may be a defendant.[53] In that unusual circumstance, the provisions of Rule 23 apply in much the same fashion as they apply to plaintiff classes, with only a few differences. One difference is that members of a defendant class are entitled to constitutional protections of notice, as well as any protections provided within Rule 23. This difference tends to have little practical impact, however, because class representatives are obligated to protect the interests of passive class members, including appropriate notice, discussed elsewhere. A more significant potential distinction between a plaintiff class and a defendant class is heightened concern to ensure that the representatives of a defendant class adequately represent the interests of the class. The concern is greater with defendant classes because, at least initially, the representatives of a defendant class are chosen by the plaintiff who is suing the class.[54]

50. *Phillips Petroleum Co. v. Shutts,* 472 U.S. 797, 105 S.Ct. 2965, 86 L.Ed.2d 628 (1985).

51. *See, e.g., Appleton Electric Co. v. Advance–United Expressways,* 494 F.2d 126, 140 (7th Cir.1974)(looking only to venue of named representatives).

52. *Phillips Petroleum Co. v. Shutts,* 472 U.S. 797, 105 S.Ct. 2965, 86 L.Ed.2d 628 (1985).

53. *See, e.g., Consolidated Rail Corp. v. Town of Hyde Park,* 47 F.3d 473 (2d Cir. 1995) (approving a defendant class and noting Rule 23 "does not require a willing representative, merely an adequate one").

54. *See, e.g., Ameritech Benefit Plan Committee v. Communication Workers of America,* 220 F.3d 814, 819 (7th Cir.2000) (defendant classes require special attention because they are "initiated by those opposed to the interests of the class").

Certification and the Merits

The question whether a district court may properly consider the merits of the case when deciding a certification motion is not fully resolved. One line of cases cites Supreme Court authority for the proposition that the merits should not be consulted.[55] However, there is significant authority, also drawing upon Supreme Court precedent, permitting and even encouraging use of the merits to make the certification decision.[56] Until the matter is finally resolved, attorneys will be required to consult local precedent.

It should be noted, however, that there is clear agreement authorizing dismissal of a case without deciding a motion for certification because the plaintiff cannot, e.g., state a cognizable claim or satisfy jurisdiction. In such circumstances the dismissal may address some feature of the merits of the case but does not address certification at all.[57]

---

55. *Eisen v. Carlisle & Jacquelin,* 417 U.S. 156, 177, 94 S.Ct. 2140, 2152, 40 L.Ed.2d 732 (1974) ("We find nothing in either the language or history of Rule 23 that gives a court any authority to conduct a preliminary inquiry into the merits of a suit in order to determine whether it may be maintained as a class action."). *See also Lienhart v. Dryvit Systems, Inc.,* 255 F.3d 138, 143 n. 2 (4th Cir.2001) (merits should not be consulted when deciding certification; however, merits may be considered when appellate court decides whether to permit appeal under Rule 23(f)); *Caridad v. Metro–North Commuter Railroad,* 191 F.3d 283, 291–92 (2d Cir.1999) ("[A] motion for class certification is not an occasion for examination of the merits of the case." Although statistical data presented by proponent of class certification may ultimately prove unpersuasive on merits of case, it may still satisfactorily demonstrate common questions of fact under Rule 23(a)(2)); *Valentino v. Carter–Wallace, Inc.,* 97 F.3d 1227, 1232 (9th Cir.1996) (merits are not part of analysis required for class certification).

56. *General Telephone Co. of Southwest v. Falcon,* 457 U.S. 147, 160, 102 S.Ct. 2364, 2372, 72 L.Ed.2d 740 (1982) ("[S]ometimes it may be necessary for the court to probe behind the pleadings before coming to rest on the certification question."); *Coopers & Lybrand v. Livesay,* 437 U.S. 463, 469 n. 12, 98 S.Ct. 2454, 2458 n. 12, 57 L.Ed.2d 351 (1978) (determination of class action may be " 'intimately involved with the merits of the claim' "). *See also, Miles v. Merrill Lynch & Co.,* 471 F.3d 24, 39 (2d Cir. 2006) (suggesting that conflicting line of holdings that bar inquiries on merits reads Supreme Court precedent incorrectly; holding that where Rule 23 inquiry and merits inquiry overlap, district court may make inquiry for purpose of Rule 23, but findings to not bind court on later decisions on merits); *Newton v. Merrill Lynch, Pierce, Fenner & Smith, Inc.,* 259 F.3d 154, 166–68 (3d Cir.2001) (*Eisen* should be taken in context; noting more qualified language of *Coopers & Lybrand,* supra; "[A] preliminary inquiry into the merits is sometimes necessary to determine whether the alleged claims can be properly resolved as a class action."); *Castano v. American Tobacco Co.,* 84 F.3d 734 (5th Cir.1996) (citing *Rhone-Poulenc,* infra, with apparent approval); *In the Matter of Rhone-Poulenc Rorer, Inc.,* 51 F.3d 1293, 1299 (7th Cir.1995) (likelihood that plaintiffs will lose should be weighed in determining whether to certify class).

57. *See, e.g., Boulware v. Crossland Mortgage Corp.,* 291 F.3d 261, 268 n. 4 (4th Cir.2002) ("Because [plaintiff] failed to state a claim as the purported named plaintiff, and because all other similarly situated plaintiffs would likewise fail to state a claim, the district court necessarily acted within its discretion in denying class certification."); *Curtin v. United Airlines, Inc.,* 275 F.3d 88, 92 (D.C. Cir.2001) (approving resolution of straightforward summary judgment motion without addressing more difficult and unnecessary question of class certification). *Cf., Todd v. Exxon Corp.* 275 F.3d 191, 202 n. 5 (2d Cir.2001) ("[D]ifficulty meeting the predominance and typicality requirements for Rule 23 certification ... does not indicate that plaintiff fails to state a claim upon which relief can be granted.").

Statutes of Limitation: Equitable Tolling

In a case based on federal question jurisdiction, it is settled that institution of the class action tolls applicable statutes of limitations for the class.[58] The statute remains in suspension until the district court denies certification.[59] If the statute resumes running, it does so from the point at which it was tolled.[60] This protection applies to parties who subsequently seek to intervene in the suit after certification has been denied.[61] Further, if the class was certified under Rule 23(b)(3) and some members of the class exercise their right to opt out of the class under Rule 23(c)(2), the statute remains tolled as to those individuals until they exercise the right to opt out.[62] This protection applies even to members of the class who were unaware of the pendency of the class litigation.[63] Moreover, equitable tolling applies to "all members of the putative class until class certification has been denied."[64]

If following denial of class certification due to a deficiency in the class itself, e.g., failure to meet the requirement of numerosity/impractability of joinder, class members who seek to file a subsequent class action will be denied the benefits of equitable tolling.[65] However, where certification is denied solely due to a deficiency in the class representatives (and not in the class itself), the cases are in conflict.[66] Attorneys must consult the local precedent and practice.

It should be noted that this doctrine of equitable tolling, though applicable to cases based on federal question jurisdiction, applies to class actions arising from state claims only when state law also

58. *American Pipe & Construction Co. v. Utah,* 414 U.S. 538, 550–51, 94 S.Ct. 756, 764–65, 38 L.Ed.2d 713 (1974).

59. *See, e.g., Hemenway v. Peabody Coal Co.,* 159 F.3d 255, 265 (7th Cir.1998) ("[C]ases have confirmed that time begins immediately, rather than after final judgment or decision on appeal."); *Armstrong v. Martin Marietta Corp.,* 138 F.3d 1374, 1378 (11th Cir.1998) (en banc) (denial by district court resumes running of statute of limitations). *Cf., Bridges v. Department of Maryland State Police,* 441 F.3d 197, 212–13 (4th Cir.2006) (statute begins to run again when court enters order denying class certification, not when representative parties abandon class through inaction); *In re Copper Antitrust Litigation,* 436 F.3d 782, 793 (7th Cir.2006) (statute of limitation resumes running when class certification is denied or party opts out of class); *Culver v. City of Milwaukee,* 277 F.3d 908, 913–14 (7th Cir. 2002) (although instant case was properly decertified and individual claim dismissed, error not to provide class members with notice of proposed dismissal under Rule 23(e) so they could, as appropriate, prevent

resumption of running and expiration of statute of limitations that had been tolled while class action was pending).

60. *American Pipe & Construction Co. v. Utah,* 414 U.S. 538, 542–43, 94 S.Ct. 756, 760–61, 38 L.Ed.2d 713 (1974) (class action filed eleven days before running of statute; six months later certification was denied; held, individual claims filed eight days after entry of order denying class status were timely).

61. *Id. at* 553.

62. *Id. at* 550–51 (statute begins to run against individuals at time they opt out).

63. *Id. at* 551.

64. *Crown, Cork & Seal Co. v. Parker,* 462 U.S. 345, 354, 103 S.Ct. 2392, 2397, 76 L.Ed.2d 628 (1983) (expanding *American Pipe* to apply to plaintiffs who file separate suits, not just those who intervene in the original suit).

65. *Yang v. Odom,* 392 F.3d 97, 104 (3d Cir.2004).

66. *Yang v. Odom,* 392 F.3d 97, 104–08 (3d Cir.2004) (collecting cases).

provides for equitable tolling. Courts reach this conclusion through application of the *Erie* doctrine,[67] discussed elsewhere in this text.

It should also be noted that for mass actions within the scope of the Class Action Fairness Act, encoded in part in § 1332(d)(11), the existing case law doctrine is now mandated by legislation.[68]

RULE 23(b). TYPES OF CLASS ACTIONS

CORE CONCEPT

Before a class action will be certified, all the requirements of case law, jurisdiction, and Rule 23(a) must be satisfied. In addition, a class will not be certified unless it also fits within one of the types of classes described in Rule 23(b).[69] Unlike the requirement that all elements of Rule 23(a) be satisfied, however, Rule 23(b) is satisfied if only one of the kinds of classes described is present.

NOTE: Although a class may be certified if it fits within only one of the Rule 23(b) categories, there are sometimes advantages to fitting within more than one of the categories. This analysis is discussed more fully immediately below and under Rule 23(c).

APPLICATIONS

Risk of Incompatible Duties for Class Opponent

A class will be certified if the opposing party will otherwise be at risk of being subjected to incompatible duties.[70] Rule 23(b)(1)(A) was invoked when the class opponent was sued by employees who, in the absence of a class action, might have obtained employment benefits for themselves that were inconsistent with the employer's obligations to other employees.[71]

Risk of Practical Impairment of Non–Parties' Interests

Rule 23(b)(1)(B) permits certification of a class if piecemeal litigation involving individual class members may as a practical matter produce injustice for class members who are not parties to

67. *See, e.g., Wade v. Danek Medical, Inc.,* 182 F.3d 281, 286–87 (4th Cir.1999) (under principles of *Erie,* state law controls; in instant case, Virginia does not provide for equitable tolling).

68. 28 U.S.C.A. § 1332(d)(11)(D).

69. *See, e.g., Parke v. First Reliance Standard Life Insurance Co.,* 368 F.3d 999, 1004 (8th Cir.2004) (advocate of class must satisfy all four requirements of Rule 23(a) plus one requirement of Rule 23(b)).

70. *Cf., Weinman v. Fidelity Capital Appreciation Fund,* 354 F.3d 1246, 1263–64 (10th Cir.2004) ("A widely recognized limitation on (b)(1)(A) certification requires that there be 'more than the mere possibility that inconsistent judgments and resolution of identical questions of law would result if numerous actions are conducted instead of one class action;' " mere fact that class opponent might win some individual cases and lose others does not meet requirements of Rule 23(b)(1)(A)).

71. *Mungin v. Florida East Coast Railway Co.,* 318 F.Supp. 720 (M.D.Fla.1970), *affirmed,* 441 F.2d 728 (5th Cir.1971). *See also Zinser v. Accufix Research Institute, Inc.,* 253 F.3d 1180 (9th Cir.2001), *opinion amended and superseded on denial of reh'g,* 273 F.3d 1266 (9th Cir.2001) (where possible relief is a fund, which would be created by defendant, to pay for future medical monitoring of plaintiffs, relief sought is primarily monetary damages–not relief that imposes inconsistent obligations on defendant–and therefore case is not suitable for certification under Rule 23(b)(1)(A)).

the individual litigation.[72] One of the most common applications of Rule 23(b)(1)(B) occurs when numerous claimants may seek relief from a limited fund and, in the absence of class certification, individual lawsuits might deplete the fund before all worthy claimants had a chance to obtain some share of the fund.[73] However, to obtain certification under Rule 23(b)(1)(B) in such circumstances, it is settled that the "limited" fund must be "limited by more than the agreement of the parties."[74]

"Incompatible Duties" Contrasted with "Risk of Practical Impairment"

Rule 23(b)(1)(A), establishing the "incompatible duties" standard, has the primary purpose of protecting the opponent of the class from the possibility of inconsistent obligations. In a situation where Rule 23(b)(1)(A) is suitable, there is less concern about the potential class members, because even if no class is certified individual members of the class can still bring their claims individually without loss to themselves. In a Rule 23(b)(1)(B) situation involving potential "practical impairment," however, failure to certify a class creates the probability that individual members will not be able to share recovery in limited resources in a proportional manner, fair to all.

Classes Seeking Final Equitable Relief

Rule 23(b)(2) permits certification of class actions where the primary relief sought is equitable in nature.[75] There are two elements to satisfy before a class may be certified under Rule 23(b)(2): the class must share a general claim against the non-class

---

72. *See, e.g., Weinman v. Fidelity Capital Appreciation Fund,* 354 F.3d 1246, 1264 (10th Cir.2004) (Rule 23(b)(1)(B) is satisfied when resolution of first individual case could be dispositive of factual and legal issues that would resolve subsequent individual cases before those litigants had a chance to pursue their claims); *McDonnell Douglas Corp. v. United States District Court for the Central District of California,* 523 F.2d 1083 (9th Cir.1975). *Flanagan v. McDonnell Douglas Corp.,* 425 U.S. 911, 96 S.Ct. 1506, 47 L.Ed.2d 761 (1976)(class certification appropriate to ensure "equitable distribution of the refund program"). *But cf., Tilley v. TJX Companies, Inc.,* 345 F.3d 34, 42 (1st Cir.2003) (certification under Rule 23(b)(1)(B) "cannot rest solely on an anticipated stare decisis effect").

73. *See, e.g., Trautz v. Weisman,* 846 F.Supp. 1160 (S.D.N.Y.1994) (classic Rule 23(b)(1)(B) case occurs when multiple claims of individuals exceed value of limited fund, and early individual suits would exhaust fund before later-filing claimants can share).

74. *Ortiz v. Fibreboard Corp.,* 527 U.S. 815, 119 S.Ct. 2295, 144 L.Ed.2d 715 (1999)

(error for district court to treat fund as limited only because parties agreed to limit claims to specified amount; before certifying class under Rule 23(b)(1)(B) district court should have examined grand total of funds actually available in event of success by plaintiffs; additionally, Supreme Court refuses to decide "whether Rule 23(b)(1)(B) may ever be used to aggregate individual tort claims"). *See also In re Simon II Litigation,* 407 F.3d 125, 138 (2d Cir.2005) (inability of class plaintiffs to identify upper limit or insufficiency of fund means plaintiffs cannot meet Rule 23(b)(1)(B) requirement that individual plaintiffs would be prejudiced by separate lawsuits); *Zinser v. Accufix Research Institute, Inc.,* 253 F.3d 1180 (9th Cir.2001), *opinion amended and superseded on denial of reh'g,* 273 F.3d 1266 (9th Cir.2001) (for certification under Rule 23(b)(1)(B) plaintiffs must prove that fund is actually limited to amount less than that for which defendant might be liable).

75. *But see Thorn v. Jefferson–Pilot Life Insurance Co.,* 445 F.3d 311, 331 (4th Cir. 2006) (Rule 23(b)(2) applies only to case involving primarily injunctive or declarato-

party;[76] and the class must seek either final injunctive or declaratory relief.   Race and gender discrimination class actions, seeking an alteration in the future behavior of the opponent of the class, are typical of the class actions certified under Rule 23(b)(2).[77]

Obtaining Damages in "Equity" Class Actions Classes

Certification of a class under Rule 23(b)(2) requires that the relief sought in the case is primarily declaratory or injunctive in nature.   However, there is no prohibition on adding pleas for damages in a (b)(2) class.   Thus it is not necessarily disabling to a Rule 23(b)(2) certification if the suit, in addition to seeking final equitable relief, also seeks damages.[78]   The key to obtaining certification under Rule 23(b)(2) is the court's determination of the relative importance of the equitable relief to the damages sought.[79]   This distinction is explained in greater detail immediately below.

NOTE: If damages are more important in the case than equitable remedies, it is likely that the suit will be certified under some

ry relief, not all forms of equitable relief; "if the Rule's drafters had intended the Rule to extend to all forms of equitable relief, the text of the Rule would say so"); *In re All-state Insurance Co.,* 400 F.3d 505 (7th Cir. 2005) (refusing certification under Rule 23(b)(2) notwithstanding that relief sought is exclusively injunctive or declaratory; noting that if certification is appropriate, Rule 23(b)(3) is preferred when individual hearings for class members may be necessary to determine causation and liability).

76. *Cf., e.g., Heffner v. Blue Cross & Blue Shield of Alabama, Inc.,* 443 F.3d 1330, 1344 (11th Cir.2006) (where each plaintiff must demonstrate individual reliance on representations in documents that are central to case, commonality that is necessary for classwide equitable relief under Rule 23(b)(2) is lacking).

77. *See, e.g., Comer v. Cisneros,* 37 F.3d 775, 796 (2d Cir.1994)("[p]attern of racial discrimination cases for injunctions against state or local officials are the 'paradigm' of [Rule 23(b)(2)] cases." [sic]). *Cf., Washington v. CSC Credit Services, Inc.,* 199 F.3d 263, 267 (5th Cir.2000) (if underlying law does not permit injunctive relief, class cannot be certified under Rule 23(b)(2)).

78. *See, e.g., Robinson v. Metro–North Commuter Railroad Co.,* 267 F.3d 147, 164 (2d Cir.2001) (rejecting "incidental damages" approach; adopting an "ad hoc" approach based on facts of particular cases, with view to determining whether value of potential injunctive or declaratory relief is predominant; such determination requires deciding whether reasonable plaintiffs, in absence of any monetary relief, would still bring suit to obtain equitable relief; and equitable relief would be necessary and appropriate if plaintiff prevailed on merits); *Kanter v. Warner–Lambert Co.,* 265 F.3d 853, 860 (9th Cir.2001) ("In Rule 23(b)(2) cases, monetary damages requests are generally allowable only if they are merely incidental to the litigation."); *James v. City of Dallas, Texas,* 254 F.3d 551 (5th Cir.2001) (class certification under Rule 23(b)(2) means "[p]laintiffs must demonstrate that their class action suit seeks predominantly injunctive relief rather than monetary damages"); *Probe v. State Teachers' Retirement System,* 780 F.2d 776, 780 (9th Cir.1986) (class certified under Rule 23(b)(2) may also seek "incidental" money damages). *See also Cooper v. Southern Co.,* 390 F.3d 695, 720 (11th Cir.2004) ("Back pay is considered equitable relief and can therefore be awarded in a case certified under Rule 23(b)(2)."). *But see, Ticor Title Insurance Co. v. Brown,* 511 U.S. 117, 119, 114 S.Ct. 1359, 1361, 128 L.Ed.2d 33 (1994) (per curiam) (suggesting in dicta the "substantial possibility" that classes seeking money damages can only be certified under Rule 23(b)(3)).

79. *See, e.g., Jefferson v. Ingersoll International, Inc.,* 195 F.3d 894, 896 (7th Cir. 1999) (use of Rule 23(b)(2) in cases involving damages is permissible only where predominant relief is an injunction or declaration, and damages are incidental to such equitable relief; incidental damages arise from wrong to class as a whole, not from circumstances that require fact finding on individual class members' cases); *Boughton v. Cotter Corp.,* 65 F.3d 823, 827 (10th

provision other than Rule 23(b)(2) or not certified at all.[80]   Alternatively, if a class is certified based on the predominance of common legal or factual questions under Rule 23(b)(3), substantial difficulties could follow.   Rule 23(b)(3) class representatives may be burdened with substantial expenses in notifying other class members of the litigation.[81]   Thus in seeking damages in a Rule 23(b)(2) class, the benefits of obtaining damages should be weighed against the possibility that the case might be certified under Rule 23(b)(3).   If notification expenses in a particular case are likely to be substantial, it might be prudent to consider whether the class should seek damages at all.[82]   Notification duties for a Rule 23(b)(3) class are discussed in Rule 23(c)(2), below.   For other notification obligations the court may impose, see Rule 23(d)(2) and (e).

Rule 23(b)(2) and Jury Trials

The Seventh Amendment to the United States Constitution normally provides a right to trial by jury in federal district courts in civil litigation where money damages are sought.[83] At the same time, in class actions certified under Rule 23(b)(2), the case must be based primarily on equitable claims, which do not normally qualify to be heard by a jury. When the Rule 23(b)(2) class action also contains a

Cir.1995)(where relief sought is primarily money, Rule 23(b)(2) class is inappropriate). *See also Lemon v. International Union of Operating Engineers, Local No. 139, AFL–CIO,* 216 F.3d 577 (7th Cir.2000) (where compensatory damages would require examination of each individual's magnitude of injury, and punitive damages would require finding that defendant was recklessly indifferent to each plaintiff's federal rights, damages are not "incidental" within meaning of Rule 23(b)(2)).

80. *See, e.g., Jefferson v. Ingersoll International, Inc.,* 195 F.3d 894, 898–99 (7th Cir.1999) (three options for cases involving damages that are not certifiable under Rule 23(b)(2):   (1) certification under Rule 23(b)(3);   (2) "divided certification," meaning a Rule 23(b)(2) class for portion of case requiring equitable relief and a Rule 23(b)(3) class for portion requiring damages;   or (3) certification of entire action under Rule 23(b)(2), but with provision, pursuant to Rule 23(d)(2) and (5), that individual class members will receive personal notice and opportunity to opt out); *Allison v. Citgo Petroleum Corp.,* 151 F.3d 402 (5th Cir.1998) (denying Rule 23(b)(2) because equitable remedies do not outweigh importance of money damages; holding that key to determination of "predomination" issue is whether request for monetary relief makes class so disparate in makeup that notice and opt-out provisions are necessary). *But see Berger v. Xerox Corp. Retire-*

ment Income Guarantee Plan, 338 F.3d 755 (7th Cir.2003) (declaratory judgment actions are usually preludes to requests for other relief (injunctive or monetary); likelihood that successful litigants may subsequently seek damages is not, of itself, fatal to effort to obtain certification under Rule 23(b)(2)).

81. *See also Bratcher v. National Standard Life Insurance Co.,* 365 F.3d 408, 417 (5th Cir.2004) ("[D]ue process requires the provision of notice where a rule 23(b)(2) class seeks monetary damages."); *Jefferson v. Ingersoll International, Inc.,* 195 F.3d 894, 896–97 (7th Cir.1999) (judgments and settlements in cases certified under rule 23(b)(2) are more susceptible to collateral attack by class members than cases controlled by rule 23(b)(3); defendants who need finality prefer Rule 23(b)(3), whose provisions for notice and opt out make judgments and settlements less vulnerable to collateral attacks).

82. *Cf., Allen v. International Truck & Engine Corp.,* 358 F.3d 469, 470 (7th Cir. 2004) (suggesting that when case involving both equitable relief and money damages is certified under Rule 23(b)(2), notice and right to opt out may still be required for damages issues).

83. *Beacon Theatres, Inc. v. Westover,* 359 U.S. 500, 510, 79 S.Ct. 948, 956, 3 L.Ed.2d 988 (1959).

plea for money damages, the combination of circumstances might seem to create a problem. However, the solution appears to be readily available. In such cases, issues relating to damages alone or to both damages and equitable relief may require trial by jury, but issues going to the equitable claims alone should be heard by the judge.[84]

Predominance of Common Legal or Factual Questions

The final possibility for certifying a class action is a determination that the questions of law or fact common to the members of the class predominate over other questions. Rule 23(b)(3) certification is often a last resort for litigants who cannot be certified under any other portion of Rule 23(b).[85] Two special requirements exist for Rule 23(b)(3) classes. Both must be satisfied to achieve certification under Rule 23(b)(3). First among these is the requirement that common questions *predominate* over individual interests.[86] As can be seen from cites contained in the immediately preceding footnote, resolution of the "predominance" analysis rests heavily on the facts

---

84. *Allen v. International Truck & Engine Corp.,* 358 F.3d 469, 471 (7th Cir. 2004).

85. *See, e.g., DeBoer v. Mellon Mortgage Co.,* 64 F.3d 1171, 1175 (8th Cir.1995) (where certification is appropriate under either Rule 23(b)(1) or (2), certification under Rule 23(b)(3) is inappropriate). *See also Murray v. GMAC Mortgage Corp.,* 434 F.3d 948, 953 (7th Cir.2006) ("Rule 23(b)(3) was designed for situations ... in which the potential recovery is too slight to support individual suits, but injury is substantial in the aggregate.").

86. *Amchem Products, Inc. v. Windsor,* 521 U.S. 591, 623, 117 S.Ct. 2231, 2250, 138 L.Ed.2d 689 (1997) (predominance issues require a "close look" at, among other factors, "difficulties likely to be encountered in the management of a class action;" predominance not satisfied if there are a number of significant questions peculiar to different categories within class or to individuals within class; exposure to different asbestos products, at different times, in different ways, for different periods of time, with differing results ranging from no injury through only symptoms of injury to grave illnesses of several different kinds, all complicated by differences in cigarette use among class members where use of cigarettes complicates injury, defeats allegation of predominance). *See, e.g., Stuebler v. Xcelera.com,* 430 F.3d 503, 507–08 (1st Cir. 2005) (in securities fraud cases brought under federal law, fraud-on-the-market theory "eliminates the need to prove individualized reliance by allowing a rebuttable pre-sumption that the plaintiff relied on the 'integrity of the market price' which reflected the misrepresentation;" however, fraud-on-the-market theory is applicable only in efficient markets; if market is inefficient, theory cannot be used); *Tardiff v. Knox County,* 365 F.3d 1, 5 (1st Cir.2004) (county policy of strip searching most or all categories of persons arrested satisfies "predominance," notwithstanding differences between cases of individual persons within those categories); *Stirman v. Exxon Corp.,* 280 F.3d 554, 564 (5th Cir.2002) ("[S]ignificant variations in state law ... defeat predominance."); *Johnston v. HBO Film Management, Inc.,* 265 F.3d 178, 190 (3d Cir.2001) ("[I]t has become well-settled that, as a general rule, an action based substantially on oral rather than written communications is inappropriate for treatment as a class action."); *Szabo v. Bridgeport Machines, Inc.,* 249 F.3d 672, 674 (7th Cir.2001) ("A nationwide class in what is fundamentally a breach of warranty action, coupled with a claim of fraud, poses serious problems about choice of law, the manageability of the suit, and thus the propriety of class certification;" noting differences in substantive laws of states, plus issues of who made fraudulent statements, where they were made, and on whose behalf); *Bolin v. Sears, Roebuck & Co.,* 231 F.3d 970, 978–79 (5th Cir.2000) (civil RICO claim cannot be certified as class action where individual reliance is an issue); *Nagel v. ADM Investor Services, Inc.,* 217 F.3d 436 (7th Cir.2000) (allegations of fraud tend to be "plaintiff-specific," and therefore issues

of particular cases.[87] There is also an important unresolved question as to whose version of the "facts"—plaintiff's or defendant's—courts should use when addressing the predominance problem. On this particular point the cases are significantly divided, and attorneys are compelled to consult the local precedent.[88]

In other Rule 23(b) classes, by contrast, there is only the requirement, stated in Rule 23(a)(2), that common questions of law or fact exist among the class members, with no requirement that the common questions predominate.[89]

Certification Requirements for Classes Where Common Questions Predominate: Superiority

The second requirement for certification under Rule 23(b)(3) is a finding that a class action is the superior means of adjudicating

common to class tend not to predominate over issues of interest to individuals); *Rutstein v. Avis Rent–A–Car Systems, Inc.,* 211 F.3d 1228 (11th Cir.2000) (in non-employment discrimination case, each plaintiff must establish: (1) membership in racial minority; (2) intent to discriminate on basis of race; and (3) discrimination that fell within scope of activity prohibited by relevant statute; held, determination of intent to discriminate on basis of race is highly fact specific, including not only defendant's general policy, but also whether individual plaintiffs were denied benefits, whether independent legitimate reasons (such as age or financial status of individual plaintiffs) for defendant's behavior existed; held, where liability rests upon individualized determinations, common questions do not predominate as required by Rule 23(b)(3)); *Castano v. American Tobacco Co.,* 84 F.3d 734, 745 (5th Cir.1996)("[A] fraud class action cannot be certified when individual reliance will be an issue;" moreover, where laws of different states will apply to different class members, "variations in state law may swamp any common issues and defeat predominance"). *Compare, e.g., Waste Management Holdings, Inc. v. Mowbray,* 208 F.3d 288, 295–96 (1st Cir.2000) (on the one hand, in a securities context, fraud on the market "may be particularly well-suited for class treatment"; additionally individualized effects of statutes of limitations should be considered in Rule 23(b)(3) evaluations, but variations in such statutes need not be a per se disqualifier of class certification), *with Broussard v. Meineke Discount Muffler Shops, Inc.,* 155 F.3d 331, 340–43 (4th Cir. 1998) (non-uniform oral representations to class members, differences in equitable tolling of statute of limitations for different class members, and differences in calcula-

tion of lost profits, all demonstrate that even the minimal requirement of commonality under rule 23(a)(2) is not satisfied). *See also, Mullen v. Treasure Chest Casino, LLC,* 186 F.3d 620, 626–27 (5th Cir.1999) (common issues of negligence and seaworthiness of vessel are "pivotal"; case invokes only federal law, so no choice of law issues; non-common issue of causation of illness will be left to second phase of litigation involving individual trials; held, requirement of predominance is satisfied).

87. *See also Tardiff v. Knox County,* 365 F.3d 1, 4 (1st Cir.2004) (noting that in the context of class actions relating to strip searches of arrested persons, lower courts have reached opposite conclusions on questions of predominance).

88. *Id.* ("It is sometimes taken for granted that the complaint's allegations are necessarily controlling; but class action machinery is expensive and in our view a court has the power to test disputed premises early on if and when the class action would be proper on one premise but not another;" collecting various appellate decisions on point).

89. *Amchem Products, Inc. v. Windsor,* 521 U.S. 591, 623, 117 S.Ct. 2231, 2250, 138 L.Ed.2d 689 (1997) (for purposes of Rule 23(b)(3), predominance requirement is "far more demanding" than commonality requirement of Rule 23(a)). *See, e.g., Hanlon v. Chrysler Corp.,* 150 F.3d 1011 (9th Cir. 1998) ("The commonality preconditions of Rule 23(a)(2) are less rigorous than the companion requirements of Rule 23(b)(3)."). *See also, Walters v. Reno,* 145 F.3d 1032 (9th Cir.1998) (no requirement under Rule 23(b)(2) that common issues predominate).

the controversy.[90]   In reaching that determination, a court is required to make four findings described in Rule 23(b)(3). The court may also address other issues that, in particular cases, are relevant to determining whether certification of a class action is the best way to process a case.[91]   The court's determination of those points will ordinarily be dispositive of a Rule 23(b)(3) class certification.   It should be noted that while the court is required to make findings on the four points listed, there is no requirement that before a class is certified, all four findings must be resolved in favor of certification. Instead, the court has discretion to weigh its findings in determining whether class certification is the superior method of litigating the controversy.

(1) *Rule 23(b)(3)(A)—Individual Interests in Separate Actions:* The court will evaluate the desire, if any, of individual litigants to pursue their own separate actions, and the net balance of interests between such individuals and the class as a whole.[92]   Because individual litigants who feel the need to control their own cases may exercise their right under Rule 23(c) to "opt out" of a Rule 23(b)(3) class, it is usually possible to certify the class and still accommodate most of the needs of such individuals.   Harmonizing individual interests with class certification would be more difficult if it was likely that so many individuals would opt out that the "class" no longer represented the bulk of its potential members.   In that circumstance, the evidence of such strong interest in individual litigation would argue strongly against certifying a Rule 23(b)(3) class.

(2) *Rule 23(b)(3)(B)—Pending Litigation:* The court will also consider the effects of any other pending litigation on the proposed class action.   If individual class members have already begun to pursue their own cases, it may be difficult to justify certification of a

---

90. *See, e.g., Gregory v. Finova Capital Corp.,* 442 F.3d 188, 191 n.3 (4th Cir.2006) ("A necessary condition to certification under Rule 23(b)(3) is the class action's superiority to all other methods for the fair and efficient adjudication of the controversy. Thus, a class cannot be certified under Rule 23(b)(3) if there is a method to which the class action is not superior.").

91. *See, e.g., Castano v. American Tobacco Co.,* 84 F.3d 734 (5th Cir.1996)(court may consider whether class action will preserve judicial resources). *See also, Hanlon v. Chrysler Corp.,* 150 F.3d 1011, 1022–23 (9th Cir.1998) (individual suits would be ineffective for members of potential class).

92. *See, e.g., Zinser v. Accufix Research Institute, Inc.,* 253 F.3d 1180 (9th Cir.2001), *opinion amended and superseded on denial of reh'g,* 273 F.3d 1266 (9th Cir.2001) ("Where damages suffered by each putative

class member are not large, this factor weighs in favor of certifying a class action;" holding claims in excess of $50,000 each— the jurisdictional amount then in effect for diversity cases—tends to undermine somewhat an allegation that the claims are small); *In re Northern District of California Dalkon Shield IUD Products Liability Litigation,* 693 F.2d 847, 856 (9th Cir.1982), *cert. denied,* 459 U.S. 1171, 103 S.Ct. 817, 74 L.Ed.2d 1015 (1983)(where class members have a strong interest in individual suits, court should incline toward refusal to certify). *See also, Heaven v. Trust Company Bank,* 118 F.3d 735, 738 (11th Cir.1997) (counterclaims against individual class members is a factor to consider in evaluating whether, under Rule 23(b)(3)(A), individual members might have interest in controlling their own cases).

Rule 23(b)(3) class on grounds of judicial economy.[93] Indeed, it is possible that such pending litigation will reach judgment before the class action, and many of the contested issues in the class action might then be resolved through application of principles of stare decisis or collateral estoppel.

(3) *Rule 23(b)(3)(C)—Progress in Class Litigation:* If the court hearing the class action has already invested enough resources in the case so that dismissal or refusal to certify the action would be inefficient, a strong argument exists in favor of certifying the class so that the action can be concentrated in the chosen forum.[94]

(4) *Rule 23(b)(3)(C)—Geography:* Another consideration that may bear on the wisdom of proceeding with the class action in the chosen forum is geography. If the case is being heard in an area of the country where the class or the evidence is concentrated, this may be an argument for continuing in the chosen forum.[95]

(5) *Rule 23(b)(3)(D)—Difficulties in Managing a Class Action:* Courts can refuse to certify if too many administrative difficulties exist in class actions. In exercising this discretion, courts consider a wide variety of factors affecting ease of administration of a case. Examples of problems in managing a class include internal disputes within a class and problems of notification of class members[96], as well as the impact that state law variations can have on management in a multi-state case.[97]

---

93. *See, e.g., City of Inglewood v. City of Los Angeles,* 451 F.2d 948, 952 n. 4 (9th Cir.1971)(directing that if party seeks a Rule 23(b)(3) class, "the court should note the fact that some 2,350 members of the class are already involved in suits against the same defendant"). *But cf., Hanlon v. Chrysler Corp.,* 150 F.3d 1011 (9th Cir. 1998) (no bar to class certification where only a few pending lawsuits may be difficult to merge into class action).

94. *Cf., e.g., In re Mid-Atlantic Toyota Antitrust Litigation,* 564 F.Supp. 1379, 1391 (D.Md.1983)("The fact that the panel on multi-district litigation has transferred all actions [to the court] indicates the desirability [of the forum].")

95. *See, e.g., Zinser v. Accufix Research Institute, Inc.,* 253 F.3d 1180 (9th Cir.2001), *opinion amended and superseded on denial of reh'g,* 273 F.3d 1266 (9th Cir.2001) (where potential plaintiffs, witnesses and evidence are spread across country, it is undesirable to concentrate litigation in instant forum unless plaintiff can demonstrate adequate justification); *Langley v. Coughlin,* 715 F.Supp. 522, 561 (S.D.N.Y. 1989) (location of "most relevant evidence" in forum is factor favoring certification under Rule 23(b)(3)(C)).

96. *See, e.g., Zinser v. Accufix Research Institute, Inc.,* 253 F.3d 1180 (9th Cir.2001), *opinion amended and superseded on denial of reh'g,* 273 F.3d 1266 (9th Cir.2001) (where pacemaker leads were implanted in different patients by different doctors in different states, producing different injuries at different times, there are too many individual issues and case management would be too difficult, notwithstanding common nucleus of facts about defendant's conduct); *Simer v. Rios,* 661 F.2d 655, 678 (7th Cir. 1981), *Simer v. United States,* 456 U.S. 917, 102 S.Ct. 1773, 72 L.Ed.2d 177 (1982)(proper to consider problems of notifying class members in deciding whether to certify class). *But cf., Williams v. Chartwell Financial Services, Ltd.,* 204 F.3d 748, 760 (7th Cir.2000) (possible need for subclasses, by itself, is insufficient ground for denying certification because a class action would be unmanageable).

97. *See, e.g., Castano v. American Tobacco Co.,* 84 F.3d 734 (5th Cir.1996)(so holding). *See also, Heaven v. Trust Company Bank,* 118 F.3d 735, 738 (11th Cir.1997) (counterclaims against individual members of class with potential liability greater than original claims might create case management problems under Rule 23(b)(3)(D)). *But*

Affirmative Defenses

The "predominance" requirement is obviously a substantial obstacle to class certification under Rule 23(b)(3). However, it appears settled that a defendant's possible affirmative defenses against claims by individual class members will not, of themselves, prevent the parties seeking class certification from meeting the requirement.[98]

RULE 23(c).   CERTIFICATION ORDER; NOTICE TO CLASS MEMBERS; JUDGMENT; ISSUES CLASSES; SUBCLASSES

CORE CONCEPT

Rules 23(a) and (b) contain most of the requirements that must be satisfied before a class may be certified. Rule 23(c), by contrast, concentrates on the procedure and timing of motions to certify and the process to be followed once a decision to certify has been made.

APPLICATIONS

Motion or Court Initiative

A party may seek certification by motion, or the court may on its own initiative make the certification decision. It should be noted that the lack of a motion to certify does not relieve the district court of its duty to make this determination, and the lack of such a motion cannot be the basis for denial of class certification.[99]

"Implied" Classes

Rule 23(c)(1), by its express terms, appears to require that the district court "must" determine whether a class should be certified. However, there is authority that a court's failure to make a formal certification ruling does not mean the case at bar cannot be a class action. If the elements required for class certification are satisfied, an "implied" class may exist notwithstanding a lack of formal certification by the district court.[100]

---

cf., *Mullen v. Treasure Chest Casino, LLC,* 186 F.3d 620, 627 (5th Cir.1999) (superiority requirement satisfied by: lack of complex choice-of-law or *Erie* problems; modest number of class members ("hundreds instead of millions"); bifurcated-trial plan; and likelihood that trial would focus on second-hand smoke as both result of poor ventilation and cause of illnesses).

98. *See, e.g., Smilow v. Southwestern Bell Mobile Systems, Inc.,* 323 F.3d 32, 39–40 (1st Cir.2003).

99. *See, e.g., Trevizo v. Adams,* 455 F.3d 1155 (10th Cir.2006) ("Rule 23(c)(1) places the onus on the court to make a determination irrespective of whether the parties have requested class action status.");

McGowan v. Faulkner Concrete Pipe Co., 659 F.2d 554, 559 (5th Cir.1981) (trial court has duty to decide suitability of class action, even if no party makes a motion).

100. *See, e.g., Doe v. Bush,* 261 F.3d 1037, 1048–49 (11th Cir.2001) ("[T]he fact that the district court failed to properly certify a class does not necessarily establish that no class exists, or that the defendants cannot be held in contempt for failing to provide class-wide relief." Plaintiffs filed certification motion in timely manner, but district court did not act; however, district court referred to plaintiffs as class and defendants behaved as opponents of class); *Navarro-Ayala v. Hernandez–Colon,* 951 F.2d 1325, 1333 (1st Cir.1991) (no notice

Timing

Rule 23(c) provides no rigid timetable for resolving the certification issue, but courts are directed to make the decision "at an early practicable time."[101]

Conditional Certification

In the past Rule 23(c)(1) permitted the court to make certification conditional upon later developments in the case. Even if the court had not expressly reserved the power, it retained authority to amend its order as events require.[102] However, Rule 23(c)(1) was

ever provided to class members, but "because this case was instituted by a complaint seeking class relief, implicitly granted class relief, and was conducted for years as a de facto class, it should and may be recognized as such"). *But see Brown v. Philadelphia Housing Authority,* 350 F.3d 338, 344 (3d Cir.2003) (rejecting doctrine of implied class certification; *Martinez–Mendoza v. Champion International Corp.,* 340 F.3d 1200 n. 37 (11th Cir.2003) (Rule 23(c)(1) requires courts to determine independently whether case should be class action, even where no party seeks a ruling on class certification); *Davis v. Hutchins,* 321 F.3d 641, 648 (7th Cir.2003) ("Class damages cannot be awarded if no class is certified.").

101. *See, e.g., Kerkhof v. MCI Worldcom, Inc.,* 282 F.3d 44, 55 (1st Cir.2002) (post-judgment certification should usually be discouraged because it "would frustrate the opt-out mechanisms for Rule 23(b)(3) classes provided in Rules 23(c)(2) and (c)(3), which were intended to avoid situations in which class members could choose to join only when judgment favored the class"; also, "a delay in adding class allegations deprives a defendant of fair warning as to the true stakes and, by eliminating mutuality, leaves the defendant liable on class claims (if he loses the summary judgment motion) without protecting him (if he wins)"); *Grandson v. University of Minnesota,* 272 F.3d 568, 574 (8th Cir.2001) (failure to seek class certification before expiration of deadline for such motions (in this case, fifteen months after complaint was filed) and failure to seek extension of time constitute grounds for striking class allegations); *Prado-Steiman v. Bush,* 221 F.3d 1266, 1273 (11th Cir.2000) ("Rule 23 contemplates that the class certification decision will be made prior to the close of discovery."); *In re Philip Morris, Inc.,* 214 F.3d 132 (2d Cir.2000) (per curiam) (district court does not have "unfettered discretion" to delay decision on class certification; usu-

ally decision will be made somewhere between end of pleadings and end of discovery (depending on facts of individual cases), but only rarely should decision be delayed until after hearing on merits); *Navarro–Ayala v. Hernandez–Colon,* 951 F.2d 1325, 1334 (1st Cir.1991)("egregious omission" for court not to move quickly on issue of class certification); *Peritz v. Liberty Loan Corp.,* 523 F.2d 349, 353 (7th Cir.1975) ("[A]mended Rule 23 requires class certification prior to a determination on the merits."). *But cf., Miami University Wrestling Club v. Miami University,* 302 F.3d 608, 616 (6th Cir.2002) ("We have consistently held that a district court is not required to rule on a motion for class certification before ruling on the merits of the case."); *Postow v. OBA Federal Savings & Loan Association,* 627 F.2d 1370, 1383–84 (D.C. Cir.1980) ("[T]he present state of the law does not necessarily preclude class certification after a judgment on the merits in Rule 23(b)(3) class actions; it suggests there may be equitable reasons for allowing post-judgment certification in some cases." Citing some other authority; holding that in instant case equitable considerations justified post-judgment decision on certification); *Cowen v. Bank United of Texas, F.S.B.,* 70 F.3d 937, 941 (7th Cir. 1995)(usually certification will be addressed before summary judgment, but facts of particular case may justify different sequence of events).

102. *See, e.g., Lyons v. Georgia-Pacific Corp. Salaried Employees Retirement Plan,* 221 F.3d 1235, 1253 n. 32 (11th Cir.2000) ("Rule 23(a) is not immutable;" court retains power under Rule 23(c) and (d) to change prior order if subsequent events make that step appropriate); *Forehand v. Florida State Hospital,* 89 F.3d 1562, 1566 (11th Cir.1996) (court may decertify class previously certified even when case was filed ten years earlier and had proceeded through trial).

amended in 2003 to remove the language authorizing conditional certification. Instead, courts are encouraged to withhold certification until the requirements of Rule 23 are met. At the same time, courts are given latitude to make a decision on certification at all times up to the time of final judgment.[103]

Defining Claims, Issues or Defenses

If a class is certified, Rule 23(c)(1)(B) directs the district court to include in the certification order a clear and complete summary of the claims, issues, and defenses subject to class treatment. However, there is some reason to believe that district courts do not always fulfill this requirement completely.[104]

Amending a Certification Order

Rule 23(c)(1)(C) authorizes a district court to alter or amend its original certification order at any time prior to final judgment on the merits.[105]

Notice

As amended in 2003, Rule 23(c)(2) establishes various notice options and/or requirements for cases certified under Rule 23. For classes certified pursuant to Rule 23(b)(1) or (2), Rule 23(c)(2)(A) authorizes – but does not require – the district court to order notice to such classes. This authority is intended to supplement the court's already existing power under Rule 23(d)(2) to issue notice in some circumstances to class members.[106] This change in Rule 23(c)(2) leaves unaltered the assumption that courts will be cautious in their use of notice to Rule 23(b)(1) and (2) classes so as, *inter alia,* not to burden the class representatives with unnecessary costs of notice.[107]

Rule 23(c)(2) also establishes special requirements for notifying class members of pending Rule 23(b)(3) actions. The reason for this provision arises from the special nature of Rule 23(b)(3) suits, in which common questions must predominate and the class suit must be superior to alternative methods of adjudication. Such suits tend to involve the least homogeneous classes. Lack of homogeneity increases the risk that informal notice of the class action may not

---

103. *See* Rule 23(c)(1) advisory committee notes to 2003 amendments.

104. *See, e.g., Wachtel v. Guardian Life Insurance Co. of America,* 453 F.3d 179, 184 (3d Cir.2006) (observing that district courts often do not fulfill this requirement adequately).

105. *See, e.g., Culpepper v. Irwin Mortgage Corp.,* 491 F.3d 1260 (11th Cir. 2007) (district court thereby retains flexibility "in light of subsequent developments in the case").

106. *See* Rule 23(c)(2) advisory committee notes to 2003 amendments. *See also Eubanks v. Billington,* 110 F.3d 87, 96 (D.C. Cir.1997) (Rule 23(d) authorizes court to permit party to opt out of class certified

under Rule 23(b)(1) or (2) "on a selective basis").

107. *See* Rule 23(c)(2) advisory committee notes to 2003 amendments (noting that classes certified under Rule 23(b)(1) or (2) have no right to opt out, reducing need for notice on that point). *See also* 15 U.S.C.A. § 78u–4 (in litigation within scope of Private Securities Litigation Reform Act of 1995, lead plaintiff must, within twenty days of filing complaint, provide publication notice in "widely circulated national business-oriented publication or wire service" of pending action and potential opportunity to serve as lead plaintiff).

flow freely within the class. To correct this problem, Rule 23(c)(2) provides that individual members must receive the "best notice practicable," which will often be mail service on all class members whose identities and addresses are known.[108]

Finally, amended Rule 23(c)(2) also requires that if a class action requires certification under both Rule 23(b)(2) and (b)(3), the usually more burdensome notice requirements required for a (b)(3) class must be satisfied for the (b)(3) class.[109]

Elements of Notice to Rule 23(b)(3) Classes

Rule 23(c)(2) specifies that notification will include the following pieces of advice: (1) "the nature of the action, (2) the definition of the class certified, (3) the class claims, issues, or defenses," (4) the right of individual members of the class to appear through counsel if they choose, (5) the right to opt out of the class and not be bound by any judgment,[110] and (6) the binding effect of a class judgment on members of the class who do not opt out.[111]

Expense of Notice

The financial burden of notification in Rule 23(b)(3) cases is generally borne by the class representatives.[112] Thus, in some cases class representatives should be selected with an eye to their financial resources as well as their dedication to the litigation. When the burden of Rule 23(b)(3) notification is onerous, the possibility of certification under another portion of Rule 23(b) should be explored.

No Requirement to "Opt In"

There is no provision in Rule 23(c) requiring class members to "opt in" or be excluded from a class.[113] Rule 23(c) contains only an "opt out" provision.

---

108. *See generally Schwarzschild v. Tse,* 69 F.3d 293, 295 (9th Cir.1995) (in general, Rule 23(c)(2) requires notice to class members before merits are adjudicated; in unusual case where summary judgment is granted prior to certification, plaintiff no longer has duty of notification). *Cf., Mirfasihi v. Fleet Mortgage Corp.,* 356 F.3d 781, 786 (7th Cir.2004) ("When individual notice is infeasible, notice by publication in a newspaper of national circulation . . . is an acceptable substitute.").

109. *See* Rule 23(c)(2) advisory committee notes to 2003 amendments.

110. *See, e.g., Abbott Laboratories, Inc. v. CVS Pharmacy, Inc.,* 290 F.3d 854, 859 (7th Cir.2002) (if party opts out, party is not bound by judgment; moreover, party cannot be "dragged back in under . . . supplemental jurisdiction"); *Sperling v. Hoffmann–LaRoche, Inc.,* 24 F.3d 463, 470 (3d Cir.1994) ("Members of a Rule 23(b)(3)

class are automatically included . . . unless they make a timely election to opt-out.").

111. *See generally Eisen v. Carlisle and Jacquelin,* 417 U.S. 156, 94 S.Ct. 2140, 40 L.Ed.2d 732 (1974).

112. *Oppenheimer Fund, Inc. v. Sanders,* 437 U.S. 340, 356-59, 98 S.Ct. 2380, 2392-93, 57 L.Ed.2d 253 (1978) (but if defendant could perform task more efficiently, burden may be shifted to defendant; also suggesting that other circumstances, not enumerated, may justify shifting cost from class representatives to defendant).

113. *Phillips Petroleum Co. v. Shutts,* 472 U.S. 797, 105 S.Ct. 2965, 86 L.Ed.2d 628 (1985) (no due process requirement to "opt in"); *Kern ex rel .Estate of Kern v. Siemens Corp.,* 393 F.3d 120, 124 (2d Cir. 2004) (Rule 23(e) contains no "opt in" provision).

Parties Bound by Judgment

Rule 23(c)(3) affords the court substantial discretion to determine the binding effect of a class action. Class actions certified under either Rule 23(b)(1) or (b)(2)(described above) have binding effect on whomever the court finds to be within the membership of the class. There is no requirement that the class members receive notice of the action.[114] Rule 23(b)(3) actions bind class members who did not opt out under Rule 23(c)(2) and whom the court defines as members.[115] Thus it is possible that persons in a (b)(3) class might not get actual notice under Rule 23(c)(2) because their names and/or addresses are unknown, yet be bound because the court found them to be members of the class.

Subclasses

Rule 23(c)(4) authorizes the court to create classes only as to particular issues. Rule 23(c)(5) authorizes the court to create subclasses within an action.[116] If subclasses are certified, each subclass is treated as an independent class for purposes of the action. The circumstances in which the court is most likely to create subclasses occur when the class members share a cause of action against a class opponent, but also experience differing interests among themselves.[117]

Classes for Settlement

Courts have certified classes created for purposes of settlement only. In such a circumstance, the court may notify potential class

114. *See, e.g., Payne v. Travenol Laboratories,* 673 F.2d 798, 812 (5th Cir.1982) (notice required only in Rule 23(b)(3) classes and at time of dismissal or settlement). *Cf., Langbecker v. Electronic Data Systems Corp.,* 476 F.3d 299, 306 (5th Cir. 2007) ("Neither a Rule 23(b)(1) or (2) class action requires notice to class members or the option to opt-out.").

115. *Eisen v. Carlisle and Jacquelin,* 417 U.S. 156, 94 S.Ct. 2140, 40 L.Ed.2d 732 (1974)(Rule 23(c)(2) requirement of notice binds all members of Rule 23(b)(3) class who do not opt out).

116. *In re Visa Check/MasterMoney Antitrust Litigation,* 280 F.3d 124, 141 (2d Cir.2001) (Individualized damages issues may be handled by "(1) bifurcating liability and damage trials with the same or different juries; (2) appointing a magistrate judge or special master to preside over individual damages proceedings; (3) decertifying the class after the liability trial and providing notice to class members concerning how they may proceed to prove damages; (4) creating subclasses; or (5) altering or amending the class.").

117. *Ortiz v. Fibreboard Corp.,* 527 U.S. 815, 119 S.Ct. 2295, 144 L.Ed.2d 715 (1999) (class comprised of holders of both present and future claims "requires subdivision into homogenous subclasses"). *See, e.g., Hawkins v. Comparet–Cassani,* 251 F.3d 1230 (9th Cir.2001) (convict can represent other convicts on Eighth Amendment claim; however, Fourth Amendment claim can be raised only by individuals not already convicted, and convict/class representative therefore lacks standing; suggesting possibility of subclasses with different subclass representatives under Rule 23(c)(4)); *Marisol A. v. Giuliani,* 126 F.3d 372, 379 (2d Cir.1997) (court emphasizes need to locate appropriate representatives for each subclass and to establish that each subclass of instant case meet requirements of Rule 23(b)(2); otherwise, describing value of subclasses as: (1) helping to focus discovery; (2) identifying claims for which there is no adequate representative, so that such claims can be dismissed; and (3) opportunity for notice to defendants of specific charges). *See also Bogosian v. Gulf Oil Corp.,* 561 F.2d 434, 456 (3d Cir.1977) (if liability is common issue, but calculation of damages is peculiar to individual members of class, court should consider limited class certification under Rule 23(c)(4)).

members of the possibility of class certification at the time the court notifies class members of the proposed settlement.[118]

RULE 23(d).   CONDUCTING THE ACTION

CORE CONCEPT

Rule 23(d) provides the court explicit authority to craft orders governing class suits.   Central to class actions is a need to protect the interests of parties who are less active than persons engaged in more conventional litigation.   At the same time, the potential administrative complexity of class actions requires that the court have tools immediately at hand to ensure that the litigation remains manageable.

APPLICATIONS

Undue Repetition of Evidence

Rule 23(d) explicitly vests the court with broad discretion to limit cumulative or repetitive evidence.

Relation to Rule 16

As amended in 2007, Rule 23(d)(2) contains two provisions. First, it authorizes alteration or amendment of any order previously issued under Rule 23(d)(1). Second, it provides that such an alteration or amendment may be combined with a pretrial order issued under Rule 16. However, even in circumstances in which orders under Rules 16 and 23(d)(2) are combined, it is settled that applications for Rule 23(d)(2) relief will be judged by a less exacting standard than the more stringent requirements for relief from a pretrial order under Rule 16.[119]

Additional Notice to Class Members

Rule 23(d)(1)(B) allows the court to order additional notice to class members to ensure fair treatment of passive members of the class.[120]   The court's authority under this provision is very broad, and encompasses discretion to order notice to the class of almost any important event in the litigation.[121]   The court may use its power in

---

118. *See, e.g., In re General Motors Corp. Pick–Up Truck Fuel Tank Products Liability Litigation,* 55 F.3d 768 (3d Cir. 1995) (standard requirements of Rule 23(a) and (b) must be met; class is typically certified formally at same time court approves settlement). *But cf., Ortiz v. Fibreboard Corp.,* 527 U.S. 815, 119 S.Ct. 2295, 144 L.Ed.2d 715 (1999) (trial court is obligated to ensure that requirements of Rule 23(a) and (b) are met; "A fairness hearing under subdivision (e) can no more swallow the preceding protective requirements of Rule 23 in a subdivision (b)(1)(B) action than in one under subdivision (b)(3).").

119. Advisory Note, Fed.R.Civ.P. 23 (2007).

120. *See, e.g., Southern Ute Indian Tribe v. Amoco Production Co.,* 2 F.3d 1023 (10th Cir.1993)(using Rule 23(d) to order representatives of defendant class—not plaintiff—to notify passive members of defendant class of pending litigation).

121. *See, e.g., Jefferson v. Ingersoll International, Inc.,* 195 F.3d 894, 898 (7th Cir.1999) (suggesting possible certification under Rule 23(b)(2), but with use of Rule 23(d)(2) and (5) to notify members of class seeking both money and equitable relief and to provide opportunity to opt out). *But see Cobell v. Kempthorne,* 455 F.3d 317, 324 (D.C. Cir. 2006) (Rule 23(d)(2) authorizes orders affecting notice of procedural matters, but provides no authority to issue or-

a variety of circumstances, including: notice to a class of pending litigation; discussion of proposed judgments; identification of class representatives to the whole class; and informing the class of key decision points in the suit so the class can participate in decisions, or evaluate opportunities to seek to participate more actively as class representatives.

Supervision of Class Representatives and Intervenors

Rule 23(d)(1)(C) provides explicit authority for the court to monitor class representatives and intervenors, and thereby supports both fair representation for the class and expeditious processing of the entire case.[122]

Rejecting Class Certification

Rule 23(d)(1)(D) allows the court to enter an order stripping a case of allegations concerning class representation. This provision is typically employed when the court has already refused, under Rule 23(c)(1), to certify the case as a class action. It may also be used if the court originally certified a class, but later altered its decision and refused certification. In either circumstance, Rule 23(d)(1)(D) contemplates that a suit denied class certification may still proceed as conventional litigation, assuming that the requirements of such litigation are satisfied.

Other Procedural Matters

Rule 23(d)(1)(E) makes explicit that the authority of the court to issue orders to process a class suit expeditiously and fairly is not limited to the other provisions of Rule 23(d).[123] In so doing, Rule 23(d)(1)(E) re-emphasizes the broad discretion a trial court enjoys in class litigation. However, in regulating communications between class lawyers or class representatives to potential class members, the court will explain with particularity the need for such regulation.[124]

Alteration of Prior Rulings

As a practical matter, Rule 23(d)'s declaration that the court may alter prior orders as necessary to the conduct of the suit means the court is not bound by its own interlocutory decisions in class actions. Thus the court enjoys almost complete flexibility to adjust class litigation as events may require. In particular, courts are prepared to change earlier orders appointing class representatives if

---

ders relating to substantive relief); *Cruz v. American Airlines, Inc.,* 356 F.3d 320, 331 (D.C. Cir.2004) (expressing doubt that Rule 23(d)(2) grants authority to order notice to a class that has not been certified).

122. *But see Cobell v. Kempthorne,* 455 F.3d 317, 323 (D.C. Cir. 2006) (Rule 23(d)(3) cannot be used to impose a condition on non-class defendant).

123. *See, e.g., Molski v. Gleich,* 318 F.3d 937, 947 (9th Cir.2003) (even with class

certified under rule 23(b)(2), "a district court may require notice and the right to opt-out under its discretionary authority provided in Rule 23(d)[(1)(C)]").

124. *Gulf Oil Co. v. Bernard,* 452 U.S. 89, 101 S.Ct. 2193, 68 L.Ed.2d 693 (1981)(requiring district court to explain the abuse such regulations are intended to address; reversing such regulations in the absence of explanation).

events show that the representatives are not protecting adequately the interests of the whole class.

RULE 23(e).   SETTLEMENT, VOLUNTARY DISMISSAL OR COMPROMISE

CORE CONCEPT

Rule 23(e) requires court approval of voluntary dismissal or compromise, and requires that proposals to settle the case be submitted to the entire class for approval.   This requirement of court supervision recognizes the fact that class actions are especially vulnerable to the possibility that the class representatives or the class attorneys may be placed in circumstances where their personal interests conflict with the interests of passive class members.   The risk of inappropriate collaboration between class representatives, or class counsel, and the class opponent is probably greatest when questions of settlement or voluntary dismissal are at issue.[125]   Rule 23(e) attempts to suppress the possibility of such conflicts by imposing a series of obligations on both the court and the parties seeking approval of the proposed settlement.

APPLICATIONS

Authority to Settle: Judicial Approval

As amended in 2003, Rule 23(e)(1)(A) expressly authorizes class representatives to settle claims, issues or defenses as appropriate.[126]   However, this authority is subject to other provisions in Rule 23(e) that have the effect of giving the power to approve or veto settlement to the district court, which in turn must solicit the views of class members before making its decision.

Comparison With Conventional Litigation

Rule 23(e) is an exception to the standard practice that parties may normally settle their disputes without the approval of the court.[127]

All Class Actions

Rule 23(e) applies to all actions certified under any portion of Rule 23(b).[128]   There is also authority that the notice requirement of

125.   *See, e.g., In re Vitamins Antitrust Class Actions,* 215 F.3d 26 (D.C. Cir.2000) (noting that "settlement dynamics" can cause even well-intentioned parties to give insufficient weight to interests of class as a whole).

126.   *See* Rule 23(e)(1)(A) advisory committee notes to 2003 amendments.

127.   *See, e.g., In re Cendant Corporation Litigation,* 264 F.3d 201, 231 (3d Cir. 2001) ("Under Rule 23(e), the District Court acts as a fiduciary guarding the rights of absent class members and must determine that the proffered settlement is

'fair, reasonable, and adequate.' "); *In re Painewebber Limited Partnerships Litigation,* 147 F.3d 132, 137 (2d Cir.1998) (plaintiff's authority to dismiss an action voluntarily under Rule 41(a)(1) is expressly subject to court's authority under Rule 23(e)). *See also, In the Matter of Cook,* 49 F.3d 263 (7th Cir.1995)(in a class action settlement involving a common fund, Rule 23(e) provides court with authority to monitor closely attorneys' fees).

128.   *See, e.g., Grimes v. Vitalink Communications Corp.,* 17 F.3d 1553, 1557 (3d Cir.1994) (duty to monitor fairness of set-

Rule 23(e) applies even in some situations where the class was decertified or never certified at all.[129]

Effect on Individual Claims

The power of the court to approve or reject settlements of class litigation does not extend to individual claims which members of the class may possess separate from the class claims. By its terms, the approval power of Rule 23(e)(1)(A) is limited to class litigation only.[130]

Notice of Proposed Settlement

As amended, Rule 23(e)(1)(C) expressly requires the district court to hold a hearing and make findings before approving a class settlement or voluntary dismissal. The findings must include a determination that the proposed course of resolution for the class action is "fair, reasonable, and adequate." [131] Within the limits of due process, courts may treat the requirements of Rule 23(e) as satisfied by less notice than, for example, the requirement of first-class mail that may accompany notice obligations under Rule 23(c)(2)(governing notice in Rule 23(b)(3) "predominance of common questions" classes).[132] Moreover, because the litigation has moved toward settlement and the class representatives can now see what the potential outcome of the suit might be, the burdens of notice when Rule 23(e) is relevant are sometimes much less onerous than the burdens established by Rule 23(c)(2).[133]

tlement is "particularly acute" in Rule 23(b)(1) and (2) class actions, because members of those classes cannot opt out of the class litigation).

129. See, e.g., Culver v. City of Milwaukee, 277 F.3d 908, 914–15 (7th Cir.2002) (acknowledging issue is "not yet definitively settled," but holding that all classes, without regard to status of certification, need notice to enable them to protect against, e.g, statute of limitations problems; but accepting contrary result if violation of Rule 23(e) is harmless). See also Doe v. Lexington–Fayette Urban County Government, 407 F.3d 755, 761 (6th Cir.2005) (noting that Culver's requirement of notice to all classes is clear majority rule). Cf., Shelton v. Pargo, Inc., 582 F.2d 1298, 1315 (4th Cir.1978) (no automatic requirement of notice to non-certified class members in the absence of collusion or unfair prejudice).

130. See Rule 23(e)(1)(A) advisory committee notes to 2003 amendments.

131. See also Rule 23(e)(1)(C) advisory committee notes to 2003 amendments.

132. See, e.g., Denney v. Deutsche Bank Securities, Inc., 443 F.3d 253, 271 (2d Cir. 2006) (Rule 23(e) authorizes court to require additional notice where appropriate, e.g., where information class members

should have in order to make a decision has changed; but court is under no blanket mandate to provide a second opt-out period under Rule 23(e)).

133. See, e.g., Wal-Mart Stores, Inc. v. Visa USA, Inc., 396 F.3d 96, 114 (2d Cir. 2005) (Rule 23(e) measures notice by reasonableness; there are no "rigid rules;" to be adequate, notice must be understandable by average class members); Gottlieb v. Wiles, 11 F.3d 1004, 1013 (10th Cir. 1993)(suggesting that notice requirements of Rule 23(e) are less rigorous than those of Rule 23(b)(3) and (c)(2)). See also Crawford v. F. Hoffman–La Roche Ltd., 267 F.3d 760, 764 (8th Cir.2001) ("[N]otice is not necessarily required if a class has not been certified."). But see, White v. Alabama, 74 F.3d 1058, 1066 n. 27 (11th Cir.1996)(newspaper ads in small type, using "legalese" that attorneys might not fully understand, did not satisfy Rule 23(e) notice requirements). See also 15 U.S.C.A. § 78u–4 (in litigation controlled by Private Securities Litigation Reform Act of 1995, notice must include, inter alia, disclosure of recovery to class members; reason for settlement; agreements or disagreements as to damages individual class members would potentially recover if class had achieved victory rather

Disclosure

As amended, Rule 23(e)(2) requires the proponents of a proposed settlement or voluntary dismissal to disclose any agreements that have been made that relate to the proposal.[134]

Settlement

The power to approve settlement of a class action lies within the court's discretion, and such decisions are rarely disturbed on appeal.[135] However, some important considerations may restrict judicial discretion. First, while the court is authorized to determine whether the settlement is fair to passive members of the class,[136] the court must still give substantial deference to a consensus of class members on the wisdom of the settlement.[137] Disregarding such a consensus is not automatically abuse of discretion, but is likely to enhance the chances that the trial court's decision will be overturned on appeal. Second, while the court must pass on the fairness of the proposal, it may not rewrite the settlement to make it conform to the court's view of a satisfactory settlement.[138] Third, the

than settlement; and likely payments to lawyers).

134. *See* Rule 23(e)(2) advisory committee notes to 2003 amendments.

135. *See, e.g., Durkin v. Shea & Gould,* 92 F.3d 1510, 1512 n. 6 (9th Cir.1996) (standard for approving settlement is whether it is "fundamentally fair, adequate, and reasonable"); *Isby v. Bayh,* 75 F.3d 1191, 1196 (7th Cir. 1996) (standard for review of district court's approval of class action settlement is abuse of discretion); *See also, Hanlon v. Chrysler Corp.,* 150 F.3d 1011 (9th Cir.1998) (for settlement approval prior to formal certification, court should make a "more probing inquiry" into terms of proposed settlement). *But see, In re Painewebber Limited Partnerships Litigation,* 147 F.3d 132 (2d Cir.1998) (notwithstanding Rule 23(e), members of potential class that is not yet certified are free to settle individual claims without court supervision; but Rule 23(e) applies once a class is certified). *But cf., Devlin v. Scardelletti,* 536 U.S. 1, 122 S.Ct. 2005, 153 L.Ed.2d 27 (2002) (class member who was not named party and who objects to settlement has right to appeal without first intervening in case; where class member has no choice to opt out of litigation, as when class was certified under, e.g., Rule 23(b)(1), the right of class members to appeal settlement has even greater force).

136. *See, e.g., Reynolds v. Beneficial National Bank,* 288 F.3d 277, 280 (7th Cir. 2002) (district court's duty in reviewing

proposed settlement is comparable "to the high duty of care that the law requires of fiduciaries"). *Hanlon v. Chrysler Corp.,* 150 F.3d 1011, 1026 (9th Cir.1998) (court should consider: "the strengths of the plaintiff's case; the risk, expense, complexity, and likely duration of further litigation; the risk of maintaining a class action status throughout the trial; the amount offered in settlement; the extent of discovery completed and the stage of the proceedings; the experience and views of counsel; ... and the reaction of the class members to the proposed settlement").

137. *See, e.g., County of Suffolk v. Long Island Lighting Co.,* 266 F.3d 131, 135 (2d Cir.2001) (notice provided to nearly one million class members; four hearings held in various places; audience numbered in hundreds; time for briefing was extended; class expert testified that settlement was fair; all expert testimony was subject to cross-examination); *Paradise v. Wells,* 686 F.Supp. 1442, 1444 (M.D.Ala.1988)(first place court should look is to views of class).

138. *Evans v. Jeff D.,* 475 U.S. 717, 726, 106 S.Ct. 1531, 1537, 89 L.Ed.2d 747 (1986)(under rule 23(e), court has authority to approve or reject settlement, but cannot impose a settlement on unwilling parties). *In re Wireless Telephone Federal Cost Recovery Fees Litigation,* 396 F.3d 922, 934 (8th Cir.2005) ("Rule 23(e) requires the court to intrude on that private consensual agreement merely to ensure that the agreement is not the product of fraud or collusion and that, taken as a whole, it is fair,

court's duty is primarily to the members of the class.[139] If persons have previously opted out of the class, the court has no power or duty to use the settlement process to address their interests.[140] Fourth, at least in class actions affected by fee shifting provisions in civil rights cases, the court has the authority and duty to review waivers of attorneys' fees that are part of a proposed settlement.[141] Finally, the court's authority to certify a class created for purposes of settlement and to approve the proposed settlement is subject to a determination that the proposed class meets the requirements of Rule 23(a) and (b).[142]

Legislation Authorizing Judicial Review of Settlements Involving "Coupons"

Congress has authorized district courts, when reviewing proposed settlements of class actions that involve an award of coupons, on motion of a party, to obtain expert testimony on the issue of the actual value to class members of coupons that are redeemed.[143] Moreover, in such cases, the court must hold a hearing and determine, in a written finding, that the settlement is fair, reasonable, and adequate to class members.[144] Finally, the court has discretion to require that a settlement provide for distribution of some portion of the value of unredeemed coupons to charitable or governmental organizations, per an agreement by the parties.[145] However, such a distribution may not be included as part of the basis for calculating attorney's fees.[146]

Protection against Loss by Class Members

In 28 U.S.C.A. § 1713, Congress provided the district court with authority to approve a proposed settlement involving a payment by

---

adequate and reasonable to all concerned.'').

139. *See, e.g., In re Cendant Corp. Litigation,* 264 F.3d 286, 295 (3d Cir.2001) (district court has no duty to assess fairness of settlement to corporate opponent of class; such issues are more properly the subject of separate shareholder derivative litigation); *Tennessee Association of Health Maintenance Organizations, Inc. v. Grier,* 262 F.3d 559, 566 (6th Cir.2001) ("[U]nder Rule 23(e), non-class members have no standing to object to a lack of notice.''). *But cf., Local No. 93, International Association of Firefighters,* 478 U.S. 501, 106 S.Ct. 3063, 92 L.Ed.2d 405 (1986) (intervenors are entitled to heard, but they have no right to a "quasi-trial" or to block the settlement by refusing to agree).

140. *See, e.g., In re Vitamins Antitrust Class Actions,* 215 F.3d 26 (D.C. Cir.2000) (non-parties "fall outside the zone of interests protected by Rule 23(e)'').

141. *Evans v. Jeff D.,* 475 U.S. 717, 728, 106 S.Ct. 1531, 1538, 89 L.Ed.2d 747 (1986).

142. *Amchem Products, Inc. v. Windsor,* 521 U.S. 591, 117 S.Ct. 2231, 138 L.Ed.2d 689 (1997). *See also Ortiz v. Fibreboard Corp.,* 527 U.S. 815, 119 S.Ct. 2295, 144 L.Ed.2d 715 (1999) (fairness hearing under Rule 23(e) cannot adequately substitute for failure of class certification movants to demonstrate that certification requirements of Rule 23(a) and (b) are met). *In re Community Bank of Northern Virginia and Guaranty National Bank of Tallahassee Second Mortgage Loan Litigation,* 418 F.3d 277, 299 (3d Cir.2005) (mere fact that settlement is "fair" does not relieve district court of duty to ensure that requirements of Rule 23(a) and (b) are met; an exception is that because settlement will not require a trial, district court may properly disregard issue of whether case will involve intractable management problems, as otherwise required by Rule 23(b)(3)(D)).

143. 28 U.S.C.A. § 1712(d).

144. 28 U.S.C.A. § 1712(e).

145. 28 U.S.C.A § 1712(e).

146. 28 U.S.C.A. § 1712(e).

members of the class to class counsel that would be a net loss to the class members. However, that authority is restricted to cases in which the court, by a written finding, concludes that nonmonetary benefits to the class "substantially" outweigh the monetary loss.[147] This provision of § 1713 is not restricted to cases involving "coupon" settlements, and appears to apply to class action settlements generally.

Protection against Geographic Discrimination

Congress has prohibited approval of proposed settlements in which some members of the class receive greater amounts of value than others based "solely" on their closer geographic ties to the location of the court hearing the case.[148] This provision appears to apply not only to "coupon" settlements but to class action settlements generally.

Additional Opportunity to Opt Out of Class

As amended, Rule 23(e)(3) provides members of classes previously certified under Rule 23(b)(3) with an additional opportunity to opt out of the proposed settlement or voluntary dismissal. The notification obligations attendant on this opportunity will be the same as those required for initial certification of a Rule 23(b)(3) class under Rule 23(c)(2)(B). There are some restrictions on this new opportunity to opt out. First, it applies only to classes certified under Rule 23(b)(3). Second, only individual class members may exercise the option to opt out if they choose. No one has standing to attempt to opt out for other members of the class.[149]

Special Provisions for "Coupon" Settlements

Congress has enacted a number of provisions that are effective in class actions in which some or all members of the class will receive their award in the form of coupons. Title 28 U.S.C.A. § 1712(a) provides that when the attorney will receive a contingency fee based on the value of the coupons, the fee shall be based on the value to class members of the coupons that are actually redeemed.[150] The effect of this provision is to reduce at least somewhat any apparent disparities between the award of contingency fees to class counsel and the nominal value of coupons to class members.

Additionally, if a proposed settlement will provide the class with coupons, but the attorney's fee is not measured solely as a contingency award, § 1712(b) provides that the additional portion of the attorney's fee shall be based on the reasonable amount of time the lawyer expended on the case.[151]

The foregoing provisions are subject to review and approval by the court. They include authorization for an appropriate fee in cases involving equitable relief. Moreover, in making calculations as to the

---

147. 28 U.S.C.A. § 1713.

148. 28 U.S.C.A. § 1714.

149. *See* Rule 23(e)(3) advisory committee notes to 2003 amendments.

150. 28 U.S.C.A. § 1712(a).

151. 28 U.S.C.A. § 1712(b)(1).

appropriate amount to be awarded as an attorney's fee, § 1712 expressly authorizes (but does not require) the use of a lodestar/multiplier method of determining fees.[152] This method of calculation is discussed at greater length on preceding pages.

If the proposed settlement contains both coupons and equitable relief, § 1712(c) provides that § 1712(a) shall govern the calculation of that portion of the attorney's fees applicable to the award of coupons, and 1712(b) shall govern the calculation of that portion of the attorney's fee attributable to considerations other than the award of coupons.[153]

Section 1712(d) provides the court with authority, upon motion of one of the parties, to obtain expert testimony on the issue of the actual value to class members of the coupons that are redeemed.[154] This provision appears to be relevant not only to calculation of an attorney's fee, but also the value and appropriateness of the settlement to the class. Judicial review of the appropriateness of a settlement to the class is discussed elsewhere in the analysis of Rule 23 and related material.

Finally, § 1712(e) authorizes the court to require that a portion of the value of unclaimed coupons be distributed to charitable or governmental organizations, as the parties choose. Such a distribution, however, cannot be used to calculate attorney's fees under § 1712.[155]

Objections to Settlement

Rule 23(e)(4) affords standing to any member of a class who wants to object to a proposed settlement or voluntary dismissal of a kind that requires judicial approval under Rule 23(e).[156] Once such an objection has been made, it can be withdrawn only with the court's approval.[157]

NOTE: Limitations on the court's discretion notwithstanding, judicial control of settlements in class litigation is still profound.[158] To ensure that the court will approve settlements the parties reach, it is probably wise to invite the court to participate in settlement discussions whenever that is practical.

Legislative Expansion of Notice Requirements for Settlement

Congress enacted a series of additional notice requirements for proposed settlements of class actions. First, within ten days of the filing of a proposed settlement with the district court, each defen-

---

152. 28 U.S.C.A. § 1712(b)(2).

153. 28 U.S.C.A. § 1712(c).

154. 28 U.S.C.A. 1712(d).

155. 28 U.S.C.A. § 1712(e).

156. *In re Rite Aid Corporate Securities Litigation,* 396 F.3d 294, 299 (3d Cir.2005) (any class member may object to a settlement governed by Rule 23(e)).

157. *See* Rule 23(e)(5) advisory committee notes to 2003 amendments (also providing examples of circumstances in which approval of withdrawal of objection may be obtained).

158. *See, e.g., Kloster v. McColl,* 350 F.3d 747, 751 (8th Cir.2003) (Rule 23(e) makes district court "fiduciary" and "guardian" of rights of passive members of class).

dant participating in the proposed settlement must serve notice of the proposed settlement, to include the following documents on both the appropriate federal official and the appropriate state official in each state in which any class member resides: (1) the complaint, amended complaint (if any), and material filed with such pleadings (unless such documents are available electronically, in which case an appropriate explanation of access to the documents will suffice); (2) notice of any scheduled hearing in the case; (3) notice of any proposed or final notification to class members of their right to seek exclusion from the case, or a statement that no such right exists, as well as a copy of the proposed settlement; (4) a copy of the final settlement; (5) a copy of any contemporaneous agreement reached between class counsel and defendants' counsel; (6) any final judgment or notice of dismissal; (7) if feasible, names of the class members residing in each state and an estimate of the proportion of the settlement likely to be distributed in each state, or if that information is not reasonably available, a reasonable estimate of such information; and (8) any written judicial opinions relating to items three through six.[159]

For purposes of this provision, the appropriate federal official is the Attorney General of the United States. The appropriate state official is that person with primary regulatory authority over the business in which the defendant engages. If there is no such person, the appropriate state official is the state attorney general. If the defendant is a federal or state depository institution, a foreign bank, or a subsidiary of any such institution, the appropriate federal official is not the Attorney General, but the person who has primary federal regulatory authority over such an entity. The appropriate state official also becomes the corresponding state official with similar regulatory authority when a defendant is a state financial institution.[160]

Presumably so that appropriate federal or state officials may participate in the settlement process, § 1715(d) provides that a final order approving a settlement may not issue until at least 90 days after the latest date of notification to federal or state officials required under § 1715(b).[161] If a class member is able to establish that the requirements of § 1715(b) were not met, the class member has the option to refuse to comply with the settlement agreement. No such option exists if the defendants have complied with § 1715(b).[162]

RULE 23(f). APPEALS

CORE CONCEPT

Rule 23(f) creates the possibility that a district court's decision granting or denying class certification could be appealed on an interlocu-

159. 28 U.S.C.A. § 1715(b).

160. 28 U.S.C.A. § 1715(a).

161. 28 U.S.C.A. § 1715(d).

162. 28 U.S.C.A. 1715(e).

tory basis. That is, the parties might not have to wait until the end of the litigation in the district court to learn whether the decision to certify (or not) would be upheld.

APPLICATIONS

2007 Amendments

The 2007 Style Project amended Rule 23(g) by transferring provisions within various subparts of subsection (g). Specifically, former Rule 23(g)(1)(B), addressing class counsel's duty of fair and adequate representation of the interests of the class, is now Rule 23(g)(4). Further, old Rule 23(g)(2)(C), addressing the inclusion of provisions about attorneys fees and nontaxable costs in the order appointing class counsel , is now Rule 23(g)(1)(D). These are not substantive changes, but they may require attorneys to be cautious to cite accurately to cases decided prior to the 2007 amendments.

Appellate Discretion

Rule 23(f) vests discretion in appellate courts to permit or deny an appeal granting or denying class certification, and circuit courts have begun to develop standards for determining whether to permit an appeal. Although their discretion is substantially uncurbed,[163] there seems to be general agreement that review under Rule 23(f) should not be a commonplace event.[164] Nevertheless, several situations arise where a circuit court is more likely than not to permit Rule 23(f) interlocutory appellate review of a class certification decision. These situations may sometimes be found together in the same case, but each by itself may justify review. First, if a denial of class certification would probably preclude any realistic chance that individual claims could be prosecuted and the district court's decision was questionable, circuits are inclined to grant review.[165] Second, if a district court's grant of class certification puts substantial pressure on a defendant to settle without regard to the merits of a case and the certification grant was questionable, review is appropriate.[166] Third, circuits generally agree that review is appropriate if it

---

163. *See, e.g., Shin v. Cobb County Board of Education,* 248 F.3d 1061, 1063–65 (11th Cir.2001) (discretion is "unfettered").

164. *See, e.g., In re Lorazepam & Clorazepate Antitrust Litigation,* 289 F.3d 98, 105 (D.C. Cir.2002) ("As is true for all the circuits, we are of the view that Rule 23(f) review should be granted rarely where a case does not fall within one of these ... categories."); *Waste Management Holdings, Inc. v. Mowbray,* 208 F.3d 288, 294 (1st Cir.2000) (court will "exercise discretion judiciously").

165. *See, e.g., In re Sumitomo Copper Litigation,* 262 F.3d 134, 140 (2d Cir.2001) (review likely if certification denial is death knell for case, and certification decision was

questionable); *Waste Management Holdings, Inc. v. Mowbray,* 208 F.3d 288, 293–94 (1st Cir.2000) (same); *Blair v. Equifax Check Services, Inc.,* 181 F.3d 832, 834 (7th Cir.1999) (same). *See also In re Lorazepam & Clorazepate Antitrust Litigation,* 289 F.3d 98, 105 (D.C. Cir.2002) (approving review that is death-knell situation for either plaintiff or defendant where the district court's decision is questionable).

166. *See, e.g., Tardiff v. Knox County,* 365 F.3d 1, 3 (1st Cir.2004) ("One reason for review is a threat of liability so large as to place on the defendant an 'irresistible pressure to settle.' "); *In re Lorazepam & Clorazepate Antitrust Litigation,* 289 F.3d 98, 106 (D.C. Cir.2002); *In re Sumitomo Copper Litigation,* 262 F.3d 134 (2d Cir.

will help develop law regarding class actions.[167] For this last possibility to apply, some circuit courts do not require that there be evidence of some error by the district court,[168] but other courts have imposed additional caveats that the development of law must be both important to the instant litigation and class action law generally, as well as unlikely to be subject to review at the termination of the case in the district court.[169]

Another possibility for obtaining review under Rule 23(f) arises if a party can demonstrate that the district court's certification decision is clear error. In that circumstance some circuits have held that review should normally occur without regard to whether other factors, such as those discussed immediately above, are present.[170]

Circuit courts that emphasize the appropriateness of appellate review in the circumstance of clear error have also adopted a slightly different characterization of the factors that other courts have used. Instead of identifying the three independent circumstances in which appellate review may be appropriate, these circuits have melded the factors together in a way that weighs all of them, plus one or two others. In such circuits Rule 23(f) petitions may be granted if consideration of these factors—taken together, not independently— justify review: (1) the "death knell" consideration, discussed above; (2) potential abuse of discretion by the district court in making its certification decision; (3) whether the appeal presents an unsettled legal question of general importance and importance in the instant litigation that might not be susceptible to review at a later point in the case; (4) the status of the case in the district court, including consideration of progress in discovery, other unresolved motions, and the passage of time since initiation of the case; and (5) the possibility that at some future time it will be clear that prompt review now was appropriate.[171] Courts that follow this approach weigh most heavily the presence of manifest error in the district court's decision. When such error is found it may be unnecessary for

2001); *Blair v. Equifax Check Services, Inc.*, 181 F.3d 832, 834 (7th Cir.1999).

167. *See, e.g., Carnegie v. Household International, Inc.*, 376 F.3d 656 (7th Cir. 2004) ("the more important the resolution of the issue is either to the particular litigation or to the general development of class action law," the greater is the likelihood that appeal will be heard).

168. *See, e.g., Blair v. Equifax Check Services, Inc.*, 181 F.3d 832, 835 (7th Cir. 1999).

169. *In re Lorazepam & Clorazepate Antitrust Litigation*, 289 F.3d 98, 105 (D.C. Cir.2002); *In re Sumitomo Copper Litigation*, 262 F.3d 134 (2d Cir.2001) (same); *Waste Management Holdings, Inc. v. Mowbray*, 208 F.3d 288, 293–94 (1st Cir.2000) (same).

170. *See, e.g., Prado–Steiman ex rel. Prado v. Bush*, 221 F.3d 1266, 1275 (11th Cir.2000) (clear error means review could be appropriate "even if none of the other factors supports granting the Rule 23(f) petition"). *See also Lienhart v. Dryvit Systems, Inc.*, 255 F.3d 138, 145–46 (4th Cir. 2001) (manifest error justifies review even where other factors are not met). *Cf., Carnegie v. Household International, Inc.*, 376 F.3d 656 (7th Cir.2004) ("the more novel the issue presented by the appeal and so the less likely that the district court's resolution of it will stand ... the stronger the case for allowing the appeal").

171. *See, e.g., Prado–Steiman v. Bush*, 221 F.3d 1266, 1274–75 n. 10 (11th Cir. 2000). *See also Lienhart v. Dryvit Systems, Inc.*, 255 F.3d 138, 146 (4th Cir.2001) (same).

the appellate court to find that the other factors favor review before granting a Rule 23(f) petition.[172]

Yet another court has adopted the three independent factors discussed above, plus the additional independent ground for review when a decision is clearly erroneous.[173]

Role of District Court; Relation to 28 U.S.C.A. § 1292

As is suggested immediately above, a determination to grant or deny an application to appeal under Rule 23(f) is vested in the court of appeals. Once a district court has granted or denied the motion for certification, its role under Rule 23(f) is minor. The district court's entry of the order on class certification starts the running of the ten days in which an application to appeal must be filed (discussed below).[174] Additionally, filing a motion for reconsideration within ten days of the district court's entry of its order tolls the running of the Rule 23(f) time limit.[175]

The extremely truncated role of district courts in Rule 23(f) cases highlights the difference between that Rule and 28 U.S.C.A. § 1292, which governs many other circumstances in which an interlocutory appeal may be sought on grounds outside the scope of Rule 23(f). In particular, § 1292 provides that the district court must agree to certify a question before it can be put before a circuit court on an interlocutory basis.[176] Further, § 1292(b) requires that the district court's certification of an interlocutory appeal includes determinations as to the importance of the appeal and the need for an expeditious ruling by the circuit court on the questions at hand. Only after the district court has made that certification may the circuit court exercise its own discretion in determining whether to accept the appeal.[177]

Time

By its terms, Rule 23(f) requires that any application for such an appeal be made to the circuit court within 10 days after the district court has entered its order granting or denying class certifi-

172. *Lienhart v. Dryvit Systems, Inc.,* 255 F.3d 138, 146 (4th Cir.2001); *Prado-Steiman v. Bush,* 221 F.3d 1266, 1275 (11th Cir.2000).

173. *Newton v. Merrill Lynch, Pierce, Fenner & Smith,* 259 F.3d 154, 165 (3d Cir.2001).

174. Fed. R. Civ. P. 23(f).

175. *See, e.g., Shin v. Cobb County Board of Education,* 248 F.3d 1061, 1064–65 (11th Cir. 2001) ("[T]he 10–day period to file a Rule 23(f) petition does not start to run until the district judge rules on the motion for reconsideration."). *But cf., Gray v. Sheahan,* 188 F.3d 891, 893 (7th Cir. 1999) (late or successive motions to reconsider the district court's certification decision do not toll the time limits of Rule 23(f)).

176. 28 U.S.C.A. § 1292(b).

177. 28 U.S.C.A. § 1292(b). *See, e.g., Jenkins v. BellSouth Corp.,* 491 F.3d 1288 (11th Cir. 2007) ("[S]ection 1292(b) does not guide our interpretation of Rule 23(f)."). *See also McNamara v. Felderhof,* 410 F.3d 277, 281 (5th Cir. 2005) (time limit of Rule 23(f) cannot be extended through untimely motion in district court for reconsideration of certification order). *Cf., Delta Airlines v. Butler,* 383 F.3d 1143, 1145 (10th Cir. 2004) (district court cannot extend time limit of Rule 23(f)).

cation.[178] It appears settled that the computation of time for Rule 23(f) is governed by Rule 6(a), which is discussed elsewhere in this text.[179]

Raising Other Issues

Rule 23(f) authorizes appeal of class certification only. In general, other issues will not be considered when the basis for appeal is Rule 23(f). Two exceptions to that practice are standing and subject matter jurisdiction, which appellate courts are willing to consider on an appeal under Rule 23(f).[180]

Relation to 28 U.S.C. § 1292

Section 1292(b) governs some of the circumstances in which a party may seek authorization for an interlocutory appeal from the decision of a district court. Section 1292(b) provides no fixed time

---

178. *Cf., Chevron U.S.A., Inc. v. School Board Vermilion Parish,* 294 F.3d 716 (5th Cir.2002) (ten day time limit of Rule 23(f) is jurisdictional and may not be waived); *Gary v. Sheahan,* 188 F.3d 891, 892 (7th Cir. 1999) (failure to seek appellate review within time limit of rule 23(f) means "appeal must wait until the final judgment"). *But see Shin v. Cobb County Board of Education,* 248 F.3d 1061, 1063–65 (11th Cir. 2001) (motion for reconsideration filed within 10 days of order granting or denying certification stays time for Rule 23(f) appeal until district court decides reconsideration motion; also, when time is calculated it excludes weekends and legal holidays, per Rule 6).

179. *See, e.g., In re Veneman,* 309 F.3d 789, 793 (D.C. Cir.2002) (appellate courts have held unanimously that Rule 6(a) controls).

180. *See, e.g., Rivera v. Wyeth–Ayerst Laboratories,* 283 F.3d 315, 319 (5th Cir. 2002) ("[S]tanding may—indeed must—be addressed even under the limits of a Rule 23(f) appeal."); *Bertulli v. Independent Association of Continental Pilots,* 242 F.3d 290, 294 (5th Cir.2001) (enunciating this general rule, but deciding that issues of standing are an exception and may be heard on a Rule 23(f) appeal); *Carter v. West Publishing Co.,* 225 F.3d 1258, 1262 (11th Cir. 2000) (under Rule 23(f) court may also evaluate standing, but not merits of case); *Prado-Steiman v. Bush,* 221 F.3d 1266, 1273 (11th Cir.2000) ("Rule 23(f) should not be a vehicle for courts of appeals to micro-manage complex class action litigation as it unfolds in the district court."). *But see McKowan Lowe & Co. v. Jasmine, Ltd.,* 295 F.3d 380 (3d Cir.2002) (refusing to review dismissal of plaintiff's underlying claims when

hearing Rule 23(f) appeal of denial of class certification; Rule 23(f) does not extend to any other type order, "even where that order has some impact on another portion of Rule 23"); *In re Lorazepam & Clorazepate Antitrust Litigation,* 289 F.3d 98, 107–08 (D.C. Cir 2002) (refusing to consider antitrust standing under Rule 23(f). "The fact that [defendant's] challenge would be dispositive of the class action is not unlike a variety of issues of law on the merits of a class action," but review of such issues "would inappropriately mix the issue of class certification with the merits of a case." However, acknowledging authority for evaluating constitutional standing under Rule 23(f); but distinguishing such cases because such standing goes to court's jurisdiction, while antitrust standing does not). *See also Lindsay v. Government Employees Insurance Co.,* 448 F.3d 416, 420 (D.C. Cir.2006) ("Because subject matter jurisdiction is a prerequisite to class certification, it is properly reviewed in a Rule 23(f) interlocutory appeal."); *Samuel-Bassett v. Kia Motors America, Inc.,* 357 F.3d 392, 395 (3d Cir.2004) (circuit court hearing Rule 23(f) issue has obligation to examine subject matter jurisdiction); *Heffner v. Blue Cross & Blue Shield of Alabama, Inc.,* 443 F.3d 1330, 1337 (11th Cir.2006) ("[W]hile a court should not determine the merits of a claim at the class certification stage, it is appropriate to 'consider the merits of the case to the degree necessary to determine whether the requirements of Rule 23 will be satisfied.' "); *Lienhart v. Dryvit Systems, Inc.,* 255 F.3d 138, 143 n. 2 (4th Cir.2001) (acknowledging that "on occasion" merits may be examined when appellate court decides whether to permit early appeal of certification issue pursuant to Rule 23(f)).

limit for seeking such an appeal. However, it appears that when an interlocutory appeal might lie under Rule 23(f), neither district courts nor potential appellants should seek interlocutory relief under § 1292(b).[181]

Stay of District Court Proceedings

If the circuit court allows an appeal under Rule 23(f), the appeal does not automatically stay proceedings in the district court.[182] Instead, a party seeking such a stay must apply to either the district court or the court of appeals.

RULE 23(g). CLASS COUNSEL

CORE CONCEPT

Rule 23(g) is an amendment to Rule 23, effective in late 2003. It governs the manner in which a court will supervise the appointment of counsel to represent the class. Previously there was no precise counterpart to Rule 23(g), but courts had previously used authority derived from Rule 23(a)(4) to develop substantial precedent guiding decisions courts had to make in this area. Additionally, the precepts adopted for class litigation in the area of securities law,[183] themselves heavily borrowed from case law, will also undoubtedly provide guidance to federal courts as they attempt to flesh out the requirements of new Rule 23(g).

APPLICATIONS

Relationship of Rule 23(a)(4) to Rule 23(g)

Until the addition of Rule 23(g), courts had routinely employed Rule 23(a)(4) (governing evaluation of whether class representatives would adequately protect class interests) to examine the adequacy of class counsel.[184] The standards developed by that case law[185] have

---

181. *Richardson Electronics, Ltd. v. Panache Broadcasting of Pennsylvania, Inc.,* 202 F.3d 957, 959 (7th Cir.2000) (When issue "is an arguable candidate for a rule 23(f) appeal, the appellants may not use § 1292(b) to circumvent the 10–day limitation in Rule 23(f). . . . Should a case arise in which a class-certification order is appealable under [§] 1292(b) but not under [Rule] 23(f), perhaps because it presents an issue that while it satisfies the criteria of the statute does not involve the merits of class certification, the appellant can protect himself by seeking the district judge's permission to take a [§] 1292(b) appeal at the same time that the appellant asks us to entertain his appeal under [Rule] 23(f).").

182. *See, e.g., Prado–Steiman v. Bush,* 221 F.3d 1266, 1273 n. 8 (11th Cir.2000) ("Rule 23(f) contemplates that in most cases discovery (at the very least, merits discovery) will continue notwithstanding

the pendency of an appeal of the class certification order.").

183. 15 U.S.C.A. § 78u–4(a)(3)(B).

184. *Amchem Products, Inc. v. Windsor,* 521 U.S. 591, 626 n. 20, 117 S.Ct. 2231, 2251 n. 20, 138 L.Ed.2d 689 (1997) ("The adequacy heading also factors in competency and conflicts of class counsel."). *See, e.g., Greisz v. Household Bank, N.A.,* 176 F.3d 1012, 1013 (7th Cir.1999) (Rule 23(a)(4) requires assessment of competence of counsel for class).

185. *See, e.g., Fymbo v. State Farm Fire and Casualty Co.,* 213 F.3d 1320, 1320–21 (10th Cir.2000) (rule 23(a)(4) prevents non-attorney from serving as pro se class representative; plaintiff's pleadings were also evidence of lack of competence); *Hanlon v. Chrysler Corp.,* 150 F.3d 1011, 1021 (9th Cir.1998) (Rule 23(a)(4) requires evaluation of counsel's ability; also, in settlement class,

been incorporated almost in their entirety into new Rule 23(g), giving courts broad discretion to inquire and evaluate the appropriateness of permitting any particular lawyers' representation of the class.

Reverse Auctions

Historically, courts have discouraged reverse auctions–"the practice whereby the defendant in a series of class actions picks the most ineffectual class lawyers to negotiate a settlement with in the hope that the district court will approve a weak settlement that will preclude other claims against the defendant." [186] Rule 23(g)(1)(C)(iii) and (g)(2)(C) now provide the court with express authority to examine and propose appropriate terms for compensation and to include those requirements as part of the order appointing class counsel. The result should be to control attorneys' fees and costs while ensuring that the class opponent is not in a position to choose, unilaterally, the lawyers who will cost the least and who may not do the best work. These portions of Rule 23(g) harmonize closely with Rule 23(h), governing awards of attorney fees. Rule 23(h) is discussed immediately below.

RULE 23(h). ATTORNEY'S FEES AND NONTAXABLE COSTS

CORE CONCEPT

Rule 23(h) governs the award of attorneys' fees in class actions. Heretofore this issue was controlled by case law as well as statutes applicable to particular kinds of class actions, such as the Private Securities Litigation Reform Act of 1995.[187] New Rule 23(h) establishes no substantive standards for determining the appropriateness of a particular fee award. Instead, it establishes a procedure by which a fee application may be made and objections to that application may be heard.

APPLICATIONS

Existing Case Law

Outside of the area of class actions, the general American approach to attorney's fees is to require each party to bear its own burden. However, class actions present a special problem, because the nature of such litigation is that the work of attorneys may enrich an entire group of people. In such a situation it would be unfair to require that the attorneys be compensated, if at all, only by

court must also examine "rationale for not pursuing further litigation"); *In re Fine Paper Antitrust Litigation*, 617 F.2d 22, 27 (3d Cir.1980) (trial judge has "constant duty" to monitor "professional competency and behavior of class counsel").

186. *Reynolds v. Beneficial National Bank*, 288 F.3d 277, 282 (7th Cir.2002). *See*

also In re Cendant Corp. Litigation, 264 F.3d 201 (3d Cir.2001) (disapproving choice of lead counsel by reverse auction in case controlled by Private Securities Litigation Reform Act).

187. 15 U.S.C.A. § 78u–4(a)(6).

those few individuals who began the litigation.[188] New Rule 23(h) recognizes that principle by permitting attorneys to petition for fees that are taxable, in appropriate cases, against the entire class.

The basis and source of such fees has depended partly on the nature of the cause of action and the judgment or settlement obtained. For example, fees might have been available from the defendant when authorized under an applicable statute.[189] When such a statute was not applicable (and usually even when it was), the district court had substantial authority to determine the method of calculating fees and the amount that would be awarded. Rule 23(h), in essence, codifies that existing practice. Thus, it is likely that for at least the near future courts will rely on precedent developed prior to enactment of Rule 24(h) to determine the appropriateness of a fee award in a particular case.

Methods of Calculation

Measurement of the appropriate amount of a fee has usually been determined through one of two methods. If a fund was available, courts have awarded the lawyers a percentage of the money available.[190] In circumstances where the court believed another approach was appropriate or where no fund was available, e.g., where the class sought injunctive relief, courts typically measured the appropriate fee through a "lodestar" approach.[191] In the context of a class action, this calculation begins by determining appropriate hourly rates for individual lawyers, which are then multiplied by the number of hours actually and reasonably expended on the project. Finally, factors such as difficulty of the case, quality of legal work, risk of failure, etc., may be used in some cases to modify the result (up or down) reached by the simple multiplication of hours and

---

188.   *See, e.g, Savoie v. Merchants Bank,* 166 F.3d 456, 460 (2d Cir.1999) ("A party whose initiative confers a benefit upon a class of people is entitled to recover its costs–including attorneys' fees–from the common fund."). *See also In re Synthroid Marketing Litigation,* 264 F.3d 712, 717 (7th Cir.2001) ("Unless a class contracts privately over attorneys' fees, lawyers in class-fund cases must petition the court for their compensation.").

189.   *See, e.g.,* 42 U.S.C.A. § 1988 (governing attorneys' fees in civil rights litigation).

190.   *Blum v. Stenson,* 465 U.S. 886, 900 n. 16, 104 S.Ct. 1541, 1550 n. 16, 79 L.Ed.2d 891 (1984) (approving calculation based on percentage of fund). *See, e.g., Hanlon v. Chrysler Corp.,* 150 F.3d 1011, 1029 (9th Cir.1998) (approving approximately 4.5% of very large fund as appropriate compensation).

191.   *See, e.g.,* 28 U.S.C.A. § 1712(b) (expressly authorizing, but not mandating, use of lodestar method to calculate attor-

ney's fees). *In re Synthroid Marketing Litigation,* 264 F.3d 712, 718 (7th Cir.2001) ("We have held repeatedly that, when deciding on appropriate fee levels in common-fund cases, courts must do their best to award counsel the market price for legal services, in light of the risk of nonpayment and the normal rate of compensation in the market at the time."); *In re Cendant Corp. PRIDES Litigation,* 243 F.3d 722, 732 (3d Cir.) (lodestar applicable when anticipated relief is too small to justify use of percentage-of-recovery method but case still has potential social benefit). *Compare, e.g., Savoie v. Merchants Bank,* 166 F.3d 456, 460 (2d Cir.1999) (suggesting that Second Circuit will use only lodestar method to determine compensation, even in cases involving common fund) *with Goldberger v. Integrated Resources, Inc.,* 209 F.3d 43, 50 (2d Cir.2000) (acknowledging that lodestar method is approved, but is not "exclusive methodology in common fund cases").

rates.[192] It should be noted that while the lodestar method has been available in many class actions, the use of so-called "risk multipliers," *e.g.*, difficulty of the case, etc., has *not* been available in class actions where a fee is imposed based on a fee shifting statute. In such cases it appears that district courts have made their lodestar calculation based only on the reasonable hourly rate multiplied by the reasonable number of hours devoted to the case.[193]

Motion Required

Rule 23(h) requires that an application for attorneys' fees must be made by motion, subject to Rule 54(d) (governing taxation of costs).

Notice

Rule 23(h) requires that the motion for fees must be served on all parties. If the motion is made by class counsel, as it typically will be, it must also "be directed to class members in a reasonable manner."

Objections, Hearing and Findings

Rule 23(h) provides that both class members and the party who may have to pay the fees have standing to object to the motion. The court has discretion—not an obligation—to hold a hearing on the motion. The court must make findings of fact and conclusions of law in a manner consistent with the requirements of Rule 52(a) (governing the court's duty in such matters when issues are tried to the court).

Special Masters and Magistrate Judges

Rule 23(h) permits the district court to refer matters relating to fees to special masters or magistrate judges.

Protection against Loss by Class Members

In 28 U.S.C.A. § 1713, Congress provided the district court with authority to approve a proposed settlement involving a payment by members of the class to class counsel that would be a net loss to the class members. However, that authority is restricted to cases in which the court, by a written finding, concludes that nonmonetary benefits to the class "substantially" outweigh the monetary loss.[194] This provision of § 1713 is not restricted to cases involving "cou-

---

192. See, e.g., *Gunter v. Ridgewood Corp.*, 223 F.3d 190, 195 n. 1 (3d Cir.2000) (factors to consider "include: (1) the size of the fund created and the number of persons benefited; (2) the presence or absence of substantial objection by members of the class to the settlement terms and/or fees requested by counsel; (3) the skill and efficiency of the attorneys involved; (4) the complexity and duration of the litigation; (5) the risk of nonpayment; (6) the amount of time devoted to the case by plaintiff's counsel; and (7) the awards in similar cases"); *Goldberger v. Integrated Resources, Inc.*, 209 F.3d 43, 53 (2d Cir.2000) (lodestar case: "[o]f course contingency risk and quality of representation must be considered in settling a reasonable fee").

193. *City of Burlington v. Dague*, 505 U.S. 557, 565–66, 112 S.Ct. 2638, 2642–43, 120 L.Ed.2d 449 (1992) (rejecting use of risk multipliers in cases using lodestar method to calculate attorneys' fees under federal fee-shifting statutes).

194. 28 U.S.C.A. § 1713.

pon" settlements, and appears to apply to class action settlements generally.

Reverse Auctions

Historically, courts have discouraged reverse auctions–"the practice whereby the defendant in a series of class actions picks the most ineffectual class lawyers to negotiate a settlement with in the hope that the district court will approve a weak settlement that will preclude other claims against the defendant." [195] Provisions of new Rule 23(g) that permit the court to consider the impact of attorneys' fees even at an early stage of the case when the court is considering appointment of class counsel are likely to further dampen enthusiasm for reverse auctions. In this area the provisions of Rule 23(h), giving the court final approval of attorneys' fees, complement the provisions of Rule 23(g) that authorize the court to restrict fees as a condition of appointment of counsel. Rule 23(g) is discussed in greater detail above.

ADDITIONAL RESEARCH REFERENCES

Wright & Miller, *Federal Practice and Procedure* §§ 1751–1805.

C.J.S. Federal Civil Procedure §§ 63–92, 170.

West's Key No. Digests, Federal Civil Procedure ☞161–189.

195. *Reynolds v. Beneficial National Bank,* 288 F.3d 277, 282 (7th Cir.2002). *See also In re Cendant Corp. Litigation,* 264 F.3d 201 (3d Cir.2001) (disapproving choice of lead counsel by reverse auction in case controlled by Private Securities Litigation Reform Act).

RULE 23.1

DERIVATIVE ACTIONS BY SHAREHOLDERS

(a) Prerequisites. This rule applies when one or more shareholders or members of a corporation or an unincorporated association bring a derivative action to enforce a right that the corporation or association may properly assert but has failed to enforce. The derivative action may not be maintained if it appears that the plaintiff does not fairly and adequately represent the interests of shareholders or members who are similarly situated in enforcing the right of the corporation or association.

(b) Pleading Requirements. The complaint must be verified and must:

(1) allege that the plaintiff was a shareholder or member at the time of the transaction complained of, or that the plaintiff's share or membership later devolved on it by operation of law;

(2) allege that the action is not a collusive one to confer jurisdiction that the court would otherwise lack; and

(3) state with particularity:

(A) any effort by the plaintiff to obtain the desired action from the directors or comparable authority and, if necessary, from the shareholders or members; and

(B) the reasons for not obtaining the action or not making the effort.

(c) Settlement, Dismissal, and Compromise. A derivative action may be settled, voluntarily dismissed, or compromised only with the court's approval. Notice of a proposed settlement, voluntary dismissal, or compromise must be given to shareholders or members in the manner that the court orders.

[Added effective July 1, 1966; amended effective August 1, 1987; April 30, 2007, effective December 1, 2007.]

——————— **2007 AMENDMENTS ROADMAP** ———————

STYLE PROJECT CHANGES: Rule 23.1 was subsectioned into three parts to aid readability. Minor stylistic alterations were made in the Rule.

NON-STYLE CHANGES: None.

NOTE: The Federal Rules "Style Project" is explained in Part III–A.

AUTHORS' COMMENTARY ON RULE 23.1

PURPOSE AND SCOPE

In a shareholder derivative suit, a shareholder sues on behalf of a corporation and/or its shareholders by alleging that the officers and directors who control the corporation will not institute the suit. In fact, often the officers and directors are themselves defendants in the derivative suit. The utility of shareholder derivative suits is balanced by the risk that this type of litigation can be used to harass corporate officers and directors into settlements favorable to the plaintiffs, at the expense of degrading corporate assets that are the common property of all shareholders. Through a series of procedural requirements not normally imposed on other kinds of litigation, Rule 23.1 attempts to preserve the social value of derivative suits, while reducing the risk of inappropriate harassment. Some of these requirements bear substantial similarity to elements of Rule 23, governing class actions.

RULE 23.1(a). DERIVATIVE ACTION

CORE CONCEPT

Rule 23.1(a) provides that shareholders or members of a corporation may bring an action on behalf of a corporation that the corporation has not asserted. Only persons who will fairly and adequately represent the interests of other shareholders or members, and who will represent the interests of other similarly situated shareholders or members, may enforce the corporation's rights.

APPLICATIONS

Applicability

For the requirements of Rule 23.1 to apply to a case, a plaintiff must be a "shareholder" or "member" seeking to enforce a right of a corporation or unincorporated association.[1] Other types of derivative claims need not meet the standards of Rule 23.1.[2]

---

[1] *See, e.g., Lefkovitz v. Wagner,* 395 F.3d 773, 776 (7th Cir.2005) ("Although most derivative suits are brought on behalf of corporations, a derivative suit can be brought on behalf of a partnership or other unincorporated form.").

[2] *Daily Income Fund, Inc. v. Fox,* 464 U.S. 523, 528, 104 S.Ct. 831, 834, 78

Subject Matter Jurisdiction

If the cause of action is based exclusively on state law, the requirements of diversity jurisdiction must be satisfied. Diversity jurisdiction and other kinds of subject matter jurisdiction are discussed at §§ 2.10–2.13. Because the corporation is normally treated as an indispensable party needed for just adjudication, alignment of the corporate entity as a plaintiff or defendant can have significant consequences for jurisdiction. Although there is no absolute rule governing this issue, it is likely that the court will not align the corporation in a way that defeats diversity jurisdiction. The courts still retain discretion in this area, however, and have on occasion aligned the corporation in a way that defeats diversity.[3]

Personal Jurisdiction

Personal jurisdiction over defendants who are natural persons is obtained in derivative suits in the same manner as in other litigation. For corporations aligned as defendants, however, Congress has enacted a special service of process provision. 28 U.S.C.A. § 1695 allows plaintiffs in shareholder derivative suits to serve process on such corporate defendants "in any district where [they are] organized or licensed to do business or ... doing business."

Venue

A special statute for derivative suits, 28 U.S.C.A. § 1401, provides that the plaintiff may sue in any judicial district where the corporation might have sued the same defendants. As a practical matter, this means § 1401 should be read in conjunction with § 1391(a) and (b), governing the venue requirements for diversity suits and many claims based on federal questions.

RULE 23.1(b). PLEADING REQUIREMENTS

CORE CONCEPT

Rule 23.1(b) identifies the special pleading requirements for derivative actions governed by Rule 23.1 and also provide that a pleading governed by Rule 23.1 must be verified.

Verification of Complaint

Complaints that initiate shareholders' derivative actions must be sworn to and notarized. This is a departure from the general

---

L.Ed.2d 645 (1984)(Rule 23.1 applies only when "a shareholder claims a right that could have been, but was not, 'asserted' by the corporation."); *see also, Kayes v. Pacific Lumber Co.,* 51 F.3d 1449, 1462–63 (9th Cir.1995). (Rule 23.1 applies narrowly; it is not applicable to "plan beneficiaries" seeking "to enforce the right of the plan against its fiduciaries").

3. *See, e.g., Liddy v. Urbanek,* 707 F.2d 1222, 1224 (11th Cir.1983)([F]inal alignment of the parties should reflect the actual antagonisms between the plaintiffs, the corporation, and the directors; held, corporation should be joined where appropriate, even when joinder will destroy diversity); *Frank v. Hadesman and Frank, Inc.,* 83 F.3d 158 (7th Cir.1996)(in derivative suit, corporation is aligned as plaintiff if shareholders have suffered harm in common; citing state law; dismissing because corporation is not diverse from defendant).

practice in federal civil procedure, which usually imposes no federal requirement for verification of a complaint. The practical impact of a verification requirement in derivative suits may be limited, however, because it is not applied in a way that prohibits a layperson from relying on competent information in bringing a derivative suit.[4] Thus, any shareholder who has undertaken a reasonable investigation, in person or through the advice of qualified persons, of the allegations in the complaint, should be able to satisfy the verification requirement without undue difficulty.[5]

Standing: Continuous Ownership Requirement

Under Rule 23.1(1), the complaint must state that the derivative suit is initiated on behalf of a person who: (1) was a shareholder at the time the cause of action arose, or who became a shareholder by operation of law from someone who had been a shareholder at that time; and (2) who remained a shareholder at the time the suit was filed.[6] If the plaintiff is divested of ownership while the suit is pending, the suit will usually be dismissed.[7] In diversity suits, these standing requirements of rule 23.1 will apparently apply even if state law might be less strict. The matter is not entirely free from doubt, however, and attorneys should consult the local practice.[8]

Collusive Attempts to Invoke Federal Jurisdiction

Rule 23.1(2) requires that the plaintiff swear that a shareholder derivative suit based on diversity jurisdiction was not brought to manufacture federal court jurisdiction on behalf of the corporation. This issue could arise only if the corporation had the same citizenship as the defendants.

4. *Surowitz v. Hilton Hotels Corp.,* 383 U.S. 363, 86 S.Ct. 845, 15 L.Ed.2d 807 (1966).

5. *See, e.g., Lewis v. Curtis,* 671 F.2d 779, 788 (3d Cir.1982) (reliance on Wall Street Journal article satisfies requirement).

6. *See, e.g., In re Bank of New York Derivative Litigation,* 320 F.3d 291, 298 (2d Cir.2003) (requiring plaintiff to own stock *"throughout* the course of the activities that constitute the *primary basis* of the complaint;" rejecting use of continuing wrong doctrine to expand definition of transaction; holding that plaintiff need not have owned stock during "the entire course of all relevants," but plaintiff must have owned stock "before the case of the allegedly wrongful conduct transpired"); *Rosenbaum v. MacAllister,* 64 F.3d 1439, 1443 n. 2 (10th Cir. 1995) (explaining requirements of contemporaneous ownership and continuing ownership; also identifying one exception to those requirements).

7. *See, e.g., Johnson v. United States,* 317 F.3d 1331, 1333–34 (Fed. Cir.2003)

(plaintiff who loses shareholder status through bankruptcy proceeding while instant lawsuit was pending loses standing upon cancellation of shares); *Schilling v. Belcher,* 582 F.2d 995, 999 (5th Cir.1978) ("It is generally held that the ownership requirement continues throughout the life of the suit and that the action will abate if the plaintiff ceases to be a shareholder before the litigation ends.").

8. *See, e.g., Kona Enterprises, Inc. v. Estate of Bishop,* 179 F.3d 767, 769 (9th Cir.1999) (holding that standing requirement of Rule 23.1 "is procedural in nature and thus applicable in diversity actions"). *But see Fagin v. Gilmartin,* 432 F.3d 276, 285 (3d Cir.2005) ("The question of whether the plaintiff is a 'shareholder' is determined by state law."); *Batchelder v. Kawamoto,* 147 F.3d 915, 917–18 (9th Cir. 1998) (where choice of law clause provided that Japanese law governed rights of interest holders, neither Rule 23.1 nor state law applied).

Pleading With Particularity

Rule 23.1 requires that certain allegations of the shareholder derivative complaint be pleaded with particularity. This means that the plaintiff must provide additional factual detail that is not normally required under the "notice pleading" policy of the Federal Rules. The requirement of particularity is usually satisfied without difficulty by plaintiffs who simply explain the facts behind their conclusory allegation.[9]

Explanation of Efforts to Encourage Corporation to Protect Its Own Interest

Rule 23.1 requires that a plaintiff allege in the complaint, "with particularity," the following facts: (1) the efforts plaintiff made, if any, to encourage those who control the corporation—shareholders, officers and/or directors—to take action; and (2) the reasons why the efforts were unsuccessful, or reasons why no effort was made.[10]

Demand: Futility

Rule 23.1 requires the plaintiff to make a demand on the corporate officers to pursue the suit. The facts of this demand must be pleaded with particularity.[11] However, plaintiffs are not entitled to discovery to establish the particular facts underlying an allegation of futility.[12]

The requirement that the plaintiff demand that the corporation bring the lawsuit may be waived, however, if it is clear from the facts of a case that such a demand would be clearly futile. Rule 23.1 requires the plaintiff to plead with particularity the facts establishing futility, but the standard by which the facts are evaluated is a matter of state law.[13]

---

9. *See, e.g., In re Abbott Laboratories Derivative Shareholders Litigation,* 325 F.3d 795, 804 (7th Cir.2003) (holding requirement satisfied when "[a]lthough plaintiffs have a conclusory paragraph in their claim of demand futility, they have also incorporated all of the detailed factual allegations"); *Stepak v. Addison,* 20 F.3d 398, 400 (11th Cir.1994)(mere allegation that law firm was "conflicted" did not satisfy requirement of particularity in Rule 23.1; but allegations that law firm defended corporate officers in criminal matters related to plaintiff's demand, and then gave advice to board about demand, satisfied requirement).

10. *Id.* at 402 (Rule 23.1 imposes "more stringent pleading requirements" than Rules 8 and 12(b)(6)). *See, e.g., Frank v. Hadesman and Frank, Inc.,* 83 F.3d 158 (7th Cir.1996) (noting plaintiff's duty to make demand on corporate board to pursue claim).

11. *See, e.g., In re Abbott Laboratories Derivative Shareholders Litigation,* 325

F.3d 795, 804 (7th Cir.2003) (holding requirement satisfied when "[a]lthough plaintiffs have a conclusory paragraph in their claim of demand futility, they have also incorporated all of the detailed factual allegations"); *Starrels v. First National Bank of Chicago,* 870 F.2d 1168, 1171 (7th Cir. 1989)(conclusory allegations adequate for standard notice pleading may not meet particularity requirements of Rule 23.1).

12. *See, e.g., In re Merck & Co. Securities, Derivative & ERISA Litigation,* 493 F.3d 393 (3d Cir. 2007) (if discovery was allowed, "shareholder plaintiffs [would] have incentive to make baseless allegations and then engage in discovery fishing expeditions").

13. *Kamen v. Kemper Financial Services, Inc.,* 500 U.S. 90, 111 S.Ct. 1711, 114 L.Ed.2d 152 (1991)(Rule 23.1 controls adequacy of pleadings. State law controls substantive standard). *See, e.g., McCall v. Scott,* 239 F.3d 808, 816 (6th Cir.2001) (demand may be excused "because either the

Special Litigation Committees

When officers of a business entity are faced with a Rule 23.1 demand to pursue a lawsuit, a typical response has been to appoint a special litigation committee to investigate the matter. In that circumstance courts will usually grant a request to stay proceedings in the derivative action until the committee can make a report recommending a course of action, *e.g.*, terminate the litigation, take it over, or authorize the original plaintiff to continue it. The court has authority to accept or reject the recommendation.[14]

Adequacy of Representation

The plaintiff in a shareholder derivative suit must be a person who will adequately represent the best interests of those—the corporation and other shareholders—on whose behalf the suit is prosecuted.[15] Perhaps because Rule 23.1 derivative suits present fewer of the case management problems associated with Rule 23 class actions, the courts seem less concerned in derivative suits with the quality and experience of the plaintiff's counsel.[16]

RULE 23.1(c). SETTLEMENT, DISMISSAL, AND COMPROMISE

CORE CONCEPT

Rule 23.1(c) provides that any settlement of a derivative action is subject to the court's approval. It also establishes a notice requirement for such settlements.

directors were incapable of making an impartial decision, or the directors wrongfully refused a demand to sue"). *See also, Boland v. Engle,* 113 F.3d 706 (7th Cir.1997) (state law determines whether demand would be futile, but Rule 23.1 requires plaintiff to provide court with information sufficient to determine whether demand is futile); *In re Evergreen Mutual Funds Fee Litigation,* 423 F.Supp.2d 249, 262–63 (S.D.N.Y.2006) (holding that none of the following, if proved, are sufficient to establish demand futility: selection of trustee by a person who would also be a defendant in the case; membership on multiple boards; substantial compensation for service (unless compensation is not justified); threat of personal liability if trustee approves lawsuit).

14. *See, e.g., Strougo v. Padegs,* 986 F.Supp. 812, 814 (S.D.N.Y.1997) (explaining process and noting courts' awareness of special litigation committee's potential bias toward protecting corporate board and officers).

15. *But see Powers v. Eichen,* 229 F.3d 1249, 1254 (9th Cir.2000) (concluding that Rule 23.1 does not offer as much protection as Rule 23; "Unlike . . . Rule 23, in shareholder derivative suits under Rule 23.1, a preliminary affirmative determination that the named plaintiffs will fairly and adequately represent the interests of the other class members is not a prerequisite to the maintenance of the action. Rather, the rule provides only that the derivative suit may not be maintained if it appears that the named shareholder does not fairly and adequately represent the other shareholders. . . . In addition, there is no opt-out provision in shareholder derivative suits. Thus, all shareholders are bound by the outcome regardless of their objections."[internal quotation marks omitted]).

16. *Cf., In re Sonus Networks, Inc. Shareholder Derivative Litigation,* 422 F.Supp.2d 281, 292 (D.Mass.2006) (inadequate representation, including fraud or collusion, will vitiate attempt to impose res judicata; however, allegation of mere failure to raise additional facts does not, by itself, constitute inadequate representation).

Settlement Subject to Court Approval

Derivative suits may not be dismissed or settled without prior judicial approval. The district court enjoys broad, but not totally unfettered, discretion to evaluate a proposed settlement.[17] In determining whether to approve a settlement, the court may consider the reaction of persons, such as other shareholders, who will be affected by the outcome of the case.[18] In theory, the court should not rewrite a proposed settlement, but should limit itself to approving or disapproving the proposal.[19] In practice, courts have substantial ability to influence the contents of a settlement by indicating what the court deems a satisfactory compromise.

Notice of Settlement

Rule 23.1 requires that the court will order notice of voluntary dismissals or proposed settlements to interested persons. The court has substantial discretion, within the circumstances of the particular case, to determine the manner in which notification will occur.[20]

Bond Requirements

Many states require that plaintiffs in derivative suits post bonds, from which the defendants will be compensated for litigation expenses if the defendants prevail. Rule 23.1 contains no such requirement. In diversity suits, however, it is settled that federal courts will enforce requirements established under state law.[21]

Numerosity Requirements

Rule 23.1 does not require that the plaintiff represent any number of similarly situated persons. Thus it will often be to the advantage of a shareholder who is one among a small group of similarly situated people to file a derivative action, rather than try to file a class action, which requires a greater number of plaintiffs.

ADDITIONAL RESEARCH REFERENCES

Wright & Miller, *Federal Practice and Procedure* §§ 1821–41.

C.J.S. Corporations §§ 397–413; Federal Civil Procedure §§ 84–91, 139, 149, 298.

West's Key No. Digests, Corporations ☞202–214.

17. *See, e.g., McDannold v. Star Bank, N.A.,* 261 F.3d 478, 488 (6th Cir.2001) (district court "enjoys wide discretion in evaluating the settlement of derivative actions").

18. *See, e.g., Bell Atlantic Corp. v. Bolger,* 2 F.3d 1304 (3d Cir.1993)("We also consider the response of other shareholders to the lawsuit.").

19. *See, e.g., United Founders Life Insurance Co. v. Consumers National Life Insurance Co.,* 447 F.2d 647, 655 (7th Cir. 1971)("The business judgment of the court is not to be substituted for that of the parties.").

20. *See, e.g., Kyriazi v. Western Electric Co.,* 647 F.2d 388, 395 (3d Cir. 1981)(manner of notification within court's discretion, provided notice satisfies dues process).

21. *Cohen v. Beneficial Industrial Loan Corp.,* 337 U.S. 541, 69 S.Ct. 1221, 93 L.Ed. 1528 (1949)(state bond requirement applicable to diversity suit); *Fagin v. Gilmartin,* 432 F.3d 276, 285 (3d Cir.2005) (same).

RULE 23.2

ACTIONS RELATING TO UNINCORPORATED ASSOCIATIONS

This rule applies to an action brought by or against the members of an unincorporated association as a class by naming certain members as representative parties. The action may be maintained only if it appears that those parties will fairly and adequately protect the interests of the association and its members. In conducting the action, the court may issue any appropriate orders corresponding with those in Rule 23(d), and the procedure for settlement, voluntary dismissal, or compromise must correspond with the procedure in Rule 23(e).

[Added effective July 1, 1966; April 30, 2007, effective December 1, 2007.]

─────────── **2007 AMENDMENTS ROADMAP** ───────────

STYLE PROJECT CHANGES: Minor stylistic changes were made.

NON-STYLE CHANGES: None.

NOTE: The Federal Rules "Style Project" is explained in Part III-A.

AUTHORS' COMMENTARY ON RULE 23.2

─────────── **PURPOSE AND SCOPE** ───────────

Rule 23.2 extends some of the procedural protections of class actions under Rule 23 and shareholder derivative suits under Rule 23.1 to members of unincorporated associations who are sued through representatives, or on whose behalf representatives have initiated suit. The three rules all address situations where persons will be affected by the outcome of suits without necessarily having an opportunity to participate fully in litigation. Rule 23.2 is devoted to ensuring that representatives of the unincorporated association's membership adequately represent the interest of the entire membership.

NOTE: Rule 23.2 does not *create* a right for representatives of an unincorporated association to sue or be sued. Rather, it governs such a suit when the applicable state or federal law provides a cause of action by or against the unincorporated association, but does not permit suit by or against the association as an entity.[1]

APPLICATIONS

Fair and Adequate Representation

The court's first concern is to ascertain whether the interests of the unincorporated association's representatives conflict with those of the association or its membership. However, the case law is divided as to whether an association's representatives in a Rule 23.2 case must meet the standards developed for adequate class representation in Rule 23(a), governing class actions.[2]

Orders Regulating Proceedings

Rule 23.2 explicitly incorporates Rule 23(d), governing the court's power to issue orders in the course of class action litigation. Because the court's authority under Rule 23(d) is broad, the effect of this incorporation is to give the trial court greater discretion to issue orders ensuring both the efficient processing of the case and substantial protection for passive members of the unincorporated association. Elements of Rule 23(d) should therefore also be consulted in the course of applying Rule 23.2.

Approval of Settlement

Rule 23.2 also explicitly incorporates Rule 23(e), which provides a court substantial authority to approve or disapprove settlements in class actions. As a practical matter, the effect is to require not only consultation of Rule 23(e), but also strong consideration of the possibility of inviting the trial judge to participate in settlement discussions whenever the discussions have advanced sufficiently to make participation practicable.

Numerosity

Rule 23.2 contains no requirement that the membership of the unincorporated association rise above some minimum number.[3] Nevertheless, counsel should investigate local precedent before proceeding with a Rule 23.2 action.

---

1. *See, e.g., Northbrook Excess and Surplus Insurance Co. v. Medical Malpractice Joint Underwriting Ass'n of Massachusetts,* 900 F.2d 476, 477 (1st Cir.1990)("Rule 23.2 provides a mechanism by which an association may sue or be sued through a representative where state law prevents the association from doing so in its own name."). *Cf., Benn v. Seventh–Day Adventist Church,* 304 F.Supp.2d 716, 723 (D.Md.2004) (most courts hold that where state law permits suit by unincorporated association as an entity, "Rule 23.2 is unavailable.").

2. *Compare Gravenstein v. Campion,* 96 F.R.D. 137, 140 (D.Alaska 1982)(Rule 23 requirements applied to Rule 23.2 lawsuit) *with* [*Curley v. Brignoli, Curley & Roberts Associates,* 915 F.2d 81, 86 (2d Cir.1990) (requirements of Rule 23(a) do not apply to cases proceeding under Rule 23.2)].

3. *See, e.g., Curley v. Brignoli, Curley & Roberts Associates,* 915 F.2d 81, 86 (2d Cir. 1990) (numerosity and other prerequisites of Rule 23(a) inapplicable in Rule 23.2 case).

Citizenship for Diversity Jurisdiction

Where an unincorporated association may sue or be sued through representatives, the established practice is to determine diversity by examining the citizenship of the representatives.[4] Thus, an unincorporated association often can create diversity jurisdiction by selecting a representative who is a citizen of a different state from the defendants (provided that the amount in controversy exceeds $75,000, exclusive of interest and costs).

Amount in Controversy

The prevailing practice in federal district courts is to determine the amount in controversy by examining the individual claims of the membership of the unincorporated association. This approach creates a substantial hurdle to achieving diversity jurisdiction. Thus, if an unincorporated association has a claim for $1,000,000, the claim would appear to exceed the more–than–$75,000 requirement by a safe margin. If, however, the association has 10,000 members, and each member has an equal share in the aggregate claim of $1,000,000, the value of the suit to each member is only one hundred dollars—well short of the threshold for diversity jurisdiction.

ADDITIONAL RESEARCH REFERENCES

Wright & Miller, *Federal Practice and Procedure* § 1861.

C.J.S. Associations §§ 8, 40–48, 51–53; Federal Civil Procedure §§ 76–93.

West's Key No. Digests, Associations ☞20(1); Federal Civil Procedure ☞186.5.

---

4. *See, e.g., Aetna Casualty & Surety Co. v. Iso–Tex, Inc.,* 75 F.3d 216, 218 (5th Cir. 1996)(diversity tested by looking to citizenship of named representatives); *Murray v. Scott,* 176 F.Supp.2d 1249 (M.D.Ala.2001) (same).

RULE 24

INTERVENTION

(a) Intervention of Right. On timely motion, the court must permit anyone to intervene who:

(1) is given an unconditional right to intervene by a federal statute; or

(2) claims an interest relating to the property or transaction that is the subject of the action, and is so situated that disposing of the action may as a practical matter impair or impede the movant's ability to protect its interest, unless existing parties adequately represent that interest.

(b) Permissive Intervention.

(1) *In General.* On timely motion, the court may permit anyone to intervene who:

(A) is given a conditional right to intervene by a federal statute; or

(B) has a claim or defense that shares with the main action a common question of law or fact.

(2) *By a Government Officer or Agency.* On timely motion, the court may permit a federal or state governmental officer or agency to intervene if a party's claim or defense is based on:

(A) a statute or executive order administered by the officer or agency; or

(B) any regulation, order, requirement, or agreement issued or made under the statute or executive order.

(3) *Delay or Prejudice.* In exercising its discretion, the court must consider whether the intervention will unduly delay or prejudice the adjudication of the original parties' rights.

(c) Notice and Pleading Required. A motion to intervene must be served on the parties as provided in Rule 5. The motion must state the grounds for intervention and be accompanied by a pleading that sets out the claim or defense for which intervention is sought.

[Amended effective March 19, 1948; October 20, 1949; July 1, 1963; July 1, 1966; August 1, 1987; December 1, 1991; April 12, 2006, effective December 1, 2006; April 30, 2007, effective December 1, 2007.]

--------------- **2007 AMENDMENTS ROADMAP** ---------------

STYLE PROJECT CHANGES: Minor language and organizational changes were made in all three subsections of Rule 24.

NON-STYLE CHANGES: The last sentence of Rule 24(c), providing that the procedure for filing and serving motions is the same without regard to the specific portion of Rule 24(a) or (b) that is being used to authorize intervention, was deleted as unnecessary.

NOTE: The Federal Rules "Style Project" is explained in Part III-A.

AUTHORS' COMMENTARY ON RULE 24

--------------- **PURPOSE AND SCOPE** ---------------

Rule 24 governs situations in which persons not already parties may intervene in existing litigation. Unlike most Rule 19 situations, where persons who are already parties seek to serve process on non-parties and conscript them into the litigation, in most Rule 24 situations the non-party seeks to join in litigation to which the non-party was not previously invited. Rule 24 attempts to balance the interest of the person seeking intervention with the burdens such intervention may impose on parties to pending suits. The Rule divides intervenors into two basic groups: those seeking intervention as of right under Rule 24(a); and those who seek the court's permission to intervene under Rule 24(b). Notwithstanding the terminology of those two portions of Rule 24, the court enjoys substantial discretion when deciding whether to permit intervention under either Rule 24(a) or Rule 24(b). There remain, however, important distinctions in the factors courts consider in exercising discretion under Rule 24(a) and Rule 24(b). Finally, while cases granting applications to intervene often declare that intervention provisions are to be construed liberally,[1] the application of Rule 24 to particular motions is not always as generous as such general statements might suggest.

NOTE: Rule 24 is another Rule that was changed substantially in 1966, thereby making much of the case law decided prior to that time unreliable.

---

1. *See, e.g., South Dakota v. United States Department of Interior,* 317 F.3d 783, 785 (8th Cir.2003) ("... Rule 24 should be liberally construed with all doubts resolved in favor of the proposed intervenor.").

RULE 24(a). INTERVENTION OF RIGHT

CORE CONCEPT

Rule 24(a) identifies two distinct circumstances in which a person may be entitled to intervene in pending litigation: where a federal statute confers a right to intervene; and where the intervenor is able to satisfy all elements for intervention as of right.[2]

APPLICATIONS

Intervenor's Choice

There is no obligation to intervene. If the requirements of intervention are met, the decision to intervene rests with the potential intervenor.[3]

Timing

Rule 24(a) explicitly imposes a "timeliness" requirement on motions to intervene.[4] However, unlike timing elements in some other Federal Rules, the actual time limits are not set out in Rule 24(a).[5] Generally speaking, courts weigh four factors in determining timeliness: (1) length of delay in seeking intervention;[6] (2) prejudicial impact of such delay on existing parties;[7] (3) prejudice to intervenor if intervention is denied; and (4) other factors affecting fairness in an individual case.[8] Thus, courts enjoy substantial discretion to make very fact-specific rulings on the timeliness of a

2. *See, e.g., United States v. City of New York,* 198 F.3d 360, 364 (2d Cir.1999) (movant must satisfy timeliness plus three elements enumerated in Rule 23(a)(2)). *See also Martin v. Wilks,* 490 U.S. 755, 109 S.Ct. 2180, 104 L.Ed.2d 835 (1989) (Rule 24 does not require intervention; it is permissive in nature, not mandatory; drawing contrast with Rule 19).

3. *See, e.g., Kourtis v. Cameron,* 419 F.3d 989 (9th Cir.2005) ("There is no duty of mandatory intervention imposed upon nonparties, and the decision not to intervene thus does not expose a nonparty to the earlier proceedings' preclusive effects."),

4. *See, e.g., Associated Builders & Contractors, Inc. v. Herman,* 166 F.3d 1248, 1257 (D.C.Cir.1999) ("If the motion was not timely, there is no need for the court to address the other factors that enter into an intervention analysis.").

5. *See, e.g., Heaton v. Monogram Credit Card Bank of Georgia,* 297 F.3d 416 (5th Cir.2002) ("There are no absolute measures of timeliness; it is determined from all the circumstances."); *United States v. Washington,* 86 F.3d 1499, 1503 (9th Cir. 1996)("[A]ny substantial lapse of time weighs heavily against intervention."); *At-*

lantic Mutual Insurance Co. v. Northwest Airlines, Inc., 24 F.3d 958, 961 (7th Cir. 1994)(timeliness means intervenor applicant must "act with dispatch").

6. *See, e.g., League of United Latin American Citizens v. Wilson,* 131 F.3d 1297, 1302 (9th Cir.1997) (27 month delay in moving to intervene makes intervention motion "an uphill battle").

7. *Cf., Effjohn International Cruise Holdings, Inc. v. A&L Sales, Inc.,* 346 F.3d 552, 561 (5th Cir.2003) (noting prejudice factor, but explaining, "[t]he inquiry for this factor is whether other parties were prejudiced *by the delay,* not whether they would be prejudiced *by the addition of the claim* (obviously, in the sense that they may obtain less, existing parties are always prejudiced by new claims) [emphasis in original]").

8. *See, e.g., MasterCard Intern. Inc. v. Visa Intern. Service Ass'n, Inc.,* 471 F.3d 377, 390–391 (2nd Cir.2006) (motion to intervene as of right in breach of contract suit was untimely where movant waited until the eve of preliminary injunctive hearing and delay would prejudice existing parties); *Heaton v. Monogram Credit Card Bank of*

Rule 24(a) motion.[9] An initial decision to reject intervention on grounds of lack of timeliness is rarely disturbed on appeal.[10] This is probably the most important kind of discretion courts possess when considering applications to intervene under Rule 24(a).

"Collateral Purpose" Exception

Some courts modify the timeliness requirement of Rule 24(a) when the purpose of the intervention application is only to modify, e.g., an existing protective order.[11] This view has not been adopted in all circuits,[12] and lawyers must consult the local precedent.

Subject Matter Jurisdiction

When a person seeks to intervene as of right, subject matter jurisdiction may be established either through an independent basis of jurisdiction (such as diversity of citizenship[13] or federal question jurisdiction[14]) or through supplemental jurisdiction.[15] However, in

Georgia, 297 F.3d 416 (5th Cir.2002); *see also, Associated Builders & Contractors, Inc. v. Herman*, 166 F.3d 1248, 1257 (D.C.Cir.1999) (unexplained failure to take clear opportunity to intervene at trial is ground for denying intervention after judgment); *Arrow v. Gambler's Supply, Inc.*, 55 F.3d 407 (8th Cir.1995)(weighing: (1) how far litigation had proceeded; (2) intervenor's prior knowledge of case; (3) reason for any delay in seeking intervention; and (4) risk of prejudice to parties. *See also Roeder v. Islamic Republic of Iran*, 333 F.3d 228, 233 (D.C. Cir.2003) (timeliness measured from point at which intervenor knew or should have know interest was directly at stake in litigation); *Jordan v. Michigan Conference of Teamsters Welfare Fund*, 207 F.3d 854, 862 (6th Cir.2000) (timeliness evaluated through five factors: "1) the point to which the suit has progressed; 2) the purpose for which the intervention is sought; 3) the length of time preceding the application during which the proposed intervenor knew or reasonably should have known of his interest in the case; 4) the prejudice to the original parties due to the proposed intervenor's failure, after he knew or reasonably should have known of his interest in the case, to apply promptly for intervention; and 5) the existence of unusual circumstances militating against or in favor of intervention;" denying intervention after judgment when intervention should have been sought earlier). *See also Acree v. Republic of Iraq*, 370 F.3d 41, 49 (D.C. Cir. 2004) ("Courts are generally reluctant to permit intervention after a suit has proceeded to final judgment, particularly where the applicant had the opportunity to intervene prior to judgment."). *But cf., Associat-*

ed Builders and Contractors, Saginaw Valley Area Chapter v. Perry, 115 F.3d 386 (6th Cir.1997) (original party's decision not to appeal may create grounds for intervention even after trial court's decision).

9. *See, e.g., Edwards v. City of Houston*, 37 F.3d 1097 (5th Cir.1994)(held, intervention in district court was properly denied, but intervention for appeal should be granted). *But see Elliott Industries Limited Partnership v. BP American Production Co.*, 407 F.3d 1091, 1103 (10th Cir.2005) ("[I]ntervention on appeal will be permitted 'only in an exceptional case for imperative reasons.' "); *Acree v. Republic of Iraq*, 370 F.3d 41, 49 (D.C. Cir.2004) ("Courts are generally reluctant to permit intervention after a suit has proceeded to final judgment, particularly where the applicant had the opportunity to intervene prior to judgment.").

10. *See, e.g., Caterino v. Barry*, 922 F.2d 37, 40 (1st Cir.1990)(trial court entitled to "substantive deference" on timeliness).

11. *See, e.g., United Nuclear Corp. v. Cranford Insurance Co.*, 905 F.2d 1424, 1427 (10th Cir.1990). *See also Pansy v. Borough of Stroudsburg*, 23 F.3d 772, 780 n. 9 (3d Cir.1994).

12. *See, e.g., Empire Blue Cross & Blue Shield of Connecticut, Inc. v. Janet Greeson's A Place for Us, Inc.*, 62 F.3d 1217, 1221 (9th Cir.1995); *Banco Popular de Puerto Rico v. Greenblatt*, 964 F.2d 1227, 1230–34 (1st Cir.1992) (refusing to modify timeliness requirement for limited purpose motion).

13. 28 U.S.C.A. § 1332.

14. 28 U.S.C.A. § 1331.

15. 28 U.S.C.A. § 1367.

circumstances where the basis for subject matter jurisdiction in the underlying case is diversity of citizenship and the intervening person is not diverse from the parties on the other side of the case, the availability of supplemental jurisdiction depends on whether the would-be intervenor will be aligned as a plaintiff or a defendant. If the intervenor will be a plaintiff, it is probable that the intervenor will not be able to employ supplemental jurisdiction.[16] If, on the other hand, the intervenor will be aligned as a defendant, supplemental jurisdiction will normally be available.[17] Where a party who is dispensable under Rule 19 and is also nondiverse seeks to intervene under Rule 24, diversity jurisdiction is not necessarily defeated.[18]

Where the original basis for jurisdiction in the underlying case is a federal question, the problem resolves itself in a more straightforward manner. In those situations, supplemental jurisdiction is routinely available without regard to the intervenor's status as a plaintiff or defendant.[19]

Subject matter jurisdiction is discussed at greater length elsewhere in this text.

Personal Jurisdiction

When a person attempts to intervene under Rule 24, that person submits to the jurisdiction of the court.[20]

Statutory Right Narrowly Construed

Rule 24(a)(1) explicitly defers to any other federal statute that confers on qualifying persons an unconditional right to intervene in pending litigation. If applicants for statutory intervention demon-

---

16. 28 U.S.C.A. § 1367(b) (in cases where original basis of jurisdiction is diversity and person intervening under Rule 24 will be aligned as a plaintiff, supplemental jurisdiction is not available). *Exxon Mobil Corp. v. Allapattah Services, Inc.*, 545 U.S. 546, ___, 125 S.Ct. 2611, 2621, 162 L.Ed.2d 502 (2005) ("Section 1367(b) withholds supplemental jurisdiction over the claims of plaintiffs who seek to intervene pursuant to Rule 24."). *But cf., Aurora Loan Services, Inc. v. Craddieth*, 442 F.3d 1018, 1025 (7th Cir.2006) (in diversity cases supplemental jurisdiction normally not available to intervenor plaintiffs; but prohibition on use of supplemental jurisdiction inapplicable where a person is "forced to intervene to protect an interest that arose during the course of a federal litigation in which he had no stake at the outset").

17. *Exxon Mobil Corp. v. Allapattah Services, Inc.*, 545 U.S. 546, ___, 125 S.Ct. 2611, 2621, 162 L.Ed.2d 502 (2005) (noting that 28 U.S.C.A. § 1367(b) does not prohib-

it use of supplemental jurisdiction in such circumstances).

18. *In re Olympic Mills Corp.*, 477 F.3d 1, 12 (1st Cir.2007) (in bankruptcy case, court reviewed case law and concluded "the weight of authority holds that claims launched by necessary but dispensable, nondiverse defendant-intervenors do not defeat the original jurisdiction (diversity) that obtained at the commencement of the action").

19. *See, e.g., Grace United Methodist Church v. City of Cheyenne*, 451 F.3d 643, 672–73 (10th Cir.2006) (for intervention of right in case originally based on federal question jurisdiction, supplemental jurisdiction is sufficient and no independent basis of jurisdiction is require).

20. *See, e.g., County Security Agency v. Ohio Department of Commerce*, 296 F.3d 477 (6th Cir.2002) (refusing to permit reservation of objections to jurisdiction made by petitioning intervenor; "a motion to intervene is fundamentally incompatible with an objection to personal jurisdiction").

strate a right to intervene under Rule 24(a)(1), they "need not show inadequacy of representation or that their interests may be impaired if not allowed to intervene" as is required for intervention under Rule 24(a)(2).[21] However, the case law demonstrates a clear judicial tendency to construe statutory intervention rights narrowly.[22] As a practical result, persons seeking to intervene under Rule 24(a) should routinely consider arguing for intervention under the "interest" test of Rule 24(a)(2)—even in circumstances where they believe they might qualify for intervention as a statutory right under Rule 24(a)(1).[23]

Amicus Curiae Briefs

There may appear to be a superficial similarity between the process of intervention and the opportunity to file an amicus curiae brief. However, courts do not equate amicus status with the rights and responsibilities of a party joined through intervention.[24]

Denying Intervention of Right—Standard of Review

On issues of the timeliness of intervention, as mentioned above, district courts enjoy substantial discretion. However, as to other substantive requirements for intervention under Rule 24(a), there is a split of authority in the courts of appeal as to the proper standard of review. Some appellate courts use a *de novo* standard;[25] others

---

21. *Ruiz v. Estelle,* 161 F.3d 814, 828 (5th Cir.1998) ("Under Rule 24(a)(1), intervenors need not even prove a 'sufficient' interest relating to the subject matter of the controversy, since Congress has already declared that interest sufficient by granting the statutory right to intervene." However, statutory intervention is still subject to a determination of timeliness, over which the district court enjoys substantial discretion.). *See also Newdow v. United States Congress,* 313 F.3d 495, 497 (9th Cir.2002) (statute granting right to intervene in instant case also imposes requirement of timely application).

22. *See, e.g., Equal Employment Opportunity Commission v. American Telephone and Telegraph Co.,* 506 F.2d 735 (3d Cir. 1974); *see also, Phar-Mor, Inc. v. Coopers & Lybrand,* 22 F.3d 1228, 1232 (3d Cir. 1994) ("[C]ourts have construed Rule 24(a)(1) narrowly; these courts have been reluctant to interpret statutes to grant an unconditional right to intervene to private parties."); *Haspel & Davis Milling & Planting Co. Ltd. v. Board Of Levee,* 493 F.3d 570 (5th Cir.2007) (State of Louisiana did not have unconditional right to intervene under 28 U.S.C. § 2403(b) because case did not challenge constitutionality of state constitution; also denied State's motion to intervene as a matter of right pursuant to

under Rule 24(a)(2) as interest was protected by party to litigation).

23. *Cf., Yorkshire v. United States,* 26 F.3d 942, 944 (9th Cir.1994) (Rule 24(a)(2) "is construed broadly in favor of the applicants").

24. *See, e.g., United States v. City of Los Angeles,* 288 F.3d 391, 400 (9th Cir. 2002) ("'[A]micus status is insufficient to protect the [petitioner for intervention's] rights because such status does not allow the [petitioner] to raise issues or arguments formally and gives it no right of appeal."); *Coalition of Arizona/New Mexico Counties for Stable Economic Growth v. Department of the Interior,* 100 F.3d 837, 844 (10th Cir.1996) ("[T]he right to file a brief as amicus curiae is no substitute for the right to intervene as a party in the action under Rule 24(a)(2).").

25. *See, e.g., Haspel & Davis Milling & Planting Co. Ltd. v. Board Of Levee,* 493 F.3d 570 (5th Cir.2007); *Sierra Club, Inc. v. Leavitt,* 488 F.3d 904, 909–910 (11th Cir. 2007); *Medical Liability Mutual. Ins. Co. v. Alan Curtis LLC,* 485 F.3d 1006, 1008 (8th Cir.2007); *United States v. BDO Seidman,* 337 F.3d 802 (7th Cir.2003) (applying de novo standard to all requirements but timeliness requirement); *Alameda Water & Sanitation District v. Browner,* 9 F.3d 88, 89

apply an "abuse of discretion" standard;[26] and sometimes a combination of the standards is employed.[27] Where applied, the *de novo* standard is less deferential to the decision of the district court.

Right to Intervene Based on Interest in Litigation

The right to intervene under Rule 24(a)(2) exists only when the court holds that a person seeking intervention has established three elements: (1) an interest in the subject matter of the pending litigation; (2) a substantial risk that the litigation will impair the interest; and (3) existing parties do not adequately protect that interest. These three elements are *not* weighing factors. *All* must be satisfied before an applicant may exercise a right to intervene under Rule 24(a)(2).[28]

Interest in the Subject Matter

The definition of an "interest" that satisfies Rule 24(a)(2) is unclear.[29] It is at least reasonably clear that a person who has an interest that by itself could be a case or controversy will meet the requirement of Rule 24(a)(2).[30] An economic interest in the subject

(10th Cir.1993)(acknowledging split of authority and applying *de novo* standard).

26. *See, e.g., DSI Associates LLC v. U.S.*, 496 F.3d 175 (2nd Cir.2007) (applying abuse of discretion standard to intervention of right and permissive intervention); *In re Sierra Club*, 945 F.2d 776, 779 (4th Cir. 1991)(explicitly adopting "abuse of discretion" standard). *But cf., Public Service Co. of New Hampshire v. Patch*, 136 F.3d 197, 204 (1st Cir.1998) (using abuse of discretion standard, but "discretion is more circumscribed when Rule 24(a) is in play").

27. *See, e.g., Northland Family Planning Clinic, Inc. v. Cox*, 487 F.3d 323, 344 (6th Cir.2007) (timeliness reviewed for abuse of discretion; other factors reviewed *de novo*); *Vollmer v. Publishers Clearing House & Campus Subscriptions, Inc.*, 248 F.3d 698, 705 (7th Cir.2001)(timeliness reviewed for abuse of discretion; other factors reviewed *de novo*).

28. *See, e.g., Purcell v. BankAtlantic Financial Corp.*, 85 F.3d 1508 (11th Cir.1996), *cert. denied*, 519 U.S. 867, 117 S.Ct. 178, 136 L.Ed.2d 118 (1996)(citing three requirements, plus timeliness); *Americans United for Separation of Church and State v. City of Grand Rapids*, 922 F.2d 303, 305 (6th Cir.1990)(intervenor must satisfy all elements). *But cf., Ross v. Marshall*, 426 F.3d 745, 753 (5th Cir.2005) (acknowledging that all elements must be met, but examination should be flexible and non-technical; "Intervention should generally be allowed where 'no one would be hurt and greater justice could be attained.' ").

29. *See, e.g., Utahns for Better Transportation v. United States Department of Transportation*, 295 F.3d 1111 (10th Cir. 2002) ("The sufficiency of an applicant's interest is a highly fact-specific determination." Also noting that "[t]here is some value in having the parties before the court so that they will be bound by the result."); *Daggett v. Commission on Governmental Ethics & Election Practices*, 172 F.3d 104, 110 (1st Cir.1999) (noting that narrow reading of interest is disfavored, "although clear outer boundaries have yet to be developed"); *United Keetoowah Band of Cherokee Indians of Okla. v. U.S.*, 480 F.3d 1318 (C.A.Fed.2007) (court held that interest satisfying Rule 24(a)(2) can not be contingent but must be of such a direct and immediate character that the party will either gain or lose by the direct legal operation and effect of the judgment; the holding is dicta as the case is decided under Rule 19).

30. *See, e.g., Aurora Loan Services, Inc. v. Craddieth*, 442 F.3d 1018, 1022 (7th Cir. 2006) ("[T]he applicant's interest must be one on which an independent federal suit could be based, consistent with Article III's requirement that only a case or controversy can be litigated in a federal court at any stage of the proceeding."). *But see Solid Waste Agency of Northern Cook County v. United States Army Corps of Engineers*, 101 F.3d 503, 507 (7th Cir.1996) ("The strongest case for intervention is not where the aspirant for intervention could file an independent suit, but where the intervenor-aspirant has no claim against the defendant

matter of the litigation may satisfy this element of the Rule.[31] A substantial privacy interest has also been found sufficient.[32] Also, if the intervening party will be legally bound by the judgment in the pending litigation, an "interest" exists that satisfies Rule 24(a)(2).[33] Other cases construe the concept of "interest" more broadly, including precedent allowing parents of schoolchildren to intervene in litigation affecting the resources available to certain schools.[34]

yet a legally protected interest that could be impaired by the suit.").

31. *See, e.g., Fund For Animals, Inc. v. Norton,* 322 F.3d 728, 733 (D.C.Cir.2003) (interest of foreign government agency in protecting flow of tourist dollars meets interest requirement of Rule 24(a)); *Utahns for Better Transportation v. United States Department of Transportation,* 295 F.3d 1111 (10th Cir.2002) ("The threat of economic injury from the outcome of the litigation undoubtedly gives a petitioner the requisite interest."); *United States v. Peoples Benefit Life Insurance Co.,* 271 F.3d 411, 416 (2d Cir.2001) (constructive trust may sometimes be sufficient interest to support intervention in forfeiture case, but not when property to be forfeited is not traceable to trust; also noting other facts that distinguish this case from constructive trust cases in which court permitted intervention); *Sierra Club v. Espy,* 18 F.3d 1202, 1207 (5th Cir.1994)(citing economic interest for intervention). *But see, Medical Liability Mutual Ins. Co. v. Alan Curtis LLC,* 485 F.3d 1006, 1008 (8th Cir.2007) (held that an economic interest in the outcome of the litigation was not itself sufficient to warrant mandatory intervention and denied intervention where only interest was to ensure sufficient resources to satisfy would-be intervenor's claim); *Mt. Hawley Insurance Co. v. Sandy Lake Properties, Inc.,* 425 F.3d 1308, 1311 (11th Cir.2005) ("legally protectable interest" is "more than an economic interest"); *Montana v. Environmental Protection Agency,* 137 F.3d 1135, 1142 (9th Cir.1998) ("[A] speculative and purely economic interest does not create a protectable interest in litigation concerning a statute that regulates environmental, not economic interests."); *Greene v. United States,* 996 F.2d 973, 976 (9th Cir.1993)(economic interest alone is insufficient); *Mountain Top Condominium Association v. Dave Stabbert Master Builder, Inc.,* 72 F.3d 361, 366 (3d Cir.1995)("mere" economic interest might be insufficient, but interest in specific fund that is at risk will satisfy "interest" requirement of Rule 24(a)(2)); *Gould v. Alleco, Inc.,* 883 F.2d 281, 285 (4th Cir.1989)

("In a sense, every company's stockholders, bondholders, directors and employees have a stake in the outcome of any litigation involving the company, but this alone is insufficient to imbue them with the degree of 'interest' required for Rule 24(a) intervention.").

32. *Doe v. Oberweis Dairy,* 456 F.3d 704, 718 (7th Cir.2006) (mother and sister of plaintiff asserting Title VII sexual harassment were entitled to intervene to contest trial court's grant of employer's motion for access to the plaintiff's psychiatric records, where mother and sister were present and participated in some of the sessions).

33. *See, e.g., Triax Co. v. TRW,* 724 F.2d 1224, 1227 (6th Cir.1984)(collateral estoppel). *See also, Mova Pharmaceutical Corp. v. Shalala,* 140 F.3d 1060, 1074 (D.C.Cir.1998) (to meet "interest" requirement of Rule 24, intervenor need only demonstrate standing to sue). *But see In re Bayshore Ford Trucks Sales, Inc.,* 471 F.3d 1233, 1248 (11th Cir.2006) (reversed district court's order granting intervention for exclusive purpose of challenging plaintiff's application for an injunction, holding Rule 24 "does not contemplate intervention for such purpose.").

34. *See, e.g., Smuck v. Hobson,* 408 F.2d 175 (D.C.Cir.1969). *See also, Roeder v. Islamic Republic of Iran,* 333 F.3d 228, 233 (D.C.Cir.2003) (interest in protecting diplomatic agreement with foreign sovereign that might be affected by litigation gave United States interest that met intervention requirement); *In re Grand Jury Subpoena,* 274 F.3d 563, 570 (1st Cir.2001) (appropriate intervention by attorney and corporate officers to attempt to quash grand jury subpoena; "[c]olorable claims of attorney-client and work product privilege qualify as sufficient interests to ground intervention as of right"); *Cotter v. Massachusetts Association of Minority Law Enforcement Officers,* 219 F.3d 31, 34–36 (1st Cir.2000) (black police officers previously promoted have interest in intervening in

Impairment of Interest

Rule 24(a)(2) declares that risk of impairment to an applicant's interest may include legal impairment, such as a risk that principles of stare decisis may apply.[35] At the same time, other practical consequences of litigation may also satisfy the "impairment" element. For example, even though a party may not, through res judicata or collateral estoppel, be bound by the judgment, a substantial risk of practical impairments can sometimes constitute sufficient risk of "impairment" to a party seeking to intervene.[36]

suit alleging racial discrimination in promotions harmful to white officers; interest is in protecting promotions of black officers; organization of officers also has interest in intervening to protect interests of black officers who are not parties to suit); *Grutter v. Bollinger,* 188 F.3d 394, 398 (6th Cir. 1999) (proposed intervenors' interest in continued use of race as factor in university admissions satisfies interest requirement of rule 24, even if interest is not a specifically protectable legal or equitable interest; " 'close cases should be resolved in favor of recognizing an interest under Rule 24(a)' "); *Loyd v. Alabama Department of Corrections,* 176 F.3d 1336, 1339 (11th Cir. 1999) (state attorney general need not demonstrate standing before intervening in lawsuit over prisoners' rights, provided that existing parties have satisfied requirement of justiciable case or controversy); *Coalition of Arizona/New Mexico Counties for Stable Economic Growth v. Department of the Interior,* 100 F.3d 837, 841 (10th Cir.1996) (granting intervention where there is little economic interest, but intervenor has interest based on involvement with issue and record of advocacy of protection of affected wildlife); *but cf., Kootenai Tribe of Idaho v. Veneman,* 313 F.3d 1094, 1108 (9th Cir. 2002) (where statute creates liability only for government, private party cannot meet rigorous standard of interest that justifies intervention; however, permissive intervention under Rule 24(b) may still be possible, because lower standard of common question of law or fact may still be met); *Standard Heating & Air Conditioning Co. v. City of Minneapolis,* 137 F.3d 567, 571 (8th Cir. 1998) (remote interests or interests requiring a sequence of events before becoming colorable do not meet requirements of Rule 24(a)); *City of Cleveland, Ohio v. Nuclear Regulatory Commission,* 17 F.3d 1515 (D.C.Cir.1994)(per curiam)(interest should be "legally protectable;" otherwise intervenor would lack standing). *See generally, Rio Grande Pipeline Co. v. Federal Energy Reg-*

ulatory Commission, 178 F.3d 533 (D.C.Cir. 1999) (noting uncertainty as to how great an interest an intervention applicant must demonstrate; making comparison to constitutional requirement of standing and citing cases). *But see Northland Family Planning Clinic, Inc. v. Cox,* 487 F.3d 323, 344 (6th Cir.2007) (public interest group which sought to intervene in suit challenging Michigan law effectively prohibiting partial-birth abortion did not have substantial legal interest to intervene as of right; group's interest pertained to the enforceability of the statute in general as opposed to a challenge to the legislative process by which the statute was enacted, which would have provide a significantly stronger legal interest).

35. *See, e.g., Sierra Club v. Espy,* 18 F.3d 1202, 1207 (5th Cir.1994)(stare decisis effect of decision is sufficient potential impairment to satisfy requirements of Rule 24(a)(2)). *See also United States v. City of Los Angeles,* 288 F.3d 391, 401 (9th Cir. 2002) (potential impairment is sufficient; no requirement that outcome will necessarily impair interest). *Compare DBSI/TRI IV Ltd. Partnership v. U.S.,* 465 F.3d 1031, 1037 (9th Cir.2006) (residents of low-income housing not entitled to intervene as of right in quiet title action brought by owners of low-income housing against the Rural Housing Service; residents failed to demonstrate that the disposition of the action might impair their interest where pending Administrative Procedure Act claim would yield the same remedy sought by intervening in the quiet title lawsuit).

36. *See, e.g., Utah Association of Counties v. Clinton,* 255 F.3d 1246, 1253 (10th Cir.2001) (question of impairment cannot be separated from question of existence of interest; moreover, " 'the court is not limited to consequences of a strictly legal nature' "); *Grutter v. Bollinger,* 188 F.3d 394, 400 (6th Cir.1999) ("minimal requirements" of impairment satisfied by likely prospect that access of minority students to

Adequate Representation by Existing Parties

Even if the person seeking intervention demonstrates that the elements of "interest" and "impairment" are satisfied, intervention under Rule 24(a)(2) will be denied if the interest at risk is represented adequately by persons already parties to the action.[37] The burden of establishing inadequate representation is on the applicant for intervention but is minimal.[38] Typically, a potential intervenor will not have great difficulty establishing a lack of adequate representation by existing parties,[39] unless the intervenor and an existing party share identical objectives.[40]

Lack of adequate representation is most easily demonstrated if the interest is not currently represented at all, or if the persons already parties have positions clearly adverse to those of the intervention applicant.[41] Moreover, a difference in tactics does not of

university will be impaired if university stops using race as criterion in admissions); *Edwards v. City of Houston,* 78 F.3d 983, 1004 (5th Cir.1996)(practical impairment is sufficient—legal impairment not required).

37. *See, e.g., Daggett v. Commission on Governmental Ethics & Election Practices,* 172 F.3d 104, 111 (1st Cir.1999) (rebuttable presumption that government's defense of validity of statute adequately represents interests of citizens who support statute); *Clark v. Putnam County,* 168 F.3d 458, 461 (11th Cir.1999) ("weak" presumption of adequate representation when "existing party seeks the same objectives as the would-be intervenor").

38. *Haspel & Davis Milling & Planting Co. Ltd. v. Board Of Levee,* 493 F.3d 570 (5th Cir.2007) (State of Louisiana could not intervene as it did not satisfy burden of showing inadequate representing by existing party; levee board could adequately defend Louisiana's anti-seizure provisions). *Also see Sierra Club, Inc. v. Leavitt,* 488 F.3d 904, 910 (11th Cir.2007) (The Florida Department of Environmental Protection could not intervene in suit alleging Clean Water Act violations as its interests were adequately represented by the Sierra Club; no evidence presented to refute "weak" presumption of adequate representation when existing party seeks the same objectives as the would-be intervenors.)

39. *Trbovich v. United Mine Workers of Americas,* 404 U.S. 528, 538 n.10, 92 S.Ct. 630, 636, 30 L.Ed.2d 686 (1972) ("The requirement of the Rule is satisfied if the applicant shows that representation of his interest 'may be' inadequate; and the burden of making that showing should be treated as minimal."); *Northeast Ohio Co-*

alition for Homeless and Service Employees Intern., 467 F.3d 999, 1008 (6th Cir.2006) (minimal burden to show interest not adequately protected met and State of Ohio allowed to intervene to defending constitutionality of Ohio's absentee ballot statute; it is sufficient to prove that existing representation may be inadequate; divergent interest shown by existing party's stated desire not to appeal court's grant of a temporary restraining order).

40. *See, e.g., B. Fernandez & Hnos., Inc. v. Kellogg USA, Inc.,* 440 F.3d 541, 546 (1st Cir.2006) ("[I]n cases where the intervenor's ultimate objective matches that of the named party, a rebuttable presumption of adequate representation applies."). *See also Gonzalez v. Arizona,* 485 F.3d 1041, 1052 (9th Cir.2007) ("very compelling showing" necessary to overcome presumption that government acting on behalf of a constituency will adequately represent that constituency, and to permit intervention).

41. *See, e.g., Twelve John Does v. District of Columbia,* 117 F.3d 571 (D.C.Cir. 1997) (existing representation is generally adequate where there is no conflicting interest between representative and would-be intervenor and where representative has ability to litigate the issues with vigor); *but cf., Supreme Beef Processors, Inc. v. United States Department of Agriculture,* 275 F.3d 432, 437–38 (5th Cir.2001) (intervenors need only show that current representation "may be" inadequate; possibility that current party's fate in Chapter 7 bankruptcy proceeding could be liquidation—which would render instant case moot—could mean intervenor might have to litigate issue all over again even though current par-

itself necessarily indicate a lack of adequate representation.[42]

Burden of Proof

Most courts require the intervenor to show that its interest is not adequately represented.[43]

ty won on those issues in district court; held, intervention justified); *Jordan v. Michigan Conference of Teamsters Welfare Fund,* 207 F.3d 854, 863 (6th Cir.2000) (movant's burden is only to show that representation "may be" inadequate, not that representation "will in fact be inadequate"; but burden of demonstrating inadequate representation not met where: "1) no collusion is shown between the existing party and the opposition; 2) the existing party does not have any interests adverse to the intervenor; and 3) the existing party has not failed in the fulfillment of its duty"); *Sierra Club v. Espy,* 18 F.3d 1202 (5th Cir.1994)(burden of demonstrating inadequate existing representation is "minimal.").

42. *See, e.g., United States v. City of Miami,* 278 F.3d 1174, 1179 (11th Cir.2002) (police associations concerned with advancement of blacks and women is adequately represented by government interest in ending discrimination for all minorities); *Massachusetts Food Association v. Massachusetts Alcoholic Beverages Control Commission,* 197 F.3d 560, 566 (1st Cir.1999) (courts generally presume that government defendant will adequately represent interest of all private defenders of relevant law "unless there is a showing to the contrary"); *Grutter v. Bollinger,* 188 F.3d 394, 401 (6th Cir.1999) (prospect that university, in defending against challenge to admissions program based partly on race, may not present evidence of its own past discrimination; minority students have therefore demonstrated that existing representation by university is inadequate); *B.H. v. McDonald,* 49 F.3d 294 (7th Cir. 1995)(party's preference to in-chamber conferences as opposed to open court hearings does not constitute inadequate representation). *But see B. Fernandez & Hnos., Inc. v. Kellogg USA, Inc.,* 440 F.3d 541, 546 (1st Cir.2006) (presumption of adequate representation not established solely by fact that existing party and intervenor are subsidiaries of same parent); *Utahns for Better Transportation v. United States Department of Transportation,* 295 F.3d 1111 (10th Cir. 2002) (burden of showing inadequacy of representation is minimal; relying on gov-

ernment creates potential conflict between government's duty to protect public interest and private interests of private intervention petitioners; also, private parties have expertise that government lacks; finally, government's silence on its intent to protect private parties is "deafening"); *United States v. City of Los Angeles,* 288 F.3d 391, 401–02 (9th Cir.2002) (presumption that government will adequately represent interests "arises when the government is acting on behalf of a constituency that it represents. ...The situation is different when the government acts as an employer, as here. ...The presumption has not been applied to parties who are antagonists in the collective bargaining process."); *Turn Key Gaming, Inc. v. Oglala Sioux Tribe,* 164 F.3d 1080, 1082 (8th Cir.1999) (lender/holder of security interest in personalty purchased with proceeds of loan has interest in outcome of lawsuit over, among other issues, whether security interest is valid; current party that was responsible for development of project financed with loan did not adequately represent security interest holder's interest because current party was subject of counterclaim; and it was conceivable that current party would settle counterclaim in way that was detrimental to validity of security interest). *See also, Public Service Co. of New Hampshire v. Patch,* 136 F.3d 197, 207 (1st Cir.1998) (intervenor need make only "minimal showing" of inadequacy of representation, but there must still be "some tangible basis" for claim of inadequacy).

43. *See, e.g., Maine v. Director, United States Fish & Wildlife Service,* 262 F.3d 13, 18 (1st Cir.2001) ("Some burden of showing inadequacy is placed on the proposed intervenor."). *Gottlieb v. Wiles,* 11 F.3d 1004, 1008 (10th Cir.1993)(would-be intervenors bear burden of showing inadequacy of representation). *But cf., Southwest Center for Biological Diversity v. Berg,* 268 F.3d 810, 819–20 (9th Cir.2001) (Circuits hold "that a district court is required to accept as true the non-conclusory allegations made in support of an intervention motion."). *See also Brennan v. New York City Board of Education,* 260 F.3d 123, 129 (2d Cir.2001)

Status of Intervenor: Standing

Assuming that an intervenor applicant satisfies the requirements of Rule 24(a)(2), the intervenor may participate as a party. However, left open is whether the intervenor, like a party, must satisfy requirements such as standing.[44] The courts are divided on this issue, and an attorney must consult local precedent.[45]

Class Action Settlements: Standing

It is settled that if a non-named class member objects in a timely manner to a proposed settlement, that member need not intervene in order to appeal the settlement.[46]

Conditional Intervention

It appears that if a court permits intervention as of right, it may impose conditions on such intervention.[47]

RULE 24(b).   PERMISSIVE INTERVENTION

CORE CONCEPT

Rule 24(b) contains provisions under which a person may move to intervene, but does not confer a right to intervene. Rule 24(b) applies a substantially more relaxed approach to motions to intervene. A person seeking permission to intervene under Rule 24(b) need not demonstrate the sort of interest required for intervention under Rule 24(a)(2). The court's discretion to reject Rule 24(b)(2) intervention applications, however, is substantially greater than its capacity to reject a Rule 24(a)(2) application.

(court cannot go to merits of case to conclude that movant's claim of interest is factually or legally weak).

44. *Diamond v. Charles,* 476 U.S. 54, 68–69, 106 S.Ct. 1697, 90 L.Ed.2d 48 (1986) (leaving undecided the question whether every intervenor must demonstrate standing in addition to the requirements of Rule 24).

45. *Compare, e.g., Building and Construction Trades Department, AFL–CIO v. Reich,* 40 F.3d 1275, 1282 (D.C.Cir. 1994)(intervenor is on "equal footing" with parties, and must satisfy standing requirements of Article III of the Constitution) *with, e.g., Newby v. Enron Corp.,* 443 F.3d 416, 422 (5th Cir.2006) (this requirement "has been construed liberally"); *Jones v. Prince George's County,* 348 F.3d 1014, 1018 (D.C. Cir.2003) ("As the Rule's plain text indicates, intervenors of right need only an 'interest' in the litigation–not a 'cause of action' or 'permission to sue.' "). *See also, Mausolf v. Babbitt,* 85 F.3d 1295 (8th Cir.1996)(collecting cases); *Dillard v. Chilton County Commission,* 495 F.3d 1324

(11th Cir.2007) (denying intervention where there was no independent standing and the original parties had entered into a consent decree); *DSI Associates LLC v. U.S.,* 496 F.3d 175 (2nd Cir.2007) (party who lacked standing under Comprehensive Crime Control Act of 1984 could not reframe claim to intervene under Rule 24).

46. *Devlin v. Scardelletti,* 536 U.S. 1, 122 S.Ct. 2005, 153 L.Ed.2d 27 (2002) (held, such a party easily satisfies standing requirement, and right to appeal is not restricted to named parties).

47. *See, e.g., Walsh v. Walsh,* 221 F.3d 204, 213 (1st Cir.2000) ("[I]t was well within the district court's discretion to limit [a person's] intervention, which took place long after trial and judgment, to a distinct legal issue that required no additional factfinding."); *Beauregard, Inc. v. Sword Services, L.L.C.,* 107 F.3d 351, 352 (5th Cir. 1997) (permitting intervention provided, *inter alia,* that intervenor agreed to seize asset and help pay cost of maintaining asset; noting contrary scholarly authority).

APPLICATIONS

Common Question of Law or Fact

The bedrock requirement for Rule 24(b)(2) permissive intervention is a demonstration by the person seeking intervention that there exists a common question of law or fact between that person's claim or defense and the pending litigation.[48]

Discretion

A district court's decision to deny permissive intervention is almost never overturned on appeal.[49]

Subject Matter Jurisdiction

Persons attempting to intervene under Rule 24(b)(2) must establish an independent basis for subject matter jurisdiction. Supplemental jurisdiction is not available to would-be permissive intervenors.[50]

Timing

Applications to intervene under Rule 24(b) must be "timely". The determination of what constitutes a timely application rests within the court's discretion in the context of the facts in a particular case.[51] Because Rule 24(b) intervention questions do not typically affect the interests of non-parties as importantly as Rule 24(a) cases, courts tend to hold motions for permissive intervention to a more rigorous standard of timeliness than would be applied to motions for intervention of right.[52]

---

48. *See, e.g., Kootenai Tribe of Idaho v. Veneman,* 313 F.3d 1094, 1108 (9th Cir. 2002) (standard for permissive intervention under rule 24(b) is common question of law or fact, not more rigorous standard of interest that may be impaired); *Griffith v. University Hospital, L.L.C.,* 249 F.3d 658, 661 (7th Cir.2001) (Rule 24(b) is appropriate way for third party to challenge protective order); *E.E.O.C. v. National Children's Center, Inc.,* 146 F.3d 1042, 1045 (D.C. Cir. 1998) (same; collecting circuit decisions). *Cf., Trans Chemical, Ltd. v. China National Machinery Import & Export Corp.,* 332 F.3d 815, 824 (5th Cir.2003) (lack of common question of law or fact means permissive intervention is inappropriate).

49. *See, e.g., Northland Family Planning Clinic, Inc. v. Cox,* 487 F.3d 323, 346 (6th Cir.2007) (denial of permissive intervention is reversed only for clear abuse of discretion by trial judge); *Purcell v. BankAtlantic Financial Corp.,* 85 F.3d 1508, 1513 (11th Cir.1996) (Rule 24(b) intervention is "wholly discretionary" even where the requirements of Rule 24(b) are satisfied);

Shea v. Angulo, 19 F.3d 343, 346 (7th Cir. 1994)(reversal of district court's decision denying permissive intervention " 'is a very rare bird indeed, so seldom seen as to be unique.' ").

50. *See, e.g., E.E.O.C. v. National Children's Center, Inc.,* 146 F.3d 1042, 1046 (D.C.Cir.1998) ("Permissive intervention . . . has always required an independent basis for jurisdiction.").

51. *See, e.g., Caterino v. Barry,* 922 F.2d 37, 40 (1st Cir.1990)(trial court entitled to "substantial deference"); *Medical Liability Mutual Ins. Co. v. Alan Curtis LLC,* 485 F.3d 1006, 1009 (8th Cir.2007) (not abuse of discretion for district court to deny permissive intervention where motion for intervention filed more than a year after underlying suit filed and shortly before discovery deadline).

52. *See, e.g., Banco Popular de Puerto Rico v. Greenblatt,* 964 F.2d 1227, 1230 (1st Cir.1992)(timeliness standard more strict for Rule 24(a) than Rule 24(b)).

Delay or Prejudice

Rule 24(b) expressly authorizes the court to deny permissive intervention if intervention will unduly delay or prejudice the pending litigation. The provision permits denial of intervention if undue delay to existing parties will result even from an arguably timely application. That might occur if the complexity added by an intervenor would prolong the litigation excessively.[53] Similarly, inappropriate prejudice to existing parties might occur if the presence of the intervenor might shift the focus of the litigation from the pending issues to those introduced by the intervenor.[54]

There is authority for the position that the "prejudice" evaluation of Rule 24(b)(2) should include an evaluation of the merits of the proposed party's claim. To the extent that the claim is duplicative or weak on its merits, the court will be inclined to give greater weight to concerns about delay or prejudice.[55]

Permissive Statutory Intervention

Fewer cases deal with permissive statutory intervention. Such statutes as exist, and which clearly contemplate permissive statutory intervention, generally accord the court authority to allow intervention by some public official such as the United States Attorney General.[56] In other circumstances it is less clear whether the statute is intended to allow intervention as of right or permissive intervention. Although the paucity of case law makes conclusions difficult, the inclination of courts to construe narrowly statutes that clearly contemplate intervention as of right may suggest that courts will be inclined to construe the uncertain statutes as authorizing permissive statutory intervention under Rule 24(b)(1) rather than statutory intervention as of right under Rule 24(a)(1). As a practical matter, that inclination provides the courts with greater opportunities to use discretion to reject an application for permissive intervention.

Standing for Non-statutory Permissive Intervention

Although a person seeking intervention under Rule 24(b)(2) need not demonstrate an "interest" within the kinds contemplated by Rule 24(a)(2), the person seeking permissive intervention must nonetheless have a sufficient stake in the litigation to satisfy ordinary requirements for standing.[57]

---

53. See, e.g., Massachusetts v. Microsoft Corp., 373 F.3d 1199 (D.C. Cir.2004) (prejudice evaluation "captures all the possible drawbacks of piling on parties," including extra cost and increased risk of error). See also Farmland Dairies v. Commissioner of New York State Department of Agriculture and Markets, 847 F.2d 1038, 1044 (2d Cir. 1988)(post-judgment intervention is disfavored).

54. See, e.g., Alaniz v. Tillie Lewis Foods, 572 F.2d 657, 659 (9th Cir.1978), (per curiam). See also Beaver v. Alaniz, 439

U.S. 837, 99 S.Ct. 123, 58 L.Ed.2d 134 (1978)(post-resolution intervention often unfairly hard on existing parties).

55. See, e.g., Massachusetts v. Microsoft Corp., 373 F.3d 1199 (D.C. Cir.2004) (but in instant case intervention is appropriate because concerns about delay or prejudice are minimal).

56. See, e.g., 42 U.S.C.A. § 2000a–3(a).

57. See, e.g., United States v. Napper, 887 F.2d 1528, 1532 (11th Cir.1989) (standing is required for both intervenors of right and permissive intervenors). But cf., In re

Permissive Intervention for Public Officials

Rule 24(b) authorizes intervention by officers or agencies if the pending litigation raises questions of law administered by the officer or agency, or questions of regulations issued by the officer or agency.[58]

Conditional Permissive Intervention

If intervention is permitted under Rule 24(b), the court has substantial authority to impose conditions on the intervention.[59]

RULE 24(c). NOTICE AND PLEADING REQUIRED

CORE CONCEPT

Rule 24(c) contains the provisions for notice and service of process of the motion to intervene. It also requires that the motion to intervene be accompanied by a pleading that identifies the claim or defense which is the basis of the attempt to intervene.

APPLICATIONS

Service of Process

The motion to intervene should be filed with the court and served on all persons already parties to the pending litigation, as provided in Rule 5.

Service of Proposed Pleading

In addition to the motion to intervene, Rule 24(c) also requires that the applicant for intervention file and serve a proposed pleading explaining the claim or defense that is the purpose of the intervention.[60] This proposed pleading should also be served consistent with the requirements of Rule 5, governing service on persons already parties.

Failure to Meet Rule 24(c) Motion and Pleading Requirements

There is a split of authority as to the consequences an intervenor should experience for failure to meet the motion and pleading requirements of Rule 24(c). An apparent majority of circuits has held that failure to comply with Rule 24(c) should not of itself

---

Vitamins Antitrust Class Actions, 215 F.3d 26 (D.C. Cir.2000) (expressing uncertainty as to whether standing is required).

58. *See, e.g., Harris v. Amoco Production Co.,* 768 F.2d 669, 680 (5th Cir.1985) (citing federal law authorizing permissive intervention for federal agency).

59. *See, e.g., Beauregard, Inc. v. Sword Services, L.L.C.,* 107 F.3d 351, 352 n. 2 (5th Cir.1997) ("It is undisputed that virtually any condition may be attached to a grant of permissive intervention.").

60. *See, e.g., Bridges v. Maryland Department State Police,* 441 F.3d 197, 208 (4th Cir.2006) (pleading gives existing parties notice of claim or defense for which intervention is sought); *Retired Chicago Police Association v. City of Chicago,* 7 F.3d 584, 595 (7th Cir.1993) (for purposes of Rule 24(c), intervenor should provide an original pleading, not merely an adoption by reference of prior pleadings; Rule 10(c), permitting adoption by reference in other situations, does not apply to pleadings required under Rule 24(c)).

disqualify the attempt to intervene.[61] A smaller number of circuits has applied the requirements more rigorously.[62]

ADDITIONAL RESEARCH REFERENCES

Wright & Miller, *Federal Practice and Procedure* §§ 1900–23.

C.J.S. Federal Civil Procedure §§ 128–155.

West's Key No. Digests, Federal Civil Procedure ☞311–345.

61. *See, e.g., Providence Baptist Church v. Hillandale Committee, Ltd.,* 425 F.3d 309, 314 (6th Cir.2005) (abuse of discretion to reject motion to intervene for failure to include pleading); *Massachusetts v. Microsoft Corp.,* 373 F.3d 1199, 1236 (D.C. Cir. 2004) (failure to include pleading with motion–procedural defects should generally be excused); *Piambino v. Bailey,* 757 F.2d 1112, 1121 (11th Cir.1985) (same failure—such "nonprejudicial technical defects" may be disregarded); *Spring Construction Co. v. Harris,* 614 F.2d 374, 376–77 (4th Cir.1980) (same); *Farina v. Mission Investment Trust,* 615 F.2d 1068, 1074 (5th Cir.1980) (objection that intervenor made no "formal petition to intervene" rejected as "excessively technical").

62. *See, e.g, Public Service Co. of New Hampshire v. Patch,* 136 F.3d 197, 205 n. 6 (1st Cir.1998) (failure to include pleading "ordinarily would warrant dismissal" of motion, but such result unnecessary in instant case because lower court rejected motion on other grounds); *Shevlin v. Schewe,* 809 F.2d 447, 450 (7th Cir.1987) (pleading must accompany motion; defect may be excusable where intervenor later remedied defect, but not in case where pleading was never filed); *Abramson v. Pennwood Investment Corp.,* 392 F.2d 759, 761 (2d Cir.1968) (reference in motion to allegations of original complaint does not meet Rule 24(c) requirement). *See also Thompson v. Boggs,* 33 F.3d 847, 858 n. 10 (7th Cir.1994) (Rule 24 motion by non-party to intervene is "proper course;" by contrast, courts do not grant motions to join when motion is made by non-party).

RULE 25

SUBSTITUTION OF PARTIES

(a) Death.

(1) *Substitution if the Claim Is Not Extinguished.* If a party dies and the claim is not extinguished, the court may order substitution of the proper party. A motion for substitution may be made by any party or by the decedent's successor or representative. If the motion is not made within 90 days after service of a statement noting the death, the action by or against the decedent must be dismissed.

(2) *Continuation Among the Remaining Parties.* After a party's death, if the right sought to be enforced survives only to or against the remaining parties, the action does not abate, but proceeds in favor of or against the remaining parties. The death should be noted on the record.

(3) *Service.* A motion to substitute, together with a notice of hearing, must be served on the parties as provided in Rule 5 and on nonparties as provided in Rule 4. A statement noting death must be served in the same manner. Service may be made in any judicial district.

(b) Incompetency. If a party becomes incompetent, the court may, on motion, permit the action to be continued by or against the party's representative. The motion must be served as provided in Rule 25(a)(3).

(c) Transfer of Interest. If an interest is transferred, the action may be continued by or against the original party unless the court, on motion, orders the transferee to be substituted in the action or joined with the original party. The motion must be served as provided in Rule 25(a)(3).

(d) Public Officers; Death or Separation from Office. An action does not abate when a public officer who is a party in an official capacity dies, resigns, or otherwise ceases to hold office while the action is pending. The officer's successor is automatically substituted as a party. Later proceedings should be in the substituted party's name, but any misnomer not affecting the parties' substantial rights must be disregarded. The court may order substitution at any time, but the absence of such an order does not affect the substitution.

[Amended effective October 20, 1949; July 19, 1961; July 1, 1963; August 1, 1987; April 30, 2007, effective December 1, 2007.]

─────────────── 2007 AMENDMENTS ROADMAP ───────────────

STYLE PROJECT CHANGES: Rule 25(a) was re-organized into three subparts. Minor changes in language were made throughout the Rule.

NON-STYLE CHANGES: Rule 25(d)(2), governing use of a public officer's name or job title when the officer is sued in an official capacity, is transferred to Rule 17, where it appears as Rule 17(d). Minor changes were made in the language of new Rule 17(d).

NOTE: The Federal Rules "Style Project" is explained in Part III-A.

AUTHORS' COMMENTARY ON RULE 25

─────────────── PURPOSE AND SCOPE ───────────────

Rule 25 prescribes the steps to employ when, in any of four distinct circumstances described in the Rule, it becomes necessary to substitute a party in a case. Rule 25 applies only to cases already pending when the substitution becomes necessary. It does not apply to substitutions in circumstances where suit has not already commenced. Such circumstances are more likely to be controlled by Rule 17, governing a person's capacity to initiate a suit.

RULE 25(a). DEATH

CORE CONCEPT

Rule 25(a) prescribes the procedure to follow for substituting a party when a plaintiff or defendant in pending litigation dies during the course of the proceedings. The Rule expressly defers to state or federal substantive law to determine whether the cause of action survives the death of the party, and is only applicable if the suit is not extinguished by the death.

APPLICATIONS

Motion for Substitution

Rule 25(a)(1) provides that any party, or the persons affiliated with the deceased party, may make a motion for substitution.[1] It is important to note that until a motion for substitution has been made and granted, the court has no authority to proceed with the deceased party's case.[2]

Service

The motion should be filed and served on all parties consistent with the requirements of Rule 5. If the circumstances are such that service on non-parties is also appropriate, the non-parties shall be served consistent with the requirements for service of a summons under Rule 4, which controls service at the beginning of a suit. Rule 25(a)(3) authorizes service of such process in any federal judicial district.

Hearing

If there is a dispute as to the appropriateness of the proposed substituted party, the court has a duty to resolve the issue and may hold a hearing before ruling on the motion.[3] The notice of hearing should be filed and served on all parties in the manner provided by Rule 5.

Time

The time in which the motion for substitution must be made is 90 days from when the death of the party is "suggested" on the record of the case. Thus, a party may have been deceased for a substantial period before a suggestion of death is made, and that fact will have no consequence for the 90–day limitation.[4]

Suggestion of Death

Death of a party is suggested by written notice on the record, which should be filed and served on all parties pursuant to Rule 5.[5] Non-party representatives of the deceased should be served pursuant to Rule 4.[6]

Failure to Move for Substitution Within 90 Days

If more than 90 days elapses following the suggestion of death without a motion for substitution, Rule 25(a)(1) provides that the

1. *See, e.g., Unicorn Tales, Inc. v. Banerjee,* 138 F.3d 467 (2d Cir.1998) (so holding; suggestion can be made by widow who is not a party, and need not be made by formally appointed representative of estate).

2. *See, e.g., Younts v. Fremont County,* 370 F.3d 748, 752 (8th Cir.2004) ("Because the deceased ... is not a proper party on appeal and no proper party has been substituted for her, we cannot address the merits of the appeal raised on [her] behalf.").

3. *See, e.g., Escareno v. Noltina Crucible and Refractory Corp.,* 139 F.3d 1456 (11th Cir.1998) (court has duty to determine whether substitute party–here an administrator of estate–was properly appointed; is-

sue in instant case was whether probate court had jurisdiction to appoint administrator).

4. *See, e.g., Grandbouche v. Lovell,* 913 F.2d 835 (10th Cir.1990). *But see, Miles, Inc. v. Scripps Clinic & Research Foundation,* 810 F.Supp. 1091, 1102 (S.D.Cal. 1993)(party who delays unreasonably in filing suggestion of death may be denied permission to substitute a party).

5. *See, e.g., Barlow v. Ground,* 39 F.3d 231, 233–34 (9th Cir.1994) (90 days does not start to run until representative of estate is properly served).

6. See, e.g., id. at 233 (requiring service on non-party representatives under Rule 4).

suit will be dismissed as to the deceased party. However, notwithstanding the apparently mandatory language of the Rule, the cases generally hold that the courts have discretion to extend the time in which a party may move for substitution.[7]

Status of Successor

A party who replaces a deceased party receives the status the deceased party possessed at the time of death. For example, if the deceased party had already consented to trial by a magistrate judge, the successor is bound by that consent.[8]

Death of a Party for Whom Substitution Cannot Be Made

Before Rule 25(a) can be employed to substitute a new party for a deceased party, the substantive law controlling the suit must allow survival of the cause of action. If the cause of action does not survive the death of a party, there can be no substitution for that party under Rule 25(a).[9] In multi-party litigation, however, it is possible that substantive law would extinguish the cause of action as to a deceased party, but that sufficient parties would remain to continue the action. In that circumstance, Rule 25(a)(2) directs that the action may continue as to surviving parties, with appropriate record made of the death.

RULE 25(b). INCOMPETENCY

CORE CONCEPT

Rule 25(b) addresses the possibility of substitution for parties who become incompetent in the course of litigation. It requires a motion to substitute a representative for the incompetent party, and it expressly adopts the same service provisions applicable to substitution for deceased parties found in Rule 25(a).

APPLICATIONS

Survival of the Action

Incompetency will not extinguish a cause of action.

Timing

Rule 25(b) contains no reference to time limitations for motions to substitute parties. There is little or no case law on the point.

---

7. *See, e.g., Continental Bank, N.A. v. Meyer,* 10 F.3d 1293, 1297 (7th Cir. 1993)(extensions of 90–day time period may be granted liberally). *But see, Kaubisch v. Weber,* 408 F.3d 540, 543 (8th Cir.2005) (acknowledging district court's discretion; but "the misapplication or misreading of the plain language of Rule 25 does not establish excusable neglect"); *Russell v. City of Milwaukee,* 338 F.3d 662, 668 (7th Cir.2003) (affirming dismissal where counsel failed to demonstrate excusable neglect).

8. *See, e.g., Brook, Weiner, Sered, Kreger & Weinberg v. Coreq, Inc.,* 53 F.3d 851, 852 (7th Cir.1995)("A successor takes over without any other change in the status of the case," and therefore decedent's consent to trial by magistrate judge binds successor.).

9. *See, e.g., Asklar v. Honeywell, Inc.,* 95 F.R.D. 419, 422 (D.Conn.1982)(substantive law, not Rule 25(a), determines whether case may proceed after death of party).

RULE 25(c).   TRANSFER OF INTEREST

CORE CONCEPT

Rule 25(c) addresses substitution in circumstances in which, during the course of the litigation, an interest is transferred from a party to another entity. It also controls the procedure for substitution when one corporate entity loses its identity through dissolution or merger with another corporate entity.

APPLICATIONS

Option to Substitute Parties

Rule 25(c) does not require that the person now holding the interest transferred be substituted for the transferor-party.[10] Instead, the Rule allows the action to continue in the name of the transferor unless the court chooses to order substitution, or joinder, of the transferee.[11] Thus the case may go to judgment without any substitution of parties having occurred, and the absence of a formal substitution will have no consequence.[12] If it is appropriate in the circumstances of the particular case, both the transferor and transferee will be bound by the court's judgment.[13]

Personal Jurisdiction

Courts generally hold that when successors in interest are joined under Rule 25(c), they are subject to the personal jurisdiction of the court simply because they are successors in interest, "without regard to whether they had any other minimum contacts." [14]

Timing

Rule 25(c) contains no time limit in which substitution must take place.

Subject Matter Jurisdiction: Relation to Rule 19

Joinder of a nondiverse party under rule 25(c) does not usually destroy diversity jurisdiction.[15] However, if the joined party was

---

10. *See, e.g., Educational Credit Management Corp. v. Bernal*, 207 F.3d 595, 598 (9th Cir.2000) (Rule 25(c) requires no action by anyone after a transfer of interest; judgment binds successor in interest even if successor is not named).

11. *See, e.g., Burka v. Aetna Life Insurance Co.*, 87 F.3d 478 (D.C.Cir.1996)(noting that Rule 25(c) affords option of replacing one party with another, or joining a person with original party).

12. *See, e.g., Arnold Graphics Industries, Inc. v. Independent Agent Center, Inc.*, 775 F.2d 38, 40 (2d Cir.1985)(enforcing judgment against successor corporation where substitution was made only after judgment).

13. *See, e.g., Luxliner P.L. Export Co. v. RDI/Luxliner, Inc.*, 13 F.3d 69, 71 (3d Cir. 1993)(even if no substitution is sought, judgment against original defendant can bind successor). *But cf., Organic Cow, L.L.C. v. Center for New England Dairy Compact Research*, 335 F.3d 66, 72 (2d Cir. 2003) ("Where ... a government entity terminates with no provision for naming a successor and with no appropriate governmental body to stand in its shoes for purposes of litigation ... there can be no substitution of parties under Rule 25.").

14. *LiButti v. United States*, 178 F.3d 114 (2d Cir.1999) (collecting other case authority).

someone who would have been indispensable under Rule 19 at the time the case was filed, joinder of a nondiverse party destroys diversity jurisdiction.[16]

Extinguishing Corporate Causes of Action

Rule 25(c) is subordinate to substantive law on the issue of survival of a cause of action after corporate reorganizations. Thus if substantive law directs that dissolution of a corporation also extinguishes the corporation's causes of action, Rule 25(c) will not save the cause of action.[17]

Status of Successor

A party who enters a case as the legal successor of a corporation receives the status which the predecessor corporation possessed at the time the successor entered the case. For example, if the predecessor corporation had already consented to trial by a magistrate judge, the successor is bound by that consent.[18]

Service of Process

If a motion to substitute parties is made under Rule 25(c), service should meet the requirements established in Rule 25(a) for motions to make substitutions for deceased parties.

Relation to Rule 17

Rule 25(c) governs transfers of interest during the pendency of a case. Rule 17(a), by contrast, governs situations in which an interest is transferred before the suit is filed.[19]

15. *Freeport-McMoRan, Inc. v. K N Energy, Inc.,* 498 U.S. 426, 428, 111 S.Ct. 858, 859, 112 L.Ed.2d 951 (1991) (per curiam) (any other result would impede "normal business transactions during the pendency of what might be lengthy litigation").

16. *Freeport–McMoRan, Inc. v. K N Energy, Inc.,* 498 U.S. 426, 111 S.Ct. 858, 112 L.Ed.2d 951 (1991)(per curiam).

17. *See, e.g., Citibank v. Grupo Catalan de Inversiones, S.A.,* 382 F.3d 29, 32–33 (1st Cir.2004) ("Rule 25 does not substantively determine what actions survive the transfer of an interest."); *ELCA Enterprises, Inc. v. Sisco Equipment Rental & Sales Inc.,* 53 F.3d 186, 190 n. 4 (8th Cir.1995)("Rule 25 does not substantively determine what actions survive the transfer of an interest; rather, it provides substitution procedures for an action that does survive."). *See also Organic Cow, L.L.C. v. Center for New England Dairy Compact Research,* 335 F.3d 66 (2d Cir.2003) (when mandate of commission

created by Congress to administer dairy compact expired without renewal, private entity could not be substituted under Rule 25(c) because private entity had no authority to perform role of commission).

18. *See, e.g., Andrews v. Lakeshore Rehabilitation Hospital,* 140 F.3d 1405, 1408 (11th Cir.1998) (where transfer of interest occurs prior to trial, Rule 25(c) is not applicable and therefore "does not save plaintiff's amendments from the statute of limitations"). *Brook, Weiner, Sered, Kreger & Weinberg v. Coreq, Inc.,* 53 F.3d 851, 852 (7th Cir.1995)("A successor takes over without any other change in the status of the case," and therefore a successor to a corporation is bound by the corporation's previous consent to trial by a magistrate judge.).

19. *See, e.g., FDIC v. Deglau,* 207 F.3d 153, 159 (3d Cir.2000) (Rule 17 governs transfers prior to filing of lawsuit; after lawsuit begins, Rule 25 governs).

RULE 25(d). PUBLIC OFFICERS; DEATH OR SEPARATION FROM OFFICE

CORE CONCEPT

Rule 25(d) governs substitution in which public officers are named parties to actions in their official capacities. It does not control substitution in suits where parties, who also happen to be public officers, are suing or being sued personally.[20] Rule 25(d) provides that if substitution of a successor to a public officer is necessary in a pending suit, the substitution shall be automatic. Rule 25(d) applies to circumstances involving death of a public officer or departure from public office for any reason.

APPLICATIONS

Motions

Because the substitution under Rule 25(d) occurs automatically, there is no need to file or serve a motion seeking the substitution.[21]

Timing

For the same reason that no motion is necessary under Rule 25(d), Rule 25(d) imposes no time requirements.

Survival of the Action

Rule 25(d) provides expressly that a suit by or against a public officer does not abate when a substitution occurs.[22]

Events Prior to Substitution: Stipulations, Admissions, Etc.

It appears settled that substitution of an official for a predecessor in office binds the successor to the results of previous events in the case as surely as if no substitution had been made.[23]

Substitutions in the Style of the Case

Rule 25(d) directs that proceedings subsequent to the substitution shall be in the name of the substituted party. However, this provision is usually no more than a formality, for no consequence

20. *See, e.g., Society of Separationists v. Pleasant Grove City,* 416 F.3d 1239 (10th Cir.2005) (absence of claims against defendants personally makes substitution of successors proper, because suit was brought against elected officials in their official capacity). *Bunn v. Conley,* 309 F.3d 1002, 1009 (7th Cir.2002) (*Bivens* claim is suit against government officer in individual (not official) capacity; thus newly appointed officer cannot be substituted for officer originally sued in individual capacity).

21. *Cheney v. United States District Court,* 541 U.S. 913, 916, 124 S.Ct. 1391, 1395, 158 L.Ed.2d 225 (2004) (substitution is automatic). *See, e.g., Negron Gaztambide v. Hernandez Torres,* 145 F.3d 410 (1st Cir. 1998) (per curiam) (new officeholders are substituted automatically for their prede-

cessors and automatically have same standing to litigate case). *See also Buczkowski v. Federal Deposit Insurance Corp.,* 415 F.3d 594, 596 (7th Cir.2005) (Rule 25(d), governing substitution of government officers in official-capacity litigation, is exception to federal practice requirement of notice that applies to substitution of other parties).

22. *See, e.g., Saldana–Sanchez v. Lopez–Gerena,* 256 F.3d 1, 10, n. 16 (1st Cir.2001) ("As Fed. R. Civ. P. 25(d)(1) makes clear, the substitution of a public official by his or her successor in an official capacity suit does not affect the underlying action.").

23. *See, e.g., Feliciano v. Rullan,* 303 F.3d 1, 7–8 (1st Cir.2002) (holding that substituted party cannot repudiate stipulations to which predecessor agreed).

attaches to erroneous use of the name of the original party—unless such error somehow has an adverse effect on the case.[24]

Order of Substitution

The court has discretion to order that a new public officer be substituted for a predecessor, but need not do so. Whatever the court decides, Rule 25(d) provides that the presence or absence of such an order does not alter the fact that the automatic substitution has already occurred.[25]

ADDITIONAL RESEARCH REFERENCES

Wright & Miller, *Federal Practice and Procedure* §§ 1951–62.

C.J.S. Federal Civil Procedure §§ 156–168 et seq.

West's Key No. Digests, Federal Civil Procedure ☞351–366, 391.

24. *See, e.g., Cable v. Ivy Tech State College,* 200 F.3d 467, 475 (7th Cir.1999) (Rule 17(d) "expressly directs that any misnomer of the parties that does not affect their substantive rights shall be disregarded even without a motion or order for substitution"); *Presbytery of New Jersey of Orthodox Presbyterian Church v. Florio,* 40 F.3d 1454, 1458 n. 4 (3d Cir.1994) (failure to amend caption to reflect election of new governor/defendant does not affect case).

25. *See, e.g., Shakman v. Democratic Organization of Cook County,* 919 F.2d 455, 456 (7th Cir.1990)(challenger who wins election against official defendant "automatically became a party to . . . consent decree").

V. DEPOSITIONS AND DISCOVERY

RULE 26

DUTY TO DISCLOSE; GENERAL PROVISIONS GOVERNING DISCOVERY

(a) Required Disclosures.

(1) *Initial Disclosure.*

(A) *In General.* Except as exempted by Rule 26(a)(1)(B) or as otherwise stipulated or ordered by the court, a party must, without awaiting a discovery request, provide to the other parties:

(i) the name and, if known, the address and telephone number of each individual likely to have discoverable information—along with the subjects of that information—that the disclosing party may use to support its claims or defenses, unless the use would be solely for impeachment;

(ii) a copy—or a description by category and location—of all documents, electronically stored information, and tangible things that the disclosing party has in its possession, custody, or control and may use to support its claims or defenses, unless the use would be solely for impeachment;

(iii) a computation of each category of damages claimed by the disclosing party—who must also make available for inspection and copying as under Rule 34 the documents or other evidentiary material, unless privileged or protected from disclosure, on which each computation is based, including materials bearing on the nature and extent of injuries suffered; and

(iv) for inspection and copying as under Rule 34, any insurance agreement under which an insurance business may be liable to satisfy all or part of a possible judgment in the action or to indemnify or reimburse for payments made to satisfy the judgment.

(B) *Proceedings Exempt from Initial Disclosure.* The following proceedings are exempt from initial disclosure:

(i) an action for review on an administrative record;

(ii) a petition for habeas corpus or any other proceeding to challenge a criminal conviction or sentence;

(iii) an action brought without an attorney by a person in the custody of the United States, a state, or a state subdivision;

(iv) an action to enforce or quash an administrative summons or subpoena;

(v) an action by the United States to recover benefit payments;

(vi) an action by the United States to collect on a student loan guaranteed by the United States;

(vii) a proceeding ancillary to a proceeding in another court; and

(viii) an action to enforce an arbitration award.

(C) *Time for Initial Disclosures—In General.* A party must make the initial disclosures at or within 14 days after the parties' Rule 26(f) conference unless a different time is set by stipulation or court order, or unless a party objects during the conference that initial disclosures are not appropriate in this action and states the objection in the proposed discovery plan. In ruling on the objection, the court must determine what disclosures, if any, are to be made and must set the time for disclosure.

(D) *Time for Initial Disclosures—For Parties Served or Joined Later.* A party that is first served or otherwise joined after the Rule 26(f) conference must make the initial disclosures within 30 days after being served or joined, unless a different time is set by stipulation or court order.

(E) *Basis for Initial Disclosure; Unacceptable Excuses.* A party must make its initial disclosures based on the information then reasonably available to it. A party is not excused from making its disclosures because it has not fully investigated the case or because it challenges the sufficiency of another party's disclosures or because another party has not made its disclosures.

(2) *Disclosure of Expert Testimony.*

(A) *In General.* In addition to the disclosures required by Rule 26(a)(1), a party must disclose to the other parties the identity of any witness it may use at trial to present evidence under Federal Rule of Evidence 702, 703, or 705.

(B) *Written Report.* Unless otherwise stipulated or ordered by the court, this disclosure must be accompanied by a written report—prepared and signed by the witness—if the witness is one retained or specially employed to provide expert testimony in the case or one whose duties as the party's employee regularly involve giving expert testimony. The report must contain:

(i) a complete statement of all opinions the witness will express and the basis and reasons for them;

(ii) the data or other information considered by the witness in forming them;

(iii) any exhibits that will be used to summarize or support them;

(iv) the witness's qualifications, including a list of all publications authored in the previous ten years;

(v) a list of all other cases in which, during the previous four years, the witness testified as an expert at trial or by deposition; and

(vi) a statement of the compensation to be paid for the study and testimony in the case.

(C) *Time to Disclose Expert Testimony.* A party must make these disclosures at the times and in the sequence that the court orders. Absent a stipulation or a court order, the disclosures must be made:

     (i) at least 90 days before the date set for trial or for the case to be ready for trial; or

     (ii) if the evidence is intended solely to contradict or rebut evidence on the same subject matter identified by another party under Rule 26(a)(2)(B), within 30 days after the other party's disclosure.

(D) *Supplementing the Disclosure.* The parties must supplement these disclosures when required under Rule 26(e).

(3) *Pretrial Disclosures.*

    (A) *In General.* In addition to the disclosures required by Rule 26(a)(1) and (2), a party must provide to the other parties and promptly file the following information about the evidence that it may present at trial other than solely for impeachment:

       (i) the name and, if not previously provided, the address and telephone number of each witness—separately identifying those the party expects to present and those it may call if the need arises;

       (ii) the designation of those witnesses whose testimony the party expects to present by deposition and, if not taken stenographically, a transcript of the pertinent parts of the deposition; and

       (iii) an identification of each document or other exhibit, including summaries of other evidence—separately identifying those items the party expects to offer and those it may offer if the need arises.

    (B) *Time for Pretrial Disclosures; Objections.* Unless the court orders otherwise, these disclosures must be made at least 30 days before trial. Within 14 days after they are made, un-

less the court sets a different time, a party may
serve and promptly file a list of the following
objections: any objections to the use under Rule
32(a) of a deposition designated by another
party under Rule 26(a)(3)(A)(ii); and any objection, together with the grounds for it, that may
be made to the admissibility of materials identified under Rule 26(a)(3)(A)(iii). An objection
not so made—except for one under Federal
Rule of Evidence 402 or 403—is waived unless
excused by the court for good cause.

(4) *Form of Disclosures.* Unless the court orders otherwise, all disclosures under Rule 26(a) must be in
writing, signed, and served.

(b) Discovery Scope and Limits.

(1) *Scope in General.* Unless otherwise limited by court
order, the scope of discovery is as follows: Parties
may obtain discovery regarding any nonprivileged
matter that is relevant to any party's claim or
defense—including the existence, description, nature, custody, condition, and location of any documents or other tangible things and the identity and
location of persons who know of any discoverable
matter. For good cause, the court may order discovery of any matter relevant to the subject matter
involved in the action. Relevant information need
not be admissible at the trial if the discovery appears reasonably calculated to lead to the discovery
of admissible evidence. All discovery is subject to the
limitations imposed by Rule 26(b)(2)(C).

(2) *Limitations on Frequency and Extent.*

(A) *When Permitted.* By order, the court may alter
the limits in these rules on the number of
depositions and interrogatories or on the length
of depositions under Rule 30. By order or local
rule, the court may also limit the number of
requests under Rule 36.

(B) *Specific Limitations on Electronically Stored Information.* A party need not provide discovery
of electronically stored information from
sources that the party identifies as not reason-

ably accessible because of undue burden or cost. On motion to compel discovery or for a protective order, the party from whom discovery is sought must show that the information is not reasonably accessible because of undue burden or cost. If that showing is made, the court may nonetheless order discovery from such sources if the requesting party shows good cause, considering the limitations of Rule 26(b)(2)(C). The court may specify conditions for the discovery.

(C) *When Required.* On motion or on its own, the court must limit the frequency or extent of discovery otherwise allowed by these rules or by local rule if it determines that:

(i) the discovery sought is unreasonably cumulative or duplicative, or can be obtained from some other source that is more convenient, less burdensome, or less expensive;

(ii) the party seeking discovery has had ample opportunity to obtain the information by discovery in the action; or

(iii) the burden or expense of the proposed discovery outweighs its likely benefit, considering the needs of the case, the amount in controversy, the parties' resources, the importance of the issues at stake in the action, and the importance of the discovery in resolving the issues.

(3) *Trial Preparation: Materials.*

(A) *Documents and Tangible Things.* Ordinarily, a party may not discover documents and tangible things that are prepared in anticipation of litigation or for trial by or for another party or its representative (including the other party's attorney, consultant, surety, indemnitor, insurer, or agent). But, subject to Rule 26(b)(4), those materials may be discovered if:

(i) they are otherwise discoverable under Rule 26(b)(1); and

(ii) the party shows that it has substantial need for the materials to prepare its case and

cannot, without undue hardship, obtain
their substantial equivalent by other
means.

(B) *Protection Against Disclosure.* If the court orders discovery of those materials, it must protect against disclosure of the mental impressions, conclusions, opinions, or legal theories of
a party's attorney or other representative concerning the litigation.

(C) *Previous Statement.* Any party or other person
may, on request and without the required showing, obtain the person's own previous statement
about the action or its subject matter. If the
request is refused, the person may move for a
court order, and Rule 37(a)(5) applies to the
award of expenses. A previous statement is either:

(i) a written statement that the person has
signed or otherwise adopted or approved; or

(ii) a contemporaneous stenographic, mechanical, electrical, or other recording—or a
transcription of it—that recites substantially verbatim the person's oral statement.

(4) *Trial Preparation: Experts.*

(A) *Expert Who May Testify.* A party may depose
any person who has been identified as an expert
whose opinions may be presented at trial. If
Rule 26(a)(2)(B) requires a report from the
expert, the deposition may be conducted only
after the report is provided.

(B) *Expert Employed Only for Trial Preparation.*
Ordinarily, a party may not, by interrogatories
or deposition, discover facts known or opinions
held by an expert who has been retained or
specially employed by another party in anticipation of litigation or to prepare for trial and who
is not expected to be called as a witness at trial.
But a party may do so only:

(i) as provided in Rule 35(b); or

(ii) on showing exceptional circumstances under which it is impracticable for the party

to obtain facts or opinions on the same subject by other means.

(C) *Payment.* Unless manifest injustice would result, the court must require that the party seeking discovery:

(i) pay the expert a reasonable fee for time spent in responding to discovery under Rule 26(b)(4)(A) or (B); and

(ii) for discovery under (B), also pay the other party a fair portion of the fees and expenses it reasonably incurred in obtaining the expert's facts and opinions.

(5) *Claiming Privilege or Protecting Trial–Preparation Materials.*

(A) *Information Withheld.* When a party withholds information otherwise discoverable by claiming that the information is privileged or subject to protection as trial-preparation material, the party must:

(i) expressly make the claim; and

(ii) describe the nature of the documents, communications, or tangible things not produced or disclosed—and do so in a manner that, without revealing information itself privileged or protected, will enable other parties to assess the claim.

(B) *Information Produced.* If information produced in discovery is subject to a claim of privilege or of protection as trial-preparation material, the party making the claim may notify any party that received the information of the claim and the basis for it. After being notified, a party must promptly return, sequester, or destroy the specified information and any copies it has; must not use or disclose the information until the claim is resolved; must take reasonable steps to retrieve the information if the party disclosed it before being notified; and may promptly present the information to the court under seal for a determination of the claim. The producing party must preserve the information until the claim is resolved.

(c) Protective Orders.

(1) *In General.* A party or any person from whom discovery is sought may move for a protective order in the court where the action is pending—or as an alternative on matters relating to a deposition, in the court for the district where the deposition will be taken. The motion must include a certification that the movant has in good faith conferred or attempted to confer with other affected parties in an effort to resolve the dispute without court action. The court may, for good cause, issue an order to protect a party or person from annoyance, embarrassment, oppression, or undue burden or expense, including one or more of the following:

(A) forbidding the disclosure or discovery;

(B) specifying terms, including time and place, for the disclosure or discovery;

(C) prescribing a discovery method other than the one selected by the party seeking discovery;

(D) forbidding inquiry into certain matters, or limiting the scope of disclosure or discovery to certain matters;

(E) designating the persons who may be present while the discovery is conducted;

(F) requiring that a deposition be sealed and opened only on court order;

(G) requiring that a trade secret or other confidential research, development, or commercial information not be revealed or be revealed only in a specified way; and

(H) requiring that the parties simultaneously file specified documents or information in sealed envelopes, to be opened as the court directs.

(2) *Ordering Discovery.* If a motion for a protective order is wholly or partly denied, the court may, on just terms, order that any party or person provide or permit discovery.

(3) *Awarding Expenses.* Rule 37(a)(5) applies to the award of expenses.

(d) Timing and Sequence of Discovery.

(1) *Timing.* A party may not seek discovery from any source before the parties have conferred as required by Rule 26(f), except in a proceeding exempted from initial disclosure under Rule 26(a)(1)(B), or when authorized by these rules, by stipulation, or by court order.

(2) *Sequence.* Unless, on motion, the court orders otherwise for the parties' and witnesses' convenience and in the interests of justice:

(A) methods of discovery may be used in any sequence; and

(B) discovery by one party does not require any other party to delay its discovery.

(e) Supplementing Disclosures and Responses.

(1) *In General.* A party who has made a disclosure under Rule 26(a)—or who has responded to an interrogatory, request for production, or request for admission—must supplement or correct its disclosure or response:

(A) in a timely manner if the party learns that in some material respect the disclosure or response is incomplete or incorrect, and if the additional or corrective information has not otherwise been made known to the other parties during the discovery process or in writing; or

(B) as ordered by the court.

(2) *Expert Witness.* For an expert whose report must be disclosed under Rule 26(a)(2)(B), the party's duty to supplement extends both to information included in the report and to information given during the expert's deposition. Any additions or changes to this information must be disclosed by the time the party's pretrial disclosures under Rule 26(a)(3) are due.

(f) Conference of the Parties; Planning for Discovery.

(1) *Conference Timing.* Except in a proceeding exempted from initial disclosure under Rule 26(a)(1)(B) or when the court orders otherwise, the parties must confer as soon as practicable—and in any event at least 21 days before a scheduling conference is to be held or a scheduling order is due under Rule 16(b).

(2) *Conference Content; Parties' Responsibilities.* In conferring, the parties must consider the nature and basis of their claims and defenses and the possibilities for promptly settling or resolving the case; make or arrange for the disclosures required by Rule 26(a)(1); discuss any issues about preserving discoverable information; and develop a proposed discovery plan. The attorneys of record and all unrepresented parties that have appeared in the case are jointly responsible for arranging the conference, for attempting in good faith to agree on the proposed discovery plan, and for submitting to the court within 14 days after the conference a written report outlining the plan. The court may order the parties or attorneys to attend the conference in person.

(3) *Discovery Plan.* A discovery plan must state the parties' views and proposals on:

(A) what changes should be made in the timing, form, or requirement for disclosures under Rule 26(a), including a statement of when initial disclosures were made or will be made;

(B) the subjects on which discovery may be needed, when discovery should be completed, and whether discovery should be conducted in phases or be limited to or focused on particular issues;

(C) any issues about disclosure or discovery of electronically stored information, including the form or forms in which it should be produced;

(D) any issues about claims of privilege or of protection as trial-preparation materials, including— if the parties agree on a procedure to assert these claims after production—whether to ask the court to include their agreement in an order;

(E) what changes should be made in the limitations on discovery imposed under these rules or by local rule, and what other limitations should be imposed; and

(F) any other orders that the court should issue under Rule 26(c) or under Rule 16(b) and (c).

(4) *Expedited Schedule.* If necessary to comply with its expedited schedule for Rule 16(b) conferences, a court may by local rule:

(A) require the parties' conference to occur less than 21 days before the scheduling conference is held or a scheduling order is due under Rule 16(b); and

(B) require the written report outlining the discovery plan to be filed less than 14 days after the parties' conference, or excuse the parties from submitting a written report and permit them to report orally on their discovery plan at the Rule 16(b) conference.

(g) Signing Disclosures and Discovery Requests, Responses, and Objections.

(1) *Signature Required; Effect of Signature.* Every disclosure under Rule 26(a)(1) or (a)(3) and every discovery request, response, or objection must be signed by at least one attorney of record in the attorney's own name—or by the party personally, if unrepresented—and must state the signer's address, e-mail address, and telephone number. By signing, an attorney or party certifies that to the best of the person's knowledge, information, and belief formed after a reasonable inquiry:

(A) with respect to a disclosure, it is complete and correct as of the time it is made; and

(B) with respect to a discovery request, response, or objection, it is:

(i) consistent with these rules and warranted by existing law or by a nonfrivolous argument for extending, modifying, or reversing existing law, or for establishing new law;

636

       (ii) not interposed for any improper purpose, such as to harass, cause unnecessary delay, or needlessly increase the cost of litigation; and

       (iii) neither unreasonable nor unduly burdensome or expensive, considering the needs of the case, prior discovery in the case, the amount in controversy, and the importance of the issues at stake in the action.

(2) *Failure to Sign.* Other parties have no duty to act on an unsigned disclosure, request, response, or objection until it is signed, and the court must strike it unless a signature is promptly supplied after the omission is called to the attorney's or party's attention.

(3) *Sanction for Improper Certification.* If a certification violates this rule without substantial justification, the court, on motion or on its own, must impose an appropriate sanction on the signer, the party on whose behalf the signer was acting, or both. The sanction may include an order to pay the reasonable expenses, including attorney's fees, caused by the violation.

[Amended December 27, 1946, effective March 19, 1948; January 21, 1963, effective July 1, 1963; February 28, 1966, effective July 1, 1966; March 30, 1970, effective July 1, 1970; April 29, 1980, effective August 1, 1980; April 28, 1983, effective August 1, 1983; March 2, 1987, effective August 1, 1987; April 22, 1993, effective December 1, 1993; April 17, 2000, effective December 1, 2000; April 12, 2006, effective December 1, 2006; April 30, 2007, effective December 1, 2007.]

2007 AMENDMENTS ROADMAP

STYLE PROJECT CHANGES: The style changes to Rule 26 were extensive. Many of the sections were broken into new subsections or renumbered, so care should be exercised when reviewing or citing to prior cases citing to individual subsections. Section 26(a)(5), which contained a list of discovery methods provided by later rules, was deleted. The reference to discovery of "books" in Rule 26(b)(1) was deleted to be consistent with the language used in other Rules, but books remain discoverable. Rule 26(b)(3) was amended to specify that a party may get a copy of the party's own statement by request–previously, the Rule only expressly made the request procedure available to nonparties. Rule 26(e) previously described the duty to supplement "to include information thereafter acquired." This language was removed to remove any doubt that the duty extends to information that was not originally produced although it was available. Rule 26(e) was also revised to consistently describe the time to supplement or correct a disclosure or discovery request as "in a timely manner," to avoid any inferred distinction between that standard and "season-ably" or "at appropriate intervals." Rule 26(g)(2) now specifically calls for striking an unsigned disclosure, correcting an oversight in the former version. Rule 26(b)(1)(B)(i) was amended to change the reference to a "good faith" argument to a "nonfrivolous" argument to be consistent with Rule 11. Active voice replaced passive voice, "must" was used instead of "shall", cumbersome and obsolete language was culled, and the language was generally simplified and clarified.

NON-STYLE CHANGES: Rule 26(g)(1) was amended to require that the signer of discovery documents provide the signer's email address and phone number as well as address. Rule 26(g)(1)(B)(i), governing the signer's certifica-tion for disclosures, discovery requests and responses, and objections, was amended to allow the assertion of a position based on a nonfrivolous argument for establishing new law.

NOTE: The Federal Rules "Style Project" is explained in Part III-A.

AUTHORS' COMMENTARY ON RULE 26

PURPOSE AND SCOPE

Rule 26 contains the general provisions governing discovery. It sets forth the general discovery procedures, controls the scope of inquiry allowed, provides for protective orders, and imposes a duty to supple-ment discovery responses. The general provisions in Rule 26 apply to the specific discovery devices in Rules 27 through 37.

NOTE: Rule 26 and the other discovery rules were substantially revised in 1970, 1993, 2000, 2006, and 2007. Therefore, great care should be exercised when citing or relying on decisions pertaining to Rule 26.

2006 AMENDMENTS: The 2006 Amendments to Rule 26 were primarily designed to refine the way that electronic data is discovered under the Rules. The specific changes are described in footnotes to each amended subsection. In addition, details of the effects of the amend-ments are described in the author commentary to Rule 26. The following is a summary of those changes:

(1) The initial disclosure provisions in Rule 26(a) were amended to require the disclosure of "electronically stored information," as well as documents and tangible things, that the party may use to support its claims or defenses.

(2) Rule 26(b)(2), which provides limitations on discovery, was amended to provide limitations related to electronic data. It provides that a party can identify sources of electronically stored information as not reasonably accessible based on burden or cost. If the parties disagree about this designation, either party can move the court for a determination. Even if the court

determines that the information is not reasonably accessible, the court may order its production for good cause shown.

(3) Rule 26(b)(5), which addresses claims of privilege, was amended to address the inadvertent production of privileged information. Under the new procedure, the producing party may notify the receiving party that privileged information had been produced. The receiving party must then either return the privileged information or provide the information to the court for a determination of the validity of the privilege.

(4) Rule 26(f), which covers the discovery conference that the parties must conduct prior to the first Rule 16 conference, was amended to require the parties to discuss the preservation of discoverable information and to add two new subsections containing additional topics that the parties must discuss at the conference and include in their report to the court:

i. disclosure and discovery of electronically stored information, including the preservation of such information, the form in which such information should be produced, and the costs associated with the production of such information.

ii. New Rule 26(f)(3)(D) requires the parties to discuss the handling of privileged information, and specifically the manner for asserting a claim of privilege after production.

RULE 26(a). REQUIRED DISCLOSURES

CORE CONCEPT

Rule 26(a) requires that parties disclose certain information automatically, without the need for discovery requests, at three points during the litigation. First, all parties must make broad initial disclosures at or shortly after they conduct the discovery meeting under Rule 26(f). Second, Rule 26(a) requires disclosures about expert testimony 90 days before trial. Third, Rule 26(a) specifies the pretrial disclosures to be made 30 days before trial. Rule 26(a) also establishes the exclusive list of available discovery methods to supplement the automatic disclosures. In general, the only discovery devices that parties may use are: depositions upon oral examination (Rules 30, 27, 28, and 32); depositions upon written questions (Rules 31, 27, 28, and 32); written interrogatories (Rule 33); production of documents and things and entry onto land for inspection (Rule 34); physical and mental inspections (Rule 35); and requests for admission (Rule 36).

RULE 26(a)(1). INITIAL DISCLOSURE

CORE CONCEPT

At the commencement of discovery, each party must disclose the identity of witnesses, a description of documents by category and location, a computation of each category of damages, and insurance information.

APPLICATIONS

2007 Amendments

The 2007 amendments substantially reorganized Rule 26(a)(1), regrouping the content into renumbered subsections. Notably, the types of actions exempt from the automatic disclosures formerly located in Rule 26(a)(1)(E) are now located in Rule 26(a)(1)(B). Care should be exercised in researching and citing pre–2008 cases referring to subsections of Rule 26(a)(1).

Time for Initial Disclosure

Parties must make their initial disclosures at or within 14 days after the discovery meeting required by Rule 26(f), unless a different time is set by court order or stipulation. Thus, Rule 26 establishes the following typical sequence for the early discovery events: first, the court schedules an initial scheduling conference; second, the parties conduct a discovery meeting at least 21 days before the court's initial scheduling conference; third, the parties make their voluntary disclosures; and fourth, the parties meet with the judge for the scheduling conference, where the timetable for the balance of the discovery events will be established. Parties joined or served after the Rule 26(f) conference must make the initial disclosures within 30 days after being joined or served, unless a different time is set by stipulation or court order.

Content of Initial Disclosure

Rule 26(a)(1) requires automatic initial disclosure of four categories of information:

> (A) *Witnesses*: Parties must disclose the name, and if known the address and telephone number,[1] of each individual likely to have discoverable information that the disclosing party may use to support its claims or defenses.[2] Parties must also identify the subjects of such information.

> (B) *Documents*: Parties must provide a copy of, or a description by category and location of, all documents, electronically stored information, and tangible things that the disclosing party may use to support its claims or defenses.[3] Except in cases with

---

1. *Scaife v. Boenne*, 191 F.R.D. 590, 594 (N.D.In.2000) (Rule 26(a)(1) contemplates disclosure of address and telephone number so the other party can contact the witnesses, if appropriate).

2. *Cummings v. General Motors Corp.*, 365 F.3d 944, 954 (10th Cir.2004) (a party is not obligated to disclose witnesses or documents, whether favorable or unfavorable, that it does not intend to use); *Intel Corp. v. VIA Technologies, Inc.*, 204 F.R.D. 450, 451–52 (N.D.Cal.2001) (witness identi-

ty must be disclosed if the witness may be used to support claims or defenses in the context of a motion or at trial, but an affidavit or declaration is work product and need not be disclosed).

3. *Lovato v. Burlington Northern and Santa Fe Ry. Co.*, 200 F.R.D. 448 (D.Colo. 2001), *rev'd on other grounds*, 201 F.R.D. 509 (D. Colo.2001) (medical records must be disclosed).

very few documents, most parties will disclose categories and locations rather than producing all the documents. Parties must provide or describe all disclosable documents in their possession, control, or custody.[4]

(C) *Damages Computations*: Each party must provide a computation of any category of damages claimed by that party.[5] Each party must also produce the non-privileged documents supporting the computation, including documents bearing on the nature and extent of injuries suffered.

(D) *Insurance*: Each party must provide all insurance policies that may provide coverage for part or all of any judgment that might be entered in the action.[6]

Additional disclosures may be required by directive.

Information to Support Claims or Defenses

Rule 26(a)(1) requires disclosure only of information and documents that the disclosing party may use to support its claims or defenses.[7] This provision dovetails with the exclusionary sanction of Rule 37(c)(1), so that a party may not use information or documents not disclosed initially or by supplement.[8]

Impeachment

Information and documents that a party may use solely for impeachment need not be disclosed.[9]

Electronic Data

Rule 26(a)(1)(A)(ii) specifically requires the disclosure of the "electronically stored information"[10] that it may use to support its claims or defenses. If electronic data is very costly or burdensome to disclose, a party may invoke the procedure under Rule 26(b)(2) (under which a party may notify the other parties that it is not

---

4. See Rule 34(a) for an explanation of the scope of documents within a party's possession, custody, or control.

5. *Williams v. Trader Pub. Co.*, 218 F.3d 481, 487 (5th Cir.2000) (damages for emotional distress are not susceptible to the type of calculation contemplated by Rule 26(a)(1)); *Morrison Knudsen Corp. v. Fireman's Fund Ins. Co.*, 175 F.3d 1221 (10th Cir.1999); *Design Strategies, Inc. v. Davis*, 367 F.Supp.2d 630 (S.D.N.Y.2005).

6. *Excelsior College v. Frye*, 233 F.R.D. 583, 585–86 (S.D.Cal.2006) ("Rule 26(a)(1)(D), merely requires the disclosure of an insurance policy or other agreement that gives rise to an insurer's obligation to indemnify or hold its insured harmless for a judgment, and does not require the production of all agreements relating to insurance"); *Gluck v. Ansett Australia Ltd.*, 204 F.R.D. 217, 222 (D.D.C.2001); *Flores v.*

Southern Peru Copper Corp., 203 F.R.D. 92 (S.D.N.Y.2001).

7. *Krause v. Buffalo and Erie County Workforce Development Consortium, Inc.*, 425 F.Supp.2d 352 (W.D.N.Y.2006).

8. The 2000 Amendment to the Advisory Committee Note to Rule 26(a)(1).

9. *Hammel v. Eau Galle Cheese Factory*, 407 F.3d 852, 869 (7th Cir.2005); *Searles v. Van Bebber*, 251 F.3d 869 (10th Cir.2001); *Lomascolo v. Otto Oldsmobile–Cadillac, Inc.*, 253 F.Supp.2d 354, 359 (N.D.N.Y. 2003) (documents must be used *solely* for impeachment).

10. The Advisory Committee Notes to the 2006 Amendments indicate that the term "electronically stored information" is consistent with the prior case law requiring the production of electronic documents and "data compilations."

collecting and disclosing certain electronic data, and then either party may ask the court to determine whether the data need be disclosed).

Excluded Proceedings

Rule 26(a)(1)(B) excludes 8 categories of proceedings from the initial disclosures:

(1) appeals from administrative proceedings;

(2) petitions for habeas corpus or like challenges to criminal convictions or sentences;

(3) pro se prisoner actions;

(4) actions to enforce or quash an administrative summons or subpoena;

(5) actions by the United States to recover benefit payments;

(6) actions by the United States to collect on student loans guaranteed by the United States;

(7) proceedings ancillary to proceedings in other courts; and

(8) actions to enforce arbitration awards.

Investigation for Initial Disclosure

The parties must make their initial disclosures based on the information then "reasonably available." Rule 26(a)(1) expressly provides that a party may not avoid the initial disclosure requirements by claiming that its investigation is not yet complete.

Failure to Disclose

Failure to make the initial disclosures required by Rule 26(a)(1) can result in the exclusion of the undisclosed witness or information,[11] unless the failure was harmless or there was substantial justification.[12]

Other Party's Failure to Disclose

A party may not refuse to make the Rule 26(a) disclosures because another party has also failed to do so.[13] Likewise, a party believing that another party's disclosure was not sufficient must nonetheless make its own disclosures.

---

11. *Wilson v. AM General Corp.*, 167 F.3d 1114 (7th Cir.1999) (rejecting claim that the witnesses were impeachment witnesses and excluding their testimony). *But see Hernandez–Torres v. Intercontinental Trading, Inc.*, 158 F.3d 43, 49 (1st Cir. 1998) (witnesses need not be listed until 30 days before trial, as required by Rule 26(a)(3)(A)(i)).

12. *Davis v. U.S. Bancorp*, 383 F.3d 761, 765 (8th Cir.2004); *Pfingston v. Ronan Engineering Co.*, 284 F.3d 999, 1005 (9th Cir.2002) (examining prejudice to the other party caused by delayed disclosure); *Trost v. Trek Bicycle Corp.*, 162 F.3d 1004 (8th Cir. 1998); *Wilkins v. Kmart Corp.*, 487 F.Supp.2d 1216 (D.Kan. 2007) (if the other party was well aware of the identity of the undisclosed witness, it may render the failure to disclose harmless).

13. *See Jacobsen v. Deseret Book Co.*, 287 F.3d 936, 954 (10th Cir.2002).

Disclosures Automatic

The initial disclosures are automatically required, without any need for a request or demand.

Stipulations Not to Disclose

The parties may stipulate to the elimination or modification of the initial disclosures, unless precluded from doing so by local rule or court order.

Form of Disclosures

The initial disclosures should be in writing, signed, and served on other parties unless otherwise directed by local rule or court order.[14] The signature constitutes a certification that the disclosure is complete and accurate under Rule 26(g)(1).

Objections

A party believing that Rule 26(a)(1) initial disclosures are "not appropriate in the circumstances of the action" may object during the Rule 26(f) discovery conference. The objection should then be stated in the Rule 26(f) discovery plan filed with the court. Disclosures are not required thereafter except as ordered by the court.[15] In ruling on the objection, the court must determine what disclosures, if any, will be made and set the time for such disclosures.

New or Late Served Parties

Parties that have not been joined or served at the time of the initial disclosures or the Rule 26(f) discovery conference must still make initial disclosures. The time for their disclosures will be 30 days from when they are served or joined, unless modified by stipulation or order. The scope of such parties' disclosures will be similar to the original parties with respect to any stipulations or court orders.[16]

RULE 26(a)(2).   DISCLOSURE OF EXPERT TESTIMONY

CORE CONCEPT

Each party must disclose the identity of its expert witnesses and produce an expert report for each expert witness.

APPLICATIONS

Which Experts

Rule 26(a)(2)(A) requires the disclosure of the identity of any person who "may be used at trial to present evidence" under the Federal Rules of Evidence governing expert testimony. Rule 26(a)(2)(B) requires an expert report for any witness "retained or

14. *See S.E.C. v. TheStreet.Com*, 273 F.3d 222, 233 (2d Cir.2001) (initial disclosures under Rule 26(a)(1) are not filed unless ordered by the court or used in a subsequent stage of the proceedings).

15. The 2000 Amendment to the Advisory Committee Note to Rule 26(a)(1).

16. The Advisory Committee Note to the 2000 Amendment to Rule 26(a)(1).

specially employed to provide expert testimony."[17]

Time for Expert Disclosure

The time for expert disclosures can be set by the court or stipulated by the parties.[18] In the absence of a court order or stipulation, the expert disclosures must be made 90 days before the trial date.[19] If the expert testimony is purely to contradict or rebut testimony disclosed by another party, then the disclosure must be made within 30 days after the disclosure by the other party.[20] Leave may be obtained to disclose an expert report for a rebuttal expert witness after the time for expert disclosures under Rule 26(a)(2).[21]

Content of Expert Disclosure

Rule 26(a)(2) requires automatic disclosure of the identity of persons who "may" testify as expert witnesses and production of a report for each such witness.

Expert Report

Each expert report must be in writing and signed by the expert,[22] and must contain: a complete statement of all the expert's opinions and the basis and reasons therefor;[23] the data and information considered by the expert, including documents provided by counsel;[24] any exhibits to be used as support for or a summary of

17. In re Ephedra Products Liability Litigation, 478 F.Supp.2d 624, 634 (S.D.N.Y. 2007) (plaintiff required to disclose the identify of, but not a report for, an expert not engaged or specially employed to provide expert testimony).

18. See Corwin v. Walt Disney Co., 475 F.3d 1239, 1252 (11th Cir. 2007) (court may set deadline for expert disclosures); Southern Union Company v. Southwest Gas Corp., 180 F.Supp.2d 1021, 1059–60 (D.Ariz.2002) (the disclosures should be sufficiently in advance of trial that opposing parties have a reasonable opportunity to prepare for effective cross examination and perhaps arrange for expert testimony from other witnesses).

19. Lutz v. Glendale Union High School, 403 F.3d 1061, 1071 (9th Cir.2005) (the 90 day period applies only in the absence of a court established deadline); School Bd. of Collier County, Fla. v. K.C., 285 F.3d 977, 981 (11th Cir.2002).

20. Primus v. United States, 389 F.3d 231, 234 (1st Cir.2004); Callahan v. A.E.V., Inc., 182 F.3d 237, 259 (3d Cir.1999) (expert witness designated as "rebuttal expert" allowed to testify during case-in-chief).

21. See Nyama v. Ashcroft, 357 F.3d 812, 816 (8th Cir.2004); Eckelkamp v. Beste, 315 F.3d 863, 872 (8th Cir.2002).

22. Gust v. Jones, 162 F.3d 587 (10th Cir.1998); In re Omeprazole Patent Litigation, 227 F.R.D. 227 (S.D.N.Y.2005) (it is the expert's report, and the party may not amend it); Trigon Ins. Co. v. United States, 204 F.R.D. 277, 292–93 (E.D.Va.2001) (the report must be prepared by the expert, but the attorney may assist); but see Jenkins v. Bartlett, 487 F.3d 482 (7th Cir. 2007) (allowing experts to adopt a letter written by another doctor as their report).

23. King v. Ford Motor Co., 209 F.3d 886, 900 (6th Cir.2000); Atkins v. County of Orange, 372 F.Supp.2d 377 (S.D.N.Y. 2005)(report must disclose underlying opinions, not merely bald conclusions as to ultimate issues); but see Thompson v. Doane Pet Care Co., 470 F.3d 1201, 1203 (6th Cir. 2006) (the expert is not limited to reading the report aloud, but can "supplement, elaborate on, [and] explain" the opinions in the report).

24. Fidelity Nat. Title Ins. Co. of New York v. Intercounty Nat. Title Ins. Co., 412 F.3d 745 (7th Cir.2005) (party must disclose all documents "considered" by the expert, without regard to the expert's document retention policy); Synthes Spine Co., L.P. v. Walden, 232 F.R.D. 460, 461–62 (E.D.Pa. 2005) (the rule requires the disclosure of all information provided to the expert, including privileged information); Colindres v.

the opinions; the qualifications of the expert and all publications authored by the expert in the past 10 years; the expert's compensation for his review and testimony; and a list of all other cases in which the expert has testified at trial or at deposition in the past 4 years.[25] The report itself should contain all the required information with considerable detail,[26] and may not satisfy Rule 26(a)(2)(B) by incorporating interrogatory answers.[27]

Failure to Disclose Report

The failure to disclose a report meeting the requirements of Rule 26(a)(2)(B) may preclude that witness from testifying, either altogether[28] or as to specific opinions not disclosed in the report.[29] Such sanctions are "automatic and mandatory" unless the party failing to disclose can show the failure was justified or harmless.[30] The courts are divided as to whether disclosure of the expert opinions or required information in deposition is a substitute for inclusion in the expert disclosure.[31]

Quietflex Mfg., 228 F.R.D. 567 (S.D.Tex. 2005) (documents "considered" by the expert must be disclosed, even if not ultimately relied upon); *Herman v. Marine Midland Bank*, 207 F.R.D. 26 (W.D.N.Y.2002) (the rule requires the disclosure of all information provided to the expert, including work product).

25. *Doblar v. Unverferth Manuf. Co., Inc.*, 185 F.R.D. 258 (D.S.D.1999) (awarding sanctions against the expert because many instances of prior testimony were not disclosed); *Coleman v. Dydula*, 190 F.R.D. 316, 318 (W.D.N.Y.1999) (the list of cases should, at a minimum, include the name of the court where the testimony occurred, the names of the parties, the case number, and whether the testimony was given at a deposition or trial); *Zic v. Italian Government Travel Office*, 130 F.Supp.2d 991, 1001 (N.D.Ill.2001) (names of the parties in other cases in which the expert has testified is sufficient, although not ideal). Cf. *Trunk v. Midwest Rubber & Supply Co.*, 175 F.R.D. 664, 665 (D.Colo.1997) (Rule 26(a)(2)(B) report does not require a party to produce reports offered by its expert witness in unrelated litigation).

26. *In re Sulfuric Acid Antitrust Litigation*, 432 F.Supp.2d 794 (N.D.Ill.2006) (part of the purpose of the expert report is to shorten, or even eliminate the need for, the expert's deposition); *Hilt v. SFC, Inc.*, 170 F.R.D. 182, 184–85 (D.Kan.1997) (report must provide the substantive rationale in detail with respect to the basis and reasons for the proffered opinions).

27. *Smith v. State Farm Fire and Casualty Co.*, 164 F.R.D. 49 (S.D.W.Va.1995).

28. *Pena–Crespo v. Puerto Rico*, 408 F.3d 10, 13–14 (1st Cir.2005); *Ortiz-Lopez v. Sociedad Espanola de Auxilio Mutuo Y Beneficiencia de Puerto Rico*, 248 F.3d 29 (1st Cir.2001).

29. *Dairy Farmers of America, Inc. v. Travelers Ins. Co.*, 391 F.3d 936, 943–44 (8th Cir.2004); *Brandt Distributing Co., Inc. v. Federal Ins. Co.*, 247 F.3d 822 (8th Cir. 2001); *Salgado v. General Motors Corp.*, 150 F.3d 735, 742 (7th Cir.1998) (expert report must contain a detailed description of expert opinions and bases therefore); *Lamarca v. United States*, 31 F.Supp.2d 110, 122–23 (E.D.N.Y.1998) (expert opinion not in report excluded even though disclosed during deposition); *Coastal Fuels of Puerto Rico v. Caribbean Petroleum Corp.*, 79 F.3d 182 (1st Cir.1996).

30. *Keach v. U.S. Trust Co.*, 419 F.3d 626, 639–40 (7th Cir.2005); *Jacobsen v. Deseret Book Co.*, 287 F.3d 936, 952–53 (10th Cir.2002) (listing factors to be considered in determining the existence of substantial justification or harmlessness).

31. *See Smith v. Tenet Healthsystem SL, Inc.*, 436 F.3d 879, 889 (8th Cir.2006) (expert could rely on x-rays disclosed at the deposition because failure to disclose in the report was harmless); *In re Sulfuric Acid Antitrust Litigation*, 432 F.Supp.2d 794 (N.D.Ill.2006) (asking about additional opinions at deposition may open the door for admission of those opinions at trial); *Olson v. Montana Rail Link, Inc.*, 227 F.R.D. 550, 552 (D.Mont.2005) (disclosure at a deposition held not sufficient); *Commercial Data Servers, Inc. v. International*

Stipulations Not to Disclose Expert Reports

The parties may stipulate to the elimination or modification of the expert report disclosures, unless precluded from doing so by local rule or court order.

Testimony is Measure, Not Witness Qualification

The expert disclosures are required if the testimony is expert in nature, not factual; expert disclosures are not required if an expert is being called to give percipient factual testimony.[32]

Experts Employed by a Party

A party must produce an expert report for any employee whose duties regularly involve giving expert testimony or who was specially employed to provide expert testimony.[33] This requirement will only apply, however, if the employee is giving expert testimony.[34]

Treating Physicians

An expert report is generally not required for a treating physician to testify regarding the treatment,[35] although a number of courts require an expert report when the treating physician will offer testimony as to causation.[36]

Always Disclose Experts Identities

In circumstances where no expert report is required, such as by stipulation, for employees whose duties do not include regularly testifying, or for treating physicians, the party must still disclose the identity of the expert witness or the witness will not be permitted to testify.[37]

Business Machines Corp., 262 F.Supp.2d 50 (S.D.N.Y.2003) (disclosure at a deposition held not sufficient).

32. *Gomez v. Rivera Rodriguez*, 344 F.3d 103, 113 (1st Cir.2003) (Rule 26(a)(2) does not encompass a percipient witness who happens to be an expert); *Gonzalez v. Executive Airlines, Inc.*, 236 F.R.D. 73 (D.Puerto Rico 2006) (the term expert pertains to those who will testify under Rule 702 of the Federal Rules of Evidence); *Indemnity Ins. Co. of North America v. American Eurocopter LLC*, 227 F.R.D. 421, 423 (M.D.N.C.2005).

33. *Prieto v. Malgor*, 361 F.3d 1313, 1318 (11th Cir.2004); *Rollins ex rel Rollins v. Barlow*, 188 F.Supp.2d 660, 661–62 (S.D.W.Va.2002) (report not required for police officer expert witness neither retained nor employed by the plaintiff); *Brown v. Best Foods*, 169 F.R.D. 385, 387 (N.D.Ala.1996) (treating physician may give expert opinion testimony without filing an expert report because the physician was not "retained or specifically employed" to render expert testimony).

34. *Watson v. United States*, ___ F.3d ___ (10th Cir. 2007) (employee allowed to

give expert testimony without expert report because he did not regularly give expert testimony); *Long v. Cottrell, Inc.*, 265 F.3d 663, 668 (8th Cir.2001) (expert report not required even though employee regularly testified for the party as an expert witness because the testimony at issue was fact testimony, not expert testimony).

35. *See Fielden v. CSX Transp., Inc.*, 482 F.3d 866, 869 (6th Cir. 2007); *Gonzalez v. Executive Airlines, Inc.*, 236 F.R.D. 73(D.Puerto Rico 2006) ("The Advisory Committee notes specifically single out treating physicians as an example of witnesses that are not bound by the written report requirement.").

36. *See Musser v. Gentiva Health Services*, 356 F.3d 751, 757 (7th Cir.2004); Indemnity Ins. Co. of North America v. American Eurocopter LLC, 227 F.R.D. 421, 423–24 (M.D.N.C.2005); *Martin v. CSX Transp., Inc.*, 215 F.R.D. 554 (S.D.Ind. 2003).

37. *Hamburger v. State Farm Mut. Auto. Ins. Co.*, 361 F.3d 875, 883, n.4 (5th Cir.2004).

Disclosures Automatic

The expert disclosures are automatically required, without any need for a request or demand.

Form of Disclosures

The expert disclosures should be in writing, signed, and served on other parties, unless otherwise directed by local rule or court order.[38] The signature constitutes a certification that the disclosure is complete and accurate under Rule 26(g)(1).

Objections to Disclosures

The court's case management order may designate a period for filing objections to the sufficiency of expert disclosures, in which case such objections are waived if not timely raised.[39] Otherwise, sanctions for an insufficient disclosure are governed by the sanctions provisions in Rule 37(c)(1).

Standard on Appeal

In reviewing a trial court's order for exclusion of expert testimony for failure to disclose, the appellate court will apply an abuse of discretion standard.[40]

RULE 26(a)(3). PRETRIAL DISCLOSURES

CORE CONCEPT

Prior to trial, each party must disclose the witnesses that may testify at trial, the deposition testimony that may be offered at trial, and the exhibits that may be offered at trial.

APPLICATIONS

2007 Amendments

The 2007 amendments reorganized Rule 26(a)(3), grouping former subsections (A) through (C) into subsections (i) through (iii) of new Rule 26(a)(3)(A). The trailing text at the end of Rule 26(a)(3) was made Rule 26(a)(3)(B). Care should be exercised in researching and citing pre–2008 cases referring to subsections of Rule 26(a)(3).

Time for Pretrial Disclosure

The time for pretrial disclosures is often set by the court. In the absence of a court order, the expert disclosures must be made 30 days before the trial date. Parties will not be required to respond to discovery requests seeking the information covered by Rule 26(a)(3) at an earlier stage in the litigation.[41]

---

38. *See S.E.C. v. TheStreet.Com*, 273 F.3d 222, 233 (2d Cir.2001) (initial disclosures under Rule 26(a)(2) are not filed unless ordered by the court or used in a subsequent stage of the proceedings).

39. *McCoy v. Whirlpool Corp.*, 214 F.R.D. 646, 648–49 (D.Kan.2003).

40. *Smith v. Tenet Healthsystem SL, Inc.*, 436 F.3d 879, 889 (8th Cir.2006); *Tompkin v. Philip Morris USA, Inc.*, 362 F.3d 882, 894–95 (6th Cir.2004).

41. *Banks v. Office of Senate Sergeant-At-Arms*, 222 F.R.D. 7, 15 (D.D.C.2004).

Content of Pretrial Disclosure

Rule 26(a)(3) requires a pretrial disclosure of the following information:

(A) *Witnesses*: Each party must disclose the name and, unless already disclosed, the address and phone number of each witness that may testify at trial. The disclosure should indicate those witnesses who are expected to testify and those who may be called if needed.

(B) *Depositions*: Each party must designate the testimony that the party intends to introduce in the form of a deposition. If the deposition was recorded other than stenographically, then the party must provide a transcript of the pertinent parts of the testimony.[42]

(C) *Exhibits*: Each party must identify all exhibits, including demonstrative or summary exhibits. The disclosure should indicate those exhibits that the party expects to introduce and those that the party may introduce if needed.

Impeachment

The pretrial disclosure is not required to include documents or testimony to be introduced solely for impeachment.[43]

Failure to Disclose

Any witnesses, depositions, or exhibits not properly disclosed under Rule 26(a)(3) may be excluded from use at trial.[44]

Objections to Deposition Testimony or Exhibits

Any objections to the use of a deposition or exhibit must be served and filed within 14 days of the disclosure of the intent to use the deposition or exhibit. The statement of the objections should state the grounds for the objections. Failure to disclose such an objection is a waiver of the objection, except for objections to relevancy under Rules 402 and 403 of the Federal Rules of Evidence. Note that the disclosure of the objection is not the same as making the objection; a party must still object when the deposition or exhibit is offered at trial.[45]

Disclosures Automatic

The pretrial disclosures are automatically required, without any need for a request or demand.

42. *Tilton v. Capital Cities/ABC, Inc.,* 115 F.3d 1471, 1478 (10th Cir.1997).

43. *Hammel v. Eau Galle Cheese Factory,* 407 F.3d 852, 869 (7th Cir.2005); *Bearint ex rel. Bearint v. Dorell Juvenile Group, Inc.,* 389 F.3d 1339, (11th Cir.2004) (party cannot admit just the rebuttal parts of an expert's testimony if no report was disclosed); *Halbasch v. Med–Data, Inc.,* 192 F.R.D. 641 (D.Or.2000) (discussing the various interpretations of "solely for impeachment"); *DeBiasio v. Illinois Central Railroad,* 52 F.3d 678 (7th Cir.1995).

44. The Advisory Committee Note to the 1993 Amendment to Rule 26.

45. The Advisory Committee Note to the 1993 Amendment to Rule 26.

Form of Disclosures

The pretrial disclosures should be in writing, signed, served on other parties, and filed with the court, unless otherwise directed by local rule or court order. The signature constitutes a certification that the disclosure is complete and accurate under Rule 26(g)(1).

RULE 26(a)(4). FORM OF DISCLOSURES

CORE CONCEPT

The automatic disclosures under Rule 26(a) should be in writing, signed, served on other parties, unless otherwise directed by local rule or court order. Only the pretrial disclosure under Rule 26(a)(3) must be filed. The signature constitutes a certification that the disclosure is complete and accurate under Rule 26(g)(1).

RULE 26(b)(1). DISCOVERY SCOPE AND LIMITS—SCOPE IN GENERAL

CORE CONCEPT

In general, discovery is allowed of any matter that is relevant to the claim or defense of any party in the pending action and is not privileged.[46] Discovery is more limited with respect to trial preparation materials, non-testifying expert witnesses, and physical or mental examinations.

APPLICATIONS

Covered Actions

The discovery rules apply to all civil actions in federal court, except for the narrow exceptions listed in Rule 81 (such as certain admiralty matters and matters in arbitration pursuant to federal statute). The Rules apply in bankruptcy proceedings, patent actions, and civil contempt proceedings. They apply in habeas corpus actions if the court grants leave to conduct discovery.

"Relevant" Defined

The term "relevant" is not defined by the Rules, but was extremely broad prior to the 2000 Amendments.[47] Courts have defined "relevant" to encompass "any matter that bears on, or that reasonably could lead to other matters that could bear on, any issue that is or may be in the case."[48] Courts also have defined "rele-

---

46. *Watts v. S.E.C.*, 482 F.3d 501, 507 (D.C.Cir. 2007); *Semien v. Life Ins. Co. of North America*, 436 F.3d 805, 813 (7th Cir. 2006); *In re EchoStar Communications Corp.*, 448 F.3d 1294 (Fed.Cir.2006).

47. *United Oil Co., Inc. v. Parts Associates, Inc.*, 227 F.R.D. 404 (D.Md.2005); *but see Food Lion, Inc. v. United Food and Commercial Workers Int'l Union*, 103 F.3d

1007, 1012–14 (D.C.Cir.1997) (finding that "relevant" did not extend to third and fourth party documents).

48. *Oil, Chemical & Atomic Workers Local Union v. N.L.R.B.*, 711 F.2d 348, 360 (D.C.Cir.1983); *Kidwiler v. Progressive Paloverde Ins. Co.*, 192 F.R.D. 193, 199 (N.D.W.Va.2000).

vant" as "germane." [49] However, although Rule 26(b)(1) continues to use the word "relevant" after the 2000 Amendments, the scope of discovery has been narrowed.[50]

Claim or Defense vs. Subject Matter

The 2000 Amendments changed the scope of discovery from matters "relevant to the subject matter involved in the pending action" to matters "relevant to the claim or defense of any party."[51] The Advisory Committee did not define the distinction, but indicated that it wants the focus of discovery to be the actual claims and defenses in the action, and does not want discovery to be used to develop new claims or defenses not already pleaded.[52] However, information such as other incidents of the same type or involving the same product or information about a party's organizational structure may be relevant to the claims in the action.[53]

Motion to Expand the Scope

For "good cause," the court may expand discovery to include matters relevant to the subject matter involved in the action.[54] This determination might be made in the context of a motion to compel a more broad response to particular discovery requests, or possibly could be raised in the Rule 26(f) discovery report and addressed during the initial status conference with the court.[55] The "good cause" standard is meant to be flexible, giving broad discretion to the court.[56]

Relevant to Potential Claims

A party may discover any matter that is relevant to any claim, issue, or defense that is pleaded in the case, regardless of which party raises the claim, issue, or defense. Discovery is not permitted as to potential additional claims or defenses, absent a court order expanding the scope of discovery.[57] Thus, discovery is permitted with respect to claims that have been challenged by a motion to dismiss or motion for summary judgment. However, if a claim has

49. *Oppenheimer Fund, Inc. v. Sanders,* 437 U.S. 340, 351, 98 S.Ct. 2380, 2389–90, 57 L.Ed.2d 253 (1978).

50. *See In re PE Corp. Securities Litigation,* 221 F.R.D. 20, 24 (D.Conn.2003); *Behler v. Hanlon,* 199 F.R.D. 553, 555 (D.Md. 2001) (amended Rule 26 is more narrow); *but see United Oil Co., Inc. v. Parts Associates, Inc.,* 227 F.R.D. 404 (D.Md.2005) (the new standard is still a broad one).

51. *See Sallis v. University of Minn.,* 408 F.3d 470, 477–78 (8th Cir.2005); *United Oil Co., Inc. v. Parts Associates, Inc.,* 227 F.R.D. 404 (D.Md.2005) (discussing the effects of the 2000 Amendments).

52. The Advisory Committee Note to the 2000 Amendment to Rule 26(b)(1). *See*

also *Sallis v. University of Minn.,* 408 F.3d 470, 477 (8th Cir.2005) (advisory committee wanted courts to be more involved in controlling discovery).

53. The Advisory Committee Note to the 2000 Amendment to Rule 26(b)(1).

54. *Klein v. AIG Trading Group Inc.,* 228 F.R.D. 418 (D.Conn.2005); *Castillo v. Norton,* 219 F.R.D. 155, 160, n.2 (D.Ariz. 2003).

55. The Advisory Committee Note to the 2000 Amendment to Rule 26(b)(1).

56. The Advisory Committee Note to the 2000 Amendment to Rule 26(b)(1).

57. The Advisory Committee Note to the 2000 Amendment to Rule 26(b)(1).

been dismissed, further discovery that is relevant to that claim only will not be allowed.[58]

Relevant vs. Admissible

Evidence need not be admissible to be relevant, and thus discoverable.[59] Rule 26(b)(1) states that relevant inadmissible evidence is discoverable if it is "reasonably calculated to lead to the discovery of admissible evidence."[60] Conversely, admissible evidence is almost always discoverable.[61]

Limitations on Discovery

The broad scope of discovery under Rule 26(b)(1) must be read in conjunction with the three limitations in Rule 26(b)(2) relating to discovery that is cumulative or unduly burdensome. Although this has been the case for years, the 2000 amendments added a specific reference in Rule 26(b)(1) to these limitations to prompt the courts to apply the limitations more vigorously.[62]

Jurisdictional Issues

Discovery is allowed with respect to jurisdictional issues.[63] Thus, parties may conduct discovery pertaining to other parties' citizenship, the amount in controversy, a party's contacts with the forum state, and other jurisdictional issues.

Location of Evidence

Rule 26(b)(1) explicitly authorizes discovery about the location and existence of documents and other evidence and about the identity and location of persons having knowledge of discoverable matters. The latter provision includes the identity of investigators hired by a party.

Matters Known to Others

A party must provide information and documents it possesses, regardless of who else possesses that information. Thus, it generally is not proper to object on the basis that the party already has the information it is requesting or that information is in the public record[64] or is otherwise available to the party[65] (although the court

---

58. *Oppenheimer Fund, Inc. v. Sanders,* 437 U.S. 340, 351, 98 S.Ct. 2380, 2389–90, 57 L.Ed.2d 253 (1978).

59. *Seattle Times Co. v. Rhinehart,* 467 U.S. 20, 104 S.Ct. 2199, 81 L.Ed.2d 17 (1984); *Klein v. AIG Trading Group Inc.,* 228 F.R.D. 418 (D.Conn.2005); *Bruggeman ex rel. Bruggeman v. Blagojevich,* 219 F.R.D. 430, 432 (N.D.Ill.2004).

60. *United States v. R&F Properties of Lake County, Inc.,* 433 F.3d 1349, 1359 (11th Cir.2005); *Glover v. South Carolina Law Enforcement Division,* 170 F.3d 411 (4th Cir.1999), *cert. dism'd,* 528 U.S. 1146, 120 S.Ct. 1005, 145 L.Ed.2d 1065 (2000).

61. *Terwilliger v. York Int'l. Corp.,* 176 F.R.D. 214, 218 (W.D.Va.1997).

62. The Advisory Committee Note to the 2000 Amendment to Rule 26(b)(1).

63. *Oppenheimer Fund, Inc. v. Sanders,* 437 U.S. 340, 351 n. 13, 98 S.Ct. 2380, 2389–90 n. 13, 57 L.Ed.2d 253 (1978).

64. *Mid-Atlantic Recycling Technologies, Inc. v. City of Vineland,* 222 F.R.D. 81 (D.N.J.2004); *Petruska v. Johns–Manville,* 83 F.R.D. 32, 35 (E.D.Pa.1979).

65. *Abrahamsen v. Trans–State Express, Inc.,* 92 F.3d 425, 428 (6th Cir.1996).

might curtail such requests as unduly burdensome in some circumstances).

Impeachment

Discovery is generally allowed of matters that would be used to impeach other parties' witnesses.[66] Thus, one normally may ask whether the responding party has any criminal convictions and may inquire as to prior statements.[67] It is less clear whether one may inquire as to what other parties will use for impeachment. The courts are divided as to whether a party may ask whether opponents are aware of any prior injuries of the party or whether opponents have surveillance movies of the party.

Discovery of Attorneys

Attorneys with discoverable facts not covered by attorney-client privilege or work product protection are subject to discovery despite being retained by one of the parties to represent it in the litigation.[68]

Privileges

Privileged matters are protected from discovery.[69] Privileges in federal court depend upon whether the action involves a state law issue before the court under diversity or supplemental jurisdiction, or whether the action involves a federal cause of action. If a state's substantive laws are being applied, that state's laws of privilege also apply,[70] except as to the attorney work product protection, which is governed by federal common law.[71] If the action is governed by federal law, then Rule 501 of the Federal Rules of Evidence applies. Essentially, Rule 501 instructs the federal courts to develop a body of federal common law privileges. When a deposition is taken in a state other than the state in which the action is pending, the analysis becomes very complicated, and depends upon each state's choice of law provisions.

Raising Claim of Privilege

The normal manner for raising a privilege is by objecting to a particular request or inquiry. For example, at a deposition, a party may orally raise an objection to an individual question, then refuse to provide the privileged information (by counsel instructing the witness not to answer). In response to interrogatories, document requests, or requests for admission, a party may make a written

---

66. *Hickman v. Taylor,* 329 U.S. 495, 511, 67 S.Ct. 385, 394, 91 L.Ed. 451 (1947); *Varga v. Rockwell International Corp.,* 242 F.3d 693, 697 (6th Cir.2001) (a party may not hold back materials responsive to a proper discovery request because it prefers to use the evidence as surprise impeachment evidence at trial).

67. *See Curro v. Watson,* 884 F.Supp. 708 (E.D.N.Y.1995)(limiting impeachment discovery to areas related to expected testimony).

68. *United Phosphorus, Ltd. v. Midland Fumigant, Inc.,* 164 F.R.D. 245 (D.Kan. 1995).

69. *In re Lott,* 424 F.3d 446, 452 (6th Cir.2005) (privileged material, even if relevant, is not discoverable); *Goodyear Tire & Rubber Co. v. Chiles Power Supply, Inc.,* 332 F.3d 976 (6th Cir.2003).

70. *Brown v. Waco Fire & Cas. Co.,* 73 F.R.D. 297 (S.D.Miss.1976).

71. *Tompkins v. R.J. Reynolds Tobacco Co.,* 92 F.Supp.2d 70 (N.D.N.Y.2000).

objection to individual questions or requests and withhold the privileged information. The objection must include sufficient information so that the court and opposing counsel can assess the applicability of the privilege.[72]

Who May Assert

Usually, a privilege may only be asserted by the person holding the privilege. Certainly, one party may not assert a privilege of a non-party witness or another party. When an attorney or doctor is deposed it is unclear who may assert the privilege—the privilege technically belongs to the client, but courts allow the attorney to assert the privilege if asked about the attorney-client communication.[73]

Waiver of Privilege

Privileges generally are waived by voluntary disclosure,[74] either during discovery or elsewhere.[75] Thus, caution should be exercised in discussing or responding to discovery requests pertaining to privileged matters.

Recalling Privileged Information

Rule 26(b)(5)(B) establishes a procedure to recall privileged information that has already been produced. A party believing that it has produced privileged information may provide a notification to the parties who have received the information. The notification should be in writing (unless circumstances do not so allow, such as in a deposition) and should be sufficiently detailed to allow the receiving parties to evaluate the claim of privilege[76] After receiving such a notification, the receiving parties must return, sequester, or destroy the specified information and all copies (including taking reasonable steps to retrieve any information that the receiving party had already disclosed to other persons). If they do not agree with the privilege assertion, they can present the information to the court under seal for a determination of the privilege claim. During the pendency of the court's review of the privilege claim, the receiving parties are prohibited from using the information and the producing party must preserve it. Alternatively, the parties can propose their own procedures for privileged information that has been produced or disclosed.

Documents Containing Privileged and Non-privileged Matters

If part of a document contains privileged matters and part does not, a party must provide the non-privileged matter, but may redact the privileged matter.

72. Rule 26(b)(5); *Burns v. Imagine Films Entertainment, Inc.*, 164 F.R.D. 589 (W.D.N.Y.1996).

73. *See Martin Marietta Materials, Inc. v. Bedford Reinforced Plastics, Inc.*, 227 F.R.D. 382, 390 (W.D.Pa.2005) (privilege belongs to the client, not to the attorney).

74. *In re Grand Jury Proceedings Subpoena to Testify to: Wine*, 841 F.2d 230, 234 (8th Cir.1988).

75. *See In re Lott*, 424 F.3d 446, 452 (6th Cir.2005) (attorney client privilege is waived when the legal advice is placed at issue).

76. The 2006 Amendment to the Advisory Committee Note to Rule 26(b)(2).

Privileged Matters to be Introduced at Trial

A majority of courts hold that a party cannot assert a privilege at the discovery stage, then introduce the privileged matter at trial.[77] Consequently, any matter intended to be introduced at trial should be produced during discovery if requested.

Particular Privileges

A detailed analysis of every potential privilege is beyond the scope of this book. The following is an overview of the most commonly asserted privileges:

- *Attorney–Client:* The attorney-client privilege applies to all confidential communications between a client and the client's attorney that occur in connection with legal representation or in the process of obtaining legal representation.[78] It applies to communications to an in-house attorney if the attorney is providing legal services. The privilege does not protect communications between one party and the attorney for another party. It does not protect documents or other physical evidence provided to the attorney (other than written communications to the attorney) or the underlying facts,[79] nor does it protect information or evidence gathered by the attorney from other sources or notes and memoranda prepared by the attorney (but see the discussion of attorney-work product under Rule 26(b)(3)).

- *Self–Incrimination:* The Fifth Amendment to the United States Constitution provides all persons (whether or not parties to a litigation) with a privilege against testifying in a manner that would tend to incriminate them.[80] The privilege applies at depositions,[81] interrogatories, requests for admission, and production of documents,[82] as well as at trial. Corporations may not assert the privilege, but corporate representatives may assert it if their testimony would incriminate them personally, regardless of whether they are testifying in their individual or representative capacities.[83] There can be no penalties or sanctions for properly exercising the Fifth Amendment privilege. However, in a civil proceeding it appears that opposing parties may comment on a party's exercise of the Fifth Amendment (in contrast to the prohibition on such comments in a criminal proceeding).[84]

77. *Doe v. Eli Lilly & Co., Inc.,* 99 F.R.D. 126, 127 (D.D.C.1983).

78. *Diversified Industries, Inc. v. Meredith,* 572 F.2d 596, 612 (8th Cir.1977); *Martin Marietta Materials, Inc. v. Bedford Reinforced Plastics, Inc.,* 227 F.R.D. 382, 392 (W.D.Pa.2005).

79. *Martin Marietta Materials, Inc. v. Bedford Reinforced Plastics, Inc.,* 227 F.R.D. 382, 392 (W.D.Pa.2005).

80. *De Vita v. Sills,* 422 F.2d 1172 (3d Cir.1970).

81. *In re Folding Carton Antitrust Litigation,* 609 F.2d 867 (7th Cir.1979).

82. *Gordon v. Federal Deposit Ins. Corp.,* 427 F.2d 578, 580 (D.C.Cir.1970).

83. *United States v. Kordel,* 397 U.S. 1, 8, 90 S.Ct. 763, 767, 25 L.Ed.2d 1 (1970).

84. *Baxter v. Palmigiano,* 425 U.S. 308, 96 S.Ct. 1551, 47 L.Ed.2d 810 (1976).

- *Governmental Privileges:* The United States and the individual States must produce all relevant, non-privileged matter, just as any other party.[85] However, the United States has some extra privileges:

  - *Governmental Informer Privilege:* The United States has a qualified privilege to refuse to reveal the identity of an informer.[86] When the privilege is asserted, the court will balance the litigant's need for the information against the government's interest in protecting its informer's identity. The privilege belongs to the government, and protects only the identity of the informer, not the information provided by the informer. The government may not assert the privilege if it intends for the informer to testify at trial.

  - *Government's Privilege for Military or State Secrets:* The United States has a qualified privilege for matters that involve military or state secrets. In order to assert the privilege, the head of the department that has control over the matter must lodge a formal claim of privilege. The court will then rule on the privilege by balancing the litigant's need against the government's interest in keeping the matter secret.[87]

  - *Government's Statutory Privilege:* Some statutes require governmental agencies and other entities to file certain documents or reports, and designate the submissions as confidential. Under these statutes, the privilege is generally absolute. A common example is income tax returns. Under the regulation,[88] the United States receives and keeps tax returns, but is not required to produce them to private litigants. Note that the privilege belongs to the United States only—the individual filing the return may be required to produce it (although other objections, such as relevance, might apply).

  - *Executive Privilege:* The Executive branch of the United States government has a general qualified privilege, grounded in the need for the executive branch to gather information. The privilege generally must be asserted by the head of the relevant department. The court will then balance the litigant's need against the governmental interest asserted.[89]

- *Other Privileges:* In some states, communications with spouses, physicians, clergy, journalists,[90] accountants, and social workers are privileged.

---

85. *United States v. Procter & Gamble Co.,* 356 U.S. 677, 681, 78 S.Ct. 983, 986, 2 L.Ed.2d 1077 (1958).

86. *Roviaro v. United States,* 353 U.S. 53, 59, 77 S.Ct. 623, 627, 1 L.Ed.2d 639 (1957).

87. *United States v. Reynolds,* 345 U.S. 1, 73 S.Ct. 528, 97 L.Ed. 727 (1953).

88. 26 C.F.R. § 301.6103(a–1(c)).

89. *United States v. Nixon,* 418 U.S. 683, 94 S.Ct. 3090, 41 L.Ed.2d 1039 (1974).

90. *In re: Madden,* 151 F.3d 125, 128 (3d Cir.1998) (recognizing qualified journal-

Burden of Proof

The party raising a privilege has the burden of establishing the existence of the privilege.[91] Likewise, a party claiming that requested discovery is not relevant has the burden to show that the discovery is outside the scope of the rules.[92]

RULE 26(b)(2).   LIMITATIONS ON FREQUENCY AND EXTENT

CORE CONCEPT

Rule 26(b)(2) provides the court with authority to limit discovery that is unreasonably cumulative or duplicative,[93] is obtainable from another source more conveniently, or is unduly burdensome[94] or expensive given the nature and circumstances of the case.[95]   The court may also limit discovery if the party seeking the discovery has had "ample opportunity" to obtain the information during prior discovery. Rule 26(b)(2)(B) also establishes a procedure for limiting the need to search for and produce electronic data if it would be unreasonably burdensome or costly to do so.

APPLICATIONS

Objections to Specific Requests

One method of asserting the limitations in Rule 26(b)(2) is by making an objection to a discovery request, such as objecting to an interrogatory or request for production as cumulative or overly burdensome.

Motion for Protective Order

A party seeking to have the use of certain discovery procedures limited should make a motion for a protective order under Rule 26(c).

---

ists' privilege); *Gonzales v. National Broadcasting Co., Inc.*, 155 F.3d 618, 626–27 (2d Cir.1998) (journalists' privilege applies only to confidential information).

91. *Heathman v. United States District Court*, 503 F.2d 1032, 1033 (9th Cir.1974); *Martin Marietta Materials, Inc. v. Bedford Reinforced Plastics, Inc.*, 227 F.R.D. 382, 389 (W.D.Pa.2005) (party asserting the privilege has the initial burden, then the burden shifts to the opposing party to establish waiver).

92. *Moss v. Blue Cross and Blue Shield of Kansas, Inc.*, 241 F.R.D. 683 (D.Kan. 2007) (when the discovery sought appears relevant, the party opposing production has the burden to establish lack of relevance; when the discovery does not appear relevant, the party seeking production has the burden to demonstrate relevance); *Simpson*

v. University of Colorado, 220 F.R.D. 354, 359 (D.Colo.2004).

93. *Bayer AG v. Betachem, Inc.*, 173 F.3d 188 (3d Cir.1999).

94. *In re Microcrystalline Cellulose Antitrust Litigation*, 221 F.R.D. 428 (E.D.Pa. 2004).

95. *See Patterson v. Avery Dennison Corp.*, 281 F.3d 676, 681–82 (7th Cir.2002) (before restricting discovery, the court should consider the totality of the circumstances, weighing the value of the material sought against the burden of providing it, and taking into account society's interest in furthering the truthseeking function); *Koch v. Koch Industries, Inc.*, 203 F.3d 1202, 1238 (10th Cir.2000) (parties are not entitled to conduct a "fishing expedition").

Limits Established by Rules

Other Rules place limits on the duration of depositions and on the number of interrogatories and depositions, which may be altered by court order.[96] These limits may also be altered by stipulation under Rule 29. The Rules do not contain any limit on the number of requests for admission, but such limits can be set by local rule, court order, or stipulation.

Electronic Data

Rule 26(b)(2)(B) establishes a procedure to provide protections when a party believes that the production of "electronically stored information" will result in unreasonable burden or cost.[97] In such cases, the party invoking the protection must identify the sources of information that it is neither searching nor producing with sufficient particularity that the requesting party can evaluate the burden and cost of producing the information.[98] If the requesting party still believes that the information should be produced, the parties must confer to see if they can resolve the issue without court intervention.[99] If an informal conference does not resolve the issue, the requesting party may file a motion to compel or the responding party may file a motion for a protective order. In either type of motion, the responding party bears the burden of showing that the information is not reasonably accessible, in terms of undue burden or cost. Even following such a showing, the court may require production of the information upon good cause shown.[100] The good cause analysis examines whether the need for the discovery outweighs the burdens and costs of production.[101] Relevant factors include the specificity of the request, the information that is or should be available from other sources, predictions of the importance of the information, the importance of the issues at stake, and the parties resources.[102]

RULE 26(b)(3).   TRIAL PREPARATION: MATERIALS

CORE CONCEPT

Rule 26(b)(3) provides limited protection to otherwise discoverable[103]

---

96. *Andamiro U.S.A. v. Konami Amusement of America, Inc.*, 2001 WL 535667 (C.D.Cal.2001) (setting forth the factors for a motion to take more than 10 depositions).

97. *See Disability Rights Council of Greater Washington v. Washington Metropolitan Transit Authority*, 242 F.R.D. 139 (D.D.C. 2007) (questioning whether a party who failed to maintain the data properly should be heard to complain that it is too burdensome to retrieve the data).

98. The 2006 Amendment to the Advisory Committee Note to Rule 26(b)(2).

99. The 2006 Amendment to the Advisory Committee Note to Rule 26(b)(2).

100. *Disability Rights Council of Greater Washington v. Washington Metropolitan Transit Authority*, 242 F.R.D. 139 (D.D.C. 2007).

101. The 2006 Amendment to the Advisory Committee Note to Rule 26(b)(2).

102. The 2006 Amendment to the Advisory Committee Note to Rule 26(b)(2); *Disability Rights Council of Greater Washington v. Washington Metropolitan Transit Authority*, 242 F.R.D. 139 (D.D.C. 2007).

103. *Reedhycalog UK, Ltd. v. Baker Hughes Oilfield Operations Inc.*, 242 F.R.D. 357, 360, n. 1 (E.D.Tex. 2007) (first step is to determine if materials are attorney-client

trial preparation and work product materials.[104] Such materials must be produced in discovery *only* when the information contained there is not reasonably available from any other source.[105] Note that the work product protection is broader than the attorney-client privilege, but is less absolute.[106]

APPLICATIONS

Documents Only

The work product protection applies only to documents[107] prepared in anticipation of litigation.[108] It does not apply to facts known or gathered relating to the litigation, which generally are discoverable.[109] It is unsettled whether the work product protection applies to compilations of documents, such as documents selected for deposition preparation.[110] The protection has been held not to apply to electronic images of documents created for use in the litigation.[111]

Prepared in Anticipation of Litigation

The work product protection applies only to documents prepared in anticipation of litigation.[112] Most courts apply the protection to documents prepared when litigation is expected but has not

communications, because work product protection only applies to documents that are otherwise discoverable).

104. *See In re Perrigo Co.*, 128 F.3d 430, 437 (6th Cir.1997) (noting that the work product doctrine creates a qualified immunity rather than a privilege).

105. Rule 26(b)(3) is essentially a codification of the principles announced by the Supreme Court in *Hickman v. Taylor*, 329 U.S. 495, 67 S.Ct. 385, 91 L.Ed. 451 (1947), which contains an excellent discussion of the work product protection. *See also In re Ford Motor Co.*, 110 F.3d 954 (3d Cir.1997).

106. *In re Sealed Case*, 107 F.3d 46, 51 (D.C.Cir.1997).

107. *In re EchoStar Communications Corp.*, 448 F.3d 1294 (Fed.Cir.2006); *In re Perrigo Co.*, 128 F.3d 430, 437 (6th Cir. 1997).

108. *Mattenson v. Baxter Healthcare Corp.*, 438 F.3d 763, 768 (7th Cir.2006) (initial purpose of the meeting does not have to be to discuss the litigation so long as the litigation is discussed); *In re Ford Motor Company*, 110 F.3d 954 (3d Cir.1997) (work product doctrine extends to materials prepared by an agent of an attorney provided that material was prepared in anticipation of litigation).

109. *See In re Cendant Corp. Securities Litigation*, 343 F.3d 658, 662 (3rd Cir.

2003); *Weiss v. National Westminster Bank, PLC*, 242 F.R.D. 33 (E.D.N.Y. 2007) (work product protection only applies to documents, not to the facts in the documents); *but see In re: Grand Jury Subpoena Dated Oct. 22, 2001*, 282 F.3d 156, 161 (2d Cir. 2002) (we see no reason why work product cannot encompass facts as well as opinions and strategy).

110. *In re Grand Jury Subpoenas Dated March 19, 2002 and August 2, 2002*, 318 F.3d 379, 385 (2nd Cir.2003); *Nutramax Laboratories, Inc. v. Twin Laboratories, Inc.*, 183 F.R.D. 458 (D.Md.1998) (containing a detailed analysis of this issue).

111. *Hines v. Widnall*, 183 F.R.D. 596 (N.D.Fla.1998).

112. *In re Sealed Case*, 146 F.3d 881, 884 (D.C.Cir.1998); *Reedhycalog UK, Ltd. v. Baker Hughes Oilfield Operations Inc.*, 242 F.R.D. 357 (E.D.Tex. 2007) (litigation need not be imminent, but litigation must have been the *"primary motivating purpose"*); *United States v. M & T Mort. Corp.*, 235 F.R.D. 11, 16 (D.D.C.2006) (" 'In anticipation of litigation' contains two related, but nevertheless distinct, concepts. One is temporal. The other is motivational."); *Southern Union Co. v. Southwest Gas Corp.*, 205 F.R.D. 542, 549 (D.Ariz.2002) ("litigation" includes administrative proceedings provided there is an opportunity for cross examination).

yet been commenced;[113] rather, to be protected, the documents must be primarily concerned with legal assistance.[114] Conversely, the protection does not apply to documents prepared in the regular course of business while litigation is pending.[115] The trend seems to be to apply the protection to documents prepared in anticipation of any litigation, not just the pending action.[116]

Investigators' Reports

The work product protection applies to reports prepared by investigators or others on behalf of a party.[117]

Parties Only

The work product protection only applies to parties and their agents.[118] Thus, if a non-party witness prepares a document for the witness's own purposes, it is generally not work product. However, when an insurance company is defending a party, the protection may extend to documents prepared by or on behalf of the insurance company.[119] The work product protection may be invoked by the party or the party's attorney.[120]

113. *Equal Employment Opportunity Commission v. Lutheran Social Services,* 186 F.3d 959 (D.C.Cir.1999); *Binks Mfg. Co. v. National Presto Industries, Inc.,* 709 F.2d 1109, 1119 (7th Cir.1983); *Navigant Consulting, Inc. v. Wilkinson,* 220 F.R.D. 467, 476–77 (N.D.Tex.2004) .

114. *In re Lernout & Hauspie Securities Litigation,* 222 F.R.D. 29 (D.Mass.2004) (litigation need not be imminent, as long as the primary motivating purpose behind the creation of the document was to aid in possible future litigation); *North Shore Gas Co. v. Elgin, Joliet & Eastern Ry. Co.,* 164 F.R.D. 59, 61 (N.D.Ill.1995); but see *In re Ford Motor Co.,* 110 F.3d 954 (3d Cir.1997) (materials deemed to be prepared in anticipation of litigation for purposes of work product protection did not necessarily include legal advice).

115. *JumpSport, Inc. v. Jumpking, Inc.,* 213 F.R.D. 329, 344 (N.D.Cal.2003); *Simon v. G.D. Searle & Co.,* 816 F.2d 397, 401 (8th Cir.1987)

116. *See Hobley v. Burge,* 433 F.3d 946, 949 (7th Cir.2006) ("A majority of courts have held ... that the privilege endures after termination of the proceedings for which the documents were created, especially if the old and new matters are related."); *In re Ford Motor Co.,* 110 F.3d 954 (3d Cir.1997) (looking to literal language of the Rule); *but see In re Grand Jury Subpoena,* 220 F.R.D. 130, 148 (D.Mass.2004) (con-taining a detailed discussion of this issue); *Burton v. R.J. Reynolds Tobacco Co.,* 177 F.R.D. 491 (D.Kan.1997) (documents must pertain to a specific claim or potential litigation, particularly for an insurance company whose entire business involves claims).

117. *See, In re: In re Grand Jury Subpoena* (Mark Torf/Torf Environmental Management), 357 F.3d 900, 907 (9th Cir.2004) (the work product doctrine applies to documents created by investigators working for attorneys, provided the documents were created in anticipation of litigation); *Grand Jury Subpoena Dated Oct. 22, 2001,* 282 F.3d 156, 161 (2d Cir.2002).

118. *Weiss v. National Westminster Bank, PLC,* 242 F.R.D. 33 (E.D.N.Y. 2007) (work product protection only applies to documents created by or for parties or their representatives); *In re Grand Jury Subpoena,* 220 F.R.D. 130, 144 (D.Mass.2004) (courts typically do not extend work product protection to documents prepared by non-parties or their agents); *Duck v. Warren,* 160 F.R.D. 80 (E.D.Va.1995)(police internal affairs investigation documents were not prepared by the party police officer being sued, and thus were not work product).

119. *See Tayler v. Travelers Ins. Co.,* 183 F.R.D. 67, 69 (N.D.N.Y.1998).

120. *Hobley v. Burge,* 433 F.3d 946, 949 (7th Cir.2006).

Obtaining Work Product

Work product is discoverable if the attorney makes a sufficient showing that there is no reasonable alternative source for the same or substantially equivalent information,[121] and that the attorney has a *substantial* need for the information.[122] For example, a party may obtain a written statement in opposing counsel's files if the witness is no longer available.[123] Similarly, there may be no substitute for photographs or statements taken shortly after an incident. Work product is also discoverable in an action where the work product is directly at issue, such as in an action for legal malpractice.[124]

Mental and Legal Impressions

The mental impressions and legal evaluations of an attorney, investigator, or claims agent (sometimes referred to as "core" or "opinion" work product) enjoy an almost absolute privilege from disclosure.[125] Thus, an attorney may redact statements reflecting mental and legal impressions from work product that must be disclosed under Rule 26(b)(3).[126] Note, however, that the protections in Rule 26(b)(3) do not apply to interrogatories, which may require the respondent to make legal conclusions requiring the application of law to facts (in other words, the responding attorney may not interpose an objection on the basis that such a legal conclusion is the attorney's work product).

Statement of a Party

A party may always obtain a copy of the party's own statement, whether a signed written statement or a recording of an oral statement.[127] A party may similarly obtain a copy of a statement by the party's agent or representative.[128] To obtain a copy of a party's statement, the party does not need to use the document request procedures in Rule 34, but instead may simply make a request under

121. *United Kingdom v. United States,* 238 F.3d 1312, 1322 (11th Cir.2001); *Hendrick v. Avis Rent A Car System, Inc.,* 916 F.Supp. 256, 261 (W.D.N.Y.1996)(expense in obtaining the information independently is a factor which may be considered by a court in determining whether to order disclosure of work product).

122. *In re EchoStar Communications Corp.,* 448 F.3d 1294 (Fed.Cir.2006); *Corley v. Rosewood Care Ctr., Inc.,* 142 F.3d 1041, 1052 (7th Cir.1998).

123. *McCoo v. Denny's Inc.,* 192 F.R.D. 675 (D.Kan.2000) (statements from witnesses who failed to appear for their depositions must be produced).

124. *Rutgard v. Haynes,* 61 F.Supp.2d 1082 (S.D.Cal.1999).

125. *Mattenson v. Baxter Healthcare Corp.,* 438 F.3d 763, 768 (7th Cir.2006); *In re EchoStar Communications Corp.,* 448 F.3d 1294 (Fed.Cir.2006); *In re Cendant Corp. Securities Litigation,* 343 F.3d 658, 663 (3rd Cir.2003); *Baker v. General Motors Corp.,* 209 F.3d 1051, 1054 (8th Cir.2000); *but see Hager v. Bluefield Regional Medical Center,* 170 F.R.D. 70, 78 (D.D.C.1997) ("near absolute protection given by courts to opinion work product must give way" when attorney is designated as an expert witness).

126. *See In re EchoStar Communications Corp.,* 448 F.3d 1294 (Fed.Cir.2006).

127. *Corley v. Rosewood Care Center, Inc. of Peoria,* 142 F.3d 1041, 1052 (7th Cir.1998); *Rofail v. United States,* 227 F.R.D. 53, 55 (E.D.N.Y.2005) (a party is entitled to obtain a copy of the statement it made, merely upon request and without any showing of any kind).

128. *Woodard v. Nabors Offshore Corp.,* 2001 WL 13339 (E.D.La.2001).

Rule 26(b)(3). A statement can either be a written statement that the party has signed or otherwise adopted or approved, or a contemporaneous verbatim recording of the person's oral statement.

Statement of a Witness

A non-party witness has a right to a copy of the witness's own statement, whether a signed written statement or a recording of an oral statement. If a party refuses to provide a witness with a copy of the witness's statement, the witness may move to compel and for sanctions under Rule 37(a)(4). Parties, in contrast, do not have an absolute right to a copy of a non-party witness's statement.[129] A party can attempt to get a copy of a witness's statement directly from the witness or by making the showing of necessity required to obtain attorney-work product.[130] A statement can either be a written statement that the party has signed or otherwise adopted or approved, or a contemporaneous verbatim recording of the person's oral statement.

Controlling Law

Unlike most privileges, the work product doctrine is controlled by federal common law, even in diversity cases.[131]

Burden of Proof

The party asserting the work product doctrine has the burden of demonstrating that the subject documents are work product.[132] The party seeking the opponent's work product then has the burden of showing the necessity of obtaining the work product.[133]

Waiver

Disclosure of documents to an adverse party, or in a manner such that an adverse party may see the documents,[134] constitutes a waiver of the work product protection with respect to those documents.[135] Disclosure of documents to a non-adverse party, such as a co-defendant, will not constitute a waiver of the work product protection if the documents fall within the scope of a proper joint

129. *Garcia v. City of El Centro*, 214 F.R.D. 587, 594–95 (S.D.Cal.2003).

130. *Garcia v. City of El Centro*, 214 F.R.D. 587, 594–95 (S.D.Cal.2003) (there is a split as to whether the mere passage of time creates a substantial need for a witness statement).

131. *Meoli v. American Medical Service of San Diego*, 287 B.R. 808, 813 (S.D.Cal. 2003).

132. *Gulf Islands Leasing, Inc. v. Bombardier Capital, Inc.*, 215 F.R.D. 466 (S.D.N.Y.2003).

133. *Ferko v. National Ass'n For Stock Car Auto Racing, Inc.*, 219 F.R.D. 396, 400 (E.D.Tex.2003); *Pippenger v. Gruppe*, 883 F.Supp. 1201 (S.D.Ind.1994).

134. *Scanlon v. Bricklayers and Allied Craftworkers, Local No. 3*, 242 F.R.D. 238 (W.D.N.Y. 2007) (inadvertent disclosure to opposing party not waiver); *United States ex rel. Bagley v. TRW, Inc.*, 212 F.R.D. 554, 560 (C.D.Cal.2003) (required disclosure of a document to the United States does not waive the attorney work product doctrine).

135. *United States v. M.I.T.*, 129 F.3d 681, 687 (1st Cir.1997) (disclosure of a contractor's documents to a Defense Contract Audit Agency constitutes disclosure to a potential adversary which forfeits work product protection for disclosed documents); *United States v. M & T Mort. Corp.*, 235 F.R.D. 11 (D.D.C.2006); *Oxyn Telecommunications, Inc. v. Onse Telecom*, 2003 WL 660848 (S.D.N.Y.2003).

defense agreement.[136] Disclosure of fact work product to a testifying expert may also constitute waiver.[137] Disclosure to a third-party who does not share a common interest in developing legal theories and analyses of documents may also constitute a waiver.[138] Note that this differs from most privileges, which are waived by disclosure to anyone, not just parties.[139] The courts are divided as to which party has the burden of proving non-waiver.[140]

Recalling Trial Preparation Materials

Rule 26(b)(5)(B) establishes a procedure to recall attorney work product that has already been produced. A party believing that it has produced work product may provide a notification to the parties who have received the work product. The notification should be in writing (unless circumstances do not so allow, such as in a deposition) and should be sufficiently detailed to allow the receiving parties to evaluate the claim of work product protection[141] After receiving such a notification, the receiving parties must return, sequester, or destroy the specified work product and all copies (including taking reasonable steps to retrieve any work product that the receiving party had already disclosed to other persons). If they do not agree with the work product assertion, they can present the work product to the court under seal for a determination of the claim. During the pendency of the court's review of the claim, the receiving parties are prohibited from using the work product and the producing party must preserve it. Alternatively, the parties can propose their own procedures for work product that has been produced or disclosed.

Discovery Stage Only

Work product may be withheld as privileged during discovery, then used at trial. Note the contrast with most other privileges, which cannot be asserted during discovery then waived at trial.

RULE 26(b)(4).   TRIAL PREPARATION: EXPERTS

CORE CONCEPT

Parties may depose expert witnesses who may testify at trial.[142] Rule 26(b)(4) allows only very limited discovery with respect to non-

136. *U.S. v. Duke Energy Corp.*, 214 F.R.D. 383, 389 (M.D.N.C.2003).

137. *Johnson v. Gmeinder*, 191 F.R.D. 638, 644 (D.Kan.2000); *see also Tennison v. City & County of San Francisco*, 226 F.R.D. 615, 621 (N.D.Cal.2005).

138. *Judicial Watch, Inc. v. U.S. Postal Service*, 297 F.Supp.2d 252, 268 (D.D.C. 2004).

139. *See In re Columbia/HCA Healthcare Corp. Billing Practices Litigation*, 293 F.3d 289, 314 (6th Cir.2002) (disclosure to

third parties does not waive the work product protection).

140. *See Granite Partners, L.P. v. Bear, Stearns & Co. Inc.*, 184 F.R.D. 49, 54 (S.D.N.Y.1999) (party making work product claim has the burden of proving non-waiver); *Johnson v. Gmeinder*, 191 F.R.D. 638, 643 (D.Kan.2000) (party claiming waiver must prove waiver).

141. The 2006 Amendment to the Advisory Committee Note to Rule 26(b)(2).

142. FRCP 26(b)(4)(A). See also *Colindres v. Quietflex Mfg.*, 228 F.R.D. 567

testifying experts.[143]

APPLICATIONS

Depositions of Experts

Parties may take the deposition of any expert witness that may testify at trial.[144]

Time for Expert Depositions

If an expert report is to be disclosed for the witness, then the deposition may not occur before the report is disclosed.

Experts Specially Retained but Not Expected to Testify

A party may obtain discovery pertaining to experts not expected to testify only upon a showing of exceptional circumstances rendering it impracticable to obtain facts or opinions on the same subject by other means.[145] Such further discovery might be allowed when the particular consulting expert was the only expert to examine evidence that is no longer available (such as a blood sample).[146]

Discovery of Examining Physician

Discovery pertaining to treating or examining health professionals is available under Rule 35(b).[147] There is a split of authority as to whether a treating physician is a fact witness or an expert witness for purposes of the provisions of Rule 26(b)(4).[148]

Experts Informally Consulted

No discovery is permitted of experts informally consulted but not retained.[149]

(S.D.Tex.2005) (the work product privilege does not apply to experts).

143. *Employer's Reinsurance Corp. v. Clarendon Nat. Ins. Co.*, 213 F.R.D. 422 (D.Kan.2003); *Agron v. Trustees of Columbia Univ.*, 176 F.R.D. 445, 449 (S.D.N.Y. 1997) (limitation on discovery is virtually inapplicable where adverse party has not objected to discovery of its expert).

144. *Lovato v. Burlington Northern and Santa Fe Ry. Co.*, 200 F.R.D. 448 (D.Colo. 2001), *rev'd on other grounds*, 201 F.R.D. 509 (D.Colo.2001).

145. *Lowery v. Circuit City Stores, Inc.*, 158 F.3d 742, 765 (4th Cir.1998), *cert. granted, judgment vacated on other grounds*, 527 U.S. 1031, 119 S.Ct. 2388, 144 L.Ed.2d 790 (1999); *Essex Builders Group, Inc. v. Amerisure Ins. Co.*, 235 F.R.D. 703 (M.D.Fla.2006). *But see American Crop Protection Ass'n v. U.S. E.P.A.*, 182 F.Supp.2d 89, 93 (D.D.C.2002) (non-testifying experts are shielded from discovery only in the action with respect to which they are consult-

ed; full discovery is permitted of their writings and opinions in subsequent matters).

146. *See, e.g., Spearman Industries, Inc. v. St. Paul Fire and Marine Ins. Co.*, 128 F.Supp.2d 1148 (N.D.Ill.2001) (describing circumstances where a party might obtain discovery from a non-testifying expert).

147. *But see Coleman v. Dydula*, 190 F.R.D. 320, 321–24 (W.D.N.Y.1999) (awarding deposition attendance fees to treating physicians under Rule 26(b)(4)).

148. *See, e.g., Kirkham v. Societe Air France*, 236 F.R.D. 9 (D.D.C.2006). *Demar v. United States*, 199 F.R.D. 617 (N.D.Ill. 2001) (treating physician not entitled to expert fees from the party noticing the physician's deposition); *Grant v. Otis Elevator Co.*, 199 F.R.D. 673, 675-76 (N.D.Okla. 2001) (treating physician entitled to expert fee compensation for deposition testimony).

149. *West Tennessee Chapter of Associated Builders and Contractors, Inc. v. City of Memphis*, 219 F.R.D. 587, 591 (W.D.Tenn.2004).

Experts Generally Retained

Full discovery is permitted regarding an expert who is a full-time employee of a party, or who was retained generally, rather than in connection with pending or anticipated litigation.[150] No expert fees are awarded in connection with such discovery.

Experts Who Witnessed or Participated in Events

Discovery pertaining to an expert who acquired his knowledge and facts through witnessing or participating in the events that form the basis for the complaint is not covered by Rule 26(b)(4), which is limited to information acquired or developed in anticipation of litigation.[151] Thus, full fact discovery is allowed regarding such experts, and no expert fees are awarded.[152]

Party Who Is an Expert

A party cannot avoid discovery or obtain expert fees by claiming to be an expert witness.

Ex Parte Communications with Experts

All communications with an opposing party's expert should be through the procedures set forth in Rule 26, such as a Rule 26(b)(4) deposition; a party should not have *ex parte* communications with an expert for another party.[153]

Testifying Expert Fees

The court must impose on the party seeking expert discovery of a testifying expert the reasonable expert fees incurred in responding to the discovery[154] unless manifest injustice would result.[155] For a deposition, the fee normally includes compensation for time testifying but not preparation time.[156] However, if the expert charges

---

150. *Dunn v. Sears, Roebuck & Co.*, 639 F.2d 1171, 1174 (5th Cir.1981); *Essex Builders Group, Inc. v. Amerisure Ins. Co.*, 235 F.R.D. 703 (M.D.Fla.2006).

151. *Battle ex rel. Battle v. Memorial Hosp. at Gulfport*, 228 F.3d 544, 551 (5th Cir.2000); *Essex Builders Group, Inc. v. Amerisure Ins. Co.*, 235 F.R.D. 703 (M.D.Fla.2006).

152. The Advisory Committee Note to Rule 26(b)(4); *Paquin v. Federal Nat'l. Mortgage Assn.*, 119 F.3d 23, 33 (D.C.Cir. 1997) (denying payment of fees for alleged experts with personal knowledge).

153. *See Sanderson v. Boddie–Noell Enterprises, Inc.*, 227 F.R.D. 448 (E.D.Va. 2005); *Sewell v. Maryland Dept. of Transp.*, 206 F.R.D. 545 (D.Md.2002).

154. *Gwin v. American River Transp. Co.*, 482 F.3d 969, 975 (7th Cir. 2007) (abuse of discretion not to award fees); *Knight v. Kirby Inland Marine Inc.*, 482 F.3d 347, 356 (5th Cir. 2007) (fees for testi-

mony at a *Daubert* hearing are not discovery fees recoverable under Rule 26); *Trepel v. Roadway Express, Inc.*, 266 F.3d 418, 426–27 (6th Cir.2001); *Haarhuis v. Kunnan Enterprises, Ltd.*, 177 F.3d 1007 (D.C.Cir. 1999) ($300 per hour for deposition, including time traveling to and from deposition, was reasonable).

155. *Research Systems Corp. v. IPSOS Publicite*, 276 F.3d 914, 920 (7th Cir.2002); *Harris v. San Jose Mercury News, Inc.*, 2006 WL 862953 (N.D.Cal.2006) (the movant, although not technically indigent, would experience undue hardship from the financial burden of paying the expert fees for the depositions).

156. *Knight v. Kirby Inland Marine Inc.*, 482 F.3d 347, 356 (5th Cir. 2007) (fees for testimony are mandatory, but fees for other discovery are within the court's discretion); *Frydman v. Department of Justice*, 852 F.Supp. 1497 (D.Kan.1994)(holding that a large lapse of time can warrant compensation for preparation time). *But see*

664

more than a "reasonable" fee, the party retaining that expert must pay over and above the "reasonable" rate for that witness' deposition by an adversary.[157] Courts are split as to whether and when treating physicians are entitled to an expert witness fee.[158]

Non-testifying Expert Fees

If discovery is sought of non-testifying experts, the court must also require the party to pay a fair share of the expenses already expended for the experts to form their opinions, in addition to the experts' fees for the time testifying or responding to the discovery.

RULE 26(b)(5).   CLAIMING PRIVILEGE OR PROTECTING TRIAL-PREPARATION MATERIALS

CORE CONCEPT

A party who withholds information based on a claim of privilege or attorney work product protection must state the claim expressly and describe the nature of the documents or information so withheld in a manner that will enable other parties to assess the claim of privilege or protection.[159] If privileged information is inadvertently produced in discovery, the producing party may notify the parties that received the information. The receiving parties must then either return the information or present the information to the court.

APPLICATIONS

Failure to State Claim of Privilege with Sufficient Specificity

If a party withholds information without properly disclosing the basis, the party may be subject to sanctions under Rule 37(b)(2), and may have waived the privilege.[160]

Privilege Log

Many courts read Rule 26(b)(5) to require a party asserting a privilege to produce a privilege log describing the documents with-

McNerney v. Archer Daniels Midland Co., 164 F.R.D. 584, 587 (W.D.N.Y.1995) (holding plaintiff's expert was entitled to charge defendant up to 4 hours time in preparing for the deposition and reviewing and signing the transcript).

157. *Frederick v. Columbia University*, 212 F.R.D. 176, 177 (S.D.N.Y.2003) (setting forth a test for reasonableness of expert fees); *Hansen v. Sea Ray Boats, Inc.*, 160 F.R.D. 166 (D.Utah 1995)(limiting the recovery of expert fees to the statutory $40.00 witness fee).

158. *See Wirtz v. Kansas Farm Bureau Services, Inc.*, 355 F.Supp.2d 1190, 1212–13 (D.Kan.2005).

159. *U.S. v. Philip Morris Inc.*, 347 F.3d 951, 954 (D.C.Cir.2003); *In re Santa Fe Intern. Corp.*, 272 F.3d 705, 710 (5th Cir.

2001) (party asserting the privilege has the burden of demonstrating its applicability); *Scanlon v. Bricklayers and Allied Craftworkers, Local No. 3*, 242 F.R.D. 238 (W.D.N.Y. 2007).

160. *Hobley v. Burge*, 433 F.3d 946, 951 (7th Cir.2006); *Anderson v. Marion County Sheriff's Dept.*, 220 F.R.D. 555, 563 (S.D.Ind.2004) ("the time to make the showing that certain information is privileged is at the time the privilege is asserted, not months later when the matter is before the Court on a motion to compel"); *Ritacca v. Abbott Laboratories*, 203 F.R.D. 332, (N.D.Ill.2001) ("Minor procedural violations, good faith attempts at compliance, and other such mitigating circumstances militate against finding waiver."); The Advisory Committee Note to the 1993 Amendment to Rule 26.

held.[161] The respondent may wait until the court rules upon pending objections before generating the privilege log if the objections pertain to the allegedly privileged documents.[162] Privileges may be waived broadly for failure to produce a privilege log[163] or specifically for any documents omitted from the privilege log.[164]

Recalling Privileged Information

Rule 26(b)(5)(B) establishes a procedure to recall privileged information that has already been produced. A party believing that it has produced privileged information may provide a notification to the parties who have received the information. The notification should be in writing (unless circumstances do not so allow, such as in a deposition) and should be sufficiently detailed to allow the receiving parties to evaluate the claim of privilege[165] After receiving such a notification, the receiving parties must return, sequester, or destroy the specified information and all copies (including taking reasonable steps to retrieve any information that the receiving party had already disclosed to other persons). If they do not agree with the privilege assertion, they can present the information to the court under seal for a determination of the privilege claim. During the pendency of the court's review of the privilege claim, the receiving parties are prohibited from using the information and the producing party must preserve it. Alternatively, the parties can propose their own procedures for privileged information that has been produced or disclosed.

Waiver of the Privilege for Recalled Information

Rule 26(b)(5)(B) does not address whether the privilege or protection is preserved for information that was disclosed and then recalled. There is substantial case law addressing this topic that is unaffected by the procedures in Rule 26(b)(5)(B).[166]

---

161. *Weiss v. National Westminster Bank, PLC*, 242 F.R.D. 33 (E.D.N.Y. 2007) (failure to include sufficient information on a privilege log can result in waiver); *United Investors Life Ins. Co. v. Nationwide Life Ins. Co.*, 233 F.R.D. 483, 486 (N.D.Miss. 2006) (a party asserting a privilege must provide sufficient information within the log so that the court and the requesting party can determine whether the log entry satisfies *each element* of the asserted privilege). *But see Burlington Northern & Santa Fe Ry. Co. v. U.S. Dist. Court for Dist. of Mont.*, 408 F.3d 1142, 1147(9th Cir.2005) (rejecting a per se rule that failure to provide a timely privilege log is a waiver of the privilege).

162. *United States v. Philip Morris Inc.*, 314 F.3d 612, 621 (D.C.Cir.2003); *see also Banks v. Office of the Senate Sergeant-at-Arms and Doorkeeper*, 226 F.R.D. 113 (D.D.C.2005) (there is no consensus as to when a privilege log must be provided).

163. *Banks v. Office of Senate Sergeant-At-Arms*, 222 F.R.D. 7, 15 (D.D.C.2004).

164. *Robinson v. Texas Auto. Dealers Ass'n*, 214 F.R.D. 432, 456 (E.D.Tex.2003), *vac'd in part*, 2003 WL 21911333 (5th Cir. 2003).

165. The 2006 Amendment to the Advisory Committee Note to Rule 26(b)(2).

166. The 2006 Amendment to the Advisory Committee Note to Rule 26(b)(2).

RULE 26(c).   PROTECTIVE ORDERS

CORE CONCEPT

The court may enter orders designed to protect the parties and witnesses during the discovery process.

APPLICATIONS

2007 Amendments

The 2007 amendments substantially reorganized Rule 26(c). The original 8 subsections are now subsections of Rule 26(c)(1), and the trailing text at the end was moved into new subsections 26(c)(2) and 26(c)(3). Care should be exercised in researching and citing pre–2008 cases referring to subsections of Rule 26(c).

Motion

Protective orders are obtained by motion filed in the district where the action is pending.[167]   In the case of a deposition that is to occur in a different district, a motion may also be filed where the deposition is to occur.[168]

Certificate of Conference

A motion for protective order must include a certification that the movant has in good faith conferred or attempted to confer with the other party in an effort to resolve the dispute without court action.[169]

Timing

Normally, the motion must be filed before the discovery is to occur, unless there is no opportunity to do so.[170]

Who May File

A motion may be made by a party or by a witness from whom discovery is sought.[171]   The motion must be brought by the individual whose interests are affected.   Thus, a party may not move for a protective order to protect the interests of another, but may move to protect the party's own interests when discovery is sought from another.

Good Cause

Protective orders are entered for "good cause." [172]   The court has almost complete discretion in determining what constitutes good

---

167. *Kirshner v. Uniden Corp. of America*, 842 F.2d 1074 (9th Cir.1988).

168. *In re: Sealed Case*, 141 F.3d 337 (D.C.Cir.1998) (non-party witness has a right to have a motion for protective order heard in the district where the deposition is to occur); The Advisory Committee Note to Rule 26(c).

169. *Avocent Redmond Corp. v. Rose Electronics, Inc.*, 242 F.R.D. 574 (W.D.Wash. 2007); *Lockwood v. City of Philadelphia*, 205 F.R.D. 448, 450 (E.D.Pa. 2002).

170. *Mims v. Central Mfrs. Mut. Ins. Co.*, 178 F.2d 56 (5th Cir.1949); *Drexel Her-itage Furnishings, Inc. v. Furniture USA, Inc.*, 200 F.R.D. 255 (M.D.N.C.2001).

171. *Silkwood v. Kerr–McGee Corp.*, 563 F.2d 433 (10th Cir.1977).

172. *Foltz v. State Farm Mut. Auto. Ins. Co.*, 331 F.3d 1122 (9th Cir.2003) (a party seeking a protective order must show, for each particular document it seeks to protect, that specific prejudice or harm will result if no protective order is granted); *Chicago Tribune Co. v. Bridgestone/Firestone, Inc.*, 263 F.3d 1304, 1310 (11th Cir. 2001) (applying the good cause standard, and rejecting the press' argument that a

cause,[173] and such determinations are rarely disturbed on appeal.[174] Rule 26(c) specifically instructs the court to limit the frequency or extent of discovery if justice so requires to protect a party or witness from annoyance, embarrassment,[175] oppression, or undue burden[176] or expense.[177] Rule 26(b)(1) instructs the court to limit the frequency or extent of discovery if: (i) the discovery sought is unreasonably cumulative or is obtainable from a more convenient or less burdensome or expensive source; (ii) the party seeking the discovery has had ample opportunity to obtain the information; or (iii) the discovery is unduly burdensome[178] or expensive taking into account the circumstances of the particular case. A court may grant a protective order prohibiting the taking of a deposition when it believes the information sought is wholly irrelevant to the issues or to prospective relief.[179] In general, the court will balance the need of the party seeking the discovery against the burden on the party responding.[180]

Burden of Proof

The party seeking the protective order has the burden of showing that good cause exists by stating particular and specific facts.[181]

Depositions

Motions for protective orders are most common in connection with depositions, because such motions are the only mechanism for challenging a deposition in advance of its occurrence. With interrogatories, document requests, and requests for admission, a party

---

compelling interest was required to keep documents from the press).

173. *Flatow v. Islamic Republic of Iran*, 308 F.3d 1065, 1074 (9th Cir.2002); *Contratto v. Ethicon, Inc.*, 227 F.R.D. 304, 308 (N.D.Cal.2005); *Wiggins v. Burge*, 173 F.R.D. 226, 229 (N.D.Ill.1997) ("In deciding whether good cause exists, the district court must balance interests involved: the harm to the party seeking the protective order and the importance of disclosure to the public.").

174. *But see Citizens First National Bank of Princeton v. Cincinnati Ins. Co.*, 178 F.3d 943, 944 (7th Cir.1999) (court must make an actual determination of good cause, and may not allow the parties to seal whatever portions of the record they choose).

175. *Miscellaneous Docket Matter #1 v. Miscellaneous Docket Matter #2*, 197 F.3d 922, 925 (8th Cir.1999).

176. *Mitchell v. Fishbein*, 227 F.R.D. 239 (S.D.N.Y.2005) (discussing the meaning of "burden").

177. *Stagman v. Ryan*, 176 F.3d 986 (7th Cir.1999).

178. *Cummings v. General Motors Corp.*, 365 F.3d 944, 954 (10th Cir.2004) (it is not enough that the discovery be burdensome, that burden must be "undue").

179. *Leighr v. Beverly Enterprises–Kansas Inc.*, 164 F.R.D. 550, 551 (D.Kan.1996).

180. *In re Sealed Case (Medical Records)*, 381 F.3d 1205, 1215–16 (D.C.Cir. 2004); *In re Wilson*, 149 F.3d 249, 252 (4th Cir.1998); *A Helping Hand, LLC v. Baltimore County, Md.*, 295 F.Supp.2d 585, 592 (D.Md.2003).

181. *Gulf Oil Co. v. Bernard*, 452 U.S. 89, 102, 101 S.Ct. 2193, 2201, 68 L.Ed.2d 693 (1981); *Kamakana v. City and County of Honolulu*, 447 F.3d 1172 (9th Cir.2006) (recognizing a heightened standard of "compelling reasons" necessary to keep documents to be attached to a dispositive motion secret); *Phillips ex rel. Estates of Byrd v. General Motors Corp.*, 307 F.3d 1206,1211, n.1 (9th Cir.2002); *Friends Of The Earth v. United States Dept. of The Interior*, 236 F.R.D. 39 (D.D.C.2006) (courts require a particular and specific demonstration of fact, as distinguished from stereotyped and conclusory statements).

can make objections to individual requests without providing a
substantive response. The onus then shifts to the party seeking the
discovery to move to compel an answer under Rule 37(a). The
scheduling of a second deposition of the same person without good
cause will generally support finding of annoyance and undue burden, and thus allow the entrance of a protective order.[182]

Types of Protective Order

Rule 26(c) lists eight kinds of protective orders, which are
discussed immediately below. The list is not exclusive, however,
and the court may make any type of protective order required by
justice.[183] The specifically enumerated categories are:

(1) *Order that Disclosure or Discovery Not be Had:* Rule
26(c)(1)(A) allows the court to order that the automatic
disclosure or requested discovery not occur. Such orders
are occasionally entered with respect to interrogatories or
document requests, since the court can examine the requests. Such orders are rarely granted with respect to
depositions.[184]

(2) *Specified Terms and Conditions:* The court can impose
terms and conditions on the automatic disclosure or the
taking of discovery under Rule 26(c)(1)(B). The court may
designate the time and location of a deposition,[185] or the
time to respond to interrogatories, document requests, or
requests for admission. The court may order the party
seeking discovery to pay the responding party's resulting
expenses.[186] The court may set deadlines for the completion
of various phases of discovery or order that discovery be
conducted in a particular sequence.[187] The court may issue a
stay of discovery.[188] The court may also modify any of the
terms and conditions in subsequent orders.[189]

(3) *Method of Discovery:* The court may restrict discovery to a
particular method (such as no depositions or depositions
only upon written questions) under Rule 26(c)(1)(C). The
general principle is that the parties may select their own
discovery methods without unnecessary interference from

---

182. *Sentry Insurance v. Shivers*, 164
F.R.D. 255, 256 (D.Kan.1996).

183. *Mitchell v. Fishbein*, 227 F.R.D.
239, 254 (S.D.N.Y.2005).

184. *Simmons Foods, Inc. v. Willis*, 191
F.R.D. 625, 630 (D.Kan.2000) (although
courts rarely grant a protective order which
totally prohibits a deposition, a request to
take the deposition of the opposing party's
counsel may justify such an order).

185. *Philadelphia Indemnity Insurance
Co. v. Federal Insurance Co*, 215 F.R.D. 492
(E.D.Pa.2003).

186. *Medtronic Sofamor Danek, Inc. v.
Michelson*, 2003 WL 21468573 (W.D.Tenn.
2003).

187. *Builders Ass'n of Greater Chicago
v. City of Chicago*, 170 F.R.D. 435, 437
(N.D.Ill.1996) (order setting the sequence of
discovery appropriate when a potentially
dispositive threshold issue has been raised).

188. *Chesney v. Valley Stream Union
Free School Dist. No. 24*, 236 F.R.D. 113
(E.D.N.Y.2006) (staying discovery pending
resolution of dispositive motions).

189. *Martin v. Reynolds Metals Corp.*,
297 F.2d 49 (9th Cir.1961).

the court.[190] Thus, most motions to restrict the discovery methods are denied unless the moving party shows special circumstances.[191]

(4) *Limit of Scope or Time:* The court may limit the scope of the automatic disclosures or discovery to specific areas of inquiry or to a specific time period.[192] The court may also stay discovery, either while a dispositive motion is pending,[193] or except with respect to a critical or threshold issue.[194] For example, if a jurisdictional dispute exists, the court may restrict discovery to the jurisdictional issues, then permit broad discovery if jurisdiction is found to exist.[195] Similarly, if liability and damages are to be tried separately, the court may restrict discovery to liability issues until the first phase of the case is complete.

(5) *Persons Present:* The court may exclude the public, the press, other witnesses, or other non-parties from a deposition or access to documents produced in discovery under Rule 26(c)(1)(E).[196] The court generally will not exclude the parties or their attorneys.

(6) *Sealed Transcript:* The court may order a deposition transcript sealed, and thus not part of the public record, under Rule 26(c)(1)(F).[197] Similar orders have been entered with respect to interrogatory answers or documents to be produced,[198] although such orders are not expressly authorized by 26(c)(1)(F).[199] Once a sealing order has been entered, parties are prohibited from disclosing to third persons information obtained pursuant to the court order. The prohibi-

190. *National Life Ins. Co. v. Hartford Acc. & Indem. Co.,* 615 F.2d 595 (3d Cir. 1980).

191. *Nguyen v. Excel Corp.,* 197 F.3d 200, 208–09 (5th Cir.1999) (for "good cause shown," court may order discovery taken by a method other than that selected by the party seeking the discovery).

192. *See* Rule 26(c)(1)(D).

193. *Johnson v. New York Univ. School of Educ.,* 205 F.R.D. 433, 434 (S.D.N.Y. 2002); *GTE Wireless v. Qualcomm, Inc.,* 192 F.R.D. 284, 285–86 (S.D.Cal.2000) (before staying discovery, the court should "take a preliminary peek" at the merits to see if there is an "immediate and clear possibility" that the dispositive motion will be granted).

194. *Vivid Technologies, Inc. v. American Science & Engineering, Inc.,* 200 F.3d 795, 804 (staying discovery on all other issues until critical issue is resolved).

195. *Orchid Biosciences, Inc. v. St. Louis University,* 198 F.R.D. 670 (S.D.Cal. 2001).

196. *Phillips v. General Motors Corp.,* 307 F.3d 1206. 1210 (9th Cir.2002) (the public generally, and the press in particular, are presumptively entitled to access to documents produced in discovery, and good cause must be demonstrated to shield document from such access); *Jones v. Circle K Stores, Inc.,* 185 F.R.D. 223 (M.D.N.C.1999).

197. *In re Estate of Martin Luther King, Jr., Inc. v. CBS, Inc.,* 184 F.Supp.2d 1353, 1362 (N.D.Ga.2002) (only the court may seal documents; the parties cannot do so by stipulation).

198. *United States v. Nine Million Forty One Thousand Five Hundred Ninety Eight Dollars and Sixty Eight Cents,* 163 F.3d 238, 250 (5th Cir.1998) (even after the record is sealed, the court may still deny a request for an unredacted copy of sealed documents).

199. *Morgan v. United States Dept. of Justice,* 923 F.2d 195 (D.C.Cir.1991).

tion does not apply, however, to information already in a party's possession when the order is entered.[200]

(7) *Confidential Information:* The court may enter an order restricting disclosure of trade secrets and confidential research, development, or commercial information[201] obtained during discovery.[202] Sealing a document is sometimes viewed as extraordinary relief, and there is a presumptive right to access to discovery in civil cases.[203] There is no absolute privilege or protection with respect to such matters.[204] The normal procedure is for the responding party to claim that certain information is confidential. Then, if the parties cannot agree to a confidentiality stipulation, the responding party can move for a protective order or the party seeking the discovery can move to compel under Rule 37(a). The party seeking the discovery will have the burden of showing that the information is relevant and needed.[205] In most cases, the discovery will be allowed, but under restricted conditions regarding further disclosure. The court can fashion any order it sees fit, limiting how the information may be used, who may see it, etc. The court may also order disclosure of limited portions of confidential information, such as ordering disclosure of the ingredients of a product, but not the formula. The court can also designate an impartial third person to examine the confidential information.

(8) *Simultaneous Exchange:* The court may order the parties to simultaneously file designated documents or information in sealed envelopes, to be opened as directed by the court.

200. *See Rodgers v. United States Steel Corp.,* 536 F.2d 1001 (3d Cir.1976); *International Prods. Corp. v. Koons,* 325 F.2d 403, 408–09 (2d Cir.1963).

201. *Phillips v. General Motors Corp.,* 289 F.3d 1117 (9th Cir.2002), *opinion amended and superseded,* 307 F.3d 1206 (9th Cir.2002) (the enumerated categories of confidential information are not exclusive, and settlement information can be protected); *Avocent Redmond Corp. v. Rose Electronics, Inc.,* 242 F.R.D. 574 (W.D.Wash. 2007) (discussing when access to trade secrets can be limited to counsel); *Drexel Heritage Furnishings, Inc. v. Furniture USA, Inc.,* 200 F.R.D. 255 (M.D.N.C. 2001) (making a distinction between trade secrets and other confidential research and commercial information).

202. *Seattle Times v. Rhinehart,* 467 U.S. 20, 104 S.Ct. 2199, 81 L.Ed.2d 17 (1984); *Surfvivor Media, Inc. v. Survivor Productions,* 406 F.3d 625, 635 (9th Cir. 2005) (documents need not be privileged to be protected); *Pearson v. Miller* 211 F.3d 57 (3d Cir.2000).

203. *Keith H. v. Long Beach Unified School Dist.,* 228 F.R.D. 652 (C.D.Cal.2005); *Loussier v. Universal Music Group, Inc.,* 214 F.R.D. 174, 176–77 (S.D.N.Y.2003).

204. *Federal Open Market Committee v. Merrill,* 443 U.S. 340, 99 S.Ct. 2800, 61 L.Ed.2d 587 (1979); *Sprinturf, Inc. v. Southwest Recreational Industries, Inc.,* 216 F.R.D. 320 (E.D.Pa.2003) (the party seeking the order must show that the information sought is a trade secret or other confidential information protected by Rule 26(c)(1)(G), and that good cause exists to prevent the disclosure of this information).

205. *Bruno & Stillman, Inc. v. Globe Newspaper Co.,* 633 F.2d 583 (1st Cir.1980); *Tailored Lighting, Inc. v. Osram Sylvania Products, Inc.,* 236 F.R.D. 146 (W.D.N.Y. 2006).

This procedure is most common in patent cases, where it can be an advantage to know an opponent's claims.

Order Compelling Discovery

If the court denies a motion for a protective order, it may at the same time issue an order compelling the discovery. Such an order can facilitate obtaining sanctions under Rule 37.

Discovery While Motion for Protective Order Pending

Technically, a motion for protective order does not automatically stay the discovery that is the subject of the motion.[206] Thus, for example, a motion for protective order to prevent a deposition should not be filed on the day of the deposition, unless it was not practical to file it sooner. However, some local rules provide for an automatic stay of the subject discovery.[207]

Expenses and Attorney Fees

The court has discretion to require the party losing a motion for protective order to pay the expenses the opposing party incurred in connection with the motion, including reasonable attorney fees, under Rule 26(c) and Rule 37(a)(4).

Motion to Vacate or Modify Protective Order

If circumstances change, a party may move to vacate or modify a protective order.[208]

Appeal of Discovery Order by Party

Discovery orders are normally interlocutory, not final, and thus not appealable until the end of the lawsuit.[209] A discovery order will be final if the underlying motion was the entire proceeding, such as with an order granting or denying a deposition to perpetuate testimony under Rule 27, an order denying discovery in aid of execution, an order granting or denying letters rogatory under Rule 28, or an order denying the deposition of a non-party that was entered in another district.[210]

Appeal of Discovery Order by Non-party

In general, non-parties cannot appeal discovery orders.[211] If the discovery is denied, they have no need to appeal. If the order is granted, their only recourse is to disobey, then appeal any contempt judgment. In limited circumstances, such as to protect the attorney

206. *Creative Solutions Group, Inc. v. Pentzer Corp.*, 199 F.R.D. 443, 444 (D.Mass. 2001) (motion to stay discovery does not stay discovery).

207. *Ecrix Corp. v. Exabyte Corp.*, 191 F.R.D. 611, 617 (D.Col.2000).

208. *Murata Mfg. Co., Ltd. v. Bel Fuse, Inc.*, 234 F.R.D. 175, (N.D.Ill.2006) (factors are "(1) the nature of the protective order, (2) the foreseeability, at the time of issuance of the order, of the modification re-

quested, (3) the parties' reliance on the order; and most significantly (4) whether good cause exists for the modification.").

209. *Cipollone v. Liggett Group, Inc.*, 785 F.2d 1108, 1116 (3d Cir.1986).

210. *United States v. Sciarra*, 851 F.2d 621, 628 (3d Cir.1988).

211. *National Super Spuds, Inc. v. New York Mercantile Exchange*, 591 F.2d 174 (2d Cir.1979). *See also In re Ford Motor Co.*, 110 F.3d 954 (3d Cir.1997).

client privilege, a non-party may be able to appeal a discovery order.[212]

Discretion of the Trial Court

The trial court enjoys considerable discretion in deciding discovery matters and may be reversed only for abuse of discretion.[213]

Appeal as Interlocutory Order

Interlocutory orders may be appealed under the Interlocutory Appeals Act of 1958, 28 U.S.C. § 1292(b), if the issues meet the criteria of the Act (such as issues that present a controlling question of law justifying immediate review).[214] Normally, discovery orders will not qualify for interlocutory review.

Appeal at Conclusion

Interlocutory discovery orders may be appealed at the conclusion of the case, and will be reviewed for abuse of discretion.[215] In general, however, it will be difficult to have a verdict overturned based upon a discovery order.

RULE 26(d). TIMING AND SEQUENCE OF DISCOVERY

CORE CONCEPT

Parties may not conduct discovery prior to their discovery conference meeting under Rule 26(f). Thereafter, each party may conduct whatever discovery that party chooses, in any sequence, regardless of the discovery undertaken by other parties. The various discovery devices may be used in any order or simultaneously.

APPLICATIONS

Commencement of Discovery

Parties may not conduct discovery prior to their discovery conference under Rule 26(f).[216] This limitation may be altered by court order or stipulation.[217]

---

212. *See United States v. Ryan*, 402 U.S. 530, 533, 91 S.Ct. 1580, 1582, 29 L.Ed.2d 85 (1971); *Perlman v. United States*, 247 U.S. 7, 38 S.Ct. 417, 62 L.Ed. 950 (1918).

213. *See Surfvivor Media, Inc. v. Survivor Productions*, 406 F.3d 625, 635 (9th Cir.2005); *Cummings v. General Motors Corp.*, 365 F.3d 944, 953 (10th Cir.2004); *Food Lion, Inc. v. United Food and Commercial Workers Int'l Union*, 103 F.3d 1007, 1012 (D.C.Cir.1997).

214. *See S.E.C. v. TheStreet.Com*, 273 F.3d 222, 228 (2d Cir.2001) (Rule 26(c) order immediately appealable if such order (1) conclusively determined the disputed question; (2) "resolved an important issue completely separate from the merits of the ac-

tion; and (3) was effectively unreviewable on appeal from a final judgment").

215. *Thomas v. International Business Machines*, 48 F.3d 478 (10th Cir.1995).

216. *Willis v. Town Of Marshall, N.C.*, 426 F.3d 251, 264, n.5 (4th Cir.2005); *Alston v. Parker*, 363 F.3d 229, 236, n.11 (3rd Cir.2004).

217. *See Semitool, Inc. v. Tokyo Electron America, Inc.*, 208 F.R.D. 273 (N.D.Cal. 2002) (applying the good cause standard to a motion to conduct discovery prior to a Rule 26(f) conference); The Advisory Committee Note to the 2000 Amendment to Rule 26(d) (the 2000 Amendment removed the option to eliminate the Rule 26(d) discovery moratorium by local rule).

Court Orders

The court may order discovery in a specified sequence or according to a schedule "for the convenience of the parties and witnesses and in the interests of justice."[218]   Such orders are authorized under Rule 26(c)(2), and are within the broad discretion of the court.[219]

Simultaneous Discovery

The parties may conduct discovery simultaneously.   There is no obligation for any party to wait until others have completed their discovery.[220]

Failure to Answer by One Party

A party is not excused from answering discovery because another party has failed to answer discovery.   The proper remedy if another party fails to answer discovery is a motion to compel under Rule 37, not a refusal to comply with valid discovery requests.

No Mutuality

There is no requirement that a party conduct discovery in a manner like that used by other parties.   Each party is free to conduct any authorized discovery in any sequence regardless of the discovery conducted by other parties.[221]

Excluded Proceedings

The moratorium on early discovery established by Rule 26(d) does not apply to the proceedings exempted from the initial disclosures and discovery conference process by Rule 26(a)(1)(E).

RULE 26(e).   SUPPLEMENTING DISCLOSURES AND RESPONSES

CORE CONCEPT

Parties have a duty to supplement automatic disclosures and discovery responses under certain limited conditions set forth in Rule 26(e).[222]   Otherwise, there is no general duty to supplement.[223]

APPLICATIONS

2007 Amendments

The 2007 amendments reorganized Rule 26(e). The provisions in Rule 26(e)(2) were moved to Rule 26(e)(1)(A), and the provisions

---

218. *Dimension Data North America, Inc. v. NetStar–1, Inc.*, 226 F.R.D. 528 (E.D.N.C.2005) (evaluating a request for expedited discovery).

219. *Doebele v. Sprint Corp.*, 2001 WL 392513 (D.Kan.2001). *But see Ortiz–Rivera v. Municipal Government of Toa Alta*, 214 F.R.D. 51, 54 (D.Puerto Rico 2003) (only the most obviously compelling reasons are sufficient to justify a departure from the rule).

220. *George C. Frey Ready–Mixed Concrete, Inc. v. Pine Hill Concrete Mix Corp.*, 554 F.2d 551 (2d Cir.1977).

221. *Keller v. Edwards*, 206 F.R.D. 412 (D.Md.2002).

222. *See, e.g., Rodowicz v. Massachusetts Mut. Life Ins. Co.*, 279 F.3d 36, 45, n.10 (1st Cir.2002).

223. *Alvariza v. Home Depot*, 240 F.R.D. 586, 590 (D.Colo. 2007) (no duty to supplement documents informally produced by agreement).

regarding supplementing expert disclosures were pulled out of Rule 26(e)(1) and made into Rule 26(e)(2). Care should be exercised in researching and citing pre–2008 cases referring to subsections of Rule 26(e).

Conditions Requiring Supplemental Responses

The following three conditions require supplemental answers:

(1) *Automatic Disclosures:* A party must at reasonable intervals supplement its initial, expert,[224] and pretrial disclosures under Rule 26(a) if the party learns that the information disclosed was incomplete or incorrect;[225]

(2) *Incorrect Response:* A party must supplement a response to an interrogatory, request for production, or request for admission that the party learns was incorrect or incomplete when made and the information has not otherwise been made known to the other parties;[226] and

(3) *Court Order:* The duty to supplement may also arise by court order.

Timing of Supplemental Responses

No specific time periods are established for the duty to supplement.[227] Instead, supplements are to be made "in a timely manner."

No Request to Supplement Needed

The obligations to supplement under Rule 26(e) are self-effectuating; there is no need to serve a request to supplement.[228] Nonetheless, a party will sometimes serve a notice to supplement if it is concerned that another party has new information that it has not yet disclosed or produced.

Supplementing Expert Discovery

The obligations to supplement described above apply to both expert reports disclosed under Rule 26(a)(2)(B)[229] and depositions of such experts. Supplemental expert information should be disclosed by the time the pretrial disclosures are made under Rule 26(a)(3), 30 days before trial unless otherwise set by the court.[230]

---

224. *Mannoia v. Farrow*, 476 F.3d 453, 457 (7th Cir. 2007); *Air Turbine Technology, Inc. v. Atlas Copco AB*, 410 F.3d 701 (Fed.Cir.2005).

225. *Klonoski v. Mahlab*, 156 F.3d 255, 268 (1st Cir.1998) (duty to supplement is broad).

226. *Colon-Millin v. Sears Roebuck De Puerto Rico, Inc.*, 455 F.3d 30, 37 (1st Cir. 2006); *Rodriguez v. Ibp, Inc.*, 243 F.3d 1221, 1229 (10th Cir.2001); *Johnson v. United Parcel Service, Inc.*, 236 F.R.D. 376 (E.D.Tenn.2006).

227. *See Luma Corp. v. Stryker Corp.*, 226 F.R.D. 536, 539 (S.D.W.Va.2005) (the absence of a court established deadline does not mean that the parties do not have to supplement).

228. *Johnson v. United Parcel Service, Inc.*, 236 F.R.D. 376 (E.D.Tenn.2006).

229. *See Brainard v. American Skandia Life Assur. Corp.*, 432 F.3d 655, 664 (6th Cir.2005); *Macaulay v. Anas*, 321 F.3d 45, 50 (1st Cir.2003); *Jacobsen v. Deseret Book Co.*, 287 F.3d 936, 951 (10th Cir.2002).

230. *U.S. S.E.C. v. Maxxon, Inc.*, 465 F.3d 1174, 1182, n.17 (10th Cir. 2006); *Reid v. Lockheed Martin Aeronautics Co.*, 205 F.R.D. 655, 662 (N.D.Ga.2001) (Rule 26(e) is not to be used to delay disclosures until

Information Already Provided

A party need not supplement a disclosure or discovery response if the other parties have already received the additional or corrective information in writing.[231]

No Other Duty

The duties described in Rule 26(e) are the only duties to supplement. Thus, an instruction in a set of interrogatories that the interrogatories are continuing or purporting to impose a duty to supplement is ineffective.

Sanctions

Failure to supplement a disclosure or discovery response is the equivalent of providing incorrect information in the initial disclosure or response. The court may exclude certain evidence[232] or claims,[233] may order a continuance and further discovery, or take any other action it deems appropriate[234] (*see* Rule 37 for a more detailed analysis of the available sanctions).

RULE 26(f). CONFERENCE OF THE PARTIES; PLANNING FOR DISCOVERY

CORE CONCEPT

The parties must confer and develop a proposed discovery plan, to be submitted to the court in writing, addressing the discovery schedule and any modifications to the limits or scope of discovery.

APPLICATIONS

2007 Amendments

The 2007 amendments substantially reorganized Rule 26(f), breaking the text into 4 new subsections, some of which have as many as 6 subsections of their own. Care should be exercised in researching and citing pre–2008 cases referring to subsections of Rule 26(f).

Time for Conference

Rule 26(f) directs that the parties confer "as soon as practicable and in any event at least 21 days before a scheduling conference is

---

30 days before trial by calling them supplements).

231. *See Westefer v. Snyder*, 422 F.3d 570, 584 (7th Cir.2005) (information provided in an affidavit did not need to also be provided in a supplemental interrogatory response); *Gutierrez v. AT & T Broadband, LLC*, 382 F.3d 725, 733 (7th Cir.2004); *Williams v. Morton*, 343 F.3d 212, 222 (3rd Cir.2003); *Troknya v. Cleveland Chiropractic Clinic*, 280 F.3d 1200, 1205 (8th Cir. 2002).

232. *W.G. Pettigrew Distributing Co. v. Borden, Inc.*, 976 F.Supp. 1043, 1050 (S.D.Tx.1996).

233. *U.S. v. Philip Morris USA, Inc.*, 219 F.R.D. 198, 200–01 (D.D.C.2004); *Loral Fairchild Corp. v. Victor Company of Japan, Ltd.*, 911 F.Supp. 76, 80 (E.D.N.Y. 1996).

234. *Townsend v. Daniel, Mann, Johnson & Mendenhall*, 196 F.3d 1140, 1151 (10th Cir.1999) (no sanction warranted where conduct not culpable and no harm to defendant).

held or a scheduling order is due under Rule 16(b)."[235] The timing of the discovery conference may be modified by local rule or court order, and specified actions may be exempted from the discovery conference requirement.

In Person Attendance

The rules do not require that the Rule 26(f) conference be conducted in person, and the parties may participate by telephone.[236] However, the court can order the parties to participate in person.

Agenda for Discovery Conference

At the discovery conference, the parties must discuss the nature and basis of their claims and defenses and the possibilities of prompt settlement or resolution of the case. They must also make or arrange for the initial automatic disclosures required by Rule 26(a)(1), discuss orders that the court should enter,[237] issues relating to preserving discoverable information,[238] and develop a proposed discovery plan, as described below. The parties may also attempt to reach a consensus as to the disputed facts alleged in the pleadings with particularity for purpose of the disclosures under Rule 26(a).

Content of Discovery Plan

The discovery plan should indicate the parties' positions or proposals concerning:

(1) *Automatic Disclosures*: Any changes to the timing, form, or requirement for disclosures under Rule 26(a).[239] The plan must explicitly state when the initial disclosures were or are to be made;

(2) *Discovery Scope and Schedule*: The likely subjects of discovery, the completion date for discovery, and any discovery that should be conducted in phases or limited to or focused on particular issues;

(3) *Electronic Information*: Issues relating to the disclosure or production of electronically stored information, including the sources of such data, the form in which it should be produced (i.e., in paper or electronic form, and if electronic, how it will be made available), and the costs of such production;

235. *Coleman v. Sears, Roebuck & Co.,* 221 F.R.D. 433 (W.D.Pa.2003).

236. The Advisory Committee Note to the 2000 Amendment to Rule 26(f) expresses a preference for in person meetings, but recognizes that the distances some counsel would have to travel and the resulting expenses may outweigh the benefits of an in person meeting.

237. *Mallinckrodt, Inc. v. Masimo Corp.,* 254 F.Supp.2d 1140, 1157 (C.D.Cal. 2003).

238. Although not specifically so limited, the 2006 Amendment to Rule 26(f) added information preservation to the agenda for the Rule 26 conference to address issues related to the preservation of electronically stored information. See the 2006 Amendment to the Advisory Committee Note to Rule 26(f) for a discussion of potential document preservation issues.

239. *In re Bristol–Myers Squibb Securities Litigation,* 205 F.R.D. 437, 440–41 (D.N.J.2002) (the discovery conference should include a discussion of what documents are available in electronic format, and the format to be used for disclosures and production of such documents).

(4) *Privilege Issues*: Issues relating to claims of privilege or work product protection, including any procedures to be used in the event of the production of privileged information (to the extend that they differ from the procedures in Rule 26(b)(2)(B));[240]

(5) *Discovery Limits*: Any changes to the discovery limits established by the Rules or by local rule, plus any additional limits; and

(6) *Other Orders*: Any other case management or protective orders proposed to the court for consideration at the court's scheduling conference.

Submission of Plan

The parties should submit to the court a written report outlining the plan within 14 days of the discovery meeting. The court may order that the discovery plan be submitted at a different time or that the plan be submitted orally at the Rule 16 conference with the court. Form 35 of the Appendix of Forms to the Rules (printed in Part IV) contains a sample report.

Good Faith Participation

Rule 26(f) places a joint obligation on the attorneys (and on unrepresented parties) to schedule the discovery conference and to attempt in good faith to agree on a proposed discovery plan and a report outlining the plan.

Excluded Proceedings

A discovery conference and discovery plan are not required in proceedings listed in Rule 26(a)(1)(B) as exempted from initial disclosures.[241] Additionally, the parties may be excused from the discovery conference and plan requirements by court order.

RULE 26(g).   SIGNING DISCLOSURES AND DISCOVERY REQUESTS, RESPONSES, AND OBJECTIONS

CORE CONCEPT

Every disclosure, request for discovery, and response or objection must be signed by at least one attorney of record. The signature constitutes a certification that to the best of the signer's knowledge, information, and belief, the document is complete and correct, and is being served for proper purposes within the Rules.

---

240. See the 2006 Amendment to the Advisory Committee Note to Rule 26(f) for a discussion of possible agreements regarding inadvertently produced privileged material, such as the "quick peek" procedure and the "clawback" procedure.

241. *See, e.g., Orbe v. True*, 201 F.Supp.2d 671 (E.D.Va.2002) (habeas corpus proceedings exempt from Rule 26(f)).

APPLICATIONS

2007 Amendments

The 2007 amendments substantially reorganized Rule 26(g). Much of the content of Rule 26(g)(2) was moved up into Rule 26(g)(1), and only the trailing text from Rule 26(g)(2) remains in that subsection. Care should be exercised in researching and citing pre–2008 cases referring to subsections of Rule 26(g).

Signature and Certification

Every disclosure, discovery request, response, or objection must be signed by at least one attorney of record (or by the party, if unrepresented).[242] The document must also state the address, e-mail address, and telephone number of the signer. The signature constitutes a certification to the best of the signer's knowledge, information, and belief formed after "reasonable inquiry"[243] that:

(A) The document is consistent with the Rules and existing law, or with a nonfrivolous argument for extension, modification, or reversal of existing law, or for establishing new law;

(B) The document is not imposed for any improper purpose, such as to harass, delay, or cause needless expense for an opponent;[244] and

(C) The discovery is not unreasonably or unduly burdensome or expensive, given the nature of the case, the discovery already conducted, the amount in controversy, and the importance of the issues at stake in the litigation.[245]

Duty of Inquiry

The signer of a discovery document is under an obligation to make a reasonable inquiry into the issues covered by his certification before signing the document.[246]

Unsigned Discovery Documents

If without substantial justification a discovery disclosure, request, response, or objection is unsigned, other parties should advise the party making the disclosure, request, response, or objection. If

---

242. *Dugan v. Smerwick Sewerage Co.*, 142 F.3d 398, 407 (7th Cir.1998).

243. *Allender v. Raytheon Aircraft Co.*, 220 F.R.D. 661, 666 (D.Kan.2004) ("counsel's unrepentant failure to consider, follow, and cite the Tenth Circuit's holding in *Biocore* also amounts to a violation of the 'reasonable inquiry' requirement of Rule 26(g)").

244. *United States v. Kouri–Perez*, 187 F.3d 1, 6 (1st Cir.1999).

245. *See Legault v. Zambarano*, 105 F.3d 24, 27 (1st Cir.1997).

246. *Green Leaf Nursery v. E.I. DuPont De Nemours and Co.*, 341 F.3d 1292, 1305 (11th Cir.2003) (the signature certifies that the lawyer has made a reasonable effort to assure that the client has provided all the information and documents available to him that are responsive to the discovery demand); *Legault v. Zambarano*, 105 F.3d 24, 28 (1st Cir.1997) (certifying attorney must make a reasonable effort to ensure that the client has provided all responsive information and documents to a discovery request); *Bernal v. All American Investment Realty, Inc.*, 479 F.Supp.2d 1291, 1333 (S.D.Fla. 2007) (signer does not certify the accuracy of the client's response, only that the signer has made a reasonable effort to ensure the accuracy and completeness).

counsel for that party fails to sign the document promptly, the unsigned document will be stricken, and no party is obligated to respond to the unsigned document.[247]

Unrepresented Parties

An unrepresented party should sign disclosures, discovery requests, responses, and objections and should list the party's address.

Automatic Disclosures

The initial disclosure (Rule 26(a)(1)) and the pretrial disclosure (Rule 26(a)(3)) must be signed by at least one attorney of record. The disclosure must also state the address of the attorney. The signature constitutes a certification to the best of the signer's knowledge, information, and belief formed after "reasonable inquiry" that the disclosure is complete and correct.[248]

Sanctions

If without a substantial justification a certification is made in violation of Rule 26(g), the court will impose an appropriate sanction[249] on the party, the attorney, or both.[250] The sanction may include expenses incurred because of the violation, including attorney fees.[251] Generally, a discovery sanction is not a final appealable order.[252]

ADDITIONAL RESEARCH REFERENCES

Wright & Miller, *Federal Practice and Procedure* §§ 2001–2052.

C.J.S. Federal Civil Procedure §§ 526–535.

West's Key No. Digests, Federal Civil Procedure ⟳1261–1278.

247. *Saria v. Massachusetts Mut. Life Ins. Co.*, 228 F.R.D. 536 (S.D.W.Va.2005).

248. *Metropolitan Opera Ass'n, Inc. v. Local 100, Hotel Employees and Restaurant Employees Intern. Union*, 212 F.R.D. 178, 222, n.28 (S.D.N.Y.2003).

249. *Bernal v. All American Investment Realty, Inc.*, 479 F.Supp.2d 1291, 1334 (S.D.Fla. 2007) (court may fashion an appropriate sanction); *PLX, Inc. v. Prosystems, Inc.*, 220 F.R.D. 291, 296 (N.D.W.Va. 2004) (court has broad discretion in determining the appropriate sanction).

250. *Maynard v. Nygren*, 332 F.3d 462 (7th Cir.2003) (attorney may not be sanctioned absent a knowing improper certification or violation of the discovery Rules); *Bernal v. All American Investment Realty,*

Inc., 479 F.Supp.2d 1291, 1334–35 (S.D.Fla. 2007); *McCoo v. Denny's Inc.*, 192 F.R.D. 675 (D.Kan.2000) (sanctions should be assessed against counsel absent evidence that the party was aware of the wrongdoing).

251. *Starlight International, Inc. v. Herlihy*, 190 F.R.D. 587 (D.Kan.1999) (containing a detailed discussion of the criteria for awarding attorney fees as a sanction); *Deese v. Springfield Thoracic and Cardiovascular Surgeons, S.C.*, 183 F.R.D. 534 (C.D.Ill. 1998) (awarding fees for attempted introduction of audio tape not properly disclosed during discovery).

252. *United States v. Kouri–Perez*, 187 F.3d 1, 6 (1st Cir.1999).

RULE 27

DEPOSITIONS TO PERPETUATE TESTIMONY

(a) Before an Action Is Filed.

(1) *Petition.* A person who wants to perpetuate testimony about any matter cognizable in a United States court may file a verified petition in the district court for the district where any expected adverse party resides. The petition must ask for an order authorizing the petitioner to depose the named persons in order to perpetuate their testimony. The petition must be titled in the petitioner's name and must show:

(A) that the petitioner expects to be a party to an action cognizable in a United States court but cannot presently bring it or cause it to be brought;

(B) the subject matter of the expected action and the petitioner's interest;

(C) the facts that the petitioner wants to establish by the proposed testimony and the reasons to perpetuate it;

(D) the names or a description of the persons whom the petitioner expects to be adverse parties and their addresses, so far as known; and

(E) the name, address, and expected substance of the testimony of each deponent.

(2) *Notice and Service.* At least 20 days before the hearing date, the petitioner must serve each expected adverse party with a copy of the petition and a notice stating the time and place of the hearing. The notice may be served either inside or outside the district or state in the manner provided in Rule 4. If that service cannot be made with reasonable diligence on an expected adverse party, the court may order service by publication or otherwise. The court must appoint an attorney to represent persons not served in the manner provided in Rule 4 and to cross-examine the deponent if an unserved person is not otherwise represented. If any expected adverse

681

party is a minor or is incompetent, Rule 17(c) applies.

(3) *Order and Examination.* If satisfied that perpetuating the testimony may prevent a failure or delay of justice, the court must issue an order that designates or describes the persons whose depositions may be taken, specifies the subject matter of the examinations, and states whether the depositions will be taken orally or by written interrogatories. The depositions may then be taken under these rules, and the court may issue orders like those authorized by Rules 34 and 35. A reference in these rules to the court where an action is pending means, for purposes of this rule, the court where the petition for the deposition was filed.

(4) *Using the Deposition.* A deposition to perpetuate testimony may be used under Rule 32(a) in any later-filed district-court action involving the same subject matter if the deposition either was taken under these rules or, although not so taken, would be admissible in evidence in the courts of the state where it was taken.

(b) Pending Appeal.

(1) *In General.* The court where a judgment has been rendered may, if an appeal has been taken or may still be taken, permit a party to depose witnesses to perpetuate their testimony for use in the event of further proceedings in that court.

(2) *Motion.* The party who wants to perpetuate testimony may move for leave to take the depositions, on the same notice and service as if the action were pending in the district court. The motion must show:

(A) the name, address, and expected substance of the testimony of each deponent; and

(B) the reasons for perpetuating the testimony.

(3) *Court Order.* If the court finds that perpetuating the testimony may prevent a failure or delay of justice, the court may permit the depositions to be taken and may issue orders like those authorized by Rules

34 and 35. The depositions may be taken and used as any other deposition taken in a pending district-court action.

(c) Perpetuation by an Action. This rule does not limit a court's power to entertain an action to perpetuate testimony.

[Amended effective March 19, 1948; October 20, 1949; July 1, 1971; August 1, 1987; April 25, 2005, effective December 1, 2005; April 30, 2007, effective December 1, 2007.]

--------------------- **2007 AMENDMENTS ROADMAP** ---------------------

STYLE PROJECT CHANGES: Rules 27(a)(1) and 27(b) were subsectioned to add organization, and orienting labels were added to the new subsections in Rule 27(b). The language was shortened and clarified, obsolete language was culled, and "must" replaced "shall".

NON-STYLE CHANGES: None.

NOTE: The Federal Rules "Style Project" is explained in Part III-A.

AUTHORS' COMMENTARY ON RULE 27

------------------------ **PURPOSE AND SCOPE** ------------------------

Sometimes it will be important to preserve or perpetuate testimony before an action is commenced or during the appeal of an action. Rule 27 provides one mechanism for perpetuating such testimony by taking a deposition.

RULE 27(a).   BEFORE AN ACTION IS FILED

CORE CONCEPT

Rule 27 is most commonly used to perpetuate testimony when there is a danger that important testimony will be lost, but for one reason or another a civil action cannot yet be commenced.

APPLICATIONS

Verified Petition

A request for a deposition under Rule 27 must be by *verified* petition (*i.e.,* a petition accompanied by a statement signed by the petitioner that the factual averments are accurate).[1]

Contents of Petition

A Rule 27 petition must contain the following:

(1) A statement that the petitioner expects to be a party to an action in federal court, but is presently unable to bring the action;

(2) A description of the subject matter of the anticipated action and the petitioner's relationship to the action;

(3) The facts that the petitioner intends to establish by the testimony, and the petitioner's need for perpetuating it;

(4) The identities and addresses of the persons expected to be adverse parties in the action; and

(5) The identity of the deponent(s) and a detailed description of the substance of their testimony.[2]

The petition must also include a proposed order describing the procedure and scope of the deposition.

Testimony Only

The general rule appears to be that one may not obtain documents or interrogatory responses under Rule 27, only deposition testimony.[3]

Certainty of Litigation Unnecessary

A party need not demonstrate that litigation is absolutely certain in order to file a motion to perpetuate; instead, the party must be found to be acting in anticipation of litigation.[4]

Need to Perpetuate

It is not necessary to show that the deponents are on their death beds. Rather, one must show that there is a danger of the testimony or evidence being lost,[5] such as when circumstances indicate that memories may fade.[6] In making this determination,

1. *In re Chester County Elec., Inc.*, 208 F.R.D. 545, 546–47 (E.D.Pa.2002).

2. *Penn Mutual Life Insurance Co. v. United States*, 68 F.3d 1371, 1374, 1376 (D.C.Cir.1995)(instructing the district court on remand of a Rule 27 ruling to require a "narrowly tailored showing of the substance" of the testimony); *In re Petition of Allegretti*, 229 F.R.D. 93, 97 (S.D.N.Y.2005) (discussing the degree of detail required).

3. *United States v. Van Rossem*, 180 F.R.D. 245, 247 (W.D.N.Y.1998). *But see Application of Deiulemar Compagnia Di Navigazione S.p.A*, 198 F.3d 473, 478, n. 5 (4th Cir.1999); *Ashafa v. City of Chicago*, 146 F.3d 459, 461 (7th Cir.1998) (Rule 27 petition for names of officers involved in an incident). *But see Pacific Technology Corp. v. Ehrenwald*, 2000 WL 1634393 (S.D.N.Y.

2000) (recognizing that Rule 27 does not allow for the obtaining of documents, but allowing it nonetheless because of the importance of the documents).

4. *Calderon v. U.S. Dist. Court*, 144 F.3d 618 (9th Cir.1998).

5. *Calderon v. U.S. Dist. Court*, 144 F.3d 618 (9th Cir.1998); *In re Ramirez*, ___ F.R.D. ___ (W.D.Tex. 2006) (conclusory statement that the petitioner believes that testimony will be lost is not sufficient); *In re Petition of Allegretti*, 229 F.R.D. 93, 98 (S.D.N.Y.2005) (concluding that the testimony of a young witness with ties to the forum was unlikely to become unavailable).

6. *Arizona v. California*, 292 U.S. 341, 54 S.Ct. 735, 78 L.Ed. 1298 (1934).

however, the deponent's age alone can present a sufficient risk the deponent will be unable to testify.[7]

Pre-Litigation Only

Once litigation has been commenced, Rule 27(a) may no longer be used to perpetuate testimony, and Rules 26 and 30 take over.[8]

Inability to Bring Suit

One requirement for petitions to perpetuate testimony under Rule 27(a) is that the movant not be able to bring a law suit.[9] One basis for such inability is a lack of sufficient information to draft the complaint under the constraints of Rule 11.[10] However, Rule 27 may not be used to uncover or discover testimony necessary to file suit,[11] and applies only where known testimony is to be preserved.[12]

Place of Filing

The petition may be filed in the district in which any of the adverse parties reside. If *all* adverse parties are both not American citizens and not residing in the United States, the petition may be filed in any district.

Notice and Service

At least 20 days prior to the hearing, the petitioner must send notice and a copy of the petition to all expected adverse parties.[13] The notice may be served in the manner provided under Rule 4. If personal service cannot be made, the court can order service by publication or otherwise. In such cases, the court must appoint an attorney to represent those not personally served. If an expected party is a minor or incompetent, then the provisions of Rule 17(c) apply.

Standard for Ruling

The court will order the deposition if it is satisfied that the perpetuation of the testimony may prevent a future failure or delay of justice.[14] The court may also make orders of the type allowable

---

7. *Penn Mutual Life Insurance Co. v. United States*, 68 F.3d 1371, 1375 (D.C.Cir. 1995); *In re Ramirez*, ___ F.R.D. ___ (W.D.Tex. 2006).

8. *19th Street Baptist Church v. St. Peters Episcopal Church*, 190 F.R.D. 345, 348 (E.D.Pa.2000).

9. *In re Town of Amenia, NY*, 200 F.R.D. 200 (S.D.N.Y.2001) (party can take a Rule 27 deposition when a declaratory judgment is technically possible but the parties are still negotiating).

10. *In the Matter of Petition of Alpha Industries, Inc.*, 159 F.R.D. 456 (S.D.N.Y. 1995).

11. *Application of Deiulemar Compagnia Di Navigazione S.p.A*, 198 F.3d 473, 485 (4th Cir.1999); *In re Ramirez*, ___ F.R.D. ___ (W.D.Tex. 2006); *In re Petition of*

Allegretti, 229 F.R.D. 93, 96 (S.D.N.Y.2005) (Rule 27 cannot be used to discover evidence for the purpose of filing a complaint).

12. *In re Ramirez*, ___ F.R.D. ___ (W.D.Tex. 2006); *In re Petition of Sheila Roberts Ford*, 170 F.R.D. 504, 507 (M.D.Ala. 1997).

13. *In re Petition of Allegretti*, 229 F.R.D. 93, 96 (S.D.N.Y.2005); *In re Chester County Elec., Inc.*, 208 F.R.D. 545, 546–47 (E.D.Pa.2002); *In re Solorio*, 192 F.R.D. 709 (D.Utah 2000) (notice is a "condition precedent" to discovery under Rule 27).

14. *In re Charter Communications, Inc., Subpoena Enforcement Matter*, 393 F.3d 771, 784 (8th Cir.2005); *19th Street Baptist Church v. St. Peters Episcopal Church*, 190 F.R.D. 345 (E.D.Pa.2000).

under Rules 34 (production of documents) and 35 (mental examinations).[15]

Conduct of the Deposition

The court must designate the deponent(s), the subject matter of the examination, and whether the deposition will be oral or written.[16] The deposition is then taken in accordance with the court order and Rules pertaining to depositions (*see* Rule 30 and Rule 31).

Scope of Deposition

An inquiry under Rule 27 may include inspection of documents and mental and physical examinations. However, the scope of a deposition under Rule 27 is often more narrow than a typical discovery deposition, and generally will be governed by the court's order.[17] In general, courts have required that the evidence to be preserved be material and competent, not merely discoverable under general discovery provisions.[18]

Use of the Transcript

A deposition taken pursuant to Rule 27 may be used in any subsequent action in federal court involving the subject matter identified in the petition, under the general terms and conditions governing use of depositions in Rule 32(a).

Subject Matter Jurisdiction

A proceeding to perpetuate testimony is not a separate civil action, and does not require its own basis for jurisdiction. However, the petition must demonstrate that the anticipated legal action will proceed in federal court.[19]

Bankruptcy Proceedings

Rule 27 does not apply in contested matters before a bankruptcy court.[20]

Appeals

A grant or denial of a Rule 27 petition is appealable as a final order.[21] It is reviewed under the abuse of discretion standard.[22]

---

15. *Lucas v. Riddle,* 2004 WL 1084719 (D.Conn.2004).

16. *Martin v. Reynolds Metals Corp.,* 297 F.2d 49, 55 (9th Cir.1961).

17. *Nevada v. O'Leary,* 63 F.3d 932, 936 (9th Cir.1995).

18. *In re Hopson Marine Transportation, Inc.,* 168 F.R.D. 560, 565 (E.D.La. 1996).

19. *Dresser Industries, Inc. v. United States,* 596 F.2d 1231 (5th Cir.1979); *In re Complaint of Financial Indemnity Co.,* 173 F.R.D. 435, 437 (W.D.La.1997) (implicit in showing that legal action will proceed in federal court is requirement that in diversity cases, petitioner must prove by a preponderance of the evidence that the amount in controversy exceeds the jurisdictional amount). *But see Application of Deiulemar Compagnia Di Navigazione S.p.A,* 198 F.3d 473, 479 (4th Cir.1999) (allowing Rule 27 discovery to preserve evidence for an arbitration).

20. *See Sweetland v. Szadkowski,* 198 B.R. 140, 141 n. 1 (Bkrtcy.D.Md.1996). *See also* Fed.Rules Bankr.Proc.Rule 9014.

21. *Martin v. Reynolds Metals Corp.,* 297 F.2d 49 (9th Cir.1961).

22. *Application of Deiulemar Compagnia Di Navigazione S.p.A,* 198 F.3d 473, 479 (4th Cir.1999); *Shore v. Acands, Inc.,* 644 F.2d 386 (5th Cir.1981).

RULE 27(b).   PENDING APPEAL

CORE CONCEPT

Rule 27 may be used while a case is on appeal, or while the period to appeal is running, to preserve testimony in the event that further proceedings are needed.[23]   A request for a deposition pending an appeal is made by motion (not petition) to the district court where the action proceeded.[24]   The motion must include the names and addresses of the deponents, the substance of their testimony, and the reasons for perpetuating their testimony.[25]   Otherwise, a motion pursuant to Rule 27(b) is subject to the notice, service, and other requirements and conditions for a petition under Rule 27(a) described immediately above.

RULE 27(c).   PERPETUATION BY AN ACTION

CORE CONCEPT

Rule 27 is not the exclusive method of perpetuating testimony.[26] Thus, for example, a deposition that would be admissible in a subsequent proceeding in state court will also be admissible in federal court, even though the offering party may not have complied with Rule 27.   Likewise, a party may preserve testimony under a method authorized by statute.

ADDITIONAL RESEARCH REFERENCES

Wright & Miller, *Federal Practice and Procedure* §§ 2071–2076.   Lisnek & Kaufman, *Depositions: Procedure, Strategy and Technique.*

C.J.S. Federal Civil Procedure §§ 544–547.

West's Key No. Digests, Federal Civil Procedure ⟲1291–1299.

23.   *See Schreier v. Weight Watchers Northeast Region, Inc.,* 872 F.Supp. 1 (E.D.N.Y.1994).

24.   *United States v. Van Rossem,* 180 F.R.D. 245, 247 (W.D.N.Y.1998) (motion to compel Rule 27 discovery denied because need to perpetuate testimony was not demonstrated).

25.   *Foy v. Dicks,* 1996 WL 745501 (E.D.Pa.1996) (petitioners' Rule 27 motion denied for failure to assert reasons why perpetuation of evidence was necessary).

26.   *See Nissei Sangyo America, Ltd. v. United States,* 31 F.3d 435 (7th Cir. 1994) (action to perpetuate foreign bank records).

RULE 28

PERSONS BEFORE WHOM DEPOSITIONS MAY BE TAKEN

(a) Within the United States.

(1) *In General.* Within the United States or a territory or insular possession subject to United States jurisdiction, a deposition must be taken before:

(A) an officer authorized to administer oaths either by federal law or by the law in the place of examination; or

(B) a person appointed by the court where the action is pending to administer oaths and take testimony.

(2) *Definition of "Officer."* The term "officer" in Rules 30, 31, and 32 includes a person appointed by the court under this rule or designated by the parties under Rule 29(a).

(b) In a Foreign Country.

(1) *In General.* A deposition may be taken in a foreign country:

(A) under an applicable treaty or convention;

(B) under a letter of request, whether or not captioned a "letter rogatory";

(C) on notice, before a person authorized to administer oaths either by federal law or by the law in the place of examination; or

(D) before a person commissioned by the court to administer any necessary oath and take testimony.

(2) *Issuing a Letter of Request or a Commission.* A letter of request, a commission, or both may be issued:

(A) on appropriate terms after an application and notice of it; and

(B) without a showing that taking the deposition in another manner is impracticable or inconvenient.

(3) *Form of a Request, Notice, or Commission.* When a letter of request or any other device is used according to a treaty or convention, it must be captioned in the form prescribed by that treaty or convention. A letter of request may be addressed "To the Appropriate Authority in [name of country]." A deposition notice or a commission must designate by name or descriptive title the person before whom the deposition is to be taken.

(4) *Letter of Request—Admitting Evidence.* Evidence obtained in response to a letter of request need not be excluded merely because it is not a verbatim transcript, because the testimony was not taken under oath, or because of any similar departure from the requirements for depositions taken within the United States.

(c) Disqualification. A deposition must not be taken before a person who is any party's relative, employee, or attorney; who is related to or employed by any party's attorney; or who is financially interested in the action.

[Amended December 27, 1946, effective March 19, 1948; January 21, 1963, effective July 1, 1963; April 29, 1980, effective August 1, 1980; March 2, 1987, effective August 1, 1987; April 22, 1993, effective December 1, 1993; April 30, 2007, effective December 1, 2007.]

—————————— **2007 AMENDMENTS ROADMAP** ——————————

STYLE PROJECT CHANGES: Sections 28(a) and (b) were subsectioned to add organization, and orienting labels were added. Cumbersome and confusing language was revised.

NON-STYLE CHANGES: None.

NOTE: The Federal Rules "Style Project" is explained in Part III-A.

AUTHORS' COMMENTARY ON RULE 28

———————————— PURPOSE AND SCOPE ————————————

Rule 28 specifies the type of person who must be present at a deposition to administer the oath and to record the testimony.

RULE 28(a).   WITHIN THE UNITED STATES

CORE CONCEPT

In the United States, or a territory or insular possession, depositions may be taken before an officer authorized to administer oaths under federal or state law.[1] Typically, a stenographer is such an officer. A deposition may also be taken before someone appointed by the court, or before a person designated by the parties pursuant to Rule 29.[2]

RULE 28(b).   IN A FOREIGN COUNTRY

CORE CONCEPT

The procedures for taking depositions in a foreign country depend upon the particular country. Some countries have treaties with the United States that facilitate such depositions. Other countries strictly prohibit such depositions altogether.

NOTE: In some countries, the taking of evidence under unauthorized procedures may subject the interrogator to severe—even criminal—sanctions. Before taking such evidence, a practitioner should consult the Hague Convention and all treaty supplements thereto.[3]

APPLICATIONS

Alternatives

Depending upon the laws of the foreign country, a deposition in a foreign country may be taken:

(1) Pursuant to any applicable treaty or convention (such as the Hague Convention described above);[4]

(2) Pursuant to a letter request (or letter rogatory), which is a formal communication between the court in which an action is proceeding and another court requesting that the testimony of a foreign witness be taken under the direction of the foreign court;[5]

(3) Upon a notice of deposition by any person authorized to administer oaths either by the laws of the foreign country or the United States; and

1. *Hudson v. Spellman High Voltage,* 178 F.R.D. 29, 32 (E.D.N.Y.1998).

2. *Popular Imports, Inc. v. Wong's Int'l Inc.,* 166 F.R.D. 276, 279–80 (E.D.N.Y. 1996).

3. The Hague Convention on the Taking of Evidence Abroad in Civil or Commercial Matters is reproduced as a note to 28 U.S.C.A. § 1781, and may also be found on WESTLAW in the IEL database, **ci(vii-b & text)**. *Also see* Lowenfeld, International Litigation and Arbitration: Selected Trea-

ties, Statutes and Rules, page 262 (1993). *See Societe Nationale Industrielle Aerospatiale v. United States District Court for the Southern District of Iowa,* 482 U.S. 522, 107 S.Ct. 2542, 96 L.Ed.2d 461 (1987).

4. *International Ins. Co. v. Caja Nacional De Ahoroo Y Seguro,* 2004 WL 555618 (N.D.Ill.2004).

5. *See Murata Mfg. Co., Ltd. v. Bel Fuse, Inc.,* 242 F.R.D. 470 (N.D.Ill. 2007).

(4) Before persons commissioned by the court, who will have power to administer an oath and hear testimony by virtue of their oaths.

Method Optional

A party seeking to depose a witness in a foreign country may use any of the methods listed in Rule 28(b) allowed by the foreign country's laws, and may even combine two or more methods.

Issuance of Letter Requests

All courts of the United States are authorized to issue letter requests or letters rogatory,[6] which are typically channeled through the United States Department of State.

Testimony Pursuant to a Letter Request

The evidence taken pursuant to a letter request varies according to the foreign country's laws. Sometimes the foreign judge examines the witness, then makes a written summary of the testimony, which is acknowledged as correct by the witness. The United States court will then decide on the weight to be given to the evidence depending upon the method of recording.

Compelling Attendance of Witness

If the witness is a party, then the witness is subject to the United States court's sanctions if the witness fails to appear as noticed. If the witness is a United States citizen, then the witness still may be subject to the United States court's subpoena power. However, if the witness is an alien, then the party will have to rely on a letter request.

RULE 28(c). DISQUALIFICATION

CORE CONCEPT

The officer at a deposition may not be a relative, employee, attorney, or counsel of any of the parties,[7] or an employee or relative of an attorney for a party, or anyone with a financial interest in the action.[8]

APPLICATIONS

Objections

Objections to the officer must be raised before the deposition starts, or as soon thereafter as the interest of the officer becomes known or should have become known, with due diligence. Otherwise, the objection is waived.[9]

6. *See United States v. Reagan*, 453 F.2d 165 (6th Cir.1971).

7. *See United States v. Washington*, 46 M.J. 477, 482 (C.A.A.F.1997) (defendant objected to the appointment of a prosecutor on the basis that he had prior prosecutorial involvement in the case).

8. *Ott v. Stipe Law Firm*, 169 F.R.D. 380, 381 (E.D.Okla.1996) (plaintiff is not permitted to administer oath).

9. See Rule 32(d)(2).

ADDITIONAL RESEARCH REFERENCES

Wright & Miller, *Federal Practice and Procedure* §§ 2081–2084.

C.J.S. Federal Civil Procedure § 593.

West's Key No. Digests, Federal Civil Procedure ⚮1371.

RULE 29

STIPULATIONS ABOUT DISCOVERY PROCEDURE

Unless the court orders otherwise, the parties may stipulate that:

(a) a deposition may be taken before any person, at any time or place, on any notice, and in the manner specified—in which event it may be used in the same way as any other deposition; and

(b) other procedures governing or limiting discovery be modified—but a stipulation extending the time for any form of discovery must have court approval if it would interfere with the time set for completing discovery, for hearing a motion, or for trial.

[Amended March 30, 1970, effective July 1, 1970; April 22, 1993, effective December 1, 1993; April 30, 2007, effective December 1, 2007.]

─────────── **2007 AMENDMENTS ROADMAP** ───────────

STYLE PROJECT CHANGES: Rule 29 was reformatted to include two subsections. Cumbersome and confusing language was revised.

NON-STYLE CHANGES: None.

NOTE: The Federal Rules "Style Project" is explained in Part III-A.

AUTHORS' COMMENTARY ON RULE 29

─────────── **PURPOSE AND SCOPE** ───────────

For their convenience, the parties may stipulate to modified procedures for taking depositions and for other discovery methods as long as the stipulation does not interfere with a hearing or trial date or the discovery deadline.

APPLICATIONS

Procedures

Rule 29 states that stipulations must be in writing.[1] Although not expressly required by Rule 29, the stipulation should be signed by the parties.[2] Stipulations under Rule 29 are self-effectuating, and do not need to be filed with the court unless they interfere with the close of discovery or any other case management deadline.[3]

Depositions

The parties may designate the person before whom a deposition will occur, and the time, location, notice requirements, and method of taking the deposition.[4] Thereafter, a deposition taken in accordance with the stipulation may be used as if taken in accordance with the provisions governing depositions in Rules 30 and 31.

Other Discovery Methods

The parties may also stipulate to any other discovery method, except that the parties need court approval to modify the time to respond to interrogatories, document requests, and requests for admission set forth in Rules 33, 34, and 36 if the extension would interfere with the court's discovery deadline or with a hearing or trial date.[5]

Court Override

The court can order that parties perform under the Rules as written, vitiating any stipulations.[6]

ADDITIONAL RESEARCH REFERENCES

Wright & Miller, *Federal Practice and Procedure* §§ 2091–2092.

C.J.S. Federal Civil Procedure § 566.

West's Key No. Digests, Federal Civil Procedure ⬤1326.

1. *In re Carney*, 258 F.3d 415, 419 (5th Cir.2001) (stipulation not effective if not in writing); *Venture Funding, Ltd. v. United States*, 190 F.R.D. 209, 212 (E.D.Mich.1999) (oral agreement that only certain documents need to be produced is unenforceable); *Pescia v. Auburn Ford–Lincoln Mercury, Inc.*, 177 F.R.D. 509, 510 (M.D.Ala.1997) (oral agreement, even though confirmed in writing, did not satisfy the requirement of Rule 29 that stipulations must be in writing).

2. *Land Ocean Logistics, Inc. v. Aqua Gulf Corp.*, 181 F.R.D. 229, 243 (W.D.N.Y. 1998) (competing unsigned stipulations are unenforceable).

3. *Cozort v. State Farm Mut. Auto. Ins. Co.*, 233 F.R.D. 674, 678 (M.D.Fla.2005).

4. *Reder Enterprises, Inc. v. Loomis, Fargo & Co. Corp.*, 490 F.Supp.2d 111 (D.Mass. 2007) (parties may stipulate that depositions be taken "at any ... place"); *Hudson v. Spellman High Voltage*, 178 F.R.D. 29, 32 (E.D.N.Y.1998).

5. *See Laborers' Pension Fund v. Blackmore Sewer Const., Inc.*, 298 F.3d 600, 605–06 (7th Cir.2002); *Jayne H. Lee, Inc. v. Flagstaff Indus. Corp.*, 173 F.R.D. 651, 654 n. 8 (D.Md.1997).

6. The Advisory Note to the 1970 amendment of Rule 29.

RULE 30

DEPOSITIONS BY ORAL EXAMINATION

(a) When a Deposition May Be Taken.

(1) *Without Leave.* A party may, by oral questions, depose any person, including a party, without leave of court except as provided in Rule 30(a)(2). The deponent's attendance may be compelled by subpoena under Rule 45.

(2) *With Leave.* A party must obtain leave of court, and the court must grant leave to the extent consistent with Rule 26(b)(2):

(A) if the parties have not stipulated to the deposition and:

(i) the deposition would result in more than 10 depositions being taken under this rule or Rule 31 by the plaintiffs, or by the defendants, or by the third-party defendants;

(ii) the deponent has already been deposed in the case; or

(iii) the party seeks to take the deposition before the time specified in Rule 26(d), unless the party certifies in the notice, with supporting facts, that the deponent is expected to leave the United States and be unavailable for examination in this country after that time; or

(B) if the deponent is confined in prison.

(b) Notice of the Deposition; Other Formal Requirements.

(1) *Notice in General.* A party who wants to depose a person by oral questions must give reasonable written notice to every other party. The notice must state the time and place of the deposition and, if known, the deponent's name and address. If the name is unknown, the notice must provide a general description sufficient to identify the person or the particular class or group to which the person belongs.

(2) *Producing Documents.* If a subpoena duces tecum is to be served on the deponent, the materials designated for production, as set out in the subpoena, must be listed in the notice or in an attachment. The notice to a party deponent may be accompanied by a request under Rule 34 to produce documents and tangible things at the deposition.

(3) *Method of Recording.*

    (A) *Method Stated in the Notice.* The party who notices the deposition must state in the notice the method for recording the testimony. Unless the court orders otherwise, testimony may be recorded by audio, audiovisual, or stenographic means. The noticing party bears the recording costs. Any party may arrange to transcribe a deposition.

    (B) *Additional Method.* With prior notice to the deponent and other parties, any party may designate another method for recording the testimony in addition to that specified in the original notice. That party bears the expense of the additional record or transcript unless the court orders otherwise.

(4) *By Remote Means.* The parties may stipulate—or the court may on motion order—that a deposition be taken by telephone or other remote means. For the purpose of this rule and Rules 28(a), 37(a)(2), and 37(b)(1), the deposition takes place where the deponent answers the questions.

(5) *Officer's Duties.*

    (A) *Before the Deposition.* Unless the parties stipulate otherwise, a deposition must be conducted before an officer appointed or designated under Rule 28. The officer must begin the deposition with an on-the-record statement that includes:

        (i) the officer's name and business address;

        (ii) the date, time, and place of the deposition;

        (iii) the deponent's name;

        (iv) the officer's administration of the oath or affirmation to the deponent; and

(v) the identity of all persons present.

(B) *Conducting the Deposition; Avoiding Distortion.* If the deposition is recorded nonstenographically, the officer must repeat the items in Rule 30(b)(5)(A)(i)–(iii) at the beginning of each unit of the recording medium. The deponent's and attorneys' appearance or demeanor must not be distorted through recording techniques.

(C) *After the Deposition.* At the end of a deposition, the officer must state on the record that the deposition is complete and must set out any stipulations made by the attorneys about custody of the transcript or recording and of the exhibits, or about any other pertinent matters.

(6) *Notice or Subpoena Directed to an Organization.* In its notice or subpoena, a party may name as the deponent a public or private corporation, a partnership, an association, a governmental agency, or other entity and must describe with reasonable particularity the matters for examination. The named organization must then designate one or more officers, directors, or managing agents, or designate other persons who consent to testify on its behalf; and it may set out the matters on which each person designated will testify. A subpoena must advise a nonparty organization of its duty to make this designation. The persons designated must testify about information known or reasonably available to the organization. This paragraph (6) does not preclude a deposition by any other procedure allowed by these rules.

(c) Examination and Cross–Examination; Record of the Examination; Objections; Written Questions.

(1) *Examination and Cross–Examination.* The examination and cross-examination of a deponent proceed as they would at trial under the Federal Rules of Evidence, except Rules 103 and 615. After putting the deponent under oath or affirmation, the officer must record the testimony by the method designated under Rule 30(b)(3)(A). The testimony must be recorded by the officer personally or by a person

acting in the presence and under the direction of the officer.

(2) *Objections.* An objection at the time of the examination—whether to evidence, to a party's conduct, to the officer's qualifications, to the manner of taking the deposition, or to any other aspect of the deposition—must be noted on the record, but the examination still proceeds; the testimony is taken subject to any objection. An objection must be stated concisely in a nonargumentative and nonsuggestive manner. A person may instruct a deponent not to answer only when necessary to preserve a privilege, to enforce a limitation ordered by the court, or to present a motion under Rule 30(d)(3).

(3) *Participating Through Written Questions.* Instead of participating in the oral examination, a party may serve written questions in a sealed envelope on the party noticing the deposition, who must deliver them to the officer. The officer must ask the deponent those questions and record the answers verbatim.

(d) Duration; Sanction; Motion to Terminate or Limit.

(1) *Duration.* Unless otherwise stipulated or ordered by the court, a deposition is limited to 1 day of 7 hours. The court must allow additional time consistent with Rule 26(b)(2) if needed to fairly examine the deponent or if the deponent, another person, or any other circumstance impedes or delays the examination.

(2) *Sanction.* The court may impose an appropriate sanction—including the reasonable expenses and attorney's fees incurred by any party—on a person who impedes, delays, or frustrates the fair examination of the deponent.

(3) *Motion to Terminate or Limit.*

(A) *Grounds.* At any time during a deposition, the deponent or a party may move to terminate or limit it on the ground that it is being conducted in bad faith or in a manner that unreasonably annoys, embarrasses, or oppresses the deponent or party. The motion may be filed in the court where the action is pending or the deposition is being taken. If the objecting deponent or party so demands, the deposition must be suspended for the time necessary to obtain an order.

(B) *Order.* The court may order that the deposition be terminated or may limit its scope and manner as provided in Rule 26(c). If terminated, the deposition may be resumed only by order of the court where the action is pending.

(C) *Award of Expenses.* Rule 37(a)(5) applies to the award of expenses.

(e) Review by the Witness; Changes.

(1) *Review; Statement of Changes.* On request by the deponent or a party before the deposition is completed, the deponent must be allowed 30 days after being notified by the officer that the transcript or recording is available in which:

(A) to review the transcript or recording; and

(B) if there are changes in form or substance, to sign a statement listing the changes and the reasons for making them.

(2) *Changes Indicated in the Officer's Certificate.* The officer must note in the certificate prescribed by Rule 30(f)(1) whether a review was requested and, if so, must attach any changes the deponent makes during the 30–day period.

(f) Certification and Delivery; Exhibits; Copies of the Transcript or Recording; Filing.

(1) *Certification and Delivery.* The officer must certify in writing that the witness was duly sworn and that the deposition accurately records the witness's testimony. The certificate must accompany the record of the deposition. Unless the court orders otherwise, the officer must seal the deposition in an envelope or package bearing the title of the action and marked "Deposition of [witness's name]" and must promptly send it to the attorney who arranged for the transcript or recording. The attorney must store it under conditions that will protect it against loss, destruction, tampering, or deterioration.

(2) *Documents and Tangible Things.*

(A) *Originals and Copies.* Documents and tangible things produced for inspection during a deposition must, on a party's request, be marked for identification and attached to the deposition. Any party may inspect and copy them. But if the person who produced them wants to keep the originals, the person may:

(i) offer copies to be marked, attached to the deposition, and then used as originals—after giving all parties a fair opportunity to verify the copies by comparing them with the originals; or

(ii) give all parties a fair opportunity to inspect and copy the originals after they are marked—in which event the originals may be used as if attached to the deposition.

(B) *Order Regarding the Originals.* Any party may move for an order that the originals be attached to the deposition pending final disposition of the case.

(3) *Copies of the Transcript or Recording.* Unless otherwise stipulated or ordered by the court, the officer must retain the stenographic notes of a deposition taken stenographically or a copy of the recording of a deposition taken by another method. When paid reasonable charges, the officer must furnish a copy of the transcript or recording to any party or the deponent.

(4) *Notice of Filing.* A party who files the deposition must promptly notify all other parties of the filing.

(g) Failure to Attend a Deposition or Serve a Subpoena; Expenses. A party who, expecting a deposition to be taken, attends in person or by an attorney may recover reasonable expenses for attending, including attorney's fees, if the noticing party failed to:

(1) attend and proceed with the deposition; or

(2) serve a subpoena on a nonparty deponent, who consequently did not attend.

[Amended January 21, 1963, effective July 1, 1963; March 30, 1970, effective July 1, 1970; March 1, 1971, effective July 1, 1971; November 20, 1972, effective July 1, 1975; April 29, 1980, effective August 1, 1980; March 2, 1987, effective August 1, 1987; April 22, 1993, effective December 1, 1993; April 17, 2000, effective December 1, 2000; April 30, 2007, effective December 1, 2007.]

--------------------- **2007 AMENDMENTS ROADMAP** ---------------------

STYLE PROJECT CHANGES: Many of the sections in Rule 30 were broken into new subsections, renumbered, or relabeled so care should be exercised when reviewing or citing to prior cases citing to individual subsections. Active voice generally replaced passive voice and cumbersome wording was culled.

NON-STYLE CHANGES: Rule 30(b)(3)(A) was revised so that any party may arrange for the transcription of a deposition, regardless of how it was recorded. The phrase "or other entity" was added to Rule 30(b)(6) so that a party may depose a representative of any type of organization, including those such as limited liability companies that were not specifically listed.

NOTE: The Federal Rules "Style Project" is explained in Part III-A.

AUTHORS' COMMENTARY ON RULE 30

--------------------- **PURPOSE AND SCOPE** ---------------------

Rule 30 sets forth the procedures for the taking of depositions by oral examination. Rule 30 must be considered in conjunction with the other discovery rules, and in particular Rule 26 governing the scope of discovery.

NOTE: Rule 30 was substantially revised in 1993, 2000, and 2007, and great care should be exercised when citing decisions pertaining to Rule 30.

RULE 30(a).   WHEN A DEPOSITION MAY BE TAKEN

CORE CONCEPT

In general, a party may take the deposition of up to 10 witnesses, party or otherwise, at any time after the parties have conducted the discovery conference under Rule 26(d).

APPLICATIONS

Persons Subject to Deposition

Rule 30 applies to parties and nonparties alike.[1] A party may even take the party's own deposition if, for example, the party will be unable to attend trial. One may also take the deposition of attorneys, including the attorneys for parties,[2] although the attorney-client privilege may protect most of an attorney's testimony. Depositions are also permitted of public officials, the United States, individual states, and other governmental subdivisions.[3]

Number of Depositions

The plaintiffs as a group are limited to 10 depositions total, by written and/or oral examination, as are the defendants and third-party defendants.[4] Subpoenas to produce documents do not count towards the 10 deposition limit.[5] It is not clear whether expert depositions count toward the limit.[6] This number may be increased by stipulation or by order of court.[7]

Repeat Depositions

Leave of court is required to depose someone a second time (although leave of court is not required to reconvene and continue a deposition that was suspended or not completed the first day).[8] This restriction arguably applies to depositions of a corporate representative under Rule 30(b)(6).[9] Leave shall be granted subject to the principles in Rule 26(b)(2), such as when the sought-after information could not have been obtained in the first deposition.[10]

When Depositions May be Conducted

Depositions generally may be taken at any time after the Rule 26(d) discovery conference and before the cut-off date for discovery

1. *CSC Holdings, Inc. v. Redisi*, 309 F.3d 988, 993 (7th Cir.2002) (a party has a general right to compel any person to appear at a deposition).

2. *Shelton v. American Motors Corp.*, 805 F.2d 1323 (8th Cir.1986); *Ellipsis, Inc. v. Color Works, Inc.*, 227 F.R.D. 496, 497 (W.D.Tenn.2005) (deposing opposing counsel is discouraged by many courts); *Prevue Pet Products, Inc. v. Avian Adventures, Inc.*, 200 F.R.D. 4135 (N.D.Ill.2001) (describing the criteria for taking the deposition of opposing counsel).

3. *United States v. Procter & Gamble Co.*, 356 U.S. 677, 78 S.Ct. 983, 2 L.Ed.2d 1077 (1958).

4. *Finova Capital Corp. v. Lawrence*, 2000 WL 1808276 (N.D.Tex.2000) (depositions of parties and nonparties alike both count towards the 10 deposition limit).

5. *Andamiro U.S.A. v. Konami Amusement of America, Inc.*, 2001 WL 535667 (C.D.Cal.2001).

6. *Express One Intern., Inc. v. Sochata*, 2001 WL 363073 (N.D.Tex.2001).

7. *Raniola v. Bratton*, 243 F.3d 610, 628 (2d Cir.2001); *Barrow v. Greenville Independent School Dist.*, 202 F.R.D. 480, 482 (N.D.Tex.2001) (magistrate judge's ruling denying leave to take more than 10 depositions reviewed on an abuse of discretion standard).

8. *In re Tutu Water Wells Contamination CERCLA Litigation*, 189 F.R.D. 153, 155 (D.Vi.1999) (balancing need for testimony against burden of second deposition); *Melhorn v. New Jersey Transit Rail Operations, Inc.*, 203 F.R.D. 176 (E.D.Pa.2001) ("Absent some showing of need or good reason for doing so, a deponent should not be required to appear for a second deposition.").

9. *See Ameristar Jet Charter, Inc. v. Signal Composites, Inc.*, 244 F.3d 189 (1st Cir.2001).

10. *Collins v. International Dairy Queen*, 189 F.R.D. 496, 498 (M.D.Ga.1999).

established by the court. Leave of court is generally required to depose someone prior to the time when the parties conduct the discovery conference under Rule 26(d).[11] An exception occurs when the deponent is expected to leave the United States. In such instances, the notice of deposition must contain a certification with the facts supporting the need for the early deposition.[12] Additionally, in proceedings listed in Rule 26(a)(1)(B) as exempt from initial disclosures, there is no preliminary waiting period for depositions.

Postjudgment Depositions

A judgment creditor is entitled to take depositions of the judgment debtor to inquire into the assets necessary to satisfy the judgment.[13]

Deponent in Prison

Leave of court must be obtained in order to take the deposition of a person confined in prison.[14]

RULE 30(b)(1).   NOTICE OF THE DEPOSITION; OTHER FORMAL REQUIREMENTS: NOTICE IN GENERAL

CORE CONCEPT

A party desiring to take a deposition must serve a written notice upon all other parties identifying the deponent and time and location of the deposition. Depositions are only admissible against parties properly noticed or actually represented at the deposition.

APPLICATIONS

2007 Amendments

The 2007 amendments substantially reorganized Rule 30(b). The portion of Rule 30(b)(1) addressing subpoenas for the production documents and things was combined with Rule 30(b)(5) to form new Rule 30(b)(2). The content of Rule 30(b)(2) and Rule 30(b)(3) pertaining to methods of recording a deposition were combined to form new Rule 30(b)(3). Rule 30(b)(7), pertaining to telephonic and remote depositions, was moved to Rule 30(b)(4). Old Rule 30(b)(4) became Rule 30(b)(5). Only Rule 30(b)(6) was immune from this reorganization. Great care should be exercised in researching and citing pre–2008 cases referring to subsections of Rule 30(b).

Content of Notice

The notice must state the time and place of the deposition. It must also state the name and address of the deponent, if known, or

---

11. *Dimension Data North America, Inc. v. NetStar–1, Inc.*, 226 F.R.D. 528, 531 (E.D.N.C.2005).

12. *19th Street Baptist Church v. St. Peters Episcopal Church*, 190 F.R.D. 345, 348 n. 5 (E.D.Pa.2000).

13. *Credit Lyonnais v. SGC International, Inc.*, 160 F.3d 428, 430 (8th Cir.1998).

14. *See Ashby v. McKenna*, 331 F.3d 1148(10th Cir.2003) (prisoner plaintiff sanctioned for refusing to participate in deposition without court order); *Davis v. Artuz*, 2001 WL 50887 (S.D.N.Y.2001).

a general description sufficient to identify the deponent. If a subpoena duces tecum (seeking documents) is to be served under Rule 45, then the notice must include a description of the documents sought.[15] There is no need to state the subject of the inquiry.

Filing of Notice

The notice need not be filed.

Notice to Party

Parties must comply with a notice of deposition or they are potentially subject to sanctions from the court.[16] A corporate party is required to produce directors, officers, and managing agents[17] pursuant to a notice of deposition; a subpoena is required for other employees.[18] Parties that believe that they should not be required to attend can file motions for protective orders.

Failure to Notify

If a party does not receive a notice of a deposition and does not appear, or is not represented at the deposition, the testimony cannot be used against that party, even if the party had actual knowledge.[19]

Notice to Non-party

A notice of deposition is not binding on a non-party. Instead, a subpoena must be issued pursuant to Rule 45 to force a non-party to attend a deposition.[20]

Reasonable Notice

Rule 30(b)(1) states that a party must give reasonable notice.[21] There is no bright line as to what is reasonable notice, and the determination is extremely fact-specific.[22] If the parties cannot agree on a mutually acceptable date, then unreasonable notice may be challenged by a motion to enlarge or shorten the time for taking the deposition by a motion for a protective order under Rule 26(c). An order vacating a deposition notice based upon unreasonable notice does not preclude further discovery with proper notice.

15. *Orleman v. Jumpking, Inc.*, 2000 WL 1114849 (D.Kan.2000) (description of documents to be produced must be attached to or included in the notice).

16. *Blazek v. Capital Recovery Associates, Inc.*, 222 F.R.D. 360, 361 (E.D.Wis. 2004) (a defaulting party deemed a party for purposes of a notice of deposition).

17. *Murata Mfg. Co., Ltd. v. Bel Fuse, Inc.*, 242 F.R.D. 470 (N.D.Ill. 2007) (managing agents generally are current employees with control or authority over day-to-day business decisions).

18. *U.S. Fidelity & Guar. Co. v. Braspetro Oil Services Co.*, 2001 WL 43607 (S.D.N.Y.2001).

19. *Lauson v. Stop–N–Go Foods, Inc.*, 133 F.R.D. 92 (W.D.N.Y.1990).

20. *Blazek v. Capital Recovery Associates, Inc.*, 222 F.R.D. 360, 361 (E.D.Wis. 2004).

21. *Howard v. Everex Systems, Inc.*, 228 F.3d 1057, 1067 (9th Cir.2000); *United States v. Philip Morris Inc.*, 312 F.Supp.2d 27 (D.D.C.2004) (3 days notice for busy professionals is not reasonable).

22. *In re Sulfuric Acid Antitrust Litigation*, 231 F.R.D. 320, 327 (N.D.Ill.2005) (10 days unreasonable in a complex case); *In re Stratosphere Corp. Securities Litigation*, 183 F.R.D. 684, 687 (D.Nev.1999) (six days notice not reasonable).

Sanctions

The sanctions for failure to appear at a deposition depend upon whether the witness is a party. Non-party witnesses may be held in contempt of court for failure to obey a subpoena. Party witnesses are subject to the sanctions described in Rule 37(d).

Place of Examination

For a party deponent, one may select any location for the deposition, subject to the party's right to move for a protective order (but see the general rules below).[23] For a non-party witness, the witness must travel up to 100 miles from the place where the witness resides, is employed, or regularly transacts business.

General Rules for Deposition Location

The court has discretion to control the location of a deposition.[24] In general, however, plaintiffs will be required to travel to the district where the suit is pending for their depositions,[25] whereas defendants can have their depositions taken where they work or live.[26] Also, in general, the deposition of a corporation occurs at its principal place of business.[27] These general principles are, of course, subject to extenuating circumstances, such as a plaintiff who is too sick to travel.

Motion for Protective Order

If a notice of deposition is facially valid, then the witness must attend or file a motion for a protective order pursuant to Rule 26(c).[28] The motion must be made before the time scheduled for the deposition, and must show good reason for the requested protection. The motion must be accompanied by a certification that the parties met prior to the filing of the motion and attempted to resolve their dispute without intervention by the court.

RULE 30(b)(2).   PRODUCING DOCUMENTS

CORE CONCEPT

A witness may be compelled to bring documents to a deposition by including a description of the documents in the notice of deposition (for a party witness) or by issuing a subpoena duces tecum under Rule

23. *New Medium Technologies LLC v. Barco N.V.*, 242 F.R.D. 460 (N.D.Ill. 2007).

24. *In re Standard Metals Corp.*, 817 F.2d 625, 628 (10th Cir.1987); *New Medium Technologies LLC v. Barco N.V.*, 242 F.R.D. 460 (N.D.Ill. 2007); *Starlight International Inc. v. Herlihy*, 186 F.R.D. 626, 644 (D.Kan. 1999) (court will consider each case on its own facts and the equities of the particular situation).

25. *United States v. Rock Springs Vista Development*, 185 F.R.D. 603 (D.Nev.1999) (wheelchair-bound out-of-state plaintiffs must travel to the forum of the suit for their depositions); *Dollar Systems, Inc. v. Tomlin*, 102 F.R.D. 93 (D.Tenn.1984).

26. *Rapoca Energy Comapny, L.P. v. Amci Export Corp.*, 199 F.R.D. 191, 193 (W.D.Va.2001).

27. *New Medium Technologies LLC v. Barco N.V.*, 242 F.R.D. 460 (N.D.Ill. 2007); *Custom Form Mfg., Inc. v. Omron Corp.*, 196 F.R.D. 333, 336 (N.D.Ind.2000).

28. *Collins v. Wayland*, 139 F.2d 677 (9th Cir.1944).

45(a)(1)(A)(iii) and including a description in the notice (for a non-party witness).[29] However, if the witness is a party, then the witness must be accorded 30 days to interpose objections to the document request[30] (the rationale being that one should not be able to circumvent the 30–day period in the document request rules by issuing a notice of deposition).[31] A deposition notice to a party may also be accompanied by a document request under Rule 34.

APPLICATIONS

2007 Amendments

The 2007 amendments substantially reorganized Rule 30(b). The portion of Rule 30(b)(1) addressing subpoenas for the production documents and things was combined with Rule 30(b)(5) to form new Rule 30(b)(2). The content of Rule 30(b)(2) and Rule 30(b)(3) pertaining to methods of recording a deposition were combined to form new Rule 30(b)(3). Rule 30(b)(7), pertaining to telephonic and remote depositions, was moved to Rule 30(b)(4). Old Rule 30(b)(4) became Rule 30(b)(5). Only Rule 30(b)(6) was immune from this reorganization. Great care should be exercised in researching and citing pre–2008 cases referring to subsections of Rule 30(b).

RULE 30(b)(3).   THE DEPOSITION; METHOD OF RECORDING

CORE CONCEPT

The notice of deposition must specify the method for recording the deposition testimony.

APPLICATIONS

2007 Amendments

The 2007 amendments substantially reorganized Rule 30(b). The portion of Rule 30(b)(1) addressing subpoenas for the production documents and things was combined with Rule 30(b)(5) to form new Rule 30(b)(2). The content of Rule 30(b)(2) and Rule 30(b)(3) pertaining to methods of recording a deposition were combined to form new Rule 30(b)(3). Rule 30(b)(7), pertaining to telephonic and remote depositions, was moved to Rule 30(b)(4). Old Rule 30(b)(4) became Rule 30(b)(5). Only Rule 30(b)(6) was immune from this reorganization. Great care should be exercised in researching and citing pre–2008 cases referring to subsections of Rule 30(b).

Methods Available

The party taking the deposition may have it recorded by audio, audio visual, or stenographic means, unless the court orders other-

---

29. *Lee v. U.S. Dept. of Justice,* 287 F.Supp.2d 15, 22 (D.D.C.2003).

30. *Howell v. Standard Motor Products, Inc.,* 2001 WL 456241 (N.D.Tex.2001).

31. *See Canal Barge Co. v. Commonwealth Edison Co.,* 2001 WL 817853

(N.D.Ill.2001) (discussing the relationship between document requests under Rule 34 and requests to bring documents to depositions).

wise.[32]   Other parties may arrange for additional methods of recording under Rule 30(b)(3)(B).

Cost of Recording

The party taking the deposition bears the cost of the party's chosen method(s) of recording.[33]

Transcript

Any party may, at its own expense, arrange for a transcript to be made of a deposition recorded by nonstenographic means.[34]

Use of Nonstenographic Depositions

In order to use a nonstenographically recorded deposition at trial or in connection with a dispositive motion, a party must submit a transcript of the portions to be introduced for the court's use.[35]

Objections

Objections to the nonstenographic recording of a deposition should be raised prior to the commencement of the deposition via a motion for protective order under Rule 26(c) or at the commencement of the deposition under Rule 30(c).[36]

Additional Methods of Recording

Any party may arrange for a method of recording a deposition in addition to that specified in the notice of deposition.   The party desiring such additional method of recording must send prior notice to all other parties and to the deponent,[37] and will bear the expense of the additional recording unless otherwise ordered by the court. Any party may arrange to transcribe a deposition.

RULE 30(b)(4).   NOTICE OF THE DEPOSITION; BY REMOTE MEANS

CORE CONCEPT

The parties may stipulate to a deposition by telephone or may move the court for an order that a deposition be taken by telephone.[38]

32. *Planned Parenthood of Columbia/Willamette, Inc. v. American Coalition of Life Activists,* 290 F.3d 1058 (9th Cir.2002) ("'nonstenographic" means audio or visual); *Banks v. Office of Senate Sergeant-at-Arms,* 241 F.R.D. 370 (D.D.C. 2007) (videotape of deposition not permitted because the party intended to use the tape for publicity, not for proper purposes).

33. *Morrison v. Reichhold Chemicals, Inc.,* 97 F.3d 460, 464 (11th Cir.1996); *Hudson v. Spellman High Voltage,* 178 F.R.D. 29 (E.D.N.Y.1998). *See also Cherry v. Champion International Corp.,* 186 F.3d 442, 448–49 (4th Cir.1999) (discussing the recovery of alternative means of recording as costs under 28 U.S.C. § 1920).

34. *Hudson v. Spellman High Voltage,* 178 F.R.D. 29 (E.D.N.Y.1998).

35. Rule 26(a)(3)(A)(ii) and Rule 32(c); *But see Hudson v. Spellman High Voltage,* 178 F.R.D. 29 (E.D.N.Y.1998) ("there is no requirement that a party taking a deposition by non-stenographic means provide a written transcript of the entire deposition to other parties.").

36. *Fanelli v. Centenary College,* 211 F.R.D. 268 (D.N.J.2002) (anxiety over videotaping not good cause sufficient to warrant a protective order).

37. *Ogden v. Keystone Residence,* 226 F.Supp.2d 588, 605 (M.D.Pa.2002).

Generally, leave to take depositions by telephone will be granted liberally.[39] Such depositions are deemed to occur in the district where the deponent is located when answering the questions,[40] and the court reporter should be in the presence of the witness, not the attorneys.[41]

APPLICATIONS

2007 Amendments

The 2007 amendments substantially reorganized Rule 30(b). The portion of Rule 30(b)(1) addressing subpoenas for the production documents and things was combined with Rule 30(b)(5) to form new Rule 30(b)(2). The content of Rule 30(b)(2) and Rule 30(b)(3) pertaining to methods of recording a deposition were combined to form new Rule 30(b)(3). Rule 30(b)(7), pertaining to telephonic and remote depositions, was moved to Rule 30(b)(4). Old Rule 30(b)(4) became Rule 30(b)(5). Only Rule 30(b)(6) was immune from this reorganization. Great care should be exercised in researching and citing pre–2008 cases referring to subsections of Rule 30(b).

RULE 30(b)(5). THE DEPOSITION; OFFICER'S DUTIES

CORE CONCEPT

At the beginning of a deposition, the officer shall place on the record administrative details identifying and describing the deposition. During the deposition, the demeanor of the witnesses shall not be distorted in the recording.

APPLICATIONS

2007 Amendments

The 2007 amendments substantially reorganized Rule 30(b). The portion of Rule 30(b)(1) addressing subpoenas for the production documents and things was combined with Rule 30(b)(5) to form new Rule 30(b)(2). The content of Rule 30(b)(2) and Rule 30(b)(3) pertaining to methods of recording a deposition were combined to form new Rule 30(b)(3). Rule 30(b)(7), pertaining to telephonic and remote depositions, was moved to Rule 30(b)(4). Old Rule 30(b)(4) became Rule 30(b)(5). Only Rule 30(b)(6) was immune from this

---

38. *Brown v. Carr*, 236 F.R.D. 311 (S.D.Tex.2006) (upon motion, the party seeking the telephone deposition has the initial burden of establishing a legitimate need for the motion; the burden then shifts to the other party to establish good cause why the deposition should not occur by telephone); *Advani Enterprises, Inc. v. Underwriters at Lloyds*, 2000 WL 1568255 (S.D.N.Y.2000) ("permission should be

granted unless an objecting party will likely be prejudiced or the method employed 'would not reasonably ensure accuracy and trustworthiness' ").

39. *Brown v. Carr*, 236 F.R.D. 311, 312 (S.D.Tex. 2006).

40. *Hudson v. Spellman High Voltage*, 178 F.R.D. 29, 32 (E.D.N.Y.1998).

41. *Aquino v. Automotive Service Industry Assoc.*, 93 F.Supp.2d 922 (N.D.Ill.2000).

reorganization. Great care should be exercised in researching and citing pre–2008 cases referring to subsections of Rule 30(b).

Statement at Deposition Beginning

The officer recording the deposition shall begin the record with a statement that includes:

A) the officer's name and business address;

B) the date, time, and place of deposition;

C) the name of the deponent;

D) the administration of the oath or affirmation to the deponent; and

E) an identification of all persons present.

If the deposition is recorded other than stenographically, then each separate tape or unit of recording must begin with the officer's name and business address, the date, time and place of the deposition, and the deponent's name.

Statement at Deposition End

The officer recording the deposition shall close the record by stating that the deposition is complete and setting forth any administrative stipulations regarding the deposition.

Witness Demeanor

The recording device should accurately and neutrally depict the witness's demeanor and appearance.

RULE 30(b)(6). THE DEPOSITION; NOTICE OR SUBPEONA DIRECTED TO AN ORGANIZATION

CORE CONCEPT

Rule 30(b)(6) allows a party to notice the deposition of a corporation, partnership,[42] association, governmental agency,[43] or other entity[44] and to specify the areas of inquiry. The named organization must then designate one or more representatives to testify as to the areas of inquiry.

APPLICATIONS

Subpoena

If the corporation or organization is not a party, then one must

---

42. *Starlight International Inc. v. Herlihy*, 186 F.R.D. 626, 638 (D.Kan.1999) (Rule 30(b)(6) applies to partnerships and joint ventures).

43. *Watts v. S.E.C.*, 482 F.3d 501, 505 (D.C.Cir. 2007); *McKesson v. Islamic Republic of Iran*, 185 F.R.D. 70 (D.D.C.1999)

(allowing a Rule 30(b)(6) deposition of Iran).

44. Advisory Committee Notes to the 2007 Amendments (the phrase "other entity" is intended to capture any type of organization not specifically listed, such as limited liability companies).

issue a subpoena to compel attendance.[45] If the corporation or organization is a party, a notice of deposition is sufficient.

Content of Notice

The notice (and the subpoena, if necessary) must state that the corporation has the duty to designate a representative, and must specify the areas of inquiry with reasonable particularity.[46]

Selection of Representatives

The representative does not have to be an officer or director of the organization, and in fact does not even need to be employed by the organization. Instead, the company has a duty to make a conscientious, good-faith effort to designate a knowledgeable representative.[47] Regardless of the status of the representative, however, the representative's testimony will be admissible against the organization and the organization must prepare the representative to testify as to the organization's collective knowledge and information.[48] If no single individual can provide the corporation's testimony as to all the designated topics, the corporation must name more than one representative.[49] Sometimes, corporate counsel are selected as the corporate representative.[50]

Particular Officer

To depose a specific officer, director, or managing agent, there is no need to use Rule 30(b)(6); a notice of deposition may be sent indicating that the individual's testimony is sought in the individual's official capacity.[51] The corporation is then subject to sanctions if the named representative fails to appear.[52] The party moving for such sanctions has the burden of proving that the individual was an officer, director, or managing agent.

Officer vs. Employee

One cannot compel the attendance at a deposition of an employee who is not an officer, director, or managing agent of the organiza-

45. See Mattel, Inc. v. Walking Mountain Productions, 353 F.3d 792, 797 (9th Cir.2003); Cates v. LTV Aerospace Corp., 480 F.2d 620 (5th Cir.1973).

46. Omegaflex, Inc. v. Parker Hannifin Corp., 425 F.Supp.2d 171 (D.Mass.2006); Tri–State Hosp. Supply Corp. v. United States, 226 F.R.D. 118, 125 (D.D.C.2005) (the phrase "including but not limited to" rendered the deposition topics overbroad); Steil v. Humana Kansas City, Inc., 197 F.R.D. 442 (D.Kan.2000).

47. Brazos River Authority v. GE Ionics, Inc., 469 F.3d 416, 433 (5th Cir. 2006); Sprint Communications Co., L.P. v. Theglobe.com, 236 F.R.D. 524 (D.Kan.2006).

48. Sprint Communications Co., L.P. v. Theglobe.com, 236 F.R.D. 524 (D.Kan.2006).

49. Tequila Centinela, S.A. de C.V. v. Bacardi & Co. Ltd., 242 F.R.D. 1 (D.D.C.

2007); Ferko v. National Ass'n for Stock Car Auto Racing, Inc., 218 F.R.D. 125, 142 (E.D.Tex.2003).

50. See In re Pioneer Hi–Bred Intern., Inc., 238 F.3d 1370, 1376 (Fed.Cir.2001) (addressing the attorney client privilege issues when counsel is designated as the corporate representative); Cartier, a Div. of Richemont North America, Inc. v. Bertone Group, Inc., 404 F.Supp.2d 573 (S.D.N.Y. 2005).

51. Cummings v. General Motors Corp., 365 F.3d 944, 953 (10th Cir.2004); Folwell v. Hernandez, 210 F.R.D. 169, 172 (M.D.N.C.2002) (Rule 30(b)(6) does not eliminate the prior Rule 30(a)(1) method of examination which permits the opposing party to select an officer, director, or managing agent for deposition).

52. Bon Air Hotel, Inc. v. Time, Inc., 376 F.2d 118 (5th Cir.1967).

tion merely by sending a notice.[53]   Such an employee may be served with a subpoena,[54] and the employee is then subject to sanctions if the employee fails to appear.   The corporation is not bound by the statements of such employees.[55]

Sanctions Against Organization

If the designated officer, director, or managing agent fails to appear for a deposition, the corporation or organization is subject to sanctions.   Likewise, if a corporation provides witnesses who cannot answer questions listed in notice of deposition, then corporation has failed to comply with its obligations under the rule and may be subject to sanctions.[56]

Scope of Testimony

The corporation or organization must select an individual or individuals who can testify to the areas specified in the notice.[57] The individual(s) must testify to all matters known or reasonably available to the corporation,[58] which may necessitate some gathering of documents and interviewing witnesses and having the individual(s) review and become familiar with the documents and information.[59] Thus, the individual will often testify to matters outside the individual's personal knowledge.[60]   The courts are divided as to whether the examination of the representative is limited to the areas of inquiry identified in the notice of deposition.[61] The testimony is not limited to facts, but can include beliefs and opinions held by the entity.[62]

Legal Matters

Many courts are reluctant to allow depositions of opposing counsel, and will closely examine notices under Rule 30(b)(6) that

53. *See Folwell v. Hernandez,* 210 F.R.D. 169, 173 (M.D.N.C.2002) (the definition of a managing agent is made on a case-by-case factual determination).

54. *Philadelphia Indem. Ins. Co. v. Federal Ins. Co.,* 215 F.R.D. 492 (E.D.Pa.2003).

55. *Burns Bros. v. The B & O No. 177,* 21 F.R.D. 142 (E.D.N.Y.1957).

56. *Reilly v. NatWest Markets Group Inc.,* 181 F.3d 253 (2d Cir.1999) (corporation precluded from offering testimony from witnesses not designated in response to Rule 30(b)(6) notice); *King v. Pratt & Whitney,* 161 F.R.D. 475 (S.D.Fla.1995).

57. *Poole v. Textron, Inc.,* 192 F.R.D. 494 (D.Md.2000) (a corporation should make a "diligent inquiry" to determine the individual(s) best suited to testify).

58. *Sprint Communications Co., L.P. v. Theglobe.com,* 236 F.R.D. 524 (D.Kan.2006) (the designee presents the corporation's position on the topic); *Media Services Group, Inc. v. Lesso, Inc.,* 45 F.Supp.2d 1237 (D.Kan.1999).

59. *Poole v. Textron, Inc.,* 192 F.R.D. 494 (D.Md.2000); *Alexander v. Federal Bureau of Investigation,* 186 F.R.D. 148 (D.D.C.1999) (listing 5 obligations of recipient of a Rule 30(b)(6) notice).

60. *PPM Finance, Inc. v. Norandal USA, Inc.,* 392 F.3d 889, 894–95 (7th Cir. 2004).

61. *See U.S. ex rel. Tiesinga v. Dianon Systems, Inc.,* 240 F.R.D. 40, 42 (D.Conn. 2006); *Starlight International Inc. v. Herlihy,* 186 F.R.D. 626, 639 (D.Kan.1999) (for questions outside the areas in the notice, the general deposition principles apply, and no sanctions attach if the witness does not know the answer).

62. *Brazos River Authority v. GE Ionics, Inc.,* 469 F.3d 416, 432 (5th Cir. 2006). *But see U.S. ex rel. Tiesinga v. Dianon Systems, Inc.,* 240 F.R.D. 40 (D.Conn. Nov 15, 2006) (representative cannot be forced to endorse an expert opinion).

are "back door" attempts to depose opposing counsel.[63]

Duty to Prepare

If the representative(s) cannot testify as to the corporation's collective information on the matters requested, then the corporation has a duty to gather the information and prepare the representative(s) so that the representatives can give complete, knowledgeable, and binding testimony.[64] Failure to adequately prepare the representative can result in sanctions.[65]

Effect of Testimony

Testimony by a Rule 30(b)(6) representative has the effect of an evidentiary admission, not a judicial admission, and thus may be controverted or explained by the party.[66] The organization may then be prohibited from using theories or information not disclosed during the Rule 30(b)(6) deposition unless the information was unavailable at the time of the deposition.[67]

RULE 30(c). EXAMINATION AND CROSS–EXAMINATION; RECORD OF THE EXAMINATION; OBJECTIONS; WRITTEN QUESTIONS

CORE CONCEPT

In general, the examination of witnesses at a deposition proceeds much like at trial, except that most objections are reserved until the testimony is offered into evidence. Objections to questions must be stated in a non-suggestive and non-argumentative manner. An attorney may not instruct a witness not to answer a question except to preserve a privilege, to suspend the privilege to seek a protective order, or to enforce a limitation on the scope of the deposition established by the court.

APPLICATIONS

2007 Amendments

The 2007 amendments reorganized Rule 30(c) and Rule 30(d). The provisions of Rule 30(c) were broken into Rules 30(c)(1) and

---

63. *See Sprint Communications Co., L.P. v. Theglobe.com,* 236 F.R.D. 524 (D.Kan.2006) (in order to avoid privilege issues, the party can designate a non-attorney and then prepare that designee to testify as to all non-privileged information); *S.E.C. v. Buntrock,* 217 F.R.D. 441, 445 (N.D.Ill.2003) (3 factor test for obtaining the deposition of opposing counsel).

64. *Brazos River Authority v. GE Ionics, Inc.,* 469 F.3d 416, 433 (5th Cir. 2006); *Sprint Communications Co., L.P. v. Theglobe.com,* 236 F.R.D. 524 (D.Kan.2006).

65. *Wilson v. Lakner,* 228 F.R.D. 524 (D.Md.2005); *Black Horse Lane Assoc., L.P.*

v. Dow Chemical Corp., 228 F.3d 275, 301–05 (3d Cir.2000).

66. *United States v. M & T Mort. Corp.,* 235 F.R.D. 11, 22 (D.D.C.2006) ("the agents' testimony is generally admissible as a statement of the corporation."); *Interstate Narrow Fabrics, Inc. v. Century USA, Inc.,* 218 F.R.D. 455, 462 (M.D.N.C.2003); *Media Services Group, Inc. v. Lesso, Inc.,* 45 F.Supp.2d 1237 (D.Kan.1999).

67. *Rainey v. American Forest and Paper Assoc., Inc.,* 26 F.Supp.2d 82, 94 (D.D.C. 1998).

30(c)(3). The provisions in Rule 30(d)(1) regarding statement of objections and instructions not to answer were moved to Rule 30(c)(2), together with some text from old Rule 30(c). The sanction provisions of Rule 30(d)(3) became Rule 30(d)(2). Finally, the provision of Rule 30(d)(4) became Rule 30(d)(3). Great care should be exercised in researching and citing pre–2008 cases referring to Rule 30(c) or Rule 30(d).

Oath or Affirmation

The officer before whom the deposition is to be taken (usually the stenographer) will put the witness on oath or affirmation at the beginning of the deposition.

Recording

The officer will also arrange to have the testimony recorded, either stenographically or otherwise (as discussed above under Rule 30(b)(3)).

Expense of Recording

The party noticing the deposition arranges for and pays the cost of recording but the other parties pay for their copies of the recording. If the party taking the deposition does not order a transcript, then any other party can order one, and the court then has discretion as to who bears the expense.[68]

Examination

Examination proceeds as at trial, with direct examination and cross-examination.[69] Unlike trial, cross-examination is not limited to matters raised on direct, although the admission at trial of the deposition transcript may be limited on that basis.

Witness's Rights

At a deposition, the witness has the same rights as at trial, and may refresh his recollection with former testimony.[70] The extent to which a witness has the right to confer with counsel during a deposition is unsettled.[71]

Refusal to Answer Question

If a witness refuses to answer a question, the examining party may suspend the proceedings to seek an order under Rule 37(a) compelling an answer or may reserve the right to move for an order to compel and proceed to other areas. The losing party to such a motion to compel may then be subject to sanctions under Rule 37(a)(5).

---

68. The Advisory Committee Note to the 1970 amendment of Rule 30(c).

69. *Sperling v. City of Kennesaw Dept.*, 202 F.R.D. 325, 329 (N.D.Ga.2001) (adverse party entitled to review and use writing used by witness to refresh recollection).

70. *See Magee v. The Paul Revere Life Ins. Co.*, 172 F.R.D. 627, 637 (E.D.N.Y. 1997) (deponent repeatedly consulted his notes to refresh his memory at the deposition).

71. *See, e.g., In re Stratosphere Corp. Securities Litigation,* 182 F.R.D. 614, 620 (D.Nev.1998) (witness not permitted to confer while a question is pending); *Hall v. Clifton Precision,* 150 F.R.D. 525, 526 (E.D.Pa.1993).

Objections to Questions

Objections must be stated in a non-suggestive manner.[72] Some objections to questions must be raised at the time of the deposition or they are waived, others are reserved until trial. The way to determine whether an objection must be made is to determine whether the examiner could rephrase the question to cure the objection. Thus, parties must object to leading questions in order to give the examiner an opportunity to ask the question in a non-leading fashion. Conversely, parties do not need to raise objections such as relevancy or competency that cannot be cured.

Instruction Not to Answer

Directions to a witness not to answer a question are only allowed in three narrow circumstances: to claim a privilege (*i.e.*, attorney client communication);[73] to enforce a court directive limiting the scope or length of the deposition;[74] or to suspend the deposition for purposes of a motion under Rule 30(d)(3) relating to improper harassing conduct.[75] Thus, it is inappropriate for counsel to instruct a witness not to answer a question on the basis of relevance,[76] on the basis that the question has been asked and answered,[77] is harassing,[78] or on the basis that the question is outside the areas of inquiry identified in the notice of deposition for a Rule 30(b)(6) deposition of a party representative.[79]

Objections to Officer or Procedures

All objections to the qualifications of the officer, to the manner of recording, or to any other procedure must be raised at the deposition and noted by the officer or they are waived.

Objections to Exhibits

Exhibits that have been objected to are taken and appended to the transcript subject to a subsequent ruling on the objection.

---

72. See the commentary to Rule 30(d), below.

73. *Moloney v. United States*, 204 F.R.D. 16, 20–21 (D.Mass.2001); *United States v. Philip Morris Inc.*, 209 F.R.D. 13, 19 (D.D.C.2002).

74. *S.E.C. v. Oakford Corp.*, 141 F.Supp.2d 435 (S.D.N.Y.2001).

75. *See Biovail Laboratories, Inc. v. Anchen Pharmaceuticals, Inc.*, 233 F.R.D. 648, 653 (C.D.Cal.2006) (Rule 30(d)(4) is the only authority allowing the interruption of a deposition); *A.W. v. I.B. Corp.*, 224 F.R.D. 20, 22 (D.Me.2004); *Cobell v. Norton*, 213 F.R.D. 16, 27 (D.D.C.2003) (counsel may not instruct the witness not to answer because the question is harassing, but only to suspend the deposition to seek a court order protecting the witness from harassment); *Mathias v. Jacobs*, 167 F.Supp.2d 606, 626 (S.D.N.Y.2001) (Rule 30(d) is the only

mechanism for redressing harassing conduct at a deposition).

76. *Resolution Trust Corp. v. Dabney*, 73 F.3d 262, 266 (10th Cir.1995); *Banks v. Office of Senate Sergeant–At–Arms*, 222 F.R.D. 1, 6 (D.D.C.2004); *Gober v. City of Leesburg*, 197 F.R.D. 519, 520 (M.D.Fla. 2000).

77. *Athridge v. Aetna Casualty and Surety Co.*, 184 F.R.D. 200, 208 (D.D.C. 1998).

78. *Redwood v. Dobson*, 476 F.3d 462, 467–68 (7th Cir. 2007); *Biovail Laboratories, Inc. v. Anchen Pharmaceuticals, Inc.*, 233 F.R.D. 648, 653 (C.D.Cal.2006).

79. *Paparelli v. Prudential Insurance Co. of America*, 108 F.R.D. 727, 730–31 (D.Mass.1985).

Procedure after Objections

After an objection to the officer recording the deposition, the manner of taking the deposition, the evidence, the conduct of a party, or any other aspect of the deposition, the deposition should continue subject to such objections.[80] Exceptions to this principle are matters like questions seeking attorney-client information, as discussed under Rule 30(c)(2).

Attendance by Other Witnesses

Other witnesses are not excluded from observing deposition absent a court order under Rule 26(c)(1)(E).[81]

Written Questions

Instead of attending a deposition in person, a party can send written questions to the party taking the deposition, who will then ask the questions to the deponent on the record.   This procedure is rarely used.

RULE 30(d).   DURATION; SANCTION;   MOTION TO TERMINATE OR LIMIT

CORE CONCEPT

The Rules provide for a 7 hour time limit on depositions, which may be extended by court order.   Rule 30(d) also provides protection from unreasonable or vexatious examination during a deposition.

APPLICATIONS

2007 Amendments

The 2007 amendments reorganized Rule 30(c) and Rule 30(d). The provisions of Rule 30(c) were broken into Rules 30(c)(1) and 30(c)(3). The provisions in Rule 30(d)(1) regarding statement of objections and instructions not to answer were moved to Rule 30(c)(2), together with some text from old Rule 30(c). The sanction provisions of Rule 30(d)(3) became Rule 30(d)(2). Finally, the provision of Rule 30(d)(4) became Rule 30(d)(3). Great care should be exercised in researching and citing pre–2008 cases referring to Rule 30(c) or Rule 30(d).

Stating Objections

Objections must be stated in a non-suggestive manner.[82]   Attorneys should not use an objection to instruct the witnesses how to

---

80. *Morales v. Zondo, Inc.*, 204 F.R.D. 50 (S.D.N.Y.2001).

81. The Advisory Committee Note to the 1993 Amendment to Rule 30; *In re Terra Int'l., Inc.*, 134 F.3d 302, 305–06 (5th Cir.1998)(party moving to exclude other witnesses must show good cause why such witnesses should not attend); *Bell ex rel.*

Estate of Bell v. Board of Educ. of County of Fayette, 225 F.R.D. 186, 195 (S.D.W.Va. 2004).

82. *Banks v. Office of Senate Sergeant-at-Arms*, 241 F.R.D. 370 (D.D.C. 2007); *Jones v. J.C. Penney's Dept. Stores, Inc.*, 228 F.R.D. 190, 197–98 (W.D.N.Y.2005).

answer (or not answer) a question.[83] However, the specific nature of the objection should be stated so that the court later can rule on the objection (*i.e.* "objection, leading" or "objection, lack of foundation").[84]

Duration of Depositions

Rule 30(d)(1) sets a time limit for depositions of 1 day of 7 hours. The time period includes only time spent examining the witness; lunch and other breaks are not counted.[85] The parties can extend or eliminate the time limitation by stipulation,[86] or can file a motion to extend the time limit for specified depositions[87] or for the case in general (discussed below).

Motion to Extend Time

A party may file a motion to extend the 1 day 7 hour limitation.[88] The court must allow additional time if needed for a "fair examination" of the witness or if the examination has been impeded or delayed by another person or by circumstances.[89] Examples of situations in which an extended deposition would be warranted include: witnesses who need interpreters; examinations covering long periods of time or numerous and/or lengthy documents (although the Advisory Committee suggests that a prerequisite might be sending the documents to the witness to review prior to the deposition); instances where documents were requested but not produced prior to the deposition; multi-party cases (if the parties have taken measures to avoid duplicative questioning); depositions in which the lawyer for the witness also wants to ask questions; depositions of expert witnesses; depositions interrupted by power outage, health emergency, or other like event; and depositions in which improper objections or other conduct by other attorneys or the witness has impeded the examination.[90] The court need not order an extended deposition if the extended deposition would be cumulative or unreasonably burdensome, as provided by Rule 26(b)(2). The burden will be on the party moving for an extension to show good cause why the extension is warranted.

83. *Calzaturficio S.C.A.R.P.A. s.p.a. v. Fabiano Shoe Co., Inc.*, 201 F.R.D. 33 (D.Mass.2001); *Quantachrome Corp. v. Micromeritics Instrument Corp.*, 189 F.R.D. 697, 700 (S.D.Fla.1999).

84. *Moloney v. United States*, 204 F.R.D. 16, 20–21 (D.Mass.2001) (certain privileges were waived because the objection did not identify those privileges).

85. The Advisory Committee Note to the 2000 Amendment to Rule 30(d).

86. *Constand v. Cosby*, 232 F.R.D. 494, 504 (E.D.Pa.2006).

87. *LaPlante v. Estano*, 226 F.R.D. 439, 439–40 (D.Conn.2005) (deposition extended because party and attorney were recalci-

trant and uncooperative during the deposition).

88. *See Dunkin' Donuts Incorporated v. Mary's Donuts, Inc.*, 206 F.R.D. 518, 522 (S.D.Fla.2002).

89. Roberson v. Bair, 242 F.R.D. 130 (D.D.C. 2007).

90. The Advisory Committee Note to the 2000 Amendment to Rule 30(d). *See also United States v. Kattar*, 191 F.R.D. 33, 38 (D.N.H.1999) (pre–2000 Amendment case in which additional time was allowed to cure improper objections and instructions not to answer).

Designated Representatives

If a corporation or entity designates more than 1 representative in response to a deposition notice under Rule 30(b)(6), the 1 day 7 hour limitation will apply separately to each representative.[91]

Sanctions for Impediment or Delay

Parties or witnesses should not engage in conduct that unreasonably impedes, delays, or otherwise frustrates a deposition.[92] When such conduct occurs, the court may impose the costs of such conduct, including attorney fees, on the party engaging in the obstructive behavior.[93] Non-party witnesses are also subject to such sanctions.

Motion to Terminate or Limit Deposition

In order to prevail on a motion to terminate or limit an examination, the moving party must demonstrate that the examination was being conducted in bad faith or in an unreasonably annoying, embarrassing, or oppressive manner.[94] The court can then order the deposition concluded or can limit the time and/or scope of the deposition,[95] and may impose upon the persons responsible an appropriate sanction, including the reasonable costs and attorney's fees incurred by any parties as a result.[96]

Which Court for Motion to Terminate

A motion under Rule 30(d)(3) may be filed either in the court where the case is pending or in the district where the deposition is occurring.

Suspension of Deposition

A party desiring to make a Rule 30(d)(3) motion may suspend the deposition for the period of time necessary to make the motion.

Expenses of Motion to Terminate

In ruling on a Rule 30(d)(3) motion, the court must consider awarding expenses to the prevailing party, in accordance with Rule 37(a)(3).[97]

---

91. The Advisory Committee Note to the 2000 Amendment to Rule 30(d)(2).

92. *Royal Maccabees Life Ins. Co. v. Malachinski*, 2001 WL 290308 (N.D.Ill.2001).

93. *See Biovail Laboratories, Inc. v. Anchen Pharmaceuticals, Inc.*, 233 F.R.D. 648, 653 (C.D.Cal.2006) (terminating a deposition without complying with the provisions of Rule 30(d)(4) is cause for sanctions); *Higginbotham v. KCS Intern., Inc.*, 202 F.R.D. 444, 458–59 (D.Md.2001) (advising the witness to leave the deposition before it was completed frustrated the fair examination of the witness, warranting sanctions); *Oleson v. Kmart Corp.*, 175 F.R.D. 570, 573

(D.Kan.1997) (extension of the length of time of the deposition caused by attorney's interference was a factor in court's decision to order sanction).

94. *Garland v. Torre*, 259 F.2d 545 (2d Cir.1958).

95. *S.E.C. v. Oakford Corp.*, 141 F.Supp.2d 435 (S.D.N.Y.2001).

96. *Hague v. Celebrity Cruises, Inc.*, 2001 WL 546519 (S.D.N.Y.2001).

97. *See Biovail Laboratories, Inc. v. Anchen Pharmaceuticals, Inc.*, 233 F.R.D. 648, 654 (C.D.Cal.2006).

Resuming Terminated Deposition

Once a deposition has been terminated by the court upon a Rule 30(d)(3) motion, it cannot be resumed or re-noticed without leave of court.

Parallel to Protective Order

A party may seek the same types of protection for a deposition under Rule 30(d) that are available under a protective order under Rule 26(c).[98] A motion for a protective order under Rule 26(c) provides similar protection before a deposition begins, at which point Rule 30(d) takes over.

RULE 30(e).   REVIEW BY THE WITNESS; CHANGES

CORE CONCEPT

The opportunity to review and correct the transcript is available upon timely request.

APPLICATIONS

Request to Review

To obtain an opportunity to review and correct the transcript, the deponent or a party must make a request prior to the completion of the deposition.

Submission of Changes

If a review is requested, the witness must submit a signed statement describing any changes within 30 days of submission by the officer.[99] The statement should state the reasons for the changes[100] and be signed by the witness. The time for submission of changes may be extended by the court upon motion.[101] Any changes that are submitted are attached to the transcript.

Changes in Form

Changes in form, such as typographic errors, are entered into the transcript with an explanation as to the reason for the change.

Changes in Substance

The courts vary as to whether and when they will allow a witness to make changes in the substance of the testimony,[102] which

---

98. *In re CFS–Related Securities Fraud Litigation*, 256 F.Supp.2d 1227, 1240 (N.D.Okla.2003) (a deposition transcript may be placed under seal under Rule 30(d)).

99. *Margo v. Weiss*, 213 F.3d 55 (2d Cir.2000); *World Impressions, Inc. v. McDonald's Corp.*, 235 F.Supp.2d 831, 840 (N.D.Ill.2002).

100. *DeLoach v. Philip Morris Companies, Inc.*, 206 F.R.D. 568 (M.D.N.C.2002).

101. *Statzer v. Town of Lebanaon, VA*, 2001 WL 604160 (W.D.Va.2001).

102. *See Reilly v. TXU Corp.*, 230 F.R.D. 486 (N.D.Tex.2005) (discussing cases going both ways); *Glenwood Farms, Inc. v. Ivey*, 229 F.R.D. 34 (D.Me.2005) ("A substantial body of case law holds that, so long as the deponent gives reasons for changes or additions to his deposition testimony under the terms of Rule 30(e) and the original testimony remains in the transcript, no action by the court is indicated"); *Banks v. Office of Senate Sergeant–At–Arms*, 222 F.R.D. 7, 9 (D.D.C.2004) (if a motion for

are also entered into the transcript with an explanation as to the reason for the change.[103] With changes in substance, the deposition can be reconvened.[104] A deponent who changes the answers may be impeached with the former answers.[105]

Failure to Submit Changes

A witness who fails to submit any changes or return the signed errata sheet within the time period allowed waives the right to make corrections to the transcript.[106]

RULE 30(f). CERTIFICATION AND DELIVERY; EXHIBITS; COPIES OF THE TRANSCRIPT OR RECORDING; FILING

CORE CONCEPT

The officer must certify that the witness was duly sworn and that the deposition transcript was a true record of the testimony given by the deponent.

APPLICATIONS

2007 Amendments

The 2007 amendments reorganized Rule 30(f). Rule 30(f)(1) was broken into Rule 30(f)(1) and Rule 30(f)(2). Rule 30(f)(2) was renumbered Rule 30(f)(3) and Rule 30(f)(3) was renumbered Rule 30(f)(4). Care should be exercised in researching and citing pre–2008 cases referring to subsections of Rule 30(f).

Certificate

The officer shall prepare a written certificate to accompany the record of the deposition.[107] The certificate should indicate that the

summary judgment has been filed, allowing the witness to modify what she said can so disrupt the movant's legal arguments that a court may hesitate to permit the change); *Burn v. Board of County Com'rs of Jackson County*, 330 F.3d 1275, 1281–82 (10th Cir. 2003) (setting forth a test for when a witness may contradict his or her deposition testimony); *Thorn v. Sundstrand Aerospace Corp.*, 207 F.3d 383, 388–89 (7th Cir.2000) (witness may not directly contradict testimony).

103. *Podell v. Citicorp Diners Club, Inc.*, 112 F.3d 98, 103 (2d Cir.1997); *Wigg v. Sioux Falls School Dist. 49–5*, 274 F.Supp.2d 1084, 1090 (D.S.D.2003), aff'd in part, rev'd in part, 382 F.3d 807 (8th Cir. 2004); *Holland v. Cedar Creek Min., Inc.*, 198 F.R.D. 651, 653 (S.D.W.Va.2001) (without an explanation for the changes, the changes are not allowed).

104. *Tingley Sys., Inc. v. CSC Consulting, Inc.*, 152 F.Supp.2d 95, 120 (D.Mass. 2001).

105. *Thorn v. Sundstrand Aerospace Corp.*, 207 F.3d 383, 388–89 (7th Cir.2000); *Podell v. Citicorp Diners Club, Inc.*, 112 F.3d 98 (2d Cir.1997) (the changes made do not replace the deponent's original answers; the original information remains part of the record and may be introduced at trial).

106. *Green v. Louisiana*, 2001 WL 474280 (E.D.La.2001).

107. *Orr v. Bank of America, NT & SA*, 285 F.3d 764, 774 (9th Cir.2002); *DIRECTV, Inc. v. Morris*, 357 F.Supp.2d 966, 972 (E.D.Tex.2004) (an affidavit of counsel is not sufficient to authenticate a deposition transcript); *Fenje v. Feld*, 301 F.Supp.2d 781, 817 (N.D.Ill.2003).

witness was sworn, that the deposition is a true and accurate record of the testimony, and whether review of the record was requested.

Filing of Transcript

Ordinarily, deposition transcripts should not be filed. However, under Rule 5(d), once a deposition is used in a proceeding, the attorney must file it.

Original Transcript

The stenographer should supply the original transcript to the party noticing the deposition in a sealed envelope, which should be preserved for use at trial.[108]

Copies of the Transcript

Any party or the deponent can obtain a copy of the recording of the deposition for a reasonable charge.[109] If the deposition was recorded stenographically and has not been transcribed, then the party seeking the transcript will normally have to pay the transcription costs, unless the court orders otherwise.

Exhibits

Upon the request of a party, a document produced at a deposition (or any other document) may be marked for identification and annexed to the deposition transcript. A copy of a document may be substituted for the original. If documents are produced at a deposition, any party has a right to inspect and copy them.

Retaining Recording

The officer should retain a copy of the transcript or recording of the deposition.

RULE 30(g). FAILURE TO ATTEND A DEPOSITION OR SERVE SUBPOENA; EXPENSES

CORE CONCEPT

The court may award expenses, including attorney fees, to a party that appears for a deposition that does not occur because either: (1) the party noticing the deposition does not attend;[110] or (2) the party fails to subpoena a witness and that witness does not appear. In both cases, the party noticing the deposition may be ordered to pay the expenses of other parties incurred as a result of appearing for the deposition.

---

108. *Barton v. City and County of Denver*, 432 F.Supp.2d 1178, 1199, n.6 (D.Colo. 2006).

109. *Rivera v. DiSabato*, 962 F.Supp. 38, 39–40 (D.N.J.1997).

110. *Frazier v. Layne Christensen Co.*, 486 F.Supp.2d 831 (W.D.Wis. 2006); *Barrett v. Brian Bemis Auto World*, 230 F.R.D. 535, 537 (N.D.Ill.2005).

ADDITIONAL RESEARCH REFERENCES

Wright & Miller, *Federal Practice and Procedure* §§ 2101–2120.

C.J.S. Federal Civil Procedure §§ 548–583 et seq., 600–644 et seq.

West's Key No. Digests, Federal Civil Procedure ⬦1311–1456.

RULE 31

DEPOSITIONS BY WRITTEN QUESTIONS

(a) When a Deposition May Be Taken.

(1) *Without Leave.* A party may, by written questions, depose any person, including a party, without leave of court except as provided in Rule 31(a)(2). The deponent's attendance may be compelled by subpoena under Rule 45.

(2) *With Leave.* A party must obtain leave of court, and the court must grant leave to the extent consistent with Rule 26(b)(2):

(A) if the parties have not stipulated to the deposition and:

(i) the deposition would result in more than 10 depositions being taken under this rule or Rule 30 by the plaintiffs, or by the defendants, or by the third-party defendants;

(ii) the deponent has already been deposed in the case; or

(iii) the party seeks to take a deposition before the time specified in Rule 26(d); or

(B) if the deponent is confined in prison.

(3) *Service; Required Notice.* A party who wants to depose a person by written questions must serve them on every other party, with a notice stating, if known, the deponent's name and address. If the name is unknown, the notice must provide a general description sufficient to identify the person or the particular class or group to which the person belongs. The notice must also state the name or descriptive title and the address of the officer before whom the deposition will be taken.

(4) *Questions Directed to an Organization.* A public or private corporation, a partnership, an association, or a governmental agency may be deposed by written questions in accordance with Rule 30(b)(6).

(5) *Questions from Other Parties.* Any questions to the deponent from other parties must be served on all parties as follows: cross-questions, within 14 days

after being served with the notice and direct questions; redirect questions, within 7 days after being served with cross-questions; and recross-questions, within 7 days after being served with redirect questions. The court may, for good cause, extend or shorten these times.

(b) Delivery to the Officer; Officer's Duties. The party who noticed the deposition must deliver to the officer a copy of all the questions served and of the notice. The officer must promptly proceed in the manner provided in Rule 30(c), (e), and (f) to:

(1) take the deponent's testimony in response to the questions;

(2) prepare and certify the deposition; and

(3) send it to the party, attaching a copy of the questions and of the notice.

(c) Notice of Completion or Filing.

(1) *Completion.* The party who noticed the deposition must notify all other parties when it is completed.

(2) *Filing.* A party who files the deposition must promptly notify all other parties of the filing.

[Amended March 30, 1970, effective July 1, 1970; March 2, 1987, effective August 1, 1987; April 22, 1993, effective December 1, 1993; April 30, 2007, effective December 1, 2007.]

───────────── **2007 AMENDMENTS ROADMAP** ─────────────

STYLE PROJECT CHANGES: All of the second level subsections of Rule 31 were labeled. The subsections in Rule 31(a)(2) and Rule 31(b) were reorganized and renumbered. The portion of Rule 31(3) addressing written depositions of an organization was broken out into new subsection 31(a)(4) and old subsection 31(a)(4) was relabeled 31(a)(5). For uniformity and readability, the person being deposed is referred to as the "deponent."

NON-STYLE CHANGES: New Rule 31(c)(1) was added to provide that the party who noticed the deposition must notify all other parties when it is completed, and the previous Rule 31(c) was relabeled 31(c)(2).

NOTE: The Federal Rules "Style Project" is explained in Part III-A.

AUTHORS' COMMENTARY ON RULE 31

──────────── PURPOSE AND SCOPE ────────────

Rule 31 contains the procedures for taking depositions through written questions.

RULE 31(a).   WHEN A DEPOSITION MAY BE TAKEN

CORE CONCEPT

Any party may take depositions by serving written questions, which are asked by the deposition officer (stenographer) and answered orally by the witness. Depositions by written question are rarely used, and their only advantage seems to be that they may be less expensive than depositions by oral question.[1]

APPLICATIONS

Notice

A party seeking to take a deposition by written questions must serve a notice on all other parties stating the name and address of the deponent, if known, or a general description sufficient to identify the deponent and providing the name or title and address of the stenographer or officer before whom the deposition will be taken.[2]

Timing of Notice

The notice of written deposition may be served at any time after the parties have conducted the discovery conference under Rule 26(d), or earlier with leave of court. In proceedings listed in Rule 26(a)(1)(B) as exempt from initial disclosures, there is no preliminary waiting period for written depositions. The latest time to conduct a deposition upon written questions will be governed by the court's scheduling order.[3]

Subpoenas

Subpoenas must be used to compel the attendance of non-party witnesses. Party witnesses and representatives of corporations are compelled to attend by virtue of the notice alone.

Service of Direct–Examination

The written deposition questions for direct examination are served upon all parties with the notice.[4]

---

1. *See Brown v. Carr*, 236 F.R.D. 311 (S.D.Tex.2006) ("If plaintiff is unable to afford to take depositions via telephone, then he may take depositions upon written questions.").

2. *Rahn v. Hawkins*, 464 F.3d 813, 821–22 (8th Cir. 2006).

3. *See Summerville v. Local 77*, 369 F.Supp.2d 648, 651 (M.D.N.C.2005) (written deposition questions are treated like other written discovery, and must be served such that the responses are due before the close of written discovery).

4. *Lenders Mortgage Services, Inc.*, 224 B.R. 707, 710 (Bkrtcy.E.D.Mo.1997).

Cross, Redirect, and Recross

Within 14 days of service of the notice and direct examination questions, any other party may serve cross-examination questions. The noticing party may then serve redirect examination questions within 7 days, and the other party may serve re-cross examination questions within 7 more days. The court may shorten or lengthen these time periods upon motion and for cause shown. All questions should be served on all parties.

Number of Depositions

The plaintiffs as a group are limited to 10 depositions total, by written and/or oral examination, as are the defendants and the third-party defendants. This number may be increased by stipulation or by leave of court.

Scope of Questions

The scope of the written deposition questions is the same as oral questions, and is controlled by Rule 26.

Persons Subject

Both parties and non-parties are subject to written depositions.[5]

Corporate Representative

A party may require a corporation or organization to designate a representative to respond to the questions, as described in detail under Rule 30(b)(6).

Repeat Depositions

Leave of court is required to depose someone a second time.[6]

Deponent in Prison

If the deponent is in prison, leave of court is required to take a written deposition.[7]

Objections

Objections to the form of a written question (*i.e.,* because it is leading) must be served in writing upon the party propounding the question within the time for serving succeeding questions and within 5 days of the last questions authorized.[8]

RULE 31(b).   DELIVERY TO THE OFFICER; OFFICER'S DUTIES

CORE CONCEPT

Once all the questions have been served, the party initiating the deposition provides all the questions to the deposition officer. The

---

5. *New Hampshire Motor Transport Ass'n v. Rowe*, 324 F.Supp.2d 231, 237 (D.Me.2004) (written deposition questions, in contrast to interrogatories, can be served on non-parties).

6. *Rahn v. Hawkins*, 464 F.3d 813, 821–22 (8th Cir. 2006).

7. *Whitehurst v. United States*, 231 F.R.D. 500, 501 (S.D.Tex.2005).

8. *See* Rule 32(d)(3)(C); *Whitehurst v. United States*, 231 F.R.D. 500, 501 (S.D.Tex.2005).

officer then promptly takes the deposition by reading the questions and recording the answers.[9] A transcript is then prepared and submitted to the witness as provided in Rule 30 governing oral depositions.

RULE 31(c). NOTICE OF COMPLETION OR FILING

CORE CONCEPT

When the deposition has been completed, the party who noticed the deposition must provide notice to all other parties. Local rules usually determine whether the officer files a sealed transcript with the court. If so, the party noticing the deposition must promptly give notice of the filing of the transcript to all other parties.

ADDITIONAL RESEARCH REFERENCES

Wright & Miller, *Federal Practice and Procedure* §§ 2131–2133.

C.J.S. Federal Civil Procedure §§ 591–592.

West's Key No. Digests, Federal Civil Procedure ☞1369–1370.

9. *See Estate of Ungar v. Palestinian*   2006).
Authority, 451 F.Supp.2d 607, 612 (S.D.N.Y.

RULE 32

USING DEPOSITIONS IN COURT PROCEEDINGS

(a) Using Depositions.

(1) *In General.* At a hearing or trial, all or part of a deposition may be used against a party on these conditions:

    (A) the party was present or represented at the taking of the deposition or had reasonable notice of it;

    (B) it is used to the extent it would be admissible under the Federal Rules of Evidence if the deponent were present and testifying; and

    (C) the use is allowed by Rule 32(a)(2) through (8).

(2) *Impeachment and Other Uses.* Any party may use a deposition to contradict or impeach the testimony given by the deponent as a witness, or for any other purpose allowed by the Federal Rules of Evidence.

(3) *Deposition of Party, Agent, or Designee.* An adverse party may use for any purpose the deposition of a party or anyone who, when deposed, was the party's officer, director, managing agent, or designee under Rule 30(b)(6) or 31(a)(4).

(4) *Unavailable Witness.* A party may use for any purpose the deposition of a witness, whether or not a party, if the court finds:

    (A) that the witness is dead;

    (B) that the witness is more than 100 miles from the place of hearing or trial or is outside the United States, unless it appears that the witness's absence was procured by the party offering the deposition;

    (C) that the witness cannot attend or testify because of age, illness, infirmity, or imprisonment;

    (D) that the party offering the deposition could not procure the witness's attendance by subpoena; or

(E) on motion and notice, that exceptional circumstances make it desirable—in the interest of justice and with due regard to the importance of live testimony in open court—to permit the deposition to be used.

(5) *Limitations on Use.*

(A) *Deposition Taken on Short Notice.* A deposition must not be used against a party who, having received less than 11 days' notice of the deposition, promptly moved for a protective order under Rule 26(c)(1)(B) requesting that it not be taken or be taken at a different time or place— and this motion was still pending when the deposition was taken.

(B) *Unavailable Deponent; Party Could Not Obtain an Attorney.* A deposition taken without leave of court under the unavailability provision of Rule 30(a)(2)(A)(iii) must not be used against a party who shows that, when served with the notice, it could not, despite diligent efforts, obtain an attorney to represent it at the deposition.

(6) *Using Part of a Deposition.* If a party offers in evidence only part of a deposition, an adverse party may require the offeror to introduce other parts that in fairness should be considered with the part introduced, and any party may itself introduce any other parts.

(7) *Substituting a Party.* Substituting a party under Rule 25 does not affect the right to use a deposition previously taken.

(8) *Deposition Taken in an Earlier Action.* A deposition lawfully taken and, if required, filed in any federal- or state-court action may be used in a later action involving the same subject matter between the same parties, or their representatives or successors in interest, to the same extent as if taken in the later action. A deposition previously taken may also be used as allowed by the Federal Rules of Evidence.

(b) Objections to Admissibility. Subject to Rules 28(b) and 32(d)(3), an objection may be made at a hearing or trial to the admission of any deposition testimony that would be inadmissible if the witness were present and testifying.

(c) Form of Presentation. Unless the court orders otherwise, a party must provide a transcript of any deposition testimony the party offers, but may provide the court with the testimony in nontranscript form as well. On any party's request, deposition testimony offered in a jury trial for any purpose other than impeachment must be presented in nontranscript form, if available, unless the court for good cause orders otherwise.

(d) Waiver of Objections.

(1) *To the Notice.* An objection to an error or irregularity in a deposition notice is waived unless promptly served in writing on the party giving the notice.

(2) *To the Officer's Qualification.* An objection based on disqualification of the officer before whom a deposition is to be taken is waived if not made:

(A) before the deposition begins; or

(B) promptly after the basis for disqualification becomes known or, with reasonable diligence, could have been known.

(3) *To the Taking of the Deposition.*

(A) *Objection to Competence, Relevance, or Materiality.* An objection to a deponent's competence—or to the competence, relevance, or materiality of testimony—is not waived by a failure to make the objection before or during the deposition, unless the ground for it might have been corrected at that time.

(B) *Objection to an Error or Irregularity.* An objection to an error or irregularity at an oral examination is waived if:

(i) it relates to the manner of taking the deposition, the form of a question or answer, the oath or affirmation, a party's conduct, or other matters that might have been corrected at that time; and

(ii) it is not timely made during the deposition.

(C) *Objection to a Written Question.* An objection to the form of a written question under Rule 31 is

729

waived if not served in writing on the party submitting the question within the time for serving responsive questions or, if the question is a recross-question, within 5 days after being served with it.

(4) *To Completing and Returning the Deposition.* An objection to how the officer transcribed the testimony—or prepared, signed, certified, sealed, endorsed, sent, or otherwise dealt with the deposition—is waived unless a motion to suppress is made promptly after the error or irregularity becomes known or, with reasonable diligence, could have been known.

[Amended March 30, 1970, effective July 1, 1970; November 20, 1972, effective July 1, 1975; April 29, 1980, effective August 1, 1980; March 2, 1987, effective August 1, 1987; April 22, 1993, effective December 1, 1993; April 30, 2007, effective December 1, 2007.]

──────────── **2007 AMENDMENTS ROADMAP** ────────────

STYLE PROJECT CHANGES: Rule 32(a) previously specified the use of depositions that were "duly filed." New Rule 32(a)(8) deletes that requirement because many depositions are no longer filed. The language in Rule 32(a) describing when depositions may be used was simplified to read "at hearing or trial." Rule 32(a) was substantially reorganized and labeled, going from 4 subparts to 8, and Rule 32(d) was relabeled and further subsectioned. Active voice generally replaced passive voice and cumbersome wording was culled.

NON-STYLE CHANGES: None.

NOTE: The Federal Rules "Style Project" is explained in Part III-A.

AUTHORS' COMMENTARY ON RULE 32
──────────── PURPOSE AND SCOPE ────────────

Rule 32 specifies the circumstances in which a deposition is admissible at trial. Any analysis, however, must always include reference to the applicable rules of evidence.

RULE 32(a). USING DEPOSITIONS

CORE CONCEPT

A deposition may be used at trial or hearing if admissible under the Federal Rules of Evidence and: it is used to impeach a witness or for any other purpose permitted by the Federal Rules of Evidence; the deposition was of an adverse party; or the witness is unavailable as defined by Rule 32(a)(4). If one party offers part of a deposition, other parties may introduce other parts.

APPLICATIONS

2007 Amendments

The 2007 amendments substantially reorganized Rule 32(a), changing it from 4 subsections to 8 subsections, so care should be exercised in researching and citing pre–2008 cases referring to subsections of Rule 32(a).

Impeachment

Rule 32(a)(1) allows the use of a deposition to impeach or contradict a witness. A party may use a deposition to impeach the party's own witness, if permitted by the applicable rules of evidence. The Federal Rules of Evidence allow the use of a prior inconsistent statement made at the deposition as substantive evidence (as opposed to for impeachment purposes only).[1]

Deposition of Adverse Party

Rule 32(a)(3) allows the deposition of an adverse party to be used for any purpose (*i.e.,* as substantive evidence or for impeachment).[2] Rule 32(a)(3) applies to the deposition of an officer, director, or managing agent of a party organization,[3] and to a representative of a party designated pursuant to a Rule 30(b)(6) deposition notice.[4]

Unavailable Non-party Witness

Under Rule 32(a)(4), the deposition of a witness may be used as substantive, non-impeachment evidence only under certain circumstances (but see Rules 801(d) and 801(d)(2) of the Federal Rules of Evidence relating to hearsay). The general requirement is that the witness be unavailable at the time of trial.[5] Rule 32(a)(4) enumerates five situations in which the deposition may be used for non-impeachment purposes:

(A) The witness is dead.[6] However, if the witness dies during the taking of the deposition, so that one party does not have a full opportunity to examine the witness, then the Court has discretion as to whether to admit the testimony;

---

1. Fed.R.Evid. 801(d); *Fiber Systems Intern., Inc. v. Roehrs*, 470 F.3d 1150, 1160 (5th Cir. 2006).

2. *C.R. Bard, Inc. v. M3 Systems Inc.*, 866 F.Supp. 362 (N.D.Ill.1994).

3. *Shanklin v. Norfolk Southern Ry. Co.*, 369 F.3d 978 (6th Cir.2004); *Palmer Coal & Rock Co. v. Gulf Oil Co. U.S.*, 524 F.2d 884 (10th Cir.1975); *Niver v. Travelers Indem. Co. of IL*, 430 F.Supp.2d 852 (N.D.Iowa 2006).

4. The Advisory Note to the 1970 amendment to former Rule 32(a)(2).

5. *Niver v. Travelers Indem. Co. of IL*, 430 F.Supp.2d 852, 866 (N.D.Iowa, 2006) (availability is evaluated at the time of the testimony).

6. *See Dellwood Farms, Inc. v. Cargill*, 128 F.3d 1122, 1128 (7th Cir.1997).

(B) The witness is more than 100 miles from the courthouse (measured "as the crow flies")[7] or outside the United States, unless it appears that the party offering the testimony procured the absence of the witness;[8]

(C) The deponent is unable to attend trial because of age,[9] sickness,[10] infirmity, or imprisonment;

(D) The party offering the deposition was unable to procure the deponent's attendance at trial by subpoena;[11] or

(E) Exceptional other circumstances.[12] In order to take advantage of the catchall in Rule 32(a)(4)(E), a party must give notice to the other party of its intent.[13] Note, however, that the general policy favoring live testimony leads to a restrictive reading of this "catch-all" clause.[14]

Otherwise Admissible Under the FRE

Rule 32(a)(1) authorizes the admission of deposition testimony that does not meet any of the three specific criteria in Rules 32(a)(1), (2), or (3), but is otherwise admissible under the Federal Rules of Evidence.[15]

Must Comply with Rules of Evidence

Once the criteria in Rule 32 for use of a deposition have been satisfied, the deposition must still be admissible under the rules of evidence.[16] The rules of evidence are applied as though the depo-

7. *Chrysler Intern. Corp. v. Chemaly*, 280 F.3d 1358, 1359 (11th Cir.2002); *Ueland v. U.S.*, 291 F.3d 993, 996 (7th Cir. 2002); *Niver v. Travelers Indem. Co. of IL*, 430 F.Supp.2d 852 (N.D.Iowa 2006) (distance should be measured at the time the deposition is offered); *Young & Associates Public Relations, L.L.C. v. Delta Air Lines, Inc.*, 216 F.R.D. 521, 524 (D.Utah 2003) (distance from the courthouse should be evaluated at all times during trial).

8. *Garcia–Martinez v. City and County of Denver*, 392 F.3d 1187, 1191–92 (10th Cir.2004); *Wilson v. Philadelphia Detention Ctr.*, 986 F.Supp. 282, 291 n. 13 (E.D.Pa. 1997).

9. *United States v. Firishchak*, 468 F.3d 1015, 1023 (7th Cir. 2006).

10. *Alphonso v. Pitney Bowes, Inc.*, 356 F.Supp.2d 442, 458–59 (D.N.J.2005); *Cognitronics Imaging Systems, Inc. v. Recognition Research Inc.*, 83 F.Supp.2d 689, 699, n. 14 (E.D.Va.2000).

11. *Griman v. Makousky*, 76 F.3d 151, 154 (7th Cir.1996)(counsel must have used reasonable diligence to secure witness' attendance).

12. *See Battle ex rel. Battle v. Memorial Hosp. at Gulfport*, 228 F.3d 544, 554 (5th Cir.2000) (videotaped deposition of physician allowed); *Hague v. Celebrity Cruises, Inc.*, 2001 WL 546519 (S.D.N.Y.2001) (courts are divided as to whether a physician's busy schedule constitutes exceptional circumstances).

13. *In re Hayes Lemmerz Intern., Inc.*, 340 B.R. 461, 468 (Bankr.D.Del.2006).

14. *Griman v. Makousky*, 76 F.3d 151, 153 (7th Cir.1996); *Young & Associates Public Relations, L.L.C. v. Delta Air Lines, Inc.*, 216 F.R.D. 521, 522–23 (D.Utah 2003).

15. *Fiber Systems Intern., Inc. v. Roehrs*, 470 F.3d 1150, 1160 (5th Cir. 2006) (transcript admissible under FRE 801(d)(1)(A)); *Bouygues Telecom, S.A. v. Tekelec*, 473 F.Supp.2d 692, 694 (E.D.N.C. 2007).

16. *Reeg v. Shaughnessy*, 570 F.2d 309 (10th Cir.1978); *Haseotes and CM Acquisitions, Inc. v. Cumberland Farms*, 216 B.R. 690, 694 (D.Mass.1997) (applying Rule 32 in bankruptcy adversary proceeding).

nent were present and testifying.[17] Thus, the effect of Rule 32 is to negate the hearsay objection.[18] Furthermore, as with any evidence, the admission of deposition testimony is subject to the Court's discretion.[19]

Use of Part of a Deposition

If a party introduces only part of a deposition, any adverse party may require the offering party to introduce additional parts necessary to clarify the offered text.[20] Such adverse parties have the right to have the additional text introduced immediately following the admission of the offered testimony.[21] The admission of the additional parts is still subject to evidentiary objections.[22]

Deposition Taken in Another Matter

A deposition from another matter may be used if the witness is unavailable and if the party against whom the testimony is offered (or the party's predecessor in interest) had an opportunity and similar motive to examine the witness at the deposition.[23]

Documents Attached to Transcript

A document attached to a deposition transcript may be used under the same circumstances as the transcript itself.[24]

Who May Use

Deposition transcripts may be used by any party, regardless of who noticed the deposition.[25]

Use of One's Own Deposition

Parties may notice their own deposition for use at trial if they know they will be "unavailable" under the provisions of Rule 32(a)(4).[26] The court will evaluate whether the party truly was "unavailable."[27]

17. *See   S.E.C.   v.   Franklin*,   348 F.Supp.2d 1159, 1162 (S.D.Cal.2004).

18. *Ueland v. United States*, 291 F.3d 993 (7th Cir.2002); *Vandenbraak v. Alfieri*, 2005 WL 1242158(D.Del.2005).

19. *Coletti v. Cudd Pressure Control*, 165 F.3d 767, 773 (10th Cir.1999) (upholding trial court's refusal to admit deposition testimony as substantive evidence).

20. *Lentomyynti Oy v. Medivac, Inc.*, 997 F.2d 364 (7th Cir.1993); *Hupp v. City of Walnut Creek*, 389 F.Supp.2d 1229, 1231, n.2 (N.D.Cal.2005); *Heary Bros. Lightning Protection Co., Inc. v. Lightning Protection Institute*, 287 F.Supp.2d 1038, 1065, n.10 (D.Ariz.2003) (other parts of the deposition transcript should be admitted "in fairness"); *Blue Cross and Blue Shield of New Jersey, Inc. v. Philip Morris, Inc.*, 199 F.R.D. 487, 489–90 (E.D.N.Y.2001).

21. *Westinghouse Electric Corp. v. Wray Equip. Corp.*, 286 F.2d 491, 494 (1st Cir.

1961); *Trepel v. Roadway Express, Inc.*, 194 F.3d 708, 710 (6th Cir.1999).

22. *See Heary Bros. Lightning Protection Co., Inc. v. Lightning Protection Institute*, 287 F.Supp.2d 1038, 1065, n.10 (D.Ariz.2003).

23. *See* Fed.R.Evid. 804(b)(1), Part X, infra; *Nippon Credit Bank, Ltd. v. Matthews*, 291 F.3d 738 (11th Cir.2002); *Clay v. Buzas*, 208 F.R.D. 636 (D.Utah 2002).

24. *Gore v. Maritime Overseas Corp.*, 256 F.Supp. 104, 119 (E.D.Pa.1966), *aff'd in part, rev'd in part on other grounds*, 378 F.2d 584 (3d Cir.1967).

25. *Savoie v. Lafourche Boat Rentals, Inc.*, 627 F.2d 722 (5th Cir.1980).

26. *Richmond v. Brooks*, 227 F.2d 490 (2d Cir.1955).

27. *Vevelstad v. Flynn*, 230 F.2d 695 (9th Cir.1956).

Against Whom/Reasonable Notice

The deposition may be used against any party who had reasonable notice of the deposition. A deposition cannot be used against a party who demonstrates that it was unable to obtain counsel to represent it at the deposition despite the exercise of diligence. Likewise, the deposition cannot be used against a party who received less than 11 days notice and who has filed a motion for a protective order that was pending at the time of the deposition.[28]

Discovery Depositions

Rule 32 does not draw any distinctions between depositions taken for discovery purposes and those taken "for use at trial."[29]

Substitution of Parties

Substitution of parties pursuant to Rule 25 (such as upon the death of a party) does not affect the use of a deposition transcript unless the substitution significantly alters the nature of the claim.

Motion for Summary Judgment

Deposition transcripts may be used in support of or in opposition to motions for summary judgment.[30] The use of depositions in connection with summary judgment is governed by Rule 56(c).

RULE 32(b).   OBJECTIONS TO ADMISSIBILITY

CORE CONCEPT

Objections to the admissibility of a deposition under Rule 32 must be made at the time the testimony is offered at trial or the objections are waived.

APPLICATIONS

Rules of Evidence

A deposition admissible under Rule 32 must also be admissible under the rules of evidence.[31] Evidentiary rulings are made as though the deponent were present and testifying.

Compare to Objections at Deposition

Objections that can be cured by rephrasing the question, such as leading questions, must be raised at the deposition or they are

28. *United States Securities Exchange Commission v. Talbot*, 430 F.Supp.2d 1029 (C.D.Cal.2006) (amended notice does not trigger the 11 day provision where the original notice put the party on notice of the date of the deposition).

29. *Manley v. Ambase Corp.*, 337 F.3d 237, 247 (2nd Cir.2003); *Niver v. Travelers Indem. Co. of IL*, 430 F.Supp.2d 852 (N.D.Iowa 2006).

30. *Carmen v. San Francisco Unified School Dist.*, 237 F.3d 1026, 1028 (9th Cir.

2001); *Beiswenger Enterprises, Corp. v. Carletta*, 46 F.Supp.2d 1297 (M.D.Fla.1999) (allowing the use of a deposition from another action to support a motion for summary judgment); *In re KZK Livestock, Inc.*, 221 B.R. 471, 475 (Bkrtcy.C.D.Ill.1998) (allowing the use of a deposition transcript that did not meet the requirements for use at trial, but did meet the requirements for an affidavit).

31. *Marshall v. Planz*, 145 F.Supp.2d 1258 (M.D.Ala.2001).

waived. These objections are covered by Rule 32(d)(3). All other objections, such as relevance,[32] capacity, etc., are reserved until the testimony is offered at trial.[33]

Non-jury Trial

In a non-jury trial, the court can admit a deposition transcript subject to future rulings on objections.

RULE 32(c). FORM OF PRESENTATION

CORE CONCEPT

Deposition testimony may be offered in stenographic or nonstenographic form. In jury trials, any party may require that the nonstenographic form be used if available.

APPLICATIONS

Nonstenographic Forms

A party expecting to use a nonstenographic form of deposition at trial must provide other parties with a transcript in advance of trial under Rule 26(a)(3)(A)(ii). When nonstenographic forms of testimony are offered, the offering party shall also provide the court a transcript.[34] Rule 32 does not authorize the submission of deposition summaries in lieu of the transcript.[35]

Jury Trials

In a jury trial, any party may require that depositions be offered in nonstenographic form if available unless the deposition is being used for impeachment or unless the court orders otherwise for good cause shown.

RULE 32(d). WAIVER OF OBJECTIONS

CORE CONCEPT

Objections to the procedures at a deposition must be asserted as soon as practicable or they are waived.

APPLICATIONS

Defects in Notice

Objections to the notice must be made in writing to the party issuing the notice,[36] unless there was no opportunity to object.[37]

---

32. *In re Stratosphere Corp. Securities Litigation*, 182 F.R.D. 614, 618 (D.Nev. 1998).

33. *Cronkrite v. Fahrbach*, 853 F.Supp. 257 (W.D.Mich.1994).

34. *Tilton v. Capital Cities*, 115 F.3d 1471, 1479 (10th Cir.1997) (a party intending to use a videotape deposition must provide a transcript).

35. *Planned Parenthood of Columbia/Willamette, Inc. v. American Coalition of Life Activists*, 290 F.3d 1058, 1117 (9th Cir.2002).

36. *State Farm Mut. Auto. Ins. Co. v. Dowdy ex rel. Dowdy*, 445 F.Supp.2d 1289, 1293 (N.D.Okla. 2006).

37. *Oates v. S.J. Groves & Sons Co.*, 248 F.2d 388 (6th Cir.1957).

Disqualification of Officer

Objections to the qualifications of the officer (*e.g.,* stenographer), which are set forth in Rule 28, must be made before the start of the deposition or they are waived.

Objections to Testimony

Objections that can be cured by rephrasing the question, such as leading questions, must be raised at the deposition.[38] These objections are covered by Rule 32(d)(3). All other objections, such as relevance,[39] capacity, etc., are reserved until the testimony is offered at trial.[40]

Objections as to Oath

Objections as to the manner of the oath or affirmation administered must be made at the time of the deposition or they are waived.[41]

Objections to Written Deposition Questions

Objections to the form of a written question (*e.g.,* because it is leading) must be served in writing upon the party propounding the question within the time for serving succeeding questions and within 5 days of the last questions authorized.

Objections as to Manner of Transcription

Objections as to the manner of transcription or as to the procedures used in correcting and signing the transcript must be made in the form of a motion to suppress, which must be made with "reasonable promptness" after the defect is discovered or should have been discovered with due diligence.[42]

ADDITIONAL RESEARCH REFERENCES

Wright & Miller, *Federal Practice and Procedure* §§ 2142–2157.

C.J.S. Federal Civil Procedure §§ 544–568, 633–638 et seq.

West's Key No. Digests, Federal Civil Procedure ☞1297, 1298, 1334, 1432–1440.

38. *Whitehurst v. United States,* 231 F.R.D. 500, 501 (S.D.Tex.2005) (a party who has not objected to a leading question at the deposition may not subsequently object to it when the deposition is introduced at trial); *Daubach v. Wnek,* 2001 WL 290181 (N.D.Ill.2001); *Boyd v. University of Maryland Med. System,* 173 F.R.D. 143, 147 n. 8 (D.Md.1997) (containing a list of the ten most common objections to the form of the question).

39. *Quantachrome Corp. v. Micromeritics Instrument Corp.,* 189 F.R.D. 697, 700

(S.D.Fla.1999); *In re Stratosphere Corp. Securities Litigation,* 182 F.R.D. 614, 618 (D.Nev.1998).

40. *State Farm Mut. Auto. Ins. Co. v. Dowdy ex rel. Dowdy,* 445 F.Supp.2d 1289, 1293 (N.D.Okla. 2006) (such objections should not be made at the deposition).

41. *Cabello v. Fernandez–Larios,* 402 F.3d 1148, 1160 (11th Cir.2005).

42. *Trade Development Bank v. Continental Ins. Co.,* 469 F.2d 35 (2d Cir.1972).

RULE 33

INTERROGATORIES TO PARTIES

(a) In General.

(1) *Number.* Unless otherwise stipulated or ordered by the court, a party may serve on any other party no more than 25 written interrogatories, including all discrete subparts. Leave to serve additional interrogatories may be granted to the extent consistent with Rule 26(b)(2).

(2) *Scope.* An interrogatory may relate to any matter that may be inquired into under Rule 26(b). An interrogatory is not objectionable merely because it asks for an opinion or contention that relates to fact or the application of law to fact, but the court may order that the interrogatory need not be answered until designated discovery is complete, or until a pretrial conference or some other time.

(b) Answers and Objections.

(1) *Responding Party.* The interrogatories must be answered:

(A) by the party to whom they are directed; or

(B) if that party is a public or private corporation, a partnership, an association, or a governmental agency, by any officer or agent, who must furnish the information available to the party.

(2) *Time to Respond.* The responding party must serve its answers and any objections within 30 days after being served with the interrogatories. A shorter or longer time may be stipulated to under Rule 29 or be ordered by the court.

(3) *Answering Each Interrogatory.* Each interrogatory must, to the extent it is not objected to, be answered separately and fully in writing under oath.

(4) *Objections.* The grounds for objecting to an interrogatory must be stated with specificity. Any ground not stated in a timely objection is waived unless the court, for good cause, excuses the failure.

(5) *Signature.* The person who makes the answers must sign them, and the attorney who objects must sign any objections.

(c) Use. An answer to an interrogatory may be used to the extent allowed by the Federal Rules of Evidence.

(d) Option to Produce Business Records. If the answer to an interrogatory may be determined by examining, auditing, compiling, abstracting, or summarizing a party's business records (including electronically stored information), and if the burden of deriving or ascertaining the answer will be substantially the same for either party, the responding party may answer by:

(1) specifying the records that must be reviewed, in sufficient detail to enable the interrogating party to locate and identify them as readily as the responding party could; and

(2) giving the interrogating party a reasonable opportunity to examine and audit the records and to make copies, compilations, abstracts, or summaries.

[Amended December 27, 1946, effective March 19, 1948; March 30, 1970, effective July 1, 1970; April 29, 1980, effective August 1, 1980; April 22, 1993, effective December 1, 1993; April 12, 2006, effective December 1, 2006; April 30, 2007, effective December 1, 2007.]

─────────── **2007 AMENDMENTS ROADMAP** ───────────

STYLE PROJECT CHANGES: The final sentence of Rule 33(a) was deleted as an unnecessary cross-reference to the discovery moratorium provisions of Rule 26(d). Former Rule 33(b)(5) was deleted as a redundant reference to the Rule 37(a) procedure for instances where a party fails to respond to an interrogatory. Former Rule 33(c) stated that an interrogatory was not "necessarily" objectionable because it involves an opinion or contention. The word "necessarily" was deleted to eliminate any implication that interrogatories might be objectionable on those grounds. The "scope" provisions of Rule 33(c) were moved to Rule 33(a)(2), and the provisions regarding responses by organizations were moved from Rule 33(a) to Rule 33(b)(1)(B). Rule 33(b) was reorganized, and Rule 33(a) and Rule 33(d) were further subsectioned. The language was generally simplified and clarified, and "must" replaced "shall."

NON-STYLE CHANGES: None.

NOTE: The Federal Rules "Style Project" is explained in Part III-A.

AUTHORS' COMMENTARY ON RULE 33

———————————— PURPOSE AND SCOPE ————————————

Rule 33 sets forth the procedures for using interrogatories. It must be read in conjunction with Rule 26, which establishes the scope of all the discovery rules.

NOTE: Rule 33 was substantially revised in 1970, 1993, 2006, and 2007, and great care should be exercised when citing decisions pertaining to Rule 33.

2006 AMENDMENTS: The 2006 Amendments to Rule 33(d) added the phrase "electronically stored information" to clarify that, when the burden is substantially the same for either party, the responding party may provide access to electronic data instead of answering the interrogatory.

RULE 33(a).   IN GENERAL

CORE CONCEPT

Any party may serve up to 25 interrogatories or questions on any other party. The scope of interrogatories is the broad discovery available under Rule 26.

APPLICATIONS

2007 Amendments

The 2007 amendments reorganized Rule 33(a), Rule 33(b), and Rule 33(c). The "scope" provisions of Rule 33(c) were moved to Rule 33(a)(2), and the provisions regarding responses by organizations were moved from Rule 33(a) to Rule 33(b)(1)(B). The subsections of Rule 33(b) were also reorganized and renumbered. Care should be exercised in researching and citing pre–2008 cases referring to Rule 30(a), Rule 33(b), or Rule 30(c).

Who May Serve

Any party may serve interrogatories.

Who May Be Served

Interrogatories are limited to parties to the action,[1] although the party need not be an adverse party. The interrogatories must be addressed to the party. Thus, if the party is a corporation, interrogatories should be addressed to the corporation, not to a corporate officer or the attorney.[2] In a class action, the courts are

---

1. *United States v. Lot 41, Berryhill Farm Estates*, 128 F.3d 1386, 1397 (10th Cir.1997); *New Hampshire Motor Transport Ass'n v. Rowe*, 324 F.Supp.2d 231, 237 (D.Me.2004) (but one may take the deposition by written examination of a non-par-ty); *Alcon Laboratories, Inc. v. Pharmacia Corp.*, 225 F.Supp.2d 340, 344 (S.D.N.Y. 2002).

2. *Holland v. Minneapolis–Honeywell Regulator Co.*, 28 F.R.D. 595 (D.D.C.1961).

split as to whether only the named representatives can be served.[3]

Time for Service

Interrogatories can be served after the parties have conducted the discovery conference under Rule 26(f),[4] or earlier with leave of court. In proceedings listed in Rule 26(a)(1)(B) as exempt from initial disclosures, there is no preliminary waiting period for interrogatories. The Rules do not set an outer limit on how late in the case interrogatories may be served, but many local rules or case management orders will set such a limit. Usually, when such a limit exists, interrogatories must be served so that the answers are due before the close of discovery.[5]

Number

Each party may serve up to 25 interrogatories,[6] including subparts,[7] on each other party.[8] Additional interrogatories may be served pursuant to a court order or stipulation.[9]

Scope of Questions

The scope of interrogatories, and all other discovery forms, is controlled by Rule 26(b).[10] The information sought must be relevant to the issues in the case, but need not be admissible evidence. Privileged information is not discoverable, and discovery is limited with respect to expert witnesses and trial preparation materials.

Form

Parties have a great deal of latitude in framing interrogatories, as long as the responding party can reasonably determine the information to include in the answer. Only rarely will a question be so ambiguous that it does not require an answer, although the responding party can limit the scope of its answer.

---

3. *Brennan v. Midwestern United Life Ins. Co.,* 450 F.2d 999 (7th Cir.1971) (unnamed members of class required to respond); *Wainwright v. Kraftco Corp.,* 54 F.R.D. 532 (N.D.Ga.1972)(unnamed members of class not required to respond).

4. *Krause v. Buffalo and Erie County Workforce Development Consortium, Inc.,* 425 F.Supp.2d 352 (W.D.N.Y.2006).

5. *Thomas v. Pacificorp,* 324 F.3d 1176, (10th Cir.2003).

6. *Allahverdi v. Regents of University of New Mexico,* 228 F.R.D. 696 (D.N.M.2005) (answering some of the interrogatories is a waiver to the objection to the number of interrogatories); *Walker v. Lakewood Condominium Owners Assoc.,* 186 F.R.D. 584, 586–89 (C.D.Cal.1999) (interrogatories count toward the limit of 25 even though the respondent objects instead of answering, and such interrogatories may not be withdrawn to allow for additional interrogatories).

7. *United States v. Diabetes Treatment Centers of America, Inc.,* 235 F.R.D. 521 (D.D.C.2006) (discussing the counting of subparts); *Swackhammer v. Sprint Corp. PCS,* 225 F.R.D. 658, 665 (D.Kan.2004) (subparts that relate to a single common theme do not count as separate interrogatories).

8. The Advisory Committee Note to the 1993 Amendment to Rule 33; *Chudasama v. Mazda Motor Corp.,* 123 F.3d 1353, 1357 (11th Cir.1997); *Nagele v. Electronic Data Systems Corp.,* 193 F.R.D. 94 (W.D.N.Y. 2000) (allowing more than 25 interrogatories where the recipient failed to object).

9. *Duncan v. Paragon Pub., Inc.,* 204 F.R.D. 127, 128 (S.D.Ind.2001); *Berry v. Rite Aid Corp.,* 2001 WL 527815 (E.D.Pa. 2001).

10. *Pulsecard, Inc. v. Discover Card Services, Inc.,* 168 F.R.D. 295, 310 (D.Kan. 1996).

Proceedings Where Interrogatories Available

Rule 33 applies to all civil actions in district court, including post-judgment proceedings (*i.e.,* interrogatories in aid-of-execution). Rule 33 does not apply to habeas proceedings.[11]

RULE 33(b). ANSWERS AND OBJECTIONS

CORE CONCEPT

The responding party must answer interrogatories separately and in writing within 30 days after service. Objections must be stated with specificity, and objections are waived if not made timely. The responding party must sign the answers and the attorney must sign any objections.

APPLICATIONS

2007 Amendments

The 2007 amendments reorganized Rule 33(a), Rule 33(b), and Rule 33(c). The "scope" provisions of Rule 33(c) were moved to Rule 33(a)(2), and the provisions regarding responses by organizations were moved from Rule 33(a) to Rule 33(b)(1)(B). The subsections of Rule 33(b) were also reorganized and renumbered. Care should be exercised in researching and citing pre–2008 cases referring to Rule 30(a), Rule 33(b), or Rule 30(c).

Answers

Each interrogatory must be answered separately and fully[12] in writing,[13] unless an objection is interposed in lieu of an answer. The answer must include all information within the party's control or known by the party's agents.[14] This includes *facts* in an attorney's possession and information supplied to the party by others.[15] If no such information is available, the answer may so state.[16] If only some information is available, that information must be provided, and may be prefaced with a statement placing the answer in context.

---

11. *Harris v. Nelson,* 394 U.S. 286, 293–94, 89 S.Ct. 1082, 1087, 22 L.Ed.2d 281 (1969); Sloan v. Pugh, 351 F.3d 1319, 1322 (10th Cir.2003).

12. *See United States v. Diabetes Treatment Centers of America, Inc.,* 235 F.R.D. 521 (D.D.C.2006) (the one-sentence vague restatement of the allegation was inadequate); *Union Pacific R. Co., a Delaware Corp. v. Larkin,* 229 F.R.D. 240 (D.N.M. 2005) (references to deposition testimony are insufficient responses).

13. *Wsol v. Fiduciary Management Associates, Inc.,* 2000 WL 748143 (N.D.Ill. 2000) (oral answers are not permitted).

14. *American Intern. Specialty Lines Ins. Co. v. NWI–I, Inc.,* 240 F.R.D. 401, 413 (N.D.Ill. 2007) (information held by former officers is not in the party's custody or control, and need not be gathered and produced); *Hansel v. Shell Oil Corp.,* 169 F.R.D. 303, 305 (E.D.Pa.1996) ("Parties must provide true, explicit, responsive, complete, and candid answers to interrogatories.").

15. *Hickman v. Taylor,* 329 U.S. 495, 504, 67 S.Ct. 385, 390, 91 L.Ed. 451 (1947).

16. *Hansel v. Shell Oil Corp.,* 169 F.R.D. 303, 305 (E.D.Pa.1996) (answer should set forth the efforts used to attempt to obtain the requested information).

Time to Answer

Answers and objections are due within 30 days of service.[17] Failure to serve a response in a timely manner (i.e. within 30 days of service) may constitute a waiver of all objections.[18] The time to answer may be extended by written agreement under Rule 29.[19]

Who Answers

The party must answer the interrogatories, not the party's attorney (although it is common practice for the attorney to draft the answers). The attorney interposes the objections. If the party is a corporation or organization, an officer or agent will answer for the corporation.[20] In this case, the attorney may answer the interrogatories as agent for the corporation.[21] The answering officer or agent need not have first-hand knowledge of the information being provided.[22] However, the responding agent's answers must provide the composite knowledge available to the party.[23] If the party is an infant, the infant's attorney or next friend may answer.[24]

Verification

When the party is an individual, the party, not the attorney,[25] must sign a verification or affidavit as to the accuracy of the answers.[26] This is one of the few exceptions to the general principle under the Federal Rules of Civil Procedure that the attorney may sign all pleadings and papers. A representative, including counsel,[27] of a corporate party may verify interrogatory answers without personal knowledge of every response by furnishing the information available to the corporation.[28]

17. *See Verkuilen v. South Shore Building & Mortgage Co.*, 122 F.3d 410, 411 (7th Cir.1997).

18. *Banks v. Office of Senate Sergeant-At-Arms*, 222 F.R.D. 7, 21 (D.D.C.2004); *Jayne H. Lee, Inc. v. Flagstaff Indus. Corp.*, 173 F.R.D. 651, 653 (D.Md.1997).

19. *Jayne H. Lee, Inc. v. Flagstaff Indus. Corp.*, 173 F.R.D. 651, 654 (D.Md. 1997).

20. *General Dynamics Corp. v. Selb Mfg. Co.*, 481 F.2d 1204 (8th Cir.1973).

21. *Wilson v. Volkswagen of America, Inc.*, 561 F.2d 494, 508 (4th Cir.1977).

22. *See Duff v. Lobdell–Emery Mfg. Co.*, 926 F.Supp. 799, 802 (N.D.Ind.1996).

23. *Law v. NCAA*, 167 F.R.D. 464, 476 (D.Kan.1996), *vacated on other grounds, Univ. of Texas at Austin v. Vratil*, 96 F.3d 1337 (10th Cir.1996).

24. *Hall v. Hague*, 34 F.R.D. 449 (D.Md. 1964).

25. *Saria v. Massachusetts Mut. Life Ins. Co.*, 228 F.R.D. 536, 538–39 (S.D.W.Va. 2005) (verification by the attorney renders the attorney a witness); *Overton v. City of Harvey*, 29 F.Supp.2d 894, 901 (N.D.Ill. 1998).

26. *Morin v. Nationwide Federal Credit Union*, 229 F.R.D. 364, 369 (D.Conn.2005) (interrogatory answers must be signed by the person making the answers); *Davidson v. Goord*, 215 F.R.D. 73, 77 (W.D.N.Y.2003); *Buffalo Carpenters Pension Fund v. CKG Ceiling and Partition Co., Inc.*, 192 F.R.D. 95 (W.D.N.Y.2000) (defendant must redraft and reserve interrogatory answers because the first response was not under oath).

27. *Rea v. Wichita Mortg. Corp.*, 747 F.2d 567 (10th Cir.1984); *Wilson v. Volkswagen of America, Inc.*, 561 F.2d 494, 508 (4th Cir.1977); *Gluck v. Ansett Australia Ltd.*, 204 F.R.D. 217, 221 (D.D.C.2001).

28. *Shepherd v. American Broadcasting Companies, Inc.*, 62 F.3d 1469, 1482 (D.C.Cir.1995).

Objections

If the responding party determines that a particular interrogatory is outside the scope of discovery, the party may object to the question in lieu of answering it. The objection must be made in writing, must state the grounds of the objection with specificity,[29] and must be signed by the attorney for the responding party.[30] Some common objections are:

- *Overly broad, unduly vague, and ambiguous:* When a question is written broadly so that it extends to information not relevant to the complaint (such as a question not limited in time to the events relevant to the complaint), the question may be overly broad.[31] When a question is susceptible to numerous meanings, it may be unduly vague and ambiguous. In general, these objections are probably not justification for refusing to answer a question altogether, but the responding party can raise the objection, then expressly limit the scope of the response.

- *Burdensome and oppressive:* In general, the responding party must produce the information available without undue effort or expense. Thus, questions that require extensive research, compilation of data, or evaluation of data may be objectionable.[32] The responding party is not required to prepare the adverse party's case. Likewise, an interrogatory that seeks a high level of detail may be overly burdensome.[33] The reasonableness of an interrogatory is within the court's discretion.

- *Privileged information:* Questions that seek information protected by the attorney-client privilege or by another privilege are objectionable. When privileged information is withheld, the responding party must explicitly state the objection and describe the nature of the information not provided sufficiently to enable other parties to assess the applicability of the privilege. Care should be exercised in responding to such interrogatories, because the privilege may be waived by revealing part or all of the privileged communication.

- *Attorney work product:* Rule 26(b)(3) provides that trial preparation materials may be discovered only upon a showing that

29. *Essex Ins. Co. v. Neely*, 236 F.R.D. 287 (N.D.W.Va.2006) (mere recitation of familiar litany that interrogatory is overly broad, burdensome, oppressive, and irrelevant does not suffice as specific objection); *Martinez v. Cornell Corrections of Texas*, 377 F.Supp.2d 1138 (D.N.M.2005); *PLX, Inc. v. Prosystems, Inc.*, 220 F.R.D. 291, 293 (N.D.W.Va.2004) (same); *Pulsecard, Inc. v. Discover Card Services, Inc.*, 168 F.R.D. 295, 303 (D.Kan.1996) ("Use of general, reserved objections is disfavored.").

30. *Sonnino v. University Kansas Hosp. Authority*, 220 F.R.D. 633, 655 (D.Kan.

2004); *Momah v. Albert Einstein Medical Center*, 164 F.R.D. 412, 417 (E.D.Pa.1996).

31. *Jewish Hospital Ass'n of Louisville v. Struck Const. Co.*, 77 F.R.D. 59 (W.D.Ky. 1978).

32. *IBP, Inc. v. Mercantile Bank of Topeka*, 179 F.R.D. 316, 321 (D.Kan.1998) (interrogatory asking for every fact and application of law to fact supporting claim held burdensome).

33. *See Cardenas v. Dorel Juvenile Group, Inc.*, 231 F.R.D. 616, 618 (D.Kan. 2005).

the party is unable to obtain the equivalent information through other means without undue hardship.[34]

- *Non-discoverable expert information:* Rule 26(b)(4) limits the scope of discovery directed towards experts. It generally requires the responding party to provide an expert report for each expert it may call as a witness, and thereafter allows other parties to depose such experts. Further discovery with respect to such witnesses is available only upon motion. Rule 26(b)(4)(B) does not allow any discovery with respect to experts not intended to be called as witnesses, absent "exceptional circumstances." [35]

- *Not calculated to lead to the discovery of admissible evidence:* Rule 26 takes a very broad approach with respect to what information is discoverable. The requested information need not be admissible, only relevant.[36]

Failure to Object Is Waiver

All grounds for objection must be specifically stated in a timely response[37] or they are waived,[38] unless excused by the court for good cause shown.[39]

Objection to Part of Interrogatory

If only part of an interrogatory is objectionable, the responding party must answer the interrogatory to the extent that it is not objectionable.[40] Thus, if an interrogatory is overly broad, it must be answered to the extent it is not overly broad.[41]

Motion for a Protective Order

As an alternative to making objections to individual questions, the responding party may make a motion for a protective order under Rule 26(c). A motion for a protective order is appropriate when most or all of a set of interrogatories is too burdensome or cumulative. The burden is on the moving party to show hardship or

---

34. *See* Rule 26(b)(3)(in-depth discussion of discovery of work product).

35. *See* Rule 26(b)(4)(in-depth discussion of discovery directed toward experts).

36. *See* Rule 26(b)(1)(in-depth discussion of the scope of discovery).

37. *Essex Ins. Co. v. Neely*, 236 F.R.D. 287 (N.D.W.Va.2006) (late filed objections deemed waived); *Swackhammer v. Sprint Corp. PCS*, 225 F.R.D. 658, 665 (D.Kan. 2004); *Starlight International, Inc. v. Herlihy*, 181 F.R.D. 494, 496 (D.Kan.1998) (objections in response served 4 days late deemed waived).

38. *India Brewing, Inc. v. Miller Brewing Co.*, 237 F.R.D. 190, 194 (E.D.Wis. 2006) (each specific objection must be asserted or it is waived); *Essex Ins. Co. v. Neely*, 236 F.R.D. 287 (N.D.W.Va.2006)

(late filed objections deemed waived); *Nagele v. Electronic Data Systems Corp.*, 193 F.R.D. 94 (W.D.N.Y.2000) (failure to object to interrogatories in excess of 25 results in waiver).

39. *Banks v. Office of Senate Sergeant–At–Arms*, 222 F.R.D. 7, 21 (D.D.C.2004); *Puricelli v. Borough of Morrisville*, 136 F.R.D. 393, 396 (E.D.Pa.1991)(failure to raise an objection with sufficient specificity within the time period prescribed by Rule 33, without an extension, may be deemed waiver).

40. *Tequila Centinela, S.A. de C.V. v. Bacardi & Co. Ltd.*, 242 F.R.D. 1 (D.D.C. 2007); *Martinez v. Cornell Corrections of Texas*, 377 F.Supp.2d 1138 (D.N.M.2005).

41. *See Walls v. International Paper Co.*, 192 F.R.D. 294 (D.Kan.2000).

injustice.[42] The motion must be accompanied by a certification that the parties met prior to the filing of the motion and attempted to resolve their dispute without intervention by the court.

Motion to Compel

If the responding party fails to answer or objects to a question, the propounding party may file a motion to compel under Rule 37(a).[43] The court will award the prevailing party its reasonable expenses, including attorney fees, incurred in connection with the motion to compel, unless the conduct of the losing party was justified (*i.e.*, not frivolous). The motion must be accompanied by a certification that good faith attempts were made to resolve discovery disputes before relief was sought from the court.

Burden of Persuasion

In a motion to compel, the burden is on the responding party (the non-moving party) to convince the court that an interrogatory is objectionable.[44]

Discretion of Court

The district court has extremely broad discretion in ruling on objections to interrogatories.[45] The court will balance the need and the burden, but will generally require an answer unless the administration of justice would be impeded.

Appeals

The court's rulings on objections to interrogatories are reviewed on an abuse of discretion standard.[46] Usually, such rulings are not final orders, and cannot be appealed until the conclusion of the case.

Sanctions for Failure to Answer

If a party files no response to an interrogatory, the court may impose certain sanctions specified in Rule 37(b)(2), such as deeming certain facts established or refusing to allow the party to oppose or support certain claims.[47] Furthermore, the court must award reasonable expenses, including attorney fees, caused by the responding party's failure to answer, unless the court finds that the failure to answer was justified.

Sanctions for Incomplete Answers or Improper Objections

If the responding party makes an incomplete answer or makes an improper objection, the propounding party can make a motion to compel under Rule 37(a). The court will award the prevailing party its reasonable expenses, including attorney fees, incurred in connection with the motion to compel, unless the conduct of the losing

---

42. *Roesberg v. Johns–Manville Corp.*, 85 F.R.D. 292 (E.D.Pa.1980).

43. *PCS Phosphate Co., Inc. v. Norfolk Southern Corp.*, 238 F.R.D. 555, 559 (E.D.N.C. 2006).

44. *See Donahay v. Palm Beach Tours & Transp., Inc.*, 242 F.R.D. 685 (S.D.Fla. 2007).

45. *Mack v. Great Atlantic and Pacific Tea Co.*, 871 F.2d 179, 186 (1st Cir.1989).

46. *Mack v. Great Atlantic and Pacific Tea Co.*, 871 F.2d 179, 186 (1st Cir.1989).

47. *See* Rule 37(d).

party was justified. If the motion is granted in part and denied in part, then the court will award expenses as it sees fit.

Sanctions for Failure to Obey Order to Answer

If, in response to a motion to compel, the court orders an answer or a more complete answer, and if the responding party fails to comply, then the court can impose the sanctions specified in Rule 37(b)(2), such as deeming certain facts established or refusing to allow the party to oppose or support certain claims. Furthermore, the court must award reasonable expenses, including attorney fees, caused by the responding party's failure to answer, unless the court finds that the failure to answer was justified.

Sanctions for Untrue Answers

If an answer is untrue, either at the time it was made or subsequently, and is not supplemented, the court may exclude certain testimony or make whatever order justice requires.

Duty to Supplement

Rule 26(e)(1)(A) provides that a party must supplement its response to an interrogatory if the party learns that the response is in some material respect incomplete or incorrect and if the additional or corrective information has not been provided to the other parties in writing or at a deposition.[48]

RULE 33(c).   USE

CORE CONCEPT

Interrogatory answers are not admissions, but generally may be used as though made in court by the party.

APPLICATIONS

2007 Amendments

The 2007 amendments reorganized Rule 33(a), Rule 33(b), and Rule 33(c). The "scope" provisions of Rule 33(c) were moved to Rule 33(a)(2), and the provisions regarding responses by organizations were moved from Rule 33(a) to Rule 33(b)(1)(B). The subsections of Rule 33(b) were also reorganized and renumbered. Care should be exercised in researching and citing pre–2008 cases referring to Rule 30(a), Rule 33(b), or Rule 30(c).

Requests for Documents

Interrogatories may not be used to obtain documents.[49] Rather, a document request must be made under Rule 34. However, interrogatories may inquire about the existence of documents and the facts contained therein. Furthermore, documents may, under cer-

---

48. *See* Rule 26(e)(1)(A).

49. *Alltmont v. United States,* 177 F.2d 971 (3d Cir.1949); *Donahay v. Palm Beach* *Tours & Transp., Inc.,* 242 F.R.D. 685 (S.D.Fla. 2007).

tain circumstances, be produced in lieu of answering an interrogatory, as discussed below under Rule 33(d).

Opinions or Contentions

Rule 33(a)(2) explicitly states that an interrogatory is not objectionable because it seeks an opinion or contention that relates to fact or the application of law to fact.[50] However, the court may order that a contention interrogatory not be answered until discovery is complete or until after the pre-trial conference is held.[51] Rule 33(a)(2) does not authorize a question that asks for a pure legal conclusion, without application to the facts.[52]

Use of Interrogatory Answers at Trial

Answers to interrogatories are treated like any other evidence, and may be offered[53] and admitted into evidence as allowed by the Federal Rules of Evidence.[54] However, the responding party is not bound by its answers, and generally may change the answers or offer evidence that is inconsistent with them.[55] They may be objected to as irrelevant, prejudicial, confusing, cumulative, or for any other applicable reason. Interrogatory answers are generally not hearsay with respect to the party making the answer because they are party admissions.[56] However, they may be hearsay if offered against another party. If only part of an answer is read, the responding party may require that other parts of the answer be admitted at the same time in order to clarify the portion offered.[57]

Answers Not Binding

Answers to interrogatories are not admissions, and a party is not bound by its answers. Thus, a party can supplement or amend its answers, and is obligated to do so under certain circumstances discussed above. Even absent an amendment, a party may take a different position at trial unless it would prejudice another party.[58]

---

50. *Weiss v. National Westminster Bank, PLC*, 242 F.R.D. 33 (E.D.N.Y. 2007); *Banks v. Office of Senate Sergeant–At–Arms*, 222 F.R.D. 7, 13 (D.D.C.2004) (a party's opinions and contentions are discoverable by interrogatory); *E.E.O.C. v. Carrols Corp.*, 215 F.R.D. 46, 54 (N.D.N.Y.2003) (contention interrogatories are most useful to narrow and sharpen issues, a major purpose of discovery).

51. *See Weiss v. National Westminster Bank, PLC*, 242 F.R.D. 33 (E.D.N.Y. 2007); (early contention interrogatories allowed); *In re Priceline.com Inc. Securities Litigation*, 233 F.R.D. 83, 87 (D.Conn.2005).

52. *United States v. Boyce*, 148 F.Supp.2d 1069 (S.D.Cal.2001) (party must respond to interrogatories because they do not go to issues of "pure law"); *Coles v. Jenkins*, 179 F.R.D. 179, 181 (W.D.Va. 1998).

53. *Cimino v. Raymark Industries, Inc.*, 151 F.3d 297, 309 (5th Cir.1998) (interroga-

tory answers are not part of the record unless formally offered into evidence).

54. *In re Exide Technologies*, 340 B.R. 222, 241 (Bankr.D.Del.2006); *Melius v. National Indian Gaming Com'n*, 2000 WL 1174994 (D.D.C.2000) (the purpose of interrogatories is not merely to gather information but also to obtain statements that can be admitted at trial).

55. *United States v. Amerigroup Illinois, Inc.*, 230 F.R.D. 538, 541 (N.D.Ill. 2005).

56. *Underberg v. United States*, 362 F.Supp.2d 1278, 1283 (D.N.M.2005).

57. *Grace & Co. v. City of Los Angeles*, 278 F.2d 771 (9th Cir.1960).

58. The Advisory Committee Note to Rule 33(b).

Opposing parties may then impeach by questioning the reason for the changed answer.

Use of Interrogatory Answers in a Summary Judgment Motion

Interrogatory answers may be used in support of or in opposition to a motion for summary judgment, as provided in Rule 56(c).[59]

RULE 33(d).   OPTION TO PRODUCE BUSINESS RECORDS

CORE CONCEPT

A party may produce business records in lieu of answering an interrogatory when the burden of extracting the requested information would be substantially equal for either party.

APPLICATIONS

Business Records Only

Only business records may be used in lieu of interrogatory answers. Thus, one cannot produce pleadings[60] or deposition transcripts[61] instead of answering an interrogatory.

Documents Must Contain Information

In order to respond to an interrogatory by producing business records, a party must state that the documents contain the requested information.[62]   It is not sufficient to state that the documents *may* contain the information.[63]

Identify Specific Documents

A party responding to an interrogatory by producing business records must provide sufficient detail so that the propounding party can identify which individual documents contain the information requested.[64]

Equal Burden

In order to respond to interrogatories by producing business records, the burden of deriving or ascertaining the answer must be

59. *Kirkpatrick v. Merit Behavioral Care Corp.*, 128 F.Supp.2d 186, 191 (D.Vt. 2000).

60. *Melius v. National Indian Gaming Com'n*, 2000 WL 1174994 (D.D.C.2000).

61. *Starlight International, Inc. v. Herlihy*, 190 F.R.D. 587 (D.Kan.1999).

62. *Bujnicki v. American Paving and Excavating, Inc.*, 2004 WL 1071736 (W.D.N.Y.2004) (to the extent that the information sought in the interrogatory is not contained in the documents produced, defendants must respond to the interrogatory); *United States S.E.C. v. Elfindepan, S.A.*, 206 F.R.D. 574, 576 (M.D.N.C.2002); *Mackey v. IBP, Inc.*, 167 F.R.D. 186, 198 (D.Kan.1996) (a party electing to produce documents must affirmatively state so under oath).

63. *Daiflon, Inc. v. Allied Chemical Corp.*, 534 F.2d 221 (10th Cir.1976).

64. *Rainbow Pioneer No. 44–18–04A v. Hawaii–Nevada Inv. Corp.*, 711 F.2d 902 (9th Cir.1983); *Lucero v. Valdez*, 240 F.R.D. 591, 595 (D.N.M. 2007) (simply referring a party to a mass of records, or offering to make a party's records generally available, is not a sufficient response); *United States v. Los Angeles County*, 235 F.R.D. 675 (E.D.Cal.2006) ("If the records are voluminous, the responding party must produce an index designed to guide the searcher to the documents responsive to the interrogatories.").

substantially equal for the requesting party and the producing party.[65] If the sufficiency of the response is challenged, the producing party will bear the burden of making this showing.[66]

Electronic Data

A party may provide access to electronically stored information instead of answering an interrogatory if, and only if, the burden of deriving the answer is equal on both parties and the responding party provides sufficient specificity such that the other party can locate the records containing the answer as easily as the responding party.[67]

Compilations, Abstracts, and Summaries

If a compilation, abstract, or summary exists of the documents containing the responsive information, then a party electing to refer to documents in lieu of answering an interrogatory must make available the compilation, abstract, or summary.[68]

Privileged Documents

A party cannot elect to produce business records and then withhold the documents as privileged in order to prevent a party from deriving an answer.[69]

Copies or Originals

The responding party may allow the propounding party to inspect and copy the originals or may make copies.[70]

Expense of Compiling Records

Under proper circumstances, the court will, upon motion for a protective order, require the propounding party to pay the cost of compiling the records.[71]

Motion to Compel

If the propounding party believes that its burden to find the answers from the records is substantially greater than that of the responding party, the propounding party can file a motion to compel an answer.[72]   Note that the court may find the burden not substantially the same, yet nonetheless deny the motion to compel, if the court finds that the burden on the responding party to answer fully would be excessive or unreasonable.[73]   The motion to compel must be accompanied by a certification that the parties met prior to the

65. *United States v. Rachel,* 289 F.Supp.2d 688, 693 (D.Md.2003); *United States S.E.C. v. Elfindepan, S.A.,* 206 F.R.D. 574, 577 (M.D.N.C.2002).

66. *United States S.E.C. v. Elfindepan, S.A.,* 206 F.R.D. 574, 577 (M.D.N.C.2002).

67. The 2006 Amendment to the Advisory Committee Note to Rule 33(d).

68. *United States v. Los Angeles County,* 235 F.R.D. 675 (E.D.Cal.2006).

69. *Ampex v. Mitsubishi Elec. Corp.,* 937 F.Supp. 352, 355 (D.Del.1996).

70. *Neal v. Siegel–Robert, Inc.,* 171 F.R.D. 264, 267 (E.D.Mo.1996).

71. *See* Rule 26(c)(detail on costs).

72. *See Matthews v. USAir, Inc.,* 882 F.Supp. 274 (N.D.N.Y.1995)(may not respond by producing documents that are unintelligible).

73. The Advisory Committee Note to the 1970 amendment of Rule 33(c).

filing of the motion and attempted to resolve their dispute without intervention by the court.

ADDITIONAL RESEARCH REFERENCES

Wright & Miller, *Federal Practice and Procedure* §§ 2161–2182.

C.J.S. Federal Civil Procedure §§ 645–695 et seq.

West's Key No. Digests, Federal Civil Procedure ⚲1471–1542.

RULE 34

PRODUCING DOCUMENTS, ELECTRONI-CALLY STORED INFORMATION, AND TANGIBLE THINGS, OR ENTERING ONTO LAND, FOR INSPECTION AND OTHER PURPOSES

(a) In General. A party may serve on any other party a request within the scope of Rule 26(b):

(1) to produce and permit the requesting party or its representative to inspect, copy, test, or sample the following items in the responding party's possession, custody, or control:

(A) any designated documents or electronically stored information—including writings, drawings, graphs, charts, photographs, sound recordings, images, and other data or data compilations—stored in any medium from which information can be obtained either directly or, if necessary, after translation by the responding party into a reasonably usable form; or

(B) any designated tangible things; or

(2) to permit entry onto designated land or other property possessed or controlled by the responding party, so that the requesting party may inspect, measure, survey, photograph, test, or sample the property or any designated object or operation on it.

(b) Procedure.

(1) *Contents of the Request.* The request:

(A) must describe with reasonable particularity each item or category of items to be inspected;

(B) must specify a reasonable time, place, and manner for the inspection and for performing the related acts; and

(C) may specify the form or forms in which electronically stored information is to be produced.

(2) *Responses and Objections.*

(A) *Time to Respond.* The party to whom the request is directed must respond in writing with-

751

in 30 days after being served. A shorter or longer time may be stipulated to under Rule 29 or be ordered by the court.

(B) *Responding to Each Item.* For each item or category, the response must either state that inspection and related activities will be permitted as requested or state an objection to the request, including the reasons.

(C) *Objections.* An objection to part of a request must specify the part and permit inspection of the rest.

(D) *Responding to a Request for Production of Electronically Stored Information.* The response may state an objection to a requested form for producing electronically stored information. If the responding party objects to a requested form—or if no form was specified in the request—the party must state the form or forms it intends to use.

(E) *Producing the Documents or Electronically Stored Information.* Unless otherwise stipulated or ordered by the court, these procedures apply to producing documents or electronically stored information:

(i) A party must produce documents as they are kept in the usual course of business or must organize and label them to correspond to the categories in the request;

(ii) If a request does not specify a form for producing electronically stored information, a party must produce it in a form or forms in which it is ordinarily maintained or in a reasonably usable form or forms; and

(iii) A party need not produce the same electronically stored information in more than one form.

(c) Nonparties. As provided in Rule 45, a nonparty may be compelled to produce documents and tangible things or to permit an inspection.

[Amended December 27, 1946, effective March 19, 1948; March 30, 1970, effective July 1, 1970; April 29, 1980, effective August 1, 1980; March 2, 1987, effective August 1, 1987;

April 30, 1991, effective December 1, 1991; April 22, 1993, effective December 1, 1993; April 12, 2006, effective December 1, 2006; April 30, 2007, effective December 1, 2007.]

─────────── 2007 AMENDMENTS ROADMAP ───────────

STYLE PROJECT CHANGES: The final sentence of Rule 34(b) was deleted as an unnecessary cross-reference to the discovery moratorium provisions of Rule 26(d). Language in former Rule 34(b) was deleted as a redundant reference to the Rule 37(a) procedure for instances where a party fails to respond to a document request. Rule 34(a) was further subsectioned and reorganized for clarity. Rule 34(b) was substantially reorganized, subsectioned, and labeled. The language was generally simplified and clarified, and "must" replaced "shall."

NON-STYLE CHANGES: None.

NOTE: The Federal Rules "Style Project" is explained in Part III-A.

───────────────────────────

AUTHORS' COMMENTARY ON RULE 34

─────────────── PURPOSE AND SCOPE ───────────────

Rule 34 sets forth the procedures for obtaining access to documents and things within the control of other parties, and for gaining entry upon other parties' land for inspection. It must be read in conjunction with Rule 26, which establishes the scope of all discovery rules.

NOTE: Rule 34 was substantially revised in 1970, 1991, 1993, 2006, and 2007, and great care should be exercised when citing decisions pertaining to Rule 34.

2006 AMENDMENTS: The 2006 Amendments to Rule 34(a) and (b) added language addressing the production of electronic data. Rule 34(a) now specifically includes "electronically stored information" among the categories of documents and things that must be produced. Rule 34(b) now has language addressing the form in which electronic data must be produced. It allows the requesting party to specify the form in which it is requesting electronic data. The responding party can then produce it in that form or object and specify the form in which it will produce the electronic data. If the requesting party does not specify the form, then the responding party must produce it in the form in which it is ordinarily maintained. Under any of these scenarios, a party need not produce electronic data in more than one form. Electronic data produced under Rule 34 must be made available for inspection, copying, testing, or sampling.

RULE 34(a).   IN GENERAL

CORE CONCEPT

The scope of document requests and other discovery under Rule 34 is the broad discovery available under Rule 26.[1] Generally, any relevant, non-privileged document is discoverable unless it was prepared in anticipation of litigation, pertains to expert witnesses, or would be unreasonably burdensome to produce.

APPLICATIONS

Documents

"Documents" is broadly defined to include all forms of recorded information. Rule 34(a) specifically lists writings, drawings, graphs, charts, photographs, phonorecords, and other data compilations. Generally, a party is not required to create documents meeting the document requests, only to produce documents already in existence.[2] A party is entitled to inspect, copy, test, or sample discoverable documents.

Electronic Data

Rule 34(a) specifically includes "electronically stored information" among the categories of documents and things that must be produced.[3] "Electronically stored information" is intended to be a broad and flexible term encompassing email and information "stored in any medium"[4] If the electronic data is not stored in a form that is reasonably accessible, Rule 34(a) requires that the producing party translate it into a reasonably usable form.[5] Rule 34(a) allows a party to make a request to inspect, copy, test, or sample the electronic data.[6]

Tangible Things

Rule 34 allows a party to inspect and copy, test, or sample tangible things relevant to the action (e.g., the allegedly defective product in a products liability case).[7]

Property

A party has the right to enter onto another party's land and inspect, measure, survey, photograph, test, or sample property or a

---

1. *Del Campo v. Kennedy*, 236 F.R.D. 454 (N.D.Cal.2006).

2. *Alexander v. F.B.I.*, 194 F.R.D. 305, 310 (D.D.C.2000); *but see Harris v. Athol–Royalston Regional School District Committee*, 200 F.R.D. 18 (D.Mass.2001) (party required to create a handwriting exemplar for examination by the opposing party's expert).

3. *See Avocent Redmond Corp. v. Rose Electronics, Inc.*, 242 F.R.D. 574 (W.D.Wash. 2007).

4. The 2006 Amendment to the Advisory Committee Note to Rule 34(a).

5. The 2006 Amendment to the Advisory Committee Note to Rule 34(a).

6. The 2006 Amendment to the Advisory Committee Note to Rule 34(a).

7. *Harris v. Athol–Royalston Regional School Dist. Committee*, 206 F.R.D. 30, 32–33 (D.Mass.2002) (fingerprint samples may be obtained under either Rule 34 or Rule 35).

designated object or operation thereon if relevant to the pending action.[8]

Parties Only

Only parties are obligated to respond to document requests.[9] "Party" is sometimes liberally construed, such as to include experts,[10] insurance companies,[11] and garnishees.[12] Note, however, that documents may be obtained from non-parties by a subpoena under Rule 45.[13]

Documents Within Party's Possession, Custody, or Control

A party must produce all discoverable documents or things responsive to a request that are in the party's possession, custody, or control.[14] Documents are deemed to be within the possession, custody, or control of a party if the party has actual possession, custody, control, or the legal right to obtain the documents on demand.[15] Documents held by the party's attorney,[16] expert,[17] insurance company,[18] accountant,[19] spouse,[20] contractor,[21] or agent[22]

---

8. *Albany Bank & Trust Co. v. Exxon Mobil Corp.*, 310 F.3d 969, 974 (7th Cir. 2002); *Baugus v. CSX Transp., Inc.*, 223 F.R.D. 469, 470 (N.D.Ohio 2004) (suggesting that it is improper to videotape the property of another party without going through the Rule 34 procedures); *Macort v. Goodwill Industries–Manasota, Inc.*, 220 F.R.D. 377, 379 (M.D.Fla.2003) (inspection of property); *Micro Chemical, Inc. v. Lextron, Inc.*, 193 F.R.D. 667, 669–70 (D.Colo. 2000) (allowing the president of the opposing party to attend the inspection of the plant, but not allowing the discovering party to alter the machine of the responding party to allow better observation of its operation).

9. *See Hobley v. Burge*, 433 F.3d 946, 949 (7th Cir.2006) (Rule 45 subpoena is the only way to get documents from a nonparty); *In re Greenwood Air Crash*, 161 F.R.D. 387 (S.D.Ind.1995)(discussion of who constitutes a "party" under Rule 34).

10. *Alper v. United States*, 190 F.R.D. 281, 283 (D.Mass.2000)(document request to the party's expert is deemed a document request to the party).

11. *See, e.g., Parrett v. Ford Motor Co.*, 47 F.R.D. 22, 24 (W.D.Mo.1968).

12. *See, e.g., Conversion Chem. Corp. v. Dr.–Ing. Max Schloetter Fabrik Fur Galvanotechnik*, 49 F.R.D. 126 (D.Conn.1969).

13. *Hobley v. Burge*, 433 F.3d 946, 949 (7th Cir.2006) (Rule 45 subpoena is the only way to get documents from a non-party).

14. *Kissinger v. Reporters Com. for Freedom of the Press*, 445 U.S. 136, 166,

100 S.Ct. 960, 976, 63 L.Ed.2d 267 (1980); *Wiwa v. Royal Dutch Petroleum Co.*, 392 F.3d 812, 821 (5th Cir.2004) (having access to documents does not render them within a party's possession, custody, or control).

15. *In Re Bankers Trust Co.*, 61 F.3d 465, 469 (6th Cir.1995); *Tequila Centinela, S.A. de C.V. v. Bacardi & Co. Ltd.*, 242 F.R.D. 1 (D.D.C. 2007); *Rosie D. v. Romney*, 256 F.Supp.2d 115, 119 (D.Mass.2003) (control may be established by the existence of a principal-agent relationship or a legal right pursuant to a contractual provision). *But see United States v. Skeddle*, 176 F.R.D. 258, 261 (N.D.Ohio 1997) ("in practice the courts have sometimes interpreted Rule 34 to require production if the party has practical ability to obtain the documents from another, irrespective of his legal entitlement to the documents").

16. *American Society For Prevention of Cruelty To Animals v. Ringling Brothers and Barnum & Bailey Circus*, 233 F.R.D. 209, 212 (D.D.C.2006) (documents held by attorney are within party's control, but subject to work product protection); *Hobley v. Burge*, 226 F.R.D. 312, 320 (N.D.Ill.2005) (documents of the party's former attorney are within the party's control).

17. *Alper v. United States*, 190 F.R.D. 281, 283 (D.Mass.2000) (documents held by the party's expert are within the party's control).

18. *Henderson v. Zurn Industries, Inc.*, 131 F.R.D. 560, 567 (S.D.Ind.1990). *But see Japan Halon Co., Ltd. v. Great Lakes Chemical Corp.*, 155 F.R.D. 626 (N.D.Ind.

19.–22.   See notes 19–22 on page 756.

are deemed to be within the party's control.   Likewise, documents held by a subsidiary, affiliated corporation, or branch office in another state may be within a party's control.[23]   Moreover, documents owned by a third person but possessed by a party are within the party's control.[24] The courts are divided as to whether a party will be deemed to have possession, custody or control of documents which the party may release by authorization, such as medical records.[25]

Duty to Search for Documents

A party must make a reasonable search of all sources reasonably likely to contain responsive documents.[26]

Documents Available From Another Source

The fact that documents are available from another source, such as public records, is not, by itself, a valid basis for objecting or refusing to produce such documents if they are within the possession, custody, or control of the responding party.[27] Depending on the circumstances, however, the availability of alternative sources for the requested documents may support an objection on the basis of undue burden.[28] A party that does not have the requested records in its possession, custody, or control will not be required to obtain those documents from public sources equally accessible to the requesting parties.[29]

1993) (subsidiary not required to obtain documents from parent in another country).

19. *Wardrip v. Hart,* 934 F.Supp. 1282, 1286 (D.Kan.1996) (financial records of defendant in possession of defendant's accountant are in defendant's control).

20. *Monroe's Estate v. Bottle Rock Power Corp.,* 2004 WL 737463 (E.D.La.2004).

21. *Mercy Catholic Medical Center v. Thompson,* 380 F.3d 142, 160 (3rd Cir. 2004).

22. *American Rock Salt Co., LLC v. Norfolk Southern Corp.,* 228 F.R.D. 426, 457 (W.D.N.Y.2004).

23. *Steele Software Systems, Corp. v. DataQuick Information Systems, Inc.,* 237 F.R.D. 561, 564–65 (D.Md. 2006); *American Rock Salt Co., LLC v. Norfolk Southern Corp.,* 228 F.R.D. 426, 457 (W.D.N.Y.2004).

24. *Societe Internationale Pour Participations Industrielles Et Commerciales, S.A. v. Rogers,* 357 U.S. 197, 78 S.Ct. 1087, 2 L.Ed.2d 1255 (1958); *Commerce and Industry Ins. Co. v. Grinnell Corp.,* 2001 WL 96377 (E.D.La.2001).

25. *See E.E.O.C. v. Thorman & Wright Corp.,* 243 F.R.D. 421 (D.Kan. 2007) (party not required to provide an authorization for his employment records); *Preservation*

Products, LLC v. Nutraceutical Clinical Laboratories Intern., Inc., 214 F.R.D. 494, 495 (N.D.Ill.2003) (plaintiff must supply authorization for SEC testimony sought by defendant); *J.J.C. v. Fridell,* 165 F.R.D. 513, 517 (D.Minn.1995) (in considering authorization for release of medical records, the court must balance the patient's right to privacy with the need for such records in obtaining a fair trial); *but see Clark v. Vega Wholesale Inc.,* 181 F.R.D. 470, 472 (D.Nev. 1998) (medical records not deemed in the plaintiff's control).

26. *See A. Farber and Partners, Inc. v. Garber,* 234 F.R.D. 186, 190 (C.D.Cal.2006).

27. *Sabouri v. Ohio Bureau of Employment Services,* 2000 WL 1620915 (S.D.Ohio 2000) (party required to produce a pleading that could also be obtained from the courthouse). *But see Bleecker v. Standard Fire Ins. Co.,* 130 F.Supp.2d 726 (E.D.N.C.2000) (discovery is not required when documents are readily obtainable by the party seeking a motion to compel).

28. *See Tequila Centinela, S.A. de C.V. v. Bacardi & Co. Ltd.,* 242 F.R.D. 1 (D.D.C. 2007).

29. *Krause v. Buffalo and Erie County Workforce Development Consortium, Inc.,* 425 F.Supp.2d 352 (W.D.N.Y.2006)

Proceedings Where Requests Available

Document requests are available in all civil actions in federal court, subject to certain narrow exceptions listed in Rule 81. Document requests are available in bankruptcy proceedings.

Procedure to Perpetuate Testimony

A party may file a motion to obtain documents in connection with an action to perpetuate testimony under Rule 27.

Procedures in Aid of Execution

Document requests may be served following the entry of judgment, as part of procedures in aid of execution.

Motion for a Protective Order

As an alternative to making objections to individual document requests, the responding party may make a motion for a protective order under Rule 26(c).[30] A motion for a protective order is appropriate when most or all of a set of document requests is too burdensome or cumulative. The burden is on the moving party to show hardship or injustice. The motion must be accompanied by a certification that the parties met prior to the filing of the motion and attempted to resolve their dispute without intervention by the court.

Contractual Agreements

Parties sometimes have previously entered into agreements defining a right to inspect designated documents (such as an agreement restricting one party's right to inspect another party's financial records for one year). Such agreements may be upheld by the court, if reasonable.

RULE 34(b). PROCEDURE

CORE CONCEPT

Any party may serve document requests on any other party,[31] who must respond in writing within 30 days.

APPLICATIONS

Who May Serve

Any party may serve document requests.

Who May Be Served

Document requests are limited to parties to the action, although the party need not be an adverse party (documents are obtained from non-parties by a subpoena under Rule 45). The document requests must be addressed to the party. Thus, if the party is a

---

30. *Minnesota Mining & Mfg. Co., Inc. v. Nippon Carbide Indus. Co., Inc.,* 171 F.R.D. 246 (D.Minn.1997).

31. *McKesson v. Islamic Republic of Iran,* 185 F.R.D. 70 (D.D.C.1999) (compel-

ling a foreign nation defendant to allow the plaintiff's expert to enter the country and conduct an inspection).

corporation, document requests should be addressed to the corporation, not to a corporate officer or the attorney. In a class action, the courts are split as to whether only the named representatives can be served.[32] Copies of the document requests should be served upon all parties.

Time for Service

Document requests can be served after the parties have conducted the discovery conference under Rule 26(f), or earlier with leave of court. In proceedings listed in Rule 26(a)(1)(B) as exempt from initial disclosures, there is no preliminary waiting period for document requests. The Rules do not set an outer limit on how late in the case document requests may be served, but many local rules or case management orders will set such a limit. Usually, when such a limit exists, document requests must be served so that the response is due before the close of discovery.[33]

Number

The Rule contains no limitation on the number of document requests.[34] Some districts have local rules limiting the number of document requests.

Designation of Documents

Documents to be produced must be designated with "reasonable particularity."[35] Rule 34(b) permits requests for categories of documents as long as the category is described with reasonable particularity.[36] Essentially, the test is whether the responding party can determine what documents to produce.

Form of Requests

A request for inspection should be a formal document[37] setting forth the items to be inspected with "reasonable particularity."[38] What constitutes "reasonable particularity" depends on the circumstances. The request should also specify a reasonable time, place, and manner for the inspection.[39] The time designated should be after the time to respond has elapsed (30 days). As an alternative, the serving party may designate "a time and manner convenient to the parties," then reach an agreement with opposing counsel. If the

---

32. *Brennan v. Midwestern United Life Ins. Co.*, 450 F.2d 999 (7th Cir.1971) (unnamed members of class required to respond); *Wainwright v. Kraftco Corp.*, 54 F.R.D. 532 (N.D.Ga.1972)(unnamed members of class not required to respond).

33. *Thomas v. Pacificorp*, 324 F.3d 1176, 1179 (10th Cir.2003).

34. *Bourguignon v. Spielvogel*, 2004 WL 743668 (D.Conn.2004).

35. *Bruggeman ex rel. Bruggeman v. Blagojevich*, 219 F.R.D. 430, 436 (N.D.Ill. 2004); *St. Paul Reinsurance Co., Ltd. v.*

Commercial Financial Corp., 198 F.R.D. 508, 514 (N.D.Iowa 2000).

36. *Goosman v. A. Duie Pyle, Inc.*, 320 F.2d 45 (4th Cir.1963).

37. *Suid v. Cigna Corp.*, 203 F.R.D. 227, 229–29 (D.Virgin Islands 2001) (letters between counsel are not document requests under Rule 34).

38. *Roebling v. Anderson*, 257 F.2d 615, 620 (D.C.Cir.1958).

39. *Southern Estate Services, Inc. v. Puritan Financial Services, Inc.*, 2000 WL 1725086 (E.D.La.2000).

request seeks electronic data, the request may, but is not required to, specify the form in which electronic data is to be produced.

Response

A party served with a document request must serve a written response[40] or move for a protective order under Rule 26(c). Otherwise, the party will be subject to the sanctions in Rule 37(d). The response may state that the request will be complied with in the manner requested. It may also state that the request will be complied with, but at some other time or place, or in some other manner. The response may also raise objections to some or all of the requests. If the request does not specify the form for production of electronic data, or if the responding party has objected to the form specified in the request, then the response must specify the form in which electronic data will be produced. Finally, the response may advise that the party has no such documents in its possession, custody, or control.[41]

Time to Answer

A written response is due within 30 days of service.[42] The time to answer may be extended by written agreement under Rule 29.[43] If the responding party intends to object to some of the document requests, the stipulation should specify that the time is extended to answer and file objections.[44] The period for responding may also be shortened or lengthened by the court, typically upon motion by one of the parties.[45]

Service of Response

The response must be served upon all parties.

Objections

If the responding party determines that a particular document request is outside the scope of discovery, the party may object to the request in lieu of producing the documents. The objection must be made in writing, must state the grounds of the objection with specificity,[46] and must be signed by the attorney for the responding party. Some common objections are:

40. *Starcher v. Correctional Medical Systems, Inc.*, 144 F.3d 418, 420–21 (6th Cir.1998), *cert. granted*, 525 U.S. 1098, 119 S.Ct. 864, 142 L.Ed.2d 716 (1999).

41. *See Fishel v. BASF*, 175 F.R.D. 525, 531 (S.D.Iowa 1997) ("Even if there are no such documents, plaintiff is entitled to a response as required by Fed.R.Civ.P. 34(b) and the Court will so order.").

42. *Jayne H. Lee, Inc. v. Flagstaff Indus. Corp.*, 173 F.R.D. 651, 654 (D.Md. 1997).

43. *Tropix, Inc. v. Lyon & Lyon*, 169 F.R.D. 3, *3–4 (D.Mass.1996).

44. *Coregis Ins. Co. v. Baratta & Fenerty, Ltd.*, 187 F.R.D. 528, 530 (E.D.Pa.1999).

45. *Ellsworth Associates v. United States*, 917 F.Supp. 841, 844 (D.D.C. 1996)(motion for expedited discovery is particularly appropriate with a claim for injunctive relief).

46. *United States v. Philip Morris Inc.*, 347 F.3d 951, 954 (D.C.Cir.2003); *Tequila Centinela, S.A. de C.V. v. Bacardi & Co. Ltd.*, 242 F.R.D. 1 (D.D.C. 2007); A. Farber and Partners, Inc. v. Garber, 234 F.R.D. 186, 188 (C.D.Cal.2006) (general boilerplate objections are ineffective).

- *Overly broad, unduly vague, and/or ambiguous:* When a document request is written broadly so that it extends to documents not relevant to the complaint (such as a request not limited in time to the events relevant to the complaint), the request may be overly broad.[47] When a request is susceptible to numerous meanings, it may be unduly vague and ambiguous. In general, these objections are probably not justification for refusing to provide documents altogether, but the responding party can raise the objection, then expressly limit the scope of the response.

- *Burdensome and oppressive:* In general, the responding party must produce the documents available without undue effort or expense. Thus, requests that require extensive research, compilation, or evaluation of documents may be objectionable.[48] The responding party is not required to prepare the adverse party's case. The reasonableness of a request is within the court's discretion.

- *Privileged information:* Requests that seek documents protected by the attorney-client privilege or by another privilege are objectionable.[49] When privileged documents are withheld, the responding party must explicitly state the objection and describe the nature of the documents not produced sufficiently to enable other parties to assess the applicability of the privilege.[50] A log of the documents withheld on the basis of privilege should be provided to the requesting party, either at the time of the responses or at a mutually agreeable time.[51] Care should be exercised in responding to such requests, because the privilege may be waived by revealing part or all of the privileged documents.

- *Attorney work product:* Rule 26(b)(3) provides that trial preparation materials may be discovered only upon a showing that the party is unable to obtain the equivalent information through other means without undue hardship.[52]

- *Non-discoverable expert information:* Rule 26(b)(4) limits the scope of discovery directed towards experts. It generally requires the responding party to provide an expert report for each expert the party may call as a witness, and thereafter allows other parties to depose such experts. Further discov-

---

47. *Westhemeco Ltd. v. New Hampshire Ins. Co.,* 82 F.R.D. 702 (S.D.N.Y.1979).

48. *Chambers v. Capital Cities/ABC,* 154 F.R.D. 63 (S.D.N.Y.1994).

49. *Tequila Centinela, S.A. de C.V. v. Bacardi & Co. Ltd.,* 242 F.R.D. 1 (D.D.C. 2007).

50. *United States v. Philip Morris Inc.,* 347 F.3d 951, 954 (D.C.Cir.2003); *Tequila Centinela, S.A. de C.V. v. Bacardi & Co. Ltd.,* 242 F.R.D. 1 (D.D.C. 2007).

51. *Burlington Northern & Santa Fe Ry. Co. v. U.S. Dist. Court for Dist. of Mont.,* 408 F.3d 1142, 1147 (9th Cir.2005) (failure to produce a privilege log within 30 days is not a per se waiver of the privilege); *Universal City Development Partners, Ltd. v. Ride & Show Engineering, Inc.,* 230 F.R.D. 688, 695 (M.D.Fla.2005); *Strougo v. Bea Associates,* 199 F.R.D. 515, 521 (S.D.N.Y.2001).

52. *See* Rule 26(b)(3)(discovery of work product).

ery with respect to such witnesses is available only upon motion. Rule 26(b)(4)(B) does not allow any discovery with respect to experts not intended to be called as witnesses, absent "exceptional circumstances." [53]

- *Not calculated to lead to the discovery of admissible evidence:* Rule 26 takes a very broad approach with respect to what information is discoverable. The requested information need not be admissible, only relevant. Information that is neither admissible nor reasonably calculated to lead to the discovery of admissible evidence, however, is not discoverable.[54]

- *Form of Electronic Data:* If the requesting party specifies a form for the production of electronic data that the responding party believes is burdensome or otherwise objectionable, Rule 34(b) specifically provides for objections to the request.

Failure to Object Is Waiver

All grounds for objection must be specifically stated in a timely[55] response or they are waived,[56] unless excused by the court for good cause shown.[57]

Objection to Part of Request

If any part of a request is objectionable, the responding party must specify the objectionable part and respond to the remaining parts.[58]

Production of Documents

The responding party has the option of allowing the serving party to inspect, copy, test, or sample the documents as they are normally kept (*i.e.,* "There is our file room.").[59] The responding party may also produce selected responsive documents, in which

53. *See* Rule 26(b)(4)(in-depth discussion of discovery directed toward experts).

54. *See* Rule 26(b)(1)(in-depth discussion of the scope of discovery).

55. *Lucero v. Valdez,* 240 F.R.D. 591, 593 (D.N.M. 2007).

56. *Essex Ins. Co. v. Neely,* 236 F.R.D. 287 (N.D.W.Va.2006) (while Rule 34 does not contain the same specificity and waiver provisions as Rule 33, the Advisory Committee notes to Rule 34 state that the procedure for Rule 34 is essentially the same as that for Rule 33); *Drexel Heritage Furnishings, Inc. v. Furniture USA, Inc.,* 200 F.R.D. 255 (M.D.N.C.2001) (waiver is implicit in Rule 34's requirement that objections be explicitly stated); *Rivera v. Kmart Corp.,* 190 F.R.D. 298, 300–01 (D.Puerto Rico 2000).

57. *Starlight International, Inc. v. Herlihy,* 181 F.R.D. 494 (D.Kan.1998) (attorney inadvertence not good cause).

58. *Martinez v. Cornell Corrections of Texas,* 377 F.Supp.2d 1138 (D.N.M.2005); *Cotracom Commodity Trading Co. v. Seaboard Corp.,* 189 F.R.D. 655, 666 (D.Kan. 1999).

59. *Doe v. District of Columbia,* 231 F.R.D. 27, 36–7 (D.D.C.2005) (producing party does not have to organize and label documents that are produced as they are kept); *Hagemeyer North America, Inc. v. Gateway Data Sciences Corp.,* 222 F.R.D. 594, 598 (E.D.Wis.2004) (documents in storage may be produced as they are stored); *but see Bonilla v. Trebol Motors Corp.,* 1997 WL 178844, *68 (D.Puerto Rico), *reversed in part, vacated in part,* 150 F.3d 88 (1st Cir.1998) (responding party may not utilize a system of record-keeping which conceals rather than discloses relevant records or which makes production of the documents excessively burdensome and costly).

case the party must organize and label them to correspond to the categories requested.[60] The responding party may make copies for the requesting party, but is not obligated to do so.

Use of Documents at Trial

Documents produced in response to document requests are treated like any other evidence, and are admissible as allowed by the rules of evidence. They may be objected to as irrelevant, prejudicial, confusing, cumulative, or any other applicable objection.

Cost of Copying

The requesting party is responsible for the cost of copying the requested documents,[61] although parties sometimes agree (formally or informally) that the responding party pays copying costs. The requesting party may inspect the produced documents before copying in order to avoid duplicative copying of documents already in the requesting party's possession.[62]

Production of Electronic Data

Rule 34(b) now has language addressing the form in which electronic data must be produced (i.e., hard copy or electronic, and if electronic, the precise manner of production). It allows, but does not require, the requesting party to specify the form in which it is requesting electronic data. The responding party can then produce it in that form or object and specify the form in which it will produce the electronic data. If the requesting party does not specify the form, then the responding party must produce it in the form in which it is ordinarily maintained or in a form that is reasonably usable. Unless the responding party is producing the data in the form specified by the requesting party, the responding party must specify the form it intends to use for production in its written response to the document request.[63] If the responding party objects to the form stated by the requesting party, or if the requesting party is not satisfied with the form specified by the responding party, then the parties must meet and confer under Rule 37(a)(2)(B).[64] Under any of these scenarios, a party need not produce electronic data in more than one form.

Limitations on Inspection

The responding party can set reasonable limitations on the time, place, and manner of an inspection.

60. *American Intern. Specialty Lines Ins. Co. v. NWI–I, Inc.*, 240 F.R.D. 401, 410 (N.D.Ill. 2007) (documents must either be produced in the manner normally maintained or organized to correspond to the requests); *Ferrito v. IKON Office Solutions, Inc.*, 2000 WL 1477188 (D.Kan.2000) (production of 2,000 pages of documents that were neither Bates stamped nor otherwise organized did not satisfy Rule 34).

61. *Obiajulu v. City of Rochester, Dept. of Law*, 166 F.R.D. 293, 297 (W.D.N.Y.1996) (plaintiff may copy documents by bringing in his own portable copying machine or by paying the defendant a reasonable copying cost.)

62. *Stiller v. Arnold*, 167 F.R.D. 68, 70 (N.D.Ind.1996).

63. The 2006 Amendment to the Advisory Committee Note to Rule 34(b).

64. The 2006 Amendment to the Advisory Committee Note to Rule 34(b).

Motion to Compel

If the responding party fails to respond to a document request or to allow an inspection, or objects to a document request, the propounding party may file a motion to compel under Rule 37(a).[65] The court will award the prevailing party its reasonable expenses, including attorney fees, incurred in connection with the motion to compel, unless the conduct of the losing party was justified (*i.e.,* not frivolous).

NOTE: Rule 37 requires the moving party to certify in writing that good faith attempts were made to resolve discovery disputes before relief was sought from the court.

Burden of Persuasion

In a motion to compel, the burden is on the responding party (the non-moving party) to convince the court that a document request is objectionable.[66]

Discretion of Court

The district court has extremely broad discretion in ruling on objections to document requests. The court will balance the need for the documents and the burden of producing them, but will generally require production unless the administration of justice would be impeded. The court may allow inspection under limited conditions, and may restrict further disclosure of sensitive documents. The court may also privately inspect the documents before ruling.

Appeals

The court's rulings on objections to document requests are reviewed on an abuse of discretion standard.[67] Usually, such rulings are not final orders, and cannot be appealed until the conclusion of the case.

Sanctions for Failure to Respond

If a party files no response to a document request, the court may impose certain sanctions under Rule 37(b)(2), such as deeming certain facts established or refusing to allow the party to oppose or support certain claims.[68] The court may also deem objections to the document request waived by the failure to file a timely response.[69] Furthermore, the court must award reasonable expenses, including attorney fees, caused by the responding party's failure to answer, unless the court finds that the failure to answer was justified.

65. Molski v. Franklin, 222 F.R.D. 433, 435 (S.D.Cal.2004); *United States v. Kattar,* 191 F.R.D. 33, 35–36 (D.N.H.1999) (such a motion must comply with the requirements of Rule 37(a)).

66. *Tequila Centinela, S.A. de C.V. v. Bacardi & Co. Ltd.,* 242 F.R.D. 1 (D.D.C. 2007).

67. *Swanner v. United States,* 406 F.2d 716, 719 (5th Cir.1969).

68. *See* Rule 37(d); *Land Ocean Logistics, Inc. v. Aqua Gulf Corp.,* 181 F.R.D. 229, 235 (W.D.N.Y.1998) (preclusion of evidence is a harsh sanction reserved for exceptional cases).

69. *Scaturro v. Warren and Sweat Manufacturing Co., Inc.,* 160 F.R.D. 44 (M.D.Pa. 1995).

Sanctions for Failure to Obey Order to Produce Documents

If, in response to a motion to compel, the court orders a party to produce certain documents, and if the responding party fails to comply, then the court can impose the sanctions specified in Rule 37(b)(2), such as deeming certain facts established or refusing to allow the party to oppose or support certain claims. Furthermore, the court must award reasonable expenses, including attorney fees, caused by the responding party's failure to produce the documents, unless the court finds that the failure was justified.

RULE 34(c).   NONPARTIES

CORE CONCEPT

Although document requests or requests for inspection cannot be served on a non-party, documents or inspections can be obtained from a non-party by a subpoena under Rule 45.[70] Furthermore, Rule 34 does not preclude an independent action for production of documents or things or for permission to enter onto land (but such actions may be unnecessary under the expanded subpoena powers in Rule 45).[71]

ADDITIONAL RESEARCH REFERENCES

Wright & Miller, *Federal Practice and Procedure* §§ 2201–2218.

C.J.S. Federal Civil Procedure §§ 696–740 et seq.

West's Key No. Digests, Federal Civil Procedure ⊚1551–1640.

70. *Hobley v. Burge*, 433 F.3d 946, 949 (7th Cir.2006) (Rule 45 subpoena is the only way to get documents from a non-party); *F.D.I.C. v. Wachovia Ins. Services, Inc.*, 241 F.R.D. 104, 107 (D.Conn. 2007); *In re Greenwood Air Crash*, 161 F.R.D. 387 (S.D.Ind.1995)(discussion of who constitutes a "party" under Rule 34).

71. *See Darbeau v. Library of Congress*, 453 F.Supp.2d 168, 171 (D.D.C. 2006); the Advisory Committee Note to the 1970 amendment to Rule 34(c).

RULE 35

PHYSICAL AND MENTAL EXAMINATIONS

(a) Order for an Examination.

(1) *In General.* The court where the action is pending may order a party whose mental or physical condition—including blood group—is in controversy to submit to a physical or mental examination by a suitably licensed or certified examiner. The court has the same authority to order a party to produce for examination a person who is in its custody or under its legal control.

(2) *Motion and Notice; Contents of the Order.* The order:

(A) may be made only on motion for good cause and on notice to all parties and the person to be examined; and

(B) must specify the time, place, manner, conditions, and scope of the examination, as well as the person or persons who will perform it.

(b) Examiner's Report.

(1) *Request by the Party or Person Examined.* The party who moved for the examination must, on request, deliver to the requester a copy of the examiner's report, together with like reports of all earlier examinations of the same condition. The request may be made by the party against whom the examination order was issued or by the person examined.

(2) *Contents.* The examiner's report must be in writing and must set out in detail the examiner's findings, including diagnoses, conclusions, and the results of any tests.

(3) *Request by the Moving Party.* After delivering the reports, the party who moved for the examination may request—and is entitled to receive—from the party against whom the examination order was issued like reports of all earlier or later examinations of the same condition. But those reports need not be delivered by the party with custody or control of the person examined if the party shows that it could not obtain them.

(4) *Waiver of Privilege.* By requesting and obtaining the examiner's report, or by deposing the examiner, the party examined waives any privilege it may have—in that action or any other action involving the same controversy—concerning testimony about all examinations of the same condition.

(5) *Failure to Deliver a Report.* The court on motion may order—on just terms—that a party deliver the report of an examination. If the report is not provided, the court may exclude the examiner's testimony at trial.

(6) *Scope.* This subdivision (b) applies also to an examination made by the parties' agreement, unless the agreement states otherwise. This subdivision does not preclude obtaining an examiner's report or deposing an examiner under other rules.

[Amended effective July 1, 1970; August 1, 1987; November 18, 1988; December 1, 1991; April 30, 2007, effective December 1, 2007.]

––––––––––––––––––– **2007 AMENDMENTS ROADMAP** –––––––––––––––––––

STYLE PROJECT CHANGES: Rule 35(a) and (b) were both reorganized and further subdivided, and new labels were added. The language was also shortened and clarified, and active voice was substituted for passive.

NON-STYLE CHANGES: None.

NOTE: The Federal Rules "Style Project" is explained in Part III-A.

AUTHORS' COMMENTARY ON RULE 35

––––––––––––––––––– PURPOSE AND SCOPE –––––––––––––––––––

Rule 35 requires a party to submit to a mental or physical examination when the party's mental or physical condition is at issue in the action. In contrast to most other discovery procedures, mental or physical examinations are available only for "good cause."

RULE 35(a). ORDER FOR AN EXAMINATION

CORE CONCEPT

Examination is compulsory only if ordered by the court. Examination will be ordered for good cause shown, which will generally exist in every case in which the plaintiff is claiming personal injuries.

APPLICATIONS

Motion

Technically, a request for examination must be made by motion, with a proposed order attached, served upon the person to be examined and all parties.[1] The motion should specify the time, place, manner, conditions, and scope of the examination and the person or persons by whom it is to be made, as well as the grounds supporting the motion.[2] Typically, however, examination is arranged by consent.

Order

If the court grants a motion for a Rule 35 examination, it must issue an order that specifies the time, place, manner, conditions, and scope of the examination and the examiner.[3] These topics are discussed individually below. The order may also include protective measures deemed appropriate by the court.[4]

Condition at Issue

Examinations for a particular condition are allowed only when that condition is in controversy.[5]

Good Cause

The court will order an examination "for good cause shown." [6] The burden of demonstrating good cause rests with the moving

---

1. *Smith v. Koplan*, 215 F.R.D. 11, 12 (D.D.C.2003).

2. *See* Roberson v. Bair, 242 F.R.D. 130 (D.D.C. 2007) (emotional distress claim places the plaintiff's condition at issue); *Cabana v. Forcier*, 200 F.R.D. 9 (D.Mass.2001) (the movant complied with Rule 35 by providing a time and place for the exam as well as the name of the examiner and a general idea of the exam's intended scope).

3. *Ziemba v. Armstrong*, 2004 WL 834685 (D.Conn.2004); *Hertenstein v. Kimberly Home Health Care, Inc.*, 189 F.R.D. 620, 623 (D.Kan.1999).

4. *Favale v. Roman Catholic Diocese of Bridgeport*, 235 F.R.D. 553, 555 (D.Conn. 2006).

5. Roberson v. Bair, 242 F.R.D. 130 (D.D.C. 2007) (emotional distress claim places the plaintiff's condition at issue);

Green v. Branson, 108 F.3d 1296, 1304 (10th Cir.1997) (denying motion by the plaintiff to have himself examined where purpose was for the plaintiff, a prisoner, to obtain treatment); *John Doe v. District of Columbia*, 229 F.R.D. 24 (D.D.C.2005) (a plaintiff claiming mental or physical injury places that condition at issue); *Bowen v. Parking Authority of City of Camden*, 214 F.R.D. 188, 193 (D.N.J.2003) ("garden variety" emotional distress claim does not put the plaintiff's mental condition at issue).

6. *Schlagenhauf v. Holder*, 379 U.S. 104, 85 S.Ct. 234, 13 L.Ed.2d 152 (1964) (describing "good cause" as a determination that must be made on a case-by-case basis); *John Doe v. District of Columbia*, 229 F.R.D. 24 (D.D.C.2005) (good cause depends on the circumstances); *Johnson v. City of Ecorse*, 137 F.Supp.2d 886, 894 (E.D.Mich.2001) ("A demonstration of good

party.[7] The requirement of good cause is not a formality; the court must genuinely balance the need for the information with the right to privacy and safety of the party.[8] In a tort action where the plaintiff seeks to recover for personal injuries, good cause will almost always be found to exist.[9] It becomes less clear when the party has not put the party's own mental or physical condition at issue.[10]

Time for Filing Motion

There is no time limit on the filing of a motion for an examination.

Who Conducts Exam

Rule 35 states that the examination may be conducted by any suitably licensed or certified examiner or examiners.[11] It does not address the selection of a particular examiner. In general, the court will allow the movant to select the examiner unless the person to be examined raises a valid objection.[12] The court may reject a particular examiner upon a showing of bias[13] or, arguably, if a person requests a doctor of the same gender. Some local rules have provisions regarding the selection of a neutral examiner.[14] The court order must designate the examiner, and may be invalid if it fails to do so.

Testimony of Examiner

The party conducting the examination may call the examiner to testify as an expert witness (assuming the criteria for expert testi-

cause requires, initially, that the desired information cannot be obtained by other means.").

7. *Doe v. District of Columbia*, 229 F.R.D. 24, 26 (D.D.C.2005); *Cauley v. Ingram Micro, Inc.*, 216 F.R.D. 241 (W.D.N.Y. 2003).

8. *Schlagenhauf v. Holder*, 379 U.S. 104, 118, 85 S.Ct. 234, 242, 13 L.Ed.2d 152 (1964); *Houghton v. M & F Fishing, Inc.*, 198 F.R.D. 666 (S.D.Cal.2001); *but see Simpson v. University of Colorado*, 220 F.R.D. 354, 362 (D.Colo.2004) (the rule is to be construed liberally in favor of granting the examination).

9. *See Chaney v. Venture Transport, Inc.*, 2004 WL 445134 (E.D.La.2004); *Nyfield v. Virgin Islands Telephone Corp.*, 2001 WL 378858 (D.Virgin Islands 2001).

10. *See Bradford Felmly v. Hills*, 222 F.R.D. 257, 258–59 (D.Virgin Islands 2004); *Ali v. Wang Labs., Inc.*, 162 F.R.D. 165 (M.D.Fla.1995).

11. *Merritt v. Stolt Offshore, Inc.*, 2004 WL 224578 (E.D.La.2004) (holding that the court may order more than one examiner,

but noting that some states hold differently); *Fischer v. Coastal Towing, Inc.*, 168 F.R.D. 199, 201 (E.D.Tex.1996) (vocational-rehabilitation expert deemed a "suitably licensed and/or certified examiner").

12. *Douponce v. Drake*, 183 F.R.D. 565, 566 (D.Colo.1998) (allowing the defendant's selected examiner despite allegations of bias); *Lahr v. Fulbright & Jaworski, L.L.P.*, 164 F.R.D. 196, 202–03 (N.D.Tex.1995).

13. *See O'Sullivan v. Rivera*, 229 F.R.D. 184 (D.N.M.2004) (the fact that the expert regularly testifies for defendants does not disqualify the expert under Rule 35); *Nyfield v. Virgin Islands Telephone Corp.*, 2001 WL 378858 (D.Virgin Islands 2001) ("There is no requirement that a Rule 35 examination be conducted by a physician wholly unconnected with either party and absent evidence of bias, Defendants should be allowed their chosen examiner.").

14. *But see Hunt v. R & B Falcon Drilling USA, Inc.*, 2000 WL 1838327 (E.D.La. 2000) (a motion for a court appointed examiner is more properly brought under Federal Rule of Evidence 706).

mony are satisfied). The courts are split as to whether the party who was examined may call the examiner as an expert.[15]

Type of Exams

The type of exams allowable depends on the circumstances of the case. Exams can include blood tests, x-rays, electrocardiograms, fingerprint analysis,[16] and other safe, medically accepted tests indicated by the condition at issue.[17] Vocational exams are also permissible under Rule 35.[18] The burden on the movant to show good cause will be greater if the tests are more invasive, painful, or burdensome, or if repeated examinations are sought. However, a party that objects to a particular test as too painful or invasive may be precluded from offering evidence of the type that would result from the test. A court may also limit testing to only those tests that have been specifically identified.[19]

Mental Examinations

Psychiatric examinations are allowable if a person's mental condition is at issue.[20] The examination may be conducted by a psychiatrist or psychologist. Courts are divided as to whether a claim for emotional distress places the plaintiff's mental condition at issue.[21]

Safety of Tests

In order to oppose a mental or physical exam on the grounds that the exam is unsafe, a party must demonstrate that the proposed test is potentially dangerous. Thereafter, the burden shifts to the party requesting the examination to show that it is both necessary and safe.[22]

Second Examinations

When permanent injuries are claimed or under other appropriate circumstances, the court may allow a second examination just

---

15. *Lehan v. Ambassador Programs, Inc.*, 190 F.R.D. 670 (E.D.Wash.2000) (discussing the various positions taken by the courts on this issue).

16. *Harris v. Athol–Royalston Regional School Dist. Committee*, 206 F.R.D. 30, 32–33 (D.Mass.2002) (fingerprint samples may be obtained under either Rule 34 or Rule 35).

17. *See Jefferys v. LRP Publications, Inc.*, 184 F.R.D. 262, 263 (E.D.Pa.1999) (allowing interview by vocational expert).

18. *See Storms v. Lowe's Home Centers, Inc.*, 211 F.R.D. 296, 297 (W.D.Va.2002); *Douris v. County of Bucks*, 2000 WL 1358481 (E.D.Pa.2000).

19. *Hirschheimer v. Associated Metals & Minerals Corp.*, 1995 WL 736901, at *4 (S.D.N.Y.1995); *contra Ragge v. MCA/Universal Studios*, 165 F.R.D. 605, 609 (C.D.Cal.1995).

20. Roberson v. Bair, 242 F.R.D. 130 (D.D.C. 2007) (emotional distress claim places the plaintiff's condition at issue). *See also Smith v. J.I. Case Corp.*, 163 F.R.D. 229, 230 (E.D.Pa.1995)(discussing four possible situations in which a party's mental condition is in controversy).

21. *See E.E.O.C. v. Grief Bros. Corp.*, 218 F.R.D. 59, 61 (W.D.N.Y. 2003) (mental examinations may be obtained where a plaintiff's allegations of emotional distress amount to more than a claim for garden variety emotional distress damages); *Ford v. Contra Costa County*, 179 F.R.D. 579, 579–80 (N.D.Cal.1998) (mere claim for emotional distress damages does not place mental condition at issue); *E.E.O.C. v. Old Western Furniture Corp.*, 173 F.R.D. 444, 445–46 (W.D.Tex.1996); *Neal v. Siegel–Robert, Inc.*, 171 F.R.D. 264 (E.D.Mo.1996).

22. *Pena v. Troup*, 163 F.R.D. 352, 353–54 (D.Colo.1995).

before trial.[23] A stronger showing of necessity is usually required for a second examination.[24]

Time and Location

The court will designate the time and location of the examination in the order. Usually, the plaintiff will be required to travel to the district where the action is pending to be examined.[25]

Cost of Examination

The moving party must pay the medical or professional expenses of the examination. The person to be examined is not compensated, however, for transportation costs[26] and lost time.

Who Is Present at Examination

The court has discretion to determine who may be present at the examination.[27] Some courts allow the person being examined by a doctor to bring his own physician, others do not.[28] It is also unsettled as to whether attorneys have a right to be present.[29]

Persons Subject to Examination

Any party is subject to examination upon motion by any other party, provided that the physical or mental condition of the party to be examined is at issue.[30] Additionally, a person who is within the control of a party is subject to examination. Thus, a parent suing on behalf of an injured child may have to produce the child for examination.[31] This principle has also been extended to a spouse when one spouse is suing for injuries to the other.[32] In such case, the party has a duty to make a good faith effort to obtain the person's presence.[33]

23. See *Galieti v. State Farm Mutual Automobile Ins. Co.*, 154 F.R.D. 262 (D.Colo.1994).

24. *Furlong v. Circle Line Statue of Liberty Ferry, Inc.*, 902 F.Supp. 65 (S.D.N.Y. 1995).

25. *Landry v. Green Bay & Western R. Co.*, 121 F.R.D. 400 (E.D.Wis.1988).

26. *McCloskey v. UPS*, 171 F.R.D. 268, 270 (D.Or.1997).

27. See *Bethel v. Dixie Homecrafters, Inc.*, 192 F.R.D. 320 (N.D. Ga.2000); *Ali v. Wang Labs., Inc.*, 162 F.R.D. 165, 168 (M.D.Fla.1995).

28. *Favale v. Roman Catholic Diocese of Bridgeport*, 235 F.R.D. 553, 555 (D.Conn. 2006) (Rule 35 does not provide for anyone to be present); *Shirsat v. Mutual Pharmaceutical Co., Inc.*, 169 F.R.D. 68, 71 (E.D.Pa. 1996).

29. *Marsch v. Rensselaer County*, 218 F.R.D. 367, 371 (N.D.N.Y.2003) (although attorneys are generally not permitted to be present during the examination, Fifth Amendment concerns dictated allowing counsel to be present); *Cabana v. Forcier*, 200 F.R.D. 9 (D.Mass.2001) (the clear majority of federal courts have refused to permit third party observers at Rule 35 examinations); *Gensbauer v. May Department Stores Co.*, 184 F.R.D. 552 (E.D.Pa.1999).

30. *Schlagenhauf v. Holder*, 379 U.S. 104, 85 S.Ct. 234, 13 L.Ed.2d 152 (1964).

31. The Advisory Committee Note to the 1970 amendment of Rule 35(a); *but see Caban v. 600 E. 21st Street Co.*, 200 F.R.D. 176 (E.D.N.Y.2001) (a guardian suing on behalf of a child is not the party or within the control of the party, and thus is not subject to examination under Rule 35).

32. *In re Certain Asbestos Cases*, 112 F.R.D. 427, 434 (N.D.Tex.1986).

33. The Advisory Committee Note to the 1970 amendment of Rule 35(a).

Sanctions

If a party fails to comply with the order, most of the sanctions in Rule 37(b)(2) are available, such as deeming certain facts established or refusing to allow the violator to oppose or support certain claims. However, contempt sanctions are not available for failure to submit to the examination.[34] If a person within the control of a party is to be examined, no sanctions apply to that person because he is not a party. The party's duty is to make a good faith effort to obtain the person's presence, and the party will be subject to the sanctions if the party fails to make the requisite good faith effort.[35]

Actions Applicable

Examinations are available in all civil actions in federal court,[36] subject to certain narrow exceptions in Rule 81. The court may also order an examination in connection with a deposition to perpetuate testimony under Rule 27.[37]

Appeal

The courts are split as to whether an order directing or refusing an examination is interlocutory, and thus generally not appealable until the end of the action or may be appealed immediately as a collateral order.[38] It is reviewed under the abuse of discretion standard.[39]

RULE 35(b). EXAMINER'S REPORT

CORE CONCEPT

Upon request by the party or person examined, the party moving for the examination must provide a copy of a detailed written report by the examiner, together with any reports of earlier examinations for the same condition.[40] Following the delivery of such a copy, the examined party must provide copies of reports of the results of any other examinations for the same condition, whether conducted before or after the Rule 35 examination.

APPLICATIONS

Examination by Agreement

The report exchanging provisions apply to examinations by agreement unless the agreement expressly provides otherwise.

34. *Sibbach v. Wilson & Co.*, 312 U.S. 1, 61 S.Ct. 422, 85 L.Ed. 479 (1941).

35. The Advisory Committee Note to the 1970 amendment of Rule 35(a).

36. *Caban v. 600 E. 21st Street Co.*, 200 F.R.D. 176 (E.D.N.Y.2001) (Rule 35 governs in diversity cases even in the face of conflicting state rules regarding examinations of parties).

37. *See* Rules 27(a)(3) and 27(b).

38. *See Goodman v. Harris County*, 443 F.3d 464, 467–68 (5th Cir.2006) (applying the factors for appeal of a collateral order to a Rule 35 order); *O'Malley v. Chrysler Corp.*, 160 F.2d 35 (7th Cir.1947).

39. *Green v. Branson*, 108 F.3d 1296, 1304 (10th Cir.1997).

40. *See Grajales–Romero v. American Airlines, Inc.*, 194 F.3d 288, 298 (1st Cir. 1999) (duty to exchange applies to an examination voluntarily submitted to by the plaintiff).

Effect of Report

Testimony by the examiner will be limited to the opinions disclosed in the report.[41]

Waiver of Privilege

A request for a report under Rule 35 acts as a waiver of the doctor-patient or psychologist-patient privilege for other examinations for the same condition.[42] Thus, the examined party may not refuse to produce other reports on the basis of privilege once the party has requested a copy of the report of the Rule 35 examination. Note that the Rule 35 waiver may be avoided by attempting to obtain the reports via another discovery rule or another procedural device.

Other Discovery Procedures

The parties may use other discovery procedures in lieu of or in addition to the report exchange procedures in Rule 35, such as document requests or depositions of the examiner.

Failure to Exchange

If either party fails to provide covered reports, the court can order production.

Failure to Draft Report

If the examiner fails to prepare or provide a report, the court may exclude the examiner's testimony.

Extraneous Material

If the report contains extraneous or unreasonably prejudicial material, the court can order certain portions excised.

Reports for Persons Under Control of Party

If a person is examined under Rule 35 because that person is in the control of a party, the party is entitled to the same reporting rights and obligations as the person would be.

ADDITIONAL RESEARCH REFERENCES

Wright & Miller, *Federal Practice and Procedure* §§ 2231–2239.

C.J.S. Federal Civil Procedure §§ 752–755.

West's Key No. Digests, Federal Civil Procedure ⚬1651–1664.

41. *Licciardi v. TIG Insurance Group,* 140 F.3d 357 (1st Cir.1998) (testimony beyond the scope of the report excluded).

42. *Cunningham v. Connecticut Mutual Life Insurance,* 845 F.Supp. 1403 (S.D.Cal. 1994).

RULE 36

REQUESTS FOR ADMISSION

(a) Scope and Procedure.

(1) *Scope.* A party may serve on any other party a written request to admit, for purposes of the pending action only, the truth of any matters within the scope of Rule 26(b)(1) relating to:

(A) facts, the application of law to fact, or opinions about either; and

(B) the genuineness of any described documents.

(2) *Form; Copy of a Document.* Each matter must be separately stated. A request to admit the genuineness of a document must be accompanied by a copy of the document unless it is, or has been, otherwise furnished or made available for inspection and copying.

(3) *Time to Respond; Effect of Not Responding.* A matter is admitted unless, within 30 days after being served, the party to whom the request is directed serves on the requesting party a written answer or objection addressed to the matter and signed by the party or its attorney. A shorter or longer time for responding may be stipulated to under Rule 29 or be ordered by the court.

(4) *Answer.* If a matter is not admitted, the answer must specifically deny it or state in detail why the answering party cannot truthfully admit or deny it. A denial must fairly respond to the substance of the matter; and when good faith requires that a party qualify an answer or deny only a part of a matter, the answer must specify the part admitted and qualify or deny the rest. The answering party may assert lack of knowledge or information as a reason for failing to admit or deny only if the party states that it has made reasonable inquiry and that the information it knows or can readily obtain is insufficient to enable it to admit or deny.

(5) *Objections.* The grounds for objecting to a request must be stated. A party must not object solely on the

ground that the request presents a genuine issue for trial.

(6) *Motion Regarding the Sufficiency of an Answer or Objection.* The requesting party may move to determine the sufficiency of an answer or objection. Unless the court finds an objection justified, it must order that an answer be served. On finding that an answer does not comply with this rule, the court may order either that the matter is admitted or that an amended answer be served. The court may defer its final decision until a pretrial conference or a specified time before trial. Rule 37(a)(5) applies to an award of expenses.

(b) Effect of an Admission; Withdrawing or Amending It. A matter admitted under this rule is conclusively established unless the court, on motion, permits the admission to be withdrawn or amended. Subject to Rule 16(e), the court may permit withdrawal or amendment if it would promote the presentation of the merits of the action and if the court is not persuaded that it would prejudice the requesting party in maintaining or defending the action on the merits. An admission under this rule is not an admission for any other purpose and cannot be used against the party in any other proceeding.

[Amended December 27, 1946, effective March 19, 1948; March 30, 1970, effective July 1, 1970; March 2, 1987, effective August 1, 1987; April 22, 1993, effective December 1, 1993; April 30, 2007, effective December 1, 2007.]

2007 AMENDMENTS ROADMAP

STYLE PROJECT CHANGES: The final sentence of the first paragraph of Rule 36(a) was deleted as an unnecessary cross-reference to the discovery moratorium provisions of Rule 26(d). An unnecessary reference to Rule 37(c) was also deleted from the second paragraph of Rule 36(a). Rule 36(a) was broken into 6 new labeled subsections, and Rule 36(b) was relabeled. "Request to admit" was substituted for "request for admission"; "must" replaced "shall"; and the language was shortened and clarified.

NON-STYLE CHANGES: None.

NOTE: The Federal Rules "Style Project" is explained in Part III-A.

AUTHORS' COMMENTARY ON RULE 36

———————————— PURPOSE AND SCOPE ————————————

Rule 36 allows each party to require other parties to admit each relevant fact not in controversy, thereby eliminating the need to produce witnesses and evidence in support of these facts. It must be read in conjunction with Rule 26, which establishes the scope of all discovery rules.

RULE 36(a). SCOPE AND PROCEDURE

CORE CONCEPT

Rule 36 establishes a procedure whereby one party serves requests for admission on another party, who must investigate and either admit, deny with specificity, or object to each requested admission.

APPLICATIONS

Who May Serve

Any party may serve requests for admission.

Who May Be Served

Requests for admission are limited to parties to the action, although the party need not be an adverse party.

Time for Service

Requests for admission can be served after the parties have conducted the discovery conference under Rule 26(f).[1] In proceedings listed in Rule 26(a)(1)(B) as exempt from initial disclosures, there is no preliminary waiting period for requests for admission. The Rules do not set an outer limit on how late in the case requests for admission may be served, and courts are split as to whether requests for admission are discovery devices subject to a general discovery cutoff.[2] However, many local rules or case management orders will set a limit for requests for admission. Usually, when such a time limit exists, requests for admission must be served so that the response is due before the specified deadline.[3]

Contents of Request

Each fact[4] or matter for which admission is requested should be

---

1. *DIRECTV, Inc. v. DeVries*, 302 F.Supp.2d 837, 838 (W.D.Mich.2004).

2. *See Jinks–Umstead v. England*, 227 F.R.D. 143, 153 (D.D.C.2005) (requests are governed by the discovery cut-off date); *Gluck v. Ansett Australia Ltd.*, 204 F.R.D. 217, 218–19 (D.D.C.2001) (discussing the split and citing cases on both sides).

3. *Laborers' Pension Fund v. Blackmore Sewer Const., Inc.*, 298 F.3d 600, 605 (7th Cir.2002).

4. *See Fisher v. Baltimore Life Ins. Co.*, 235 F.R.D. 617 (N.D.W.Va.2006) (a request for an admission that seeks the application of law to fact is proper); Disability Rights Council v. Wash. Metro. Area, 234 F.R.D. 1, 3 (D.D.C.2006) (a request to admit a pure matter of law is improper).

set forth in a separate paragraph.[5] All facts that are part of the request should be set forth in the request—it is improper to incorporate facts by reference to other text.

Scope

The scope of requests for admission is the broad discovery available under Rule 26.[6] Generally, any relevant, non-privileged matter is covered unless it was prepared in anticipation of litigation or pertains to expert witnesses. The requests may pertain to any issue that is or may be in the case, including the ultimate facts at issue,[7] the application of law to fact,[8] jurisdiction, or the statute of limitations.

Number

Rule 36 contains no limitation on the number of requests for admission. Some districts have local rules limiting the number of requests.

Authenticity of Documents

A request may ask that the genuineness or authenticity of a document be admitted.[9] If so, a copy of the document should be attached, unless already provided.

Who Must Receive Copies

All parties must be served with a copy of the requests for admissions.

Time to Answer

A written response is due within 30 days of service. The time to answer may be extended by written agreement under Rule 29.[10] Additionally, the court has discretion to lengthen or shorten the time in which a party must respond.[11]

Service of Response

Copies of the response should be served on the propounding party and all other parties, unless the court has ordered otherwise.

---

5. *See United States v. Los Angeles County,* 235 F.R.D. 675 (E.D.Cal.2006) (requests for admission should not contain compound, conjunctive, or disjunctive statements).

6. *Johnson v. Royal Coal Co.,* 326 F.3d 421, 424, n.2 (4th Cir.2003); *City of Rome v. United States,* 450 F.Supp. 378 (D.D.C. 1978), *affirmed,* 446 U.S. 156, 100 S.Ct. 1548, 64 L.Ed.2d 119 (1980).

7. *In re Carney,* 258 F.3d 415, 419 (5th Cir.2001). *But see North Louisiana Rehabilitation Center, Inc. v. United States,* 179 F.Supp.2d 658, 663 (W.D.La.2001) (allowing withdrawal of an admission because the ultimate issues are better decided on the merits).

8. *In re Carney,* 258 F.3d 415, 419 (5th Cir.2001).

9. *Booth Oil Site Administrative Group v. Safety–Kleen Corporation,* 194 F.R.D. 76, 80 (W.D.N.Y.2000).

10. *Simien v. Chemical Waste Management, Inc.,* 30 F.Supp.2d 939, 941, n. 1 (W.D.La.1998).

11. *Manatt v. Union Pacific R.R. Co.,* 122 F.3d 514, 517 (8th Cir.1997); *A. Farber & Partners, Inc. v. Garber,* 237 F.R.D. 250, 257 (C.D.Cal. 2006) (responses served 2 days late deemed timely).

Form of Response

The response should be in writing and signed by the party or the attorney.[12] It should be a single document organized in numbered paragraphs to correspond to the requests.

Responses

The responding party essentially has four possible responses to a request for admission. The party can admit the request (in part or in full), deny the request (in part or in full), set forth reasons why the party cannot admit or deny the request, or object to the request (by a specific objection or by a motion for a protective order).

Duty to Supplement

Rule 26(e) imposes a duty to supplement a denial or statement of inability to admit or deny if the party learns that the original response is in some material respect incomplete or incorrect, and if the additional or corrective information has not been provided to the other parties in writing or at a deposition.[13]

Denials

A denial must specifically address the substance of the requested admission.[14] The denial may be as simple as the single word "denied,"[15] or may be a longer sentence, but may not sidestep the request or be evasive.[16] If the propounding party feels that the denial is not sufficiently specific, the party can move the court to determine the sufficiency of the denial. If the court deems the denial not sufficiently specific, it can deem the denial an admission or order a more specific answer.

Partial Denial

If the responding party believes that part of a requested admission is accurate and part is not, the proper response is to admit the accurate portion and deny the balance.[17]

Inability to Admit or Deny

If the responding party is genuinely unable to admit or deny the requested admission, the party can so state, but must describe in detail why after reasonable inquiry the party cannot admit or

12. The Advisory Committee Note to Rule 36(a).

13. *See House v. Giant of Maryland LLC*, 232 F.R.D. 257, 259 (E.D.Va.2005).

14. The Advisory Committee Note to Rule 36(a); *Fisher v. Baltimore Life Ins. Co.*, 235 F.R.D. 617 (N.D.W.Va.2006) (the denial must "meet the substance of the requested admission"); *ATD Corp. v. Lydall, Inc.*, 159 F.3d 534, 548 (Fed.Cir.1998).

15. *Caruso v. Coleman Co.*, 1995 WL 347003 (E.D.Pa.1995); *Wanke v. Lynn's Transp. Co.*, 836 F.Supp. 587 (N.D.Ind. 1993).

16. *Asea, Inc. v. Southern Pac. Transp. Co.*, 669 F.2d 1242, 1245 (9th Cir.1981) (evasive denial may be deemed an admission); *United States v. Los Angeles County*, 235 F.R.D. 675 (E.D.Cal.2006) ("When the purpose and significance of a request are reasonably clear, courts do not permit denials based on an overly-technical reading of the request.").

17. *ATD Corp. v. Lydall, Inc.*, 159 F.3d 534, 549 (Fed.Cir.1998); *Henry v. Champlain Enterprises, Inc.*, 212 F.R.D. 73, 78 (N.D.N.Y.2003).

deny.[18] A general statement that the responding party has insufficient information to respond will be treated as an insufficient answer, and upon motion the court will treat the answer as an admission or will order a further answer.[19]

Objections

Objections must be made in writing within the time allowed for answering. If answering some requests and objecting to others, the objections should be included in the document containing the answers. Typical grounds for objections to requests for admission are:

- *Privilege:* If a response requires the disclosure of privileged matters, it is objectionable.[20] *See* Rule 26 (discussion of commonly asserted privileges).

- *Vague or Ambiguous:* A request may be objectionable if it is so vague or ambiguous that the responding party cannot answer it.

- *Outside the Scope of Discovery:* Rule 36 is limited to relevant matters, as defined by Rule 26. Thus, if a requested admission is irrelevant to the issues that are or may be in the case, it is objectionable.[21]

Improper Objections

An improper objection is not the same as an admission, and the proper response to an improper objection is to file a motion to compel a further response.[22] It is irrelevant who has the burden of proof with respect to the matter for which admission is requested. Likewise, a party cannot refuse to answer a request on the basis that the serving party already knows the answer. Similarly, a party cannot refuse to answer a request on the basis that it pertains to ultimate facts in the case or facts for proof at trial.[23]

Opinions and Conclusions

Rule 36 explicitly states that a request for admission is not objectionable because it involves an opinion or contention that

18. *United States v. Los Angeles County,* 235 F.R.D. 675 (E.D.Cal.2006); *Taborn v. Unknown Officers,* 2001 WL 138908 (N.D.Ill.2001) (reasonable inquiry includes investigation and inquiry of any of defendant's officers, administrators, agents, employees, servants, enlisted or other personnel who may have information which may lead to or furnish the necessary and appropriate response); *Uniden America Corp. v. Ericsson Inc.,* 181 F.R.D. 302, 303 (M.D.N.C.1998) (respondent may even have a duty to make an inquiry of third parties).

19. *City of Rome v. United States,* 450 F.Supp. 378 (D.D.C.1978), *affirmed,* 446 U.S. 156, 100 S.Ct. 1548, 64 L.Ed.2d 119 (1980).

20. *United States v. One Tract of Real Property Together With all Buildings, Improvements, Appurtenances, and Fixtures,* 95 F.3d 422, 428 (6th Cir.1996).

21. *But see Bell v. Domino's Pizza, Inc.,* 2000 WL 1780266 (D.D.C.2000) (relevance concerns are diminished with requests for admission because they cannot be used in any other proceeding).

22. *Butler v. Oak Creek–Franklin School Dist.,* 172 F.Supp.2d 1102, 1122, n.9 (E.D.Wis.2001).

23. *Taborn v. Unknown Officers,* 2001 WL 138908 (N.D.Ill.2001); the Advisory Committee Note to Rule 36(a).

relates to fact or the application of law to fact.[24] Rule 36 does not authorize a request that requires a pure legal conclusion, without application to the facts.[25]

Motion for a Protective Order

As an alternative to making objections to individual requests for admission, the responding party may make a motion for a protective order under Rule 26(c). A motion for a protective order is appropriate when most or all of a set of requests is objectionable. The motion must be accompanied by a certification that the parties met prior to the filing of the motion and attempted to resolve their dispute without intervention of the court.

Failure to Respond

Failure to respond in a timely fashion is deemed an admission.[26] The court has discretion to allow a party to submit responses after the allowed time for a response.[27]

Motion to Determine Sufficiency

If a party believes that a response is insufficient or that an objection is improper, the party can move the court to determine the sufficiency of the answer.[28] Note that "insufficient" refers to the specificity of the response, not whether the response is correct or in good faith.[29] The burden will be on the party raising an objection to show that the objection was proper.[30] If the court determines that the answer was insufficient, it can deem the answer an admission or can order a more complete answer.[31] The court may also defer ruling until later in the pretrial proceedings.[32]

Expenses of Motion to Determine Sufficiency

The party losing a motion to determine the sufficiency of a response pays the other party's expenses, including a reasonable

---

24. *Marchand v. Mercy Medical Center,* 22 F.3d 933 (9th Cir.1994); *Miller v. Holzmann,* 240 F.R.D. 1, 4–5 (D.D.C. 2006).

25. *Miller v. Holzmann,* 240 F.R.D. 1, 4–5 (D.D.C. 2006); *Tulip Computers Intern., B.V. v. Dell Computer Corp.,* 210 F.R.D. 100, 108 (D.Del.2002).

26. *Walsh v. McCain Foods, Ltd.,* 81 F.3d 722, 726 (7th Cir.1996); *Switchmusic.com, Inc. v. U.S. Music Corp.,* 416 F.Supp.2d 812, 817 (C.D.Cal.2006) (no motion is necessary–unanswered requests are automatically deemed admitted); *Kansas City Cable Partners ex rel. Time Warner Entertainment Co., L.P. v. Espy,* 250 F.Supp.2d 1296, 1297 (D.Kan.2003).

27. *Banks v. Office of the Senate Sergeant-at-Arms and Doorkeeper,* 226 F.R.D. 113, 118 (D.D.C.2005) (the rule is not applied woodenly); *A. Farber & Partners, Inc. v. Garber,* 237 F.R.D. 250, 257 (C.D.Cal. 2006) (responses served 2 days late deemed timely).

28. *Disability Rights Council v. Wash. Metro. Area,* 234 F.R.D. 1, 3 (D.D.C.2006) (a motion to determine the sufficiency of a response is the mechanism for having an inadequate response deemed an admission); *Tri–State Hosp. Supply Corp. v. United States,* 226 F.R.D. 118, 138 (D.D.C.2005); *In re Heritage Bond Litigation,* 220 F.R.D. 624, 626 (C.D.Cal.2004).

29. *Foretich v. Chung,* 151 F.R.D. 3 (D.D.C.1993).

30. *Moses v. Halstead,* 236 F.R.D. 667, 680 (D.Kan. 2006).

31. *See Ruran v. Beth El Temple of West Hartford, Inc.,* 226 F.R.D. 165, 168 (D.Conn.2005); *Security Ins. Co. of Hartford v. DHL Worldwide Exp. NV,* 2001 WL 55460 (N.D.Ill.2001).

32. The Advisory Committee Note to Rule 36(a).

attorney fee, incurred in connection with the motion, pursuant to Rule 37(a)(5).[33]

Sanctions

The sanctions available depend upon the conduct of the responding party. The sanction for failure to respond is that the requests are deemed admitted.[34] The sanction for improperly denying a request is that the responding party will be required to pay the costs of the other party incurred in proving the matter, including attorney fees, under Rule 37(c).[35] The sanction for an insufficient answer or improper objection is that the response may be deemed an admission, plus the responding party will be liable for the other party's expenses in bringing the motion, including a reasonable attorney fee. The sanctions for failing to obey a court order to make a further response are the sanctions set forth in Rule 37(b)(2), such as deeming certain facts established or refusing to allow the party to oppose or support certain claims. Furthermore, the court must award reasonable expenses, including attorney fees, caused by the responding party's failure to comply with the order, unless the court finds that the failure was justified. Sanctions can be awarded against the party under Rule 37(c) and/or against the attorney under Rule 26(g).[36]

Appeals

The court's rulings on the sufficiency of and objections to requests for admissions are reviewed under an abuse of discretion standard. Usually, such rulings are not final orders, and cannot be appealed until the conclusion of the case.

RULE 36(b). EFFECT OF AN ADMISSION; WITHDRAWING OR AMENDING IT

CORE CONCEPT

An admission is deemed conclusively established unless the court permits withdrawal or amendment of the admission.[37]

APPLICATIONS

Proceedings Covered

An admission is only binding within the action in which the

33. *Epling v. UCB Films, Inc.*, 2000 WL 1466216 (D.Kan.2000).

34. *Weiss v. National Westminster Bank, PLC*, 242 F.R.D. 33 (E.D.N.Y. 2007).

35. *House v. Giant of Maryland LLC*, 232 F.R.D. 257, 260 (E.D.Va.2005); *National Semiconductor Corp. v. Ramtron International Corp.*, 265 F.Supp.2d 71 (D.D.C. 2003).

36. *Johnson International Co. v. Jackson National Life Ins. Co.*, 19 F.3d 431 (8th Cir.1994).

37. *Tate v. Farmland Industries, Inc.*, 268 F.3d 989, 998–99 (10th Cir.2001); *Switchmusic.com, Inc. v. U.S. Music Corp.*, 416 F.Supp.2d 812, 817 (C.D.Cal.2006); *T. Rowe Price Small–Cap Fund, Inc. v. Oppenheimer & Co., Inc.*, 174 F.R.D. 38, 44 (S.D.N.Y.1997) ("Rule 36 responses become, in effect, sworn evidence that is binding upon the respondent at trial.").

request was served.[38] An admission may be introduced at trial or in the context of a motion, such as a motion for summary judgment.[39]

Evidentiary Objections

Admissions are still subject to evidentiary objections at trial, such as hearsay.[40] However, adverse parties can use the exception to the hearsay rule for admissions of party opponents.[41]

Party Making Admission

The party making the admission may not introduce it at trial.[42]

Coparties Not Bound

An admission will only be binding on the admitting party and will not be binding on any coparties.[43]

Withdrawal

A party may move to withdraw or amend an admission.[44] The court may allow withdrawal or amendment when it will aid in the resolution of the matter on the merits and when the party who obtained the admission will not be prejudiced by the amendment or withdrawal.[45] Normally, changed circumstances or honest error will be valid grounds.[46] Amendment or withdrawal will not be allowed where prejudice will result to the opponent from reliance on the admission.[47] The court has broad discretion in ruling on motions to

---

38. *American Civil Liberties Union v. The Florida Bar*, 999 F.2d 1486 (11th Cir. 1993); *Bell v. Domino's Pizza, Inc.*, 2000 WL 1780266 (D.D.C.2000).

39. *See Universal City Studios Productions LLLP v. Bigwood*, 441 F.Supp.2d 185, 187 (D.Me. 2006); *Switchmusic.com, Inc. v. U.S. Music Corp.*, 416 F.Supp.2d 812, 817 (C.D.Cal.2006).

40. *Walsh v. McCain Foods Ltd.*, 81 F.3d 722, 726 (7th Cir.1996).

41. *Id.*

42. *In re Air Crash*, 982 F.Supp. 1060, 1067 (D.S.C.1996), *aff'd*, 105 F.3d 1042 (5th Cir.1997).

43. *Becerra v. Asher*, 921 F.Supp. 1538, 1544 (S.D.Tex.1996).

44. *In re Carney*, 258 F.3d 415, 419 (5th Cir.2001) (discussing the standards for a motion to withdraw an admission). *Kalis v. Colgate–Palmolive Co.*, 231 F.3d 1049, 1059 (7th Cir.2000) (the proper procedural vehicle to withdraw admissions is a motion under Rule 36(b)).

45. *Raiser v. Utah County*, 409 F.3d 1243, 1246 (10th Cir.2005) (inconvenience does not constitute prejudice); *Gallegos v. City of Los Angeles*, 308 F.3d 987, 993 (9th Cir.2002) (The prejudice relates to the difficulty a party may face in proving its case,

such as problems caused by the unavailability of key witnesses, or the sudden need to obtain evidence with respect to the questions previously deemed admitted); *Perez v. Miami–Dade County*, 297 F.3d 1255, 1265 (11th Cir.2002), *cert. denied*, 537 U.S. 1193, 123 S.Ct. 1291, 154 L.Ed.2d 1028 (2003) (a district court abuses its discretion in denying a motion to withdraw or amend admissions when it applies some other criterion beyond the two-part test—or grossly misapplies the two-part test—in making its ruling).

46. *See ADM Agri–Industries, Ltd. v. Harvey*, 200 F.R.D. 467 (M.D.Ala.2001) (courts should be reluctant to deny motions to withdraw or amend when final disposition of the case may result from mere discovery noncompliance rather than the merits).

47. *Sonoda v. Cabrera*, 255 F.3d 1035, 1039 (9th Cir.2001) (prejudice refers to the difficulty the non-moving party will have in proving its case, such as by the unavailability of witnesses related to the delay); *In re: Durability Inc.*, 212 F.3d 551 (10th Cir. 2000) (the court's focus in a motion to withdraw an admission is the prejudice on the opposing party, not on the excuse of the moving party).

withdraw or amend admissions.[48]

Binding Nature of Formal Admissions

A matter formally admitted under Rule 36 is conclusively established.[49] In contrast, an informal, extrajudicial admission is evidence, but not conclusive.[50]

Proof of Admission by Failure to Answer

In order to use the failure to answer as an admission, the offering party must prove service of the requests and the failure to answer.[51]

ADDITIONAL RESEARCH REFERENCES

Wright & Miller, *Federal Practice and Procedure* §§ 2251–2265.

C.J.S. Federal Civil Procedure §§ 756–774 et seq.

West's Key No. Digests, Federal Civil Procedure ☞1671–1686.

48. *Conlon v. U.S.*, 474 F.3d 616, 621 (9th Cir. 2007) (Rule 36(b) is permissive, not mandatory); *Raiser v. Utah County*, 409 F.3d 1243, 1245–46 (10th Cir.2005).

49. *Central Admixture Pharmacy Services, Inc. v. Advanced Cardiac Solutions, P.C.*, 482 F.3d 1347, 1352 (Fed.Cir. 2007); *Switchmusic.com, Inc. v. U.S. Music Corp.*, 416 F.Supp.2d 812, 817 (C.D.Cal.2006) (admission under Rule 36 cannot be overcome by offering contradictory affidavits).

50. *Murrey v. United States*, 73 F.3d 1448, 1455 (7th Cir.1996).

51. *Gilbert v. General Motors Corp.*, 133 F.2d 997 (2d Cir.1943), *cert. denied,* 319 U.S. 743, 63 S.Ct. 1031, 87 L.Ed. 1700 (1943).

RULE 37

FAILURE TO MAKE DISCLOSURES OR TO COOPERATE IN DISCOVERY; SANCTIONS

(a) Motion for an Order Compelling Disclosure or Discovery.

(1) *In General.* On notice to other parties and all affected persons, a party may move for an order compelling disclosure or discovery. The motion must include a certification that the movant has in good faith conferred or attempted to confer with the person or party failing to make disclosure or discovery in an effort to obtain it without court action.

(2) *Appropriate Court.* A motion for an order to a party must be made in the court where the action is pending. A motion for an order to a nonparty must be made in the court where the discovery is or will be taken.

(3) *Specific Motions.*

(A) *To Compel Disclosure.* If a party fails to make a disclosure required by Rule 26(a), any other party may move to compel disclosure and for appropriate sanctions.

(B) *To Compel a Discovery Response.* A party seeking discovery may move for an order compelling an answer, designation, production, or inspection. This motion may be made if:

(i) a deponent fails to answer a question asked under Rule 30 or 31;

(ii) a corporation or other entity fails to make a designation under Rule 30(b)(6) or 31(a)(4);

(iii) a party fails to answer an interrogatory submitted under Rule 33; or

(iv) a party fails to respond that inspection will be permitted—or fails to permit inspection—as requested under Rule 34.

(C) *Related to a Deposition.* When taking an oral deposition, the party asking a question may complete or adjourn the examination before moving for an order.

(4) *Evasive or Incomplete Disclosure, Answer, or Response.* For purposes of this subdivision (a), an evasive or incomplete disclosure, answer, or response must be treated as a failure to disclose, answer, or respond.

(5) *Payment of Expenses; Protective Orders.*

(A) *If the Motion Is Granted (or Disclosure or Discovery Is Provided After Filing).* If the motion is granted—or if the disclosure or requested discovery is provided after the motion was filed—the court must, after giving an opportunity to be heard, require the party or deponent whose conduct necessitated the motion, the party or attorney advising that conduct, or both to pay the movant's reasonable expenses incurred in making the motion, including attorney's fees. But the court must not order this payment if:

(i) the movant filed the motion before attempting in good faith to obtain the disclosure or discovery without court action;

(ii) the opposing party's nondisclosure, response, or objection was substantially justified; or

(iii) other circumstances make an award of expenses unjust.

(B) *If the Motion Is Denied.* If the motion is denied, the court may issue any protective order authorized under Rule 26(c) and must, after giving an opportunity to be heard, require the movant, the attorney filing the motion, or both to pay the party or deponent who opposed the motion its reasonable expenses incurred in opposing the motion, including attorney's fees. But the court must not order this payment if the motion was substantially justified or other circumstances make an award of expenses unjust.

(C) *If the Motion Is Granted in Part and Denied in Part.* If the motion is granted in part and de-

784

nied in part, the court may issue any protective order authorized under Rule 26(c) and may, after giving an opportunity to be heard, apportion the reasonable expenses for the motion.

(b) Failure to Comply with a Court Order.

(1) *Sanctions in the District Where the Deposition Is Taken.* If the court where the discovery is taken orders a deponent to be sworn or to answer a question and the deponent fails to obey, the failure may be treated as contempt of court.

(2) *Sanctions in the District Where the Action Is Pending.*

     (A) *For Not Obeying a Discovery Order.* If a party or a party's officer, director, or managing agent—or a witness designated under Rule 30(b)(6) or 31(a)(4)—fails to obey an order to provide or permit discovery, including an order under Rule 26(f), 35, or 37(a), the court where the action is pending may issue further just orders. They may include the following:

         (i) directing that the matters embraced in the order or other designated facts be taken as established for purposes of the action, as the prevailing party claims;

         (ii) prohibiting the disobedient party from supporting or opposing designated claims or defenses, or from introducing designated matters in evidence;

         (iii) striking pleadings in whole or in part;

         (iv) staying further proceedings until the order is obeyed;

         (v) dismissing the action or proceeding in whole or in part;

         (vi) rendering a default judgment against the disobedient party; or

         (vii) treating as contempt of court the failure to obey any order except an order to submit to a physical or mental examination.

     (B) *For Not Producing a Person for Examination.* If a party fails to comply with an order under

Rule 35(a) requiring it to produce another person for examination, the court may issue any of the orders listed in Rule 37(b)(2)(A)(i)–(vi), unless the disobedient party shows that it cannot produce the other person.

(C) *Payment of Expenses.* Instead of or in addition to the orders above, the court must order the disobedient party, the attorney advising that party, or both to pay the reasonable expenses, including attorney's fees, caused by the failure, unless the failure was substantially justified or other circumstances make an award of expenses unjust.

(c) Failure to Disclose, to Supplement an Earlier Response, or to Admit.

(1) *Failure to Disclose or Supplement.* If a party fails to provide information or identify a witness as required by Rule 26(a) or (e), the party is not allowed to use that information or witness to supply evidence on a motion, at a hearing, or at a trial, unless the failure was substantially justified or is harmless. In addition to or instead of this sanction, the court, on motion and after giving an opportunity to be heard:

(A) may order payment of the reasonable expenses, including attorney's fees, caused by the failure;

(B) may inform the jury of the party's failure; and

(C) may impose other appropriate sanctions, including any of the orders listed in Rule 37(b)(2)(A)(i)–(vi).

(2) *Failure to Admit.* If a party fails to admit what is requested under Rule 36 and if the requesting party later proves a document to be genuine or the matter true, the requesting party may move that the party who failed to admit pay the reasonable expenses, including attorney's fees, incurred in making that proof. The court must so order unless:

(A) the request was held objectionable under Rule 36(a);

(B) the admission sought was of no substantial importance;

(C) the party failing to admit had a reasonable ground to believe that it might prevail on the matter; or

(D) there was other good reason for the failure to admit.

(d) Party's Failure to Attend Its Own Deposition, Serve Answers to Interrogatories, or Respond to a Request for Inspection.

(1) *In General.*

(A) *Motion; Grounds for Sanctions.* The court where the action is pending may, on motion, order sanctions if:

(i) a party or a party's officer, director, or managing agent—or a person designated under Rule 30(b)(6) or 31(a)(4)—fails, after being served with proper notice, to appear for that person's deposition; or

(ii) a party, after being properly served with interrogatories under Rule 33 or a request for inspection under Rule 34, fails to serve its answers, objections, or written response.

(B) *Certification.* A motion for sanctions for failing to answer or respond must include a certification that the movant has in good faith conferred or attempted to confer with the party failing to act in an effort to obtain the answer or response without court action.

(2) *Unacceptable Excuse for Failing to Act.* A failure described in Rule 37(d)(1)(A) is not excused on the ground that the discovery sought was objectionable, unless the party failing to act has a pending motion for a protective order under Rule 26(c).

(3) *Types of Sanctions.* Sanctions may include any of the orders listed in Rule 37(b)(2)(A)(i)–(vi). Instead of or in addition to these sanctions, the court must require the party failing to act, the attorney advising that party, or both to pay the reasonable expenses, including attorney's fees, caused by the failure, unless the failure was substantially justified or other circumstances make an award of expenses unjust.

(e) Failure to Provide Electronically Stored Information. Absent exceptional circumstances, a court may not impose sanctions under these rules on a party for failing to provide electronically stored information lost as a result of the routine, good-faith operation of an electronic information system.

(f) Failure to Participate in Framing a Discovery Plan. If a party or its attorney fails to participate in good faith in developing and submitting a proposed discovery plan as required by Rule 26(f), the court may, after giving an opportunity to be heard, require that party or attorney to pay to any other party the reasonable expenses, including attorney's fees, caused by the failure.

[Amended December 29, 1948, effective October 20, 1949; March 30, 1970, effective July 1, 1970; April 29, 1980, effective August 1, 1980; amended by Pub.L. 96–481, Title II, § 205(a), October 21, 1980, 94 Stat. 2330, effective October 1, 1981; amended March 2, 1987, effective August 1, 1987; April 22, 1993, effective December 1, 1993; April 17, 2000, effective December 1, 2000; April 12, 2006, effective December 1, 2006; April 30, 2007, effective December 1, 2007.]

--------- **2007 AMENDMENTS ROADMAP** ---------

STYLE PROJECT CHANGES: Rule 37 was extensively reorganized, subsectioned, and relabeled. Former Rule 37(e), which had been abrogated, was deleted altogether, and Rules 37(f) and 37(g) were renumbered 37(e) and 37(f). The language was also shortened and clarified; active voice was substituted for passive; and "must" replaced "shall."

NON-STYLE CHANGES: None.

NOTE: The Federal Rules "Style Project" is explained in Part III-A.

AUTHORS' COMMENTARY ON RULE 37
--------- **PURPOSE AND SCOPE** ---------

Rule 37 contains the mechanisms for enforcing the provisions of the other discovery rules by imposing sanctions on parties who violate the Rules. In general, obtaining sanctions is a two-step process in which a party must first obtain an order compelling discovery under Rule 37(a), then move for sanctions under Rule 37(b) for failure to comply with the order. If, however, the responding party totally fails to respond to an entire discovery request, the sanctions may be available immediately.

NOTE: Rule 37 was revised in 1993, 2000, 2006, and 2007, and care should be exercised when citing case law pertaining to Rule 37.

2006 AMENDMENTS: The 2006 Amendments to Rule 37 added new subsection (f) addressing electronically stored data. It provides that a party normally cannot be sanctioned for failing to produce electronic data that is lost as a result of the routine operation of the computer system.

RULE 37(a). MOTION FOR AN ORDER COMPELLING DISCLOSURE OR DISCOVERY

CORE CONCEPT

The first step in obtaining sanctions is to make a motion for an order compelling the discovery sought.[1] A motion to compel is filed after the opponent fails to make the automatic disclosures required by Rule 26(a), fails to respond to discovery served pursuant to the discovery rules, or makes an improper or incomplete disclosure or discovery response.

APPLICATIONS

Procedures

Motions to compel are served on all parties and filed with the court. There is no set time limit for filing a motion to compel, and the court will consider delay in filing the motion and the procedural posture of the case in deciding whether a motion to compel is timely.[2]

Certification of Conference

The motion to compel must be accompanied by a certification that the movant has in good faith conferred or attempted to confer with the other party or person in an effort to resolve the dispute without court action.[3]

Which Court

The proper court in which to file a motion to compel depends on the location and status of the person that is the subject of the

---

1. *Helfand v. Gerson*, 105 F.3d 530, 536 (9th Cir.1997) (failure to bring a motion to compel is a waiver of any future objections).

2. *PCS Phosphate Co., Inc. v. Norfolk Southern Corp.*, 238 F.R.D. 555, 558 (E.D.N.C. 2006) (close of discovery often considered deadline for motions to compel where no deadline expressly set); *United States v. MWI Corp.*, 232 F.R.D. 14, 17 (D.D.C.2005) (motion to compel responses to discovery served 2 years earlier deemed timely where no motion for summary judgment pending and no trial date set).

3. *Naviant Marketing Solutions, Inc. v. Larry Tucker, Inc.*, 339 F.R.D. 180 (3rd Cir. 2003); *LaFleur v. Teen Help*, 342 F.3d 1145, 1152 (10th Cir.2003); *Payless Shoesource Worldwide, Inc. v. Target Corp.*, 237 F.R.D. 666, 670–71 (D.Kan. 2006) (certificate should describe efforts to resolve the dispute, which means more than faxing or mailing a letter to the opposing party); *but see Oleson v. Kmart Corp.*, 175 F.R.D. 570, 571 (D.Kan.1997) (entertaining a motion for sanctions where the correspondence between the parties indicated that the dispute would not have been resolved by additional efforts to confer).

motion. If the individual or entity is a party, then a motion to compel must be filed in the court where the action is pending.[4] If the motion to compel pertains to a non-party witness, pursuant to a subpoena for deposition or to produce documents, then only the court issuing the subpoena can enforce it through the court's contempt powers.[5]

Expenses

In general, the victorious party in a motion to compel is entitled to recover its expenses, including a reasonable attorney fee,[6] from the losing party.[7] The movant is also entitled to expenses if the respondent provides a disclosure or discovery response after the motion was filed.[8] The award of expenses by the court is mandatory unless the movant failed to confer with the respondent in good faith prior to filing the motion or the losing party demonstrates that its conduct was "substantially justified,"[9] or if other circumstances render an award of expenses "unjust."[10]

- *Substantially Justified:* Good faith generally does not equate to substantial justification; the losing party must demonstrate some unsettled issue of law or like circumstance.[11] The burden is on the losing party to show that the party's behavior was "substantially justified."

- *Opportunity to be Heard*: The court must provide the non-moving party with an opportunity to be heard, either orally or in writing.[12]

4. *United States v. Diabetes Treatment Centers of America, Inc.*, 444 F.3d 462, 468, n.2 (6th Cir.2006).

5. *United States v. Diabetes Treatment Centers of America, Inc.*, 444 F.3d 462, 468 (6th Cir.2006); *see also* Rule 45 (discussing subpoenas). *But see Platypus Wear, Inc. v. K.D. Co.*, 905 F.Supp. 808, 810 (S.D.Cal. 1995)(holding that a disputed claim of privilege should be presented to the court where the action is pending regardless of the location of the deposition).

6. *Kister v. District of Columbia*, 229 F.R.D. 326, 330 (D.D.C.2005) (attorney may only bill hours to the adversary that would properly be billed to the attorney's own client); *Cobell v. Norton*, 231 F.Supp.2d 295 (D.D.C.2002) (discussing the calculation of a reasonable attorney fee).

7. *See Interactive Products Corp. v. a2z Mobile Office Solutions, Inc.*, 326 F.3d 687, 700 (6th Cir.2003) (motion for leave to take depositions deemed motion to compel, and expenses awarded against unsuccessful movant); *A. Farber and Partners, Inc. v. Garber*, 234 F.R.D. 186, 194 (C.D.Cal.2006); *Stein v. Foamex Intern., Inc.*, 204 F.R.D.

270, 271 (E.D.Pa.2001) (court may not reduce the amount of attorney fees awarded if the amount claimed is demonstrated to be reasonable).

8. *Tuszkiewicz v. Allen–Bradley Co., Inc.*, 172 F.R.D. 396, 398 (E.D.Wis.1997).

9. *Australian Gold, Inc. v. Hatfield*, 436 F.3d 1228, 1244 (10th Cir.2006); *Dukes v. Georgia*, 428 F.Supp.2d 1298 (N.D.Ga. 2006).

10. *Rickels v. City of South Bend, Ind.*, 33 F.3d 785 (7th Cir.1994); *PLX, Inc. v. Prosystems, Inc.*, 220 F.R.D. 291, 298 (N.D.W.Va.2004) (the losing party has the burden of showing that fees should not be awarded).

11. *Pierce v. Underwood*, 487 U.S. 552, 565, 108 S.Ct. 2541, 2550, 101 L.Ed.2d 490 (1988) (motion is substantially justified if it raises an issue about which there is a genuine dispute, or if reasonable people could differ as to the appropriateness of the contested action); *Doe v. Lexington–Fayette Urban County Government*, 407 F.3d 755, 765 (6th Cir.2005).

12. *Kister v. District of Columbia*, 229 F.R.D. 326, 329, n.2 (D.D.C.2005) (written

- *Who Pays Expenses:* The court may impose the expenses on the party, the attorney, or both.[13]

- *Motion Granted in Part:* If a motion to compel is granted in part and denied in part, the court may apportion the expenses as it sees fit.[14]

- *Non-parties:* The expense provisions apply only to certain motions involving non-parties.[15] Fees will be awarded in connection with a non-party making a motion to obtain a copy of the non-party's statement. A non-party may be required to pay expenses incurred because of the non-party's failure to attend a deposition if a court order had already been entered compelling the non-party's attendance.

- *Applicable Discovery Motions:* The expense provisions apply to all but a small group of discovery motions. The expense provisions do *not* apply to: Rule 27—(petition to perpetuate testimony); Rule 28(b)—(application for a commission or letter rogatory to take a deposition in a foreign country); Rule 30(a)—(motion for leave of court to take a deposition); Rule 30(d)(1)—(motion to enlarge or shorten the time for taking a deposition); Rule 33(b)(2)—(motion that a shorter or longer time be allowed to answer interrogatories); Rule 34(b)(2)(A)—(motion that a shorter or longer time be allowed to serve a response to a request for inspection); Rule 35(a)(2)—(motion to compel a physical or mental examination); Rule 35(b)(5)—(motion to compel delivery of report of a physical or mental examination); Rule 37(c)(2)—(motion to assess expenses for failure to make requested admission); and Rule 45(c)(2)(B)(i)—(motion to compel deponent to permit inspection and copying of documents and things subpoenaed for deposition).[16]

- *Fees From United States:* Attorney fees can be awarded against the United States.[17]

- *Appeal of Fee Award:* An award of attorney fees under Rule 37(a)(5) is not a final, appealable order.[18]

submissions provide an opportunity to be heard); *Swackhammer v. Sprint Corp. PCS,* 225 F.R.D. 658, 666–67 (D.Kan.2004).

13. *A. Farber & Partners, Inc. v. Garber,* 237 F.R.D. 250, 257 (C.D.Cal. 2006) (fees awarded jointly against party and attorney); *Hoffman v. United Parcel Service, Inc.,* 206 F.R.D. 506, 507 (D.Kan.2002) (fees should be imposed on the person or entity responsible for the sanctionable conduct).

14. *Export Worldwide, Ltd. v. Knight,* 241 F.R.D. 259, 268 (W.D.Tex. 2006) (parties each bear their costs when motion granted in part); *Sonnino v. University Kansas Hosp. Authority,* 220 F.R.D. 633, 656 (D.Kan.2004).

15. *Athridge v. Aetna Casualty and Surety Co.,* 184 F.R.D. 200, 208 (D.D.C. 1998); *Cuthbertson v. Excel Industries, Inc.,* 179 F.R.D. 599, 602 (D.Kan.1998) (non-party who appeared voluntarily at a deposition without subpoena was not subject to the court's jurisdiction or to sanctions).

16. *Wright, Miller & Marcus, Federal Practice and Procedure:* Civil 2d § 2288.

17. *United States v. Horn,* 29 F.3d 754 (1st Cir.1994)(fees may be assessed against the United States as a sanction); *Cook v. Watt,* 597 F.Supp. 552 (D.Alaska 1984).

18. *Cunningham v. Hamilton County, Ohio,* 527 U.S. 198, 200, 119 S.Ct. 1915, 1917, 144 L.Ed.2d 184 (1999) (fee award

Basis for Motion to Compel

Generally, a motion to compel may only be filed after a discovery request has been properly served and the opposing party has failed to respond. A motion to compel may be filed after a witness improperly refuses to answer a deposition question.[19] A party cannot bring a motion to compel where the subject is not a discovery request to which the other party has not adequately responded.[20]

Evasive or Incomplete Answer

Rule 37(a)(4) states that an evasive or incomplete answer or disclosure is treated as a failure to answer or disclose.[21]

Motion Denied

If a motion to compel is denied, the court can at the same time enter a protective order under Rule 26(c).

RULE 37(b).　FAILURE TO COMPLY WITH A COURT ORDER

CORE CONCEPT

The sanctions listed in Rule 37(b) become available if a party or deponent fails to obey a court order regarding discovery. The court has broad discretion to impose one or more[22] of the listed sanctions or any other sanction it deems appropriate.[23]

APPLICATIONS

Order Prerequisite

The court may not impose sanctions under Rule 37(b) unless it has already issued a discovery order with which a party or deponent has failed to comply.[24] The order may be pursuant to a motion to compel under Rule 37(a) or may be issued in a discovery conference

against attorney is not immediately appealable even if attorney has withdrawn).

19. *Cabana v. Forcier*, 200 F.R.D. 9 (D.Mass.2001).

20. *Mitchell v. National R.R. Passenger Corp.*, 217 F.R.D. 53, 57–58 (D.D.C.2003) (prevailing party not entitled to expenses under Rule 37(a) where motion was to take additional depositions).

21. *International Broth. of Elec. Workers, Local Union No. 545 v. Hope Elec. Corp.*, 380 F.3d 1084, 1105 (8th Cir.2004); *Dotson v. Bravo*, 321 F.3d 663, 667 (7th Cir.2003) (incomplete or evasive responses to interrogatories can support dismissal of the entire action).

22. *Young v. Office of U.S. Senate Sergeant at Arms*, 217 F.R.D. 61, 65, n.2 (D.D.C.2003) (the sanctions are not mutually exclusive)

23. *Anderson v. Foundation for Advancement, Education and Employment of American Indians*, 155 F.3d 500, 504 (4th Cir.1998).

24. *In re: Williams*, 156 F.3d 86, 89 n. 1 (1st Cir.1998); *Nike Inc. v. Wolverine World Wide, Inc.*, 43 F.3d 644 (Fed.Cir.1994)(oral order sufficient to support sanctions); *United States v. Matusoff Rental Co.*, 204 F.R.D. 396, 398 (S.D.Ohio 2001). *But see Monsanto Co. v. Ralph*, 382 F.3d 1374, 1382 (Fed.Cir. 2004) (district court has the inherent power under Rule **37** to sanction abuses of the judicial process irrespective of the existence of any particular order); *Dotson v. Bravo*, 202 F.R.D. 559, 570 (N.D.Ill.2001) (a prior order is not required when extreme discovery abuses have occurred).

under Rule 26(f).[25] Note, however, that the court may impose certain sanctions under Rules 37(c) and 37(d) without having first issued a discovery order, under the circumstances discussed below.

Exception to Order Prerequisite

Courts occasionally use Rule 37 to impose sanctions for inappropriate conduct that does not fall within a specific provision of Rule 37 (i.e., not following an order as provided by Rule 37(b) or under the circumstances listed in Rules 37(c) or (d)).[26]

Sanctions by Court Where Deposition to Occur

If a non-party witness fails to comply with an order to appear and be sworn in for a deposition or an order to answer a question at a deposition, the court in the district where the deposition was to occur may treat the failure as a contempt of court under Rule 37(b)(1).[27]

Sanctions by Court Where Action Pending

Rule 37(b)(2) lists specific categories of sanctions that may be imposed by the court where the action is pending on a party (or an officer, director, or managing agent of a party)[28] who fails to obey an order to permit or provide discovery. The court has broad discretion to impose any sanction or combination of sanctions it deems appropriate,[29] including the following listed sanctions:

- *Deem Facts Established:* The court may deem as established the facts that the moving party was seeking to establish.[30] Thus, where an individual claiming to be totally disabled refused to submit to a physical examination, the court deemed it established that he was not totally disabled.[31]

25. *Lipscher v. LRP Publications, Inc.,* 266 F.3d 1305, 1322–23 (11th Cir.2001) (Rule 37(b) sanctions not available for violation of a protective order under Rule 26(c)), *but see Paul Revere Life Ins. Co. v. Jafari,* 206 F.R.D. 126, 127 (D.Md.2002) (allowing sanctions for violation of a protective order). *Buffalo Carpenters Pension Fund v. CKG Ceiling and Partition Co., Inc.,* 192 F.R.D. 95 (W.D.N.Y.2000) (sanctions may be imposed for failure to comply with any discovery order, not just an order under Rule 37(a)).

26. *Monsanto Co. v. Ralph,* 382 F.3d 1374, 1382 (Fed.Cir.2004) (district court has the inherent power under Rule 37 to sanction abuses of the judicial process irrespective of the existence of any particular order); *Clark Const. Group, Inc. v. City of Memphis,* 229 F.R.D. 131 (W.D.Tenn.2005).

27. *In re: Sealed Case,* 141 F.3d 337 (D.C.Cir.1998).

28. *United States v. Diabetes Treatment Centers of America, Inc.,* 444 F.3d 462, 468, n.3 (6th Cir.2006).

29. *McDowell v. Government of Dist. of Columbia,* 233 F.R.D. 192, 200–01 (D.D.C. 2006) (the sanctions must be proportionate to the offense).

30. *Insurance Corp. of Ireland, Ltd. v. Compagnie des Bauxites de Guinee,* 456 U.S. 694, 102 S.Ct. 2099, 72 L.Ed.2d 492 (1982)(deeming personal jurisdiction established as a discovery sanction); *Compaq Computer Corp. v. Ergonome Inc.,* 387 F.3d 403, 412 (5th Cir.2004); *Navellier v. Sletten,* 262 F.3d 923, 947–48 (9th Cir.2001) (deeming breach of duty established when witness failed to answer questions at a deposition after being ordered to do so); *Knowlton v. Teltrust Phones, Inc.,* 189 F.3d 1177, 1182 (10th Cir.1999) (deeming certain facts established can be tantamount to summary judgment, triggering a higher level of scrutiny).

31. *McMullen v. Travelers Ins. Co.,* 278 F.2d 834 (9th Cir.1960).

- *Prohibit Evidence:* The court may refuse to allow the disobedient party to introduce certain matters into evidence, or to support or oppose certain claims.[32] Thus, where a party failed to comply with discovery orders regarding damages, the party was precluded from offering evidence as to its damages.[33]

- *Strike Pleadings:* The court may strike any pleading or portion of a pleading.[34]

- *Issue Stay:* The court may stay further proceedings until the order is obeyed.[35]

- *Dispositive Ruling:* In extreme situations, the court may dismiss an action or portions of the action.[36] The court may also enter judgment against the disobedient party.[37]

- *Contempt:* The court may treat the failure to obey its order as a contempt of court,[38] with the exception of a failure to submit to a mental or physical examination (which is punishable by other sanctions, but not as contempt).[39]

List Not Exclusive

The court is not limited to the sanctions listed in Rule 37(b)(2), and may make any order that is "just." [40] In practice, however, courts generally have imposed only those sanctions listed.

32. *In re TMI Litigation*, 193 F.3d 613, 721 (3d Cir.1999) (listing the factors for the exclusion of evidence); *Trilogy Communications, Inc. v. Times Fiber Communications, Inc.*, 109 F.3d 739, 745 (Fed.Cir.1997) (barring expert testimony submitted after due date for expert reports had passed); *Melendez v. Illinois Bell Tel. Co.*, 79 F.3d 661, 671–72 (7th Cir.1996)(barring expert's testimony concerning the validity of a standardized cognitive ability test when the party failed to disclose that there was an ongoing project to revise the test).

33. *Ware v. Rodale Press, Inc.*, 322 F.3d 218 (3rd Cir.2003).

34. *See Creative Gifts, Inc. v. UFO*, 235 F.3d 540, 544 (10th Cir.2000).

35. Rule 37(b)(2)(A)(iv).

36. *Malot v. Dorado Beach Cottages Associates*, 478 F.3d 40, 44 (1st Cir. 2007) (disregard of court orders qualifies as extreme behavior); *Phillips v. Cohen*, 400 F.3d 388, 402 (6th Cir.2005) (listing factors to be considered before imposing the drastic sanction of dismissal); *Bay Fireworks, Inc. v. Frenkel & Co., Inc.*, 359 F.Supp.2d 257, 262 (E.D.N.Y.2005) (dismissal pursuant to Rule 37 deemed on the merits and with prejudice). *See also Atchison, Topeka and Santa Fe Railway Co. v. Hercules Inc.*, 146 F.3d 1071, 1074 (9th Cir.1998) (court may not dismiss a separate but related action).

37. *Connecticut General Life Ins. Co. v. New Images of Beverly Hills*, 482 F.3d 1091, 1096–96 (9th Cir. 2007) (listing 5 factors for imposing sanction of default); *Chrysler Corp. v. Carey*, 186 F.3d 1016, 1022 (8th Cir.1999).

38. *Serra Chevrolet, Inc. v. General Motors Corp.*, 446 F.3d 1137 (11th Cir.2006); *General Ins. Co. v. Eastern Consol. Util., Inc.*, 126 F.3d 215, 220 (3d Cir.1997) (a nonparty may be held in contempt of court for violating an order requiring the nonparty to produce documents and attend a deposition); *Maynard v. Nygren*, 332 F.3d 462, 470 (7th Cir.2003) (fines are permissible sanctions); *Jones v. J.C. Penney's Dept. Stores, Inc.*, 228 F.R.D. 190, 198 (W.D.N.Y. 2005) (attorney held in contempt for conduct during deposition in violation of order).

39. Rule 37(b)(2)(A)(vii).

40. *Valley Engineers Inc. v. Electric Engineering Co.*, 158 F.3d 1051, 1056 (9th Cir.1998) (justice is the central factor in a sanctions order under rule 37(b)); *Harris v. City of Philadelphia*, 47 F.3d 1311 (3d Cir. 1995); *Thompson v. U.S. Dept. of Housing*

Sanctions Under 28 U.S.C. § 1927

Sanctions may also be available against a party who "multiplies the proceedings in any case unreasonably and vexatiously" under 28 U.S.C. § 1927.[41]

Failure to Produce Another for Examination

If a party fails to comply with an order to produce another for a mental or physical examination, the party is subject to the same sanctions that would apply if the party failed to appear, unless the party can show that the party was unable to produce the individual.[42]

Multiple Sanctions

The court may impose any combination of sanctions it deems appropriate.[43]

Expenses

The court will also require the party not complying with the court order and/or the party's attorney[44] to pay all expenses, including a reasonable attorney fee, incurred by the moving party as a result of the failure to comply.[45] This includes expenses incurred in the motion for sanctions, but not expenses incurred in obtaining the order compelling the discovery (although these expenses may be recoverable under Rule 37(a) as discussed above). The court must award such expenses unless it finds that the failure was "substantially justified" or that other circumstances exist that would make the award "unjust."[46] The amount of monetary damages must be related to the expenses incurred as a result of the violations.[47]

Corporate Representative

The court may also impose sanctions on a party that is a corporation or organization if its officer, director, managing agent, or designated representative fails to obey an order.[48] The party

and Urban Development, 219 F.R.D. 93, 101 (D.Md.2003) (list of sanctions is non-exclusive).

41. *See Atkins v. Fischer*, 232 F.R.D. 116, 127 (D.D.C.2005).

42. *Societe Internationale v. Rogers,* 357 U.S. 197, 78 S.Ct. 1087, 2 L.Ed.2d 1255 (1958).

43. *See O'Neill v. AGWI Lines*, 74 F.3d 93 (5th Cir.1996)(dismissing the action and imposing attorney's fees).

44. *Stuart I. Levin & Associates, P.A. v. Rogers*, 156 F.3d 1135, 1140 (11th Cir. 1998); *Heath v. F/V ZOLOTOI*, 221 F.R.D. 545 (W.D.Wash.2004).

45. *Ofoedu v. St. Francis Hosp.*, 234 F.R.D. 26, 33 (D.Conn.2006) (expense reimbursement is the mildest sanction); *Knox v.*

Palestine Liberation Organization, 229 F.R.D. 65 (S.D.N.Y.2005) (party against whom expenses are sought must have an opportunity to challenge the expenses); *Watkins & Son Pet Supplies v. Iams Co.*, 197 F.Supp.2d 1030, 1032 (S.D.Ohio 2002) (attorney fees must be reasonable); *Cobell v. Babbitt*, 188 F.R.D. 122, 125 (D.D.C.1999) (discussing the calculation of the attorney fees award).

46. *U.S. v. One 1999 Forty Seven Foot Fountain Motor Vessel*, 240 F.R.D. 695, 697 (S.D.Fla. 2007).

47. *Tollett v. City of Kemah*, 285 F.3d 357 (5th Cir.2002) (discussing the method of proving attorney fees); *Martin v. Brown*, 63 F.3d 1252, 1263–64 (3d Cir.1995).

48. *Bon Air Hotel, Inc. v. Time, Inc.,* 376 F.2d 118 (5th Cir.1967).

noticing the deposition will have the burden of showing that the person had the necessary relationship to the corporation.

Waiver of Sanctions

A party might be deemed to have waived its rights to sanctions by not strictly enforcing the order, such as by failing to make attempts to schedule a physical examination[49] or by failing to bring a motion for sanctions in a reasonable period of time.[50]

Conflicts with Regulations

Where compliance with a discovery order would force a party to violate a federal agency regulation, compliance with the discovery order will be excused.[51]

Appeals

Sanctions orders are normally interlocutory orders not immediately appealable, but sometimes may be appealed under the collateral order doctrine.[52] The entry of sanctions under Rule 37(b) is reviewed under the abuse of discretion standard.[53] A claim that the sanction violated the due process clause is reviewed *de novo*.[54]

RULE 37(c). FAILURE TO DISCLOSE, TO SUPPLEMENT AN EARLIER RESPONSE, OR TO ADMIT

CORE CONCEPT

If a party improperly fails to make the automatic disclosures under Rule 26(a) or makes false or misleading disclosures, or if a party fails to supplement a prior discovery response as required by Rule 26(e)(1), the party is subject to a variety of sanctions. If a party improperly fails to admit a matter, Rule 37(c) imposes on that party the cost to the other party in proving the matter.

APPLICATIONS

Failure to Disclose

If a party fails to make the automatic disclosures under Rule

49. *Hinson v. Michigan Mut. Liability Co.*, 275 F.2d 537 (5th Cir.1960).

50. *United States Fidelity & Guar. Co. v. Baker Material Handling, Corp.*, 62 F.3d 24, 29 (1st Cir.1995); *Tolliver v. Federal Republic of Nigeria*, 265 F.Supp.2d 873 (W.D.Mich.2003).

51. *In re Bankers Trust Co.*, 61 F.3d 465, 469–70 (6th Cir.1995).

52. *United States v. Diabetes Treatment Centers of America, Inc.*, 444 F.3d 462, 472 (6th Cir.2006).

53. *Serra Chevrolet, Inc. v. General Motors Corp.*, 446 F.3d 1137 (11th Cir.2006); *Chimie v. PPG Industries, Inc.*, 402 F.3d

1371, 1381 (Fed.Cir.2005) (listing factors for abuse of discretion); *International Broth. of Elec. Workers, Local Union No. 545 v. Hope Elec. Corp.*, 380 F.3d 1084, 1105 (8th Cir.2004) (sanction of default judgment will be scrutinized more carefully because of the severity of the sanction, but the standard is still abuse of discretion); *Computer Task Group, Inc. v. Brotby*, 364 F.3d 1112, 1115 (9th Cir.2004) (sanctions reversed only if appellate court has a definite and firm conviction that the trial court committed a clear error of judgment).

54. *Serra Chevrolet, Inc. v. General Motors Corp.*, 446 F.3d 1137 (11th Cir.2006).

26(a)[55] in a timely manner[56] or makes false or misleading disclosures, the party will not be permitted to use at trial or in a motion[57] the documents, information,[58] or witnesses[59] not properly disclosed, unless the party had "substantial justification"[60] or the failure was harmless.[61]

Failure to Supplement

If a party fails to supplement its automatic disclosures or to supplement a prior discovery response as required under Rule 26(e)(1), the party will not be permitted to use at trial the documents, information, opinions,[62] or witnesses not properly disclosed, unless the party had "substantial justification" or the failure was harmless.[63]

Additional Sanctions

In addition to or in lieu of[64] precluding the evidence, upon motion and after an opportunity to be heard,[65] the court may impose additional sanctions, including:

- payment of reasonable expenses, including attorney and/or

---

55. *Alvariza v. Home Depot*, 240 F.R.D. 586, 590 (D.Colo. 2007) (Rule 37(c) sanctions do not apply to informal agreements to disclose, only to the formal Rule 26(a) disclosure process).

56. *Trost v. Trek Bicycle Corp.*, 162 F.3d 1004, 1008 (8th Cir.1998) (failure to disclose in a timely manner is equivalent to failure to disclose); *Johnson v. United Parcel Service, Inc.*, 236 F.R.D. 376 (E.D.Tenn. 2006) (the exclusion of undisclosed evidence is automatic and mandatory unless nondisclosure was justified or harmless).

57. *Shepard v. Frontier Communications Services, Inc.*, 92 F.Supp.2d 279 (S.D.N.Y.2000).

58. *City of Moses Lake v. U.S.*, 472 F.Supp.2d 1220, 1228 (E.D.Wash. 2007) (exclusion of damages information not disclosed).

59. *Musser v. Gentiva Health Services*, 356 F.3d 751, 758 (7th Cir.2004); *Maritime-Ontario Freight Lines, Ltd. v. STI Holdings, Inc.*, 481 F.Supp.2d 963, 972 (W.D.Wis. 2007).

60. *Gagnon v. Teledyne Princeton, Inc.*, 437 F.3d 188, 195–96 (1st Cir.2006); *McCarthy v. Option One Mortg. Corp.*, 362 F.3d 1008, 1012 (7th Cir.2004).

61. *Gagnon v. Teledyne Princeton, Inc.*, 437 F.3d 188, 197 (1st Cir.2006) (describing factors for harmlessness); *Primrose Operating Co. v. National American Ins. Co.*, 382 F.3d 546, 563–64 (5th Cir.2004) (same); *Sommer v. Davis*, 317 F.3d 686, 692 (6th

Cir.2003) (harmless involves an honest mistake on the part of a party coupled with sufficient knowledge on the part of the other party); *Wilson v. Bradlees of New England, Inc.*, 250 F.3d 10 (1st Cir.2001) (mandatory preclusion is the required sanction in the ordinary case); Saudi *v. Valmet–Appleton, Inc.*, 219 F.R.D. 128, 132, n.5 (E.D.Wis.2003) (the 2000 Amendment that replaced "shall" with "is" was stylistic, and did not lessen the mandatory nature of the sanctions).

62. *Air Turbine Technology, Inc. v. Atlas Copco AB*, 410 F.3d 701, 711–12 (Fed. Cir.2005); *Southern States Rack And Fixture, Inc. v. Sherwin–Williams Co.*, 318 F.3d 592, 595–96 (4th Cir.2003)

63. *Primrose Operating Co. v. National American Ins. Co.*, 382 F.3d 546, 563–64 (5th Cir.2004) (describing factors for determining whether a failure was harmless); *Payless Shoesource Worldwide, Inc. v. Target Corp.*, 237 F.R.D. 666, 676–77 (D.Kan. 2006).

64. *Dura Automotive Systems of Indiana, Inc. v. CTS Corp.*, 285 F.3d 609, 615–16 (7th Cir.2002) (additional sanctions may be imposed in lieu of evidence exclusion only if the failure to disclose was substantially justified).

65. *Paladin Associates, Inc. v. Montana Power Co.*, 328 F.3d 1145, 1164–65 (9th Cir.2003)(the opportunity to submit briefs was an opportunity to be heard).

expert fees, caused by the failure;[66]

● informing the jury of the failure to make the disclosure;[67]

● deeming certain matters established;

● precluding the non-disclosing party from supporting or opposing designated claims or defenses;[68]

● striking pleadings or portions thereof;[69]

● staying the action pending proper disclosure; or

● dismissing or entering judgment as to part or all of the action.[70]

The court has broad discretion in awarding sanctions under Rule 37(c), and its decision will be reviewed for abuse of that discretion.[71]

Sanctions Apply at Trial, Hearing, or Motion

The information or witnesses not properly disclosed are most commonly excluded from trial, but also may be excluded from a hearing or motion for summary judgment.[72]

Failure to Admit

If a party fails to admit a matter that another party subsequently proves at trial,[73] the other party can move after trial for its reasonable expenses, including a reasonable attorney fee, incurred in proving the matter.[74] The court must then award expenses unless one of the following four conditions exists:

(1) The request was objectionable;[75]

66. *Speedplay, Inc. v. Bebop, Inc.*, 211 F.3d 1245, 1260 (Fed.Cir.2000).

67. *Central States Indus. Supply, Inc. v. McCullough*, 279 F.Supp.2d 1005, 1025 (N.D.Iowa 2003); *Tarlton v. Cumberland County Correctional Facility*, 192 F.R.D. 165 (D.N.J.2000).

68. *Patterson v. State Auto. Mut. Ins. Co.*, 105 F.3d 1251, 1252 (8th Cir.1997) (expert's testimony about his unannounced second visit to site was precluded due to prejudice on opposing party).

69. *Second Chance Body Armor, Inc. v. American Body Armor, Inc.*, 177 F.R.D. 633, 637 (N.D.Ill.1998).

70. *Maynard v. Nygren*, 332 F.3d 462, 467–68 (7th Cir.2003) (dismissal is a draconian sanction, and the circuit court will be vigilant in reviewing a dismissal sanction); *Signature Combs, Inc. v. U.S.*, 222 F.R.D. 343, 345 (W.D.Tenn.2004) (listing factors that must be considered before imposing sanction of dismissal).

71. *Gagnon v. Teledyne Princeton, Inc.*, 437 F.3d 188, 191 (1st Cir.2006); *Tisdale v.* *Federal Exp. Corp.*, 415 F.3d 516 (6th Cir. 2005) (listing factors for abuse of discretion).

72. *Gagnon v. Teledyne Princeton, Inc.*, 437 F.3d 188, 199 (1st Cir.2006) (motion for summary judgment based on lack of any expert testimony following exclusion based on untimely expert disclosure); *Poulis–Minott v. Smith*, 388 F.3d 354, 358 (1st Cir. 2004).

73. *Joseph v. Fratar*, 197 F.R.D. 20 (D.Mass.2000) (motion for expenses for improper failure to admit may not be made until after trial).

74. *Bradshaw v. Thompson*, 454 F.2d 75 (6th Cir.1972); *House v. Giant of Maryland LLC*, 232 F.R.D. 257, 260 (E.D.Va.2005) (party is not required to meet and confer or file a pre-trial motion in order to obtain sanctions for an improper failure to admit); *National Semiconductor Corp. v. Ramtron International Corp.*, 265 F.Supp.2d 71 (D.D.C.2003).

75. *Russo v. Baxter Healthcare Corp.*, 51 F.Supp.2d 70, 78 (D.R.I.1999).

(2) The admission sought was of no substantial importance, such as when the proof of the matter was trivial;[76]

(3) The party refusing to admit had reasonable grounds to believe that it would be successful on the matter;[77] or

(4) Other good reasons exist for the failure to admit, such as a genuine inability to determine the truth of the matter.[78]

Party Only

Expenses and fees under Rule 37(c) may be awarded against the party only, not against the attorney, in contrast to other provisions of Rule 37.[79]

Improper Statement of Inability to Admit

The sanctions in Rule 37(c) apply to an improper statement of inability to admit or deny, as well as to an improper denial.

Failure to Respond to Requests for Admissions

The sanctions in Rule 37(c) do not apply to a failure to respond to a request for admissions because such a failure is deemed an admission.[80]

Explanation of Sanctions

The court order must state the basis for its decision to impose sanctions so that the appellate court can conduct a meaningful review.[81]

RULE 37(d). PARTY'S FAILURE TO ATTEND ITS OWN DEPOSITION, SERVE ANSWERS TO INTERROGATORIES, OR RESPOND TO A REQUEST FOR INSPECTION

CORE CONCEPT

Rule 37(d) provides that upon motion sanctions are immediately available against a party who completely fails to participate in the discovery process.

76. *Read-Rite Corp. v. Burlington Air Express, Inc.*, 183 F.R.D. 545, 547 (N.D.Cal. 1998).

77. *Mutual Service Ins. Co. v. Frit Industries, Inc.*, 358 F.3d 1312, 1326 (11th Cir.2004) (the true test is not whether a party prevailed at trial, but whether it acted reasonably in believing that it might prevail); *Washington State Dep't of Transp. v. Washington Natural Gas Co.*, 59 F.3d 793, 805–06 (9th Cir.1995); *Caruthers v. Proctor & Gamble Manufacturing Co.*, 177 F.R.D. 667, 669 (D.Kan.1998).

78. *Maynard v. Nygren*, 332 F.3d 462, 470 (7th Cir.2003) (attorneys can be sanctioned for failure-to-disclose violations under Rule 26(g)(3)).

79. *Apex Oil Co. v. Belcher Co. of New York, Inc.*, 855 F.2d 1009, 1013–14 (2d Cir. 1988).

80. *West Ky. Coal Co. v. Walling*, 153 F.2d 582, 587 (6th Cir.1946).

81. *Mutual Service Ins. Co. v. Frit Industries, Inc.*, 358 F.3d 1312, 1326 (11th Cir.2004) ("'[I]n cases invoking the sanction power of Rule 37 the district court must 'clearly state its reasons so that meaningful review may be had on appeal.' '"); *but see Umbenhower v. Copart, Inc.*, 222 F.R.D. 672, 675 (D.Kan.2004) (court need not make explicit findings regarding substantial justification or harmlessness).

APPLICATIONS

When Available

Sanctions under Rule 37(d) are available when the party fails to appear for the party's deposition after being served with proper notice,[82] fails to answer or object to properly-served interrogatories,[83] or fails to serve a written response to a properly-served request to inspect documents or things.[84] Thus, a court order is not a prerequisite to sanctions under Rule 37(d).[85] Rule 37(d) does not specify when the motion for sanctions must be filed, but some courts have held that the motion must be filed without "unreasonable delay,"[86] or before the entry of judgment.[87]

Certification of Conference

A motion for sanctions under Rule 37(d) for failure to respond to interrogatories or requests for inspection must include a certification that the movant has in good faith conferred or attempted to confer with the other party or person in an effort to obtain a response without court action.[88] Note that this requirement does not apply to the failure to appear for a deposition.[89]

Sanctions

Rule 37(d) states that the court may impose whatever sanctions as are "just,"[90] including those listed in Rule 37(b)(2)(A),[91] which are essentially the sanctions discussed above except for contempt of court sanctions.[92] The court has broad discretion in deciding what sanction to impose, and an award of sanctions is reviewed for abuse of discretion.[93] The court can consider all the circumstances, such

---

82. *Colindres v. QuitFlex Mfg.*, 235 F.R.D. 347 (S.D.Tex.2006); *Haraway v. National Ass'n For Stock Car Auto Racing, Inc.*, 213 F.R.D. 161, 165 (D.Del.2003).

83. *Roney v. Starwood Hotels & Resorts Worldwide, Inc.*, 236 F.R.D. 346 (E.D.Mich. 2006); *Jayne H. Lee, Inc. v. Flagstaff Indus. Corp.*, 173 F.R.D. 651, 653 (D.Md.1997).

84. *Alvariza v. Home Depot*, 240 F.R.D. 586, 590 (D.Colo. 2007) (Rule 37(c) sanctions do not apply to informal agreements to provide documents, only to properly served Rule 34 document requests); *Roney v. Starwood Hotels & Resorts Worldwide, Inc.*, 236 F.R.D. 346 (E.D.Mich.2006).

85. *Guidry v. Continental Oil Co.*, 640 F.2d 523, 533 (5th Cir.1981); *Inmuno Vital, Inc. v. Telemundo Group, Inc.*, 203 F.R.D. 561, 566 (S.D.Fla.2001).

86. *See Lancaster v. Independent School District No. 5*, 149 F.3d 1228, 1237 (10th Cir.1998).

87. *See Mercy v. County of Suffolk*, 748 F.2d 52, 55–56 (2d Cir.1984).

88. *Black Horse Lane Assoc., L.P. v. Dow Chemical Corp.*, 228 F.3d 275, 301 (3d Cir.2000).

89. *Grand Oaks, Inc. v. A.W. Anderson*, 175 F.R.D. 247, 250 (N.D.Miss.1997).

90. *Coan v. Hutter*, 207 B.R. 981, 986 (Bkrtcy.D.Conn.1997).

91. *Panaderia La Diana, Inc. v. Salt Lake City Corp.*, 342 F.Supp.2d 1013, 1030 (D.Utah 2004) (dismissal is an appropriate sanction when a plaintiff fails to appear for the plaintiff's deposition).

92. *See Bishop v. First Mississippi Financial Group, Inc.*, 221 F.R.D. 461 (S.D.Miss.2004) (dismissal for failure to appear at depositions and respond to motions); *Viswanathan v. Scotland County Bd. of Educ.*, 165 F.R.D. 50 (M.D.N.C. 1995)(dismissing action after claimant failed to appear at a scheduled deposition three times), *affirmed*, 76 F.3d 377 (4th Cir.1996).

93. *Black Horse Lane Assoc., L.P. v. Dow Chemical Corp.*, 228 F.3d 275, 301 (3d Cir.2000); *Webb v. District of Columbia*, 146 F.3d 964 (D.C.Cir.1998).

as whether the failure was accidental or in bad faith in determining the sanctions to impose.[94]

Expenses

The court must require that the party failing to participate in discovery and/or the party's attorney pay the resulting expenses of the other party, including a reasonable attorney fee.[95] The court must award such expenses unless it finds that the failure was "substantially justified"[96] or that other circumstances exist that would make the award "unjust."[97] The award of expenses can be in addition to or instead of other sanctions.

Objections to Discovery/Protective Order

It is not a defense to a motion for sanctions under Rule 37(d) to argue that the discovery request was objectionable.[98] The proper response to an objectionable discovery request is to file a motion for a protective order under Rule 26(c), not to ignore the discovery request.[99]

Court Order

Although a court order is not a prerequisite to a motion for sanctions under Rule 37(d), the motion may still be brought if the party failing to participate in discovery had been ordered to participate.[100]

Procedure

A motion for sanctions under Rule 37(d) is filed in the court in which the action is pending.

Corporate Representative

A corporation or organization that is a party is subject to the sanctions in Rule 37(d) if its officer, director, managing agent, or person designated to testify under Rule 30(b)(6) fails to appear for a deposition after being properly noticed.[101] Likewise, if a party re-

94. *In re Sumitomo Copper Litigation,* 204 F.R.D. 58, 60–61 (S.D.N.Y.2001) (case dismissed based on willful failure to appear at deposition).

95. *Hyde & Drath v. Baker,* 24 F.3d 1162 (9th Cir.1994).

96. *Telluride Management Solutions, Inc. v. Telluride Investment Group,* 55 F.3d 463 (9th Cir.1995)(good faith but incorrect belief that the action had been dismissed was not sufficient to excuse absence from a deposition); *Lee v. Walters,* 172 F.R.D. 421, 429 (D.Or.1997).

97. *Miller v. International Paper Co.,* 408 F.2d 283, 292–94 (5th Cir.1969).

98. *International Broth. of Elec. Workers, Local Union No. 545 v. Hope Elec. Corp.,* 380 F.3d 1084, 1106 (8th Cir.2004); *Magee v. Paul Revere Life Ins.Co.,* 178 F.R.D. 33, 38 (E.D.N.Y.1998).

99. *Ferko v. National Ass'n for Stock Car Auto Racing, Inc.,* 218 F.R.D. 125, 143–44 (E.D.Tex.2003).

100. *Independent Productions Corp. v. Loew's Inc.,* 283 F.2d 730 (2d Cir.1960).

101. *Atlantic Cape Fisheries v. Hartford Fire Ins. Co.,* 509 F.2d 577 (1st Cir.1975); *Precisionflow Technologies, Inc. v. CVD Equipment Corp.,* 140 F.Supp.2d 195, (N.D.N.Y.2001) (corporation that agrees to produce employees sanctioned when employees do not appear for their depositions); *Starlight International Inc. v. Herlihy,* 186 F.R.D. 626, 639 (D.Kan.1999) (producing an unprepared witness is tantamount to not producing any witness at all); *but see Stone v. Morton Int'l, Inc.,* 170 F.R.D. 498, 503 (D.Utah 1997) (questioning the ability to sanction a corporation for failure of its officer to appear).

fuses to designate a representative, the party will be subject to sanctions under Rule 37(d).[102] In extreme cases, a party who produces an unprepared or inappropriate representative may also be subject to sanctions under Rule 37(d).[103]

Party Who Refuses to Be Sworn In

A party appearing at the designated time but who refuses to be sworn in generally is not subject to Rule 37(d) sanctions.[104]

Refusal to Answer Specific Questions

A party who appears and is sworn in, but who then refuses to answer a specific question or questions is not subject to sanctions under Rule 37(d). The proper procedure is for the party taking the deposition to move to compel answers under Rule 37(a), then move for sanctions under Rule 37(b) if the party still refuses to answer.[105] The same result is reached with respect to evasive or incomplete answers. However, if the party refuses to answer all or substantially all of the questions, Rule 37(d) will apply.[106]

Continuation of Deposition

Sanctions under Rule 37(d) do not apply to a party who fails to appear for the continuation of a deposition if the date of the continuation was not specified in a notice.[107]

Incomplete Response to Interrogatories or Document Requests

Rule 37(d) only applies if the party fails altogether to serve a response to interrogatories or document requests. If the party serves an incomplete or evasive response, the proper procedure is a motion to compel under Rule 37(a), then a motion for sanctions under Rule 37(b) if the party does not comply with the court order.[108]

Failure to Preserve Evidence

Dismissal may be imposed as a sanction against parties who bring actions with knowledge that their own actions, or actions of a

---

102. *Ferko v. National Ass'n for Stock Car Auto Racing, Inc.*, 218 F.R.D. 125, 133 (E.D.Tex.2003).

103. *Ferko v. National Ass'n for Stock Car Auto Racing, Inc.*, 218 F.R.D. 125, 142–43 (E.D.Tex.2003) (if the representative is not knowledgeable about the designated subject matter, the appearance is, for all practical purposes, no appearance at all).

104. *Aziz v. Wright*, 34 F.3d 587 (8th Cir.1994).

105. *Independent Productions Corp. v. Loew's Inc.*, 283 F.2d 730 (2d Cir.1960).

106. *Black Horse Lane Assoc., L.P. v. Dow Chemical Corp.*, 228 F.3d 275, 301 (3d Cir.2000) (producing an unprepared Rule 30(b)(6) corporate representative is tantamount to not producing a witness at all); *Starlight International Inc. v. Herlihy*, 186 F.R.D. 626, 639 (D.Kan.1999) (producing an unprepared witness is tantamount to not producing any witness at all). *But see Garcia v. Senkowski*, 919 F.Supp. 609, 613–14 (N.D.N.Y.1996)(denying sanction of dismissal where deponent appeared, refused to answer questions orally, but submitted written answers).

107. *Miller v. International Paper Co.*, 408 F.2d 283, 292–294 (5th Cir.1969).

108. *Fjelstad v. American Honda Motor Co., Inc.*, 762 F.2d 1334 (9th Cir.1985).

third party, have caused the spoliation or loss of key pieces of evidence which render defense of the action difficult.[109]

Compliance After Motion

Once a motion for sanctions has been filed, the non-participating party cannot avoid sanctions by responding to the discovery request. However, the court can consider that conduct in deciding what sanctions to impose.[110]

RULE 37(e). FAILURE TO PROVIDE ELECTRONICALLY STORED INFORMATION

CORE CONCEPT

Rule 37(e) recognizes that certain types of electronically stored information are lost during the regular operation of a computer system. It prohibits the imposition of sanctions for failure to produce such lost information, in the absence of exceptional circumstances.

APPLICATIONS

2007 Amendments

The 2007 amendments deleted former abrogated Rule 37(e) and renumbered former Rule 37(f) as Rule 37(e). Care should be exercised in researching and citing pre–2008 cases referring to Rule 37(e) or Rule 37(f).

Data Lost Through Routine Operation

A party is generally protected from sanctions for data that is lost through the routine operation of a computer system. An example of the type of data that is contemplated by this provision is the metadata (or data about data) that computers automatically store such as the last time a document was opened. Each time the document is opened, the information that was stored in that field is deleted and replaced by new data. A party would not likely be sanctioned for the loss of the data about when a document was last opened.[111]

Good Faith

The protections in Rule 37(e) are expressly limited to the good faith operation of the computer system. Thus, a party cannot exploit the Rule 37(e) protections to deliberately delete relevant information.[112]

Suspending Routine Operation

Under certain circumstances, a party must suspend those features of its computer system that result in the routine loss of

---

109. *Thiele v. Oddy's Auto and Marine, Inc.*, 906 F.Supp. 158, 161–62 (W.D.N.Y. 1995).

110. *Antico v. Honda of Camden*, 85 F.R.D. 34, 36 (E.D.Pa.1979).

111. See The 2006 Amendment to the Advisory Committee Note to former Rule 37(f).

112. See The 2006 Amendment to the Advisory Committee Note to former Rule 37(f).

information.[113] A party wishing to require another party to preserve electronic data can write a letter to the party placing it on notice that the electronic data may be relevant and should be preserved, or can seek a preservation order from the court.[114]

RULE 37(f). FAILURE TO PARTICIPATE IN FRAMING A DISCOVERY PLAN

CORE CONCEPT

If a party fails to participate in developing a proposed discovery plan as required by Rule 26(f), the court may, after opportunity for a hearing, require the party failing to participate to pay the expenses of the other party, including a reasonable attorney fee, caused by the failure.

APPLICATIONS

2007 Amendments

The 2007 amendments deleted former abrogated Rule 37(e) and renumbered former Rule 37(g) as Rule 37(f). Care should be exercised in researching and citing pre–2008 cases referring to Rule 37(e) or Rule 37(g).

ADDITIONAL RESEARCH REFERENCES

Wright & Miller, *Federal Practice and Procedure* §§ 2281–2293.

C.J.S. Federal Civil Procedure §§ 535–547, 640–644, 694, 695, 748–774.

West's Key No. Digests, Federal Civil Procedure ⬤1278, 1299, 1451–1456, 1537–1542, 1636–1640, 1663–1664, 1685.

113. See The 2006 Amendment to the Advisory Committee Note to former Rule 37(f) (such obligation may arise by common law, statute, regulation, or court order).

114. See The 2006 Amendment to the Advisory Committee Note to former Rule 37(f).

VI. TRIALS

RULE 38

RIGHT TO A JURY TRIAL; DEMAND

(a) Right Preserved. The right of trial by jury as declared by the Seventh Amendment to the Constitution—or as provided by a federal statute—is preserved to the parties inviolate.

(b) Demand. On any issue triable of right by a jury, a party may demand a jury trial by:

(1) serving the other parties with a written demand— which may be included in a pleading—no later than 10 days after the last pleading directed to the issue is served; and

(2) filing the demand in accordance with Rule 5(d).

(c) Specifying Issues. In its demand, a party may specify the issues that it wishes to have tried by a jury; otherwise, it is considered to have demanded a jury trial on all the issues so triable. If the party has demanded a jury trial on only some issues, any other party may—within 10 days after being served with the demand or within a shorter time ordered by the court—serve a demand for a jury trial on any other or all factual issues triable by jury.

(d) Waiver; Withdrawal. A party waives a jury trial unless its demand is properly served and filed. A proper demand may be withdrawn only if the parties consent.

(e) Admiralty and Maritime Claims. These rules do not create a right to a jury trial on issues in a claim that is an admiralty or maritime claim under Rule 9(h).

[Amended February 28, 1966, effective July 1, 1966; March 2, 1987, effective August 1, 1987; April 22, 1993, effective December 1, 1993; April 30, 2007, effective December 1, 2007.]

─────────── **2007 AMENDMENTS ROADMAP** ───────────

STYLE PROJECT CHANGES: The language in Rule 38 was shortened and clarified; active voice was substituted for passive; and "jury trial" replaced "trial by jury."

NON-STYLE CHANGES: None.

NOTE: The Federal Rules "Style Project" is explained in Part III-A.

AUTHORS' COMMENTARY ON RULE 38

———————————— PURPOSE AND SCOPE ————————————

Rule 38 governs the parties' right to a trial by jury and how the parties exercise their right to such a trial. Rule 38 essentially serves two functions: (1) Rules 38(a) and 38(e) describe the issues for which the parties have a right to a jury trial; and (2) Rules 38(b), 38(c), and 38(d) control the procedural aspects of making a jury trial demand and the consequences of failing to do so.

NOTE: The right to a jury trial is waived unless a jury trial demand is served within 10 days of the answer or last pleading.

RULE 38(a).   RIGHT PRESERVED

CORE CONCEPT

Rule 38 essentially codifies the Constitution's Seventh Amendment, which provides that the parties have a right to trial by jury for all suits at law with more than $20.00 in controversy.[1]

APPLICATIONS

Law vs. Equity

Under Rule 38, one has a right to a jury in all actions that historically would have been tried at law, such as actions for damages, but no right to a jury in actions that historically would have been tried in the courts of equity, such as actions for specific performance[2] or injunctive relief.[3]

Declaratory Judgment Actions

The right to a jury trial is preserved in declaratory judgment actions. If the issues would have been triable by a jury had something other than declaratory relief been sought, a right to a jury trial exists in a declaratory judgment action.[4]

---

1. *International Financial Services Corp. v. Chromas Technologies Canada, Inc.*, 356 F.3d 731, 735 (7th Cir.2004) (there is a right to a jury trial where either the Seventh Amendment or an ordinary statute of the United States so requires); *GTFM, LLC v. TKN Sales, Inc.*, 257 F.3d 235, 239–40 (2d Cir.2001).

2. *See Tull v. United States*, 481 U.S. 412, 417, 107 S.Ct. 1831, 1835, 95 L.Ed.2d 365 (1987); *Parklane Hosiery Co. v. Shore*, 439 U.S. 322, 99 S.Ct. 645, 58 L.Ed.2d 552 (1979).

3. *National Ass'n For Advancement of Colored People v. Acusport Corp.*, 226 F.Supp.2d 391, 397 (E.D.N.Y.2002).

4. *See Simler v. Conner*, 372 U.S. 221,

Individual Issues

The right to a jury trial is evaluated claim by claim, not for the entire case.[5] If one claim triable at law is present in the case, then the parties have a right to a jury trial on that claim; whether the primary or principal claim is legal or equitable is immaterial.[6]

Policy Favors Jury Trials

There is a strong policy in favor of jury trials, so courts will tend to allow jury trials if it is unclear whether an issue historically would have been triable at law.[7]

Governing Law

Federal law generally governs whether an issue is legal or equitable, not state law.[8] The determination of whether a party has a right to a jury trial is a legal determination subject to de novo review.[9]

Right Depends on Facts

The court bases its rulings on the issues raised by the *facts* alleged in the pleadings, not on the labels used by the parties.[10]

Jury Issues First

When there are jury and non-jury issues or claims present, the jury first determines the jury trial issues, then the court resolves any remaining issues. Any factual findings made by the jury are then binding on the court when trying the non-jury issues. The court may also conduct completely separate trials of jury and non-jury issues.[11]

Procedural Posture

The procedural device by which the parties arrive at court is irrelevant; legal issues are tried by jury even if the claims are brought under the historically equitable joinder provisions such as class actions, derivative actions, and intervention.[12]

83 S.Ct. 609, 9 L.Ed.2d 691 (1963); *Beacon Theatres, Inc. v. Westover*, 359 U.S. 500, 79 S.Ct. 948, 3 L.Ed.2d 988 (1959); *Esso Standard Oil Co. v. Zayas*, 352 F.Supp.2d 165, 170 (D.Puerto Rico 2005).

5. *Bleecker v. Standard Fire Ins. Co.*, 130 F.Supp.2d 726, 737 (E.D.N.C.2000).

6. *Beacon Theatres, Inc. v. Westover*, 359 U.S. 500, 79 S.Ct. 948, 3 L.Ed.2d 988 (1959).

7. *Beacon Theatres, Inc. v. Westover*, 359 U.S. 500, 79 S.Ct. 948, 3 L.Ed.2d 988 (1959).

8. *Simler v. Conner,* 372 U.S. 221, 83 S.Ct. 609, 9 L.Ed.2d 691 (1963); *International Financial Services Corp. v. Chromas Technologies Canada, Inc.*, 356 F.3d 731,

735 (7th Cir.2004) (even where a district court is applying the substantive law of a state, federal procedural law controls the question of whether there is a right to a jury trial).

9. *Indiana Lumbermens Mutual Ins. Co. v. Timberland Pallet and Lumber Co., Inc.*, 195 F.3d 368, 374 (8th Cir.1999).

10. *Dairy Queen, Inc. v. Wood,* 369 U.S. 469, 82 S.Ct. 894, 8 L.Ed.2d 44 (1962); *California Scents v. Surco Products, Inc.*, 406 F.3d 1102, 1106 (9th Cir.2005).

11. *Beacon Theatres, Inc. v. Westover,* 359 U.S. 500, 79 S.Ct. 948, 3 L.Ed.2d 988 (1959).

12. *Ross v. Bernhard,* 396 U.S. 531, 90 S.Ct. 733, 24 L.Ed.2d 729 (1970).

RULE 38(b).   DEMAND

CORE CONCEPT

Any party may make a jury trial demand.   The demand then applies to all parties for the duration of the case.[13]

APPLICATIONS

Form of Demand

The jury trial demand should be in writing,[14] and can be part of pleading[15] or a separate signed document. Rule 38 does not require any particular language or placement, so long as the intent to demand a jury is clear.[16]   To avoid timing problems, it is advisable to include the jury demand on the complaint or answer.   Note that it is probably not sufficient to indicate a jury trial on the civil coversheet or legal backer.[17] Likewise, a jury trial demand in a motion is probably not effective.[18]

Timing

A party wishing a jury trial for an issue must *serve* a jury trial demand within 10 days after service of the last pleading raising or responding to that issue.[19]   Normally, the last pleading is the answer to the pleading raising the issue.[20]   The party must then *file* the jury trial demand within a reasonable time, as provided in Rule

13. *Kramer v. Banc of America Securities, LLC*, 355 F.3d 961, 967 (7th Cir.2004).

14. *U.S. Leather, Inc. v. Mitchell Mfg. Group, Inc.*, 276 F.3d 782, 790 (6th Cir. 2002) (oral jury demand during proceedings before a magistrate judge deemed insufficient).

15. *Metzger v. City of Leawood*, 144 F.Supp.2d 1225 (D.Kan.2001) ("While it is not desirable to bury the demand in the text of the pleading, plaintiff is correct in stating that demand may be incorporated in a pleading.").

16. *Lutz v. Glendale Union High School*, 403 F.3d 1061, 1063 (9th Cir.2005) (local rule requiring a particular placement is unenforceable, test is whether a careful reader would understand that a jury trial had been demanded).

17. *Johnson v. Dalton*, 57 F.Supp.2d 958, 959 (C.D.Cal.1999). *But see Wright v. Lewis*, 76 F.3d 57, 59 (2d Cir.1996)(a jury trial demand on a civil cover sheet can satisfy Rule 38(b) if the cover sheet is served).

18. *Bogosian v. Woloohojian Realty Corp.*, 323 F.3d 55, 62 (1st Cir.2003); *Hunt*

v. HEB Fed. Credit Union, 215 B.R. 505, 509 (Bkrtcy.W.D.Tex.1997) (jury trial demand contained in a motion to withdraw reference to bankruptcy court is not effective).

19. *Marshall v. Knight*, 445 F.3d 965, 970, n.5 (7th Cir.2006) (jury demand may be made not later than 10 days after *service*); *Burns v. Lawther,* 44 F.3d 960 (11th Cir.1995) (look to Rule 7 for definition of pleading); *Triad Elec. & Controls, Inc. v. Power Sys. Eng'g, Inc.*, 117 F.3d 180, 195 (5th Cir.1997); *In re Apponline.Com., Inc.*, 303 B.R. 723 (E.D.N.Y.2004) (an amended complaint revives the right to a jury demand only if it adds new issues for which there is a right to a jury trial).

20. *See Shelton v. Consumer Products Safety Com'n*, 277 F.3d 998, 1011 (8th Cir. 2002) (amended complaint does not trigger a new period to file a jury demand for issues raised in the original complaint); *United States v. California Mobile Home Park Management Co.*, 107 F.3d 1374, 1378 (9th Cir.1997) ("last pleading" is the answer to the intervenor's complaint, rather than the answer to the original complaint filed); *Tropez v. Veneman*, 2004 WL 574733 (E.D.La.2004).

5(d).[21]   If a jury trial demand is served after the 10th day, the court has discretion to consider the demand.[22]

Service

To be effective, the jury demand must be served on other parties within the 10 day time limit of Rule 38(b).[23] If the last pleading was served by mail, then all parties other than the party serving the last pleading may add an additional three days to the mailing date.[24]

Other Parties

Once one party has made a jury demand, the other parties are entitled to rely on that demand and do not need to file jury demands of their own.[25]

Amendments

An amended or supplemental pleading does not restart the jury trial demand clock for issues raised in the original pleading.[26]   The focus is the issue, not the remedy.[27]   Therefore, if the original complaint seeks specific performance of a breached contract and the amended complaint adds a damages claim arising out of the same breach, under the majority approach, the parties do not have the right to demand a jury trial 10 days after service of the amended complaint, unless the court directs the party to make such a demand.[28]

Removal

The removing party may make a jury trial demand within 10 days of filing the petition.[29]   Others may make demands within 10 days of service of the petition.   If a pleading is filed after the

21.   *Harrington v. Wilber*, 384 F.Supp.2d 1321, 1324 (S.D.Iowa 2005).

22.   *Zivkovic v. Southern California Edison Co.*, 302 F.3d 1080, (9th Cir.2002) (the district court's discretion is narrow and does not permit a court to grant relief when the failure to make a timely demand results from an oversight or inadvertence, such as a good faith mistake with respect to the deadline for demanding a jury trial); *Members v. Paige,* 140 F.3d 699 (7th Cir.1998) (district judge may require a litigant who requests an untimely jury trial to offer a reason for not meeting the deadline); *Miller v. Merrill Lynch Credit Corp.*, 2004 WL 813029 (D.Conn.2004) (a court's discretion to permit a late jury demand is somewhat broader in removed cases than original actions).

23.   *Harrington v. Wilber*, 384 F.Supp.2d 1321, 1324 (S.D.Iowa 2005); *Ruiz v. Rodriguez*, 206 F.R.D. 501, 503–04 (E.D.Cal. 2002).

24.   *See* Rule 6(e).

25.   *California Scents v. Surco Products, Inc.*, 406 F.3d 1102, 1106 (9th Cir.2005).

26.   *Huff v. Dobbins, Fraker, Tennant, Joy & Perlstein*, 243 F.3d 1086 (7th Cir. 2001).

27.   *See Westchester Day School v. Village of Mamaroneck*, 363 F.Supp.2d 667, 670 (S.D.N.Y.2005); *National Union Fire Ins., Co. of Pittsburgh, Pa. v. L.E. Myers Co. Group*, 928 F.Supp. 394, 396 (S.D.N.Y. 1996).

28.   *See, e.g., California Scents v. Surco Products, Inc.*, 406 F.3d 1102, 1106 (9th Cir.2005); *Hostrop v. Board of Jr. College Dist. No. 515*, 523 F.2d 569 (7th Cir.1975).

29.   *Polywell Intern., Inc. v. Hauppauge Computer Works, Inc.*, 2003 WL 22176616 (N.D.Tex.2003); *Avne Systems, Ltd. v. Marketsource Corp.*, 191 F.R.D. 56, 57 (S.D.N.Y.2000) (greater leniency is appropriate in cases originally filed in state court); *Williams v. J.F.K. Int'l Carting Co.*, 164 F.R.D. 340, 341–42 (S.D.N.Y.1996).

petition, then all parties have 10 days from service of the pleading.[30] If, prior to removal, a party has made a jury demand in accordance with state procedures or has made a jury demand that would satisfy federal requirements,[31] or if state procedures do not require an express demand, then no jury demand is necessary following removal.[32]

Objections to Jury Trial Demand

A party objecting to a jury trial demand may challenge it by filing a motion to strike. The Rules do not specify a time limit for moving to strike a jury trial demand.[33]

Appeals

A party that believes that the court has incorrectly denied its right to a jury trial may either seek a Writ of Mandamus or take an appeal after final judgment.[34]

RULE 38(c).   SPECIFYING ISSUES

CORE CONCEPT

A party may limit a jury trial demand to specific issues.[35]   Other parties then have 10 days to make a jury trial demand for remaining issues.

NOTE: A demand that does not specify individual issues is deemed a demand for a jury trial on all issues that are properly triable to a jury.[36]

RULE 38(d).   WAIVER; WITHDRAWAL

CORE CONCEPT

Failure to serve and file a timely jury trial demand is a waiver of the right, even if the failure was inadvertent.[37]

30.   *See* Rule 81(c); *Lutz v. Glendale Union High School*, 403 F.3d 1061, 1063 (9th Cir.2005).

31.   *Lutz v. Glendale Union High School*, 403 F.3d 1061, 1063 (9th Cir.2005); *Wyatt v. Hunt Plywood Co., Inc.*, 297 F.3d 405, 415, n.26 (5th Cir.2002).

32.   Rule 81(c); *Williams v. J.F.K. Int'l Carting Co.*, 164 F.R.D. 340, 341–42 (S.D.N.Y.1996)(failure to make a demand by the deadline set by the court constitutes waiver).

33.   *Jones-Hailey v. Corp. of TVA*, 660 F.Supp. 551, 553 (E.D.Tenn.1987) (motion to strike jury trial demand allowed one month before trial because Rule 38 contains no time limit).

34.   *Dairy Queen, Inc. v. Wood*, 369 U.S. 469, 82 S.Ct. 894, 8 L.Ed.2d 44 (1962);

California Scents v. Surco Products, Inc., 406 F.3d 1102, 1106 (9th Cir.2005) (the erroneous denial of a jury trial is subject to harmless error analysis).

35.   *Athridge v. Iglesias*, 2003 WL 23100036 (D.D.C.2003).

36.   *See Allison v. Citgo Petroleum*, 151 F.3d 402 (5th Cir.1998); *Zirlin v. Village of Scarsdale*, 365 F.Supp.2d 477, 483 (S.D.N.Y.2005).

37.   *Bogosian v. Woloohojian Realty Corp.*, 323 F.3d 55, 62 (1st Cir.2003) (cursory objection to bench trial cannot resurrect a waived jury trial right); *Garcia-Ayala v. Lederle Parenterals, Inc.*, 212 F.3d 638, 645 (1st Cir.2000) (the right to a jury trial is constitutionally protected and casual waivers are not to be presumed); *Synovus Trust Co., N.A. v. Honda Motor Co., Ltd.*, 223

APPLICATIONS

Waiver Following Demand

A party making timely jury trial demand waives that right if the party participates in a non-jury trial without objecting.[38]

Withdrawal of Demand

Once a jury trial demand has been made, it cannot be withdrawn except with the consent of all parties.[39] Note, however, that if the case develops such that the right to a jury trial no longer exists, the court can designate the case as non-jury without the consent of the party initially making the jury demand.[40]

RULE 38(e). ADMIRALTY AND MARITIME CLAIMS

CORE CONCEPT

Rule 38 does not create a right to a jury trial for admiralty or maritime claims.[41] However, jury trials in an admiralty claim are not forbidden.[42]

ADDITIONAL RESEARCH REFERENCES

Wright & Miller, *Federal Practice and Procedure* §§ 2301–2322.

C.J.S. Admiralty §§ 216–218; Federal Civil Procedure §§ 943–950; Juries §§ 9, 11, 84–113 et seq.

West's Key No. Digests, Admiralty ⟜80; Jury ⟜9–37.

F.R.D. 699, 702 (M.D.Ga.2004) (the right to trial by jury should not be deemed waived absent exceptional circumstances).

38. *Bostic v. Goodnight*, 443 F.3d 1044, 1047 (8th Cir.2006); *Thompson v. Mahre*, 110 F.3d 716, 721 (9th Cir.1997); *but see United States v. California Mobile Home Park Management Co.*, 107 F.3d 1374, 1379–80 (9th Cir.1997) (plaintiff's filing a continuing demand for a jury trial and objecting several times prior to trial was sufficient to preserve her right to a jury trial even though she went to bench trial and did not object at trial); *Jennings v. McCormick*, 154 F.3d 542, 545 (5th Cir.1998) (participation in bench trial by a *pro se* party is not a waiver).

39. *Middle Tennessee News Co., Inc. v. Charnel of Cincinnati, Inc.*, 250 F.3d 1077

(7th Cir.2001); *Allison v. Citgo Petroleum*, 151 F.3d 402 (5th Cir.1998).

40. *Kramer v. Banc of America Securities, LLC*, 355 F.3d 961, 968 (7th Cir.2004).

41. *See Fitzgerald v. U. S. Lines Co.*, 374 U.S. 16, 83 S.Ct. 1646, 10 L.Ed.2d 720 (1963); *Becker v. Tidewater, Inc.*, 405 F.3d 257, 259 (5th Cir.2005); *Foulk v. Donjon Marine Co., Inc.*, 144 F.3d 252 (3d Cir. 1998); *Windsor Mount Joy Mut. Ins. Co. v. Johnson*, 264 F.Supp.2d 158 (D.N.J.2003); *Group Therapy, Inc. v. White*, 280 F.Supp.2d 21, 32 (W.D.N.Y.2003).

42. *See American River Transp. Co., Inc. v. Paragon Marine Services, Inc.*, 329 F.3d 946, 947 (8th Cir.2003).

RULE 39

TRIAL BY JURY OR BY THE COURT

(a) When a Demand Is Made. When a jury trial has been demanded under Rule 38, the action must be designated on the docket as a jury action. The trial on all issues so demanded must be by jury unless:

(1) the parties or their attorneys file a stipulation to a nonjury trial or so stipulate on the record; or

(2) the court, on motion or on its own, finds that on some or all of those issues there is no federal right to a jury trial.

(b) When No Demand Is Made. Issues on which a jury trial is not properly demanded are to be tried by the court. But the court may, on motion, order a jury trial on any issue for which a jury might have been demanded.

(c) Advisory Jury; Jury Trial by Consent. In an action not triable of right by a jury, the court, on motion or on its own:

(1) may try any issue with an advisory jury; or

(2) may, with the parties' consent, try any issue by a jury whose verdict has the same effect as if a jury trial had been a matter of right, unless the action is against the United States and a federal statute provides for a nonjury trial.

—————————— **2007 AMENDMENTS ROADMAP** ——————————

STYLE PROJECT CHANGES: The subsections in Rule 39 were relabeled, and Rules 39(a) and (c) were further subsectioned. The language in Rule 39 was shortened, clarified, and reorganized; active voice was substituted for passive; and "jury trial" replaced "trial by jury."

NON-STYLE CHANGES: None.

AUTHORS' COMMENTARY ON RULE 39

─────────────── PURPOSE AND SCOPE ───────────────

Rule 39 describes the mechanisms for allocating issues for trial by jury or non-jury (other than by filing a jury trial demand pursuant to Rule 38). Rule 39 also covers advisory juries.

RULE 39(a). WHEN A DEMAND IS MADE

CORE CONCEPT

Once a jury trial has been demanded, the docket will be so designated and the claim will be tried to a jury unless the parties stipulate otherwise or the court determines that no right to a jury trial exists under the Constitution or federal statute.[1]

APPLICATIONS

Stipulations

The parties may stipulate to a non-jury trial, even if a timely jury trial demand has been filed.[2] The parties may also stipulate to trial by the court of specific issues.[3] Such a stipulation should be clear and unambiguous,[4] and must be made either:

- in writing and filed with the court;[5] or
- orally in open court and entered in the record.[6]

Striking Improper Jury Demand

When a party has filed a jury trial demand for an equity claim, the court should order a non-jury trial, either *sua sponte*[7] or upon motion.[8]

Jury Verdict Binding

If a trial occurs before a jury following a jury trial demand, the verdict is binding and may not be treated as advisory.

1. *South Port Marine, LLC v. Gulf Oil Ltd. Partnership*, 234 F.3d 58, 62 (1st Cir. 2000); *Bordeau v. Saginaw Control & Engineering, Inc.*, 477 F.Supp.2d 797, 799 (E.D.Mich. 2007).

2. *Clark v. Runyon*, 218 F.3d 915, 917–18 (8th Cir.2000).

3. *Gaworski v. ITT Commercial Finance Corp.*, 17 F.3d 1104 (8th Cir.1994).

4. *Hupp v. Siroflex of America*, 159 F.R.D. 29 (S.D.Tex.1994)(failure to object is not a stipulation).

5. *Garcia-Ayala v. Lederle Parenterals, Inc.*, 212 F.3d 638, 645 (1st Cir.2000).

6. *Fuller v. City of Oakland, Cal.*, 47 F.3d 1522 (9th Cir.1995).

7. *Tegal Corp. v. Tokyo Electron America, Inc.*, 257 F.3d 1331, 1341 (Fed.Cir. 2001); *Kennedy v. Alabama State Board of Education*, 78 F.Supp.2d 1246, 1259 (M.D.Ala.2000).

8. *Kramer v. Banc of America Securities*, LLC, 355 F.3d 961, 967–68 (7th Cir. 2004); *Lamberty v. Premier Millwork and Lumber Co., Inc.*, 329 F.Supp.2d 737, 744 (E.D.Va.2004); *General Instrument Corp. of Del. v. Nu–Tek Elecs. & Mfg., Inc.*, 1996 WL 184794 (E.D.Pa.1996) (holding that a party may unilaterally revoke a demand for a jury trial where a jury trial is not a matter of right).

Waiver

Participating in a bench trial without objection may constitute a waiver of the right to a jury trial, even if a timely demand has been filed.[9]

RULE 39(b).   WHEN NO DEMAND IS MADE

CORE CONCEPT

Claims for which no party has filed a jury trial demand are tried by the court.

APPLICATIONS

No Jury Without Demand or Motion

The court may not impanel a jury without a demand or motion,[10] except in an advisory capacity.[11]

Rules Governing Trial by Court

Other Rules govern the procedures for trial by the court. *See* Rule 41(b)(pertaining to involuntary dismissal), Rule 43(c)(pertaining to offers of proof), Rule 52 (pertaining to findings of fact), Rules 53(b) and (e)(2)(pertaining to reference to a master), Rule 58 (pertaining to entry of judgments), and Rule 59(c)(pertaining to grounds for a new trial).

Motion for Jury Trial

When a jury demand is omitted or filed out-of-time, the court, upon motion[12] and in its discretion, may order a jury trial of claims for which a jury trial could properly have been made.[13] Courts are split on the standard for granting such motions.[14] On appeal, rulings

---

9. *United States v. Rangel de Aguilar,* 308 F.3d 1134, 1138 (10th Cir.2002) (allowing waiver of jury trial right by oral stipulation entered in the record); *Wilcher v. City of Wilmington,* 139 F.3d 366 (3d Cir.1998).

10. *Sartin v. Cliff's Drilling Co.,* 2004 WL 551209 (E.D.La.2004) (Rule 39(b) requires a motion by a party; the court may not employ Rule 39(b) of its own initiative).

11. *Swofford v. B & W, Inc.,* 336 F.2d 406, 409 (5th Cir.1964).

12. *Sartin v. Cliff's Drilling Co.,* 2004 WL 551209 (E.D.La.2004) (Rule 39(b) requires a motion by a party; the court may not employ Rule 39(b) of its own initiative).

13. *United States Securities and Exchange Commission v. The Infinity Group Co.,* 212 F.3d 180 (3d Cir.2000); *Harrington v. Wilber,* 384 F.Supp.2d 1321, 1324 (S.D.Iowa 2005) (setting forth factors for a motion for jury trial; *Pyramid Co. of Holyoke v. Homeplace Stores Two, Inc.,* 175 F.R.D. 415, 421 (D.Mass.1997) (motion

must be done formally, be well supported, and be addressed to the trial judge in whose discretion the decision resides).

14. *See Ruiz v. Rodriguez,* 206 F.R.D. 501 (E.D.Cal.2002) (discussing the different standards applied by various courts); *Green Construction Co. v. Kansas Power & Light Co.,* 1 F.3d 1005 (10th Cir.1993)(jury trial should be granted in the absence of strong and compelling reasons to the contrary); *Pacific Fisheries Corp. v. HIH Cas. & General Ins., Ltd.,* 239 F.3d 1000, 1002 (9th Cir.2001) (discretion to grant an untimely jury trial is narrow, and does not permit a court to grant relief when the failure to make a timely demand results from an oversight or inadvertence); *Members v. Paige,* 140 F.3d 699, 703 (7th Cir.1998) (court may request a reason the deadline has not been met and then approach the "application under Rule 39(b) with an open mind and an eye to the factual situation of that particular case, rather than with a fixed policy").

on motions for jury trials are reviewed under the abuse of discretion standard.[15]

RULE 39(c).   ADVISORY JURY;
JURY TRIAL BY CONSENT

CORE CONCEPT

The judge may impanel an advisory jury if the case will not be tried to a binding jury.

APPLICATIONS

Verdict Non-binding

The judge is the ultimate trier of fact as to equitable claims,[16] and has complete discretion to adopt or reject the verdict of an advisory jury.[17]

Findings of Fact and Conclusions of Law

The court must make its own findings of fact and conclusions of law in cases tried with an advisory jury.[18]

Broad Discretion

The court has broad discretion as to whether to impanel an advisory jury.[19]

Binding Jury With Consent

If no claims at law are present, the judge still may impanel a normal, binding jury with the consent (either express or by failure to object) of *all* parties.[20] Consent of the parties does not require the judge to empanel a jury, it merely gives the court the discretion to do so.[21] The exception to this rule is that certain statutes prohibit

15. *Mile High Industries v. Cohen*, 222 F.3d 845, 855 (10th Cir.2000).

16. *N.A.A.C.P. v. AcuSport, Inc.*, 271 F.Supp.2d 435, 469 (E.D.N.Y.2003) (the judge in an equitable action is the ultimate trier of fact even when the judge has invoked the discretionary right to empanel an advisory jury).

17. *Hyde Properties v. McCoy*, 507 F.2d 301 (6th Cir.1974); *Hine v. Mineta*, 238 F.Supp.2d 497, 499 (E.D.N.Y.2003) (it is wholly within the discretion of the trial court whether to accept or reject in whole or in part the verdict of the advisory jury).

18. Rule 52(a); *Kolstad v. American Dental Assoc.*, 108 F.3d 1431, 1440 (D.C.Cir.1997).

19. *Kramer v. Banc of America Securities, LLC*, 355 F.3d 961, 968, n.2 (7th Cir. 2004); *Indiana Lumbermens Mutual Ins.*

Co. v. Timberland Pallet and Lumber Co., Inc., 195 F.3d 368, 374 (8th Cir.1999) (district court's discretion is not unlimited); *Hamm v. Nasatka Barriers, Inc.*, 166 F.R.D. 1, 2 (D.D.C.1996) (permitting the use of an advisory jury in a case where the United States was the defendant).

20. *See Broadnax v. City of New Haven*, 415 F.3d 265 (2nd Cir.2005) (failure to object to a trial before a jury is the equivalent of consenting); *Pals v. Schepel Buick & GMC Truck, Inc.*, 220 F.3d 495, 501 (7th Cir.2000); *Crane v. Green & Freedman Baking Co., Inc.*, 134 F.3d 17, 22 (1st Cir.1998); *Barry v. Carnival Corp.*, 424 F.Supp.2d 1354, 1358 (S.D.Fla.2006) (advisory jury may be impaneled in admiralty case with all parties' consent).

21. *Ed Peters Jewelry Co., Inc. v. C & J Jewelry Co., Inc.*, 215 F.3d 182 (1st Cir. 2000).

jury trials in specified actions against the United States.[22]

Mixed Legal and Equitable Issues

In a case in which a jury trial has been demanded as to some of the claims (or if the right to a jury trial exists as to only some of the claims), the court may consider the equitable claims as being submitted to the jury on an advisory basis.[23]

Advisory Jury With Legal Claims

Rule 39(c) states that a judge may impanel an advisory jury "[i]n all actions not triable of right by a jury. . . ."[24] Some courts construe this language broadly to include any action for which the right has not been exercised.

ADDITIONAL RESEARCH REFERENCES

Wright & Miller, *Federal Practice and Procedure* §§ 2323–2350.

C.J.S. Federal Civil Procedure §§ 933, 946, 1028–1030; Juries §§ 11, 91–98.

West's Key No. Digests, Federal Civil Procedure ☞1991, 2251, 2252; Jury ☞25(1), 28(6).

22. *See Palischak v. Allied Signal Aerospace Co.*, 893 F.Supp. 341, 342 (D.N.J. 1995).

23. *Everest Capital Ltd. v. Everest Funds Management, L.L.C.*, 393 F.3d 755, 762 (8th Cir.2005).

24. *Mota v. University of Texas Houston Health Science Center*, 261 F.3d 512, 526, n. 45 (5th Cir.2001) (although front pay was equitable remedy to be decided by the court, an advisory jury could be empaneled); *Epstein v. Kalvin–Miller Intern., Inc.*, 2000 WL 1761052 (S.D.N.Y.2000) (court of its own initiative has the right to try issue with advisory jury where the claim was not triable of right by a jury, even when parties not given notice of the advisory jury in advance of trial).

RULE 40

SCHEDULING CASES FOR TRIAL

Each court must provide by rule for scheduling trials. The court must give priority to actions entitled to priority by a federal statute.

─────────────── **2007 AMENDMENTS ROADMAP** ───────────────

STYLE PROJECT CHANGES: The language in Rule 40 was shorted and clarified.

NON-STYLE CHANGES: Rule 40 was amended so that the method for scheduling trials would be determined at the local level, without limitations in the Federal Rules.

NOTE: The Federal Rules "Style Project" is explained in Part III-A.

AUTHORS' COMMENTARY ON RULE 40
─────────────── **PURPOSE AND SCOPE** ───────────────

Rule 40 allows individual district courts to formulate their own rules for placing cases on the trial calendar.

APPLICATIONS

Broad Discretion

Individual judges have broad discretion in enforcing the district court's rules regarding assignment of cases. They may give precedence to cases of public importance or cases in which delay will cause hardship.[1]

Precedence by Statute

Some statutes provide for precedence for actions brought thereunder.

Motion for Continuance

The trial judge has great discretion in ruling on motions for continuance.[2]

---

1. *Clinton v. Jones*, 520 U.S. 681, 707–708, 117 S.Ct. 1636, 1650–51, 137 L.Ed.2d 945 (1997) (the court abused its discretion in deferring trial until after president left office).

2. *Clinton v. Jones*, 520 U.S. 681, 706–707, 117 S.Ct. 1636, 1650–51, 137 L.Ed.2d 945 (1997).

ADDITIONAL RESEARCH REFERENCES

Wright & Miller, *Federal Practice and Procedure* §§ 2351–2352.

C.J.S. Federal Civil Procedure § 934.

West's Key No. Digests, Federal Civil Procedure ⊙1993–1994.

RULE 41

DISMISSAL OF ACTIONS

(a) Voluntary Dismissal.

   (1) *By the Plaintiff.*

      (A) *Without a Court Order.* Subject to Rules 23(e), 23.1(c), 23.2, and 66 and any applicable federal statute, the plaintiff may dismiss an action without a court order by filing:

         (i) a notice of dismissal before the opposing party serves either an answer or a motion for summary judgment; or

         (ii) a stipulation of dismissal signed by all parties who have appeared.

      (B) *Effect.* Unless the notice or stipulation states otherwise, the dismissal is without prejudice. But if the plaintiff previously dismissed any federal-or state-court action based on or including the same claim, a notice of dismissal operates as an adjudication on the merits.

   (2) *By Court Order; Effect.* Except as provided in Rule 41(a)(1), an action may be dismissed at the plaintiff's request only by court order, on terms that the court considers proper. If a defendant has pleaded a counterclaim before being served with the plaintiff's motion to dismiss, the action may be dismissed over the defendant's objection only if the counterclaim can remain pending for independent adjudication. Unless the order states otherwise, a dismissal under this paragraph (2) is without prejudice.

(b) Involuntary Dismissal; Effect. If the plaintiff fails to prosecute or to comply with these rules or a court order, a defendant may move to dismiss the action or any claim against it. Unless the dismissal order states otherwise, a dismissal under this subdivision (b) and any dismissal not under this rule—except one for lack of jurisdiction, improper venue, or failure to join a party under Rule 19—operates as an adjudication on the merits.

(c) Dismissing a Counterclaim, Crossclaim, or Third–Party Claim. This rule applies to a dismissal of any counterclaim, crossclaim, or third-party claim. A claimant's voluntary dismissal under Rule 41(a)(1)(A)(i) must be made:

(1) before a responsive pleading is served; or

(2) if there is no responsive pleading, before evidence is introduced at a hearing or trial.

(d) Costs of a Previously Dismissed Action. If a plaintiff who previously dismissed an action in any court files an action based on or including the same claim against the same defendant, the court:

(1) may order the plaintiff to pay all or part of the costs of that previous action; and

(2) may stay the proceedings until the plaintiff has complied.

[Amended effective March 19, 1948; July 1, 1963; July 1, 1966; July 1, 1968; August 1, 1987; December 1, 1991; April 30, 2007, effective December 1, 2007.]

2007 AMENDMENTS ROADMAP

STYLE PROJECT CHANGES: Rule 41(a)(1) was amended to clarify that voluntary dismissal of class actions is subject to Rule 23.1(c) and Rule 23.2, as well as to Rule 23(e), curing an historical oversight. Rules 41(a), (c), and (d) were further subsectioned, and headings were added or revised throughout. The language in Rule 41 was shortened and clarified; active voice was substituted for passive; and cumbersome language was culled.

NON-STYLE CHANGES: None.

NOTE: The Federal Rules "Style Project" is explained in Part III-A.

AUTHORS' COMMENTARY ON RULE 41

PURPOSE AND SCOPE

Rule 41 controls the procedural aspects and effects of dismissals. It addresses both voluntary and involuntary dismissals, as well as the plaintiff's ability to initiate another action based on the same cause of action.

NOTE: The second voluntary dismissal by the plaintiff acts as an adjudication on the merits and will bar subsequent actions based on the same claims.

RULE 41(a)(1).   VOLUNTARY DISMISSAL;
BY THE PLAINTIFF

CORE CONCEPT

The plaintiff may dismiss an action without consent of the court either by stipulation of all parties or unilaterally if the defendant has not yet filed an answer or motion for summary judgment.[1]

APPLICATIONS

Timing

Unless stipulated to by all parties, a plaintiff may file a notice of dismissal under Rule 41(a)(1) only if the defendant has not yet served an answer or motion for summary judgment.[2] Otherwise, a plaintiff must file a motion under Rule 41(a)(2).[3]

Notice of Dismissal

Dismissal under Rule 41(a)(1) is achieved by filing a *notice* of dismissal, not by motion, and no court order is required.[4] The notice is effective when filed,[5] but must be served on all parties pursuant to Rule 5(a).

Notice Unconditional

A notice of dismissal must be unconditional[6] and unequivocal[7] in both dismissals by the plaintiff and by stipulation, although the parties may privately impose conditions (such as the payment of a sum of money) on their participation in a stipulation for dismissal.

Effect of Dismissal

A voluntary dismissal leaves the situation as if the lawsuit had never been filed, unless the dismissal is specified as with prejudice.[8]

1. *Wilson v. City of San Jose*, 111 F.3d 688, 692 (9th Cir.1997); *SmithKline Beecham Corp. v. Pentech Pharmaceuticals, Inc.*, 261 F.Supp.2d 1002, 1004 (N.D.Ill.2003).

2. *RFR Industries, Inc. v. Century Steps, Inc.*, 477 F.3d 1348, 1351–52 (Fed.Cir. 2007) (answer that had been filed and faxed but not properly served did not preclude a voluntary dismissal); *ITV Direct, Inc. v. Healthy Solutions, LLC*, 445 F.3d 66, 70 (1st Cir.2006); *Arndt v. UBS AG*, 342 F.Supp.2d 132, 137 (E.D.N.Y.2004) (motion to dismiss does not prevent notice of dismissal).

3. *GF Gaming Corp. v. City of Black Hawk, Colo.*, 405 F.3d 876, 887–88 (10th Cir.2005).

4. *In re Matthews*, 395 F.3d 477, 480 (4th Cir.2005); *Torres v. Walker*, 356 F.3d 238, 243 (2nd Cir.2004).

5. *Marques v. Federal Reserve Bank of Chicago*, 286 F.3d 1014, 1018 (7th Cir.2002)

(a judgment entered after a proper voluntary dismissal is void); *Commercial Space Management Co., Inc. v. The Boeing Co., Inc.*, 193 F.3d 1074, 1076 (9th Cir.1999) (once the notice of dismissal is filed, the court loses jurisdiction over the action). *But see University of South Alabama v. American Tobacco Co.*, 168 F.3d 405, 409 (11th Cir.1999) (dismissal not effective where court did not have subject matter jurisdiction and motion to remand was pending).

6. *Hyde Constr. Co. v. Koehring Co.*, 388 F.2d 501, 507 (10th Cir.1968); *Scam Instrument Corp. v. Control Data Corp.*, 458 F.2d 885 (7th Cir.1972).

7. *Carter v. Beverly Hills Sav. and Loan Ass'n*, 884 F.2d 1186 (9th Cir.1989).

8. *Harvey Specialty & Supply, Inc. v. Anson Flowline Equipment Inc.*, 434 F.3d 320, 324 (5th Cir.2005); *In re Matthews*, 395 F.3d 477, 480 (4th Cir.2005); *Gambale*

A voluntary dismissal that is specified as with prejudice is given the same res judicata effect as any other judgment.[9]

Absolute Right

Generally, the right to voluntarily dismiss an action is considered absolute, not requiring assent by the court or opposing parties.[10] Likewise, the court cannot impose conditions in connection with a voluntary dismissal[11] (although it can do so under Rule 41(a)(2)).[12]

Stipulation

A stipulation for dismissal must be signed by all parties who have appeared in the action or it is not effective.[13]

Dismissal Without Prejudice (Two Dismissal Rule)

Dismissals by stipulation are presumed without prejudice unless they specify otherwise.[14] Dismissals unilaterally by the plaintiff are governed by the Two Dismissal Rule: the first voluntary dismissal of a given claim is without prejudice; the second dismissal acts as a final adjudication on the merits and will preclude a third action based on the same claim.[15]

v. Deutsche Bank AG, 377 F.3d 133, 139 (2nd Cir.2004) (a voluntary dismissal deprives the court of jurisdiction over the matter); Scheinblum v. Lauderdale County Bd. of Supervisors, 350 F.Supp.2d 743; 745–46 (S.D.Miss.2004) (dismissal as to non-diverse plaintiffs allows diversity jurisdiction); but see Macheska v. Thomson Learning, 347 F.Supp.2d 169, 179 (M.D.Pa.2004) (court retains jurisdiction to award costs or fees).

9. Norfolk Southern Corp. v. Chevron, U.S.A., Inc., 371 F.3d 1285 (11th Cir.2004); but see Headwaters Inc. v. U.S. Forest Service, 399 F.3d 1047, (9th Cir.2005) (although dismissals under Rule 41 are commonly denominated adjudications "on the merits," only a judgment that actually passes directly on the substance of a particular claim before the court triggers the doctrine of res judicata or claim preclusion).

10. Marques v. Federal Reserve Bank of Chicago, 286 F.3d 1014, 1017 (7th Cir.2002) (a party does not need a good reason, or even a sane reason, for a voluntary dismissal); American Soccer Co., Inc. v. Score First Enterprises, 187 F.3d 1108, 1111 (9th Cir. 1999) (the amount of time and effort expended does not affect the plaintiff's right to a voluntary dismissal).

11. Commercial Space Management Co., Inc. v. The Boeing Co., Inc., 193 F.3d 1074, 1076 (9th Cir.1999); Hester Industries, Inc. v. Tyson Foods, Inc., 160 F.3d 911, 916 (2d Cir.1998).

12. Commercial Space Management Co., Inc. v. The Boeing Co., Inc., 193 F.3d 1074, 1078 (9th Cir.1999).

13. Mutual Assignment and Indemnification Co. v. Lind–Waldock & Co., LLC, 364 F.3d 858, 860 (7th Cir.2004); Camacho v. Mancuso, 53 F.3d 48 (4th Cir. 1995)(stipulation of dismissal ssigned by the plaintiff only is not effective even though all parties admit that they consented); Byrd v. Howse Implement Co., Inc., 227 F.R.D. 692, 694 (M.D.Ala.2005) (dismissal stipulation must be signed by all defendants); but see Role v. Eureka Lodge No. 434, I.A. of M & A.W. AFL–CIO, 402 F.3d 314, 318 (2nd Cir.2005) ("a voluntary, clear, explicit, and unqualified stipulation of dismissal entered into by the parties in court and on the record is enforceable even if the agreement is never reduced to writing, signed, or filed").

14. Bowers v. National Collegiate Athletic Ass'n, 346 F.3d 402, 413 (3rd Cir. 2003); West v. Macht, 197 F.3d 1185, 1188 (7th Cir.1999).

15. Murray v. Conseco, Inc., 467 F.3d 602, 605 (7th Cir. 2006) (dismissal for lack of subject matter does not implicate the Two Dismissal Rule); American Cyanamid Co. v. Capuano, 381 F.3d 6, 17 (1st Cir. 2004) (two dismissal rule applies only to the defendants of the dismissed actions or those in privity); ASX Investment Corp. v. Newton, 183 F.3d 1265, 1267–68 (11th Cir.1999)

Dismissal With Prejudice

A dismissal stipulation may specifically provide that dismissal is with prejudice.[16]

Actions in State Court

The Two Dismissal Rule applies to actions filed in state court on the first occasion. However, if the second action is filed and dismissed in state court, it will not trigger the Two Dismissal Rule [17] unless the state has a similar rule.[18] Once an action is barred in federal court by the Two Dismissal Rule, it will also be barred in state court.

Statute of Limitations

An action dismissed without prejudice does not toll the statute of limitations.[19]

Class Actions, Receivers, etc.

Rule 41 is expressly subject to the provisions of Rule 23(e)(requiring court approval for the dismissal of a class action)[20] and Rule 66 (governing cases in which a receiver has been appointed). Rule 41 also may not apply in other statutorily controlled areas, such as stockholders' derivative actions.[21] Rule 41 does apply to appeals of certain proceedings to a federal court, such as an appeal of a decision by the Board of Veterans' Appeals.[22]

Removal

Rule 41 applies with equal force to cases removed from state court.[23]

Rule 12 Motions

In general, a motion to dismiss pursuant to Rule 12(b) for failure to state a claim or for lack of jurisdiction or venue does not terminate the plaintiff's unilateral right to dismiss.[24] An exception may arise if the court has held extensive hearings on the motion,[25] or converted the motion to dismiss into a motion for summary judgment.[26]

(Two Dismissal Rule does not count a dismissal by court order under Rule 41(a)(2)).

16. *Norfolk Southern Corp. v. Chevron, U.S.A., Inc.*, 371 F.3d 1285 (11th Cir.2004) (a stipulation of dismissal with prejudice is given the same res judicata effect as any other judgment).

17. *Rader v. Baltimore & O.R. Co.*, 108 F.2d 980 (7th Cir.1940).

18. *Manning v. South Carolina Dept. of Highway and Public Transp.*, 914 F.2d 44 (4th Cir.1990).

19. *Beck v. Caterpillar Inc.*, 50 F.3d 405 (7th Cir.1995).

20. *Crawford v. F. Hoffman–La Roche Ltd.*, 267 F.3d 760, 764 (8th Cir.2001); *In re Painewebber Limited Partnerships Litigation*, 147 F.3d 132, 137 (2d Cir.1998).

21. *Baker v. America's Mortgage Servicing, Inc.*, 58 F.3d 321 (7th Cir.1995).

22. *Graves v. Principi*, 294 F.3d 1350 (Fed.Cir.2002).

23. *Grivas v. Parmelee Transp. Co.*, 207 F.2d 334 (7th Cir.1953).

24. *Manze v. State Farm Ins. Co.*, 817 F.2d 1062, 1066 (3d Cir.1987).

25. *Harvey Aluminum, Inc. v. American Cyanamid Co.*, 203 F.2d 105 (2d Cir.1953).

26. *Swedberg v. Marotzke*, 339 F.3d 1139 (9th Cir.2003); *Hamm v. Rhone–Poulenc Rorer Pharmaceuticals, Inc.*, 187 F.3d

Dismissal of Part of Action

Courts differ as to the proper procedural mechanism for voluntarily dismissing part of an action. The majority allow voluntary dismissal of part of an action by notice pursuant to Rule 41.[27] Some courts require a motion to amend pursuant to Rule 15(a).[28] A third party plaintiff may voluntarily dismiss the third party complaint under Rule 41(a)(1).[29]

Costs and Fees

Following a voluntary dismissal under Rule 41, the district court retains jurisdiction over the matter such that the court may award costs to the defendant.[30] The defendant is not considered the prevailing party following a voluntary dismissal pursuant to Rule 41(a)(1) for purposes of statutes governing the award of attorney fees to the prevailing party.[31]

Enforcement of Settlement Agreement

Normally, a federal court does not have jurisdiction over an action to enforce the terms of a settlement agreement. In order to vest the court with such jurisdiction, the parties can include language in their Rule 41(a)(1)(ii) stipulation for dismissal providing that the court will retain jurisdiction for purposes of enforcing the settlement agreement.[32]

Appeals

The first voluntary dismissal under Rule 41(a)(1) is normally not considered a final order and thus not appealable.[33] The second dismissal, however, is a final, appealable order.[34]

941, 950 (8th Cir.1999); *Finley Lines Joint Protective Bd. Unit 200 v. Norfolk So. Corp.*, 109 F.3d 993 (4th Cir.1997).

27. See *Bowers v. National Collegiate Athletic Ass'n*, 346 F.3d 402, 413 (3rd Cir. 2003) (allowing dismissal of part of a third party complaint); *Commercial Space Management Co., Inc. v. The Boeing Co., Inc.*, 193 F.3d 1074, 1079 (9th Cir.1999) (stipulation of dismissal as to some defendants); *Public Interest Research Group of New Jersey, Inc. v. Windall*, 51 F.3d 1179 (3d Cir. 1995).

28. See *Gobbo Farms & Orchards v. Poole Chem. Co.*, 81 F.3d 122, 123 (10th Cir.1996)(holding that a voluntary dismissal must be for all claims within an action); *Sudnick v. Department of Defense*, 474 F.Supp.2d 91, 95, n.3 (D.D.C. 2007) (same); *Vogel v. American Kiosk Management*, 371 F.Supp.2d 122, 129 (D.Conn.2005).

29. *Century Mfg. Co., Inc. v. Central Transport Intern., Inc.*, 209 F.R.D. 647 (D.Mass.2002).

30. *Sequa Corp. v. Cooper*, 245 F.3d 1036, 1037 (8th Cir.2001).

31. See *RFR Industries, Inc. v. Century Steps, Inc.*, 477 F.3d 1348, 1351–52 (Fed. Cir. 2007) (the defendant not the prevailing party for purposes of 35 U.S.C. § 285).

32. *Kokkonen v. Guardian Life Ins. Co. of Am.*, 511 U.S. 375, 378–81, 114 S.Ct. 1673, 1675-1677, 128 L.Ed.2d 391 (1994); *Municipality of San Juan v. Rullan*, 318 F.3d 26, 30 (1st Cir.2003); *Lopez Morales v. Hospital Hermanos Melendez, Inc.*, 460 F.Supp.2d 288, 293–94 (D.Puerto Rico 2006).

33. *Versa Products, Inc. v. Home Depot, USA, Inc.*, 387 F.3d 1325, (11th Cir.2004); *State Treasurer of the State of Michigan v. Barry*, 168 F.3d 8, 11 (11th Cir.1999).

34. *Muzikowski v. Paramount Pictures Corp.*, 322 F.3d 918, 923–24 (7th Cir.2003).

RULE 41(a)(2). BY COURT ORDER; EFFECT

CORE CONCEPT

Except as provided in Rule 41(a)(1) above (dismissal by stipulation or before an answer or motion for summary judgment has been filed), dismissal of an action must be by court order.[35]

APPLICATIONS

Prejudice

A dismissal by order of court can be with or without prejudice.[36] A court order granting voluntary dismissal is presumed to be without prejudice unless it explicitly specifies otherwise.[37]

Discretion of Court

The decision whether to grant or deny the plaintiff's motion for voluntary dismissal is within the sound discretion of the court,[38] although some courts hold that the court had no discretion to deny a motion to dismiss *with prejudice* (reasoning that it is unfair to force an unwilling plaintiff to go to trial).[39] A court should grant a Rule 41(a)(2) motion for voluntary dismissal unless a defendant can show that it will suffer some plain legal prejudice as a result.[40] In general, courts are more likely to grant motions for voluntary dismissal at earlier stages of the litigation.[41]

Conditions

The court may include terms and conditions in its order granting voluntary dismissal in order to prevent prejudice to the defendant.[42] These conditions may be proposed by the parties or *sua*

35. *Wilson v. City of San Jose,* 111 F.3d 688, 692 (9th Cir.1997); *Home American Credit, Inc. v. Investors Title Ins. Co.,* 199 F.R.D. 563, 564–65 (E.D.N.C.2001) (leave of court is required for a dismissal once the defendant has answered or filed a motion for summary judgment).

36. *See, e.g., Minnesota Mining And Mfg. Co. v. Barr Laboratories, Inc.,* 289 F.3d 775, 779 (Fed.Cir.2002).

37. *LeBlang Motors, Ltd. v. Subaru of America, Inc.,* 148 F.3d 680, 687 (7th Cir. 1998) (dismissal deemed with prejudice even though the defendant's motion only asked for dismissal without prejudice); *Palmieri v. Defaria,* 88 F.3d 136, 140 (2d Cir. 1996).

38. *Walter Kidde Portable Equipment, Inc. v. Universal Sec. Instruments, Inc.,* 479 F.3d 1330, 1336 (Fed.Cir. 2007) (dismissal within the court's discretion as long as there is no impairment of the defendant's rights); *Camilli v. Grimes,* 436 F.3d 120, 123 (2nd Cir.2006).

39. *Smoot v. Fox,* 340 F.2d 301 (6th Cir.1964).

40. *Brown v. Baeke,* 413 F.3d 1121, 1124 (10th Cir.2005) (listing factors for evaluating prejudice); *County of Santa Fe, N.M. v. Public Service Co. of New Mexico,* 311 F.3d 1031, 1047 (10th Cir.2002) (the important aspect is whether the opposing party will suffer prejudice); *Echols ex rel. Pitman v. EBA Krug & Priester GmbH & Co.,* 225 F.R.D. 518, 519 (E.D.N.C.2005).

41. *See Jones v. Simek,* 193 F.3d 485, 491 (7th Cir.1999); *Virgil v. Montgomery,* 353 F.Supp.2d 620 (E.D.N.C.2005); *Berry v. General Star National Ins. Co.,* 190 F.R.D. 697, 698 (M.D.Ala.2000).

42. *Walter Kidde Portable Equipment, Inc. v. Universal Sec. Instruments, Inc.,* 479 F.3d 1330, 1336 (Fed.Cir. 2007); *Elbaor v. Tripath Imaging, Inc.,* 279 F.3d 314, 316, n.1 (5th Cir.2002) ("Rule 41(a)(2), which is designed to protect non-movants from prejudice occasioned by unconditional dismiss-

sponte by the court.[43]   Examples of such conditions include the payment of costs[44] and/or attorney fees,[45] the production of specified documents,[46] making the dismissal with prejudice,[47] and an agreement not to assert specified claims in another action.   If the plaintiff is unhappy with the conditions imposed by the court, the plaintiff may decline the dismissal.[48]

Counterclaims

If the defendant has filed a counterclaim, then the plaintiff cannot dismiss the action against the defendant's objections unless the counterclaim can remain pending for adjudication.[49]   The defendant may dismiss its own counterclaim in the same manner that Rule 41 provides for dismissal of the plaintiff's claims.[50]

Dismissal of Part of Action

The plaintiff may dismiss some, but not all, of the defendants.[51]   Courts differ as to the proper procedural mechanism for voluntarily dismissing part of an action after an answer or summary judgment motion has been filed.[52]   Some courts allow voluntary dismissal by

als, is not a proper mechanism to punish non-compliance with court orders.'').

43.   *Brown v. Baeke,* 413 F.3d 1121, 1123 (10th Cir.2005) (some conditions proposed by the plaintiff, and others added by the court).

44.   *Chavez v. Illinois State Police,* 251 F.3d 612 (7th Cir.2001); *Williams v. Peralta Community College Dist.,* 227 F.R.D. 538, 540 (N.D.Cal.2005) (listing factors for deciding whether to award costs); *ACEquip, Ltd. v. Am. Eng'g Corp.,* 219 F.R.D. 44, 46 (D.Conn.2003) (deciding not to award costs, but requiring that any future action be filed in the same court).

45.   *Steinert v. Winn Group, Inc.,* 440 F.3d 1214, 1222 (10th Cir.2006) (when dismissal is *without* prejudice, attorney fees should only be awarded in extreme circumstances); *Brown v. Local 58, Int'l Bhd. of Elec. Workers,* 76 F.3d 762, 766–67 (6th Cir.1996); *Hinfin Realty Corp. v. The Pittston Co.,* 212 F.R.D. 461, 462 (E.D.N.Y. 2002) (courts often grant fee awards when a plaintiff dismisses a suit without prejudice under Rule 41(a)(2)); *BD v. Debuono,* 193 F.R.D. 117 (S.D.N.Y.2000) (attorney fees awarded only where conduct of the plaintiff was in bad faith or vexatious).

46.   *In re Vitamins Antitrust Litigation,* 198 F.R.D. 296 (D.D.C.2000) (dismissal conditioned on the plaintiff responding to outstanding document requests and interrogatories).

47.   *Shady Records, Inc. v. Source Enterprises, Inc.,* 371 F.Supp.2d 394, 396

(S.D.N.Y.2005) (dismissal required to be with prejudice where trial two weeks away); *Elbaor v. Tripath Imaging, Inc.,* 279 F.3d 314, 316, n.1 (5th Cir.2002) (the court may require the dismissal to be with prejudice to protect the defendant, but not to punish the plaintiff).

48.   *Elbaor v. Tripath Imaging, Inc.,* 279 F.3d 314, 320 (5th Cir.2002); *Babcock v. McDaniel,* 148 F.3d 797, 799 (7th Cir.1998) (if the plaintiff moves for dismissal without prejudice, the court may not dismiss with prejudice without offering the plaintiff an opportunity withdraw the motion).

49.   *See Walter Kidde Portable Equipment, Inc. v. Universal Sec. Instruments, Inc.,* 479 F.3d 1330, 1336 (Fed.Cir. 2007); *Esso Standard Oil Co. (Puerto Rico) v. Rodriguez–Perez,* 455 F.3d 1 (1st Cir.2006).

50.   *eCash Technologies, Inc. v. Guagliardo,* 127 F.Supp.2d 1069, 1081–82 (C.D.Cal.2000).

51.   *Disabled in Action of Pennsylvania v. Southeastern Pennsylvania Transp. Authority,* 224 F.R.D. 601, 605 (E.D.Pa.2004); *Protocomm Corp. v. Novell, Inc.,* 171 F.Supp.2d 459, 471 (E.D.Pa.2001)(dismissal of some defendants is permissible even in the presence of cross-claims).

52.   *See Jet, Inc. v. Sewage Aeration Systems,* 223 F.3d 1360, 1364 (Fed.Cir.2000) (Rule 41(a)(2) and Rule 15(a) are functionally interchangeable); *State Treasurer of State of Michigan v. Barry,* 168 F.3d 8, 18 (11th Cir.1999).

court order pursuant to Rule 41(a)(2).[53] Some courts require a motion to amend pursuant to Rule 15(a).[54]

Enforcement of Settlement Agreement

Normally, a federal court does not have jurisdiction over an action to enforce the terms of a settlement and stipulated dismissal.[55] In order to vest the district court with such jurisdiction, the court may, at its discretion, make the parties' compliance with a settlement agreement part of its dismissal order.[56]

Circumvention of Rule 39(b)

A district court may not use Rule 41(a)(2) to allow an untimely jury demand (by dismissal, then refiling a new complaint with a jury demand) if it would be prohibited from doing so under Rule 39(b), as that would introduce an unnecessary conflict between the two federal rules.[57]

Appeal

The Plaintiff normally cannot appeal the granting or denial of a motion for voluntary dismissal.[58] However, mandamus will lie if the motion was to dismiss with prejudice.[59] The plaintiff may be able to appeal the granting of its own motion to dismiss if the court imposes conditions on the dismissal that prejudice the plaintiff and to which the plaintiff has not acquiesced.[60] The plaintiff may not appeal prior rulings in an action if the action is dismissed without prejudice.[61] The defendant may appeal a notice of voluntary dismissal[62] or an order granting a motion for voluntary dismissal.[63]

---

53. See *Transwitch Corp. v. Galazar Networks, Inc.*, 377 F.Supp.2d 284 (D.Mass. 2005) (allowing motion for voluntary dismissal of all claims and substitution of new claims under Rule 42).

54. See *Boyce v. Augusta–Richmond County*, 111 F.Supp.2d 1363, 1374 (S.D.Ga. 2000).

55. *Solv-Ex Corp. v. Quillen*, 186 F.R.D. 313, 315 (S.D.N.Y.1999); *Lee v. Runyon*, 18 F.Supp.2d 649, 653 (E.D.Tex.1998).

56. *Kokkonen v. Guardian Life Ins. Co. of America*, 511 U.S. 375, 114 S.Ct. 1673, 128 L.Ed.2d 391 (1994); *Bragg v. Robertson*, 54 F.Supp.2d 653, 662–63 (S.D.W.Va.1999).

57. *Russ v. Standard Ins. Co.*, 120 F.3d 988, 990 (9th Cir.1997); *but see Hoffmann v. Alside, Inc.*, 596 F.2d 822, 823 (8th Cir. 1979).

58. See *Briseno v. Ashcroft*, 291 F.3d 377 (5th Cir.2002).

59. *In re International Business Machines Corp.*, 687 F.2d 591 (2d Cir.1982).

60. See *Versa Products, Inc. v. Home Depot, USA, Inc.*, 387 F.3d 1325, (11th Cir. 2004); *Chavez v. Illinois State Police*, 251 F.3d 612 (7th Cir.2001); *Belle-Midwest, Inc. v. Missouri Property & Casualty Ins. Guarantee Ass'n*, 56 F.3d 977 (8th Cir.1995).

61. *Martens v. Thomann*, 273 F.3d 159, 183 (2d Cir.2001) ("interlocutory orders should not ordinarily merge with a final judgment dismissing an action for failure to prosecute"); *Chappelle v. Beacon Communications Corp.*, 84 F.3d 652, 654 (2d Cir. 1996).

62. *Harvey Aluminum, Inc. v. American Cyanamid Co.*, 203 F.2d 105 (2d Cir.1953).

63. *Pontenberg v. Boston Scientific Corp.*, 252 F.3d 1253 (11th Cir.2001) (order granting dismissal is reviewed under the abuse of discretion standard).

RULE 41(b). INVOLUNTARY DISMISSAL; EFFECT

CORE CONCEPT

Rule 41(b) governs two types of involuntary dismissals: dismissal for failure to prosecute; and dismissal for failure to comply with other Rules or with a court order.

NOTE: Rule 41(b) was amended in 1991, and care should be exercised when citing decisions pertaining to Rule 41(b).

APPLICATIONS

Disfavored

Involuntary dismissal is within the discretion of the court,[64] but is disfavored and is granted sparingly.[65]

Failure to Prosecute

The court may dismiss for failure to prosecute *sua sponte* or upon motion.[66] Local Rules frequently specify the conditions for dismissal based on inactivity (typically, lack of activity for a period of one year).[67]

Failure to Comply With Rules or With Order

The court may grant a motion for involuntary dismissal or dismiss an action *sua sponte* based on the plaintiff's failure to comply with the Rules or with a court order.[68] For example, the plaintiff may risk involuntary dismissal by persistently refusing to file a pretrial statement. To determine whether dismissal is an appropriate sanction for violation of a particular Rule, the practitioner should also review the author commentary and case law discussing that Rule.[69]

---

64. *Bishop v. Lewis*, 155 F.3d 1094, 1096 (9th Cir.1998).

65. *LeSane v. Hall's Sec. Analyst, Inc.*, 239 F.3d 206, 209 (2d Cir.2001) (involuntary dismissal is a harsh remedy to be utilized only in extreme situations, particularly when *pro se* plaintiffs are involved); *Hunt v. City of Minneapolis, Minnesota*, 203 F.3d 524, 527 (8th Cir.2000) (involuntary dismissal should be used when lesser sanctions prove futile); *Tunica–Biloxi Indians of Louisiana v. Pecot*, 227 F.R.D. 271, 278 (W.D.La.2005) (dismissals with prejudice will be affirmed only upon a showing of a clear record of delay or contumacious conduct by the plaintiff, and where lesser sanctions would not serve the best interest of justice).

66. *Sealed Appellant v. Sealed Appellee*, 452 F.3d 415, 417 (5th Cir.2006) (there must be a clear record of delay or contumacious conduct by the plaintiff); *James v. McDonald's Corp.*, 417 F.3d 672 (7th Cir. 2005); *Pomales v. Celulares Telefonica, Inc.*, 342 F.3d 44, 50, n.5 (1st Cir.2003) (warning is not strictly required before dismissal, but

without a warning, the circumstances must show knowledge of the potential consequences of the party's conduct); *Aura Lamp & Lighting Inc. v. International Trading Corp.*, 325 F.3d 903, 908 (7th Cir.2003) (setting forth the factors for involuntary dismissal for failure to prosecute).

67. *See Wagner v. Ashcroft*, 214 F.R.D. 78 (N.D.N.Y.2003).

68. *Slack v. McDaniel*, 529 U.S. 473, 120 S.Ct. 1595, 146 L.Ed.2d 542 (2000); *Holly v. Anderson*, 467 F.3d 1120, 1121 (8th Cir. 2006) (court may dismiss sua sponte for failure to comply with its orders); *Doe v. Cassel*, 403 F.3d 986, 990 (8th Cir.2005) (the sanction needs to be proportionate to the transgression); *Wynder v. McMahon*, 360 F.3d 73, 78 (2nd Cir.2004) (court may not dismiss based on failure to comply with an order that imposes requirements greater than those authorized by the Rules).

69. *See, e.g., Bowling v. Hasbro, Inc.*, 403 F.3d 1373, 1375–76 (Fed.Cir.2005) (Rule 4(m) does not permit dismissal with prejudice); *Jackson v. City of New York*, 22 F.3d 71 (2d Cir.1994).

With Prejudice

Involuntary dismissals are presumed to be with prejudice unless the court specifies otherwise.[70] Additionally, involuntary dismissal under Rule 41(b) and dismissals not under Rule 41 (other than dismissals for lack of jurisdiction,[71] lack of venue,[72] or failure to join a party under Rule 19) operate as adjudications on the merits for purposes of res judicata or collateral estoppel.[73]

Motion Formalities

If the defendant makes the motion for involuntary dismissal at the close of plaintiff's case, it may be oral and without notice. Otherwise, the defendant must comply with the normal procedural formalities.

Dismissal Under Other Rules

Rule 41(b) governs only the two specified types of involuntary dismissal. Other types of dismissal are addressed elsewhere, such as in Rule 12(b), governing dismissal for reasons such as failure to state a claim and lack of jurisdiction.[74]

Appeal

The plaintiff may appeal an involuntary dismissal as a final order.[75] The order will be reviewed under the abuse of discretion standard.[76]

---

70. *Payne v. Brake*, 439 F.3d 198, 204 (4th Cir.2006); *Styskal v. Weld County Bd. of County Com'rs*, 365 F.3d 855, 858–59 (10th Cir.2004); *Owens v. Kaiser Foundation Health Plan, Inc.*, 244 F.3d 708, 714 (9th Cir.2001) (dismissal for failure to prosecute acts as an adjudication on the merits). *Cf. Criales v. American Airlines, Inc.*, 105 F.3d 93, 95 (2d Cir.1997) (dismissal for failure to exhaust state or administrative remedies is usually without prejudice).

71. *Brereton v. Bountiful City Corp.*, 434 F.3d 1213, 1216–17 (10th Cir.2006); *Intera Corp. v. Henderson*, 428 F.3d 605, 620 (6th Cir.2005) (rule applies with equal effect to personal and subject matter jurisdiction); *Matosantos Commercial Corp. v. Applebee's Intern., Inc.*, 245 F.3d 1203, 1209 (10th Cir.2001) (noting that the first adjudication will have estoppel effect as to the jurisdictional issues actually determined by the court).

72. *See Vasquez v. Bridgestone/Firestone, Inc.*, 325 F.3d 665, 678 (5th Cir.2003) (dismissal for forum non conveniens is not dismissal for lack of venue, and this is a dismissal with prejudice).

73. *See Semtek Intern. Inc. v. Lockheed Martin Corp.*, 531 U.S. 497, 121 S.Ct. 1021, 149 L.Ed.2d 32 (2001) (Rule 41 determines that the dismissal is on the merits, but in diversity cases, state law then determines the preclusive effect of the dismissal on another action); *Hells Canyon Preservation Council v. U.S. Forest Service*, 403 F.3d 683, 687 (9th Cir.2005); *Orca Yachts, L.L.C. v. Mollicam, Inc.*, 287 F.3d 316, 319 (4th Cir.2002).

74. *See Blue Cross and Blue Shield of Ala. v. Fondren*, 966 F.Supp. 1093, 1097 (M.D.Ala.1997) (case due to be dismissed for lack of subject matter jurisdiction is due to be dismissed without prejudice).

75. *Wynder v. McMahon*, 360 F.3d 73, 76 (2nd Cir.2004) (a dismissal without prejudice that does not give leave to amend and closes the case is a final, appealable order); *Rodgers v. Curators of the Univ. of Missouri*, 135 F.3d 1216, 1219 (8th Cir.1998) (applying an abuse of discretion standard).

76. *Ruiz-Rosa v. Rullan*, 485 F.3d 150, 153 (1st Cir. 2007); *Rivera Diaz v. American Airlines, Inc.*, 433 F.3d 120, 123 (1st Cir.2005).

RULE 41(c).   DISMISSING A COUNTERCLAIM, CROSSCLAIM, OR THIRD-PARTY CLAIM

CORE CONCEPT

The provisions of Rule 41 apply to counterclaims, crossclaims, and third-party claims with equal force.[77] For example, the right to unilateral voluntary dismissal ends with the filing of a responsive pleading or motion for summary judgment directed toward the counterclaim, crossclaim, or third-party claim.

RULE 41(d).   COSTS OF A PREVIOUSLY DISMISSED ACTION

CORE CONCEPT

If a plaintiff who has already *voluntarily* dismissed an action commences another action on the same claim, the court, in its discretion, can stay the second action until the plaintiff[78] pays such costs of the first action as the court deems appropriate.[79] The courts are split as to whether an award of costs under Rule 41(d) may include attorneys fees.[80]

ADDITIONAL RESEARCH REFERENCES

Wright & Miller, *Federal Practice and Procedure* §§ 2361–2376.

C.J.S. Federal Civil Procedure §§ 486, 775–819 et seq., 839–869 et seq.

West's Key No. Digests, Federal Civil Procedure ☞1691–1715, 1721–1729, 1741, 1758–1765, 1821–1842.

77. *Orca Yachts, L.L.C. v. Mollicam, Inc.*, 287 F.3d 316, 319 (4th Cir.2002).

78. *Duffy v. Ford Motor Co.*, 218 F.3d 623, 636 (6th Cir.2000) (Rule 41(d) discusses the imposition of costs upon the plaintiffs, not counsel).

79. *Pontenberg v. Boston Scientific Corp.*, 252 F.3d 1253 (11th Cir.2001) (Rule 41(d) authorizes the district court to require the plaintiff to pay the defendant's costs of the dismissed action upon refiling the action); *Rogers v. Wal–Mart Stores, Inc.*, 230 F.3d 868, 874 (6th Cir.2000) (part of the purpose of Rule 41(d) is to avoid forum shopping; it is not necessary to show bad

faith or vexatious conduct); *Siepel v. Bank of America, N.A.*, 239 F.R.D. 558, 563 (E.D.Mo. 2006) (same).

80. *See Rogers v. Wal–Mart Stores, Inc.*, 230 F.3d 868, 875 (6th Cir.2000) (noting the split and determining that fees are not available in the 6th Circuit); *Esposito v. Piatrowski*, 223 F.3d 497 (7th Cir.2000) (attorneys fees may be recovered only when an underlying statute defines costs as including attorneys fees); *Siepel v. Bank of America, N.A.*, 239 F.R.D. 558, 563 (E.D.Mo. 2006) (noting the split and allowing the recovery of fees).

RULE 42

CONSOLIDATION; SEPARATE TRIALS

(a) Consolidation. If actions before the court involve a common question of law or fact, the court may:

(1) join for hearing or trial any or all matters at issue in the actions;

(2) consolidate the actions; or

(3) issue any other orders to avoid unnecessary cost or delay.

(b) Separate Trials. For convenience, to avoid prejudice, or to expedite and economize, the court may order a separate trial of one or more separate issues, claims, crossclaims, counterclaims, or third-party claims. When ordering a separate trial, the court must preserve any federal right to a jury trial.

[Amended effective July 1, 1966; April 30, 2007, effective December 1, 2007.]

--------------- 2007 AMENDMENTS ROADMAP ---------------

STYLE PROJECT CHANGES: Rule 42(a) was further subsectioned. The language in Rule 42 was simplified and shortened, and cumbersome language was culled.

NON-STYLE CHANGES: None.

NOTE: The Federal Rules "Style Project" is explained in Part III-A.

AUTHORS' COMMENTARY ON RULE 42

--------------- PURPOSE AND SCOPE ---------------

Rule 42 allows the court to control the manner in which the cases on its docket are tried; the court may consolidate several actions into a single proceeding or may conduct separate trials of various issues within a single action.

RULE 42(a).   CONSOLIDATION

CORE CONCEPT

When actions pending[1] before the court share common issues of law or fact, the court can consolidate the actions, either completely or for limited proceedings or stages.[2]

APPLICATIONS

Court's Discretion

In deciding whether to consolidate actions, the court should balance the savings to the judicial system against the possible inconvenience, delay, or prejudice to the parties.[3] The court has broad discretion in this balancing process,[4] and does not need the parties' consent.[5]

Common Issues Necessary

Although the court has broad discretion, it may not consolidate actions that do not share common issues of law or fact.[6]

Limited Consolidation

The court may consolidate actions for all purposes, for pretrial proceedings only, or for specified hearings or issues.

Actions in Different Districts

Actions in different districts may not be consolidated. However, if actions are pending in different districts that ought to be consolidated, the actions may be transferred to a single district, then consolidated, as provided in 28 U.S.C.A. § 1407.

Actions Remain Separate

In general, consolidated actions retain their separate identity.[7] Thus, the pleadings will remain separate and the court will enter

---

1. *Mourik Intern. B.V. v. Reactor Services Intern., Inc.*, 182 F.Supp.2d 599, 602 (S.D.Tex.2002) (the case must be properly pending before the court to be consolidated; an improperly removed case could not be consolidated).

2. *Lewis v. ACB Bus. Services Inc.*, 135 F.3d 389, 412 (6th Cir.1998).

3. *Arnold v. Eastern Air Lines, Inc.*, 681 F.2d 186, 193 (4th Cir.1982); *Commonwealth Land Title Ins. Co. v. IDC Properties, Inc.*, 482 F.Supp.2d 203, 206 (D.R.I. 2007) (listing the factors to be considered).

4. *Young v. Augusta, Ga. Through DeVaney*, 59 F.3d 1160, 1168 (11th Cir.1995); *Scarborough v. National Ass'n of Sur. Bond Producers*, 474 F.Supp.2d 64, 70–71 (D.D.C. 2007).

5. *Connecticut General Life Ins. Co. v. Sun Life Assurance Co. Of Canada*, 210

F.3d 771 (7th Cir.2000); *Disher v. Citigroup Global Markets, Inc.*, 486 F.Supp.2d 790 (S.D.Ill. 2007).

6. *Malcolm v. National Gypsum Co.*, 995 F.2d 346 (2d Cir.1993); *Cruickshank v. Clean Seas Co.*, 402 F.Supp.2d 328, 330 (D.Mass.2005); *Philips Electronics North America Corp. v. Contec Corp.*, 220 F.R.D. 415, 418 (D.Del.2004); *Saudi Basic Industries Corp. v. Exxonmobil Corp.*, 194 F.Supp.2d 378, 416 (D.N.J.2002), *order vac'd in part*, 364 F.3d 102 (3d Cir.2004) (Rule 42(a) does not require that the cases be identical, merely that there be a common question of law or fact).

7. *Boardman Petroleum, Inc. v. Federated Mut. Ins. Co.*, 135 F.3d 750, 752 (11th Cir.1998); *Lewis v. ACB Bus. Services, Inc.*, 135 F.3d 389, 412 (6th Cir.1998); *State v.*

separate judgments in each action. However, the court can order that briefs and rulings apply to all consolidated cases.[8]

Conflicts of Interest

Consolidation may be improper if it aligns parties who have conflicting interests.[9]

Arbitration

Many courts do not permit consolidation of arbitrations unless there is an express provision in the arbitration agreements providing for consolidation.[10]

Procedures

Consolidation is achieved by motion of any party or by the court *sua sponte*.[11] Local rules may determine to which judge a motion to consolidate should be presented if the matters are pending before different judges.[12] Once actions have been consolidated, the court manages the proceedings. In unusual circumstances, the court may appoint one counsel as lead or liaison counsel.

Appeals

An order granting or denying a motion for consolidation is not appealable as a final judgment,[13] although mandamus may be available under extreme circumstances.[14]

RULE 42(b). SEPARATE TRIALS

CORE CONCEPT

The court may conduct separate trials of any claim or issue.[15]

APPLICATIONS

Court's Discretion

In deciding whether to order separate trials, the court should balance the savings to the judicial system against the possible

---

Microsoft Corp., 209 F.Supp.2d 132 (D.D.C. 2002) (consolidation does not make the parties to one action parties to the other).

8. *Specht v. Netscape Communications Corp.*, 150 F.Supp.2d 585, 586, n.1 (S.D.N.Y.2001).

9. *Dupont v. Southern Pac. Co.*, 366 F.2d 193 (5th Cir.1966); *Atkinson v. Roth*, 297 F.2d 570 (3d Cir.1961).

10. *Champ v. Siegel Trading Co.*, 55 F.3d 269, 274 (7th Cir.1995); *but see Office & Professional Employees Intern. Union, AFL–CIO v. Sea–Land Service, Inc.*, 210 F.3d 117, 123 (2d Cir.2000) (developing common law of labor contracts empowered district court to consolidate two arbitration proceedings without consideration of whether such consolidation was authorized by Fed.R.Civ.P. 42(a)).

11. *Tucker v. Kenney,* 994 F.Supp. 412 (E.D.N.Y.1998) (court may order consolidation upon its own motion, and the consent of the parties is not required).

12. *Stewart v. O'Neill*, 225 F.Supp.2d 16, 21 (D.D.C.2002) (local rule providing that the motion to consolidate should be presented in the matter first filed).

13. *NAACP of Louisiana v. Michot*, 480 F.2d 547, 548 (5th Cir.1973).

14. *In re Repetitive Stress Injury Litigation*, 11 F.3d 368 (2d Cir.1993).

15. *Simon v. Philip Morris Inc.*, 200 F.R.D. 21, 27 (E.D.N.Y.2001) (the court may order a separate trial of any claim, cross-claim, counterclaim, or third-party claim, or of any separate issue or of any number of claims, cross-claims, counterclaims, third-party claims, or issues).

inconvenience, delay, or prejudice to the parties.[16]　The court has broad discretion in this balancing process.[17]

Burden of Proof

The burden is on the moving party to demonstrate that bifurcation is justified even in cases where bifurcation is not uncommon.[18]

Single Action

A separation under Rule 42 separates aspects of the action for trial, but the aspects remain part of a single action, and result in a single judgment.[19] This contrasts with claims that are severed pursuant to Rule 21.[20]

Liability and Damages

The most common instance of separate trials is when the court first conducts a trial as to liability, then as to damages if necessary.[21]

Separate Trials for Each Defendant

The court may order separate trials for each defendant, particularly if one is in bankruptcy, as long as the defendants are not indispensable parties.[22]

Procedure

The court may order separate trials *sua sponte* or by motion of any party.

Federal Law Controls

Bifurcated trials are permissible under Rule 42 even when the state law would prohibit bifurcation.[23]

Jury Trials

The procedures for separate trials do not affect the parties'

---

16. *Lindsey v. Prive Corp.*, 161 F.3d 886, 892 (5th Cir.1998); *Quintanilla v. City of Downey*, 84 F.3d 353, 356 (9th Cir.1996); *Niver v. Travelers Indem. Co. of IL*, 430 F.Supp.2d 852, 871–72 (N.D.Iowa 2006) (describing the factors for bifurcation).

17. *M2 Software, Inc., a Delaware corporation v. Madacy Entertainment, a corporation*, 421 F.3d 1073, 1088 (9th Cir.2005); *American Trim, L.L.C. v. Oracle Corp.*, 383 F.3d 462, 474 (6th Cir.2004); *Houseman v. United States Aviation Underwriters*, 171 F.3d 1117 (7th Cir.1999).

18. *Svege v. Mercedes–Benz Credit Corporation*, 329 F.Supp.2d 283, 284 (D.Conn. 2004) (bifurcation is the exception, not the rule, and the movant must justify it); *Real v. Bunn–O–Matic Corp.*, 195 F.R.D. 618, 620 (N.D.Ill.2000) (the party seeking bifurcation has the burden of demonstrating that judicial economy would be served and that no party would be prejudiced by separate trials); *Industrias Metalicas Marva,*

Inc. v. Lausell, 172 F.R.D. 1, 2 (D.P.R.1997) (bifurcation is not and should not be routine, but should be encouraged where experienced has demonstrated its worth).

19. *White v. ABCO Engineering Corp.*, 199 F.3d 140, 145 (3d Cir.1999); *Reid v. General Motors Corp.*, 240 F.R.D. 260, 263 (E.D.Tex. 2007); *Hecht v. City of New York*, 217 F.R.D. 148, 149–50 (S.D.N.Y.2003).

20. *Rice v. Sunrise Express, Inc.*, 209 F.3d 1008, 1014–16 (7th Cir.2000); *Reid v. General Motors Corp.*, 240 F.R.D. 260, 263 (E.D.Tex. 2007) (explaining the distinction between Rule 42(b) and Rule 21).

21. *See Gafford v. General Electric Co.*, 997 F.2d 150 (6th Cir.1993); *Colon ex rel. Molina v. Bic USA, Inc.*, 199 F.Supp.2d 53, 97–98 (S.D.N.Y.2001).

22. *Hecht v. City of New York*, 217 F.R.D. 148, 150 (S.D.N.Y.2003).

23. *Oulds v. Principal Mutual Life Ins. Co.*, 6 F.3d 1431 (10th Cir.1993).

rights to a jury trial.[24] Separate trials may be conducted before one jury or different juries.[25] If there are jury and non-jury claims present, the jury claims may have to be tried first, so that the court does not make factual findings that should properly have been made by the jury.

State Law Claims

The court may conduct a separate trial of an issue over which it could not exercise independent jurisdiction. Thus, if a court exercised supplemental jurisdiction over a state law claim that otherwise could not have been brought as a separate action, the court may at the trial stage conduct a separate trial for that state law claim.[26]

Appeals

An order granting or denying a motion for bifurcation is not appealable as a final judgment, although mandamus may be available under extreme circumstances.[27] The decision ultimately may be reviewed under the "abuse of discretion" standard.[28]

ADDITIONAL RESEARCH REFERENCES

Wright & Miller, *Federal Practice and Procedure* §§ 2381–2392.

C.J.S. Federal Civil Procedure §§ 611, 916–918.

West's Key No. Digests, Federal Civil Procedure ⟜8–9, 1953–1965.

24. *Danjaq LLC v. Sony Corp.*, 263 F.3d 942, 961–62 (9th Cir.2001) (in ordering separate trials, the court must "always preserv[e] inviolate the right of trial by jury as declared by the Seventh Amendment to the Constitution").

25. *See Reid v. General Motors Corp.*, 240 F.R.D. 260, 263 (E.D.Tex. 2007) (separate juries should not be allowed to pass on overlapping issues of fact because of the risk of inconsistent verdicts).

26. *Travelers Indem. Co. v. Miller Mfg. Co.*, 276 F.2d 955 (6th Cir.1960).

27. *See In re Repetitive Stress Injury Litigation*, 11 F.3d 368 (2d Cir.1993).

28. *Palace Exploration Co. v. Petroleum Development Co.*, 316 F.3d 1110, 1118–19 (10th Cir.2003); *Athey v. Farmers Ins. Exchange*, 234 F.3d 357, 362 (8th Cir.2000).

RULE 43

TAKING TESTIMONY

(a) In Open Court. At trial, the witnesses' testimony must be taken in open court unless a federal statute, the Federal Rules of Evidence, these rules, or other rules adopted by the Supreme Court provide otherwise. For good cause in compelling circumstances and with appropriate safeguards, the court may permit testimony in open court by contemporaneous transmission from a different location.

(b) Affirmation Instead of an Oath. When these rules require an oath, a solemn affirmation suffices.

(c) Evidence on a Motion. When a motion relies on facts outside the record, the court may hear the matter on affidavits or may hear it wholly or partly on oral testimony or on depositions.

(d) Interpreter. The court may appoint an interpreter of its choosing; fix reasonable compensation to be paid from funds provided by law or by one or more parties; and tax the compensation as costs.

[Amended effective July 1, 1966; July 1, 1975; August 1, 1987, December 1, 1996; April 30, 2007, effective December 1, 2007.]

─────────────── **2007 AMENDMENTS ROADMAP** ───────────────

STYLE PROJECT CHANGES: Abrogated sections 43(b) and 43(c) were deleted, and subsequent sections were renumbered. The language in Rule 43 was simplified and shortened, and active voice replaced passive.

NON-STYLE CHANGES: None.

NOTE: The Federal Rules "Style Project" is explained in Part III-A.

AUTHORS' COMMENTARY ON RULE 43

─────────────── **PURPOSE AND SCOPE** ───────────────

Rule 43, formerly entitled "Evidence" was largely supplanted by the Federal Rules of Evidence. The remaining provisions govern the manner in which testimony is taken, the manner in which evidence is presented in support of motions, and the use of interpreters. A discussion of the Federal Rules of Evidence is beyond the scope of this book.

RULE 43(a). IN OPEN COURT

CORE CONCEPT

There is a preference in federal court for testimony taken in open court.[1] All testimony shall be in such form unless otherwise authorized by the Federal Rules of Evidence,[2] federal statute, or Supreme Court rule, or if stipulated by the parties.[3]

APPLICATIONS

Live Testimony

The Rules place a strong emphasis on live testimony taken in open court.[4] Rule 43(a) reflects the permissible use of other forms of communication, such as writing or sign language, if the witness cannot speak.[5]

Remote Testimony

Rule 43(a) allows the transmitting of testimony from a different location.[6] However, the Rules continue to emphasize live testimony in court, and transmitted testimony is permitted only for good cause shown in compelling circumstances.[7] In cases where remote testimony is to be used, the court must employ appropriate safeguards to protect the procedure and the parties' interests.[8] Transmitted testimony might be allowed when unexpected circumstances, such as an accident or illness, render a witness unable to appear in court.[9]

---

1. *In re Stevinson*, 194 B.R. 509, 511 (D.Colo.1996) (approving use of written direct testimony and live cross-examination).

2. *Kuntz v. Sea Eagle Diving Adventures Corp.*, 199 F.R.D. 665, 667 (D.Hawai'i 2001) (Federal Rules of Evidence authorize the submission of testimony by affidavit).

3. *Charlton Mem. Hosp. v. Sullivan*, 816 F.Supp. 50 (D.Mass.1993); *Saverson v. Levitt*, 162 F.R.D. 407, 408 (D.D.C.1995).

4. *Rusu v. U.S. I.N.S.*, 296 F.3d 316 (4th Cir.2002); *In re Vioxx Products Liability Litigation*, 414 F.Supp.2d 574 (E.D.La. 2006).

5. The Advisory Committee Note to the 1996 Amendment to Rule 43.

6. *Beltran–Tirado v. I.N.S.*, 213 F.3d 1179, 1185–86 (9th Cir.2000) (rejecting a due process challenge to telephonic testimony); *In re Vioxx Products Liability Litigation*, 414 F.Supp.2d 574 (E.D.La.2006) ("there has been an increasing trend by federal courts allowing and by legal commentators advocating for the use of contemporaneous transmission of trial testimony").

7. *See In re Vioxx Products Liability Litigation*, 414 F.Supp.2d 574 (E.D.La.2006) (listing the factors for considering remote testimony); *F.T.C. v. Swedish Match North America, Inc.*, 197 F.R.D. 1, 2 (D.D.C.2000) (serious inconvenience to the witness constitutes good cause); *United States v. Gigante*, 971 F.Supp. 755 (E.D.N.Y.1997), *aff'd*, 166 F.3d 75 (2d Cir.1999) (recognizing the use of televised presentation of evidence under Rule 43).

8. *F.T.C. v. Swedish Match North America, Inc.*, 197 F.R.D. 1 (D.D.C.2000) (in assessing the safeguards of remote testimony, the courts focus on whether the testimony was made in open court, under oath, and whether the opportunity for cross examination was available).

9. The Advisory Committee Note to the 1996 Amendment to Rule 43.

RULE 43(b). AFFIRMATION INSTEAD OF AN OATH

CORE CONCEPT

A party who, for religious reasons or otherwise, chooses not to take an oath, may make a "solemn affirmation" instead.[10]

APPLICATIONS

2007 Amendments

The 2007 amendments deleted former abrogated Rules 43(b) and (c) and renumbered former Rule 43(d) as Rule 43(b). Care should be exercised in researching and citing pre–2008 cases referring to Rule 43(b) or Rule 43(d).

RULE 43(c). EVIDENCE ON A MOTION

CORE CONCEPT

A party may submit affidavits in support of or in opposition to a motion in order to demonstrate facts not found in the record.[11] The court, in its discretion, may order oral evidence taken[12] or may request deposition transcripts when a motion is based on facts not of record.[13] The court may also consider a motion solely on the parties' written submissions.[14] The court may also consider preliminary injunction applications under Rule 43(c).[15]

APPLICATIONS

2007 Amendments

The 2007 amendments deleted former abrogated Rules 43(b) and (c) and renumbered former Rule 43(e) as Rule 43(c). Care should be exercised in researching and citing pre–2008 cases referring to Rule 43(c) or Rule 43(e).

---

10. *Doe v. Phillips*, 81 F.3d 1204 (2d Cir.1996).

11. *Valentin v. Hospital Bella Vista*, 254 F.3d 358, 364 (1st Cir.2001); *Spurlock v. Lawson*, 881 F.Supp. 436, 438 (E.D.Ark. 1995)(evidence not in the record considered in ruling on a motion for new trial); *Tiberi v. CIGNA Ins. Co.*, 40 F.3d 110 (5th Cir. 1994)(holding that faxed affidavits are admissible).

12. *March v. Levine*, 249 F.3d 462 (6th Cir.2001) (oral testimony is not favored in summary judgment proceedings due to the well founded reluctance to turn a summary judgment hearing into a trial); *Thompson v. Mahre,* 110 F.3d 716, 719 (9th Cir.1997)

(district courts may in their discretion "sparingly and with great care" take oral testimony under Rule 43(e) on a summary judgment motion); *PAR Microsystems, Inc. v. Pinnacle Dev. Corp.,* 995 F.Supp. 655 (N.D.Tex.1997) (oral testimony permitted only when a controlling credibility question is presented).

13. *Smith v. Oakland County Circuit Court*, 344 F.Supp.2d 1030, 1051 (E.D.Mich. 2004)

14. *Sunseri v. Macro Cellular Partners,* 412 F.3d 1247, 1248 (11th Cir.2005).

15. *Jones v. Bush*, 122 F.Supp.2d 713, 715 (N.D.Tex.2000).

RULE 43(d).   INTERPRETER

CORE CONCEPT

The court may, in its discretion, appoint an interpreter,[16] who then should take an oath or affirmation that the translation will be accurate. If an interpreter is appointed, the court may determine the interpreter's fees. The court may order that one party pay the fees, and may award the fees as costs after the conclusion of the trial.

APPLICATIONS

2007 Amendments

The 2007 amendments deleted former abrogated Rules 43(b) and (c) and renumbered former Rule 43(f) as Rule 43(d). Care should be exercised in researching and citing pre–2008 cases referring to Rule 43(d) or Rule 43(f).

ADDITIONAL RESEARCH REFERENCES

Wright & Miller, *Federal Practice and Procedure* §§ 2401–2417.

C.J.S. Courts § 1–110; Federal Civil Procedure §§ 368, 373, 935; Witnesses §§ 320–326.

West's Key No. Digests, Courts ⊶56; Federal Civil Procedure ⊶921, 2011; Witnesses ⊶227, 228, 230.

16. *Pedraza v. Phoenix,* 1994 WL 177285 (S.D.N.Y.1994)(no right to a court-ordered translation of pre-trial motions).

RULE 44

PROVING AN OFFICIAL RECORD

(a) Means of Proving.

(1) *Domestic Record.* Each of the following evidences an official record—or an entry in it—that is otherwise admissible and is kept within the United States, any state, district, or commonwealth, or any territory subject to the administrative or judicial jurisdiction of the United States:

(A) an official publication of the record; or

(B) a copy attested by the officer with legal custody of the record—or by the officer's deputy—and accompanied by a certificate that the officer has custody. The certificate must be made under seal:

(i) by a judge of a court of record in the district or political subdivision where the record is kept; or

(ii) by any public officer with a seal of office and with official duties in the district or political subdivision where the record is kept.

(2) *Foreign Record.*

(A) *In General.* Each of the following evidences a foreign official record—or an entry in it—that is otherwise admissible:

(i) an official publication of the record; or

(ii) the record—or a copy—that is attested by an authorized person and is accompanied either by a final certification of genuineness or by a certification under a treaty or convention to which the United States and the country where the record is located are parties.

(B) *Final Certification of Genuineness.* A final certification must certify the genuineness of the signature and official position of the attester or of any foreign official whose certificate of genuineness relates to the attestation or is in a

840

chain of certificates of genuineness relating to the attestation. A final certification may be made by a secretary of a United States embassy or legation; by a consul general, vice consul, or consular agent of the United States; or by a diplomatic or consular official of the foreign country assigned or accredited to the United States.

(C) *Other Means of Proof.* If all parties have had a reasonable opportunity to investigate a foreign record's authenticity and accuracy, the court may, for good cause, either:

(i) admit an attested copy without final certification; or

(ii) permit the record to be evidenced by an attested summary with or without a final certification.

(b) Lack of a Record. A written statement that a diligent search of designated records revealed no record or entry of a specified tenor is admissible as evidence that the records contain no such record or entry. For domestic records, the statement must be authenticated under Rule 44(a)(1). For foreign records, the statement must comply with (a)(2)(C)(ii).

(c) Other Proof. A party may prove an official record—or an entry or lack of an entry in it—by any other method authorized by law.

[Amended effective July 1, 1966; August 1, 1987; December 1, 1991; April 30, 2007, effective December 1, 2007.]

──────────── **2007 AMENDMENTS ROADMAP** ────────────

STYLE PROJECT CHANGES: Rule 44(a) was further subsectioned and labels were added or revised. Provisions were reorganized, language was simplified and clarified, and cumbersome phrasing was culled.

NON-STYLE CHANGES: None.

NOTE: The Federal Rules "Style Project" is explained in Part III-A.

AUTHORS' COMMENTARY ON RULE 44

PURPOSE AND SCOPE

Rule 44 describes certain methods for authenticating official records of the United States or foreign governments. It also provides methods to demonstrate the absence of a particular official document or record.

RULE 44(a)(1). MEANS OF PROVING; DOMESTIC RECORD

CORE CONCEPT

An official record kept within the United States is authenticated if it is an official publication or if it is a copy of an official record which is attested to by the legal custodian and accompanied by a certificate made by a judge or public officer with a seal of office.

APPLICATIONS

Official Record

"Official record" is not a defined term, but includes such documents as weather bureau records, records of conviction, tax returns, marriage and birth certificates, and selective service files. "Official" does not mean "public"; the public need not have access to "official records."

No Summaries

The Rule applies only to the record itself, not to summaries of the contents of the record.

Authentication Only

Rule 44 only *authenticates* records. It does not render the records immune from other objections, such as hearsay (but see the exception to the hearsay rule for official records), nor does it govern the import of those records.[1]

Entries in Record

The Rule applies equally to entire records or individual entries.

Official Publication

When a document has been printed by government authority, its authenticity is established.

Documents Kept in the United States

Rule 44 applies to all official federal, state, or local records physically maintained within the United States or within territories subject to United States jurisdiction, not just to United States official records. Thus, it includes foreign government records maintained in the United States.

---

1. *Moreno v. Macaluso*, 844 F.Supp. 736   (M.D.Fla.1994).

Attested Copy

A copy of an official record may be attested to by the officer having legal custody of the record or by the officer's deputy.

Certificate

The attested copy must be accompanied by a certificate that the attesting individual has custody of the record. The certificate must be made by a judge in the district or political subdivision in which the document is kept, or by a public official with duties in the district or political subdivision in which the document is kept, provided that the official has a seal of office and authenticates the certificate with that seal.[2]

RULE 44(a)(2). MEANS OF PROVING; FOREIGN RECORD

CORE CONCEPT

A foreign official record may be authenticated in essentially the same manner as a domestic record (described immediately above), with some minor variations.

APPLICATIONS

Official Publication

As with a domestic official record, official publications of foreign official records are self-authenticating.[3]

Attested Copy With Certificate

A foreign official record may be attested to by any person authorized by the laws of that country to attest records if the signature is certified by a secretary of embassy or legation, consul general, consul, vice consul or consular agent of the United States, or a diplomatic or consular official of the foreign country assigned or accredited to the United States.[4] The certification will not be necessary if the United States and the foreign country are signatories to a treaty providing for proof of foreign records without a certification and the foreign record is submitted in accordance with the treaty.[5] In particular, see the Hague Public Documents Convention,[6] and the Convention Abolishing the Requirement of Legalization for Foreign Public Documents.[7]

2. *Espinoza v. Immigration & Naturalization Service*, 45 F.3d 308 (9th Cir.1995).

3. *Construction Drilling, Inc. v. Chusid*, 63 F.Supp.2d 509 514 (D.N.J.1999).

4. *United States v. Squillacote*, 221 F.3d 542 (4th Cir.2000), *cert. denied*, 532 U.S. 971, 121 S.Ct. 1601, 149 L.Ed.2d 468 (2001) (the certification may be a separate document—the Rule does not require that the document itself be signed).

5. *United States v. Pintado–Isiordia*, 448 F.3d 1155, 1157 (9th Cir.2006) (Mexican birth certificate self-authenticating); *Ocean Rig ASA v. Safra National Bank of New York*, 72 F.Supp.2d 193, 204–05 (S.D.N.Y.1999).

6. Reprinted in *Martindale Hubbell*, International Law Digests. *See also Jiang v. Gonzales*, 474 F.3d 25, 29, n.4 (1st Cir. 2007).

7. The Convention Abolishing the Re-

Chain of Certificate

An attestation may also be certified via a chain of certifications, as long as the chain leads to one of the officials listed above.[8]

Attested Copy Without Certificate

The court has discretion to admit an attested copy of a foreign official record without a certificate if all parties have had a reasonable opportunity to investigate the authenticity and accuracy of the record, or for good cause.[9]

RULE 44(b). LACK OF A RECORD

CORE CONCEPT

One may prove the absence of a particular record with a written statement that after diligent search, no record or entry of the specified nature exists. The statement must be authenticated in the same manner as for an official record.

RULE 44(c). OTHER PROOF

CORE CONCEPT

The methods in Rule 44 are not exclusive. Quite often, an official will testify as to the authenticity of an official record. Similarly, certain documents are self-authenticating under Rule 902 of the Federal Rules of Evidence.

ADDITIONAL RESEARCH REFERENCES

Wright & Miller, *Federal Practice and Procedure* §§ 2431–2437.

C.J.S. Evidence § 634 et seq.

West's Key No. Digests, Evidence ⇐366.

quirement of Legalization for Foreign Public Documents may be found on WESTLAW in the IEL database, **ci(vii-c & text)**.

8. *See United States v. Squillacote*, 221 F.3d 542 (4th Cir.2000), *cert. denied*, 532 U.S. 971, 121 S.Ct. 1601, 149 L.Ed.2d 468 (2001) (second official certified identity of first official and that first official was authorized to attest to the authenticity of the documents).

9. *Batista v. Ashcroft*, 270 F.3d 8, 17, n.8 (1st Cir.2001).

RULE 44.1

DETERMINING FOREIGN LAW

A party who intends to raise an issue about a foreign country's law must give notice by a pleading or other writing. In determining foreign law, the court may consider any relevant material or source, including testimony, whether or not submitted by a party or admissible under the Federal Rules of Evidence. The court's determination must be treated as a ruling on a question of law.

[Added effective July 1, 1966; amended effective July 1, 1975; August 1, 1987; April 30, 2007, effective December 1, 2007.]

─────────── **2007 AMENDMENTS ROADMAP** ───────────

STYLE PROJECT CHANGES: The language in Rule 44.1 was clarified, and "must" replaced "shall."

NON-STYLE CHANGES: None.

NOTE: The Federal Rules "Style Project" is explained in Part III-A.

AUTHORS' COMMENTARY ON RULE 44.1

─────────── PURPOSE AND SCOPE ───────────

Rule 44.1 contains the provisions for raising and determining issues concerning the law of a foreign country. A party must give notice of its intent to raise an issue of foreign law. Thereafter, the judge will determine the applicable law of the foreign country.

NOTE: Rule 44.1 (which became effective in 1966) presents a significant diversion from past law, so be wary of citing any authority before 1966.

APPLICATIONS

Notice of Foreign Law Issue

A party must give written notice to the court and all other parties of its intent to raise an issue concerning foreign law.[1] The

---

1. *DP Aviation v. Smiths Industries Aerospace and Defense Systems Ltd.*, 268 F.3d 829, 846 (9th Cir.2001) (presenting a detailed analysis of what constitutes suffi-

notice should specify the issues or claims purportedly governed by foreign law, but need not state the specific provisions of the foreign law. Failure to provide the required notice of intent to raise an issue concerning foreign law can result in a waiver of the right to raise the issue.[2]

Form of Notice

The notice may be included in a pleading or may be a separate document.[3]

Timing for Notice

Rule 44.1 does not set a specific time for filing the notice. If the notice is a separate document, it should be served as soon as possible to give a reasonable opportunity to all parties to prepare.[4] If not already raised, issues of foreign law are sometimes raised at the pretrial conference.[5]

Party Giving Notice

Notice is normally given by the party whose claim or defense is based on foreign law, but may be raised by any party. If parties believe that a different foreign law applies from the law raised by another party, they should issue separate notices.

Court Determines Foreign Law

The determination of foreign law is now considered a matter of law,[6] not a matter of fact, and is therefore made by the court.[7]

Materials Used by the Court

The court may consider any relevant material or source to determine foreign law,[8] regardless of whether it is admissible.[9] A

cient notice); *Weiss v. National Westminster Bank, PLC*, 242 F.R.D. 33 (E.D.N.Y. 2007).

2. *In re Magnetic Audiotape Antitrust Litigation*, 334 F.3d 204(2d Cir.2003).

3. *Local 875 I.B.T. Pension Fund v. Pollack*, 992 F.Supp. 545 (E.D.N.Y.1998) (raising issue of foreign law in reply papers is not sufficient notice under Rule 44.1); *see also Canadian Imperial Bank of Commerce v. Saxony Carpet Co.*, 899 F.Supp. 1248, 1253 (S.D.N.Y.1995)(raising issues of foreign law in motion papers was adequate notice).

4. *See Rationis Enterprises Inc. of Panama v. Hyundai Mipo Dockyard Co., Ltd.*, 426 F.3d 580, 2005 A.M.C. 2516 (2nd Cir.(N.Y.) Oct 17, 2005) (Rule 44.1 deliberately does not provide a specific time period); *Club Car, Inc. v. Club Car (Quebec) Import, Inc.*, 362 F.3d 775, 782 (11th Cir. 2004) (notice 2 weeks before trial held reasonable); *Mutual Service Ins. Co. v. Frit Industries, Inc.*, 358 F.3d 1312, 1321 (11th Cir.2004) (notice at pretrial conference held reasonable); *Thyssen Steel Co. v. M/V Kavo*

Yerakas, 911 F.Supp. 263, 266 (S.D.Tex. 1996)(holding that notice of intent to rely on foreign law served after the case was remanded was sufficient).

5. *But see Whirlpool Fin. Corp. v. Sevaux*, 96 F.3d 216, 221 (7th Cir.1996) (choice-of-law issue is waived if party brings it up after summary judgment is rendered).

6. *Pazcoguin v. Radcliffe*, 292 F.3d 1209 (9th Cir.2002); *Weiss v. National Westminster Bank, PLC*, 242 F.R.D. 33 (E.D.N.Y. 2007).

7. *U.S. Fidelity and Guar. Co. v. Braspetro Oil Services Co.*, 369 F.3d 34 (2nd Cir.2004); *S.E.C. v. Dunlap*, 253 F.3d 768 (4th Cir.2001).

8. *Ferrostaal, Inc. v. M/V Sea Phoenix*, 447 F.3d 212, 216 (3rd Cir.2006); *Prewitt Enterprises, Inc. v. Organization of Petroleum Exporting Countries*, 353 F.3d 916, 924, n.11 (11th Cir.2003).

9. *Aon Financial Products, Inc. v. Societe Generale*, 476 F.3d 90, 101 (2nd Cir. 2007); *General Star Nat. Ins. Co. v. Admin-*

common method of proving foreign law is through expert testimony[10] and treatises.[11] The court may also do its own research[12] or seek the aid of an expert witness to help in the interpretation of foreign law.[13]

Absence of Proof

In the absence of proof of foreign law, the court may presume that the foreign law would be the same as local law.[14]

Summary Judgment

As an issue of law, a determination of foreign law is appropriate for summary judgment.[15]

Applies in All Cases

Rule 44.1 applies in diversity cases and federal question cases. Note, however, that the state conflict of law rules will determine *which* laws apply in diversity cases. Rule 44.1 is implicated only after the court has determined that a foreign country's laws apply.

Appellate Review

Determinations of foreign law are legal determinations fully reviewable by the Courts of Appeals.[16] However, a ruling as to foreign law is interlocutory, and cannot be immediately appealed. If the trial court has not determined the foreign law, the appellate

istratia Asigurarilor de Stat, 289 F.3d 434, 439 (6th Cir.2002).

10. *Primavera Familienstifung v. Askin*, 130 F.Supp.2d 450, 520, n.73 (S.D.N.Y. 2001) (courts may consider the statements of foreign attorneys on issues affected by foreign law); *Consorcio Rive, S.A. de C.V. v. Briggs of Cancun, Inc.*, 2001 WL 46875 (E.D.La.2001) (testimony of foreign attorney admitted to prove foreign law).

11. *See Access Telecom, Inc. v. MCI Telecommunications Corp.*, 197 F.3d 694, 713 (5th Cir.1999).

12. *Ferrostaal, Inc. v. M/V Sea Phoenix*, 447 F.3d 212, 216 (3rd Cir.2006); *Getty Petroleum Marketing, Inc. v. Capital Terminal Co.*, 391 F.3d 312, 326, n.20 (1st Cir.2004) (court may do its own research, but may also insist that the parties present a full analysis); *Brockmeyer v. May*, 361 F.3d 1222, 1241 (9th Cir.2004) (courts may reject even the uncontradicted conclusions of an expert witness and reach their own decisions on the basis of independent examination of foreign legal authorities).

13. *In re Agent Orange Product Liability Litigation*, 373 F.Supp.2d 7, 18 (E.D.N.Y. 2005) (court has broad discretion to rely on expert testimony to interpret foreign law);

ID Sec. Systems Canada, Inc. v. Checkpoint Systems, Inc., 198 F.Supp.2d 598, 623 (E.D.Pa.2002); *Thomson Consumer Elec., Inc. v. Innovatron, S.A.*, 3 F.Supp.2d 49 (D.D.C.1998) (no express hierarchy of sources exists for questions of foreign law).

14. *Ferrostaal, Inc. v. M/V Sea Phoenix*, 447 F.3d 212, 216 (3rd Cir.2006); *Minebea Co., Ltd. v. Papst*, 444 F.Supp.2d 68, 185 (D.D.C. 2006) (when both parties have failed to prove foreign law, the court may say that the parties have acquiesced in the application of local law).

15. *McKesson HBOC, Inc. v. Islamic Republic of Iran*, 271 F.3d 1101, 1108 (D.C.Cir.2001); *Kim v. Co-op. Centrale Raiffeisen–Boerenleebank B.A.*, 364 F.Supp.2d 346, 349 (S.D.N.Y.2005) (disputes as to foreign law do not preclude summary judgment); *Korea Life Ins. Co., Ltd. v. Morgan Guar. Trust Co. of New York*, 269 F.Supp.2d 424 (S.D.N.Y.2003).

16. *Ferrostaal, Inc. v. M/V Sea Phoenix*, 447 F.3d 212, 216 (3rd Cir.2006) (the appellate court may consider materials not considered by the trial court); *U.S. Fidelity and Guar. Co. v. Braspetro Oil Services Co.*, 369 F.3d 34, 53 (2nd Cir.2004).

court will generally remand, rather than determine foreign law in the first instance.[17]

ADDITIONAL RESEARCH REFERENCES

Wright & Miller, *Federal Practice and Procedure* §§ 2441–2447.

C.J.S. Evidence §§ 12–26.

West's Key No. Digests, Evidence ⚲37, 51.

17. *Yavuz v. 61 MM, Ltd.*, 465 F.3d 418, 431 (10th Cir. 2006).

RULE 45

SUBPOENA

(a) In General.

(1) *Form and Contents.*

(A) *Requirements—In General.* Every subpoena must:

(i) state the court from which it issued;

(ii) state the title of the action, the court in which it is pending, and its civil-action number;

(iii) command each person to whom it is directed to do the following at a specified time and place: attend and testify; produce designated documents, electronically stored information, or tangible things in that person's possession, custody, or control; or permit the inspection of premises; and

(iv) set out the text of Rule 45(c) and (d).

(B) *Command to Attend a Deposition—Notice of the Recording Method.* A subpoena commanding attendance at a deposition must state the method for recording the testimony.

(C) *Combining or Separating a Command to Produce or to Permit Inspection; Specifying the Form for Electronically Stored Information.* A command to produce documents, electronically stored information, or tangible things or to permit the inspection of premises may be included in a subpoena commanding attendance at a deposition, hearing, or trial, or may be set out in a separate subpoena. A subpoena may specify the form or forms in which electronically stored information is to be produced.

(D) *Command to Produce; Included Obligations.* A command in a subpoena to produce documents, electronically stored information, or tangible things requires the responding party to permit inspection, copying, testing, or sampling of the materials.

(2) *Issued from Which Court.* A subpoena must issue as follows:

    (A) for attendance at a hearing or trial, from the court for the district where the hearing or trial is to be held;

    (B) for attendance at a deposition, from the court for the district where the deposition is to be taken; and

    (C) for production or inspection, if separate from a subpoena commanding a person's attendance, from the court for the district where the production or inspection is to be made.

(3) *Issued by Whom.* The clerk must issue a subpoena, signed but otherwise in blank, to a party who requests it. That party must complete it before service. An attorney also may issue and sign a subpoena as an officer of:

    (A) a court in which the attorney is authorized to practice; or

    (B) a court for a district where a deposition is to be taken or production is to be made, if the attorney is authorized to practice in the court where the action is pending.

(b) Service.

(1) *By Whom; Tendering Fees; Serving a Copy of Certain Subpoenas.* Any person who is at least 18 years old and not a party may serve a subpoena. Serving a subpoena requires delivering a copy to the named person and, if the subpoena requires that person's attendance, tendering the fees for 1 day's attendance and the mileage allowed by law. Fees and mileage need not be tendered when the subpoena issues on behalf of the United States or any of its officers or agencies. If the subpoena commands the production of documents, electronically stored information, or tangible things or the inspection of premises before trial, then before it is served, a notice must be served on each party.

(2) *Service in the United States.* Subject to Rule 45(c)(3)(A)(ii), a subpoena may be served at any place:

      (A) within the district of the issuing court;

      (B) outside that district but within 100 miles of the place specified for the deposition, hearing, trial, production, or inspection;

      (C) within the state of the issuing court if a state statute or court rule allows service at that place of a subpoena issued by a state court of general jurisdiction sitting in the place specified for the deposition, hearing, trial, production, or inspection; or

      (D) that the court authorizes on motion and for good cause, if a federal statute so provides.

  (3) *Service in a Foreign Country.* 28 U.S.C. § 1783 governs issuing and serving a subpoena directed to a United States national or resident who is in a foreign country.

  (4) *Proof of Service.* Proving service, when necessary, requires filing with the issuing court a statement showing the date and manner of service and the names of the persons served. The statement must be certified by the server.

(c) Protecting a Person Subject to a Subpoena.

  (1) *Avoiding Undue Burden or Expense; Sanctions.* A party or attorney responsible for issuing and serving a subpoena must take reasonable steps to avoid imposing undue burden or expense on a person subject to the subpoena. The issuing court must enforce this duty and impose an appropriate sanction—which may include lost earnings and reasonable attorney's fees—on a party or attorney who fails to comply.

  (2) *Command to Produce Materials or Permit Inspection.*

      (A) *Appearance Not Required.* A person commanded to produce documents, electronically stored information, or tangible things, or to permit the inspection of premises, need not appear in person at the place of production or inspection unless also commanded to appear for a deposition, hearing, or trial.

(B) *Objections.* A person commanded to produce documents or tangible things or to permit inspection may serve on the party or attorney designated in the subpoena a written objection to inspecting, copying, testing or sampling any or all of the materials or to inspecting the premises—or to producing electronically stored information in the form or forms requested. The objection must be served before the earlier of the time specified for compliance or 14 days after the subpoena is served. If an objection is made, the following rules apply:

    (i) At any time, on notice to the commanded person, the serving party may move the issuing court for an order compelling production or inspection.

    (ii) These acts may be required only as directed in the order, and the order must protect a person who is neither a party nor a party's officer from significant expense resulting from compliance.

(3) *Quashing or Modifying a Subpoena.*

    (A) *When Required.* On timely motion, the issuing court must quash or modify a subpoena that:

        (i) fails to allow a reasonable time to comply;

        (ii) requires a person who is neither a party nor a party's officer to travel more than 100 miles from where that person resides, is employed, or regularly transacts business in person—except that, subject to Rule 45(c)(3)(B)(iii), the person may be commanded to attend a trial by traveling from any such place within the state where the trial is held;

        (iii) requires disclosure of privileged or other protected matter, if no exception or waiver applies; or

        (iv) subjects a person to undue burden.

    (B) *When Permitted.* To protect a person subject to or affected by a subpoena, the issuing court may, on motion, quash or modify the subpoena if it requires:

(i) disclosing a trade secret or other confidential research, development, or commercial information;

(ii) disclosing an unretained expert's opinion or information that does not describe specific occurrences in dispute and results from the expert's study that was not requested by a party; or

(iii) a person who is neither a party nor a party's officer to incur substantial expense to travel more than 100 miles to attend trial.

(C) *Specifying Conditions as an Alternative.* In the circumstances described in Rule 45(c)(3)(B), the court may, instead of quashing or modifying a subpoena, order appearance or production under specified conditions if the serving party:

(i) shows a substantial need for the testimony or material that cannot be otherwise met without undue hardship; and

(ii) ensures that the subpoenaed person will be reasonably compensated.

(d) Duties in Responding to a Subpoena.

(1) *Producing Documents or Electronically Stored Information.* These procedures apply to producing documents or electronically stored information:

(A) *Documents.* A person responding to a subpoena to produce documents must produce them as they are kept in the ordinary course of business or must organize and label them to correspond to the categories in the demand.

(B) *Form for Producing Electronically Stored Information Not Specified.* If a subpoena does not specify a form for producing electronically stored information, the person responding must produce it in a form or forms in which it is ordinarily maintained or in a reasonably usable form or forms.

(C) *Electronically Stored Information Produced in Only One Form.* The person responding need not produce the same electronically stored information in more than one form.

(D) *Inaccessible Electronically Stored Information.* The person responding need not provide discovery of electronically stored information from sources that the person identifies as not reasonably accessible because of undue burden or cost. On motion to compel discovery or for a protective order, the person responding must show that the information is not reasonably accessible because of undue burden or cost. If that showing is made, the court may nonetheless order discovery from such sources if the requesting party shows good cause, considering the limitations of Rule 26(b)(2)(C). The court may specify conditions for the discovery.

(2) *Claiming Privilege or Protection.*

(A) *Information Withheld.* A person withholding subpoenaed information under a claim that it is privileged or subject to protection as trial-preparation material must:

(i) expressly make the claim; and

(ii) describe the nature of the withheld documents, communications, or tangible things in a manner that, without revealing information itself privileged or protected, will enable the parties to assess the claim.

(B) *Information Produced.* If information produced in response to a subpoena is subject to a claim of privilege or of protection as trial-preparation material, the person making the claim may notify any party that received the information of the claim and the basis for it. After being notified, a party must promptly return, sequester, or destroy the specified information and any copies it has; must not use or disclose the information until the claim is resolved; must take reasonable steps to retrieve the information if the party disclosed it before being notified; and may promptly present the information

854

to the court under seal for a determination of the claim. The person who produced the information must preserve the information until the claim is resolved.

(e) Contempt. The issuing court may hold in contempt a person who, having been served, fails without adequate excuse to obey the subpoena. A nonparty's failure to obey must be excused if the subpoena purports to require the nonparty to attend or produce at a place outside the limits of Rule 45(c)(3)(A)(ii).

[Amended effective March 19, 1948; October 20, 1949; July 1, 1970; August 1, 1980; August 1, 1985; August 1, 1987; December 1, 1991; April 25, 2005, effective December 1, 2005; April 12, 2006, effective December 1, 2006; April 30, 2007, effective December 1, 2007.]

2007 AMENDMENTS ROADMAP

STYLE PROJECT CHANGES: The references to obtaining "books" in Rule 45 were deleted to be consistent with the language used in other Rules, but books remain obtainable by subpoena. Rule 45(b)(1) was amended to provide that notice of a subpoena to produce documents or for inspection must be served on other parties prior to service upon the person subject to the subpoena. The cross-reference to Rule 5(b) was also eliminated. Section 45(d)(2), regarding the assertion of privilege, was rewritten to parallel the language in Rule 26(b)(5) on the same topic. The language in Rule 45 was extensively reorganized, resubsectioned, and relabeled, and care should be exercised in researching or citing to the subsections of Rule 45. The language was simplified and clarified, and active voice replaced passive voice.

NON-STYLE CHANGES: None.

NOTE: The Federal Rules "Style Project" is explained in Part III-A.

AUTHORS' COMMENTARY ON RULE 45

PURPOSE AND SCOPE

Rule 45 governs subpoenas, both for discovery purposes and for hearings or trial. It addresses subpoenas *ad testificandum,* pertaining to testimony, and subpoenas *duces tecum,* pertaining to documents.

2006 AMENDMENTS: The 2006 Amendments to Rule 45 were primarily designed to refine the way that electronic data is obtained. The specific changes are described in footnotes to each amended subsection. In addition, details of the effects of the amendments are described in the author commentary to Rule 45. The following is a summary of those changes:

(1) The provisions in Rule 45 were amended to require the production of "electronically stored information" that is responsive to the subpoena. The responding person must make such electronically stored information available for testing and sampling, as well as inspection and copying.

(2) New Rule 45(d)(1)(B) discusses the form in which electronic data must be produced. The discovering party can specify the form in the subpoena. In the absence of a specification, the responding person must produce the data in the form it is ordinarily maintained or in a reasonably usable form.

(3) New Rule 45(d)(1)(C) provides that the responding person will not be required to produce electronic data in more than one form.

(4) New Rule 45(d)(1)(D) protects the producing person from undue burden or cost related to electronic data. If a person declines to produce electronic data under this provision, then if a motion to compel or quash is filed, the person have the burden of showing that the information is not reasonably accessible because of burden or cost. The burden then shifts to the responding party to show good cause why it nonetheless should obtain the information. In ruling on the motion, the court can impose conditions on the production of the electronic data.

(5) New Rule 45(d)(2)(B) contains provisions addressing the production of privileged information. Under the new procedure, a person or party seeking to invoke the privilege may notify the receiving party that privileged information had been produced. The receiving party must then either return the privileged information or provide the information to the court for a determination of the validity of the privilege.

RULE 45(a).   IN GENERAL

CORE CONCEPT

Parties to legal proceedings have the power to obtain a subpoena compelling a witness to appear and testify at a designated time and location.[1]

APPLICATIONS

Issued by Clerk

A subpoena may be issued by the clerk of court. The clerk will issue subpoenas with the name of the recipient left blank, to be filled in by the party.

---

1. *Gomez v. Gates*, 25 F.3d 761 (9th Cir.1994) ("when the subpoena is ad testifi- candum, there can be no pinch hitters.").

Issued by Attorney

A subpoena may also be issued by an attorney, acting as an officer of the court.[2] To be effective, the subpoena must be signed by the issuing attorney.[3] An attorney may issue a subpoena on behalf of any court before which the attorney is authorized to practice. An attorney may also issue a subpoena on behalf of a court where a deposition is to occur, provided that the deposition pertains to a matter pending in a court where the attorney is authorized to practice. This applies equally to attorneys admitted *pro hac vice* (for one matter only).

Which Court

A subpoena commanding attendance at a trial or hearing shall be issued from the court in which the trial is to occur. A subpoena for attendance at a deposition shall be issued from the court for the district in which the deposition is to occur, bearing the same case name and number as the case in the court where trial is to occur.[4] If the subpoena is issued from a court other than that where the action is pending, it is not necessary to open a new action with a miscellaneous docket number in the court issuing the subpoena unless it becomes necessary to move to enforce the subpoena. If a separate subpoena is issued commanding the production of documents or an inspection of premises, the subpoena shall issue from the court for the district in which the production or inspection is to occur.[5]

Subject Matter Jurisdiction

In order to issue a valid, enforceable subpoena in a lawsuit, the lawsuit must properly be before a federal court with subject matter jurisdiction.[6]

Contents

Every subpoena should:

(1) state the name of the court issuing the subpoena;

(2) state the name of the court where the action is pending;

(3) contain the caption and civil action number of the case;[7]

2. *Highland Tank & Mfg. Co. v. PS Intern.*, Inc., 227 F.R.D. 374, 380 (W.D.Pa. 2005) (subpoena issued by an attorney has the same force and effect as one issued by the clerk); *United States v. Santiago–Lugo*, 904 F.Supp. 43, 46 (D.P.R.1995).

3. *Atlantic Inv. Management, LLC v. Millennium Fund I, Ltd.*, 212 F.R.D. 395, 397 (N.D.Ill.2002) (lack of signature waived by conduct of recipient).

4. *Amgen Inc. v. Kidney Center of Delaware County, Ltd.*, 879 F.Supp. 878 (N.D.Ill. 1995).

5. *Dynegy Midstream Services v. Trammochem*, 451 F.3d 89, 95 (2nd Cir.2006); *Mabe v. San Bernardino County, Dept. of Public Social Services*, 237 F.3d 1101, 1112 (9th Cir.2001); *Cusumano v. Microsoft Corp.*, 162 F.3d 708, 711 (1st Cir.1998) (motion to compel docketed as an independent matter in court where documents were to be produced); *In re Subpoena To University of North Carolina at Chapel Hill*, 367 F.Supp.2d 945, 957–58 (M.D.N.C.2005) (a district court cannot issue a subpoena to a non-party for the production of documents located in another district).

6. *Olcott v. Delaware Flood Co.*, 76 F.3d 1538, 1552 (10th Cir.1996).

7. *U.S. v. Patiwana*, 267 F.Supp.2d 301 (E.D.N.Y.2003) (enforcing subpoena despite failure to include a civil action number).

(4) command the recipient to appear and give testimony, to produce for inspection the documents or things described in the subpoena or in an attachment thereto,[8] or to permit inspection of premises, at a designated time and location; and

(5) recite the language in subsections (c) and (d) of Rule 45.[9]

NOTE: Blank subpoenas generally are available at the clerk's office and will include the requisite language.

Scope

The scope of documents or information that can be obtained by subpoena is the same as the scope of discovery generally under Rule 26.[10]

Multiple Commands

A subpoena to produce documents or to inspect premises may be issued separately or joined with a command to appear to testify.

Number

There is no limit on the number of subpoenas in a civil action.

Time

Courts are split as to whether subpoenas are subject to the discovery deadline established by the court, with the majority not allowing subpoenas after the deadline.[11]

Documents

Witnesses may be compelled to produce all documents which they possess, have custody of, *or control*.[12] Thus, a corporation must produce documents in the possession of its agent, attorney, or subsidiary, even if these documents are located outside the district.[13]

---

8. *Orleman v. Jumpking, Inc.*, 2000 WL 1114849 (D.Kan.2000); *Insituform Technologies, Inc. v. Cat Contracting, Inc.*, 168 F.R.D. 630, 633 (N.D.Ill.1996).

9. *Elam v. Ryder Automotive Operations, Inc.*, 179 F.R.D. 413, 415 (W.D.N.Y. 1998) (subpoena enforced despite omission of language from Rule 45(c) and (d) based on absence of real prejudice); *Anderson v. Government of the Virgin Islands*, 180 F.R.D. 284 (D.Vi.1998).

10. *Gonzales v. Google, Inc.*, 234 F.R.D. 674, 679 (N.D.Cal.2006); *Graham v. Casey's General Stores*, 206 F.R.D. 251, 253–54 (S.D.Ind.2002).

11. *Dreyer v. GACS Inc.*, 204 F.R.D. 120, 122–23 (N.D.Ind.2001).

12. *Hay Group, Inc. v. E.B.S. Acquisition Corp.*, 360 F.3d 404, 408 (3rd Cir. 2004); *In re: Citric Acid Litigation*, 191 F.3d 1090, 1106–07 (9th Cir.1999) ("control" is defined as the legal right to obtain docu-

ments upon demand); *Power Integrations, Inc. v. Fairchild Semiconductor Intern., Inc.*, 233 F.R.D. 143, 145 (D.Del.2005) (same); *Insituform Technologies, Inc. v. Cat Contracting, Inc.*, 168 F.R.D. 630, 633 (N.D.Ill.1996) (subpoena recipient must produce all existing documents within its control, but is not required to create documents).

13. *See In re Automotive Refinishing Paint*, 229 F.R.D. 482 (E.D.Pa.2005) (documents outside the court's jurisdiction must be produced if the party is served within the court's jurisdiction); *Crafton v. U.S. Specialty Ins. Co.*, 218 F.R.D. 175, 177 (E.D.Ark.2003) (quashing document subpoena served on a corporate agent in one state where documents and corporate headquarters were in a different state more than 100 miles from service).

Electronic Data

Rule 45 expressly allows for the party issuing the subpoena to request to inspect, copy, sample, or test electronic data.

- *Form of Electronic Data:* Rule 45(d)(1)(B) allows, but does not require, the requesting party to specify the form in which it is requesting electronic data (i.e., hard copy or electronic, and if electronic, the precise manner of production). If the requesting party does not specify the form, then the responding person must produce it in the form in which it is ordinarily maintained or in a form that is reasonably usable. In any event, a person need not produce electronic data in more than one form.

- *Undue Burden or Cost:* If the responding person believes that the production of electronic data from certain sources will cause undue burden or cost, the person can, in lieu of producing the documents, identify those sources.[14] If a motion to compel or quash is filed, the responding person will have the burden of showing that production would cause undue burden or cost. The burden would then shift to the requesting party to show good cause why the data should be produced nonetheless.

Inspection, Testing, or Sampling

A subpoena may be used to obtain inspection, testing, or sampling of the property, documents, or electronic data of a non-party.[15]

Asserting Privileges

The recipient of a subpoena *duces tecum* may refuse to produce privileged documents. If the issuing party contests the asserted privilege, that party can request that the court conduct an *in camera* inspection of such documents.

Recalling Privileged Information

Rule 45(d)(2)(B) establishes a procedure to recall privileged information that has already been produced. Anyone believing that a person has produced privileged information in response to a subpoena may provide a notification to the parties who have received the information. After receiving such a notification, the receiving parties must return, sequester, or destroy the specified information and all copies (including taking reasonable steps to retrieve any information that the receiving party had already disclosed to other persons). If they do not agree with the privilege assertion, they can present the information to the court under seal for a determination of the privilege claim. During the pendency of the court's review of the privilege claim, the receiving parties are prohibited from using the information and the producing party must preserve it.

---

14. Rule 45(d)(1)(D).

15. *Fitzpatrick v. Arco Marine, Inc.*, 199 F.R.D. 663, 664 (C.D.Cal.2001) (allowing inspection of a non-party's ship).

Challenge

The proper method for challenging a subpoena that requires personal attendance is by motion to quash. The court can modify or quash the subpoena if it is unreasonable or oppressive.[16] Expense is not a reason to quash, but the court may condition compliance on the advancement of the expenses of complying by the issuing party.[17] A motion to quash may only be brought by the witness; the parties do not have standing to bring the motion on behalf of the witness.[18] If the subpoena is issued in one district for an action pending in another district, a motion to quash should be brought in the court issuing the subpoena.[19] In addition, if the subpoena is for a deposition, the witness may move for a protective order under the discovery provisions in Rule 26(c). If the subpoena is for the production of documents only, the recipient may serve written objections on the issuer within 14 days of receipt of the subpoena, or before the date for production if sooner than 14 days from receipt of the subpoena.[20] After serving written objections, the recipient does not need to produce the documents unless the serving party successfully brings a motion to compel.

Parties

A subpoena is not necessary to take the deposition of a party or an officer, director, or managing agent of a party, or to compel a party to produce documents;[21] a notice of deposition pursuant to Rules 30(b) and 31(a) is sufficient.[22]

Corporations

In deposing a corporation, one may describe the information sought in the subpoena (or notice) and require the corporation to designate a representative qualified to testify about the designated issues.[23]

United States

As a general rule, agencies and representatives of the United States must comply with subpoenas.[24]

---

16. *Ariel v. Jones,* 693 F.2d 1058 (11th Cir.1982).

17. *SEC v. Arthur Young & Co.,* 584 F.2d 1018 (D.C.Cir.1978).

18. *Brown v. Braddick,* 595 F.2d 961, 967 (5th Cir.1979).

19. *In re: Sealed Case,* 141 F.3d 337, 340 (D.C.Cir.1998).

20. *See* Rule 45(c) below.

21. *Dixon v. Ford Motor Credit Co.,* 2000 WL 1182274 (E.D.La.2000) (Rule 34, not Rule 45, provides the proper way for a party to obtain documents from another party).

22. *COMSAT Corp. v. National Science Foundation,* 190 F.3d 269, 278 (4th Cir.

1999); but see *First City, Texas–Houston, N.A. v. Rafidain Bank,* 197 F.R.D. 250, 254 (S.D.N.Y.2000) (nothing in the Rules prevents issuing a subpoena to a party).

23. *Price Waterhouse LLP v. First American Corp.,* 182 F.R.D. 56, 61 (S.D.N.Y.1998).

24. *Yousuf v. Samantar,* 451 F.3d 248, 251–53 (D.C.Cir.2006) (agencies of the United States are persons who must respond to subpoenas); *Linder v. Calero–Portocarrero,* 251 F.3d 178 (D.C.Cir.2001); but see *United States v. Diabetes Treatment Centers of America, Inc.,* 235 F.R.D. 521, 528 (D.D.C.2006).

RULE 45(b).   SERVICE

CORE CONCEPT

Subpoenas may be served by any non-party not under the age of 18.

APPLICATIONS

Personal Service

The courts are divided as to whether service of a subpoena must be personal, in-hand service, or can be accomplished by delivery to the recipient's residence or place of business.[25]

Proof of Service

If necessary, service can be proved by filing a statement of the date and manner of service, certified by the person making service, with the clerk of the court issuing the subpoena.

Deadline for Subpoenas

Rule 45 does not establish any cutoff or deadline for serving subpoenas. However, a subpoena for a deposition or for the production of documents may be governed by the discovery deadline.[26]

Not on Lawyer

Service upon the witness's lawyer is not sufficient.

Corporations

Service on the agent of a corporation is sufficient to obtain service on the corporation.[27]

Expenses

If the recipient's attendance is commanded, service must be accompanied by the tender of the fees and expenses for a 1–day appearance, unless the issuing party is the United States or officer or agency thereof.[28] There is no requirement to tender witness fees and expenses when the subpoena is only for the production of

---

25. *Hall v. Sullivan*, 229 F.R.D. 501 (D.Md.2005) (discussing the split in authority); *Hall v. Sullivan*, 229 F.R.D. 501, 502 (D.Md.2005) (subpoena for production of documents does not require in-hand service); *Catskill Development, L.L.C. v. Park Place Entertainment Corp.*, 206 F.R.D. 78, 84, n.5 (S.D.N.Y.2002); *King v. Crown Plastering Corp.*, 170 F.R.D. 355, 356 (E.D.N.Y. 1997) ("personal service" does not necessarily mean in hand delivery); *United States v. Philip Morris Inc.*, 312 F.Supp.2d 27 (D.D.C.2004). *But see Doe v. Hersemann*, 155 F.R.D. 630 (N.D.Ind.1994) (certified mail satisfies Rule 45(b)(1) as delivery by a non-party adult).

26. *See Alper v. United States*, 190 F.R.D. 281, 283 (D.Mass.2000).

27. *Sabatier v. Barnes*, 2001 WL 175234 (E.D.La.2001) (service on a secretary or receptionist is technically sufficient, but not advisable); *In re: Motorsports Merchandise Antitrust Litigation*, 186 F.R.D. 344 (W.D.Va.1999) (look to Rule 4 to determine proper service on a corporation).

28. *In re Dennis*, 330 F.3d 696, 704–05 (5th Cir.2003) (Rule 45(b)(1) requires simultaneous tendering of witness fees and the reasonably estimated mileage allowed by law with service of a subpoena; mileage need not be precise, only a reasonable estimate); *In re Hunt*, 238 F.3d 1098, 1100 (9th Cir.2001) (subpoena quashed because service not accompanied by witness fee and mileage).

documents, and no witness is commanded to appear.[29]   The amount of fees and expenses is controlled by 28 U.S.C.A. § 1821.[30]

Place of Service

A subpoena may be served at any place within the district,[31] at any place within 100 miles of the hearing, deposition, production, or trial,[32] or at any place within the state where a subpoena could be served under state law.[33]   The 100–mile limit is extended by statute under some circumstances,[34] such as in some bankruptcy proceedings.

Service in Multiparty, Multiforum Actions

When jurisdiction of the district court is based in whole or in part on the multiparty, multiforum statute,[35] a subpoena for attendance at a hearing or trial may, if authorized by the court upon motion for good cause shown, be served at any place within the United States, or anywhere outside the United States if otherwise permitted by law.[36] The court may impose terms and conditions on service under this provision.[37]

Foreign Countries

Under certain circumstances, a witness subject to the jurisdiction of the court may be in a foreign country.   The procedure for issuing a subpoena to such a witness is governed by 28 U.S.C.A. § 1783 (The Walsh Act), which provides for the issuance of such a subpoena if the court finds that the witness's testimony or documents are "necessary in the interest of justice," and it is not possible to obtain the testimony or documents by other means.   The person serving such a subpoena must advance the recipient estimated travel expenses.

NOTE: The Walsh Act, 28 U.S.C.A. § 1783, only governs issuing a subpoena to a trial witness.   Rule 30 discusses when foreign witnesses may be deposed.

---

29. *United States E.E.O.C. v. Laidlaw Waste, Inc.*, 934 F.Supp. 286, 290 n.6 (N.D.Ill.1996).

30. 28 U.S.C.A. § 1821 is reprinted in this book. *See also Fisher v. Ford Motor Co.*, 178 F.R.D. 195 (N.D.Ohio 1998).

31. *In re Automotive Refinishing Paint*, 229 F.R.D. 482 (E.D.Pa.2005) (the critical location is the place where the documents are to be produced, not where they are maintained).

32. *See Gipson v. Wells Fargo Bank, N.A.*, 239 F.R.D. 280, 281 (D.D.C. 2006) (offer to take deposition by telephone does not allow subpoena of witness located more than 100 miles away); *In re Automotive Refinishing Paint*, 229 F.R.D. 482 (E.D.Pa. 2005) (the critical location is the place

where the documents are to be produced, not where they are maintained).

33. *Vass v. Volvo Trucks North America, Inc.*, 304 F.Supp.2d 851, 857 (S.D.W.Va. 2004); *In re Security Life Ins. Co. of America*, 228 F.3d 865, 871 (8th Cir.2000) (100 mile limitation does not apply to a subpoena for documents); *Robertson v. Kiamichi Railroad Co., L.L.C.*, 42 F.Supp.2d 651 (E.D.Tex.1999).

34. *Dynegy Midstream Services v. Trammochem*, 451 F.3d 89, 95 (2nd Cir. 2006).

35. 28 U.S.C. § 1369.

36. 28 U.S.C. § 1783.

37. 28 U.S.C. § 1783.

Service on Other Parties

If the subpoena is for a deposition, a notice of deposition must be served on all parties pursuant to Rule 30 or 31. If the subpoena requires the production of documents or inspection of premises, notice must be served upon all parties prior to service on the recipient so that they may assert any privileges or objections and may obtain the same or additional documents.[38]

Arbitrations

The federal courts can enforce subpoenas issued by arbitrators under the provisions of the Federal Arbitration Act, 9 U.S.C. § 1 *et seq.*[39]

RULE 45(c). PROTECTING A PERSON SUBJECT TO A SUBPOENA

CORE CONCEPT

An attorney has a duty not to issue a subpoena for improper purposes or to impose undue burden on the recipient of the subpoena. Rule 45(c) also provides mechanisms for recipients of subpoenas to challenge the subpoenas.

NOTE: The cautionary language in Rule 45(c) *must* be reprinted on every subpoena.

APPLICATIONS

Duty to Avoid Undue Burden

An attorney issuing a subpoena has a duty to avoid causing undue burden or expense on the recipient.[40]

Compensation for Respondent

If compliance with a subpoena would require the disclosure of a trade secret or other business confidential information, would require the disclosure of an unretained expert's opinion or information,[41] or would cause undue burden[42] or expense, the court issuing the subpoena will shift some or all of the costs to the party issuing

38. *Butler v. Biocore Medical Technologies, Inc.,* 348 F.3d 1163, 1173 (10th Cir. 2003); *Judson Atkinson Candies, Inc. v. Latini–Hohberger Dhimantec,* 476 F.Supp.2d 913, 928–29 (N.D.Ill. 2007) (describing standard for quashing and for imposing sanctions); *Mid-Atlantic Constructors Inc. v. Stone & Webster Const., Inc.,* 231 F.R.D. 465, 467 (E.D.Pa.2005) (Rule 45(b) clearly requires prior notice to opposing counsel).

39. *Festus & Helen Stacy Foundation, Inc. v. Merrill Lynch, Pierce Fenner, & Smith Inc.,* 432 F.Supp.2d 1375, 1377–78 (N.D.Ga.2006).

40. *Northwestern Memorial Hosp. v. Ashcroft,* 362 F.3d 923, 938 (7th Cir.2004);

Federal Deposit Ins. Corp. v. Garner, 126 F.3d 1138, 1145–46 (9th Cir.1997); *Liberty Mut. Ins. Co. v. Diamante,* 194 F.R.D. 20, 23 (D.Mass.2000) (good faith is not sufficient, but rather the issue is whether the issuing party took reasonable steps to avoid imposing undue burden or expense on the person subject to the subpoena).

41. *Klay v. All Defendants,* 425 F.3d 977, 983–84 (11th Cir.2005) (compensation could include the value of the intellectual property provided to the recipient).

42. *Flatow v. Islamic Republic of Iran,* 201 F.R.D. 5, 8 (D.D.C.2001) (describing test for evaluating undue burden).

the subpoena,[43] or otherwise provide for reasonable compensation.[44] The compensation may include wages lost because of the improperly issued subpoena, and may also include attorney fees.[45]

Attendance by Person Producing Documents

A person subpoenaed to produce documents or things or to permit an inspection need not actually appear at the designated time, as long as the person complies with the subpoena.

Objection to Subpoena to Produce Documents

A person subpoenaed to produce documents or things or to permit an inspection may serve an objection to all or part of the subpoena within fourteen days after service of the subpoena (or before the time designated in the subpoena, if sooner).[46] Objections to subpoenas are customarily made by letter.[47] All grounds for objection should be asserted or they may be waived.[48] Once an objection has been served on the party issuing the subpoena, the subpoena recipient is not obligated to comply with the subpoena.[49] Failure to serve timely objections may constitute a waiver of objections to the subpoena other than objections relating to service.[50] Only non-parties may serve objections; parties must contest a subpoena by a motion to quash or modify.[51]

Motion to Compel

If a subpoena recipient serves an objection to the subpoena, the serving party may file a motion to compel in the court from which the subpoena was issued.[52] The motion must be served on the subpoena recipient. In ruling on such a motion, the court will protect non-parties from "significant" expense.[53] Respondents to

43. *Heidelberg Americas, Inc. v. Tokyo Kikai Seisakusho, Ltd.*, 333 F.3d 38 (1st Cir.2003) (a court "shall" quash or modify a subpoena if the subpoena subjects a person to undue burden); *In re Law Firms of McCourts and McGrigor Donald*, 2001 WL 345233 (S.D.N.Y.2001) (the court is required to protect the non-party from undue burden or expense, but that does not mean that the non-party cannot absorb some of the cost of compliance).

44. *Dravo Corp. v. Liberty Mut. Ins. Co.*, 160 F.R.D. 123 (D.Neb.1995).

45. *Mattel, Inc. v. Walking Mountain Productions*, 353 F.3d 792, 814 (9th Cir. 2003).

46. *McCabe v. Ernst & Young, LLP*, 221 F.R.D. 423 (D.N.J.2004); *McCoy v. Southwest Airlines Co., Inc.*, 211 F.R.D. 381, 384 (C.D.Cal.2002) (only the nonparty can prevent disclosure by objection; the party to whom the subpoenaed records pertain cannot simply object).

47. *See Tuite v. Henry*, 98 F.3d 1411, 1416 (D.C.Cir.1996).

48. *DG Acquisition Corp. v. Dabah*, 151 F.3d 75, 81 (2d Cir.1998); *In re Corso*, 328 B.R. 375 (E.D.N.Y.2005) (recipient must raise all objections at one time so that discovery does not become a game); *McCoy v. Southwest Airlines Co., Inc.*, 211 F.R.D. 381, 385 (C.D.Cal.2002).

49. *Pamida, Inc. v. E.S. Originals, Inc.*, 281 F.3d 726, 732 (8th Cir.2002).

50. *Judicial Watch, Inc. v. U.S. Dept. of Commerce*, 196 F.R.D. 1, 2 (D.D.C.2000).

51. *Moon v. SCP Pool Corp.*, 232 F.R.D. 633, 636 (C.D.Cal.2005)

52. *United States v. Diabetes Treatment Centers of America, Inc.*, 444 F.3d 462, 468 (6th Cir.2006); *McCabe v. Ernst & Young, LLP*, 221 F.R.D. 423 (D.N.J.2004).

53. *See Klay v. All Defendants*, 425 F.3d 977, 984 (11th Cir.2005); *McCabe v. Ernst & Young, LLP*, 221 F.R.D. 423 (D.N.J. 2004); *First American Corp. v. Price Waterhouse LLP*, 184 F.R.D. 234, 238 (S.D.N.Y. 1998) (respondent awarded expenses plus a portion of attorney's fees).

motions to compel should raise the issue of expenses or risk waiver.[54] Some courts and local rules require counsel for the moving party to make a reasonable effort to confer with opposing counsel prior to filing a motion to compel.[55]

Motion to Quash or Modify

A subpoena recipient[56] may move to quash a subpoena in the court from which the subpoena was issued.[57] If the court finds the subpoena objectionable,[58] it may either quash it altogether or modify it to cure the objection.[59] The motion must be "timely" filed, and should certainly be filed before the subpoena's return date.[60] Failure to file a motion to quash may constitute a waiver of objections to the subpoena.[61] A motion to quash is normally filed in the district where the subpoena was issued, but the court where the matter is pending also has the authority to issue protective orders and generally control the scope of discovery.[62] Some courts and local rules require counsel for the moving party to make a reasonable effort to confer with opposing counsel prior to filing a motion to quash.[63] Rule 45(c)(3) lists situations in which a subpoena will be quashed or modified:

(1) *Time to Comply:* Rule 45(c)(3)(A)(i) requires that the subpoena recipient be provided reasonable time to comply.[64]

---

54. *First American Corp. v. Price Waterhouse LLP*, 184 F.R.D. 234, 238–39 (S.D.N.Y.1998).

55. *See Boukadoum v. Hubanks*, 239 F.R.D. 427, 429–30 (D.Md. 2006); *Medical Components, Inc. v. Classic Medical, Inc.*, 210 F.R.D. 175, 178 (M.D.N.C.2002).

56. *Sterling Merchandising, Inc. v. Nestle, S.A.*, 470 F.Supp.2d 77, 81 (D.Puerto Rico 2006) (only the recipient of a subpoena may move to quash, unless the movant is asserting its privilege).

57. *Pamida, Inc. v. E.S. Originals, Inc.*, 281 F.3d 726, 729, n.3 (8th Cir.2002).

58. *Stock v. Integrated Health Plan, Inc.*, 241 F.R.D. 618 (S.D.Ill. 2007) (court had wide discretion as to what is objectionable, and can quash a subpoena seeking irrelevant information, as well as for the reasons listed in Rule 45(c)(3)(A)).

59. *Wiwa v. Royal Dutch Petroleum Co.*, 392 F.3d 812, 818 (5th Cir.2004) (modifying a subpoena is generally preferable to quashing it); *CSC Holdings, Inc. v. Redisi*, 309 F.3d 988, 993 (7th Cir.2002).

60. *See Sterling Merchandising, Inc. v. Nestle, S.A.*, 470 F.Supp.2d 77, 81 (D.Puerto Rico 2006) ("timely" is not defined in the Rule, and is subject to interpretation); *First City, Texas–Houston, N.A. v. Rafidain Bank*, 197 F.R.D. 250, 254 (S.D.N.Y.2000)

(objections raised more than one year after respondent held in contempt were waived).

61. *In re Flat Glass Antitrust Litigation*, 288 F.3d 83, 90 (3d Cir.2002) (failure to file motion to quash constitutes waiver of objections to manner of service of subpoena).

62. *GFL Advantage Fund, LTD v. Colkitt*, 216 F.R.D. 189 (D.D.C.2003); *Static Control Components, Inc. v. Darkprint Imaging*, 201 F.R.D. 431, 437 (M.D.N.C.2001); *Goodyear Tire & Rubber Co. v. Kirk's Tire & Auto Servicenter of Haverstraw, Inc.*, 211 F.R.D. 658, 660 (D.Kan.2003) (it is within the discretion of the court that issued the subpoena to transfer motions involving the subpoena to the district in which the action is pending); *but see In re Subpoenas Served on Wilmer, Cutler & Pickering and Goodwin Proctor LLP*, 255 F.Supp.2d 1, 2 (D.D.C.2003) (a district court has no authority to transfer a Rule 45(c) motion to the district in which the underlying litigation is pending).

63. *See Hill v. Wheatland Waters, Inc.*, 327 F.Supp.2d 1294, 1298, n.5 (D.Kan. 2004); *In re Bennett Funding Group, Inc.*, 259 B.R. 243, 250 (N.D.N.Y.2001); *Smith v. Midland Brake, Inc.*, 162 F.R.D. 683, 685 (D.Kan.1995).

64. *Washington v. Thurgood Marshall Academy*, 230 F.R.D. 18 (D.D.C.2005) (29

(2) *Distance to Travel:* Rule 45(c)(3)(A)(ii) provides for the quashing of a subpoena requiring a person not a party or officer of a party[65] to travel too far. Generally, such a person must travel up to 100 miles.[66] When the subpoena is for trial, such a person must travel anywhere within the state.[67] These distances are measured from any place that the person resides, is employed, or regularly transacts business.[68] Thus, a non-party witness must attend a deposition if his residence or place of employment is within 100 miles of the deposition location.

(3) *Privileged Matters:* Rule 45(c)(3)(A)(iii) provides that a subpoena may be quashed if it requires the disclosure of privileged or other protected matters.[69]

(4) *Undue Burden:* Rule 45(c)(3)(A)(iv) provides that a subpoena may be quashed if it subjects the recipient to undue burden.[70] This provision is sometimes used as justification for imposing the non-party's expenses on the party issuing the subpoena to cure the undue burden on the non-party.[71]

days was reasonable time to comply with subpoena to produce documents); *Paul v. Stewart Enterprises, Inc.*, 2000 WL 1171120 (E.D.La.2000) (one business day's notice is clearly unreasonable in light of the requirement in Rule 45(c)(2)(B) that a subpoenaed person be permitted 14 days to object); *United States v. Woods*, 931 F.Supp. 433, 442 n. 3 (E.D.Va.1996) (obtaining subpoenas 7 days before the hearing was not a reasonable enough time to comply).

65. *See In re Vioxx Products Liability Litigation*, 414 F.Supp.2d 574 (E.D.La. 2006); *Herbert Ltd. Partnership v. Electronic Arts Inc.*, 325 F.Supp.2d 282, 290 (S.D.N.Y.2004) (Rule 45(c)(3)(A)(ii) does not specify whether it applies to employees of a party who are not officers, and the courts are split).

66. *In re Edelman*, 295 F.3d 171, 174 (2nd Cir.2002).

67. *Zimmer Enterprises, Inc. v. Atlandia Imports, Inc.*, 478 F.Supp.2d 983, 991–92 (S.D.Ohio 2007) (offer to pay travel expenses does not cure distance problem).

68. *See Cooper Tire & Rubber Co. v. Farese*, 423 F.3d 446, 452 (5th Cir.2005); *Idlewild Creek Ltd. Partnership v. Travelers Property Cas.*, 2000 WL 1717566 (D.Me. 2000); *Price Waterhouse LLP v. First American Corp.*, 182 F.R.D. 56, 62 (S.D.N.Y. 1998) (when the subpoena seeks a corporate representative, travel distance is measured for the representative, not the corporation).

69. *Horace Mann Ins. Co. v. Nationwide Mut. Ins. Co.*, 240 F.R.D. 44, 46 (D.Conn. 2007) (party asserting the privilege must produce a privilege log); *Kitzmiller v. Dover Area School Dist.*, 379 F.Supp.2d 680 (M.D.Pa.2005) (reporters required to testify regardless of assertion of reporter's privilege).

70. *Positive Black Talk Inc. v. Cash Money Records, Inc.*, 394 F.3d 357, 377–78 (5th Cir.2004) (requiring an expert to testify in the face of a potential conflict of interest was an unreasonable burden); *Northwestern Memorial Hosp. v. Ashcroft*, 362 F.3d 923, 927 (7th Cir.2004) (balancing the burden and the need for the information); *Jones v. Hirschfeld*, 219 F.R.D. 71 (S.D.N.Y.2003) (court is particularly sensitive to burden when subpoena served on high ranking government official); *Linder v. Department of Defense*, 133 F.3d 17, 24 (D.C.Cir.1998); *Flatow v. The Islamic Republic of Iran*, 196 F.R.D. 203, 206–07 (D.D.C.2000) (undue burden can be identified through looking at factors such as relevance, the need of the party for the documents, the breadth of the document request, the time period covered by it, the particularity with which the documents are described and the burden imposed).

71. *See Medical Components, Inc. v. Classic Medical, Inc.*, 210 F.R.D. 175, 179 (M.D.N.C.2002).

Substantial Need of Serving Party

Rule 45(c)(3)(B) lists circumstances in which a subpoena will be quashed unless the serving party shows a "substantial need" for the testimony, documents, or inspection. In such cases, the court will condition compliance on the serving party compensating the recipient. These circumstances are:

(1) *Trade Secrets:* Rule 45(c)(3)(B)(i) provides limited protection for trade secrets and other confidential research, development, and commercial information.[72]

(2) *Unretained Experts:* Rule 45(c)(3)(B)(ii) provides limited protection for experts who have not been retained, so that parties cannot obtain their testimony without paying their fees.[73]

(3) *Undue Travel:* Rule 45(c)(3)(B)(iii) provides limited protection to persons who are not parties or officers of parties who would incur substantial expenses to travel more than 100 miles to attend trial.[74]

Appellate Review

Motions to compel and motions to quash are reviewed for abuse of discretion.[75]

RULE 45(d).   DUTIES IN RESPONDING TO A SUBPOENA

CORE CONCEPT

Documents may be produced as they are normally kept or may be separated and organized. When privileges are asserted, the privilege must be expressly described.

NOTE: The cautionary language in Rule 45(d) *must* be reprinted on every subpoena.

APPLICATIONS

Production of Documents

The scope of production under a subpoena is the same as the scope for discovery generally under Rule 26.[76] The responding party

72. *Mattel, Inc. v. Walking Mountain Productions*, 353 F.3d 792, 814 (9th Cir. 2003); *Hobley v. Burge*, 223 F.R.D. 499, 505 (N.D.Ill.2004) (newspaper reporter's notes are confidential research); *In re Vitamins Antitrust Litigation*, 267 F.Supp.2d 738 (S.D.Ohio 2003).

73. *U.S. ex rel. Tiesinga v. Dianon Systems, Inc.*, 240 F.R.D. 40, 42, n.2 (D.Conn. 2006); *Express One Intern., Inc. v. Sochata*, 2001 WL 363073 (N.D.Tex.2001) (witness was an employee who has not consented to

serve as an expert and cannot be forced to testify as an expert).

74. *Kisser v. Coalition for Religious Freedom*, 1995 WL 590169 (E.D.Pa. 1995)(ordering party to reimburse non-party for reasonable attorney's fees and travel expenses).

75. *Wiwa v. Royal Dutch Petroleum Co.*, 392 F.3d 812, 817 (5th Cir.2004).

76. *Stock v. Integrated Health Plan, Inc.*, 241 F.R.D. 618 (S.D.Ill. 2007); *Trans-*

has the option of allowing the serving party to inspect and copy the documents where they are normally kept (*e.g.,* "There is our file room.")[77]   The responding party may also collect the responsive documents and organize and label them to correspond to the categories requests.   The responding party may make copies for the requesting party, but is not obligated to do so.

Electronic Data

Rule 45 expressly allows for the party issuing the subpoena to request to inspect, copy, sample, or test electronic data.

- *Form of Electronic Data:* Rule 45(d)(1)(B) allows, but does not require, the requesting party to specify the form in which it is requesting electronic data (i.e., hard copy or electronic, and if electronic, the precise manner of production). If the requesting party does not specify the form, then the responding person must produce it in the form in which it is ordinarily maintained or in a form that is reasonably usable. In any event, a person need not produce electronic data in more than one form.

- *Undue Burden or Cost:* If the responding person believes that the production of electronic data from certain sources will cause undue burden or cost, the person can, in lieu of producing the documents, identify those sources.[78] If a motion to compel or quash is filed, the responding person will have the burden of showing that production would cause undue burden or cost.[79] The burden would then shift to the requesting party to show good cause why the data should be produced nonetheless.[80] In such cases, the court may specify conditions for the production, such as payment of the expenses of the production by the requesting party.[81]

Asserting a Privilege

When the subpoena recipient seeks to withhold information that is privileged, the recipient must expressly claim the privilege and describe the nature of the documents, communications, or things not produced in sufficient detail that the court and parties can assess the privilege.[82] The party asserting the privilege should provide a

cor, Inc. v. Furney Charters, Inc., 212 F.R.D. 588, 591, n.4 (D.Kan.2003).

77. *In re Copper Market Antitrust Litigation,* 200 F.R.D. 213 (S.D.N.Y.2001).

78. *Guy Chemical Co., Inc. v. Romaco AG,* 243 F.R.D. 310 (N.D.Ind. 2007).

79. *Guy Chemical Co., Inc. v. Romaco AG,* 243 F.R.D. 310 (N.D.Ind. 2007).

80. *Guy Chemical Co., Inc. v. Romaco AG,* 243 F.R.D. 310 (N.D.Ind. 2007) (good cause exists where no other source exists for the information).

81. *Guy Chemical Co., Inc. v. Romaco AG,* 243 F.R.D. 310 (N.D.Ind. 2007).

82. *In re Subpoena Duces Tecum Issued to Commodity Futures Trading Com'n,* 439 F.3d 740, 751 (D.C.Cir.2006) (a privilege log generally satisfies Rule 45(d)(2)); *In re Grand Jury Subpoena,* 274 F.3d 563, 575–76 (1st Cir.2001); *Horace Mann Ins. Co. v. Nationwide Mut. Ins. Co.,* 240 F.R.D. 44, 47 (D.Conn. 2007) (party asserting the privilege must produce a timely and detailed privilege log).

detailed privilege log at the time of asserting the privilege or within a reasonable time thereafter.[83]

Recalling Privileged Information

Rule 45(d)(2)(B) establishes a procedure to recall privileged information that has already been produced. Anyone believing that a person has produced privileged information in response to a subpoena may provide a notification to the parties who have received the information. After receiving such a notification, the receiving parties must return, sequester, or destroy the specified information and all copies (including taking reasonable steps to retrieve any information that the receiving party had already disclosed to other persons). If they do not agree with the privilege assertion, they can present the information to the court under seal for a determination of the privilege claim. During the pendency of the court's review of the privilege claim, the receiving parties are prohibited from using the information and the producing party must preserve it.

RULE 45(e).   CONTEMPT

CORE CONCEPT

Failure to obey a valid subpoena without adequate excuse is a contempt of the court issuing the subpoena.[84] However, sanctions may not be available without a court order compelling compliance.[85]

APPLICATIONS

Challenge to Subpoena

If a party believes that a subpoena is not valid, the proper response is a motion to quash or a motion for a protective order. *See* Rule 26(c). If the motion is unsuccessful and the party disobeys the subpoena nonetheless, the party can also raise validity grounds again at the contempt proceedings.[86] However, if the lawsuit is not before a federal court with subject matter jurisdiction, the subpoena will not be enforceable and a disobedient recipient is not subject to contempt sanctions.[87]

Due Process

Before sanctions may be imposed on a person charged with contempt under Rule 45, due process requires that the person receive notice and an opportunity to be heard.[88]

83. *Horace Mann Ins. Co. v. Nationwide Mut. Ins. Co.,* 240 F.R.D. 44, 47 (D.Conn. 2007) (discussing what qualifies as a reasonable period of time).

84. *Blackmer v. United States,* 284 U.S. 421, 52 S.Ct. 252, 76 L.Ed. 375 (1932); *Dynegy Midstream Services v. Trammochem,* 451 F.3d 89, 95 (2nd Cir.2006); *In re Sealed Case,* 141 F.3d 337, 341 (D.C.Cir. 1998).

85. *Cruz v. Meachum,* 159 F.R.D. 366 (D.Conn.1994).

86. *United States v. Ryan,* 402 U.S. 530, 533, 91 S.Ct. 1580, 1582, 29 L.Ed.2d 85 (1971).

87. *Olcott v. Delaware Flood Co.,* 76 F.3d 1538, 1552 (10th Cir.1996).

88. *In re Corso,* 328 B.R. 375 (E.D.N.Y. 2005).

Adequate Excuse

Inability to comply is an adequate excuse.[89]   The fact that the subpoena would require the recipient to travel greater distances than those listed in Rule 45(c)(3)(A)(iii) is also an adequate excuse.[90] Likewise, a timely objection to the subpoena is an adequate excuse.[91] Preferring to work instead of comply with the subpoena is not an adequate excuse.[92]

Appeal

Orders pertaining to subpoenas are ordinarily interlocutory, and thus not appealable.   An exception exists when one district clerk issues a discovery subpoena for an action proceeding in another district, and that subpoena is quashed.   Such an order is immediately appealable as a final order.[93]   To be reversed, an order pertaining to a subpoena must be plainly arbitrary.

ADDITIONAL RESEARCH REFERENCES

Wright & Miller, *Federal Practice and Procedure* §§ 2451–2463.

C.J.S. Federal Civil Procedure §§ 582–583 et seq., 644; Witnesses §§ 13–27 et seq.

West's Key No. Digests, Federal Civil Procedure ☞1353–1354, 1456; Witnesses ☞7–16, 21.

89. *Fisher v. Marubeni Cotton Corp.*, 526 F.2d 1338, 1342 (8th Cir.1975); *Tranchant v. Environmental Monitoring Service, Inc.*, 2001 WL 617426 (E.D.La.2001) ("For a person to be held in contempt for failing to produce documents, it must be proven that the documents actually exist.").

90. *See Hillard v. Guidant Corp.*, 76 F.Supp.2d 566, 570 (M.D.Pa.1999); *National Property Investors VIII v. Shell Oil Co.*, 917 F.Supp. 324, 328 (D.N.J.1995).

91. *Flatow v. Islamic Republic of Iran*, 196 F.R.D. 203, 208 (D.D.C.2000).

92. *Higginbotham v. KCS Intern., Inc.*, 202 F.R.D. 444, 455 (D.Md.2001).

93. *CF & I Steel Corp. v. Mitsui & Co. (U.S.A.), Inc.*, 713 F.2d 494 (9th Cir.1983); *Horizons Titanium Corp. v. Norton*, 290 F.2d 421 (1st Cir.1961).

RULE 46

OBJECTING TO A RULING OR ORDER

A formal exception to a ruling or order is unnecessary. When the ruling or order is requested or made, a party need only state the action that it wants the court to take or objects to, along with the grounds for the request or objection. Failing to object does not prejudice a party who had no opportunity to do so when the ruling or order was made.

[Amended effective August 1, 1987; April 30, 2007, effective December 1, 2007.]

———————— **2007 AMENDMENTS ROADMAP** ————————

STYLE PROJECT CHANGES: The title of rule 46 was revised, and the language in Rule 46 was clarified and simplified.

NON-STYLE CHANGES: None.

NOTE: The Federal Rules "Style Project" is explained in Part III-A.

AUTHORS' COMMENTARY ON RULE 46

———————— **PURPOSE AND SCOPE** ————————

Rule 46 abolishes the formality of noting "exceptions" when the court overrules an objection or takes some action contrary to a request.[1]

NOTE: An attorney still needs to voice an objection to a court's ruling in the first instance; Rule 46 only relieves the need to note exceptions to the court's ruling.

APPLICATIONS

Applies to All Stages

Rule 46 applies to all stages of a trial, from voir dire through jury instructions. The attorney must object even to questions asked by the judge, although the appeals court may be more lenient about the form and timing of such objections.

---

1. *Kasper v. Saint Mary of Nazareth Hospital*, 135 F.3d 1170, 1175 (7th Cir. 1998).

Form of Objection

In order to preserve an issue for appeal, an attorney must state the particular grounds upon which the objection rests.[2] It is not sufficient to state simply, "objection," or to make a general objection. The primary purpose of the specificity requirement is to apprise the court of the litigant's position so that the court can correct its ruling if appropriate.[3] Consequently, if the grounds are obvious to the trial judge, an appellate court may overlook a lack of specificity.[4] If the judge's ruling is ambiguous, a party cannot challenge it on appeal without first attempting to have the judge clarify the ruling.[5]

Exceptions

It is not necessary to note an exception or take any other action to preserve a properly raised but overruled objection.[6]

Failure to Object

In general, failure to object to a ruling or issue constitutes a waiver of the ruling or issue.[7] Rule 46 provides that an attorney need not object if there is no opportunity to do so.[8] Additionally, the appeals court may consider on appeal an issue to which no objection was asserted when the basis was so clear that no objection was necessary, such as when the attorney has already objected to the same evidence.[9] Also, the appellate court may overlook the lack of an objection if the error was so fundamental that it caused a miscarriage of justice.[10]

Unsuccessful Motion in Limine

If a party files an unsuccessful motion in limine where the exclusion of certain evidence is sought, that party does not have to formally object at trial when the evidence in question is introduced as long as two conditions are met: (1) the party filed a written pre-trial motion setting forth reasons and case citations in support of the request that the evidence be excluded; and (2) the district court

2. *Ramey v. District 141, Intern. Ass'n of Machinists and Aerospace Workers,* 378 F.3d 269, 281 (2nd Cir.2004) (a party seeking to preserve an objection must make known to the court the party's objection to the action of the court and the grounds therefore); *Kasper v. Saint Mary of Nazareth Hospital,* 135 F.3d 1170, 1176 (7th Cir.1998).

3. *Kasper v. Saint Mary of Nazareth Hospital,* 135 F.3d 1170, 1176 (7th Cir. 1998); *In re Wedtech Corp.,* 196 B.R. 274, 277 (Bankr.S.D.N.Y.1996).

4. *New England Newspaper Pub. Co. v. Bonner,* 68 F.2d 880 (1st Cir.1934).

5. *Kasper v. Saint Mary of Nazareth Hospital,* 135 F.3d 1170, 1176 (7th Cir. 1998).

6. *Jacques v. DiMarzio, Inc.,* 386 F.3d 192, 200–01 (2nd Cir.2004)(formal exceptions to rulings of the court are unnecessary as long as the party makes known its objection and the basis for it at the time the district court rules); *Fogarty v. Near North Insurance Brokerage, Inc.,* 162 F.3d 74, 81 (2d Cir.1998).

7. *See Krieger v. Fadely,* 211 F.3d 134 (D.C.Cir.2000).

8. *Boeing Co. v. Cascade Corp.,* 207 F.3d 1177, 1191 n. 46 (9th Cir.2000).*Angelo v. Armstrong World Industries, Inc.,* 11 F.3d 957 (10th Cir.1993).

9. *Beech Aircraft Corp. v. Rainey,* 488 U.S. 153, 109 S.Ct. 439, 102 L.Ed.2d 445 (1988).

10. *Sibbach v. Wilson & Co.,* 312 U.S. 1, 16, 61 S.Ct. 422, 427, 85 L.Ed. 479 (1941).

made a "definitive" ruling with no suggestion that it would reconsider the matter at trial.[11]

ADDITIONAL RESEARCH REFERENCES

Wright & Miller, *Federal Practice and Procedure* §§ 2471–2473.

C.J.S. Federal Civil Procedure §§ 370 et seq., 941–942.

West's Key No. Digests, Federal Civil Procedure ⟾928, 2017–2019.

---

11. *Walden v. Georgia–Pacific Corp.,* 126 F.3d 506, 518 (3d Cir.1997). *See also Inter Medical Supplies, Ltd. v. EBI Medical Systems, Inc.,* 181 F.3d 446, 455 (3d Cir. 1999) (objection unnecessary following motion in limine where the court has made a definitive ruling on the issue and is unlikely to reconsider).

RULE 47

SELECTING JURORS

(a) Examining Jurors. The court may permit the parties or their attorneys to examine prospective jurors or may itself do so. If the court examines the jurors, it must permit the parties or their attorneys to make any further inquiry it considers proper, or must itself ask any of their additional questions it considers proper.

(b) Peremptory Challenges. The court must allow the number of peremptory challenges provided by 28 U.S.C. § 1870.

(c) Excusing a Juror. During trial or deliberation, the court may excuse a juror for good cause.

[Amended effective July 1, 1966; December 1, 1991; April 30, 2007, effective December 1, 2007.]

―――――――――――― **2007 AMENDMENTS ROADMAP** ――――――――――――

STYLE PROJECT CHANGES: The sections of Rule 47 were renamed, and the language was clarified and simplified. Active voice replaced passive voice, and "must" replaced "shall".

NON-STYLE CHANGES: None.

NOTE: The Federal Rules "Style Project" is explained in Part III-A.

AUTHORS' COMMENTARY ON RULE 47

―――――――――――― **PURPOSE AND SCOPE** ――――――――――――

Rule 47 addresses the examination of prospective jurors (voir dire) and contains provisions for alternate jurors.

RULE 47(a). EXAMINING OF JURORS

CORE CONCEPT

The court and/or the parties may ask prospective jurors questions in order to determine bias and to enable the parties to exercise their peremptory challenges in a meaningful manner.

APPLICATIONS

Scope of Examinations

The court has broad discretion with respect to the scope of voir dire.[1] It may conduct the examination itself or allow the parties to do so. If the court conducts the examination, the parties may submit proposed questions, which the court may ask if it deems them proper.[2] In exercising its discretion, the court must allow sufficient questioning so that the selection process is meaningful.

Challenges for Cause

Challenges for cause are ruled on by the court. The party making the challenge has the burden of persuading the court. Partiality is the main grounds for such challenges. Parties can challenge the entire panel or the selection process. Such challenges should be made at the time of jury selection, not in a motion for new trial.[3]

Qualifications for Jurors

The qualifications for jurors is governed by the Jury Selection and Service Act of 1968, 28 U.S.C. § 1861 *et seq.* Essentially, jurors must be United States citizens, have resided in the district for at least one year, must meet minimum literacy requirements and be fluent in English, must be mentally and physically capable of service, and must be free from pending charges or past convictions of crimes punishable by imprisonment for more than 2 years.

Excluded Groups

The Jury Selection and Service Act of 1968 also provides for the establishment of certain groups who are precluded or excused from serving. Generally, these include: persons providing vital services (such as members of the armed services and policemen); persons for whom service would be a particular hardship (such as sole proprietors, mothers with young children, persons with gravely ill family members); and those excluded by the court for partiality or because they are likely to be disruptive.

Conduct of Jurors

The court has great latitude with respect to such issues as note taking by jurors, sequestration, questions by the jury, etc.

Alternate Jurors

Alternate jurors are no longer used in civil trials in federal court.[4]

---

1. *Smith v. Vicorp, Inc.*, 107 F.3d 816, 817 (10th Cir.1997).

2. *Smith v. Tenet Healthsystem SL, Inc.*, 436 F.3d 879, 884 (8th Cir.2006); *Butler v. City of Camden, City Hall*, 352 F.3d 811, 815 (3rd Cir.2003).

3. *Atlas Roofing Mfg. Co. v. Parnell*, 409 F.2d 1191 (5th Cir.1969).

4. The Advisory Committee Note to the 1991 Amendments to Rule 47 and Rule 48; *Delaney v. Detella*, 2004 WL 525007 (N.D.Ill. 2004).

RULE 47(b).   PEREMPTORY CHALLENGES

CORE CONCEPT

Rule 47(b) provides that peremptory challenges are governed by 28 U.S.C.A. § 1870, which provides that each party has 3 peremptory challenges, and generally need not give any explanation for using those challenges. Peremptory challenges are not constitutionally protected fundamental rights, but are merely one means to the constitutional end of an impartial jury and a fair trial.[5] When there are multiple plaintiffs or defendants, the court may require them to exercise the challenges collectively or may allow additional challenges.[6]

APPLICATIONS

Improper Grounds

It is improper to use a peremptory challenge to exclude a juror on the basis of race[7] or gender.[8]

RULE 47(c).   EXCUSING A JUROR

CORE CONCEPT

The court may excuse a juror for reasons of sickness, family emergency, juror misconduct, or for other "good cause shown."[9] A juror's refusal to join the majority is not grounds for excuse.[10]

APPLICATIONS

Considerations for Excuse

Characteristics of a juror to be scrutinized pursuant to Rule 47(c) include not only spoken words, but gestures and attitudes in order to ensure the jury's impartiality and competence.[11]

ADDITIONAL RESEARCH REFERENCES

Wright & Miller, *Federal Practice and Procedure* §§ 2481–2485. Bennett & Hirschhorn, Bennett's *Guide to Jury Selection and Trial Dynamics in Civil and Criminal Litigation.*

C.J.S. Juries §§ 208–250 et seq., 251–285 et seq.

West's Key No. Digests, Jury ⬷83–142.

5. *United States v. Allen–Brown*, 243 F.3d 1293, 1299 (11th Cir.2001), *cert. denied*, 534 U.S. 1010, 122 S.Ct. 496, 151 L.Ed.2d 407 (2001); *see also Rahn v. Hawkins*, 464 F.3d 813, 819 (8th Cir. 2006) (declining to vacate a verdict where trial court erroneously gave each side 2 peremptory challenges).

6. *Polec v. Northwest Airlines, Inc.*, 86 F.3d 498, 518–519 (6th Cir.1996).

7. *Edmonson v. Leesville Concrete Co.*, 500 U.S. 614, 111 S.Ct. 2077, 114 L.Ed.2d 660 (1991).

8. *Montanez v. Puerto Rico Police Department*, 33 F.Supp.2d 106, 108 (D.Puerto Rico 1999).

9. *See Harris v. Folk Construction Co.*, 138 F.3d 365, 371 (8th Cir.1998); *Interpool Limited v. Patterson*, 874 F.Supp. 616 (S.D.N.Y.1995)(juror excused because of important business trip).

10. *See Murray v. Laborers Union Local No. 324*, 55 F.3d 1445, 1450–51 (9th Cir. 1995).

11. *Harris v. Folk Construction Co.*, 138 F.3d 365, 371 (8th Cir.1998).

RULE 48

NUMBER OF JURORS; VERDICT

A jury must initially have at least 6 and no more than 12 members, and each juror must participate in the verdict unless excused under Rule 47(c). Unless the parties stipulate otherwise, the verdict must be unanimous and be returned by a jury of at least 6 members.

[Amended effective December 1, 1991; April 30, 2007, effective December 1, 2007.]

─────────────── **2007 AMENDMENTS ROADMAP** ───────────────

STYLE PROJECT CHANGES: The title of Rule 48 was revised, and the language was clarified and simplified. Active voice replaced passive voice, and "must" replaced "shall".

NON-STYLE CHANGES: None.

NOTE: The Federal Rules "Style Project" is explained in Part III-A.

AUTHORS' COMMENTARY ON RULE 48

─────────────── **PURPOSE AND SCOPE** ───────────────

The court may select any number of jurors from 6 to 12, inclusive. Unless the parties stipulate otherwise, the verdict must be unanimous.

APPLICATIONS

Verdicts Normally Unanimous

Absent a stipulation, verdicts must be unanimous.[1] However, verdicts are considered unanimous even if 1 or more jurors reluctantly joins just to reach a verdict.[2] If a jury reports being unable to reach a unanimous verdict, the majority of the courts allow an instruction to the jury to deliberate further to attempt to break the deadlock.[3]

---

1. *Jazzabi v. Allstate Ins. Co.*, 278 F.3d 979, 985 (9th Cir.2002) (jury must be unanimous as to affirmative defense as well as ultimate verdict); *Robinson v. Cattaraugus County*, 147 F.3d 153, 161 (2d Cir.1998).

2. *See Cary v. Allegheny Technologies Inc.*, 267 F.Supp.2d 43 (W.D.Pa.2003) (allowing a charge to the jury about the benefits of reaching a verdict).

3. *Cary v. Allegheny Technologies Inc.*, 267 F.Supp.2d 442, 446 (W.D.Pa.2003) (the

Polling the Jury

A party may demand that the jury be polled to verify that the verdict is unanimous. If 1 or more jurors dissents, the court may require the jury to deliberate further or may declare a mistrial. Polling must occur before the verdict is recorded and the jury is discharged.

Excused Jurors

If a juror is excused for illness or other reason under Rule 47(c), a unanimous verdict among the remaining jurors will be valid if at least 6 jurors remain.[4] If fewer than 6 remain, the parties may consent to allow the trial or deliberations to continue and to then be bound by the verdict.[5]

Stipulations

By stipulation, the parties can agree that a unanimous decision is not necessary, and that the decision of a specified majority will be taken as the decision of the jury.[6] The parties may also stipulate to fewer than 6 jurors.[7]

Alternate Jurors

Alternate jurors are not used in civil trials in federal court.[8]

Advisory Jury

It does not appear that the provisions of Rule 48 regarding unanimity pertain to advisory juries.[9]

ADDITIONAL RESEARCH REFERENCES

Wright & Miller, *Federal Practice and Procedure* §§ 2491–2492. Bennett & Hirschhorn, Bennett's *Guide to Jury Selection and Trial Dynamics in Civil and Criminal Litigation.*

C.J.S. Federal Civil Procedure §§ 995 et seq.; Juries § 4.

West's Key No. Digests, Federal Civil Procedure ☞2191; Jury ☞4.

"vast majority" of the courts allow supplemental "Allen" instructions to civil juries).

4. *Weaver v. Blake,* 454 F.3d 1087 (10th Cir.2006).

5. *Meyers v. Wal–Mart Stores, East, Inc.,* 257 F.3d 625, 633 (6th Cir.2001) (approving a trial with 4 jurors based on the parties' stipulation, and noting that a bench trial is essentially a stipulation to trial before zero jurors); *N.A.A.C.P v. Acusport, Inc.,* 253 F.Supp.2d 459 (E.D.N.Y.2003).

6. *Baxter Healthcare Corp. v. Spectramed, Inc.,* 49 F.3d 1575 (Fed.Cir.1995);

Cook v. Rockwell Intern. Corp., 428 F.Supp.2d 1152, 1154 (D.Colo.2006); *NAACP v. AcuSport, Inc.,* 271 F.Supp.2d 435 (E.D.N.Y.2003).

7. *Meyers v. Wal–Mart Stores, East, Inc.,* 77 F.Supp.2d, 826, 827 (E.D.Mich.1999) (both parties stipulated to 4 jurors).

8. The Advisory Committee Note to the 1991 Amendments to Rule 47 and Rule 48; *Delaney v. Detella,* 2004 WL 525007 (N.D.Ill.2004).

9. *N.A.A.C.P v. Acusport, Inc.,* 253 F.Supp.2d 459 (E.D.N.Y.2003).

RULE 49

SPECIAL VERDICT; GENERAL VERDICT AND QUESTIONS

(a) Special Verdict.

(1) *In General.* The court may require a jury to return only a special verdict in the form of a special written finding on each issue of fact. The court may do so by:

   (A) submitting written questions susceptible of a categorical or other brief answer;

   (B) submitting written forms of the special findings that might properly be made under the pleadings and evidence; or

   (C) using any other method that the court considers appropriate.

(2) *Instructions.* The court must give the instructions and explanations necessary to enable the jury to make its findings on each submitted issue.

(3) *Issues Not Submitted.* A party waives the right to a jury trial on any issue of fact raised by the pleadings or evidence but not submitted to the jury unless, before the jury retires, the party demands its submission to the jury. If the party does not demand submission, the court may make a finding on the issue. If the court makes no finding, it is considered to have made a finding consistent with its judgment on the special verdict.

(b) General Verdict with Answers to Written Questions.

(1) *In General.* The court may submit to the jury forms for a general verdict, together with written questions on one or more issues of fact that the jury must decide. The court must give the instructions and explanations necessary to enable the jury to render a general verdict and answer the questions in writing, and must direct the jury to do both.

(2) *Verdict and Answers Consistent.* When the general verdict and the answers are consistent, the court

must approve, for entry under Rule 58, an appropriate judgment on the verdict and answers.

(3) *Answers Inconsistent with the Verdict.* When the answers are consistent with each other but one or more is inconsistent with the general verdict, the court may:

(A) approve, for entry under Rule 58, an appropriate judgment according to the answers, notwithstanding the general verdict;

(B) direct the jury to further consider its answers and verdict; or

(C) order a new trial.

(4) *Answers Inconsistent with Each Other and the Verdict.* When the answers are inconsistent with each other and one or more is also inconsistent with the general verdict, judgment must not be entered; instead, the court must direct the jury to further consider its answers and verdict, or must order a new trial.

[Amended effective July 1, 1963; August 1, 1987; April 30, 2007, effective December 1, 2007.]

───────── **2007 AMENDMENTS ROADMAP** ─────────

STYLE PROJECT CHANGES: Rules 49(a) and (b) were subsectioned, and labels were added and amended. The language was clarified and simplified, active voice replaced passive voice, and "must" replaced "shall".

NON-STYLE CHANGES: None.

NOTE: The Federal Rules "Style Project" is explained in Part III-A.

AUTHORS' COMMENTARY ON RULE 49

───────── PURPOSE AND SCOPE ─────────

Rule 49 provides mechanisms for directing specific questions to the jury. There are 2 alternative methods: special verdicts, which allow the jury to make findings as to each issue of fact; and written interrogatories which, together with a general verdict, allow the parties to verify that the jury is applying the law to the facts in the manner instructed by the court.

RULE 49(a). SPECIAL VERDICT

CORE CONCEPT

The court may require the jury to return special verdicts as to each factual issue, instead of a general verdict in favor of one party.[1]

APPLICATIONS

Comparison With General Verdict

A general verdict is a single statement disposing of the entire case ("We find in favor of the defendant.").[2] Special verdicts ask the jury to decide specific factual questions ("At the time of the accident, the vehicle was proceeding at an excessive rate of speed.").[3]

Court's Discretion

The court has virtually absolute discretion as to the use of special verdicts.[4] This discretion extends to determining the content and layout of the verdict form, and any interrogatories submitted to the jury, provided the questions asked are reasonably capable of an interpretation that would allow the jury to address all factual issues essential to judgment.[5] Generally, special verdicts are more appropriate in complex cases.[6] Special verdicts are also valuable when the status of the law is uncertain because if the trial court is reversed on the law, sufficient special verdicts may render a new trial unnecessary.

Scope of Questions

The special verdicts should fairly present the case, and should cover all factual issues.[7] Although special verdicts should not ask purely legal questions, they sometimes will contain a mixture of law and fact.

1. *Lee v. Coss*, 39 F.Supp.2d 170 (D.Conn.1999).

2. *Mason v. Ford Motor Co., Inc.*, 307 F.3d 1271, 1274 (11th Cir.2002).

3. *Zhang v. American Gem Seafoods, Inc.*, 339 F.3d 1020, 1031 (9th Cir.2003) (comparing special and general verdicts); *Lavin v. Emery Air Freight Corp.*, 980 F.Supp. 93, 98 (D.Conn.1997), *aff'd*, 141 F.3d 1151 (2d Cir.1998) (court looks to two factors when determining whether a verdict is general or special, its own intent and the substantive charge given).

4. *See International Ground Transp. v. Mayor And City Council Of Ocean City,* MD, 475 F.3d 214, 223 (4th Cir. 2007); *Santos v. Posadas De Puerto Rico Associates, Inc.*, 452 F.3d 59, 65 (1st Cir.2006).

5. *United States v. Real Property Located at 20832 Big Rock Drive, Malibu, CA 90265*, 51 F.3d 1402, 1408 (9th Cir.1995).

6. *Dinco v. Dylex Ltd.*, 111 F.3d 964, 969 (1st Cir.1997).

7. *Santos v. Posadas De Puerto Rico Associates, Inc.*, 452 F.3d 59, 65 (1st Cir.2006); *Broadcast Satellite Intern., Inc. v. National Digital Television Center, Inc.*, 323 F.3d 339, 342 (5th Cir.2003).

Form of Questions

Special verdicts may take different forms. Sometimes the questions will require the jury to write a brief answer (such as "yes" or "no"). Sometimes alternative special verdicts will be written out, and the jury need only choose one alternative.

Instructions to Jury

Rule 49(a) requires the court to give the jury sufficient instructions so that they can determine each issue before them.[8] When an issue before the jury involves mixed questions of fact and law, the court must give instructions as to the applicable law.[9]

Omission of Issues

If the court submits special verdicts to the jury and omits a question of fact raised by the pleadings or evidence, each party must object to the omission before the jury retires or that party waives the right to a jury trial on that issue (note that one party cannot rely on the objection of another party).[10] As to issues not submitted to the jury and not objected to, the court may make a finding.[11] If the court merely issues a general verdict, the court will be deemed to have ruled in a consistent fashion on issues not submitted to the jury.[12]

Return of Verdict

The jury's verdicts must be certain, unequivocal, and consistent. If there is a construction of the verdicts that renders them consistent, it will be adopted.[13] Otherwise, the court may require the jury to deliberate further[14] or may declare a mistrial. The court may not, however, make findings contrary to the jury verdict.[15]

Failure to Find

If the jury fails to unanimously agree on some of the answers to special interrogatories, the judge has several available procedures

---

8. *Romano v. Howarth*, 998 F.2d 101 (2d Cir.1993). *But see Aerotech Resources, Inc. v. Dodson Aviation, Inc.*, 191 F.Supp.2d 1209, 1220 (D.Kan.2002) (with special interrogatories, the jury makes findings of fact as to each contested fact, then the court applies the law to those facts, so instructions of the law to the jury are unnecessary).

9. *Manufacturers Hanover Trust Co. v. Drysdale Sec. Corp.*, 801 F.2d 13, 26 (2d Cir.1986); *Tights, Inc. v. Acme–McCrary Corp.*, 541 F.2d 1047, 1061 (4th Cir.1976).

10. *See Ross v. Marshall*, 426 F.3d 745, 762 (5th Cir.2005); *Becker v. Poling Transp. Corp.*, 356 F.3d 381, 390 (2nd Cir.2004); *Reynolds v. City of Chicago*, 296 F.3d 524 (7th Cir.2002).

11. *Roberts v. Karimi*, 251 F.3d 404, 407–08 (2d Cir.2001); *Ramos v. Davis & Geck, Inc.*, 224 F.3d 30, 32 (1st Cir.2000)

(issue must be raised by the pleadings); *Parrish v. Sollecito*, 280 F.Supp.2d 145, 158 (S.D.N.Y.2003).

12. *Ansin v. River Oaks Furniture, Inc.*, 105 F.3d 745, 756 (1st Cir.1997).

13. *Technical Resource Services, Inc. v. Dornier Medical Sys.*, 134 F.3d 1458, 1464 (11th Cir.1998) (test to be applied in reconciling potential conflicts between the jury's answers is whether the answers may fairly be said to represent a logical and probable decision on the relevant issues as submitted).

14. *Selgas v. American Airlines, Inc.*, 858 F.Supp. 316 (D.P.R.1994), *aff'd in part, vac'd in part*, 69 F.3d 1205 (1st Cir.1995).

15. *Ramos v. Davis & Geck, Inc.*, 224 F.3d 30, 32 (1st Cir.2000).

prior to dismissing the jury. The judge can: resubmit the interrogatories to the jury for further deliberations; ask the parties if they would be willing to accept the majority responses; enter judgment on the basis of the unanimous interrogatory answers if they are dispositive; declare the entire case a mistrial; or order a partial retrial of the issues not unanimously agreed upon.[16]

Objections

Objections to the instructions to the jury should be made before the jury retires.[17] Objections to the jury's responses or to the verdict to be entered based on the jury's responses should be made, if possible, before the jury is discharged. Failure to do so may result in a waiver of the objections.[18]

Law Governing

The use of special verdicts or interrogatories is a procedural issue governed by federal law, not by state law.[19]

Appellate Review

The standard for reviewing the court's use of special verdicts depends on the issue under appeal. The court's decision to use special verdicts is reviewed under the "abuse of discretion" standard.[20] The threshold determination that the jury returned a general verdict inconsistent with its answers to special interrogatories is a mixed question of law and fact subject to plenary review.[21]

RULE 49(b). GENERAL VERDICT WITH ANSWERS TO WRITTEN QUESTIONS

CORE CONCEPT

The court may submit to the jury a general verdict[22] and written interrogatories about specific factual issues.

16. *Baxter Healthcare Corp. v. Spectramed, Inc.*, 49 F.3d 1575 (Fed.Cir.1995), *cert. denied*, 516 U.S. 906, 116 S.Ct. 272, 133 L.Ed.2d 194 (1995).

17. *Austin v. Paramount Parks, Inc.*, 195 F.3d 715, 725 (4th Cir.1999); *Wilson v. Maritime Overseas Corp.*, 150 F.3d 1, 6 (1st Cir.1998).

18. *L & W, Inc. v. Shertech, Inc.*, 471 F.3d 1311, 1319 (Fed.Cir. 2006); *Marcano-Rivera v. Pueblo International, Inc.*, 232 F.3d 245, 253 n.4 (1st Cir.2000). *But see Johnson v. Ablt Trucking Co., Inc.*, 412 F.3d 1138, 1141 (10th Cir.2005)(failure to object to inconsistent special verdicts before the jury is discharged is not a waiver); *Heno v. Sprint/United Management Co.*, 208 F.3d 847, 851 (10th Cir.2000) (a party is not required to object to inconsistent special

verdicts before the jury retires in order to preserve the issue for a subsequent motion to the court).

19. *Affiliated FM Ins. Co. v. Neosho Construction Co., Inc.*, 192 F.R.D. 662, 673 (D. Kan.2000); *Dewitt v. Smith*, 152 F.R.D. 162 (W.D.Ark.1993).

20. *Bills v. Aseltine*, 52 F.3d 596 (6th Cir.1995); *Davis v. Ford Motor Co.*, 128 F.3d 631, 633 (8th Cir.1997).

21. *Wilbur v. Correctional Services Corp.*, 393 F.3d 1192, 1200 (11th Cir.2004).

22. *Zhang v. American Gem Seafoods, Inc.*, 339 F.3d 1020 (9th Cir.2003) (the Rules do not define general verdicts, but they imply that general verdicts do not involve factual findings but rather ultimate legal conclusions).

APPLICATIONS

Purpose

Written interrogatories can serve 2 functions. First they focus the jury's attention on important factual issues and insure that the general verdict is consistent with the factual findings. Second, if the court is subsequently reversed on a legal issue, a new trial may be avoided if the interrogatories contain sufficient findings.

Court's Discretion

As with special verdicts, the court has virtually absolute discretion with respect to the use of written interrogatories to the jury and with respect to the format of the questions.[23] The court also has broad discretion in evaluating the consistency of the interrogatories and the general verdict, and in selecting the remedy for any inconsistencies as described below.[24]

Content of Interrogatories

Because there is a general verdict, the content of the interrogatories is not as critical as with special verdicts—every issue need not be covered. A special interrogatory should address an issue or issues of fact, the resolution of which is necessary to the verdict.[25]

Interrogatory Answers and Verdict Consistent

If the general verdict is consistent with the interrogatory answers, then the court will enter judgment accordingly. Any ambiguity will be resolved in favor of consistency.[26]

Interrogatory Answers and Verdict Not Consistent

If the interrogatory answers are internally consistent but not consistent with the general verdict,[27] the court has 3 options: it can order the jury to deliberate further;[28] it can enter judgment based on the interrogatories if they are sufficient;[29] or it can declare a mistrial.[30] The court may not enter judgment based on the general verdict in the face of inconsistent interrogatory answers (although judgment may be proper if the inconsistent interrogatory response

---

23. *Micrel, Inc. v. TRW, Inc.*, 486 F.3d 866 (6th Cir. 2007); *JGR, Inc. v. Thomasville Furniture Indust., Inc.*, 370 F.3d 519 (6th Cir.2004); *Cruz v. Town of Cicero, Ill.*, 275 F.3d 579, 591 (7th Cir.2001); *Hostetler v. Consol. Rail Corp.*, 123 F.3d 387, 393 (6th Cir.1997).

24. *Beard v. Flying J. Inc.*, 116 F.Supp.2d 1077, 1088 (S.D.Iowa 2000), *aff'd in part, rev'd in part*, 266 F.3d 792 (8th Cir. 2001).

25. *U.S. ex rel. Tyson v. Amerigroup Illinois, Inc.*, ___ F.Supp.2d ___ (N.D.Ill. 2007).

26. *Turyna v. Martam Construction Co., Inc.*, 83 F.3d 178, 181 (7th Cir.1996).

27. *Wilbur v. Correctional Services Corp.*, 393 F.3d 1192, 1200 (11th Cir.2004) (a verdict contains an inconsistency if answers given by the jury may not fairly be said to represent a logical and probable decision on the relevant issues as submitted).

28. *Kerman v. City of New York*, 261 F.3d 229, 244 (2d Cir.2001).

29. *Zhang v. American Gem Seafoods, Inc.*, 339 F.3d 1020, 1038 (9th Cir.2003).

30. *See Intermatic Inc. v. Lamson & Sessions Co.*, 273 F.3d 1355, 1369 (Fed.Cir. 2001).

goes to a different issue or is not necessary for the judgment).[31]   If the interrogatory answers are internally inconsistent and inconsistent with the general verdict, the court can order further deliberations or declare a mistrial, but cannot enter judgment.[32]   A party believing that the interrogatory answers are inconsistent with the general verdict should place an objection on the record to avoid waiving the objection.[33]

Inconsistent Interrogatories

When the interrogatory answers are internally inconsistent, the court may order the jury to deliberate further or may order a new trial.[34]

Inconsistent General Verdicts

When general verdicts on different claims are inconsistent, a court may not simply mold one of the two verdicts to be consistent with the other. Faced with inconsistent general verdicts, the court may take one of four approaches: (1) "in certain circumstances, . . . allow the verdict to stand;" (2) "attempt to read the verdict in a manner that will resolve the inconsistencies;" (3) "resubmit the question to the jury;" or (4) "order an entirely new trial."[35]

Objections to Interrogatories

The courts are divided as to whether objections to interrogatories are waived unless raised before the jury retires.[36]

ADDITIONAL RESEARCH REFERENCES

Wright & Miller, *Federal Practice and Procedure* §§ 2501–2513. Bennett & Hirschhorn, Bennett's *Guide to Jury Selection and Trial Dynamics in Civil and Criminal Litigation.*

C.J.S. Federal Civil Procedure §§ 1009–1027 et seq.

West's Key No. Digests, Federal Civil Procedure ⊘2211–2220, 2231–2242.

31. *Armstrong ex rel. Armstrong v. Brookdale University Hospital and Medical Center,* 425 F.3d 126, 135 (2nd Cir.2005).

32. *King v. Ford Motor Co.,* 209 F.3d 886 (6th Cir.2000) (court has broad discretion as to whether to send the jury out for further deliberations or order a new trial); *Loughman v. Consol–Pennsylvania Coal Company,* 6 F.3d 88 (3d Cir.1993).

33. *See Johnson v. Ablt Trucking Co., Inc.,* 412 F.3d 1138, 1141 (10th Cir.2005); *Wilbur v. Correctional Services Corp.,* 393 F.3d 1192, 1200 (11th Cir.2004) (formal objection not necessary when the court has already indicated that it recognizes the inconsistency).

34. *Wilbur v. Correctional Services Corp.,* 393 F.3d 1192, 1204 (11th Cir.2004) (court has wide discretion as to which option to employ); *Zhang v. American Gem Seafoods, Inc.,* 339 F.3d 1020, 1038 (9th

Cir.2003); *King v. Ford Motor Co.,* 209 F.3d 886, 895 (6th Cir.2000) (the court has wide discretion as to which option to employ).

35. *Mosley v. Wilson,* 102 F.3d 85, 90–91 (3d Cir.1996) (quoting *Los Angeles v. Heller,* 475 U.S. 796, 106 S.Ct. 1571, 89 L.Ed.2d 806 (1986)) (internal quotes omitted).

36. *Correia v. Fitzgerald,* 354 F.3d 47, 57 (1st Cir.2003) (failure to object to an alleged inconsistency while the jury is still in the box forfeits a party's objection, subject only to the possibility of relief for plain error); *Mason v. Ford Motor Co., Inc.,* 307 F.3d 1271, 1274 (11th Cir.2002) (if the jury rendered inconsistent general verdicts, failure to object timely waives that inconsistency as a basis for seeking retrial); *Fleet National Bank v. Anchor Media Television, Inc., KOVR,* 831 F.Supp. 16 (D.R.I.1993).

RULE 50

JUDGMENT AS A MATTER OF LAW IN A JURY TRIAL; RELATED MOTION FOR A NEW TRIAL; CONDITIONAL RULING

(a) Judgment as a Matter of Law.

(1) *In General.* If a party has been fully heard on an issue during a jury trial and the court finds that a reasonable jury would not have a legally sufficient evidentiary basis to find for the party on that issue, the court may:

(A) resolve the issue against the party; and

(B) grant a motion for judgment as a matter of law against the party on a claim or defense that, under the controlling law, can be maintained or defeated only with a favorable finding on that issue.

(2) *Motion.* A motion for judgment as a matter of law may be made at any time before the case is submitted to the jury. The motion must specify the judgment sought and the law and facts that entitle the movant to the judgment.

(b) Renewing the Motion After Trial; Alternative Motion for a New Trial.

If the court does not grant a motion for judgment as a matter of law made under Rule 50(a), the court is considered to have submitted the action to the jury subject to the court's later deciding the legal questions raised by the motion. No later than 10 days after the entry of judgment—or if the motion addresses a jury issue not decided by a verdict, no later than 10 days after the jury was discharged—the movant may file a renewed motion for judgment as a matter of law and may include an alternative or joint request for a new trial under Rule 59. In ruling on the renewed motion, the court may:

(1) allow judgment on the verdict, if the jury returned a verdict;

(2) order a new trial; or

(3) direct the entry of judgment as a matter of law.

(c) Granting the Renewed Motion; Conditional Ruling on a Motion for a New Trial.

(1) *In General.* If the court grants a renewed motion for judgment as a matter of law, it must also conditionally rule on any motion for a new trial by determining whether a new trial should be granted if the judgment is later vacated or reversed. The court must state the grounds for conditionally granting or denying the motion for a new trial.

(2) *Effect of a Conditional Ruling.* Conditionally granting the motion for a new trial does not affect the judgment's finality; if the judgment is reversed, the new trial must proceed unless the appellate court orders otherwise. If the motion for a new trial is conditionally denied, the appellee may assert error in that denial; if the judgment is reversed, the case must proceed as the appellate court orders.

(d) Time for a Losing Party's New–Trial Motion. Any motion for a new trial under Rule 59 by a party against whom judgment as a matter of law is rendered must be filed no later than 10 days after the entry of the judgment.

(e) Denying the Motion for Judgment as a Matter of Law; Reversal on Appeal. If the court denies the motion for judgment as a matter of law, the prevailing party may, as appellee, assert grounds entitling it to a new trial should the appellate court conclude that the trial court erred in denying the motion. If the appellate court reverses the judgment, it may order a new trial, direct the trial court to determine whether a new trial should be granted, or direct the entry of judgment.

[Amended January 21, 1963, effective July 1, 1963; March 2, 1987, effective August 1, 1987; April 30, 1991, effective December 1, 1991; April 22, 1993, effective December 1, 1993; April 27, 1995, effective December 1, 1995; April 12, 2006, effective December 1, 2006; April 30, 2007, effective December 1, 2007.]

─────────────── **2007 AMENDMENTS ROADMAP** ───────────────

STYLE PROJECT CHANGES: The amendments to Rule 50(b) were intended in part to clarify that, if the court denies a motion for judgment as a matter of law, either actively or otherwise, and the case is submitted to the jury, the court is considered to have reserved the right to determine the legal questions raised by the motion after the jury verdict. Former Rule 50(c)(2) was renumbered Rule 50(d) and former Rule 50(d) was renumbered Rule 50(e). Newly numbered Rule 50(e) was amended to provide that an appellate court can direct the entry of judgment if it reverses judgment, consistent with *Weisgram v. Marley Co.*, 528 U.S. 440, 120 S.Ct. 1011, 145 L.Ed.2d 958 (2000). Rule 50(b) was shortened and simplified. Rule 50(c) was further subsectioned, and orienting labels were added. The language was generally reorganized and simplified, active voice replaced passive voice, and "must" replaced "shall".

NON-STYLE CHANGES: None.

NOTE: The Federal Rules "Style Project" is explained in Part III-A.

AUTHORS' COMMENTARY ON RULE 50

PURPOSE AND SCOPE

Rule 50 contains the provisions governing motions for judgment as a matter of law during and following jury trials. These remedies are generally available when the evidence in the record could not reasonably support a particular verdict.

NOTE: A motion for judgment after trial must be filed within 10 days of entry of the verdict.

2006 AMENDMENTS: The 2006 Amendments refine the procedures under Rule 50 for asserting a motion for new trial. They eliminate the language requiring a party to renew a motion for judgment as a matter of law at the close of evidence as a prerequisite to filing a post trial motion under Rule 50(b). The 2006 Amendments also add a provision allowing a party 10 days from the discharge of the jury to file a post-trial motion under Rule 50(b) if the party's prior motion for judgment as a matter of law addressed an issue that was not decided by the verdict.

RULE 50(a). JUDGMENT AS A MATTER OF LAW

CORE CONCEPT

Rule 50(a) allows the court to take a case away from the jury by entering a judgment if there is not sufficient evidence to raise a genuine factual controversy.[1]

APPLICATIONS

Content of Motion

A motion for judgment as a matter of law must state the judgment sought (*i.e.,* the counts or issues upon which judgment is

---

1. *Wimmer v. Suffolk County Police Dept.*, 176 F.3d 125, 134 (2d Cir.1999); *CVI/* *Beta Ventures, Inc. v. Tura LP*, 112 F.3d 1146, 1152 (Fed.Cir.1997).

sought) and the law and facts supporting the judgment.[2]

Form and Timing of Motion

A motion for judgment as a matter of law may be made orally or in writing, but must be made on the record.[3] The motion may be made after the opposing party has been fully heard on an issue, at any time before submission of the case to the jury.[4] Such motions are typically made at the close of the plaintiff's case (by the defendant), at the close of the record, or both.

Subject of Motion

A motion for judgment as a matter of law may seek judgment on entire claims or defenses or on specific issues that are not wholly dispositive of a claim or defense.[5]

Opportunity to Cure

A major purpose of the motion is to call a deficiency in the evidence to the attention of the court so the opposing counsel may cure the defect.[6] The court then has a duty to apprise the non-moving party of the materiality of the dispositive fact and provide that party with an opportunity to present any available evidence.[7]

Sufficiency of Evidence

The sufficiency of the evidence is an issue of law to be determined by the judge.[8] The primary consideration is whether the evidence in the record could properly support a particular verdict.[9] The court must view all evidence in the light most favorable to the party opposing the motion; [10] it may not make credibility determina-

---

2. *Smith v. Northwest Fin. Acceptance, Inc.*, 129 F.3d 1408, 1415 (10th Cir.1997); *Zeigler v. Fisher–Price, Inc.*, 302 F.Supp.2d 999, 1007 (N.D.Iowa 2004) (although the grounds do not have to be stated with technical precision, the movant must give fair notice to the court of the grounds for the motion); Frazier v. Boyle, 206 F.R.D. 480, 490–91 (E.D.Wis.2002).

3. *Ross v. Rhodes Furniture, Inc.*, 146 F.3d 1286, 1289 (11th Cir.1998).

4. *Bristol v. Board of County Com'rs of County of Clear Creek*, 281 F.3d 1148, 1163 (10th Cir.2002), *vac'd in part on reh'g en banc*, 312 F.3d 1213 (10th Cir.2002); *Wolfgang v. Mid–America Motorsports, Inc.*, 111 F.3d 1515, 1521 (10th Cir.1997).

5. *Ross v. Rhodes Furniture, Inc.*, 146 F.3d 1286, 1289–90 (11th Cir.1998) (grounds for motion must be clear from the record so that the appeals court can ensure that setting aside the verdict would not be a surprise to the non-movant); *Chesapeake Paper Products Co. v. Stone & Webster Engineering Corp.*, 51 F.3d 1229, 1236 (4th Cir.1995).

6. *Laborers' Pension Fund v. A & C Environmental, Inc.*, 301 F.3d 768, 775 (7th Cir.2002).

7. *Waters v. Young*, 100 F.3d 1437, 1441 (9th Cir.1996) (adding that the court's duty is especially important when confronted with pro se litigants).

8. *Lange v. Penn Mut. Life Ins. Co.*, 843 F.2d 1175, 1181 (9th Cir.1988).

9. *Anderson v. Liberty Lobby, Inc.*, 477 U.S. 242, 106 S.Ct. 2505, 91 L.Ed.2d 202 (1986); *Acevedo-Garcia v. Monroig*, 351 F.3d 547, 565 (1st Cir.2003); *Murray v. Chicago Transit Authority*, 252 F.3d 880 (7th Cir.2001) (the test for a Rule 50 motion is whether there is no legally sufficient evidentiary basis for a reasonable jury to find for the non-moving party on the issues that are the subject of the motion).

10. *Galloway v. United States*, 319 U.S. 372, 63 S.Ct. 1077, 87 L.Ed. 1458 (1943); *Filipovich v. K & R Exp. Systems, Inc.*, 391 F.3d 859, 863 (7th Cir.2004); *Cobb v. Pozzi*, 363 F.3d 89, 101 (2nd Cir.2004) (essentially, the standard for a Rule 50 motion is the same as the standard for a summary judgment motion under Rule 56).

tions or weigh the evidence.[11] However, the court may disregard testimony that is opposed to undisputed physical facts.[12] Moreover, a "mere scintilla" of evidence is not sufficient.[13]

Inferences

The court must draw all reasonable inferences from the evidence that favor the party opposing the motion.[14] Thus, even if all the facts are undisputed, a motion for judgment as a matter of law will still be denied if the evidence is susceptible of conflicting inferences.[15] However, inferences created by statute or doctrine, such as *res ipsa loquitur,* may raise different issues requiring specific research.

Jury Trials Only

Rule 50 applies only to binding jury cases.[16] The appropriate motion in non-jury trials and trials with an advisory jury is a motion for judgment on partial findings under Rule 52(c).[17]

Motions Held Under Consideration

The court is under no obligation to grant a motion for judgment as a matter of law even if the record supports the motion. Courts often allow the jury to reach a verdict in order to minimize the likelihood of needing a new trial, if the court enters a judgment contrary to the verdict that is overturned on appeal, then enter judgment contrary to the verdict if the verdict is unsupported by sufficient evidence.[18]

---

11. *Jackson v. State of Alabama State Tenure Com'n,* 405 F.3d 1276, 1281 (11th Cir.2005); *This Is Me, Inc. v. Taylor,* 157 F.3d 139, 142 (2d Cir.1998); *Andrade v. Jamestown Housing Authority,* 82 F.3d 1179, 1186 (1st Cir.1996); *Ziemba v. Armstrong,* 433 F.Supp.2d 248 (D.Conn.2006).

12. *See, e.g., O'Connor v. Pennsylvania R.R. Co.,* 308 F.2d 911 (2d Cir.1962) (testimony about snowfall disregarded when contrary to the records of the Weather Bureau); *Grant v. Cia Anonima Venezolana de Navegacion,* 228 F.Supp. 232 (E.D.La.1964), *affirmed,* 343 F.2d 757 (5th Cir.1965) (testimony that a winch was operated electrically disregarded when a physical inspection showed that the winch was operated hydraulically).

13. *A.B. Small Co. v. Lamborn & Co.,* 267 U.S. 248, 254, 45 S.Ct. 300, 303, 69 L.Ed. 597 (1925); *Filipovich v. K & R Exp. Systems, Inc.,* 391 F.3d 859, 863 (7th Cir. 2004); *DP Solutions, Inc. v. Rollins, Inc.,* 353 F.3d 421, 427 (5th Cir.2003).

14. *Laxton v. Gap Inc.,* 333 F.3d 572, 577 (5th Cir.2003). *Green v. Administrators of Tulane Educational Fund,* 284 F.3d 642,

652 (5th Cir.2002); *Ziemba v. Armstrong,* 433 F.Supp.2d 248 (D.Conn.2006); *Zirlin v. Village of Scarsdale,* 365 F.Supp.2d 477, 483 (S.D.N.Y.2005).

15. *Daniels v. Twin Oaks Nursing Home,* 692 F.2d 1321, 1325 (11th Cir.1982); *but see Everett v. Verizon Wireless, Inc.,* 361 F.Supp.2d 698 (N.D.Ohio 2005) (where there are two possible inferences and no factual basis to pick one over the other, the court may enter judgment against the party with the burden of proof).

16. *Federal Ins. Co. v. HPSC, Inc.,* 480 F.3d 26, 32 (1st Cir. 2007); *Nieto v. Kapoor,* 268 F.3d 1208, 1217 (10th Cir.2001).

17. *Federal Ins. Co. v. HPSC, Inc.,* 480 F.3d 26, 32 (1st Cir. 2007); *Northeast Drilling, Inc. v. Inner Space Services, Inc.,* 243 F.3d 25, 37 (1st Cir.2001).

18. *Colonial Lincoln–Mercury, Inc. v. Musgrave,* 749 F.2d 1092, 1098 (4th Cir. 1984); *United States v. Singleton,* 702 F.2d 1159, 1172 (D.C.Cir.1983).

Motion Granted

If the court grants a motion for judgment as a matter of law, it will enter the appropriate verdict without involvement of the jury.

Motion Denied

If the motion for judgment as a matter of law is denied, the defendant may put on evidence. However, if the plaintiff's case lacked a certain element and that element is brought out during the defendant's case, the deficiency will be cured.[19]

Who May Make Motion

Both defendants and plaintiffs may make motions for judgment as a matter of law. Thus, if the plaintiff enters evidence sufficient to support each element of the plaintiff's case and that evidence is not contradicted during the defendant's case, the plaintiff will be entitled to a judgment as a matter of law.[20] In addition, the judge may grant a judgment as a matter of law *sua sponte*.[21]

Prerequisite to Appeal

A motion for judgment as a matter of law at the close of the record is a prerequisite to challenging the sufficiency of the evidence on appeal.[22] Note, however, that appellate issues other than those relating to the sufficiency of the evidence are not affected.[23] An exception to this principle occurs if the verdict constitutes plain error on the face of the record, and a miscarriage of justice would result if the verdict remained in effect.[24]

Standard of Review

On appeal, the appellate court applies the same standard as the district court, without deference to the ruling of the trial judge.[25]

RULE 50(b). RENEWING THE MOTION AFTER TRIAL; ALTERNATIVE MOTION FOR A NEW TRIAL

CORE CONCEPT

The court can enter a judgment that is inconsistent with the jury's verdict if it determines that the verdict was not supported by the evidence. However, a prerequisite to a motion for judgment after trial is

19. *Trustees of University of Pa. v. Lexington Ins. Co.,* 815 F.2d 890, 903 (3d Cir. 1987); *Peterson v. Hager,* 724 F.2d 851, 854 (10th Cir.1984).

20. *Hurd v. American Hoist & Derrick Co.,* 734 F.2d 495, 499 (10th Cir.1984); *Walter E. Heller & Co. v. Video Innovations, Inc.,* 730 F.2d 50, 54 (2d Cir.1984).

21. *American & Foreign Ins. Co. v. Bolt,* 106 F.3d 155, 160 (6th Cir.1997).

22. *Unitherm Food Systems, Inc. v. Swift–Eckrich, Inc.,* 546 U.S. 394, 126 S.Ct. 980, 987, 163 L.Ed.2d 974 (2006); *Federal Ins. Co. v. HPSC, Inc.,* 480 F.3d 26, 32 (1st Cir. 2007).

23. *Ruyle v. Continental Oil Co.,* 44 F.3d 837 (10th Cir.1994).

24. *Stephenson v. Doe,* 332 F.3d 68, 75–76 (2nd Cir.2003).

25. *Barnes v. City of Cincinnati,* 401 F.3d 729, 736 (6th Cir.2005) (district court's denial of a motion for judgment as a matter of law or a renewed motion for judgment as a matter of law is reviewed *de novo*); *Cobb v. Pozzi,* 363 F.3d 89, 101 (2nd Cir.2004).

a motion for a judgment as a matter of law at the close of the record.[26]

APPLICATIONS

Content of Motion

A motion for judgment after trial must state the grounds for relief,[27] and may include only those grounds raised in the motion for judgment as a matter of law.[28]

Timing

The motion must be filed not later than 10 days after the *entry* of the judgment[29] (not the notice of entry of the judgment). If the jury does not return a verdict, such as with a mistrial, or if the subject of the motion for judgment as a matter of law was an issue not decided by the verdict, the parties have 10 days from the discharge of the jury.[30] This strict time limit cannot be enlarged.[31]

Same Standard as Rule 50(a)

A renewed motion for judgment as a matter of law under Rule 50(b) is evaluated under the same standard as the initial motion under Rule 50(a) filed at the close of evidence; the motion will be denied if the evidence in the record could properly support the verdict, viewing the evidence, and all inferences, in the light most favorable to the non-moving party.[32] This standard is discussed in more detail in the commentary to Rule 50(a) above.

26. *Graves v. City of Coeur D'Alene*, 339 F.3d 828 (9th Cir.2003) (failure to raise lack of a Rule 50(a) motion was a waiver of the defect); *Nichols v. Ashland Hosp. Corp.*, 251 F.3d 496, 502, n.1 (4th Cir.2001).

27. *Andreas v. Volkswagen of America, Inc.*, 336 F.3d 789 (8th Cir.2003) (Rule 50(b) motion must put the court and the parties on notice of the issues being raised).

28. *Ross v. Rhodes Furniture, Inc.*, 146 F.3d 1286, 1289–90 (11th Cir.1998) (grounds for motion must be clear from the record so that the appeals court can ensure that setting aside the verdict would not be a surprise to the non-movant); *Staley v. Bridgestone/Firestone, Inc.*, 106 F.3d 1504, 1508 (10th Cir.1997).

29. *Green v. Administrators of Tulane Educational Fund*, 284 F.3d 642, 652 (5th Cir.2002) (Rule 50(b) motion timely when delivered to the clerk's office within 10 days even though the clerks did not file the motion until after 10 days); *Fruit of the Loom, Inc. v. American Marketing Enterprises, Inc.*, 192 F.3d 73, 75–76 (2d Cir. 1999).

30. Rule 50(b) is silent about the deadline for filing a post-trial motion if a judgment is not entered. However, the best in-terpretation is that the 10 day limit also applies when judgment is not entered, such as with a mistrial. *See Wiehoff v. GTE Directories Corp.*, 851 F.Supp. 1322 (D. Minn. 1993), *affirmed in part, reversed in part*, 61 F.3d 588 (8th Cir.1995) (stating without discussion that a rule 50(b) motion may be filed 10 days after the jury has been discharged following a mistrial). The 2006 Amendments to Rule 50(b) clarify that the parties have 10 days following the discharge of the jury to make a Rule 50(b) post-trial motion if the motion for judgment as a matter of law addressed an issue that was not decided by the verdict.

31. *Goodman v. Bowdoin College*, 380 F.3d 33, 47 (1st Cir.2004); *Andreas v. Volkswagen of America, Inc.*, 336 F.3d 789 (8th Cir.2003); *Hodge ex rel. Skiff v. Hodge*, 269 F.3d 155, 157 (2d Cir.2001).

32. *See Alphamed Pharmaceuticals Corp. v. Arriva Pharmaceuticals, Inc.*, 432 F.Supp.2d 1319, 1333 (S.D.Fla.2006); *Lopez v. Aramark Uniform & Career Apparel, Inc.*, 426 F.Supp.2d 914, 937 (N.D.Iowa 2006).

Rule 59 Motion for New Trial

A Rule 50(b) motion is often combined with a motion for new trial under Rule 59(a).[33]

Motion During Trial a Prerequisite

A party cannot make a motion for judgment after trial unless it has filed a motion for judgment as a matter of law.[34] Moreover, the post trial motion is limited to the issues raised in the pre-verdict motion.[35] If there was no motion for judgment as a matter of law but the evidence does not support the verdict, the court can order a new trial.[36]

Motion for a New Trial

A party may join a motion for a new trial with a motion for judgment after trial, or request a new trial in the alternative.[37] The standard is the same as with a motion for new trial under Rule 59; the motion will be granted if the verdict is contrary to the clear weight of the evidence. A new trial is favored over a judgment contrary to the verdict when it appears that the party could present sufficient evidence to support the verdict at a future date.

Rulings

If the jury returned a verdict, the court may allow the verdict to stand, order a new trial, or direct entry of judgment as a matter of law. If no verdict was returned, the court may order a new trial or direct the entry of judgment as a matter of law. When a motion for new trial is joined with a motion for judgment after trial, Rule 50 specifically requires that the court rule on both motions.

Appeals

Rulings on motions for judgment after trial are final, appealable orders. In contrast, an order granting a new trial may not be a final, appealable order.[38] On appeal, legal determinations are reviewed de novo.[39] In diversity cases, questions of evidence sufficiency are reviewed under the standard used by the forum state. When there is a federal question, evidence sufficiency is reviewed in a light most favorable to the non-moving party and motions are granted

33. *See, e.g., Frazier v. Boyle*, 206 F.R.D. 480 (E.D.Wis.2002); *Pickett v. Detella*, 163 F.Supp.2d 999 (N.D.Ill.2001).

34. *Rinehimer v. Cemcolift, Inc.*, 292 F.3d 375 (3d Cir.2002); *but see Minnesota Supply Co. v. Raymond Corp.*, 472 F.3d 524, 535–36 (8th Cir. 2006) (failure to renew the motion not a waiver when the court advised the party that there was no need to renew the motion).

35. *Freund v. Nycomed Amersham*, 347 F.3d 752, 761 (9th Cir.2003). *American & Foreign Ins. Co. v. Bolt*, 106 F.3d 155, 160 (6th Cir.1997) (holding a judge may not *sua*

sponte raise a new issue in a Rule 50(b) motion).

36. *Johnson v. New York, N.H. & H.R. Co.*, 344 U.S. 48, 54, 73 S.Ct. 125, 128, 97 L.Ed. 77 (1952).

37. *Willis v. State Farm Fire and Cas. Co.*, 219 F.3d 715 (8th Cir.2000) (moved for judgment as a matter of law and, in the alternative, for a new trial).

38. *Binder v. Long Island Lighting Co.*, 57 F.3d 193 (2d Cir.1995).

39. *Diaz-Fonseca v. Puerto Rico*, 451 F.3d 13, 26 (1st Cir.2006); *Graves v. City of Coeur D'Alene*, 339 F.3d 828 (9th Cir.2003).

only when reasonable minds could not come to a conclusion other than the one favoring the movant.[40]

RULE 50(c). GRANTING THE RENEWED MOTION; CONDITIONAL RULINGS ON A MOTION FOR A NEW TRIAL

CORE CONCEPT

If the court grants a motion for judgment as a matter of law after trial and a motion for a new trial was also filed, the court will make a conditional ruling on the motion for a new trial.[41]

APPLICATIONS

Rulings Conditional on Reversal

The trial court's rulings on the motion for a new trial are applicable if the appeals court reverses the granting of the judgment after trial.[42] In that case, the appeals court will generally enter the original verdict or order a new trial, depending on the trial court's conditional ruling. However, the appeals court also may review the trial court's conditional ruling on the motion for a new trial.

Granting of Both Motions

If the trial court grants both a motion for judgment notwithstanding the verdict and a motion for a new trial, the ruling on the motion for a new trial is automatically deemed conditional.

Failure to Issue a Conditional Ruling

If a court fails to issue a conditional ruling, the appellate court has the authority to either remand to the trial court to decide the new trial motion or decide the new trial motion itself.[43]

RULE 50(d). TIME FOR A LOSING PARTY'S NEW-TRIAL MOTION

CORE CONCEPT

If the court grants a motion for judgment after trial, the party against whom judgment was entered may file a motion for a new trial no later than 10 days after the entry of judgment, pursuant to Rule 59.

40. *K & T Enterprises, Inc. v. Zurich Ins. Co.*, 97 F.3d 171, 175–176 (6th Cir. 1996).

41. *Christopher v. Florida*, 449 F.3d 1360, 1365 (11th Cir.2006); *Rhone Poulenc Rorer Pharmaceuticals, Inc. v. Newman Glass Works*, 112 F.3d 695, 698 (3d Cir. 1997).

42. *Fioto v. Manhattan Woods Golf Enterprises, LLC.*, 304 F.Supp.2d 541 (S.D.N.Y.2004).

43. *Acosta v. San Francisco*, 83 F.3d 1143, 1149 (9th Cir.1996); *but see Christopher v. Florida*, 449 F.3d 1360, 1365, n.3 (11th Cir.2006) (where the appellant fails to pursue a new trial on appeal, the court will consider the issue abandoned).

APPLICATIONS

2007 Amendments

The 2007 amendments renumbered former Rule 50(c)(2) as Rule 50(d). Care should be exercised in researching and citing pre–2008 cases referring to Rule 50(c)(2) or Rule 50(d).

RULE 50(e).   DENYING THE MOTION FOR JUDGMENT AS A MATTER OF LAW; REVERSAL ON APPEAL

CORE CONCEPT

If the losing party appeals the denial of a motion for judgment after trial, the prevailing party may on appeal assert grounds for a new trial in the event that the court reverses the denial of the motion for judgment after trial. If the appellate court does reverse, it may order the entry of judgment, order a new trial, or remand to the trial court to determine whether a new trial is warranted.

APPLICATIONS

2007 Amendments

The 2007 amendments renumbered former Rule 50(d) as Rule 50(e). Care should be exercised in researching and citing pre–2008 cases referring to Rule 50(d) or Rule 50(e).

ADDITIONAL RESEARCH REFERENCES

Wright & Miller, *Federal Practice and Procedure* §§ 2521–2540.

C.J.S. Federal Civil Procedure §§ 958–977 et seq., 1034, 1089, 1093, 1219–1226 et seq.

West's Key No. Digests, Federal Civil Procedure ⊙⇒2111–2156, 2601–2610.

RULE 51

INSTRUCTIONS TO THE JURY; OBJECTIONS; PRESERVING A CLAIM OF ERROR

(a) Requests.

(1) *Before or at the Close of the Evidence.* At the close of the evidence or at any earlier reasonable time that the court orders, a party may file and furnish to every other party written requests for the jury instructions it wants the court to give.

(2) *After the Close of the Evidence.* After the close of the evidence, a party may:

(A) file requests for instructions on issues that could not reasonably have been anticipated by an earlier time that the court set for requests; and

(B) with the court's permission, file untimely requests for instructions on any issue.

(b) Instructions. The court:

(1) must inform the parties of its proposed instructions and proposed action on the requests before instructing the jury and before final jury arguments;

(2) must give the parties an opportunity to object on the record and out of the jury's hearing before the instructions and arguments are delivered; and

(3) may instruct the jury at any time before the jury is discharged.

(c) Objections.

(1) *How to Make.* A party who objects to an instruction or the failure to give an instruction must do so on the record, stating distinctly the matter objected to and the grounds for the objection.

(2) *When to Make.* An objection is timely if:

(A) a party objects at the opportunity provided under Rule 51(b)(2); or

(B) a party was not informed of an instruction or action on a request before that opportunity to object, and the party objects promptly after learning that the instruction or request will be, or has been, given or refused.

(d) Assigning Error; Plain Error.

(1) *Assigning Error.* A party may assign as error:

(A) an error in an instruction actually given, if that party properly objected; or

(B) a failure to give an instruction, if that party properly requested it and—unless the court rejected the request in a definitive ruling on the record—also properly objected.

(2) *Plain Error.* A court may consider a plain error in the instructions that has not been preserved as required by Rule 51(d)(1) if the error affects substantial rights.

[Amended effective August 1, 1987; March 27, 2003, effective December 1, 2003; April 30, 2007, effective December 1, 2007.]

──────────── **2007 AMENDMENTS ROADMAP** ────────────

STYLE PROJECT CHANGES: Orienting headings were added, and the language was simplified and clarified.

NON-STYLE CHANGES: None.

NOTE: The Federal Rules "Style Project" is explained in Part III-A.

AUTHORS' COMMENTARY ON RULE 51

──────────── **PURPOSE AND SCOPE** ────────────

Before the jury retires to deliberate, the judge must instruct the jury as to the law that they are to apply. The parties have an opportunity to request that certain instructions be given, and to object to the instructions given and to the instructions not given.

NOTE: Rule 51 was substantially revised in 2003. The amendments reorganized Rule 51 into 4 subparts, and codified much of the case law that had evolved under Rule 51.

RULE 51(a). REQUESTS

CORE CONCEPT

The parties may submit proposed jury instructions to the court. Proposed instructions are submitted at the close of the evidence, or at such earlier time as directed by the court.

APPLICATIONS

Timing of Requests

Requests for jury instructions are normally made at the close of the evidence, or earlier if the court so directs.[1] If the court has set a time before the close of evidence for submission of requests for instructions, a party may submit additional requests for instructions after the close of evidence on issues that could not have been anticipated when the requests were submitted.[2] Note, however, that local rules may set the time for making requests for jury instructions. The court, in its discretion, may consider untimely requests.[3]

Form and Content of Requests

Requests normally should be reasonably neutral statements of the law governing the case, and not overly argumentative. Requests are usually written, although they can be oral.

Service

Requests for instruction must be furnished to every other party.[4]

RULE 51(b). INSTRUCTIONS

CORE CONCEPT

The court must inform the parties of its proposed instructions before instructing the jury and before the parties' final arguments to the jury, and must give the parties an opportunity to object on the record and out of the jury's hearing.

APPLICATIONS

Rulings on Requests

The court is required to inform the parties of its rulings on the jury instruction requests before the closing arguments, so that the counsel may adjust their closings accordingly. Failure to do so, however, will not be grounds for a new trial unless it is prejudicial.[5]

---

1. *Potthast v. Metro–North Railroad Co.*, 400 F.3d 143, 153 (2nd Cir.2005).

2. *Potthast v. Metro–North Railroad Co.*, 400 F.3d 143, 153 (2nd Cir.2005); Rule 51(a)(2)(A).

3. Rule 51(a)(2)(B).

4. Rule 51(a)(1).

5. *Delano v. Kitch*, 542 F.2d 550 (10th Cir.1976), *opinion clarified*, 554 F.2d 1004 (10th Cir.1977).

Form and Procedure for Instructions

Instructions are given to the jury in open court at any time after trial begins and before the jury is discharged.[6] The judge may repeat portions of the charge or give a supplemental charge at the jury's request, but must afford the parties notice and an opportunity to be present for such additional instruction. The judge may submit a written charge to the jury, although it is not commonly done.

Content of Instructions

The court should give an instruction on every material issue in the case. The instruction should clearly and understandably convey the status of the applicable law. There is no particular wording or order mandated, and the judge need not use the language requested by the parties. Narrowly-tailored instructions are favored over broad statements of the law.

Deadlocked Jury

In the civil context, the judge may instruct a jury claiming to be deadlocked to make further attempts to reach a verdict. The judge may not, however, coerce reluctant jurors to join the majority.

Comments on Evidence

The court, in its discretion, may comment on the evidence and even focus the jury's attention on certain portions of the evidence. If the judge does so, the judge must make it clear to the jury that they, not the judge, are the ultimate fact finders.

Opportunity to Object

The court must give the parties an opportunity to raise objections to the instructions on the record and out of the hearing of the jury before the instructions and closing arguments are delivered.[7] If the court fails to give an opportunity to raise the objections, parties with objections should request such an opportunity. However, if instructions are reread or the jury is given additional instructions, an objection may be raised at that time.[8]

RULE 51(c). OBJECTIONS

CORE CONCEPT

Objections to the instructions must be made on the record[9] with a statement of the grounds when the court provides and opportunity for such objections.[10]

---

6. Rule 51(b)(3).

7. *See Niemiec v. Union Pacific Railroad Co.,* 449 F.3d 854, 857 (8th Cir.2006); *Club Car, Inc. v. Club Car (Quebec) Import, Inc.,* 362 F.3d 775, 782 (11th Cir.2004).

8. *Barrett v. Orange County Human Rights Commission,* 194 F.3d 341, 349 (2d Cir.1999).

9. *Colon-Millin v. Sears Roebuck De Puerto Rico, Inc.,* 455 F.3d 30 (1st Cir.2006)

(judge's statement that the parties could rely on objections asserted earlier in chambers did not relieve them of the obligation to state the objections on the record); *Positive Black Talk Inc. v. Cash Money Records, Inc.,* 394 F.3d 357, 368 (5th Cir.2004) (off the record objections, no matter how clear and detailed, cannot satisfy Rule 51).

10. *Sherman v. Kasotakis,* 314 F.Supp.2d 843 (N.D.Iowa 2004).

APPLICATIONS

Content of Objection

The objection must be stated with sufficient clarity and specificity that the judge can understand the nature of the objection and remedy the problem if the judge agrees.[11] Any appeal must be based upon issues so raised in an objection.[12]

Time of Objections

A party must object to the content of the instructions at the opportunity provided by the court before the instructions and closing arguments are delivered[13], even if the party has previously raised and attempted to preserve the same objection.[14] If a party was not informed of an instruction or action on a request for an instruction prior to the opportunity to object provided by the court, the party may object promptly upon learning that the instruction was or would be given or refused.[15]

Formal Objection on the Record

Objections to jury instructions must be on the record; objections made off the record in chambers are not effective.[16] It is not sufficient to have proposed an instruction that the court does not give.[17]

11. *Colon-Millin v. Sears Roebuck De Puerto Rico, Inc.*, 455 F.3d 30 (1st Cir.2006) (references to the instruction numbers was not specific enough); *Bitler v. A.O. Smith Corp.*, 391 F.3d 1114, 1127–28 (10th Cir. 2004) (a general objection is not sufficient to reserve issues for appeal).

12. *Royal Maccabees Life Ins. Co. v. Choren*, 393 F.3d 1175, 1179 (10th Cir. 2005); *Schobert v. Illinois Dept. of Transp.*, 304 F.3d 725, 729 (7th Cir.2002); *FHS Properties Limited Partnership v. BC Associates*, 175 F.3d 81, 87 (1st Cir.1999).

13. Rule 51(c)(2)(A). *See also Niemiec v. Union Pacific Railroad Co.*, 449 F.3d 854, 857 (8th Cir.2006); *Flynn v. AK Peters, Ltd.*, 377 F.3d 13, 25 (1st Cir.2004) (if the court does not provide an opportunity to object before the instructions are given, the party must still place an objection on the record as soon as practicable); *Moba, B.V. v. Diamond Automation, Inc.*, 325 F.3d 1306, 1314 (Fed.Cir.2003); *Greene v. Safeway Stores, Inc.*, 210 F.3d 1237 (10th Cir.2000).

14. *Torres–Rivera v. O'Neill–Cancel*, 406 F.3d 43, 49–50 (1st Cir.2005) (party

must object at the time of the instructions even if the party previously proposed the instruction that the court declined to give); *Gray v. Genlyte Group, Inc.*, 289 F.3d 128, 134 (1st Cir.2002) (it is not enough to refer back to previously raised objections); *Libbey–Owens–Ford Company v. Insurance Company of North America*, 9 F.3d 422 (6th Cir.1993)(objections were waived even though the trial court told the parties that previously raised objections were preserved); *but see Lighting & Power Services, Inc. v. Roberts*, 354 F.3d 817, 820 (8th Cir. 2004) (finding that plaintiff's counsel's fully explained in-chambers objections satisfied Rule 51); *Smith v. Borough of Wilkinsburg*, 147 F.3d 272, 276 (3d Cir.1998) (a definitive ruling rejecting a proposed instruction preserves the issue for appeal).

15. Rule 51(c)(2)(B).

16. *See Franklin Prescriptions, Inc. v. New York Times Co.*, 424 F.3d 336, 339 (3rd Cir.2005).

17. *Franklin Prescriptions, Inc. v. New York Times Co.*, 424 F.3d 336, 339 (3rd Cir.2005).

Failure to Object

If a party fails to object to an instruction before the jury begins deliberations and the court has not already made a definitive ruling on the record regarding the subject instruction,[18] the party loses the right to challenge the instruction on appeal.[19] Some courts will undertake appellate review in the absence of a timely objection if the party never had an opportunity to object,[20] but most courts strictly require a timely objection on the record.[21] Similarly, some courts will undertake appellate review in the absence of a timely objection if an objection would have been a pointless formality.[22] Thus, as a general matter, if a party does not make a timely objection, it is limited to objections of plain error under Rule 51(d).

RULE 51(d). ASSIGNING ERROR; PLAIN ERROR

CORE CONCEPT

A party may base an appeal on an instruction if the party made a proper objection pursuant to Rule 51(c) or upon plain error.

APPLICATIONS

Issues On Appeal

In general, a party may only raise on appeal issues regarding the instructions given that the party properly raised as objections pursuant to Rule 51(c).[23] A party may only raise on appeal an issue regarding an instruction not given if the party made a proper request for the instruction and either the court made a definitive

---

18. The 2003 amendment to Rule 51 provided that a party need not object to an instruction if the court has made a definitive ruling on the issue on the record. See also Colon–Millin v. Sears Roebuck De Puerto Rico, Inc., 455 F.3d 30 (1st Cir. 2006).

19. *Melford Olsen Honey, Inc. v. Adee,* 452 F.3d 956 (8th Cir.2006); *Baron v. Suffolk County Sheriff's Dept.,* 402 F.3d 225, 235 (1st Cir.2005); *Kanida v. Gulf Coast Medical Personnel LP,* 363 F.3d 568, 580 (5th Cir.2004).

20. *Schmitz v. Canadian Pacific Ry. Co.,* 454 F.3d 678 (7th Cir.2006) (judge changed the instructions without notifying the parties).

21. *See Colon-Millin v. Sears Roebuck De Puerto Rico, Inc.,* 455 F.3d 30 (1st Cir. 2006) (judge's statement that the parties could rely on objections asserted earlier in chambers did not relieve them of the obligation to state the objections on the record); *Monroe v. City of Phoenix, Ariz.,* 248 F.3d 851, 858 (9th Cir.2001).

22. *See Collegenet, Inc. v. Applyyourself, Inc.,* 418 F.3d 1225 (Fed.Cir.2005) (where the district court is aware of the party's concerns and further objection would be unavailing, a futile formal objection is not required); *Riverwood Intern. Corp. v. R.A. Jones & Co., Inc.,* 324 F.3d 1346, 1353 (Fed.Cir.2003) (no need to object when issue had already been briefed and objection would have been futile); *Monroe v. City of Phoenix, Ariz.,* 248 F.3d 851, 858 (9th Cir. 2001) (an objection may be a pointless formality when: (1) throughout the trial the party argued the disputed matter with the court; (2) it is clear from the record that the court knew the party's grounds for disagreement with the instruction; and (3) the party offered an alternative instruction).

23. *Fisher v. City of San Jose,* 475 F.3d 1049, 1072 (9th Cir. 2007); *Connelly v. Hyundai Motor Co.,* 351 F.3d 535, 544 (1st Cir.2003) (an objection on one ground does not preserve appellate review of a different ground).

ruling on the record rejecting the request[24] or the party made a proper objection regarding the omitted instruction.[25]

Plain Error

The appeals court generally will review only issues to which there was a timely objection, but may, under extreme circumstances when justice demands, reverse even if no objections were made when an instruction contains plain error.[26] Additionally, the appeals court may consider an issue not preserved by objection where there has been a supervening change in the law.[27]

Appellate Review

Whether a jury instruction is legally erroneous is a question of law.[28] On appeal, the court reads the instructions as a whole and considers them in light of the entire charge to the jury.[29] There is a presumption that the jury followed the instructions[30] and that an erroneous instruction was prejudicial.[31]

ADDITIONAL RESEARCH REFERENCES

Wright & Miller, *Federal Practice and Procedure* §§ 2551–2558. Devitt, Blackmar, Wolff & O'Malley, *Federal Jury Practice and Instructions.*

C.J.S. Federal Civil Procedure §§ 983–994 et seq.

West's Key No. Digests, Federal Civil Procedure ⚷2171–2185.

24. *Colon-Millin v. Sears Roebuck De Puerto Rico, Inc.,* 455 F.3d 30, 40, n.7 (1st Cir. 2006).

25. Rule 51(d)(1)(B). *See also Murphy Oil USA, Inc. v. Wood,* 438 F.3d 1008, 1014–15 (10th Cir.2006).

26. *Ammons-Lewis v. Metropolitan Water Reclamation Dist. of Greater Chicago,* 488 F.3d 739 (7th Cir. 2007); *Diaz-Fonseca v. Puerto Rico,* 451 F.3d 13, 36 (1st Cir. 2006) (listing the factors for plain error); *Higbee v. Sentry Ins. Co.,* 440 F.3d 408, 409 (7th Cir.2006) (courts should be guided by the principles of plain error in the criminal context).

27. *See Cadena v. Pacesetter Corp.,* 224 F.3d 1203, 1212 (10th Cir.2000); *Anixter v.*

Home–Stake Production Company, 77 F.3d 1215, 1230–31 (10th Cir.1996).

28. *Advanced Display Systems, Inc. v. Kent State University,* 212 F.3d 1272, 1282 (Fed.Cir.2000).

29. *Schmitz v. Canadian Pacific Ry. Co.,* 454 F.3d 678 (7th Cir.2006); *Advanced Display Systems, Inc. v. Kent State University,* 212 F.3d 1272, 1282 (Fed.Cir.2000).

30. Rule 51(d)(2). *See also Pittman v. Littlefield,* 438 F.2d 659, 662 (1st Cir.1971).

31. *United States v. River Rouge Improvement Co.,* 269 U.S. 411, 421, 46 S.Ct. 144, 148, 70 L.Ed. 339 (1926).

RULE 52

FINDINGS AND CONCLUSIONS BY THE COURT; JUDGMENT ON PARTIAL FINDINGS

(a) Findings and Conclusions.

(1) *In General.* In an action tried on the facts without a jury or with an advisory jury, the court must find the facts specially and state its conclusions of law separately. The findings and conclusions may be stated on the record after the close of the evidence or may appear in an opinion or a memorandum of decision filed by the court. Judgment must be entered under Rule 58.

(2) *For an Interlocutory Injunction.* In granting or refusing an interlocutory injunction, the court must similarly state the findings and conclusions that support its action.

(3) *For a Motion.* The court is not required to state findings or conclusions when ruling on a motion under Rule 12 or 56 or, unless these rules provide otherwise, on any other motion.

(4) *Effect of a Master's Findings.* A master's findings, to the extent adopted by the court, must be considered the court's findings.

(5) *Questioning the Evidentiary Support.* A party may later question the sufficiency of the evidence supporting the findings, whether or not the party requested findings, objected to them, moved to amend them, or moved for partial findings.

(6) *Setting Aside the Findings.* Findings of fact, whether based on oral or other evidence, must not be set aside unless clearly erroneous, and the reviewing court must give due regard to the trial court's opportunity to judge the witnesses' credibility.

(b) Amended or Additional Findings. On a party's motion filed no later than 10 days after the entry of judgment, the court may amend its findings—or make additional findings—and may amend the judgment ac-

cordingly. The motion may accompany a motion for a new trial under Rule 59.

(c) Judgment on Partial Findings. If a party has been fully heard on an issue during a nonjury trial and the court finds against the party on that issue, the court may enter judgment against the party on a claim or defense that, under the controlling law, can be maintained or defeated only with a favorable finding on that issue. The court may, however, decline to render any judgment until the close of the evidence. A judgment on partial findings must be supported by findings of fact and conclusions of law as required by Rule 52(a).

[Amended December 27, 1946, effective March 19, 1948; January 21, 1963, effective July 1, 1963; April 28, 1983, effective August 1, 1983; April 29, 1985, effective August 1, 1985; April 30, 1991, effective December 1, 1991; April 22, 1993, effective December 1, 1993; April 27, 1995, effective December 1, 1995; April 30, 2007, effective December 1, 2007.]

——————— **2007 AMENDMENTS ROADMAP** ———————

STYLE PROJECT CHANGES: Rule 52(a)(3) was amended to provide that the court does not need to make findings when deciding motions, except as otherwise provided by the Rules. Rule 52(a) previously only expressly excepted the situations provided by Rule 52(c). The reference in Rule 52(c) to entering "judgment as a matter of law" was amended simply to refer to "judgment" to clarify that it was not a reference to the provisions in Rule 50 concerning judgment as a matter of law in jury cases. Rule 52(a) was subdivided into 5 subparts, with Rule 52(a)(5) combining provisions from Rule 52(a) and Rule 52(b). Orienting labels were added, provisions were reorganized, active voice replaced passive voice, "must" replaced "shall", and the language was generally simplified and clarified.

NON-STYLE CHANGES: None.

NOTE: The Federal Rules "Style Project" is explained in Part III-A.

AUTHORS' COMMENTARY ON RULE 52

——————— PURPOSE AND SCOPE ———————

Following a non-jury trial, Rule 52 requires that the trial judge make findings of fact and conclusions of law. Rule 52 also sets forth the standard of review for such findings, and allows the judge to enter judgment during the trial if a party fails to carry its burden of proof.

RULE 52(a).   FINDINGS AND CONCLUSIONS

CORE CONCEPT

The trial judge shall explicitly state findings of fact and conclusions of law upon which the judge bases the verdict. Findings of fact will not be disturbed on appeal unless clearly erroneous. Conclusions of law are fully reviewable on appeal.

APPLICATIONS

2007 Amendments

The 2007 amendments moved the text from Rule 52(b) providing that a party may challenge the sufficiency of the evidentiary support for the court's findings after the findings are made regardless of whether the party previously took any positions on the findings into new Rule 52(a)(5). Care should be exercised in researching and citing pre–2008 cases referring to Rule 52(a) or Rule 52(b).

Findings Mandatory

The requirement that the judge make findings of fact and conclusions of law is mandatory, and cannot be waived.[1] The parties do not need to request findings.

Content of Findings

The findings must be sufficient to indicate the factual basis for the ultimate conclusion,[2] and permit meaningful appellate review,[3] but need not address all the evidence presented at trial.[4] The court need not make findings on uncontested or stipulated facts.[5]

Proposed Findings and Conclusions

The court may require the parties to submit proposed findings of fact and conclusions of law,[6] although the court's wholesale adoption of the prevailing party's submission is discouraged.[7]

---

1. See Golden Blount, Inc. v. Robert H. Peterson Co., 365 F.3d 1054, 1060–61 (Fed. Cir.2004); Francis v. Goodman, 81 F.3d 5, 8 (1st Cir.1996).

2. OCI Wyoming, L.P. v. PacifiCorp, 479 F.3d 1199, 1203 (10th Cir. 2007). American Canoe Ass'n v. Murphy Farms, Inc., 326 F.3d 505, 522 (4th Cir.2003).

3. Folger Coffee Co. v. Olivebank, 201 F.3d 632, 635 (5th Cir.2000); Duffie v. Deere & Co., 111 F.3d 70, 73 (8th Cir.1997) (without findings of fact, a trial court's conclusions are considered suspect).

4. See OCI Wyoming, L.P. v. PacifiCorp, 479 F.3d 1199, 1203 (10th Cir. 2007) (court does not need to set out its findings in "excruciating detail"). But see Kidd v. Illinois State Police, 167 F.3d 1084, 1101 (7th Cir.1999) (court should address conflicting testimony in its findings); League of United Latin American Citizens, Council No. 4434 v. Clements, 986 F.2d 728 (5th Cir.1993) (the court should address all substantial evidence contrary to its opinion).

5. Simeonoff v. Hiner, 249 F.3d 883, 891 (9th Cir.2001) ("We will affirm the district court if . . . there can be no genuine dispute about omitted findings").

6. American River Trans. Co. v. Kavo Kaliakra SS, 148 F.3d 446, 449 (5th Cir. 1998)(proposed findings adopted by the court are entitled to the same deference as findings crafted by the court).

7. McLennan v. American Eurocopter Corp., Inc., 245 F.3d 403, 409 (5th Cir.2001) ("the district court's decision to adopt one

Proceedings Covered by Rule 52

Rule 52 requires findings of fact and conclusions of law in non-jury trials, trials with advisory juries,[8] proceedings for preliminary or permanent injunctions,[9] and when the court grants a motion for dismissal after the plaintiff has presented evidence pursuant to Rule 52(c).[10] Rule 52 does not apply to motions for summary judgment under Rule 56,[11] motions under Rule 12(b)[12] (such as motions to dismiss), motions for attorney fees,[13] or any other motion other than a motion for judgment on partial findings under Rule 52(c).[14] Likewise, findings are not required for actions before administrative agencies that submit reports and recommendations to the district court,[15] or in proceedings where the district court reviews rulings made by the bankruptcy court.

Findings in Jury Trials

In jury trials, Rule 52 applies to any issues decided by the court instead of the jury. The court must also make findings of fact and conclusions of law in a case tried before an advisory jury.[16]

Injunctions

The court must make findings of fact and conclusions of law when ruling on a motion for a preliminary injunction.[17] If a

party's proposed findings and conclusions without change may cause us to approach such findings with greater caution, and as a consequence to apply the standard of review more rigorously"); *Counihan v. Allstate Ins. Co.*, 194 F.3d 357, 365 (2d Cir.1999).

8. *OCI Wyoming, L.P. v. PacifiCorp*, 479 F.3d 1199, 1203 (10th Cir. 2007).

9. *See Prairie Band of Potawatomi Indians v. Pierce*, 253 F.3d 1234, 1245 (10th Cir.2001); *Ciena Corp. v. Jarrard*, 203 F.3d 312 (4th Cir.2000); *but see Dresser–Rand Co. v. Virtual Automation Inc.*, 361 F.3d 831, 847 (5th Cir.2004) (findings not required at when addressing a request for a permanent injunction at the conclusion of a jury trial).

10. *Nieto v. Kapoor*, 268 F.3d 1208, 1217 (10th Cir.2001).

11. *Grossman v. Berman*, 241 F.3d 65, 68 (1st Cir.2001) (on a motion for summary judgment, a trial court has no obligation either to make specific findings of fact or to elaborate upon its view of the controlling legal principles); *but see Holly D. v. California Institute of Technology*, 339 F.3d 1158, 1180 (9th Cir.2003) (Rule 52(a) does not relieve a court of the burden of stating its reasons somewhere in the record when its underlying holdings would otherwise be ambiguous).

12. *Souza v. Pina*, 53 F.3d 423 (1st Cir. 1995)(noting that, although not required, findings would be helpful).

13. *W.G. v. Senatore*, 18 F.3d 60 (2d Cir.1994)(suggesting that findings regarding attorney fees would have been helpful, even though not required); *but see Kelly v. Golden*, 352 F.3d 344, 352 (8th Cir.2003) (when awarding attorney fees, the court must make findings).

14. *Microfinancial, Inc. v. Premier Holidays Intern., Inc.*, 385 F.3d 72, 76 (1st Cir. 2004) (Rule 52 does not apply to a motion to stay); *Enzo Biochem, Inc. v. Calgene, Inc.*, 188 F.3d 1362, 1379 (Fed.Cir.1999).

15. *But see Muller v. First Unum Life Ins. Co.*, 341 F.3d 119, 124 (2nd Cir.2003) (findings are required in ruling on a motion for judgment on the administrative record).

16. *Kolstad v. American Dental Ass'n*, 108 F.3d 1431, 1440 (D.C.Cir.1997). *See also*, Rule 39(c) and the author commentary discussing advisory juries.

17. *Bonnell v. Lorenzo*, 241 F.3d 800 (6th Cir.2001); *Hoechst Diafoil Co. v. Nan Ya Plastics Corp.*, 174 F.3d 411 (4th Cir. 1999) (findings help the parties understand the grounds for the court's ruling and permits the appellate court to conduct a meaningful review); *Blackhawk Industries Products Group Unlimited, LLc. v. U.S. General*

temporary restraining order is to be extended beyond the period allowed by Rule 65, it becomes a preliminary injunction and findings are required.[18] In ruling on a permanent injunction, the court must make findings if the ruling hinges on factual issues,[19] but the court will not be bound by findings made at the preliminary injunction stage.[20] Findings are not required in ruling on a motion to dissolve an injunction.[21]

Failure to Make Sufficient Findings

The appellate court may vacate and remand if the trial court's findings of fact are insufficient.[22] The appellate court may also direct the trial judge to order a new trial[23] or hearing to supplement the record.[24] The appellate court may also decide the appeal on the record, if possible.[25]

Form

The findings of fact may be a separate document or may be included in an opinion.[26] The court may also make its findings orally on the record.[27] If the court makes separate findings, then on appeal those findings control over any contradictory factual statements in an opinion.[28]

Objections

Rule 52 explicitly states that there is no need to request findings of fact and that no objection is necessary on the basis that the evidence does not support the findings.

Services Admin., 348 F.Supp.2d 649, 655 (E.D.Va.2004).

18. *Hoechst Diafoil Co. v. Nan Ya Plastics Corp.*, 174 F.3d 411 (4th Cir.1999).

19. *Alberti v. Cruise*, 383 F.2d 268 (4th Cir.1967); *but see Dresser–Rand Co. v. Virtual Automation Inc.*, 361 F.3d 831, 847 (5th Cir.2004) (findings not required at when addressing a request for a permanent injunction at the conclusion of a jury trial).

20. *TEC Engineering Corp. v. Budget Molders Supply, Inc.*, 82 F.3d 542, 545 (1st Cir.1996).

21. *Baltimore & O. R. Co. v. Chicago River & I.R. Co.*, 170 F.2d 654 (7th Cir. 1948).

22. *Hatahley v. United States*, 351 U.S. 173, 76 S.Ct. 745, 100 L.Ed. 1065 (1956); *Supermercados Econo, Inc. v. Integrand Assurance Co.*, 375 F.3d 1, 3–4 (1st Cir.2004) (matter remanded for further findings of fact and conclusions of law); *Federal Trade Com'n. v. Enforma Natural Products, Inc.*, 362 F.3d 1204, 1212 (9th Cir.2004).

23. *Andre v. Bendix Corp.*, 774 F.2d 786, 801 (7th Cir.1985).

24. *Cordova v. Cox*, 351 F.2d 269 (10th Cir.1965).

25. *United States v. $242,484.00*, 389 F.3d 1149, 1154 (11th Cir.2004) (decided appeals on the merits where the district court has not even entered any findings on each separate factual issue so long as "a complete understanding of the issues" is possible); *E.E.O.C. v. Severn Trent Services, Inc.*, 358 F.3d 438, 442 (7th Cir.2004) (the absence of explanation can be forgiven when the justification for the injunction is clear from the record).

26. *See In re Hongisto*, 293 B.R. 45 (N.D.Cal.2003).

27. *Federal Trade Com'n. v. Enforma Natural Products, Inc.*, 362 F.3d 1204, 1212 (9th Cir.2004); *Ciena Corp. v. Jarrard*, 203 F.3d 312, 321 (4th Cir.2000).

28. *Snow Machines, Inc. v. Hedco, Inc.*, 838 F.2d 718, 727 (3d Cir.1988).

Record on Appeal

On appeal, the record includes the court's findings. Courts are divided as to whether the record includes proposed but not adopted findings.

Standard of Review

Findings of fact are presumed correct, and are only disturbed if clearly erroneous.[29] "Clearly erroneous" has been defined by the Supreme Court as when, after reviewing all of the evidence, the appeals court is "left with the definite and firm conviction that a mistake has been committed."[30] The appellate court's deference for findings is not quite as strong as for jury verdicts, but findings are not set aside merely because the appellate court would have decided differently.[31] Conclusions of law are reviewed de novo.[32] Courts are split as to whether mixed questions of law and fact are reviewed under the clearly erroneous standard or de novo.[33] The court's awards of damages or equitable remedies are reviewed for abuse of discretion.[34]

Prerequisites for Appeal

Challenges to the sufficiency of the evidence supporting the findings in a non-jury trial may be made on appeal, even absent an objection to the findings, motion to amend the findings, or motion for partial findings before the district court.[35] However, challenges other than to the sufficiency of the evidence may need to be raised at the trial level to be raised on appeal. For example, a motion under Rule 52(b) to request additional findings may be a prerequisite to basing an appeal on the lack of such findings.[36] Likewise, a

29. *See Hurley v. Irish–American Gay, Lesbian and Bisexual Group of Boston*, 515 U.S. 557, 115 S.Ct. 2338, 132 L.Ed.2d 487 (1995); *S.E.C. v. Washington Inv. Network*, 475 F.3d 392, 399 (D.C.Cir. 2007); *New Windsor Volunteer Ambulance Corps, Inc. v. Meyers*, 442 F.3d 101, 112 (2nd Cir.2006) (if there are two permissible views of the evidence, the factfinder's choice cannot be clearly erroneous).

30. *United States v. U.S. Gypsum Co.*, 333 U.S. 364, 395, 68 S.Ct. 525, 541, 92 L.Ed. 746 (1948); *United States v. Zajanck-auskas*, 441 F.3d 32, 37 (1st Cir.2006); *Carnes Co. v. Stone Creek Mechanical, Inc.*, 412 F.3d 845, 855 (7th Cir.2005); *Presley v. U.S. Postal Service*, 317 F.3d 167, 174 (2nd Cir.2003).

31. *See Moorer v. Baptist Memorial Health Care System*, 398 F.3d 469, 478 (6th Cir.2005); *Nelson-Salabes, Inc. v. Morning-side Development, LLC*, 284 F.3d 505, 512 (4th Cir.2002); *Damon v. Sun Co., Inc.*, 87 F.3d 1467, 1472 (1st Cir.1996) (but, find-

ings of fact based on errors of law receive diminished respect).

32. *S.E.C. v. Washington Inv. Network*, 475 F.3d 392, 399 (D.C.Cir. 2007); *Hammel v. Eau Galle Cheese Factory*, 407 F.3d 852, 861 (7th Cir.2005).

33. *See Phansalkar v. Andersen Wein-roth & Co., L.P.*, 344 F.3d 184, 199 (2nd Cir.2003) (de novo); *Ringling Bros.-Barnum & Bailey Combined Shows, Inc. v. Utah Division of Travel Development*, 170 F.3d 449, 461 (4th Cir.1999) (clearly erroneous).

34. *Triple Five of Minnesota, Inc. v. Simon*, 404 F.3d 1088, 1095 (8th Cir.2005) (equitable remedies); *Bucheit v. Palestine Liberation Organization*, 388 F.3d 346, 351 (D.C.Cir.2004) (damages).

35. Rule 52(a)(5); *Glaverbel Societe Anonyme v. Northlake Marketing & Supply, Inc.*, 45 F.3d 1550 (Fed.Cir.1995).

36. *See Northeast Drilling, Inc. v. Inner Space Services, Inc.*, 243 F.3d 25, 35 (1st Cir.2001).

party may not be permitted to first raise objections to the form of the finding on appeal.[37]

Review of Credibility Determinations

Appellate courts are particularly hesitant to set aside findings based on evaluations of witness credibility.[38] The same applies to expert testimony,[39] except for evidentiary rulings such as foundation and methodology. On the other hand, findings based solely on documents in the record may not be accorded quite such high deference.[40]

Review of Inferences

Inferences from the evidence are reviewed under the same standard as any factual finding; the judge's inferences will not be disturbed unless clearly erroneous, in contrast to the summary judgment standard under which inferences are drawn in favor of the non-moving party.[41]

Review of Mixed Fact and Law

Often findings or conclusions by the trial court are actually mixtures of fact and law. Such mixed holdings are generally fully reviewable, and not subject to the "clearly erroneous" standard.[42] However, the line between issues of fact and law is often blurry. The appellate court will not rely on the trial court's label, but will determine on its own whether a holding is factual or legal.

Review of Findings of Master

If the report and recommendation of a master is adopted, those findings are subject to the same standard as the court's findings.[43] The standard of review is less clear when the trial court rejects or modifies the master's findings.

37. *Miller v. Bittner*, 985 F.2d 935 (8th Cir.1993).

38. *Pinkston v. Madry*, 440 F.3d 879; 890 (7th Cir.2006); *EIMSKIP v. Atlantic Fish Market, Inc.*, 417 F.3d 72 (1st Cir. 2005); *Adzick v. UNUM Life Ins. Co. of America*, 351 F.3d 883, 889 (8th Cir.2003) (findings based on credibility can virtually never be clear error); *but see Doe v. Menefee*, 391 F.3d 147, 164 (2nd Cir.2004) (court cannot insulate its findings from review by couching them as credibility determinations).

39. *Graver Tank & Mfg. Co. v. Linde Air Prods. Co.*, 336 U.S. 271, 274, 69 S.Ct. 535, 537, 93 L.Ed. 672 (1949).

40. *Taylor Corp. v. Four Seasons Greetings, LLC*, 403 F.3d 958, 965 (8th Cir.2005) (deference applies to oral and documentary evidence, but is particularly strong for oral testimony); *Hall v. Nat'l Gypsum Co.*, 105 F.3d 225, 228 (5th Cir.1997); *but see Shire US Inc. v. Barr Laboratories, Inc.*, 329 F.3d 348, 352 (3d Cir.2003) (the clearly erroneous standard applies to the district court's factual findings whether based on oral or documentary evidence).

41. *United States v. U.S. Gypsum Co.*, 333 U.S. 364, 68 S.Ct. 525, 92 L.Ed. 746 (1948); *Pinkston v. Madry*, 440 F.3d 879; 890 (7th Cir.2006).

42. *Muller v. Committee on Special Education of East Islip Union Free School District*, 145 F.3d 95, 102 (2d Cir.1998); *Hirschfeld v. Spanakos*, 104 F.3d 16, 19 (2d Cir.1997).

43. *See Summers v. Howard University*, 374 F.3d 1188, 1196 (D.C.Cir.2004); *Accu-Soft Corp. v. Palo*, 237 F.3d 31, 39 (1st Cir.2001); *Berger v. Iron Workers Reinforced Rodmen, Local 201*, 170 F.3d 1111, 1119 (D.C.Cir.1999).

RULE 52(b). AMENDED OR ADDITIONAL FINDINGS

CORE CONCEPT

Upon motion, the court may amend its findings and/or judgment.

APPLICATIONS

2007 Amendments

The 2007 amendments moved the text from Rule 52(b) providing that a party may challenge the sufficiency of the evidentiary support for the court's findings after the findings are made regardless of whether the party previously took any positions on the findings into new Rule 52(a)(5). Care should be exercised in researching and citing pre–2008 cases referring to Rule 52(a) or Rule 52(b).

Timing

Motions to amend the findings must be filed no later than 10 days after entry of judgment.[44] This time period is absolute, and cannot be enlarged by the court.[45] The motion may be filed before entry of judgment.

Grounds

Proper grounds for a Rule 52(b) motion to amend include newly discovered evidence,[46] a change in the law, or a manifest error of fact or law by the trial court.[47] A Rule 52(b) motion to amend should not merely relitigate old issues or rehear the merits of the case.[48] A party may move to amend the findings of fact even if the modified or additional findings in effect reverse the judgment.[49] Once a motion to amend has been filed, the court can amend any findings it deems appropriate, regardless of the issues raised in the motion.[50]

Tolls Appeal Period

The filing of a motion to amend the findings tolls the running of the time to file an appeal.[51] The appeal clock starts over when the court enters an order granting or denying the motion to amend.

---

44. *Golden Blount, Inc. v. Robert H. Peterson Co.*, 438 F.3d 1354, 1358 (Fed.Cir. 2006); *Cayuga Indian Nation of New York v. Pataki*, 188 F.Supp.2d 223, 229–30 (N.D.N.Y.2002).

45. *Martin v. Monumental Life Ins. Co.*, 240 F.3d 223, 237–38 (3d Cir.2001).

46. *See Draim v. Virtual Geosatellite Holdings, Inc.*, 241 F.R.D. 48, 50 (D.D.C. 2007) (evidence that was merely not offered into evidence does not support a Rule 52(b) motion to amend).

47. *Pro Edge L.P. v. Gue*, 377 F.Supp.2d 694 (N.D.Iowa 2005); *Sherman v. Kasotakis*, 314 F.Supp.2d 843 (N.D.Iowa 2004); *Padilla v. Miller*, 143 F.Supp.2d 479, 487 (M.D.Pa.2001).

48. *Oneida Indian Nation of New York v. Madison County*, 235 F.R.D. 559, 561 (N.D.N.Y.2006); *Pro Edge L.P. v. Gue*, 377 F.Supp.2d 694 (N.D.Iowa 2005); *Gutierrez v. Ashcroft*, 289 F.Supp.2d 555, 561 (D.N.J. 2003).

49. *Golden Blount, Inc. v. Robert H. Peterson Co.*, 438 F.3d 1354, 1358 (Fed.Cir. 2006) (if the trial court has entered an erroneous judgment, it should correct it).

50. *Golden Blount, Inc. v. Robert H. Peterson Co.*, 438 F.3d 1354, 1358 (Fed.Cir. 2006).

51. *Weyant v. Okst*, 198 F.3d 311, 314–15 (2d Cir.1999).

RULE 52(c).   JUDGMENT ON PARTIAL FINDINGS

CORE CONCEPT

At any time in a non-jury trial after a party has presented all its evidence with respect to a particular issue, the court may enter judgment against that party if the evidence failed to persuade the judge.[52]

APPLICATIONS

Proceedings Applicable

Rule 52(c) applies only in non-jury trials.[53]   The parallel for jury trials is a judgment as a matter of law under Rule 50(a).[54]

Timing of Motion

A Rule 52(c) motion may be made at any time after all the evidence has been presented on a particular topic;[55] although motions for judgment on partial findings are typically made at the close of the opposing party's case,[56] the movant technically does not need to wait until the opposing party has rested.[57]

Standard for Granting

The trial judge rules on motions for judgment on partial findings as a final factfinder, reviewing all evidence presented thus far without presumptions in favor of either party.[58]   The judge grants the motion if, upon the evidence already presented, the judge would find against the party that has already presented evidence and in favor of the moving party.

Scope of Judgment

The judge will enter judgment on the claim or issue that is the subject of the motion and on any other claim, issue, counterclaim, crossclaim, or third-party claim that is determined by the outcome of the issue that is the subject of the motion.

Findings of Fact

If the judge grants a motion for judgment on partial findings,

---

52. *Macia v. Microsoft Corp.*, 335 F.Supp.2d 507, 511 (D.Vt.2004); *Lamarca v. United States*, 31 F.Supp.2d 110, 123 (E.D.N.Y.1998) (judgment on partial findings may be rendered in favor of plaintiffs or defendants).

53. *Fillmore v. Page*, 358 F.3d 496, 502–03 (7th Cir.2004); *Northeast Drilling, Inc. v. Inner Space Services, Inc.*, 243 F.3d 25, 35 (1st Cir.2001).

54. *Federal Ins. Co. v. HPSC, Inc.*, 480 F.3d 26, 32 (1st Cir. 2007) (motion for judgment as a matter of law in a non-jury trial treated as a motion for judgment on partial findings under Rule 52(c)).

55. *First Virginia Banks, Inc. v. BP Exploration & Oil, Inc.*, 206 F.3d 404, 407 (4th Cir.2000) (Rule 52 does not create a right to introduce all the evidence on a topic that the party wishes; the court may exclude evidence if cumulative or not probative).

56. *See, e.g., Pinkston v. Madry*, 440 F.3d 879, 885–86 (7th Cir.2006).

57. *Cajun Electric Power Cooperative, Inc. v. Gulf States Utilities Company*, 848 F.Supp. 71 (M.D.La.1994).

58. *Ortloff v. U.S.*, 335 F.3d 652, 660 (7th Cir.2003) (contrasting the standard under Rule 52(c) to the standard under Rule 52(a)); *Geddes v. Northwest Missouri State University*, 49 F.3d 426 (8th Cir.1995); *Wechsler v. Hunt Health Systems, Ltd.*, 330 F.Supp.2d 383, 433 (S.D.N.Y.2004).

the judge must make findings of fact pursuant to Rule 52(a).[59]

Deferred Ruling

The judge, in an exercise of discretion, may defer ruling until all evidence has been presented.[60]

Appeals

The appeals court will review judgments on partial findings under the "clearly erroneous" standard because such findings represent the judge's factual determinations.[61] Conclusions of law are reviewed *de novo*.[62] The appeals court will probably review all the evidence in the record. Thus, if the motion is denied and the defendant elects to offer evidence, the plaintiff may be able to cure the purported deficiency in its case. Judgments on partial findings under Rule 52(c) are reviewed under the same standard as the court's findings under Rule 52(a), which is discussed in more detail above.

ADDITIONAL RESEARCH REFERENCES

Wright & Miller, *Federal Practice and Procedure* §§ 2571–2591.

C.J.S. Federal Civil Procedure §§ 1036–1056 et seq.

West's Key No. Digests, Federal Civil Procedure ⚲2261–2293.

59. *Burger v. New York Inst. of Technology*, 94 F.3d 830, 835 (2d Cir.1996) (explaining that a "one-sentence statement in no way constitutes the requisite findings under Rule 52"); *Quantachrome Corp. v. Micromeritics Instrument Corp.*, 97 F.Supp.2d 1181 (S.D. Fla.2000).

60. *United States v. Davis*, 20 F.Supp.2d 326, 331 (D.R.I.1998), *aff'd in part, remanded in part*, 261 F.3d 1 (1st Cir.2001).

61. *Pinkston v. Madry*, 440 F.3d 879, 888 (7th Cir.2006); *Samson v. Apollo Resources, Inc.*, 242 F.3d 629, 633 (5th Cir. 2001).

62. *Marina Bay Realty Trust LLC v. U.S.*, 407 F.3d 418, 423 (1st Cir.2005); *Mullin v. Town of Fairhaven*, 284 F.3d 31, 36 (1st Cir.2002).

RULE 53

MASTERS

(a) Appointment.

(1) *Scope.* Unless a statute provides otherwise, a court may appoint a master only to:

(A) perform duties consented to by the parties;

(B) hold trial proceedings and make or recommend findings of fact on issues to be decided without a jury if appointment is warranted by:

(i) some exceptional condition; or

(ii) the need to perform an accounting or resolve a difficult computation of damages; or

(C) address pretrial and posttrial matters that cannot be effectively and timely addressed by an available district judge or magistrate judge of the district.

(2) *Disqualification.* A master must not have a relationship to the parties, attorneys, action, or court that would require disqualification of a judge under 28 U.S.C. § 455, unless the parties, with the court's approval, consent to the appointment after the master discloses any potential grounds for disqualification.

(3) *Possible Expense or Delay.* In appointing a master, the court must consider the fairness of imposing the likely expenses on the parties and must protect against unreasonable expense or delay.

(b) Order Appointing a Master.

(1) *Notice.* Before appointing a master, the court must give the parties notice and an opportunity to be heard. Any party may suggest candidates for appointment.

(2) *Contents.* The appointing order must direct the master to proceed with all reasonable diligence and must state:

(A) the master's duties, including any investigation or enforcement duties, and any limits on the master's authority under Rule 53(c);

    (B) the circumstances, if any, in which the master may communicate ex parte with the court or a party;

    (C) the nature of the materials to be preserved and filed as the record of the master's activities;

    (D) the time limits, method of filing the record, other procedures, and standards for reviewing the master's orders, findings, and recommendations; and

    (E) the basis, terms, and procedure for fixing the master's compensation under Rule 53(g).

  (3) *Issuing.* The court may issue the order only after:

    (A) the master files an affidavit disclosing whether there is any ground for disqualification under 28 U.S.C. § 455; and

    (B) if a ground is disclosed, the parties, with the court's approval, waive the disqualification.

  (4) *Amending.* The order may be amended at any time after notice to the parties and an opportunity to be heard.

(c) Master's Authority.

  (1) *In General.* Unless the appointing order directs otherwise, a master may:

    (A) regulate all proceedings;

    (B) take all appropriate measures to perform the assigned duties fairly and efficiently; and

    (C) if conducting an evidentiary hearing, exercise the appointing court's power to compel, take, and record evidence.

  (2) *Sanctions.* The master may by order impose on a party any noncontempt sanction provided by Rule 37 or 45, and may recommend a contempt sanction against a party and sanctions against a nonparty.

(d) Master's Orders. A master who issues an order must file it and promptly serve a copy on each party. The clerk must enter the order on the docket.

(e) Master's Reports. A master must report to the court as required by the appointing order. The master must file the report and promptly serve a copy on each party, unless the court orders otherwise.

(f) Action on the Master's Order, Report, or Recommendations.

(1) *Opportunity for a Hearing; Action in General.* In acting on a master's order, report, or recommendations, the court must give the parties notice and an opportunity to be heard; may receive evidence; and may adopt or affirm, modify, wholly or partly reject or reverse, or resubmit to the master with instructions.

(2) *Time to Object or Move to Adopt or Modify.* A party may file objections to—or a motion to adopt or modify—the master's order, report, or recommendations no later than 20 days after a copy is served, unless the court sets a different time.

(3) *Reviewing Factual Findings.* The court must decide de novo all objections to findings of fact made or recommended by a master, unless the parties, with the court's approval, stipulate that:

(A) the findings will be reviewed for clear error; or

(B) the findings of a master appointed under Rule 53(a)(1)(A) or (C) will be final.

(4) *Reviewing Legal Conclusions.* The court must decide de novo all objections to conclusions of law made or recommended by a master.

(5) *Reviewing Procedural Matters.* Unless the appointing order establishes a different standard of review, the court may set aside a master's ruling on a procedural matter only for an abuse of discretion.

(g) Compensation.

(1) *Fixing Compensation.* Before or after judgment, the court must fix the master's compensation on the basis and terms stated in the appointing order, but the court may set a new basis and terms after giving notice and an opportunity to be heard.

(2) *Payment.* The compensation must be paid either:

(A) by a party or parties; or

(B) from a fund or subject matter of the action within the court's control.

(3) *Allocating Payment.* The court must allocate payment among the parties after considering the nature and amount of the controversy, the parties' means, and the extent to which any party is more responsible than other parties for the reference to a master. An interim allocation may be amended to reflect a decision on the merits.

(h) Appointing a Magistrate Judge. A magistrate judge is subject to this rule only when the order referring a matter to the magistrate judge states that the reference is made under this rule.

[Amended February 28, 1966, effective July 1, 1966; April 28, 1983, effective August 1, 1983; March 2, 1987, effective August 1, 1987; April 30, 1991, effective December 1, 1991; April 22, 1993, effective December 1, 1993; March 27, 2003, effective December 1, 2003; April 30, 2007, effective December 1, 2007.]

───────── **2007 AMENDMENTS ROADMAP** ─────────

STYLE PROJECT CHANGES: Rules 53(b)(3) and 53(c) were subsectioned. The provisions of Rule 53(d) were moved to Rule 53(c)(1)(C), and the provisions in the sections following former Rule 53(d) were renumbered accordingly. Orienting labels were added, and the language otherwise received minor modifications to add clarity.

NON-STYLE CHANGES: None.

NOTE: The Federal Rules "Style Project" is explained in Part III-A.

AUTHORS' COMMENTARY ON RULE 53

───────── **PURPOSE AND SCOPE** ─────────

Rule 53 provides the procedures governing the reference of designated aspects of an action to a master.

NOTE: Rule 53 was substantially revised in 2003 to reflect changing practices in using masters. The amendment recognizes that special masters are used for a variety of pretrial and post-trial functions as well as to conduct trials. The amendment also changes the standard of review for findings of fact by a master.

RULE 53(a).   APPOINTMENT

CORE CONCEPT

The court in which an action is pending may appoint a special master to conduct trials in limited circumstances and to conduct certain pretrial and post-trial functions.

APPLICATIONS

Functions Performed by Master

Rule 53 defines three categories of functions that a master may perform:

- Duties consented to by the parties;[1]

- Hold trial proceedings and make recommended findings of fact on non-jury issues if the appointment is warranted by an exceptional condition or by the need to perform an accounting or resolve a difficult computation of damages;[2]

- or address pretrial[3] or post-trial matters[4] if they cannot be addressed effectively and timely by the court

Jury Trials

The 2003 Amendments eliminated the use of masters in matters to be tried to a jury unless the parties consent.[5]

Ineligible Persons

One cannot be master if related to the parties, the action, or the court under the same standards that govern disqualification of a judge set forth in 28 U.S.C. § 455.[6] The clerk of court and the clerk's deputies are also ineligible. The parties can waive this restriction with the court's approval.[7]

Court's Discretion—Fairness

In determining whether to appoint a master, the court must consider the fairness of imposing the cost of the master's compensation on the parties and the effects of delay.[8] The court has discretion

---

1. Rule 53(a)(1)(A). *See also Cremin v. Merrill Lynch, Pierce, Fenner & Smith, Inc.,* 328 F.Supp.2d 865, 869 (N.D.Ill.2004).

2. Rule 53(a)(1)(B). *See also Beazer East, Inc. v. Mead Corp.,* 412 F.3d 429, 441 (3rd Cir.2005) (equitable allocation under CERCLA is not a computation of damages and thus may not be referred to a special master).

3. Rule 53(a)(1)(C). *See also* The Advisory Committee Note to the 2003 Amendment to Rule 53 ("A pretrial master should be appointed only when the need is clear.").

4. Rule 53(a)(1)(C). *See also* The Advisory Committee Note to the 2003 Amendment

to Rule 53 (reliance on a master is appropriate when a complex decree requires ongoing policing).

5. The Advisory Committee Note to the 2003 Amendments to Rule 53.

6. *In re Kensington Intern. Ltd.,* 353 F.3d 211, 222 (3rd Cir.2003).

7. *See United States v. Michigan,* 234 F.R.D. 636 (E.D.Mich.2006).

8. Rule 53(a)(3). *See also Gaddis v. United States,* 381 F.3d 444, 462 (5th Cir. 2004).

917

as to whether to refer a matter to a master,[9] but reference should be the exception, not the rule.[10] The court also has discretion to refuse to appoint a master even if the parties have consented.[11]

Magistrate Judges

The court may appoint a United States Magistrate Judge to serve as a special master.[12] The provisions regarding compensation do not apply when a United States Magistrate Judge is designated to serve as a special master.

Common References

References are most common in patent, trademark, and copyright actions. They are also used occasionally to supervise discovery, following summary judgment on liability when the damages are difficult to calculate, and to oversee compliance.[13]

RULE 53(b). ORDER APPOINTING A MASTER

CORE CONCEPT

A master is appointed by an order setting forth the duties and parameters of the reference.

APPLICATIONS

Notice and Opportunity to Be Heard

The court must give notice of the proposed appointment of a master to the parties and provide an opportunity to be heard before appointing the master.[14] Written submissions will provide an "opportunity to be heard" unless the circumstances require live testimony.[15]

Candidates for Appointment

A party may suggest candidates for appointment as master.[16]

Contents of Order

The order appointing a master must:

9. *Middle Tennessee News Co., Inc. v. Charnel of Cincinnati, Inc.*, 250 F.3d 1077 (7th Cir.2001) ("The district court did not need the consent of the parties to refer "complicated" issues to an independent accountant under Rule 53."); *United States v. State of Washington*, 157 F.3d 630, 660 (9th Cir.1998).

10. *United States v. State of Wash.*, 135 F.3d 618, 646 (9th Cir.1998), *amended and superseded on denial of rehearing*, 157 F.3d 630 (9th Cir.1998).

11. The Advisory Committee Note to the 2003 Amendments to Rule 53.

12. *Securities and Exchange Commission v. AMX, International, Inc.*, 872 F.Supp. 1541 (N.D.Tex.1994).

13. *See United States v. Microsoft Corp.*, 147 F.3d 935, (D.C.Cir.1998) (discussing the "well established tradition allowing use of special masters to oversee compliance.").

14. Rule 53(b)(1). *See also Amgen, Inc. v. Hoechst Marion Roussel, Inc.*, 339 F.Supp.2d 202, 221 (D.Mass.2004), *vac'd and remanded on other grounds*, 457 F.3d 1293 (Fed.Cir.2006).

15. The Advisory Committee Note to the 2003 Amendment to Rule 53.

16. Rule 53(b)(1).

- Direct the master to proceed with all reasonable diligence;[17]
- State the master's duties and any limits on the master's authority;[18]
- State the circumstances, if any, in which the master may communicate *ex parte* with the court or a party;[19]
- State the nature of the materials to be preserved and filed as the record of the master's activities;[20]
- State the time limits, methods of filing the record, other procedures, and standards for reviewing the master's orders, findings, and recommendations;[21] and
- State the basis, terms, and procedures for determining the master's compensation under Rule 53(g).[22]

Affidavit re Disqualification

Before the court can enter the order appointing the master, the master must file an affidavit disclosing whether there is any ground for disqualification under 28 U.S.C. § 455.[23] If a ground for disqualification is disclosed, the court may not enter the order unless the parties have consented with the court's approval to waive the disqualification.[24]

Amendment of Order

The order appointing the master may be amended at any time after notice to the parties and an opportunity to be heard.[25]

Challenging Reference

The proper method for contesting a reference is a motion to amend, vacate or revoke the reference.[26] Failure to make such a motion may be deemed a consent or waiver.[27] If the motion to vacate is denied, the disgruntled party may attempt to compel the court to vacate by a writ of mandamus.[28] Orders of reference are interlocutory, and may not be appealed directly, but may be appealed at the conclusion of the district court proceedings.[29]

---

17. Rule 53(b)(2).

18. Rule 53(b)(2)(A). *See also Horn v. McQueen*, 353 F.Supp.2d 785, 850 (W.D.Ky. 2004).

19. Rule 53(b)(2)(B). *See also* The Advisory Committee Note to the 2003 Amendment to Rule 53 (ordinarily, the order should prohibit *ex parte* communications).

20. Rule 53(b)(2)(C). *See also* The Advisory Committee Note to the 2003 Amendment to Rule 53 (a basic requirement is that the master must make and file a complete record of the evidence considered in making or recommending findings of fact).

21. Rule 53(b)(2)(D).

22. Rule 53(b)(2)(E).

23. Rule 53(b)(3).

24. Rule 53(b)(3).

25. Rule 53(b)(4).

26. *Fajardo Shopping Center, S.E. v. Sun Alliance Ins. Co. of Puerto Rico, Inc.*, 167 F.3d 1, 6 (1st Cir.1999).

27. *Fajardo Shopping Center, S.E. v. Sun Alliance Ins. Co. of Puerto Rico, Inc.*, 167 F.3d 1, 6 (1st Cir.1999); *Spaulding v. University of Washington*, 740 F.2d 686, 693 (9th Cir.1984).

28. *La Buy v. Howes Leather Co.*, 352 U.S. 249, 77 S.Ct. 309, 1 L.Ed.2d 290 (1957); *United States v. Microsoft Corp.*, 147 F.3d 935 (D.C.Cir.1998).

29. *Sierra Club v. Clifford*, 257 F.3d 444 (5th Cir.2001).

RULE 53(c). MASTER'S AUTHORITY

CORE CONCEPT

Absent specific limitations in the order appointing the master, the master has all powers necessary to perform the referred matters, including the powers necessary to regulate the proceedings, rule on evidentiary issues, place witnesses under oath, and examine witnesses.[30] The master has discretion as to what procedures to employ, with the only requirement being that when the master determines that a hearing is necessary, the master shall make a record of the evidence offered and excluded in the same manner and subject to the same limitations as provided in the Federal Rules of Evidence for a non-jury trial.[31] The court has the duty to oversee the special master's performance of his duties to ensure that they are appropriately discharged.[32]

APPLICATIONS

2007 Amendments

The 2007 amendments moved the provisions of Rule 53(d) to Rule 53(c)(1)(C), and the provisions in the sections following former Rule 53(d) were renumbered accordingly. Care should be exercised in researching and citing pre–2008 cases referring to Rule 53(c) or Rule 53(d).

Sanctions

The master may impose on a party any non-contempt sanction provided by Rule 37 or 45. The master may also recommend contempt sanctions against a party and sanctions against a non-party.

Evidentiary Hearings

Unless otherwise limited by the order appointing the master, the master may exercise the powers of the court to compel (by subpoena under Rule 45), take, and record evidence.

RULE 53(d). MASTER'S ORDERS

CORE CONCEPT

A master who makes an order must file the order with the clerk and promptly serve a copy on each party. The clerk must enter the order on the docket.

APPLICATIONS

2007 Amendments

The 2007 amendments moved the provisions of Rule 53(d) to Rule 53(c)(1)(C), and the subsequent sections were renumbered

---

30. *United States v. Clifford Matley Family Trust*, 354 F.3d 1154, 1159 (9th Cir.2004) (the order referring the case is the source and the limit of the master's duties and powers); *Laube v. Campbell*, 333 F.Supp.2d 1234, 1240 (M.D.Ala.2004).

31. *United States v. Clifford Matley Family Trust*, 354 F.3d 1154, 1159 (9th Cir.2004).

32. *Cordoza v. Pacific States Steel Corp.*, 320 F.3d 989, 999 (9th Cir.2003) (court has the duty to reduce special master's compensation if appropriate).

accordingly. Rule 53(e) was renumbered as Rule 53(d). Care should be exercised in researching and citing pre–2008 cases referring to Rule 53(d) or Rule 53(e).

RULE 53(e). MASTER'S REPORTS

CORE CONCEPT

A master must prepare reports as directed by the order of appointment. The master must file such reports with the clerk and promptly serve a copy upon each party unless the court directs otherwise.[33]

APPLICATIONS

2007 Amendments

The 2007 amendments moved the provisions of Rule 53(d) to Rule 53(c)(1)(C), and the subsequent sections were renumbered accordingly. Rule 53(f) was renumbered as Rule 53(e). Care should be exercised in researching and citing pre–2008 cases referring to Rule 53(e) or Rule 53(f).

Supporting Materials

The master should provide all portions of the record that the master deems relevant to the report. The parties may seek to designate additional materials from the record, and may seek to supplement the record. The court may provide that additional materials from the record be filed.[34]

Sealed Report

Sealing of the report from public access may be appropriate, particularly with respect to pre-trial and post-trial masters. A report detailing a continuing or failed settlement effort is one example of a report that might be sealed.[35]

RULE 53(f). ACTION ON THE MASTER'S ORDER, REPORT, OR RECOMMENDATIONS

CORE CONCEPT

Rule 53(f) sets forth the procedures for the court to act on the masters report and the standards by which the court should review the report.

APPLICATIONS

2007 Amendments

The 2007 amendments moved the provisions of Rule 53(d) to Rule 53(c)(1)(C), and the subsequent sections were renumbered

---

33. *See Schaefer Fan Co., Inc. v. J & D Mfg.*, 265 F.3d 1282, 1289 (Fed.Cir.2001); *In re Latex Glove Products Liability Litigation*, 2004 WL 1118691 (E.D.Pa.2004).

34. The Advisory Committee Note to the 2003 Amendment to Rule 53.

35. The Advisory Committee Note to the 2003 Amendment to Rule 53.

accordingly. Rule 53(g) was renumbered as Rule 53(f). Care should be exercised in researching and citing pre–2008 cases referring to Rule 53(f) or Rule 53(g).

Actions by the Court

When considering an order, report, or recommendation from a master, the court may adopt or affirm, modify, reject or reverse in whole or in part, or resubmit to the master with instructions.[36]

Opportunity to be Heard

Before taking action on an order, report, or recommendation from a master, the court must provide the parties with an opportunity to be heard.[37] Written submissions will provide an "opportunity to be heard" unless the circumstances require live testimony.[38]

Time for Objections

A party may file objections to the master's order, report, or recommendations no later than 20 days from the time the order, report, or recommendations are served, unless the court sets a different time. The parties may also file a motion to adopt or modify the order, report, or recommendations in the same time frame.[39] This time period is not jurisdictional, and the court has the authority to consider a late objection or motion.[40]

Findings of Fact

Absent a stipulation otherwise,[41] the court must decide *de novo* all objections to findings of fact made or recommended by a master.[42] The court may also review *de novo* findings of fact made or recommended by a master in the absence of an objection.[43] The parties may stipulate, with the court's consent, that the master's findings of fact will only be reviewed for clear error.[44] The parties may also stipulate, with the court's consent, that the master's findings of fact will be final if the master was appointed by consent or was appointed to address pretrial or post-trial matters.[45] The court may withdraw its consent to a stipulation for clear error

36. Rule 53(g)(1). *See also In re Omeprazole Patent Litigation*, 227 F.R.D. 227, 229 (S.D.N.Y.2005).

37. *United States v. Fairway Capital Corp.*, 433 F.Supp.2d 226 (D.R.I.2006); *Doe ex rel. Doe v. Keala*, 361 F.Supp.2d 1171, 1177 (D.Hawai'i 2005).

38. The Advisory Committee Note to the 2003 Amendment to Rule 53.

39. Rule 53(f)(2).

40. *See Wallace v. Skadden, Arps, Slate, Meagher & Flom, LLP*, 362 F.3d 810, 816 (D.C.Cir.2004); The Advisory Committee Note to the 2003 Amendment to Rule 53.

41. *AgGrow Oils, L.L.C. v. National Union Fire Ins. Co. of Pittsburgh*, PA, 276 F.Supp.2d 999, 1005 (D.N.D.2003) (when the parties stipulate that a master's find-

ings of fact shall be final, the district court shall only consider questions of law).

42. *Guardian Pipeline, L.L.C. v. 950.80 Acres of Land*, 486 F.Supp.2d 741 (N.D.Ill. 2007); *United States v. Fairway Capital Corp.*, 433 F.Supp.2d 226 (D.R.I.2006).

43. The Advisory Committee Note to the 2003 Amendment to Rule 53.

44. Rule 53(f)(3)(A). *See also* The Advisory Committee Note to the 2003 Amendment to Rule 53 (suggesting that clear error review is more likely to be appropriate with respect to findings that do not go to the merits of the claims or defenses, such as findings of fact going to a privilege issue); *Grace v. City of Detroit*, 341 F.Supp.2d 709, 714 (E.D.Mich.2004).

45. Rule 53(f)(3)(B).

review or finality, may reopen the opportunity for the parties to object.[46]

Conclusions of Law

The court must decide *de novo* all objections to conclusions of law made or recommended by a master.[47]

Procedural Matters

In the absence of a different standard set by the order of appointment, the court reviews a master's ruling on a procedural matter for abuse of discretion.[48]

Appeals

The report of the master is not appealable until adopted by the court. Thereafter, the report of the master becomes the findings of the court and is appealable under the same "clearly erroneous" standard used for all findings of fact by the court, as set forth in Rule 52.[49]

RULE 53(g). COMPENSATION

CORE CONCEPT

The court sets the compensation for a master. The master's compensation will be allocated among the parties or taken from the subject matter of the litigation.

APPLICATIONS

2007 Amendments

The 2007 amendments moved the provisions of Rule 53(d) to Rule 53(c)(1)(C), and the subsequent sections were renumbered accordingly. Rule 53(h) was renumbered as Rule 53(g). Care should be exercised in researching and citing pre–2008 cases referring to Rule 53(g) or Rule 53(h).

Amount of Compensation

The court fixes the compensation for a master,[50] and the amount will not be disturbed on appeal absent an abuse of discretion.[51] The court may also require the posting of a bond to secure

---

46. The Advisory Committee Note to the 2003 Amendment to Rule 53.

47. *United States v. Fairway Capital Corp.*, 433 F.Supp.2d 226 (D.R.I.2006); *JCW Investments, Inc. v. Novelty, Inc.*, 366 F.Supp.2d 688, 689–90 (N.D.Ill.2005); *United States v. KPMG LLP*, 316 F.Supp.2d 30 (D.D.C.2004).

48. Rule 53(f)(5). *See also* The Advisory Committee Note to the 2003 Amendment to Rule 53 (suggesting that the abuse of discretion standard may be more searching for a master's rulings than an appellate court

exercises over a district court); *Doe ex rel. Doe v. Keala*, 361 F.Supp.2d 1171, 1177 (D.Hawai'i 2005).

49. *See Summers v. Howard University*, 374 F.3d 1188, 1195 (D.C.Cir.2004); *Charter Oak Fire Ins. Co. v. Hedeen & Companies*, 280 F.3d 730, 738 (7th Cir.2002).

50. *Cordoza v. Pacific States Steel Corp.*, 320 F.3d 989, 999 (9th Cir.2003) (court has the duty to reduce special master's compensation if appropriate).

51. *Roy v. County of Lexington, South Carolina*, 141 F.3d 533 (4th Cir.1998).

payment of the fee or require the payment of the fee into escrow.[52] The amount of compensation will be controlled by the order of appointment,[53] but the court may set a new basis and terms after notice to the parties and an opportunity to be heard.[54]

Source of Compensation

The court may impose the master's fee upon either party or may apportion it among the parties.[55] The court may also direct that the fee be paid from any fund[56] or subject matter of the action in the custody of the court.

Allocation Among Parties

If the compensation is to be paid by the parties, the court must allocate the compensation among the parties. The court should consider the nature and amount of the controversy, the parties' financial means, and the extent to which any party is more responsible for the reference to the master.[57] The court may make interim allocations and may adjust the interim allocation later to reflect the decision on the merits.[58]

Collection of Compensation

The master may obtain a writ of execution against a party not paying his share of the master's fee. The master may not withhold the report to obtain payment.

RULE 53(h).   APPOINTING A MAGISTRATE JUDGE

CORE CONCEPT

The provisions of Rule 53 do not pertain to matters referred to magistrate judges unless the order of reference specifically states that it is made pursuant to Rule 53.[59]

APPLICATIONS

2007 Amendments

The 2007 amendments moved the provisions of Rule 53(d) to Rule 53(c)(1)(C), and the subsequent sections were renumbered accordingly. Rule 53(i) was renumbered as Rule 53(h). Care should be exercised in researching and citing pre–2008 cases referring to Rule 53(h) or Rule 53(i).

52. *Allapattah Services, Inc. v. Exxon Corp.*, 157 F.Supp.2d 1291, 1325 (S.D.Fla. 2001).

53. *Gaddis v. United States*, 381 F.3d 444, 462 (5th Cir.2004).

54. Rule 53(g)(1).

55. *See Gaddis v. United States*, 381 F.3d 444, 462 (5th Cir.2004). *Roy v. County of Lexington, S.C.*, 141 F.3d 533, 549 (4th Cir.1998); *Hook v. State of Arizona*, 907 F.Supp. 1326, 1336–37 (D.Ariz. 1995)(charging special master fees against Arizona despite a state statute purporting to insulate the state from such fees).

56. *See Six L's Packing Co., Inc. v. Post & Taback, Inc.*, 132 F.Supp.2d 306, 309 (S.D.N.Y.2001).

57. Rule 53(g)(3).

58. Rule 53(g)(3).

59. *See Wallace v. Skadden, Arps, Slate, Meagher & Flom, LLP*, 362 F.3d 810, 814–16 (D.C.Cir.2004); *Gonzalez v. Rakkas*, 846 F.Supp. 229 (E.D.N.Y.1994).

ADDITIONAL RESEARCH REFERENCES

Wright & Miller, *Federal Practice and Procedure* §§ 2601–2615.

C.J.S. Federal Civil Procedure §§ 890–904; United States Commissioners § 3.

West's Key No. Digests, Federal Civil Procedure ⊶1871–1908; United States Magistrates ⊶14.

VII. JUDGMENT

RULE 54

JUDGMENT; COSTS

(a) Definition; Form. "Judgment" as used in these rules includes a decree and any order from which an appeal lies. A judgment should not include recitals of pleadings, a master's report, or a record of prior proceedings.

(b) Judgment on Multiple Claims or Involving Multiple Parties. When an action presents more than one claim for relief—whether as a claim, counterclaim, cross-claim, or third-party claim—or when multiple parties are involved, the court may direct entry of a final judgment as to one or more, but fewer than all, claims or parties only if the court expressly determines that there is no just reason for delay. Otherwise, any order or other decision, however designated, that adjudicates fewer than all the claims or the rights and liabilities of fewer than all the parties does not end the action as to any of the claims or parties and may be revised at any time before the entry of a judgment adjudicating all the claims and all the parties' rights and liabilities.

(c) Demand for Judgment; Relief to Be Granted. A default judgment must not differ in kind from, or exceed in amount, what is demanded in the pleadings. Every other final judgment should grant the relief to which each party is entitled, even if the party has not demanded that relief in its pleadings.

(d) Costs; Attorney's Fees.

    (1) *Costs Other Than Attorney's Fees.* Unless a federal statute, these rules, or a court order provides otherwise, costs—other than attorney's fees—should be allowed to the prevailing party. But costs against the United States, its officers, and its agencies may be imposed only to the extent allowed by law. The clerk may tax costs on 1 day's notice. On motion served within the next 5 days, the court may review the clerk's action.

    (2) *Attorney's Fees.*

(A) *Claim to Be by Motion.* A claim for attorney's fees and related nontaxable expenses must be made by motion unless the substantive law requires those fees to be proved at trial as an element of damages.

(B) *Timing and Contents of the Motion.* Unless a statute or a court order provides otherwise, the motion must:

(i) be filed no later than 14 days after the entry of judgment;

(ii) specify the judgment and the statute, rule, or other grounds entitling the movant to the award;

(iii) state the amount sought or provide a fair estimate of it; and

(iv) disclose, if the court so orders, the terms of any agreement about fees for the services for which the claim is made.

(C) *Proceedings.* Subject to Rule 23(h), the court must, on a party's request, give an opportunity for adversary submissions on the motion in accordance with Rule 43(c) or 78. The court may decide issues of liability for fees before receiving submissions on the value of services. The court must find the facts and state its conclusions of law as provided in Rule 52(a).

(D) *Special Procedures by Local Rule; Reference to a Master or a Magistrate Judge.* By local rule, the court may establish special procedures to resolve fee-related issues without extensive evidentiary hearings. Also, the court may refer issues concerning the value of services to a special master under Rule 53 without regard to the limitations of Rule 53(a)(1), and may refer a motion for attorney's fees to a magistrate judge under Rule 72(b) as if it were a dispositive pretrial matter.

(E) *Exceptions.* Subparagraphs (A)–(D) do not apply to claims for fees and expenses as sanctions for violating these rules or as sanctions under 28 U.S.C. § 1927.

[Amended December 27, 1946, effective March 19, 1948; April 17, 1961, effective July 19, 1961; March 2, 1987, effective August 1, 1987; April 22, 1993, effective December 1, 1993; amended April 29, 2002, effective December 1, 2002; March 27, 2003, effective December 1, 2003; April 30, 2007, effective December 1, 2007.]

─────────── **2007 AMENDMENTS ROADMAP** ───────────

STYLE PROJECT CHANGES: Limited new subsectioning was added (but only to subpart 54(d)(2)), and a few new labels were included. Confusing use of "shall" was replaced by "must" or "should", depending on context. Redundant "express direction for the entry of judgment" reduced to "direct entry of final judgment". Active voice replaced passive voice. Class member rights to object to fee awards are placed more appropriately in Rule 23(h). Rule 54(d)(2)(c) now simply cross-references back to that Rule for content.

NON-STYLE CHANGES: None.

NOTE: The Federal Rules "Style Project" is explained in Part III-A.

AUTHORS' COMMENTARY ON RULE 54

─────────── **PURPOSE AND SCOPE** ───────────

Rule 54 defines the term "judgment", discusses the limits of recovery on a judgment, and allows the taxation of costs. The Rule also permits the federal court to enter judgment as to one adjudicated claim or the adjudicated rights of one party, and thus permit an immediate appeal from that otherwise incomplete judgment.

RULE 54(a). DEFINITION AND FORM OF "JUDGMENT"

CORE CONCEPT

A judgment is any appealable decree or order.

APPLICATIONS

Definition

To be a "judgment" within the meaning of Rule 54(a), the court's order or decree must be a ruling from which an appeal can be taken.[1] Ordinarily, this requires "some clear and unequivocal

---

1. *See Brown v. Local 58, Int'l Bhd. of Elec. Workers, AFL–CIO,* 76 F.3d 762, 767 (6th Cir.1996)(whether order is a "judgment" is determined by whether an appeal could be taken from the order); *Maristuen v. National States Ins. Co.,* 57 F.3d 673, 679 (8th Cir.1995) (judgment defined to include any decree or order from which an appeal lies); *National Basketball Ass'n v. Minnesota Professional Basketball, Ltd. P'ship,* 56

manifestation" by the district court that, at least as far as that court is concerned, the case is closed.[2] A ruling that partially adjudicates a claim or is an otherwise non-final order will not usually qualify as a judgment.[3]

Appears Alone

To avoid confusion and uncertainty about what is (and is not) a "judgment", it should appear alone. It should not include recitals of the pleadings, a report from a master, or a record of prior proceedings.[4] It should, instead, be set forth in a separate document containing nothing of substance other than the judgment.[5]

RULE 54(b). JUDGMENT ON MULTIPLE CLAIMS OR INVOLVING MULTIPLE PARTIES

CORE CONCEPT

A judgment entered as to fewer than all claims or all parties in a lawsuit is not immediately appealable. Instead, the appeal must generally await the entry of judgment as to all remaining claims and parties. However, the district court can make a final adjudication of such claims or parties "final", and thus immediately appealable, by expressly determining that no just cause exists to delay the appeal and by directing the entry of judgment.

APPLICATIONS

Purpose

Separate, piecemeal appeals during a single litigation are often inefficient and uneconomical, and thus are contrary to the historic federal policy favoring one appeal on all issues at the conclusion of the lawsuit.[6] Rule 54(b) determinations allowing immediate appeal

F.3d 866, 872 (8th Cir.1995)(definition of judgment encompasses interlocutory orders appealable as of right, such as preliminary injunction rulings); *Balla v. Idaho State Bd. of Corrections*, 869 F.2d 461, 466 (9th Cir.1989)(noting that Rule 54 encompasses final judgments and appealable interlocutory orders). *See also United States v. Haynes*, 158 F.3d 1327, 1329 (D.C.Cir.1998) (holding that order denying Rule 60(b) motion is a "judgment" under Rule 54(a)).

2. *See Diaz–Reyes v. Fuentes–Ortiz*, 471 F.3d 299, 301 (1st Cir. 2006).

3. *See Dishman v. UNUM Life Ins. Co. of America*, 269 F.3d 974, 990–91 (9th Cir. 2001) (holding that post-judgment interest does not begin to accrue when district court enters a partial or non-final judgment because the ruling doesn't qualify under Rule 54(a)); *Resolution Trust Corp. v. O'Bear, Overholser, Smith & Huffer*, 886 F.Supp. 658, 671 n. 11 (N.D. Ind. 1995) (summary

judgment granted as to less than entire claim is not a "judgment" but merely a partial, pretrial adjudication of certain issues). *But cf.* Rule 54(b); *infra* Authors' Commentary to Rule 54(b) (a judgment that fully adjudicates one distinct part of a lawsuit may qualify as an immediately-appealable judgment, even though the remainder of the lawsuit continues).

4. *See* Rule 54(a).

5. *See* Rule 58(a); *infra* Authors' Commentary to Rule 58(a).

6. *See Reiter v. Cooper*, 507 U.S. 258, 263, 113 S.Ct. 1213, 1217, 122 L.Ed.2d 604 (1993); *Curtiss-Wright Corp. v. General Elec. Co.*, 446 U.S. 1, 8, 100 S.Ct. 1460, 1464–65, 64 L.Ed.2d 1 (1980). *Cf. Williams v. County of Westchester*, 171 F.3d 98, 102 (2d Cir.1999) (holding that interlocutory orders are, by their nature, subject to modification or adjustment by the trial court prior

permit exceptions from this general policy for those infrequent instances where awaiting a final judgment would be unduly harsh or unjust.[7]

"Certification" Nomenclature

Often in the case law, the Rule 54(b) determination procedure is described as a "certification". One court of appeals has counseled against this nomenclature as a "misnomer born of confusion".[8] The term "certification" is also used to describe the procedure for seeking immediate appellate review of interlocutory orders under 28 U.S.C. § 1292(b). Conversely, a Rule 54(b) determination, if granted, effectively severs what becomes a *final* judgment (albeit as to one or more but fewer than all claims or parties) from the remaining claims and parties in the case.[9]

Prerequisites to Rule 54(b) Judgments

In evaluating whether to grant a Rule 54(b) determination, the district courts function somewhat like a "dispatcher".[10] The district courts must decide whether three prerequisites for an immediately appealable partial judgment exist:

- **1: *Multiple Claims or Parties Fully Resolved:*** To be eligible for immediate appeal under Rule 54(b), an adjudication must *either* (a) finally resolve at least one claim or (b) finally resolve the rights and liabilities of at least one party. A claim or a party's interest *must* be adjudicated to finality, such that there is nothing more to do on that claim or for that party but await the conclusion of the remaining portions of the litigation.[11] This limitation is a pivotal one. Rule 54(b) does not alter the normal rules of appellate finality for individual claims, and no appeal may be taken from district

to the entry of a final judgment adjudicating the claims to which they pertain).

7. *See O'Bert ex rel. Estate of O'Bert v. Vargo,* 331 F.3d 29, 40–41 (2d Cir.2003); *Oklahoma Turnpike Auth. v. Bruner,* 259 F.3d 1236, 1241–42 (10th Cir.2001); *In re Southeast Banking Corp.,* 69 F.3d 1539, 1547 (11th Cir.1995); *PYCA Indus. v. Harrison County Waste Water Mgmt. Dist.,* 81 F.3d 1412, 1421 (5th Cir.1996).

8. *See James v. Price Stern Sloan, Inc.,* 283 F.3d 1064, 1067–68 n. 6 (9th Cir.2002).

9. *See James v. Price Stern Sloan, Inc.,* 283 F.3d 1064, 1067–68 n. 6 (9th Cir.2002) ("Referring to a Rule 54(b) severance order as a 'certification' misleadingly brings to mind the kind of rigorous judgment embodied in the section 1292(b) certification process. In reality, issuance of a Rule 54(b) order is a fairly routine act that is reversed only in the rarest instances").

10. *See Curtiss-Wright Corp. v. General Elec. Co.,* 446 U.S. 1, 8, 100 S.Ct. 1460, 1464, 64 L.Ed.2d 1 (1980); *Lloyd Noland*

Found., Inc. v. Tenet Health Care Corp., 483 F.3d 773, 777–78 (11th Cir. 2007); *Berckeley Inv. Group, Ltd. v. Colkitt,* 455 F.3d 195, 202 (3d Cir.2006); *Ultra–Precision Mfg. Ltd. v. Ford Motor Co.,* 338 F.3d 1353, 1357 (Fed.Cir.2003).

11. *See Curtiss-Wright Corp. v. General Elec. Co.,* 446 U.S. 1, 7, 100 S.Ct. 1460, 1464, 64 L.Ed.2d 1 (1980); *In re Air Crash at Belle Harbor, N.Y. on Nov. 12, 2001,* 490 F.3d 99, 108–09 (2d Cir. 2007). *Lloyd Noland Found., Inc. v. Tenet Health Care Corp.,* 483 F.3d 773, 777–78 (11th Cir. 2007). *See Compagnie De Reassurance D'Ile de France v. New England Reinsurance Corp.,* 57 F.3d 56, 69 n. 11 (1st Cir. 1995)(although the "better practice" requires that counterclaims be denied explicitly, court held that where district court's intention to do so was apparent from other rulings, all claims were deemed to be fully adjudicated for Rule 54(b) purposes).

court rulings on any particular claim until the court finally resolves that claim.[12] Thus, for example, if an affirmative defense to a claim otherwise completely adjudicated would still remain for trial, the claim has not been finally resolved and immediate appeal is improper.[13]

- *"Claim Defined":* A "claim" has been defined to include all legal grounds based on closely related facts.[14] Multiple claims exist where each claim is factually separate and independent,[15] where each claim could be enforced separately,[16] where there is more than one potential recovery, or where different types of relief are requested.[17] If, however, only one recovery is possible (even though several legal theories are offered to support that same recovery) or if alternative recoveries either substantially overlap or are mutually exclusive, the partial adjudication of such claims cannot be immediately appealed under Rule 54(b).[18] One test of a claim's separability asks whether that claim so overlaps the claims that remain for trial such that an appeal at the end of the case on the retained claims would compel the court to retrace the same ground it would have addressed had the first claim received a Rule 54(b) determination; if so, then the Rule 54(b) determination should be denied.[19]

12. *See Ultra-Precision Mfg. Ltd. v. Ford Motor Co.*, 338 F.3d 1353, 1357 (Fed. Cir.2003); *Information Resources, Inc. v. Dun & Bradstreet Corp.*, 294 F.3d 447, 451–52 (2d Cir.2002); *In re Lull Corp.*, 52 F.3d 787, 788 (8th Cir.1995). *See also N.W. Enters. Inc. v. City of Houston*, 352 F.3d 162, 179 (5th Cir.2003) (Rule 54(b) judgment improper where district court only authorized appeal of elements of claims, and not entire claims), *modified in part on reh'g on other grounds*, 372 F.3d 333 (5th Cir.2004).

13. *See Waldorf v. Shuta*, 142 F.3d 601, 611 (3d Cir.1998).

14. *See Jordan v. Pugh*, 425 F.3d 820, 827 (10th Cir.2005); *Lowery v. Federal Exp. Corp.*, 426 F.3d 817, 820 (6th Cir.2005); *Greenwell v. Aztar Indiana Gaming Corp.*, 268 F.3d 486, 490 (7th Cir.2001).

15. *See Seatrain Shipbuilding Corp. v. Shell Oil Co.*, 444 U.S. 572, 100 S.Ct. 800, 63 L.Ed.2d 36 (1980); *Advanced Magnetics, Inc. v. Bayfront Partners, Inc.*, 106 F.3d 11, 16 n. 21 (2d Cir.1997). *See Lawyers Title Ins. Corp. v. Dearborn Title Corp.*, 118 F.3d 1157 (7th Cir.1997) (noting that test for "separate claims" is whether the claim at issue so overlaps the claims remaining that any appeal at the end of the case on the remaining claims would require the appel-

late court to cover the same ground addressed on the Rule 54(b) appeal).

16. *See Advanced Magnetics, Inc. v. Bayfront Partners, Inc.*, 106 F.3d 11, 16 n. 21 (2d Cir.1997); *Rieser v. Baltimore & Ohio R.R.*, 224 F.2d 198 (2d Cir.1955). *Cf. General Acquisition, Inc. v. GenCorp., Inc.*, 23 F.3d 1022, 1028 (6th Cir.1994)(if the action seeks to vindicate only one legal right, but merely alleges several elements of damage, only one claim is presented and Rule 54(b) does not apply).

17. *See Advanced Magnetics, Inc. v. Bayfront Partners, Inc.*, 106 F.3d 11, 16 n. 21 (2d Cir.1997); *In re Southeast Banking Corp.*, 69 F.3d 1539, 1547 (11th Cir.1995) (if more than one possible recovery exists or if different sorts of recoveries are sought, the claims are "separately enforceable" under Rule 54(b), even though the claims may arise from a single transaction or occurrence).

18. *See Lloyd Noland Found., Inc. v. Tenet Health Care Corp.*, 483 F.3d 773, 780 (11th Cir. 2007); *Lowery v. Federal Exp. Corp.*, 426 F.3d 817, 820 (6th Cir.2005); *Lottie v. West American Ins. Co.*, 408 F.3d 935, 939 (7th Cir.2005).

19. *See Lottie v. West American Ins. Co.*, 408 F.3d 935, 938–39 (7th Cir.2005). *Accord*

- *Multiple Parties:* As the text of Rule 54(b) makes clear, absent the determination allowed under this rule, the dismissal of one defendant in a multi-defendant case is not immediately appealable.[20] A named, but unserved, defendant will typically not be considered a "party" for the purpose of applying this Rule.[21]

- *2: No Just Cause for Delay:* The district court must state, in clear and unmistakable language, that there is no just cause to delay the appeal of the adjudicated claim or the adjudicated rights and liabilities of a party. This determination ordinarily can be made only where delay in appealing presents some risk of hardship or injustice that would be avoided by an immediate appellate review, where a plaintiff could be prejudiced by a delay in recovering a monetary judgment, or where an expensive, duplicative trial could be avoided by reviewing a dismissed claim promptly before the remaining claims reach trial.[22] Whether "just cause" exists is a determination made on a case-by-case basis.[23] Certain criteria guide the court's consideration:

  - The relationship between adjudicated and unadjudicated claims;

  - The possibility that the need for appellate review might be mooted by future developments in the district court;

  - The possibility that the district court might be obligated to consider the same issue on a later occasion;

  - The presence (or absence) of a claim or counterclaim that could result in a set-off against the judgment now sought to be made final and appealed; and

  - Other factors, including delay, economic and solvency concerns, shortening of trial time, frivolity of competing claims, and expense.[24]

  Thus, for example, a Rule 54(b) determination may be proper where, among other factors, the appellate resolution

Jordan v. Pugh, 425 F.3d 820, 827 (10th Cir.2005).

20. *See Morton Int'l, Inc. v. A.E. Staley Mfg. Co.*, 460 F.3d 470 (3d Cir.2006).

21. *See Cambridge Holdings Group, Inc. v. Federal Ins. Co.*, 489 F.3d 1356, 1360–61 (D.C.Cir. 2007); *Raiser v. Utah County*, 409 F.3d 1243, 1245 n.2 (10th Cir. 2005); *Kane Enters. v. MacGregor (USA) Inc.*, 322 F.3d 371, 374 n.1 (5th Cir.2003); *Gomez v. Gov't of V.I.*, 882 F.2d 733, 736 (3d Cir.1989); *Young v. Mount Hawley Ins. Co.*, 864 F.2d 81, 83 (8th Cir.1988); *Insinga v. LaBella*, 817 F.2d 1469, 1470 (11th Cir. 1987); *Leonhard v. United States*, 633 F.2d 599, 608 (2d Cir.1980).

22. *See Advanced Magnetics, Inc. v. Bayfront Partners, Inc.*, 106 F.3d 11, 16 (2d Cir.1997).

23. *See Sears, Roebuck & Co. v. Mackey*, 351 U.S. 427, 76 S.Ct. 895, 100 L.Ed. 1297 (1956). *See also Doe v. City of Chicago*, 360 F.3d 667, 673 (7th Cir.2004) (ruling that there was "just reason for delay" and, thus, Rule 54(b) relief was not available, where factual development of certain claim was necessary).

24. *See Lowery v. Federal Exp. Corp.*, 426 F.3d 817, 821–22 (6th Cir.2005); *Akers v. Alvey*, 338 F.3d 491, 495 (6th Cir.2003); *Waldorf v. Shuta*, 142 F.3d 601, 609 (3d Cir.1998).

could facilitate a global settlement.[25] Conversely, a Rule 54(b) determination is likely to be improper where the litigation itself, and the contested claim resolution, is routine and would inevitably return to the trial court on essentially the same set of facts.[26]

● *3: Entry of Judgment:* In clear and unmistakable language, the district court must also direct that judgment is entered as to that one claim or one party.[27]

Use of "Magic Language"

There is some authority for the proposition that the district court need not expressly incant the phrase "no just reason for delay" in order to permit a Rule 54(b) appeal, so long as the trial judge's intent to proceed under Rule 54(b) is unmistakably clear from the order and/or the record.[28] But this view is not universal.[29]

> *Abandoned Claims*: A district court's judgment that resolves some open claims, but leaves others unaddressed, may still be deemed to be final (even without the inclusion of the "magic language"), if the court had fairly concluded that the unaddressed claims were abandoned and did not need to be addressed further.[30]

Explanation by the District Court

In its order entering a Rule 54(b) judgment, the district court must clearly and cogently explain why it has concluded that an immediate appellate review of the order is advisable,[31] or those

25. *See Lowery v. Federal Exp. Corp.*, 426 F.3d 817, 828 (6th Cir.2005).

26. *See Wood v. GCC Bend, LLC*, 422 F.3d 873, 878 (9th Cir.2005). *See also Credit Francais Int'l, S.A. v. Bio–Vita, Ltd.*, 78 F.3d 698, 707 (1st Cir.1996) (early appeal is particularly suspect when the appellants remain litigants before the trial court).

27. *Blackman v. District of Columbia*, 456 F.3d 167, 175-76 (D.C.Cir.2006) (must be an express direction for entry of judgment); *Berckeley Inv. Group, Ltd. v. Colkitt*, 455 F.3d 195, 202 (3d Cir.2006) (must be a final judgment on the merits); *Jordan v. Pugh*, 425 F.3d 820, 826 (10th Cir.2005) (must be a final decision on at least one claim); *Wood v. GCC Bend, LLC*, 422 F.3d 873, 878 (9th Cir.2005) (must render a final judgment).

28. *See Carringer v. Tessmer*, 253 F.3d 1322, 1324 n.1 (11th Cir.2001); *Briargrove Shopping Ctr. Joint Venture v. Pilgrim Enters., Inc.*, 170 F.3d 536, 539 (5th Cir.1999). *But cf. Berckeley Inv. Group, Ltd. v. Colkitt*, 259 F.3d 135, 141–42 (3d Cir.2001). *See also Downie v. City of Middleburg Heights*, 301

F.3d 688, 693 (6th Cir.2002) (district court need not enter partial final judgment in its certification, but it must recognize that such a partial final judgment has been entered).

29. *See Blackman v. District of Columbia*, 456 F.3d 167, 175-76 (D.C.Cir.2006) (trial court must make *express* determination that there is no just reason for delay and *express* direction for the entry of judgment; absent such statements, Rule 54(b) treatment must be reversed on appeal).

30. *See DIRECTV, Inc. v. Budden*, 420 F.3d 521 (5th Cir.2005).

31. *See Lowery v. Federal Exp. Corp.*, 426 F.3d 817, 821–22 (6th Cir.2005) (trial court must "spell out its reasons"); *Stockman's Water Co., LLC v. Vaca Partners, L.P.*, 425 F.3d 1263, 1265 (10th Cir.2005) (trial court must "clearly articulate" its reasons and "make careful statements based on the record"); *O'Bert ex rel. Estate of O'Bert v. Vargo*, 331 F.3d 29, 42 (2d Cir.2003) (court ordinarily must offer reasoned, yet brief, explanation); *Federal Home Loan Mortgage Corp. v. Scottsdale*

reasons must be readily apparent from the record.[32] The district court should not simply reprint, in boilerplate, the formula of the Rule.[33] The court of appeals may, in the absence of such a written explanation, dismiss the appeal as inappropriately allowed under Rule 54(b).[34] Although dismissal of the appeal is permitted (and perhaps even likely) without a corresponding explanation from the trial court, dismissal is not compulsory; the failure to offer a written explanation is *not* a jurisdictional defect that *compels* the appeal's dismissal.[35]

Duty of Counsel in Explanation Requirement

In moving for a Rule 54(b) determination, the courts expect counsel, as officers of the court and advocates for an immediate appeal, to assist the district court by making appropriate submissions that express the reasons for and basis of a Rule 54(b) determination.[36]

Burden of Proof

The moving party bears the burden of establishing that a partial judgment should be entered under Rule 54(b).[37]

Discretion of District Judge

The court is not *required* to enter a final judgment in an action involving multiple parties where the court resolves claims involving

---

Ins. Co., 316 F.3d 431, 440 (3d Cir.2003) (court should clearly articulate reasons and factors underlying decision to permit Rule 54(b) appeal).

32. *See Mercado v. Ritz–Carlton San Juan Hotel, Spa & Casino*, 410 F.3d 41, 45 & 45 n.5 (1st Cir.2005) (although "not condon[ing]" absence of explicit facts and reasoning justifying determination, court finds circumstances plainly support appeal from partial judgment); *O'Bert ex rel. Estate of O'Bert v. Vargo*, 331 F.3d 29, 41 (2d Cir. 2003) (noting that courts, on "rare occasions", have excused full explanations where reasons for Rule 54(b) entry were obvious and remand would only unnecessarily delay appeal process); *Cooper Power Sys., Inc. v. Union Carbide Chemicals & Plastics Co.*, 123 F.3d 675, 679 n. 1 (7th Cir.1997) (commenting that court failed to set forth explicitly its reasons for certification, but those reasons were apparent from record which incorporated rationale of litigant's motion for Rule 54(b) order).

33. *See Akers v. Alvey*, 338 F.3d 491, 495 (6th Cir.2003); *O'Bert ex rel. Estate of O'Bert v. Vargo*, 331 F.3d 29, 41 (2d Cir. 2003); *Federal Home Loan Mortgage Corp. v. Scottsdale Ins. Co.*, 316 F.3d 431, 440 (3d Cir.2003).

34. *See Smith ex rel. Smith v. Half Hollow Hills Cent. Sch. Dist.*, 298 F.3d 168, 171

(2d Cir.2002) (dismissing appeal, ruling that district courts must not "merely repeat the formulaic language" of Rule 54(b), but must offer "a brief, reasoned explanation" for the decision to allow an immediate appeal); *Advanced Magnetics, Inc. v. Bayfront Partners, Inc.*, 106 F.3d 11, 16 n. 21 (2d Cir.1997) (holding that trial court's failure to offer appropriate explanation is basis for dismissal).

35. *See Carter v. City of Philadelphia*, 181 F.3d 339 (3d Cir.1999) (not jurisdictional). *See also Smith ex rel. Smith v. Half Hollow Hills Cent. Sch. Dist.*, 298 F.3d 168, 171 (2d Cir.2002) (noting that, under rare certain circumstances, the reason for certification may be sufficiently obvious that no explanation is required and the court of appeals is able to provide meaningful review without an explanation from the trial judge of why certification was deemed appropriate).

36. *See Federal Home Loan Mortgage Corp. v. Scottsdale Ins. Co.*, 316 F.3d 431, 441–42 (3d Cir.2003)

37. *See Braswell Shipyards, Inc. v. Beazer East, Inc.*, 2 F.3d 1331, 1335 (4th Cir.1993); *Anthuis v. Colt Indus. Operating Corp.*, 971 F.2d 999, 1003 (3d Cir.1992).

less than all parties or less than all claims.[38] To the contrary, whether to enter a judgment under Rule 54(b) is reserved for the sound discretion of the district judge.[39] Indeed, such judgments are contrary to the historic federal policy against piecemeal appeals, particularly during a period when the courts of appeals' caseload has grown faster than any other segment of the federal bench.[40] For this reason, Rule 54(b) orders are not granted routinely,[41] or merely with the hope of avoiding a trial,[42] or as an accommodation to counsel.[43] Instead, the district court must carefully balance the needs of the parties for an immediate appeal against the interest of efficient management of the litigation.[44]

Determination by Trial Judge Is *Not* Conclusive on Court of Appeals

That the district judge allowed a ruling for an immediate appeal under Rule 54(b) is not wholly dispositive. The courts of appeals will still review the matter to ensure that the trial judge allowed a ruling that was eligible for immediate review under the Rule.[45]

Procedure for Obtaining Rule 54(b) Determination

The Rule sets no defined procedure for obtaining a determination under Rule 54(b). The district court may grant such a determi-

---

38. *See generally Ruiz v. Blentech Corp.,* 89 F.3d 320, 323 (7th Cir.1996) (court has two options in placing into final form individual orders in multi-party cases: Rule 54(b) finality order or final order disposing of all claims respecting all parties).

39. *See Curtiss–Wright Corp. v. General Elec. Co.,* 446 U.S. 1, 100 S.Ct. 1460, 64 L.Ed.2d 1 (1980). *See also Sears, Roebuck & Co. v. Mackey,* 351 U.S. 427, 437, 76 S.Ct. 895, 900, 100 L.Ed. 1297 (1956)(noting that discretion lies primarily with the district court "as the one most likely to be familiar with the case and with any justifiable reasons for delay"); *Wood v. GCC Bend, LLC,* 422 F.3d 873, 878 (9th Cir.2005); *Akers v. Alvey,* 338 F.3d 491, 495 (6th Cir.2003); *Federal Home Loan Mortgage Corp. v. Scottsdale Ins. Co.,* 316 F.3d 431, 440 (3d Cir.2003).

40. *See In re Southeast Banking Corp.,* 69 F.3d 1539, 1548 (11th Cir.1995). *See also Reiter v. Cooper,* 507 U.S. 258, 263, 113 S.Ct. 1213, 1218, 122 L.Ed.2d 604 (1993); *Curtiss-Wright Corp. v. General Elec. Co.,* 446 U.S. 1, 8, 100 S.Ct. 1460, 1465, 64 L.Ed.2d 1 (1980); *Soliday v. Miami County,* 55 F.3d 1158, 1163 (6th Cir.1995) (reiterating that Rule 54(b) does not permit the piecemeal review of claims, nor should it be used indiscriminately).

41. *See Curtiss–Wright Corp. v. General Elec. Co.,* 446 U.S. 1, 10, 100 S.Ct. 1460, 1466, 64 L.Ed.2d 1 (1980)(writing that

sound judicial administration does not require that Rule 54(b) requests be granted routinely). *See also Guerrero v. J.W. Hutton, Inc.,* 458 F.3d 830 (8th Cir.2006); *O'Bert ex rel. Estate of O'Bert v. Vargo,* 331 F.3d 29, 40–41 (2d Cir.2003).

42. *See Credit Francais Int'l, S.A. v. Bio–Vita, Ltd.,* 78 F.3d 698, 706 (1st Cir. 1996)(possibility of avoiding a trial is "rarely, if ever, a self-sufficient basis for a Rule 54(b) certification").

43. *See also Guerrero v. J.W. Hutton, Inc.,* 458 F.3d 830 (8th Cir.2006); *Braswell Shipyards, Inc. v. Beazer East, Inc.,* 2 F.3d 1331, 1335 (4th Cir.1993).

44. *See L.B. Foster Co. v. America Piles, Inc.,* 138 F.3d 81, 86 (2d Cir.1998) (certification should be reserved for "the infrequent harsh case" where danger exists for hardship or injustice through delay, which could be alleviated by immediate appeal); *PYCA Indus. v. Harrison County Waste Water Mgmt. Dist.,* 81 F.3d 1412, 1421 (5th Cir.1996)(certification should be granted only where some danger of hardship or injustice through delay exists); *General Acquisition, Inc. v. GenCorp., Inc.,* 23 F.3d 1022, 1027 (6th Cir.1994).

45. *See Schudel v. General Elec. Co.,* 120 F.3d 991, 994 (9th Cir.1997); *Ebrahimi v. City of Huntsville Bd. of Educ.,* 114 F.3d 162, 166 (11th Cir.1997).

nation *sua sponte* to accompany the order at issue. Alternatively, the parties may separately move the district court under Rule 54(b) to grant a determination. The time for making such a motion is not specified in the Rule. Prudent practitioners will seek a Rule 54(b) determination promptly, and within the familiar 10–day period allotted for alterations or amendments to "judgments". Although Rule 54(b) motions are technically not motions seeking Rule 59 or Rule 60 relief (and, thus, might not fall within the ambit of the 10–day limit), this type of prompt action is consistent with the moving party's claim that the order qualifies as an immediate "judgment" under the Rule and comports with the Rule 54(b) objective of permitting some piecemeal appeals where delay would be unduly harsh or unjust.[46] If an appeal is taken prior to the district court's determination under Rule 54(b), most Circuits have ruled that the belated determination will "ripen" an otherwise improper appeal, so long as the determination issues prior to the date the court of appeals considers the appeal.[47]

Effect of Rule 54(b) Judgments

Once a Rule 54(b) judgment is entered, the time for appeal on that judgment begins to run,[48] as does post-judgment interest.[49] Note, however, that some courts have ruled that the time for appeal following a Rule 54(b) determination can begin to run even earlier, before entry on the docket–on the date the order granting Rule 54(b) relief was signed and mailed to the parties.[50] Accordingly, prudent counsel should file their appeal promptly after the Rule 54(b) order is served.

Effect of Dismissals Without Rule 54(b) Judgment

Unless the court enters a separate judgment under Rule 54(b), litigants in a multi-party case who are dismissed may technically remain in the case until the final resolution of all claims as to all parties. Dismissed litigants are, however, entitled to rely on the dismissal until notified that they have been rejoined as parties. Thus, until notified otherwise, dismissed litigants need not participate in discovery, in pretrial proceedings, or in the trial itself.[51]

---

46. There does not appear to be published case law resolving this issue, a factor that all the more urgently counsels in favor of prompt action by the moving party.

47. *See, e.g., Barrett ex rel. Estate of Barrett v. United States,* 462 F.3d 28, 34–35 (1st Cir. 2006); *United States v. Brown,* 348 F.3d 1200, 1206 (10th Cir.2003); *Lewis v. B.F. Goodrich Co.,* 850 F.2d 641 (10th Cir. 1988); *Tidler v. Eli Lilly & Co.,* 824 F.2d 84, 85–87 (D.C. Cir.1987) (per curiam).

48. *See FDIC v. Tripati,* 769 F.2d 507 (8th Cir.1985).

49. *See* 28 U.S.C.A. § 1961; *Hooks v. Washington Sheraton Corp.,* 642 F.2d 614 (D.C.Cir.1980).

50. *See Silivanch v. Celebrity Cruises, Inc.,* 333 F.3d 355, 364–65 (2d Cir.2003) (commenting that "[t]here is no requirement that such a certification be docketed in order for it to become effective", and thus the order became effective, and the appeal period began to run, when the order "was signed and mailed to the parties"). *But cf. Brown v. Mississippi Valley State Univ.,* 311 F.3d 328, 331–32 (5th Cir.2002) (noting that, for purposes of Rule 4 of the Federal Rules of Appellate Procedure 4, judgment becomes final on the date Rule 54(b) determination is entered).

Scope of "Determination"

On appeal following a Rule 54(b) determination, the court of appeals will confine its review only to those specific rulings for which determination was granted. All other rulings by the district court will not be examined during the interlocutory appeal.[52]

No "Tag–Along" Partial Appeals

A decision to permit an immediate appeal of one part of a litigation is not, by itself, sufficient justification to grant Rule 54(b) relief for another part.[53]

Appealability of Denials of Rule 54(b) Requests

Allowing immediate appellate review of "partial" final judgments is a practice that departs from the federal courts' traditional opposition to piecemeal appeals. Rule 54(b), thus, represents an unusual exception to this settled policy. Predictably, the courts reject attempts to immediately challenge denials of Rule 54(b) determinations as premature and unappealable until a final ruling is entered on the merits.[54]

Sua Sponte Review on Appeal

Even if the appealing litigants do not challenge a Rule 54(b) determination, the court of appeals lacks appellate jurisdiction if the determination was improper; consequently, the appeals court will consider the propriety of a Rule 54(b) determination *sua sponte*.[55]

Adversary Proceedings in Bankruptcy Require Determination

The majority view holds that litigants who lose and then seek to immediately appeal from an adversary proceeding ruling in bankruptcy are required to obtain a Rule 54(b) determination from the trial court in order to press the appeal.[56]

Rule 54(b) and Tax Court Rulings

Although there is some division of authority on the point, recent case law supports the application of Rule 54(b) procedures to partial rulings by the United States Tax Court.[57]

---

51. *See Bennett v. Pippin*, 74 F.3d 578, 587 (5th Cir.1996).

52. *See Monsanto Co. v. McFarling*, 363 F.3d 1336, 1343 n.1 (Fed.Cir.2004); *New Castle County v. Hartford Accident & Indemnity Co.*, 933 F.2d 1162, 1178 n. 33 (3d Cir.1991).

53. *See O'Bert ex rel. Estate of O'Bert v. Vargo*, 331 F.3d 29, 43 (2d Cir.2003).

54. *See United Indus. v. Eimco Process Equip. Co.*, 61 F.3d 445, 448 (5th Cir.1995).

55. *See Lowery v. Federal Exp. Corp.*, 426 F.3d 817, 820 (6th Cir.2005).

56. *See In re Boca Arena, Inc.*, 184 F.3d 1285 (11th Cir.1999).

57. *See New York Football Giants, Inc. v. C.I.R.*, 349 F.3d 102, 106–07 (3d Cir. 2003) (so holding, and surveying division among Circuits).

RULE 54(c).   DEMAND FOR JUDGMENT; RELIEF TO BE GRANTED

CORE CONCEPT

The district court generally must grant all the relief to which the prevailing party is entitled, whether or not such relief was requested in the pleadings. Pleadings serve as "guides" to the nature of the case, but the lawsuit is ultimately measured by what is pleaded and proven, not merely by what was demanded.[58]   In default judgments, however, the district court may not award relief beyond that sought in the complaint.

APPLICATIONS

Default Judgments

Because a non-appearing defendant may be relying on the demand (or WHEREFORE) clause contained in the complaint, a plaintiff may not receive a default judgment for more than the amount sought in the complaint.[59]

Non-default Judgments

Where the defendant has answered or otherwise appeared to defend the lawsuit, a plaintiff may receive a judgment for an amount greater or less than that sought in the complaint,[60] and containing types of relief not mentioned in the complaint's demand clause.[61]   It is the court's duty to grant generally all appropriate relief.[62]

Limitations on Awarding Relief Beyond What Was Demanded

Although the court is entitled to award all relief to which a party is entitled, even if not demanded in the pleadings, this entitlement is not unbounded. It does not license the federal courts with untethered roaming authority, permitting them generally to provide a remedy for all wrongs.[63] The rule is designed to protect a pleader against clumsy drafting and prevent, through a mere technical misstep, depriving the pleader of a deserved recovery; it is not, however, meant to allow the pleader to recover on claims never alleged.[64] Thus, a party may not recover on issues not presented to

58. *See Minyard Enters. v. Southeastern Chem. & Solvent Co.*, 184 F.3d 373 (4th Cir.1999); *Baker v. John Morrell & Co.*, 266 F.Supp.2d 909, 929 (N.D.Iowa 2003).

59. *See Scala v. Moore McCormack Lines, Inc.*, 985 F.2d 680, 683 (2d Cir.1993); *Appleton Elec. Co. v. Graves Truck Line*, 635 F.2d 603 (7th Cir.1980).

60. *See Avitia v. Metropolitan Club of Chicago, Inc.*, 49 F.3d 1219, 1229 (7th Cir. 1995)(holding that, except for "special damages" under Rule 9(g), plaintiffs are not obligated to itemize their damages in their complaints); *Stineman v. Fontbonne College,* 664 F.2d 1082 (8th Cir.1981).

61. *See Holt Civic Club v. Tuscaloosa*, 439 U.S. 60, 65–66, 99 S.Ct. 383, 387–388, 58 L.Ed.2d 292 (1978) (writing that federal courts should not dismiss meritorious constitutional claims because the pleadings specify one remedy, rather than another, appropriate one). *See also People for Ethical Treatment of Animals, Inc. v. Gittens*, 396 F.3d 416, 420–21 (D.C.Cir.2005); *In re Bennett*, 298 F.3d 1059, 1069–70 (9th Cir.2002).

62. *See Felce v. Fiedler*, 974 F.2d 1484, 1501 (7th Cir.1992)(noting that Rule 54(c) is to be liberally construed so that there is no doubt but that the court must grant whatever relief is appropriate). *See Feldman v. Philadelphia Housing Auth.*, 43 F.3d 823, 832 (3d Cir.1994)(commenting that nature of relief is "determined by the merits of the case, not by the pleadings").

63. *See Knight v. Alabama*, 476 F.3d 1219, 1229 n.19 (11th Cir. 2007)

64. *See USX Corp. v. Barnhart*, 395 F.3d 161, 165 (3d Cir.2004).

and not actually litigated before the factfinder, nor may the party recover relief which has been lost due to failures in the pleadings or failure in proof.[65] Nor may a litigant obtain relief from a particular defendant unless relief of some kind has first been sought from that defendant,[66] or where the award would otherwise be unfairly prejudicial or unjust.[67] (Thus, pleaders usually will not be permitted to manipulatively "cap" their claims in order to achieve some procedural advantage, and then rely on the courts' ability to grant them all "entitled" relief to receive through the backdoor an un-capped remedy.[68]) A remedy that none of the parties desire, however, will not be forced upon them.[69] Moreover, a party will generally be held bound by representations made during a pretrial conference or in a pretrial order that had outlined the claims in the case and the relief requested.[70]

- *Types of Unpleaded Relief Permitted:* Courts have, for example, permitted litigants to recover punitive damages[71] and attorney's fees[72] where those remedies were not expressly sought in the complaints, in appropriate cases.

65. *See Old Republic Ins. Co. v. Employers Reinsurance Corp.*, 144 F.3d 1077, 1080 (7th Cir.1998) (trial court may not award relief upon theory not properly raised at trial); *Gilbane Bldg. Co. v. Federal Reserve Bank*, 80 F.3d 895, 904 (4th Cir. 1996)(alternative relief only permitted where the factfinder has found all factual conclusions necessary to support that relief); *Rodriguez v. Doral Mortgage Corp.*, 57 F.3d 1168, 1173 (1st Cir. 1995)(commenting that the thesis of Rule 54(c) is "hollow at its core", because the Rule creates no entitlement to any relief based on issues not presented to and tried before the factfinder).

66. *See Powell v. National Bd. of Med. Examiners*, 364 F.3d 79, 86 (2d Cir.2004); *NAACP v. United States Sugar Corp.*, 84 F.3d 1432, 1438 (D.C.Cir.1996).

67. *See Powell v. National Bd. of Med. Examiners*, 364 F.3d 79, 86 (2d Cir.2004); *Pinkley, Inc. v. City of Frederick*, 191 F.3d 394, 400 (4th Cir.1999). *See also United Phosphorus, Ltd. v. Midland Fumigant, Inc.*, 205 F.3d 1219, 1235 (10th Cir.2000) (although jury award exceeding relief requested does not invalidate jury's award, remittitur may be necessary to avoid a double recovery).

68. *See Morgan v. Gay*, 471 F.3d 469, 476–77 (3d Cir. 2006) (construing Class Action Fairness Act of 2005 (CAFA), Pub.L. No. 109–2, 119 Stat. 4 (2005) (codified in scattered sections of 28 U.S.C.)), *petition for*

cert. filed, 75 U.S.L.W. 3622 (U.S. May 3, 2007) (No. 06–1471); *De Aguilar v. Boeing Co.*, 47 F.3d 1404, 1410 (5th Cir.1995) (construing removal jurisdiction).

69. *See Minyard Enters. v. Southeastern Chem. & Solvent Co.*, 184 F.3d 373, 386 n. 14 (4th Cir.1999).

70. *See Walker v. Anderson Elec. Connectors*, 944 F.2d 841, 844 (11th Cir. 1991)(limiting plaintiff to the relief demanded at the pretrial conference, and finding no conflict between Rule 54(c) and requirement that plaintiff set forth, at the pretrial conference, all relief sought). *See also Seven Words LLC v. Network Solutions*, 260 F.3d 1089, 1098 (9th Cir.2001) (where damages claim was made years into litigation, after various representations that only declaratory and injunctive relief was sought, after a motion to dismiss, and only days before oral argument on appeal, court joins other courts of appeals in declining to read damages claim into complaint).

71. *See Bowles v. Osmose Utilities Servs., Inc.*, 443 F.3d 671, 675 (8th Cir. 2006); *Griffith Labs. U.S.A., Inc. v. Pomper*, 607 F.Supp. 999, 1001 (S.D.N.Y.1985).

72. *See Sea–Land Serv., Inc. v. Murrey & Son's Co.*, 824 F.2d 740, 745 (9th Cir. 1987); *Black v. O'Haver*, 567 F.2d 361, 370–71 (10th Cir.1977); *Inland Dredging Co. v. Panama City Port Auth.*, 406 F.Supp.2d 1277, 1280 (N.D.Fla.2005).

Prejudgment Interest

If prejudgment interest is authorized under the applicable substantive law, the court will award it even if it has not been expressly demanded in the pleadings.[73]

RULE 54(d).   COSTS AND ATTORNEY'S FEES

CORE CONCEPT

The district court may, in its discretion, award costs to the prevailing party in a lawsuit, unless an express provision regarding costs is made by federal statute or court rule. Prevailing parties have 14 days from entry of judgment to seek attorney's fees and other nontaxable expenses, in cases where such recoveries are permitted.

APPLICATIONS

"Prevailing Party" Defined

A prevailing plaintiff is generally one who succeeds on some significant issue in the litigation and thereby achieves some of the benefit sought in filing the lawsuit.[74] Thus, a prevailing plaintiff is one who obtains relief that materially alters the parties' legal relationship by modifying the behavior of the defendant in a way that directly benefits the plaintiff.[75] A judgment for *any* amount of damages necessarily modifies the defendant's behavior to the plaintiff's benefit, thus a plaintiff who obtains even nominal damages may still become a prevailing party.[76] A litigant need not succeed on all issues to qualify as a prevailing party.[77]

A prevailing defendant is one who defeats the litigation and obtains a denial of relief. Thus, a dismissal, with prejudice and on the merits, of all claims against a defendant will generally make that defendant a prevailing party.[78]

---

73. *See, e.g., Baker v. John Morrell & Co.,* 266 F.Supp.2d 909, 931 n.4 (N.D.Iowa 2003); *J.A. McDonald, Inc. v. Waste Sys. Int'l Moretown Landfill, Inc.,* 247 F.Supp.2d 542, 546 (D.Vt.2002); *Stanford Square, L.L.C. v. Nomura Asset Capital Corp.,* 232 F.Supp.2d 289, 290–91 (S.D.N.Y.2002).

74. *Cf. Texas State Teachers Ass'n v. Garland Independent Sch. Dist.,* 489 U.S. 782, 791–92, 109 S.Ct. 1486, 1493–94, 103 L.Ed.2d 866 (1989)(applying definition in civil rights litigation under 42 U.S.C.A. § 1988); *Hensley v. Eckerhart,* 461 U.S. 424, 433, 103 S.Ct. 1933, 1939, 76 L.Ed.2d 40 (1983)(same); *Andretti v. Borla Performance Indus., Inc.,* 426 F.3d 824, 835 (6th Cir.2005).

75. *See Buckhannon Bd. & Care Home, Inc. v. West Va. Dep't of Health & Human Res,* 532 U.S. 598, 605, 121 S.Ct. 1835, 1840, 149 L.Ed.2d 855 (2001); *Farrar v.*

Hobby, 506 U.S. 103, 111–13, 113 S.Ct. 566, 573, 121 L.Ed.2d 494 (1992); *Dattner v. ConAgra Foods, Inc.,* 458 F.3d 98 (2d Cir. 2006); *Andretti v. Borla Performance Indus., Inc.,* 426 F.3d 824, 835 (6th Cir.2005).

76. *See Farrar v. Hobby,* 506 U.S. 103, 111–13, 113 S.Ct. 566, 573, 121 L.Ed.2d 494 (1992); *Barber v. T.D. Williamson, Inc.,* 254 F.3d 1223, 1234 (10th Cir.2001).

77. *See Kemin Foods, L.C. v. Pigmentos Vegetales Del Centro S.A. de C.V.,* 464 F.3d 1339, 1347 (Fed.Cir. 2006). *See also Fireman's Fund Ins. Co. v. Tropical Shipping & Const. Co.,* 254 F.3d 987, 1012–13 (11th Cir.2001) (noting precedent supporting an award of costs where the prevailing party obtains a judgment "on even a fraction of the claims advanced").

78. *See Power Mosfet Techs, L.L.C. v. Siemens AG,* 378 F.3d 1396 (Fed.Cir.2004) (prevailing party is one who "wins com-

Generally, there are no prevailing parties if the case is dismissed for lack of jurisdiction[79] or *forum non conveniens.*[80]

A litigation who is deemed a "prevailing party" for purposes of awarding attorney's fees is likewise a "prevailing party" for purposes of taxing costs.[81]

Against Whom May Costs Be Taxed

Under Rule 54(d), costs may be taxed only against the non-prevailing party; costs may not be taxed under this Rule against counsel for a litigant.[82]

Types of Taxable Costs

The types of costs that can be taxed in favor of the prevailing party in a federal litigation are set by statute.[83]   These costs include:

1. Clerk and U.S. Marshal fees;[84]

2. Deposition expenses, when the transcript is received in evidence or was otherwise reasonably necessary for the trial[85] (conversely, transcripts taken solely for discovery, or of witnesses who are withdrawn or precluded, are likely not taxable[86]); allowable deposition expenses may include costs for videotape depositions; [87]

3. Printing fees;

pletely on every claim at issue", and thus party who "had all claims against it dismissed with prejudice" so qualifies); *Weaver v. Toombs*, 948 F.2d 1004 (6th Cir.1991)(a dismissal, whether on the merits or not, defines the defendant as the prevailing party).

79. *See Miles v. California*, 320 F.3d 986, 988 (9th Cir.2003).

80. *See Dattner v. ConAgra Foods, Inc.*, 458 F.3d 98 (2d Cir.2006).

81. *See Dattner v. ConAgra Foods, Inc.*, 458 F.3d 98 (2d Cir.2006); *Tunison v. Continental Airlines Corp.*, 162 F.3d 1187, 1189–90 (D.C.Cir.1998); *Manildra Milling Corp. v. Ogilvie Mills, Inc.*, 76 F.3d 1178, 1180 n. 1 (Fed.Cir.1996).

82. *See In re Cardizem CD Antitrust Litig.*, 481 F.3d 355, 359–60 (6th Cir. 2007); *Wilder v. GL Bus Lines*, 258 F.3d 126, 127–31 (2d Cir.2001).

83. *See* 28 U.S.C.A. § 1920. *See also* 28 U.S.C.A. §§ 1911–31 (defining costs provisions generally). In addition, the Rules allow costs to be taxed in other instances: when an attorney violates Rule 11, conducts discovery improperly in violation of Rule 37, or rejects unwisely an offer of settlement under Rule 68.

84. *See Winniczek v. Nagelberg*, 400 F.3d 503, 504–05 (7th Cir.2005) (allowing docketing fee to be taxed).

85. *See Smith v. Tenet Healthsys. SL, Inc.*, 436 F.3d 879, 889–90 (8th Cir.2006); *Summit Tech., Inc. v. Nidek Co.*, 435 F.3d 1371, 1378–80 (Fed.Cir.2006); *Mitchell v. City of Moore, Oklahoma*, 218 F.3d 1190 (10th Cir.2000). *See also Virginia Panel Corp. v. Mac Panel Co.*, 887 F.Supp. 880, 886 (W.D.Va.1995)(cost of daily copies of trial transcripts is recoverable if daily copy is "indispensable", and not a convenience for counsel).

86. *See Marmo v. Tyson Fresh Meats, Inc.*, 457 F.3d 748 (8th Cir.2006).

87. *See BDT Prods., Inc. v. Lexmark Int'l, Inc.*, 405 F.3d 415, 419–20 (6th Cir. 2005); *Tilton v. Capital Cities/ABC, Inc.*, 115 F.3d 1471, 1477–79 (10th Cir.1997); *Garonzik v. Whitman Diner*, 910 F.Supp. 167, 170–71 (D.N.J.1995)(allowing recovery of recording and playback costs for videotape depositions). *But cf. Cherry v. Champion Int'l Corp.*, 186 F.3d 442 (4th Cir.1999) (although costs of video depositions may be taxed, prevailing party must make a showing why *both* the transcript and the video deposition were "necessary").

4. Witness fees and witnesses' travel and subsistence expenses, where the witnesses' testimony was material, relevant, and reasonably necessary to the case; [88]

5a. Fees to "exemplify" documents (which may include reimbursement for many methods of illustration, including models, charts, graphs, and sometimes even computerized presentation systems[89]);

5b. Fees to print copies of papers necessary for use in the case[90] (which may, in appropriate circumstances, include the electronic scanning and imaging of documents[91]); although courts may not obligate parties to track copies with page-by-page precision, the bill of costs must show a calculation that is reasonably accurate under the circumstances.[92]

6. Certain docket fees;[93] and

7. Fees for court-appointed experts and interpreters.[94]

Types of Costs That Will Not Be Taxed

The district court may not tax costs under Rule 54(d) that are not authorized by statute or court rule.[95] Thus, in the absence of an

88. See Marmo v. Tyson Fresh Meats, Inc., 457 F.3d 748 (8th Cir.2006); Rank v. Balshy, 590 F.Supp. 787 (M.D.Pa.1984).

89. See Cefalu v. Village of Elk Grove, 211 F.3d 416, 427–28 (7th Cir.2000) (affirming reimbursement for cost of computerized, multi-media system used to present exhibits to jury). But cf. Kohus v. Toys R US, Inc., 282 F.3d 1355, 1357–61 (Fed.Cir. 2002) (reversing award of $12,950 for video model/animation as unauthorized under federal law); Arcadian Fertilizer, L.P. v. MPW Indus. Services, Inc., 249 F.3d 1293, 1297 (11th Cir.2001) (refusing reimbursement for videotape exhibits and computer animation, since they are not "copies of paper" or "exemplifications").

90. See BDT Prods., Inc. v. Lexmark Int'l, Inc., 405 F.3d 415, 419–20 (6th Cir. 2005); Concord Boat Corp. v. Brunswick Corp., 309 F.3d 494, 497–98 (8th Cir.2002), mandate amended, 318 F.3d 1156 (8th Cir. 2003) (allowing costs for photocopies "necessarily obtained for use in the case"); Cengr v. Fusibond Piping Sys., Inc., 135 F.3d 445, 455 (7th Cir.1998) (rejecting party's objection to $12.60 copying as "border[ing] on dopiness"); Jones v. Unisys Corp., 54 F.3d 624, 633 (10th Cir.1995)(fees for copies of papers "necessarily obtained for use in the case").

91. See BDT Prods., Inc. v. Lexmark Int'l, Inc., 405 F.3d 415, 420 (6th Cir.2005)

92. See Summit Tech., Inc. v. Nidek Co., 435 F.3d 1371, 1378–80 (Fed.Cir.2006).

93. See BDT Prods., Inc. v. Lexmark Int'l, Inc., 405 F.3d 415, 419–20 (6th Cir. 2005).

94. See BDT Prods., Inc. v. Lexmark Int'l, Inc., 405 F.3d 415, 419 (6th Cir.2005) (taxing translator fees). Guardians ad litem may be taxed as costs. See Gaddis v. United States, 381 F.3d 444 (5th Cir.2004) (court may award guardian ad litem fees as court costs, even against government); Kollsman, a Div. of Sequa Corp. v. Cohen, 996 F.2d 702 (4th Cir.1993)(noting that such costs may be taxed); Hull v. United States, 971 F.2d 1499 (10th Cir. 1992)(noting that taxing guardian ad litem expenses depends on role of guardian). Fees and expenses to a Special Master are also recoverable costs. See also Hook v. Arizona, 907 F.Supp. 1326, 1339 (D.Ariz. 1995), aff'd, 73 F.3d 369 (9th Cir. 1995)(Table).

95. See Arlington Cent. Sch. Bd. of Educ. v. Murphy, ___ U.S. ___, ___, 126 S.Ct. 2455, 2461–62, 165 L.Ed.2d 526 (2006); Mathews v. Crosby, 480 F.3d 1265, 1276 (11th Cir. 2007); In re Cardizem CD Antitrust Litig., 481 F.3d 355, 359 (6th Cir. 2007); United States v. Bevilacqua, 447 F.3d 124, 128 (1st Cir.2006).

express legal authority otherwise, courts generally may *not* tax as costs the fees and expenses of expert witnesses (beyond the modest travel and subsistence expenses noted above for witnesses generally);[96] computer-assisted legal research;[97] trial consultants who prepared computer animations, videos, powerpoint slides, and graphic illustrations;[98] postage, overnight courier, and similar messenger or delivery services;[99] telephone calls;[100] facsimile transmissions;[101] paralegals;[102] travel, lodging, transportation, and parking;[103] mediation;[104] or post-trial / pre-appeal costs (like supersedeas bond premiums).[105]

Attorney's Fees as Costs

In the absence of a federal statute to the contrary, attorney's fees may not be taxed as costs beyond the modest provisions set forth in 28 U.S.C.A. § 1923.[106]

Exception: Attorney's fees, however, may be taxed against a common fund generated in a class action or shareholders' derivative action.[107] Attorney's fees may also be taxed where a party instituted, defended, or conducted litigation in bad faith.[108]

Diversity Jurisdiction Cases

Federal law governs the taxation of costs in the district courts, even where the district court's jurisdiction is premised on diversity

96. *See Arlington Cent. Sch. Bd. of Educ. v. Murphy,* ___ U.S. ___, 126 S.Ct. 2455, 165 L.Ed.2d 526 (2006); *W. Va. Univ. Hosps. v. Casey,* 499 U.S. 83, 102, 111 S.Ct. 1138, 113 L.Ed.2d 68 (1991); *Crawford Fitting Co. v. J.T. Gibbons, Inc.,* 482 U.S. 437, 439, 107 S.Ct. 2494, 96 L.Ed.2d 385 (1987).

97. *See Jones v. Unisys Corp.,* 54 F.3d 624, 633 (10th Cir.1995); *Garshman Co. v. General Elec. Co.,* 993 F.Supp. 25, 29 (D.Mass.1998), *aff'd,* 176 F.3d 1 (1st Cir. 1999).

98. *See Summit Tech., Inc. v. Nidek Co.,* 435 F.3d 1371, 1374–75 (Fed.Cir.2006). *But see Marmo v. Tyson Fresh Meats, Inc.,* 457 F.3d 748 (8th Cir.2006) (taxing as "copying and exemplification" costs the expenses for graphic and visual aids, and other materials prepared for electronic display).

99. *See Smith v. Tenet Healthsys. SL, Inc.,* 436 F.3d 879, 889–90 (8th Cir.2006); *O'Bryhim v. Reliance Standard Life Ins. Co.,* 997 F.Supp. 728, 737–38 (E.D.Va.1998), *aff'd,* 188 F.3d 502 (4th Cir.1999).

100. *See O'Bryhim v. Reliance Standard Life Ins. Co.,* 997 F.Supp. 728, 737–38 (E.D.Va.1998), *aff'd,* 188 F.3d 502 (4th Cir. 1999); *Ortega v. IBP Inc.,* 883 F.Supp. 558, 562–63 (D.Kan.1995).

101. *See O'Bryhim v. Reliance Standard Life Ins. Co.,* 997 F.Supp. 728, 737–38 (E.D.Va.1998), *aff'd,* 188 F.3d 502 (4th Cir. 1999); *Garshman Co. v. General Elec. Co.,* 993 F.Supp. 25, 29 (D.Mass.1998), *aff'd,* 176 F.3d 1 (1st Cir.1999).

102. *See Thomas v. Treasury Mgmt. Ass'n,* 158 F.R.D. 364, 372 (D.Md.1994).

103. *See O'Bryhim v. Reliance Standard Life Ins. Co.,* 997 F.Supp. 728, 737–38 (E.D.Va.1998), *aff'd,* 188 F.3d 502 (4th Cir. 1999); *Garshman Co. v. General Elec. Co.,* 993 F.Supp. 25, 29 (D.Mass.1998), *aff'd,* 176 F.3d 1 (1st Cir.1999).

104. *See Brisco–Wade v. Carnahan,* 297 F.3d 781, 782 (8th Cir.2002).

105. *See Republic Tobacco Co. v. North Atlantic Trading Co.,* 481 F.3d 442, 447–48 (7th Cir. 2007).

106. *See Alyeska Pipeline Serv. Co. v. Wilderness Soc'y,* 421 U.S. 240, 95 S.Ct. 1612, 44 L.Ed.2d 141 (1975).

107. *See Mills v. Electric Auto–Lite Co.,* 396 U.S. 375, 90 S.Ct. 616, 24 L.Ed.2d 593 (1970).

108. *See Chambers v. NASCO, Inc.,* 501 U.S. 32, 111 S.Ct. 2123, 115 L.Ed.2d 27 (1991).

of citizenship.[109]

Discretion of District Court

Rule 54(d) provides that costs shall be taxed "as of course".[110] The courts have interpreted this mandate to create a presumption in favor of the award of costs in favor of the prevailing party,[111] but reserving for the district judge the discretion to deny costs in appropriate circumstances.[112] A "sound basis" is needed to overcome this presumption.[113] If the court chooses not to award costs to a prevailing party, the court must explain its good reasons for not doing so.[114] An implied or implicit justification will ordinarily be insufficient to sustain the denial on appeal.[115]

Reasons for Denying Costs

The proper exercise of a trial court's discretion to deny costs may hinge on whether the costs are of a type authorized by law and whether the costs pay for materials necessarily obtained for use in the case.[116] Costs may be denied, for example, where both parties partially prevail in the litigation,[117] where a prevailing plaintiff fails

---

109. *See Humann v. KEM Elec. Co-op., Inc.,* ___ F.3d ___, ___, 2007 WL 2296411, at *3 (8th Cir. 2007); *Gobbo Farms & Orchards v. Poole Chem. Co.,* 81 F.3d 122, 123 (10th Cir.1996).

110. *See Miles v. California,* 320 F.3d 986, 988 (9th Cir.2003); *Concord Boat Corp. v. Brunswick Corp.,* 309 F.3d 494, 497–98 (8th Cir.2002), *mandate amended,* 318 F.3d 1156 (8th Cir.2003). *See also In re Paoli R.R. Yard PCB Litig.,* 221 F.3d 449 (3d Cir.2000) (tracing history of award of costs from English inception).

111. *See Delta Air Lines, Inc. v. August,* 450 U.S. 346, 352, 101 S.Ct. 1146, 1150, 67 L.Ed.2d 287 (1981); *Mathews v. Crosby,* 480 F.3d 1265, 1276 (11th Cir. 2007); *Thompson v. Wal–Mart Stores, Inc.,* 472 F.3d 515, 517 (8th Cir. 2006); *Rivera v. City of Chicago,* 469 F.3d 631, 634–35 (7th Cir. 2006); *Knology, Inc. v. Insight Commc'ns Co.,* 460 F.3d 722 (6th Cir.2006).

112. *See Crawford Fitting Co. v. J. T. Gibbons, Inc.,* 482 U.S. 437, 107 S.Ct. 2494, 96 L.Ed.2d 385 (1987); *Farmer v. Arabian American Oil Co.,* 379 U.S. 227, 85 S.Ct. 411, 13 L.Ed.2d 248 (1964); *Rivera v. City of Chicago,* 469 F.3d 631, 634–35 (7th Cir. 2006); *Knology, Inc. v. Insight Commc'ns Co.,* 460 F.3d 722 (6th Cir.2006).

113. *See Mathews v. Crosby,* 480 F.3d 1265, 1277 (11th Cir. 2007) .

114. *See Thompson v. Wal–Mart Stores, Inc.,* 472 F.3d 515, 517 (8th Cir. 2006); *McInnis v. Fairfield Communities, Inc.,* 458 F.3d 1129 (10th Cir.2006); *Pacheco v. Mine-*

ta, 448 F.3d 783, 794 (5th Cir.2006); *Holton v. City of Thomasville Sch. Dist.,* 425 F.3d 1325, 1355–56 (11th Cir.2005). *See also Allison v. Bank One–Denver,* 289 F.3d 1223, 1248–49 (10th Cir.2002) (trial court abuses its discretion when it rests its ruling on an erroneous legal conclusion or where no rational basis supports the ruling).

115. *See Holton v. City of Thomasville Sch. Dist.,* 425 F.3d 1325, 1355–56 (11th Cir.2005).

116. *See Allison v. Bank One–Denver,* 289 F.3d 1223, 1248 (10th Cir.2002).

117. *See Kemin Foods, L.C. v. Pigmentos Vegetales Del Centro S.A. de C.V.,* 464 F.3d 1339, 1348 (Fed.Cir. 2006) (courts may, but are not required to, apportion costs according to parties' relative success); *Barber v. T.D. Williamson, Inc.,* 254 F.3d 1223, 1234–35 (10th Cir.2001) (where prevailing party has been only partially successful, some courts have chosen to apportion costs among parties or to reduce size of prevailing party's award); *Perlman v. Zell,* 185 F.3d 850 (7th Cir.1999) (plaintiff's modest recovery (in relation to original demand) implies that defendants won more of the dispute than they lost, and therefore award of costs could be refused); *Cherry v. Champion Int'l Corp.,* 186 F.3d 442 (4th Cir.1999) (limited value of prevailing party's victory could justify denying award of costs); *AeroTech, Inc. v. Estes,* 110 F.3d 1523, 1526 (10th Cir.1997) (costs may be denied when the prevailing party only partially succeeds); *Amarel v. Connell,* 102

to prove that federal jurisdiction was proper (either because plaintiff fails to recover the $75,000 jurisdictional minimum in a diversity case or because plaintiff fails to win on the federal question counts),[118] where the prevailing party needlessly prolongs the litigation or otherwise acts in bad faith,[119] or, perhaps, where the losing party is unable to pay or would be rendered indigent by paying,[120] or is incarcerated,[121] or where the prevailing party's recovery was nominal or "substantially less" than what was sought,[122] where a voluntarily dismissal is entered but only after first obtaining some modicum of relief,[123] or where there would be some other "injustice" in approving an award of costs.[124]   Generally, a district court may not deny costs simply upon a finding that the case was brought and litigated in "good faith" and without a vexatious motive,[125] because a significant disparity exists between the parties' financial re-

F.3d 1494, 1523 (9th Cir.1996) (district court may require each party to bear their own costs in the event of a mixed judgment); *Testa v. Village of Mundelein*, 89 F.3d 443, 447 (7th Cir.1996)(in viewed of mixed outcome, district court did not abuse its discretion in requiring each party to bear its own costs).

118. See *Miles v. California*, 320 F.3d 986, 988 (9th Cir.2003); *Perlman v. Zell*, 185 F.3d 850 (7th Cir.1999).

119. See *Farrar v. Hobby*, 506 U.S. 103, 115–16, 113 S.Ct. 566, 575, 121 L.Ed.2d 494 (1992)(commenting that, having considered the amount and nature of the plaintiff's success on the merits, district courts may award modest fees or no fees at all); *Champion Produce, Inc. v. Ruby Robinson Co.*, 342 F.3d 1016, 1022 (9th Cir.2003); *Mother & Father v. Cassidy*, 338 F.3d 704, 708 (7th Cir.2003) (costs can be denied for party's misconduct); *In re Paoli R.R. Yard PCB Litig.*, 221 F.3d 449, 468 (3d Cir.2000) (prevailing party's "unclean hands" is relevant factor for consideration); *Cherry v. Champion Int'l Corp.*, 186 F.3d 442, 446 (4th Cir. 1999) ("misconduct by the prevailing party worthy of a penalty" may justify denial of costs).

120. See *Rivera v. City of Chicago*, 469 F.3d 631, 634–35 (7th Cir. 2006) (indigency may be considered); *Champion Produce, Inc. v. Ruby Robinson Co.*, 342 F.3d 1016, 1022 (9th Cir.2003) (losing party's "limited financial resources" may be considered); *Lampkins v. Thompson*, 337 F.3d 1009, 1017 (8th Cir.2003) (party's indigency properly considered); *Chapman v. AI Transport*, 229 F.3d 1012, 1039 (11th Cir.2000) (noting that non-prevailing party's financial status is factor to be considered, but court must

first require substantial documentation of true inability to pay costs); *In re Paoli R.R. Yard PCB Litig.*, 221 F.3d 449 (3d Cir.2000) (commenting that "most important" factor is defeated party's indigency or inability to pay which may, but need not automatically, excuse taxation of costs). *But see Rodriguez v. Whiting Farms, Inc.*, 360 F.3d 1180, 1190–91 (10th Cir.2004) (finding no error in district court's rejection of party's indigency as possible justification to deny costs).

121. See *Lampkins v. Thompson*, 337 F.3d 1009, 1017 (8th Cir.2003).

122. See *Champion Produce, Inc. v. Ruby Robinson Co.*, 342 F.3d 1016, 1022–23 (9th Cir.2003).

123. See *Knology, Inc. v. Insight Commc'ns Co.*, 460 F.3d 722 (6th Cir.2006).

124. See *Cherry v. Champion Int'l Corp.*, 186 F.3d 442 (4th Cir.1999). *See also Barber v. T.D. Williamson, Inc.*, 254 F.3d 1223, 1234–35 (10th Cir.2001) (noting that courts have refused to award costs where neither side entirely prevailed, both sides prevailed, or litigation resulted from fault on both parties).

125. See *Pacheco v. Mineta*, 448 F.3d 783, 794–95 (5th Cir.2006) (surveying views from various Circuits), *petition for cert. filed*, 75 U.S.L.W. 3066 (U.S. Aug. 3, 2006) (No. 06–199); *In re Paoli R.R. Yard PCB Litig.*, 221 F.3d 449, 454 (3d Cir.2000); *Cherry v. Champion Int'l Corp.*, 186 F.3d 442 (4th Cir.1999); *National Information Servs., Inc. v. TRW, Inc.*, 51 F.3d 1470, 1471–72 (9th Cir.1995). *But see Champion Produce, Inc. v. Ruby Robinson Co.*, 342 F.3d 1016, 1022 (9th Cir.2003) (whether losing party litigated in good faith could be considered).

sources,[126] because a heavy taxation would deter the poor from seeking redress,[127] because the case was "complex" or a "close call",[128] because the prevailing party had rejected the defendant's Rule 68 offer of judgment,[129] or because the case involved significant matters in the public interest.[130] In many cases, the district court will also be precluded from denying costs merely because the prevailing party failed to pray for them in a pleading.[131]

Note, however, that the Circuits are not always uniform in their approaches to these various factors.[132] Indeed, one court of appeals

126. See In re Paoli R.R. Yard PCB Litig., 221 F.3d 449 (3d Cir.2000) (rejecting relative wealth of parties as relevant factor); Cherry v. Champion Int'l Corp., 186 F.3d 442 (4th Cir.1999) (rejecting "comparative economic power" argument, noting that it would frequently favor defendant, thus ignoring plain language of Rule and undermining foundation of legal system that justice is administered to all equally, regardless of wealth or status). But see Jack Russell Terrier Network v. American Kennel Club, Inc., 407 F.3d 1027, 1038 (9th Cir. 2005) (lack of financial resources by one party and substantial profit by other may justify denying costs).

127. See Smith v. Tenet Healthsystem SL, Inc., 436 F.3d 879, 889–90 (8th Cir. 2006).

128. See In re Paoli R.R. Yard PCB Litig., 221 F.3d 449 (3d Cir.2000) (complexity or closeness of issues not appropriate factors for consideration); National Information Servs., Inc. v. TRW, Inc., 51 F.3d 1470, 1473 (9th Cir.1995)(rejecting view that costs may be denied in cases presenting "close and difficult" legal issues); Klein v. Grynberg, 44 F.3d 1497, 1506 (10th Cir. 1995)(rejecting premise that costs may be denied because litigation was complex or lengthy). See also Rodriguez v. Whiting Farms, Inc., 360 F.3d 1180, 1190–91 (10th Cir.2004) (finding no error in district court's rejection of claim that case involved "close and difficult call" as possible justification to deny costs). Note, however, that the case law in this area is not developing uniformly. See Champion Produce, Inc. v. Ruby Robinson Co., 342 F.3d 1016, 1022 (9th Cir.2003) ("close and difficult" issues in case may be considered); Cherry v. Champion Int'l Corp., 186 F.3d 442 (4th Cir.1999) (commenting that factors that could justify denying award of costs include the closeness and difficulty of the issues decided); Luckey v. Baxter Healthcare Corp., 183 F.3d 730 (7th Cir.1999) (observing that

district judge might require each side to bear its own costs when the case is close, or when the side with the better position loses on a technicality).

129. See Champion Produce, Inc. v. Ruby Robinson Co., 342 F.3d 1016, 1022–24 (9th Cir.2003).

130. See Mitchell v. City of Moore, Oklahoma, 218 F.3d 1190 (10th Cir.2000) (presumption in favor of awarding costs applies even where prevailing party is defendant in civil rights case); Cherry v. Champion Int'l Corp., 186 F.3d 442 (4th Cir.1999) (holding that presumptive award of costs cannot be defeated on the basis of the nature of the underlying litigation). But see Champion Produce, Inc. v. Ruby Robinson Co., 342 F.3d 1016, 1022 (9th Cir.2003) ("the chilling effect of imposing ... high costs on future civil rights litigants" may be considered, as well as whether the case involved "a landmark issue of national importance"). Stanley v. University of So. Cal., 178 F.3d 1069, 1079 (9th Cir.1999) (directing courts, in civil rights cases, to consider plaintiff's financial resources and amount of cost so as to avoid unnecessarily chilling civil rights litigation; "Without civil rights litigants who are willing to test the boundaries of our laws, we would not have made much of the progress that has occurred in this nation since Brown v. Board of Educ.").

131. See Flynn v. AK Peters, Ltd., 377 F.3d 13, 26 (1st Cir.2004) (right to attorney's fees not waived where prayer for fees not listed as "special damages" in complaint); Port of Stockton v. Western Bulk Carrier KS, 371 F.3d 1119, 1121–22 (9th Cir.2004) (same effect).

132. See Knology, Inc. v. Insight Commc'ns Co., 460 F.3d 722 (6th Cir.2006) (factors that may justify denying costs include losing party's good faith, difficulty of case, winning party's behavior, and necessity of costs).

has explained that denying costs is "in the nature of a severe penalty" and, as such, the party opposing the taxing of costs will be obligated to offer a reason why the prevailing party ought to be "penalized" by a refusal of costs.[133]

Burden of Proof

The burden of proving the amount of compensable costs and expenses lies with the party seeking those costs.[134] Once the prevailing party demonstrates the amount of its costs and that they fall within an allowable category of taxable costs, the prevailing party enjoys the "strong presumption" that its costs will be awarded "in full measure".[135] The party opposing the award of costs bears the burden of demonstrating that the award would be improper.[136]

Taxing Costs For or Against the United States

The United States may be awarded costs in the same manner as any prevailing party.[137] Costs may be taxed against the United States in accordance with the list set forth in 28 U.S.C.A. § 1920,[138] except that in non-tort actions, the district court may refuse to tax costs upon a finding that the United States' position was substantially justified or where special circumstances make an award of costs unjust.[139]

Taxing Costs Against States

Some courts have construed the Eleventh Amendment to the United States Constitution as prohibiting a district court's right to tax costs against a State.[140] To ensure that costs may be so taxed against a State, the court will consult the source of the substantive law under which the suit is brought to determine whether provision is made for such an award of costs against a State.

Costs in Pauper Actions

The district court may, in its discretion, permit a civil litigant, criminal defendant, or appellant to proceed without the prepayment of costs upon receiving an affidavit showing an inability to pay costs.[141]

Procedure for Obtaining Award of Non–Attorney's Fee Costs

To obtain an award of costs, the prevailing party must file a "Bill of Costs" with the clerk (the district court may have a

---

133. *See Rodriguez v. Whiting Farms, Inc.,* 360 F.3d 1180, 1190–91 (10th Cir. 2004).

134. *See Allison v. Bank One–Denver,* 289 F.3d 1223, 1248–49 (10th Cir.2002).

135. *See Concord Boat Corp. v. Brunswick Corp.,* 309 F.3d 494, 497–98 (8th Cir. 2002), *mandate amended,* 318 F.3d 1156 (8th Cir.2003).

136. *See BDT Prods., Inc. v. Lexmark Int'l, Inc.,* 405 F.3d 415, 420 (6th Cir.2005); *Rodriguez v. Whiting Farms, Inc.,* 360 F.3d 1180, 1190–91 (10th Cir.2004); *Save Our Valley v. Sound Transit,* 335 F.3d 932, 944–45 (9th Cir.2003).

137. *See E.E.O.C. v. W & O, Inc.,* 213 F.3d 600, 620 (11th Cir.2000); *United States v. Lynd,* 349 F.2d 785 (5th Cir.1965).

138. *See* 28 U.S.C.A. § 1920.

139. *See* 28 U.S.C.A. § 2412.

140. *See Alyeska Pipeline Serv. Co. v. Wilderness Soc'y,* 421 U.S. 240, 269 n. 44, 95 S.Ct. 1612, 1627 n. 44, 44 L.Ed.2d 141 (1975).

141. *See* 28 U.S.C.A. § 1915.

preprinted form for this purpose). The Bill of Costs must be verified by affidavit. The clerk may tax costs on one-day notice. Within 5 days thereafter, a disappointed party may seek court review of the clerk's assessment. Some courts have ruled that a failure to seek review within this 5–day period waives the losing party's right to challenge the award.[142] Other courts have noted that the time period is not jurisdictional and untimely objections may, in the trial court's discretion, be considered.[143] The district court is authorized to conduct a *de novo* review of the clerk's assessments.[144] Costs may be taxed against multiple losing parties either in allocated amounts or jointly and severally.[145] The time for filing a Bill of Costs is typically regulated by local court rule, but usually is set after the court has rendered its decision in the case.[146]

Procedure for Obtaining Award of Attorney's Fees

Where an award of attorney's fees is appropriate, Rule 54(d)(2) fixes the procedure for obtaining an award of such fees and related non-taxable expenses. This procedure does *not* apply to attorney's fees recoverable as an element of damages (*e.g.*, under terms of a contract) or to fees and expenses awarded as sanctions.[147] The procedure follows:

1. *Motion Required:* The prevailing party must apply for such an award by motion. The motion must: (a) specify the judgment; (b) identify the legal source authorizing such an award of fees or expenses; and (c) state the amount, or a fair estimate of the amount, of the requested award.[148]

   Court-Implemented Settlements: In cases where a settlement must be implemented by the court, the district court may also require that the motion disclose any fee agreement affecting the litigation.

2. *Time for Service:* Ordinarily, the motion must be served within 14 days after entry of judgment. This deadline helps both to ensure that the opponent receives proper notice of the fees claim and to promote a prompt fees ruling from the district court, thus permitting simultaneous appellate re-

---

142. *See Ahlberg v. Chrysler Corp.*, 481 F.3d 630, 638–39 (8th Cir. 2007); *Bloomer v. UPS, Inc.*, 337 F.3d 1220, 1221 (10th Cir.2003); *Cooper v. Eagle River Mem'l Hosp., Inc.*, 270 F.3d 456, 464 (7th Cir. 2001); *Walker v. California*, 200 F.3d 624, 626 (9th Cir.1999); *Prince v. Poulos*, 876 F.2d 30, 34 (5th Cir.1989).

143. *See Corwin v. Walt Disney Co.*, 475 F.3d 1239, 1254 (11th Cir. 2007); *In re Paoli R.R. Yard PCB Litig.*, 221 F.3d 449 (3d Cir.2000).

144. *See In re Paoli R.R. Yard PCB Litig.*, 221 F.3d 449 (3d Cir.2000).

145. *In re Paoli R.R. Yard PCB Litig.*, 221 F.3d 449 (3d Cir.2000).

146. *See S.A. Healy Co. v. Milwaukee Metropolitan Sewerage Dist.*, 60 F.3d 305 (7th Cir.1995)(commenting that because Rule 54(d) specifies no uniform national deadline for filing Bills of Costs, such timing is typically governed by local court rules).

147. *See Carolina Power & Light Co. v. Dynegy Marketing & Trade*, 415 F.3d 354, 358–59 (4th Cir.2005); *United Indus. v. Simon–Hartley, Ltd.*, 91 F.3d 762, 766 (5th Cir.1996).

148. *See* Rule 54(d)(2)(A)-(2)(B). *See also United Indus. v. Simon–Hartley, Ltd.*, 91 F.3d 762, 766–67 (5th Cir.1996).

view of both the merits and the fees award.[149]   Failure to
serve within this allotted time constitutes a waiver of a
party's right to recover such fees or expenses.[150] Nevertheless, because the 14–day time period is not jurisdictional,
some courts have held that the district judge may exercise
discretion to extend the time period.[151] Most courts also
agree that this 14–day period does not begin to run until
post-trial motions under Rules 50(b), 52(b), or 59 are resolved.[152]

● *Amended Judgments:* Amended judgments are "judgments" just the same, and the 14–day period will run from
them as well.[153]

● *Local Rules & Standing Orders:* Practitioners must
carefully consult the applicable local rules on Rule 54(d)
attorneys fee motions. This 14–day period may be modified
"by statute or order of the court".[154] Several courts have
ruled that local rules which adopt longer periods for making
attorney's fee motions qualify as "standing orders" and,
thus, are authorized modifications of the 14–day period.[155]

3. *Time for Filing*: Originally, Rule 54(d) required that a
motion for attorney's fees must be *both* served and filed
within 14 days. This requirement was changed in the 2002
amendments to the Rule. Now, filing must be made, as with
any other document under Rule 5(d), "within a reasonable
time after service".[156]

4. *Opponent's Response:* Upon request, the court must provide
the opponent with the opportunity to present evidence in
opposition to the requested award.

149. *See United Indus. v. Simon–Hartley, Ltd.*, 91 F.3d 762, 766 (5th Cir.1996).

150. *See In re Veritas Software Corp.
Secs. Litig.*, 496 F.3d 962, ___, 2007 WL
2120274, at *8—*9 (9th Cir. 2007); *United
Indus. v. Simon–Hartley, Ltd.*, 91 F.3d 762,
767 (5th Cir.1996); *Mathews v. Lancaster
General Hosp.*, 87 F.3d 624, 642 n. 12 (3d
Cir.1996). *But cf. Johnson v. Lafayette Fire
Fighters Ass'n Local 472*, 51 F.3d 726, 729
(7th Cir.1995)(holding that local court rule,
as a uniform "order of court", modified the
14–day period set forth in Rule 54(d)(2)(B)).

151. *See Green v. Administrators of Tulane Educ. Fund*, 284 F.3d 642, 664 (5th
Cir.2002); *Amarel v. Connell*, 102 F.3d 1494
(9th Cir.1996). *See also Tancredi v. Metropolitan Life Ins.*, 378 F.3d 220, 227–28 (2d
Cir.2004) (before extension to 14–day deadline may be granted, trial court must find
"excusable neglect").

152. *See Bailey v. County of Riverside*,
414 F.3d 1023, 1024 (9th Cir.2005); *Miltimore Sales, Inc. v. Int'l Rectifier, Inc.*, 412

F.3d 685, 689 (6th Cir.2005); *Members First
Fed. Credit Union v. Members First Credit
Union*, 244 F.3d 806, 807 (11th Cir.2001);
Weyant v. Okst, 198 F.3d 311, 314 (2d Cir.
1999).

153. *See Quigley v. Rosenthal*, 427 F.3d
1232, 1236–37 (10th Cir.2005).

154. *See Rule 54(d)(2)(B).*

155. *See Miltimore Sales, Inc. v. Int'l
Rectifier, Inc.*, 412 F.3d 685, 692 (6th Cir.
2005); *Planned Parenthood of Cent. New
Jersey v. Attorney General of New Jersey*,
297 F.3d 253, 259–61 (3d Cir.2002); *Green
v. Administrators of Tulane Educ. Fund*,
284 F.3d 642, 664 (5th Cir.2002).

156. *See* Rule 5(d). *See also* Rule
54(d)(2)(B) advisory committee note to 2002
amendments (noting deletion of 14–day filing requirement "to establish a parallel
with Rules 50, 52, and 59. Service continues
to be required under Rule 5(a)").

5. *Court's Delegation:* The court may enlist the help of a Special Master for setting the proper value to be awarded for the attorney services provided. The court may also refer the entire motion to a magistrate judge for a Report & Recommendation (akin to dispositive pretrial matters).

6. *Court's Ruling:* In ruling on a Rule 54(d)(2) motion, the court must issue findings of fact and conclusions of law as required under Rule 52(a), and must issue a separate judgment as required under Rule 58. The court may, at its option, bifurcate its consideration of the motion to resolve liability issues first, before considering the amount of an appropriate award.

7. *Additional Procedures By Local Rule:* Rule 54(d)(2) permits the district courts to promulgate local rules to govern procedures for claims without the need for extensive evidentiary hearings.[157]

Effect of an Attorney's Fees Motion on Judgment's "Finality"

The filing of a Rule 54(d)(2) motion for an award of attorney's fees does not ordinarily affect the finality of the underlying judgment.[158] However, when a *timely* motion for fees is made and so long as no notice of appeal has yet been filed (or become effective), the district court may enter an order directing that the fees motion be deemed to have the same effect as a timely Rule 59 motion and, thereby, toll the time for taking an appeal until after the motion is resolved.[159] This extension option applies only to fees motions, not to the taxation of costs.[160]

ADDITIONAL RESEARCH REFERENCES

Wright & Miller, *Federal Practice and Procedure* §§ 2651–79.

C.J.S. Federal Civil Procedure §§ 1105–1120 et seq., 1236; Federal Courts § 293(17).

West's Key No. Digests, Federal Civil Procedure ☞2391–2399, 2571–2587, 2721–2742.5; Federal Courts ☞660.

157. Local rules *must* be consulted on this point. The advisory committee notes suggest that, by local rule, the district courts may even adopt schedules listing customary attorney's fees or factors that affect attorney's fees within a particular legal community. *See* Rule 54(d)(2)(D) advisory committee note.

158. *See* Rule 58(c)(1). *See also Moody Nat'l Bank of Galveston v. GE Life & Annuity Assur. Co.*, 383 F.3d 249 (5th Cir.2004).

159. *See* Rule 58(c)(2). *See also Moody Nat'l Bank of Galveston v. GE Life & Annuity Assur. Co.*, 383 F.3d 249 (5th Cir.2004).

160. *See Moody Nat'l Bank of Galveston v. GE Life & Annuity Assur. Co.*, 383 F.3d 249 (5th Cir.2004).

RULE 55

DEFAULT; DEFAULT JUDGMENT

(a) Entering a Default. When a party against whom a judgment for affirmative relief is sought has failed to plead or otherwise defend, and that failure is shown by affidavit or otherwise, the clerk must enter the party's default.

(b) Entering a Default Judgment.

(1) *By the Clerk.* If the plaintiff's claim is for a sum certain or a sum that can be made certain by computation, the clerk—on the plaintiff's request, with an affidavit showing the amount due—must enter judgment for that amount and costs against a defendant who has been defaulted for not appearing and who is neither a minor nor an incompetent person.

(2) *By the Court.* In all other cases, the party must apply to the court for a default judgment. A default judgment may be entered against a minor or incompetent person only if represented by a general guardian, conservator, or other like fiduciary who has appeared. If the party against whom a default judgment is sought has appeared personally or by a representative, that party or its representative must be served with written notice of the application at least 3 days before the hearing. The court may conduct hearings or make referrals—preserving any federal statutory right to a jury trial—when, to enter or effectuate judgment, it needs to:

(A) conduct an accounting;

(B) determine the amount of damages;

(C) establish the truth of any allegation by evidence; or

(D) investigate any other matter.

(c) Setting Aside a Default or a Default Judgment. The court may set aside an entry of default for good cause, and it may set aside a default judgment under Rule 60(b).

(d) Judgment Against the United States. A default judgment may be entered against the United States, its officers, or its agencies only if the claimant establishes a claim or right to relief by evidence that satisfies the court.

[Amended effective August 1, 1987; April 30, 2007, effective December 1, 2007.]

——————————— 2007 AMENDMENTS ROADMAP ———————————

STYLE PROJECT CHANGES: Former Rule 55(d) was deleted as redundant (the first part of that Rule deemed incomplete and repetitive, and the second part deemed an unnecessary reminder of material found elsewhere). Old Rule 55(e) was repositioned as new Rule 55(d). The phrase "as provided by these Rules" was deleted from Rule 55(a) as improperly implying that the Clerk should default a party who showed an intent to defend, even if the type of showing was not specifically listed in the Rules. In Rule 55(c), "good cause" remained the standard for setting aside a default, but the standard for setting aside default judgments now merely references Rule 60(b). Limited new subsectioning was added (but only to subpart 55(b)). "Must" replaced "shall", and "minor" replaced "infant".

NON-STYLE CHANGES: None.

NOTE: The Federal Rules "Style Project" is explained in Part III-A.

AUTHORS' COMMENTARY ON RULE 55

——————————— PURPOSE AND SCOPE ———————————

Rule 55 sets the procedure for defaults and default judgments in the federal courts. Because default judgments are not favored by the courts, Rule 55 also defines the procedure for setting aside defaults and default judgments.

RULE 55(a). ENTERING A DEFAULT

CORE CONCEPT

Upon motion of a party, the clerk of court may enter a default against a party who has failed to plead or otherwise defend.

APPLICATIONS

Distinguished From Default Judgment

The clerk's entry of a party's default is the official recognition that the party is in default.[1] The entry of default is a prerequisite

---

1. *See New York Life Ins. Co. v. Brown,* 84 F.3d 137, 141 (5th Cir.1996)(entry of

for the entry of judgment upon that default.[2]   It is, in effect, akin to a finding of liability with the entry of final judgment yet to come.[3] Thus, there are two stages in a default proceeding—the establishment of the default itself, followed by the entry of a default judgment.[4]

Prerequisites

The party against whom the default is entered must have been properly served with process, and the district court must enjoy subject matter jurisdiction and either personal or quasi-in-rem/in-rem jurisdiction over the defaulting party.[5]   The clerk must also be satisfied, by the moving party's affidavit or otherwise, that the defaulting party has failed to plead or otherwise defend.[6]

Contested Motions for Entry of Default

Where a motion for entry of default is opposed by a party who has entered an appearance, the courts may, in considering the contested motion, apply the criteria guiding motions to set aside a default.[7]

Effect of Entry of Default

A defaulting party is deemed to have admitted all well-pleaded allegations of the complaint.[8] This greatly limits a defendant's ability to defend the lawsuit. A defendant in default is ordinarily foreclosed from raising any defenses other than a challenge to the legal sufficiency of the pleading to support a cognizable judgment, the adequacy of service of process, and the propriety of the court's jurisdiction.[9]

default is made by clerk, once default established by affidavit or otherwise, after which application can be made for judgment upon that default); *Pinaud v. County of Suffolk*, 52 F.3d 1139, 1152 n. 11 (2d Cir. 1995)(noting crucial distinction between entry of default and entry of default judgment; entry of default is essentially a formal matter, and is not a judgment).

2.   *See New York v. Green*, 420 F.3d 99, 104 (2d Cir.2005); *Johnson v. Dayton Elec. Mfg. Co.*, 140 F.3d 781, 783 (8th Cir.1998); *Inman v. American Home Furniture Placement, Inc.*, 120 F.3d 117 (8th Cir.1997).

3.   *See Alameda v. Secretary of Health, Educ. & Welfare*, 622 F.2d 1044, 1048 n. 3 (1st Cir.1980).

4.   *See In re Catt*, 368 F.3d 789, 793 (7th Cir.2004).

5.   *See Maryland State Firemen's Ass'n v. Chaves*, 166 F.R.D. 353 (D.Md. 1996)(noting that it is "axiomatic" that process must be properly served before a default or a default judgment may be entered); *Dahl v. Kanawha Investment Holding Co.*, 161 F.R.D. 673 (N.D.Iowa 1995)(as precondition for entry of default or default

judgment, movant must show that proper service was made on defendants).

6.   *See New York Life Ins. Co. v. Brown*, 84 F.3d 137, 141 (5th Cir.1996)(entry of default is made by clerk, once default established by affidavit or otherwise); *Martin v. Coughlin*, 895 F.Supp. 39 (N.D.N.Y.1995).

7.   *See* Rule 55(c). *See also Schmir v. Prudential Ins. Co.*, 220 F.R.D. 4, 5 (D.Me. 2004) (applying Rule 55(c) factors, namely (1) whether default was willful, (2) prejudice to adversary, (3) whether meritorious defense is presented, (4) nature of explanation for default, (5) good faith of parties, (6) amount of money involved, (7) timing of motion, and (8) general philosophy favoring decisions on merits).

8.   *See D.H. Blair & Co., Inc. v. Gottdiener*, 462 F.3d 95, 107 (2d Cir. 2006); *In re The Home Restaurants, Inc.*, 285 F.3d 111, 114 (1st Cir.2002); *Adkins v. Teseo*, 180 F.Supp.2d 15, 17 (D.D.C.2001).

9.   *See Tyco Fire & Sec., LLC v. Alcocer*, 218 Fed.Appx. 860, 863–64 (11th Cir. 2007).

Appealability

Entry of default is an interlocutory order, from which an immediate appeal ordinarily cannot be taken.[10]

RULE 55(b).   ENTERING A DEFAULT JUDGMENT

CORE CONCEPT

Where the defendant has defaulted for failing to appear and the moving party has submitted evidence by affidavit establishing damages in a sum certain or in a sum that can be made certain by computation, the clerk of court may enter a default judgment upon motion. In all other cases, the *court* (and *not* the clerk of court) may enter a default judgment.

APPLICATIONS

Defendant's "Appearance"

A defendant "appears" in the action by making some presentation or submission to the court (*e.g.,* serving a responsive pleading, filing an entry of appearance, serving a Rule 12 motion to dismiss, or having counsel attend a conference on the client's behalf).[11] Some courts have taken an even wider view,[12] ruling that "appearing" within the meaning of Rule 55(b) is defined broadly and is not necessarily limited to a formal filing in court.[13] In those courts, informal acts such as correspondence or telephone calls between counsel can constitute the requisite appearance,[14] as can engaging in settlement negotiations under certain circumstances.[15] Given the judicial philosophy disfavoring default judgments, the courts may search to find that an appearance has occurred.[16] Nevertheless,

---

10. *See In re Lam*, 192 F.3d 1309, 1311 (9th Cir.1999); *Ackra Direct Mktg. Corp. v. Fingerhut Corp.*, 86 F.3d 852, 855 (8th Cir. 1996).

11. *See Sun Bank of Ocala v. Pelican Homestead & Savings Ass'n*, 874 F.2d 274, 276 (5th Cir.1989) (filing motion to dismiss constitutes "appearing"); *Hudson v. North Carolina*, 158 F.R.D. 78, 80 (E.D.N.C. 1994) (same); *Lutwin v. City of New York*, 106 F.R.D. 502, 504 n.1 (S.D.N.Y.1985) (attendance at conference sufficient to "appear"), *aff'd*, 795 F.2d 1004 (2d Cir.1986) (Table).

12. *See New York v. Green*, 420 F.3d 99, 105 (2d Cir.2005) (noting division among the Circuits on the issue).

13. *See Silverman v. RTV Communications Group, Inc.*, 2002 WL 483421, at *3 (S.D.N.Y.2002) (holding that appearance "is broadly defined and is not limited to a formal court filing"). *See also Rogers v. Hartford Life & Accident Ins. Co.*, 167 F.3d 933, 936–37 (5th Cir.1999) (noting that Fifth Circuit does not construe "appeared"

as requiring the filing of responsive papers or actual in-court actions by the defendant). *But see Zuelzke Tool & Eng'g Co. v. Anderson Die Castings, Inc.*, 925 F.2d 226, 230 (7th Cir.1991) (rejecting informal contacts approach); *Town & Country Kids, Inc. v. Protected Venture Investment Trust #1, Inc.*, 178 F.R.D. 453, 455 (E.D.Va.1998) (holding that, for purposes of Rule 55(b), parties "appear" in action only where they make a presentation or submission to the court).

14. *See Sun Bank of Ocala v. Pelican Homestead & Savings Ass'n*, 874 F.2d 274, 276–77 (5th Cir.1989). *See generally New York v. Green*, 420 F.3d 99 (2d Cir.2005) (noting prevailing view, that informal contacts, like telephone calls, may suffice provided there is "clear intention to defend").

15. *See S.E.C. v. Getanswers, Inc.*, 219 F.R.D. 698, 700 (S.D.Fla.2004).

16. *See Franchise Holding II, LLC. v. Huntington Restaurants Group, Inc.*, 375 F.3d 922, 927 (9th Cir.2004).

merely accepting or waiving service of process will not qualify as "appearing" within the meaning of this Rule.[17]

The Appearance 3–Day Rule

If a default judgment is being sought against a party who has "appeared" (as that term is used in Rule 55(b)), that party must be served with *written* notice of the application for a default judgment at least 3 days before the hearing.[18]

Default Judgment by Clerk

The clerk may only enter a default judgment where the following three prerequisites are met:

1. The defendant was defaulted because of a failure to appear; and

2. The defendant is not a minor or incompetent person; and

3. The moving party submits an affidavit establishing that the amount due is either a sum certain or a sum that can be made certain by computation.

   - *"Sum Certain" Defined:* A claim is not a "sum certain" under Rule 55 unless there is no doubt as to the amount that must be awarded.[19] The definition contemplates a context in which, once liability is established, the amount due is beyond question (such as actions on money judgments or negotiable instruments).[20] This standard is not met where some portion of damages, such as "reasonable" attorney's fees or punitive damages, still needs to be determined.[21]

Default Judgment by Court

In all other circumstances, the court may enter the default judgment:

1. Where the defendant has "appeared", in which case the appearing defendant must be served with written notice of the application for default judgment at least 3 days before any hearing on the application;[22]

17. *See Rogers v. Hartford Life & Accident Ins. Co.,* 167 F.3d 933, 936–37 (5th Cir.1999).

18. *See* Rule 55(b)(2).

19. *See Franchise Holding II, LLC. v. Huntington Restaurants Group, Inc.,* 375 F.3d 922, 928–29 (9th Cir.2004); *KPS & Assocs., Inc. v. Designs By FMC, Inc.,* 318 F.3d 1, 19–20 (1st Cir.2003).

20. *See KPS & Assocs., Inc. v. Designs By FMC, Inc.,* 318 F.3d 1, 19–20 (1st Cir. 2003)

21. *See Dailey v. R & J Commercial Contracting,* 2002 WL 484988, at *3 (S.D.Ohio 2002) (error for clerk to enter requested judgment involving punitive damages); *Combs v. Coal & Mineral Management Servs., Inc.,* 105 F.R.D. 472 (D.D.C. 1984).

22. *See Canal Ins. Co. v. Dale Ashmore,* 61 F.3d 15 (8th Cir.1995)(abuse of discretion to fail to set aside default judgment where defendant never received notice); *D.B. v. Bloom,* 896 F.Supp. 166 (D.N.J. 1995)(court must be satisfied that party received notice of motion).

2. Where the defendant is a minor or incompetent person, in which case a default judgment may be entered only if the minor or incompetent is represented;

3. Where the amount due is not certain, in which case the court may conduct a hearing, bench trial, or jury trial to assess damages; [23]

> *Note:* The court may either conduct an evidentiary hearing,[24] or may choose to rely simply on affidavits or other documentary evidence.[25] Whether to convene a hearing is a decision committed to the trial judge's discretion.[26] So long as there is a proper basis for awarding the damages specified in the default judgment, a hearing is not necessarily required.[27] If an evidentiary hearing is convened, the party seeking default bears the burden of proof[28], and the pleading's allegations regarding the amount of damages are not presumed true.[29] All reasonable inferences from the evidence offered, however, are drawn in the moving party's favor.[30]

4. Where the defendant has been defaulted for a reason other than a failure to appear.

Note: The entry of a default deprives a defendant of the right to contest the factual allegations of the complaint (unless the default is set aside),[31] but does not prevent the defendant from appearing to challenge the amount of damages.

23. *See S.E.C. v. Smyth*, 420 F.3d 1225, 1231-32 (11th Cir.2005) (although not compulsively required in all contexts, evidentiary hearing often necessary to determine damages); *Chudasama v. Mazda Motor Corp.*, 123 F.3d 1353, 1364 n.27 (11th Cir. 1997) (commenting that where amount of damages is disputed, only court—after determining the amount of damages—may enter default judgment); *Wing v. East River Chinese Restaurant*, 884 F.Supp. 663, 669 (E.D.N.Y.1995)(unless amount of damages is certain, court required to make independent determination of sum to be awarded; factors for court's consideration include amount potentially involved, whether material factual issues exist, whether default is "largely technical", prejudice to the movant, harshness of judgment, likelihood that default would be set aside).

24. *See Cablevision Sys. New York City Corp. v. Lokshin*, 980 F.Supp. 107, 111–12 (E.D.N.Y.1997); *In re Crazy Eddie Secs. Litig.*, 948 F.Supp. 1154, 1160 (E.D.N.Y. 1996).

25. *See Time Warner Cable of New York City v. Foote*, 2002 WL 1267993, at *4 (E.D.N.Y.2002); *Cablevision Sys. New York*

City Corp. v. Lokshin, 980 F.Supp. 107, 111–12 (E.D.N.Y.1997); *In re Crazy Eddie Secs. Litig.*, 948 F.Supp. 1154, 1160 (E.D.N.Y.1996).

26. *See DIRECTV, Inc. v. Huynh*, 318 F.Supp.2d 1122, 1129 (M.D.Ala.2004); *In re Crazy Eddie Secs. Litig.*, 948 F.Supp. 1154, 1160 (E.D.N.Y.1996).

27. *See Directv, Inc. v. Griffin*, 290 F.Supp.2d 1340, 1343–44 (M.D.Fla.2003).

28. *See In re Catt*, 368 F.3d 789, 793 (7th Cir.2004); *Oberstar v. F.D.I.C.*, 987 F.2d 494, 505 n. 9 (8th Cir.1993); *In re Crazy Eddie Secs. Litig.*, 948 F.Supp. 1154, 1160 (E.D.N.Y.1996).

29. *See In re Catt*, 368 F.3d 789, 793 (7th Cir.2004).

30. *See Time Warner Cable of New York City v. Foote*, 2002 WL 1267993, at *4 (E.D.N.Y.2002); *In re Crazy Eddie Secs. Litig.*, 948 F.Supp. 1154, 1160 (E.D.N.Y. 1996).

31. *See Ramos–Falcon v. Autoridad de Energia Electrica*, 301 F.3d 1, 2 (1st Cir. 2002) (if court examines complaint, it may

Default in Multiple Defendant Cases

Where the plaintiff alleges joint liability against multiple defendants or the defendants have closely related defenses, the default of one defendant usually will not result in a judgment against that defendant. Instead, the court will allow the lawsuit to proceed as to the other, non-defaulting defendants. The result in the litigation (*e.g.*, judgment for plaintiff or judgment for defendants) will then simply be entered as to the defaulting defendant as well.[32]

Defaulting Defendants in the Military

The federal Soldiers' and Sailors' Civil Relief Act of 1940[33] prohibits the entry of any federal or State judgment by default against absent military defendants, unless the court first appoints counsel to represent the absent defendants' interests. Often, the court may simply stay a lawsuit against the absent military defendants until their return.

Note: In seeking a default judgment, a plaintiff must either set forth facts showing that the defaulting defendant is not in the military or provide an affidavit attesting to that fact.

Limitation on Default Judgments

No judgment by default can be greater in amount or different in kind from the demand contained in the complaint.[34]

Discretion of District Court

Judgments by default are disfavored and are never granted as a matter of right.[35] Whether to enter a judgment by default is a decision entrusted to the sound discretion of the district court.[36] Thus, a defendant's default does not necessarily entitle the plaintiff to an automatic default judgment.[37] Before exercising their discretion and entering a default judgment, courts may examine the standards for setting aside a default.[38]

---

take all well-pleaded factual allegations as true).

32. *See Frow v. De La Vega*, 82 U.S. (15 Wall.) 552, 21 L.Ed. 60 (1872). *But see Whelan v. Abell*, 953 F.2d 663 (D.C.Cir. 1992) (construing *Frow* narrowly to hold that a default order that is inconsistent with a judgment on the merits must be set aside only where the liability is actually "joint" (i.e., where the theory of recovery would render all defendants (even the defaulting defendant) liable if any one of the defendants is liable)); *In re Uranium Antitrust Litig.*, 617 F.2d 1248, 1257–58 (7th Cir.1980) (same); *Douglas v. Metro Rental Servs., Inc.*, 827 F.2d 252 (7th Cir. 1987)(same); *Martin v. Coughlin*, 895 F.Supp. 39 (N.D.N.Y.1995)(same, and noting Second Circuit view that it is "most unlikely" that *Frow* principle survived promulgation of Rule 54(b)).

33. 50 U.S.C.A.App. § 501.

34. *See* Rule 54(c).

35. *See Kauffman v. Cal Spas*, 37 F.Supp.2d 402, 404 (E.D.Pa.1999); *Patray v. Northwest Publ'g, Inc.*, 931 F.Supp. 865, 868 (S.D.Ga.1996).

36. *See Bender Shipbuilding & Repair Co., Inc. v. Vessel DRIVE OCEAN V*, 123 F.Supp.2d 1201, 1208 (S.D.Cal.1998); *Patray v. Northwest Publ'g, Inc.*, 931 F.Supp. 865, 868 (S.D.Ga.1996); *D.B. v. Bloom*, 896 F.Supp. 166 (D.N.J.1995).

37. *See Philip Morris USA, Inc. v. Castworld Prods., Inc.*, 219 F.R.D. 494, 498 (C.D.Cal.2003).

38. *See Philip Morris USA, Inc. v. Castworld Prods., Inc.*, 219 F.R.D. 494, 498 (C.D.Cal.2003).

Appealability

The entry of a judgment by default is a final order, and is subject to immediate appeal.[39] Although often, upon the entry of a default judgment, the defaulted litigant will move the district court for relief from the default under Rule 55(c) and Rule 60(b), this is not required. Because a default judgment is a final order, the defaulted litigant may appeal at once.[40] Note, however, that the appellate review is an abuse of discretion standard.[41]

RULE 55(c). SETTING ASIDE DEFAULT OR A DEFAULT JUDGMENT

CORE CONCEPT

The court may set aside the entry of default for good cause, and may vacate a judgment by default in accordance with Rule 60(b) (which governs some of the grounds upon which a party may seek relief from the judgment).

APPLICATIONS

Setting Aside a Default

Rule 55(c) authorizes the district courts, "for good cause", to set aside the entry of a default.[42] Not susceptible to a precise definition, "good cause" has been labeled a liberal and "mutable" standard, one that varies from situation to situation.[43] This "good cause", however, is not "good cause" for the defendant's mistake, but rather "good cause" justifying the court's decision to set the default aside.[44]

In many jurisdictions, "good cause" alone is not sufficient. Instead, the courts examine various equitable criteria in determining whether to set aside a default. These criteria include: (1) proof that the default was not willful or culpable;[45] (2) prompt action by the defaulting party to correct the default;[46] (3) the existence of a

---

39. *See Ackra Direct Mktg. Corp. v. Fingerhut Corp.*, 86 F.3d 852, 855 n. 3 (8th Cir.1996).

40. *See Pecarsky v. Galaxiworld.com Ltd.*, 249 F.3d 167, 170–71 (2d Cir. 2001).

41. *See Pecarsky v. Galaxiworld.com Ltd.*, 249 F.3d 167, 171 (2d Cir. 2001).

42. *See African Methodist Episcopal Church, Inc. v. Ward*, 185 F.3d 1201, 1202 (11th Cir.1999) (noting that district court may set aside entry of default only if good reason is provided).

43. *See Compania Interamericana Export–Import, S.A. v. Compania Dominicana de Aviacion*, 88 F.3d 948, 951 (11th Cir. 1996).

44. *See Sims v. EGA Prods., Inc.*, 475 F.3d 865, 868 (7th Cir. 2007).

45. *See SEC v. McNulty*, 137 F.3d 732, 738 (2d Cir.1998) (explaining that "willfulness" refers to more than merely negligent or careless conduct, but may be found where conduct was egregious and not adequately explained). *See also Burrell v. Henderson*, 434 F.3d 826, 831–32 (6th Cir. 2006); *Franchise Holding II, LLC. v. Huntington Restaurants Group, Inc.*, 375 F.3d 922, 925–26 (9th Cir.2004).

46. *See Payne ex rel. Estate of Calzada v. Brake*, 439 F.3d 198, 204 (4th Cir.2006); *Effjohn Int'l Cruise Holdings, Inc. v. A&L Sales, Inc.*, 346 F.3d 552, 563 (5th Cir. 2003); *KPS & Assocs., Inc. v. Designs By FMC, Inc.*, 318 F.3d 1, 12 (1st Cir.2003).

meritorious defense;[47] (4) an absence of prejudice to the opponent;[48] (5) whether the default resulted from a good faith mistake in following a rule of procedure;[49] (6) the nature of the defendant's explanation for defaulting;[50] (7) the amount in controversy;[51] (8) the availability of effective alternative sanctions;[52] and (9) whether entry of a default would produce a harsh or unfair result.[53] Each particular consideration need not necessarily be satisfied,[54] and the list is generally seen as non-exhaustive, intended instead to serve only as a series of indicators of circumstances that could warrant setting aside a default.[55] Such determinations are necessarily case-specific, and are made in a "practical, commonsense manner, without rigid

47. *See Payne ex rel. Estate of Calzada v. Brake*, 439 F.3d 198, 204 (4th Cir.2006); *Burrell v. Henderson*, 434 F.3d 826, 831–32 (6th Cir.2006); *Franchise Holding II, LLC. v. Huntington Restaurants Group, Inc.*, 375 F.3d 922, 925–26 (9th Cir.2004).

48. *See SEC v. McNulty*, 137 F.3d 732, 740 (2d Cir.1998) (noting prejudice element, but clarifying that mere absence of prejudice would not automatically entitle defaulting party to relief); *East Coast Express, Inc. v. Ruby, Inc.*, 162 F.R.D. 37 (E.D.Pa. 1995)(prejudice means a loss of evidence or the impairment of plaintiff's ability to press claim; prejudice not established merely by showing that litigation will continue absent default); *Mathon v. Marine Midland Bank, N.A.*, 875 F.Supp. 986, 992 (E.D.N.Y. 1995)(noting that real prejudice is indicated by loss of evidence, unavailability of witnesses, or roadblocks to discovery). *See also Payne ex rel. Estate of Calzada v. Brake*, 439 F.3d 198, 204 (4th Cir.2006); *Burrell v. Henderson*, 434 F.3d 826, 831–32 (6th Cir.2006); *Franchise Holding II, LLC. v. Huntington Restaurants Group, Inc.*, 375 F.3d 922, 925–26 (9th Cir.2004). Note that the practical reality that, absent default, the moving party would be required to litigate on the merits ordinarily does *not* qualify as "prejudice" within the meaning of Rule 55(c). *See Thiemann v. Electrical Insulation Suppliers, Inc.*, 180 F.R.D. 200, 201 (D.P.R.1998).

49. *See KPS & Assocs., Inc. v. Designs By FMC, Inc.*, 318 F.3d 1, 12 (1st Cir.2003); *Conetta v. National Hair Care Ctrs., Inc.*, 186 F.R.D. 262, 268–69 (D.R.I.1999).

50. *See KPS & Assocs., Inc. v. Designs By FMC, Inc.*, 318 F.3d 1, 12 (1st Cir.2003).

51. *See KPS & Assocs., Inc. v. Designs By FMC, Inc.*, 318 F.3d 1, 12 (1st Cir.2003); *Compania Interamericana Export–Import, S.A. v. Compania Dominicana de Aviacion*, 88 F.3d 948, 951 (11th Cir.1996).

52. *See Payne ex rel. Estate of Calzada v. Brake*, 439 F.3d 198, 204–05 (4th Cir. 2006); *Kauffman v. Cal Spas*, 37 F.Supp.2d 402, 404 (E.D.Pa.1999).

53. *See Richardson v. Nassau County*, 184 F.R.D. 497, 501 (E.D.N.Y.1999); *Canfield v. VSH Restaurant Corp.*, 162 F.R.D. 431 (N.D.N.Y.1995).

54. *See Franchise Holding II, LLC. v. Huntington Restaurants Group, Inc.*, 375 F.3d 922, 926 (9th Cir.2004) (commenting that factors are disjunctive, and motion for relief could be denied if any factor was true); *Conetta v. National Hair Care Ctrs., Inc.*, 186 F.R.D. 262, 268–69 (D.R.I.1999) (commenting that no precise formula is required, and each case will turn on its own particular facts). *But see Messick v. Toyota Motor Mfg., Ky., Inc.*, 45 F.Supp.2d 578, 582 (E.D.Ky.1999) (holding that movant *must* independently satisfy each of three factors—absence of culpability, absence of prejudice to the adversary, and existence of meritorious defense).

55. *See Effjohn Int'l Cruise Holdings, Inc. v. A&L Sales, Inc.*, 346 F.3d 552, 563 (5th Cir.2003) (noting factors are non-exclusive, and "are to be regarded simply as a means to identify good cause"); *KPS & Assocs., Inc. v. Designs By FMC, Inc.*, 318 F.3d 1, 12 (1st Cir.2003) (noting court will consider "panoply of relevant equitable factors"); *Fink v. Swisshelm*, 185 F.R.D. 353 (D.Kan.1999) (commenting that factors are not talismanic, and others may be considered); *Richardson v. Nassau County*, 184 F.R.D. 497, 501 (E.D.N.Y.1999) (same effect). *But cf. Conetta v. National Hair Care Ctrs., Inc.*, 186 F.R.D. 262, 269 (D.R.I.1999) (court may deny vacation where party claims to have simply "misplaced" the legal papers, to have negligently ignored deadlines, or to have avoided the case in the hope it "would all go away").

adherence to, or undue reliance upon, a mechanical formula".[56] Note, however, that some courts conclude that the first criterion (willfulness) can, by itself, justify ending the inquiry and preserving the default.[57]

> *Note:* In practice, any of the grounds that justify vacating a default judgment will likely also constitute adequate "good cause" to warrant setting aside the entry of a default. This "good cause" test is more lenient than the Rule 60(b) standard,[58] however, and some circumstances that might not justify relief from judgment under Rule 60(b) could still permit the setting aside of the entry of default under Rule 55(c) (*e.g.,* illness of counsel, mistake of counsel).

Vacating a Judgment by Default

Once a judgment is entered upon a party's default, the task of vacating it becomes more difficult.[59] The court may vacate a default judgment if (1) the defaulting party meets the "good cause" test noted above, *and also* (2) satisfies one of the Rule 60(b) reasons for vacating a judgment (*i.e.,* mistake, inadvertence, surprise, excusable neglect, newly discovered evidence, misconduct by an adverse party, void judgment, or satisfied or discharged judgment).[60] Default judgments are "the biggest weapon in the district court's armory", and may be useful in reining in recalcitrant parties or penalizing prejudicial tactics.[61] Such judgments generally are not appropriate where the misstep does not prejudice the adversary but costs the erring party an otherwise certain victory.[62] The time for filing such motions is set forth in Rule 60(b).

Discretion of District Court

Defaults and default judgments are disfavored, as such remedies are inconsistent with the federal courts' preference for resolving

---

56. *See KPS & Assocs., Inc. v. Designs By FMC, Inc.,* 318 F.3d 1, 12 (1st Cir.2003).

57. *See Lacy v. Sitel Corp.,* 227 F.3d 290, 291 (5th Cir.2000) (commenting that a finding of intentional failure of responsive pleadings ends the need for further findings).

58. *See Sims v. EGA Prods., Inc.,* 475 F.3d 865, 868 (7th Cir. 2007); *Dennis Garberg & Assocs., Inc. v. Pack–Tech Int'l Corp.,* 115 F.3d 767, 775 n. 6 (10th Cir. 1997); *American Alliance Ins. Co. v. Eagle Ins. Co.,* 92 F.3d 57 (2d Cir.1996).

59. *See Brand Scaffold Builders, Inc. v. Puerto Rico Elec. Power Auth.,* 364 F.Supp.2d 50, 54 (D.P.R.2005) (noting that Rule 55(c) "good cause" standard is "lower and more easily overcome" than requirements for relief from judgment under Rule 60).

60. *See Brien v. Kullman Indus.,* 71 F.3d 1073, 1077 (2d Cir.1995) (noting factors including willfulness, the existence of a meritorious defense, and the level of prejudice to the non-defaulting party); *Enron Oil Corp. v. Diakuhara,* 10 F.3d 90, 96 (2d Cir.1993)(noting that factors for vacating a default judgment are largely the same as those for setting aside a default, except that the courts apply the factors more rigorously in cases of default judgments); *O'Brien v. R.J. O'Brien & Assocs., Inc.,* 998 F.2d 1394 (7th Cir.1993)(same); *East Coast Express, Inc. v. Ruby, Inc.,* 162 F.R.D. 37 (E.D.Pa. 1995)(court must consider defendant's meritorious defense, prejudice to plaintiff, culpability of defendant's conduct, and effectiveness of other sanctions).

61. *See Mommaerts v. Hartford Life & Acc. Ins. Co.,* 472 F.3d 967, 967–69 (7th Cir. 2007).

62. *See Mommaerts v. Hartford Life & Acc. Ins. Co.,* 472 F.3d 967, 969–69 (7th Cir. 2007).

disputes on their merits.[63]   Thus, defaults are extreme sanctions[64] reserved for rare occasions, the "good faith" criteria are applied generously,[65] and doubts are resolved in favor of lifting the default.[66] Whether to set aside the entry of default or vacate a default judgment is left to the discretion of the district judge.[67]

RULE 55(d).   DEFAULT JUDGMENT AGAINST THE UNITED STATES

CORE CONCEPT

No default judgment may be entered against the United States or any federal agency or officer, unless the plaintiff establishes, by evidence satisfactory to the court, a claim or right to relief.

APPLICATIONS

2007 Amendments

Old Rule 55(d) ("Plaintiffs, Counterclaimants, Cross–Claimants") was deleted in 2007 as unnecessary. The first sentence of this former Rule incompletely listed those who could move for default judgments, and the second sentence merely cross-referenced to Rule 54(c)'s allowable scope of judgments. The content of former Rule 55(e) has now been moved up to Rule 55(d). Practitioners searching for pre–2007 interpretations of this Rule should bear this repositioning in mind in doing their research. Current Rule 55(d) was, until 2007, old Rule 55(e).

Policy

The entry of default judgments against the United States is not favored.   The courts reason that federal taxpayers (on whom the burden of paying the default judgment would ultimately rest) should not be called upon to pay a penalty imposed as the consequence of the neglect of some government official, if to do so would cause a windfall to the litigant.[68]

63. *See Enron Oil Corp. v. Diakuhara*, 10 F.3d 90, 95–96 (2d Cir.1993); *United States on Behalf of and for Use of Time Equip. Rental & Sales, Inc. v. Harre*, 983 F.2d 128, 130 (8th Cir.1993);. *Richardson v. Nassau County*, 184 F.R.D. 497, 501 (E.D.N.Y.1999) (in deciding Rule 55(c) motion, court must be mindful of longstanding preference in the federal courts that litigation disputes be resolved on their merits).

64. *See Mommaerts v. Hartford Life & Acc. Ins. Co.*, 472 F.3d 967–69 (7th Cir. 2007); *D.B. v. Bloom*, 896 F.Supp. 166 (D.N.J.1995). *See also Martin v. Coughlin*, 895 F.Supp. 39, 42 (N.D.N.Y.1995)(default judgment is extreme sanction, and "a weapon of last, and not first, resort").

65. *See Martin v. Coughlin*, 895 F.Supp. 39 (N.D.N.Y.1995).

66. *See Powerserve Int'l, Inc. v. Lavi*, 239 F.3d 508, 514 (2d Cir.2001); *Lacy v. Sitel Corp.*, 227 F.3d 290, 291 (5th Cir. 2000); *Enron Oil Corp. v. Diakuhara*, 10 F.3d 90, 96 (2d Cir.1993).

67. *See Payne ex rel. Estate of Calzada v. Brake*, 439 F.3d 198, 204 (4th Cir.2006); *O.J. Distrib., Inc. v. Hornell Brewing Co.*, 340 F.3d 345, 353 (6th Cir.2003); *Bailey v. United Airlines*, 279 F.3d 194, 204 (3d Cir. 2002).

68. *See Compania Interamericana Export–Import, S.A. v. Compania Dominicana de Aviacion*, 88 F.3d 948, 951 (11th Cir. 1996); *ABI Investment Group v. FDIC*, 860 F.Supp. 911, 914 (D.N.H.1994).   The Foreign Sovereign Immunities Act, 28 U.S.C.A. § 1608(e), provides foreign sovereigns with

Applies Only to Judgments, Not Defaults

Although default judgments may not be entered against the United States, the default itself may be entered.[69]

Claim-or-Right-to-Relief Inquiry

The court's inquiry to determine whether the plaintiff has a claim or a right-to-relief against the United States (and, thus, should be entitled to seek a default judgment) does not necessarily require a hearing, or either more or different evidence than would otherwise be received.[70] (However, at least one court has ruled that the burden for default against the United States is "higher", and requires a demonstration of an evidentiary basis that is legally sufficient for a reasonable jury to find for the plaintiff.[71]) Instead, the courts assume a flexible approach in determining the procedures necessary to conduct this inquiry.[72]

Foreign Governments

By statute, Congress requires that this same "satisfies-the-court" standard be applied in actions against foreign governments, foreign political subdivisions, and foreign agencies and instrumentalities.[73]

ADDITIONAL RESEARCH REFERENCES

Wright & Miller, *Federal Practice and Procedure* §§ 2681–2702.

C.J.S. Federal Civil Procedure §§ 1122–1134 et seq.

West's Key No. Digests, Federal Civil Procedure ⚷2411–2455.

this same protection against default judgments in federal courts. *See Commercial Bank of Kuwait v. Rafidain Bank*, 15 F.3d 238, 242 (2d Cir.1994); *Nationsbank of Florida v. Banco Exterior de Espana*, 867 F.Supp. 167, 174 (S.D.N.Y. 1994)(commenting that court's preference for denying motion for default judgment is particularly strong where the defendant is a foreign sovereign; when foreign sovereign defaults, movant bears the burden to show sufficient evidence that default judgment is appropriate).

69. *See Alameda v. Secretary of Health, Educ. & Welfare*, 622 F.2d 1044, 1048 (1st Cir.1980)(noting that default may be entered, and commenting that the exemption from default judgments "heightens" the United States' obligation to cooperate with the court).

70. *See Commercial Bank of Kuwait v. Rafidain Bank*, 15 F.3d 238, 242 (2d Cir. 1994).

71. *See Smith ex rel. Smith v. Islamic Emirate of Afghanistan*, 262 F.Supp.2d 217, 223–24 (S.D.N.Y.2003).

72. *See Gadoury v. United States*, 187 B.R. 816, 822 (D.R.I.1995).

73. *See* 28 U.S.C.A. § 1608(e). *See also Weininger v. Castro*, 462 F.Supp.2d 457, 491 n.28 (S.D.N.Y. 2006).

RULE 56

SUMMARY JUDGMENT

(a) By a Claiming Party. A party claiming relief may move, with or without supporting affidavits, for summary judgment on all or part of the claim. The motion may be filed at any time after:

    (1) 20 days have passed from commencement of the action; or

    (2) the opposing party serves a motion for summary judgment.

(b) By a Defending Party. A party against whom relief is sought may move at any time, with or without supporting affidavits, for summary judgment on all or part of the claim.

(c) Serving the Motion; Proceedings. The motion must be served at least 10 days before the day set for the hearing. An opposing party may serve opposing affidavits before the hearing day. The judgment sought should be rendered if the pleadings, the discovery and disclosure materials on file, and any affidavits show that there is no genuine issue as to any material fact and that the movant is entitled to judgment as a matter of law.

(d) Case Not Fully Adjudicated on the Motion.

    (1) *Establishing Facts.* If summary judgment is not rendered on the whole action, the court should, to the extent practicable, determine what material facts are not genuinely at issue. The court should so determine by examining the pleadings and evidence before it and by interrogating the attorneys. It should then issue an order specifying what facts—including items of damages or other relief—are not genuinely at issue. The facts so specified must be treated as established in the action.

    (2) *Establishing Liability.* An interlocutory summary judgment may be rendered on liability alone, even if there is a genuine issue on the amount of damages.

(e) Affidavits; Further Testimony.

    (1) *In General.* A supporting or opposing affidavit must be made on personal knowledge, set out facts that

963

would be admissible in evidence, and show that the affiant is competent to testify on the matters stated. If a paper or part of a paper is referred to in an affidavit, a sworn or certified copy must be attached to or served with the affidavit. The court may permit an affidavit to be supplemented or opposed by depositions, answers to interrogatories, or additional affidavits.

(2) *Opposing Party's Obligation to Respond.* When a motion for summary judgment is properly made and supported, an opposing party may not rely merely on allegations or denials in its own pleading; rather, its response must—by affidavits or as otherwise provided in this rule—set out specific facts showing a genuine issue for trial. If the opposing party does not so respond, summary judgment should, if appropriate, be entered against that party.

(f) When Affidavits Are Unavailable. If a party opposing the motion shows by affidavit that, for specified reasons, it cannot present facts essential to justify its opposition, the court may:

(1) deny the motion;

(2) order a continuance to enable affidavits to be obtained, depositions to be taken, or other discovery to be undertaken; or

(3) issue any other just order.

(g) Affidavit Submitted in Bad Faith. If satisfied that an affidavit under this rule is submitted in bad faith or solely for delay, the court must order the submitting party to pay the other party the reasonable expenses, including attorney's fees, it incurred as a result. An offending party or attorney may also be held in contempt.

[Amended effective March 19, 1948; July 1, 1963; August 1, 1987; April 30, 2007, effective December 1, 2007.]

─────────── **2007 AMENDMENTS ROADMAP** ───────────

STYLE PROJECT CHANGES: The familiar summary judgment standard ("no genuine issue as to any material fact", with the moving party "entitled to judgment as a matter of law") was retained without change. The incomplete listings in Rule 56(a) and Rule 56(b) of specific litigants who could seek summary judgment was culled, and replaced with more generic language. Rule 56(c)'s scope of the permitted summary judgment record now expressly includes Rule 26 disclosure materials. Partial summary adjudications on liability-alone was moved from Rule 56(c) to Rule 56(d), which in turn was restructured into "factual" and "liability" partial adjudications. Rule 56(d)'s language was also conformed to the Rule 56(c) standard. Rule 56(e) and Rule 56(f) were subsectioned, and new labels were added. "Shall" was replaced by "must" or "should", depending on context.

NON-STYLE CHANGES: Old references in Rule 56(c) and Rule 56(d) that summary judgment "shall" be granted were changed to "should" (and the emphatic "forthwith" was deleted from Rule 56(c)). The drafters intend these revisions to better reflect the district court's discretion to grant (or not grant) summary judgment even when the literal terms for such relief are otherwise satisfied, albeit (they note) that such discretion ought to be exercised sparingly.

NOTE: The Federal Rules "Style Project" is explained in Part III-A.

AUTHORS' COMMENTARY ON RULE 56

PURPOSE AND SCOPE

Rule 56 sets the procedure by which a party may request or oppose either full or partial summary judgment, and the standards the federal courts consider when ruling on motions for summary judgment.

COMPARISONS WITH OTHER RULES OF ADJUDICATION

Dismissals and Judgments on the Pleadings: When granting a dismissal under Rule 12(b)(6) or a judgment on the pleadings under Rule 12(c), the district judge generally examines only the allegations contained in the non-moving party's pleadings to determine whether the averments of law and fact, if true, are legally sufficient. In contrast, a motion for summary judgment under Rule 56 permits the district judge to consult not only the pleadings, but also any affidavits, depositions, interrogatory answers, admissions, Rule 26 disclosures, and other evidence to determine whether any factual dispute exists between the parties.

> *Note:* A motion to dismiss under Rule 12(b)(6) for failing to state a claim upon which relief can be granted and a motion for judgment on the pleadings under Rule 12(c) will be converted into a Rule 56 motion for summary judgment if the court considers matters outside the pleadings in ruling on the motion.[1]

1. *See* Rule 12(d). *See also supra* Au-   thors' Commentary to Rule 12(d).

Judgments as a Matter of Law: The prerequisites for and effects of summary judgments are much the same as judgments as a matter of law, entered under Rule 50 (the federal equivalent of a "directed verdict").[2] Both motions test for whether, on the evidence then before the court, a reasonable jury could return a verdict in the nonmoving party's favor. Both motions, if granted, will result in a "judgment" in the movant's favor. The difference between the motions is largely one of timing. Summary judgment motions are filed before trial begins and are supported by pleadings, Rule 26 disclosures, discovery responses, affidavits, deposition excerpts, documents, and other "cold" evidence. Conversely, motions for judgment as a matter of law are made during trial, after the close of the plaintiff's case (and, possibly, the defendant's case), with the trial judge having listened to a full, live evidentiary presentation. Thus, Rule 50 motions challenge whether there is any need for the trial—then underway—to reach the jury deliberation stage; Rule 56 motions challenge whether there is any need to convene a trial at all.

RULE 56(a)–(b).   PARTIES WHO MAY MAKE MOTION

CORE CONCEPT

Motions for summary judgment may be filed in any federal court action—whether at law or equity—by any claiming or defending party, including the United States, its agencies and officers.

APPLICATIONS

Motions by Claiming Parties

Summary judgment is not only a defensive tool; claimants can move for summary judgment on their own claims as well.[3] There is a timing restriction on motions by claimants, however. Claimants must wait to file such motions until 20 days after the lawsuit was commenced or immediately after the defendant files her motion for summary judgment, whichever is earlier.[4]

Motions by Defending Parties

Defending parties may move for summary judgment at any

---

2. *See Anderson v. Liberty Lobby, Inc.,* 477 U.S. 242, 250–51, 106 S.Ct. 2505, 2511, 91 L.Ed.2d 202 (1986) (noting that summary judgment standard "mirrors the standard for a directed verdict under Federal Rule of Civil Procedure 50(a), which is that the trial judge must direct a verdict if, under the governing law, there can be but one reasonable conclusion as to the verdict").

3. *See Bouchat v. Baltimore Ravens Football Club, Inc.,* 346 F.3d 514, 521 (4th Cir.2003).

4. *See G & G Fire Sprinklers, Inc. v. Bradshaw,* 136 F.3d 587 (9th Cir.1998),

amended and superseded on other grounds, 156 F.3d 893 (9th Cir.1998), *vacated on other grounds,* 526 U.S. 1061, 119 S.Ct. 1450, 143 L.Ed.2d 538 (1999)(rejecting argument that plaintiff's motion for summary judgment was "premature" when it was filed more than 20 days after lawsuit was commenced and no motion under Rule 56(f) was pending); *United States v. Cannabis Cultivators Club,* 5 F.Supp.2d 1086 (N.D.Cal.1998) (ruling that plaintiff's motion for summary judgment was premature where it was filed at the same time as the lawsuit itself).

time.[5] Note, however, that the case law is unclear whether moving for summary judgment tolls the time for filing an answer to the complaint.[6] The filing of an answer is clearly not, however, a prerequisite for filing a summary judgment motion.[7]

Motions by Both Parties (Cross–Motions)

Both parties may seek summary judgment in the same action, with "cross-motions" under Rule 56.[8]

Motions by Others

Summary judgment is available only when one party is formally asserting a claim against, or defending against a claim formally asserted by, another party. The rights of parties can only be resolved by summary judgment if claims or defenses are already pending.[9]

Time for Making Motion

A motion for summary judgment can be made at almost any time. A claiming party can make a motion "at any time" after the first 20 days from commencement or after service of the adversary's motion for summary judgment.[10] A defending party can make a motion "at any time".[11] The defending party need not file an answer before moving for summary judgment,[12] although the tolling effect of such a motion is not at all certain.[13] Notwithstanding this breadth, the propriety of filing a motion for summary judgment on the eve of trial has been questioned.[14] Moreover, some courts have attempted to restraining the timing of a restrain a litigant's right to file with pretrial docket scheduling orders under Rule 16. The validity of such restraint (squarely at odds with the language of the Rule itself) has been questioned.[15]

5. *See Jefferson v. Chattanooga Pub. Co.*, 375 F.3d 461, 463 (6th Cir.2004); *Alexander v. Pathfinder, Inc.*, 189 F.3d 735, 744 (8th Cir.1999); *Mattei v. Mattei*, 126 F.3d 794, 807 (6th Cir.1997); *Brill v. Lante Corp.*, 119 F.3d 1266 (7th Cir.1997).

6. *Compare Poe v. Cristina Copper Mines, Inc.*, 15 F.R.D. 85 (D.Del. 1953)(holding that summary judgment motion does not automatically toll the period for answering) *with Rashidi v. Albright*, 818 F.Supp. 1354 (D.Nev.1993)(holding that summary judgment motion will toll the period for answering), *aff'd*, 39 F.3d 1188 (9th Cir.1994)(table).

7. *See HS Resources, Inc. v. Wingate*, 327 F.3d 432, 440 (5th Cir.2003).

8. *See B.F. Goodrich Co. v. U.S. Filter Corp.*, 245 F.3d 587, 593 (6th Cir. 2001) (noting standards for deciding cross-motions for summary judgment). *See also infra* Authors' Commentary to Rule 56(c) ("**Stipulated Facts and Cross Motions**").

9. *See Scottsdale Ins. Co. v. Knox Park Const., Inc.*, 488 F.3d 680, 685 (5th Cir. 2007).

10. *See* Rule 56(a).

11. *See* Rule 56(b).

12. *See Marquez v. Cable One, Inc.*, 463 F.3d 1118, 1120–21 (10th Cir. 2006).

13. *See* Rule 12(a) (establishing pre-answer tolling only for Rule 12(b) motions). *See also 10A Charles Alan Wright, Arthur R. Miller, Mary Kay Kane, Federal Practice & Procedure* § 2718, at 303–04 (3d ed. 1998) (opining that Rule 12(a) tolling ought to apply to a pre-answer summary judgment motion).

14. *See Johnson v. United States*, 460 F.3d 616, 620 (5th Cir. 2006) (discussing this debate).

15. *See Johnson v. United States*, 460 F.3d 616 (5th Cir.2006) (finding it "questionable" whether scheduling orders can impose such limits, but not deciding the issue).

Time for Responding to Motion

The non-moving party must be served with the motion papers at least 10 days before any hearing or disposition on the motion.[16] The purpose of this 10–day notice rule is to allow non-moving parties a specific period of time in which to marshal their resources and offer into the summary judgment record additional materials and arguments.[17] The 10–day period is an essential and mandatory component of the Rule, and not a mere technicality.[18] However, if the non-moving party has had ample opportunity to oppose the motion, or if the 10–day period would not have developed additional materials that could have defeated summary judgment, a failure to provide the 10–day notice may be deemed harmless error and excused.[19]

"Premature" Motions

Recent appellate courts seem to have rejected the notion that a summary judgment motion (the timing of which otherwise comports with Rule 56(a) or Rule 56(b)) can be "premature" simply because it was filed before discovery is completed or even begun.[20] Such a conclusion is somewhat at odds with the Supreme Court's admonition in 1986 that summary judgment may be granted only after the

---

16. See Smith v. School Bd. of Orange County, 487 F.3d 1361, 1367–68 (11th Cir. 2007); Ross v. University of Texas at San Antonio, 139 F.3d 521, 527 (5th Cir.1998); Employers Ins. of Wausau v. Petroleum Specialties, Inc., 69 F.3d 98, 105 (6th Cir.1995); Whiting v. Maiolini, 921 F.2d 5 (1st Cir. 1990).

17. See Restigouche, Inc. v. Town of Jupiter, 59 F.3d 1208, 1213 (11th Cir.1995); United States v. Houston Pipeline Co., 37 F.3d 224, 228 (5th Cir.1994)(purpose is to allow nonmoving party time "to put its best foot forward").

18. See Smith v. School Bd. of Orange County, 487 F.3d 1361, 1367–68 (11th Cir. 2007); Celestine v. Petroleos de Venezuella SA, 266 F.3d 343, 350 (5th Cir.2001); Beaird v. Seagate Tech., Inc., 145 F.3d 1159, 1165 (10th Cir.1998); Employers Ins. of Wausau v. Petroleum Specialties, Inc., 69 F.3d 98, 105 (6th Cir.1995).

19. See Celestine v. Petroleos de Venezuella SA, 266 F.3d 343, 350 (5th Cir.2001) (failure to give 10–days notice may be harmless if non-moving party admits that no additional evidence would be offered or if appellate court evaluates all additional evidence and finds no genuine issue of material fact); Restigouche, Inc. v. Town of Jupiter, 59 F.3d 1208, 1213 (11th Cir. 1995)(violation of notice period deemed harmless where supplemental materials

would not have prevented entry of summary judgment); In re Harris Pine Mills, 44 F.3d 1431, 1439–40 (9th Cir. 1995)(commenting that although court may not ordinarily enter relief under Rule 56 without 10 days notice and an opportunity to oppose, judgment may be entered without notice if losing party has had a full and fair opportunity to address the issues implicated in the motion).

20. See, e.g., Alholm v. American Steamship Co., 144 F.3d 1172, 1177 (8th Cir.1998) (noting that Rule 56 does not require that discovery be closed before motion can be heard); G & G Fire Sprinklers, Inc. v. Bradshaw, 136 F.3d 587 (9th Cir. 1998), amended and superseded on other grounds, 156 F.3d 893 (9th Cir.1998), vacated on other grounds, 526 U.S. 1061, 119 S.Ct. 1450, 143 L.Ed.2d 538 (1999) (rejecting argument that plaintiff's motion for summary judgment was "premature" when it was filed more than 20 days after lawsuit was commenced and no motion under Rule 56(f) was pending); Brill v. Lante Corp., 119 F.3d 1266, 1275 (7th Cir.1997) (commenting that plaintiff's argument that summary judgment should not have been granted while discovery remained open is an argument that "hardly concerns us because a party can file a motion for summary judgment at any time, indeed, even before discovery has begun").

nonmoving party has had an "adequate time for discovery".[21] It would seem, at least, that pre-discovery summary judgments should more appropriately be the exception, rather than the rule.[22]

RULE 56(c).   SERVING THE MOTION; PROCEEDING

Core Concept

The district court may enter summary judgment when the motion papers, affidavits, and other evidence submitted to the court show that no genuine issue exists as to any material fact, and that the moving party is entitled to judgment as a matter of law.

APPLICATIONS

Purpose of Summary Judgment

The purpose of summary judgment is to isolate, and then terminate, claims and defenses that are factually unsupported.[23] The Supreme Court has emphasized that summary judgment is not to be viewed as a disfavored technical shortcut, but rather as an integral component of the Federal Rules.[24]   Summary judgment motions must be resolved not only with an appropriate regard for the rights of those asserting claims and defenses to have their positions heard by a factfinder, but also with due regard for the rights of persons opposing such claims and defenses to demonstrate, under this Rule and *before* trial, that the claims and defenses have no factual basis.[25]   Thus, a party moving for summary judgment forces the opponent to come forward with at least one sworn averment of fact essential to that opponent's claims or defenses, before the time-consuming process of litigation will continue.[26] The non-moving party must do this by setting forth "specific facts"

21. *Celotex Corp. v. Catrett*, 477 U.S. 317, 322, 106 S.Ct. 2548, 2552, 91 L.Ed.2d 265 (1986). *Accord Jefferson v. Chattanooga Pub. Co.*, 375 F.3d 461, 463 (6th Cir.2004).

22. *See Patton v. General Signal Corp.*, 984 F.Supp. 666, 670 (W.D.N.Y.1997) (commenting that "pre-discovery summary judgment remains the exception rather than the rule, and will be 'granted only in the clearest of cases' "). *See also Doe v. Abington Friends Sch.*, 480 F.3d 252, 257 (3d Cir. 2007) ("'well established'" that opposing party must be given "adequate opportunity to obtain discovery"); *Information Handling Servs., Inc. v. Defense Automated Printing Servs.*, 338 F.3d 1024, 1032 (D.C.Cir.2003) (commenting that summary judgment is ordinarily proper only when plaintiff has had adequate time for discovery); *Miller v. Wolpoff & Abramson, L.L.P.*, 321 F.3d 292, 303–04 (2d Cir.2003) (pre-discovery summary judgment granted in only rarest cases); *Vaughn v. United States*

Small Bus. Admin., 65 F.3d 1322, 1325 n. 1 (6th Cir.1995) (defendant's summary judgment motion cannot ordinarily be considered until the plaintiff has had the opportunity to conduct discovery).

23. *See Celotex Corp. v. Catrett*, 477 U.S. 317, 323–24, 106 S.Ct. 2548, 2552–53, 91 L.Ed.2d 265 (1986).

24. *See Celotex Corp. v. Catrett*, 477 U.S. 317, 327, 106 S.Ct. 2548, 2554, 91 L.Ed.2d 265 (1986).

25. *See Celotex Corp. v. Catrett*, 477 U.S. 317, 327, 106 S.Ct. 2548, 2554, 91 L.Ed.2d 265 (1986).

26. *See Lujan v. National Wildlife Fed'n*, 497 U.S. 871, 888–89, 110 S.Ct. 3177, 3188–89, 111 L.Ed.2d 695 (1990). *See also Al–Zubaidy v. TEK Indus., Inc.*, 406 F.3d 1030, 1036 (8th Cir.2005) ("Evidence, not contentions, avoids summary judgment").

showing that there is a genuine issue requiring a trial.[27] If that party is unable to make that showing, the law requires entry of a judgment in favor of the moving party.[28] Thus, as one court has ably described it, a Rule 56 motion is "essentially 'put up or shut up' time for the non-moving party."[29]

> *Seventh Amendment Jury Rights:* A proper entry of summary judgment does not violate the nonmoving party's constitutional right under the Seventh Amendment to a trial by jury; a properly entered Rule 56 judgment means that no triable issue exists to be submitted to a jury.[30]

Standards for Granting or Denying Summary Judgment

Summary judgment should be rendered when, after an adequate period for discovery,[31] a party is unable to show a genuine issue as to a material fact on which that party will bear the burden of proof at trial, so long as judgment against that party is appropriate as a matter of law.[32]

> *Genuine Issue:* A "genuine issue" exists where the evidence before the court is of such a nature that a rational factfinder could find in favor of the non-moving party.[33] This standard parallels the test for judgment as a matter of law under Rule 50(a): a mere "scintilla" of evidence, or evidence that is only "colorable" or is not sufficiently probative, is not enough to defeat summary judgment.[34] Likewise, positing a factual scenario that is clearly contradicted by the summary judgment record will not suffice.[35] Moreover, a party theorizing a factually improbable claim or defense will be required to present more persuasive evidence than might otherwise be necessary to stave

---

27. See *Beard v. Banks*, ___ U.S. ___, ___, 126 S.Ct. 2572, 2578, 165 L.Ed.2d 697 (2006).

28. See *Beard v. Banks*, ___ U.S. ___, ___, 126 S.Ct. 2572, 2578, 165 L.Ed.2d 697 (2006).

29. See *Berckeley Inv. Group, Ltd. v. Colkitt*, 455 F.3d 195, 201 (3d Cir.2006).

30. See *Shannon v. Graves*, 257 F.3d 1164, 1167 (10th Cir.2001) (citing *Fidelity & Deposit Co. v. United States*, 187 U.S. 315, 319–20, 23 S.Ct. 120, 121-122, 47 L.Ed. 194 (1902)).

31. See *Celotex Corp. v. Catrett*, 477 U.S. 317, 322, 106 S.Ct. 2548, 2552, 91 L.Ed.2d 265 (1986); *Doe v. Abington Friends Sch.*, 480 F.3d 252, 257 (3d Cir. 2007). *See also supra* Authors' Commentary to Rule 56(a)-(b) ("**'Premature' Motions**") (discussion of pre-discovery motions for summary judgment).

32. See *Beard v. Banks*, ___ U.S. ___, ___, 126 S.Ct. 2572, 2578, 165 L.Ed.2d 697

(2006); *Department of Commerce v. U.S. House of Representatives*, 525 U.S. 316, 327, 119 S.Ct. 765, 772, 142 L.Ed.2d 797 (1999); *Nebraska v. Wyoming*, 507 U.S. 584, 589, 113 S.Ct. 1689, 1694, 123 L.Ed.2d 317 (1993); *Celotex Corp. v. Catrett*, 477 U.S. 317, 322, 106 S.Ct. 2548, 2552, 91 L.Ed.2d 265 (1986).

33. See *Scott v. Harris*, ___ U.S. ___, ___, 127 S.Ct. 1776, 167 L.Ed.2d 686 (2007); *Anderson v. Liberty Lobby, Inc.*, 477 U.S. 242, 247–252, 106 S.Ct. 2505, 91 L.Ed.2d 202 (1986); *Matsushita Elec. Indus. Co. v. Zenith Radio Corp.*, 475 U.S. 574, 586–587, 106 S.Ct. 1348, 89 L.Ed.2d 538 (1986).

34. See *Anderson v. Liberty Lobby, Inc.*, 477 U.S. 242, 247–252, 106 S.Ct. 2505, 91 L.Ed.2d 202 (1986).

35. See *Scott v. Harris*, ___ U.S. ___, ___, 127 S.Ct. 1776, 167 L.Ed.2d 686 (2007) (court should not adopt plaintiff's version of high-speed auto chase that was "blatantly contradicted" by unchallenged videotape evidence).

off summary judgment.[36] Conversely, if summary judgment is not appropriate, the mere fact that the supporting affidavits are uncontroverted will not justify granting the motion.[37] Even though no opposing evidentiary material is presented, summary judgment will be denied, where the evidence presented in support of the motion fails to demonstrate the absence of a genuine issue.[38]

> *Controlling Legal Standard:* The court will test for a "genuine issue" through the prism of the applicable controlling legal standard—the quantum and quality of proof necessary to support liability under the claims raised. Thus, if the plaintiff must prove its case by clear and convincing evidence, the court will assess whether the evidence in the summary judgment record would allow a rational factfinder to find for the plaintiff by that standard of clear and convincing evidence.[39]

Material Fact: Whether a fact is "material" hinges on the substantive law at issue. A fact is "material" if it might affect the outcome of the case.[40] Disputes over irrelevant or unnecessary facts are insufficient to defeat a motion for summary judgment.[41]

Appropriate As A Matter Of Law: Judgment is appropriate "as a matter of law" when the nonmoving party has failed to make an adequate showing on an essential element of her case, as to which she has the burden of proof.[42]

Predominantly Legal Disputes

Summary judgment is often especially appropriate in cases where the remaining unresolved disputes are primarily legal, rather

---

36. *See Matsushita Elec. Indus. Co. v. Zenith Radio Corp.*, 475 U.S. 574, 587, 106 S.Ct. 1348, 1356, 89 L.Ed.2d 538 (1986).

37. *See Edwards v. Aguillard*, 482 U.S. 578, 595, 107 S.Ct. 2573, 96 L.Ed.2d 510 (1987).

38. *See Torres–Rosado v. Rotger–Sabat*, 335 F.3d 1, 9 (1st Cir.2003).

39. *See Anderson v. Liberty Lobby, Inc.*, 477 U.S. 242, 254, 106 S.Ct. 2505, 2513, 91 L.Ed.2d 202 (1986).

40. *See Anderson v. Liberty Lobby, Inc.*, 477 U.S. 242, 248, 106 S.Ct. 2505, 2510, 91 L.Ed.2d 202 (1986). *See also Wright ex rel. Trust Co. of Kansas v. Abbott Labs., Inc.*, 259 F.3d 1226, 1231–32 (10th Cir.2001) ("material" if, under substantive law, fact is "essential to the proper disposition of the claim"); *Hoffman-Dombrowski v. Arlington Int'l Racecourse, Inc.*, 254 F.3d 644, 650 (7th Cir.2001) ("material" if fact "might

affect the outcome of the suit under the governing law").

41. *See Anderson v. Liberty Lobby, Inc.*, 477 U.S. 242, 248, 106 S.Ct. 2505, 2510, 91 L.Ed.2d 202 (1986). *See also Scott v. Harris*, ___ U.S. ___, ___, 127 S.Ct. 1776, 167 L.Ed.2d 686 (2007); *State Auto. Ins. Co. v. Lawrence*, 358 F.3d 982, 985 (8th Cir.2004).

42. *See Cleveland v. Policy Mgmt. Sys. Corp.*, 526 U.S. 795, 804, 119 S.Ct. 1597, 1603, 143 L.Ed.2d 966 (1999); *Celotex Corp. v. Catrett*, 477 U.S. 317, 323, 106 S.Ct. 2548, 2552, 91 L.Ed.2d 265 (1986); *Waterhouse v. District of Columbia*, 298 F.3d 989, 922 (D.C.Cir.2002). *See also Young Dental Mfg. Co., Inc. v. Q3 Special Prods., Inc.*, 112 F.3d 1137, 1141 (Fed.Cir.1997) (even if material facts remain disputed, summary judgment may be proper if, after all inferences are drawn in the nonmoving party's favor, the moving party is entitled to judgment as a matter of law).

than factual in nature.[43]

Discretion of District Court

The 2007 amendments emphasize the breadth of the district court's discretion when resolving a summary judgment motion. The court *must* deny summary judgment when a genuine issue of material fact remains to be tried, or where the moving party is not entitled to a judgment as a matter of law.[44] The court also may not decide the motion on the basis of clearly erroneous findings of fact, an improper application of the law, or an erroneous legal standard (ergo, the abuse of discretion standard).[45] In all other contexts, the court enjoys some measure of discretion to grant or deny the motion.[46] For example, summary judgment may be denied where the factual records are "disturbingly thin" or "contain gaps" that could be resolved by readily obtainable evidence,[47] where the court concludes that a fuller factual development is necessary[48] or where there is some particular reason to believe that the wiser course would be to proceed to trial.[49]

Warning to Unrepresented Parties

Before summary judgment may be entered against unrepresented litigants, some courts require that the unrepresented party first be expressly informed of the consequences that may follow from failing to come forward with contradicting evidence (*e.g.*, the party must be told he or she cannot rely merely on the allegations of the pleadings, and risks dismissal in doing so).[50] Other courts recognize this special warning duty, but only in the context of incarcerated unrepresented parties.[51] As to nonprisoner unrepresented parties, those courts would require no special warning.[52]

---

43. *See Koehn v. Indian Hills Cmty. Coll.*, 371 F.3d 394, 396 (8th Cir.2004).

44. *See* Rule 56 advisory committee note to 2007 amendments.

45. *See In re Brown*, 342 F.3d 620, 633 (6th Cir. 2003).

46. *See* Rule 56 advisory committee note to 2007 amendments (citing *Kennedy v. Silas Mason Co.*, 334 U.S. 249, 256–57, 68 S.Ct. 1031, 92 L.Ed. 1347 (1948)). *But cf. Beard v. Banks*, ___ U.S. ___, ___, 126 S.Ct. 2572, 2578, 165 L.Ed.2d 697 (2006) (noting that, if the non-moving party is unable to demonstrate a genuine issue of material fact, the law "requires" entry of a judgment in favor of the moving party).

47. *See Spratt v. Rhode Island Dep't of Corrections*, 482 F.3d 33, 43 (1st Cir. 2007).

48. *See Kennedy v. Silas Mason Co.*, 334 U.S. 249, 68 S.Ct. 1031, 92 L.Ed. 1347 (1948).

49. *See Anderson v. Liberty Lobby, Inc.*, 477 U.S. 242, 255, 106 S.Ct. 2505, 2513, 91 L.Ed.2d 202 (1986).

50. *See United States v. Ninety Three Firearms*, 330 F.3d 414, 427 (6th Cir.2003) (collecting cases); *Bryant v. Madigan*, 84 F.3d 246, 248 (7th Cir.1996) (Posner, J.).

51. *See United States v. Ninety Three Firearms*, 330 F.3d 414, 427–28 (6th Cir. 2003).

52. *See United States v. Ninety Three Firearms*, 330 F.3d 414, 428 (6th Cir.2003) (citing other precedent in concluding that this distinction "was only fair because parties choosing to have counsel 'must bear the risk of their attorney's mistakes,' and thus, 'a litigant who chooses himself as a legal representative should be treated no differently' ").

Burden of Proof

The party moving for summary judgment always has the burden of persuasion on such a motion. The burden of going forward, however, shifts during the motion process.

The moving party must first make a prima facie showing that summary judgment is appropriate under Rule 56. This does not require the moving party to disprove the opponent's claims or defenses.[53] Instead, this prima facie burden is discharged simply by pointing out for the court an absence of evidence in support of the non-moving party's claims or defenses.[54] The burden of going forward then shifts to the non-moving party to show, by affidavit or otherwise, that a genuine issue of material fact remains for the factfinder to resolve.[55] The non-moving party must carry this burden as to each essential element on which she bears the burden of proof.[56] Thus, once this summary judgment stage arrives, the non-moving party is not saved by merely recounting the generous notice-pleading standards of the federal courts.[57] She must show evidence.[58] A party does *not* meet this burden simply by theorizing a "plausible scenario" in support of the party's claims, when that proffered scenario conflicts with direct, contrary evidence.[59]

The burden of uncovering the existence or absence of a disputed issue of material fact will rarely shift to the trial judge. Most courts that have considered the issue have ruled that the trial judge is not generally obligated to conduct an independent review of the record, sifting through the often voluminous record, unguided, searching for a genuine issue of fact sufficient to defeat summary judgment.[60] In fact, even though courts enjoy the discretion to conduct such independent reviews, they are cautioned to be wary in doing so, mindful of their limited, neutral roles and vigilant against transforming into advocates for any party.[61] Not all courts agree, however. Some courts seem to hold that the district judge has such an independent

53. *See Edwards v. Aguillard,* 482 U.S. 578, 595, 107 S.Ct. 2573, 96 L.Ed.2d 510 (1987); *Celotex Corp. v. Catrett,* 477 U.S. 317, 323, 106 S.Ct. 2548, 2553, 91 L.Ed.2d 265 (1986).

54. *See Celotex Corp. v. Catrett,* 477 U.S. 317, 106 S.Ct. 2548, 2553, 91 L.Ed.2d 265 (1986).

55. *See Celotex Corp. v. Catrett,* 477 U.S. 317, 106 S.Ct. 2548, 91 L.Ed.2d 265 (1986). *See also Beard v. Banks,* ___ U.S. ___, ___, 126 S.Ct. 2572, 2578, 165 L.Ed.2d 697 (2006).

56. *See Wheeler v. Aventis Pharms.,* 360 F.3d 853, 857 (8th Cir.2004).

57. *See Tucker v. Union of Needletrades, Indus. & Textile Employees,* 407 F.3d 784, 788 (6th Cir.2005).

58. *See Al–Zubaidy v. TEK Indus., Inc.,* 406 F.3d 1030, 1036 (8th Cir.2005) ("Evi-

dence, not contentions, avoids summary judgment").

59. *See Scott v. Harris,* ___ U.S. ___, ___, 127 S.Ct. 1769, 1774–76, 167 L.Ed.2d 686 (2007); *Swanson v. Leggett & Platt, Inc.,* 154 F.3d 730, 733 (7th Cir.1998).

60. *See Winters v. Fru–Con Inc.,* ___ F.3d ___, ___, 2007 WL 2377386, at *6 (7th Cir. 2007); *Chicago Title Ins. Corp. v. Magnuson,* 487 F.3d 985, 995 (6th Cir. 2007); *Adams v. Travelers Indem. Co.,* 465 F.3d 156, 164 (5th Cir. 2006); *Amnesty America v. Town of West Hartford,* 288 F.3d 467, 470 (2d Cir.2002); *Carmen v. San Francisco Unified Sch. Dist.,* 237 F.3d 1026, 1030–31 (9th Cir.2001); *Jackson v. Finnegan, Henderson, Farabow, Garrett & Dunner,* 101 F.3d 145, 154 (D.C.Cir.1996).

61. *See Adler v. Wal–Mart Stores, Inc.,* 144 F.3d 664, 672 (10th Cir. 1998).

obligation generally,[62] or must conduct such an independent search in certain cases, such as those involving the First Amendment.[63]

Doubts and Inferences

In ruling on a motion for summary judgment, the court will never weigh the evidence or find the facts.[64] Instead, the court's role under Rule 56 is narrowly limited to assessing the threshold issue of whether a genuine issue exists as to material facts requiring a trial.[65] Thus, the evidence of the non-moving party will be believed as true, all doubts will be resolved against the moving party, all evidence will be construed in the light most favorable to the non-moving party, and all reasonable inferences will be drawn in the non-moving party's favor.[66]

"Reasonable" inferences are inferences reasonably drawn from all the facts then before the court, after sifting through the universe of all possible inferences the facts could support. "Reasonable" inferences are not necessarily more probable or likely than other inferences that might tilt in the moving party's favor. Instead, so long as more than one reasonable inference can be drawn, and one inference creates a genuine issue of material fact, the trier of fact is entitled to decide which inference to believe and summary judgment is not appropriate.[67]

Ordinarily, an appropriately supported summary judgment motion cannot be defeated by inferences that are unreasonable or improbable, allegations that are conclusory, or rank speculation.[68] Nor will a motion be defeated by a posited factual scenario that is clearly contradicted by the summary judgment record,[69] or by the

---

62. See Stepanischen v. Merchants Despatch Trans. Corp., 722 F.2d 922, 931 (1st Cir.1983) (holding that Rule 56(c) imposes on trial courts the duty to examine all evidence "on file").

63. See Summum v. Duchesne City, 482 F.3d 1263, 1268 (10th Cir. 2007) (because case involved First Amendment interests, "we have an obligation to conduct an independent review of the record and to examine constitutional facts and conclusions of law de novo"); Andersen v. McCotter, 100 F.3d 723, 725 (10th Cir. 1996) (same).

64. See Baranski v. Fifteen Unknown Agents of Bureau of Alcohol, Tobacco & Firearms, 452 F.3d 433, 451 (6th Cir.2006).

65. See Anderson v. Liberty Lobby, Inc., 477 U.S. 242, 249, 106 S.Ct. 2505, 2510, 91 L.Ed.2d 202 (1986).

66. See Beard v. Banks, ___ U.S. ___, ___, 126 S.Ct. 2572, 2578, 165 L.Ed.2d 697 (2006); Hunt v. Cromartie, 526 U.S. 541, 550–55, 119 S.Ct. 1545, 1551–52, 143

L.Ed.2d 731 (1999); Eastman Kodak Co. v. Image Technical Servs., Inc., 504 U.S. 451, 456, 112 S.Ct. 2072, 2076, 119 L.Ed.2d 265 (1992); Anderson v. Liberty Lobby, Inc., 477 U.S. 242, 255, 106 S.Ct. 2505, 2513, 91 L.Ed.2d 202 (1986); Adickes v. S.H. Kress & Co., 398 U.S. 144, 157–59, 90 S.Ct. 1598, 1608–09, 26 L.Ed.2d 142 (1970).

67. See Hunt v. Cromartie, 526 U.S. 541, 552, 119 S.Ct. 1545, 1552, 143 L.Ed.2d 731 (1999); Patterson & Wilder Const. Co., Inc. v. United States, 226 F.3d 1269, 1273 (11th Cir.2000).

68. See Caban Hernandez v. Philip Morris USA, Inc., 486 F.3d 1, 8 (1st Cir. 2007); Mulloy v. Acushnet Co., 460 F.3d 141 (1st Cir.2006); Ellis v. England, 432 F.3d 1321, 1326 (11th Cir.2005).

69. See Scott v. Harris, ___ U.S. ___, ___, 127 S.Ct. 1776, 167 L.Ed.2d 686 (2007) (court should not adopt plaintiff's version of high-speed auto chase that was "blatantly contradicted" by unchallenged videotape evidence).

mere promise from the non-moving party that she will later demonstrate the falsity of the moving party's facts.[70] "Evidence, not contentions, avoids summary judgment,"[71] and non-moving parties must arrive brandishing more than "a cardboard sword".[72]

Credibility Questions

The court will not weigh the credibility of witnesses or other evidence in ruling on a motion for summary judgment.[73] Evaluating credibility, weighing evidence, and drawing factual inferences are all functions reserved for the jury.[74] However, simply lobbing broad, conclusory attacks on a witness's credibility is not enough to defeat summary judgment.[75]

State of Mind Questions

Summary judgment is never automatically foreclosed merely because a person's state of mind (such as motive, knowledge, intent, good faith or bad faith, malice, fraud, conspiracy, or consent) is at issue.[76] But such cases will seldom lend themselves to a summary disposition because questions of credibility will ordinarily abound.[77] Thus, summary judgment is used "sparingly" and "seldom granted" in cases involving peculiarly intensive state of mind questions such as employment actions, discrimination claims, and antitrust cases.[78]

---

70. *See Island Software & Computer Serv., Inc. v. Microsoft Corp.*, 413 F.3d 257, 261–62 (2d Cir.2005).

71. *See Al–Zubaidy v. TEK Indus., Inc.*, 406 F.3d 1030, 1036 (8th Cir.2005).

72. *See Calvi v. Knox County*, 470 F.3d 422, 426 (1st Cir. 2006).

73. *See Baranski v. Fifteen Unknown Agents of Bureau of Alcohol, Tobacco & Firearms*, 452 F.3d 433, 451 (6th Cir.2006).

74. *See Anderson v. Liberty Lobby, Inc.*, 477 U.S. 242, 255, 106 S.Ct. 2505, 2513, 91 L.Ed.2d 202 (1986).

75. *See Island Software & Computer Serv., Inc. v. Microsoft Corp.*, 413 F.3d 257, 261–62 (2d Cir.2005).

76. *See Quinones v. Buick*, 436 F.3d 284, 289 (1st Cir.2006); *Ward v. Bechtel Corp.*, 102 F.3d 199, 202 (5th Cir.1997); *Ennis v. National Ass'n of Business & Educational Radio, Inc.*, 53 F.3d 55, 62 (4th Cir.1995).

77. *See Hutchinson v. Proxmire*, 443 U.S. 111, 99 S.Ct. 2675, 61 L.Ed.2d 411 (1979). *See also Graham v. Long Island R.R.*, 230 F.3d 34, 38 (2d Cir.2000) (commenting that summary judgment is used "sparingly" where intent and state of mind are implicated); *EMI Catalogue Partnership v. Hill, Holliday, Connors, Cosmopulos Inc.*,

228 F.3d 56, 61 (2d Cir.2000) ("caution" must be observed with issues involving defendant's intent); *Seamons v. Snow*, 206 F.3d 1021, 1027–28 (10th Cir.2000) (noting that grant of summary judgment is "especially questionable" in cases delving into party's state of mind); *United States ex rel. Cantekin v. University of Pittsburgh*, 192 F.3d 402, 411 (3d Cir.1999) (noting "basic rule" that state of mind issues typically should not be decided on summary judgment).

78. *See, e.g., Smith Wholesale Co. v. R.J. Reynolds Tobacco Co.*, 477 F.3d 854, 862 (6th Cir. 2007) (summary judgment disfavored, but not precluded, in antitrust litigation), *petition for cert. filed,* 75 U.S.L.W. 3646 (U.S. May 29, 2007) (No. 06–1578); *Peterson v. Scott County*, 406 F.3d 515, 521 (8th Cir.2005) ("seldom" granted in employment discrimination cases); *Feingold v. New York*, 366 F.3d 138, 148–49 (2d Cir. 2004) ("sparingly" in discrimination cases); *Ashley Creek Phosphate Co. v. Chevron USA, Inc.*, 315 F.3d 1245, 1253 (10th Cir. 2003) ("sparingly" in antitrust cases). *But cf. PepsiCo, Inc. v. Coca–Cola Co.*, 315 F.3d 101, 104–05 (2d Cir.2002) (noting that summary judgment is "particularly favored" in antitrust cases due to the risk that protracted litigation will chill pro-competitive market forces).

Form of Motion

Motions for summary judgment generally must be in writing.[79] Local rules may prescribe the briefing requirements for summary judgment motions, and these rules should always be consulted before briefing. In some judicial districts, the local rules may also require the moving parties to compile a list of all material facts they believe are not in dispute, and require non-moving parties to submit a counterstatement listing material facts they believe to be disputed.[80] Such requirements have been enforced strictly, and practitioners should take care to notice these district-specific obligations when consulting the local rules.[81]

Materials Accompanying the Motion

A moving party may choose to submit the motion papers alone, or may supplement the motion with affidavits, pleadings, deposition transcripts, interrogatory answers, admissions, stipulations, transcripts from another proceeding, oral testimony, authenticated exhibits, other proper exhibits, and anything of which the court may properly take judicial notice. To be considered, the facts generally contained in these materials must be admissible or usable at trial, although for purposes of summary judgment, the facts generally need not be presented to the court in a form admissible at trial.[82]

79. *See National Fire Ins. v. Bartolazo,* 27 F.3d 518, 520 (11th Cir.1994); *Hanson v. Polk County Land, Inc.,* 608 F.2d 129, 131 (5th Cir.1979).

80. *See, e.g.,* M.D. Pa. Loc. R. 56.1 ("Upon any motion for summary judgment pursuant to Fed.R.Civ.P. 56, there shall be filed with the motion a separate, short and concise statement of the material facts, in numbered paragraphs, as to which the moving party contends there is no genuine issue to be tried. The papers opposing a motion for summary judgment shall include a separate, short and concise statement of the material facts, responding to the numbered paragraphs set forth in the statement required in the foregoing paragraph, as to which it is contended that there exists a genuine issue to be tried."). *See also* D. Conn. Loc. R. 56(a) (same effect); M.D. Ga. Loc. R. 56 (same effect); W.D. Mo. Loc. R. 56.1(a) (same effect); M.D. Tenn. Loc. R. 56.01(b)-(c) (same effect).

81. *See, e.g., A.M. Capen's Co. v. American Trading & Production Corp.,* 202 F.3d 469, 472 (1st Cir.2000) (finding that trial court properly admitted uncontested facts when non-moving party failed to comply with local rules in opposing motion with proper format); *Jackson v. Finnegan, Henderson, Farabow, Garrett & Dunner,* 101 F.3d 145, 154 (D.C.Cir.1996) (citing local rule, deeming "admitted" all facts which the nonmoving party did not dispute when filing its counterstatement); *Buchanan v. Sherrill,* 51 F.3d 227, 228–29 (10th Cir.1995)(citing local court practice requiring concise statements regarding disputed and undisputed facts); *Johnson v. Gudmundsson,* 35 F.3d 1104, 1108 (7th Cir.1994)(noting court's strict enforcement of local rule requiring statement); *Professional Programs Group v. Department of Commerce,* 29 F.3d 1349, 1353 (9th Cir.1994)(noting local rule requiring non-moving party to file genuine issue statement).

82. *See Trevizo v. Adams,* 455 F.3d 1155, 1160 (10th Cir.2006); *Miller v. Glenn Miller Prods., Inc.,* 454 F.3d 975, 988 (9th Cir.2006); *Cottrill v. MFA, Inc.,* 443 F.3d 629, 635–36 (8th Cir.2006); *Stinnett v. Iron Works Gym/Executive Health SPA, Inc.,* 301 F.3d 610, 613 (7th Cir.2002). *See also Celotex Corp. v. Catrett,* 477 U.S. 317, 324, 106 S.Ct. 2548, 2553, 91 L.Ed.2d 265 (1986)(commenting that party need not depose its own witnesses in order to defeat a summary judgment motion). Indeed, the most frequently submitted support on a summary judgment motion—affidavits—will rarely (if ever) be admissible at trial in the absence of the affiant.

Documents and Other Exhibits: Documents (even documents obtained through discovery) do not automatically become part of a summary judgment record merely because they are cited in a supporting memorandum.[83] Rather, most courts require that documents submitted with summary judgment motions be attached to a Rule 56(e) affidavit that, upon personal knowledge, both identifies and authenticates each document.[84] The language of Rule 56(e) tends to support imposing this requirement.[85] Documents that fail to satisfy this affidavit authentication requirement may be properly disregarded by those courts when analyzing the pending motion.[86]

Party Admissions: Admissions by a party—whether express (intentional acknowledgment) or through default (*e.g.*, where a party fails to deny Rule 36 requests for admission)—are considered conclusive as to the matters admitted, cannot be contradicted by affidavit or otherwise, and can support a grant of summary judgment.[87]

Transcribed Oral Testimony: Deposition testimony may be used to support a motion for summary judgment, so long as the testimony meets the competence and admissibility requirements of Rule 56(e).[88]

Live Oral Testimony: Entertaining live oral testimony in conjunction with a summary judgment motion is rare and problematic. Because the summary judgment procedure is intended to offer a speedy resolution when the material facts are undisputed, and because the trial court may not, under Rule 56, resolve any facts that remain disputed, oral testimony in summary judgment proceedings will only be granted "sparingly" and "with great care".[89]

Briefs: The court may consider concessions in a party's brief or during oral argument in gauging whether a genuine issue of material fact exists; otherwise, however, the parties' briefs are not evidence.[90]

83. *See Hoffman v. Applicators Sales & Serv., Inc.*, 439 F.3d 9, 15 (1st Cir.2006).

84. *See Article II Gun Shop, Inc. v. Gonzales*, 441 F.3d 492, 496 (7th Cir.2006); *Hoffman v. Applicators Sales & Serv., Inc.*, 439 F.3d 9, 15 (1st Cir.2006); *Woods v. City of Chicago*, 234 F.3d 979, 988 (7th Cir. 2000); *Stuart v. General Motors Corp.*, 217 F.3d 621, 635 n. 20 (8th Cir.2000); *Carmona v. Toledo*, 215 F.3d 124, 131 (1st Cir. 2000).

85. *See* Rule 56(e)(1)("If a paper or part of a paper is referred to in an affidavit, a sworn or certified copy must be attached to or served with the affidavit.").

86. *See Stuart v. General Motors Corp.*, 217 F.3d 621, 635 n.20 (8th Cir.2000); *Car-*

mona v. Toledo, 215 F.3d 124, 131 (1st Cir.2000).

87. *See In re Carney*, 258 F.3d 415, 420 (5th Cir.2001).

88. *See Carmen v. San Francisco Unified Sch. Dist.*, 237 F.3d 1026, 1028 n.4 (9th Cir.2001).

89. *See Seamons v. Snow*, 206 F.3d 1021, 1025–26 (10th Cir.2000).

90. *See Orson, Inc. v. Miramax Film Corp.*, 79 F.3d 1358, 1372 (3d Cir. 1996)(legal memoranda and oral argument are not evidence and cannot create a factual dispute that prevents summary judgment); *American Title Ins. Co. v. Lacelaw Corp.*, 861 F.2d 224, 226–27 (9th Cir.1988)(noting that district court, in its discretion, may

Responding to the Motion

When the moving party supplements the motion by affidavit or other material, the non-moving party cannot respond with mere allegations or denials,[91] nor may the non-moving party rest on mere assertions made in pleadings, legal memoranda, or oral argument.[92] Instead, the non-moving party must show, by affidavit, deposition testimony, or otherwise, that a genuine issue of material fact remains for trial.[93] The non-moving party will generally receive at least 10 days in which to respond.[94]

Uncontested Summary Judgment Motions

Summary judgment will not be entered automatically if the non-moving party fails to file an opposition to the motion.[95] Summary judgment may be granted only if it is appropriate to do so.[96] Consequently, although it is assuredly a dangerous practice to fail to oppose a summary judgment motion, even uncontested motions must be examined carefully by the district court to determine whether no genuine issue of material fact remains and whether judgment is appropriate as a matter of law.[97] The trial court may not accept as true the moving party's itemization of undisputed facts; instead, the court must satisfy itself that the evidence in the summary judgment record supports this relief.[98] This does not necessarily require the court to review all evidentiary materials on file, but it must at least review those materials supporting the motion itself.[99] Moreover, the district court's order should recount

consider statements of fact contained in summary judgment briefing as party admissions for Rule 56 purposes); *Stallard v. United States*, 12 F.3d 489, 496 n. 27 (5th Cir.1994)(noting same practice).

91. *See First Nat'l Bank v. Cities Serv. Co.*, 391 U.S. 253, 289, 88 S.Ct. 1575, 1592, 20 L.Ed.2d 569 (1968).

92. *See Berckeley Inv. Group, Ltd. v. Colkitt*, 455 F.3d 195, 201 (3d Cir.2006).

93. *See Millar v. Houghton*, 115 F.3d 348, 350 (5th Cir.1997). *See also* Rule 56(e); *Anderson v. Liberty Lobby, Inc.*, 477 U.S. 242, 257, 106 S.Ct. 2505, 2514, 91 L.Ed.2d 202 (1986).

94. *See supra* Authors' Commentary to Rule 56(a)-(b) (" **Time for Responding to Motion**' "). *See also* Rule 56(f) (providing for extensions of time in which to respond for certain discovery).

95. *See De La Vega v. San Juan Star, Inc.*, 377 F.3d 111, 115–16 (1st Cir.2004); *Vermont Teddy Bear Co. v. 1–800 Beargram Co.*, 373 F.3d 241, 244–46 (2d Cir.2004); *United States v. One Piece of Real Prop. Located at 5800 SW 74th Ave., Miami, Fla.*, 363 F.3d 1099, 1101–02 (11th Cir.2004).

96. *See* Rule 56(c) (summary judgment entered only if no genuine issue of material

facts exists *and* movant is entitled to judgment); Rule 56(e) ("If the opposing party does not so respond, summary judgment should, *if appropriate*, shall be entered against that party") (emphasis added). *See also Adams v. Travelers Indem. Co.*, 465 F.3d 156 (5th Cir. 2006) (finding no abuse of discretion in treating motion as uncontested, but in applying Rule 56 standards to determine that summary judgment was improper); *United States v. One Piece of Real Prop. Located at 5800 SW 74th Ave., Miami, Fla.*, 363 F.3d 1099, 1101 (11th Cir.2004) (noting that summary judgment, even when unopposed, may be entered only when appropriate).

97. *See Aguiar-Carrasquillo v. Agosto–Alicea*, 445 F.3d 19, 25 (1st Cir.2006); *Vermont Teddy Bear Co. v. 1–800 Beargram Co.*, 373 F.3d 241, 244–46 (2d Cir.2004).

98. *See Vermont Teddy Bear Co. v. 1–800 Beargram Co.*, 373 F.3d 241, 244 (2d Cir.2004).

99. *See United States v. One Piece of Real Prop. Located at 5800 SW 74th Ave., Miami, Fla.*, 363 F.3d 1099, 1101–02 (11th Cir.2004).

that it addressed the underlying motion on its merits.[100]

New Evidence in Reply

If the moving party introduces new evidence in a reply brief or memoranda, the trial court should not accept and consider the new evidence without first affording the non-moving party an opportunity to respond.[101]

Hearings and Oral Argument

Although the district court may, in its discretion, entertain a hearing or oral argument on the Rule 56 motion, hearings and oral argument are not obligatory.[102]

Multiple Summary Judgment Motions

The district court may permit a second motion for summary judgment, especially where there has been an intervening change in the controlling law, where new evidence has become available or the factual record has otherwise expanded through discovery, or where a clear need arises to correct a manifest injustice.[103]

Stipulated Facts and Cross Motions

If the parties stipulate to the facts, obviously no genuine dispute as to material facts then exists for a factfinder to resolve.[104]   Never-

100. *See United States v. One Piece of Real Prop. Located at 5800 SW 74th Ave., Miami, Fla.*, 363 F.3d 1099, 1101–02 (11th Cir.2004).

101. *See Seay v. Tennessee Valley Auth.*, 339 F.3d 454, 481–82 (6th Cir.2003); *Beaird v. Seagate Tech., Inc.*, 145 F.3d 1159, 1163–65 (10th Cir.1998).

102. *See* Rule 78(b) (authorizing determination of motions without oral argument). *See Johnson v. United States*, 460 F.3d 616, 620 (5th Cir. 2006); *Cruz v. Melecio*, 204 F.3d 14, 19 (1st Cir.2000) (refusing to vacate summary judgment in absence of oral argument, holding that summary judgment upon written submissions only is neither "fundamentally unfair" nor a denial of due process). *See also AD/SAT, Div. of Skylight, Inc. v. Associated Press*, 181 F.3d 216, 226 (2d Cir.1999); *McCormack v. Citibank, N.A.*, 100 F.3d 532, 541 (8th Cir.1996); *L.S.T., Inc. v. Crow*, 49 F.3d 679, 684 n. 9 (11th Cir.1995); *Cray Commc'ns, Inc. v. Novatel Computer Sys., Inc.*, 33 F.3d 390, 396 (4th Cir.1994); *Kennedy v. Meacham*, 540 F.2d 1057, 1061 n. 3 (10th Cir.1976).

103. *See Garvin v. Wheeler*, 304 F.3d 628, 632 (7th Cir.2002); *Whitford v. Boglino*, 63 F.3d 527, 530 (7th Cir.1995). *See also Lexicon, Inc. v. Safeco Ins. Co.*, 436 F.3d 662, 670 n.6 (6th Cir.2006) (permitting renewed or successive motions where factual record has expanded); *Enlow v. Tishom-*

ingo County, 962 F.2d 501, 506 (5th Cir. 1992) (successive summary judgment motion allowed when new facts were presented by amended pleading); *Williamsburg Wax Museum, Inc. v. Historic Figures, Inc.*, 810 F.2d 243, 251 (D.C.Cir.1987)(noting that subsequent motion for summary judgment premised upon expanded record is always permitted); *Shearer v. Homestake Mining Co.*, 727 F.2d 707, 709 (8th Cir. 1984)(finding no error in permitting second or renewed motion based upon substantial discovery of facts not previously before the court). *Gulezian v. Drexel Univ.*, 1999 WL 200675, at *2 (E.D.Pa.1999) (noting that courts may entertain successive summary judgment motions, particularly when parties have expanded factual record on which summary judgment is sought); *Holloman v. Neily*, 1998 WL 828413, at *1 (E.D.Pa.1998) (same); *Bank One, Texas, N.A. v. FDIC*, 16 F.Supp.2d 698, 715 (N.D.Tex.1998) (noting possibility of summary judgment on subsequent motion). *See also Gann v. Fruehauf Corp.*, 52 F.3d 1320, 1324 (5th Cir. 1995)(reversing district court's sanctioning of counsel for filing a second motion for summary judgment where arguments presented in both motions differed).

104. *See Centennial Ins. Co. v. Ryder Truck Rental, Inc.*, 149 F.3d 378 (5th Cir. 1998); *Miyazawa v. City of Cincinnati*, 45 F.3d 126, 127 (6th Cir.1995); *Luden's Inc.*

theless, the summary judgment standard remains the same. The court must draw inferences from the stipulated facts, and resolve those inferences in favor of the non-moving party.[105] Cross-motions for summary judgment are also examined under the usual Rule 56 standards.[106] Each cross-motion must be evaluated on its own merits, with the court viewing all facts and reasonable inferences in the light most favorable to the nonmoving party.[107] Thus, the mere fact that cross motions have been filed does not, by itself, necessarily justify the entry of a summary judgment,[108] nor will the denial of one cross-motion compel the grant of the other cross-motion.[109]

Entry of Summary Judgment in Favor of *Non-Moving Party*

In unusual circumstances, the trial court may not only deny the moving party's motion for summary judgment, but may enter summary judgment in favor of the non-moving party (even though that party has not sought such relief). Such judgments are generally only entered if the court is convinced that the factual record is fully developed, that the non-moving party is "clearly" entitled to judgment, and that entry of the judgment would not result in procedural prejudice to the moving party.[110] Because such motions are, in effect, *sua sponte* motions for summary judgment, the trial court should generally abide by the standards for entry of *sua sponte* relief.[111]

v. Local Union No. 6 of Bakery, Confectionery & Tobacco Workers' Int'l Union of America, 28 F.3d 347, 353 (3d Cir.1994).

105. See Leebaert v. Harrington, 332 F.3d 134, 138–39 (2d Cir.2003); Luden's Inc. v. Local Union No. 6 of Bakery, Confectionery & Tobacco Workers' Int'l Union of America, 28 F.3d 347, 353 (3d Cir.1994). But see United Paperworkers Int'l Union Local 14, AFL–CIO–CLC v. International Paper Co., 64 F.3d 28, 31 (1st Cir. 1995)(noting that summary judgment standard may be modified where dispute arrives as a "case stated"; in that instance, trial judge is free to engage in certain factfinding, including the drawing of inferences). But see also United States Fidelity & Guaranty Co. v. Planters Bank & Trust Co., 77 F.3d 863, 866 (5th Cir.1996)(noting that court of appeals recognizes a "hint of a distinction" between the standard applied in jury cases and an arguably more lenient standard in certain non-jury cases).

106. See Latin American Music Co. v. Archdiocese of San Juan of Roman Catholic & Apostolic Church, __ F.3d __, __, 2007 WL 2326817, at *3 (1st Cir. 2007); Bronx Household of Faith v. Board of Educ. of City of New York, 492 F.3d 89, 96–97 (2d Cir. 2007); Spectrum Health Continuing Care Group v. Anna Marie Bowling Irrecoverable Trust Dated June 27, 2002, 410 F.3d 304, 309 (6th Cir.2005).

107. See Diaz v. Prudential Ins. Co. of America, __ F.3d __, __, 2007 WL 2389773, at *2 (7th Cir. 2007); Bronx Household of Faith v. Board of Educ. of City of New York, 492 F.3d 89, 96–97 (2d Cir. 2007); Appoloni v. United States, 450 F.3d 185, 189 (6th Cir.2006); Cross Med. Prods., Inc. v. Medtronic Sofamor Danek, Inc., 424 F.3d 1293, 1302 (Fed.Cir.2005).

108. See Spectrum Health Continuing Care Group v. Anna Marie Bowling Irrecoverable Trust Dated June 27, 2002, 410 F.3d 304, 309 (6th Cir.2005); Atlantic Richfield Co. v. Farm Credit Bank of Wichita, 226 F.3d 1138, 1148 (10th Cir.2000); Wightman v. Springfield Terminal Ry. Co., 100 F.3d 228, 230 (1st Cir.1996).

109. See Christian Heritage Academy v. Oklahoma Secondary Sch. Activities Ass'n, 483 F.3d 1025, 1030 (10th Cir. 2007).

110. See Faustin v. City of Denver, 423 F.3d 1192, 1198–99 (10th Cir.2005); E.C. Ernst, Inc. v. General Motors Corp., 537 F.2d 105, 109 (5th Cir.1976).

111. See Madewell v. Downs, 68 F.3d 1030, 1049 (8th Cir.1995) (commenting that liability of the nonmoving party was "derivative" of the motion, such that when motion leaves no genuine issue of material fact as to the *nonmoving* party's right to summary judgment, *sua sponte* summary judgment is proper). See also infra Authors'

Before granting such relief, it must find that entering summary judgment is both proper and is procedurally sound (that its entry does not offend fundamental fairness).[112]

Sua Sponte Motions

The court may enter summary judgment *sua sponte*.[113] The case law, however, cautions great care in the grant of *sua sponte* summary judgments.[114] In practice, *sua sponte* summary judgments should be unnecessary because the trial court may always invite a party to file a summary judgment motion.[115] Where the court considers entering a *sua sponte* judgment, it must first ensure that proper advance notice of this intention (at least 10 days) has been made.[116] A litigant must appreciate that he is the "target" of a summary judgment inquiry, and possess that motivation when preparing the response.[117] The court must also confirm that the litigants have a full and fair opportunity to respond.[118] Discovery must either be completed or clearly be of no further benefit.[119] These notice-and-opportunity requirements apply even when the *sua sponte* summary judgment is entered against a party who, herself, has moved for summary judgment.[120] An order granting summary judgment *sua sponte* without notice will generally be reversed unless

Commentary to Rule 56(c) ("**Sua Sponte Motions**").

112. *See Caswell v. City of Detroit Housing Com'n*, 418 F.3d 615 (6th Cir.2005); *John G. Alden, Inc. of Mass. v. John G. Alden Ins. Agency of Fla., Inc.*, 389 F.3d 21, 25 (1st Cir.2004).

113. *See Celotex Corp. v. Catrett*, 477 U.S. 317, 326, 106 S.Ct. 2548, 2554, 91 L.Ed.2d 265 (1986)(noting district court's right to enter *sua sponte* motions under Rule 56); *Couden v. Duffy*, 446 F.3d 483, 500 (3d Cir.2006); *Brown v. Raymond Corp.*, 432 F.3d 640, 649 (6th Cir.2005); *United States v. Hoyts Cinemas Corp.*, 380 F.3d 558 (1st Cir.2004); *Gibson v. Mayor of Wilmington*, 355 F.3d 215, 222 (3d Cir. 2004). *But cf. Baker v. Metropolitan Life Ins. Co.*, 364 F.3d 624, 632 (5th Cir.2004) (commenting that *sua sponte* summary judgment may not be granted "on grounds not requested by the moving party").

114. *See First American Kickapoo Operations, L.L.C. v. Multimedia Games, Inc.*, 412 F.3d 1166, 1170 (10th Cir.2005) (practice is "not encourage[d]"); *Ramsey v. Coughlin*, 94 F.3d 71, 74 (2d Cir. 1996)("great care"); *Goldstein v. Fidelity & Guaranty Ins. Underwriters, Inc.*, 86 F.3d 749, 751 (7th Cir.1996)("special caution" warranted with this "just a bit risky" practice, which the court of appeals does not want to encourage); *Employers Ins. of Wau-*

sau v. Petroleum Specialties, Inc., 69 F.3d 98, 105 (6th Cir.1995)("discourage[d]").

115. *See Goldstein v. Fidelity & Guaranty Ins. Underwriters, Inc.*, 86 F.3d 749, 751 (7th Cir.1996).

116. *See Figg v. Russell*, 433 F.3d 593, 597 (8th Cir.2006); *First American Kickapoo Operations, L.L.C. v. Multimedia Games, Inc.*, 412 F.3d 1166, 1170 (10th Cir.2005); *John G. Alden, Inc. of Mass. v. John G. Alden Ins. Agency of Fla., Inc.*, 389 F.3d 21, 25 (1st Cir.2004). *But cf. Enowmbitang v. Seagate Tech., Inc.*, 148 F.3d 970 (8th Cir.1998) (holding that trial court may grant *sua sponte* summary judgment without prior notice for failure to state claim upon which relief may be granted).

117. *See John G. Alden, Inc. of Mass. v. John G. Alden Ins. Agency of Fla., Inc.*, 389 F.3d 21, 25 (1st Cir.2004).

118. *See Couden v. Duffy*, 446 F.3d 483, 500 (3d Cir.2006); *Pourghoraishi v. Flying J, Inc.*, 449 F.3d 751, 765 (7th Cir.2006); *Figg v. Russell*, 433 F.3d 593, 597 (8th Cir.2006); *Brown v. Raymond Corp.*, 432 F.3d 640, 649 (6th Cir.2005).

119. *See Sanchez v. Triple–S Mgmt., Corp.*, 492 F.3d 1, 7–8 (1st Cir. 2007); *Ramsey v. Coughlin*, 94 F.3d 71, 74 (2d Cir. 1996).

120. *See Bridgeway Corp. v. Citibank*, 201 F.3d 134, 139–40 (2d Cir.2000).

the nonmoving party has waived this right or unless it is clear that the non-moving party suffered no prejudice (*e.g.*, because there was no additional evidence for the record or because none of the evidence would create a genuine issue of material fact).[121] Other courts have excused this notice and response requirement where three criteria are met: the summary judgment record is fully developed, there is no prejudice to the non-moving party, and the decision rests on a purely legal issue.[122]

Any objection to this procedural error must be appropriately preserved for appeal, however. Thus, filing a motion for reconsideration that contests a *sua sponte* grant of summary judgment, but that omits from that motion a challenge to the procedural propriety of the order, will be reviewed narrowly for "plain error" only.[123]

Effect of Summary Judgment Rulings—"Law Of The Case"

The "law of the case" doctrine holds that when a court decides upon a rule of law, that decision should generally control the same issues throughout the subsequent stages in the same case.[124] It is based on the sound, salutary policy of judicial finality—that all litigation should come to an end.[125] This is a prudential doctrine; it guides and influences the court's exercise of discretion, but it does not limit the court's jurisdiction or power.[126] Because *denials* of summary judgment generally do nothing more than acknowledge that a genuine issue of material fact remains for trial, such denials are typically not accorded any preclusive effect nor do they become "law of the case".[127] Moreover, a denial of a Rule 12(b)(6) motion to dismiss is ordinarily not accorded preclusive effect on a later Rule 56 motion for summary judgment because the "relevant legal factors" on each motion are different; motions to dismiss test the facial adequacy of the allegations, whereas motions for summary judgment examine the evidence gathered in the course of discovery.[128]

---

121. *See Vives v. Fajardo*, 472 F.3d 19, 22 (1st Cir. 2007); *Schwan-Stabilo Cosmetics GmbH & Co. v. Pacificlink Int'l Corp.*, 401 F.3d 28, 33 (2d Cir.2005); *Ward v. Utah*, 398 F.3d 1239, 1245–46 (10th Cir. 2005).

122. *See Gibson v. Mayor of Wilmington*, 355 F.3d 215, 222 (3d Cir.2004).

123. *See Love v. National Med. Enters.*, 230 F.3d 765, 771 (5th Cir.2000).

124. *See Arizona v. California*, 460 U.S. 605, 618, 103 S.Ct. 1382, 1391, 75 L.Ed.2d 318 (1983).

125. *See Lyons v. Fisher*, 888 F.2d 1071 (5th Cir.1989). *See also Gindes v. United States*, 740 F.2d 947, 949 (Fed.Cir.1984) (commenting that doctrine rests upon important public policy litigants do not enjoy the right to cover the same ground twice, hoping that passage of time or changes in court's composition will alter outcome).

126. *See Arizona v. California*, 460 U.S. 605, 618, 103 S.Ct. 1382, 1391, 75 L.Ed.2d 318 (1983); *Sejman v. Warner–Lambert Co.*, 845 F.2d 66, 68–69 (4th Cir.1988).

127. *See Switzerland Cheese Assoc., Inc. v. E. Horne's Market, Inc.*, 385 U.S. 23, 25, 87 S.Ct. 193, 17 L.Ed.2d 23 (1966); *Rigby v. Damant*, 486 F.3d 692, 692–93 (1st Cir. 2007); *Murphy v. Missouri Dep't of Corrections*, 372 F.3d 979, 986 (8th Cir.2004); *Kovacevich v. Kent State Univ.*, 224 F.3d 806 (6th Cir.2000). *But see Federal Ins. Co. v. Scarsella Bros.*, 931 F.2d 599, 601 n. 4 (9th Cir.1991) (holding that doctrine is not amenable to such broad generalizations, and may apply to summary judgment denials when trial court intends to resolve definitively the legal questions in issue).

128. *See Robbins v. Wilkie*, 433 F.3d 755, 764–65 (10th Cir.2006), *cert. granted,*

Pro Se Motions

In considering summary judgment motions involving *pro se* litigants, the courts construe liberally the *pro se* party's pleadings, but are not obligated to act as the party's advocate.[129]

Appealability

Ordinarily, an order denying a party's motion for summary judgment is interlocutory and, therefore, not immediately appealable.[130] Conversely, an order granting summary judgment is appealable only when it constitutes the "final order" in the case.[131]

Exceptions: Practitioners must be wary. Exceptions to these general rules are numerous. For example, if the motion asserts questions of immunity from suit, a denial of summary judgment may be immediately appealable.[132] Similarly, a denial of a cross-motion for summary judgment may be immediately appealable along with a challenge to that portion of the cross-motion that was granted.[133]

Effect of Non–Appealable Summary Judgment Denials: Because such rulings only determine that a genuine issue of material fact remains for trial, denials of summary judgment motions ordinarily do not merge into the final judgment and, therefore, are typically not independently appealable even where the case proceeds to trial and a later appeal.[134]

127 S. Ct. 722, 166 L. Ed. 2d 559 (U.S. 2006) and *judgment vac'd,* 497 F.3d 1122 (10th Cir. 2007).

129. *See Cardoso v. Calbone,* 490 F.3d 1194, 1197 (10th Cir. 2007). *See also supra* Authors' Commentary to Rule 8(e) (**"Pleadings Drafted by Laypersons"**).

130. *See Wachtel v. Health Net, Inc.,* 482 F.3d 225, 228 (3d Cir. 2007); *Chesher v. Neyer,* 477 F.3d 784, 793 (6th Cir. 2007); *Ambrose v. Young,* 474 F.3d 1070, 1074 (8th Cir. 2007); *Jones v. Parmley,* 465 F.3d 46, 54 (2d Cir. 2006); *Valdizan v. Rivera–Hernandez,* 445 F.3d 63, 64 (1st Cir.2006); *M. Eagles Tool Warehouse, Inc. v. Fisher Tooling Co.,* 439 F.3d 1335, 1344 (Fed.Cir.2006).

131. *See Santaella v. Metropolitan Life Ins. Co.,* 123 F.3d 456, 461 (7th Cir.1997). *See also* 28 U.S.C.A. § 1291. *But see* 28 U.S.C.A. § 1292 (permitting certification by district court of interlocutory orders); Rule 54(b)(permitting entry of partial judgment that resolves one claim or all rights of one party).

132. *See Swint v. Chambers County Comm'n,* 514 U.S. 35, 115 S.Ct. 1203, 131 L.Ed.2d 60 (1995)(district court orders denying summary judgment not immediately appealable unless appellant raised qualified immunity defense); *Mitchell v. Forsyth,* 472 U.S. 511, 530, 105 S.Ct. 2806, 2817, 86 L.Ed.2d 411 (1985)(same). *See also Chesher v. Neyer,* 477 F.3d 784, 793 (6th Cir. 2007); *Ambrose v. Young,* 474 F.3d 1070, 1074 (8th Cir. 2007); *Jones v. Parmley,* 465 F.3d 46, 54 (2d Cir. 2006). *But cf. Jones v. City of Jackson,* 203 F.3d 875, 878 (5th Cir.2000) (even with immunity motions, summary judgment denials are not immediately appealable if disputed and material factual issues are present).

133. *See Padfield v. AIG Life Ins. Co.,* 290 F.3d 1121, 1124 (9th Cir.2002); *National Coalition For Students With Disabilities Educ. v. Allen,* 152 F.3d 283 (4th Cir.1998); *McIntosh v. Scottsdale Ins. Co.,* 992 F.2d 251, 253 (10th Cir.1993).

134. *See Iacobucci v. Boulter,* 193 F.3d 14, 22 (1st Cir.1999).

RULE 56(d). CASE NOT FULLY ADJUDICATED ON THE MOTION

CORE CONCEPT

The court may enter a summary ruling on the issue of liability alone, even though a genuine issue of material fact exists as to damages. The court may also summarily resolve other individual issues as to which there remain no genuine issue of material fact. The courts are divided on the question of whether a litigant may make a separate motion under Rule 56(d), or whether Rule 56(d) relief is instead a mechanism available only to the court following an unsuccessful motion for a full summary judgment.

APPLICATIONS

2007 Amendments

A portion of current Rule 56(d) was located previously in Rule 56(c). That portion (relating to partial summary adjudications on the issue of liability alone) was moved in the 2007 amendments to Rule 56(d) to create an omnibus partial adjudication rule. Now, both the provisions for partial summary adjudication on facts (placed in Rule 56(d)(1)) and on liability (placed in Rule 56(d)(2)) are positioned in one sub-Rule. Practitioners searching for pre–2007 interpretations of this Rule should bear this repositioning in mind in doing their research. Current Rule 56(d)(2) was, until 2007, the last sentence of old Rule 56(d)(1).

Purpose of Partial Summary Adjudications

Where a summary judgment is not possible (or not requested) and the dispute will have to go to trial, the district court is nevertheless permitted to declare certain facts—those which it determines appear without substantial controversy—as established for purposes of the case.[135] Partial summary adjudications allow the trial court to salvage some constructive result from its efforts in ruling upon an otherwise denied summary judgment motion.[136] Partial summary adjudications accelerate litigations by narrowing the triable issues and resolving—before trial—those matters involving no genuine issues of material fact.[137]

Partial Adjudication on Facts or Liability

The trial court may partially adjudicate issues of fact or liability.[138] Partial factual adjudications may include items of damage. Any partial factual adjudications should be made after the court exam-

---

135. *See FDIC v. Massingill*, 24 F.3d 768 (5th Cir.1994), *opinion supplemented*, 30 F.3d 601 (5th Cir.1994); *City of Los Angeles v. County of Kern*, __ F.Supp.2d __, __, 2007 WL 2326825, at *9 (C.D.Cal. 2007); *Algie v. RCA Global Commc'ns, Inc.*, 891 F.Supp. 875, 882–83 (S.D.N.Y.1994), *aff'd*, 60 F.3d 956 (2d Cir.1995); .

136. *See Patrick Schaumburg Autos., Inc. v. Hanover Ins. Co.*, 452 F.Supp.2d 857, 867 (N.D.Ill. 2006); *Access Solutions Int'l,*

Inc. v. Data/Ware Dev't, Inc., 70 F.Supp.2d 92, 95–96 (D.R.I.1999); *National Union Fire Ins. Co. of Pittsburgh v. L.E. Myers Co. Group*, 937 F.Supp. 276, 285 (S.D.N.Y. 1996).

137. *See National Union Fire Ins. Co. of Pittsburgh v. L.E. Myers Co. Group*, 937 F.Supp. 276, 285 (S.D.N.Y.1996).

138. *See* Rule 56(d)(1) (facts); Rule 56(d)(2) (liability).

ines the pleadings and evidence, and after "interrogating the attorneys".[139]

Separate Motions Under Rule 56(d)

The language of Rule 56(d) seems to imply that partial summary adjudication is what a court may enter following its decision that a motion for full summary judgment must be denied. The meaning of this implication has divided the courts.[140] Some courts, relying on this implication, have ruled that a litigant may *not* file a separate motion for partial summary adjudication under this Rule, but may only seek full summary judgment under Rules 56(a) or (b),[141] or alternatively, that any such independent motion may only be made "in the wake" of such an unsuccessful full motion.[142] Other courts reject this reasoning, and permit the filing of distinct motions for partial summary adjudication.[143]

Standards for Granting or Denying Partial Summary Adjudication

In resolving a motion for partial summary adjudication, the court will apply the same standards and criteria used for evaluating full motions for summary judgment.[144] The burden of demonstrating an entitlement to partial summary adjudication lies with the moving party, and borrows the same burden-of-going-forward shift from Rule 56(c).[145]

District Court's Discretion

Similar to motions for "full" summary judgment, the district judge has the discretion (subject to the familiar summary judgment standards generally) to defer a partial adjudication ruling until the proper time arrives for making a complete adjudication on all issues in the case.[146]

---

139. *See* Rule 56(d)(1).

140. *See Beaty v. Republic of Iraq,* 480 F.Supp.2d 60, 100 (D.D.C. Mar. 20, 2007) (discussing division), *motion to certify appeal granted,* 2007 WL 1169333 (D.D.C. Apr. 19, 2007).

141. *See, e.g., LaPrade v. Abramson,* Civ. A. No. 97–0010, 2006 WL 3469532, at *8 (D.D.C. 2006); *Patrick Schaumburg Autos., Inc. v. Hanover Ins. Co.,* 452 F.Supp.2d 857, 867 (N.D.Ill. 2006); *Sears, Roebuck & Co. v. Sears Realty Co.,* 932 F.Supp. 392, 410 (N.D.N.Y.1996); *SFM Corp. v. Sundstrand Corp.,* 102 F.R.D. 555, 558 (N.D.Ill. 1984); *Warner v. United States,* 698 F.Supp. 877, 878 (S.D.Fla.1988); *Arado v. Gen. Fire Extinguisher Corp.,* 626 F.Supp. 506, 509 (N.D.Ill.1985). *See also Coffman v. Fed. Labs., Inc.,* 171 F.2d 94, 98 (3d Cir.1949) (motion not proper for a portion of a claim); *Biggins v. Oltmer Iron Works,* 154 F.2d 214, 216 (7th Cir.1946) (same).

142. *See Kendall McGaw Labs., Inc. v. Cmty. Mem'l Hosp.,* 125 F.R.D. 420, 421 (D.N.J.1989).

143. *See, e.g., Zapata Hermanos Sucesores, S.A. v. Hearthside Baking Co., Inc.,* 313 F.3d 385, 391 (7th Cir.2003); *McDonnell v. Cardiothoracic & Vascular Surgical Assoc., Inc.,* Civ. A. No. C2–03–0079, 2004 WL 1234138, at *1–*3 (S.D.Ohio 2004); *Northeast Ill. Reg'l Commuter R.R. Corp. v. Kiewit Western Co.,* 396 F.Supp.2d 913, 921 (N.D.Ill.2005); *In re Doctors Hosp. of Hyde Park,* 330 B.R. 689, 698 (N.D.Ill.2005); *Russell v. Enter. Rent–A–Car Co. of R.I.,* 160 F.Supp.2d 239, 249 (D.R.I.2001).

144. *See California v. Campbell,* 138 F.3d 772, 780 (9th Cir.1998); *Green v. Sun Life Assur. Co.,* 383 F.Supp.2d 1224, 1226 (C.D.Cal.2005); *Russell v. Enterprise Rent–A–Car Co. of Rhode Island,* 160 F.Supp.2d 239, 249 (D.R.I.2001).

145. *See Green v. Sun Life Assur. Co.,* 383 F.Supp.2d 1224, 1226 (C.D.Cal.2005).

146. *See Patrick Schaumburg Autos., Inc. v. Hanover Ins. Co.,* 452 F.Supp.2d 857, 867 (N.D.Ill. 2006); *Colasanto v. Life Ins. Co. of North America,* 100 F.3d 203, 210

Effect of Partial Summary Adjudications—"Law Of The Case"

Partial summary adjudications are not "judgments" and do not become "final orders" until the district court enters a judgment disposing of the entire case.[147] Nevertheless, such adjudications are still rulings on a "dispositive motion",[148] and will be accorded treatment as "law of the case".[149] Thus, the parties are entitled to rely on the conclusiveness of the partial summary adjudication[150] and, absent good reason for doing so, the district court will not generally revisit or alter the issues adjudicated under Rule 56(d).[151] Nevertheless, such partial adjudications are not immutable and have no *res judicata* effect; they may, under appropriate circumstances, be revisited.[152] If the court later decides that good reasons exist to alter a partial summary adjudication, the court must so inform the parties and permit them an opportunity to present evidence concerning any of the revisited issues.[153]

Appealability

Ordinarily, rulings that grant[154] or deny[155] partial summary adjudications are considered interlocutory, subject to revision by the district court, and thus not immediately appealable. This rule is, however, subject to exceptions.[156]

(1st Cir.1996); *Department of Toxic Substances Control v. Interstate Non–Ferrous Corp.*, 99 F.Supp.2d 1123, 1125 (E.D.Cal. 2000).

147. *See Alberty-Velez v. Corporacion de Puerto Rico Para La Difusion Publica*, 361 F.3d 1, 6 n.5 (1st Cir.2004); *Burkhart v. Washington Metro. Area Transit Auth.*, 112 F.3d 1207, 1215–16 (D.C.Cir.1997).

148. *See Burkhart v. Washington Metro. Area Transit Auth.*, 112 F.3d 1207, 1215–16 (D.C.Cir.1997).

149. *See Burge v. Parish of St. Tammany*, 187 F.3d 452, 467 (5th Cir.1999); *Carr v. O'Leary*, 167 F.3d 1124, 1126 (7th Cir. 1999); *Palmer v. Fox Software, Inc.*, 107 F.3d 415, 419 (6th Cir.1997).

150. *See Huss v. King Co.*, 338 F.3d 647, 650–51 (6th Cir.2003); *Leddy v. Standard Drywall, Inc.*, 875 F.2d 383, 386 (2d Cir.1989).

151. *See Carr v. O'Leary*, 167 F.3d 1124, 1126 (7th Cir.1999).

152. *See Alberty-Velez v. Corporacion de Puerto Rico Para La Difusion Publica*, 361 F.3d 1, 6 n.5 (1st Cir.2004); *Burge v. Parish of St. Tammany*, 187 F.3d 452, 467 (5th Cir.1999).

153. *See Alberty-Velez v. Corporacion de Puerto Rico Para La Difusion Publica*, 361 F.3d 1, 6 n.5 (1st Cir.2004); *Huss v. King Co.*, 338 F.3d 647, 650–51 (6th Cir.2003). *See also Joseph P. Caulfield & Assocs., Inc. v. Litho Prods., Inc.*, 155 F.3d 883, 888 (7th Cir.1998) (holding that proper procedure to seek a revisitation of the adjudicated issues is to file a motion to vacate the ruling and request either that the issues be added to the trial or that they be resolved as a matter of law in favor of the moving party).

154. *See Alternate Fuels, Inc. v. Cabanas*, 435 F.3d 855, 860 (8th Cir.2006); *Lovejoy-Wilson v. NOCO Motor Fuel, Inc.*, 263 F.3d 208, 219 n.6 (2d Cir.2001); *CAE Screenplates Inc. v. Heinrich Fiedler GmbH & Co.*, 224 F.3d 1308 (Fed.Cir.2000); *Bower v. Federal Express Corp.*, 473 F.Supp.2d 814, 819 (W.D.Tenn. 2006).

155. *See American Airlines, Inc. v. Herman*, 176 F.3d 283, 288 (5th Cir.1999); *Burns-Vidlak ex rel. Burns v. Chandler*, 165 F.3d 1257 (9th Cir.1999).

156. *See supra* Authors' Commentary to Rule 56(c) ("**Appealability**").

RULE 56(e).   AFFIDAVITS AND OTHER TESTIMONY IN SUMMARY JUDGMENT PRACTICE

CORE CONCEPT

When submitted to support or oppose a summary judgment motion, an affidavit must be sworn, must be based on personal knowledge, must set forth facts that would be admissible at time of trial, and must establish the affiant's competence to testify.

APPLICATIONS

When Affidavits or Other Materials Are Required

When a summary judgment motion is supported with affidavits or other material, the non-moving party cannot rely on mere allegations or denials found in his own pleadings.   Rather, the non-moving party must demonstrate, by affidavit, deposition testimony, or otherwise, that a genuine issue of material fact remains for trial.[157]

Affidavit Prerequisites

To be considered on a motion for summary judgment, an affidavit must satisfy four prerequisites: it must be sworn; it must be based upon personal knowledge; it must state specific facts admissible in evidence at time of trial; and it must be offered by a competent affiant.   In ruling upon a motion for summary judgment, the court generally will not ordinarily consider affidavits that fail to satisfy these prerequisites.[158] If, however, the opposing party fails to object to an improper affidavit, the decision to consider it might not be reversible error.[159]

> *Sworn:* A summary judgment affidavit must be "sworn".[160] A statement verified under 28 U.S.C.A. § 1746 meets this "sworn" requirement.[161]

> *Personal Knowledge:* A summary judgment affidavit must be made on personal knowledge.[162]   Affidavits based on "informa-

157.   *See* Rule 56(e)(2).

158.   *See Collins v. Seeman,* 462 F.3d 757, 760 n.1 (7th Cir. 2006); *Briggs v. Potter,* 463 F.3d 507, 512 (6th Cir. 2006); *Patterson v. County of Oneida,* 375 F.3d 206, 219 (2d Cir.2004); *Lantec, Inc. v. Novell, Inc.,* 306 F.3d 1003, 1019 (10th Cir.2002). *But see Ruby v. Springfield R–12 Pub. Sch. Dist.,* 76 F.3d 909, 912 n. 8 (8th Cir. 1996)(absent motion to strike or other timely objection, district judge may consider a document which fails to conform to Rule 56(e)'s formal requirements).

159.   *See Capobianco v. City of New York,* 422 F.3d 47, 55 (2d Cir.2005).

160.   *See Adickes v. S.H. Kress & Co.,* 398 U.S. 144, 158 n.17, 90 S.Ct. 1598, 1609 n.17, 26 L.Ed.2d 142 (1970); *Woloszyn v. County of Lawrence,* 396 F.3d 314, 323 (3d Cir.2005); *Markel v. Board of Regents of Univ. of Wisc. Sys.,* 276 F.3d 906, 912 (7th

Cir.2002). *Cf. Collins v. Seeman,* 462 F.3d 757, 760 n.1 (7th Cir. 2006) (rejecting unsworn written witness summaries); *Watts v. Kroger Co.,* 170 F.3d 505, 508 (5th Cir. 1999) (same, for handwritten statements); *Chaiken v. VV Publ'g Corp. d/b/a Village Voice,* 119 F.3d 1018 (2d Cir.1997) (same, for unsworn letters do not meet prerequisites); *Berwick Grain Co. v. Illinois Dep't of Agric.,* 116 F.3d 231, 234 (7th Cir.1997) (same, for unsworn transcript of witness interview).

161.   *See infra* Authors' Commentary to Rule 56(e) ("**Verifications**").

162.   *See Argo v. Blue Cross & Blue Shield of Kansas, Inc.,* 452 F.3d 1193, 1200 (10th Cir.2006); *Brainard v. American Skandia Life Assur. Corp.,* 432 F.3d 655, 667 (6th Cir.2005); *Nieves-Luciano v. Hernandez–Torres,* 397 F.3d 1, 5 (1st Cir.2005). *Cf. Leary v. Dalton,* 58 F.3d 748, 754 (1st

tion and belief"—facts that the affiant *believes* are true, but does not *know* are true—are not proper.[163]   Likewise, inferences and opinions must be premised on first-hand observations or personal experience.[164] An affidavit will not be rejected merely because it is a self-serving recitation by the party herself (indeed, it would make little sense for a party to submit one that was not self-serving).[165] But the self-serving affirmations must be more than mere conclusions or unsupported inferences; in other words, such affidavits must aver specific facts and otherwise satisfy the requirements of this Rule.[166]

Specific Admissible Facts: A summary judgment affidavit must also contain specific facts[167] which, in turn, must be admissible in evidence at time of trial.[168] For most courts, it is not necessary that the evidence be submitted in a *form* that would be admissible at trial (indeed, most summary judgment motions are supported and opposed by affidavit evidence); so long as the offered evidence may ultimately be presented at trial in an admissible form, it can be considered in ruling upon the motion.[169]   Thus, hearsay statements,[170] conclusory averments,[171]

Cir.1995)(ruling that "cursory submissions" do not satisfy the "specific facts" showing necessary to defeat a motion for summary judgment).

163. *See Automatic Radio Mfg. Co. v. Hazeltine Research Inc.*, 339 U.S. 827, 831, 70 S.Ct. 894, 896, 94 L.Ed. 1312 (1950); *Argo v. Blue Cross & Blue Shield of Kansas, Inc.*, 452 F.3d 1193, 1200 (10th Cir. 2006); *Ellis v. England*, 432 F.3d 1321, 1326 (11th Cir.2005).

164. *See Briggs v. Potter*, 463 F.3d 507, 512 (6th Cir. 2006); *Argo v. Blue Cross & Blue Shield of Kansas, Inc.*, 452 F.3d 1193, 1200 (10th Cir.2006). *See also Payne v. Pauley*, 337 F.3d 767, 772 (7th Cir.2003) (personal knowledge may include reasonable inferences grounded in observation or other first-hand experience; they may not be "flights of fancy, speculations, hunches, intuitions, or rumors about matters remote from that experience").

165. *See S.E.C. v. Phan*, ___ F.3d ___, ___, 2007 WL 2429365, at *10 (9th Cir. 2007); *Velazquez-Garcia v. Horizon Lines of Puerto Rico, Inc.*, 473 F.3d 11, 18 (1st Cir. 2007).

166. *See S.E.C. v. Phan*, ___ F.3d ___, ___, 2007 WL 2429365, at *10 (9th Cir. 2007); *Velazquez-Garcia v. Horizon Lines of Puerto Rico, Inc.*, 473 F.3d 11, 18 (1st Cir. 2007).

167. *See Moore v. J.B. Hunt Transport, Inc.*, 221 F.3d 944 (7th Cir.2000); *Santiago-*

Ramos v. Centennial P.R. Wireless Corp., 217 F.3d 46, 53 (1st Cir.2000); *Doren v. Battle Creek Health Sys.*, 187 F.3d 595, 598–99 (6th Cir.1999).

168. *See Trevizo v. Adams*, 455 F.3d 1155, 1160 (10th Cir.2006); *Miller v. Glenn Miller Prods., Inc.*, 454 F.3d 975, 988 (9th Cir.2006); *Phillips v. Jasper County Jail*, 437 F.3d 791, 796 (8th Cir.2006); *Security Ins. Co. v. Old Dominion Freight Line Inc.*, 391 F.3d 77, 84–85 (2d Cir.2004).

169. *See Trevizo v. Adams*, 455 F.3d 1155, 1160 (10th Cir.2006); *Argo v. Blue Cross & Blue Shield of Kansas, Inc.*, 452 F.3d 1193, 1199 (10th Cir.2006).

170. *See Davila v. Corporacion De Puerto Rico Para La Difusion Publica*, ___ F.3d ___, ___, 2007 WL 2253531, at *7 (1st Cir. 2007); *Argo v. Blue Cross & Blue Shield of Kansas, Inc.*, 452 F.3d 1193, 1199 (10th Cir.2006); *Cottrill v. MFA, Inc.*, 443 F.3d 629, 635–36 (8th Cir.2006); *Patterson v. County of Oneida*, 375 F.3d 206, 219 (2d Cir.2004).   *But see J.F. Feeser, Inc. v. Serv-A-Portion, Inc.*, 909 F.2d 1524, 1542 (3d Cir.1990)(noting Third Circuit rule that hearsay evidence produced in an affidavit opposing summary judgment may be considered if the out-of-court declarant could later present the evidence through direct testimony at trial).

171. *See Scaife v. Cook County*, 446 F.3d 735, 740 (7th Cir.2006); *Patterson v. County of Oneida*, 375 F.3d 206, 219 (2d Cir.2004); *Lantec, Inc. v. Novell, Inc.*, 306

unfounded self-serving declarations,[172] speculation or conjecture,[173] and inadmissible expert opinions[174] are generally improper in Rule 56(e) affidavits. A party's promise that he or she has certain unidentified "additional evidence", which will be produced at trial, is insufficient to avoid summary judgment.[175]

Competence: The summary judgment affidavit must demonstrate that the affiant is competent to testify as to the facts contained in the affidavit.[176] Competence to testify may be inferred from the affidavits themselves.[177] Ordinarily, statements of counsel in a memorandum of law are not competent to support or oppose that litigant's own summary judgment position.[178]

"Acquired" Competence: It might not be possible, in all circumstances, for the affiant to "acquire" competence and personal knowledge she otherwise lacks by merely reviewing documents relevant to the matter at issue.[179]

Verifications

For purposes of Rule 56(e), the federal courts will accept verified statements made under the penalties of perjury in lieu of an

F.3d 1003, 1019 (10th Cir.2002). *See Lujan v. National Wildlife Fed'n*, 497 U.S. 871, 888, 110 S.Ct. 3177, 3188, 111 L.Ed.2d 695 (1990)(noting that object of Rule 56 is not to replace conclusory averments in a pleading with conclusory allegations in an affidavit).

172. *See Evans v. Techs. Applications & Serv. Co.*, 80 F.3d 954, 962 (4th Cir.1996); *Hall v. Bellmon*, 935 F.2d 1106, 1111 (10th Cir.1991). *See also In re Kaypro*, 218 F.3d 1070, 1075 (9th Cir.2000) ("self-serving" affidavit is not necessarily disqualified, so long as foundation was adequate); *Delange v. Dutra Const. Co.*, 183 F.3d 916 (9th Cir.1999) (when nonmoving party relies only on his own affidavit to oppose summary judgment, his affidavit may not be conclusory or unsupported by factual data).

173. *See Stagman v. Ryan*, 176 F.3d 986, 995 (7th Cir.1999).

174. *See Bryant v. Farmers Ins. Exchange*, 432 F.3d 1114, 1122–23 (10th Cir. 2005) (expert opinion testimony may not be considered unless affiant has been designated as an expert for trial); *Ruffin v. Shaw Indus., Inc.*, 149 F.3d 294 (4th Cir.1998) (because expert's opinions are inadmissible under Supreme Court's *Daubert* test, expert's affidavits and deposition testimony cannot be considered on summary judgment motion).

175. *See Geske & Sons, Inc. v. NLRB*, 103 F.3d 1366, 1376 (7th Cir.1997); *Roche v. John Hancock Mut. Life Ins. Co.*, 81 F.3d 249, 253 (1st Cir.1996).

176. *See Security Ins. Co. v. Old Dominion Freight Line Inc.*, 391 F.3d 77, 84–85 (2d Cir.2004); *Lantec, Inc. v. Novell, Inc.*, 306 F.3d 1003, 1019 (10th Cir.2002); *Markel v. Board of Regents of Univ. of Wisc. Sys.*, 276 F.3d 906, 912 (7th Cir.2002).

177. *See Barthelemy v. Air Lines Pilots Ass'n*, 897 F.2d 999, 1018 (9th Cir. 1990)(noting that affiant's competence could be inferred from position with the company).

178. *See Orson, Inc. v. Miramax Film Corp.*, 79 F.3d 1358, 1372 (3d Cir. 1996)(noting that legal memoranda and oral argument are not evidence and cannot independently create a genuine issue of disputed fact sufficient to preclude summary judgment); *Lopez v. Corporacion Azucarera de Puerto Rico*, 938 F.2d 1510, 1516 n. 11 (1st Cir.1991).

179. *See Hernandez–Santiago v. Ecolab, Inc.*, 397 F.3d 30, 35 (1st Cir.2005) (affidavit that represented merely the "review of relevant manufacturing and sales records" not sufficient, where affiant did not attest that he conducted or supervised review or had personal knowledge of results of review).

affidavit.[180]　Thus, verified complaints (ordinarily not required under the Rules) may be treated as summary judgment "affidavits",[181] so long as they otherwise satisfy the Rule 56(e) prerequisites.[182]

Affidavits to Authenticate Summary Judgment Documents and Exhibits

Parties may submit documents and other exhibits to support or oppose motions for summary judgment. Most courts require that those documents be attached to a Rule 56(e) affidavit that, upon personal knowledge, both identifies and authenticates each document.[183] Documents that fail to satisfy this affidavit authentication requirement may be properly disregarded by those courts when analyzing the pending motion.[184]

"Vouching" Risk with Summary Judgment Affidavits

At least one court has ruled that a party offering a Rule 56(e) affidavit effectively concedes that the affidavit qualifies for consideration under the Rule (that is, that the statements made are sworn, made upon personal knowledge, factually specific and admissible, and competent). The court may properly deny a party's later, pretrial *in limine* motion to strike testimony that the same moving party had earlier itself offered in support of a summary judgment brief, especially where the *in limine* motion purports to challenge an aspect of the testimony that the proffering party had earlier implicitly conceded.[185]

Contradictory Sworn Evidence from Same Party

Most courts have embraced the "sham affidavit" rule, which provides that a party ordinarily cannot defeat summary judgment by

180.　*See* 28 U.S.C.A. § 1746; *Neal v. Kelly*, 963 F.2d 453, 457 (D.C.Cir.1992). *See also Winterrowd v. Nelson*, 480 F.3d 1181, 1183 n.3 (9th Cir. 2007) (permitting *pro se* plaintiff to convert brief into affidavit with an attached penalty-of-perjury swearing).

181.　*See Monahan v. New York City Dep't of Corrections*, 214 F.3d 275, 292 (2d Cir.2000); *Ford v. Wilson*, 90 F.3d 245, 247 (7th Cir.1996) (though not "condon[ing] the practice," court holds that verifying the complaint converts the pleading into an affidavit, and it is immaterial that the verification was not captioned "affidavit"); *Hayes v. Marriott*, 70 F.3d 1144, 1148 (10th Cir.1995)(same).

182.　*See Schroeder v. McDonald*, 55 F.3d 454, 460 (9th Cir.1995) (verified complaint may be considered as opposing affidavit if based on personal knowledge and if it sets forth specific, admissible facts). *But see Lantec, Inc. v. Novell, Inc.*, 306 F.3d 1003, 1019 (10th Cir.2002) (district court properly refused to consider verified complaint as summary judgment affidavit where its allegations were merely conclusory).

183.　*See Article II Gun Shop, Inc. v. Gonzales*, 441 F.3d 492, 496 (7th Cir.2006); *Hoffman v. Applicators Sales & Serv., Inc.*, 439 F.3d 9, 15 (1st Cir.2006); *Orr v. Bank of America, NT & SA*, 285 F.3d 764, 773–74 (9th Cir.2002).

184.　*See Scott v. Edinburg*, 346 F.3d 752, 759–60 & 760 n.7 (7th Cir.2003); *Citizens for Better Forestry v. United Stated Dep't of Agric.*, 341 F.3d 961, 972 n.7 (9th Cir.2003).

185.　*See Williams v. Trader Pub'g Co.*, 218 F.3d 481, 485 (5th Cir.2000) (in an employment case, party offered affidavits of certain male employees to support its summary judgment position, then later attempted to argue that the testimony of these same male employees was inadmissible because the male employees were not in situations "nearly identical" to the plaintiff; court ruled that the testimony was properly admitted because defendant, by introducing this same evidence at the summary judgment stage, contended that the evidence would be relevant and admissible at trial).

simply denying, in an affidavit, a statement that the party had earlier admitted in a sworn statement. To create a genuine issue for trial sufficient to defeat summary judgment, the party must, in addition to the denial itself, offer an explanation for the inconsistency that the district court finds adequate to allow a reasonable juror to *both* accept the current denial and yet still assume either the truth of, or the party's good faith belief in, the earlier sworn statement.[186] Where, however, the original statement was truly ambiguous, and the later affidavit serves to clarify the testimony, the subsequent statement may be accepted.[187]

Striking Affidavits

A party may move to strike a Rule 56 affidavit. In resolving such motions, the courts use "a scalpel, not a butcher knife".[188] Only those improper portions of an affidavit are disallowed; all properly stated facts are allowed.[189] Moreover, if a party fails to move to strike an improper affidavit or improper portions thereof, the objection is waived.[190]

RULE 56(f).   WHEN AFFIDAVITS ARE UNAVAILABLE

CORE CONCEPT

Once a motion for summary judgment is filed, the non-moving party must prove to the court that a genuine and material factual dispute exists to defeat summary judgment. If the non-moving party is still conducting valuable discovery or for some other reason is not yet ready or able to make that showing, he or she may file an affidavit explaining why a ruling on summary judgment should be postponed. The court, in its discretion, may then grant a temporary reprieve if the affidavit of reasons is persuasive.

186. *See Cleveland v. Policy Mgmt. Sys. Corp.*, 526 U.S. 795, 804, 119 S.Ct. 1597, 1603, 143 L.Ed.2d 966 (1999); *Galvin v. Eli Lilly & Co.*, 488 F.3d 1026, 1030 (D.C.Cir. 2007). *See also Bausman v. Interstate Brands Corp.*, 50 F.Supp.2d 1028 (D.Kan. 1999) (conflicting affidavit can only be disregarded if court determines it was merely an attempt to create "sham fact issue"), *aff'd in part, rev'd in part*, 252 F.3d 1111 (10th Cir.2001).

187. *See Galvin v. Eli Lilly & Co.*, 488 F.3d 1026, 1030 (D.C.Cir. 2007); *Selenke v. Medical Imaging of Colorado*, 248 F.3d 1249, 1258 (10th Cir.2001).

188. *See Perez v. Volvo Car Corp.*, 247 F.3d 303, 315–16 (1st Cir.2001).

189. *See Perez v. Volvo Car Corp.*, 247 F.3d 303, 315–16 (1st Cir.2001); *Hollander v. American Cyanamid Co.*, 172 F.3d 192, 198 (2d Cir.1999); *Evans v. Technologies Applications & Serv. Co.*, 80 F.3d 954, 962 (4th Cir.1996).

190. *See Ruby v. Springfield R–12 Pub. Sch. Dist.*, 76 F.3d 909, 912 n. 8 (8th Cir. 1996)(absent motion to strike or other timely objection, district judge may consider a document which fails to conform to Rule 56(e)'s formal requirements); *In re Unisys Sav. Plan Litig.*, 74 F.3d 420, 437 n. 12 (3d Cir.1996), (party waived objection to form of affidavit by failing to move to strike or otherwise object); *Humane Soc'y of United States v. Babbitt*, 46 F.3d 93, 96 n. 5 (D.C.Cir.1995)(agreeing with sister circuits that Rule 56(e) defects are deemed waived if motion to strike not filed in the district court); *Casas Office Machs., Inc. v. Mita Copystar America, Inc.*, 42 F.3d 668, 682 (1st Cir.1994)(commenting that, absent motion to strike (which specifies objectionable portions of affidavit and grounds for challenge), objections to Rule 56(e) affidavit are deemed waived).

APPLICATIONS

Affidavit Requirement for Motion

Some courts will not consider a Rule 56(f) request unless it is accompanied by a sworn affidavit.[191] Other courts, in appropriate circumstances, will excuse the failure to submit a formal affidavit where all other necessary information has been supplied.[192]

Formal Request Requirement for Motion

A party seeking a Rule 56(f) postponement of a summary judgment ruling must make that request specifically, and plainly ask the trial court to defer ruling on a then-pending motion until discovery is completed.[193] A footnoted request contained in a summary judgment brief will not qualify under this Rule.[194]

Substantive Requirements for Motion

Although relief under this Rule is often and liberally granted, it does not come automatically.[195] Before the courts will postpone a summary judgment ruling pending further discovery, the courts will generally require a Rule 56(f) movant to make three showings: (1) a description of the particular discovery the movant intends to seek; (2) an explanation showing how that discovery would preclude the entry of summary judgment; and (3) a statement justifying why this discovery had not been or could not have been obtained earlier.[196] Although the affidavit (or, where permitted, a non-affidavit submission) need not contain evidentiary facts,[197] the showing made in the

191. See Doe v. Abington Friends Sch., 480 F.3d 252, 255 n.3 (3d Cir. 2007); Hackworth v. Progressive Casualty Ins. Co., 468 F.3d 722, 732 (10th Cir. 2006); Ball v. Union Carbide Corp., 376 F.3d 554, 561 (6th Cir.2004); American Chiropractic Ass'n v. Trigon Healthcare, Inc., 367 F.3d 212, 237 (4th Cir.2004); Di Benedetto v. Pan Am World Serv., Inc., 359 F.3d 627, 630 (2d Cir.2004). See also Pastore v. Bell Tel. Co. of Pa., 24 F.3d 508 (3d Cir.1994)(noting that affidavit requirement ensures that Rule 56(f) protection is being invoked in good faith and provides trial court with the showing necessary to assess the merits of the party's opposition to the motion).

192. See Hernandez–Santiago v. Ecolab, Inc., 397 F.3d 30, 35 n.3 (1st Cir.2005) (failure to comply with affidavit rule can, in appropriate circumstances, be excused as technical error); Cacevic v. City of Hazel Park, 226 F.3d 483, 488–89 (6th Cir.2000) (noting practice by other courts to permit Rule 56(f) request by form other than affidavit); Stults v. Conoco, Inc., 76 F.3d 651, 657–58 (5th Cir.1996) (affidavit form not required).

193. See Been v. O.K. Indus., Inc., 495 F.3d 1217, 1235 (10th Cir. 2007); Hack-

worth v. Progressive Casualty Ins. Co., 468 F.3d 722, 732 (10th Cir. 2006); Velez v. Awning Windows, Inc., 375 F.3d 35, 40 (1st Cir.2004).

194. See Allen v. Sybase, Inc., 468 F.3d 642, 662 (10th Cir. 2006).

195. See Been v. O.K. Indus., Inc., 495 F.3d 1217, 1235 (10th Cir. 2007); Allen v. CSX Transp., Inc., 325 F.3d 768, 775 (6th Cir.2003).

196. See Doe v. Abington Friends Sch., 480 F.3d 252, 255 n.3 (3d Cir. 2007); Hackworth v. Progressive Casualty Ins. Co., 468 F.3d 722, 732 (10th Cir. 2006); Adams v. Travelers Indem. Co., 465 F.3d 156, 162 (5th Cir. 2006); Adorno v. Crowley Towing & Transp. Co., 443 F.3d 122, 128 (1st Cir. 2006); Tatum v. City of San Francisco, 441 F.3d 1090, 1100 (9th Cir.2006); Exigent Tech., Inc. v. Atrana Solutions, Inc., 442 F.3d 1301, 1310 (Fed.Cir.2006).

197. See Price ex rel. Price v. Western Resources, Inc., 232 F.3d 779, 783–84 (10th Cir.2000).

affidavit must be specific—vague or baldly conclusory statements will not suffice.[198] Moreover, the affidavit containing these showings must be authoritative (that is, it must be taken by someone with first-hand knowledge of the statements made).[199] The court is unlikely to grant such a request where the moving party has not been diligent in beginning discovery; the request must verify that the moving party has been diligent in pursuing discovery.[200] If the moving party fails to adequately make any of these showings, the court may deny the requested postponement and rule upon the pending summary judgment motion.[201]

When Rule 56(f) Formalities May Not Be Required

There is some tension between an absolute requirement that a Rule 56(f) affidavit be filed and the established principle that summary judgment is only properly entered after an adequate time for discovery.[202] To reconcile this tension, some courts have held that a postponement in entering summary judgment may still be appropriate, even in the absence of a Rule 56(f) affidavit, where the nonmoving party adequately notifies the trial court that summary judgment is premature and that additional discovery is necessary, and where the nonmoving party—through no fault of her own—has had little or no opportunity for discovery.[203] Practitioners should be cautioned against relying on this case-specific liberalizing approach, however; even in those cases where this approach is followed, the court has "hasten[ed] to add that parties who ignore Rule 56(f)'s affidavit requirement do so at their peril".[204]

---

198. *See Adams v. Travelers Indem. Co.*, 465 F.3d 156, 162 (5th Cir. 2006); *Trask v. Franco*, 446 F.3d 1036, 1042 (10th Cir. 2006); *Messina v. Krakower*, 439 F.3d 755, 762 (D.C.Cir.2006); *Ball v. Union Carbide Corp.*, 376 F.3d 554, 561 (6th Cir.2004).

199. *See C.B. Trucking, Inc. v. Waste Management, Inc.*, 137 F.3d 41, 44 n. 2 (1st Cir.1998). *But cf. Simas v. First Citizens' Fed. Credit Union*, 170 F.3d 37, 46 n. 4 (1st Cir.1999) (although movant must attest to personal knowledge of recited grounds, statement need not be presented in form admissible at trial, so long as it rises sufficiently above mere speculation; thus, reliance on hearsay is not necessarily a dispositive defect under Rule 56(f)).

200. *See Velez v. Awning Windows, Inc.*, 375 F.3d 35, 40 (1st Cir.2004); *Chance v. Pac–Tel Teletrac Inc.*, 242 F.3d 1151, 1161 n.6 (9th Cir.2001); *Beattie v. Madison County Sch. Dist.*, 254 F.3d 595, 606 (5th Cir.2001).

201. *See Cervantes v. Jones*, 188 F.3d 805 (7th Cir.1999) (affirming denial of Rule 56(f) motion where excuse for failing to conduct the deposition earlier was a desire to refrain from beginning discovery in order to "foster an atmosphere conducive to set-

tlement"); *Kelly v. Marcantonio*, 187 F.3d 192 (1st Cir.1999) (affirming denial of motion where party failed to specify any material evidence that they would likely uncover if given additional discovery); *In re Silicon Graphics Inc. Secs. Litig.*, 183 F.3d 970 (9th Cir.1999) (noting that failure to comply with Rule 56(f) requirements is proper ground for denying discovery and proceeding to summary judgment); *Stanback v. Best Diversified Prods., Inc.*, 180 F.3d 903, 911 (8th Cir.1999) (noting that where "party fails to carry burden under Rule 56(f), postponement of summary judgment ruling is not justified"); *Byrd v. United States EPA*, 174 F.3d 239, 248 n. 8 (D.C.Cir.1999) (affirming denial where movant, without more, alleged merely that "there may well be" evidence helpful to the claim).

202. *See Celotex Corp. v. Catrett*, 477 U.S. 317, 322, 106 S.Ct. 2548, 2552, 91 L.Ed.2d 265 (1986) (setting forth principle).

203. *See Harrods Ltd. v. Sixty Internet Domain Names*, 302 F.3d 214, 244 (4th Cir.2002).

204. *See Harrods Ltd. v. Sixty Internet Domain Names*, 302 F.3d 214, 246 n. 19 (4th Cir.2002) (making comment, and "reit-

Postponing Very Early Filed Motions for Summary Judgment

When a summary judgment motion is filed very early in the litigation, before a realistic opportunity for discovery, courts generally grant Rule 56(f) postponements freely.[205] In such cases, summary judgment should be refused as a matter of course,[206] with exceptions permitted in only rare cases.[207] With such early filed motions, the courts recognize that the Rule 56(f) affiant may not be capable of framing its postponement request with great specificity.[208]

Timing

A Rule 56(f) motion to postpone a summary judgment ruling must be made in a timely fashion, which generally means before the party files a response to the pending motion or, in any event, prior to any scheduled oral argument on the motion.[209] A party may not wait until after the court rules on the main Rule 56 motion. Thus, a party may not attempt to defeat the summary judgment motion on its merits and, if an adverse ruling is entered, then seek the Rule 56(f) extension for discovery in an effort to pursue reconsideration.[210]

Burden on the Movant

The party moving to postpone the summary judgment ruling bears the burden of demonstrating the requisite basis for relief under Rule 56(f).[211]

District Court's Discretion and Options

Whether to grant or deny a Rule 56(f) postponement is committed to the district court's discretion.[212] In ruling, the district court must balance the moving party's need for the requested discovery against the burden the discovery and delay will place on the oppos-

---

erat[ing] that our court expects full compliance with Rule 56(f)"). *See also Bradley v. United States*, 299 F.3d 197, 207 (3d Cir. 2002) (noting "strong presumption against a finding of constructive compliance with Rule 56(f)").

205. *See Burlington No. Santa Fe R. Co. v. Assiniboine & Sioux Tribes of Fort Peck Reservation*, 323 F.3d 767, 773–74 (9th Cir.2003).

206. *See Anderson v. Liberty Lobby, Inc.*, 477 U.S. 242, 250 n.5, 106 S.Ct. 2505, 91 L.Ed.2d 202 (1986); *Been v. O.K. Indus., Inc.*, 495 F.3d 1217, 1235 (10th Cir. 2007).

207. *See Miller v. Wolpoff & Abramson, L.L.P.*, 321 F.3d 292, 303–04 (2d Cir.2003).

208. *See Burlington No. Santa Fe R. Co. v. Assiniboine & Sioux Tribes of Fort Peck Reservation*, 323 F.3d 767, 773–74 (9th Cir.2003) (noting that affiant cannot be expected to frame motion with great specificity as to nature of discovery likely to develop

useful information because ground for such specificity has not yet been laid).

209. *See Adorno v. Crowley Towing & Transp. Co.*, 443 F.3d 122, 127–28 (1st Cir. 2006).

210. *See Been v. O.K. Indus., Inc.*, 495 F.3d 1217, 1235 (10th Cir. 2007); *Hackworth v. Progressive Casualty Ins. Co.*, 468 F.3d 722, 732–33 (10th Cir. 2006); *Rodriguez–Cuervos v. Wal–Mart Stores, Inc.*, 181 F.3d 15, 23 (1st Cir.1999).

211. *See Summers v. Leis*, 368 F.3d 881, 887 (6th Cir.2004); *Chance v. Pac–Tel Teletrac Inc.*, 242 F.3d 1151, 1161 n.6 (9th Cir. 2001); *Stanback v. Best Diversified Prods., Inc.*, 180 F.3d 903, 911 (8th Cir.1999).

212. *See Ball v. Union Carbide Corp.*, 376 F.3d 554, 561 (6th Cir.2004); *Chance v. Pac–Tel Teletrac Inc.*, 242 F.3d 1151, 1161 n.6 (9th Cir.2001); *Beattie v. Madison County Sch. Dist.*, 254 F.3d 595, 606 (5th Cir.2001).

ing party.[213] Ordinarily, such requests are construed and granted liberally;[214] denying properly made and supported motions is "disfavored".[215] On the basis of the party's meritorious Rule 56(f) showings, the district court may: (1) deny the motion for summary judgment; (2) grant a continuance to allow affidavits to be prepared and submitted; (3) permit discovery; or (4) make any other order as is just. If the court is presented with a Rule 56(f) motion, it may not proceed to decide the summary judgment motion without first considering and ruling upon the Rule 56(f) request.[216]

RULE 56(g). AFFIDAVITS SUBMITTED IN BAD FAITH

CORE CONCEPT

If the district court concludes that an affidavit submitted under Rule 56(c) or Rule 56(f) was presented in bad faith or solely for purposes of delay, the court must order the offending party to pay reasonable expenses incurred by the party's adversary (including attorney's fees) as a result of the improper affidavits.

APPLICATIONS

Prerequisites of Bad Faith or Delay

Rarely invoked or granted,[217] this Rule requires the court to compensate an adversary who confronted affidavits submitted either in bad faith or for purposes of delay.[218] Merely because one party disbelieves the other party is not a basis for invoking this Rule,[219] nor is the Rule automatically invoked merely because the affidavit conflicts with the affiant's prior sworn testimony.[220] Instead, the Rule has been granted in "particularly egregious" circumstances[221]

213. *See Harbert Int'l, Inc. v. James,* 157 F.3d 1271, 1280 (11th Cir.1998).

214. *See Doe v. Abington Friends Sch.,* 480 F.3d 252, 257 (3d Cir. 2007); *Culwell v. City of Fort Worth,* 468 F.3d 868, 871 (5th Cir. 2006). *See also Simas v. First Citizens' Fed. Credit Union,* 170 F.3d 37, 46 n. 4 (1st Cir.1999) (when all Rule 56(f) preconditions are met, a "strong presumption arises in favor of relief").

215. *See Ingle ex rel. Estate of Ingle v. Yelton,* 439 F.3d 191, 196 (4th Cir. 2006).

216. *See Doe v. Abington Friends Sch.,* 480 F.3d 252, 257 (3d Cir. 2007).

217. *See Fort Hill Builders, Inc. v. National Grange Mut. Ins. Co.,* 866 F.2d 11, 16 (1st Cir.1989).

218. *See In re Gioioso,* 979 F.2d 956 (3d Cir.1992)(noting that once bad faith is found, court is obligated to assess costs and fees).

219. *See Moorer v. Grumman Aerospace Corp.,* 964 F.Supp. 665, 676 (E.D.N.Y.1997), *aff'd,* 162 F.3d 1148 (2d Cir.1998).

220. *See Turner v. Baylor Richardson Med. Ctr.,* 476 F.3d 337, 349 (5th Cir. 2007); *Becton v. Starbucks Corp.,* 491 F.Supp.2d 737, 743 (S.D.Ohio 2007); *Bausman v. Interstate Brands Corp.,* 50 F.Supp.2d 1028 (D.Kan.1999), *aff'd in part, rev'd in part,* 252 F.3d 1111 (10th Cir.2001) (conflicting affidavit can only be disregarded if court determines it was merely an attempt to create "sham fact issue"). *See also Cleveland v. Policy Management Sys. Corp.,* 526 U.S. 795, 804, 119 S.Ct. 1597, 1603, 143 L.Ed.2d 966 (1999) (party ordinarily cannot defeat summary judgment by simply denying, in an affidavit, a statement that the party had earlier admitted in a sworn statement unless an adequate explanation for the inconsistency is offered).

221. *See Fort Hill Builders, Inc. v. National Grange Mut. Ins. Co.,* 866 F.2d 11, 16 (1st Cir.1989).

where the district court finds that the affidavit was, in fact, submitted in bad faith or with the purpose of delay.[222] Little case law exists to guide the court's assessment of "bad faith" under the Rule, and the courts possess wide discretion in making this analysis.[223] Courts have found "bad faith" to be egregious conduct (*e.g.*, averring perjurious or blatantly false allegations or facts) related and necessary to issues central to the disposition of the case.[224] If the improper affidavit is not considered in resolving the summary judgment motion, sanctions under Rule 56(g) may be deemed inappropriate.[225]

Prescribed Remedies For Bad Faith Affidavits

When a court determines that an affidavit has been presented in bad faith, the court will order the presenting party to reimburse its adversaries for all expenses—including attorney's fees—attributable to the additional litigation generated by the bad faith affidavit.[226] The relief is mandatory–once the court finds that the affidavit was presented in bad faith or solely for purpose of delay, compensation to the responding party is not discretionary and must be awarded.[227]

Improper Affidavits May Be Stricken

In addition to sanctioning the submitting party, the court also has discretion to strike sham summary judgment affidavits.[228]

Other Penalties

In addition to the sanctions permitted under Rule 56(g), the court may also hold the attorney and the offending party in con-

---

222. *See Klein v. Stahl GMBH & Co. Maschinefabrik*, 185 F.3d 98, 110 (3d Cir. 1999) (bad faith required); *Murray v. Board of Educ. of New York*, 111 F.Supp.2d 349 (S.D.N.Y.2000) (same); *Rogers v. AC Humko Corp.*, 56 F.Supp.2d 972 (W.D.Tenn. 1999) (granting sanctions where affiant made a representation upon personal knowledge, relating to a crucial issue, in a manner favorable to his employer, which later proved to be false, and where representation was not a simple mistake but either a highly reckless representation of an important fact or a deliberate and calculated misrepresentation abetted by counsel and designed to thwart justice); *Hunt v. Tektronix, Inc.*, 952 F.Supp. 998, 1010 (W.D.N.Y.1997) (denying sanctions where affiant's actions, though "unfortunate", were not deliberately taken in bad faith); *Feltner v. Partyka*, 945 F.Supp. 1188, 1192 (N.D.Ind.1996) (denying sanctions where affiant, although technically deficient, was not "willful[ly]" deficient).

223. *See Turner v. Baylor Richardson Med. Ctr.*, 476 F.3d 337, 349 (5th Cir. 2007); *Cobell v. Norton*, 214 F.R.D. 13, 20 (D.D.C.2003).

224. *See Fort Hill Builders, Inc. v. National Grange Mut. Ins. Co.*, 866 F.2d 11, 16 (1st Cir.1989); *Boggs v. Die Fliedermaus,*

LLP, 286 F.Supp.2d 291, 302 (S.D.N.Y. 2003); *Jaisan, Inc. v. Sullivan*, 178 F.R.D. 412, 415–16 (S.D.N.Y.1998).

225. *See, e.g., Wilson v. Maricopa County*, 463 F.Supp.2d 987, 1000 (D.Ariz. 2006); *Structural Polymer Group, Ltd. v. Zoltek Corp.*, 2006 WL 2802202, at *2 (E.D.Mo. 2006); *SAT Int'l Corp. v. Great White Fleet (US) Ltd.*, 2006 WL 661042, at *13 (S.D.N.Y.2006); *Laney v. American Equity Inv. Life Ins. Co.*, 243 F.Supp.2d 1347, 1358 (M.D.Fla.2003).

226. *See Klein v. Stahl GMBH & Co. Maschinefabrik*, 185 F.3d 98, 110 (3d Cir. 1999).

227. *See* Rule 56(g) (during the 2007 style project amendments to this Rule, the verb "shall" was replaced by "must", confirming the nondiscretionary obligation). *See also Scott v. Metropolitan Health Corp.*, 2007 WL 1028853, at *26 (6th Cir. 2007); *Cobell v. Norton*, 214 F.R.D. 13, 20 (D.D.C. 2003).

228. *See Bausman v. Interstate Brands Corp.*, 50 F.Supp.2d 1028 (D.Kan.1999), *aff'd in part, rev'd in part*, 252 F.3d 1111 (10th Cir.2001).

tempt of court,[229] and false swearing to the court could also give rise to criminal penalties.[230] The Rule does not authorize any other penalty (such as the punitive granting of summary judgment against the presenter of the improper affidavit).[231]

Affidavits from *Pro Se* Litigants

Some courts apply the affidavit sanction rule more gently in cases involving affidavits submitted by *pro se* litigants.[232]

Affidavits Made in Non–Summary Judgment Settings

By its terms, this Rule applies only to affidavits presented in the summary judgment context. Affidavits submitted for other purposes, or in support of relief under other Rules, are not subject to Rule 56(g).[233]

ADDITIONAL RESEARCH REFERENCES

Wright & Miller, *Federal Practice and Procedure* §§ 2711–2742.

C.J.S. Federal Civil Procedure §§ 1135–1187 et seq., 1189–1216 et seq.

West's Key No. Digests, Federal Civil Procedure ☞2461–2559.

229. *See Klein v. Stahl GMBH & Co. Maschinefabrik*, 185 F.3d 98, 110 (3d Cir. 1999).

230. *See* 18 U.S.C.A. § 1623 (prescribing that person who makes a knowingly false material declaration to a court is subject to a $10,000 fine, five years in prison, or both).

231. *See Stovall v. Lakanu*, 2006 WL 3350686, at *7 (D.Minn. 2006).

232. *See Boggs v. Die Fliedermaus, LLP*, 286 F.Supp.2d 291, 302 (S.D.N.Y. 2003) (finding sanctions inappropriate where litigant appeared *pro se*, no bad faith evidence existed, there had not been repeated unmeritorious filings, and no prior warnings to litigant had been given by the court).

233. *See McCarley v. Household Fin. Corp. III*, 2007 WL 1100330, at *2 (M.D.Ala. 2007).

RULE 57

DECLARATORY JUDGMENT

These rules govern the procedure for obtaining a declaratory judgment under 28 U.S.C. § 2201. Rules 38 and 39 govern a demand for a jury trial. The existence of another adequate remedy does not preclude a declaratory judgment that is otherwise appropriate. The court may order a speedy hearing of a declaratory-judgment action.

[Amended effective October 20, 1949; April 30, 2007, effective December 1, 2007.]

───────────── 2007 AMENDMENTS ROADMAP ─────────────

STYLE PROJECT CHANGES: Modest, general language simplification throughout. No new subsectioning, and no new labels.

NON-STYLE CHANGES: None.

NOTE: The Federal Rules "Style Project" is explained in Part III-A.

AUTHORS' COMMENTARY ON RULE 57

───────────── PURPOSE AND SCOPE ─────────────

Rule 57 permits parties to obtain a declaratory judgment to determine their rights and obligations in cases involving actual controversies. The Rule operates in conjunction with the federal Declaratory Judgment Act, 28 U.S.C.A. §§ 2201–02.

APPLICATIONS

Purpose

A declaratory judgment declares the rights and obligations of litigants. Its purpose is to afford litigants an early opportunity to resolve their federal disputes so as to avoid the threat of impending litigation,[1] and obtain both clarity in their legal relationships and the ability to make responsible decisions about their future.[2] It provides a practical solution to instances in which the adversary's interests may be well served by delaying the commencement of the

───────────────────────────

1. *See Biodiversity Legal Found. v. Badgley,* 309 F.3d 1166, 1172 (9th Cir. 2002).

2. *See Surrick v. Killion,* 449 F.3d 520, 529 (3d Cir.2006).

very lawsuit at issue.[3] As such, it provides a procedural vehicle for "clearing the air".[4] This procedure is particularly useful for defendants confronting numerous lawsuits, who may seek declaratory relief to avoid a multiplicity of actions and achieve an adequate, expedient, and comparably inexpensive declaration of rights.[5]

Relationship between Rule 57 and Declaratory Judgment Act

Courts have held that the federal Declaratory Judgment Act, 28 U.S.C.A. §§ 2201–02, is "mirrored by" and "functionally equivalent to" Rule 57.[6]

The Constitutional Requirements: Subject Matter Jurisdiction, Actual Controversy, and Ripeness

Subject Matter Jurisdiction. A plaintiff seeking declaratory relief must establish an independent basis for the district court's subject matter jurisdiction (*e.g.,* diversity of citizenship or federal question).[7] Neither Rule 57 nor the Declaratory Judgment Act expands the court's jurisdiction; these provisions only provide a declaratory remedy in cases properly brought in federal court.[8]

Note: In federal question cases, the district courts will apply the "well-pleaded complaint" rule to assess whether the plaintiff's action involves a federal question. Thus, where the federal nature of plaintiff's claim comes only from plaintiff's anticipation that the defendant will assert a federal defense, the court is likely to find that the plaintiff's claim lacks subject matter jurisdiction.[9]

Actual Controversy. The district court may only enter a declaratory judgment where the dispute between the parties is definite and concrete, affecting the parties' adverse legal interests with sufficient immediacy as to justify relief.[10] No declaratory

---

3. *See BP Chems. Ltd. v. Union Carbide Corp.,* 4 F.3d 975, 977 (Fed.Cir.1993).

4. *See Microchip Tech. Inc. v. Chamberlain Group, Inc.,* 441 F.3d 936, 943 (Fed. Cir.2006).

5. *See Biodiversity Legal Found. v. Badgley,* 309 F.3d 1166, 1172 (9th Cir. 2002).

6. *See Ernst & Young v. Depositors Econ. Prot. Corp.,* 45 F.3d 530, 534 n.8 (1st Cir.1995).

7. For further discussion on this point, see Part II of this text §§ 2.10–2.13 on subject matter jurisdiction.

8. *See Schilling v. Rogers,* 363 U.S. 666, 677, 80 S.Ct. 1288, 1295, 4 L.Ed.2d 1478 (1960)(commenting that the Act is not an independent source of federal jurisdiction); *Aetna Life Ins. Co. v. Haworth,* 300 U.S. 227, 240, 57 S.Ct. 461, 463, 81 L.Ed. 617 (1937)(writing that Act is only procedural). *See also TIG Ins. Co. v. Reliable Research Co.,* 334 F.3d 630, 634 (7th Cir.2003); *Hey-*

don *v. MediaOne of S.E. Mich., Inc.,* 327 F.3d 466, 470 (6th Cir.2003).

9. *See Public Serv. Comm'n v. Wycoff Co.,* 344 U.S. 237, 73 S.Ct. 236, 97 L.Ed. 291 (1952). *See also Skelly Oil Co. v. Phillips Petroleum Co.,* 339 U.S. 667, 673, 70 S.Ct. 876, 880, 94 L.Ed. 1194 (1950)("It would turn into the federal courts a vast amount of litigation indubitably arising under State law, in the sense that the right to be vindicated was State-created, if a suit for a declaration of rights could be brought into the federal courts merely because an anticipated defense derived from federal law").

10. *See MedImmune, Inc. v. Genentech, Inc.,* __ U.S. __, __, 127 S.Ct. 764, 771, 166 L.Ed.2d 604 (2007); *Maryland Cas. Co. v. Pacific Coal & Oil Co.,* 312 U.S. 270, 61 S.Ct. 510, 85 L.Ed. 826 (1941); *Aetna Life Ins. Co. v. Haworth,* 300 U.S. 227, 57 S.Ct. 461, 81 L.Ed. 617 (1937). *Cf. Calderon v. Ashmus,* 523 U.S. 740, 118 S.Ct. 1694, 140 L.Ed.2d 970 (1998) (holding that declarato-

judgment may be entered where the parties' dispute is hypothetical, abstract, or academic.[11]

Note: The Supreme Court has confirmed that declaratory relief is available where the plaintiff is threatened by adverse government action, and has noted (without criticism) that the lower federal courts have long agreed that declaratory relief is available where the plaintiff is threatened by adverse action from a private party.[12]

Ripeness. The actual controversy requirement obligates the court to determine that the case is "ripe" for adjudication.[13] This "ripeness" must remain throughout the lawsuit. Thus, the district court must decide at the time it is about to enter judgment whether an actual controversy still exists between the parties. Thus, even if an actual controversy existed at the time the lawsuit was filed, the court will not enter a declaratory judgment if later events ended the controversy and the dispute has become moot.[14]

Note: The courts recognize an exception to this mootness limitation where the plaintiff is able to show a substantial likelihood that the dispute will re-occur in the future.[15]

The Prudential Concerns: Exercise of the District Court's Discretion

Declaratory relief is never automatic. The courts have no "unflagging duty" to hear declaratory judgment cases.[16] Whether to grant or deny declaratory relief is vested in the sound discretion of the district court.[17] This discretion, though wide, is not boundless;

---

ry judgments cannot be sought merely for the purpose of testing the validity of a defense that a State may possibly raise in some future, as yet unfiled habeas proceeding).

11. *See MedImmune, Inc. v. Genentech, Inc.,* ___ U.S. ___, ___, 127 S.Ct. 764, 771, 166 L.Ed.2d 604 (2007).

12. *See MedImmune, Inc. v. Genentech, Inc.,* ___ U.S. ___, ___, 127 S.Ct. 764, 772–73, 166 L.Ed.2d 604 (2007).

13. *See Surrick v. Killion,* 449 F.3d 520, 527 (3d Cir.2006); *Pic-A-State Pa., Inc. v. Reno,* 76 F.3d 1294, 1298 (3d Cir.1996).

14. *See Preiser v. Newkirk,* 422 U.S. 395, 95 S.Ct. 2330, 45 L.Ed.2d 272 (1975); *Golden v. Zwickler,* 394 U.S. 103, 89 S.Ct. 956, 22 L.Ed.2d 113 (1969). *See also Prier v. Steed,* 456 F.3d 1209, 1213 (10th Cir.2006); *Bauer v. Texas,* 341 F.3d 352, 358 (5th Cir.2003).

15. *See Super Tire Eng'g Co. v. McCorkle,* 416 U.S. 115, 94 S.Ct. 1694, 40 L.Ed.2d 1 (1974); *Malowney v. Federal Collection Deposit Group,* 193 F.3d 1342, 1347 (11th Cir.1999) (holding that declaratory judg-

ment remedy is only proper where plaintiffs assert a reasonable expectation that injury will continue or will be repeated in the future).

16. *See Diaz–Fonseca v. Puerto Rico,* 451 F.3d 13, 39 (1st Cir.2006).

17. *See MedImmune, Inc. v. Genentech, Inc.,* ___ U.S. ___, ___, 127 S.Ct. 764, 776, 166 L.Ed.2d 604 (2007); *Provident Tradesmens Bank & Trust Co. v. Patterson,* 390 U.S. 102, 88 S.Ct. 733, 19 L.Ed.2d 936 (1968). *See also Wilton v. Seven Falls Co.,* 515 U.S. 277, 281, 115 S.Ct. 2137, 2140, 132 L.Ed.2d 214 (1995)(noting that, even when subject matter jurisdiction prerequisites are otherwise satisfied, district courts enjoy discretion to determine whether, in what circumstances, to entertain declaratory judgment action); *Hewitt v. Helms,* 482 U.S. 755, 762, 107 S.Ct. 2672, 2676, 96 L.Ed.2d 654 (1987) ("The fact that a court can enter a declaratory judgment does not mean that it should"); *Public Serv. Comm'n v. Wycoff Co.,* 344 U.S. 237, 241, 73 S.Ct. 236, 239, 97 L.Ed. 291 (1952)(noting that the declaratory judgment statute "is an enabling act,

the district court may not refuse on "whim or personal disinclination" to hear a declaratory judgment action, but must instead base its refusal on good reason.[18] If the court decides not to entertain the declaratory proceeding, it may either stay or dismiss the federal action, and may enter such an order before trial or after all arguments come to a close.[19]

Factors for Court's Consideration

To decide whether to entertain a declaratory judgment action, courts may consider various factors, including whether the declaratory judgment proceeding will resolve the controversy, whether such a proceeding would serve a useful purpose in clarifying the legal relations in dispute, whether the proceeding is being initiated for the purpose of forum shopping, "racing to res judicata", or to procedurally "fence" with the opponent, whether the declaratory judgment action would be inequitable to the allegedly injured party, whether a State court action is already pending in which the controversy could be fully litigated, whether the district court would increase friction between federal and State court systems by hearing the case or would otherwise encroach upon State jurisdiction, whether some alternate relief might be better or more effective, and whether the federal court is a convenient forum for parties and witnesses and would otherwise serve the interests of judicial economy.[20]

> *Note:* When another lawsuit involving the same dispute is pending in state court, the district judge may defer to the State forum, particularly where the State case was filed first.[21]

which confers a discretion on the courts rather than an absolute right upon the litigant"); *Brillhart v. Excess Ins. Co.*, 316 U.S. 491, 494, 62 S.Ct. 1173, 1175, 86 L.Ed. 1620 (1942) (vesting discretion).

18. *See Public Affairs Assocs., Inc. v. Rickover*, 369 U.S. 111, 112, 82 S.Ct. 2137, 2143, 132 L.E.2d 214 (1995); *Nautilus Ins. Co. v. Winchester Homes, Inc.*, 15 F.3d 371, 375 (4th Cir.1994).

19. *See Wilton v. Seven Falls Co.*, 515 U.S. 277, 287, 115 S.Ct. 2137, 2143, 132 L.Ed.2d 214 (1995).

20. *See, e.g., Bituminous Cas. Corp. v. J & L Lumber Co.*, 373 F.3d 807, 813 (6th Cir.2004) (listing several factors for consideration); *St. Paul Fire & Marine Ins. Co. v. Runyon*, 53 F.3d 1167, 1169 (10th Cir. 1995)(same). *See Igartua-De La Rosa v. United States*, 417 F.3d 145, 149 (1st Cir. 2005) (cautioning that declaratory relief to be exercised with "great circumspection" when matters of public moment are involved); *Ameritas Variable Life Ins. Co. v.*

Roach, 411 F.3d 1328, 1330–32 (11th Cir. 2005) (noting concern for abstention on state-law claims in face of parallel State court litigation); *International Ass'n of Entrepreneurs of America v. Angoff*, 58 F.3d 1266, 1270 (8th Cir.1995)(noting reluctance to grant such relief where the action is filed to obtain a "tactical advantage" over an opponent or to open an otherwise closed avenue into federal court by asserting what is essentially a defensive action, reactive to State court litigations); *BASF Corp. v. Symington*, 50 F.3d 555, 558–59 (8th Cir. 1995)(emphasizing that declaratory judgment actions may merit closer inspection to ensure that the plaintiff is not simply forum shopping, and such proceedings may be refused where the plaintiff asserts principally an affirmative defense in a declaratory judgment action brought to deny an injured party its otherwise proper choice of forum and time for suit).

21. *See Geni–Chlor Int'l, Inc. v. Multisonics Dev't Corp.*, 580 F.2d 981 (9th Cir. 1978).

Statement of Circumstances Supporting Declaratory Judgment

If a party contests the prudence of the district court's exercise of discretion to hear a declaratory judgment claim, the court must articulate the factual circumstances supporting the award of declaratory relief.[22]

Realignment of the Parties

In determining whether to grant a declaratory judgment, the courts may realign the parties in order to reflect the nature of the actual, underlying controversy.[23] In making this determination, the courts may consider the underlying purposes of declaratory relief, the parties' respective burdens of proof, and the best, clearest method for presenting evidence to the jury.[24] Where both sides will carry proof burdens at trial, realignment may properly be refused.[25]

Burden of Proof

A party seeking a declaratory judgment bears the burden of proving the existence of an actual case or controversy.[26] But the courts are divided on the question of the merits burden of proof in declaratory judgment actions. Because a declaratory judgment plaintiff often seeks a determination that the defendant lacks some type of right that, had defendant filed suit first, the defendant would bear the burden of proving, some courts permit a shift in the burden of proof.[27] Practitioners should consult their local rules and substantive case law on this issue.

Type of Relief Available

The court may grant a successful plaintiff whatever relief is warranted by the evidence, regardless of the demand in the plaintiff's complaint. The Declaratory Judgment Act provides that further relief can be awarded after reasonable notice and hearing. The courts, for example, possess "broad power" to make damages awards in declaratory judgment actions where appropriate.[28]

> *Note:* The Eleventh Amendment ordinarily does not preclude declaratory judgment proceedings instituted against State officials.[29]

22. *See Government Employees Ins. Co. v. Dizol*, 133 F.3d 1220, 1225 (9th Cir.1998).

23. *See BASF Corp. v. Symington*, 50 F.3d 555, 557 (8th Cir.1995).

24. *See Fresenius Med. Care Holdings, Inc. v. Baxter Int'l, Inc.*, 2006 WL 1646110, at *1 (N.D.Cal.2006).

25. *See Anheuser–Busch, Inc. v. John Labatt Ltd.*, 89 F.3d 1339, 1344 (8th Cir. 1996); *L–3 Commc'ns Corp. v. OSI Sys., Inc.*, 418 F.Supp.2d 380, 383 (S.D.N.Y. 2005).

26. *See Cardinal Chem. Co. v. Morton Int'l, Inc.*, 508 U.S. 83, 94, 113 S.Ct. 1967, 1974, 124 L.Ed.2d 1 (1993); *Hosein v. Gonzales*, 452 F.3d 401, 404 (5th Cir.2006).

27. *See Reliance Life Ins. Co. v. Burgess*, 112 F.2d 234 (8th Cir.1940). *See also*

American Eagle Ins. Co. v. Thompson, 85 F.3d 327, 331 (8th Cir.1996)(burden remains on the party asserting the affirmative on an issue); *Utah Farm Bureau Ins. Co. v. Dairyland Ins. Co.*, 634 F.2d 1326 (10th Cir.1980)(noting divergent views on burden of proof in declaratory judgment actions); *Fireman's Fund Ins. Co. v. Videfreeze Corp.*, 540 F.2d 1171 (3d Cir.1976).

28. *See United Teacher Assocs. Ins. Co. v. Union Labor Life Ins. Co.*, 414 F.3d 558, 570 (5th Cir.2005); *BancInsure, Inc. v. BNC Nat'l Bank, N.A.*, 263 F.3d 766, 772 (8th Cir.2001).

29. *See Native Village of Noatak v. Blatchford*, 38 F.3d 1505, 1513–14 (9th Cir. 1994).

The Existence of Other Possible Remedies

With one exception, declaratory relief is not foreclosed merely by showing that an adequate remedy other than a declaratory judgment exists.[30] A declaratory judgment may be entered whether or not further relief is sought or could have been awarded.[31] However, the existence of another, adequate remedy may convince the district court to exercise its discretion to deny declaratory relief in favor of some better or more effective remedy.[32] Moreover, where declaratory relief will not terminate the controversy, but further remedies will be sought in a different or subsequent proceeding, the declaratory judgment can be refused.[33]

> *The One Exception:* Where a special statutory proceeding has been provided to adjudicate a special type of case, declaratory relief may not be awarded. Such proceedings include petitions for habeas corpus and motions to vacate criminal sentences, proceedings under the Civil Rights Act of 1964, and certain administrative proceedings.[34]

Partial Remedy

If it exercises its discretion to hear a declaratory judgment case, the trial court is not obligated to rule on every issue presented. The court may, instead, properly choose to decide some of the issues raised and decline to decide others.[35]

Any Party May Seek Declaratory Judgment

Any party who has an interest in an actual controversy has standing to seek a declaratory judgment.

Who Declaratory Judgments Benefit

Ordinarily, a declaratory judgment is effective only as to the plaintiffs who obtained it. Often, however, such relief has far broader ramifications (such as in cases declaring the invalidity of a statute or patent).

---

30. *See Exxon Shipping Co. v. Airport Depot Diner, Inc.,* 120 F.3d 166 (9th Cir. 1997). *But see National Private Truck Council, Inc. v. Oklahoma Tax Com'n,* 515 U.S. 582, 589, 115 S.Ct. 2351, 2356, 132 L.Ed.2d 509 (1995)(commenting that the availability of an adequate remedy at law makes declaratory relief unwarranted).

31. *See Powell v. McCormack,* 395 U.S. 486, 89 S.Ct. 1944, 23 L.Ed.2d 491 (1969); *Nautilus Ins. Co. v. Winchester Homes, Inc.,* 15 F.3d 371, 379 (4th Cir.1994).

32. *See Universal Underwriters Serv. Corp. v. Melson,* 953 F.Supp. 385, 388 (M.D.Ala.1996).

33. *See* Rule 57 advisory committee note ("A declaratory judgment is appropriate when it will 'terminate the controversy' giving rise to the proceeding. ... When declaratory relief will not be effective in settling the controversy, the court may decline to grant it.").

34. *See New York Times Co. v. Gonzales,* 459 F.3d 160, 166 (2d Cir. 2006).

35. *See Henglein v. Colt Indus. Operating Corp.,* 260 F.3d 201, 210–11 (3d Cir. 2001).

Rules of Procedure

All rules of procedure applicable generally to civil lawsuits apply in a declaratory judgment action.[36]

Expedited Treatment

The district court may order a speedy hearing in declaratory judgment cases, and may move such cases to the top of the court's calendar.

Jury Trial

The right to a jury trial is preserved in declaratory judgment actions. If the issues would have been triable by a jury had something other than declaratory relief been sought, a right to a jury trial exists.[37]

Common Uses

Declaratory judgments are often used in insurance disputes to determine the validity of a policy, the extent of coverage, the insurance company's duty to defend, or a waiver of conditions.[38] Declaratory judgments are also commonly used in patent, copyright, and trademark cases to determine such questions as patent validity and patent infringement.[39] Declaratory judgments can be also be sought to determine a party's immunity status.[40]

Cautious Uses

The district court frequently will refrain from declaratory relief in cases involving important public issues, where the concreteness of a monetary or injunctive dispute is more advisable.[41] The district judge will also often deny declaratory relief that would act to interfere with a State criminal prosecution.[42]

Improper Uses

Declaratory relief is generally not available to merely adjudicate past conduct or to proclaim that one litigant is liable to another.[43] It

36. *See Cloverland–Green Spring Dairies, Inc. v. Pennsylvania Milk Mktg. Bd.,* 298 F.3d 201, 210 n. 12 (3d Cir.2002) (noting that standards for granting summary judgment in declaratory judgment case are same as for all other types of relief).

37. *See Simler v. Conner,* 372 U.S. 221, 83 S.Ct. 609, 9 L.Ed.2d 691 (1963); *Beacon Theatres, Inc. v. Westover,* 359 U.S. 500, 79 S.Ct. 948, 3 L.Ed.2d 988 (1959). *See also Marseilles Hydro Power, LLC v. Marseilles Land & Water Co.,* 299 F.3d 643, 649 (7th Cir.2002) (if declaratory judgment action fits into none of existing equitable patterns, but is instead an "inverted law suit") (a claim by a litigant who, at common law, would have been a defendant, then a jury right exists; if, however, the action is the counterpart of an equity suit, no jury right exists); *Owens-Illinois, Inc. v. Lake Shore*

Land Co., 610 F.2d 1185, 1189 (3d Cir. 1979) (same).

38. *See, e.g., Aetna Life Ins. Co. v. Haworth,* 300 U.S. 227, 57 S.Ct. 461, 81 L.Ed. 617 (1937).

39. *See Verizon Commc'ns, Inc. v. Inverizon Int'l, Inc.,* 295 F.3d 870, 873 (8th Cir. 2002); *Phillips Plastics Corp. v. Kato Hatsujou Kabushiki Kaisha,* 57 F.3d 1051, 1053–54 (Fed.Cir.1995).

40. *See In re B–727 Aircraft Serial No. 21010,* 272 F.3d 264, 270 (5th Cir.2001).

41. *See Public Affairs Assocs., Inc. v. Rickover,* 369 U.S. 111, 82 S.Ct. 580, 7 L.Ed.2d 604 (1962).

42. *See Samuels v. Mackell,* 401 U.S. 66, 91 S.Ct. 764, 27 L.Ed.2d 688 (1971).

43. *See Corliss v. O'Brien,* 200 Fed. Appx. 80, 84–85 (3d Cir. 2006).

is also not available where a special statutory proceeding has been provided to adjudicate a special type of case.[44] And it is often not available in federal and State tax cases, particularly where State law provides for efficient tax challenges and remedies, and where the action contests the constitutionality of a State tax provision.

> *Exception:* Congress allows declaratory judgment remedies in cases brought under Section 7428 of the Internal Revenue Code (relating to the status and classification of certain organizations for tax purposes) and Sections 505 and 1146 of the Bankruptcy Code (relating to determinations of tax liability in bankruptcy cases).

Appealability

Whether a declaratory judgment order is immediately appealable depends upon the nature of the court's ruling. Once the court disposes of all the issues presented in the declaratory judgment action (either by ruling upon them or by declining to rule upon them), the resulting declaratory judgment becomes complete, final, and appealable.[45] Conversely, if the court enters an order resolving certain of the issues presented, but expressly leaves open for later resolution other issues in the case, the order is merely interlocutory and, therefore, not immediately appealable under the final order doctrine.[46]

ADDITIONAL RESEARCH REFERENCES:

Wright & Miller, *Federal Practice and Procedure* §§ 2751–2771.

C.J.S. Declaratory Judgments §§ 1–24 et seq., 25–75, 76–126, 127–142 et seq., 143–165.

West's Key No. Digests, Declaratory Judgment ⊘1–395.

ADDITIONAL RESEARCH REFERENCES

Wright & Miller, *Federal Practice and Procedure* §§ 2781–2787.

C.J.S. Federal Civil Procedure §§ 1227–1231 et seq.

West's Key No. Digests, Federal Civil Procedure ⊘2621–2628.

44. *See New York Times Co. v. Gonzales*, 459 F.3d 160, 166 (2d Cir. 2006) (such proceedings include petitions for habeas corpus and motions to vacate criminal sentences, proceedings under the Civil Rights Act of 1964, and certain administrative proceedings).

45. *See Henglein v. Colt Indus. Operating Corp.*, 260 F.3d 201, 211 (3d Cir.2001).

46. *See Henglein v. Colt Indus. Operating Corp.*, 260 F.3d 201, 211 (3d Cir.2001).

RULE 58

ENTERING JUDGMENT

(a) Separate Document. Every judgment and amended judgment must be set out in a separate document, but a separate document is not required for an order disposing of a motion:

(1) for judgment under Rule 50(b);

(2) to amend or make additional findings under Rule 52(b);

(3) for attorney's fees under Rule 54;

(4) for a new trial, or to alter or amend the judgment, under Rule 59; or

(5) for relief under Rule 60.

(b) Entering Judgment.

(1) *Without the Court's Direction.* Subject to Rule 54(b) and unless the court orders otherwise, the clerk must, without awaiting the court's direction, promptly prepare, sign, and enter the judgment when:

(A) the jury returns a general verdict;

(B) the court awards only costs or a sum certain; or

(C) the court denies all relief.

(2) *Court's Approval Required.* Subject to Rule 54(b), the court must promptly approve the form of the judgment, which the clerk must promptly enter, when:

(A) the jury returns a special verdict or a general verdict with answers to written questions; or

(B) the court grants other relief not described in this subdivision (b).

(c) Time of Entry. For purposes of these rules, judgment is entered at the following times:

(1) if a separate document is not required, when the judgment is entered in the civil docket under Rule 79(a); or

   (2) if a separate document is required, when the judg-
       ment is entered in the civil docket under Rule 79(a)
       and the earlier of these events occurs:

       (A) it is set out in a separate document; or

       (B) 150 days have run from the entry in the civil
           docket.

(d) Request for Entry. A party may request that judgment be set out in a separate document as required by
Rule 58(a).

(e) Cost or Fee Awards. Ordinarily, the entry of judgment
may not be delayed, nor the time for appeal extended, in
order to tax costs or award fees. But if a timely motion
for attorney's fees is made under Rule 54(d)(2), the
court may act before a notice of appeal has been filed
and become effective to order that the motion have the
same effect under Federal Rule of Appellate Procedure
4(a)(4) as a timely motion under Rule 59.

[Amended December 27, 1946, effective March 19, 1948; January 21, 1963, effective July 1,
1963; April 22, 1993, effective December 1, 1993; April 29, 2002, effective December 1,
2002; April 30, 2007, effective December 1, 2007.]

2007 AMENDMENTS ROADMAP

   STYLE PROJECT CHANGES: This Rule had been substantially rewritten
in 2002, and the new language changes are modest. However, the cumbersome
structure of Rule 58(a) was thinned by dividing Rules 58(a)(1) and 58(a)(2) into
separate subparts. To make room for that separation, old Rules 58(b) and 58(c)
were repositioned (into new Rules 58(c) and 58(e), respectively). "General verdict
accompanied by interrogatories" was replaced with "general verdict with answers to written questions", to conform to changes made elsewhere in the Rules.

   NON-STYLE CHANGES: None.

   NOTE: The Federal Rules "Style Project" is explained in Part III-A.

AUTHORS' COMMENTARY ON RULE 58

PURPOSE AND SCOPE

   Rule 58 sets the procedure by which the district court enters
judgments on its docket records. The date a judgment is "entered" on

the district court docket triggers the time for making post-trial motions, for taking an appeal, and for executing on the relief awarded.

RULE 58(a). SEPARATE DOCUMENT

CORE CONCEPT

To avoid uncertainty about when the clock for taking an appeal begins to tick, the district courts are required to set forth most judgments (and amended judgments) in a "separate document".

APPLICATIONS

2007 Amendments

The overly-long Rule 58(a) was separated into two subparts in the 2007 amendments. The current Rule 58(a) now contains only the "separate document" rule, and the procedure for entering judgment has now been shifted to new Rule 58(b). Practitioners searching for pre–2007 interpretations of this Rule should bear this repositioning in mind in doing their research. Current Rule 58(b) now contains what, until 2007, was the second paragraph of old Rule 58(a).

Contents of Judgment

The judgment document must clearly state which parties are entitled to what relief.[1]

Transferring Judgments to Another Judicial District

A judgment for money or property entered by one federal district court may be transferred to, and executed upon in, another district court. Such transfers are accomplished by filing a certified copy of the judgment in the new district court *after* the judgment has become final after appeal, by the expiration of time for appeal, or when, still pending appeal, the court so orders for good cause.[2] The transferred judgment will have the same effect as any other judgment entered in the new district.[3]

The "Old" Separate Document Rule

Prior to 2002, a judgment was required to be (1) set forth in writing, (2) in a "separate document", and (3) entered on the docket. These requirements were intended to create a "bright line" for litigants and the courts in determining when finality attached and, thus, when the period for seeking an appeal began.[4] To abate any uncertainty as to when the appeal "clock" would start ticking,

---

1. *See Citizens Elec. Corp. v. Bituminous Fire & Marine Ins. Co.*, 68 F.3d 1016, 1021(7th Cir.1995)(proper judgments say who is liable for how much, then stop).

2. *See Stanford v. Utley*, 341 F.2d 265 (8th Cir.1965).

3. *See* 28 U.S.C.A. § 1963.

4. *See Fogade v. ENB Revocable Trust*, 263 F.3d 1274, 1285–86 (11th Cir.2001); *United States v. Haynes*, 158 F.3d 1327, 1329 (D.C.Cir.1998).

the courts generally applied these requirements mechanically.[5] Until each requirement was met, the judgment was not deemed to have been entered[6] and the time for filing an appeal would not begin to run.[7]

What resulted was a significant body of interpretative case law construing the "separate document" requirement, and deciding what, if any, effect it would have on the appeal period. Some cases explained how rulings orally announced from the bench[8] or included within the text of a minute-order, a memorandum, or a written opinion[9] could not qualify as "judgments" under Rule 58. Other cases explained how a little, but not much, collateral discussion by the trial court might be overlooked when included on the "judgment" document.[10] Still other cases explained that the "separate document" requirement could be waived because it was not jurisdictional.[11] Some courts determined that waiver could occur by express agreement of the parties[12] or by failing to timely object.[13] In still other instances, the courts would simply excuse a "separate document" failure entirely where the circumstances made it plain that the court's decision was final.[14]

Ultimately, a split developed among the Circuits over how to address the nagging spectre of an appeal period being postponed indefinitely by the failure to meet the requirements of a "separate document" judgment.[15]

5. See Trotter v. Regents of Univ. of New Mexico, 219 F.3d 1179 (10th Cir.2000).

6. See United States v. Indrelunas, 411 U.S. 216, 93 S.Ct. 1562, 36 L.Ed.2d 202 (1973); Miller v. Marriott Int'l, Inc., 300 F.3d 1061, 1064–65 (9th Cir.2002); Constitution Bank v. Tubbs, 68 F.3d 685, 692 n. 7 (3d Cir.1995).

7. See Fogade v. ENB Revocable Trust, 263 F.3d 1274, 1286 (11th Cir.2001); Trotter v. Regents of Univ. of New Mexico, 219 F.3d 1179 (10th Cir.2000).

8. Atlantic Richfield Co. v. Monarch Leasing Co., 84 F.3d 204 (6th Cir.1996).

9. See United States v. Johnson, 254 F.3d 279, 285 (D.C.Cir.2001); Transit Mgmt. of S.E. La., Inc. v. Group Ins. Admin., Inc., 226 F.3d 376, 382 (5th Cir.2000).

10. See Kidd v. District of Columbia, 206 F.3d 35, 39 (D.C.Cir.2000); Pacific Employers Ins. Co. v. Domino's Pizza, Inc., 144 F.3d 1270, 1278 (9th Cir.1998).

11. See Bankers Trust Co. v. Mallis, 435 U.S. 381, 98 S.Ct. 1117, 55 L.Ed.2d 357 (1978); Henglein v. Colt Indus. Operating Corp., 260 F.3d 201, 209 n.5 (3d Cir.2001).

12. See Pohl v. United Airlines, Inc., 213 F.3d 336, 338 (7th Cir.2000).

13. See American Disability Ass'n, Inc. v. Chmielarz, 289 F.3d 1315, 1318 n. 1 (11th Cir.2002); Puerto Rico Aqueduct & Sewer Auth. v. Constructora Lluch, Inc., 169 F.3d 68, 76 (1st Cir.1999).

14. See Allison v. Bank One–Denver, 289 F.3d 1223, 1232–33 (10th Cir.2002); First Ins. Funding Corp. v. Federal Ins. Co., 284 F.3d 799, 804 n. 3 (7th Cir.2002). See also Quinn v. Haynes, 234 F.3d 837, 843 (4th Cir.2000) (separate-document requirement may be excused where (1) trial court evidenced its intent that order constituted final decision in the case, (2) judgment was docketed by the clerk, and (3) no objection was made to the procedural violation); Reynolds v. Golden Corral Corp., 213 F.3d 1344, 1347 n. 2 (11th Cir.2000) (same).

15. Compare White v. Fair, 289 F.3d 1, 6 (1st Cir.2002) (noting court rule that waiver will be inferred where a party fails to act within 3 months to resolve a separate document failure) with Hammack v. Baroid Corp., 142 F.3d 266, 270 (5th Cir.1998) (rejecting First Circuit's 3–month inferred waiver rule); United States v. Haynes, 158 F.3d 1327, 1330–31 (D.C.Cir.1998) (same); Rubin v. Schottenstein, Zox & Dunn, 143 F.3d 263, 270 (6th Cir.1998) (en banc) (same).

The Current Separate Document Rule

The underlying purpose of the current Rule 58 remains the same: the separate document requirement is designed to ensure that litigants are alerted to the entry of judgment and to the starting of the clock for post-verdict motions or an appeal.[16] As before, the Rule achieves this goal by insisting on a "clear line of demarcation" between a judgment and an opinion or memorandum.[17] The Rule mandates an extraordinarily austere approach to drafting judgments: a body of the proper judgment should state the relief granted and little else.[18] This austerity should make clear for the parties when the appeal time has begun.[19] When extraneous text offends the separate document requirement, and when it does not, remains a question for the courts.[20] The postponement period for the appeals clock is now capped.[21]

When a "Separate Document" is *Not* Required

A separate document is not required for an order disposing of a Rule 50(b) renewed motion for judgment after trial, a Rule 52(b) motion to amend or make additional findings of fact, a Rule 54(d) motion for attorney's fees, a Rule 59 motion for new trial or to alter or amend a judgment, or a Rule 60 motion for relief from a judgment or order.[22]

What Qualifies as a "Separate Document"?

Except for five exempted instances set out in the Rule's text,[23] every judgment and amended judgment (as well as partial dispositions under Rule 54(b)[24]) must be labeled "judgment" and must be set forth on a separate document.[25] Neither a judicial memorandum or opinion[26] nor marginal entry orders[27] nor minute orders[28] satisfy this requirement; indeed, even an otherwise qualifying order that is mistakenly stapled to the end of a memorandum opinion will fail this separateness requirement.[29] Likewise, a judgment that is en-

---

16. *See Bankers Trust Co. v. Mallis,* 435 U.S. 381, 384, 98 S.Ct. 1117, 55 L.Ed.2d 357 (1978) (per curiam); *Whitaker v. Garcetti,* 486 F.3d 572, 579–80 (9th Cir. 2007); *Bailey v. Potter,* 478 F.3d 409, 411 (D.C.Cir. 2007).

17. *See In re Cendant Corp. Secs. Litig.,* 454 F.3d 235, 243 (3d Cir.2006).

18. *See In re Cendant Corp. Secs. Litig.,* 454 F.3d 235, 245 (3d Cir.2006).

19. *See In re Cendant Corp. Secs. Litig.,* 454 F.3d 235, 245 (3d Cir.2006).

20. *See* Rule 58 advisory committee notes to 2002 amendment (noting that Forms 31 and 32 "provide examples" of a proper separate document judgment). The Appendix of Forms is reprinted in Part IV of this text.

21. *See infra* Authors' Commentary to Rule 58(c)

22. *See* Rule 58(a)(1).

23. *See* Rule 58(a)(1)-(a)(5). *See also infra* Authors' Commentary to Rule 58(a) (**"When a 'Separate Document' is *Not* Required"**).

24. *See In re Cendant Corp. Secs. Litig.,* 454 F.3d 235, 240 n.2 (3d Cir.2006).

25. *See* Rule 58(a). *See also Silivanch v. Celebrity Cruises, Inc.,* 333 F.3d 355, 363 (2d Cir.2003) (must be labeled a "judgment").

26. *See Silivanch v. Celebrity Cruises, Inc.,* 333 F.3d 355, 363 (2d Cir.2003).

27. *See Inland Bulk Transfer Co. v. Cummins Engine Co.,* 332 F.3d 1007, 1015 n.7 (6th Cir.2003).

28. *See ABF Capital Corp. v. Osley,* 414 F.3d 1061, 1065 (9th Cir.2005).

29. *See Alinsky v. United States,* 415 F.3d 639, 643 (7th Cir.2005).

cumbered with extraneous text, such as an "extensive" recitation of legal reasoning, analysis, facts, or procedural history, fails the separateness requirement.[30] Thus, to qualify as a "separate document", the judgment must (1) be a self-contained, separate document, (2) state the relief granted, and (3) omit the reasoning used by the district court to dispose of pending motions (which should, instead, be contained in the court's opinion).[31] There remains, however, a division among the Circuits as to whether a document marked "order" can ever qualify as a separate document "judgment" under this Rule.[32]

- *Two Documents?:* The majority view holds that the separate document requirement can, in appropriate circumstances, be met even if there is only one document (such as when the court's reasoning and analysis was conveyed orally, during oral argument or a hearing).[33]

- *Actual or Implied Clarity:* The fact that the litigants knew, or should have known, that the contested order was intended to serve as a final judgment will not excuse a failure to meet the separateness requirement.[34] Debating over a "known-or-should-have-known" standard is precisely what Rule 58 is designed to avoid. As one court wrote: "Rule 58 is a touch-the-base requirement that lays perception aside".[35]

Effect of the "Separate Document" Requirement

The "separate document" requirement is designed to create protection, not traps.[36] An appellant can always waive the right to receive a judgment on a "separate document", and file an early appeal from a judgment that fails to meet this requirement.[37]

---

30. *See In re Cendant Corp. Secs. Litig.,* 454 F.3d 235, 243 (3d Cir.2006).

31. *See In re Cendant Corp. Secs. Litig.,* 454 F.3d 235, 241 (3d Cir.2006); *Selkridge v. United of Omaha Life Ins. Co.,* 360 F.3d 155, 160 n.2 (3d Cir.2004). *See also Local Union No. 1992 of Int'l Bhd. of Elec. Workers v. Okonite Co.,* 358 F.3d 278, 284–85 (3d Cir.2004) (separate document requirement satisfied where order was self-contained and separate from opinion, had separate caption, was separately (not consecutively) paginated, was separately signed, was separately file-stamped, and was separately docketed).

32. *See Local Union No. 1992 of Int'l Bhd. of Elec. Workers v. Okonite Co.,* 358 F.3d 278, 285–86 (3d Cir.2004) (finding "order" may qualify, and discussing case law); *United States v. Johnson,* 254 F.3d 279, 285–86 & 286 n.7 (D.C.Cir.2001) (same); *Mirpuri v. ACT Mfg., Inc.,* 212 F.3d 624, 628–29 (1st Cir.2000) (same). *See also* Rule

54(a) (defining "judgment" to include "a decree and any order from which an appeal lies"). *But see Kanematsu–Gosho Ltd. v. M/T Messiniaki Aigli,* 805 F.2d 47, 48–49 (2d Cir.1986) (per curiam) ("order" does not qualify as judgment).

33. *See In re Cendant Corp. Secs. Litig.,* 454 F.3d 235, 241–42 (3d Cir.2006).

34. *See In re Cendant Corp. Secs. Litig.,* 454 F.3d 235, 241 n.4 (3d Cir.2006).

35. *See In re Cendant Corp. Secs. Litig.,* 454 F.3d 235, 241 n.4 (3d Cir.2006).

36. *See Bankers Trust Co. v. Mallis,* 435 U.S. 381, 386, 98 S.Ct. 1117, 55 L.Ed.2d 357 (1978) (per curiam) (requirement is to be "interpreted to prevent loss of the right of appeal, not to facilitate loss"); *Bailey v. Potter,* 478 F.3d 409, 411 (D.C.Cir. 2007) (same).

37. *See Bankers Trust Co. v. Mallis,* 435 U.S. 381, 384, 98 S.Ct. 1117, 1119, 55 L.Ed.2d 357 (1978); *Long v. County of Los*

Choosing not to wait until full compliance with the "separate document" requirement will not affect the validity of the appeal.[38] In other words, the "clock" for a timely appeal does not begin running until the judgment is placed in a "separate document" (unless, of course, the judgment is exempt from this requirement), or the capped outside time period set by the Rule expires.[39] During this time, the district court would never lose its jurisdiction over the case.[40] Nevertheless, while the appellant is permitted to wait (until either the "separate document" requirement is met or the outside time period runs), she is not obligated to wait.[41]

- *Appellee Cannot Stop Appeal:* An appellee cannot oppose an appellant's early appeal in order to insist that the appellant first return to the district court to demand compliance with the ministerial act of preparing a "separate document" judgment.[42] If the appellant elects to waive her right to a "separate document" and immediately appeal, the appellee cannot stop her.

- *Other Means of Waiver:* Other conduct, like filing a Rule 60 motion for relief from a non-separate-document judgment, may also constitute a waiver of the "separate document" requirement.[43]

- *Practitioners' Safe Harbor:* Because these early appeals are permitted, the effect grants the appellant a safe harbor. Consequently, when in doubt whether a "separate document" has been filed or not, the practitioner may always file an appeal.[44]

RULE 58(b). ENTERING JUDGMENT

CORE CONCEPT

Judgments on a general verdict, for sums certain or costs, or that deny relief may be entered by the clerk. All other judgments must be entered by the court.

Angeles, 442 F.3d 1178, 1184 n.3 (9th Cir. 2006); *Public Water Supply Dist. No. 8 of Clay County v. City of Kearney,* 401 F.3d 930, 933 (8th Cir.2005); *de Jesus–Mangual v. Rodriguez,* 383 F.3d 1, 5 (1st Cir.2004).

38. *See Whitaker v. Garcetti,* 486 F.3d 572, 579–80 (9th Cir. 2007); *Bailey v. Potter,* 478 F.3d 409, 411 (D.C.Cir. 2007).

39. *See Shalala v. Schaefer,* 509 U.S. 292, 113 S.Ct. 2625, 125 L.Ed.2d 239 (1993) (decided under pre–2002 amendment, but noting that trial court's failure to enter judgment on a separate document kept the time for appeal open). *See also Cambridge Holdings Group, Inc. v. Federal Ins. Co.,* 489 F.3d 1356, 1364 (D.C.Cir. 2007); *In re Cendant Corp. Secs. Litig.,* 454 F.3d 235,

245 (3d Cir.2006); *Borrero v. City of Chicago,* 456 F.3d 698, 701 (7th Cir.2006).

40. *See Fogade v. ENB Revocable Trust,* 263 F.3d 1274, 1286 (11th Cir.2001).

41. *See* Rule 58(c); *see also infra* Authors' Commentary to Rule 58(c).

42. *See Bailey v. Potter,* 478 F.3d 409, 411 (D.C.Cir. 2007); *Peng v. Mei Chin Penghu,* 335 F.3d 970, 975 n.4 (9th Cir. 2003).

43. *See Casey v. Albertson's Inc.,* 362 F.3d 1254, 1256–59 (9th Cir.2004).

44. *See In re Cendant Corp. Secs. Litig.,* 454 F.3d 235, 245 (3d Cir.2006); *Borrero v. City of Chicago,* 456 F.3d 698, 701 (7th Cir.2006).

APPLICATIONS

2007 Amendments

The overly-long Rule 58(a) was separated into two subparts in the 2007 amendments. The current Rule 58(a) now contains only the "separate document" rule, and the procedure for entering judgment has now been shifted to new Rule 58(b). The former content of Rule 58(b), "Time of Entry", was repositioned to new Rule 58(c). Practitioners searching for pre–2007 interpretations of this Rule should bear this repositioning in mind in doing their research. Current Rule 58(b) was, until 2007, the second paragraph of old Rule 58(a).

Entry of Judgment

Unless it is a "partial" final judgment under Rule 54(b),[45] all federal judgments are entered either by the clerk or by the court:

By The Clerk: Unless the court otherwise orders, the clerk of court must, without awaiting any further direction from the court, promptly prepare, sign, and enter judgment when (i) the jury returns a general verdict, (ii) the court awards only costs or a sum certain, or (iii) the court denies all relief.[46]

By The Court: The court must review and promptly approve the form of judgment (which the clerk then must promptly enter) when (i) the jury returns a special verdict or a general verdict accompanied by interrogatories, or (ii) the court grants other relief not described above.[47]

RULE 58(c). TIME OF ENTRY

CORE CONCEPT

Judgments are deemed to be entered when they are placed on the civil docket, unless a "separate document" is required. In those cases, the judgments are deemed entered either when the "separate document" requirement is met or 150–days after placement on the civil docket (whichever is earlier).

APPLICATIONS

2007 Amendments

To accommodate the separating of old Rule 58(a), the former content of Rule 58(b), "Time of Entry", has been repositioned to new Rule 58(c). The former content of Rule 58(c), "Cost or Fee Awards", was repositioned to new Rule 58(e). Practitioners search-

---

45. *See* Rule 54(b) (permitting court to direct the entry of final judgment "as to one or more but fewer than all of the claims or parties only upon an express determination that there is no just reason for delay and upon an express direction for the entry of judgment").

46. *See* Rule 58(b)(1). *See also Otis v. City of Chicago,* 29 F.3d 1159, 1163 (7th Cir.1994) (observing that Rule 58 places on clerk of court the onus of preparing the judgment).

47. *See* Rule 58(b)(2).

ing for pre–2007 interpretations of this Rule should bear this repositioning in mind in doing their research. Current Rule 58(c) was,
until 2007, old Rule 58(b).

Computing "Entry of Judgment" Date

A judgment must always be entered on the docket.[48] To avoid
the uncertainty created by the old "separate document" requirement (which could, theoretically, have allowed for months or years
to pass before the appeals clock might begin to run)[49], the current
Rule now imposes an outside time limit for triggering the appeal
period:

When Separate Document Required: If a separate document is
required, the judgment is deemed to be entered when (1) it is
entered in the civil docket *and* (2) it is actually set forth on a
qualifying separate document *or* 150 days passes after the entry
in the civil docket, whichever occurs earlier.[50]

When Separate Document Not Required: If a separate document
is not required (*i.e.*, involving a qualifying Rule 50(b), 52(b),
54(d), 59, or 60 motion), the judgment is deemed to be entered
when it is entered in the civil docket.[51]

Disregarding the 150–Day Cap

The 150–day outside time limit should be disregarded where it
serves no purpose to apply it.[52] Thus, for example, assessing the
propriety of an appeal from a collateral order should *not* be complicated by the separate document requirement.[53] To the contrary,
appeal periods for collateral orders should start to run when the
collateral order is entered, and should not await either the creation
of a separate document or the passing of 150 days.[54]

Entry in the Civil Docket

The date the clerk enters the judgment "in the civil docket" is
the trigger for calculating time under Rule 58(c). The clerk is
obligated by Rule 79(a) to make this entry.[55] This ministerial,
administrative duty is distinct from the Rule 58(b)(2) duty of the
court to approve a "separate document" judgment before it is
deemed a true Rule 58 judgment. Administratively, the clerk may
properly record a judgment in the civil docket, even though that

---

48. *See* Rule 79 (providing for entries on
the official court docket).

49. *See Burnley v. City of San Antonio,*
470 F.3d 189, 195 (5th Cir. 2006) (noting
that 2002 amendments to Rule 58 were
designed to ensure that appeal time "does
not linger on indefinitely").

50. *See* Rule 58(c)(2). *See Funk v.
LFLM Defendants,* 382 F.3d 1058, 1064
(10th Cir.2004); *Freudensprung v. Offshore
Tech. Servs., Inc.,* 379 F.3d 327 (5th Cir.
2004).

51. *See* Rule 58(c)(1).

52. *See* Rule 58 advisory committee
notes to 2002 amendments.

53. *See* Rule 58 advisory committee
notes to 2002 amendments.

54. *See* Rule 58 advisory committee
notes to 2002 amendments.

55. *See* Rule 79(a)(1) (clerk must maintain the civil docket); Rule 79(a)(2)(C)
(judgments must be entered chronologically
in the civil docket).

judgment fails the "separate document" requirement (and, thus, will not start the appeal clock ticking).[56]

RULE 58(d). REQUEST FOR ENTRY

CORE CONCEPT

Because entry of judgment in a "separate document" has serious procedural consequences (for, among other things, the time for appealing), a party may request the court to prepare one.

APPLICATIONS

Former Prohibition on Attorney–Prepared Judgments

Before the 2002 amendments, Rule 58 prohibited attorneys from drafting and submitting proposed forms of judgment, unless directed to do so by the court.[57] This prohibition was designed to avoid delays encountered by such drafting and submission and to avoid occasionally inept drafting results.[58]

Party's Request to Prompt a "Separate Document"

A party may request the district court to enter a "separate document" judgment. Allowing such requests was intended to help protect a party's need to ensure that timing periods are promptly triggered for motions, appeals, and enforcement procedures.[59] Thus, a party may make such a request in order to cure a "separate document" problem with an existing judgment (and, thus, trigger the running of the appeals clock),[60] to seek a Rule 54(b) determination that would permit an immediate partial judgment appeal,[61] or to quicken the pace for enforcement.[62] Such a request can also be made by a party who suffers a dismissal *without prejudice*, and who wishes to appeal that dismissal rather than attempt to re-plead.[63]

RULE 58(e). COST OR FEE AWARDS

CORE CONCEPT

To facilitate a single, consolidated appeal from both a merits ruling and a ruling on an award of attorney's fees, the district court may allow

56. *See Burnley v. City of San Antonio*, 470 F.3d 189, 194–96 (5th Cir. 2006).

57. *See* Rule 58 (former language: "Attorneys shall not submit forms of judgment except upon direction of the court, and these directions shall not be given as a matter of course").

58. *See* Rule 58 advisory committee notes to 2002 amendment. *See also Matteson v. United States*, 240 F.2d 517, 519 (2d Cir.1956) (commenting that earlier practice of having lawyers prepare form of judgment caused delay in the entry of judgment and forced the court to sift through "the normal excess of detail supplied by zealous advo-

cates in their natural desire to press home all conceivable ad hoc advantages from the judgment").

59. *See* Rule 58(d) advisory committee notes to 2002 amendment.

60. *See In re Carolina Tobacco Co.*, 2007 WL 1541507, at *1 (D.Or. 2007).

61. *See Cook v. Avi Casino Enter., Inc.*, 2006 WL 3694859, at *1 (D.Ariz. 2006).

62. *See Uhl v. Komatsu Forklift Co.*, 466 F.Supp.2d 899, 911 (E.D.Mich. 2006).

63. *See Parker v. Google, Inc.*, 2007 WL 1989660, at *2 (3d Cir. 2007).

the pending (but yet undecided) attorney's fees motion to suspend the time for finality.

APPLICATIONS

2007 Amendments

To accommodate the separating of old Rule 58(a), the former content of Rule 58(c), "Cost or Fee Awards", has been repositioned to new Rule 58(e). Practitioners searching for pre–2007 interpretations of this Rule should bear this repositioning in mind in doing their research. Current Rule 58(e) was, until 2007, old Rule 58(c).

General Rule

Generally, the entry of final judgment (and, thus, the triggering of the clock for taking an appeal) is neither delayed nor extended while the district court considers requests to tax costs or award attorney's fees.[64] A Rule 58(e) motion offers an exception to this practice.

Effect of a Rule 58(e) Order

In order to allow a consolidated appeal of both its merits judgment and its ruling on attorney's fees, the district court may, in its discretion, enter an order under Rule 58(e) that treats a pending motion for an award of attorney's fees as the equivalent of a Rule 59 motion.[65] (*Note:* the court may only enter such an order if the fees motion has already been filed.[66]) If the court enters such an order, the time for appealing will not begin to run until the court decides the pending fees motion.[67] The court must, however, actually enter the Rule 58(e) order; the mere fact that a litigant has asked the court to enter such an order is not sufficient to toll.[68]

Prerequisites for a Rule 58(e) Order

The court may enter a Rule 58(e) order only if: (1) the motion for fees is pending and has been timely made (*i.e.*, within 14 days after entry of judgment),[69] (2) no effective notice of appeal has yet been made, and (3) a timely notice of appeal is still possible (*i.e.*, the

---

64. *See* Rule 58(e). *See also Richards v. Government of V.I.*, 579 F.2d 830 (3d Cir. 1978).

65. *See* Rule 58(e). *See also Burnley v. City of San Antonio*, 470 F.3d 189, 199 (5th Cir. 2006) (noting purpose); *Gilda Marx, Inc. v. Wildwood Exercise, Inc.*, 85 F.3d 675, 680 n. 5 (D.C.Cir.1996)(from the perspective of the appellate courts, it is obviously desirable to have merits appeals and fees order appeals decided together).

66. *See Robinson v. City of Harvey*, 489 F.3d 864, 868 (7th Cir. 2007) (finding it "clear that the time for appeal cannot be extended in anticipation of a fee petition").

67. *See Wikol ex rel. Wikol v. Birmingham Pub. Schs. Bd. of Educ.*, 360 F.3d 604,

607–08 (6th Cir.2004); *Deboard v. Sunshine Mining & Refining Co.*, 208 F.3d 1228, 1236 (10th Cir.2000).

68. *See Stephanie–Cardona LLC v. Smith's Food & Drug Ctrs., Inc.*, 476 F.3d 701, 705 (9th Cir. 2007). *See also Wikol ex rel. Wikol v. Birmingham Pub. Schs. Bd. of Educ.*, 360 F.3d 604, 609–10 (6th Cir. 2004) (criticizing confusing former language of Rule 58).

69. *See Cooper v. Pentecost*, 77 F.3d 829 (5th Cir.1996)(noting that 14–day period for petitioning for fee award does not begin to run until judgment is entered in a separate document).

time for appealing has not already expired).[70] An order under Rule 58(e) must satisfy the "separate document" requirement.[71]

When the Order is *Not* Proper

The practical effect of a Rule 58(e) motion is to delay the arrival of finality and, with it, the time for taking an appeal from the court's order. The reason why district courts are authorized to grant this postponement is efficiency: to permit a simultaneous, joint appeal from both the trial court's judgment on the merits and its ruling on attorney's fees.[72] If that goal cannot be attained, no Rule 58(e) postponement order is proper. Thus, if an appeal has already been taken from the merits ruling, if the attorney's fees motion has already been ruled upon, or if the merits judgment has already become unappealable (*e.g.*, if the appeal time has already expired), the district court has no reason or authority to issue such a postponement order.[73]

Order Cannot Apply When Fees Are Part of the Claim Itself

The district court may not grant a Rule 58(e) postponement when the fees are an integral part of the underlying substantive claim, such as where the fees are sought as an element of damages pursuant to a contract that authorizes fees. Ordinarily, no final judgment is even possible in such a case until the fees issue (considered to be core damages) is resolved.[74]

Order Applies Only to Fees, Not Costs

A postponement of finality under Rule 58(e) is, by its terms, only applicable to attorney's fee awards; finality cannot be suspended while costs are being taxed.[75]

ADDITIONAL RESEARCH REFERENCES

Wright & Miller, *Federal Practice and Procedure* §§ 2781–2787.

C.J.S. Federal Civil Procedure §§ 1227–1231 et seq.

West's Key No. Digests, Federal Civil Procedure ⟐2621–2628.

70. *See Mendes Junior Int'l Co. v. Banco do Brasil, S.A.*, 215 F.3d 306 (2d Cir. 2000) (the filing of a fees-and-costs motion cannot rescue an otherwise out-of-time appeal; if the 30–day appeal clock has run, a ruling on the fees-and-costs motion will not revive the time to appeal).

71. *See Deboard v. Sunshine Mining & Refining Co.*, 208 F.3d 1228, 1237 (10th Cir.2000).

72. *See Burnley v. City of San Antonio*, 470 F.3d 189, 199 (5th Cir. 2006).

73. *See Burnley v. City of San Antonio*, 470 F.3d 189, 199 (5th Cir. 2006). *See also Robinson v. City of Harvey*, 489 F.3d 864, 868–69 (7th Cir. 2007) (appeal period must still be live at time of order; order may not "revive" an already-expired appeal period).

74. *See Carolina Power & Light Co. v. Dynegy Mktg. & Trade*, 415 F.3d 354, 359 (4th Cir. 2005) (holding that unresolved claim for *substantive* attorneys fees prevents entry of judgment); *Maristuen v. National Sales Ins. Co.*, 57 F.3d 673, 678 (8th Cir. 1995) (award of specific sum in attorney's fees required for final order where such award was integral part of claim, such as bad faith claim).

75. *See Moody Nat'l Bank of Galveston v. GE Life & Annuity Assur. Co.*, 383 F.3d 249, 253 (5th Cir.2004).

RULE 59

NEW TRIAL; ALTERING OR AMENDING A JUDGMENT

(a) In General.

(1) *Grounds for New Trial.* The court may, on motion, grant a new trial on all or some of the issues—and to any party—as follows:

(A) after a jury trial, for any reason for which a new trial has heretofore been granted in an action at law in federal court; or

(B) after a nonjury trial, for any reason for which a rehearing has heretofore been granted in a suit in equity in federal court.

(2) *Further Action After a Nonjury Trial.* After a nonjury trial, the court may, on motion for a new trial, open the judgment if one has been entered, take additional testimony, amend findings of fact and conclusions of law or make new ones, and direct the entry of a new judgment.

(b) Time to File a Motion for a New Trial. A motion for a new trial must be filed no later than 10 days after the entry of judgment.

(c) Time to Serve Affidavits. When a motion for a new trial is based on affidavits, they must be filed with the motion. The opposing party has 10 days after being served to file opposing affidavits; but that period may be extended for up to 20 days, either by the court for good cause or by the parties' stipulation. The court may permit reply affidavits.

(d) New Trial on the Court's Initiative or for Reasons Not in the Motion. No later than 10 days after the entry of judgment, the court, on its own, may order a new trial for any reason that would justify granting one on a party's motion. After giving the parties notice and an opportunity to be heard, the court may grant a timely motion for a new trial for a reason not stated in the motion. In either event, the court must specify the reasons in its order.

(e) **Motion to Alter or Amend a Judgment.** A motion to alter or amend a judgment must be filed no later than 10 days after the entry of the judgment.

[Amended effective March 19, 1948; July 1, 1966; April 27, 1995, effective December 1, 1995; April 30, 2007, effective December 1, 2007.]

―――――――――― **2007 AMENDMENTS ROADMAP** ――――――――――

STYLE PROJECT CHANGES: Rule 59(a) was subsectioned, its language was simplified, and new labels were added. Rule 59 received few other notable changes. "Must" replaced "shall", and "reasons" replaced "grounds".

NON-STYLE CHANGES: None.

NOTE: The Federal Rules "Style Project" is explained in Part III-A.

AUTHORS' COMMENTARY ON RULE 59

―――――――――― **PURPOSE AND SCOPE** ――――――――――

When appropriate to prevent a miscarriage of justice, the district court may set aside a verdict and order a new trial or, alternatively, alter or amend a judgment. A party moving for either a new trial or an order altering or amending a judgment must file such a motion no later than 10 days after the judgment is entered. The district court may *not* extend this 10 day period.

RULE 59(a). NON TRIALS, GENERALLY

CORE CONCEPT

In both jury and bench trials, the court may grant a new trial for any reason for which new trials (jury trials) or rehearings (bench trials) were formerly granted, such as where the verdict is against the weight of the evidence or is either excessive or inadequate, where probative evidence is newly discovered, or where conduct by the court, counsel, or the jury improperly influenced the deliberative process.

APPLICATIONS

Procedure

Motions for new trial are usually made in writing and must state with particularity the grounds for relief.

Discretion of District Court

Whether the circumstances justify the granting of a new trial is a decision left to the sound discretion of the trial judge.[1] So broad is this discretion in certain contexts, that one court has described it as "virtually unassailable on appeal".[2] In exercising this discretion, the trial judge may reopen a judgment, hear additional testimony, and amend (or make new) findings of fact and conclusions of law.[3]

Grounds for New Trials

Rule 59(a) provides no list of proper reasons for which new trials may be granted, and relies instead upon historical practice.[4] What historically justified a new trial in an action at law in the federal courts, may now warrant a new trial following a jury verdict; what historically justified a rehearing in a suit in equity in the federal courts, may now warrant a new trial following a bench decision.[5] The courts have recognized that new trials may be properly granted in at least the following circumstances:

- *Verdict Against the Weight of Evidence:* when the district court concludes that the factfinder's verdict is against the "clear" or "great" weight of the evidence, and a new trial is therefore necessary to prevent a miscarriage of justice;[6]

- *Verdict is Excessive or Inadequate:* when the district court determines that the amount of the verdict is so unreasonable that it shocks the conscience;[7]

1. *See Gasperini v. Ctr. for Humanities, Inc.,* 518 U.S. 415, 433, 116 S.Ct. 2211, 2222, 135 L.Ed.2d 659 (1996) ("the authority of trial judges to grant new trials ... is large"); *Allied Chem. Corp. v. Daiflon, Inc.,* 449 U.S. 33, 101 S.Ct. 188, 66 L.Ed.2d 193 (1980)(noting that the authority to grant a new trial "is confided almost entirely to the exercise of discretion on the part of the trial court"). *See also Bell v. Johnson,* 404 F.3d 997, 1002 (6th Cir.2005); *Rivera Castillo v. Autokirey, Inc.,* 379 F.3d 4 (1st Cir.2004); *Manley v. Ambase Corp.,* 337 F.3d 237, 244–45 (2d Cir.2003).

2. *See Children's Broad. Corp. v. Walt Disney Co.,* 357 F.3d 860, 867 (8th Cir. 2004). *See also Gasperini v. Ctr. for Humanities, Inc.,* 518 U.S. 415, 433, 116 S.Ct. 2211, 2222, 135 L.Ed.2d 659 (1996) ("the authority of trial judges to grant new trials ... is large").

3. *See Defenders of Wildlife v. Bernal,* 204 F.3d 920, 928–29 (9th Cir.2000).

4. *See Molski v. M.J. Cable, Inc.,* 481 F.3d 724, 729 (9th Cir. 2007).

5. *See* Rule 59(a)(1).

6. *See Byrd v. Blue Ridge Rural Elec. Cooperative, Inc.,* 356 U.S. 525, 540, 78 S.Ct. 893, 902, 2 L.Ed.2d 953 (1958); *Molski v. M.J. Cable, Inc.,* 481 F.3d 724, 729–30 (9th Cir. 2007); *Mitchell v. Boelcke,* 440 F.3d 300, 303 (6th Cir.2006); *Rivera Castillo v. Autokirey, Inc.,* 379 F.3d 4 (1st Cir. 2004). *See also Latino v. Kaizer,* 58 F.3d 310, 314 (7th Cir.1995)(ruling that jury's verdict should be accorded greater deference under Rule 59 in cases involving simple issues with highly disputed facts, than in cases involving complex issues with facts that are not as disputed).

7. *See Mitchell v. Boelcke,* 440 F.3d 300, 303 (6th Cir.2006). *See also Rivera Castillo v. Autokirey, Inc.,* 379 F.3d 4, 13 (1st Cir. 2004) (exceed "any rational appraisal or estimate of the damage that could be based on the evidence before the jury"); *Eiland v. Westinghouse Elec. Corp.,* 58 F.3d 176, 183 (5th Cir.1995)("contrary to right reason" or "entirely disproportionate to the injury sustained"). *But see Gasperini v. Center for Humanities, Inc.,* 518 U.S. 415, 116 S.Ct. 2211, 135 L.Ed.2d 659 (1996) (citing the *Erie* doctrine in applying New York's state law standard for judging "excessiveness", where state standard differed from federal "shocks the conscience" benchmark).

"Remittitur": If the court decides that the verdict is excessive, the court may offer the verdict winner a reduction—called a "remittitur"—in exchange for the court's denial of a motion for a new trial.[8] If the verdict winner accepts the court's offer, the verdict winner waives the right of appeal.[9] If remitted, the jury's verdict will usually be reduced to the maximum amount the jury could have awarded without being excessive.[10] A trial court's decision on remittitur is accorded wide discretion, given that judge's ability to hear the testimony and assess the demeanor of the witnesses; a trial court's ruling that denies remittitur will be overturned on appeal only where the verdict is found to be so grossly excessive that the outcome is "monstrous or shocking".[11]

"Additur": If the court finds that the verdict is inadequate, the court may *not* offer the verdict winner an increase in verdict size—called an "additur"—in exchange for the court's denial of a motion for new trial. Where the verdict is inadequate, the court's only option is ordering a new trial.[12]

• *Newly Discovered Evidence:* when the district court learns of a party's newly discovered evidence. To entitle the moving party to a new trial, the "newly discovered evidence" generally: (1) must have existed as of the time of trial; (2) must have been excusably overlooked by the moving party, notwithstanding the moving party's due diligence in attempting to discover it; (3) must be admissible; and (4) must be likely to alter the trial's outcome.[13] In addition to a new trial under Rule 59, newly discovered evidence may also entitle the moving party to relief from judgment under Rule 60(b)(2);

8. *See Linn v. United Plant Guard Workers of America, Local 114*, 383 U.S. 53, 65–66, 86 S.Ct. 657, 664–65, 15 L.Ed.2d 582 (1966) (if damages award is excessive, trial judge has the "duty" to require a remittitur or grant a new trial); *Cline v. Wal–Mart Stores, Inc.*, 144 F.3d 294, 305 n. 2 (4th Cir.1998) (describing remittitur procedure and Seventh Amendment concerns); *Atlas Food Sys. & Servs., Inc. v. Crane Nat'l Vendors, Inc.*, 99 F.3d 587, 593 (4th Cir. 1996) (noting remittitur's history); *Tingley Sys., Inc. v. Norse Sys., Inc.*, 49 F.3d 93, 96 (2d Cir.1995)(instructing that district courts, upon finding jury verdict to be excessive, may order a new trial, may order a partial new trial limited to damages, or may offer to deny the new trial motion on the condition that plaintiff accepts damages in reduced amount). Note, however, that the court ordinarily may not reduce plaintiff's damages award without first offering plaintiff a new trial. *See In re Joint Eastern & Southern Dist. Asbestos Litig.*, 52 F.3d 1124, 1139 (2d Cir.1995).

9. *See Donovan v. Penn Shipping Co.*, 429 U.S. 648, 97 S.Ct. 835, 51 L.Ed.2d 112 (1977)(per curiam).

10. *See Eiland v. Westinghouse Elec. Corp.*, 58 F.3d 176, 183 (5th Cir.1995). *See Earl v. Bouchard Transp. Co.*, 917 F.2d 1320, 1328–30 (2d Cir.1990)(adopting same rule, but discussing the three views on remittitur and scholarly commentary's preferences).

11. *See Hite v. Vermeer Mfg. Co.*, 446 F.3d 858, 869–70 (8th Cir.2006).

12. *See Dimick v. Schiedt*, 293 U.S. 474, 55 S.Ct. 296, 79 L.Ed. 603 (1935)(finding that additur violates Constitution's Seventh Amendment right to a jury verdict).

13. *See Colon-Millin v. Sears Roebuck De Puerto Rico, Inc.*, 455 F.3d 30, 36 n.4 (1st Cir.2006); *Advanced Display Sys., Inc. v. Kent State Univ.*, 212 F.3d 1272, 1284 (Fed.Cir.2000); *Defenders of Wildlife v. Bernal*, 204 F.3d 920, 928–29 (9th Cir.2000); *Peacock v. Board of Sch. Comm'rs*, 721 F.2d 210 (7th Cir.1983).

- *Improper Conduct by Counsel or the Court:* when improper conduct by either an attorney or the court unfairly influenced the verdict;[14]

- *Improper Conduct Affecting the Jury:* when the jury verdict was not unanimous or was facially inconsistent, or when the jury was improperly influenced,[15] or when an erroneous jury instruction likely misled or confused the jury.[16] Note, however, that after the verdict is returned, jurors may not impeach or alter their verdict except to testify as to improper, extrinsic influences.[17]

Prejudice

Trial errors may only give rise to a new trial if they affect the substantive rights of the parties and are not cured by the trial judge's cautionary instructions to the jury.[18]

Waiver

A party may not seek a new trial on grounds not brought contemporaneously to the trial judge's attention.[19] The courts recognize a narrow exception to this waiver rule where a trial error is so fundamental that gross injustice would result were it not corrected.

Bench Trials

If a new trial is awarded following a bench trial, the district court may, upon retrial, open a judgment already entered, hear additional testimony, revise or add findings of fact and conclusions of law, and direct the entry of a new judgment.[20]

Partial New Trials

The court may grant a partial new trial limited only to certain issues, provided the error justifying the new trial did not affect the

14. *See Wharf v. Burlington Northern R. Co.,* 60 F.3d 631 (9th Cir.1995)(granting new trial where counsel permitted district court to read to the jury an untruthful stipulated fact concerning plaintiff); *Aggarwal v. Ponce Sch. of Med.,* 837 F.2d 17 (1st Cir.1988)(before conduct of judge will warrant a new trial, the moving party must be "so seriously prejudiced as to be deprived of a fair trial"); *City of Cleveland v. Peter Kiewit Sons' Co.,* 624 F.2d 749 (6th Cir. 1980)(moving for new trial where counsel injected into trial notion that insurance company would pay any award).

15. *Cf. Parker v. Gladden,* 385 U.S. 363, 87 S.Ct. 468, 17 L.Ed.2d 420 (1966)(per curiam)(statement by bailiff that defendant was a "wicked fellow" who was guilty, and that the higher courts would correct a guilty verdict if it was wrong).

16. *See Susan Wakeen Doll Co. v. Ashton Drake Galleries,* 272 F.3d 441, 452 (7th Cir.2001).

17. *See Carson v. Polley,* 689 F.2d 562 (5th Cir.1982); *Smallwood v. Pearl Brewing Co.,* 489 F.2d 579 (5th Cir.1974).

18. *See* Rule 61 (directing that harmless errors are to be disregarded).

19. *See United States v. Walton,* 909 F.2d 915 (6th Cir.1990). *But cf. Pulla v. Amoco Oil Co.,* 72 F.3d 648, 656 (8th Cir. 1995)(party may move for new trial under Rule 59 "based on the overwhelming evidence contrary to the verdict without ever previously raising such an objection").

20. *See* Rule 59(a)(2).

determination of the remaining issues[21], and provided that the singular issue for retrial is so clearly distinct and separate from all other issues that a retrial of it alone will not be unjust.[22] If, however, the trial court concludes that passion influenced the jury, a partial new trial on the issue of damages alone is ordinarily improper; the court must instead order a new trial on all issues.[23] When a partial new trial is granted, those portions of the original judgment that were not set aside by the court become part of the single, ultimate judgment following the new trial. Most commonly, courts have granted partial new trials on damages, following an error-free trial on liability issues, but partial new trials can be granted as to any "separable matter".[24]

Appealability

An order granting a new trial is generally interlocutory and not immediately appealable, absent a showing that the court lacked authority to enter the order.[25] An order denying a new trial is also usually not immediately appealable because the party's proper appeal is often an appeal from the final judgment, not from the denial of a new trial.[26] Note that even ultimate appellate review of denials of new trials may be further limited by Seventh Amendment constitutional concerns.[27]

RULE 59(b). TIME TO FILE A MOTION FOR A NEW TRIAL

CORE CONCEPT

A party must file a motion for new trial within 10 days after the entry of judgment.

APPLICATIONS

10 Days to File Motion for New Trial

A party seeking a new trial must *file* the Rule 59 motion within

21. *See Anderson v. Siemens Corp.*, 335 F.3d 466, 475–76 (5th Cir.2003); *Eximco, Inc. v. Trane Co.*, 737 F.2d 505 (5th Cir. 1984).

22. *See Gasoline Prods. v. Champlin Refining Co.*, 283 U.S. 494, 500, 51 S.Ct. 513, 515, 75 L.Ed. 1188 (1931); *Armstrong v. Burdette Tomlin Mem. Hosp.*, 438 F.3d 240, 253 (3d Cir.2006); *Anderson v. Siemens Corp.*, 335 F.3d 466, 475–76 (5th Cir.2003).

23. *See Sanford v. Crittenden Mem'l Hosp.*, 141 F.3d 882, 885 (8th Cir.1998).

24. *See Rice v. Community Health Ass'n*, 203 F.3d 283, 290 (4th Cir.2000).

25. *See Allied Chem. Corp. v. Daiflon, Inc.*, 449 U.S. 33, 101 S.Ct. 188, 66 L.Ed.2d 193 (1980); *Schudel v. General Elec. Co.*, 120 F.3d 991, 994–95 (9th Cir.1997).

26. *See, e.g., Clark v. Heidrick*, 150 F.3d 912 (8th Cir.1998) (in absence of exceptional circumstances, orders denying motion for new trial are not immediately appealable); *Bethel v. McAllister Bros., Inc.*, 81 F.3d 376, 382 (3d Cir.1996)(order granting new trial is interlocutory and therefore nonappealable; but once new trial is complete, appellate court may review Rule 59 order).

27. *See Jocks v. Tavernier*, 316 F.3d 128, 137 (2d Cir.2003) (commenting that district court's determination that jury's verdict was not against weight of evidence is not reviewable on appeal due to limitations imposed by Seventh Amendment).

10 days after the district court enters its judgment on the docket.[28]

Amended Judgments

Where an amended judgment is filed and alters the legal rights or obligations of the parties, a new 10–day period for filing Rule 59 motions might be triggered.[29]

Early Motions

A party may move for a new trial before the formal entry of judgment and at any time during the 10 days following the entry of judgment.

No Extensions or Waiver

This 10–day period may not be extended by court order or waived by the parties.[30] An old and rarely-invoked common law exception used to rescue untimely appeals (the "unique circumstances" doctrine) has now been formally rejected by the Supreme Court.[31] Nor will the fact that one party moves for relief under Rule 59 excuse all other parties seeking such relief from timely filing separately.[32] Although the 10–day limitation is mandatory, courts may consider untimely Rule 59 motions as requests for relief under Rule 60.[33]

3–Day Service Extension Does *Not* Apply

Rule 6(d) extends a party's time for acting by 3 days if the relevant time period is dated from service by mail, electronic service, or certain other service methods. Because Rule 59(b) requires *filing* (not service) no later than 10 days after entry of judgment, this 3–day service extension does not apply.[34]

Timely Motion Tolls Appeal Period

A timely-filed motion for a new trial delays the finality of the underlying judgment and tolls the time for appeal. Originally, a notice of appeal, filed prematurely before the trial court had ruled upon a pending motion for a new trial, would have been deemed a

---

28. *See Schudel v. General Elec. Co.*, 120 F.3d 991 (9th Cir.1997) (noting that Rule 59, as amended in 1995, requires that such motions be filed, not served, within 10 days following entry of judgment).

29. *See Walker v. Bain*, 257 F.3d 660, 670 (6th Cir.2001).

30. Rule 6(b). *See Schneider ex rel. Estate of Schneider v. Fried*, 320 F.3d 396, 402–03 (3d Cir.2003); *Lichtenberg v. Besicorp Group Inc.*, 204 F.3d 397, 401 (2d Cir.2000).

31. *See Bowles v. Russell*, ___ U.S. ___, ___, 127 S.Ct. 2360, 2366, 168 L.Ed.2d 96 (2007) (denouncing doctrine as "illegitimate", overruling prior case law, and emphasizing "that the timely filing of a notice of appeal in a civil case is a jurisdictional requirement").

32. *See Hertz Corp. v. Alamo Rent–A–Car, Inc.*, 16 F.3d 1126 (11th Cir.1994).

33. *See Feathers v. Chevron U.S.A., Inc.*, 141 F.3d 264, 268 (6th Cir.1998) (where party failed to file timely Rule 59 motion, court appropriately could consider motion under Rule 60).

34. *See Cavaliere v. Allstate Ins. Co.*, 996 F.2d 1111, 1112–14 (11th Cir.1993). *See also Adams v. Trustees of N.J. Brewery Employees' Pension Trust Fund*, 29 F.3d 863, 870–71 (3d Cir.1994)(applying same reasoning in construing Rule 59(e)); *Derrington–Bey v. District of Columbia Dep't of Corrections*, 39 F.3d 1224, 1225 (D.C.Cir. 1994) (same).

"nullity".[35] Under recent amendments to Federal Rule of Appellate Procedure 4(a)(4), a prematurely filed appeal is now treated as filed as of the date the trial court ultimately disposes of the pending Rule 59 motion.[36]

- *Tolling Applies to All Parties:* A timely filed Rule 59 motion tolls the time for appeal for all parties.[37]

Motion Filed After Notice of Appeal

The filing of a notice of appeal is jurisdictional; once filed, the district court is divested of jurisdiction over those aspects of the case implicated in the appeal, and jurisdiction is conferred upon the court of appeals.[38] Consequently, a party seeking to move the district court for a new trial after a notice of appeal has been filed must file a motion with the district judge, and the judge may then request a remand of the case from the court of appeals.[39]

RULE 59(c). TIME TO SERVE AFFIDAVITS

CORE CONCEPT

A party may support a motion for new trial with affidavits. In such a case, the supporting affidavits must be filed with the motion. Opposing affidavits may be filed 10 days thereafter, unless an additional period not to exceed 20 days is permitted by the court for good cause or by stipulated agreement of the parties.

RULE 59(d). NEW TRIAL ON THE COURT'S INITIATIVE OR FOR OTHER REASONS NOT IN THE MOTION

CORE CONCEPT

The court may grant a new trial entirely on its own initiative, or, upon reviewing a party's motion, may grant a new trial for a reason not stated in the moving papers.

APPLICATIONS

Grounds

The court may grant a new trial for any reason that a party

---

35. *See Griggs v. Provident Consumer Discount Co.*, 459 U.S. 56, 61, 103 S.Ct. 400, 403, 74 L.Ed.2d 225 (1982)(per curiam). *Accord Acosta v. Louisiana Dep't of Health & Human Resources*, 478 U.S. 251, 254, 106 S.Ct. 2876, 2877, 92 L.Ed.2d 192 (1986).

36. *See* Fed. R. App. P. 4(a)(4)(B). *See also New Windsor Volunteer Ambulance Corps, Inc. v. Meyers*, 442 F.3d 101, 120 (2d Cir.2006); *Leader Nat'l Ins. Co. v. Industrial Indemn. Ins. Co.*, 19 F.3d 444 (9th Cir. 1994)(noting that, after 1993 amendment,

appeal is no longer a nullity but is merely held in abeyance).

37. *See New Windsor Volunteer Ambulance Corps, Inc. v. Meyers*, 442 F.3d 101, 120 (2d Cir.2006).

38. *See Griggs v. Provident Consumer Discount Co.*, 459 U.S. 56, 58, 103 S.Ct. 400, 402, 74 L.Ed.2d 225 (1982)(per curiam).

39. *See Hattersley v. Bollt*, 512 F.2d 209 (3d Cir.1975).

could have permissibly requested by motion.[40]

Time

A court that intends to grant a new trial on its own initiative must do so within 10 days after the entry of judgment. When a court receives a motion, but decides to grant a new trial for reasons not specified in the motion, the timing is less clear. One court has held that this 10–day requirement does not apply to such rulings.[41]

Granting on Different Grounds

When a court decides to grant a new trial for reasons different from those set forth in the moving party's papers, the court must give the parties notice of this intention and an opportunity to be heard.

Nature of Order

When the court grants a motion for a new trial on its own initiative or on grounds different from those stated in a party's motion papers, the order must specify the grounds for the court's decision.

RULE 59(e).   MOTION TO ALTER OR AMEND A JUDGMENT

CORE CONCEPT

The court may alter or amend its judgment upon motion by a party.

APPLICATIONS

Purpose

The purpose of Rule 59(e) is to provide the district court with a means for correcting errors that may have "crept into the proceeding", while that court still holds jurisdiction over the case.[42] It thus gives the trial court the opportunity to resolve its own mistakes (if it believes it made any).[43]

Grounds

No listing of proper grounds for altering or amending a judgment is included in the language of Rule 59(e), and federal case law has been left to fill in that void.[44] Broadly, a motion to alter or amend a judgment is appropriate where it seeks a re-examination of matters properly encompassed within the trial court's motions to decision on the merits.[45] The case law acknowledges four grounds

---

40. *See Pryer v. C.O. 3 Slavic*, 251 F.3d 448, 453 (3d Cir.2001) (noting principle, and ruling that new trial may be granted where verdict is against the great weight of the evidence).

41. *See Kelly v. Moore*, 376 F.3d 481, 484 (5th Cir.2004).

42. *See Sosebee v. Astrue*, 494 F.3d 583, 589 (7th Cir. 2007).

43. *See Zinkand v. Brown*, 478 F.3d 634, 637 (4th Cir. 2007).

44. *See Zinkand v. Brown*, 478 F.3d 634, 636–37 (4th Cir. 2007).

45. *See White v. New Hampshire Dep't of Employment Sec.*, 455 U.S. 445, 451, 102 S.Ct. 1162, 1166, 71 L.Ed.2d 325 (1982).

that justify altering or amending a judgment: to incorporate an intervening change in the law,[46] to reflect new evidence not available at the time of trial,[47] to correct a clear legal error,[48] and to prevent a manifest injustice.[49] Thus, for example, a Rule 59(e) motion is appropriate where the court misunderstood the facts, a party's arguments, or the controlling law,[50] where the original judgment failed to provide that relief which the court found a party entitled to receive,[51] or where the party seeks a post-judgment award of pre-judgment interest.[52]

District Court's Discretion

The decision whether to alter or amend a judgment is generally committed to the discretion of the trial judge.[53] Exercising this discretion calls upon the court to balance two competing interests— the need to bring litigation to a close and the need to render just rulings based on all the facts.[54] However, this liberal discretion standard does not apply to Rule 59(e) motions seeking review of a grant of summary judgment; as to those motions, a *de novo* standard

---

46. *See Zinkand v. Brown*, 478 F.3d 634, 636–37 (4th Cir. 2007); *Henderson v. Walled Lake Consol. Schs.*, 469 F.3d 479, 496 (6th Cir. 2006); *Messina v. Krakower*, 439 F.3d 755, 758 (D.C.Cir.2006); *In re Benjamin Moore & Co.*, 318 F.3d 626, 629 (5th Cir.2002).

47. *See Zinkand v. Brown*, 478 F.3d 634, 636–37 (4th Cir. 2007); *Greyhound Lines, Inc. v. Wade*, 485 F.3d 1032, 1036 (8th Cir. 2007); *Henderson v. Walled Lake Consol. Schs.*, 469 F.3d 479, 496 (6th Cir. 2006); *Messina v. Krakower*, 439 F.3d 755, 758 (D.C.Cir.2006); *Bell v. Board of County Com'rs Of Jefferson County*, 451 F.3d 1097, 1102 (10th Cir.2006). *See generally Greyhound Lines, Inc. v. Wade*, 485 F.3d 1032, 1036 (8th Cir. 2007) (party must show (1) evidence was discovered after trial, (2) exercise of due diligence to discover it earlier, (3) evidence is material, not merely cumulative or impeaching, (4) evidence would probably produce different result).

48. *See Zinkand v. Brown*, 478 F.3d 634, 636–37 (4th Cir. 2007); *Henderson v. Walled Lake Consol. Schs.*, 469 F.3d 479, 496 (6th Cir. 2006); *Messina v. Krakower*, 439 F.3d 755, 758 (D.C.Cir.2006); *Munafo v. Metropolitan Transp. Auth.*, 381 F.3d 99, 105 (2d Cir.2004).

49. *See Zinkand v. Brown*, 478 F.3d 634, 636–37 (4th Cir. 2007); *Henderson v. Walled Lake Consol. Schs.*, 469 F.3d 479, 496 (6th Cir. 2006); *Messina v. Krakower*, 439 F.3d 755, 758 (D.C.Cir.2006); *John G. Alden, Inc. of Mass. v. John G. Alden Ins. Agency of Fla., Inc.*, 389 F.3d 21, 25 (1st

Cir.2004). *See also Ford Motor Credit Co. v. Bright*, 34 F.3d 322, 324 (5th Cir.1994)(in considering Rule 59(e) motion, court may take into account attorney's conduct). *But cf. Frietsch v. Refco, Inc.*, 56 F.3d 825, 828 (7th Cir.1995)(affirming refusal to consider affidavit filed after dismissal; Rule 59(e) does not "enable a party to complete presenting his case after the court has ruled against him").

50. *See Servants of Paraclete v. Does*, 204 F.3d 1005, 1012 (10th Cir.2000).

51. *See Continental Cas. Co. v. Howard*, 775 F.2d 876 (7th Cir.1985).

52. *See Osterneck v. Ernst & Whinney*, 489 U.S. 169, 109 S.Ct. 987, 103 L.Ed.2d 146 (1989). *But see Buchanan v. Stanships, Inc.*, 485 U.S. 265, 108 S.Ct. 1130, 99 L.Ed.2d 289 (1988)(seeking an allowance of costs under Rule 54(d) is not appropriate for a Rule 59(e) motion, because such costs are collateral to the merits of the action); *White v. New Hampshire Dep't of Employment Sec.*, 455 U.S. 445, 102 S.Ct. 1162, 71 L.Ed.2d 325 (1982)(seeking an award of attorney's fees is not appropriate for a Rule 59(e) motion).

53. *See Minton v. National Ass'n of Secs. Dealers, Inc.*, 336 F.3d 1373, 1379 (5th Cir.2003); *Zivitz v. Greenberg*, 279 F.3d 536, 539 (7th Cir.2002); *Callantine v. Staff Builders, Inc.*, 271 F.3d 1124, 1134 (8th Cir.2001); *Vaughn v. Lawrenceburg Power Sys.*, 269 F.3d 703, 710 (6th Cir.2001).

54. *See Templet v. HydroChem Inc.*, 367 F.3d 473, 478–79 (5th Cir.2004).

applies.[55] This sort of reconsideration of a judgment is an extraordinary remedy and is used only sparingly.[56]

10 Days to File Motion to Alter or Amend a Judgment

A party seeking to alter or amend a judgment must *file* the motion within 10 days after the judgment is entered in the civil docket.[57]

No Extensions

The court may not grant a party any extensions to this 10-day rule.[58] An untimely Rule 59(e) motion may be deemed a nullity.[59] However, there is developing case law that when an untimely Rule 59(e) motion is filed, but not objected to by the non-moving party, the timeliness objection may be deemed forfeited through waiver.[60]

3–Day Service Extension Does Not Apply

Rule 6(e) extends a party's time for acting by 3 days if the relevant time period is to begin upon service by mail, electronic service, or certain other means of service. Because Rule 59(e) requires *filing* (not service) no later than 10 days after entry of judgment, this 3–day service extension does not apply.[61]

Prisoner Plaintiffs

The prisoner "mailbox rule" has been adopted by some courts for Rule 59(e) motions. Consequently, a *pro se* prisoner's papers may be deemed filed when deposited with the post office.[62]

Motion Tolls Appeal Period

Like Rule 59 motions for new trial, a timely-filed Rule 59(e) motion to alter or amend the judgment tolls the time for appeal.[63]

55. *See Cockrel v. Shelby County Sch. Dist.*, 270 F.3d 1036, 1047 (6th Cir.2001).

56. *See Templet v. HydroChem Inc.*, 367 F.3d 473, 479 (5th Cir.2004).

57. *See Schudel v. General Elec. Co.*, 120 F.3d 991 (9th Cir.1997) (noting that Rule 59, as amended in 1995, requires that such motions be filed, not served, within 10 days following entry of judgment), *cert. denied*, 523 U.S. 1094, 118 S.Ct. 1560, 140 L.Ed.2d 792 (1998). *See also Life Ins. Co. of North America v. Von Valtier*, 116 F.3d 279, 282–83 (7th Cir.1997) (considering motion to be timely filed where it was delivered to district court, as required by standing chambers order, but trial judge delayed in transmitting motion to clerk's office for formal filing).

58. *See* Rule 6(b). *See also Morris v. Unum Life Ins. Co.*, 430 F.3d 500, 502 (1st Cir.2005); *Weitz v. Lovelace Health Sys., Inc.*, 214 F.3d 1175, 1179 (10th Cir.2000); *Wight v. Bankamerica Corp.*, 219 F.3d 79, 84 (2d Cir.2000).

59. *See Morris v. Unum Life Ins. Co.*, 430 F.3d 500, 502 (1st Cir.2005).

60. *See National Ecological Found. v. Alexander*, 496 F.3d 466, 474–475 (6th Cir. 2007) (relying on two recent Supreme Court cases, *Eberhart v. Untied States*, 546 U.S. 12, 126 S.Ct. 403, 163 L.Ed.2d 14 (2005) (per curiam) and *Kontrick v. Ryan*, 540 U.S. 443, 124 S.Ct. 906, 157 L.Ed.2d 867 (2004)).

61. *See Albright v. Virtue*, 273 F.3d 564, 567 (3d Cir.2001); *FHC Equities, L.L.C. v. MBL Life Assur. Corp.*, 188 F.3d 678 (6th Cir.1999). *See also Cavaliere v. Allstate Ins. Co.*, 996 F.2d 1111, 1112–14 (11th Cir. 1993)(applying same reasoning in construing Rule 59(b)).

62. *See Edwards v. United States*, 266 F.3d 756, 758 (7th Cir.2001).

63. *See, e.g., Bass v. United States Dep't of Agriculture*, 211 F.3d 959, 962 (5th Cir. 2000); *Innovative Home Health Care, Inc. v. P.T.-O.T. Assocs. of Black Hills*, 141 F.3d 1284, 1286 (8th Cir.1998).

A prematurely filed appeal during the pendency of a Rule 59(e) motion is held in abeyance until the date the district court resolves the pending motion.[64] An untimely Rule 59(e) motion will not toll the time for appeal,[65] nor, generally, will a second or later Rule 59(e) motion when multiple such motions are filed.[66] However, in rare instances, the trial court's ruling on a Rule 59(e) motion will change "matters of substance" or resolve a "genuine ambiguity" in court's original order and, in those infrequent cases, a new judgment is recognized, from which a new Rule 59(e) motion (with appeal-period tolling effect) may be filed.[67]

"Particularity" Requirement for Motion

All Rule 59(e) motions must satisfy the "particularity" require-ment of Rule 7(b)(1).[68] Failure to do so may have dire consequences, including a loss of appeal-period tolling. Thus, a "skeleton" motion that fails to alert the court or the other litigants of the grounds for which an alteration or amendment is sought may be deemed improp-er and, thus, ineffective in tolling the appeal period.[69]

> *Appeal Must Name Correct Order:* The filing of a timely, proper Rule 59(e) motion can toll the time for filing an appeal from the original underlying *merits* ruling, and not just from the court's disposition of the Rule 59(e) motion itself.[70] However, to benefit from that *merits* tolling effect, the litigant must list the *merits* ruling on the Notice of Appeal (in addition to any other orders from which the appeal is taken).[71] Although the appellate courts will liberally construe the Notice of Appeal to give effect to the parties' intentions if clearly obvious (and in the absence of prejudice to the adversary),[72] litigants have been cautioned by

---

64. *See* Fed. R. App. P. 4(a)(4)(as amended Dec. 1, 1993); *Andrews v. E.I. Du Pont De Nemours & Co.*, 447 F.3d 510, 515 (7th Cir.2006); *Schroeder v. McDonald*, 55 F.3d 454, 458 (9th Cir.1995)(applying Fed. R.App.P. 4(a)(4) to Rule 59(e) motion).

65. *See Garcia-Velazquez v. Frito Lay Snacks Caribbean*, 358 F.3d 6, 9 (1st Cir. 2004); *Panhorst v. United States*, 241 F.3d 367, 370 (4th Cir.2001); *Wight v. Bankam-erica Corp.*, 219 F.3d 79, 84 (2d Cir.2000).

66. *See Acevedo–Villalobos v. Hernan-dez*, 22 F.3d 384 (1st Cir.1994).

67. *See Andrews v. E.I. Du Pont De Nemours & Co.*, 447 F.3d 510, 516 (7th Cir.2006) (noting exception, and stating that test is "whether the district court dis-turbed or revised legal rights settled in the original . . . order").

68. *See Intera Corp. v. Henderson*, 428 F.3d 605, 611 (6th Cir.2005).

69. *See Talano v. Northwestern Med. Faculty Found., Inc.*, 273 F.3d 757, 760–61 (7th Cir.2001) ("if a party could file a skele-

ton motion and later fill it in, the purpose of the time limitation would be defeated").

70. *See Chamorro v. Puerto Rican Cars, Inc.*, 304 F.3d 1, 3 (1st Cir.2002).

71. *See Chamorro v. Puerto Rican Cars, Inc.*, 304 F.3d 1, 3 (1st Cir.2002) (an appeal taken only from the order denying the Rule 59(e) motion will generally not be consid-ered an appeal from the underlying merits judgment); *Correa v. Cruisers, a Div. of KCS Int'l, Inc.*, 298 F.3d 13, 21 n. 3 (1st Cir.2002) (same).

72. *See Chamorro v. Puerto Rican Cars, Inc.*, 304 F.3d 1, 3 (1st Cir.2002) (comment-ing that "formalism is not obligatory", and Notice will be construed liberally and exam-ined in the context of the record as a whole, "with a recognition that the core purpose of a notice of appeal is to 'facilitate a proper decision on the merits' "); *Correa v. Cruis-ers, a Div. of KCS Int'l, Inc.*, 298 F.3d 13, 21 n. 3 (1st Cir.2002) (same effect).

the courts "that such rescue missions are not automatic, and litigants will do well to draft notices of appeal with care".[73]

Motions for "Reconsideration"

The Rules do not expressly recognize motions for "reconsideration".[74] Instead, such motions are treated typically as motions to alter or amend a judgment under Rule 59(e) or motions for relief from judgments or orders under Rule 60(b). Often, whether a "reconsideration" motion is governed by Rule 59(e) or Rule 60(b) will depend on the date it is filed. If filed within the 10–day period set for Rule 59(e) motions, the "reconsideration" will generally be treated under Rule 59(e).[75] Otherwise, the courts will ordinarily examine the motion under Rule 60(b).[76] In either case, however, the applicable legal analysis will depend on the grounds asserted for the relief requested.[77]

Motions for "reconsideration" will not be granted absent "highly unusual circumstances."[78] Such motions do not provide litigants with an opportunity for a "second bite at the apple"[79] or allow them, like Emperor Nero, to "fiddle as Rome burns",[80] or license a litigation "game of hopscotch", in which parties switch from one legal theory to a new one "like a bee in search of honey".[81] In other words, motions for reconsideration are not vehicles for relitigating old issues.[82] But nor are they motions for "initial consideration".[83]

73. See Chamorro v. Puerto Rican Cars, Inc., 304 F.3d 1, 3 (1st Cir.2002).

74. See Computerized Thermal Imaging, Inc. v. Bloomberg, L.P., 312 F.3d 1292, 1296 n.3 (10th Cir.2002); Bass v. United States Dep't of Agriculture, 211 F.3d 959, 962 (5th Cir.2000).

75. See Global Naps, Inc. v. Verizon New England, Inc., 489 F.3d 13, 25 (1st Cir. 2007); Allender v. Raytheon Aircraft Co., 439 F.3d 1236, 1242 (10th Cir.2006); Texas A&M Research Found. v. Magna Transp., Inc., 338 F.3d 394, 400 (5th Cir.2003).

76. See Allender v. Raytheon Aircraft Co., 439 F.3d 1236, 1242 (10th Cir.2006); Texas A&M Research Found. v. Magna Transp., Inc., 338 F.3d 394, 400 (5th Cir. 2003); Dudley ex rel. Estate of Patton v. Penn–America Ins. Co., 313 F.3d 662, 675 (2d Cir.2002).

77. See Jennings v. Rivers, 394 F.3d 850, 855 (10th Cir.2005) (because litigant sought relief based upon attorney mistake, motion filed within 10 days would nevertheless be evaluated under Rule 60(b)(1)).

78. See McDowell v. Calderon, 197 F.3d 1253, 1255 (9th Cir.1999). See also United States ex rel. Becker v. Westinghouse Savannah River Co., 305 F.3d 284, 290 (4th Cir. 2002) (simple disagreement with the court's ruling will not support Rule 59(e) relief).

79. See Sequa Corp. v. GBJ Corp., 156 F.3d 136 (2d Cir.1998); Bhatnagar v. Surrendra Overseas Ltd., 52 F.3d 1220, 1231 (3d Cir.1995); Senza–Gel Corp. v. Seiffhart, 803 F.2d 661, 664 (Fed.Cir.1986).

80. Vasapolli v. Rostoff, 39 F.3d 27, 36 (1st Cir.1994)(Selya, J.)("Unlike the Emperor Nero, litigants cannot fiddle as Rome burns. A party who sits in silence, withholds potentially relevant information, allows his opponent to configure the summary judgment record, and acquiesces in a particular choice of law does so at his peril").

81. See Cochran v. Quest Software, Inc., 328 F.3d 1, 11 (1st Cir.2003) (noting that litigants "frame the issues in a case before the trial court rules" and, once framed, should not be permitted to switch from theory to theory thereafter).

82. See Sigsworth v. City of Aurora, 487 F.3d 506, 512 (7th Cir. 2007); Michael Linet, Inc. v. Village of Wellington, 408 F.3d 757, 759 (11th Cir.2005); Templet v. Hydro-Chem Inc., 367 F.3d 473, 478–79 (5th Cir. 2004).

83. See National Ecological Found. v. Alexander, 496 F.3d 466, 477 (6th Cir. 2007).

Courts properly decline to consider new arguments or new evidence on reconsideration where those arguments or evidence were available earlier.[84]

Motions to Include Prejudgment Interest

Generally, motions to amend to include an award of either mandatory or discretionary prejudgment interest are treated under this Rule and, thus, must be sought within 10 days of entry of the judgment or be deemed waived.[85]

ADDITIONAL RESEARCH REFERENCES

Wright & Miller, *Federal Practice and Procedure* §§ 2801–21.

C.J.S. Federal Civil Procedure §§ 1061–1103 et seq., 1233–1251 et seq.

West's Key No. Digests, Federal Civil Procedure ☞2311–2377, 2641–2662.

84. *See Sigsworth v. City of Aurora*, 487 F.3d 506, 512 (7th Cir. 2007); *K.C.1986 Ltd. P'ship v. Reade Mfg.*, 472 F.3d 1009, 1016 (8th Cir. 2007); *Marks 3 Zet–Ernst Marks GmBh & Co. KG v. Presstek, Inc.*, 455 F.3d 7, 15–16 (1st Cir.2006); *Michael Linet, Inc. v. Village of Wellington*, 408 F.3d 757, 759 (11th Cir.2005); *Templet v. HydroChem Inc.*, 367 F.3d 473, 478–79 (5th Cir.2004).

85. *See Osterneck v. Ernst & Whinney*, 489 U.S. 169, 173–78, 109 S.Ct. 987, 989–82, 103 L.Ed.2d 146 (1989) (mandatory prejudgment interest); *McCalla v. Royal MacCabees Life Ins. Co.*, 369 F.3d 1128, 1130–34 (9th Cir.2004) (mandatory prejudgment interest); *Crowe v. Bolduc*, 365 F.3d 86, 92–93 (1st Cir.2004) (mandatory or discretionary prejudgment interest).

RULE 60

RELIEF FROM A JUDGMENT OR ORDER

(a) Corrections Based on Clerical Mistakes; Oversights and Omissions. The court may correct a clerical mistake or a mistake arising from oversight or omission whenever one is found in a judgment, order, or other part of the record. The court may do so on motion or on its own, with or without notice. But after an appeal has been docketed in the appellate court and while it is pending, such a mistake may be corrected only with the appellate court's leave.

(b) Grounds for Relief from a Final Judgment, Order, or Proceeding. On motion and just terms, the court may relieve a party or its legal representative from a final judgment, order, or proceeding for the following reasons:

(1) mistake, inadvertence, surprise, or excusable neglect;

(2) newly discovered evidence that, with reasonable diligence, could not have been discovered in time to move for a new trial under Rule 59(b);

(3) fraud (whether previously called intrinsic or extrinsic), misrepresentation, or misconduct by an opposing party;

(4) the judgment is void;

(5) the judgment has been satisfied, released or discharged; it is based on an earlier judgment that has been reversed or vacated; or applying it prospectively is no longer equitable; or

(6) any other reason that justifies relief.

(c) Timing and Effect of the Motion.

(1) *Timing.* A motion under Rule 60(b) must be made within a reasonable time—and for reasons (1), (2), and (3) no more than a year after the entry of the judgment or order or the date of the proceeding.

(2) *Effect on Finality.* The motion does not affect the judgment's finality or suspend its operation.

(d) Other Powers to Grant Relief. This rule does not limit a court's power to:

(1) entertain an independent action to relieve a party from a judgment, order, or proceeding;

(2) grant relief under 28 U.S.C. § 1655 to a defendant who was not personally notified of the action; or

(3) set aside a judgment for fraud on the court.

(e) Bills and Writs Abolished. The following are abolished: bills of review, bills in the nature of bills of review, and writs of coram nobis, coram vobis, and audita querela.

[Amended effective March 19, 1948; October 20, 1949; August 1, 1987; April 30, 2007, effective December 1, 2007.]

--------------------- 2007 AMENDMENTS ROADMAP ---------------------

STYLE PROJECT CHANGES: Rule 60(a) was modestly reworded (although as recrafted, the power of the district court to correct clerical errors following the taking of an appeal, but before docketing in the appeals court, is now less obvious. Presumably, that authority remains unaffected by these "style" amendments.) Rule 60(b) was subsectioned into four parts, each of which follows in the order of the original Rule's language. Labels and further subsectioning were added to each new part. The final sentence of the old Rule 60(b), which noted that the procedure for obtaining judgment relief was to be limited to that permitted by the Civil Rules or by an independent action, was omitted as unnecessary.

NON-STYLE CHANGES: None.

NOTE: The Federal Rules "Style Project" is explained in Part III-A.

AUTHORS' COMMENTARY ON RULE 60

--------------------- PURPOSE AND SCOPE ---------------------

The district judge may grant relief from a judgment or order to correct clerical errors or in circumstances justifying an alteration of the judgment or order. Motions to correct clerical errors may be made at any time. Motions for relief from judgment founded on other reasons must be made within a "reasonable" time after the judgment is entered and, in some cases, no later than 1 year after the judgment is entered. Motions for relief on the basis that the judgment is void may be made at any time.

RULE 60(a). CORRECTION BASED ON CLERICAL MISTAKES, OVERSIGHTS AND OMISSIONS

CORE CONCEPT

The district court, on its own initiative or on motion of a party, may correct clerical errors in judgments, orders, or other parts of the record, as well as errors arising from oversight or omission.

APPLICATIONS

Procedure

Motions to correct clerical errors are made to the district court that rendered the judgment sought to be corrected, rather than to any court where such a judgment may have been transferred.

Sua Sponte Corrections

The court *sua sponte* may raise clerical errors for correction.[1] Before doing so, however, the court must provide the parties with fair notice of its intention, allow them the opportunity to present their positions, and assure itself that no significant prejudice would follow from correcting the errors.[2]

Types of Qualifying Errors

Rule 60(a) is reserved for "clerical mistakes" or "mistakes arising from oversight or omission". Because the district courts enjoy the broadest discretion in correcting these types of mistakes, accurately defining them is essential. Most simply, the distinction lies with intent. Where the judgment, as entered, fails to reflect the original intention of the court, the error can be corrected with Rule 60(a).[3] Conversely, where the judgment was entered accurately, but ought to have been done differently, Rule 60(a) does not apply.[4] Rule 60(a) errors are minor and ministerial ones, not substantively factual or legal.[5] This is a distinction between "blunders in execution"

---

1. *See In re West Texas Mktg. Corp.*, 12 F.3d 497, 503 n. 4 (5th Cir.1994).

2. *See Day v. McDonough*, 547 U.S. 198, ___, 126 S.Ct. 1675, 1684, 164 L.Ed.2d 376 (2006).

3. *See Bowen Inv., Inc. v. Carneiro Donuts, Inc.*, 490 F.3d 27, 29 (1st Cir. 2007); *Robert Lewis Rosen Assocs., Ltd. v. Webb*, 473 F.3d 498, 504–05 (2d Cir. 2007).

4. *See Blue Cross & Blue Shield Ass'n v. American Express Co.*, 467 F.3d 634, 637 (7th Cir. 2006) (noting that Rule 60(a) "cannot be used to change language that was poorly chosen, as opposed to incorrectly

transcribed", and instead "allows a court to correct records to show what *was* done, rather than change them to reflect what *should have been* done").

5. *See In re West Texas Mktg. Corp.*, 12 F.3d 497, 504–05 (5th Cir.1994)("As long as the intentions of the parties are clearly defined and all the court need do is employ a judicial eraser to obliterate a mechanical or mathematical mistake, the modification will be allowed" under Rule 60(a)). *See, e.g. Pfizer Inc. v. Uprichard*, 422 F.3d 124, 129-30 (3d Cir.2005) (inclusion of prejudgment interest proper, but order to sign set-

and "a change of mind".[6] Where the error lies in accurately reducing the court's original intentions to paper, a Rule 60(a) motion is appropriate; however, where the written order accurately captures the court's intentions, but that ruling is allegedly in error, a Rule 60(a) motion is not proper.[7]

Whose Errors

Relief under Rule 60(a) is not limited to clerical mistakes committed only by the clerk; the Rule applies to mistakes by the court, the parties, and the jury as well.[8] Most inadvertent errors may be corrected under Rule 60(a), if the correction would cause the ruling to reflect not a new and later intention of the court, but merely to conform the order to the court's original intention.[9]

Time for Correction

The district court may correct clerical errors even after an appeal is taken;[10] however, once the case is docketed in the appellate court the district court may correct clerical errors only upon leave of the court of appeals.

Implications for Appeal

Historically, whether a party's post-entry motion was a motion to alter or amend under Rule 59(e) or a motion for relief under Rule 60 had great appellate significance—Rule 59(e) motions tolled the

tlement agreement was not); *United States v. Mosbrucker*, 340 F.3d 664, 665–67 (8th Cir.2003) (permitting correction to note true status of easement tract); *Big Bear Lodging Ass'n v. Snow Summit, Inc.*, 182 F.3d 1096 (9th Cir.1999) (to clarify whether court ruled on pending state law claims); *Rezzonico v. H & R Block, Inc.*, 182 F.3d 144 (2d Cir.1999) (used to correct district court's omission of word "not" from judgment); *Hale Container Line, Inc. v. Houston Sea Packing Co.*, 137 F.3d 1455, 1474 (11th Cir.1998) (correcting damages award containing erroneous mathematical computation); *McNamara v. City of Chicago*, 138 F.3d 1219, 1221 (7th Cir.1998) (replacing "Chicago Police Department" with "Chicago Fire Department" in one sentence of opinion); *Kosnoski v. Howley*, 33 F.3d 376, 379 (4th Cir.1994) (correcting a calculation, based upon earlier determined formula, to fix the total amount of judgment).

6. *See Harman v. Harper*, 7 F.3d 1455, 1457 (9th Cir.1993). *See also In re Walter*, 282 F.3d 434, 440–41 (6th Cir.2002) (citing quotation with approval).

7. *See Lowe v. McGraw–Hill Cos.*, 361 F.3d 335, 341 (7th Cir.2004) ("defining element" is that litigants knew error "was by pure inadvertence, rather than a mistaken exercise of judgment"); *United States v. Mosbrucker*, 340 F.3d 664, 666 (8th Cir. 2003) (Rule 60(a) permits correction to reflect "what was understood, intended, and agreed upon by parties and court"); *In re Craddock*, 149 F.3d 1249, 1254 n. 4, (10th Cir.1998) (holding that Rule 60(a) can be invoked where "the thing spoken, written or recorded is not what the person intended to speak, write or record"; Rule may not be used "to correct something that was deliberately done but later discovered to be wrong"). *See also In re Transtexas Gas Corp.*, 303 F.3d 571, 581 (5th Cir.2002); *In re Walter*, 282 F.3d 434, 440–41 (6th Cir. 2002). Hodge ex rel. Skiff v. Hodge, 269 F.3d 155, 158 (2d Cir.2001).

8. *See Day v. McDonough*, 547 U.S. 198, 210–11, 126 S.Ct. 1675, 1684, 164 L.Ed.2d 376 (2006); *In re Walter*, 282 F.3d 434, 440–41 (6th Cir.2002); *In re West Texas Mktg. Corp.*, 12 F.3d 497, 503–04 (5th Cir.1994); *Pattiz v. Schwartz*, 386 F.2d 300 (8th Cir. 1968).

9. *See Robert Lewis Rosen Assocs., Ltd. v. Webb*, 473 F.3d 498, 505 n.11 (2d Cir. 2007).

10. *See In re U.S. Healthcare, Inc.*, 193 F.3d 151, 158 n. 2 (3d Cir.1999).

time for appeal, but Rule 60 motions did not.[11] This effect was changed in a recent amendment to the Federal Rules of Appellate Procedure. Now, Rule 60 motions (like Rule 59(e) motions) will toll the appeal period, but only so long as those motions are filed within 10 days after judgment is entered.[12] Conversely, Rule 60 motions filed beyond the 10–day period will not toll the time for appeal.[13]

Nature of Appellate Review

An appeal from a district court order denying relief under Rule 60(a) implicates only the propriety of that denial, and not the underlying merits of the contested judgment itself.[14]

RULE 60(b). OTHER GROUNDS FOR RELIEF

CORE CONCEPT

In its discretion, the district court may grant a motion for relief from a final judgment, order, or proceeding for various enumerated reasons.

APPLICATIONS

Purpose

The purpose of permitting substantive relief from a judgment or order is to allow the federal courts to strike the proper balance between two often conflicting principles—that litigation must be brought to a final close and that justice must be done.[15]

Reasons for Granting Substantive Relief

Rule 60(b) provides five specified reasons for which substantive (non-clerical) relief may be granted, and adds a sixth catch-all category for reasons not otherwise specifically listed.

Reason 1—Mistake, Inadvertence, Surprise, or Excusable Neglect

Relief from a judgment or order may be granted for mistakes by any person, not just a party.[16] This category permits relief where the order or judgment results from such circumstances as an inability to consult with counsel,[17] a misunderstanding regarding the duty to

11. See Fed. R. App. P. 4(a)(4)(A)(vi) advisory committee notes to 1993 amendment.

12. See Fed. R. App. P. 4(a)(4)(A)(vi). But see Hodge ex rel. Skiff v. Hodge, 269 F.3d 155, 158 (2d Cir.2001) (citing authorities, and holding that Rule 60(a) motion does not extend time for filing post-judgment motions).

13. See American Fed'n of Grain Millers, Local 24 v. Cargill, Inc., 15 F.3d 726, 728 (7th Cir.1994); Harman v. Harper, 7 F.3d 1455, 1457 (9th Cir.1993).

14. See Paddington Partners v. Bouchard, 34 F.3d 1132, 1147 (2d Cir.1994).

15. See Smalls v. United States, 471 F.3d 186, 191 (D.C.Cir. 2006); Coltec Indus., Inc. v. Hobgood, 280 F.3d 262, 271 (3d Cir.2002). See generally Gonzalez v. Crosby, 545 U.S. 524, 529, 125 S.Ct. 2641, 2646, 162 L.Ed.2d 480 (2005) (noting that Rule 60(b)'s "whole purpose is to make an exception to finality").

16. See Associates Discount Corp. v. Goldman, 524 F.2d 1051 (3d Cir.1975).

17. See Falk v. Allen, 739 F.2d 461 (9th Cir.1984).

appear,[18] a failure to receive service,[19] or, in some circumstances, an attorney's negligent failure to meet a deadline.[20] (Note, however, that not all courts recognize attorney negligence as capable of qualifying under this category, and those that do impose a heavy standard for doing so.[21])

The standard for relief under this category is a demanding one.[22] Whether relief is appropriate is assessed on a case-by-case analysis: not every error or omission in the course of litigation will qualify as "excusable neglect",[23] nor will routine carelessness[24], a lack of diligence,[25] a confusion concerning the Rules,[26] or a party's misunderstanding of the consequences of her actions (even after advice of counsel) qualify for relief.[27] Moreover, otherwise careful clients can be penalized for omissions of their careless attorneys.[28] As a threshold showing, the moving party must demonstrate that the error made did not result from his or her own culpable conduct.[29] To qualify as "excusable neglect", the conduct is tested against an equitable standard, one that weighs the totality of the circumstances;[30] among the factors the courts consider in this analysis are: (1) prejudice to the opponent; (2) length of delay and impact on the proceedings; (3) reason for the delay; and (4) the moving party's good faith.[31] The "reason-for-delay" factor is characterized

18. *See Ellingsworth v. Chrysler,* 665 F.2d 180 (7th Cir.1981).

19. *See Blois v. Friday,* 612 F.2d 938 (5th Cir.1980).

20. *See United States v. $23,000 in U.S. Currency,* 356 F.3d 157, 164 (1st Cir.2004); *Robb v. Norfolk & Western Ry. Co.,* 122 F.3d 354 (7th Cir.1997).

21. *See Latshaw v. Trainer Wortham & Co.,* 452 F.3d 1097, 1101 (9th Cir.2006) (surveying other Circuits, and ruling that Rule 60(b)(1) does not remedy erroneous legal advice (even innocent carelessness) of counsel, explaining that "[s]uch mistakes are more appropriately addressed through malpractice claims"); *Robb v. Norfolk & Western Ry. Co.,* 122 F.3d 354, 361–63 (7th Cir.1997) (noting that Circuit discontinues its "hard-and-fast" rule barring application of Rule to attorney negligence, but sternly cautioning counsel against expecting such relief to be granted automatically). *See also Acevedo–Garcia v. Vera–Monroig,* 368 F.3d 49, 54 (1st Cir.2004); *McCurry ex rel. Turner v. Adventist Health Sys./Sunbelt, Inc.,* 298 F.3d 586, 595 (6th Cir.2002).

22. *See United States v. $23,000 in U.S. Currency,* 356 F.3d 157, 164 (1st Cir.2004).

23. *See Rodgers v. Wyoming Attorney Gen.,* 205 F.3d 1201, 1206 (10th Cir.2000) (party who simply misunderstands the legal consequences of his deliberate acts might not be deemed excusably neglectful). *See*

also Robinson v. Armontrout, 8 F.3d 6, 7 (8th Cir.1993)(party's and attorney's failure to object does not justify relief).

24. *See Noah v. Bond Cold Storage,* 408 F.3d 1043, 1045 (8th Cir.2005); *Easley v. Kirmsee,* 382 F.3d 693, 698 (7th Cir.2004); *Negron v. Celebrity Cruises, Inc.,* 316 F.3d 60, 62 (1st Cir.2003).

25. *See Aguiar–Carrasquillo v. Agosto–Alicea,* 445 F.3d 19, 28 (1st Cir.2006).

26. *See Noah v. Bond Cold Storage,* 408 F.3d 1043, 1045 (8th Cir.2005); *United States v. $23,000 in U.S. Currency,* 356 F.3d 157, 164 (1st Cir.2004).

27. *See Cashner v. Freedom Stores, Inc.,* 98 F.3d 572, 577–78 (10th Cir.1996).

28. *See Easley v. Kirmsee,* 382 F.3d 693, 698 (7th Cir.2004); *United States v. Reyes,* 307 F.3d 451, 456 (6th Cir.2002).

29. *See Weiss v. St. Paul Fire & Marine Ins. Co.,* 283 F.3d 790, 794 (6th Cir.2002).

30. *See Nara v. Frank,* 488 F.3d 187, 193–94 (3d Cir. 2007).

31. *See In re Guidant Corp. Implantable Defibrillators Prods. Liab. Litig.,* 496 F.3d 863, ___ (8th Cir. 2007); *Nara v. Frank,* 488 F.3d 187, 193–94 (3d Cir. 2007); *Burrell v. Henderson,* 434 F.3d 826, 832–33 (6th Cir. 2006); *Laurino v. Syringa General Hosp.,* 279 F.3d 750, 753 (9th Cir.2002).

as the "key" factor for this analysis.[32]

Note: This provision has been applied for seeking relief under Rule 60(b) from default judgments, and, so applied, generally obligates the moving party to show good cause for defaulting, quick action in correcting the default, and the existence of a meritorious defense.[33]

Reason 2—Newly Discovered Evidence

Relief from an order or judgment may also be granted on the basis of new evidence where: (1) the evidence has been newly discovered since trial, (2) the moving party was diligent in discovering the new evidence, (3) the new evidence is not merely cumulative or impeaching, (4) the new evidence is material, and (5) in view of the new evidence, a new trial would probably produce a different result.[34] Implicit in these elements is the recognition that the evidence must be evidence of facts that were in existence at the time of trial (though not discovered until after trial).[35] Moreover (and implicitly), the newly discovered evidence must be both admissible and credible.[36] These requirements are strictly enforced.[37] If the movant fails to meet *any* of these prerequisites, the Rule 60(b)(2) motion may be denied.[38] Relief under this category is considered an "extraordinary remedy" to be granted only in exceptional circumstances.[39]

Note: The same principles apply whether relief is sought for this reason under Rule 59 or Rule 60(b).[40]

Reason 3—Fraud, Misrepresentation, Other Adversary Misconduct

Relief from a judgment or order may be permitted on the basis of misconduct where: (1) the moving party possessed a meritorious claim at trial, (2) the adverse party engaged in fraud, misrepresentation, or other misconduct, and (3) the adverse party's conduct prevented the moving party from fully and fairly presenting its case

---

32. *See In re Guidant Corp. Implantable Defibrillators Prods. Liab. Litig.*, 496 F.3d 863, ___ (8th Cir. 2007).

33. *See Warfield v. Byron*, 436 F.3d 551, 556 (5th Cir.2006); *Burrell v. Henderson*, 434 F.3d 826, 831–32 (6th Cir.2006); *York v. Green*, 420 F.3d 99 (2d Cir.2005).

34. *See Moron-Barradas v. Dep't of Educ. of Puerto Rico*, 488 F.3d 472, 482 (1st Cir. 2007); *Zurich North America v. Matrix Serv., Inc.*, 426 F.3d 1281, 1290 (10th Cir. 2005); *Hesling v. CSX Transp.*, Inc., 396 F.3d 632, 639 (5th Cir.2005).

35. *See General Universal Sys., Inc. v. Lee*, 379 F.3d 131 (5th Cir.2004); *Betterbox Commcn's Ltd. v. BB Tech., Inc.*, 300 F.3d 325 (3d Cir.2002).

36. *See Goldstein v. MCI WorldCom*, 340 F.3d 238, 257 (5th Cir.2003).

37. *See Waddell v. Hendry County Sheriff's Office*, 329 F.3d 1300, 1309 (11th Cir. 2003).

38. *See Jones v. Lincoln Elec. Co.*, 188 F.3d 709 (7th Cir.1999) (commenting that if any of these prerequisites is not satisfied, Rule 60(b)(2) motion must fail); *McCormack v. Citibank, N.A.*, 100 F.3d 532, 542 (8th Cir.1996) (commenting that even if movant could meet many prerequisites, he would fail to meet at least one).

39. *See Jones v. Lincoln Elec. Co.*, 188 F.3d 709 (7th Cir.1999).

40. *See Jones v. Aero/Chem Corp.*, 921 F.2d 875 (9th Cir.1990).

during trial.[41] This category is reserved for judgments that were unfairly obtained, not at those that are claimed to be just factually in error.[42] Indeed, an actual factual error in the judgment may not even be required.[43] This provision is remedial, and is liberally construed.[44] In appropriate cases, relief under this category may be granted to remedy belatedly uncovered misconduct during discovery, but only where the challenged behavior substantially interfered with the moving party's ability to fully and fairly try the case.[45] Ordinarily, relief under this category is reserved for instances where the fraud was committed by the adversary (and not by the party's own counsel or other non-adversaries).[46] Further, the fraud must generally have been perpetrated in the course of litigation, and not, for example, during the course of an underlying commercial transaction.[47] A party's entitlement to relief must be proven by clear and convincing evidence.[48]

> *Note:* Some courts will presume or infer the third element (substantial interference with the ability to fully and fairly prepare) where the misconduct is proven to be knowing or deliberate.[49]

Reason 4—Void Judgment

Relief may also be granted where the judgment or order is void, whether because the court lacked jurisdiction over the subject matter, lacked personal jurisdiction over the parties, acted in some manner inconsistent with constitutional due process, or otherwise acted beyond the powers granted to it under the law.[50] When a

41. *See Hutchins v. Zoll Med. Corp.*, 492 F.3d 1377, 1385–86 (Fed.Cir. 2007); *Aguiar-Carrasquillo v. Agosto–Alicea*, 445 F.3d 19, 28 (1st Cir.2006); *United States v. Metropolitan St. Louis Sewer Dist.*, 440 F.3d 930, 935 (8th Cir.2006); *Hesling v. CSX Transp., Inc.*, 396 F.3d 632, 641 (5th Cir.2005); *State Street Bank & Trust Co. v. Inversiones Errazuriz Limitada*, 374 F.3d 158, 176 (2d Cir.2004). *See also Assmann v. Fleming*, 159 F.2d 332 (8th Cir.1947) (noting possibility of relief, irrespective of whether the fraud is considered "extrinsic" or "intrinsic").

42. *See General Universal Sys., Inc. v. Lee*, 379 F.3d 131, 156 (5th Cir.2004).

43. *See Hesling v. CSX Transp., Inc.*, 396 F.3d 632, 641 (5th Cir.2005) (proof that withheld information would have altered outcome is not required, because Rule "is aimed at judgments which were unfairly obtained, not at those which are factually incorrect").

44. *See Hesling v. CSX Transp., Inc.*, 396 F.3d 632, 641 (5th Cir.2005).

45. *See General Universal Sys., Inc. v. Lee*, 379 F.3d 131 (5th Cir.2004); *Summers*

v. Howard Univ., 374 F.3d 1188, 1193 (D.C.Cir.2004); *Cummings v. General Motors Corp.*, 365 F.3d 944, 955 (10th Cir. 2004).

46. *See Latshaw v. Trainer Wortham & Co.*, 452 F.3d 1097, 1102 (9th Cir.2006).

47. *See Roger Edwards, LLC v. Fiddes & Son Ltd.*, 427 F.3d 129, 134 (1st Cir. 2005).

48. *See Hutchins v. Zoll Med. Corp.*, 492 F.3d 1377, 1385–86 (Fed.Cir. 2007); *Cox Nuclear Pharmacy, Inc. v. CTI, Inc.*, 478 F.3d 1303, 1314 (11th Cir. 2007); *Muniz v. Rovira–Martino*, 453 F.3d 10, 12 (1st Cir. 2006); *United States v. Metropolitan St. Louis Sewer Dist.*, 440 F.3d 930, 935 (8th Cir.2006).

49. *See Aguiar–Carrasquillo v. Agosto–Alicea*, 445 F.3d 19, 28 (1st Cir.2006).

50. *See Grace v. Bank Leumi Trust Co.*, 443 F.3d 180, 193 (2d Cir.2006); *Wendt v. Leonard*, 431 F.3d 410, 412–13 (4th Cir. 2005); *Callon Petroleum Co. v. Frontier Ins. Co.*, 351 F.3d 204, 208 (5th Cir.2003).

motion challenges a judgment as void, the district court lacks discretion: either the judgment is void (in which case relief must be granted) or it is not.[51] As interpreted by the courts, however, the definition of a "void" judgment is a narrow one. A ruling alleged to be simply wrong is not "void",[52] nor is a judgment that is merely "voidable" (based on the existence of a particular defense or objection).[53] Instead, a judgment is deemed "void" only if the exercise of jurisdiction is "egregious" and represents a "clear usurpation of power", where no arguable ground for jurisdiction existed.[54]

Reason 5—Changed Circumstances

Relief from a judgment or order may also be granted where the circumstances justifying the ruling have changed, such as (1) when the judgment is satisfied, released, or discharged, (2) where a prior judgment on which the present judgment is based has been reversed or otherwise vacated, or (3) in any other circumstance where the continued enforcement of the judgment would be inequitable (*e.g.*, a change in legislative or decisional law, or a change in critical facts).[55] This encompasses the traditional power invested in a court of equity to modify its decree when appropriate in view of changed circumstances.[56] In evaluating such motions, the courts consider whether a substantial change in circumstances or law has occurred since the contested order was entered, whether complying with the contested order would cause extreme and unexpected hardship, and whether a

51. *See United States v. Three Hundred Fifty–Three Thousand Six Hundred Dollars, in U.S. Currency*, 463 F.3d 812, 813 (8th Cir. 2006); *Central Vermont Pub. Serv. Corp. v. Herbert*, 341 F.3d 186, 189 (2d Cir.2003); *Carter v. Fenner*, 136 F.3d 1000, 1005 (5th Cir.1998).

52. *See United States v. Buck*, 281 F.3d 1336, 1344 (10th Cir.2002); *United States v. Berke*, 170 F.3d 882, 883 (9th Cir.1999); *Eberhardt v. Integrated Design & Const., Inc.*, 167 F.3d 861, 871 (4th Cir.1999).

53. *See Days Inns Worldwide, Inc. v. Patel*, 445 F.3d 899, 906–08 (6th Cir.2006) (distinguishing between void ab initio and voidable).

54. *See Wendt v. Leonard*, 431 F.3d 410, 412–13 (4th Cir.2005); *Central Vermont Pub. Serv. Corp. v. Herbert*, 341 F.3d 186, 190 (2d Cir.2003); *In re G.A.D., Inc.*, 340 F.3d 331, 336 (6th Cir.2003).

55. *See Agostini v. Felton*, 521 U.S. 203, 117 S.Ct. 1997, 138 L.Ed.2d 391 (1997) (allowing relief under Rule 60(b)(5) to alter permanent injunction in light of Supreme Court's decision to overrule earlier constitutional precedent on which injunction was based); *Rufo v. Inmates of Suffolk County Jail*, 502 U.S. 367, 112 S.Ct. 748, 116 L.Ed.2d 867 (1992)(parties seeking a modification of an order entered by consent bear the burden of demonstrating a "significant change" in circumstances to warrant relief from the decree). *See also Reynolds v. McInnes*, 338 F.3d 1221, 1227 (11th Cir. 2003) (modification may be warranted where significant time has passed since order was entered and, despite defendants' efforts, objectives of original agreement have not been met); *Maraziti v. Thorpe*, 52 F.3d 252, 254 (9th Cir.1995)(noting that nearly every court order causes some reverberations into the future, and mere "continuing consequences" do not equate with the "prospective application" required under Rule 60(b)(5); instead, standard for Rule 60(b)(5) is whether judgment is "executory" or implicates "supervision of changing conduct or conditions"); *Valentine Sugars, Inc. v. Sudan*, 34 F.3d 320, 321–22 (5th Cir.1994)(modification under Rule 60(b)(5) is granted cautiously and only when dangers have almost disappeared, moving party is experiencing significantly extreme and unexpected hardship and oppression, and movant's case is unanswerable).

56. *See Frew ex rel. Frew v. Hawkins*, 540 U.S. 431, 441–42, 124 S.Ct. 899, 905–06, 157 L.Ed.2d 855 (2004).

good reason for modification exists.[57] The proposed modification must be "suitably tailored" to meet the new legal or factual circumstances.[58] Relief under the "changed circumstances" category is only available where there is a prospective effect to the challenged judgment;[59] the mere fact that a ruling will have future collateral estoppel effect (something obviously common to many rulings)[60] or otherwise causes "some reverberations into the future"[61] does not provide the requisite "prospective" effect necessary for relief under this provision. Ordinarily, money judgments will not possess the required "prospective" effect because the set nature of the monetary outlay provides the finality.[62] However, the "satisfied, released, or discharged" clause is often invoked by parties seeking to have a judgment satisfied by the court, due to an ongoing dispute with the judgment holder over the judgment.[63]

> *Note:* The Supreme Court has confirmed that the lower courts should not apply Rule 60(b)(5) in *anticipation* of the Supreme Court's overruling of an earlier precedent. To the contrary, the Supreme Court instructs that where one of its precedents applies directly to the circumstances at hand, even though the precedent's reasoning has been undermined by other opinions, the lower courts should nevertheless follow the precedent and leave to the Supreme Court the prerogative of overruling its own decisions.[64]

Reason 6—In the Interests of Justice

Finally, relief from a judgment or order may be permitted to further the interests of justice if such relief will not affect the substantial rights of the parties. This "catch-all" category is reserved for extraordinary circumstances.[65] Relief under this Rule is

---

57. *See United States v. Kayser–Roth Corp.*, 272 F.3d 89, 95 (1st Cir.2001); *Parton v. White*, 203 F.3d 552, 555 (8th Cir. 2000).

58. *See Reynolds v. McInnes*, 338 F.3d 1221 (11th Cir.2003).

59. *See Prudential Ins. Co. v. National Park Med. Ctr., Inc.*, 413 F.3d 897, 903 (8th Cir.2005).

60. *See Coltec Indus., Inc. v. Hobgood*, 280 F.3d 262, 271–72 (3d Cir.2002) ("If this [collateral estoppel argument] were enough to satisfy Rule 60(b)(5)'s threshold requirement, then the Rule's requirement of 'prospective application' would be meaningless").

61. *See Kalamazoo River Study Group v. Rockwell Int'l Corp.*, 355 F.3d 574, 587–88 (6th Cir.2004).

62. *See Kalamazoo River Study Group v. Rockwell Int'l Corp.*, 355 F.3d 574, 587–88 (6th Cir.2004).

63. *See Zamani v. Carnes*, 491 F.3d 990, 995–96 (9th Cir. 2007).

64. *See Agostini v. Felton*, 521 U.S. 203, 117 S.Ct. 1997, 138 L.Ed.2d 391 (1997). *See also Cano v. Baker*, 435 F.3d 1337, 1341–43 (11th Cir.2006) (rejecting, on similar grounds, Rule 60(b)(5)'s use by former abortion plaintiff who sought to revisit her earlier abortion rights decision as wrongly decided in light of intervening medical evidence).

65. *See, e.g., Gonzalez v. Crosby*, 545 U.S. 524, 535, 125 S.Ct. 2641, 2649, 162 L.Ed.2d 480 (2005); *In re Guidant Corp. Implantable Defibrillators Prods. Liab. Litig.*, 496 F.3d 863, 868 (8th Cir. 2007); *Kramer v. Gates*, 481 F.3d 788, 791–92 (D.C.Cir. 2007); *Delay v. Gordon*, 475 F.3d 1039, 1044–45 (9th Cir. 2007).

"exceedingly rare".[66] It does offer an unsuccessful litigant an opportunity "to take a mulligan".[67] Seeking relief under this Rule also generally requires a showing of actual injury and the presence of circumstances beyond the movant's control that prevented timely action to protect her interests.[68] There is also some authority for the conclusion that this Rule is limited to setting aside a judgment or order, and may not be used to grant affirmative relief.[69]

> *Note:* The "catch-all" category and the preceding five specific categories are mutually exclusive. If the reason for which relief is sought fits within one of the five specific categories (even though the facts fail to meet the prerequisites for that relief (*e.g.*, the neglect is not truly excusable, the time period for seeking relief under that Rule provision has passed, etc.)), the catch-all category will not permit relief.[70] "Something more" is required, and, given the breadth of the reasons captured by Rule 60(b)(1) through (b)(5), there is an understandably thin volume of cases explaining when that "something more" will be present to warrant relief under Rule 60(b)(6).[71] Note, however, that some older cases have ruled that Rule 60(b)(6) may be proper where a defaulted client seeks relief from judgment on the basis of extremely gross negligence of counsel.[72]

Burden of Proof

The party seeking relief from a judgment or order bears the burden of demonstrating that the prerequisites for such relief are satisfied.[73]

Discretion of District Judge

Whether to grant relief under Rule 60(b) is left to the discretion of the trial court, and will not be disturbed on appeal unless that discretion has been abused.[74] In the case of "void" judgments

---

66. *See In re Guidant Corp. Implantable Defibrillators Prods. Liab. Litig.*, 496 F.3d 863, 868 (8th Cir. 2007). *See also Kramer v. Gates*, 481 F.3d 788, 791–92 (D.C.Cir. 2007) (used "sparingly").

67. *See Kramer v. Gates*, 481 F.3d 788, 792 (D.C.Cir. 2007).

68. *See Delay v. Gordon*, 475 F.3d 1039, 1044–45 (9th Cir. 2007).

69. *See Delay v. Gordon*, 475 F.3d 1039, 1044–45 (9th Cir. 2007).

70. *See Liljeberg v. Health Servs. Acquisition Corp.*, 486 U.S. 847, 108 S.Ct. 2194, 100 L.Ed.2d 855 (1988). *See also Ford Motor Co. v. Mustangs Unlimited, Inc.*, 487 F.3d 465, 468 (6th Cir. 2007); *Kramer v. Gates*, 481 F.3d 788, 791–92 (D.C.Cir. 2007); *Delay v. Gordon*, 475 F.3d 1039, 1044–45 (9th Cir. 2007); *Arrieta v. Battaglia*, 461 F.3d 861, 865 (7th Cir.2006).

71. *See Ford Motor Co. v. Mustangs Unlimited, Inc.*, 487 F.3d 465, 468 (6th Cir. 2007).

72. *See Community Dental Servs. v. Tani*, 282 F.3d 1164, 1169 (9th Cir.2002) (neglect must be "so gross that it is inexcusable"); *Shepard Claims Serv., Inc. v. William Darrah & Assocs.*, 796 F.2d 190, 195 (6th Cir.1986); *Boughner v. Secretary of Health, Educ. & Welfare*, 572 F.2d 976, 978 (3d Cir.1978); *L.P. Steuart, Inc. v. Matthews*, 329 F.2d 234, 235 (D.C.Cir.1964).

73. *See McCurry ex rel. Turner v. Adventist Health Sys./Sunbelt, Inc.*, 298 F.3d 586, 592 (6th Cir.2002).

74. *See McCurry ex rel. Turner v. Adventist Health Sys./Sunbelt, Inc.*, 298 F.3d 586, 592 (6th Cir.2002); *Provident Life & Acc. Ins. Co. v. Goel*, 274 F.3d 984, 997 (5th Cir.2001); *Davila-Alvarez v. Escuela de*

attacked under Rule 60(b)(4), however, the district court's discretion is almost illusory, if it exists at all. True "void" judgments are "legal nullities", and the court's refusal to vacate such judgments is a *per se* abuse of discretion.[75]

Procedure

Motions under this Rule should be made to the court that rendered the judgment.[76] Absent a local rule dictating otherwise, the court is not required to convene a hearing on Rule 60(b) motions, but may choose to do so in its discretion.[77] The court generally does not need to enter findings of fact and conclusions of law to grant Rule 60(b) relief.[78]

Who May Seek Relief

Relief under this Rule may be requested by a party, the party's legal representative,[79] or one in privity with a party.[80]

Sua Sponte Motions

The Circuits are divided on whether a district court may, on its own initiative, grant relief from a judgment or order under Rule 60(b).[81] When such *sua sponte* relief is permitted, the courts generally demand that the parties receive notice and an opportunity to be heard before the relief is ordered.[82]

RULE 60(c). TIMING AND EFFECT OF MOTION

CORE CONCEPT

Medicina Universidad Central Del Caribe, 257 F.3d 58, 63–64 (1st Cir.2001).

75. *See, e.g., United States v. Three Hundred Fifty–Three Thousand Six Hundred Dollars, in U.S. Currency,* 463 F.3d 812, 813 (8th Cir. 2006); *Central Vermont Pub. Serv. Corp. v. Herbert,* 341 F.3d 186, 189 (2d Cir.2003); *Jackson v. FIE Corp.,* 302 F.3d 515, 522 (5th Cir.2002).

76. *See Board of Trustees, Sheet Metal Workers' Nat'l Pension Fund v. Elite Erectors, Inc.,* 212 F.3d 1031, 1034 (7th Cir. 2000).

77. *See Atkinson v. Prudential Property Co.,* 43 F.3d 367, 374 (8th Cir.1994).

78. *See Atkinson v. Prudential Property Co.,* 43 F.3d 367, 374 (8th Cir.1994).

79. *See In re El Paso Refinery, LP,* 37 F.3d 230, 234 (5th Cir.1994) (defining phrase "party's legal representative" as person standing in the place, and in the stead, of another (such as an heir at law), who either holds position tantamount to that of the party, or whose legal rights were so tied to the party that his or her rights were directly affected by final judgment).

80. *See Eyak Native Village v. Exxon Corp.,* 25 F.3d 773 (9th Cir.1994).

81. *See Pierson v. Dormire,* 484 F.3d 486, 491–92 (8th Cir. 2007) (describing Circuit split). *Compare United States v. Pauley,* 321 F.3d 578, 581 & 581 n.1 (6th Cir.2003) (no *sua sponte* relief) *and Dow v. Baird,* 389 F.2d 882, 884–85 (10th Cir.1968) (same) *with Pierson v. Dormire,* 484 F.3d 486, 491–92 (8th Cir. 2007) (*sua sponte* relief permitted); *Fort Knox Music Inc. v. Baptiste,* 257 F.3d 108, 111 (2d Cir.2001) (same) *and Kingvision Pay–Per–View Ltd. v. Lake Alice Bar,* 168 F.3d 347, 351 (9th Cir.1999) (same) *and McDowell v. Celebrezze,* 310 F.2d 43, 44 (5th Cir.1962) (same); *United States v. Jacobs,* 298 F.2d 469, 472 (4th Cir.1961) (same).

82. *See Pierson v. Dormire,* 484 F.3d 486, 492 (8th Cir. 2007); *Fort Knox Music Inc. v. Baptiste,* 257 F.3d 108, 111 (2d Cir. 2001); *Kingvision Pay–Per–View Ltd. v. Lake Alice Bar,* 168 F.3d 347, 352 (9th Cir. 1999).

Relief under Rule 60(b) must be sought within a "reasonable" time after entry of the challenged judgment or order, except for three grounds which specify a 1–year time limit (from which no extensions may be granted). Making a motion under this Rule has no effect on finality.

APPLICATIONS

2007 Amendments

Former Rule 60(b) was subsectioned in the 2007 amendments, into new Rules 60(b), 60(c), 60(d), and 60(e). The new subsections follow in the same order as the content was presented in the old Rule 60(b). Practitioners searching for pre–2007 interpretations of this Rule should bear this repositioning in mind in doing their research. Current Rule 60(c) was, until 2007, a portion of old Rule 60(b).

The "Reasonable" Time Grounds

Relief from a judgment or order that is sought under either Reason 5 ("changed circumstances") or Reason 6 ("interests of justice") must be made "within a reasonable time" after entry of the judgment or order being challenged.[83] The courts determine whether the time of filing is "reasonable" on a case-by-case basis, by examining the prejudice to the party opposing the motion and whether the moving party had good reason for not acting sooner.[84]

The "Void" Judgment Ground

Relief from a "void" judgment or order can be sought at any time:[85] Laches and similar finality principles generally have no effect on void judgments; the courts have held that the mere passage of time will not convert a void judgment into a proper one.[86] However, if a party attacks the court's jurisdiction and loses on that issue, the question of jurisdiction becomes *res judicata* and, accordingly, the judgment is not void; the party's only recourse in such a case is a proper, timely merits appeal, not relief under Rule 60(b).[87]

The 1–Year Time Grounds

Seeking relief from a judgment or order under any one of the three remaining Rule 60(b) grounds for relief must be done within 1 year from entry of the challenged ruling. Thus, this 1–year time limit applies to Reason 1 ("mistake, inadvertence, surprise"),[88]

---

83. See Rule 60(c)(1).

84. See Venture Indus. Corp. v. Autoliv ASP, Inc., 457 F.3d 1322 (Fed.Cir.2006); In re G.A.D., Inc., 340 F.3d 331, 334–35 (6th Cir.2003); Old Republic Ins. Co. v. Pacific Fin. Servs. of America, Inc., 301 F.3d 54, 59 (2d Cir.2002).

85. See Grace v. Bank Leumi Trust Co., 443 F.3d 180, 190 (2d Cir.2006); Jackson v. FIE Corp., 302 F.3d 515, 523–24 (5th Cir. 2002); Hertz Corp. v. Alamo Rent–A–Car, Inc., 16 F.3d 1126, 1130 (11th Cir.1994).

86. See Jackson v. FIE Corp., 302 F.3d 515, 523–24 (5th Cir.2002); United States v. One Toshiba Color Television, 213 F.3d 147, 157–58 (3d Cir.2000).

87. See Durfee v. Duke, 375 U.S. 106, 84 S.Ct. 242, 11 L.Ed.2d 186 (1963); American Surety Co. v. Baldwin, 287 U.S. 156, 53 S.Ct. 98, 77 L.Ed. 231 (1932).

88. See The Tool Box, Inc. v. Ogden City Corp., 419 F.3d 1084 (10th Cir.2005) (noting one-year time limit is "absolute"). See also In re G.A.D., Inc., 340 F.3d 331, 334 (6th Cir.2003).

Reason 2 ("newly discovered evidence"),[89] and Reason 3 ("fraud, misrepresentation, other adversary misconduct").[90] Note that this 1–year time limit for Reason 3, fraud, is "absolute", and is not tolled during the pendency of an appeal from the same judgment.[91]

No Extensions

Where the 1-year time limit is specified in Rule 60(c), the district court lacks the authority to extend the time for bringing a motion.[92] However, there is developing case law that when an untimely Rule 60(b) motion is filed, but not objected to by the non-moving party, the timeliness objection may be deemed forfeited through waiver.[93]

Enforceability of Judgment

Rule 60(b) provides that a judgment challenged under that Rule remains valid and enforceable unless and until the Rule 60(b) motion is granted.[94]

Effect of Appeals

Ordinarily, taking an appeal does not extend the Rule 60(c) 1–year or "reasonable" time limits.[95] However, a Rule 60 motion filed within 10 days after entry of the judgment will toll the time for taking an appeal.[96] Otherwise, a Rule 60(b) motion filed more than 10 days following entry of judgment will generally not postpone the finality of the judgment and the appeal period begins to run.[97] In such cases, a pending Rule 60(b) motion does not prevent an otherwise proper notice of appeal from conferring jurisdiction on the appellate court.[98] Once an appeal is taken, the district court's ability to act on Rule 60(b) motions is limited. Although the district court may *deny* such motions, it may not *grant* them without a remand from the court of appeals.[99] If the district court is inclined to grant a Rule 60(b) motion during the pendency of an appeal, the

---

89. *See In re G.A.D., Inc.*, 340 F.3d 331, 334 (6th Cir.2003).

90. *See In re G.A.D., Inc.*, 340 F.3d 331, 334 (6th Cir.2003).

91. *See King v. First American Investigations, Inc.*, 287 F.3d 91, 94 (2d Cir.2002).

92. *See* Rule 60(b)(2). *See also Wilburn v. Robinson*, 480 F.3d 1140, 1147–48 (D.C.Cir. 2007) (noting that court may not extend); *The Tool Box, Inc. v. Ogden City Corp.*, 419 F.3d 1084 (10th Cir.2005) (noting one-year time limit is "absolute" in Rule 60(b)(1) cases).

93. *See Wilburn v. Robinson*, 480 F.3d 1140, 1147–48 (D.C.Cir. 2007).

94. *See* Rule 60(c)(2). *See also Balark v. City of Chicago*, 81 F.3d 658, 663 (7th Cir. 1996) (Rule 60(b) order "operates prospectively only").

95. *See Cashner v. Freedom Stores, Inc.*, 98 F.3d 572, 579 n. 4 (10th Cir.1996).

96. *See* Fed. R. App. P. 4(a)(4)(A)(vi). *See also Wilburn v. Robinson*, 480 F.3d 1140, 1144 (D.C.Cir. 2007).

97. *See Carpenter v. Williams,* 86 F.3d 1015 (10th Cir.1996)(Rule 60(b) motion filed more than ten days after district court dismissed case does not toll time for filing notice of appeal).

98. *See Hatfield v. Board of County Comm'rs*, 52 F.3d 858, 861 (10th Cir.1995).

99. *See Fobian v. Storage Tech. Corp.*, 164 F.3d 887, 890–91 (4th Cir.1999); *Cashner v. Freedom Stores, Inc.*, 98 F.3d 572, 579 n. 4 (10th Cir.1996). *See also Brooks v. Celeste*, 16 F.3d 104, 108 (6th Cir.1994) (noting that once notice of appeal is filed, district court will generally lack jurisdiction to consider Rule 60(b) motions), *vacated on other grounds on reconsideration*, 39 F.3d 125 (6th Cir.1994).

court should issue a brief memorandum so notifying the movant, and the movant, thereafter, should seek a limited remand of the appeal for that purpose.[100]

Nature of Appellate Review

An appeal from a district court order denying relief under Rule 60(b) implicates only the propriety of that denial, and not the underlying merits of the contested judgment itself.[101]

RULE 60(d). OTHER POWERS TO GRANT RELIEF

CORE CONCEPT

Although Rule 60(a) and Rule 60(b) give the district courts specific Rule-based authority to grant relief from judgments and orders, the courts also enjoy other vehicles for granting such relief as well.

APPLICATIONS

2007 Amendments

Former Rule 60(b) was subsectioned in the 2007 amendments, into new Rules 60(b), 60(c), 60(d), and 60(e). The new subsections follow in the same order as the content was presented in the old Rule 60(b). Practitioners searching for pre–2007 interpretations of this Rule should bear this repositioning in mind in doing their research. Current Rule 60(d) was, until 2007, a portion of old Rule 60(b).

Relief by an Independent Action

Litigants may also seek relief from a judgment or order by filing an "independent action", a proceeding that sounds in equity.[102] Independent actions are completely distinct from a motion under Rule 60.[103] Independent actions are permitted in only exceptional cases to prevent grave miscarriages of justice.[104] An independent action may be maintained where:

(1) the judgment should not, in good conscience, be enforced;

(2) a good defense exists to the plaintiff's lawsuit;

(3) fraud, accident, or mistake prevented the defendant from obtaining the benefit of the good defense;

(4) the defendant is free of fault and negligence; *and*

---

100. *See Davis v. Yageo Corp.*, 481 F.3d 661, 685 (9th Cir. 2007) (detailing remand procedures). *See also Mahone v. Ray*, 326 F.3d 1176, 1180 (11th Cir.2003); *Morse v. McWhorter*, 290 F.3d 795, 799 (6th Cir. 2002); *Fobian v. Storage Tech. Corp.*, 164 F.3d 887, 890–91 (4th Cir.1999).

101. *See Browder v. Director*, 434 U.S. 257, 263 n. 7, 98 S.Ct. 556, 560 n. 7, 54 L.Ed.2d 521 (1978).

102. *See United States v. Beggerly*, 524 U.S. 38, 118 S.Ct. 1862, 141 L.Ed.2d 32 (1998).

103. *See Herring v. United States*, 424 F.3d 384, 389 (3d Cir.2005).

104. *See United States v. Beggerly*, 524 U.S. 38, 118 S.Ct. 1862, 141 L.Ed.2d 32 (1998); *Middleton v. McDonald*, 388 F.3d 614, 618 (8th Cir.2004); *Appling v. State Farm Mut. Auto. Ins. Co.*, 340 F.3d 769, 780 (9th Cir.2003).

(5) there is no adequate remedy at law.[105]

The Rule 60(c) time limits do not apply to independent actions in equity.[106] If the independent action is filed in the same court that granted the judgment, supplemental jurisdiction exists—regardless of diversity or federal question jurisdiction.[107]

Relief by Section 1655 of the Judiciary Code

Congress has, by statute, created a procedure for the enforcement and the removal of liens, incumbrances, and clouds upon the title to real or personal property. The statute provides a means for notifying the affected defendant of the pending proceeding. If, however, the defendant does not receive proper notification, he may act within 1 year to have the judgment lifted and appear to defend (provided he pays costs assessed by the court).[108]

Relief due to Fraud on the Court

Finally, the district court also possesses the inherent power to grant relief where the judgment or order is obtained through a fraud on the court.[109] No time limits apply.[110] The court may grant the relief on its own initiative or on motion. Such fraud must be proven by clear and convincing evidence.[111]

> *Note:* To constitute as a fraud on the court, the alleged misconduct must be something more than fraud among the litigants. Instead, the misconduct must be an assault on the integrity of the judicial process, which defiles the court itself or is perpetrated by officers of the court in such a manner that the impartial system of justice fails to function.[112] Fraud in the discovery process, to the extent it meets this standard, can support an independent action.[113]

105. *See In re West Texas Mktg. Corp.,* 12 F.3d 497, 503 n. 3 (5th Cir.1994)(listing criteria); *Great Coastal Express, Inc. v. International Bhd. of Teamsters, Chauffeurs, Warehousemen & Helpers of America,* 675 F.2d 1349, 1358 (4th Cir.1982)(same).

106. *See Robinson v. Volkswagenwerk AG,* 56 F.3d 1268, 1274 (10th Cir.1995); *In re West Texas Mktg. Corp.,* 12 F.3d 497, 503 n. 3 (5th Cir.1994).

107. *See United States v. Beggerly,* 524 U.S. 38, 118 S.Ct. 1862, 141 L.Ed.2d 32 (1998); *Cresswell v. Sullivan & Cromwell,* 922 F.2d 60, 70 (2d Cir.1990).

108. *See* 28 U.S.C.A. § 1655.

109. *Universal Oil Prods. Co. v. Root Refining Co.,* 328 U.S. 575, 66 S.Ct. 1176, 90 L.Ed. 1447 (1946); *Hazel–Atlas Glass Co. v. Hartford–Empire Co.,* 322 U.S. 238, 64 S.Ct. 997, 88 L.Ed. 1250 (1944).

110. *See King v. First American Investigations, Inc.,* 287 F.3d 91, 95 (2d Cir.2002).

111. *See King v. First American Investigations, Inc.,* 287 F.3d 91, 95 (2d Cir.2002).

112. *See Roger Edwards, LLC v. Fiddes & Son Ltd.,* 427 F.3d 129, 133 (1st Cir. 2005); *Appling v. State Farm Mut. Auto. Ins. Co.,* 340 F.3d 769, 780 (9th Cir.2003). *King v. First American Investigations, Inc.,* 287 F.3d 91, 95 (2d Cir.2002). *See also Baltia Air Lines, Inc. v. Transaction Management, Inc.,* 98 F.3d 640, 642 (D.C.Cir. 1996) (citing bribery of a judge or an attorney's knowing participation in the presentation of perjured testimony).

113. *See Appling v. State Farm Mut. Auto. Ins. Co.,* 340 F.3d 769, 780 (9th Cir. 2003).

RULE 60(e). BILLS AND WRITS ABOLISHED

CORE CONCEPT

The old common law writs of coram nobis, coram vobis, audita querela, and bills of review are abolished in civil proceedings.[114] Filings under these ancient writs may be treated by the courts as motions for relief under Rule 60(b).[115]

ADDITIONAL RESEARCH REFERENCES

Wright & Miller, *Federal Practice and Procedure* §§ 2851–73.

C.J.S. Federal Civil Procedure §§ 368, 373, 1233–1251 et seq.

West's Key No. Digests, Federal Civil Procedure ☞921, 2641–2662.

114. At the old common law, a writ of coram nobis (if sought at the King's Bench) or writ of coram vobis (if sought in the Courts of Common Pleas) were the procedural tools to correct errors of fact by petitioning to bring before the court certain facts which, if known earlier, would have prevented the entry of judgment. *See* 18 Am. Jur. 2d *Coram Nobis & Allied Statutory Remedies* §§ 1–2 (1985). A person against whom execution has issued or was about to issue could seek a writ of audita querela to prevent execution where the execution would be contrary to justice. *See* 7 Am. Jur. 2d *Audita Querela* § 1 (1997). Finally, a bill of review was a new action, filed in equity, that sought the correction, reversal, alteration, or explanation of a decree issued in an earlier proceeding. *See* 27A Am. Jur. 2d *Equity* § 256 (1996). Each of these ancient writs—in civil actions only—have been abolished by the Federal Rules.

115. *See Green v. White*, 319 F.3d 560, 563 n.1 (3d Cir.2003) (treating request for writ in the nature of a writ of coram nobis as motion under Rule 60(b)).

RULE 61

HARMLESS ERROR

Unless justice requires otherwise, no error in admitting or excluding evidence—or any other error by the court or a party—is ground for granting a new trial, for setting aside a verdict, or for vacating, modifying, or otherwise disturbing a judgment or order. At every stage of the proceeding, the court must disregard all errors and defects that do not affect any party's substantial rights.

―――――――――― 2007 AMENDMENTS ROADMAP ――――――――――

STYLE PROJECT CHANGES: The densely complex first sentence of this Rule was reworded. The bulky "inconsistent with substantial justice" standard was thinned to "justice requires".

NON-STYLE CHANGES: None.

NOTE: The Federal Rules "Style Project" is explained in Part III-A.

AUTHORS' COMMENTARY ON RULE 61

―――――――――― PURPOSE AND SCOPE ――――――――――

Rule 61 codifies the principle that "harmless" errors by the district court—those errors that do not affect the parties' substantial rights—will not justify a new trial, setting aside a verdict, or vacating, modifying, or otherwise disturbing the court's order.

APPLICATIONS

Standard for "Harmlessness"

Rule 61 defines a harmless error as one that does not affect the substantial rights of the parties or does not defeat substantial justice.[1] But an error will not be discounted as harmless if the court is left with a grave doubt as to whether the error had a substantial influence in the ultimate result.[2] A more exacting definition is

―――――――――――――――――――――――――――――

1. Rule 61. *See Brandt v. Vulcan, Inc.,* 30 F.3d 752 (7th Cir.1994)(harmless error calls into question the fundamental fairness of the trial).

2. *See Krulewitch v. United States,* 336 U.S. 440, 444–45, 69 S.Ct. 716, 718–19, 93 L.Ed. 790 (1949)(defining harmlessness in criminal context); *Sims v. Great American*

probably impossible, just as it is impossible to ignore the subjectivity inherent in the inquiry itself.[3] Some baseline principles exist, however. In testing for harmlessness, the court considers the entire record, and applies the standard on a case-by-case basis.[4] Every reasonable possibility of prejudice need not be disproved.[5] At its core, the harmless error inquiry asks whether the trial error "affected the outcome of a case to the substantial disadvantage of the losing party".[6] Unsurprisingly, this risk is considered greater in close cases, than in more one-sided cases.[7]

Burden of Proof

The party moving for relief bears the burden of establishing that a trial error affected that party's substantial rights and, thus, was not harmless.[8] (Note, however, that the standard for harmlessness (as articulated by some courts) seems to suppose that harm is presumed, rather than proved.[9])

Applies to All Errors

The harmless error rule applies to all types of errors, including most constitutional errors. The courts of appeals review rulings of

Life Ins. Co., 469 F.3d 870, 886 (10th Cir. 2006) (court must reverse unless it finds that jury's verdict more probably than not was unaffected by error); *General Motors Corp. v. New A.C. Chevrolet, Inc.*, 263 F.3d 296, 329 (3d Cir.2001) (non-constitutional legal errors are harmless if it is "highly probable that the error did not affect the judgment"); *Nieves-Villanueva v. Soto–Rivera*, 133 F.3d 92, 102 (1st Cir.1997) (court assumes error affected the verdict if court is in "grave doubt" about its effect on verdict). *See also Barber v. Ruth*, 7 F.3d 636, 641 (7th Cir.1993)(in bench trial, trial error is harmless if the record indicates that trial court would have reached the same judgment regardless of the error).

3. *See United States v. O'Keefe*, 169 F.3d 281, 287 n. 5 (5th Cir.1999) (citing formulations by Judge Traynor and Justice Rutledge as among the clearest formulations) (citing 11 Charles Alan Wright, Arthur R. Miller, & Mary Kay Kane, *Federal Practice & Procedure* § 2883, at 445–47 (2d ed. 1995)). *Cf.* Roger Traynor, *The Riddle of Harmless Error* 35 (1970) ("[U]nless the appellate court believes it highly probable that the error did not affect the judgment, it should reverse"); *Kotteakos v. United States*, 328 U.S. 750, 760, 66 S.Ct. 1239, 1245, 90 L.Ed. 1557 (1946) (Rutledge, J.) ("Do not be technical, where technicality does not really hurt the party whose rights in the trial and in its outcome the technicality affects").

4. *See Sims v. Great American Life Ins. Co.*, 469 F.3d 870, 886 (10th Cir. 2006); *Nieves-Villanueva v. Soto–Rivera*, 133 F.3d 92, 102 (1st Cir.1997); *Brewer v. Jeep Corp.*, 724 F.2d 653 (8th Cir.1983).

5. *See General Motors Corp. v. New A.C. Chevrolet, Inc.*, 263 F.3d 296, 329 (3d Cir. 2001).

6. *See United States v. O'Keefe*, 169 F.3d 281, 287 n. 5 (5th Cir.1999). *See also Muldrow ex rel. Estate of Muldrow v. Re–Direct, Inc.*, 493 F.3d 160, 168 (D.C.Cir. 2007); *Pelletier v. Main St. Textiles, LP*, 470 F.3d 48, 52–53 (1st Cir. 2006); *SR Int'l Bus. Ins. Co., Ltd. v. World Trade Ctr. Props., LLC*, 467 F.3d 107, 119 (2d Cir. 2006).

7. *See Sims v. Great American Life Ins. Co.*, 469 F.3d 870, 886 (10th Cir. 2006).

8. *See Palmer v. Hoffman*, 318 U.S. 109, 116, 63 S.Ct. 477, 481–82, 87 L.Ed. 645 (1943)(moving party bears the burden of showing resulting prejudice); *SR Int'l Bus. Ins. Co., Ltd. v. World Trade Ctr. Props., LLC*, 467 F.3d 107, 119 (2d Cir. 2006) (same); *Dresser-Rand Co. v. Virtual Automation Inc.*, 361 F.3d 831, 842 (5th Cir. 2004) (same).

9. *See Sims v. Great American Life Ins. Co.*, 469 F.3d 870, 886 (10th Cir. 2006) (court must reverse unless it finds that jury's verdict was, more probably than not, unaffected by error).

the district courts under this standard as well.[10]

Federal Law Controls

Under *Erie* principles,[11] the federal (not State) construction of the harmless error rule usually controls where the federal and State standards are inconsistent.[12]

Errors in Rulings on Pleadings

Technical errors in pleadings will generally be discounted as harmless.[13] Likewise, errors in granting parties the right to intervene are not overturned unless they affected the substantial rights of the parties.[14]

Errors in Ruling on Motions

The same "substantial rights" standard applies to errors in ruling upon motions. Thus, the improper dismissal of co-defendants may be deemed harmless where the plaintiffs, for other reasons, were already barred from any recovery,[15] and the improper dismissal of counterclaims may be deemed harmless where those same claims could be readily asserted in another proceeding.[16] Similarly, in ruling upon a motion for summary judgment, the improper consideration of unsworn and inadmissible exhibits may be deemed harmless where that error is, in context, unlikely to have been prejudicial.[17]

Errors in Admitting or Excluding Evidence

The district court enjoys broad discretion to admit or exclude evidence.[18] Errors in such rulings are harmless if the party raises no objection,[19] if the evidence wrongfully admitted or excluded was cumulative,[20] if adequate curative instructions are given[21], or if the rulings are otherwise determined not to have caused substantial

---

10. *See* 28 U.S.C.A. § 2111 (fixing harmlessness standard for appeals). *See also McDonough Power Equip., Inc. v. Greenwood*, 464 U.S. 548, 554, 104 S.Ct. 845, 849, 78 L.Ed.2d 663 (1984)(noting that appellate courts must act in accordance with the salutary policy embodied in Rule 61); *General Motors Corp. v. New A.C. Chevrolet, Inc.*, 263 F.3d 296, 329 n.18 (3d Cir.2001) (same).

11. *See Erie R.R. v. Tompkins*, 304 U.S. 64, 58 S.Ct. 817, 82 L.Ed. 1188 (1938)(in diversity cases, the federal courts will apply federal rules of procedure but State substantive law). *See* discussion of the *Erie* Doctrine in Part II of this text.

12. *See Sokol Crystal Prods., Inc. v. DSC Commc'ns Corp.*, 15 F.3d 1427 (7th Cir.1994); *Smith v. Chesapeake & Ohio Ry.*, 778 F.2d 384 (7th Cir.1985).

13. *See Toth v. Corning Glass Works*, 411 F.2d 912 (6th Cir.1969)(refusal to strike a pleading's claim deemed harmless).

14. *See Prete v. Bradbury*, 438 F.3d 949, 959–60 (9th Cir.2006).

15. *See Lippoldt v. Cole*, 468 F.3d 1204, 1221 (10th Cir. 2006).

16. *See Walter Kidde Portable Equip., Inc. v. Universal Sec. Instruments, Inc.*, 479 F.3d 1330, 1340 (Fed.Cir. 2007).

17. *See Harnden v. Jayco, Inc.*, 496 F.3d 579, 583 (6th Cir. 2007).

18. *See Kight v. Auto Zone, Inc.*, 494 F.3d 727, 732–733 (8th Cir. 2007); *Nimely v. City of New York*, 414 F.3d 381, 399–400 (2d Cir.2005); *United States v. Kim*, 111 F.3d 1351, 1363 (7th Cir.1997).

19. *See Abrams v. Lightolier Inc.*, 50 F.3d 1204, 1213 (3d Cir.1995); *Sokol Crystal Prods., Inc. v. DSC Commc'ns Corp.*, 15 F.3d 1427, 1435 (7th Cir.1994).

20. *See In re Air Crash Disaster*, 86 F.3d 498, 531 (6th Cir.1996); *La Crosse County v. Gershman, Brickner & Bratton, Inc.*, 982 F.2d 1171, 1175 (7th Cir.1993).

21. *See Grizzle v. Travelers Health Network, Inc.*, 14 F.3d 261, 269 (5th Cir. 1994)(court must consider curative instructions when assessing harmlessness). In

prejudice or to have substantially influenced the jury.[22] However, evidentiary rulings that affected the substantial rights of a party are *not* harmless, and the rulings must be reversed.[23] Thus, if the trial evidence is not sufficient to support the verdict without the wrongfully admitted evidence, the ruling is prejudicial.[24] In making this "harmlessness" evaluation, the court considers the centrality of the evidence and the prejudicial effect of the inclusion or exclusion of the evidence.[25] The court also examines whether other evidence is "sufficiently strong" to support a conclusion that the evidentiary error had no effect on the outcome.[26] The courts often begin with a "presumption of prejudice"[27]–thus, only if the court can say "with fair assurance" that the judgment was not substantially affected by the wrongfully admitted or excluded evidence, the error will be considered harmless.[28] The courts are particularly careful in discounting an error as harmless in close cases.[29]

> *Expert Testimony:* This same harmless error standard applies to challenges to expert testimony as well.[30]

> *Effect of Multiple Errors:* Although each individual evidentiary error might not, standing alone, have affected a party's substantial rights, the court may find that the collective effect of

ruling on the effect of the curative instructions, a court will assume that the jury obeyed the court and followed its instructions. *Trademark Research Corp. v. Maxwell Online, Inc.*, 995 F.2d 326, 340 (2d Cir.1993). *Compare Davidson v. Smith*, 9 F.3d 4 (2d Cir.1993)(improper testimony not cured by trial instructions) *with Trademark Research Corp. v. Maxwell Online, Inc.*, 995 F.2d 326 (2d Cir.1993) (trial error deemed cured by court's instructions).

22. *See Muldrow ex rel. Estate of Muldrow v. Re–Direct, Inc.*, 493 F.3d 160, 168 (D.C.Cir. 2007); *Fort v. C.W. Keller Trucking, Inc.*, 330 F.3d 1006 1013 (7th Cir. 2003); *Blake v. Pellegrino*, 329 F.3d 43, 49 (1st Cir.2003); *Anderson v. WBMG–42*, 253 F.3d 561, 563 (11th Cir.2001). *See also Hynes v. Coughlin*, 79 F.3d 285, 291 (2d Cir.1996)(tests for whether improperly admitted evidence substantially influenced the jury include: examining whether evidence was unimportant in relation to all other issues jury considered, whether evidence bore on an issue that was plainly critical to the jury's deliberations, and whether the evidence was emphasized during jury argument).

23. *See Kight v. Auto Zone, Inc.*, 494 F.3d 727, 732–733 (8th Cir. 2007); *Becker v. ARCO Chem. Co.*, 207 F.3d 176, 180 (3d Cir.2000); *Costantino v. David M. Herzog, M.D., P.C.*, 203 F.3d 164, 174 (2d Cir.2000).

24. *See S.E.C. v. Happ*, 392 F.3d 12, 28 (1st Cir.2004); *Havrum v. United States*, 204 F.3d 815, 818 (8th Cir.2000).

25. *See Nieves–Villanueva v. Soto–Rivera*, 133 F.3d 92, 102 (1st Cir.1997).

26. *See Goebel v. Denver & Rio Grande W. R.R. Co.*, 215 F.3d 1083, 1089 (10th Cir.2000).

27. *See Jerden v. Amstutz*, 430 F.3d 1231, 1240–41 (9th Cir.2005).

28. *See Pelletier v. Main St. Textiles, LP*, 470 F.3d 48, 52–53 (1st Cir. 2006); *Tesser v. Board of Educ. of City Sch. Dist. of New York*, 370 F.3d 314, 319–20 (2d Cir.2004); *Blake v. Pellegrino*, 329 F.3d 43, 49 (1st Cir.2003). *See also Mihailovich v. Laatsch*, 359 F.3d 892, 913–14 (7th Cir. 2004) (errors in evidence satisfy standard only if significant chance exists that errors affected trial's outcome); *Goodman v. Pennsylvania Turnpike Com'n*, 293 F.3d 655, 667 (3d Cir.2002) (evidentiary admission error is harmless, and not grounds for reversal, if it is "highly probable" that jury would have reached same result otherwise).

29. *See Sims v. Great American Life Ins. Co.*, 469 F.3d 870, 886 (10th Cir. 2006); *Nimely v. City of New York*, 414 F.3d 381, 400 (2d Cir.2005).

30. *See Dresser–Rand Co. v. Virtual Automation Inc.*, 361 F.3d 831, 842 (5th Cir. 2004).

multiple evidentiary errors deprived the moving party of a fair trial.[31]

Errors in Jury Instructions

Jury instructions must be considered in their entirety.[32] If the charging errors would not have changed the trial result,[33] or if the parties waived the errors by failing to timely object,[34] challenges to jury instructions will be rejected as harmless.[35] Conversely, if the jury may have based their verdict on an erroneous instruction, a new trial is warranted.[36]

Errors in Ruling on Counsel's Conduct During Trial

Misconduct by counsel during trial will be deemed harmless unless the court determines that the misconduct affected the verdict.[37]

Errors in Bench Judgments

A court's error in applying a method of damages valuation (one to which there was no testimony or other record basis) may be

31. *See Jerden v. Amstutz*, 430 F.3d 1231, 1240–41 (9th Cir.2005); *Gomez v. Rivera Rodriguez*, 344 F.3d 103, 118 (1st Cir. 2003); *Phoenix Assocs. III v. Stone*, 60 F.3d 95, 105 (2d Cir.1995); *Kopf v. Skyrm*, 993 F.2d 374, 381 (4th Cir.1993).

32. *See Elwell v. University Hosps. Home Care Servs.*, 276 F.3d 832, 844 (6th Cir.2002); *Dadian v. Village of Wilmette*, 269 F.3d 831, 839 (7th Cir.2001).

33. *See Richards v. Relentless, Inc.*, 341 F.3d 35, 48 (1st Cir.2003) (new trial necessary only if instruction error could have affected jury's deliberation); *Elwell v. University Hosps. Home Care Servs.*, 276 F.3d 832, 844 (6th Cir.2002) (assessing ruling in context of instructions as a whole, ruling "harmless because risk of jury confusion was minimal"); *Dadian v. Village of Wilmette*, 269 F.3d 831, 839 (7th Cir.2001) (testing whether instructions, as a whole, sufficiently informed jury correctly as to applicable law and thus did not affect substantial rights of parties).

34. *See Foley v. Commonwealth Elec. Co.*, 312 F.3d 517, 520 (1st Cir.2002) (if party properly objects to jury instruction, harmless error Rule 61 applies; if proper objection not made, plain error rule applies which requires proof of: (1) error, (2) that error was plain, (3) that error likely altered outcome, and (4) that error was sufficiently fundamental to threaten fairness, integrity, or public reputation of judicial proceedings).

35. *See Terminate Control Corp., Nu-Life Const. Corp. v. Horowitz*, 28 F.3d 1335

(2d Cir.1994)(jury instructions warrant a new trial only if the court is persuaded, based on the record as a whole, that the error was prejudicial or the charge was highly confusing).

36. *See Dossett v. First State Bank*, 399 F.3d 940, 950 (8th Cir.2005) (ruling was not harmless where it eliminated potentially viable avenue to establish liability); *S.E.C. v. Yun*, 327 F.3d 1263, 1282 (11th Cir.2003) (granting new trial due to court's erroneous jury instruction, reinforced in counsel's closing argument); *Jannotta v. Subway Sandwich Shops, Inc.*, 125 F.3d 503, 515 (7th Cir.1997) (holding that instructional error was not harmless if it provided jury with inadequate understanding of the law and caused prejudice to the complaining party); *Coleman v. B–G Maintenance Mgmt. of Colo., Inc.*, 108 F.3d 1199, 1204–05 (10th Cir.1997)(because the jury, in all probability, based its verdict on erroneous instruction, jury's verdict must be reversed).

37. *Cf.* Rule 39(c)(relating to advisory juries). *See Peterson v. Willie*, 81 F.3d 1033, 1036 (11th Cir.1996)(noting that statements made during oral arguments will not constitute reversible error unless they are plainly unwarranted and clearly injurious); *Westfarm Assocs. Ltd. Partnership v. Washington Suburban Sanitary Com'n*, 66 F.3d 669, 685 n. 10 (4th Cir. 1995)(inappropriate allusion made during closing argument, followed by proper instructions from the court, is not basis for reversal).

deemed harmless if the effect of the error caused no prejudice.[38]

Error in Granting or Denying Jury Trial

The court's mistaken decision to grant a jury trial is generally harmless error,[39] but an improper denial of a jury trial is usually grounds for reversal.[40]

ADDITIONAL RESEARCH REFERENCES

Wright & Miller, *Federal Practice and Procedure* §§ 2881–88.

C.J.S. Federal Civil Procedure §§ 1062–1100 et seq., 1241–1247 et seq.

West's Key No. Digests, Federal Civil Procedure ⊙2333–2353, 2651–2656.

38. *See United States v. 191.07 Acres of Land*, 482 F.3d 1132, 1137 (9th Cir. 2007) (finding valuation error was harmless as to appellants because it resulted in a higher award than appellants (using other method) would otherwise have received).

39. *See Mateyko v. Felix*, 924 F.2d 824, 828 (9th Cir.1990). *See also Venture Properties, Inc. v. First Southern Bank,* 79 F.3d 90, 92 (8th Cir.1996)(movant demonstrated no prejudice from court's decision to conduct a jury trial rather than a bench trial).

40. *See Burns v. Lawther*, 53 F.3d 1237, 1241–42 (11th Cir.1995) (harmless error rule may be applied to improper denials of trial by jury, but only if the issues could have been resolved by summary judgment or judgment as a matter of law); *King v. United Benefit Fire Ins. Co.,* 377 F.2d 728, 731 (10th Cir.1967)(denial will be deemed harmless where only a question of law is involved or where a verdict for the movant would have been set aside). *See also Sailor v. Hubbell, Inc.,* 4 F.3d 323 (4th Cir. 1993)(denial of jury trial harmless if it did not affect party's rights, such as where no reasonable jury could have found in that party's favor).

RULE 62

STAY OF PROCEEDINGS TO ENFORCE A JUDGMENT

(a) Automatic Stay; Exceptions for Injunctions, Receiverships, and Patent Accountings. Except as stated in this rule, no execution may issue on a judgment, nor may proceedings be taken to enforce it, until 10 days have passed after its entry. But unless the court orders otherwise, the following are not stayed after being entered, even if an appeal is taken:

(1) an interlocutory or final judgment in an action for an injunction or a receivership; or

(2) a judgment or order that directs an accounting in an action for patent infringement.

(b) Stay Pending the Disposition of a Motion. On appropriate terms for the opposing party's security, the court may stay the execution of a judgment—or any proceedings to enforce it—pending disposition of any of the following motions:

(1) under Rule 50, for judgment as a matter of law;

(2) under Rule 52(b), to amend the findings or for additional findings;

(3) under Rule 59, for a new trial or to alter or amend a judgment; or

(4) under Rule 60, for relief from a judgment or order.

(c) Injunction Pending an Appeal. While an appeal is pending from an interlocutory order or final judgment that grants, dissolves, or denies an injunction, the court may suspend, modify, restore, or grant an injunction on terms for bond or other terms that secure the opposing party's rights. If the judgment appealed from is rendered by a statutory three-judge district court, the order must be made either:

(1) by that court sitting in open session; or

(2) by the assent of all its judges, as evidenced by their signatures.

(d) Stay with Bond on Appeal. If an appeal is taken, the appellant may obtain a stay by supersedeas bond, except in an action described in Rule 62(a)(1) or (2). The bond may be given upon or after filing the notice of appeal or after obtaining the order allowing the appeal. The stay takes effect when the court approves the bond.

(e) Stay Without Bond on an Appeal by the United States, Its Officers, or Its Agencies. The court must not require a bond, obligation, or other security from the appellant when granting a stay on an appeal by the United States, its officers, or its agencies or on an appeal directed by a department of the federal government.

(f) Stay in Favor of a Judgment Debtor Under State Law. If a judgment is a lien on the judgment debtor's property under the law of the state where the court is located, the judgment debtor is entitled to the same stay of execution the state court would give.

(g) Appellate Court's Power Not Limited. This rule does not limit the power of the appellate court or one of its judges or justices:

(1) to stay proceedings—or suspend, modify, restore, or grant an injunction—while an appeal is pending; or

(2) to issue an order to preserve the status quo or the effectiveness of the judgment to be entered.

(h) Stay with Multiple Claims or Parties. A court may stay the enforcement of a final judgment entered under Rule 54(b) until it enters a later judgment or judgments, and may prescribe terms necessary to secure the benefit of the stayed judgment for the party in whose favor it was entered.

[Amended effective March 19, 1948; October 20, 1949; July 19, 1961; August 1, 1987; April 30, 2007, effective December 1, 2007.]

──────────── **2007 AMENDMENTS ROADMAP** ────────────

STYLE PROJECT CHANGES: Minor changes in language were made throughout the Rule. Minor changes in the titles of subsections were also made. Within some subsections, additional subparagraphs were added and numbered to aid readability.

NON-STYLE CHANGES: The last sentence of old Rule 62(a), which had heretofore provided that Rule 62(c) governed suspension, modification, restoration, or grant of an injunction while an appeal was pending, was deleted as unnecessary.

AUTHORS' COMMENTARY ON RULE 62

——————————— PURPOSE AND SCOPE ———————————

Rule 62 provides for stays to prevent the enforcement of judgments pending post-trial motions and appeals.

NOTE: Except for a ten-day stay immediately following entry of judgment as provided by Rule 62(a), post-trial motions and appeals do not automatically stay enforcement of judgments.

RULE 62(a). AUTOMATIC STAY; EXCEPTIONS FOR INJUNCTIONS, RECEIVERSHIPS, AND PATENT ACCOUNTINGS

CORE CONCEPT

The automatic stay postpones enforcement of a judgment for ten days from the date of entry of the judgment. However, Rule 62(a) provides no automatic stay in three circumstances: (1) an interlocutory or final judgment in an action for an injunction; (2) an interlocutory or final judgment in a receivership action; and (3) a judgment or order directing an accounting in an action for infringement of letters patent.

APPLICATIONS

Effect

An automatic stay will prevent the enforcement of the judgment, but the stay will not affect the appealability of the judgment or the running of the appeal time.[1] Additionally, the judgment has *res judicata* effect during the pendency of the appeal.[2]

Judgments Covered

The automatic stay applies to any judgment defined in Rule 54(a).[3]

Expiration of Stay Period

Once the automatic stay period expires, a party may seek enforcement of the judgment.[4]

---

1. FED.R.APP.P. 4(a).

2. *See, e.g., Fish Market Nominee Corp. v. Pelofsky,* 72 F.3d 4, 7 (1st Cir. 1995)(noting distinction between bar to enforcing judgment and absence of bar to *res judicata*).

3. *But cf., Arnold v. Garlock, Inc.,* 278 F.3d 426, 437 (5th Cir.2001) (remand of pending case to state court is not final judgment and therefore Rule 62 has no applicability to remands).

4. *See, e.g., Acevedo–Garcia v. Vera–Monroig,* 368 F.3d 49, 58 (1st Cir.2004)

Armed Services Personnel

The Soldiers and Sailors Civil Relief Act of 1940, 50 U.S.C.A. §§ 203–04, Appendix §§ 523–24, provides that a court may stay the execution of any judgment entered against a person in the military service, or vacate or stay an attachment or garnishment.

Relation to Rule 6(a)

Although there is little authority on point, it appears that for purposes of 10–day stays under Rule 62(a), time shall be computed under the standards of Rule 6(a).[5]

RULE 62(b). STAY PENDING THE DISPOSITION OF A MOTION

CORE CONCEPT

After judgment, a court has discretion to order a stay while it considers post-trial motions. The court also has discretion to establish conditions for the security of the adverse party during the pendency of the stay.

APPLICATIONS

Security

The court has discretion not only to order a stay pending post-trial motions, but may order the movant to post security, including the amount of the judgment and interest, during the period of the stay. The court may also require the bond to include costs and damages for delay or any other loss that may result during the period of the stay. Additionally, the court may order the movant to provide written notice to the opposing parties of any material disposition of the movant's assets.

Effect of Denial

When the court denies a stay pending disposition of a post trial motion, judgment is binding (and may be enforced) until vacated by the court or reversed on appeal.

Procedure

The filing of post-trial motions does not stay execution of the judgment or the proceeding in execution. Hence, a party should assert the motion for stay before the end of the 10–day automatic stay period, provided under Rule 62(a). Once the motion for stay is made, the court has discretion to stay execution or enforcement of the judgment pending disposition of the post-trial motions.

("The federal rules contemplate that, absent a stay, a victorious plaintiff may execute on the judgment even while an appeal of that judgment is pending.").

5. *See, e.g., KRW Sales, Inc. v. Kristel Corp.,* 154 F.R.D. 186, 188 (N.D.Ill. 1994)(computing 10 days for purposes of Rule 62(a) under standards of Rule 6(a)).

RULE 62(c). INJUNCTION PENDING AN APPEAL

CORE CONCEPT

Rule 62(c) authorizes the district judge or a district court of three judges having granted, dissolved, or denied a preliminary or final injunction to stay its decision or grant other interim relief pending appeal.[6]

NOTE: There are no automatic stays in injunction actions. Injunction actions may be stayed only by court order. The district court has discretion to determine whether to grant a stay.[7]

APPLICATIONS

Scope

Rule 62(c) expressly covers interlocutory as well as final judgments in injunction cases and applies to cases where the court has denied an injunction as well as granted an injunction. However, the district court may not dissolve an injunction that has been appealed. Instead, the court may only modify the injunction while it is being appealed, with the purpose of maintaining the status quo.[8]

Time for Motion

A party should make a motion to stay an injunction immediately after the notice of appeal has been filed and may make this motion at any time while the appeal is pending.[9]

Which Court

The movant should first assert the motion in the district court. If the district court denies relief or the district court provides inadequate relief, the movant may assert the motion in the court of appeals.[10] Where submission to a panel would prejudice the mov-

6. See also A & M Records, Inc. v. Napster, Inc., 284 F.3d 1091, 1099 (9th Cir. 2002) (Rule 62(c) "authorizes a district court to continue supervising compliance with the injunction." Affirming district court's decision to continue to supervise defendant's compliance with injunction.).

7. See, e.g., LiButti v. United States, 178 F.3d 114, 121 (2d Cir.1999) ("It has been long-established law that simply filing an appeal from the grant or denial of an injunction—absent a stay of further proceedings—does not enjoin the operative effect of the trial court's ruling from which the appeal is taken.").

8. See, e.g., Mayweathers v. Newland, 258 F.3d 930, 935 (9th Cir.2001) (filing of notice of appeal generally strips district court of jurisdiction over case, but Rule 62(c) is exception; under Rule 62(c) district court may issue second injunction while first injunction is under appeal–provided that new injunction does not change status quo); Natural Resources Defense Council v. Southwest Marine, Inc., 242 F.3d 1163,

1166 (9th Cir.2001) (Rule 62(c) gives district court authority only to take steps to maintain status quo while case is pending on appeal; district court has no authority to re-visit the merits of case on appeal). But cf., Pro–Edge, L.P. v. Gue, 419 F.Supp.2d 1064, 1077 (N.D. Iowa 2006) ("It is settled that the pendency of [an appeal of a grant of a preliminary injunction] does not divest a district court of jurisdiction to proceed with other aspects of the case.").

9. See, e.g., Credit Suisse First Boston Corp. v. Grunwald, 400 F.3d 1119, 1124 (9th Cir.2005) (motion may be made "at any time before entry of a final judgment"); Minnesota Humane Society v. Clark, 184 F.3d 795, 797 (8th Cir.1999) (denial of preliminary injunction that was sought to bar removal and killing of geese should have caused plaintiff to seek prompt appeal under 28 U.S.C. § 1292 and request for injunction pending appeal).

10. FED.R.APP. 8(a). See Rakovich v. Wade, 834 F.2d 673, 675 (7th Cir. 1987)(movant should first seek relief in dis-

ant, the motion can be made to a single judge of the court of appeals.[11] In extraordinary circumstances, pending disposition of an application for writ of certiorari and during the pendency of an appeal to the court of appeals [12] or from a final judgment of the court of appeals,[13] a single justice of the Supreme Court, sitting as a single Circuit Justice, may take any action provided in Rule 62(g).[14] In addition, a judge of the court rendering the judgment may grant a stay on application for writ of certiorari to the Supreme Court.[15]

Requirements

Rule 62(c) authorizes the court to issue a stay to maintain the status quo or the effectiveness of the final judgment during the pendency of an appeal. When a party makes a motion under Rule 62(c), the courts will require the movant to show the following elements: [16] (a) a strong likelihood of success on the merits of the appeal; (b) that unless the motion is granted the movant will suffer irreparable injury; (c) no substantial harm will come to other interested parties; and (d) a grant of the motion will not harm the public interest. The courts have often balanced the irreparable injury to the movant if the court did not issue the stay against the harm the stay would cause to the other parties and to the public. The governing considerations are the same whether the party applies to the district court or to the appellate courts under Rule 62(g).

Requirements of Order

An injunctive order issued pursuant to Rule 62(c) must set forth the reasons for its issuance and be specific in its terms in compliance with the requirements of Rule 65(d).

Security for Stay

The court may order the movant to post security during the period of the stay or the injunction.

Three Judge District Court

When a district court of three judges, sitting by statute, renders judgment in an injunction case, a motion to that judgment should be addressed to all three judges. Such a court may only issue a stay pending an appeal in open court or by signature of all three judges.

trict court; if district court denies relief, movant may then seek stay in court of appeals).

11. FED.R.APP. 8(a).

12. *Atiyeh v. Capps,* 449 U.S. 1312, 101 S.Ct. 829, 66 L.Ed.2d 785 (1981)(per Justice Rehnquist).

13. *Graddick v. Newman,* 453 U.S. 928, 102 S.Ct. 4, 69 L.Ed.2d 1025 (1981); *Holtzman v. Schlesinger,* 414 U.S. 1304, 94 S.Ct. 1, 38 L.Ed.2d 18 (1973)(per Justice Marshall).

14. 28 U.S.C.A. § 1651(a); U.S.Sup. Ct.R. 23.

15. 28 U.S.C.A. 2101(f).

16. *See, e.g., Michigan Coalition of Radioactive Material Users, Inc. v. Griepentrog,* 945 F.2d 150, 153 (6th Cir.1991); *Cuomo v. United States Nuclear Regulatory Commission,* 772 F.2d 972, 974 (D.C. Cir. 1985) (per curiam) (citing same four factors; also noting "[A] movant need not always establish a high probability of success on the merits. Probability of success is inversely proportional to the degree of irreparable injury evidenced. A stay may be granted with either a high probability of success and some injury, or *vice versa*.") .

RULE 62(d). STAY WITH BOND UPON APPEAL

CORE CONCEPT

The act of appealing a judgment does not automatically create a stay of the judgment pending appeal.[17] However, a party may obtain a stay by filing a supersedeas bond with the court (*i.e.,* a bond posted as security against an appeal) that is approved by the court. Unless state law provides otherwise (as described in Rule 62(f)), Rule 62(d) governs the only circumstances in which a party may obtain a stay of enforcement of a money judgment pending appeal,[18] beyond the automatic 10–day period provided by Rule 62(a).

APPLICATIONS

Stay as of Right

By posting a supersedeas bond with the court and upon approval of the bond by the court, a party may obtain a stay upon appeal as a matter of course.[19]

Amount of Bond

The amount of the bond will usually be an amount sufficient to satisfy the judgment plus interest.[20] The court may also require the bond to include costs,[21] plus any damages for delay. The court has the discretion to provide a lesser amount or other types of security.[22] Local rule may provide the amount required.

Alternatives to Bond

Although Rule 62(d) speaks only of bonds, courts may permit "other forms of judgment guarantee." [23]

---

17. *See, e.g., Correa v. Cruisers,* 298 F.3d 13, 29 (1st Cir.2002) ("[T]here is no requirement that the judgment become final before it can be enforced.").

18. *See, e.g., Cleveland Hair Clinic, Inc. v. Puig,* 104 F.3d 123, 125 (7th Cir. 1997)(Rule 62(d) stay may also prevent enforcement of final decision to sanction parties and attorney for misconduct in case; applicability of Rule 62(d) not limited to circumstances involving only judgments).

19. *See, e.g., Hoban v. Washington Metropolitan Area Transit Authority,* 841 F.2d 1157, 1159 (D.C.Cir.1988) (per curiam)(posting bond under Rule 62(d) creates stay). *But see, National Labor Relations Board v. Westphal,* 859 F.2d 818, 819 (9th Cir.1988)(Rule 62(d) stay as of right limited to money judgments; no right to stay order enforcing subpoenas).

20. *See, e.g., Strong v. Laubach,* 443 F.2d 1297, 1299 (10th Cir.2006) (bond "is usually for the full amount of the judgment").

21. F.R.A.P. 7.

22. *See, e.g., Olcott v. Delaware Flood Co.,* 76 F.3d 1538, 1559 (10th Cir. 1996)(bond normally equals amount of judgment; trial court, however, has discretion to require lesser amount; but no discretion, apparently to require bond in amount greater than judgment). *Dillon v. City of Chicago,* 866 F.2d 902 (7th Cir. 1988)(identifying circumstances when other guarantees are appropriate).

23. *See, e.g., Arban v. West Publishing Corp.,* 345 F.3d 390, 409 (6th Cir.2003) (bond that meets requirements of Rule 62(d) entitles party to stay as of right; however, even in absence of bond, court has discretion to issue stay); *Dale M. v. Board of Education,* 237 F.3d 813, 815 (7th Cir. 2001) (judgment debtor who pays judgment and does not choose to post bond under Rule 62(d) has not rendered appeal moot and is entitled to repayment of judgment if reversed); *In the Matter of Carlson,* 224

Deadline for Posting Bond

Rule 62(d) permits the bond to be posted at the time a party files a notice of appeal (or receives permission to appeal), or later. However, because the stay does not become effective until the court approves the bond, it is wise to post the bond within the 10–day period of the automatic stay provided by Rule 62(a).[24]

Actions Not Stayed

Rule 62(d), by its own terms, does not apply to the three circumstances enunciated in Rule 62(a). Those circumstances are: judgments in injunction actions; judgments in receivership actions; and judgments requiring an accounting in patent infringement cases. In such cases an appealing party may not post a bond and obtain a stay of judgment under Rule 62(d).

Judgments for Damages and Injunctions

If a party seeks to use Rule 62(d) to stay a judgment by which the court ordered both money damages and equitable relief, the stay under Rule 62(d) is effective only to stop enforcement of the damage award.[25] Unless the appealing party can persuade the court to stay the injunction under Rule 62(c), the injunction portion of the judgment may be enforced pending appeal.

Failure to Post Bond

Failure to post bond under Rule 62(d) does not affect a party's right to appeal.[26] However, in the absence of a stay ordered

---

F.3d 716, 719 (7th Cir.2000) (waiver of bond requirement "is appropriate only if the appellant has a clearly demonstrated ability to satisfy the judgment if the appeal is unsuccessful and there is no other concern that the appellee's rights will be compromised by a failure adequately to secure the judgment"); *FDIC v. Ann–High Associates*, 129 F.3d 113 (2d Cir.1997) (per curiam) (court has discretion to waive bond requirement "if the appellant provides an acceptable alternative means of securing the judgment"); *Olympia Equipment Leasing Corp. v. Western Union Telegraph Co.*, 786 F.2d 794, 796 (7th Cir.1986) ("[A]n inflexible requirement of a bond would be inappropriate in two sorts of case: where the defendant's ability to pay the judgment is so plain that the cost of the bond would be a waste of money; and–the opposite case, one of increasing importance in an age of titanic damage judgments–where the requirement would put the defendant's other creditors in undue jeopardy.").

24. *But see, Equal Employment Opportunity Commission v. Clear Lake Dodge*, 25 F.3d 265, 273 (5th Cir.1994)(Rule 62(d) permits posting of bond at or after filing notice

of appeal; thus, to post bond prior to appealing is inappropriate).

25. *N.L.R.B. v. Westphal*, 859 F.2d 818 (9th Cir.1988)(Rule 62(d) cannot stay injunctions). *But cf., Venus Lines Agency v. CVG Industria Venezolana De Aluminio, C.A.*, 210 F.3d 1309, 1313 (11th Cir.2000) (per curiam) (seizure of property to secure enforcement of any award issued in pending arbitration proceeding; held, determination that stay is justified in circumstances of a non-money judgment depends on following factors: "(1) whether the stay applicant has made a strong showing that [it] is likely to succeed on the merits; (2) whether the applicant will be irreparably injured absent a stay; (3) whether the issuance of a stay will substantially injure the other parties interested in the proceeding; and (4) where the public interest lies"; brackets in original).

26. *See, e.g., Porco v. Trustees of Indiana University*, 453 F.3d 390, 394 (7th Cir. 2006) (failure to obtain stay under Rule 62(d) does not ordinarily moot appeal); *In re American President Lines, Inc.*, 779 F.2d 714, 718 (D.C.Cir.1985)(per curiam)(failure to post bond leaves appellant vulnerable to enforcement of judgment, but does not forfeit right of appeal).

pursuant to Rule 62(d), an adverse party may enforce a judgment while the appeal is pending,[27] which sometimes may render the appeal moot.[28]

It should be noted that while Rule 62(d) mandates a stay when an appropriate supersedeas bond is filed, some courts may grant stays notwithstanding the absence of a bond.[29] To determine which courts follow this practice, attorneys are advised to consult local practice.

Impact of Appeal by Prevailing Party

If the prevailing party also appeals some facet of a district court's judgment, there is some conflict in the cases as to whether the judgment debtor must post a bond to stay execution of judgment pending the judgment debtor's appeal.[30] Attorneys are urged to consult local precedent.

Relation to Rule 11

Inappropriate use of Rule 62(d) bonds may be grounds for sanctions under Rule 11.

RULE 62(e).   STAY WITHOUT BOND ON AN APPEAL BY THE UNITED STATES, ITS OFFICERS, OR ITS AGENCIES

CORE CONCEPT

The United States is not required to post a bond to obtain a stay of the enforcement of a judgment pending appeal.   This exemption also

---

27. *See, e.g., Eurasia International, Ltd. v. Holman Shipping Co.,* 411 F.3d 578, 585 (5th Cir.2005) (failure to post bond means no automatic stay may issue; bond requirement not met by filing motion to stay that was contingent on filing bond); *In re American President Lines, Inc.,* 779 F.2d 714, 718 (D.C. Cir.1985) (per curiam) (failure to post bond leaves appellant vulnerable to enforcement of judgment, but does not forfeit right of appeal).

28. *But see Strong v. Laubach,* 443 F.3d 1297, 1299 (10th Cir.2006) (judgment debtor who does not post bond may nonetheless appeal; upon successful appeal, district court may (on motion or sua sponte) order disgorgement of benefit previously obtained by judgment creditor; but in such circumstances, risk that judgment creditor is insolvent falls on judgment debtor).

29. *See, e.g., Federal Prescription Service, Inc. v. American Pharmaceutical Association,* 636 F.2d 755, 759 (D.C. Cir. 1980) ("[The Rule] speaks only to stays granted as a matter of right, it does not speak to stays granted by the court in accordance with its discretion;" collecting cases);

Southeast Booksellers Association v. McMaster, 233 F.R.D. 456, 458 (D.S.C.2006) ("Rule 62(d) does not address, and hence does not preclude, issuance of a stay on the basis of some lesser bond, or indeed, no bond.").

30. *Compare Tennessee Valley Authority v. Atlas Machine and Iron Works, Inc.,* 803 F.2d 794, 797 (4th Cir.1986) (appeal by prevailing party suspends judgment; thus losing party need not post supersedeas bond to prevent execution on judgment while losing party's appeal is pending), *with Trustmark Insurance Co. v. Gallucci,* 193 F.3d 558–59 (1st Cir.1999) (noting split of authority; concluding that appeal by prevailing party eliminates obligation of judgment debtor to post bond under Rule 62(d) to stay execution of money judgment only when basis of prevailing party's appeal is inconsistent with enforcement of judgment; requiring bond when prevailing party's appeal was only for denial of pre-judgment interest, which is not inconsistent with immediate enforcement of judgment).

extends to officers and agents of the United States government, and any party acting under the direction of any department or agency of the government, as provided by 28 U.S.C.A. § 2408.

RULE 62(f). STAY IN FAVOR OF A JUDGMENT DEBTOR UNDER STATE LAW

CORE CONCEPT

When the judgment creates a lien upon the debtor's property and the judgment debtor is entitled to a stay under applicable state law, the district court shall stay the enforcement of the judgment to the same extent that state law directs a state court to enter a stay.[31] The court has no discretion to deny such a stay.[32] Moreover, while the normal practice anticipates that the judgment debtor will file a motion for a stay, there appears to be no requirement for such a motion and the stay can become effective even in the absence of a motion.[33]

RULE 62(g). APPELLATE COURT'S POWER NOT LIMITED

CORE CONCEPT

The provisions of Rule 62 apply only to district courts, and do not limit appellate courts.

RULE 62(h). STAY WITH MULTIPLE CLAIMS OR PARTIES

CORE CONCEPT

When a court issues a partial judgment under Rule 54(b), it may allow immediate enforcement of the partial judgment or it may stay enforcement of the partial judgment pending a further adjudication.

APPLICATIONS

Time for Filing

A party must make a motion for stay upon partial judgment after the entry of the partial judgment and during the ten-day automatic stay period.

---

31. See, e.g., Hoban v. Washington Metropolitan Area Transit Authority, 841 F.2d 1157, 1159 (D.C.Cir.1988)(per curiam)(if state law authorizes stay without requiring a supersedeas bond, stay imposed under rule 62(f) must also be unencumbered by bond).

32. Cf., Rodriguez–Vazquez v. Lopez–Martinez, 345 F.3d 13, 14 (1st Cir.2003) ("Our own inclination is to think that where a lien can be procured [under state law] by minor ministerial acts, this minor

burden on the judgment-creditor should not preclude a stay under Rule 62(f)." Citing division of authority in district courts).

33. See, e.g., Whitehead v. Food Max of Mississippi, Inc., 332 F.3d 796, 804–05 (5th Cir.2003) (en banc) (no requirement for a formal motion to grant a Rule 62(f) stay; if sanctions under Rule 11 are appropriate because prevailing party violated stay, the absence of a Rule 62(f) motion does not prevent imposition).

Standards for Granting a Stay

The court has discretion to decide a motion for stay, balancing the equities of the parties and considering the administration of the case.[34]

Independent Actions

When a court consolidates several independent actions and renders judgment on one of the independent actions, this is not considered a partial judgment under Rule 54(b), and a stay will not be granted under Rule 62(h).[35]

Posting of Security

When issuing a stay of a particular judgment, the court may require security to be posted to secure that part of the judgment.[36]

ADDITIONAL RESEARCH REFERENCES

Wright & Miller, *Federal Practice and Procedure: Civil 2d* §§ 2901–20.

C.J.S. Federal Civil Procedure § 1263; Federal Courts § 294(1–5) et seq.

West's Key No. Digests, Federal Civil Procedure ⚷2700; Federal Courts ⚷684–687.

34. *See, e.g., North Penn Transfer, Inc. v. Maple Press Co.,* 176 B.R. 372, 375–77 (M.D.Pa.1995)(judgment for plaintiff on unpaid shipping charges stayed under Rule 62(h) so that defendant can challenge reasonableness of shipping rates before regulatory agency; citing possibility that immediate enforcement of judgment would make defendant insolvent). *See also ITV Direct, Inc. v. Healthy Solutions, L.L.C.,* 445 F.3d 66 (1st Cir.2006) (party may also preserve claim and argue for reversal on appeal).

35. *In re Massachusetts Helicopter Airlines, Inc.,* 469 F.2d 439, 442 (1st Cir. 1972)(Rule 62(h) applicable only to circumstances governed by Rule 54(b); independent actions cannot be stayed under Rule 62(h)).

36. *Curtiss-Wright Corp. v. General Electric Co.,* 446 U.S. 1, 13, 100 S.Ct. 1460, 64 L.Ed.2d 1 (1990) ("[W]e assume it would be within the power of the District Court to protect all parties by having the losing party deposit the amount of the judgment with the court.").

RULE 63

JUDGE'S INABILITY TO PROCEED

If a judge conducting a hearing or trial is unable to proceed, any other judge may proceed upon certifying familiarity with the record and determining that the case may be completed without prejudice to the parties. In a hearing or a nonjury trial, the successor judge must, at a party's request, recall any witness whose testimony is material and disputed and who is available to testify again without undue burden. The successor judge may also recall any other witness.

[Amended effective August 1, 1987; December 1, 1991; April 30, 2007, effective December 1, 2007.]

─────────────── **2007 AMENDMENTS ROADMAP** ───────────────

STYLE PROJECT CHANGES: Cumbersome wording was revised. "Must" replaced "shall".

NON-STYLE CHANGES: None.

NOTE: The Federal Rules "Style Project" is explained in Part III-A.

AUTHORS' COMMENTARY ON RULE 63
─────────────── **PURPOSE AND SCOPE** ───────────────

When a judge withdraws after a trial or hearing begins, any other judge of the court may proceed with the case. The successor judge will read the pertinent portions of the record, certify familiarity with that record, and then decide whether he or she may proceed with the case without causing prejudice to the parties. In a non-jury hearing or trial format, if the successor judge proceeds with the case, he or she must recall any witnesses requested by the parties, if their testimony is material and disputed and where the witnesses are available to testify again without undue burden. In addition, the successor judge may recall any witnesses in order to become more familiar with the record.

APPLICATIONS

Caution in Relying on Pre–1992 Case Law

Rule 63 was substantially amended in late 1991 to expand the Rule's scope and to alter certain interpretations given to the Rule by the courts. Decisions that predate the 1991 amendment should be cited with due care.[1]

Conditions for Inability to Proceed

A judge's withdrawal must rest on compelling reasons, such as sickness, death, or other disability, including recusal and disqualification.[2] A judge may not withdraw for personal convenience.[3]

Statement of Grounds for Withdrawal

The withdrawing judge must state on the record the reasons for his or her withdrawal.[4]

Timing of Substitution

The original text of Rule 63 implied that, once a trial or hearing had begun, district judges could not be substituted unless the departing judge had already filed findings of fact and conclusions of law. The courts embraced this implication and, unless the parties stipulated otherwise, required new trials where the departing judge had not filed the findings and conclusions.[5]

This "negative inference" mandate ascribed to Rule 63 was abolished in 1991. Citing the increasing length of trials in federal court and the expected concomitant increase in the number of trials interrupted by a judge's disability,[6] the drafters provided that a substitution may be made after trial commences and even in the absence of filed findings and conclusions, if the replacement judge (1) can certify his or her familiarity with the proceedings in the case to date, and (2) can continue the proceedings without prejudicing the parties.

Certifying Familiarity With the Record

Once a trial or hearing has begun, no substitute judge can replace a departing judge without first "certifying familiarity with the record".[7] It is this certification procedure that ensures that Due

---

1. *But see Zand v. Commissioner,* 143 F.3d 1393, 1400 (11th Cir.1998) (court may look to pre–1991 decisions for guidance given facts of particular case).

2. *See* Rule 63 advisory committee notes to 1991 amendment. *See also* 28 U.S.C. §§ 144 & 455 (providing for disqualification of judges).

3. *See* Rule 63 advisory committee notes to 1991 amendment.

4. *See* Rule 63 advisory committee notes to 1991 amendment.

5. *See, e.g., In re Higginbotham,* 917 F.2d 1130, 1132 (8th Cir.1990); *Olle v. Henry & Wright Corp.,* 910 F.2d 357, 361 (6th Cir.1990); *Home Placement Serv., Inc. v. Providence Journal Co.,* 819 F.2d 1199, 1202 (1st Cir.1987); *Whalen v. Ford Motor Credit Co.,* 684 F.2d 272, 274 n. 5 (4th Cir.1982), *cert. denied,* 459 U.S. 910, 103

S.Ct. 216, 74 L.Ed.2d 172 (1982); *Thompson v. Sawyer,* 678 F.2d 257, 268–69 (D.C.Cir.1982); *Arrow-Hart, Inc. v. Philip Carey Co.,* 552 F.2d 711, 713 (6th Cir.1977).

6. *See* Rule 63 advisory committee notes to 1991 amendment. *See also Mergentime Corp. v. Washington Metro. Area Transit Auth.,* 166 F.3d 1257, 1262 (D.C.Cir.1999) (noting motivation for Rule change, and commenting that successor judges may now take over at any point after the trial begins, subject to certain additional responsibilities imposed upon the successor judges).

7. *See Maritimes & Northeast Pipeline, L.L.C. v. 0.714 Acres of Land, More or Less, in Danvers, Mass.,* 2007 WL 2461054, at *1 (D.Mass. 2007) (successor judge certification).

Process is not violated when the case resumes.[8] Although an express "certification" is plainly preferred,[9] the court of appeals will likely not reverse in the absence of an express certification so long as the successor judge's statements confirm compliance with the record familiarity requirement.[10] This certification requirement obligates the substitute judge to read and consider all relevant portions of the record.[11] What portions of the record the successor judge is required to learn depends upon the nature of the successor judge's role in the case. For example, if the successor judge inherits a jury trial before the evidence has closed, she must become familiar with the entire record so as to properly rule upon relevance-based evidentiary objections; but if the successor judge inherits the case after the entry of verdict or judgment, she need only review those portions of the record relevant to the particular issues challenged by post-trial motions.[12]

Prerequisite for Substitution

In order for a judge to be substituted, there must be an available transcript or a videotape to permit the replacement judge to become familiar with the proceedings that occurred prior to the substitution. The Committee Notes encourage the prompt preparation of the trial or videotape transcript, so as to prevent delaying the jury longer than necessary.[13]

Jury Trials

In a jury trial, the parties do not have the right to insist that a witness be recalled.[14] Instead, if the successor judge can certify familiarity with the record and can determine that the proceedings are able to be completed without prejudice to the parties, nothing more is required.[15] Should she choose to do so, however, the successor judge has the discretion to recall a witness in her own right.[16]

Bench Trials

In a non-jury trial, the parties can insist that the successor judge recall a witness whose testimony is material and disputed *and* who is available to testify again:[17]

8. *See Patelco Credit Union v. Sahni,* 262 F.3d 897, 905 (9th Cir.2001).

9. *See, e.g., Vescio v. Merchants Bank,* 272 B.R. 413, 420 (D.Vt.2001) ("The Court hereby certifies pursuant to Fed.R.Civ.P. 63 that it has reviewed the transcript of the trial, together with the exhibits, and that the proceedings in this case may be completed without prejudice to the parties").

10. *See Bisbal-Ramos v. City of Mayaguez,* 467 F.3d 16, 26 (1st Cir. 2006); *Mergentime Corp. v. Washington Metro. Area Transit Auth.,* 166 F.3d 1257, 1265 (D.C.Cir.1999).

11. *See Mergentime Corp. v. Washington Metro. Area Transit Auth.,* 166 F.3d 1257, 1265 (D.C.Cir.1999); *Canseco v. United States,* 97 F.3d 1224, 1226 (9th Cir.1996) (as amended Dec. 18, 1996).

12. *See Mergentime Corp. v. Washington Metro. Area Transit Auth.,* 166 F.3d 1257, 1265 (D.C.Cir.1999).

13. *See* Rule 63 advisory committee notes to 1991 amendment.

14. *See Jackson v. Alabama State Tenure Com'n,* 405 F.3d 1276, 1286–87 (11th Cir.2005).

15. *See Jackson v. Alabama State Tenure Com'n,* 405 F.3d 1276, 1287 (11th Cir. 2005).

16. *See* Rule 63.

17. *See* Rule 63. *See also Jackson v. Alabama State Tenure Com'n,* 405 F.3d 1276, 1286–87 (11th Cir.2005).

(1) *Testimony of Available Witness:* When a witness is available, the successor judge may decide to hear the witness' testimony if the testimony is material or disputed. It may be error for the court to decline to hear the testimony of a witness whose credibility is material to a finding of fact, particularly if a party so requests.[18]

(2) *Testimony of Unavailable Witness:* If a witness has become unavailable, such that a subpoena to compel testimony at trial is unavailable, the successor judge can consider the testimony recorded at trial or, if the testimony was not material or not disputed, may choose not to hear the testimony at all.[19]

Previously Litigated Issues

Unless the controlling law has changed, the successor judge will not ordinarily revisit rulings made by the withdrawing judge. However, the successor judge is required to consider and rule upon allegations of trial error properly raised in post-trial motions.[20]

Option To Enter Summary Judgment

If, after reviewing the trial transcript, the court decides that no credibility determinations are required and that one party is entitled to a judgment as a matter of law, summary judgment can be entered as an alternative to the successor judge "stepping into the shoes" of the unavailable trial judge.[21]

Removed Cases

Where the parties or issues permit a belated removal of a State court proceeding, the federal court may enter judgment upon the State court jury's verdict.[22]

Waiver of Right to Object to New Judge

Following the departure of the original judge, the litigants may be deemed to have waived any objection to the case's reassignment to a new judge if the litigants fail either to timely seek a new trial or

---

18. *See* Rule 63 advisory committee notes to 1991 amendment. *See also Mergentime Corp. v. Washington Metro. Area Transit Auth.*, 166 F.3d 1257, 1266 (D.C.Cir. 1999) (holding that, upon request of party, district court must recall any witness whose testimony is material and disputed and who, without undue burden, is available to testify again); *Canseco v. United States*, 97 F.3d 1224, 1227 (9th Cir.1996) (as amended Dec. 18, 1996) (where credibility of witness is questioned, and where sufficiency of the evidence hinges on that witness's testimony and credibility cannot be determined from the record, substitute judge must recall the witness, if available without undue burden, and make own credibility determination); *Chemoil Holding Co. v. Delta Commodities,*

Inc., 1998 WL 474216, at *2 (E.D.La.1998) (recalling witnesses where litigation involved factual disputes necessitating credibility determinations).

19. *See* Rule 63 advisory committee notes to 1991 amendment.

20. *See Mergentime Corp. v. Washington Metro. Area Transit Auth.*, 166 F.3d 1257, 1263 (D.C.Cir.1999) (holding that successor judge may not refuse to consider post-trial motions out of deference to the original judge).

21. *See Patelco Credit Union v. Sahni*, 262 F.3d 897, 906 (9th Cir.2001).

22. *See Sweeney v. Resolution Trust Corp.*, 16 F.3d 1, 5–6 (1st Cir.1994).

timely object to a reassignment.[23] Minimally, a failure to object will likely relegate the appellate court to the very forgiving "plain error" standard of review.[24]

ADDITIONAL RESEARCH REFERENCES

Wright & Miller, *Federal Practice and Procedure: Civil 2d* §§ 2921–30.

C.J.S. Judges §§ 35–68.

West's Key No. Digests, Judges ⊶21, 32.

23. *See Zand v. Commissioner*, 143 F.3d 1393, 1400 (11th Cir.1998) (ruling that parties had "cleverly tiptoe[d]" across a "procedural tightrope", refusing to consent to a reassignment while, simultaneously, failing to seek the added expense of a retrial; therefore, an unfavorable verdict by the successor judge could not be challenged under Rule 63).

24. *See Bisbal–Ramos v. City of Mayaguez*, 467 F.3d 16, 26 (1st Cir. 2006).

VIII.   PROVISIONAL AND FINAL REMEDIES

RULE 64

SEIZING A PERSON OR PROPERTY

(a) Remedies Under State Law—In General. At the commencement of and throughout an action, every remedy is available that, under the law of the state where the court is located, provides for seizing a person or property to secure satisfaction of the potential judgment. But a federal statute governs to the extent it applies.

(b) Specific Kinds of Remedies. The remedies available under this rule include the following—however designated and regardless of whether state procedure requires an independent action:

- arrest;

- attachment;

- garnishment;

- replevin;

- sequestration; and

- other corresponding or equivalent remedies.

───────── **2007 AMENDMENTS ROADMAP** ─────────

STYLE PROJECT CHANGES: Minor changes were made in the title of the Rule and in some language within the Rule. The Rule was divided into two subsections (heretofore it had been a single paragraph), each with an individual subtitle. New Rule 64(b) also contains six "bullet" subparts, which aid readability but do not change the substance of the Rule.

NON-STYLE CHANGES: New Rule 64 no longer expressly provides that the Civil Rules govern an action in which a remedy is sought under Rule 64. That provision was considered redundant in light of the provision of Rule 1 (applying Civil Rules to "all civil actions") and Rule 81(c)(1) (applying Civil Rules to all removed actions).

NOTE: The Federal Rules "Style Project" is explained in Part III-A.

AUTHORS' COMMENTARY ON RULE 64

―――――――――― PURPOSE AND SCOPE ――――――――――

After the commencement of an action and until the time of judgment, Rule 64 provides means by which a claimant may seek an order of court to seize a person or property in order to secure satisfaction of the eventual judgment. Relief under Rule 64 is infrequently granted and should be infrequently sought.

RULE 64(a). REMEDIES UNDER STATE LAW—IN GENERAL

CORE CONCEPT

Rule 64(a) provides that federal courts possess the same remedies for seizing a person or property that are available to a state court in the state where the federal court is located. However, Rule 64(a) provides that if a federal statute is applicable, it governs in place of state law.

APPLICATIONS

Time to Seek an Order

At any time after the commencement of an action and until the time of judgment,[1] a party may assert an ancillary claim in the pending action or file an independent action to seize property under Rule 64.

Sources of Remedies

The claimant must seek the applicable federal remedy, if a specific federal remedy exists.[2] The Advisory Committee Notes to Rule 64 list some of the federal remedies. Otherwise, the movant may choose any provisional remedy under applicable state law.[3]

RULE 64(b). SPECIFIC KINDS OF REMEDIES

CORE CONCEPT

Rule 64(b) provides a non-exclusive list of remedies available to a federal court, without regard to how a state may designated those

---

1. *See, e.g., Rosen v. Cascade International, Inc.,* 21 F.3d 1520, 1530 (11th Cir. 1994)(Rule 64 authorizes prejudgment attachment in some situations); *But see, Credit Managers Association of Southern California v. Kennesaw Life and Accident Insurance Co.,* 25 F.3d 743, 750 (9th Cir. 1994)(permitting use of Rule 64 to satisfy existing judgment; but Rule 64 deferred to state law, which prohibited satisfaction on instant facts).

2. *See, e.g., Hoult v. Hoult,* 373 F.3d 47, 54 (1st Cir.2004) ("federal statute governs to the extent applicable").

3. *See, e.g., Goya Foods, Inc. v. Wallack Management Co.,* 290 F.3d 63, 70 (1st Cir. 2002) ("By its terms [Rule 64] allows a federal court to borrow provisional remedies created by state law."); *Stephens v. National Distillers and Chemical Corp.,* 69 F.3d 1226, 1228 n. 2 (2d Cir.1995) (noting that Rule 64 incorporates state remedies).

remedies. It also provides that a district court may use those remedies without the need to follow state rules that may otherwise require an independent enforcement action.

Method for Obtaining Relief

Where a federal remedy exists, the procedure for obtaining relief will be provided by the relevant statute and the Rules. When relief is sought under a state remedy, state law generally supplies the procedures, except to the extent that the Rules apply. The method for obtaining relief will vary from state to state and district to district. However, in all cases a U.S. Marshal rather than a state officer would seize the goods or property.

Jurisdiction

Procedures under Rule 64 whether asserted in a pending action or in an independent action do not require a separate basis of subject matter jurisdiction.[4]

Constitutional Limitations

The seizure of a person or property without notice or a prior hearing may often be a violation of constitutional due process.[5]

Relation to Rule 65

It now appears settled that in cases involving only money damages on an unsecured claim, a party may not use Rule 65 (governing preliminary injunctions and temporary restraining orders) to obtain a prejudgment injunction aimed at preventing dissipation of assets. Instead, such relief must be sought under other provisions, such as Rule 64's authorization to use state law prejudgment attachment provisions.[6] However, if the lawsuit also seeks equitable relief, the district court is not restricted by Rule 64 and may still grant a prejudgment injunction that freezes specific assets that are the subject of a restitution or recission claim or that preserves the power of the court to grant final injunctive relief.[7]

---

4. *Cf., Skevofilax v. Quigley,* 810 F.2d 378 (3d Cir.1987).

5. *North Georgia Finishing, Inc. v. Di–Chem, Inc.,* 419 U.S. 601, 95 S.Ct. 719, 42 L.Ed.2d 751 (1975) (*Fuentes v. Shevin* is weakened); *Mitchell v. W.T. Grant Co.,* 416 U.S. 600, 94 S.Ct. 1895, 40 L.Ed.2d 406 (1974); *Fuentes v. Shevin,* 407 U.S. 67, 92 S.Ct. 1983, 32 L.Ed.2d 556 (1972).

6. *Grupo Mexicano de Desarrollo, S.A. v. Alliance Bond Fund, Inc.,* 527 U.S. 308, 330–31, 119 S.Ct. 1961, 1968–75, 144 L.Ed.2d 319 (1999) (in case involving only general creditor seeking damages at law and with no lien in specific property of defendant, Rule 65 may not be used to obtain prejudgment injunction because, *inter alia,* such use of Rule 65 would render Rule 64 "a virtual irrelevance. Why go

through the trouble of complying with local attachment and garnishment standards when this all-purpose prejudgment injunction is available?").

7. *See, e.g., United States ex rel. Rahman v. Oncology Associates,* 198 F.3d 489, 495–97 (4th Cir.1999) (explaining relationship of *Grupo Mexicano* to earlier Supreme Court precedent authorizing use of prejudgment injunction in equity cases; also noting that equity court "has enhanced authority when the public interest is involved"). *See also De Beers Consolidated Mines, Ltd. v. United States,* 325 U.S. 212, 219, 65 S.Ct. 1130, 1133–34, 89 L.Ed. 1566 (1945) ("A preliminary injunction is always appropriate to grant intermediate relief of the same character as that which may be granted finally"; however, in instant case property

Armed Services Personnel

Provisional relief under Rule 64 is subject to the Soldiers' and Sailors' Civil Relief Act of 1940, 50 U.S.C.A. §§ 203, 204, Appendix §§ 523, 524, which prohibits seizure of the assets of absent military personnel in many circumstances.

Execution

A plaintiff who recovers judgment is entitled to an execution sale of the previously seized property in satisfaction of the judgment.

ADDITIONAL RESEARCH REFERENCES

Wright & Miller, *Federal Practice and Procedure: Civil 2d* §§ 2931–40.

C.J.S. Federal Civil Procedure §§ 233–241, 1271.

West's Key No. Digests, Federal Civil Procedure ☞581–590, 601–610.

affected by injunction lies outside issues of case; also noting, *inter alia,* that relief government requested was not available under Rule 64); *Deckert v. Independence Shares Corp.,* 311 U.S. 282, 289, 61 S.Ct. 229, 233, 85 L.Ed. 189 (1940) (in case where equita-ble remedy of recission is sought, district court has authority to issue prejudgment injunction freezing assets as means of pre-serving status quo pending final outcome of case).

RULE 65

INJUNCTIONS AND RESTRAINING ORDERS

(a) Preliminary Injunction.

(1) *Notice.* The court may issue a preliminary injunction only on notice to the adverse party.

(2) *Consolidating the Hearing with the Trial on the Merits.* Before or after beginning the hearing on a motion for a preliminary injunction, the court may advance the trial on the merits and consolidate it with the hearing. Even when consolidation is not ordered, evidence that is received on the motion and that would be admissible at trial becomes part of the trial record and need not be repeated at trial. But the court must preserve any party's right to a jury trial.

(b) Temporary Restraining Order.

(1) *Issuing Without Notice.* The court may issue a temporary restraining order without written or oral notice to the adverse party or its attorney only if:

(A) specific facts in an affidavit or a verified complaint clearly show that immediate and irreparable injury, loss, or damage will result to the movant before the adverse party can be heard in opposition; and

(B) the movant's attorney certifies in writing any efforts made to give notice and the reasons why it should not be required.

(2) *Contents; Expiration.* Every temporary restraining order issued without notice must state the date and hour it was issued; describe the injury and state why it is irreparable; state why the order was issued without notice; and be promptly filed in the clerk's office and entered in the record. The order expires at the time after entry—not to exceed 10 days—that the court sets, unless before that time the court, for good cause, extends it for a like period or the adverse party consents to a longer extension. The

reasons for an extension must be entered in the record.

(3) *Expediting the Preliminary–Injunction Hearing.* If the order is issued without notice, the motion for a preliminary injunction must be set for hearing at the earliest possible time, taking precedence over all other matters except hearings on older matters of the same character. At the hearing, the party who obtained the order must proceed with the motion; if the party does not, the court must dissolve the order.

(4) *Motion to Dissolve.* On 2 days' notice to the party who obtained the order without notice—or on shorter notice set by the court—the adverse party may appear and move to dissolve or modify the order. The court must then hear and decide the motion as promptly as justice requires.

(c) Security. The court may issue a preliminary injunction or a temporary restraining order only if the movant gives security in an amount that the court considers proper to pay the costs and damages sustained by any party found to have been wrongfully enjoined or restrained. The United States, its officers, and its agencies are not required to give security.

(d) Contents and Scope of Every Injunction and Restraining Order.

(1) *Contents.* Every order granting an injunction and every restraining order must:

(A) state the reasons why it issued;

(B) state its terms specifically; and

(C) describe in reasonable detail—and not by referring to the complaint or other document—the act or acts restrained or required.

(2) *Persons Bound.* The order binds only the following who receive actual notice of it by personal service or otherwise:

(A) the parties;

(B) the parties' officers, agents, servants, employees, and attorneys; and

(C) other persons who are in active concert or participation with anyone described in Rule 65(d)(2)(A) or (B).

(e) Other Laws Not Modified. These rules do not modify the following:

(1) any federal statute relating to temporary restraining orders or preliminary injunctions in actions affecting employer and employee;

(2) 28 U.S.C. § 2361, which relates to preliminary injunctions in actions of interpleader or in the nature of interpleader; or

(3) 28 U.S.C. § 2284, which relates to actions that must be heard and decided by a three-judge district court.

(f) Copyright Impoundment. This rule applies to copyright-impoundment proceedings.

[Amended effective March 19, 1948; October 20, 1949; July 1, 1966; August 1, 1987; April 23, 2001, effective December 1, 2001; April 30, 2007, effective December 1, 2007.]

───────────── **2007 AMENDMENTS ROADMAP** ─────────────

STYLE PROJECT CHANGES: Minor changes were made in the title of the Rule and in some language within the Rule. Subsections (b), (d), and (e) were broken into additional subparagraphs to aid readability.

NON-STYLE CHANGES: The last sentence of old Rule 65, providing expressly that Rule 65.1 applies to a surety upon a bond or undertaking governed by Rule 65, was deleted as redundant. Additionally, a perceived ambiguity in old Rule 65(d) was corrected. The perception was that old Rule 65(d) did not literally provide that a party or its various agents had to receive actual notice before the party could be bound by an injunction. New Rule 65(d)(2) clarifies that ambiguity by expressing the established principle that actual notice must be provided. Finally, new Rule 65(d)(2) expresses more clearly the established principle that an injunction may be enforced against persons not parties or agents of a party, but who act in concert with such parties or agents and who receive actual notice.

NOTE: The Federal Rules "Style Project" is explained in Part III-A.

───────────────────────────────

AUTHORS' COMMENTARY ON RULE 65

───────────── **PURPOSE AND SCOPE** ─────────────

Rule 65 establishes the procedural requirements for obtaining a temporary restraining order or a preliminary injunction. It is important to note that although a party must satisfy the procedures of Rule 65 before a court will grant such injunctive relief, the substantive requirements for an injunction are separate from and additional to Rule 65, and they must also be satisfied.[1]

The substantive requirements for injunctions are found predominantly in federal case law, as well as federal statutes authorizing injunctions in certain circumstances and limiting their applicability in others. Although there can be substantial variations in the requirements from one circuit to another, courts deciding whether to grant an injunction generally weigh some or all of the following factors: (1) whether the potential harm to the person seeking injunctive relief is irreparable,[2] *i.e.,* whether such harm could be cured through an award of money damages instead of an injunction;[3] (2) whether the person against whom an injunction would be entered would be harmed excessively by the injunction; (3) whether, and to what extent, the grant or denial of an injunction would affect interests of third persons, including public interests; and (4) when a motion for a temporary restraining order or a preliminary injunction is before the court, whether the person seeking such relief is likely to prevail on the merits when the case comes to trial.[4]

1. *See, e.g. United States v. Cohen,* 152 F.3d 321, 324 (4th Cir.1998) ("[Rule] 65 is not a source of power for a district court to enter an injunction. Rather, it regulates the issuance of injunctions otherwise authorized.").

2. *See, e.g., Rodriguez v. DeBuono,* 175 F.3d 227, 235 (2d Cir.1999) (per curiam) (noting that both preliminary and permanent injunction require a showing of irreparable harm; however, standard for obtaining preliminary injunction is nevertheless more stringent, because moving party must also demonstrate "imminence" of harm, which is not required for grant of permanent injunction). *But cf., Prayze FM v. Federal Communications Commission,* 214 F.3d 245, 250 (2d Cir.2000) (where government seeks preliminary injunction for violation of statute irreparable nature of injury is rebuttably presumed; distinguishing private injunction claims).

3. *Cf., Grupo Mexicano de Desarrollo, S.A. v. Alliance Bond Fund, Inc.,* 527 U.S. 308, 119 S.Ct. 1961, 144 L.Ed.2d 319 (1999) (in action for money damages on contract claim district court lacks jurisdiction to issue preliminary injunction preventing defendants' transfer of assets prior to judgment). *See also Lakeview Technology, Inc. v. Robinson,* 446 F.3d 655 (7th Cir.2006) (if issue is whether the person to be enjoined will be able to pay damages in the absence of an injunction, the issue may be neutral-

ized if that person provides a "non-injunction" bond that will compensate opponent if no injunction is granted and opponent is thereby damaged).

4. *See, e.g., Prairie Band of Potawatomi Indians v. Pierce,* 253 F.3d 1234 (10th Cir. 2001) (citing all four factors, but observing that if party seeking preliminary relief can establish last three factors, application of first factor is "less strict"); *United States v. Power Engineering Co.,* 191 F.3d 1224, 1230 (10th Cir.1999) (citing use of all four factors; also noting that "[a] mandatory preliminary injunction (*i.e.,* one that directs a party to act) imposes an even heavier burden on [the movant] of showing that the four factors ... weigh heavily and compellingly in movant's favor"). *But cf., Heideman v. South Salt Lake City,* 348 F.3d 1182, 1189 (10th Cir.2003) (if movant can show that latter three "harm" factors tip "*decidedly*" in its favor, it is entitled to a "somewhat relaxed" burden on probability of success standard; however, no such leniency applies to application for injunction against government action undertaken in public interest); *New Comm Wireless Services, Inc. v. SprintCom, Inc.,* 287 F.3d 1, 9 (1st Cir. 2002) ("The sine qua non of this four-part inquiry is likelihood of success on the merits: if the moving party cannot demonstrate that he is likely to succeed in his quest, the remaining factors become matters of idle curiosity.").

NOTE: It is important to keep in mind that most of Rule 65 applies only to requests for preliminary relief. With the exception of Rule 65(d), discussed below, Rule 65 has no application to grants or denials of permanent injunctions.[5]

RULE 65(a). PRELIMINARY INJUNCTION

CORE CONCEPT

Rule 65(a) contains two distinct concepts. The first portion of the Rule ensures that courts will not grant applications for preliminary injunctions until affected parties receive notice and an opportunity to oppose the proposed preliminary injunction. The second part of Rule 65(a) provides that the court may consolidate an application for a preliminary injunction with a trial on the merits, to the extent that consolidation is feasible under the facts of the particular case.

APPLICATIONS

Purpose

The purpose of a preliminary injunction is usually to maintain the status quo until the merits of a case can be decided.[6] Courts grant preliminary injunctions ordering an alteration of the status quo only in unusual circumstances where the merits clearly favor one party over another.[7] A preliminary injunction can only apply during the pendency of the case, at the end of which the court may consider whether to enter a permanent injunction.

Relation to Rule 64

It now appears settled that in cases involving only money damages on an unsecured claim, a party may not use Rule 65 (governing preliminary injunctions and temporary restraining orders) to obtain a prejudgment injunction aimed at preventing dissipation of assets. Instead, such relief must be sought under other provisions, such as Rule 64's authorization to use state law prejudgment attachment provisions.[8] However, if the lawsuit also seeks

---

5. *See, e.g., United States v. Criminal Sheriff, Parish of Orleans,* 19 F.3d 238 (5th Cir.1994)(Rule 65 does not apply to permanent injunctions).

6. *See, e.g., Resolution Trust Corp. v. Cruce,* 972 F.2d 1195, 1198 (10th Cir. 1992)(primary purpose of preliminary injunction is to preserve status quo).

7. *See, e.g., Dominion Video Satellite, Inc. v. EchoStar Satellite Corp.,* 269 F.3d 1149, 1154–55 (10th Cir.2001) (movant has "heightened burden of showing that the traditional four factors weigh heavily and compellingly in its favor before obtaining a preliminary injunction. . . . The heightened

burden applies to preliminary injunctions that (1) disturb the status quo, (2) mandatory rather than prohibitory, or (3) provide the movant substantially all the relief it could feasibly attain after a full trial on the merits. . . . This court disfavors such injunctions."); *Aoude v. Mobil Oil Corp.,* 862 F.2d 890, 893 (1st Cir.1988)("[On] the peculiar facts of this case, the preliminary injunction is not vulnerable to attack even if it is seen as changing the status quo.").

8. *Grupo Mexicano de Desarrollo, S.A. v. Alliance Bond Fund, Inc.,* 527 U.S. 308, 330–31, 119 S.Ct. 1961, 1968–75, 144 L.Ed.2d 319 (1999) (in case involving only general creditor seeking damages at law

equitable relief, the district court is not restricted by Rule 64 and may still grant a prejudgment injunction that freezes specific assets that are the subject of a restitution or recission claim or that preserves the power of the court to grant final injunctive relief.[9]

Comparison With Temporary Restraining Order

A temporary restraining order is also directed at freezing circumstances in place until further action can be taken. However, in certain circumstances discussed below, Rule 65(b) permits a temporary restraining order to issue without notice to the opposing party. Temporary restraining orders issued without notice are effective for no more than ten days, and may be extended without the consent of the opposing party only once, for a maximum of ten additional days. Courts often use temporary restraining orders to maintain the status quo until there is an opportunity for a fuller hearing on a motion for a preliminary injunction.[10]

Appeal

A court's decision to grant, deny, dissolve, continue, or modify a preliminary injunction is immediately appealable of right pursuant to 28 U.S.C.A. § 1292(a)(1).[11]

(1). NOTICE

Contents of Notice

Rule 65(a)(1) prohibits issuance of a preliminary injunction without notice to the opposing party.[12] However, the Rule contains no provisions governing what constitutes adequate notice. Generally, courts require at a minimum that opposing parties be served with copies of the motion for a preliminary injunction and any supporting

---

and with no lien in specific property of defendant, Rule 65 may not be used to obtain prejudgment injunction because, *inter alia,* such use of Rule 65 would render Rule 64 "a virtual irrelevance. Why go through the trouble of complying with local attachment and garnishment standards when this all-purpose prejudgment injunction is available?").

9. *See, e.g., United States ex rel. Rahman v. Oncology Associates,* 198 F.3d 489, 495–97 (4th Cir.1999) (explaining relationship of *Grupo Mexicano* to earlier Supreme Court precedent authorizing use of prejudgment injunction in equity cases; also noting that equity court "has enhanced authority when public interest is involved"). *See also De Beers Consolidated Mines, Ltd. v. United States,* 325 U.S. 212, 219, 65 S.Ct. 1130, 1133–34, 89 L.Ed. 1566 (1945) ("A preliminary injunction is always appropriate to grant intermediate relief of the same character as that which may be granted finally"; however, in instant case property af-

fected by injunction lies outside issues of case; also noting, *inter alia,* that relief government requested was not available under Rule 64); *Deckert v. Independence Shares Corp.,* 311 U.S. 282, 289, 61 S.Ct. 229, 233, 85 L.Ed. 189 (1940) (in case where equitable remedy of recission is sought, district court has authority to issue prejudgment injunction freezing assets as means of preserving status quo pending final outcome of case).

10. *See, e.g., Hospital Resource Personnel, Inc. v. United States,* 860 F.Supp. 1554, 1556 (S.D.Ga.1994)(granting restraining order so that court can "conduct a thorough inquiry" on injunction).

11. *See, e.g., Nutrasweet Co. v. Vit–Mar Enterprises, Inc.,* 112 F.3d 689 (3d Cir.1997) (so noting).

12. *Cf., Western Water Management, Inc. v. Brown,* 40 F.3d 105, 109 (5th Cir. 1994)(prohibiting modification of injunction in absence of notice).

documents, along with notification of the date of a proposed hearing.[13]

Scope of Hearing

Rule 65 requires that the court hold a hearing before granting or refusing a preliminary injunction. However, the scope of such a hearing is subject to the discretion of the trial court.[14]

Timing of Service

A motion for a preliminary injunction should meet the timeliness requirements of Rule 6(d), which generally provides that motions should be served no less than five days before the date of a proposed hearing on the motion.[15]

(2). CONSOLIDATION OF HEARING WITH TRIAL ON MERITS

Standard for Consolidation

The court has discretion to consolidate the preliminary injunction hearing with the trial on the merits.[16] Parties seeking a quick

---

13. *Granny Goose Foods, Inc. v. Brotherhood of Teamsters & Auto Truck Drivers Local No. 70,* 415 U.S. 423, 433 n. 7, 94 S.Ct. 1113, 1122, 39 L.Ed.2d 435 (1974) (same day notice is inadequate; distinguishing between less formal notice requirements of restraining order versus requirement of Rule 65(a) that "implies a hearing in which the defendant is given a fair opportunity to oppose the application and to prepare for such opposition"). *See, e.g., Wyandotte Nation v. Sebelius,* 443 F.3d 1247, 1253 (10th Cir.2006) (rejecting need to give minimum five days notice, but holding that failure of district court to give notice that injunction was being considered was "obvious violation of Rule 65 and is a clear abuse of discretion"); *PCI Transportation, Inc. v. Fort Worth & Western Railroad Co.,* 418 F.3d 535 (5th Cir.2005) (where facts are disputed, parties are entitled to fair hearing); *United States v. Microsoft Corp.,* 147 F.3d 935 (D.C.Cir.1998) (held, preliminary injunction entered without adequate notice; plaintiff's request for contempt citation, arising from previous consent decree, did not constitute adequate notice because standards for contempt and for preliminary injunction are different); *Parker v. Ryan,* 960 F.2d 543, 544 (5th Cir. 1992) (notice should provide opponent with at least a fair opportunity to prepare opposition; generally such notice "should comply with Rule 6(d), which requires five days notice before a hearing on a motion"). *But cf., Dominion Video Satellite, Inc. v. Echo-Star Satellite Corp.,* 269 F.3d 1149, 1154 (10th Cir.2001) (noting that most circuits have not incorporated Rule 6(d)'s five day

notice requirement into Rule 65(a)(1)); holding that three days was sufficient in circumstances of instant case; *Harris County, Texas v. CarMax Auto Superstores, Inc.,* 177 F.3d 306 (5th Cir.1999) (notice under Rule 65(a)(1) should normally comply with Rule 6(d), which normally requires notice of at least five days; in apparent dicta, however, court observed that while defendant received only three days formal notice, defendant had "ample" informal notice; court also observed that at hearing, defendant called witnesses, presented exhibits, engaged in vigorous cross-examination, and never sought postponement of hearing).

14. *See, e.g., McDonald's Corp. v. Robertson,* 147 F.3d 1301, 1311–13 (11th Cir. 1998) ("Rule 65 does not [always] require an evidentiary hearing;" undisputed material facts require no hearing, but "bitterly disputed" facts do; in cases where facts are clear but dispute exists as to which important inferences to draw, trial court has substantial discretion as to whether to hold evidentiary hearing); *Campbell Soup Co. v. Giles,* 47 F.3d 467 (1st Cir.1995) (sometimes it is acceptable to consider documentary evidence only; evidentiary hearing may be curtailed or eliminated when speedy decision is required); *Schulz v. Williams,* 38 F.3d 657, 658 (2d Cir.1994) (per curiam)(parties entitled only to "reasonable opportunity" to contest evidence).

15. *Cf., e.g., Gomperts v. Chase,* 404 U.S. 1237, 92 S.Ct. 16, 30 L.Ed.2d 30 (1971)(Douglas, J., in chambers)(three days insufficient to prepare for or implement preliminary injunction).

decision in the case may consent to consolidation, because Rule 65(a)(2) provides that the schedule for the trial will be advanced to the date of the preliminary injunction hearing. However, the tactical consequences that can follow from such an approach should not be overlooked.[17] If the case on the merits is not yet ripe for trial, as when discovery is not yet completed, courts will not consolidate the trial with the preliminary injunction hearing.[18]

Timing of Order to Consolidate

Rule 65(a)(2) permits the court to order consolidation before or after commencement of the hearing on the preliminary injunction. This authorization is construed to mean that courts will not order consolidation unless all parties had adequate warning of the possibility of consolidation and a reasonable opportunity to prepare their positions on the merits.[19]

Preliminary Injunction Evidence

If the court decides not to consolidate the preliminary injunction hearing with trial on the merits, evidence presented at the hearing is nonetheless preserved as part of the record. Significantly, Rule 65(a)(2) provides that the evidence need not be repeated for trial and may be used as it was inserted in the record of the hearing, consistent with the rules of evidence.[20]

---

16. *See, e.g., American Train Dispatchers Department of the Brotherhood of Locomotive Engineers v. Fort Smith Railroad Co.,* 121 F.3d 267, 270 (7th Cir.1997) (so holding; noting also that district court must provide parties with "clear and unambiguous notice" of intent to do so). *See also Teva Pharmaceuticals USA, Inc. v. Food & Drug Administration,* 441 F.3d 1, 3 (D.C. Cir.2006) (permitting consolidation of hearing on preliminary injunction with motion for summary judgment).

17. *See, e.g., Rodriguez v. DeBuono,* 175 F.3d 227, 235 (2d Cir.1999) (per curiam) (standard for permanent injunction is less stringent than standard for preliminary injunction because, *e.g.,* motion for permanent injunction does not have to demonstrate potential for "imminent" irreparable harm, while motion for preliminary injunction must make such a showing).

18. *Pughsley v. 3750 Lake Shore Drive Cooperative Building,* 463 F.2d 1055, 1057 (7th Cir.1972)("A litigant applying for a preliminary injunction should seldom be required either to forego discovery in order to seek emergency relief, or to forego a prompt application for an injunction in order to prepare adequately for trial.").

19. *University of Texas v. Camenisch,* 451 U.S. 390, 101 S.Ct. 1830, 68 L.Ed.2d 175 (1981)(parties entitled to clear notice of intent to consolidate so that parties can prepare). *See also, American Train Dispatchers of International Brotherhood of Locomotive Engineers v. Fort Smith Railroad Co.,* 121 F.3d 267 (7th Cir.1997) ("Because different standards of proof may apply in the hearing than in the trial, parties must be given a clear chance to object or to propose special procedures for the consolidation."). *But cf., Aponte v. Calderon,* 284 F.3d 184, 190 (1st Cir.2002) (although notice must be early enough "to allow the parties time to assemble and present their evidence," an objection to lack of timely notice is lost if a "party does not object contemporaneously with the court's notice of consolidation"); *Campaign for Family Farms v. Glickman,* 200 F.3d 1180, 1186 (8th Cir.2000) (When dealing "with a purely legal issue on a fixed administrative standard ... a district court may properly reach the merits in such a case without expressly ordering consolidation under Rule 65 and without giving the parties adequate notice.").

20. *Dupuy v. Samuels,* 423 F.3d 714, 722 n. 3 (7th Cir.2005).

Trial by Jury

Rule 65(a)(2) directs that it be construed so that consolidation and/or preservation of evidence for trial does not interfere with a party's right to a jury trial. Thus, if the court decides a motion for a preliminary injunction by ruling on some issues of fact, evidence presented on those issues of fact is preserved for trial. However, the trier of fact at trial is not bound by the previous findings of fact made by the court in the preliminary injunction hearing.[21]

Modifying or Dissolving a Preliminary Injunction

Although Rule 65(a) is silent on the matter, a preliminary injunction can be modified or dissolved on motion of party who demonstrates that the purpose of the injunction has been fulfilled.[22] Thus, a preliminary injunction not to interfere with the destruction of a derelict building is fulfilled when the building is destroyed.

RULE 65(b).   TEMPORARY RESTRAINING ORDER

CORE CONCEPT

Rule 65(b) provides the procedure for obtaining a temporary restraining order. Although the Rule permits a party to obtain a temporary restraining order without first providing notice to opposing parties, it restricts such relief to circumstances where it is clear that notice was not feasible, and limits the duration of such restraining orders to a maximum of twenty days.

APPLICATIONS

Purpose

The purpose of a temporary restraining order is generally to hold the status quo in place until the court has an opportunity to hear a request for fuller relief, such as a preliminary injunction.[23]

Comparison With Preliminary Injunction

A preliminary injunction is also usually directed at freezing circumstances in place until there is greater opportunity to hear the merits of a case.[24] However, a preliminary injunction cannot be issued unless all parties are provided with notice of the motion for such relief, whereas it is possible in some circumstances to obtain a

21. *University of Texas v. Camenisch,* 451 U.S. 390, 395, 101 S.Ct. 1830, 1834, 68 L.Ed.2d 175 (1981) ("[F]indings of fact and conclusions of law made by a court granting a preliminary injunction are not binding at trial on the merits.").

22. *United States v. United Shoe Machinery Corp.,* 391 U.S. 244, 88 S.Ct. 1496, 20 L.Ed.2d 562 (1968). See also, *Favia v. Indiana University of Pennsylvania,* 7 F.3d 332, 337 (3d Cir.1993) (modification proper only when change of circumstances makes continuation of original order inequitable).

23. *See, e.g., Hospital Resource Personnel, Inc. v. United States,* 860 F.Supp. 1554, 1556 (S.D.Ga.1994)(granting temporary restraining order to preserve status quo until hearing on preliminary or permanent injunction).

24. *See, e.g., CMM Cable Rep., Inc. v. Ocean Coast Properties, Inc.,* 48 F.3d 618, 620 (1st Cir.1995)("The purpose of a preliminary injunction is to preserve the status quo," pending full adjudication later.).

temporary restraining order without first providing notice to opposing parties. Preliminary injunctions may be effective for the pendency of the case, whereas temporary restraining orders issued without notice are effective, with a single renewal, for a maximum of twenty days.[25] When courts grant temporary restraining orders, it is often with an eye to holding a prompt hearing on a motion for a preliminary injunction.[26] In one respect, temporary restraining orders are identical to preliminary injunctions, i.e., the substantive requirements for both (discussed above) are identical.[27]

Order Without Notice to Opposing Party

Although much of Rule 65(b) is devoted to the circumstances in which a party may obtain a temporary restraining order without first notifying opponents of the motion, it is important to note that such ex parte temporary restraining orders are disfavored.[28] Before granting one, the court will search the facts carefully to ascertain the need for ex parte relief, and will require that the party seeking relief satisfy *all* the requirements in Rule 65 for a temporary restraining order, as well as substantive prerequisites in case law governing such equitable remedies as restraining orders and injunctions.[29]

Oral Notice

The preferred method of notice for a temporary restraining order is formal service of written documents upon the opposing party. However, the court has substantial discretion to approve lesser notice.[30] Additionally, Rule 65(b) provides that if written notice is impractical, a party seeking relief under the Rule should attempt to notify the adversary orally.

Orders Issuing Without Prior Notice

Rule 65(b) permits issuance of a temporary restraining order without prior notice to the opposing party, but imposes two additional requirements before such an order is granted: proof of

---

25. *Cf., Bennett v. Medtronic, Inc.,* 285 F.3d 801, 804 (9th Cir.2002) (if district court's order exceeds time limits of temporary restraining order, order should be reviewed under standards of preliminary injunction).

26. *Granny Goose Foods, Inc. v. Brotherhood of Teamsters and Auto Truck Drivers Local No. 70 of Alameda County,* 415 U.S. 423, 94 S.Ct. 1113, 39 L.Ed.2d 435 (1974).

27. *See, e.g., Bieros v. Nicola,* 857 F.Supp. 445, 446 (E.D.Pa.1994)("The standards for a temporary restraining order are the same as those for a preliminary injunction.").

28. *See, e.g., Reno Air Racing Association v. McCord,* 452 F.3d 1126, 1131 (9th

Cir.2006) ("[C]ircumstances justifying the issuance of an ex parte order are extremely limited."); *Redken Laboratories v. Levin,* 843 F.2d 226, 228 (6th Cir.1988) (Ex parte temporary restraining orders "often [exact] manifest injustices.").

29. *See, e.g., Phillips v. Chas. Schreiner Bank,* 894 F.2d 127, 131 (5th Cir. 1990)(noting "stringent restrictions" of Rule 65(b) on ex parte temporary restraining orders).

30. *Cf., People of Illinois ex rel. Hartigan v. Peters,* 871 F.2d 1336, 1340 (7th Cir.1989)("[w]e leave the question of what constitutes sufficient notice primarily to the district court's discretion.").

irreparable injury and a statement of the efforts made to notify the opposing party.

Irreparable Injury

Rule 65(b)(1) requires a party to show by affidavit or verified complaint the irreparable injury that will occur if the order is not granted until the opposing parties are notified and have an opportunity to appear.[31]

(1) *Affidavit or Complaint:* The quality and detail required in an affidavit or complaint vary substantially, but the explanation should be sufficient for the court to understand the risk of irreparable injury, along with other relevant facts that will help the court understand the need for prompt action.[32]

(2) *Irreparable Injury:* The concept of what constitutes irreparable injury is so flexible as to be elusive. However, it seems clear that a party can demonstrate that the loss likely to occur if an ex parte temporary restraining order is not issued is an irreparable loss when the damages will be of a nature as are difficult to calculate.[33] Thus, substantial risk of lost future profits or business reputation might constitute irreparable injury. Alternatively, if the loss will be of a nature that the courts normally consider beyond compensation by money, however calculated, the injury is likely to be irreparable. Thus, risk of damage to unique property, such as land, might also meet the standard of irreparable injury.

Efforts to Notify Adversary

Rule 65(b)(2) requires that an applicant for a temporary restraining order explain, in writing, whatever efforts have been made to notify the opposing party, and the reasons why no further efforts at notification before issuance of the order are justified. Although the Rule does not literally require that an applicant make efforts to notify an adversary, the court may treat failure to make efforts that would have been reasonable as a ground for denying the motion for a temporary restraining order.[34]

Date and Time of Issuance

If a party is able to obtain a temporary restraining order without first providing notice to opposing parties, Rule 65(b) requires that the order be indorsed with the date and time it was issued. This indorsement is significant because it begins the running of the ten-day period, discussed below, for which the order is effective.

---

31. *See, e.g., American Can Co. v. Mansukhani,* 742 F.2d 314, 321–24 (7th Cir. 1984)(failure to comply with Rule 65(b)(1) is abuse of discretion).

32. *See, e.g., Id.*

33. *Cf., In re Arthur Treacher's Franchisee Litigation,* 689 F.2d 1137, 1145 (3d Cir.1982)("we have never upheld an injunction where the claimed injury constituted a loss of money, a loss capable of recoupment in a proper action at law.").

34. *See, e.g., American Can Co. v. Mansukhani,* 742 F.2d 314, 321–24 (7th Cir. 1984)(failure to make reasonable efforts make grant of order an abuse of discretion).

Filing With Clerk

Once an order is issued without prior notice, it must be filed "forthwith" with the clerk of court and entered as part of the record of the case.

Explanation of Injury and Lack of Notice

The court's temporary restraining order will explain the apprehended irreparable injury in detail sufficient to inform an appellate court,[35] and will also explain the reasons why the court found it necessary to issue the order without first hearing from opposing parties.

Duration of Temporary Restraining Order

If an order issues under Rule 65(b) without prior notice to opposing parties, the order will expire no later than ten days after issuance.[36] The court may provide for expiration of the order in a lesser period. Additionally, even temporary restraining orders issued with notice cannot continue indefinitely unless they meet the standards required for preliminary injunctions.[37]

Consent to Extension

If the opposing party consents to an extension of the temporary restraining order, the order may be extended for any length of time to which the parties agree.[38]

Judicial Extension of Time

Temporary restraining orders issued without prior notice may be extended by judicial order for an additional period not greater than the length of time in the original order, and in no event for more than ten additional days.

Obtaining an Extension

A party seeking judicial extension of an order must move for the extension within the time limitation of the original order, and must show good cause for the extension. Good cause might be a continuation of the circumstances of irreparable injury that justified the

---

35. *See, e.g., Ben David v. Travisono,* 495 F.2d 562, 564–65 (1st Cir. 1974)("Expansive" injunction against "brutalization" of prisoners must be based on "express findings that the prohibited conduct is likely").

36. *Cf., CVI/Beta Ventures, Inc. v. Custom Optical Frames, Inc.,* 859 F.Supp. 945, 948 (D.Md.1994)(but if order issues only after notice to opponent, order may extend for longer period; order is then analogous to preliminary injunction).

37. *See, e.g., United States v. Crawford,* 329 F.3d 131, 137 (2d Cir.2003) (where temporary restraining order was unambiguous as to its continuing nature and was originally granted only upon notice and

hearing, it properly continued beyond time limit as a preliminary injunction). *But cf., Chicago United Industries, Ltd. v. City of Chicago,* 445 F.3d 940, 946 (7th Cir.2006) (notwithstanding the literal language of Rule 65(b), all temporary restraining orders are subject to the 20 day limit, not merely "without notice" temporary restraining orders; but "without notice" restraining orders are subject to additional restrictions; citing other cases).

38. *See, e.g., In re Arthur Treacher's Franchise Litigation,* 689 F.2d 1150 (3d Cir. 1982); *Cf., Hudson v. Barr,* 3 F.3d 970, 973 (6th Cir.1993)(noting that temporary restraining order can be extended beyond 20 days only with consent of parties).

original order, or such new circumstances as the temporary restraining order produced. For example, if the court is considering issuance of a preliminary injunction, extension of a temporary restraining order might be appropriate to allow the court more time to decide the preliminary injunction question.

Recording of Reasons for Extension

If a temporary restraining order is extended, Rule 65(b) provides that the court must record its reasons for granting the extension.[39]

Timing of Hearing on Preliminary Injunction

If the court grants a temporary restraining order without prior notice to opposing parties, Rule 65(b) directs that a hearing on a motion for a preliminary injunction will be held "at the earliest possible time." The preliminary injunction hearing must move to the head of the court's docket, second only to preliminary injunction matters that are already pending.

Failure to Seek a Preliminary Injunction

If a party obtained a temporary restraining order without prior notice, and then fails to pursue an application for a preliminary injunction at the scheduled hearing, the court will terminate the temporary restraining order.

Motion to Modify or Dissolve Order

Like preliminary injunctions, temporary restraining orders may be modified or dissolved on motion of a party. Grounds for dissolution include a demonstration that the purpose of the order has been fulfilled. An order may also be modified or dissolved if the court is persuaded that the circumstances requiring the order have changed.

Notice

A party subject to a temporary restraining order issued without prior notice may move to dissolve or modify the order. Rule 65(b) requires that the moving party provide other parties at least two days notice of a hearing on the motion to dissolve, unless the court permits less notice.

Timing of Hearing

Rule 65(b) establishes no time limit within which the court must hear a motion to dissolve or modify a temporary restraining order, but the Rule clearly encourages a prompt hearing, "as expeditiously as the ends of justice require."

Appeal

Generally, a court's decision to grant, deny, modify, continue, or dissolve a temporary restraining order is not appealable.[40]

---

39. *But cf., Reliance Insurance Co. v. Mast Construction Co.,* 159 F.3d 1311, 1316 (10th Cir.1998) (extension of expiration date of order does not require that operative language of order must be restated; it is sufficient that extension incorporated by reference such language as was previously laid out when order was originally granted).

40. *See, e.g., In re Lorillard Tobacco Co.,* 370 F.3d 982, 986 (9th Cir.2004) (tem-

RULE 65(c). SECURITY

CORE CONCEPT

Rule 65(c) requires that, as a condition of granting a preliminary injunction or temporary restraining order, the court must impose a bond or other security.[41] The party bound by the injunction or order is entitled to recover damages from the posted security if the injunction or order is subsequently found to have been erroneously granted. The court retains substantial discretion to determine the amount of the security.

APPLICATIONS

Mandatory Security

Although the language of Rule 65(c) seems to direct a court to impose a bond, many cases treat the decision to impose a bond as a matter of discretion for the court.[42]

Timing

If a bond is required, it must be posted when the court grants a preliminary injunction or temporary restraining order.[43] There is no requirement to post security when a party initially seeks such relief.

porary restraining orders "are generally not appealable as of right"); *Robinson v. Lehman,* 771 F.2d 772, 782 (3d Cir.1985) (temporary restraining order not appealable unless denial of order effectively decides the case).

41. *Cf., Mead Johnson & Co. v. Abbott Laboratories,* 209 F.3d 1032, 1033 (7th Cir. 2000) (per curiam) (posting bond may be required to obtain preliminary injunction, but "posting a bond is [still] voluntary"; if party chooses to do so, party can decline to pay bond and drop the suit).

42. *Snider v. Temple University,* 502 U.S. 1032, 112 S.Ct. 873, 116 L.Ed.2d 778 (1992) (sometimes a strict reading of bond requirement may be "inappropriate"). *See, e.g., Doctor's Associates, Inc. v. Stuart,* 85 F.3d 975 (2d Cir.1996)(affirming district court's decision not to require bond); *Moltan Co. v. Eagle-Picher Industries, Inc.,* 55 F.3d 1171, 1176 (6th Cir.1995)("While we recognize that the language of Rule 65(c) appears to be mandatory, and that many circuits have so interpreted it, the rule in our circuit has long been that the district court possesses discretion over whether to require the posting of security"); *Sprint Communications Co. v. CAT Communica-*

tions International, Inc., 335 F.3d 235 n.4 (3d Cir.2003) (suggesting that exceptions to bond requirement are rare). *See also Ty, Inc. v. Publications International, Inc.,* 292 F.3d 512, 516 (7th Cir.2002) (bond requirement of Rule 65(c) applies only to temporary restraining order or preliminary injunction, ... "not for a permanent injunction").

43. *See, e.g., Massachusetts Mutual Life Insurance Co. v. Associated Dry Goods Corp.,* 786 F.Supp. 1403, 1419 (N.D.Ind. 1992)(bond covering loss is "precondition" to injunction, imposed upon grant of order). *But Compare Kos Pharmaceuticals, Inc. v. Andrix Corp.,* 369 F.3d 700, 728 (3d Cir. 2004) (court should determine amount of bond by evaluation of potential financial damages; however, decision to grant injunction should be separate from determination of bond amount), *with Corning, Inc. v. PicVue Electronics, Ltd.,* 365 F.3d 156, 158 (2d Cir.2004) ("While it might have been within the discretion of the district court to decide that, under the circumstances, no security was required, ... the district court was required to make this determination before it entered the preliminary injunction.").

Amount of Security

The maximum amount of security that may be required is the court's estimate of the potential loss to a party proximately caused by erroneous issuance of the injunction or order.[44] The court has discretion to require posting of lesser amounts than the bound party's estimated potential loss.[45] In practice, that means in some cases the court may limit security to a nominal amount, if such a small sum is in the interest of justice.[46]

Requests for Increase in Bond

If a party believes the amount designated for the bond is insufficient to cover damages, the party may seek an increase in the bond during the time when the preliminary relief is in effect—or when the preliminary remedy has been lifted, but might still be re-imposed. However, once an injunction or restraining order has been reversed and will not be replaced, the amount of the bond cannot be increased.[47]

Standard for "Wrongfully Enjoined"

A party has been wrongfully enjoined "if it is ultimately found that the enjoined party had at all times the right to do the enjoined act." [48]

---

44. *See, e.g., Hoechst Diafoil Co. v. Nan Ya Plastics Corp.,* 174 F.3d 411, 421 (4th Cir.1999) (court must impose bond of an amount that considers magnitude of both defendant's potential loss and plaintiff's potential enrichment, as well as likelihood that harm will actually occur; citing authority for bond amount of zero if no evidence supported likelihood of harm). *But cf., Connecticut General Life Insurance Co. v. New Images of Beverly Hills,* 321 F.3d 878, 883 (9th Cir.2003) (party affected by injunction has obligation to present evidence that bond in a particular amount is needed).

45. *See, e.g., GoTo.com, Inc. v. Walt Disney Co.,* 202 F.3d 1199, 1211 (9th Cir.2000) (refusing to raise bond from $25,000 to $20,000,000; noting discretion of district court and practical result); *International Association of Machinists and Aerospace Workers v. Eastern Airlines, Inc.,* 925 F.2d 6 (1st Cir.1991)(district court has "substantial discretion" to set terms of bond).

46. *See, e.g., Davis v. Mineta,* 302 F.3d 1104 (10th Cir.2002) ("Ordinarily, where a party is seeking to vindicate the public interest served by [federal environmental law], a minimal bond amount should be considered."); *Cronin v. United States Department of Agriculture,* 919 F.2d 439, 445 (7th Cir.1990)(citing circuits that require only nominal bonds in environmental cases). *But see, Mead Johnson & Co. v.* *Abbott Laboratories,* 201 F.3d 883, 888 (7th Cir.2000) ("When setting the amount of security, district courts should err on the high side"; partly because bond acts to limit damages recoverable); *MacDonald v. Chicago Park District,* 132 F.3d 355, 358 (7th Cir.1997) (per curiam) (finding error in imposition of $100 bond on plaintiff of modest means; loss to defendant is potentially much larger).

47. *See, e.g., Mead Johnson & Co. v. Abbott Laboratories,* 209 F.3d 1032, 1033 (7th Cir.2000) (per curiam) ("To permit changes in the bond after an injunction's reversal would be to overturn the rule [that recoverable damages are limited to amount of the bond] in fact, if not in name.").

48. *Blumenthal v. Merrill Lynch, Pierce, Fenner & Smith, Inc.,* 910 F.2d 1049, 1054 (2d Cir.1990). *See also Global NAPS, Inc. v. Verizon New England, Inc.,* 489 F.3d 13, 22 (1st Cir. 2007) (adopting majority view; rejecting contrary view that injunction is wrongful only if grant of injunction was abuse of discretion); *Milan Express, Inc. v. Averitt Express, Inc.,* 254 F.3d 966 (11th Cir.2001) (elements are: (1) wrongfully enjoined; and (2) proximately caused damage). *But see H & R Block, Inc. v. McCaslin,* 541 F.2d 1098, 1099–1100 (5th Cir. 1976) (per curiam) (where injunction issued on basis of good faith claims and district court did not

Damages Recoverable

An injured party's maximum recovery is generally limited to the amount of the bond.[49] However, a party may pursue an independent action for malicious prosecution in the unusual cases where the elements of that tort are satisfied.[50]

Actions Involving the United States

Rule 65(c) exempts the United States, its officers, and agencies from the obligation to post security.

Relation to Rule 65.1

Rule 65.1 governs the procedure by which a party may seek recovery against security posted pursuant to Rule 65(c).

"Non–Injunction" Bonds

As is explained immediately above, Rule 65(c) governs the circumstances in which a bond requirement may be imposed as a prerequisite to the imposition of a preliminary injunction or temporary restraining order. A "non-injunction" bond, by contrast, addresses a very different situation.

One of the underlying elements a court considers in determining if it should grant equitable relief is whether, in the absence of such relief, irreparable harm may be done to the unsuccessful moving party. Such harm may arise in a number of circumstances— including the possibility that while activities by one party may cause damage to the other that would normally give rise to monetary relief, such relief is unobtainable because the wrongdoer is penniless or, at least, unlikely to be able to pay the damages that might arise.[51] When such a possibility is before a district court, therefore, the court is entitled to consider whether harm that could arise from its refusal to grant injunctive relief is "irreparable," notwithstanding that a legal remedy is nominally available. That would, of course, weigh in favor of granting the injunction or temporary restraining order.

A "non-injunction" bond is one possible response to that situation by the party opposing a motion for injunctive relief. As a means of establishing that potential damage to the moving party is not irreparable because the opposing party is impoverished or unable to pay for damages, the opposing party may offer a "non-injunction"

---

abuse discretion, later finding that injunction wrongfully issue did not establish liability on bond for party that obtained injunction).

49. *W.R. Grace & Co. v. Local Union 759, International Union of United Rubber, Cork, Linoleum & Plastic Workers of America,* 461 U.S. 757, 770, 103 S.Ct. 2177, 2185, 76 L.Ed.2d 298 (1983) ("A party injured by the issuance of an injunction later determined to be erroneous has no action for damages in the absence of a bond."). *See, e.g., Coyne–Delany Co. v. Capital Develop-*

ment Board, 717 F.2d 385, 393–94 (7th Cir. 1983)(bond is a ceiling on damages, except where plaintiff acted in bad faith).

50. *Meyers v. Block,* 120 U.S. 206, 211, 7 S.Ct. 525, 528, 30 L.Ed. 642 (1887)(bond sets limit of recovery, in absence of suit for malicious prosecution).

51. *See generally Lakeview Technology, Inc. v. Robinson,* 446 F.3d 655 (7th Cir. 2006). *See also* Author's Commentary on Rule 65.

bond or other financial guarantee that would compensate the moving party if the motion for injunctive relief is denied and the moving party later suffers monetary loss. Thus, the "non-injunction" bond may play almost the opposite role of a bond issued pursuant to Rule 65(c).[52]

RULE 65(d). CONTENTS AND SCOPE OF EVERY INJUNCTION AND RESTRAINING ORDER

CORE CONCEPT

Rule 65(d) governs the information that must be contained in injunctions and temporary restraining orders. The Rule also describes categories of persons who are bound by an injunction or order.

APPLICATIONS

Reasons for Issuance

The injunction or order must contain an explanation of the reasons for its issuance. However, failure of a district court to provide such an explanation does not, of itself, mandate reversal of the grant of the injunction.[53] A sufficient explanation will state specifically the facts found by the court as well as the conclusions of law upon which the court's decision is based.[54] An explanation of the reason for the court's action is usually direct, without excessive detail.

Relation to Rule 52

Alongside the Rule 65(d) requirement of reasons for issuance of an injunction or restraining order, Rule 52(a) provides that district courts must make findings of fact and conclusions of law when granting or denying a request for an interlocutory injunction.[55] This issue is discussed in greater detail under Rule 52.

---

52. *See, e.g., Lakeview Technology, Inc. v. Robinson*, 446 F.3d 655 (7th Cir.2006) ("A 'non-injunctive' bond ... is the flip side of an injunction bond under Rule 65(c).").

53. *See, e.g., Test Masters Educational Services, Inc. v. Singh*, 428 F.3d 559, 577 (5th Cir.2005) (failure to make express findings does not require reversal or vacation of injunction, but it does force circuit court to examine record "to determine if sufficient evidence supports the issuance of injunctive relief").

54. *Schmidt v. Lessard*, 414 U.S. 473, 476, 94 S.Ct. 713, 715, 38 L.Ed.2d 661 (1974) ("The specificity provisions of Rule 65(d) are no mere technical requirements. The Rule was designed to prevent uncertainty and confusion on the part of those faced with injunction orders, and to avoid the possible founding of a contempt citation on a decree too vague to be understood.").

But *cf., EEOC v. Severn Trent Services, Inc.*, 358 F.3d 438, 442 (7th Cir.2004) ("The explanation can be oral rather than written ... and the absence of explanation can be forgiven when the justification for the injunction is clear from the record.").

55. *See, e.g., Prairie Band of Potawatomi Indians v. Pierce*, 253 F.3d 1234 (10th Cir.2001) ("[W]ithout adequate findings of fact and conclusions of law, appellate review is in general not possible."). But *cf., Knapp Shoes, Inc. v. Sylvania Shoe Manufacturing Corp.*, 15 F.3d 1222, 1228 (1st Cir.1994) ("conclusory findings are not enough, [but court may make] brief, definite, pertinent findings and conclusions upon the contested matters; there is no necessity for over-elaboration of detail or particularization of facts" [internal quotation marks omitted]).

Description of Acts Proscribed: Requirement of Writing

Rule 65(d) ordinarily requires that the injunction or order describe the prohibited acts with sufficient detail and clarity so that a layperson who was bound by the order could distinguish between acts that were permitted and acts the injunction or order prohibited.[56] Thus, a court will ordinarily not use highly technical language unless there is no other way to describe the acts and the parties affected are likely to be uniquely capable of understanding such language.

Part of the requirement of describing with reasonable precision the prohibited conduct is a companion requirement that the court's order must be reduced to writing.[57]

Incorporation by Reference

The Rule specifically provides that prohibited acts *may not* be described only by reference to the complaint or other documents in the action.[58] However, some courts hold that Rule 65(d) is satisfied if

---

56. *See, e.g., Fortyune v. American Multi–Cinema, Inc.,* 364 F.3d 1075, 1087 (9th Cir.2004) (district court has no duty to explain *how* to enforce injunction, only to explain what must or must not be done); *A & M Records, Inc. v. Napster, Inc.,* 284 F.3d 1091, 1097 (9th Cir.2002) ("We do not set aside injunctions under [Rule 65(d)] 'unless they are so vague that they have no reasonably specific meaning.' "); *Prairie Band of Potawatomi Indians v. Pierce,* 253 F.3d 1234 (10th Cir.2001) (finding sufficient specificity in order barring state from enforcing state motor vehicle registration and titling laws against vehicles registered and titled under tribal motor vehicle code; use of words "applying" and "enforcing" in instant context are clear; "Rule 65(d) does not require the impossible."); *Power v. Summers,* 226 F.3d 815, 819 (7th Cir.2000) (prohibition on "retaliation" against plaintiffs who are suing for alleged violation of free speech rights is not unduly vague); *CPC International, Inc. v. Skippy, Inc.,* 214 F.3d 456, 459 (4th Cir.2000) (order that tells defendant with specificity what to remove from website but provides no clear reason for the redaction violates Rule 65(d)); *Burton v. City of Belle Glade,* 178 F.3d 1175 (11th Cir.1999) (enjoining city to abstain from racial discrimination in annexation policies does "no more than instruct the City to 'obey the law' " and therefore does not meet specificity requirement of Rule 65(d)); *Reliance Insurance Co. v. Mast Construction Co.,* 159 F.3d 1311, 1316 (10th Cir.1998) (temporary restraining order blocking transfer of assets of bank account in which "defendants have or maintain an interest" is sufficiently specific under Rule 65(d); "interest" is not ambiguous "when used to describe rights in a bank account"); *PMC, Inc. v. Sherwin–Williams Co.,* 151 F.3d 610, 619 (7th Cir.1998) (injunction requiring defendant to take "full responsibility" for cleanup of toxic waste site is "hopelessly vague;" defendant should bear no risk of responsibility for past or future pollution caused by others; remanded for redrafting); *IDS Life Insurance Co. v. SunAmerica Life Insurance Co.,* 136 F.3d 537, 543 (7th Cir.1998) (injunction prohibiting encouragement of "unlawful insurance practices" is vacated; but district court may try to reformulate injunction more precisely); *Peregrine Myanmar, Ltd. v. Segal,* 89 F.3d 41 (2d Cir.1996)(prohibition against "spurious" lawsuits is overbroad, unless district court on remand can define that term more precisely). *Cf., Dupuy v. Samuels,* 465 F.3d 757, 759 (7th Cir. 2006) (where injunction violates Rule 65(b), but its "core . . . is clear enough to be enforceable," injunction can be enforced as to prohibitions within injunction that are clear).

57. *See, e.g., Lau v. Meddaugh,* 229 F.3d 121, 123 (2d Cir.2000) (failure to memorialize order is reversible error).

58. *See, e.g., Advent Electronics, Inc. v. Buckman,* 112 F.3d 267 (7th Cir.1997) (order must state reasons for issuance and specific terms "without reference to another document"); *Dunn v. New York State Department of Labor,* 47 F.3d 485 (2d Cir. 1995)(unacceptable to incorporate consent decree from related case; because consent

a document specifically describing the prohibited acts is "physically appended" to the injunction order.[59]

Persons Bound

Rule 65(d) describes the categories of persons subject to an injunction or order: (1) parties;[60] (2) their officers, agents, servants, employees, and attorneys;[61] and (3) other persons "in active concert or participation with [parties]." [62]

Notice to Persons Bound

No one is bound by an injunction or order until that person receives fair notice of the judicial act. However, formal notice, in the form of service of documents, is not necessarily required to bind a party or those in privity with a party. A party or a person in a close relationship with a party may be bound if they simply have actual knowledge of the injunction or order.[63]

Personal Jurisdiction

Persons outside the jurisdiction of the court are not subject to its orders.[64] For a further discussion of jurisdiction over persons and things, see §§ 2.2–2.10.

decree can be modified, incorporation of such decree risks confusion in instant case).

59. *LeBlanc-Sternberg v. Fletcher,* 143 F.3d 748 (2d Cir.1998). *See also Reno Air Racing Association, Inc. v. McCord,* 452 F.3d 1126, 1132–33 (9th Cir. 2006) (permitting incorporation by reference in "limited scenarios" where document is physically attached to injunction).

60. *See, e.g., United States v. Vitek Supply Corp.,* 151 F.3d 580 (7th Cir.1998) (Rule 65(d) extends scope of injunction to bind alter egos); *Hernandez v. O'Malley,* 98 F.3d 293, 294 (7th Cir.1996) (injunction against public official also applies to successor in office).

61. *See, e.g., Whiting v. Marathon County Sheriff's Department,* 382 F.3d 700, 704 (7th Cir.2004) (attorney bound by no-contact order issued against client); *Planned Parenthood of Columbia/Willamette, Inc. v. American Coalition of Life Activists,* 290 F.3d 1058, 1088 n. 19 (9th Cir. 2002) (en banc) (individual employee/agent of party is appropriately within scope of injunction); *American Civil Liberties Union v. Johnson,* 194 F.3d 1149 (10th Cir.1999) (preliminary injunction against enforcement by governor and attorney general of criminal statute also binds state's district attorneys). *But cf., Doctor's Associates, Inc. v. Reinert & Duree,* 191 F.3d 297, 302–303 (2d Cir.1999) (violation of Rule 65(d) to enjoin preliminarily franchisees of defen-

dant who are not parties to current litigation in federal court from pursuing their separate claims in state court).

62. *Regal Knitwear Co. v. National Labor Relations Board,* 324 U.S. 9, 65 S.Ct. 478, 89 L.Ed. 661 (1945). *But cf., R.M.S. Titanic, Inc. v. Haver,* 171 F.3d 943, 957–58 (4th Cir.1999) (shipping company that agreed to transport enjoined party to site of sunken vessel is not in privity with party prohibited from approaching or photographing wreckage); *Additive Controls & Measurement Systems, Inc. v. Flowdata, Inc.,* 96 F.3d 1390, 1395 (Fed.Cir.1996) ("Having a relationship to an enjoined party of the sort set forth in Rule 65(d) exposes a non-party to contempt for assisting the party to violate the injunction, but does not justify granting injunctive relief against the non-party in its separate capacity.").

63. *Spallone v. United States,* 493 U.S. 265, 110 S.Ct. 625, 107 L.Ed.2d 644 (1990).

64. *See, e.g., R.M.S. Titanic, Inc. v. Haver,* 171 F.3d 943, 957–58 (4th Cir.1999) ("[A] party cannot obtain injunctive relief against another without first obtaining in personam jurisdiction over that person or someone in legal privity with that person."); *Parker v. Ryan,* 960 F.2d 543, 546 (5th Cir.1992)(nonparty acting independently of defendant is not subject to court's jurisdiction under Rule 65(d)). *But see, Waffenschmidt v. MacKay,* 763 F.2d 711, 714 (5th Cir.1985) (nonparties residing out-

Persons in Active Concert

This broad category of persons who may be subject to an injunction or order is necessarily fact-specific in application.[65]   Generally, however, assignees who take an interest from a party with actual or constructive notice of an injunction or order prohibiting that party from performing a certain act relating to the interest may also be barred from performing the act.[66]

Permanent Injunctions

Unlike other provisions of Rule 65, Rule 65(d) does not refer only to preliminary injunctions or temporary restraining orders. Thus, Rule 65(d)'s provisions for a satisfactory explanation of the court's decision, an adequate description of prohibited acts, and the categories of persons bound by an injunction or order apply equally to permanent injunctions.[67]

Standing to Enforce Permanent Injunction

As is described above, there are many circumstances in which persons who are not parties may nonetheless be bound by an injunction. However, only those who are parties to a lawsuit have standing to seek enforcement of a final injunction.[68]

Failure to Comply with Injunction or Order

Persons within the categories of Rule 65(d) who have notice of an injunction or order and who do not comply are subject to the court's power of contempt.[69]

RULE 65(e).   OTHER LAWS NOT MODIFIED

CORE CONCEPT

side territorial jurisdiction are nevertheless subject to court's jurisdiction if they intentionally and knowingly aid and abet violation of court's order).

65.   *See, e.g., Reliance Insurance Co. v. Mast Construction Co.,* 84 F.3d 372 (10th Cir.1996)(nonparties bound include alter egos, and also those "with actual notice" who assist defendant or privy in violation of order); *United States v. International Brotherhood of Teamsters, Chauffeurs, Warehousemen and Helpers of America, AFL-CIO,* 964 F.2d 180, 184 (2d Cir. 1992)(whether a person is bound "always depends on the precise relationship of that person to the underlying litigation").

66.   *Regal Knitwear Co. v. National Labor Relations Board,* 324 U.S. 9, 65 S.Ct. 478, 89 L.Ed. 661 (1945). *See, e.g., Chicago Truck Drivers v. Brotherhood Labor Leasing,* 207 F.3d 500, 507–08 (8th Cir.2000) (non-party who is sole shareholder, corporate officer and agent of corporations easily falls within scope of Rule 65(d) for purposes

of contempt; however, such non-party has no personal liability for payment obligations of corporations when non-party has not been sued in underlying litigation).

67.   *See, e.g., Reich v. ABC/York–Estes Corp.,* 64 F.3d 316, 320 (7th Cir.1995) (holding that failure to comply with Rule 65(d) meant no permanent injunction existed).

68.   *See, e.g., Planned Parenthood of Idaho, Inc. v. Wasden,* 376 F.3d 908 (9th Cir.2004) ("Only a proper party to an action can enforce an injunction that results from a final judgment.").

69.   *Gunn v. University Committee to End the War in Viet Nam,* 399 U.S. 383, 90 S.Ct. 2013, 26 L.Ed.2d 684 (1970). *See also, Reliance Insurance Co. v. Mast Construction Co.,* 84 F.3d 372, 376 (10th Cir. 1996)("Generally speaking, a person who violates an injunction or temporary restraining order during its pendency is subject to a compensatory civil contempt judgment.").

Rule 65(e) provides that nothing in Rule 65 shall be construed to modify statutes relating to labor relations, interpleader actions, or actions subject to the jurisdiction of a three-judge court.

APPLICATION

Alterations to Courts' Injunctive Power

In each of the three areas of law addressed by Rule 65(e)—labor law, statutory interpleader, and three-judge courts—federal statutes alter the typical power of courts to issue injunctions and restraining orders. Rule 65(e) makes clear that when those statutes are applicable to a case and conflict with a provision of Rule 65, the statute governs.

RULE 65(f). COPYRIGHT IMPOUNDMENT

CORE CONCEPT

Rule 65(f), scheduled to become effective on December 1, 2001 unless Congress acts prior to that date, provides that other provisions of Rule 65 apply to copyright impoundment proceedings.

ADDITIONAL RESEARCH REFERENCES

Wright & Miller, *Federal Practice and Procedure* §§ 2941–62.

C.J.S. Injunctions §§ 4–54, 60–110, 111–158, 160–206, 213–263, 264–314, 320–341.

West's Key No. Digests, Injunction ⟳132–188.

RULE 65.1

PROCEEDINGS AGAINST A SURETY

Whenever these rules (including the Supplemental Rules for Admiralty or Maritime Claims and Asset Forfeiture Actions) require or allow a party to give security, and security is given through a bond or other undertaking with one or more sureties, each surety submits to the court's jurisdiction and irrevocably appoints the court clerk as its agent for receiving service of any papers that affect its liability on the bond or undertaking. The surety's liability may be enforced on motion without an independent action. The motion and any notice that the court orders may be served on the court clerk, who must promptly mail a copy of each to every surety whose address is known.

[Added effective July 1, 1966; amended effective August 1, 1987; April 12, 2006, effective December 1, 2006; April 30, 2007, effective December 1, 2007.]

––––––––––––––– **2007 AMENDMENTS ROADMAP** –––––––––––––––

STYLE PROJECT CHANGES: Minor changes were made in the title of the Rule and in language within the Rule.

NON-STYLE CHANGES: None.

NOTE: The Federal Rules "Style Project" is explained in Part III-A.

AUTHORS' COMMENTARY ON RULE 65.1

––––––––––––––– PURPOSE AND SCOPE –––––––––––––––

Rule 65.1 provides a summary procedure by which parties can enforce their rights against a surety who has posted security.

APPLICATIONS

Scope

Rule 65.1 applies to proceedings to enforce a surety's liability on an appeal bond, a supersedeas bond, or an injunction bond posted pursuant to Rule 65(c). The Rule also applies when the Supplemental Rules for Certain Admiralty and Maritime Claims require the posting of bond. Finally, Rule 65.1 applies to the satisfaction of provisional remedies under Rule 64, when state law requires a bond.

Injunction Bonds: Rebuttable Presumption

The majority of courts hold that a party wrongfully enjoined under Rule 65 enjoys a rebuttable presumption in favor of recovering provable damages up to the limit of any bond required under Rule 65(c). Only in "rare cases" will the wrongfully enjoined party not be entitled to recovery on the bond.[1]

Alternative Procedures

Rule 65.1 is not the only means by which a party can seek to collect on a bond. Instead of employing the Rule, a party may bring an independent action against the surety in a state or federal court.[2]

Motion for Judgment

The appropriate method for seeking to collect from a surety under Rule 65.1 is a motion for judgment on the bond.[3]

Timing

Generally, a party may seek recovery under Rule 65.1 once the court has terminated or altered the relief that the bond secured. Thus, if a court determines that a preliminary injunction was improvidently granted, or was of excessive scope, the party previously enjoined may then move against the bond for damages.[4]

Consent to Personal Jurisdiction

Rule 65.1 provides that when a surety posts a bond or other security, the surety submits to the personal jurisdiction of the court for purposes of any litigation relating to liability on the bond.[5] Personal jurisdiction is discussed further earlier in this text.

Service of Process

Upon posting bond, a surety also irrevocably appoints the clerk of court as the surety's agent to receive service of process in matters relating to liability on the bond.

---

1. *Nintendo of America, Inc. v. Lewis Galoob Toys, Inc.,* 16 F.3d 1032, 1039 (9th Cir.1994) (presumption in favor of recovery of proven damages). *But cf., Bass v. First Pacific Networks, Inc.,* 219 F.3d 1052, 1053 (9th Cir.2000) (attorney's fees allegedly incurred in collecting on bond under Rule 65.1 cannot be recovered under that Rule; contrary state law is irrelevant to bond enforcement under Rule 65.1).

2. *See, e.g., Alabama ex rel. Siegelman v. United States Environmental Protection Agency,* 925 F.2d 385, 388 (11th Cir. 1991)(permitting independent action when bond is unavailable). *See also De Boer Structures (U.S.A.), Inc. v. Shaffer Tent & Awning Co.,* 187 F.Supp.2d 910, 925 (S.D.Ohio 2001) (noting that appointment of receiver is extraordinary remedy justified only in extreme situations).

3. *See, e.g., Global NAPS, Inc. v. Verizon New England, Inc.,* 489 F.3d 13, 20 (1st Cir. 2007) (enforcement on motion is appropriate; no need to file independent action); *Lyrick Studios, Inc. v. Big Idea Products, Inc.,* 420 F.3d 388 (5th Cir.2005) (noting that motion is appropriate, obviating need for separate actions).

4. *See, e.g., American Bible Society v. Blount,* 446 F.2d 588, 595 n. 12 (3d Cir. 1971)(liability on bond arises after defendant prevails on merits).

5. *See, e.g., Instant Air Freight Co. v. C.F. Air Freight, Inc.,* 882 F.2d 797, 804 (3d Cir.1989)(noting that Rule 65.1 requires that surety submit to jurisdiction of court).

Notice

A party seeking to collect on a bond should serve the motion on the clerk of court, along with such other notice as the court may require. Rule 65.1 requires that the clerk shall "forthwith" mail copies of the documents to all affected sureties whose addresses are known.

Injunction Staying Enforcement

Although Rule 65.1 is intended to provide an expeditious means of recovering damages from a bond, there are situations in which Rule 65.1 proceedings will be stayed. In particular, if a court enjoins proceedings against the bond, the injunction must be obeyed until it is modified or dissolved.[6]

Collecting From Principals

Although Rule 65.1 addresses the means by which a party may seek damages on a surety's bond or other undertaking, courts also permit the use of Rule 65.1 for similar relief against a surety's principal.[7]

Subject Matter Jurisdiction

If a party seeks in the original action to collect against a bond under Rule 65.1, the court will have supplemental jurisdiction over the claim.[8] If a party seeks to enforce a bond in an independent action, the court has subject matter jurisdiction under 28 U.S.C.A. § 1352, governing independent actions on bonds posted pursuant to federal law.[9] Subject matter jurisdiction is discussed further at §§ 2.10–2.13.

ADDITIONAL RESEARCH REFERENCES

Wright & Miller, *Federal Practice and Procedure* §§ 2971–74.

C.J.S. Federal Civil Procedure §§ 1273–1295.

West's Key No. Digests, Federal Civil Procedure ⊙=2732–2733.

6. *Celotex Corp. v. Edwards,* 514 U.S. 300, 115 S.Ct. 1493, 131 L.Ed.2d 403 (1995)(notwithstanding Rule 65.1, a bankruptcy court's injunction may stay collection from a debtor's surety until injunction is modified or dissolved).

7. *See, e.g., Willis v. Celotex Corp.,* 970 F.2d 1292 (4th Cir.1992)(Rule 65.1 permits recovery against both surety and principal). *See also Lyrick Studios, Inc. v. Big Idea Productions, Inc.,* 420 F.3d 388, 396–97 (5th Cir.2005) (party had enforced surety's liability on motion without filing independent action; held, when party later lost on appeal, surety also had no need to file separate action and could instead recover on motion).

8. *See, e.g., Buddy Systems, Inc. v. Exer–Genie, Inc.,* 545 F.2d 1164, 1166 (9th Cir.1976) (jurisdiction over collection against bond exists until bond is discharged).

9. *See, e.g., Milan Express, Inc. v. Averitt Express, Inc.,* 208 F.3d 975, 980 (11th Cir.2000) (28 U.S.C. § 1352 provides jurisdiction over claims against injunction bond issued under Rule 65; further, claim for damages in excess of bond, based on allegation of bad faith, could be heard under supplemental jurisdiction of court, 28 U.S.C. § 1367).

RULE 66

RECEIVERS

These rules govern an action in which the appointment of a receiver is sought or a receiver sues or is sued. But the practice in administering an estate by a receiver or a similar court-appointed officer must accord with the historical practice in federal courts or with a local rule. An action in which a receiver has been appointed may be dismissed only by court order.

[Amended effective March 19, 1948; October 20, 1949; April 30, 2007, effective December 1, 2007.]

———————————— **2007 AMENDMENTS ROADMAP** ————————————

STYLE PROJECT CHANGES: The three sentences of former Rule 66 were inverted to promote greater readability. Cumbersome wording was revised. "Must" replaced "shall".

NON-STYLE CHANGES: None.

NOTE: The Federal Rules "Style Project" is explained in Part III-A.

AUTHORS' COMMENTARY ON RULE 66

———————————— **PURPOSE AND SCOPE** ————————————

Rule 66 provides that, when appointed by district courts, federal equity receivers shall administer estates in accordance with prior federal practice and local court rules. Once an equity receiver is appointed in a particular lawsuit, the action may not thereafter be dismissed without the court's prior approval.

APPLICATIONS

Role of Federal Equity Receiver

Receivership is an extraordinary equitable remedy, justified only in extreme circumstances.[1] Federal courts appoint equity receivers to assume custody, control, and management of property that either

---

1. *See Hollywood Healthcare Corp. v. Deltec, Inc.*, 2004 WL 1118610, at *10 (D.Minn. May 17, 2004); *Sumpter v. United States*, 314 F.Supp.2d 684, 690 (E.D.Mich. 2004).

is presently involved or is likely to become involved in litigation.[2] The receiver is charged to preserve the property, and any rents or profits the property earns, until a final disposition by the court.[3] Although typically appointed only to care for property, a federal equity receiver may be appointed where other, extraordinary circumstances compel intimate judicial supervision.[4]

- *Officer of the Court:* An equity receiver is not an agent of any of the parties to the litigation. Instead, the receiver is deemed to be an officer of the court.[5]

- *Auxiliary Remedy Only:* The appointment of a receiver is not permitted as an end in itself; receivers are only appointed as an auxiliary remedy necessary to some other, primary requested relief.[6]

Administration of Estates By Receivers

Traditional federal practice and, where promulgated, local court rules guide a federal equity receiver in administering the receivership property.[7]

- *State Law:* The substantive law of the State in which the receivership property is located dictates the manner in which the receiver must manage and operate the receivership property.[8]

Federal Rules Control Litigations Involving Receivers

The Rules govern all actions in which a party seeks the appointment of a federal equity receiver, as well as all actions brought by or against the receiver once appointed.[9]

2. *See Gilchrist v. General Elec. Capital Corp.*, 262 F.3d 295, 302 (4th Cir.2001) (noting that federal courts have equity power to appoint receivers and administer receiverships).

3. *See Liberte Capital Group, LLC v. Capwill*, 462 F.3d 543, 551 (6th Cir. 2006).

4. *See Morgan v. McDonough*, 540 F.2d 527 (1st Cir.1976)(affirming appointment of federal receiver for public high school, to implement desegregation orders). *See also De Boer Structures (U.S.A.), Inc. v. Shaffer Tent & Awning Co.*, 187 F.Supp.2d 910, 925 (S.D.Ohio 2001) (noting that appointment of receiver is extraordinary remedy justified only in extreme situations).

5. *See Liberte Capital Group, LLC v. Capwill*, 462 F.3d 543, 551 (6th Cir. 2006); *Hollywood Healthcare Corp. v. Deltec, Inc.*, 2004 WL 1118610, at *9 (D.Minn. 2004); *Federal Home Loan Mortgage Corp. v. Spark Tarrytown, Inc.*, 829 F.Supp. 82, 85 n. 6 (S.D.N.Y.1993).

6. *See Gordon v. Washington*, 295 U.S. 30, 37 n. 4, 55 S.Ct. 584, 588 n. 4, 79 L.Ed.

1282 (1935)("A receivership is only a means to reach some legitimate end sought through the exercise of the power of a court of equity. It is not an end in itself"); *See also Sumpter v. United States*, 314 F.Supp.2d 684, 690 (E.D.Mich.2004); *New York Life Ins. Co. v. Watt West Inv. Corp.*, 755 F.Supp. 287, 291 n. 6 (E.D.Cal. 1991)(commenting that appointment of receiver is ancillary remedy).

7. *See Liberte Capital Group, LLC v. Capwill*, 462 F.3d 543, 551 (6th Cir. 2006).

8. *See* 28 U.S.C.A. § 959(b). *See also Gilchrist v. General Elec. Capital Corp.*, 262 F.3d 295, 302 (4th Cir.2001); *Federal Home Loan Mortgage Corp. v. Spark Tarrytown, Inc.*, 829 F.Supp. 82, 85 (S.D.N.Y.1993).

9. *See Phelan v. Middle States Oil Corp.*, 210 F.2d 360 (2d Cir.1954), aff'd, 220 F.2d 593 (2d Cir.1955); *Terry v. June*, 359 F.Supp.2d 510, 518–19 (W.D.Va.2005); *World Fuel Servs. Corp. v. Moorehead*, 229 F.Supp.2d 584, 596 (N.D.Tex.2002); *Varsames v. Palazzolo*, 96 F.Supp.2d 361, 365 (S.D.N.Y.2000).

Appointment of Receivers

Rule 66 does not create a substantive right to the appointment of a receiver; a statute or general principle of equity must first justify the appointment. Federal law controls whether an equity receiver should be appointed, even in a diversity case.[10]

- *Who May Seek An Appointment:* The appointment of a receiver may be requested by any person having a legally recognized right to the property—a mere interest or claim to the property will not be sufficient to justify the appointment of a receiver.[11] Receivers are appointed frequently at the request of secured creditors, mortgagees, judgment creditors, and plaintiffs in shareholder derivative actions.[12]

- *Prerequisites for Appointment:* The appointment of a receiver is an extraordinary remedy, available only upon a clear showing that a receivership is essential to protect the property from some threatened loss or injury pending a final disposition by the court.[13] Thus, the court may consider the following factors in deciding whether an appointment is necessary:
  - the existence of a valid claim by the party seeking the appointment;
  - the imminent nature of any danger to the property, to its concealment or removal, or to its value;
  - the adequacy of other legal remedies;
  - the lack of a less drastic equitable remedy;
  - the plaintiff's probable success in the lawsuit and the risk of irreparable injury to the property;
  - whether the defendant has engaged, or may engage, in any fraudulent actions with respect to the property;
  - the likelihood that appointing the receiver will do more good than harm; *and*
  - whether the potential harm to the plaintiff outweighs the injury to others.[14]

---

10. *See National P'ship Inv. Corp. v. National Housing Dev't Corp.,* 153 F.3d 1289, 1291–92 (11th Cir.1998); *Aviation Supply Corp. v. R.S.B.I. Aerospace, Inc.,* 999 F.2d 314, 317 (8th Cir.1993); *Hollywood Healthcare Corp. v. Deltec, Inc.,* 2004 WL 1118610, at *9 (D.Minn. May 17, 2004); *Sumpter v. United States,* 314 F.Supp.2d 684, 690 (E.D.Mich.2004).

11. *See Santibanez v. Wier McMahon & Co.,* 105 F.3d 234, 241 (5th Cir.1997) (appointments sought by judgment creditors); *Piambino v. Bailey,* 757 F.2d 1112 (11th Cir.1985); *Mintzer v. Arthur L. Wright & Co.,* 263 F.2d 823 (3d Cir.1959).

12. *See Santibanez v. Wier McMahon & Co.,* 105 F.3d 234, 241 (5th Cir.1997) (appointments sought by judgment creditors).

13. *See Gordon v. Washington,* 295 U.S. 30, 55 S.Ct. 584, 79 L.Ed. 1282 (1935); *Aviation Supply Corp. v. R.S.B.I. Aerospace, Inc.,* 999 F.2d 314, 317 (8th Cir.1993); *Hollywood Healthcare Corp. v. Deltec, Inc.,* 2004 WL 1118610, at *10 (D.Minn. May 17, 2004); *Sumpter v. United States,* 314 F.Supp.2d 684, 690 (E.D.Mich.2004); *World Fuel Servs. Corp. v. Moorehead,* 229 F.Supp.2d 584, 596 (N.D.Tex.2002); *Varsames v. Palazzolo,* 96 F.Supp.2d 361, 365 (S.D.N.Y.2000).

14. *See Santibanez v. Wier McMahon & Co.,* 105 F.3d 234, 241–42 (5th Cir.1997);

Each factor need not be satisfied, so long as the court determines that its review favors the receiver's appointment.[15] Courts have held that the existence of an express contractual right to the appointment of a receiver, along with adequate *prima facie* evidence of default, can suffice to justify appointment.[16]

Consent to Appointment

The court may appoint a receiver where the defendant both admits liability for the claim asserted in the litigation and consents to the appointment of a receiver—provided that there has been no improper attempt by the parties to collusively manufacture federal jurisdiction.[17]

Discretion of the District Court

Whether to appoint a receiver lies within the district judge's sound discretion.[18]

Who May Be Appointed

The court may appoint as the receiver any person deemed capable of serving in that capacity. Ordinarily, this requires the appointment of someone who is indifferent between the parties.[19] Federal law prevents the judge from appointing as a receiver any person related to the judge by consanguinity within the fourth degree,[20] a clerk or deputy of the court (absent special circumstances),[21] or a federal employee or person employed by the appointing judge.[22]

Aviation Supply Corp. v. R.S.B.I. Aerospace, Inc., 999 F.2d 314, 317 (8th Cir.1993); *Hollywood Healthcare Corp. v. Deltec, Inc.,* 2004 WL 1118610, at *9—*10 (D.Minn. May 17, 2004); *Fleet Business Credit, L.L.C. v. Wings Rests., Inc.,* 291 B.R. 550, 556 (N.D.Okla.2003); *Pioneer Capital Corp. v. Environamics Corp.,* 2003 WL 345349, at *9 (D.Me.2003) (decision of Magistrate Judge), *aff'd,* 2003 WL 1923765 (D.Me.2003); *World Fuel Servs. Corp. v. Moorehead,* 229 F.Supp.2d 584, 596 (N.D.Tex.2002); *De Boer Structures (U.S.A.), Inc. v. Shaffer Tent & Awning Co.,* 187 F.Supp.2d 910, 925 (S.D.Ohio 2001); *Varsames v. Palazzolo,* 96 F.Supp.2d 361, 365 (S.D.N.Y.2000); *Select Creations, Inc. v. Paliafito America, Inc.,* 828 F.Supp. 1301, 1367 (E.D.Wis.1992); *RTC v. Fountain Circle Assocs. Ltd. Partnership,* 799 F.Supp. 48, 50–51 (N.D.Ohio 1992).

15. *See Fleet Bus. Credit, L.L.C. v. Wings Rests., Inc.,* 291 B.R. 550, 556 (N.D.Okla.2003) (appointing receiver where "several of the factors weigh in favor of the propriety of appointing a receiver").

16. *See Pioneer Capital Corp. v. Environamics Corp.,* 2003 WL 345349, at *9 (D.Me.2003) (decision of Magistrate Judge), *aff'd,* 2003 WL 1923765 (D.Me.2003).

17. *See In re Reisenberg,* 208 U.S. 90, 28 S.Ct. 219, 52 L.Ed. 403 (1908).

18. *See Santibanez v. Wier McMahon & Co.,* 105 F.3d 234, 241 (5th Cir.1997); *De Boer Structures (U.S.A.), Inc. v. Shaffer Tent & Awning Co.,* 187 F.Supp.2d 910, 925 (S.D.Ohio 2001); *Varsames v. Palazzolo,* 96 F.Supp.2d 361, 365 (S.D.N.Y.2000); *Insussary v. Adminstaff Cos., Inc.,* 1999 WL 305102, at *1–*2 (S.D.N.Y.1999).

19. *See Liberte Capital Group, LLC v. Capwill,* 462 F.3d 543, 551 n.2 (6th Cir. 2006).

20. 28 U.S.C.A. § 458; 18 U.S.C.A. § 1910.

21. 28 U.S.C.A. § 957.

22. 28 U.S.C.A. § 958.

Place of Appointment

Because the appointment of a receiver is a type of *in rem* proceeding, the appointing court must enjoy a strong relationship to the contemplated receivership: a substantial portion of the defendant's business must be conducted in the host district, or a substantial portion of the anticipated receivership property must be located within the host district.

- *Conflicting Claims to Jurisdiction:* If two courts of concurrent and coordinate jurisdiction (*e.g.,* two federal courts) attempt to assert a claim to the same property, the court where the legal papers are first filed assumes exclusive jurisdiction, irrespective of whether its receiver is the first to obtain physical possession of the property.

If the two courts are not of the same or concurrent jurisdiction (*e.g.,* one State and one federal court), and where the subject matter in the one litigation is not the same as in the other litigation, or where no constructive possession of the property is obtained through the filing, the court whose receiver first obtains actual possession of the property assumes exclusive jurisdiction.[23]

Notice of Appointment

Generally, the court gives notice to all parties before appointing an equity receiver. But where notice is impractical or self-defeating, or where the appointment must be made immediately, the court enjoys the power to appoint a receiver *ex parte*.[24]

Effect of Appointment

Once a receiver is appointed and gives the bond required by the court, the court and the receiver obtain exclusive jurisdiction of all of the defendant's property, no matter where it is kept.[25] To obtain such jurisdiction over property outside the appointing district, the receiver must first file a copy of the complaint and appointment order in that foreign district.[26]

Actions by Receivers

A federal equity receiver is authorized to commence and prosecute any action necessary to accomplish the objectives of the receivership.[27] The receiver may be directed to bring suit on specific instructions from the court, or the receiver may independently institute lawsuits pursuant to the receiver's general duties of receiving, controlling, and managing the receivership property.

23. *See Harkin v. Brundage,* 276 U.S. 36, 48 S.Ct. 268, 72 L.Ed. 457 (1928).

24. *See Arkansas Louisiana Gas Co. v. Kroeger,* 303 F.2d 129 (5th Cir.1962).

25. *See Liberte Capital Group, LLC v. Capwill,* 462 F.3d 543, 551 (6th Cir. 2006).

26. 28 U.S.C.A. § 754.

27. *See Gilchrist v. General Elec. Capital Corp.,* 262 F.3d 295, 302 (4th Cir.2001) (noting that, when appointed, federal equity receivers may sue and be sued as provided by federal law).

- *May Sue In Any Jurisdiction:* The receiver may bring suit in any federal district, including those districts outside the court in which the receiver was formally appointed.[28]

- *Equitable Defenses*: Receivers are deemed to have stepped into the shoes of the persons or entities for whom they act. Thus, absent statutory provisions dictating otherwise, defenses that could be asserted against the original plaintiff are equally available against the plaintiff's equity receiver. However, equitable defenses (such as unclean hands) that could be asserted against the original plaintiff might not be effective against the receiver.[29]

Actions Against Receivers

A person may sue an equity receiver, without leave of court, for any of the receiver's actions taken after the receiver was appointed and during the receiver's management and operation of the receivership property.[30]

- *Leave of Court Needed:* Leave of court is required before the receiver may be sued for claims that arise from the property owner's actions or for claims that do not challenge the receiver's actions since appointment. To protect the assets (and to avoid their diminution by the costs of defending lawsuits), the receivership court may issue a blanket injunction staying all litigation against the receiver and entities under the receiver's control.[31] Although claimants are entitled to have their claims heard, the court enjoys broad control over the time and manner of those proceedings.[32] Intentionally interfering with a receivership in violation of such an injunction is punishable as contempt.[33]

- *Subject to Court's General Equity Power:* Suits against receivers remain subject to the court's general equity powers, which the court may exercise to achieve the ends of justice.

Jurisdiction in Actions Involving Receivers

Receivers may only sue or be sued when the district court would enjoy subject matter jurisdiction over the dispute.

- *Diversity Cases:* In diversity jurisdiction cases, the citizenship of the appointed receiver is examined to determine whether

---

28. 28 U.S.C.A. § 754.

29. *See FDIC v. O'Melveny & Myers*, 61 F.3d 17 (9th Cir.1995)(commenting that while party may be denied right or defense due to its misdeeds, the same punishment should not be imposed upon innocent receiver who assumes control pursuant to court order or by operation of law).

30. 28 U.S.C.A. § 959(a). *See Gilchrist v. General Elec. Capital Corp.*, 262 F.3d 295, 301 (4th Cir.2001) (noting that, when

appointed, federal equity receivers may sue and be sued as provided by federal law).

31. *See Liberte Capital Group, LLC v. Capwill*, 462 F.3d 543, 551–52 (6th Cir. 2006).

32. *See Liberte Capital Group, LLC v. Capwill*, 462 F.3d 543, 552 (6th Cir. 2006).

33. *See Liberte Capital Group, LLC v. Capwill*, 462 F.3d 543, 552 (6th Cir. 2006).

complete diversity exists.[34]

- *Federal Question Cases:* The district court's act of appointing a federal receiver probably will suffice to vest that district court with subject matter jurisdiction over actions brought by or against the receiver in that district.[35] Thus, when instituted in the appointing district, suits by the receiver intended to accomplish the objectives of the receivership are deemed ancillary to the appointing court's subject matter jurisdiction.[36] Likewise, suits may be maintained against the receiver in the receiver's appointing district even though no independent basis for subject matter jurisdiction is present.[37]

- *Outside Appointing District:* Suits by or against receivers instituted outside the appointing district will generally require an independent basis for federal subject matter jurisdiction.[38]

Dismissal of Actions Involving Receivers

After the court appoints a receiver in a litigation, the parties may not thereafter dismiss the litigation without first obtaining the court's approval.[39] This requirement protects against a waste of the court's time in unnecessarily establishing a receivership.

Vacating or Terminating the Receivership

The district court may vacate the order appointing the receiver or terminate the receivership when the objectives of the receivership have been obtained or the need for the receiver has abated.

Appeals

The district court's decision to appoint a receiver may be immediately appealed.[40] The court of appeals will review the appointment under the lenient abuse of discretion standard. If the appointment is found to have been improvident, the court of appeals may reverse and tax the costs and expenses incurred in the receivership on the persons who procured the receivership.[41]

Orders refusing to wind up the receivership or that otherwise have the effect of either ousting persons from their property or injuring the property may also be immediately appealed.[42]

All other orders involving receivers may only be appealed after entry of a final order.

---

34. *See Barber v. Powell,* 135 F.2d 728 (4th Cir.1943).

35. *See Gay v. Ruff,* 292 U.S. 25, 54 S.Ct. 608, 78 L.Ed. 1099 (1934).

36. *See Pope v. Louisville, N.A. & C. Ry. Co.,* 173 U.S. 573, 19 S.Ct. 500, 43 L.Ed. 814 (1899); *Haile v. Henderson Nat'l Bank,* 657 F.2d 816 (6th Cir.1981).

37. *See Rouse v. Hornsby,* 161 U.S. 588, 16 S.Ct. 610, 40 L.Ed. 817 (1896); *Robinson*

v. Michigan Consolidated Gas Co., 918 F.2d 579 (6th Cir.1990).

38. *See United States v. Franklin Nat'l Bank,* 512 F.2d 245 (2d Cir.1975).

39. *See* Rule 66.

40. 28 U.S.C.A. § 1292(a)(2).

41. *See Tucker v. Baker,* 214 F.2d 627 (5th Cir.1954).

42. 28 U.S.C.A. § 1292(a)(2).

ADDITIONAL RESEARCH REFERENCES

Wright & Miller, *Federal Practice and Procedure* §§ 2981–86.

C.J.S. Mechanics Liens § 214; Receivers §§ 1–30 et seq., 52–103 et seq., 105–150 et seq., 163–208 et seq., 227–256 et seq., 283–325 et seq., 365–411 et seq., 418–431 et seq.

West's Key No. Digests, Receivers ⛏1–220.

RULE 67

DEPOSIT INTO COURT

(a) Depositing Property. If any part of the relief sought is a money judgment or the disposition of a sum of money or some other deliverable thing, a party—on notice to every other party and by leave of court—may deposit with the court all or part of the money or thing, whether or not that party claims any of it. The depositing party must deliver to the clerk a copy of the order permitting deposit.

(b) Investing and Withdrawing Funds. Money paid into court under this rule must be deposited and withdrawn in accordance with 28 U.S.C. §§ 2041 and 2042 and any like statute. The money must be deposited in an interest-bearing account or invested in a court-approved, interest-bearing instrument.

[Amended effective October 20, 1949; August 1, 1983; April 30, 2007, effective December 1, 2007.]

--------------------- 2007 AMENDMENTS ROADMAP ---------------------

STYLE PROJECT CHANGES: Old Rule 67 was a single paragraph. New Rule 67 is partitioned into two subsections, with their own subtitles. Minor language changes were also made to aid readability.

NON-STYLE CHANGES: None.

NOTE: The Federal Rules "Style Project" is explained in Part III-A.

AUTHORS' COMMENTARY ON RULE 67

--------------------- PURPOSE AND SCOPE ---------------------

Rule 67 governs the circumstances in which a court may accept deposits of money and other personal assets pending the outcome of a case.

RULE 67(a). DEPOSITING PROPERTY

CORE CONCEPT

Rule 67(a) authorizes the court, in its discretion, to accept deposits of money or some other deliverable property in cases where such assets are at issue in the case.

APPLICATIONS

Common Uses

Parties have used Rule 67 in cases concerning Rule 22 and statutory interpleader[1] and when Rule 62 provides for security as a condition of a stay pending appeal.[2] Rule 67 has no applicability to payments permitted or ordered in criminal cases.[3]

Time for Deposit

A party may move pursuant to Rule 67 at any time during an action.

Stakeholder's Decision

Rule 67 provides the holder of a disputed asset with an opportunity to seek relief from the burden of safeguarding the asset. However, it provides no authority for another party to demand surrender of the asset.[4]

Leave of Court

Deposits may only be made with leave of court, on motion and with notice to all other parties.[5] If funds are actually deposited with the court, one effect may be to stop the accrual of interest on claims until the case is decided.[6]

Content of Motion

In the motion, the movant should state that opposing parties dispute the ownership of the property or money as well as the

---

1. *See, e.g., Southtrust Bank of Florida, N.A. v. Wilson,* 971 F.Supp. 539, 542 (M.D.Fla.1997) (using Rule 67 to accept deposit in interpleader case).

2. *Cf., e.g., Kotsopoulos v. Asturia Shipping Co.,* 467 F.2d 91, 94 (2d Cir.1972) (by paying amount of judgment into court, party can stop running of interest against that party during pendency of appeal).

3. *See, e.g., United States v. Sun Growers of California,* 212 F.3d 603, 606 (D.C.Cir.2000) (Rule 67 applies "only to civil actions.").

4. *See, e.g., Cajun Electric Power Cooperative, Inc. v. Riley Stoker Corp.,* 901 F.2d 441, 444–45 (5th Cir.1990) ("The ... purpose [of Rule 67] is to relieve the depositor of responsibility for the fund in dispute

while the parties hash out their differences with respect to it.").

5. *See, e.g., Alstom Caribe, Inc. v. Geo. P. Reintjes Co.,* 484 F.3d 106, 113–14 (1st Cir. 2007) (noting court's discretion to accept deposit is limited to cases where there is genuine dispute as to entitlement to funds, and dispute is still alive at time of motion to make deposit; deposit with court may be appropriate even when some claimants to funds are not parties to action); *Garrick v. Weaver,* 888 F.2d 687, 694 (10th Cir.1989) (court has discretion to decide whether to accept payment).

6. *See, e.g., Cajun Electric Power Cooperative, Inc. v. Riley Stoker Corp.,* 901 F.2d 441, 445 (5th Cir.1990) (so noting).

particular reasons for making the deposit, such as to avoid responsibility for the property or money.

Method of Deposit

When the court grants leave to make the deposit, the party must serve the order on the clerk of court at the time of making the deposit.

RULE 67(b). INVESTING AND WITHDRAWING FUNDS

CORE CONCEPT

Rule 67(b) identifies the relevant statutes governing deposits and withdrawals, and also provides that money paid into court under Rule 67 must be deposited in a court-approved interest bearing account.

Administration of Deposit

The clerk of court must invest any money paid into the court in an interest-bearing account or in an interest-bearing instrument approved by the court in the name and to the credit of the court.

Withdrawal of Deposit

A person seeking the money deposited in court must make a motion asserting a judgment or any other document establishing that person's judicially defined interest in the deposit. The court may not disburse any deposit until it establishes ownership by court order, unless the parties have stipulated to the ownership of the property under the direction of the court.[7]

The Merits

Rule 67 provides a potential safe haven for an asset until a court determines rights in the asset. However, Rule 67 does not of itself offer a forum for adjudicating such rights. The question of the merits is reserved for some separate proceeding.[8]

Deposit Not Claimed

If the deposit is not claimed by the person entitled to the deposit for five years from the date of adjudication or from the date of deposit when the asset deposited is not in dispute, the asset will be transferred to the U.S. Treasury in the name of and to the credit of the United States.[9]

7. *But cf., Craig's Stores of Texas, Inc. v. Bank of Louisiana*, 402 F.3d 522, 524 (5th Cir.2005) (where money was deposited in court in a proceeding which court was subsequently found to be lacking in jurisdiction, court could not distribute funds as it deemed just; instead, court had to return funds to party who made deposit).

8. *See, e.g., LTV Corp. v. Gulf States Steel, Inc. of Alabama*, 969 F.2d 1050, 1063 (D.C.Cir.1992) (Rule 67 " 'provides a place of safekeeping for disputed funds pending the resolution of a legal dispute, but it cannot be used as a means of altering the contractual relationships and legal duties of the parties.' ").

9. 28 U.S.C.A. § 2042.

ADDITIONAL RESEARCH REFERENCES

Wright & Miller, *Federal Practice and Procedure* §§ 2991–3000.

C.J.S. Deposits in Court §§ 1–9.

West's Key No. Digests, Deposits in Court ⮞1–12.

RULE 68

OFFER OF JUDGMENT

(a) Making an Offer; Judgment on an Accepted Offer. More than 10 days before the trial begins, a party defending against a claim may serve on an opposing party an offer to allow judgment on specified terms, with the costs then accrued. If, within 10 days after being served, the opposing party serves written notice accepting the offer, either party may then file the offer and notice of acceptance, plus proof of service. The clerk must then enter judgment.

(b) Unaccepted Offer. An unaccepted offer is considered withdrawn, but it does not preclude a later offer. Evidence of an unaccepted offer is not admissible except in a proceeding to determine costs.

(c) Offer After Liability Is Determined. When one party's liability to another has been determined but the extent of liability remains to be determined by further proceedings, the party held liable may make an offer of judgment. It must be served within a reasonable time— but at least 10 days—before a hearing to determine the extent of liability.

(d) Paying Costs After an Unaccepted Offer. If the judgment that the offeree finally obtains is not more favorable than the unaccepted offer, the offeree must pay the costs incurred after the offer was made.

[Amended effective March 19, 1948; July 1, 1966; August 1, 1987; April 30, 2007, effective December 1, 2007.]

——————— **2007 AMENDMENTS ROADMAP** ———————

STYLE PROJECT CHANGES: Old Rule 68 was a single paragraph. New Rule 68 is partitioned into four subsections, with their own subtitles. Minor language changes were also made to aid readability.

NON-STYLE CHANGES: None.

NOTE: The Federal Rules "Style Project" is explained in Part III-A.

AUTHORS' COMMENTARY ON RULE 68

———————————— PURPOSE AND SCOPE ————————————

Rule 68 governs the circumstances in which a party defending against a claim for money damages or property may seek to resolve the claim by offering to allow judgment against that party for a specified amount of money or property. The Rule also establishes the consequences when a party does not accept an offer of judgment.

RULE 68(a). MAKING AN OFFER; JUDGMENT ON AN ACCEPTED OFFER

CORE CONCEPT

Rule 68(a) establishes the time limit for making an offer of judgment. It also provides that the offer and proof of service will be filed with the court only if the opposing party accepts the offer. Finally, it provides that an accept offer requires the clerk of court to enter judgment.

APPLICATIONS

Contents of Offer

An offer of judgment must be for a specified dollar amount or specified property.[1] Rule 68 provides that the offer must include an offer to pay costs accrued by the claiming party prior to receipt of the offer of judgment.[2] In practice, however, if the offer provides a specified amount for costs or provides that costs are included, the offer satisfies the requirements of the Rule. The court may add an amount for costs only when the offer does not provide for costs.[3]

Relation to Rule 54

Rule 54(d) provides that the party who prevails in a lawsuit is entitled to costs "as of course" unless some other provision of

---

1. *See, e.g., Basha v. Mitsubishi Motor Credit of America, Inc.,* 336 F.3d 451 (5th Cir.2003) (offer that proposed to settle all claims but did not quantify damages could not meet Rule 68 requirements); *Marryshow v. Flynn,* 986 F.2d 689, 691 (4th Cir. 1993) (offer must be for "specified amount").

2. *See, e.g., McCain v. Detroit II Auto Finance Center,* 378 F.3d 561 (6th Cir.2004) (defendant's silence on costs means they are recoverable by plaintiff).

3. *Marek v. Chesny,* 473 U.S. 1, 105 S.Ct. 3012, 87 L.Ed.2d 1 (1985). *But compare, Stewart v. Professional Computer Centers, Inc.,* 148 F.3d 937 (8th Cir.1998) (defendant made offer to cover "any and all

counts;" plaintiff had sought attorneys' fees and costs in complaint; held, facts were open to more than one interpretation, and therefore no valid offer and acceptance had occurred; judgment based on Rule 68 must therefore be vacated), *with Webb v. James,* 147 F.3d 617 (7th Cir.1998) (defendants' offer did not mention costs; held, plaintiff entitled to attorneys' fees and costs under applicable law; principles of contract recision should not apply to situations involving Rule 68). *See also Hennessy v. Daniels Law Office,* 270 F.3d 551, 553–54 (8th Cir. 2001) (where accepted offer is silent as to attorney's fees and no parol evidence exists to resolve ambiguity, defendant is liable for attorney's fees; using contract principle to construe ambiguity against offeror).

federal law or the federal rules intervenes.[4] When Rule 68 is applicable, it is a provision of the federal rules that overrides Rule 54(d) and can create a situation where a non-prevailing party may recover costs.[5]

Offering Judgment

The appropriate method of offering judgment is to serve a written offer upon the party whose claim is at issue.[6] Although the Rule does not strictly require it, standard practice is to serve copies of the offer upon all other parties to the case. However, until an offer is accepted by the claiming party, it is inappropriate to file a copy of the offer with the clerk's office.[7]

Ambiguities: Ordinary Contract Analysis

In accordance with ordinary rules of contract law, ambiguities in Rule 68 offers are construed against the offeror.[8]

Timing of Offer

To be effective under Rule 68, an offer of judgment must be served on the party prosecuting a claim at least 11 days before the beginning of a trial. However, if the trial is a bifurcated proceeding, in which liability only is established in a first hearing, a timely offer of judgment may be served after a determination of liability but not less than 10 days before a damages hearing begins.[9]

Method of Accepting an Offer

The appropriate method for accepting an offer of judgment is by written notice of acceptance to the party who made the offer. It is

---

4. Fed.R.Civ.P. 54(d).

5. See, e.g., Payne v. Milwaukee County, 288 F.3d 1021, 1027 (7th Cir.2002).

6. See, e.g., Driver Music Co. v. Commercial Union Insurance Cos., 94 F.3d 1428, 1432 (10th Cir.1996) (Rule 68 contemplates that offer will be in writing); Magnuson v. Video Yesteryear, 85 F.3d 1424, 1429 (9th Cir.1996)(absent demonstrated special need or consent of opposing party, service by fax or federal express is ineffective service).

7. See, e.g., Kason v. Amphenol Corp., 132 F.R.D. 197 (N.D.Ill.1990) ("[N]o filing is permitted at the time of tender.").

8. See, e.g., Andretti v. Borla Performance Industries, Inc., 426 F.3d 824, 837 (6th Cir.2005) ("[W]e should apply general contract principles to interpret Rule 68 offers of judgment."); Arbor Hill Concerned Citizens Neighborhood Association v. County of Albany, 369 F.3d 91, 95 (2d Cir.2004) (mere promise that is dependent on will or inclination of promisor is not an offer of a mutually binding contract and therefore cannot be an offer of judgment); Hennessy v. Daniels Law Office, 270 F.3d 551, 553–54

(8th Cir.2001) (where accepted offer is silent as to attorney's fees and no parol evidence exists to resolve ambiguity, defendant is liable for attorney's fees; using contract principle to construe ambiguity against offeror). Gavoni v. Dobbs House, Inc., 164 F.3d 1071, 1077 (7th Cir.1999) (unapportioned offer of $10,000 to three defendants is ineffective to trigger Rule 68; burden is on defendant to make offer with precision); Herrington v. County of Sonoma, 12 F.3d 901 (9th Cir.1993)(additionally, extrinsic evidence is admissible to clarify ambiguities). See also Nordby v. Anchor Hocking Packaging Co., 199 F.3d 390, 392 (7th Cir. 1999) (additional reasons for construing ambiguities against offeror are that "plaintiff is being asked to give up his right to a trial" and that ambiguities mean plaintiff "can't make an intelligent choice whether to accept [the offer]–and [unlike ordinary contracts] there are consequences either way").

9. Delta Air Lines v. August, 450 U.S. 346, 101 S.Ct. 1146, 67 L.Ed.2d 287 (1981).

standard practice to serve copies of such notice on all other parties to the case.

Terms of Acceptance

The offer must be accepted in its entirety, or it is deemed rejected.[10]

RULE 68(b). UNACCEPTED OFFER

CORE CONCEPT

Rule 68(b) provides that unaccepted offers are deemed withdrawn, though it remains possible for a party to make a subsequent offer. Unaccepted offers are not admissible in court, except in a proceeding to determine costs.

Timing of Acceptance

A party has 10 days after receipt of service of the written offer to accept the offer of judgment.[11] If the offer is not accepted within the 10–day period, Rule 68 treats the offer as withdrawn, and it cannot thereafter be accepted. However, it is possible for the party that made the offer to renew the offer, or make a different offer, in which event the 10–day period for acceptance begins to run again.

Offers by Plaintiff

Unless a plaintiff is defending against a counterclaim or a crossclaim, as described in Rules 13 and 14, a plaintiff cannot make an offer of judgment.[12] Only parties defending against claims may use Rule 68 to make offers of judgment.[13]

Offer for Full Amount of Claim

It is settled that if a Rule 68 offer of judgment is made for the full amount of relief sought or for the full amount of recovery authorized by statute, the case is ended.[14] Courts differ only as to

10. *See, e.g., Whitcher v. Town of Matthews,* 136 F.R.D. 582, 585 (W.D.N.C.1991). (Plaintiffs cannot both accept offer as to money damages and continue action as to equitable relief). *But cf., Gordon v. Gouline,* 81 F.3d 235 (D.C.Cir.1996) (acceptance is effective even when conditioned upon approval of bankruptcy court).

11. *See, e.g., Perkins v. U.S. West Communications, Inc.,* 138 F.3d 336 (8th Cir. 1998) (defendant filed motion for summary judgment; while motion was pending, defendant made offer of judgment under Rule 68; two days after offer of judgment was made, court granted defendant's summary judgment motion; plaintiff, upon notice of grant of summary judgment, accepted Rule 68 offer; held, acceptance bound defendant, notwithstanding grant of summary judgment; possible different result if defendant had conditioned offer of judgment on

court's denial of summary judgment motion).

12. *Delta Air Lines v. August,* 450 U.S. 346, 101 S.Ct. 1146, 67 L.Ed.2d 287 (1981).

13. *See, e.g., Garcia v. Wal–Mart Stores, Inc.,* 209 F.3d 1170, 1176 (10th Cir.2000) ("Rule 68 governs only defendants' costs."). *Cf., Amati v. City of Woodstock,* 176 F.3d 952, 958 (7th Cir.1999) ("A plaintiff has no right to demand a Rule 68 offer."). *But cf., S.A. Healy Co. v. Milwaukee Metropolitan Sewerage District,* 60 F.3d 305, 310–12 (7th Cir.1995) (Rule 68 permits offers only by parties defending claims, but in diversity case, state law permitting plaintiff's offer of settlement may be applied).

14. *See, e.g., Zimmerman v. Bell,* 800 F.2d 386, 390 (4th Cir.1986) (dismissing securities fraud claim where defendant offered full amount of relief sought); *Sam-*

whether the plaintiff should simply be forced to accept the offer[15] or whether the outcome is mandated by the resulting disappearance of subject matter jurisdiction (for lack of a case or controversy).[16]

Entering Final Judgment: Judicial Discretion

If the party prosecuting a claim accepts the offer of judgment, Rule 68 permits either party to file the offer and notice of acceptance, along with proof of service, with the clerk of court. Rule 68 then directs that the clerk shall enter judgment consistent with the offer and acceptance.[17]

Once the offer, notice of acceptance and proof of service are filed with the court, the court must normally enter judgment.[18] Except in circumstances where the literal language of Rule 68 conflicts with some other requirement of federal law, the court has no discretion to refuse to enter judgment.[19]

Determining Whether Judgment is "More Favorable"

In cases involving only money damages, it is usually not difficult to calculate whether the judgment a party won is more favorable than an earlier offer of judgment. However, where a party obtains an injunction as part of a favorable judgment, the calculation can be more challenging.[20] Nevertheless, it appears settled that in determining whether a judgment is more favorable than an earlier offer of judgment, the value of an injunction granted should be included in the calculation.[21]

Equitable Claims Only

Rule 68 generally applies to offers of specific sums or specific property. Typically the Rule is not used to resolve claims in equity

---

sung Electronics Co. v. Rambus, Inc., 398 F.Supp.2d 470, 484 (E.D.Va.2005) (once full offer is made no case or controversy remains).

15. *See, e.g., Wilner v. OSI Collection Services, Inc.,* 198 F.R.D. 393, 395 (S.D.N.Y. 2001) (asserting power to compel plaintiff to accept offer).

16. *See, e.g., Abrams v. Interco, Inc.,* 719 F.2d 23, 32–33 (2d Cir.1983) (asserting lack of subject matter jurisdiction).

17. *See, e.g., Parental Guide of Texas, Inc. v. Thomson, Inc.,* 446 F.3d 1265, 1270 (Fed.Cir.2006) ("[T]he entry of judgment 'is generally a ministerial act and can be performed by the clerk without any input from the court or a jury.' ").

18. *See, e.g., Webb v. James,* 147 F.3d 617, 621 (7th Cir.1998).

19. *See, e.g., Parental Guide of Texas, Inc. v. Thomson, Inc.,* 446 F.3d 1265, 1270 (Fed. Cir.2006) ("[U]nder Rule 68, the terms of a judgment are agreed upon by the parties; the court has no input or discretion

to alter or modify any of the terms."); *Ramming v. Natural Gas Pipeline Co.,* 390 F.3d 366, 371 (5th Cir.2004) (duty of court to review settlement of class action under Rule 23 provides exception to Rule 68; same result, slightly different reasoning, when case involves plea for injunctive relief).

20. *See, e.g., Andretti v. Borla Performance Industries, Inc.,* 426 F.3d 824, 837 (6th Cir.2005) ("comparing the value of damages to an injunction is like comparing apples and oranges," but courts must sometimes do so in situations governed by Rule 68).

21. *See, e.g., Reiter v. MTA New York City Transit Authority,* 457 F.3d 224 (2d Cir.2006) ("Nothing in the language of Rule 68 suggests that a final judgment that contains equitable relief is inherently less favorable than a Rule 68 offer that contains monetary relief."); *Andretti v. Borla Performance Industries, Inc.,* 426 F.3d 824, 837 (6th Cir.2005) ("[M]oney damages [need not be] the only measure of whether a plaintiff has obtained a 'more favorable' judgment under Rule 68.").

where a party seeks only an injunction, but Rule 68 itself does not expressly prohibit such an application.[22]

Revocation

It appears settled that except in exceptional circumstances a Rule 68 offer cannot be revoked during the 10 days provided by the Rule.[23] This conclusion is an exception to the general rule that principles of contract law apply to construe a Rule 68 offer and acceptance.[24]

Consequences of Nonacceptance

The consequences of nonacceptance of an offer under Rule 68 depend on the outcome of the litigation. Once final judgment is entered, if the party that did not accept the offer has won a judgment greater than the amount in the offer of judgment, the refusal of the offer has no consequence whatever.[25] If, however, the nonaccepting party receives a favorable final judgment, but for less than the amount in the offer of judgment—Rule 68 requires the nonaccepting party to pay the offering party's costs incurred after the offer was made.[26] Rule 68 may thus permit a party that has made an offer of judgment, and then loses the case, to recover some costs from the prevailing party. To that extent, Rule 68 provides a possible exception to Rule 54(d), which provides that the prevailing party ordinarily will collect costs from the losing party.

Relation to Rule 23

Rule 23 governs class actions. If a plaintiff has sought to have a case certified as a class action, it appears that a Rule 68 offer of

22. *See, e.g., Chathas v. Local 134 IBEW,* 233 F.3d 508, 511 (7th Cir.2000) ("Rule 68 offers are much more common in money cases than in equity cases, but nothing in the rule forbids its use in the latter type of case.").

23. *See, e.g., Richardson v. National Railroad Passenger Corp.,* 49 F.3d 760, 764 (D.C.Cir.1995) (noting that courts treat offers as irrevocable for 10 days). *Cf., Perkins v. U.S. West Communications, Inc.,* 138 F.3d 336 (8th Cir.1998) (revocation permitted only for "good cause").

24. *See, e.g., Herrington v. County of Sonoma,* 12 F.3d 901, 907 (9th Cir.1993) (Rule 68 is subject to standard rules of contract construction.).

25. *See, e.g., Brown v. Lester E. Cox, Medical Centers,* 286 F.3d 1040, 1047 (8th Cir.2002) (plaintiff refused offer of judgment and then won judgment greater than offer; held, plaintiff's right to attorney's fees established by applicable federal civil rights law was therefore unaffected by refusal).

26. *See, e.g., Payne v. Milwaukee County,* 288 F.3d 1021, 1025 (7th Cir.2002) (civil rights case; prevailing plaintiff who won less than offer of judgment is not entitled to recovery attorney's fees that would otherwise have been available under federal civil rights law); *Haworth v. Nevada,* 56 F.3d 1048 (9th Cir.1995) (plaintiff recovering less than offer of judgment cannot recover costs incurred after offer, and must pay defendant's post-offer costs). *See also Pouillon v. Little,* 326 F.3d 713, 715 (6th Cir. 2003) (Rule 68 offer that was not accepted retains cost-shifting effect after plaintiff got reversal on appeal of original loss and won nominal amount upon remand). *Cf., Berkla v. Corel Corp.,* 302 F.3d 909, 922 (9th Cir. 2002) (prevailing party won less than rejected offer, but offer did not satisfy elements of Rule 68; held, prevailing party could not be denied costs that would otherwise have been awarded if no offer had been made); *Ortiz v. Regan,* 980 F.2d 138, 141 (2d Cir. 1992) (defendant made settlement offer which did not satisfy Rule 68; held, plaintiff's rejection could not be used to reduce fee award that would otherwise have been made).

judgment for the full statutory amount of the individual plaintiff's claim cannot be used to render the putative class action moot.[27]

Additionally, when an offer of judgment is made in a case that has been certified as a class action, it may appear that the authority of a district judge to review and approve proposed settlements (found in Rule 23) is in conflict with the provision of Rule 68 that the court has no authority to approve or reject an offer of judgment that meets the requirements of Rule 68. However, the case law seems to establish clearly that, when applicable, Rule 23 is an exception to the limitations Rule 68 imposes on a court.[28]

When Defendant Prevails

If an opponent of a claim makes an offer of judgment that is not accepted, and if the offeror then wins the case, Rule 68 has *no* effect. Rule 68 is applied, if at all, only when an offer is not accepted, and then the offeree obtains judgment—but for less than the amount of the offer.[29]

RULE 68(c). OFFER AFTER LIABILITY IS DETERMINED

CORE CONCEPT

Rule 68(c) permits an offer after liability is determined, but the amount of liability has not been established. Such an offer must be served at least ten days before the date of a hearing on the extent of liability.

Offer to Multiple Plaintiffs

If a defendant makes an offer of judgment to more than one plaintiff in the same case, the offer must itemize the proposed

27. *See, e.g., Carroll v. United Compucred Collections, Inc.,* 399 F.3d 620, 625 (6th Cir.2005) (in instant case motion for class certification was pending but not yet decided when offer of judgment was made; if complaint could be rendered moot by use of Rule 68, court could never reach class action even in cases where class certification would be appropriate); *Weiss v. Regal Collections,* 385 F.3d 337, 348 (3d Cir.2004) (same, but making exception for "undue delay" in filing motion for class certification).

28. *See, e.g., Ramming v. Natural Gas Pipeline Co.,* 390 F.3d 366, 371 (5th Cir. 2004) (duty of court to review settlement of class actions under Rule 23 provides exception to Rule 68; same result when case involves plea for injunctive relief).

29. *Delta Air Lines v. August,* 450 U.S. 346, 352, 101 S.Ct. 1146, 1150, 67 L.Ed.2d 287 (1981). *See also, Payne v. Milwaukee County,* 288 F.3d 1021, 1025 (7th Cir.2002) ("Had [plaintiff] not prevailed in some significant sense, [defendant] would be con-

fined to Rule 54(d), and rule 68 would simply have no application."). *MRO Communications, Inc. v. AT&T Corp.,* 197 F.3d 1276, 1280 (9th Cir.1999) (under *Delta Air Lines* "Rule 68 is inapplicable in a case in which the defendant obtains judgment"); *Amati v. City of Woodstock,* 176 F.3d 952, 957 (7th Cir.1999) ("Rule 68 bites only when the plaintiff wins but wins less than the defendant's offer of judgment."); *Louisiana Power & Light Co. v. Kellstrom,* 50 F.3d 319, 333 (5th Cir.1995) ("If a plaintiff takes nothing ... Rule 68 does not apply." (citing *Delta Air Lines*)). *But see McCauley v. Trans Union, L.L.C.,* 402 F.3d 340, 341–42 (2d Cir.2005) (where plaintiff has rejected offer of judgment that included full dollar amount at issue but also included a denial of liability of defendant, proper remedy is to enter default judgment for full dollar amount, plus costs; judgment will contain no record of liability of defendant).

payment to each plaintiff. If the offer does not identify the proposed allocation of money among the plaintiffs, the defendant will not collect costs even if the plaintiffs' final judgment is for less than the offer.[30]

Joint Offer from Multiple Defendants

When more than one defendant makes an offer of judgment to a plaintiff, the defendants should be careful to make clear the proportion of the offer being made by each defendant. Failure to provide more than an unapportioned joint offer creates a significant possibility that, if one of the defendants is somehow excused but another is found liable, the offeror/defendants will not meet their burden of demonstrating that the offer was more favorable than the judgment the plaintiff later obtained.[31]

Settled Cases

The literal language of Rule 68 bars its use to award costs in cases that settle without going to judgment. Less certain is the result when the parties settle, and the court enters judgment on the settlement.[32] Attorneys are advised to consult local practice.

Offer of Judgment as Evidence

Rule 68 provides that if an offer of judgment is not accepted, the offer may not be used as evidence at trial. The only use to which a nonaccepted offer of judgment may be put is to establish the consequences, if any, to the nonaccepting party when final judgment is entered in the case.

---

30. *See, e.g., Gavoni v. Dobbs House, Inc.,* 164 F.3d 1071, 1075–77 (7th Cir.1999) (defendant has burden of showing that offer was more favorable than final judgment; defendant also has burden of making offer clear, and plaintiffs are entitled to "a clear baseline from which [they] may evaluate the merits of their case relative to the value of the offer").

31. *See, e.g., Harbor Motor Co. v. Arnell Chevrolet–Geo, Inc.,* 265 F.3d 638, 647–49 (7th Cir.2001) (one defendant won at trial, but other lost; held, plaintiff could not have estimated with any confidence what portion of offer was attributable to losing defendant, so offer was ineffective; acknowledging possibility that on different facts court might be able to calculate the share of an unapportioned offer to ascribe to each of several defendants; "We need not go so far as to conclude ... that Rule 68 always requires an exact delineation of the manner in which damages are to be apportioned among multiple parties."); *Johnston v. Penrod Drilling Co.,* 803 F.2d 867, 870 (5th

Cir.1986) (plaintiff settled with one defendant, won judgment against another; held, offer of judgment and judgment actually obtained could not be compared because "settlement may have ... had an effect on the damage award;" noting different result if plaintiff's judgment had been won against both defendants). *Cf., Tai Van Le v. University of Pennsylvania,* 321 F.3d 403, 408 (3d Cir.2003) (distinguishing results in other cases where it was not as clear as in instant case that all payments, whether pursuant to Rule 68 or judgment on merits, would be made by one defendant who had duty of indemnification to other defendant).

32. *Compare, e.g., Equal Employment Opportunity Commission v. Hamilton Standard Division, United Technologies Corp.,* 637 F.Supp. 1155, 1158 (D.Conn. 1986)(refusing to apply Rule 68 to case ending in settlement and stipulated dismissal), *with Lang v. Gates,* 36 F.3d 73, 77 (9th Cir.1994) (approving application of Rule 68 to order enforcing settlement).

RULE 68(d). PAYING COSTS AFTER AN UNACCEPTED OFFER

CORE CONCEPT

Rule 68(d) establishes the consequences when an offer has been rejected and the offeree subsequently obtains a judgment that is not more favorable than the offer. In that circumstance the offeree must pay costs incurred by the offering party after the offer was made. As is noted under Rule 68(c) above, however, the offeree has no obligation to pay costs if the offeree loses the case.

Attorney Fees

Rule 68 is silent as to whether a nonaccepting party may be required to pay another party's attorney fees as part of the other party's "costs". However, it is settled that Rule 68 does not itself create a right to recover attorney fees.[33] Instead, Rule 68 authorizes recovery of attorney fees from a nonaccepting party—who subsequently received a final judgment less favorable than the offer of judgment—if some other provision of federal law permits recovery of attorney fees.[34] Thus, if a defendant who was sued on a federal civil rights claim made an offer of judgment that was not accepted, and the defendant then lost on the merits (but for less than the offer of judgment), the defendant might be entitled to recover costs that included attorney fees if federal civil rights law included attorney fees within the range of recoverable costs.[35] Moreover, if the statute normally awarded fees to a prevailing plaintiff (who recovered less than the offer), the court has authority to reduce the attorney fees award to the plaintiff.[36]

---

33. *See, e.g., McCain v. Detroit II Auto Finance Center,* 378 F.3d 561 (6th Cir.2004) ("[T]he only way in which Rule 68 directly implicates awards of attorney's fees is in situations where such fees are made an element of 'costs'—whether by statute . . . or as a matter of contract."); *Poteete v. Capital Engineering, Inc.,* 185 F.3d 804, 807 (7th Cir.1999) ("Rule 68 does not entitle a defendant to recover his attorneys' fees." (citing extensive authority)).

34. *See, e.g., Wilson v. Nomura Securities International, Inc.,* 361 F.3d 86, 89 (2d Cir.2004) ("Where the underlying statute defines 'costs' to include attorney's fees . . . such fees are 'costs' for purposes of Rule 68.").

35. *Marek v. Chesny,* 473 U.S. 1, 105 S.Ct. 3012, 87 L.Ed.2d 1 (1985). *Harbor Motor Co. v. Arnell Chevrolet–Geo, Inc.,* 265 F.3d 638, 646 (7th Cir.2001) (agreeing with *Crossman,* infra, that in cases controlled by fee provision of copyright law "only prevailing parties can receive attorney's fees pursuant to rule 68;" defendant who lost case for less than offer of judgment therefore cannot recover attorney's fees; acknowledging different result in *Jordan v. Time,*

Inc., infra); *Crossman v. Marcoccio,* 806 F.2d 329, 333–34 (1st Cir.1986) (where underlying copyright statute awards attorney's fees only to prevailing party, defendant who lost case—but for amount less than offer of judgment—cannot recover attorney's fee because defendant did not prevail in case). *Cf., Haworth v. Nevada,* 56 F.3d 1048 (9th Cir.1995)(because relevant federal statute did not include attorney fees in costs, attorney fees could not be shifted by Rule 68). *But see Jordan v. Time, Inc.,* 111 F.3d 102, 105 (11th Cir.1997) (requiring plaintiff in copyright case who obtained judgment for less than offer of judgment to pay defendant's costs and fees incurred after offer was made).

36. *See, e.g., Dalal v. Alliant Techsystems, Inc.,* 182 F.3d 757 (10th Cir.1999) (affirming reduced award of attorney fees for legal work done between date of offer of judgment and date of judgment; acknowledging lack of precise formula for making calculation); *Haworth v. Nevada,* 56 F.3d 1048 (9th Cir.1995)(reducing plaintiff's recovery of attorney fees because judgment was for less than the offer of judgment).

Multiple Offers

Rule 68 explicitly permits a party whose previous offer of judgment was not accepted to continue making offers, provided that the offers are served more than 10 days before the beginning of a trial.

ADDITIONAL RESEARCH REFERENCES

Wright & Miller, *Federal Practice and Procedure* §§ 3001–10.   Lisnek, *Effective Negotiation and Mediation, A Lawyer's Guide.*

C.J.S. Federal Civil Procedure § 1276.

West's Key No. Digests, Federal Civil Procedure ☜2725.

RULE 69

EXECUTION

(a) In General.

    (1) *Money Judgment; Applicable Procedure.* A money judgment is enforced by a writ of execution, unless the court directs otherwise. The procedure on execution—and in proceedings supplementary to and in aid of judgment or execution—must accord with the procedure of the state where the court is located, but a federal statute governs to the extent it applies.

    (2) *Obtaining Discovery.* In aid of the judgment or execution, the judgment creditor or a successor in interest whose interest appears of record may obtain discovery from any person—including the judgment debtor—as provided in these rules or by the procedure of the state where the court is located.

(b) Against Certain Public Officers. When a judgment has been entered against a revenue officer in the circumstances stated in 28 U.S.C. § 2006, or against an officer of Congress in the circumstances stated in 2 U.S.C. § 118, the judgment must be satisfied as those statutes provide.

[Amended effective October 20, 1949; July 1, 1970; August 1, 1987; April 30, 2007, effective December 1, 2007.]

--------------- 2007 AMENDMENTS ROADMAP ---------------

    STYLE PROJECT CHANGES: Rule 69(a) was partitioned into two subparts to aid readability. Minor language changes were made throughout Rule 69 to aid readability.

    NON-STYLE CHANGES: Rule 69(b) was amended to provide that execution of a judgment against a revenue officer, pursuant to either 28 U.S.C.A. § 2006 or 2 U.S.C.A. § 118, must be satisfied only as those statutes authorize. Previous language left an ambiguity as to whether such a judgment might sometimes be properly executed against the officer or the officer's property.

NOTE: The Federal Rules "Style Project" is explained in Part III-A.

AUTHORS' COMMENTARY ON RULE 69

─────────── PURPOSE AND SCOPE ───────────

Rule 69 provides a mechanism for executing money judgments entered by a federal court. Rule 69 also provides for the execution of judgments entered against district directors of the Internal Revenue Service and officers of Congress.

───

RULE 69(a).   IN GENERAL

CORE CONCEPT

Rule 69(a) provides for the enforcement of money judgments generally through a writ of execution. If enforcement of a money judgment requires ancillary litigation, state law will usually control such litigation unless a federal statute otherwise provides.[1] However, discovery to enforce a money judgment may be conducted pursuant to either the federal discovery rules or the discovery rules of the forum state.

APPLICATIONS

Scope

Rule 69 only applies to an execution of a money judgment entered by a federal court[2] and has no application to state court judgments or other types of judgments.

Subject Matter Jurisdiction

Efforts to collect judgments under Rule 69 fall within the supplemental jurisdiction of district courts.[3]

Supplementing or Supplanting State Procedure

Although Rule 69(a) directs a district court to use state procedure,[4] it also provides that the court may "direct otherwise." At

---

1. *See, e.g., United States v. Little,* 52 F.3d 495 (4th Cir.1995)(holding that Rule 69(a) requires application of state law governing enforcement of judgments). *But cf., Apparel Art International, Inc. v. Amertex Enterprises, Ltd.,* 48 F.3d 576 (1st Cir. 1995)(Rule 69 requires application of state procedure on execution; however, Rule 69 does not require use of "general state procedural law," such as state doctrine on res judicata).

2. *See, e.g., United States v. Timilty,* 148 F.3d 1, 4 (1st Cir.1998) (enforcement of judgment imposing criminal fine in favor of United States is also controlled by, *inter alia,* Rule 69(a)).

3. *See, e.g., Kokkonen v. Guardian Life Insurance Co.,* 511 U.S. 375, 379, 114 S.Ct. 1673, 1676, 128 L.Ed.2d 391 (1994) (ancil-

lary jurisdiction permits district court, *inter alia,* to "vindicate its authority, and effectuate its decrees"); *Yang v. City of Chicago,* 137 F.3d 522, 525 (7th Cir.1998) (citing to extensive authority). *But cf., Sandlin v. Corporate Interiors, Inc.,* 972 F.2d 1212, 1217 (10th Cir.1992) (if enforcement proceeding is an attempt to collect judgment from nonparty on theory distinct from theory underlying judgment, "an independent basis for federal jurisdiction must exist").

4. *Peacock v. Thomas,* 516 U.S. 349, 359 n. 7, 116 S.Ct. 862, 869 n. 7, 133 L.Ed.2d 817 (1996)("Rule 69(a) ... permits judgment creditors to use any execution method consistent with [state] practice and procedure."). *See, e.g., In re Levander,* 180 F.3d 1114, 1120 (9th Cir.1999) (if state law allows amendment of judgment to add addi-

the same time, federal courts apparently have authority to supplement such procedure with federal practice when necessary.[5] Indeed, if state law is an obstacle to enforcement, federal courts may even be able to disregard state practice.[6] Finally, Rule 69(a) explicitly provides that any applicable federal statute supplants state law.[7]

Stay of Enforcement

Rule 62(a) directs that a federal money judgment may not be executed upon until 10 days after entry of judgment. The court may further stay execution of the final judgment when an appeal is properly taken or when the court reviews post-trial motions, as provided by Rule 62.[8]

Time for Enforcement

State law will determine the time limitation of the writ of execution and how the time limitation may be extended.

Source of Remedies

A party seeking execution of a money judgment may use any applicable federal statute. Federal remedies for executions in aid of judgments are listed at 28 U.S.C.A. §§ 2001 *et seq.* See also the Advisory Committee Notes to Rule 69. Additionally, a party may use any of the provisional remedies of the forum state at the time the remedy is sought, such as garnishment, arrest, mandamus, contempt, or the appointment of a receiver. When a state remedy is utilized, a party need only comply substantially with the provisions

tional judgment debtor, federal court may do so under Rule 69(a)). *Cf., United International Holdings, Inc. v. Wharf Holdings, Ltd.,* 210 F.3d 1207, 1235 (10th Cir.2000), *affirmed,* 532 U.S. 588, 121 S.Ct. 1776, 149 L.Ed.2d 845 (2001) (no requirement to make findings of fact before applying Rule 69 unless federal statute or state rules on execution of judgments provides otherwise).

5. *See, e.g., United States v. Harkins Builders, Inc.,* 45 F.3d 830, 833 (4th Cir. 1995)(Rule 69(a) permits use of federal procedure to further "the federal policy of affording judgment creditors the right to a writ of execution to enforce money judgments in federal courts."). *But see, Credit Suisse v. United States District Court for the Central District of California,* 130 F.3d 1342, 1344 (9th Cir.1997) (Rule 69(a) authorizes only a writ of execution; it provides no authority for court to order payment into court); *Aetna Casualty & Surety Co. v. Markarian,* 114 F.3d 346, 349 (1st Cir.1997) ("The 'otherwise' clause is narrowly construed. ...It does not authorize enforcement of a civil money judgment by methods other than a writ of execution, except [in

unusual circumstances];" vacating writ that required judgment debtor to surrender passport).

6. *See, e.g., Hankins v. Finnel,* 964 F.2d 853, 860 (8th Cir.1992) ("Where state law fails to supply the necessary procedure, or actually stands in the way of enforcement, the district court may take the necessary steps to ensure compliance with its judgment."). *But see, Credit Suisse v. United States District Court for the Central District of California,* 130 F.3d 1342, 1344 (9th Cir. 1997) (where state law requires service of a notice of levy on the branch office where defendant holds account—and that branch is not within state—service is ineffective).

7. *See, e.g., Rubin v. Islamic Republic of Iran,* 408 F.Supp.2d 549, 553 (N.D.Ill.2005) (where Foreign Sovereign Immunity Act, 28 U.S.C.A. § 1602 *et seq.,* is applicable, its provisions supplant otherwise applicable state law).

8. *Cf., Acevedo–Garcia v. Vera–Monroig,* 296 F.3d 13 (1st Cir.2002) ("Absent a stay on some ground, plaintiffs are free to seek execution of the judgment pursuant to Fed. R. Civ. P. 69.").

of the state remedy.[9]

Registering a Judgment in District Outside Forum State

A judgment for money or property entered by any district court may be registered in any other district court by filing a certified copy of such judgment in the other district after the judgment has become final.[10] A judgment that has been registered has the same effect as the original judgment and may be enforced as would any other judgment. However, a potentially important result of registering a judgment in federal court that was previously awarded in a different federal court in a different state is that the law of the enforcing state—not the judgment state—will normally control.[11]

Writ of Execution

A writ of execution is a writ to enforce a judgment by the seizure and sale of property of the debtor in satisfaction of the judgment.

Enforcement of Judgment

Upon obtaining the writ of execution, the judgment creditor may serve the writ on the U.S. Marshal or state officer, who will then execute, by attachment or otherwise, the property of the judgment debtor in the possession of third parties, and may have the judgment debtor's property sold at an execution sale. The specific procedures for obtaining a writ of execution and executing on the property of the judgment debtor will depend upon the remedy sought and will vary from state to state and district to district.

Discovery

A party seeking to enforce a judgment may use either the federal or the state discovery rules [12] to uncover information concerning assets of the debtor and to aid in execution of the judgment. Rule 69(a) expressly provides that such discovery may be directed toward "any person," including persons not parties to the lawsuit.[13]

9. *Duchek v. Jacobi,* 646 F.2d 415, 417 (9th Cir.1981); (state law requiring that enforcement proceedings be held in state court may properly be disregarded).

10. 28 U.S.C.A. § 1963.

11. *See, e.g., Condaire, Inc. v. Allied Piping, Inc.,* 286 F.3d 353, 357–58 (6th Cir. 2002) (collecting other cases on point). *Cf., Gagan v. Monroe,* 269 F.3d 871, 873 (7th Cir.2001) (judgment in Indiana federal district court; when defendant did not pay, plaintiff sought Rule 69 enforcement in Indiana district court; held, because property to be executed upon was in Arizona, Indiana state law required use of Arizona law to determine whether property was subject to execution).

12. *See, e.g., Natural Gas Pipeline Co. of America v. Energy Gathering, Inc.,* 2 F.3d 1397, 1403 (5th Cir.1993) (post-judgment

discovery may follow federal pre-trial discovery or applicable state discovery law).

13. *See, e.g., Credit Lyonnais, S.A. v. SGC International, Inc.,* 160 F.3d 428, 430 (8th Cir.1998) (Under Rule 69(a) and applicable state procedure, "[a] party may depose almost anyone, including corporations, who may provide relevant information."). *Cf., Falicia v. Advanced Tenant Services, Inc.,* 235 F.R.D. 5, 7–8 (D.D.C. 2006) (judgment creditors entitled to acquire information from non-parties about concealed assets of judgment debtors; general rule discouraging forced disclosure of assets of non-parties is overcome when there is reason to question good faith of transfer of assets from debtor to non-party); *See also Estate of Ungar v. Palestinian Authority,* 400 F.Supp.2d 541 (S.D.N.Y. 2005) (use of Rule 69 to subpoena non-

Property Subject to Levy

State law will designate the property of the judgment debtor which may be levied upon in satisfaction of the judgment.

Fees and Costs

Fees for writs, subpoenas, keeping attached property, seizing or levying on property, and for the sale of property may be taxed as costs.[14]

RULE 69(b). AGAINST CERTAIN PUBLIC OFFICERS

CORE CONCEPT

If a district director of the Internal Revenue Service—a "collector" of revenue—or an officer of Congress has obtained a certificate of probable cause, a judgment entered against such district director[15] or officer[16] for damages resulting from any of the individual's official acts, or for the recovery of any money exacted by or paid to the individual and subsequently paid into the Treasury may only be executed against the United States Treasury, and not against the individual's property.

APPLICATIONS

District Director

"District director" is defined as any district director of the Internal Revenue Service, former district director, or personal representative of a deceased district director.

Obtaining Certificate of Probable Cause

When a judgment creditor seeks to enforce a judgment, the district director or the officer of Congress may apply to the court for a certificate of probable cause. Upon such application, the court will determine whether the director or officer acted with probable and reasonable cause in performing their proper governmental duties. If the court so finds, the court will issue a certificate of probable cause.

Effect of Certificate

The certificate of probable cause converts the action to one against the United States, extinguishing the personal liability of the individual. Subsequently, the judgment creditor may serve the certificate of probable cause, along with the judgment, on the United States Treasury. The Treasury will pay the amount of the judgment.

---

parties is subject to long-arm statute of forum state or applicable federal law on nationwide personal jurisdiction).

14. 28 U.S.C.A. § 1921.

15. 28 U.S.C.A. § 2006 (Internal Revenue Officer).

16. 2 U.S.C.A. § 118 (18 Stat. 401)(Officer of Congress).

ADDITIONAL RESEARCH REFERENCES

Wright & Miller, *Federal Practice and Procedure* §§ 3011–3020.

C.J.S. Federal Civil Procedure §§ 1254–1272 et seq.

West's Key No. Digests, Federal Civil Procedure ⇨2691–2714.

RULE 70

ENFORCING A JUDGMENT FOR A SPECIFIC ACT

(a) Party's Failure to Act; Ordering Another to Act. If a judgment requires a party to convey land, to deliver a deed or other document, or to perform any other specific act and the party fails to comply within the time specified, the court may order the act to be done—at the disobedient party's expense—by another person appointed by the court. When done, the act has the same effect as if done by the party.

(b) Vesting Title. If the real or personal property is within the district, the court—instead of ordering a conveyance—may enter a judgment divesting any party's title and vesting it in others. That judgment has the effect of a legally executed conveyance.

(c) Obtaining a Writ of Attachment or Sequestration. On application by a party entitled to performance of an act, the clerk must issue a writ of attachment or sequestration against the disobedient party's property to compel obedience.

(d) Obtaining a Writ of Execution or Assistance. On application by a party who obtains a judgment or order for possession, the clerk must issue a writ of execution or assistance.

(e) Holding in Contempt. The court may also hold the disobedient party in contempt.

[April 30, 2007, effective December 1, 2007.]

——————— 2007 AMENDMENTS ROADMAP ———————

STYLE PROJECT CHANGES: Rule 70, previously a single paragraph, has been subdivided into five subsections, each with its own new title. Minor language changes were made to aid readability.

NON-STYLE CHANGES: None.

NOTE: The Federal Rules "Style Project" is explained in Part III-A.

AUTHORS' COMMENTARY ON RULE 70

─────────── PURPOSE AND SCOPE ───────────

Rule 70 provides that the court may convey property or perform any other specific act, when a party ordered to convey property or perform a specific act fails to comply.

───────────────────────────────

RULE 70(a). PARTY'S FAILURE TO ACT; ORDERING ANOTHER TO ACT

CORE CONCEPT

Rule 70(a) provides that if a judgment includes a requirement that a party transfer property or perform some other act, the court may appoint a person to do the act if the party fails to do so. Such appointment will be at the expense of the non-performing party and will carry the same legal result as if the party had performed the act.

APPLICATIONS

Scope

Rule 70 "applies only to parties who have failed to perform specific acts pursuant to a judgment."[1]

RULE 70(b). VESTING TITLE

CORE CONCEPT

Rule 70(b) provides that if property to be transferred pursuant to judgment is located within the district where the court sits, the court may simply enter judgment transferring title, without going through the process of appointing a person to do the act.

Property Within the District

If a party has failed to obey a court order pertaining to real or personal property physically located within the district in which the court sits, the court may order title transferred directly from the disobedient party to the prevailing party.

---

1. *See, e.g., Analytical Engineering, Inc. v. Baldwin Filters, Inc.,* 425 F.3d 443, 449 (7th Cir.2005) ("Rule 70 gives the district court a discrete and limited power to deal with parties who thwart final judgments by refusing to comply with orders to perform specific acts."); *Westlake North Property Owners Association v. City of Thousand Oaks,* 915 F.2d 1301, 1304 (9th Cir.1990) (party's attorneys cannot be sanctioned under Rule 70). *Cf., McAlpin v. Lexington 76* *Auto Truck Stop, Inc.,* 229 F.3d 491, 504 (6th Cir.2000) (where judgment contained only one term of twenty-page settlement and otherwise dismissed case, court had no authority under Rule 70 to enforce terms of settlement not incorporated in judgment). *But see Peterson v. Highland Music, Inc.,* 140 F.3d 1313, 1323 (9th Cir.1998) (nonparties who aid parties in defying judgment are also subject to Rule 70; upholding contempt citation).

Property Outside the District

If the real or personal property is not physically located within the district in which the court sits, the court must appoint a person to convey the property. The act performed by the appointed party has the full effect as it if it were executed by the disobedient party.

Timing

Rule 70 applies to the enforcement of court orders after the entry of judgment and after the time for performing the ordered action has elapsed.[2]

Content of Motion

In a written motion, the movant should allege with specificity the disobedient party's noncompliance, as well as the relief sought to remedy noncompliance.

RULE 70(c). OBTAINING A WRIT OF ATTACHMENT OR SEQUESTRATION

CORE CONCEPT

Rule 70(c) provides that a party entitled to performance of an act may obtain a writ of sequestration or attachment to ensure performance.

Alternative Enforcement Remedies

The court may enforce a judgment by requiring a party to convey property or perform a specific act through the following remedies.

Upon proper motion to the clerk of court, a prevailing party may obtain a writ of attachment or sequestration authorizing seizure of the disobedient party's property or money until that party complies with a judgment.

Costs Against Disobedient Party

A court may tax against the disobedient party the costs of transferring the property or performing the specific act.

RULE 70(d). OBTAINING A WRIT OF EXECUTION OR ASSISTANCE

CORE CONCEPT

Rule 70(d) provides that a party who has obtained a judgment or order for possession of property may apply for a write of execution or assistance. Upon proper application, it is the duty of the clerk to issue such a writ.

Upon a proper motion to the clerk of court, a party may obtain a writ of assistance to enforce the delivery of property to the person

---

2. *See, e.g., Barmat, Inc. v. United States,* 159 F.R.D. 578, 582 (N.D.Ga. 1994)(Rule 70 "is operative only after entry of judgment").

entitled to the property under a judgment against a party who refuses to surrender possession.

RULE 70(e). HOLDING IN CONTEMPT

CORE CONCEPT

Rule 70(e) provides that in addition to other remedies available under Rule 70, the court has authority to hold disobedient parties in contempt.

In addition to other remedies under Rule 70, the court retains the authority to enforce a judgment directing the performance of a specific act by finding the disobedient party in contempt of court.[3]

ADDITIONAL RESEARCH REFERENCES

Wright & Miller, *Federal Practice and Procedure* §§ 3021–3030.

C.J.S. Assistance, Writ of §§ 3, 4; Contempt § 12; Federal Civil Procedure §§ 1254–1260 et seq.

West's Key No. Digests, Assistance, Writ of ⚷2; Contempt ⚷20; Federal Civil Procedure ⚷2691, 2695.

3. *See, e.g., McMahan & Co. v. Po Folks, Inc.,* 206 F.3d 627, 634 (6th Cir.2000) ("[U]nder Fed.R.Civ.P. 70, a party may be held in civil contempt for violating a gar-   nishment order.").

RULE 71

ENFORCING RELIEF FOR OR AGAINST A NONPARTY

When an order grants relief for a nonparty or may be enforced against a nonparty, the procedure for enforcing the order is the same as for a party.

[Amended effective August 1, 1987; April 30, 2007, effective December 1, 2007.]

--------------------- **2007 AMENDMENTS ROADMAP** ---------------------

STYLE PROJECT CHANGES: Minor changes were made in the title of the Rule. Other language changes were made that shortened the length of the Rule, without changing the substance of the Rule.

NON-STYLE CHANGES: None.

NOTE: The Federal Rules "Style Project" is explained in Part III-A.

AUTHORS' COMMENTARY ON RULE 71

--------------------- **PURPOSE AND SCOPE** ---------------------

Rule 71 provides for the enforcement of a court order by any person (including a non-party) in whose favor an order has been entered. Additionally, Rule 71 provides for the enforcement of a court order against a non-party when such enforcement is otherwise lawful.

APPLICATIONS

In Favor of a Non-party

A court order may be enforced by a non-party when that person shares an identity of interest with a prevailing party or is an intended beneficiary of the court order with the right to enforce it.[1]

---

1. *See, e.g., Brennan v. Nassau County,* 352 F.3d 60, 65 (2d Cir.2003) (suggesting that motion to compel may be suitable means of employing Rule 71; but also noting that non-parties must be able to meet requirements of standing); *Beckett v. Air Line Pilots Association,* 995 F.2d 280, 287–88 (D.C.Cir.1993)(Rule 71 permits intended beneficiaries of consent decree to sue to enforce decree; incidental third-party beneficiaries do not have such standing). *See also, Washington Hospital v. White,* 889 F.2d 1294, 1299 (3d Cir.1989)(third-party beneficiary has standing under Rule 71 to enforce court-ordered stipulation of dismissal); *SEC v. Prudential Securities, Inc.,* 136 F.3d 153, 159 (D.C.Cir.1998) ("The test is not ... only whether the contracting par-

Thus, an assignee of a party who prevailed in a dispute concerning the title of property is entitled under Rule 71 to enforce a judgment in the same manner as the assignor.[2]

Against a Non-party

A court order may be enforced against a non-party when that person's interests are so closely related to a losing party's interests that enforcement against that non-party is not unfair.[3] When enforcing a judgment against non-parties, Rule 71 is explicitly restricted to circumstances where enforcement does not violate due process and is otherwise lawful.[4]

ADDITIONAL RESEARCH REFERENCES

Wright & Miller, *Federal Practice and Procedure* §§ 3031–3040.

C.J.S. Federal Civil Procedure § 1107.

West's Key No. Digests, Federal Civil Procedure ⊗2394.

ties intended to confer a benefit directly on the third parties, but also whether the parties intended the third party to be able to sue to protect that benefit.'').

2. *See, e.g., Peterson v. Highland Music, Inc.,* 140 F.3d 1313 (9th Cir.1998) (citing rule 71 as authority to hold non-parties in contempt).

3. *See, e.g., Irwin v. Mascott,* 370 F.3d 924, 931–32 (9th Cir.2004) (Rule 71 permits use of contempt power of court to enforce order against non-party who has notice of injunction).

4. *See, e.g., LiButti v. United States,* 178 F.3d 114 (2d Cir.1999) (enforcement of a judgment against a person who is a successor in interest to a party requires that the court first obtain personal jurisdiction over the successor in interest).

IX. SPECIAL PROCEEDINGS

RULE 71.1

CONDEMNING REAL OR PERSONAL PROPERTY

(a) Applicability of Other Rules. These rules govern proceedings to condemn real and personal property by eminent domain, except as this rule provides otherwise.

(b) Joinder of Properties. The plaintiff may join separate pieces of property in a single action, no matter whether they are owned by the same persons or sought for the same use.

(c) Complaint.

(1) *Caption.* The complaint must contain a caption as provided in Rule 10(a). The plaintiff must, however, name as defendants both the property—designated generally by kind, quantity, and location—and at least one owner of some part of or interest in the property.

(2) *Contents.* The complaint must contain a short and plain statement of the following:

(A) the authority for the taking;

(B) the uses for which the property is to be taken;

(C) a description sufficient to identify the property;

(D) the interests to be acquired; and

(E) for each piece of property, a designation of each defendant who has been joined as an owner or owner of an interest in it.

(3) *Parties.* When the action commences, the plaintiff need join as defendants only those persons who have or claim an interest in the property and whose names are then known. But before any hearing on compensation, the plaintiff must add as defendants all those persons who have or claim an interest and whose names have become known or can be found by a reasonably diligent search of the records, considering both the property's character and value and the interests to be acquired. All others may be made

1133

defendants under the designation "Unknown Owners."

(4) *Procedure.* Notice must be served on all defendants as provided in Rule 71.1(d), whether they were named as defendants when the action commenced or were added later. A defendant may answer as provided in Rule 71.1(e). The court, meanwhile, may order any distribution of a deposit that the facts warrant.

(5) *Filing; Additional Copies.* In addition to filing the complaint, the plaintiff must give the clerk at least one copy for the defendants' use and additional copies at the request of the clerk or a defendant.

(d) Process.

(1) *Delivering Notice to the Clerk.* On filing a complaint, the plaintiff must promptly deliver to the clerk joint or several notices directed to the named defendants. When adding defendants, the plaintiff must deliver to the clerk additional notices directed to the new defendants.

(2) *Contents of the Notice.*

(A) *Main Contents.* Each notice must name the court, the title of the action, and the defendant to whom it is directed. It must describe the property sufficiently to identify it, but need not describe any property other than that to be taken from the named defendant. The notice must also state:

(i) that the action is to condemn property;

(ii) the interest to be taken;

(iii) the authority for the taking;

(iv) the uses for which the property is to be taken;

(v) that the defendant may serve an answer on the plaintiff's attorney within 20 days after being served with the notice;

(vi) that the failure to so serve an answer constitutes consent to the taking and to the court's authority to proceed with the action and fix the compensation; and

(vii) that a defendant who does not serve an answer may file a notice of appearance.

(B) *Conclusion.* The notice must conclude with the name, telephone number, and e-mail address of the plaintiff's attorney and an address within the district in which the action is brought where the attorney may be served.

(3) *Serving the Notice.*

(A) *Personal Service.* When a defendant whose address is known resides within the United States or a territory subject to the administrative or judicial jurisdiction of the United States, personal service of the notice (without a copy of the complaint) must be made in accordance with Rule 4.

(B) *Service by Publication.*

(i) A defendant may be served by publication only when the plaintiff's attorney files a certificate stating that the attorney believes the defendant cannot be personally served, because after diligent inquiry within the state where the complaint is filed, the defendant's place of residence is still unknown or, if known, that it is beyond the territorial limits of personal service. Service is then made by publishing the notice—once a week for at least three successive weeks—in a newspaper published in the county where the property is located or, if there is no such newspaper, in a newspaper with general circulation where the property is located. Before the last publication, a copy of the notice must also be mailed to every defendant who cannot be personally served but whose place of residence is then known. Unknown owners may be served by publication in the same manner by a notice addressed to "Unknown Owners."

(ii) Service by publication is complete on the date of the last publication. The plaintiff's attorney must prove publication and mailing by a certificate, attach a printed copy of the published notice, and mark on the copy the newspaper's name and the dates of publication.

(4) *Effect of Delivery and Service.* Delivering the notice to the clerk and serving it have the same effect as serving a summons under Rule 4.

(5) *Proof of Service; Amending the Proof or Notice.* Rule 4(*l*) governs proof of service. The court may permit the proof or the notice to be amended.

(e) Appearance or Answer.

(1) *Notice of Appearance.* A defendant that has no objection or defense to the taking of its property may serve a notice of appearance designating the property in which it claims an interest. The defendant must then be given notice of all later proceedings affecting the defendant.

(2) *Answer.* A defendant that has an objection or defense to the taking must serve an answer within 20 days after being served with the notice. The answer must:

(A) identify the property in which the defendant claims an interest;

(B) state the nature and extent of the interest; and

(C) state all the defendant's objections and defenses to the taking.

(3) *Waiver of Other Objections and Defenses; Evidence on Compensation.* A defendant waives all objections and defenses not stated in its answer. No other pleading or motion asserting an additional objection or defense is allowed. But at the trial on compensation, a defendant—whether or not it has previously appeared or answered—may present evidence on the amount of compensation to be paid and may share in the award.

(f) Amending Pleadings. Without leave of court, the plaintiff may—as often as it wants—amend the complaint at any time before the trial on compensation. But no amendment may be made if it would result in a dismissal inconsistent with Rule 71.1(i)(1) or (2). The plaintiff need not serve a copy of an amendment, but must serve notice of the filing, as provided in Rule 5(b), on every affected party who has appeared and, as provided in Rule 71.1(d), on every affected party who has not appeared. In addition, the plaintiff must give the clerk at least one copy of each amendment for the defendants' use, and additional copies at the request of the clerk or a defendant. A defendant may appear or answer in the time and manner and with the same effect as provided in Rule 71.1(e).

(g) Substituting Parties. If a defendant dies, becomes incompetent, or transfers an interest after being joined, the court may, on motion and notice of hearing, order that the proper party be substituted. Service of the motion and notice on a nonparty must be made as provided in Rule 71.1(d)(3).

(h) Trial of the Issues.

    (1) *Issues Other Than Compensation; Compensation.* In an action involving eminent domain under federal law, the court tries all issues, including compensation, except when compensation must be determined:

        (A) by any tribunal specially constituted by a federal statute to determine compensation; or

        (B) if there is no such tribunal, by a jury when a party demands one within the time to answer or within any additional time the court sets, unless the court appoints a commission.

    (2) *Appointing a Commission; Commission's Powers and Report.*

        (A) *Reasons for Appointing.* If a party has demanded a jury, the court may instead appoint a three-person commission to determine compensation because of the character, location, or quantity of the property to be condemned or for other just reasons.

        (B) *Alternate Commissioners.* The court may appoint up to two additional persons to serve as alternate commissioners to hear the case and replace commissioners who, before a decision is filed, the court finds unable or disqualified to perform their duties. Once the commission renders its final decision, the court must discharge any alternate who has not replaced a commissioner.

(C) *Examining the Prospective Commissioners.* Before making its appointments, the court must advise the parties of the identity and qualifications of each prospective commissioner and alternate, and may permit the parties to examine them. The parties may not suggest appointees, but for good cause may object to a prospective commissioner or alternate.

(D) *Commission's Powers and Report.* A commission has the powers of a master under Rule 53(c). Its action and report are determined by a majority. Rule 53(d), (e), and (f) apply to its action and report.

(i) Dismissal of the Action or a Defendant.

(1) *Dismissing the Action.*

(A) *By the Plaintiff.* If no compensation hearing on a piece of property has begun, and if the plaintiff has not acquired title or a lesser interest or taken possession, the plaintiff may, without a court order, dismiss the action as to that property by filing a notice of dismissal briefly describing the property.

(B) *By Stipulation.* Before a judgment is entered vesting the plaintiff with title or a lesser interest in or possession of property, the plaintiff and affected defendants may, without a court order, dismiss the action in whole or in part by filing a stipulation of dismissal. And if the parties so stipulate, the court may vacate a judgment already entered.

(C) *By Court Order.* At any time before compensation has been determined and paid, the court may, after a motion and hearing, dismiss the action as to a piece of property. But if the plaintiff has already taken title, a lesser interest, or possession as to any part of it, the court must award compensation for the title, lesser interest, or possession taken.

(2) *Dismissing a Defendant.* The court may at any time dismiss a defendant who was unnecessarily or improperly joined.

(3) *Effect.* A dismissal is without prejudice unless otherwise stated in the notice, stipulation, or court order.

(j) Deposit and Its Distribution.

(1) *Deposit.* The plaintiff must deposit with the court any money required by law as a condition to the exercise of eminent domain and may make a deposit when allowed by statute.

(2) *Distribution; Adjusting Distribution.* After a deposit, the court and attorneys must expedite the proceedings so as to distribute the deposit and to determine and pay compensation. If the compensation finally awarded to a defendant exceeds the amount distributed to that defendant, the court must enter judgment against the plaintiff for the deficiency. If the compensation awarded to a defendant is less than the amount distributed to that defendant, the court must enter judgment against that defendant for the overpayment.

(k) Condemnation Under a State's Power of Eminent Domain. This rule governs an action involving eminent domain under state law. But if state law provides for trying an issue by jury—or for trying the issue of compensation by jury or commission or both—that law governs.

(*l*) Costs. Costs are not subject to Rule 54(d).

[Adopted April 30, 1951, effective August 1, 1951; amended January 21, 1963, effective July 1, 1963; April 29, 1985, effective August 1, 1985; March 2, 1987, effective August 1, 1987; April 25, 1988, effective August 1, 1988; amended by Pub.L. 100–690, Title VII, § 7050, November 18, 1988, 102 Stat. 4401 (although amendment by Pub.L. 100–690 could not be executed due to prior amendment by Court order which made the same change effective August 1, 1988); amended April 22, 1993, effective December 1, 1993; March 27, 2003, effective December 1, 2003; April 30, 2007, effective December 1, 2007.]

2007 AMENDMENTS ROADMAP

STYLE PROJECT CHANGES: Old Rule 71(a) was retitled as Rule 71.1. It should be noted that while this change is intended to be stylistic only, it will require attorneys researching cases decided prior to application of the new amendments to approach their cites with care. Additionally, subsections (c), (d), (e), (h), (i), and (j) were further partitioned to aid readability. Other minor language changes were made in the titles of subsections and in the text.

NON-STYLE CHANGES: None.

NOTE: The Federal Rules "Style Project" is explained in Part III-A.

AUTHORS' COMMENTARY ON RULE 71.1
PURPOSE AND SCOPE

Rule 71.1 provides a uniform set of rules for the condemnation of real and personal property under the federal and state powers of eminent domain.

RULE 71.1(a).   APPLICABILITY OF OTHER RULES

CORE CONCEPT

Rule 71.1(a) directs that, unless specifically otherwise provided in Rule 71.1, the General Civil Rules govern the procedure for the condemnation of real and personal property under the power of eminent domain.

APPLICATIONS

Condemnation of Personal Property

Rule 71.1 applies to the condemnation of personal property as an appurtenance to real property or as the sole object of the proceeding.[1]

Inverse Condemnation Proceedings

Rule 71.1 does not apply to inverse condemnation proceedings. An inverse condemnation "is a cause of action by which a landowner recovers just compensation from the government for a taking of his or her property when condemnation proceedings have not been instituted."[2] An important difference between an inverse condemnation and a direct condemnation governed by Rule 71.1 is that there

---

1. *See,* 42 U.S.C.A. §§ 1805, 1811, 1813 (Atomic Energy Act); 50 U.S.C.A. § 79 (nitrates); 50 U.S.C.A. §§ 161–166 (helium gas).

2. *KLK, Inc. v. United States Department of the Interior,* 35 F.3d 454, 455 n. 1 (9th Cir.1994)(Rule 71.1 applicable only to "traditional" condemnation, not inverse condemnation).

is no right to a jury trial on any issue—not even compensation—in an inverse condemnation proceeding.[3]

Supplementary Condemnation Statutes

Rule 71.1 does not affect supplementary condemnation statutes, such as the Declaration of Taking Act,[4] which permit the Federal Government to take private property for public use under the power of eminent domain.

Uniformity of Procedure

Rule 71.1 makes the procedure for condemnation of property under all statutes uniform.

Choice of Law

Federal condemnation is strictly governed by federal law and precedent. State law only defines the nature of the real or personal property interest, such as the meaning of property, defining what is taken, or determining the ownership of land.

Condemnation Under State Law

A district court may entertain condemnation proceedings under state law, as provided by Rule 71.1(k).

Jurisdiction and Venue

The district courts have original jurisdiction over proceedings to condemn real property for the use of the United States, its agencies, or departments.[5] Venue will be in the district court of the district in which the real property is located or, if located in different districts in the same state, in any such districts.[6]

Rule 71.1 and the Other Rules

In cases where Rule 71.1 does not provide a procedure concerning litigation, the court will apply other applicable Rules, such as the discovery Rules.[7]

RULE 71.1(b).   JOINDER OF PROPERTIES

CORE CONCEPT

Rule 71.1(b) permits condemnation of separate properties, including properties belonging to different owners, or properties for different public uses in the same court action.[8] Only in exceptional circumstances is the court required to conduct separate trials. To eliminate jury

---

3. *See, e.g., United States v. 191.07 Acres of Land,* 482 F.3d 1132, 1136 (9th Cir. 2007) (in inverse proceeding, compensation is determined by bench trial).

4. 40 U.S.C.A. §§ 248a–258e.

5. 28 U.S.C.A. § 1358.

6. 28 U.S.C.A. § 1403.

7. *See also East Tennessee Natural Gas Co. v. Sage,* 361 F.3d 808, 828–29 (4th

Cir.2004) (approving use of Rule 65 to obtain preliminary injunction enabling early occupation of land).

8. *See, e.g., McLaughlin v. Mississippi Power Co.,* 376 F.3d 344 (5th Cir.2004) (also noting that joinder of properties under Rule 71.1 is "much broader" than joinder of parties under Rules 19 and 20 and joinder of claims under Rule 18).

confusion over the relative value of properties, the court may separate the evidence concerning the damages sustained by each owner.

RULE 71.1(c). COMPLAINT

CORE CONCEPT

The requirements for a complaint under Rule 71.1(c) are different from those in an ordinary civil action. In the complaint's caption, Rule 71.1(c) requires the plaintiff to name as defendants both the property and at least one of the owners. Rule 71.1(c) does not require the plaintiff to serve a summons and a complaint on the defendants; rather the clerk of court arranges for notice to all defendants as provided in Rule 71.1(d). However, prior to a hearing on compensation, the plaintiff must join all defendants who can be ascertained from a reasonably diligent search of the records.

APPLICATIONS

Caption

The complaint's caption must include the name of the court, the title of the action, the docket number, and the name of the type of pleading being presented.[9] The caption must name as defendants both the property and at least one of the owners. The plaintiff will name the property as the defendant by stating the kind, quantity, and location of the property.

Contents of Complaint

The complaint must contain a short and plain statement of:

(1) the authority for the taking;

(2) the use for which the property is to be taken;[10]

(3) a description of the property sufficient for identification;[11]

(4) the interests to be acquired; and

(5) for each separate piece of property, the owners who have been joined as defendants or who have some interest.

Filing of Complaint and Notice

The plaintiff must file the complaint with the clerk and provide the clerk with at least one copy for the defendants. Upon the request of the clerk or the defendants, the plaintiff must furnish additional copies. This practice differs from the normal practice under Rule 4, which requires the plaintiff to serve a summons and a copy of the complaint on the defendants.

---

9. *See,* Official Form 29.

10. *See, e.g., City of Arlington v. Gold-dust Twins Realty Corp.,* 41 F.3d 960, 964 (5th Cir.1994)(Rule 71.1(c) requires condemning authority to state purpose for which condemnation is sought).

11. *See, e.g., Southern Natural Gas Co. v. Land, Cullman County,* 197 F.3d 1368, 1375 (11th Cir.1999) (a legal description and plat map showing location of pipeline and related easements "easily" satisfies Rule 71A(c)(2)).

Joining Parties at Commencement

At the commencement of an action, the condemnor must join as defendants all persons or entities of title record having or claiming an interest in the property whose names are then known. All other persons unascertained or unknown shall be made parties as defendants by description if their names are unknown.

Joining of Interested Parties Prior to Hearing

Prior to a hearing involving compensation, the condemnor must add as defendants all persons who have an interest whose identities can be ascertained by a reasonably diligent search of the records,[12] and also those whose names have been learned. "Reasonably diligent" search means the type of search a title searcher would undertake, but the extent of the search required will depend upon the character and value of the property involved and the interests to be acquired. Property owners joined after the commencement of the action must be served with notice by the clerk and allowed to answer.

Failure to Join a Party

There are no indispensable parties in a condemnation action. Therefore, the failure to join a party will not defeat the condemnor's title to the land because a condemnation action is an action *in rem*.[13] If the condemnor fails to join a party, the omitted party may have the right to sue for compensation in the Claims Court after the condemnation is completed.[14]

RULE 71.1(d).   PROCESS

CORE CONCEPT

Rule 71.1(d) directs that the clerk will deliver a notice of the complaint to a marshal or specially appointed person who will make personal service on the defendants.

APPLICATIONS

Content of Notice

Each notice must state:

(1) the court;

(2) the title of the action;

(3) the name of the defendant to whom it is directed;

---

12. *See, e.g., Cadorette v. United States,* 988 F.2d 215, 224 (1st Cir.1993)(Rule 71A(c) requires government to make an affirmative search for "lost" heirs).

13. *Fulcher v. United States,* 632 F.2d 278, 282 (4th Cir.1980); ("Persons not identified ... can be impleaded as unknown.").

14. *See, e.g., United States v. 194.08 Acres of Land,* 135 F.3d 1025, 1035 n. 8

(5th Cir.1998) (failure to join party or give required notice does not invalidate taking; such failure only preserves right of unjoined interested party to challenge taking). *Cadorette v. United States,* 988 F.2d 215, 225 (1st Cir.1993)(person not joined may seek compensation in Claims Court through the device of a takings claim).

(4) the nature of the action (condemning property);

(5) a description of the property sufficient for its identification;

(6) the interest to be taken;

(7) the authority for the taking;

(8) the uses for which the property is being taken;

(9) the time for answering the complaint (the defendant may serve an answer upon the plaintiff's attorney within twenty days after the service of the notice);

(10) the penalty for failing to answer (a consent to the taking, permitting the court to proceed to hear the action and fix compensation); and

(11) that any defendant who chooses not to file an answer may nevertheless file a notice of appearance.

The notice must, finally, include the name, telephone number, and e-mail address of the plaintiff's attorney as well as an address within the district in which the suit is brought where that attorney may be served.

Preparation of Notice

The plaintiff may prepare joint or separate notices. However, one notice must be delivered to each named defendant and need contain a description of only that property taken from the particular defendant to whom it is directed.

Filing of Notice

The plaintiff's attorney will prepare a notice and deliver it to the clerk with the complaint. Subsequently, the clerk will file and enter the complaint in the record and deliver a notice of the complaint (but not a copy of the complaint itself) to the marshal or specially-appointed person for service.

Persons Requiring Notice

At the commencement of the case, the clerk need only provide notice to persons whose names are in the complaint. Property owners joined after the filing of the complaint must be served with notice and allowed to answer.

Service

Personal service of the notice (but without copies of the complaint) shall be made in accordance with Rule 4 upon each defendant who resides within the United States or its territories or insular possessions and whose residence is known.

Service By Publication

(1) *Persons Served by Publication:* A plaintiff may make service by publication on three types of defendants:[15]

---

15. *See, e.g., United States v. 499.472 Acres of Land More or Less, in Brazoria* County, Texas, 701 F.2d 545, 551 (5th Cir. 1983)(publication service permissible only

(a) owners who do not reside in the United States, its territories, or insular possessions, and who, therefore, are beyond the territorial limits of personal service;

(b) owners within the state in which the complaint is filed whose place of residence is unknown after a diligent search of the records; and

(c) unknown owners.

(2) *Publication:* The plaintiff must publish the notice in a newspaper in the county where the land is located. When no newspaper exists in the county where the land is located, the plaintiff must publish the notice in a newspaper having a circulation in the area where the land is located. The plaintiff must publish the notice once a week for at least three successive weeks.

(3) *Proof of Publication:* When a plaintiff wishes to make proof of service by publication, the plaintiff's attorney must file with the court a certificate stating that the defendant cannot be served personally because the defendant's residence is beyond the personal service limits or after diligent inquiry defendant's residence is unknown. The plaintiff's attorney must attach to the certificate a printed copy of the published notice marked with the name of the newspaper and the dates of publication.

(4) *Defendants Who Cannot Be Served But Residence Known:* A defendant who cannot be personally served but whose place of residence is known must be mailed a copy of the notice prior to the date of the last publication. Service is complete on the date of the last publication.

RULE 71.1(e).   APPEARANCE OR ANSWER

CORE CONCEPT

A defendant may respond to a condemnation complaint in two ways. If the defendant intends to either contest the taking or make objections to the complaint, the defendant must file an answer. Alternatively, if the defendant has no defenses or objections to the taking, the defendant simply serves a notice of appearance designating the property in which the defendant has an interest. However, regardless of whether the defendant files an answer or an appearance, a defendant may present evidence at the hearing on compensation and share in the award.[16]

APPLICATIONS

Answer

The answer is the only document in which defenses or objections may be asserted.[17] Unlike most answers to complaints in

in the explicit circumstances described in Rule 71.1(d)).

16. *See, e.g., Bank One Texas, N.A. v. United States,* 157 F.3d 397 (5th Cir.1998).

17. *See, e.g., Washington Metropolitan Area Transit Authority v. Precision Small Engines,* 227 F.3d 224, 228 n. 2 (4th Cir. 2000) (except for amount of compensation,

ordinary civil actions, the defendant must make specific allegations. In the answer the defendant must identify the property, the defendant's interest in the property, and the defenses to the taking. After filing an answer, the defendant is entitled to receive notice of all of the proceedings affecting the defendant.

Counterclaims and Crossclaims

An answer may not contain a counterclaim or crossclaim.[18] A counterclaim must be brought in a separate action in the district court or the Court of Claims.

Timing of Answer

Within 20 days of service of the notice, the defendant must answer the complaint. This response period may be enlarged by motion, as provided by Rule 6(b).

Appearance

When the defendant has no defenses or objections to the taking or to the complaint, the defendant may serve a notice of appearance. The notice of appearance should designate the property in which the defendant claims an interest. When a defendant has filed an appearance, the defendant is entitled to receive notice of all of the proceedings affecting the defendant.

RULE 71.1(f). AMENDING PLEADINGS

CORE CONCEPT

Before the trial on the issue of just compensation, a plaintiff may amend the complaint multiple times without leave of court. However, except as provided by Rule 71.1(i), the plaintiff may not amend the complaint to remove the names of defendants or claims. Within 20 days of the notice of each amended complaint, the defendant is entitled to file one amended answer as of right.

APPLICATIONS

Procedure for Amending Complaint

The plaintiff may amend the complaint by filing with the clerk the amended pleading and by serving notice of the amended pleading on each defendant. The plaintiff need not serve a copy of the amended pleading itself on defendants, a practice that differs from normal civil actions. Instead, if a defendant or the clerk requests additional copies of the amended complaint, the plaintiff must provide the clerk with additional copies.

Service to Persons Who Have Not Entered an Appearance

The plaintiff should serve notice of an amended complaint on

---

defenses or objections not raised in answer are waived; "Simply put, no other pleading besides the answer is contemplated.").

18. *See, e.g., United States v. Certain Land Situated in the City of Detroit,* 361 F.3d 305, 308 (6th Cir.2004) ("A district court lacks jurisdiction to hear counterclaims against the United States in condemnation cases.").

persons who have not entered an appearance.[19]

RULE 71.1(g).   SUBSTITUTING PARTIES

CORE CONCEPT

Upon proper motion and notice of hearing, the court may order the substitution of parties when a defendant dies or becomes incompetent, or transfers an interest after the defendant's joinder. If a new party is substituted, the plaintiff must serve a copy of the motion and notice of hearing on the new party, as provided by Rule 71.1(d). Rule 25, governing substitution of parties in most civil actions, does not apply to condemnation actions.

RULE 71.1(h).   TRIAL OF THE ISSUES

CORE CONCEPT

All issues other than the issue of compensation will be decided by the court. The issue of compensation will be decided by either a special tribunal, a commission, a jury, or the court, in condemnation actions instituted by the federal or state government under powers of eminent domain. Federal law may require the issue of compensation to be decided by a tribunal specially constituted by Congress. When any party demands a trial by jury, the court will decide whether to conduct a jury trial or to appoint a commission to decide the issue of compensation.

> **NOTE:** If a commission is appointed to decide the issue of compensation, the commission must issue a report. Within 10 days after service of the commission report, parties must make and serve on the other parties and the court their objections to the report.

APPLICATIONS

Trial by Jury

When any party demands a trial by jury, the court may conduct a jury trial or may appoint a commission to decide the issue of compensation. However, there is no constitutional right to a trial by jury in condemnation cases,[20] and the jury in such cases may

---

19. *See,* Rule 71.1(d).

20. *United States v. Reynolds,* 397 U.S. 14, 18, 90 S.Ct. 803, 806, 25 L.Ed.2d 12 (1970). ("[I]t has long been settled that there is no constitutional right to a jury in eminent domain cases."). *See, e.g., United States v. Certain Land Situated in the City of Detroit,* 450 F.3d 205 (6th Cir.2006) (no constitutional right to trial by jury in eminent domain proceedings; instead, Rule 71.1(h) authorizes, but does not require, the district court to convene a jury to decide the single issue of just compensation; other issues, such as whether certain property was within the original scope of a project, are to be decided by the judge). *See also Southern Natural Gas Co. v. Land, Cullman County,* 197 F.3d 1368, 1373 (11th Cir.1999) (condemnation action pursuant to Natural Gas Act, 15 U.S.C. § 717 *et seq.*; notwithstanding provision in Natural Gas Act providing that condemnation procedure shall conform as closely as possible to state law, Rule 71.1(h) permits district court to appoint commission in place of jury; held, Rule 71.1(h) supercedes applicable provisions of Natural Gas Act).

decide only the issue of compensation.[21]

(1) *Time for Demand:* Within the time allowed for the answer to the condemnation complaint (20 days of service of the notice of the complaint, unless an enlargement of time has extended the period) or a further time fixed by the court, any party may demand a trial by jury.

(2) *Procedure for Trial by Jury:* The trial of a condemnation action is similar to any other civil proceeding involving a trial by jury. However, the judge will determine all issues other than the amount of compensation.[22]

Trial by Commission

(1) *Appointment of Commission:* When a party demands a trial by jury, the court has discretion to appoint a commission to decide the issue of compensation rather than conducting a trial by jury.[23] Although the court is not required to make findings of fact to support its determination to appoint a commission, for purposes of appellate review the court will often state in writing its reasons for appointing a commission.

(a) *Conditions for Reference to Commission:* Courts have appointed commissions for such reasons as: local preference or habit, the preference of the Justice Department, the distance of the property from the courthouse, the complexity of the issues, the character of the land, the nature of the interest or the number of tracts taken, the need for numerous jury trials, the desirability of uniform awards, or to prevent discrimination.

(2) *Number of Commissioners:* A commission is generally composed of three persons. The court may appoint two alternate commissioners to sit at the hearing with the other commissioners.

(3) *Appointment of Commissioners:* The parties may suggest nominees as potential commissioners. Usually, the court will appoint commissioners and alternate commissioners. Often, the court will appoint a lawyer or ex-judge as chair of the commission and one real estate person as a member. After appointing the commissioners, the court will advise the parties of the identity and qualifications of each prospective commissioner and alternate commissioner. The parties may examine the commissioners and may, for valid cause, object to the appointment of any commissioner.

21. *See, e.g., United States v. Certain Land Situated in the City of Detroit,* 450 F.3d 205, 208 (6th Cir.2006) (jury decides only narrow issue of compensation). *See also United States v. 191.07 Acres of Land,* 482 F.3d 1132, 1136 (9th Cir. 2007) (in inverse proceeding compensation is determined by bench trial).

22. *See, e.g., United States v. 4.0 Acres of Land,* 175 F.3d 1133 (9th Cir.1999) (jury's sole function is to determine amount of compensation).

23. *But cf., United States v. 320.0 Acres of Land,* 605 F.2d 762, 828 (5th Cir.1979) (acknowledging some contrary authority but holding that "a commission is to be used only for exceptional cases" such as large tracts of land held by many small landowners or tracts too distant for jury to view); *Questar Southern Trails Pipeline Co. v. 4.26 Acres of Land,* 194 F.Supp.2d 1192, 1193 (D.N.M.2002) (in 10th Circuit "jury trial is . . . still the standard").

(4) *Reformation and Revocation of Commission:* When the court believes the judgment of the commission has been affected by bias, the court may reform the commission by replacing some or all of the commissioners.[24] When justice so requires, such as instances of undue delay, the court may vacate the reference to the commission.

(5) *Procedure for Trial by Commission:*

(a) *Powers:* The commission will only try the issue of compensation; all other issues will be decided by the court. The commission has the same powers as a master in a non-jury trial. Proceedings before the commission are governed by Rule 53(c). The commission may regulate its proceedings, require the production of all documents, rule on the admissibility of evidence, call and examine witnesses, and permit the witnesses to be examined by the parties. These powers will be regulated indirectly by the court through its instructions to the commission in the order of reference.

(b) *Instructions:* In its order of reference, the trial judge will instruct the commissioners as to such issues as: the qualifications of expert witnesses, the weight to be given to other opinions of evidence, competent evidence of value, the best evidence of value, the manner of the hearing and the method of conducting it, the right to view the property, the limited purpose of viewing, and the kind of evidence which is inadmissible and the manner of ruling on the admissibility of evidence.

(c) *Admission of Evidence:* Although the court will control the kind of evidence which is admissible, the commission will apply the Federal Rules of Evidence when ruling on the admissibility of the evidence.

(1) *View of Property:* When necessary or conducive to a proper determination of compensation and when not inconvenient or the cause of undue delay or expense, the commission may view the property.

(6) *Findings and Report of Commission:* A majority of the commissioners will decide the amount of compensation to award, and the commission will submit a report. The findings and the report of the commission will follow the provisions of Rule 53(e)(2). In its report, the commission must clearly show a factual basis for its finding, but need not make detailed findings. A suitable commission report will state what evidence and what measure of damages the commission accepted and why the commission reached its award.[25]

---

24. *But cf., City of Stilwell, Oklahoma v. Ozarks Rural Electric Cooperative Corp.,* 166 F.3d 1064, 1069 (10th Cir.1999) (commissioners need not have "complete and absolute impartiality;" no error in appointment of either customer of cooperative's competitor (owned by city) or owner-member bers of cooperative, especially when virtually every resident in area used utility services of one or another of the parties).

25. *See, United States v. Merz,* 376 U.S. 192, 198, 84 S.Ct. 639, 643, 11 L.Ed.2d 629 (1964) (conclusory findings are unaccepta-

(7) *Objection to Commission Report:* Within 10 days after service of the commission's report, a party must make and file with the court and serve on all other parties objections to the report.[26] The party objecting to the report retains the burden of demonstrating that the report is erroneous.

(8) *Trial Court Review of Commission Report:* The trial court must adopt the report of the commission unless it finds the report to be clearly erroneous.[27] A trial court may find the report clearly erroneous when there was a substantial error in the proceedings, when the report is unsupported by substantial evidence, against the clear weight of the evidence,[28] or involves a misapplication of law. Courts have also found commission reports clearly erroneous when the award was grossly inadequate. When the trial court finds the report clearly erroneous, the court may examine the testimony and make its own judgment or it may recommit the matter to the commission with instructions.[29]

(9) *Commissioners' Compensation:* Commissioners will be compensated in reasonable relation to the services rendered (i.e., the bar association's minimum fee schedule). The commissioners' compensation will be charged to the condemnor and may be included in the damage award, not taxed as costs against the award.

(10) *Appellate Court Review of Commission or Court Decision:* An appellate court reviews the judgment of a trial court under a clearly erroneous standard.[30]

RULE 71.1(i). DISMISSAL OF THE ACTION OR A DEFENDANT

CORE CONCEPT

The procedures for dismissal depend on the posture of the proceedings. Prior to a hearing or declaration of taking, the action may be dismissed as of right. Where the government files a declaration of taking, acquires an interest, acquires title, or takes possession of the property before the entry of judgment, neither the plaintiff nor the court may dismiss an action, except by stipulation of the parties.[31] After the entry

---

ble; commissioners should explain reasoning, what evidence was used, etc.).

26. *See,* Rule 53(e)(2).

27. *United States v. Merz,* 376 U.S. 192, 198, 84 S.Ct. 639, 643, 11 L.Ed.2d 629 (1964)(adopting "clearly erroneous" standard).

28. *Georgia Power Co. v. 138.30 Acres of Land,* 596 F.2d 644 (5th Cir.1979), *rehearing ordered,* 602 F.2d 1243 (5th Cir.1979), *vacated on other grounds,* 617 F.2d 1112 (5th Cir.1980).

29. *See, e.g., Southern Natural Gas Co. v. Land, Cullman County,* 197 F.3d 1368, 1375 (11th Cir.1999) (district court has dis-

cretion to recommit matter to commission or to hear additional evidence itself).

30. *See, e.g., United States v. 179.26 Acres of Land in Douglas County, Kansas,* 644 F.2d 367, 373 (10th Cir.1981)(applying clearly erroneous standard).

31. *Kirby Forest Industries, Inc. v. United States,* 467 U.S. 1, 12 n. 18, 104 S.Ct. 2187, 2195 n. 18, 81 L.Ed.2d 1 (1984) (Rule 71.1(i)(1)(C) bars dismissal by court if government has acquired interest in property—court must first hold compensation hearing).

of judgment the court has discretion to vacate the judgment upon the stipulation of the parties.

APPLICATIONS

Dismissal

(1) *As of Right:* Before a hearing on compensation has begun and before the plaintiff has filed a declaration of taking as provided by statute, acquired title, acquired an interest, or taken possession of the property, the plaintiff may dismiss the action by filing a notice of dismissal stating a brief description of the property.

(2) *By Stipulation:* Before the entry of a judgment vesting plaintiff with title, an interest, or possession of the property, the parties may stipulate to a dismissal in whole or in part without an order of the court. After judgment, the parties may stipulate to a dismissal and the court may vacate the judgment and revest title in the defendant.

(3) *By Court Order:* When the hearing on compensation has begun, but the plaintiff has not filed a declaration of taking, acquired title, acquired an interest, or taken possession, the court will decide whether to grant a voluntary dismissal.[32] However, when the hearing has begun and the plaintiff has filed a declaration of taking, acquired title, acquired an interest, or taken possession, the court must award just compensation for the possession, title, or the interest taken, unless stipulated otherwise by the parties.[33]

Dismissal of Improperly and Unnecessarily Joined Parties

At any time, upon a motion or *sua sponte,* the court may dismiss a defendant who has no interest but has been unnecessarily or improperly joined.

Dismissal Without Prejudice

Unless stated in the order or the stipulation, a dismissal of a condemnation proceeding is without prejudice.

RULE 71.1(j).   DEPOSIT AND ITS DISTRIBUTION

CORE CONCEPT

Rule 71.1(j) describes the procedure for the deposit of money with the court when required or permitted by statute. State substantive law will determine the amount to be deposited in state eminent domain actions, while federal substantive law will determine the amount to be deposited in federal eminent domain actions.

---

32. *See, e.g., United States v. 4,970 Acres of Land,* 130 F.3d 712, 714–15 (5th Cir.1997) (if jury has returned verdict but government has not yet engaged in specified acts, government may buy property by tendering the amount of the verdict or may move to dismiss condemnation action; if government sought dismissal of action, court then would have discretion to dismiss; "Condemnation is a means by which the sovereign may find out what any piece of property will cost.").

33. *See, e.g., Id. at* 715.

APPLICATIONS

The Declaration of Taking Act

The Declaration of Taking Act supplements the procedure under Rule 71.1(j), relating to the deposit and distribution in eminent domain cases. Under the Act, upon the filing of a declaration of taking and a deposit of the estimated compensation with the court, title immediately vests in the federal government.

(1) *Time for Filing:* A declaration of taking may be brought at the commencement of the condemnation action and at any time before a judgment.

(2) *Certification:* The chief of the government department or bureau acquiring the land will certify that the land is within the value prescribed by Congress.

(3) *Surrender of Possession; Encumbrances:* Upon the filing of a declaration of taking, the court will fix the time and the terms upon which the parties in possession will surrender possession of the property to the plaintiff. The court may also make orders concerning encumbrances, liens, rents, taxes, assessments, insurance, etc.

(4) *Amount of Award:* The judgment will include 6 percent interest from the date of the taking to the date of the award. However, no interest will be ordered on money paid into the court. When the court or the jury awards an amount greater than the deposit, the court will enter judgment against the plaintiff and in favor of the defendant for the difference plus 6 percent interest.[34] When the court or the jury awards an amount less than the deposit, the court will enter judgment against the defendant and in favor of the plaintiff for the amount of overpayment. When the deposit exceeds the award the plaintiff will obtain the excess deposit from the clerk.[35]

(5) *Deposit and Distribution:* At the time of the taking and the deposit into the court, the court may order distribution of the deposit to the known defendants.[36]

(6) *Appellate Review:* A transfer of title is not a final appealable judgment until a final judgment on compensation has been entered.[37]

---

34. *United States v. 9.20 Acres of Land, More or Less, Situate in Polk County, State of Iowa,* 638 F.2d 1123 (8th Cir.1981) (deposit insufficient). *See also,* 40 U.S.C.A. § 258a.

35. *United States v. Featherston,* 325 F.2d 539, 541 (10th Cir.1963)(if deposit exceeds award, government can get excess from the clerk or sue landowner if landowner received excess).

36. *See,* Rule 71A(c)(2). *See also,* 40 U.S.C.A. § 258a. *Cf., United States v. 8.0 Acres of Land,* 197 F.3d 24, 29 n. 1 (1st Cir.1999) (when United States has taken title to condemned land, it has no standing to participate in proceedings relating to distribution of compensation award once amount of award has been determined; however, when other parties initiate appeal, United States may properly seek to have district court judgment affirmed and to offer government's advice on distribution; citing Rule 71.1(j) provision dealing with expediting distribution of money deposited).

37. *Catlin v. United States,* 324 U.S. 229, 65 S.Ct. 631, 89 L.Ed. 911 (1945) (appeal must await final judgment).

RULE 71.1(k).   CONDEMNATION UNDER A STATE'S POWER OF EMINENT DOMAIN

CORE CONCEPT

Although most federal court eminent domain cases will involve the federal power of eminent domain, a state may institute an eminent domain action in a federal district court when diversity of citizenship exists between the plaintiff (condemnor) and the defendant (landowner) and the amount in controversy exceeds $75,000, exclusive of interest and costs.   Similarly, a defendant (landowner) may remove a state eminent domain action to federal district court when the condemnor initiates the suit and the defendant (landowner) is not a citizen of the state in which the action is brought, and the amount in controversy exceeds $75,000, exclusive of interest and costs.[38]   These state eminent domain actions must be brought in the federal district court for the district in which the land is situated.

APPLICATIONS

Choice of Law

The federal court will apply the procedure described in Rule 71.1.   The court will apply state substantive condemnation law.

Trial by Jury

In state eminent domain cases, the court will follow state law provisions for trial by jury or a commission.[39]

Collateral Attack of State Court Judgment

A party may not bring a federal court action challenging a state court judgment in a state eminent domain action.

RULE 71.1(*l*).   COSTS

CORE CONCEPT

Rule 71.1(*l*) governs the assessment of costs in condemnation proceedings decided pursuant to Rule 71.1.   The normal expenses of the proceeding will be charged to the condemnor.   Expenses incurred in the distribution of the award are charged to the condemnee.

APPLICATIONS

Costs Paid by Condemnor

The condemnor shall pay the normal expenses such as the bills for publication of notice, commissioners' fees, the cost of transporting commissioners and jurors for a view, fees for attorneys representing defendants who have failed to answer, and witness' fees.   These expenses shall be charged to the government and, when

---

38.   28 U.S.C.A. § 1441(a), (b).

39.   *West, Inc. v. United States,* 374 F.2d 218, 224 n. 3 (5th Cir.1967)(Rule 71.1(k))

applies when state has condemned property and diversity jurisdiction causes case to be in federal court).

1153

required, be included as damages in the award but will not be taxed against the award, except to the extent permitted by law.[40] In addition, the condemnor shall pay for the expenses of a commissioner who records the deed and executes the conveyance.

Expenses of Distribution

Expenses incurred in the distribution of the award, such as ascertaining the identity of the distributees and deciding between conflicting claimants, are chargeable against the award.[41]

ADDITIONAL RESEARCH REFERENCES

Wright & Miller, *Federal Practice and Procedure* §§ 3041–3056.

C.J.S. Eminent Domain §§ 209–251 et seq., 267–315 et seq., 319–366 et seq., 373–386 et seq.

West's Key No. Digests, Eminent Domain ⊗166–265(5).

40. *See,* Advisory Committee Note to Rule 71.1(*l*).

41. *See,* Advisory Committee Note to Rule 71.1(*l*)

RULE 72

MAGISTRATE JUDGES: PRETRIAL ORDER

(a) Nondispositive Matters. When a pretrial matter not dispositive of a party's claim or defense is referred to a magistrate judge to hear and decide, the magistrate judge must promptly conduct the required proceedings and, when appropriate, issue a written order stating the decision. A party may serve and file objections to the order within 10 days after being served with a copy. A party may not assign as error a defect in the order not timely objected to. The district judge in the case must consider timely objections and modify or set aside any part of the order that is clearly erroneous or is contrary to law.

(b) Dispositive Motions and Prisoner Petitions.

(1) *Findings and Recommendations.* A magistrate judge must promptly conduct the required proceedings when assigned, without the parties' consent, to hear a pretrial matter dispositive of a claim or defense or a prisoner petition challenging the conditions of confinement. A record must be made of all evidentiary proceedings and may, at the magistrate judge's discretion, be made of any other proceedings. The magistrate judge must enter a recommended disposition, including, if appropriate, proposed findings of fact. The clerk must promptly mail a copy to each party.

(2) *Objections.* Within 10 days after being served with a copy of the recommended disposition, a party may serve and file specific written objections to the proposed findings and recommendations. A party may respond to another party's objections within 10 days after being served with a copy. Unless the district judge orders otherwise, the objecting party must promptly arrange for transcribing the record, or whatever portions of it the parties agree to or the magistrate judge considers sufficient.

(3) *Resolving Objections.* The district judge must determine de novo any part of the magistrate judge's disposition that has been properly objected to. The district judge may accept, reject, or modify the rec-

ommended disposition; receive further evidence; or return the matter to the magistrate judge with instructions.

[Former Rule 72 abrogated December 4, 1967, effective July 1, 1968; new Rule 72 adopted April 28, 1983, effective August 1, 1983; amended April 30, 1991, effective December 1, 1991; April 22, 1993, effective December 1, 1993; April 30, 2007, effective December 1, 2007.]

―――――――― **2007 AMENDMENTS ROADMAP** ――――――――

STYLE PROJECT CHANGES: Minor changes were made in the title and language of Rule 72. Rule 72(b), previously treated as two paragraphs, is now subdivided into three subparts.

NON-STYLE CHANGES: None.

NOTE: The Federal Rules "Style Project" is explained in Part III-A.

AUTHORS' COMMENTARY ON RULE 72

―――――――― **PURPOSE AND SCOPE** ――――――――

Rule 72 provides that a district judge may refer pretrial, trial, and post-trial matters to a magistrate judge without the consent of the parties under the court's additional duties jurisdiction, as provided by 28 U.S.C.A. § 636(b)(3). A district judge may also refer prisoner petitions challenging conditions of confinement for consideration by a magistrate judge.

NOTE: Rule 72(a) was significantly amended as of December 31, 1991.

RULE 72(a).   NONDISPOSITIVE MATTERS

CORE CONCEPT

A district judge may refer, without the consent of the parties,[1] pretrial matters nondispositive of a claim or a defense to a magistrate judge. Such decisions of the magistrate judge may be appealed to the district court for review on a standard of clear error or contrary to law.

NOTE: A party must file written objections to the magistrate judge's order within 10 days after being served with a copy of the order.

―――――――――――

1. *Holder v. Holder,* 392 F.3d 1009, 1022 (9th Cir.2004) (noting absence of re-   quirement for consent).

Failure to make a timely objection may constitute a waiver of appellate review of the magistrate judge's order.[2]

APPLICATIONS

Nondispositive Pretrial Matters

A nondispositive pretrial matter is a matter which is collateral and nonessential to a full disposition of the petitioner's claim and the defendant's liability, such as: (1) motions relating to discovery matters; (2) a motion for sanctions for noncompliance with a discovery order;[3] (3) motions to add claims; and (4) a motion to join a counterclaim. It is unclear whether a magistrate judge may impose sanctions under Rule 72(a) for violations of Rule 11 (governing sanctions for inappropriate pleadings, motions and other papers) or may only recommend such sanctions to the district court pursuant to Rule 72(b).[4]

Dispositive Sanction Not Imposed

If a motion seeks a sanction that would be dispositive, but the magistrate judge denies the motion, the matter is not considered dispositive. Instead, the standard of review is provided by Rule 72(a) (clearly erroneous or contrary to law), rather than Rule 72(b)(de novo review upon the record).[5]

Magistrate Judge's Authority

When appropriate, and to aid further proceedings, Rule 72 authorizes a magistrate judge to enter a written order on the record that constitutes a final adjudication regarding nondispositive pretrial matters, subject to review on appeal by the district court.

Magistrate Judge's Ruling

A magistrate judge's ruling on a pretrial matter on referral from a district judge will follow the Rules. When a magistrate judge

---

2. *See, e.g., Phinney v. Wentworth Douglas Hospital,* 199 F.3d 1, 4 (1st Cir.1999) (Rule 72(a) objection to magistrate judge's order must contain all claims of error; claims of error not raised before district judge cannot be raised in circuit court); *Simpson v. Lear Astronics Corp.,* 77 F.3d 1170, 1174 (9th Cir.1996) ("[A] party who fails to file timely objections to a magistrate judge's nondispositive order ... forfeits its right to appellate review."); *International Surplus Lines Insurance Co. v. Wyoming Coal Refining Systems, Inc.,* 52 F.3d 901, 904 (10th Cir.1995)(failure to make timely objection constitutes waiver). *But see Spence v. Superintendent, Great Meadow Correctional Facility,* 219 F.3d 162, 174 (2d Cir.2000) (exception to time limit for arguments with "substantial merit" or existence of plain error in magistrate judge's ruling); *Kruger v. Apfel,* 214 F.3d 784, 786–87 (7th Cir.2000) (10 day time limit is not jurisdictional; where appeal is only a few days late

and opposing party experienced no unfair prejudice, district court should consider objections to magistrate judge's recommendation de novo; moreover, separate from party's objection, district court should examine recommendation of magistrate judge for clear error).

3. *See, e.g., Hutchinson v. Pfeil,* 105 F.3d 562, 566 (10th Cir.1997) (magistrate judge may impose sanctions in discovery as nondispositive matter).

4. *See, e.g., Alpern v. Lieb,* 38 F.3d 933, 935 (7th Cir.1994) (citing conflicting cases; holding that Rule 72(a) does not confer such authority on magistrate judges). *But cf., Hutchinson v. Pfeil,* 208 F.3d 1180, 1184 n. 7 (10th Cir.2000) (refusing to decide issue).

5. *See, e.g., Gomez v. Martin Marietta Corp.,* 50 F.3d 1511 (10th Cir.1995)(decision not to impose dispositive sanction alters standard of review).

decides a nondispositive pretrial matter, the order becomes effective when made, and requires no further action by the district judge.

Review of Nondispositive Pretrial Matter

The district judge who assigned the case retains ultimate authority over the case and shall modify or set aside any portion of the magistrate judge's order found to be clearly erroneous or contrary to law.[6] Even if no objections are presented, the district judge may rehear or reconsider the matter *sua sponte*.

Implicit Affirmation of Magistrate Judge's Decision

If a party objects to the ruling of a magistrate judge, but the district court does not expressly rule on some part of the objections, in appropriate circumstances the district court's action may be treated as a denial of those objections.[7]

Failure to Object

When a party fails to file a timely objection to a magistrate judge's ruling under Rule 72(a), that party's right to seek review of the magistrate judge's ruling is greatly curtailed. However, it is settled that even in that circumstance the district court retains authority to evaluate the matter.[8]

Review by Court of Appeals

A party may not appeal directly to the Court of Appeals from a magistrate judge's nondispositive pretrial order.[9]

RULE 72(b). DISPOSITIVE MOTIONS AND PRISONER PETITIONS

CORE CONCEPT

When a dispositive matter is referred to a magistrate judge, the magistrate judge will conduct evidentiary hearings and submit a recommendation, and when appropriate, submit proposed findings of fact to the district judge. If a party makes a timely written objection to the proposed findings and recommendation of the magistrate judge, the

---

6. *See, e.g., Hall v. Norfolk Southern Railway Co.,* 469 F.3d 590, 595 (7th Cir. 2006) ("[D]istrict judges are to review nondispositive motions for clear error.").

7. *See, e.g., Miller v. Automobile Club of New Mexico, Inc.,* 420 F.3d 1098, 1117 (10th Cir.2005) (where record indicated district court had considered all materials, "we may properly construe a district court's failure to address arguments raised in a Rule 72(a) objection 'as an implicit denial of those arguments' and a refusal to overrule the magistrate judge's order.").

8. *See, e.g., Allen v. Sybase, Inc.,* 468 F.3d 642, 658 (10th Cir. 2006) ("[A] Party's

failure to seek timely review does not strip a district court of its power to revisit the issue.").

9. *See, e.g., United States v. Gonzalez–Ramirez,* 350 F.3d 731, 733 (8th Cir.2003) (no right to appeal to circuit court unless district court has already reviewed magistrate judge's order after objection to order); *Simpson v. Lear Astronics Corp.,* 77 F.3d 1170, 1173–74 (9th Cir.1996) (if party does not object to district court, and if district court does not therefore hear the issue, finding of magistrate judge under Rule 72(a) cannot be appealed to circuit court).

district judge must make a *de novo* review of the record.[10]

NOTE: A party must file specific, written objections to the magistrate judge's findings and recommendation within 10 days after being served with a copy of the recommended disposition. Failure to make timely objection constitutes a waiver of the right to review of the magistrate judge's findings and recommendation.[11]

APPLICATIONS

Matters Considered Dispositive

The following matters are deemed dispositive by statute:[12] (1) a motion for injunctive relief; (2) a motion for judgment on the pleadings; (3) a motion for summary judgment; (4) a motion to dismiss or permit maintenance of a class action; (5) a motion to dismiss for failure to state a claim upon which relief may be granted; or (6) a motion for involuntary dismissal.[13] The following matters may also be considered dispositive: (1) an application to proceed *in forma pauperis*;[14] (2) a motion to amend a pleading;[15] (3) a motion for attorney's fees;[16] and (4) an order remanding a removed case to state court.[17] It is unclear whether sanctions for violations of Rule 11 (governing pleadings, motions and other papers) is within a magistrate judge's authority under Rule 72(a), or whether the magistrate judge may only make a recommendation to the district judge under Rule 72(b).[18]

Dispositive Sanction Not Imposed

If a motion seeks a sanction that would be dispositive, but the magistrate judge denies the motion, the matter is not considered

---

10. 28 U.S.C.A. § 636(b)(1)(C). *See also, Rajaratnam v. Moyer*, 47 F.3d 922, 925 n. 8 (7th Cir.1995)(de novo review does not require new trial; only a fresh look at issues to which objection has been raised). *But cf., Taylor v. Farrier*, 910 F.2d 518, 521 (8th Cir.1990)("in conducting [de novo] review, the district court must, at a minimum, listen to a tape recording or read a transcript of the evidentiary hearing.").

11. *See International Surplus Lines Insurance Co. v. Wyoming Coal Refining Systems, Inc.*, 52 F.3d 901, 904 (10th Cir. 1995)(failure to make timely objection constitutes waiver).

12. 28 U.S.C.A. § 636(b)(1)(A).

13. *See, e.g., Bennett v. General Caster Service of N. Gordon Co.*, 976 F.2d 995, 997 (6th Cir.1992)(identifying similar list and noting that list is "nonexhaustive").

14. *See, e.g., Woods v. Dahlberg*, 894 F.2d 187, 187 (6th Cir.1990) (per curiam)(motion to proceed in forma pauperis is dispositive, and therefore magistrate judge may only make recommendation).

15. *Lundy v. Adamar of New Jersey, Inc.*, 34 F.3d 1173, 1183 (3d Cir.1994) (mo-

tion to amend is dispositive of statute of limitations defense).

16. *See, e.g., Massey v. City of Ferndale*, 7 F.3d 506 (6th Cir.1993)(motion for attorney's fees is dispositive); *but see Merritt v. International Brotherhood of Boilermakers*, 649 F.2d 1013, 1016–18 (5th Cir.1981)(post-judgment award of attorney's fees as sanction for misconduct in pre-trial discovery is non-dispositive; held, pre-trial discovery issues are inherently non-dispositive matters).

17. *Vogel v. United States Office Products Co.*, 258 F.3d 509, 515 (6th Cir.2001) (also collecting other examples of dispositive motions); *First Union Mortgage Corp. v. Smith*, 229 F.3d 992, 996 (10th Cir.2000).

18. *See, e.g., Alpern v. Lieb*, 38 F.3d 933, 935 (7th Cir.1994) (citing conflicting cases; holding that Rule 72(a) does not confer such authority on magistrate judges). *But cf., Hutchinson v. Pfeil*, 208 F.3d 1180, 1184 n. 7 (10th Cir.2000) (refusing to decide issue).

dispositive. Instead, the standard of review is provided by Rule 72(a) (clearly erroneous or contrary to law), rather than Rule 72(b)(de novo review upon the record).[19]

Habeas Corpus

Rule 72(b) does not extend to habeas corpus petitions. Habeas corpus petitions are governed by specific statutes.[20]

Procedure for Dispositive Pretrial Matters

A magistrate judge has substantial discretion to conduct hearings on dispositive matters. The magistrate judge shall make a record of all evidentiary proceedings, but has discretion whether to keep a record of non-evidentiary proceedings. The magistrate judge shall submit a recommendation for disposition of the matter to the district judge who assigned the case to the magistrate judge. When appropriate, the magistrate judge shall submit proposed findings of fact with the recommendation. The clerk of the court is required to mail copies of the magistrate judge's recommendation and findings of fact to all parties.

Obligation to Order Transcript

A party objecting to the magistrate judge's recommended disposition should promptly arrange for the transcription of the record or portions of the record agreed upon by the parties or as directed by the magistrate judge, unless directed otherwise by the district judge.

Response to Objections

A party may respond to another party's objections within 10 days after service of a copy of the objections.[21]

De Novo Review of Dispositive Motions by District Judge

Upon proper objection, the district judge who assigned the motion to the magistrate judge shall make a *de novo* determination. After making a *de novo* review of the ruling, a district judge may accept, reject, or modify the recommended disposition or recommit the matter to the magistrate judge with instructions.

A district judge, under the *de novo* review standard, is not required to conduct a new hearing, but is required to make a new examination of the issues upon which specific, written objections were based, either on the record, through the recall of witnesses, or by receiving additional testimony.[22]

---

19. *See, e.g., Gomez v. Martin Marietta Corp.,* 50 F.3d 1511 (10th Cir.1995)(decision not to impose dispositive sanction alters standard of review).

20. 28 U.S.C.A. §§ 2254, 2255.

21. *See, e.g., United States v. Mora,* 135 F.3d 1351, 1357 (10th Cir.1998).

22. *See, e.g., Taylor v. Farrier,* 910 F.2d 518, 520 (8th Cir.1990) (de novo review of record requires study of transcript or tape recording). *See also Garcia v. City of Albu-*

querque, 232 F.3d 760, 766 (10th Cir. 2000) (Rule 72(b) does not require district court to make specific findings, only a de novo review of record); *Borden v. Secretary of Health & Human Services,* 836 F.2d 4, 6 (1st Cir. 1987) ("We hold categorically that an unsuccessful party is not entitled as of right to de novo review by the judge of an argument never seasonably raised before the magistrate."). *But cf., Carpet Group International v. Oriental Rug Importers Association, Inc.,* 227 F.3d 62, 72 (3d Cir.2000)

Failure to Object and Untimely Objections

The courts are split on whether and to what extent the district judge is obligated to review a magistrate judge's recommendation absent a timely objection.[23]

Waiver of Right to Appeal

A party who fails to file a timely objection to the district judge regarding the magistrate judge's findings or recommendations waives the party's right to appeal the issue to the court of appeals.[24]

ADDITIONAL RESEARCH REFERENCES

Wright & Miller, *Federal Practice and Procedure* §§ 3076.1–3076.9.

C.J.S. United States Commissioners § 3.

West's Key No. Digests, United States Magistrates ⟲15–31.

(district judge has discretion to consider additional evidence not presented to magistrate judge).

23. *See, e.g., Conetta v. National Hair Care Centers, Inc.,* 236 F.3d 67, 73 (1st Cir.2001) (even in absence of timely objection to final action by magistrate judge, Rule 72(b) requires district court to "adapt, reject, or modify the recommendation before there is any final judgment"); *But see Diamond v. Colonial Life & Accident Insurance Co.,* 416 F.3d 310 (4th Cir.2005) ("[I]n the absence of a timely filed objection, a district court need not conduct a de novo review, but instead must 'only satisfy itself that there is no clear error on the fact of the record in order to accept the recommendation.' "); *Diaz v. Oklahoma,* ___ Fed.

Appx. ___, 2005 WL 1519116 (10th Cir. 2005) ("Failure to file a specific objection ... constitutes a waiver of appellate review."); *Federal Deposit Insurance Corp. v. Hillcrest Associates,* 66 F.3d 566, 569 (2d Cir.1995) (failure to make timely objection acts as waiver; very narrow exception to that general rule in pro se cases); *Douglass v. United Services Automobile Association,* 79 F.3d 1415 (5th Cir.1996)(court need only determine absence of clear error); *Park Motor Mart, Inc. v. Ford Motor Co.,* 616 F.2d 603 (1st Cir.1980)(no obligation).

24. *See, e.g., Phillips v. General Motors Corp.,* 307 F.3d 1206, 1210 (9th Cir.2002) (failure to file timely appeal is waiver of right to appeal to appellate court).

RULE 73

MAGISTRATE JUDGES: TRIAL BY CONSENT; APPEAL

(a) Trial by Consent. When authorized under 28 U.S.C. § 636(c), a magistrate judge may, if all parties consent, conduct a civil action or proceeding, including a jury or nonjury trial. A record must be made in accordance with 28 U.S.C. § 636(c)(5).

(b) Consent Procedure.

    (1) *In General.* When a magistrate judge has been designated to conduct civil actions or proceedings, the clerk must give the parties written notice of their opportunity to consent under 28 U.S.C. § 636(c). To signify their consent, the parties must jointly or separately file a statement consenting to the referral. A district judge or magistrate judge may be informed of a party's response to the clerk's notice only if all parties have consented to the referral.

    (2) *Reminding the Parties About Consenting.* A district judge, magistrate judge, or other court official may remind the parties of the magistrate judge's availability, but must also advise them that they are free to withhold consent without adverse substantive consequences.

    (3) *Vacating a Referral.* On its own for good cause—or when a party shows extraordinary circumstances—the district judge may vacate a referral to a magistrate judge under this rule.

(c) Appealing a Judgment. In accordance with 28 U.S.C. § 636(c)(3), an appeal from a judgment entered at a magistrate judge's direction may be taken to the court of appeals as would any other appeal from a district-court judgment.

[Former Rule 73 abrogated December 4, 1967, effective July 1, 1968; new Rule 73 adopted April 28, 1983, effective August 1, 1983; amended March 2, 1987, effective August 1, 1987; April 22, 1993, effective December 1, 1993, April 11, 1997, effective December 1, 1997; April 30, 2007, effective December 1, 2007.]

—————————— **2007 AMENDMENTS ROADMAP** ——————————

STYLE PROJECT CHANGES: Minor changes were made in the title of the Rule and its subsections. The three paragraphs of subsection (b), previously unnumbered and untitled, now have numbers and titles to aid readability. Minor language changes were made throughout the text of the Rule. Reference to Rule 73(d), previously abrogated in 1997, was deleted entirely.

NON-STYLE CHANGES: None.

NOTE: The Federal Rules "Style Project" is explained in Part III-A.

AUTHORS' COMMENTARY ON RULE 73

PURPOSE AND SCOPE

Rule 73 provides that, upon consent of the parties, a district judge may refer cases to a magistrate judge for trial or final disposition. Rule 73 also provides for the district judge to vacate the reference to the magistrate judge's ruling.

RULE 73(a). TRIAL BY CONSENT

CORE CONCEPT

By local rule or by order of court, and with the consent of the parties, a magistrate judge may be designated with case-dispositive or final judgment authority to conduct any or all of the proceedings in a jury or non-jury case. In such cases, the magistrate judge has all of the powers of a district judge, except the power of contempt. A local rule providing that magistrate judges may hear case-dispositive proceedings may not restrict the types of cases a magistrate judge may hear.

APPLICATIONS

Preserving the Record

The magistrate judge must decide by what means the record should be preserved, such as verbatim by a court reporter, by electronic sound, or by shorthand. When deciding the means of preservation of the record, the magistrate judge may consider the complexity of the case, the likelihood of appeal, the costs of the record, and time constraints.

Contempt

Magistrate judges may not hold contempt hearings. Instead, the magistrate judge will certify the facts of the contempt to the district judge and serve an order to show cause why a contempt citation should not be issued upon the alleged disobedient party. Subsequently, the district judge in a summary proceeding will hear the evidence of the contemptuous act and may punish the disobedient party.[1]

RULE 73(b).   CONSENT PROCEDURE

CORE CONCEPT

The clerk of court handles the procedures for obtaining the parties' consent to trial before a magistrate judge, isolating the district judge from the consenting process. All parties must make a free and voluntary consent to having a magistrate judge preside over their trial.[2]

APPLICATIONS

Consent Procedure

To prevent the district judge from exercising any influence over the decision by the parties and to prevent the district judge from knowing who may have opposed the reference, the clerk of court administers the complete consent procedure.

Notification

At the time the action is filed, the clerk of court notifies the parties in writing of their option to proceed before a magistrate judge.[3]

Time for Consent

The time for indicating a party's consent or lack of consent is set generally by local rule or court order.[4]

Acceptance

Parties indicate their consent by submitting completed consent forms supplied by the clerk of court.[5]

Voluntariness of Consent

Most courts have local rules to ensure the voluntariness and willingness of consent, such as preventing the clerk of court from notifying litigants that their case will be heard sooner by a magistrate judge or that they will receive an experienced magistrate judge. Neither the district judge, the magistrate judge, nor the clerk of court may attempt to persuade the parties to consent to a trial before a magistrate judge. The parties must clearly and unambigu-

---

1. 28 U.S.C.A. § 636(e).

2. 28 U.S.C.A. § 636(c)(2).

3. 28 U.S.C.A. § 636(c)(2).

4. *See, e.g., Rembert v. Apfel,* 213 F.3d 1331, 1335 n. 1 (11th Cir.2000) ("Parties can consent even after judgment."); *Drake v. Minnesota Mineral & Manufacturing Co.,* 134 F.3d 878, 883 (7th Cir.1998) (good consent even after appellate oral argument). *But see Hajek v. Burlington Northern Railroad Co.,* 186 F.3d 1105, 1108 (9th Cir. 1999) (consent in appellate brief is ineffective); *Archie v. Christian,* 808 F.2d 1132

(5th Cir.1987)(en banc)(consent must be given before trial begins—rule of 5th Circuit).

5. *But see Roell v. Withrow,* 538 U.S. 580, 581, 123 S.Ct. 1696, 1699, 155 L.Ed.2d 775 (2003) (noting normal requirement of written consent, but holding that where non-consenting parties appear before magistrate without making further objection, magistrate has jurisdiction; fact of inferred consent satisfies requirement of Rule 73(b)).

ously consent to a magistrate judge.[6] A mere acquiesence or failure to object does not constitute consent.[7]

Consequence of Failure to Consent

If a magistrate judge hears a case without the consent of the parties, the resulting judgment is a "nullity."[8]

Additional Parties and Consent

In general, local rules will control the time within which new parties must exercise their right to consent. The clerk of court will notify new parties of their right to consent in the same manner as the original parties. When an additional party is joined who does not consent to the participation of the magistrate judge, the district judge must hear the case.[9]

Vacating the Reference to a Magistrate by the District Judge

The court may, for good cause shown on its own motion, or under extraordinary circumstances shown by any party, vacate its reference of a civil matter to a magistrate judge.[10] For example, it has been held that a district judge may vacate a proceeding from a magistrate judge when the magistrate judge is faced with extraordinary questions of law with possibly wide precedential effect.[11] This power may not be used routinely to vacate certain categories of cases from a magistrate judge.[12] The court retains this power, notwithstanding the consent of all parties to trial before a magistrate judge.

---

6. *See, e.g., Hajek v. Burlington Northern Railroad,* 186 F.3d 1105, 1108 (9th Cir. 1999) (party's response to proposed referral to magistrate judge that " 'at this time the Defendant does not believe any special procedures are required or are appropriate' " is "far from 'clear and unambiguous' "). *Alaniz v. California Processors, Inc.,* 690 F.2d 717, 720 (9th Cir.1982)(per curiam)(holding that consent must be clear and unambiguous). *Cf., Aldrich v. Bowen,* 130 F.3d 1364, 1365 (9th Cir.1997) (in the absence of written consent in the record, magistrate judge lacked jurisdiction to hear case). *But see Kadonsky v. United States,* 216 F.3d 499, 502 (5th Cir.2000) (sufficient consent where party signed document "evincing his willingness to proceed before a magistrate judge;" use of particular written form is not required for consent); *Rembert v. Apfel,* 213 F.3d 1331, 1335 (11th Cir.2000) ("Although consent must be 'express and on the record,' it need not necessarily be written.").

7. *See, e.g., Hajek v. Burlington Northern Railroad,* 186 F.3d 1105, 1108 (9th Cir. 1999) (local rule provided that failure to object to referral to magistrate judge was

consent to referral; held, local rule is invalid); *In re Marriage of Nasca,* 160 F.3d 578, 579 (9th Cir.1998) (" 'consent by failure to object' " does not provide magistrate judge with authority under Rule 73(b); appellate court raised issue *sua sponte*); *Caprera v. Jacobs,* 790 F.2d 442, 444 (5th Cir. 1986)(consent cannot be inferred from parties' conduct; "consent to proceed before a magistrate [must] be explicit").

8. *Binder v. Gillespie,* 184 F.3d 1059, 1063 (9th Cir.1999).

9. *See, e.g., New York Chinese TV Programs, Inc. v. U.E. Enterprises, Inc.,* 996 F.2d 21, 24 (2d Cir.1993)(intervenors must also consent, even when joined after magistrate judge begins to hear case).

10. 28 U.S.C.A. § 636(c)(6).

11. *Gomez v. Harris,* 504 F.Supp. 1342, 1345 (D.Alaska 1981)(reference vacated in case with "controlling question of law and a thicket of procedural difficulties").

12. *See,* S.Report No. 74, 96th Cong., 1st Sess. 14 (1979)(WESTLAW: LH database, **ti(senate + 5 96–74)**).

RULE 73(c).　APPEALING A JUDGMENT

CORE CONCEPT

The appeal procedure provides that a party make a direct appeal of a magistrate judge's final judgment to the Court of Appeals in the same manner as a judgment from the district court.[13]

ADDITIONAL RESEARCH REFERENCES

Wright & Miller, *Federal Practice and Procedure* §§ 3077.1–3077.5.

C.J.S. United States Commissioners § 3.

West's Key No. Digests, United States Magistrates ⬥12–13, 24–31.

---

13. *See, e.g., Dluhos v. Floating & Abandoned Vessel, Known as "New York,"* 162 F.3d 63, 67 (2d Cir.1998) (consent to trial before magistrate judge waives any appeal to district judge; appeal is to circuit court).

RULE 74*

METHOD OF APPEAL FROM MAGISTRATE TO DISTRICT JUDGE UNDER TITLE 28, U.S.C. § 636(c)(4) AND RULE 73(d)

[ABROGATED]

——————————— **2007 AMENDMENTS ROADMAP** ———————————

STYLE PROJECT CHANGES: None. Rule 74 was abrogated in 1997, and is preserved only for possible future use. However, the word "abrogated," heretofore appearing in brackets after the Rule number, is now deleted.

NON-STYLE CHANGES: None.

NOTE: The Federal Rules "Style Project" is explained in Part III-A.

RULE 75*

PROCEEDINGS ON APPEAL FROM MAGISTRATE TO DISTRICT JUDGE UNDER RULE 73(d)

[ABROGATED]

——————————— **2007 AMENDMENTS ROADMAP** ———————————

STYLE PROJECT CHANGES: None. Rule 75 was abrogated in 1997, and is preserved only for possible future use. However, the word "abrogated," heretofore appearing in brackets after the Rule number, is now deleted.

NON-STYLE CHANGES: None.

NOTE: The Federal Rules "Style Project" is explained in Part III-A.

* Rules 73(d) and 74–76 provided that when a magistrate judge hears a case, the parties could choose to appeal to either the district court or the court of appeals. However, in 1997 the so-called "optional appeal route" to the district court was abolished by Congress. Accordingly, the Supreme Court abrogated Rules 73(d) and 74–76 effective in December, 1997. Henceforth appeals from trials conducted by magistrate judges shall be made only to the appropriate court of appeals.

RULE 76*

JUDGMENT OF THE DISTRICT JUDGE ON THE APPEAL UNDER RULE 73(d) AND COSTS

[ABROGATED]

─────────── **2007 AMENDMENTS ROADMAP** ───────────

STYLE PROJECT CHANGES: None. Rule 76 was abrogated in 1997, and is preserved only for possible future use. However, the word "abrogated," heretofore appearing in brackets after the Rule number, is now deleted.

NON-STYLE CHANGES: None.

NOTE: The Federal Rules "Style Project" is explained in Part III-A.

X. DISTRICT COURTS AND CLERKS

RULE 77

CONDUCTING BUSINESS; CLERK'S AUTHORITY; NOTICE OF AN ORDER OR JUDGMENT

(a) When Court Is Open. Every district court is considered always open for filing any paper, issuing and returning process, making a motion, or entering an order.

(b) Place for Trial and Other Proceedings. Every trial on the merits must be conducted in open court and, so far as convenient, in a regular courtroom. Any other act or proceeding may be done or conducted by a judge in chambers, without the attendance of the clerk or other court official, and anywhere inside or outside the district. But no hearing—other than one ex parte—may be conducted outside the district unless all the affected parties consent.

(c) Clerk's Office Hours; Clerk's Orders.

    (1) *Hours.* The clerk's office—with a clerk or deputy on duty—must be open during business hours every day except Saturdays, Sundays, and legal holidays. But a court may, by local rule or order, require that the office be open for specified hours on Saturday or a particular legal holiday other than one listed in Rule 6(a)(4)(A).

    (2) *Orders.* Subject to the court's power to suspend, alter, or rescind the clerk's action for good cause, the clerk may:

        (A) issue process;

        (B) enter a default;

        (C) enter a default judgment under Rule 55(b)(1); and

        (D) act on any other matter that does not require the court's action.

(d) Serving Notice of an Order or Judgment.

    (1) *Service.* Immediately after entering an order or judgment, the clerk must serve notice of the entry, as provided in Rule 5(b), on each party who is not in

default for failing to appear. The clerk must record the service on the docket. A party also may serve notice of the entry as provided in Rule 5(b).

(2) *Time to Appeal Not Affected by Lack of Notice.* Lack of notice of the entry does not affect the time for appeal or relieve—or authorize the court to relieve— a party for failing to appeal within the time allowed, except as allowed by Federal Rule of Appellate Procedure (4)(a).

[Amended effective March 19, 1948; July 1, 1963; July 1, 1968; July 1, 1971; August 1, 1987; December 1, 1991; April 23, 2001, effective December 1, 2001; April 30, 2007, effective December 1, 2007.]

2007 AMENDMENTS ROADMAP

STYLE PROJECT CHANGES: Rules 77(c) and 77(d) were subsectioned, and orienting labels were added or revised. Obsolete language was culled, "must" replaced "shall", like provisions were grouped together, and the language was clarified.

NON-STYLE CHANGES: None.

NOTE: The Federal Rules "Style Project" is explained in Part III-A.

AUTHORS' COMMENTARY ON RULE 77

PURPOSE AND SCOPE

Rule 77 contains a variety of provisions pertaining to the operations of the district court and the clerk's office. It provides that the court is always "open," and sets forth the times that the clerk's office is open. It also states that trials and hearings shall be conducted in the courtroom. Finally, Rule 77 controls notice of judgments and orders.

RULE 77(a).   WHEN COURT IS OPEN

CORE CONCEPT

The district courts are deemed open at all times for the purposes of filing papers, issuing process, and the like.[1] This does not mean that the

---

1. *In re Bradshaw*, 283 B.R. 814, 817 (1st Cir.BAP 2002) (the guiding principle is that clerks of court must be available in some fashion twenty-four hours a day).

clerk's office will be manned and open at all times.[2] Rather, papers may be filed after hours by delivering them to the clerk or a deputy clerk, depositing them in a designated receptacle provided by the clerk and authorized by local rule,[3] or even leaving them with a judge under exceptional circumstances.[4] However, filing is not accomplished merely by delivery to the clerk's office without delivering the paper to a proper officer or otherwise using an established method of after-hours filing.[5]

RULE 77(b). PLACE FOR TRIAL AND OTHER PROCEEDINGS

CORE CONCEPT

All trials must be conducted in open court, and in a regular courtroom to the extent practicable. Other proceedings, such as status conferences, pretrial conferences, etc., may be conducted in chambers or some other location.[6] However, no hearing, other than one *ex parte,* may be held outside the district without consent of all parties.

RULE 77(c). CLERK'S OFFICE HOURS; CLERK'S ORDERS

CORE CONCEPT

The clerk's office must be open at minimum during working hours on all days except weekends and holidays. The hours may be expanded by local rule. The clerk's office has the power to take certain acts, such as entering default judgments and process to execute judgments.[7] Such actions by the clerk's office are reviewable by the court and may be suspended, altered, or rescinded upon cause shown.[8]

RULE 77(d). SERVING NOTICE OF AN ORDER OR JUDGMENT

CORE CONCEPT

The clerk's office must send notice of the entry of judgment to all parties who have entered appearances in the manner set forth in Rule

2. *Stone Street Capital, Inc. v. Mc-Donald's Corp.*, 300 F.Supp.2d 345, 348, n.4 (D.Md.2003); *In re Bradshaw*, 283 B.R. 814, 818 (1st Cir.BAP 2002); *McIntosh v. Antonino*, 71 F.3d 29, 35 (1st Cir.1995).

3. *Ticketmaster Corp. v. Tickets.Com, Inc.*, 2000 WL 525390, 2000 (C.D.Cal.2000) (a drop box is one method to accommodate the fact that the court shall be deemed always open).

4. *Turner v. City of Newport*, 887 F.Supp. 149 (E.D.Ky.1995)(deposit in post office box of clerk deemed filing).

5. *McIntosh v. Antonino*, 71 F.3d 29, 35 (1st Cir.1995); *In the Matter of the Com-*plaint of Fisherman's Wharf Fillet, Inc., 83 F.Supp.2d 651, 657 (E.D.Va.1999) (after hours facsimile is not adequate filing).

6. *B.H. v. McDonald*, 49 F.3d 294 (7th Cir.1995); *Crumrine v. NEG Micon USA, Inc.*, 104 F.Supp.2d 1123, 1126 (N.D.Iowa 2000) (court could be held at any courthouse within the district even without the consent of the parties).

7. *United States v. Laws*, 352 F.Supp.2d 707, 709 (E.D.Va.2004) (writ of garnishment).

8. *Brady v. United States*, 211 F.3d 499 (9th Cir.2000) (clerk's entry of default may be set aside for cause shown).

5(b).[9]   However, the failure of the clerk to do so does not necessarily increase the time for appeal[10] (but note that the appellate courts may extend the time for appeal and may consider the failure of the clerk to send notice).[11]   A party who wants to insure that all parties have notice of the judgment (and thus that the time for appeal has commenced running) may serve the notice by mail[12] as provided in Rule 5.[13]

ADDITIONAL RESEARCH REFERENCES

Wright & Miller, *Federal Practice and Procedure* §§ 3081–3084.

C.J.S. Courts § 236; Federal Civil Procedure §§ 915 et seq., 1213; Federal Courts §§ 302 et seq.

West's Key No. Digests, Clerk of Courts ⟜1; Federal Civil Procedure ⟜1951, 2628; Federal Courts ⟜971.

9. *Poole v. Family Court of New Castle County*, 368 F.3d 263 (3rd Cir.2004); *Arai v. American Bryce Ranches Inc.*, 316 F.3d 1066, 1068 (9th Cir.2003); *Nguyen v. Southwest Leasing and Rental Inc.*, 282 F.3d 1061, 1064–65 (9th Cir.2002) (Rule 77(d) contemplates that the notice will be in writing); *Dempster v. Dempster*, 404 F.Supp.2d 445, 448 (E.D.N.Y.2005) (service by email pursuant to electronic docketing system is sufficient).

10. *Jackson v. Crosby*, 375 F.3d 1291, 1294 (11th Cir.2004); *Jackson v. Crosby*, 375 F.3d 1291, 1294 (11th Cir.2004); *Poole v. Family Court of New Castle County*, 368 F.3d 263 (3rd Cir.2004); *In re City of Memphis*, 293 F.3d 345 (6th Cir.2002).

11. *Nguyen v. Southwest Leasing and Rental Inc.*, 282 F.3d 1061, 1065–66 (9th Cir.2002) (Rule 77(d) must be read in conjunction with Rule 4(a)(6) of the Federal Rules of Appellate Procedure); *In re Stein*, 197 F.3d 421, 424–25 (9th Cir.1999).

12. *Ryan v. First Unum Life Ins. Co.*, 174 F.3d 302, 304–05 (2d Cir.1999) (service must be by mail, not by hand delivery).

13. *Resendiz v. Dretke*, 452 F.3d 356, 358, n.3 (5th Cir.2006) (only formal service pursuant to Rule 5(b) constitutes notice); *Bass v. United States Dept. Of Agriculture*, 211 F.3d 959 (5th Cir.2000); *Nunley v. City of Los Angeles*, 52 F.3d 792 (9th Cir.1995).

RULE 78

HEARING MOTIONS; SUBMISSION ON BRIEFS

(a) Providing a Regular Schedule for Oral Hearings. A court may establish regular times and places for oral hearings on motions.

(b) Providing for Submission on Briefs. By rule or order, the court may provide for submitting and determining motions on briefs, without oral hearings.

[Amended effective August 1, 1987; April 30, 2007, effective December 1, 2007.]

──────────── **2007 AMENDMENTS ROADMAP** ────────────

STYLE PROJECT CHANGES: The language *requiring* each district court to establish regular times for hearing motions was modified to *allow* the establishment of such regular times. Rule 78 was subdivided into 78(a) and 78(b), and orienting labels were added.

NON-STYLE CHANGES: The sentence in Rule 78 referring to the judge issuing an order to advance, conduct, and hear an action was deleted because Rule 16 addresses these issues.

NOTE: The Federal Rules "Style Project" is explained in Part III-A.

AUTHORS' COMMENTARY ON RULE 78

──────────── **SCOPE AND PURPOSE** ────────────

Rule 78 allows each district to enact local rules establishing regular motion days for the presentation of motions requiring a hearing. However, judges may conduct oral arguments on motions at other times. Furthermore, the districts or individual judges may also provide that motions are to be determined on briefs only, without oral argument.

RULE 78(a). PROVIDING A REGULAR SCHEDULE FOR ORAL HEARINGS

CORE CONCEPT

The court may establish regular times for hearing arguments, but also may hear arguments at any time or place on notice that the court considers reasonable.

RULE 78(b). PROVIDING FOR SUBMISSION ON BRIEFS

CORE CONCEPT

The court may decide motions on the papers, without oral argument.[1]

ADDITIONAL RESEARCH REFERENCES

Wright & Miller, *Federal Practice and Procedure* §§ 3091.

C.J.S. Federal Civil Procedure § 933.

West's Key No. Digests, Federal Civil Procedure 1991.

---

1. *United States v. Peninsula Communications, Inc.*, 287 F.3d 832, 839 (9th Cir. 2002); *Willis v. Pacific Maritime Association*, 244 F.3d 675, 684, n.2 (9th Cir.2001); *Jetton v. McDonnell Douglas Corp.*, 121 F.3d 423, 427 (8th Cir.1997); *Coleman v. Hartford Life Ins. Co.*, 432 F.Supp.2d 1030, 1031 (C.D.Cal.2006); *Love v. The Mail on Sunday*, 473 F.Supp.2d 1052 (C.D.Cal. 2007).

RULE 79

RECORDS KEPT BY THE CLERK

(a) Civil Docket.

    (1) *In General.* The clerk must keep a record known as the "civil docket" in the form and manner prescribed by the Director of the Administrative Office of the United States Courts with the approval of the Judicial Conference of the United States. The clerk must enter each civil action in the docket. Actions must be assigned consecutive file numbers, which must be noted in the docket where the first entry of the action is made.

    (2) *Items to be Entered.* The following items must be marked with the file number and entered chronologically in the docket:

        (A) papers filed with the clerk;

        (B) process issued, and proofs of service or other returns showing execution; and

        (C) appearances, orders, verdicts, and judgments.

    (3) *Contents of Entries; Jury Trial Demanded.* Each entry must briefly show the nature of the paper filed or writ issued, the substance of each proof of service or other return, and the substance and date of entry of each order and judgment. When a jury trial has been properly demanded or ordered, the clerk must enter the word "jury" in the docket.

(b) Civil Judgments and Orders. The clerk must keep a copy of every final judgment and appealable order; of every order affecting title to or a lien on real or personal property; and of any other order that the court directs to be kept. The clerk must keep these in the form and manner prescribed by the Director of the Administrative Office of the United States Courts with the approval of the Judicial Conference of the United States.

(c) Indexes; Calendars. Under the court's direction, the clerk must:

    (1) keep indexes of the docket and of the judgments and orders described in Rule 79(b); and

(2) prepare calendars of all actions ready for trial, distinguishing jury trials from nonjury trials.

(d) Other Records. The clerk must keep any other records required by the Director of the Administrative Office of the United States Courts with the approval of the Judicial Conference of the United States.

[Amended effective March 19, 1948; October 20, 1949; July 1, 1963; April 30, 2007, effective December 1, 2007.]

--------------- **2007 AMENDMENTS ROADMAP** ---------------

STYLE PROJECT CHANGES: Rules 79(a) and 79(b) were subdivisioned and orienting labels were added. Obsolete language was culled, "must" replaced "shall", and the language was clarified.

NON-STYLE CHANGES: None.

NOTE: The Federal Rules "Style Project" is explained in Part III-A.

AUTHORS' COMMENTARY ON RULE 79

--------------- PURPOSE AND SCOPE ---------------

Rule 79 governs the record keeping duties of the district court clerk's office.

RULE 79(a).   CIVIL DOCKET

CORE CONCEPT

The clerk shall keep a civil docket, which is a descriptive, chronological listing of each pleading, motion, order, etc., filed in the case. The docket may be maintained manually or electronically.[1]

APPLICATIONS

Description

The docket should contain a brief description of each entry.[2]

---

1. *Active Products Corp. v. A.H. Choitz & Co. Inc.*, 163 F.R.D. 274, 280–81 (N.D.Ind.1995).

2. *United States v. Alcantara*, 396 F.3d 189, 200 (2nd Cir.2005) (even a motion filed

Entries should be entered chronologically[3] and should show the dates on which orders or judgments are entered.[4]

Jury vs. Non-jury

The docket should indicate if the case is to be tried before a jury.

Judgments

Judgments are not effective until entered on the docket.[5] Under Rule 58, a judgment must be a separate document.[6]

Briefs

In general, briefs are not part of the record, so they are not filed and are not entered on the docket.

Time of Entry

Rule 79 does not specify the time for making entries in the docket. However, the parties' rights will not be prejudiced by a delay in entry on the docket.

RULE 79(b).   CIVIL JUDGMENTS AND ORDERS

CORE CONCEPT

Rule 79(b) requires the clerk's office to retain a copy of every final judgment, appealable order, order creating a lien on property, and any other order as directed by the court.

RULE 79(c).   INDEXES; CALENDARS

CORE CONCEPT

Rule 79(c) requires the clerk's office to maintain an index or indices of the civil docket and of every civil judgment, appealable order, order creating a lien on property, and other order as directed by the court. The clerk's office must also maintain a calendar of all actions ready for trial. This calendar will indicate whether the matter is to be tried jury or non-jury.

under seal should be reflected in the docket).

3. *Casey v. Long Island R. Co.*, 406 F.3d 142, 148 (2nd Cir.2005); *Goode v. Winkler*, 252 F.3d 242 (2d Cir.2001) (criticizing the district court for not arranging the docket strictly chronologically).

4. *Connecticut ex rel. Blumenthal v. Crotty*, 346 F.3d 84, 92 (2nd Cir.2003) (the operative date is the date the order is entered onto the docket, not the date the order is signed or dated); *Houston v. Greiner*, 174 F.3d 287 (2d Cir.1999) (computerized docketing system that did not list a date for each entry violates Rule 79).

5. *Long v. County of Los Angeles*, 442 F.3d 1178, 1184, n.3 (9th Cir.2006); *United States v. Fiorelli*, 337 F.3d 282 (3d Cir. 2003) (although an order may be signed by the district court, received by the clerk, and entered in the docket on different days, the entry date controls).

6. *Dieser v. Continental Cas. Co.*, 440 F.3d 920, 926, n.6 (8th Cir.2006); *Jackson v. Albany Appeal Bureau Unit*, 442 F.3d 51, 53, n.1 (2nd Cir.2006); *United States v. Johnson*, 254 F.3d 279, 286 (D.C.Cir.2001).

RULE 79(d). OTHER RECORDS

CORE CONCEPT

The Administrative Office of the United States may direct that the clerk's offices maintain other books and records.

ADDITIONAL RESEARCH REFERENCES

Wright & Miller, *Federal Practice and Procedure* §§ 3101–3107.

C.J.S. Federal Civil Procedure §§ 933, 1227 et seq.

West's Key No. Digests, Federal Civil Procedure ⬿1991, 2621.

RULE 80

STENOGRAPHIC TRANSCRIPT AS EVIDENCE

If stenographically reported testimony at a hearing or trial is admissible in evidence at a later trial, the testimony may be proved by a transcript certified by the person who reported it.

[Amended effective March 19, 1948; April 30, 2007, effective December 1, 2007.]

------------ **2007 AMENDMENTS ROADMAP** ------------

STYLE PROJECT CHANGES: Abrogated Rules 80(a) and 80(b) were deleted, and Rule 80(c) was renumbered 80(a). The title of Rule 80 was revised, and the language was clarified.

NON-STYLE CHANGES: None.

NOTE: The Federal Rules "Style Project" is explained in Part III-A.

AUTHORS' COMMENTARY ON RULE 80

------------ **PURPOSE AND SCOPE** ------------

Rule 80 pertains to the use of testimony at one trial or hearing as evidence at a subsequent hearing or trial. The rule provides that a transcript certified by an official court reporter is proof of the prior testimony.[1]

ADDITIONAL RESEARCH REFERENCES

Wright & Miller, *Federal Practice and Procedure* §§ 3121–3122.

C.J.S. Evidence §§ 629–633 et seq., 652 et seq.

West's Key No. Digests, Evidence ☜332(1, 4), 340.

1. *Orr v. Bank of America, NT & SA,* scripts not properly certified not admitted). 285 F.3d 764, 776 (9th Cir.2002) (tran-

XI. GENERAL PROVISIONS

RULE 81

APPLICABILITY OF THE RULES IN GENERAL; REMOVED ACTIONS

(a) Applicability to Particular Proceedings.

(1) *Prize Proceedings.* These rules do not apply to prize proceedings in admiralty governed by 10 U.S.C. §§ 7651–7681.

(2) *Bankruptcy.* These rules apply to bankruptcy proceedings to the extent provided by the Federal Rules of Bankruptcy Procedure.

(3) *Citizenship.* These rules apply to proceedings for admission to citizenship to the extent that the practice in those proceedings is not specified in federal statutes and has previously conformed to the practice in civil actions. The provisions of 8 U.S.C. § 1451 for service by publication and for answer apply in proceedings to cancel citizenship certificates.

(4) *Special Writs.* These rules apply to proceedings for habeas corpus and for quo warranto to the extent that the practice in those proceedings:

(A) is not specified in a federal statute, the Rules Governing Section 2254 Cases, or the Rules Governing Section 2255 Cases; and

(B) has previously conformed to the practice in civil actions.

(5) *Proceedings Involving a Subpoena.* These rules apply to proceedings to compel testimony or the production of documents through a subpoena issued by a United States officer or agency under a federal statute, except as otherwise provided by statute, by local rule, or by court order in the proceedings.

(6) *Other Proceedings.* These rules, to the extent applicable, govern proceedings under the following laws, except as these laws provide other procedures:

(A) 7 U.S.C. §§ 292, 499g(c), for reviewing an order of the Secretary of Agriculture;

1180

(B) 9 U.S.C., relating to arbitration;

(C) 15 U.S.C. § 522, for reviewing an order of the Secretary of the Interior;

(D) 15 U.S.C. § 715d(c), for reviewing an order denying a certificate of clearance;

(E) 29 U.S.C. §§ 159, 160, for enforcing an order of the National Labor Relations Board;

(F) 33 U.S.C. §§ 918, 921, for enforcing or reviewing a compensation order under the Longshore and Harbor Workers' Compensation Act; and

(G) 45 U.S.C. § 159, for reviewing an arbitration award in a railway-labor dispute.

(b) Scire Facias and Mandamus. The writs of scire facias and mandamus are abolished. Relief previously available through them may be obtained by appropriate action or motion under these rules.

(c) Removed Actions.

(1) *Applicability.* These rules apply to a civil action after it is removed from a state court.

(2) *Further Pleading.* After removal, repleading is unnecessary unless the court orders it. A defendant who did not answer before removal must answer or present other defenses or objections under these rules within the longest of these periods:

(A) 20 days after receiving—through service or otherwise—a copy of the initial pleading stating the claim for relief;

(B) 20 days after being served with the summons for an initial pleading on file at the time of service; or

(C) 5 days after the notice of removal is filed.

(3) *Demand for a Jury Trial.*

(A) *As Affected by State Law.* A party who, before removal, expressly demanded a jury trial in accordance with state law need not renew the demand after removal. If the state law did not require an express demand for a jury trial, a party need not make one after removal unless the court orders the parties to do so within a

1181

specified time. The court must so order at a party's request and may so order on its own. A party who fails to make a demand when so ordered waives a jury trial.

(B) *Under Rule 38.* If all necessary pleadings have been served at the time of removal, a party entitled to a jury trial under Rule 38 must be given one if the party serves a demand within 10 days after:

(i) it files a notice of removal; or

(ii) it is served with a notice of removal filed by another party.

(d) Law Applicable.

(1) *State Law.* When these rules refer to state law, the term "law" includes the state's statutes and the state's judicial decisions.

(2) *District of Columbia.* The term "state" includes, where appropriate, the District of Columbia. When these rules provide for state law to apply, in the District Court for the District of Columbia:

(A) the law applied in the District governs; and

(B) the term "federal statute" includes any Act of Congress that applies locally to the District.

[Amended effective December 28, 1939; March 19, 1948; October 20, 1949; August 1, 1951; July 1, 1963; July 1, 1966; July 1, 1968; July 1, 1971; August 1, 1987; April 23, 2001, effective December 1, 2001; April 29, 2002, effective December 1, 2002; April 30, 2007, effective December 1, 2007.]

—————————— **2007 AMENDMENTS ROADMAP** ——————————

STYLE PROJECT CHANGES: Rule 81(c) was revised to reflect the amendment of the removal provisions in 28 U.S.C. § 1446(a) that changed the nomenclature from "petition for removal" to "notice of removal." Former Rule 81(e) defined the law of a state to include only statutes and case law interpreting the statutes. That language was revised to also include other types of case law. Former Rule 81(f) was deleted because it pertained to the office of district director of internal revenue, which was abolished by restructuring under the Internal Revenue Service Restructuring and Reform Act of 1998. Abrogated Rule 81(d) was deleted, and Rule 81(f) was renumbered Rule 81(d). Abrogated Rule 81(a)(7) was also deleted. Rule 81(a)(6), Rule 81(c), and new Rule 81(d) were subsectioned, and orienting labels were added throughout. Like provisions were grouped together, obsolete language was culled, and the language was generally simplified and clarified.

NON-STYLE CHANGES: None.

NOTE: The Federal Rules "Style Project" is explained in Part III-A.

AUTHORS' COMMENTARY ON RULE 81

──────────── PURPOSE AND SCOPE ────────────

Rule 81 specifies whether the Federal Rules of Civil Procedure apply in various proceedings. It also specifies how the Rules operate in the District of Columbia, contains some provisions governing removed actions, abolishes the Writs of Mandamus and Scire Facias, and defines "Officer of the United States."

RULE 81(a). APPLICABILITY TO PARTICULAR PROCEEDINGS APPLICABLE

CORE CONCEPT

Rule 81(a) lists specific proceedings to which the Rules apply and identifies specific proceedings to which the Rules do not apply.

APPLICATIONS

Not Applicable[1]

Rule 81(a) provides that the Rules do not apply to:

- Prize Proceedings in Admiralty;[2]
- Proceedings to Review Orders of the Secretary of Agriculture;[3]
- Proceedings to Review Orders of the Secretary of the Interior;[4]
- Proceedings to Review Orders of the Petroleum Control Boards;[5] and
- Proceedings to Enforce Orders of the National Labor Relations Board.[6]

Applicable

The Rules supplement the statutory procedures for the following:

1. Rule 81(a) exempted copyright proceedings and mental health proceedings in the United States District Court for the District of Columbia from the Rules. These exemptions were removed by the 2001 amendments to Rule 81(a).

2. Rule 81(a)(1).

3. Rule 81(a)(6)(A). *Riccelli's Produce, Inc. v. Horton Tomato Co., Inc.*, 155 F.R.D. 411 (N.D.N.Y.1994).

4. Rule 81(a)(6)(C).

5. Rule 81(a)(6)(D).

6. Rule 81(a)(6)(E).

- Bankruptcy Proceedings, to the extent provided by the Bankruptcy Rules;[7]

- Admission to Citizenship Proceedings;[8]

- Habeas Corpus Proceedings;[9]

- Quo Warranto Proceedings;[10]

- Proceedings for Enforcement or Review of Compensation Orders under the Longshoremen's and Harbor Workers' Compensation Act;[11] and

- Proceedings to enforce subpoenas to testify or to produce documents issued by agencies of the United States.[12]

Arbitrations

In proceedings arbitrated under federal statute, the Rules generally act as default provisions, applying when no arbitration rule addresses the procedural issue.[13]

Habeas Corpus

Prior to the 2002 Amendments, Rule 81(a)(2) contained specific procedures relating to writs of habeas corpus. Those procedures were eliminated by the 2002 Amendments to eliminate the inconsistency between the procedures in Rule 81(a)(2) and in Sections 2254 and 2255.[14]

RULE 81(b). SCIRE FACIAS AND MANDAMUS

CORE CONCEPT

Rule 81(b) abolishes the Writs of Scire Facias (a writ with a variety of functions such as reviving a judgment[15] or effecting execution) and Mandamus (a writ compelling an official to take an action).[16]

7. Rule 81(a)(2). *Chrysler Financial Corp. v. Powe*, 312 F.3d 1241, 1243, n.1 (11th Cir.2002); *Ben–Baruch v. Island Properties*, 362 B.R. 565 (E.D.N.Y. 2007).

8. Rule 81(a)(3); *Chan v. Gantner*, 464 F.3d 289, 295 (2nd Cir. 2006).

9. Rule 81(a)(4). *Mayle v. Felix*, 545 U.S. 644, ___, 125 S.Ct. 2562, 2569, 162 L.Ed.2d 582 (2005); *U.S. v. Nelson*, 465 F.3d 1145, 1147 (10th Cir. 2006); *Caldwell v. Dretke*, 429 F.3d 521, 527–28 (5th Cir.2005).

10. Rule 81(a)(4).

11. Rule 81(a)(6)(F); *Galle v. Director, Office of Workers' Compensation Programs*, 246 F.3d 440, 447 (5th Cir.2001); *Pleasant-El v. Oil Recovery Co., Inc.*, 148 F.3d 1300, 1302 (11th Cir.1998).

12. Rule 81(a)(5); *Martin v. Bally's Park Place Hotel & Casino*, 983 F.2d 1252 (3d Cir.1993); *N.L.R.B. v. Cable Car Advertisers, Inc.*, 319 F.Supp.2d 991 (N.D.Cal.2004).

13. Rule 81(a)(6)(B); *D.H. Blair & Co., Inc. v. Gottdiener*, 462 F.3d 95, 108 (2nd Cir. 2006); *IFC Interconsult, AG v. Safeguard Intern. Partners, LLC.*, 438 F.3d 298, 307 (3rd Cir.2006).

14. The Advisory Committee Note to the 2002 Amendment to Rule 81. *See also Gonzalez v. Crosby*, 545 U.S. 524, ___, 125 S.Ct. 2641, 2646, 162 L.Ed.2d 480 (2005); *U.S. v. Nelson*, 465 F.3d 1145, 1147 (10th Cir. 2006).

15. *TDK Electronics Corp. v. Draiman*, 321 F.3d 677, 680 (7th Cir.2003)(although the writ of *scire facias* is abolished, revival or reentry of a judgment is obtainable by a more modern motion).

16. *Badier v. Gonzales*, 475 F.Supp.2d 1294, 1298 (N.D.Ga. 2006); *SBA Communications, Inc. v. Zoning Commission of Town of Brookfield*, 96 F.Supp.2d 139 (D.Conn. 2000).

APPLICATIONS

District Court Only

Rule 81(b) abolishes the Writs in the district court only. Thus, a Court of Appeals, under appropriate circumstances, may issue a Writ of Mandamus to a district judge under Rule 21 of the Federal Rules of Appellate Procedure.[17]

Relief Not Abolished

Only the Writs themselves are abolished. The relief sought may be available through some other motion or proceeding.[18]

RULE 81(c). REMOVED ACTIONS

CORE CONCEPT

Rule 81(c) provides that the Rules apply to actions commenced in state court and removed to federal court.[19] It also contains procedures governing removed actions.

APPLICATIONS

Rules Apply After Removal

The Rules only apply to pleadings or motions filed after the removal.[20] Thus, Rules governing the form of pleadings would not apply to pleadings filed in state court prior to removal.[21]

Time to Answer

If the defendant has not yet answered at the time of removal, the defendant may file an answer either by the latest of 5 days (excluding weekends and holidays) from the date of removal,[22] or 20

---

17. *In re Nagy*, 89 F.3d 115, 116–17 (2d Cir.1996). *But see In re Campbell*, 264 F.3d 730, 731 (7th Cir.2001) (declining to issue writ of mandamus to state court).

18. *In re Cheney*, 406 F.3d 723, 728–29 (D.C.Cir.2005) (mandamus like relief can be obtained through a mandatory injunction); *Simmat v. United States Bureau of Prisons*, 413 F.3d 1225, 1235 (10th Cir.2005) (mandamus relief otherwise available); *TDK Electronics Corp. v. Draiman*, 321 F.3d 677, 680 (7th Cir.2003)(although the writ of *scire facias* is abolished, revival or reentry of a judgment is obtainable by a more modern motion).

19. *S. Wallace Edwards & Sons, Inc. v. Cincinnati Ins. Co.*, 353 F.3d 367, 374, n.4 (4th Cir.2003); *Lee v. City of Beaumont*, 12 F.3d 933 (9th Cir.1993).

20. *D.H. Blair & Co., Inc. v. Gottdiener*, 462 F.3d 95, 101–02 (2nd Cir. 2006); *Castleberry v. Goldome Credit Corp.*, 408 F.3d 773, 784 (11th Cir.2005); *Pacific Employers*

Ins. Co. v. Sav-a-Lot of Winchester, 291 F.3d 392 (6th Cir.2002).

21. *See Romo v. Gulf Stream Coach, Inc.*, 250 F.3d 1119 (7th Cir.2001) ("The Federal Rules make clear that they do not apply to filings in state court, even if the case is later removed to federal court."); *Prazak v. Local 1 Intern. Union of Bricklayers & Allied Crafts*, 233 F.3d 1149, 1152–53 (9th Cir.2000); *Griffen v. City of Oklahoma City*, 3 F.3d 336, (10th Cir.1993)(holding that Rule 11 sanctions do not apply to a complaint filed in state court and removed to federal court); *but see Levine v. McLeskey*, 881 F.Supp. 1030, 1048 (E.D.Va.1995), *affirmed in part, vacated in part*, 164 F.3d 210 (4th Cir.1998).

22. *D.H. Blair & Co., Inc. v. Gottdiener*, 462 F.3d 95, 102 (2nd Cir. 2006); *Norsyn, Inc. v. Desai*, 351 F.3d 825, 828 (8th Cir. 2003); *Veryfine Products, Inc. v. Phlo Corp.*, 124 F.Supp.2d 16, 21 (D.Mass.2000) (discussing the counting of the 5 day period).

days from service of the original pleading, if the pleading has been filed, whichever is later.[23] Note, however, that the act of removal alone does not trigger an obligation to answer a complaint that has not yet been properly served.[24]

Repleading Unnecessary

Unless the court orders otherwise, pleadings filed while the action was in state court do not need to be repleaded after removal to federal court.[25]

Jury Demand

If a jury trial demand has been properly made in state court, no new demand is necessary.[26] If no jury trial demand was made in state court and if all pleadings were filed in state court, the parties may nonetheless make a jury trial demand within 10 days of removal to federal court.[27] The 10 days are measured from filing the removal petition in the case of the petitioner and from service of the petition for all other parties. If no express jury trial demand is required under state law, none will be required in the removed action unless the court so directs.[28] If a jury demand was made in the state court proceedings that does not meet the state requirements but does satisfy federal requirements, it can be accepted by the federal court.[29] There remain some scenarios that are not covered by Rule 81(c). In New York, jury demands may be made shortly before trial. In such cases, the court will have discretion to allow a late jury demand.[30]

RULE 81(d).   LAW APPLICABLE

CORE CONCEPT

Rule 81(d) provides that, in general, when the Rules refer to "states," they include the District of Columbia.[31] Thus, when the Rules refer to the law of the state in which the court sits, the United States District Court for the District of Columbia uses the law applied in the

23. *Murphy Bros., Inc. v. Michetti Pipe Stringing, Inc.*, 526 U.S. 344, 346, 119 S.Ct. 1322, 1325, 143 L.Ed.2d 448 (1999); *Silva v. City of Madison*, 69 F.3d 1368, 1371 (7th Cir.1995)(only proper service triggers the 20 day period to answer).

24. *Norsyn, Inc. v. Desai*, 351 F.3d 825, 829 (8th Cir.2003).

25. *Kuehl v. Federal Deposit Insurance Corp.*, 8 F.3d 905 (1st Cir.1993); *Sapiro v. Encompass Ins.*, 221 F.R.D. 513 (N.D.Cal. 2004).

26. *Lutz v. Glendale Union High School*, 403 F.3d 1061, 1063–64 (9th Cir. 2005); *Winter v. Minnesota Mutual Life Ins. Co.*, 199 F.3d 399, 406 (7th Cir.1999); *Marcella v. Brandywine Hospital*, 47 F.3d 618 (3d Cir.1995).

27. *Lutz v. Glendale Union High School*, 403 F.3d 1061, 1063–64 (9th Cir. 2005); *Ajnoha v. JC Penney Life Ins. Co.*, 480 F.Supp.2d 663, 676 (E.D.N.Y. 2007).

28. *Bruns v. Amana*, 131 F.3d 761, 762 (8th Cir.1997).

29. *Wyatt v. Hunt Plywood Co., Inc.*, 297 F.3d 405, 415 (5th Cir.2002).

30. *See* Rule 38(b); *Ajnoha v. JC Penney Life Ins. Co.*, 480 F.Supp.2d 663, 676–77 (E.D.N.Y. 2007). *Breedlove v. Cabou*, 296 F.Supp.2d 253, 278 (N.D.N.Y.2003).

31. *United States Intern. Trade Com'n v. ASAT, Inc.*, 411 F.3d 245, 250 (D.C.Cir. 2005); *Pharmachemie B.V. v. Pharmacia S.p.A.*, 934 F.Supp. 484 (D.Mass.1996).

District of Columbia. Rule 81(d) also defines the phrase "law of a state" as including statutes and judicial decisions.

APPLICATIONS

2007 Amendments

The 2007 amendments eliminated abrogated Rule 81(d) and Rule 81(e) was renumbered as Rule 81(d). Care should be exercised in researching and citing pre–2008 cases referring to Rule 81(d) or Rule 81(e).

ADDITIONAL RESEARCH REFERENCES

Wright & Miller, *Federal Practice and Procedure* §§ 3131–3134.

C.J.S. Federal Civil Procedure §§ 7–23 et seq.

West's Key No. Digests, Federal Civil Procedure ⊶31–44.

RULE 82

JURISDICTION AND VENUE UNAFFECTED

These rules do not extend or limit the jurisdiction of the district courts or the venue of actions in those courts. An admiralty or maritime claim under Rule 9(h) is not a civil action for purposes of 28 U.S.C. §§ 1391–1392.

[Amended effective October 20, 1949; July 1, 1966; April 23, 2001, effective December 1, 2001; April 30, 2007, effective December 1, 2007.]

──────────── 2007 AMENDMENTS ROADMAP ────────────

STYLE PROJECT CHANGES: Minor revisions to Rule 82 were made for clarity and consistency.

NON-STYLE CHANGES: None.

NOTE: The Federal Rules "Style Project" is explained in Part III-A.

AUTHORS' COMMENTARY ON RULE 82

──────────── PURPOSE AND SCOPE ────────────

Jurisdiction and venue are determined by statute (as discussed in separate sections of this book) and are not affected by the Rules.[1]

APPLICATIONS

Subject Matter Jurisdiction Only

As a general matter, the Rules do not extend the court's subject matter jurisdiction. This principle is limited to *subject matter* jurisdiction (*i.e.,* the type of case a district court can hear), not *personal* jurisdiction (*i.e.,* which parties must appear and defend themselves).[2] Likewise, the Rules contain timing requirements that are often

---

1. *Henderson v. United States*, 517 U.S. 654, 116 S.Ct. 1638, 134 L.Ed.2d 880 (1996); *Canatella v. California*, 404 F.3d 1106, 1113 (9th Cir.2005); *Easter v. American West Financial*, 381 F.3d 948, 963 (9th Cir.2004); *United States v. Eleven Vehicles, Their Equipment and Accessories*, 200 F.3d 203, 216 (3d Cir.2000).

2. *See Chambers Medical Foundation v. Chambers*, 236 F.R.D. 299 (W.D.La.2006); *In re National Century Financial Enterprises, Inc., Inv. Litigation*, 323 F.Supp.2d 861 (S.D.Ohio 2004).

described as "jurisdictional" but do not affect the court's subject matter jurisdiction.[3]

Joinder

The Rules actually do affect subject matter jurisdiction in that they govern the joinder of ancillary claims and parties.[4]

Admiralty and Maritime Cases

Rule 82 also provides that admiralty and maritime cases are not considered civil actions for purposes of the venue statutes.[5] Admiralty and maritime cases generally have separate venue provisions to facilitate suing seamen wherever they may be found.[6]

ADDITIONAL RESEARCH REFERENCES

Wright & Miller, *Federal Practice and Procedure* §§ 3141–3142.

C.J.S. Federal Civil Procedure § 19.

West's Key No. Digests, Federal Civil Procedure ⌾40.

3. *Kontrick v. Ryan*, 540 U.S. 443, 124 S.Ct. 906, 157 L.Ed.2d 867 (U.S.2004) ("the filing deadlines prescribed in Bankruptcy Rules 4004 and 9006(b)(3) are claim-processing rules that do not delineate what cases bankruptcy courts are competent to adjudicate"); *Brickwood Contractors, Inc. v. Datanet Engineering, Inc.*, 369 F.3d 385 (4th Cir.2004) (courts are said to be without jurisdiction to consider an untimely motion under Rule 59); *American Canoe Ass'n, Inc. v. City Of Attalla*, 363 F.3d 1085, 1088 (11th Cir.2004) (application of Rule 6(a)'s computational rules presents no offense to Rule 82).

4. *See Lunney v. U.S.*, 319 F.3d 550, 556–57 (2nd Cir.2003).

5. *See Sunbelt Corp. v. Noble, Denton & Associates, Inc.*, 5 F.3d 28 (3d Cir.1993); *Empty Barge Lines II, Inc. v. DREDGE LEONARD FISHER*, 441 F.Supp.2d 786 (E.D.Tex.2006); *Holmes v. Energy Catering Services, LLC*, 270 F.Supp.2d 882 (S.D.Tex. 2003).

6. *See Empty Barge Lines II, Inc. v. DREDGE LEONARD FISHER*, 441 F.Supp.2d 786 (E.D.Tex.2006); *Holmes v. Energy Catering Services, LLC*, 270 F.Supp.2d 882, 885 (S.D.Tex.2003); *Denson v. United States*, 99 F.Supp.2d 792, 793 (S.D.Tex.2000).

RULE 83

RULES BY DISTRICT COURTS; JUDGE'S DIRECTIVES

(a) Local Rules.

(1) *In General.* After giving public notice and an opportunity for comment, a district court, acting by a majority of its district judges, may adopt and amend rules governing its practice. A local rule must be consistent with—but not duplicate—federal statutes and rules adopted under 28 U.S.C. §§ 2072 and 2075, and must conform to any uniform numbering system prescribed by the Judicial Conference of the United States. A local rule takes effect on the date specified by the district court and remains in effect unless amended by the court or abrogated by the judicial council of the circuit. Copies of rules and amendments must, on their adoption, be furnished to the judicial council and the Administrative Office of the United States Courts and be made available to the public.

(2) *Requirement of Form.* A local rule imposing a requirement of form must not be enforced in a way that causes a party to lose any right because of a nonwillful failure to comply.

(b) Procedure When There Is No Controlling Law.
A judge may regulate practice in any manner consistent with federal law, rules adopted under 28 U.S.C. §§ 2072 and 2075, and the district's local rules. No sanction or other disadvantage may be imposed for noncompliance with any requirement not in federal law, federal rules, or the local rules unless the alleged violator has been furnished in the particular case with actual notice of the requirement.

[Amended effective August 1, 1985; April 27, 1995, effective December 1, 1995; April 30, 2007, effective December 1, 2007.]

——————— **2007 AMENDMENTS ROADMAP** ———————

STYLE PROJECT CHANGES: Obsolete language was culled, active voice replaced passive voice, "must" replaced "shall", and other minor revisions to Rule 83 were made for clarity and consistency.

NON-STYLE CHANGES: None.

NOTE: The Federal Rules "Style Project" is explained in Part III-A.

AUTHORS' COMMENTARY ON RULE 83

PURPOSE AND SCOPE

Rule 83 authorizes the districts to develop local rules that are "consistent" with the Federal Rules.

RULE 83(a).   LOCAL RULES

CORE CONCEPT

Rule 83(a) provides that each district court can develop local rules. These local rules must be consistent with the federal rules, both in substance and in numbering.   Local rules pertaining to matters of form cannot be enforced in a manner that prejudices the substantive rights of a party.

APPLICATIONS

Consistent with Federal Rules

Local rule must be consistent with, and not duplicative of,[1] Acts of Congress[2] and the Federal Rules.[3] Additionally, numbering must be consistent with the Federal Rules.

Typical Local Rules

Local rules can cover a wide variety of topics, and vary greatly in number and scope from district to district.   Some typical local rules address:

1. *United States v. Galiczynski,* 44 F.Supp.2d 707 (E.D.Pa.1999).

2. *D'Iorio v. Majestic Lanes, Inc.,* 370 F.3d 354 (3d Cir.2004); *Weibrecht v. Southern Illinois Transfer, Inc.,* 241 F.3d 875, 879 (7th Cir.2001)(to the extent a local rule conflicts with a federal statute, the local rule must be held invalid).

3. *U.S. v. Comprehensive Drug Testing, Inc.,* 473 F.3d 915, 927 (9th Cir. 2006) (where a local rule conflicts with a federal rule, the federal rule prevails); *Dattner v.*

ConAgra Foods, Inc., 458 F.3d 98 (2nd Cir. 2006); *NEPSK, Inc. v. Town of Houlton,* 283 F.3d 1, 7 (1st Cir.2002) (a district court cannot enforce its local rules in a way that conflicts with the Federal Rules of Civil Procedure); *Stern v. United States District Court for the District of Massachusetts,* 214 F.3d 4 (1st Cir.2000) ("Even if a local rule does not contravene the text of a national rule, the former cannot survive if it subverts the latter's purpose.").

- Admission to practice before the district courts;[4]

- Admission *Pro Hac Vice;*

- Procedures for disbarment;

- Security for court costs;

- Creation of divisions within the district;

- Form and number of copies of pleadings and briefs;

- Period of time for process;

- Manner for presentation of motions;[5]

- Notice for constitutional challenges to acts of Congress;

- Continuances;

- Discovery procedures;

- Pretrial and status conferences, including pretrial statements;

- Impartial medical examinations;

- Courtroom rules and regulations, including the use of cameras and recording equipment;

- Size, selection, and instruction of the jury;

- Handling and marking of exhibits;

- Entry of judgment; and

- Motions for new trials.

Effect of Local Rule

A valid local rule has the effect of law,[6] and must be obeyed.[7] The court has authority to impose sanctions when a party violates the court's local rules.[8] However, a local rule imposing a requirement of form (as opposed to substance) may not be enforced in a manner that causes a party to lose rights for a "nonwillful" violation.[9] Thus, a party should not be deprived of a right to a jury trial because it is unaware of or forgets a local rule requiring jury demands to be noted in the caption of pleadings.[10]

---

4. *See In re Poole,* 222 F.3d 618, 621 (9th Cir.2000)

5. *Miltimore Sales, Inc. v. International Rectifier, Inc.,* 412 F.3d 685, 693 (6th Cir. 2005) (motions for attorneys fees); *Jetton v. McDonnell Douglas Corp.,* 121 F.3d 423, 426 (8th Cir.1997); *Goltz v. Univ. of Notre Dame,* 177 F.R.D. 638 (N.D.Ind.1997) (one purpose of local rules is to further the administration of justice by mandating that motions for summary judgment be properly briefed).

6. *U.S. v. Comprehensive Drug Testing, Inc.,* 473 F.3d 915, 927 (9th Cir. 2006) (local rules are laws of the United States); *Jetton v. McDonnell Douglas Corp.,* 121 F.3d 423, 426 (8th Cir.1997) (local rule has "the force of law" and the parties are charged with

knowledge of the district court's rules the same as with knowledge of the Federal Rules and all federal law).

7. *Weil v. Neary,* 278 U.S. 160, 169, 49 S.Ct. 144, 148, 73 L.Ed. 243 (1929).

8. *Carmona v. Wright,* 233 F.R.D. 270, 275 (N.D.N.Y.2006); *Nick v. Morgan's Foods, Inc.,* 99 F.Supp.2d 1056, 1061 (E.D.Mo.2000).

9. *Thompson v. Doane Pet Care Co.,* 470 F.3d 1201, 1204, n.3 (6th Cir. 2006); *Cordray v. 135–80 Travel Plaza, Inc.,* 356 F.Supp.2d 1011, 1015, n.6 (D.Neb.2005).

10. The Advisory Committee Note to the 1995 amendment to Rule 83.

Promulgation of Local Rules

Local rules are adopted pursuant to the procedures in the Rules Enabling Act.[11]

Public Comment

Before a local rule may be enacted, it must be published for comment by the public.[12]

Copies

Local rules are included in West's court rules pamphlets for most states. A copy of the local rules can also be obtained from the clerk's office for a nominal fee. Additionally, Rule 83 provides that the district must submit a copy of the local rules to the Administrative Office of the United States Courts.[13]

Bankruptcy

Local rules do not apply to proceedings in Bankruptcy.[14]

RULE 83(b). PROCEDURE WHEN THERE IS NO CONTROLLING LAW

CORE CONCEPT

The judges may regulate proceedings before them as they see fit, so long the court's rules are consistent with federal law, the Federal Rules, and local rules.[15]

APPLICATIONS

Orders Consistent with Other Rules

Individual judges' standing orders or requirements must be consistent with Acts of Congress, the Federal Rules, and local rules.[16]

Parties Must have Actual Notice of Court Requirements

The court may not sanction or "disadvantage" a party for noncompliance with a requirement not found in federal law, federal rules, or local rules unless that party has been furnished in the particular case with actual notice of the requirement.[17] Actual

---

11. 28 U.S.C. § 2071(b); *In re Dorner,* 343 F.3d 910, 913 (7th Cir.2003).

12. *In re Dorner,* 343 F.3d 910, 913 (7th Cir.2003). *Antoine v. Atlas Turner, Inc.,* 66 F.3d 105, 108 (6th Cir.1995).

13. *Dais v. Lane Bryant, Inc.,* 2000 WL 869489 (S.D.N.Y.2000).

14. *In re Flanagan,* 999 F.2d 753 (3d Cir.1993).

15. *See Carnes v. Zamani,* 488 F.3d 1057, 1059 (9th Cir. 2007) (the judge's power under Rule 83(b) to regulate the practice in the court only applies where there is no other controlling law); *Amnesty America v.*

Town of West Hartford, 288 F.3d 467, 470–71 (2d Cir.2002) (district court may regulate motion practice in any manner consistent with federal law and the federal rules).

16. *In re Dorner,* 343 F.3d 910, 913 (7th Cir.2003).

17. *Massachusetts Institute of Technology and Electronics For Imaging, Inc. v. Abacus Software,* 462 F.3d 1344, 1359 (Fed. Cir. 2006); *Amnesty America v. Town of West Hartford,* 288 F.3d 467, 471 (2d Cir. 2002); *Carroll v. Jaques Admiralty Law Firm,* 110 F.3d 290, 293 (5th Cir.1997)(but, the rule does not eliminate a court's inher-

notice can be provided with a copy of the judge's requirements or by an order referencing the judge's standing order and indicating how copies can be obtained.[18]

ADDITIONAL RESEARCH REFERENCES

Wright & Miller, *Federal Practice and Procedure* §§ 3151–3155.

C.J.S. Federal Civil Procedure § 21.

West's Key No. Digests, Federal Civil Procedure ⚷25.

ent power to sanction for intentional disruption of the discovery process).

18. The Advisory Committee Note to the 1995 amendment to Rule 83.

RULE 84

FORMS

The forms in the Appendix suffice under these rules and illustrate the simplicity and brevity that these rules contemplate.

[Amended effective March 19, 1948; April 30, 2007, effective December 1, 2007.]

───────── **2007 AMENDMENTS ROADMAP** ─────────

STYLE PROJECT CHANGES: Minor revisions to Rule 84 were made for clarity and consistency.

NON-STYLE CHANGES: None.

NOTE: The Federal Rules "Style Project" is explained in Part III-A.

AUTHORS' COMMENTARY ON RULE 84

───────── **PURPOSE AND SCOPE** ─────────

The Rules contain an Appendix of Forms that contains 82 forms, including complaints, answers, motions, discovery requests, and notices of appeal. The forms were completely rewritten in the 2007 amendments, and are intended to indicate the simplicity and brevity that are acceptable under in federal court.[1] The official forms cannot be challenged under the Rules[2] (although they can be challenged with substantive legal defenses, such as immunities).[3]

ADDITIONAL RESEARCH REFERENCES

Wright & Miller, *Federal Practice and Procedure* §§ 3161–3162.

C.J.S. Federal Civil Procedure § 251.

West's Key No. Digests, Federal Civil Procedure ⚼625–627.

1. *General Elec. Capital Corp. v. Posey,* 415 F.3d 391, 396 (5th Cir.2005); *Educadores Puertorriquenos en Accion v. Hernandez,* 367 F.3d 61, 68 (1st Cir.2004); *In re Total Containment, Inc.,* 335 B.R. 589, 600, n.2 (Bankr.E.D.Pa.2005); *Hutton v. Priddy's Auction Galleries, Inc.,* 275 F.Supp.2d 428 (S.D.N.Y.2003).

2. *Guidry v. United States Tobacco Co., Inc.,* 188 F.3d 619, 632 (5th Cir.1999) (the forms in the Appendix of Forms are sufficient under the Rules); *Reis Robotics USA, Inc. v. Concept Industries, Inc.,* 462 F.Supp.2d 897, 905 (N.D.Ill. 2006) (defendant may use the affirmative defenses included in the forms).

3. *See Atchinson v. District of Columbia,* 73 F.3d 418, 423 (D.C.Cir.1996).

RULE 85

TITLE

These rules may be cited as the Federal Rules of Civil Procedure.

───────── **2007 AMENDMENTS ROADMAP** ─────────

STYLE PROJECT CHANGES: Minor revisions to Rule 85 were made for clarity and consistency.

NON-STYLE CHANGES: None.

NOTE: The Federal Rules "Style Project" is explained in Part III-A.

AUTHORS' COMMENTARY ON RULE 85

───────── **PURPOSE AND SCOPE** ─────────

The full title of the Rules is the "Federal Rules of Civil Procedure." The Rules should be cited as "Fed.R.Civ.P. ___."

ADDITIONAL RESEARCH REFERENCES

Wright & Miller, *Federal Practice and Procedure* § 3171.

C.J.S. Federal Civil Procedure §§ 7 et seq.

West's Key No. Digests, Federal Civil Procedure ☞31.

RULE 86

EFFECTIVE DATES

(a) In General. These rules and any amendments take effect at the time specified by the Supreme Court, subject to 28 U.S.C. § 2074. They govern:

(1) proceedings in an action commenced after their effective date; and

(2) proceedings after that date in an action then pending unless:

    (A) the Supreme Court specifies otherwise; or

    (B) the court determines that applying them in a particular action would be infeasible or work an injustice.

(b) December 1, 2007 Amendments. If any provision in Rules 1–5.1, 6–73, or 77–86 conflicts with another law, priority in time for the purpose of 28 U.S.C. § 2072(b) is not affected by the amendments taking effect on December 1, 2007.

[Amended effective March 19, 1948; October 20, 1949; July 19, 1961; July 1, 1963; April 30, 2007, effective December 1, 2007.]

———————— **2007 AMENDMENTS ROADMAP** ————————

STYLE PROJECT CHANGES: The subparts of Rule 86 providing a list of the effective dates of the original Civil Rules and the amendments through 1963 were deleted as no longer useful. Instead, Rule 86(a) now addresses the effective date of the Rules and any amendments. New Rule 86(b) clarifies the relationship of the December 1, 2007 amendments to other laws for purposes of applying the "supersession" clause in 28 U.S.C. § 2072(b). The supersession clause turns on the priority in time between the Rules and another law. Rule 86(b) provides that the non-substantive changes to every Rule in the 2007 amendments do not affect that priority-in-time analysis.

NON-STYLE CHANGES: None.

NOTE: The Federal Rules "Style Project" is explained in Part III-A.

AUTHORS' COMMENTARY ON RULE 86

——————————— PURPOSE AND SCOPE ———————————

Rule 86 lists the effective dates of the Rules and certain of the amendments. Amendments typically become effective 90 days after transmittal to Congress.

APPLICATIONS

RULE 86(a). IN GENERAL

CORE CONCEPT

In general, amendments to the Rules will apply to all actions filed after the effective date of the amendments, and to proceedings in actions filed before the effective date unless the Supreme Court has specified otherwise or if the court determines that application of an amended provision would not be feasible or would work an injustice.[1]

RULE 86(b). DECEMBER 1, 2007 AMENDMENTS

CORE CONCEPT

Rule 86(b) addresses the interplay between the 2007 amendments to the Rules and the supersession clause in 28 U.S.C. § 2072(b). The supersession clause says that laws in conflict with one or more of the Rules shall have no further force and effect after such Rules have taken effect. In essence, the Rules are deemed to have superseded existing inconsistent laws. Because the supersession clause focuses on priority in time between the Rules and other laws, Rule 86(b) provides that the non-substantive changes to every Rule in the 2007 amendments do not affect the priority in time analysis.

ADDITIONAL RESEARCH REFERENCES

Wright & Miller, *Federal Practice and Procedure* §§ 3181–3182.

C.J.S. Federal Civil Procedure §§ 7 et seq.

West's Key No. Digests, Federal Civil Procedure ⚷31.

1. *Ultra-Temp Corp. v. Advanced Vacuum Systems, Inc.*, 194 F.R.D. 378, 380, n.5 (D.Mass.2000); *Eastman Kodak Co. v. Knight*, 1994 WL 258538 (D.N.H.1994).

SUPPLEMENTAL RULES FOR ADMIRALTY OR MARITIME CLAIMS AND ASSET FORFEITURE ACTIONS

Adopted February 28, 1966, effective July 1, 1966

The former Rules of Practice in Admiralty and Maritime Cases, promulgated by the Supreme Court on December 6, 1920, effective March 7, 1921, as revised, amended and supplemented, were rescinded, effective July 1, 1966.

Including Amendments effective December 1, 2006

RULE A

SCOPE OF RULES

(1) These Supplemental Rules apply to:

(A) the procedure in admiralty and maritime claims within the meaning of Rule 9(h) with respect to the following remedies:

(i) maritime attachment and garnishment,

(ii) actions in rem,

(iii) possessory, petitory, and partition actions, and

(iv) actions for exoneration from or limitation of liability;

(B) forfeiture actions in rem arising from a federal statute; and

(C) the procedure in statutory condemnation proceedings analogous to maritime actions in rem, whether within the admiralty and maritime jurisdiction or not. Except as otherwise provided, references in these Supplemental Rules to actions in rem include such analogous statutory condemnation proceedings.

(2) The Federal Rules of Civil Procedure also apply to the foregoing proceedings except to the extent that they are inconsistent with these Supplemental Rules.

[Added Feb. 28, 1966, eff. July 1, 1966; April 12, 2006, effective December 1, 2006.]

RULE B

IN PERSONAM ACTIONS: ATTACHMENT AND GARNISHMENT

(1) When Available; Complaint, Affidavit, Judicial Authorization, and Process. In an in personam action:

(a) If a defendant is not found within the district when a verified complaint praying for attachment and the affidavit required by Rule B(1)(b) are filed, a verified complaint may contain a prayer for process to attach the defendant's tangible or intangible personal property—up to the amount sued for—in the hands of garnishees named in the process.

(b) The plaintiff or the plaintiff's attorney must sign and file with the complaint an affidavit stating that, to the affiant's knowledge, or on information and belief, the defendant cannot be found within the district. The court must review the complaint and affidavit and, if the conditions of this Rule B appear to exist, enter an order so stating and authorizing process of attachment and garnishment. The clerk may issue supplemental process enforcing the court's order upon application without further court order.

(c) If the plaintiff or the plaintiff's attorney certifies that exigent circumstances make court review impracticable, the clerk must issue the summons and process of attachment and garnishment. The plaintiff has the burden in any post-attachment hearing under Rule E(4)(f) to show that exigent circumstances existed.

(d)(i) If the property is a vessel or tangible property on board a vessel, the summons, process, and any supplemental process must be delivered to the marshal for service.

(ii) If the property is other tangible or intangible property, the summons, process, and any supplemental process must be delivered to a person or organization authorized to serve it, who may be (A) a marshal; (B) someone under contract with the United States; (C) someone specially appointed by the court for that purpose; or, (D) in an action brought by the United States, any officer or employee of the United States.

(e) The plaintiff may invoke state-law remedies under Rule 64 for seizure of person or property for the purpose of securing satisfaction of the judgment.

(2) Notice to Defendant. No default judgment may be entered except upon proof—which may be by affidavit—that:

(a) the complaint, summons, and process of attachment or garnishment have been served on the defendant in a manner authorized by Rule 4;

(b) the plaintiff or the garnishee has mailed to the defendant the complaint, summons, and process of attachment or garnishment, using any form of mail requiring a return receipt; or

(c) the plaintiff or the garnishee has tried diligently to give notice of the action to the defendant but could not do so.

(3) Answer.

(a) By Garnishee. The garnishee shall serve an answer, together with answers to any interrogatories served with the complaint, within 20 days after service of process upon the garnishee. Interrogatories to the garnishee may be served with the complaint without leave of court. If the garnishee refuses or neglects to answer on oath as to the debts, credits, or effects of the defendant in the garnishee's hands, or any interrogatories concerning such debts, credits, and effects that may be propounded by the plaintiff, the court may award compulsory process against the garnishee. If the garnishee admits any debts, credits, or effects, they shall be held in the garnishee's hands or paid into the registry of the court, and shall be held in either case subject to the further order of the court.

(b) By Defendant. The defendant shall serve an answer within 30 days after process has been executed, whether by attachment of property or service on the garnishee.

[Added Feb. 28, 1966, eff. July 1, 1966, and amended Apr. 29, 1985, effective Aug. 1, 1985; Mar. 2, 1987, effective Aug. 1, 1987; April 17, 2000, effective December 1, 2000; April 25, 2005, effective December 1, 2005.]

RULE C

IN REM ACTIONS: SPECIAL PROVISIONS

(1) When Available. An action in rem may be brought:

(a) To enforce any maritime lien;

(b) Whenever a statute of the United States provides for a maritime action in rem or a proceeding analogous thereto.

Except as otherwise provided by law a party who may proceed in rem may also, or in the alternative, proceed in personam against any person who may be liable.

Statutory provisions exempting vessels or other property owned or possessed by or operated by or for the United States from arrest or seizure are not affected by this rule. When a statute so provides, an action against the United States or an instrumentality thereof may proceed on in rem principles.

(2) Complaint. In an action in rem the complaint must:

(a) be verified;

(b) describe with reasonable particularity the property that is the subject of the action; and

(c) state that the property is within the district or will be within the district while the action is pending.

(3) Judicial Authorization and Process.

(a) Arrest Warrant.

(i) The court must review the complaint and any supporting papers. If the conditions for an in rem action appear to exist, the court must issue an order directing the clerk to issue a warrant for the arrest of the vessel or other property that is the subject of the action.

(ii) If the plaintiff or the plaintiff's attorney certifies that exigent circumstances make court review impracticable, the clerk must promptly issue a summons and a warrant for the arrest of the vessel or other property that is the subject of the action. The plaintiff has the burden in any post-arrest hearing under Rule E(4)(f) to show that exigent circumstances existed.

(b) Service.

  (i) If the property that is the subject of the action is a vessel or tangible property on board a vessel, the warrant and any supplemental process must be delivered to the marshal for service.

  (ii) If the property that is the subject of the action is other property, tangible or intangible, the warrant and any supplemental process must be delivered to a person or organization authorized to enforce it, who may be: (A) a marshal; (B) someone under contract with the United States; (C) someone specially appointed by the court for that purpose; or, (D) in an action brought by the United States, any officer or employee of the United States.

(c) Deposit in Court. If the property that is the subject of the action consists in whole or in part of freight, the proceeds of property sold, or other intangible property, the clerk must issue—in addition to the warrant—a summons directing any person controlling the property to show cause why it should not be deposited in court to abide the judgment.

(d) Supplemental Process. The clerk may upon application issue supplemental process to enforce the court's order without further court order.

(4) Notice. No notice other than execution of process is required when the property that is the subject of the action has been released under Rule E(5). If the property is not released within 10 days after execution, the plaintiff must promptly—or within the time that the court allows—give public notice of the action and arrest in a newspaper designated by court order and having general circulation in the district, but publication may be terminated if the property is released before publication is completed. The notice must specify the time under Rule C(6) to file a statement of interest in or right against the seized property and to answer. This rule does not affect the notice requirements in an action to foreclose a preferred ship mortgage under 46 U.S.C. §§ 31301 et seq., as amended.

(5) Ancillary Process. In any action in rem in which process has been served as provided by this rule, if any part of the property that is the subject of the action has not been brought within the control of the court because it has been removed or sold, or because it is intangible property in the hands of a person who has not been served with process, the court may, on motion, order any person having possession or control of such property or its proceeds to show cause why it should not be delivered into the custody of the marshal or other person or organization having a warrant for the arrest of the property, or paid into court to abide the judgment; and, after hearing, the court may enter such judgment as law and justice may require.

(6) Responsive Pleading; Interrogatories.

    (a) Maritime Arrests and Other Proceedings.

        (i) a [sic; text begins so in original] person who asserts a right of possession or any ownership interest in the property that is the subject of the action must file a verified statement of right or interest:

           (A) within 10 days after the execution of process, or

           (B) within the time that the court allows;

        (ii) the statement of right or interest must describe the interest in the property that supports the person's demand for its restitution or right to defend the action;

        (iii) an agent, bailee, or attorney must state the authority to file a statement of right or interest on behalf of another; and

        (iv) a person who asserts a right of possession or any ownership interest must serve an answer within 20 days after filing the statement of interest or right.

(b) Interrogatories. Interrogatories may be served with the complaint in an in rem action without leave of court. Answers to the interrogatories must be served with the answer to the complaint.

[Added Feb. 28, 1966, eff. Jul. 1, 1966, and amended Apr. 29, 1985, effective Aug. 1, 1985; Mar. 2, 1987, effective Aug. 1, 1987; Apr. 30, 1991, effective Dec. 1, 1991; April 17, 2000, effective December 1, 2000; April 29, 2002, effective December 1, 2002; April 25, 2005, effective December 1, 2005; April 12, 2006, effective December 1, 2006.]

RULE D

POSSESSORY, PETITORY, AND PARTITION ACTIONS

In all actions for possession, partition, and to try title maintainable according to the course of the admiralty practice with respect to a vessel, in all actions so maintainable with respect to the possession of cargo or other maritime property, and in all actions by one or more part owners against the others to obtain security for the return of the vessel from any voyage undertaken without their consent, or by one or more part owners against the others to obtain possession of the vessel for any voyage on giving security for its safe return, the process shall be by a warrant of arrest of the vessel, cargo, or other property, and by notice in the manner provided by Rule B(2) to the adverse party or parties.

[Added Feb. 28, 1966, eff. Jul. 1, 1966.]

RULE E

ACTIONS IN REM AND QUASI IN REM: GENERAL PROVISIONS

(1) Applicability. Except as otherwise provided, this rule applies to actions in personam with process of maritime attachment and garnishment, actions in rem, and petitory, possessory, and partition actions, supplementing Rules B, C, and D.

(2) Complaint; Security.

(a) *Complaint.* In actions to which this rule is applicable the complaint shall state the circumstances from

1205

which the claim arises with such particularity that the defendant or claimant will be able, without moving for a more definite statement, to commence an investigation of the facts and to frame a responsive pleading.

(b) *Security for Costs.*   Subject to the provisions of Rule 54(d) and of relevant statutes, the court may, on the filing of the complaint or on the appearance of any defendant, claimant, or any other party, or at any later time, require the plaintiff, defendant, claimant, or other party to give security, or additional security, in such sum as the court shall direct to pay all costs and expenses that shall be awarded against the party by any interlocutory order or by the final judgment, or on appeal by any appellate court.

(3) Process.

(a) In admiralty and maritime proceedings process in rem or of maritime attachment and garnishment may be served only within the district.

(b) Issuance and Delivery. Issuance and delivery of process in rem, or of maritime attachment and garnishment, shall be held in abeyance if the plaintiff so requests.

(4) Execution of Process; Marshal's Return; Custody of Property; Procedures for Release.

(a) *In General.*   Upon issuance and delivery of the process, or, in the case of summons with process of attachment and garnishment, when it appears that the defendant cannot be found within the district, the marshal or other person or organization having a warrant shall forthwith execute the process in accordance with this subdivision (4), making due and prompt return.

(b) *Tangible Property.*   If tangible property is to be attached or arrested, the marshal or other person or organization having the warrant shall take it into the marshal's possession for safe custody.   If the character or situation of the property is such that the taking of actual possession is impracticable, the marshal or other person executing the process shall affix a copy thereof to the property in a conspicuous

place and leave a copy of the complaint and process
with the person having possession or the person's
agent. In furtherance of the marshal's custody of
any vessel the marshal is authorized to make a
written request to the collector of customs not to
grant clearance to such vessel until notified by the
marshal or deputy marshal or by the clerk that the
vessel has been released in accordance with these
rules.

(c) *Intangible Property*. If intangible property is to be
attached or arrested the marshal or other person or
organization having the warrant shall execute the
process by leaving with the garnishee or other obligor a copy of the complaint and process requiring
the garnishee or other obligor to answer as provided
in Rules B(3)(a) and C(6); or the marshal may
accept for payment into the registry of the court the
amount owed to the extent of the amount claimed
by the plaintiff with interest and costs, in which
event the garnishee or other obligor shall not be
required to answer unless alias process shall be
served.

(d) *Directions With Respect to Property in Custody*.
The marshal or other person or organization having
the warrant may at any time apply to the court for
directions with respect to property that has been
attached or arrested, and shall give notice of such
application to any or all of the parties as the court
may direct.

(e) *Expenses of Seizing and Keeping Property; Deposit*.
These rules do not alter the provisions of Title 28,
U.S.C., § 1921, as amended, relative to the expenses
of seizing and keeping property attached or arrested
and to the requirement of deposits to cover such
expenses.

(f) *Procedure for Release From Arrest or Attachment*.
Whenever property is arrested or attached, any person claiming an interest in it shall be entitled to a
prompt hearing at which the plaintiff shall be required to show why the arrest or attachment should
not be vacated or other relief granted consistent
with these rules. This subdivision shall have no

application to suits for seamen's wages when process is issued upon a certification of sufficient cause filed pursuant to Title 46, U.S.C. §§ 603 and 604 or to actions by the United States for forfeitures for violation of any statute of the United States.

(5) Release of Property.

(a) *Special Bond.* Whenever process of maritime attachment and garnishment or process in rem is issued the execution of such process shall be stayed, or the property released, on the giving of security, to be approved by the court or clerk, or by stipulation of the parties, conditioned to answer the judgment of the court or of any appellate court. The parties may stipulate the amount and nature of such security. In the event of the inability or refusal of the parties so to stipulate the court shall fix the principal sum of the bond or stipulation at an amount sufficient to cover the amount of the plaintiff's claim fairly stated with accrued interest and costs; but the principal sum shall in no event exceed (i) twice the amount of the plaintiff's claim or (ii) the value of the property on due appraisement, whichever is smaller. The bond or stipulation shall be conditioned for the payment of the principal sum and interest thereon at 6 per cent per annum.

(b) *General Bond.* The owner of any vessel may file a general bond or stipulation, with sufficient surety, to be approved by the court, conditioned to answer the judgment of such court in all or any actions that may be brought thereafter in such court in which the vessel is attached or arrested. Thereupon the execution of all such process against such vessel shall be stayed so long as the amount secured by such bond or stipulation is at least double the aggregate amount claimed by plaintiffs in all actions begun and pending in which such vessel has been attached or arrested. Judgments and remedies may be had on such bond or stipulation as if a special bond or stipulation had been filed in each of such actions. The district court may make necessary orders to carry this rule into effect, particularly as to the giving of proper notice of any action against or attachment of a vessel for which a general bond has been filed. Such bond or stipulation shall be indorsed by the clerk with a minute of the actions wherein process is so stayed. Further security may be required by the court at any time.

If a special bond or stipulation is given in a particular case, the liability on the general bond or stipulation shall cease as to that case.

(c) *Release by Consent or Stipulation; Order of Court or Clerk; Costs.* Any vessel, cargo, or other property in the custody of the marshal or other person or organization having the warrant may be released forthwith upon the marshal's acceptance and approval of a stipulation, bond, or other security, signed by the party on whose behalf the property is detained or the party's attorney and expressly authorizing such release, if all costs and charges of the court and its officers shall have first been paid. Otherwise no property in the custody of the marshal, other person or organization having the warrant, or other officer of the court shall be released without an order of the court; but such order may be entered as of course by the clerk, upon the giving of approved security as provided by law and these rules, or upon the dismissal or discontinuance of the action; but the marshal or other person or organization having the warrant shall not deliver any property so released until the costs and charges of the officers of the court shall first have been paid.

(d) *Possessory, Petitory, and Partition Actions.* The foregoing provisions of this subdivision (5) do not apply to petitory, possessory, and partition actions. In such cases the property arrested shall be released only by order of the court, on such terms and conditions and on the giving of such security as the court may require.

(6) Reduction or Impairment of Security. Whenever security is taken the court may, on motion and hearing, for good cause shown, reduce the amount of security given; and if the surety shall be or become insufficient, new or additional sureties may be required on motion and hearing.

(7) Security on Counterclaim.

(a) When a person who has given security for damages in the original action asserts a counterclaim that arises from the transaction or occurrence that is the subject of the original action, a plaintiff for whose benefit the security has been given must give security for damages demanded in the counterclaim unless the court for cause shown, directs otherwise. Proceedings on the original claim must be stayed until this security is given unless the court directs otherwise.

(b) The plaintiff is required to give security under Rule E(7)(a) when the United States or its corporate instrumentality counterclaims and would have been required to give security to respond in damages if a private party but is relieved by law from giving security.

(8) Restricted Appearance. An appearance to defend against an admiralty and maritime claim with respect to which there has issued process in rem, or process of attachment and garnishment, may be expressly restricted to the defense of such claim, and in that event is not an appearance for the purposes of any other claim with respect to which such process is not available or has not been served.

(9) Disposition of Property; Sales.

(a) Interlocutory Sales; Delivery.

(i) On application of a party, the marshal, or other person having custody of the property, the court may order all or part of the property sold—with the sales proceeds, or as much of them as will satisfy the judgment, paid into court to await further orders of the court—if:

(A) the attached or arrested property is perishable, or liable to deterioration, decay, or injury by being detained in custody pending the action;

(B) the expense of keeping the property is excessive or disproportionate; or

(C) there is an unreasonable delay in securing release of the property.

(ii) In the circumstances described in Rule E(9)(a)(i), the court, on motion by a defendant or a person filing a statement of interest or right under Rule C(6), may order that the property, rather than being sold, be delivered to the movant upon giving security under these rules.

(b) *Sales; Proceeds.* All sales of property shall be made by the marshal or a deputy marshal, or by other person or organization having the warrant, or by any other person assigned by the court where the marshal or other person or organization having the warrant is a party in interest; and the proceeds of sale shall be forthwith paid into the registry of the court to be disposed of according to law.

(10) Preservation of Property. When the owner or another person remains in possession of property attached or arrested under the provisions of Rule E(4)(b) that permit execution of process without taking actual possession, the court, on a party's motion or on its own, may enter any order necessary to preserve the property and to prevent its removal.

[Added Feb. 28, 1966, eff. Jul. 1, 1966, and amended Apr. 29, 1985, effective Aug. 1, 1985; Mar. 2, 1987, effective Aug. 1, 1987; Apr. 30, 1991, effective Dec. 1, 1991; April 17, 2000, effective December 1, 2000; April 12, 2006, effective December 1, 2006.]

RULE F

LIMITATION OF LIABILITY

(1) Time for Filing Complaint; Security. Not later than six months after receipt of a claim in writing, any vessel owner may file a complaint in the appropriate district court, as provided in subdivision (9) of this rule, for limitation of liability pursuant to statute. The owner (a) shall deposit with the court, for the benefit of claimants, a sum equal to the amount or value of the owner's interest in the vessel and pending freight, or approved security therefor, and in addition such sums, or approved security therefor, as the court may from time to time fix as necessary to carry out the provisions of the statutes as amended; or (b) at the owner's option shall transfer to a trustee to be appointed by the court, for the benefit of claimants, the owner's interest in the vessel and pending freight, together with such sums, or approved security therefor, as the court may from time to time fix as necessary to carry out the provisions of the statutes as amended. The plaintiff shall also give security for costs and, if the plaintiff elects to give security, for interest at the rate of 6 percent per annum from the date of the security.

(2) Complaint. The complaint shall set forth the facts on the basis of which the right to limit liability is asserted and all facts necessary to enable the court to determine the amount to which the owner's liability shall be limited. The complaint may demand exoneration from as well as limitation of liability. It shall state the voyage if any, on which the demands sought to be limited arose, with the date and place of its termination; the amount of all demands including all unsatisfied liens or claims of lien, in contract or in tort or otherwise, arising on that voyage, so far as known to the plaintiff, and what actions and proceedings, if any, are pending thereon; whether the vessel was damaged, lost, or abandoned, and, if so, when and where; the value of the vessel at the close of the voyage or, in case of wreck, the value of her wreckage, strippings, or proceeds, if any, and where and in whose possession they are; and the amount of any pending freight recovered or recoverable. If the plaintiff elects to transfer the plaintiff's interest in the vessel to a trustee, the complaint must further show any prior paramount liens thereon, and what voyages or trips, if any, she has made since the voyage or trip on which the claims sought to be limited arose, and any existing liens arising upon any such subsequent voyage or trip, with the amounts and causes thereof, and the names and addresses of the lienors, so far as known; and whether the vessel sustained any injury upon or by reason of such subsequent voyage or trip.

(3) Claims Against Owner; Injunction. Upon compliance by the owner with the requirements of subdivision (1) of this rule all claims and proceedings against the owner or the owner's property with respect to the matter in question shall cease. On application of the plaintiff the court shall enjoin the further prosecution of any action or proceeding against the plaintiff or the plaintiff's property with respect to any claim subject to limitation in the action.

(4) Notice to Claimants. Upon the owner's compliance with subdivision (1) of this rule the court shall issue a notice to all persons asserting claims with respect to which the complaint seeks limitation, admonishing them to file their respective claims with the clerk of the court and to serve on the attorneys for the plaintiff a copy thereof on or before a date to be named in the notice. The date so fixed shall not be less than 30 days after issuance of the notice. For cause shown, the court may enlarge the time within which claims may be filed. The notice shall be published in such newspaper or newspapers as the court may direct once a week for four successive weeks prior to the date fixed for the filing of claims. The plaintiff not later than the day of second publication shall also mail a copy of the notice to every person known to have made any claim against the vessel or the plaintiff arising out of the voyage or trip on which the claims sought to be limited arose. In cases involving death a copy of such notice shall be mailed to the decedent at the decedent's last known address, and also to any person who shall be known to have made any claim on account of such death.

(5) Claims and Answer. Claims shall be filed and served on or before the date specified in the notice provided for in subdivision (4) of this rule. Each claim shall specify the facts upon which the claimant relies in support of the claim, the items thereof, and the dates on which the same accrued. If a claimant desires to contest either the right to exoneration from or the right to limitation of liability the claimant shall file and serve an answer to the complaint unless the claim has included an answer.

(6) Information to Be Given Claimants. Within 30 days after the date specified in the notice for filing claims, or within such time as the court thereafter may allow, the plaintiff shall mail to the attorney for each claimant (or if the claimant has no attorney to the claimant) a list setting forth (a) the name of each claimant, (b) the name and address of the claimant's attorney (if the claimant is known to have one), (c) the nature of the claim, i.e., whether property loss, property damage, death, personal injury etc., and (d) the amount thereof.

(7) Insufficiency of Fund or Security. Any claimant may by motion demand that the funds deposited in court or the security given by the plaintiff be increased on the ground that they are less than the value of the plaintiff's interest in the vessel and pending freight. Thereupon the court shall cause due appraisement to be made of the value of the plaintiff's interest in the vessel and pending freight; and if the court finds that the deposit or security is either insufficient or excessive it shall order its increase or reduction. In like manner any claimant may demand that the deposit or security be increased on the ground that it is insufficient to carry out the provisions of the statutes relating to claims in respect of loss of life or bodily injury; and, after notice and hearing, the court may similarly order that the deposit or security be increased or reduced.

(8) Objections to Claims: Distribution of Fund. Any interested party may question or controvert any claim without filing an objection thereto. Upon determination of liability the fund deposited or secured, or the proceeds of the vessel and pending freight, shall be divided pro rata, subject to all relevant provisions of law, among the several claimants in proportion to the amounts of their respective claims, duly proved, saving, however, to all parties any priority to which they may be legally entitled.

(9) Venue; Transfer. The complaint shall be filed in any district in which the vessel has been attached or arrested to answer for any claim with respect to which the plaintiff seeks to limit liability; or, if the vessel has not been attached or arrested, then in any district in which the owner has been sued with respect to any such claim. When the vessel has not been attached or arrested to answer the matters aforesaid, and suit has not been commenced against the owner, the proceedings may be had in the district in which the vessel may be, but if the vessel is not within any district and no suit has been commenced in any district, then the complaint may be filed in any district. For the convenience of parties and witnesses, in the interest of justice, the court may transfer the action to any district; if venue is wrongly laid the court shall dismiss or, if it be in the interest of justice, transfer the action to any district in which it could have been brought. If the vessel shall have been sold, the proceeds shall represent the vessel for the purposes of these rules.

[Added Feb. 28, 1966, eff. Jul. 1, 1966, and amended Mar. 2, 1987, effective Aug. 1, 1987.]

RULE G

FORFEITURE ACTIONS IN REM

(1) Scope. This rule governs a forfeiture action in rem arising from a federal statute. To the extent that this rule does not address an issue, Supplemental Rules C and E and the Federal Rules of Civil Procedure also apply.

(2) Complaint. The complaint must:

    (a) be verified;

    (b) state the grounds for subject-matter jurisdiction, in rem jurisdiction over the defendant property, and venue;

    (c) describe the property with reasonable particularity;

    (d) if the property is tangible, state its location when any seizure occurred and—if different—its location when the action is filed;

    (e) identify the statute under which the forfeiture action is brought; and

    (f) state sufficiently detailed facts to support a reasonable belief that the government will be able to meet its burden of proof at trial.

(3) Judicial Authorization and Process.

    (a) Real Property. If the defendant is real property, the government must proceed under 18 U.S.C. § 985.

    (b) Other Property; Arrest Warrant. If the defendant is not real property:

        (i) the clerk must issue a warrant to arrest the property if it is in the government's possession, custody, or control;

        (ii) the court—on finding probable cause—must issue a warrant to arrest the property if it is not in the government's possession, custody, or control and is not subject to a judicial restraining order; and

(iii) a warrant is not necessary if the property is subject to a judicial restraining order.

(c) Execution of Process.

(i) The warrant and any supplemental process must be delivered to a person or organization authorized to execute it, who may be: (A) a marshal or any other United States officer or employee; (B) someone under contract with the United States; or (C) someone specially appointed by the court for that purpose.

(ii) The authorized person or organization must execute the warrant and any supplemental process on property in the United States as soon as practicable unless:

(A) the property is in the government's possession, custody, or control; or

(B) the court orders a different time when the complaint is under seal, the action is stayed before the warrant and supplemental process are executed, or the court finds other good cause.

(iii) The warrant and any supplemental process may be executed within the district or, when authorized by statute, outside the district.

(iv) If executing a warrant on property outside the United States is required, the warrant may be transmitted to an appropriate authority for serving process where the property is located.

(4) Notice.

(a) Notice by Publication.

(i) When Publication Is Required. A judgment of forfeiture may be entered only if the government has published notice of the action within a reasonable time after filing the complaint or at a time the court orders. But notice need not be published if:

(A) the defendant property is worth less than $1,000 and direct notice is sent under Rule G(4)(b) to every person the government can reasonably identify as a potential claimant; or

(B) the court finds that the cost of publication exceeds the property's value and that other means of notice would satisfy due process.

(ii) Content of the Notice. Unless the court orders otherwise, the notice must:

(A) describe the property with reasonable particularity;

(B) state the times under Rule G(5) to file a claim and to answer; and

(C) name the government attorney to be served with the claim and answer.

(iii) Frequency of Publication. Published notice must appear:

(A) once a week for three consecutive weeks; or

(B) only once if, before the action was filed, notice of nonjudicial forfeiture of the same property was published on an official internet government forfeiture site for at least 30 consecutive days, or in a newspaper of general circulation for three consecutive weeks in a district where publication is authorized under Rule G(4)(a)(iv).

(iv) Means of Publication. The government should select from the following options a means of publication reasonably calculated to notify potential claimants of the action:

(A) if the property is in the United States, publication in a newspaper generally circulated in the district where the action is filed, where the property was seized, or where property that was not seized is located;

(B) if the property is outside the United States, publication in a newspaper generally circulated in a district where the action is filed, in a newspaper generally circulated in the country where the property is located, or in legal notices published and generally circulated in the country where the property is located; or

(C) instead of (A) or (B), posting a notice on an official internet government forfeiture site for at least 30 consecutive days.

(b) Notice to Known Potential Claimants.

(i) Direct Notice Required. The government must send notice of the action and a copy of the complaint to any person who reasonably appears to be a potential claimant on the facts known to the government before the end of the time for filing a claim under Rule G(5)(a)(ii)(B).

(ii) Content of the Notice. The notice must state:

(A) the date when the notice is sent;

(B) a deadline for filing a claim, at least 35 days after the notice is sent;

(C) that an answer or a motion under Rule 12 must be filed no later than 20 days after filing the claim; and

(D) the name of the government attorney to be served with the claim and answer.

(iii) Sending Notice.

(A) The notice must be sent by means reasonably calculated to reach the potential claimant.

(B) Notice may be sent to the potential claimant or to the attorney representing the potential claimant with respect to the seizure of the property or in a related investigation, administrative forfeiture proceeding, or criminal case.

(C) Notice sent to a potential claimant who is incarcerated must be sent to the place of incarceration.

(D) Notice to a person arrested in connection with an offense giving rise to the forfeiture who is not incarcerated when notice is sent may be sent to the address that person last gave to the agency that arrested or released the person.

(E) Notice to a person from whom the property was seized who is not incarcerated when notice is sent may be sent to the last address that person gave to the agency that seized the property.

(iv) When Notice Is Sent. Notice by the following means is sent on the date when it is placed in the mail, delivered to a commercial carrier, or sent by electronic mail.

(v) Actual Notice. A potential claimant who had actual notice of a forfeiture action may not oppose or seek relief from forfeiture because of the government's failure to send the required notice.

(5) Responsive Pleadings.

(a) Filing a Claim.

(i) A person who asserts an interest in the defendant property may contest the forfeiture by filing a claim in the court where the action is pending. The claim must:

(A) identify the specific property claimed;

(B) identify the claimant and state the claimant's interest in the property;

(C) be signed by the claimant under penalty of perjury; and

(D) be served on the government attorney designated under Rule G(4)(a)(ii)(C) or (b)(ii)(D).

(ii) Unless the court for good cause sets a different time, the claim must be filed:

(A) by the time stated in a direct notice sent under Rule G(4)(b);

(B) if notice was published but direct notice was not sent to the claimant or the claim-

1219

ant's attorney, no later than 30 days after final publication of newspaper notice or legal notice under Rule G(4)(a) or no later than 60 days after the first day of publication on an official internet government forfeiture site; or

(C) if notice was not published and direct notice was not sent to the claimant or the claimant's attorney:

(1) if the property was in the government's possession, custody, or control when the complaint was filed, no later than 60 days after the filing, not counting any time when the complaint was under seal or when the action was stayed before execution of a warrant issued under Rule G(3)(b); or

(2) if the property was not in the government's possession, custody, or control when the complaint was filed, no later than 60 days after the government complied with 18 U.S.C. § 985(c) as to real property, or 60 days after process was executed on the property under Rule G(3).

(iii) A claim filed by a person asserting an interest as a bailee must identify the bailor, and if filed on the bailor's behalf must state the authority to do so.

(b) Answer. A claimant must serve and file an answer to the complaint or a motion under Rule 12 within 20 days after filing the claim. A claimant waives an objection to in rem jurisdiction or to venue if the objection is not made by motion or stated in the answer.

(6) Special Interrogatories.

(a) Time and Scope. The government may serve special interrogatories limited to the claimant's identity and relationship to the defendant property without the court's leave at any time after the claim is filed and before discovery is closed. But if the claimant serves a motion to dismiss the action, the government must serve the interrogatories within 20 days after the motion is served.

(b) Answers or Objections. Answers or objections to these interrogatories must be served within 20 days after the interrogatories are served.

(c) Government's Response Deferred. The government need not respond to a claimant's motion to dismiss the action under Rule G(8)(b) until 20 days after the claimant has answered these interrogatories.

(7) Preserving, Preventing Criminal Use, and Disposing of Property; Sales.

(a) Preserving and Preventing Criminal Use of Property. When the government does not have actual possession of the defendant property the court, on motion or on its own, may enter any order necessary to preserve the property, to prevent its removal or encumbrance, or to prevent its use in a criminal offense.

(b) Interlocutory Sale or Delivery.

(i) Order to Sell. On motion by a party or a person having custody of the property, the court may order all or part of the property sold if:

(A) the property is perishable or at risk of deterioration, decay, or injury by being detained in custody pending the action;

(B) the expense of keeping the property is excessive or is disproportionate to its fair market value;

(C) the property is subject to a mortgage or to taxes on which the owner is in default; or

(D) the court finds other good cause.

(ii) Who Makes the Sale. A sale must be made by a United States agency that has authority to sell the property, by the agency's contractor, or by any person the court designates.

(iii) Sale Procedures. The sale is governed by 28 U.S.C. § § 2001, 2002, and 2004, unless all parties, with the court's approval, agree to the

sale, aspects of the sale, or different procedures.

(iv) Sale Proceeds. Sale proceeds are a substitute
res subject to forfeiture in place of the property
that was sold. The proceeds must be held in an
interest-bearing account maintained by the
United States pending the conclusion of the
forfeiture action.

(v) Delivery on a Claimant's Motion. The court
may order that the property be delivered to the
claimant pending the conclusion of the action if
the claimant shows circumstances that would
permit sale under Rule G(7)(b)(i) and gives
security under these rules.

(c) Disposing of Forfeited Property. Upon entry of
a forfeiture judgment, the property or proceeds from
selling the property must be disposed of as provided
by law.

(8) Motions.

**(a) Motion To Suppress Use of the Property as
Evidence.** If the defendant property was seized, a
party with standing to contest the lawfulness of the
seizure may move to suppress use of the property as
evidence. Suppression does not affect forfeiture of
the property based on independently derived evidence.

(b) Motion To Dismiss the Action.

(i) A claimant who establishes standing to contest
forfeiture may move to dismiss the action under
Rule 12(b).

(ii) In an action governed by 18 U.S.C.
§ 983(a)(3)(D) the complaint may not be dismissed on the ground that the government did
not have adequate evidence at the time the
complaint was filed to establish the forfeitabili-
ty of the property. The sufficiency of the complaint is governed by Rule G(2).

(c) Motion To Strike a Claim or Answer.

(i) At any time before trial, the government may
move to strike a claim or answer:

(A) for failing to comply with Rule G(5) or (6), or

(B) because the claimant lacks standing.

(ii) The motion:

(A) must be decided before any motion by the claimant to dismiss the action; and

(B) may be presented as a motion for judgment on the pleadings or as a motion to determine after a hearing or by summary judgment whether the claimant can carry the burden of establishing standing by a preponderance of the evidence.

(d) Petition To Release Property.

(i) If a United States agency or an agency's contractor holds property for judicial or nonjudicial forfeiture under a statute governed by 18 U.S.C. § 983(f), a person who has filed a claim to the property may petition for its release under § 983(f).

(ii) If a petition for release is filed before a judicial forfeiture action is filed against the property, the petition may be filed either in the district where the property was seized or in the district where a warrant to seize the property issued. If a judicial forfeiture action against the property is later filed in another district—or if the government shows that the action will be filed in another district—the petition may be transferred to that district under 28 U.S.C. § 1404.

(e) Excessive Fines. A claimant may seek to mitigate a forfeiture under the Excessive Fines Clause of the Eighth Amendment by motion for summary judgment or by motion made after entry of a forfeiture judgment if:

(i) the claimant has pleaded the defense under Rule 8; and

(ii) the parties have had the opportunity to conduct civil discovery on the defense.

(9) Trial. Trial is to the court unless any party demands trial by jury under Rule 38.

(Added Apr. 12, 2006, eff. Dec. 1, 2006.)

PART IV

APPENDIX OF FORMS

(See Rule 84)

Table of Forms

Introductory Statement.

INTRODUCTORY STATEMENT

1. The following forms are intended for illustration only. They are limited in number. No attempt is made to furnish a manual of forms. Each form assumes the action to be brought in the Southern District of New York. If the district in which an action is brought has divisions, the division should be indicated in the caption.

2. Except where otherwise indicated each pleading, motion, and other paper should have a caption similar to that of the summons, with the designation of the particular paper substituted for the word "Summons". In the caption of the summons and in the caption of the complaint all parties must be named but in other pleadings and papers, it is sufficient to state the name of the first party on either side, with an appropriate indication of other parties. See Rules 4(b), 7(b)(2), and 10(a).

3. In Form 3 and the forms following, the words, "Allegation of jurisdiction," are used to indicate the appropriate allegation in Form 2.

4. Each pleading, motion, and other paper is to be signed in his individual name by at least one attorney of record (Rule 11). The attorney's name is to be followed by his address as indicated in Form 3. In forms following Form 3 the signature and address are not indicated.

5. If a party is not represented by an attorney, the signature and address of the party are required in place of those of the attorney.

FORM 1

CAPTION

(Use on every summons, complaint, answer, motion, or other document.)

United States District Court
for the
_____ **District of** _____

A B, Plaintiff   )
)
v.   )
)   Civil Action No. _____
C D, Defendant   )
)
v.   )
)
E F, Third–Party Defendant   )
        (Use if needed.)   )

(Name of Document)

(Added Apr. 20, 2007, eff. Dec. 1. 2007.)

FORM 2
DATE, SIGNATURE, ADDRESS, E–MAIL ADDRESS, AND TELEPHONE NUMBER

(Use at the conclusion of pleadings and other papers that require a signature.)

Date _____

_____
(Signature of the attorney or unrepresented party)

_____
(Printed name)

_____
(Address)

_____
(E-mail address)

_____
(Telephone number)

(Added Apr. 20, 2007, eff. Dec. 1. 2007.)

FORM 3
SUMMONS

(Caption—See Form 1.)

To *name the defendant*:

A lawsuit has been filed against you.

Within 20 days after service of this summons on you (not counting the day you received it), you must serve on the plaintiff an answer to the attached complaint or a motion under Rule 12 of the Federal Rules of Civil Procedure. The answer or motion must be served on the plaintiff's attorney, _____, whose address is _____. If you fail to do so, judgment by default will be entered against you for the relief demanded in the complaint. You also must file your answer or motion with the court.

Date _____

_____
Clerk of Court

(Court Seal)

(Use 60 days if the defendant is the United States or a United States agency, or is an officer or employee of the United States allowed 60 days by Rule 12(a)(3).)

(Added Apr. 20, 2007, eff. Dec. 1. 2007.)

FORM 4
SUMMONS ON A THIRD–PARTY COMPLAINT

(Caption—See Form 1.)

To *name the third-party defendant*:

A lawsuit has been filed against defendant _____, who as third-party plaintiff is making this claim against you to pay part or all of what [he] may owe to the plaintiff _____.

Within 20 days after service of this summons on you (not counting the day you received it), you must serve on the plaintiff and on the defendant an answer to the attached third-party complaint or a motion under Rule 12 of the Federal Rules of Civil Procedure. The answer or motion must be served on the defendant's attorney, _____ , whose address is _____ , and also on the plaintiff's attorney, _____ , whose address is _____ . If you fail to do so, judgment by default will be entered against you for the relief demanded in the third-party complaint. You also must file the answer or motion with the court and serve it on any other parties.

A copy of the plaintiff's complaint is also attached. You may—but are not required to—respond to it.

Date _____

_____
Clerk of Court

(Court Seal)

(Added Apr. 20, 2007, eff. Dec. 1. 2007.)

FORM 5

NOTICE OF A LAWSUIT AND REQUEST TO WAIVE SERVICE OF A SUMMONS

(Caption—See Form 1.)

To (*name the defendant—or if the defendant is a corporation, partner-ship, or association name an officer or agent authorized to receive service*):

Why are you getting this?

A lawsuit has been filed against you, or the entity you represent, in this court under the number shown above. A copy of the complaint is attached.

This is not a summons, or an official notice from the court. It is a request that, to avoid expenses, you waive formal service of a summons by signing and returning the enclosed waiver. To avoid these expenses, you must return the signed waiver within (*give at least 30 days or at least 60 days if the defendant is outside any judicial district of the United States*) from the date shown below, which is the date this notice was sent. Two copies of the waiver form are enclosed, along with a stamped, self-addressed envelope or other prepaid means for returning one copy. You may keep the other copy.

What happens next?

If you return the signed waiver, I will file it with the court. The action will then proceed as if you had been served on the date the waiver is filed, but no summons will be served on you and you will have 60 days from the date this notice is sent (see the date below) to answer the complaint (or 90 days if this notice is sent to you outside any judicial district of the United States).

If you do not return the signed waiver within the time indicated, I will arrange to have the summons and complaint served on you. And I will ask the court to require you, or the entity you represent, to pay the expenses of making service.

Please read the enclosed statement about the duty to avoid unnecessary expenses.

I certify that this request is being sent to you on the date below.

(Date and sign—See Form 2.)

(Added Apr. 20, 2007, eff. Dec. 1. 2007.)

FORM 6

WAIVER OF THE SERVICE OF SUMMONS

(Caption—See Form 1.)

To *name the plaintiff's attorney or the unrepresented plaintiff*:

I have received your request to waive service of a summons in this action along with a copy of the complaint, two copies of this waiver form, and a prepaid means of returning one signed copy of the form to you.

I, or the entity I represent, agree to save the expense of serving a summons and complaint in this case.

I understand that I, or the entity I represent, will keep all defenses or objections to the lawsuit, the court's jurisdiction, and the venue of the action, but that I waive any objections to the absence of a summons or of service.

I also understand that I, or the entity I represent, must file and serve an answer or a motion under Rule 12 within 60 days from _____, the date when this request was sent (or 90 days if it was sent outside the United States). If I fail to do so, a default judgment will be entered against me or the entity I represent.

(Date and sign—See Form 2.)

(Attach the following to Form 6.)

Duty to Avoid Unnecessary Expenses of Serving a Summons

Rule 4 of the Federal Rules of Civil Procedure requires certain defendants to cooperate in saving unnecessary expenses of serving a summons and complaint. A defendant who is located in the United States and who fails to return a signed waiver of service requested by a plaintiff located in the United States will be required to pay the expenses of service, unless the defendant shows good cause for the failure.

"Good cause" does *not* include a belief that the lawsuit is groundless, or that it has been brought in an improper venue, or that the court has no jurisdiction over this matter or over the defendant or the defendant's property.

If the waiver is signed and returned, you can still make these and all other defenses and objections, but you cannot object to the absence of a summons or of service.

If you waive service, then you must, within the time specified on the waiver form, serve an answer or a motion under Rule 12 on the plaintiff and file a copy with the court. By signing and returning the waiver form, you are allowed more time to respond than if a summons had been served.

(Added Apr. 20, 2007, eff. Dec. 1. 2007.)

FORM 7

STATEMENT OF JURISDICTION

a. (*For diversity-of-citizenship jurisdiction.*) The plaintiff is [a citizen of <u>Michigan</u>] [a corporation incorporated under the laws of <u>Michigan</u> with its principal place of business in <u>Michigan</u>]. The defendant is [a citizen of <u>New York</u>] [a corporation incorporated under the laws of <u>New York</u> with its principal place of business in <u>New York</u>]. The amount in controversy, without interest and costs, exceeds the sum or value specified by 28 U.S.C. § 1332.

b. (*For federal-question jurisdiction.*) This action arises under [the United States Constitution, *specify the article or amendment and the section*] [a United States treaty *specify*] [a federal statute, ___ U.S.C. § ___].

c.   (*For a claim in the admiralty or maritime jurisdiction.*) This is a case of admiralty or maritime jurisdiction. (*To invoke admiralty status under Rule 9(h) use the following:* This is an admiralty or maritime claim within the meaning of Rule 9(h).)

(Added Apr. 20, 2007, eff. Dec. 1. 2007.)

FORM 8

STATEMENT OF REASONS FOR OMITTING A PARTY

(If a person who ought to be made a party under Rule 19(a) is not named, include this statement in accordance with Rule 19(c).)

This complaint does not join as a party *name* who [is not subject to this court's personal jurisdiction] [cannot be made a party without depriving this court of subject-matter jurisdiction] because *state the reason.*

(Added Apr. 20, 2007, eff. Dec. 1. 2007.)

FORM 9

STATEMENT NOTING A PARTY'S DEATH

(Caption—See Form 1.)

In accordance with Rule 25(a) *name the person,* who is [a party to this action] [a representative of or successor to the deceased party], notes the death during the pendency of this action of *name,* [*describe as party* in this action].

(Date and sign—See Form 2.)

(Added Apr. 20, 2007, eff. Dec. 1. 2007.)

FORM 10

COMPLAINT TO RECOVER A SUM CERTAIN

(Caption—See Form 1.)

1.   (Statement of Jurisdiction—See Form 7.)

*(Use one or more of the following as appropriate
and include a demand for judgment.)*

(a) On a Promissory Note

2.   On *date*, the defendant executed and delivered a note promising to pay the plaintiff on *date* the sum of $_____ with interest at the rate of __ percent. A copy of the note [is attached as Exhibit A] [is summarized as follows: _____].

3.   The defendant has not paid the amount owed.

(b) On an Account

2.   The defendant owes the plaintiff $_____ according to the account set out in Exhibit A.

(c) For Goods Sold and Delivered

2. The defendant owes the plaintiff $_____ for goods sold and delivered by the plaintiff to the defendant from *date* to *date* .

(d) For Money Lent

2. The defendant owes the plaintiff $_____ for money lent by the plaintiff to the defendant on *date*.

(e) For Money Paid by Mistake

2. The defendant owes the plaintiff $_____ for money paid by mistake to the defendant on *date* under these circumstances: *describe with particularity in accordance with Rule 9(b)*.

(f) For Money Had and Received

2. The defendant owes the plaintiff $_____ for money that was received from *name* on *date* to be paid by the defendant to the plaintiff.

Demand for Judgment

Therefore, the plaintiff demands judgment against the defendant for $_____, plus interest and costs.

(Date and sign—See Form 2.)

(Added Apr. 20, 2007, eff. Dec. 1. 2007.)

FORM 11

COMPLAINT FOR NEGLIGENCE

(Caption—See Form 1.)

1. (Statement of Jurisdiction—See Form 7.)

2. On *date*, at *place*, the defendant negligently drove a motor vehicle against the plaintiff.

3. As a result, the plaintiff was physically injured, lost wages or income, suffered physical and mental pain, and incurred medical expenses of $_____.

Therefore, the plaintiff demands judgment against the defendant for $_____, plus costs.

(Date and sign—See Form 2.)

(Added Apr. 20, 2007, eff. Dec. 1. 2007.)

FORM 12

COMPLAINT FOR NEGLIGENCE WHEN THE PLAINTIFF DOES NOT KNOW WHO IS RESPONSIBLE

(Caption—See Form 1.)

1. (Statement of Jurisdiction—See Form 7.)

2. On *date*, at *place*, defendant *name* or defendant *name* or both of them willfully or recklessly or negligently drove, or caused to be driven, a motor vehicle against the plaintiff.

3. As a result, the plaintiff was physically injured, lost wages or income, suffered mental and physical pain, and incurred medical expenses of $_____.

Therefore, the plaintiff demands judgment against one or both defendants for $_____, plus costs.

(Date and sign—See Form 2.)

(Added Apr. 20, 2007, eff. Dec. 1. 2007.)

FORM 13
COMPLAINT FOR NEGLIGENCE UNDER THE FEDERAL EMPLOYERS' LIABILITY ACT

(Caption—See Form 1.)

1. (Statement of Jurisdiction—See Form 7.)

2. At the times below, the defendant owned and operated in interstate commerce a railroad line that passed through a tunnel located at _____.

3. On *date*, the plaintiff was working to repair and enlarge the tunnel to make it convenient and safe for use in interstate commerce.

4. During this work, the defendant, as the employer, negligently put the plaintiff to work in a section of the tunnel that the defendant had left unprotected and unsupported.

5. The defendant's negligence caused the plaintiff to be injured by a rock that fell from an unsupported portion of the tunnel.

6. As a result, the plaintiff was physically injured, lost wages or income, suffered mental and physical pain, and incurred medical expenses of $_____.

Therefore, the plaintiff demands judgment against the defendant for $_____, and costs.

(Date and sign—See Form 2.)

(Added Apr. 20, 2007, eff. Dec. 1. 2007.)

FORM 14
COMPLAINT FOR DAMAGES UNDER THE MERCHANT MARINE ACT

(Caption—See Form 1.)

1. (Statement of Jurisdiction—See Form 7.)

2. At the times below, the defendant owned and operated the vessel *name* and used it to transport cargo for hire by water in interstate and foreign commerce.

3. On *date*, at *place*, the defendant hired the plaintiff under seamen's articles of customary form for a voyage from _____ to _____ and return at a wage of $_____ a month and found, which is equal to a shore worker's wage of $_____ a month.

1233

4. On *date*, the vessel was at sea on the return voyage. (*Describe the weather and the condition of the vessel.*)

5. (*Describe as in Form 11 the defendant's negligent conduct.*)

6. As a result of the defendant's negligent conduct and the unseaworthiness of the vessel, the plaintiff was physically injured, has been incapable of any gainful activity, suffered mental and physical pain, and has incurred medical expenses of $_____.

Therefore, the plaintiff demands judgment against the defendant for $_____, plus costs.

(Date and signSee Form 2.)

(Added Apr. 20, 2007, eff. Dec. 1. 2007.)

FORM 15
COMPLAINT FOR THE CONVERSION OF PROPERTY

(Caption—See Form 1.)

1. (Statement of Jurisdiction—See Form 7.)

2. On *date* , at *place* , the defendant converted to the defendant's own use property owned by the plaintiff. The property converted consists of *describe* .

3. The property is worth $_____.

Therefore, the plaintiff demands judgment against the defendant for $_____, plus costs.

(Date and sign—See Form 2.)

(Added Apr. 20, 2007, eff. Dec. 1. 2007.)

FORM 16
THIRD-PARTY COMPLAINT

(Caption—See Form 1.)

1. Plaintiff *name* has filed against defendant *name* a complaint, a copy of which is attached.

2. (*State grounds entitling defendant's name to recover from third-party defendant's name for (all or an identified share) of any judgment for plaintiff's name against defendant's name.*)

Therefore, the defendant demands judgment against *third-party defendant's name* for *all or an identified share* of sums that may be adjudged against the defendant in the plaintiff's favor.

(Date and sign—See Form 2.)

(Added Apr. 20, 2007, eff. Dec. 1. 2007.)

FORM 17
COMPLAINT FOR SPECIFIC PERFORMANCE
OF A CONTRACT TO CONVEY LAND

(Caption—See Form 1.)

1. (Statement of Jurisdiction—See Form 7.)

2. On *date*, the parties agreed to the contract [attached as Exhibit A] [summarize the contract].

3. As agreed, the plaintiff tendered the purchase price and requested a conveyance of the land, but the defendant refused to accept the money or make a conveyance.

4. The plaintiff now offers to pay the purchase price.

Therefore, the plaintiff demands that:

(a) the defendant be required to specifically perform the agreement and pay damages of $_____, plus interest and costs, or

(b) if specific performance is not ordered, the defendant be required to pay damages of $_____, plus interest and costs.

(Date and sign—See Form 2.)

(Added Apr. 20, 2007, eff. Dec. 1. 2007.)

FORM 18
COMPLAINT FOR PATENT INFRINGEMENT

(Caption—See Form 1.)

1. (Statement of Jurisdiction—See Form 7.)

2. On   *date* , United States Letters Patent No. _____ were issued to the plaintiff for an invention in an *electric motor*. The plaintiff owned the patent throughout the period of the defendant's infringing acts and still owns the patent.

3. The defendant has infringed and is still infringing the Letters Patent by making, selling, and using *electric motors* that embody the patented invention, and the defendant will continue to do so unless enjoined by this court.

4. The plaintiff has complied with the statutory requirement of placing a notice of the Letters Patent on all *electric motors* it manufactures and sells and has given the defendant written notice of the infringement.

Therefore, the plaintiff demands:

(a) a preliminary and final injunction against the continuing infringement;

(b) an accounting for damages; and

(c) interest and costs.

(Date and sign—See Form 2.)

(Added Apr. 20, 2007, eff. Dec. 1. 2007.)

FORM 19
COMPLAINT FOR COPYRIGHT INFRINGEMENT
AND UNFAIR COMPETITION

(Caption—See Form 1.)

1. (Statement of Jurisdiction—See Form 7.)

2. Before *date*, the plaintiff, a United States citizen, wrote a book entitled _____.

3. The book is an original work that may be copyrighted under United States law. A copy of the book is attached as Exhibit A.

4. Between *date* and *date*, the plaintiff applied to the copyright office and received a certificate of registration dated _____ and identified as *date, class, number*.

5. Since *date*, the plaintiff has either published or licensed for publication all copies of the book in compliance with the copyright laws and has remained the sole owner of the copyright.

6. After the copyright was issued, the defendant infringed the copyright by publishing and selling a book entitled _____, which was copied largely from the plaintiff's book. A copy of the defendant's book is attached as Exhibit B.

7. The plaintiff has notified the defendant in writing of the infringement.

8. The defendant continues to infringe the copyright by continuing to publish and sell the infringing book in violation of the copyright, and further has engaged in unfair trade practices and unfair competition in connection with its publication and sale of the infringing book, thus causing irreparable damage.

Therefore, the plaintiff demands that:

(a) until this case is decided the defendant and the defendant's agents be enjoined from disposing of any copies of the defendant's book by sale or otherwise;

(b) the defendant account for and pay as damages to the plaintiff all profits and advantages gained from unfair trade practices and unfair competition in selling the defendant's book, and all profits and advantages gained from infringing the plaintiff's copyright (but no less than the statutory minimum);

(c) the defendant deliver for impoundment all copies of the book in the defendant's possession or control and deliver for destruction all infringing copies and all plates, molds, and other materials for making infringing copies;

(d) the defendant pay the plaintiff interest, costs, and reasonable attorney's fees; and

(e) the plaintiff be awarded any other just relief.

(Date and sign—See Form 2.)

(Added Apr. 20, 2007, eff. Dec. 1. 2007.)

FORM 20
COMPLAINT FOR INTERPLEADER
AND DECLARATORY RELIEF

(Caption—See Form 1.)

1. (Statement of Jurisdiction—See Form 7.)

2. On *date* , the plaintiff issued a life insurance policy on the life of *name* with *name* as the named beneficiary.

3. As a condition for keeping the policy in force, the policy required payment of a premium during the first year and then annually.

4. The premium due on *date* was never paid, and the policy lapsed after that date.

5. On *date* , after the policy had lapsed, both the insured and the named beneficiary died in an automobile collision.

6. Defendant *name* claims to be the beneficiary in place of *name* and has filed a claim to be paid the policy's full amount.

7. The other two defendants are representatives of the deceased persons' estates. Each defendant has filed a claim on behalf of each estate to receive payment of the policy's full amount.

8. If the policy was in force at the time of death, the plaintiff is in doubt about who should be paid.

Therefore, the plaintiff demands that:

(a) each defendant be restrained from commencing any action against the plaintiff on the policy;

(b) a judgment be entered that no defendant is entitled to the proceeds of the policy or any part of it, but if the court determines that the policy was in effect at the time of the insured's death, that the defendants be required to interplead and settle among themselves their rights to the proceeds, and that the plaintiff be discharged from all liability except to the defendant determined to be entitled to the proceeds; and

(c) the plaintiff recover its costs.

(Date and sign—See Form 2.)

(Added Apr. 20, 2007, eff. Dec. 1. 2007.)

FORM 21
COMPLAINT ON A CLAIM FOR A DEBT AND TO SET ASIDE A FRAUDULENT CONVEYANCE UNDER RULE 18(b)

(Caption—See Form 1.)

1. (Statement of Jurisdiction—See Form 7.)

2. On *date* , defendant *name* signed a note promising to pay to the plaintiff on *date* the sum of $＿＿＿＿ with interest at the rate of ＿＿ percent. [The pleader may, but need not, attach a copy or plead the note verbatim.]

3. Defendant *name* owes the plaintiff the amount of the note and interest.

4. On *date* , defendant *name* conveyed all defendant's real and personal property *if less than all, describe it fully* to defendant *name* for the purpose of defrauding the plaintiff and hindering or delaying the collection of the debt.

Therefore, the plaintiff demands that:

(a) judgment for $_____, plus costs, be entered against defendant(s) *name(s)* ; and

(b) the conveyance to defendant *name* be declared void and any judgment granted be made a lien on the property.

(Date and sign—See Form 2.)

(Added Apr. 20, 2007, eff. Dec. 1. 2007.)

FORM 30
ANSWER PRESENTING DEFENSES UNDER RULE 12(b)

(Caption—See Form 1.)

Responding to Allegations in the Complaint

1. Defendant admits the allegations in paragraphs _____.

2. Defendant lacks knowledge or information sufficient to form a belief about the truth of the allegations in paragraphs _____.

3. Defendant admits *identify part of the allegation* in paragraph _____ and denies or lacks knowledge or information sufficient to form a belief about the truth of the rest of the paragraph.

Failure to State a Claim

4. The complaint fails to state a claim upon which relief can be granted.

Failure to Join a Required Party

5. If there is a debt, it is owed jointly by the defendant and *name* who is a citizen of _____. This person can be made a party without depriving this court of jurisdiction over the existing parties.

Affirmative Defense—Statute of Limitations

6. The plaintiff's claim is barred by the statute of limitations because it arose more than _____ years before this action was commenced.

Counterclaim

7. *(Set forth any counterclaim in the same way a claim is pleaded in a complaint. Include a further statement of jurisdiction if needed.)*

Crossclaim

8. *(Set forth a crossclaim against a coparty in the same way a claim is pleaded in a complaint. Include a further statement of jurisdiction if needed.)*

(Date and sign—See Form 2.)

(Added Apr. 20, 2007, eff. Dec. 1. 2007.)

FORM 31

ANSWER TO A COMPLAINT FOR MONEY HAD AND RECEIVED WITH A COUNTERCLAIM FOR INTERPLEADER

(Caption—See Form 1.)

Response to the Allegations in the Complaint
(See Form 30.)

Counterclaim for Interpleader

1. The defendant received from *name* a deposit of $_____.

2. The plaintiff demands payment of the deposit because of a purported assignment from *name* , who has notified the defendant that the assignment is not valid and who continues to hold the defendant responsible for the deposit.

Therefore, the defendant demands that:

    (a) *name* be made a party to this action;

    (b) the plaintiff and *name* be required to interplead their respective claims;

    (c) the court decide whether the plaintiff or *name* or either of them is entitled to the deposit and discharge the defendant of any liability except to the person entitled to the deposit; and

    (d) the defendant recover costs and attorney's fees.

(Date and sign—See Form 2.)

(Added Apr. 20, 2007, eff. Dec. 1. 2007.)

FORM 40

MOTION TO DISMISS UNDER RULE 12(b) FOR LACK OF JURISDICTION, IMPROPER VENUE, INSUFFICIENT SERVICE OF PROCESS, OR FAILURE TO STATE A CLAIM

(Caption—See Form 1.)

The defendant moves to dismiss the action because:

1. the amount in controversy is less than the sum or value specified by 28 U.S.C. § 1332;

2. the defendant is not subject to the personal jurisdiction of this court;

3. venue is improper (this defendant does not reside in this district and no part of the events or omissions giving rise to the claim occurred in the district);

4. the defendant has not been properly served, as shown by the attached affidavits of _____; or

5. the complaint fails to state a claim upon which relief can be granted.

(Date and sign—See Form 2.)

(Added Apr. 20, 2007, eff. Dec. 1. 2007.)

FORM 41
MOTION TO BRING IN A THIRD–PARTY DEFENDANT

(Caption—See Form 1.)

The defendant, as third-party plaintiff, moves for leave to serve on *name* a summons and third-party complaint, copies of which are attached.

(Date and sign—See Form 2.)

(Added Apr. 20, 2007, eff. Dec. 1. 2007.)

FORM 42
MOTION TO INTERVENE AS A DEFENDANT
UNDER RULE 24

(Caption—See Form 1.)

1. *name* moves for leave to intervene as a defendant in this action and to file the attached answer.

    (*State grounds under Rule 24(a) or (b).*)

2. The plaintiff alleges patent infringement. We manufacture and sell to the defendant the articles involved, and we have a defense to the plaintiff's claim.

3. Our defense presents questions of law and fact that are common to this action.

(Date and sign—See Form 2.)

[An Intervener's Answer must be attached. See Form 30.]

(Added Apr. 20, 2007, eff. Dec. 1. 2007.)

FORM 50
REQUEST TO PRODUCE DOCUMENTS AND
TANGIBLE THINGS, OR TO ENTER
ONTO LAND UNDER RULE 34

(Caption—See Form 1.)

The plaintiff *name* requests that the defendant *name* respond within ___ days to the following requests:

1. To produce and permit the plaintiff to inspect and copy and to test or sample the following documents, including electronically stored information:

    (*Describe each document and the electronically stored information, either individually or by category.*)

    (*State the time, place, and manner of the inspection and any related acts.*)

2. To produce and permit the plaintiff to inspect and copy—and to test or sample—the following tangible things:

(Describe each thing, either individually or by category.)

(State the time, place, and manner of the
inspection and any related acts.)

3. To permit the plaintiff to enter onto the following land to inspect, photograph, test, or sample the property or an object or operation on the property.

(Describe the property and each object or operation.)

(State the time and manner of the inspection and any related acts.)

(Date and sign—See Form 2.)

(Added Apr. 20, 2007, eff. Dec. 1. 2007.)

FORM 51
REQUEST FOR ADMISSIONS UNDER RULE 36

(Caption—See Form 1.)

The plaintiff *name* asks the defendant *name* to respond within 30 days to these requests by admitting, for purposes of this action only and subject to objections to admissibility at trial:

1. The genuineness of the following documents, copies of which [are attached] [are or have been furnished or made available for inspection and copying].

(List each document.)

2. The truth of each of the following statements:

(List each statement.)

(Date and sign—See Form 2.)

(Added Apr. 20, 2007, eff. Dec. 1. 2007.)

FORM 52
REPORT OF THE PARTIES' PLANNING MEETING

(Caption—See Form 1.)

1. The following persons participated in a Rule 26(f) conference on *date* by *state the method of conferring* :

(e.g., name representing the plaintiff.)

2. Initial Disclosures. The parties [have completed] [will complete by *date*] the initial disclosures required by Rule 26(a)(1).

3. Discovery Plan. The parties propose this discovery plan:

(Use separate paragraphs or subparagraphs if the parties disagree.)

(a) Discovery will be needed on these subjects: *(describe.)*

(b) (Dates for commencing and completing discovery, including discovery to be commenced or completed before other discovery.)

(c) (Maximum number of interrogatories by each party to another party, along with the dates the answers are due.)

    (d) (Maximum number of requests for admission, along with the dates responses are due.)

    (e) (Maximum number of depositions by each party.)

    (f) (Limits on the length of depositions, in hours.)

    (g) (Dates for exchanging reports of expert witnesses.)

    (h) (Dates for supplementations under Rule 26(e).)

4. Other Items:

    (a) (A date if the parties ask to meet with the court before a scheduling order.)

    (b) (Requested dates for pretrial conferences.)

    (c) (Final dates for the plaintiff to amend pleadings or to join parties.)

    (d) (Final dates for the defendant to amend pleadings or to join parties.)

    (e) (Final dates to file dispositive motions.)

    (f) (State the prospects for settlement.)

    (g) (Identify any alternative dispute resolution procedure that may enhance settlement prospects.)

    (h) (Final dates for submitting Rule 26(a)(3) witness lists, designations of witnesses whose testimony will be presented by deposition, and exhibit lists.)

    (i) (Final dates to file objections under Rule 26(a)(3).)

    (j) (Suggested trial date and estimate of trial length.)

    (k) (Other matters.)

(Date and sign—See Form 2.)

(Added Apr. 20, 2007, eff. Dec. 1. 2007.)

FORM 60
NOTICE OF CONDEMNATION

(Caption—See Form 1.)

To *name the defendant*.

1. A complaint in condemnation has been filed in the United States District Court for the _____ District of _____, to take property to use for *purpose*. The interest to be taken is *describe*. The court is located in the United States courthouse at this address: _____.

2. The property to be taken is described below. You have or claim an interest in it.

(*Describe the property.*)

3. The authority for taking this property is *cite*.

4. If you want to object or present any defense to the taking you must serve an answer on the plaintiff's attorney within 20 days

[after being served with this notice] [from (insert the date of the last publication of notice)]. Send your answer to this address: _____.

5. Your answer must identify the property in which you claim an interest, state the nature and extent of that interest, and state all your objections and defenses to the taking. Objections and defenses not presented are waived.

6. If you fail to answer you consent to the taking and the court will enter a judgment that takes your described property interest.

7. Instead of answering, you may serve on the plaintiff's attorney a notice of appearance that designates the property in which you claim an interest. After you do that, you will receive a notice of any proceedings that affect you. Whether or not you have previously appeared or answered, you may present evidence at a trial to determine compensation for the property and share in the overall award.

(Date and sign—See Form 2.)

(Added Apr. 20, 2007, eff. Dec. 1. 2007.)

FORM 61

COMPLAINT FOR CONDEMNATION

(Caption—See Form 1; name as defendants
the property and at least one owner.)

1. (Statement of Jurisdiction—See Form 7.)

2. This is an action to take property under the power of eminent domain and to determine just compensation to be paid to the owners and parties in interest.

3. The authority for the taking is _____.

4. The property is to be used for _____.

5. The property to be taken is (*describe in enough detail for identification—or attach the description and state "is described in Exhibit A, attached"*).

6. The interest to be acquired is _____.

7. The persons known to the plaintiff to have or claim an interest in the property are: _____. (*For each person include the interest claimed.*)

8. There may be other persons who have or claim an interest in the property and whose names could not be found after a reasonably diligent search. They are made parties under the designation "Unknown Owners."

Therefore, the plaintiff demands judgment:

(a) condemning the property;

(b) determining and awarding just compensation; and

(c) granting any other lawful and proper relief.

(Date and sign—See Form 2.)

(Added Apr. 20, 2007, eff. Dec. 1. 2007.)

FORM 70

JUDGMENT ON A JURY VERDICT

(Caption—See Form 1.)

This action was tried by a jury with Judge _____ presiding, and the jury has rendered a verdict.

It is ordered that:

[the plaintiff *name* recover from the defendant *name* the amount of $_____ with interest at the rate of __ %, along with costs.]

[the plaintiff recover nothing, the action be dismissed on the merits, and the defendant *name* recover costs from the plaintiff *name*.]

Date _____   _____
                                      Clerk of Court

(Added Apr. 20, 2007, eff. Dec. 1. 2007.)

FORM 71

JUDGMENT BY THE COURT WITHOUT A JURY

(Caption—See Form 1.)

This action was tried by Judge _____ without a jury and the following decision was reached:

It is ordered that [the plaintiff *name* recover from the defendant *name* the amount of $_____, with prejudgment interest at the rate of __%, postjudgment interest at the rate of __%, along with costs.] [the plaintiff recover nothing, the action be dismissed on the merits, and the defendant *name* recover costs from the plaintiff *name*.]

Date _____   _____
                                      Clerk of Court

(Added Apr. 20, 2007, eff. Dec. 1. 2007.)

FORM 80

NOTICE OF A MAGISTRATE JUDGE'S AVAILABILITY

1. A magistrate judge is available under title 28 U.S.C. § 636(c) to conduct the proceedings in this case, including a jury or nonjury trial and the entry of final judgment. But a magistrate judge can be assigned only if all parties voluntarily consent.

2. You may withhold your consent without adverse substantive consequences. The identity of any party consenting or withholding consent will not be disclosed to the judge to whom the case is assigned or to any magistrate judge.

3. If a magistrate judge does hear your case, you may appeal directly to a United States court of appeals as you would if a district judge heard it.

A form called *Consent to an Assignment to a United States Magistrate Judge* is available from the court clerk's office.

(Added Apr. 20, 2007, eff. Dec. 1. 2007.)

FORM 81

CONSENT TO AN ASSIGNMENT TO A MAGISTRATE JUDGE

(Caption—See Form 1.)

I voluntarily consent to have a United States magistrate judge conduct all further proceedings in this case, including a trial, and order the entry of final judgment. (Return this form to the court clerk—not to a judge or magistrate judge.)

Date _____ _____

Signature of the Party

(Added Apr. 20, 2007, eff. Dec. 1. 2007.)

FORM 82

ORDER OF ASSIGNMENT TO A MAGISTRATE JUDGE

With the parties' consent it is ordered that this case be assigned to United States Magistrate Judge _____ of this district to conduct all proceedings and enter final judgment in accordance with 28 U.S.C. § 636(c).

Date _____ _____

United States District Judge

(Added Apr. 20, 2007, eff. Dec. 1. 2007.)

PART V

MULTIDISTRICT LITIGATION

Table of Sections

§ 5.1 Introduction

Congress created the Judicial Panel on Multidistrict Litigation in the late 1960's in response to the challenge of efficiently and effectively managing related, protracted, and complex civil cases that were being filed in various federal courts throughout the Nation.[1] At that time, nearly 2,000 separate but related electrical equipment antitrust cases were pending in 36 different federal judicial districts.[2] To manage these numerous distinct but related antitrust cases, Chief Justice Earl Warren appointed an advisory "Coordinating Committee for Multiple Litigation" which invited counsel and district court judges to attend hearings on how to economically supervise these electrical equipment litigations.[3]

The Committee prepared and recommended more than 40 "national pretrial orders" for the cases, which were then entered voluntarily by the judges in most of the districts where these electrical equipment antitrust cases were pending.[4] The orders established a coordinated system of national pretrial discovery, including a central document depository available to all parties and the conduct of depositions on a coordinated, nationwide schedule.[5]

This voluntary, advisory procedure was so successful that Congress established a statutory, national multidistrict litigation court in 1968 with affirmative authority to direct the transfer of multidistrict civil cases that involve one or more common questions of fact to a single federal district for the purpose of consolidated or coordinated nationwide pretrial proceedings.[6] This specialized court, entitled the "Judicial Panel on Multidistrict Litigation", comprises 7 circuit and district court judges, designated from time to time by the Chief Justice, no 2 of whom may come from the same Circuit.[7] The Judicial Panel is authorized to transfer cases for pretrial multidistrict litigation—or "MDL"—treatment

---

1. *See* 28 U.S.C. § 1407.

2. *See* Robert A. Cahn, *A Look at the Judicial Panel on Multidistrict Litigation*, 72 F.R.D. 211, 211 (1976).

3. *See* id. at 211–12.

4. *See* id. at 212.

5. *See* id.

6. *See* 28 U.S.C. § 1407(a).

7. *See* 28 U.S.C. § 1407(d).

upon three findings: (a) that civil cases, then pending in different federal judicial districts, involve one or more common questions of fact, and that coordinated or consolidated pretrial proceedings, centralized before a single district court, (b) will be for the convenience of parties and witnesses and (c) will promote the just and efficient conduct of the lawsuits.[8] Once these prerequisite findings have been made, MDL transfer to a central judicial district is appropriate, even if subject matter jurisdiction or venue would otherwise be improper there over the transferred cases.[9]

MDL treatment may be initiated by the Judicial Panel on its own initiative or upon motion by a party in any action believed to qualify for this type of coordination or consolidation.[10] If MDL treatment is granted by the Judicial Panel, the general procedure is as follows: a single judicial district and federal judge is selected by the Judicial Panel as the MDL court for all the cases; all qualifying federal lawsuits are then transferred to that federal judge for pretrial purposes;[11] the MDL judge presides over and manages a nationwide, coordinated discovery and pretrial procedures program; and, in the event the cases are not disposed of or settled by the MDL judge by the close of the pretrial stage, the lawsuits are each transferred back to their original districts for trial.[12] The MDL judge may rule on case-dispositive motions, and consequently may grant motions to dismiss both on substantive grounds[13] and for failures to abide by court scheduling orders and procedures.[14]

Remands are made by the Judicial Panel (not by the transferee judge), although the transferee judge retains a vital role in the remand back to the original forum by notifying the Judicial Panel (typically through a *"Suggestion to Remand"*) that the coordinated or consolidated proceedings have been concluded.[15] The Judicial Panel *must* remand when the coordinated or consolidated proceedings have concluded, but *may*, in its "unusually broad discretion", remand when all that remains to be accomplished is case-specific.[16] Thus, this MDL treatment is a vehicle for pretrial—and only pretrial—coordination and consolidation.[17]

---

8. *See* 28 U.S.C. § 1407(a). *See also Pinney v. Nokia, Inc.*, 402 F.3d 430, 451 (4th Cir.2005).

9. *See Pinney v. Nokia, Inc.*, 402 F.3d 430, 451–52 (4th Cir.2005).

10. *See* 28 U.S.C. § 1407(c).

11. *See Boomer v. AT & T Corp.*, 309 F.3d 404, 413 (7th Cir.2002) (noting that multidistrict transfer order is effective only when filed in the office of the clerk in the transferee district).

12. *See* 28 U.S.C. § 1407(a). *See also Lexecon Inc. v. Milberg Weiss Bershad Hynes & Lerach*, 523 U.S. 26, 32, 118 S.Ct. 956, 961, 140 L.Ed.2d 62 (1998) (holding that MDL judge cannot ordinarily "self-transfer" unresolved MDL cases to herself for post-pretrial resolution on the merits); *In re Collins*, 233 F.3d 809 (3d Cir.2000)

(refusing to disturb MDL practice of transferring back only compensatory damage asbestos claims to origination district, while retaining punitive damages claims in MDL).

13. *See In re African–American Slave Descendants Litig.*, 471 F.3d 754, 754–57 & 763 (7th Cir. 2006), *petition for cert. filed*, 75 U.S.L.W. 3638 (U.S. May 14, 2007) (No. 06–1533).

14. *See In re Guidant Corp. Implantable Defibrillators Prods. Liab. Litig.*, __ F.3d __, __, 2007 WL 2189069, at *2 (8th Cir. 2007).

15. *See In re Wilson*, 451 F.3d 161, 165 & 165 n.5 (3d Cir.2006).

16. *See In re Wilson*, 451 F.3d 161, 172–73 (3d Cir.2006).

17. *See In re Patenaude*, 210 F.3d 135, 142 (3d Cir.2000) (noting that MDL statute limits transferee court to only proceedings

The MDL procedure endeavors to achieve the economical use of the federal judiciary and the resolution of similar complex civil cases with the least cost and disruption to the parties and witnesses. During the coordinated or consolidated pretrial MDL proceedings, the MDL judge will typically look to the Federal Judicial Center's *Manual for Complex Litigation* as a primary resource for guiding the nationwide proceedings.[18] With those guidelines in mind, documents are generally produced only once for hundreds or thousands of cases, with responsive documents made available to all parties at a centralized document depository. Interrogatories and requests for admissions are served on behalf of an entire series of related cases. Witnesses and parties, whose testimony is relevant to perhaps thousands of different cases, are deposed only once (or at least far less often than otherwise would be the case) by a select group of lead or liaison counsel. Throughout the MDL process, the transferee judge generally possesses the power to act not only on behalf of the transferee district, but also with the powers of a district judge in every district from which the consolidated cases have been transferred.[19]

The MDL judge's discretion is broad and commensurate with the enormous task of managing a large litigation involving numerous litigants from across the country and posing substantial legal questions implicating pleading, discovery, expert, timeliness, choice of law, cognizable claim, and causation issues.[20] This authority encompasses the power to rule on motions relating to subpoenas issued from other judicial districts, including motions to quash.[21] But, although broad, the MDL judge's discretion is not unbounded; the judge may not, in the cause of efficiency and docketing progress, engage in "assembly-line justice".[22]

Appeals from the MDL judge's pretrial orders typically are taken to the Court of Appeals for the Circuit that encompasses the MDL judge's district.[23] However, when the MDL judge's order implicates a ruling compelling or sanctioning a non-party located outside the MDL judge's district, the appeal is generally taken to the Court of Appeals for the Circuit embracing the district of the foreign discovery event.[24]

that are (1) coordinated or consolidated and (2) pretrial. *See also id.* at 144 (commenting that "pretrial" is interpreted broadly to mean all judicial proceedings that occur before trial).

18. For an excellent annotated and commentary-laden version of this essential MDL resource, see David Herr's *Annotated Manual for Complex Litigation Third* (Thomson West, revised annually). Multidistrict litigation under § 1407 is also discussed in detail in Wright, Miller & Cooper, *Federal Practice and Procedure* §§ 3861–68 (West Group).

19. *See In re Flat Glass Antitrust Litig.,* 288 F.3d 83, 90 n. 12 (3d Cir.2002).

20. *See In re Guidant Implantable Defibrillators Prods. Liab. Litig.,* 496 F.3d 863,

867 (8th Cir. 2007); *In re Phenylpropanolamine (PPA) Prods. Liab. Litig.,* 460 F.3d 1217, 1231-32 (9th Cir.2006).

21. *See In re Clients & Former Clients of Baron & Budd, P.C.,* 478 F.3d 670 (5th Cir. 2007) (per curiam).

22. *See In re Phenylpropanolamine (PPA) Prods. Liab. Litig.,* 460 F.3d 1217, 1250 (9th Cir.2006) (affirming in part and reversing in part dismissals for non-compliance with discovery orders).

23. *See United States ex rel. Pogue v. Diabetes Treatment Ctrs. of America, Inc.,* 444 F.3d 462, 467 (6th Cir.2006).

24. *See United States ex rel. Pogue v. Diabetes Treatment Ctrs. of America, Inc.,* 444 F.3d 462, 467-68 (6th Cir.2006).

Over the years, MDL pretrial treatment has been granted in many different types of lawsuits,[25] including national products liability cases,[26] airplane disaster and other large calamity cases,[27] antitrust cases,[28] patent cases,[29] copyright cases, and trademark cases. In its first 27 years of use, the statutory multidistrict litigation procedure has been applied to more than 39,000 federal civil cases, of which more than 90% were resolved in the MDL and prior to trial.[30]

For the reader's convenience, both the MDL statute itself and the Rules of Practice as promulgated by the Judicial Panel on Multidistrict Litigation are reprinted below. For a more extensive treatment of MDL practice, see David F. Herr, *Multidistrict Litigation Manual: Practice Before The Judicial Panel On Multidistrict Litigation* (Thompson–West revised annually).

§ 5.2 The Federal Multidistrict Litigation Statute, 28 U.S.C.A. § 1407

§ 1407. Multidistrict litigation

(a) When civil actions involving one or more common questions of fact are pending in different districts, such actions may be transferred to any district for coordinated or consolidated pretrial proceedings. Such transfers shall be made by the judicial panel on multidistrict litigation authorized by this section upon its determination that transfers for such proceedings will be for the convenience of parties and witnesses and will promote the just and efficient conduct of such actions. Each action so

25. *See* Robert A. Cahn, *A Look at the Judicial Panel on Multidistrict Litigation*, 72 F.R.D. 211, 214 (1976). *See also In re Columbia/HCA Healthcare Corp. Billing Practices Litig.*, 93 F.Supp.2d 876 (M.D.Tenn.2000) (MDL treatment for illegal billing practices claims).

26. *See, e.g., In re Diet Drugs (Phentermine, Fenfluramine, Dexfenfluramine) Prods. Liab. Litig.*, 990 F.Supp. 834 (J.P.M.L.1998) (MDL No. 1203); *In re Temporomandibular Joint (TMJ) Implants Prods. Liab. Litig.*, 844 F.Supp. 1553 (J.P.M.L.1994) (MDL No. 1001); *In re "Factor VIII or IX Concentrate Blood Products", Prod. Liab. Litig.*, 853 F.Supp. 454 (J.P.M.L.1993) (MDL No. 986); *In re Pantopaque Prods. Liab. Litig.*, 787 F.Supp. 229 (J.P.M.L.1992) (MDL No. 920).

27. *See, e.g., In re Air Crash Disaster at Sioux City, Iowa, on July 19, 1989*, 128 F.R.D. 131 (J.P.M.L.1989) (MDL No. 817); *In re Air Disaster at Lockerbie, Scotland, on Dec. 21, 1988*, 709 F.Supp. 231 (J.P.M.L. 1989) (MDL No. 799), *aff'd*, 16 F.3d 513 (2d Cir.1994); *In re Air Crash Disaster At Stapleton Int'l Airport, Denver Colo. on Nov. 15, 1987*, 683 F.Supp. 266 (J.P.M.L.1988) (MDL No. 751); *In re Air Disaster Near Brunswick, Ga., on Apr. 5, 1991*, 794 F.Supp. 393 (J.P.M.L.1992) (MDL No. 930); *In re Fire Disaster at Dupont Plaza Hotel, San Juan, Puerto Rico, on Dec.31, 1986*, 660 F.Supp. 982 (J.P.M.L.1987) (MDL No. 721).

28. *See, e.g., In re Copper Antitrust Litig.*, 98 F.Supp.2d 1039 (W.D.Wis.2000) (MDL No. 1303); *In Re Baseball Bat Antitrust Litig.*, 112 F.Supp.2d 1175 (2000) (MDL No. 1249); *In re Wirebound Boxes Antitrust Litig.*, 1988 WL 216816 (J.P.M.L. 1988) (MDL No. 793); *In re West Coast Bakery Flour Antitrust Litig.*, 368 F.Supp. 808 (J.P.M.L.1974) (MDL No. 146); *In re Professional Hockey Antitrust Litig.*, 369 F.Supp. 1117 (J.P.M.L.1974) (MDL No. 119); *In re Wheat Farmers Antitrust Class Action Litig.*, 366 F.Supp. 1087 (J.P.M.L. 1973) (MDL No. 129).

29. *See, e.g., In re Phonometrics, Inc., Elec. Long Distance Call Cost Computers & Recorder Patent Litig.*, 1997 WL 83673 (J.P.M.L.1997) (MDL No. 1141).

30. *See Lexecon Inc. v. Milberg Weiss Bershad Hynes & Lerach*, 523 U.S. 26, 32, 118 S.Ct. 956, 961, 140 L.Ed.2d 62 (1998).

transferred shall be remanded by the panel at or before the conclusion of such pretrial proceedings to the district from which it was transferred unless it shall have been previously terminated: *Provided, however,* That the panel may separate any claim, cross-claim, counter-claim, or third-party claim and remand any of such claims before the remainder of the action is remanded.

(b) Such coordinated or consolidated pretrial proceedings shall be conducted by a judge or judges to whom such actions are assigned by the judicial panel on multidistrict litigation. For this purpose, upon request of the panel, a circuit judge or a district judge may be designated and assigned temporarily for service in the transferee district by the Chief Justice of the United States or the chief judge of the circuit, as may be required, in accordance with the provisions of chapter 13 of this title. With the consent of the transferee district court, such actions may be assigned by the panel to a judge or judges of such district. The judge or judges to whom such actions are assigned, the members of the judicial panel on multidistrict litigation, and other circuit and district judges designated when needed by the panel may exercise the powers of a district judge in any district for the purpose of conducting pretrial depositions in such coordinated or consolidated pretrial proceedings.

(c) Proceedings for the transfer of an action under this section may be initiated by—

　(i) the judicial panel on multidistrict litigation upon its own initiative, or

　(ii) motion filed with the panel by a party in any action in which transfer for coordinated or consolidated pretrial proceedings under this section may be appropriate. A copy of such motion shall be filed in the district court in which the moving party's action is pending.

The panel shall give notice to the parties in all actions in which transfers for coordinated or consolidated pretrial proceedings are contemplated, and such notice shall specify the time and place of any hearing to determine whether such transfer shall be made. Orders of the panel to set a hearing and other orders of the panel issued prior to the order either directing or denying transfer shall be filed in the office of the clerk of the district court in which a transfer hearing is to be or has been held. The panel's order of transfer shall be based upon a record of such hearing at which material evidence may be offered by any party to an action pending in any district that would be affected by the proceedings under this section, and shall be supported by findings of fact and conclusions of law based upon such record. Orders of transfer and such other orders as the panel may make thereafter shall be filed in the office of the clerk of the district court of the transferee district and shall be effective when thus filed. The clerk of the transferee district court shall forthwith transmit a certified copy of the panel's order to transfer to the clerk of the district court from which the action is being transferred. An order denying transfer shall be filed in each district wherein there is a case pending in which the motion for transfer has been made.

(d) The judicial panel on multidistrict litigation shall consist of seven circuit and district judges designated from time to time by the Chief Justice of the United States, no two of whom shall be from the same circuit. The concurrence of four members shall be necessary to any action by the panel.

(e) No proceedings for review of any order of the panel may be permitted except by extraordinary writ pursuant to the provisions of title 28, section 1651, United States Code. Petitions for an extraordinary writ to review an order of the panel to set a transfer hearing and other orders of the panel issued prior to the order either directing or denying transfer shall be filed only in the court of appeals having jurisdiction over the district in which a hearing is to be or has been held. Petitions for an extraordinary writ to review an order to transfer or orders subsequent to transfer shall be filed only in the court of appeals having jurisdiction over the transferee district. There shall be no appeal or review of an order of the panel denying a motion to transfer for consolidated or coordinated proceedings.

(f) The panel may prescribe rules for the conduct of its business not inconsistent with Acts of Congress and the Federal Rules of Civil Procedure.

(g) Nothing in this section shall apply to any action in which the United States is a complainant arising under the antitrust laws. "Antitrust laws" as used herein include those acts referred to in the Act of October 15, 1914, as amended (38 Stat. 730; 15 U.S.C. 12), and also include the Act of June 19, 1936 (49 Stat. 1526; 15 U.S.C. 13, 13a, and 13b) and the Act of September 26, 1914, as added March 21, 1938 (52 Stat. 116, 117; 15 U.S.C. 56); but shall not include section 4A of the Act of October 15, 1914, as added July 7, 1955 (69 Stat. 282; 15 U.S.C. 15a).

(h) Notwithstanding the provisions of section 1404 or subsection (f) of this section, the judicial panel on multidistrict litigation may consolidate and transfer with or without the consent of the parties, for both pretrial purposes and for trial, any action brought under section 4C of the Clayton Act.

(Added Pub.L. 90–296, § 1, Apr. 29, 1968, 82 Stat. 109, and amended Pub.L. 94–435, Title III, § 303, Sept. 30, 1976, 90 Stat. 1396.)

§ 5.3 Rules of Procedure of the Judicial Panel on Multi-district Litigation (Including amendments received to October 1, 2007)

I. GENERAL RULES/RULE FOR MULTIDISTRICT
LITIGATION UNDER 28 U.S.C. § 1407

I. GENERAL RULES/RULES FOR MULTIDISTRICT LITIGATION UNDER 28 U.S.C. § 1407

Rule 1.1.   Definitions

As used in these Rules "Panel" means the members of the Judicial Panel on Multidistrict Litigation appointed by the Chief Justice of the United States pursuant to Section 1407, Title 28, United States Code.

"Clerk of the Panel" means the official appointed by the Panel to act as Clerk of the Panel and shall include those deputized by the Clerk of the Panel to perform or assist in the performance of the duties of the Clerk of the Panel.

"Chairman" means the Chairman of the Judicial Panel on Multidistrict Litigation appointed by the Chief Justice of the United States pursuant to Section 1407, or the member of the Panel designated by the Panel to act as Chairman in the absence or inability of the appointed Chairman.

A "tag-along action" refers to a civil action pending in a district court and involving common questions of fact with actions previously transferred under Section 1407.

(Added May 3, 1993, eff. July 1, 1993, and amended Sept. 1, 1998, eff. Nov. 2, 1998; Apr. 2, 2001, eff. Apr. 2, 2001.)

Rule 1.2.   Practice

Where not fixed by statute or rule, the practice shall be that heretofore customarily followed by the Panel.

(Added May 3, 1993, eff. July 1, 1993, and amended Sept. 1, 1998, eff. Nov. 2, 1998; Apr. 2, 2001, eff. Apr. 2, 2001.)

Rule 1.3.   Failure to Comply with Rules

The Clerk of the Panel may, when a paper submitted for filing is not in compliance with the provisions of these Rules, advise counsel of the deficiencies and a date for full compliance. If full compliance is not accomplished within the established time, the non-complying paper shall nonetheless be filed by the Clerk of the Panel but it may be stricken by order of the Chairman of the Panel.

(Added May 3, 1993, eff. July 1, 1993, and amended Sept. 1, 1998, eff. Nov. 2, 1998; Apr. 2, 2001, eff. Apr. 2, 2001.)

Rule 1.4.   Admission to Practice Before the Panel and Representation in Transferred Actions

Every member in good standing of the Bar of any district court of the United States is entitled without condition to practice before the Judicial Panel on Multidistrict Litigation. Any attorney of record in any action transferred under Section 1407 may continue to represent his or her client in any district court of the United States to which such action is transferred. Parties to any action transferred under Section 1407 are not required to obtain local counsel in the district to which such action is transferred.

(Added May 3, 1993, eff. July 1, 1993, and amended Sept. 1, 1998, eff. Nov. 2, 1998; Apr. 2, 2001, eff. Apr. 2, 2001.)

Rule 1.5.   Effect of the Pendency of an Action Before the Panel

The pendency of a motion, order to show cause, conditional transfer order or conditional remand order before the Panel concerning transfer or remand of an action pursuant to 28 U.S.C. § 1407 does not affect or suspend orders and pretrial proceedings in the district court in which the action is pending and does not in any way limit the pretrial jurisdiction of that court. A transfer or remand pursuant to 28 U.S.C. § 1407 shall be effective when the transfer or remand order is filed in the office of the clerk of the district court of the transferee district.

(Added May 3, 1993, eff. July 1, 1993, and amended Sept. 1, 1998, eff. Nov. 2, 1998; Apr. 2, 2001, eff. Apr. 2, 2001.)

Rule 1.6.   Transfer of Files

(a) Upon receipt of a certified copy of a transfer order from the clerk of the transferee district court, the clerk of the transferor district court shall forward to the clerk of the transferee district court the complete original file and a certified copy of the docket sheet for each transferred action.

(b) If an appeal is pending, or a notice of appeal has been filed, or leave to appeal has been sought under 28 U.S.C. § 1292(b) or a petition for an extraordinary writ is pending, in any action included in an order of transfer under 28 U.S.C. § 1407, and the original file or parts thereof have been forwarded to the court of appeals, the clerk of the transferor district court shall notify the clerk of the court of appeals of the order of transfer and secure the original file long enough to prepare and transmit to the clerk of the transferee district court a certified copy of all papers contained in the original file and a certified copy of the docket sheet.

(c) If the transfer order provides for the separation and simultaneous remand of any claim, cross-claim, counterclaim, or third-party claim, the clerk of the transferor district court shall retain the original file and shall prepare and transmit to the clerk of the transferee district court a certified copy of the docket sheet and copies of all papers except those relating exclusively to separated and remanded claims.

(d) Upon receipt of an order to remand from the Clerk of the Panel, the transferee district court shall prepare and send to the clerk of the transferor district court the following:

(i) a certified copy of the individual docket sheet for each action being remanded;

(ii) a certified copy of the master docket sheet, if applicable;

(iii) the entire file for each action being remanded, as originally received from the transferor district court and augmented as set out in this rule;

(iv) a certified copy of the final pretrial order, if applicable; and

(v) a "record on remand" to be composed of those parts of the files and records produced during coordinated or consolidated pretrial proceedings which have been stipulated to or designated by counsel as being necessary for any or all proceedings to be conducted following remand. It shall be the responsibility of counsel originally preparing or filing any document to be included in the "record on remand" to furnish on request sufficient copies to the clerk of the transferee district court.

(e) The Clerk of the Panel shall be notified when any files have been transmitted pursuant to this Rule.

(Added May 3, 1993, eff. July 1, 1993, and amended Sept. 1, 1998, eff. Nov. 2, 1998; Apr. 2, 2001, eff. Apr. 2, 2001.)

Rule 5.1. Keeping Records and Files

(a) The records and files of the Panel shall be kept by the Clerk of the Panel at the offices of the Panel. Records and files may be temporarily or permanently removed to such places at such times as the Panel or the Chairman of the Panel shall direct. The Clerk of the Panel may charge fees, as prescribed by the Judicial Conference of the United States, for duplicating records and files. Records and files may be transferred whenever appropriate to the Federal Records Center.

(b) In order to assist the Panel in carrying out its functions, the Clerk of the Panel shall obtain the complaints and docket sheets in all actions under consideration for transfer under 28 U.S.C. § 1407 from the clerk of each district court wherein such actions are pending. The Clerk of the Panel shall similarly obtain any other pleadings and orders that could affect the Panel's decision under 28 U.S.C. § 1407.

(Added May 3, 1993, eff. July 1, 1993, and amended Sept. 1, 1998, eff. Nov. 2, 1998; Apr. 2, 2001, eff. Apr. 2, 2001.)

Rule 5.11.   Place of Filing of Papers

All papers for consideration by the Panel shall be submitted for filing to the Clerk of the Panel by mailing or delivering to:

Clerk of the Panel Judicial Panel on Multidistrict Litigation

Thurgood Marshall Federal Judiciary Building

One Columbus Circle, N.E., Room G–255, North Lobby

Washington, D.C. 20002–8004

No papers shall be left with or mailed to a Judge of the Panel.

(Added May 3, 1993, eff. July 1, 1993, and amended Sept. 1, 1998, eff. Nov. 2, 1998; Apr. 2, 2001, eff. Apr. 2, 2001.)

Rule 5.12.   Manner of Filing of Papers

(a) An original of the following papers shall be submitted for filing to the Clerk of the Panel: a proof of service pursuant to Rule 5.2(a) and (b) of these Rules, a notice of appearance pursuant to Rule 5.2(c) and (d) of these Rules, a corporate disclosure statement pursuant to Rule 5.3 of these Rules, a status notice pursuant to Rules 7.2(f), 7.3(e) and 7.4(b) of these Rules, a notice of opposition pursuant to Rules 7.4(c) and 7.6(f)(ii) of these Rules, a notice of related action pursuant to Rules 7.2(i), 7.3(a) and 7.5(e) of these Rules, an application for extension of time pursuant to Rule 6.2 of these Rules, or a notice of presentation or waiver of oral argument pursuant to Rule 16.1(d) of these Rules. An original and eleven copies of all other papers shall be submitted for filing to the Clerk of the Panel. The Clerk of the Panel may require that additional copies also be submitted for filing.

(b) When papers are submitted for filing, the Clerk of the Panel shall endorse thereon the date for filing.

(c) Copies of motions for transfer of an action or actions pursuant to 28 U.S.C. § 1407 shall be filed in each district court in which an action is pending that will be affected by the motion. Copies of a motion for remand pursuant to 28 U.S.C. § 1407 shall be filed in the Section 1407 transferee district court in which any action affected by the motion is pending.

(d) Papers requiring only an original may be faxed to the Panel office with prior approval of the Clerk of the Panel. No papers requiring multiple copies shall be accepted via fax.

(Added May 3, 1993, eff. July 1, 1993, and amended Sept. 1, 1998, eff. Nov. 2, 1998; Apr. 2, 2001, eff. Apr. 2, 2001.)

Rule 5.13.   Filing of Papers: Computer Generated Disk Required

(a) Whenever an original paper and eleven copies is required to be submitted for filing to the Clerk of the Panel pursuant to Rule 5.12(a) of these Rules, and where a party is represented by counsel, one copy of that paper must also be submitted on a computer readable disk and shall be filed at the time the party's paper is filed. The disk shall contain the entire paper exclusive of computer non-generated exhibits. The label of the disk shall include i) "MDL #___," ii) an abbreviated version of the MDL descriptive title, or other appropriate descriptive title, if not yet designated by the Panel, iii) the identity of the type of paper being filed (i.e. motion, response, reply, etc.), iv) the name of the counsel who signed the paper, and v) the first named represented party on the paper.

(b) The paper must be on a 3 1/2 inch disk in WordPerfect for Windows format.

(c) One copy of the disk may be served on each party separately represented by counsel. If a party chooses to serve a copy of the disk, the proof of service, as required by Rule 5.2 of these Rules, must indicate service of the paper in both paper and electronic format.

(d) A party may be relieved from the requirements of this Rule by submitting a written application for a waiver, in a timely manner in advance of submission of the paper, certifying that compliance with the Rule would impose undue hardship, that the text of the paper is not available on disk, or that other unusual circumstances preclude compliance with this Rule. The requirements of this Rule shall not apply to parties appearing pro se. Papers embraced by this Rule and submitted by counsel after June 1, 2000 without a computer disk copy or Panel-approved waiver of the requirements of this Rule shall be governed by Rule 1.3 of these Rules.

(Added May 22, 2000, eff. June 1, 2000, and amended Apr. 2, 2001, eff. Apr. 2, 2001.)

Rule 5.2. Service of Papers Filed

(a) All papers filed with the Clerk of the Panel shall be accompanied by proof of previous or simultaneous service on all other parties in all actions involved in the litigation. Service and proof of service shall be made as provided in Rules 5 and 6 of the Federal Rules of Civil Procedure. The proof of service shall indicate the name and complete address of each person served and shall indicate the party represented by each. If a party is not represented by counsel, the proof of service shall indicate the name of the party and the party's last known address. The proof of service shall indicate why any person named as a party in a constituent complaint was not served with the Section 1407 pleading. The original proof of service shall be filed with the Clerk of the Panel and copies thereof shall be sent to each person included within the proof of service. After the "Panel Service List" described in subsection (d) of this Rule has been received from the Clerk of the Panel, the "Panel Service List" shall be utilized for service of responses to motions and all other filings. In such instances, the "Panel Service List" shall be attached to the proof of service and shall be supplemented in the proof of service in the event of the presence of additional parties or subsequent corrections relating to any party, counsel or address already on the "Panel Service List."

(b) The proof of service pertaining to motions for transfer of actions pursuant to 28 U.S.C. § 1407 shall certify that copies of the motions have been mailed or otherwise delivered for filing to the clerk of each district court in which an action is pending that will be affected by the motion. The proof of service pertaining to a motion for remand pursuant to 28 U.S.C. § 1407 shall certify that a copy of the motion has been mailed or otherwise delivered for filing to the clerk of the Section 1407 transferee district court in which any action affected by the motion is pending.

(c) Within eleven days of filing of a motion to transfer, an order to show cause or a conditional transfer order, each party or designated attorney shall notify the Clerk of the Panel, in writing, of the name and address of the attorney designated to receive service of all pleadings, notices, orders and other papers relating to practice before the Judicial Panel on Multidistrict Litigation. Only one attorney shall be designated for each party. Any party not represented by counsel shall be served by mailing such pleadings to the party's last known address. Requests for an extension of time to file the designation of attorney shall not be granted except in extraordinary circumstances.

(d) In order to facilitate compliance with subsection (a) of this Rule, the Clerk of the Panel shall prepare and serve on all counsel and parties not represented by counsel, a "Panel Service List" containing the names and addresses of the designated attorneys and the party or parties they represent in the actions under consideration by the Panel and the names and addresses of the parties not represented by counsel in the actions under consideration by the Panel. After the "Panel Service List" has been received from the Clerk of the Panel, notice of subsequent corrections relating to any party, counsel or address on the "Panel Service List" shall be served on all other parties in all actions involved in the litigation.

(e) If following transfer of any group of multidistrict litigation, the transferee district court appoints liaison counsel, this Rule shall be satisfied by serving each party in each affected action and all liaison counsel. Liaison counsel designated by the transferee district court shall receive copies of all Panel orders concerning their particular litigation and shall be responsible for distribution to the parties for whom he or she serves as liaison counsel.

(Added May 3, 1993, eff. July 1, 1993, and amended Sept. 1, 1998, eff. Nov. 2, 1998; Apr. 2, 2001, eff. Apr. 2, 2001.)

Rule 5.3. Corporate Disclosure Statement

(a) Any nongovernmental corporate party to a matter before the Panel shall file a statement identifying all its parent corporations and listing any publicly held company that owns 10% or more of the party's stock.

(b) A party shall file the corporate disclosure statement within eleven days of the filing of a motion to transfer or remand, an order to show cause, or a motion to vacate a conditional transfer order or a conditional remand order.

(c) Once a corporate disclosure statement by a party has been filed in an MDL docket pursuant to subsection (b) of this Rule, such a party is required to update the statement to reflect any change in the information therein i) until the matter before the Panel is decided, and ii) within eleven days of the filing of any subsequent motion to transfer or remand, order to show cause, or motion to vacate a conditional transfer order or a conditional remand order in that docket.

(Added Apr. 2, 2001, eff. Apr. 2, 2001.)

Rule 6.2.   Applications for Extensions of Time

Any application for an extension of time to file a pleading or perform an act required by these Rules must be in writing, must request a specific number of additional days and may be acted upon by the Clerk of the Panel. Such an application will be evaluated in relation to the impact on the Panel's calendar as well as on the basis of the reasons set forth in support of the application. Any party aggrieved by the Clerk of the Panel's action on such application may submit its objections to the Panel for consideration. Absent exceptional circumstances, no extensions of time shall be granted to file a notice of opposition to either a conditional transfer order or a conditional remand order. All applications for extensions of time shall be filed and served in conformity with Rules 5.12, 5.2 and 7.1 of these Rules.

(Added May 3, 1993, eff. July 1, 1993, and amended Sept. 1, 1998, eff. Nov. 2, 1998; Apr. 2, 2001, eff. Apr. 2, 2001.)

Rule 7.1.   Form of Papers Filed

(a) Averments in any motion seeking action by the Panel shall be made in numbered paragraphs, each of which shall be limited, as far as practicable, to a statement of a single factual averment.

(b) Responses to averments in motions shall be made in numbered paragraphs, each of which shall correspond to the number of the paragraph of the motion to which the responsive paragraph is directed. Each responsive paragraph shall admit or deny wholly or in part the averment of the motion, and shall contain the respondent's version of the subject matter when the averment or the motion is not wholly admitted.

(c) Each pleading filed shall be:

(i) flat and unfolded;

(ii) plainly written, typed in double space, printed or prepared by means of a duplicating process, without erasures or interlineations which materially deface it;

(iii) on opaque, unglazed, white paper (not onionskin);

(iv) approximately 8–1/2 x 11 inches in size; and

(v) fastened at the top-left corner without side binding or front or back covers.

(d) The heading on the first page of each pleading shall commence not less than three inches from the top of the page. Each pleading shall bear the heading "Before the Judicial Panel on Multidistrict Litigation," the identification "MDL Docket No.___" and the descriptive title designated by the Panel for the litigation involved. If the Panel has not yet designated a title, an appropriate descriptive title shall be used.

(e) The final page of each pleading shall contain the name, address and telephone number of the attorney or party in active charge of the case. Each attorney shall also include the name of each party represented.

(f) Except with the approval of the Panel, each brief submitted for filing with the Panel shall be limited to twenty pages, exclusive of exhibits. Absent exceptional circumstances, motions to exceed page limits shall not be granted.

(g) Exhibits exceeding a cumulative total of 50 pages shall be fastened separately from the accompanying pleading.

(h) Proposed Panel orders shall not be submitted with papers for filing.

(Added May 3, 1993,eff. July 1, 1993, and amended Sept. 1, 1998, eff. Nov. 2, 1998; Apr. 2, 2001, eff. Apr. 2, 2001.)

Rule 7.2. Motion Practice

(a) All requests for action by the Panel under 28 U.S.C. § 1407 shall be made by written motion. Every motion shall be accompanied by:

> **(i)** a brief in support thereof in which the background of the litigation and factual and legal contentions of the movant shall be concisely stated in separate portions of the brief with citation of applicable authorities; and

> **(ii)** a schedule giving

>> **(A)** the complete name of each action involved, listing the full name of each party included as such on the district court's docket sheet, not shortened by the use of references such as "et al." or "etc.";

>> **(B)** the district court and division in which each action is pending;

>> **(C)** the civil action number of each action; and

>> **(D)** the name of the judge assigned each action, if known.

(b) The Clerk of the Panel shall notify recipients of a motion of the filing date, caption, MDL docket number, briefing schedule and pertinent Panel policies.

(c) Within twenty days after filing of a motion, all other parties shall file a response thereto. Failure of a party to respond to a motion shall be treated as that party's acquiescence to the action requested in the motion.

(d) The movant may, within five days after the lapse of the time period for filing responsive briefs, file a single brief in reply to any opposition.

(e) Motions, their accompaniments, responses, and replies shall also be governed by Rules 5.12, 5.2 and 7.1 of these Rules.

(f) With respect to any action that is the subject of Panel consideration, counsel shall promptly notify the Clerk of the Panel of any development that would partially or completely moot the matter before the Panel.

(g) A joinder in a motion shall not add any action to the previous motion.

(h) Once a motion is filed, any other pleading that purports to be a "motion" in the docket shall be filed by the Clerk of the Panel as a response unless the "motion" adds an action. The Clerk of the Panel, upon designating such a pleading as a motion, shall acknowledge that designation by the distribution of a briefing schedule to all parties in the docket. Response time resulting from an additional motion shall ordinarily be extended only to those parties directly affected by the additional motion. An accelerated briefing schedule for the additional motion may be set by the Clerk of the Panel to conform with the hearing session schedule established by the Chairman.

(i) Any party or counsel in a new group of actions under consideration by the Panel for transfer under Section 1407 shall promptly notify the Clerk of the Panel of any potential tag-along action in which that party is also named or in which that counsel appears.

(Added May 3, 1993, eff. July 1, 1993, and amended Sept. 1, 1998, eff. Nov. 2, 1998; Apr. 2, 2001, eff. Apr. 2, 2001.)

Rule 7.3. Show Cause Orders

(a) When transfer of multidistrict litigation is being considered on the initiative of the Panel pursuant to 28 U.S.C. § 1407(c)(i), an order shall be filed by the Clerk of the Panel directing the parties to show cause why the action or actions should not be transferred for coordinated or consolidated pretrial proceedings. Any party or counsel in such actions shall promptly notify the Clerk of the Panel of any other federal district court actions related to the litigation encompassed by the show cause order. Such notification shall be made for additional actions pending at the time of the issuance of the show cause order and whenever new actions are filed.

(b) Any party may file a response to the show cause order within twenty days of the filing of said order unless otherwise provided for in the order. Failure of a party to respond to a show cause order shall be treated as that party's acquiescence to the Panel action contemplated in the order.

(c) Within five days after the lapse of the time period for filing a response, any party may file a reply limited to new matters.

(d) Responses and replies shall be filed and served in conformity with Rules 5.12, 5.2 and 7.1 of these Rules.

(e) With respect to any action that is the subject of Panel consideration, counsel shall promptly notify the Clerk of the Panel of any development that would partially or completely moot the matter before the Panel.

(Added May 3, 1993, eff. July 1, 1993, and amended Sept. 1, 1998, eff. Nov. 2, 1998; Apr. 2, 2001, eff. Apr. 2, 2001.)

Rule 7.4. Conditional Transfer Orders for "Tag–Along Actions"

(a) Upon learning of the pendency of a potential "tag-along action," as defined in Rule 1.1 of these Rules, an order may be entered by the Clerk of the Panel transferring that action to the previously designated transferee district court on the basis of the prior hearing session(s) and for the reasons expressed in previous opinions and orders of the Panel in the litigation. The Clerk of the Panel shall serve this order on each party to the litigation but, in order to afford all parties the opportunity to oppose transfer, shall not send the order to the clerk of the transferee district court for fifteen days from the entry thereof.

(b) Parties to an action subject to a conditional transfer order shall notify the Clerk of the Panel within the fifteen-day period if that action is no longer pending in its transferor district court.

(c) Any party opposing the transfer shall file a notice of opposition with the Clerk of the Panel within the fifteen-day period. If a notice of opposition is received by the Clerk of the Panel within this fifteen-day period, the Clerk of the Panel shall not transmit said order to the clerk of the transferee district court until further order of the Panel. The Clerk of the Panel shall notify the parties of the briefing schedule.

(d) Within fifteen days of the filing of its notice of opposition, the party opposing transfer shall file a motion to vacate the conditional transfer order and brief in support thereof. The Chairman of the Panel shall set the motion for the next appropriate hearing session of the Panel. Failure to file and serve a motion and brief shall be treated as withdrawal of the opposition and the Clerk of the Panel shall forthwith transmit the order to the clerk of the transferee district court.

(e) Conditional transfer orders do not become effective unless and until they are filed with the clerk of the transferee district court.

(f) Notices of opposition and motions to vacate such orders of the Panel and responses thereto shall be governed by Rules 5.12, 5.2, 7.1 and 7.2 of these Rules.

(Added May 3, 1993, eff. July 1, 1993, and amended Sept. 1, 1998, eff. Nov. 2, 1998; Apr. 2, 2001, eff. Apr. 2, 2001.)

Rule 7.5.   Miscellaneous Provisions Concerning "Tag–Along Actions"

(a) Potential "tag-along actions" filed in the transferee district require no action on the part of the Panel and requests for assignment of such actions to the Section 1407 transferee judge should be made in accordance with local rules for the assignment of related actions.

(b) Upon learning of the pendency of a potential "tag-along action" and having reasonable anticipation of opposition to transfer of that action, the Panel may direct the Clerk of the Panel to file a show cause order, in accordance with Rule 7.3 of these Rules, instead of a conditional transfer order.

(c) Failure to serve one or more of the defendants in a potential "tag-along action" with the complaint and summons as required by Rule 4 of the Federal Rules of Civil Procedure does not preclude transfer of such action under Section 1407. Such failure, however, may be submitted by such a defendant as a basis for opposing the proposed transfer if prejudice can be shown. The inability of the Clerk of the Panel to serve a conditional transfer order on all plaintiffs or defendants or their counsel shall not render the transfer of the action void but can be submitted by such a party as a basis for moving to remand as to such party if prejudice can be shown.

(d) A civil action apparently involving common questions of fact with actions under consideration by the Panel for transfer under Section 1407, which was either not included in a motion under Rule 7.2 of these Rules, or was included in such a motion that was filed too late to be included in the initial hearing session, will ordinarily be treated by the Panel as a potential "tag-along action."

(e) Any party or counsel in actions previously transferred under Section 1407 or under consideration by the Panel for transfer under Section 1407 shall promptly notify the Clerk of the Panel of any potential "tag-along actions" in which that party is also named or in which that counsel appears.

(Added May 3, 1993, eff. July 1, 1993, and amended Sept. 1, 1998, eff. Nov. 2, 1998; Apr. 2, 2001, eff. Apr. 2, 2001.)

Rule 7.6. Termination and Remand

In the absence of unusual circumstances—

(a) Actions terminated in the transferee district court by valid judgment, including but not limited to summary judgment, judgment of dismissal and judgment upon stipulation, shall not be remanded by the Panel and shall be dismissed by the transferee district court. The clerk of the transferee district court shall send a copy of the order terminating the action to the Clerk of the Panel but shall retain the original files and records unless otherwise directed by the transferee judge or by the Panel.

(b) Each action transferred only for coordinated or consolidated pretrial proceedings that has not been terminated in the transferee district court shall be remanded by the Panel to the transferor district for trial. Actions that were originally filed in the transferee district require no action by the Panel to be reassigned to another judge in the transferee district at the conclusion of the coordinated or consolidated pretrial proceedings affecting those actions.

(c) The Panel shall consider remand of each transferred action or any separable claim, cross-claim, counterclaim or third-party claim at or before the conclusion of coordinated or consolidated pretrial proceedings on

   (i) motion of any party,

   (ii) suggestion of the transferee district court, or

   (iii) the Panel's own initiative, by entry of an order to show cause, a conditional remand order or other appropriate order.

(d) The Panel is reluctant to order remand absent a suggestion of remand from the transferee district court. If remand is sought by motion of a party, the motion shall be accompanied by:

   (i) an affidavit reciting

(**A**) whether the movant has requested a suggestion of remand from the transferee district court, how the court responded to any request, and, if no such request was made, why;

(**B**) whether all common discovery and other pretrial proceedings have been completed in the action sought to be remanded, and if not, what remains to be done; and

(**C**) whether all orders of the transferee district court have been satisfactorily complied with, and if not, what remains to be done; and

(**ii**) a copy of the transferee district court's final pretrial order, where such order has been entered.

Motions to remand and responses thereto shall be governed by Rules 5.12, 5.2, 7.1 and 7.2 of these Rules.

(**e**) When an order to show cause why an action or actions should not be remanded is entered pursuant to subsection (c), paragraph (iii) of this Rule, any party may file a response within twenty days of the filing of said order unless otherwise provided for in the order. Within five days of filing of a party's response, any party may file a reply brief limited to new matters. Failure of a party to respond to a show cause order regarding remand shall be treated as that party's acquiescence to the remand. Responses and replies shall be filed and served in conformity with Rules 5.12, 5.2 and 7.1 of these Rules.

(**f**) Conditional Remand Orders.

(**i**) When the Panel has been advised by the transferee district judge, or otherwise has reason to believe, that pretrial proceedings in the litigation assigned to the transferee district judge are concluded or that remand of an action or actions is otherwise appropriate, an order may be entered by the Clerk of the Panel remanding the action or actions to the transferor district court. The Clerk of the Panel shall serve this order on each party to the litigation but, in order to afford all parties the opportunity to oppose remand, shall not send the order to the clerk of the transferee district court for fifteen days from the entry thereof.

(**ii**) Any party opposing the remand shall file a notice of opposition with the Clerk of the Panel within the fifteen-day period. If a notice of opposition is received by the Clerk of the Panel within this fifteen-day period, the Clerk of the Panel shall not transmit said order to the clerk of the transferee district court until further order of the Panel. The Clerk of the Panel shall notify the parties of the briefing schedule.

(**iii**) Within fifteen days of the filing of its notice of opposition, the party opposing remand shall file a motion to vacate the conditional remand order and brief in support thereof. The Chairman of the Panel shall set the motion for the next appropriate hearing session of the Panel. Failure to file and serve a motion and brief shall be treated as a withdrawal of the opposition and the Clerk of the Panel shall forthwith transmit the order to the clerk of the transferee district court.

(iv) Conditional remand orders do not become effective unless and until they are filed with the clerk of the transferee district court.

(v) Notices of opposition and motions to vacate such orders of the Panel and responses thereto shall be governed by Rules 5.12, 5.2, 7.1 and 7.2 of these Rules.

(g) Upon receipt of an order to remand from the Clerk of the Panel, the parties shall furnish forthwith to the transferee district clerk a stipulation or designation of the contents of the record or part thereof to be remanded and furnish the transferee district clerk all necessary copies of any pleading or other matter filed so as to enable the transferee district clerk to comply with the order of remand.

(Added May 3, 1993, eff. July 1, 1993, and amended Sept. 1, 1998, eff. Nov. 2, 1998; Apr. 2, 2001, eff. Apr. 2, 2001.)

Rule 16.1.   Hearing Sessions and Oral Argument

(a) Hearing sessions of the Panel for the presentation of oral argument and consideration of matters taken under submission without oral argument shall be held as ordered by the Panel. The Panel shall convene whenever and wherever desirable or necessary in the judgment of the Chairman. The Chairman shall determine which matters shall be considered at each hearing session and the Clerk of the Panel shall give notice to counsel for all parties involved in the litigation to be so considered of the time, place and subject matter of such hearing session.

(b) Each party filing a motion or a response to a motion or order of the Panel under Rules 7.2, 7.3, 7.4 or 7.6 of these Rules may file simultaneously therewith a separate statement limited to one page setting forth reasons why oral argument should, or need not, be heard. Such statements shall be captioned "Reasons Why Oral Argument Should [Need Not] Be Heard," and shall be filed and served in conformity with Rules 5.12 and 5.2 of these Rules.

(c) No transfer or remand determination regarding any action pending in the district court shall be made by the Panel when any party timely opposes such transfer or remand unless a hearing session has been held for the presentation of oral argument except that the Panel may dispense with oral argument if it determines that:

(i) the dispositive issue(s) have been authoritatively decided; or

(ii) the facts and legal arguments are adequately presented in the briefs and record, and the decisional process would not be significantly aided by oral argument.

Unless otherwise ordered by the Panel, all other matters before the Panel, such as a motion for reconsideration, shall be considered and determined upon the basis of the papers filed.

(d) In those matters in which oral argument is not scheduled by the Panel, counsel shall be promptly advised. If oral argument is scheduled in a matter the Clerk of the Panel may require counsel for all parties who wish to make or to waive oral argument to file and serve notice to that effect within a stated time in conformity with Rules 5.12 and 5.2 of these Rules. Failure to do so shall be deemed a waiver of oral argument by that party. If oral argument is scheduled but not attended by a party, the matter shall not be rescheduled and that party's position shall be treated as submitted for decision by the Panel on the basis of the papers filed.

(e) Except for leave of the Panel on a showing of good cause, only those parties to actions scheduled for oral argument who have filed a motion or written response to a motion or order shall be permitted to appear before the Panel and present oral argument.

(f) Counsel for those supporting transfer or remand under Section 1407 and counsel for those opposing such transfer or remand are to confer separately prior to the oral argument for the purpose of organizing their arguments and selecting representatives to present all views without duplication.

(g) Unless otherwise ordered by the Panel, a maximum of twenty minutes shall be allotted for oral argument in each matter. The time shall be divided equally among those with varying viewpoints. Counsel for the moving party or parties shall generally be heard first.

(h) So far as practicable and consistent with the purposes of Section 1407, the offering of oral testimony before the Panel shall be avoided. Accordingly, oral testimony shall not be received except upon notice, motion and order of the Panel expressly providing for it.

(i) After an action or group of actions has been set for a hearing session, consideration of such action(s) may be continued only by order of the Panel on good cause shown.

(Added May 3, 1993, eff. July 1, 1993, and amended Sept. 1, 1998, eff. Nov. 2, 1998; Apr. 2, 2001, eff. Apr. 2, 2001.)

II. RULES FOR MULTICIRCUIT PETITIONS FOR REVIEW UNDER 28 U.S.C. § 2112(a)(3)

Rule 17.1. Random Selection

(a) Upon filing a notice of multicircuit petitions for review, the Clerk of the Panel or designated deputy shall randomly select a circuit court of appeals from a drum containing an entry for each circuit wherein a constituent petition for review is pending. Multiple petitions for review pending in a single circuit shall be allotted only a single entry in the drum. This random selection shall be witnessed by the Clerk of the Panel or a designated deputy other than the random selector. Thereafter, an order on behalf of the Panel shall be issued, signed by the random selector and the witness,

(i) consolidating the petitions for review in the court of appeals for the circuit that was randomly selected; and

(ii) designating that circuit as the one in which the record is to be filed pursuant to Rules 16 and 17 of the Federal Rules of Appellate Procedure.

(b) A consolidation of petitions for review shall be effective when the Panel's consolidation order is filed at the offices of the Panel by the Clerk of the Panel.

(Added May 3, 1993, eff. July 1, 1993, and amended Sept. 1, 1998, eff. Nov. 2, 1998; Apr. 2, 2001, eff. Apr. 2, 2001.)

Rule 25.1.   Filing of Notices

(a) An original of a notice of multicircuit petitions for review pursuant to 28 U.S.C. § 2112(a)(3) shall be submitted for filing to the Clerk of the Panel by the affected agency, board, commission or officer. The term "agency" as used in Section II of these Rules shall include agency, board, commission or officer.

(b) All notices of multicircuit petitions for review submitted by the affected agency for filing with the Clerk of the Panel shall embrace exclusively petitions for review filed in the courts of appeals within ten days after issuance of an agency order and received by the affected agency from the petitioners within that ten-day period.

(c) When a notice of multicircuit petitions for review is submitted for filing to the Clerk of the Panel, the Clerk of the Panel shall file the notice and endorse thereon the date of filing.

(d) Copies of notices of multicircuit petitions for review shall be filed by the affected agency with the clerk of each circuit court of appeals in which a petition for review is pending that is included in the notice.

(Added May 3, 1993, eff. July 1, 1993, and amended Sept. 1, 1998, eff. Nov. 2, 1998; Apr. 2, 2001, eff. Apr. 2, 2001.)

Rule 25.2.   Accompaniments to Notices

(a) All notices of multicircuit petitions for review shall be accompanied by:

(i) a copy of each involved petition for review as the petition for review is defined in 28 U.S.C. § 2112(a)(2); and

(ii) a schedule giving

(A) the date of the relevant agency order;

(B) the case name of each petition for review involved;

(C) the circuit court of appeals in which each petition for review is pending;

(D) the appellate docket number of each petition for review;

(E) the date of filing by the court of appeals of each petition for review; and

(F) the date of receipt by the agency of each petition for review.

(b) The schedule in Subsection (a)(ii) of this Rule shall also be governed by Rules 25.1, 25.3 and 25.4(a) of these Rules.

(Added May 3, 1993, eff. July 1, 1993, and amended Sept. 1, 1998, eff. Nov. 2, 1998; Apr. 2, 2001, eff. Apr. 2, 2001.)

Rule 25.3.   Service of Notices

(a) All notices of multicircuit petitions for review shall be accompanied by proof of service by the affected agency on all other parties in all petitions for review included in the notice. Service and proof of service shall be made as provided in Rule 25 of the Federal Rules of Appellate Procedure. The proof of service shall state the name and address of each person served and shall indicate the party represented by each. If a party is not represented by counsel, the proof of service shall indicate the name of the party and his or her last known address. The original proof of service shall be submitted by the affected agency for filing with the Clerk of the Panel and copies thereof shall be sent by the affected agency to each person included within the proof of service.

(b) The proof of service pertaining to notices of multicircuit petitions for review shall certify that copies of the notices have been mailed or otherwise delivered by the affected agency for filing to the clerk of each circuit court of appeals in which a petition for review is pending that is included in the notice.

(Added May 3, 1993, eff. July 1, 1993, and amended Sept. 1, 1998, eff. Nov. 2, 1998; Apr. 2, 2001, eff. Apr. 2, 2001.)

Rule 25.4. Form of Notices

(a) Each notice of multicircuit petitions for review shall be

    (i) flat and unfolded;

    (ii) plainly written, typed in double space, printed or prepared by means of a duplicating process, without erasures or interlineations which materially deface it;

    (iii) on opaque, unglazed white paper (not onionskin);

    (iv) approximately 8–1/2 x 11 inches in size; and

    (v) fastened at the top-left corner without side binding or front or back covers.

(b) The heading on the first page of each notice of multicircuit petitions for review shall commence not less that three inches from the top of the page. Each notice shall bear the heading "Notice to the Judicial Panel on Multidistrict Litigation of Multicircuit Petitions for Review," followed by a brief caption identifying the involved agency, the relevant agency order, and the date of the order.

(c) The final page of each notice of multicircuit petitions for review shall contain the name, address and telephone number of the individual or individuals who submitted the notice on behalf of the agency.

(Added May 3, 1993, eff. July 1, 1993, and amended Sept. 1, 1998, eff. Nov. 2, 1998; Apr. 2, 2001, eff. Apr. 2, 2001.)

Rule 25.5. Service of Panel Consolidation Order

(a) The Clerk of the Panel shall serve the Panel's consolidation order on the affected agency through the individual or individuals, as identified in Rule 25.4(c) of these Rules, who submitted the notice of multicircuit petitions for review on behalf of the agency.

(b) That individual or individuals, or anyone else designated by the agency, shall promptly serve the Panel's consolidation order on all other parties in all petitions for review included in the Panel's consolidation order, and shall promptly submit a proof of that service to the Clerk of the Panel. Service and proof of that service shall also be governed by Rule 25.3 of these Rules.

(c) The Clerk of the Panel shall serve the Panel's consolidation order on the clerks of all circuit courts of appeals that were among the candidates for the Panel's random selection.

(Added May 3, 1993, eff. July 1, 1993, and amended Sept. 1, 1998, eff. Nov. 2, 1998; Apr. 2, 2001, eff. Apr. 2, 2001.)

PART VI

APPELLATE PROCEDURE

Table of Sections

§ 6.1   Introduction

The rules and procedures for appealing a district court's judgment or order are no longer included in the Federal Rules of Civil Procedure, as they once were. Since 1968, these rules and procedures have been set forth in the "Federal Rules of Appellate Procedure", as supplemented by the local rules adopted by each of the various courts of appeals.

In-depth, rule-by-rule commentary regarding the federal appeals rules is beyond the scope of this text. However, the following preview of federal appellate procedure is included for the practitioner's reference. This preview is intended only to orient the practitioner to the general procedures governing appeals in the federal courts; this section is *not* a substitute for careful study of both the Federal Rules of Appellate Procedure and the local rules applicable to the pertinent court of appeals.

§ 6.2   Step One: Appealability

CORE CONCEPT

Not every order entered by a federal district judge is immediately appealable to the courts of appeals. Instead, litigants are generally required to wait until the lawsuit is completed in the district court—until there is a "final order" in the case—before an appeal from any of the district court's rulings may be taken.[1] This "finality" doctrine was

---

1. *See Digital Equip. Corp. v. Desktop Direct, Inc.*, 511 U.S. 863, 868, 114 S.Ct. 1992, 1996, 128 L.Ed.2d 842 (1994)(noting federal court practice that litigants are entitled to only a single appeal in their case, that this single appeal is deferred until the district court enters its final judgment, and that the appeal may include claims of trial error from every stage of the litigation).

designed to limit the expense, delays, burdens, and inefficiencies of repeated, successive appeals in a single case.[2] Important exceptions to this finality or "final order" doctrine exist, however.

> *NOTE:* Practitioners must exercise great care in determining an order's immediate appealability. When an order is immediately appealable, a delay in taking the appeal may forever foreclose the right of appeal. When an order is not immediately appealable, the premature filing of an appeal may be dismissed summarily.

APPLICATIONS

Threshold Nature of Appellate Jurisdiction

Federal appellate jurisdiction is not assumed, nor can it be waived by the parties' failure to assert the absence of jurisdiction. Instead, the courts of appeals have a separate, special obligation to confirm the presence of appellate jurisdiction, even where the parties to the appeal are prepared to concede it.[3] Moreover, if the appellate court independently determines that the trial court lacked subject matter jurisdiction over the dispute, the court of appeals has jurisdiction over the appeal for the limited purpose of correcting the jurisdictional error only.[4]

Final Orders

Congress has vested the courts of appeals with jurisdiction to hear appeals from all "final orders" of the district courts.[5] Final orders are, thus, immediately appealable to the courts of appeals. A final order is a ruling that "ends the litigation on the merits and leaves nothing for the court to do but execute the judgment."[6]

---

2. The finality, or "final order", doctrine has several objectives. It codifies the deference the appellate courts owe to the trial courts as forums that are obligated to first decide the many questions of law and fact arising at trial. The doctrine thus protects the independence of the district judges. The doctrine also avoids the obstruction to proper appellate review that would come from permitting successive appeals from the many rulings issued in a litigation, from the date the complaint is served until final judgment is entered. The doctrine thus promotes judicial efficiency. *See Firestone Tire & Rubber Co. v. Risjord,* 449 U.S. 368, 374, 101 S.Ct. 669, 673, 66 L.Ed.2d 571 (1981). *See also Cobbledick v. United States,* 309 U.S. 323, 325, 60 S.Ct. 540, 541, 84 L.Ed. 783 (1940)(judicial administration's "momentum would be arrested by permitting separate reviews of the component elements in a unified cause").

3. *See Bender v. Williamsport Area Sch. Dist.,* 475 U.S. 534, 541, 106 S.Ct. 1326, 1331, 89 L.Ed.2d 501 (1986).

4. *See Bender v. Williamsport Area Sch. Dist.,* 475 U.S. 534, 541, 106 S.Ct. 1326, 1331, 89 L.Ed.2d 501 (1986).

5. *See* 28 U.S.C.A. § 1291.

6. *See Van Cauwenberghe v. Biard,* 486 U.S. 517, 521–22, 108 S.Ct. 1945, 1949, 100 L.Ed.2d 517 (1988)(quoting *Catlin v. United States,* 324 U.S. 229, 233, 65 S.Ct. 631, 633, 89 L.Ed. 911 (1945)). *Accord Cunningham v. Hamilton County,* 527 U.S. 198, 201–03, 119 S.Ct. 1915, 1919–20, 144 L.Ed.2d 184 (1999) (same, holding that order imposing sanctions on attorney for discovery abuses (under Federal Rules of Civil Procedure) was not a final order from which appeal would lie). *See Behrens v. Pelletier,* 516 U.S. 299, 304, 116 S.Ct. 834, 838, 133 L.Ed.2d 773 (1996)(commenting that finality prevents consideration of rulings that remain subject to revision).

Interlocutory Orders

Interlocutory orders are all other interim rulings by the district courts—rulings that do not end the litigation and that contemplate some type of further action by the trial judge. Interlocutory orders are generally not appealable immediately to the courts of appeals. Review of interlocutory orders must ordinarily wait until the district court enters its final order on the merits of the litigation. Under well-settled appellate tenets, litigants may, while appealing a final order, challenge all the preceding rulings previously entered by the trial court.[7]

There are statutory and case law exceptions to and "constructions" of the final order rule.

Partial Final Orders (Rule 54(b))

Ordinarily, a judgment as to less than all claims in a lawsuit, or as to less than all parties in a lawsuit, is not immediately appealable until all other claims affecting all other parties are finally resolved. However, the district court may, in the exercise of its discretion, convert such "partial" judgments into immediately appealable final orders by (a) finally resolving at least one claim or the rights and liabilities of at least one party, (b) expressly declaring that no just cause exists to delay the appeal from such a ruling, and (c) directing the entry of judgment on the ruling.[8] The purpose, prerequisites, and procedure for such immediately appealable "partial" judgments are discussed earlier in this text.[9]

Permitted Interlocutory Appeals (28 U.S.C. § 1292(a))

Certain rulings involving federal injunctions, receiverships, and admiralty orders are immediately appealable to the courts of appeals, notwithstanding that the rulings do not qualify as "final orders":

> *Injunctions:* Interlocutory orders that grant, continue, modify, refuse, or dissolve injunctions, or that refuse to dissolve or modify injunctions are appealable immediately.[10] This is considered a "narrowly tailored exception" to the general policy disfavoring piecemeal appeals.[11] (For purposes of appellate jurisdiction, an immediately appealable interlocutory injunction order has three features: (1) it is a court's clearly defined, understandable directive that a party act or refrain from acting, (2) it is enforceable through contempt, and (3) it gives some or all of the substantive relief sought in the complaint.[12])

7. *See Exxon Corp. v. St. Paul Fire & Marine Ins. Co.*, 129 F.3d 781, 784 (5th Cir.1997).

8. *See* Rule 54(b).

9. *See supra* Authors' Commentary to Rule 54(b).

10. 28 U.S.C.A. § 1292(a)(1).

11. *See Sahu v. Union Carbide Corp.*, 475 F.3d 465, 467 (2d Cir. 2007). *See also Carson v. Am. Brands, Inc.*, 450 U.S. 79, 84,

101 S.Ct. 993, 67 L.Ed.2d 59 (1981) (interlocutory appeals prohibited unless litigants can show that district court's interlocutory order might have "serious, perhaps irreparable, consequence" and that only effective challenge to order is by immediate appeal).

12. *See Alabama v. United States Army Corps of Eng'rs*, 424 F.3d 1117, 1128–29 (11th Cir.2005).

Receivers: Interlocutory orders that appoint receivers, or refuse orders to wind up receiverships or take steps to accomplish those purposes (*i.e.,* directing disposals of property) are appealable immediately.[13]

Admiralty: Decrees that determine the rights and liabilities of parties to admiralty cases in which appeals from final decrees are allowed, are appealable immediately.[14]

Discretionary Interlocutory Appeals (28 U.S.C. § 1292(b))

The district court may, in the exercise of its discretion,[15] choose to certify certain non-final, interlocutory orders as eligible for immediate appellate review.[16] The district court's certification does *not* require the court of appeals to immediately hear the appeal; instead, whether to entertain an immediate appeal from a certified interlocutory order remains subject to the court of appeals' discretion.[17] In fact, the court of appeals may deny the certified appeal "for any reason, including docket congestion".[18]

Certification by the district judge is not routinely granted, and such certified immediate appeals are reserved for "exceptional" cases,[19] and are "hen's teeth rare".[20] Liberal grants of interlocutory appeals are "bad policy", and threaten the appropriate division of responsibility between federal trial and appellate courts.[21] The purpose of the procedure is to avoid protracted litigation, to assure the quick resolution of complicated legal issues, and to allow appellate review of ephemeral questions of law that could be lost in the context of a complete and final record.[22] The procedure was not intended to serve a mere error-correction function.[23]

---

13. 28 U.S.C.A. § 1292(a)(2).

14. 28 U.S.C.A. § 1292(a)(3).

15. *See Swint v. Chambers County Comm'n,* 514 U.S. 35, 47, 115 S.Ct. 1203, 1210, 131 L.Ed.2d 60 (1995) (noting that Congress conferred upon district courts the "first line discretion to allow interlocutory appeals").

16. *See* 28 U.S.C.A. § 1292(b).

17. *See* 28 U.S.C.A. § 1292(b). *See also Van Cauwenberghe v. Biard,* 486 U.S. 517, 530, 108 S.Ct. 1945, 1953, 100 L.Ed.2d 517 (1988) (noting that Court of Appeals may, in its discretion, determine that certified order warrants immediate review); *Coopers & Lybrand v. Livesay,* 437 U.S. 463, 475, 98 S.Ct. 2454, 2461, 57 L.Ed.2d 351 (1978) (noting that even if the district court certifies the order, the appellant must still persuade the Court of Appeals that "exceptional circumstances" justify hearing the appeal immediately); *Tidewater Oil Co. v. United States,* 409 U.S. 151, 173 n. 50, 93 S.Ct. 408, 421 n. 50, 34 L.Ed.2d 375 (1972) (noting Court of Appeals' discretion).

18. *Coopers & Lybrand v. Livesay,* 437 U.S. 463, 475, 98 S.Ct. 2454, 2461, 57 L.Ed.2d 351 (1978).

19. *See Caterpillar Inc. v. Lewis,* 519 U.S. 61, 74, 117 S.Ct. 467, 475, 136 L.Ed.2d 437 (1996) (commenting that "[r]outine resort to § 1292(b) requests would hardly comport with Congress' design to reserve interlocutory review for 'exceptional' cases while generally retaining for the federal courts a firm final judgment rule"); *Coopers & Lybrand v. Livesay,* 437 U.S. 463, 475, 98 S.Ct. 2454, 2461, 57 L.Ed.2d 351 (1978) ("exceptional circumstances" must exist).

20. *See Camacho v. Puerto Rico Ports Auth.,* 369 F.3d 570, 573 (1st Cir. 2004).

21. *See Moorman v. UnumProvident Corp.,* 464 F.3d 1260, 1272 (11th Cir. 2006).

22. *See Weber v. United States,* 484 F.3d 154, 159 (2d Cir. 2007).

23. *See Weber v. United States,* 484 F.3d 154, 159 n.3 (2d Cir. 2007).

To qualify for certification, the district court must state in writing:

(1) That the order in question involves a "controlling question of law" (which generally means a question of "pure law", which the appellate court can resolve "quickly and cleanly" without laboring over the record[24]—such as the meaning of a regulatory, statutory, or constitutional provision or common law doctrine,[25] the resolution of which is *likely* (although not necessarily certain) to affect the future course of the litigation[26]); and

(2) There is "substantial ground for difference of opinion" on the legal issue the order resolves (which generally means either that there is conflicting legal authority on the disputed issue or that the issue is a particularly difficult or uncertain one of first impression);[27] and

(3) An immediate appeal from the interlocutory order may "materially advance" the ultimate termination of the litigation (which generally means that immediate appeal may avoid expensive and protracted litigation).[28]

24. *See McFarlin v. Conseco Servs., LLC*, 381 F.3d 1251, 1258 (11th Cir. 2004); *id.* at 1259 ("The legal question must be stated at a high enough level of abstraction to lift the question out of the details of the evidence or facts of a particular case and give it general relevance to other cases in the same area of law.").

25. *See Ahrenholz v. Board of Trustees of Univ. of Ill.*, 219 F.3d 674, 676 (7th Cir.2000).

26. *See Sokaogon Gaming Enter. Corp. v. Tushie–Montgomery Assocs., Inc.*, 86 F.3d 656, 659 (7th Cir.1996) ("controlling" if issue's resolution is "quite likely" to affect further course of litigation); *In re Baker & Getty Fin. Servs., Inc.*, 954 F.2d 1169, 1172 n. 8 (6th Cir.1992) (to be "controlling", all that must be shown is that issue's resolution on appeal could materially affect outcome of litigation in trial court); *Klinghoffer v. S.N.C. Achille Lauro Ed Altri– Gestione Motonave Achille Lauro in Amministrazione Straordinaria*, 921 F.2d 21, 24 (2d Cir.1990) ("controlling" if reversal on appeal would terminate lawsuit). *See also Katz v. Carte Blanche Corp.*, 496 F.2d 747, 755 (3d Cir.1974) ("controlling" means "serious to the conduct of the litigation, either practically or legally", and saving of district court's time and litigants' money are "highly relevant" factors).

27. *See McFarlin v. Conseco Servs., LLC*, 381 F.3d 1251, 1258 (11th Cir. 2004) (same); *White v. Nix*, 43 F.3d 374, 378 (8th Cir.1994) ("substantial ground for disagree-

ment" could be shown by sufficient number of conflicting and contradictory opinions); *In re Baker & Getty Fin. Servs., Inc.*, 954 F.2d 1169, 1172 (6th Cir.1992) (split among Circuits on issue); *Klinghoffer v. S.N.C. Achille Lauro Ed Altri–Gestione Motonave Achille Lauro in Amministrazione Straordinaria*, 921 F.2d 21, 25 (2d Cir.1990) (difficult issues of first impression). *But cf. In re Flor*, 79 F.3d 281, 284 (2d Cir.1996) (holding that mere presence of disputed issue of first impression is not, by itself, sufficient to show substantial ground for difference of opinion).

28. *See McFarlin v. Conseco Servs., LLC*, 381 F.3d 1251, 1259 (11th Cir. 2004) (resolution would "avoid a trial or otherwise substantially shorten the litigation"). *See also White v. Nix*, 43 F.3d 374, 378–79 (8th Cir.1994) (when case will proceed in substantially similar manner regardless of decision on appeal, Court of Appeals' review will not "materially advance" termination of litigation); *People Who Care v. Rockford Bd. of Educ. Dist. No. 205*, 921 F.2d 132, 134 (7th Cir.1991) (commenting that it was "hard to see how resolving the dispute one way or the other could 'materially advance the ultimate termination of the litigation' "); *Klinghoffer v. S.N.C. Achille Lauro Ed Altri–Gestione Motonave Achille Lauro in Amministrazione Straordinaria*, 921 F.2d 21, 25 (2d Cir.1990) (if Court of Appeals rules that jurisdiction is absent over one defendant, ruling would greatly assist litigation's ultimate termination).

The moving party must satisfy *all* of these criteria; unless each criterion is meet, the trial judge cannot grant the Rule 1292(b) certification.[29] If certification is granted, the trial judge generally should specify what question of law it finds to be "controlling"— although a failure to do so is not necessarily dispositive.[30] Certification is jurisdictional; if certification is not granted, the court of appeals lacks authority to hear the appeal under Section 1292(b).[31]

A party may move the district court for such a certification. There is no express time limit for seeking the trial judge to grant a Section 1292(b) certification, although unreasonably dilatory requests may be denied by the trial judge or refused by the courts of appeals.[32] If granted by the district judge, the party may petition the court of appeals within 10 days thereafter for permission to immediately appeal the certified question.[33] The scope of the appellate review is limited to the certified order. The court may not reach beyond that order to consider other, uncertified rulings by the trial judge.[34] But the court of appeals may address any issue that is "fairly included" within the certified order itself; review is limited by the order that is certified, not by the precise question found to be controlling.[35]

Collateral Order Doctrine

In addition to the Rule and statutory exceptions to the "final order" limitation, the Supreme Court has developed the common law "collateral order" doctrine, which recognizes that certain impor-

29. *See Ahrenholz v. Board of Trustees of Univ. of Ill.*, 219 F.3d 674, 676 (7th Cir.2000).

30. *See McFarlin v. Conseco Servs., LLC*, 381 F.3d 1251, 1264 (11th Cir. 2004) ("Given our caseload, when the district court hands us an entire case to sort through for ourselves we are likely to hand it right back. If the district court is unsure about which of the questions, if any, that are answered by its order qualify for certification under § 1292(b), it should not certify the order for review. If convinced that a particular question does qualify, the district court should tell us which question it is.").

31. *See In re Ford Motor Co., Bridgestone/Firestone North American Tire, LLC*, 344 F.3d 648, 654–55 (7th Cir. 2003) (noting jurisdictional nature, and how most courts hold that mandamus is not proper to compel district court to certify).

32. *See Richardson Elecs., Ltd. v. Panache Broad. of Pa., Inc.*, 202 F.3d 957, 958 (7th Cir.2000). *See also Ahrenholz v. Board of Trustees of Univ. of Ill.*, 219 F.3d 674, 675–76 (7th Cir.2000) (commenting that pe-

titions for certification must be filed in the district court within a "reasonable time" after the contested order is entered).

33. *See* 28 U.S.C.A. § 1292(b); Fed. R. App. P. 5. The district court may, in certain circumstances, rescue a party's failure to petition within 10 days by vacating and re-entering the certification order. Generally, this is permitted when the moving party is blameless and the delay is caused by the court itself or by a failure to timely receive the certification order. *See In re City of Memphis*, 293 F.3d 345, 348–50 (6th Cir. 2002) (discussing process and National case law on point).

34. *See Yamaha Motor Corp., U.S.A. v. Calhoun*, 516 U.S. 199, 205, 116 S.Ct. 619, 623, 133 L.Ed.2d 578 (1996).

35. *See Yamaha Motor Corp. v. Calhoun*, 516 U.S. 199, 205, 116 S.Ct. 619, 623, 133 L.Ed.2d 578 (1996) ("it is the order that is appealable, and not the controlling question identified by the district court"). *Accord Moorman v. UnumProvident Corp.*, 464 F.3d 1260, 1272 (11th Cir. 2006); *NVE, Inc. v. Dep't of Health & Human Servs.*, 436 F.3d 182, 196 (3d Cir.2006).

tant legal rulings—concededly collateral to the litigation's underlying merits—may nevertheless be deemed "final" and eligible for immediate appellate review. To qualify under the collateral order doctrine, the district court's order must:

(1) Be conclusive on the issue sought to be immediately appealed; and

(2) Resolve an "important question" that is completely separate from the underlying merits; and

(3) Be effectively unreviewable if the appeal were to await a final order on the merits.[36]

A failure to satisfy even one of these three requirements defeats the use of the collateral order doctrine.[37]

The collateral order exception represents a narrow, common law construction of the final order doctrine.[38] It is applied stringently and is never permitted to "swallow" the federal courts' general prohibition against piecemeal appeals.[39] Although collateral orders typically involve a claimed right to "avoid" trial (a right which would be lost and effectively unappealable later), the Supreme Court has rejected the notion that this characteristic alone justifies collateral order treatment.[40] Instead, the Court has ruled that true collateral orders are those that would imperil "a substantial public interest" if not immediately reviewed.[41]

Other Exceptions

Orders may be deemed immediately appealable for other special, common law reasons. For example, certain interlocutory orders may also be appealable immediately where they resolve the rights of one party to the potentially irreparable injury of another party.[42] The extensive case law that explains and defines the precise reach of these other, common law exceptions to the final order doctrine is beyond the scope of this text. When in doubt, practitioners should carefully research whether a particular district court ruling qualifies for immediate appellate review.

36. *See Will v. Hallock,* ___ U.S. ___, ___, 126 S.Ct. 952, 956, 163 L.Ed.2d 836 (2006); *Coopers & Lybrand v. Livesay,* 437 U.S. 463, 468–69, 98 S.Ct. 2454, 2457–58, 57 L.Ed.2d 351 (1978); *Cohen v. Beneficial Indus. Loan Corp.,* 337 U.S. 541, 546, 69 S.Ct. 1221, 1226, 93 L.Ed. 1528 (1949). *Accord Sell v. United States,* 539 U.S. 166, 176, 123 S.Ct. 2174, 2182, 156 L.Ed.2d 197 (2003); *Cunningham v. Hamilton County,* 527 U.S. 198, 201–203, 119 S.Ct. 1915, 1919–20, 144 L.Ed.2d 184 (1999).

37. *See Gulfstream Aerospace Corp. v. Mayacamas Corp.,* 485 U.S. 271, 276, 108 S.Ct. 1133, 99 L.Ed.2d 296 (1988).

38. *See Houston Cmty. Hosp. v. Blue Cross & Blue Shield of Tex., Inc.,* 481 F.3d 265, 268 (5th Cir. 2007).

39. *See Digital Equip. Corp. v. Desktop Direct, Inc.,* 511 U.S. 863, 868, 114 S.Ct. 1992, 1996, 128 L.Ed.2d 842 (1994).

40 *See Will v. Hallock,* ___ U.S. ___, ___, 126 S.Ct. 952, 958, 163 L.Ed.2d 836 (2006).

41 *See Will v. Hallock,* ___ U.S. ___, ___, 126 S.Ct. 952, 959, 163 L.Ed.2d 836 (2006) (offering, as examples, the need to respect the separation of powers, to preserve the efficiency of government and the initiative of its officials, to respect a State's dignitary interests, and to mitigate the government's advantage over the individual).

42. *See Forgay v. Conrad,* 47 U.S. (6 How.) 201, 201, 12 L.Ed. 404 (1848)(allowing immediate appeal from order directing delivery of property to appellee).

Federal Courts §§ 290(1)–291(5) et seq.

West's Key No. Digests, Federal Courts ⊙551–600.

§ 6.3   Step Two: Time for Taking an Appeal

CORE CONCEPT

In civil cases, an appeal generally must be taken within 30 days after the entry of the disputed judgment or order.[43] This time for appeal is mandatory and jurisdictional.[44] Except for extensions narrowly permitted by the Rules of Appellate Procedure, the time period may not be waived, even for good cause shown.[45] A failure to file a timely appeal will forfeit that party's right of appeal.

APPLICATIONS

Dated From "Entry" of Judgment or Order

For purposes of timeliness on appeal, a judgment or order is "entered" when the formal judgment is filed by the district court in accordance with Federal Rule of Civil Procedure 58 and entered by the district court on its docket in accordance with Federal Rule of Civil Procedure 79(a).[46]

> *Note:* The "separate document" requirement of Rule 58 was significantly amended in 2002, and case law precedent decided before that amendment must be cited with great care.[47] When the "separate document" requirement applies, the time for appeal will not begin to run until the "separate document" prerequisite is satisfied or the 150–day period expires.[48] However, the Rules now contain this 150–day outside time limit to prevent litigants from having "forever" to appeal.[49]

When United States Is a Party

When the United States or a federal officer or agency is a party to the litigation, the parties have 60 days after the entry of the

---

43. Fed. R. App. P. 4(a)(1)(A). *See Selkridge v. United of Omaha Life Ins. Co.*, 360 F.3d 155, 160–61 (3d Cir.2004).

44. *See Browder v. Director, Dep't of Corrections*, 434 U.S. 257, 264, 98 S.Ct. 556, 560, 54 L.Ed.2d 521 (1978); *Dieser v. Continental Cas. Co.*, 440 F.3d 920, 923 (8th Cir. 2006); *Intera Corp. v. Henderson*, 428 F.3d 605, 611 (6th Cir. 2005).

45 *See Benn v. First Judicial Dist. of Pa.*, 426 F.3d 233, 237 (3d Cir. 2005).

46. Fed. R. App. P. 4(a)(7). *Cf. Selletti v. Carey*, 173 F.3d 104, 109 (2d Cir.1999) (although appeal was taken more than 30 days after order was entered, appeal was never-theless proper where district court had never entered separate judgment on the docket, as Rule 58 requires).

47. *See* Authors' Commentary to Rule 58 (discussing text and effect of 2002 amendments to Rule 58's "separate document" requirement).

48. *See* Rule 58. *See also Freudensprung v. Offshore Tech. Servs., Inc.*, 379 F.3d 327, 337 (5th Cir.2004).

49. *See Cambridge Holdings Group, Inc. v. Federal Ins. Co.*, 489 F.3d 1356, 1363 (D.C.Cir. 2007); *Burnley v. City of San Antonio*, 470 F.3d 189, 195 (5th Cir. 2006).

disputed judgment or order in which to take an appeal.[50] This 60–day period applies to all parties in the case—the federal parties as well as all others.

When United States Is *Not* a Party

In all other cases, the parties have 30 days after the entry of the disputed judgment or order in which to take an appeal.[51]

When Opponent Appeals

After one party takes an appeal, all other parties to the litigation have at least 14 days thereafter in which to take their own appeals.[52] The parties receive the benefit of this 14–day "extension" period even if the original notice of appeal is defective or otherwise is dismissed.[53]

Some courts of appeals have ruled that this 14–day period is mandatory and jurisdictional—if the time period lapses, the right to cross-appeal is irretrievably lost.[54] Other courts of appeals take a different view. These courts conclude that the 14–day period is simply "proper procedure", but not jurisdictional; they reason that appellate jurisdiction was already properly invoked with the filing of the *original* notice of appeal (*i.e.*, the one to which the cross-notice would be filed) and, thus, the court enjoys the authority to adjudicate fully the entire appeal before it.[55] These courts would permit the 14–day period to be excused in a proper circumstance.

Computing Time For Taking Appeal

The period within which an appeal must be taken is calculated according to the counting method set in the federal appellate rules. The period[56] is calculated: (1) by *excluding* the day of the event that triggers the period; and (2) by *including* the last day of the period *unless* the last day is a Saturday, Sunday, legal holiday, or day on which weather or other conditions make the clerk's office inaccessible.[57]

50. Fed. R. App. P. 4(a)(1)(B).

51. Fed. R. App. P. 4(a)(1)(A).

52. Fed. R. App. P. 4(a)(3)(party may file notice of appeal within 14 days after first notice of appeal was filed or within the 30 or 60 day period prescribed in Rule 4(a), whichever period is longer).

53. *See In re Julien Co.*, 146 F.3d 420, 423 (6th Cir.1998) (applying 14–day extension rule even where first appeal was dismissed for lack of standing).

54. *See Johnson v. Teamsters Local 559*, 102 F.3d 21, 29 (1st Cir.1996); *EF Operating Corp. v. American Bldgs.*, 993 F.2d 1046, 1049 n. 1 (3d Cir.1993); *Francis v. Clark Equip. Co.*, 993 F.2d 545, 552–53 (6th Cir.1993).

55. *See Mendocino Env'l Ctr. v. Mendocino County*, 192 F.3d 1283, 1297 (9th Cir.

1999); *Texport Oil Co. v. M/V Amolyntos*, 11 F.3d 361, 366 (2d Cir.1993).

56. If any appeal period is ever 6 days or less, the period is further modified by the federal appellate rules by *excluding* all intermediate Saturdays, Sundays, and legal holidays. *See* Fed. R. App. P. 26(a)(2).

57. *See* Fed. R. App. P. 26(a). *See also Keyser v. Sacramento City Unified Sch. Dist.*, 238 F.3d 1132, 1135 (9th Cir.) (ruling that 30th day of appeal period, which would have been Friday, November 26, 1999, was deemed extended until Monday, November 29, because the California clerk's office was officially closed on Friday (day after Thanksgiving), and appeal period cannot expire on a Saturday or Sunday), *amended and superseded on other grounds*, 265 F.3d 741 (9th Cir.2001).

Suspending Time For Appeal by Filing Post–Trial Motions

The timely filing of certain post-trial motions will suspend the time for appeal.[58] The post-trial motions that qualify for this suspension effect are:

- Motions for judgment as a matter of law, under Federal Rule of Civil Procedure 50(b);

- Motions to alter or supplement findings of fact, under Federal Rule of Civil Procedure 52(b);

- Motions for attorney's fees, under Federal Rule of Civil Procedure 54(d), but only if the district court extends the time for appeal in accordance with Federal Rule of Civil Procedure 58; and

- Motions to alter or amend the judgment, under Federal Rule of Civil Procedure 59;

- Motions for a new trial, under Federal Rule of Civil Procedure 59; and

- Motions for relief from a judgment or order, under Federal Rule of Civil Procedure 60, but only if such motion is served within 10 days after entry of judgment.

These motions need not be successful in order to extend the appeal period.[59] But the motions must be filed timely; an untimely filed post-trial motion will *not* suspend the appeal time.[60] (There is, however, developing case law that when such an untimely motion is filed, but not objected to by the non-moving party, the timeliness objection may be deemed forfeited through waiver.[61]) Once the district court grants or denies the post-trial motion, the time for appeal begins to run.

Explicit or Implicit Post–Trial Rulings as Appellate Trigger

The courts of appeals are divided on the issue of whether the district court must *expressly* rule on all pending post-trial motions before the appeal clock resumes ticking. The majority rule holds that the appeal time remains tolled until the trial court explicitly grants or denies the pending post-trial motions.[62] The minority view holds that the appeal period begins to run as soon as the district court enters the judgment (interpreting the entry as an implicit denial of the post-trial motions).[63]

58. *See* Fed. R. App. P. 4(a)(4)(A).

59. *See Urso v. United States*, 72 F.3d 59, 61 (7th Cir.1995).

60. *See Panhorst v. United States*, 241 F.3d 367, 370 (4th Cir.2001).

61. *See Wilburn v. Robinson*, 480 F.3d 1140, 1147–48 (D.C.Cir. 2007).

62. *See Havird Oil Co. v. Marathon Oil Co.*, 149 F.3d 283 (4th Cir.1998) (holding that district court must explicitly dispose of all outstanding post-trial motions before appeal period resumes).

63. *See Dunn v. Truck World, Inc.*, 929 F.2d 311, 313 (7th Cir.1991) (holding that entry of judgment is implicitly the order denying a post-trial motion).

Successive Post–Trial Motions

Most courts of appeals have ruled that after the time for appeal has been *once* extended by the filing of a tolling post-trial motion, the appeal period can not be suspended *again* by the filing of a *subsequent* post-trial motion.[64]

Extensions of Time by District Court for Filing an Appeal

The district court may extend the time for appeal only in two narrow circumstances–(1) for excusable neglect/good cause or (2) when there is a failure to receive the order.

- *Excusable Neglect* or *Good Cause:* Upon a showing of either excusable neglect or good cause, the district court may briefly extend the time for appeal.[65] To obtain such an extension, the movant *must* seek the extension within the original 30–day appeal period itself or within 30 days after the original appeal period expires.[66] The district court may only extend the time for appeal for 30 days after the original appeal period expires, or for 10 days after the order granting the motion for extension is granted, whichever time is later.[67] The presence of *either* excusable neglect or good cause can justify an extension by the district court.[68]

- *Excusable Neglect Defined:* Excusable neglect applies in circumstances involving fault, and seeks an extension typically made necessary by something that should have been within the movant's control.[69] Whether the neglect is "excusable" is a determination vested to the district court's discretion.[70] In evaluating whether "excusable neglect" exists, the courts will assess the risk of prejudice to the non-moving party, the length of the delay, the delay's potential impact on the

64. *See Andrews v. E.I. Du Pont De Nemours & Co.*, 447 F.3d 510, 515–16 (7th Cir.2006); *Johnson v. Teamsters Local 559*, 102 F.3d 21, 29–30 (1st Cir.1996); *Glinka v. Maytag Corp.*, 90 F.3d 72 (2d Cir.1996).

65. *See* Fed. R. App. P. 4(a)(5).

66. *See* Fed.R.App.P. 4(a)(5). *See also Cohen v. Empire Blue Cross & Blue Shield*, 142 F.3d 116, 118 (2d Cir.1998) (holding that district court lacks jurisdiction to grant extension that is not filed within 30–day grace period).

67. Fed.R.App.P. 4(a)(5)(C). *Cf. Harris v. Ballard*, 158 F.3d 1164, 1166 (11th Cir. 1998) (holding that 30–day extension runs from date original appeal expires, *not* 30 days from date extension motion is granted).

68. *See* Fed. R. App. P. 4(a)(5)(A). *See also id.* advisory committee notes to 2002 amendments. *See also Gibbons v. United States*, 317 F.3d 852, 854 n.3 (8th Cir.2003) (noting that either is sufficient, and observing that the recent Rule amendment cor-

rected an earlier, contrary interpretation that "good cause" applied to motions filed before original deadline expired and "excusable neglect" applied during the 30 days thereafter).

69. *See* Fed. R. App. P. 4(a)(5)(A) advisory committee notes to 2002 amendments.

70. *See Gibbons v. United States*, 317 F.3d 852, 853–54 (8th Cir.2003); *Farthing v. City of Shawnee*, 39 F.3d 1131, 1134 n. 1 (10th Cir.1994). The courts of appeals are divided on the standard to be applied to Rule 4(a)(5) motions for extensions. The majority view holds that "good cause" is required to justify extension motions filed before the expiration of the original timely appeal period, and "excusable neglect" is required to warrant an extension sought after the expiration of the time period. *See Virella–Nieves v. Briggs & Stratton Corp.*, 53 F.3d 451, 453 (1st Cir. 1995)(summarizing majority view).

proceedings, the reason for the delay and (especially whether that reason was within the reasonable control of the moving party), and the moving party's good faith.[71] These factors are not given equal weight–the excuse offered for the delay often has the greatest impact.[72] The "excusable neglect" analysis thus generally requires something more than an attorney's busy caseload or an oversight in consulting or a misreading of the procedural rules to justify an extension of the time for appeal.[73]

- *Good Cause Defined:* Good cause applies in circumstances where there is no fault (excusable or otherwise), and seeks an extension typically made necessary by something that was not within the movant's control.[74]

- *Failure to Receive Order:* If the district court determines that a party entitled to notice of the entry of a judgment or order did not timely receive such notice, the court may extend the time for appeal, but only under the following conditions:

  - *Party's non-receipt within 21 days:* The court must first find that the party did not receive formal Rule 77(d) notice within 21 days after entry of the judgment or order;[75] *and*

  - *Party promptly moved to reopen the appeal period*: The non-noticed party must promptly move the district court

71. *See Pioneer Inv. Servs. Co. v. Brunswick Assocs. Ltd. P'ship*, 507 U.S. 380, 395, 113 S.Ct. 1489, 1498, 123 L.Ed.2d 74 (1993)(assessing "excusable neglect" in bankruptcy rules context). *See also Bishop v. Corsentino*, 371 F.3d 1203, 1206–07 (10th Cir. 2004) (listing factors).

72. *See Gibbons v. United States*, 317 F.3d 852, 854 (8th Cir.2003).

73. *See Midwest Employers Cas. Co. v. Williams*, 161 F.3d 877, 879–80 (5th Cir. 1998) (holding that misinterpretations of the Federal Rules could constitute excusable neglect in a "rare case", where the Rule at issue is unambiguous, district court's determination that neglect was inexcusable is "virtually unassailable"); *Advanced Estimating Sys., Inc. v. Riney*, 130 F.3d 996, 998 (11th Cir.1997) (holding that counsel's misunderstanding of a procedural rule's plain language cannot qualify as such excusable neglect); *United States v. Vaccaro*, 51 F.3d 189, 191 (9th Cir.1995) (commenting that inadvertence or mistake by counsel will not qualify as excusable neglect); *Weinstock v. Cleary, Gottlieb, Steen & Hamilton*, 16 F.3d 501, 503 (2d Cir.1994)(noting that "excusable neglect" is never satisfied by a showing of an inability or refusal to read and comprehend the plain language of the Federal Rules); *Gochis v. Allstate Ins. Co.*, 16 F.3d 12, 14 (1st Cir.1994)(to constitute "excusable neglect", the moving party must demonstrate unique or extraordinary circumstances warranting an extension). *Cf. Zipperer v. School Bd. of Seminole County*, 111 F.3d 847, 849–50 (11th Cir.1997) (finding excusable neglect where notice was filed one-day late, having been mailed to the Court, by in-State mailing, six days before filing, noting that normal mail delivery is three days).

74. *See* Fed. R. App. P. 4(a)(5)(A) advisory committee notes to 2002 amendments. *See also Bishop v. Corsentino*, 371 F.3d 1203, 1207 (10th Cir.2004).

75. *See* Fed. R. App. P. 4(a)(6)(A). The 2005 amendments to Rule 4(a) make clear that this 21–day trigger requires actual, formal notice under Rule 77(d). Thus, if no formal Rule 77(d) notice was served within 21 days, but the party nevertheless receives informal notice of the entry, an extension of the appeal time may still be sought. *See* Fed. R. App. P. 4(a)(6)(A) advisory committee note (2005).

to reopen the appeal period within 7 days after receiving or observing written notice of the entry from any source;[76] *and*

- *Party moved no later than 180 days after entry:* The maximum window for an appeal extension can never last longer than 180 days (thus obligating practitioners to routinely check the court dockets, even when no formal notice has been received);[77] *and*

- *No party is prejudiced by the extension:* The court must find that no party would be prejudiced by granting an appeal period extension;[78] *and*

- *Actual extension may last only 14 days:* If an extension is granted, it will compel the non-noticed party to file the appeal within 14 days.[79]

The burden of demonstrating non-receipt rests with the moving party.[80] Evidence that the order was properly mailed creates a presumption of receipt, but this presumption may be defeated by the moving party's specific factual denial of receipt; the district court, in such cases, will assess the proof and make a considered factual determination on the question of receipt or non-receipt.[81] Motions for extensions due to non-receipt are committed to the district court's discretion.[82] In exercising that discretion, the district court may deny this extension even where the litigant otherwise satisfies the technical elements of the extension rule (provided, of course, that the basis for the court's denial is something other than the district court's own assessment of the merits of the appeal).[83] The moving party is ordinarily not required to demonstrate "excusable neglect" in order to justify such relief.[84]

76. *See* Fed. R. App. P. 4(a)(6)(B). The extension window will start to run on the day the party receives or observes "written" notice from "any source" (*e.g.*, by fax, e-mail, viewing a website entry, etc.), and will last for only 7 days. *See* Fed. R. App. P. 4(a)(6)(B) advisory committee note (2005). Oral notice, "no matter how specific, reliable, or unequivocal", will not start the 7-day period running. *Id.*

77. *See* Fed. R. App. P. 4(a)(6)(B).

78. *See* Fed. R. App. P. 4(a)(6)(C).

79. *See* Fed. R. App. P. 4(a)(6).

80. *See Nunley v. City of Los Angeles,* 52 F.3d 792, 795 (9th Cir.1995).

81. *See Nunley v. City of Los Angeles,* 52 F.3d 792, 796 (9th Cir.1995)(noting that, once specific factual denial of receipt is made, district court can give no further weight to presumption of receipt). *Cf. Benavides v. Bureau of Prisons,* 79 F.3d 1211,

1214 (D.C.Cir.1996)(holding that 7-day period does not begin to run until party receives notice of the judgment's or order's entry "directly 'from the clerk or any party'"; inquiry notice of an order, from a second-hand source not connected with the dispute, does not begin the 7-day period).

82. *See* Fed. R. App. P. 4(a)(6)("The district court ... *may* extend the time for filing a notice of appeal ...")(emphasis added).

83. *See Kuhn v. Sulzer Orthopedics, Inc.,* — F.3d —, —, 2007 WL 2287742, at *3 (6th Cir. 2007); *Arai v. American Bryce Ranches Inc.,* 316 F.3d 1066, 1069–71 (9th Cir.2003).

84. *See Benavides v. Bureau of Prisons,* 79 F.3d 1211, 1214 (D.C.Cir.1996)(showings of excusable neglect and good cause are not required because the court supposes that the party's tardiness is not his or her fault;

Note: This 180–day extension rule provides the *exclusive* method for extensions based on a party's failure to receive notice of the judgment or order. Seeking relief from orders under other rules, such as Rule 60(b), cannot be used to circumvent this 180–day limitation.[85]

Extensions of Time by Court of Appeals for Filing an Appeal

The courts of appeals may not grant litigants an extension of the time for appeal under any circumstances.[86]

Premature Appeals

A notice of appeal is *not* necessarily fatally defective merely because it is filed too quickly. If the notice is filed after the district court announces its decision, but before the judgment or order is formally entered, the notice of appeal may be held in abeyance and deemed "filed" on the day the district court formally enters the judgment or order (at least as to orders that would be immediately appealable upon entry).[87] This rule, however, will likely not apply to orders that are clearly interlocutory and, thus, would not be immediately appealable upon entry.[88]

If the notice of appeal is filed after the district court formally enters the judgment or order, but before the district court rules upon those types of post-trial motions that suspend the time for appeal, the notice is deemed to lie dormant. The notice will become effective on the date the trial court rules on the outstanding post-trial motions.[89]

if the party is at fault (e.g., by negligently failing to notify the clerk of a change of address), the court may deny relief).

85. *See Vencor Hosps., Inc. v. Standard Life & Acc. Ins. Co.,* 279 F.3d 1306, 1310 (11th Cir.2002).

86. Fed. R. App. P. 26(b). *See Burnley v. City of San Antonio,* 470 F.3d 189, 192–93 (5th Cir. 2006); *Delta Airlines v. Butler,* 383 F.3d 1143, 1145 (10th Cir. 2004).

87. Fed. R. App. P. 4(a)(2). *See FirsTier Mortg. Co. v. Investors Mortg. Ins. Co.,* 498 U.S. 269, 276, 111 S.Ct. 648, 112 L.Ed.2d 743 (1991).

88. *See FirsTier Mortg. Co. v. Investors Mortg. Ins. Co.,* 498 U.S. 269, 276, 111 S.Ct. 648, 652, 112 L.Ed.2d 743 (1991). *Barrett ex rel. Estate of Barrett v. United States,* 462 F.3d 28, 34 (1st Cir.2006); *Carter v. Ashland, Inc.,* 450 F.3d 795, 796–97 (8th Cir. 2006); *Dieser v. Continental Cas. Co.,* 440 F.3d 920, 924 (8th Cir. 2006) *But cf. Cape May Greene, Inc. v. Warren,* 698 F.2d 179, 184–85 (3d Cir.1983) (distinguishing be-

tween unalterably interlocutory orders (such as discovery orders) and orders that, although interlocutory, would become final upon entry of judgment).

89. Fed. R. App. P. 4(a)(4)(B). *See Schroeder v. McDonald,* 55 F.3d 454, 458 (9th Cir.1995)(noting that prematurely filed notice of appeal is held in abeyance and become effective upon date of entry of order resolving Rule 59(e) post-trial motion); *United States v. One Hundred Twenty–Four Thousand Eight Hundred Thirteen Dollars ($124,813) in United States Currency,* 53 F.3d 108, 110 (5th Cir.1995)(ruling that claimant's notice of appeal would be treated as dormant until date post-judgment motion was decided). This Rule represents a change in earlier practice, which before 1993 held that a notice of appeal was a "nullity" if prematurely filed while post-trial motions remained pending. *See also Leader Nat'l Ins. Co. v. Industrial Indem. Ins. Co.,* 19 F.3d 444, 445 (9th Cir. 1994)(noting 1993 amendment's change to practice).

ADDITIONAL RESEARCH REFERENCES

C.J.S. Federal Courts §§ 293(5–17) et seq.

West's Key No. Digests, Federal Courts ⟶652–660.40.

§ 6.4   Step Three: Procedure for Taking an Appeal

CORE CONCEPT

A federal appeal is taken by filing a notice of appeal with the district court. Thus, there are essentially two "modest tasks" that must be completed before an appeal is properly taken: the appellants must give proper "notice" of their intent to appeal and they must deliver that notice "in time".[90]

APPLICATIONS

Contents of Notice of Appeal

A notice of appeal is typically a simple, one-page form that contains the case caption, specifies the party or parties taking the appeal, designates the challenged judgment or order, and identifies the court to which the appeal is taken.[91] Thus, the essential contents of a notice of appeal are three: (1) naming the party or parties taking the appeal; (2) naming the court to which the appeal is taken; and (3) naming the order that is being appealed.[92] The notice of appeal need not identify the appellees[93] nor should it contain the appealing party's assignment of errors or legal arguments.

- *Naming All Parties:* The parties to the appeal should each be individually named.[94] The failure to name each appealing party is dangerous practice.[95] The courts of appeals will only permit appeals from parties actually named on the notice and from parties whose intent to appeal is "objectively clear" from the notice.[96] Thus, for

---

90. *See Isert v. Ford Motor Co.*, 461 F.3d 756, 758 (6th Cir.2006).

91. Fed. R. App. P. 3(c)(1). *See* Fed. R. App. P. Appendix, Form 1.

92. *See Isert v. Ford Motor Co.*, 461 F.3d 756, 758 (6th Cir.2006); *Berrey v. Asarco Inc.*, 439 F.3d 636, 642 (10th Cir. 2006).

93. *See MIF Realty L.P. v. Rochester Assocs.*, 92 F.3d 752, 758 (8th Cir.1996) (Rules do not require specific listing of all appellees called upon to respond to the appeal); *Crawford v. Roane*, 53 F.3d 750, 752 (6th Cir.1995)(same).

94. *See* Fed. R. App. P. 3(c)(1)(A).

95. *See Agee v. Paramount Communications, Inc.*, 114 F.3d 395 (2d Cir.1997) (following entry of award of attorney's fees and costs against *both* party and party's attorney, party's attorney lost right to appeal where the notice of appeal listed only party as appellant).

96. Fed. R. App. P. 3(c)(4) & 1993 advisory committee note. *See Pugh v. Goord*, 345 F.3d 121, 124 n.2 (2d Cir. 2003) (although names of all appellants did not appear in caption, their names did appear in notice and, thus, were "objectively clear"); *Garcia v. Wash*, 20 F.3d 608 (5th Cir. 1994)(noting that appellant's references were sufficiently clear to show that appellant intended to appeal). This provision marks a change from earlier practice, which held that the failure to specifically name all appealing parties (for example, with the use of grouping phrases such as "et al.") pre-

example, using the phrase *"et al."* to describe the members of a certified class action should be adequate to appeal on behalf of all class members.[97] Even in that instance, however, the courts prefer a clearer designation of the identities of the appealing parties.[98]

- *Naming All Parts of Order Appealed From:* Each part of a separable judgment or separable order appealed from must be named.[99] Ordinarily, an appeal taken from the final judgment itself will support appellate review of all earlier interlocutory orders in the case,[100] so long as the intent to appeal from each particular interlocutory order is clear.[101] However, if a party chooses to state in the Notice of Appeal an intention to appeal from a particular order or ruling (*e.g.*, appealing from the order of November 10 granting summary judgment), the court of appeals may rule that the party has *not* also appealed from other rulings in the same case.[102] To ease the harsh effect of

cluded those parties' rights to appeal. *See also Spain v. Board of Educ. of Meridian Community Unit Sch. Dist. No. 101*, 214 F.3d 925, 929 (7th Cir.2000) (permitting appeal by "Mr. Spain" because, although not named in body of notice of appeal, his intent to appeal was otherwise clear from notice). *Cf. Torres v. Oakland Scavenger Co.*, 487 U.S. 312, 108 S.Ct. 2405, 101 L.Ed.2d 285 (1988).

97. *See Air Line Pilots Ass'n v. Continental Airlines*, 125 F.3d 120 (3d Cir.1997) (finding term "the LPP Claimants" sufficient to adequately identify appellants), *cert. denied*, 522 U.S. 1114, 118 S.Ct. 1049, 140 L.Ed.2d 113 (1998); *Olenhouse v. Commodity Credit Corp.*, 42 F.3d 1560, 1572 (10th Cir.1994)(commenting that use of phrase "et al." to identify group of appellants is discouraged, but where class has been certified, phrase provides ample notice for appeal on behalf of class). *Cf. Murphy v. Keystone Steel & Wire Co.*, 61 F.3d 560 (7th Cir.1995)(in class action, court had appellate jurisdiction only over named plaintiffs because only they were listed in the notice of appeal, and no other objective notice existed that the appeal was intended to be taken on behalf of the entire class).

98. *See Olenhouse v. Commodity Credit Corp.*, 42 F.3d 1560, 1572 n. 19 (10th Cir. 1994)(observing that the preferred means of identifying a class of appellants is by naming a designated member "as representative of the class").

99. *See* Fed. R. App. P. 3(c)(1)(B).

100. *See Newman v. Federal Exp. Corp.*, 266 F.3d 401, 404 (6th Cir.2001) (noting

that appeal from final judgment draws into question all prior non-final rulings and orders); *Trust Co. of La. v. N.N.P. Inc.*, 104 F.3d 1478, 1485–86 (5th Cir.1997) (commenting that appeal from final judgment preserves all prior orders intertwined with final judgment).

101. *See Lolli v. County of Orange*, 351 F.3d 410, 414–15 (9th Cir. 2003) (appellant presumed to appeal from merits of summary judgment motion, and not just denial of reconsideration). *Cf. C & S Acquisitions Corp. v. Northwest Aircraft, Inc.*, 153 F.3d 622 (8th Cir.1998) (principle did not apply where notice failed to give sufficient notice of intent to appeal separate, distinct issues).

102. *See Parkhill v. Minnesota Mut. Life Ins. Co.*, 286 F.3d 1051, 1058 (8th Cir.2002) (appeals from one order do not inherently imply intent to appeal from all other orders in case, and notice that manifests appeal from specific district court order precludes appellant from challenging other unlisted orders); *Newman v. Federal Exp. Corp.*, 266 F.3d 401, 404 (6th Cir.2001) (if appellant chooses to designate specific orders in Notice, only those determinations are appealed); *Trust Co. of La. v. N.N.P. Inc.*, 104 F.3d 1478, 1485–86 (5th Cir.1997) (court may not hear challenges to other rulings or orders not specified in notice, if party designates particular orders only and not final judgment); *MCI Telecomms. Corp. v. Teleconcepts, Inc.*, 71 F.3d 1086, 1092 (3d Cir.1995) (noting that court does not acquire jurisdiction over issues not designated in appeal).

this application, some courts of appeals will allow added information supplied in the party's "Docketing Statement" to supplement (and, perhaps, rescue) an otherwise insufficiently detailed Notice of Appeal.[103]

- *Naming Court of Appeals:* The notice of appeal must identify the specific court to which the appeal is being taken.[104]

Errors in Notice of Appeal

The appellate rules prescribing the contents of a notice of appeal are jurisdictional in nature,[105] although these rules are construed liberally.[106] Thus, appeal papers that are "technically at variance with the letter of Rule 3" may be excused if the appellant's actions are otherwise the functional equivalent of what the rules require.[107] The courts will apply an "intent" rule, testing whether the litigant's intention to seek appellate review is objectively clear; a litigant's subjective motivation is not dispositive.[108] Thus, where the litigant's intentions are clear, and the adversary has not been misled or otherwise prejudiced, the court of appeals may overlook a technical mistake.[109] An adversary is unlikely to be deemed misled or prejudiced if the appellant resolved any lack of clarity in the opening brief and the adversary thereby had notice and an opportunity to brief in response.[110] Nevertheless, whether the litigants comply

103. *See Trotter v. Regents of Univ. of N.M.,* 219 F.3d 1179, 1184 (10th Cir.2000) (holding that timely filed docketing statement that "clearly" describes the appellate issues will be accepted as the "functional equivalent" of a proper notice of appeal).

104. *See* Fed. R. App. P. 3(c)(1)(C). *Bradley v. Work,* 154 F.3d 704 (7th Cir. 1998). *But cf. United States v. Treto–Haro,* 287 F.3d 1000, 1002 n.1 (10th Cir.2002) (failure to name correct court will not warrant dismissal where intention to appeal to a certain court of appeals may be reasonably inferred from notice and where defect did not materially mislead appellee); *Dillon v. United States,* 184 F.3d 556 (6th Cir. 1999) (holding that where appeal may only be taken to one court, appeal is not defective merely because Notice of Appeal fails to name particular appellate court).

105. *See Smith v. Barry,* 502 U.S. 244, 248, 112 S.Ct. 678, 681, 116 L.Ed.2d 678 (1992); *Isert v. Ford Motor Co.,* 461 F.3d 756, 759 (6th Cir.2006).

106. *See Marie v. Allied Home Mortg. Corp.,* 402 F.3d 1, 8 (1st Cir. 2005); *Bogart v. Chapell,* 396 F.3d 548, 555 (4th Cir. 2005). *See also Isert v. Ford Motor Co.,* 461 F.3d 756, 763 (6th Cir.2006) ("Courts can, and should, work overtime to excuse errors of form but they cannot simultaneously excuse errors of form *and* function without

assuming authority to waive compliance with the Rules altogether."); *In re National Warranty Ins. Risk Retention Group,* 384 F.3d 959, 964 (8th Cir. 2004) ("We do not strictly construe the contents of the notice of appeal").

107. *See Smith v. Barry,* 502 U.S. 244, 248, 112 S.Ct. 678, 681, 116 L.Ed.2d 678 (1992); *Torres v. Oakland Scavenger Co.,* 487 U.S. 312, 316–17, 108 S.Ct. 2405, 2408, 101 L.Ed.2d 285 (1988). *See also Becker v. Montgomery,* 532 U.S. 757, 121 S.Ct. 1801, 149 L.Ed.2d 983 (2001) (holding that failure to timely sign the notice of appeal did not compel dismissal of the appeal; the error was curable and a timely signature was not a jurisdictional failing; *Isert v. Ford Motor Co.,* 461 F.3d 756, 759 (6th Cir.2006); *Berrey v. Asarco Inc.,* 439 F.3d 636, 642 (10th Cir. 2006).

108. *See Rinaldo v. Corbett,* 256 F.3d 1276, 1278–79 (11th Cir.2001).

109. *See Marie v. Allied Home Mortg. Corp.,* 402 F.3d 1, 8 (1st Cir. 2005); *Bogart v. Chapell,* 396 F.3d 548, 555 (4th Cir. 2005); *In re Nat'l Warranty Ins. Risk Retention Group,* 384 F.3d 959, 964 (8th Cir. 2004).

110. *See Bogart v. Chapell,* 396 F.3d 548, 555 (4th Cir. 2005).

literally or functionally, the rules must be satisfied before a court of appeals may entertain the appeal.[111]

Privacy Protection for Personal Data Identifiers

The vulnerability of electronically-accessible court files to privacy and security mischief prompted the adoption of special redaction and sealing privileges for certain civil cases.[112] In cases where these privileges applied at the district court level, the privileges will extend to the appeal as well.[113]

Notice Must Be *Filed* Timely

The notice of appeal must be actually filed with the clerk of court within the time allotted under the Rules for taking an appeal. Mailing the notice to the court or serving the notice on other parties is not sufficient.

> *Filing by Pro Se Prisoners:* A notice of appeal is deemed to be "filed" when a *pro se* prisoner deposits the notice into the prison's internal mail system.[114]

Place of Filing

A notice of appeal is filed with the clerk of the district court from which the appeal is taken.[115] However, mistakenly filing the notice with the court of appeals will *not* defeat the appeal. If the notice is filed with the court of appeals within the permitted time for taking an appeal, the appeals court clerk will note the date of filing and send the notice to the clerk of the district court.[116]

Electronic Filing

Each individual court of appeals may (but is not obligated to) permit the electronic filing of appeal papers.[117] In fact, the Appellate Rules now authorize a court of appeals to *require* electronic filing, so long as reasonable exceptions are allowed for litigants for whom such electronic filing would impose a hardship.[118]

Service Not Required

The appealing party need not serve the notice of appeal on all other parties; this service is made by the clerk of court.[119] The clerk's failure to serve the notice, however, does not defeat the appeal.[120]

> *Service Copies to the Court:* Although the appellant does not actually serve the notice of appeal on the other

---

111. *See Smith v. Barry,* 502 U.S. 244, 248, 112 S.Ct. 678, 681, 116 L.Ed.2d 678 (1992).

112. *See* Rule 5.2. *See also supra* Authors' Commentary to Rule 5.2.

113. *See* Fed. R. App. P. 25(a)(5).

114. Fed. R. App. P. 4(c)(requiring accompanying notarized statement or declaration).

115. Fed. R. App. P. 3(a).

116. Fed. R. App. P. 4(d).

117 *See* Fed. R. App. P. 25(a)(2)(D).

118 *See* Fed. R. App. P. 25(a)(2)(D) and advisory committee note to 2006 amendments.

119. Fed. R. App. P. 3(d)(1).

120. Fed. R. App. P. 3(d)(3).

parties, the appellant is required to provide the clerk's office with sufficient copies of the notice for service.[121]

Joint Appeals

Joint appeals may be taken by two or more parties whose similar interests make such joinder practicable.[122] Each plaintiff, however, must file a timely notice of appeal. The fact that some similarly situated plaintiffs timely appealed is immaterial; the appeal of each plaintiff must be appropriately noticed to the court.[123]

Consolidated Appeals

Upon its own motion or by motion of a party, the court of appeals may consolidate the appeals of different parties.[124]

Fees

The appealing party must pay to the district court both the district court fee for appeal and the court of appeals' docket fee.[125]

ADDITIONAL RESEARCH REFERENCES

Federal Courts §§ 282–301(48) et seq.

West's Key No. Digests, Federal Courts ⬤521–956.

§ 6.5   Step Four: Stays Pending Appeal

CORE CONCEPT

A party may seek a stay of judgment by filing such an application with the district court. In applications *not* involving stays of injunctions, receiverships, or accountings in patent infringement actions, a party may request a stay pending appeal by filing a supersedeas bond. Stay applications must be filed timely and, generally, initially in the district court.

APPLICATIONS

10–Day "Automatic" Stay

For a period of 10 days after a judgment is entered, the parties are barred from executing upon the judgment or pursuing further proceedings for its enforcement.[126] This automatic stay does *not* apply to judgments involving injunctions, judgments in receivership actions, or judgments or orders directing accountings in patent infringement actions.

Time to Apply for Stay

Applications for stay generally should be filed at the earliest possible opportunity. Because the automatic stay does not apply in

---

121. Fed. R. App. P. 3(a)(1).

122. Fed. R. App. P. 3(b)(1).

123. *See Wooden v. Board of Regents of Univ. Sys. of Ga.*, 247 F.3d 1262, 1273 (11th Cir.2001).

124. Fed. R. App. P. 3(b)(2).

125. Fed. R. App. P. 3(e).

126. *See* Rule 62(a).

certain injunction, receivership, and patent infringement circumstances, appellants in those cases do not enjoy the automatic 10–day stay period and the time for execution and enforcement will immediately arrive. Even in automatic stay cases, supersedeas bonds must first be approved by the court before any stay is effective.[127] Consequently, a delay in seeking a stay will expose the defeated party to execution and enforcement of the judgment.

Where to Apply for Stay

Ordinarily, stays pending appeal must be filed first with the district court.[128] Only in those circumstances where applying in the district court is not practicable, or where the district court has denied the request or failed to grant all the relief requested, may a party request a stay in the court of appeals.[129]

Procedure for Stay Applications in the District Court

In cases that do not involve injunctions, receivers, or accountings in patent infringement cases, the posting of a supersedeas bond—after it has been approved by the court—will stay execution and enforcement of the judgment.[130]

In cases involving injunctions, the district court may, in its discretion, grant a stay of the injunction pending appeal.[131] To obtain such a stay, the moving party must generally make the traditional showing required for any injunction: strong likelihood of success on the merits, irreparable injury, no substantial harm to others, and no damage to the public interest.[132] The court may condition such a stay upon the posting of a bond or other appropriate security.[133]

Procedure for Stay Applications in the Court of Appeals

In applying for a stay in the court of appeals, the moving party must make several showings in the motion papers:[134]

a. *Proceedings Before Trial Court:* The motion must show why a stay application cannot be practicably directed to the district judge, or that the district judge has denied a stay or failed to grant all the relief requested (the district court's reasons must be set forth); *and*

b. *Reasons for Relief:* The motion must show the reasons for the relief requested, and set forth the facts relied upon in support of that showing. Relevant parts of the record shall be included and, where the facts relied upon are subject to dispute, supporting affidavits or other sworn statements shall also be included; *and*

---

127. *See* Rule 62(d).

128. *See* Fed. R. App. P. 8(a)(1).

129. *See* Fed. R. App. P. 8(a)(2).

130. *See* Rule 62(d).

131. *See* Rule 62(c).

132. *See supra* Author's Commentary to Rule 62(c).

133. *See* Rule 62(c).

134. *See* Fed. R. App. P. 8(a)(2)(A)–(2)(D).

c. *Reasonable Notice:* Reasonable notice of the motion shall be given to the non-moving party; *and*

d. *Disposition:* The motion will ordinarily be resolved by a panel or division of the court, unless exceptional circumstances justify submitting the motion to a single judge; *and*

e. *Bond or Security:* If the motion is granted, the court of appeals can condition the stay upon the filing in the district court of a bond or other appropriate security.[135]

§ 6.6   Step Five: The Appeal Process

CORE CONCEPT

Once the appeal is timely filed, the court of appeals will mail to each party a briefing notice that will schedule the filing of an Appellant's Brief, an Appellee's Brief, and an Appellant's Reply Brief. Thereafter, the court of appeals may schedule oral argument, the case will be submitted, and a written disposition on appeal will be filed.

APPLICATIONS

Effect of Appeal

Once the appeal is taken, jurisdiction over the case passes from the district court to the court of appeals.[136] The district court thereafter enjoys only the narrow power to perform ministerial functions, issue stays and injunctions pending appeal, and, in certain instances, award counsel fees. An appeal from a final judgment generally draws into question (and thus will permit appellate review of) all non-final rulings and orders that preceded the judgment.[137]

Compliance With Schedule and Procedures

Failure to comply with the court of appeals' schedule and procedures is ground for such action as the court of appeals deems appropriate, including denial of right to participate in oral argument or even dismissal of the appeal itself.[138]

Designation of the Record and Statement of Issues

The "record" on appeal consists of (1) the original papers and exhibits filed in the trial court, (2) the transcript, and (3) a certified copy of docket entries.[139] The "record" encompasses not just those exhibits admitted into evidence, but may include items presented for admission and denied by the district court.[140] Within 10 days after

---

135. *See* Fed. R. App. P. 8(a)(2)(E).

136. *See Griggs v. Provident Consumer Discount Co.,* 459 U.S. 56, 58, 103 S.Ct. 400, 402, 74 L.Ed.2d 225 (1982)(noting that notice of appeal is an event of jurisdictional significance, conferring jurisdiction on the Court of Appeals and divesting the district court of control over those aspects of the litigation involved in the appeal).

137. *See National Ecological Found. v. Alexander,* ___ F.3d ___, ___, 2007 WL 2213278, at *7 (6th Cir. 2007); *Trust Co. of La. v. N.N.P. Inc.,* 104 F.3d 1478, 1485–86 (5th Cir. 1997).

138. *See* Fed. R. App. P. 3(a)(2).

139. *See Morton Int'l, Inc. v. A.E. Staley Mfg. Co.,* 343 F.3d 669, 682 (3d Cir.2003).

140. *See Morton Int'l, Inc. v. A.E. Staley Mfg. Co.,* 343 F.3d 669, 682 (3d Cir.2003).

filing the notice of appeal, the appealing party must order those portions of the transcript that are necessary for the appeal. Unless the appellant orders the entire transcript, the appellant must, during this same 10–day period, file a statement of the issues for appeal and a list of the intended contents of the Appendix. The appellee may thereafter serve a counter-designation of additional portions of the transcript to be included.[141]

> *Note*: Some districts have promulgated Local Rules requiring the appellant to transcribe the entire proceedings.[142] Practitioners should be diligent in consulting their local rules for guidance on this point.

Briefing Procedures

Briefing procedures are generally set in the Federal Rules of Appellate Procedure, but additional provisions vary by Local Rules among the different courts of appeals. The practitioner should always consult the Local Rules for these additional procedures.

Content of Appellate Briefs:	Rule 28
Filing/Service of Briefs:	Rules 25 & 31
Content of Cross-Appeal Briefs	Rule 28.1
Form of Briefs/Appendix:	Rule 32
Appendix to the Briefs:	Rule 30

Briefing Privacy

Special redaction and sealing privileges may be applied to certain civil cases in the district court (*e.g.*, social security numbers, taxpayer identification numbers, financial account numbers, birth years, and full names of minors may be presented in an abbreviated form).[143] In cases where these privileges applied at the district court level, the privileges will extend to the appeal as well.[144]

Briefing Reminders

The "Do's" and "Don't's" of effective appellate briefing could fill volumes. Several common oversights, however, are worth special mention:

Corporate Disclosure Statement: The Appellate Rules require each non-governmental corporate party in every civil case to file a statement identifying each of its parent corporations and all publicly-held companies that own 10% or more of the party's stock, and to supplement that statement whenever the necessary information changes.[145] The Rules require that this Statement be reprinted

---

141. *See* Fed. R. App. P. 10, 11, & 30.

142. *See* E.D.Pa. Loc. R. 7.1(e)(requiring moving party to order "a transcript of the trial"); *Bongard v. Korn*, 1993 WL 39267 (E.D.Pa.1993)("the whole transcript is to be ordered rather than a mere portion of the trial transcript as the particular party requesting post-trial relief unilaterally deems necessary").

143. *See* Rule 5.2. *See also supra* Authors' Commentary to Rule 5.2.

144. *See* Fed. R. App. P. 25(a)(5).

145. Fed. R. App. P. 26.1(a).

in front of the Table of Contents in that party's opening brief, even if the Statement has already been filed with the Court of Appeals.[146]

Footnote Restrictions: Some courts of appeals have adopted local rules that severely limit the use of footnotes in appellate briefs.[147] Practitioners should be careful to consult their court of appeals' local rules to be certain their briefs comply with these restrictions.

Citing "Unpublished" Decisions: For years, many courts of appeals forbade the citation of "unpublished", "non-precedential", "not-for-publication", or similarly labeled decisions. An amendment to the Appellate Rules, effective January 1, 2007, invalidates this local practice. Courts of appeals may no longer prohibit or discourage the citation of such decisions[148] (although litigants citing such opinions that are not publicly accessible through a commercial, legal research service, or court database must file and serve copies).[149] The amendment, however, is a narrow one; it does not restrict a court of appeals from *issuing* decisions bearing those labels, nor does it prescribe what effect the court must give (or not give) to such decisions.[150] The amendment merely addresses the question of citation.

Oral Argument

Oral argument is permitted generally unless the appeal is frivolous, the dispositive issues were authoritatively decided, or the decisional process would not be significantly aided by argument because the facts and legal arguments are adequately set forth in the briefs.[151] The length, scheduling, and location of argument is set by the particular court of appeals.

> *Note:* The parties cannot postpone oral argument by stipulation; postponement can occur only upon court order.

§ 6.7 Step Six: Appeals To The United States Supreme Court

CORE CONCEPT

A party enjoys an appeal as of right to the United States Supreme Court in only very few circumstances. In all other cases, the Supreme Court has the discretion whether to permit or refuse appeals to the Court. In practice, only a small handful of the many thousands of requests for Supreme Court review are granted each year.

---

146. Fed. R. App. P. 26.1(b).

147. *See* 3d Cir. Loc. App. R. 32.2(a)("Excessive footnotes in briefs are discouraged. Footnotes shall be printed in the same size type utilized in the text.").

148 Fed. R. App. P. 32.1(a). *See also id.* advisory committee note to 2006 amendment.

149 Fed. R. App. P. 32.1(b). *See also id.* advisory committee note to 2006 amendment.

150 Fed. R. App. P. 32.1. *See also id.* advisory committee note to 2006 amendment.

151. Fed. R. App. P. 34(a)(2).

APPLICATIONS

Appeals As Of Right; Time to File

Whenever a specially convened three-judge district court panel declares any Act of Congress to be unconstitutional, a direct appeal may be taken to the Supreme Court.[152] Such appeals must be filed within 30 days of the date the district court's order is entered.[153] Congress may permit other direct appeals from the district courts, and such appeals must also be filed within 30 days of the district court's action.[154]

Discretionary Appeals; Time to File

The Supreme Court may, in its discretion, grant a party appellate review from other federal and State court rulings. Supreme Court review of federal appellate court decisions may be sought by petitioning for a Writ of Certiorari[155] or by seeking a certification from the court of appeals.[156] The Supreme Court may, in its discretion, also grant a Writ of Certiorari to review of decisions from the highest court of any State, but only where (a) a federal treaty or statute is drawn into question, (b) a State statute is drawn into question on federal grounds, or (c) any title, right, privilege, or immunity is specially set up or claimed under federal law.[157]

Petitions for Writs of Certiorari from federal court of appeals rulings must be filed with the Supreme Court within 90 days after the entry of the disputed judgment or decree.[158] Petitions for Writs from qualifying State court rulings must also be filed with the Supreme Court within 90 days after the entry of the disputed judgment or decree.[159]

Considerations in Granting Writs of Certiorari

The Supreme Court Rules provide a non-controlling, non-exhaustive list of the types of "compelling reasons" that may prompt the Supreme Court to grant a Writ of Certiorari:

(1) A conflict among the federal Circuits on an "important matter";

(2) A conflict between a federal court of appeals and the highest court of a State on an "important federal question";

(3) A ruling by a court of appeals that "so far departed from the accepted and usual course of judicial proceedings" (or that

---

152. *See* 28 U.S.C.A. § 1253.

153. *See* 28 U.S.C.A. § 2102(a).

154. *See* 28 U.S.C.A. § 2102(b).

155. *See* 28 U.S.C.A. § 1254(1). In Latin, "certiorari" means "to be informed of"; such writs of certiorari are of common law origin, and were (and are) issued by a higher court to a lower court requiring that the certified record in a case be delivered for review. *See Black's Law Dictionary* 207 (5th ed. 1979).

156. *See* 28 U.S.C.A. § 1254(2).

157. *See* 28 U.S.C.A. § 1257.

158. *See* 28 U.S.C.A. § 2101(c); U.S. S. Ct. R. 13(1), (3). *See also id.* (permitting Supreme Court, for good cause shown, to extend this 90–day period for another 60 days); U.S. S. Ct. R. 13(5) (same).

159. *See* 28 U.S.C. § 2101(d); U.S. S. Ct. R. 13(1), (3).

sanctions such a departure by a lower court) that the Supreme Court's "supervisory power" is called for;

(4) A ruling by the highest court of a State that conflicts with the decision of another State's highest court or a federal court of appeals on an "important federal question"; or

(5) A ruling by a State court or a federal court of appeals that decides "an important question of federal law that has not been, but should be," settled by the Supreme Court, or that decides "an important federal question in a way that conflicts with relevant decisions" of the Supreme Court.[160]

§ 6.8 *Federal Rules of Appellate Procedure* (Effective July 1, 1968; amendments effective December 1, 2007)

160. *See* U.S. S. Ct. R. 10(a)-(c).

TITLE I. APPLICABILITY OF RULES

RULE 1. SCOPE OF RULES; TITLE

(a) Scope of Rules.

(1) These rules govern procedure in the United States courts of appeals.

(2) When these rules provide for filing a motion or other document in the district court, the procedure must comply with the practice of the district court.

(b) [Abrogated]

(c) Title. These rules are to be known as the Federal Rules of Appellate Procedure.

RULE 2. SUSPENSION OF RULES

On its own or a party's motion, a court of appeals may—to expedite its decision or for other good cause—suspend any provision of these rules in a particular case and order proceedings as it directs, except as otherwise provided in Rule 26(b).

TITLE II. APPEAL FROM A JUDGMENT OR ORDER OF A DISTRICT COURT

RULE 3. APPEAL AS OF RIGHT—HOW TAKEN

(a) Filing the Notice of Appeal.

(1) An appeal permitted by law as of right from a district court to a court of appeals may be taken only by filing a notice of appeal with the district clerk within the time allowed by Rule 4. At the time of filing, the appellant must furnish the clerk with enough copies of the notice to enable the clerk to comply with Rule 3(d).

(2) An appellant's failure to take any step other than the timely filing of a notice of appeal does not affect the validity of the appeal, but is ground only for the court of appeals to act as it considers appropriate, including dismissing the appeal.

(3) An appeal from a judgment by a magistrate judge in a civil case is taken in the same way as an appeal from any other district court judgment.

(4) An appeal by permission under 28 U.S.C. § 1292(b) or an appeal in a bankruptcy case may be taken only in the manner prescribed by Rules 5 and 6, respectively.

(b) Joint or Consolidated Appeals.

(1) When two or more parties are entitled to appeal from a district-court judgment or order, and their interests make joinder practicable, they may file a joint notice of appeal. They may then proceed on appeal as a single appellant.

(2) When the parties have filed separate timely notices of appeal, the appeals may be joined or consolidated by the court of appeals.

(c) Contents of the Notice of Appeal.

(1) The notice of appeal must:

(A) specify the party or parties taking the appeal by naming each one in the caption or body of the notice, but an attorney representing more than one party may describe those parties with such terms as "all plaintiffs," "the defendants," "the plaintiffs A, B, et al.," or "all defendants except X";

(B) designate the judgment, order, or part thereof being appealed; and

(C) name the court to which the appeal is taken.

(2) A pro se notice of appeal is considered filed on behalf of the signer and the signer's spouse and minor children (if they are parties), unless the notice clearly indicates otherwise.

(3) In a class action, whether or not the class has been certified, the notice of appeal is sufficient if it names one person qualified to bring the appeal as representative of the class.

(4) An appeal must not be dismissed for informality of form or title of the notice of appeal, or for failure to name a party whose intent to appeal is otherwise clear from the notice.

(5) Form 1 in the Appendix of Forms is a suggested form of a notice of appeal.

(d) Serving the Notice of Appeal.

(1) The district clerk must serve notice of the filing of a notice of appeal by mailing a copy to each party's counsel of record—excluding the appellant's—or, if a party is proceeding pro se, to the party's last known address. When a defendant in a criminal case appeals, the clerk must also serve a copy of the notice of appeal on the defendant, either by personal service or by mail addressed to the defendant. The clerk must promptly send a copy of the notice of appeal and of the docket entries—and any later docket entries—to the clerk of the court of appeals named in the notice. The district clerk must note, on each copy, the date when the notice of appeal was filed.

(2) If an inmate confined in an institution files a notice of appeal in the manner provided by Rule 4(c), the district clerk must also note the date when the clerk docketed the notice.

(3) The district clerk's failure to serve notice does not affect the validity of the appeal. The clerk must note on the docket the names of the parties to whom the clerk mails copies, with the date of mailing. Service is sufficient despite the death of a party or the party's counsel.

(e) Payment of Fees. Upon filing a notice of appeal, the appellant must pay the district clerk all required fees. The district clerk receives the appellate docket fee on behalf of the court of appeals.

RULE 3.1 APPEAL FROM A JUDGMENT OF A MAGISTRATE JUDGE IN A CIVIL CASE [ABROGATED]

RULE 4. APPEAL AS OF RIGHT—WHEN TAKEN

(a) Appeal in a Civil Case.

(1) Time for Filing a Notice of Appeal.

(A) In a civil case, except as provided in Rules 4(a)(1)(B), 4(a)(4), and 4(c), the notice of appeal required by Rule 3 must be filed with the district clerk within 30 days after the judgment or order appealed from is entered.

(B) When the United States or its officer or agency is a party, the notice of appeal may be filed by any party within 60 days after the judgment or order appealed from is entered.

(C) An appeal from an order granting or denying an application for a writ of error *coram nobis* is an appeal in a civil case for purposes of Rule 4(a).

(2) Filing Before Entry of Judgment. A notice of appeal filed after the court announces a decision or order—but before the entry of the judgment or order—is treated as filed on the date of and after the entry.

(3) Multiple Appeals. If one party timely files a notice of appeal, any other party may file a notice of appeal within 14 days after the date when the first notice was filed, or within the time otherwise prescribed by this Rule 4(a), whichever period ends later.

(4) Effect of a Motion on a Notice of Appeal.

(A) If a party timely files in the district court any of the following motions under the Federal Rules of Civil Procedure, the time to file an appeal runs for all parties from the entry of the order disposing of the last such remaining motion:

(i) for judgment under Rule 50(b);

(ii) to amend or make additional factual findings under Rule 52(b), whether or not granting the motion would alter the judgment;

(iii) for attorney's fees under Rule 54 if the district court extends the time to appeal under Rule 58;

(iv) to alter or amend the judgment under Rule 59;

(v) for a new trial under Rule 59; or

(vi) for relief under Rule 60 if the motion is filed no later than 10 days after the judgment is entered.

(B)(i) If a party files a notice of appeal after the court announces or enters a judgment—but before it disposes of any motion listed in Rule 4(a)(4)(A)—the notice becomes effective to appeal a judgment or order, in whole or in part, when the order disposing of the last such remaining motion is entered.

(ii) A party intending to challenge an order disposing of any motion listed in Rule 4(a)(4)(A), or a judgment altered or amended upon such a motion, must file a notice of appeal, or an amended notice of appeal—in compliance with Rule 3(c)—within the time prescribed by this Rule measured from the entry of the order disposing of the last such remaining motion.

(iii) No additional fee is required to file an amended notice.

(5) Motion for Extension of Time.

(A) The district court may extend the time to file a notice of appeal if:

(i) a party so moves no later than 30 days after the time prescribed by this Rule 4(a) expires; and

(ii) regardless of whether its motion is filed before or during the 30 days after the time prescribed by this Rule 4(a) expires, that party shows excusable neglect or good cause.

(B) A motion filed before the expiration of the time prescribed in Rule 4(a)(1) or (3) may be ex parte unless the court requires otherwise. If the motion is filed after the expiration of the prescribed time, notice must be given to the other parties in accordance with local rules.

(C) No extension under this Rule 4(a)(5) may exceed 30 days after the prescribed time or 10 days after the date when the order granting the motion is entered, whichever is later.

(6) Reopening the Time to File an Appeal. The district court may reopen the time to file an appeal for a period of 14 days after the date when its order to reopen is entered, but only if all the following conditions are satisfied:

(A) the court finds that the moving party did not receive notice under Federal Rule of Civil Procedure 77(d) of the entry of the judgment or order sought to be appealed within 21 days after entry;

(B) the motion is filed within 180 days after the judgment or order is entered or within 7 days after the moving party receives notice under Federal Rule of Civil Procedure 77(d) of the entry, whichever is earlier; and

(C) the court finds that no party would be prejudiced.

(7) Entry Defined.

(A) A judgment or order is entered for purposes of this Rule 4(a):

    (i) if Federal Rule of Civil Procedure 58(a)(1) does not require a separate document, when the judgment or order is entered in the civil docket under Federal Rules of Civil Procedure 79(a); or

    (ii) if Federal Rule of Civil Procedure 58(a)(1) requires a separate document, when the judgment or order is entered in the civil docket under Federal Rule of Civil Procedure 79(a) and when the earlier of these events occurs:

- the judgment or order is set forth on a separate document, or

- 150 days have run from entry of the judgment or order in the civil docket under Federal Rule of Civil Procedure 79(a).

(B) A failure to set forth a judgment or order on a separate document when required by Federal Rule of Civil Procedure 58(a)(1) does not affect the validity of an appeal from that judgment or order.

(b) Appeal in a Criminal Case.

(1) Time for Filing a Notice of Appeal.

(A) In a criminal case, a defendant's notice of appeal must be filed in the district court within 10 days after the later of:

    (i) the entry of either the judgment or the order being appealed; or

    (ii) the filing of the government's notice of appeal.

(B) When the government is entitled to appeal, its notice of appeal must be filed in the district court within 30 days after the later of:

(i) the entry of the judgment or order being appealed; or

(ii) the filing of a notice of appeal by any defendant.

(2) Filing Before Entry of Judgment. A notice of appeal filed after the court announces a decision, sentence, or order—but before the entry of the judgment or order—is treated as filed on the date of and after the entry.

(3) Effect of a Motion on a Notice of Appeal.

(A) If a defendant timely makes any of the following motions under the Federal Rules of Criminal Procedure, the notice of appeal from a judgment of conviction must be filed within 10 days after the entry of the order disposing of the last such remaining motion, or within 10 days after the entry of the judgment of conviction, whichever period ends later. This provision applies to a timely motion:

(i) for judgment of acquittal under Rule 29;

(ii) for a new trial under Rule 33, but if based on newly discovered evidence, only if the motion is made no later than 10 days after the entry of the judgment; or

(iii) for arrest of judgment under Rule 34.

(B) A notice of appeal filed after the court announces a decision, sentence, or order—but before it disposes of any of the motions referred to in Rule 4(b)(3)(A)—becomes effective upon the later of the following:

(i) the entry of the order disposing of the last such remaining motion; or

(ii) the entry of the judgment of conviction.

(C) A valid notice of appeal is effective—without amendment—to appeal from an order disposing of any of the motions referred to in Rule 4(b)(3)(A).

(4) Motion for Extension of Time. Upon a finding of excusable neglect or good cause, the district court may—before or after the time has expired, with or without motion and notice—extend the time to file a notice of appeal for a period not to exceed 30 days from the expiration of the time otherwise prescribed by this Rule 4(b).

(5) Jurisdiction. The filing of a notice of appeal under this Rule 4(b) does not divest a district court of jurisdiction to correct a sentence under Federal Rule of Criminal Procedure 35(c), nor does the filing of a motion under 35(c) affect the validity of a notice of appeal filed before entry of the order disposing of the motion. The filing of a motion under Federal Rule of Criminal Procedure 35(a) does not suspend the time for filing a notice of appeal from a judgment of conviction.

(6) Entry Defined. A judgment or order is entered for purposes of this Rule 4(b) when it is entered on the criminal docket.

(c) Appeal by an Inmate Confined in an Institution.

(1) If an inmate confined in an institution files a notice of appeal in either a civil or a criminal case, the notice is timely if it is deposited in the institution's internal mail system on or before the last day for filing. If an institution has a system designed for legal mail, the inmate must use that system to receive the benefit of this rule. Timely filing may be shown by a declaration in compliance with 28 U.S.C. § 1746 or by a notarized statement, either of which must set forth the date of deposit and state that first-class postage has been prepaid.

(2) If an inmate files the first notice of appeal in a civil case under this Rule 4(c), the 14–day period provided in Rule 4(a)(3) for another party to file a notice of appeal runs from the date when the district court dockets the first notice.

(3) When a defendant in a criminal case files a notice of appeal under this Rule 4(c), the 30–day period for the government to file its notice of appeal runs from the entry of the judgment or order appealed from or from the district court's docketing of the defendant's notice of appeal, whichever is later.

(d) Mistaken Filing in the Court of Appeals. If a notice of appeal in either a civil or a criminal case is mistakenly filed in the court of appeals, the clerk of that court must note on the notice the date when it was received and send it to the district clerk. The notice is then considered filed in the district court on the date so noted.

RULE 5. APPEAL BY PERMISSION

(a) Petition for Permission to Appeal.

(1) To request permission to appeal when an appeal is within the court of appeals' discretion, a party must file a petition for permission to appeal. The petition must be filed with the circuit clerk with proof of service on all other parties to the district-court action.

(2) The petition must be filed within the time specified by the statute or rule authorizing the appeal or, if no such time is specified, within the time provided by Rule 4(a) for filing a notice of appeal.

(3) If a party cannot petition for appeal unless the district court first enters an order granting permission to do so or stating that the necessary conditions are met, the district court may amend its order, either on its own or in response to a party's motion, to include the required permission or statement. In that event, the time to petition runs from entry of the amended order.

(b) Contents of the Petition; Answer or Cross–Petition; Oral Argument.

(1) The petition must include the following:

    (A) the facts necessary to understand the question presented;

    (B) the question itself;

    (C) the relief sought;

    (D) the reasons why the appeal should be allowed and is authorized by a statute or rule; and

    (E) an attached copy of:

        (i) the order, decree, or judgment complained of and any related opinion or memorandum, and

        (ii) any order stating the district court's permission to appeal or finding that the necessary conditions are met.

    (2) A party may file an answer in opposition or a cross-petition within 7 days after the petition is served.

    (3) The petition and answer will be submitted without oral argument unless the court of appeals orders otherwise.

    (c) Form of Papers; Number of Copies. All papers must conform to Rule 32(c)(2). Except by the court's permission, a paper must not exceed 20 pages, exclusive of the disclosure statement, the proof of service, and the accompanying documents required by Rule 5(b)(1)(E). An original and 3 copies must be filed unless the court requires a different number by local rule or by order in a particular case.

    (d) Grant of Permission; Fees; Cost Bond; Filing the Record.

    (1) Within 10 days after the entry of the order granting permission to appeal, the appellant must:

    (A) pay the district clerk all required fees; and

    (B) file a cost bond if required under Rule 7.

    (2) A notice of appeal need not be filed. The date when the order granting permission to appeal is entered serves as the date of the notice of appeal for calculating time under these rules.

    (3) The district clerk must notify the circuit clerk once the petitioner has paid the fees. Upon receiving this notice, the circuit clerk must enter the appeal on the docket. The record must be forwarded and filed in accordance with Rules 11 and 12(c).

RULE 5.1 APPEAL BY LEAVE UNDER 28 U.S.C. § 636(c)(5) [ABROGATED]

RULE 6. APPEAL IN A BANKRUPTCY CASE FROM A FINAL JUDGMENT, ORDER, OR DECREE OF A DISTRICT COURT OR BANKRUPTCY APPELLATE PANEL

    (a) Appeal From a Judgment, Order, or Decree of a District Court Exercising Original Jurisdiction in a Bankruptcy Case. An appeal to a court of appeals from a final judgment, order, or decree of a district court exercising jurisdiction under 28 U.S.C. § 1334 is taken as any other civil appeal under these rules.

    (b) Appeal From a Judgment, Order, or Decree of a District Court or Bankruptcy Appellate Panel Exercising Appellate Jurisdiction in a Bankruptcy Case.

(1) Applicability of Other Rules. These rules apply to an appeal to a court of appeals under 28 U.S.C. § 158(d) from a final judgment, order, or decree of a district court or bankruptcy appellate panel exercising appellate jurisdiction under 28 U.S.C. § 158(a) or (b). But there are 3 exceptions:

(A) Rules 4(a)(4), 4(b), 9, 10, 11, 12(b), 13–F20, 22–23, and 24(b) do not apply;

(B) the reference in Rule 3(c) to "Form 1 in the Appendix of Forms" must be read as a reference to Form 5; and

(C) when the appeal is from a bankruptcy appellate panel, the term "district court," as used in any applicable rule, means "appellate panel."

(2) Additional Rules. In addition to the rules made applicable by Rule 6(b)(1), the following rules apply:

(A) Motion for rehearing.

(i) If a timely motion for rehearing under Bankruptcy Rule 8015 is filed, the time to appeal for all parties runs from the entry of the order disposing of the motion. A notice of appeal filed after the district court or bankruptcy appellate panel announces or enters a judgment, order, or decree—but before disposition of the motion for rehearing—becomes effective when the order disposing of the motion for rehearing is entered.

(ii) Appellate review of the order disposing of the motion requires the party, in compliance with Rules 3(c) and 6(b)(1)(B), to amend a previously filed notice of appeal. A party intending to challenge an altered or amended judgment, order, or decree must file a notice of appeal or amended notice of appeal within the time prescribed by Rule 4—excluding Rules 4(a)(4) and 4(b)—measured from the entry of the order disposing of the motion.

(iii) No additional fee is required to file an amended notice.

(B) The record on appeal.

(i) Within 10 days after filing the notice of appeal, the appellant must file with the clerk possessing the record assembled in accordance with Bankruptcy Rule 8006—and serve on the appellee—a statement of the issues to be presented on appeal and a designation of the record to be certified and sent to the circuit clerk.

(ii) An appellee who believes that other parts of the record are necessary must, within 10 days after being served with the appellant's designation, file with the clerk and serve on the appellant a designation of additional parts to be included.

(iii) The record on appeal consists of:

* the redesignated record as provided above;

* the proceedings in the district court or bankruptcy appellate panel; and

* a certified copy of the docket entries prepared by the clerk under Rule 3(d).

(C) Forwarding the record.

(i) When the record is complete, the district clerk or bankruptcy appellate panel clerk must number the documents constituting the record and send them promptly to the circuit clerk together with a list of the documents correspondingly numbered and reasonably identified. Unless directed to do so by a party or the circuit clerk, the clerk will not send to the court of appeals documents of unusual bulk or weight, physical exhibits other than documents, or other parts of the record designated for omission by local rule of the court of appeals. If the exhibits are unusually bulky or heavy, a party must arrange with the clerks in advance for their transportation and receipt.

(ii) All parties must do whatever else is necessary to enable the clerk to assemble and forward the record. The court of appeals may provide by rule or order that a certified copy of the docket entries be sent in place of the redesignated record, but any party may request at any time during the pendency of the appeal that the redesignated record be sent.

(D) Filing the record. Upon receiving the record—or a certified copy of the docket entries sent in place of the redesignated record—the circuit clerk must file it and immediately notify all parties of the filing date.

RULE 7. BOND FOR COSTS ON APPEAL IN A CIVIL CASE

In a civil case, the district court may require an appellant to file a bond or provide other security in any form and amount necessary to ensure payment of costs on appeal. Rule 8(b) applies to a surety on a bond given under this rule.

RULE 8. STAY OR INJUNCTION PENDING APPEAL

(a) Motion for Stay.

(1) Initial Motion in the District Court. A party must ordinarily move first in the district court for the following relief:

(A) a stay of the judgment or order of a district court pending appeal;

(B) approval of a supersedeas bond; or

(C) an order suspending, modifying, restoring, or granting an injunction while an appeal is pending.

(2) Motion in the Court of Appeals; Conditions on Relief. A motion for the relief mentioned in Rule 8(a)(1) may be made to the court of appeals or to one of its judges.

(A) The motion must:

(i) show that moving first in the district court would be impracticable; or

(ii) state that, a motion having been made, the district court denied the motion or failed to afford the relief requested and state any reasons given by the district court for its action.

(B) The motion must also include:

(i) the reasons for granting the relief requested and the facts relied on;

(ii) originals or copies of affidavits or other sworn statements supporting facts subject to dispute; and

(iii) relevant parts of the record.

(C) The moving party must give reasonable notice of the motion to all parties.

(D) A motion under this Rule 8(a)(2) must be filed with the circuit clerk and normally will be considered by a panel of the court. But in an exceptional case in which time requirements make that procedure impracticable, the motion may be made to and considered by a single judge.

(E) The court may condition relief on a party's filing a bond or other appropriate security in the district court.

(b) Proceeding Against a Surety. If a party gives security in the form of a bond or stipulation or other undertaking with one or more sureties, each surety submits to the jurisdiction of the district court and irrevocably appoints the district clerk as the surety's agent on whom any papers affecting the surety's liability on the bond or undertaking may be served. On motion, a surety's liability may be enforced in the district court without the necessity of an independent action. The motion and any notice that the district court prescribes may be served on the district clerk, who must promptly mail a copy to each surety whose address is known.

(c) Stay in a Criminal Case. Rule 38 of the Federal Rules of Criminal Procedure governs a stay in a criminal case.

RULE 9. RELEASE IN A CRIMINAL CASE

(a) Release Before Judgment of Conviction.

(1) The district court must state in writing, or orally on the record, the reasons for an order regarding the release or detention of a defendant in a criminal case. A party appealing from the order must file with the court of appeals a copy of the district court's order and the court's statement of reasons as soon as practicable after filing the notice of appeal. An appellant who questions the factual basis for the district court's order must file a transcript of the release proceedings or an explanation of why a transcript was not obtained.

(2) After reasonable notice to the appellee, the court of appeals must promptly determine the appeal on the basis of the papers,

affidavits, and parts of the record that the parties present or the court requires. Unless the court so orders, briefs need not be filed.

(3) The court of appeals or one of its judges may order the defendant's release pending the disposition of the appeal.

(b) Release After Judgment of Conviction. A party entitled to do so may obtain review of a district-court order regarding release after a judgment of conviction by filing a notice of appeal from that order in the district court, or by filing a motion in the court of appeals if the party has already filed a notice of appeal from the judgment of conviction. Both the order and the review are subject to Rule 9(a). The papers filed by the party seeking review must include a copy of the judgment of conviction.

(c) Criteria for Release. The court must make its decision regarding release in accordance with the applicable provisions of 18 U.S.C. §§ 3142, 3143, and 3145(c).

RULE 10. THE RECORD ON APPEAL

(a) Composition of the Record on Appeal. The following items constitute the record on appeal:

(1) the original papers and exhibits filed in the district court;

(2) the transcript of proceedings, if any; and

(3) a certified copy of the docket entries prepared by the district clerk.

(b) The Transcript of Proceedings.

(1) Appellant's Duty to Order. Within 10 days after filing the notice of appeal or entry of an order disposing of the last timely remaining motion of a type specified in Rule 4(a)(4)(A), whichever is later, the appellant must do either of the following:

(A) order from the reporter a transcript of such parts of the proceedings not already on file as the appellant considers necessary, subject to a local rule of the court of appeals and with the following qualifications:

(i) the order must be in writing;

(ii) if the cost of the transcript is to be paid by the United States under the Criminal Justice Act, the order must so state; and

(iii) the appellant must, within the same period, file a copy of the order with the district clerk; or

(B) file a certificate stating that no transcript will be ordered.

(2) Unsupported Finding or Conclusion. If the appellant intends to urge on appeal that a finding or conclusion is unsupported by the evidence or is contrary to the evidence, the appellant must include in the record a transcript of all evidence relevant to that finding or conclusion.

(3) Partial Transcript. Unless the entire transcript is ordered:

(A) the appellant must—within the 10 days provided in Rule 10(b)(1)—file a statement of the issues that the appellant intends to present on the appeal and must serve on the appellee a copy of both the order or certificate and the statement;

(B) if the appellee considers it necessary to have a transcript of other parts of the proceedings, the appellee must, within 10 days after the service of the order or certificate and the statement of the issues, file and serve on the appellant a designation of additional parts to be ordered; and

(C) unless within 10 days after service of that designation the appellant has ordered all such parts, and has so notified the appellee, the appellee may within the following 10 days either order the parts or move in the district court for an order requiring the appellant to do so.

(4) Payment. At the time of ordering, a party must make satisfactory arrangements with the reporter for paying the cost of the transcript.

(c) Statement of the Evidence When the Proceedings Were Not Recorded or When a Transcript Is Unavailable. If the transcript of a hearing or trial is unavailable, the appellant may prepare a statement of the evidence or proceedings from the best available means, including the appellant's recollection. The statement must be served on the appellee, who may serve objections or proposed amendments within 10 days after being served. The statement and any objections or proposed amendments must then be submitted to the district court for settlement and approval. As settled and approved, the statement must be included by the district clerk in the record on appeal.

(d) Agreed Statement as the Record on Appeal. In place of the record on appeal as defined in Rule 10(a), the parties may prepare, sign, and submit to the district court a statement of the case showing how the issues presented by the appeal arose and were decided in the district court. The statement must set forth only those facts averred and proved or sought to be proved that are essential to the court's resolution of the issues. If the statement is truthful, it—together with any additions that the district court may consider necessary to a full presentation of the issues on appeal—must be approved by the district court and must then be certified to the court of appeals as the record on appeal. The district clerk must then send it to the circuit clerk within the time provided by Rule 11. A copy of the agreed statement may be filed in place of the appendix required by Rule 30.

(e) Correction or Modification of the Record.

(1) If any difference arises about whether the record truly discloses what occurred in the district court, the difference must be submitted to and settled by that court and the record conformed accordingly.

(2) If anything material to either party is omitted from or misstated in the record by error or accident, the omission or mis-

statement may be corrected and a supplemental record may be certified and forwarded:

(A) on stipulation of the parties;

(B) by the district court before or after the record has been forwarded; or

(C) by the court of appeals.

(3) All other questions as to the form and content of the record must be presented to the court of appeals.

RULE 11. FORWARDING THE RECORD

(a) **Appellant's Duty.** An appellant filing a notice of appeal must comply with Rule 10(b) and must do whatever else is necessary to enable the clerk to assemble and forward the record. If there are multiple appeals from a judgment or order, the clerk must forward a single record.

(b) **Duties of Reporter and District Clerk.**

(1) **Reporter's Duty to Prepare and File a Transcript.** The reporter must prepare and file a transcript as follows:

(A) Upon receiving an order for a transcript, the reporter must enter at the foot of the order the date of its receipt and the expected completion date and send a copy, so endorsed, to the circuit clerk.

(B) If the transcript cannot be completed within 30 days of the reporter's receipt of the order, the reporter may request the circuit clerk to grant additional time to complete it. The clerk must note on the docket the action taken and notify the parties.

(C) When a transcript is complete, the reporter must file it with the district clerk and notify the circuit clerk of the filing.

(D) If the reporter fails to file the transcript on time, the circuit clerk must notify the district judge and do whatever else the court of appeals directs.

(2) **District Clerk's Duty to Forward.** When the record is complete, the district clerk must number the documents constituting the record and send them promptly to the circuit clerk together with a list of the documents correspondingly numbered and reasonably identified. Unless directed to do so by a party or the circuit clerk, the district clerk will not send to the court of appeals documents of unusual bulk or weight, physical exhibits other than documents, or other parts of the record designated for omission by local rule of the court of appeals. If the exhibits are unusually bulky or heavy, a party must arrange with the clerks in advance for their transportation and receipt.

(c) **Retaining the Record Temporarily in the District Court for Use in Preparing the Appeal.** The parties may stipulate, or the district court on motion may order, that the district clerk retain the record temporarily for the parties to use in preparing the papers on appeal. In that event the district clerk must certify to the circuit clerk that the record on appeal is complete. Upon receipt of the appellee's brief, or earlier if the court orders or the parties agree, the appellant must request the district clerk to forward the record.

(d) [Abrogated.]

(e) Retaining the Record by Court Order.

(1) The court of appeals may, by order or local rule, provide that a certified copy of the docket entries be forwarded instead of the entire record. But a party may at any time during the appeal request that designated parts of the record be forwarded.

(2) The district court may order the record or some part of it retained if the court needs it while the appeal is pending, subject, however, to call by the court of appeals.

(3) If part or all of the record is ordered retained, the district clerk must send to the court of appeals a copy of the order and the docket entries together with the parts of the original record allowed by the district court and copies of any parts of the record designated by the parties.

(f) Retaining Parts of the Record in the District Court by Stipulation of the Parties. The parties may agree by written stipulation filed in the district court that designated parts of the record be retained in the district court subject to call by the court of appeals or request by a party. The parts of the record so designated remain a part of the record on appeal.

(g) Record for a Preliminary Motion in the Court of Appeals. If, before the record is forwarded, a party makes any of the following motions in the court of appeals:

* for dismissal;

* for release;

* for a stay pending appeal;

* for additional security on the bond on appeal or on a supersedeas bond; or

* for any other intermediate order—

the district clerk must send the court of appeals any parts of the record designated by any party.

RULE 12. DOCKETING THE APPEAL; FILING A REPRESENTATION STATEMENT; FILING THE RECORD

(a) Docketing the Appeal. Upon receiving the copy of the notice of appeal and the docket entries from the district clerk under Rule 3(d), the circuit clerk must docket the appeal under the title of the district-court action and must identify the appellant, adding the appellant's name if necessary.

(b) Filing a Representation Statement. Unless the court of appeals designates another time, the attorney who filed the notice of appeal must, within 10 days after filing the notice, file a statement with the circuit clerk naming the parties that the attorney represents on appeal.

(c) Filing the Record, Partial Record, or Certificate. Upon receiving the record, partial record, or district clerk's certificate as provided in Rule 11, the circuit clerk must file it and immediately notify all parties of the filing date.

TITLE III. REVIEW OF A DECISION OF THE UNITED STATES TAX COURT

RULE 13. REVIEW OF A DECISION OF THE TAX COURT

(a) How Obtained; Time for Filing Notice of Appeal.

(1) Review of a decision of the United States Tax Court is commenced by filing a notice of appeal with the Tax Court clerk within 90 days after the entry of the Tax Court's decision. At the time of filing, the appellant must furnish the clerk with enough copies of the notice to enable the clerk to comply with Rule 3(d). If one party files a timely notice of appeal, any other party may file a notice of appeal within 120 days after the Tax Court's decision is entered.

(2) If, under Tax Court rules, a party makes a timely motion to vacate or revise the Tax Court's decision, the time to file a notice of appeal runs from the entry of the order disposing of the motion or from the entry of a new decision, whichever is later.

(b) Notice of Appeal; How Filed.
The notice of appeal may be filed either at the Tax Court clerk's office in the District of Columbia or by mail addressed to the clerk. If sent by mail the notice is considered filed on the postmark date, subject to § 7502 of the Internal Revenue Code, as amended, and the applicable regulations.

(c) Contents of the Notice of Appeal; Service; Effect of Filing and Service.
Rule 3 prescribes the contents of a notice of appeal, the manner of service, and the effect of its filing and service. Form 2 in the Appendix of Forms is a suggested form of a notice of appeal.

(d) The Record on Appeal; Forwarding; Filing.

(1) An appeal from the Tax Court is governed by the parts of Rules 10, 11, and 12 regarding the record on appeal from a district court, the time and manner of forwarding and filing, and the docketing in the court of appeals. References in those rules and in Rule 3 to the district court and district clerk are to be read as referring to the Tax Court and its clerk.

(2) If an appeal from a Tax Court decision is taken to more than one court of appeals, the original record must be sent to the court named in the first notice of appeal filed. In an appeal to any other court of appeals, the appellant must apply to that other court to make provision for the record.

RULE 14. APPLICABILITY OF OTHER RULES TO THE REVIEW OF A TAX COURT DECISION

All provisions of these rules, except Rules 4–9, 15–20, and 22–23, apply to the review of a Tax Court decision.

TITLE IV. REVIEW OR ENFORCEMENT OF AN ORDER OF AN ADMINISTRATIVE AGENCY, BOARD, COMMISSION, OR OFFICER

RULE 15. REVIEW OR ENFORCEMENT OF AN AGENCY ORDER—HOW OBTAINED; INTERVENTION

(a) Petition for Review; Joint Petition.

(1) Review of an agency order is commenced by filing, within the time prescribed by law, a petition for review with the clerk of a court of appeals authorized to review the agency order. If their interests make joinder practicable, two or more persons may join in a petition to the same court to review the same order.

(2) The petition must:

(A) name each party seeking review either in the caption or the body of the petition—using such terms as "et al.," "petitioners," or "respondents" does not effectively name the parties;

(B) name the agency as a respondent (even though not named in the petition, the United States is a respondent if required by statute); and

(C) specify the order or part thereof to be reviewed.

(3) Form 3 in the Appendix of Forms is a suggested form of a petition for review.

(4) In this rule "agency" includes an agency, board, commission, or officer; "petition for review" includes a petition to enjoin, suspend, modify, or otherwise review, or a notice of appeal, whichever form is indicated by the applicable statute.

(b) Application or Cross–Application to Enforce an Order; Answer; Default.

(1) An application to enforce an agency order must be filed with the clerk of a court of appeals authorized to enforce the order. If a petition is filed to review an agency order that the court may enforce, a party opposing the petition may file a cross-application for enforcement.

(2) Within 20 days after the application for enforcement is filed, the respondent must serve on the applicant an answer to the application and file it with the clerk. If the respondent fails to answer in time, the court will enter judgment for the relief requested.

(3) The application must contain a concise statement of the proceedings in which the order was entered, the facts upon which venue is based, and the relief requested.

(c) Service of the Petition or Application. The circuit clerk must serve a copy of the petition for review, or an application or cross-application to enforce an agency order, on each respondent as prescribed by Rule 3(d), unless a different manner of service is prescribed by statute. At the time of filing, the petitioner must:

(1) serve, or have served, a copy on each party admitted to participate in the agency proceedings, except for the respondents;

(2) file with the clerk a list of those so served; and

(3) give the clerk enough copies of the petition or application to serve each respondent.

(d) Intervention. Unless a statute provides another method, a person who wants to intervene in a proceeding under this rule must file a motion for leave to intervene with the circuit clerk and serve a copy on all parties. The motion—or other notice of intervention authorized by statute—must be filed within 30 days after the petition for review is filed and must contain a concise statement of the interest of the moving party and the grounds for intervention.

(e) Payment of Fees. When filing any separate or joint petition for review in a court of appeals, the petitioner must pay the circuit clerk all required fees.

RULE 15.1 BRIEFS AND ORAL ARGUMENT IN A NATIONAL LABOR RELATIONS BOARD PROCEEDING

In either an enforcement or a review proceeding, a party adverse to the National Labor Relations Board proceeds first on briefing and at oral argument, unless the court orders otherwise.

RULE 16. THE RECORD ON REVIEW OR ENFORCEMENT

(a) Composition of the Record. The record on review or enforcement of an agency order consists of:

(1) the order involved;

(2) any findings or report on which it is based; and

(3) the pleadings, evidence, and other parts of the proceedings before the agency.

(b) Omissions From or Misstatements in the Record. The parties may at any time, by stipulation, supply any omission from the record or correct a misstatement, or the court may so direct. If necessary, the court may direct that a supplemental record be prepared and filed.

RULE 17. FILING THE RECORD

(a) Agency to File; Time for Filing; Notice of Filing. The agency must file the record with the circuit clerk within 40 days after being served with a petition for review, unless the statute authorizing review provides otherwise, or within 40 days after it files an application for enforcement unless the respondent fails to answer or the court orders otherwise. The court may shorten or extend the time to file the record. The clerk must notify all parties of the date when the record is filed.

(b) Filing—What Constitutes.

(1) The agency must file:

(A) the original or a certified copy of the entire record or parts designated by the parties; or

(B) a certified list adequately describing all documents, transcripts of testimony, exhibits, and other material constituting the record, or describing those parts designated by the parties.

(2) The parties may stipulate in writing that no record or certified list be filed. The date when the stipulation is filed with the circuit clerk is treated as the date when the record is filed.

(3) The agency must retain any portion of the record not filed with the clerk. All parts of the record retained by the agency are a part of the record on review for all purposes and, if the court or a party so requests, must be sent to the court regardless of any prior stipulation.

RULE 18. STAY PENDING REVIEW

(a) Motion for a Stay.

(1) Initial Motion Before the Agency. A petitioner must ordinarily move first before the agency for a stay pending review of its decision or order.

(2) Motion in the Court of Appeals. A motion for a stay may be made to the court of appeals or one of its judges.

(A) The motion must:

(i) show that moving first before the agency would be impracticable; or

(ii) state that, a motion having been made, the agency denied the motion or failed to afford the relief requested and state any reasons given by the agency for its action.

(B) The motion must also include:

(i) the reasons for granting the relief requested and the facts relied on;

(ii) originals or copies of affidavits or other sworn statements supporting facts subject to dispute; and

(iii) relevant parts of the record.

(C) The moving party must give reasonable notice of the motion to all parties.

(D) The motion must be filed with the circuit clerk and normally will be considered by a panel of the court. But in an exceptional case in which time requirements make that procedure impracticable, the motion may be made to and considered by a single judge.

(b) Bond. The court may condition relief on the filing of a bond or other appropriate security.

RULE 19. SETTLEMENT OF A JUDGMENT ENFORCING AN AGENCY ORDER IN PART

When the court files an opinion directing entry of judgment enforcing the agency's order in part, the agency must within 14 days file with the clerk and serve on each other party a proposed judgment conforming to the opinion. A party who disagrees with the agency's proposed judgment must within 7 days file with the clerk and serve the agency with a proposed judgment that the party believes conforms to the opinion. The court will settle the judgment and direct entry without further hearing or argument.

RULE 20. APPLICABILITY OF RULES TO THE REVIEW OR ENFORCEMENT OF AN AGENCY ORDER

All provisions of these rules, except Rules 3–14 and 22–23, apply to the review or enforcement of an agency order. In these rules, "appellant" includes a petitioner or applicant, and "appellee" includes a respondent.

TITLE V. EXTRAORDINARY WRITS

RULE 21. WRITS OF MANDAMUS AND PROHIBITION, AND OTHER EXTRAORDINARY WRITS

(a) Mandamus or Prohibition to a Court: Petition, Filing, Service, and Docketing.

(1) A party petitioning for a writ of mandamus or prohibition directed to a court must file a petition with the circuit clerk with proof of service on all parties to the proceeding in the trial court. The party must also provide a copy to the trial-court judge. All parties to the proceeding in the trial court other than the petitioner are respondents for all purposes.

(2)(A) The petition must be titled "In re [name of petitioner]."

(B) The petition must state:

(i) the relief sought;

(ii) the issues presented;

(iii) the facts necessary to understand the issue presented by the petition; and

(iv) the reasons why the writ should issue.

(C) The petition must include a copy of any order or opinion or parts of the record that may be essential to understand the matters set forth in the petition.

(3) Upon receiving the prescribed docket fee, the clerk must docket the petition and submit it to the court.

(b) Denial; Order Directing Answer; Briefs; Precedence.

(1) The court may deny the petition without an answer. Otherwise, it must order the respondent, if any, to answer within a fixed time.

(2) The clerk must serve the order to respond on all persons directed to respond.

(3) Two or more respondents may answer jointly.

(4) The court of appeals may invite or order the trial-court judge to address the petition or may invite an amicus curiae to do so. The trial-court judge may request permission to address the petition but may not do so unless invited or ordered to do so by the court of appeals.

(5) If briefing or oral argument is required, the clerk must advise the parties, and when appropriate, the trial-court judge or amicus curiae.

(6) The proceeding must be given preference over ordinary civil cases.

(7) The circuit clerk must send a copy of the final disposition to the trial-court judge.

(c) Other Extraordinary Writs. An application for an extraordinary writ other than one provided for in Rule 21(a) must be made by filing a petition with the circuit clerk with proof of service on the respondents. Proceedings on the application must conform, so far as is practicable, to the procedures prescribed in Rule 21(a) and (b).

(d) Form of Papers; Number of Copies. All papers must conform to Rule 32(c)(2). Except by the court's permission, a paper must not exceed 30 pages, exclusive of the disclosure statement, the proof of service, and the accompanying documents required by Rule 21(a)(2)(C). An original and 3 copies must be filed unless the court requires the filing of a different number by local rule or by order in a particular case.

TITLE VI. HABEAS CORPUS; PROCEEDINGS IN FORMA PAUPERIS

RULE 22. HABEAS CORPUS AND SECTION 2255 PROCEEDINGS

(a) Application for the Original Writ. An application for a writ of habeas corpus must be made to the appropriate district court. If made to a circuit judge, the application must be transferred to the appropriate district court. If a district court denies an application made or transferred to it, renewal of the application before a circuit judge is not permitted. The applicant may, under 28 U.S.C. § 2253, appeal to the court of appeals from the district court's order denying the application.

(b) Certificate of Appealability.

(1) In a habeas corpus proceeding in which the detention complained of arises from process issued by a state court, or in a 28 U.S.C. § 2255 proceeding, the applicant cannot take an appeal unless a circuit justice or a circuit or district judge issues a certificate of appealability under 28 U.S.C. § 2253(c). If an applicant files a notice of appeal, the district judge who rendered the judgment must either issue a certificate of appealability or state why a certificate should not issue. The district clerk must send the certificate or statement to the court of appeals with the notice of appeal and the file of the district-court proceedings. If the district judge has denied the certificate, the applicant may request a circuit judge to issue the certificate.

(2) A request addressed to the court of appeals may be considered by a circuit judge or judges, as the court prescribes. If no express request for a certificate is filed, the notice of appeal constitutes a request addressed to the judges of the court of appeals.

(3) A certificate of appealability is not required when a state or its representative or the United States or its representative appeals.

RULE 23. CUSTODY OR RELEASE OF A PRISONER IN A HABEAS CORPUS PROCEEDING

(a) Transfer of Custody Pending Review. Pending review of a decision in a habeas corpus proceeding commenced before a court, justice, or judge of the United States for the release of a prisoner, the person having custody of the prisoner must not transfer custody to another unless a transfer is directed in accordance with this rule. When, upon application, a custodian shows the need for a transfer, the court, justice, or judge rendering the decision under review may authorize the transfer and substitute the successor custodian as a party.

(b) Detention or Release Pending Review of Decision Not to Release. While a decision not to release a prisoner is under review, the court or judge rendering the decision, or the court of appeals, or the Supreme Court, or a judge or justice of either court, may order that the prisoner be:

(1) detained in the custody from which release is sought;

(2) detained in other appropriate custody; or

(3) released on personal recognizance, with or without surety.

(c) Release Pending Review of Decision Ordering Release. While a decision ordering the release of a prisoner is under review, the prisoner must—unless the court or judge rendering the decision, or the court of appeals, or the Supreme Court, or a judge or justice of either court orders otherwise—be released on personal recognizance, with or without surety.

(d) Modification of the Initial Order on Custody. An initial order governing the prisoner's custody or release, including any recognizance or surety, continues in effect pending review unless for special reasons shown to the court of appeals or the Supreme Court, or to a judge or justice of either court, the order is modified or an independent order regarding custody, release, or surety is issued.

RULE 24. PROCEEDING IN FORMA PAUPERIS

(a) Leave to Proceed in Forma Pauperis.

(1) Motion in the District Court. Except as stated in Rule 24(a)(3), a party to a district-court action who desires to appeal in forma pauperis must file a motion in the district court. The party must attach an affidavit that:

(A) shows in the detail prescribed by Form 4 of the Appendix of Forms, the party's inability to pay or to give security for fees and costs;

(B) claims an entitlement to redress; and

(C) states the issues that the party intends to present on appeal.

(2) Action on the Motion. If the district court grants the motion, the party may proceed on appeal without prepaying or giving security for fees and costs, unless a statute provides otherwise. If the district court denies the motion, it must state its reasons in writing.

(3) Prior Approval. A party who was permitted to proceed in forma pauperis in the district-court action, or who was determined to be financially unable to obtain an adequate defense in a criminal case, may proceed on appeal in forma pauperis without further authorization, unless:

(A) the district court—before or after the notice of appeal is filed—certifies that the appeal is not taken in good faith or finds that the party is not otherwise entitled to proceed in forma pauperis and states in writing its reasons for the certification or finding; or

(B) a statute provides otherwise.

(4) Notice of District Court's Denial. The district clerk must immediately notify the parties and the court of appeals when the district court does any of the following:

(A) denies a motion to proceed on appeal in forma pauperis;

(B) certifies that the appeal is not taken in good faith; or

(C) finds that the party is not otherwise entitled to proceed in forma pauperis.

(5) Motion in the Court of Appeals. A party may file a motion to proceed on appeal in forma pauperis in the court of appeals within 30 days after service of the notice prescribed in Rule 24(a)(4). The motion must include a copy of the affidavit filed in the district court and the district court's statement of reasons for its action. If no affidavit was filed in the district court, the party must include the affidavit prescribed by Rule 24(a)(1).

(b) Leave to Proceed in Forma Pauperis on Appeal or Review of an Administrative–Agency Proceeding. When an appeal or review of a proceeding before an administrative agency, board, commission, or officer (including for the purpose of this rule the United States Tax Court) proceeds directly in a court of appeals, a party may file in the court of appeals a motion for leave to proceed on appeal in forma pauperis with an affidavit prescribed by Rule 24(a)(1).

(c) Leave to Use Original Record. A party allowed to proceed on appeal in forma pauperis may request that the appeal be heard on the original record without reproducing any part.

TITLE VII. GENERAL PROVISIONS

RULE 25. FILING AND SERVICE

(a) Filing.

(1) Filing with the Clerk. A paper required or permitted to be filed in a court of appeals must be filed with the clerk.

(2) Filing: Method and Timeliness.

(A) In general. Filing may be accomplished by mail addressed to the clerk, but filing is not timely unless the clerk receives the papers within the time fixed for filing.

(B) A brief or appendix. A brief or appendix is timely filed, however, if on or before the last day for filing, it is:

    (i) mailed to the clerk by First–Class Mail, or other class of mail that is at least as expeditious, postage prepaid; or

    (ii) dispatched to a third-party commercial carrier for delivery to the clerk within 3 calendar days.

(C) Inmate filing. A paper filed by an inmate confined in an institution is timely if deposited in the institution's internal mailing system on or before the last day for filing. If an institution has a system designed for legal mail, the inmate must use that system to receive the benefit of this rule. Timely filing may be shown by a declaration in compliance with 28 U.S.C. § 1746 or by a notarized statement, either of which must set forth the date of deposit and state that first-class postage has been prepaid.

(D) Electronic filing. A court of appeals may by local rule permit or require papers to be filed, signed, or verified by electronic means that are consistent with technical standards, if any, that the Judicial Conference of the United States establishes. A local rule may require filing by electronic means only if reasonable exceptions are allowed. A paper filed by electronic means in compliance with a local rule constitutes a written paper for the purpose of applying these rules.

(3) Filing a Motion with a Judge. If a motion requests relief that may be granted by a single judge, the judge may permit the motion to be filed with the judge; the judge must note the filing date on the motion and give it to the clerk.

(4) Clerk's Refusal of Documents. The clerk must not refuse to accept for filing any paper presented for that purpose solely because it is not presented in proper form as required by these rules or by any local rule or practice.

(5) Privacy Protection. An appeal in a case whose privacy protection was governed by Federal Rule of Bankruptcy Procedure 9037, Federal Rule of Civil Procedure 5.2, or Federal Rule of Criminal Procedure 49.1 is governed by the same rule on appeal. In all other proceedings, privacy protection is governed by Federal Rule of Civil Procedure 5.2, except that Federal Rule of Criminal Procedure 49.1 governs when an extraordinary writ is sought in a criminal case.

(b) Service of All Papers Required. Unless a rule requires service by the clerk, a party must, at or before the time of filing a paper, serve a copy on the other parties to the appeal or review. Service on a party represented by counsel must be made on the party's counsel.

(c) Manner of Service.

(1) Service may be any of the following:

(A) personal, including delivery to a responsible person at the office of counsel;

(B) by mail;

(C) by third-party commercial carrier for delivery within 3 calendar days; or

(D) by electronic means, if the party being served consents in writing.

(2) If authorized by local rule, a party may use the court's transmission equipment to make electronic service under Rule 25(c)(1)(D).

(3) When reasonable considering such factors as the immediacy of the relief sought, distance, and cost, service on a party must be by a manner at least as expeditious as the manner used to file the paper with the court.

(4) Service by mail or by commercial carrier is complete on mailing or delivery to the carrier. Service by electronic means is complete on transmission, unless the party making service is notified that the paper was not received by the party served.

(d) Proof of Service.

(1) A paper presented for filing must contain either of the following:

(A) an acknowledgment of service by the person served; or

(B) proof of service consisting of a statement by the person who made service certifying:

(i) the date and manner of service;

(ii) the names of the persons served; and

(iii) their mail or electronic addresses, facsimile numbers, or the addresses of the places of delivery, as appropriate for the manner of service.

(2) When a brief or appendix is filed by mailing or dispatch in accordance with Rule 25(a)(2)(B), the proof of service must also state the date and manner by which the document was mailed or dispatched to the clerk.

(3) Proof of service may appear on or be affixed to the papers filed.

(e) **Number of Copies.** When these rules require the filing or furnishing of a number of copies, a court may require a different number by local rule or by order in a particular case.

RULE 26. COMPUTING AND EXTENDING TIME

(a) **Computing Time.** The following rules apply in computing any period of time specified in these rules or in any local rule, court order, or applicable statute:

(1) Exclude the day of the act, event, or default that begins the period.

(2) Exclude intermediate Saturdays, Sundays, and legal holidays when the period is less than 11 days, unless stated in calendar days.

(3) Include the last day of the period unless it is a Saturday, Sunday, legal holiday, or—if the act to be done is filing a paper in court—a day on which the weather or other conditions make the clerk's office inaccessible.

(4) As used in this rule, "legal holiday" means New Year's Day, Martin Luther King, Jr.'s Birthday, Washington's Birthday, Memorial Day, Independence Day, Labor Day, Columbus Day, Veterans' Day, Thanksgiving Day, Christmas Day, and any other day declared a holiday by the President, Congress, or the state in which is located either the district court that rendered the challenged judgment or order, or the circuit clerk's principal office.

(b) **Extending Time.** For good cause, the court may extend the time prescribed by these rules or by its order to perform any act, or may permit an act to be done after that time expires. But the court may not extend the time to file:

(1) a notice of appeal (except as authorized in Rule 4) or a petition for permission to appeal; or

(2) a notice of appeal from or a petition to enjoin, set aside, suspend, modify, enforce, or otherwise review an order of an admin-

istrative agency, board, commission, or officer of the United States, unless specifically authorized by law.

(c) Additional Time after Service. When a party is required or permitted to act within a prescribed period after a paper is served on that party, 3 calendar days are added to the prescribed period unless the paper is delivered on the date of service stated in the proof of service. For purposes of this Rule 26(c), a paper that is served electronically is not treated as delivered on the date of service stated in the proof of service.

RULE 26.1 CORPORATE DISCLOSURE STATEMENT

(a) Who Must File. Any nongovernmental corporate party to a proceeding in a court of appeals must file a statement that identifies any parent corporation and any publicly held corporation that owns 10% or more of its stock or states that there is no such corporation.

(b) Time for Filing; Supplemental Filing. A party must file the Rule 26.1(a) statement with the principal brief or upon filing a motion, response, petition, or answer in the court of appeals, whichever occurs first, unless a local rule requires earlier filing. Even if the statement has already been filed, the party's principal brief must include the statement before the table of contents. A party must supplement its statement whenever the information that must be disclosed under Rule 26.1(a) changes.

(c) Number of Copies. If the Rule 26.1(a) statement is filed before the principal brief, or if a supplemental statement is filed, the party must file an original and 3 copies unless the court requires a different number by local rule or by order in a particular case.

RULE 27. MOTIONS

(a) In General.

(1) Application for Relief. An application for an order or other relief is made by motion unless these rules prescribe another form. A motion must be in writing unless the court permits otherwise.

(2) Contents of a Motion.

(A) Grounds and relief sought. A motion must state with particularity the grounds for the motion, the relief sought, and the legal argument necessary to support it.

(B) Accompanying documents.

(i) Any affidavit or other paper necessary to support a motion must be served and filed with the motion.

(ii) An affidavit must contain only factual information, not legal argument.

(iii) A motion seeking substantive relief must include a copy of the trial court's opinion or agency's decision as a separate exhibit.

(C) Documents barred or not required.

(i) A separate brief supporting or responding to a motion must not be filed.

(ii) A notice of motion is not required.

(iii) A proposed order is not required.

(3) Response.

(A) Time to file. Any party may file a response to a motion; Rule 27(a)(2) governs its contents. The response must be filed within 8 days after service of the motion unless the court shortens or extends the time. A motion authorized by Rules 8, 9, 18, or 41 may be granted before the 8–day period runs only if the court gives reasonable notice to the parties that it intends to act sooner.

(B) Request for affirmative relief. A response may include a motion for affirmative relief. The time to respond to the new motion, and to reply to that response, are governed by Rule 27(a)(3)(A) and (a)(4). The title of the response must alert the court to the request for relief.

(4) Reply to Response. Any reply to a response must be filed within 5 days after service of the response. A reply must not present matters that do not relate to the response.

(b) Disposition of a Motion for a Procedural Order. The court may act on a motion for a procedural order—including a motion under Rule 26(b)—at any time without awaiting a response, and may, by rule or by order in a particular case, authorize its clerk to act on specified types of procedural motions. A party adversely affected by the court's, or the clerk's, action may file a motion to reconsider, vacate, or modify that action. Timely opposition filed after the motion is granted in whole or in part does not constitute a request to reconsider, vacate, or modify the disposition; a motion requesting that relief must be filed.

(c) Power of a Single Judge to Entertain a Motion. A circuit judge may act alone on any motion, but may not dismiss or otherwise determine an appeal or other proceeding. A court of appeals may provide by rule or by order in a particular case that only the court may act on any motion or class of motions. The court may review the action of a single judge.

(d) Form of Papers; Page Limits; and Number of Copies.

(1) Format.

(A) Reproduction. A motion, response, or reply may be reproduced by any process that yields a clear black image on light paper. The paper must be opaque and unglazed. Only one side of the paper may be used.

(B) Cover. A cover is not required but there must be a caption that includes the case number, the name of the court, the title of the case, and a brief descriptive title indicating the purpose of the motion and identifying the party or parties for whom it is filed. If a cover is used, it must be white.

(C) Binding. The document must be bound in any manner that is secure, does not obscure the text, and permits the document to lie reasonably flat when open.

(D) Paper size, line spacing, and margins. The document must be on 8½ by 11 inch paper. The text must be double-spaced, but quotations more than two lines long may be indented and single-spaced. Headings and footnotes may be single-spaced. Margins must be at least one inch on all four sides. Page numbers may be placed in the margins, but no text may appear there.

(E) Typeface and type styles. The document must comply with the typeface requirements of Rule 32(a)(5) and the type-style requirements of Rule 32(a)(6).

(2) Page Limits. A motion or a response to a motion must not exceed 20 pages, exclusive of the corporate disclosure statement and accompanying documents authorized by Rule 27(a)(2)(B), unless the court permits or directs otherwise. A reply to a response must not exceed 10 pages.

(3) Number of Copies. An original and 3 copies must be filed unless the court requires a different number by local rule or by order in a particular case.

(e) Oral Argument. A motion will be decided without oral argument unless the court orders otherwise.

RULE 28. BRIEFS

(a) Appellant's Brief. The appellant's brief must contain, under appropriate headings and in the order indicated:

(1) a corporate disclosure statement if required by Rule 26.1;

(2) a table of contents, with page references;

(3) a table of authorities—cases (alphabetically arranged), statutes, and other authorities—with references to the pages of the brief where they are cited;

(4) a jurisdictional statement, including:

(A) the basis for the district court's or agency's subject-matter jurisdiction, with citations to applicable statutory provisions and stating relevant facts establishing jurisdiction;

(B) the basis for the court of appeals' jurisdiction, with citations to applicable statutory provisions and stating relevant facts establishing jurisdiction;

(C) the filing dates establishing the timeliness of the appeal or petition for review; and

(D) an assertion that the appeal is from a final order or judgment that disposes of all parties' claims, or information establishing the court of appeals' jurisdiction on some other basis;

(5) a statement of the issues presented for review;

(6) a statement of the case briefly indicating the nature of the case, the course of proceedings, and the disposition below;

(7) a statement of facts relevant to the issues submitted for review with appropriate references to the record (see Rule 28(e));

(8) a summary of the argument, which must contain a succinct, clear, and accurate statement of the arguments made in the body of the brief, and which must not merely repeat the argument headings;

(9) the argument, which must contain:

(A) appellant's contentions and the reasons for them, with citations to the authorities and parts of the record on which the appellant relies; and

(B) for each issue, a concise statement of the applicable standard of review (which may appear in the discussion of the issue or under a separate heading placed before the discussion of the issues);

(10) a short conclusion stating the precise relief sought; and

(11) the certificate of compliance, if required by Rule 32(a)(7).

(b) Appellee's Brief. The appellee's brief must conform to the requirements of Rule 28(a)(1)-(9) and (11), except that none of the following need appear unless the appellee is dissatisfied with the appellant's statement:

(1) the jurisdictional statement;

(2) the statement of the issues;

(3) the statement of the case;

(4) the statement of the facts; and

(5) the statement of the standard of review.

(c) Reply Brief. The appellant may file a brief in reply to the appellee's brief. Unless the court permits, no further briefs may be filed. A reply brief must contain a table of contents, with page references, and a table of authorities—cases (alphabetically arranged), statutes, and other authorities—with references to the pages of the reply brief where they are cited.

(d) References to Parties. In briefs and at oral argument, counsel should minimize use of the terms "appellant" and "appellee." To make briefs clear, counsel should use the parties' actual names or the designations used in the lower court or agency proceeding, or such descriptive terms as "the employee," "the injured person," "the taxpayer," "the ship," "the stevedore."

(e) References to the Record. References to the parts of the record contained in the appendix filed with the appellant's brief must be to the pages of the appendix. If the appendix is prepared after the briefs are filed, a party referring to the record must follow one of the methods detailed in Rule 30(c). If the original record is used under Rule 30(f) and is not consecutively paginated, or if the brief refers to an unreproduced part of the record, any reference must be to the page of the original document. For example:

* Answer p. 7;

* Motion for Judgment p. 2;

* Transcript p. 231.

Only clear abbreviations may be used. A party referring to evidence whose admissibility is in controversy must cite the pages of the appendix or of the transcript at which the evidence was identified, offered, and received or rejected.

(f) Reproduction of Statutes, Rules, Regulations, etc. If the court's determination of the issues presented requires the study of statutes, rules, regulations, etc., the relevant parts must be set out in the brief or in an addendum at the end, or may be supplied to the court in pamphlet form.

(g) [Reserved]

(h) [Reserved]

(i) Briefs in a Case Involving Multiple Appellants or Appellees. In a case involving more than one appellant or appellee, including consolidated cases, any number of appellants or appellees may join in a brief, and any party may adopt by reference a part of another's brief. Parties may also join in reply briefs.

(j) Citation of Supplemental Authorities. If pertinent and significant authorities come to a party's attention after the party's brief has been filed—or after oral argument but before decision—a party may promptly advise the circuit clerk by letter, with a copy to all other parties, setting forth the citations. The letter must state the reasons for the supplemental citations, referring either to the page of the brief or to a point argued orally. The body of the letter must not exceed 350 words. Any response must be made promptly and must be similarly limited.

RULE 28.1 CROSS–APPEALS

(a) Applicability. This rule applies to a case in which a cross-appeal is filed. Rules 28(a)-(c), 31(a)(1), 32(a)(2), and 32(a)(7)(A)-(B) do not apply to such a case, except as otherwise provided in this rule.

(b) Designation of Appellant. The party who files a notice of appeal first is the appellant for the purposes of this rule and Rules 30 and 34. If notices are filed on the same day, the plaintiff in the proceeding below is the appellant. These designations may be modified by the parties' agreement or by court order.

(c) Briefs. In a case involving a cross-appeal:

(1) Appellant's Principal Brief. The appellant must file a principal brief in the appeal. That brief must comply with Rule 28(a).

(2) Appellee's Principal and Response Brief. The appellee must file a principal brief in the cross-appeal and must, in the same brief, respond to the principal brief in the appeal. That appellee's brief must comply with Rule 28(a), except that the brief need not include a statement of the case or a statement of the facts unless the appellee is dissatisfied with the appellant's statement.

(3) Appellant's Response and Reply Brief. The appellant must file a brief that responds to the principal brief in the cross-appeal and may, in the same brief, reply to the response in the appeal. That brief must comply with Rule 28(a)(2)–(9) and (11), except that none of the following need appear unless the appellant is dissatisfied with the appellee's statement in the cross-appeal:

(A) the jurisdictional statement;

(B) the statement of the issues;

(C) the statement of the case;

(D) the statement of the facts; and

(E) the statement of the standard of review.

(4) Appellee's Reply Brief. The appellee may file a brief in reply to the response in the crossappeal. That brief must comply with Rule 28(a)(2)–(3) and (11) and must be limited to the issues presented by the cross-appeal.

(5) No Further Briefs. Unless the court permits, no further briefs may be filed in a case involving a cross-appeal.

(d) Cover. Except for filings by unrepresented parties, the cover of the appellant's principal brief must be blue; the appellee's principal and response brief, red; the appellant's response and reply brief, yellow; the appellee's reply brief, gray; an intervenor's or amicus curiae's brief, green; and any supplemental brief, tan. The front cover of a brief must contain the information required by Rule 32(a)(2).

(e) Length.

(1) Page Limitation. Unless it complies with Rule 28.1(e)(2) and (3), the appellant's principal brief must not exceed 30 pages; the appellee's principal and response brief, 35 pages; the appellant's response and reply brief, 30 pages; and the appellee's reply brief, 15 pages.

(2) Type–Volume Limitation.

(A) The appellant's principal brief or the appellant's response and reply brief is acceptable if:

(i) it contains no more than 14,000 words;

or

(ii) it uses a monospaced face and contains no more than 1,300 lines of text.

(B) The appellee's principal and response brief is acceptable if:

(i) it contains no more than 16,500 words;

or

(ii) it uses a monospaced face and contains no more than 1,500 lines of text.

(C) The appellee's reply brief is acceptable if it contains no more than half of the type volume specified in Rule 28.1(e)(2)(A).

(3) Certificate of Compliance. A brief submitted under Rule 28.1(e)(2) must comply with Rule 32(a)(7)(C).

(f) Time to Serve and File a Brief. Briefs must be served and filed as follows:

(1) the appellant's principal brief, within 40 days after the record is filed;

(2) the appellee's principal and response brief, within 30 days after the appellant's principal brief is served;

(3) the appellant's response and reply brief, within 30 days after the appellee's principal and response brief is served; and

(4) the appellee's reply brief, within 14 days after the appellant's response and reply brief is served, but at least 3 days before argument unless the court, for good cause, allows a later filing.

RULE 29. BRIEF OF AN AMICUS CURIAE

(a) When Permitted. The United States or its officer or agency, or a State, Territory, Commonwealth, or the District of Columbia may file an amicus-curiae brief without the consent of the parties or leave of court. Any other amicus curiae may file a brief only by leave of court or if the brief states that all parties have consented to its filing.

(b) Motion for Leave to File. The motion must be accompanied by the proposed brief and state:

(1) the movant's interest; and

(2) the reason why an amicus brief is desirable and why the matters asserted are relevant to the disposition of the case.

(c) Contents and Form. An amicus brief must comply with Rule 32. In addition to the requirements of Rule 32, the cover must identify the party or parties supported and indicate whether the brief supports affirmance or reversal. If an amicus curiae is a corporation, the brief must include a disclosure statement like that required of parties by Rule 26.1. An amicus brief need not comply with Rule 28, but must include the following:

(1) a table of contents, with page references;

(2) a table of authorities—cases (alphabetically arranged), statutes and other authorities—with references to the pages of the brief where they are cited;

(3) a concise statement of the identity of the amicus curiae, its interest in the case, and the source of its authority to file;

(4) an argument, which may be preceded by a summary and which need not include a statement of the applicable standard of review; and

(5) a certificate of compliance, if required by Rule 32(a)(7).

(d) Length. Except by the court's permission, an amicus brief may be no more than one-half the maximum length authorized by these rules for a party's principal brief. If the court grants a party permission to file a longer brief, that extension does not affect the length of an amicus brief.

(e) Time for Filing. An amicus curiae must file its brief, accompanied by a motion for filing when necessary, no later than 7 days after the principal brief of the party being supported is filed. An amicus curiae that does not support either party must file its brief no later than 7 days after the appellant's or petitioner's principal brief is filed. A court may grant leave for later filing, specifying the time within which an opposing party may answer.

(f) Reply Brief. Except by the court's permission, an amicus curiae may not file a reply brief.

(g) Oral Argument. An amicus curiae may participate in oral argument only with the court's permission.

RULE 30. APPENDIX TO THE BRIEFS

(a) Appellant's Responsibility.

(1) Contents of the Appendix. The appellant must prepare and file an appendix to the briefs containing:

(A) the relevant docket entries in the proceeding below;

(B) the relevant portions of the pleadings, charge, findings, or opinion;

(C) the judgment, order, or decision in question; and

(D) other parts of the record to which the parties wish to direct the court's attention.

(2) Excluded Material. Memoranda of law in the district court should not be included in the appendix unless they have independent relevance. Parts of the record may be relied on by the court or the parties even though not included in the appendix.

(3) Time to File; Number of Copies. Unless filing is deferred under Rule 30(c), the appellant must file 10 copies of the appendix with the brief and must serve one copy on counsel for each party separately represented. An unrepresented party proceeding in forma pauperis must file 4 legible copies with the clerk, and one copy must be served on counsel for each separately represented party. The court may by local rule or by order in a particular case require the filing or service of a different number.

(b) All Parties' Responsibilities.

(1) Determining the Contents of the Appendix. The parties are encouraged to agree on the contents of the appendix. In the absence of an agreement, the appellant must, within 10 days after the record is filed, serve on the appellee a designation of the parts of the record the appellant intends to include in the appendix and a statement of the issues the appellant intends to present for review.

The appellee may, within 10 days after receiving the designation, serve on the appellant a designation of additional parts to which it wishes to direct the court's attention. The appellant must include the designated parts in the appendix. The parties must not engage in unnecessary designation of parts of the record, because the entire record is available to the court. This paragraph applies also to a cross-appellant and a cross-appellee.

(2) Costs of Appendix. Unless the parties agree otherwise, the appellant must pay the cost of the appendix. If the appellant considers parts of the record designated by the appellee to be unnecessary, the appellant may advise the appellee, who must then advance the cost of including those parts. The cost of the appendix is a taxable cost. But if any party causes unnecessary parts of the record to be included in the appendix, the court may impose the cost of those parts on that party. Each circuit must, by local rule, provide for sanctions against attorneys who unreasonably and vexatiously increase litigation costs by including unnecessary material in the appendix.

(c) Deferred Appendix.

(1) Deferral Until After Briefs Are Filed. The court may provide by rule for classes of cases or by order in a particular case that preparation of the appendix may be deferred until after the briefs have been filed and that the appendix may be filed 21 days after the appellee's brief is served. Even though the filing of the appendix may be deferred, Rule 30(b) applies; except that a party must designate the parts of the record it wants included in the appendix when it serves its brief, and need not include a statement of the issues presented.

(2) References to the Record.

(A) If the deferred appendix is used, the parties may cite in their briefs the pertinent pages of the record. When the appendix is prepared, the record pages cited in the briefs must be indicated by inserting record page numbers, in brackets, at places in the appendix where those pages of the record appear.

(B) A party who wants to refer directly to pages of the appendix may serve and file copies of the brief within the time required by Rule 31(a), containing appropriate references to pertinent pages of the record. In that event, within 14 days after the appendix is filed, the party must serve and file copies of the brief, containing references to the pages of the appendix in place of or in addition to the references to the pertinent pages of the record. Except for the correction of typographical errors, no other changes may be made to the brief.

(d) Format of the Appendix. The appendix must begin with a table of contents identifying the page at which each part begins. The relevant docket entries must follow the table of contents. Other parts of the record must follow chronologically. When pages from the transcript of proceedings are placed in the appendix, the transcript page numbers must be shown in brackets immediately before the included pages. Omissions in the text of papers or of the transcript must be indicated by asterisks. Immaterial formal matters (captions, subscriptions, acknowledgments, etc.) should be omitted.

(e) Reproduction of Exhibits. Exhibits designated for inclusion in the appendix may be reproduced in a separate volume, or volumes, suitably indexed. Four copies must be filed with the appendix, and one copy must be served on counsel for each separately represented party. If a transcript of a proceeding before an administrative agency, board, commission, or officer was used in a district-court action and has been designated for inclusion in the appendix, the transcript must be placed in the appendix as an exhibit.

(f) Appeal on the Original Record Without an Appendix. The court may, either by rule for all cases or classes of cases or by order in a particular case, dispense with the appendix and permit an appeal to proceed on the original record with any copies of the record, or relevant parts, that the court may order the parties to file.

RULE 31. SERVING AND FILING BRIEFS

(a) Time to Serve and File a Brief.

(1) The appellant must serve and file a brief within 40 days after the record is filed. The appellee must serve and file a brief within 30 days after the appellant's brief is served. The appellant may serve and file a reply brief within 14 days after service of the appellee's brief but a reply brief must be filed at least 3 days before argument, unless the court, for good cause, allows a later filing.

(2) A court of appeals that routinely considers cases on the merits promptly after the briefs are filed may shorten the time to serve and file briefs, either by local rule or by order in a particular case.

(b) Number of Copies. Twenty-five copies of each brief must be filed with the clerk and 2 copies must be served on each unrepresented party and on counsel for each separately represented party. An unrepresented party proceeding in forma pauperis must file 4 legible copies with the clerk, and one copy must be served on each unrepresented party and on counsel for each separately represented party. The court may by local rule or by order in a particular case require the filing or service of a different number.

(c) Consequence of Failure to File. If an appellant fails to file a brief within the time provided by this rule, or within an extended time, an appellee may move to dismiss the appeal. An appellee who fails to file a brief will not be heard at oral argument unless the court grants permission.

RULE 32. FORM OF BRIEFS, APPENDICES, AND OTHER PAPERS

(a) Form of a Brief.

(1) Reproduction.

(A) A brief may be reproduced by any process that yields a clear black image on light paper. The paper must be opaque and unglazed. Only one side of the paper may be used.

(B) Text must be reproduced with a clarity that equals or exceeds the output of a laser printer.

(C) Photographs, illustrations, and tables may be reproduced by any method that results in a good copy of the original; a glossy finish is acceptable if the original is glossy.

(2) Cover. Except for filings by unrepresented parties, the cover of the appellant's brief must be blue; the appellee's, red; an intervenor's or amicus curiae's, green; any reply brief, gray; and any supplemental brief, tan. The front cover of a brief must contain:

(A) the number of the case centered at the top;

(B) the name of the court;

(C) the title of the case (see Rule 12(a));

(D) the nature of the proceeding (e.g., Appeal, Petition for Review) and the name of the court, agency, or board below;

(E) the title of the brief, identifying the party or parties for whom the brief is filed; and

(F) the name, office address, and telephone number of counsel representing the party for whom the brief is filed.

(3) Binding. The brief must be bound in any manner that is secure, does not obscure the text, and permits the brief to lie reasonably flat when open.

(4) Paper Size, Line Spacing, and Margins. The brief must be on 8½ by 11 inch paper. The text must be double-spaced, but quotations more than two lines long may be indented and single-spaced. Headings and footnotes may be single-spaced. Margins must be at least one inch on all four sides. Page numbers may be placed in the margins, but no text may appear there.

(5) Typeface. Either a proportionally spaced or a monospaced face may be used.

(A) A proportionally spaced face must include serifs, but sans-serif type may be used in headings and captions. A proportionally spaced face must be 14–point or larger.

(B) A monospaced face may not contain more than 10½ characters per inch.

(6) Type Styles. A brief must be set in a plain, roman style, although italics or boldface may be used for emphasis. Case names must be italicized or underlined.

(7) Length.

(A) Page limitation. A principal brief may not exceed 30 pages, or a reply brief 15 pages, unless it complies with Rule 32(a)(7)(B) and (C).

(B) Type-volume limitation.

(i) A principal brief is acceptable if:

* it contains no more than 14,000 words; or

* it uses a monospaced face and contains no more than 1,300 lines of text.

(ii) A reply brief is acceptable if it contains no more than half of the type volume specified in Rule 32(a)(7)(B)(i).

(iii) Headings, footnotes, and quotations count toward the word and line limitations. The corporate disclosure statement, table of contents, table of citations, statement with respect to oral argument, any addendum containing statutes, rules or regulations, and any certificates of counsel do not count toward the limitation.

(C) Certificate of compliance.

(i) A brief submitted under Rules 28.1(e)(2) or 32(a)(7)(B) must include a certificate by the attorney, or an unrepresented party, that the brief complies with the type-volume limitation. The person preparing the certificate may rely on the word or line count of the word-processing system used to prepare the brief. The certificate must state either:

● the number of words in the brief; or

● the number of lines of monospaced type in the brief.

(ii) Form 6 in the Appendix of Forms is a suggested form of a certificate of compliance. Use of Form 6 must be regarded as sufficient to meet the requirements of Rules 28.1(e)(3) and 32(a)(7)(C)(i).

(b) Form of an Appendix. An appendix must comply with Rule 32(a)(1), (2), (3), and (4), with the following exceptions:

(1) The cover of a separately bound appendix must be white.

(2) An appendix may include a legible photocopy of any document found in the record or of a printed judicial or agency decision.

(3) When necessary to facilitate inclusion of odd-sized documents such as technical drawings, an appendix may be a size other than 8½ by 11 inches, and need not lie reasonably flat when opened.

(c) Form of Other Papers.

(1) Motion. The form of a motion is governed by Rule 27(d).

(2) Other Papers. Any other paper, including a petition for panel rehearing and a petition for hearing or rehearing en banc, and any response to such a petition, must be reproduced in the manner prescribed by Rule 32(a), with the following exceptions:

(A) A cover is not necessary if the caption and signature page of the paper together contain the information required by Rule 32(a)(2). If a cover is used, it must be white.

(B) Rule 32(a)(7) does not apply.

(d) Signature. Every brief, motion, or other paper filed with the court must be signed by the party filing the paper or, if the party is represented, by one of the party's attorneys.

(e) Local Variation. Every court of appeals must accept documents that comply with the form requirements of this rule. By local rule or order in a particular case a court of appeals may accept documents that do not meet all of the form requirements of this rule.

RULE 32.1 CITING JUDICIAL DISPOSITIONS

(a) Citation Permitted. A court may not prohibit or restrict the citation of federal judicial opinions, orders, judgments, or other written dispositions that have been:

(i) designed as "unpublished," "not for publication," "non-precedential," "not precedent," or the like; and

(ii) issued on or after January 1, 2007.

(b) Copies Required. If a party cites a federal judicial opinion, order, judgment, or other written disposition that is not available in a publicly accessible electronic database, the party must file and serve a copy of that opinion, order, judgment, or disposition with the brief or other paper in which it is cited.

RULE 33. APPEAL CONFERENCES

The court may direct the attorneys—and, when appropriate, the parties—to participate in one or more conferences to address any matter that may aid in disposing of the proceedings, including simplifying the issues and discussing settlement. A judge or other person designated by the court may preside over the conference, which may be conducted in person or by telephone. Before a settlement conference, the attorneys must consult with their clients and obtain as much authority as feasible to settle the case. The court may, as a result of the conference, enter an order controlling the course of the proceedings or implementing any settlement agreement.

RULE 34. ORAL ARGUMENT

(a) In General.

(1) Party's Statement. Any party may file, or a court may require by local rule, a statement explaining why oral argument should, or need not, be permitted.

(2) Standards. Oral argument must be allowed in every case unless a panel of three judges who have examined the briefs and record unanimously agrees that oral argument is unnecessary for any of the following reasons:

(A) the appeal is frivolous;

(B) the dispositive issue or issues have been authoritatively decided; or

(C) the facts and legal arguments are adequately presented in the briefs and record, and the decisional process would not be significantly aided by oral argument.

(b) Notice of Argument; Postponement. The clerk must advise all parties whether oral argument will be scheduled, and, if so, the date, time, and place for it, and the time allowed for each side. A motion to postpone the argument or to allow longer argument must be filed reasonably in advance of the hearing date.

(c) Order and Contents of Argument. The appellant opens and concludes the argument. Counsel must not read at length from briefs, records, or authorities.

(d) Cross–Appeals and Separate Appeals. If there is a cross-appeal, Rule 28.1(b) determines which party is the appellant and which is the appellee for purposes of oral argument. Unless the court directs otherwise, a cross-appeal or separate appeal must be argued when the initial appeal is argued. Separate parties should avoid duplicative argument.

(e) Nonappearance of a Party. If the appellee fails to appear for argument, the court must hear appellant's argument. If the appellant fails to appear for argument, the court may hear the appellee's argument. If neither party appears, the case will be decided on the briefs, unless the court orders otherwise.

(f) Submission on Briefs. The parties may agree to submit a case for decision on the briefs, but the court may direct that the case be argued.

(g) Use of Physical Exhibits at Argument; Removal. Counsel intending to use physical exhibits other than documents at the argument must arrange to place them in the courtroom on the day of the argument before the court convenes. After the argument, counsel must remove the exhibits from the courtroom, unless the court directs otherwise. The clerk may destroy or dispose of the exhibits if counsel does not reclaim them within a reasonable time after the clerk gives notice to remove them.

RULE 35. EN BANC DETERMINATION

(a) When Hearing or Rehearing En Banc May Be Ordered. A majority of the circuit judges who are in regular active service and who are not disqualified may order that an appeal or other proceeding be heard or reheard by the court of appeals en banc. An en banc hearing or rehearing is not favored and ordinarily will not be ordered unless:

(1) en banc consideration is necessary to secure or maintain uniformity of the court's decisions; or

(2) the proceeding involves a question of exceptional importance.

(b) Petition for Hearing or Rehearing En Banc. A party may petition for a hearing or rehearing en banc.

(1) The petition must begin with a statement that either:

(A) the panel decision conflicts with a decision of the United States Supreme Court or of the court to which the petition is addressed (with citation to the conflicting case or cases) and consideration by the full court is therefore necessary to secure and maintain uniformity of the court's decisions; or

(B) the proceeding involves one or more questions of exceptional importance, each of which must be concisely stated; for example, a petition may assert that a proceeding presents a question of exceptional importance if it involves an issue on which the panel decision conflicts with the authoritative decisions of every other United States Court of Appeals that has addressed the issue.

(2) Except by the court's permission, a petition for an en banc hearing or rehearing must not exceed 15 pages, excluding material not counted under Rule 32.

(3) For purposes of the page limit in Rule 35(b)(2), if a party files both a petition for panel rehearing and a petition for rehearing en banc, they are considered a single document even if they are filed separately, unless separate filing is required by local rule.

(c) Time for Petition for Hearing or Rehearing En Banc. A petition that an appeal be heard initially en banc must be filed by the date when the appellee's brief is due. A petition for a rehearing en banc must be filed within the time prescribed by Rule 40 for filing a petition for rehearing.

(d) Number of Copies. The number of copies to be filed must be prescribed by local rule and may be altered by order in a particular case.

(e) Response. No response may be filed to a petition for an en banc consideration unless the court orders a response.

(f) Call for a Vote. A vote need not be taken to determine whether the case will be heard or reheard en banc unless a judge calls for a vote.

RULE 36. ENTRY OF JUDGMENT; NOTICE

(a) Entry. A judgment is entered when it is noted on the docket. The clerk must prepare, sign, and enter the judgment:

(1) after receiving the court's opinion—but if settlement of the judgment's form is required, after final settlement; or

(2) if a judgment is rendered without an opinion, as the court instructs.

(b) Notice. On the date when judgment is entered, the clerk must serve on all parties a copy of the opinion—or the judgment, if no opinion was written—and a notice of the date when the judgment was entered.

RULE 37. INTEREST ON JUDGMENT

(a) When the Court Affirms. Unless the law provides otherwise, if a money judgment in a civil case is affirmed, whatever interest is allowed by law is payable from the date when the district court's judgment was entered.

(b) When the Court Reverses. If the court modifies or reverses a judgment with a direction that a money judgment be entered in the district court, the mandate must contain instructions about the allowance of interest.

RULE 38. FRIVOLOUS APPEAL—DAMAGES AND COSTS

If a court of appeals determines that an appeal is frivolous, it may, after a separately filed motion or notice from the court and reasonable opportunity to respond, award just damages and single or double costs to the appellee.

RULE 39. COSTS

(a) Against Whom Assessed. The following rules apply unless the law provides or the court orders otherwise:

(1) if an appeal is dismissed, costs are taxed against the appellant, unless the parties agree otherwise;

(2) if a judgment is affirmed, costs are taxed against the appellant;

(3) if a judgment is reversed, costs are taxed against the appellee;

(4) if a judgment is affirmed in part, reversed in part, modified, or vacated, costs are taxed only as the court orders.

(b) Costs For and Against the United States. Costs for or against the United States, its agency, or officer will be assessed under Rule 39(a) only if authorized by law.

(c) Costs of Copies. Each court of appeals must, by local rule, fix the maximum rate for taxing the cost of producing necessary copies of a brief or appendix, or copies of records authorized by Rule 30(f). The rate must not exceed that generally charged for such work in the area where the clerk's office is located and should encourage economical methods of copying.

(d) Bill of Costs: Objections; Insertion in Mandate.

(1) A party who wants costs taxed must—within 14 days after entry of judgment—file with the circuit clerk, with proof of service, an itemized and verified bill of costs.

(2) Objections must be filed within 10 days after service of the bill of costs, unless the court extends the time.

(3) The clerk must prepare and certify an itemized statement of costs for insertion in the mandate, but issuance of the mandate must not be delayed for taxing costs. If the mandate issues before costs are finally determined, the district clerk must—upon the circuit clerk's request—add the statement of costs, or any amendment of it, to the mandate.

(e) Costs on Appeal Taxable in the District Court. The following costs on appeal are taxable in the district court for the benefit of the party entitled to costs under this rule:

(1) the preparation and transmission of the record;

(2) the reporter's transcript, if needed to determine the appeal;

(3) premiums paid for a supersedeas bond or other bond to preserve rights pending appeal; and

(4) the fee for filing the notice of appeal.

RULE 40. PETITION FOR PANEL REHEARING

(a) Time to File; Contents; Answer; Action by the Court if Granted.

(1) Time. Unless the time is shortened or extended by order or local rule, a petition for panel rehearing may be filed within 14 days after entry of judgment. But in a civil case, if the United States or its officer or agency is a party, the time within which any party may seek rehearing is 45 days after entry of judgment, unless an order shortens or extends the time.

(2) Contents. The petition must state with particularity each point of law or fact that the petitioner believes the court has overlooked or misapprehended and must argue in support of the petition. Oral argument is not permitted.

(3) Answer. Unless the court requests, no answer to a petition for panel rehearing is permitted. But ordinarily rehearing will not be granted in the absence of such a request.

(4) Action by the Court. If a petition for panel rehearing is granted, the court may do any of the following:

(A) make a final disposition of the case without reargument;

(B) restore the case to the calendar for reargument or resubmission; or

(C) issue any other appropriate order.

(b) Form of Petition; Length. The petition must comply in form with Rule 32. Copies must be served and filed as Rule 31 prescribes. Unless the court permits or a local rule provides otherwise, a petition for panel rehearing must not exceed 15 pages.

RULE 41. MANDATE: CONTENTS; ISSUANCE
AND EFFECTIVE DATE; STAY

(a) Contents. Unless the court directs that a formal mandate issue, the mandate consists of a certified copy of the judgment, a copy of the court's opinion, if any, and any direction about costs.

(b) When Issued. The court's mandate must issue 7 calendar days after the time to file a petition for rehearing expires, or 7 calendar days after entry of an order denying a timely petition for panel rehearing, petition for rehearing en banc, or motion for stay of mandate, whichever is later. The court may shorten or extend the time.

(c) Effective Date. The mandate is effective when issued.

(d) Staying the Mandate.

(1) On Petition for Rehearing or Motion. The timely filing of a petition for panel rehearing, petition for rehearing en banc, or motion for stay of mandate, stays the mandate until disposition of the petition or motion, unless the court orders otherwise.

(2) Pending Petition for Certiorari.

(A) A party may move to stay the mandate pending the filing of a petition for a writ of certiorari in the Supreme Court. The motion must be served on all parties and must show that the certiorari petition would present a substantial question and that there is good cause for a stay.

(B) The stay must not exceed 90 days, unless the period is extended for good cause or unless the party who obtained the stay files a petition for the writ and so notifies the circuit clerk in writing within the period of the stay. In that case, the stay continues until the Supreme Court's final disposition.

(C) The court may require a bond or other security as a condition to granting or continuing a stay of the mandate.

(D) The court of appeals must issue the mandate immediately when a copy of a Supreme Court order denying the petition for writ of certiorari is filed.

RULE 42. VOLUNTARY DISMISSAL

(a) Dismissal in the District Court. Before an appeal has been docketed by the circuit clerk, the district court may dismiss the appeal on the filing of a stipulation signed by all parties or on the appellant's motion with notice to all parties.

(b) Dismissal in the Court of Appeals. The circuit clerk may dismiss a docketed appeal if the parties file a signed dismissal agreement specifying how costs are to be paid and pay any fees that are due. But no mandate or other process may issue without a court order. An appeal may be dismissed on the appellant's motion on terms agreed to by the parties or fixed by the court.

RULE 43. SUBSTITUTION OF PARTIES

(a) Death of a Party.

(1) After Notice of Appeal Is Filed. If a party dies after a notice of appeal has been filed or while a proceeding is pending in the court of appeals, the decedent's personal representative may be substituted as a party on motion filed with the circuit clerk by the representative or by any party. A party's motion must be served on the representative in accordance with Rule 25. If the decedent has no representative, any party may suggest the death on the record, and the court of appeals may then direct appropriate proceedings.

(2) Before Notice of Appeal Is Filed—Potential Appellant. If a party entitled to appeal dies before filing a notice of appeal, the decedent's personal representative—or, if there is no personal representative, the decedent's attorney of record—may file a notice of appeal within the time prescribed by these rules. After the notice of appeal is filed, substitution must be in accordance with Rule 43(a)(1).

(3) Before Notice of Appeal Is Filed—Potential Appellee. If a party against whom an appeal may be taken dies after entry of a judgment or order in the district court, but before a notice of appeal is filed, an appellant may proceed as if the death had not occurred. After the notice of appeal is filed, substitution must be in accordance with Rule 43(a)(1).

(b) Substitution for a Reason Other Than Death. If a party needs to be substituted for any reason other than death, the procedure prescribed in Rule 43(a) applies.

(c) Public Officer: Identification; Substitution.

(1) Identification of Party. A public officer who is a party to an appeal or other proceeding in an official capacity may be described as a party by the public officer's official title rather than by name. But the court may require the public officer's name to be added.

(2) Automatic Substitution of Officeholder. When a public officer who is a party to an appeal or other proceeding in an official capacity dies, resigns, or otherwise ceases to hold office, the action does not abate. The public officer's successor is automatically substituted as a party. Proceedings following the substitution are to be in the name of the substituted party, but any misnomer that does not affect the substantial rights of the parties may be disregarded. An order of substitution may be entered at any time, but failure to enter an order does not affect the substitution.

RULE 44. CASE INVOLVING A CONSTITUTIONAL QUESTION WHEN THE UNITED STATES OR THE RELEVANT STATE IS NOT A PARTY

(a) Constitutional Challenge to Federal Statute. If a party questions the constitutionality of an Act of Congress in a proceeding in which the United States or its agency, officer, or employee is not a party in an official capacity, the questioning party must give written notice to the circuit clerk immediately upon the filing of the record or as soon as the question is raised in the court of appeals. The clerk must then certify that fact to the Attorney General.

(b) Constitutional Challenge to State Statute. If a party questions the constitutionality of a statute of a State in a proceeding in which that State or its agency, officer, or employee is not a party in an official capacity, the questioning party must give written notice to the circuit clerk immediately upon the filing of the record or as soon as the question is raised in the court of appeals. The clerk must then certify that fact to the attorney general of the State.

RULE 45. CLERK'S DUTIES

(a) General Provisions.

(1) Qualifications. The circuit clerk must take the oath and post any bond required by law. Neither the clerk nor any deputy clerk may practice as an attorney or counselor in any court while in office.

(2) When Court Is Open. The court of appeals is always open for filing any paper, issuing and returning process, making a motion, and entering an order. The clerk's office with the clerk or a deputy in attendance must be open during business hours on all days except Saturdays, Sundays, and legal holidays. A court may provide by local rule or by order that the clerk's office be open for specified hours on Saturdays or on legal holidays other than New Year's Day, Martin Luther King, Jr.'s Birthday, Washington's Birthday, Memorial Day, Independence Day, Labor Day, Columbus Day, Veterans' Day, Thanksgiving Day, and Christmas Day.

(b) Records.

(1) The Docket. The circuit clerk must maintain a docket and an index of all docketed cases in the manner prescribed by the Director of the Administrative Office of the United States Courts. The clerk must record all papers filed with the clerk and all process, orders, and judgments.

(2) Calendar. Under the court's direction, the clerk must prepare a calendar of cases awaiting argument. In placing cases on the calendar for argument, the clerk must give preference to appeals in criminal cases and to other proceedings and appeals entitled to preference by law.

(3) Other Records. The clerk must keep other books and records required by the Director of the Administrative Office of the United States Courts, with the approval of the Judicial Conference of the United States, or by the court.

(c) Notice of an Order or Judgment. Upon the entry of an order or judgment, the circuit clerk must immediately serve a notice of entry on each party, with a copy of any opinion, and must note the date of service on the docket. Service on a party represented by counsel must be made on counsel.

(d) Custody of Records and Papers. The circuit clerk has custody of the court's records and papers. Unless the court orders or instructs otherwise, the clerk must not permit an original record or paper to be taken from the clerk's office. Upon disposition of the case, original papers constituting the record on appeal or review must be returned to the court or agency from which they were received. The clerk must preserve a copy of any brief, appendix, or other paper that has been filed.

RULE 46. ATTORNEYS

(a) Admission to the Bar.

(1) Eligibility. An attorney is eligible for admission to the bar of a court of appeals if that attorney is of good moral and professional character and is admitted to practice before the Supreme Court of the United States, the highest court of a state, another United States court of appeals, or a United States district court (including the district courts for Guam, the Northern Mariana Islands, and the Virgin Islands).

(2) Application. An applicant must file an application for admission, on a form approved by the court that contains the applicant's personal statement showing eligibility for membership. The applicant must subscribe to the following oath or affirmation: "I, _____, do solemnly swear [or affirm] that I will conduct myself as an attorney and counselor of this court, uprightly and according to law; and that I will support the Constitution of the United States."

(3) Admission Procedures. On written or oral motion of a member of the court's bar, the court will act on the application. An applicant may be admitted by oral motion in open court. But, unless the court orders otherwise, an applicant need not appear before the court to be admitted. Upon admission, an applicant must pay the clerk the fee prescribed by local rule or court order.

(b) Suspension or Disbarment.

(1) Standard. A member of the court's bar is subject to suspension or disbarment by the court if the member:

(A) has been suspended or disbarred from practice in any other court; or

(B) is guilty of conduct unbecoming a member of the court's bar.

(2) Procedure. The member must be given an opportunity to show good cause, within the time prescribed by the court, why the member should not be suspended or disbarred.

(3) Order. The court must enter an appropriate order after the member responds and a hearing is held, if requested, or after the time prescribed for a response expires, if no response is made.

(c) Discipline.
A court of appeals may discipline an attorney who practices before it for conduct unbecoming a member of the bar or for failure to comply with any court rule. First, however, the court must afford the attorney reasonable notice, an opportunity to show cause to the contrary, and, if requested, a hearing.

RULE 47. LOCAL RULES BY COURTS OF APPEALS

(a) Local Rules.

(1) Each court of appeals acting by a majority of its judges in regular active service may, after giving appropriate public notice and opportunity for comment, make and amend rules governing its practice. A generally applicable direction to parties or lawyers regarding practice before a court must be in a local rule rather than an internal operating procedure or standing order. A local rule must be consistent with—but not duplicative of—Acts of Congress and rules adopted under 28 U.S.C. § 2072 and must conform to any uniform numbering system prescribed by the Judicial Conference of the United States. Each circuit clerk must send the Administrative Office of the United States Courts a copy of each local rule and internal operating procedure when it is promulgated or amended.

(2) A local rule imposing a requirement of form must not be enforced in a manner that causes a party to lose rights because of a nonwillful failure to comply with the requirement.

(b) Procedure When There Is No Controlling Law. A court of appeals may regulate practice in a particular case in any manner consistent with federal law, these rules, and local rules of the circuit. No sanction or other disadvantage may be imposed for noncompliance with any requirement not in federal law, federal rules, or the local circuit rules unless the alleged violator has been furnished in the particular case with actual notice of the requirement.

RULE 48. MASTERS

(a) Appointment; Powers. A court of appeals may appoint a special master to hold hearings, if necessary, and to recommend factual findings and disposition in matters ancillary to proceedings in the court. Unless the order referring a matter to a master specifies or limits the master's powers, those powers include, but are not limited to, the following:

(1) regulating all aspects of a hearing;

(2) taking all appropriate action for the efficient performance of the master's duties under the order;

(3) requiring the production of evidence on all matters embraced in the reference; and

(4) administering oaths and examining witnesses and parties.

(b) Compensation. If the master is not a judge or court employee, the court must determine the master's compensation and whether the cost is to be charged to any party.

§ 6.9 Appendix of Forms to the *Federal Rules of Appellate Procedure*

1. Notice of Appeal to a Court of Appeals From a Judgment or Order of a District Court.
2. Notice of Appeal to a Court of Appeals From a Decision of the United States Tax Court.
3. Petition for Review of Order of an Agency, Board, Commission or Officer.
4. Affidavit Accompanying Motion for Permission to Appeal In Forma Pauperis.
5. Notice of Appeal to a Court of Appeals from a Judgment or Order of a District Court or a Bankruptcy Appellate Panel.

Form 1. Notice of Appeal to a Court of Appeals From a Judgment or Order of a District Court

United States District Court for the _____ District of _____
File Number _____

A.B., Plaintiff	)	
	)	
v	)	Notice of Appeal
	)	
C.D., Defendant	)	

Notice is hereby given that [*(here name all parties taking the appeal)*, (plaintiffs) (defendants) in the above named case,[1]] hereby appeal to the United States Court of Appeals for the _____ Circuit (from the final judgment) (from an order (describing it)) entered in this action on the _____ day of _____, 19__.

(s) _____

Attorney for [_____]

[Address: _____]

1. See Rule 3(c) for permissible ways of identifying appellants.

Form 2. Notice of Appeal to a Court of Appeals From a Decision of the United States Tax Court

UNITED STATES TAX COURT Washington, D.C.

A.B., Petitioner	)	
	)	
v.	)	Docket No. _____
	)	
Commissioner of Internal Revenue,	)	
Respondent	)	

Notice of Appeal

Notice is hereby given that [*here name all parties taking the appeal*[1]], hereby appeals to the United States Court of Appeals for the _____ Circuit from (that part of) the decision of this court entered in the above captioned proceeding on the _____ day of _____, 19__ (relating to _____).

(s) _____

Counsel for [_____]

[Address: _____]

---

1. See Rule 3(c) for permissible ways of identifying appellants.

Form 3. Petition for Review of Order of an Agency, Board, Commission or Officer

United States Court of Appeals for the _____ Circuit

A.B., Petitioner   )
)
v.   ) Petition for Review
)
XYZ Commission, Respondent)

[*(here name all parties bringing the petition* [1]*)*] hereby petitions the court for review of the Order of the XYZ Commission (describe the order) entered on _____, 19__.

[(s)] _____

Attorney for Petitioners

Address: _____

---

1. See Rule 15.

Form 4. Affidavit Accompanying Motion for Permission to Appeal In Forma Pauperis

United States District Court for the _____ District of _____

A.B., Plaintiff

v.   **Case No.** _____

__**C.D., Defendant**_____

Affidavit in Support of Motion

I swear or affirm under penalty of perjury that, because of my poverty, I cannot prepay the docket fees of my appeal or post a bond for them. I believe I am entitled to redress. I swear or affirm under penalty of perjury under United States laws that my answers on this form are true and correct. (28 U.S.C. § 1746; 18 U.S.C. § 1621.)

Instructions

Complete all questions in this application and then sign it. Do not leave any blanks: if the answer to a question is "0," "none," or "not applicable (N/A)," write in that response. If you need more space to answer a question or to explain your answer, attach a separate sheet of paper identified with your name, your case's docket number, and the question number.

Signed: _____ Date: _____

My issues on appeal are:

1. For both you and your spouse estimate the average amount of money received from each of the following sources during the past 12 months. Adjust any amount that was received weekly, biweekly, quarterly, semiannually, or annually to show the monthly rate. Use gross amounts, that is, amounts before any deductions for taxes or otherwise.

Income source	Average monthly amount during the past 12 months You	Amount expected next month You
Employment	$_____	$_____
Self-employment	$_____	$_____
Income from real property (such as rental income)	$_____	$_____
Interest and dividends	$_____	$_____
Gifts	$_____	$_____
Alimony	$_____	$_____
Child support	$_____	$_____
Retirement (such as social security, pensions, annuities, insurance)	$_____	$_____
Disability (such as social security, insurance payments)	$_____	$_____
Unemployment payments	$_____	$_____
Public-assistance (such as welfare)	$_____	$_____
Other (specify):_____	$_____	$_____
Total monthly income:	$_____	$_____

2. *List your employment history, most recent employer first. (Gross monthly pay is before taxes or other deductions.)*

Employer	Address	Dates of employment	Gross monthly pay
_____	_____	_____	_____
_____	_____	_____	_____
_____	_____	_____	_____

3. *List your spouse's employment history, most recent employer first. (Gross monthly pay is before taxes or other deductions.)*

Employer	Address	Dates of employment	Gross monthly pay
_____	_____	_____	_____
_____	_____	_____	_____
_____	_____	_____	_____

4. *How much cash do you and your spouse have?* $_____

Below, state any money you or your spouse have in bank accounts or in any other financial institution.

Financial institution	Type of account	Amount you have	Amount your spouse has
_____	_____	$_____	$_____
_____	_____	$_____	$_____
_____	_____	$_____	$_____

If you are a prisoner, you must attach a statement certified by the appropriate institutional officer showing all receipts, expenditures, and balances during the last six months in your institutional accounts. If you have multiple accounts, perhaps because you have been in multiple institutions, attach one certified statement of each account.

5. *List the assets, and their values, which you own or your spouse owns. Do not list clothing and ordinary household furnishings.*

Home (Value)	Other real (Value) estate	Motor vehicle (Value) #1
_____	_____	Make & year: _____
_____	_____	Model: _____
_____	_____	Registration #: _____

Motor (Value) vehicle #2	**Other assets** (Value)	**Other assets** (Value)
Make & year: __	_____	_____
Model: _____	_____	_____
Reg. #: _____	_____	_____

6. *State every person, business, or organization owing you or your spouse money, and the amount owed.*

Person owing you or your spouse money	Amount owed to you	Amount owed to your spouse
_____	_____	_____
_____	_____	_____
_____	_____	_____

7. *State the persons who rely on you or your spouse for support.*

Name	Relationship	Age
_____	_____	_____
_____	_____	_____
_____	_____	_____

8. *Estimate the average monthly expenses of you and your family. Show separately the amounts paid by your spouse. Adjust any payments that are made weekly, biweekly, quarterly, semiannually, or annually to show the monthly rate.*

	You	**Your Spouse**
Rent or home-mortgage payment (include lot rented for mobile home)	$_____	$_____
Are real-estate taxes included? ___ Yes ___ No		
Is property insurance included? ___ Yes ___ No		
Utilities (electricity, heating fuel, water, sewer, and Telephone)	$_____	$_____
Home maintenance (repairs and upkeep)	$_____	$_____
Food	$_____	$_____
Clothing	$_____	$_____
Laundry and dry-cleaning	$_____	$_____
Medical and dental expenses	$_____	$_____
Transportation (not including motor vehicle payments)	$_____	$_____
Recreation, entertainment, newspapers, magazines, etc.	$_____	$_____
Insurance (not deducted from wages or included in Mortgage payments)	$_____	$_____
Homeowner's or renter's	$_____	$_____
Life	$_____	$_____
Health	$_____	$_____
Motor Vehicle	$_____	$_____
Other: _____	$_____	$_____
Taxes (not deducted from wages or included in Mortgage payments) (specify): _____	$_____	$_____
Installment payments	$_____	$_____
Motor Vehicle	$_____	$_____
Credit card (name): _____	$_____	$_____
Department store (name): _____	$_____	$_____
Other: _____	$_____	$_____
Alimony, maintenance, and support paid to others	$_____	$_____
Regular expenses for operation of business, profession, or farm (attach detailed statement)	$_____	$_____
Other (specify): _____	$_____	$_____
Total monthly expenses:	$_____	$_____

9. *Do you expect any major changes to your monthly income or expenses or in your assets or liabilities during the next 12 months?*

___ Yes ___ No   If yes, describe on an attached sheet.

10. *Have you paid—or will you be paying—an attorney any money for services in connection with this case, including the completion of this form?* ___ Yes ___ No

If yes, how much? $_____
If yes, state the attorney's name, address, and telephone number:

_____
_____
_____

11. *Have you paid—or will you be paying—anyone other than an attorney (such as a paralegal or a typist) any money for services in connection with this case, including the completion of this form?*

___ Yes ___ No
If yes, how much? $_____
If yes, state the person's name, address, and telephone number:

_____
_____
_____

12. *Provide any other information that will help explain why you cannot pay the docket fees for your appeal.*

13. *State the address of your legal residence.*

_____
_____

Your daytime phone number: (___) _____
Your age: _____ Your years of schooling: _____
Your social-security number: _____

Form 5.   Notice of Appeal to a Court of Appeals from a Judgment or Order of a District Court or a Bankruptcy Appellate Panel

United States District Court for the . . . .
District of . . . .

In re	)
	)
———————————,	)
Debtor	)
	) File No. _____
———————————,	)
Plaintiff	)
	)
v.	)

)
———————————,)
)
Defendant)

Notice of Appeal to United States Court of
Appeals for the . . . . Circuit

. . . ., the plaintiff [or defendant or other party] appeals to the United States Court of Appeals for the . . . . Circuit from the final judgment [or order or decree] of the district court for the district of . . . . [or bankruptcy appellate panel of the . . . . circuit], entered in this case on . . . ., 19 . . . [here describe the judgment, order, or decree] . . . .

The parties to the judgment [or order or decree] appealed from and the names and addresses of their respective attorneys are as follows:

Dated ——————————————
Signed ——————————————
Attorney for Appellant
Address: ——————————————

——————————————

Form 6. Certificate of Compliance With Rule 32(a)

Certificate of Compliance With Type–Volume Limitation,
Typeface Requirements, and Type Style Requirements

1. This brief complies with the type-volume limitation of Fed. R. App. P. 32(a)(7)(B) because:

☐ this brief contains [*state the number of*] words, excluding the parts of the brief exempted by Fed. R. App. P. 32(a)(7)(B)(iii), or

☐ this brief uses a monospaced typeface and contains [*state the number of*] lines of text, excluding the parts of the brief exempted by Fed. R. App. P. 32(a)(7)(B)(iii).

2. This brief complies with the typeface requirements of Fed. R. App. P. 32(a)(5) and the type style requirements of Fed. R. App. P. 32(a)(6) because:

☐ this brief has been prepared in a proportionally spaced typeface using [*state name and version of word processing program*] in [*state font size and name of type style*], or

☐ this brief has been prepared in a monospaced typeface using [*state name and version of word processing program*] with [*state number of characters per inch and name of type style*].

(s)——————————————

Attorney for ————————————
Dated: ————————————

Charles A. Wright, Arthur R. Miller, & Edward H. Cooper, *Federal Practice and Procedure* §§ 3945–4000.

ADDITIONAL RESEARCH REFERENCES

David G. Knibb, *Federal Court of Appeals Manual: A Manual on Practice in the United States Court of Appeals.*

Charles A. Wright, Arthur R. Miller, & Edward H. Cooper, *Federal Practice and Procedure* §§ 3945–4000.

Federal Courts §§ 291(1)–301(48) et seq.

West's Key No. Digests, Federal Courts ⊷741–956.

ADDITIONAL RESEARCH REFERENCES

C.J.S. Federal Civil Procedure §§ 14 to 27.

Federal Procedural Forms.

West's Key Number Digest, Federal Courts.

PART VII

ADVISORY COMMITTEE NOTES

§ 7.1 Introduction to the Committee Notes—The Civil Rules' "Legislative History"

The United States Supreme Court promulgated the original Federal Rules of Civil Procedure on December 20, 1937, and the Rules first became effective nine months later in September 1938. In the years since the original Rules took effect, the Supreme Court has amended the Rules many times, most recently in April 2007 with changes made effective as of December 1, 2007.

The Supreme Court delegated the task of drafting the original Rules and their subsequent amendments to an Advisory Committee on Civil Rules, comprised of federal and State judges, practicing attorneys, law professors, and Department of Justice representatives. At the time the original Rules were drafted, and with every subsequent proposed amendment, the Advisory Committee has prepared "Advisory Committee Notes" that accompany each draft.

Today, these Advisory Committee Notes constitute the principal source of "legislative history" for construing and interpreting the Federal Rules of Civil Procedure.[1] As one court observed, the Notes "constitute[ ] a comment on the part of the best informed body, on the subject of the scope of the Federal Rules—namely, the Committee which formulated them—and, as such, cannot be treated otherwise than with great respect".[2] The Supreme Court credits the Committee Notes as a "respected source of scholarly commentary"[3], and has instructed that the

1. *See Use of Notes And Statements of Advisory Committee In Construction Of Rules,* 2 Fed. R. Serv. 632 (1940)(and as supplemented in 3 Fed. R. Serv. 663). *See also United States v. Hayes,* 983 F.2d 78, 82 (7th Cir.1992) (commenting that Notes are analogous to legislative history, and are used to clarify "legislative intent"); *United States v. Brackeen,* 969 F.2d 827, 830 (9th Cir.1992)(noting that, in construing Federal Rules of Evidence, the courts look to the Advisory Committee Notes as "legitimate sources of legislative history"); *Reed v. Binder,* 165 F.R.D. 424, 427 (D.N.J.1996) (noting that Committee Notes "provide something akin to a legislative history of the Rules").

2. *United States v. 720 Bottles Labeled 2 Fl. Oz. * * * Plantation Pure Vanilla Extract, Etc.,* 3 F.R.D. 466, 467 (E.D.N.Y. 1944)(Byers, J.).

3. *Tome v. United States,* 513 U.S. 150, 159, 115 S.Ct. 696, 702, 130 L.Ed.2d 574 (1995)(noting that author of specific Committee Note was "a distinguished commentator on the law of evidence, and he and members of the Committee consulted and considered the views, criticisms, and suggestions of the academic community in preparing the Notes"). *See also Williamson v. United States,* 512 U.S. 594, 614, 114 S.Ct. 2431, 2441, 129 L.Ed.2d 476 (1994) (Kennedy, J., concurring) ("When as here the text of a Rule of Evidence does not answer a question that must be answered in order to apply the Rule, and when the Advisory Committee's Note does answer the question, our practice indicates that we should pay attention to the Advisory Committee's Note.").

Notes are properly afforded "weight"[4] and thus provide "a useful guide"[5] in discerning the meaning of the Rules. The Supreme Court considers the Notes to be "relevant evidence of the drafters' intent as to the meaning" of the Rules,[6] especially when the Rule language is enacted precisely as the Advisory Committee had proposed.[7] Likewise, the later Advisory Committees' commentary on Rule amendments is entitled to similar weight.[8]

Although a formidable authority for construing the Rules, the Advisory Committee itself has acknowledged that its Notes are *not* binding on the courts:

> [S]tatements in the notes as to the purpose or effect of the rules, can have no greater force than the reasons which may be adduced to support them. The notes are not part of the rules, and the Supreme Court has not approved or otherwise assumed responsibility for them. They have no official sanction, and can have no controlling weight with the courts, when applying the rules in litigated cases.[9]

Thus, while the Advisory Committee Notes constitute persuasive authority for construing and interpreting the Rules, the Notes are not control-

4. *Mississippi Publ'g Corp. v. Murphree*, 326 U.S. 438, 444, 66 S.Ct. 242, 245, 90 L.Ed. 185 (1946). *See also Torres v. Oakland Scavenger Co.*, 487 U.S. 312, 315, 108 S.Ct. 2405, 2408, 101 L.Ed.2d 285 (1988); *Schiavone v. Fortune*, 477 U.S. 21, 31, 106 S.Ct. 2379, 2385, 91 L.Ed.2d 18 (1986)(superseded by Rule amendment on other grounds). *Accord United States v. Means*, 133 F.3d 444, 449 (6th Cir.1998) (Notes are "due some deference" by the courts); *Scott-Harris v. City of Fall River*, 134 F.3d 427, 433 (1st Cir.1997) (Notes entitled to weight in interpreting federal rules of practice and procedure), *rev'd on other grounds*, 118 S.Ct. 966 (1998); *Johnson v. Gmeinder*, 191 F.R.D. 638, 646 (D.Kan.2000) (Committee's construction is "of weight" and should be given "due deference"); *In re Southern Ohio Correctional Facility*, 166 F.R.D. 391, 396 (S.D.Ohio 1996) (Committee's construction is of weight in determining meaning of the Rules); *In re Cluff*, 313 B.R. 323, 333 n.24 (Bankr.D.Utah 2004) ("entitled to weight in determining Congressional purpose"); *In re Grossman*, 80 B.R. 311, 314 n. 9 (Bankr. E.D.Pa.1987) (holding that Committee Notes are properly used as aids to interpreting the Rules).

5. *Tome v. United States*, 513 U.S. 150, 159, 115 S.Ct. 696, 702, 130 L.Ed.2d 574 (1995). *Accord Esposito v. United States*, 368 F.3d 1271, 1275 (10th Cir. 2004) (courts looks to Notes "to provide parame-

ters" for Rule's application); *United States v. Orlandez–Gamboa*, 320 F.3d 328, 331 n.2 (2d Cir.2003) ("useful guide"); *United States v. Navarro*, 169 F.3d 228, 237 (5th Cir. 1999) ("instructive"); *Waters v. Young*, 100 F.3d 1437, 1441 (9th Cir.1996)(Committee Note guides interpretation of Rules); *In re Outboard Marine Corp.*, 359 B.R. 893, 900 (Bankr.N.D.Ill. 2007) ("useful guide"); *In re Sulfuric Acid Antitrust Litig.*, 235 F.R.D. 646, 650 (N.D.Ill.2006) ("informative"); *JumpSport, Inc. v. Jumpking, Inc.*, 213 F.R.D. 329, 344 n.12 (N.D.Cal.2003) ("important sources of guidance"); *United States v. Chan*, 184 F.Supp.2d 337, 343 (S.D.N.Y.2002) ("helpful guide"); *BCCI Holdings (Luxembourg), Societe Anonyme v. Khalil*, 184 F.R.D. 3, at 6 (D.D.C.1999) (same).

6. *Libretti v. United States*, 516 U.S. 29, 41, 116 S.Ct. 356, 364, 133 L.Ed.2d 271 (1995).

7. *See United States v. Vonn*, 535 U.S. 55, 64 n.6, 122 S.Ct. 1043, 1049 n.6, 152 L.Ed.2d 90 (2002). *See also United States v. Hodge*, 412 F.3d 479, 489 (3d Cir. 2005).

8. *See United States v. Anderson*, 942 F.2d 606, 611–12 (9th Cir.1991)(noting that Committee Notes "explain the purpose and intent of the proposed rule changes").

9. *See* Introductory Statement for Original Notes to Federal Rules of Civil Procedure.

ling.[10] Like statutory legislative history, the Committee Notes should be relied upon principally to dispel an ambiguity in the text of a Rule and may never be used to contradict or supplant a Rule's plain meaning.[11] In this way, the Notes can help "supplement any deficiency" in the "explicit" language of the Rules, and, as such, may be appropriately relied upon.[12] Moreover, if contrary rulings render incorrect or unjust results, courts may disregard the Notes.[13]

The text of the original Advisory Committee Notes, and the Notes that accompanied each of the judicially promulgated amendments are reprinted below.

§ 7.2   Full Text of the Advisory Committee Notes

I. SCOPE OF RULES—ONE FORM OF ACTION

Rule 1.   Scope and Purpose of Rules

1937 ADOPTION

1. Rule 81 states certain limitations in the application of these rules to enumerated special proceedings.

2. The expression "district courts of the United States" appearing in the statute authorizing the Supreme Court of the United States to promulgate rules of civil procedure does not include the district courts held in the territories and insular possessions. See *Mookini et al.* v. *United States,* 1938, 303 U.S. 201, 58 S.Ct. 543, 82 L.Ed. 748.

3. These rules are drawn under the authority of the Act of June 19, 1934, U.S.C., Title 28, § 2072, formerly § 723b (Rules in actions at law; Supreme Court authorized to make), and § 2072, formerly § 723c (Union of equity and action at law rules; power of Supreme Court) and also other grants of rule making power to the Court. See Clark and Moore, A New Federal Civil Procedure—I, The Background, 44 Yale L.J. 387, 391 (1935). Under § 2072, formerly § 723b after the rules have taken effect all laws in conflict

---

10. *See Burnley v. City of San Antonio,* 470 F.3d 189, 193 (5th Cir. 2006) (though not determinative, they are "of weight"); *Ross v. Marshall,* 426 F.3d 745, 752 n.13 (5th Cir.2005) ("do not have the force of law", but are "instructive"); *Moody Nat'l Bank of Galveston v. GE Life & Annuity Assur. Co.,* 383 F.3d 249, 253 (5th Cir. 2004) (same); *United States v. Hayes,* 983 F.2d 78, 82 (7th Cir.1992) ("not binding"); *JumpSport, Inc. v. Jumpking, Inc.,* 213 F.R.D. 329, 344 n.12 (N.D.Cal.2003) ("not binding legal authority—at least until incorporated into law by authoritative judicial opinions"); *Reed v. Binder,* 165 F.R.D. 424, 427 (D.N.J.1996)(commenting that Committee Notes are "a very important source of information" which are given "considerable weight", but which are not conclusive); *United States v. Downin,* 884 F.Supp. 1474, 1479 (E.D.Cal.1995)(noting that Committee Notes are "of weight" in construing the Rules, but they "are not determinative"); *C.J. Wieland & Son Dairy Prods. Co. v. Wickard,* 4 F.R.D. 250, 252 (E.D.Wis.1945).

11. *See Whitehouse v. United States Dist. Ct. for Dist. of R.I.,* 53 F.3d 1349, 1365 (1st Cir.1995)(although Committee Notes are of weight, they cannot alter the unambiguous language of a Federal Rule); *United States v. Nahodil,* 36 F.3d 323, 328 (3d Cir.1994)(commenting that Committee Notes "are due some deference", but they may not be permitted to contradict a Rule's express language); *City of Merced v. Fields,* 997 F.Supp. 1326, 1337 (E.D.Cal.1998) (Rules must be given plain meaning; only if Rule requires interpretation should court refer to Notes); *United States v. Downin,* 884 F.Supp. 1474, 1479 (E.D.Cal. 1995)(noting that Committee Notes remain extrinsic sources and, where Rule's language is unambiguous, that language is conclusive and reliance on extrinsic sources is not necessary).

12.   *See Thompson v. Greene,* 427 F.3d 263, 269 (4th Cir.2005).

13. *See United States v. Hayes,* 983 F.2d 78, 82 (7th Cir.1992) ("We have not hesitated to rule in contradiction with committee notes when contrary rulings rendered incorrect or unjust results".)

therewith are of no further force or effect. In accordance with § 2072, formerly § 723c, the Court has united the general rules prescribed for cases in equity with those in actions at law so as to secure one form of civil action and procedure for both. See Rule 2 (One Form of Action). For the former practice in equity and at law see U.S.C., Title 28, §§ 2071 and 2073, formerly §§ 723 and 730 (conferring power on the Supreme Court to make rules of practice in equity) and the Equity Rules promulgated thereunder; U.S.C., Title 28, formerly § 724 (Conformity Act); former Equity Rule 22 (Action at Law Erroneously Begun as Suit in Equity—Transfer); former Equity Rule 23 (Matters Ordinarily Determinable at Law When Arising in Suit in Equity to be Disposed of Therein); U.S.C., Title 28, former §§ 397 (Amendments to pleadings when case brought to wrong side of court), and 398 (Equitable defenses and equitable relief in actions at law).

4. With the second sentence compare U.S.C., Title 28, former § 777 (Defects of form; amendments), former § 767 (Amendment of process); former Equity Rule 19 (Amendments Generally).

1948 AMENDMENT

The amendment effective October 20, 1949, substituted the words "United States district courts" for the words "district courts of the United States."

1966 AMENDMENT

This is the fundamental change necessary to effect unification of the civil and admiralty procedure. Just as the 1938 rules abolished the distinction between actions at law and suits in equity, this change would abolish the distinction between civil actions and suits in admiralty. See also Rule 81.

1993 AMENDMENT

The purpose of this revision, adding the words "and administered" to the second sentence, is to recognize the affirmative duty of the court to exercise the authority conferred by these rules to ensure that civil litigation is resolved not only fairly, but also without undue cost or delay. As officers of the court, attorneys share this responsibility with the judge to whom the case is assigned.

2007 AMENDMENT

The language of Rule 1 has been amended as part of the general restyling of the Civil Rules to make them more easily understood and to make style and terminology consistent throughout the rules. These changes are intended to be stylistic only.

The merger of law, equity, and admiralty practice is complete. There is no need to carry forward the phrases that initially accomplished the merger.

The former reference to "suits of a civil nature" is changed to the more modern "civil actions and proceedings." This change does not affect such questions as whether the Civil Rules apply to summary proceedings created by statute. See *SEC v. McCarthy*, 322 F.3d 650 (9th Cir. 2003); *see also New Hampshire Fire Ins. Co. v. Scanlon*, 362 U.S. 404 (1960).

The Style Project

The Civil Rules are the third set of the rules to be restyled. The restyled Rules of Appellate Procedure took effect in 1998. The restyled Rules of Criminal Procedure took effect in 2002. The restyled Rules of Civil Procedure apply the same general drafting guidelines and principles used in restyling the Appellate and Criminal Rules.

1. General Guidelines

Guidance in drafting, usage, and style was provided by Bryan Garner, *Guidelines for Drafting and Editing Court Rules*, Administrative Office of the United States Courts (1996) and Bryan Garner, *Dictionary of Modern Legal Usage* (2d ed. 1995). *See also* Joseph Kimble, *Guiding Principles for Restyling the Civil Rules*, in *Preliminary Draft of Proposed Style Revision of the Federal Rules of Civil Procedure*, at x (Feb. 2005) (available at http://www.uscourts.gov/rules/Prelim_draft_proposed_pt1.pdf).

2. Formatting Changes

Many of the changes in the restyled Civil Rules result from using format to achieve clearer presentation. The rules are broken down into constituent parts, using progressively indented subparagraphs with headings and substituting vertical for horizontal lists. "Hanging indents" are used throughout. These formatting changes make the structure of the rules graphic and make the restyled rules easier to read and understand even when the words are not changed. Rule 14(a) illustrates the benefits of formatting changes.

3. Changes to Reduce Inconsistent, Ambiguous, Redundant, Repetitive, or Archaic Words

The restyled rules reduce the use of inconsistent terms that say the same thing in different ways. Because different words are presumed to have different meanings, such inconsistencies can result in confusion. The restyled rules reduce inconsistencies by using the same words to express the same meaning. For example, consistent expression is achieved without affecting meaning by the changes from "infant" in many rules to "minor" in all rules; from "upon motion or on its own initiative" in Rule 4(m) and variations in many other rules to "on motion or on its own"; and from "deemed" to "considered" in Rules 5(c), 12(e), and elsewhere. Some variations of expression have been carried forward when the context made that appropriate. As an example, "stipulate," "agree," and "consent" appear throughout the rules, and "written" qualifies these words in some places but not others. The number of variations has been reduced, but at times the former words were carried forward. None of the changes, when made, alters the rule's meaning.

The restyled rules minimize the use of inherently ambiguous words. For example, the word "shall" can mean "must," "may," or something else, depending on context. The potential for confusion is exacerbated by the fact that "shall" is no longer generally used in spoken or clearly written English. The restyled rules replace "shall" with "must," "may," or "should," depending on which one the context and established interpretation make correct in each rule.

The restyled rules minimize the use of redundant "intensifiers." These are expressions that attempt to add emphasis, but instead state the obvious and create negative implications for other rules. "The court in its discretion may" becomes "the court may"; "unless the order expressly directs otherwise" becomes "unless the court orders otherwise." The absence of intensifiers in the restyled rules does not change their substantive meaning. For example, the absence of the word "reasonable" to describe the written notice of foreign law required in Rule 44.1 does not mean that "unreasonable" notice is permitted.

The restyled rules also remove words and concepts that are outdated or redundant. The reference to "at law or in equity" in Rule 1 has become redundant with the merger of law and equity. Outdated words and concepts include the reference to "demurrers, pleas, and exceptions" in Rule 7(c); the reference to "mesne" process in Rule 77(c); and the reference in Rule 81(f) to a now-abolished official position.

The restyled rules remove a number of redundant cross-references. For example, Rule 8(b) states that a general denial is subject to the obligations of Rule 11, but all pleadings are subject to Rule 11. Removing such cross-references does not defeat application of the formerly cross-referenced rule.

4. Rule Numbers

The restyled rules keep the same rule numbers to minimize the effect on research. Subdivisions have been rearranged within some rules to achieve greater clarity and simplicity. The only change that moves one part of a rule to another is the transfer of former Rule 25(d)(2) to Rule 17(d). The restyled rules include a comparison chart to make it easy to identify transfers of provisions between subdivisions and redesignations of some subdivisions.

5. Other Changes

The style changes to the rules are intended to make no changes in substantive meaning. A very small number of minor technical amendments that arguably do change meaning were approved separately from the restyled rules, but become effective at the same time. An example is adding "e-mail address" to the information that must be included in pleadings. These minor changes occur in Rules 4(k), 9(h), 11(a), 14(b), 16(c)(1), 26(g)(1), 30(b), 31, 40, 71.1, and 78.

Rule 2.   One Form of Action

1937 ADOPTION

1. This rule modifies U.S.C., Title 28, former § 384 (Suits in equity, when not sustainable). U.S.C., Title 28, §§ 2071–2073, formerly §§ 723 and 730 (conferring power on the Supreme Court to make rules of practice in equity), are unaffected in so far as they relate to the rule making power in admiralty. These sections, together with § 2072, formerly § 723b (Rules in actions at law; Supreme Court authorized to make) are continued in so far as they are not inconsistent with § 2072, formerly § 723c (Union of equity and action at law rules; power of Supreme Court). See Note 3 to Rule 1. U.S.C., Title 28, former §§ 724 (Conformity Act), 397 (Amendments to pleadings when case

brought to wrong side of court) and 398 (Equitable defenses and equitable relief in actions at law) are superseded.

2.   Reference to actions at law or suits in equity in all statutes should now be treated as referring to the civil action prescribed in these rules.

3.   This rule follows in substance the usual introductory statements to code practices which provide for a single action and mode of procedure, with abolition of forms of action and procedural distinctions.   Representative statutes are N.Y.Code 1848, Laws 1848, ch. 379, § 62;   N.Y.C.P.A.1937, § 8;   Calif.Code Civ.Proc. 1937, § 307;   2 Minn.Stat.Ann.1945, § 540.01;   2 Wash.Rev.Stat.Ann. Remington, 1932, §§ 153, 255.

2007 AMENDMENT

The language of Rule 2 has been amended as part of the general restyling of the Civil Rules to make them more easily understood and to make style and terminology consistent throughout the rules. These changes are intended to be stylistic only.

II.   COMMENCEMENT OF ACTION; SERVICE OF PROCESS, PLEADINGS, MOTIONS AND ORDERS

Rule 3.   Commencement of Action

1937 ADOPTION

1.   Rule 5(e) defines what constitutes filing with the court.

2.   This rule governs the commencement of all actions, including those brought by or against the United States or an officer or agency thereof, regardless of whether service is to be made personally pursuant to Rule 4(d), or otherwise pursuant to Rule 4(e).

3.   With this rule compare former Equity Rule 12 (Issue of Subpoena—Time for Answer) and the following statutes (and other similar statutes) which provide a similar method for commencing an action:

U.S.C., Title 28 former:

§ 45 (District courts; practice and procedure in certain cases under interstate commerce laws)

§ 762 (Petition in suit against United States)

§ 766 (Partition suits where United States is tenant in common or joint tenant)

4.   This rule provides that the first step in an action is the filing of the complaint. Under Rule 4(a) this is to be followed forthwith by issuance of a summons and its delivery to an officer for service.   Other rules providing for dismissal for failure to prosecute suggest a method available to attack unreasonable delay in prosecuting an action after it has been commenced.   When a federal or state statute of limitations is pleaded as a defense, a question may arise under this rule whether the mere filing of the complaint stops the running of the statute, or whether any further step is required, such as, service of the summons and complaint or their delivery to the marshal for service.   The answer to this question may depend on whether it is competent for the Supreme Court, exercising the power to make rules of procedure without affecting substantive rights, to vary the operation of statutes of limitations.   The requirement of Rule 4(a) that the clerk shall forthwith issue the summons and deliver it to the marshal for service will reduce the chances of such a question arising.

2007 AMENDMENT

The caption of Rule 3 has been amended as part of the general restyling of the Civil Rules to make them more easily understood and to make style and terminology consistent throughout the rules. These changes are intended to be stylistic only.

Rule 4.   Summons

1937 ADOPTION

Note to Subdivision (a).   With the provision permitting additional summons upon request of the plaintiff, compare former Equity Rule 14 (Alias Subpoena) and the last sentence of former Equity Rule 12 (Issue of Subpoena—Time for Answer).

Note to Subdivision (b). This rule prescribes a form of summons which follows substantially the requirements stated in former Equity Rules 12 (Issue of Subpoena—Time for Answer) and 7 (Process, Mesne and Final).

U.S.C., Title 28, § 1691, formerly § 721 (Sealing and testing of writs) is substantially continued in so far as it applies to a summons, but its requirements as to teste of process are superseded. U.S.C., Title 28, former § 722 (Teste of Process, day of) is superseded.

See Rule 12(a) for a statement of the time within which the defendant is required to appear and defend.

Note to subdivision (c). This rule does not affect U.S.C., Title 28, § 547, formerly § 503, as amended June 15, 1935 (Marshals; duties) and such statutes as the following in so far as they provide for service of process by a marshal, but modifies them in so far as they may imply service by a marshal only:

U.S.C., Title 15:

§ 5 (Bringing in additional parties)(Sherman Act)

§ 10 (Bringing in additional parties)

§ 25 (Restraining violations; procedure)

U.S.C., Title 28, former:

§ 45 (Practice and procedure in certain cases under the interstate commerce laws)

Compare former Equity Rule 15 (Process, by Whom Served).

Note to Subdivision (d). Under this rule the complaint must always be served with the summons.

Paragraph (1). For an example of a statute providing for service upon an agent of an individual see U.S.C., Title 28, §§ 1400, 1694, formerly § 109, (Patent cases).

Paragraph (3). This enumerates the officers and agents of a corporation or of a partnership or other unincorporated association upon whom service of process may be made, and permits service of process only upon the officers, managing or general agents, or agents authorized by appointment or by law, of the corporation, partnership or unincorporated association against which the action is brought. See *Christian* v. *International Ass'n of Machinists*, D.C.Ky.1925, 7 F.2d 481 and *Singleton* v. *Order of Railway Conductors of America*, D.C.Ill.1935, 9 F.Supp. 417. Compare *Operative Plasterers' and Cement Finishers' International Ass'n of the United States and Canada v. Case*, App.D.C.1937, 93 F.2d 56.

For a statute authorizing service upon a specified agent and requiring mailing to the defendant, see U.S.C., Title 6, § 7 (Surety companies as sureties; appointment of agents; service of process).

Paragraphs (4) and (5) provide a uniform and comprehensive method of service for all actions against the United States or an officer or agency thereof. For statutes providing for such service, see U.S.C., Title 7, §§ 217 (Proceedings for suspension of orders) 499k (Injunctions; application of injunction laws governing orders of Interstate Commerce Commission), 608c(15)(B)(Court review of ruling of Secretary of Agriculture), and 855 (making § 608c(15)(B) applicable to orders of the Secretary of Agriculture as to handlers of anti-hog-cholera serum and hog-cholera virus); U.S.C., Title 26, § 3679 (Bill in chancery to clear title to realty on which the United States has a lien for taxes); U.S.C., Title 28, former § 45 (District Courts; practice and procedure in certain cases under the interstate commerce laws) former § 763 (Petition in suit against the United States; service; appearance by district attorney), § 2409, formerly § 766 (Partition suits where United States is tenant in common or joint tenant), § 2410, formerly § 902 (Foreclosure of mortgages or other liens on property in which the United States has an interest). These and similar statutes are modified in so far as they prescribe a different method of service or dispense with the service of a summons.

For the Equity Rule on service, see [former] Equity Rule 13, Manner of Serving Subpoena.

Note to Subdivision (e). The provisions for the service of a summons or of notice or of an order in lieu of summons contained in U.S.C., Title 8, § 1451, formerly § 465 (Cancellation of certificates of citizenship fraudulently or illegally procured)(service by publication in accordance with state law); U.S.C., Title 28, § 1655, formerly § 118 (Absent defendants in suits to enforce liens); U.S.C., Title 35, § 72a (Jurisdiction of District Court of United States for the District of Columbia in certain equity suits where adverse parties reside elsewhere) (service by publication against parties residing in foreign countries); U.S.C., Title 38, § 445 (Action against the United States on a veteran's contract of insurance)(parties not inhabitants of or not found within the district may be served with an order of the court, personally or by publication) and similar statutes are continued by this rule. Title 24, § 378 of the Code of the District of Columbia (Publication against non-resident; those absent for six months; unknown heirs or devisees; for divorce or in rem; actual service beyond District) is continued, by this rule.

Note to Subdivision (f). This rule enlarges to some extent the present rule as to where service may be made. It does not, however, enlarge the jurisdiction of the district courts.

U.S.C., Title 28, § 1392, formerly § 113 (Suits in States containing more than one district)(where there are two or more defendants residing in different districts), former § 115 (Suits of a local nature), § 1392, formerly § 116 (Property in different districts in same state), former § 838 (Executions run in all districts of state); U.S.C., Title 47, § 13 (Action for damages against a railroad or telegraph company whose officer or agent in control of a telegraph line refuses or fails to operate such line in a certain manner—"upon any agent of the company found in such state"); U.S.C., Title 49, § 321(c)(Requiring designation of a process agent by interstate motor carriers and in case of failure so to do, service may be made upon any agent in the state) and similar statutes, allowing the running of process throughout a state, are substantially continued.

U.S.C., Title 15, § 5 (Bringing in additional parties)(Sherman Act), 25 (Restraining violations; procedure); U.S.C., Title 28, § 2321, formerly § 44 (Procedure in certain cases under interstate commerce laws; service of processes of court), §§ 754, 1692, formerly § 117 (Property in different states in same circuit; jurisdiction of receiver), § 2413, formerly § 839 (Executions; run in every State and Territory) and similar statutes, providing for the running of process beyond the territorial limits of a state, are expressly continued.

Note to Subdivision (g). With the second sentence compare former Equity Rule 15 (Process, by Whom Served).

Note to Subdivision (h). This rule substantially continues U.S.C., Title 28, former § 767 (Amendment of process).

1963 AMENDMENT

Subdivision (b). Under amended subdivision (e) of this rule, an action may be commenced against a nonresident of the State in which the district court is held by complying with State procedures. Frequently the form of the summons or notice required in these cases by State law differs from the Federal form of summons described in present subdivision (b) and exemplified in Form 1. To avoid confusion, the amendment of subdivision (b) states that a form of summons or notice, corresponding "as nearly as may be" to the State form, shall be employed. See also a corresponding amendment of Rule 12(a) with regard to the time to answer.

Subdivision (d)(4). This paragraph, governing service upon the United States, is amended to allow the use of certified mail as an alternative to registered mail for sending copies of the papers to the Attorney General or to a United States officer or agency. Cf. N.J. Rule 4:5–2. See also the amendment of Rule 30(f)(1).

Subdivision (d)(7). Formerly a question was raised whether this paragraph, in the context of the rule as a whole, authorized service in original Federal actions pursuant to State statutes permitting service on a State official as a means of bringing a nonresident motorist defendant into court. It was argued in *McCoy* v. *Siler*, 205 F.2d 498, 501–2 (3d Cir.)(concurring opinion), cert. denied, 346 U.S. 872, 74 S.Ct. 120, 98 L.Ed. 380 (1953), that the effective service in those cases occurred not when the State official was served but when notice was given to the defendant outside the State, and that subdivision (f)(Territorial limits of effective service), as then worded, did not authorize out-of-State service. This contention found little support. A considerable number of cases held the service to be good, either by fixing upon the service on the official within the State as the effective service, thus satisfying the wording of subdivision (f) as it then stood, see *Holbrook* v. *Cafiero*, 18 F.R.D. 218 (D.Md.1955); *Pasternack* v. *Dalo*, 17 F.R.D. 420 (W.D.Pa.1955); cf. *Super Prods. Corp.* v. *Parkin*, 20 F.R.D. 377 (S.D.N.Y.1957), or by reading paragraph (7) as not limited by subdivision (f). See *Giffin* v. *Ensign*, 234 F.2d 307 (3d Cir.1956); 2 Moore's Federal Practice, ¶ 4.19 (2d ed. 1948); 1 Barron & Holtzoff, Federal Practice & Procedure § 182.1 (Wright ed. 1960); Comment, 27 U. of Chi.L.Rev. 751 (1960). See also *Olberding* v. *Illinois Central R. R.*, 201 F.2d 582 (6th Cir.), rev'd on other grounds, 346 U.S. 338, 74 S.Ct. 83, 98 L.Ed. 39 (1953); *Feinsinger* v. *Bard*, 195 F.2d 45 (7th Cir.1952).

An important and growing class of State statutes base personal jurisdiction over nonresidents on the doing of acts or on other contacts within the State, and permit notice to be given the defendant outside the State without any requirement of service on a local

State official. See, e.g., Ill.Ann.Stat., c. 110, §§ 16, 17 (Smith-Hurd 1956); Wis. Stat. § 262.06 (1959). This service, employed in original Federal actions pursuant to paragraph (7), has also been held proper. See *Farr & Co.* v. *Cia. Intercontinental De Nav. De Cuba*, 243 F.2d 342 (2d Cir.1957); *Kappus* v. *Western Hills Oil, Inc.*, 24 F.R.D. 123 (E.D.Wis. 1959); *Star* v. *Rogalny*, 162 F.Supp. 181 (E.D.Ill.1957). It has also been held that the clause of paragraph (7) which permits service "in the manner prescribed by the law of the state," etc., is not limited by subdivision (c) requiring that service of all process be made by certain designated persons. See *Farr & Co.* v. *Cia. Intercontinental De Nav. De Cuba*, supra. But cf. *Sappia* v. *Lauro Lines*, 130 F.Supp. 810 (S.D.N.Y.1955).

The salutary results of these cases are intended to be preserved. See paragraph (7), with a clarified reference to State law, and amended subdivisions (e) and (f).

Subdivision (e). For the general relation between subdivisions (d) and (e), see 2 Moore, supra, ¶ 4.32.

The amendment of the first sentence inserting the word "thereunder" supports the original intention that the "order of court" must be authorized by a specific United States statute. See 1 Barron & Holtzoff, supra, at 731. The clause added at the end of the first sentence expressly adopts the view taken by commentators that, if no manner of service is prescribed in the statute or order, the service may be made in a manner stated in Rule 4. See 2 Moore, supra, ¶ 4.32, at 1004; Smit, International Aspects of Federal Civil Procedure, 61 Colum.L.Rev. 1031, 1036–39 (1961). But see Commentary, 5 Fed. Rules Serv. 791 (1942).

Examples of the statutes to which the first sentence relates are 28 U.S.C. § 2361 (Interpleader; process and procedure); 28 U.S.C. § 1655 (Lien enforcement; absent defendants).

The second sentence, added by amendment, expressly allows resort in original Federal actions to the procedures provided by State law for effecting service on nonresident parties (as well as on domiciliaries not found within the State). See, as illustrative, the discussion under amended subdivision (d)(7) of service pursuant to State nonresident motorist statutes and other comparable State statutes. Of particular interest is the change brought about by the reference in this sentence to State procedures for commencing actions against nonresidents by attachment and the like, accompanied by notice. Although an action commenced in a State court by attachment may be removed to the Federal court if ordinary conditions for removal are satisfied, see 28 U.S.C. § 1450; *Rorick* v. *Devon Syndicate, Ltd.*, 307 U.S. 299, 59 S.Ct. 877, 83 L.Ed. 1303 (1939); *Clark* v. *Wells*, 203 U.S. 164, 27 S.Ct. 43, 51 L.Ed. 138 (1906), there has heretofore been no provision recognized by the courts for commencing an original Federal civil action by attachment. See Currie, Attachment and Garnishment in the Federal Courts, 59 Mich.L.Rev. 337 (1961), arguing that this result came about through historical anomaly, Rule 64, which refers to attachment, garnishment, and similar procedures under State law, furnishes only provisional remedies in actions otherwise validly commenced. See *Big Vein Coal Co.* v. *Read*, 229 U.S. 31, 33 S.Ct. 694, 57 L.Ed. 1053 (1913); *Davis* v. *Ensign–Bickford Co.*, 139 F.2d 624 (8th Cir.1944); 7 Moore's Federal Practice ¶ 64.05 (2d ed. 1954); 3 Barron & Holtzoff, Federal Practice & Procedure § 1423 (Wright ed. 1958); but cf. Note, 13 So.Calif.L.Rev. 361 (1940). The amendment will now permit the institution of original Federal actions against nonresidents through the use of familiar State procedures by which property of these defendants is brought within the custody of the court and some appropriate service is made upon them.

The necessity of satisfying subject-matter jurisdictional requirements and requirements of venue will limit the practical utilization of these methods of effecting service. Within those limits, however, there appears to be no reason for denying plaintiffs means of commencing actions in Federal courts which are generally available in the State courts. See 1 Barron & Holtzoff, supra, at 374–80; Nordbye, Comments on Proposed Amendments to Rules of Civil Procedure for the United States District Courts, 18 F.R.D. 105, 106 (1956); Note, 34 Corn.L.Q. 103 (1948); Note, 13 So.Calif.L.Rev. 361 (1940).

If the circumstances of a particular case satisfy the applicable Federal law (first sentence of Rule 4(e), as amended) and the applicable State law (second sentence), the party seeking to make the service may proceed under the Federal or the State law, at his option.

See also amended Rule 13(a), and the Advisory Committee's Note thereto.

Subdivision (f). The first sentence is amended to assure the effectiveness of service outside the territorial limits of the State in all the cases in which any of the rules authorize service beyond those boundaries. Besides the preceding provisions of Rule 4, see Rule 71A(d)(3). In addition, the new second sentence of the subdivision permits effective service within a limited area outside the State in certain special situations, namely, to bring in additional parties to a counterclaim or cross-claim (Rule 13(h)), impleaded parties (Rule 14), and indispensable or conditionally necessary parties to a pending action (Rule 19); and to secure compliance with an order of commitment for civil contempt. In those situations effective service can be made at points not more than 100 miles distant from the courthouse in which the action is commenced, or to which it is assigned or transferred for trial.

The bringing in of parties under the 100-mile provision in the limited situations enumerated is designed to promote the objective of enabling the court to determine entire controversies. In the light of present-day facilities for communication and travel, the territorial range of the service allowed, analogous to that which applies to the service of a subpoena under Rule 45(e)(1), can hardly work hardship on the parties summoned. The provision will be especially useful in metropolitan areas spanning more than one State. Any requirements of subject-matter jurisdiction and venue will still have to be satisfied as to the parties brought in, although these requirements will be eased in some instances when the parties can be regarded as "ancillary." See *Pennsylvania R.R.* v. *Erie Avenue Warehouse Co.*, 302 F.2d 843 (3d Cir.1962); *Dery* v. *Wyer*, 265 F.2d 804 (2d Cir.1959); *United Artists Corp.* v. *Masterpiece Productions, Inc.*, 221 F.2d 213 (2d Cir.1955); *Lesnik* v. *Public Industrials Corp.*, 144 F.2d 968 (2d Cir.1944); *Vaughn* v. *Terminal Transp. Co.*, 162 F.Supp. 647 (E.D.Tenn.1957); and compare the fifth paragraph of the Advisory Committee's Note to Rule 4(e), as amended. The amendment is but a moderate extension of the territorial reach of Federal process and has ample practical justification. See 2 Moore, supra, § 4.01[13] (Supp.1960); 1 Barron & Holtzoff, supra, § 184; Note, 51 Nw.U.L.Rev. 354 (1956). But cf. Nordbye, Comments on Proposed Amendments to Rules of Civil Procedure for the United States District Courts, 18 F.R.D. 105, 106 (1956).

As to the need for enlarging the territorial area in which orders of commitment for civil contempt may be served, see *Graber* v. *Graber*, 93 F.Supp. 281 (D.D.C.1950); *Teele Soap Mfg. Co.* v. *Pine Tree Products Co., Inc.*, 8 F.Supp. 546 (D.N.H.1934); *Mitchell* v. *Dexter*, 244 Fed. 926 (1st Cir.1917); *In re Graves*, 29 Fed. 60 (N.D.Iowa 1886).

As to the Court's power to amend subdivisions (e) and (f) as here set forth, see *Mississippi Pub. Corp.* v. *Murphree*, 326 U.S. 438, 66 S.Ct. 242, 90 L.Ed. 185 (1946).

Subdivision (i). The continual increase of civil litigation having international elements makes it advisable to consolidate, amplify, and clarify the provisions governing service upon parties in foreign countries. See generally Jones, International Judicial Assistance: Procedural Chaos and a Program for Reform, 62 Yale L.J. 515 (1953); Longley, Serving Process, Subpoenas and Other Documents in Foreign Territory, Proc. A.B.A., Sec.Int'l & Comp.L. 34 (1959); Smit, International Aspects of Federal Civil Procedure, 61 Colum.L.Rev. 1031 (1961).

As indicated in the opening lines of new subdivision (i), referring to the provisions of subdivision (e), the authority for effecting foreign service must be found in a statute of the United States or a statute or rule of court of the State in which the district court is held providing in terms or upon proper interpretation for service abroad upon persons not inhabitants of or found within the State. See the Advisory Committee's Note to amended Rule 4(d)(7) and Rule 4(e). For examples of Federal and State statutes expressly authorizing such service, see 8 U.S.C. § 1451(b); 35 U.S.C. §§ 146, 293; Me.Rev.Stat., ch. 22, § 70 (Supp.1961); Minn.Stat.Ann. § 303.13 (1947); N.Y.Veh. & Tfc.Law § 253. Several decisions have construed statutes to permit service in foreign countries, although the matter is not expressly mentioned in the statutes. See, e.g., *Chapman* v. *Superior Court*, 162 Cal.App.2d 421, 328 P.2d 23 (Dist.Ct.App.1958); *Sperry* v. *Fliegers*, 194 Misc. 438, 86 N.Y.S.2d 830 (Sup.Ct.1949); *Ewing* v. *Thompson*, 233 N.C. 564, 65 S.E.2d 17 (1951); *Rushing* v. *Bush*, 260 S.W.2d 900 (Tex.Ct.Civ.App.1953). Federal and State statutes authorizing service on nonresidents in such terms as to warrant the interpretation that service abroad is permissible include 15 U.S.C. §§ 77v(a), 78aa, 79y; 28 U.S.C. § 1655; 38 U.S.C. § 784(a); Ill.Ann.Stat., c. 110, §§ 16, 17 (Smith-Hurd 1956); Wis.Stat. § 262.06 (1959).

Under **subdivisions (e) and (i),** when authority to make foreign service is found in a Federal statute or statute or rule of court of a State, it is always sufficient to carry out the service in the manner indicated therein. Subdivision (i) introduces considerable further flexibility by permitting the foreign service and return thereof to be carried out in any of a number of other alternative ways that are also declared to be sufficient. Other aspects of foreign service continue to be governed by the other provisions of Rule 4. Thus, for example, subdivision (i) effects no change in the form of the summons, or the issuance of separate or additional summons, or the amendment of service.

Service of process beyond the territorial limits of the United States may involve difficulties not encountered in the case of domestic service. Service abroad may be considered by a foreign country to require the performance of judicial, and therefore "sovereign," acts within its territory, which that country may conceive to be offensive to its policy or contrary to its law. See Jones, supra, at 537. For example, a person not qualified to serve process according to the law of the foreign country may find himself subject to sanctions if he attempts service therein. See Inter-American Juridical Committee, Report on Uniformity of Legislation on International Cooperation in Judicial Procedures 20 (1952). The enforcement of a judgment in the foreign country in which the service was made may be embarrassed or prevented if the service did not comport with the law of that country. See ibid.

One of the purposes of **subdivision (i)** is to allow accommodation to the policies and procedures of the foreign country. It is emphasized, however, that the attitudes of foreign countries vary considerably and that the question of recognition of United States judgments abroad is complex. Accordingly, if enforcement is to be sought in the country of service, the foreign law should be examined before a choice is made among the methods of service allowed by subdivision (i).

Subdivision (i)(1). Subparagraph (a) of paragraph (1), permitting service by the method prescribed by the law of the foreign country for service on a person in that country in a civil action in any of its courts of general jurisdiction, provides an alternative that is likely to create least objection in the place of service and also is likely to enhance the possibilities of securing ultimate enforcement of the judgment abroad. See Report on Uniformity of Legislation on International Cooperation in Judicial Procedures, supra.

In certain foreign countries service in aid of litigation pending in other countries can lawfully be accomplished only upon request to the foreign court, which in turn directs the service to be made. In many countries this has long been a customary way of accomplishing the service. See *In re Letters Rogatory Out of First Civil Court of City of Mexico*, 261 Fed. 652 (S.D.N.Y.1919); Jones, supra, at 543; Comment, 44 Colum.L.Rev. 72 (1944); Note, 58 Yale L.J. 1193 (1949). Subparagraph (B) of paragraph (1), referring to a letter rogatory, validates this method. A proviso, applicable to this subparagraph and the preceding one, requires, as a safeguard, that the service made shall be reasonably calculated to give actual notice of the proceedings to the party. See *Milliken* v. *Meyer*, 311 U.S. 457, 61 S.Ct. 339, 85 L.Ed. 278 (1940).

Subparagraph (C) of paragraph (1), permitting foreign service by personal delivery on individuals and corporations, partnerships, and associations, provides for a manner of service that is not only traditionally preferred, but also is most likely to lead to actual notice. Explicit provision for this manner of service was thought desirable because a number of Federal and State statutes permitting foreign service do not specifically provide for service by personal delivery abroad, see e.g., 35 U.S.C. §§ 146, 293; 46 U.S.C. § 1292; Calif.Ins.Code § 1612; N.Y.Veh. & Tfc.Law § 253, and it also may be unavailable under the law of the country in which the service is made.

Subparagraph (D) of paragraph (1), permitting service by certain types of mail, affords a manner of service that is inexpensive and expeditious, and requires a minimum of activity within the foreign country. Several statutes specifically provide for service in a foreign country by mail, e.g., Hawaii Rev.Laws §§ 230–31, 230–32 (1955); Minn.Stat.Ann. § 303.13 (1947); N.Y.Civ.Prac.Act, § 229–b; N.Y.Veh. & Tfc.Law § 253, and it has been sanctioned by the courts even in the absence of statutory provision specifying that form of service. *Zurini* v. *United States*, 189 F.2d 722 (8th Cir.1951); *United States* v. *Cardillo*, 135 F.Supp. 798 (W.D.Pa.1955); *Autogiro Co.* v. *Kay Gyroplanes, Ltd.*, 55 F.Supp. 919 (D.D.C.1944). Since the reliability of postal service may vary from country to country, service by mail is proper only when it is addressed to the party to be served and a form of mail requiring a signed receipt is used. An additional safeguard is provided by the requirement that the mailing be attended to by the clerk of the court. See also the provisions of paragraph (2) of this subdivision (i) regarding proof of service by mail.

Under the applicable law it may be necessary, when the defendant is an infant or incompetent person, to deliver the summons and complaint to a guardian, committee, or similar fiduciary. In such a case it would be advisable to make service under subparagraph (A), (B), or (E).

Subparagraph (E) of paragraph (1) adds flexibility by permitting the court by order to tailor the manner of service to fit the necessities of a particular case or the peculiar requirements of the law of the country in which the service is to be made. A similar provision appears in a number of statutes, e.g., 35 U.S.C. §§ 146, 293; 38 U.S.C. § 784(a); 46 U.S.C. § 1292.

The next-to-last sentence of paragraph (1) permits service under (C) and (E) to be made by any person who is not a party and is not less than 18 years of age or who is designated by court order or by the foreign court. Cf. Rule 45(c); N.Y.Civ.Prac.Act §§ 233, 235. This alternative increases the possibility that the plaintiff will be able to find a process server who can proceed unimpeded in the foreign country; it also may improve the chances of enforcing the judgment in the country of service. Especially is the alternative valuable when authority for the foreign service is found in a statute or rule of court that limits the group of eligible process servers to designated officials or special appointees who, because directly connected with another "sovereign," may be particularly offensive to the foreign country. See generally Smit, supra, at 1040–41. When recourse is had to subparagraph (A) or (B) the identity of the process server always will be determined by the law of the foreign country in which the service is made.

The last sentence of paragraph (1) sets forth an alternative manner for the issuance and transmission of the summons for service. After obtaining the summons from the clerk, the plaintiff must ascertain the best manner of delivering the summons and complaint to the person, court, or officer who will make the service. Thus the clerk is not burdened with the task of determining who is permitted to serve process under the law of a particular country or the appropriate governmental or nongovernmental channel for forwarding a letter rogatory. Under (D), however, the papers must always be posted by the clerk.

Subdivision (i)(2). When service is made in a foreign country, paragraph (2) permits methods for proof of service in addition to those prescribed by subdivision (g). Proof of service in accordance with the law of the foreign country is permitted because foreign process servers, unaccustomed to the form or the requirement of return of service prevalent in the United States, have on occasion been unwilling to execute the affidavit required by Rule 4(g). See *Jones, supra*, at 537; *Longley, supra*, at 35. As a corollary of the alternate manner of service in subdivision (i)(1)(E), proof of service as directed by order of the court is permitted. The special provision for proof of service by mail is intended as an additional safeguard when that method is used. On the type of evidence of delivery that may be satisfactory to a court in lieu of a signed receipt, see *Aero Associates, Inc.* v. *La Metropolitana*, 183 F.Supp. 357 (S.D.N.Y.1960).

1966 AMENDMENT

The wording of Rule 4(f) is changed to accord with the amendment of Rule 13(h) referring to Rule 19 as amended.

1980 AMENDMENT

Subdivision (a). This is a technical amendment to conform this subdivision with the amendment of subdivision (c).

Subdivision (c). The purpose of this amendment is to authorize service of process to be made by any person who is authorized to make service in actions in the courts of general jurisdiction of the state in which the district court is held or in which service is made.

There is a troublesome ambiguity in Rule 4. Rule 4(c) directs that all process is to be served by the marshal, by his deputy, or by a person specially appointed by the court. But Rule 4(d)(7) authorizes service in certain cases "in the manner prescribed by the law of the state in which the district court is held. ..." And Rule 4(e), which authorizes service beyond the state and service in quasi in rem cases when state law permits such service, directs that "service may be made ... under the circumstances and in the manner prescribed in the [state] statute or rule." State statutes and rules of the kind referred to in Rule 4(d)(7) and Rule 4(e) commonly designate the persons who are to make the service provided for, e.g., a sheriff or a plaintiff. When that is so, may the persons so designated by state law make service, or is service in all cases to be made by a marshal or by one specially appointed under present Rule 4(c)? The commentators have noted the ambiguity and have suggested the desirability of an amendment. See 2 Moore's Federal Practice ¶ 4.08 (1974); Wright & Miller, Federal Practice and Procedure: Civil § 1092 (1969). And the ambiguity has given rise to unfortunate results. See *United States for Use of Tanos* v. *St. Paul Mercury Ins. Co.*, 361 F.2d 838 (5th Cir.1966); *Veeck* v. *Commodity Enterprises, Inc.*, 487 F.2d 423 (9th Cir.1973).

The ambiguity can be resolved by specific amendments to Rules 4(d)(7) and 4(e), but the Committee is of the view that there is no reason why Rule 4(c) should not generally authorize service of process in all cases by anyone authorized to make service in the courts of general jurisdiction of the state in which the district court is held or in which service is made. The marshal continues to be the obvious, always effective officer for service of process.

1987 AMENDMENT

The amendments are technical. No substantive change is intended.

1993 AMENDMENT

SPECIAL NOTE: Mindful of the constraints of the Rules Enabling Act, the Committee calls the attention of the Supreme Court and Congress to new subdivision (k)(2). Should this limited extension of service be disapproved, the Committee nevertheless recommends adoption of the balance of the rule, with subdivision (k)(1) becoming simply subdivision (k). The Committee Notes would be revised to eliminate references to subdivision (k)(2). [Edit. note: Subd. (k)(2) was not disapproved.]

Purposes of Revision. The general purpose of this revision is to facilitate the service of the summons and complaint. The revised rule explicitly authorizes a means for service of the summons and complaint on any defendant. While the methods of service so authorized always provide appropriate notice to persons against whom claims are made, effective service under this rule does not assure that personal jurisdiction has been established over the defendant served.

First, the revised rule authorizes the use of any means of service provided by the law not only of the forum state, but also of the state in which a defendant is served, unless the defendant is a minor or incompetent.

Second, the revised rule clarifies and enhances the cost-saving practice of securing the assent of the defendant to dispense with actual service of the summons and complaint. This practice was introduced to the rule in 1983 by an act of Congress authorizing "service-by-mail," a procedure that effects economic service with cooperation of the defendant. Defendants that magnify costs of service by requiring expensive service not necessary to achieve full notice of an action brought against them are required to bear the wasteful costs. This provision is made available in actions against defendants who cannot be served in the districts in which the actions are brought.

Third, the revision reduces the hazard of commencing an action against the United States or its officers, agencies, and corporations. A party failing to effect service on all the offices of the United States as required by the rule is assured adequate time to cure defects in service.

Fourth, the revision calls attention to the important effect of the Hague Convention and other treaties bearing on service of documents in foreign countries and favors the use of internationally agreed means of service. In some respects, these treaties have facilitated service in foreign countries but are not fully known to the bar.

Finally, the revised rule extends the reach of federal courts to impose jurisdiction over the person of all defendants against whom federal law claims are made and who can be constitutionally subjected to the jurisdiction of the courts of the United States. The present territorial limits on the effectiveness of service to subject a defendant to the jurisdiction of the court over the defendant's person are retained for all actions in which there is a state in which personal jurisdiction can be asserted consistently with state law and the Fourteenth Amendment. A new provision enables district courts to exercise jurisdiction, if permissible under the Constitution and not precluded by statute, when a federal claim is made against a defendant not subject to the jurisdiction of any single state.

The revised rule is reorganized to make its provisions more accessible to those not familiar with all of them. Additional subdivisions in this rule allow for more captions; several overlaps among subdivisions are eliminated; and several disconnected provisions are removed, to be relocated in a new Rule 4.1.

The Caption of the Rule. Prior to this revision, Rule 4 was entitled "Process" and applied to the service of not only the summons but also other process as well, although these are not covered by the revised rule. Service of process in eminent domain proceedings is governed by Rule 71A. Service of a subpoena is governed by Rule 45, and service of papers such as orders, motions, notices, pleadings, and other documents is governed by Rule 5.

The revised rule is entitled "Summons" and applies only to that form of legal process. Unless service of the summons is waived, a summons must be served whenever a person is joined as a party against whom a claim is made. Those few provisions of the former rule which relate specifically to service of process other than a summons are relocated in Rule 4.1 in order to simplify the text of this rule.

Subdivision (a). Revised subdivision (a) contains most of the language of the former subdivision (b). The second sentence of the former subdivision (b) has been stricken, so that the federal court summons will be the same in all cases. Few states now employ distinctive requirements of form for a summons and the applicability of such a requirement in federal court can only serve as a trap for an unwary party or attorney. A sentence is added to this subdivision authorizing an amendment of a summons. This sentence replaces the rarely used former subdivision 4(h). *See* 4A Wright & Miller, *Federal Practice and Procedure* § 1131 (2d ed. 1987).

Subdivision (b). Revised subdivision (b) replaces the former subdivision (a). The revised text makes clear that the responsibility for filling in the summons falls on the plaintiff, not the clerk of the court. If there are multiple defendants, the plaintiff may secure issuance of a summons for each defendant, or may serve copies of a single original bearing the names of multiple defendants if the addressee of the summons is effectively identified.

Subdivision (c). Paragraph (1) of revised subdivision (c) retains language from the former subdivision (d)(1). Paragraph (2) retains language from the former subdivision (a), and adds an appropriate caution regarding the time limit for service set forth in subdivision (m).

The 1983 revision of Rule 4 relieved the marshals' offices of much of the burden of serving the summons. Subdivision (c) eliminates the requirement for service by the marshal's office in actions in which the party seeking service is the United States. The United States, like other civil litigants, is now permitted to designate any person who is 18 years of age and not a party to serve its summons.

The court remains obligated to appoint a marshal, a deputy, or some other person to effect service of a summons in two classes of cases specified by statute: actions brought *in forma pauperis* or by a seaman. 28 U.S.C. §§ 1915, 1916. The court also retains discretion to appoint a process server on motion of a party. If a law enforcement presence appears to be necessary or advisable to keep the peace, the court should appoint a marshal or deputy or other official person to make the service. The Department of Justice may also call upon the Marshals Service to perform services in actions brought by the United States. 28 U.S.C. § 651.

Subdivision (d). This text is new, but is substantially derived from the former subdivisions (c)(2)(C) and (D), added to the rule by Congress in 1983. The aims of the provision are to eliminate the costs of service of a summons on many parties and to foster cooperation among adversaries and counsel. The rule operates to impose upon the defendant those costs that could have been avoided if the defendant had cooperated reasonably in the manner prescribed. This device is useful in dealing with defendants who are furtive, who reside in places not easily reached by process servers, or who are outside the United States and can be served only at substantial and unnecessary expense. Illustratively, there is no useful purpose achieved by requiring a plaintiff to comply with all the formalities of service in a foreign country, including costs of translation, when suing a defendant manufacturer, fluent in English, whose products are widely distributed in the United States. *See Bankston v. Toyota Motor Corp.*, 889 F.2d 172 (8th Cir.1989).

The former text described this process as service-by-mail. This language misled some plaintiffs into thinking that service could be effected by mail without the affirmative cooperation of the defendant. *E.g., Gulley v. Mayo Foundation,* 886 F.2d 161 (8th Cir.1989). It is more accurate to describe the communication sent to the defendant as a request for a waiver of formal service.

The request for waiver of service may be sent only to defendants subject to service under subdivision (e), (f), or (h). The United States is not expected to waive service for the reason that its mail receiving facilities are inadequate to assure that the notice is actually received by the correct person in the Department of Justice. The same principle is applied to agencies, corporations, and officers of the United States and to other governments and entities subject to service under subdivision (j). Moreover, there are policy reasons why governmental entities should not be confronted with the potential for bearing costs of service in cases in which they ultimately prevail. Infants or incompetent persons likewise are not called upon to waive service because, due to their presumed inability to understand the request and its consequences, they must generally be served through fiduciaries.

It was unclear whether the former rule authorized, mailing of a request for "acknowledgement of service" to defendants outside the forum state. *See* 1 R. Casad, *Jurisdiction in Civil Actions* (2d Ed.) 5–29, 30 (1991) and cases cited. But, as Professor Casad observed, there was no reason not to employ this device in an effort to obtain service outside the state, and there are many instances in which it was in fact so used, with respect both to defendants within the United States and to defendants in other countries.

The opportunity for waiver has distinct advantages to a foreign defendant. By waiving service, the defendant can reduce the costs that may ultimately be taxed against it if unsuccessful in the lawsuit, including the sometimes substantial expense of translation that may be wholly unnecessary for defendants fluent in English. Moreover, a foreign defendant that waives service is afforded substantially more time to defend against the action than if it had been formally served: under Rule 12, a defendant ordinarily has only 20 days after service in which to file its answer or raise objections by motion, but by signing a waiver it is allowed 90 days after the date the request for waiver was mailed in which to submit its defenses. Because of the additional time needed for mailing and the unreliability of some foreign mail services, a period of 60 days (rather than the 30 days required for domestic transmissions) is provided for a return of a waiver sent to a foreign country.

It is hoped that, since transmission of the notice and waiver forms is a private nonjudicial act, does not purport to effect service, and is not accompanied by any summons or directive from a court, use of the procedure will not offend foreign sovereignties, even those that have withheld their assent to formal service by mail or have objected to the "service-by-mail" provisions of the former rule. Unless the addressee consents, receipt of the request under the revised rule does not give rise to any obligation to answer the lawsuit, does not provide a basis for default judgment, and does not suspend the statute of limitations in those states where the period continues to run until service. Nor are there any adverse consequences to a foreign defendant, since the provisions for shifting the expense of service to a defendant that declines to waive service apply only if the plaintiff and defendant are both located in the United States.

With respect to a defendant located in a foreign country like the United Kingdom, which accepts documents in English, whose Central Authority acts promptly in effecting service, and whose policies discourage its residents from waiving formal service, there will be little reason for a plaintiff to send the notice and request under subdivision (d) rather than use convention methods. On the other hand, the procedure offers significant potential benefits to a plaintiff when suing a defendant that, though fluent in English, is located in a country where, as a condition to formal service under a convention, documents must be translated into another language or where formal service will be otherwise costly or time-consuming.

Paragraph (1) is explicit that a timely waiver of service of a summons does not prejudice the right of a defendant to object by means of a motion authorized by Rule 12(b)(2) to the absence of jurisdiction over the defendant's person, or to assert other defenses that may be available. The only issues eliminated are those involving the sufficiency of the summons or the sufficiency of the method by which it is served.

Paragraph (2) states what the present rule implies: the defendant has a duty to avoid costs associated with the service of a summons not needed to inform the defendant regarding the commencement of an action. The text of the rule also sets forth the requirements for a Notice and Request for Waiver sufficient to put the cost-shifting provision in place. These requirements are illustrated in Forms 1A and 1B, which replace the former Form 18–A.

Paragraph (2)(A) is explicit that a request for waiver of service by a corporate defendant must be addressed to a person qualified to receive service. The general mail rooms of large organizations cannot be required to identify the appropriate individual recipient for an institutional summons.

Paragraph (2)(B) permits the use of alternatives to the United States mails in sending the Notice and Request. While private messenger services or electronic communications may be more expensive than the mail, they may be equally reliable and on occasion more convenient to the parties. Especially with respect to transmissions to foreign countries, alternative means may be desirable, for in some countries facsimile transmission is the most efficient and economical means of communication. If electronic means such as facsimile transmission are employed, the sender should maintain a record of the transmission to assure proof of transmission if receipt is denied, but a party receiving such a transmission has a duty to cooperate and cannot avoid liability for the resulting cost of formal service if the transmission is prevented at the point of receipt.

A defendant failing to comply with a request for waiver shall be given an opportunity to show good cause for the failure, but sufficient cause should be rare. It is not a good cause for failure to waive service that the claim is unjust or that the court lacks jurisdiction. Sufficient cause not to shift the cost of service would exist, however, if the defendant did not receive the request or was insufficiently literate in English to understand it. It should be noted that the provisions for shifting the cost of service apply only if the plaintiff and the defendant are both located in the United States, and accordingly a foreign defendant need not show "good cause" for its failure to waive service.

Paragraph (3) extends the time for answer if, before being served with process, the defendant waives formal service. The extension is intended to serve as an inducement to waive service and to assure that a defendant will not gain any delay by declining to waive service and thereby causing the additional time needed to effect service. By waiving service, a defendant is not called upon to respond to the complaint until 60 days from the date the notice was sent to it—90 days if the notice was sent to a foreign country—rather than within the 20 day period from date of service specified in Rule 12.

Paragraph (4) clarifies the effective date of service when service is waived; the provision is needed to resolve an issue arising when applicable law requires service of process to toll the statute of limitations. *E.g., Morse v. Elmira Country Club,* 752 F.2d 35 (2d Cir.1984). *Cf. Walker v. Armco Steel Corp.,* 446 U.S. 740, 100 S.Ct. 1978, 64 L.Ed.2d 659 (1980).

The provisions in former subdivision (c)(2)(C)(ii) of this rule may have been misleading to some parties. Some plaintiffs, not reading the rule carefully, supposed that receipt by the defendant of the mailed complaint had the effect both of establishing the jurisdiction of the court over the defendant's person and of tolling the statute of limitations in actions in which service of the summons is required to toll the limitations period. The revised rule is clear that, if the waiver is not returned and filed, the limitations period under such a law is not tolled and the action will not otherwise proceed until formal service of process is effected.

Some state limitations laws may toll an otherwise applicable statute at the time when the defendant receives notice of the action. Nevertheless, the device of requested waiver of service is not suitable if a limitations period which is about to expire is not tolled by filing the action. Unless there is ample time, the plaintiff should proceed directly to the formal methods for service identified in subdivisions (e), (f), or (h).

The procedure of requesting waiver of service should also not be used if the time for service under subdivision (m) will expire before the date on which the waiver must be returned. While a plaintiff has been allowed additional time for service in that situation, *e.g., Prather v. Raymond Constr. Co.,* 570 F.Supp. 278 (N.D.Ga.1983), the court could refuse a request for additional time unless the defendant appears to have evaded service pursuant to subdivision (e) or (h). It may be noted that the presumptive time limit for service under subdivision (m) does not apply to service in a foreign country.

Paragraph (5) is a cost-shifting provision retained from the former rule. The costs that may be imposed on the defendant could include, for example, the cost of the time of a process server required to make contact with a defendant residing in a guarded apartment house or residential development. The paragraph is explicit that the costs of enforcing the cost-shifting provision are themselves recoverable from a defendant who fails to return the waiver. In the absence of such a provision, the purpose of the rule would be frustrated by the cost of its enforcement, which is likely to be high in relation to the small benefit secured by the plaintiff.

Some plaintiffs may send a notice and request for waiver and, without waiting for return of the waiver, also proceed with efforts to effect formal service on the defendant. To discourage this practice, the cost-shifting provisions in paragraphs (2) and (5) are limited to costs of effecting service incurred after the time expires for the defendant to return the waiver. Moreover, by returning the waiver within the time allowed and before being served with process, a defendant receives the benefit of the longer period for responding to the complaint afforded for waivers under paragraph (3).

Subdivision (e). This subdivision replaces former subdivisions (c)(2)(C)(i) and (d)(1). It provides a means for service of summons on individuals within a judicial district of the United States. Together with subdivision (f), it provides for service on persons anywhere, subject to constitutional and statutory constraints.

Service of the summons under this subdivision does not conclusively establish the jurisdiction of the court over the person of the defendant. A defendant may assert the territorial limits of the court's reach set forth in subdivision (k), including the constitutional limitations that may be imposed by the Due Process Clause of the Fifth Amendment.

Paragraph (1) authorizes service in any judicial district in conformity with state law. This paragraph sets forth the language of former subdivision (c)(2)(C)(i), which authorized the use of the law of the state in which the district court sits, but adds as an alternative the use of the law of the state in which the service is effected.

Paragraph (2) retains the text of the former subdivision (d)(1) and authorizes the use of the familiar methods of personal or abode service or service on an authorized agent in any judicial district.

To conform to these provisions, the former subdivision (e) bearing on proceedings against parties not found within the state is stricken. Likewise stricken is the first sentence of the former subdivision (f), which had restricted the authority of the federal process server to the state in which the district court sits.

Subdivision (f). This subdivision provides for service on individuals who are in a foreign country, replacing the former subdivision (i) that was added to Rule 4 in 1963. Reflecting the pattern of Rule 4 in incorporating state law limitations on the exercise of jurisdiction over persons, the former subdivision (i) limited service outside the United States to cases in which extraterritorial service was authorized by state or federal law. The new rule eliminates the requirement of explicit authorization. On occasion, service in a foreign country was held to be improper for lack of statutory authority. *E.g., Martens v. Winder,* 341 F.2d 197 (9th Cir.), *cert. denied,* 382 U.S. 937, 86 S.Ct. 391, 15 L.Ed.2d 349 (1965). This authority, however, was found to exist by implication. *E.g., SEC v. VTR, Inc.,* 39 F.R.D. 19 (S.D.N.Y.1966). Given the substantial increase in the number of international transactions and events that are the subject of litigation in federal courts, it is appropriate to infer a general legislative authority to effect service on defendants in a foreign country.

A secondary effect of this provision for foreign service of a federal summons is to facilitate the use of federal long-arm law in actions brought to enforce the federal law against defendants who cannot be served under any state law but who can be constitutionally subjected to the jurisdiction of the federal court. Such a provision is set forth in paragraph (2) of subdivision (k) of this rule, applicable only to persons not subject to the territorial jurisdiction of any particular state.

Paragraph (1) gives effect to the Hague Convention on the Service Abroad of Judicial and Extrajudicial Documents, which entered into force for the United States on February 10, 1969. See 28 U.S.C.A., Fed.R.Civ.P. 4 (Supp.1986). This Convention is an important means of dealing with problems of service in a foreign country. *See generally* 1 B. Ristau, *International Judicial Assistance* §§ 4–1–1 to 4–5–2 (1990). Use of the Convention procedures, when available, is mandatory if documents must be transmitted abroad to effect service. *See Volkswagenwerk Aktiengesellschaft v. Schlunk,* 486 U.S. 694, 108 S.Ct. 2104, 100 L.Ed.2d 722 (1988)(noting that voluntary use of these procedures may be desirable even when service could constitutionally be effected in another manner); J. Weis, *The Federal Rules and the Hague Conventions: Concerns of Conformity and Comity,* 50 *U.Pitt.L.Rev.* 903 (1989). Therefore, this paragraph provides that, when service is to be effected outside a judicial district of the United States, the methods of service appropriate under an applicable treaty shall be employed if available and if the treaty so requires.

The Hague Convention furnishes safeguards against the abridgment of rights of parties through inadequate notice. Article 15 provides for verification of actual notice or a demonstration that process was served by a method prescribed by the internal laws of the foreign state before a default judgment may be entered. Article 16 of the Convention also enables the judge to extend the time for appeal after judgment if the defendant shows a lack of adequate notice either to defend or to appeal the judgment, or has disclosed a prima facie case on the merits.

The Hague Convention does not specify a time within which a foreign country's Central Authority must effect service, but Article 15 does provide that alternate methods may be used if a Central Authority does not respond within six months. Generally, a Central Authority can be expected to respond much more quickly than that limit might permit, but there have been occasions when the signatory state was dilatory or refused to cooperate for substantive reasons. In such cases, resort may be had to the provision set forth in subdivision (f)(3).

Two minor changes in the text reflect the Hague Convention. First, the term "letter of request" has been added. Although these words are synonymous with "letter rogatory," "letter of request" is preferred in modern usage. The provision should not be interpreted to authorize use of a letter of request when there is in fact no treaty obligation on the receiving country to honor such a request from this country or when the United States does not extend diplomatic recognition to the foreign nation. Second, the passage formerly found in subdivision (i)(1)(B), "when service in either case is reasonably calculated to give actual notice," has been relocated.

Paragraph (2) provides alternative methods for use when internationally agreed methods are not intended to be exclusive, or where there is no international agreement applicable. It contains most of the language formerly set forth in subdivision (i) of the rule. Service by methods that would violate foreign law is not generally authorized. Subparagraphs (A) and (B) prescribe the more appropriate methods for conforming to local practice or using a local authority. Subparagraph (C) prescribes other methods authorized by the former rule.

Paragraph (3) authorizes the court to approve other methods of service not prohibited by international agreements. The Hague Convention, for example, authorizes special forms of service in cases of urgency if convention methods will not permit service within the time required by the circumstances. Other circumstances that might justify the use of additional methods include the failure of the foreign country's Central Authority to effect service within the six-month period provided by the Convention, or the refusal of the Central Authority to serve a complaint seeking punitive damages or to enforce the antitrust laws of the United States. In such cases, the court may direct a special method of service not explicitly authorized by international agreement if not prohibited by the agreement. Inasmuch as our Constitution requires that reasonable notice be given, an earnest effort should be made to devise a method of communication that is consistent with due process and minimizes offense to foreign law. A court may in some instances specially authorize use of ordinary mail. *Cf. Levin v. Ruby Trading Corp.,* 248 F.Supp. 537 (S.D.N.Y.1965).

Subdivision (g). This subdivision retains the text of former subdivision (d)(2). Provision is made for service upon an infant or incompetent person in a foreign country.

Subdivision (h). This subdivision retains the text of former subdivision (d)(3), with changes reflecting those made in subdivision (e). It also contains the provisions for service on a corporation or association in a foreign country, as formerly found in subdivision (i).

Frequent use should be made of the Notice and Request procedure set forth in subdivision (d) in actions against corporations. Care must be taken, however, to address the request to an individual officer or authorized agent of the corporation. It is not effective use of the Notice and Request procedure if the mail is sent undirected to the mail room of the organization.

Subdivision (i). This subdivision retains much of the text of former subdivisions (d)(4) and (d)(5). Paragraph (1) provides for service of a summons on the United States; it amends former subdivision (d)(4) to permit the United States attorney to be served by registered or certified mail. The rule does not authorize the use of the Notice and Request procedure of revised subdivision (d) when the United States is the defendant. To assure proper handling of mail in the United States attorney's office, the authorized mail service must be specifically addressed to the civil process clerk of the office of the United States attorney.

Paragraph (2) replaces former subdivision (d)(5). Paragraph (3) saves the plaintiff from the hazard of losing a substantive right because of failure to comply with the complex requirements of multiple service under this subdivision. That risk has proved to be more than nominal. *E.g., Whale v. United States,* 792 F.2d 951 (9th Cir.1986). This provision should be read in connection with the provisions of subdivision (c) of Rule 15 to preclude the loss of substantive rights against the United States or its agencies, corporations, or officers resulting from a plaintiff's failure to correctly identify and serve all the persons who should be named or served.

Subdivision (j). This subdivision retains the text of former subdivision (d)(6) without material change. The waiver-of-service provision is also inapplicable to actions against governments subject to service pursuant to this subdivision.

The revision adds a new paragraph (1) referring to the statute governing service of a summons on a foreign state and its political subdivisions, agencies, and instrumentalities, the Foreign Sovereign Immunities Act of 1976, 28 U.S.C. § 1608. The caption of the subdivision reflects that change.

Subdivision (k). This subdivision replaces the former subdivision (f), with no change in the title. Paragraph (1) retains the substance of the former rule in explicitly authorizing the exercise of personal jurisdiction over persons who can be reached under state long-arm law, the "100–mile bulge" provision added in 1963, or the federal interpleader act. Paragraph (1)(D) is new, but merely calls attention to federal legislation that may provide for nationwide or even world-wide service of process in cases arising under particular federal laws. Congress has provided for nationwide service of process and full exercise of territorial jurisdiction by all district courts with respect to specified federal actions. *See* 1 R. Casad, *Jurisdiction in Civil Actions* (2d Ed.) chap. 5 (1991).

Paragraph (2) is new. It authorizes the exercise of territorial jurisdiction over the person of any defendant against whom is made a claim arising under any federal law if that person is subject to personal jurisdiction in no state. This addition is a companion to the amendments made in revised subdivisions (e) and (f).

This paragraph corrects a gap in the enforcement of federal law. Under the former rule, a problem was presented when the defendant was a non-resident of the United States having contacts with the United States sufficient to justify the application of United States law and to satisfy federal standards of forum selection, but having insufficient contact with any single state to support jurisdiction under state long-arm legislation or meet the requirements of the Fourteenth Amendment limitation on state court territorial jurisdiction. In such cases, the defendant was shielded from the enforcement of federal law by the fortuity of a favorable limitation on the power of state courts, which was incorporated into the federal practice by the former rule. In this respect, the revision responds to the suggestion of the Supreme Court made in *Omni Capital Int'l v. Rudolf Wolff & Co., Ltd.,* 484 U.S. 97, 111 (1987).

There remain constitutional limitations on the exercise of territorial jurisdiction by federal courts over persons outside the United States. These restrictions arise from the Fifth Amendment rather than from the Fourteenth Amendment, which limits state-court reach and which was incorporated into federal practice by the reference to state law in the text of the former subdivision (e) that is deleted by this revision. The Fifth Amendment requires that any defendant have affiliating contacts with the United States sufficient to justify the exercise of personal jurisdiction over that party. *Cf. Wells Fargo & Co. v. Wells Fargo Express Co.,* 556 F.2d 406, 418 (9th Cir.1977). There also may be a further Fifth Amendment constraint in that a plaintiff's forum selection might be so inconvenient to a defendant that it would be a denial of "fair play and substantial justice" required by the due process clause, even though the defendant had significant affiliating contacts with the United States. *See DeJames v. Magnificence Carriers,* 654 F.2d 280, 286 n. 3 (3d Cir.), *cert. denied,* 454 U.S. 1085, 102 S.Ct. 642, 70 L.Ed.2d 620 (1981). *Compare World–Wide Volkswagen Corp. v. Woodson,* 444 U.S. 286, 293–294 (1980); *Insurance Corp. of Ireland v. Compagnie des Bauxites de Guinee,* 456 U.S. 694, 702–03 (1982); *Burger King Corp. v. Rudzewicz,* 471 U.S. 462, 476–78 (1985); *Asahi Metal Indus. v. Superior Court of Cal., Solano County,* 480 U.S. 102, 108–13 (1987). *See generally* R. Lusardi, *Nationwide Service of Process: Due Process Limitations on the Power of the Sovereign,* 33 Vill.L.Rev. 1 (1988).

This provision does not affect the operation of federal venue legislation. *See generally* 28 U.S.C. § 1391. Nor does it affect the operation of federal law providing for the change of venue. 28 U.S.C. §§ 1404, 1406. The availability of transfer for fairness and convenience under § 1404 should preclude most conflicts between the full exercise of territorial jurisdiction permitted by this rule and the Fifth Amendment requirement of "fair play and substantial justice."

The district court should be especially scrupulous to protect aliens who reside in a foreign country from forum selections so onerous that injustice could result. "[G]reat care and reserve should be exercised when extending our notions of personal jurisdiction into the international field." *Asahi Metal Indus. v. Superior Court of Cal., Solano County,* 480 U.S. 102, 115 (1987), quoting *United States v. First Nat'l City Bank,* 379 U.S. 378, 404 (1965)(Harlan, J., dissenting).

This narrow extension of the federal reach applies only if a claim is made against the defendant under federal law. It does not establish personal jurisdiction if the only claims are those arising under state law or the law of another country, even though there might be diversity or alienage subject matter jurisdiction as to such claims. If, however, personal jurisdiction is established under this paragraph with respect to a federal claim, then 28 U.S.C. § 1367(a) provides supplemental jurisdiction over related claims against that defendant, subject to the court's discretion to decline exercise of that jurisdiction under 28 U.S.C. § 1367(c).

Subdivision (*l*). This subdivision assembles in one place all the provisions of the present rule bearing on proof of service. No material change in the rule is effected. The provision that proof of service can be amended by leave of court is retained from the former subdivision (h). *See generally* 4A Wright & Miller, *Federal Practice and Procedure* § 1132 (2d ed. 1987).

Subdivision (m). This subdivision retains much of the language of the present subdivision (j).

The new subdivision explicitly provides that the court shall allow additional time if there is good cause for the plaintiff's failure to effect service in the prescribed 120 days, and authorizes the court to relieve a plaintiff of the consequences of an application of this subdivision even if there is no good cause shown. Such relief formerly was afforded in some cases, partly in reliance on Rule 6(b). Relief may be justified, for example, if the applicable statute of limitations would bar the refiled action, or if the defendant is evading service or conceals a defect in attempted service. *E.g., Ditkof v. Owens–Illinois, Inc.,* 114 F.R.D. 104 (E.D.Mich.1987). A specific instance of good cause is set forth in paragraph (3) of this rule, which provides for extensions if necessary to correct oversights in compliance with the requirements of multiple service in actions against the United States or its officers, agencies, and corporations. The district court should also take care to protect *pro se* plaintiffs from consequences of confusion or delay attending the resolution of an *in forma pauperis* petition. *Robinson v. America's Best Contacts & Eyeglasses,* 876 F.2d 596 (7th Cir.1989).

The 1983 revision of this subdivision referred to the "party on whose behalf such service was required," rather than to the "plaintiff," a term used generically elsewhere in this rule to refer to any party initiating a claim against a person who is not a party to the action. To simplify the text, the revision returns to the usual practice in the rule of referring simply to the plaintiff even though its principles apply with equal force to defendants who may assert claims against non-parties under Rules 13(h), 14, 19, 20, or 21.

Subdivision (n). This subdivision provides for in rem and quasi-in-rem jurisdiction. Paragraph (1) incorporates any requirements of 28 U.S.C. § 1655 or similar provisions bearing on seizures or liens.

Paragraph (2) provides for other uses of quasi-in-rem jurisdiction but limits its use to exigent circumstances. Provisional remedies may be employed as a means to secure jurisdiction over the property of a defendant whose person is not within reach of the court, but occasions for the use of this provision should be rare, as where the defendant is a fugitive or assets are in imminent danger of disappearing. Until 1963, it was not possible under Rule 4 to assert jurisdiction in a federal court over the property of a defendant not personally served. The 1963 amendment to subdivision (e) authorized the use of state law procedures authorizing seizures of assets as a basis for jurisdiction. Given the liberal availability of long-arm jurisdiction, the exercise of power quasi-in-rem has become almost an anachronism. Circumstances too spare to affiliate the defendant to the forum state sufficiently to support long-arm jurisdiction over the defendant's person are also inadequate to support seizure of the defendant's assets fortuitously found within the state. *Shaffer v. Heitner,* 433 U.S. 186, 97 S.Ct. 2569, 53 L.Ed.2d 683 (1977).

2000 AMENDMENT

Paragraph (2)(B) is added to Rule 4(i) to require service on the United States when a United States officer or employee is sued in an individual capacity for acts or omissions occurring in connection with duties performed on behalf of the United States. Decided cases provide uncertain guidance on the question whether the United States must be served in such actions. *See Vaccaro v. Dobre,* 81 F.3d 854, 856–857 (9th Cir.1996); *Armstrong v. Sears,* 33 F.3d 182, 185–187 (2d Cir.1994); *Ecclesiastical Order of the Ism of Am v. Chasin,* 845 F.2d 113, 116 (6th Cir.1988); *Light v. Wolf,* 816 F.2d 746 (D.C.Cir.1987); *see also Simpkins v. District of Columbia,* 108 F.3d 366, 368–369 (D.C.Cir.1997). Service on the United States will help to protect the interest of the individual defendant in securing representation by the United States, and will expedite the process of determining whether the United States will provide representation. It has been understood that the individual defendant must be served as an individual defendant, a requirement that is made explicit. Invocation of the individual service provisions of subdivisions (e), (f), and (g) invokes also the waiver- of-service provisions of subdivision (d).

Paragraph 2(B) reaches service when an officer or employee of the United States is sued in an individual capacity "for acts or omissions occurring in connection with the performance of duties on behalf of the United States." This phrase has been chosen as a functional phrase that can be applied without the occasionally distracting associations of such phrases as "scope of employment," "color of office," or "arising out of the employment." Many actions are brought against individual federal officers or employees of the United States for acts or omissions that have no connection whatever to their governmental roles. There is no reason to require service on the United States in these actions. The connection to federal employment that requires service on the United States must be determined as a practical matter, considering whether the individual defendant has reasonable grounds to look to the United States for assistance and whether the United States has reasonable grounds for demanding formal notice of the action.

An action against a former officer or employee of the United States is covered by paragraph (2)(B) in the same way as an action against a present officer or employee. Termination of the relationship between the individual defendant and the United States does not reduce the need to serve the United States.

Paragraph (3) is amended to ensure that failure to serve the United States in an action governed by paragraph 2(B) does not defeat an action. This protection is adopted because there will be cases in which the plaintiff reasonably fails to appreciate the need to serve the United States . There is no requirement, however, that the plaintiff show that the failure to serve the United States was reasonable. A reasonable time to effect service on the United States must be allowed after the failure is pointed out. An additional change ensures that if the United States or United States attorney is served in an action governed by paragraph 2(A), additional time is to be allowed even though no officer, employee, agency, or corporation of the United States was served.

GAP Report

The most important changes were made to ensure that no one would read the seemingly independent provisions of paragraphs 2(A) and 2(B) to mean that service must be made twice both on the United States and on the United States employee when the employee is sued in both official and individual capacities. The word "only" was added in subparagraph (A) and the new phrase "whether or not the officer or employee is sued also in an individual capacity" was inserted in subparagraph (B).

Minor changes were made to include "Employees" in the catch-line for subdivision (i), and to add "or employee" in paragraph 2(A). Although it may seem awkward to think of suit against an employee in an official capacity, there is no clear definition that separates "officers" from "employees" for this purpose. The published proposal to amend Rule 12(a)(3) referred to actions against an employee sued in an official capacity, and it seemed better to make the rules parallel by adding "employee" to Rule 4(i)(2)(A) than by deleting it from Rule 12(a)(3)(A).

2007 AMENDMENT

The language of Rule 4 has been amended as part of the general restyling of the Civil Rules to make them more easily understood and to make style and terminology consistent throughout the rules. These changes are intended to be stylistic only.

Rule 4(d)(1)(C) corrects an inadvertent error in former Rule 4(d)(2)(G). The defendant needs two copies of the waiver form, not an extra copy of the notice and request.

Rule 4(g) changes "infant" to "minor." "Infant" in the present rule means "minor." Modern word usage suggests that "minor" will better maintain the intended meaning. The same change from "infant" to "minor" is made throughout the rules. In addition, subdivision (f)(3) is added to the description of methods of service that the court may order; the addition ensures the evident intent that the court not order service by means prohibited by international agreement.

Rule 4(i)(4) corrects a misleading reference to "the plaintiff" in former Rule 4(i)(3). A party other than a plaintiff may need a reasonable time to effect service. Rule 4(i)(4) properly covers any party.

Former Rule 4(j)(2) refers to service upon an "other governmental organization subject to suit." This is changed to "any other state-created governmental organization that is subject to suit." The change entrenches the meaning indicated by the caption ("Serving a Foreign, State, or Local Government"), and the invocation of state law. It excludes any risk that this rule might be read to govern service on a federal agency, or other entities not created by state law.

The former provision describing service on interpleader claimants [former (k)(1)(C)] is deleted as redundant in light of the general provision in (k)(1)(C) recognizing personal jurisdiction authorized by a federal statute.

Rule 4.1. Service of Other Process

1993 ADOPTION

This is a new rule. Its purpose is to separate those few provisions of the former Rule 4 bearing on matters other than service of a summons to allow greater textual clarity in Rule 4. Subdivision (a) contains no new language.

Subdivision (b) replaces the final clause of the penultimate sentence of the former subdivision 4(f), a clause added to the rule in 1963. The new rule provides for nationwide service of orders of civil commitment enforcing decrees of injunctions issued to compel compliance with federal law. The rule makes no change in the practice with respect to the enforcement of injunctions or decrees not involving the enforcement of federally-created rights.

Service of process is not required to notify a party of a decree or injunction, or of an order that the party show cause why that party should not be held in contempt of such an order. With respect to a party who has once been served with a summons, the service of the decree or injunction itself or of an order to show cause can be made pursuant to Rule 5. Thus, for example, an injunction may be served on a party through that person's attorney. *Chagas v. United States,* 369 F.2d 643 (5th Cir.1966). The same is true for service of an order to show cause. *Waffenschmidt v. MacKay,* 763 F.2d 711 (5th Cir.1985).

The new rule does not affect the reach of the court to impose criminal contempt sanctions. Nationwide enforcement of federal decrees and injunctions is already available with respect to criminal contempt: a federal court may effect the arrest of a criminal contemnor anywhere in the United States, 28 U.S.C. § 3041, and a contemnor when arrested may be subject to removal to the district in which punishment may be imposed. Fed.R.Crim.P. 40. Thus, the present law permits criminal contempt enforcement against a contemnor wherever that person may be found.

The effect of the revision is to provide a choice of civil or criminal contempt sanctions in those situations to which it applies. Contempt proceedings, whether civil or criminal, must be brought in the court that was allegedly defied by a contumacious act. *Ex parte Bradley,* 74 U.S. (7 Wall) 364, 19 L.Ed. 214 (1869). This is so even if the offensive conduct or inaction occurred outside the district of the court in which the enforcement proceeding must be conducted. *E.g., McCourtney v. United States,* 291 Fed. 497 (8th Cir.), *cert. denied,* 263 U.S. 714, 44 S.Ct. 134, 68 L.Ed. 520 (1923). For this purpose, the rule as before does not distinguish between parties and other persons subject to contempt sanctions by reason of their relation or connection to parties.

2007 AMENDMENT

The language of Rule 4.1 has been amended as part of the general restyling of the Civil Rules to make them more easily understood and to make style and terminology consistent throughout the rules. These changes are intended to be stylistic only.

Rule 5.   Service and Filing of Pleadings and Other Papers

1937 ADOPTION

Note to Subdivisions (a) and (b). Compare 2 Minn.Stat. (1927) §§ 9240, 9241, 9242; N.Y.C.P.A. (1937) §§ 163, 164 and N.Y.R.C.P. (1937) Rules 20, 21; 2 Wash.Rev.Stat. Ann. (Remington, 1932) §§ 244–249.

Note to Subdivision (d). Compare the present practice under former Equity Rule 12 (Issue of Subpoena—Time for Answer).

1963 AMENDMENT

The words "affected thereby," stricken out by the amendment, introduced a problem of interpretation. See 1 Barron & Holtzoff, Federal Practice & Procedure 760–61 (Wright ed. 1960). The amendment eliminates this difficulty and promotes full exchange of information among the parties by requiring service of papers on all the parties to the action, except as otherwise provided in the rules. See also subdivision (c) of Rule 5. So, for example, a third-party defendant is required to serve his answer to the third-party complaint not only upon the defendant but also upon the plaintiff. See amended Form 22–A and the Advisory Committee's Note thereto.

As to the method of serving papers upon a party whose address is unknown, see Rule 5(b).

1970 AMENDMENT

The amendment makes clear that all papers relating to discovery which are required to be served on any party must be served on all parties, unless the court orders otherwise. The present language expressly includes notices and demands, but it is not explicit as to answers or responses as provided in Rules 33, 34, and 36. Discovery papers may be voluminous or the parties numerous, and the court is empowered to vary the requirement if in a given case it proves needlessly onerous.

In actions begun by seizure of property, service will at times have to be made before the absent owner of the property has filed an appearance. For example, a prompt deposition may be needed in a maritime action in rem. See Rules 30(a) and 30(b)(2) and the related notes. A provision is added authorizing service on the person having custody or possession of the property at the time of its seizure.

1980 AMENDMENT

Subdivision (d). By the terms of this rule and Rule 30(f)(1) discovery materials must be promptly filed, although it often happens that no use is made of the materials after they are filed. Because the copies required for filing are an added expense and the large volume of discovery filings presents serious problems of storage in some districts, the Committee in 1978 first proposed that discovery materials not be filed unless on order of the court or for use in the proceedings. But such materials are sometimes of interest to those who may have no access to them except by a requirement of filing, such as members of a class, litigants similarly situated, or the public generally. Accordingly, this amendment and a change in Rule 30(f)(1) continue the requirement of filing but make it subject to an order of the court that discovery materials not be filed unless filing is requested by the court or is effected by parties who wish to use the materials in the proceeding.

1987 AMENDMENT

The amendments are technical. No substantive change is intended.

1991 AMENDMENT

Subdivision (d). This subdivision is amended to require that the person making service under the rule certify that service has been effected. Such a requirement has generally been imposed by local rule.

Having such information on file may be useful for many purposes, including proof of service if an issue arises concerning the effectiveness of the service. The certificate will generally specify the date as well as the manner of service, but parties employing private delivery services may sometimes be unable to specify the date of delivery. In the latter circumstance, a specification of the date of transmission of the paper to the delivery service may be sufficient for the purposes of this rule.

Subdivision (e). The words *"pleading and other"* are stricken as unnecessary. Pleadings are papers within the meaning of the rule. The revision also accommodates the development of the use of facsimile transmission for filing.

Several local district rules have directed the office of the clerk to refuse to accept for filing papers not conforming to certain requirements of form imposed by local rules or practice. This is not a suitable role for the office of the clerk, and the practice exposes litigants to the hazards of time bars; for these reasons, such rules are proscribed by this revision. The enforcement of these rules and of the local rules is a role for a judicial officer. A clerk may of course advise a party or counsel that a particular instrument is not in proper form, and may be directed to so inform the court.

1993 AMENDMENT

This is a technical amendment, using the broader language of Rule 25 of the Federal Rules of Appellate Procedure. The district court—and the bankruptcy court by virtue of a cross-reference in Bankruptcy Rule 7005—can, by local rule, permit filing not only by facsimile transmissions but also by other electronic means, subject to standards approved by the Judicial Conference.

The present Rule 5(e) has authorized filing by facsimile or other electronic means on two conditions. The filing must be authorized by local rule. Use of this means of filing must be authorized by the Judicial Conference of the United States and must be consistent with standards established by the Judicial Conference. Attempts to develop Judicial Conference standards have demonstrated the value of several adjustments in the rule.

The most significant change discards the requirement that the Judicial Conference authorize local electronic filing rules. As before, each district may decide for itself whether it has the equipment and personnel required to establish electronic filing, but a district that wishes to establish electronic filing need no longer await Judicial Conference action.

The role of Judicial Conference standards is clarified by specifying that the standards are to govern technical matters. Technical standards can provide nationwide uniformity, enabling ready use of electronic filing without pausing to adjust for the otherwise inevitable variations among local rules. Judicial Conference adoption of technical standards should prove superior to specification in these rules. Electronic technology has advanced with great speed. The process of adopting Judicial Conference standards should prove speedier and more flexible in determining the time for the first uniform standards, in adjusting standards at appropriate intervals, and in sparing the Supreme Court and Congress the need to consider technological details. Until Judicial Conference standards are adopted, however, uniformity will occur only to the extent that local rules deliberately seek to copy other local rules.

It is anticipated that Judicial Conference standards will govern such technical specifications as data formatting, speed of transmission, means to transmit copies of supporting documents, and security of communication. Perhaps more important, standards must be established to assure proper maintenance and integrity of the record and to provide appropriate access and retrieval mechanisms. Local rules must address these issues until Judicial Conference standards are adopted.

The amended rule also makes clear the equality of filing by electronic means with written filings. An electronic filing that complies with the local rule satisfies all requirements for filing on paper, signature, or verification. An electronic filing that otherwise satisfies the requirements of 28 U.S.C. s 1746 need not be separately made in writing. Public access to electronic filings is governed by the same rules as govern written filings.

The separate reference to filing by facsimile transmission is deleted. Facsimile transmission continues to be included as an electronic means.

1996 AMENDMENT

The present Rule 5(e) has authorized filing by facsimile or other electronic means on two conditions. The filing must be authorized by local rule. Use of this means of filing must be authorized by the Judicial Conference of the United States and must be consistent with standards established by the Judicial Conference. Attempts to develop Judicial Conference standards have demonstrated the value of several adjustments in the rule.

The most significant change discards the requirement that the Judicial Conference authorize local electronic filing rules. As before, each district may decide for itself whether it has the equipment and personnel required to establish electronic filing, but a district that wishes to establish electronic filing need no longer await Judicial Conference action.

The role of Judicial Conference standards is clarified by specifying that the standards are to govern technical matters. Technical standards can provide nationwide uniformity, enabling ready use of electronic filing without pausing to adjust for the otherwise inevitable variations among local rules. Judicial Conference adoption of technical standards should prove superior to specification in these rules. Electronic technology has advanced with great speed. The process of adopting Judicial Conference standards should prove speedier and more flexible in determining the time for the first uniform standards, in adjusting standards at appropriate intervals, and in sparing the Supreme Court and Congress the need to consider technological details. Until Judicial Conference standards are adopted, however, uniformity will occur only to the extent that local rules deliberately seek to copy other local rules.

It is anticipated that Judicial Conference standards will govern such technical specifications as data formatting, speed of transmission, means to transmit copies of supporting documents, and security of communication. Perhaps more important, standards must be established to assure proper maintenance and integrity of the record and to provide appropriate access and retrieval mechanisms. Local rules must address these issues until Judicial Conference standards are adopted.

The amended rule also makes clear the equality of filing by electronic means with written filings. An electronic filing that complies with the local rule satisfies all requirements for filing on paper, signature, or verification. An electronic filing that otherwise satisfies the requirements of 28 U.S.C. § 1746 need not be separately made in writing. Public access to electronic filings is governed by the same rules as govern written filings.

The separate reference to filing by facsimile transmission is deleted. Facsimile transmission continues to be included as an electronic means.

2000 AMENDMENT

Subdivision (d). Rule 5(d) is amended to provide that disclosures under Rule 26(a)(1) and (2), and discovery requests and responses under Rules 30, 31, 33, 34, and 36 must not be filed until they are used in the action. "Discovery requests" includes deposition notices and "discovery responses" includes objections. The rule supersedes and invalidates local rules that forbid, permit, or require filing of these materials before they are used in the action. The former Rule 26(a)(4) requirement that disclosures under Rule 26(a)(1) and (2) be filed has been removed. Disclosures under Rule 26(a)(3), however, must be promptly filed as provided in Rule 26(a)(3). Filings in connection with Rule 35 examinations, which involve a motion proceeding when the parties do not agree, are unaffected by these amendments.

Recognizing the costs imposed on parties and courts by required filing of discovery materials that are never used in an action, Rule 5(d) was amended in 1980 to authorize court orders that excuse filing. Since then, many districts have adopted local rules that excuse or forbid filing. In 1989 the Judicial Conference Local Rules Project concluded that these local rules were inconsistent with Rule 5(d), but urged the Advisory Committee to consider amending the rule. *Local Rules Project* at 92 (1989). The Judicial Conference of the Ninth Circuit gave the Committee similar advice in 1997. The reality of nonfiling reflected in these local rules has even been assumed in drafting the national rules. In 1993, Rule 30(f)(1) was amended to direct that the officer presiding at a deposition file it with the court or send it to the attorney who arranged for the transcript or recording. The Committee Note explained that this alternative to filing was designed for "courts which direct that depositions not be automatically filed." Rule 30(f)(1) has been amended to conform to this change in Rule 5(d).

Although this amendment is based on widespread experience with local rules, and confirms the results directed by these local rules, it is designed to supersede and invalidate local rules. There is no apparent reason to have different filing rules in different districts. Even if districts vary in present capacities to store filed materials that are not used in an action, there is little reason to continue expending court resources for this purpose. These costs and burdens would likely change as parties make increased use of audio- and videotaped depositions. Equipment to facilitate review and reproduction of such discovery materials may prove costly to acquire, maintain, and operate.

The amended rule provides that discovery materials and disclosures under Rule 26(a)(1) and (a)(2) must not be filed until they are "used in the proceeding." This phrase is meant to refer to proceedings in court. This filing requirement is not triggered by "use" of discovery materials in other discovery activities, such as depositions. In connection with proceedings in court, however, the rule is to be interpreted broadly; any use of discovery materials in court in connection with a motion, a pretrial conference under Rule 16, or otherwise, should be interpreted as use in the proceeding.

Once discovery or disclosure materials are used in the proceeding, the filing requirements of Rule 5(d) should apply to them. But because the filing requirement applies only with regard to materials that are used, only those parts of voluminous materials that are actually used need be filed. Any party would be free to file other pertinent portions of materials that are so used. *See* Fed. R. Evid. 106; *cf.* Rule 32(a)(4). If the parties are unduly sparing in their submissions, the court may order further filings. By local rule, a court could provide appropriate direction regarding the filing of discovery materials, such as depositions, that are used in proceedings.

"Shall" is replaced by "must" under the program to conform amended rules to current style conventions when there is no ambiguity.

GAP Report

The Advisory Committee recommends no changes to either the amendments to Rule 5(d) or the Committee Note as published.

2001 AMENDMENT

Rule 5(b) is restyled.

Rule 5(b)(1) makes it clear that the provision for service on a party's attorney applies only to service made under Rules 5(a) and 77(d). Service under Rules 4, 4.1, 45(b), and 71A(d)(3)—as well as rules that invoke those rules—must be made as provided in those rules.

Subparagraphs (A), (B), and (C) of Rule 5(b)(2) carry forward the method-of-service provisions of former Rule 5(b).

Subparagraph (D) of Rule 5(b)(2) is new. It authorizes service by electronic means or any other means, but only if consent is obtained from the person served. The consent must be express, and cannot be implied from conduct. Early experience with electronic filing as authorized by Rule 5(d) is positive, supporting service by electronic means as well. Consent is required, however, because it is not yet possible to assume universal entry into the world of electronic communication. Subparagraph (D) also authorizes service by nonelectronic means. The Rule 5(b)(2)(B) provision making mail service complete on mailing is extended in subparagraph (D) to make service by electronic means complete on transmission; transmission is effected when the sender does the last act that must be performed by the sender. Service by other agencies is complete on delivery to the designated agency.

Finally, subparagraph (D) authorizes adoption of local rules providing for service through the court. Electronic case filing systems will come to include the capacity to make service by using the court's facilities to transmit all documents filed in the case. It may prove most efficient to establish an environment in which a party can file with the court, making use of the court's transmission facilities to serve the filed paper on all other parties. Transmission might be by such means as direct transmission of the paper, or by transmission of a notice of filing that includes an electronic link for direct access to the paper. Because service is under subparagraph (D), consent must be obtained from the persons served.

Consent to service under Rule 5(b)(2)(D) must be in writing, which can be provided by electronic means. Parties are encouraged to specify the scope and duration of the consent. The specification should include at least the persons to whom service should be made, the appropriate address or location for such service—such as the e-mail address or facsimile machine number, and the format to be used for attachments. A district court may establish a registry or other facility that allows advance consent to service by specified means for future actions.

Rule 6(e) is amended to allow additional time to respond when service is made under Rule 5(b)(2)(D). The additional time does not relieve a party who consents to service under Rule 5(b)(2)(D) of the responsibilities to monitor the facility designated for receiving service and to provide prompt notice of any address change.

Paragraph (3) addresses a question that may arise from a literal reading of the provision that service by electronic means is complete on transmission. Electronic communication is rapidly improving, but lawyers report continuing failures of transmission, particularly with respect to attachments. Ordinarily the risk of non-receipt falls on the person being served, who has consented to this form of service. But the risk should not extend to situations in which the person attempting service learns that the attempted service in fact did not reach the person to be served. Given actual knowledge that the attempt failed, service is not effected. The person attempting service must either try again or show circumstances that justify dispensing with service.

Paragraph (3) does not address the similar questions that may arise when a person attempting service learns that service by means other than electronic means in fact did not reach the person to be served. Case law provides few illustrations of circumstances in which a person attempting service actually knows that the attempt failed but seeks to act as if service had been made. This negative history suggests there is no need to address these problems in Rule 5(b)(3). This silence does not imply any view on these issues, nor on the circumstances that justify various forms of judicial action even though service has not been made.

Changes Made After Publication and Comments

Rule 5(b)(2)(D) was changed to require that consent be "in writing."

Rule 5(b)(3) is new. The published proposal did not address the question of failed service in the text of the rule. Instead, the Committee Note included this statement: "As with other modes of service, however, actual notice that the transmission was not received defeats the presumption of receipt that arises from the provision that service is complete on transmission. The sender must take additional steps to effect service. Service by other agencies is complete on delivery to the designated agency." The addition of paragraph (3) was prompted by consideration of the draft Appellate *Rule 25(c)* that was prepared for the meeting of the Appellate Rules Advisory Committee. This draft provided: "Service by electronic means is complete on transmission, unless the party making service is notified that the paper was not received." Although Appellate *Rule 25(c)* is being prepared for publication and comment, while Civil Rule 5(b) has been published and otherwise is ready to recommend for adoption, it seemed desirable to achieve some parallel between the two rules.

The draft Rule 5(b)(3) submitted for consideration by the Advisory Committee covered all means of service except for leaving a copy with the clerk of the court when the person to be served has no known address. It was not limited to electronic service for fear that a provision limited to electronic service might generate unintended negative implications as to service by other means, particularly mail. This concern was strengthened by a small number of opinions that say that service by mail is effective, because complete on mailing, even when the person making service has prompt actual notice that the mail was not delivered. The Advisory Committee voted to limit Rule 5(b)(3) to service by electronic means because this means of service is relatively new, and seems likely to miscarry more frequently than service by post. It was suggested during the Advisory Committee meeting that the question of negative implication could be addressed in the Committee Note. There was little discussion of this possibility. The Committee Note submitted above includes a "no negative implications" paragraph prepared by the Reporter for consideration by the Standing Committee.

The Advisory Committee did not consider at all a question that was framed during the later meeting of the Appellate Rules Advisory Committee. As approved by the Advisory

Committee, Rule 5(b)(3) defeats service by electronic means "if the party making service learns that the attempted service did not reach the person to be served." It says nothing about the time relevant to learning of the failure. The omission may seem glaring. Curing the omission, however, requires selection of a time. As revised, proposed Appellate *Rule 25(c)* requires that the party making service learn of the failure within three calendar days. The Appellate Rules Advisory Committee will have the luxury of public comment and another year to consider the desirability of this short period. If Civil Rule 5(b) is to be recommended for adoption now, no such luxury is available. This issue deserves careful consideration by the Standing Committee.

Several changes are made in the Committee Note. (1) It requires that consent "be express, and cannot be implied from conduct." This addition reflects a more general concern stimulated by a reported ruling that an e-mail address on a firm's letterhead implied consent to email service. (2) The paragraph discussing service through the court's facilities is expanded by describing alternative methods, including an "electronic link." (3) There is a new paragraph that states that the requirement of written consent can be satisfied by electronic means, and that suggests matters that should be addressed by the consent. (4) A paragraph is added to note the additional response time provided by amended Rule 6(e). (5) The final two paragraphs address newly added Rule 5(b)(3). The first explains the rule that electronic service is not effective if the person making service learns that it did not reach the person to be served. The second paragraph seeks to defeat any negative implications that might arise from limiting Rule 5(b)(3) to electronic service, not mail, not other means consented to such as commercial express service, and not service on another person on behalf of the person to be served.

Rule 6(e)

The Advisory Committee recommended that no change be made in Civil Rule 6(e) to reflect the provisions of Civil Rule 5(b)(2)(D) that, with the consent of the person to be served, would allow service by electronic or other means. Absent change, service by these means would not affect the time for acting in response to the paper served. Comment was requested, however, on the alternative that would allow an additional 3 days to respond. The alternative Rule 6(e) amendments are cast in a form that permits ready incorporation in the Bankruptcy Rules. Several of the comments suggest that the added three days should be provided. Electronic transmission is not always instantaneous, and may fail for any of a number of reasons. It may take three days to arrange for transmission in readable form. Providing added time to respond will not discourage people from asking for consent to electronic transmission, and may encourage people to give consent. The more who consent, the quicker will come the improvements that will make electronic service ever more attractive. Consistency with the Bankruptcy Rules will be a good thing, and the Bankruptcy Rules Advisory Committee believes the additional three days should be allowed.

2006 AMENDMENT

Amended Rule 5(e) acknowledges that many courts have required electronic filing by means of a standing order, procedures manual, or local rule. These local practices reflect the advantages that courts and most litigants realize from electronic filing. Courts that mandate electronic filing recognize the need to make exceptions when requiring electronic filing imposes a hardship on a party. Under amended Rule 5(e), a local rule that requires electronic filing must include reasonable exceptions, but Rule 5(e) does not define the scope of those exceptions. Experience with the local rules that have been adopted and that will emerge will aid in drafting new local rules and will facilitate gradual convergence on uniform exceptions, whether in local rules or in an amended Rule 5(e).

2007 AMENDMENT

The language of Rule 5 has been amended as part of the general restyling of the Civil Rules to make them more easily understood and to make style and terminology consistent throughout the rules. These changes are intended to be stylistic only.

Rule 5(a)(1)(E) omits the former reference to a designation of record on appeal. Appellate Rule 10 is a self-contained provision for the record on appeal, and provides for service.

Former Rule 5(b)(2)(D) literally provided that a local rule may authorize use of the court's transmission facilities to make service by non-electronic means agreed to by the parties. That was not intended. Rule 5(b)(3) restores the intended meaning—court transmission facilities can be used only for service by electronic means.

Rule 5(d)(2)(B) provides that "a" judge may accept a paper for filing, replacing the reference in former Rule 5(e) to "the" judge. Some courts do not assign a designated judge to each case, and it may be important to have another judge accept a paper for filing even when a case is on the individual docket of a particular judge. The ministerial acts of accepting the paper, noting the time, and transmitting the paper to the court clerk do not interfere with the assigned judge's authority over the action.

Rule 5.1. Constitutional Challenge to a Statute—Notice, Certification, and Intervention

2006 ADOPTION

Rule 5.1 implements 28 U.S.C. § 2403, replacing the final three sentences of Rule 24(c). New Rule 5.1 requires a party that files a pleading, written motion, or other paper drawing in question the constitutionality of a federal or state statute to file a notice of constitutional question and serve it on the United States Attorney General or state attorney general. The party must promptly file and serve the notice of constitutional question. This notice requirement supplements the court's duty to certify a constitutional challenge to the United States Attorney General or state attorney general. The notice of constitutional question will ensure that the attorney general is notified of constitutional challenges and has an opportunity to exercise the statutory right to intervene at the earliest possible point in the litigation. The court's certification obligation remains, and is the only notice when the constitutionality of a federal or state statute is drawn in question by means other than a party's pleading, written motion, or other paper.

Moving the notice and certification provisions from Rule 24(c) to a new rule is designed to attract the parties' attention to these provisions by locating them in the vicinity of the rules that require notice by service and pleading.

Rule 5.1 goes beyond the requirements of § 2403 and the former Rule 24(c) provisions by requiring notice and certification of a constitutional challenge to any federal or state statute, not only those "affecting the public interest." It is better to assure, through notice, that the attorney general is able to determine whether to seek intervention on the ground that the act or statute affects a public interest. Rule 5.1 refers to a "federal statute," rather than the § 2403 reference to an "Act of Congress," to maintain consistency in the Civil Rules vocabulary. In Rule 5.1 "statute" means any congressional enactment that would qualify as an "Act of Congress."

Unless the court sets a later time, the 60–day period for intervention runs from the time a party files a notice of constitutional question or from the time the court certifies a constitutional challenge, whichever is earlier. Rule 5.1(a) directs that a party promptly serve the notice of constitutional question. The court may extend the 60–period on its own or on motion. One occasion for extension may arise if the court certifies a challenge under § 2403 after a party files a notice of constitutional question. Pretrial activities may continue without interruption during the intervention period, and the court retains authority to grant interlocutory relief. The court may reject a constitutional challenge to a statute at any time. But the court may not enter a final judgment holding a statute unconstitutional before the attorney general has responded or the intervention period has expired without response. This rule does not displace any of the statutory or rule procedures that permit dismissal of all or part of an action—including a constitutional challenge—at any time, even before service of process.

2007 AMENDMENT

The language of Rule 5.1 has been amended as part of the general restyling of the Civil Rules to make them more easily understood and to make style and terminology consistent throughout the rules. These changes are intended to be stylistic only.

Rule 5.2. Privacy Protection For Filings Made with the Court

2007 ADOPTION

The rule is adopted in compliance with section 205(c)(3) of the E–Government Act of 2002, Public Law 107–347. Section 205(c)(3) requires the Supreme Court to prescribe rules "to protect privacy and security concerns relating to electronic filing of documents and the public availability ... of documents filed electronically." The rule goes further than the E–Government Act in regulating paper filings even when they are not converted to electronic form. But the number of filings that remain in paper form is certain to diminish over time. Most districts scan paper filings into the electronic case file, where they become available to the public in the same way as documents initially filed in electronic form. It is electronic availability, not the form of the initial filing, that raises the privacy and security concerns addressed in the E–Government Act.

The rule is derived from and implements the policy adopted by the Judicial Conference in September 2001 to address the privacy concerns resulting from public access to electronic case files. See http://www.privacy.uscourts.gov/Policy.htm. The Judicial Conference policy is that documents in case files generally should be made available electronically to the same extent they are available at the courthouse, provided that certain "personal data identifiers" are not included in the public file.

While providing for the public filing of some information, such as the last four digits of an account number, the rule does not intend to establish a presumption that this information never could or should be protected. For example, it may well be necessary in individual cases to prevent remote access by nonparties to any part of an account number or social security number. It may also be necessary to protect information not covered by the redaction requirement—such as driver's license numbers and alien registration numbers—in a particular case. In such cases, protection may be sought under subdivision (d) or (e). Moreover, the Rule does not affect the protection available under other rules, such as Civil Rules 16 and 26(c), or under other sources of protective authority.

Parties must remember that any personal information not otherwise protected by sealing or redaction will be made available over the internet. Counsel should notify clients of this fact so that an informed decision may be made on what information is to be included in a document filed with the court.

The clerk is not required to review documents filed with the court for compliance with this rule. The responsibility to redact filings rests with counsel and the party or non-party making the filing.

Subdivision (c) provides for limited public access in Social Security cases and immigration cases. Those actions are entitled to special treatment due to the prevalence of sensitive information and the volume of filings. Remote electronic access by nonparties is limited to the docket and the written dispositions of the court unless the court orders otherwise. The rule contemplates, however, that nonparties can obtain full access to the case file at the courthouse, including access through the court's public computer terminal.

Subdivision (d) reflects the interplay between redaction and filing under seal. It does not limit or expand the judicially developed rules that govern sealing. But it does reflect the possibility that redaction may provide an alternative to sealing.

Subdivision (e) provides that the court can by order in a particular case for good cause require more extensive redaction than otherwise required by the Rule. Nothing in this subdivision is intended to affect the limitations on sealing that are otherwise applicable to the court.

Subdivision (f) allows a person who makes a redacted filing to file an unredacted document under seal. This provision is derived from section 205(c)(3)(iv) of the E–Government Act.

Subdivision (g) allows the option to file a register of redacted information. This provision is derived from section 205(c)(3)(v) of the E–Government Act, as amended in 2004. In accordance with the E–Government Act, subdivision (g) refers to "redacted" information. The term "redacted" is intended to govern a filing that is prepared with abbreviated identifiers in the first instance, as well as a filing in which a personal identifier is edited after its preparation.

Subdivision (h) allows a person to waive the protections of the rule as to that person's own personal information by filing it unsealed and in unredacted form. One may wish to waive the protection if it is determined that the costs of redaction outweigh the benefits to privacy. If a person files an unredacted identifier by mistake, that person may seek relief from the court.

Trial exhibits are subject to the redaction requirements of Rule 5.2 to the extent they are filed with the court. Trial exhibits that are not initially filed with the court must be redacted in accordance with the rule if and when they are filed as part of an appeal or for other reasons.

Rule 6. Time

1937 ADOPTION

Note to Subdivisions (a) and (b). These are amplifications along lines common in state practices, of former Equity Rule 80 (Computation of Time—Sundays and Holidays) and of the provisions for enlargement of time found in former Equity Rules 8 (Enforcement of Final Decrees) and 16 (Defendant to Answer—Default—Decree Pro Confesso). See also Rule XIII, Rules and Forms in Criminal Cases, 1934, 292 U.S. 661, 666. Compare Ala.Code Ann. (Michie, 1928) § 13 and former Law Rule 8 of the Rules of the Supreme Court of the District of Columbia (1924), superseded in 1929 by Law Rule 8, Rules of the District Court of the United States for the District of Columbia (1937).

Note to Subdivision (c). This eliminates the difficulties caused by the expiration of terms of court. Such statutes as U.S.C., Title 28, former § 12 (Trials not discontinued by new term) are not affected. Compare Rules of the United States District Court of Minnesota, Rule 25 (Minn.Stat. (Mason, Supp. 1936), p. 1089).

Note to Subdivision (d). Compare 2 Minn.Stat. (Mason, 1927) § 9246; N.Y.R.C.P. (1937) Rules 60 and 64.

1946 AMENDMENT

Note to Subdivision (b). The purpose of the amendment is to clarify the finality of judgments. Prior to the advent of the Federal Rules of Civil Procedure, the general rule that a court loses jurisdiction to disturb its judgments, upon the expiration of the term at which they were entered, had long been the classic device which (together with the statutory limits on the time for appeal) gave finality to judgments. See note to Rule 73(a). Rule 6(c) abrogates that limit on judicial power. That limit was open to many objections, one of them being inequality of operation because, under it, the time for vacating a judgment rendered early in a term was much longer than for a judgment rendered near the end of the term.

The question to be met under Rule 6(b) is: how far should the desire to allow correction of judgments be allowed to postpone their finality? The rules contain a number of provisions permitting the vacation or modification of judgments on various grounds. Each of these rules contains express time limits on the motions for granting of relief. Rule 6(b) is a rule of general application giving wide discretion to the court to enlarge these time limits or revive them after they have expired, the only exceptions stated in the original rule being a prohibition against enlarging the time specified in Rule 59(b) and (d) for making motions for or granting new trials, and a prohibition against enlarging the time fixed by law for taking an appeal. It should also be noted that Rule 6(b) itself contains no limitation of time within which the court may exercise its discretion, and since the expiration of the term does not end its power, there is now no time limit on the exercise of its discretion under Rule 6(b).

Decisions of lower federal courts suggest that some of the rules containing time limits which may be set aside under Rule 6(b) are Rules 25, 50(b), 52(b), 60(b), and 73(g).

In a number of cases the effect of Rule 6(b) on the time limitations of these rules has been considered. Certainly the rule is susceptible of the interpretation that the court is given the power in its discretion to relieve a party from failure to act within the times specified in any of these other rules, with only the exceptions stated in Rule 6(b), and in some cases the rule has been so construed.

With regard to Rule 25(a) for substitution, it was held in *Anderson* v. *Brady*, E.D.Ky.1941, 1 F.R.D. 589, 4 Fed.Rules Service 25a.1, Case 1, and in *Anderson* v. *Yungkau*, C.C.A.6, 1946, 153 F.2d 685, certiorari granted 328 U.S. 829, 66 S.Ct. 1025, 90 L.Ed. 1606, that under Rule 6(b) the court had no authority to allow substitution of parties after the expiration of the limit fixed in Rule 25(a).

As to Rules 50(b) for judgments notwithstanding the verdict and 52(b) for amendment of findings and vacation of judgment, it was recognized in *Leishman* v. *Associated Wholesale Electric Co.*, 1943, 318 U.S. 203, 63 S.Ct. 543, 87 L.Ed. 714, that Rule 6(b) allowed the district court to enlarge the time to make a motion for amended findings and judgment beyond the limit expressly fixed in Rule 52(b). See *Coca-Cola* v. *Busch*, E.D.Pa.1943, 7 Fed.Rules Service, 59b.2, Case 4. Obviously, if the time limit in Rule 52(b) could be set aside under rule 6(b), the time limit in Rule 50(b) for granting judgment notwithstanding the verdict (and thus vacating the judgment entered "forthwith" on the verdict) likewise could be set aside.

As to Rule 59 on motions for a new trial, it has been settled that the time limits in Rule 59(b) and (d) for making motions for or granting new trial could not be set aside under Rule 6(b), because Rule 6(b) expressly refers to Rule 59, and forbids it. See *Safeway Stores, Inc.* v. *Coe*, 1943, 136 F.2d 771, 78 U.S.App.D.C. 19; *Jusino* v. *Morales & Tio*, C.C.A.1, 1944, 139 F.2d 946; *Coca–Cola Co.* v. *Busch*, E.D.Pa.1942, 7 Fed.Rules Service 59b.2, Case 4; *Petersen* v. *Chicago, Great Western Ry. Co.*, D.Neb.1943, 3 F.R.D. 346, 7 Fed.Rules Service 59b.2, Case 1; *Leishman* v. *Associated Wholesale Electric Co.*, 1943, 318 U.S. 203, 63 S.Ct. 543, 87 L.Ed. 714.

As to Rule 60(b) for relief from a judgment, it was held in *Schram* v. *O'Connor*, E.D.Mich.1941, 5 Fed.Rules Serv. 6b.31, Case 1, 2 F.R.D. 192, s.c., 5 Fed.Rules Serv. 6b.31, Case 2, 2 F.R.D. 192, that the six-months time limit in original Rule 60(b) for making a motion for relief from a judgment for surprise, mistake, or excusable neglect could be set aside under Rule 6(b). The contrary result was reached in *Wallace* v. *United States*, C.C.A.2, 1944, 142 F.2d 240, certiorari denied 323 U.S. 712, 65 S.Ct. 37, 89 L.Ed. 573; *Reed* v. *South Atlantic Steamship Co. of Del.*, D.Del.1942, 2 F.R.D. 475, 6 Fed.Rules Serv. 60b.31, Case 1.

As to Rule 73(g), fixing the time for docketing an appeal, it was held in *Ainsworth* v. *Gill Glass & Fixture Co.*, C.C.A.3, 1939, 104 F.2d 83, that under Rule 6(b) the district court, upon motion made after the expiration of the forty-day period, stated in Rule 73(g), but before the expiration of the ninety-day period therein specified, could permit the docketing of the appeal on a showing of excusable neglect. The contrary was held in *Mutual Benefit Health & Accident Ass'n* v. *Snyder*, C.C.A.6, 1940, 109 F.2d 469 and in *Burke* v. *Canfield*, 1940, 111 F.2d 526, 72 App.D.C. 127.

The amendment of Rule 6(b) now proposed is based on the view that there should be a definite point where it can be said a judgment is final; that the right method of dealing with the problem is to list in Rule 6(b) the various other rules whose time limits may not be set aside, and then, if the time limit in any of those other rules is too short, to amend that other rule to give a longer time. The further argument is that rule 6(c) abolished the long standing device to produce finality in judgments through expiration of the term, and since that limitation on the jurisdiction of courts to set aside their own judgments has been removed by rule 6(c), some other limitation must be substituted or judgments never can be said to be final.

In this connection reference is made to the established rule that if a motion for new trial is seasonably made, the mere making or pendency of the motion destroys the finality of the judgment, and even though the motion is ultimately denied, the full time for appeal starts anew from the date of denial. Also, a motion to amend the findings under Rule 52(b) has the same effect on the time for appeal. *Leishman* v. *Associated Wholesale Electric Co.*, 1943, 318 U.S. 203, 63 S.Ct. 543, 87 L.Ed. 714. By the same reasoning a motion for judgment under Rule 50(b), involving as it does the vacation of a judgment entered "forthwith" on the verdict (Rule 58), operates to postpone, until an order is made, the running of the time for appeal. The Committee believes that the abolition by Rule 6(c) of the old rule that a court's power over its judgments ends with the term, requires a substitute limitation, and that unless Rule 6(b) is amended to prevent enlargement of the times specified in Rules 50(b), 52(b) and 60(b), and the limitation as to Rule 59(b) and (d) is retained, no one can say when a judgment is final. This is also true with regard to proposed Rule 59(e), which authorizes a motion to alter or amend a judgment, hence that rule is also included in the enumeration in amended Rule 6(b). In consideration of the amendment, however, it should be noted that Rule 60(b) is also to be amended so as to lengthen the six-months period originally prescribed in that rule to one year.

As to Rule 25 on substitution, while finality is not involved, the limit there fixed should be controlling. That rule, as amended, gives the court power, upon showing of a reasonable excuse, to permit substitution after the expiration of the two-year period.

As to Rule 73(g), it is believed that the conflict in decisions should be resolved and not left to further litigation, and that the rule should be listed as one whose limitation may not be set aside under Rule 6(b).

As to Rule 59(c), fixing the time for serving affidavits on motion for new trial, it is believed that the court should have authority under Rule 6(b) to enlarge the time, because, once the motion for new trial is made the judgment no longer has finality, and the extension of time for affidavits thus does not of itself disturb finality.

Other changes proposed in Rule 6(b) are merely clarifying and conforming. Thus "request" is substituted for "application" in clause (1) because an application is defined as a motion under Rule 7(b). The phrase "extend the time" is substituted for "enlarge the period" because the former is a more suitable expression and relates more clearly to both clauses (1) and (2). The final phrase in Rule 6(b), "or the period for taking an appeal as provided by law", is deleted and a reference to Rule 73(a) inserted, since it is proposed to state in that rule the time for appeal to a circuit court of appeals, which is the only appeal governed by the Federal Rules, and allows an extension of time. See Rule 72.

Subdivision (c). The purpose of this amendment is to prevent reliance upon the continued existence of a term as a source of power to disturb the finality of a judgment upon grounds other than those stated in these rules. See *Hill* v. *Hawes*, 1944, 320 U.S. 520, 64 S.Ct. 334, 88 L.Ed. 283; *Boaz* v. *Mutual Life Ins. Co. of New York*, C.C.A.8, 1944, 146 F.2d 321; *Bucy* v. *Nevada Construction Co.*, C.C.A.9, 1942, 125 F.2d 213.

1963 AMENDMENT

Subdivision (a). This amendment is related to the amendment of Rule 77(c) changing the regulation of the days on which the clerk's office shall be open.

The wording of the first sentence of Rule 6(a) is clarified and the subdivision is made expressly applicable to computing periods of time set forth in local rules.

Saturday is to be treated in the same way as Sunday or a "legal holiday" in that it is not to be included when it falls on the last day of a computed period, nor counted as an intermediate day when the period is less than 7 days. "Legal holiday" is defined for purposes of this subdivision and amended Rule 77(c). Compare the definition of "holiday" in 11 U.S.C. § 1(18); also 5 U.S.C. § 86a; Executive Order No. 10358, "Observance of Holidays," June 9, 1952, 17 Fed.Reg. 5269. In the light of these changes the last sentence of the present subdivision, dealing with half holidays, is eliminated.

With Saturdays and State holidays made "dies non" in certain cases by the amended subdivision, computation of the usual 5-day notice of motion or the 2-day notice to dissolve or modify a temporary restraining order may work out so as to cause embarrassing delay in urgent cases. The delay can be obviated by applying to the court to shorten the time, see Rules 6(d) and 65(b).

Subdivision (b). The prohibition against extending the time for taking action under Rule 25 (Substitution of parties) is eliminated. The only limitation of time provided for in amended Rule 25 is the 90-day period following a suggestion upon the record of the death of a party within which to make a motion to substitute the proper parties for the deceased party. See Rule 25(a)(1), as amended, and the Advisory Committee's Note thereto. It is intended that the court shall have discretion to enlarge that period.

1966 AMENDMENT

P.L. 88–139, § 1, 77 Stat. 248, approved on October 16, 1963, amended 28 U.S.C. § 138 to read as follows: "The district court shall not hold formal terms." Thus Rule 6(c) is rendered unnecessary, and it is rescinded.

1967 AMENDMENT

The amendment eliminates the references to Rule 73, which is to be abrogated.

1971 AMENDMENT

The amendment adds Columbus Day to the list of legal holidays to conform the subdivision to the Act of June 28, 1968, 82 Stat. 250, which constituted Columbus Day a legal holiday effective after January 1, 1971.

The Act, which amended Title 5, U.S.C. § 6103(a), changes the day on which certain holidays are to be observed. Washington's Birthday, Memorial Day and Veterans Day are to be observed on the third Monday in February, the last Monday in May and the fourth Monday in October, respectively, rather than, as heretofore, on February 22, May 30, and November 11, respectively, Columbus Day is to be observed on the second Monday in October. New Year's Day, Independence Day, Thanksgiving Day and Christmas continue to be observed on the traditional days.

1983 AMENDMENT

Subdivision (b). The amendment confers finality upon the judgments of magistrates by foreclosing enlargement of the time for appeal except as provided in new Rule 74(a)(20 day period for demonstration of excusable neglect).

1985 AMENDMENT

Rule 6(a) is amended to acknowledge that weather conditions or other events may render the clerk's office inaccessible one or more days. Parties who are obliged to file something with the court during that period should not be penalized if they cannot do so. The amendment conforms to changes made in Federal Rule of Criminal Procedure 45(a), effective August 1, 1982.

The Rule also is amended to extend the exclusion of intermediate Saturdays, Sundays, and legal holidays to the computation of time periods less than 11 days. Under the current version of the Rule, parties bringing motions under rules with 10-day periods could have as few as 5 working days to prepare their motions. This hardship would be especially acute in the case of Rules 50(b) and (c)(2), 52(b), and 59(b), (d), and (e), which may not be enlarged at the discretion of the court. See Rule 6(b). If the exclusion of Saturdays,

Sundays, and legal holidays will operate to cause excessive delay in urgent cases, the delay can be obviated by applying to the court to shorten the time. See Rule 6(b).

The Birthday of Martin Luther King, Jr., which becomes a legal holiday effective in 1986, has been added to the list of legal holidays enumerated in the Rule.

1987 AMENDMENT

The amendments are technical. No substantive change is intended.

1999 AMENDMENT

The reference to Rule 74(a) is stricken from the catalogue of time periods that cannot be extended by the district court. The change reflects the 1997 abrogation of Rule 74(a).

2001 AMENDMENT

The additional three days provided by Rule 6(e) is extended to the means of service authorized by the new paragraph (D) added to Rule 5(b), including—with the consent of the person served—service by electronic or other means. The three-day addition is provided as well for service on a person with no known address by leaving a copy with the clerk of the court.

2005 AMENDMENT

Rule 6(e) is amended to remove any doubt as to the method for extending the time to respond after service by mail, leaving with the clerk of court, electronic means, or other means consented to by the party served. Three days are added after the prescribed period otherwise expires under Rule 6(a). Intermediate Saturdays, Sundays, and legal holidays are included in counting these added three days.

If the third day is a Saturday, Sunday, or legal holiday, the last day to act is the next day that is not a Saturday, Sunday, or legal holiday. The effect of invoking the day when the prescribed period would otherwise expire under Rule 6(a) can be illustrated by assuming that the thirtieth day of a thirty-day period is a Saturday. Under Rule 6(a) the period expires on the next day that is not a Sunday or legal holiday. If the following Monday is a legal holiday, under Rule 6(a) the period expires on Tuesday. Three days are then added—Wednesday, Thursday, and Friday as the third and final day to act. If the period prescribed expires on a Friday, the three added days are Saturday, Sunday, and Monday, which is the third and final day to act unless it is a legal holiday. If Monday is a legal holiday, the next day that is not a legal holiday is the third and final day to act.

Application of Rule 6(e) to a period that is less than eleven days can be illustrated by a paper that is served by mailing on a Friday. If ten days are allowed to respond, intermediate Saturdays, Sundays, and legal holidays are excluded in determining when the period expires under Rule 6(a). If there is no legal holiday, the period expires on the Friday two weeks after the paper was mailed. The three added Rule 6(e) days are Saturday, Sunday, and Monday, which is the third and final day to act unless it is a legal holiday. If Monday is a legal holiday, the next day that is not a legal holiday is the final day to act.

2007 AMENDMENT

The language of Rule 6 has been amended as part of the general restyling of the Civil Rules to make them more easily understood and to make style and terminology consistent throughout the rules. These changes are intended to be stylistic only.

III.   PLEADINGS AND MOTIONS

Rule 7.   Pleadings Allowed; Form of Motions

1937 ADOPTION

1. A provision designating pleadings and defining a motion is common in the State Practice Acts. See Smith-Hurd Ill.Stats. ch. 110, § 156 (Designation and order of pleadings); 2 Minn.Stat. (Mason, 1927) § 9246 (Definition of motion); and N.Y.C.P.A. (1937) § 113 (Definition of motion). Former Equity Rules 18 (Pleadings—Technical Forms Abrogated), 29 (Defenses—How Presented), and 33 (Testing Sufficiency of Defense) abolished technical forms of pleading, demurrers and pleas, and exceptions for insufficiency of an answer.

2. **Note to Subdivision (a).** This preserves the substance of former Equity Rule 31 (Reply—When Required—When Cause at Issue). Compare the English practice, English

Rules under the Judicature Act (The Annual Practice, 1937) O. 23, r. r. 1, 2 (Reply to counterclaim; amended, 1933, to be subject to the rules applicable to defenses, O. 21). See O. 21, r. r. 1–14; O. 27, r. 13 (When pleadings deemed denied and put in issue). Under the codes the pleadings are generally limited. A reply is sometimes required to an affirmative defense in the answer. 1 Colo.Stat.Ann. (1935) § 66; Ore.Code Ann. (1930) §§ 1–614, 1–616. In other jurisdictions no reply is necessary to an affirmative defense in the answer, but a reply may be ordered by the court. N.C.Code Ann. (1935) § 525; 1 S.D.Comp.Laws (1929) § 2357. A reply to a counterclaim is usually required. Ark.Civ.Code (Crawford, 1934) §§ 123–125; Wis.Stat. (1935) §§ 263.20, 263.21. U.S.C.A., Title 28, former § 45 (District courts; practice and procedure in certain cases) is modified in so far as it may dispense with a reply to a counterclaim.

For amendment of pleadings, see Rule 15 dealing with amended and supplemental pleadings.

3. All statutes which use the words "petition", "bill of complaint", "plea", "demurrer", and other such terminology are modified in form by this rule.

1946 AMENDMENT

Note. This amendment [to subdivision (a)] eliminates any question as to whether the compulsory reply, where a counterclaim is pleaded, is a reply only to the counterclaim or is a general reply to the answer containing the counterclaim. The Commentary, Scope of Reply where Defendant Has Pleaded Counterclaim, 1939, 1 Fed.Rules Serv. 672; *Fort Chartres and Ivy Landing Drainage and Levee District No. 5* v. *Thompson*, E.D.Ill.1945, 8 Fed.Rules Serv. 13.32, Case 1.

1963 AMENDMENT

Certain redundant words are eliminated and the subdivision is modified to reflect the amendment of Rule 14(a) which in certain cases eliminates the requirement of obtaining leave to bring in a third-party defendant.

1983 AMENDMENT

One of the reasons sanctions against improper motion practice have been employed infrequently is the lack of clarity of Rule 7. That rule has stated only generally that the pleading requirements relating to captions, signing, and other matters of form also apply to motions and other papers. The addition of Rule 7(b)(3) makes explicit the applicability of the signing requirement and the sanctions of Rule 11, which have been amplified.

2007 AMENDMENT

The language of Rule 7 has been amended as part of the general restyling of the Civil Rules to make them more easily understood and to make style and terminology consistent throughout the rules. These changes are intended to be stylistic only.

Former Rule 7(a) stated that "there shall be * * * an answer to a cross-claim, if the answer contains a cross-claim * * *." Former Rule 12(a)(2) provided more generally that "[a] party served with a pleading stating a cross-claim against that party shall serve an answer thereto * * *." New Rule 7(a) corrects this inconsistency by providing for an answer to a crossclaim.

For the first time, Rule 7(a)(7) expressly authorizes the court to order a reply to a counterclaim answer. A reply may be as useful in this setting as a reply to an answer, a third-party answer, or a crossclaim answer.

Former Rule 7(b)(1) stated that the writing requirement is fulfilled if the motion is stated in a written notice of hearing. This statement was deleted as redundant because a single written document can satisfy the writing requirements both for a motion and for a Rule 6(c)(1) notice.

The cross-reference to Rule 11 in former Rule 7(b)(3) is deleted as redundant. Rule 11 applies by its own terms. The force and application of Rule 11 are not diminished by the deletion.

Former Rule 7(c) is deleted because it has done its work. If a motion or pleading is described as a demurrer, plea, or exception for insufficiency, the court will treat the paper as if properly captioned.

Rule 7.1.   Disclosure Statement

2002 ADOPTION

Rule 7.1 is drawn from Rule 26.1 of the Federal Rules of Appellate Procedure, with changes to adapt to the circumstances of district courts that dictate different provisions for the time of filing, number of copies, and the like. The information required by Rule 7.1(a) reflects the "financial interest" standard of Canon 3C(1)(c) of the Code of Conduct for United States Judges. This information will support properly informed disqualification decisions in situations that call for automatic disqualification under Canon 3C(1)(c). It does not cover all of the circumstances that may call for disqualification under the financial interest standard, and does not deal at all with other circumstances that may call for disqualification.

Although the disclosures required by Rule 7.1(a) may seem limited, they are calculated to reach a majority of the circumstances that are likely to call for disqualification on the basis of financial information that a judge may not know or recollect. Framing a rule that calls for more detailed disclosure will be difficult. Unnecessary disclosure requirements place a burden on the parties and on courts. Unnecessary disclosure of volumes of information may create a risk that a judge will overlook the one bit of information that might require disqualification, and also may create a risk that unnecessary disqualifications will be made rather than attempt to unravel a potentially difficult question. It has not been feasible to dictate more detailed disclosure requirements in Rule 7.1(a).

Rule 7.1 does not prohibit local rules that require disclosures in addition to those required by Rule 7.1. Developing experience with local disclosure practices and advances in electronic technology may provide a foundation for adopting more detailed disclosure requirements by future amendments of Rule 7.1.

2007 AMENDMENT

The language of Rule 7.1 has been amended as part of the general restyling of the Civil Rules to make them more easily understood and to make style and terminology consistent throughout the rules. These changes are intended to be stylistic only.

Rule 8.   General Rules of Pleading

1937 ADOPTION

Note to Subdivision (a). See former Equity Rules 25 (Bill of Complaint—Contents), and 30 (Answer—Contents—Counterclaim). Compare 2 Ind.Stat.Ann. (Burns, 1933) §§ 2–1004, 2–1015; 2 Ohio Gen.Code Ann. (Page, 1926) §§ 11305, 11314; Utah Rev.Stat.Ann. (1933) §§ 104–7–2, 104–9–1.

See Rule 19(c) for the requirement of a statement in a claim for relief of the names of persons who ought to be parties and the reason for their omission.

See Rule 23(b) for particular requirements as to the complaint in a secondary action by shareholders.

Note to Subdivision (b). 1. This rule supersedes the methods of pleading prescribed in U.S.C., Title 19, § 508 (Persons making seizures pleading general issue and proving special matter); U.S.C. Title 35, former § 40d (Proving under general issue, upon notice, that a statement in application for an extended patent is not true), § 282, formerly § 69 (Pleading and proof in actions for infringement) and similar statutes.

2. This rule is, in part, former Equity Rule 30 (Answer—Contents—Counterclaim), with the matter on denials largely from the Connecticut practice. See Conn. Practice Book (1934) §§ 107, 108, and 122; Conn.Gen.Stat. (1930) §§ 5508–5514. Compare the English practice, English Rules Under the Judicature Act (The Annual Practice, 1937) O. 19, r. r. 17–20.

Note to Subdivision (c). This follows substantially English Rules Under the Judicature Act (The Annual Practice, 1937) O. 19, r. 15 and N.Y.C.P.A. (1937) § 242, with "surprise" omitted in this rule.

Note to Subdivision (d). The first sentence is similar to former Equity Rule 30 (Answer—Contents—Counterclaim). For the second sentence see former Equity Rule 31 (Reply—When Required—When Cause at Issue). This is similar to English Rules Under the Judicature Act (The Annual Practice, 1937) O. 19, r. r. 13, 18; and to the practice of the States.

Note to Subdivision (e). This rule is an elaboration upon former Equity Rule 30 (Answer—Contents—Counterclaim), plus a statement of the actual practice under some codes. Compare also former Equity Rule 18 (Pleadings—Technical Forms Abrogated). See Clark, Code Pleading (1928), pp. 171–4, 432–5; Hankin, Alternative and Hypothetical Pleading (1924), 33 Yale L.J. 365.

Note to Subdivision (f). A provision of like import is of frequent occurrence in the codes. Smith-Hurd Ill.Stats. ch. 110, § 157(3); 2 Minn.Stat. (Mason, 1927) § 9266; N.Y.C.P.A. (1937) § 275; 2 N.D.Comp.Laws Ann. (1913) § 7458.

1966 AMENDMENT

The change here is consistent with the broad purposes of unification.

1987 AMENDMENT

The amendments are technical. No substantive change is intended.

2007 AMENDMENT

The language of Rule 8 has been amended as part of the general restyling of the Civil Rules to make them more easily understood and to make style and terminology consistent throughout the rules. These changes are intended to be stylistic only.

The former Rule 8(b) and 8(e) cross-references to Rule 11 are deleted as redundant. Rule 11 applies by its own terms. The force and application of Rule 11 are not diminished by the deletion.

Former Rule 8(b) required a pleader denying part of an averment to "specify so much of it as is true and material and * * * deny only the remainder." "[A]nd material" is deleted to avoid the implication that it is proper to deny something that the pleader believes to be true but not material.

Deletion of former Rule 8(e)(2)'s "whether based on legal, equitable, or maritime grounds" reflects the parallel deletions in Rule 1 and elsewhere. Merger is now successfully accomplished.

Rule 9. Pleading Special Matters

1937 ADOPTION

Note to Subdivision (a). Compare former Equity Rule 25 (Bill of Complaint—Contents) requiring disability to be stated; Utah Rev.Stat.Ann. (1933) § 104–13–15, enumerating a number of situations where a general averment of capacity is sufficient. For provisions governing averment of incorporation, see 2 Minn.Stat. (Mason, 1927) § 9271; N.Y.R.C.P. (1937) Rule 93; 2 N.D.Comp.Laws Ann. (1913) § 7981 et seq.

Note to Subdivision (b). See English Rules Under the Judicature Act (The Annual Practice, 1937) O. 19, r. 22.

Note to Subdivision (c). The codes generally have this or a similar provision. See English Rules Under the Judicature Act (The Annual Practice, 1937) O. 19, r. 14; 2 Minn.Stat. (Mason, 1927) § 9273; N.Y.R.C.P. (1937) Rule 92; 2 N.D.Comp.Laws Ann. (1913) § 7461; 2 Wash.Rev.Stat.Ann. (Remington, 1932) § 288.

Note to Subdivision (e). The rule expands the usual code provisions on pleading a judgment by including judgments or decisions of administrative tribunals and foreign courts. Compare Ark.Civ.Code (Crawford, 1934) § 141; 2 Minn.Stat. (Mason, 1927) § 9269; N.Y.R.C.P. (1937) Rule 95; 2 Wash.Rev.Stat.Ann. (Remington, 1932) § 287.

1966 AMENDMENT

Certain distinctive features of the admiralty practice must be preserved for what are now suits in admiralty. This raises the question: After unification, when a single form of action is established, how will the counterpart of the present suit in admiralty be identifiable? In part the question is easily answered. Some claims for relief can only be suits in admiralty, either because the admiralty jurisdiction is exclusive or because no nonmaritime ground of federal jurisdiction exists. Many claims, however, are cognizable by the district courts whether asserted in admiralty or in a civil action, assuming the existence of a nonmaritime ground of jurisdiction. Thus at present the pleader has power to determine procedural consequences by the way in which he exercises the classic privilege given by the saving-to-suitors clause (28 U.S.C. § 1333) or by equivalent statutory provisions. For example, a longshoreman's claim for personal injuries suffered by reason of the unseaworthiness of a vessel may be asserted in a suit in admiralty or, if diversity of citizenship exists, in a civil action. One of the important procedural consequences is that in the civil action either party may demand a jury trial, while in the suit in admiralty there is no right to jury trial except as provided by statute.

It is no part of the purpose of unification to inject a right to jury trial into those admiralty cases in which that right is not provided by statute. Similarly as will be more specifically noted below, there is no disposition to change the present law as to interlocutory appeals in admiralty, or as to the venue of suits in admiralty; and, of course, there is no disposition to inject into the civil practice as it now is the distinctively maritime remedies (maritime attachment and garnishment, actions in rem, possessory, petitory and partition actions and limitation of liability). The unified rules must therefore provide some device for preserving the present power of the pleader to determine whether these historically maritime procedures shall be applicable to his claim or not; the pleader must be afforded some means of designating his claim as the counterpart of the present suit in admiralty, where its character as such is not clear.

The problem is different from the similar one concerning the identification of claims that were formerly suits in equity. While that problem is not free from complexities, it is broadly true that the modern counterpart of the suit in equity is distinguishable from the former action at law by the character of the relief sought. This mode of identification is possible in only a limited category of admiralty cases. In large numbers of cases the relief sought in admiralty is simple money damages, indistinguishable from the remedy afforded by the common law. This is true, for example, in the case of the longshoreman's action for personal injuries stated above. After unification has abolished the distinction between civil actions and suits in admiralty, the complaint in such an action would be almost completely ambiguous as to the pleader's intentions regarding the procedure invoked. The allegation of diversity of citizenship might be regarded as a clue indicating an intention to proceed as at present under the saving-to-suitors clause; but this, too, would be ambiguous if there were also reference to the admiralty jurisdiction, and the pleader ought not be required to forego mention of all available jurisdictional grounds.

Other methods of solving the problem were carefully explored, but the Advisory Committee concluded that the preferable solution is to allow the pleader who now has power to determine procedural consequences by filing a suit in admiralty to exercise that power under unification, for the limited instances in which procedural differences will remain, by a simple statement in his pleading to the effect that the claim is an admiralty or maritime claim.

The choice made by the pleader in identifying or in failing to identify his claim as an admiralty or maritime claim is not an irrevocable election. The rule provides that the amendment of a pleading to add or withdraw an identifying statement is subject to the principles of Rule 15.

1968 AMENDMENT

The amendment eliminates the reference to Rule 73 which is to be abrogated and transfers to Rule 9(h) the substance of Subsection (h) of Rule 73 which preserved the right to an interlocutory appeal in admiralty cases which is provided by 28 U.S.C. § 1292(a)(3).

1970 AMENDMENT

The reference to Rule 26(a) is deleted, in light of the transfer of that subdivision to Rule 30(a) and the elimination of the de bene esse procedure therefrom. See the Advisory Committee's note to Rule 30(a).

1987 AMENDMENT

The amendment is technical. No substantive change is intended.

1997 AMENDMENT

Section 1292(a)(3) of the Judicial Code provides for appeal from "[i]nterlocutory decrees of * * * district courts * * * determining the rights and liabilities of the parties to admiralty cases in which appeals from final decrees are allowed."

Rule 9(h) was added in 1966 with the unification of civil and admiralty procedure. Civil Rule 73(h) was amended at the same time to provide that the § 1292(a)(3) reference "to admiralty cases shall be construed to mean admiralty and maritime claims within the meaning of Rule 9(h)." This provision was transferred to Rule 9(h) when the Appellate Rules were adopted.

A single case can include both admiralty or maritime claims and nonadmiralty claims or parties. This combination reveals an ambiguity in the statement in present Rule 9(h) that an admiralty "claim" is an admiralty "case." An order "determining the rights and liabilities of the parties" within the meaning of § 1292(a)(3) may resolve only a nonadmiralty claim, or may simultaneously resolve interdependent admiralty and nonadmirality claims. Can appeal be taken as to the nonadmiralty matter, because it is part of a case that includes an admiralty claim, or is appeal limited to the admiralty claim?

The courts of appeals have not achieved full uniformity in applying the § 1292(a)(3) requirement that an order "determin[e] the rights and liabilities of the parties." It is common to assert that the statute should be construed narrowly, under the general policy that exceptions to the final judgment rule should be construed narrowly. This policy would suggest that the ambiguity should be resolved by limiting the interlocutory appeal right to orders that determine the rights and liabilities of the parties to an admiralty claim.

A broader view is chosen by this amendment for two reasons. The statute applies to admiralty "cases," and may itself provide for appeal from an order that disposes of a nonadmiralty claim that is joined in a single case with an admiralty claim. Although a rule of court may help to clarify and implement a statutory grant of jurisdiction, the line is not always clear between permissible implementation and impermissible withdrawal of jurisdiction. In addition, so long as an order truly disposes of the rights and liabilities of the parties within the meaning of § 1292(a)(3), it may prove important to permit appeal as to the nonadmiralty claim. Disposition of the nonadmiralty claim, for example, may make it unnecessary to consider the admiralty claim and have the same effect on the case and parties as disposition of the admiralty claim. Or the admiralty and nonadmiralty claims may be interdependent. An illustration is provided by *Roco Carriers, Ltd. v. M/V Nurnberg Express*, 899 F.2d 1292 (2d Cir.1990). Claims for losses of ocean shipments were made against two defendants, one subject to admiralty jurisdiction and the other not. Summary judgment was granted in favor of the admiralty defendant and against the nonadmiralty defendant. The nonadmiralty defendant's appeal was accepted, with the explanation that the determination of its liability was "integrally linked with the determination of non-liability" of the admiralty defendant, and that "section 1292(a)(3) is not limited to admiralty *claims;* instead, it refers to admiralty *cases.*" 899 F.2d at 1297. The advantages of permitting appeal by the nonadmiralty defendant would be particularly clear if the plaintiff had appealed the summary judgment in favor of the admiralty defendant.

It must be emphasized that this amendment does not rest on any particular assumptions as to the meaning of the § 1292(a)(3) provision that limits interlocutory appeal to orders that determine the rights and liabilities of the parties. It simply reflects the conclusion that so long as the case involves an admiralty claim and an order otherwise meets statutory requirements, the opportunity to appeal should not turn on the circumstance that the order does—or does not—dispose of an admiralty claim. No attempt is made to invoke the authority conferred by 28 U.S.C. § 1292(e) to provide by rule for appeal of an interlocutory decision that is not otherwise provided for by other subsections of § 1292.

2006 AMENDMENT

Rule 9(h) is amended to conform to the changed title of the Supplemental Rules.

2007 AMENDMENT

The language of Rule 9 has been amended as part of the general restyling of the Civil Rules to make them more easily understood and to make style and terminology consistent throughout the rules. These changes are intended to be stylistic only.

Rule 15 governs pleading amendments of its own force. The former redundant statement that Rule 15 governs an amendment that adds or withdraws a Rule 9(h) designation as an admiralty or maritime claim is deleted. The elimination of paragraph (2) means that "(3)" will be redesignated as "(2)" in Style Rule 9(h).

Rule 10. Form of Pleadings

1937 ADOPTION

The first sentence is derived in part from the opening statement of former Equity Rule 25 (Bill of Complaint—Contents). The remainder of the rule is an expansion in conformity with usual state provisions. For numbered paragraphs and separate statements, see Conn.Gen.Stat., 1930, § 5513 Smith-Hurd Ill.Stats. ch. 110, § 157(2); N.Y.R.C.P., (1937) Rule 90. For incorporation by reference, see N.Y.R.C.P., (1937) Rule 90. For written instruments as exhibits, see Smith-Hurd Ill.Stats. ch. 110, § 160.

2007 AMENDMENT

The language of Rule 10 has been amended as part of the general restyling of the Civil Rules to make them more easily understood and to make style and terminology consistent throughout the rules. These changes are intended to be stylistic only.

Rule 11. Signing of Pleadings, Motions, and Other Papers; Representations to Court; Sanctions

1937 ADOPTION

This is substantially the content of former Equity Rules 24 (Signature of Counsel) and 21 (Scandal and Impertinence) consolidated and unified. Compare former Equity Rule 36 (Officers Before Whom Pleadings Verified). Compare to similar purposes, English Rules Under the Judicature Act (The Annual Practice, 1937) O. 19, r. 4, and *Great Australian Gold Mining Co.* v. *Martin, L. R.*, 5 Ch.Div. 1, 10 (1877). Subscription of pleadings is required in many codes. 2 Minn.Stat. (Mason, 1927) § 9265; N.Y.R.C.P. (1937) Rule 91; 2 N.D.Comp.Laws Ann. (1913) § 7455.

This rule expressly continues any statute which requires a pleading to be verified or accompanied by an affidavit, such as:

U.S.C., Title 28 former:

§ 381 (Preliminary injunctions and temporary restraining orders).

§ 762 (Suit against the United States).

U.S.C., Title 28, former § 829 (now § 1927)(Costs; attorney liable for, when) is unaffected by this rule.

For complaints which must be verified under these rules, see Rules 23(b) (Secondary Action by Shareholders) and 65 (Injunctions).

For abolition of the rule in equity that the averments of an answer under oath must be overcome by the testimony of two witnesses or of one witness sustained by corroborating circumstances. See Pa.Stat.Ann. (Purdon, 1931) see 12 P.S.Pa., § 1222; for the rule in equity itself, see *Greenfield* v. *Blumenthal*, 69 F.2d 294 (C.C.A. 3d.1934).

1983 AMENDMENT

Since its original promulgation, Rule 11 has provided for the striking of pleadings and the imposition of disciplinary sanctions to check abuses in the signing of pleadings. Its provisions have always applied to motions and other papers by virtue of incorporation by reference in Rule 7(b)(2). The amendment and the addition of Rule 7(b)(3) expressly confirms this applicability.

Experience shows that in practice Rule 11 has not been effective in deterring abuses. See 6 Wright & Miller, Federal Practice and Procedure: Civil § 1334 (1971). There has been considerable confusion as to (1) the circumstances that should trigger striking a pleading or motion or taking disciplinary action, (2) the standard of conduct expected of attorneys who sign pleadings and motions, and (3) the range of available and appropriate sanctions. See Rodes, Ripple & Mooney, Sanctions Imposable for Violations of the Federal Rules of Civil Procedure 64–65, Federal Judicial Center (1981). The new language is intended to reduce the reluctance of courts to impose sanctions, see Moore, Federal Practice ¶ 7.05, at 1547, by emphasizing the responsibilities of the attorney and reenforcing those obligations by the imposition of sanctions.

The amended rule attempts to deal with the problem by building upon and expanding the equitable doctrine permitting the court to award expenses, including attorney's fees, to a litigant whose opponent acts in bad faith in instituting or conducting litigation. See, e.g., Roadway Express, Inc. v. Piper, 447 U.S. 752 (1980); Hall v. Cole, 412 U.S. 1, 5 (1973). Greater attention by the district courts to pleading and motion abuses and the imposition of sanctions when appropriate, should discourage dilatory or abusive tactics and help to streamline the litigation process by lessening frivolous claims or defenses.

The expanded nature of the lawyer's certification in the fifth sentence of amended Rule 11 recognizes that the litigation process may be abused for purposes other than delay. See, e.g., Browning Debenture Holders' Committee v. DASA Corp., 560 F.2d 1078 (2d Cir.1977).

The words "good ground to support" the pleading in the original rule were interpreted to have both factual and legal elements. See, e.g., Heart Disease Research Foundation v. General Motors Corp., 15 Fed.R.Serv.2d 1517, 1519 (S.D.N.Y.1972). They have been replaced by a standard of conduct that is more focused.

The new language stresses the need for some prefiling inquiry into both the facts and the law to satisfy the affirmative duty imposed by the rule. The standard is one of reasonableness under the circumstances. See Kinee v. Abraham Lincoln Fed. Sav. & Loan Ass'n, 365 F.Supp. 975 (E.D.Pa.1973). This standard is more stringent than the original good-faith formula and thus it is expected that a greater range of circumstances will trigger its violation. See Nemeroff v. Abelson, 620 F.2d 339 (2d Cir.1980).

The rule is not intended to chill an attorney's enthusiasm or creativity in pursuing factual or legal theories. The court is expected to avoid using the wisdom of hindsight and should test the signer's conduct by inquiring what was reasonable to believe at the time the pleading, motion, or other paper was submitted. Thus, what constitutes a reasonable inquiry may depend on such factors as how much time for investigation was available to the signer; whether he had to rely on a client for information as to the facts underlying the pleading, motion, or other paper; whether the pleading, motion, or other paper was based on a plausible view of the law; or whether he depended on forwarding counsel or another member of the bar.

The rule does not require a party or an attorney to disclose privileged communications or work product in order to show that the signing of the pleading, motion, or other paper is substantially justified. The provisions of Rule 26(c), including appropriate orders after in camera inspection by the court, remain available to protect a party claiming privilege or work product protection.

Amended Rule 11 continues to apply to anyone who signs a pleading, motion, or other paper. Although the standard is the same for unrepresented parties, who are obliged themselves to sign the pleadings, the court has sufficient discretion to take account of the special circumstances that often arise in pro se situations. See Haines v. Kerner, 404 U.S. 519 (1972).

The provision in the original rule for striking pleadings and motions as sham and false has been deleted. The passage has rarely been utilized, and decisions thereunder have tended to confuse the issue of attorney honesty with the merits of the action. See generally Risinger, Honesty in Pleading and its Enforcement: Some "Striking" Problems with Fed.R.Civ.P. 11, 61 Minn.L.Rev. 1 (1976). Motions under this provision generally present issues better dealt with under Rules 8, 12, or 56. See Murchison v. Kirby, 27 F.R.D. 14 (S.D.N.Y.1961); 5 Wright & Miller, Federal Practice and Procedure: Civil § 1334 (1969).

The former reference to the inclusion of scandalous or indecent matter, which is itself strong indication that an improper purpose underlies the pleading, motion, or other paper, also has been deleted as unnecessary. Such matter may be stricken under Rule 12(f) as well as dealt with under the more general language of amended Rule 11.

The text of the amended rule seeks to dispel apprehensions that efforts to obtain enforcement will be fruitless by insuring that the rule will be applied when properly invoked. The word "sanctions" in the caption, for example, stresses a deterrent orientation in dealing with improper pleadings, motions or other papers. This corresponds to the approach in imposing sanctions for discovery abuses. See National Hockey League v. Metropolitan Hockey Club, 427 U.S. 639 (1976)(per curiam). And the words "shall impose" in the last sentence focus the court's attention on the need to impose sanctions for pleading and motion abuses. The court, however, retains the necessary flexibility to deal appropriately with violations of the rule. It has discretion to tailor sanctions to the particular facts of the case, with which it should be well acquainted.

The reference in the former text to wilfulness as a prerequisite to disciplinary action has been deleted. However, in considering the nature and severity of the sanctions to be imposed, the court should take account of the state of the attorney's or party's actual or presumed knowledge when the pleading or other paper was signed. Thus, for example, when a party is not represented by counsel, the absence of legal advice is an appropriate factor to be considered.

Courts currently appear to believe they may impose sanctions on their own motion. See North American Foreign Trading Corp. v. Zale Corp., 83 F.R.D. 293 (S.D.N.Y.1979). Authority to do so has been made explicit in order to overcome the traditional reluctance of courts to intervene unless requested by one of the parties. The detection and punishment of a violation of the signing requirement, encouraged by the amended rule, is part of the court's responsibility for securing the system's effective operation.

If the duty imposed by the rule is violated, the court should have the discretion to impose sanctions on either the attorney, the party the signing attorney represents, or both, or on an unrepresented party who signed the pleading, and the new rule so provides. Although Rule 11 has been silent on the point, courts have claimed the power to impose sanctions on an attorney personally, either by imposing costs or employing the contempt technique. See 5 Wright & Miller, Federal Practice and Procedure: Civil § 1334 (1969); 2A Moore, Federal Practice ¶ 11.02, at 2104 n.8. This power has been used infrequently. The amended rule should eliminate any doubt as to the propriety of assessing sanctions against the attorney.

Even though it is the attorney whose signature violates the rule, it may be appropriate under the circumstances of the case to impose a sanction on the client. See Browning Debenture Holders' Committee v. DASA Corp., supra. This modification brings Rule 11 in line with practice under Rule 37, which allows sanctions for abuses during discovery to be imposed upon the party, the attorney, or both.

A party seeking sanctions should give notice to the court and the offending party promptly upon discovering a basis for doing so. The time when sanctions are to be imposed rests in the discretion of the trial judge. However, it is anticipated that in the case of pleadings the sanctions issue under Rule 11 normally will be determined at the end of the litigation, and in the case of motions at the time when the motion is decided or shortly thereafter. The procedure obviously must comport with due process requirements. The particular format to be followed should depend on the circumstances of the situation and the severity of the sanction under consideration. In many situations the judge's participation in the proceedings provides him with full knowledge of the relevant facts and little further inquiry will be necessary.

To assure that the efficiencies achieved through more effective operation of the pleading regimen will not be offset by the cost of satellite litigation over the imposition of sanctions, the court must to the extent possible limit the scope of sanction proceedings to the record. Thus, discovery should be conducted only by leave of the court, and then only in extraordinary circumstances.

Although the encompassing reference to "other papers" in new Rule 11 literally includes discovery papers, the certification requirement in that context is governed by proposed new Rule 26(g). Discovery motions, however, fall within the ambit of Rule 11.

1987 AMENDMENT

The amendments are technical. No substantive change is intended.

1993 AMENDMENT

Purpose of revision. This revision is intended to remedy problems that have arisen in the interpretation and application of the 1983 revision of the rule. For empirical examination of experience under the 1983 rule, see, *e.g.,* New York State Bar Committee on Federal Courts, *Sanctions and Attorneys' Fees* (1987); T. Willging, *The Rule 11 Sanctioning Process* (1989); American Judicature Society, *Report of the Third Circuit Task Force on Federal Rule of Civil Procedure 11* (S. Burbank ed., 1989); E. Wiggins, T. Willging, and D. Stienstra, *Report on Rule 11* (Federal Judicial Center 1991). For book-length analyses of the case law, see G. Joseph, *Sanctions: The Federal Law of Litigation Abuse* (1989); J. Solovy, *The Federal Law of Sanctions* (1991); G. Vairo, *Rule 11 Sanctions: Case Law Perspectives and Preventive Measures* (1991).

The rule retains the principle that attorneys and pro se litigants have an obligation to the court to refrain from conduct that frustrates the aims of Rule 1. The revision broadens the scope of this obligation, but places greater constraints on the imposition of sanctions and should reduce the number of motions for sanctions presented to the court. New subdivision (d) removes from the ambit of this rule all discovery requests, responses, objections, and motions subject to the provisions of Rule 26 through 37.

Subdivision (a). Retained in this subdivision are the provisions requiring signatures on pleadings, written motions, and other papers. Unsigned papers are to be received by the Clerk, but then are to be stricken if the omission of the signature is not corrected promptly after being called to the attention of the attorney or pro se litigant. Correction can be made by signing the paper on file or by submitting a duplicate that contains the signature. A court may require by local rule that papers contain additional identifying information regarding the parties or attorneys, such as telephone numbers to facilitate facsimile transmissions, though, as for omission of a signature, the paper should not be rejected for failure to provide such information.

The sentence in the former rule relating to the effect of answers under oath is no longer needed and has been eliminated. The provision in the former rule that signing a paper constitutes a certificate that it has been read by the signer also has been eliminated as unnecessary. The obligations imposed under subdivision (b) obviously require that a pleading, written motion, or other paper be read before it is filed or submitted to the court.

Subdivisions (b) and (c). These subdivisions restate the provisions requiring attorneys and pro se litigants to conduct a reasonable inquiry into the law and facts before signing pleadings, written motions, and other documents, and prescribing sanctions for violation of these obligations. The revision in part expands the responsibilities of litigants to the court, while providing greater constraints and flexibility in dealing with infractions of the rule. The rule continues to require litigants to "stop-and-think" before initially making legal or factual contentions. It also, however, emphasizes the duty of candor by subjecting litigants to potential sanctions for insisting upon a position after it is no longer tenable and by generally providing protection against sanctions if they withdraw or correct contentions after a potential violation is called to their attention.

The rule applies only to assertions contained in papers filed with or submitted to the court. It does not cover matters arising for the first time during oral presentations to the court, when counsel may make statements that would not have been made if there had been more time for study and reflection. However, a litigant's obligations with respect to the contents of these papers are not measured solely as of the time they are filed with or submitted to the court, but include reaffirming to the court and advocating positions contained in those pleadings and motions after learning that they cease to have any merit. For example, an attorney who during a pretrial conference insists on a claim or defense should be viewed as "presenting to the court" that contention and would be subject to the obligations of subdivision (b) measured as of that time. Similarly, if after a notice of removal is filed, a party urges in federal court the allegations of a pleading filed in state court (whether as claims, defenses, or in disputes regarding removal or remand), it would be viewed as "presenting"—and hence certifying to the district court under Rule 11—those allegations.

The certification with respect to allegations and other factual contentions is revised in recognition that sometimes a litigant may have good reason to believe that a fact is true or false but may need discovery, formal or informal, from opposing parties or third persons to gather and confirm the evidentiary basis for the allegation. Tolerance of factual contentions in initial pleadings by plaintiffs or defendants when specifically identified as made on information and belief does not relieve litigants from the obligation to conduct an appropriate investigation into the facts that is reasonable under the circumstances; it is not a license to join parties, make claims, or present defenses without any factual basis or justification. Moreover, if evidentiary support is not obtained after a reasonable opportunity for further investigation or discovery, the party has a duty under the rule not to persist with that contention. Subdivision (b) does not require a formal amendment to pleadings for which evidentiary support is not obtained, but rather calls upon a litigant not thereafter to advocate such claims or defenses.

The certification is that there is (or likely will be) "evidentiary support" for the allegation, not that the party will prevail with respect to its contention regarding the fact. That summary judgment is rendered against a party does not necessarily mean, for purposes of this certification, that it had no evidentiary support for its position. On the other hand, if a party has evidence with respect to a contention that would suffice to defeat a motion for summary judgment based thereon, it would have sufficient "evidentiary support" for purposes of Rule 11.

Denials of factual contentions involve somewhat different considerations. Often, of course, a denial is premised upon the existence of evidence contradicting the alleged fact. At other times a denial is permissible because, after an appropriate investigation, a party has no information concerning the matter or, indeed, has a reasonable basis for doubting the credibility of the only evidence relevant to the matter. A party should not deny an allegation it knows to be true; but it is not required, simply because it lacks contradictory evidence, to admit an allegation that it believes is not true.

The changes in subdivisions (b)(3) and (b)(4) will serve to equalize the burden of the rule upon plaintiffs and defendants, who under Rule 8(b) are in effect allowed to deny allegations by stating that from their initial investigation they lack sufficient information to form a belief as to the truth of the allegation. If, after further investigation or discovery, a denial is no longer warranted, the defendant should not continue to insist on that denial. While sometimes helpful, formal amendment of the pleadings to withdraw an allegation or denial is not required by subdivision (b).

Arguments for extensions, modifications, or reversals of existing law or for creation of new law do not violate subdivision (b)(2) provided they are "nonfrivolous." This establishes an objective standard, intended to eliminate any "empty-head pure-heart" justification for patently frivolous arguments. However, the extent to which a litigant has researched the issues and found some support for its theories even in minority opinions, in law review articles, or through consultation with other attorneys should certainly be taken into account in determining whether paragraph (2) has been violated. Although arguments for a change of law are not required to be specifically so identified, a contention that is so identified should be viewed with greater tolerance under the rule.

The court has available a variety of possible sanctions to impose for violations, such as striking the offending paper; issuing an admonition, reprimand, or censure; requiring participation in seminars or other educational programs; ordering a fine payable to the court; referring the matter to disciplinary authorities (or, in the case of government attorneys, to the Attorney General, Inspector General, or agency head), etc. *See Manual for Complex Litigation, Second,* § 42.3. The rule does not attempt to enumerate the factors a court should consider in deciding whether to impose a sanction or what sanctions would be appropriate in the circumstances; but, for emphasis, it does specifically note that a sanction may be nonmonetary as well as monetary. Whether the improper conduct was willful, or negligent; whether it was part of a pattern of activity, or an isolated event; whether it infected the entire pleading, or only one particular count or defense; whether the person has engaged in similar conduct in other litigation; whether it was intended to injure; what effect it had on the litigation process in time or expense; whether the responsible person is trained in the law; what amount, given the financial resources of the responsible person, is needed to deter that person from repetition in the same case; what amount is needed to deter similar activity by other litigants: all of these may in a particular case be proper considerations. The court has significant discretion in determining what sanctions, if any, should be imposed for a violation, subject to the principle that the sanctions should not be more severe than reasonably necessary to deter repetition of the conduct by the offending person or comparable conduct by similarly situated persons.

Since the purpose of Rule 11 sanctions is to deter rather than to compensate, the rule provides that, if a monetary sanction is imposed, it should ordinarily be paid into court as a penalty. However, under unusual circumstances, particularly for (b)(1) violations, deterrence may be ineffective unless the sanction not only requires the person violating the rule to make a monetary payment, but also directs that some or all of this payment be made to those injured by the violation. Accordingly, the rule authorizes the court, if requested in a motion and if so warranted, to award attorney's fees to another party. Any such award to another party, however, should not exceed the expenses and attorneys' fees for the services directly and unavoidably caused by the violation of the certification requirement. If, for example, a wholly unsupportable count were included in a multi-count complaint or counterclaim for the purpose of needlessly increasing the cost of litigation to an impecunious adversary, any award of expenses should be limited to those directly caused by inclusion of the improper count, and not those resulting from the filing of the complaint or answer itself. The award should not provide compensation for services that could have been avoided by an earlier disclosure of evidence or an earlier challenge to the groundless claims or defenses. Moreover, partial reimbursement of fees may constitute a sufficient deterrent with respect to violations by persons having modest financial resources. In cases brought under statutes providing for fees to be awarded to prevailing parties, the court should not employ cost-shifting under this rule in a manner that would be inconsistent with the standards that govern the statutory award of fees, such as stated in *Christiansburg Garment Co. v. EEOC,* 434 U.S. 412 (1978).

The sanction should be imposed on the persons—whether attorneys, law firms, or parties—who have violated the rule or who may be determined to be responsible for the violation. The person signing, filing, submitting, or advocating a document has a nondelegable responsibility to the court, and in most situations is the person to be sanctioned for a violation. Absent exceptional circumstances, a law firm is to be held also responsible when, as a result of a motion under subdivision (c)(1)(A), one of its partners, associates, or employees is determined to have violated the rule. Since such a motion may be filed only if the offending paper is not withdrawn or corrected within 21 days after service of the motion, it is appropriate that the law firm ordinarily be viewed as jointly responsible under established principles of agency. This provision is designed to remove the restrictions of the former rule. *Cf. Pavelic & LeFlore v. Marvel Entertainment Group,* 493 U.S. 120, 110 S.Ct. 456, 107 L.Ed.2d 438 (1989)(1983 version of Rule 11 does not permit sanctions against law firm of attorney signing groundless complaint).

The revision permits the court to consider whether other attorneys in the firm, co-counsel, other law firms, or the party itself should be held accountable for their part in causing a violation. When appropriate, the court can make an additional inquiry in order to determine whether the sanction should be imposed on such persons, firms, or parties either in addition to or, in unusual circumstances, instead of the person actually making the presentation to the court. For example, such an inquiry may be appropriate in cases involving governmental agencies or other institutional parties that frequently impose substantial restrictions on the discretion of individual attorneys employed by it.

Sanctions that involve monetary awards (such as a fine or an award of attorney's fees) may not be imposed on a represented party for causing a violation of subdivision (b)(2), involving frivolous contentions of law. Monetary responsibility for such violations is more properly placed solely on the party's attorneys. With this limitation, the rule should not be subject to attack under the Rules Enabling Act. *See Willy v. Coastal Corp.,* 503 U.S. 131, 112 S.Ct. 1076, 117 L.Ed.2d 280 (1992); *Business Guides, Inc. v. Chromatic Communications Enter. Inc.,* 498 U.S. 533, 111 S.Ct. 922, 112 L.Ed.2d 1140 (1991). This restriction does not limit the court's power to impose sanctions or remedial orders that may have collateral financial consequences upon a party, such as dismissal of a claim, preclusion of a defense, or preparation of amended pleadings.

Explicit provision is made for litigants to be provided notice of the alleged violation and an opportunity to respond before sanctions are imposed. Whether the matter should be decided solely on the basis of written submissions or should be scheduled for oral argument (or, indeed, for evidentiary presentation) will depend on the circumstances. If the court imposes a sanction, it must, unless waived, indicate its reasons in a written order or on the record; the court should not ordinarily have to explain its denial of a motion for sanctions. Whether a violation has occurred and what sanctions, if any, to impose for a violation are matters committed to the discretion of the trial court; accordingly, as under current law, the standard for appellate review of these decisions will be for abuse of discretion. *See Cooter & Gell v. Hartmarx Corp.,* 496 U.S. 384, 110 S.Ct. 2447, 110 L.Ed.2d 359 (1990)(noting, however, that an abuse would be established if the court based its ruling on an erroneous view of the law or on a clearly erroneous assessment of the evidence).

The revision leaves for resolution on a case-by-case basis, considering the particular circumstances involved, the question as to when a motion for violation of Rule 11 should be served and when, if filed, it should be decided. Ordinarily the motion should be served promptly after the inappropriate paper is filed, and, if delayed too long, may be viewed as untimely. In other circumstances, it should not be served until the other party has had a reasonable opportunity for discovery. Given the "safe harbor" provisions discussed below, a party cannot delay serving its Rule 11 motion until conclusion of the case (or judicial rejection of the offending contention).

Rule 11 motions should not be made or threatened for minor, inconsequential violations of the standards prescribed by subdivision (b). They should not be employed as a discovery device or to test the legal sufficiency or efficacy of allegations in the pleadings; other motions are available for those purposes. Nor should Rule 11 motions be prepared to emphasize the merits of a party's position, to exact an unjust settlement, to intimidate an adversary into withdrawing contentions that are fairly debatable, to increase the costs of litigation, to create a conflict of interest between attorney and client, or to seek disclosure of matters otherwise protected by the attorney-client privilege or the work-product doctrine. As under the prior rule, the court may defer its ruling (or its decision as to the identity of the persons to be sanctioned) until final resolution of the case in order to avoid immediate conflicts of interest and to reduce the disruption created if a disclosure of attorney-client communications is needed to determine whether a violation occurred or to identify the person responsible for the violation.

The rule provides that requests for sanctions must be made as a separate motion, *i.e.,* not simply included as an additional prayer for relief contained in another motion. The motion for sanctions is not, however, to be filed until at least 21 days (or such other period as the court may set) after being served. If, during this period, the alleged violation is corrected, as by withdrawing (whether formally or informally) some allegation or contention, the motion should not be filed with the court. These provisions are intended to provide a type of "safe harbor" against motions under Rule 11 in that a party will not be subject to sanctions on the basis of another party's motion unless, after receiving the motion, it refuses to withdraw that position or to acknowledge candidly that it does not currently have evidence to support a specified allegation. Under the former rule, parties were sometimes reluctant to abandon a questionable contention lest that be viewed as evidence of a violation of Rule 11; under the revision, the timely withdrawal of a contention will protect a party against a motion for sanctions.

To stress the seriousness of a motion for sanctions and to define precisely the conduct claimed to violate the rule, the revision provides that the "safe harbor" period begins to run only upon service of the motion. In most cases, however, counsel should be expected to give informal notice to the other party, whether in person or by a telephone call or letter, of a potential violation before proceeding to prepare and serve a Rule 11 motion.

As under former Rule 11, the filing of a motion for sanctions is itself subject to the requirements of the rule and can lead to sanctions. However, service of a cross motion under Rule 11 should rarely be needed since under the revision the court may award to the person who prevails on a motion under Rule 11—whether the movant or the target of the motion—reasonable expenses, including attorney's fees, incurred in presenting or opposing the motion.

The power of the court to act on its own initiative is retained, but with the condition that this be done through a show cause order. This procedure provides the person with notice and an opportunity to respond. The revision provides that a monetary sanction imposed after a court-initiated show cause order be limited to a penalty payable to the court and that it be imposed only if the show cause order is issued before any voluntary dismissal or an agreement of the parties to settle the claims made by or against the litigant. Parties settling a case should not be subsequently faced with an unexpected order from the court leading to monetary sanctions that might have affected their willingness to settle or voluntarily dismiss a case. Since show cause orders will ordinarily be issued only in situations that are akin to a contempt of court, the rule does not provide a "safe harbor" to a litigant for withdrawing a claim, defense, etc., after a show cause order has been issued on the court's own initiative. Such corrective action, however, should be taken into account in deciding what—if any—sanction to impose if, after consideration of the litigant's response, the court concludes that a violation has occurred.

Subdivision (d). Rules 26(g) and 37 establish certification standards and sanctions that apply to discovery disclosures, requests, responses, objections, and motions. It is appropriate that Rules 26 through 37, which are specially designed for the discovery process, govern such documents and conduct rather than the more general provisions of Rule 11. Subdivision (d) has been added to accomplish this result.

Rule 11 is not the exclusive source for control of improper presentations of claims, defenses, or contentions. It does not supplant statutes permitting awards of attorney's fees to prevailing parties or alter the principles governing such awards. It does not inhibit the court in punishing for contempt, in exercising its inherent powers, or in imposing sanctions, awarding expenses, or directing remedial action authorized under other rules or under 28 U.S.C. § 1927. *See Chambers v. NASCO,* 501 U.S. 32 (1991). *Chambers* cautions, however, against reliance upon inherent powers if appropriate sanctions can be imposed under provisions such as Rule 11, and the procedures specified in Rule 11—notice, opportunity to respond, and findings—should ordinarily be employed when imposing a sanction under the court's inherent powers. Finally, it should be noted that Rule 11 does not preclude a party from initiating an independent action for malicious prosecution or abuse of process.

2007 AMENDMENT

The language of Rule 11 has been amended as part of the general restyling of the Civil Rules to make them more easily understood and to make style and terminology consistent throughout the rules. These changes are intended to be stylistic only.

Providing an e-mail address is useful, but does not of itself signify consent to filing or service by e-mail.

Rule 12. Defenses and Objections—When and How Presented—By Pleading or Motion—Motion for Judgment on the Pleadings

1937 ADOPTION

Note to Subdivision (a). 1. Compare former Equity Rules 12 (Issue of Subpoena—Time for Answer) and 31 (Reply—When Required—When Cause at Issue); 4 Mont.Rev. Codes Ann. (1935) §§ 9107, 9158; N.Y.C.P.A. (1937) § 263; N.Y.R.C.P. (1937) Rules 109–111.

2. U.S.C., Title 28, § 507, formerly § 763 (Petition in action against United States; service; appearance by district attorney) provides that the United States as a defendant shall have 60 days within which to answer or otherwise defend. This and other statutes which provide 60 days for the United States or an officer or agency thereof to answer or otherwise defend are continued by this rule. In so far as any statutes not excepted in Rule 81 provide a different time for a defendant to defend, such statutes are modified. See U.S.C., Title 28, former § 45 (District courts; practice and procedure in certain cases under the interstate commerce laws)(30 days).

3. Compare the last sentence of former Equity Rule 29 (Defenses—How Presented) and N.Y.C.P.A., 1937, § 283. See rule 15(a) for time within which to plead to an amended pleading.

Note to Subdivisions (b) and (d). 1. See generally former Equity Rules 29 (Defenses—How Presented), 33 (Testing Sufficiency of Defense), 43 (Defect of Parties—Resisting Objection), and 44 (Defect of Parties—Tardy Objection); N.Y.C.P.A., 1937, §§ 277–280; N.Y.R.C.P., 1937, Rules 106–112; English Rules Under the Judicature Act (The Annual Practice, 1937) O. 25, r.r. 1–4; Clark, Code Pleading, 1928, pp. 371–381.

2. For provisions authorizing defenses to be made in the answer or reply see English Rules Under the Judicature Act (The Annual Practice, 1937) O. 25, r.r. 1–4; 1 Miss.Code Ann., 1930, §§ 378, 379. Compare former Equity Rule 29 (Defenses—How Presented); U.S.C., Title 28, former § 45 (District Courts; practice and procedure in certain cases under the interstate commerce laws). U.S.C., Title 28, former § 45, substantially continued by this rule, provides: "No replication need be filed to the answer, and objections to the sufficiency of the petition or answer as not setting forth a cause of action or defense must be taken at the final hearing or by motion to dismiss the petition based on said grounds, which motion may be made at any time before answer is filed." Compare Calif.Code Civ.Proc. (Deering, 1937) § 433; 4 Nev.Comp.Laws (Hillyer, 1929) § 8600. For provisions that the defendant may demur and answer at the same time, see Calif.Code Civ.Proc. (Deering, 1937) § 431; 4 Nev.Comp.Laws (Hillyer, 1929) § 8598.

3. Former Equity Rule 29 (Defenses—How Presented) abolished demurrers and provided that defenses in point of law arising on the face of the bill should be made by motion to dismiss or in the answer, with further provision that every such point of law going to the whole or material part of the cause or causes stated might be called up and disposed of before final hearing "at the discretion of the court." Likewise many state practices have abolished the demurrer, or retain it only to attack substantial and not formal defects. See 6 Tenn.Code Ann. (Williams, 1934) § 8784; Ala.Code Ann. (Michie, 1928) § 9479; 2 Mass.Gen.Laws (Ter.Ed., 1932) ch. 231, §§ 15–18; Kansas Gen.Stat.Ann. (1935) §§ 60–705, 60–706.

Note to Subdivision (c). Compare former Equity Rule 33 (Testing Sufficiency of Defense); N.Y.R.C.P. (1937) Rules 111 and 112.

Note to Subdivisions (e) and (f). Compare former Equity Rules 20 (Further and Particular Statement in Pleading May Be Required) and 21 (Scandal and Impertinence); English Rules Under the Judicature Act (The Annual Practice, 1937) O. 19, r. r. 7, 7a, 7b, 8; 4 Mont.Rev.Codes Ann. (1935) §§ 9166, 9167; N.Y.C.P.A. (1937) § 247; N.Y.R.C.P. (1937) Rules 103, 115, 116, 117; Wyo.Rev.Stat.Ann. (Courtright, 1931) §§ 89–1033, 89–1034.

Note to Subdivision (g). Compare Rules of the District Court of the United States for the District of Columbia (1937) former Equity Rule 11; N.M.Rules of Pleading, Practice and Procedure, 38 N.M.Rep. vii [105–408] (1934); Wash.Gen.Rules of the Superior Courts, 1 Wash.Rev.Stat.Ann. (Remington, 1932) p. 160, Rule VI(e) and (f).

Note to Subdivision (h). Compare Calif.Code Civ.Proc. (Deering, 1937) § 434; 2 Minn.Stat. (Mason, 1927) § 9252; N.Y.C.P.A. (1937) §§ 278 and 279; Wash.Gen.Rules of the Superior Courts, 1 Wash.Rev.Stat.Ann. (Remington, 1932) p. 160, Rule VI(e). This rule continues U.S.C., Title 28, former § 80 (Dismissal or remand)(of action over which district court lacks jurisdiction), while U.S.C., Title 28, former § 399 (Amendments to show diverse citizenship) is continued by Rule 15.

1946 AMENDMENT

Note to Subdivision (a). Various minor alterations in language have been made to improve the statement of the rule. All references to bills of particulars have been stricken in accordance with changes made in subdivision (e).

Subdivision (b). The addition of defense (7), "failure to join an indispensable party", cures an omission in the rules, which are silent as to the mode of raising such failure. See Commentary, Manner of Raising Objection of Non-Joinder of Indispensable Party, 1940, 2 Fed.Rules Serv. 658, and, 1942, 5 Fed.Rules Serv. 820. In one case, *United States* v. *Metropolitan Life Ins. Co.*, E.D.Pa.1941, 36 F.Supp. 399, the failure to join an indispensable party was raised under Rule 12(c).

Rule 12(b)(6), permitting a motion to dismiss for failure of the complaint to state a claim on which relief can be granted, is substantially the same as the old demurrer for failure of a pleading to state a cause of action. Some courts have held that as the rule by its terms refers to statements in the complaint, extraneous matter on affidavits, depositions or otherwise, may not be introduced in support of the motion, or to resist it. On the other hand, in many cases the district courts have permitted the introduction of such material. When these cases have reached circuit courts of appeals in situations where the extraneous material so received shows that there is no genuine issue as to any material question of fact and that on the undisputed facts as disclosed by the affidavits or depositions, one party or the other is entitled to judgment as a matter of law, the circuit courts, properly enough, have been reluctant to dispose of the case merely on the face of the pleading, and in the interest of prompt disposition of the action have made a final disposition of it. In dealing with such situations the Second Circuit has made the sound suggestion that whatever its label or original basis, the motion may be treated as a motion for summary judgment and disposed of as such. *Samara* v. *United States*, C.C.A.2, 1942, 129 F.2d 594, certiorari denied 317 U.S. 686, 63 S.Ct. 258, 87 L.Ed. 549; *Boro Hall Corp.* v. *General Motors Corp.*, C.C.A.2, 1942, 124 F.2d 822, certiorari denied 317 U.S. 695, 63 S.Ct. 436, 87 L.Ed. 556. See, also, *Kithcart* v. *Metropolitan Life Ins. Co.*, C.C.A.8, 1945, 150 F.2d 997.

It has also been suggested that this practice could be justified on the ground that the federal rules permit "speaking" motions. The Committee entertains the view that on motion under Rule 12(b)(6) to dismiss for failure of the complaint to state a good claim, the trial court should have authority to permit the introduction of extraneous matter, such as may be offered on a motion for summary judgment, and if it does not exclude such matter the motion should then be treated as a motion for summary judgment and disposed of in the manner and on the conditions stated in Rule 56 relating to summary judgments, and, of course, in such a situation, when the case reaches the circuit court of appeals, that court should treat the motion in the same way. The Committee believes that such practice, however, should be tied to the summary judgment rule. The term "speaking motion" is not mentioned in the rules, and if there is such a thing its limitations are undefined. Where extraneous matter is received, by tying further proceedings to the summary judgment rule the courts have a definite basis in the rules for disposing of the motion.

The Committee emphasizes particularly the fact that the summary judgment rule does not permit a case to be disposed of by judgment on the merits on affidavits, which disclose a conflict on a material issue of fact, and unless this practice is tied to the summary judgment rule, the extent to which a court, on the introduction of such extraneous matter, may resolve questions of fact on conflicting proof would be left uncertain.

The decisions dealing with this general situation may be generally grouped as follows: (1) cases dealing with the use of affidavits and other extraneous material on motions; (2) cases reversing judgments to prevent final determination on mere pleading allegations alone.

Under group (1) are: *Boro Hall Corp.* v. *General Motors Corp.*, C.C.A.2, 1942, 124 F.2d 822, certiorari denied 317 U.S. 695, 63 S.Ct. 436, 87 L.Ed. 556; *Gallup* v. *Caldwell*, C.C.A.3, 1941, 120 F.2d 90; *Central Mexico Light & Power Co.* v. *Munch*, C.C.A.2, 1940, 116 F.2d 85; *National War Labor Board* v. *Montgomery Ward & Co.*, 1944, 144 F.2d 528, 79 U.S.App.D.C. 200, certiorari denied 323 U.S. 774, 65 S.Ct. 134, 89 L.Ed. 619; *Urquhart* v. *American-La France Foamite Corp.*, 1944, 144 F.2d 542, 79 U.S.App.D.C. 219; *Samara* v. *United States*, C.C.A.2, 1942, 129 F.2d 594; *Cohen* v. *American Window Glass Co.*, C.C.A.2, 1942, 126 F.2d 111; *Sperry Products Inc.* v. *Association of American Railroads*, C.C.A.2, 1942, 132 F.2d 408; *Joint Council Dining Car Employees Local 370* v. *Delaware, Lackawanna and Western R. Co.*, C.C.A.2, 1946, 157 F.2d 417; *Weeks* v. *Bareco Oil Co.*, C.C.A.7, 1941, 125 F.2d 84; *Carroll* v. *Morrison Hotel Corp.*, C.C.A.7, 1945, 149 F.2d 404; *Victory* v. *Manning*, C.C.A.3, 1942, 128 F.2d 415; *Locals No. 1470, No. 1469, and No. 1512 of International Longshoremen's Association* v. *Southern Pacific Co.*, C.C.A.5, 1942, 131 F.2d 605; *Lucking* v. *Delano*, C.C.A.6, 1942, 129 F.2d 283; *San Francisco Lodge No. 68 of International Association of Machinists* v. *Forrestal*, Cal.1944, 58 F.Supp. 466; *Benson* v. *Export Equipment Corp.*, 1945, 164 P.2d 380, 49 N.M. 356, construing New Mexico rule identical with Rule 12(b)(6); *F. E. Myers & Bros. Co.* v. *Goulds Pumps, Inc.*, N.Y.1946, 9 Fed.Rules Serv. 12b, 5 F.R.D. 132-33 Case 2. Cf. *Kohler* v. *Jacobs*, C.C.A.5, 1943, 138 F.2d 440; *Cohen* v. *United States*, C.C.A.8, 1942, 129 F.2d 733.

Under group (2) are: *Sparks* v. *England*, C.C.A.8, 1940, 113 F.2d 579; *Continental Collieries, Inc.* v. *Shober*, C.C.A.3, 1942, 130 F.2d 631; *Downey* v. *Palmer*, C.C.A.2, 1940, 114 F.2d 116; *DeLoach* v. *Crowley's Inc.*, C.C.A.5, 1942, 128 F.2d 378; *Leimer* v. *State Mutual Life Assurance Co. of Worcester, Mass.*, C.C.A.8, 1940, 108 F.2d 302; *Rossiter* v. *Vogel*, C.C.A.2, 1943, 134 F.2d 908, compare s.c., C.C.A.2, 1945, 148 F.2d 292; *Karl Kiefer Machine Co.* v. *United States Bottlers Machinery Co.*, C.C.A.7, 1940, 113 F.2d 356; *Chicago Metallic Mfg. Co.* v. *Edward Katzinger Co.*, C.C.A.7, 1941, 123 F.2d 518; *Louisiana Farmers' Protective Union, Inc.* v. *Great Atlantic & Pacific Tea Co. of America, Inc.*, C.C.A.8, 1942, 131 F.2d 419; *Publicity Bldg. Realty Corp.* v. *Hannegan*, C.C.A.8, 1943, 139 F.2d 583; *Dioguardi* v. *Durning*, C.C.A.2, 1944, 139 F.2d 774; *Package Closure Corp.* v. *Sealright Co., Inc.*, C.C.A.2, 1944, 141 F.2d 972; *Tahir Erk* v. *Glenn L. Martin Co.*, C.C.A.4, 1941, 116 F.2d 865; *Bell* v. *Preferred Life Assurance Society of Montgomery, Ala.*, 1943, 320 U.S. 238, 64 S.Ct. 5, 88 L.Ed. 15.

The addition at the end of subdivision (b) makes it clear that on a motion under Rule 12(b)(6) extraneous material may not be considered if the court excludes it, but that if the court does not exclude such material the motion shall be treated as a motion for summary judgment and disposed of as provided in Rule 56. It will also be observed that if a motion under Rule 12(b)(6) is thus converted into a summary judgment motion, the amendment insures that both parties shall be given a reasonable opportunity to submit affidavits and extraneous proofs to avoid taking a party by surprise through the conversion of the motion into a motion for summary judgment. In this manner and to this extent the amendment regularizes the practice above described. As the courts are already dealing with cases in this way, the effect of this amendment is really only to define the practice carefully and apply the requirements of the summary judgment rule in the disposition of the motion.

Subdivision (c). The sentence appended to subdivision (c) performs the same function and is grounded on the same reasons as the corresponding sentence added in subdivision (b).

Subdivision (d). The change here was made necessary because of the addition of defense (7) in subdivision (b).

Subdivision (e). References in this subdivision to a bill of particulars have been deleted, and the motion provided for is confined to one for more definite statement to be obtained only in cases where the movant cannot reasonably be required to frame an answer or other responsive pleading to the pleading in question. With respect to preparations for trial, the party is properly relegated to the various methods of examination and discovery provided in the rules for that purpose. *Slusher* v. *Jones*, Ky.1943, 7 Fed.Rules Serv. 12e.231, Case 5, 3 F.R.D. 168; *Best Foods, Inc.* v. *General Mills, Inc.*, D.Del.1943, 7 Fed.Rules Serv. 12e.231, Case 7, 3 F.R.D. 275; *Braden* v. *Callaway*, Tenn.1943, 8 Fed.Rules Serv. 12e.231, Case 1 ("... most courts ... conclude that the definiteness required is only such as will be sufficient for the party to prepare responsive pleadings"). Accordingly, the reference to the 20 day time limit has also been eliminated, since the purpose of this present provision is to state a time period where the motion for a bill is made for the purpose of preparing for trial.

Rule 12(e) as originally drawn has been the subject of more judicial rulings than any other part of the rules, and has been much criticized by commentators, judges and members of the bar. See general discussion and cases cited in 1 Moore's Federal Practice, 1938, Cum.Supplement, § 12.07, under "Page 657"; also, Holtzoff, New Federal Procedure and the Courts, 1940, 35–41. And compare vote of Second Circuit Conference of Circuit and District Judges, June 1940, recommending the abolition of the bill of particulars; *Sun Valley Mfg. Co.* v. *Mylish*, Pa.1944, 8 Fed.Rules Serv. 12e.231, Case 6 ("Our experience . . . has demonstrated not only that 'the office of the bill of particulars is fast becoming obsolete' . . 27 but that in view of the adequate discovery procedure available under the Rules, motions for bills of particulars should be abolished altogether."); *Walling* v. *American Steamship Co.*, N.Y.1945, 4 F.R.D. 355, 8 Fed.Rules Serv. 12e.244, Case 8 (". . . the adoption of the rule was ill advised. It has led to confusion, duplication and delay.") The tendency of some courts freely to grant extended bills of particulars has served to neutralize any helpful benefits derived from Rule 8, and has overlooked the intended use of the rules on depositions and discovery. The words "or to prepare for trial"—eliminated by the proposed amendment—have sometimes been seized upon as grounds for compulsory statement in the opposing pleading of all the details which the movant would have to meet at the trial. On the other hand, many courts have in effect read these words out of the rule. See *Walling* v. *Alabama Pipe Co.*, Mo.1942, 3 F.R.D. 159, 6 Fed.Rules Serv. 12e.244, Case 7; *Fleming* v. *Mason & Dixon Lines, Inc.*, Tenn.1941, 42 F.Supp. 230; *Kellogg Co.* v. *National Biscuit Co.*, N.J.1941, 38 F.Supp. 643; *Brown* v. *H. L. Green Co.*, N.Y.1943, 7 Fed.Rules Serv. 12e.231, Case 6; *Pedersen* v. *Standard Accident Ins. Co.*, Mo.1945, 8 Fed.Rules Serv. 12e.231, Case 8; *Bowles* v. *Ohse*, Neb.1945, 4 F.R.D. 403, 9 Fed.Rules Serv. 12e.231, Case 1; *Klages* v. *Cohen*, N.Y.1945, 9 Fed.Rules Serv. 8a.25, Case 4; *Bowles* v. *Lawrence*, Mass.1945, 8 Fed.Rules Serv. 12e.231, Case 19; *McKinney Tool Mfg. Co.* v. *Hoyt*, Ohio 1945, 9 Fed.Rules Serv. 12e.235, Case 1; *Bowles* v. *Jack*, Minn.1945, 5 F.R.D. 1, 9 Fed.Rules Serv. 12e.244, Case 9. And it has been urged from the bench that the phrase be stricken, *Poole* v. *White*, W.Va.1941, 5 Fed.Rules Serv. 12e.231, Case 4, 2 F.R.D. 40. See also *Bowles* v. *Gabel*, Mo.1946, 9 Fed.Rules Serv. 12e.244, Case 10. ("The courts have never favored that portion of the rules which undertook to justify a motion of this kind for the purpose of aiding counsel in preparing his case for trial.").

Subdivision (f). This amendment affords a specific method of raising the insufficiency of a defense, a matter which has troubled some courts, although attack has been permitted in one way or another. See *Dysart* v. *Remington-Rand, Inc.*, Conn.1939, 31 F.Supp. 296; *Eastman Kodak Co.* v. *McAuley*, N.Y.1941, 4 Fed.Rules Serv. 12f.21, Case 8, 2

F.R.D. 21; *Schenley Distillers Corp.* v. *Renken*, S.C.1940, 34 F.Supp. 678; *Yale Transport Corp.* v. *Yellow Truck & Coach Mfg. Co.*, N.Y.1944, 3 F.R.D. 440; *United States* v. *Turner Milk Co.*, Ill.1941, 4 Fed.Rules Serv. 12b.51, Case 3, 1 F.R.D. 643; *Teiger* v. *Stephan Oderwald, Inc.*, N.Y.1940, 31 F.Supp. 626; *Teplitzky* v. *Pennsylvania R. Co.*, Ill.1941, 38 F.Supp. 535; *Gallagher* v. *Carroll*, N.Y.1939, 27 F.Supp. 568; *United States* v. *Palmer*, N.Y.1939, 28 F.Supp. 936. And see *Indemnity Ins. Co. of North America* v. *Pan American Airways, Inc.*, N.Y.1944, 58 F.Supp. 338; Commentary, Modes of Attacking Insufficient Defenses in the Answer, 1939, 1 Fed.Rules Serv. 669, 1940, 2 Fed.Rules Serv. 640.

Subdivision (g). The change in title conforms with the companion provision in subdivision (h).

The alteration of the "except" clause requires that other than provided in subdivision (h) a party who resorts to a motion to raise defenses specified in the rule, must include in one motion all that are then available to him. Under the original rule defenses which could be raised by motion were divided into two groups which could be the subjects of two successive motions.

Subdivision (h). The addition of the phrase relating to indispensable parties is one of necessity.

1963 AMENDMENT

This amendment conforms to the amendment of Rule 4(e). See also the Advisory Committee's Note to amended Rule 4(b).

1966 AMENDMENT

Subdivision (b)(7). The terminology of this subdivision is changed to accord with the amendment of Rule 19. See the Advisory Committee's Note to Rule 19, as amended, especially the third paragraph therein before the caption "Subdivision (c)."

Subdivision (g). Subdivision (g) has forbidden a defendant who makes a preanswer motion under this rule from making a further motion presenting any defense or objection which was available to him at the time he made the first motion and which he could have included, but did not in fact include therein. Thus if the defendant moves before answer to dismiss the complaint for failure to state a claim, he is barred from making a further motion presenting the defense of improper venue, if that defense was available to him when he made his original motion. Amended subdivision (g) is to the same effect. This required consolidation of defenses and objections in a Rule 12 motion is salutary in that it works against piecemeal consideration of a case. For exceptions to the requirement of consolidation, see the last clause of subdivision (g), referring to new subdivision (h)(2).

Subdivision (h). The question has arisen whether an omitted defense which cannot be made the basis of a second motion may nevertheless be pleaded in the answer. Subdivision (h) called for waiver of "* * * defenses and objections which he [defendant] does not present * * * by motion * * * or, if he has made no motion, in his answer * * *." If the clause "if he has made no motion," was read literally, it seemed that the omitted defense was waived and could not be pleaded in the answer. On the other hand, the clause might be read as adding nothing of substance to the preceding words; in that event it appeared that a defense was not waived by reason of being omitted from the motion and might be set up in the answer. The decisions were divided. Favoring waiver, see *Keefe* v. *Derounian*, 6 F.R.D. 11 (N.D.Ill.1946); *Elbinger* v. *Precision Metal Workers Corp.*, 18 F.R.D. 467 (E.D.Wis.1956); see also *Rensing* v. *Turner Aviation Corp.*, 166 F.Supp. 790 (N.D.Ill.1958); *P Beiersdorf & Co.* v. *Duke Laboratories, Inc.*, 10 F.R.D. 282 (S.D.N.Y.1950); *Neset* v. *Christensen*, 92 F.Supp. 78 (E.D.N.Y.1950). Opposing waiver, see *Phillips* v. *Baker*, 121 F.2d 752 (9th Cir.1941); *Crum* v. *Graham*, 32 F.R.D. 173 (D.Mont. 1963)(regretfully following the Phillips case); see also *Birnbaum* v. *Birrell*, 9 F.R.D. 72 (S.D.N.Y.1948); *Johnson* v. *Joseph Schlitz Brewing Co.*, 33 F.Supp. 176 (E.D.Tenn.1940); cf. *Carter* v. *American Bus Lines, Inc.*, 22 F.R.D. 323 (D.Neb.1958).

Amend subdivision (h)(1)(A) eliminates the ambiguity and states that certain specified defenses which were available to a party when he made a preanswer motion, but which he omitted from the motion, are waived. The specified defenses are lack of jurisdiction over the person, improper venue, insufficiency of process, and insufficiency of service of process (see Rule 12(b)(2)–(5)). A party who by motion invites the court to pass upon a threshold defense should bring forward all the specified defenses he then has and thus allow the court to do a reasonably complete job. The waiver reinforces the policy of subdivision (g) forbidding successive motions.

By amended subdivision (h)(1)(B), the specified defenses, even if not waived by the operation of (A), are waived by the failure to raise them by a motion under Rule 12 or in the responsive pleading or any amendment thereof to which the party is entitled as a matter of course. The specified defenses are of such a character that they should not be delayed and brought up for the first time by means of an application to the court to amend the responsive pleading.

Since the language of the subdivisions is made clear, the party is put on fair notice of the effect of his actions and omissions and can guard himself against unintended waiver. It is to be noted that while the defenses specified in subdivision (h)(1) are subject to waiver as there provided, the more substantial defenses of failure to state a claim upon which relief can be granted, failure to join a party indispensable under Rule 19, and failure to state a legal defense to a claim (see Rule 12(b)(6), (7), (f)), as well as the defense of lack of jurisdiction over the subject matter (see Rule 12(b)(1)), are expressly preserved against waiver by amended subdivision (h)(2) and (3).

1987 AMENDMENT

The amendments are technical. No substantive change is intended.

1993 AMENDMENT

Subdivision (a) is divided into paragraphs for greater clarity, and paragraph (1)(B) is added to reflect amendments to Rule 4. Consistent with Rule 4(d)(3), a defendant that timely waives service is allowed 60 days from the date the request was mailed in which to respond to the complaint, with an additional 30 days afforded if the request was sent out of the country. Service is timely waived if the waiver is returned within the time specified in the request (30 days after the request was mailed, or 60 days if mailed out of the country) and before being formally served with process. Sometimes a plaintiff may attempt to serve a defendant with process while also sending the defendant a request for waiver of service; if the defendant executes the waiver of service within the time specified and before being served with process, it should have the longer time to respond afforded by waiving service.

The date of sending the request is to be inserted by the plaintiff on the face of the request for waiver and on the waiver itself. This date is used to measure the return day for the waiver form, so that the plaintiff can know on a day certain whether formal service of process will be necessary; it is also a useful date to measure the time for answer when service is waived. The defendant who returns the waiver is given additional time for answer in order to assure that it loses nothing by waiving service of process.

2000 AMENDMENT

Rule 12(a)(3)(B) is added to complement the addition of Rule 4(i)(2)(B). The purposes that underlie the requirement that service be made on the United States in an action that asserts individual liability of a United States officer or employee for acts occurring in connection with the performance of duties on behalf of the United States also require that the time to answer be extended to 60 days. Time is needed for the United States to determine whether to provide representation to the defendant officer or employee. If the United States provides representation, the need for an extended answer period is the same as in actions against the United States, a United States agency, or a United States officer sued in an official capacity.

An action against a former officer or employee of the United States is covered by subparagraph (3)(B) in the same way as an action against a present officer or employee. Termination of the relationship between the individual defendant and the United States does not reduce the need for additional time to answer.

GAP Report

No changes are recommended for Rule 12 as published.

2007 AMENDMENT

The language of Rule 12 has been amended as part of the general restyling of the Civil Rules to make them more easily understood and to make style and terminology consistent throughout the rules. These changes are intended to be stylistic only.

Former Rule 12(a)(4)(A) referred to an order that postpones disposition of a motion "until the trial on the merits." Rule 12(a)(4) now refers to postponing disposition "until trial." The new expression avoids the ambiguity that inheres in "trial on the merits," which may become confusing when there is a separate trial of a single issue or another event different from a single all-encompassing trial.

Rule 13. Counterclaim and Cross-Claim

1937 ADOPTION

1. This is substantially former Equity Rule 30 (Answer—Contents—Counterclaim), broadened to include legal as well as equitable counterclaims.

2. Compare the English practice, English Rules Under the Judicature Act (The Annual Practice, 1937) O. 19, r. r. 2 and 3, and O. 21, r. r. 10–17; *Beddall* v. *Maitland,* L.R. 17 Ch.Div. 174, 181, 182 (1881).

3. Certain states have also adopted almost unrestricted provisions concerning both the subject matter of and the parties to a counterclaim. This seems to be the modern tendency. Ark.Civ.Code (Crawford, 1934) §§ 117 (as amended) and 118; N.J.S.A. 2:27–137, 2:27–139, 2:27–141; N.Y.C.P.A. (1937) §§ 262, 266, 267 (all as amended, Laws of 1936, ch. 324), 268, 269, and 271; Wis.Stat. (1935) § 263.14(1)(c).

4. Most codes do not expressly provide for a counterclaim in the reply. Clark, Code Pleading (1928), p. 486, Ky.Codes (Carroll, 1932) Civ.Pract. § 98 does provide, however, for such counterclaim.

5. The provisions of this rule respecting counterclaims are subject to Rule 82 (Jurisdiction and Venue Unaffected). For a discussion of federal jurisdiction and venue in regard to counterclaims and cross-claims, see Shulman and Jaegerman, Some Jurisdictional Limitations in Federal Procedure (1936), 45 Yale L.J. 393, 410 et seq.

6. This rule does not affect such statutes of the United States as U.S.C., Title 28, §§ 1332, 1345, 1357, formerly § 41(1)(United States as plaintiff; civil suits at common law and in equity), relating to assigned claims in actions based on diversity of citizenship.

7. If the action proceeds to judgment without the interposition of a counterclaim as required by subdivision (a) of this rule, the counterclaim is barred. See *American Mills Co.* v. *American Surety Co.,* 1922, 260 U.S. 360, 43 S.Ct. 149, 67 L.Ed. 306; *Marconi Wireless Telegraph Co.* v. *National Electric Signalling Co.,* N.Y.1913, 206 F. 295; Hopkins, Federal Equity Rules (8th ed., 1933), p. 213; Simkins, Federal Practice (1934), p. 663.

8. For allowance of credits against the United States see U.S.C., Title 26, Int.Rev. Code, § 3772 (a)(1)(2)(b)(Suits for refunds of internal revenue taxes—limitations); U.S.C., Title 28, § 2406, formerly §§ 774 (Suits by United States against individuals; credits), 775 (Suits under postal laws; credits); U.S.C., Title 31, § 227 (Offsets against judgments and claims against United States).

1946 AMENDMENT

Note to Subdivision (a). The use of the word "filing" was inadvertent. The word "serving" conforms with subdivision (e) and with usage generally throughout the rules.

The removal of the phrase "not the subject of a pending action" and the addition of the new clause at the end of the subdivision is designed to eliminate the ambiguity noted in *Prudential Insurance Co. of America* v. *Saxe,* 1943, 134 F.2d 16, 77 U.S.App.D.C. 144, 33–34, certiorari denied 319 U.S. 745, 63 S.Ct. 1033, 87 L.Ed. 1701. The rewording of the subdivision in this respect insures against an undesirable possibility presented under the original rule whereby a party having a claim which would be the subject of a compulsory counterclaim could avoid stating it as such by bringing an independent action in another court after the commencement of the federal action but before serving his pleading in the federal action.

Subdivision (g). The amendment is to care for a situation such as where a second mortgagee is made defendant in a foreclosure proceeding and wishes to file a cross-complaint against the mortgagor in order to secure a personal judgment for the indebtedness and foreclose his lien. A claim of this sort by the second mortgagee may not necessarily arise out of the transaction or occurrence that is the subject matter of the original action under the terms of Rule 13(g).

Subdivision (h). The change clarifies the interdependence of Rules 13(i) and 54(b).

1963 AMENDMENT

When a defendant, if he desires to defend his interest in property, is obliged to come in and litigate in a court to whose jurisdiction he could not ordinarily be subjected, fairness suggests that he should not be required to assert counterclaims, but should rather be permitted to do so at his election. If, however, he does elect to assert a counterclaim, it seems fair to require him to assert any other which is compulsory within the meaning of Rule 13(a). Clause (2), added by amendment to Rule 13(a), carries out this idea. It will apply to various cases described in Rule 4(e), as amended, where service is effected through attachment or other process by which the court does not acquire jurisdiction to render a personal judgment against the defendant. Clause (2) will also apply to actions commenced in State courts jurisdictionally grounded on attachment or the like, and removed to the Federal courts.

1966 AMENDMENT

Rule 13(h), dealing with the joinder of additional parties to a counterclaim or cross-claim, has partaken of some of the textual difficulties of Rule 19 on necessary joinder of parties. See Advisory Committee's Note to Rule 19, as amended; cf. 3 Moore's Federal Practice, par. 13.39 (2d ed. 1963), and Supp. thereto; 1A Barron & Holtzoff, Federal Practice and Procedure § 399 (Wright ed. 1960). Rule 13(h) has also been inadequate in failing to call attention to the fact that a party pleading a counterclaim or cross-claim may join additional persons when the conditions for permissive joinder of parties under Rule 20 are satisfied.

The amendment of Rule 13(h) supplies the latter omission by expressly referring to Rule 20, as amended, and also incorporates by direct reference the revised criteria and procedures of Rule 19, as amended. Hereafter, for the purpose of determining who must or may be joined as additional parties to a counterclaim or cross-claim, the party pleading the claim is to be regarded as a plaintiff and the additional parties as plaintiffs or defendants as the case may be, and amended Rules 19 and 20 are to be applied in the usual fashion. See also Rules 13(a)(compulsory counterclaims) and 22 (interpleader).

The amendment of Rule 13(h), like the amendment of Rule 19, does not attempt to regulate Federal jurisdiction or venue. See Rule 82. It should be noted, however, that in some situations the decisional law has recognized "ancillary" Federal jurisdiction over counterclaims and cross-claims and "ancillary" venue as to parties to these claims.

1987 AMENDMENT

The amendments are technical. No substantive change is intended.

2007 AMENDMENT

The language of Rule 13 has been amended as part of the general restyling of the Civil Rules to make them more easily understood and to make style and terminology consistent throughout the rules. These changes are intended to be stylistic only.

The meaning of former Rule 13(b) is better expressed by deleting "not arising out of the transaction or occurrence that is the subject matter of the opposing party's claim." Both as a matter of intended meaning and current practice, a party may state as a permissive counterclaim a claim that does grow out of the same transaction or occurrence as an opposing party's claim even though one of the exceptions in Rule 13(a) means the claim is not a compulsory counterclaim.

Rule 14. Third Party Practice

1937 ADOPTION

Third-party impleader is in some aspects a modern innovation in law and equity although well known in admiralty. Because of its many advantages a liberal procedure with respect to it has developed in England, in the federal admiralty courts, and in some American state jurisdictions. See English Rules Under the Judicature Act (The Annual Practice, 1937) O. 16A, r. r. 1–13; United States Supreme Court Admiralty Rules (1920), Rule 56 (Right to Bring in Party Jointly Liable); 12 P.S.Pa.Ann. (1936) § 141; Wis.Stat. (1935) §§ 260.19, 260.20; N.Y.C.P.A. (1937) §§ 193(2), 211(a). Compare La.Code Pract. (Dart, 1932) §§ 378–388. For the practice in Texas as developed by judicial decision, see *Lottman* v. *Cuilla,* Tex.1926, 288 S.W. 123, 126. For a treatment of this subject see Gregory, Legislative Loss Distribution in Negligence Actions (1936); Shulman and Jaegerman, Some Jurisdictional Limitations on Federal Procedure (1936), 45 Yale L.J. 393, 417 et seq.

Third-party impleader under the former conformity act has been applied in actions at law in the federal courts. *Lowry and Co., Inc.* v. *National City Bank of New York,* N.Y.1928, 28 F.2d 895; *Yellow Cab Co. of Philadelphia* v. *Rodgers,* C.C.A.3, 1932, 61 F.2d 729.

1946 AMENDMENT

Note. The provisions in rule 14(a) which relate to the impleading of a third party who is or may be liable to the plaintiff have been deleted by the proposed amendment. It has been held that under rule 14(a) the plaintiff need not amend his complaint to state a claim against such third party if he does not wish to do so. *Satink* v. *Holland Township,* N.J.1940, 31 F.Supp. 229, noted, 1940, 88 U.Pa.L.Rev. 751; *Connelly* v. *Bender,* Mich.1941, 36 F.Supp. 368; *Whitmire* v. *Partin,* Tenn.1941, 2 F.R.D. 83, 5 Fed.Rules Serv. 14a.513, Case 2; *Crim* v. *Lumbermen's Mutual Casualty Co.,* D.C.1939, 26 F.Supp. 715; *Carbola Chemical Co., Inc.* v. *Trundle,* N.Y.1943, 3 F.R.D. 502, 7 Fed.Rules Serv. 14a.224, Case 1; *Roadway Express, Inc.* v. *Automobile Ins. Co. of Hartford, Conn.,* Ohio 1945, 8 Fed.Rules Serv. 14a.513, Case 3. In *Delano* v. *Ives,* Pa.1941, 40 F.Supp. 672, the court said: "... the weight of authority is to the effect that a defendant cannot compel the plaintiff, who has sued him, to sue also a third party whom he does not wish to sue, by tendering in a third party complaint the third party as an additional defendant directly liable to the plaintiff." Thus impleader here amounts to no more than a mere offer of a party to the plaintiff, and if he rejects it, the attempt is a time-consuming futility. See *Satink* v. *Holland Township, supra; Malkin* v. *Arundel Corp.,* Md.1941, 36 F.Supp. 948; also Koenigsberger, Suggestions for Changes in the Federal Rules of Civil Procedure, 1941, 4 Fed.Rules Serv. 1010. But cf. *Atlantic Coast Line R. Co.* v. *United States Fidelity & Guaranty Co.,* Ga.1943, 52 F.Supp. 177.

Moreover, in any case where the plaintiff could not have joined the third party originally because of jurisdictional limitations such as lack of diversity of citizenship, the majority view is that any attempt by the plaintiff to amend his complaint and assert a claim against the impleaded third party would be unavailing. *Hoskie* v. *Prudential Ins. Co. of America,* N.Y.1941, 39 F.Supp. 305; *Johnson* v. *G. J. Sherrard Co.,* Mass.1941, 5 Fed.Rules Serv. 14a.511, Case 1, 2 F.R.D. 164; *Thompson* v. *Cranston,* N.Y.1942, 6 Fed.Rules Serv. 14a.511, Case 1, 2 F.R.D. 270, affirmed, C.C.A.2d, 132 F.2d 631, certiorari denied 1943, 319 U.S. 741, 63 S.Ct. 1028, 87 L.Ed. 1698; *Friend* v. *Middle Atlantic Transportation Co.,* C.C.A.2, 1946, 153 F.2d 778, certiorari denied 328 U.S. 865, 66 S.Ct. 1370, 90 L.Ed. 1635; *Herrington* v. *Jones,* La.1941, 5 Fed.Rules Serv. 14a.511, Case 2, 2 F.R.D. 108; *Banks* v. *Employers' Liability Assurance Corp.,* Mo.1943, 7 Fed.Rules Serv. 14a.11, Case 2; *Saunders* v. *Baltimore & Ohio R. Co.,* W.Va.1945, 9 Fed.Rules Serv. 14a.62, Case 2; *Hull* v. *United States Rubber Co.,* Mich.1945, 9 Fed.Rules Serv. 14a.62, Case 3. See also concurring opinion of Circuit Judge Minton in *People of State of Illinois for Use of Trust Co. of Chicago* v. *Maryland Casualty Co.,* C.C.A.7, 1942, 132 F.2d 850, 853. Contra: *Sklar* v. *Hayes,* Pa.1941, 4 Fed.Rules Serv. 14a.511, Case 2, 1 F.R.D. 594. Discussion of the problem will be found in Commentary, Amendment of Plaintiff's Pleading to Assert Claim Against Third-Party Defendant, 1942, 5 Fed.Rules Serv. 811; Commentary, Federal Jurisdiction in Third-Party Practice, 1943, 6 Fed.Rules Serv. 766; Holtzoff, Some Problems Under Federal Third-Party Practice, 1941, 3 La.L.Rev. 408, 419–420; 1 Moore's Federal Practice, 1938, Cum.Supplement § 14.08. For these reasons therefore, the words "or to the plaintiff" in the first sentence of subdivision (a) have been removed by the amendment; and in conformance therewith the words "the plaintiff" in the second sentence of the subdivision, and the words "or to the third-party plaintiff" in the concluding sentence thereof have likewise been eliminated.

The third sentence of Rule 14(a) has been expanded to clarify the right of the third-party defendant to assert any defenses which the third-party plaintiff may have to the plaintiff's claim. This protects the impleaded third-party defendant where the third-party plaintiff fails or neglects to assert a proper defense to the plaintiff's action. A new sentence has also been inserted giving the third-party defendant the right to assert directly against the original plaintiff any claim arising out of the transaction or occurrence that is the subject matter of the plaintiff's claim against the third-party plaintiff. This permits all claims arising out of the same transaction or occurrence to be heard and determined in the same action. See *Atlantic Coast Line R. Co.* v. *United States Fidelity & Guaranty Co.,* Ga.1943, 52 F.Supp. 177. Accordingly, the next to the last sentence of subdivision (a) has also been revised to make clear that the plaintiff may, if he desires, assert directly against the third-party defendant either by amendment or by a new pleading any claim he may have against him arising out of the transaction or occurrence that is the subject matter of the plaintiff's claim against the third-party plaintiff. In such a case, the third-party defendant then is entitled to assert the defenses, counter-claims and cross-claims provided in Rules 12 and 13.

The sentence reading "The third-party defendant is bound by the adjudication of the third-party plaintiff's liability to the plaintiff, as well as of his own to the plaintiff, or to the third-party plaintiff" has been stricken from Rule 14(a), not to change the law, but because the sentence states a rule of substantive law which is not within the scope of a procedural rule. It is not the purpose of the rules to state the effect of a judgment.

The elimination of the words "the third-party plaintiff, or any other party" from the second sentence of Rule 14(a), together with the insertion of the new phrases therein, are not changes of substance but are merely for the purpose of clarification.

1963 AMENDMENT

Under the amendment of the initial sentences of the subdivision, a defendant as a third-party plaintiff may freely and without leave of court bring in a third-party defendant if he files the third-party complaint not later than 10 days after he serves his original answer. When the impleader comes so early in the case, there is little value in requiring a preliminary ruling by the court on the propriety of the impleader.

After the third-party defendant is brought in, the court has discretion to strike the third-party claim if it is obviously unmeritorious and can only delay or prejudice the disposition of the plaintiff's claim, or to sever the third-party claim or accord it separate trial if confusion or prejudice would otherwise result. This discretion, applicable not merely to the cases covered by the amendment where the third-party defendant is brought in without leave, but to all impleaders under the rule, is emphasized in the next-to-last sentence of the subdivision, added by amendment.

In dispensing with leave of court for an impleader filed not later than 10 days after serving the answer, but retaining the leave requirement for impleaders sought to be effected thereafter, the amended subdivision takes a moderate position on the lines urged by some commentators, see Note, 43 Minn.L.Rev. 115 (1958); cf. Pa.R.Civ.P. 2252–53 (60 days after service on the defendant); Minn.R.Civ.P. 14.01 (45 days). Other commentators would dispense with the requirement of leave regardless of the time when impleader is effected, and would rely on subsequent action by the court to dismiss the impleader if it would unduly delay or complicate the litigation or would be otherwise objectionable. See 1A Barron & Holtzoff, Federal Practice & Procedure 649–50 (Wright ed. 1960); Comment, 58 Colum.L.Rev. 532, 546 (1958); cf. N.Y.Civ.Prac.Act § 193–a; Me.R.Civ.P. 14. The amended subdivision preserves the value of a preliminary screening, through the leave procedure, of impleaders attempted after the 10-day period.

The amendment applies also when an impleader is initiated by a third-party defendant against a person who may be liable to him, as provided in the last sentence of the subdivision.

1966 AMENDMENT

Rule 14 was modeled on Admiralty Rule 56. An important feature of Admiralty Rule 56 was that it allowed impleader not only of a person who might be liable to the defendant by way of remedy over, but also of any person who might be liable to the plaintiff. The importance of this provision was that the defendant was entitled to insist that the plaintiff proceed to judgment against the third-party defendant. In certain cases this was a valuable implementation of a substantive right. For example, in a case of ship collision where a finding of mutual fault is possible, one shipowner, if sued alone, faces the prospect of an absolute judgment for the full amount of the damage suffered by an innocent third-party; but if he can implead the owner of the other vessel, and if mutual fault is found, the judgment against the original defendant will be in the first instance only for a moiety of the damages; liability for the remainder will be conditioned on the plaintiff's inability to collect from the third-party defendant.

This feature was originally incorporated in Rule 14, but was eliminated by the amendment of 1946, so that under the amended rule a third party could not be impleaded on the basis that he might be liable to the plaintiff. One of the reasons for the amendment was that the Civil Rule, unlike the Admiralty Rule, did not require the plaintiff to go to judgment against the third-party defendant. Another reason was that where jurisdiction depended on diversity of citizenship the impleader of an adversary having the same citizenship as the plaintiff was not considered possible.

Retention of the admiralty practice in those cases that will be counterparts of a suit in admiralty is clearly desirable.

1987 AMENDMENT

The amendments are technical. No substantive change is intended.

2000 AMENDMENT

Subdivisions (a) and (c) are amended to reflect revisions in Supplemental Rule C(6).

GAP Report

Rule B(1)(a) was modified by moving "in an in personam action" out of paragraph (a) and into the first line of subdivision (1). This change makes it clear that all paragraphs of subdivision (1) apply when attachment is sought in an in personam action. Rule B(1)(d) was modified by changing the requirement that the clerk deliver the summons and process to the person or organization authorized to serve it. The new form requires only that the summons and process be delivered, not that the clerk effect the delivery. This change conforms to present practice in some districts and will facilitate rapid service. It matches the spirit of Civil Rule 4(b), which directs the clerk to issue the summons "to the plaintiff for service on the defendant." A parallel change is made in Rule C(3)(b).

2006 AMENDMENT

Rule 14 is amended to conform to changes in designating the paragraphs of Supplemental Rule C(6).

2007 AMENDMENT

The language of Rule 14 has been amended as part of the general restyling of the Civil Rules to make them more easily understood and to make style and terminology consistent throughout the rules. These changes are intended to be stylistic only.

Former Rule 14 twice refers to counterclaims under Rule 13. In each case, the operation of Rule 13(a) depends on the state of the action at the time the pleading is filed. If plaintiff and third-party defendant have become opposing parties because one has made a claim for relief against the other, Rule 13(a) requires assertion of any counterclaim that grows out of the transaction or occurrence that is the subject matter of that claim. Rules 14(a)(2)(B) and (a)(3) reflect the distinction between compulsory and permissive counterclaims.

A plaintiff should be on equal footing with the defendant in making third-party claims, whether the claim against the plaintiff is asserted as a counterclaim or as another form of claim. The limit imposed by the former reference to "counterclaim" is deleted.

Rule 15. Amended and Supplemental Pleadings

1937 ADOPTION

See generally for the present federal practice, former Equity Rules 19 (Amendments Generally), 28 (Amendment of Bill as of Course), 32 (Answer to Amended Bill), 34 (Supplemental Pleading), and 35 (Bills of Revivor and Supplemental Bills—Form); U.S.C., Title 28, § 1653, formerly § 399 (Amendments to show diverse citizenship) and former § 777 (Defects of form; amendments). See English Rules Under the Judicature Act (The Annual Practice, 1937) O. 28, r. r. 1–13; O. 20, r. 4; O. 24, r. r. 1–3.

Note to Subdivision (a). The right to serve an amended pleading once as of course is common. 4 Mont.Rev.Codes Ann. (1935) § 9186; 1 Ore.Code Ann. (1930) § 1–904; 1 S.C.Code (Michie, 1932) § 493; English Rules Under the Judicature Act (The Annual Practice, 1937) O. 28, r. 2. Provision for amendment of pleading before trial, by leave of court, is in almost every code. If there is no statute the power of the court to grant leave is said to be inherent. Clark, Code Pleading, 1928, pp. 498, 509.

Note to Subdivision (b). Compare former Equity Rule 19 (Amendments Generally) and code provisions which allow an amendment "at any time in furtherance of justice," (e.g., Ark. Civ.Code (Crawford, 1934) § 155) and which allow an amendment of pleadings to conform to the evidence, where the adverse party has not been misled and prejudiced (e.g., N.M.Stat.Ann. (Courtright, 1929) §§ 105–601, 105–602).

Note to Subdivision (c). "Relation back" is a well recognized doctrine of recent and now more frequent application. Compare Ala.Code Ann. (Michie, 1928) § 9513; Smith-Hurd Ill.Stats. ch. 110, § 170(2); 2 Wash.Rev.Stat.Ann. (Remington, 1932) § 308–3(4). See U.S.C., Title 28, § 1653, formerly § 399 (Amendments to show diverse citizenship) for a provision for "relation back".

Note to Subdivision (d). This is an adaptation of former Equity Rule 34 (Supplemental Pleading).

1963 AMENDMENT

Rule 15(d) is intended to give the court broad discretion in allowing a supplemental pleading. However, some cases, opposed by other cases and criticized by the commentators, have taken the rigid and formalistic view that where the original complaint fails to state a claim upon which relief can be granted, leave to serve a supplemental complaint must be denied. See *Bonner* v. *Elizabeth Arden, Inc.,* 177 F.2d 703 (2d Cir.1949); *Bowles* v. *Senderowitz,* 65 F.Supp. 548 (E.D.Pa.), rev'd on other grounds, 158 F.2d 435 (3d Cir.1946), cert. denied, *Senderowitz* v. *Fleming,* 330 U.S. 848, 67 S.Ct. 1091, 91 L.Ed. 1292 (1947); cf. *La Salle Nat. Bank* v. *222 East Chestnut St. Corp.,* 267 F.2d 247 (7th Cir.), cert. denied, 361 U.S. 836, 80 S.Ct. 88, 4 L.Ed.2d 77 (1959). But see *Camilla Cotton Oil Co.* v.

Spencer Kellogg & Sons, 257 F.2d 162 (5th Cir.1958); *Genuth* v. *National Biscuit Co.,* 81 F.Supp. 213 (S.D.N.Y.1948), app. dism., 177 F.2d 962 (2d Cir.1949); 3 Moore's Federal Practice ¶ 15.01 [5] (Supp.1960); 1A Barron & Holtzoff, Federal Practice & Procedure 820–21 (Wright ed. 1960). Thus plaintiffs have sometimes been needlessly remitted to the difficulties of commencing a new action even though events occurring after the commencement of the original action have made clear the right to relief.

Under the amendment the court has discretion to permit a supplemental pleading despite the fact that the original pleading is defective. As in other situations where a supplemental pleading is offered, the court is to determine in the light of the particular circumstances whether filing should be permitted, and if so, upon what terms. The amendment does not attempt to deal with such questions as the relation of the statute of limitations to supplemental pleadings, the operation of the doctrine of laches, or the availability of other defenses. All these questions are for decision in accordance with the principles applicable to supplemental pleadings generally. Cf. *Blau* v. *Lamb,* 191 F.Supp. 906 (S.D.N.Y.1961); *Lendonsol Amusement Corp.* v. *B. & Q. Assoc., Inc.,* 23 F.R.Serv. 15d.3, Case 1 (D.Mass.1957).

1966 AMENDMENT

Rule 15(c) is amplified to state more clearly when an amendment of a pleading changing the party against whom a claim is asserted (including an amendment to correct a misnomer or misdescription of a defendant) shall "relate back" to the date of the original pleading.

The problem has arisen most acutely in certain actions by private parties against officers or agencies of the United States. Thus an individual denied social security benefits by the Secretary of Health, Education, and Welfare may secure review of the decision by bringing a civil action against that officer within sixty days. 42 U.S.C. § 405(g)(Supp. III, 1962). In several recent cases the claimants instituted timely action but mistakenly named as defendant the United States, the Department of HEW, the "Federal Security Administration" (a nonexistent agency), and a Secretary who had retired from the office nineteen days before. Discovering their mistakes, the claimants moved to amend their complaints to name the proper defendant; by this time the statutory sixty-day period had expired. The motions were denied on the ground that the amendment "would amount to the commencement of a new proceeding and would not relate back in time so as to avoid the statutory provision * * * that suit be brought within sixty days * * * " *Cohn* v. *Federal Security Adm.,* 199 F.Supp. 884, 885 (W.D.N.Y.1961); see also *Cunningham* v. *United States,* 199 F.Supp. 541 (W.D.Mo.1958); *Hall* v. *Department of HEW,* 199 F.Supp. 833 (S.D.Tex.1960); *Sandridge* v. *Folsom, Secretary of HEW,* 200 F.Supp. 25 (M.D.Tenn. 1959). [The Secretary of Health, Education, and Welfare has approved certain ameliorative regulations under 42 U.S.C. § 405(g). See 29 Fed.Reg. 8209 (June 30, 1964); Jacoby, The Effect of Recent Changes in the Law of "Nonstatutory" Judicial Review, 53 Geo.L.J. 19, 42–43 (1964); see also *Simmons* v. *United States Dept. HEW,* 328 F.2d 86 (3d Cir.1964).]

Analysis in terms of "new proceeding" is traceable to *Davis* v. *L. L. Cohen & Co.,* 268 U.S. 638, 45 S.Ct. 633, 69 L.Ed. 1129 (1925), and *Mellon* v. *Arkansas Land & Lumber Co.,* 275 U.S. 460, 48 S.Ct. 150, 72 L.Ed. 372 (1928), but those cases antedate the adoption of the Rules which import different criteria for determining when an amendment is to "relate back". As lower courts have continued to rely on the Davis and Mellon cases despite the contrary intent of the Rules, clarification of Rule 15(c) is considered advisable.

Relation back is intimately connected with the policy of the statute of limitations. The policy of the statute limiting the time for suit against the Secretary of HEW would not have been offended by allowing relation back in the situations described above. For the government was put on notice of the claim within the stated period—in the particular instances, by means of the initial delivery of process to a responsible government official (see Rule 4(d)(4) and (5)). In these circumstances, characterization of the amendment as a new proceeding is not responsive to the reality, but is merely question-begging; and to deny relation back is to defeat unjustly the claimant's opportunity to prove his case. See the full discussion by Byse, Suing the "Wrong" Defendant in Judicial Review of Federal Administrative Action: Proposals for Reform, 77 Harv.L.Rev. 40 (1963); see also Ill.Civ. P.Act § 46(4).

Much the same question arises in other types of actions against the government (see *Byse,* supra, at 45 n. 15). In actions between private parties, the problem of relation back of amendments changing defendants has generally been better handled by the courts, but incorrect criteria have sometimes been applied, leading sporadically to doubtful results. See 1A Barron & Holtzoff, Federal Practice & Procedure § 451 (Wright ed. 1960); 1 id. § 186 (1960); 2 id. § 543 (1961); 3 Moore's Federal Practice, par. 15.15 (Cum.Supp.1962);

Annot., Change in Party After Statute of Limitations Has Run, 8 A.L.R.2d 6 (1949). Rule 15(c) has been amplified to provide a general solution. An amendment changing the party against whom a claim is asserted relates back if the amendment satisfies the usual condition of Rule 15(c) of "arising out of the conduct * * * set forth * * * in the original pleading," and if, within the applicable limitations period, the party brought in by amendment, first, received such notice of the institution of the action—the notice need not be formal—that he would not be prejudiced in defending the action, and, second, knew or should have known that the action would have been brought against him initially had there not been a mistake concerning the identity of the proper party. Revised Rule 15(c) goes on to provide specifically in the government cases that the first and second requirements are satisfied when the government has been notified in the manner there described (see Rules 4(d)(4) and (5)). As applied to the government cases, revised Rule 15(c) further advances the objectives of the 1961 amendment of Rule 25(d)(substitution of public officers).

The relation back of amendments changing plaintiffs is not expressly treated in revised Rule 15(c) since the problem is generally easier. Again the chief consideration of policy is that of the statute of limitations, and the attitude taken in revised Rule 15(c) toward change of defendants extends by analogy to amendments changing plaintiffs. Also relevant is the amendment of Rule 17(a)(real party in interest). To avoid forfeitures of just claims, revised Rule 17(a) would provide that no action shall be dismissed on the ground that it is not prosecuted in the name of the real party in interest until a reasonable time has been allowed for correction of the defect in the manner there stated.

1987 AMENDMENT

The amendments are technical. No substantive change is intended.

1991 AMENDMENT

The rule has been revised to prevent parties against whom claims are made from taking unjust advantage of otherwise inconsequential pleading errors to sustain a limitations defense.

Paragraph (c)(1). This provision is new. It is intended to make it clear that the rule does not apply to preclude any relation back that may be permitted under the applicable limitations law. Generally, the applicable limitations law will be state law. If federal jurisdiction is based on the citizenship of the parties, the primary reference is the law of the state in which the district court sits. *Walker v. Armco Steel Corp.,* 446 U.S. 740, 100 S.Ct. 1978, 64 L.Ed.2d 659 (1980). If federal jurisdiction is based on a federal question, the reference may be to the law of the state governing relations between the parties. *E.g., Board of Regents v. Tomanio,* 446 U.S. 478, 100 S.Ct. 1790, 64 L.Ed.2d 440 (1980). In some circumstances, the controlling limitations law may be federal law. *E.g., West v. Conrail, Inc.,* 481 U.S. 35, 107 S.Ct. 1538, 95 L.Ed.2d 32 (1987). Cf. *Burlington Northern R. Co. v. Woods,* 480 U.S. 1, 107 S.Ct. 967, 94 L.Ed.2d 1 (1987); *Stewart Organization v. Ricoh,* 487 U.S. 22, 108 S.Ct. 2239, 101 L.Ed.2d 22 (1988). Whatever may be the controlling body of limitations law, if that law affords a more forgiving principle of relation back than the one provided in this rule, it should be available to save the claim. Accord, *Marshall v. Mulrenin,* 508 F.2d 39 (1st Cir.1974). If *Schiavone v. Fortune,* 477 U.S. 21, 106 S.Ct. 2379, 91 L.Ed.2d 18 (1986) implies the contrary, this paragraph is intended to make a material change in the rule.

Paragraph (c)(3). This paragraph has been revised to change the result in *Schiavone v. Fortune, supra,* with respect to the problem of a misnamed defendant. An intended defendant who is notified of an action within the period allowed by Rule 4(m) for service of a summons and complaint may not under the revised rule defeat the action on account of a defect in the pleading with respect to the defendant's name, provided that the requirements of clauses (A) and (B) have been met. If the notice requirement is met within the Rule 4(m) period, a complaint may be amended at any time to correct a formal defect such as a misnomer or misidentification. On the basis of the text of the former rule, the Court reached a result in *Schiavone v. Fortune* that was inconsistent with the liberal pleading practices secured by Rule 8. See Bauer, Schiavone: *An Un-Fortune-ate Illustration of the Supreme Court's Role as Interpreter of the Federal Rules of Civil Procedure,* 63 NOTRE DAME L.REV. 720 (1988); Brussack, *Outrageous Fortune: The Case for Amending Rule 15(c) Again,* 61 S.CAL.L.REV. 671 (1988); Lewis, *The Excessive History of Federal Rule 15(c) and Its Lessons for Civil Rules Revision,* 86 MICH.L.REV. 1507 (1987).

In allowing a name-correcting amendment within the time allowed by Rule 4(m) [subdivision (m) in Rule 4 was a proposed subdivision which was withdrawn by the Supreme Court], this rule allows not only the 120 days specified in that rule, but also any additional time resulting from any extension ordered by the court pursuant to that rule, as may be granted, for example, if the defendant is a fugitive from service of the summons.

This revision, together with the revision of Rule 4(i) [revision to subdivision (i) in Rule 4 was a proposed revision which was withdrawn by the Supreme Court] with respect to the failure of a plaintiff in an action against the United States to effect timely service on all the appropriate officials, is intended to produce results contrary to those reached in *Gardner v. Gartman,* 880 F.2d 797 (4th Cir.1989), *Rys v. U.S. Postal Service,* 886 F.2d 443 (1st Cir.1989), *Martin's Food & Liquor, Inc. v. U.S. Dept. of Agriculture,* 14 F.R.S.3d 86 (N.D.Ill.1988). *But cf. Montgomery v. United States Postal Service,* 867 F.2d 900 (5th Cir.1989), *Warren v. Department of the Army,* 867 F.2d 1156 (8th Cir.1989); *Miles v. Department of the Army,* 881 F.2d 777 (9th Cir.1989), *Barsten v. Department of the Interior,* 896 F.2d 422 (9th Cir.1990); *Brown v. Georgia Dept. of Revenue,* 881 F.2d 1018 (11th Cir.1989).

1993 AMENDMENT

The amendment conforms the cross reference to Rule 4 to the revision of that rule.

2007 AMENDMENT

The language of Rule 15 has been amended as part of the general restyling of the Civil Rules to make them more easily understood and to make style and terminology consistent throughout the rules. These changes are intended to be stylistic only.

Former Rule 15(c)(3)(A) called for notice of the "institution" of the action. Rule 15(c)(1)(C)(i) omits the reference to "institution" as potentially confusing. What counts is that the party to be brought in have notice of the existence of the action, whether or not the notice includes details as to its "institution."

Rule 16.   Pretrial Conferences; Scheduling; Management

1937 ADOPTION

1.   Similar rules of pre-trial procedure are now in force in Boston, Cleveland, Detroit, and Los Angeles, and a rule substantially like this one has been proposed for the urban centers of New York state.   For a discussion of the successful operation of pre-trial procedure in relieving the congested condition of trial calendars of the courts in such cities and for the proposed New York plan, see A Proposal for Minimizing Calendar Delay in Jury Cases (Dec. 1936—published by the New York Law Society); Pre-Trial Procedure and Administration, Third Annual Report of the Judicial Council of the State of New York (1937), pages 207–243; Report of the Commission on the Administration of Justice in New York State (1934), pp. (288)–(290).   See also Pre-trial Procedure in the Wayne Circuit Court, Detroit, Michigan, Sixth Annual Report of the Judicial Council of Michigan (1936), pp. 63–75; and Sunderland, The Theory and Practice of Pre-trial Procedure (Dec. 1937) 36 Mich.L.Rev. 215–226, 21 J.Am.Jud.Soc. 125.   Compare the English procedure known as the "summons for directions," English Rules Under the Judicature Act (The Annual Practice, 1937) O. 38a; and a similar procedure in New Jersey, N.J.S.A. 2:27–135, 2:27–136, 2:27–160; N.J. Supreme Court Rules, 2 N.J.Misc.Rep. (1924) 1230, Rules 94, 92, 93, 95 (the last three as amended 1933, 11 N.J.Misc.Rep. (1933) 955, N.J.S.A. Tit. 2).

2.   Compare the similar procedure under Rule 56(d)(Summary Judgment—Case Not Fully Adjudicated on Motion).   Rule 12(g)(Consolidation of Motions), by requiring to some extent the consolidation of motions dealing with matters preliminary to trial, is a step in the same direction.   In connection with clause (5) of this rule, see Rules 53(b)(Masters; Reference) and 53(e)(3)(Master's Report: In Jury Actions).

1983 AMENDMENT

Introduction

Rule 16 has not been amended since the Federal Rules were promulgated in 1938.   In many respects, the rule has been a success.   For example, there is evidence that pretrial conferences may improve the quality of justice rendered in the federal courts by sharpening the preparation and presentation of cases, tending to eliminate trial surprise, and improving, as well as facilitating, the settlement process.   See 6 Wright & Miller, *Federal Practice and Procedure: Civil* § 1522 (1971).   However, in other respects particularly with regard to case management, the rule has not always been as helpful as it might have been.   Thus there has been a widespread feeling that amendment is necessary to encourage pretrial management that meets the needs of modern litigation.   See *Report of the National Commission for the Review of Antitrust Laws and Procedures* (1979).

Major criticism of Rule 16 has centered on the fact that its application can result in over-regulation of some cases and under-regulation of others. In simple, run-of-the-mill cases, attorneys have found pretrial requirements burdensome. It is claimed that over-administration leads to a series of mini-trials that result in a waste of an attorney's time and needless expense to a client. Pollack, *Pretrial Procedures More Effectively Handled*, 65 F.R.D. 475 (1974). This is especially likely to be true when pretrial proceedings occur long before trial. At the other end of the spectrum, the discretionary character of Rule 16 and its orientation toward a single conference late in the pretrial process has led to under-administration of complex or protracted cases. Without judicial guidance beginning shortly after institution, these cases often become mired in discovery.

Four sources of criticism of pretrial have been identified. First, conferences often are seen as a mere exchange of legalistic contentions without any real analysis of the particular case. Second, the result frequently is nothing but a formal agreement on minutiae. Third, the conferences are seen as unnecessary and time-consuming in cases that will be settled before trial. Fourth, the meetings can be ceremonial and ritualistic, having little effect on the trial and being of minimal value, particularly when the attorneys attending the sessions are not the ones who will try the case or lack authority to enter into binding stipulations. See generally *McCargo v. Hedrick*, 545 F.2d 393 (4th Cir.1976); Pollack, *Pretrial Procedures More Effectively Handled*, 65 F.R.D. 475 (1974); Rosenberg, *The Pretrial Conference and Effective Justice* 45 (1964).

There also have been difficulties with the pretrial orders that issue following Rule 16 conferences. When an order is entered far in advance of trial, some issues may not be properly formulated. Counsel naturally are cautious and often try to preserve as many options as possible. If the judge who tries the case did not conduct the conference, he could find it difficult to determine exactly what was agreed to at the conference. But any insistence on a detailed order may be too burdensome, depending on the nature or posture of the case.

Given the significant changes in federal civil litigation since 1938 that are not reflected in Rule 16, it has been extensively rewritten and expanded to meet the challenges of modern litigation. Empirical studies reveal that when a trial judge intervenes personally at an early stage to assume judicial control over a case and to schedule dates for completion by the parties of the principal pretrial steps, the case is disposed of by settlement or trial more efficiently and with less cost and delay than when the parties are left to their own devices. Flanders, *Case Management and Court Management in United States District Courts* 17, Federal Judicial Center (1977). Thus, the rule mandates a pretrial scheduling order. However, although scheduling and pretrial conferences are encouraged in appropriate cases, they are not mandated.

Discussion

Subdivision (a); Pretrial Conferences; Objectives. The amended rule makes scheduling and case management an express goal of pretrial procedure. This is done in Rule 16(a) by shifting the emphasis away from a conference focused solely on the trial and toward a process of judicial management that embraces the entire pretrial phase, especially motions and discovery. In addition, the amendment explicitly recognizes some of the objectives of pretrial conferences and the powers that many courts already have assumed. Rule 16 thus will be a more accurate reflection of actual practice.

Subdivision (b); Scheduling and Planning. The most significant change in Rule 16 is the mandatory scheduling order described in Rule 16(b), which is based in part on Wisconsin Civil Procedure Rule 802.10. The idea of scheduling orders is not new. It has been used by many federal courts. See, *e.g.*, Southern District of Indiana, Local Rule 19.

Although a mandatory scheduling order encourages the court to become involved in case management early in the litigation, it represents a degree of judicial involvement that is not warranted in many cases. Thus, subdivision (b) permits each district court to promulgate a local rule under Rule 83 exempting certain categories of cases in which the burdens of scheduling orders exceed the administrative efficiencies that would be gained. See Eastern District of Virginia, Local Rule 12(1). Logical candidates for this treatment include social security disability matters, habeas corpus petitions, forfeitures, and reviews of certain administrative actions.

A scheduling conference may be requested either by the judge, a magistrate when authorized by district court rule, or a party within 120 days after the summons and complaint are filed. If a scheduling conference is not arranged within that time and the case is not exempted by local rule, a scheduling order must be issued under Rule 16(b), after some communication with the parties, which may be by telephone or mail rather than in person. The use of the term "judge" in subdivision (b) reflects the Advisory Committee's judgment that it is preferable that this task should be handled by a district judge rather than a magistrate, except when the magistrate is acting under 28 U.S.C. § 636(c). While personal supervision by the trial judge is preferred, the rule, in recognition of the impracticality or difficulty of complying with such a requirement in some districts, authorizes a district by local rule to delegate the duties to a magistrate. In order to formulate a practicable scheduling order, the judge, or a magistrate when authorized by district court rule, and attorneys are required to develop a timetable for the matters listed in Rule 16(b)(1)–(3). As indicated in Rule 16(b)(4)–(5), the order may also deal with a wide range of other matters. The rule is phrased permissively as to clauses (4) and (5), however, because scheduling these items at an early point may not be feasible or appropriate. Even though subdivision (b) relates only to scheduling, there is no reason why some of the procedural matters listed in Rule 16(c) cannot be addressed at the same time, at least when a scheduling conference is held.

Item (1) assures that at some point both the parties and the pleadings will be fixed, by setting a time within which joinder of parties shall be completed and the pleadings amended.

Item (2) requires setting time limits for interposing various motions that otherwise might be used as stalling techniques.

Item (3) deals with the problem of procrastination and delay by attorneys in a context in which scheduling is especially important—discovery. Scheduling the completion of discovery can serve some of the same functions as the conference described in Rule 26(f).

Item (4) refers to setting dates for conferences and for trial. Scheduling multiple pretrial conferences may well be desirable if the case is complex and the court believes that a more elaborate pretrial structure, such as that described in the *Manual for Complex Litigation,* should be employed. On the other hand, only one pretrial conference may be necessary in an uncomplicated case.

As long as the case is not exempted by local rule, the court must issue a written scheduling order even if no scheduling conference is called. The order, like pretrial orders under the former rule and those under new Rule 16(c), normally will "control the subsequent course of the action." See Rule 16(e). After consultation with the attorneys for the parties and any unrepresented parties—a formal motion is not necessary—the court may modify the schedule on a showing of good cause if it cannot reasonably be met despite the diligence of the party seeking the extension. Since the scheduling order is entered early in the litigation, this standard seems more appropriate than a "manifest injustice" or "substantial hardship" test. Otherwise, a fear that extensions will not be granted may encourage counsel to request the longest possible periods for completing pleading, joinder, and discovery. Moreover, changes in the court's calendar sometimes will oblige the judge or magistrate when authorized by district court rule to modify the scheduling order.

The district courts undoubtedly will develop several prototype scheduling orders for different types of cases. In addition, when no formal conference is held, the court may obtain scheduling information by telephone, mail, or otherwise. In many instances this will result in a scheduling order better suited to the individual case than a standard order, without taking the time that would be required by a formal conference.

Rule 16(b) assures that the judge will take some early control over the litigation, even when its character does not warrant holding a scheduling conference. Despite the fact that the process of preparing a scheduling order does not always bring the attorneys and judge together, the fixing of time limits serves

> to stimulate litigants to narrow the areas of inquiry and advocacy to those they believe are truly relevant and material. Time limits not only compress the amount of time for litigation, they should also reduce the amount of resources invested in litigation. Litigants are forced to establish discovery priorities and thus to do the most important work first.

Report of the National Commission for the Review of Antitrust Laws and Procedures 28 (1979).

Thus, except in exempted cases, the judge or a magistrate when authorized by district court rule will have taken some action in every case within 120 days after the complaint is filed that notifies the attorneys that the case will be moving toward trial. Subdivision (b) is reenforced by subdivision (f), which makes it clear that the sanctions for violating a scheduling order are the same as those for violating a pretrial order.

Subdivision (c); Subjects to be Discussed at Pretrial Conferences. This subdivision expands upon the list of things that may be discussed at a pretrial conference that appeared in original Rule 16. The intention is to encourage better planning and management of litigation. Increased judicial control during the pretrial process accelerates the processing and termination of cases. Flanders, *Case Management and Court Management in United States District Courts,* Federal Judicial Center (1977). See also *Report of the National Commission for the Review of Antitrust Laws and Procedures* (1979).

The reference in Rule 16(c)(1) to "formulation" is intended to clarify and confirm the court's power to identify the litigable issues. It has been added in the hope of promoting efficiency and conserving judicial resources by identifying the real issues prior to trial, thereby saving time and expense for everyone. See generally *Meadow Gold Prods. Co. v. Wright,* 278 F.2d 867 (D.C.Cir.1960). The notion is emphasized by expressly authorizing the elimination of frivolous claims or defenses at a pretrial conference. There is no reason to require that this await a formal motion for summary judgment. Nor is there any reason for the court to wait for the parties to initiate the process called for in Rule 16(c)(1).

The timing of any attempt at issue formulation is a matter of judicial discretion. In relatively simple cases it may not be necessary or may take the form of a stipulation between counsel or a request by the court that counsel work together to draft a proposed order.

Counsel bear a substantial responsibility for assisting the court in identifying the factual issues worthy of trial. If counsel fail to identify an issue for the court, the right to have the issue tried is waived. Although an order specifying the issues is intended to be binding, it may be amended at trial to avoid manifest injustice. See Rule 16(e). However, the rule's effectiveness depends on the court employing its discretion sparingly.

Clause (6) acknowledges the widespread availability and use of magistrates. The corresponding provision in the original rule referred only to masters and limited the function of the reference to the making of "findings to be used as evidence" in a case to be tried to a jury. The new text is not limited and broadens the potential use of a magistrate to that permitted by the Magistrate's Act.

Clause (7) explicitly recognizes that it has become commonplace to discuss settlement at pretrial conferences. Since it obviously eases crowded court dockets and results in savings to the litigants and the judicial system, settlement should be facilitated at as early a stage of the litigation as possible. Although it is not the purpose of Rule 16(b)(7) to impose settlement negotiations on unwilling litigants, it is believed that providing a neutral forum for discussing the subject might foster it. See Moore's *Federal Practice* ¶ 16.17; 6 Wright & Miller, *Federal Practice and Procedure: Civil* § 1522 (1971). For instance, a judge to whom a case has been assigned may arrange, on his own motion or at a party's request, to have settlement conferences handled by another member of the court or by a magistrate. The rule does not make settlement conferences mandatory because they would be a waste of time in many cases. See Flanders, *Case Management and Court Management in the United States District Courts,* 39, Federal Judicial Center (1977). Requests for a conference from a party indicating a willingness to talk settlement normally should be honored, unless thought to be frivolous or dilatory.

A settlement conference is appropriate at any time. It may be held in conjunction with a pretrial or discovery conference, although various objectives of pretrial management, such as moving the case toward trial, may not always be compatible with settlement negotiations, and thus a separate settlement conference may be desirable. See 6 Wright & Miller, *Federal Practice and Procedure: Civil* § 1522, at p. 571 (1971).

In addition to settlement, Rule 16(c)(7) refers to exploring the use of procedures other than litigation to resolve the dispute. This includes urging the litigants to employ adjudicatory techniques outside the courthouse. See, for example, the experiment described in Green, Marks & Olson, *Settling Large Case Litigation: An Alternative Approach,* 11 Loyola of L.A. L.Rev. 493 (1978).

Rule 16(c)(10) authorizes the use of special pretrial procedures to expedite the adjudication of potentially difficult or protracted cases. Some district courts obviously have done so for many years. See Rubin, *The Managed Calendar: Some Pragmatic Suggestions About Achieving the Just, Speedy and Inexpensive Determination of Civil Cases in Federal Courts,* 4 Just. Sys. J. 135 (1976). Clause 10 provides an explicit authorization for such procedures and encourages their use. No particular techniques have been described; the Committee felt that flexibility and experience are the keys to efficient management of complex cases. Extensive guidance is offered in such documents as the *Manual for Complex Litigation.*

The rule simply identifies characteristics that make a case a strong candidate for special treatment. The four mentioned are illustrative, not exhaustive, and overlap to some degree. But experience has shown that one or more of them will be present in every protracted or difficult case and it seems desirable to set them out. See Kendig, *Procedures for Management of Non-Routine Cases,* 3 Hofstra L.Rev. 701 (1975).

The last sentence of subdivision (c) is new. See Wisconsin Civil Procedure Rule 802.11(2). It has been added to meet one of the criticisms of the present practice described earlier and insure proper preconference preparation so that the meeting is more than a ceremonial or ritualistic event. The reference to "authority" is not intended to insist upon the ability to settle the litigation. Nor should the rule be read to encourage the judge conducting the conference to compel attorneys to enter into stipulations or to make admissions that they consider to be unreasonable, that touch on matters that could not normally have been anticipated to arise at the conference, or on subjects of a dimension that normally require prior consultation with and approval from the client.

Subdivision (d); Final Pretrial Conference. This provision has been added to make it clear that the time between any final pretrial conference (which in a simple case may be the only pretrial conference) and trial should be as short as possible to be certain that the litigants make substantial progress with the case and avoid the inefficiency of having that preparation repeated when there is a delay between the last pretrial conference and trial. An optimum time of 10 days to two weeks has been suggested by one federal judge. Rubin, *The Managed Calendar: Some Pragmatic Suggestions About Achieving the Just, Speedy and Inexpensive Determination of Civil Cases in Federal Courts,* 4 Just. Sys. J. 135, 141 (1976). The Committee, however, concluded that it would be inappropriate to fix a precise time in the rule, given the numerous variables that could bear on the matter. Thus the timing has been left to the court's discretion.

At least one of the attorneys who will conduct the trial for each party must be present at the final pretrial conference. At this late date there should be no doubt as to which attorney or attorneys this will be. Since the agreements and stipulations made at this final conference will control the trial, the presence of lawyers who will be involved in it is especially useful to assist the judge in structuring the case, and to lead to a more effective trial.

Subdivision (e); Pretrial Orders. Rule 16(e) does not substantially change the portion of the original rule dealing with pretrial orders. The purpose of an order is to guide the course of the litigation and the language of the original rule making that clear has been retained. No compelling reason has been found for major revision, especially since this portion of the rule has been interpreted and clarified by over forty years of judicial decisions with comparatively little difficulty. See 6 Wright & Miller, *Federal Practice and Procedure: Civil* §§ 1521–30 (1971). Changes in language therefore have been kept to a minimum to avoid confusion.

Since the amended rule encourages more extensive pretrial management than did the original, two or more conferences may be held in many cases. The language of Rule 16(e) recognizes this possibility and the corresponding need to issue more than one pretrial order in a single case.

Once formulated, pretrial orders should not be changed lightly; but total inflexibility is undesirable. See, *e.g., Clark v. Pennsylvania R.R. Co.,* 328 F.2d 591 (2d Cir.1964). The exact words used to describe the standard for amending the pretrial order probably are less important than the meaning given them in practice. By not imposing any limitation on the ability to modify a pretrial order, the rule reflects the reality that in any process of continuous management what is done at one conference may have to be altered at the next. In the case of the final pretrial order, however, a more stringent standard is called for and the words "to prevent manifest injustice," which appeared in the original rule, have been retained. They have the virtue of familiarity and adequately describe the restraint the trial judge should exercise.

Many local rules make the plaintiff's attorney responsible for drafting a proposed pretrial order, either before or after the conference. Others allow the court to appoint any of the attorneys to perform the task, and others leave it to the court. See Note, *Pretrial Conference: A Critical Examination of Local Rules Adopted by Federal District Courts,* 64 Va.L.Rev. 467 (1978). Rule 16 has never addressed this matter. Since there is no consensus about which method of drafting the order works best and there is no reason to believe that nationwide uniformity is needed, the rule has been left silent on the point. See *Handbook for Effective Pretrial Procedure,* 37 F.R.D. 225 (1964).

Subdivision (f); Sanctions. Original Rule 16 did not mention the sanctions that might be imposed for failing to comply with the rule. However, courts have not hesitated to enforce it by appropriate measures. See, *e.g., Link v. Wabash R. Co.,* 370 U.S. 626 (1962)(district court's dismissal under Rule 41(b) after plaintiff's attorney failed to appear at a pretrial conference upheld); *Admiral Theatre Corp. v. Douglas Theatre,* 585 F.2d 877 (8th Cir.1978)(district court has discretion to exclude exhibits or refuse to permit the testimony of a witness not listed prior to trial in contravention of its pretrial order).

To reflect that existing practice, and to obviate dependence upon Rule 41(b) or the court's inherent power to regulate litigation, *cf. Societe Internationale Pour Participations Industrielles et Commerciales, S.A. v. Rogers,* 357 U.S. 197, 78 S.Ct. 1087, 2 L.Ed.2d 1255 (1958), Rule 16(f) expressly provides for imposing sanctions on disobedient or recalcitrant parties, their attorneys, or both in four types of situations. Rodes, Ripple & Mooney, *Sanctions Imposable for Violations of the Federal Rules of Civil Procedure* 65–67, 80–84, Federal Judicial Center (1981). Furthermore, explicit reference to sanctions reenforces the rule's intention to encourage forceful judicial management.

Rule 16(f) incorporates portions of Rule 37(b)(2), which prescribes sanctions for failing to make discovery. This should facilitate application of Rule 16(f), since courts and lawyers already are familiar with the Rule 37 standards. Among the sanctions authorized by the new subdivision are: preclusion order, striking a pleading, staying the proceeding, default judgment, contempt, and charging a party, his attorney, or both with the expenses, including attorney's fees, caused by noncompliance. The contempt sanction, however, is only available for a violation of a court order. The references in Rule 16(f) are not exhaustive.

As is true under Rule 37(b)(2), the imposition of sanctions may be sought by either the court or a party. In addition, the court has discretion to impose whichever sanction it feels is appropriate under the circumstances. Its action is reviewable under the abuse-of-discretion standard. See *National Hockey League v. Metropolitan Hockey Club, Inc.,* 427 U.S. 639, 96 S.Ct. 2778, 49 L.Ed.2d 747 (1976).

1987 AMENDMENT

The amendments are technical. No substantive change is intended.

1993 AMENDMENT

Subdivision (b). One purpose of this amendment is to provide a more appropriate deadline for the initial scheduling order required by the rule. The former rule directed that the order be entered within 120 days from the filing of the complaint. This requirement has created problems because Rule 4(m) allows 120 days for service and ordinarily at least one defendant should be available to participate in the process of formulating the scheduling order. The revision provides that the order is to be entered within 90 days after the date a defendant first appears (whether by answer or by a motion under Rule 12) or, if earlier (as may occur in some actions against the United States or if service is waived under Rule 4), within 120 days after service of the complaint on a defendant. The longer time provided by the revision is not intended to encourage unnecessary delays in entering the scheduling order. Indeed, in most cases the order can and should be entered at a much earlier date. Rather, the additional time is intended to alleviate problems in multi-defendant cases and should ordinarily be adequate to enable participation by all defendants initially named in the action.

In many cases the scheduling order can and should be entered before this deadline. However, when setting a scheduling conference, the court should take into account the effect this setting will have in establishing deadlines for the parties to meet under revised Rule 26(f) and to exchange information under revised Rule 26(a)(1). While the parties are expected to stipulate to additional time for making their disclosures when warranted by the circumstances, a scheduling conference held before defendants have had time to learn much about the case may result in diminishing the value of the Rule 26(f) meeting, the parties' proposed discovery plan, and indeed the conference itself.

New paragraph (4) has been added to highlight that it will frequently be desirable for the scheduling order to include provisions relating to the timing of disclosures under Rule 26(a). While the initial disclosures required by Rule 26(a)(1) will ordinarily have been made before entry of the scheduling order, the timing and sequence for disclosure of expert testimony and of the witnesses and exhibits to be used at trial should be tailored to the circumstances of the case and is a matter that should be considered at the initial scheduling conference. Similarly, the scheduling order might contain provisions modifying the extent of discovery (*e.g.,* number and length of depositions) otherwise permitted under these rules or by a local rule.

The report from the attorneys concerning their meeting and proposed discovery plan, as required by revised Rule 26(f), should be submitted to the court before the scheduling order is entered. Their proposals, particularly regarding matters on which they agree, should be of substantial value to the court in setting the timing and limitations on discovery and should reduce the time of the court needed to conduct a meaningful conference under Rule 16(b). As under the prior rule, while a scheduling order is mandated, a scheduling conference is not. However, in view of the benefits to be derived from the litigants and a judicial officer meeting in person, a Rule 16(b) conference should, to the extent practicable, be held in all cases that will involve discovery.

This subdivision, as well as subdivision (c)(8), also is revised to reflect the new title of United States Magistrate Judges pursuant to the Judicial Improvements Act of 1990.

Subdivision (c). The primary purposes of the changes in subdivision (c) are to call attention to the opportunities for structuring of trial under Rules 42, 50, and 52 and to eliminate questions that have occasionally been raised regarding the authority of the court to make appropriate orders designed either to facilitate settlement or to provide for an efficient and economical trial. The prefatory language of this subdivision is revised to clarify the court's power to enter appropriate orders at a conference notwithstanding the objection of a party. Of course settlement is dependent upon agreement by the parties and, indeed, a conference is most effective and productive when the parties participate in a spirit of cooperation and mindful of their responsibilities under Rule 1.

Paragraph (4) is revised to clarify that in advance of trial the court may address the need for, and possible limitations on, the use of expert testimony under Rule 702 of the Federal Rules of Evidence. Even when proposed expert testimony might be admissible under the standards of Rules 403 and 702 of the evidence rules, the court may preclude or limit such testimony if the cost to the litigants—which may include the cost to adversaries of securing testimony on the same subjects by other experts—would be unduly expensive given the needs of the case and the other evidence available at trial.

Paragraph (5) is added (and the remaining paragraphs renumbered) in recognition that use of Rule 56 to avoid or reduce the scope of trial is a topic that can, and often should, be considered at a pretrial conference. Renumbered paragraph (11) enables the court to rule on pending motions for summary adjudication that are ripe for decision at the time of the conference. Often, however, the potential use of Rule 56 is a matter that arises from discussions during a conference. The court may then call for motions to be filed.

Paragraph (6) is added to emphasize that a major objective of pretrial conferences should be to consider appropriate controls on the extent and timing of discovery. In many cases the court should also specify the times and sequence for disclosure of written reports from experts under revised Rule 26(a)(2)(B) and perhaps direct changes in the types of experts from whom written reports are required. Consideration should also be given to possible changes in the timing or form of the disclosure of trial witnesses and documents under Rule 26(a)(3).

Paragraph (9) is revised to describe more accurately the various procedures that, in addition to traditional settlement conferences, may be helpful in settling litigation. Even if a case cannot immediately be settled, the judge and attorneys can explore possible use of alternative procedures such as mini-trials, summary jury trials, mediation, neutral evaluation, and nonbinding arbitration that can lead to consensual resolution of the dispute without a full trial on the merits. The rule acknowledges the presence of statutes and local rules or plans that may authorize use of some of these procedures even when not agreed to by the parties. See 28 U.S.C. §§ 473(a)(6), 473(b)(4), 651–58; Section 104(b)(2), Pub.L. 101–650. The rule does not attempt to resolve questions as to the extent a court would be authorized to require such proceedings as an exercise of its inherent powers.

The amendment of paragraph (9) should be read in conjunction with the sentence added to the end of subdivision (c), authorizing the court to direct that, in appropriate cases, a responsible representative of the parties be present or available by telephone during a conference in order to discuss possible settlement of the case. The sentence refers to participation by a party or its representative. Whether this would be the individual party, an officer of a corporate party, a representative from an insurance carrier, or someone else would depend on the circumstances. Particularly in litigation in which governmental agencies or large amounts of money are involved, there may be no one with on-the-spot settlement authority, and the most that should be expected is access to a person who would have a major role in submitting a recommendation to the body or board with ultimate decision-making responsibility. The selection of the appropriate representative should ordinarily be left to the party and its counsel. Finally, it should be noted that the unwillingness of a party to be available, even by telephone, for a settlement conference may be a clear signal that the time and expense involved in pursuing settlement is likely to be unproductive and that personal participation by the parties should not be required.

The explicit authorization in the rule to require personal participation in the manner stated is not intended to limit the reasonable exercise of the court's inherent powers, *e.g.*, *G. Heileman Brewing Co. v. Joseph Oat Corp.*, 871 F.2d 648 (7th Cir.1989), or its power to require party participation under the Civil Justice Reform Act of 1990. See 28 U.S.C. § 473(b)(5)(civil justice expense and delay reduction plans adopted by district courts may include requirement that representatives "with authority to bind [parties] in settlement discussions" be available during settlement conferences).

New paragraphs (13) and (14) are added to call attention to the opportunities for structuring of trial under Rule 42 and under revised Rules 50 and 52.

Paragraph (15) is also new. It supplements the power of the court to limit the extent of evidence under Rules 403 and 611(a) of the Federal Rules of Evidence, which typically would be invoked as a result of developments during trial. Limits on the length of trial established at a conference in advance of trial can provide the parties with a better opportunity to determine priorities and exercise selectivity in presenting evidence than when limits are imposed during trial. Any such limits must be reasonable under the circumstances, and ordinarily the court should impose them only after receiving appropriate submissions from the parties outlining the nature of the testimony expected to be presented through various witnesses, and the expected duration of direct and cross-examination.

2006 AMENDMENT

The amendment to Rule 16(b) is designed to alert the court to the possible need to address the handling of discovery of electronically stored information early in the litigation if such discovery is expected to occur. Rule 26(f) is amended to direct the parties to discuss discovery of electronically stored information if such discovery is contemplated in the action. Form 35 is amended to call for a report to the court about the results of this discussion. In many instances, the court's involvement early in the litigation will help avoid difficulties that might otherwise arise.

Rule 16(b) is also amended to include among the topics that may be addressed in the scheduling order any agreements that the parties reach to facilitate discovery by minimizing the risk of waiver of privilege or work-product protection. Rule 26(f) is amended to add to the discovery plan the parties' proposal for the court to enter a case-management or other order adopting such an agreement. The parties may agree to various arrangements. For example, they may agree to initial provision of requested materials without waiver of privilege or protection to enable the party seeking production to designate the materials desired or protection for actual production, with the privilege review of only those materials to follow. Alternatively, they may agree that if privileged or protected information is inadvertently produced, the producing party may by timely notice assert the privilege or protection and obtain return of the materials without waiver. Other arrangements are possible. In most circumstances, a party who receives information under such an arrangement cannot assert that production of the information waived a claim of privilege or of protection as trial-preparation material.

An order that includes the parties' agreement may be helpful in avoiding delay and excessive cost in discovery. *See Manual for Complex Litigation* (4th) § 11.446. Rule 16(b)(6) recognizes the propriety of including such agreements in the court's order. The rule does not provide the court with authority to enter such a case-management or other order without party agreement, or limit the court's authority to act on motion.

2007 AMENDMENT

The language of Rule 16 has been amended as part of the general restyling of the Civil Rules to make them more easily understood and to make style and terminology consistent throughout the rules. These changes are intended to be stylistic only.

When a party or its representative is not present, it is enough to be reasonably available by any suitable means, whether telephone or other communication device.

HISTORICAL NOTES

Change of Name

Reference to United States magistrate or to magistrate deemed to refer to United States magistrate judge pursuant to section 321 of Pub.L. 101–650, set out as a note under section 631 of this title.

IV. PARTIES

Rule 17.   Parties Plaintiff and Defendant; Capacity

1937 ADOPTION

Note to Subdivision (a). The real party in interest provision, except for the last clause which is new, is taken verbatim from former Equity Rule 37 (Parties Generally—

Intervention), except that the word "expressly" has been omitted. For similar provisions see N.Y.C.P.A., 1937, § 210; Wyo.Rev.Stat.Ann., 1931, §§ 89–501, 89–502, 89–503; English Rules Under the Judicature Act (The Annual Practice, 1937) O. 16, r. 8. See, also former Equity Rule 41 (Suit to Execute Trusts of Will—Heir as Party). For examples of statutes of the United States providing particularly for an action for the use or benefit of another in the name of the United States, see U.S.C., Title 40, § 270b (Suit by persons furnishing labor and material for work on public building contracts * * * may sue on a payment bond, "in the name of the United States for the use of the person suing"); and U.S.C., Title 25, § 201 (Penalties under laws relating to Indians—how recovered). Compare U.S.C., Title 26, Int.Rev.Code [1939], § 3745(c)(Suits for penalties, fines, and forfeitures, under this title, where not otherwise provided for, to be in name of United States).

Note to Subdivision (b). For capacity see generally Clark and Moore, A New Federal Civil Procedure—II. Pleadings and Parties, 44 Yale L.J. 1291, 1312–1317, 1935, and specifically *Coppedge* v. *Clinton*, C.C.A.10, 1934, 72 F.2d 531 (natural person); *David Lupton's Sons Co.* v. *Automobile Club of America*, 1912, 32 S.Ct. 711, 225 U.S. 489, 56 L.Ed. 1177, , Ann.Cas.1914A, 699 (corporation); *Puerto Rico* v. *Russell & Co.*, 1933, 288 U.S. 476, 53 S.Ct. 447, 77 L.Ed. 903, (unincorporated assn.); *United Mine Workers of America* v. *Coronado Coal Co.*, 1922, 42 assn. S.Ct. 570, 259 U.S. 344, 42 S.Ct. 570, 66 L.Ed. 975, 27 A.L.R. 762 (federal substantive right enforced against unincorporated association by suit against the association in its common name without naming all its members as parties). This rule follows the existing law as to such associations, as declared in the case last cited above. Compare *Moffat Tunnel League* v. *United States*, 289 U.S. 113, 53 S.Ct. 543, 77 L.Ed. 1069 (1933). See note to Rule 23, clause (1).

Note to Subdivision (c). The provision for infants and incompetent persons is substantially former Equity Rule 70 (Suits by or Against Incompetents) with slight additions. Compare the more detailed English provisions, English Rules Under the Judicature Act (The Annual Practice, 1937) O. 16, r. r. 16–21.

1946 AMENDMENT

Note. The new matter [in subdivision (b)] makes clear the controlling character of Rule 66 regarding suits by or against a federal receiver in a federal court.

1948 AMENDMENT

The amendment effective October 20, 1949, deleted the words "Rule 66" at the end of subdivision (b) and substituted the words "Title 28, U.S.C., §§ 754 and 959(a)."

1966 AMENDMENT

The minor change in the text of the rule is designed to make it clear that the specific instances enumerated are not exceptions to, but illustrations of, the rule. These illustrations, of course, carry no negative implication to the effect that there are not other instances of recognition as the real party in interest of one whose standing as such may be in doubt. The enumeration is simply of cases in which there might be substantial doubt as to the issue but for the specific enumeration. There are other potentially arguable cases that are not excluded by the enumeration. For example, the enumeration states that the promisee in a contract for the benefit of a third party may sue as real party in interest; it does not say, because it is obvious, that the third-party beneficiary may sue (when the applicable law gives him that right.)

The rule adds to the illustrative list of real parties in interest a bailee—meaning, of course, a bailee suing on behalf of the bailor with respect to the property bailed. (When the possessor of property other than the owner sues for an invasion of the possessory interest he is the real party in interest.) The word "bailee" is added primarily to preserve the admiralty practice whereby the owner of a vessel as bailee of the cargo, or the master of the vessel as bailee of both vessel and cargo, sues for damage to either property interest or both. But there is no reason to limit such a provision to maritime situations. The owner of a warehouse in which household furniture is stored is equally entitled to sue on behalf of the numerous owners of the furniture stored. Cf. *Gulf Oil Corp.* v. *Gilbert*, 330 U.S. 501, 67 S.Ct. 839, 91 L.Ed. 1055 (1947).

The provision that no action shall be dismissed on the ground that it is not prosecuted in the name of the real party in interest until a reasonable time has been allowed, after the objection has been raised, for ratification, substitution, etc., is added simply in the interests of justice. In its origin the rule concerning the real party in interest was permissive in purpose: it was designed to allow an assignee to sue in his own name. That having been accomplished, the modern function of the rule in its negative aspect is simply to protect the defendant against a subsequent action by the party actually entitled to recover, and to insure generally that the judgment will have its proper effect as res judicata.

This provision keeps pace with the law as it is actually developing. Modern decisions are inclined to be lenient when an honest mistake has been made in choosing the party in whose name the action is to be filed—in both maritime and nonmaritime cases. See *Levinson* v. *Deupree*, 345 U.S. 648, 73 S.Ct. 914, 97 L.Ed.2d 1319 (1953); *Link Aviation, Inc.* v. *Downs*, 325 F.2d 613 (D.C.Cir.1963). The provision should not be misunderstood or distorted. It is intended to prevent forfeiture when determination of the proper party to sue is difficult or when an understandable mistake has been made. It does not mean, for example, that, following an airplane crash in which all aboard were killed, an action may be filed in the name of John Doe (a fictitious person), as personal representative of Richard Roe (another fictitious person), in the hope that at a later time the attorney filing the action may substitute the real name of the real personal representative of a real victim, and have the benefit of suspension of the limitation period. It does not even mean, when an action is filed by the personal representative of John Smith, of Buffalo, in the good faith belief that he was aboard the flight, that upon discovery that Smith is alive and well, having missed the fatal flight, the representative of James Brown, of San Francisco, an actual victim, can be substituted to take advantage of the suspension of the limitation period. It is, in cases of this sort, intended to insure against forfeiture and injustice—in short, to codify in broad terms the salutary principle of *Levinson* v. *Deupree*, 345 U.S. 648, 73 S.Ct. 914, 97 L.Ed.2d 1319 (1953), and *Link Aviation, Inc.* v. *Downs*, 325 F.2d 613 (D.C.Cir.1963).

1987 AMENDMENT

The amendments are technical. No substantive change is intended.

1988 AMENDMENT

The amendment is technical. No substantive change is intended.

2007 AMENDMENT

The language of Rule 17 has been amended as part of the general restyling of the Civil Rules to make them more easily understood and to make style and terminology consistent throughout the rules. These changes are intended to be stylistic only.

Rule 17(d) incorporates the provisions of former Rule 25(d)(2), which fit better with Rule 17.

Rule 18.   Joinder of Claims and Remedies

1937 ADOPTION

Note to Subdivision (a). 1. Recent development, both in code and common law states, has been toward unlimited joinder of actions. See Smith-Hurd Ill.Stats. ch. 110, § 168; N.J.S.A. 2:27–37, as modified by N.J.Sup.Ct.Rules, Rule 21, 2 N.J.Misc. 1208 (1924); N.Y.C.P.A. (1937) § 258 as amended by Laws of 1935, ch. 339.

2. This provision for joinder of actions has been patterned upon former Equity Rule 26 (Joinder of Causes of Action) and broadened to include multiple parties. Compare the English practice, English Rules Under the Judicature Act (The Annual Practice, 1937) O. 18, r. r. 1–9 (noting rules 1 and 6). The earlier American codes set forth classes of joinder, following the now abandoned New York rule. See N.Y.C.P.A. § 258 before amended in 1935; Compare Kan.Gen.Stat.Ann. (1935) § 60–601; Wis.Stat. (1935) § 263.04 for the more liberal practice.

3. The provisions of this rule for the joinder of claims are subject to Rule 82 (Jurisdiction and Venue Unaffected). For the jurisdictional aspects of joinder of claims, see Shulman and Jaegerman. Some Jurisdictional Limitations on Federal Procedure (1936), 45 Yale L.J. 393, 397–410. For separate trials of joined claims, see rule 42(b).

Note to Subdivision (b). This rule is inserted to make it clear that in a single action a party should be accorded all the relief to which he is entitled regardless of whether it is legal or equitable or both. This necessarily includes a deficiency judgment in foreclosure actions formerly provided for in former Equity Rule 10 (Decree for Deficiency in Foreclosures, Etc.). In respect to fraudulent conveyances the rule changes the former rule requiring a prior judgment against the owner (*Braun* v. *American Laundry Mach. Co.*, N.Y.1932, 56 F.2d 197) to conform to the provisions of the Uniform Fraudulent Conveyance Act, §§ 9 and 10. See McLaughlin, Application of the Uniform Fraudulent Conveyance Act, 46 Harv.L.Rev. 404, 444 (1933).

1966 AMENDMENT

The Rules "proceed upon the theory that no inconvenience can result from the joinder of any two or more matters in the pleadings, but only from trying two or more matters together which have little or nothing in common." Sunderland, The New Federal Rules, 45 W.Va.L.Q. 5, 13 (1938); see Clark, Code Pleading 58 (2d ed. 1947). Accordingly, Rule 18(a) has permitted a party to plead multiple claims of all types against an opposing party, subject to the court's power to direct an appropriate procedure for trying the claims. See Rules 42(b), 20(b), 21.

The liberal policy regarding joinder of claims in the pleadings extends to cases with multiple parties. However, the language used in the second sentence of Rule 18(a)—"if the requirements of Rules 19 [necessary joinder of parties], 20 [permissive joinder of parties], and 22 [interpleader] are satisfied"—has led some courts to infer that the rules regulating joinder of parties are intended to carry back to Rule 18(a) and to impose some special limits on joinder of claims in multiparty cases. In particular, Rule 20(a) has been read as restricting the operation of Rule 18(a) in certain situations in which a number of parties have been permissively joined in an action. In *Federal Housing Admr.* v. *Christianson*, 26 F.Supp. 419 (D.Conn.1939), the indorsee of two notes sued the three comakers of one note, and sought to join in the action a count on a second note which had been made by two of the three defendants. There was no doubt about the propriety of the joinder of the three parties defendant, for a right to relief was being asserted against all three defendants which arose out of a single "transaction" (the first note) and a question of fact or law "common" to all three defendants would arise in the action. See the text of Rule 20(a). The court, however, refused to allow the joinder of the count on the second note, on the ground that this right to relief, assumed to arise from a distinct transaction, did not involve a question common to all the defendants but only two of them. For analysis of the Christianson case and other authorities, see 2 Barron & Holtzoff, Federal Practice & Procedure, § 533.1 (Wright ed. 1961); 3 Moore's Federal Practice, par. 18.04[3] (2d ed. 1963).

If the court's view is followed, it becomes necessary to enter at the pleading stage into speculations about the exact relation between the claim sought to be joined against fewer than all the defendants properly joined in the action, and the claims asserted against all the defendants. Cf. Wright, Joinder of Claims and Parties Under Modern Pleading Rules, 36 Minn.L.Rev. 580, 605–06 (1952). Thus if it could be found in the Christianson situation that the claim on the second note arose out of the same transaction as the claim on the first or out of a transaction forming part of a "series," and that any question of fact or law with respect to the second note also arose with regard to the first, it would be held that the claim on the second note could be joined in the complaint. See 2 Barron & Holtzoff, supra, at 199; see also id. at 198 n. 60.4; cf. 3 Moore's Federal Practice, supra, at 1811. Such pleading niceties provide a basis for delaying and wasteful maneuver. It is more compatible with the design of the Rules to allow the claim to be joined in the pleading, leaving the question of possible separate trial of that claim to be later decided. See 2 Barron & Holtzoff, supra, § 533.1; Wright, supra, 36 Minn.L.Rev. at 604–11; Developments in the Law—Multiparty Litigation in the Federal Courts, 71 Harv. 874, 970–71 (1958); Commentary, Relation Between Joinder of Parties and Joinder of Claims, 5 F.R.Serv. 822 (1942). It is instructive to note that the court in the Christianson case, while holding that the claim on the second note could not be joined as a matter of pleading, held open the possibility that both claims would later be consolidated for trial under Rule 42(a). See 26 F.Supp. 419.

Rule 18(a) is now amended not only to overcome the Christianson decision and similar authority, but also to state clearly, as a comprehensive proposition, that a party asserting a claim (an original claim, counterclaim, cross-claim, or third-party claim) may join as many claims as he has against an opposing party. See *Noland Co., Inc.* v. *Graver Tank & Mfg. Co.*, 301 F.2d 43, 49–51 (4th Cir.1962); but cf. *C. W. Humphrey Co.* v. *Security Alum. Co.*, 31 F.R.D. 41 (E.D.Mich.1962). This permitted joinder of claims is not affected by the fact that there are multiple parties in the action. The joinder of parties is governed by other rules operating independently.

It is emphasized that amended Rule 18(a) deals only with pleading. As already indicated, a claim properly joined as a matter of pleading need not be proceeded with together with the other claims if fairness or convenience justifies separate treatment.

Amended Rule 18(a), like the rule prior to amendment, does not purport to deal with questions of jurisdiction or venue which may arise with respect to claims properly joined as a matter of pleading. See Rule 82.

See also the amendment of Rule 20(a) and the Advisory Committee's Note thereto.

Free joinder of claims and remedies is one of the basic purposes of unification of the admiralty and civil procedure. The amendment accordingly provides for the inclusion in the rule of maritime claims as well as those which are legal and equitable in character.

1987 AMENDMENT

The amendments are technical. No substantive change is intended.

2007 AMENDMENT

The language of Rule 18 has been amended as part of the general restyling of the Civil Rules to make them more easily understood and to make style and terminology consistent throughout the rules. These changes are intended to be stylistic only.

Modification of the obscure former reference to a claim "heretofore cognizable only after another claim has been prosecuted to a conclusion" avoids any uncertainty whether Rule 18(b)'s meaning is fixed by retrospective inquiry from some particular date.

Rule 19.   Joinder of Persons Needed for Just Adjudication

1937 ADOPTION

Note to Subdivision (a). The first sentence with verbal differences (e. g., "united" interest for "joint" interest) is to be found in former Equity Rule 37 (Parties Generally—Intervention). Such compulsory joinder provisions are common. Compare Alaska Comp. Laws (1933) § 3392 (containing in same sentence a "class suit" provision); Wyo.Rev.Stat. Ann. (Courtright, 1931) § 89–515 (immediately followed by "class suit" provisions, § 89–516). See also former Equity Rule 42 (Joint and Several Demands). For example of a proper case for involuntary plaintiff, see *Independent Wireless Telegraph Co.* v. *Radio Corp. of America*, 1926, 269 U.S. 459, 46 S.Ct. 166, 70 L.Ed. 357.

The joinder provisions of this rule are subject to Rule 82 (Jurisdiction and Venue Unaffected).

Note to Subdivision (b). For the substance of this rule see former Equity Rule 39 (Absence of Persons Who Would be Proper Parties) and U.S.C., Title 28, § 1391, formerly § 111 (When part of several defendants cannot be served); *Camp* v. *Gress*, 1919, 250 U.S. 308, 39 S.Ct. 478, 63 L.Ed. 997. See also the second and third sentences of former Equity Rule 37 (Parties Generally—Intervention).

Note to Subdivision (c). For the substance of this rule see the fourth subdivision of former Equity Rule 25 (Bill of Complaint—Contents).

1966 AMENDMENT
GENERAL CONSIDERATIONS

Whenever feasible, the persons materially interested in the subject of an action—see the more detailed description of these persons in the discussion of new subdivision (a) below—should be joined as parties so that they may be heard and a complete disposition made. When this comprehensive joinder cannot be accomplished—a situation which may be encountered in Federal courts because of limitations on service of process, subject matter jurisdiction, and venue—the case should be examined pragmatically and a choice made between the alternatives of proceeding with the action in the absence of particular interested persons, and dismissing the action.

Even if the court is mistaken in its decision to proceed in the absence of an interested person, it does not by that token deprive itself of the power to adjudicate as between the parties already before it through proper service of process. But the court can make a legally binding adjudication only between the parties actually joined in the action. It is true that an adjudication between the parties before the court may on occasion adversely affect the absent person as a practical matter, or leave a party exposed to a later inconsistent recovery by the absent person. These are factors which should be considered in deciding whether the action should proceed, or should rather be dismissed; but they do not themselves negate the court's power to adjudicate as between the parties who have been joined.

DEFECTS IN THE ORIGINAL RULE

The foregoing propositions were well understood in the older equity practice, see Hazard, Indispensable Party: The Historical Origin of a Procedural Phantom, 61 Colum.L.Rev. 1254 (1961), and Rule 19 could be and often was applied in consonance with them. But experience showed that the rule was defective in its phrasing and did not point clearly to the proper basis of decision.

Textual defects.—(1) The expression "persons * * * who ought to be parties if complete relief is to be accorded between those already parties," appearing in original subdivision (b), was apparently intended as a description of the persons whom it would be desirable to join in the action, all questions of feasibility of joinder being put to one side; but it was not adequately descriptive of those persons.

(2) The word "indispensable," appearing in original subdivision (b), was apparently intended as an inclusive reference to the interested persons in whose absence it would be advisable, all factors having been considered, to dismiss the action. Yet the sentence implied that there might be interested persons, not "indispensable," in whose absence the action ought also to be dismissed. Further, it seemed at least superficially plausible to equate the word "indispensable" with the expression "having a joint interest," appearing in subdivision (a). See *United States* v. *Washington Inst. of Tech., Inc.,* 138 F.2d 25, 26 (3d Cir.1943); cf. *Chidester* v. *City of Newark,* 162 F.2d 598 (3d Cir.1947). But persons holding an interest technically "joint" are not always so related to an action that it would be unwise to proceed without joining all of them, whereas persons holding an interest not technically "joint" may have this relation to an action. See Reed, Compulsory Joinder of Parties in Civil Actions, 55 Mich.L.Rev. 327, 356 ff., 483 (1957).

(3) The use of "indispensable" and "joint interest" in the context of original Rule 19 directed attention to the technical or abstract character of the rights or obligations of the persons whose joinder was in question, and correspondingly distracted attention from the pragmatic considerations which should be controlling.

(4) The original rule, in dealing with the feasibility of joining a person as a party to the action, besides referring to whether the person was "subject to the jurisdiction of the court as to both service of process and venue," spoke of whether the person could be made a party "without depriving the court of jurisdiction of the parties before it." The second quoted expression used "jurisdiction" in the sense of the competence of the court over the subject matter of the action, and in this sense the expression was apt. However, by a familiar confusion, the expression seems to have suggested to some that the absence from the lawsuit of a person who was "indispensable" or "who ought to be [a] part[y]" itself deprived the court of the power to adjudicate as between the parties already joined. See *Samuel Goldwyn, Inc.* v. *United Artists Corp.,* 113 F.2d 703, 707 (3d Cir.1940); *McArthur* v. *Rosenbaum Co. of Pittsburgh,* 180 F.2d 617, 621 (3d Cir.1950); cf. *Calcote* v. *Texas Pac. Coal & Oil Co.,* 157 F.2d 216 (5th Cir.1946), cert. denied, 329 U.S. 782, 67 S.Ct. 205, 91 L.Ed. 671 (1946), noted in 56 Yale L.J. 1088 (1947); Reed, supra, 55 Mich.L.Rev. at 332–34.

Failure to point to correct basis of decision. The original rule did not state affirmatively what factors were relevant in deciding whether the action should proceed or be dismissed when joinder of interested persons was infeasible. In some instances courts did not undertake the relevant inquiry or were misled by the "jurisdiction" fallacy. In other instances there was undue preoccupation with abstract classifications of rights or obligations, as against consideration of the particular consequences of proceeding with the action and the ways by which these consequences might be ameliorated by the shaping of final relief or other precautions.

Although these difficulties cannot be said to have been general analysis of the cases showed that there was good reason for attempting to strengthen the rule. The literature also indicated how the rule should be reformed. See Reed, supra (discussion of the important case of *Shields* v. *Barrow,* 17 How. (58 U.S.) 130 (1854), appears at 55 Mich.L.Rev. p. 340 ff.); Hazard, supra; N.Y. Temporary Comm. on Courts, First Preliminary Report, Legis.Doc.1957, No. 6(b), pp. 28, 233; N. Y. Judicial Council, Twelfth Ann.Rep., Legis.Doc.1946, No. 17, p. 163; Joint Comm. on Michigan Procedural Revision, Final Report, Pt. III, p. 69 (1960); Note, Indispensable Parties in the Federal Courts, 65 Harv.L.Rev. 1050 (1952); Developments in the Law—Multiparty Litigation in the Federal Courts, 71 Harv.L.Rev. 874, 879 (1958); Mich.Gen. Court Rules, R. 205 (effective Jan. 1, 1963); N.Y.Civ.Prac.Law & Rules, § 1001 (effective Sept. 1, 1963).

THE AMENDED RULE

New subdivision (a) defines the persons whose joinder in the action is desirable. Clause (1) stresses the desirability of joining those persons in whose absence the court would be obliged to grant partial or "hollow" rather than complete relief to the parties before the court. The interests that are being furthered here are not only those of the parties, but also that of the public in avoiding repeated lawsuits on the same essential subject matter. Clause (2)(i) recognizes the importance of protecting the person whose joinder is in question against the practical prejudice to him which may arise through a disposition of the action in his absence. Clause (2)(ii) recognizes the need for considering whether a party may be left, after the adjudication, in a position where a person not joined can subject him to a double or otherwise inconsistent liability. See Reed, supra, 55 Mich.L.Rev. at 330, 338; Note, supra, 65 Harv.L.Rev. at 1052–57; Developments in the Law, supra, 71 Harv.L.Rev. at 881–85.

The subdivision (a) definition of persons to be joined is not couched in terms of the abstract nature of their interests—"joint," "united," "separable," or the like. See N.Y. Temporary Comm. on Courts, First Preliminary Report, supra; Developments in the Law, supra, at 880. It should be noted particularly, however, that the description is not at variance with the settled authorities holding that a tortfeasor with the usual "joint-and-several" liability is merely a permissive party to an action against another with like liability. See 3 Moore's Federal Practice 2153 (2d ed. 1963); 2 Barron & Holtzoff, Federal Practice & Procedure § 513.8 (Wright ed. 1961). Joinder of these tortfeasors continues to be regulated by Rule 20; compare Rule 14 on third-party practice.

If a person as described in subdivision (a)(1)–(2) is amenable to service of process and his joinder would not deprive the court of jurisdiction in the sense of competence over the action, he should be joined as a party; and if he has not been joined, the court should order him to be brought into the action. If a party joined has a valid objection to the venue and chooses to assert it, he will be dismissed from the action.

Subdivision (b).—When a person as described in subdivision (a)(1)–(2) cannot be made a party, the court is to determine whether in equity and good conscience the action should proceed among the parties already before it, or should be dismissed. That this decision is to be made in the light of pragmatic considerations has often been acknowledged by the courts. See *Roos* v. *Texas Co.*, 23 F.2d 171 (2d Cir.1927), cert. denied, 277 U.S. 587, 48 S.Ct. 434, 72 L.Ed. 1001 (1928); *Niles–Bement–Pond Co.* v. *Iron Moulders' Union*, 254 U.S. 77, 80, 41 S.Ct. 39, 65 L.Ed. 145 (1920). The subdivision sets out four relevant considerations drawn from the experience revealed in the decided cases. The factors are to a certain extent overlapping, and they are not intended to exclude other considerations which may be applicable in particular situations.

The first factor brings in a consideration of what a judgment in the action would mean to the absentee. Would the absentee be adversely affected in a practical sense, and if so, would the prejudice be immediate and serious, or remote and minor? The possible collateral consequences of the judgment upon the parties already joined are also to be appraised. Would any party be exposed to a fresh action by the absentee, and if so, how serious is the threat? See the elaborate discussion in Reed, supra; cf. *A. L. Smith Iron Co.* v. *Dickson*, 141 F.2d 3 (2d Cir.1944); *Caldwell Mfg. Co.* v. *Unique Balance Co.*, 18 F.R.D. 258 (S.D.N.Y.1955).

The second factor calls attention to the measures by which prejudice may be averted or lessened. The "shaping of relief" is a familiar expedient to this end. See, e. g., the award of money damages in lieu of specific relief where the latter might affect an absentee adversely. *Ward* v. *Deavers*, 203 F.2d 72 (D.C.Cir.1953); *Miller & Lux, Inc.* v. *Nickel*, 141 F.Supp. 41 (N.D.Cal.1956). On the use of "protective provisions," see *Roos* v. *Texas Co.*, supra; *Atwood* v. *Rhode Island Hosp. Trust Co.*, 275 Fed. 513, 519 (1st Cir.1921), cert. denied, 257 U.S. 661, 42 S.Ct. 270, 66 L.Ed. 422 (1922); cf. *Stumpf* v. *Fidelity Gas Co.*, 294 F.2d 886 (9th Cir.1961); and the general statement in *National Licorice Co.* v. *National Labor Relations Board*, 309 U.S. 350, 363, 60 S.Ct. 569, 84 L.Ed. 799 (1940).

Sometimes the party is himself able to take measures to avoid prejudice. Thus a defendant faced with a prospect of a second suit by an absentee may be in a position to bring the latter into the action by defensive interpleader. See *Hudson* v. *Newell*, 172 F.2d 848, 852 mod., 174 F.2d 546 (5th Cir.1949); *Gauss* v. *Kirk*, 198 F.2d 83, 86 (D.C.Cir.1952); *Abel* v. *Brayton Flying Service, Inc.*, 248 F.2d 713, 716 (5th Cir.1957)(suggestion of possibility of counterclaim under Rule 13(h)); cf. *Parker Rust–Proof Co.* v. *Western Union Tel. Co.*, 105 F.2d 976 (2d Cir.1939), cert. denied, 308 U.S. 597 (1939). So also the absentee may sometimes be able to avert prejudice to himself by voluntarily appearing in the action or intervening on an ancillary basis. See Developments in the Law, supra, 71 Harv.L.Rev. at 882; Annot., Intervention or Subsequent Joinder of Parties as Affecting Jurisdiction of Federal Court Based on Diversity of Citizenship, 134 A.L.R. 335 (1941); *Johnson* v. *Middleton*, 175 F.2d 535 (7th Cir.1949); *Kentucky Nat. Gas Corp.* v. *Duggins*, 165 F.2d 1011 (6th Cir.1948); *McComb* v. *McCormack*, 159 F.2d 219 (5th Cir.1947). The court should consider whether this, in turn, would impose undue hardship on the absentee (For the possibility of the court's informing an absentee of the pendency of the action, see comment under subdivision (c) below.)

The third factor—whether an "adequate" judgment can be rendered in the absence of a given person—calls attention to the extent of the relief that can be accorded among the parties joined. It meshes with the other factors, especially the "shaping of relief" mentioned under the second factor. Cf. *Kroese* v. *General Steel Castings Corp.,* 179 F.2d 760 (3d Cir.1950), cert. denied, 339 U.S. 983, 70 S.Ct. 1026, 94 L.Ed. 1386 (1950).

The fourth factor, looking to the practical effects of a dismissal, indicates that the court should consider whether there is any assurance that the plaintiff, if dismissed, could sue effectively in another forum where better joinder would be possible. See *Fitzgerald* v. *Haynes,* 241 F.2d 417, 420 (3d Cir.1957); *Fouke* v. *Schenewerk,* 197 F.2d 234, 236 (5th Cir.1952); cf. *Warfield* v. *Marks,* 190 F.2d 178 (5th Cir.1951).

The subdivision uses the word "indispensable" only in a conclusory sense, that is, a person is "regarded as indispensable" when he cannot be made a party and, upon consideration of the factors above mentioned, it is determined that in his absence it would be preferable to dismiss the action, rather than to retain it.

A person may be added as a party at any stage of the action on motion or on the court's initiative (see Rule 21); and a motion to dismiss, on the ground that a person has not been joined and justice requires that the action should not proceed in his absence, may be made as late as the trial on the merits (see Rule 12(h)(2), as amended; cf. Rule 12(b)(7), as amended). However, when the moving party is seeking dismissal in order to protect himself against a later suit by the absent person (subdivision (a)(2)(ii)), and is not seeking vicariously to protect the absent person against a prejudicial judgment (subdivision (a)(2)(i)), his undue delay in making the motion can properly be counted against him as a reason for denying the motion. A joinder question should be decided with reasonable promptness, but decision may properly be deferred if adequate information is not available at the time. Thus the relationship of an absent person to the action, and the practical effects of an adjudication upon him and others, may not be sufficiently revealed at the pleading stage; in such a case it would be appropriate to defer decision until the action was further advanced. Cf. Rule 12(d).

The amended rule makes no special provision for the problem arising in suits against subordinate Federal officials where it has often been set up as a defense that some superior officer must be joined. Frequently this defense has been accompanied by or intermingled with defenses of sovereign community or lack of consent of the United States to suit. So far as the issue of joinder can be isolated from the rest, the new subdivision seems better adapted to handle it than the predecessor provision. See the discussion in *Johnson* v. *Kirkland,* 290 F.2d 440, 446–47 (5th Cir.1961)(stressing the practical orientation of the decisions); *Shaughnessy* v. *Pedreiro,* 349 U.S. 48, 54, 75 S.Ct. 591, 99 L.Ed. 868 (1955). Recent legislation, P.L. 87–748, 76 Stat. 744, approved October 5, 1962, adding §§ 1361, 1391(e) to Title 28, U.S.C., vests original jurisdiction in the District Courts over actions in the nature of mandamus to compel officials of the United States to perform their legal duties, and extends the range of service of process and liberalizes venue in these actions. If, then, it is found that a particular official should be joined in the action, the legislation will make it easy to bring him in.

Subdivision (c) parallels the predecessor subdivision (c) of Rule 19. In some situations it may be desirable to advise a person who has not been joined of the fact that the action is pending, and in particular cases the court in its discretion may itself convey this information by directing a letter or other informal notice to the absentee.

Subdivision (d) repeats the exception contained in the first clause of the predecessor subdivision (a).

1987 AMENDMENT

The amendments are technical. No substantive change is intended.

2007 AMENDMENT

The language of Rule 19 has been amended as part of the general restyling of the Civil Rules to make them more easily understood and to make style and terminology consistent throughout the rules. These changes are intended to be stylistic only.

Former Rule 19(b) described the conclusion that an action should be dismissed for inability to join a Rule 19(a) party by carrying forward traditional terminology: "the absent person being thus regarded as indispensable." "Indispensable" was used only to express a conclusion reached by applying the tests of Rule 19(b). It has been discarded as redundant.

Rule 20.   Permissive Joinder of Parties
1937 ADOPTION

The provisions for joinder here stated are in substance the provisions found in England, California, Illinois, New Jersey, and New York. They represent only a moderate expansion of the present federal equity practice to cover both law and equity actions.

With this rule compare also former Equity Rules 26 (Joinder of Causes of Action), 37 (Parties Generally—Intervention), 40 (Nominal Parties), and 42 (Joint and Several Demands).

The provisions of this rule for the joinder of parties are subject to rule 82 (Jurisdiction and Venue Unaffected).

Note to Subdivision (a). The first sentence is derived from English Rules Under the Judicature Act (The Annual Practice, 1937) O. 16, r. 1. Compare Calif.Code Civ.Proc. (1937) §§ 378, 379a; Smith-Hurd Ill.Stats. ch. 110, §§ 147–148; N.J.S.A. 2:27–24, 2:27–25, 2:27–38; N.Y.C.P.A. (1937) §§ 209, 211. The second sentence is derived from English Rules Under the Judicature Act (The Annual Practice, 1937) O. 16, r. 4. The third sentence is derived from O. 16, r. 5, and the fourth from O. 16, r. r. 1 and 4.

Note to Subdivision (b). This is derived from English Rules Under the Judicature Act (The Annual Practice, 1937) O. 16, r. r. 1 and 5.

1966 AMENDMENT

See the amendment of Rule 18(a) and the Advisory Committee's Note thereto. It has been thought that a lack of clarity in the antecedent of the word "them," as it appeared in two places in Rule 20(a), contributed to the view, taken by some courts, that this rule limited the joinder of claims in certain situations of permissive party-joinder. Although the amendment of Rule 18(a) should make clear that this view is untenable, it has been considered advisable to amend Rule 20(a) to eliminate any ambiguity. See 2 Barron & Holtzoff, Federal Practice & Procedure 202 (Wright Ed. 1961).

A basic purpose of unification of admiralty and civil procedure is to reduce barriers to joinder; hence the reference to "any vessel," etc.

1987 AMENDMENT

The amendments are technical. No substantive change is intended.

2007 AMENDMENT

The language of Rule 20 has been amended as part of the general restyling of the Civil Rules to make them more easily understood and to make style and terminology consistent throughout the rules. These changes are intended to be stylistic only.

Rule 21. Misjoinder and Non-Joinder of Parties

1937 ADOPTION

See English Rules Under the Judicature Act (The Annual Practice, 1937) O. 16, r. 11. See also former Equity Rules 43 (Defect of Parties—Resisting Objection) and 44 (Defect of Parties—Tardy Objection).

For separate trials see Rules 13(i)(Counterclaims and Cross-Claims: Separate Trials; Separate Judgments), 20(b)(Permissive Joinder of Parties: Separate Trials), and 42(b)(Separate Trials, generally) and the note to the latter rule.

2007 AMENDMENT

The language of Rule 21 has been amended as part of the general restyling of the Civil Rules to make them more easily understood and to make style and terminology consistent throughout the rules. These changes are intended to be stylistic only.

Rule 22. Interpleader

1937 ADOPTION

The first paragraph provides for interpleader relief along the newer and more liberal lines of joinder in the alternative. It avoids the confusion and restrictions that developed around actions of strict interpleader and actions in the nature of interpleader. Compare *John Hancock Mutual Life Insurance Co.* v. *Kegan et al.,* D.C.Md.1938, 22 F.Supp. 326. It does not change the rules on service of process, jurisdiction, and venue, as established by judicial decision.

The second paragraph allows an action to be brought under the recent interpleader statute when applicable. By this paragraph all remedies under the statute are continued, but the manner of obtaining them is in accordance with these rules. For temporary restraining orders and preliminary injunctions under this statute, see Rule 65(e).

This rule substantially continues such statutory provisions as U.S.C., Title 38, § 445 (Actions on claims; jurisdiction; parties; procedure; limitation; witnesses; definitions)(actions upon veterans' contracts of insurance with the United States), providing for interpleader by the United States where it acknowledges indebtedness under a contract of insurance with the United States; U.S.C., Title 49, § 97 (Interpleader of conflicting claimants)(by carrier which has issued bill of lading). See Chafee, The Federal Interpleader Act of 1936: I and II (1936), 45 Yale L.J. 963, 1161.

1948 AMENDMENT

The amendment effective October 20, 1949, substituted the reference to "Title 28, U.S.C., §§ 1335, 1397, and 2361," at the end of the first sentence of paragraph (2), in lieu of the reference to "Section 24(26) of the Judicial Code, as amended, U.S.C., Title 28, § 41(26)." The amendment also substituted the words "those provisions" in the second sentence of paragraph (2) for the words "that section."

1987 AMENDMENT

The amendment is technical. No substantive change is intended.

2007 AMENDMENT

The language of Rule 22 has been amended as part of the general restyling of the Civil Rules to make them more easily understood and to make style and terminology consistent throughout the rules. These changes are intended to be stylistic only.

Rule 23. Class Actions

1937 ADOPTION

Note to Subdivision (a). This is a substantial restatement of former Equity Rule 38 (Representatives of Class) as that rule has been construed. It applies to all actions, whether formerly denominated legal or equitable. For a general analysis of class actions, effect of judgment, and requisites of jurisdiction see Moore, Federal Rules of Civil Procedure: Some Problems Raised by the Preliminary Draft, 25 Georgetown L.J. 551, 570 et seq., 1937; Moore and Cohn, Federal Class Actions, 32 Ill.L.Rev. 307, 1937; Moore and Cohn, Federal Class Actions—Jurisdiction and Effect of Judgment, 32 Ill.L.Rev. 555–567, 1938; Lesar, Class Suits and the Federal Rules, 22 Minn.L.Rev. 34, 1937; cf. Arnold and James, Cases on Trials, Judgments and Appeals, 1936, 175; and see Blume, Jurisdictional Amount in Representative Suits, 15 Minn.L.Rev. 501, 1931.

The general test of former Equity Rule 38 (Representatives of Class) that the question should be "one of common or general interest to many persons constituting a class so numerous as to make it impracticable to bring them all before the court," is a common test. For states which require the two elements of a common or general interest and numerous persons, as provided for in former Equity Rule 38, see Del.Ch. Rule 113; Fla.Comp.Gen.Laws Ann. (Supp., 1936) § 4918(7); Georgia Code, 1933, § 37–1002, and see English Rules Under the Judicature Act (The Annual Practice, 1937) O. 16, r. 9. For statutory provisions providing for class actions when the question is one of common or general interest or when the parties are numerous, see Ala.Code Ann. (Michie, 1928) § 5701; 2 Ind.Stat.Ann. (Burns, 1933) § 2–220; N.Y.C.P.A.1937, § 195; Wis.Stat.1935, § 260.12. These statutes have, however, been uniformly construed as though phrased in the conjunctive. See *Garfein* v. *Stiglitz*, 260 Ky. 430, 86 S.W.2d 155, 1935. The rule adopts the test of former Equity Rule 38, but defines what constitutes a "common or general interest". Compare with code provisions which make the action dependent upon the propriety of joinder of the parties. See Blume, The "Common Questions" Principle in the Code Provision for Representative Suits, 30 Mich.L.Rev. 878, 1932. For discussion of what constitutes "numerous persons" see Wheaton, Representative Suits Involving Numerous Litigants, 19 Corn.L.Q. 399 (1934); Note, 36 Harv.L.Rev. 89 (1922).

Clause (1). Joint, Common, or Secondary Right. This clause is illustrated in actions brought by or against representatives of an unincorporated association. See *Oster* v. *Brotherhood of Locomotive Firemen and Enginemen*, 1921, 114 A. 377, 271 Pa. 419; *Pickett* v. *Walsh*, 1906, 78 N.E. 753, 192 Mass. 572, 6 L.R.A.,N.S. 1067; *Colt* v. *Hicks*, 1932, 179 N.E. 335, 97 Ind.App. 177. Compare rule 17(b) as to when an unincorporated association has capacity to sue or be sued in its common name; *United Mine Workers of America* v. *Coronado Coal Co.*, 1922, 259 U.S. 344, 42 S.Ct. 570, 66 L.Ed. 975, 27 A.L.R. 762 (an unincorporated association was sued as an entity for the purpose of enforcing against it a federal substantive right); Moore, Federal Rules of Civil Procedure: Some Problems Raised by the Preliminary Draft, 25 Georgetown L.J. 551, 566 (for discussion of jurisdictional requisites when an unincorporated association sues or is sued in its common name and jurisdiction is founded upon diversity of citizenship). For an action brought by representatives of one group against representatives of another group for distribution of a fund held by an unincorporated association, see *Smith* v. *Swormstedt,* 1853, 14 L.Ed. 942, 16 How. 288. Compare *Christopher et al.* v. *Brusselback,* 1938, 302 U.S. 500, 58 S.Ct. 350, 82 L.Ed. 388.

For an action to enforce rights held in common by policyholders against the corporate issuer of the policies, see *Supreme Tribe of Ben Hur* v. *Cauble,* 1921, 255 U.S. 356, 41 S.Ct. 338, 65 L.Ed. 673. See also *Terry* v. *Little,* 1880, 101 U.S. 216, 25 L.Ed. 864; *John A. Roebling's Sons Co.* v. *Kinnicutt,* D.C.N.Y.1917, 248 F. 596, dealing with the right held in common by creditors to enforce the statutory liability of stockholders.

Typical of a secondary action is a suit by stockholders to enforce a corporate right. For discussion of the general nature of these actions see *Ashwander* v. *Tennessee Valley Authority,* 1936, 297 U.S. 288, 56 S.Ct. 466, 80 L.Ed. 688; Glenn, The Stockholder's Suit—Corporate and Individual Grievances, 33 Yale L.J. 580 (1924); McLaughlin, Capacity of Plaintiff-Stockholder to Terminate a Stockholder's Suit, 46 Yale L.J. 421 (1937). See also Subdivision (b) of this rule which deals with Shareholder's Action; Note, 15 Minn.L.Rev. 453 (1931).

Clause (2). A creditor's action for liquidation or reorganization of a corporation is illustrative of this clause. An action by a stockholder against certain named defendants as representatives of numerous claimants presents a situation converse to the creditor's action.

Clause (3). See *Everglades Drainage League* v. *Napoleon Broward Drainage Dist.,* D.C.Fla.1918, 253 F. 246; *Gramling* v. *Maxwell,* D.C.N.C.1931, 52 F.2d 256, approved in 1932, 30 Mich.L.Rev. 624; *Skinner* v. *Mitchell,* 1921, 197 P. 569, 108 Kan. 861; *Duke of Bedford* v. *Ellis,* 1901, A.C. 1, for class actions when there were numerous persons and there was only a question of law or fact common to them; and see Blume, The "Common Questions" Principle in the Code Provision for Representative Suits, 30 Mich.L.Rev. 878 (1932).

Note to Subdivision (b). This is former Equity Rule 27 (Stockholder's Bill) with verbal changes. See also *Hawes* v. *Oakland,* 1882, 104 U.S. 450, 26 L.Ed. 827 and former Equity Rule 94, promulgated January 23, 1882, 104 U.S. IX.

Note to Subdivision (c). See McLaughlin, Capacity of Plaintiff-Stockholder to Terminate a Stockholder's Suit, 46 Yale L.J. 421 (1937).

SUPPLEMENTARY NOTE OF ADVISORY COMMITTEE REGARDING THIS RULE

Note. Subdivision (b), relating to secondary actions by shareholders, provides among other things, that in such an action the complainant "shall aver (1) that the plaintiff was a shareholder at the time of the transaction of which he complains or that his share thereafter devolved on him by operation of law * * *".

As a result of the decision in *Erie R. Co.* v. *Tompkins,* 1938, 304 U.S. 64, 58 S.Ct. 817, 82 L.Ed. 1188 (decided April 25, 1938, after this rule was promulgated by the Supreme Court, though before it took effect) a question has arisen as to whether the provision above quoted deals with a matter of substantive right or is a matter of procedure. If it is a matter of substantive law or right, then under *Erie R. Co.* v. *Tompkins,* clause (1) may not be validly applied in cases pending in states whose local law permits a shareholder to maintain such actions, although not a shareholder at the time of the transactions complained of. The Advisory Committee, believing the question should be settled in the courts, proposes no change in Rule 23 but thinks rather that the situation should be explained in an appropriate note.

The rule has a long history. In *Hawes* v. *Oakland,* 1882, 104 U.S. 450, 26 L.Ed. 827, the Court held that a shareholder could not maintain such an action unless he owned shares at the time of the transactions complained of, or unless they devolved on him by operation of law. At that time the decision in *Swift* v. *Tyson,* 1842, 41 U.S. 1, 10 L.Ed. 865, 16 Peters 1, was the law, and the federal courts considered themselves free to establish their own principles of equity jurisprudence, so the Court was not in 1882 and has not been, until *Erie R. Co.* v. *Tompkins* in 1938, concerned with the question whether *Hawes* v. *Oakland* dealt with substantive right or procedure.

Following the decision in *Hawes* v. *Oakland,* and at the same term, the Court, to implement its decision, adopted former Equity Rule 94, which contained the same provision above quoted from Rule 23 F.R.C.P. The provision in former Equity Rule 94 was later embodied in former Equity Rule 27, of which the present Rule 23 is substantially a copy.

In *City of Quincy* v. *Steel,* 1887, 120 U.S. 241, 245, 7 S.Ct. 520, 30 L.Ed. 624, the Court referring to *Hawes* v. *Oakland* said: "In order to give effect to the principles there laid down, this Court at that term adopted [former] Rule 94 of the rules of practice for courts of equity of the United States."

Some other cases dealing with former Equity Rules 94 or 27 prior to the decision in *Erie R. Co.* v. *Tompkins* are *Dimpfel* v. *Ohio & Miss. R. R.,* 1884, 110 U.S. 209, 3 S.Ct. 573, 28 L.Ed. 121; *Illinois Central R. Co.* v. *Adams,* 1901, 180 U.S. 28, 34, 21 S.Ct. 251, 45 L.Ed. 410; *Venner* v. *Great Northern Ry.,* 1908, 209 U.S. 24, 30, 28 S.Ct. 328, 52 L.Ed. 666; *Jacobson* v. *General Motors Corp.,* N.Y.1938, 22 F.Supp. 255, 257. These cases generally treat *Hawes* v. *Oakland* as establishing a "principle" of equity, or as dealing not with jurisdiction but with the "right" to maintain an action, or have said that the defense under the equity rule is analogous to the defense that the plaintiff has no "title" and results in a dismissal "for want of equity."

Those state decisions which held that a shareholder acquiring stock after the event may maintain a derivative action are founded on the view that it is a right belonging to the shareholder at the time of the transaction and which passes as a right to the subsequent purchaser. See *Pollitz* v. *Gould,* 1911, 94 N.E. 1088, 202 N.Y. 11.

The first case arising after the decision in *Erie R. Co.* v. *Tompkins* in which this problem was involved, was *Summers* v. *Hearst,* N.Y.1938, 23 F.Supp. 986. It concerned former Equity Rule 27, as Federal Rule 23 was not then in effect. In a well considered opinion Judge Leibell reviewed the decisions and said: "The federal cases that discuss this section of [former] Rule 27 support the view that it states a principle of substantive law." He quoted *Pollitz* v. *Gould,* 1911, 94 N.E. 1088, 202 N.Y. 11, as saying that the United States Supreme Court "seems to have been more concerned with establishing this rule as one of practice than of substantive law" but that "whether it be regarded as establishing a principle of law or a rule of practice, this authority has been subsequently followed in the United States courts."

He then concluded that, although the federal decisions treat the equity rule as "stating a principle of substantive law", if "[former] Equity Rule 27 is to be modified or revoked in view of *Erie R. Co.* v. *Tompkins,* it is not the province of this Court to suggest it, much less impliedly to follow that course by disregarding the mandatory provisions of the Rule."

Some other federal decisions since 1938 touch the question.

In *Piccard* v. *Sperry Corporation,* N.Y.1941, 36 F.Supp. 1006, 1009–10, affirmed without opinion, C.C.A.2d 1941, 120 F.2d 328, a shareholder, not such at the time of the transactions complained of, sought to intervene. The court held an intervenor was as much subject to Rule 23 as an original plaintiff; and that the requirement of Rule 23(b) was "a matter of practice," not substance, and applied in New York where the state law was otherwise, despite *Erie R. Co.* v. *Tompkins.* In *York* v. *Guaranty Trust Co. of New York,* C.C.A.2, 1944, 143 F.2d 503, reversed on other grounds 326 U.S. 99, 65 S.Ct. 1464, 89 L.Ed. 2079, the court said: "Restrictions on the bringing of stockholders' actions, such as those imposed by F.R.C.P. 23(b) or other state statutes are procedural," citing the Picard and other cases.

In *Gallup* v. *Caldwell,* C.C.A.3, 1941, 120 F.2d 90, 95, arising in New Jersey, the point was raised but not decided, the court saying that it was not satisfied that the then New Jersey rule differed from Rule 23(b), and that "under the circumstances the proper course was to follow Rule 23(b)."

In *Mullins* v. *DeSoto Securities Co.,* La.1942, 45 F.Supp. 871, 878, the point was not decided, because the court found the Louisiana rule to be the same as that stated in Rule 23(b).

In *Toebelman* v. *Missouri–Kansas Pipe Line Co.,* Del.1941, 41 F.Supp. 334, 340, the court dealt only with another part of rule 23(b), relating to prior demands on the stockholders and did not discuss *Erie R. Co.* v. *Tompkins* or its effect on the rule.

In *Perrott* v. *United States Banking Corp.,* Del.1944, 53 F.Supp. 953, it appeared that the Delaware law does not require the plaintiff to have owned shares at the time of the transaction complained of. The court sustained Rule 23(b), after discussion of the authorities, saying:

"It seems to me the rule does not go beyond procedure. * * * Simply because a particular plaintiff cannot qualify as a proper party to maintain such an action does not destroy or even whittle at the cause of action. The cause of action exists until a qualified plaintiff can get it started in a federal court."

In *Bankers Nat. Corp. v. Barr,* N.Y.1945, 9 Fed.Rules Serv. 23b.11, Case 1, the court held Rule 23(b) to be one of procedure, but that whether the plaintiff was a stockholder was a substantive question to be settled by state law.

The New York rule, as stated in *Pollitz v. Gould,* supra, has been altered by an act of the New York Legislature, Chapter 667, Laws of 1944, effective April 9, 1944, General Corporation Law, § 61, which provides that "in any action brought by a shareholder in the right of a * * * corporation, it must appear that the plaintiff was a stockholder at the time of the transaction of which he complains, or that his stock thereafter devolved upon him by operation of law." At the same time a further and separate provision was enacted, requiring under certain circumstances the giving of security for reasonable expenses and attorney's fees, to which security the corporation in whose right the action is brought and the defendants therein may have recourse. (Chapter 668, Laws of 1944, effective April 9, 1944, General Corporation Law, § 61–b.) These provisions are aimed at so-called "strike" stockholders' suits and their attendant abuses. *Shielcrawt v. Moffett,* 1945, 61 N.E.2d 435, 294 N.Y. 180; *Noel Associates, Inc. v. Merrill,* 1944, 53 N.Y.S.2d 143, 184 Misc. 646.

Insofar as § 61 is concerned, it has been held that the section is procedural in nature. *Klum v. Clinton Trust Co.,* 1944, 48 N.Y.S.2d 267, 183 Misc. 340; *Noel Associates, Inc.* v. *Merrill,* supra. In the latter case the court pointed out that "The 1944 amendment to Section 61 rejected the rule laid down in the Pollitz case and substituted, in place thereof, in its precise language, the rule which has long prevailed in the Federal Courts and which is now Rule 23(b) * * *". There is, nevertheless, a difference of opinion regarding the application of the statute to pending actions. See *Klum v. Clinton Trust Co.,* supra (applicable); *Noel Associates, Inc. v. Merrill,* supra (inapplicable).

With respect to § 61–B, which may be regarded as a separate problem, *Noel Associates, Inc.* v. *Merrill,* supra, it has been held that even though the statute is procedural in nature—a matter not definitely decided—the Legislature evinced no intent that the provisions should apply to actions pending when it became effective. *Shielcrawt v. Moffett,* supra. As to actions instituted after the effective date of the legislation, the constitutionality of § 61–b is in dispute. See *Wolf* v. *Atkinson,* 1944, 49 N.Y.S.2d 703, 182 Misc. 675 (constitutional); *Citron* v. *Mangel Stores Corp.,* Sup.Ct.1944, 50 N.Y.S.2d 416 (unconstitutional); Zlinkoff, The American Investor and the Constitutionality of Section 61–B of the New York General Corporation Law, 1945, 54 Yale L.J. 352.

New Jersey also enacted a statute, similar to Chapters 667 and 668 of the New York Law. See P.L.1945, Ch. 131, R.S.Cum.Supp. 14:3–15. The New Jersey provision similar to Chapter 668, § 61–B, differs, however, in that it specifically applies retroactively. It has been held that this provision is procedural and hence will not govern a pending action brought against a New Jersey corporation in the New York courts. *Shielcrawt v. Moffett,* 1945, 56 N.Y.S.2d 134, 184 Misc. 1074.

See, also generally, 2 Moore's Federal Practice, 1938, 2250–2253, and Cum.Supplement § 23.05.

The decisions here discussed show that the question is a debatable one, and that there is respectable authority for either view, with a recent trend towards the view that Rule 23(b)(1) is procedural. There is reason to say that the question is one which should not be decided by the Supreme Court ex parte, but left to await a judicial decision in a litigated case, and that in the light of the material in this note, the only inference to be drawn from a failure to amend rule 23(b) would be that the question is postponed to await a litigated case.

The Advisory Committee is unanimously of the opinion that this course should be followed.

If, however, the final conclusion is that the rule deals with a matter of substantive right, then the rule should be amended by adding a provision that Rule 23(b)(1) does not apply in jurisdictions where state law permits a shareholder to maintain a secondary action, although he was not a shareholder at the time of the transactions of which he complains.

1966 AMENDMENT

Difficulties with the original rule. The categories of class actions in the original rule were defined in terms of the abstract nature of the rights involved: the so-called "true" category was defined as involving "joint, common, or secondary rights"; the "hybrid" category, as involving "several" rights related to "specific property"; the "spurious" category, as involving "several" rights affected by a common question and related to common relief. It was thought that the definitions accurately described the situations amenable to the class-suit device, and also would indicate the proper extent of the judgment in each category, which would in turn help to determine the res judicata effect of the judgment if questioned in a later action. Thus the judgments in "true" and "hybrid" class actions would extend to the class (although in somewhat different ways); the judgment in a "spurious" class action would extend only to the parties including intervenors. See Moore, Federal Rules of Civil Procedure: Some Problems Raised by the Preliminary Draft, 25 Geo.L.J. 551, 570–76 (1937).

In practice the terms "joint," "common," etc., which were used as the basis of the Rule 23 classification proved obscure and uncertain. See Chafee, Some Problems of Equity 245–46, 256–57 (1950); Kalven & Rosenfield, The Contemporary Function of the Class Suit, 8 U. of Chi.L.Rev. 684, 707 & n. 73 (1941); Keeffe, Levy & Donovan, Lee Defeats Ben Hur, 33 Corn.L.Q. 327, 329–36 (1948); Developments in the Law: Multiparty Litigation in the Federal Courts, 71 Harv.L.Rev. 874, 931 (1958); Advisory Committee's Note to Rule 19, as amended. The courts had considerable difficulty with these terms. See, e.g., *Gullo* v. *Veterans' Co–op Housing Assn.,* 13 F.R.D. 11 (D.D.C.1952); *Shipley* v. *Pittsburgh & L. E. R. Co.,* 70 F.Supp. 870 (W.D.Pa.1947); *Deckert* v. *Independence Shares Corp.,* 27 F.Supp. 763 (E.D.Pa.1939), rev'd, 108 F.2d 51 (3d Cir.1939), rev'd, 311 U.S. 282, 61 S.Ct. 229, 85 L.Ed. 189 (1940), on remand, 39 F.Supp. 592 (E.D.Pa.1941), rev'd sub nom. *Pennsylvania Co. for Ins. on Lives* v. *Deckert,* 123 F.2d 979 (3d Cir.1941)(see Chafee, supra, at 264–65).

Nor did the rule provide an adequate guide to the proper extent of the judgments in class actions. First, we find instances of the courts classifying actions as "true" or intimating that the judgments would be decisive for the class where these results seemed appropriate but were reached by dint of depriving the word "several" of coherent meaning. See, e.g., *System Federation No. 91* v. *Reed,* 180 F.2d 991 (6th Cir.1950); *Wilson* v. *City of Paducah,* 100 F.Supp. 116 (W.D.Ky.1951); *Citizens Banking Co.* v. *Monticello State Bank,* 143 F.2d 261 (8th Cir.1944); *Redmond* v. *Commerce Trust Co.,* 144 F.2d 140 (8th Cir.1944), cert. denied, 323 U.S. 776, 65 S.Ct. 187, 89 L.Ed. 620 (1944); *United States* v. *American Optical Co.,* 97 F.Supp. 66 (N.D.Ill.1951); *National Hairdressers' & C. Assn.* v. *Philad Co.,* 34 F.Supp. 264 (D.Del.1940); 41 F.Supp. 701 (D.Del.1941), aff'd mem., 129 F.2d 1020 (3d Cir.1942). Second, we find cases classified by the courts as "spurious" in which, on a realistic view, it would seem fitting for the judgments to extend to the class. See, e.g., *Knapp* v. *Bankers Sec. Corp.,* 17 F.R.D. 245 (E.D.Pa.1954), aff'd 230 F.2d 717 (3d Cir.1956); *Giesecke* v. *Denver Tramway Corp.,* 81 F.Supp. 957 (D.Del.1949); *York* v. *Guaranty Trust Co.,* 143 F.2d 503 (2d Cir.1944), rev'd on grounds not here relevant, 326 U.S. 99, 65 S.Ct. 1464, 89 L.Ed. 2079 (1945)(see Chafee, supra, at 208); cf. *Webster Eisenlohr, Inc.* v. *Kalodner,* 145 F.2d 316, 320 (3d Cir.1944), cert. denied, 325 U.S. 867, 65 S.Ct. 1404, 89 L.Ed. 1986 (1945). But cf. the early decisions, *Duke of Bedford* v. *Ellis,* [1901] A.C. 1; *Sheffield Waterworks* v. *Yeomans,* L.R. 2 Ch.App. 8 (1866); *Brown* v. *Vermuden,* 1 Ch.Cas. 272, 22 Eng.Rep. 796 (1676).

The "spurious" action envisaged by original Rule 23 was in any event an anomaly because, although denominated a "class" action and pleaded as such, it was supposed not to adjudicate the rights or liabilities of any person not a party. It was believed to be an advantage of the "spurious" category that it would invite decisions that a member of the "class" could, like a member of the class in a "true" or "hybrid" action, intervene on an ancillary basis without being required to show an independent basis of Federal jurisdiction, and have the benefit of the date of the commencement of the action for purposes of the statute of limitations. See 3 Moore's Federal Practice, pars. 23.10[1], 23.12 (2d ed. 1963). These results were attained in some instances but not in others. On the statute of limitations, see *Union Carbide & Carbon Corp.* v. *Nisley,* 300 F.2d 561 (10th Cir.1961), pet. cert. dism., 371 U.S. 801, 83 S.Ct. 13, 9 L.Ed.2d 46 (1962); but cf. *P. W. Husserl, Inc.* v. *Simplicity Pattern Co.,* 25 F.R.D. 264 (S.D.N.Y.1960); *Athas* v. *Day,* 161 F.Supp. 916 (D.Colo.1958). On ancillary intervention, see *Amen* v. *Black,* 234 F.2d 12 (10th Cir.1956), cert. granted, 352 U.S. 888, 77 S.Ct. 127, 1 L.Ed.2d 84 (1956), dism. on stip., 355 U.S. 600, 78 S.Ct. 530, 2 L.Ed.2d 523 (1958); but cf. *Wagner* v. *Kemper,* 13 F.R.D. 128 (W.D.Mo. 1952). The results, however, can hardly depend upon the mere appearance of a "spurious" category in the rule; they should turn on more basic considerations. See discussion of subdivision (c)(1) below.

Finally, the original rule did not squarely address itself to the question of the measures that might be taken during the course of the action to assure procedural fairness, particularly giving notice to members of the class, which may in turn be related in some instances to the extension of the judgment to the class. See Chafee, supra, at 230–31; Keeffe, Levy & Donovan, supra; Developments in the Law, supra, 71 Harv.L.Rev. at 937–38; Note Binding Effect of Class Actions, 67 Harv.L.Rev. 1059, 1062–65 (1954); Note, Federal Class Actions: A Suggested Revision of Rule 23, 46 Colum.L.Rev. 818, 833–36 (1946); Mich.Gen.Court R. 208.4 (effective Jan. 1, 1963); Idaho R.Civ.P. 23(d); Minn. R.Civ.P. 23.04; N.Dak.R.Civ.P. 23(d).

The amended rule describes in more practical terms the occasions for maintaining class actions; provides that all class actions maintained to the end as such will result in judgments including those whom the court finds to be members of the class, whether or not the judgment is favorable to the class; and refers to the measures which can be taken to assure the fair conduct of these actions.

Subdivision (a) states the prerequisites for maintaining any class action in terms of the numerousness of the class making joinder of the members impracticable, the existence of questions common to the class, and the desired qualifications of the representative parties. See Weinstein, Revision of Procedure: Some Problems in Class Actions, 9 Buffalo L.Rev. 433, 458–59 (1960); 2 Barron & Holtzoff, Federal Practice & Procedure § 562, at 265, § 572, at 351–52 (Wright ed. 1961). These are necessary but not sufficient conditions for a class action. See, e.g., *Giordano* v. *Radio Corp. of Am.,* 183 F.2d 558, 560 (3d Cir.1950); *Zachman* v. *Erwin,* 186 F.Supp. 681 (S.D.Tex.1959); *Baim & Blank, Inc.* v. *Warren–Connelly Co., Inc.,* 19 F.R.D. 108 (S.D.N.Y.1956). Subdivision (b) describes the additional elements which in varying situations justify the use of a class action.

Subdivision (b)(1). The difficulties which would be likely to arise if resort were had to separate actions by or against the individual members of the class here furnish the reasons for, and the principal key to, the propriety and value of utilizing the class-action device. The considerations stated under clauses (A) and (B) are comparable to certain of the elements which define the persons whose joinder in an action is desirable as stated in Rule 19(a), as amended. See amended Rule 19(a)(2)(i) and (ii), and the Advisory Committee's Note thereto; Hazard, Indispensable Party: The Historical Origin of a Procedural Phantom, 61 Colum.L.Rev. 1254, 1259–60 (1961); cf. 3 Moore, supra, par. 23.08 at 3435.

Clause (A): One person may have rights against, or be under duties toward, numerous persons constituting a class, and be so positioned that conflicting or varying adjudications in lawsuits with individual members of the class might establish incompatible standards to govern his conduct. The class action device can be used effectively to obviate the actual or virtual dilemma which would thus confront the party opposing the class. The matter has been stated thus: "The felt necessity for a class action is greatest when the courts are called upon to order or sanction the alteration of the status quo in circumstances such that a large number of persons are in a position to call on a single person to alter the status quo, or to complain if it is altered, and the possibility exists that [the] actor might be called upon to act in inconsistent ways." Louisell & Hazard, Pleading and Procedure: State and Federal 719 (1962); see *Supreme Tribe of Ben Hur* v. *Cauble,* 255 U.S. 356, 366–67, 41 S.Ct. 338, 65 L.Ed. 673 (1921). To illustrate: Separate actions by individuals against a municipality to declare a bond issue invalid or condition or limit it, to prevent or limit the making of a particular appropriation or to compel or invalidate an assessment, might create a risk of inconsistent or varying determinations. In the same way, individual litigations of the rights and duties of riparian owners, or of landowners' rights and duties respecting a claimed nuisance, could create a possibility of incompatible adjudications. Actions by or against a class provide a ready and fair means of achieving unitary adjudication. See *Maricopa County Mun.Water Con. Dist.* v. *Looney,* 219 F.2d 529 (9th Cir.1955); *Rank* v. *Krug,* 142 F.Supp. 1, 154–59 (S.D.Cal.1956), on app., *State of California* v. *Rank,* 293 F.2d 340, 348 (9th Cir.1961); *Gart* v. *Cole,* 263 F.2d 244 (2d Cir.1959), cert. denied 359 U.S. 978, 79 S.Ct. 898, 3 L.Ed.2d 929 (1959); cf. *Martinez* v. *Maverick Cty. Water Con. & Imp. Dist.,* 219 F.2d 666 (5th Cir.1955); 3 Moore, supra, par. 23.11[2], at 3458–59.

Clause (B): This clause takes in situations where the judgment in a nonclass action by or against an individual member of the class, while not technically concluding the other members, might do so as a practical matter. The vice of an individual action would lie in the fact that the other members of the class, thus practically concluded, would have had no representation in the lawsuit. In an action by policy holders against a fraternal benefit association attacking a financial reorganization of the society, it would hardly have been practical, if indeed it would have been possible, to confine the effects of a validation of the reorganization to the individual plaintiffs. Consequently a class action was called for with adequate representation of all members of the class. See *Supreme Tribe of Ben Hur* v. *Cauble,* 255 U.S. 356, 41 S.Ct. 338, 65 L.Ed. 673 (1921); *Waybright* v. *Columbian Mut. Life Ins. Co.,* 30 F.Supp. 885 (W.D.Tenn.1939); cf. *Smith* v. *Swormstedt,* 16 How. (57 U.S.) 288 (1853). For much the same reason actions by shareholders to compel the declaration of a dividend, the proper recognition and handling of redemption or pre-emption rights, or the like (or actions by the corporation for corresponding declarations of rights), should ordinarily be conducted as class actions, although the matter has been much obscured by the insistence that each shareholder has an individual claim. See *Knapp* v. *Bankers Securities Corp.,* 17 F.R.D. 245 (E.D.Pa.1954), aff'd, 230 F.2d 717 (3d Cir.1956); *Giesecke* v. *Denver Tramway Corp.,* 81 F.Supp. 957 (D.Del.1949); *Zahn* v. *Transamerica Corp.,* 162 F.2d 36 (3d Cir.1947); *Speed* v. *Transamerica Corp.,* 100 F.Supp. 461 (D.Del.1951); *Sobel*

v. *Whittier Corp.,* 95 F.Supp. 643 (E.D.Mich.1951), app. dism., 195 F.2d 361 (6th Cir.1952); *Goldberg* v. *Whittier Corp.,* 111 F.Supp. 382 (E.D.Mich.1953); *Dann* v. *Studebaker–Packard Corp.,* 288 F.2d 201 (6th Cir.1961); *Edgerton* v. *Armour & Co.,* 94 F.Supp. 549 (S.D.Cal. 1950); *Ames* v. *Mengel Co.,* 190 F.2d 344 (2d Cir.1951). These shareholders' actions are to be distinguished from derivative actions by shareholders dealt with in new Rule 23.1. The same reasoning applies to an action which charges a breach of trust by an indenture trustee or other fiduciary similarly affecting the members of a larger class of security holders or other beneficiaries, and which requires an accounting or like measures to restore the subject of the trust. See *Boesenberg* v. *Chicago T. & T. Co.,* 128 F.2d 245 (7th Cir.1942); *Citizens Banking Co.* v. *Monticello State Bank,* 143 F.2d 261 (8th Cir.1944); *Redmond* v. *Commerce Trust Co.,* 144 F.2d 140 (8th Cir.1944), cert. denied, 323 U.S. 776, 65 S.Ct. 187, 89 L.Ed. 620 (1944); cf. *York* v. *Guaranty Trust Co.,* 143 F.2d 503 (2d Cir.1944), rev'd on grounds not here relevant, 326 U.S. 99, 65 S.Ct. 1464, 89 L.Ed. 2079 (1945).

In various situations an adjudication as to one or more members of the class will necessarily or probably have an adverse practical effect on the interests of other members who should therefore be represented in the lawsuit. This is plainly the case when claims are made by numerous persons against a fund insufficient to satisfy all claims. A class action by or against representative members to settle the validity of the claims as a whole, or in groups, followed by separate proof of the amount of each valid claim and proportionate distribution of the fund, meets the problem. Cf. *Dickinson* v. *Burnham,* 197 F.2d 973 (2d Cir.1952), cert. denied, 344 U.S. 875, 73 S.Ct. 169, 97 L.Ed. 678 (1952); 3 Moore, supra, at par. 23.09. The same reasoning applies to an action by a creditor to set aside a fraudulent conveyance by the debtor and to appropriate the property to his claim, when the debtor's assets are insufficient to pay all creditors' claims. See *Heffernan* v. *Bennett & Armour,* 110 Cal.App.2d 564, 243 P.2d 846 (1952); cf. *City & County of San Francisco* v. *Market Street Ry.,* 95 Cal.App.2d 648, 213 P.2d 780 (1950). Similar problems, however, can arise in the absence of a fund either present or potential. A negative or mandatory injunction secured by one of a numerous class may disable the opposing party from performing claimed duties toward the other members of the class or materially affect his ability to do so. An adjudication as to movie "clearances and runs" nominally affecting only one exhibitor would often have practical effects on all the exhibitors in the same territorial area. Cf. *United States* v. *Paramount Pictures, Inc.,* 66 F.Supp. 323, 341–46 (S.D.N.Y.1946); 334 U.S. 131, 144–48, 68 S.Ct. 915, 92 L.Ed. 1260 (1948). Assuming a sufficiently numerous class of exhibitors, a class action would be advisable. (Here representation of subclasses of exhibitors could become necessary; see subdivision (c)(3)(B).)

Subdivision (b)(2). This subdivision is intended to reach situations where a party has taken action or refused to take action with respect to a class, and final relief of an injunctive nature or of a corresponding declaratory nature, settling the legality of the behavior with respect to the class as a whole, is appropriate. Declaratory relief "corresponds" to injunctive relief when as a practical matter it affords injunctive relief or serves as a basis for later injunctive relief. The subdivision does not extend to cases in which the appropriate final relief relates exclusively or predominantly to money damages. Action or inaction is directed to a class within the meaning of this subdivision even if it has taken effect or is threatened only as to one or a few members of the class, provided it is based on grounds which have general application to the class.

Illustrative are various actions in the civil-rights field where a party is charged with discriminating unlawfully against a class, usually one whose members are incapable of specific enumeration. See *Potts* v. *Flax,* 313 F.2d 284 (5th Cir.1963); *Bailey* v. *Patterson,* 323 F.2d 201 (5th Cir.1963), cert. denied, 376 U.S. 910, 84 S.Ct. 666, 11 L.Ed.2d 609 (1964); *Brunson* v. *Board of Trustees of School District No. 1, Clarendon Cty., S.C.,* 311 F.2d 107 (4th Cir.1962), cert. denied, 373 U.S. 933, 83 S.Ct. 1538, 10 L.Ed.2d 690 (1963); *Green* v. *School Bd. of Roanoke, Va.,* 304 F.2d 118 (4th Cir.1962); *Orleans Parish School Bd.* v. *Bush,* 242 F.2d 156 (5th Cir.1957), cert. denied, 354 U.S. 921, 77 S.Ct. 1380, 1 L.Ed.2d 1436 (1957); *Mannings* v. *Board of Public Inst. of Hillsborough County, Fla.,* 277 F.2d 370 (5th Cir.1960); *Northcross* v. *Board of Ed. of City of Memphis,* 302 F.2d 818 (6th Cir.1962), cert. denied, 370 U.S. 944, 82 S.Ct. 1586, 8 L.Ed.2d 810 (1962); *Frasier* v. *Board of Trustees of Univ. of N. C.,* 134 F.Supp. 589 (M.D.N.C.1955, 3-judge court), aff'd, 350 U.S. 979, 76 S.Ct. 467, 100 L.Ed. 848 (1956). Subdivision (b)(2) is not limited to civil-rights cases. Thus an action looking to specific or declaratory relief could be brought by a numerous class of purchasers, say retailers of a given description, against a seller alleged to have undertaken to sell to that class at prices higher than those set for other purchasers, say retailers of another description, when the applicable law forbids such a pricing differential. So also a patentee of a machine, charged with selling or licensing the machine on condition that purchasers or licensees also purchase or obtain licenses to use an ancillary unpatented machine, could be sued on a class basis by a numerous group of purchasers or licensees, or by a numerous group of competing sellers or licensors of the unpatented machine, to test the legality of the "tying" condition.

Subdivision (b)(3). In the situations to which this subdivision relates, class-action treatment is not as clearly called for as in those described above, but it may nevertheless be convenient and desirable depending upon the particular facts. Subdivision (b)(3) encompasses those cases in which a class action would achieve economies of time, effort, and expense, and promote uniformity of decision as to persons similarly situated, without sacrificing procedural fairness or bringing about other undesirable results. Cf. Chafee, supra, at 201.

The court is required to find, as a condition of holding that a class action may be maintained under this subdivision, that the questions common to the class predominate over the questions affecting individual members. It is only where this predominance exists that economies can be achieved by means of the class-action device. In this view, a fraud perpetrated on numerous persons by the use of similar misrepresentations may be an appealing situation for a class action, and it may remain so despite the need, if liability is found, for separate determination of the damages suffered by individuals within the class. On the other hand, although having some common core, a fraud case may be unsuited for treatment as a class action if there was material variation in the representations made or in the kinds or degrees of reliance by the persons to whom they were addressed. See *Oppenheimer* v. *F. J. Young & Co., Inc.*, 144 F.2d 387 (2d Cir.1944); *Miller* v. *National City Bank of N. Y.*, 166 F.2d 723 (2d Cir.1948); and for like problems in other contexts, see *Hughes* v. *Encyclopaedia Britannica*, 199 F.2d 295 (7th Cir.1952); *Sturgeon* v. *Great Lakes Steel Corp.*, 143 F.2d 819 (6th Cir.1944). A "mass accident" resulting in injuries to numerous persons is ordinarily not appropriate for a class action because of the likelihood that significant questions, not only of damages but of liability and defenses of liability, would be present, affecting the individuals in different ways. In these circumstances an action conducted nominally as a class action would degenerate in practice into multiple lawsuits separately tried. See *Pennsylvania R.R.* v. *United States,* 111 F.Supp. 80 (D.N.J.1953); cf. Weinstein, supra, 9 Buffalo L.Rev. at 469. Private damage claims by numerous individuals arising out of concerted antitrust violations may or may not involve predominating common questions. See *Union Carbide & Carbon Corp.* v. *Nisley,* 300 F.2d 561 (10th Cir.1961), pet. cert. dism., 371 U.S. 801, 83 S.Ct. 13, 9 L.Ed.2d 46 (1962); cf. *Weeks* v. *Bareco Oil Co.,* 125 F.2d 84 (7th Cir.1941); *Kainz* v. *Anheuser–Busch, Inc.,* 194 F.2d 737 (7th Cir.1952); *Hess* v. *Anderson, Clayton & Co.,* 20 F.R.D. 466 (S.D.Cal.1957).

That common questions predominate is not itself sufficient to justify a class action under subdivision (b)(3), for another method of handling the litigious situation may be available which has greater practical advantages. Thus one or more actions agreed to by the parties as test or model actions may be preferable to a class action; or it may prove feasible and preferable to consolidate actions. Cf. Weinstein, supra, 9 Buffalo L.Rev. at 438–54. Even when a number of separate actions are proceeding simultaneously, experience shows that the burdens on the parties and the courts can sometimes be reduced by arrangements for avoiding repetitious discovery or the like. Currently the Coordinating Committee on Multiple Litigation in the United States District Courts (a subcommittee of the Committee on Trial Practice and Technique of the Judicial Conference of the United States) is charged with developing methods for expediting such massive litigation. To reinforce the point that the court with the aid of the parties ought to assess the relative advantages of alternative procedures for handling the total controversy, subdivision (b)(3) requires, as a further condition of maintaining the class action, that the court shall find that that procedure is "superior" to the others in the particular circumstances.

Factors (A)–(D) are listed, non-exhaustively, as pertinent to the findings. The court is to consider the interests of individual members of the class in controlling their own litigations and carrying them on as they see fit. See *Weeks* v. *Bareco Oil Co.*, 125 F.2d 84, 88–90, 93–94 (7th Cir.1941)(anti-trust action); see also *Pentland* v. *Dravo Corp.*, 152 F.2d 851 (3d Cir.1945), and Chafee, supra, at 273–75, regarding policy of Fair Labor Standards Act of 1938, § 16(b), 29 U.S.C. § 216(b), prior to amendment by Portal-to-Portal Act of 1947, § 5(a). [The present provisions of 29 U.S.C. § 216(b) are not intended to be affected by Rule 23, as amended.]

In this connection the court should inform itself of any litigation actually pending by or against the individuals. The interests of individuals in conducting separate lawsuits may be so strong as to call for denial of a class action. On the other hand, these interests may be theoretic rather than practical; the class may have a high degree of cohesion and prosecution of the action through representatives would be quite unobjectionable, or the amounts at stake for individuals may be so small that separate suits would be impracticable. The burden that separate suits would impose on the party opposing the class, or upon the court calendars, may also fairly be considered. (See the discussion, under subdivision (c)(2) below, of the right of members to be excluded from the class upon their request.)

Also pertinent is the question of the desirability of concentrating the trial of the claims in the particular forum by means of a class action, in contrast to allowing the claims to be litigated separately in forums to which they would ordinarily be brought. Finally, the court should consider the problems of management which are likely to arise in the conduct of a class action.

Subdivision (c)(1). In order to give clear definition to the action, this provision requires the court to determine, as early in the proceedings as may be practicable, whether an action brought as a class action is to be so maintained. The determination depends in each case on satisfaction of the terms of subdivision (a) and the relevant provisions of subdivision (b).

An order embodying a determination can be conditional; the court may rule, for example, that a class action may be maintained only if the representation is improved through intervention of additional parties of a stated type. A determination once made can be altered or amended before the decision on the merits if, upon fuller development of the facts, the original determination appears unsound. A negative determination means that the action should be stripped of its character as a class action. See subdivision (d)(4). Although an action thus becomes a nonclass action, the court may still be receptive to interventions before the decision on the merits so that the litigation may cover as many interests as can be conveniently handled; the questions whether the intervenors in the nonclass action shall be permitted to claim "ancillary" jurisdiction or the benefit of the date of the commencement of the action for purposes of the statute of limitations are to be decided by reference to the laws governing jurisdiction and limitations as they apply in particular contexts.

Whether the court should require notice to be given to members of the class of its intention to make a determination, or of the order embodying it, is left to the court's discretion under subdivision (d)(2).

Subdivision (c)(2) makes special provision for class actions maintained under subdivision (b)(3). As noted in the discussion of the latter subdivision, the interests of the individuals in pursuing their own litigations may be so strong here as to warrant denial of a class action altogether. Even when a class action is maintained under subdivision (b)(3), this individual interest is respected. Thus the court is required to direct notice to the members of the class of the right of each member to be excluded from the class upon his request. A member who does not request exclusion may, if he wishes, enter an appearance in the action through his counsel; whether or not he does so, the judgment in the action will embrace him.

The notice, setting forth the alternatives open to the members of the class, is to be the best practicable under the circumstances, and shall include individual notice to the members who can be identified through reasonable effort. (For further discussion of this notice, see the statement under subdivision (d)(2) below.)

Subdivision (c)(3). The judgment in a class action maintained as such to the end will embrace the class, that is, in a class action under subdivision (b)(1) or (b)(2), those found by the court to be class members; in a class action under subdivision (b)(3), those to whom the notice prescribed by subdivision (c)(2) was directed, excepting those who requested exclusion or who are ultimately found by the court not to be members of the class. The judgment has this scope whether it is favorable or unfavorable to the class. In a (b)(1) or (b)(2) action the judgment "describes" the members of the class, but need not specify the individual members; in a (b)(3) action the judgment "specifies" the individual members who have been identified and described the others.

Compare subdivision (c)(4) as to actions conducted as class actions only with respect to particular issues. Where the class-action character of the lawsuit is based solely on the existence of a "limited fund," the judgment, while extending to all claims of class members against the fund, has ordinarily left unaffected the personal claims of nonappearing members against the debtor. See 3 Moore, supra, par. 23.11[4].

Hitherto, in a few actions conducted as "spurious" class actions and thus nominally designed to extend only to parties and others intervening before the determination of liability, courts have held or intimated that class members might be permitted to intervene after a decision on the merits favorable to their interests, in order to secure the benefits of the decision for themselves, although they would presumably be unaffected by an unfavorable decision. See, as to the propriety of this so-called "one-way" intervention in "spurious" actions, the conflicting views expressed in *Union Carbide & Carbon Corp.* v. *Nisley*, 300 F.2d 561 (10th Cir.1961), pet. cert. dism., 371 U.S. 801, 83 S.Ct. 13, 9 L.Ed.2d 46

(1962); *York* v. *Guaranty Trust Co.*, 143 F.2d 503, 529 (2d Cir.1944), rev'd on grounds not here relevant, 326 U.S. 99, 65 S.Ct. 1464, 89 L.Ed. 2079 (1945); *Pentland* v. *Dravo Corp.*, 152 F.2d 851, 856 (3d Cir.1945); *Speed* v. *Transamerica Corp.*, 100 F.Supp. 461, 463 (D.Del.1951); *State Wholesale Grocers* v. *Great Atl. & Pac. Tea Co.*, 24 F.R.D. 510 (N.D.Ill.1959); *Alabama Ind. Serv. Stat. Assn.* v. *Shell Pet. Corp.*, 28 F.Supp. 386, 390 (N.D.Ala.1939); *Tolliver* v. *Cudahy Packing Co.*, 39 F.Supp. 337, 339 (E.D.Tenn.1941); *Kalven & Rosenfield*, supra, 8 U. of Chi.L.Rev. 684 (1941); Comment, 53 Nw.U.L.Rev. 627, 632–33 (1958); Developments in the Law, supra, 71 Harv.L.Rev. at 935; 2 Barron & Holtzoff, supra, § 568; but cf. *Lockwood* v. *Hercules Powder Co.*, 7 F.R.D. 24, 28–29 (W.D.Mo.1947); *Abram* v. *San Joaquin Cotton Oil Co.*, 46 F.Supp. 969, 976–77 (S.D.Cal. 1942); Chafee, supra, at 280, 285; 3 Moore, supra, par. 23.12, at 3476. Under proposed subdivision (c)(3), one-way intervention is excluded; the action will have been early determined to be a class or nonclass action, and in the former case the judgment, whether or not favorable, will include the class, as above stated.

Although thus declaring that the judgment in a class action includes the class, as defined, subdivision (c)(3) does not disturb the recognized principle that the court conducting the action cannot predetermine the res judicata effect of the judgment; this can be tested only in a subsequent action. See Restatement, Judgments § 86, comment (h), § 116 (1942). The court, however, in framing the judgment in any suit brought as a class action, must decide what its extent or coverage shall be, and if the matter is carefully considered, questions of res judicata are less likely to be raised at a later time and if raised will be more satisfactorily answered. See Chafee, supra, at 294; Weinstein, supra, 9 Buffalo L.Rev. at 460.

Subdivision (c)(4). This provision recognizes that an action may be maintained as a class action as to particular issues only. For example, in a fraud or similar case the action may retain its "class" character only through the adjudication of liability to the class; the members of the class may thereafter be required to come in individually and prove the amounts of their respective claims.

Two or more classes may be represented in a single action. Where a class is found to include subclasses divergent in interest, the class may be divided correspondingly, and each subclass treated as a class.

Subdivision (d) is concerned with the fair and efficient conduct of the action and lists some types of orders which may be appropriate.

The court should consider how the proceedings are to be arranged in sequence, and what measures should be taken to simplify the proof and argument. See subdivision (d)(1). The orders resulting from this consideration, like the others referred to in subdivision (d), may be combined with a pretrial order under Rule 16, and are subject to modification as the case proceeds.

Subdivision (d)(2) sets out a non-exhaustive list of possible occasions for orders requiring notice to the class. Such notice is not a novel conception. For example, in "limited fund" cases, members of the class have been notified to present individual claims after the basic class decision. Notice has gone to members of a class so that they might express any opposition to the representation, see *United States* v. *American Optical Co.*, 97 F.Supp. 66 (N.D.Ill.1951), and 1950–51 CCH Trade Cases 64573–74 (par. 62869); cf. *Weeks* v. *Bareco Oil Co.*, 125 F.2d 84, 94 (7th Cir.1941), and notice may encourage interventions to improve the representation of the class. Cf. *Oppenheimer* v. *F. J. Young & Co.*, 144 F.2d 387 (2d Cir.1944). Notice has been used to poll members on a proposed modification of a consent decree. See record in *Sam Fox Publishing Co.* v. *United States*, 366 U.S. 683, 81 S.Ct. 1309, 6 L.Ed.2d 604 (1961).

Subdivision (d)(2) does not require notice at any stage, but rather calls attention to its availability and invokes the court's discretion. In the degree that there is cohesiveness or unity in the class and the representation is effective, the need for notice to the class will tend toward a minimum. These indicators suggest that notice under subdivision (d)(2) may be particularly useful and advisable in certain class actions maintained under subdivision (b)(3), for example, to permit members of the class to object to the representation. Indeed, under subdivision (c)(2), notice must be ordered, and is not merely discretionary, to give the members in a subdivision (b)(3) class action an opportunity to secure exclusion from the class. This mandatory notice pursuant to subdivision (c)(2), together with any discretionary notice which the court may find it advisable to give under subdivision (d)(2), is designed to fulfill requirements of due process to which the class action procedure is of course subject. See *Hansberry* v. *Lee*, 311 U.S. 32, 61 S.Ct. 115, 85 L.Ed. 22 (1940); *Mullane* v. *Central Hanover Bank & Trust Co.*, 339 U.S. 306, 70 S.Ct. 652, 94 L.Ed. 865 (1950); cf. *Dickinson* v. *Burnham*, 197 F.2d 973, 979 (2d Cir.1952), and studies cited at 979 n. 4; see also *All American Airways, Inc.* v. *Elderd*, 209 F.2d 247, 249

(2d Cir.1954); *Gart* v. *Cole*, 263 F.2d 244, 248–49 (2d Cir.1959), cert. denied, 359 U.S. 978, 79 S.Ct. 898, 3 L.Ed.2d 929 (1959).

Notice to members of the class, whenever employed under amended Rule 23, should be accommodated to the particular purpose but need not comply with the formalities for service of process. See Chafee, supra, at 230–31; *Brendle* v. *Smith*, 7 F.R.D. 119 (S.D.N.Y.1946). The fact that notice is given at one stage of the action does not mean that it must be given at subsequent stages. Notice is available fundamentally "for the protection of the members of the class or otherwise for the fair conduct of the action" and should not be used merely as a device for the undesirable solicitation of claims. See the discussion in *Cherner* v. *Transitron Electronic Corp.*, 201 F.Supp. 934 (D.Mass.1962); *Hormel* v. *United States*, 17 F.R.D. 303 (S.D.N.Y.1955).

In appropriate cases the court should notify interested government agencies of the pendency of the action or of particular steps therein.

Subdivision (d)(3) reflects the possibility of conditioning the maintenance of a class action, e.g., on the strengthening of the representation, see subdivision (c)(1) above; and recognizes that the imposition of conditions on intervenors may be required for the proper and efficient conduct of the action.

As to orders under **subdivision (d)(4)**, see subdivision (c)(1) above.

Subdivision (e) requires approval of the court, after notice, for the dismissal or compromise of any class action.

1987 AMENDMENT

The amendments are technical. No substantive change is intended.

1998 AMENDMENT

Subdivision (f). This permissive interlocutory appeal provision is adopted under the power conferred by 28 U.S.C. § 1292(e). Appeal from an order granting or denying class certification is permitted in the sole discretion of the court of appeals. No other type of Rule 23 order is covered by this provision. The court of appeals is given unfettered discretion whether to permit the appeal, akin to the discretion exercised by the Supreme Court in acting on a petition for certiorari. This discretion suggests an analogy to the provision in 28 U.S.C. § 1292(b) for permissive appeal on certification by a district court. Subdivision (f), however, departs from the § 1292(b) model in two significant ways. It does not require that the district court certify the certification ruling for appeal, although the district court often can assist the parties and court of appeals by offering advice on the desirability of appeal. And it does not include the potentially limiting requirements of § 1292(b) that the district court order "involve[] a controlling question of law as to which there is substantial ground for difference of opinion and that an immediate appeal from the order may materially advance the ultimate termination of the litigation."

The courts of appeals will develop standards for granting review that reflect the changing areas of uncertainty in class litigation. The Federal Judicial Center study supports the view that many suits with class-action allegations present familiar and almost routine issues that are no more worthy of immediate appeal than many other interlocutory rulings. Yet several concerns justify expansion of present opportunities to appeal. An order denying certification may confront the plaintiff with a situation in which the only sure path to appellate review is by proceeding to final judgment on the merits of an individual claim that, standing alone, is far smaller than the costs of litigation. An order granting certification, on the other hand, may force a defendant to settle rather than incur the costs of defending a class action and run the risk of potentially ruinous liability. These concerns can be met at low cost by establishing in the court of appeals a discretionary power to grant interlocutory review in cases that show appeal-worthy certification issues.

Permission to appeal may be granted or denied on the basis of any consideration that the court of appeals finds persuasive. Permission is most likely to be granted when the certification decision turns on a novel or unsettled question of law, or when, as a practical matter, the decision on certification is likely dispositive of the litigation.

The district court, having worked through the certification decision, often will be able to provide cogent advice on the factors that bear on the decision whether to permit appeal. This advice can be particularly valuable if the certification decision is tentative. Even as to a firm certification decision, a statement of reasons bearing on the probable benefits and costs of immediate appeal can help focus the court of appeals decision, and may persuade the disappointed party that an attempt to appeal would be fruitless.

The 10–day period for seeking permission to appeal is designed to reduce the risk that attempted appeals will disrupt continuing proceedings. It is expected that the courts of appeals will act quickly in making the preliminary determination whether to permit appeal. Permission to appeal does not stay trial court proceedings. A stay should be sought first from the trial court. If the trial court refuses a stay, its action and any explanation of its views should weigh heavily with the court of appeals.

Appellate Rule 5 has been modified to establish the procedure for petitioning for leave to appeal under subdivision (f).

Changes Made after Publication (GAP Report)

No changes were made in the text of Rule 23(f) as published.

Several changes were made in the published Committee Note. (1) References to 28 U.S.C. § 1292(b) interlocutory appeals were revised to dispel any implication that the restrictive elements of § 1292(b) should be read into Rule 23(f). New emphasis was placed on court of appeals discretion by making explicit the analogy to certiorari discretion. (2) Suggestions that the new procedure is a "modest" expansion of appeal opportunities, to be applied with "restraint," and that permission "almost always will be denied when the certification decision turns on case-specific matters of fact and district court discretion," were deleted. It was thought better simply to observe that courts of appeals will develop standards "that reflect the changing areas of uncertainty in class litigation."

2003 AMENDMENT

Subdivision (c). Subdivision (c) is amended in several respects. The requirement that the court determine whether to certify a class "as soon as practicable after commencement of an action" is replaced by requiring determination "at an early practicable time." The notice provisions are substantially revised.

Paragraph (1). Subdivision (c)(1)(A) is changed to require that the determination whether to certify a class be made "at an early practicable time." The "as soon as practicable" exaction neither reflect s prevailing practice nor captures the many valid reasons that may justify deferring the initial certification decision. See Willging, Hooper & Niemic, Empirical Study of Class Actions in Four Federal District Courts: Final Report to the Advisory Committee on Civil Rules 26–36 (Federal Judicial Center 1996).

Time may be needed to gather information necessary to make the certification decision. Although an evaluation of the probable outcome on the merits is not properly part of the certification decision, discovery in aid of the certification decision often includes information required to identify the nature of the issues that actually will be presented at trial. In this sense it is appropriate to conduct controlled discovery into the "merits," limited to those aspects relevant to making the certification decision on an informed basis. Active judicial supervision may be required to achieve the most effective balance that expedites an informed certification determination without forcing an artificial and ulti-mately wasteful division between "certification discovery" and "merits discovery." A critical need is to determine how the case will be tried. An increasing number of courts require a party requesting class certification to present a "trial plan" that describes the issues likely to be presented at trial and tests whether they are susceptible of class-wide proof. See Manual For Complex Litigation Third, § 21.213, p. 44; § 30.11, p. 214; § 30.12, p. 215.

Other considerations may affect the timing of the certification decision. The party opposing the class may prefer to win dismissal or summary judgment as to the individual plaintiffs without certification and without binding the class that might have been certified. Time may be needed to explore designation of class counsel under Rule 23(g), recognizing that in many cases the need to progress toward the certification determination may require designation of interim counsel under Rule 23(g)(2)(A).

Although many circumstances may justify deferring the certification decision, active management may be necessary to ensure that the certification decision is not unjustifiably delayed.

Subdivision (c)(1)(C) reflects two amendments. The provision that a class certification "may be conditional" is deleted. A court that is not satisfied that the requirements of Rule 23 have been met should refuse certification until they have been met. The provision that permits alteration or amendment of an order granting or denying class certification is amended to set the cut-off point at final judgment rather than "the decision on the merits." This change avoids the possible ambiguity in referring to "the decision on the merits." Following a determination of liability, for example, proceedings to define the remedy may demonstrate the need to amend the class definition or subdivide the class. In this setting the final judgment concept is pragmatic. It is not the same as the concept used for appeal purposes, but it should be flexible, particularly in protract ed litigation.

The authority to amend an order under Rule 23(c)(1) before final judgment does not restore the practice of "one-way intervention" that was rejected by the 1966 revision of Rule 23. A determination of liability after certification, however, may show a need to amend the class definition. Decertification may be warranted after further proceedings.

If the definition of a class certified under Rule 23(b)(3) is altered to include members who have not been afforded notice and an opportunity to request exclusion, notice— including an opportunity to request exclusion—must be directed to the new class members under Rule 23(c)(2)(B).

Paragraph (2). The first change made in Rule 23(c)(2) is to call attention to the court's authority—already established in part by Rule 23(d)(2)—to direct notice of certification to a Rule 23(b)(1) or (b)(2) class. The present rule expressly requires notice only in actions certified under Rule 23(b)(3). Members of classes certified under Rules 23(b)(1) or (b)(2) have interests that may deserve protection by notice.

The authority to direct notice to class members in a (b)(1) or (b)(2) class action should be exercised with care. For several reasons, there may be less need for notice than in a (b)(3) class action. There is no right to request exclusion from a (b)(1) or (b)(2) class. The characteristics of the class may reduce the need for formal notice. The cost of providing notice, moreover, could easily cripple actions that do not seek damages. The court may decide not to direct notice after balancing the risk that notice costs may deter the pursuit of class relief against the benefits of notice.

When the court does direct certification notice in a (b)(1) or (b)(2) class action, the discretion and flexibility established by subdivision (c)(2)(A) extend to the method of giving notice. Notice facilitates the opportunity to participate. Notice calculated to reach a significant number of class members often will protect the interests of all. Informal methods may prove effective. A simple posting in a place visited by many class members, directing attention to a source of more detailed information, may suffice. The court should consider the costs of notice in relation to the probable reach of inexpensive methods.

If a Rule 23(b)(3) class is certified in conjunction with a (b)(2) class, the (c)(2)(B) notice requirements must be satisfied as to the (b)(3) class.

The direction that class-certification notice be couched in plain, easily understood language is a reminder of the need to work unremittingly at the difficult task of communicating with class members. It is difficult to provide information about most class actions that is both accurate and easily understood by class members who are not themselves lawyers. Factual uncertainty, legal complexity, and the complication of class-action procedure raise the barriers high. The Federal Judicial Center has created illustrative clear-notice forms that provide a helpful starting point for actions similar to those described in the forms.

Subdivision (e). Subdivision (e) is amended to strengthen the process of reviewing proposed class-action settlements. Settlement may be a desirable means of resolving a class action. But court review and approval are essential to assure adequate representation of class members who have not participated in shaping the settlement.

Paragraph (1). Subdivision (e)(1)(A) expressly recognizes the power of a class representative to settle class claims, issues, or defenses.

Rule 23(e)(1)(A) resolves the ambiguity in former Rule 23(e)'s reference to dismissal or compromise of "a class action." That language could be—and at times was—read to require court approval of settlements with putative class representatives that resolved only individual claims. See Manual for Complex Litigation Third, § 30.41. The new rule requires approval only if the claims, issues, or defenses of a certified class are resolved by a settlement, voluntary dismissal, or compromise.

Subdivision (e)(1)(B) carries forward the notice requirement of present Rule 23(e) when the settlement binds the class through claim or issue preclusion; notice is not required when the settlement binds only the individual class representatives. Notice of a settlement binding on the class is required either when the settlement follows class certification or when the decisions on certification and settlement proceed simultaneously.

Reasonable settlement notice may require individual notice in the manner required by Rule 23(c)(2)(B) for certification notice to a Rule 23(b)(3) class. Individual notice is appropriate, for example, if class members are required to take action—such as filing claims—to participate in the judgment, or if the court orders a settlement opt-out opportunity under Rule 23(e)(3).

Subdivision (e)(1)(C) confirms and mandates the already common practice of holding hearings as part of the process of approving settlement, voluntary dismissal, or compromise that would bind members of a class.

Subdivision (e)(1)(C) states the standard for approving a proposed settlement that would bind class members. The settlement must be fair, reasonable, and adequate. A helpful review of many factors that may deserve consideration is provided by In re: Prudential Ins. Co. America Sales Practice Litigation Agent Actions, 148 F.3d 283, 316–324 (3d Cir. 1998). Further guidance can be found in the Manual for Complex Litigation.

The court must make findings that support the conclusion that the settlement is fair, reasonable, and adequate. The findings must be set out in sufficient detail to explain to class members and the appellate court the factors that bear on applying the standard.

Settlement review also may provide an occasion to review the cogency of the initial class definition. The terms of the settlement themselves, or objections, may reveal divergent interests of class members and demonstrate the need to redefine the class or to designate subclasses. Redefinition of a class certified under Rule 23(b)(3) may require notice to new class members under Rule 23(c)(2)(B). See Rule 23(c)(1)(C).

Paragraph (2). Subdivision (e)(2) requires parties seeking approval of a settlement, voluntary dismissal, or compromise under Rule 23(e)(1) to file a statement identifying any agreement made in connection with the settlement. This provision does not change the basic requirement that the parties disclose all terms of the settlement or compromise that the court must approve under Rule 23(e)(1). It aims instead at related undertakings that, although seemingly separate, may have influenced the terms of the settlement by trading away possible advantages for the class in return for advantages for others. Doubts should be resolved in favor of identification.

Further inquiry into the agreements identified by the parties should not become the occasion for discovery by the parties or objectors. The court may direct the parties to provide to the court or other parties a summary or copy of the full terms of any agreement identified by the parties. The court also may direct the parties to provide a summary or copy of any agreement not identified by the parties that the court considers relevant to its review of a proposed settlement. In exercising discretion under this rule, the court may act in steps, calling first for a summary of any agreement that may have affected the settlement and then for a complete version if the summary does not provide an adequate basis for review. A direction to disclose a summary or copy of an agreement may raise concerns of confidentiality. Some agreements may include information that merits protection against general disclosure. And the court must provide an opportunity to claim work-product or other protections.

Paragraph (3). Subdivision (e)(3) authorizes the court to refuse to approve a settlement unless the settlement affords class members a new opportunity to request exclusion from a class certified under Rule 23(b)(3) after settlement terms are known. An agreement by the parties themselves to permit class members to elect exclusion at this point by the settlement agreement may be one factor supporting approval of the settlement. Often there is an opportunity to opt out at this point because the class is certified and settlement is reached in circumstances that lead to simultaneous notice of certification and notice of settlement. In these cases, the basic opportunity to elect exclusion applies without further complication. In some cases, particularly if settlement appears imminent at the time of certification, it may be possible to achieve equivalent protection by deferring notice and the opportunity to elect exclusion until actual settlement terms are known. This approach avoids the cost and potential confusion of providing two notices and makes the single notice more meaningful. But notice should not be delayed unduly after certification in the hope of settlement.

Rule 23(e)(3) authorizes the court to refuse to approve a settlement unless the settlement affords a new opportunity to elect exclusion in a case that settles after a certification decision if the earlier opportunity to elect exclusion provided with the certification notice has expired by the time of the settlement notice. A decision to remain in the class is likely to be more carefully considered and is better informed when settlement terms are known.

The opportunity to request exclusion from a proposed settlement is limited to members of a (b)(3) class. Exclusion may be requested only by individual class members; no class member may purport to opt out other class members by way of another class action.

The decision whether to approve a settlement that does not allow a new opportunity to elect exclusion is confided to the court's discretion. The court may make this decision before directing notice to the class under Rule 23(e)(1)(B) or after the Rule 23(e)(1)(C) hearing. Many factors may influence the court's decision. Among these are changes in the information available to class members since expiration of the first opportunity to request exclusion, and the nature of the individual class members' claims.

The terms set for permitting a new opportunity to elect exclusion from the proposed settlement of a Rule 23(b)(3) class action may address concerns of potential misuse. The court might direct, for example, that class members who elect exclusion are bound by rulings on the merits made before the settlement was proposed for approval. Still other terms or conditions may be appropriate.

Paragraph (4). Subdivision (e)(4) confirms t he right of class members to object to a proposed settlement, voluntary dismissal, or compromise. The right is defined in relation to a disposition that, because it would bind the class, requires court approval under subdivision (e)(1)(C).

Subdivision (e)(4)(B) requires court approval for withdrawal of objections made under subdivision (e)(4)(A). Review follows automatically if the objections are withdrawn on terms that lead to modification of the settlement with the class. Review also is required if the objector formally withdraws the objections. If the objector simply abandons pursuit of the objection, the court may inquire into the circumstances.

Approval under paragraph (4)(B) may be given or denied with little need for further inquiry if the objection and the disposition go only to a protest that the individual treatment afforded the objector under the proposed settlement is unfair because of factors that distinguish the objector from other class members. Different considerations may apply if the objector has protested that the proposed settlement is not fair, reasonable, or adequate on grounds that apply generally to a class or subclass. Such objections, which purport to represent class-wide interests, may augment the opportunity for obstruction or delay. If such objections are surrendered on terms that do not affect the class settlement or the objector's participation in the class settlement, the court often can approve withdrawal of the objections without elaborate inquiry.

Once an objector appeals, control of the proceeding lies in the court of appeals. The court of appeals may undertake review and approval of a settlement with the objector, perhaps as part of appeal settlement procedures, or may remand to the district court to take advantage of the district court's familiarity with the action and settlement.

Subdivision (g). Subdivision (g) is new. It responds to the reality that the selection and activity of class counsel are often critically important to the successful handling of a class action. Until now, courts have scrutinized proposed class counsel as well as the class representative under Rule 23(a)(4). This experience has recognized the importance of judicial evaluation of the proposed lawyer for the class, and this new subdivision builds on that experience rather than introducing an entirely new element into the class certification process. Rule 23(a)(4) will continue to call for scrutiny of the proposed class representative, while this subdivision will guide the court in assessing proposed class counsel as part of the certification decision. This subdivision recognizes the importance of class counsel, states the obligation to represent the interests of the class, and provides a framework for selection of class counsel. The procedure and standards for appointment vary depending on whether there are multiple applicants to be class counsel. The new subdivision also provides a method by which the court may make directions from the outset about the potential fee award to class counsel in the event the action is successful.

Paragraph (1) sets out the basic requirement that class counsel be appointed if a class is certified and articulates the obligation of class counsel to represent the interests of the class, as opposed to the potentially conflicting interests of individual class members. It also sets out the factors the court should consider in assessing proposed class counsel.

Paragraph (1)(A) requires that the court appoint class counsel to represent the class. Class counsel must be appointed for all classes, including each subclass that the court certifies to represent divergent interests.

Paragraph (1)(A) does not apply if "a statute provides otherwise." This recognizes that provisions of the Private Securities Litigation Reform Act of 1995, Pub. L. No. 104–67, 109 Stat. 737 (1995) (codified in various sections of 15 U.S.C.), contain directives that bear on selection of a lead plaintiff and the retention of counsel. This subdivision does not purport to supersede or to affect the interpretation of those provisions, or any similar provisions of other legislation.

Paragraph 1(B) recognizes t hat t he primary responsibility of class counsel, resulting from appointment as class counsel, is to represent the best interests of the class. The rule thus establishes the obligation of class counsel, an obligation that may be different from the customary obligations of counsel to individual clients. Appointment as class counsel means that the primary obligation of counsel is to the class rather than to any individual members of it. The class representatives do not have an unfettered right to "fire" class counsel. In the same vein, the class representatives cannot command class counsel to accept or reject a settlement proposal. To the contrary, class counsel must determine whether seeking the court's approval of a settlement would be in the best interests of the class as a whole.

Paragraph (1)(C) articulates the basic responsibility of the court to appoint class counsel who will provide the adequate representation called for by paragraph (1)(B). It identifies criteria that must be considered and invites the court to consider any other pertinent matters. Although couched in terms of the court's duty, the listing also informs counsel seeking appointment about the topics that should be addressed in an application for appointment or in the motion for class certification.

The court may direct potential class counsel to provide additional information about the topics mentioned in paragraph (1)(C) or about any other relevant topic. For example, the court may direct applicants to inform the court concerning any agreements about a prospective award of attorney fees or nontaxable costs, as such agreements may sometimes be significant in the selection of class counsel. The court might also direct that potential class counsel indicate how parallel litigation might be coordinated or consolidated with t he action before the court.

The court may also direct counsel to propose terms for a potential award of attorney fees and nontaxable costs. Attorney fee awards are an important feature of class action practice, and attention to this subject from the outset may often be a productive technique. Paragraph (2)(C) therefore authorizes the court to provide directions about attorney fees and costs when appointing class counsel. Because there will be numerous class actions in which this information is not likely to be useful, the court need not consider it in all class actions.

Some information relevant to class counsel appointment may involve matters that include adversary preparation in a way that should be shielded from disclosure to other parties. An appropriate protective order may be necessary to preserve confidentiality.

In evaluating prospective class counsel, the court should weigh all pertinent factors. No single factor should necessarily be determinative in a given case. For example, the resources counsel will commit to the case must be appropriate to its needs, but the court should be careful not to limit consideration t o lawyers with the greatest resources.

If, after review of all applicants, the court concludes that none would be satisfactory class counsel, it may deny class certification, reject all applications, recommend that an application be modified, invite new applications, or make any other appropriate order regarding selection and appointment of class counsel.

Paragraph (2). This paragraph sets out the procedure that should be followed in appointing class counsel. Although it affords substantial flexibility, it provides the framework for appointment of class counsel in all class actions. For counsel who filed the action, the materials submitted in support of the motion for class certification may suffice to justify appointment so long as the information described in paragraph (g)(1)(C) is included. If there are other applicants, they ordinarily would file a formal application detailing their suitability for the position.

In a plaintiff class action the court usually would appoint as class counsel only an attorney or attorneys who have sought appointment. Different considerations may apply in defendant class actions.

The rule states that the court should appoint "class counsel." In many instances, the applicant will be an individual attorney. In other cases, however, an entire firm, or perhaps numerous attorneys who are not otherwise affiliated but are collaborating on the action will apply. No rule of thumb exists to determine when such arrangements are appropriate; the court should be alert to the need for adequate staffing of the case, but also to the risk of overstaffing or an ungainly counsel structure.

Paragraph (2)(A) authorizes the court to designate interim counsel during the pre-certification period if necessary to protect the interests of the putative class. Rule 23(c)(1)(B) directs that the order certifying the class include appointment of class counsel. Before class certification, however, it will usually be important for an attorney to take action to prepare for the certification decision. The amendment to Rule 23(c)(1) recognizes that some discovery is often necessary for that determination. It also may be important to make or respond to motions before certification. Settlement may be discussed before certification. Ordinarily, such work is handled by the lawyer who filed the action. In some cases, however, there may be rivalry or uncertainty that makes formal designation of interim counsel appropriate. Rule 23(g)(2)(A) authorizes the court to designate interim counsel to act on behalf of the putative class before the certification decision is made. Failure to make the formal designation does not prevent the attorney who filed the action from proceeding in it. Whether or not formally designated interim counsel, an attorney who acts on behalf of the class before certification must act in the best interests of the class as a whole. For example, an attorney who negotiates a pre-certification settlement must seek a settlement that is fair, reasonable, and adequate for the class.

Rule 23(c)(1) provides that the court should decide whether to certify the class "at an early practicable time," and directs that class counsel should be appointed in the order certifying the class. In some cases, it may be appropriate for the court to allow a reasonable period after commencement of the action for filing applications to serve as class counsel. The primary ground for deferring appointment would be that there is reason to anticipate competing applications to serve as class counsel. Examples might include instances in which more than one class action has been filed, or in which other attorneys have filed individual actions on behalf of putative class members. The purpose of facilitating competing applications in such a case is to afford the best possible representation for the class. Another possible reason for deferring appointment would be that the initial applicant was found inadequate, but it seems appropriate to permit additional applications rather than deny class certification.

Paragraph (2)(B) states the basic standard the court should use in deciding whether to certify the class and appoint class counsel in the single applicant situation—that the applicant be able to provide the representation called for by paragraph (1)(B) in light of the factors identified in paragraph (1)(C).

If there are multiple adequate applicants, paragraph (2)(B) directs the court to select the class counsel best able to represent the interests of the class. This decision should also be made using the factors outlined in paragraph (1)(C), but in the multiple applicant situation the court is to go beyond scrutinizing the adequacy of counsel and make a comparison of the strengths of the various applicants. As with the decision whether to appoint the sole applicant for the posit ion, no single factor should be dispositive in selecting class counsel in cases in which there are multiple applicants. The fact that a given attorney filed the instant action, for example, might not weigh heavily in the decision if that lawyer had not done significant work identifying or investigating claims. Depending on the nature of the case, one important consideration might be the applicant's existing attorney-client relationship with the proposed class representative.

Paragraph (2)(C) builds on the appointment process by authorizing the court to include provisions regarding attorney fees in the order appointing class counsel. Courts may find it desirable to adopt guidelines for fees or nontaxable costs, or to direct class counsel to report to the court at regular intervals on the efforts undertaken in the action, to facilitate the court's later determination of a reasonable attorney fee.

Subdivision (h). Subdivision (h) is new. Fee awards are a powerful influence on the way attorneys initiate, develop, and conclude class actions. Class action attorney fee awards have heretofore been handled, along with all other attorney fee awards, under Rule 54(d)(2), but that rule is not addressed to the particular concerns of class actions. This subdivision is designed to work in tandem with new subdivision (g) on appointment of class counsel, which may afford an opportunity for the court to provide an early framework for an eventual fee award, or for monitoring the work of class counsel during the pendency of the action.

Subdivision (h) applies to "an action certified as a class action." This includes cases in which there is a simultaneous proposal for class certification and settlement even though technically the class may not be certified unless the court approves the settlement pursuant to review under Rule 23(e). When a settlement is proposed for Rule 23(e) approval, either after certification or with a request for certification, notice to class members about class counsel's fee motion would ordinarily accompany the notice to the class about the settlement proposal itself.

This subdivision does not undertake to create new grounds for an award of attorney fees or nontaxable costs. Instead, it applies when such awards are authorized by law or by agreement of the parties. Against that background, it provides a format for all awards of attorney fees and nontaxable costs in connection with a class action, not only the award to class counsel. In some situations, there may be a basis for making an award to other counsel whose work produced a beneficial result for the class, such as attorneys who acted for the class before certification but were not appointed class counsel, or attorneys who represented objectors to a proposed settlement under Rule 23(e) or to the fee motion of class counsel. Other situations in which fee awards are authorized by law or by agreement of the parties may exist.

This subdivision authorizes an award of "reasonable" attorney fees and nontaxable costs. This is the customary term for measurement of fee awards in cases in which counsel may obtain an award of fees under the "common fund" theory that applies in many class actions, and is used in many fee-shifting statutes. Depending on the circumstances, courts have approached the determination of what is reasonable in different ways. In particular, there is some variation among courts about whether in "common fund" cases the court should use the lodestar or a percentage method of determining what fee is reasonable. The rule does not attempt to resolve the question whether the lodestar or percentage approach should be viewed as preferable.

Active judicial involvement in measuring fee awards is singularly important to the proper operation of the class-action process. Continued reliance on caselaw development of fee-award measures does not diminish the court's responsibility. In a class action, the district court must ensure that the amount and mode of payment of attorney fees are fair and proper whether the fees come from a common fund or are otherwise paid. Even in the absence of objections, the court bears this responsibility.

Courts discharging this responsibility have looked to a variety of factors. One fundamental focus is the result actually achieved for class members, a basic consideration in any case in which fees are sought on the basis of a benefit achieved for class members. The Private Securities Litigation Reform Act of 1995 explicitly makes this factor a cap for a fee award in actions to which it applies. See 15 U.S.C. §§ 77z–1(a)(6); 78u–4(a)(6) (fee award should not exceed a "reasonable percentage of the amount of any damages and prejudgment interest actually paid to the class"). For a percentage approach to fee measurement, results achieved is the basic starting point.

In many instances, the court may need to proceed with care in assessing the value conferred on class members. Settlement regimes that provide for future payments, for example, may not result in significant actual payments to class members. In this connection, the court may need to scrutinize the manner and operation of any applicable claims procedure. In some cases, it may be appropriate to defer some portion of the fee award until actual payouts to class members are known. Settlements involving nonmonetary provisions for class members also deserve careful scrutiny to ensure that these provisions have actual value to the class. On occasion the court's Rule 23(e) review will provide a solid basis for t his sort of evaluation, but in any event it is also important to assessing the fee award for the class.

At the same time, it is important to recognize that in some class actions the monetary relief obtained is not the sole determinant of an appropriate attorney fees award. Cf. Blanchard v. Bergeron, 489 U.S. 87, 95 (1989) (cautioning in an individual case against an "undesirable emphasis" on "the importance of the recovery of damages in civil rights litigation" that might "shortchange efforts to seek effective injunctive or declaratory relief").

Any directions or orders made by the court in connection with appointing class counsel under Rule 23(g) should weigh heavily in making a fee award under this subdivision.

Courts have also given weight to agreements among the parties regarding the fee motion, and to agreements between class counsel and others about the fees claimed by the motion. Rule 54(d)(2)(B) provides: "If directed by the court, the motion shall also disclose the terms of any agreement with respect to fees to be paid for the services for which claim is made." The agreement by a settling party not to oppose a fee application up to a certain amount, for example, is worthy of consideration, but the court remains responsible to determine a reasonable fee. "Side agreements" regarding fees provide at least perspective pertinent to an appropriate fee award.

In addition, courts may take account of the fees charged by class counsel or other attorneys for representing individual claimants or objectors in the case. In determining a fee for class counsel, the court's objective is to ensure an overall fee that is fair for counsel and equitable within the class. In some circumstances individual fee agreements between class counsel and class members might have provisions inconsistent with those goals, and the court might determine that adjustments in the class fee award were necessary as a result.

Finally, it is important to scrutinize separately the application for an award covering nontaxable costs. If costs were addressed in the order appointing class counsel, those directives should be a presumptive starting point in determining what is an appropriate award.

Paragraph (1). Any claim for an award of attorney fees must be sought by motion under Rule 54(d)(2), which invokes the provisions for timing of appeal in Rule 58 and Appellate Rule 4. Owing to the distinctive features of class action fee motions, however, the provisions of t his subdivision control disposition of fee motions in class actions, while Rule 54(d)(2) applies to matters not addressed in this subdivision.

The court should direct when the fee motion must be filed. For motions by class counsel in cases subject to court review of a proposed settlement under Rule 23(e), it would be important to require the filing of at least the initial motion in time for inclusion of information about the motion in the notice to the class about the proposed settlement that is required by Rule 23(e). In cases litigated to judgment, the court might also order class counsel's motion to be filed promptly so that notice to the class under t his subdivision (h) can be given.

Besides service of the motion on all parties, notice of class counsel's motion for attorney fees must be "directed to the class in a reasonable manner." Because members of the class have an interest in the arrangements for payment of class counsel whether that payment comes from the class fund or is made directly by another party, notice is required in all instances. In cases in which settlement approval is contemplated under Rule 23(e), notice of class counsel's fee motion should be combined with notice of the proposed settlement, and the provision regarding notice to the class is parallel to the requirements for notice under Rule 23(e). In adjudicated class actions, the court may calibrate the notice to avoid undue expense.

Paragraph (2). A class member and any party from whom payment is sought may object to the fee motion. Other parties—for example, nonsettling defendants—may not object because they lack a sufficient interest in the amount the court awards. The rule does not specify a time limit for making an objection. In setting the date objections are due, the court should provide sufficient time after the full fee motion is on file to enable potential objectors to examine the motion.

The court may allow an objector discovery relevant to the objections. In determining whether to allow discovery, the court should weigh the need for the information against the cost and delay that would attend discovery. See Rule 26(b)(2). One factor in determining whether to authorize discovery is the completeness of the material submitted in support of the fee motion, which depends in part on the fee measurement standard applicable to the case. If the motion provides thorough information, the burden should be on the objector to justify discovery to obtain further information.

Paragraph (3). Whether or not there are formal objections, the court must determine whether a fee award is justified and, if so, set a reasonable fee. The rule does not require a formal hearing in all cases. The form and extent of a hearing depend on the circumstances of the case. The rule does require findings and conclusions under Rule 52(a).

Paragraph (4). By incorporating Rule 54(d)(2), this provision gives the court broad authority to obtain assistance in determining the appropriate amount to award. In deciding whether to direct submission of such questions to a special master or magistrate judge, the court should give appropriate consideration to the cost and delay that such a process might entail.

2007 AMENDMENT

The language of Rule 23 has been amended as part of the general restyling of the Civil Rules to make them more easily understood and to make style and terminology consistent throughout the rules. These changes are intended to be stylistic only.

Amended Rule 23(d)(2) carries forward the provisions of former Rule 23(d) that recognize two separate propositions. First, a Rule 23(d) order may be combined with a pretrial order under Rule 16. Second, the standard for amending the Rule 23(d) order continues to be the more open-ended standard for amending Rule 23(d) orders, not the more exacting standard for amending Rule 16 orders.

As part of the general restyling, intensifiers that provide emphasis but add no meaning are consistently deleted. Amended Rule 23(f) omits as redundant the explicit reference to court of appeals discretion in deciding whether to permit an interlocutory appeal. The omission does not in any way limit the unfettered discretion established by the original rule.

Rule 23.1. Derivative Actions by Shareholders

1966 ADDITION

A derivative action by a shareholder of a corporation or by a member of an unincorporated association has distinctive aspects which require the special provisions set forth in the new rule. The next-to-the-last sentence recognizes that the question of adequacy of representation may arise when the plaintiff is one of a group of shareholders or members. Cf. 3 Moore's Federal Practice, par. 23.08 (2d ed. 1963).

The court has inherent power to provide for the conduct of the proceedings in a derivative action, including the power to determine the course of the proceedings and require that any appropriate notice be given to shareholders or members.

1987 AMENDMENT

The amendments are technical. No substantive change is intended.

2007 AMENDMENT

The language of Rule 23.1 has been amended as part of the general restyling of the Civil Rules to make them more easily understood and to make style and terminology consistent throughout the rules. These changes are intended to be stylistic only.

Rule 23.2. Actions Relating to Unincorporated Associations

1966 ADDITION

Although an action by or against representatives of the membership of an unincorporated association has often been viewed as a class action, the real or main purpose of this characterization has been to give "entity treatment" to the association when for formal reasons it cannot sue or be sued as a jural person under Rule 17(b). See Louisell & Hazard, Pleading and Procedure: State and Federal 718 (1962); 3 Moore's Federal Practice, par. 23.08 (2d ed. 1963); Story, J. in *West* v. *Randall*, 29 Fed.Cas. 718, 722–23, No. 17,424 (C.C.D.R.I.1820); and, for examples, *Gibbs* v. *Buck*, 307 U.S. 66, 59 S.Ct. 725, 83 L.Ed. 1111 (1939); *Tunstall* v. *Brotherhood of Locomotive F. & E.*, 148 F.2d 403 (4th Cir.1945); *Oskoian* v. *Canuel*, 269 F.2d 311 (1st Cir.1959). Rule 23.2 deals separately with these actions, referring where appropriate to Rule 23.

2007 AMENDMENT

The language of Rule 23.2 has been amended as part of the general restyling of the Civil Rules to make them more easily understood and to make style and terminology consistent throughout the rules. These changes are intended to be stylistic only.

Rule 24. Intervention

1937 ADOPTION

The right to intervene given by the following and similar statutes is preserved, but the procedure for its assertion is governed by this rule:

U.S.C., Title 28, former:

§ 45a (Special attorneys; participation by Interstate Commerce Commission; intervention)(in certain cases under interstate commerce laws)

§ 48 (Suits to be against United States; intervention by United States)

§ 401 (Intervention by United States; constitutionality of Federal statute)

U.S.C., Title 40:

§ 276a–2(b)(Bonds of contractors for public buildings or works; rights of persons furnishing labor and materials).

Compare with the last sentence of former Equity Rule 37 (Parties Generally—Intervention). This rule amplifies and restates the present federal practice at law and in equity. For the practice in admiralty see Admiralty Rules 34 (How Third Party May Intervene) and 42 (Claims Against Proceeds in Registry). See generally Moore and Levi, Federal Intervention: I The Right to Intervene and Reorganization (1936), 45 Yale L.J. 565. Under the codes two types of intervention are provided, one for the recovery of specific real or personal property (2 Ohio Gen.Code Ann. (Page, 1926) § 11263; Wyo.Rev. Stat.Ann. (Courtright, 1931) § 89–522), and the other allowing intervention generally when the applicant has an interest in the matter in litigation (1 Colo.Stat.Ann. (1935) Code Civ.Proc. § 22; La.Code Pract. (Dart, 1932) Arts. 389–394; Utah Rev.Stat.Ann. (1933) § 104–3–24). The English intervention practice is based upon various rules and decisions and falls into the two categories of absolute right and discretionary right. For the absolute right see English Rules Under the Judicature Act (The Annual Practice, 1937) O. 12, r. 24 (admiralty), r. 25 (land), r. 23 (probate); O. 57, r. 12 (execution); J.A. (1925) §§ 181, 182, 183(2)(divorce); *In re Metropolitan Amalgamated Estates, Ltd.*, (1912) 2 Ch. 497 (receivership); *Wilson* v. *Church*, 9 Ch.D. 552 (1878)(representative action). For the discretionary right see O. 16, r. 11 (nonjoinder) and *Re Fowler*, 142 L.T.Jo. 94 (Ch.1916), *Vavasseur* v. *Krupp*, 9 Ch.D. 351 (1878)(persons out of the jurisdiction).

1946 AMENDMENT

Note to Subdivision (a). The addition to subdivision (a)(3) covers the situation where property may be in the actual custody of some other officer or agency—such as the Secretary of the Treasury—but the control and disposition of the property is lodged in the court wherein the action is pending.

Subdivision (b). The addition in subdivision (b) permits the intervention of governmental officers or agencies in proper cases and thus avoids exclusionary constructions of the rule. For an example of the latter, see Matter of Bender Body Co., Ref. Ohio 1942, 47 F.Supp. 224, app'd as moot, N.E. Ohio 1942, 47 F.Supp. 224, 234, holding that the Administrator of the Office of Price Administration, then acting under the authority of an Executive Order of the President, could not intervene in a bankruptcy proceeding to protest the sale of assets above ceiling prices. Compare, however, *Securities and Exchange Commission* v. *United States Realty & Improvement Co.*, 1940, 310 U.S. 434, 60 S.Ct. 1044, 84 L.Ed. 1293, where permissive intervention of the Commission to protect the public interest in an arrangement proceeding under Chapter XI of the Bankruptcy Act was upheld. See also dissenting opinion in *Securities and Exchange Commission* v. *Long Island Lighting Co.*, C.C.A.2d 1945, 148 F.2d 252, judgment vacated as moot and case remanded with direction to dismiss complaint, 1945, 325 U.S. 833, 65 S.Ct. 1085, 89 L.Ed. 1961. For discussion see Commentary, Nature of Permissive Intervention Under Rule 24b, 1940, 3 Fed.Rules Serv. 704; Berger, Intervention by Public Agencies in Private Litigation in the Federal Courts, 1940, 50 Yale L.J. 65.

Regarding the construction of subdivision (b)(2), see *Allen Calculators, Inc.*, v. *National Cash Register Co.*, 1944, 322 U.S. 137, 64 S.Ct. 905, 88 L.Ed. 1188.

1948 AMENDMENT

The amendment effective Oct. 20, 1949, substituted the reference to "Title 28, U.S.C., § 2403" at the end of subdivision (c) for the reference to "the Act of August 24, 1937, c. 754, § 1."

1963 AMENDMENT

This amendment conforms to the amendment of Rule 5(a). See the Advisory Committee's Note to that amendment.

1966 AMENDMENT

In attempting to overcome certain difficulties which have arisen in the application of present Rule 24(a)(2) and (3), this amendment draws upon the revision of the related Rules 19 (joinder of persons needed for just adjudication) and 23 (class actions), and the reasoning underlying that revision.

Rule 24(a)(3) as amended in 1948 provided for intervention of right where the applicant established that he would be adversely affected by the distribution or disposition of property involved in an action to which he had not been made a party. Significantly, some decided cases virtually disregarded the language of this provision. Thus Professor Moore states: "The concept of a fund has been applied so loosely that it is possible for a court to find a fund in almost any in personam action." 4 Moore's Federal Practice, par. 24.09[3], at 55 (2d ed. 1962), and see, e.g., *Formulabs, Inc.* v. *Hartley Pen Co.*, 275 F.2d 52 (9th Cir.1960). This development was quite natural, for Rule 24(a)(3) was unduly restricted. If an absentee would be substantially affected in a practical sense by the determination made in an action, he should, as a general rule, be entitled to intervene, and his right to do so should not depend on whether there is a fund to be distributed or otherwise disposed of. Intervention of right is here seen to be a kind of counterpart to Rule 19(a)(2)(i) on joinder of persons needed for a just adjudication: where, upon motion of a party in an action, an absentee should be joined so that he may protect his interest which as a practical matter may be substantially impaired by the disposition of the action, he ought to have a right to intervene in the action on his own motion. See Louisell & Hazard, Pleading and Procedure: State and Federal 749–50 (1962).

The general purpose of original Rule 24(a)(2) was to entitle an absentee, purportedly represented by a party, to intervene in the action if he could establish with fair probability that the representation was inadequate. Thus, where an action is being prosecuted or defended by a trustee, a beneficiary of the trust should have a right to intervene if he can show that the trustee's representation of his interest probably is inadequate; similarly a member of a class should have the right to intervene in a class action if he can show the inadequacy of the representation of his interest by the representative parties before the court.

1446

Original Rule 24(a)(2), however, made it a condition of intervention that "the applicant is or may be bound by a judgment in the action," and this created difficulties with intervention in class actions. If the "bound" language was read literally in the sense of res judicata, it could defeat intervention in some meritorious cases. A member of a class to whom a judgment in a class action extended by its terms (see Rule 23(c)(3), as amended) might be entitled to show in a later action, when the judgment in the class action was claimed to operate as res judicata against him, that the "representative" in the class action had not in fact adequately represented him. If he could make this showing, the class-action judgment might be held not to bind him. See *Hansberry* v. *Lee*, 311 U.S. 32, 61 S.Ct. 115, 85 L.Ed. 22 (1940). If a class member sought to intervene in the class action proper, while it was still pending, on grounds of inadequacy of representation, he could be met with the argument: if the representation was in fact inadequate, he would not be "bound" by the judgment when it was subsequently asserted against him as res judicata, hence he was not entitled to intervene; if the representation was in fact adequate, there was no occasion or ground for intervention. See *Sam Fox Publishing Co.*, v. *United States*, 366 U.S. 683, 81 S.Ct. 1309, 6 L.Ed.2d 604 (1961); cf. *Sutphen Estates, Inc.* v. *United States*, 342 U.S. 19, 72 S.Ct. 14, 96 L.Ed. 19 (1951). This reasoning might be linguistically justified by original Rule 24(a)(2); but it could lead to poor results. Compare the discussion in *International M. & I. Corp.* v. *Von Clemm*, 301 F.2d 857 (2d Cir.1962); *Atlantic Refining Co.* v. *Standard Oil Co.*, 304 F.2d 387 (D.C.Cir.1962). A class member who claims that his "representative" does not adequately represent him, and is able to establish that proposition with sufficient probability, should not be put to the risk of having a judgment entered in the action which by its terms extends to him, and be obliged to test the validity of the judgment as applied to his interest by a later collateral attack. Rather he should, as a general rule, be entitled to intervene in the action.

The amendment provides that an applicant is entitled to intervene in an action when his position is comparable to that of a person under Rule 19(a)(2)(i), as amended, unless his interest is already adequately represented in the action by existing parties. The Rule 19(a)(2)(i) criterion imports practical considerations, and the deletion of the "bound" language similarly frees the rule from undue preoccupation with strict considerations of res judicata.

The representation whose adequacy comes into question under the amended rule is not confined to formal representation like that provided by a trustee for his beneficiary or a representative party in a class action for a member of the class. A party to an action may provide practical representation to the absentee seeking intervention although no such formal relationship exists between them, and the adequacy of this practical representation will than have to be weighed. See *International M. & I. Corp.* v. *Von Clemm*, and *Atlantic Refining Co.* v. *Standard Oil Co.*, both supra; *Wolpe* v. *Poretsky*, 144 F.2d 505 (D.C.Cir. 1944), cert. denied, 323 U.S. 777, 65 S.Ct. 190, 89 L.Ed. 621 (1944); cf. *Ford Motor Co.* v. *Bisanz Bros.*, 249 F.2d 22 (8th Cir.1957); and generally, Annot., 84 A.L.R.2d 1412 (1961).

An intervention of right under the amended rule may be subject to appropriate conditions or restrictions responsive among other things to the requirements of efficient conduct of the proceedings.

1987 AMENDMENT

The amendments are technical. No substantive change is intended.

1991 AMENDMENT

Language is added to bring Rule 24(c) into conformity with the statute cited, resolving some confusion reflected in district court rules. As the text provides, counsel challenging the constitutionality of legislation in an action in which the appropriate government is not a party should call the attention of the court to its duty to notify the appropriate governmental officers. The statute imposes the burden of notification on the court, not the party making the constitutional challenge, partly in order to protect against any possible waiver of constitutional rights by parties inattentive to the need for notice. For this reason, the failure of a party to call the court's attention to the matter cannot be treated as a waiver.

2006 AMENDMENT

New Rule 5.1 replaces the final three sentences of Rule 24(c), implementing the provisions of 28 U.S.C. § 2403. Section 2403 requires notification to the Attorney General of the United States when the constitutionality of an Act of Congress is called in question, and to the state attorney general when the constitutionality of a state statute is drawn into question.

2007 AMENDMENT

The language of Rule 24 has been amended as part of the general restyling of the Civil Rules to make them more easily understood and to make style and terminology consistent throughout the rules. These changes are intended to be stylistic only.

The former rule stated that the same procedure is followed when a United States statute gives a right to intervene. This statement is deleted because it added nothing.

Rule 25. Substitution of Parties

1937 ADOPTION

Note to Subdivision (a). 1. The first paragraph of this rule is based upon former Equity Rule 45 (Death of Party—Revivor) and U.S.C., Title 28, former § 778 (Death of parties; substitution of executor or administrator). The *scire facias* procedure provided for in the statute cited is superseded and the writ is abolished by Rule 81(b). Paragraph two states the content of U.S.C., Title 28, former § 779 (Death of one of several plaintiffs or defendants). With these two paragraphs compare generally English Rules Under the Judicature Act (The Annual Practice, 1937) O. 17, r. r. 1–10.

2. This rule modifies U.S.C., Title 28, former §§ 778 (Death of parties; substitution of executor or administrator), 779 (Death of one of several plaintiffs or defendants), and 780 (Survival of actions, suits, or proceedings, etc.), in so far as they differ from it.

Note to Subdivisions (b) and (c). These are a combination and adaptation of N.Y.C.P.A. (1937) § 83 and Calif.Code Civ.Proc. (1937) § 385; see also 4 Nev.Comp.Laws (Hillyer, 1929) § 8561.

Note to Subdivision (d). With the first and last sentences compare U.S.C., Title 28, former § 780 (Survival of actions, suits, or proceedings, etc.). With the second sentence of this subdivision compare *Ex parte La Prade*, 1933, 289 U.S. 444, 53 S.Ct. 682, 77 L.Ed. 1311.

1948 AMENDMENT

The amendment effective October 19, 1949, inserted the words, "the Canal Zone, a territory, an insular possession," in the first sentence of subdivision (d), and, in the same sentence, after the phrase "or other governmental agency," deleted the words, "or any other officer specified in the Act of February 13, 1925, c. 229, § 11 (43 Stat. 941), formerly section 780 of this title."

1961 AMENDMENT

Subdivision (d)(1). Present Rule 25(d) is generally considered to be unsatisfactory. 4 Moore's Federal Practice ¶ 25.01[7] (2d ed. 1950); Wright, Amendments to the Federal Rules: The Function of a Continuing Rules Committee, 7 Vand.L.Rev. 521, 529 (1954); Developments in the Law—Remedies Against the United States and Its Officials, 70 Harv.L.Rev. 827, 931–34 (1957). To require, as a condition of substituting a successor public officer as a party to a pending action, that an application be made with a showing that there is substantial need for continuing the litigation, can rarely serve any useful purpose and fosters a burdensome formality. And to prescribe a short, fixed time period for substitution which cannot be extended even by agreement, see *Snyder* v. *Buck,* 340 U.S. 15, 19, 71 S.Ct. 93, 95 L.Ed. 15 (1950), with the penalty of dismissal of the action, "makes a trap for unsuspecting litigants which seems unworthy of a great government." *Vibra Brush Corp.* v. *Schaffer,* 256 F.2d 681, 684 (2d Cir.1958). Although courts have on occasion found means of undercutting the rule, e. g. *Acheson* v. *Furusho,* 212 F.2d 284 (9th Cir.1954)(substitution of defendant officer unnecessary on theory that only a declaration of status was sought), it has operated harshly in many instances, e. g. *Snyder* v. *Buck,* supra; *Poindexter* v. *Folsom,* 242 F.2d 516 (3d Cir.1957).

Under the amendment, the successor is automatically substituted as a party without an application or showing of need to continue the action. An order of substitution is not required, but may be entered at any time if a party desires or the court thinks fit.

The general term "public officer" is used in preference to the enumeration which appears in the present rule. It comprises Federal, State, and local officers.

The expression "in his official capacity" is to be interpreted in its context as part of a simple procedural rule for substitution; care should be taken not to distort its meaning by mistaken analogies to the doctrine of sovereign immunity from suit or the Eleventh Amendment. The amended rule will apply to all actions brought by public officers for the government, and to any action brought in form against a named officer, but intrinsically against the government or the office or the incumbent thereof whoever he may be from time to time during the action. Thus the amended rule will apply to actions against officers to compel performance of official duties or to obtain judicial review of their orders. It will also apply to actions to prevent officers from acting in excess of their authority or under authority not validly conferred, cf. *Philadelphia Co.* v. *Stimson,* 223 U.S. 605, 32 S.Ct. 340, 56 L.Ed. 570 (1912), or from enforcing unconstitutional enactments, cf. *Ex parte Young,* 209 U.S. 123, 28 S.Ct. 441, 52 L.Ed. 714 (1908); *Ex parte La Prade,* 289 U.S. 444, 53 S.Ct. 682, 77 L.Ed. 1311 (1933). In general it will apply whenever effective relief would call for corrective behavior by the one then having official status and power, rather than one who has lost that status and power through ceasing to hold office. Cf. *Land* v. *Dollar,* 330 U.S. 731, 67 S.Ct. 1009, 91 L.Ed. 1209 (1947); *Larson* v. *Domestic & Foreign Commerce Corp.,* 337 U.S. 682, 69 S.Ct. 1457, 93 L.Ed. 1628 (1949). Excluded from the operation of the amended rule will be the relatively infrequent actions which are directed to securing money judgments against the named officers enforceable against their personal assets; in these cases Rule 25(a)(1), not Rule 25(d), applies to the question of substitution. Examples are actions against officers seeking to make them pay damages out of their own pockets for defamatory utterances or other misconduct in some way related to the office, see *Barr* v. *Matteo,* 360 U.S. 564, 79 S.Ct. 1335, 3 L.Ed.2d 1434 (1959); *Howard* v. *Lyons,* 360 U.S. 593, 79 S.Ct. 1331, 3 L.Ed.2d 1454 (1959); *Gregoire* v. *Biddle,* 177 F.2d 579 (2d Cir.1949), cert. denied, 339 U.S. 949, 70 S.Ct. 803, 94 L.Ed. 1363 (1950). Another example is the anomalous action for a tax refund against a collector of internal revenue, see *Ignelzi* v. *Granger,* 16 F.R.D. 517 (W.D.Pa.1955), 28 U.S.C. § 2006, 4 Moore, supra, ¶ 25.05, p. 531; but see 28 U.S.C. § 1346(a)(1), authorizing the bringing of such suits against the United States rather than the officer.

Automatic substitution under the amended rule, being merely a procedural device for substituting a successor for a past officeholder as a party, is distinct from and does not affect any substantive issues which may be involved in the action. Thus a defense of immunity from suit will remain in the case despite a substitution.

Where the successor does not intend to pursue the policy of his predecessor which gave rise to the lawsuit, it will be open to him, after substitution, as plaintiff to seek voluntary dismissal of the action, or as defendant to seek to have the action dismissed as moot or to take other appropriate steps to avert a judgment or decree. Contrast *Ex parte La Prade,* supra; *Allen* v. *Regents of the University System,* 304 U.S. 439, 58 S.Ct. 980, 82 L.Ed. 1448 (1938); *McGrath* v. *National Assn. of Mfgrs.,* 344 U.S. 804, 73 S.Ct. 31, 97 L.Ed. 627 (1952); *Danenberg* v. *Cohen,* 213 F.2d 944 (7th Cir.1954).

As the present amendment of Rule 25(d)(1) eliminates a specified time period to secure substitution of public officers, the reference in Rule 6(b)(regarding enlargement of time) to Rule 25 will no longer apply to these public-officer substitutions.

As to substitution on appeal, the rules of the appellate courts should be consulted.

Subdivision (d)(2). This provision, applicable in "official capacity" cases as described above, will encourage the use of the official title without any mention of the officer individually, thereby recognizing the intrinsic character of the action and helping to eliminate concern with the problem of substitution. If for any reason it seems desirable to add the individual's name, this may be done upon motion or on the court's initiative; thereafter the procedure of amended Rule 25(d)(1) will apply if the individual named ceases to hold office.

For examples of naming the officer or title rather than the officeholder, see *Annot.,* 102 A.L.R. 943, 948–52; *Comment,* 50 Mich.L.Rev. 443, 450 (1952); cf. 26 U.S.C. § 7484. Where an action is brought by or against a board or agency with continuity of existence, it has been often decided that there is no need to name the individual members and substitution is unnecessary when the personnel changes. 4 Moore, supra, ¶ 25.09, p. 536. The practice encouraged by amended Rule 25(d)(2) is similar.

1963 AMENDMENT

Present Rule 25(a)(1), together with present Rule 6(b), results in an inflexible requirement that an action be dismissed as to a deceased party if substitution is not carried out within a fixed period measured from the time of the death. The hardships and inequities of this unyielding requirement plainly appear from the cases. See, e. g., *Anderson* v. *Yungkau,* 329 U.S. 482, 67 S.Ct. 428, 91 L.Ed. 436 (1947); *Iovino* v. *Waterson,* 274 F.2d 41 (1959), cert. denied, *Carlin* v. *Iovino,* 362 U.S. 949, 80 S.Ct. 860, 4 L.Ed.2d 867 (1960); *Perry* v. *Allen,* 239 F.2d 107 (5th Cir.1956); *Starnes* v. *Pennsylvania R. R.,* 26 F.R.D. 625 (E.D.N.Y.), aff'd per curiam, 295 F.2d 704 (2d Cir.1961), cert. denied, 369 U.S. 813, 82 S.Ct. 688, 7 L.Ed.2d 612 (1962); *Zdanok* v. *Glidden Co.,* 28 F.R.D. 346 (S.D.N.Y.

1961). See also 4 Moore's Federal Practice ¶ 25.01[9] (Supp.1960); 2 Barron & Holtzoff, Federal Practice & Procedure § 621, at 420–21 (Wright ed. 1961).

The amended rule establishes a time limit for the motion to substitute based not upon the time of the death, but rather upon the time information of the death is provided by means of a suggestion of death upon the record, i. e., service of a statement of the fact of the death. Cf. Ill.Ann.Stat., c. 110, § 54(2)(Smith-Hurd 1956). The motion may not be made later than 90 days after the service of the statement unless the period is extended pursuant to Rule 6(b), as amended. See the Advisory Committee's Note to amended Rule 6(b). See also the new Official Form 30.

A motion to substitute may be made by any party or by the representative of the deceased party without awaiting the suggestion of death. Indeed, the motion will usually be so made. If a party or the representative of the deceased party desires to limit the time within which another may make the motion, he may do so by suggesting the death upon the record.

A motion to substitute made within the prescribed time will ordinarily be granted, but under the permissive language of the first sentence of the amended rule ("the court may order") it may be denied by the court in the exercise of a sound discretion if made long after the death—as can occur if the suggestion of death is not made or is delayed—and circumstances have arisen rendering it unfair to allow substitution. Cf. *Anderson* v. *Yungkau,* supra, 329 U.S. at 485, 486, 67 S.Ct. at 430, 431, 91 L.Ed. 436, where it was noted under the present rule that settlement and distribution of the estate of a deceased defendant might be so far advanced as to warrant denial of a motion for substitution even though made within the time limit prescribed by that rule. Accordingly, a party interested in securing substitution under the amended rule should not assume that he can rest indefinitely awaiting the suggestion of death before he makes his motion to substitute.

1987 AMENDMENT

The amendments are technical. No substantive change is intended.

2007 AMENDMENT

The language of Rule 25 has been amended as part of the general restyling of the Civil Rules to make them more easily understood and to make style and terminology consistent throughout the rules. These changes are intended to be stylistic only.

V. DEPOSITIONS AND DISCOVERY

ADVISORY COMMITTEE'S EXPLANATORY STATEMENT CONCERNING 1970 AMENDMENTS OF THE DISCOVERY RULES

This statement is intended to serve as a general introduction to the amendments of Rules 26–37, concerning discovery, as well as related amendments of other rules. A separate note of customary scope is appended to amendments proposed for each rule. This statement provides a framework for the consideration of individual rule changes.

CHANGES IN THE DISCOVERY RULES

The discovery rules, as adopted in 1938, were a striking and imaginative departure from tradition. It was expected from the outset that they would be important, but experience has shown them to play an even larger role than was initially foreseen. Although the discovery rules have been amended since 1938, the changes were relatively few and narrowly focused, made in order to remedy specific defects. The amendments now proposed reflect the first comprehensive review of the discovery rules undertaken since 1938. These amendments make substantial changes in the discovery rules. Those summarized here are among the more important changes.

Scope of Discovery. New provisions are made and existing provisions changed affecting the scope of discovery: (1) The contents of insurance policies are made discoverable (Rule 26(b)(2)). (2) A showing of good cause is no longer required for discovery of documents and things and entry upon land (Rule 34). However, a showing of need is required for discovery of "trial preparation" materials other than a party's discovery of his own statement and a witness' discovery of his own statement; and protection is afforded against disclosure in such documents of mental impressions, conclusions, opinions, or legal theories concerning the litigation. (Rule 26(b)(3)). (3) Provision is made for discovery with respect to experts retained for trial preparation, and particularly those experts who will be called to testify at trial (Rule 26(b)(4)). (4) It is provided that interrogatories and requests for admission are not objectionable simply because they relate to matters of opinion or contention, subject of course to the supervisory power of the court (Rules 33(b), 36(a)). (5) Medical examination is made available as to certain nonparties. (Rule 35(a)).

Mechanics of Discovery. A variety of changes are made in the mechanics of the discovery process, affecting the sequence and timing of discovery, the respective obligations of the parties with respect to requests, responses, and motions for court orders, and the related powers of the court to enforce discovery requests and to protect against their abusive use. A new provision eliminates the automatic grant of priority in discovery to one side (Rule 26(d)). Another provides that a party is not under a duty to supplement his responses to requests for discovery, except as specified (Rule 26(e)).

Other changes in the mechanics of discovery are designed to encourage extrajudicial discovery with a minimum of court intervention. Among these are the following: (1) The requirement that a plaintiff seek leave of court for early discovery requests is eliminated or reduced, and motions for a court order under Rule 34 are made unnecessary. Motions under Rule 35 are continued. (2) Answers and objections are to be served together and an enlargement of the time for response is provided. (3) The party seeking discovery, rather than the objecting party, is made responsible for invoking judicial determination of discovery disputes not resolved by the parties. (4) Judicial sanctions are tightened with respect to unjustified insistence upon or objection to discovery. These changes bring Rules 33, 34, and 36 substantially into line with the procedure now provided for depositions.

Failure to amend Rule 35 in the same way is based upon two considerations. First, the Columbia Survey (described below) finds that only about 5 percent of medical examinations require court motions, of which about half result in court orders. Second and of greater importance, the interest of the person to be examined in the privacy of his person was recently stressed by the Supreme Court in *Schlagenhauf* v. *Holder*, 379 U.S. 104, 85 S.Ct. 234, 13 L.Ed.2d 152 (1964). The court emphasized the trial judge's responsibility to assure that the medical examination was justified, particularly as to its scope.

Rearrangement of Rules. A limited rearrangement of the discovery rules has been made, whereby certain provisions are transferred from one rule to another. The reasons for this rearrangement are discussed below in a separate section of this statement and the details are set out in a table at the end of this statement.

Optional Procedures. In two instances, new optional procedures have been made available. A new procedure is provided to a party seeking to take the deposition of a corporation or other organization (Rule 30(b)(6)). A party on whom interrogatories have been served requesting information derivable from his business records may under specified circumstances produce the records rather than give answers (Rule 33(c)).

Other Changes. This summary of changes is by no means exhaustive. Various changes have been made in order to improve, tighten, or clarify particular provisions, to resolve conflicts in the case law, and to improve language. All changes, whether mentioned here or not, are discussed in the appropriate note for each rule.

A FIELD SURVEY OF DISCOVERY PRACTICE

Despite widespread acceptance of discovery as an essential part of litigation, disputes have inevitably arisen concerning the values claimed for discovery and abuses alleged to exist. Many disputes about discovery relate to particular rule provisions or court decisions and can be studied in traditional fashion with a view to specific amendment. Since discovery is in large measure extrajudicial, however, even these disputes may be enlightened by a study of discovery "in the field." And some of the larger questions concerning discovery can be pursued only by a study of its operation at the law office level and in unreported cases.

The Committee, therefore, invited the Project for Effective Justice of Columbia Law School to conduct a field survey of discovery. Funds were obtained from the Ford Foundation and the Walter E. Meyer Research Institute of Law, Inc. The survey was carried on under the direction of Prof. Maurice Rosenberg of Columbia Law School. The Project for Effective Justice has submitted a report to the Committee entitled "Field Survey of Federal Pretrial Discovery" (hereafter referred to as the Columbia Survey). The Committee is deeply grateful for the benefit of this extensive undertaking and is most appreciative of the cooperation of the Project and the funding organizations. The Committee is particularly grateful to Professor Rosenberg who not only directed the survey but has given much time in order to assist the Committee in assessing the results.

The Columbia Survey concludes, in general, that there is no empirical evidence to warrant a fundamental change in the philosophy of the discovery rules. No widespread or profound failings are disclosed in the scope or availability of discovery. The costs of discovery do not appear to be oppressive, as a general matter, either in relation to ability to pay or to the stakes of the litigation. Discovery frequently provides evidence that would not otherwise be available to the parties and thereby makes for a fairer trial or settlement. On the other hand, no positive evidence is found that discovery promotes settlement.

More specific findings of the Columbia Survey are described in other Committee notes, in relation to particular rule provisions and amendments. Those interested in more detailed information may obtain it from the Project for Effective Justice.

REARRANGEMENT OF THE DISCOVERY RULES

The present discovery rules are structured entirely in terms of individual discovery devices, except for Rule 27 which deals with perpetuation of testimony, and Rule 37 which provides sanctions to enforce discovery. Thus, Rules 26 and 28 to 32 are in terms addressed only to the taking of a deposition of a party or third person. Rules 33 to 36 then deal in succession with four additional discovery devices: Written interrogatories to parties, production for inspection of documents and things, physical or mental examination and requests for admission.

Under the rules as promulgated in 1938, therefore, each of the discovery devices was separate and self-contained. A defect of this arrangement is that there is no natural location in the discovery rules for provisions generally applicable to all discovery or to several discovery devices. From 1938 until the present, a few amendments have applied a discovery provision to several rules. For example, in 1948, the scope of deposition discovery in Rule 26(b) and the provision for protective orders in Rule 30(b) were incorporated by reference in Rules 33 and 34. The arrangement was adequate so long as there were few provisions governing discovery generally and these provisions were relatively simple.

As will be seen, however, a series of amendments are now proposed which govern most or all of the discovery devices. Proposals of a similar nature will probably be made in the future. Under these circumstances, it is very desirable, even necessary, that the discovery rules contain one rule addressing itself to discovery generally.

Rule 26 is obviously the most appropriate rule for this purpose. One of its subdivisions, Rule 26(b), in terms governs only scope of deposition discovery, but it has been expressly incorporated by reference in Rules 33 and 34 and is treated by courts as setting a general standard. By means of a transfer to Rule 26 of the provisions for protective orders now contained in Rule 30(b), and a transfer from Rule 26 of provisions addressed exclusively to depositions, Rule 26 is converted into a rule concerned with discovery generally. It becomes a convenient vehicle for the inclusion of new provisions dealing with the scope, timing, and regulation of discovery. Few additional transfers are needed. See table showing rearrangement of rules, set out below.

There are, to be sure, disadvantages in transferring any provision from one rule to another. Familiarity with the present pattern, reinforced by the references made by prior court decisions and the various secondary writings about the rules, is not lightly to be sacrificed. Revision of treatises and other reference works is burdensome and costly. Moreover, many States have adopted the existing pattern as a model for their rules.

On the other hand, the amendments now proposed will in any event require revision of texts and reference works as well as reconsideration by States following the Federal model. If these amendments are to be incorporated in an understandable way, a rule with general discovery provisions is needed. As will be seen, the proposed rearrangement produces a more coherent and intelligible pattern for the discovery rules taken as a whole. The difficulties described are those encountered whenever statutes are reexamined and revised. Failure to rearrange the discovery rules now would freeze the present scheme, making future change even more difficult.

TABLE SHOWING REARRANGEMENT OF RULES

Existing Rule No.	New Rule No.
26(a)	30(a), 31(a)
26(c)	30(c)
26(d)	32(a)
26(e)	32(b)
26(f)	32(c)
30(a)	30(b)
30(b)	26(c)
32	32(d)

Rule 26. General Provisions Governing Discovery; Duty of Disclosure

1937 ADOPTION

Note to Subdivision (a). This rule freely authorizes the taking of depositions under
the same circumstances and by the same methods whether for the purpose of discovery or
for the purpose of obtaining evidence. Many states have adopted this practice on account
of its simplicity and effectiveness, safeguarding it by imposing such restrictions upon the
subsequent use of the deposition at the trial or hearing as are deemed advisable. See
Ark.Civ.Code (Crawford, 1934) §§ 606–607; Calif.Code Civ.Proc. (Deering, 1937) § 2021; 1
Colo.Stat.Ann. (1935) Code Civ.Proc. § 376; Idaho Code Ann. (1932) § 16–906; Ill.Rules of
Pract., Rule 19 (Smith-Hurd Ill.Stats. c. 110, § 259.19); Smith-Hurd Ill.Stats. c. 51, § 24;
2 Ind.Stat.Ann. (Burns, 1933) §§ 2–1501, 2–1506; Ky.Codes (Carroll, 1932) Civ.Pract.
§ 557; 1 Mo.Rev.Stat. (1929) § 1753; 4 Mont.Rev.Codes Ann. (1935) § 10645; Neb.Comp.
Stat. (1929) ch. 20, §§ 1246–7; 4 Nev.Comp.Laws (Hillyer, 1929) § 9001; 2 N.H.Pub.Laws
(1926) ch. 337, § 1; N.C.Code Ann. (1935) § 1809; 2 N.D.Comp.Laws Ann. (1913)
§§ 7889–7897; 2 Ohio Gen.Code Ann. (Page, 1926) §§ 11525–6; 1 Ore.Code Ann. (1930)
tit. 9, § 1503; 1 S.D.Comp.Laws (1929) §§ 2713–16; Vernon's Ann.Civ.Stats.Tex. arts.
3738, 3752, 3769; Utah Rev.Stat.Ann. (1933) § 104–51–7; Wash.Rules of Practice adopted
by the Supreme Ct., Rule 8, 2 Wash.Rev.Stat.Ann. (Remington, 1932) § 308–8; W.Va.Code
(1931) ch. 57, art. 4, § 1. Compare former Equity Rules 47 (Depositions—To be Taken in
Exceptional Instances); 54 (Depositions Under Revised Statutes, Sections 863, 865, 866,
867—Cross-Examination); 58 (Discovery—Interrogatories—Inspection and Production of
Documents—Admission of Execution or Genuineness).

This and subsequent rules incorporate, modify, and broaden the provisions for depositions under U.S.C., Title 28, former §§ 639 (Depositions *de bene esse* ; when and where
taken; notice), 640 (Same; mode of taking). 641 (Same; transmission to court), 644
(Depositions under *dedimus potestatem* and *in perpetuam*), 646 (Deposition under *dedimus
potestatem*; how taken). These statutes are superseded in so far as they differ from this
and subsequent rules. U.S.C., Title 28, § 643 (Depositions; taken in mode prescribed by
State laws) is superseded by the third sentence of Subdivision (a).

While a number of states permit discovery only from parties or their agents, others
either make no distinction between parties or agents of parties and ordinary witnesses, or
authorize the taking of ordinary depositions, without restriction, from any persons who
have knowledge of relevant facts. See Ark.Civ.Code (Crawford, 1934) §§ 606–607; 1 Idaho
Code Ann. (1932) § 16–906; Ill.Rules of Pract., Rule 19 (Smith-Hurd Ill.Stats. c. 110,
§ 259.19); Smith-Hurd Ill.Stats. c. 51, § 24; 2 Ind.Stat.Ann. (Burns, 1933) § 2–1501;
Ky.Codes (Carroll, 1932) Civ.Pract. §§ 554–558; 2 Md.Ann.Code (Bagby, 1924) Art. 35,
§ 21; 2 Minn.Stat. (Mason, 1927) § 9820; Mo.St.Ann. §§ 1753, 1759, pp. 4023, 4026;
Neb.Comp.Stat. (1929) ch. 20, §§ 1246–7; 2 N.H.Pub.Laws (1926) ch. 337, § 1; 2
N.D.Comp.Laws Ann. (1913) § 7897; 2 Ohio Gen.Code Ann. (Page, 1926) §§ 11525–6; 1
S.D.Comp.Laws (1929) §§ 2713–16; Vernon's Ann.Civil Stats.Tex. arts. 3738, 3752, 3769;
Utah Rev.Stat.Ann. (1933) § 104–51–7; Wash.Rules of Practice adopted by Supreme Ct.,
Rule 8, 2 Wash.Rev.Stat.Ann. (Remington, 1932) § 308–8; W.Va.Code (1931) ch. 57, art. 4,
§ 1.

The more common practice in the United States is to take depositions on notice by the
party desiring them, without any order from the court, and this has been followed in these
rules. See Calif.Code Civ.Proc. (Deering, 1937) § 2031; 2 Fla.Comp.Gen.Laws Ann. (1927)
§§ 4405–7; 1 Idaho Code Ann. (1932) § 16–902; Ill.Rules of Pract., Rule 19 (Smith-Hurd
Ill.Stats. c. 110, § 259.19); Smith-Hurd Ill.Stats. c. 51, § 24; 2 Ind.Stat.Ann. (Burns, 1933)
§ 2–1502; Kan.Gen.Stat.Ann. (1935) § 60–2827; Ky.Codes (Carroll, 1932) Civ.Pract.
§ 565; 2 Minn.Stat. (Mason, 1927) § 9820; Mo.St.Ann. § 1761, p. 4029; 4 Mont.Rev.Codes
Ann. (1935) § 10651; Nev.Comp.Laws (Hillyer, 1929) § 9002; N.C.Code Ann. (1935)
§ 1809; 2 N.D.Comp.Laws Ann. (1913) § 7895; Utah Rev.Stat.Ann. (1933) § 104–51–8.

Note to Subdivision (b). While the old chancery practice limited discovery to facts
supporting the case of the party seeking it, this limitation has been largely abandoned by
modern legislation. See Ala.Code Ann. (Michie, 1928) §§ 7764–7773; 2 Ind.Stat.Ann.
(Burns, 1933) §§ 2–1028, 2–1506, 2–1728—2–1732; Iowa Code (1935) § 11185; Ky.Codes
(Carroll, 1932) Civ.Pract. §§ 557, 606(8); La.Code Pract. (Dart, 1932) arts. 347–356; 2
Mass.Gen.Laws (Ter.Ed., 1932) ch. 231, §§ 61–67; Mo.St.Ann. §§ 1753, 1759, pp. 4023,
4026; Neb.Comp.Stat. (1929) §§ 20–1246, 20–1247; 2 N.H.Pub.Laws (1926) ch. 337, § 1;
2 Ohio Gen.Code Ann. (Page, 1926) §§ 11497, 11526; Vernon's Ann.Civ.Stats.Tex. arts.
3738, 3753, 3769; Wis.Stat. (1935) § 326.12; Ontario Consol.Rules of Pract. (1928) Rules
237–347; Quebec Code of Civ.Proc. (Curran, 1922) §§ 286–290.

Note to Subdivisions (d), (e), and (f). The restrictions here placed upon the use of depositions at the trial or hearing are substantially the same as those provided in U.S.C., Title 28, former § 641, for depositions taken, *de bene esse*, with the additional provision that any deposition may be used when the court finds the existence of exceptional circumstances. Compare English Rules Under the Judicature Act (The Annual Practice, 1937) O. 37, r. 18 (with additional provision permitting use of deposition by consent of the parties). See also former Equity Rule 64 (Former Depositions, Etc. May be Used Before Master); and 2 Minn.Stat. (Mason, 1927) § 9835 (Use in a subsequent action of a deposition filed in a previously dismissed action between the same parties and involving the same subject matter).

1946 AMENDMENT

Note to Subdivision (a). The amendment eliminates the requirement of leave of court for the taking of a deposition except where a plaintiff seeks to take a deposition within 20 days after the commencement of the action. The retention of the requirement where a deposition is sought by a plaintiff within 20 days of the commencement of the action protects a defendant who has not had an opportunity to retain counsel and inform himself as to the nature of the suit; the plaintiff, of course, needs no such protection. The present rule forbids the plaintiff to take a deposition, without leave of court, before the answer is served. Sometimes the defendant delays the serving of an answer for more than 20 days, but as 20 days are sufficient time for him to obtain a lawyer, there is no reason to forbid the plaintiff to take a deposition without leave merely because the answer has not been served. In all cases, Rule 30(a) empowers the court, for cause shown, to alter the time of the taking of a deposition, and Rule 30(b) contains provisions giving ample protection to persons who are unreasonably pressed. The modified practice here adopted is along the line of that followed in various states. See e. g., 8 Mo.Rev.Stat.Ann.1939, § 1917; 2 Burns' Ind.Stat.Ann.1933, § 2–1506.

Subdivision (b). The amendments to subdivision (b) make clear the broad scope of examination and that it may cover not only evidence for use at the trial but also inquiry into matters in themselves inadmissible as evidence but which will lead to the discovery of such evidence. The purpose of discovery is to allow a broad search for facts, the names of witnesses, or any other matters which may aid a party in the preparation or presentation of his case. *Engl v. Aetna Life Ins. Co.*, C.C.A.2, 1943, 139 F.2d 469; *Mahler v. Pennsylvania R. Co.*, N.Y.1945, 8 Fed.Rules Serv. 33.351, Case 1. In such a preliminary inquiry admissibility at trial should not be the test as to whether the information sought is within the scope of proper examination. Such a standard unnecessarily curtails the utility of discovery practice. Of course, matters entirely without bearing either as direct evidence or as leads to evidence are not within the scope of inquiry, but to the extent that the examination develops useful information, it functions successfully as an instrument of discovery, even if it produces no testimony directly admissible. *Lewis v. United Air Lines Transport Corp.*, Conn.1939, 27 F.Supp. 946; *Engl v. Aetna Life Ins. Co.*, supra; *Mahler v. Pennsylvania R. Co.*, supra; *Bloomer v. Sirian Lamp Co.*, Del.1944, 8 Fed.Rules Serv. 26b.31, Case 3; *Rosseau v. Langley*, N.Y.1945, 9 Fed.Rules Serv. 34.41, Case 1 (Rule 26 contemplates "examinations not merely for the narrow purpose of adducing testimony which may be offered in evidence but also for the broad discovery of information which may be useful in preparation for trial."); *Olson Transportation Co. v. Socony-Vacuum Co.*, Wis.1944, 8 Fed.Rules Serv. 34.41, Case 2 ("... the Rules ... permit 'fishing' for evidence as they should."); Note, 1945, 45 Col.L.Rev. 482. Thus hearsay, while inadmissible itself, may suggest testimony which properly may be proved. Under Rule 26(b) several cases, however, have erroneously limited discovery on the basis of admissibility, holding that the word "relevant" in effect meant "material and competent under the rules of evidence". *Poppino v. Jones Store Co.*, Mo.1940, 1 F.R.D. 215, 3 Fed.Rules Serv. 26b.5, Case 1; *Benevento v. A & P Food Stores, Inc.*, N.Y.1939, 26 F.Supp. 424. Thus it has been said that inquiry might not be made into statements or other matters which, when disclosed, amounted only to hearsay. See *Maryland, for Use of Montvila v. Pan–American Bus Lines, Inc.*, Md.1940, 1 F.R.D. 213, 3 Fed.Rules Serv. 26b.211, Case 3; *Gitto v. "Italia", Societa Anonima Di Navigazione*, N.Y.1940, 31 F.Supp. 567; *Rose Silk Mills Inc. v. Insurance Co. of North America*, N.Y.1939, 29 F.Supp. 504; *Colpak v. Hetterick*, N.Y.1941, 40 F.Supp. 350; *Matthies v. Peter F. Connolly Co.*, N.Y.1941, 6 Fed.Rules Serv. 30a.22, Case 1, 2 F.R.D. 277; *Matter of Examination of Citizens Casualty Co. of New York*, N.Y.1942, 3 F.R.D. 171, 7 Fed.Rules Serv. 26b.211, Case 1; *United States v. Silliman*, N.J.1944, 8 Fed.Rules Serv. 26b.52, Case 1. The contrary and better view, however, has often been stated. See, e. g., *Engl v. Aetna Life Ins. Co.*, supra; *Stevenson v. Melady*, N.Y.1940, 3 Fed.Rules Serv. 26b.31, Case 1, 1 F.R.D. 329; *Lewis v. United Air Lines Transport Corp.*, supra; *Application of Zenith Radio Corp.*, Pa.1941, 4 Fed.Rules Serv. 30b.21, Case 1, 1 F.R.D. 627; *Steingut v. Guaranty Trust Co. of New York*, N.Y.1941, 1 F.R.D. 723, 4

Fed.Rules Serv. 26b.5, Case 2; *De Seversky v. Republic Aviation Corp.*, N.Y.1941, 2 F.R.D. 183, 5 Fed.Rules Serv. 26b.31, Case 5; *Moore v. George A. Hormel & Co.*, N.Y.1942, 6 Fed.Rules Serv. 30b.41, Case 1, 2 F.R.D. 340; *Hercules Powder Co. v. Rohm & Haas Co.*, Del.1943, 7 Fed.Rules Serv. 45b.311, Case 2, 3 F.R.D. 302; *Bloomer v. Sirian Lamp Co.*, supra; *Crosby Steam Gage & Valve Co. v. Manning, Maxwell & Moore, Inc.*, Mass.1944, 8 Fed.Rules Serv. 26b.31, Case 1; *Patterson Oil Terminals, Inc. v. Charles Kurz & Co., Inc.*, Pa.1945, 9 Fed.Rules Serv. 33.321, Case 2; *Pueblo Trading Co. v. Reclamation Dist. No. 1500*, Cal.1945, 9 Fed.Rules Serv. 33.321, Case 4, 4 F.R.D. 471. See also discussion as to the broad scope of discovery in *Hoffman v. Palmer*, C.C.A.2, 1942, 129 F.2d 976, 995–997, affirmed 318 U.S. 109, 63 S.Ct. 477, 87 L.Ed. 645; Note, 1945, 45 Col.L.Rev. 482.

1963 AMENDMENT

This amendment conforms to the amendment of Rule 28(b). See the next-to-last paragraph of the Advisory Committee's Note to that amendment.

1966 AMENDMENT

The requirement that the plaintiff obtain leave of court in order to serve notice of taking of a deposition within 20 days after commencement of the action gives rise to difficulties when the prospective deponent is about to become unavailable for examination. The problem is not confined to admiralty, but has been of special concern in that context because of the mobility of vessels and their personnel. When Rule 26 was adopted as Admiralty Rule 30A in 1961, the problem was alleviated by permitting depositions *de bene esse*, for which leave of court is not required. See Advisory Committee's Note to Admiralty Rule 30A (1961).

A continuing study is being made in the effort to devise a modification of the 20-day rule appropriate to both the civil and admiralty practice to the end that Rule 26(a) shall state a uniform rule applicable alike to what are now civil actions and suits in admiralty. Meanwhile, the exigencies of maritime litigation require preservation, for the time being at least, of the traditional *de bene esse* procedure for the post-unification counterpart of the present suit in admiralty. Accordingly, the amendment provides for continued availability of that procedure in admiralty and maritime claims within the meaning of Rule 9(h).

1970 AMENDMENT

A limited rearrangement of the discovery rules is made, whereby certain rule provisions are transferred, as follows: Existing Rule 26(a) is transferred to Rules 30(a) and 31(a). Existing Rule 26(c) is transferred to Rule 30(c). Existing Rules 26(d), (e), and (f) are transferred to Rule 32. Revisions of the transferred provisions, if any, are discussed in the notes appended to Rules 30, 31, and 32. In addition, Rule 30(b) is transferred to Rule 26(c). The purpose of this rearrangement is to establish Rule 26 as a rule governing discovery in general. (The reasons are set out in the Advisory Committee's explanatory statement.)

Subdivision (a)—Discovery Devices. This is a new subdivision listing all of the discovery devices provided in the discovery rules and establishing the relationship between the general provisions of Rule 26 and the specific rules for particular discovery devices. The provision that the frequency of use of these methods is not limited confirms existing law. It incorporates in general form a provision now found in Rule 33.

Subdivision (b)—Scope of Discovery. This subdivision is recast to cover the scope of discovery generally. It regulates the discovery obtainable through any of the discovery devices listed in Rule 26(a).

All provisions as to scope of discovery are subject to the initial qualification that the court may limit discovery in accordance with these rules. Rule 26(c)(transferred from 30(b)) confers broad powers on the courts to regulate or prevent discovery even though the materials sought are within the scope of 26(b), and these powers have always been freely exercised. For example, a party's income tax return is generally held not privileged, 2A Barron & Holtzoff, Federal Practice and Procedure, § 65.2 (Wright ed. 1961), and yet courts have recognized that interests in privacy may call for a measure of extra protection. *E.g., Wiesenberger* v. *W. E. Hutton & Co.*, 35 F.R.D. 556 (S.D.N.Y.1964). Similarly, the courts have in appropriate circumstances protected materials that are primarily of an impeaching character. These two types of materials merely illustrate the many situations, not capable of governance by precise rule, in which courts must exercise judgment. The new subsections in Rule 26(d) do not change existing law with respect to such situations.

Subdivision (b)(1)—In General. The language is changed to provide for the scope of discovery in general terms. The existing subdivision, although in terms applicable only to depositions, is incorporated by reference in existing Rules 33 and 34. Since decisions as to relevance to the subject matter of the action are made for discovery purposes well in advance of trial, a flexible treatment of relevance is required and the making of discovery, whether voluntary or under court order, is not a concession or determination of relevance for purposes of trial. *Cf.* 4 Moore's Federal Practice ¶ 26–16[1] (2d ed. 1966).

Subdivision (b)(2)—Insurance Policies. Both the cases and commentators are sharply in conflict on the question whether defendant's liability insurance coverage is subject to discovery in the usual situation when the insurance coverage is not itself admissible and does not bear on another issue in the case. Examples of Federal cases requiring disclosure and supporting comments: *Cook* v. *Welty*, 253 F.Supp. 875 (D.D.C. 1966)(cases cited); *Johanek* v. *Aberle*, 27 F.R.D. 272 (D.Mont.1961); Williams, Discovery of Dollar Limits in Liability Policies in Automobile Tort Cases, 10 Ala.L.Rev. 355 (1958); Thode, Some Reflections on the 1957 Amendments to the Texas Rules, 37 Tex.L.Rev. 33, 40–42 (1958). Examples of Federal cases refusing disclosure and supporting comments: *Bisserier* v. *Manning*, 207 F.Supp. 476 (D.N.J.1962); *Cooper* v. *Stender*, 30 F.R.D. 389 (E.D.Tenn.1962); Frank, Discovery and Insurance, Coverage, 1959 Ins.L.J. 281; Fournier, Pre-trial Discovery of Insurance Coverage and Limits, 28 Ford.L.Rev. 215 (1959).

The division in reported cases is close. State decisions based on provisions similar to the federal rules are similarly divided. See cases collected in 2A Barron & Holtzoff, Federal Practice and Procedure § 647.1, nn. 45.5, 45.6 (Wright ed. 1961). It appears to be difficult if not impossible to obtain appellate review of the issue. Resolution by rule amendment is indicated. The question is essentially procedural in that it bears upon preparation for trial and settlement before trial, and courts confronting the question, however they have decided it, have generally treated it as procedural and governed by the rules.

The amendment resolves this issue in favor of disclosure. Most of the decisions denying discovery, some explicitly, reason from the text of Rule 26(b) that it permits discovery only of matters which will be admissible in evidence or appear reasonably calculated to lead to such evidence; they avoid considerations of policy, regarding them as foreclosed. See *Bisserier* v. *Manning*, supra. Some note also that facts about a defendant's financial status are not discoverable as such, prior to judgment with execution unsatisfied, and fear that, if courts hold insurance coverage discoverable, they must extend the principle to other aspects of the defendant's financial status. The cases favoring disclosure rely heavily on the practical significance of insurance in the decisions lawyers make about settlement and trial preparation. In *Clauss* v. *Danker*, 264 F.Supp. 246 (S.D.N.Y.1967), the court held that the rules forbid disclosure but called for an amendment to permit it.

Disclosure of insurance coverage will enable counsel for both sides to make the same realistic appraisal of the case, so that settlement and litigation strategy are based on knowledge and not speculation. It will conduce to settlement and avoid protracted litigation in some cases, though in others it may have an opposite effect. The amendment is limited to insurance coverage, which should be distinguished from any other facts concerning defendant's financial status (1) because insurance is an asset created specifically to satisfy the claim; (2) because the insurance company ordinarily controls the litigation; (3) because information about coverage is available only from defendant or his insurer; and (4) because disclosure does not involve a significant invasion of privacy.

Disclosure is required when the insurer "may be liable" on part or all of the judgment. Thus, an insurance company must disclose even when it contests liability under the policy, and such disclosure does not constitute a waiver of its claim. It is immaterial whether the liability is to satisfy the judgment directly or merely to indemnify or reimburse another after he pays the judgment.

The provision applies only to persons "carrying on an insurance business" and thus covers insurance companies and not the ordinary business concern that enters into a contract of indemnification. *Cf.* N.Y.Ins.Law § 41. Thus, the provision makes no change in existing law on discovery of indemnity agreements other than insurance agreements by persons carrying on an insurance business. Similarly, the provision does not cover the business concern that creates a reserve fund for purposes of self-insurance.

For some purposes other than discovery, an application for insurance is treated as a part of the insurance agreement. The provision makes clear that, for discovery purposes, the application is not to be so treated. The insurance application may contain personal and financial information concerning the insured, discovery of which is beyond the purpose of this provision.

In no instance does disclosure make the facts concerning insurance coverage admissible in evidence.

Subdivision (b)(3)—Trial Preparation: Materials. Some of the most controversial and vexing problems to emerge from the discovery rules have arisen out of requests for the production of documents or things prepared in anticipation of litigation or for trial. The existing rules make no explicit provision for such materials. Yet, two verbally distinct doctrines have developed, each conferring a qualified immunity on these materials—the "good cause" requirement in Rule 34 (now generally held applicable to discovery of documents via deposition under Rule 45 and interrogatories under Rule 33) and the work-product doctrine of *Hickman* v. *Taylor*, 329 U.S. 495, 67 S.Ct. 385, 91 L.Ed. 451 (1947). Both demand a showing of justification before production can be had, the one of "good cause" and the other variously described in the *Hickman* case: "necessity or justification," "denial * * * would unduly prejudice the preparation of petitioner's case," or "cause hardship or injustice" 329 U.S. at 509–510.

In deciding the *Hickman* case, the Supreme Court appears to have expressed a preference in 1947 for an approach to the problem of trial preparation materials by judicial decision rather than by rule. Sufficient experience has accumulated, however, with lower court applications of the *Hickman* decision to warrant a reappraisal.

The major difficulties visible in the existing case law are (1) confusion and disagreement as to whether "good cause" is made out by a showing of relevance and lack of privilege, or requires an additional showing of necessity, (2) confusion and disagreement as to the scope of the *Hickman* work-product doctrine, particularly whether it extends beyond work actually performed by lawyers, and (3) the resulting difficulty of relating the "good cause" required by Rule 34 and the "necessity or justification" of the work-product doctrine, so that their respective roles and the distinctions between them are understood.

Basic Standard.—Since Rule 34 in terms requires a showing of "good cause" for the production of all documents and things, whether or not trial preparation is involved, courts have felt that a single formula is called for and have differed over whether a showing of relevance and lack of privilege is enough or whether more must be shown. When the facts of the cases are studied, however, a distinction emerges based upon the type of materials. With respect to documents not obtained or prepared with an eye to litigation, the decisions, while not uniform, reflect a strong and increasing tendency to relate "good cause" to a showing that the documents are relevant to the subject matter of the action. *E.g.*, *Connecticut Mutual Life Ins. Co.* v. *Shields*, 17 F.R.D. 273 (S.D.N.Y.1955), with cases cited; *Houdry Process Corp.* v. *Commonwealth Oil Refining Co.*, 24 F.R.D. 58 (S.D.N.Y.1959); see *Bell* v. *Commercial Ins. Co.*, 280 F.2d 514, 517 (3d Cir.1960). When the party whose documents are sought shows that the request for production is unduly burdensome or oppressive, courts have denied discovery for lack of "good cause" although they might just as easily have based their decision on the protective provisions of existing Rule 30(b)(new Rule 26(c)). *E.g.*, *Lauer* v. *Tankrederi*, 39 F.R.D. 334 (E.D.Pa.1966).

As to trial-preparation materials, however, the courts are increasingly interpreting "good cause" as requiring more than relevance. When lawyers have prepared or obtained the materials for trial, all courts require more than relevance; so much is clearly commanded by *Hickman*. But even as to the preparatory work of nonlawyers, while some courts ignore work-product and equate "good cause" with relevance, *e.g.*, *Brown* v. *New York, N. H. & H. R. R.*, 17 F.R.D. 324 (S.D.N.Y.1955), the more recent trend is to read "good cause" as requiring inquiry into the importance of and need for the materials as well as into alternative sources for securing the same information. In *Guilford Nat'l Bank* v. *Southern Ry.*, 297 F.2d 921 (4th Cir.1962), statements of witnesses obtained by claim agents were held not discoverable because both parties had had equal access to the witnesses at about the same time, shortly after the collision in question. The decision was based solely on Rule 34 and "good cause"; the court declined to rule on whether the statements were work-products. The court's treatment of "good cause" is quoted at length and with approval in *Schlagenhauf* v. *Holder*, 379 U.S. 104, 117–118, 85 S.Ct. 234, 13 L.Ed.2d 152 (1964). See also *Mitchell* v. *Bass*, 252 F.2d 513 (8th Cir.1958); *Hauger* v. *Chicago, R. I. & Pac. R. R.*, 216 F.2d 501 (7th Cir.1954); *Burke* v. *United States*, 32 F.R.D. 213 (E.D.N.Y.1963). While the opinions dealing with "good cause" do not often draw an explicit distinction between trial preparation materials and other materials, in fact an overwhelming proportion of the cases in which a special showing is required are cases involving trial preparation materials.

The rules are amended by eliminating the general requirement of "good cause" from Rule 34 but retaining a requirement of a special showing for trial preparation materials in this subdivision. The required showing is expressed, not in terms of "good cause" whose generality has tended to encourage confusion and controversy, but in terms of the elements of the special showing to be made: substantial need of the materials in the preparation of the case and inability without undue hardship to obtain the substantial equivalent of the materials by other means.

These changes conform to the holdings of the cases, when viewed in light of their facts. Apart from trial preparation, the fact that the materials sought are documentary does not in and of itself require a special showing beyond relevance and absence of privilege. The protective provisions are of course available, and if the party from whom production is sought raises a special issue of privacy (as with respect to income tax returns or grand jury minutes) or points to evidence primarily impeaching, or can show serious burden or expense, the court will exercise its traditional power to decide whether to issue a protective order. On the other hand, the requirement of a special showing for discovery of trial preparation materials reflects the view that each side's informal evaluation of its case should be protected, that each side should be encouraged to prepare independently, and that one side should not automatically have the benefit of the detailed preparatory work of the other side. See Field and McKusick, Maine Civil Practice 264 (1959).

Elimination of a "good cause" requirement from Rule 34 and the establishment of a requirement of a special showing in this subdivision will eliminate the confusion caused by having two verbally distinct requirements of justification that the courts have been unable to distinguish clearly. Moreover, the language of the subdivision suggests the factors which the courts should consider in determining whether the requisite showing has been made. The importance of the materials sought to the party seeking them in preparation of his case and the difficulty he will have obtaining them by other means are factors noted in the *Hickman* case. The courts should also consider the likelihood that the party, even if he obtains the information by independent means, will not have the substantial equivalent of the documents the production of which he seeks.

Consideration of these factors may well lead the court to distinguish between witness statements taken by an investigator, on the one hand, and other parts of the investigative file, on the other. The court in *Southern Ry.* v. *Lanham*, 403 F.2d 119 (5th Cir.1968), while it naturally addressed itself to the "good cause" requirements of Rule 34, set forth as controlling considerations the factors contained in the language of this subdivision. The analysis of the court suggests circumstances under which witness statements will be discoverable. The witness may have given a fresh and contemporaneous account in a written statement while he is available to the party seeking discovery only a substantial time thereafter. *Lanham, supra* at 127–128; *Guilford, supra* at 926. Or he may be reluctant or hostile. *Lanham, supra* at 128–129; *Brookshire* v. *Pennsylvania RR*, 14 F.R.D. 154 (N.D.Ohio 1953); *Diamond* v. *Mohawk Rubber Co.*, 33 F.R.D. 264 (D.Colo. 1963). Or he may have a lapse of memory. *Tannenbaum* v. *Walker*, 16 F.R.D. 570 (E.D.Pa.1954). Or he may probably be deviating from his prior statement. *Cf. Hauger* v. *Chicago, R. I. & Pac. RR*, 216 F.2d 501 (7th Cir.1954). On the other hand, a much stronger showing is needed to obtain evaluative materials in an investigator's reports. *Lanham, supra* at 131–133; *Pickett* v. *L. R. Ryan, Inc.*, 237 F.Supp. 198 (E.D.S.C.1965).

Materials assembled in the ordinary course of business, or pursuant to public requirements unrelated to litigation, or for other nonlitigation purposes are not under the qualified immunity provided by this subdivision. *Goosman* v. *A. Duie Pyle, Inc.*, 320 F.2d 45 (4th Cir.1963); *cf. United States* v. *New York Foreign Trade Zone Operators, Inc.*, 304 F.2d 792 (2d Cir.1962). No change is made in the existing doctrine, noted in the *Hickman* case, that one party may discover relevant facts known or available to the other party, even though such facts are contained in a document which is not itself discoverable.

Treatment of Lawyers; Special Protection of Mental Impressions, Conclusions, Opinions, and Legal Theories Concerning the Litigation.—The courts are divided as to whether the work-product doctrine extends to the preparatory work only of lawyers. The *Hickman* case left this issue open since the statements in that case were taken by a lawyer. As to courts of appeals compare *Alltmont* v. *United States*, 177 F.2d 971, 976 (3d Cir.1949), *cert. denied*, 339 U.S. 967, 70 S.Ct. 999, 94 L.Ed. 1375 (1950)(*Hickman* applied to statements obtained by FBI agents on theory it should apply to "all statements of prospective witnesses which a party has obtained for his trial counsel's use"), with *Southern Ry.* v. *Campbell*, 309 F.2d 569 (5th Cir.1962)(statements taken by claim agents not work-product), and *Guilford Nat'l Bank* v. *Southern Ry.*, 297 F.2d 921 (4th Cir.1962)(avoiding issue of work-product as to claim agents, deciding case instead under Rule 34 "good cause"). Similarly, the district courts are divided on statements obtained by claim agents, compare, *e.g., Brown* v. *New York, N. H. & H. R. R.*, 17 F.R.D. 324 (S.D.N.Y.1955) with *Hanke* v. *Milwaukee Electric Ry. & Transp. Co.*, 7 F.R.D. 540 (E.D.Wis.1947); Investigators, compare *Burke* v. *United States*, 32 F.R.D. 213 (E.D.N.Y. 1963) with *Snyder* v. *United States*, 20 F.R.D. 7 (E.D.N.Y.1956); and Insurers, compare *Gottlieb* v. *Bresler*, 24 F.R.D. 371 (D.D.C.1959) with *Burns* v. *Mulder*, 20 F.R.D. 605 (E.D.Pa.1957). See 4 Moore's Federal Practice ¶ 26.23[8.1] (2d ed. 1966); 2A Barron & Holtzoff, Federal Practice and Procedure § 652.2 (Wright ed. 1961).

A complication is introduced by the use made by courts of the "good cause" requirement of Rule 34, as described above. A court may conclude that trial preparation materials are not work-product because not the result of lawyer's work and yet hold that they are not producible because "good cause" has not been shown. *Cf. Guilford Nat'l Bank v. Southern Ry.*, 297 F.2d 921 (4th Cir.1962), cited and described above. When the decisions on "good cause" are taken into account, the weight of authority affords protection of the preparatory work of both lawyers and nonlawyers (though not necessarily to the same extent) by requiring more than a showing of relevance to secure production.

Subdivision (b)(3) reflects the trend of the cases by requiring a special showing, not merely as to materials prepared by an attorney, but also as to materials prepared in anticipation of litigation or preparation for trial by or for a party or any representative acting on his behalf. The subdivision then goes on to protect against disclosure of the mental impressions, conclusions, opinions, or legal theories concerning the litigation of an attorney or other representative of a party. The *Hickman* opinion drew special attention to the need for protecting an attorney against discovery of memoranda prepared from recollection of oral interviews. The courts have steadfastly safeguarded against disclosure of lawyers' mental impressions and legal theories, as well as mental impressions and subjective evaluations of investigators and claim-agents. In enforcing this provision of the subdivision, the courts will sometimes find it necessary to order disclosure of a document but with portions deleted.

Rules 33 and 36 have been revised in order to permit discovery calling for opinions, contentions, and admissions relating not only to fact but also to the application of law to fact. Under those rules, a party and his attorney or other representative may be required to disclose, to some extent, mental impressions, opinions, or conclusions. But documents or parts of documents containing these matters are protected against discovery by this subdivision. Even though a party may ultimately have to disclose in response to interrogatories or requests to admit, he is entitled to keep confidential documents containing such matters prepared for internal use.

Party's Right to Own Statement.—An exception to the requirement of this subdivision enables a party to secure production of his own statement without any special showing. The cases are divided. Compare, *e.g., Safeway Stores, Inc.* v. *Reynolds*, 176 F.2d 476 (D.C.Cir.1949); *Shupe* v. *Pennsylvania R. R.*, 19 F.R.D. 144 (W.D.Pa.1956); with *e.g., New York Central R. R.* v. *Carr*, 251 F.2d 433 (4th Cir.1957); *Belback* v. *Wilson Freight Forwarding Co.*, 40 F.R.D. 16 (W.D.Pa.1966).

Courts which treat a party's statement as though it were that of any witness overlook the fact that the party's statement is, without more, admissible in evidence. Ordinarily, a party gives a statement without insisting on a copy because he does not yet have a lawyer and does not understand the legal consequences of his actions. Thus, the statement is given at a time when he functions at a disadvantage. Discrepancies between his trial testimony and earlier statement may result from lapse of memory or ordinary inaccuracy; a written statement produced for the first time at trial may give such discrepancies a prominence which they do not deserve. In appropriate cases the court may order a party to be deposed before his statement is produced. *E.g., Smith* v. *Central Linen Service Co.*, 39 F.R.D. 15 (D.Md.1966); *McCoy* v. *General Motors Corp.*, 33 F.R.D. 354 (W.D.Pa.1963).

Commentators strongly support the view that a party be able to secure his statement without a showing. 4 Moore's Federal Practice ¶ 26.23[8.4] (2d ed. 1966); 2A Barron & Holtzoff, Federal Practice and Procedure § 652.3 (Wright ed. 1961); see also Note, Developments in the Law—Discovery, 74 Harv.L.Rev. 940, 1039 (1961). The following states have by statute or rule taken the same position: *Statutes*: Fla.Stat.Ann. § 92.33; Ga.Code Ann. § 38–2109(b); La.Stat.Ann.R.S. 13:3732; Mass.Gen.Laws Ann. c. 271, § 44; Minn.Stat.Ann. § 602.01; N.Y.C.P.L.R. § 3101(e); *Rules*: Mo.R.C.P. 56.01(a); N.Dak.R.C.P. 34(b); Wyo.R.C.P. 34(b); *cf.* Mich.G.C.R. 306.2.

In order to clarify and tighten the provision on statements by a party, the term "statement" is defined. The definition is adapted from 18 U.S.C. § 3500(e)(Jencks Act). The statement of a party may of course be that of plaintiff or defendant, and it may be that of an individual or of a corporation or other organization.

Witness' Right to Own Statement.—A second exception to the requirement of this subdivision permits a non-party witness to obtain a copy of his own statement without any special showing. Many, though not all, of the considerations supporting a party's right to obtain his statement apply also to the non-party witness. Insurance companies are increasingly recognizing that a witness is entitled to a copy of his statement and are modifying their regular practice accordingly.

Subdivision (b)(4)—Trial Preparation: Experts. This is a new provision dealing with discovery of information (including facts and opinions) obtained by a party from an expert retained by that party in relation to litigation or obtained by the expert and not yet transmitted to the party. The subdivision deals separately with those experts whom the party expects to call as trial witnesses and with those experts who have been retained or specially employed by the party but who are not expected to be witnesses. It should be noted that the subdivision does not address itself to the expert whose information was not acquired in preparation for trial but rather because he was an actor or viewer with respect to transactions or occurrences that are part of the subject matter of the lawsuit. Such an expert should be treated as an ordinary witness.

Subsection (b)(4)(A) deals with discovery of information obtained by or through experts who will be called as witnesses at trial. The provision is responsive to problems suggested by a relatively recent line of authorities. Many of these cases present intricate and difficult issues as to which expert testimony is likely to be determinative. Prominent among them are food and drug, patent, and condemnation cases. See, *e.g., United States* v. *Nysco Laboratories, Inc.,* 26 F.R.D. 159, 162 (E.D.N.Y.1960)(food and drug); *E. I. du Pont De Nemours & Co.* v. *Phillips Petroleum Co.,* 24 F.R.D. 416, 421 (D.Del.1959)(patent); *Cold Metal Process Co.* v. *Aluminum Co. of America,* 7 F.R.D. 425 (N.D.Ohio 1947), aff'd, *Sachs* v. *Aluminum Co. of America,* 167 F.2d 570 (6th Cir.1948)(same); *United States* v. *50.34 Acres of Land,* 13 F.R.D. 19 (E.D.N.Y.1952)(condemnation).

In cases of this character, a prohibition against discovery of information held by expert witnesses produces in acute form the very evils that discovery has been created to prevent. Effective cross-examination of an expert witness requires advance preparation. The lawyer even with the help of his own experts frequently cannot anticipate the particular approach his adversary's expert will take or the data on which he will base his judgment on the stand. McGlothlin, Some Practical Problems in Proof of Economic, Scientific, and Technical Facts, 23 F.R.D 467, 478 (1958). A California study of discovery and pretrial in condemnation cases notes that the only substitute for discovery of experts' valuation materials is "lengthy—and often fruitless—cross-examination during trial," and recommends pretrial exchange of such material. Calif.Law Rev.Comm'n, Discovery in Eminent Domain Proceedings 707–710 (Jan. 1963). Similarly, effective rebuttal requires advance knowledge of the line of testimony of the other side. If the latter is foreclosed by a rule against discovery, then the narrowing of issues and elimination of surprise which discovery normally produces are frustrated.

These considerations appear to account for the broadening of discovery against experts in the cases cited where expert testimony was central to the case. In some instances, the opinions are explicit in relating expanded discovery to improved cross-examination and rebuttal at trial. *Franks* v. *National Dairy Products Corp.,* 41 F.R.D. 234 (W.D.Tex.1966); *United States* v. *23.76 Acres,* 32 F.R.D. 593 (D.Md.1963); see also an unpublished opinion of Judge Hincks, quoted in *United States* v. *48 Jars, etc.,* 23 F.R.D. 192, 198 (D.D.C.1958). On the other hand, the need for a new provision is shown by the many cases in which discovery of expert trial witnesses is needed for effective cross-examination and rebuttal, and yet courts apply the traditional doctrine and refuse disclosure. *E.g., United States* v. *Certain Parcels of Land,* 25 F.R.D. 192 (N.D.Cal.1959); *United States* v. *Certain Acres,* 18 F.R.D. 98 (M.D.Ga.1955).

Although the trial problems flowing from lack of discovery of expert witnesses are most acute and noteworthy when the case turns largely on experts, the same problems are encountered when a single expert testifies. Thus, subdivision (b)(4)(A) draws no line between complex and simple cases, or between cases with many experts and those with but one. It establishes by rule substantially the procedure adopted by decision of the court in *Knighton* v. *Villian & Fassio,* 39 F.R.D. 11 (D.Md.1965). For a full analysis of the problem and strong recommendations to the same effect, see Friedenthal, Discovery and Use of an Adverse Party's Expert Information, 14 Stan.L.Rev. 455, 485–488 (1962); Long, Discovery and Experts under the Federal Rules of Civil Procedure, 38 F.R.D. 111 (1965).

Past judicial restrictions on discovery of an adversary's expert, particularly as to his opinions, reflect the fear that one side will benefit unduly from the other's better preparation. The procedure established in subsection (b)(4)(A) holds the risk to a minimum. Discovery is limited to trial witnesses, and may be obtained only at a time when the parties know who their expert witnesses will be. A party must as a practical matter prepare his own case in advance of that time, for he can hardly hope to build his case out of his opponent's experts.

Subdivision (b)(4)(A) provides for discovery of an expert who is to testify at the trial. A party can require one who intends to use the expert to state the substance of the testimony that the expert is expected to give. The court may order further discovery, and it has ample power to regulate its timing and scope and to prevent abuse. Ordinarily, the order for further discovery shall compensate the expert for his time, and may compensate the party who intends to use the expert for past expenses reasonably incurred in obtaining facts or opinions from the expert. Those provisions are likely to discourage abusive practices.

Subdivision (b)(4)(B) deals with an expert who has been retained or specially employed by the party in anticipation of litigation or preparation for trial (thus excluding an expert who is simply a general employee of the party not specially employed on the case), but who is not expected to be called as a witness. Under its provisions, a party may discover facts known or opinions held by such an expert only on a showing of exceptional circumstances under which it is impracticable for the party seeking discovery to obtain facts or opinions on the same subject by other means.

Subdivision (b)(4)(B) is concerned only with experts retained or specially consulted in relation to trial preparation. Thus the subdivision precludes discovery against experts who were informally consulted in preparation for trial, but not retained or specially employed. As an ancillary procedure, a party may on a proper showing require the other party to name experts retained or specially employed, but not those informally consulted.

These new provisions of subdivision (b)(4) repudiate the few decisions that have held an expert's information privileged simply because of his status as an expert, *e.g., American Oil Co.* v. *Pennsylvania Petroleum Products Co.*, 23 F.R.D. 680, 685–686 (D.R.I.1959). See Louisell, Modern California Discovery 315–316 (1963). They also reject as ill-considered the decisions which have sought to bring expert information within the work-product doctrine. See *United States* v. *McKay*, 372 F.2d 174, 176–177 (5th Cir.1967). The provisions adopt a form of the more recently developed doctrine of "unfairness". See *e.g., United States* v. *23.76 Acres of Land*, 32 F.R.D. 593, 597 (D.Md.1963); Louisell, *supra*, at 317–318; 4 Moore's Federal Practice ¶ 26.24 (2d ed. 1966).

Under subdivision (b)(4)(C), the court is directed or authorized to issue protective orders, including an order that the expert be paid a reasonable fee for time spent in responding to discovery, and that the party whose expert is made subject to discovery be paid a fair portion of the fees and expenses that the party incurred in obtaining information from the expert. The court may issue the latter order as a condition of discovery, or it may delay the order until after discovery is completed. These provisions for fees and expenses meet the objection that it is unfair to permit one side to obtain without cost the benefit of an expert's work for which the other side has paid, often a substantial sum. *E.g., Lewis* v. *United Air Lines Transp. Corp.*, 32 F.Supp. 21 (W.D.Pa.1940); *Walsh* v. *Reynolds Metals Co.*, 15 F.R.D. 376 (D.N.J.1954). On the other hand, a party may not obtain discovery simply by offering to pay fees and expenses. *Cf. Boynton* v. *R. J. Reynolds Tobacco Co.*, 36 F.Supp. 593 (D.Mass.1941).

In instances of discovery under subdivision (b)(4)(B), the court is directed to award fees and expenses to the other party, since the information is of direct value to the discovering party's preparation of his case. In ordering discovery under (b)(4)(A)(ii), the court has discretion whether to award fees and expenses to the other party; its decision should depend upon whether the discovering party is simply learning about the other party's case or is going beyond this to develop his own case. Even in cases where the court is directed to issue a protective order, it may decline to do so if it finds that manifest injustice would result. Thus, the court can protect, when necessary and appropriate, the interests of an indigent party.

Subdivision (c)—Protective Orders. The provisions of existing Rule 30(b) are transferred to this subdivision (c), as part of the rearrangement of Rule 26. The language has been changed to give it application to discovery generally. The subdivision recognizes the power of the court in the district where a deposition is being taken to make protective orders. Such power is needed when the deposition is being taken far from the court where the action is pending. The court in the district where the deposition is being taken may, and frequently will, remit the deponent or party to the court where the action is pending.

In addition, drafting changes are made to carry out and clarify the sense of the rule. Insertions are made to avoid any possible implication that a protective order does not extend to "time" as well as to "place" or may not safeguard against "undue burden or expense."

The new reference to trade secrets and other confidential commercial information reflects existing law. The courts have not given trade secrets automatic and complete immunity against disclosure, but have in each case weighed their claim to privacy against the need for disclosure. Frequently, they have been afforded a limited protection. See *e.g., Covey Oil Co.* v. *Continental Oil Co.*, 340 F.2d 993 (10th Cir.1965); *Julius M. Ames Co.* v. *Bostitch, Inc.*, 235 F.Supp. 856 (S.D.N.Y.1964).

The subdivision contains new matter relating to sanctions. When a motion for a protective order is made and the court is disposed to deny it, the court may go a step further and issue an order to provide or permit discovery. This will bring the sanctions of Rule 37(b) directly into play. Since the court has heard the contentions of all interested persons, an affirmative order is justified. See Rosenberg, Sanctions to Effectuate Pretrial Discovery, 58 Col.L.Rev. 480, 492–493 (1958). In addition, the court may require the payment of expenses incurred in relation to the motion.

Subdivision (d)—Sequence and Priority. This new provision is concerned with the sequence in which parties may proceed with discovery and with related problems of timing. The principal effects of the new provision are first, to eliminate any fixed priority in the sequence of discovery, and second, to make clear and explicit the court's power to establish priority by an order issued in a particular case.

A priority rule developed by some courts, which confers priority on the party who first serves notice of taking a deposition, is unsatisfactory in several important respects:

First, this priority rule permits a party to establish a priority running to all depositions as to which he has given earlier notice. Since he can on a given day serve notice of taking many depositions he is in a position to delay his adversary's taking of depositions for an inordinate time. Some courts have ruled that deposition priority also permits a party to delay his answers to interrogatories and production of documents. *E.g., E. I. duPont de Nemours & Co.* v. *Phillips Petroleum Co.*, 23 F.R.D. 237 (D.Del.1959); *but cf. Sturdevant* v. *Sears, Roebuck & Co.*, 32 F.R.D. 426 (W.D.Mo.1963).

Second, since notice is the key to priority, if both parties wish to take depositions first a race results. See *Caldwell–Clements, Inc.* v. *McGraw–Hill Pub. Co.*, 11 F.R.D. 156 (S.D.N.Y.1951)(description of tactics used by parties). But the existing rules on notice of deposition create a race with runners starting from different positions. The plaintiff may not give notice without leave of court until 20 days after commencement of the action, whereas the defendant may serve notice at any time after commencement. Thus, a careful and prompt defendant can almost always secure priority. This advantage of defendants is fortuitous, because the purpose of requiring plaintiff to wait 20 days is to afford defendant an opportunity to obtain counsel, not to confer priority.

Third, although courts have ordered a change in the normal sequence of discovery on a number of occasions, *e.g., Kaeppler* v. *James H. Matthews & Co.*, 200 F.Supp. 229 (E.D.Pa.1961); *Park & Tilford Distillers Corp.* v. *Distillers Co.*, 19 F.R.D. 169 (S.D.N.Y. 1956) and have at all times avowed discretion to vary the usual priority, most commentators are agreed that courts in fact grant relief only for "the most obviously compelling reasons." 2A Barron & Holtzoff, Federal Practice and Procedure 44–47 (Wright ed. 1961); see also Younger, Priority of Pretrial Examination in the Federal Courts—A Comment, 34 N.Y.U.L.Rev. 1271 (1959); Freund, The Pleading and Pretrial of an Antitrust Claim, 46 Corn.L.Q. 555, 564 (1964). Discontent with the fairness of actual practice has been evinced by other observers. Comment, 59 Yale L.J. 117, 134–136 (1949); Yudkin, Some Refinements in Federal Discovery Procedure, 11 Fed.B.J. 289, 296–297 (1951); Developments in the Law-Discovery, 74 Harv.L.Rev. 940, 954–958 (1961).

Despite these difficulties, some courts have adhered to the priority rule, presumably because it provides a test which is easily understood and applied by the parties without much court intervention. It thus permits deposition discovery to function extrajudicially, which the rules provide for and the courts desire. For these same reasons, courts are reluctant to make numerous exceptions to the rule.

The Columbia Survey makes clear that the problem of priority does not affect litigants generally. It found that most litigants do not move quickly to obtain discovery. In over half of the cases, both parties waited at least 50 days. During the first 20 days after commencement of the action—the period when defendant might assure his priority by noticing depositions—16 percent of the defendants acted to obtain discovery. A race could not have occurred in more than 16 percent of the cases and it undoubtedly occurred in fewer. On the other hand, five times as many defendants as plaintiffs served notice of deposition during the first 19 days. To the same effect, see Comment, Tactical Use and Abuse of Depositions Under the Federal Rules, 59 Yale L.J. 117, 134 (1949).

These findings do not mean, however, that the priority rule is satisfactory or that a problem of priority does not exist. The court decisions show that parties do battle on this issue and carry their disputes to court. The statistics show that these court cases are not typical. By the same token, they reveal that more extensive exercise of judicial discretion to vary the priority will not bring a flood of litigation, and that a change in the priority rule will in fact affect only a small fraction of the cases.

It is contended by some that there is no need to alter the existing priority practice. In support, it is urged that there is no evidence that injustices in fact result from present practice and that, in any event, the courts can and do promulgate local rules, as in New

York, to deal with local situations and issue orders to avoid possible injustice in particular cases.

Subdivision (d) is based on the contrary view that the rule of priority based on notice is unsatisfactory and unfair in its operation. Subdivision (d) follows an approach adapted from Civil Rule 4 of the District Court for the Southern District of New York. That rule provides that starting 40 days after commencement of the action, unless otherwise ordered by the court, the fact that one party is taking a deposition shall not prevent another party from doing so "concurrently." In practice, the depositions are not usually taken simultaneously; rather, the parties work out arrangements for alternation in the taking of depositions. One party may take a complete deposition and then the other, or, if the depositions are extensive, one party deposes for a set time, and then the other. See *Caldwell–Clements, Inc.* v. *McGraw–Hill Pub. Co.*, 11 F.R.D. 156 (S.D.N.Y.1951).

In principle, one party's initiation of discovery should not wait upon the other's completion, unless delay is dictated by special considerations. Clearly the principle is feasible with respect to all methods of discovery other than depositions. And the experience of the Southern District of New York shows that the principle can be applied to depositions as well. The courts have not had an increase in motion business on this matter. Once it is clear to lawyers that they bargain on an equal footing, they are usually able to arrange for an orderly succession of depositions without judicial intervention. Professor Moore has called attention to Civil Rule 4 and suggested that it may usefully be extended to other areas. 4 Moore's Federal Practice 1154 (2d ed. 1966).

The court may upon motion and by order grant priority in a particular case. But a local court rule purporting to confer priority in certain classes of cases would be inconsistent with this subdivision and thus void.

Subdivision (e)—Supplementation of Responses. The rules do not now state whether interrogatories (and questions at deposition as well as requests for inspection and admissions) impose a "continuing burden" on the responding party to supplement his answers if he obtains new information. The issue is acute when new information renders substantially incomplete or inaccurate an answer which was complete and accurate when made. It is essential that the rules provide an answer to this question. The parties can adjust to a rule either way, once they know what it is. See 4 Moore's Federal Practice ¶ 33.25[4] (2d ed. 1966).

Arguments can be made both ways. Imposition of a continuing burden reduces the proliferation of additional sets of interrogatories. Some courts have adopted local rules establishing such a burden. E.g., E.D.Pa.R. 20(f), quoted in *Taggart* v. *Vermont Transp. Co.*, 32 F.R.D. 587 (E.D.Pa.1963); D.Me.R. 15(c). Others have imposed the burden by decision. *E.g., Chenault* v. *Nebraska Farm Products, Inc.*, 9 F.R.D. 529, 533 (D.Neb.1949). On the other hand, there are serious objections to the burden, especially in protracted cases. Although the party signs the answers, it is his lawyer who understands their significance and bears the responsibility to bring answers up to date. In a complex case all sorts of information reaches the party, who little understands its bearing on answers previously given to interrogatories. In practice, therefore, the lawyer under a continuing burden must periodically recheck all interrogatories and canvass all new information. But a full set of new answers may no longer be needed by the interrogating party. Some issues will have been dropped from the case, some questions are now seen as unimportant, and other questions must in any event be reformulated. See *Novick* v. *Pennsylvania R. R.*, 18 F.R.D. 296, 298 (W.D.Pa.1955).

Subdivision (e) provides that a party is not under a continuing burden except as expressly provided. Cf. Note, 68 Harv.L.Rev. 673, 677 (1955). An exception is made as to the identity of persons having knowledge of discoverable matters, because of the obvious importance to each side of knowing all witnesses and because information about witnesses routinely comes to each lawyer's attention. Many of the decisions on the issue of a continuing burden have in fact concerned the identity of witnesses. An exception is also made as to expert trial witnesses in order to carry out the provisions of Rule 26(b)(4). See *Diversified Products Corp.* v. *Sports Center Co.*, 42 F.R.D. 3 (D.Md.1967).

Another exception is made for the situation in which a party, or more frequently his lawyer, obtains actual knowledge that a prior response is incorrect. This exception does not impose a duty to check the accuracy of prior responses, but it prevents knowing concealment by a party or attorney. Finally, a duty to supplement may be imposed by order of the court in a particular case (including an order resulting from a pretrial conference) or by agreement of the parties. A party may of course make a new discovery request which requires supplementation of prior responses.

The duty will normally be enforced, in those limited instances where it is imposed, through sanctions imposed by the trial court, including exclusion of evidence, continuance, or other action, as the court may deem appropriate.

1980 AMENDMENT

Subdivision (f). This subdivision is new. There has been widespread criticism of abuse of discovery. The Committee has considered a number of proposals to eliminate abuse, including a change in Rule 26(b)(1) with respect to the scope of discovery and a change in Rule 33(a) to limit the number of questions that can be asked by interrogatories to parties.

The Committee believes that abuse of discovery, while very serious in certain cases, is not so general as to require such basic changes in the rules that govern discovery in all cases. A very recent study of discovery in selected metropolitan districts tends to support its belief. P. Connolly, E. Holleman, & M. Kuhlman, Judicial Controls and the Civil Litigative Process: Discovery (Federal Judicial Center, 1978). In the judgment of the Committee abuse can best be prevented by intervention by the court as soon as abuse is threatened.

To this end this subdivision provides that counsel who has attempted without success to effect with opposing counsel a reasonable program or plan for discovery is entitled to the assistance of the court.

It is not contemplated that requests for discovery conferences will be made routinely. A relatively narrow discovery dispute should be resolved by resort to Rules 26(c) or 37(a), and if it appears that a request for a conference is in fact grounded in such a dispute, the court may refer counsel to those rules. If the court is persuaded that a request is frivolous or vexatious, it can strike it. See Rules 11 and 7(b)(2).

A number of courts routinely consider discovery matters in preliminary pretrial conferences held shortly after the pleadings are closed. This subdivision does not interfere with such a practice. It authorizes the court to combine a discovery conference with a pretrial conference under Rule 16 if a pretrial conference is held sufficiently early to prevent or curb abuse.

1983 AMENDMENT

Excessive discovery and evasion or resistance to reasonable discovery requests pose significant problems. Recent studies have made some attempt to determine the sources and extent of the difficulties. See Brazil, *Civil Discovery: Lawyers' Views of its Effectiveness, Principal Problems and Abuses,* American Bar Foundation (1980); Connolly, Holleman & Kuhlman, *Judicial Controls and the Civil Litigative Process: Discovery,* Federal Judicial Center (1978); Ellington, *A Study of Sanctions for Discovery Abuse,* Department of Justice (1979); Schroeder & Frank, *The Proposed Changes in the Discovery Rules,* 1978 Ariz. St. L.J. 475.

The purpose of discovery is to provide a mechanism for making relevant information available to the litigants. "Mutual knowledge of all the relevant facts gathered by both parties is essential to proper litigation." *Hickman v. Taylor,* 329 U.S. 495, 507, 67 S.Ct. 385, 91 L.Ed. 451 (1947). Thus the spirit of the rules is violated when advocates attempt to use discovery tools as tactical weapons rather than to expose the facts and illuminate the issues by overuse of discovery or unnecessary use of defensive weapons or evasive responses. All of this results in excessively costly and time-consuming activities that are disproportionate to the nature of the case, the amount involved, or the issues or values at stake.

Given our adversary tradition and the current discovery rules, it is not surprising that there are many opportunities if not incentives, for attorneys to engage in discovery that, although authorized by the broad, permissive terms of the rules, nevertheless results in delay. See Brazil, *The Adversary Character of Civil Discovery: A Critique and Proposals for Change,* 31 Vand.L.Rev. 1259 (1978). As a result, it has been said that the rules have "not infrequently [been] exploited to the disadvantage of justice." *Herbert v. Lando,* 441 U.S. 153, 179, 99 S.Ct. 1635, 60 L.Ed.2d 115 (1979) (Powell, J., concurring). These practices impose costs on an already overburdened system and impede the fundamental goal of the "just, speedy, and inexpensive determination of every action." Fed.R.Civ.P. 1.

Subdivision (a); Discovery Methods. The deletion of the last sentence of Rule 26(a)(1), which provided that unless the court ordered otherwise under Rule 26(c) "the frequency of use" of the various discovery methods was not to be limited, is an attempt to address the problem of duplicative, redundant, and excessive discovery and to reduce it. The amendment, in conjunction with the changes in Rule 26(b)(1), is designed to encourage district judges to identify instances of needless discovery and to limit the use of the various discovery devices accordingly. The question may be raised by one of the parties, typically on a motion for a protective order, or by the court on its own initiative. It is entirely appropriate to consider a limitation on the frequency of use of discovery at a discovery conference under Rule 26(f) or at any other pretrial conference authorized by these rules. In considering the discovery needs of a particular case, the court should consider the factors described in Rule 26(b)(1).

Subdivision (b); Discovery Scope and Limits. Rule 26(b)(1) has been amended to add a sentence to deal with the problem of over-discovery. The objective is to guard against redundant or disproportionate discovery by giving the court authority to reduce the amount of discovery that may be directed to matters that are otherwise proper subjects of inquiry. The new sentence is intended to encourage judges to be more aggressive in identifying and discouraging discovery overuse. The grounds mentioned in the amended rule for limiting discovery reflect the existing practice of many courts in issuing protective orders under Rule 26(c). See, *e.g., Carlson Cos. v. Sperry & Hutchinson Co.*, 374 F.Supp. 1080 (D.Minn.1973); *Dolgow v. Anderson,* 53 F.R.D. 661 (E.D.N.Y.1971); *Mitchell v. American Tobacco Co.,* 33 F.R.D. 262 (M.D.Pa.1963); *Welty v. Clute,* 1 F.R.D. 446 (W.D.N.Y.1940). On the whole, however, district judges have been reluctant to limit the use of the discovery devices. See, *e.g., Apco Oil Corp.* v. *Certified Transp., Inc.,* 46 F.R.D. 428 (W.D.Mo.1969). See generally 8 Wright & Miller, *Federal Practice and Procedure: Civil* §§ 2036, 2037, 2039, 2040 (1970).

The first element of the standard, Rule 26(b)(1)(i), is designed to minimize redundancy in discovery and encourage attorneys to be sensitive to the comparative costs of different methods of securing information. Subdivision (b)(1)(ii) also seeks to reduce repetitiveness and to oblige lawyers to think through their discovery activities in advance so that full utilization is made of each deposition, document request, or set of interrogatories. The elements of Rule 26(b)(1)(iii) address the problem of discovery that is disproportionate to the individual lawsuit as measured by such matters as its nature and complexity, the importance of the issues at stake in a case seeking damages, the limitations on a financially weak litigant to withstand extensive opposition to a discovery program or to respond to discovery requests, and the significance of the substantive issues, as measured in philosophic, social, or institutional terms. Thus the rule recognizes that many cases in public policy spheres, such as employment practices, free speech, and other matters, may have importance far beyond the monetary amount involved. The court must apply the standards in an even-handed manner that will prevent use of discovery to wage a war of attrition or as a device to coerce a party, whether financially weak or affluent.

The rule contemplates greater judicial involvement in the discovery process and thus acknowledges the reality that it cannot always operate on a self-regulating basis. See Connolly, Holleman & Kuhlman, *Judicial Controls and the Civil Litigative Process: Discovery* 77, Federal Judicial Center (1978). In an appropriate case the court could restrict the number of depositions, interrogatories, or the scope of a production request. But the court must be careful not to deprive a party of discovery that is reasonably necessary to afford a fair opportunity to develop and prepare the case.

The court may act on motion, or its own initiative. It is entirely appropriate to resort to the amended rule in conjunction with a discovery conference under Rule 26(f) or one of the other pretrial conferences authorized by the rules.

Subdivision (g); Signing of Discovery Requests, Responses, and Objections. Rule 26(g) imposes an affirmative duty to engage in pretrial discovery in a responsible manner that is consistent with the spirit and purposes of Rules 26 through 37. In addition, Rule 26(g) is designed to curb discovery abuse by explicitly encouraging the imposition of sanctions. The subdivision provides a deterrent to both excessive discovery and evasion by imposing a certification requirement that obliges each attorney to stop and think about the legitimacy of a discovery request, a response thereto, or an objection. The term "response" includes answers to interrogatories and to requests to admit as well as responses to production requests.

If primary responsibility for conducting discovery is to continue to rest with the litigants, they must be obliged to act responsibly and avoid abuse. With this in mind, Rule 26(g), which parallels the amendments to Rule 11, requires an attorney or unrepresented party to sign each discovery request, response, or objection. Motions relating to discovery are governed by Rule 11. However, since a discovery request, response, or objection usually deals with more specific subject matter than motions or papers, the elements that must be certified in connection with the former are spelled out more completely. The signature is a certification of the elements set forth in Rule 26(g).

Although the certification duty requires the lawyer to pause and consider the reasonableness of his request, response, or objection, it is not meant to discourage or restrict necessary and legitimate discovery. The rule simply requires that the attorney make a reasonable inquiry into the factual basis of his response, request, or objection.

The duty to make a "reasonable inquiry" is satisfied if the investigation undertaken by the attorney and the conclusions drawn therefrom are reasonable under the circumstances. It is an objective standard similar to the one imposed by Rule 11. See the Advisory Committee Note to Rule 11. See also *Kinee v. Abraham Lincoln Fed. Sav. & Loan Ass'n,* 365 F.Supp. 975 (E.D.Pa.1973). In making the inquiry, the attorney may rely on assertions by the client and on communications with other counsel in the case as long as that reliance is appropriate under the circumstances. Ultimately what is reasonable is a matter for the court to decide on the totality of the circumstances.

Rule 26(g) does not require the signing attorney to certify the truthfulness of the client's factual responses to a discovery request. Rather, the signature certifies that the lawyer has made a reasonable effort to assure that the client has provided all the information and documents available to him that are responsive to the discovery demand. Thus, the lawyer's certification under Rule 26(g) should be distinguished from other signature requirements in the rules, such as those in Rules 30(e) and 33.

Nor does the rule require a party or an attorney to disclose privileged communications or work product in order to show that a discovery request, response, or objection is substantially justified. The provisions of Rule 26(c), including appropriate orders after *in camera* inspection by the court, remain available to protect a party claiming privilege or work product protection.

The signing requirement means that every discovery request, response, or objection should be grounded on a theory that is reasonable under the precedents or a good faith belief as to what should be the law. This standard is heavily dependent on the circumstances of each case. The certification speaks as of the time it is made. The duty to supplement discovery responses continues to be governed by Rule 26(e).

Concern about discovery abuse has led to widespread recognition that there is a need for more aggressive judicial control and supervision. *ACF Industries, Inc. v. EEOC,* 439 U.S. 1081, 99 S.Ct. 865, 59 L.Ed.2d 52 (1979)(certiorari denied) (Powell, J., dissenting). Sanctions to deter discovery abuse would be more effective if they were diligently applied "not merely to penalize those whose conduct may be deemed to warrant such a sanction, but to deter those who might be tempted to such conduct in the absence of such a deterrent." *National Hockey League v. Metropolitan Hockey Club,* 427 U.S. 639, 643, 96 S.Ct. 2778, 49 L.Ed.2d 747 (1976). See also Note, *The Emerging Deterrence Orientation in the Imposition of Discovery Sanctions,* 91 Harv.L.Rev. 1033 (1978). Thus the premise of Rule 26(g) is that imposing sanctions on attorneys who fail to meet the rule's standards will significantly reduce abuse by imposing disadvantages therefor.

Because of the asserted reluctance to impose sanctions on attorneys who abuse the discovery rules, see Brazil, *Civil Discovery: Lawyers' Views of its Effectiveness, Principal Problems and Abuses,* American Bar Foundation (1980); Ellington, *A Study of Sanctions for Discovery Abuse,* Department of Justice (1979), Rule 26(g) makes explicit the authority judges now have to impose appropriate sanctions and requires them to use it. This authority derives from Rule 37, 28 U.S.C. § 1927, and the court's inherent power. See *Roadway Express, Inc. v. Piper,* 447 U.S. 752, 100 S.Ct. 2455, 65 L.Ed.2d 488 (1980); *Martin v. Bell Helicopter Co.,* 85 F.R.D. 654, 661–62 (D.Col.1980); Note, *Sanctions Imposed by Courts on Attorneys Who Abuse the Judicial Process,* 44 U.Chi.L.Rev. 619 (1977). The new rule mandates that sanctions be imposed on attorneys who fail to meet the standards established in the first portion of Rule 26(g). The nature of the sanction is a matter of judicial discretion to be exercised in light of the particular circumstances. The court may take into account any failure by the party seeking sanctions to invoke protection under Rule 26(c) at an early stage in the litigation.

The sanctioning process must comport with due process requirements. The kind of notice and hearing required will depend on the facts of the case and the severity of the sanction being considered. To prevent the proliferation of the sanction procedure and to avoid multiple hearings, discovery in any sanction proceeding normally should be permitted only when it is clearly required by the interests of justice. In most cases the court will be aware of the circumstances and only a brief hearing should be necessary.

1987 AMENDMENT

The amendments are technical. No substantive change is intended.

1993 AMENDMENT

Subdivision (a). Through the addition of paragraphs (1)–(4), this subdivision imposes on parties a duty to disclose, without awaiting formal discovery requests, certain basic information that is needed in most cases to prepare for trial or make an informed decision about settlement. The rule requires all parties (1) early in the case to exchange information regarding potential witnesses, documentary evidence, damages, and insurance, (2) at an appropriate time during the discovery period to identify expert witnesses and provide a detailed written statement of the testimony that may be offered at trial through specially retained experts, and (3) as the trial date approaches to identify the particular evidence that may be offered at trial. The enumeration in Rule 26(a) of items to be disclosed does not prevent a court from requiring by order or local rule that the parties disclose additional information without a discovery request. Nor are parties precluded from using traditional discovery methods to obtain further information regarding these matters, as for example asking an expert during a deposition about testimony given in other litigation beyond the four-year period specified in Rule 26(a)(2)(B).

A major purpose of the revision is to accelerate the exchange of basic information about the case and to eliminate the paper work involved in requesting such information, and the rule should be applied in a manner to achieve those objectives. The concepts of imposing a duty of disclosure were set forth in Brazil, *The Adversary Character of Civil Discovery: A Critique and Proposals for Change,* 31 *Vand.L.Rev.* 1348 (1978), and Schwarzer, *The Federal Rules, the Adversary Process, and Discovery Reform,* 50 *U.Pitt.L.Rev.* 703, 721–23 (1989).

The rule is based upon the experience of district courts that have required disclosure of some of this information through local rules, court-approved standard interrogatories, and standing orders. Most have required pretrial disclosure of the kind of information described in Rule 26(a)(3). Many have required written reports from experts containing information like that specified in Rule 26(a)(2)(B). While far more limited, the experience of the few state and federal courts that have required pre-discovery exchange of core information such as is contemplated in Rule 26(a)(1) indicates that savings in time and expense can be achieved, particularly if the litigants meet and discuss the issues in the case as a predicate for this exchange and if a judge supports the process, as by using the results to guide further proceedings in the case. Courts in Canada and the United Kingdom have for many years required disclosure of certain information without awaiting a request from an adversary.

Paragraph (1). As the functional equivalent of court-ordered interrogatories, this paragraph requires early disclosure, without need for any request, of four types of information that have been customarily secured early in litigation through formal discovery. The introductory clause permits the court, by local rule, to exempt all or particular types of cases from these disclosure requirement *[sic]* or to modify the nature of the information to be disclosed. It is expected that courts would, for example, exempt cases like Social Security reviews and government collection cases in which discovery would not be appropriate or would be unlikely. By order the court may eliminate or modify the disclosure requirements in a particular case, and similarly the parties, unless precluded by order or local rule, can stipulate to elimination or modification of the requirements for that case. The disclosure obligations specified in paragraph (1) will not be appropriate for all cases, and it is expected that changes in these obligations will be made by the court or parties when the circumstances warrant.

Authorization of these local variations is, in large measure, included in order to accommodate the Civil Justice Reform Act of 1990, which implicitly directs districts to experiment during the study period with differing procedures to reduce the time and expense of civil litigation. The civil justice delay and expense reduction plans adopted by the courts under the Act differ as to the type, form, and timing of disclosures required. Section 105(c)(1) of the Act calls for a report by the Judicial Conference to Congress by December 31, 1995, comparing experience in twenty of these courts; and section 105(c)(2)(B) contemplates that some changes in the Rules may then be needed. While these studies may indicate the desirability of further changes in Rule 26(a)(1), these changes probably could not become effective before December 1998 at the earliest. In the meantime, the present revision puts in place a series of disclosure obligations that, unless a court acts affirmatively to impose other requirements or indeed to reject all such requirements for the present, are designed to eliminate certain discovery, help focus the discovery that is needed, and facilitate preparation for trial or settlement.

Subparagraph (A) requires identification of all persons who, based on the investigation conducted thus far, are likely to have discoverable information relevant to the factual disputes between the parties. All persons with such information should be disclosed, whether or not their testimony will be supportive of the position of the disclosing party.

As officers of the court, counsel are expected to disclose the identity of those persons who may be used by them as witnesses or who, if their potential testimony were known, might reasonably be expected to be deposed or called as a witness by any of the other parties. Indicating briefly the general topics on which such persons have information should not be burdensome, and will assist other parties in deciding which depositions will actually be needed.

Subparagraph (B) is included as a substitute for the inquiries routinely made about the existence and location of documents and other tangible things in the possession, custody, or control of the disclosing party. Although, unlike subdivision (a)(3)(C), an itemized listing of each exhibit is not required, the disclosure should describe and categorize, to the extent identified during the initial investigation, the nature and location of potentially relevant documents and records, including computerized data and other electronically-recorded information, sufficiently to enable opposing parties (1) to make an informed decision concerning which documents might need to be examined, at least initially, and (2) to frame their document requests in a manner likely to avoid squabbles resulting from the wording of the requests. As with potential witnesses, the requirement for disclosure of documents applies to all potentially relevant items then known to the party, whether or not supportive of its contentions in the case.

Unlike subparagraphs (C) and (D), subparagraph (B) does not require production of any documents. Of course, in cases involving few documents a disclosing party may prefer to provide copies of the documents rather than describe them, and the rule is written to afford this option to the disclosing party. If, as will be more typical, only the description is provided, the other parties are expected to obtain the documents desired by proceeding under Rule 34 or through informal requests. The disclosing party does not, by describing documents under subparagraph (B), waive its right to object to production on the basis of privilege or work product protection, or to assert that the documents are not sufficiently relevant to justify the burden or expense of production.

The initial disclosure requirements of subparagraphs (A) and (B) are limited to identification of potential evidence "relevant to disputed facts alleged with particularity in the pleadings." There is no need for a party to identify potential evidence with respect to allegations that are admitted. Broad, vague, and conclusory allegations sometimes tolerated in notice pleading—for example, the assertion that a product with many component parts is defective in some unspecified manner—should not impose upon responding parties the obligation at that point to search for and identify all persons possibly involved in, or all documents affecting, the design, manufacture, and assembly of the product. The greater the specificity and clarity of the allegations in the pleadings, the more complete should be the listing of potential witnesses and types of documentary evidence. Although paragraphs (1)(A) and (1)(B) by their terms refer to the factual disputes defined in the pleadings, the rule contemplates that these issues would be informally refined and clarified during the meeting of the parties under subdivision (f) and that the disclosure obligations would be adjusted in the light of these discussions. The disclosure requirements should, in short, be applied with common sense in light of the principles of Rule 1, keeping in mind the salutary purposes that the rule is intended to accomplish. The litigants should not indulge in gamesmanship with respect to the disclosure obligations.

Subparagraph (C) imposes a burden of disclosure that includes the functional equivalent of a standing Request for Production under Rule 34. A party claiming damages or other monetary relief must, in addition to disclosing the calculation of such damages, make available the supporting documents for inspection and copying as if a request for such materials had been made under Rule 34. This obligation applies only with respect to documents then reasonably available to it and not privileged or protected as work product. Likewise, a party would not be expected to provide a calculation of damages which, as in many patent infringement actions, depends on information in the possession of another party or person.

Subparagraph (D) replaces subdivision (b)(2) of Rule 26, and provides that liability insurance policies be made available for inspection and copying. The last two sentences of that subdivision have been omitted as unnecessary, not to signify any change of law. The disclosure of insurance information does not thereby render such information admissible in evidence. See Rule 411, Federal Rules of Evidence. Nor does subparagraph (D) require disclosure of applications for insurance, though in particular cases such information may be discoverable in accordance with revised subdivision (a)(5).

Unless the court directs a different time, the disclosures required by subdivision (a)(1) are to be made at or within 10 days after the meeting of the parties under subdivision (f). One of the purposes of this meeting is to refine the factual disputes with respect to which disclosures should be made under paragraphs (1)(A) and (1)(B), particularly if an answer has not been filed by a defendant, or, indeed, to afford the parties an opportunity to modify by stipulation the timing or scope of these obligations. The time of this meeting is generally left to the parties provided it is held at least 14 days before a scheduling conference is held or before a scheduling order is due under Rule 16(b). In cases in which no scheduling conference is held, this will mean that the meeting must ordinarily be held within 75 days after a defendant has first appeared in the case and hence that the initial disclosures would be due no later than 85 days after the first appearance of a defendant.

Before making its disclosures, a party has the obligation under subdivision (g)(1) to make a reasonable inquiry into the facts of the case. The rule does not demand an exhaustive investigation at this stage of the case, but one that is reasonable under the circumstances, focusing on the facts that are alleged with particularity in the pleadings. The type of investigation that can be expected at this point will vary based upon such factors as the number and complexity of the issues; the location, nature, number, and availability of potentially relevant witnesses and documents; the extent of past working relationships between the attorney and the client, particularly in handling related or similar litigation; and of course how long the party has to conduct an investigation, either before or after filing of the case. As provided in the last sentence of subdivision (a)(1), a party is not excused from the duty of disclosure merely because its investigation is incomplete. The party should make its initial disclosures based on the pleadings and the information then reasonably available to it. As its investigation continues and as the issues in the pleadings are clarified, it should supplement its disclosures as required by subdivision (e)(1). A party is not relieved from its obligation of disclosure merely because another party has not made its disclosures or has made an inadequate disclosure.

It will often be desirable, particularly if the claims made in the complaint are broadly stated, for the parties to have their Rule 26(f) meeting early in the case, perhaps before a defendant has answered the complaint or had time to conduct other than a cursory investigation. In such circumstances, in order to facilitate more meaningful and useful initial disclosures, they can and should stipulate to a period of more than 10 days after the meeting in which to make these disclosures, at least for defendants who had no advance notice of the potential litigation. A stipulation at an early meeting affording such a defendant at least 60 days after receiving the complaint in which to make its disclosures under subdivision (a)(1)—a period that is two weeks longer than the time formerly specified for responding to interrogatories served with a complaint—should be adequate and appropriate in most cases.

Paragraph (2). This paragraph imposes an additional duty to disclose information regarding expert testimony sufficiently in advance of trial that opposing parties have a reasonable opportunity to prepare for effective cross examination and perhaps arrange for expert testimony from other witnesses. Normally the court should prescribe a time for these disclosures in a scheduling order under Rule 16(b), and in most cases the party with the burden of proof on an issue should disclose its expert testimony on that issue before other parties are required to make their disclosures with respect to that issue. In the absence of such a direction, the disclosures are to be made by all parties at least 90 days before the trial date or the date by which the case is to be ready for trial, except that an additional 30 days is allowed (unless the court specifies another time) for disclosure of expert testimony to be used solely to contradict or rebut the testimony that may be presented by another party's expert. For a discussion of procedures that have been used to enhance the reliability of expert testimony, see M. Graham, *Expert Witness Testimony and the Federal Rules of Evidence: Insuring Adequate Assurance of Trustworthiness,* 1986 *U.Ill.L.Rev.* 90.

Paragraph (2)(B) requires that persons retained or specially employed to provide expert testimony, or whose duties as an employee of the party regularly involve the giving of expert testimony, must prepare a detailed and complete written report, stating the testimony the witness is expected to present during direct examination, together with the reasons therefor. The information disclosed under the former rule in answering interrogatories about the "substance" of expert testimony was frequently so sketchy and vague that it rarely dispensed with the need to depose the expert and often was even of little help in preparing for a deposition of the witness. Revised Rule 37(c)(1) provides an incentive for full disclosure; namely, that a party will not ordinarily be permitted to use on direct examination any expert testimony not so disclosed. Rule 26(a)(2)(B) does not preclude counsel from providing assistance to experts in preparing the reports, and indeed, with experts such as automobile mechanics, this assistance may be needed. Nevertheless, the report, which is intended to set forth the substance of the direct examination, should be written in a manner that reflects the testimony to be given by the witness and it must be signed by the witness.

The report is to disclose the data and other information considered by the expert and any exhibits or charts that summarize or support the expert's opinions. Given this obligation of disclosure, litigants should no longer be able to argue that materials furnished to their experts to be used in forming their opinions—whether or not ultimately relied upon by the expert—are privileged or otherwise protected from disclosure when such persons are testifying or being deposed.

Revised subdivision (b)(4)(A) authorizes the deposition of expert witnesses. Since depositions of experts required to prepare a written report may be taken only after the report has been served, the length of the deposition of such experts should be reduced, and in many cases the report may eliminate the need for a deposition. Revised subdivision (e)(1) requires disclosure of any material changes made in the opinions of an expert from whom a report is required, whether the changes are in the written report or in testimony given at a deposition.

For convenience, this rule and revised Rule 30 continue to use the term "expert" to refer to those persons who will testify under Rule 702 of the Federal Rules of Evidence with respect to scientific, technical, and other specialized matters. The requirement of a written report in paragraph (2)(B), however, applies only to those experts who are retained or specially employed to provide such testimony in the case or whose duties as an employee of a party regularly involve the giving of such testimony. A treating physician, for example, can be deposed or called to testify at trial without any requirement for a written report. By local rule, order, or written stipulation, the requirement of a written report may be waived for particular experts or imposed upon additional persons who will provide opinions under Rule 702.

Paragraph (3). This paragraph imposes an additional duty to disclose, without any request, information customarily needed in final preparation for trial. These disclosures are to be made in accordance with schedules adopted by the court under Rule 16(b) or by special order. If no such schedule is directed by the court, the disclosures are to be made at least 30 days before commencement of the trial. By its terms, rule 26(a)(3) does not require disclosure of evidence to be used solely for impeachment purposes; however, disclosure of such evidence—as well as other items relating to conduct of trial—may be required by local rule or a pretrial order.

Subparagraph (A) requires the parties to designate the persons whose testimony they may present as substantive evidence at trial, whether in person or by deposition. Those who will probably be called as witnesses should be listed separately from those who are not likely to be called but who are being listed in order to preserve the right to do so if needed because of developments during trial. Revised Rule 37(c)(1) provides that only persons so listed may be used at trial to present substantive evidence. This restriction does not apply unless the omission was "without substantial justification" and hence would not bar an unlisted witness if the need for such testimony is based upon developments during trial that could not reasonably have been anticipated—e.g., a change of testimony.

Listing a witness does not obligate the party to secure the attendance of the person at trial, but should preclude the party from objecting if the person is called to testify by another party who did not list the person as a witness.

Subparagraph (B) requires the party to indicate which of these potential witnesses will be presented by deposition at trial. A party expecting to use at trial a deposition not recorded by stenographic means is required by revised Rule 32 to provide the court with a transcript of the pertinent portions of such depositions. This rule requires that copies of the transcript of a nonstenographic deposition be provided to other parties in advance of trial for verification, an obvious concern since counsel often utilize their own personnel to prepare transcripts from audio or video tapes. By order or local rule, the court may require that parties designate the particular portions of stenographic depositions to be used at trial.

Subparagraph (C) requires disclosure of exhibits, including summaries (whether to be offered in lieu of other documentary evidence or to be used as an aid in understanding such evidence), that may be offered as substantive evidence. The rule requires a separate listing of each such exhibit, though it should permit voluminous items of a similar or standardized character to be described by meaningful categories. For example, unless the court has otherwise directed, a series of vouchers might be shown collectively as a single exhibit with their starting and ending dates. As with witnesses, the exhibits that will probably be offered are to be listed separately from those which are unlikely to be offered but which are listed in order to preserve the right to do so if needed because of developments during trial. Under revised Rule 37(c)(1) the court can permit use of unlisted documents the need for which could not reasonably have been anticipated in advance of trial.

Upon receipt of these final pretrial disclosures, other parties have 14 days (unless a different time is specified by the court) to disclose any objections they wish to preserve to the usability of the deposition testimony or to the admissibility of the documentary evidence (other than under Rules 402 and 403 of the Federal Rules of Evidence). Similar provisions have become commonplace either in pretrial orders or by local rules, and significantly expedite the presentation of evidence at trial, as well as eliminate the need to have available witnesses to provide "foundation" testimony for most items of documentary evidence. The listing of a potential objection does not constitute the making of that objection or require the court to rule on the objection; rather, it preserves the right of the party to make the objection when and as appropriate during trial. The court may, however, elect to treat the listing as a motion "in limine" and rule upon the objections in advance of trial to the extent appropriate.

The time specified in the rule for the final pretrial disclosures is relatively close to the trial date. The objective is to eliminate the time and expense in making these disclosures of evidence and objections in those cases that settle shortly before trial, while affording a reasonable time for final preparation for trial in those cases that do not settle. In many cases, it will be desirable for the court in a scheduling or pretrial order to set an earlier time for disclosures of evidence and provide more time for disclosing potential objections.

Paragraph (4). This paragraph prescribes the form of disclosures. A signed written statement is required, reminding the parties and counsel of the solemnity of the obligations imposed; and the signature on the initial or pretrial disclosure is a certification under subdivision (g)(1) that it is complete and correct as of the time when made. Consistent with Rule 5(d), these disclosures are to be filed with the court unless otherwise directed. It is anticipated that many courts will direct that expert reports required under paragraph (2)(B) not be filed until needed in connection with a motion or for trial.

Paragraph (5). This paragraph is revised to take note of the availability of revised Rule 45 for inspection from non-parties of documents and premises without the need for a deposition.

Subdivision (b). This subdivision is revised in several respects. First, former paragraph (1) is subdivided into two paragraphs for ease of reference and to avoid renumbering of paragraphs (3) and (4). Textual changes are then made in new paragraph (2) to enable the court to keep tighter rein on the extent of discovery. The information explosion of recent decades has greatly increased both the potential cost of wide-ranging discovery and the potential for discovery to be used as an instrument for delay or oppression. Amendments to Rules 30, 31, and 33 place presumptive limits on the number of depositions and interrogatories, subject to leave of court to pursue additional discovery. The revisions in Rule 26(b)(2) are intended to provide the court with broader discretion to impose additional restrictions on the scope and extent of discovery and to authorize courts that develop case tracking systems based on the complexity of cases to increase or decrease by local rule the presumptive number of depositions and interrogatories allowed in particular types or classifications of cases. The revision also dispels any doubt as to the power of the court to impose limitations on the length of depositions under Rule 30 or on the number of requests for admission under Rule 36.

Second, former paragraph (2), relating to insurance, has been relocated as part of the required initial disclosures under subdivision (a)(1)(D), and revised to provide for disclosure of the policy itself.

Third, paragraph (4)(A) is revised to provide that experts who are expected to be witnesses will be subject to deposition prior to trial, conforming the norm stated in the rule to the actual practice followed in most courts, in which depositions of experts have become standard. Concerns regarding the expense of such depositions should be mitigated by the fact that the expert's fees for the deposition will ordinarily be borne by the party taking the deposition. The requirement under subdivision (a)(2)(B) of a complete and detailed report of the expected testimony of certain forensic experts may, moreover, eliminate the need for some such depositions or at least reduce the length of the depositions. Accordingly, the deposition of an expert required by subdivision (a)(2)(B) to provide a written report may be taken only after the report has been served.

Paragraph (4)(C), bearing on compensation of experts, is revised to take account of the changes in paragraph (4)(A).

Paragraph (5) is a new provision. A party must notify other parties if it is withholding materials otherwise subject to disclosure under the rule or pursuant to a discovery request because it is asserting a claim of privilege or work product protection. To withhold materials without such notice is contrary to the rule, subjects the party to sanctions under Rule 37(b)(2), and may be viewed as a waiver of the privilege or protection.

The party must also provide sufficient information to enable other parties to evaluate the applicability of the claimed privilege or protection. Although the person from whom the discovery is sought decides whether to claim a privilege or protection, the court ultimately decides whether, if this claim is challenged, the privilege or protection applies. Providing information pertinent to the applicability of the privilege or protection should reduce the need for in camera examination of the documents.

The rule does not attempt to define for each case what information must be provided when a party asserts a claim of privilege or work product protection. Details concerning time, persons, general subject matter, etc., may be appropriate if only a few items are withheld, but may be unduly burdensome when voluminous documents are claimed to be privileged or protected, particularly if the items can be described by categories. A party can seek relief through a protective order under subdivision (c) if compliance with the requirement for providing this information would be an unreasonable burden. In rare circumstances some of the pertinent information affecting applicability of the claim, such as the identity of the client, may itself be privileged; the rule provides that such information need not be disclosed.

The obligation to provide pertinent information concerning withheld privileged materials applies only to items "otherwise discoverable." If a broad discovery request is made—for example, for all documents of a particular type during a twenty year period—and the responding party believes in good faith that production of documents for more than the past three years would be unduly burdensome, it should make its objection to the breadth of the request and, with respect to the documents generated in that three year period, produce the unprivileged documents and describe those withheld under the claim of privilege. If the court later rules that documents for a seven year period are properly discoverable, the documents for the additional four years should then be either produced (if not privileged) or described (if claimed to be privileged).

Subdivision (c). The revision requires that before filing a motion for a protective order the movant must confer—either in person or by telephone—with the other affected parties in a good faith effort to resolve the discovery dispute without the need for court intervention. If the movant is unable to get opposing parties even to discuss the matter, the efforts in attempting to arrange such a conference should be indicated in the certificate.

Subdivision (d). This subdivision is revised to provide that formal discovery—as distinguished from interviews of potential witnesses and other informal discovery—not commence until the parties have met and conferred as required by subdivision (f). Discovery can begin earlier if authorized under Rule 30(a)(2)(C)(deposition of person about to leave the country) or by local rule, order, or stipulation. This will be appropriate in some cases, such as those involving requests for a preliminary injunction or motions challenging personal jurisdiction. If a local rule exempts any types of cases in which discovery may be needed from the requirement of a meeting under Rule 26(f), it should specify when discovery may commence in those cases.

The meeting of counsel is to take place as soon as practicable and in any event at least 14 days before the date of the scheduling conference under Rule 16(b) or the date a scheduling order is due under Rule 16(b). The court can assure that discovery is not unduly delayed either by entering a special order or by setting the case for a scheduling conference.

Subdivision (e). This subdivision is revised to provide that the requirement for supplementation applies to all disclosures required by subdivisions (a)(1)–(3). Like the former rule, the duty, while imposed on a "party," applies whether the corrective information is learned by the client or by the attorney. Supplementations need not be made as each new item of information is learned but should be made at appropriate intervals during the discovery period, and with special promptness as the trial date approaches. It may be useful for the scheduling order to specify the time or times when supplementations should be made.

The revision also clarifies that the obligation to supplement responses to formal discovery requests applies to interrogatories, requests for production, and requests for admissions, but not ordinarily to deposition testimony. However, with respect to experts from whom a written report is required under subdivision (a)(2)(B), changes in the opinions expressed by the expert whether in the report or at a subsequent deposition are subject to a duty of supplemental disclosure under subdivision (e)(1).

The obligation to supplement disclosures and discovery responses applies whenever a party learns that its prior disclosures or responses are in some material respect incomplete or incorrect. There is, however, no obligation to provide supplemental or corrective information that has been otherwise made known to the parties in writing or during the discovery process, as when a witness not previously disclosed is identified during the taking of a deposition or when an expert during a deposition corrects information contained in an earlier report.

Subdivision (f). This subdivision was added in 1980 to provide a party threatened with abusive discovery with a special means for obtaining judicial intervention other than through discrete motions under Rules 26(c) and 37(a). The amendment envisioned a two-step process: first, the parties would attempt to frame a mutually agreeable plan; second, the court would hold a "discovery conference" and then enter an order establishing a schedule and limitations for the conduct of discovery. It was contemplated that the procedure, an elective one triggered on request of a party, would be used in special cases rather than as a routine matter. As expected, the device has been used only sparingly in most courts, and judicial controls over the discovery process have ordinarily been imposed through scheduling orders under Rule 16(b) or through rulings on discovery motions.

The provisions relating to a conference with the court are removed from subdivision (f). This change does not signal any lessening of the importance of judicial supervision. Indeed, there is a greater need for early judicial involvement to consider the scope and timing of the disclosure requirements of Rule 26(a) and the presumptive limits on discovery imposed under these rules or by local rules. Rather, the change is made because the provisions addressing the use of conferences with the court to control discovery are more properly included in Rule 16, which is being revised to highlight the court's powers regarding the discovery process.

The desirability of some judicial control of discovery can hardly be doubted. Rule 16, as revised, requires that the court set a time for completion of discovery and authorizes various other orders affecting the scope, timing, and extent of discovery and disclosures. Before entering such orders, the court should consider the views of the parties, preferably by means of a conference, but at the least through written submissions. Moreover, it is desirable that the parties' proposals regarding discovery be developed through a process where they meet in person, informally explore the nature and basis of the issues, and discuss how discovery can be conducted most efficiently and economically.

As noted above, former subdivision (f) envisioned the development of proposed discovery plans as an optional procedure to be used in relatively few cases. The revised rule directs that in all cases not exempted by local rule or special order the litigants must meet in person and plan for discovery. Following this meeting, the parties submit to the court their proposals for a discovery plan and can begin formal discovery. Their report will assist the court in seeing that the timing and scope of disclosures under revised Rule 26(a) and the limitations on the extent of discovery under these rules and local rules are tailored to the circumstances of the particular case.

To assure that the court has the litigants' proposals before deciding on a scheduling order and that the commencement of discovery is not delayed unduly, the rule provides that the meeting of the parties take place as soon as practicable and in any event at least 14 days before a scheduling conference is held or before a scheduling order is due under Rule 16(b). (Rule 16(b) requires that a scheduling order be entered within 90 days after the first appearance of a defendant or, if earlier, within 120 days after the complaint has been served on any defendant.) The obligation to participate in the planning process is imposed on all parties that have appeared in the case, including defendants who, because of a pending Rule 12 motion, may not have yet filed an answer in the case. Each such party should attend the meeting, either through one of its attorneys or in person if unrepresented. If more parties are joined or appear after the initial meeting, an additional meeting may be desirable.

Subdivision (f) describes certain matters that should be accomplished at the meeting and included in the proposed discovery plan. This listing does not exclude consideration of other subjects, such as the time when any dispositive motions should be filed and when the case should be ready for trial.

The parties are directed under subdivision (a)(1) to make the disclosures required by that subdivision at or within 10 days after this meeting. In many cases the parties should use the meeting to exchange, discuss, and clarify their respective disclosures. In other cases, it may be more useful if the disclosures are delayed until after the parties have discussed at the meeting the claims and defenses in order to define the issues with respect to which the initial disclosures should be made. As discussed in the Notes to subdivision (a)(1), the parties may also need to consider whether a stipulation extending this 10–day period would be appropriate, as when a defendant would otherwise have less than 60 days after being served in which to make its initial disclosure. The parties should also discuss at the meeting what additional information, although not subject to the disclosure requirements, can be made available informally without the necessity for formal discovery requests.

The report is to be submitted to the court within 10 days after the meeting and should not be difficult to prepare. In most cases counsel should be able to agree that one of them will be responsible for its preparation and submission to the court. Form 35 has been added in the Appendix to the Rules, both to illustrate the type of report that is contemplated and to serve as a checklist for the meeting.

The litigants are expected to attempt in good faith to agree on the contents of the proposed discovery plan. If they cannot agree on all aspects of the plan, their report to the court should indicate the competing proposals of the parties on those items, as well as the matters on which they agree. Unfortunately, there may be cases in which, because of disagreements about time or place or for other reasons, the meeting is not attended by all parties or, indeed, no meeting takes place. In such situations, the report—or reports—should describe the circumstances and the court may need to consider sanctions under Rule 37(g).

By local rule or special order, the court can exempt particular cases or types of cases from the meet-and-confer requirement of subdivision (f). In general this should include any types of cases which are exempted by local rule from the requirement for a scheduling order under Rule 16(b), such as cases in which there will be no discovery (*e.g.,* bankruptcy appeals and reviews of social security determinations). In addition, the court may want to exempt cases in which discovery is rarely needed (*e.g.,* government collection cases and proceedings to enforce administrative summonses) or in which a meeting of the parties might be impracticable (*e.g.,* actions by unrepresented prisoners). Note that if a court exempts from the requirements for a meeting any types of cases in which discovery may be needed, it should indicate when discovery may commence in those cases.

Subdivision (g). Paragraph (1) is added to require signatures on disclosures, a requirement that parallels the provisions of paragraph (2) with respect to discovery requests, responses, and objections. The provisions of paragraph (3) have been modified to be consistent with Rules 37(a)(4) and 37(c)(1); in combination, these rules establish sanctions for violation of the rules regarding disclosures and discovery matters. Amended Rule 11 no longer applies to such violations.

2000 AMENDMENT

Purposes of amendments. The Rule 26(a)(1) initial disclosure provisions are amended to establish a nationally uniform practice. The scope of the disclosure obligation is narrowed to cover only information that the disclosing party may use to support its position. In addition, the rule exempts specified categories of proceedings from initial disclosure, and permits a party who contends that disclosure is not appropriate in the circumstances of the case to present its objections to the court, which must then determine whether disclosure should be made. Related changes are made in Rules 26(d) and (f).

The initial disclosure requirements added by the 1993 amendments permitted local rules directing that disclosure would not be required or altering its operation. The inclusion of the "opt out" provision reflected the strong opposition to initial disclosure felt in some districts, and permitted experimentation with differing disclosure rules in those districts that were favorable to disclosure. The local option also recognized that—partly in response to the first publication in 1991 of a proposed disclosure rule—many districts had adopted a variety of disclosure programs under the aegis of the Civil Justice Reform Act. It was hoped that developing experience under a variety of disclosure systems would support eventual refinement of a uniform national disclosure practice. In addition, there was hope that local experience could identify categories of actions in which disclosure is not useful.

A striking array of local regimes in fact emerged for disclosure and related features introduced in 1993. *See* D. Stienstra, *Implementation of Disclosure in United States District Courts, With Specific Attention to Courts' Responses to Selected Amendments to Federal Rule of Civil Procedure 26* (Federal Judicial Center, March 30, 1998) (describing and categorizing local regimes). In its final report to Congress on the CJRA experience, the Judicial Conference recommended reexamination of the need for national uniformity, particularly in regard to initial disclosure. Judicial Conference, *Alternative Proposals for Reduction of Cost and Delay: Assessment of Principles, Guidelines and Techniques,* 175 F.R.D. 62, 98 (1997).

At the Committee's request, the Federal Judicial Center undertook a survey in 1997 to develop information on current disclosure and discovery practices. *See* T. Willging, J. Shapard, D. Stienstra & D. Miletich, *Discovery and Disclosure Practice, Problems, and Proposals for Change* (Federal Judicial Center, 1997). In addition, the Committee convened two conferences on discovery involving lawyers from around the country and received reports and recommendations on possible discovery amendments from a number of bar groups. Papers and other proceedings from the second conference are published in 39 Boston Col. L. Rev. 517–840 (1998).

The Committee has discerned widespread support for national uniformity. Many lawyers have experienced difficulty in coping with divergent disclosure and other practices as they move from one district to another. Lawyers surveyed by the Federal Judicial Center ranked adoption of a uniform national disclosure rule second among proposed rule changes (behind increased availability of judges to resolve discovery disputes) as a means to reduce litigation expenses without interfering with fair outcomes. *Discovery and Disclosure Practice, supra*, at 44–45. National uniformity is also a central purpose of the Rules Enabling Act of 1934, as amended, 28 U.S.C. §§ 2072–2077.

These amendments restore national uniformity to disclosure practice. Uniformity is also restored to other aspects of discovery by deleting most of the provisions authorizing local rules that vary the number of permitted discovery events or the length of depositions. Local rule options are also deleted from Rules 26(d) and (f).

Subdivision(a)(1). The amendments remove the authority to alter or opt out of the national disclosure requirements by local rule, invalidating not only formal local rules but also informal "standing" orders of an individual judge or court that purport to create exemptions from—or limit or expand—the disclosure provided under the national rule. *See* Rule 83. Case-specific orders remain proper, however, and are expressly required if a party objects that initial disclosure is not appropriate in the circumstances of the action. Specified categories of proceedings are excluded from initial disclosure under subdivision (a)(1)(E). In addition, the parties can stipulate to forgo disclosure, as was true before. But even in a case excluded by subdivision (a)(1)(E) or in which the parties stipulate to bypass disclosure, the court can order exchange of similar information in managing the action under Rule 16.

The initial disclosure obligation of subdivisions (a)(1)(A) and (B) has been narrowed to identification of witnesses and documents that the disclosing party may use to support its claims or defenses. "Use" includes any use at a pretrial conference, to support a motion, or at trial. The disclosure obligation is also triggered by intended use in discovery, apart from use to respond to a discovery request; use of a document to question a witness during a deposition is a common example. The disclosure obligation attaches both to witnesses and documents a party intends to use and also to witnesses and to documents the party intends to use if—in the language of Rule 26(a)(3)—"the need arises."

A party is no longer obligated to disclose witnesses or documents, whether favorable or unfavorable, that it does not intend to use. The obligation to disclose information the party may use connects directly to the exclusion sanction of Rule 37(c)(1). Because the disclosure obligation is limited to material that the party may use, it is no longer tied to particularized allegations in the pleadings. Subdivision (e)(1), which is unchanged, requires supplementation if information later acquired would have been subject to the disclosure requirement. As case preparation continues, a party must supplement its disclosures when it determines that it may use a witness or document that it did not previously intend to use.

The disclosure obligation applies to "claims and defenses," and therefore requires a party to disclose information it may use to support its denial or rebuttal of the allegations, claim, or defense of another party. It thereby bolsters the requirements of Rule 11(b)(4), which authorizes denials "warranted on the evidence," and disclosure should include the identity of any witness or document that the disclosing party may use to support such denials.

Subdivision (a)(3) presently excuses pretrial disclosure of information solely for impeachment. Impeachment information is similarly excluded from the initial disclosure requirement.

Subdivisions (a)(1)(C) and (D) are not changed. Should a case be exempted from initial disclosure by Rule 26(a)(1)(E) or by agreement or order, the insurance information described by subparagraph (D) should be subject to discovery, as it would have been under the principles of former Rule 26(b)(2), which was added in 1970 and deleted in 1993 as redundant in light of the new initial disclosure obligation.

New subdivision (a)(1)(E) excludes eight specified categories of proceedings from initial disclosure. The objective of this listing is to identify cases in which there is likely to be little or no discovery, or in which initial disclosure appears unlikely to contribute to the effective development of the case. The list was developed after a review of the categories excluded by local rules in various districts from the operation of Rule 16(b) and the conference requirements of subdivision (f). Subdivision (a)(1)(E) refers to categories of "proceedings" rather than categories of "actions" because some might not properly be labeled " actions." Case designations made by the parties or the clerk's office at the time of filing do not control application of the exemptions. The descriptions in the rule are generic and are intended to be administered by the parties—and, when needed, the courts—with the flexibility needed to adapt to gradual evolution in the types of proceedings that fall within these general categories. The exclusion of an action for review on an administrative record, for example, is intended to reach a proceeding that is framed as an " appeal" based solely on an administrative record. The exclusion should not apply to a proceeding in a form that commonly permits admission of new evidence to supplement the record. Item (vii), excluding a proceeding ancillary to proceedings in other courts, does not refer to bankruptcy proceedings; application of the Civil Rules to bankruptcy proceedings is determined by the Bankruptcy Rules.

Subdivision (a)(1)(E) is likely to exempt a substantial proportion of the cases in most districts from the initial disclosure requirement. Based on 1996 and 1997 case filing statistics, Federal Judicial Center staff estimate that, nationwide, these categories total approximately one-third of all civil filings.

The categories of proceedings listed in subdivision (a)(1)(E) are also exempted from the subdivision (f) conference requirement and from the subdivision (d) moratorium on discovery. Although there is no restriction on commencement of discovery in these cases, it is not expected that this opportunity will often lead to abuse since there is likely to be little or no discovery in most such cases. Should a defendant need more time to respond to discovery requests filed at the beginning of an exempted action, it can seek relief by motion under Rule 26(c) if the plaintiff is unwilling to defer the due date by agreement.

Subdivision (a)(1)(E)'s enumeration of exempt categories is exclusive. Although a case-specific order can alter or excuse initial disclosure, local rules or "standing" orders that purport to create general exemptions are invalid. *See* Rule 83.

The time for initial disclosure is extended to 14 days after the subdivision (f) conference unless the court orders otherwise. This change is integrated with corresponding changes requiring that the subdivision (f) conference be held 21 days before the Rule 16(b) scheduling conference or scheduling order, and that the report on the subdivision (f) conference be submitted to the court 14 days after the meeting. These changes provide a more orderly opportunity for the parties to review the disclosures, and for the court to consider the report. In many instances, the subdivision (f) conference and the effective preparation of the case would benefit from disclosure before the conference, and earlier disclosure is encouraged.

The presumptive disclosure date does not apply if a party objects to initial disclosure during the subdivision (f) conference and states its objection in the subdivision (f) discovery plan. The right to object to initial disclosure is not intended to afford parties an opportunity to "opt out" of disclosure unilaterally. It does provide an opportunity for an objecting party to present to the court its position that disclosure would be "inappropriate in the circumstances of the action." Making the objection permits the objecting party to present the question to the judge before any party is required to make disclosure. The court must then rule on the objection and determine what disclosures—if any—should be made. Ordinarily, this determination would be included in the Rule 16(b) scheduling order, but the court could handle the matter in a different fashion. Even when circumstances warrant suspending some disclosure obligations, others—such as the damages and insurance information called for by subdivisions (a)(1)(C) and (D)—may continue to be appropriate.

The presumptive disclosure date is also inapplicable to a party who is "first served or otherwise joined" after the subdivision (f) conference. This phrase refers to the date of service of a claim on a party in a defensive posture (such as a defendant or third-party defendant), and the date of joinder of a party added as a claimant or an intervenor. Absent court order or stipulation, a new party has 30 days in which to make its initial disclosures. But it is expected that later-added parties will ordinarily be treated the same as the original parties when the original parties have stipulated to forgo initial disclosure, or the court has ordered disclosure in a modified form.

Subdivision (a)(3). The amendment to Rule 5(d) forbids filing disclosures under subdivisions (a)(1) and (a)(2) until they are used in the proceeding, and this change is reflected in an amendment to subdivision (a)(4) . Disclosures under subdivision (a)(3), however, may be important to the court in connection with the final pretrial conference or otherwise in preparing for trial. The requirement that objections to certain matters be filed points up the court's need to be provided with these materials. Accordingly, the requirement that subdivision (a)(3) materials be filed has been moved from subdivision (a)(4) to subdivision (a)(3), and it has also been made clear that they—and any objections—should be filed "promptly."

Subdivision (a)(4). The filing requirement has been removed from this subdivision. Rule 5(d) has been amended to provide that disclosures under subdivisions (a)(1) and (a)(2) must not be filed until used in the proceeding. Subdivision (a)(3) has been amended to require that the disclosures it directs, and objections to them, be filed promptly. Subdivision (a)(4) continues to require that all disclosures under subdivisions (a)(1), (a)(2), and (a)(3) be in writing, signed, and served.

"Shall" is replaced by "must" under the program to conform amended rules to current style conventions when there is no ambiguity.

GAP Report

The Advisory Committee recommends that the amendments to Rules 26(a)(1)(A) and (B) be changed so that initial disclosure applies to information the disclosing party "may use to support" its claims or defenses. It also recommends changes in the Committee Note to explain that disclosure requirement. In addition, it recommends inclusion in the Note of further explanatory matter regarding the exclusion from initial disclosure provided in new Rule 26(a)(1)(E) for actions for review on an administrative record and the impact of these exclusions on bankruptcy proceedings. Minor wording improvements in the Note are also proposed.

Subdivision (b)(1). In 1978, the Committee published for comment a proposed amendment, suggested by the Section of Litigation of the American Bar Association, to refine the scope of discovery by deleting the "subject matter" language. This proposal was withdrawn, and the Committee has since then made other changes in the discovery rules to address concerns about overbroad discovery. Concerns about costs and delay of discovery have persisted nonetheless, and other bar groups have repeatedly renewed similar proposals for amendment to this subdivision to delete the "subject matter" language. Nearly one-third of the lawyers surveyed in 1997 by the Federal Judicial Center endorsed narrowing the scope of discovery as a means of reducing litigation expense without interfering with fair case resolutions. *Discovery and Disclosure Practice, supra,* at 44–45 (1997). The Committee has heard that in some instances, particularly cases involving large quantities of discovery, parties seek to justify discovery requests that sweep far beyond the claims and defenses of the parties on the ground that they nevertheless have a bearing on the "subject matter" involved in the action.

The amendments proposed for subdivision (b)(1) include one element of these earlier proposals but also differ from these proposals in significant ways. The similarity is that the amendments describe the scope of party- controlled discovery in terms of matter relevant to the claim or defense of any party. The court, however, retains authority to order discovery of any matter relevant to the subject matter involved in the action for good cause. The amendment is designed to involve the court more actively in regulating the breadth of sweeping or contentious discovery. The Committee has been informed repeatedly by lawyers that involvement of the court in managing discovery is an important method of controlling problems of inappropriately broad discovery. Increasing the availability of judicial officers to resolve discovery disputes and increasing court management of discovery were both strongly endorsed by the attorneys surveyed by the Federal Judicial Center. *See Discovery and Disclosure Practice, supra,* at 44. Under the amended provisions, if there is an objection that discovery goes beyond material relevant to the parties' claims or defenses, the court would become involved to determine whether the discovery is relevant to the claims or defenses and, if not, whether good cause exists for authorizing it so long as it is relevant to the subject matter of the action. The good-cause standard warranting broader discovery is meant to be flexible.

The Committee intends that the parties and the court focus on the actual claims and defenses involved in the action. The dividing line between information relevant to the claims and defenses and that relevant only to the subject matter of the action cannot be defined with precision. A variety of types of information not directly pertinent to the incident in suit could be relevant to the claims or defenses raised in a given action. For example, other incidents of the same type, or involving the same product, could be properly discoverable under the revised standard. Information about organizational arrangements or filing systems of a party could be discoverable if likely to yield or lead to the discovery of admissible information. Similarly, information that could be used to impeach a likely witness, although not otherwise relevant to the claims or defenses, might be properly discoverable. In each instance, the determination whether such information is discoverable because it is relevant to the claims or defenses depends on the circumstances of the pending action.

The rule change signals to the court that it has the authority to confine discovery to the claims and defenses asserted in the pleadings, and signals to the parties that they have no entitlement to discovery to develop new claims or defenses that are not already identified in the pleadings. In general, it is hoped that reasonable lawyers can cooperate to manage discovery without the need for judicial intervention. When judicial intervention is invoked, the actual scope of discovery should be determined according to the reasonable needs of the action. The court may permit broader discovery in a particular case depending on the circumstances of the case, the nature of the claims and defenses, and the scope of the discovery requested.

The amendments also modify the provision regarding discovery of information not admissible in evidence. As added in 1946, this sentence was designed to make clear that otherwise relevant material could not be withheld because it was hearsay or otherwise inadmissible. The Committee was concerned that the "reasonably calculated to lead to the discovery of admissible evidence" standard set forth in this sentence might swallow any other limitation on the scope of discovery. Accordingly, this sentence has been amended to clarify that information must be relevant to be discoverable, even though inadmissible, and that discovery of such material is permitted if reasonably calculated to lead to the discovery of admissible evidence. As used here, "relevant" means within the scope of discovery as defined in this subdivision, and it would include information relevant to the subject matter involved in the action if the court has ordered discovery to that limit based on a showing of good cause.

Finally, a sentence has been added calling attention to the limitations of subdivision (b)(2)(i), (ii), and (iii). These limitations apply to discovery that is otherwise within the scope of subdivision (b)(1). The Committee has been told repeatedly that courts have not implemented these limitations with the vigor that was contemplated. *See 8 Federal Practice & Procedure* § 2008.1 at 121. This otherwise redundant cross-reference has been added to emphasize the need for active judicial use of subdivision (b)(2) to control excessive discovery. *Cf. Crawford-El v. Britton*, 118 S.Ct. 1584, 1597 (1998) (quoting Rule 26(b)(2)(iii) and stating that "Rule 26 vests the trial judge with broad discretion to tailor discovery narrowly").

GAP Report

The Advisory Committee recommends changing the rule to authorize the court to expand discovery to any "matter"—not "information"—relevant to the subject matter involved in the action. In addition, it recommends additional clarifying material in the Committee Note about the impact of the change on some commonly disputed discovery topics, the relationship between cost-bearing under Rule 26(b)(2) and expansion of the scope of discovery on a showing of good cause, and the meaning of "relevant" in the revision to the last sentence of current subdivision (b)(1). In addition, some minor clarifications of language changes have been proposed for the Committee Note .

Subdivision (b)(2). Rules 30, 31, and 33 establish presumptive national limits on the numbers of depositions and interrogatories. New Rule 30(d)(2) establishes a presumptive limit on the length of depositions. Subdivision (b)(2) is amended to remove the previous permission for local rules that establish different presumptive limits on these discovery activities. There is no reason to believe that unique circumstances justify varying these nationally-applicable presumptive limits in certain districts. The limits can be modified by court order or agreement in an individual action, but "standing" orders imposing different presumptive limits are not authorized. Because there is no national rule limiting the number of Rule 36 requests for admissions, the rule continues to authorize local rules that impose numerical limits on them. This change is not intended to interfere with differentiated case management in districts that use this technique by case-specific order as part of their Rule 16 process.

Subdivision (d). The amendments remove the prior authority to exempt cases by local rule from the moratorium on discovery before the subdivision (f) conference, but the categories of proceedings exempted from initial disclosure under subdivision (a)(1)(E) are excluded from subdivision (d). The parties may agree to disregard the moratorium where it applies, and the court may so order in a case, but "standing" orders altering the moratorium are not authorized.

Subdivision (f). As in subdivision (d), the amendments remove the prior authority to exempt cases by local rule from the conference requirement. The Committee has been informed that the addition of the conference was one of the most successful changes made in the 1993 amendments, and it therefore has determined to apply the conference requirement nationwide. The categories of proceedings exempted from initial disclosure under subdivision (a)(1)(E) are exempted from the conference requirement for the reasons that warrant exclusion from initial disclosure. The court may order that the conference need not occur in a case where otherwise required, or that it occur in a case otherwise exempted by subdivision (a)(1)(E). "Standing" orders altering the conference requirement for categories of cases are not authorized.

The rule is amended to require only a "conference" of the parties, rather than a "meeting." There are important benefits to face-to-face discussion of the topics to be covered in the conference, and those benefits may be lost if other means of conferring were routinely used when face-to- face meetings would not impose burdens. Nevertheless, geographic conditions in some districts may exact costs far out of proportion to these benefits. The amendment allows the court by case-specific order to require a face-to- face meeting, but "standing" orders so requiring are not authorized.

As noted concerning the amendments to subdivision (a)(1), the time for the conference has been changed to at least 21 days before the Rule 16 scheduling conference, and the time for the report is changed to no more than 14 days after the Rule 26(f) conference. This should ensure that the court will have the report well in advance of the scheduling conference or the entry of the scheduling order.

Since Rule 16 was amended in 1983 to mandate some case management activities in all courts, it has included deadlines for Completing these tasks to ensure that all courts do so within a reasonable time. Rule 26(f) was fit into this scheme when it was adopted in 1993. It was never intended, however, that the national requirements that certain activities be completed by a certain time should delay case management in districts that move much faster than the national rules direct, and the rule is therefore amended to permit such a court to adopt a local rule that shortens the period specified for the completion of these tasks.

"Shall" is replaced by "must," "does," or an active verb under the program to conform amended rules to current style conventions when there is no ambiguity.

GAP Report

The Advisory Committee recommends adding a sentence to the published amendments to Rule 26(f) authorizing local rules shortening the time between the attorney conference and the court's action under Rule 16(b), and addition to the Committee Note of explanatory material about this change to the rule. This addition can be made without republication in response to public comments.

2006 AMENDMENT

Subdivision (a). Rule 26(a)(1)(B) is amended to parallel Rule 34(a) by recognizing that a party must disclose electronically stored information as well as documents that it may use to support its claims or defenses. The term "electronically stored information" has the same broad meaning in Rule 26(a)(1) as in Rule 34(a). This amendment is consistent with the 1993 addition of Rule 26(a)(1)(B). The term "data compilations" is deleted as unnecessary because it is a subset of both documents and electronically stored information.

Subdivision (a)(1)(E). Civil forfeiture actions are added to the list of exemptions from Rule 26(a)(1) disclosure requirements. These actions are governed by new Supplemental Rule G. Disclosure is not likely to be useful.

Subdivision (b)(2). The amendment to Rule 26(b)(2) is designed to address issues raised by difficulties in locating, retrieving, and providing discovery of some electronically stored information. Electronic storage systems often make it easier to locate and retrieve information. These advantages are properly taken into account in determining the reasonable scope of discovery in a particular case. But some sources of electronically stored information can be accessed only with substantial burden and cost. In a particular case, these burdens and costs may make the information on such sources not reasonably accessible.

It is not possible to define in a rule the different types of technological features that may affect the burdens and costs of accessing electronically stored information. Information systems are designed to provide ready access to information used in regular ongoing activities. They also may be designed so as to provide ready access to information that is not regularly used. But a system may retain information on sources that are accessible only by incurring substantial burdens or costs. Subparagraph (B) is added to regulate discovery from such sources.

Under this rule, a responding party should produce electronically stored information that is relevant, not privileged, and reasonably accessible, subject to the (b)(2)(C) limitations that apply to all discovery. The responding party must also identify, by category or type, the sources containing potentially responsive information that it is neither searching nor producing. The identification should, to the extent possible, provide enough detail to enable the requesting party to evaluate the burdens and costs of providing the discovery and the likelihood of finding responsive information on the identified sources.

A party's identification of sources of electronically stored information as not reasonably accessible does not relieve the party of its common-law or statutory duties to preserve evidence. Whether a responding party is required to preserve unsearched sources of potentially responsive information that it believes are not reasonably accessible depends on the circumstances of each case. It is often useful for the parties to discuss this issue early in discovery.

The volume of—and the ability to search—much electronically stored information means that in many cases the responding party will be able to produce information from reasonably accessible sources that will fully satisfy the parties' discovery needs. In many circumstances the requesting party should obtain and evaluate the information from such sources before insisting that the responding party search and produce information contained on sources that are not reasonably accessible. If the requesting party continues to seek discovery of information from sources identified as not reasonably accessible, the parties should discuss the burdens and costs of accessing and retrieving the information, the needs that may establish good cause for requiring all or part of the requested discovery even if the information sought is not reasonably accessible, and conditions on obtaining and producing the information that may be appropriate.

If the parties cannot agree whether, or on what terms, sources identified as not reasonably accessible should be searched and discoverable information produced, the issue may be raised either by a motion to compel discovery or by a motion for a protective order. The parties must confer before bringing either motion. If the parties do not resolve the issue and the court must decide, the responding party must show that the identified sources of information are not reasonably accessible because of undue burden or cost. The requesting party may need discovery to test this assertion. Such discovery might take the form of requiring the responding party to conduct a sampling of information contained on the sources identified as not reasonably accessible; allowing some form of inspection of such sources; or taking depositions of witnesses knowledgeable about the responding party's information systems.

Once it is shown that a source of electronically stored information is not reasonably accessible, the requesting party may still obtain discovery by showing good cause, considering the limitations of Rule 26(b)(2)(C) that balance the costs and potential benefits of discovery. The decision whether to require a responding party to search for and produce information that is not reasonably accessible depends not only on the burdens and costs of doing so, but also on whether those burdens and costs can be justified in the circumstances of the case. Appropriate considerations may include: (1) the specificity of the discovery request; (2) the quantity of information available from other and more easily accessed sources; (3) the failure to produce relevant information that seems likely to have existed but is no longer available on more easily accessed sources; (4) the likelihood of finding relevant, responsive information that cannot be obtained from other, more easily accessed sources; (5) predictions as to the importance and usefulness of the further information; (6) the importance of the issues at stake in the litigation; and (7) the parties' resources.

The responding party has the burden as to one aspect of the inquiry—whether the identified sources are not reasonably accessible in light of the burdens and costs required to search for, retrieve, and produce whatever responsive information may be found. The requesting party has the burden of showing that its need for the discovery outweighs the burdens and costs of locating, retrieving, and producing the information. In some cases, the court will be able to determine whether the identified sources are not reasonably accessible and whether the requesting party has shown good cause for some or all of the discovery, consistent with the limitations of Rule 26(b)(2)(C), through a single proceeding or presentation. The good-cause determination, however, may be complicated because the court and parties may know little about what information the sources identified as not reasonably accessible might contain, whether it is relevant, or how valuable it may be to the litigation. In such cases, the parties may need some focused discovery, which may include sampling of the sources, to learn more about what burdens and costs are involved in accessing the information, what the information consists of, and how valuable it is for the litigation in light of information that can be obtained by exhausting other opportunities for discovery.

The good-cause inquiry and consideration of the Rule 26(b)(2)(C) limitations are coupled with the authority to set conditions for discovery. The conditions may take the form of limits on the amount, type, or sources of information required to be accessed and produced. The conditions may also include payment by the requesting party of part or all of the reasonable costs of obtaining information from sources that are not reasonably accessible. A requesting party's willingness to share or bear the access costs may be weighed by the court in determining whether there is good cause. But the producing party's burdens in reviewing the information for relevance and privilege may weigh against permitting the requested discovery.

The limitations of Rule 26(b)(2)(C) continue to apply to all discovery of electronically stored information, including that stored on reasonably accessible electronic sources.

Subdivision (b)(5). The Committee has repeatedly been advised that the risk of privilege waiver, and the work necessary to avoid it, add to the costs and delay of discovery. When the review is of electronically stored information, the risk of waiver, and the time and effort required to avoid it, can increase substantially because of the volume of electronically stored information and the difficulty in ensuring that all information to be produced has in fact been reviewed. Rule 26(b)(5)(A) provides a procedure for a party that has withheld information on the basis of privilege or protection as trial-preparation material to make the claim so that the requesting party can decide whether to contest the claim and the court can resolve the dispute. Rule 26(b)(5)(B) is added to provide a procedure for a party to assert a claim of privilege or trial-preparation material protection after information is produced in discovery in the action and, if the claim is contested, permit any party that received the information to present the matter to the court for resolution.

Rule 26(b)(5)(B) does not address whether the privilege or protection that is asserted after production was waived by the production. The courts have developed principles to determine whether, and under what circumstances, waiver results from inadvertent production of privileged or protected information. Rule 26(b)(5)(B) provides a procedure for presenting and addressing these issues. Rule 26(b)(5)(B) works in tandem with Rule 26(f), which is amended to direct the parties to discuss privilege issues in preparing their discovery plan, and which, with amended Rule 16(b), allows the parties to ask the court to include in an order any agreements the parties reach regarding issues of privilege or trial-preparation material protection. Agreements reached under Rule 26(f)(4) and orders including such agreements entered under Rule 16(b)(6) may be considered when a court determines whether a waiver has occurred. Such agreements and orders ordinarily control if they adopt procedures different from those in Rule 26(b)(5)(B).

A party asserting a claim of privilege or protection after production must give notice to the receiving party. That notice should be in writing unless the circumstances preclude it. Such circumstances could include the assertion of the claim during a deposition. The notice should be as specific as possible in identifying the information and stating the basis for the claim. Because the receiving party must decide whether to challenge the claim and may sequester the information and submit it to the court for a ruling on whether the claimed privilege or protection applies and whether it has been waived, the notice should be sufficiently detailed so as to enable the receiving party and the court to understand the basis for the claim and to determine whether waiver has occurred. Courts will continue to examine whether a claim of privilege or protection was made at a reasonable time when delay is part of the waiver determination under the governing law.

After receiving notice, each party that received the information must promptly return, sequester, or destroy the information and any copies it has. The option of sequestering or destroying the information is included in part because the receiving party may have incorporated the information in protected trial-preparation materials. No receiving party may use or disclose the information pending resolution of the privilege claim. The receiving party may present to the court the questions whether the information is privileged or protected as trial-preparation material, and whether the privilege or protection has been waived. If it does so, it must provide the court with the grounds for the privilege or protection specified in the producing party's notice, and serve all parties. In presenting the question, the party may use the content of the information only to the extent permitted by the applicable law of privilege, protection for trial-preparation material, and professional responsibility.

If a party disclosed the information to nonparties before receiving notice of a claim of privilege or protection as trial-preparation material, it must take reasonable steps to retrieve the information and to return it, sequester it until the claim is resolved, or destroy it.

Whether the information is returned or not, the producing party must preserve the information pending the court's ruling on whether the claim of privilege or of protection is properly asserted and whether it was waived. As with claims made under Rule 26(b)(5)(A), there may be no ruling if the other parties do not contest the claim.

Subdivision (f). Rule 26(f) is amended to direct the parties to discuss discovery of electronically stored information during their discovery-planning conference. The rule focuses on "issues relating to disclosure or discovery of electronically stored information"; the discussion is not required in cases not involving electronic discovery, and the amendment imposes no additional requirements in those cases. When the parties do anticipate disclosure or discovery of electronically stored information, discussion at the outset may avoid later difficulties or ease their resolution.

When a case involves discovery of electronically stored information, the issues to be addressed during the Rule 26(f) conference depend on the nature and extent of the contemplated discovery and of the parties' information systems. It may be important for the parties to discuss those systems, and accordingly important for counsel to become familiar with those systems before the conference. With that information, the parties can develop a discovery plan that takes into account the capabilities of their computer systems. In appropriate cases identification of, and early discovery from, individuals with special knowledge of a party's computer systems may be helpful.

The particular issues regarding electronically stored information that deserve attention during the discovery planning stage depend on the specifics of the given case. *See Manual for Complex Litigation* (4th) § 40.25(2) (listing topics for discussion in a proposed order regarding meet-and-confer sessions). For example, the parties may specify the topics for such discovery and the time period for which discovery will be sought. They may identify the various sources of such information within a party's control that should be searched for electronically stored information. They may discuss whether the information is reasonably accessible to the party that has it, including the burden or cost of retrieving and reviewing the information. *See* Rule 26(b)(2)(B). Rule 26(f)(3) explicitly directs the parties to discuss the form or forms in which electronically stored information might be produced. The parties may be able to reach agreement on the forms of production, making discovery more efficient. Rule 34(b) is amended to permit a requesting party to specify the form or forms in which it wants electronically stored information produced. If the requesting party does not specify a form, Rule 34(b) directs the responding party to state the forms it intends to use in the production. Early discussion of the forms of production may facilitate the application of Rule 34(b) by allowing the parties to determine what forms of production will meet both parties' needs. Early identification of disputes over the forms of production may help avoid the expense and delay of searches or productions using inappropriate forms.

Rule 26(f) is also amended to direct the parties to discuss any issues regarding preservation of discoverable information during their conference as they develop a discovery plan. This provision applies to all sorts of discoverable information, but can be particularly important with regard to electronically stored information. The volume and dynamic nature of electronically stored information may complicate preservation obligations. The ordinary operation of computers involves both the automatic creation and the automatic deletion or overwriting of certain information. Failure to address preservation issues early in the litigation increases uncertainty and raises a risk of disputes.

The parties' discussion should pay particular attention to the balance between the competing needs to preserve relevant evidence and to continue routine operations critical to ongoing activities. Complete or broad cessation of a party's routine computer operations could paralyze the party's activities. *Cf. Manual for Complex Litigation* (4th) § 11.422 ("A blanket preservation order may be prohibitively expensive and unduly burdensome for parties dependent on computer systems for their day-to-day operations.") The parties should take account of these considerations in their discussions, with the goal of agreeing on reasonable preservation steps.

The requirement that the parties discuss preservation does not imply that courts should routinely enter preservation orders. A preservation order entered over objections should be narrowly tailored. Ex parte preservation orders should issue only in exceptional circumstances.

Rule 26(f) is also amended to provide that the parties should discuss any issues relating to assertions of privilege or of protection as trial-preparation materials, including whether the parties can facilitate discovery by agreeing on procedures for asserting claims of privilege or protection after production and whether to ask the court to enter an order that includes any agreement the parties reach. The Committee has repeatedly been advised about the discovery difficulties that can result from efforts to guard against waiver of privilege and work-product protection. Frequently parties find it necessary to spend large amounts of time reviewing materials requested through discovery to avoid waiving privilege. These efforts are necessary because materials subject to a claim of privilege or protection are often difficult to identify. A failure to withhold even one such item may result in an argument that there has been a waiver of privilege as to all other privileged materials on that subject matter. Efforts to avoid the risk of waiver can impose substantial costs on the party producing the material and the time required for the privilege review can substantially delay access for the party seeking discovery.

These problems often become more acute when discovery of electronically stored information is sought. The volume of such data, and the informality that attends use of e-mail and some other types of electronically stored information, may make privilege determinations more difficult, and privilege review correspondingly more expensive and time consuming. Other aspects of electronically stored information pose particular difficulties for privilege review. For example, production may be sought of information automatically included in electronic files but not apparent to the creator or to readers. Computer programs may retain draft language, editorial comments, and other deleted matter (sometimes referred to as "embedded data" or "embedded edits") in an electronic file but not make them apparent to the reader. Information describing the history, tracking, or management of an electronic file (sometimes called "metadata") is usually not apparent to the reader viewing a hard copy or a screen image. Whether this information should be produced may be among the topics discussed in the Rule 26(f) conference. If it is, it may need to be reviewed to ensure that no privileged information is included, further complicating the task of privilege review.

Parties may attempt to minimize these costs and delays by agreeing to protocols that minimize the risk of waiver. They may agree that the responding party will provide certain requested materials for initial examination without waiving any privilege or protection—sometimes known as a "quick peek." The requesting party then designates the documents it wishes to have actually produced. This designation is the Rule 34 request. The responding party then responds in the usual course, screening only those documents actually requested for formal production and asserting privilege claims as provided in Rule 26(b)(5)(A). On other occasions, parties enter agreements—sometimes called "clawback agreements"—that production without intent to waive privilege or protection should not be a waiver so long as the responding party identifies the documents mistakenly produced, and that the documents should be returned under those circumstances. Other voluntary arrangements may be appropriate depending on the circumstances of each litigation. In most circumstances, a party who receives information under such an arrangement cannot assert that production of the information waived a claim of privilege or of protection as trial-preparation material.

Although these agreements may not be appropriate for all cases, in certain cases they can facilitate prompt and economical discovery by reducing delay before the discovering party obtains access to documents, and by reducing the cost and burden of review by the producing party. A case-management or other order including such agreements may further facilitate the discovery process. Form 35 is amended to include a report to the court about any agreement regarding protections against inadvertent forfeiture or waiver of privilege or protection that the parties have reached, and Rule 16(b) is amended to recognize that the court may include such an agreement in a case-management or other order. If the parties agree to entry of such an order, their proposal should be included in the report to the court.

Rule 26(b)(5)(B) is added to establish a parallel procedure to assert privilege or protection as trial-preparation material after production, leaving the question of waiver to later determination by the court.

2007 AMENDMENT

The language of Rule 26 has been amended as part of the general restyling of the Civil Rules to make them more easily understood and to make style and terminology consistent throughout the rules. These changes are intended to be stylistic only.

Former Rule 26(a)(5) served as an index of the discovery methods provided by later rules. It was deleted as redundant. Deletion does not affect the right to pursue discovery in addition to disclosure.

Former Rule 26(b)(1) began with a general statement of the scope of discovery that appeared to function as a preface to each of the five numbered paragraphs that followed. This preface has been shifted to the text of paragraph (1) because it does not accurately reflect the limits embodied in paragraphs (2), (3), or (4), and because paragraph (5) does not address the scope of discovery.

The reference to discovery of "books" in former Rule 26(b)(1) was deleted to achieve consistent expression throughout the discovery rules. Books remain a proper subject of discovery.

Amended Rule 26(b)(3) states that a party may obtain a copy of the party's own previous statement "on request." Former Rule 26(b)(3) expressly made the request procedure available to a nonparty witness, but did not describe the procedure to be used by a party. This apparent gap is closed by adopting the request procedure, which ensures that a party need not invoke Rule 34 to obtain a copy of the party's own statement.

Rule 26(e) stated the duty to supplement or correct a disclosure or discovery response "to include information thereafter acquired." This apparent limit is not reflected in practice; parties recognize the duty to supplement or correct by providing information that was not originally provided although it was available at the time of the initial disclosure or response. These words are deleted to reflect the actual meaning of the present rule.

Former Rule 26(e) used different phrases to describe the time to supplement or correct a disclosure or discovery response. Disclosures were to be supplemented "at appropriate intervals." A prior discovery response must be "seasonably * * * amend[ed]." The fine distinction between these phrases has not been observed in practice. Amended Rule 26(e)(1)(A) uses the same phrase for disclosures and discovery responses. The party must supplement or correct "in a timely manner."

Former Rule 26(g)(1) did not call for striking an unsigned disclosure. The omission was an obvious drafting oversight. Amended Rule 26(g)(2) includes disclosures in the list of matters that the court must strike unless a signature is provided "promptly * * * after being called to the attorney's or party's attention."

Former Rule 26(b)(2)(A) referred to a "good faith" argument to extend existing law. Amended Rule 26(b)(1)(B)(i) changes this reference to a "nonfrivolous" argument to achieve consistency with Rule 11(b)(2).

As with the Rule 11 signature on a pleading, written motion, or other paper, disclosure and discovery signatures should include not only a postal address but also a telephone number and electronic-mail address. A signer who lacks one or more of those addresses need not supply a nonexistent item.

Rule 11(b)(2) recognizes that it is legitimate to argue for establishing new law. An argument to establish new law is equally legitimate in conducting discovery.

Rule 27. Depositions Before Action or Pending Appeal

1937 ADOPTION

Note to Subdivision (a). This rule offers a simple method of perpetuating testimony in cases where it is usually allowed under equity practice or under modern statutes. See *Arizona* v. *California*, 1934, 292 U.S. 341, 54 S.Ct. 735, 78 L.Ed. 1298; *Todd Engineering Dry Dock and Repair Co.* v. *United States*, C.C.A.5, 1929, 32 F.2d 734; *Hall* v. *Stout*, 4 Del.Ch. 269 (1871). For comparable state statutes see Ark.Civ.Code (Crawford, 1934) §§ 666–670; Calif.Code Civ.Proc. (Deering, 1937) 2083–2089; Smith-Hurd Ill.Stats. c. 51, §§ 39–46; Iowa Code (1935) §§ 11400–11407; 2 Mass.Gen.Laws (Ter.Ed., 1932) ch. 233, §§ 46–63; N.Y.C.P.A. (1937) § 295; Ohio Gen.Code Ann. (Throckmorton, 1936) §§ 12216–12222; Va.Code Ann. (Michie, 1936) § 6235; Wis.Stat. (1935) §§ 326.27–326.29. The appointment of an attorney to represent absent parties or parties not personally notified, or a guardian ad litem to represent minors and incompetents, is provided for in several of the above statutes.

Note to Subdivision (b). This follows the practice approved in *Richter* v. *Union Trust Co.*, 1885, 115 U.S. 55, 5 S.Ct. 1162, 29 L.Ed. 345, by extending the right to perpetuate testimony to cases pending an appeal.

Note to Subdivision (c). This preserves the right to employ a separate action to perpetuate testimony under U.S.C., Title 28, former § 644 (Depositions under *dedimus potestatem* and *in perpetuum*) as an alternate method.

1946 AMENDMENT

Note. Since the second sentence in subdivision (a)(3) refers only to depositions, it is arguable that Rules 34 and 35 are inapplicable in proceedings to perpetuate testimony. The new matter [in subdivision (a)(3) and (b)] clarifies. A conforming change is also made in subdivision (b).

1948 AMENDMENT

The amendment effective October 1949, substituted the words "United States district court" in subdivision (a)(1) and (4) in place of the words "district court of the United States."

1971 AMENDMENT

The reference intended in this subdivision is to the rule governing the use of depositions in court proceedings. Formerly Rule 26(d), that rule is now Rule 32(a). The subdivision is amended accordingly.

1987 AMENDMENT

The amendments are technical.   No substantive change is intended.

2005 AMENDMENT

The outdated cross-reference to former Rule 4(d) is corrected to incorporate all Rule 4 methods of service. Former Rule 4(d) has been allocated to many different subdivisions of Rule 4. Former Rule 4(d) did not cover all categories of defendants or modes of service, and present Rule 4 reaches further than all of former Rule 4. But there is no reason to distinguish between the different categories of defendants and modes of service encompassed by Rule 4. Rule 4 service provides effective notice. Notice by such means should be provided to any expected adverse party that comes within Rule 4.

Other changes are made to conform Rule 27(a)(2) to current style conventions.

2007 AMENDMENT

The language of Rule 27 has been amended as part of the general restyling of the Civil Rules to make them more easily understood and to make style and terminology consistent throughout the rules. These changes are intended to be stylistic only.

Rule 28.   Persons Before Whom Depositions May Be Taken

1937 ADOPTION

In effect this rule is substantially the same as U.S.C., Title 28, former § 639 (Depositions *de bene esse* ; when and where taken: notice).   U.S.C., Title 28, former § 642 (Depositions, acknowledgments, and affidavits taken by notaries public) does not conflict with Subdivision (a).

1946 AMENDMENT

Note.   The added language [in subdivision (a)] provides for the situation, occasionally arising, when depositions must be taken in an isolated place where there is no one readily available who has the power to administer oaths and take testimony according to the terms of the rule as originally stated.   In addition, the amendment affords a more convenient method of securing depositions in the case where state lines intervene between the location of various witnesses otherwise rather closely grouped.   The amendment insures that the person appointed shall have adequate power to perform his duties.   It has been held that a person authorized to act in the premises, as, for example, a master, may take testimony outside the district of his appointment.   *Consolidated Fastener Co.* v. *Columbian Button & Fastener Co.*, C.C.N.Y.1898, 85 Fed. 54; *Mathieson Alkali Works* v. *Arnold Hoffman & Co.*, C.C.A.1, 1929, 31 F.2d 1.

1963 AMENDMENT

The amendment of clause (1) is designed to facilitate depositions in foreign countries by enlarging the class of persons before whom the depositions may be taken on notice. The class is no longer confined, as at present, to a secretary of embassy or legation, consul general, consul, vice consul, or consular agent of the United States.   In a country that regards the taking of testimony by a foreign official in aid of litigation pending in a court of another country as an infringement upon its sovereignty, it will be expedient to notice depositions before officers of the country in which the examination is taken.   See generally Symposium Letters Rogatory (Grossman ed. 1956); Doyle, Taking Evidence by Deposition and Letters Rogatory and Obtaining Documents in Foreign Territory.   Proc.A.B.A., Sec. Int'l & Comp.L. 37 (1959); Heilpern, Procuring Evidence Abroad, 14 Tul.L.Rev. 29 (1939); Jones, International Judicial Assistance: Procedural Chaos and a Program for Reform, 62 Yale L.J. 515, 526–29 (1953); Smit. International Aspects of Federal Civil Procedure.   61 Colum.L.Rev. 1031, 1056–58 (1961).

Clause (2) of amended subdivision (b), like the corresponding provision of subdivision (a) dealing with depositions taken in the United States, makes it clear that the appointment of a person by commission in itself confers power upon him to administer any necessary oath.

It has been held that a letter rogatory will not be issued unless the use of a notice or commission is shown to be impossible or impractical.   See, *e.g., United States* v. *Matles*, 154 F.Supp. 574 (E.D.N.Y.1957); *The Edmund Fanning*, 89 F.Supp. 282 (E.D.N.Y.1950); *Branyan* v. *Koninklijke Luchtvaart Maatschappij*, 13 F.R.D. 425 (S.D.N.Y.1953).   See also *Ali Akber Kiachif* v. *Philco International Corp.*, 10 F.R.D. 277 (S.D.N.Y.1950).   The intent of the fourth sentence of the amended subdivision is to overcome this judicial antipathy and to permit a sound choice between depositions under a letter rogatory and on notice or by commission in the light of all the circumstances. In a case in which the foreign country will compel a witness to attend or testify in aid of a letter rogatory but not in aid of a commission, a letter rogatory may be preferred on the ground that it is less expensive to execute, even if there is plainly no need for compulsive process. A letter rogatory may also be preferred when it cannot be demonstrated that a witness will be recalcitrant or when the witness states that he is willing to testify voluntarily, but the contingency exists that he will change his mind at the last moment. In the latter case, it may be advisable to issue both a commission and a letter rogatory, the latter to be executed if the former fails. The choice between a letter rogatory and a commission may be conditioned by other factors, including the nature and extent of the assistance that the foreign country will give to the execution of either.

In executing a letter rogatory the courts of other countries may be expected to follow their customary procedure for taking testimony. See *United States* v. *Paraffin Wax*, 2255 Bags, 23 F.R.D. 289 (E.D.N.Y.1959). In many non-common-law countries the judge questions the witness, sometimes without first administering an oath, the attorneys put any supplemental questions either to the witness or through the judge, and the judge dictates a summary of the testimony, which the witness acknowledges as correct. See *Jones, supra*, at 530–32; *Doyle, supra*, at 39–41. The last sentence of the amended subdivision provides, contrary to the implications of some authority, that evidence recorded in such a fashion need not be excluded on that account. See *The Mandu*, 11 F.Supp. 845 (E.D.N.Y.1935). But cf. *Nelson* v. *United States*, 17 Fed.Cas. 1340 (No. 10,-116)(C.C.D.Pa.1816); *Winthrop* v. *Union Ins. Co.*, 30 Fed.Cas. 376 (No. 17901)(C.C.D.Pa.1807). The specific reference to the lack of an oath or a verbatim transcript is intended to be illustrative. Whether or to what degree the value or weight of the evidence may be affected by the method of taking or recording the testimony is left for determination according to the circumstances of the particular case, cf. *Uebersee Finanz–Korporation, A. G.* v. *Brownell*, 121 F.Supp. 420 (D.D.C.1954); *Danisch* v. *Guardian Life Ins. Co.*, 19 F.R.D. 235 (S.D.N.Y.1956); the testimony may indeed be so devoid of substance or probative value as to warrant its exclusion altogether.

Some foreign countries are hostile to allowing a deposition to be taken in their country, especially by notice or commission, or to lending assistance in the taking of a deposition. Thus compliance with the terms of amended subdivision (b) may not in all cases ensure completion of a deposition abroad. Examination of the law and policy of the particular foreign country in advance of attempting a deposition is therefore advisable. See 4 Moore's Federal Practice ¶¶ 28.05–28.08 (2d ed. 1950).

1980 AMENDMENT

The amendments are clarifying.

1987 AMENDMENT

The amendment is technical. No substantive change is intended.

1993 AMENDMENT

This revision is intended to make effective use of the Hague Convention on the Taking of Evidence Abroad in Civil or Commercial Matters, and of any similar treaties that the United States may enter into in the future which provide procedures for taking depositions abroad. The party taking the deposition is ordinarily obliged to conform to an applicable treaty or convention if an effective deposition can be taken by such internationally approved means, even though a verbatim transcript is not available or testimony cannot be taken under oath. For a discussion of the impact of such treaties upon the discovery process, and of the application of principles of comity upon discovery in countries not signatories to a convention, see *Société Nationale Industrielle Aérospatiale v. United States District Court*, 482 U.S. 522, 107 S.Ct. 2542, 96 L.Ed.2d 461 (1987).

The term "letter of request" has been substituted in the rule for the term "letter rogatory" because it is the primary method provided by the Hague Convention. A letter rogatory is essentially a form of letter of request. There are several other minor changes that are designed merely to carry out the intent of the other alterations.

2007 AMENDMENT

The language of Rule 28 has been amended as part of the general restyling of the Civil Rules to make them more easily understood and to make style and terminology consistent throughout the rules. These changes are intended to be stylistic only.

Rule 29.   Stipulations Regarding Discovery Procedure

1970 AMENDMENT

There is no provision for stipulations varying the procedures by which methods of discovery other than depositions are governed. It is common practice for parties to agree on such variations, and the amendment recognizes such agreements and provides a formal mechanism in the rules for giving them effect. Any stipulation varying the procedures may be superseded by court order, and stipulations extending the time for response to discovery under Rules 33, 34, and 36 require court approval.

1993 AMENDMENT

This rule is revised to give greater opportunity for litigants to agree upon modifications to the procedures governing discovery or to limitations upon discovery. Counsel are encouraged to agree on less expensive and time-consuming methods to obtain information, as through voluntary exchange of documents, use of interviews in lieu of depositions, etc. Likewise, when more depositions or interrogatories are needed than allowed under these rules or when more time is needed to complete a deposition than allowed under a local rule, they can, by agreeing to the additional discovery, eliminate the need for a special motion addressed to the court.

Under the revised rule, the litigants ordinarily are not required to obtain the court's approval of these stipulations. By order or local rule, the court can, however, direct that its approval be obtained for particular types of stipulations; and, in any event, approval must be obtained if a stipulation to extend the 30–day period for responding to interrogatories, requests for production, or requests for admissions would interfere with dates set by the court for completing discovery, for hearing of a motion, or for trial.

2007 AMENDMENT

The language of Rule 29 has been amended as part of the general restyling of the Civil Rules to make them more easily understood and to make style and terminology consistent throughout the rules. These changes are intended to be stylistic only.

Rule 30.   Depositions Upon Oral Examination

1937 ADOPTION

Note to Subdivision (a). This is in accordance with common practice. See U.S.C., Title 28, former § 639 (Depositions *de bene esse* ; when and where taken; notice), the relevant provisions of which are incorporated in this rule; West's Ann.Code Civ.Proc. § 2031; and statutes cited in respect to notice in the Note to Rule 26(a). The provision for enlarging or shortening the time of notice has been added to give flexibility to the rule.

Note to Subdivisions (b) and (d). These are introduced as a safeguard for the protection of parties and deponents on account of the unlimited right of discovery given by Rule 26.

Note to Subdivisions (c) and (e). These follow the general plan of former Equity Rule 51 (Evidence Taken Before Examiners, Etc.) and U.S.C., Title 28, former § 640 (Depositions *de bene esse* ; mode of taking), and former § 641 (Same; transmission to court), but are more specific. They also permit the deponent to require the officer to make changes in the deposition if the deponent is not satisfied with it. See also former Equity Rule 50 (Stenographer—Appointment—Fees.)

Note to Subdivision (f). Compare former Equity Rule 55 (Depositions Deemed Published When Filed.)

Note to Subdivision (g). This is similar to 2 Minn.Stat. (Mason, 1927) § 9833, but is more extensive.

1963 AMENDMENT

This amendment corresponds to the change in Rule 4(d)(4). See Advisory Committee's Note to that amendment.

1970 AMENDMENT

Subdivision (a). This subdivision contains the provisions of existing Rule 26(a), transferred here as part of the rearrangement relating to Rule 26. Existing Rule 30(a) is transferred to 30(b). Changes in language have been made to conform to the new arrangement.

This subdivision is further revised in regard to the requirement of leave of court for taking a deposition. The present procedure, requiring a plaintiff to obtain leave of court if he serves notice of taking a deposition within 20 days after commencement of the action, is changed in several respects. First, leave is required by reference to the time the deposition is to be taken rather than the date of serving notice of taking. Second, the 20-day period is extended to 30 days and runs from the service of summons and complaint on any defendant, rather than the commencement of the action. Cf. Ill.S.Ct.R. 19–1, S–H Ill.Ann.Stat. § 101.19–1. Third, leave is not required beyond the time that defendant initiates discovery, thus showing that he has retained counsel. As under the present practice, a party not afforded a reasonable opportunity to appear at a deposition, because he has not yet been served with process, is protected against use of the deposition at trial against him. See Rule 32(a), transferred from 26(d). Moreover, he can later redepose the witness if he so desires.

The purpose of requiring the plaintiff to obtain leave of court is, as stated by the Advisory Committee that proposed the present language of Rule 26(a), to protect "a defendant who has not had an opportunity to retain counsel and inform himself as to the nature of the suit." Note to 1948 amendment of Rule 26(a), quoted in 3A Barron & Holtzoff, Federal Practice and Procedure 455–456 (Wright ed. 1958). In order to assure defendant of this opportunity, the period is lengthened to 30 days. This protection, however, is relevant to the time of taking the deposition, not to the time that notice is served. Similarly, the protective period should run from the service of process rather than the filing of the complaint with the court. As stated in the note to Rule 26(d), the courts have used the service of notice as a convenient reference point for assigning priority in taking depositions, but with the elimination of priority in new Rule 26(d) the reference point is no longer needed. The new procedure is consistent in principle with the provisions of Rules 33, 34, and 36 as revised.

Plaintiff is excused from obtaining leave even during the initial 30-day period if he gives the special notice provided in subdivision (b)(2). The required notice must state that the person to be examined is about to go out of the district where the action is pending and more than 100 miles from the place of trial, or out of the United States, or on a voyage to sea, and will be unavailable for examination unless deposed within the 30-day period. These events occur most often in maritime litigation, when seamen are transferred from one port to another or are about to go to sea. Yet, there are analogous situations in nonmaritime litigation, and although the maritime problems are more common, a rule limited to claims in the admiralty and maritime jurisdiction is not justified.

In the recent unification of the civil and admiralty rules, this problem was temporarily met through addition in Rule 26(a) of a provision that depositions *de bene esse* may continue to be taken as to admiralty and maritime claims within the meaning of Rule 9(h). It was recognized at the time that "a uniform rule applicable alike to what are now civil actions and suits in admiralty" was clearly preferable, but the *de bene esse* procedure was adopted "for the time being at least." See Advisory Committee's Note in Report of the Judicial Conference: Proposed Amendments to Rules of Civil Procedure 43–44 (1966).

The changes in Rule 30(a) and the new Rule 30(b)(2) provide a formula applicable to ordinary civil as well as maritime claims. They replace the provision for depositions *de bene esse*. They authorize an early deposition without leave of court where the witness is about to depart and, unless his deposition is promptly taken, (1) it will be impossible or very difficult to depose him before trial or (2) his deposition can later be taken but only with substantially increased effort and expense. *Cf. S. S. Hai Chang,* 1966 A.M.C. 2239 (S.D.N.Y.1966), in which the deposing party is required to prepay expenses and counsel fees of the other party's lawyer when the action is pending in New York and depositions are to be taken on the West Coast. Defendant is protected by a provision that the deposition cannot be used against him if he was unable through exercise of diligence to obtain counsel to represent him.

The distance of 100 miles from place of trial is derived from the *de bene esse* provision and also conforms to the reach of a subpoena of the trial court, as provided in Rule 45(e). See also S.D.N.Y.Civ.R. 5(a). Some parts of the *de bene esse* provision are omitted from Rule 30(b)(2). Modern deposition practice adequately covers the witness who lives more than 100 miles away from place of trial. If a witness is aged or infirm, leave of court can be obtained.

Subdivision (b). Existing Rule 30(b) on protective orders has been transferred to Rule 26(c), and existing Rule 30(a) relating to the notice of taking deposition has been transferred to this subdivision. Because new material has been added, subsection numbers have been inserted.

1488

Subdivision (b)(1). If a subpoena duces tecum is to be served, a copy thereof or a designation of the materials to be produced must accompany the notice. Each party is thereby enabled to prepare for the deposition more effectively.

Subdivision (b)(2). This subdivision is discussed in the note to subdivision (a), to which it relates.

Subdivision (b)(3). This provision is derived from existing Rule 30(a), with a minor change of language.

Subdivision (b)(4). In order to facilitate less expensive procedures, provision is made for the recording of testimony by other than stenographic means—*e.g.*, by mechanical, electronic, or photographic means. Because these methods give rise to problems of accuracy and trustworthiness, the party taking the deposition is required to apply for a court order. The order is to specify how the testimony is to be recorded, preserved, and filed, and it may contain whatever additional safeguards the court deems necessary.

Subdivision (b)(5). A provision is added to enable a party, through service of notice, to require another party to produce documents or things at the taking of his deposition. This may now be done as to a nonparty deponent through use of a subpoena duces tecum as authorized by Rule 45, but some courts have held that documents may be secured from a party only under Rule 34. See 2A Barron & Holtzoff, Federal Practice and Procedure § 644.1 n. 83.2, § 792 n. 16 (Wright ed. 1961). With the elimination of "good cause" from Rule 34, the reason for this restrictive doctrine has disappeared. *Cf.* N.Y.C.P.L.R. § 3111.

Whether production of documents or things should be obtained directly under Rule 34 or at the deposition under this rule will depend on the nature and volume of the documents or things. Both methods are made available. When the documents are few and simple, and closely related to the oral examination, ability to proceed via this rule will facilitate discovery. If the discovering party insists on examining many and complex documents at the taking of the deposition, thereby causing undue burdens on others, the latter may, under Rules 26(c) or 30(d), apply for a court order that the examining party proceed via Rule 34 alone.

Subdivision (b)(6). A new provision is added, whereby a party may name a corporation, partnership, association, or governmental agency as the deponent and designate the matters on which he requests examination, and the organization shall then name one or more of its officers, directors, or managing agents, or other persons consenting to appear and testify on its behalf with respect to matters known or reasonably available to the organization. *Cf.* Alberta, Sup.Ct.R. 255. The organization may designate persons other than officers, directors, and managing agents, but only with their consent. Thus, an employee or agent who has an independent or conflicting interest in the litigation—for example, in a personal injury case—can refuse to testify on behalf of the organization.

This procedure supplements the existing practice whereby the examining party designates the corporate official to be deposed. Thus, if the examining party believes that certain officials who have not testified pursuant to this subdivision have added information, he may depose them. On the other hand, a court's decision whether to issue a protective order may take account of the availability and use made of the procedures provided in this subdivision.

The new procedure should be viewed as an added facility for discovery, one which may be advantageous to both sides as well as an improvement in the deposition process. It will reduce the difficulties not encountered in determining, prior to the taking of a deposition, whether a particular employee or agent is a "managing agent." See Note, Discovery Against Corporations Under the Federal Rules, 47 Iowa L.Rev. 1006–1016 (1962). It will curb the "bandying" by which officers or managing agents of a corporation are deposed in turn but each disclaims knowledge of facts that are clearly known to persons in the organization and thereby to it. *Cf. Haney* v. *Woodward & Lothrop, Inc.,* 330 F.2d 940, 944 (4th Cir.1964). The provision should also assist organizations which find that an unnecessarily large number of their officers and agents are being deposed by a party uncertain of who in the organization has knowledge. Some courts have held that under the existing rules a corporation should not be burdened with choosing which person is to appear for it. *E.g., United States* v. *Gahagan Dredging Corp.,* 24 F.R.D. 328, 329 (S.D.N.Y.1958). This burden is not essentially different from that of answering interrogatories under Rule 33, and is in any case lighter than that of an examining party ignorant of who in the corporation has knowledge.

Subdivision (c). A new sentence is inserted at the beginning, representing the transfer of existing Rule 26(c) to this subdivision. Another addition conforms to the new provision in subdivision (b)(4).

The present rule provides that transcription shall be carried out unless all parties waive it. In view of the many depositions taken from which nothing useful is discovered, the revised language provides that transcription is to be performed if any party requests it. The fact of the request is relevant to the exercise of the court's discretion in determining who shall pay for transcription.

Parties choosing to serve written questions rather than participate personally in an oral deposition are directed to serve their questions on the party taking the deposition, since the officer is often not identified in advance. Confidentiality is preserved, since the questions may be served in a sealed envelope.

Subdivision (d). The assessment of expenses incurred in relation to motions made under this subdivision (d) is made subject to the provisions of Rule 37(a). The standards for assessment of expenses are more fully set out in Rule 37(a), and these standards should apply to the essentially similar motions of this subdivision.

Subdivision (e). The provision relating to the refusal of a witness to sign his deposition is tightened through insertion of a 30-day time period.

Subdivision (f)(1). A provision is added which codifies in a flexible way the procedure for handling exhibits related to the deposition and at the same time assures each party that he may inspect and copy documents and things produced by a nonparty witness in response to a subpoena duces tecum. As a general rule and in the absence of agreement to the contrary or order of the court, exhibits produced without objection are to be annexed to and returned with the deposition, but a witness may substitute copies for purposes of marking and he may obtain return of the exhibits. The right of the parties to inspect exhibits for identification and to make copies is assured. *Cf.* N.Y.C.P.L.R. § 3116(c).

1971 AMENDMENT

The subdivision permits a party to name a corporation or other form of organization as a deponent in the notice of examination and to describe in the notice the matters about which discovery is desired. The organization is then obliged to designate natural persons to testify on its behalf. The amendment clarifies the procedure to be followed if a party desires to examine a non-party organization through persons designated by the organization. Under the rules, a subpoena rather than a notice of examination is served on a non-party to compel attendance at the taking of a deposition. The amendment provides that a subpoena may name a non-party organization as the deponent and may indicate the matters about which discovery is desired. In that event, the non-party organization must respond by designating natural persons, who are then obliged to testify as to matters known or reasonably available to the organization. To insure that a non-party organization that is not represented by counsel has knowledge of its duty to designate, the amendment directs the party seeking discovery to advise of the duty in the body of the subpoena.

1972 AMENDMENT

Subdivision (c). Existing Rule 43(b), which is to be abrogated, deals with the use of leading questions, the calling, interrogation, impeachment, and scope of cross-examination of adverse parties, officers, etc. These topics are dealt with in many places in the Rules of Evidence. Moreover, many pertinent topics included in the Rules of Evidence are not mentioned in Rule 43(b), e.g. privilege. A reference to the Rules of Evidence generally is therefore made in subdivision (c) of Rule 30.

1980 AMENDMENT

Subdivision (b)(4). It has been proposed that electronic recording of depositions be authorized as a matter of course, subject to the right of a party to seek an order that a deposition be recorded by stenographic means. The Committee is not satisfied that a case has been made for a reversal of present practice. The amendment is made to encourage parties to agree to the use of electronic recording of depositions so that conflicting claims with respect to the potential of electronic recording for reducing costs of depositions can be appraised in the light of greater experience. The provision that the parties may stipulate that depositions may be recorded by other than stenographic means seems implicit in Rule 29. The amendment makes it explicit. The provision that the stipulation or order shall designate the person before whom the deposition is to be taken is added to encourage the naming of the recording technician as that person, eliminating the necessity of the presence of one whose only function is to administer the oath. See Rules 28(a) and 29.

Subdivision (b)(7). Depositions by telephone are now authorized by Rule 29 upon stipulation of the parties. The amendment authorizes that method by order of the court.

The final sentence is added to make it clear that when a deposition is taken by telephone it is taken in the district and at the place where the witness is to answer the questions rather than that where the questions are propounded.

Subdivision (f)(1). For the reasons set out in the Note following the amendment of Rule 5(d), the court may wish to permit the parties to retain depositions unless they are to be used in the action. The amendment of the first paragraph permits the court to so order.

The amendment of the second paragraph is clarifying. The purpose of the paragraph is to permit a person who produces materials at a deposition to offer copies for marking and annexation to the deposition. Such copies are a "substitute" for the originals, which are not to be marked and which can thereafter be used or even disposed of by the person who produces them. In the light of that purpose, the former language of the paragraph had been justly termed "opaque." Wright & Miller, Federal Practice and Procedure: Civil § 2114.

1987 AMENDMENT

The amendments are technical. No substantive change is intended.

1993 AMENDMENT

Subdivision (a). Paragraph (1) retains the first and third sentences from the former subdivision (a) without significant modification. The second and fourth sentences are relocated.

Paragraph (2) collects all provisions bearing on requirements of leave of court to take a deposition.

Paragraph (2)(A) is new. It provides a limit on the number of depositions the parties may take, absent leave of court or stipulation with the other parties. One aim of this revision is to assure judicial review under the standards stated in Rule 26(b)(2) before any side will be allowed to take more than ten depositions in a case without agreement of the other parties. A second objective is to emphasize that counsel have a professional obligation to develop a mutual cost-effective plan for discovery in the case. Leave to take additional depositions should be granted when consistent with the principles of Rule 26(b)(2), and in some cases the ten-per-side limit should be reduced in accordance with those same principles. Consideration should ordinarily be given at the planning meeting of the parties under Rule 26(f) and at the time of a scheduling conference under Rule 16(b) as to enlargements or reductions in the number of depositions, eliminating the need for special motions.

A deposition under Rule 30(b)(6) should, for purposes of this limit, be treated as a single deposition even though more than one person may be designated to testify.

In multi-party cases, the parties on any side are expected to confer and agree as to which depositions are most needed, given the presumptive limit on the number of depositions they can take without leave of court. If these disputes cannot be amicably resolved, the court can be requested to resolve the dispute or permit additional depositions.

Paragraph (2)(B) is new. It requires leave of court if any witness is to be deposed in the action more than once. This requirement does not apply when a deposition is temporarily recessed for convenience of counsel or the deponent or to enable additional materials to be gathered before resuming the deposition. If significant travel costs would be incurred to resume the deposition, the parties should consider the feasibility of conducting the balance of the examination by telephonic means.

Paragraph (2)(C) revises the second sentence of the former subdivision (a) as to when depositions may be taken. Consistent with the changes made in Rule 26(d), providing that formal discovery ordinarily not commence until after the litigants have met and conferred as directed in revised Rule 26(f), the rule requires leave of court or agreement of the parties if a deposition is to be taken before that time (except when a witness is about to leave the country).

Subdivision (b). The primary change in subdivision (b) is that parties will be authorized to record deposition testimony by nonstenographic means without first having to obtain permission of the court or agreement from other counsel.

Former subdivision (b)(2) is partly relocated in subdivision (a)(2)(C) of this rule. The latter two sentences of the first paragraph are deleted, in part because they are redundant to Rule 26(g) and in part because Rule 11 no longer applies to discovery requests. The second paragraph of the former subdivision (b)(2), relating to use of depositions at trial where a party was unable to obtain counsel in time for an accelerated deposition, is relocated in Rule 32.

New paragraph (2) confers on the party taking the deposition the choice of the method of recording, without the need to obtain prior court approval for one taken other than stenographically. A party choosing to record a deposition only by videotape or audiotape should understand that a transcript will be required by Rule 26(a)(3)(B) and Rule 32(c) if the deposition is later to be offered as evidence at trial or on a dispositive motion under Rule 56. Objections to the nonstenographic recording of a deposition, when warranted by the circumstances, can be presented to the court under Rule 26(c).

Paragraph (3) provides that other parties may arrange, at their own expense, for the recording of a deposition by a means (stenographic, visual, or sound) in addition to the method designated by the person noticing the deposition. The former provisions of this paragraph, relating to the court's power to change the date of a deposition, have been eliminated as redundant in view of Rule 26(c)(2).

Revised paragraph (4) requires that all depositions be recorded by an officer designated or appointed under Rule 28 and contains special provisions designed to provide basic safeguards to assure the utility and integrity of recordings taken other than stenographically.

Paragraph (7) is revised to authorize the taking of a deposition not only by telephone but also by other remote electronic means, such as satellite television, when agreed to by the parties or authorized by the court.

Subdivision (c). Minor changes are made in this subdivision to reflect those made in subdivision (b) and to complement the new provisions of subdivision (d)(1), aimed at reducing the number of interruptions during depositions.

In addition, the revision addresses a recurring problem as to whether other potential deponents can attend a deposition. Courts have disagreed, some holding that witnesses should be excluded through invocation of Rule 615 of the evidence rules, and others holding that witnesses may attend unless excluded by an order under Rule 26(c)(5). The revision provides that other witnesses are not automatically excluded from a deposition simply by the request of a party. Exclusion, however, can be ordered under Rule 26(c)(5) when appropriate; and, if exclusion is ordered, consideration should be given as to whether the excluded witnesses likewise should be precluded from reading, or being otherwise informed about, the testimony given in the earlier depositions. The revision addresses only the matter of attendance by potential deponents, and does not attempt to resolve issues concerning attendance by others, such as members of the public or press.

Subdivision (d). The first sentence of new paragraph (1) provides that any objections during a deposition must be made concisely and in a non-argumentative and non-suggestive manner. Depositions frequently have been unduly prolonged, if not unfairly frustrated, by lengthy objections and colloquy, often suggesting how the deponent should respond. While objections may, under the revised rule, be made during a deposition, they ordinarily should be limited to those that under Rule 32(d)(3) might be waived if not made at that time, *i.e.,* objections on grounds that might be immediately obviated, removed, or cured, such as to the form of a question or the responsiveness of an answer. Under Rule 32(b), other objections can, even without the so-called "usual stipulation" preserving objections, be raised for the first time at trial and therefore should be kept to a minimum during a deposition.

Directions to a deponent not to answer a question can be even more disruptive than objections. The second sentence of new paragraph (1) prohibits such directions except in the three circumstances indicated: to claim a privilege or protection against disclosure (*e.g.,* as work product), to enforce a court directive limiting the scope or length of permissible discovery, or to suspend a deposition to enable presentation of a motion under paragraph (3).

Paragraph (2) is added to this subdivision to dispel any doubts regarding the power of the court by order or local rule to establish limits on the length of depositions. The rule also explicitly authorizes the court to impose the cost resulting from obstructive tactics that unreasonably prolong a deposition on the person engaged in such obstruction. This sanction may be imposed on a non-party witness as well as a party or attorney, but is otherwise congruent with Rule 26(g).

It is anticipated that limits on the length of depositions prescribed by local rules would be presumptive only, subject to modification by the court or by agreement of the parties. Such modifications typically should be discussed by the parties in their meeting under Rule 26(f) and included in the scheduling order required by Rule 16(b). Additional time, moreover, should be allowed under the revised rule when justified under the principles stated in Rule 26(b)(2). To reduce the number of special motions, local rules should ordinarily permit—and indeed encourage—the parties to agree to additional time, as when, during the taking of a deposition, it becomes clear that some additional examination is needed.

Paragraph (3) authorizes appropriate sanctions not only when a deposition is unreasonably prolonged, but also when an attorney engages in other practices that improperly frustrate the fair examination of the deponent, such as making improper objections or giving directions not to answer prohibited by paragraph (1). In general, counsel should not engage in any conduct during a deposition that would not be allowed in the presence of a judicial officer. The making of an excessive number of unnecessary objections may itself constitute sanctionable conduct, as may the refusal of an attorney to agree with other counsel on a fair apportionment of the time allowed for examination of a deponent or a refusal to agree to a reasonable request for some additional time to complete a deposition, when that is permitted by the local rule or order.

Subdivision (e). Various changes are made in this subdivision to reduce problems sometimes encountered when depositions are taken stenographically. Reporters frequently have difficulties obtaining signatures—and the return of depositions—from deponents. Under the revision pre-filing review by the deponent is required only if requested before the deposition is completed. If review is requested, the deponent will be allowed 30 days to review the transcript or recording and to indicate any changes in form or substance. Signature of the deponent will be required only if review is requested and changes are made.

Subdivision (f). Minor changes are made in this subdivision to reflect those made in subdivision (b). In courts which direct that depositions not be automatically filed, the reporter can transmit the transcript or recording to the attorney taking the deposition (or ordering the transcript or record), who then becomes custodian for the court of the original record of the deposition. Pursuant to subdivision (f)(2), as under the prior rule, any other party is entitled to secure a copy of the deposition from the officer designated to take the deposition; accordingly, unless ordered or agreed, the officer must retain a copy of the recording or the stenographic notes.

2000 AMENDMENT

Subdivision (d). Paragraph (1) has been amended to clarify the terms regarding behavior during depositions. The references to objections " to evidence" and limitations "on evidence" have been removed to avoid disputes about what is "evidence" and whether an objection is to, or a limitation is on, discovery instead. It is intended that the rule apply to any objection to a question or other issue arising during a deposition, and to any limitation imposed by the court in connection with a deposition, which might relate to duration or other matters.

The current rule places limitations on instructions that a witness not answer only when the instruction is made by a "party." Similar limitations should apply with regard to anyone who might purport to instruct a witness not to answer a question. Accordingly, the rule is amended to apply the limitation to instructions by any person. The amendment is not intended to confer new authority on nonparties to instruct witnesses to refuse to answer deposition questions. The amendment makes it clear that, whatever the legitimacy of giving such instructions, the nonparty is subject to the same limitations as parties.

Paragraph (2) imposes a presumptive durational limitation of one day of seven hours for any deposition. The Committee has been informed that overlong depositions can result in undue costs and delays in some circumstances. This limitation contemplates that there will be reasonable breaks during the day for lunch and other reasons, and that the only time to be counted is the time occupied by the actual deposition. For purposes of this durational limit, the deposition of each person designated under Rule 30(b)(6) should be considered a separate deposition. The presumptive duration may be extended, or otherwise altered, by agreement. Absent agreement, a court order is needed. The party seeking a court order to extend the examination, or otherwise alter the limitations, is expected to show good cause to justify such an order.

Parties considering extending the time for a deposition—and courts asked to order an extension—might consider a variety of factors. For example, if the witness needs an interpreter, that may prolong the examination. If the examination will cover events occurring over a long period of time, that may justify allowing additional time. In cases in which the witness will be questioned about numerous or lengthy documents, it is often desirable for the interrogating party to send copies of the documents to the witness sufficiently in advance of the deposition so that the witness can become familiar with them. Should the witness nevertheless not read the documents in advance, thereby prolonging the deposition, a court could consider that a reason for extending the time limit. If the examination reveals that documents have been requested but not produced, that may justify further examination once production has occurred. In multi-party cases, the need for each party to examine the witness may warrant additional time, although duplicative questioning should be avoided and parties with similar interests should strive to designate one lawyer to question about areas of common interest. Similarly, should the lawyer for the witness want to examine the witness, that may require additional time. Finally, with regard to expert witnesses, there may more often be a need for additional time—even after the submission of the report required by Rule 26(a)(2)—for full exploration of the theories upon which the witness relies.

It is expected that in most instances the parties and the witness will make reasonable accommodations to avoid the need for resort to the court. The limitation is phrased in terms of a single day on the assumption that ordinarily a single day would be preferable to a deposition extending over multiple days; if alternative arrangements would better suit the parties, they may agree to them. It is also assumed that there will be reasonable breaks during the day. Preoccupation with timing is to be avoided.

The rule directs the court to allow additional time where consistent with Rule 26(b)(2) if needed for a fair examination of the deponent. In addition, if the deponent or another person impedes or delays the examination, the court must authorize extra time. The amendment makes clear that additional time should also be allowed where the examination is impeded by an "other circumstance," which might include a power outage, a health emergency, or other event.

In keeping with the amendment to Rule 26(b)(2), the provision added in 1993 granting authority to adopt a local rule limiting the time permitted for depositions has been removed. The court may enter a case-specific order directing shorter depositions for all depositions in a case or with regard to a specific witness. The court may also order that a deposition be taken for limited periods on several days.

Paragraph (3) includes sanctions provisions formerly included in paragraph (2). It authorizes the court to impose an appropriate sanction on any person responsible for an impediment that frustrated the fair examination of the deponent. This could include the deponent, any party, or any other person involved in the deposition. If the impediment or delay results from an "other circumstance" under paragraph (2), ordinarily no sanction would be appropriate.

Former paragraph (3) has been renumbered (4) but is otherwise unchanged .

Subdivision (f)(1): This subdivision is amended because Rule 5(d) has been amended to direct that discovery materials, including depositions, ordinarily should not be filed. The rule already has provisions directing that the lawyer who arranged for the transcript or recording preserve the deposition. Rule 5(d) provides that, once the deposition is used in the proceeding, the attorney must file it with the court.

"Shall" is replaced by "must" or "may" under the program to conform amended rules to current style conventions when there is no ambiguity.

GAP Report

The Advisory Committee recommends deleting the requirement in the published proposed amendments that the deponent consent to extending a deposition beyond one day, and adding an amendment to Rule 30(f)(1) to conform to the published amendment to Rule 5(d) regarding filing of depositions. It also recommends conforming the Committee Note with regard to the deponent veto, and adding material to the Note to provide direction on computation of the durational limitation on depositions, to provide examples of situations in which the parties might agree—or the court order—that a deposition be extended, and to make clear that no new authority to instruct a witness is conferred by the amendment. One minor wording improvement in the Note is also suggested.

2007 AMENDMENT

The language of Rule 30 has been amended as part of the general restyling of the Civil Rules to make them more easily understood and to make style and terminology consistent throughout the rules. These changes are intended to be stylistic only.

The right to arrange a deposition transcription should be open to any party, regardless of the means of recording and regardless of who noticed the deposition.

"[O]ther entity" is added to the list of organizations that may be named as deponent. The purpose is to ensure that the deposition process can be used to reach information known or reasonably available to an organization no matter what abstract fictive concept is used to describe the organization. Nothing is gained by wrangling over the place to fit into current rule language such entities as limited liability companies, limited partnerships, business trusts, more exotic common-law creations, or forms developed in other countries.

Rule 31. Depositions Upon Written Questions

1937 ADOPTION

This rule is in accordance with common practice. In most of the states listed in the Note to Rule 26(a), provisions similar to this rule will be found in the statutes which in their respective statutory compilations follow those cited in the Note to Rule 26(a).

1970 AMENDMENT

Confusion is created by the use of the same terminology to describe both the taking of a deposition upon "written interrogatories" pursuant to this rule and the serving of "written interrogatories" upon parties pursuant to Rule 33. The distinction between these two modes of discovery will be more readily and clearly grasped through substitution of the word "questions" for "interrogatories" throughout this rule.

Subdivision (a). A new paragraph is inserted at the beginning of this subdivision to conform to the rearrangement of provisions in Rules 26(a), 30(a), and 30(b).

The revised subdivision permits designation of the deponent by general description or by class or group. This conforms to the practice for depositions on oral examination.

The new procedure provided in Rule 30(b)(6) for taking the deposition of a corporation or other organization through persons designated by the organization is incorporated by reference.

The service of all questions, including cross, redirect, and recross, is to be made on all parties. This will inform the parties and enable them to participate fully in the procedure.

The time allowed for service of cross, redirect, and recross questions has been extended. Experience with the existing time limits shows them to be unrealistically short. No special restriction is placed on the time for serving the notice of taking the deposition and the first set of questions. Since no party is required to serve cross questions less than 30 days after the notice and questions are served, the defendant has sufficient time to obtain counsel. The court may for cause shown enlarge or shorten the time.

Subdivision (d). Since new Rule 26(c) provides for protective orders with respect to all discovery, and expressly provides that the court may order that one discovery device be used in place of another, subdivision (d) is eliminated as unnecessary.

1987 AMENDMENT

The amendments are technical. No substantive change is intended.

1993 AMENDMENT

Subdivision (a). The first paragraph of subdivision (a) is divided into two subparagraphs, with provisions comparable to those made in the revision of Rule 30. Changes are made in the former third paragraph, numbered in the revision as paragraph (4), to reduce the total time for developing cross-examination, redirect, and recross questions from 50 days to 28 days.

2007 AMENDMENT

The language of Rule 31 has been amended as part of the general restyling of the Civil Rules to make them more easily understood and to make style and terminology consistent throughout the rules. These changes are intended to be stylistic only.

The party who noticed a deposition on written questions must notify all other parties when the deposition is completed, so that they may make use of the deposition. A deposition is completed when it is recorded and the deponent has either waived or exercised the right of review under Rule 30(e)(1).

Rule 32. Use of Depositions in Court Proceedings

1937 ADOPTION

This rule is in accordance with common practice. In most of the states listed in the note to Rule 26, provisions similar to this rule will be found in the statutes which in their respective statutory compilations follow those cited in the note to Rule 26.

1970 AMENDMENT

As part of the rearrangement of the discovery rules, existing subdivisions (d), (e), and (f) of Rule 26 are transferred to Rule 32 as new subdivisions (a), (b), and (c). The provisions of Rule 32 are retained as subdivision (d) of Rule 32 with appropriate changes in the lettering and numbering of subheadings. The new rule is given a suitable new title. A beneficial byproduct of the rearrangement is that provisions which are naturally related to one another are placed in one rule.

A change is made in new Rule 32(a), whereby it is made clear that the rules of evidence are to be applied to depositions offered at trial as though the deponent were then present and testifying at trial. This eliminates the possibility of certain technical hearsay objections which are based, not on the contents of deponent's testimony, but on his absence from court. The language of present Rule 26(d) does not appear to authorize these technical objections, but it is not entirely clear. Note present Rule 26(e), transferred to Rule 32(b); see 2A Barron & Holtzoff, Federal Practice and Procedure 164–166 (Wright ed. 1961).

An addition in Rule 32(a)(2) provides for use of a deposition of a person designated by a corporation or other organization, which is a party, to testify on its behalf. This complements the new procedure for taking the deposition of a corporation or other organization provided in Rules 30(b)(6) and 31(a). The addition is appropriate, since the deposition is in substance and effect that of the corporation or other organization which is a party.

A change is made in the standard under which a party offering part of a deposition in evidence may be required to introduce additional parts of the deposition. The new standard is contained in a proposal made by the Advisory Committee on Rules of Evidence. See Rule 1–07 and accompanying Note, Preliminary Draft of Proposed Rules of Evidence for the United States District Courts and Magistrates 21–22 (March, 1969).

References to other rules are changed to conform to the rearrangement, and minor verbal changes have been made for clarification. The time for objecting to written questions served under Rule 31 is slightly extended.

1972 AMENDMENT

Subdivision (c). The concept of "making a person one's own witness" appears to have had significance principally in two respects: impeachment and waiver of incompetency. Neither retains any vitality under the Rules of Evidence. The old prohibition against impeaching one's own witness is eliminated by Evidence Rule 607. The lack of recognition in the Rules of Evidence of state rules of incompetency in the Dead Man's area renders it unnecessary to consider aspects of waiver arising from calling the incompetent party-witness. Subdivision (c) is deleted because it appears to be no longer necessary in the light of the Rules of Evidence.

1980 AMENDMENT

Subdivision (a)(1). Rule 801(d) of the Federal Rules of Evidence permits a prior inconsistent statement of a witness in a deposition to be used as substantive evidence. And Rule 801(d)(2) makes the statement of an agent or servant admissible against the principal under the circumstances described in the Rule. The language of the present subdivision is, therefore, too narrow.

Subdivision (a)(4). The requirement that a prior action must have been dismissed before depositions taken for use in it can be used in a subsequent action was doubtless an oversight, and the courts have ignored it. See Wright & Miller, Federal Practice and Procedure: Civil § 2150. The final sentence is added to reflect the fact that the Federal Rules of Evidence permit a broader use of depositions previously taken under certain circumstances. For example, Rule 804(b)(1) of the Federal Rules of Evidence provides that if a witness is unavailable, as that term is defined by the rule, his deposition in any earlier proceeding can be used against a party to the prior proceeding who had an opportunity and similar motive to develop the testimony of the witness.

1987 AMENDMENT

The amendment is technical. No substantive change is intended.

1993 AMENDMENT

Subdivision (a). The last sentence of revised subdivision (a) not only includes the substance of the provisions formerly contained in the second paragraph of Rule 30(b)(2), but adds a provision to deal with the situation when a party, receiving minimal notice of a proposed deposition, is unable to obtain a court ruling on its motion for a protective order seeking to delay or change the place of the deposition. Ordinarily a party does not obtain protection merely by the filing of a motion for a protective order under Rule 26(c); any protection is dependent upon the court's ruling. Under the revision, a party receiving less than 11 days notice of a deposition can, provided its motion for a protective order is filed promptly, be spared the risks resulting from nonattendance at the deposition held before its motion is ruled upon. Although the revision of Rule 32(a) covers only the risk that the deposition could be used against the non-appearing movant, it should also follow that, when the proposed deponent is the movant, the deponent would have "just cause" for failing to appear for purposes of Rule 37(d)(1). Inclusion of this provision is not intended to signify that 11 days' notice is the minimum advance notice for all depositions or that greater than 10 days should necessarily be deemed sufficient in all situations.

Subdivision (c). This new subdivision, inserted at the location of a subdivision previously abrogated, is included in view of the increased opportunities for video-recording and audio-recording of depositions under revised Rule 30(b). Under this rule a party may offer deposition testimony in any of the forms authorized under Rule 30(b) but, if offering it in a nonstenographic form, must provide the court with a transcript of the portions so offered. On request of any party in a jury trial, deposition testimony offered other than for impeachment purposes is to be presented in a nonstenographic form if available, unless the court directs otherwise. Note that under Rule 26(a)(3)(B) a party expecting to use nonstenographic deposition testimony as substantive evidence is required to provide other parties with a transcript in advance of trial.

2007 AMENDMENT

The language of Rule 32 has been amended as part of the general restyling of the Civil Rules to make them more easily understood and to make style and terminology consistent throughout the rules. These changes are intended to be stylistic only.

Former Rule 32(a) applied "[a]t the trial or upon the hearing of a motion or an interlocutory proceeding." The amended rule describes the same events as "a hearing or trial."

The final paragraph of former Rule 32(a) allowed use in a later action of a deposition "lawfully taken and duly filed in the former action." Because of the 2000 amendment of Rule 5(d), many depositions are not filed. Amended Rule 32(a)(8) reflects this change by excluding use of an unfiled deposition only if filing was required in the former action.

Rule 33.   Interrogatories to Parties

1937 ADOPTION

This rule restates the substance of former Equity Rule 58 (Discovery—Interrogatories—Inspection and Production of Documents—Admission of Execution or Genuineness), with modifications to conform to these rules.

1946 AMENDMENT

Note. The added second sentence in the first paragraph of Rule 33 conforms with a similar change in Rule 26(a) and will avoid litigation as to when the interrogatories may be served. Original rule 33 does not state the times at which parties may serve written interrogatories upon each other. It has been the accepted view, however, that the times were the same in Rule 33 as those stated in Rule 26(a). *United States* v. *American Solvents & Chemical Corp. of California*, Del.1939, 30 F.Supp. 107; *Sheldon* v. *Great Lakes Transit Corp.*, N.Y.1942, 2 F.R.D. 272, 5 Fed.Rules Serv. 33.11, Case 3; *Musher Foundation, Inc.*, v. *Alba Trading Co.*, N.Y.1941, 42 F.Supp. 281, 2 Moore's Federal Practice, 1938, 2621. The time within which leave of court must be secured by a plaintiff has been fixed at 10 days, in view of the fact that a defendant has 10 days within which to make objections in any case, which should give him ample time to engage counsel and prepare.

Further in the first paragraph of Rule 33, the word "service" is substituted for "delivery" in conformance with the use of the word "serve" elsewhere in the rule and generally throughout the rules. See also Note to Rule 13(a) herein. The portion of the rule dealing with practice on objections has been revised so as to afford a clearer statement of the procedure. The addition of the words "to interrogatories to which objection is made" insures that only the answers to the objectionable interrogatories may be deferred, and that the answers to interrogatories not objectionable shall be forthcoming within the time prescribed in the rule. Under the original wording, answers to all interrogatories may be withheld until objections, sometimes to but a few interrogatories, are determined.

The amendment expedites the procedure of the rule and serves to eliminate the strike value of objections to minor interrogatories. The elimination of the last sentence of the original rule is in line with the policy stated subsequently in this note.

The added second paragraph in Rule 33 contributes clarity and specificity as to the use and scope of interrogatories to the parties. The field of inquiry will be as broad as the scope of examination under Rule 26(b). There is no reason why interrogatories should be more limited than depositions, particularly when the former represent an inexpensive means of securing useful information. See *Hoffman* v. *Wilson Line, Inc.,* Pa.1946, 9 Fed.Rules Serv. 33.514, Case 2; *Brewster* v. *Technicolor, Inc.,* N.Y.1941, 2 F.R.D. 186, 5 Fed.Rules Serv. 33.319, Case 3; *Kingsway Press, Inc.* v. *Farrell Publishing Corp.,* N.Y. 1939, 30 F.Supp. 775. Under present Rule 33 some courts have unnecessarily restricted the breadth of inquiry on various grounds. See *Auer* v. *Hershey Creamery Co.,* N.J.1939, 2 Fed.Rules Serv. 33.31, Case 2, 1 F.R.D. 14; *Tudor* v. *Leslie,* Mass.1940, 1 F.R.D. 448, 4 Fed.Rules Serv. 33.324, Case 1. Other courts have read into the rule the requirement that interrogation should be directed only towards "important facts", and have tended to fix a more or less arbitrary limit as to the number of interrogatories which could be asked in any case. See *Knox* v. *Alter,* Pa.1942, 2 F.R.D. 337, 6 Fed.Rules Serv. 33.352, Case 1; *Byers Theaters, Inc.* v. *Murphy,* Va.1940, 3 Fed.Rules Serv. 33.31, Case 3, 1 F.R.D. 286; *Coca-Cola Co.* v. *Dixi–Cola Laboratories, Inc.,* Md.1939, 30 F.Supp. 275. See also comment on these restrictions in Holtzoff, Instruments of Discovery under Federal Rules of Civil Procedure, 1942, 41 Mich.L.Rev. 205, 216–217. Under amended Rule 33, the party interrogated is given the right to invoke such protective orders under Rule 30(b) as are appropriate to the situation. At the same time, it is provided that the number of or number of sets of interrogatories to be served may not be limited arbitrarily or as a general policy to any particular number, but that a limit may be fixed only as justice requires to avoid annoyance, expense, embarrassment or oppression in individual cases. The party interrogated, therefore, must show the necessity for limitation on that basis. It will be noted that in accord with this change the last sentence of the present rule, restricting the sets of interrogatories to be served, has been stricken. In *J. Schoeneman, Inc.* v. *Brauer,* Mo.1940, 1 F.R.D. 292, 3 Fed.Rules Serv. 33.31, Case 2, the court said: "Rule 33 * * * has been interpreted * * * as being just as broad in its implications as in the case of depositions * * * It makes no difference therefore, how many interrogatories are propounded. If the inquiries are pertinent the opposing party cannot complain." To the same effect, see *Canuso* v. *City of Niagara Falls,* N.Y.1945, 8 Fed.Rules Serv. 33.352, Case 1; *Hoffman* v. *Wilson Line, Inc.,* supra.

By virtue of express language in the added second paragraph of Rule 33, as amended, any uncertainty as to the use of the answers to interrogatories is removed. The omission of a provision on this score in the original rule has caused some difficulty. See e.g., *Bailey* v. *New England Mutual Life Ins. Co.,* Cal.1940, 1 F.R.D. 494, 4 Fed.Rules Serv. 33.46, Case 1.

The second sentence of the second paragraph in Rule 33, as amended, concerns the situation where a party wishes to serve interrogatories on a party after having taken his deposition, or vice versa. It has been held that an oral examination of a party, after the submission to him and answer of interrogatories, would be permitted. *Howard* v. *State Marine Corp.,* N.Y.1940, 4 Fed.Rules Serv. 33.62, Case 1, 1 F.R.D. 499; *Stevens* v. *Minder Construction Co.,* N.Y.1943, 3 F.R.D. 498, 7 Fed.Rules Serv. 30b.31, Case 2. But objections have been sustained to interrogatories served after the oral deposition of a party had been taken. *McNally* v. *Simons,* N.Y.1940, 3 Fed.Rules Serv. 33.61, Case 1, 1 F.R.D. 254; *Currier* v. *Currier,* N.Y.1942, 3 F.R.D. 21, 6 Fed.Rules Serv. 33.61, Case 1, Rule 33, as amended, permits either interrogatories after a deposition or a deposition after interrogatories. It may be quite desirable or necessary to elicit additional information by the inexpensive method of interrogatories where a deposition has already been taken. The party to be interrogated, however, may seek a protective order from the court under Rule 30(b) where the additional deposition or interrogation works a hardship or injustice on the party from whom it is sought.

1970 AMENDMENT

Subdivision (a). The mechanics of the operation of Rule 33 are substantially revised by the proposed amendment, with a view to reducing court intervention. There is general agreement that interrogatories spawn a greater percentage of objections and motions than any other discovery device. The Columbia Survey shows that, although half of the litigants resorted to depositions and about one-third used interrogatories, about 65 percent of the objections were made with respect to interrogatories and 26 percent related to depositions. See also Speck, The Use of Discovery in United States District Courts, 60 Yale L.J. 1132, 1144, 1151 (1951); Note, 36 Minn.L.Rev. 364, 379 (1952).

The procedures now provided in Rule 33 seem calculated to encourage objections and court motions. The time periods now allowed for responding to interrogatories—15 days for answers and 10 days for objections—are too short. The Columbia Survey shows that tardy response to interrogatories is common, virtually expected. The same was reported in Speck, *supra*, 60 Yale L.J. 1132, 1144. The time pressures tend to encourage objections as a means of gaining time to answer.

The time for objections is even shorter than for answers, and the party runs the risk that if he fails to object in time he may have waived his objections. *E.g., Cleminshaw* v. *Beech Aircraft Corp.,* 21 F.R.D. 300 (D.Del.1957); See 4 Moore's Federal Practice, ¶ 33.27 (2d ed. 1966); 2A Barron & Holtzoff, Federal Practice and Procedure 372–373 (Wright ed. 1961). It often seems easier to object than to seek an extension of time. Unlike Rules 30(d) and 37(a), Rule 33 imposes no sanction of expenses on a party whose objections are clearly unjustified.

Rule 33 assures that the objections will lead directly to court, through its requirement that they be served with a notice of hearing. Although this procedure does not preclude an out-of-court resolution of the dispute, the procedure tends to discourage informal negotiations. If answers are served and they are thought inadequate, the interrogating party may move under Rule 37(a) for an order compelling adequate answers. There is no assurance that the hearing on objections and that on inadequate answers will be heard together.

The amendment improves the procedure of Rule 33 in the following respects:

(1) The time allowed for response is increased to 30 days and this time period applies to both answers and objections, but a defendant need not respond in less than 45 days after service of the summons and complaint upon him. As is true under existing law, the responding party who believes that some parts or all of the interrogatories are objectionable may choose to seek a protective order under new Rule 26(c) or may serve objections under this rule. Unless he applies for a protective order, he is required to serve answers or objections in response to the interrogatories, subject to the sanctions provided in Rule 37(d). Answers and objections are served together, so that a response to each interrogatory is encouraged, and any failure to respond is easily noted.

(2) In view of the enlarged time permitted for response, it is no longer necessary to require leave of court for service of interrogatories. The purpose of this requirement—that defendant have time to obtain counsel before a response must be made—is adequately fulfilled by the requirement that interrogatories be served upon a party with or after service of the summons and complaint upon him.

Some would urge that the plaintiff nevertheless not be permitted to serve interrogatories with the complaint. They fear that a routine practice might be invited, whereby form interrogatories would accompany most complaints. More fundamentally, they feel that, since very general complaints are permitted in present-day pleading, it is fair that the defendant have a right to take the lead in serving interrogatories. (These views apply also to Rule 36.) The amendment of Rule 33 rejects these views, in favor of allowing both parties to go forward with discovery, each free to obtain the information he needs respecting the case.

(3) If objections are made, the burden is on the interrogating party to move under Rule 37(a) for a court order compelling answers, in the course of which the court will pass on the objections. The change in the burden of going forward does not alter the existing obligation of an objecting party to justify his objections. *E.g., Pressley* v. *Boehlke,* 33 F.R.D. 316 (W.D.N.C.1963). If the discovering party asserts that an answer is incomplete or evasive, again he may look to Rule 37(a) for relief, and he should add this assertion to his motion to overrule objections. There is no requirement that the parties consult informally concerning their differences, but the new procedure should encourage consultation, and the court may by local rule require it.

The proposed changes are similar in approach to those adopted by California in 1961. See Calif.Code Civ.Proc. § 2030(a). The experience of the Los Angeles Superior Court is informally reported as showing that the California amendment resulted in a significant reduction in court motions concerning interrogatories. Rhode Island takes a similar approach. See R. 33, R.I.R.Civ.Proc. Official Draft, p. 74 (Boston Law Book Co.).

A change is made in subdivision (a) which is not related to the sequence of procedures. The restriction to "adverse" parties is eliminated. The courts have generally construed this restriction as precluding interrogatories unless an issue between the parties is disclosed by the pleadings—even though the parties may have conflicting interests. *E.g., Mozeika* v. *Kaufman Construction Co.,* 25 F.R.D. 233 (E.D.Pa.1960) (plaintiff and third-party defendant); *Biddle* v. *Hutchinson,* 24 F.R.D. 256 (M.D.Pa.1959)(codefendants). The resulting distinctions have often been highly technical. In *Schlagenhauf* v. *Holder,* 379

U.S. 104, 85 S.Ct. 234, 13 L.Ed.2d 152 (1964), the Supreme Court rejected a contention that examination under Rule 35 could be had only against an "opposing" party, as not in keeping "with the aims of a liberal, nontechnical application of the Federal Rules." 379 U.S. at 116. Eliminating the requirement of "adverse" parties from Rule 33 brings it into line with all other discovery rules.

A second change in subdivision (a) is the addition of the term "governmental agency" to the listing of organizations whose answers are to be made by any officer or agent of the organization. This does not involve any change in existing law. Compare the similar listing in Rule 30(b)(6).

The duty of a party to supplement his answers to interrogatories is governed by a new provision in Rule 26(c).

Subdivision (b). There are numerous and conflicting decisions on the question whether and to what extent interrogatories are limited to matters "of fact," or may elicit opinions, contentions, and legal conclusions. Compare, *e.g., Payer, Hewitt & Co.* v. *Bellanca Corp.,* 26 F.R.D. 219 (D.Del.1960)(opinions bad); *Zinsky* v. *New York Central R. R.,* 36 F.R.D. 680 (N.D.Ohio 1964)(factual opinion or contention good, but legal theory bad); *United States* v. *Carter Products, Inc.,* 28 F.R.D. 373 (S.D.N.Y.1961)(factual contentions and legal theories bad) with *Taylor* v. *Sound Steamship Lines, Inc.,* 100 F.Supp. 388 (D.Conn.1951)(opinions good); *Bynum* v. *United States,* 36 F.R.D. 14 (E.D.La. 1964)(contentions as to facts constituting negligence good). For lists of the many conflicting authorities, see 4 Moore's Federal Practice ¶ 33.17 (2d ed. 1966); 2A Barron & Holtzoff, *Federal Practice and Procedure* § 768 (Wright ed. 1961).

Rule 33 is amended to provide that an interrogatory is not objectionable merely because it calls for an opinion or contention that relates to fact or the application of law to fact. Efforts to draw sharp lines between facts and opinions have invariably been unsuccessful, and the clear trend of the cases is to permit "factual" opinions. As to requests for opinions or contentions that call for the application of law to fact, they can be most useful in narrowing and sharpening the issues, which is a major purpose of discovery. See *Diversified Products Corp.* v. *Sports Center Co.,* 42 F.R.D. 3 (D.Md.1967); Moore, *supra* ; Field & McKusick, *Maine Civil Practice* § 26.18 (1959). On the other hand, under the new language interrogatories may not extend to issues of "pure law," *i.e.,* legal issues unrelated to the facts of the case. *Cf. United States* v. *Maryland & Va. Milk Producers Assn., Inc.,* 22 F.R.D. 300 (D.D.C.1958).

Since interrogatories involving mixed questions of law and fact may create disputes between the parties which are best resolved after much or all of the other discovery has been completed, the court is expressly authorized to defer an answer. Likewise, the court may delay determination until pretrial conference, if it believes that the dispute is best resolved in the presence of the judge.

The principal question raised with respect to the cases permitting such interrogatories is whether they reintroduce undesirable aspects of the prior pleading practice, whereby parties were chained to misconceived contentions or theories, and ultimate determination on the merits was frustrated. See James, *The Revival of Bills of Particulars under the Federal Rules,* 71 Harv.L.Rev. 1473 (1958). But there are few if any instances in the recorded cases demonstrating that such frustration has occurred. The general rule governing the use of answers to interrogatories is that under ordinary circumstances they do not limit proof. See, *e.g., McElroy* v. *United Air Lines, Inc.,* 21 F.R.D. 100 (W.D.Mo. 1957); *Pressley* v. *Boehlke,* 33 F.R.D. 316, 317 (W.D.N.C.1963). Although in exceptional circumstances reliance on an answer may cause such prejudice that the court will hold the answering party bound to his answer, *e.g., Zielinski* v. *Philadelphia Piers, Inc.,* 139 F.Supp. 408 (E.D.Pa.1956), the interrogating party will ordinarily not be entitled to rely on the unchanging character of the answers he receives and cannot base prejudice on such reliance. The rule does not affect the power of a court to permit withdrawal or amendment of answers to interrogatories.

The use of answers to interrogatories at trial is made subject to the rules of evidence. The provisions governing use of depositions, to which Rule 33 presently refers, are not entirely apposite to answers to interrogatories, since deposition practice contemplates that all parties will ordinarily participate through cross-examination. See 4 Moore's *Federal Practice* ¶ 33.29[1] (2d ed. 1966).

Certain provisions are deleted from subdivision (b) because they are fully covered by new Rule 26(c) providing for protective orders and Rules 26(a) and 26(d). The language of the subdivision is thus simplified without any change of substance.

Subdivision (c). This is a new subdivision, adopted from Calif.Code Civ.Proc. § 2030(c), relating especially to interrogatories which require a party to engage in burdensome or expensive research into his own business records in order to give an answer. The subdivision gives the party an option to make the records available and place the burden of research of the party who seeks the information. "This provision, without undermining the liberal scope of interrogatory discovery, places the burden of discovery upon its potential benefitee," Louisell, *Modern California Discovery,* 124–125 (1963), and alleviates a problem which in the past has troubled Federal courts. See Speck, The Use of Discovery in United States District Courts, 60 Yale L.J. 1132, 1142–1144 (1951). The interrogating party is protected against abusive use of this provision through the requirement that the burden of ascertaining the answer be substantially the same for both sides. A respondent may not impose on an interrogating party a mass of records as to which research is feasible only for one familiar with the records. At the same time, the respondent unable to invoke this subdivision does not on that account lose the protection available to him under new Rule 26(c) against oppressive or unduly burdensome or expensive interrogatories. And even when the respondent successfully invokes the subdivision, the court is not deprived of its usual power, in appropriate cases, to require that the interrogating party reimburse the respondent for the expense of assembling his records and making them intelligible.

1980 AMENDMENT

Subdivision (c). The Committee is advised that parties upon whom interrogatories are served have occasionally responded by directing the interrogating party to a mass of business records or by offering to make all of their records available, justifying the response by the option provided by this subdivision. Such practices are an abuse of the option. A party who is permitted by the terms of this subdivision to offer records for inspection in lieu of answering an interrogatory should offer them in a manner that permits the same direct and economical access that is available to the party. If the information sought exists in the form of compilations, abstracts or summaries then available to the responding party, those should be made available to the interrogating party. The final sentence is added to make it clear that a responding party has the duty to specify, by category and location, the records from which answers to interrogatories can be derived.

1993 AMENDMENT

Purpose of Revision. The purpose of this revision is to reduce the frequency and increase the efficiency of interrogatory practice. The revision is based on experience with local rules. For ease of reference, subdivision (a) is divided into two subdivisions and the remaining subdivisions renumbered.

Subdivision (a). Revision of this subdivision limits interrogatory practice. Because Rule 26(a)(1)(3) requires disclosure of much of the information previously obtained by this form of discovery, there should be less occasion to use it. Experience in over half of the district courts has confirmed that limitations on the number of interrogatories are useful and manageable. Moreover, because the device can be costly and may be used as a means of harassment, it is desirable to subject its use to the control of the court consistent with the principles stated in Rule 26(b)(2), particularly in multi-party cases where it has not been unusual for the same interrogatory to be propounded to a party by more than one of its adversaries.

Each party is allowed to serve 25 interrogatories upon any other party, but must secure leave of court (or a stipulation from the opposing party) to serve a larger number. Parties cannot evade this presumptive limitation through the device of joining as "subparts" questions that seek information about discrete separate subjects. However, a question asking about communications of a particular type should be treated as a single interrogatory even though it requests that the time, place, persons present, and contents be stated separately for each such communication.

As with the number of depositions authorized by Rule 30, leave to serve additional interrogatories is to be allowed when consistent with Rule 26(b)(2). The aim is not to prevent needed discovery, but to provide judicial scrutiny before parties make potentially excessive use of this discovery device. In many cases it will be appropriate for the court to permit a larger number of interrogatories in the scheduling order entered under Rule 16(b).

Unless leave of court is obtained, interrogatories may not be served prior to the meeting of the parties under Rule 26(f).

When a case with outstanding interrogatories exceeding the number permitted by this rule is removed to federal court, the interrogating party must seek leave allowing the additional interrogatories, specify which twenty-five are to be answered, or resubmit interrogatories that comply with the rule. Moreover, under Rule 26(d), the time for response would be measured from the date of the parties' meeting under Rule 26(f). See Rule 81(c), providing that these rules govern procedures after removal.

Subdivision (b). A separate subdivision is made of the former second paragraph of subdivision (a). Language is added to paragraph (1) of this subdivision to emphasize the duty of the responding party to provide full answers to the extent not objectionable. If, for example, an interrogatory seeking information about numerous facilities or products is deemed objectionable, but an interrogatory seeking information about a lesser number of facilities or products would not have been objectionable, the interrogatory should be answered with respect to the latter even though an objection is raised as to the balance of the facilities or products. Similarly, the fact that additional time may be needed to respond to some questions (or to some aspects of questions) should not justify a delay in responding to those questions (or other aspects of questions) that can be answered within the prescribed time.

Paragraph (4) is added to make clear that objections must be specifically justified, and that unstated or untimely grounds for objection ordinarily are waived. Note also the provisions of revised Rule 26(b)(5), which require a responding party to indicate when it is withholding information under a claim of privilege or as trial preparation materials.

These provisions should be read in light of Rule 26(g), authorizing the court to impose sanctions on a party and attorney making an unfounded objection to an interrogatory.

Subdivisions (c) and (d). The provisions of former subdivisions (b) and (c) are renumbered.

2006 AMENDMENT

Rule 33(d) is amended to parallel Rule 34(a) by recognizing the importance of electronically stored information. The term "electronically stored information" has the same broad meaning in Rule 33(d) as in Rule 34(a). Much business information is stored only in electronic form; the Rule 33(d) option should be available with respect to such records as well.

Special difficulties may arise in using electronically stored information, either due to its form or because it is dependent on a particular computer system. Rule 33(d) allows a responding party to substitute access to documents or electronically stored information for an answer only if the burden of deriving the answer will be substantially the same for either party. Rule 33(d) states that a party electing to respond to an interrogatory by providing electronically stored information must ensure that the interrogating party can locate and identify it "as readily as can the party served," and that the responding party must give the interrogating party a "reasonable opportunity to examine, audit, or inspect" the information. Depending on the circumstances, satisfying these provisions with regard to electronically stored information may require the responding party to provide some combination of technical support, information on application software, or other assistance. The key question is whether such support enables the interrogating party to derive or ascertain the answer from the electronically stored information as readily as the responding party. A party that wishes to invoke Rule 33(d) by specifying electronically stored information may be required to provide direct access to its electronic information system, but only if that is necessary to afford the requesting party an adequate opportunity to derive or ascertain the answer to the interrogatory. In that situation, the responding party's need to protect sensitive interests of confidentiality or privacy may mean that it must derive or ascertain and provide the answer itself rather than invoke Rule 33(d).

2007 AMENDMENT

The language of Rule 33 has been amended as part of the general restyling of the Civil Rules to make them more easily understood and to make style and terminology consistent throughout the rules. These changes are intended to be stylistic only.

The final sentence of former Rule 33(a) was a redundant cross-reference to the discovery moratorium provisions of Rule 26(d). Rule 26(d) is now familiar, obviating any need to carry forward the redundant cross-reference.

Former Rule 33(b)(5) was a redundant reminder of Rule 37(a) procedure and is omitted as no longer useful.

Former Rule 33(c) stated that an interrogatory "is not necessarily objectionable merely because an answer * * * involves an opinion or contention * * *." "[I]s not necessarily" seemed to imply that the interrogatory might be objectionable merely for this reason. This implication has been ignored in practice. Opinion and contention interrogatories are used routinely. Amended Rule 33(a)(2) embodies the current meaning of Rule 33 by omitting "necessarily."

Rule 34. **Production of Documents and Things and Entry Upon Land for Inspection and Other Purposes**

1937 ADOPTION

In England orders are made for the inspection of documents, English Rules Under the Judicature Act (The Annual Practice, 1937) O. 31, r. r. 14, et seq., or for the inspection of tangible property or for entry upon land, O. 50, r. 3. Michigan provides for inspection of damaged property when such damage is the ground of the action. Mich.Court Rules Ann. (Searl, 1933) Rule 41, § 2.

Practically all states have statutes authorizing the court to order parties in possession or control of documents to permit other parties to inspect and copy them before trial. See Ragland, Discovery Before Trial (1932) Appendix, p. 267, setting out the statutes.

Compare former Equity Rule 58 (Discovery—Interrogatories—Inspection and Production of Documents—Admission of Execution or Genuineness)(fifth paragraph).

1946 AMENDMENT

Note. The changes in clauses (1) and (2) correlate the scope of inquiry permitted under Rule 34 with that provided in Rule 26(b), and thus remove any ambiguity created by the former differences in language. As stated in *Olson Transportation Co.* v. *Socony-Vacuum Oil Co.,* E.D.Wis.1944, 8 Fed.Rules Serv. 34.41, Case 2 "* * * Rule 34 is a direct and simple method of discovery." At the same time the addition of the words following the term "parties" makes certain that the person in whose custody, possession, or control the evidence reposes may have the benefit of the applicable protective orders stated in Rule 30(b). This change should be considered in the light of the proposed expansion of Rule 30(b).

An objection has been made that the word "designated" in Rule 34 has been construed with undue strictness in some district court cases so as to require great and impracticable specificity in the description of documents, papers, books, etc., sought to be inspected. The Committee, however, believes that no amendment is needed, and that the proper meaning of "designated" as requiring specificity has already been delineated by the Supreme Court. See *Brown* v. *United States,* 1928, 276 U.S. 134, 143, 48 S.Ct. 288, 290, 72 L.Ed. 500 ("The subpoena * * * specifies * * * with reasonable particularity the subjects to which the documents called for related."); *Consolidated Rendering Co.* v. *Vermont,* 1908, 207 U.S. 541, 543–544, 28 S.Ct. 178, 179, 52 L.Ed. 327 ("We see no reason why all such books, papers and correspondence which related to the subject of inquiry, and were described with reasonable detail, should not be called for and the company directed to produce them. Otherwise, the State would be compelled to designate each particular paper which it desired, which presupposes an accurate knowledge of such papers, which the tribunal desiring the papers would probably rarely, if ever, have.").

1970 AMENDMENT

Rule 34 is revised to accomplish the following major changes in the existing rule: (1) to eliminate the requirement of good cause; (2) to have the rule operate extrajudicially; (3) to include testing and sampling as well as inspecting or photographing tangible things; and (4) to make clear that the rule does not preclude an independent action for analogous discovery against persons not parties.

Subdivision (a). Good cause is eliminated because it has furnished an uncertain and erratic protection to the parties from whom production is sought and is now rendered unnecessary by virtue of the more specific provisions added to Rule 26(b) relating to materials assembled in preparation for trial and to experts retained or consulted by parties.

The good cause requirement was originally inserted in Rule 34 as a general protective provision in the absence of experience with the specific problems that would arise thereunder. As the note to Rule 26(b)(3) on trial preparation materials makes clear, good cause has been applied differently to varying classes of documents, though not without confusion. It has often been said in court opinions that good cause requires a consideration of need for the materials and of alternative means of obtaining them, i.e., something more than relevance and lack of privilege. But the overwhelming proportion of the cases in which the formula of good cause has been applied to require a special showing are those involving trial preparation. In practice, the courts have not treated documents as having a special immunity to discovery simply because of their being documents. Protection may be afforded to claims of privacy or secrecy or of undue burden or expense under what is now Rule 26(c)(previously Rule 30(b)). To be sure, an appraisal of "undue" burden inevitably entails consideration of the needs of the party seeking discovery. With special provisions added to govern trial preparation materials and experts, there is no longer any occasion to retain the requirement of good cause.

The revision of Rule 34 to have it operate extrajudicially, rather than by court order, is to a large extent a reflection of existing law office practice. The Columbia Survey shows that of the litigants seeking inspection of documents or things, only about 25 percent filed motions for court orders. This minor fraction nevertheless accounted for a significant number of motions. About half of these motions were uncontested and in almost all instances the party seeking production ultimately prevailed. Although an extrajudicial procedure will not drastically alter existing practice under Rule 34—it will conform to it in most cases—it has the potential of saving court time in a substantial though proportionately small number of cases tried annually.

The inclusion of testing and sampling of tangible things and objects or operations on land reflects a need frequently encountered by parties in preparation for trial. If the operation of a particular machine is the basis of a claim for negligent injury, it will often be necessary to test its operating parts or to sample and test the products it is producing. *Cf.* Mich.Gen.Ct.R. 310.1(1)(1963)(testing authorized).

The inclusive description of "documents" is revised to accord with changing technology. It makes clear that Rule 34 applies to electronic data compilations from which information can be obtained only with the use of detection devices, and that when the data can as a practical matter be made usable by the discovering party only through respondent's devices, respondent may be required to use his devices to translate the data into usable form. In many instances, this means that respondent will have to supply a printout of computer data. The burden thus placed on respondent will vary from case to case, and the courts have ample power under Rule 26(c) to protect respondent against undue burden or expense, either by restricting discovery or requiring that the discovering party pay costs. Similarly, if the discovering party needs to check the electronic source itself, the court may protect respondent with respect to preservation of his records, confidentiality of nondiscoverable matters, and costs.

Subdivision (b). The procedure provided in Rule 34 is essentially the same as that in Rule 33, as amended, and the discussion in the note appended to that rule is relevant to Rule 34 as well. Problems peculiar to Rule 34 relate to the specific arrangements that must be worked out for inspection and related acts of copying, photographing, testing, or sampling. The rule provides that a request for inspection shall set forth the items to be inspected either by item or category, describing each with reasonable particularity, and shall specify a reasonable time, place, and manner of making the inspection.

Subdivision (c). Rule 34 as revised continues to apply only to parties. Comments from the bar make clear that in the preparation of cases for trial it is occasionally necessary to enter land or inspect large tangible things in the possession of a person not a party, and that some courts have dismissed independent actions in the nature of bills in equity for such discovery on the ground that Rule 34 is preemptive. While an ideal solution to this problem is to provide for discovery against persons not parties in Rule 34, both the jurisdictional and procedural problems are very complex. For the present, this subdivision makes clear that Rule 34 does not preclude independent actions for discovery against persons not parties.

1980 AMENDMENT

Subdivision (b). The Committee is advised that, "It is apparently not rare for parties deliberately to mix critical documents with others in the hope of obscuring significance." Report of the Special Committee for the Study of Discovery Abuse, Section of Litigation of the American Bar Association (1977) 22. The sentence added by this subdivision follows the recommendation of the Report.

1987 AMENDMENT

The amendment is technical. No substantive change is intended.

1991 AMENDMENT

This amendment reflects the change effected by revision of Rule 45 to provide for subpoenas to compel non-parties to produce documents and things and to submit to inspections of premises. The deletion of the text of the former paragraph is not intended to preclude an independent action for production of documents or things or for permission to enter upon land, but such actions may no longer be necessary in light of this revision.

1993 AMENDMENT

The rule is revised to reflect the change made by Rule 26(d), preventing a party from seeking formal discovery prior to the meeting of the parties required by Rule 26(f). Also, like a change made in Rule 33, the rule is modified to make clear that, if a request for production is objectionable only in part, production should be afforded with respect to the unobjectionable portions.

When a case with outstanding requests for production is removed to federal court, the time for response would be measured from the date of the parties' meeting. See Rule 81(c), providing that these rules govern procedures after removal.

2006 AMENDMENT

Subdivision (a). As originally adopted, Rule 34 focused on discovery of "documents" and "things." In 1970, Rule 34(a) was amended to include discovery of data compilations, anticipating that the use of computerized information would increase. Since then, the growth in electronically stored information and in the variety of systems for creating and storing such information has been dramatic. Lawyers and judges interpreted the term "documents" to include electronically stored information because it was obviously improper to allow a party to evade discovery obligations on the basis that the label had not kept pace with changes in information technology. But it has become increasingly difficult to say that all forms of electronically stored information, many dynamic in nature, fit within the traditional concept of a "document." Electronically stored information may exist in dynamic databases and other forms far different from fixed expression on paper. Rule 34(a) is amended to confirm that discovery of electronically stored information stands on equal footing with discovery of paper documents. The change clarifies that Rule 34 applies to information that is fixed in a tangible form and to information that is stored in a medium from which it can be retrieved and examined. At the same time, a Rule 34 request for production of "documents" should be understood to encompass, and the response should include, electronically stored information unless discovery in the action has clearly distinguished between electronically stored information and "documents."

Discoverable information often exists in both paper and electronic form, and the same or similar information might exist in both. The items listed in Rule 34(a) show different ways in which information may be recorded or stored. Images, for example, might be hard-copy documents or electronically stored information. The wide variety of computer systems currently in use, and the rapidity of technological change, counsel against a limiting or precise definition of electronically stored information. Rule 34(a)(1) is expansive and includes any type of information that is stored electronically. A common example often sought in discovery is electronic communications, such as e-mail. The rule covers—either as documents or as electronically stored information—information "stored in any medium," to encompass future developments in computer technology. Rule 34(a)(1) is intended to be broad enough to cover all current types of computer-based information, and flexible enough to encompass future changes and developments.

References elsewhere in the rules to "electronically stored information" should be understood to invoke this expansive approach. A companion change is made to Rule 33(d), making it explicit that parties choosing to respond to an interrogatory by permitting access to responsive records may do so by providing access to electronically stored information. More generally, the term used in Rule 34(a)(1) appears in a number of other amendments, such as those to Rules 26(a)(1), 26(b)(2), 26(b)(5)(B), 26(f), 34(b), 37(f), and 45. In each of these rules, electronically stored information has the same broad meaning it has under Rule 34(a)(1). References to "documents" appear in discovery rules that are not amended, including Rules 30(f), 36(a), and 37(c)(2). These references should be interpreted to include electronically stored information as circumstances warrant.

The term "electronically stored information" is broad, but whether material that falls within this term should be produced, and in what form, are separate questions that must be addressed under Rules 26(b), 26(c), and 34(b).

The Rule 34(a) requirement that, if necessary, a party producing electronically stored information translate it into reasonably usable form does not address the issue of translating from one human language to another. *See In re Puerto Rico Elect. Power Auth.*, 687 F.2d 501, 504–510 (1st Cir.1982).

Rule 34(a)(1) is also amended to make clear that parties may request an opportunity to test or sample materials sought under the rule in addition to inspecting and copying them. That opportunity may be important for both electronically stored information and hard-copy materials. The current rule is not clear that such testing or sampling is authorized; the amendment expressly permits it. As with any other form of discovery, issues of burden and intrusiveness raised by requests to test or sample can be addressed under Rules

26(b)(2) and 26(c). Inspection or testing of certain types of electronically stored information or of a responding party's electronic information system may raise issues of confidentiality or privacy. The addition of testing and sampling to Rule 34(a) with regard to documents and electronically stored information is not meant to create a routine right of direct access to a party's electronic information system, although such access might be justified in some circumstances. Courts should guard against undue intrusiveness resulting from inspecting or testing such systems.

Rule 34(a)(1) is further amended to make clear that tangible things must—like documents and land sought to be examined—be designated in the request.

Subdivision (b). Rule 34(b) provides that a party must produce documents as they are kept in the usual course of business or must organize and label them to correspond with the categories in the discovery request. The production of electronically stored information should be subject to comparable requirements to protect against deliberate or inadvertent production in ways that raise unnecessary obstacles for the requesting party. Rule 34(b) is amended to ensure similar protection for electronically stored information.

The amendment to Rule 34(b) permits the requesting party to designate the form or forms in which it wants electronically stored information produced. The form of production is more important to the exchange of electronically stored information than of hard-copy materials, although a party might specify hard copy as the requested form. Specification of the desired form or forms may facilitate the orderly, efficient, and cost-effective discovery of electronically stored information. The rule recognizes that different forms of production may be appropriate for different types of electronically stored information. Using current technology, for example, a party might be called upon to produce word processing documents, e-mail messages, electronic spreadsheets, different image or sound files, and material from databases. Requiring that such diverse types of electronically stored information all be produced in the same form could prove impossible, and even if possible could increase the cost and burdens of producing and using the information. The rule therefore provides that the requesting party may ask for different forms of production for different types of electronically stored information.

The rule does not require that the requesting party choose a form or forms of production. The requesting party may not have a preference. In some cases, the requesting party may not know what form the producing party uses to maintain its electronically stored information, although Rule 26(f)(3) is amended to call for discussion of the form of production in the parties' prediscovery conference.

The responding party also is involved in determining the form of production. In the written response to the production request that Rule 34 requires, the responding party must state the form it intends to use for producing electronically stored information if the requesting party does not specify a form or if the responding party objects to a form that the requesting party specifies. Stating the intended form before the production occurs may permit the parties to identify and seek to resolve disputes before the expense and work of the production occurs. A party that responds to a discovery request by simply producing electronically stored information in a form of its choice, without identifying that form in advance of the production in the response required by Rule 34(b), runs a risk that the requesting party can show that the produced form is not reasonably usable and that it is entitled to production of some or all of the information in an additional form. Additional time might be required to permit a responding party to assess the appropriate form or forms of production.

If the requesting party is not satisfied with the form stated by the responding party, or if the responding party has objected to the form specified by the requesting party, the parties must meet and confer under Rule 37(a)(2)(B) in an effort to resolve the matter before the requesting party can file a motion to compel. If they cannot agree and the court resolves the dispute, the court is not limited to the forms initially chosen by the requesting party, stated by the responding party, or specified in this rule for situations in which there is no court order or party agreement.

If the form of production is not specified by party agreement or court order, the responding party must produce electronically stored information either in a form or forms in which it is ordinarily maintained or in a form or forms that are reasonably usable. Rule 34(a) requires that, if necessary, a responding party "translate" information it produces into a "reasonably usable" form. Under some circumstances, the responding party may need to provide some reasonable amount of technical support, information on application software, or other reasonable assistance to enable the requesting party to use the information. The rule does not require a party to produce electronically stored information in the form it which it is ordinarily maintained, as long as it is produced in a reasonably usable form. But the option to produce in a reasonably usable form does not mean that a responding party is free to convert electronically stored information from the form in which it is ordinarily maintained to a different form that makes it more difficult or burdensome for the requesting party to use the information efficiently in the litigation. If the responding party ordinarily maintains the information it is producing in a way that makes it searchable by electronic means, the information should not be produced in a form that removes or significantly degrades this feature.

Some electronically stored information may be ordinarily maintained in a form that is not reasonably usable by any party. One example is "legacy" data that can be used only by superseded systems. The questions whether a producing party should be required to convert such information to a more usable form, or should be required to produce it at all, should be addressed under Rule 26(b)(2)(B).

Whether or not the requesting party specified the form of production, Rule 34(b) provides that the same electronically stored information ordinarily need be produced in only one form.

2007 AMENDMENT

The language of Rule 34 has been amended as part of the general restyling of the Civil Rules to make them more easily understood and to make style and terminology consistent throughout the rules. These changes are intended to be stylistic only.

The final sentence in the first paragraph of former Rule 34(b) was a redundant cross-reference to the discovery moratorium provisions of Rule 26(d). Rule 26(d) is now familiar, obviating any need to carry forward the redundant cross-reference.

The redundant reminder of Rule 37(a) procedure in the second paragraph of former Rule 34(b) is omitted as no longer useful.

Rule 35. Physical and Mental Examinations of Persons

1937 ADOPTION

Physical examination of parties before trial is authorized by statute or rule in a number of states. See Ariz.Rev.Code Ann. (Struckmeyer, 1928) § 4468; Mich. Court Rules Ann. (Searl, 1933) Rule 41, § 2; 2 N.J.Comp.Stat. (1910); N.Y.C.P.A. (1937) § 306; 1 S.D.Comp.Laws (1929) § 2716A; 3 Wash.Rev.Stat.Ann. (Remington, 1932) § 1230–1.

Mental examination of parties is authorized in Iowa. Iowa Code (1935) ch. 491–F1. See McCash, The Evolution of the Doctrine of Discovery and Its Present Status in Iowa, 20 Ia.L.Rev. 68 (1934).

The constitutionality of legislation providing for physical examination of parties was sustained in *Lyon* v. *Manhattan Railway Co.*, 1894, 37 N.E. 113, 142 N.Y. 298, and *McGovern* v. *Hope*, 1899, 42 A. 830, 63 N.J.L. 76. In *Union Pacific Ry. Co.* v. *Botsford*, 1891, 141 U.S. 250, 11 S.Ct. 1000, 35 L.Ed. 734, it was held that the court could not order the physical examination of a party in the absence of statutory authority. But in *Camden and Suburban Ry. Co.* v. *Stetson*, 1900, 177 U.S. 172, 20 S.Ct. 617, 44 L.Ed. 721 where there was statutory authority for such examination, derived from a state statute made operative by the conformity act, the practice was sustained. Such authority is now found in the present rule made operative by the Act of June 19, 1934, c. 651, U.S.C., Title 28, § 2072, formerly §§ 723b (Rules in actions at law; Supreme Court authorized to make) and 723c (Union of equity and action at law rules; power of Supreme Court).

1970 AMENDMENT

Subdivision (a). Rule 35(a) has hitherto provided only for an order requiring a party to submit to an examination. It is desirable to extend the rule to provide for an order against the party for examination of a person in his custody or under his legal control. As appears from the provisions of amended Rule 37(b)(2) and the comment under that rule, an order to "produce" the third person imposes only an obligation to use good faith, efforts to produce the person.

The amendment will settle beyond doubt that a parent or guardian suing to recover for injuries to a minor may be ordered to produce the minor for examination. Further, the amendment expressly includes blood examination within the kinds of examinations that can be ordered under the rule. See *Beach* v. *Beach*, 114 F.2d 479 (D.C.Cir.1940), Provisions similar to the amendment have been adopted in at least 10 States; Calif.Code Civ.Proc. § 2032; Ida.R.Civ.P. 35; Ill. S–H Ann. c. 110A, § 215; Md.R.P. 420; Mich.Gen. Ct.R. 311; Minn.R.Civ.P. 35; Mo.Vern.Ann.R.Civ.P. 60.01; N.Dak.R.Civ.P. 35; N.Y.C.P.L. § 3121; Wyo.R.Civ.P. 35.

1507

The amendment makes no change in the requirements of Rule 35 that, before a court order may issue the relevant physical or mental condition must be shown to be "in controversy" and "good cause" must be shown for the examination. Thus, the amendment has no effect on the recent decision of the Supreme Court in *Schlagenhauf* v. *Holder*, 379 U.S. 104, 85 S.Ct. 234, 13 L.Ed.2d 152 (1964), stressing the importance of these requirements and applying them to the facts of the case. The amendment makes no reference to employees of a party. Provisions relating to employees in the State statutes and rules cited above appear to have been virtually unused.

Subdivision (b)(1). This subdivision is amended to correct an imbalance in Rule 35(b)(1) as heretofore written. Under that text, a party causing a Rule 35(a) examination to be made is required to furnish to the party examined, on request, a copy of the examining physician's report. If he delivers this copy, he is in turn entitled to receive from the party examined reports of all examinations of the same condition previously or later made. But the rule has not in terms entitled the examined party to receive from the party causing the Rule 35(a) examination any reports of earlier examinations of the same condition to which the latter may have access. The amendment cures this defect. See La.Stat.Ann., Civ.Proc. art 1495 (1960); Utah R.Civ.P. 35(c).

The amendment specifies that the written report of the examining physician includes results of all tests made, such as results of X-rays and cardiograms. It also embodies changes required by the broadening of Rule 35(a) to take in persons who are not parties.

Subdivision (b)(3). This new subdivision removes any possible doubt that reports of examination may be obtained although no order for examination has been made under Rule 35(a). Examinations are very frequently made by agreement, and sometimes before the party examined has an attorney. The courts have uniformly ordered that reports be supplied, see 4 Moore's Federal Practice ¶ 35.06, n. 1 (2d ed. 1966); 2A Barron & Holtzoff, Federal Practice and Procedure § 823, n. 22 (Wright ed. 1961), and it appears best to fill the technical gap in the present rule.

The subdivision also makes clear that reports of examining physicians are discoverable not only under Rule 35(b), but under other rules as well. To be sure, if the report is privileged, then discovery is not permissible under any rule other than Rule 35(b) and it is permissible under Rule 35(b) only if the party requests a copy of the report of examination made by the other party's doctor. *Sher* v. *De Haven*, 199 F.2d 777 (D.C.Cir.1952), *cert. denied* 345 U.S. 936, 73 S.Ct. 797, 97 L.Ed. 1363 (1953). But if the report is unprivileged and is subject to discovery under the provisions of rules other than Rule 35(b)—such as Rules 34 or 26(b)(3) or (4)—discovery should not depend upon whether the person examined demands a copy of the report. Although a few cases have suggested the contrary, *e.g., Galloway* v. *National Dairy Products Corp.*, 24 F.R.D. 362 (E.D.Pa.1959), the better considered district court decisions hold that Rule 35(b) is not preemptive. *E.g., Leszynski* v. *Russ*, 29 F.R.D. 10, 12 (D.Md.1961) and cases cited. The question was recently given full consideration in *Buffington* v. *Wood*, 351 F.2d 292 (3d Cir.1965), holding that Rule 35(b) is not preemptive.

1987 AMENDMENT

The amendments are technical. No substantive change is intended.

1991 AMENDMENT

The revision authorizes the court to require physical or mental examinations conducted by any person who is suitably licensed or certified.

The rule was revised in 1988 by Congressional enactment to authorize mental examinations by licensed clinical psychologists. This revision extends that amendment to include other certified or licensed professionals, such as dentists or occupational therapists, who are not physicians or clinical psychologists, but who may be well-qualified to give valuable testimony about the physical or mental condition that is the subject of dispute.

The requirement that the examiner be *suitably* licensed or certified is a new requirement. The court is thus expressly authorized to assess the credentials of the examiner to assure that no person is subjected to a court-ordered examination by an examiner whose testimony would be of such limited value that it would be unjust to require the person to undergo the invasion of privacy associated with the examination. This authority is not wholly new, for under the former rule, the court retained discretion to refuse to order an examination, or to restrict an examination. 8 WRIGHT & MILLER, FEDERAL PRACTICE & PROCEDURE § 2234 (1986 Supp.). The revision is intended to encourage the exercise of this discretion, especially with respect to examinations by persons having narrow qualifications.

The court's responsibility to determine the suitability of the examiner's qualifications applies even to a proposed examination by a physician. If the proposed examination and testimony calls for an expertise that the proposed examiner does not have, it should not be ordered, even if the proposed examiner is a physician. The rule does not, however, require that the license or certificate be conferred by the jurisdiction in which the examination is conducted.

2007 AMENDMENT

The language of Rule 35 has been amended as part of the general restyling of the Civil Rules to make them more easily understood and to make style and terminology consistent throughout the rules. These changes are intended to be stylistic only.

Rule 36. Requests for Admission

1937 ADOPTION

Compare similar rules: Former Equity Rule 58 (last paragraph, which provides for the admission of the execution and genuineness of documents); English Rules Under the Judicature Act (The Annual Practice, 1937) O. 32; Ill.Rev.Stat. (1937) ch. 110, § 182 and Rule 18 (Ill.Rev.Stat. (1937) ch. 110, § 259.18); 2 Mass.Gen.Laws (Ter.Ed., 1932) ch. 231, § 69; Mich. Court Rules Ann. (Searl, 1933) Rule 42; N.J.Comp.Stat. (2 Cum.Supp. 1911–1924); N.Y.C.P.A. (1937) §§ 322, 323; Wis.Stat. (1935) § 327.22.

1946 AMENDMENT

Note. The first change in the first sentence of Rule 36(a) and the addition of the new second sentence, specifying when requests for admissions may be served, bring Rule 36 in line with amended Rules 26(a) and 33. There is no reason why these rules should not be treated alike. Other provisions of Rule 36(a) give the party whose admissions are requested adequate protection.

The second change in the first sentence of the rule [subdivision (a)] removes any uncertainty as to whether a party can be called upon to admit matters of fact other than those set forth in relevant documents described in and exhibited with the request. In *Smyth v. Kaufman*, C.C.A.2, 1940, 114 F.2d 40, it was held that the word "therein", now stricken from the rule [said subdivision] referred to the request and that a matter of fact not related to any document could be presented to the other party for admission or denial. The rule of this case is now clearly stated.

The substitution of the word "served" for "delivered" in the third sentence of the amended rule [said subdivision] is in conformance with the use of the word "serve" elsewhere in the rule and generally throughout the rules. See also notes to Rules 13(a) and 33 herein. The substitution [in said subdivision] of "shorter or longer" for "further" will enable a court to designate a lesser period than 10 days for answer. This conforms with a similar provision already contained in Rule 33.

The addition of clause (2) [in said subdivision] specifies the method by which a party may challenge the propriety of a request to admit. There has been considerable difference of judicial opinion as to the correct method, if any, available to secure relief from an allegedly improper request. See Commentary, Methods of Objecting to Notice to Admit, 1942, 5 Fed.Rules Serv. 835; *International Carbonic Engineering Co. v. Natural Carbonic Products, Inc.*, S.D.Cal.1944, 57 F.Supp. 248. The changes in clause (1) are merely of a clarifying and conforming nature.

The first of the added last two sentences [in said subdivision] prevents an objection to a part of a request from holding up the answer, if any, to the remainder. See similar proposed change in Rule 33. The last sentence strengthens the rule by making the denial accurately reflect the party's position. It is taken, with necessary changes, from Rule 8(b).

1970 AMENDMENT

Rule 36 serves two vital purposes, both of which are designed to reduce trial time. Admissions are sought, first to facilitate proof with respect to issues that cannot be eliminated from the case, and secondly, to narrow the issues by eliminating those that can be. The changes made in the rule are designed to serve these purposes more effectively. Certain disagreements in the courts about the proper scope of the rule are resolved. In addition, the procedural operation of the rule is brought into line with other discovery procedures, and the binding effect of an admission is clarified. See generally Finman, The Request for Admissions in Federal Civil Procedure, 71 Yale L.J. 371 (1962).

Subdivision (a). As revised, the subdivision provides that a request may be made to admit any matters within the scope of Rule 26(b) that relate to statements or opinions of fact or of the application of law to fact. It thereby eliminates the requirement that the matters be "of fact." This change resolves conflicts in the court decisions as to whether a request to admit matters of "opinion" and matters involving "mixed law and fact" is proper under the rule. As to "opinion," compare, *e.g., Jackson Buff Corp.* v. *Marcelle*, 20 F.R.D. 139 (E.D.N.Y.1957); *California* v. *The S. S. Jules Fribourg*, 19 F.R.D. 432 (N.D.Cal. 1955), with *e.g., Photon, Inc.* v. *Harris Intertype, Inc.*, 28 F.R.D. 327 (D.Mass.1961); *Hise* v. *Lockwood Grader Corp.*, 153 F.Supp. 276 (D.Neb.1957). As to "mixed law and fact" the majority of courts sustain objections, *e.g., Minnesota Mining and Mfg. Co.* v. *Norton Co.*, 36 F.R.D. 1 (N.D.Ohio 1964), but *McSparran* v. *Hanigan*, 225 F.Supp. 628 (E.D.Pa.1963) is to the contrary.

Not only is it difficult as a practical matter to separate "fact" from "opinion," see 4 Moore's Federal Practice ¶ 36.04 (2d ed. 1966); cf. 2A Barron & Holtzoff, Federal Practice and Procedure 317 (Wright ed. 1961), but an admission on a matter of opinion may facilitate proof or narrow the issues or both. An admission of a matter involving the application of law to fact may, in a given case, even more clearly narrow the issues. For example, an admission that an employee acted in the scope of his employment may remove a major issue from the trial. In *McSparran* v. *Hanigan, supra*, plaintiff admitted that "the premises on which said accident occurred, were occupied or under the control" of one of the defendants, 225 F.Supp. at 636. This admission, involving law as well as fact, removed one of the issues from the lawsuit and thereby reduced the proof required at trial. The amended provision does not authorize requests for admissions of law unrelated to the facts of the case.

Requests for admission involving the application of law to fact may create disputes between the parties which are best resolved in the presence of the judge after much or all of the other discovery has been completed. Power is therefore expressly conferred upon the court to defer decision until a pretrial conference is held or until a designated time prior to trial. On the other hand, the court should not automatically defer decision; in many instances, the importance of the admission lies in enabling the requesting party to avoid the burdensome accumulation of proof prior to the pretrial conference.

Courts have also divided on whether an answering party may properly object to request for admission as to matters which that party regards as "in dispute". Compare, *e.g., Syracuse Broadcasting Corp.* v. *Newhouse*, 271 F.2d 910, 917 (2d Cir.1959); *Driver* v. *Gindy Mfg. Corp.*, 24 F.R.D. 473 (E.D.Pa.1959); with *e.g., McGonigle* v. *Baxter*, 27 F.R.D. 504 (E.D.Pa.1961); *United States* v. *Ehbauer*, 13 F.R.D. 462 (W.D.Mo.1952). The proper response in such cases is an answer. The very purpose of the request is to ascertain whether the answering party is prepared to admit or regards the matter as presenting a genuine issue for trial. In his answer, the party may deny, or he may give as his reason for inability to admit or deny the existence of a genuine issue. The party runs no risk of sanctions if the matter is genuinely in issue since Rule 37(c) provides a sanction of costs only when there are no good reasons for a failure to admit.

On the other hand, requests to admit may be so voluminous and so framed that the answering party finds the task of identifying what is in dispute and what is not unduly burdensome. If so, the responding party may obtain a protective order under Rule 26(c). Some of the decisions sustaining objections on "disputability" grounds could have been justified by the burdensome character of the requests. See *e.g., Syracuse Broadcasting Corp.* v. *Newhouse, supra.*

Another sharp split of authority exists on the question whether a party may base his answer on lack of information or knowledge without seeking out additional information. One line of cases has held that a party may answer on the basis of such knowledge as he has at the time he answers. *E.g., Jackson Buff Corp.* v. *Marcelle*, 20 F.R.D. 139 (E.D.N.Y.1957); *Sladek* v. *General Motors Corp.*, 16 F.R.D. 104 (S.D.Iowa 1954). A larger group of cases, supported by commentators, has taken the view that if the responding party lacks knowledge, he must inform himself in reasonable fashion. *E.g., Hise* v. *Lockwood Grader Corp.*, 153 F.Supp. 276 (D.Neb.1957); *E. H. Tate Co.* v. *Jiffy Enterprises, Inc.*, 16 F.R.D. 571 (E.D.Pa.1954); Finman, *supra*, 71 Yale L.J. 371, 404–409; 4 Moore's Federal Practice ¶ 36.04 (2d ed. 1966); 2A Barron & Holtzoff, Federal Practice and Procedure 509 (Wright ed. 1961).

The rule as revised adopts the majority view, as in keeping with a basic principle of the discovery rules that a reasonable burden may be imposed on the parties when its discharge will facilitate preparation for trial and ease the trial process. It has been argued against this view that one side should not have the burden of "proving" the other side's case. The revised rule requires only that the answering party make reasonable inquiry and secure such knowledge and information as are readily obtainable by him. In most instances, the investigation will be necessary either to his own case or to preparation for rebuttal. Even when it is not, the information may be close enough at hand to be "readily obtainable." Rule 36 requires only that the party state that he has taken these steps. The sanction for failure of a party to inform himself before he answers lies in the award of costs after trial, as provided in Rule 37(c).

The requirement that the answer to a request for admission be sworn is deleted, in favor of a provision that the answer be signed by the party or by his attorney. The provisions of Rule 36 make it clear that admissions function very much as pleadings do. Thus, when a party admits in part and denies in part, his admission is for purposes of pending action only and may not be used against him in any other proceeding. The broadening of the rule to encompass mixed questions of law and fact reinforces this feature. Rule 36 does not lack a sanction for false answers; Rule 37(c) furnishes an appropriate deterrent.

The existing language describing the available grounds for objection to a request for admission is eliminated as neither necessary nor helpful. The statement that objection may be made to any request which is "improper" adds nothing to the provisions that the party serve an answer or objection addressed to each matter and that he state his reasons for any objection. None of the other discovery rules sets forth grounds for objection, except so far as all are subject to the general provisions of Rule 26.

Changes are made in the sequence of procedures in Rule 36 so that they conform to the new procedures in Rules 33 and 34. The major changes are as follows:

(1) The normal time for response to a request for admissions is lengthened from 10 to 30 days, conforming more closely to prevailing practice. A defendant need not respond, however, in less than 45 days after service of the summons and complaint upon him. The court may lengthen or shorten the time when special situations require it.

(2) The present requirement that the plaintiff wait 10 days to serve requests without leave of court is eliminated. The revised provision accords with those in Rules 33 and 34.

(3) The requirement that the objecting party move automatically for a hearing on his objection is eliminated, and the burden is on the requesting party to move for an order. The change in the burden of going forward does not modify present law on burden of persuasion. The award of expenses incurred in relation to the motion is made subject to the comprehensive provisions of Rule 37(a)(4).

(4) A problem peculiar to Rule 36 arises if the responding party serves answers that are not in conformity with the requirements of the rule—for example, a denial is not "specific," or the explanation of inability to admit or deny is not "in detail." Rule 36 now makes no provision for court scrutiny of such answers before trial, and it seems to contemplate that defective answers bring about admissions just as effectively as if no answer had been served. Some cases have so held. *E.g., Southern Ry. Co.* v. *Crosby*, 201 F.2d 878 (4th Cir.1953); *United States* v. *Laney*, 96 F.Supp. 482 (E.D.S.C.1951).

Giving a defective answer the automatic effect of an admission may cause unfair surprise. A responding party who purported to deny or to be unable to admit or deny will for the first time at trial confront the contention that he has made a binding admission. Since it is not always easy to know whether a denial is "specific" or an explanation is "in detail," neither party can know how the court will rule at trial and whether proof must be prepared. Some courts, therefore, have entertained motions to rule on defective answers. They have at times ordered that amended answers be served, when the defects were technical, and at other times have declared that the matter was admitted. *E.g., Woods* v. *Stewart*, 171 F.2d 544 (5th Cir.1948); *SEC* v. *Kaye, Real & Co.*, 122 F.Supp. 639 (S.D.N.Y.1954); *Sieb's Hatcheries, Inc.* v. *Lindley*, 13 F.R.D. 113 (W.D.Ark.1952). The rule as revised conforms to the latter practice.

Subdivision (b). The rule does not now indicate the extent to which a party is bound by his admission. Some courts view admissions as the equivalent of sworn testimony. *E.g., Ark–Tenn Distributing Corp.* v. *Breidt*, 209 F.2d 359 (3d Cir.1954); *United States* v. *Lemons*, 125 F.Supp. 686 (W.D.Ark.1954); 4 Moore's *Federal Practice* ¶ 36.08 (2d ed. 1966 Supp.). At least in some jurisdictions a party may rebut his own testimony, *e.g., Alamo* v. *Del Rosario*, 98 F.2d 328 (D.C.Cir.1938), and by analogy an admission made pursuant to Rule 36 may likewise be thought rebuttable. The courts in *Ark-Tenn* and *Lemons, supra*, reasoned in this way, although the results reached may be supported on different grounds. In *McSparran* v. *Hanigan*, 225 F.Supp. 628, 636–637 (E.D.Pa.1963), the court held that an admission is conclusively binding, though noting the confusion created by prior decisions.

The new provisions give an admission a conclusively binding effect, for purposes only of the pending action, unless the admission is withdrawn or amended. In form and substance a Rule 36 admission is comparable to an admission in pleadings or a stipulation drafted by counsel for use at trial, rather than to an evidentiary admission of a party. Louisell, *Modern California Discovery* § 8.07 (1963); 2A Barron & Holtzoff, *Federal Practice and Procedure* § 838 (Wright ed. 1961). Unless the party securing an admission can depend on its binding effect, he cannot safely avoid the expense of preparing to prove the very matters on which he has secured the admission, and the purpose of the rule is defeated. *Field & McKusick, Maine Civil Practice* § 36.4 (1959); Finman, *supra*, 71 Yale L.J. 371, 418–426; Comment, 56 Nw.U.L.Rev. 679, 682–683 (1961).

Provision is made for withdrawal or amendment of an admission. This provision emphasizes the importance of having the action resolved on the merits, while at the same time assuring each party that justified reliance on an admission in preparation for trial will not operate to his prejudice. *Cf. Moosman* v. *Joseph P. Blitz, Inc.*, 358 F.2d 686 (2d Cir.1966).

1987 AMENDMENT

The amendments are technical. No substantive change is intended.

1993 AMENDMENT

The rule is revised to reflect the change made by Rule 26(d), preventing a party from seeking formal discovery until after the meeting of the parties required by Rule 26(f).

2007 AMENDMENT

The language of Rule 36 has been amended as part of the general restyling of the Civil Rules to make them more easily understood and to make style and terminology consistent throughout the rules. These changes are intended to be stylistic only.

The final sentence of the first paragraph of former Rule 36(a) was a redundant cross-reference to the discovery moratorium provisions of Rule 26(d). Rule 26(d) is now familiar, obviating any need to carry forward the redundant cross-reference. The redundant reminder of Rule 37(c) in the second paragraph was likewise omitted.

Rule 37. Failure to Make Disclosure or Cooperate in Discovery: Sanctions

1937 ADOPTION

The provisions of this rule authorizing orders establishing facts or excluding evidence or striking pleadings, or authorizing judgments of dismissal or default, for refusal to answer questions or permit inspection or otherwise make discovery, are in accord with *Hammond Packing Co.* v. *Arkansas*, 1909, 212 U.S. 322, 29 S.Ct. 370, 53 L.Ed. 530, 15 Ann.Cas. 645, which distinguishes between the justifiable use of such measures as a means of compelling the production of evidence, and their unjustifiable use, as in *Hovey* v. *Elliott*, 1897, 167 U.S. 409, 17 S.Ct. 841, 42 L.Ed. 215, for the mere purpose of punishing for contempt.

1948 AMENDMENT

The amendment effective October 1949, substituted the reference to "Title 28, U.S.C., § 1783" in subdivision (e) for the reference to "the Act of July 3, 1926, c. 762, § 1 (44 Stat. 835), U.S.C., Title 28, § 711."

1970 AMENDMENT

Rule 37 provides generally for sanctions against parties or persons unjustifiably resisting discovery. Experience has brought to light a number of defects in the language of the rule as well as instances in which it is not serving the purposes for which it was designed. See Rosenberg, *Sanctions to Effectuate Pretrial Discovery*, 58 Col.L.Rev. 480 (1958). In addition, changes being made in other discovery rules require conforming amendments to Rule 37.

Rule 37 sometimes refers to a "failure" to afford discovery and at other times to a "refusal" to do so. Taking note of this dual terminology, courts have imported into "refusal" a requirement of "willfulness." See *Roth* v. *Paramount Pictures Distributing Corp.*, 8 F.R.D. 31 (W.D.Pa.1948); *Campbell* v. *Johnson*, 101 F.Supp. 705, 707 (S.D.N.Y. 1951). In *Societe Internationale* v. *Rogers*, 357 U.S. 197, 78 S.Ct. 1087, 2 L.Ed.2d 1255 (1958), the Supreme Court concluded that the rather random use of these two terms in Rule 37 showed no design to use them with consistently distinctive meanings, that "refused" in Rule 37(b)(2) meant simply a failure to comply, and that willfulness was relevant only to the selection of sanctions, if any, to be imposed. Nevertheless, after the decision in *Societe*, the court in *Hinson* v. *Michigan Mutual Liability Co.*, 275 F.2d 537 (5th Cir.1960) once again ruled that "refusal" required willfulness. Substitution of "failure" for "refusal" throughout Rule 37 should eliminate this confusion and bring the rule into harmony with the *Societe Internationale* decision. See Rosenberg, *supra*, 58 Col.L.Rev. 480, 489–490 (1958).

Subdivision (a). Rule 37(a) provides relief to a party seeking discovery against one who, with or without stated objections, fails to afford the discovery sought. It has always fully served this function in relation to depositions, but the amendments being made to Rules 33 and 34 give Rule 37(a) added scope and importance. Under existing Rule 33, a party objecting to interrogatories must make a motion for court hearing on his objections. The changes now made in Rules 33 and 37(a) make it clear that the interrogating party must move to compel answers, and the motion is provided for in Rule 37(a). Existing Rule 34, since it requires a court order prior to production of documents or things or permission to enter on land, has no relation to Rule 37(a). Amendments of Rules 34 and 37(a) create a procedure similar to that provided for Rule 33.

Subdivision (a)(1). This is a new provision making clear to which court a party may apply for an order compelling discovery. Existing Rule 37(a) refers only to the court in which the deposition is being taken; nevertheless, it has been held that the court where the action is pending has "inherent power" to compel a party deponent to answer. *Lincoln Laboratories, Inc.* v. *Savage Laboratories, Inc.*, 27 F.R.D. 476 (D.Del.1961). In relation to Rule 33 interrogatories and Rule 34 requests for inspection, the court where the action is pending is the appropriate enforcing tribunal. The new provision eliminates the need to resort to inherent power by spelling out the respective roles of the court where the action is pending and the court where the deposition is taken. In some instances, two courts are available to a party seeking to compel answers from a party deponent. The party seeking discovery may choose the court to which he will apply, but the court has power to remit the party to the other court as a more appropriate forum.

Subdivision (a)(2). This subdivision contains the substance of existing provisions of Rule 37(a) authorizing motions to compel answers to questions put at depositions and to interrogatories. New provisions authorize motions for orders compelling designation under Rules 30(b)(6) and 31(a) and compelling inspection in accordance with a request made under Rule 34. If the court denies a motion, in whole or part, it may accompany the denial with issuance of a protective order. Compare the converse provision in Rule 26(c).

Subdivision (a)(3). This new provision makes clear that an evasive or incomplete answer is to be considered, for purposes of subdivision (a), a failure to answer. The courts have consistently held that they have the power to compel adequate answers. *E.g., Cone Mills Corp.* v. *Joseph Bancroft & Sons Co.*, 33 F.R.D. 318 (D.Del.1963). This power is recognized and incorporated into the rule.

Subdivision (a)(4). This subdivision amends the provisions for award of expenses, including reasonable attorney's fees, to the prevailing party or person when a motion is made for an order compelling discovery. At present, an award of expenses is made only if the losing party or person is found to have acted without substantial justification. The change requires that expenses be awarded unless the conduct of the losing party or person is found to have been substantially justified. The test of "substantial justification" remains, but the change in language is intended to encourage judges to be more alert to abuses occurring in the discovery process.

On many occasions, to be sure, the dispute over discovery between the parties is genuine, though ultimately resolved one way or the other by the court. In such cases, the losing party is substantially justified in carrying the matter to court. But the rules should deter the abuse implicit in carrying or forcing a discovery dispute to court when no genuine dispute exists. And the potential or actual imposition of expenses is virtually the sole formal sanction in the rules to deter a party from pressing to a court hearing frivolous requests for or objections to discovery.

The present provision of Rule 37(a) that the court shall require payment if it finds that the defeated party acted without "substantial justification" may appear adequate, but in fact it has been little used. Only a handful of reported cases include an award of expenses, and the Columbia Survey found that in only one instance out of about 50 motions decided under Rule 37(a) did the court award expenses. It appears that the courts do not utilize the most important available sanction to deter abusive resort to the judiciary.

The proposed change provides in effect that expenses should ordinarily be awarded unless a court finds that the losing party acted justifiably in carrying his point to court. At the same time, a necessary flexibility is maintained, since the court retains the power to find that other circumstances make an award of expenses unjust—as where the prevailing party also acted unjustifiably. The amendment does not significantly narrow the discretion of the court, but rather presses the court to address itself to abusive practices. The present provision that expenses may be imposed upon either the party or his attorney or both is unchanged. But it is not contemplated that expenses will be imposed upon the attorney merely because the party is indigent.

Subdivision (b). This subdivision deals with sanctions for failure to comply with a court order. The present captions for subsections (1) and (2) entitled, "Contempt" and "Other Consequences," respectively, are confusing. One of the consequences listed in (2) is the arrest of the party, representing the exercise of the contempt power. The contents of the subsections show that the first authorizes the sanction of contempt (and no other) by the court in which the deposition is taken, whereas the second subsection authorizes a variety of sanctions, including contempt, which may be imposed by the court in which the action is pending. The captions of the subsections are changed to reflect their contents.

The scope of Rule 37(b)(2) is broadened by extending it to include any order "to provide or permit discovery," including orders issued under Rules 37(a) and 35. Various rules authorize orders for discovery—*e.g.*, Rule 35(b)(1), Rule 26(c) as revised, Rule 37(d). See Rosenberg, *supra*, 58 Col.L.Rev. 480, 484–486. Rule 37(b)(2) should provide comprehensively for enforcement of all these orders. *Cf. Societe Internationale* v. *Rogers*, 357 U.S. 197, 207, 78 S.Ct. 1087, 1093, 2 L.Ed.2d 1255 (1958). On the other hand, the reference to Rule 34 is deleted to conform to the changed procedure in that rule.

A new subsection (E) provides that sanctions which have been available against a party for failure to comply with an order under Rule 35(a) to submit to examination will now be available against him for his failure to comply with a Rule 35(a) order to produce a third person for examination, unless he shows that he is unable to produce the person. In this context, "unable" means in effect "unable in good faith." See *Societe Internationale* v. *Rogers*, 357 U.S. 197, 78 S.Ct. 1087, 2 L.Ed.2d 1255 (1958).

Subdivision (b)(2) is amplified to provide for payment of reasonable expenses caused by the failure to obey the order. Although Rules 37(b)(2) and 37(d) have been silent as to award of expenses, courts have nevertheless ordered them on occasion. *E.g., United Sheeplined Clothing Co.* v. *Arctic Fur Cap Corp.*, 165 F.Supp. 193 (S.D.N.Y.1958); *Austin Theatre, Inc.* v. *Warner Bros. Pictures, Inc.*, 22 F.R.D. 302 (S.D.N.Y.1958). The provision places the burden on the disobedient party to avoid expenses by showing that his failure is justified or that special circumstances make an award of expenses unjust. Allocating the burden in this way conforms to the changed provisions as to expenses in Rule 37(a), and is particularly appropriate when a court order is disobeyed.

An added reference to directors of a party is similar to a change made in subdivision (d) and is explained in the note to that subdivision. The added reference to persons designated by a party under Rules 30(b)(6) or 31(a) to testify on behalf of the party carries out the new procedure in those rules for taking a deposition of a corporation or other organization.

Subdivision (c). Rule 37(c) provides a sanction for the enforcement of Rule 36 dealing with requests for admission. Rule 36 provides the mechanism whereby a party may obtain from another party in appropriate instances either (1) an admission, or (2) a sworn and specific denial or (3) a sworn statement "setting forth in detail the reasons why he cannot truthfully admit or deny." If the party obtains the second or third of these responses, in proper form, Rule 36 does not provide for a pretrial hearing on whether the response is warranted by the evidence thus far accumulated. Instead, Rule 37(c) is intended to provide posttrial relief in the form of a requirement that the party improperly refusing the admission pay the expenses of the other side in making the necessary proof at trial.

Rule 37(c), as now written, addresses itself in terms only to the sworn denial and is silent with respect to the statement of reasons for an inability to admit or deny. There is no apparent basis for this distinction, since the sanction provided in Rule 37(c) should deter all unjustified failures to admit. This omission in the rule has caused confused and diverse treatment in the courts. One court has held that if a party give inadequate reasons, he should be treated before trial as having denied the request, so that Rule 37(c) may apply. *Bertha Bldg. Corp.* v. *National Theaters Corp.*, 15 F.R.D. 339 (E.D.N.Y.1954). Another has held that the party should be treated as having admitted the request. *Heng Hsin Co.* v. *Stern, Morgenthau & Co.*, 20 Fed.Rules Serv. 36a.52, Case 1 (S.D.N.Y. Dec. 10, 1954). Still another has ordered a new response, without indicating what the outcome should be if the new response were inadequate. *United States Plywood Corp.* v. *Hudson Lumber Co.*, 127 F.Supp. 489, 497–498 (S.D.N.Y.1954). See generally Finman, *The Request for Admissions in Federal Civil Procedure*, 71 Yale L.J. 371, 426–430 (1962). The amendment eliminates this defect in Rule 37(c) by bringing within its scope all failures to admit.

Additional provisions in Rule 37(c) protect a party from having to pay expenses if the request for admission was held objectionable under Rule 36(a) or if the party failing to admit had reasonable ground to believe that he might prevail on the matter. The latter provision emphasizes that the true test under Rule 37(c) is not whether a party prevailed at trial but whether he acted reasonably in believing that he might prevail.

Subdivision (d). The scope of subdivision (d) is broadened to include responses to requests for inspection under Rule 34, thereby conforming to the new procedures of Rule 34.

Two related changes are made in subdivision (d): the permissible sanctions are broadened to include such orders "as are just"; and the requirement that the failure to appear or respond be "wilful" is eliminated. Although Rule 37(d) in terms provides for only three sanctions, all rather severe, the courts have interpreted it as permitting softer sanctions than those which it sets forth. *E.g., Gill* v. *Stolow*, 240 F.2d 669 (2d Cir.1957); *Saltzman* v. *Birrel*, 156 F.Supp. 538 (S.D.N.Y.1957); 2A Barron & Holtzoff, *Federal Practice and Procedure* 554–557 (Wright ed. 1961). The rule is changed to provide the greater flexibility as to sanctions which the cases show is needed.

The resulting flexibility as to sanctions eliminates any need to retain the requirement that the failure to appear or respond be "wilful." The concept of "wilful failure" is at best subtle and difficult, and the cases do not supply a bright line. Many courts have imposed sanctions without referring to willfulness. *E.g., Milewski* v. *Schneider Transportation Co.*, 238 F.2d 397 (6th Cir.1956); *Dictograph Products, Inc.* v. *Kentworth Corp.*, 7 F.R.D. 543 (W.D.Ky.1947). In addition, in view of the possibility of light sanctions, even a negligent failure should come within Rule 37(d). If default is caused by counsel's ignorance of Federal practice, *cf. Dunn* v. *Pennsylvania R. R.*, 96 F.Supp. 597 (N.D.Ohio 1951), or by his preoccupation with another aspect of the case, *cf. Maurer–Neuer, Inc.* v. *United Packinghouse Workers*, 26 F.R.D. 139 (D.Kan.1960), dismissal of the action and default judgment are not justified, but the imposition of expenses and fees may well be. "Willfulness" continues to play a role, along with various other factors, in the choice of sanctions. Thus, the scheme conforms to Rule 37(b) as construed by the Supreme Court in *Societe Internationale* v. *Rogers*, 357 U.S. 197, 208, 78 S.Ct. 1087, 1094, 2 L.Ed.2d 1255 (1958).

A provision is added to make clear that a party may not properly remain completely silent even when he regards a notice to take his deposition or a set of interrogatories or requests to inspect as improper and objectionable. If he desires not to appear or not to respond, he must apply for a protective order. The cases are divided on whether a protective order must be sought. Compare *Collins* v. *Wayland*, 139 F.2d 677 (9th Cir.1944), *cert. den.* 322 U.S. 744, 64 S.Ct. 1151, 88 L.Ed. 1576; *Bourgeois* v. *El Paso Natural Gas Co.*, 20 F.R.D. 358 (S.D.N.Y.1957); *Loosley* v. *Stone*, 15 F.R.D. 373 (S.D.Ill. 1954), with *Scarlatos* v. *Kulukundis*, 21 F.R.D. 185 (S.D.N.Y.1957); *Ross* v. *True Temper Corp.*, 11 F.R.D. 307 (N.D.Ohio 1951). Compare also Rosenberg, *supra*, 58 Col.L.Rev. 480, 496 (1958) with 2A Barron & Holtzoff, Federal Practice and Procedure 530–531 (Wright ed. 1961). The party from whom discovery is sought is afforded, through Rule 26(c), a fair and effective procedure whereby he can challenge the request made. At the same time, the total noncompliance with which Rule 37(d) is concerned may impose severe inconvenience or hardship on the discovering party and substantially delay the discovery process. *Cf.* 2B Barron & Holtzoff, Federal Practice and Procedure 306–307 (Wright ed. 1961)(response to a subpoena).

The failure of an officer or managing agent of a party to make discovery as required by present Rule 37(d) is treated as the failure of the party. The rule as revised provides similar treatment for a director of a party. There is slight warrant for the present distinction between officers and managing agents on the one hand and directors on the other. Although the legal power over a director to compel his making discovery may not be as great as over officers or managing agents, *Campbell* v. *General Motors Corp.*, 13 F.R.D. 331 (S.D.N.Y.1952), the practical differences are negligible. That a director's interests are normally aligned with those of his corporation is shown by the provisions of old Rule 26(d)(2), transferred to 32(a)(2)(deposition of director of party may be used at trial by an adverse party for any purpose) and of Rule 43(b)(director of party may be treated at trial as a hostile witness on direct examination by any adverse party). Moreover, in those rare instances when a corporation is unable through good faith efforts to compel a director to make discovery, it is unlikely that the court will impose sanctions. *Cf. Societe Internationale* v. *Rogers*, 357 U.S. 197, 78 S.Ct. 1087, 2 L.Ed.2d 1255 (1958).

Subdivision (e). The change in the caption conforms to the language of 28 U.S.C. § 1783, as amended in 1964.

Subdivision (f). Until recently, costs of a civil action could be awarded against the United States only when expressly provided by Act of Congress, and such provision was rarely made. See H.R.Rep.No. 1535, 89th Cong., 2d Sess., 2–3 (1966). To avoid any conflict with this doctrine, Rule 37(f) has provided that expenses and attorney's fees may not be imposed upon the United States under Rule 37. See 2A Barron & Holtzoff, *Federal Practice and Procedure* 857 (Wright ed.1961).

A major change in the law was made in 1966, 80 Stat. 308, 28 U.S.C. § 2412 (1966), whereby a judgment for costs may ordinarily be awarded to the prevailing party in any civil action brought by or against the United States. Costs are not to include the fees and expenses of attorneys. In light of this legislative development, Rule 37(f) is amended to permit the award of expenses and fees against the United States under Rule 37, but only to the extent permitted by statute. The amendment brings Rule 37(f) into line with present and future statutory provisions.

1980 AMENDMENT

Subdivision (b)(2). New Rule 26(f) provides that if a discovery conference is held, at its close the court shall enter an order respecting the subsequent conduct of discovery. The amendment provides that the sanctions available for violation of other court orders respecting discovery are available for violation of the discovery conference order.

Subdivision (e). Subdivision (e) is stricken. Title 28, U.S.C. § 1783 no longer refers to sanctions. The subdivision otherwise duplicates Rule 45(e)(2).

Subdivision (g). New Rule 26(f) imposes a duty on parties to participate in good faith in the framing of a discovery plan by agreement upon the request of any party. This subdivision authorizes the court to award to parties who participate in good faith in an attempt to frame a discovery plan the expenses incurred in the attempt if any party or his attorney fails to participate in good faith and thereby causes additional expense.

Failure of United States to Participate in Good Faith in Discovery. Rule 37 authorizes the court to direct that parties or attorneys who fail to participate in good faith in the discovery process pay the expenses, including attorneys' fees, incurred by other parties as a result of that failure. Since attorneys' fees cannot ordinarily be awarded against the United States (28 U.S.C. § 2412), there is often no practical remedy for the misconduct of its officers and attorneys. However, in the case of a government attorney who fails to participate in good faith in discovery, nothing prevents a court in an appropriate case from giving written notification of that fact to the Attorney General of the United States and other appropriate heads of offices or agencies thereof.

1987 AMENDMENT

The amendments are technical. No substantive change is intended.

1993 AMENDMENT

Subdivision (a). This subdivision is revised to reflect the revision of Rule 26(a), requiring disclosure of matters without a discovery request.

Pursuant to new subdivision (a)(2)(A), a party dissatisfied with the disclosure made by an opposing party may under this rule move for an order to compel disclosure. In providing for such a motion, the revised rule parallels the provisions of the former rule dealing with failures to answer particular interrogatories. Such a motion may be needed when the information to be disclosed might be helpful to the party seeking the disclosure but not to the party required to make the disclosure. If the party required to make the disclosure would need the material to support its own contentions, the more effective enforcement of the disclosure requirement will be to exclude the evidence not disclosed, as provided in subdivision (c)(1) of this revised rule.

Language is included in the new paragraph and added to the subparagraph (B) that requires litigants to seek to resolve discovery disputes by informal means before filing a motion with the court. This requirement is based on successful experience with similar local rules of court promulgated pursuant to Rule 83.

The last sentence of paragraph (2) is moved into paragraph (4).

Under revised paragraph (3), evasive or incomplete disclosures and responses to interrogatories and production requests are treated as failures to disclose or respond. Interrogatories and requests for production should not be read or interpreted in an artificially restrictive or hypertechnical manner to avoid disclosure of information fairly covered by the discovery request, and to do so is subject to appropriate sanctions under subdivision (a).

Revised paragraph (4) is divided into three subparagraphs for ease of reference, and in each the phrase "after opportunity for hearing" is changed to "after affording an opportunity to be heard" to make clear that the court can consider such questions on written submissions as well as on oral hearings.

Subparagraph (A) is revised to cover the situation where information that should have been produced without a motion to compel is produced after the motion is filed but before it is brought on for hearing. The rule also is revised to provide that a party should not be awarded its expenses for filing a motion that could have been avoided by conferring with opposing counsel.

Subparagraph (C) is revised to include the provision that formerly was contained in subdivision (a)(2) and to include the same requirement of an opportunity to be heard that is specified in subparagraphs (A) and (B).

Subdivision (c). The revision provides a self-executing sanction for failure to make a disclosure required by Rule 26(a), without need for a motion under subdivision (a)(2)(A).

Paragraph (1) prevents a party from using as evidence any witnesses or information that, without substantial justification, has not been disclosed as required by Rules 26(a) and 26(e)(1). This automatic sanction provides a strong inducement for disclosure of material that the disclosing party would expect to use as evidence, whether at a trial, at a hearing, or on a motion, such as one under Rule 56. As disclosure of evidence offered solely for impeachment purposes is not required under those rules, this preclusion sanction likewise does not apply to that evidence.

Limiting the automatic sanction to violations "without substantial justification," coupled with the exception for violations that are "harmless," is needed to avoid unduly harsh penalties in a variety of situations: *e.g.,* the inadvertent omission from a Rule 26(a)(1)(A) disclosure of the name of a potential witness known to all parties; the failure to list as a trial witness a person so listed by another party; or the lack of knowledge of a pro se litigant of the requirement to make disclosures. In the latter situation, however, exclusion would be proper if the requirement for disclosure had been called to the litigant's attention by either the court or another party.

Preclusion of evidence is not an effective incentive to compel disclosure of information that, being supportive of the position of the opposing party, might advantageously be concealed by the disclosing party. However, the rule provides the court with a wide range of other sanctions—such as declaring specified facts to be established, preventing contradictory evidence, or, like spoliation of evidence, allowing the jury to be informed of the fact of nondisclosure—that, though not self-executing, can be imposed when found to be warranted after a hearing. The failure to identify a witness or document in a disclosure statement would be admissible under the Federal Rules of Evidence under the same principles that allow a party's interrogatory answers to be offered against it.

Subdivision (d). This subdivision is revised to require that, where a party fails to file any response to interrogatories or a Rule 34 request, the discovering party should informally seek to obtain such responses before filing a motion for sanctions.

The last sentence of this subdivision is revised to clarify that it is the pendency of a motion for protective order that may be urged as an excuse for a violation of subdivision (d). If a party's motion has been denied, the party cannot argue that its subsequent failure to comply would be justified. In this connection, it should be noted that the filing of a motion under Rule 26(c) is not self-executing—the relief authorized under that rule depends on obtaining the court's order to that effect.

Subdivision (g). This subdivision is modified to conform to the revision of Rule 26(f).

2000 AMENDMENT

Subdivision (c)(1). When this subdivision was added in 1993 to direct exclusion of materials not disclosed as required, the duty to supplement discovery responses pursuant to Rule 26(e)(2) was omitted. In the face of this omission, courts may rely on inherent power to sanction for failure to supplement as required by Rule 26(e)(2), *see 8 Federal Practice & Procedure* § 2050 at 607–09, but that is an uncertain and unregulated ground for imposing sanctions. There is no obvious occasion for a Rule 37(a) motion in connection with failure to supplement, and ordinarily only Rule 37(c)(1) exists as rule-based authority for sanctions if this supplementation obligation is violated.

The amendment explicitly adds failure to comply with Rule 26(e)(2) as a ground for sanctions under Rule 37(c)(1), including exclusion of withheld materials. The rule provides that this sanction power only applies when the failure to supplement was "without substantial justification." Even if the failure was not substantially justified, a party should be allowed to use the material that was not disclosed if the lack of earlier notice was harmless.

"Shall" is replaced by "is" under the program to conform amended rules to current style conventions when there is no ambiguity.

GAP Report

The Advisory Committee recommends that the published amendment proposal be modified to state that the exclusion sanction can apply to failure "to amend a prior response to discovery as required by Rule 26(e)(2)." In addition, one minor phrasing change is recommended for the Committee Note.

2006 AMENDMENT

Subdivision (f). Subdivision (f) is new. It focuses on a distinctive feature of computer operations, the routine alteration and deletion of information that attends ordinary use. Many steps essential to computer operation may alter or destroy information, for reasons that have nothing to do with how that information might relate to litigation. As a result, the ordinary operation of computer systems creates a risk that a party may lose potentially discoverable information without culpable conduct on its part. Under Rule 37(f), absent exceptional circumstances, sanctions cannot be imposed for loss of electronically stored information resulting from the routine, good-faith operation of an electronic information system.

Rule 37(f) applies only to information lost due to the "routine operation of an electronic information system"—the ways in which such systems are generally designed, programmed, and implemented to meet the party's technical and business needs. The "routine operation" of computer systems includes the alteration and overwriting of information, often without the operator's specific direction or awareness, a feature with no direct counterpart in hard-copy documents. Such features are essential to the operation of electronic information systems.

Rule 37(f) applies to information lost due to the routine operation of an information system only if the operation was in good faith. Good faith in the routine operation of an information system may involve a party's intervention to modify or suspend certain features of that routine operation to prevent the loss of information, if that information is subject to a preservation obligation. A preservation obligation may arise from many sources, including common law, statutes, regulations, or a court order in the case. The good faith requirement of Rule 37(f) means that a party is not permitted to exploit the routine operation of an information system to thwart discovery obligations by allowing that operation to continue in order to destroy specific stored information that it is required to preserve. When a party is under a duty to preserve information because of pending or reasonably anticipated litigation, intervention in the routine operation of an information system is one aspect of what is often called a "litigation hold." Among the factors that bear on a party's good faith in the routine operation of an information system are the steps the party took to comply with a court order in the case or party agreement requiring preservation of specific electronically stored information.

Whether good faith would call for steps to prevent the loss of information on sources that the party believes are not reasonably accessible under Rule 26(b)(2) depends on the circumstances of each case. One factor is whether the party reasonably believes that the information on such sources is likely to be discoverable and not available from reasonably accessible sources.

The protection provided by Rule 37(f) applies only to sanctions "under these rules." It does not affect other sources of authority to impose sanctions or rules of professional responsibility.

This rule restricts the imposition of "sanctions." It does not prevent a court from making the kinds of adjustments frequently used in managing discovery if a party is unable to provide relevant responsive information. For example, a court could order the responding party to produce an additional witness for deposition, respond to additional interrogatories, or make similar attempts to provide substitutes or alternatives for some or all of the lost information.

2007 AMENDMENT

The language of Rule 37 has been amended as part of the general restyling of the Civil Rules to make them more easily understood and to make style and terminology consistent throughout the rules. These changes are intended to be stylistic only.

VI. TRIALS

Rule 38.   Jury Trial of Right

1937 ADOPTION

This rule provides for the preservation of the constitutional right of trial by jury as directed in the enabling act (act of June 19, 1934, 48 Stat. 1064, U.S.C., Title 28, former § 2072, formerly § 723c), and it and the next rule make definite provision for claim and waiver of jury trial, following the method used in many American states and in England and the British Dominions. Thus the claim must be made at once on initial pleading or appearance under Ill.Rev.Stat. (1937) ch. 110, § 188; 6 Tenn.Code Ann. (Williams, 1934) § 8734; compare Wyo.Rev.Stat.Ann. (1931) § 89–1320 (with answer or reply); within 10 days after the pleadings are completed or the case is at issue under 2 Conn.Gen.Stat. (1930) § 5624; Hawaii Rev.Laws (1935) § 4101; 2 Mass.Gen.Laws (Ter.Ed.1932) ch. 231, § 60; 3 Mich.Comp.Laws (1929) § 14263; Mich. Court Rules Ann. (Searl, 1933) Rule 33 (15 days); England (until 1933) O. 36, r. r. 2 and 6; and Ontario Jud. Act (1927) § 57(1)(4 days, or, where prior notice of trial, 2 days from such notice); or at a definite time varying under different codes, from 10 days before notice of trial to 10 days after notice, or, as in many, when the case is called for assignment, Ariz.Rev.Code Ann. (Struckmeyer, 1928) § 3802; Calif.Code Civ.Proc. (Deering, 1937) § 631, par. 4; Iowa Code (1935) § 10724; 4 Nev.Comp.Laws (Hillyer, 1929) § 8782; N.M.Stat.Ann. (Courtright, 1929) § 105–814; N.Y.C.P.A. (1937) § 426, subdivision 5 (applying to New York, Bronx, Richmond, Kings, and Queens Counties); R.I.Pub.Laws (1929), ch. 1327, amending R.I.Gen.Laws (1923) ch. 337, § 6; Utah Rev.Stat.Ann. (1933) § 104–23–6; 2 Wash.Rev.Stat.Ann. (Remington, 1932) § 316; England (4 days after notice of trial), Administration of Justice Act (1933) § 6 and amended rule under the Judicature Act (The Annual Practice, 1937), O. 36, r. 1; Australia High Court Procedure Act (1921) § 12, Rules, O. 33, r. 2; Alberta Rules of Ct. (1914) 172, 183, 184; British Columbia Sup.Ct.Rules (1925) O. 36, r. r. 2, 6, 11, and 16; New Brunswick Jud. Act (1927) O. 36, r. r. 2 and 5. See James Trial by Jury and the New Federal Rules of Procedure (1936), 45 Yale L.J. 1022.

Rule 81(c) provides for claim for jury trial in removed actions.

The right to trial by jury as declared in U.S.C., Title 28, § 1873, formerly § 770 (Trial of issues of fact; by jury; exceptions), and similar statutes, is unaffected by this rule. This rule modifies U.S.C., Title 28, former § 773 (Trial of issues of fact; by court).

1966 AMENDMENT

See Note to Rule 9(h), supra.

1987 AMENDMENT

The amendments are technical. No substantive change is intended.

1993 AMENDMENT

Language requiring the filing of a jury demand as provided in subdivision (d) is added to subdivision (b) to eliminate an apparent ambiguity between the two subdivisions. For proper scheduling of cases, it is important that jury demands not only be served on other parties, but also be filed with the court.

2007 AMENDMENT

The language of Rule 38 has been amended as part of the general restyling of the Civil Rules to make them more easily understood and to make style and terminology consistent throughout the rules. These changes are intended to be stylistic only.

Rule 39.   Trial by Jury or by the Court

1937 ADOPTION

The provisions for express waiver of jury trial found in U.S.C., Title 28, former § 773 (Trial of issues of fact; by court) are incorporated in this rule. See Rule 38, however, which extends the provisions for waiver of jury. U.S.C., Title 28, former § 772 (Trial of issues of fact; in equity in patent causes) is unaffected by this rule. When certain of the issues are to be tried by jury and others by the court, the court may determine the sequence in which such issues shall be tried. See *Liberty Oil Co.* v. *Condon Nat. Bank*, 260 U.S. 235, 43 S.Ct. 118, 67 L.Ed. 232 (1922).

A discretionary power in the courts to send issues of fact to the jury is common in state procedure. Compare Calif.Code Civ.Proc. (Deering, 1937) § 592; 1 Colo.Stat.Ann. (1935) Code Civ.Proc., Ch. 12, § 191; Conn.Gen.Stat. (1930) § 5625; 2 Minn.Stat. (Mason, 1927) § 9288; 4 Mont.Rev.Codes Ann. (1935) § 9327; N.Y.C.P.A. (1937) § 430; 2 Ohio Gen.Code Ann. (Page, 1926) § 11380; 1 Okla.Stat.Ann. (Harlow, 1931) § 351 [12 Okl.St.Ann. § 557]; Utah Rev.Stat.Ann. (1933) § 104–23–5; 2 Wash.Rev.Stat.Ann. (Remington, 1932) § 315; Wis.Stat. (1935) § 270.07. See former Equity Rule 23 (Matters Ordinarily Determinable at Law When Arising in Suit in Equity to be Disposed of Therein) and U.S.C., Title 28, former § 772 (Trial of issues of fact; in equity in patent causes); *Colleton Merc. Mfg. Co.* v. *Savannah River Lumber Co.*, C.C.A.4, 1922, 280 F. 358; *Fed. Res. Bk. of San Francisco* v. *Idaho Grimm Alfalfa Seed Growers' Ass'n,*, C.C.A.9, 1925, 8 F.2d 922, certiorari denied 270 U.S. 646, 46 S.Ct. 347, 70 L.Ed. 778; *Watt* v. *Starke*, 1879, 101 U.S. 247, 25 L.Ed. 826.

2007 AMENDMENT

The language of Rule 39 has been amended as part of the general restyling of the Civil Rules to make them more easily understood and to make style and terminology consistent throughout the rules. These changes are intended to be stylistic only.

Rule 40. Assignment of Cases for Trial

1937 ADOPTION

U.S.C., Title 28, former § 769 (Notice of case for trial) is modified. See former Equity Rule 56 (On Expiration of Time for Depositions, Case Goes on Trial Calendar). See also former Equity Rule 57 (Continuances).

For examples of statutes giving precedence, see U.S.C., Title 28, formerly § 47 (now §§ 1253, 2101, 2325)(Injunctions as to orders of Interstate Commerce Commission); formerly § 380 (now §§ 1253, 2101, 2284) (Injunctions alleged unconstitutionality of state statutes); formerly § 380a (now §§ 1253, 2101, 2284)(Same; Constitutionality of federal statute); former § 768 (Priority of cases where a state is party); Title 15, § 28 (Antitrust laws; suits against monopolies expedited); Title 22, § 240 (Petition for restoration of property seized as munitions of war, etc.); and Title 49, § 44 (Proceedings in equity under interstate commerce laws; expedition of suits).

2007 AMENDMENT

The language of Rule 40 has been amended as part of the general restyling of the Civil Rules to make them more easily understood and to make style and terminology consistent throughout the rules. These changes are intended to be stylistic only.

The best methods for scheduling trials depend on local conditions. It is useful to ensure that each district adopts an explicit rule for scheduling trials. It is not useful to limit or dictate the provisions of local rules.

Rule 41. Dismissal of Actions

1937 ADOPTION

Note to Subdivision (a). Compare Ill.Rev.Stat. (1937) c. 110, § 176, and English Rules Under the Judicature Act (The Annual Practice, 1937) O. 26.

Provisions regarding dismissal in such statutes as U.S.C., Title 8, § 164 (Jurisdiction of district courts in immigration cases) and U.S.C., Title 31, § 232 (Liability of persons making false claims against United States; suits) are preserved by paragraph (1).

Note to Subdivision (b). This provides for the equivalent of a nonsuit on motion by the defendant after the completion of the presentation of evidence by the plaintiff. Also, for actions tried without a jury, it provides the equivalent of the directed verdict practice for jury actions which is regulated by Rule 50.

1946 AMENDMENT

Note to Subdivision (a). The insertion of the reference to Rule 66 correlates Rule 41(a)(1) with the express provisions concerning dismissal set forth in amended Rule 66 on receivers.

The change in Rule 41(a)(1)(i) gives the service of a motion for summary judgment by the adverse party the same effect in preventing unlimited dismissal as was originally given only to the service of an answer. The omission of reference to a motion for summary judgment in the original rule was subject to criticism. 3 Moore's Federal Practice, 1938, 3037–3038, n. 12. A motion for summary judgment may be forthcoming prior to answer, and if well taken will eliminate the necessity for an answer. Since such a motion may require even more research and preparation than the answer itself, there is good reason why the service of the motion, like that of the answer, should prevent a voluntary dismissal by the adversary without court approval.

The word "generally" has been stricken from Rule 41(a)(1)(ii) in order to avoid confusion and to conform with the elimination of the necessity for special appearance by original Rule 12(b).

Subdivision (b). In some cases tried without a jury, where at the close of plaintiff's evidence the defendant moves for dismissal under Rule 41(b) on the ground that plaintiff's evidence is insufficient for recovery, the plaintiff's own evidence may be conflicting or present questions of credibility. In ruling on the defendant's motion, questions arise as to the function of the judge in evaluating the testimony and whether findings should be made if the motion is sustained. Three circuits hold that as the judge is the trier of the facts in such a situation his function is not the same as on a motion to direct a verdict, where the jury is the trier of the facts, and that the judge in deciding such a motion in a non-jury case may pass on conflicts of evidence and credibility, and if he performs that function of evaluating the testimony and grants the motion on the merits, findings are required. *Young* v. *United States,* C.C.A.9, 1940, 111 F.2d 823; *Gary Theatre Co.* v. *Columbia Pictures Corporation,* C.C.A.7, 1941, 120 F.2d 891; *Bach* v. *Friden Calculating Machine Co., Inc.,* C.C.A.6, 1945, 148 F.2d 407. Cf. *Mateas* v. *Fred Harvey, a Corporation,* C.C.A.9, 1945, 146 F.2d 989. The Third Circuit has held that on such a motion the function of the court is the same as on a motion to direct in a jury case, and that the court should only decide whether there is evidence which would support a judgment for the plaintiff, and therefore, findings are not required by Rule 52. *Federal Deposit Insurance Corp.* v. *Mason,* C.C.A.3, 1940, 115 F.2d 548; *Schad* v. *Twentieth Century-Fox Film Corp.,* C.C.A.3, 1943, 136 F.2d 991. The added sentence in Rule 41(b) incorporates the view of the Sixth, Seventh and Ninth Circuits. See also 3 Moore's Federal Practice, 1938, Cum.Supplement § 41.03, under "Page 3045"; Commentary, The Motion to Dismiss in Non-Jury Cases, 1946, 9 Fed.Rules Serv., Comm.Pg. 41b.14.

1963 AMENDMENT

Under the present text of the second sentence of this subdivision, the motion for dismissal at the close of the plaintiff's evidence may be made in a case tried to a jury as well as in a case tried without a jury. But, when made in a jury-tried case, this motion overlaps the motion for a directed verdict under Rule 50(a), which is also available in the same situation. It has been held that the standard to be applied in deciding the Rule 41(b) motion at the close of the plaintiff's evidence in a jury-tried case is the same as that used upon a motion for a directed verdict made at the same stage; and, just as the court need not make findings pursuant to Rule 52(a) when it directs a verdict, so in a jury-tried case it may omit these findings in granting the Rule 41(b) motion. See generally *O'Brien* v. *Westinghouse Electric Corp.,* 293 F.2d 1, 5–10 (3d Cir.1961).

As indicated by the discussion in the *O'Brien* case, the overlap has caused confusion. Accordingly, the second and third sentences of Rule 41(b) are amended to provide that the motion for dismissal at the close of the plaintiff's evidence shall apply only to non-jury cases (including cases tried with an advisory jury). Hereafter the correct motion in jury-tried cases will be the motion for a directed verdict. This involves no change of substance. It should be noted that the court upon a motion for a directed verdict may in appropriate circumstances deny that motion and grant instead a new trial, or a voluntary dismissal without prejudice under Rule 41(a)(2). See 6 Moore's Federal Practice ¶ 59.08[5] (2d ed. 1954); cf. *Cone* v. *West Virginia Pulp & Paper Co.,* 330 U.S. 212, 217, 67 S.Ct. 752, 755, 91 L.Ed. 849 (1947).

The first sentence of Rule 41(b), providing for dismissal for failure to prosecute or to comply with the Rules or any order of court, and the general provisions of the last sentence remain applicable in jury as well as non-jury cases.

The amendment of the last sentence of Rule 41(b) indicates that a dismissal for lack of an indispensable party does not operate as an adjudication on the merits. Such a dismissal does not bar a new action, for it is based merely "on a plaintiff's failure to comply with a precondition requisite to the Court's going forward to determine the merits of his substantive claim." See *Costello* v. *United States,* 365 U.S. 265, 284–288, 81 S.Ct. 534, 544–546, 5 L.Ed.2d 551 & n. 5 (1961); *Mallow* v. *Hinde,* 6 L.Ed. 599, 12 Wheat. (25 U.S.) 193 (1827); Clark, *Code Pleading* 602 (2d ed. 1947); Restatement of Judgments § 49, comm. a, b (1942). This amendment corrects an omission from the rule and is consistent with an earlier amendment, effective in 1948, adding "the defense of failure to join an indispensable party" to clause (1) of Rule 12(h).

1966 AMENDMENT

The terminology is changed to accord with the amendment of Rule 19. See that amended rule and the Advisory Committee's Note thereto.

1968 AMENDMENT

The amendment corrects an inadvertent error in the reference to amended Rule 23.

1987 AMENDMENT

The amendment is technical. No substantive change is intended.

1991 AMENDMENT

Language is deleted that authorized the use of this rule as a means of terminating a non-jury action on the merits when the plaintiff has failed to carry a burden of proof in presenting the plaintiff's case. The device is replaced by the new provisions of Rule 52(c), which authorize entry of judgment against the defendant as well as the plaintiff, and earlier than the close of the case of the party against whom judgment is rendered. A motion to dismiss under Rule 41 on the ground that a plaintiff's evidence is legally insufficient should now be treated as a motion for judgment on partial findings as provided in Rule 52(c).

2007 AMENDMENT

The language of Rule 41 has been amended as part of the general restyling of the Civil Rules to make them more easily understood and to make style and terminology consistent throughout the rules. These changes are intended to be stylistic only.

When Rule 23 was amended in 1966, Rules 23.1 and 23.2 were separated from Rule 23. Rule 41(a)(1) was not then amended to reflect the Rule 23 changes. In 1968 Rule 41(a)(1) was amended to correct the cross-reference to what had become Rule 23(e), but Rules 23.1 and 23.2 were inadvertently overlooked. Rules 23.1 and 23.2 are now added to the list of exceptions in Rule 41(a)(1)(A). This change does not affect established meaning. Rule 23.2 explicitly incorporates Rule 23(e), and thus was already absorbed directly into the exceptions in Rule 41(a)(1). Rule 23.1 requires court approval of a compromise or dismissal in language parallel to Rule 23(e) and thus supersedes the apparent right to dismiss by notice of dismissal.

Rule 42.   Consolidation; Separate Trials

1937 ADOPTION

Subdivision (a) is based upon U.S.C. Title 28, former § 734 (Orders to save costs; consolidation of causes of like nature) but in so far as the statute differs from this rule, it is modified.

For comparable statutes dealing with consolidation see Ark.Dig.Stat. (Crawford & Moses, 1921) § 1081; Cal.Code Civ.Proc. § 1048; N.M.Stat.Ann. (Courtright, 1929), § 105–828; N.Y.C.P.A. (1937) §§ 96, 96a, and 97; American Judicature Society, Bulletin XIV, (1919) Art. 26.

For severance or separate trials, see Calif.Code Civ.Proc. § 1048; N.Y.C.P.A. (1937) § 96; American Judicature Society, Bulletin XIV (1919) Art. 3, § 2 and Art. 10, § 10. See also the third sentence of former Equity Rule 29 (Defenses—How Presented) providing for discretionary separate hearing and disposition before trial of pleas in bar or abatement, and see also Rule 12(d) of these rules for preliminary hearings of defenses and objections.

For the entry of separate judgments, see Rule 54(b)(Judgment at Various Stages).

1966 AMENDMENT

In certain suits in admiralty separation for trial of the issues of liability and damages (or of the extent of liability other than damages, such as salvage and general average) has been conducive to expedition and economy, especially because of the statutory right to interlocutory appeal in admiralty cases (which is of course preserved by these Rules). While separation of issues for trial is not to be routinely ordered, it is important that it be encouraged where experience has demonstrated its worth. Cf. Weinstein, Routine Bifurcation of Negligence Trials, 14 Vand.L.Rev. 831 (1961).

In cases (including some cases within the admiralty and maritime jurisdiction) in which the parties have a constitutional or statutory right of trial by jury, separation of issues may give rise to problems. See *e.g., United Air Lines, Inc.* v. *Wiener*, 286 F.2d 302

(9th Cir.1961). Accordingly, the proposed change in Rule 42 reiterates the mandate of Rule 38 respecting preservation of the right to jury trial.

2007 AMENDMENT

The language of Rule 42 has been amended as part of the general restyling of the Civil Rules to make them more easily understood and to make style and terminology consistent throughout the rules. These changes are intended to be stylistic only.

Rule 43. Taking of Testimony

1937 ADOPTION

Note to Subdivision (a). The first sentence is a restatement of the substance of U.S.C., Title 28, former § 635 (Proof in common-law actions), formerly § 637 (now §§ 2072, 2073)(Proof in equity and admiralty), and former Equity Rule 46 (Trial—Testimony Usually Taken in Open Court—Rulings on Objections to Evidence). This rule abolishes in patent and trademark actions, the practice under former Equity Rule 48 of setting forth in affidavits the testimony in chief of expert witnesses whose testimony is directed to matters of opinion. The second and third sentences on admissibility of evidence and Subdivision (b) on contradiction and cross-examination modify U.S.C., Title 28, formerly § 725 (now § 1652) (Laws of states as rules of decision) insofar as that statute has been construed to prescribe conformity to state rules of evidence. Compare Callihan and Ferguson, *Evidence and the new Federal Rules of Civil Procedure,* 45 Yale L.J. 622 (1936), and *Same* : 2, 47 Yale L.J. 195 (1937). The last sentence modifies to the extent indicated U.S.C., Title 28, § 631 (Competency of witnesses governed by State laws).

Note to Subdivision (b). See 4 Wigmore on Evidence (2d ed., 1923) § 1885 et seq.

Note to Subdivision (c). See former Equity Rule 46 (Trial—Testimony Usually Taken in Open Court—Rulings on Objections to Evidence). With the last sentence compare *Dowagiac Mfg. Co.* v. *Lochren,* 143 Fed. 211 (C.C.A. 8 1906). See also *Blease* v. *Garlington,* 92 U.S. 1, 23 L.Ed. 521 (1876); *Nelson* v. *United States,* 201 U.S. 92, 114, 26 S.Ct. 358, 365, 50 L.Ed. 673 (1906); *Unkle* v. *Wills,* 281 Fed. 29 (8th.Cir.1922).

See Rule 61 for harmless error in either the admission or exclusion of evidence.

Note to Subdivision (d). See former Equity Rule 78 (Affirmation in Lieu of Oath) and U.S.C. Title 1, § 1 (Words importing singular number, masculine gender, etc.; extended application), providing for affirmation in lieu of oath.

SUPPLEMENTARY NOTE ON ADVISORY COMMITTEE REGARDING RULES 43 AND 44

Note. These rules have been criticized and suggested improvements offered by commentators. 1 Wigmore on Evidence, 3d ed. 1940, 200–204; Green, The Admissibility of Evidence Under the Federal Rules, 1941, 55 Harv.L.Rev. 197. Cases indicate, however, that the rule is working better than these commentators had expected. *Boerner* v. *United States,* C.C.A.2d, 1941, 117 F.2d 387, cert. den., 1941, 313 U.S. 587, 61 S.Ct. 1120, 85 L.Ed. 1542; *Mosson* v. *Liberty Fast Freight Co.,* C.C.A.2d, 1942, 124 F.2d 448; *Hartford Accident & Indemnity Co.* v. *Olivier,* C.C.A. 5th, 1941, 123 F.2d 709; *Anzano* v. *Metropolitan Life Ins. Co. of New York,* C.C.A.3d, 1941, 118 F.2d 430; *Franzen* v. *E. I. DuPont De Nemours & Co.,* C.C.A.3d, 1944, 146 F.2d 837; *Fakouri* v. *Cadais,* C.C.A. 5th, 1945, 147 F.2d 667; *In re C. & P. Co.,* S.D.Cal.1945, 63 F.Supp. 400, 408. But cf. *United States* v. *Aluminum Co. of America,* S.D.N.Y.1938, 1 Fed.Rules Serv. 43a.3, Case 1; Note, 1946, 46 Col.L.Rev. 267. While consideration of a comprehensive and detailed set of rules of evidence seems very desirable, it has not been feasible for the Committee so far to undertake this important task. Such consideration should include the adaptability to federal practice of all or parts of the proposed Code of Evidence of the American Law Institute. See Armstrong, Proposed Amendments to Federal Rules of Civil Procedure, 4 F.R.D. 124, 137–138.

1966 AMENDMENT

Note to Subdivision (f). This new subdivision authorizes the court to appoint interpreters (including interpreters for the deaf), to provide for their compensation, and to tax the compensation as costs. Compare proposed subdivision (b) of Rule 28 of the Federal Rules of Criminal Procedure.

1972 AMENDMENTS

Rule 43, entitled Evidence, has heretofore served as the basic rule of evidence for civil cases in federal courts. Its very general provisions are superseded by the detailed provisions of the new Rules of Evidence. The original title and many of the provisions of the rule are, therefore, no longer appropriate.

Subdivision (a). The provision for taking testimony in open court is not duplicated in the Rules of Evidence and is retained. Those dealing with admissibility of evidence and competency of witnesses, however, are no longer needed or appropriate since those topics are covered at large in the Rules of Evidence. They are accordingly deleted. The language is broadened, however, to take account of acts of Congress dealing with the taking of testimony, as well as of the Rules of Evidence and any other rules adopted by the Supreme Court.

Subdivision (b). The subdivision is no longer needed or appropriate since the matters with which it deals are treated in the Rules of Evidence. The use of leading questions, both generally and in the interrogation of an adverse party or witness identified with him, is the subject of Evidence Rule 611(c). Who may impeach is treated in Evidence Rule 607, and scope of cross-examination is covered in Evidence Rule 611(b). The subdivision is accordingly deleted.

Subdivision (c). Offers of proof and making a record of excluded evidence are treated in Evidence Rule 103. The subdivision is no longer needed or appropriate and is deleted.

1987 AMENDMENT

The amendment is technical. No substantive change is intended.

1996 AMENDMENT

Rule 43(a) is revised to conform to the style conventions adopted for simplifying the present Civil Rules. The only intended changes of meaning are described below.

The requirement that testimony be taken "orally" is deleted. The deletion makes it clear that testimony of a witness may be given in open court by other means if the witness is not able to communicate orally. Writing or sign language are common examples. The development of advanced technology may enable testimony to be given by other means. A witness unable to sign or write by hand may be able to communicate through a computer or similar device.

Contemporaneous transmission of testimony from a different location is permitted only on showing good cause in compelling circumstances. The importance of presenting live testimony in court cannot be forgotten. The very ceremony of trial and the presence of the factfinder may exert a powerful force for truthtelling. The opportunity to judge the demeanor of a witness face-to- face is accorded great value in our tradition. Transmission cannot be justified merely by showing that it is inconvenient for the witness to attend the trial.

The most persuasive showings of good cause and compelling circumstances are likely to arise when a witness is unable to attend trial for unexpected reasons, such as accident or illness, but remains able to testify from a different place. Contemporaneous transmission may be better than an attempt to reschedule the trial, particularly if there is a risk that other—and perhaps more important—witnesses might not be available at a later time.

Other possible justifications for remote transmission must be approached cautiously. Ordinarily depositions, including video depositions, provide a superior means of securing the testimony of a witness who is beyond the reach of a trial subpoena, or of resolving difficulties in scheduling a trial that can be attended by all witnesses. Deposition procedures ensure the opportunity of all parties to be represented while the witness is testifying. An unforeseen need for the testimony of a remote witness that arises during trial, however, may establish good cause and compelling circumstances. Justification is particularly likely if the need arises from the interjection of new issues during trial or from the unexpected inability to present testimony as planned from a different witness.

Good cause and compelling circumstances may be established with relative ease if all parties agree that testimony should be presented by transmission. The court is not bound by a stipulation, however, and can insist on live testimony. Rejection of the parties' agreement will be influenced, among other factors, by the apparent importance of the testimony in the full context of the trial.

A party who could reasonably foresee the circumstances offered to justify transmission of testimony will have special difficulty in showing good cause and the compelling nature of the circumstances. Notice of a desire to transmit testimony from a different location should be given as soon as the reasons are known, to enable other parties to arrange a deposition, or to secure an advance ruling on transmission so as to know whether to prepare to be present with the witness while testifying.

No attempt is made to specify the means of transmission that may be used. Audio transmission without video images may be sufficient in some circumstances, particularly as to less important testimony. Video transmission ordinarily should be preferred when the cost is reasonable in relation to the matters in dispute, the means of the parties, and the circumstances that justify transmission. Transmission that merely produces the equivalent of a written statement ordinarily should not be used.

Safeguards must be adopted that ensure accurate identification of the witness and that protect against influence by persons present with the witness. Accurate transmission likewise must be assured.

Other safeguards should be employed to ensure that advance notice is given to all parties of foreseeable circumstances that may lead the proponent to offer testimony by transmission. Advance notice is important to protect the opportunity to argue for attendance of the witness at trial. Advance notice also ensures an opportunity to depose the witness, perhaps by video record, as a means of supplementing transmitted testimony.

2007 AMENDMENT

The language of Rule 43 has been amended as part of the general restyling of the Civil Rules to make them more easily understood and to make style and terminology consistent throughout the rules. These changes are intended to be stylistic only.

Rule 44. Proof of Official Record

1937 ADOPTION

This rule provides a simple and uniform method of proving public records, and entry or lack of entry therein, in all cases including those specifically provided for by statutes of the United States. Such statutes are not superseded, however, and proof may also be made according to their provisions whenever they differ from this rule.

Some of those statutes are:

U.S.C., Title 28, former:

§ 661 (Copies of department or corporation records and papers; admissibility; seal)

§ 662 (Same; in office of General Counsel of the Treasury)

§ 663 (Instruments and papers of Comptroller of Currency; admissibility)

§ 664 (Organization certificates of national banks; admissibility)

§ 665 (Transcripts from books of Treasury in suits against delinquents; admissibility)

§ 666 (Same; certificate by Secretary or Assistant Secretary)

§ 670 (Admissibility of copies of statements of demands by Post Office Department)

§ 671 (Admissibility of copies of post office records and statement of accounts)

§ 672 (Admissibility of copies of records in General Land Office)

§ 673 (Admissibility of copies of records, and so forth, of Patent Office)

§ 674 (Copies of foreign letters patent as prima facie evidence)

§ 675 (Copies of specifications and drawings of patents admissible)

§ 676 (Extracts from Journals of Congress admissible when injunction of secrecy removed)

§ 677 (Copies of records in offices of United States consuls admissible)

§ 678 (Books and papers in certain district courts)

§ 679 (Records in clerks' offices, western district of North Carolina)

§ 680 (Records in clerks' offices of former district of California)

§ 681 (Original records lost or destroyed; certified copy admissible)

§ 682 (Same; when certified copy not obtainable)

§ 685 (Same; certified copy of official papers)

§ 687 (Authentication of legislative acts; proof of judicial proceedings of State)

§ 688 (Proofs of records in offices not pertaining to courts)

§ 689 (Copies of foreign records relating to land titles)

§ 695 (Writings and records made in regular course of business; admissibility)

§ 695e (Foreign documents on record in public offices; certification)

U.S.C., Title 1:

§ 112 (Statutes at large; contents; admissibility in evidence)

§ 113 ("Little and Brown's" edition of laws and treaties competent evidence of Acts of Congress)

§ 204 (Codes and supplements as establishing prima facie the laws of United States and District of Columbia, etc.)

§ 208 (Copies of supplements to Code of Laws of United States and of District of Columbia Code and supplements; conclusive evidence of original)

U.S.C., Title 5:

§ 490 (Records of Department of Interior; authenticated copies as evidence)

U.S.C., Title 6:

§ 7 (Surety Companies as sureties; appointment of agents; service of process)

U.S.C., Title 8:

§ 9a (Citizenship of children of persons naturalized under certain laws; repatriation of native-born women married to aliens prior to September 22, 1922; copies of proceedings)

§ 1443 (Regulations for execution of naturalization laws; certified copies of papers as evidence)

§ 1443 (Certifications of naturalization records; authorization; admissibility as evidence)

U.S.C., Title 11:

§ 44(d), (e), (f), (g) (Bankruptcy court proceedings and orders as evidence)

U.S.C., Title 15:

§ 127 (Trade-mark records in Patent Office; copies as evidence)

U.S.C., Title 20:

§ 52 (Smithsonian Institution; evidence of title to site and buildings)

U.S.C., Title 25:

§ 6 (Bureau of Indian Affairs; seal; authenticated and certified documents; evidence)

U.S.C., Title 31:

§ 46 (Laws governing General Accounting Office; copies of books, records, etc., thereof as evidence)

U.S.C., Title 38:

§ 11g (Seal of Veterans' Administration; authentication of copies of records)

U.S.C., Title 40:

§ 238 (National Archives; seal; reproduction of archives; fee; admissibility in evidence of reproductions)

§ 270c (Bonds of contractors for public works; right of person furnishing labor or material to copy of bond)

U.S.C., Title 43:

§§ 57–59 (Copies of land surveys, etc., in certain states and districts admissible as evidence)

§ 83 (General Land Office registers and receivers; transcripts of records as evidence)

U.S.C., Title 46:

§ 823 (Records of Maritime Commission; copies; publication of reports; evidence)

U.S.C., Title 47:

§ 154(m) (Federal Communications Commission; copies of reports and decisions as evidence)

§ 412 (Documents filed with Federal Communications Commission as public records; prima facie evidence; confidential records)

U.S.C., Title 49:

§ 14(3) (Interstate Commerce Commission reports and decisions; printing and distribution of copies)

§ 16(13) (Copies of schedules, tariffs, etc., filed with Interstate Commerce Commission as evidence)

§ 19a(i) (Valuation of property of carriers by Interstate Commerce Commission; final published valuations as evidence)

SUPPLEMENTARY NOTE OF ADVISORY COMMITTEE
REGARDING RULES 43 AND 44

For supplementary note of Advisory Committee on this rule, see note under Rule 43.

1966 AMENDMENT

Subdivision (a)(1). These provisions on proof or official records kept within the United States are similar in substance to those heretofore appearing in Rule 44. There is a more exact description of the geographical areas covered. An official record kept in one of the areas enumerated qualifies for proof under subdivision (a)(1) even though it is not a United States official record. For example, an official record kept in one of these areas by a government in exile falls within subdivision (a)(1). It also falls within subdivision (a)(2) which may be availed of alternatively. *Cf. Banco de Espana v. Federal Reserve Bank*, 114 F.2d 438 (2d Cir.1940).

Subdivision (a)(2). Foreign official records may be proved, as heretofore, by means of official publications thereof. See *United States v. Aluminum Co. of America*, 1 F.R.D. 71 (S.D.N.Y.1939). Under this rule a document that, on its face, appears to be an official publication, is admissible, unless a party opposing its admission into evidence shows that it lacks that character.

The rest of subdivision (a)(2) aims to provide greater clarity, efficiency, and flexibility in the procedure for authenticating copies of foreign official records.

The reference to attestation by "the officer having the legal custody of the record," hitherto appearing in Rule 44, has been found inappropriate for official records kept in foreign countries where the assumed relation between custody and the authority to attest does not obtain. See 2B Barron & Holtzoff, Federal Practice & Procedure § 992 (Wright ed. 1961). Accordingly it is provided that an attested copy may be obtained from any person authorized by the law of the foreign country to make the attestation without regard to whether he is charged with responsibility for maintaining the record or keeping it in his custody.

Under Rule 44 a United States foreign service officer has been called on to certify to the authority of the foreign official attesting the copy as well as the genuineness of his signature and his official position. See Schlesinger, Comparative Law 57 (2d ed. 1959); Smit, International Aspects of Federal Civil Procedure, 61 Colum.L.Rev. 1031, 1063 (1961); 22 C.F.R. § 92.41(a), (e)(1958). This has created practical difficulties. For example, the question of the authority of the foreign officer might raise issues of foreign law which were beyond the knowledge of the United States officer. The difficulties are met under the amended rule by eliminating the element of the authority of the attesting foreign official from the scope of the certifying process, and by specifically permitting use of the chain-certificate method. Under this method, it is sufficient if the original attestation purports to have been issued by an authorized person and is accompanied by a certificate of another foreign official whose certificate may in turn be followed by that of a foreign official of higher rank. The process continues until a foreign official is reached as to whom the United States foreign service official (or a diplomatic or consular officer of the foreign country assigned or accredited to the United States) has adequate information upon which to base a "final certification." See *New York Life Ins. Co. v. Aronson*, 38 F.Supp. 687 (W.D.Pa.1941); 22 C.F.R. § 92.37 (1958).

The final certification (a term used in contradistinction to the certificates prepared by the foreign officials in a chain) relates to the incumbency and genuineness of signature of the foreign official who attested the copy of the record or, where the chain-certificate method is used, of a foreign official whose certificate appears in the chain, whether that certificate is the last in the chain or not. A final certification may be prepared on the basis of material on file in the consulate or any other satisfactory information.

Although the amended rule will generally facilitate proof of foreign official records, it is recognized that in some situations it may be difficult or even impossible to satisfy the basic requirements of the rule. There may be no United States consul in a particular foreign country; the foreign officials may not cooperate, peculiarities may exist or arise hereafter in the law or practice of a foreign country. See *United States v. Grabina*, 119 F.2d 863 (2d Cir.1941); and, generally, Jones, International Judicial Assistance: Procedural Chaos and a Program for Reform, 62 Yale L.J. 515, 548–49 (1953). Therefore the final sentence of subdivision (a)(2) provides the court with discretion to admit an attested copy of a record without a final certification, or an attested summary of a record with or without a final certification. See Rep. of Comm. on Comparative Civ. Proc. & Prac., Proc. A.B.A., Sec. Int'l & Comp. L. 123, 130–131 (1952); Model Code of evidence §§ 517, 519 (1942). This relaxation should be permitted only when it is shown that the party has been unable to satisfy the basic requirements of the amended rule despite his reasonable efforts. Moreover, it is specially provided that the parties must be given a reasonable opportunity in these cases to examine into the authenticity and accuracy of the copy or summary.

Subdivision (b). This provision relating to proof of lack of record is accommodated to the changes made in subdivision (a).

Subdivision (c). The amendment insures that international agreements of the United States are unaffected by the rule. Several consular conventions contain provisions for reception of copies or summaries of foreign official records. See e.g., Consular Conv. with Italy, May 8, 1878, art. X, 20 Stat. 725, T.S. No. 178 (Dept. State 1878). See also 28 U.S.C. §§ 1740–42, 1745; *Fakouri v. Cadais*, 149 F.2d 321 (5th Cir.1945), cert. denied, 326 U.S. 742, 66 S.Ct. 54, 90 L.Ed. 443 (1945); 5 Moore's Federal Practice, par. 44.05 (2d ed. 1951).

1987 AMENDMENT

The amendments are technical. No substantive change is intended.

1991 AMENDMENT

The amendment to paragraph (a)(1) strikes the references to specific territories, two of which are no longer subject to the jurisdiction of the United States, and adds a generic term to describe governments having a relationship with the United States such that their official records should be treated as domestic records.

The amendment to paragraph (a)(2) adds a sentence to dispense with the final certification by diplomatic officers when the United States and the foreign country where the record is located are parties to a treaty or convention that abolishes or displaces the requirement. In that event the treaty or convention is to be followed. This changes the former procedure for authenticating foreign official records only with respect to records from countries that are parties to the Hague Convention Abolishing the Requirement of Legalization for Foreign Public Documents. Moreover, it does not affect the former practice of attesting the records, but only changes the method of certifying the attestation.

The Hague Public Documents Convention provides that the requirement of a final certification is abolished and replaced with a model *apostille,* which is to be issued by officials of the country where the records are located. See Hague Public Documents Convention, Arts. 2–4. The *apostille* certifies the signature, official position, and seal of the attesting officer. The authority who issues the *apostille* must maintain a register or card index showing the serial number of the *apostille* and other relevant information recorded on it. A foreign court can then check the serial number and information on the *apostille* with the issuing authority in order to guard against the use of fraudulent *apostilles.* This system provides a reliable method for maintaining the integrity of the authentication process, and the *apostille* can be accorded greater weight than the normal authentication procedure because foreign officials are more likely to know the precise capacity under their law of the attesting officer than would an American official. See generally Comment, *The United States and the Hague Convention Abolishing the Requirement of Legalization for Foreign Public Documents,* 11 HARV. INT'L L.J. 476, 482, 488 (1970).

2007 AMENDMENT

The language of Rule 44 has been amended as part of the general restyling of the Civil Rules to make them more easily understood and to make style and terminology consistent throughout the rules. These changes are intended to be stylistic only.

Rule 44.1.   Determination of Foreign Law

1966 ADDITIONS

Rule 44.1 is added by amendment to furnish Federal courts with a uniform and effective procedure for raising and determining an issue concerning the law of a foreign country.

To avoid unfair surprise, the first sentence of the new rule requires that a party who intends to raise an issue of foreign law shall give notice thereof. The uncertainty under Rule 8(a) about whether foreign law must be pleaded—compare *Siegelman v. Cunard White Star, Ltd.*, 221 F.2d 189 (2d Cir.1955), and *Pedersen v. United States*, 191 F.Supp. 95 (D.Guam 1961), with *Harrison v. United Fruit Co.*, 143 F.Supp. 598 (S.D.N.Y.1956)—is eliminated by the provision that the notice shall be "written" and "reasonable." It may, but need not be, incorporated in the pleadings. In some situations the pertinence of foreign law is apparent from the outset; accordingly the necessary investigation of that law will have been accomplished by the party at the pleading stage, and the notice can be given conveniently in the pleadings. In other situations the pertinence of foreign law may remain doubtful until the case is further developed. A requirement that notice of foreign law be given only through the medium of the pleadings would tend in the latter instances to force the party to engage in a peculiarly burdensome type of investigation which might turn out to be unnecessary; and correspondingly the adversary would be forced into a possible wasteful investigation. The liberal provisions for amendment of the pleadings afford help if the pleadings are used as the medium of giving notice of the foreign law; but it seems best to permit a written notice to be given outside of and later than the pleadings, provided the notice is reasonable.

The new rule does not attempt to set any definite limit on the party's time for giving the notice of an issue of foreign law; in some cases the issue may not become apparent until the trial and notice then given may still be reasonable. The stage which the case had reached at the time of the notice, the reason proffered by the party for his failure to give earlier notice, and the importance to the case as a whole of the issue of foreign law sought to be raised, are among the factors which the court should consider in deciding a question of the reasonableness of a notice. If notice is given by one party it need not be repeated by any other and serves as a basis for presentation of material on the foreign law by all parties.

The second sentence of the new rule describes the materials to which the court may resort in determining an issue of foreign law. Heretofore the district courts, applying Rule 43(a), have looked in certain cases to State law to find the rules of evidence by which the content of foreign-country law is to be established. The State laws vary; some embody procedures which are inefficient, time consuming and expensive. See, generally, Nussbaum, Proving the Law of Foreign Countries, 3 Am.J.Comp.L. 60 (1954). In all events the ordinary rules of evidence are often inapposite to the problem of determining foreign law and have in the past prevented examination of material which could have provided a proper basis for the determination. The new rule permits consideration by the court of any relevant material, including testimony, without regard to its admissibility under Rule 43. Cf. N.Y. Civ. Prac. Law & Rules, R. 4511 (Effective Sept. 1, 1963); 2 Va. Code Ann. tit. 8, § 8–273; 2 W. Va. Code Ann. § 5711.

In further recognition of the peculiar nature of the issue of foreign law, the new rule provides that in determining this law the court is not limited by material presented by the parties; it may engage in its own research and consider any relevant material thus found. The court may have at its disposal better foreign law materials than counsel have presented, or may wish to reexamine and amplify material that has been presented by counsel in partisan fashion or in insufficient detail. On the other hand, the court is free to insist on a complete presentation by counsel.

There is no requirement that the court give formal notice to the parties of its intention to engage in its own research on an issue of foreign law which has been raised by them, or of its intention to raise and determine independently an issue not raised by them. Ordinarily the court should inform the parties of material it has found diverging substantially from the material which they have presented; and in general the court should give the parties an opportunity to analyze and counter new points upon which it proposes to rely. See Schlesinger, Comparative Law 142 (2d ed. 1959); Wyzanski, A Trial Judge's Freedom and Responsibility, 65 Harv.L.Rev. 1281, 1296 (1952); cf. *Siegelman* v. *Cunard White Star, Ltd.*, supra, 221 F.2d at 197. To require, however, that the court give formal notice from time to time as it proceeds with its study of the foreign law would add an element of undesirable rigidity to the procedure for determining issues of foreign law.

The new rule refrains from imposing an obligation on the court to take "judicial notice" of foreign law because this would put an extreme burden on the court in many cases; and it avoids use of the concept of "judicial notice" in any form because of the uncertain meaning of that concept as applied to foreign law. See, e.g., Stern, Foreign Law in the Courts: Judicial Notice and Proof, 45 Calif.L.Rev. 23, 43 (1957). Rather the rule provides flexible procedures for presenting and utilizing material on issues of foreign law by which a sound result can be achieved with fairness to the parties.

Under the third sentence, the court's determination of an issue of foreign law is to be treated as a ruling on a question of "law," not "fact," so that appellate review will not be narrowly confined by the "clearly erroneous" standard of Rule 52(a). *Cf. Uniform Judicial Notice of Foreign Law Act* § 3; Note, 72 Harv.L.Rev. 318 (1958).

The new rule parallels Article IV of the Uniform Interstate and International Procedure Act, approved by the Commissioners on Uniform State Laws in 1962, except that section 4.03 of Article IV states that "[t]he court, not the jury" shall determine foreign law. The new rule does not address itself to this problem, since the Rules refrain from allocating functions as between the court and the jury. See Rule 38(a). It has long been thought, however, that the jury is not the appropriate body to determine issues of foreign law. See, e.g., Story, Conflict of Laws, § 638 (1st ed. 1834, 8th ed. 1883); 1 Greenleaf, Evidence, § 486 (1st ed. 1842, 16th ed. 1899); 4 Wigmore, Evidence § 2558 (1st ed. 1905); 9 id. § 2558 (3d ed. 1940). The majority of the States have committed such issues to determination by the court. See Article 5 of the Uniform Judicial Notice of Foreign Law Act, adopted by twenty-six states, 9A U.L.A. 318 (1957)(Suppl.1961, at 134); N.Y.Civ.Prac.Law & Rules, R. 4511 (effective Sept. 1, 1963); Wigmore, loc. cit. And Federal courts that have considered the problem in recent years have reached the same conclusion without reliance on statute. See *Jansson* v. *Swedish American Line*, 185 F.2d 212, 216 (1st Cir.1950); *Bank of Nova Scotia* v. *San Miguel*, 196 F.2d 950, 957, n. 6 (1st Cir.1952); *Liechti* v. *Roche*, 198 F.2d 174 (5th Cir.1952); *Daniel Lumber Co.* v. *Empresas Hondurenas, S.A.*, 215 F.2d 465 (5th Cir.1954).

1972 AMENDMENT

Since the purpose of the provision is to free the judge, in determining foreign law, from any restrictions imposed by evidence rules, a general reference to the Rules of Evidence is appropriate and is made.

1987 AMENDMENT

The amendment is technical. No substantive change is intended.

2007 AMENDMENT

The language of Rule 44.1 has been amended as part of the general restyling of the Civil Rules to make them more easily understood and to make style and terminology consistent throughout the rules. These changes are intended to be stylistic only.

Rule 45. Subpoena

1937 ADOPTION

This rule applies to subpoenas *ad testificandum* and *duces tecum* issued by the district courts for attendance at a hearing or a trial, or to take depositions. It does not apply to the enforcement of subpoenas issued by administrative officers and commissions pursuant to statutory authority. The enforcement of such subpoenas by the district courts is regulated by appropriate statutes. Many of these statutes do not place any territorial limits on the validity of subpoenas so issued, but provide that they may be served anywhere within the United States. Among such statutes are the following:

U.S.C., Title 7, §§ 222 and 511n (Secretary of Agriculture)

U.S.C., Title 15, § 49 (Federal Trade Commission)

U.S.C., Title 15, §§ 77v(b), 78u(c), 79r(d)(Securities and Exchange Commission)

U.S.C., Title 16, §§ 797(g) and 825f (Federal Power Commission)

U.S.C., Title 19, § 1333(b)(Tariff Commission)

U.S.C., Title 22, §§ 268, 270d and 270e (International Commissions, etc.)

U.S.C., Title 26, §§ 614, 619(b) [see 7456] (Board of Tax Appeals)

U.S.C., Title 26, § 1523(a) [see 7608] (Internal Revenue Officers)

U.S.C., Title 29, § 161 (Labor Relations Board)

U.S.C., Title 33, § 506 (Secretary of Army)

U.S.C., Title 35, §§ 54 to 56 [now 24] (Patent Office proceedings)

U.S.C., Title 38, [former] § 133 (Veterans' Administration)

U.S.C., Title 41, § 39 (Secretary of Labor)

U.S.C., Title 45, § 157 Third. (h)(Board of Arbitration under Railway Labor Act)

U.S.C., Title 45, § 222(b)(Investigation Commission under Railroad Retirement Act of 1935)

U.S.C., Title 46, § 1124(b)(Maritime Commission)

U.S.C., Title 47, § 409(c) and (d)(Federal Communications Commission)

U.S.C., Title 49, § 12(2) and (3)(Interstate Commerce Commission)

U.S.C., Title 49, § 173a [see 1484] (Secretary of Commerce)

Note to Subdivisions (a) and (b). These simplify the form of subpoena as provided in U.S.C., Title 28, former § 655 (Witnesses; subpoena; form; attendance under); and broaden U.S.C., Title 28, former § 636 (Production of books and writings) to include all actions, and to extend to any person. With the provision for relief from an oppressive or unreasonable subpoena *duces tecum*, compare N.Y.C.P.A. (1937) § 411.

Note to Subdivision (c). This provides for the simple and convenient method of service permitted under many state codes; e.g., N.Y.C.P.A. (1937) §§ 220, 404, J.Ct.Act, § 191; 3 Wash.Rev.Stat.Ann. (Remington, 1932) § 1218. Compare Equity Rule 15 (Process, by Whom Served).

For statutes governing fees and mileage of witnesses see:

U.S.C., Title 28, former sections:

§ 600a [now 1871] (Per diem; mileage)

§ 600c [now 1821, 1823] (Amount per diem and mileage for witnesses; subsistence)

§ 600d [former] (Fees and mileage in certain states)

§ 601 [former] (Witnesses; fees; enumeration)

§ 602 [now 1824] (Fees and mileage of jurors and witnesses)

§ 603 [see Title 5, §§ 5515, 5537] (No officer of court to have witness fees)

Note to Subdivision (d). The method provided in paragraph (1) for the authorization of the issuance of subpoenas has been employed in some districts. See *Henning v. Boyle*, N.Y.1901, 112 F. 397. The requirement of an order for the issuance of a subpoena *duces tecum* is in accordance with U.S.C., Title 28, former § 647 (Deposition under *dedimus potestatem* ; subpoena *duces tecum*). The provisions of paragraph (2) are in accordance with common practice. See U.S.C., Title 28, former § 648 (Deposition under *dedimus potestatem* ; witnesses, when required to attend); N.Y.C.P.A. (1937) § 300; 1 N.J.Rev.Stat. (1937) 2:27–174.

Note to Subdivision (e). The first paragraph continues the substance of U.S.C., Title 28, [former] § 654 (Witnesses; subpoenas; may run into another district). Compare U.S.C., Title 11, [former] § 69 (Referees in bankruptcy; contempts before)(production of books and writings) which is not affected by this rule. For examples of statutes which allow the court, upon proper application and cause shown, to authorize the clerk of the court to issue a subpoena for a witness who lives in another district and at a greater distance than 100 miles from the place of the hearing or trial, see:

U.S.C., Title 15:

§ 23 (Suits by United States; subpoenas for witnesses)(under anti-trust laws).

U.S.C., Title 38:

§ 445 [now 784] (Actions on claims; jurisdiction; parties; procedure; limitation; witnesses; definitions)(Veterans' insurance contracts).

The second paragraph continues the present procedure applicable to certain witnesses who are in foreign countries. See U.S.C., Title 28, §§ 711 [now 1783] (Letters rogatory to take testimony of witness, addressed to court of foreign country; failure of witness to appear; subpoena) and former § 713 [now 1783] (Service of Subpoena on witness in foreign country).

Note to Subdivision (f). Compare [former] Equity Rule 52 (Attendance of Witnesses Before Commissioner, Master, or Examiner).

1946 AMENDMENT

Note to Subdivision (b). The added words, "or tangible things" in subdivision (b) merely make the rule for the subpoena duces tecum at the trial conform to that of subdivision (d) for the subpoena at the taking of depositions. The insertion of the words "or modify" in clause (1) affords desirable flexibility.

Subdivision (d). The added last sentence of amended subdivision (d)(1) properly gives the subpoena for documents or tangible things the same scope as provided in Rule 26(b), thus promoting uniformity. The requirement in the last sentence of original Rule 45(d)(1)—to the effect that leave of court should be obtained for the issuance of such a subpoena—has been omitted. This requirement is unnecessary and oppressive on both counsel and court, and it had been criticized by district judges. There is no satisfactory reason for a differentiation between a subpoena for the production of documentary evidence by a witness at a trial (Rule 45(a)) and for the production of the same evidence at the taking of a deposition. Under this amendment, the person subpoenaed may obtain the protection afforded by any of the orders permitted under Rule 30(b) or Rule 45(b). See *Application of Zenith Radio Corp.*, Pa.1941, 4 F.Rules Serv. 30b.21, Case 1, 1 F.R.D. 627; *Fox v. House*, Okla.1939, 29 F.Supp. 673; *United States of America for the Use of Tilo Roofing Co., Inc. v. J. Slotnik Co.*, Conn.1944, 3 F.R.D. 408.

The changes in subdivision (d)(2) give the court the same power in the case of residents of the district as is conferred in the case of non-residents, and permit the court to fix a place for attendance which may be more convenient and accessible for the parties than that specified in the rule.

1948 AMENDMENT

The amendment effective October 1949, substituted the reference to "Title 28, U.S.C., § 1783" at the end of subdivision (e)(2) for the reference to "the Act of July 3, 1926, c. 762, §§ 1, 3 (44 Stat. 835), U.S.C., Title 28, § 713."

1970 AMENDMENT

At present when a subpoena duces tecum is issued to a deponent, he is required to produce the listed materials at the deposition, but is under no clear compulsion to permit their inspection and copying. This results in confusion and uncertainty before the time the deposition is taken, with no mechanism provided whereby the court can resolve the matter. Rule 45(d)(1), as revised, makes clear that the subpoena authorizes inspection and copying of the materials produced. The deponent is afforded full protection since he can object, thereby forcing the party serving the subpoena to obtain a court order if he wishes to inspect and copy. The procedure is thus analogous to that provided in Rule 34.

The changed references to other rules conform to changes made in those rules. The deletion of words in the clause describing the proper scope of the subpoena conforms to a change made in the language of Rule 34. The reference to Rule 26(b) is unchanged but encompasses new matter in that subdivision. The changes make it clear that the scope of discovery through a subpoena is the same as that applicable to Rule 34 and the other discovery rules.

1980 AMENDMENT

Subdivision (d)(1). The amendment defines the term "proof of service" as used in the first sentence of the present subdivision. For want of a definition, the district court clerks have been obliged to fashion their own, with results that vary from district to district. All that seems required is a simple certification on a copy of the notice to take a deposition that the notice has been served on every other party to the action. That is the proof of service required by Rule 25(d) of both the Federal Rules of Appellate Procedure and the Supreme Court Rules.

Subdivision (e)(1). The amendment makes the reach of a subpoena of a district court at least as extensive as that of the state courts of general jurisdiction in the state in which the district court is held. Under the present rule the reach of a district court subpoena is often greater, since it extends throughout the district. No reason appears why it should be less, as it sometimes is because of the accident of district lines. Restrictions upon the reach of subpoenas are imposed to prevent undue inconvenience to witnesses. State statutes and rules of court are quite likely to reflect the varying degrees of difficulty and expense attendant upon local travel.

1985 AMENDMENT

Present Rule 45(d)(2) has two sentences setting forth the territorial scope of deposition subpoenas. The first sentence is directed to depositions taken in the judicial district in which the deponent resides; the second sentence addresses situations in which the deponent is not a resident of the district in which the deposition is to take place. The Rule, as currently constituted, creates anomalous situations that often cause logistical problems in conducting litigation.

The first sentence of the present Rule states that a deponent may be required to attend only in the *county* wherein that person resides or is employed or transacts business in person, that is, where the person lives or works. Under this provision a deponent can be compelled, without court order, to travel from one end of that person's home county to the other, no matter how far that may be. The second sentence of the Rule is somewhat more flexible, stating that someone who does not reside in the district in which the deposition is to be taken can be required to attend in the county where the person is served with the subpoena, *or* within 40 miles from the place of service.

Under today's conditions there is no sound reason for distinguishing between residents of the district or county in which a deposition is to be taken and nonresidents, and the Rule is amended to provide that any person may be subpoenaed to attend a deposition within a specified radius from that person's residence, place of business, or where the person was served. The 40-mile radius has been increased to 100 miles.

1987 AMENDMENT

The amendments are technical. No substantive change is intended.

1991 AMENDMENT

Purposes of Revision. The purposes of this revision are (1) to clarify and enlarge the protections afforded persons who are required to assist the court by giving information or evidence; (2) to facilitate access outside the deposition procedure provided by Rule 30 to documents and other information in the possession of persons who are not parties; (3) to facilitate service of subpoenas for depositions or productions of evidence at places distant from the district in which an action is proceeding; (4) to enable the court to compel a witness found within the state in which the court sits to attend trial; (5) to clarify the organization of the text of the rule.

Subdivision (a). This subdivision is amended in seven significant respects.

First, Paragraph (a)(3) modifies the requirement that a subpoena be issued by the clerk of court. Provision is made for the issuance of subpoenas by attorneys as officers of the court. This revision perhaps culminates an evolution. Subpoenas were long issued by specific order of the court. As this became a burden to the court, general orders were made authorizing clerks to issue subpoenas on request. Since 1948, they have been issued in blank by the clerk of any federal court to any lawyer, the clerk serving as stationer to the bar. In allowing counsel to issue the subpoena, the rule is merely a recognition of present reality.

Although the subpoena is in a sense the command of the attorney who completes the form, defiance of a subpoena is nevertheless an act in defiance of a court order and exposes the defiant witness to contempt sanctions. In *ICC v. Brimson*, 154 U.S. 447, 14 S.Ct. 1125, 38 L.Ed. 1047 (1894), the Court upheld a statute directing federal courts to issue subpoenas to compel testimony before the ICC. In *CAB v. Hermann*, 353 U.S. 322, 77 S.Ct. 804, 1 L.Ed.2d 852 (1957), the Court approved as established practice the issuance of administrative subpoenas as a matter of absolute agency right. And in *NLRB v. Warren Co.*, 350 U.S. 107, 76 S.Ct. 185, 100 L.Ed. 96 (1955), the Court held that the lower court had no discretion to withhold sanctions against a contemnor who violated such subpoenas. The 1948 revision of Rule 45 put the attorney in a position similar to that of the administrative agency, as a public officer entitled to use the court's contempt power to investigate facts in dispute. Two courts of appeals have touched on the issue and have described lawyer-issued subpoenas as mandates of the court. *Waste Conversion, Inc. v. Rollins Environmental Services (NJ), Inc.*, 893 F.2d 605 (3d Cir.1990); *Fisher v. Marubeni Cotton Corp.*, 526 F.2d 1338, 1340 (8th Cir.1975). Cf. *Young v. United States ex rel. Vuitton et Fils S.A.*, 481 U.S. 787, 821, 107 S.Ct. 2124, 2145, 95 L.Ed.2d 740 (1987)(Scalia, J., concurring). This revision makes the rule explicit that the attorney acts as an officer of the court in issuing and signing subpoenas.

Necessarily accompanying the evolution of this power of the lawyer as officer of the court is the development of increased responsibility and liability for the misuse of this power. The latter development is reflected in the provisions of subdivision (c) of this rule, and also in the requirement imposed by paragraph (3) of this subdivision that the attorney issuing a subpoena must sign it.

Second, Paragraph (a)(3) authorizes attorneys in distant districts to serve as officers authorized to issue commands in the name of the court. Any attorney permitted to represent a client in a federal court, even one admitted pro haec vice, has the same authority as a clerk to issue a subpoena from any federal court for the district in which the subpoena is served and enforced. In authorizing attorneys to issue subpoenas from distant courts, the amended rule effectively authorizes service of a subpoena anywhere in the United States by an attorney representing any party. This change is intended to ease the administrative burdens of inter-district law practice. The former rule resulted in delay and expense caused by the need to secure forms from clerks' offices some distance from the place at which the action proceeds. This change does not enlarge the burden on the witness.

Pursuant to Paragraph (a)(2), a subpoena for a deposition must still issue from the court in which the deposition or production would be compelled. Accordingly, a motion to quash such a subpoena if it overbears the limits of the subpoena power must, as under the previous rule, be presented to the court for the district in which the deposition would occur. Likewise, the court in whose name the subpoena is issued is responsible for its enforcement.

Third, in order to relieve attorneys of the need to secure an appropriate seal to affix to a subpoena issued as an officer of a distant court, the requirement that a subpoena be under seal is abolished by the provisions of Paragraph (a)(1).

Fourth, Paragraph (a)(1) authorizes the issuance of a subpoena to compel a non-party to produce evidence independent of any deposition. This revision spares the necessity of a deposition of the custodian of evidentiary material required to be produced. A party seeking additional production from a person subject to such a subpoena may serve an additional subpoena requiring additional production at the same time and place.

Fifth, Paragraph (a)(2) makes clear that the person subject to the subpoena is required to produce materials in that person's control whether or not the materials are located within the district or within the territory within which the subpoena can be served. The non-party witness is subject to the same scope of discovery under this rule as that person would be as a party to whom a request is addressed pursuant to Rule 34.

Sixth, Paragraph (a)(1) requires that the subpoena include a statement of the rights and duties of witnesses by setting forth in full the text of the new subdivisions (c) and (d).

Seventh, the revised rule authorizes the issuance of a subpoena to compel the inspection of premises in the possession of a non-party. Rule 34 has authorized such inspections of premises in the possession of a party as discovery compelled under Rule 37, but prior practice required an independent proceeding to secure such relief ancillary to the federal proceeding when the premises were not in the possession of a party. Practice in some states has long authorized such use of a subpoena for this purpose without apparent adverse consequence.

Subdivision (b). Paragraph (b)(1) retains the text of the former subdivision (c) with minor changes.

The reference to the United States marshal and deputy marshal is deleted because of the infrequency of the use of these officers for this purpose. Inasmuch as these officers meet the age requirement, they may still be used if available.

A provision requiring service of prior notice pursuant to Rule 5 of compulsory pretrial production or inspection has been added to paragraph (b)(1). The purpose of such notice is to afford other parties an opportunity to object to the production or inspection, or to serve a demand for additional documents or things. Such additional notice is not needed with respect to a deposition because of the requirement of notice imposed by Rule 30 or 31. But when production or inspection is sought independently of a deposition, other parties may need notice in order to monitor the discovery and in order to pursue access to any information that may or should be produced.

Paragraph (b)(2) retains language formerly set forth in subdivision (e) and extends its application to subpoenas for depositions or production.

Paragraph (b)(3) retains language formerly set forth in paragraph (d)(1) and extends its applications to subpoenas for trial or hearing or production.

Subdivision (c). This provision is new and states the rights of witnesses. It is not intended to diminish rights conferred by Rules 26–37 or any other authority.

Paragraph (c)(1) gives specific application to the principle stated in Rule 26(g) and specifies liability for earnings lost by a non-party witness as a result of a misuse of the subpoena. No change in existing law is thereby effected. Abuse of a subpoena is an actionable tort, *Board of Ed. v. Farmingdale Classroom Teachers Ass'n,* 38 N.Y.2d 397, 380 N.Y.S.2d 635, 343 N.E.2d 278 (1975), and the duty of the attorney to the non-party is also embodied in Model Rule of Professional Conduct 4.4. The liability of the attorney is correlative to the expanded power of the attorney to issue subpoenas. The liability may include the cost of fees to collect attorneys' fees owed as a result of a breach of this duty.

Paragraph (c)(2) retains language from the former subdivision (b) and paragraph (d)(1). The 10–day period for response to a subpoena is extended to 14 days to avoid the complex calculations associated with short time periods under Rule 6 and to allow a bit more time for such objections to be made.

A non-party required to produce documents or materials is protected against significant expense resulting from involuntary assistance to the court. This provision applies, for example, to a non-party required to provide a list of class members. The court is not required to fix the costs in advance of production, although this will often be the most satisfactory accommodation to protect the party seeking discovery from excessive costs. In some instances, it may be preferable to leave uncertain costs to be determined after the materials have been produced, provided that the risk of uncertainty is fully disclosed to the discovering party. See, *e.g., United States v. Columbia Broadcasting System, Inc.,* 666 F.2d 364 (9th Cir.1982).

Paragraph (c)(3) explicitly authorizes the quashing of a subpoena as a means of protecting a witness from misuse of the subpoena power. It replaces and enlarges on the former subdivision (b) of this rule and tracks the provisions of Rule 26(c). While largely repetitious, this rule is addressed to the witness who may read it on the subpoena, where it is required to be printed by the revised paragraph (a)(1) of this rule.

Subparagraph (c)(3)(A) identifies those circumstances in which a subpoena must be quashed or modified. It restates the former provisions with respect to the limits of mandatory travel that are set forth in the former paragraphs (d)(2) and (e)(1), with one important change. Under the revised rule, a federal court can compel a witness to come from any place in the state to attend trial, whether or not the local state law so provides. This extension is subject to the qualification provided in the next paragraph, which authorizes the court to condition enforcement of a subpoena compelling a non-party witness to bear substantial expense to attend trial. The traveling non-party witness may be entitled to reasonable compensation for the time and effort entailed.

Clause (c)(3)(A)(iv) requires the court to protect all persons from undue burden imposed by the use of the subpoena power. Illustratively, it might be unduly burdensome to compel an adversary to attend trial as a witness if the adversary is known to have no personal knowledge of matters in dispute, especially so if the adversary would be required to incur substantial travel burdens.

Subparagraph (c)(3)(B) identifies circumstances in which a subpoena should be quashed unless the party serving the subpoena shows a substantial need and the court can devise an appropriate accommodation to protect the interests of the witness. An additional circumstance in which such action is required is a request for costly production of documents; that situation is expressly governed by subparagraph (b)(2)(B).

Clause (c)(3)(B)(i) authorizes the court to quash, modify, or condition a subpoena to protect the person subject to or affected by the subpoena from unnecessary or unduly harmful disclosures of confidential information. It corresponds to Rule 26(c)(7).

Clause (c)(3)(B)(ii) provides appropriate protection for the intellectual property of the non-party witness; it does not apply to the expert retained by a party, whose information is subject to the provisions of Rule 26(b)(4). A growing problem has been the use of subpoenas to compel the giving of evidence and information by unretained experts. Experts are not exempt from the duty to give evidence, even if they cannot be compelled to prepare themselves to give effective testimony, *e.g., Carter–Wallace, Inc. v. Otte,* 474 F.2d 529 (2d Cir.1972), but compulsion to give evidence may threaten the intellectual property of experts denied the opportunity to bargain for the value of their services. See generally Maurer, *Compelling the Expert Witness: Fairness and Utility Under the Federal Rules of Civil Procedure,* 19 GA.L.REV. 71 (1984); Note, *Discovery and Testimony of Unretained Experts,* 1987 DUKE L.J. 140. Arguably the compulsion to testify can be regarded as a "taking" of intellectual property. The rule establishes the right of such persons to withhold their expertise, at least unless the party seeking it makes the kind of showing required for a conditional denial of a motion to quash as provided in the final sentence of subparagraph (c)(3)(B); that requirement is the same as that necessary to secure work product under Rule 26(b)(3) and gives assurance of reasonable compensation. The Rule thus approves the accommodation of competing interests exemplified in *United States v. Columbia Broadcasting System Inc.*, 666 F.2d 364 (9th Cir.1982). See also *Wright v. Jeep Corporation*, 547 F.Supp. 871 (E.D.Mich.1982).

As stated in *Kaufman v. Edelstein*, 539 F.2d 811, 822 (2d Cir.1976), the district court's discretion in these matters should be informed by "the degree to which the expert is being called because of his knowledge of facts relevant to the case rather than in order to give opinion testimony; the difference between testifying to a previously formed or expressed opinion and forming a new one; the possibility that, for other reasons, the witness is a unique expert; the extent to which the calling party is able to show the unlikelihood that any comparable witness will willingly testify; and the degree to which the witness is able to show that he has been oppressed by having continually to testify...."

Clause (c)(3)(B)(iii) protects non-party witnesses who may be burdened to perform the duty to travel in order to provide testimony at trial. The provision requires the court to condition a subpoena requiring travel of more than 100 miles on reasonable compensation.

Subdivision (d). This provision is new. Paragraph (d)(1) extends to non-parties the duty imposed on parties by the last paragraph of Rule 34(b), which was added in 1980.

Paragraph (d)(2) is new and corresponds to the new Rule 26(b)(5) [paragraph (5) in Rule 26(b) was a proposed paragraph which was withdrawn by the Supreme Court]. Its purpose is to provide a party whose discovery is constrained by a claim of privilege or work product protection with information sufficient to evaluate such a claim and to resist if it seems unjustified. The person claiming a privilege or protection cannot decide the limits of that party's own entitlement.

A party receiving a discovery request who asserts a privilege or protection but fails to disclose that claim is at risk of waiving the privilege or protection. A person claiming a privilege or protection who fails to provide adequate information about the privilege or protection claim to the party seeking the information is subject to an order to show cause why the person should not be held in contempt under subdivision (e). Motions for such orders and responses to motions are subject to the sanctions provisions of Rules 7 and 11.

A person served a subpoena that is too broad may be faced with a burdensome task to provide full information regarding all that person's claims to privilege or work product protection. Such a person is entitled to protection that may be secured through an objection made pursuant to paragraph (c)(2).

Subdivision (e). This provision retains most of the language of the former subdivision (f).

"Adequate cause" for a failure to obey a subpoena remains undefined. In at least some circumstances, a non-party might be guilty of contempt for refusing to obey a subpoena even though the subpoena manifestly overreaches the appropriate limits of the subpoena power. *E.g., Walker v. City of Birmingham*, 388 U.S. 307, 87 S.Ct. 1824, 18 L.Ed.2d 1210 (1967). But, because the command of the subpoena is not in fact one uttered by a judicial officer, contempt should be very sparingly applied when the non-party witness has been overborne by a party or attorney. The language added to subdivision (f) is intended to assure that result where a non-party has been commanded, on the signature of an attorney, to travel greater distances than can be compelled pursuant to this rule.

2005 AMENDMENT

This amendment closes a small gap in regard to notifying witnesses of the manner for recording a deposition. A deposition subpoena must state the method for recording the testimony.

Rule 30(b)(2) directs that the party noticing a deposition state in the notice the manner for recording the testimony, but the notice need not be served on the deponent. The deponent learns of the recording method only if the deponent is a party or is informed by a party. Rule 30(b)(3) permits another party to designate an additional method of recording with prior notice to the deponent and the other parties. The deponent thus has notice of the recording method when an additional method is designated. This amendment completes the notice provisions to ensure that a nonparty deponent has notice of the recording method when the recording method is described only in the deposition notice.

A subpoenaed witness does not have a right to refuse to proceed with a deposition due to objections to the manner of recording. But under rare circumstances, a nonparty witness might have a ground for seeking a protective order under Rule 26(c) with regard to the manner of recording or the use of the deposition if recorded in a certain manner. Should such a witness not learn of the manner of recording until the deposition begins, undesir-

1536

able delay or complication might result. Advance notice of the recording method affords an opportunity to raise such protective issues.

Other changes are made to conform Rule 45(a)(2) to current style conventions.

2006 AMENDMENTS

Rule 45 is amended to conform the provisions for subpoenas to changes in other discovery rules, largely related to discovery of electronically stored information. Rule 34 is amended to provide in greater detail for the production of electronically stored information. Rule 45(a)(1)(C) is amended to recognize that electronically stored information, as defined in Rule 34(a), can also be sought by subpoena. Like Rule 34(b), Rule 45(a)(1) is amended to provide that the subpoena can designate a form or forms for production of electronic data. Rule 45(c)(2) is amended, like Rule 34(b), to authorize the person served with a subpoena to object to the requested form or forms. In addition, as under Rule 34(b), Rule 45(d)(1)(B) is amended to provide that if the subpoena does not specify the form or forms for electronically stored information, the person served with the subpoena must produce electronically stored information in a form or forms in which it is usually maintained or in a form or forms that are reasonably usable. Rule 45(d)(1)(C) is added to provide that the person producing electronically stored information should not have to produce the same information in more than one form unless so ordered by the court for good cause.

As with discovery of electronically stored information from parties, complying with a subpoena for such information may impose burdens on the responding person. Rule 45(c) provides protection against undue impositions on nonparties. For example, Rule 45(c)(1) directs that a party serving a subpoena "shall take reasonable steps to avoid imposing undue burden or expense on a person subject to the subpoena," and Rule 45(c)(2)(B) permits the person served with the subpoena to object to it and directs that an order requiring compliance "shall protect a person who is neither a party nor a party's officer from significant expense resulting from" compliance. Rule 45(d)(1)(D) is added to provide that the responding person need not provide discovery of electronically stored information from sources the party identifies as not reasonably accessible, unless the court orders such discovery for good cause, considering the limitations of Rule 26(b)(2)(C), on terms that protect a nonparty against significant expense. A parallel provision is added to Rule 26(b)(2).

Rule 45(a)(1)(B) is also amended, as is Rule 34(a), to provide that a subpoena is available to permit testing and sampling as well as inspection and copying. As in Rule 34, this change recognizes that on occasion the opportunity to perform testing or sampling may be important, both for documents and for electronically stored information. Because testing or sampling may present particular issues of burden or intrusion for the person served with the subpoena, however, the protective provisions of Rule 45(c) should be enforced with vigilance when such demands are made. Inspection or testing of certain types of electronically stored information or of a person's electronic information system may raise issues of confidentiality or privacy. The addition of sampling and testing to Rule 45(a) with regard to documents and electronically stored information is not meant to create a routine right of direct access to a person's electronic information system, although such access might be justified in some circumstances. Courts should guard against undue intrusiveness resulting from inspecting or testing such systems.

Rule 45(d)(2) is amended, as is Rule 26(b)(5), to add a procedure for assertion of privilege or of protection as trial-preparation materials after production. The receiving party may submit the information to the court for resolution of the privilege claim, as under Rule 26(b)(5)(B).

Other minor amendments are made to conform the rule to the changes described above.

2007 AMENDMENT

The language of Rule 45 has been amended as part of the general restyling of the Civil Rules to make them more easily understood and to make style and terminology consistent throughout the rules. These changes are intended to be stylistic only.

The reference to discovery of "books" in former Rule 45(a)(1)(C) was deleted to achieve consistent expression throughout the discovery rules. Books remain a proper subject of discovery.

Former Rule 45(b)(1) required "prior notice" to each party of any commanded production of documents and things or inspection of premises. Courts have agreed that notice must be given "prior" to the return date, and have tended to converge on an interpretation that requires notice to the parties before the subpoena is served on the person commanded to produce or permit inspection. That interpretation is adopted in amended Rule 45(b)(1) to give clear notice of general present practice.

The language of former Rule 45(d)(2) addressing the manner of asserting privilege is replaced by adopting the wording of Rule 26(b)(5). The same meaning is better expressed in the same words.

Rule 46. Exceptions Unnecessary

1937 ADOPTION

Abolition of formal exceptions is often provided by statute. See Ill.Rev.Stat. (1937), ch. 110, § 204; Neb.Comp.Stat. (1929) § 20–1139; N.M.Stat.Ann. (Courtright, 1929) § 105–830; 2 N.D.Comp.Laws Ann. (1913) § 7653; Ohio Code Ann. (Throckmorton, 1936) § 11560; 1 S.D.Comp.Laws (1929) § 2542; Utah Rev.Stat.Ann. (1933) §§ 104–39–2, 104–24–18; Va.Rules of Court, Rule 22, 163 Va. v. xii (1935); Wis.Stat. (1935) § 270.39. Compare N.Y.C.P.A. (1937) §§ 583, 445, and 446, all as amended by L.1936, ch. 915. Rule 51 deals with objections to the court's instructions to the jury.

U.S.C., Title 28, former § 776 (Bill of exceptions; authentication; signing of by judge) and former § 875 (Review of findings in cases tried without a jury) are superseded insofar as they provide for formal exceptions, and a bill of exceptions.

1987 AMENDMENT

The amendments are technical. No substantive change is intended.

2007 AMENDMENT

The language of Rule 46 has been amended as part of the general restyling of the Civil Rules to make them more easily understood and to make style and terminology consistent throughout the rules. These changes are intended to be stylistic only.

Rule 47. Selection of Jurors

1937 ADOPTION

Note to Subdivision (a). This permits a practice found very useful by federal trial judges. For an example of a state practice in which the examination by the court is supplemented by further inquiry by counsel see Rule 27 of the Code of Rules for the District Courts of Minnesota, 186 Minn. xxxiii (1932), 3 Minn.Stat. (Mason, Supp.1936) Appendix 4, p. 1062.

Note to Subdivision (b). The provision for an alternate juror is one often found in modern state codes. See N.C.Code (1935) § 2330(a); Ohio Gen.Code Ann. (Page, Supp. 1926–1935) § 11419–47; Pa.Stat.Ann. (Purdon, Supp.1936) Title 17, § 1153; compare U.S.C., Title 28, § 417a (Alternate jurors in criminal trials); 1 N.J.Rev.Stat. (1937) 2:91A–1, 2:91A–2, 2:91A–3.

Provisions for qualifying, drawing, and challenging of jurors are found in U.S.C., Title 28, former:

§ 411 (Qualifications and exemptions)

§ 412 (Manner of drawing)

§ 413 (Apportioned in district)

§ 415 (Not disqualified because of race or color)

§ 416 (Venire; service and return)

§ 417 (Talesmen for petit jurors)

§ 418 (Special juries)

§ 423 (Jurors not to serve more than once a year)

§ 424 (Challenges)

and D.C.Code (1930) Title 18, §§ 341–360 (Juries and Jury Commission) and Title 6, § 366 (Peremptory challenges).

1966 AMENDMENT

The revision of this subdivision brings it into line with the amendment of Rule 24(c) of the Federal Rules of Criminal Procedure. That rule previously allowed four alternate jurors, as contrasted with the two allowed in civil cases, and the amendments increase the number to a maximum of six in all cases. The Advisory Committee's Note to amended Criminal Rule 24(c) points to experience demonstrating that four alternates may not be enough in some lengthy criminal trials; and the same may be said of civil trials. The Note adds:

"The words 'or are found to be' are added to the second sentence to make clear that an alternate juror may be called in the situation where it is first discovered during the trial that a juror was unable or disqualified to perform his duties at the time he was sworn."

1991 AMENDMENT

Subdivision (b). The former provision for alternate jurors is stricken and the institution of the alternate juror abolished.

The former rule reflected the long-standing assumption that a jury would consist of exactly twelve members. It provided for additional jurors to be used as substitutes for jurors who are for any reason excused or disqualified from service after the commencement of the trial. Additional jurors were traditionally designated at the outset of the trial, and excused at the close of the evidence if they had not been promoted to full service on account of the elimination of one of the original jurors.

The use of alternate jurors has been a source of dissatisfaction with the jury system because of the burden it places on alternates who are required to listen to the evidence but denied the satisfaction of participating in its evaluation.

Subdivision (c). This provision makes it clear that the court may in appropriate circumstances excuse a juror during the jury deliberations without causing a mistrial. Sickness, family emergency or juror misconduct that might occasion a mistrial are examples of appropriate grounds for excusing a juror. It is not grounds for the dismissal of a juror that the juror refuses to join with fellow jurors in reaching a unanimous verdict.

2007 AMENDMENT

The language of Rule 47 has been amended as part of the general restyling of the Civil Rules to make them more easily understood and to make style and terminology consistent throughout the rules. These changes are intended to be stylistic only.

Rule 48.   Number of Jurors—Participation in Verdict

1937 ADOPTION

For provisions in state codes, compare Utah Rev.Stat.Ann. (1933) § 48–0–5 (In civil cases parties may agree in open court on lesser number of jurors); 2 Wash.Rev.Stat.Ann. (Remington, 1932) § 323 (Parties may consent to any number of jurors not less than three).

1991 AMENDMENT

The former rule was rendered obsolete by the adoption in many districts of local rules establishing six as the standard size for a civil jury.

It appears that the minimum size of a jury consistent with the Seventh Amendment is six. *Cf. Ballew v. Georgia*, 435 U.S. 223, 98 S.Ct. 1029, 55 L.Ed.2d 234 (1978)(holding that a conviction based on a jury of less than six is a denial of due process of law). If the parties agree to trial before a smaller jury, a verdict can be taken, but the parties should not other than in exceptional circumstances be encouraged to waive the right to a jury of six, not only because of the constitutional stature of the right, but also because smaller juries are more erratic and less effective in serving to distribute responsibility for the exercise of judicial power.

Because the institution of the alternate juror has been abolished by the proposed revision of Rule 47, it will ordinarily be prudent and necessary, in order to provide for sickness or disability among jurors, to seat more than six jurors. The use of jurors in excess of six increases the representativeness of the jury and harms no interest of a party. *Ray v. Parkside Surgery Center*, 13 F.R.Serv. 585 (6th Cir.1989).

If the court takes the precaution of seating a jury larger than six, an illness occurring during the deliberation period will not result in a mistrial, as it did formerly, because all seated jurors will participate in the verdict and a sufficient number will remain to render a unanimous verdict of six or more.

In exceptional circumstances, as where a jury suffers depletions during trial and deliberation that are greater than can reasonably be expected, the parties may agree to be bound by a verdict rendered by fewer than six jurors. The court should not, however, rely upon the availability of such an agreement, for the use of juries smaller than six is problematic for reasons fully explained in *Ballew v. Georgia*, supra.

2007 AMENDMENT

The language of Rule 48 has been amended as part of the general restyling of the Civil Rules to make them more easily understood and to make style and terminology consistent throughout the rules. These changes are intended to be stylistic only.

Rule 49.   Special Verdicts and Interrogatories

1937 ADOPTION

The Federal courts are not bound to follow state statutes authorizing or requiring the court to ask a jury to find a special verdict or to answer interrogatories. *Victor–American Fuel Co.* v. *Peccarich,* 209 Fed. 568 (C.C.A. 8th., 1913), cert. den. 232 U.S. 727, 34 S.Ct. 603, 58 L.Ed. 817 (1914); *Spokane and I. E. R. Co.* v. *Campbell,* 217 Fed. 518 (C.C.A. 9th., 1914), affd. 241 U.S. 497, 36 S.Ct. 683, 60 L.Ed. 1125 (1916); Simkins, *Federal Practice* (1934) § 186. The power of a territory to adopt by statute the practice under Subdivision (b) has been sustained. *Walker* v. *New Mexico and Southern Pacific R. R.,* 165 U.S. 593, 17 S.Ct. 421, 41 L.Ed. 837 (1897); *Southwestern Brewery and Ice Co.* v. *Schmidt,* 226 U.S. 162, 33 S.Ct. 68, 57 L.Ed. 170 (1912).

Compare Wis.Stat. (1935) §§ 270.27, 270.28 and 270.30; Green, A New Development in Jury Trial (1927), 13 A.B.A.J. 715; Morgan, A Brief History of Special Verdicts and Special Interrogatories, 1923, 32 Yale L.J. 575.

The provisions of U.S.C., Title 28, formerly § 400(3)(now §§ 2201, 2202) (Declaratory judgments authorized; procedure) permitting the submission of issues of fact to a jury are covered by this rule.

1963 AMENDMENT

This amendment conforms to the amendment of Rule 58. See the Advisory Committee's Note to Rule 58, as amended.

1987 AMENDMENT

The amendments are technical. No substantive change is intended.

2007 AMENDMENT

The language of Rule 49 has been amended as part of the general restyling of the Civil Rules to make them more easily understood and to make style and terminology consistent throughout the rules. These changes are intended to be stylistic only.

Rule 50.   Judgment as a Matter of Law in Jury Trials; Alternative Motion for New Trial; Conditional Rulings

1937 ADOPTION

Note to Subdivision (a). The present federal rule is changed to the extent that the formality of an express reservation of rights against waiver is no longer necessary. See *Sampliner* v. *Motion Picture Patents Co.,* 254 U.S. 233, 41 S.Ct. 79, 65 L.Ed. 240 (1920); *Union Indemnity Co.* v. *United States,* 74 F.2d 645 (C.C.A. 6th., 1935). The requirement that specific grounds for the motion for a directed verdict must be stated settles a conflict in the federal cases. See Simkins, Federal Practice (1934) § 189.

Note to Subdivision (b). For comparable state practice upheld under the conformity act, see *Baltimore and Carolina Line* v. *Redman,* 295 U.S. 654, 55 S.Ct. 890, 79 L.Ed. 1636 (1935); compare *Slocum* v. *New York Life Ins. Co.,,* 228 U.S. 364, 33 S.Ct. 523, 57 L.Ed. 879, Ann.Cas. 1914D, 1029 (1913).

See *Northern Ry. Co.* v. *Page,* 274 U.S. 65, 47 S.Ct. 491, 71 L.Ed. 929 (1927), following the Massachusetts practice of alternative verdicts, explained in Thorndike, *Trial by Jury in United States Courts,* 26 Harv.L.Rev. 732 (1913). See also Thayer, Judicial Administration, 63 U. of Pa.L.Rev. 585, 600–601, and note 32 (1915); Scott, Trial by Jury and the Reform of Civil Procedure, 31 Harv.L.Rev. 669, 685 (1918); Comment, 34 Mich.L.Rev. 93, 98 (1935).

1963 AMENDMENT

Subdivision (a). The practice, after the court has granted a motion for a directed verdict, of requiring the jury to express assent to a verdict they did not reach by their own deliberations serves no useful purpose and may give offense to the members of the jury. See 2B Barron & Holtzoff, Federal Practice & Procedure § 1072, at 367 (Wright ed. 1961); Blume, Origin and Development of the Directed Verdict, 48 Mich.L.Rev. 555, 582–85, 589–90 (1950). The final sentence of the subdivision, added by amendment, provides that the court's order granting a motion for a directed verdict is effective in itself, and that no action need be taken by the foreman or other members of the jury. See Ariz.R.Civ.P. 50(c); cf. Fed.R.Crim.P. 29(a). No change is intended in the standard to be applied in deciding the motion. To assure this interpretation, and in the interest of simplicity, the traditional term, "directed verdict," is retained.

Subdivision (b). A motion for judgment notwithstanding the verdict will not lie unless it was preceded by a motion for a directed verdict made at the close of all the evidence.

The amendment of the second sentence of this subdivision sets the time limit for making the motion for judgment n. o. v. at 10 days after the entry of judgment, rather than 10 days after the reception of the verdict. Thus the time provision is made consistent with that contained in Rule 59(b)(time for motion for new trial) and Rule 52(b)(time for motion to amend findings by the court).

Subdivision (c) deals with the situation where a party joins a motion for a new trial with his motion for judgment n. o. v., or prays for a new trial in the alternative, and the motion for judgment n. o. v. is granted. The procedure to be followed in making rulings on the motion for the new trial, and the consequences of the rulings thereon, were partly set out in *Montgomery Ward & Co.* v. *Duncan,* 311 U.S. 243, 253, 61 S.Ct. 189, 195, 85 L.Ed. 147 (1940), and have been further elaborated in later cases. See *Cone* v. *West Virginia Pulp & Paper Co.,* 330 U.S. 212, 67 S.Ct. 752, 91 L.Ed. 849 (1947); *Globe Liquor Co., Inc.* v. *San Roman,* 332 U.S. 571, 68 S.Ct. 246, 92 L.Ed. 177 (1948); *Fountain* v. *Filson,* 336 U.S. 681, 69 S.Ct. 754, 93 L.Ed. 971 (1949); *Johnson* v. *New York, N. H. & H. R. R. Co.,* 344 U.S. 48, 73 S.Ct. 125, 97 L.Ed. 77 (1952). However, courts as well as counsel have often misunderstood the procedure, and it will be helpful to summarize the proper practice in the text of the rule. The amendments do not alter the effects of a jury verdict or the scope of appellate review.

In the situation mentioned, **subdivision (c)(1)** requires that the court make a "conditional" ruling on the new-trial motion, i.e., a ruling which goes on the assumption that the motion for judgment n. o. v. was erroneously granted and will be reversed or vacated; and the court is required to state its grounds for the conditional ruling. **Subdivision (c)(1)** then spells out the consequences of a reversal of the judgment in the light of the conditional ruling on the new-trial motion.

If the motion for new trial has been conditionally granted, and the judgment is reversed, "the new trial shall proceed unless the appellate court has otherwise ordered." The party against whom the judgment n. o. v. was entered below may, as appellant, besides seeking to overthrow that judgment, also attack the conditional grant of the new trial. And the appellate court, if it reverses the judgment n. o. v., may in an appropriate case also reverse the conditional grant of the new trial and direct that judgment be entered on the verdict. See *Bailey* v. *Slentz,* 189 F.2d 406 (10th Cir.1951); *Moist Cold Refrigerator Co.* v. *Lou Johnson Co.,* 249 F.2d 246 (9th Cir.1957), cert. denied, 356 U.S. 968, 78 S.Ct. 1008, 2 L.Ed.2d 1074 (1958); *Peters* v. *Smith,* 221 F.2d 721 (3d Cir.1955); *Dailey* v. *Timmer,* 292 F.2d 824 (3d Cir. 1961), explaining *Lind* v. *Schenley Industries, Inc.,* 278 F.2d 79 (3d Cir.), cert. denied, 364 U.S. 835, 81 S.Ct. 58, 5 L.Ed.2d 60 (1960); *Cox* v. *Pennsylvania R. R.,* 120 A.2d 214 (D.C.Mun.Ct.App.1956); 3 Barron & Holtzoff, Federal Practice & Procedure § 1302.1 at 346–47 (Wright ed. 1958); 6 Moore's Federal Practice ¶ 59.16 at 3915 n. 8a (2d ed. 1954).

If the motion for a new trial has been conditionally denied, and the judgment is reversed, "subsequent proceedings shall be in accordance with the order of the appellate court." The party in whose favor judgment n. o. v. was entered below may, as appellee, besides seeking to uphold that judgment, also urge on the appellate court that the trial court committed error in conditionally denying the new trial. The appellee may assert this error in his brief, without taking a cross-appeal. Cf. *Patterson* v. *Pennsylvania R. R.,* 238 F.2d 645, 650 (6th Cir.1956); *Hughes* v. *St. Louis Nat. L. Baseball Club, Inc.,* 359 Mo. 993, 997, 224 S.W.2d 989, 992 (1949). If the appellate court concludes that the judgment cannot stand, but accepts the appellee's contention that there was error in the conditional denial of the new trial, it may order a new trial in lieu of directing the entry of judgment upon the verdict.

Subdivision (c)(2), which also deals with the situation where the trial court has granted the motion for judgment n. o. v., states that the verdict-winner may apply to the trial court for a new trial pursuant to Rule 59 after the judgment n. o. v. has been entered against him. In arguing to the trial court in opposition to the motion for judgment n. o. v., the verdict-winner may, and often will, contend that he is entitled, at the least, to a new trial, and the court has a range of discretion to grant a new trial or (where plaintiff won the verdict) to order a dismissal of the action without prejudice instead of granting judgment n. o. v. See *Cone* v. *West Virginia Pulp & Paper Co., supra,* 330 U.S. at 217, 218, 67 S.Ct. at 755, 756, 91 L.Ed. 849. Subdivision (c)(2) is a reminder that the verdict-winner is entitled, even after entry of judgment n. o. v. against him, to move for a new trial in the usual course. If in these circumstances the motion is granted, the judgment is superseded.

In some unusual circumstances, however, the grant of the new-trial motion may be only conditional, and the judgment will not be superseded. See the situation in *Tribble* v. *Bruin,* 279 F.2d 424 (4th Cir.1960)(upon a verdict for plaintiff, defendant moves for and obtains judgment n. o. v.; plaintiff moves for a new trial on the ground of inadequate damages; trial court might properly have granted plaintiff's motion, conditional upon reversal of the judgment n. o. v.).

Even if the verdict-winner makes no motion for a new trial, he is entitled upon his appeal from the judgment n. o. v. not only to urge that that judgment should be reversed and judgment entered upon the verdict, but that errors were committed during the trial which at the least entitle him to a new trial.

Subdivision (d) deals with the situation where judgment has been entered on the jury verdict, the motion for judgment n. o. v. and any motion for a new trial having been denied by the trial court. The verdict-winner, as appellee, besides seeking to uphold the judgment may urge upon the appellate court that in case the trial court is found to have erred in entering judgment on the verdict, there are grounds for granting him a new trial instead of directing the entry of judgment for his opponent. In appropriate cases the appellate court is not precluded from itself directing that a new trial be had. See *Weade* v. *Dichmann, Wright & Pugh, Inc.,* 337 U.S. 801, 69 S.Ct. 1326, 93 L.Ed. 1704 (1949). Nor is it precluded in proper cases from remanding the case for a determination by the trial court as to whether a new trial should be granted. The latter course is advisable where the grounds urged are suitable for the exercise of trial court discretion.

Subdivision (d) does not attempt a regulation of all aspects of the procedure where the motion for judgment n. o. v. and any accompanying motion for a new trial are denied, since the problems have not been fully canvassed in the decisions and the procedure is in some respects still in a formative stage. It is, however, designed to give guidance on certain important features of the practice.

1987 AMENDMENT

The amendments are technical. No substantive change is intended.

1991 AMENDMENT

Subdivision (a). The revision of this subdivision aims to facilitate the exercise by the court of its responsibility to assure the fidelity of its judgment to the controlling law, a responsibility imposed by the Due Process Clause of the Fifth Amendment. *Cf. Galloway* v. *United States,* 319 U.S. 372, 63 S.Ct. 1077, 87 L.Ed. 1458 (1943).

The revision abandons the familiar terminology of *direction of verdict* for several reasons. The term is misleading as a description of the relationship between judge and jury. It is also freighted with anachronisms some of which are the subject of the text of former subdivision (a) of this rule that is deleted in this revision. Thus, it should not be necessary to state in the text of this rule that a motion made pursuant to it is not a waiver of the right to jury trial, and only the antiquities of directed verdict practice suggest that it might have been. The term "judgment as a matter of law" is an almost equally familiar term and appears in the text of Rule 56; its use in Rule 50 calls attention to the relationship between the two rules. Finally, the change enables the rule to refer to preverdict and post-verdict motions with a terminology that does not conceal the common identity of two motions made at different times in the proceeding.

If a motion is denominated a motion for directed verdict or for judgment notwithstanding the verdict, the party's error is merely formal. Such a motion should be treated as a motion for judgment as a matter of law in accordance with this rule.

Paragraph (a)(1) articulates the standard for the granting of a motion for judgment as a matter of law. It effects no change in the existing standard. That existing standard was not expressed in the former rule, but was articulated in long-standing case law. *See generally* Cooper, *Directions for Directed Verdicts: A Compass for Federal Courts,* 55 MINN.L.REV. 903 (1971). The expressed standard makes clear that action taken under the rule is a performance of the court's duty to assure enforcement of the controlling law and is not an intrusion on any responsibility for factual determinations conferred on the jury by the Seventh Amendment or any other provision of federal law. Because this standard is also used as a reference point for entry of summary judgment under 56(a), it serves to link the two related provisions.

The revision authorizes the court to perform its duty to enter judgment as a matter of law at any time during the trial, as soon as it is apparent that either party is unable to carry a burden of proof that is essential to that party's case. Thus, the second sentence of paragraph (a)(1) authorizes the court to consider a motion for judgment as a matter of law as soon as a party has completed a presentation on a fact essential to that party's case. Such early action is appropriate when economy and expedition will be served. In no event, however, should the court enter judgment against a party who has not been apprised of the materiality of the dispositive fact and been afforded an opportunity to present any available evidence bearing on that fact. In order further to facilitate the exercise of the authority provided by this rule, Rule 16 is also revised [not revised as of date of this commentary] to encourage the court to schedule an order of trial that proceeds first with a presentation on an issue that is likely to be dispositive, if such an issue is identified in the course of pretrial. Such scheduling can be appropriate where the court is uncertain whether favorable action should be taken under Rule 56. Thus, the revision affords the court the alternative of denying a motion for summary judgment while scheduling a separate trial of the issue under Rule 42(b) or scheduling the trial to begin with a presentation on that essential fact which the opposing party seems unlikely to be able to maintain.

Paragraph (a)(2) retains the requirement that a motion for judgment be made prior to the close of the trial, subject to renewal after a jury verdict has been rendered. The purpose of this requirement is to assure the responding party an opportunity to cure any deficiency in that party's proof that may have been overlooked until called to the party's attention by a late motion for judgment. Cf. *Farley Transp. Co. v. Santa Fe Trail Transp. Co.,* 786 F.2d 1342 (9th Cir.1985)("If the moving party is then permitted to make a later attack on the evidence through a motion for judgment notwithstanding the verdict or an appeal, the opposing party may be prejudiced by having lost the opportunity to present additional evidence before the case was submitted to the jury"); *Benson v. Allphin,* 786 F.2d 268 (7th Cir.1986)("the motion for directed verdict at the close of all the evidence provides the nonmovant an opportunity to do what he can to remedy the deficiencies in his case . . ."); *McLaughlin v. The Fellows Gear Shaper Co.,* 786 F.2d 592, 4 F.R.Serv.3d 607 (3d Cir.1986)(per Adams, J., dissenting: "This Rule serves important practical purposes in ensuring that neither party is precluded from presenting the most persuasive case possible and in preventing unfair surprise after a matter has been submitted to the jury"). At one time, this requirement was held to be of constitutional stature, being compelled by the Seventh Amendment. Cf. *Slocum v. New York Life Insurance Co.,* 228 U.S. 364, 33 S.Ct. 523, 57 L.Ed. 879 (1913). But cf. *Baltimore & Carolina Line v. Redman,* 295 U.S. 654, 55 S.Ct. 890, 79 L.Ed. 1636 (1935).

The second sentence of paragraph (a)(2) does impose a requirement that the moving party articulate the basis on which a judgment as a matter of law might be rendered. The articulation is necessary to achieve the purpose of the requirement that the motion be made before the case is submitted to the jury, so that the responding party may seek to correct any overlooked deficiencies in the proof. The revision thus alters the result in cases in which courts have used various techniques to avoid the requirement that a motion for a directed verdict be made as a predicate to a motion for judgment notwithstanding the verdict. E.g., *Benson v. Allphin,* 786 F.2d 268 (7th Cir.1986)("this circuit has allowed something less than a formal motion for directed verdict to preserve a party's right to move for judgment notwithstanding the verdict"). *See generally* 9 WRIGHT & MILLER, FEDERAL PRACTICE AND PROCEDURE § 2537 (1971 and Supp.). The information required with the motion may be supplied by explicit reference to materials and argument previously supplied to the court.

This subdivision deals only with the entry of judgment and not with the resolution of particular factual issues as a matter of law. The court may, as before, properly refuse to instruct a jury to decide an issue if a reasonable jury could on the evidence presented decide that issue in only one way.

Subdivision (b). This provision retains the concept of the former rule that the post-verdict motion is a renewal of an earlier motion made at the close of the evidence. One purpose of this concept was to avoid any question arising under the Seventh Amendment. *Montgomery Ward & Co. v. Duncan,* 311 U.S. 243, 61 S.Ct. 189, 85 L.Ed. 147 (1940). It remains useful as a means of defining the appropriate issue posed by the post-verdict motion. A post-trial motion for judgment can be granted only on grounds advanced in the pre-verdict motion. *E.g., Kutner Buick, Inc. v. American Motors Corp.*, 868 F.2d 614 (3d Cir.1989).

Often it appears to the court or to the moving party that a motion for judgment as a matter of law made at the close of the evidence should be reserved for a post-verdict decision. This is so because a jury verdict for the moving party moots the issue and because a preverdict ruling gambles that a reversal may result in a new trial that might have been avoided. For these reasons, the court may often wisely decline to rule on a motion for judgment as a matter of law made at the close of the evidence, and it is not inappropriate for the moving party to suggest such a postponement of the ruling until after the verdict has been rendered.

In ruling on such a motion, the court should disregard any jury determination for which there is no legally sufficient evidentiary basis enabling a reasonable jury to make it. The court may then decide such issues as a matter of law and enter judgment if all other material issues have been decided by the jury on the basis of legally sufficient evidence, or by the court as a matter of law.

The revised rule is intended for use in this manner with Rule 49. Thus, the court may combine facts established as a matter of law either before trial under Rule 56 or at trial on the basis of the evidence presented with other facts determined by the jury under instructions provided under Rule 49 to support a proper judgment under this rule.

This provision also retains the former requirement that a post-trial motion under the rule must be made within 10 days after entry of a contrary judgment. The renewed motion must be served and filed as provided by Rule 5. A purpose of this requirement is to meet the requirements of F.R.App.P. 4(a)(4).

Subdivision (c). Revision of this subdivision conforms the language to the change in diction set forth in subdivision (a) of this revised rule.

Subdivision (d). Revision of this subdivision conforms the language to that of the previous subdivisions.

1993 AMENDMENT

This technical amendment corrects an ambiguity in the text of the 1991 revision of the rule, which, as indicated in the Notes, was not intended to change the existing standards under which "directed verdicts" could be granted. This amendment makes clear that judgments as a matter of law in jury trials may be entered against both plaintiffs and defendants and with respect to issues or defenses that may not be wholly dispositive of a claim or defense.

1995 AMENDMENT

The only change, other than stylistic, intended by this revision is to prescribe a uniform explicit time for filing of post-judgment motions under this rule—no later than 10 days after entry of the judgment. Previously, there was an inconsistency in the wording of Rules 50, 52, and 59 with respect to whether certain post-judgment motions had to be filed, or merely served, during that period. This inconsistency caused special problems when motions for a new trial were joined with other post-judgment motions. These motions affect the finality of the judgment, a matter often of importance to third persons as well as the parties and the court. The Committee believes that each of these rules should be revised to require filing before end of the 10-day period. Filing is an event that can be determined with certainty from court records. The phrase "no later than" is used—rather than "within"—to include post-judgment motions that sometimes are filed before actual entry of the judgment by the clerk. It should be noted that under Rule 6(a) Saturdays, Sundays, and legal holidays are excluded in measuring the 10-day period, and that under Rule 5 the motions when filed are to contain a certificate of service on other parties.

2006 AMENDMENT

The language of Rule 50(a) has been amended as part of the general restyling of the Civil Rules to make them more easily understood and to make style and terminology consistent throughout the rules. These changes are intended to be stylistic only.

Rule 50(b) is amended to permit renewal of any Rule 50(a) motion for judgment as a matter of law, deleting the requirement that a motion be made at the close of all the evidence. Because the Rule 50(b) motion is only a renewal of the preverdict motion, it can be granted only on grounds advanced in the preverdict motion. The earlier motion informs the opposing party of the challenge to the sufficiency of the evidence and affords a clear opportunity to provide additional evidence that may be available. The earlier motion also alerts the court to the opportunity to simplify the trial by resolving some issues, or even all issues, without submission to the jury. This fulfillment of the functional needs that underlie present Rule 50(b) also satisfies the Seventh Amendment. Automatic reservation of the legal questions raised by the motion conforms to the decision in *Baltimore & Carolina Line v. Redman*, 297 U.S. 654 (1935).

This change responds to many decisions that have begun to move away from requiring a motion for judgment as a matter of law at the literal close of all the evidence. Although the requirement has been clearly established for several decades, lawyers continue to overlook it. The courts are slowly working away from the formal requirement. The amendment establishes the functional approach that courts have been unable to reach under the present rule and makes practice more consistent and predictable.

Many judges expressly invite motions at the close of all the evidence. The amendment is not intended to discourage this useful practice.

Finally, an explicit time limit is added for making a posttrial motion when the trial ends without a verdict or with a verdict that does not dispose of all issues suitable for resolution by verdict. The motion must be made no later than 10 days after the jury was discharged.

2007 AMENDMENTS

The language of Rule 50 has been amended as part of the general restyling of the Civil Rules to make them more easily understood and to make style and terminology consistent throughout the rules. These changes are intended to be stylistic only.

Former Rule 50(b) stated that the court reserves ruling on a motion for judgment as a matter of law made at the close of all the evidence "[i]f, for any reason, the court does not grant" the motion. The words "for any reason" reflected the proposition that the reservation is automatic and inescapable. The ruling is reserved even if the court explicitly denies the motion. The same result follows under the amended rule. If the motion is not granted, the ruling is reserved.

Amended Rule 50(e) identifies the appellate court's authority to direct the entry of judgment. This authority was not described in former Rule 50(d), but was recognized in *Weisgram v. Marley Co.*, 528 U.S. 440 (2000), and in *Neely v. Martin K. Eby Construction Company*, 386 U.S. 317 (1967). When Rule 50(d) was drafted in 1963, the Committee Note stated that "[s]ubdivision (d) does not attempt a regulation of all aspects of the procedure where the motion for judgment n.o.v. and any accompanying motion for a new trial are denied * * *." Express recognition of the authority to direct entry of judgment does not otherwise supersede this caution.

Rule 51. Instructions to Jury: Objection

1937 ADOPTION

Supreme Court Rule 8 requires exceptions to the charge of the court to the jury which shall distinctly state the several matters of law in the charge to which exception is taken. Similar provisions appear in the rules of the various Circuit Courts of Appeals.

1987 AMENDMENT

Although Rule 51 in its present form specifies that the court shall instruct the jury only after the arguments of the parties are completed, in some districts (typically those in states where the practice is otherwise) it is common for the parties to stipulate to instruction before the arguments. The purpose of the amendment is to give the court discretion to instruct the jury either before or after argument. Thus, the rule as revised will permit resort to the long-standing federal practice or to an alternative procedure, which has been praised because it gives counsel the opportunity to explain the instructions, argue their application to the facts and thereby give the jury the maximum assistance in determining the issues and arriving at a good verdict on the law and the evidence. As an ancillary benefit, this approach aids counsel by supplying a natural outline so that arguments may be directed to the essential fact issues which the jury must decide. See generally Raymond, *Merits and Demerits of the Missouri System of Instructing Juries*, 5 St. Louis U.L.J. 317 (1959). Moreover, if the court instructs before an argument, counsel then know the precise words the court has chosen and need not speculate as to the words the court will later use in its instructions. Finally, by instructing ahead of argument the court has the attention of the jurors when they are fresh and can give their full attention to the court's instructions. It is more difficult to hold the attention of jurors after lengthy arguments.

2003 AMENDMENT

Rule 51 is revised to capture many of the interpretations that have emerged in practice. The revisions in text will make uniform the conclusions reached by a majority of decisions on each point. Additions also are made to cover some practices that cannot now be anchored in the text of Rule 51.

Scope. Rule 51 governs instructions to the trial jury on the law that governs the verdict. A variety of other instructions cannot practicably be brought within Rule 51. Among these instructions are preliminary instructions to a venire, and cautionary or limiting instructions delivered in immediate response to events at trial.

Requests. Subdivision (a) governs requests. Apart from the plain error doctrine recognized in subdivision (d)(2), a court is not obliged to instruct the jury on issues raised by the evidence unless a party requests an instruction. The revised rule recognizes the court's authority to direct that requests be submitted before trial.

The close-of-the-evidence deadline may come before trial is completed on all potential issues. Trial may be formally bifurcated or may be sequenced in some less formal manner. The close of the evidence is measured by the occurrence of two events: completion of all intended evidence on an identified phase of the trial and impending submission to the jury with instructions.

The risk in directing a pretrial request deadline is that trial evidence may raise new issues or reshape issues the parties thought they had understood. Courts need not insist on pretrial requests in all cases. Even if the request time is set before trial or early in the trial, subdivision (a)(2)(A) permits requests after the close of the evidence to address issues that could not reasonably have been anticipated at the earlier time for requests set by the court.

Subdivision (a)(2)(B) expressly recognizes the court's discretion to act on an untimely request. The most important consideration in exercising the discretion confirmed by subdivision (a)(2)(B) is the importance of the issue to the case—the closer the issue lies to the "plain error" that would be recognized under subdivision (d)(2), the better the reason to give an instruction. The cogency of the reason for failing to make a timely request also should be considered. To be considered under subdivision (a)(2)(B) a request should be made before final instructions and before final jury arguments. What is a "final" instruction and argument depends on the sequence of submitting the case to the jury. If separate portions of the case are submitted to the jury in sequence, the final arguments and final instructions are those made on submitting to the jury the portion of the case addressed by the arguments and instructions.

Instructions. Subdivision (b)(1) requires the court to inform the parties, before instructing the jury and before final jury arguments related to the instruction, of the proposed instructions as well as the proposed action on instruction requests. The time limit is addressed to final jury arguments to reflect the practice that allows interim argument s during trial in complex cases; it may not be feasible to develop final instructions before such interim arguments. It is enough that counsel know of the intended instructions before making final arguments addressed to the issue. If the trial is sequenced or bifurcated, the final arguments addressed to an issue may occur before the close of the entire trial.

Subdivision (b)(2) complements subdivision (b)(1) by carrying forward the opportunity to object established by present Rule 51. It makes explicit the opportunity to object on the record, ensuring a clear memorial of the objection.

Subdivision (b)(3) reflects common practice by authorizing instructions at any time after trial begins and before the jury is discharged.

Objections. Subdivision (c) states the right to object to an instruction or the failure to give an instruction. It carries forward the formula of present Rule 51 requiring that the objection state distinctly the matter objected to and the grounds of the objection, and makes explicit the requirement that the objection be made on the record. The provisions on the time to object make clear that it is timely to object promptly after learning of an instruction or action on a request when the court has not provided advance information as required by subdivision (b)(1). The need to repeat a request by way of objection is continued by new subdivision (d)(1)(B) except where the court made a definitive ruling on the record.

Preserving a claim of error and plain error. Many cases hold that a proper request for a jury instruction is not alone enough to preserve the right to appeal failure to give the instruction. The request must be renewed by objection. This doctrine is appropriate when the court may not have sufficiently focused on the request, or may believe that the request has been granted in substance although in different words. But this doctrine may also prove a trap for the unwary who fail to add an objection after the court has made it clear that the request has been considered and rejected on the merits.

Subdivision (d)(1)(B) establishes authority to review the failure to grant a timely request, despite a failure to add an objection, when the court has made a definitive ruling on the record rejecting the request.

Many circuits have recognized that an error not preserved under Rule 51 may be reviewed in exceptional circumstances. The language adopted to capture these decisions in subdivision (d)(2) is borrowed from Criminal Rule 52. Although the language is the same, the context of civil litigation often differs from the context of criminal prosecution; actual application of the plain-error standard takes account of the differences. The Supreme Court has summarized application of Criminal Rule 52 as involving four elements: (1) there must be an error; (2) the error must be plain; (3) the error must affect substantial rights; and (4) the error must seriously affect the fairness, integrity, or public reputation of judicial proceedings. Johnson v. U.S., 520 U.S. 461, 466–467, 469–470 (1997). (The Johnson case quoted the fourth element from its decision in a civil action, U.S. v. Atkinson, 297 U.S. 157, 160 (1936): "In exceptional circumstances, especially in criminal cases, appellate courts, in the public interest, may, of their own motion, notice errors to which no exception has been taken, if the errors are obvious, or if they otherwise substantially affect the fairness, integrity, or public reputation of judicial proceedings.")

The court's duty to give correct jury instructions in a civil action is shaped by at least four factors.

The factor most directly implied by a "plain" error rule is the obviousness of the mistake. The importance of the error is a second major factor. The costs of correcting an error reflect a third factor that is affected by a variety of circumstances. In a case that seems close to the fundamental error line, account also may be taken of the impact a verdict may have on nonparties.

2007 AMENDMENTS

The language of Rule 51 has been amended as part of the general restyling of the Civil Rules to make them more easily understood and to make style and terminology consistent throughout the rules. These changes are intended to be stylistic only.

Rule 52.   Findings by the Court; Judgment on Partial Findings

1937 ADOPTION

See Former Equity Rule 70½, as amended Nov. 25, 1935, (Findings of Fact and Conclusions of Law) and U.S.C., Title 28, former § 764 (Opinion, findings, and conclusions in action against United States) which are substantially continued in this rule. The provisions of U.S.C., Title 28, former §§ 773 (Trial of issues of fact; by court) and 875 (Review in cases tried without a jury) are superseded in so far as they provide a different method of finding facts and a different method of appellate review. The rule stated in the third sentence of **Subdivision (a)** accords with the decisions on the scope of the review in modern federal equity practice. It is applicable to all classes of findings in cases tried without a jury whether the finding is of a fact concerning which there was conflict of testimony, or of a fact deduced or inferred from uncontradicted testimony. See *Silver King Coalition Mines Co.* v. *Silver King Consolidated Mining Co.*, C.C.A.8, 1913, 204 F. 166, certiorari denied 229 U.S. 624, 33 S.Ct. 1051, 57 L.Ed. 1356; *Warren* v. *Keep,* 1894, 155 U.S. 265, 15 S.Ct. 83, 39 L.Ed. 144; *Furrer* v. *Ferris,* 1892, 145 U.S. 132, 12 S.Ct. 821, 36 L.Ed. 649; *Tilghman* v. *Proctor,* 1888, 125 U.S. 136, 149, 8 S.Ct. 894, 901, 31 L.Ed. 664; *Kimberly* v. *Arms,* 1889, 129 U.S. 512, 524, 9 S.Ct. 355, 359, 32 L.Ed. 764. Compare *Kaeser & Blair, Inc.* v. *Merchants' Ass'n,* C.C.A.6, 1933, 64 F.2d 575, 576; *Dunn* v. *Trefry,* C.C.A.1, 1919, 260 F. 147, 148.

In the following states findings of fact are required in all cases tried without a jury (waiver by the parties being permitted as indicated at the end of the listing): Arkansas, Civ.Code (Crawford, 1934) § 364; California, Code Civ.Proc. (Deering, 1937) §§ 632, 634; Colorado, 1 Stat.Ann. (1935) Code Civ.Proc. §§ 232, 291 (in actions before referees or for possession of and damages to land); Connecticut, Gen.Stats. §§ 5660, 5664; Idaho, 1 Code Ann. (1932) §§ 7–302 through 7–305; Massachusetts (equity cases), 2 Gen.Laws (Ter.Ed., 1932) ch. 214, § 23; Minnesota, 2 Stat. (Mason, 1927) § 9311; Nevada, 4 Comp.Laws (Hillyer, 1929) §§ 8783–8784; New Jersey, Sup.Ct.Rule 113, 2 N.J.Misc. 1197, 1239 (1924); New Mexico, Stat.Ann. (Courtright, 1929) § 105–813; North Carolina, Code (1935) § 569; North Dakota, 2 Comp.Laws Ann. (1913) § 7641; Oregon, 2 Code Ann. (1930) § 2–502; South Carolina, Code (Michie, 1932) § 649; South Dakota, 1 Comp.Laws (1929) §§ 2525–2526; Utah, Rev.Stat.Ann. (1933) §§ 104–26–2, 104–26–3; Vermont (where jury trial waived), Pub.Laws (1933) § 2069; Washington, 2 Rev.Stat.Ann. (Remington, 1932) § 367; Wisconsin, Stat. (1935) § 270.33. The parties may waive this requirement for findings in California, Idaho, North Dakota, Nevada, New Mexico, Utah, and South Dakota.

In the following states the review of findings of fact in all non-jury cases, including jury waived cases, is assimilated to the equity review: Alabama, Code Ann. (Michie, 1928) §§ 9498, 8599; California, Code Civ.Proc. (Deering, 1937) § 956a; but see 20 Calif.Law Rev. 171 (1932); Colorado, *Johnson* v. *Kountze,* 1895, 43 P. 445, 21 Colo. 486, semble; Illinois, *Baker* v. *Hinrichs,* 1934, 194 N.E. 284, 359 Ill. 138; *Weininger* v. *Metropolitan Fire Ins. Co.,* 1935, 195 N.E. 420, 359 Ill. 584, 98 A.L.R. 169; Minnesota, *State Bank of Gibbon* v. *Walter,* 1926, 208 N.W. 423, 167 Minn. 37, 38; *Waldron* v. *Page,* 1934, 253 N.W. 894, 191 Minn. 302; New Jersey, N.J.S.A. 2:27–241, 2–27–363, as interpreted in *Bussy* v. *Hatch,* 1920, 111 A. 546, 95 N.J.L. 56; New York, *York Mortgage Corporation* v. *Clotar Const. Corp.,* 1930, 172 N.E. 265, 254 N.Y. 128, 133; North Dakota, Comp.Laws Ann. (1913) § 7846, as amended by N.D.Laws 1933, c. 208; *Milnor Holding Co.* v. *Holt,* 1933, 248 N.W. 315, 63 N.D. 362, 370; Oklahoma, *Wichita Mining and Improvement Co.* v. *Hale,* 1908, 94 P. 530, 20 Okl. 159, 167; South Dakota, *Randall* v. *Burk Township,* 4 S.D. 337, 57 N.W. 4 (1893); Texas, *Custard* v. *Flowers,* 1929, 14 S.W.2d 109; Utah, Rev.Stat.Ann. (1933) § 104–41–5; Vermont, *Roberge* v. *Troy,* 1933, 105 Vt. 134, 163 A. 770; Washington, 2 Rev.Stat.Ann. (Remington, 1932) §§ 309–316; *McCullough* v. *Puget Sound Realty Associates,* 1913, 136 Pac. 1146, 76 Wash. 700, but see *Cornwall* v. *Anderson,* 1915, 148 P. 1, 85 Wash. 369; West Virginia, *Kinsey* v. *Carr,* 1906, 55 S.E. 1004, 60 W.Va. 449, semble; Wisconsin, Stat. (1935) § 251.09; *Campbell* v. *Sutliff,* 1927, 214 N.W. 374, 193 Wis. 370; *Gessler* v. *Erwin Co.,* 1924, 193 N.W. 363, 182 Wis. 315.

For examples of an assimilation of the review of findings of fact in cases tried without a jury to the review at law as made in several states, see Clark and Stone, Review of Findings of Fact, 4 U. of Chi.L.Rev. 190, 215 (1937).

1946 AMENDMENT

Note to Subdivision (a). The amended rule makes clear that the requirement for findings of fact and conclusions of law thereon applies in a case with an advisory jury. This removes an ambiguity in the rule as originally stated, but carries into effect what has been considered its intent. 3 Moore's Federal Practice, 1938, 3119. *Hurwitz* v. *Hurwitz,* 1943, 136 F.2d 796, 78 U.S.App.D.C. 66.

The two sentences added at the end of Rule 52(a) eliminate certain difficulties which have arisen concerning findings and conclusions. The first of the two sentences permits findings of fact and conclusions of law to appear in an opinion or memorandum of decision. See, e.g., *United States* v. *One 1941 Ford Sedan,* Tex.1946, 65 F.Supp. 84. Under original Rule 52(a) some courts have expressed the view that findings and conclusions could not be incorporated in an opinion. *Detective Comics, Inc.* v. *Bruns Publications,* N.Y.1939, 28 F.Supp. 399; *Pennsylvania Co. for Insurance on Lives & Granting Annuities* v. *Cincinnati & L. E. R. Co.,* Ohio 1941, 43 F.Supp. 5; *United States* v. *Aluminum Co. of America,* N.Y.1941, 2 F.R.D. 224, 5 Fed.Rules Serv. 52a.11, Case 3; see also s. c., 44 F.Supp. 97. But, to the contrary, see *Wellman* v. *United States,* Mass.1938, 25 F.Supp. 868; *Cook* v. *United States,* Mass.1939, 26 F.Supp. 253; *Proctor* v. *White,* Mass.1939, 28 F.Supp. 161; *Green Valley Creamery, Inc.* v. *United States,* C.C.A.1, 1939, 108 F.2d 342. See also *Matton Oil Transfer Corp.* v. *The Dynamic,* C.C.A.2, 1941, 123 F.2d 999; *Carter Coal Co.* v. *Litz,* C.C.A.4, 1944, 140 F.2d 934; *Woodruff* v. *Heiser,* C.C.A.10, 1945, 150 F.2d 869; *Coca Cola Co.* v. *Busch,* Pa.1943, 7 Fed.Rules Serv. 59b.2, Case 4; Oglebay, Some Developments in Bankruptcy Law, 1944, 18 J. of Nat'l Ass'n of Ref. 68, 69. Findings of fact aid in the process of judgment and in defining for future cases the precise limitations of the issues and the determination thereon. Thus they not only aid the appellate court on review, *Hurwitz* v. *Hurwitz,* 1943, 136 F.2d 796, 78 U.S.App.D.C. 66, but they are an important factor in the proper application of the doctrines of res judicata and estoppel by judgment. Nordbye, Improvements in Statement of Findings of Fact and Conclusions of Law, 1 F.R.D. 25, 26–27; *United States* v. *Forness,* C.C.A.2, 1942, 125 F.2d 928, certiorari denied 316 U.S. 694, 62 S.Ct. 1293, 86 L.Ed. 1764. These findings should represent the judge's own determination and not the long, often argumentative statements of successful counsel. *United States* v. *Forness,* supra: *United States* v. *Crescent Amusement Co.,* 1944, 323 U.S. 173, 65 S.Ct. 254, 89 L.Ed. 160. Consequently, they should be a part of the judge's opinion and decision, either stated therein or stated separately. *Matton Oil Transfer Corp.* v. *The Dynamic,* supra. But the judge need only make brief, definite, pertinent findings and conclusions upon the contested matters; there is no necessity for over-elaboration of detail or particularization of facts. *United States* v. *Forness,* supra; *United States* v. *Crescent Amusement Co.,* supra. See also *Petterson Lighterage & Towing Corp.* v. *New York Central R. Co.,* C.C.A.2d, 1942, 126 F.2d 992; *Brown Paper Mill Co., Inc.* v. *Irwin,* C.C.A.8, 1943,

134 F.2d 337; *Allen Bradley Co.* v. *Local Union No. 3, I. B. E. W.,* C.C.A.2, 1944, 145 F.2d 215, reversed on other grounds 325 U.S. 797, 65 S.Ct. 1533, 89 L.Ed. 1939; *Young* v. *Murphy,* Ohio 1946, 9 Fed.Rules Serv. 52a.11, Case 2.

The last sentence of Rule 52(a) as amended will remove any doubt that findings and conclusions are unnecessary upon decision of a motion, particularly one under Rule 12 or Rule 56, except as provided in amended Rule 41(b). As so holding, see *Thomas* v. *Peyser,* App.D.C.1941, 118 F.2d 369; *Schad* v. *Twentieth Century-Fox Corp.,* C.C.A.3, 1943, 136 F.2d 991; *Prudential Ins. Co. of America* v. *Goldstein,* N.Y.1942, 43 F.Supp. 767; *Somers Coal Co.* v. *United States,* Ohio 1942, 2 F.R.D. 532, 6 Fed.Rules Serv. 52a.1, Case 1; *Pen–Ken Oil & Gas Corp.* v. *Warfield Natural Gas Co.,* Ky.1942, 2 F.R.D. 355, 5 Fed.Rules Serv. 52a.1, Case 3; also Commentary, Necessity of Findings of Fact, 1941, 4 Fed.Rules Serv. 936.

1963 AMENDMENT

This amendment conforms to the amendment of Rule 58. See the Advisory Committee's Note to Rule 58, as amended.

1983 AMENDMENT

Rule 52(a) has been amended to revise its penultimate sentence to provide explicitly that the district judge may make the findings of fact and conclusions of law required in nonjury cases orally. Nothing in the prior text of the rule forbids this practice, which is widely utilized by district judges. See Christensen, *A Modest Proposal for Immeasurable Improvement,* 64 A.B.A.J. 693 (1978). The objective is to lighten the burden on the trial court in preparing findings in nonjury cases. In addition, the amendment should reduce the number of published district court opinions that embrace written findings.

1985 AMENDMENT

Rule 52(a) has been amended (1) to avoid continued confusion and conflicts among the circuits as to the standard of appellate review of findings of fact by the court, (2) to eliminate the disparity between the standard of review as literally stated in Rule 52(a) and the practice of some courts of appeals, and (3) to promote nationwide uniformity. See Note, *Rule 52(a): Appellate Review of Findings of Fact Based on Documentary or Undisputed Evidence,* 49 Va.L.Rev. 506, 536 (1963).

Some courts of appeal have stated that when a trial court's findings do not rest on demeanor evidence and evaluation of a witness' credibility, there is no reason to defer to the trial court's findings and the appellate court more readily can find them to be clearly erroneous. See, e.g., *Marcum* v. *United States,* 621 F.2d 142, 144–45 (5th Cir.1980). Others go further, holding that appellate review may be had without application of the "clearly erroneous" test since the appellate court is in as good a position as the trial court to review a purely documentary record. See, e.g., *Atari, Inc.* v. *North American Philips Consumer Electronics Corp.,* 672 F.2d 607, 614 (7th Cir.), *cert. denied,* 459 U.S. 880, 103 S.Ct. 176, 74 L.Ed.2d 145 (1982); *Lydle* v. *United States,* 635 F.2d 763, 765 n. 1 (6th Cir.1981); *Swanson* v. *Baker Indus., Inc.,* 615 F.2d 479, 483 (8th Cir.1980); *Taylor* v. *Lombard,* 606 F.2d 371, 372 (2d Cir.1979), *cert. denied,* 445 U.S. 946, 100 S.Ct. 1346, 63 L.Ed.2d 781 (1980); *Jack Kahn Music Co.* v. *Baldwin Piano & Organ Co.,* 604 F.2d 755, 758 (2d Cir.1979); *John R. Thompson Co.* v. *United States,* 477 F.2d 164, 167 (7th Cir.1973).

A third group has adopted the view that the "clearly erroneous" rule applies in all nonjury cases even when findings are based solely on documentary evidence or on inferences from undisputed facts. See, e.g., *Maxwell* v. *Sumner,* 673 F.2d 1031, 1036 (9th Cir.), *cert. denied,* 459 U.S. 976, 103 S.Ct. 313, 74 L.Ed.2d 291 (1982); *United States* v. *Texas Education Agency,* 647 F.2d 504, 506–07 (5th Cir.1981), *cert. denied,* 454 U.S. 1143, 102 S.Ct. 1002, 71 L.Ed.2d 295 (1982); *Constructora Maza, Inc.* v. *Banco de Ponce,* 616 F.2d 573, 576 (1st Cir.1980); *In re Sierra Trading Corp.,* 482 F.2d 333, 337 (10th Cir.1973); *Case* v. *Morrisette,* 475 F.2d 1300, 1306–07 (D.C.Cir.1973).

The commentators also disagree as to the proper interpretation of the Rule. *Compare* Wright, *The Doubtful Omniscience of Appellate Courts,* 41 Minn.L.Rev. 751, 769–70 (1957)(language and intent of Rule support view that "clearly erroneous" test should apply to all forms of evidence), *and* 9 C. Wright & A. Miller, *Federal Practice and Procedure: Civil § 2587,* at 740 (1971)(language of the Rule is clear), *with* 5A J. Moore, *Federal Practice* ¶ 52.04, 2687–88 (2d ed. 1982)(Rule as written supports broader review of findings based on non-demeanor testimony).

The Supreme Court has not clearly resolved the issue. See, *Bose Corp. v. Consumers Union of United States, Inc.*, 466 U.S. 485, 498, 104 S.Ct. 1949, 1958, 80 L.Ed.2d 502 (1984); *Pullman–Standard v. Swint*, 456 U.S. 273, 293, 102 S.Ct. 1781, 1792, 72 L.Ed.2d 66 (1982); *United States v. General Motors Corp.*, 384 U.S. 127, 141 n. 16, 86 S.Ct. 1321, 1328 n. 16, 16 L.Ed.2d 415 (1966); *United States v. United States Gypsum Co.*, 333 U.S. 364, 394–96, 68 S.Ct. 525, 541–542, 92 L.Ed. 746 (1948).

The principal argument advanced in favor of a more searching appellate review of findings by the district court based solely on documentary evidence is that the rationale of Rule 52(a) does not apply when the findings do not rest on the trial court's assessment of credibility of the witnesses but on an evaluation of documentary proof and the drawing of inferences from it, thus eliminating the need for any special deference to the trial court's findings. These considerations are outweighed by the public interest in the stability and judicial economy that would be promoted by recognizing that the trial court, not the appellate tribunal, should be the finder of the facts. To permit courts of appeals to share more actively in the fact-finding function would tend to undermine the legitimacy of the district courts in the eyes of litigants, multiply appeals by encouraging appellate retrial of some factual issues, and needlessly reallocate judicial authority.

1991 AMENDMENT

Subdivision (c) is added. It parallels the revised Rule 50(a), but is applicable to non-jury trials. It authorizes the court to enter judgment at any time that it can appropriately make a dispositive finding of fact on the evidence.

The new subdivision replaces part of Rule 41(b), which formerly authorized a dismissal at the close of the plaintiff's case if the plaintiff had failed to carry an essential burden of proof. Accordingly, the reference to Rule 41 formerly made in subdivision (a) of this rule is deleted.

As under the former Rule 41(b), the court retains discretion to enter no judgment prior to the close of the evidence.

Judgment entered under this rule differs from a summary judgment under Rule 56 in the nature of the evaluation made by the court. A judgment on partial findings is made after the court has heard all the evidence bearing on the crucial issue of fact, and the finding is reversible only if the appellate court finds it to be "clearly erroneous." A summary judgment, in contrast, is made on the basis of facts established on account of the absence of contrary evidence or presumptions; such establishments of fact are rulings on questions of law as provided in Rule 56(a) and are not shielded by the "clear error" standard of review.

1993 AMENDMENT

This technical amendment corrects an ambiguity in the text of the 1991 revision of the rule, similar to the revision being made to Rule 50. This amendment makes clear that judgments as a matter of law in nonjury trials may be entered against both plaintiffs and defendants and with respect to issues or defenses that may not be wholly dispositive of a claim or defense.

1995 AMENDMENT

The only change, other than stylistic, intended by this revision is to require that any motion to amend or add findings after a nonjury trial must be filed no later than 10 days after entry of the judgment. Previously, there was an inconsistency in the wording of Rules 50, 52, and 59 with respect to whether certain post-judgment motions had to be filed, or merely served, during that period. This inconsistency caused special problems when motions for a new trial were joined with other post-judgment motions. These motions affect the finality of the judgment, a matter often of importance to third persons as well as the parties and the court. The Committee believes that each of these rules should be revised to require filing before end of the 10–day period. Filing is an event that can be determined with certainty from court records. The phrase "no later than" is used—rather than "within"—to include post-judgment motions that sometimes are filed before actual entry of the judgment by the clerk. It should be noted that under Rule 6(a) Saturdays, Sundays, and legal holidays are excluded in measuring the 10–day period, and that under Rule 5 the motions when filed are to contain a certificate of service on other parties.

2007 AMENDMENTS

The language of Rule 52 has been amended as part of the general restyling of the Civil Rules to make them more easily understood and to make style and terminology consistent throughout the rules. These changes are intended to be stylistic only.

Former Rule 52(a) said that findings are unnecessary on decisions of motions "except as provided in subdivision (c) of this rule." Amended Rule 52(a)(3) says that findings are unnecessary "unless these rules provide otherwise." This change reflects provisions in other rules that require Rule 52 findings on deciding motions. Rules 23(e), 23(h), and 54(d)(2)(C) are examples.

Amended Rule 52(a)(5) includes provisions that appeared in former Rule 52(a) and 52(b). Rule 52(a) provided that requests for findings are not necessary for purposes of review. It applied both in an action tried on the facts without a jury and also in granting or refusing an interlocutory injunction. Rule 52(b), applicable to findings "made in actions tried without a jury," provided that the sufficiency of the evidence might be "later questioned whether or not in the district court the party raising the question objected to the findings, moved to amend them, or moved for partial findings." Former Rule 52(b) did not explicitly apply to decisions granting or refusing an interlocutory injunction. Amended Rule 52(a)(5) makes explicit the application of this part of former Rule 52(b) to interlocutory injunction decisions.

Former Rule 52(c) provided for judgment on partial findings, and referred to it as "judgment as a matter of law." Amended Rule 52(c) refers only to "judgment," to avoid any confusion with a Rule 50 judgment as a matter of law in a jury case. The standards that govern judgment as a matter of law in a jury case have no bearing on a decision under Rule 52(c).

Rule 53.   Masters

1937 ADOPTION

Note to Subdivision (a). This is a modification of former Equity Rule 68 (Appointment and Compensation of Masters).

Note to Subdivision (b). This is substantially the first sentence of former Equity Rule 59 (Reference to Master—Exceptional, Not Usual) extended to actions formerly legal. See *Ex parte Peterson*, 1920, 253 U.S. 300, 40 S.Ct. 543, 64 L.Ed. 919.

Note to Subdivision (c). This is former Equity Rules 62 (Powers of Master) and 65 (Claimants Before Master Examinable by Him) with slight modifications. Compare former Equity Rules 49 (Evidence Taken Before Examiners, Etc.) and 51. (Evidence Taken Before Examiners, Etc.).

Note to Subdivision (d). (1) This is substantially a combination of the second sentence of former Equity Rule 59 (Reference to Master—Exceptional, Not Usual) and former Equity Rule 60 (Proceedings Before Master). Compare former Equity Rule 53 (Notice of Taking Testimony Before Examiner, Etc.).

(2) This is substantially former Equity Rule 52 (Attendance of Witnesses Before Commissioner, Master, or Examiner).

(3) This is substantially former Equity Rule 63 (Form of Accounts Before Master).

Note to Subdivision (e). This contains the substance of former Equity Rules 61 (Master's Report—Documents Identified but not Set Forth), 61½ (Master's Report—Presumption as to Correctness—Review), and 66 (Return of Master's Report—Exceptions—Hearing), with modifications as to the form and effect of the report and for inclusion of reports by auditors, referees, and examiners, and references in actions formerly legal. Compare former Equity Rules 49 (Evidence Taken Before Examiners, Etc.) and 67 (Costs on Exceptions to Master's Report). See *Camden* v. *Stuart*, 1892, 144 U.S. 104, 12 S.Ct. 585, 36 L.Ed. 363; *Ex parte Peterson,* 1920, 253 U.S. 300, 40 S.Ct. 543, 64 L.Ed. 919.

1966 AMENDMENT

These changes are designed to preserve the admiralty practice whereby difficult computations are referred to a commissioner or assessor, especially after an interlocutory judgment determining liability. As to separation of issues for trial see Rule 42(b).

1983 AMENDMENT

Subdivision (a). The creation of full-time magistrates, who serve at government expense and have no nonjudicial duties competing for their time, eliminates the need to appoint standing masters. Thus the prior provision in Rule 53(a) authorizing the appointment of standing masters is deleted. Additionally, the definition of "master" in subdivision (a) now eliminates the superseded office of commissioner.

The term "special master" is retained in Rule 53 in order to maintain conformity with 28 U.S.C. § 636(b)(2), authorizing a judge to designate a magistrate "to serve as a special master pursuant to the applicable provisions of this title and the Federal Rules of Civil Procedure for the United States District Courts." Obviously, when a magistrate serves as a special master, the provisions for compensation of masters are inapplicable, and the amendment to subdivision (a) so provides.

Although the existence of magistrates may make the appointment of outside masters unnecessary in many instances, see, *e.g., Gautreaux v. Chicago Housing Authority,* 384 F.Supp. 37 (N.D.Ill.1974), mandamus denied *sub nom., Chicago Housing Authority v. Austin,* 511 F.2d 82 (7th Cir.1975); *Avco Corp. v. American Tel. & Tel. Co.,* 68 F.R.D. 532 (S.D.Ohio 1975), such masters may prove useful when some special expertise is desired or when a magistrate is unavailable for lengthy and detailed supervision of a case.

Subdivision (b). The provisions of 28 U.S.C. § 636(b)(2) not only permit magistrates to serve as masters under Rule 53(b) but also eliminate the exceptional condition requirement of Rule 53(b) when the reference is made with the consent of the parties. The amendment to subdivision (b) brings Rule 53 into harmony with the statute by exempting magistrates, appointed with the consent of the parties, from the general requirement that some exceptional condition requires the reference. It should be noted that subdivision (b) does not address the question, raised in recent decisional law and commentary, as to whether the exceptional condition requirement is applicable when *private masters* who are not magistrates are appointed with the consent of the parties. See Silberman, *Masters and Magistrates Part II: The American Analogue,* 50 N.Y.U.L.Rev. 1297, 1354 (1975).

Subdivision (c). The amendment recognizes the abrogation of Federal Rule 43(c) by the Federal Rules of Evidence.

Subdivision (f). The new subdivision responds to confusion flowing from the dual authority for references of pretrial matters to magistrates. Such references can be made, with or without the consent of the parties, pursuant to Rule 53 or under 28 U.S.C. § 636(b)(1)(A) and (b)(1)(B). There are a number of distinctions between references made under the statute and under the rule. For example, under the statute nondispositive pretrial matters may be referred to a magistrate, without consent, for final determination with reconsideration by the district judge if the magistrate's order is clearly erroneous or contrary to law. Under the rule, however, the appointment of a master, without consent of the parties, to supervise discovery would require some exceptional condition (Rule 53(b)) and would subject the proceedings to the report procedures of Rule 53(e). If an order of reference does not clearly articulate the source of the court's authority the resulting proceedings could be subject to attack on grounds of the magistrate's noncompliance with the provisions of Rule 53. This subdivision therefore establishes a presumption that the limitations of Rule 53 are not applicable unless the reference is specifically made subject to Rule 53.

A magistrate serving as a special master under 28 U.S.C. § 636(b)(2) is governed by the provisions of Rule 53, with the exceptional condition requirement lifted in the case of a consensual reference.

1987 AMENDMENT

The amendments are technical. No substantive change is intended.

1991 AMENDMENT

The purpose of the revision is to expedite proceedings before a master. The former rule required only a filing of the master's report, with the clerk then notifying the parties of the filing. To receive a copy, a party would then be required to secure it from the clerk. By transmitting directly to the parties, the master can save some efforts of counsel. Some local rules have previously required such action by the master.

1993 AMENDMENT

This revision is made to conform the rule to changes made by the Judicial Improvements Act of 1990.

2003 AMENDMENT

Rule 53 is revised extensively to reflect changing practices in using masters. From the beginning in 1938, Rule 53 focused primarily on special masters who perform trial functions. Since then, however, courts have gained experience with masters appointed to perform a variety of pretrial and post-trial functions. See Willging, Hooper, Leary, Miletich, Reagan, & Shapard, Special Masters' Incidence and Activity (Federal Judicial Center 2000). This revised Rule 53 recognizes that in appropriate circumstances masters may properly be appointed to perform these functions and regulates such appointments. Rule 53 continues to address trial masters as well, but permits appointment of a trial master in an action to be tried to a jury only if the parties consent. The new rule clarifies the provisions that govern the appointment and function of masters for all purposes. Rule 53(g) also changes the standard of review for findings of fact made or recommended by a master. The core of the original Rule 53 remains, including its prescription that appointment of a master must be the exception and not the rule.

Special masters are appointed in many circumstances outside the Civil Rules. Rule 53 applies only to proceedings that Rule 1 brings within its reach.

Subdivision (a)(1). District judges bear primary responsibility for the work of their courts. A master should be appointed only in limited circumstances. Subdivision (a)(1) describes three different standards, relating to appointments by consent of the parties, appointments for trial duties, and appointments for pretrial or post-trial duties.

Consent Masters. Subparagraph (a)(1)(A) authorizes appointment of a master with the parties' consent. Party consent does not require that the court make the appointment; the court retains unfettered discretion to refuse appointment.

Trial Masters. Use of masters for the core functions of trial has been progressively limited. These limits are reflected in the provisions of subparagraph (a)(1)(B) that restrict appointments to exercise trial functions. The Supreme Court gave clear direction to this trend in La Buy v. Howes Leather Co., 352 U.S. 249 (1957); earlier roots are sketched in Los Angeles Brush Mfg. Corp. v. James, 272 U.S. 701 (1927). As to nonjury trials, this trend has developed through elaboration of the "exceptional condition" requirement in present Rule 53(b). This phrase is retained, and will continue to have the same force as it has developed. Although the provision that a reference "shall be the exception and not the rule" is deleted, its meaning is embraced for this setting by the exceptional condition requirement.

Subparagraph (a)(1)(B)(ii) carries forward the approach of present Rule 53(b), which exempts from the "exceptional condition" requirement "matters of account and of difficult computation of damages." This approach is justified only as to essentially ministerial determinations that require mastery of much detailed information but that do not require extensive determinations of credibility.

Evaluations of witness credibility should only be assigned to a trial master when justified by an exceptional condition.

The use of a trial master without party consent is abolished as to matters to be decided by a jury unless a statute provides for this practice.

Abolition of the direct power to appoint a trial master as t o issues to be decided by a jury leaves the way free to appoint a trial master with the consent of all parties. A trial master should be appointed in a jury case, with consent of the parties and concurrence of the court, only if the parties waive jury trial with respect to the issues submitted to the master or if the master's findings are to be submitted to the jury as evidence in the manner provided by former Rule 53(e)(3). In no circumstance may a master be appointed to preside at a jury trial.

The central function of a trial master is to preside over an evidentiary hearing on the merits of the claims or defenses in the action. This function distinguishes the trial master from most functions of pretrial and post-trial masters. If any master is to be used for such matters as a preliminary injunction hearing or a determination of complex damages issues, for example,

the master should be a trial master. The line, however, is not distinct. A pretrial master might well conduct an evidentiary hearing on a discovery dispute, and a post-trial master might conduct evidentiary hearings on questions of compliance.

Rule 53 has long provided authority to report the evidence without recommendations in nonjury trials. This authority is omitted from Rule 53(a)(1)(B). In some circumstances a master may be appointed under Rule 53(a)(1)(A) or (C) to take evidence and report without recommendations.

For nonjury cases, a master also may be appointed to assist the court in discharging trial duties other than conducting an evidentiary hearing.

Pretrial and Post–Trial Masters. Subparagraph (a)(1)(C) authorizes appointment of a master to address pretrial or post-trial matters. Appointment is limited t o matters t hat cannot be addressed effectively and in a timely fashion by an available district judge or magistrate judge of the district. A master's pretrial or post-trial duties may include matters that could be addressed by a judge, such as reviewing discovery documents for privilege, or duties t hat might not be suitable for a judge. Some forms of settlement negotiations, investigations, or administration of an organization are familiar examples of duties that a judge might not feel free to undertake.

Magistrate Judges. Particular attention should be paid to the prospect that a magistrate judge may be available for special assignments. United States magistrate judges are authorized by statute to perform many pretrial functions in civil actions. 28 U.S.C. § 636(b)(1). Ordinarily a district judge who delegates these functions should refer them to a magistrate judge acting as magistrate judge.

There is statutory authority to appoint a magistrate judge as special master. 28 U.S.C. § 636(b)(2). In special circumstances, or when expressly authorized by a statute other than § 636(b)(2), it may be appropriate to appoint a magistrate judge as a master when needed to perform functions outside those listed in § 636(b)(1). There is no apparent reason to appoint a magistrate judge to perform as master duties that could be performed in the role of magistrate judge. Party consent is required for trial before a magistrate judge, moreover, and this requirement should not be undercut by resort to Rule 53 unless specifically authorized by statute; see 42 U.S.C. § 2000e–5(f)(5).

Pretrial Masters. The appointment of masters to participate in pretrial proceedings has developed extensively over the last two decades as some district courts have felt the need for additional help in managing complex litigation. This practice is not well regulated by present Rule 53, which focuses on masters as trial participants. Rule 53 is amended to confirm the authority to appoint—and to regulate the use of—pretrial masters.

A pretrial master should be appointed only when the need is clear. Direct judicial performance of judicial functions may be particularly important in cases that involve important public issues or many parties. At the extreme, a broad delegation of pretrial responsibility as well as a delegation of trial responsibilities can run afoul of Article III.

A master also may be appointed to address matters that blur the divide between pretrial and trial functions. The court's responsibility to interpret patent claims as a matter of law, for example, may be greatly assisted by appointing a master who has expert knowledge of the field in which the patent operates. Review of the master's findings will be de novo under Rule 53(g)(4), but the advantages of initial determination by a master may make the process more effective and timely than disposition by the judge acting alone. Determination of foreign law may present comparable difficulties. The decision whether to appoint a master to address such matters is governed by subdivision (a)(1)(C), not the trial-master provisions of subdivision (a)(1)(B).

Post–Trial Masters. Courts have come to rely on masters to assist in framing and enforcing complex decrees. Present Rule 53 does not directly address this practice. Amended Rule 53 authorizes appointment of post-trial masters for these and similar purposes. The constraint of subdivision (a)(1)(C) limits this practice to cases in which the master's duties cannot be performed effectively and in a timely fashion by an available district judge or magistrate judge of the district.

Reliance on a master is appropriate when a complex decree requires complex policing, particularly when a party has proved resistant or intransigent. This practice has been recognized by the Supreme Court, see Local 28, Sheet Metal Workers' Internat. Assn. v. EEOC, 478 U.S. 421, 481–482 (1986). The master's role in enforcement may extend to investigation in ways that are quite unlike the traditional role of judicial officers in an adversary system.

Expert Witness Overlap. This rule does not address the difficulties that arise when a single person is appointed to perform overlapping roles as master and as court-appointed expert witness under Evidence Rule 706. Whatever combination of functions is involved, the Rule 53(a)(1)(B) limit that confines trial masters to issues to be decided by the court does not apply to a person who also is appointed as an expert witness under Evidence Rule 706.

Subdivision (a)(2) and (3). Masters are subject to the Code of Conduct for United States Judges, with exceptions spelled out in the Code. Special care must be taken to ensure that there is no actual or apparent conflict of interest involving a master. The standard of disqualification is established by 28 U.S.C. § 455. The affidavit required by Rule 53(b)(3) provides an important source of information about possible grounds for disqualification, but careful inquiry should be made at the time of making t he initial appointment. The disqualification standards established by § 455 are strict. Because a master is not a public judicial officer, it may be appropriate to permit the parties to consent to appointment of a particular person as master in circumstances that would require disqualification of a judge. The judge must be careful to ensure that no party feels any pressure to consent, but with such assurances—and with the judge's own determination that there is no troubling conflict of interests or disquieting appearance of impropriety—consent may justify an otherwise barred appointment.

One potential disqualification issue is peculiar to the master's role. It may happen that a master who is an attorney represents a client whose litigation is assigned to the judge who appointed the attorney as master. Other parties to the litigation may fear that the attorney-master will gain special respect from the judge. A flat prohibition on appearance before the appointing judge during the time of service as master, however, might in some circumstances unduly limit t he opportunity to make a desirable appointment. These matters may be regulated to some extent by state rules of professional responsibility. The question of present conflicts, and t he possibility of future conflicts, can be considered at the time of appointment. Depending on the circumstances, the judge may consider it appropriate to impose a non-appearance condition on the lawyer-master, and perhaps on the master's firm as well.

Subdivision (b). The order appointing a pretrial master is vitally important in informing the master and the parties about the nature and extent of the master's duties and authority. Care must be taken to make the order as precise as possible. The parties must be given notice and opportunity to be heard on the question whether a master should be appointed and on the terms of the appointment. To the extent possible, the notice should describe the master's proposed duties, time to complete the duties, standards of review, and compensation. Often it will be useful to engage the parties in the process of identifying the master, inviting nominations, and reviewing potential candidates. Party involvement may be particularly useful if a pretrial master is expected to promote settlement.

The hearing requirement of Rule 53(b)(1) can be satisfied by an opportunity to make written submissions unless the circumstances require live testimony.

Rule 53(b)(2) requires precise designation of the master's duties and authority. Clear identification of any investigating or enforcement duties is particularly important. Clear delineation of topics for any reports or recommendations is also an important part of this process. And it is important to protect against delay by establishing a time schedule for performing the assigned duties. Early designation of the procedure for fixing the master's compensation also may provide useful guidance to the parties.

Ex parte communications between a master and the court present troubling questions. Ordinarily the order should prohibit such communications, assuring that the parties know where authority is lodged at each step of the proceedings. Prohibiting ex parte communications between master and court also can enhance the role of a settlement master by assuring the parties that settlement can be fostered by confidential revelations that will not be shared with the court. Yet there may be circumstances in which the master's role is enhanced by the opportunity for ex parte communications with the court. A master assigned to help coordinate multiple proceedings, for example, may benefit from off-the-record exchanges with the court about logistical matters. The rule does not directly regulate these matters. It requires only that the court exercise its discretion and address the topic in the order of appointment.

Similarly difficult questions surround ex part e communications between a master and the parties. Ex parte communications may be essential in seeking to advance settlement. Ex parte communications also may prove useful in other settings, as with in camera review of documents to resolve privilege questions.

In most settings, however, ex parte communications with the parties should be discouraged or prohibited. The rule requires that the court address the topic in the order of appointment.

Subdivision (b)(2)(C) provides that the appointment order must state the nature of the materials to be preserved and filed as the record of the master's activities, and (b)(2)(D) requires that the order state the method of filing the record. It is not feasible to prescribe the nature of the record without regard to the nature of the master's duties. The records appropriate to discovery duties may be different from those appropriate to encouraging settlement, investigating possible violations of a complex decree, or making recommendations for trial findings. A basic requirement, however, is that the master must make and file a complete record of the evidence considered in making or recommending findings of fact on the basis of evidence. The order of appointment should routinely include this requirement unless the nature of the appointment precludes any prospect that the master will make or recommend evidence-based findings of fact. In some circumstances it may be appropriate for a party to file materials directly with the court as provided by Rule 5(e), but in many circumstances filing with the court may be inappropriate. Confidentiality is important with respect to many materials that may properly be considered by a master. Materials in the record can be transmitted to the court, and filed, in connection with review of a master's order, report, or recommendations under subdivisions (f) and (g). Independently of review proceedings, the court may direct filing of any materials that it wishes to make part of the public record.

The provision in subdivision (b)(2)(D) that the order must state the standards for reviewing the master's orders, findings, or recommendations is a reminder of t he provisions of subdivision (g)(3) that recognize stipulations for review less searching than the presumptive requirement of de novo decision by the court. Subdivision (b)(2)(D) does not authorize the court to supersede the limits of subdivision (g)(3).

In setting the procedure for fixing the master's compensation, it is useful at the outset to establish specific guidelines to control total expense. The court has power under subdivision (h) to change the basis and terms for determining compensation after notice to the parties.

Subdivision (b)(3) permits entry of the order appointing a master only after the master has filed an affidavit disclosing whether there is any ground for

disqualification under 28 U.S.C. § 455. If the affidavit discloses a possible ground for disqualification, the order can enter only if the court determines that there is no ground for disqualification or if the parties, knowing of the ground for disqualification, consent with the court's approval to waive the disqualification.

The provision in Rule 53(b)(4) for amending the order of appointment is as import ant as the provisions for the initial order. Anything that could be done in the initial order can be done by amendment. The hearing requirement can be satisfied by an opportunity to make written submissions unless the circumstances require live testimony.

Subdivision (c). Subdivision (c) is a simplification of the provisions scattered throughout present Rule 53. It is intended to provide the broad and flexible authority necessary to discharge the master's responsibilities. The most important delineation of a master's authority and duties is provided by the Rule 53(b) appointing order.

Subdivision (d). The subdivision (d) provisions for evidentiary hearings are reduced from t he extensive provisions in current Rule 53. This simplification of the rule is not intended to diminish the authority that may be delegated to a master. Reliance is placed on the broad and general terms of subdivision (c).

Subdivision (e). Subdivision (e) provides that a master's order must be filed and entered on the docket. It must be promptly served on the parties, a task ordinarily accomplished by mailing or other means as permitted by Rule 5(b). In some circumstances it may be appropriate to have the clerk's office assist the master in mailing the order to the parties.

Subdivision (f). Subdivision (f) restates some of the provisions of present Rule 53(e)(1). The report is the master's primary means of communication with the court. The materials to be provided to support review of the report will depend on the nature of the report. The master should provide all portions of the record preserved under Rule 53(b)(2)(C) that the master deems relevant to the report. The parties may designate additional materials from the record, and may seek permission to supplement the record with evidence. The court may direct that additional materials from the record be provided and filed. Given the wide array of tasks that may be assigned to a pretrial master, there may be circumstances that justify sealing a report or review record against public access—a report on continuing or failed settlement efforts is the most likely example. A post-trial master may be assigned duties in formulating a decree that deserve similar protection. Such circumstances may even justify denying access to the report or review materials by the parties, although this step should be taken only for the most compelling reasons. Sealing is much less likely to be appropriate with respect to a trial master's report.

Before formally making an order, report, or recommendations, a master may find it helpful to circulate a draft to the parties for review and comment. The usefulness of this practice depends on the nature of the master's proposed action.

Subdivision (g). The provisions of subdivision (g)(1), describing the court's powers to afford a hearing, take evidence, and act on a master's order, report, or recommendations are drawn from present Rule 53(e)(2), but are not limited, as present Rule 53(e)(2) is limited, to the report of a trial master in a nonjury action. The requirement that the court must afford an opportunity to be heard can be satisfied by taking written submissions when the court acts on the report without taking live testimony.

The subdivision (g)(2) time limits for objecting to—or seeking adoption or modification of—a master's order, report, or recommendations, are important. They are not jurisdictional. Although a court may properly refuse to entertain untimely review proceedings, the court may excuse the failure to seek timely review. The basic time period is lengthened to

20 days because the present 10–day period may be too short to permit thorough study and response to a complex report dealing with complex litigation. If no party asks the court to act on a master's report, the court is free to adopt the master's action or to disregard it at any relevant point in the proceedings.

Subdivision (g)(3) establishes the standards of review for a master's findings of fact or recommended findings of fact. The court must decide de novo all objections to findings of fact made or recommended by the master unless the parties stipulate, with the court's consent, t hat t he findings will be reviewed for clear error or—with respect to a master appointed on the parties' consent or appointed to address pretrial or post-trial matters— that the findings will be final. Clear-error review is more likely to be appropriate with respect to findings that do not go to the merits of the underlying claims or defenses, such as findings of fact bearing on a privilege objection to a discovery request. Even if no objection is made, the court is free to decide the facts de novo; to review for clear error if an earlier approved stipulation provided clear-error review; or to withdraw its consent to a stipulation for clear-error review or finality, and then to decide de novo. If the court withdraws its consent to a stipulation for finality or clear-error review, it may reopen the opportunity to object.

Under Rule 53(g)(4), the court must decide de novo all objections to conclusions of law made or recommended by a master. As with findings of fact, the court also may decide conclusions of law de novo when no objection is made.

Apart from factual and legal questions, masters often make determinations that, when made by a trial court, would be treated as matters of procedural discretion. The court may set a standard for review of such matters in the order of appointment, and may amend the order to establish the standard. If no standard is set by the original or amended order appointing the master, review of procedural matters is for abuse of discretion. The subordinate role of the master means that the trial court's review for abuse of discretion may be more searching than the review that an appellate court makes of a trial court.

If a master makes a recommendation on any matter that does not fall within Rule 53(g)(3), (4), or (5), the court may act on the recommendation under Rule 53(g)(1).

Subdivision (h). The need to pay compensation is a substantial reason for care in appointing private persons as masters.

Payment of the master's fees must be allocated among the parties and any property or subject-matter within the court's control. The amount in controversy and the means of the parties may provide some guidance in making the allocation. The nature of the dispute also may be important—parties pursuing matters of public interest, for example, may deserve special protection. A party whose unreasonable behavior has occasioned the need to appoint a master, on the other hand, may properly be charged all or a major portion of the master's fees. It may be proper to revise an interim allocation after decision on the merits. The revision need not await a decision that is final for purposes of appeal, but may be made to reflect disposition of a substantial portion of the case.

The basis and terms for fixing compensation should be stated in the order of appointment. The court retains power to alter the initial basis and terms, after notice and an opportunity to be heard, but should protect the parties against unfair surprise.

The provision of former Rule 53(a) that the "provision for compensation shall not apply when a United States Magistrate Judge is designated to serve as a master" is deleted as unnecessary. Other provisions of law preclude compensation.

Subdivision (i). Rule 53(i) carries forward unchanged former Rule 53(f).

2007 AMENDMENTS

The language of Rule 53 has been amended as part of the general restyling of the Civil Rules to make them more easily understood and to make style and terminology consistent throughout the rules. These changes are intended to be stylistic only.

VII. JUDGMENT

Rule 54.   Judgments; Costs

1937 ADOPTION

Note to Subdivision (a). The second sentence is derived substantially from former Equity Rule 71 (Form of Decree).

Note to Subdivision (b). This provides for the separate judgment of equity and code practice. See Wis.Stat. (1935) § 270.54; Compare N.Y.C.P.A. (1937) § 476.

Note to Subdivision (c). For the limitation on default contained in the first sentence, see 2 N.D.Comp.Laws Ann. (1913) § 7680; N.Y.C.P.A. (1937) § 479. Compare English Rules Under the Judicature Act (The Annual Practice, 1937) O. 13, r.r. 3–12. The remainder is a usual code provision. It makes clear that a judgment should give the relief to which a party is entitled, regardless of whether it is legal or equitable or both. This necessarily includes the deficiency judgment in foreclosure cases formerly provided for by Equity Rule 10 (Decree for Deficiency in Foreclosures, Etc.).

Note to Subdivision (d). For the present rule in common law actions, see *Ex parte Peterson,* 253 U.S. 300, 40 S.Ct. 543, 64 L.Ed. 919 (1920); Payne, *Costs in Common Law Actions in the Federal Courts* (1935), 21 Va.L.Rev. 397.

The provisions as to costs in actions *in forma pauperis* contained in U.S.C., Title 28, former §§ 832–836 are unaffected by this rule. Other sections of U.S.C., Title 28, which are unaffected by this rule are: former §§ 815 (Costs; plaintiff not entitled to, when), 821 (Costs; infringement of patent; disclaimer), 825 (Costs; several actions), 829 (Costs; attorney liable for, when), and 830 (Costs; bill of; taxation).

The provisions of the following and similar statutes as to costs against the United States and its officers and agencies are specifically continued:

U.S.C., Title 15, §§ 77v(a), 78aa, 79y (Securities and Exchange Commission)

U.S.C., Title 16, § 825p (Federal Power Commission)

U.S.C., Title 26, §§ 3679(d) and 3745(d)(Internal revenue actions)

U.S.C., Title 26, § 3770(b)(2)(Reimbursement of costs of recovery against revenue officers)

U.S.C., Title 28, former § 817 (Internal revenue actions)

U.S.C., Title 28, former § 836 (United States—actions *in forma pauperis*)

U.S.C., Title 28, former § 842 (Actions against revenue officers)

U.S.C., Title 28, former § 870 (United States—in certain cases)

U.S.C., Title 28, former § 906 (United States—foreclosure actions)

U.S.C., Title 47, § 401 (Communications Commission)

The provisions of the following and similar statutes as to costs are unaffected:

U.S.C., Title 7, § 210(f)(Actions for damages based on an order of the Secretary of Agriculture under Stockyards Act)

U.S.C., Title 7, § 499g(c)(Appeals from reparations orders of Secretary of Agriculture under Perishable Commodities Act)

U.S.C., Title 8, § 45 (Action against district attorneys in certain cases)

U.S.C., Title 15, § 15 (Actions for injuries due to violation of antitrust laws)

U.S.C., Title 15, § 72 (Actions for violation of law forbidding importation or sale of articles at less than market value or wholesale prices)

U.S.C., Title 15, § 77k (Actions by persons acquiring securities registered with untrue statements under Securities Act of 1933)

U.S.C., Title 15, § 78i(e)(Certain actions under the Securities Exchange Act of 1934)

U.S.C., Title 15, § 78r (Similar to 78i(e))

U.S.C., Title 15, § 96 (Infringement of trade-mark—damages)

U.S.C., Title 15, § 99 (Infringement of trade-mark—injunctions)

U.S.C., Title 15, § 124 (Infringement of trade-mark—damages)

U.S.C., Title 19, § 274 (Certain actions under customs law)

U.S.C., Title 30, § 32 (Action to determine right to possession of mineral lands in certain cases)

U.S.C., Title 31, §§ 232 and 234 (Action for making false claims upon United States)

U.S.C., Title 33, § 926 (Actions under Harbor Workers' Compensation Act)

U.S.C., Title 35, § 67 (Infringement of patent—damages)

U.S.C., Title 35, § 69 (Infringement of patent—pleading and proof)

U.S.C., Title 35, § 71 (Infringement of patent—when specification too broad)

U.S.C., Title 45, § 153p (Actions for non-compliance with an order of National R. R. Adjustment Board for payment of money)

U.S.C., Title 46, § 38 (Action for penalty for failure to register vessel)

U.S.C., Title 46, § 829 (Action based on non-compliance with an order of Maritime Commission for payment of money)

U.S.C., Title 46, § 941 (Certain actions under Ship Mortgage Act)

U.S.C., Title 46, § 1227 (Actions for damages for violation of certain provisions of the Merchant Marine Act, 1936)

U.S.C., Title 47, § 206 (Actions for certain violations of Communications Act of 1934)

U.S.C., Title 49, § 16(2)(Action based on non-compliance with an order of I.C.C. for payment of money)

1946 AMENDMENT

Note. The historic rule in the federal courts has always prohibited piecemeal disposal of litigation and permitted appeals only from final judgments except in those special instances covered by statute. *Hohorst v. Hamburg–American Packet Co.,* 1893, 148 U.S. 262, 13 S.Ct. 590, 37 L.Ed. 443; *Rexford v. Brunswick–Balke–Collender Co.,* 1913, 228 U.S. 339, 33 S.Ct. 515, 57 L.Ed. 864; *Collins v. Miller,* 1920, 252 U.S. 364, 40 S.Ct. 347, 64 L.Ed. 616. Rule 54(b) was originally adopted in view of the wide scope and possible content of the newly created "civil action" in order to avoid the possible injustice of a delay in judgment of a distinctly separate claim to await adjudication of the entire case. It was not designed to overturn the settled federal rule stated above, which, indeed, has more recently been reiterated in *Catlin v. United States,* 1945, 324 U.S. 229, 65 S.Ct. 631, 89 L.Ed. 911. See also *United States v. Florian,* 1941, 312 U.S. 656, 61 S.Ct. 713, 85 L.Ed. 1105; *Reeves v. Beardall,* 1942, 316 U.S. 283, 62 S.Ct. 1085, 86 L.Ed. 1478.

Unfortunately, this was not always understood, and some confusion ensued. Hence situations arose where district courts made a piecemeal disposition of an action and entered what the parties thought amounted to a judgment, although a trial remained to be had on other claims similar or identical with those disposed of. In the interim the parties did not know their ultimate rights, and accordingly took an appeal, thus putting the finality of the partial judgment in question. While most appellate courts have reached a result generally in accord with the intent of the rule, yet there have been divergent precedents and division of views which have served to render the issues more clouded to the parties appellant. It hardly seems a case where multiplicity of precedents will tend to remove the problem from debate. The problem is presented and discussed in the following cases: *Atwater v. North American Coal Corp.,* C.C.A.2, 1940, 111 F.2d 125; *Rosenblum v. Dingfelder,* C.C.A.2, 1940, 111 F.2d 406; *Audi-Vision, Inc. v. RCA Mfg. Co., Inc.,* C.C.A.2, 1943, 136 F.2d 621; *Zalkind v. Scheinman,* C.C.A.2, 1943, 139 F.2d 895; *Oppenheimer v. F. J. Young & Co., Inc.,* C.C.A.2, 1944, 144 F.2d 387; *Libbey-Owens-Ford Glass Co. v. Sylvania Industrial Corp.,* C.C.A.2, 1946, 154 F.2d 814, certiorari denied 328 U.S. 859, 66 S.Ct. 1353, 90 L.Ed. 1630; *Zarati Steamship Co. v. Park Bridge Corp.,* C.C.A.2, 1946, 154 F.2d 377; *Baltimore and Ohio R. Co. v. United Fuel Gas Co.,* C.C.A.4, 1946, 154 F.2d 545; *Jefferson Electric Co. v. Sola Electric Co.,* C.C.A.7, 1941, 122 F.2d 124; *Leonard v. Socony-Vacuum Oil Co.,* C.C.A.7, 1942, 130 F.2d 535; *Markham v. Kasper,* C.C.A.7, 1945, 152 F.2d 270; *Hanney v. Franklin Fire Ins. Co. of Philadelphia,* C.C.A.9, 1944, 142 F.2d 864; *Toomey v. Toomey,* 1945, 149 F.2d 19, 80 U.S.App.D.C. 77.

In view of the difficulty thus disclosed, the Advisory Committee in its two preliminary drafts of proposed amendments attempted to redefine the original rule with particular stress upon the interlocutory nature of partial judgments which did not adjudicate all claims arising out of a single transaction or occurrence. This attempt appeared to meet with almost universal approval from those of the profession commenting upon it, although there were, of course, helpful suggestions for additional changes in language or clarification of detail. But cf. Circuit Judge Frank's dissenting opinion in *Libbey-Owens-Ford Glass Co. v. Sylvania Industrial Corp.,* supra, n.21 of the dissenting opinion. The Committee, however, became convinced on careful study of its own proposals that the seeds of ambiguity still remained, and that it had not completely solved the problem of piecemeal appeals. After extended consideration, it concluded that a retention of the older federal rule was desirable and that this rule needed only the exercise of a discretionary power to afford a remedy in the infrequent harsh case to provide a simple, definite, workable rule. This is afforded by amended Rule 54(b). It re-establishes an ancient policy with clarity and precision. For the possibility of staying execution where not all claims are disposed of under Rule 54(b), see amended Rule 62(h).

This rule permitting appeal, upon the trial court's determination of "no just reason for delay," from a judgment upon one or more but less than all the claims in an action, has generally been given a sympathetic construction by the courts and its validity is settled. *Reeves* v. *Beardall,* 316 U.S. 283, 62 S.Ct. 1085, 86 L.Ed. 1478 (1942); *Sears, Roebuck & Co.* v. *Mackey,* 351 U.S. 427, 76 S.Ct. 895, 100 L.Ed. 1297 (1956); *Cold Metal Process Co.* v. *United Engineering & Foundry Co.,* 351 U.S. 445, 76 S.Ct. 904, 100 L.Ed. 1311 (1956).

A serious difficulty has, however, arisen because the rule speaks of claims but nowhere mentions parties. A line of cases has developed in the circuits consistently holding the rule to be inapplicable to the dismissal, even with the requisite trial court determination, of one or more but less than all defendants jointly charged in an action, i. e. charged with various forms of concerted or related wrongdoing or related liability. See *Mull* v. *Ackerman,* 279 F.2d 25 (2d Cir.1960); *Richards* v. *Smith,* 276 F.2d 652 (5th Cir.1960); *Hardy* v. *Bankers Life & Cas. Co.,* 222 F.2d 827 (7th Cir.1955); *Steiner* v. *20th Century–Fox Film Corp.,* 220 F.2d 105 (9th Cir.1955). For purposes of Rule 54(b) it was arguable that there were as many "claims" as there were parties defendant and that the rule in its present text applied where less than all of the parties were dismissed, cf. *United Artist Corp.* v. *Masterpiece Productions, Inc.,* 221 F.2d 213, 215 (2d Cir.1955); *Bowling Machines, Inc.* v. *First Nat. Bank,* 283 F.2d 39 (1st Cir.1960); but the Courts of Appeals are now committed to an opposite view.

The danger of hardship through delay of appeal until the whole action is concluded may be at least as serious in the multiple-parties situations as in multiple-claims cases, see *Pabellon* v. *Grace Line, Inc.,* 191 F.2d 169, 179 (2d Cir.1951), cert. denied, 342 U.S. 893, 72 S.Ct. 201, 96 L.Ed. 669 (1951), and courts and commentators have urged that Rule 54(b) be changed to take in the former. See *Reagan* v. *Traders & General Ins. Co.,* 255 F.2d 845 (5th Cir.1958); *Meadows* v. *Greyhound Corp.,* 235 F.2d 233 (5th Cir.1956); *Steiner* v. *20th Century–Fox Film Corp.,* supra; 6 Moore's Federal Practice ¶ 54.34[2] (2d ed. 1953); 3 Barron & Holtzoff, *Federal Practice & Procedure* § 1193.2 (Wright ed. 1958); *Developments in the Law—Multiparty Litigation,* 71 Harv.L.Rev. 874, 981 (1958); Note, 62 Yale L.J. 263, 271 (1953); Ill.Ann.Stat. ch. 110, § 50(2)(Smith-Hurd 1956). The amendment accomplishes this purpose by referring explicitly to parties.

There has been some recent indication that interlocutory appeal under the provisions of 28 U.S.C. § 1292(b), added in 1958, may now be available for the multiple-parties cases here considered. See *Jaftex Corp.* v. *Randolph Mills, Inc.,* 282 F.2d 508 (2d Cir.1960). The Rule 54(b) procedure seems preferable for those cases, and § 1292(b) should be held inapplicable to them when the rule is enlarged as here proposed. See *Luckenbach Steamship Co., Inc.* v. *H. Muehlstein & Co., Inc.,* 280 F.2d 755, 757 (2d Cir.1960); 1 Barron & Holtzoff, supra, § 58.1, p. 321 (Wright ed. 1960).

The amendment is technical. No substantive change is intended.

Subdivision (d). This revision adds paragraph (2) to this subdivision to provide for a frequently recurring form of litigation not initially contemplated by the rules—disputes over the amount of attorneys' fees to be awarded in the large number of actions in which prevailing parties may be entitled to such awards or in which the court must determine the fees to be paid from a common fund. This revision seeks to harmonize and clarify procedures that have been developed through case law and local rules.

Paragraph (1). Former subdivision (d), providing for taxation of costs by the clerk, is renumbered as paragraph (1) and revised to exclude applications for attorneys' fees.

Paragraph (2). This new paragraph establishes a procedure for presenting claims for attorneys' fees, whether or not denominated as "costs." It applies also to requests for reimbursement of expenses, not taxable as costs, when recoverable under governing law incident to the award of fees. *Cf. West Virginia Univ. Hosp.* v. *Casey,* 499 U.S. 83 (1991), holding, prior to the Civil Rights Act of 1991, that expert witness fees were not recoverable under 42 U.S.C. § 1988. As noted in subparagraph (A), it does not, however, apply to fees recoverable as an element of damages, as when sought under the terms of a contract; such damages typically are to be claimed in a pleading and may involve issues to be resolved by a jury. Nor, as provided in subparagraph (E), does it apply to awards of fees as sanctions authorized or mandated under these rules or under 28 U.S.C. § 1927.

Subparagraph (B) provides a deadline for motions for attorneys' fees—14 days after final judgment unless the court or a statute specifies some other time. One purpose of this provision is to assure that the opposing party is informed of the claim before the time for appeal has elapsed. Prior law did not prescribe any specific time limit on claims for attorneys' fees. *White v. New Hampshire Dep't of Employment Sec.,* 455 U.S. 445, 102 S.Ct. 1162, 71 L.Ed.2d 325 (1982). In many nonjury cases the court will want to consider attorneys' fee issues immediately after rendering its judgment on the merits of the case. Note that the time for making claims is specifically stated in some legislation, such as the Equal Access to Justice Act, 28 U.S.C. § 2412(d)(1)(B)(30–day filing period).

Prompt filing affords an opportunity for the court to resolve fee disputes shortly after trial, while the services performed are freshly in mind. It also enables the court in appropriate circumstances to make its ruling on a fee request in time for any appellate review of a dispute over fees to proceed at the same time as review on the merits of the case.

Filing a motion for fees under this subdivision does not affect the finality or the appealability of a judgment, though revised Rule 58 provides a mechanism by which prior to appeal the court can suspend the finality to resolve a motion for fees. If an appeal on the merits of the case is taken, the court may rule on the claim for fees, may defer its ruling on the motion, or may deny the motion without prejudice, directing under subdivision (d)(2)(B) a new period for filing after the appeal has been resolved. A notice of appeal does not extend the time for filing a fee claim based on the initial judgment, but the court under subdivision (d)(2)(B) may effectively extend the period by permitting claims to be filed after resolution of the appeal. A new period for filing will automatically begin if a new judgment is entered following a reversal or remand by the appellate court or the granting of a motion under Rule 59.

The rule does not require that the motion be supported at the time of filing with the evidentiary material bearing on the fees. This material must of course be submitted in due course, according to such schedule as the court may direct in light of the circumstances of the case. What is required is the filing of a motion sufficient to alert the adversary and the court that there is a claim for fees and the amount of such fees (or a fair estimate).

If directed by the court, the moving party is also required to disclose any fee agreement, including those between attorney and client, between attorneys sharing a fee to be awarded, and between adversaries made in partial settlement of a dispute where the settlement must be implemented by court action as may be required by Rules 23(e) and 23.1 or other like provisions. With respect to the fee arrangements requiring court approval, the court may also by local rule require disclosure immediately after such arrangements are agreed to. *E.g.,* Rule 5 of United States District Court for the Eastern District of New York; *cf. In re "Agent Orange" Product Liability Litigation (MDL 381),* 611 F.Supp. 1452, 1464 (E.D.N.Y.1985).

In the settlement of class actions resulting in a common fund from which fees will be sought, courts frequently have required that claims for fees be presented in advance of hearings to consider approval of the proposed settlement. The rule does not affect this practice, as it permits the court to require submissions of fee claims in advance of entry of judgment.

Subparagraph (C) assures the parties of an opportunity to make an appropriate presentation with respect to issues involving the evaluation of legal services. In some cases, an evidentiary hearing may be needed, but this is not required in every case. The amount of time to be allowed for the preparation of submissions both in support of and in opposition to awards should be tailored to the particular case.

The court is explicitly authorized to make a determination of the liability for fees before receiving submissions by the parties bearing on the amount of an award. This option may be appropriate in actions in which the liability issue is doubtful and the evaluation issues are numerous and complex.

The court may order disclosure of additional information, such as that bearing on prevailing local rates or on the appropriateness of particular services for which compensation is sought.

On rare occasion, the court may determine that discovery under Rules 26–37 would be useful to the parties. *Compare* Rules Governing Section 2254 Cases in the U.S. District Courts, Rule 6. *See* Note, *Determining the Reasonableness of Attorneys' Fees—the Discoverability of Billing Records,* 64 *B.U.L.Rev.* 241 (1984). In complex fee disputes, the court may use case management techniques to limit the scope of the dispute or to facilitate the settlement of fee award disputes.

Fee awards should be made in the form of a separate judgment under Rule 58 since such awards are subject to review in the court of appeals. To facilitate review, the paragraph provides that the court set forth its findings and conclusions as under Rule 52(a), though in most cases this explanation could be quite brief.

Subparagraph (D) explicitly authorizes the court to establish procedures facilitating the efficient and fair resolution of fee claims. A local rule, for example, might call for matters to be presented through affidavits, or might provide for issuance of proposed findings by the court, which would be treated as accepted by the parties unless objected to within a specified time. A court might also consider establishing a schedule reflecting customary fees or factors affecting fees within the community, as implicitly suggested by Justice O'Connor in *Pennsylvania v. Delaware Valley Citizens' Council,* 483 U.S. 711, 733, 107 S.Ct. 3078, 3091, 97 L.Ed.2d 585 (1987) (O'Connor, J., concurring)(how particular markets compensate for contingency). *Cf. Thompson v. Kennickell,* 710 F.Supp. 1 (D.D.C. 1989) (use of findings in other cases to promote consistency). The parties, of course, should be permitted to show that in the circumstances of the case such a schedule should not be applied or that different hourly rates would be appropriate.

The rule also explicitly permits, without need for a local rule, the court to refer issues regarding the amount of a fee award in a particular case to a master under Rule 53. The district judge may designate a magistrate judge to act as a master for this purpose or may refer a motion for attorneys' fees to a magistrate judge for proposed findings and recommendations under Rule 72(b). This authorization eliminates any controversy as to whether such references are permitted under Rule 53(b) as "matters of account and of difficult computation of damages" and whether motions for attorneys' fees can be treated as the equivalent of a dispositive pretrial matter that can be referred to a magistrate judge. For consistency and efficiency, all such matters might be referred to the same magistrate judge.

Subparagraph (E) excludes from this rule the award of fees as sanctions under these rules or under 28 U.S.C. § 1927.

2002 AMENDMENT

Subdivision (d)(2)(C) is amended to delete the requirement that judgment on a motion for attorney fees be set forth in a separate document. This change complements the amendment of Rule 58(a)(1), which deletes the separate document requirement for an order disposing of a motion for attorney fees under Rule 54. These changes are made to support amendment of Rule 4 of the Federal Rules of Appellate Procedure. It continues to be important that a district court make clear its meaning when it intends an order to be the final disposition of a motion for attorney fees.

The requirement in subdivision (d)(2)(B) that a motion for attorney fees be not only filed but also served no later than 14 days after entry of judgment is changed to require filing only, to establish a parallel with Rules 50, 52, and 59. Service continues to be required under Rule 5(a).

2003 AMENDMENT

Rule 54(d)(2)(D) is revised to reflect amendments to Rule 53.

2007 AMENDMENTS

The language of Rule 54 has been amended as part of the general restyling of the Civil Rules to make them more easily understood and to make style and terminology consistent throughout the rules. These changes are intended to be stylistic only.

The words "or class member" have been removed from Rule 54(d)(2)(C) because Rule 23(h)(2) now addresses objections by class members to attorney-fee motions. Rule 54(d)(2)(C) is amended to recognize that Rule 23(h) now controls those aspects of attorney-fee motions in class actions to which it is addressed.

Rule 55. Default

1937 ADOPTION

This represents the joining of the equity decree *pro confesso* (former Equity Rules 12 (Issue of Subpoena—Time for Answer), 16 (Defendant to Answer—Default—Decree *Pro Confesso*), 17 (Decree *Pro Confesso* to be Followed by Final Decree—Setting Aside Default), 29 (Defenses—How Presented), 31 (Reply—When Required—When Cause at Issue)) and the judgment by default now governed by U.S.C., Title 28, former § 724 (Conformity Act). For dismissal of an action for failure to comply with these rules or any order of the court, see Rule 41(b).

Note to Subdivision (a). The provision for the entry of default comes from the Massachusetts practice, 2 Mass.Gen. Laws (Ter.Ed., 1932) ch. 231, § 57. For affidavit of default, see 2 Minn.Stat. (Mason, 1927) § 9256.

Note to Subdivision (b). The provision in paragraph (1) for the entry of judgment by the clerk when plaintiff claims a sum certain is found in the N.Y.C.P.A. (1937) § 485, in Calif.Code Civ.Proc. (Deering, 1937) § 585(1), and in Conn. Practice Book (1934) § 47. For provisions similar to paragraph (2), compare Calif.Code, *supra*, § 585(2); N.Y.C.P.A. (1937) § 490; 2 Minn.Stat. (Mason, 1927) § 9256(3); 2 Wash.Rev.Stat.Ann. (Remington, 1932) § 411(2); U.S.C., Title 28, § 1874, formerly § 785 (Action to recover forfeiture in bond) and similar statutes are preserved by the last clause of paragraph (2).

Note to Subdivision (e). This restates substantially the last clause of U.S.C., Title 28, former § 763 (Action against the United States under the Tucker Act). As this rule governs in all actions against the United States, U.S.C., Title 28, former § 45 (Practice and procedure in certain cases under the interstate commerce laws) and similar statutes are modified in so far as they contain anything inconsistent therewith.

SUPPLEMENTARY NOTE OF ADVISORY COMMITTEE REGARDING THIS RULE

Note. The operation of Rule 55(b)(Judgment) is directly affected by the Soldiers' and Sailors' Civil Relief Act of 1940, 50 U.S.C., Appendix, § 501 et seq. Section 200 of the Act [50 U.S.C.A. Appendix, § 520] imposes specific requirements which must be fulfilled before a default judgment can be entered, e.g., *Ledwith* v. *Storkan*, D.Neb.1942, 6 Fed.Rule Serv. 60b.24, Case 2, 2 F.R.D. 539, and also provides for the vacation of a judgment in certain circumstances. See discussion in Commentary, Effect of Conscription Legislation on the Federal Rules, 1940, 3 Fed.Rules Serv. 725; 3 Moore's Federal Practice, 1938, Cum.Supplement § 55.02.

1987 AMENDMENT

The amendments are technical. No substantive change is intended.

2007 AMENDMENTS

The language of Rule 55 has been amended as part of the general restyling of the Civil Rules to make them more easily understood and to make style and terminology consistent throughout the rules. These changes are intended to be stylistic only.

Former Rule 55(a) directed the clerk to enter a default when a party failed to plead or otherwise defend "as provided by these rules." The implication from the reference to defending "as provided by these rules" seemed to be that the clerk should enter a default even if a party did something showing an intent to defend, but that act was not specifically described by the rules. Courts in fact have rejected that implication. Acts that show an intent to defend have frequently prevented a default even though not connected to any particular rule. "[A]s provided by these rules" is deleted to reflect Rule 55(a)'s actual meaning.

Amended Rule 55 omits former Rule 55(d), which included two provisions. The first recognized that Rule 55 applies to described claimants. The list was incomplete and unnecessary. Rule 55(a) applies Rule 55 to any party against whom a judgment for affirmative relief is requested. The second provision was a redundant reminder that Rule 54(c) limits the relief available by default judgment.

Rule 56.   Summary Judgment

1937 ADOPTION

This rule is applicable to all actions, including those against the United States or an officer or agency thereof.

Summary judgment procedure is a method for promptly disposing of actions in which there is no genuine issue as to any material fact. It has been extensively used in England for more than 50 years and has been adopted in a number of American states. New York, for example, has made great use of it. During the first nine years after its adoption there, the records of New York county alone show 5,600 applications for summary judgments. Report of the Commission on the Administration of Justice in New York State (1934), p. 383. See also Third Annual Report of the Judicial Council of the State of New York (1937), p. 30.

In England it was first employed only in cases of liquidated claims, but there has been a steady enlargement of the scope of the remedy until it is now used in actions to recover land or chattels and in all other actions at law, for liquidated or unliquidated claims, except for a few designated torts and breach of promise of marriage. English Rules Under the Judicature Act (The Annual Practice, 1937) O. 3, r. 6; Orders 14, 14A, and 15; see also O. 32, r. 6, authorizing an application for judgment at any time upon admissions. In Michigan (3 Comp.Laws (1929) § 14260) and Illinois (Smith-Hurd Ill.Stats. c. 110, §§ 181, 259.15, 259.16), it is not limited to liquidated demands. New York (N.Y.R.C.P. (1937) Rule 113; see also Rule 107) has brought so many classes of actions under the operation of the rule that the Commission on Administration of Justice in New York State (1934) recommend that all restrictions be removed and that the remedy be available "in any action" (p. 287). For the history and nature of the summary judgment procedure and citations of state statutes, see Clark and Samenow, The Summary Judgment (1929), 38 Yale L.J. 423.

Note to Subdivision (d). See Rule 16 (Pre-Trial Procedure; Formulating Issues) and the **Note** thereto.

Note to Subdivisions (e) and (f). These are similar to rules in Michigan. Mich. Court Rules Ann. (Searl, 1933) Rule 30.

1946 AMENDMENT

Note to Subdivision (a). The amendment allows a claimant to move for a summary judgment at any time after the expiration of 20 days from the commencement of the action or after service of a motion for summary judgment by the adverse party. This will normally operate to permit an earlier motion by the claimant than under the original rule, where the phrase "at any time after the pleading in answer thereto has been served" operates to prevent a claimant from moving for summary judgment, even in a case clearly proper for its exercise, until a formal answer has been filed. Thus in *Peoples Bank* v. *Federal Reserve Bank of San Francisco,* Cal. 1944, 58 F.Supp. 25, the plaintiff's countermotion for a summary judgment was stricken as premature, because the defendant had not filed an answer. Since Rule 12(a) allows at least 20 days for an answer, that time plus the 10 days required in Rule 56(c) means that under original Rule 56(a) a minimum period of 30 days necessarily has to elapse in every case before the claimant can be heard on his right to a summary judgment. An extension of time by the court or the service of preliminary motions of any kind will prolong that period even further. In many cases this merely represents unnecessary delay. See *United States* v. *Adler's Creamery, Inc.,* C.C.A.2, 1939, 107 F.2d 987. The changes are in the interest of more expeditious litigation. The 20-day period, as provided, gives the defendant an opportunity to secure counsel and determine a course of action. But in a case where the defendant himself makes a motion for summary judgment within that time, there is no reason to restrict the plaintiff and the amended rule so provides.

Subdivision (c). The amendment of Rule 56(c), by the addition of the final sentence, resolves a doubt expressed in *Sartor* v. *Arkansas Natural Gas Corp.,* 1944, 321 U.S. 620, 64 S.Ct. 724, 88 L.Ed. 967. See also Commentary, Summary Judgment as to Damages, 1944, 7 Fed. Rules Serv. 974; *Madeirense do Brasil S/A* v. *Stulman–Emrick Lumber Co.,* C.C.A.2d, 1945, 147 F.2d 399, certiorari denied 325 U.S. 861, 65 S.Ct. 1201, 89 L.Ed. 1982. It makes clear that although the question of recovery depends on the amount of damages, the summary judgment rule is applicable and summary judgment may be granted in a proper case. If the case is not fully adjudicated it may be dealt with as provided in subdivision (d) of Rule 56, and the right to summary recovery determined by a preliminary order, interlocutory in character, and the precise amount of recovery left for trial.

Subdivision (d). Rule 54(a) defines "judgment" as including a decree and "any order from which an appeal lies." Subdivision (d) of Rule 56 indicates clearly, however, that a partial summary "judgment" is not a final judgment, and, therefore, that it is not appealable, unless in the particular case some statute allows an appeal from the interlocutory order involved. The partial summary judgment is merely a pretrial adjudication that certain issues shall be deemed established for the trial of the case. This adjudication is more nearly akin to the preliminary order under Rule 16, and likewise serves the purpose of speeding up litigation by eliminating before trial matters wherein there is no genuine issue of fact. See *Leonard* v. *Socony-Vacuum Oil Co.,* C.C.A.7, 1942, 130 F.2d 535; *Biggins* v. *Oltmer Iron Works,* C.C.A.7, 1946, 154 F.2d 214, 3 Moore's Federal Practice, 1938, 3190–3192. Since interlocutory appeals are not allowed, except where specifically provided by statute, see 3 Moore, op. cit. supra, 3155–3156, this interpretation is in line with that policy, *Leonard* v. *Socony-Vacuum Oil Co.,* supra. See also *Audi-Vision, Inc.* v. *RCA Mfg. Co.,* C.C.A.2, 1943, 136 F.2d 621; *Toomey* v. *Toomey,* App.D.C. 1945, 149 F.2d 19, 80 U.S.App.D.C. 77; *Biggins* v. *Oltmer Iron Works,* supra; *Catlin* v. *United States,* 1945, 324 U.S. 229, 65 S.Ct. 631, 89 L.Ed. 911.

1963 AMENDMENT

Subdivision (c). By the amendment "answers to interrogatories" are included among the materials which may be considered on motion for summary judgment. The phrase was inadvertently omitted from the rule, see 3 Barron & Holtzoff, Federal Practice & Procedure 159–60 (Wright ed. 1958), and the courts have generally reached by interpretation the result which will hereafter be required by the text of the amended rule. See Annot., 74 A.L.R.2d 984 (1960).

Subdivision (e). The words "answers to interrogatories" are added in the third sentence of this subdivision to conform to the amendment of subdivision (c).

The last two sentences are added to overcome a line of cases, chiefly in the Third Circuit, which has impaired the utility of the summary judgment device. A typical case is as follows: A party supports his motion for summary judgment by affidavits or other evidentiary matter sufficient to show that there is no genuine issue as to a material fact. The adverse party, in opposing the motion, does not produce any evidentiary matter, or produces some but not enough to establish that there is a genuine issue for trial. Instead, the adverse party rests on averments of his pleadings which on their face present an issue. In this situation Third Circuit cases have taken the view that summary judgment must be denied, at least if the averments are "well-pleaded," and not suppositious, conclusory, or ultimate. See *Frederick Hart & Co., Inc.* v. *Recordgraph Corp.,* 169 F.2d 580 (3d Cir.1948); *United States ex rel. Kolton* v. *Halpern,* 260 F.2d 590 (3d Cir.1958); *United States ex rel. Nobles* v. *Ivey Bros. Constr. Co., Inc.,* 191 F.Supp. 383 (D.Del.1961); *Jamison* v. *Pennsylvania Salt Mfg. Co.,* 22 F.R.D. 238 (W.D.Pa.1958); *Bunny Bear, Inc.* v. *Dennis Mitchell Industries,* 139 F.Supp. 542 (E.D.Pa.1956); *Levy* v. *Equitable Life Assur. Society,* 18 F.R.D. 164 (E.D.Pa.1955).

The very mission of the summary judgment procedure is to pierce the pleadings and to assess the proof in order to see whether there is a genuine need for trial. The Third Circuit doctrine, which permits the pleadings themselves to stand in the way of granting an otherwise justified summary judgment, is incompatible with the basic purpose of the rule. See 6 Moore's Federal Practice 2069 (2d ed. 1953); 3 Barron & Holtzoff, supra, § 1235.1.

It is hoped that the amendment will contribute to the more effective utilization of the salutary device of summary judgment.

The amendment is not intended to derogate from the solemnity of the pleadings. Rather it recognizes that, despite the best efforts of counsel to make his pleadings accurate, they may be overwhelmingly contradicted by the proof available to his adversary.

Nor is the amendment designed to affect the ordinary standards applicable to the summary judgment motion. So, for example: Where an issue as to a material fact cannot be resolved without observation of the demeanor of witnesses in order to evaluate their credibility, summary judgment is not appropriate. Where the evidentiary matter in support of the motion does not establish the absence of a genuine issue, summary judgment must be denied even if no opposing evidentiary matter is presented. And summary judgment may be inappropriate where the party opposing it shows under subdivision (f) that he cannot at the time present facts essential to justify his opposition.

1987 AMENDMENT

The amendments are technical. No substantive change is intended.

2007 AMENDMENTS

The language of Rule 56 has been amended as part of the general restyling of the Civil Rules to make them more easily understood and to make style and terminology consistent throughout the rules. These changes are intended to be stylistic only.

Former Rule 56(a) and (b) referred to summary-judgment motions on or against a claim, counterclaim, or crossclaim, or to obtain a declaratory judgment. The list was incomplete. Rule 56 applies to third-party claimants, intervenors, claimants in interpleader, and others. Amended Rule 56(a) and (b) carry forward the present meaning by referring to a party claiming relief and a party against whom relief is sought.

Former Rule 56(c), (d), and (e) stated circumstances in which summary judgment "shall be rendered," the court "shall if practicable" ascertain facts existing without substantial controversy, and "if appropriate, shall" enter summary judgment. In each place "shall" is changed to "should." It is established that although there is no discretion to enter summary judgment when there is a genuine issue as to any material fact, there is discretion to deny summary judgment when it appears that there is no genuine issue as to any material fact. *Kennedy* v. *Silas Mason Co.,* 334 U.S. 249, 256–257 (1948). Many lower court decisions are gathered in 10A Wright, Miller & Kane, Federal Practice & Procedure: Civil 3d, § 2728. "Should" in amended Rule 56(c) recognizes that courts will seldom exercise the discretion to deny summary judgment when there is no genuine issue as to any material fact. Similarly sparing exercise of this discretion is appropriate under Rule 56(e)(2). Rule 56(d)(1), on the other hand, reflects the more open-ended discretion to decide whether it is practicable to determine what material facts are not genuinely at issue.

Former Rule 56(d) used a variety of different phrases to express the Rule 56(c) standard for summary judgment—that there is no genuine issue as to any material fact. Amended Rule 56(d) adopts terms directly parallel to Rule 56(c).

Rule 57. Declaratory Judgments

1937 ADOPTION

The fact that a declaratory judgment may be granted "whether or not further relief is or could be prayed" indicates that declaratory relief is alternative or cumulative and not exclusive or extraordinary. A declaratory judgment is appropriate when it will "terminate the controversy" giving rise to the proceeding. Inasmuch as it often involves only an issue of law on undisputed or relatively undisputed facts, it operates frequently as a summary proceeding, justifying docketing the case for early hearing as on a motion, as provided for in California (Code Civ.Proc. (Deering, 1937) § 1062a), Michigan (3 Comp.Laws (1929) § 13904), and Kentucky (Codes (Carroll, 1932) Civ.Prac. § 639a–3).

The "controversy" must necessarily be "of a justiciable nature, thus excluding an advisory decree upon a hypothetical state of facts." *Ashwander* v. *Tennessee Valley Authority,* 1936, 297 U.S. 288, 325, 56 S.Ct. 466, 473, 80 L.Ed. 688, 699. The existence or non-existence of any right, duty, power, liability, privilege, disability, or immunity or of any fact upon which such legal relations depend, or of a status, may be declared. The petitioner must have a practical interest in the declaration sought and all parties having an interest therein or adversely affected must be made parties or be cited. A declaration may not be rendered if a special statutory proceeding has been provided for the adjudication of some special type of case, but general ordinary or extraordinary legal remedies, whether regulated by statute or not, are not deemed special statutory proceedings.

When declaratory relief will not be effective in settling the controversy, the court may decline to grant it. But the fact that another remedy would be equally effective affords no ground for declining declaratory relief. The demand for relief shall state with precision the declaratory judgment desired, to which may be joined a demand for coercive relief, cumulatively or in the alternative; but when coercive relief only is sought but is deemed ungrantable or inappropriate, the court may *sua sponte,* if it serves a useful purpose, grant instead a declaration of rights. *Hasselbring* v. *Koepke,* 1933, 248 N.W. 869, 263 Mich. 466, 93 A.L.R. 1170. Written instruments, including ordinances and statutes, may be construed before or after breach at the petition of a properly interested party, process being served on the private parties or public officials interested. In other respects the Uniform Declaratory Judgment Act affords a guide to the scope and function of the federal act. Compare *Aetna Life Insurance Co.* v. *Haworth,* 1937, 300 U.S. 227, 57 S.Ct. 461, 81 L.Ed. 617, 108 A.L.R. 1000; *Nashville, Chattanooga & St. Louis Ry.* v. *Wallace,* 1933, 288 U.S. 249, 53 S.Ct. 345, 77 L.Ed. 730, 87 A.L.R. 1191; *Gully, Tax Collector* v. *Interstate Natural Gas Co.,* 82 F.2d 145 (C.C.A. 5, 1936); *Ohio Casualty Ins. Co.* v. *Plummer,* Tex.1935, 13 F.Supp. 169; Borchard, Declaratory Judgments (1934), *passim.*

1948 AMENDMENT

The Amendment effective October 1949, substituted the reference to "Title 28, U.S.C., § 2201" in the first sentence for the reference to "Section 274(d) of the Judicial Code, as amended, U.S.C., Title 28, § 400."

2007 AMENDMENTS

The language of Rule 57 has been amended as part of the general restyling of the Civil Rules to make them more easily understood and to make style and terminology consistent throughout the rules. These changes are intended to be stylistic only.

Rule 58. Entry of Judgment

1937 ADOPTION

See Wis.Stat.1935, § 270.31 (judgment entered forthwith on verdict of jury unless otherwise ordered), § 270.65 (where trial is by the court, entered by direction of the court), § 270.63 (entered by clerk on judgment on admitted claim for money). Compare 1 Idaho

Code Ann.1932, § 7–1101, and 4 Mont.Rev.Codes Ann.1935, § 9403, which provides that judgment in jury cases be entered by clerk within 24 hours after verdict unless court otherwise directs. Conn.Practice Book 1934, § 200, provides that all judgments shall be entered within one week after rendition. In some States such as Washington, 2 Rev.Stat.Ann.Remington, 1932, § 431, in jury cases the judgment is entered two days after the return of verdict to give time for making motion for new trial; § 435 (*ibid.*), provides that all judgments shall be entered by the clerk, subject to the court's direction.

1946 AMENDMENT

Note. The reference to Rule 54(b) is made necessary by the amendment of that rule.

Two changes have been made in Rule 58 in order to clarify the practice. The substitution of the more inclusive phrase "all relief be denied" for the words "there be no recovery", makes it clear that the clerk shall enter the judgment forthwith in the situations specified without awaiting the filing of a formal judgment approved by the court. The phrase "all relief be denied" covers cases such as the denial of a bankrupt's discharge and similar situations where the relief sought is refused but there is literally no denial of a "recovery".

The addition of the last sentence in the rule emphasizes that judgments are to be entered promptly by the clerk without waiting for the taxing of costs. Certain district court rules, for example, Civil Rule 22 of the Southern District of New York—until its annulment Oct. 1, 1945, for conflict with this rule—and the like rule of the Eastern District of New York, are expressly in conflict with this provision, although the federal law is of long standing and well settled. *Fowler* v. *Hamill,* 1891, 139 U.S. 549, 11 S.Ct. 663, 35 L.Ed. 266; *Craig* v. *The Hartford,* C.C.Cal.1856, Fed.Cas.No.3,333; *Tuttle* v. *Claflin,* C.C.A.2, 1895, 66 F. 7, certiorari denied 166 U.S. 721, 17 S.Ct. 992, 41 L.Ed. 1187; *Prescott & A. C. Ry. Co.* v. *Atchison, T. & S. F. R. Co.,* C.C.A.2, 1897, 84 F. 213; *Stallo* v. *Wagner,* C.C.A.2, 1917, 245 F. 636, 639–40; *Brown* v. *Parker,* C.C.A.8, 1899, 97 F. 446; *Allis-Chalmers* v. *United States,* C.C.A.7, 1908, 162 F. 679. And this applies even though state law is to the contrary. *United States* v. *Nordbye,* C.C.A.8, 1935, 75 F.2d 744, 746, certiorari denied 296 U.S. 572, 56 S.Ct. 103, 80 L.Ed. 404. Inasmuch as it has been held that failure of the clerk thus to enter judgment is a "misprision" "not to be excused", *The Washington,* C.C.A.2, 1926, 16 F.2d 206, such a district court rule may have serious consequences for a district court clerk. Rules of this sort also provide for delay in entry of the judgment contrary to Rule 58. See *Commissioner of Internal Revenue* v. *Bedford's Estate,* 1945, 325 U.S. 283, 65 S.Ct. 1157, 89 L.Ed. 1611.

1963 AMENDMENT

Under the present rule a distinction has sometimes been made between judgments on general jury verdicts, on the one hand, and, on the other, judgments upon decisions of the court that a party shall recover only money or costs or that all relief shall be denied. In the first situation, it is clear that the clerk should enter the judgment without awaiting a direction by the court unless the court otherwise orders. In the second situation it was intended that the clerk should similarly enter the judgment forthwith upon the court's decision; but because of the ... separate listing in the rule, and the use of the phrase "upon receipt of the direction," the rule has sometimes been interpreted as requiring the clerk to await a separate direction of the court. All these judgments are usually uncomplicated, and should be handled in the same way. The amended rule accordingly deals with them as a single group in clause (1)(substituting the expression "only a sum certain" for the present expression "only money"), and requires the clerk to prepare, sign, and enter them forthwith, without awaiting court direction, unless the court makes a contrary order. (The clerk's duty is ministerial and may be performed by a deputy clerk in the name of the clerk. See 28 U.S.C. § 956; cf. *Gilbertson* v. *United States,* 168 Fed. 672 (7th Cir.1909).) The more complicated judgments described in clause (2) must be approved by the court before they are entered.

Rule 58 is designed to encourage all reasonable speed in formulating and entering the judgment when the case has been decided. Participation by the attorneys through the submission of forms of judgment involves needless expenditure of time and effort and promotes delay, except in special cases where counsel's assistance can be of real value. See *Matteson* v. *United States,* 240 F.2d 517, 518–19 (2d Cir.1956). Accordingly, the amended rule provides that attorneys shall not submit forms of judgment unless directed to do so by the court. This applies to the judgments mentioned in clause (2) as well as clause (1).

Hitherto some difficulty has arisen, chiefly where the court has written an opinion or memorandum containing some apparently directive or dispositive words, e.g., "the plaintiff's motion [for summary judgment] is granted," see *United States* v. *F. & M. Schaefer*

Brewing Co., 356 U.S. 227, 229, 78 S.Ct. 674, 676, 2 L.Ed.2d 721 (1958). Clerks on occasion have viewed these opinions or memoranda as being in themselves a sufficient basis for entering judgment in the civil docket as provided by Rule 79(a). However, where the opinion or memorandum has not contained all the elements of a judgment or where the judge has later signed a formal judgment, it has become a matter of doubt whether the purported entry of judgment was effective, starting the time running for post-verdict motions and for the purpose of appeal. See id.; and compare *Blanchard v. Commonwealth Oil Co.*, 294 F.2d 834 (5th Cir.1961); *United States v. Higginson*, 238 F.2d 439 (1st Cir.1956); *Danzig v. Virgin Isle Hotel, Inc.*, 278 F.2d 580 (3d Cir.1960); *Sears v. Austin*, 282 F.2d 340 (9th Cir.1960), with *Matteson v. United States*, supra; *Erstling v. Southern Bell Tel. & Tel. Co.*, 255 F.2d 93 (5th Cir.1958); *Barta v. Oglala Sioux Tribe*, 259 F.2d 553 (8th Cir.1958), cert. denied, 358 U.S. 932, 79 S.Ct. 320, 3 L.Ed.2d 304 (1959); *Beacon Fed. S. & L. Assn. v. Federal Home L. Bank Bd.*, 266 F.2d 246 (7th Cir.), cert. denied, 361 U.S. 823, 80 S.Ct. 70, 4 L.Ed.2d 67 (1959); *Ram v. Paramount Film D. Corp.*, 278 F.2d 191 (4th Cir.1960).

The amended rule eliminates these uncertainties by requiring that there be a judgment set out on a separate document—distinct from any opinion or memorandum—which provides the basis for the entry of judgment. That judgments shall be on separate documents is also indicated in Rule 79(b); and see General Rule 10 of the U. S. District Courts for the Eastern and Southern Districts of New York; *Ram v. Paramount Film D. Corp.*, supra, at 194.

See the amendment of Rule 79(a) and the new specimen forms of judgment, Forms 31 and 32.

See also Rule 55(b)(1) and (2) covering the subject of judgments by default.

1993 AMENDMENT

Ordinarily the pendency or post-judgment filing of a claim for attorney's fees will not affect the time for appeal from the underlying judgment. *See Budinich v. Becton Dickinson & Co.*, 486 U.S. 196, 108 S.Ct. 1717, 100 L.Ed.2d 178 (1988). Particularly if the claim for fees involves substantial issues or is likely to be affected by the appellate decision, the district court may prefer to defer consideration of the claim for fees until after the appeal is resolved. However, in many cases it may be more efficient to decide fee questions before an appeal is taken so that appeals relating to the fee award can be heard at the same time as appeals relating to the merits of the case. This revision permits, but does not require, the court to delay the finality of the judgment for appellate purposes under revised Fed.R.App.P. 4(a) until the fee dispute is decided. To accomplish this result requires entry of an order by the district court before the time a notice of appeal becomes effective for appellate purposes. If the order is entered, the motion for attorney's fees is treated in the same manner as a timely motion under Rule 59.

2002 AMENDMENT

Rule 58 has provided that a judgment is effective only when set forth on a separate document and entered as provided in Rule 79(a). This simple separate document requirement has been ignored in many cases. The result of failure to enter judgment on a separate document is that the time for making motions under Rules 50, 52, 54(d)(2)(B), 59, and some motions under Rule 60, never begins to run. The time to appeal under Appellate Rule 4(a) also does not begin to run. There have been few visible problems with respect to Rule 50, 52, 54(d)(2)(B), 59, or 60 motions, but there have been many and horridly confused problems under Appellate Rule 4(a). These amendments are designed to work in conjunction with Appellate Rule 4(a) to ensure that appeal time does not linger on indefinitely, and to maintain the integration of the time periods set for Rules 50, 52, 54(d)(2)(B), 59, and 60 with Appellate Rule 4(a).

Rule 58(a) preserves the core of the present separate document requirement, both for the initial judgment and for any amended judgment. No attempt is made to sort through the confusion that some courts have found in addressing the elements of a separate document. It is easy to prepare a separate document that recites the terms of the judgment without offering additional explanation or citation of authority. Forms 31 and 32 provide examples.

Rule 58 is amended, however, to address a problem that arises under Appellate Rule 4(a). Some courts treat such orders as those that deny a motion for new trial as a "judgment," so that appeal time does not start to run until the order is entered on a separate document. Without attempting to address the question whether such orders are appealable, and thus judgments as defined by Rule 54(a), the amendment provides that entry on a separate document is not required for an order disposing of the motions listed in

Appellate Rule 4(a). The enumeration of motions drawn from the Appellate Rule 4(a) list is generalized by omitting details that are important for appeal time purposes but that would unnecessarily complicate the separate document requirement. As one example, it is not required that any of the enumerated motions be timely. Many of the enumerated motions are frequently made before judgment is entered. The exemption of the order disposing of the motion does not excuse the obligation to set forth the judgment itself on a separate document. And if disposition of the motion results in an amended judgment, the amended judgment must be set forth on a separate document.

Rule 58(b) discards the attempt to define the time when a judgment becomes "effective." Taken in conjunction with the Rule 54(a) definition of a judgment to include "any order from which an appeal lies," the former Rule 58 definition of effectiveness could cause strange difficulties in implementing pretrial orders that are appealable under interlocutory appeal provisions or under expansive theories of finality. Rule 58(b) replaces the definition of effectiveness with a new provision that defines the time when judgment is entered. If judgment is promptly set forth on a separate document, as should be done when required by Rule 58(a)(1), the new provision will not change the effect of Rule 58. But in the cases in which court and clerk fail to comply with this simple requirement, the motion time periods set by Rules 50, 52, 54, 59, and 60 begin to run after expiration of 150 days from entry of the judgment in the civil docket as required by Rule 79(a).

A companion amendment of Appellate Rule 4(a)(7) integrates these changes with the time to appeal.

The new all-purpose definition of the entry of judgment must be applied with common sense to other questions that may turn on the time when judgment is entered. If the 150–day provision in Rule 58(b)(2)(B)—designed to integrate the time for post-judgment motions with appeal time—serves no purpose, or would defeat the purpose of another rule, it should be disregarded. In theory, for example, the separate document requirement continues to apply to an interlocutory order that is appealable as a final decision under collateral-order doctrine. Appealability under collateral-order doctrine should not be complicated by failure to enter the order as a judgment on a separate document—there is little reason to force trial judges to speculate about the potential appealability of every order, and there is no means to ensure that the trial judge will always reach the same conclusion as the court of appeals. Appeal time should start to run when the collateral order is entered without regard to creation of a separate document and without awaiting expiration of the 150 days provided by Rule 58(b)(2). Drastic surgery on Rules 54(a) and 58 would be required to address this and related issues, however, and it is better to leave this conundrum to the pragmatic disregard that seems its present fate. The present amendments do not seem to make matters worse, apart from one false appearance. If a pretrial order is set forth on a separate document that meets the requirements of Rule 58(b), the time to move for reconsideration seems to begin to run, perhaps years before final judgment. And even if there is no separate document, the time to move for reconsideration seems to begin 150 days after entry in the civil docket. This apparent problem is resolved by Rule 54(b), which expressly permits revision of all orders not made final under Rule 54(b) "at any time before the entry of judgment adjudicating all the claims and the rights and liabilities of all the parties."

New Rule 58(d) replaces the provision that attorneys shall not submit forms of judgment except on direction of the court. This provision was added to Rule 58 to avoid the delays that were frequently encountered by the former practice of directing the attorneys for the prevailing party to prepare a form of judgment, and also to avoid the occasionally inept drafting that resulted from attorney-prepared judgments. See *11 Wright, Miller & Kane, Federal Practice & Procedure: Civil 2d, § 2786.* The express direction in Rule 58(a)(2) for prompt action by the clerk, and by the court if court action is required, addresses this concern. The new provision allowing any party to move for entry of judgment on a separate document will protect all needs for prompt commencement of the periods for motions, appeals, and execution or other enforcement.

2007 AMENDMENTS

The language of Rule 58 has been amended as part of the general restyling of the Civil Rules to make them more easily understood and to make style and terminology consistent throughout the rules. These changes are intended to be stylistic only.

Rule 59. New Trials; Amendment of Judgments

1937 ADOPTION

This rule represents an amalgamation of the petition for rehearing of former Equity Rule 69 (Petition for Rehearing) and the motion for new trial of 28 U.S.C., § 2111, formerly § 391 (New trials; harmless error), made in the light of the experience and provision of the code States. Compare Calif.Code Civ.Proc., Deering, 1937, §§ 656–663a, 28 U.S.C., § 2111, formerly § 391 (New trials; harmless error) is thus substantially continued in this rule. U.S.C., Title 28, former § 840 (Executions; stay on conditions) is modified in so far as it contains time provisions inconsistent with **Subdivision (b)**. For the effect of the motion for new trial upon the time for taking an appeal see *Morse v. United States*, 1926, 270 U.S. 151, 46 S.Ct. 241, 70 L.Ed. 518; *Aspen Mining and Smelting Co. v. Billings*, 1893, 150 U.S. 31, 14 S.Ct. 4, 37 L.Ed. 986.

For partial new trials which are permissible under **Subdivision (a)**, see *Gasoline Products Co., Inc. v. Champlin Refining Co.*, 1931, 283 U.S. 494, 51 S.Ct. 513, 75 L.Ed. 1188; *Schuerholz v. Roach*, C.C.A.4, 1932, 58 F.2d 32; *Simmons v. Fish*, 1912, 97 N.E. 102, 210 Mass. 563, Am.Ann.Cas. 1912D, 588 (sustaining and recommending the practice and citing federal cases and cases in accord from about sixteen states and contra from three States). The procedure in several States provides specifically for partial new trials. Ariz.Rev.Code Ann., Struckmeyer, 1928, § 3852; Calif.Code Civ.Proc., Deering, 1937, §§ 657, 662; Smith-Hurd Ill.Stats., 1937, c. 110, § 216 (Par. (f)); Md.Ann.Code, Bagby, 1924, Art. 5, §§ 25, 26; Mich.Court Rules Ann., Searl, 1933, Rule 47, § 2; Miss.Sup.Ct. Rule 12, 161 Miss. 903, 905, 1931; N.J.Sup.Ct.Rules 131, 132, 147, 2 N.J.Misc. 1197, 1246–1251, 1255, 1924, 2 N.D.Comp.Laws Ann., 1913, § 7844, as amended by N.D.Laws 1927, ch. 214.

1946 AMENDMENT

Note to Subdivision (b). With the time for appeal to a circuit court of appeals reduced in general to 30 days by the proposed amendment of Rule 73(a), the utility of the original "except" clause, which permits a motion for a new trial on the ground of newly discovered evidence to be made before the expiration of the time for appeal, would have been seriously restricted. It was thought advisable, therefore, to take care of this matter in another way. By amendment of Rule 60(b), newly discovered evidence is made the basis for relief from a judgment, and the maximum time limit has been extended to one year. Accordingly the amendment of Rule 59(b) eliminates the "except" clause and its specific treatment of newly discovered evidence as a ground for a motion for new trial. This ground remains, however, as a basis for a motion for new trial served not later than 10 days after the entry of judgment. See also Rule 60(b).

As to the effect of a motion under subdivision (b) upon the running of appeal time, see amended Rule 73(a) and Note.

Subdivision (e). This subdivision has been added to care for a situation such as that arising in *Boaz v. Mutual Life Ins. Co. of New York*, C.C.A.8, 1944, 146 F.2d 321, and makes clear that the district court possesses the power asserted in that case to alter or amend a judgment after its entry. The subdivision deals only with alteration or amendment of the original judgment in a case and does not relate to a judgment upon motion as provided in Rule 50(b). As to the effect of a motion under subdivision (e) upon the running of appeal time, see amended Rule 73(a) and Note.

The title of Rule 59 has been expanded to indicate the inclusion of this subdivision.

1966 AMENDMENT

By narrow interpretation of Rule 59(b) and (d), it has been held that the trial court is without power to grant a motion for a new trial, timely served, by an order made more than 10 days after the entry of judgment, based upon a ground not stated in the motion but perceived and relied on by the trial court sua sponte. *Freid v. McGrath*, 133 F.2d 350 (D.C.Cir.1942); *National Farmers Union Auto. & Cas. Co. v. Wood*, 207 F.2d 659 (10th Cir.1953); *Bailey v. Slentz*, 189 F.2d 406 (10th Cir.1951); *Marshall's U. S. Auto Supply, Inc. v. Cashman*, 111 F.2d 140 (10th Cir.1940), cert. denied, 311 U.S. 667, 61 S.Ct. 26, 85 L.Ed. 428 (1940); but see *Steinberg v. Indemnity Ins. Co.*, 36 F.R.D. 253 (E.D.La.1964).

The result is undesirable. Just as the court has power under Rule 59(d) to grant a new trial of its own initiative within the 10 days, so it should have power, when an effective new trial motion has been made and is pending, to decide it on grounds thought meritorious by the court although not advanced in the motion. The second sentence added by amendment to Rule 59(d) confirms the court's power in the latter situation, with provision that the parties be afforded a hearing before the power is exercised. See 6 Moore's Federal Practice, par. 59.09[2] (2d ed. 1953).

In considering whether a given ground has or has not been advanced in the motion made by the party, it should be borne in mind that the particularity called for in stating the grounds for a new trial motion is the same as that required for all motions by Rule 7(b)(1). The latter rule does not require ritualistic detail but rather a fair indication to court and counsel of the substance of the grounds relied on. See *Lebeck v. William A. Jarvis, Inc.*, 250 F.2d 285 (3d Cir.1957); *Tsai v. Rosenthal*, 297 F.2d 614 (8th Cir.1961); *General Motors Corp. v. Perry*, 303 F.2d 544 (7th Cir.1962); *cf. Grimm v. California Spray-Chemical Corp.*, 264 F.2d 145 (9th Cir.1959); *Cooper v. Midwest Feed Products Co.*, 271 F.2d 177 (8th Cir.1959).

1995 AMENDMENT

The only change, other than stylistic, intended by this revision is to add explicit time limits for filing motions for a new trial, motions to alter or amend a judgment, and affidavits opposing a new trial motion. Previously, there was an inconsistency in the wording of Rules 50, 52, and 59 with respect to whether certain post-judgment motions had to be filed, or merely served, during the prescribed period. This inconsistency caused special problems when motions for a new trial were joined with other post-judgment motions. These motions affect the finality of the judgment, a matter often of importance to third persons as well as the parties and the court. The Committee believes that each of these rules should be revised to require filing before end of the 10–day period. Filing is an event that can be determined with certainty from court records. The phrase "no later than" is used—rather than "within"—to include post-judgment motions that sometimes are filed before actual entry of the judgment by the clerk. It should be noted that under Rule 5 the motions when filed are to contain a certificate of service on other parties. It also should be noted that under Rule 6(a) Saturdays, Sundays, and legal holidays are excluded in measuring the 10–day period, but that Bankruptcy Rule 9006(a) excludes intermediate Saturdays, Sundays, and legal holidays only in computing periods less than 8 days.

2007 AMENDMENTS

The language of Rule 59 has been amended as part of the general restyling of the Civil Rules to make them more easily understood and to make style and terminology consistent throughout the rules. These changes are intended to be stylistic only.

Rule 60. Relief From Judgment or Order

1937 ADOPTION

Note to Subdivision (a). See former Equity Rule 72 (Correction of Clerical Mistakes in Orders and Decrees); Mich. Court Rules Ann. (Searl, 1933) Rule 48, § 3; 2 Wash.Rev.Stat.Ann. (Remington, 1932) § 464(3); Wyo.Rev.Stat.Ann., (Courtright, 1931) § 89–2301(3). For an example of a very liberal provision for the correction of clerical errors and for amendment after judgment, see Va.Code Ann. (Michie, 1936) §§ 6329, 6333.

Note to Subdivision (b). Application to the court under this subdivision does not extend the time for taking an appeal, as distinguished from the motion for new trial. This section is based upon Calif.Code Civ.Proc. (Deering, 1937) § 473. See also N.Y.C.P.A., 1937, § 108; 2 Minn.Stat., Mason, 1927, § 9283.

For the independent action to relieve against mistake, etc. see Dobie, Federal Procedure, pages 760–765, compare 639; and Simkins, Federal Practice, ch. CXXI, pp. 820–830, and ch. CXXII, pp. 831–834, compare § 214.

1946 AMENDMENT

Note to Subdivision (a). The amendment incorporates the view expressed in *Perlman v. 322 West Seventy–Second Street Co., Inc.*, C.C.A.2, 1942, 127 F.2d 716, 3 Moore's Federal Practice, 1938, 3276, and further permits correction after docketing, with leave of the appellate court. Some courts have thought that upon the taking of an appeal the district court lost its power to act. See *Schram v. Safety Investment Co.*, Mich.1942, 45 F.Supp. 636; also *Miller v. United States*, C.C.A.7, 1940, 114 F.2d 267.

Note to Subdivision (b). When promulgated, the rules contained a number of provisions, including those found in Rule 60(b), describing the practice by a motion to obtain relief from judgments, and these rules, coupled with the reservation in Rule 60(b) of the right to entertain a new action to relieve a party from a judgment, were generally supposed to cover the field. Since the rules have been in force, decisions have been rendered that the use of bills of review, coram nobis, or audita querela, to obtain relief from final judgments is still proper, and that various remedies of this kind still exist although they are not mentioned in the rules and the practice is not prescribed in the rules. It is obvious that the rules should be complete in this respect and define the practice with respect to any existing rights or remedies to obtain relief from final judgments. For extended discussion of the old common law writs and equitable remedies, the interpretation of Rule 60, and proposals for change, see Moore and Rogers, Federal Relief from Civil Judgments, 1946, 55 Yale L.J. 623. See also 3 Moore's Federal Practice, 1938, 3254 et seq.; Commentary, Effect of Rule 60b on Other Methods of Relief From Judgment, 1941, 4 Fed.Rules Serv. 942, 945; *Wallace v. United States*, C.C.A.2, 1944, 142 F.2d 240, certiorari denied 323 U.S. 712, 65 S.Ct. 37, 89 L.Ed. 573.

The reconstruction of Rule 60(b) has for one of its purposes a clarification of this situation. Two types of procedure to obtain relief from judgments are specified in the rules as it is proposed to amend them. One procedure is by motion in the court and in the action in which the judgment was rendered. The other procedure is by a new or independent action to obtain relief from a judgment, which action may or may not be begun in the court which rendered the judgment. Various rules, such as the one dealing with a motion for new trial and for amendment of judgments, Rule 59, one for amended findings, Rule 52, and one for judgment notwithstanding the verdict, Rule 50(b), and including the provisions of Rule 60(b) as amended, prescribe the various types of cases in which the practice by motion is permitted. In each case there is a limit upon the time within which resort to a motion is permitted, and this time limit may not be enlarged under Rule 6(b). If the right to make a motion is lost by the expiration of the time limits fixed in these rules, the only other procedural remedy is by a new or independent action to set aside a judgment upon those principles which have heretofore been applied in such an action. Where the independent action is resorted to, the limitations of time are those of laches or statutes of limitations. The Committee has endeavored to ascertain all the remedies and types of relief heretofore available by coram nobis, coram vobis, audita querela, bill of review, or bill in the nature of a bill of review. See Moore and Rogers, Federal Relief from Civil Judgments, 1946, 55 Yale L.J. 623, 659–682. It endeavored then to amend the rules to permit, either by motion or by independent action, the granting of various kinds of relief from judgments which were permitted in the federal courts prior to the adoption of these rules, and the amendment concludes with a provision abolishing the use of bills of review and the other common law writs referred to, and requiring the practice to be by motion or by independent action.

To illustrate the operation of the amendment, it will be noted that under Rule 59(b) as it now stands, without amendment, a motion for new trial on the ground of newly discovered evidence is permitted within ten days after the entry of the judgment, or after that time upon leave of the court. It is proposed to amend Rule 59(b) by providing that under that rule a motion for new trial shall be served not later than ten days after the entry of the judgment, whatever the ground be for the motion, whether error by the court or newly discovered evidence. On the other hand, one of the purposes of the bill of review in equity was to afford relief on the ground of newly discovered evidence long after the entry of the judgment. Therefore, to permit relief by a motion similar to that heretofore obtained on bill of review, Rule 60(b) as amended permits an application for relief to be made by motion, on the ground of newly discovered evidence, within one year after judgment. Such a motion under Rule 60(b) does not affect the finality of the judgment, but a motion under Rule 59, made within 10 days, does affect finality and the running of the time for appeal.

If these various amendments, including principally those to Rule 60(b), accomplish the purpose for which they are intended, the federal rules will deal with the practice in every sort of case in which relief from final judgments is asked, and prescribe the practice. With reference to the question whether, as the rules now exist, relief by coram nobis, bills of review, and so forth, is permissible, the generally accepted view is that the remedies are still available, although the precise relief obtained in a particular case by use of these ancillary remedies is shrouded in ancient lore and mystery. See *Wallace v. United States*, C.C.A.2, 1944, 142 F.2d 240, certiorari denied 323 U.S. 712, 65 S.Ct. 37, 89 L.Ed. 573; *Fraser v. Doing*, App.D.C.1942, 130 F.2d 617; *Jones v. Watts*, C.C.A.5, 1944, 142 F.2d 575; *Preveden v. Hahn*, N.Y.1941, 36 F.Supp. 952; *Cavallo v. Agwilines, Inc.*, N.Y.1942, 6 Fed.Rules Serv. 60b.31, Case 2, 2 F.R.D. 526; *McGinn v. United States*, D.Mass.1942, 6 Fed.Rules Serv. 60b.51, Case 3, 2 F.R.D. 562; *City of Shattuck, Oklahoma ex rel. Versluis v. Oliver*, Okl.1945, 8 Fed.Rules Serv. 60b.31, Case 3; Moore and Rogers, Federal Relief from Civil Judgments, 1946, 55 Yale L.J. 623, 631–653; 3 Moore's Federal Practice, 1938, 3254 et seq.; Commentary Effect of Rule 60b on Other Methods of Relief from Judgments, op. cit. supra. Cf. *Norris v. Camp*, C.C.A.10, 1944, 144 F.2d 1; *Reed v. South Atlantic Steamship Co. of Delaware*, Del.1942, 2 F.R.D. 475, 6 Fed.Rules Serv. 60b.31, Case 1; *Laughlin v. Berens*, D.C.1945, 8 Fed.Rules Serv. 60b.51, Case 1, 73 W.L.R. 209.

The transposition of the words "the court" and the addition of the word "and" at the beginning of the first sentence are merely verbal changes. The addition of the qualifying word "final" emphasizes the character of the judgments, orders or proceedings from which Rule 60(b) affords relief; and hence interlocutory judgments are not brought within the restrictions of the rule, but rather they are left subject to the complete power of the court rendering them to afford such relief from them as justice requires.

The qualifying pronoun "his" has been eliminated on the basis that it is too restrictive, and that the subdivision should include the mistake or neglect of others which may be just as material and call just as much for supervisory jurisdiction as where the judgment is taken against the party through *his* mistake, inadvertence, etc.

Fraud, whether intrinsic or extrinsic, misrepresentation, or other misconduct of an adverse party are express grounds for relief by motion under amended subdivision (b). There is no sound reason for their exclusion. The incorporation of fraud and the like within the scope of the rule also removes confusion as to the proper procedure. It has been held that relief from a judgment obtained by extrinsic fraud could be secured by motion within a "reasonable time," which might be after the time stated in the rule had run. *Fiske v. Buder*, C.C.A.8, 1942, 125 F.2d 841; see also inferentially *Bucy v. Nevada Construction Co.*, C.C.A.9, 1942, 125 F.2d 213. On the other hand, it has been suggested that in view of the fact that fraud was omitted from original Rule 60(b) as a ground for relief, an independent action was the only proper remedy. Commentary, Effect of Rule 60b on Other Methods of Relief From Judgment, 1941, 4 Fed.Rules Serv. 942, 945. The amendment settles this problem by making fraud an express ground for relief by motion; and under the saving clause, fraud may be urged as a basis for relief by independent action insofar as established doctrine permits. See Moore and Rogers Federal Relief from Civil Judgments, 1946, 55 Yale L.J. 623, 653–659; 3 Moore's Federal Practice, 1938, 3267 et seq. And the rule expressly does not limit the power of the court, when fraud has been perpetrated upon it, to give relief under the saving clause. As an illustration of this situation, see *Hazel–Atlas Glass Co. v. Hartford–Empire Co.*, 1944, 322 U.S. 238, 64 S.Ct. 997, 88 L.Ed. 1250.

The time limit for relief by motion in the court and in the action in which the judgment was rendered has been enlarged from six months to one year.

It should be noted that Rule 60(b) does not assume to define substantive law as to the grounds for vacating judgments, but merely prescribes the practice in proceedings to obtain relief. It should also be noted that under § 200(4) of the Soldiers' and Sailors' Civil Relief Act of 1940, 50 U.S.C., Appendix, § 501 et seq. [§ 520(4)], a judgment rendered in any action or proceeding governed by the section may be vacated under certain specified circumstances upon proper application to the court.

1948 AMENDMENT

The amendment effective October 1949, substituted the reference to "Title 28, U.S.C., § 1655," in the next to the last sentence of subdivision (b), for the reference to "Section 57 of the Judicial Code, U.S.C., Title 28, § 118."

1987 AMENDMENT

The amendment is technical. No substantive change is intended.

2007 AMENDMENTS

The language of Rule 60 has been amended as part of the general restyling of the Civil Rules to make them more easily understood and to make style and terminology consistent throughout the rules. These changes are intended to be stylistic only.

The final sentence of former Rule 60(b) said that the procedure for obtaining any relief from a judgment was by motion as prescribed in the Civil Rules or by an independent action. That provision is deleted as unnecessary. Relief continues to be available only as provided in the Civil Rules or by independent action.

Rule 61. Harmless Error

1937 ADOPTION

A combination of U.S.C., Title 28, § 2111, former § 391 (New trials; harmless error) and former § 777 (Defects of form; amendments) with modifications. See *McCandless v. United States*, 1936, 298 U.S. 342, 56 S.Ct. 764, 80 L.Ed. 1205. Compare former Equity Rule 72 (Correction of Clerical Mistakes in Orders and Decrees); and last sentence of former Equity Rule 46 (Trial—Testimony Usually Taken in Open Court—Rulings on Objections to Evidence). For the last sentence see the last sentence of former Equity Rule 19 (Amendments Generally).

2007 AMENDMENTS

The language of Rule 61 has been amended as part of the general restyling of the Civil Rules to make them more easily understood and to make style and terminology consistent throughout the rules. These changes are intended to be stylistic only.

Rule 62. Stay of Proceedings to Enforce a Judgment

1937 ADOPTION

Note to Subdivision (a). The first sentence states the substance of the last sentence of U.S.C., Title 28, former § 874 (Supersedeas). The remainder of the subdivision states the substance of the last clause of U.S.C., Title 28, § 1292, formerly § 227 (Appeals in proceedings for injunctions; receivers; and admiralty), and of §§ 1292, 2107, formerly § 227a (Appeals in suits in equity for infringement of letters patent for inventions; stay of proceedings for accounting), but extended to include final as well as interlocutory judgments.

Note to Subdivision (b). This modifies U.S.C., Title 28, former § 840 (Executions; stay on conditions).

Note to Subdivision (c). Compare former Equity Rule 74 (Injunction Pending Appeal); and *Cumberland Telephone and Telegraph Co. v. Louisiana Public Service Commission*, 1922, 260 U.S. 212, 43 S.Ct. 75, 67 L.Ed. 217. See Simkins, Federal Practice (1934), § 916, in regard to the effect of appeal on injunctions and the giving of bonds. See U.S.C., Title 6 (Official and Penal Bonds) for bonds by surety companies. For statutes providing for a specially constituted district court of three judges, see:

U.S.C., Title 7:

§ 217 (Proceedings for suspension of orders of Secretary of Agriculture under Stockyards Act)—by reference.

§ 499k (Injunctions; application of injunction laws governing orders of Interstate Commerce Commission to orders of Secretary of Agriculture under Perishable Commodities Act)—by reference.

U.S.C., Title 15:

§ 28 (Antitrust laws; suits against monopolies expedited)

U.S.C., Title 28 former:

§ 47 (Injunctions as to orders of Interstate Commerce Commission, etc.)

§ 380 (Injunctions; alleged unconstitutionality of State statutes)

§ 380a (Same; constitutionality of federal statute)

U.S.C., Title 49:

§ 44 (Suits in equity under interstate commerce laws; expedition of suits)

Note to Subdivision (d). This modifies U.S.C., Title 28, former § 874 (Supersedeas). See Rule 36(2), Rules of the Supreme Court of the United States, which governs supersedeas bonds on direct appeals to the Supreme Court, and Rule 73(d), of these rules, which governs supersedeas bonds on appeals to a circuit court of appeals. The provisions governing supersedeas bonds in both kinds of appeals are substantially the same.

Note to Subdivision (e). This states the substance of U.S.C., Title 28, § 2408, formerly § 870 (Bond; not required of the United States).

Note to Subdivision (f). This states the substance of U.S.C., Title 28, former § 841 (Executions; stay of one term) with appropriate modification to conform to the provisions of Rule 6(c) as to terms of court.

1946 AMENDMENT

Note to Subdivision (a). [This subdivision not amended]. Sections 203 and 204 of the Soldiers' and Sailors' Civil Relief Act of 1940, 50 U.S.C., Appendix, § 501 et seq. [§§ 523, 524], provide under certain circumstances for the issuance and continuance of a stay of execution of any judgment or order entered against a person in military service. See *Bowsman v. Peterson*, Neb.1942, 45 F.Supp. 741. Section 201 of the Act [50 U.S.C., App. § 521] permits under certain circumstances the issuance of a stay of any action or proceeding at any stage thereof, where either the plaintiff or defendant is a person in military service. See also note to Rule 64 herein.

Subdivision (b). This change was necessary because of the proposed addition to Rule 59 of subdivision (e).

Subdivision (h). In proposing to revise Rule 54(b), the Committee thought it advisable to include a separate provision in Rule 62 for stay of enforcement of a final judgment in cases involving multiple claims.

1948 AMENDMENT

The amendment effective October 1949, deleted at the end of subdivision (g) the following language which originally appeared after the word "entered": "and these rules do not supersede the provisions of Section 210 of the Judicial Code, as amended, U.S.C., Title 28, former § 47a, or of other statutes of the United States to the effect that stays pending appeals to the Supreme Court may be granted only by that court or a justice thereof."

1961 AMENDMENT

The amendment adopted Apr. 17, 1961, effective July 19, 1961, eliminated words "on some but not all of the claims presented in the action" which followed "final judgment."

1987 AMENDMENT

The amendment is technical. No substantive change is intended.

2007 AMENDMENTS

The language of Rule 62 has been amended as part of the general restyling of the Civil Rules to make them more easily understood and to make style and terminology consistent throughout the rules. These changes are intended to be stylistic only.

The final sentence of former Rule 62(a) referred to Rule 62(c). It is deleted as an unnecessary. Rule 62(c) governs of its own force.

Rule 63. Inability of a Judge to Proceed

1937 ADOPTION

This rule adapts and extends the provisions of U.S.C., Title 28, former § 776 (Bill of exceptions; authentication; signing of by judge) to include all duties to be performed by the judge after verdict or judgment. The statute is therefore superseded.

1987 AMENDMENT

The amendments are technical. No substantive change is intended.

1991 AMENDMENT

The revision substantially displaces the former rule. The former rule was limited to the disability of the judge, and made no provision for disqualification or possible other reasons for the withdrawal of the judge during proceedings. In making provision for other circumstances, the revision is not intended to encourage judges to discontinue participation in a trial for any but compelling reasons. Cf. *United States v. Lane,* 708 F.2d 1394, 1395–1397 (9th Cir.1983). Manifestly, a substitution should not be made for the personal convenience of the court, and the reasons for a substitution should be stated on the record.

The former rule made no provision for the withdrawal of the judge during the trial, but was limited to disqualification after trial. Several courts concluded that the text of the former rule prohibited substitution of a new judge prior to the points described in the rule, thus requiring a new trial, whether or not a fair disposition was within reach of a substitute judge. *E.g., Whalen v. Ford Motor Credit Co.,* 684 F.2d 272 (4th Cir.1982, en banc) *cert. denied,* 459 U.S. 910, 103 S.Ct. 216, 74 L.Ed.2d 172 (1982)(jury trial); *Arrow–Hart, Inc. v. Philip Carey Co.,* 552 F.2d 711 (6th Cir.1977)(non-jury trial). *See generally* Comment, *The Case of the Dead Judge: Fed.R.Civ.P. 63: Whalen v. Ford Motor Credit Co.,* 67 MINN.L.REV. 827 (1983).

The increasing length of federal trials has made it likely that the number of trials interrupted by the disability of the judge will increase. An efficient mechanism for completing these cases without unfairness is needed to prevent unnecessary expense and delay. To avoid the injustice that may result if the substitute judge proceeds despite unfamiliarity with the action, the new Rule provides, in language similar to Federal Rule of Criminal Procedure 25(a), that the successor judge must certify familiarity with the record and determine that the case may be completed before that judge without prejudice to the parties. This will necessarily require that there be available a transcript or a videotape of the proceedings prior to substitution. If there has been a long but incomplete jury trial, the prompt availability of the transcript or videotape is crucial to the effective use of this rule, for the jury cannot long be held while an extensive transcript is prepared without prejudice to one or all parties.

The revised text authorizes the substitute judge to make a finding of fact at a bench trial based on evidence heard by a different judge. This may be appropriate in limited circumstances. First, if a witness has become unavailable, the testimony recorded at trial can be considered by the successor judge pursuant to F.R.Ev. 804, being equivalent to a recorded deposition available for use at trial pursuant to Rule 32. For this purpose, a witness who is no longer subject to a subpoena to compel testimony at trial is unavailable. Secondly, the successor judge may determine that particular testimony is not material or is not disputed, and so need not be reheard. The propriety of proceeding in this manner may be marginally affected by the availability of a videotape record; a judge who has reviewed a trial on videotape may be entitled to greater confidence in his or her ability to proceed.

The court would, however, risk error to determine the credibility of a witness not seen or heard who is available to be recalled. Cf. *Anderson v. City of Bessemer City NC*, 470 U.S. 564, 575, 105 S.Ct. 1504, 1512, 84 L.Ed.2d 518 (1985); *Marshall v. Jerrico Inc.*, 446 U.S. 238, 242, 100 S.Ct. 1610, 1613, 64 L.Ed.2d 182 (1980). See also *United States v. Raddatz*, 447 U.S. 667, 100 S.Ct. 2406, 65 L.Ed.2d 424 (1980).

2007 AMENDMENTS

The language of Rule 63 has been amended as part of the general restyling of the Civil Rules to make them more easily understood and to make style and terminology consistent throughout the rules. These changes are intended to be stylistic only.

VIII. PROVISIONAL AND FINAL REMEDIES
NOTES OF ADVISORY COMMITTEE ON RULES 1991 AMENDMENT

The purpose of the revision is to divide this chapter of the Rules into two. No substantive change is effected.

Rule 64.   Seizure of Person or Property
1937 ADOPTION

This rule adopts the existing federal law, except that it specifies the applicable state law to be that of the time when the remedy is sought. Under U.S.C., Title 28, former § 726 (Attachments as provided by state laws) the plaintiff was entitled to remedies by attachment or other process which were on June 1, 1872, provided by the applicable state law, and the district courts might, from time to time, by general rules, adopt such state laws as might be in force. This statute is superseded as are district court rules which are rendered unnecessary by the rule.

Lis pendens. No rule concerning *lis pendens* is stated, for this would appear to be a matter of substantive law affecting state laws of property. It has been held that in the absence of a state statute expressly providing for the recordation of notice of the pendency of federal actions, the commencement of a federal action is notice to all persons affected. *King v. Davis*, Va.1903, 137 F. 198. It has been held, however, that when a state statute does so provide expressly, its provisions are binding. *United States v. Calcasieu Timber Co.*, C.C.A.5, 1916, 236 F. 196.

For statutes of the United States on attachment, see, e.g.:

U.S.C., Title 28 former:

§ 737   (Attachment in postal suits)

§ 738   (Attachment; application for warrant)

§ 739   (Attachment; issue of warrant)

§ 740   (Attachment; trial of ownership of property)

§ 741   (Attachment; investment of proceeds of attached property)

§ 742   (Attachment; publication of attachment)

§ 743   (Attachment; personal notice of attachment)

§ 744   (Attachment; discharge; bond)

§ 745   (Attachment; accrued rights not affected)

§ 746   (Attachments dissolved in conformity with State laws)

For statutes of the United States on garnishment, see, e.g.:

U.S.C., Title 28 former:

§ 748   (Garnishees in suits by United States against a corporation)

§ 749   (Same; issue tendered on denial of indebtedness)

§ 750   (Same; garnishee failing to appear)

For statutes of the United States on arrest, see, e.g.:

U.S.C., Title 28 former:

§ 376   (Writs of ne exeat)

§ 755   (Special bail in suits for duties and penalties)

§ 756   (Defendant giving bail in one district and committed in another)

§ 757   (Defendant giving bail in one district and committed in another; defendant held until judgment in first suit)

§ 758   (Bail and affidavits; taking by commissioners)

§ 759   (Calling of bail in Kentucky)

§ 760   (Clerks may take bail de bene esse)

§ 843   (Imprisonment for debt)

§ 844   (Imprisonment for debt; discharge according to State laws)

§ 845   (Imprisonment for debt; jail limits)

For statutes of the United States on replevin, see, e.g.:

U.S.C., Title 28:

§ 2463, formerly § 747 (Replevy of property taken under revenue laws).

SUPPLEMENTARY NOTE OF ADVISORY COMMITTEE REGARDING THIS RULE

Note. Sections 203 and 204 of the Soldiers' and Sailors' Civil Relief Act of 1940, 50 U.S.C., Appendix, §§ 523 and 524, provide under certain circumstances for the issuance and continuance of a stay of the execution of any judgment entered against a person in military service, or the vacation or stay of any attachment or garnishment directed against such person's property, money, or debts in the hands of another. See also note to Rule 62 herein.

2007 AMENDMENTS

The language of Rule 64 has been amended as part of the general restyling of the Civil Rules to make them more easily understood and to make style and terminology consistent throughout the rules. These changes are intended to be stylistic only.

Former Rule 64 stated that the Civil Rules govern an action in which any remedy available under Rule 64(a) is used. The Rules were said to govern from the time the action is commenced if filed in federal court, and from the time of removal if removed from state court. These provisions are deleted as redundant. Rule 1 establishes that the Civil Rules apply to all actions in a district court, and Rule 81(c)(1) adds reassurance that the Civil Rules apply to a removed action "after it is removed."

Rule 65. Injunctions

1937 ADOPTION

Note to Subdivisions (a) and (b). These are taken from U.S.C., Title 28, former § 381 (Injunctions; preliminary injunctions and temporary restraining orders).

Note to Subdivision (c). Except for the last sentence, this is substantially U.S.C., Title 28, former § 382 (Injunctions; security on issuance of). The last sentence continues the following and similar statutes which expressly except the United States or an officer or agency thereof from such security requirements: U.S.C., Title 15, §§ 77t(b), 78u(e), and 79r(f)(Securities and Exchange Commission). It also excepts the United States or an officer or agency thereof from such security requirements in any action in which a restraining order or interlocutory judgment of injunction issues in its favor whether there is an express statutory exception from such security requirements or not.

See U.S.C., Title 6 (Official and Penal Bonds) for bonds by surety companies.

Note to Subdivision (d). This is substantially U.S.C., Title 28, former § 383 (Injunctions; requisites of order; binding effect).

Note to Subdivision (e). The words "relating to temporary restraining orders and preliminary injunctions in actions affecting employer and employee" are words of description and not of limitation.

Compare former Equity Rule 73 (Preliminary Injunctions and Temporary Restraining Orders) which is substantially equivalent to the statutes.

For other statutes dealing with injunctions which are continued, see e.g.:

U.S.C., Title 28, former:

§ 46 (Suits to enjoin orders of Interstate Commerce Commission to be against United States)

§ 47 (Injunctions as to orders of Interstate Commerce Commission; appeal to Supreme Court; time for taking)

§ 378 (Injunctions; when granted)

§ 379 (Injunctions; stay in State courts)

§ 380 (Injunctions; alleged unconstitutionality of State statutes; appeal to Supreme Court)

§ 380a (Injunctions; constitutionality of Federal statute; application for hearing; appeal to Supreme Court)

U.S.C., Title 7:

§ 216 (Court proceedings to enforce orders; injunction)

§ 217 (Proceedings for suspension of orders)

U.S.C., Title 15:

§ 4 (Jurisdiction of courts; duty of district attorney; procedure)

§ 25 (Restraining violations; procedure)

§ 26 (Injunctive relief for private parties; exceptions)

§ 77t(b) (Injunctions and prosecution of offenses)

1946 AMENDMENT

Note. It has been held that in actions on preliminary injunction bonds the district court has discretion to grant relief in the same proceeding or to require the institution of a new action on the bond. *Russell v. Farley*, 1881, 105 U.S. 433, 466, 26 L.Ed. 1060. It is believed, however, that in all cases the litigant should have a right to proceed on the bond in the same proceeding, in the manner provided in Rule 73(f) for a similar situation. The paragraph added to Rule 65(c) insures this result and is in the interest of efficiency. There is no reason why Rules 65(c) and 73(f) should operate differently. Compare § 50, sub. n of the Bankruptcy Act, 11 U.S.C. § 78, sub. n, under which actions on all bonds furnished pursuant to the Act may be proceeded upon summarily in the bankruptcy court. See 2 Collier on Bankruptcy, 14th ed. by Moore and Oglebay, 1853–1854.

1948 AMENDMENT

The amendment effective October 1949, changed subdivision (e) in the following respects: in the first clause the amendment substituted the words "any statute of the United States" for the words "the Act of October 15, 1914, ch. 323, §§ 1 and 20 (38 Stat. 730), U.S.C., Title 29, §§ 52 and 53, or the Act of March 23, 1932, ch. 90 (47 Stat. 70), U.S.C., Title 29, ch. 6"; in the second clause of subdivision (e) the amendment substituted the reference to "Title 28, U.S.C., § 2361" for the reference to "Section 24(26) of the Judicial Code as amended, U.S.C., Title 28, § 41(26)"; and the third clause was amended to read "Title 28, U.S.C., § 2284," etc., as at present, instead of "the Act of August 24, 1937, ch. 754, § 3, relating to actions to enjoin the enforcement of acts of Congress."

1966 AMENDMENT

Subdivision (a)(2). This new subdivision provides express authority for consolidating the hearing of an application for a preliminary injunction with the trial on the merits. The authority can be exercised with particular profit when it appears that a substantial part of evidence offered on the application will be relevant to the merits and will be presented in such form as to qualify for admission on the trial proper. Repetition of evidence is thereby avoided. The fact that the proceedings have been consolidated should cause no delay in the disposition of the application for the preliminary injunction, for the evidence will be directed in the first instance to that relief, and the preliminary injunction, if justified by the proof, may be issued in the course of the consolidated proceedings. Furthermore, to consolidate the proceedings will tend to expedite the final disposition of the action. It is believed that consolidation can be usefully availed of in many cases.

The subdivision further provides that even when consolidation is not ordered, evidence received in connection with an application for a preliminary injunction which would be admissible on the trial on the merits forms part of the trial record. This evidence need not be repeated on the trial. On the the other hand, repetition is not altogether prohibited. That would be impractical and unwise. For example, a witness testifying comprehensively on the trial who has previously testified upon the application for a preliminary injunction might sometimes be hamstrung in telling his story if he could not go over some part of his prior testimony to connect it with his present testimony. So also, some repetition of testimony may be called for where the trial is conducted by a judge who did not hear the application for the preliminary injunction. In general, however, repetition can be avoided with an increase of efficiency in the conduct of the case and without any distortion of the presentation of evidence by the parties.

Since an application for a preliminary injunction may be made in an action in which, with respect to all or part of the merits, there is a right to trial by jury, it is appropriate to add the caution appearing in the last sentence of the subdivision. In such a case the jury will have to hear all the evidence bearing on its verdict, even if some part of the evidence has already been heard by the judge alone on the application for the preliminary injunction.

The subdivision is believed to reflect the substance of the best current practice and introduces no novel conception.

Subdivision (b). In view of the possibly drastic consequence of a temporary restraining order, the opposition should be heard, if feasible, before the order is granted. Many judges have properly insisted that, when time does not permit of formal notice of the application to the adverse party, some expedient, such as telephonic notice to the attorney for the adverse party, be resorted to if this can reasonably be done. On occasion, however, temporary restraining orders have been issued without any notice when it was feasible for some fair, although informal, notice to be given. See the emphatic criticisms in *Pennsylvania R. Co. v. Transport Workers Union*, 278 F.2d 693, 694 (3d Cir.1960); *Arvida Corp. v. Sugarman*, 259 F.2d 428, 429 (2d Cir.1958); *Lummus Co. v. Commonwealth Oil Ref. Co., Inc.*, 297 F.2d 80, 83 (2d Cir.1961), cert. denied, 368 U.S. 986, 82 S.Ct. 601, 7 L.Ed.2d 524 (1962).

Heretofore the first sentence of subdivision (b), in referring to a notice "served" on the "adverse party" on which a "hearing" could be held, perhaps invited the interpretation that the order might be granted without notice if the circumstances did not permit of a formal hearing on the basis of a formal notice. The subdivision is amended to make it plain that informal notice, which may be communicated to the attorney rather than the adverse party, is to be preferred to no notice at all.

Before notice can be dispensed with, the applicant's counsel must give his certificate as to any efforts made to give notice and the reasons why notice should not be required. This certificate is in addition to the requirement of an affidavit or verified complaint setting forth the facts as to the irreparable injury which would result before the opposition could be heard.

The amended subdivision continues to recognize that a temporary restraining order may be issued without any notice when the circumstances warrant.

Subdivision (c). Original Rules 65 and 73 contained substantially identical provisions for summary proceedings against sureties on bonds required or permitted by the rules. There was fragmentary coverage of the same subject in the Admiralty Rules. Clearly, a single comprehensive rule is required, and is incorporated as Rule 65.1.

1987 AMENDMENT

The amendments are technical. No substantive change is intended.

2001 AMENDMENT

New subdivision (f) is added in conjunction with abrogation of the antiquated Copyright Rules of Practice adopted for proceedings under the 1909 Copyright Act. Courts have naturally turned to Rule 65 in response to the apparent inconsistency of the former

Copyright Rules with the discretionary impoundment procedure adopted in 1976, 17 U.S.C. § 503(a). Rule 65 procedures also have assuaged well-founded doubts whether the Copyright Rules satisfy more contemporary requirements of due process. See, e.g., Religious Technology Center v. Netcom On–Line Communication Servs., Inc., 923 F.Supp. 1231, 1260–1265 (N.D.Cal.1995); Paramount Pictures Corp. v. Doe, 821 F.Supp. 82 (E.D.N.Y. 1993); WPOW, Inc. v. MRLJ Enterprises, 584 F.Supp. 132 (D.D.C.1984).

A common question has arisen from the experience that notice of a proposed impoundment may enable an infringer to defeat the court's capacity to grant effective relief. Impoundment may be ordered on an ex parte basis under subdivision (b) if the applicant makes a strong showing of the reasons why notice is likely to defeat effective relief. Such no-notice procedures are authorized in trademark infringement proceedings, see 15 U.S.C. § 1116(d), and courts have provided clear illustrations of the kinds of showings that support ex parte relief. See Matter of Vuitton et Fils S.A., 606 F.2d 1 (2d Cir.1979); Vuitton v. White, 945 F.2d 569 (3d Cir.1991). In applying the tests for no-notice relief, the court should ask whether impoundment is necessary, or whether adequate protection can be had by a less intrusive form of no-notice relief shaped as a temporary restraining order.

This new subdivision (f) does not limit use of trademark procedures in cases that combine trademark and copyright claims. Some observers believe that trademark procedures should be adopted for all copyright cases, a proposal better considered by Congressional processes than by rulemaking processes.

Changes Made After Publication and Comments

No change has been made.

2007 AMENDMENTS

The language of Rule 65 has been amended as part of the general restyling of the Civil Rules to make them more easily understood and to make style and terminology consistent throughout the rules. These changes are intended to be stylistic only.

The final sentence of former Rule 65(c) referred to Rule 65.1. It is deleted as unnecessary. Rule 65.1 governs of its own force.

Rule 65(d)(2) clarifies two ambiguities in former Rule 65(d). The former rule was adapted from former 28 U.S.C. § 363, but omitted a comma that made clear the common doctrine that a party must have actual notice of an injunction in order to be bound by it. Amended Rule 65(d) restores the meaning of the earlier statute, and also makes clear the proposition that an injunction can be enforced against a person who acts in concert with a party's officer, agent, servant, employee, or attorney.

Rule 65.1.   Security: Proceedings Against Sureties

1966 ADDITION

See Note to Rule 65.

1987 AMENDMENT

The amendments are technical. No substantive change is intended.

2006 AMENDMENT

Rule 65.1 is amended to conform to the changed title of the Supplemental Rules.

2007 AMENDMENTS

The language of Rule 65.1 has been amended as part of the general restyling of the Civil Rules to make them more easily understood and to make style and terminology consistent throughout the rules. These changes are intended to be stylistic only.

Rule 66.   Receivers Appointed by Federal Courts

1946 AMENDMENT

Note. The title of Rule 66 has been expanded to make clear the subject of the rule, i. e., federal equity receivers.

The first sentence added to Rule 66 prevents a dismissal by any party, after a federal equity receiver has been appointed, except upon leave of court. A party should not be permitted to oust the court and its officer without the consent of that court. See Civil Rule 31(e), Eastern District of Washington.

The second sentence added at the beginning of the rule deals with suits by or against a federal equity receiver. The first clause thereof eliminates the formal ceremony of an ancillary appointment before suit can be brought by a receiver, and is in accord with the more modern state practice, and with more expeditious and less expensive judicial administration. 2 Moore's Federal Practice, 1938, 2088–2091. For the rule necessitating ancillary appointment, see *Sterrett v. Second Nat. Bank*, 1918, 248 U.S. 73, 39 S.Ct. 27, 63 L.Ed. 135; *Kelley v. Queeney*, W.D.N.Y.1941, 41 F.Supp. 1015; see also *McCandless v. Furlaud*, 1934, 293 U.S. 67, 55 S.Ct. 42, 79 L.Ed. 202. This rule has been extensively criticized. First, Extraterritorial Powers of Receivers, 1932, 27 Ill.L.Rev. 271; Rose, Extraterritorial Actions by Receivers, 1933, 17 Minn.L.Rev. 704; Laughlin, The Extraterritorial Powers of Receivers, 1932, 45 Harv.L.Rev. 429; Clark and Moore, A New Federal Civil Procedure—II, Pleadings and Parties, 1935, 44 Yale L.J.1291, 1312–1315; Note, 1932, 30 Mich.L.Rev. 1322. See also comment in *Bicknell v. Lloyd-Smith*, C.C.A.2, 1940, 109 F.2d 527, certiorari denied 311 U.S. 650, 61 S.Ct. 15, 85 L.Ed. 416. The second clause of the sentence merely incorporates the well-known and general rule that, absent statutory authorization, a federal receiver cannot be sued without leave of the court which appointed him, applied in the federal courts since *Barton v. Barbour*, 1881, 104 U.S. 126, 26 L.Ed. 672. See also 1 Clark on Receivers, 2d ed., § 549. Under 28 U.S.C., § 959, formerly § 125, leave of court is unnecessary when a receiver is sued "in respect of any act or transaction of his in carrying on the business" connected with the receivership property, but such suit is subject to the general equity jurisdiction of the court in which the receiver was appointed, so far as justice necessitates.

Capacity of a state court receiver to sue or be sued in federal court is governed by Rule 17(b).

The last sentence added to Rule 66 assures the application of the rules in all matters except actual administration of the receivership estate itself. Since this implicitly carries with it the applicability of those rules relating to appellate procedure, the express reference thereto contained in Rule 66 has been stricken as superfluous. Under Rule 81(a)(1) the rules do not apply to bankruptcy proceedings except as they may be made applicable by order of the Supreme Court. Rule 66 is applicable to what is commonly known as a federal "chancery" or "equity" receiver, or similar type of court officer. It is not designed to regulate or affect receivers in bankruptcy, which are governed by the Bankruptcy Act and the General Orders. Since the Federal Rules are applicable in bankruptcy by virtue of General Orders in Bankruptcy 36 and 37 only to the extent that they are not inconsistent with the Bankruptcy Act or the General Orders, Rule 66 is not applicable to bankruptcy receivers. See 1 Collier on Bankruptcy, 14th ed. by Moore and Oglebay, ¶¶ 2.23–2.36.

1948 AMENDMENT

The amendment effective October 1949, deleted a sentence which formerly appeared immediately following the first sentence and which read as follows: "A receiver shall have the capacity to sue in any district court without ancillary appointment; but actions against a receiver may not be commenced without leave of the court appointing him except when authorized by a statute of the United States."

2007 AMENDMENTS

The language of Rule 66 has been amended as part of the general restyling of the Civil Rules to make them more easily understood and to make style and terminology consistent throughout the rules. These changes are intended to be stylistic only.

Rule 67. Deposit in Court

1937 ADOPTION

This rule provides for deposit in court generally, continuing similar special provisions contained in such statutes as U.S.C., Title 28, §§ 1335, 1397, 2361, formerly § 41(26)(Original jurisdiction of bills of interpleader, and of bills in the nature of interpleader). See generally *Howard v. United States*, 1902, 184 U.S. 676, 22 S.Ct. 543, 46 L.Ed. 754; United States Supreme Court Admiralty Rules (1920), Rules 37 (Bringing Funds into Court), 41 (Funds in Court Registry), and 42 (Claims Against Proceeds in Registry). With the first sentence, compare English Rules Under the Judicature Act (The Annual Practice, 1937) O. 22, r. 1(1).

1948 AMENDMENT

The amendment effective October 1949 substituted the reference to "Title 28, U.S.C., §§ 2041, and 2042" for the reference to "Sections 995 and 996, Revised Statutes, as amended, U.S.C., Title 28, §§ 851, 852." The amendment also added the words "as amended" following the citation of the Act of June 26, 1934, c. 756, § 23, and, in the parenthetical citation immediately following, added the reference to "58 Stat. 845."

1983 AMENDMENT

Rule 67 has been amended in three ways. The first change is the addition of the clause in the first sentence. Some courts have construed the present rule to permit deposit only when the party making it claims no interest in the fund or thing deposited. *E.g., Blasini–Stern v. Beech–Nut Life Savers Corp.,* 429 F.Supp. 533 (D.Puerto Rico 1975); *Dinkins v. General Aniline & Film Corp.,* 214 F.Supp. 281 (S.D.N.Y.1963). However, there are situations in which a litigant may wish to be relieved of responsibility for a sum or thing, but continue to claim an interest in all or part of it. In these cases the deposit-in-court procedure should be available; in addition to the advantages to the party making the deposit, the procedure gives other litigants assurance that any judgment will be collectable. The amendment is intended to accomplish that.

The second change is the addition of a requirement that the order of deposit be served on the clerk of the court in which the sum or thing is to be deposited. This is simply to assure that the clerk knows what is being deposited and what his responsibilities are with respect to the deposit. The latter point is particularly important since the rule as amended contemplates that deposits will be placed in interest-bearing accounts; the clerk must know what treatment has been ordered for the particular deposit.

The third change is to require that any money be deposited in an interest-bearing account or instrument approved by the court.

2007 AMENDMENTS

The language of Rule 67 has been amended as part of the general restyling of the Civil Rules to make them more easily understood and to make style and terminology consistent throughout the rules. These changes are intended to be stylistic only.

Rule 68.   Offer of Judgment

1937 ADOPTION

See 2 Minn.Stat. (Mason, 1927) § 9323; 4 Mont.Rev.Codes Ann. (1935) § 9770; N.Y.C.P.A. (1937) § 177.

For the recovery of costs against the United States, see Rule 54(d).

1946 AMENDMENT

Note. The third sentence of Rule 68 has been altered to make clear that evidence of an unaccepted offer is admissible in a proceeding to determine the costs of the action but is not otherwise admissible.

The two sentences substituted for the deleted last sentence of the rule assure a party the right to make a second offer where the situation permits—as, for example, where a prior offer was not accepted but the plaintiff's judgment is nullified and a new trial ordered, whereupon the defendant desires to make a second offer. It is implicit, however, that as long as the case continues—whether there be a first, second or third trial—and the defendant makes no further offer, his first and only offer will operate to save him the costs from the time of that offer if the plaintiff ultimately obtains a judgment less than the sum offered. In the case of successive offers not accepted, the offeror is saved the costs incurred after the making of the offer which was equal to or greater than the judgment ultimately obtained. These provisions should serve to encourage settlements and avoid protracted litigation.

The phrase "before the trial begins," in the first sentence of the rule, has been construed in *Cover v. Chicago Eye Shield Co.,* C.C.A.7, 1943, 136 F.2d 374, certiorari denied 320 U.S. 749, 64 S.Ct. 53, 88 L.Ed. 445.

1966 AMENDMENT

This logical extension of the concept of offer of judgment is suggested by the common admiralty practice of determining liability before the amount of liability is determined.

1987 AMENDMENT

The amendments are technical. No substantive change is intended.

The language of Rule 68 has been amended as part of the general restyling of the Civil Rules to make them more easily understood and to make style and terminology consistent throughout the rules. These changes are intended to be stylistic only.

Rule 69. Execution

1937 ADOPTION

Note to Subdivision (a). This follows in substance U.S.C., Title 28, former § 727 (Executions as provided by State laws) and former § 729 (Proceedings in vindication of civil rights), except that, as in the similar case of attachments (see note to Rule 64), the rule specifies the applicable State law to be that of the time when the remedy is sought, and thus renders unnecessary, as well as supersedeas, local district court rules.

Statutes of the United States on execution, when applicable, govern under this rule. Among these are:

U.S.C., Title 12:

§ 91   (Transfers by bank and other acts in contemplation of insolvency)

§ 632   (Jurisdiction of United States district courts in cases arising out of foreign banking jurisdiction where Federal reserve bank a party)

U.S.C., Title 19:

§ 199   (Judgments for customs duties, how payable)

U.S.C., Title 26:

§ 1610(a)   (Surrender of property subject to distraint)

U.S.C., Title 28, former:

§ 122   (Creation of new district or transfer of territory; lien)

§ 350   (Time for making application for appeal or certiorari; stay pending application for certiorari)

§ 489   (District Attorneys; reports to Department of Justice)

§ 574   (Marshals, fees enumerated)

§ 786   (Judgments for duties; collected in coin)

§ 811   (Interest on judgments)

§ 838   (Executions; run in all districts of State)

§ 839   (Executions; run in every State and Territory)

§ 840   (Executions; stay on conditions), as modified by Rules 62(b)

§ 841   (Executions; stay of one term), as modified by Rule 62(f)

§ 842   (Executions; against officers of revenue in cases of probable cause), as incorporated in Subdivision (b) of this rule

§ 843   (Imprisonment for debt)

§ 844   (Imprisonment for debt; discharge according to State laws)

§ 845   (Imprisonment for debt; jail limits)

§ 846   (Fieri Facias; appraisal of goods; appraisers)

§ 847   (Sales; real property under order or decree)

§ 848   (Sales; personal property under order or decree)

§ 849   (Sales; necessity of notice)

§ 850   (Sales; death of marshal after levy or after sale)

§ 869   (Bond in former error and on appeal) as incorporated in Rule 73(c)

§ 874   (Supersedeas), as modified by Rules 62(d) and 73(d)

U.S.C., Title 31:

§ 195   (Purchase on execution)

U.S.C., Title 33:

§ 918   (Collection of defaulted payments)

U.S.C., Title 49:

§ 74(g) (Causes of action arising out of Federal control of railroads; execution and other process)

Special statutes of the United States on exemption from execution are also continued. Among these are:

U.S.C., Title 2:

§ 118 (Actions against officers of Congress for official acts)

U.S.C., Title 5:

§ 729 (Federal employees retirement annuities not subject to assignment, execution, levy, or other legal process)

U.S.C., Title 10:

§ 610 (Exemption of enlisted men from arrest on civil process)

U.S.C., Title 22, former:

§ 21(h) (Foreign service retirement and disability system; establishment; rules and regulations; annuities; nonassignable; exemption from legal process)

U.S.C., Title 33:

§ 916 (Assignment and exemption from claims of creditors) Longshoremen's and Harbor-workers' Compensation Act

U.S.C., Title 38:

§ 54 (Attachment, levy or seizure of moneys due pensioners prohibited)

§ 393 (Army and Navy Medal of Honor Roll; pensions additional to other pensions; liability to attachment, etc.) Compare Title 34, § 365(c) (Medal of Honor Roll; special pension to persons enrolled)

§ 618 (Benefits exempt from seizure under process and taxation; no deductions for indebtedness to United States)

U.S.C., Title 43:

§ 175 (Exemption from execution of homestead land)

U.S.C., Title 48:

§ 1371o (Panama Canal and railroad retirement annuities, exemption from execution and so forth)

SUPPLEMENTARY NOTE OF ADVISORY COMMITTEE REGARDING THIS RULE

Note. With respect to the provisions of the Soldiers' and Sailors' Civil Relief Act of 1940, 50 U.S.C. Appendix, § 501 et seq., see Notes to Rules 62 and 64 herein.

1948 AMENDMENT

The amendment effective October 1949 substituted the citation of "Title 28, U.S.C. § 2006" in subdivision (b) in place of the citation to "Section 989, Revised Statutes, U.S.C. Title 28, § 842".

1970 AMENDMENT

The amendment assures that, in aid of execution on a judgment, all discovery procedures provided in the rules are available and not just discovery via the taking of a deposition. Under the present language, one court has held that Rule 34 discovery is unavailable to the judgment creditor. *M. Lowenstein & Sons, Inc.* v. *American Underwear Mfg. Co.,* 11 F.R.D. 172 (E.D.Pa.1951). Notwithstanding the language, and relying heavily on legislative history referring to Rule 33, the Fifth Circuit has held that a judgment creditor may invoke Rule 33 interrogatories. *United States* v. *McWhirter,* 376 F.2d 102 (5th Cir.1967). But the court's reasoning does not extend to discovery except as provided in Rules 26–33. One commentator suggests that the existing language might properly be stretched to all discovery, 7 Moore's Federal Practice ¶ 69.05[1] (2d ed. 1966), but another believes that a rules amendment is needed. 3 Barron & Holtzoff, Federal Practice and Procedure 1484 (Wright ed. 1958). Both commentators and the court in *McWhirter* are clear that, as a matter of policy, Rule 69 should authorize the use of all discovery devices provided in the rules.

1987 AMENDMENT

The amendments are technical. No substantive change is intended.

2007 Amendments

The language of Rule 69 has been amended as part of the general restyling of the Civil Rules to make them more easily understood and to make style and terminology consistent throughout the rules. These changes are intended to be stylistic only.

Amended Rule 69(b) incorporates directly the provisions of 2 U.S.C. § 118 and 28 U.S.C. § 2006, deleting the incomplete statement in former Rule 69(b) of the circumstances in which execution does not issue against an officer.

Rule 70.   Judgment for Specific Acts; Vesting Title

1937 ADOPTION

Compare former Equity Rules 7 (Process, Mesne and Final), 8 (Enforcement of Final Decrees), and 9 (Writ of Assistance). To avoid possible confusion, both old and new denominations for attachment (sequestration) and execution (assistance) are used in this rule. Compare with the provision in this rule that the judgment may itself vest title, 6 Tenn.Ann.Code (Williams, 1934) § 10594; 2 Conn.Gen.Stat. (1930) § 5455; N.M.Stat.Ann. (Courtright, 1929) § 117–117; 2 Ohio Gen.Code Ann. (Page, 1926) § 11590; and England, Supreme Court of Judicature Act (1925) § 47.

2007 AMENDMENTS

The language of Rule 70 has been amended as part of the general restyling of the Civil Rules to make them more easily understood and to make style and terminology consistent throughout the rules. These changes are intended to be stylistic only.

Rule 71.   Process in Behalf of and Against Persons Not Parties

1937 ADOPTION

Compare former Equity Rule 11 (Process in Behalf of and Against Persons Not Parties). Compare also *Terrell* v. *Allison,* 1875, 22 L.Ed. 634, 21 Wall. 289; *Farmers' Loan and Trust Co.* v. *Chicago and A. Ry. Co.,* C.C.Ind.1890, 44 F. 653; *Robert Findlay Mfg. Co.* v. *Hygrade Lighting Fixture Corp.,* N.Y.1923, 288 F. 80; *Thompson* v. *Smith,* C.C.Minn. 1870, Fed.Cas.No.13,977.

1987 AMENDMENT

The amendments are technical. No substantive change is intended.

2007 AMENDMENTS

The language of Rule 71 has been amended as part of the general restyling of the Civil Rules to make them more easily understood and to make style and terminology consistent throughout the rules. These changes are intended to be stylistic only.

IX.   SPECIAL PROCEEDINGS

NOTES OF ADVISORY COMMITTEE ON RULES 1991 ADDITION

This chapter heading is to be inserted between Rule 71 and Rule 71A.

Rule 71A.   Condemnation of Property

1951 ADDITION

The Court will remember that at its conference on December 2, 1948, the discussion was confined to subdivision (h) of the rule (* * *), the particular question being whether the tribunal to award compensation should be a commission or a jury in cases where the Congress has not made specific provision on the subject. The Advisory Committee was agreed from the outset that a rule should not be promulgated which would overturn the decision of the Congress as to the kind of tribunal to fix compensation, provided that the system established by Congress was found to be working well. We found two instances where the Congress had specified the kind of tribunal to fix compensation. One case was the District of Columbia (U.S.C., Title 40, §§ 361–386 (now D.C.Code, 1951 Ed., Title 16– 619 to 16–644)) where a rather unique system exists under which the court is required in all cases to order the selection of a "jury" of five from among not less than twenty names drawn from "the special box provided by law." They must have the usual qualifications of jurors and in addition must be freeholders of the District and not in the service of the United States or the District. That system has been in effect for many years, and our inquiry revealed that it works well under the conditions prevailing in the District, and is satisfactory to the courts of the District, the legal profession and to property owners.

The other instance is that of the Tennessee Valley Authority, where the act of Congress (U.S.C. Title 16, § 831x), provides that compensation is fixed by three disinterested commissioners appointed by the court, whose award goes before the District Court for confirmation or modification. The Advisory Committee made a thorough inquiry into the practical operation of the TVA commission system. We obtained from counsel for the TVA the results of their experience, which afforded convincing proof that the commission system is preferable under the conditions affecting TVA and that the jury system would not work satisfactorily. We then, under date of February 6, 1947, wrote every Federal judge who had ever sat in a TVA condemnation case, asking his views as to whether the commission system is satisfactory and whether a jury system should be preferred. Of 21 responses from the judges 17 approved the commission system and opposed the substitution of a jury system for the TVA. Many of the judges went further and opposed the use of juries in any condemnation cases. Three of the judges preferred the jury system, and one dealt only with the TVA provision for a three judge district court. The Advisory Committee has not considered abolition of the three judge requirement of the TVA Act, because it seemed to raise a question of jurisdiction, which cannot be altered by rule. Nevertheless the Department of Justice continued its advocacy of the jury system for its asserted expedition and economy; and others favored a uniform procedure. In consequence of these divided counsels the Advisory Committee was itself divided, but in its May 1948 Report to the Court recommended the following rule as approved by a majority (* * *):

(h) Trial. If the action involves the exercise of the power of eminent domain under the law of the United States, any tribunal specially constituted by an Act of Congress governing the case for the trial of the issue of just compensation shall be the tribunal for the determination of that issue; but if there is no such specially constituted tribunal any party may have a trial by jury of the issue of just compensation by filing a demand therefor within the time allowed for answer or within such further time as the court may fix. Trial of all issues shall otherwise be by the court.

The effect of this was to preserve the existing systems in the District of Columbia and in TVA cases, but to provide for a jury to fix compensation in all other cases.

Before the Court's conference of December 2, 1948, the Chief Justice informed the Committee that the Court was particularly interested in the views expressed by Judge John Paul, Judge of the United States District Court for the Western District of Virginia, in a letter from him to the chairman of the Advisory Committee, dated February 13, 1947. Copies of all the letters from judges who had sat in TVA cases had been made available to the Court, and this letter from Judge Paul is one of them. Judge Paul strongly opposed jury trials and recommended the commission system in large projects like the TVA, and his views seemed to have impressed the Court and to have been the occasion for the conference.

The reasons which convinced the Advisory Committee that the use of commissioners instead of juries is desirable in TVA cases were these:

1. The TVA condemns large areas of land of similar kind, involving many owners. Uniformity in awards is essential. The commission system tends to prevent discrimination and provide for uniformity in compensation. The jury system tends to lack of uniformity. Once a reasonable and uniform standard of values for the area has been settled by a commission, litigation ends and settlements result.

2. Where large areas are involved many small landowners reside at great distances from the place where a court sits. It is a great hardship on humble people to have to travel long distances to attend a jury trial. A commission may travel around and receive the evidence of the owner near his home.

3. It is impracticable to take juries long distances to view the premises.

4. If the cases are tried by juries the burden on the time of the courts is excessive.

These considerations are the very ones Judge Paul stressed in his letter. He pointed out that they applied not only to the TVA but to other large governmental projects, such as flood control, hydroelectric power, reclamation, national forests, and others. So when the representatives of the Advisory Committee appeared at the Court's conference December 2, 1948, they found it difficult to justify the proposed provision in subdivision (h) of the rule that a jury should be used to fix compensation in all cases where Congress had not specified the tribunal. If our reasons for preserving the TVA system were sound, provision for a jury in similar projects of like magnitude seemed unsound.

Aware of the apparent inconsistency between the acceptance of the TVA system and the provision for a jury in all other cases, the members of the Committee attending the conference of December 2, 1948, then suggested that in the other cases the choice of jury or commission be left to the discretion of the District Court, going back to a suggestion previously made by Committee members and reported at page 15 of the Preliminary Draft of June 1947. They called the attention of the Court to the fact that the entire Advisory Committee had not been consulted about this suggestion and proposed that the draft be returned to the Committee for further consideration, and that was done.

The proposal we now make for subdivision (h) is as follows:

(h) Trial. If the action involves the exercise of the power of eminent domain under the law of the United States, any tribunal specially constituted by an Act of Congress governing the case for the trial of the issue of just compensation shall be the tribunal for the determination of that issue; but if there is no such specially constituted tribunal any party may have a trial by jury of the issue of just compensation by filing a demand therefor within the time allowed for answer or within such further time as the court may fix, unless the court in its discretion orders that, because of the character, location, or quantity of the property to be condemned, or for other reasons in the interest of justice, the issue of compensation shall be determined by a commission of three persons appointed by it. If a commission is appointed it shall have the powers of a master provided in subdivision (c) of Rule 53 and proceedings before it shall be governed by the provisions of paragraphs (1) and (2) of subdivision (d) of Rule 53. Its action and report shall be determined by a majority and its findings and report shall have the effect, and be dealt with by the court in accordance with the practice, prescribed in paragraph (2) of subdivision (e) of Rule 53. Trial of all issues shall otherwise be by the court.

In the 1948 draft the Committee had been almost evenly divided as between jury or commission and that made it easy for us to agree on the present draft. It would be difficult to state in a rule the various conditions to control the District Court in its choice and we have merely stated generally the matters which should be considered by the District Court.

The rule as now drafted seems to meet Judge Paul's objection. In large projects like the TVA the court may decide to use a commission. In a great number of cases involving only sites for buildings or other small areas, where use of a jury is appropriate, a jury may be chosen. The District Court's discretion may also be influenced by local preference or habit, and the preference of the Department of Justice and the reasons for its preference will doubtless be given weight. The Committee are convinced that there are some types of cases in which use of a commission is preferable and others in which a jury may be appropriately used, and that it would be a mistake to provide that the same kind of tribunal should be used in all cases. We think the available evidence clearly leads to that conclusion.

When this suggestion was made at the conference of December 2, 1948, representatives of the Department of Justice opposed it, expressing opposition to the use of a commission in any case. Their principal ground for opposition to commissions was then based on the assertion that the commission system is too expensive because courts allow commissioners too large compensation. The obvious answer to that is that the compensation of commissioners ought to be fixed or limited by law, as was done in the TVA Act, and the agency dealing with appropriations—either the Administrative Office or some other interested department of the government—should correct that evil, if evil there be, by obtaining such legislation. Authority to promulgate rules of procedure does not include power to fix compensation of government employees. The Advisory Committee is not convinced that even without such legislation the commission system is more expensive than the jury system. The expense of jury trials includes not only the per diem and mileage of the jurors impaneled for a case but like items for the entire venire. In computing cost of jury trials, the salaries of court officials, judges, clerks, marshals and deputies must be considered. No figures have been given to the Committee to establish that the cost of the commission system is the greater.

We earnestly recommend the rule as now drafted for promulgation by the Court, in the public interest.

The Advisory Committee have given more time to this rule, including time required for conferences with the Department of Justice to hear statements of its representatives, than has been required by any other rule. The rule may not be perfect but if faults develop in practice they may be promptly cured. Certainly the present conformity system is atrocious.

Under state practices, just compensation is normally determined by one of three methods: by commissioners; by commissioners with a right of appeal to and trial de novo before a jury; and by a jury, without a commission. A trial to the court or to the court including a master are, however, other methods that are occasionally used. Approximately 5 states use only commissioners; 23 states use commissioners with a trial de novo before a jury; and 18 states use only the jury. This classification is advisedly stated in approximate terms, since the same state may utilize diverse methods, depending upon different types of condemnations or upon the locality of the property, and since the methods used in a few states do not permit of a categorical classification. To reject the proposed rule and leave the situation as it is would not satisfy the views of the Department of Justice. The Department and the Advisory Committee agree that the use of a commission, with appeal to a jury, is a wasteful system.

The Department of Justice has a voluminous "Manual on Federal Eminent Domain," the 1940 edition of which has 948 pages with an appendix of 73 more pages. The title page informs us the preparation of the manual was begun during the incumbency of Attorney General Cummings, was continued under Attorney General Murphy, and completed during the incumbency of Attorney General Jackson. The preface contains the following statement:

It should also be mentioned that the research incorporated in the manual would be of invaluable assistance in the drafting of a new uniform code, or rules of court, for federal condemnation proceedings, which are now greatly confused, not only by the existence of over seventy federal statutes governing condemnations for different purposes—statutes which sometimes conflict with one another—but also by the countless problems occasioned by the requirements of conformity to state law. Progress of the work has already demonstrated that the need for such reform exists.

It is not surprising that more than once Attorneys General have asked the Advisory Committee to prepare a federal rule and rescue the government from this morass.

The Department of Justice has twice tried and failed to persuade the Congress to provide that juries shall be used in all condemnation cases. The debates in Congress show that part of the opposition to the Department of Justice's bills came from representatives opposed to jury trials in all cases, and in part from a preference for the conformity system. Our present proposal opens the door for district judges to yield to local preferences on the subject. It does much for the Department's points of view. It is a great improvement over the present so-called conformity system. It does away with the wasteful "double" system prevailing in 23 states where awards by commissions are followed by jury trials.

Aside from the question as to the choice of a tribunal to award compensation, the proposed rule would afford a simple and improved procedure.

We turn now to an itemized explanation of the other changes we have made in the 1948 draft. Some of these result from recent amendments to the Judicial Code. Others result from a reconsideration by the Advisory Committee of provisions which we thought could be improved.

1. In the amended Judicial Code, the district courts are designated as "United States District Courts" instead of "District Courts of the United States," and a corresponding change has been made in the rule.

2. After the 1948 draft was referred back to the committee, the provision in subdivision (c)(2), relating to naming defendants, * * * which provided that the plaintiff shall add as defendants all persons having or claiming an interest in that property whose names can be ascertained by a search of the records to the extent commonly made by competent searchers of title in the vicinity "in light of the type and value of the property involved," the phrase in quotation marks was changed to read, "in the light of the character and value of the property involved and the interests to be acquired."

The Department of Justice made a counter proposal * * * that there be substituted the words "reasonably diligent search of the records, considering the type." When the American Bar Association thereafter considered the draft, it approved the Advisory Committee's draft of this subdivision, but said that it had no objection to the Department's suggestion. Thereafter, in an effort to eliminate controversy, the Advisory Committee accepted the Department's suggestion as to (c)(2), using the word "character" instead of the word "type."

The Department of Justice also suggested that in subdivision (d)(3)(ii) relating to service by publication, the search for a defendant's residence as a preliminary to publication be limited to the state in which the complaint is filed. Here again the American Bar Association's report expressed the view that the Department's suggestion was unobjectionable and the Advisory Committee thereupon adopted it.

3. Subdivision (k) of the 1948 draft is as follows:

(k) Condemnation Under a State's Power of Eminent Domain. If the action involves the exercise of the power of eminent domain under the law of a state, the practice herein prescribed may be altered to the extent necessary to observe and enforce any condition affecting the substantial rights of a litigant attached by the state law to the exercise of the state's power of eminent domain.

Occasionally condemnation cases under a state's power of eminent domain reach a United States District Court because of diversity of citizenship. Such cases are rare, but provision should be made for them.

The 1948 draft of (k) required a district court to decide whether a provision of state law specifying the tribunal to award compensation is or is not a "condition" attached to the exercise of the state's power. On reconsideration we concluded that it would be wise to redraft (k) so as to avoid that troublesome question. As to conditions in state laws which affect the substantial rights of a litigant, the district courts would be bound to give them effect without any rule on the subject. Accordingly we present two alternative revisions. One suggestion supported by a majority of the Advisory Committee is as follows:

(k) Condemnation Under a State's Power of Eminent Domain. The practice herein prescribed governs in actions involving the exercise of the power of eminent domain under the law of a state, provided that if the state law makes provision for trial of any issue by jury, or for trial of the issue of compensation by jury or commission or both, that provision shall be followed.

The other is as follows:

(k) Condemnation Under a State's Power of Eminent Domain. The practice herein prescribed governs in actions involving the exercise of the power of eminent domain under the law of a state, provided that if the state law gives a right to a trial by jury such a trial shall in any case be allowed to the party demanding it within the time permitted by these rules, and in that event no hearing before a commission shall be had.

The first proposal accepts the state law as to the tribunals to fix compensation, and in that respect leaves the parties in precisely the same situation as if the case were pending in a state court, including the use of a commission with appeal to a jury, if the state law so provides. It has the effect of avoiding any question as to whether the decisions in *Erie R. Co.* v. *Tompkins* and later cases have application to a situation of this kind.

The second proposal gives the parties a right to a jury trial if that is provided for by state law, but prevents the use of both commission and jury. Those members of the Committee who favor the second proposal do so because of the obvious objections to the double trial with a commission and appeal to a jury. As the decisions in *Erie R. Co.* v. *Tompkins* and later cases may have a bearing on this point, and the Committee is divided, we think both proposals should be placed before the Court.

4. The provision * * * of the 1948 draft * * * prescribing the effective date of the rule was drafted before the recent amendment of the Judicial Code on that subject. On May 10, 1950, the President approved an act which amended section 2072 of Title 28, United States Code, to read as follows:

Such rules shall not take effect until they have been reported to Congress by the Chief Justice at or after the beginning of a regular session thereof but not later than the first day of May, and until the expiration of 90 days after they have been thus reported.

To conform to the statute now in force, we suggest a provision as follows:

Effective Date. This Rule 71A and the amendment to Rule 81(a) will take effect on August 1, 1951. Rule 71A governs all proceedings in actions brought after it takes effect and also all further proceedings in actions then pending, except to the extent that in the opinion of the court its application in a particular action pending when the rule takes effect would not be feasible or would work injustice, in which event the former procedure applies.

If the rule is not reported to Congress by May 1, 1951, this provision must be altered.

5. We call attention to the fact that the proposed rule does not contain a provision for the procedure to be followed in order to exercise the right of the United States to take immediate possession or title, when the condemnation proceeding is begun. There are several statutes conferring such a right which are cited in the original notes to the May 1948 draft * * *. The existence of this right is taken into account in the rule. In paragraph (c)(2), * * * it is stated: "Upon the commencement of the action, the plaintiff need join as defendants only the persons having or claiming an interest in the property whose names are then known." That is to enable the United States to exercise the right to immediate title or possession without the delay involved in ascertaining the

names of all interested parties. The right is also taken into account in the provision relating to dismissal (paragraph (i), subdivisions (1), (2), and (3), * * *); also in paragraph (j) relating to deposits and their distribution.

The Advisory Committee considered whether the procedure for exercising the right should be specified in the rule and decided against it, as the procedure now being followed seems to be giving no trouble, and to draft a rule to fit all the statutes on the subject might create confusion.

The American Bar Association has taken an active interest in a rule for condemnation cases. In 1944 its House of Delegates adopted a resolution which among other things resolved:

That before adoption by the Supreme Court of the United States of any redraft of the proposed rule, time and opportunity should be afforded to the bar to consider and make recommendations concerning any such redraft.

Accordingly, in 1950 the revised draft was submitted to the American Bar Association and its section of real property, probate and trust law appointed a committee to consider it. That committee was supplied with copies of the written statement from the Department of Justice giving the reasons relied on by the Department for preferring a rule to use juries in all cases. The Advisory Committee's report was approved at a meeting of the section of real property law, and by the House of Delegates at the annual meeting of September 1950. The American Bar Association report gave particular attention to the question whether juries or commissions should be used to fix compensation, approved the Advisory Committee's solution appearing in their latest draft designed to allow use of commissions in projects comparable to the TVA, and rejected the proposal for use of juries in all cases.

In November 1950 a committee of the Federal Bar Association, the chairman of which was a Special Assistant to the Attorney General, made a report which reflected the attitude of the Department of Justice on the condemnation rule.

Aside from subdivision (h) about the tribunal to award compensation the final draft of the condemnation rule here presented has the approval of the American Bar Association and, we understand, the Department of Justice, and we do not know of any opposition to it. Subdivision (h) has the unanimous approval of the Advisory Committee and has been approved by the American Bar Association. The use of commissions in TVA cases, and, by fair inference, in cases comparable to the TVA, is supported by 17 out of 20 judges who up to 1947 had sat in TVA cases. The legal staff of the TVA has vigorously objected to the substitution of juries for commissions in TVA cases. We regret to report that the Department of Justice still asks that subdivision (h) be altered to provide for jury trials in all cases where Congress has not specified the tribunal. We understand that the Department approves the proposal that the system prevailing in 23 states for the "double" trial, by commission with appeal to and trial de novo before a jury, should be abolished, and also asks that on demand a jury should be substituted for a commission, in those states where use of a commission alone is now required. The Advisory Committee has no evidence that commissions do not operate satisfactorily in the case of projects comparable to the TVA.

ORIGINAL REPORT

General Statement. 1. Background. When the Advisory Committee was formulating its recommendations to the Court concerning rules of procedure, which subsequently became the Federal Rules of 1938, the Committee concluded at an early stage not to fix the procedure in condemnation cases. This is a matter principally involving the exercise of the federal power of eminent domain, as very few condemnation cases involving the state's power reach the United States District Courts. The Committee's reasons at that time were that inasmuch as condemnation proceedings by the United States are governed by statutes of the United States, prescribing different procedure for various agencies and departments of the government, or, in the absence of such statutes, by local state practice under the Conformity Act (40 U.S.C., [former] sec. 258), it would be extremely difficult to draft a uniform rule satisfactory to the various agencies and departments of the government and to private parties; and that there was no general demand for a uniform rule. The Committee continued in that belief until shortly before the preparation of the April 1937 Draft of the Rules, when the officials of the Department of Justice having to do with condemnation cases urgently requested the Committee to propose rules on this subject. The Committee undertook the task and drafted a Condemnation Rule which appeared for the first time as Rule 74 of the April 1937 Draft. After the publication and distribution of this initial draft many objections were urged against it by counsel for various governmental agencies, whose procedure in condemnation cases was prescribed by federal statutes. Some of these agencies wanted to be excepted in whole or in part from the operation of the uniform rule proposed in April 1937. And the Department of Justice changed its position and stated that it preferred to have government condemnations conducted by local attorneys familiar with the state practice, which was applied under the Conformity Act where the Acts of Congress do not prescribe the practice; that it preferred to work under the Conformity Act without a uniform rule of procedure. The profession generally showed little interest in the proposed uniform rule. For these reasons the Advisory Committee in its Final Report to the Court in November 1937 proposed that all of Rule 74 be stricken and that the Federal Rules be made applicable only to appeals in condemnation cases. See note to Rule 74 of the Final Report.

Some six or seven years later when the Advisory Committee was considering the subject of amendments to the Federal Rules both government officials and the profession generally urged the adoption of some uniform procedure. This demand grew out of the volume of condemnation proceedings instituted during the war, and the general feeling of dissatisfaction with the diverse condemnation procedures that were applicable in the federal courts. A strongly held belief was that both the sovereign's power to condemn and the property owner's right to compensation could be promoted by a simplified rule. As a consequence the Committee proposed a Rule 71A on the subject of condemnation in its Preliminary Draft of May 1944. In the Second Preliminary Draft of May 1945 this earlier proposed Rule 71A was, however, omitted. The Committee did not then feel that it had sufficient time to prepare a revised draft satisfactory to it which would meet legitimate objections made to the draft of May 1944. To avoid unduly delaying the proposed amendments to existing rules the Committee concluded to proceed in the regular way with the preparation of the amendments to these rules and deal with the question of a condemnation rule as an independent matter. As a consequence it made no recommendations to the Court on condemnation in its Final Report of Proposed Amendments of June 1946; and the amendments which the Court adopted in December 1946 did not deal with condemnation. After concluding its task relative to amendments, the Committee returned to a consideration of eminent domain, its proposed Rule 71A of May 1944, the suggestions and criticisms that had been presented in the interim, and in June 1947 prepared and distributed to the profession another draft of a proposed condemnation rule. This draft contained several alternative provisions, specifically called attention to and asked for opinion relative to these matters, and in particular as to the constitution of the tribunal to award compensation. The present draft was based on the June 1947 formulation in light of the advice of the profession on both matters of substance and form.

2. Statutory Provisions. The need for a uniform condemnation rule in the federal courts arises from the fact that by various statutes Congress has prescribed diverse procedures for certain condemnation proceedings, and, in the absence of such statutes, has prescribed conformity to local state practice under 40 U.S.C. § 258. This general conformity adds to the diversity of procedure since in the United States there are multifarious methods of procedure in existence. Thus in 1931 it was said that there were 269 different methods of judicial procedure in different classes of condemnation cases and 56 methods of nonjudicial or administrative procedure. First Report of Judicial Council of Michigan, 1931, § 46, pp. 55–56. These numbers have not decreased. Consequently, the general requirement of conformity to state practice and procedure, particularly where the condemnor is the United States, leads to expense, delay and uncertainty. In advocacy of a uniform federal rule, see Armstrong, Proposed Amendments to Federal Rules for Civil Procedure 1944, 4 F.R.D. 124, 134; id., Report of the Advisory Committee on Federal Rules of Civil Procedure Recommending Amendments, 1946, 5 F.R.D. 339, 357.

There are a great variety of Acts of Congress authorizing the exercise of the power of eminent domain by the United States and its officers and agencies. These statutes for the most part do not specify the exact procedure to be followed, but where procedure is prescribed, it is by no means uniform.

The following are instances of Acts which merely authorize the exercise of the power without specific declaration as to the procedure:

U.S.C., Title 16:

§ 404c–11 (Mammoth Cave National Park; acquisition of lands, interests in lands or other property for park by the Secretary of the Interior).

§ 426d (Stones River National Park; acquisition of land for parks by the Secretary of the Army).

§ 450aa (George Washington Carver National Monument; acquisition of land by the Secretary of the Interior).

§ 517 (National forest reservation; title to lands to be acquired by the Secretary of Agriculture).

U.S.C., Title 42:

§§ 1805(b)(5), 1813(b)(Atomic Energy Act).

The following are instances of Acts which authorized condemnation and declare that the procedure is to conform with that of similar actions in state courts:

U.S.C., Title 16:

§ 423k (Richmond National Battlefield Park; acquisition of lands by the Secretary of the Interior).

§ 714 (Exercise by water power licensee of power of eminent domain).

U.S.C., Title 24:

§ 78 (Condemnation of land for the former National Home for Disabled Volunteer Soldiers).

U.S.C., Title 33:

§ 591 (Condemnation of lands and materials for river and harbor improvement by the Secretary of the Army).

U.S.C., Title 40:

§ 257 (Condemnation of realty for sites for public building and for other public uses by the Secretary of the Treasury authorized).

§ 258 (Same procedure).

U.S.C., Title 50:

§ 171 (Acquisition of land by the Secretary of the Army for national defense).

§ 172 (Acquisition of property by the Secretary of the Army, etc., for production of lumber).

§ 632 App. (Second War Powers Act, 1942; acquisition of real property for war purposes by the Secretary of the Army, the Secretary of the Navy and others).

The following are Acts in which a more or less complete code of procedure is set forth in connection with the taking:

U.S.C., Title 16:

§ 831x (Condemnation by Tennessee Valley Authority).

U.S.C., Title 40:

§§ 361–386 (now D.C. Code, 1951 Ed., Title 16–619 to 16–644)(Acquisition of lands in District of Columbia for use of United States; condemnation).

3. Adjustment of Rule to Statutory Provisions. While it was apparent that the principle of uniformity should be the basis for a rule to replace the multiple diverse procedures set out above, there remained a serious question as to whether an exception could properly be made relative to the method of determining compensation. Where Congress had provided for conformity to state law the following were the general methods in use: an initial determination by commissioners, with appeal to a judge; an initial award, likewise made by commissioners, but with the appeal to a jury; and determination by a jury without a previous award by commissioners. In two situations Congress had specified the tribunal to determine the issue of compensation: condemnation by the Tennessee Valley Authority; and condemnation in the District of Columbia. Under the TVA procedure the initial determination of value is by three disinterested commissioners, appointed by the court, from a locality other than the one in which the land lies. Either party may except to the award of the commission; in that case the exceptions are to be heard by three district judges (unless the parties stipulate for a lesser number), with a right of appeal to the circuit court of appeals. The TVA is a regional agency. It is faced with the necessity of acquiring a very substantial acreage within a relatively small area, and charged with the task of carrying on within the Tennessee Valley and in cooperation with the local people a permanent program involving navigation and flood control, electric power, soil conservation, and general regional development. The success of this program is partially dependent upon the good will and cooperation of the people of the Tennessee Valley, and this in turn partially depends upon the land acquisition program. Disproportionate awards among landowners would create dissatisfaction and ill will. To secure uniformity in treatment Congress provided the rather unique procedure of the three-judge court to review de novo the initial award of the commissioners. This procedure has worked to the satisfaction of the property owners and the TVA. A full statement of the TVA position and experience is set forth in Preliminary Draft to Proposed Rule to Govern Condemnation Cases (June, 1947) 15–19. A large majority of the district judges with experience under this procedure approve it, subject to some objection to the requirement for a three-judge district court to review commissioners' awards. A statutory three-judge requirement is, however, jurisdictional and must be strictly followed. *Stratton v. St. Louis, Southwestern Ry. Co.*, 1930, 282 U.S. 10, 51 S.Ct. 8, 75 L.Ed. 135; *Ayrshire Collieries Corp. v. United States*, 1947, 331 U.S. 132, 67 S.Ct. 1168, 91 L.Ed. 1391. Hence except insofar as the TVA statute itself authorizes the parties to stipulate for a court of less than three judges, the requirement must be followed, and would seem to be beyond alteration by court rule even if change were thought desirable. Accordingly the TVA procedure is retained for the determination of compensation in TVA condemnation cases. It was also thought desirable to retain the specific method Congress had prescribed for the District of Columbia, which is a so-called jury of five appointed by the court. This is a local matter and the specific treatment accorded by Congress has given local satisfaction.

Aside from the foregoing limited exceptions dealing with the TVA and the District of Columbia, the question was whether a uniform method for determining compensation should be a commission with appeal to a district judge, or a commission with appeal to a jury, or a jury without a commission. Experience with the commission on a nationwide basis, and in particular with the utilization of a commission followed by an appeal to a jury, has been that the commission is time consuming and expensive. Furthermore, it is largely a futile procedure where it is preparatory to jury trial. Since in the bulk of states a land owner is entitled eventually to a jury trial, since the jury is a traditional tribunal for the determination of questions of value, and since experience with juries has proved satisfactory to both government and land owner, the right to jury trial is adopted as the general rule. Condemnation involving the TVA and the District of Columbia are the two exceptions. See Note to Subdivision (h), infra.

Note to Subdivision (a). As originally promulgated the Federal rules governed appeals in condemnation proceedings but were not otherwise applicable. Rule 81(a)(7). Pre-appeal procedure, in the main, conformed to state procedure. See statutes and discussion, supra. The purpose of Rule 71A is to provide a uniform procedure for condemnation in the federal district courts, including the District of Columbia. To achieve this purpose Rule 71A prescribes such specialized procedure as is required by condemnation proceedings, otherwise it utilizes the general framework of the Federal Rules where specific detail is unnecessary. The adoption of Rule 71A, of course, renders paragraph (7) of Rule 81(a) unnecessary.

The promulgation of a rule for condemnation procedure is within the rule-making power. The Enabling Act [Act of June 19, 1934, c. 651, §§ 1, 2 (48 Stat. 1064), 28 U.S.C., former §§ 723b, 723c, now § 2072] gives the Supreme Court "the power to prescribe, by general rules * * * the forms of process, writs, pleadings, and motions, and the practice and procedure in civil actions at law." Such rules, however, must not abridge, enlarge, or modify substantive rights. In *Kohl v. United States*, 1875, 91 U.S. 367, 23 L.Ed. 449, a proceeding instituted by the United States to appropriate land for a postoffice site under a statute enacted for such purpose, the Supreme Court held that "a proceeding to take land in virtue of the government's eminent domain, and determining the compensation to be made for it, is * * * a suit at common law, when initiated in a court." See, also, *Madisonville Traction Co. v. St. Bernard Mining Co.*, 1905, 196 U.S. 239, 25 S.Ct. 251, 49 L.Ed. 462, infra, under subdivision (k). And the Conformity Act, 40 U.S.C., § 258, which is superseded by Rule 71A, deals only with "practice, pleadings, forms and proceedings and not with matters of substantive laws." *United States v. 243.22 Acres of Land in Village of Farmingdale, Town of Babylon, Suffolk County, N.Y.*, D.C.N.Y.1942, 43 F.Supp. 561, affirmed 129 F.2d 678, certiorari denied 317 U.S. 698, 63 S.Ct. 441, 87 L.Ed. 558.

Rule 71A affords a uniform procedure for all cases of condemnation invoking the national power of eminent domain, and, to the extent stated in subdivision (k), for cases invoking a state's power of eminent domain; and supplants all statutes prescribing a different procedure. While the almost exclusive utility of the rule is for the condemnation of real property, it also applies to the condemnation of personal property, either as an incident to real property or as the sole object of the proceeding, when permitted or required by statute. See 38 U.S.C., § 438j (World War Veterans' Relief Act); 42 U.S.C., §§ 1805, 1811, 1813 (Atomic Energy Act); 50 U.S.C., § 79 (Nitrates Act); 50 U.S.C., §§ 161–166 (Helium Gas Act). Requisitioning of personal property with the right in the owner to sue the United States, where the compensation cannot be agreed upon (see 42 U.S.C., § 1813, supra, for example) will continue to be the normal method of acquiring personal property and Rule 71A in no way interferes with or restricts any such right. Only where the law requires or permits the formal procedure of condemnation to be utilized will the rule have any applicability to the acquisition of personal property.

Rule 71A is not intended to and does not supersede the Act of February 26, 1931, c. 307, §§ 1–5 (46 Stat. 1421), 40 U.S.C., §§ 258a–258e, which is a supplementary condemnation statute, permissive in its nature and designed to permit the prompt acquisition of title by the United States, pending the condemnation proceeding, upon a deposit in court. See *United States v. 76,800 Acres, More or Less, of Land, in Bryan and Liberty Counties, Ga.*, D.C.Ga.1942, 44 F.Supp. 653; *United States v. 17,280 Acres of Land, More or Less, Situated in Saunders County, Neb.*, D.C.Neb.1942, 47 F.Supp. 267. The same is true insofar as the following or any other statutes authorize the acquisition of title or the taking of immediate possession:

U.S.C., Title 33:

§ 594 (When immediate possession of land may be taken; for a work of river and harbor improvements).

U.S.C., Title 42:

§ 1813(b) (When immediate possession may be taken under Atomic Energy Act).

U.S.C., Title 50:

§ 171 (Acquisition of land by the Secretary of the Army for national defense).

§ 632 App. (Second War Powers Act, 1942; Acquisition of real property for war purposes by the Secretary of the Army, the Secretary of the Navy, and others).

Note to Subdivision (b). This subdivision provides for broad joinder in accordance with the tenor of other rules such as Rule 18. To require separate condemnation proceedings for each piece of property separately owned would be unduly burdensome and would serve no useful purpose. And a restriction that only properties may be joined which are to be acquired for the same public use would also cause difficulty. For example, a unified project to widen a street, construct a bridge across a navigable river, and for the construction of approaches to the level of the bridge on both sides of the river might involve acquiring property for different public uses. Yet it is eminently desirable that the plaintiff may in one proceeding condemn all the property interests and rights necessary to carry out this project. Rule 21 which allows the court to sever and proceed separately with any claim against a party, and Rule 42(b) giving the court broad discretion to order separate trials give adequate protection to all defendants in condemnation proceedings.

Note to Subdivision (c). Since a condemnation proceeding is in rem and since a great many property owners are often involved, paragraph (1) requires the property to be named and only one of the owners. In other respects the caption will contain the name of the court, the title of the action, file number, and a designation of the pleading as a complaint in accordance with Rule 10(a).

Since the general standards of pleading are stated in other rules, paragraph (2) prescribes only the necessary detail for condemnation proceedings. Certain statutes allow the United States to acquire title or possession immediately upon commencement of an action. See the Act of February 26, 1931, c. 307, §§ 1–5 (46 Stat. 1421), 40 U.S.C., §§ 258a–258e, supra; and 33 U.S.C., § 594, 42 U.S.C., § 1813(b), 50 U.S.C., §§ 171, 632, supra. To carry out the purpose of such statutes and to aid the condemnor in instituting the action even where title is not acquired at the outset, the plaintiff is initially required to join as defendants only the persons having or claiming an interest in the property whose names are then known. This in no way prejudices the property owner, who must eventually be joined as a defendant, served with process, and allowed to answer before there can be any hearing involving the compensation to be paid for his piece of property. The rule requires the plaintiff to name all persons having or claiming an interest in the property of whom the plaintiff has learned and, more importantly, those appearing of record. By charging the plaintiff with the necessity to make "a search of the records of the extent commonly made by competent searchers of title in the vicinity in light of the type and value of the property involved" both the plaintiff and property owner are protected. Where a short term interest in property of little value is involved, as a two or three year easement over a vacant land for purposes of ingress and egress to other property, a search of the records covering a long period of time is not required. Where on the other hand fee simple title in valuable property is being condemned the search must necessarily cover a much longer period of time and be commensurate with the interests involved. But even here the search is related to the type made by competent title searchers in the vicinity. A search that extends back to the original patent may be feasible in some midwestern and western states and be proper under certain circumstances. In the Atlantic seaboard states such a search is normally not feasible nor desirable. There is a common sense business accommodation of what title searchers can and should do. For state statutes requiring persons appearing as owners or otherwise interested in the property to be named as defendants, see 3 Colo.Stat.Ann., 1935, c. 61, § 2; Ill.Ann.Stat., Smith–Hurd, c. 47, § 2; 1 Iowa Code, 1946, § 472.3; Kans.Stat.Ann., 1935, § 26–101; 2 Mass.Laws Ann., 1932, c. 80A, § 4; 7 Mich.Stat.Ann., 1936, § 8.2; 2 Minn.Stat., Mason, 1927, § 6541; 20 N.J.Stat. Ann., 1939, § 1–2; 3 Wash.Revised Stat., Remington, 1932, Title 6, § 891. For state provisions allowing persons whose names are not known to be designated under the descriptive term of "unknown owner", see Hawaii Revised Laws, 1945, c. 8, § 310 ("Such [unknown] defendant may be joined in the petition under a fictitious name."); Ill.Ann. Stat., Smith–Hurd, c. 47, § 2 ("Persons interested, whose names are unknown, may be made parties defendant by the description of the unknown owners; * * *"); Maryland Code Ann., 1939, Art. 33A, § 1 ("In case any owner or owners is or are not known, he or they may be described in such petition as the unknown owner or owners, or the unknown heir or heirs of a deceased owner."); 2 Mass.Laws Ann., 1932, c. 80A, § 4 ("Persons not in being, unascertained or unknown who may have an interest in any of such land shall be made parties respondent by such description as seems appropriate, * * *"); New Mex. Stat.Ann., 1941, § 25–901 ("the owners * * * shall be parties defendant, by name, if the names are known, and by description of the unknown owners of the land therein described, if their names are unknown."); Utah Code Ann., 1943, § 104–61–7 ("The names of all owners and claimants of the property, if known, or a statement that they are unknown who must be styled defendants").

The last sentence of paragraph (2) enables the court to expedite the distribution of a deposit, in whole or in part, as soon as pertinent facts of ownership, value and the like are established. See also subdivision (j).

The signing of the complaint is governed by Rule 11.

Note to Subdivision (d). In lieu of a summons, which is the initial process in other civil actions under Rule 4(a), subdivision (d) provides for a notice which is to contain sufficient information so that the defendant in effect obtains the plaintiff's statement of his claim against the defendant to whom the notice is directed. Since the plaintiff's attorney is an officer of the court and to prevent unduly burdening the clerk of the court, paragraph (1) of subdivision (d) provides that plaintiff's attorney shall prepare and deliver a notice or notices to the clerk. Flexibility is provided by the provision for joint or several notices and for additional notices. Where there are only a few defendants it may be convenient to prepare but one notice directed to all the defendants. In other cases where there are many defendants it will be more convenient to prepare two or more notices; but in any event a notice must be directed to each named defendant. Paragraph (2) provides that the notice is to be signed by the plaintiff's attorney. Since the notice is to be delivered to the clerk, the issuance of the notice will appear of record in the court. The clerk should forthwith deliver the notice or notices for service to the marshal or to a person specially appointed to serve the notice. Rule 4(a). The form of the notice is such that, in addition to informing the defendant of the plaintiff's statement of claim, it tells the defendant precisely what his rights are. Failure on the part of the defendant to serve an answer constitutes a consent to the taking and to the authority of the court to proceed to fix compensation therefor, but it does not preclude the defendant from presenting evidence as to the amount of compensation due him or in sharing the award of distribution. See subdivision (e); Form 28.

While under Rule 4(f) the territorial limits of a summons are normally the territorial limits of the state in which the district court is held, the territorial limits for personal service of a notice under Rule 71A(d)(3) are those of the nation. This extension of process is here proper since the aim of the condemnation proceeding is not to enforce any personal liability and the property owner is helped not imposed upon, by the best type of service possible. If personal service cannot be made either because the defendant's whereabouts cannot be ascertained, or, if ascertained, the defendant cannot be personally served, as where he resides in a foreign country such as Canada or Mexico, then service by publication is proper. The provisions for this type of service are set forth in the rule and are in no way governed by 28 U.S.C., § 118.

Note to Subdivision (e). Departing from the scheme of Rule 12, subdivision (e) requires all defenses and objections to be presented in an answer and does not authorize a preliminary motion. There is little need for the latter in condemnation proceedings. The general standard of pleading is governed by other rules, particularly Rule 8, and this subdivision (e) merely prescribes what matters the answer should set forth. Merely by appearing in the action a defendant can receive notice of all proceedings affecting him. And without the necessity of answering a defendant may present evidence as to the amount of compensation due him, and he may share in the distribution of the award. See also subdivision (d)(2); Form 28.

Note to Subdivision (f). Due to the number of persons who may be interested in the property to be condemned, there is a likelihood that the plaintiff will need to amend his complaint, perhaps many times, to add new parties or state new issues. This subdivision recognizes that fact and does not burden the court with applications by the plaintiff for leave to amend. At the same time all defendants are adequately protected; and their need to amend the answer is adequately protected by Rule 15 which is applicable by virtue of subdivision (a) of this Rule 71A.

Note to Subdivision (g). A condemnation action is a proceeding in rem. Commencement of the action as against a defendant by virtue of his joinder pursuant to subdivision (c)(2) is the point of cut-off and there is no mandatory requirement or substitution because of a subsequent change of interest, although the court is given ample power to require substitution. Rule 25 is inconsistent with subdivision (g) and hence inapplicable. Accordingly, the time periods of Rule 25 do not govern to require dismissal nor to prevent substitution.

Note to Subdivision (h). This subdivision prescribes the method for determining the issue of just compensation in cases involving the federal power of eminent domain. The method of jury trial provided by subdivision (h) will normally apply in cases involving the state power by virtue of subdivision (k).

Congress has specially constituted a tribunal for the trial of the issue of just compensation in two instances: condemnation under the Tennessee Valley Authority Act; and condemnation in the District of Columbia. These tribunals are retained for reasons set forth in the General Statement: 3. Adjustment of Rule to Statutory Provisions, supra. Subdivision (h) also has prospective application so that if Congress should create another special tribunal, that tribunal will determine the issue of just compensation. Subject to these exceptions the general method of trial of that issue is to be by jury if any party demands it, otherwise that issue, as well as all other issues, are to be tried by the court.

As to the TVA procedure that is continued, U.S.C., Title 16, § 831x requires that three commissioners be appointed to fix the compensation; that exceptions to their award are to be heard by three district judges (unless the parties stipulate for a lesser number) and that the district judges try the question de novo; that an appeal to the circuit court of appeals may be taken within 30 days from the filing of the decision of the district judges; and that the circuit court of appeals shall on the record fix compensation "without regard to the awards of findings theretofore made by the commissioners or the district judges." The mode of fixing compensation in the District of Columbia, which is also continued, is prescribed in U.S.C., Title 40, §§ 361–386. Under § 371 the court is required in all cases to order the selection of a jury of five from among not less than 20 names, drawn "from the special box provided by law." They must have the usual qualifications of jurors and in addition must be freeholders of the District, and not in the service of the United States or the District. A special oath is administered to the chosen jurors. The trial proceeds in the ordinary way, except that the jury is allowed to separate after they have begun to consider their verdict.

There is no constitutional right to jury trial in a condemnation proceeding, *Bauman v. Ross*, 1897, 167 U.S. 548, 17 S.Ct. 966, 42 L.Ed. 270. See, also, Hines, Does the Seventh Amendment to the Constitution of the United States Require Jury Trials in all Condemnation Proceedings?, 1925, 11 Va.L.Rev. 505; Blair, Federal Condemnation Proceedings and the Seventh Amendment, 1927, 41 Harv.L.Rev. 29; 3 Moore's Federal Practice, 1938, 3007. Prior to Rule 71A, jury trial in federal condemnation proceedings was however, enjoyed under the general conformity statute, 40 U.S.C., § 258, in states which provided for jury trial. See generally, 2 Lewis, Eminent Domain, 3d ed. 1909, §§ 509, 510; 3 Moore, op. cit. supra. Since the general conformity statute is superseded by Rule 71A, see supra under subdivision (a), and since it was believed that the rule to be substituted should likewise give a right to jury trial, subdivision (h) establishes that method as the general one for determining the issue of just compensation.

Note to Subdivision (i). Both the right of the plaintiff to dismiss by filing a notice of dismissal and the right of the court to permit a dismissal are circumscribed to the extent that where the plaintiff has acquired the title or a lesser interest or possession, viz., any property interest for which just compensation should be paid, the action may not be dismissed, without the defendant's consent, and the property owner remitted to another court, such as the Court of Claims, to recover just compensation for the property right taken. Circuity of action is thus prevented without increasing the liability of the plaintiff to pay just compensation for any interest that is taken. Freedom of dismissal is accorded, where both the condemnor and condemnee agree, up to the time of the entry of judgment vesting plaintiff with title. And power is given to the court, where the parties agree, to vacate the judgment and thus revest title in the property owner. In line with Rule 21, the court may at any time drop a defendant who has been unnecessarily or improperly joined as where it develops that he has no interest.

Note to Subdivision (j). Whatever the substantive law is concerning the necessity of making a deposit will continue to govern. For statutory provisions concerning deposit in court in condemnation proceedings by the United States, see U.S.C., Title 40, § 258a; U.S.C., Title 33, § 594—acquisition of title and possession statutes referred to in note to subdivision (a), supra. If the plaintiff is invoking the state's power of eminent domain the necessity of deposit will be governed by the state law. For discussion of such law, see 1

Nichols, Eminent Domain, 2d ed. 1917, §§ 209–216. For discussion of the function of deposit and the power of the court to enter judgment in cases both of deficiency and overpayment, see *United States v. Miller*, 1943, 317 U.S. 369, 63 S.Ct. 276, 87 L.Ed. 336, 147 A.L.R. 55, rehearing denied 318 U.S. 798, 63 S.Ct. 557, 87 L.Ed. 1162 (judgment in favor of plaintiff for overpayment ordered).

The court is to make distribution of the deposit as promptly as the facts of the case warrant. See also subdivision (c)(2).

Note to Subdivision (k). While the overwhelming number of cases that will be brought in the federal courts under this rule will be actions involving the federal power of eminent domain, a small percentage of cases may be instituted in the federal court or removed thereto on the basis of diversity or alienage which will involve the power of eminent domain under the law of a state. See *Boom Co. v. Patterson*, 1878, 98 U.S. 403, 25 L.Ed. 206; *Searl v. School District No. 2*, 1888, 124 U.S. 197, 8 S.Ct. 460, 31 L.Ed. 415; *Madisonville Traction Co. v. Saint Bernard Mining Co.*, 1905, 196 U.S. 239, 25 S.Ct. 251, 49 L.Ed. 462. In the Madisonville case, and in cases cited therein, it has been held that condemnation actions brought by state corporations in the exercise of a power delegated by the state might be governed by procedure prescribed by the laws of the United States, whether the cases were begun in or removed to the federal court. See, also, *Franzen v. Chicago, M. & St. P. Ry. Co.*, C.C.A.7th, 1921, 278 F. 370, 372.

Any condition affecting the substantial right of a litigant attached by state law is to be observed and enforced, such as making a deposit in court where the power of eminent domain is conditioned upon so doing. (See also subdivision (j)). Subject to this qualification, subdivision (k) provides that in cases involving the state power of eminent domain, the practice prescribed by other subdivisions of Rule 71A shall govern.

Note to Subdivision (*l*). Since the condemnor will normally be the prevailing party and since he should not recover his costs against the property owner, Rule 54(d), which provides generally that costs shall go to the prevailing party, is made inapplicable. Without attempting to state what the rule on costs is, the effect of subdivision (*l*) is that costs shall be awarded in accordance with the law that has developed in condemnation cases. This has been summarized as follows: "Costs of condemnation proceedings are not assessable against the condemnee, unless by stipulation he agrees to assume some or all of them. Such normal expenses of the proceeding as bills for publication of notice, commissioners' fees, the cost of transporting commissioners and jurors to take a view, fees for attorneys to represent defendants who have failed to answer, and witness' fees, are properly charged to the government, though not taxed as costs. Similarly, if it is necessary that a conveyance be executed by a commissioner, the United States pay his fees and those for recording the deed. However, the distribution of the award is a matter in which the United States has no legal interest. Expenses incurred in ascertaining the identity of distributees and deciding between conflicting claimants are properly chargeable against the award, not against the United States, although United States attorneys are expected to aid the court in such matters as amici curiae." Lands Division Manual 861. For other discussion and citation, see *Grand River Dam Authority v. Jarvis*, C.C.A.10th, 1942, 124 F.2d 914. Costs may not be taxed against the United States except to the extent permitted by law. *United States v. 125.71 Acres of Land in Loyalhanna Tp., Westmoreland County, Pa.*, D.C.Pa.1944, 54 F.Supp. 193; Lands Division Manual 859. Even if it were thought desirable to allow the property owner's costs to be taxed against the United States, this is a matter for legislation and not court rule.

1963 AMENDMENT

This amendment conforms to the amendment of Rule 4(f).

1985 AMENDMENT

Rule 71A(h) provides that except when Congress has provided otherwise, the issue of just compensation in a condemnation case may be tried by a jury if one of the parties so demands, unless the court in its discretion orders the issue determined by a commission of three persons. In 1980, the Comptroller General of the United States in a Report to Congress recommended that use of the commission procedure should be encouraged in order to improve and expedite the trial of condemnation cases. The Report noted that long delays were being caused in many districts by such factors as crowded dockets, the precedence given criminal cases, the low priority accorded condemnation matters, and the high turnover of Assistant United States Attorneys. The Report concluded that revising Rule 71A to make the use of the commission procedure more attractive might alleviate the situation.

Accordingly, Rule 71A(h) is being amended in a number of respects designed to assure the quality and utility of a Rule 71A commission. First, the amended Rule will give the court discretion to appoint, in addition to the three members of a commission, up to two additional persons as alternate commissioners who would hear the case and be available, at any time up to the filing of the decision by the three-member commission, to replace any commissioner who becomes unable or disqualified to continue. The discretion to appoint alternate commissioners can be particularly useful in protracted cases, avoiding expensive retrials that have been required in some cases because of the death or disability of a commissioner. Prior to replacing a commissioner an alternate would not be present at, or participate in, the commission's deliberations.

Second, the amended Rule requires the court, before appointment, to advise the parties of the identity and qualifications of each prospective commissioner and alternate. The court then may authorize the examination of prospective appointees by the parties and each party has the right to challenge for cause. The objective is to insure that unbiased and competent commissioners are appointed.

The amended Rule does not prescribe a qualification standard for appointment to a commission, although it is understood that only persons possessing background and ability to appraise real estate valuation testimony and to award fair and just compensation on the basis thereof would be appointed. In most situations the chairperson should be a lawyer and all members should have some background qualifying them to weigh proof of value in the real estate field and, when possible, in the particular real estate market embracing the land in question.

The amended Rule should give litigants greater confidence in the commission procedure by affording them certain rights to participate in the appointment of commission members that are roughly comparable to the practice with regard to jury selection. This is accomplished by giving the court permission to allow the parties to examine prospective commissioners and by recognizing the right of each party to object to the appointment of any person for cause.

1987 AMENDMENT

The amendments are technical. No substantive change is intended.

1988 AMENDMENT

The amendment is technical. No substantive change is intended.

1993 AMENDMENT

The references to the subdivisions of Rule 4 are deleted in light of the revision of that rule.

2003 AMENDMENT

The references to specific subdivisions of Rule 53 are deleted or revised to reflect amendments of Rule 53.

2007 AMENDMENTS

The language of Rule 71A has been amended as part of the general restyling of the Civil Rules to make them more easily understood and to make style and terminology consistent throughout the rules. These changes are intended to be stylistic only.

Former Rule 71A has been redesignated as Rule 71.1 to conform to the designations used for all other rules added with the original numbering system.

Rule 71.1(e) allows a defendant to appear without answering. Former form 28 (now form 60) includes information about this right in the Rule 71.1(d)(2) notice. It is useful to confirm this practice in the rule.

The information that identifies the attorney is changed to include telephone number and electronic-mail address, in line with similar amendments to Rules 11(a) and 26(g)(1).

Rule 72. Magistrate Judges; Pretrial Orders

1983 ADDITION

Subdivision (a). This subdivision addresses court-ordered referrals of nondispositive matters under 28 U.S.C. § 636(b)(1)(A). The rule calls for a written order of the magistrate's disposition to preserve the record and facilitate review. An oral order read into the record by the magistrate will satisfy this requirement.

No specific procedures or timetables for raising objections to the magistrate's rulings on nondispositive matters are set forth in the Magistrates Act. The rule fixes a 10-day period in order to avoid uncertainty and provide uniformity that will eliminate the confusion that might arise if different periods were prescribed by local rule in different districts. It also is contemplated that a party who is successful before the magistrate will be afforded an opportunity to respond to objections raised to the magistrate's ruling.

The last sentence of subdivision (a) specifies that reconsideration of a magistrate's order, as provided for in the Magistrates Act, shall be by the district judge to whom the case is assigned. This rule does not restrict experimentation by the district courts under 28 U.S.C. § 636(b)(3) involving references of matters other than pretrial matters, such as appointment of counsel, taking of default judgments, and acceptance of jury verdicts when the judge is unavailable.

Subdivision (b). This subdivision governs court-ordered referrals of dispositive pretrial matters and prisoner petitions challenging conditions of confinement, pursuant to statutory authorization in 28 U.S.C. § 636(b)(1)(B). This rule does not extend to habeas corpus petitions, which are covered by the specific rules relating to proceedings under Sections 2254 and 2255 of Title 28.

This rule implements the statutory procedures for making objections to the magistrate's proposed findings and recommendations. The 10-day period, as specified in the statute, is subject to Rule 6(e) which provides for an additional 3-day period when service is made by mail. Although no specific provision appears in the Magistrates Act, the rule specifies a 10-day period for a party to respond to objections to the magistrate's recommendation.

Implementing the statutory requirements, the rule requires the district judge to whom the case is assigned to make a de novo determination of those portions of the report, findings, or recommendations to which timely objection is made. The term "de novo" signifies that the magistrate's findings are not protected by the clearly erroneous doctrine, but does not indicate that a second evidentiary hearing is required. See *United States v. Raddatz,* 417 [447] U.S. 667 (1980). See also Silberman, *Masters and Magistrates Part II: The American Analogue,* 50 N.Y.U.L.Rev. 1297, 1367 (1975). When no timely objection is filed, the court need only satisfy itself that there is no clear error on the face of the record in order to accept the recommendation. See *Campbell v. United States Dist. Court,* 501 F.2d 196, 206 (9th Cir.1974), cert. denied, 419 U.S. 879, 95 S.Ct. 143, 42 L.Ed.2d 119, quoted in House Report No. 94–1609, 94th Cong. 2d Sess. (1976) at 3. Compare *Park Motor Mart, Inc. v. Ford Motor Co.,* 616 F.2d 603 (1st Cir.1980). Failure to make timely objection to the magistrate's report prior to its adoption by the district judge may constitute a waiver of appellate review of the district judge's order. See *United States v. Walters,* 638 F.2d 947 (6th Cir.1981).

1991 AMENDMENT

This amendment is intended to eliminate a discrepancy in measuring the 10 days for serving and filing objections to a magistrate's action under subdivisions (a) and (b) of this Rule. The rule as promulgated in 1983 required objections to the magistrate's handling of nondispositive matters to be served and filed within 10 days of entry of the order, but required objections to dispositive motions to be made within 10 days of being served with a copy of the recommended disposition. Subdivision (a) is here amended to conform to subdivision (b) to avoid any confusion or technical defaults, particularly in connection with magistrate orders that rule on both dispositive and nondispositive matters.

The amendment is also intended to assure that objections to magistrate's orders that are not timely made shall not be considered. *Compare* Rule 51.

1993 AMENDMENT

This revision is made to conform the rule to changes made by the Judicial Improvements Act of 1990.

2007 AMENDMENTS

The language of Rule 72 has been amended as part of the general restyling of the Civil Rules to make them more easily understood and to make style and terminology consistent throughout the rules. These changes are intended to be stylistic only.

Rule 73.   Magistrate Judges; Trial by Consent and Appeal

1983 ADDITION

Subdivision (a). This subdivision implements the broad authority of the 1979 amendments to the Magistrates Act, 28 U.S.C. § 636(c), which permit a magistrate to sit in lieu of a district judge and exercise civil jurisdiction over a case, when the parties consent. See McCabe, *The Federal Magistrate Act of 1979,* 16 Harv.J.Legis. 343, 364–79 (1979). In order to exercise this jurisdiction, a magistrate must be specially designated under 28 U.S.C. § 636(c)(1) by the district court or courts he serves. The only exception to a magistrate's exercise of civil jurisdiction, which includes the power to conduct jury and nonjury trials and decide dispositive motions, is the contempt power. A hearing on contempt is to be conducted by the district judge upon certification of the facts and an order to show cause by the magistrate. See 28 U.S.C. § 639(e). In view of 28 U.S.C. § 636(c)(1) and this rule, it is unnecessary to amend Rule 58 to provide that the decision of a magistrate is a "decision by the court" for the purposes of that rule and a "final decision of the district court" for purposes of 28 U.S.C. § 1291 governing appeals.

Subdivision (b). This subdivision implements the blind consent provision of 28 U.S.C. § 636(c)(2) and is designed to ensure that neither the judge nor the magistrate attempts to induce a party to consent to reference of a civil matter under this rule to a magistrate. See House Rep. No. 96–444, 96th Cong. 1st Sess. 8 (1979).

The rule opts for a uniform approach in implementing the consent provision by directing the clerk to notify the parties of their opportunity to elect to proceed before a magistrate and by requiring the execution and filing of a consent form or forms setting forth the election. However, flexibility at the local level is preserved in that local rules will determine how notice shall be communicated to the parties, and local rules will specify the time period within which an election must be made.

The last paragraph of subdivision (b) reiterates the provision in 28 U.S.C. § 636(c)(6) for vacating a reference to the magistrate.

Subdivision (c). Under 28 U.S.C. § 636(c)(3), the normal route of appeal from the judgment of a magistrate—the only route that will be available unless the parties otherwise agree in advance—is an appeal by the aggrieved party "directly to the appropriate United States court of appeals from the judgment of the magistrate in the same manner as an appeal from any other judgment of a district court." The quoted statutory language indicates Congress' intent that the same procedures and standards of appealability that govern appeals from district court judgments govern appeals from magistrates' judgments.

Subdivision (d). 28 U.S.C. § 636(c)(4) offers parties who consent to the exercise of civil jurisdiction by a magistrate an alternative appeal route to that provided in subdivision (c) of this rule. This optional appellate route was provided by Congress in recognition of the fact that not all civil cases warrant the same appellate treatment. In cases where the amount in controversy is not great and there are no difficult questions of law to be resolved, the parties may desire to avoid the expense and delay of appeal to the court of appeals by electing an appeal to the district judge. See McCabe, *The Federal Magistrate Act of 1979,* 16 Harv.J.Legis. 343, 388 (1979). This subdivision provides that the parties may elect the optional appeal route at the time of reference to a magistrate. To this end, the notice by the clerk under subdivision (b) of this rule shall explain the appeal option and the corollary restriction on review by the court of appeals. This approach will avoid later claims of lack of consent to the avenue of appeal. The choice of the alternative appeal route to the judge of the district court should be made by the parties in their forms of consent. Special appellate rules to govern appeals from a magistrate to a district judge appear in new Rules 74 through 76.

1987 AMENDMENT

The amendment is technical. No substantive change is intended.

1993 AMENDMENT

This revision is made to conform the rule to changes made by the Judicial Improvements Act of 1990. The Act requires that, when being reminded of the availability of a magistrate judge, the parties be advised that withholding of consent will have no "adverse substantive consequences." They may, however, be advised if the withholding of consent will have the adverse procedural consequence of a potential delay in trial.

1997 AMENDMENT

The Federal Courts Improvement Act of 1996 repealed the former provisions of 28 U.S.C. § 636(c)(4) and (5) that enabled parties that had agreed to trial before a magistrate judge to agree also that appeal should be taken to the district court. Rule 73 is amended to conform to this change. Rules 74, 75, and 76 are abrogated for the same reason. The portions of Form 33 and Form 34 that referred to appeals to the district court also are deleted.

2007 AMENDMENTS

The language of Rule 73 has been amended as part of the general restyling of the Civil Rules to make them more easily understood and to make style and terminology consistent throughout the rules. These changes are intended to be stylistic only.

Rule 74. Method of Appeal From Magistrate Judge to District Judge Under Title 28, U.S.C. § 636(c)(4) and Rule 73(d)

ABROGATED

2007 AMENDMENT

Rule 74 was abrogated in 1997 to reflect repeal of the statute providing for appeal from a magistrate judge's judgment to the district court. The rule number is reserved for possible future use.

Rule 75. Proceedings on Appeal from Magistrate Judge to District Judge under Rule 73(d)

ABROGATED

2007 AMENDMENT

Rule 75 was abrogated in 1997 to reflect repeal of the statute providing for appeal from a magistrate judge's judgment to the district court. The rule number is reserved for possible future use.

Rule 76. Judgment of the District Judge on the Appeal under Rule 73(d) and Costs

ABROGATED

2007 AMENDMENT

Rule 76 was abrogated in 1997 to reflect repeal of the statute providing for appeal from a magistrate judge's judgment to the district court. The rule number is reserved for possible future use.

X. DISTRICT COURTS AND CLERKS

Rule 77. District Courts and Clerks

1937 ADOPTION

This rule states the substance of U.S.C., Title 28, § 452, formerly § 13 (Courts open as courts of admiralty and equity). Compare former Equity Rules 1 (District Court Always Open For Certain Purposes—Orders at Chambers), 2 (Clerk's Office Always Open, Except, Etc.), 4 (Notice of Orders), and 5 (Motions Grantable of Course by Clerk).

1946 AMENDMENT

Note. Rule 77(d) has been amended to avoid such situations as the one arising in *Hill v. Hawes*, 1944, 320 U.S. 520, 64 S.Ct. 334, 88 L.Ed. 283. In that case, an action instituted in the District Court for the District of Columbia, the clerk failed to give notice of the entry of a judgment for defendant as required by Rule 77(d). The time for taking an appeal then was 20 days under Rule 10 of the Court of Appeals (later enlarged by amendment to thirty days), and due to lack of notice of the entry of judgment the plaintiff failed to file his notice of appeal within the prescribed time. On this basis the trial court vacated the original judgment and then re-entered it, whereupon notice of appeal was filed. The Court of

Appeals dismissed the appeal as taken too late. The Supreme Court, however, held that although Rule 77(d) did not purport to attach any consequence to the clerk's failure to give notice as specified, the terms of the rule were such that the appellant was entitled to rely on it, and the trial court in such a case, in the exercise of a sound discretion, could vacate the former judgment and enter a new one, so that the appeal would be within the allowed time.

Because of Rule 6(c), which abolished the old rule that the expiration of the term ends a court's power over its judgment, the effect of the decision in *Hill v. Hawes* is to give the district court power, in its discretion and without time limit, and long after the term may have expired, to vacate a judgment and reenter it for the purpose of reviving the right of appeal. This seriously affects the finality of judgments. See also proposed Rule 6(c) and note; proposed Rule 60(b) and note; and proposed Rule 73(a) and note.

Rule 77(d) as amended makes it clear that notification by the clerk of the entry of a judgment has nothing to do with the starting of the time for appeal; that time starts to run from the date of entry of judgment and not from the date of notice of the entry. Notification by the clerk is merely for the convenience of litigants. And lack of such notification in itself has no effect upon the time for appeal; but in considering an application for extension of time for appeal as provided in Rule 73(a), the court may take into account, as one of the factors affecting its decision, whether the clerk failed to give notice as provided in Rule 77(d), or the party failed to receive the clerk's notice. It need not, however, extend the time for appeal merely because the clerk's notice was not sent or received. It would, therefore, be entirely unsafe for a party to rely on absence of notice from the clerk of the entry of a judgment, or to rely on the adverse party's failure to serve notice of the entry of a judgment. Any party may, of course, serve timely notice of the entry of a judgment upon the adverse party and thus preclude a successful application, under Rule 73(a), for the extension of the time for appeal.

1963 AMENDMENT

Subdivision (c). The amendment authorizes closing of the clerk's office on Saturday as far as civil business is concerned. However, a district court may require its clerk's office to remain open for specified hours on Saturdays or "legal holidays" other than those enumerated ("Legal holiday" is defined in Rule 6(a), as amended.) The clerk's offices of many district courts have customarily remained open on some of the days appointed as holidays by State law. This practice could be continued by local rule or order.

Subdivision (d). This amendment conforms to the amendment of Rule 5(a). See the Advisory Committee's Note to that amendment.

1968 AMENDMENT

The provisions of Rule 73(a) are incorporated in Rule 4(a) of the Federal Rules of Appellate Procedure.

1971 AMENDMENT

The amendment adds Columbus Day to the list of legal holidays. See the Note accompanying the amendment of Rule 6(a).

1987 AMENDMENT

The amendments are technical. No substantive change is intended. The Birthday of Martin Luther King, Jr. is added to the list of national holidays in Rule 77.

1991 AMENDMENT

This revision is a companion to the concurrent amendment to Rule 4 of the Federal Rules of Appellate Procedure. The purpose of the revisions is to permit district courts to ease strict sanctions now imposed on appellants whose notices of appeal are filed late because of their failure to receive notice of entry of a judgment. See, e.g. *Tucker v. Commonwealth Land Title Ins. Co.*, 800 F.2d 1054 (11th Cir.1986); *Ashby Enterprises, Ltd. v. Weitzman, Dym & Associates*, 780 F.2d 1043 (D.C.Cir.1986); *In re OPM Leasing Services, Inc.*, 769 F.2d 911 (2d Cir.1985); *Spika v. Village of Lombard, Ill.*, 763 F.2d 282 (7th Cir.1985); *Hall v. Community Mental Health Center of Beaver County*, 772 F.2d 42 (3d Cir.1985); *Wilson v. Atwood v. Stark*, 725 F.2d 255 (5th Cir. en banc), *cert. dismissed*, 468 U.S. 1222, 105 S.Ct. 17, 82 L.Ed.2d 912 (1984); *Case v. BASF Wyandotte*, 737 F.2d 1034 (Fed.Cir.1984), *cert. denied*, 469 U.S. 982, 105 S.Ct. 386, 83 L.Ed.2d 321 (1984); *Hensley v. Chesapeake & Ohio R.R. Co.*, 651 F.2d 226 (4th Cir.1981); *Buckeye Cellulose Corp. v. Braggs Electric Construction Co.*, 569 F.2d 1036 (8th Cir.1978).

Failure to receive notice may have increased in frequency with the growth in the caseload in the clerks' offices. The present strict rule imposes a duty on counsel to maintain contact with the court while a case is under submission. Such contact is more difficult to maintain if counsel is outside the district, as is increasingly common, and can be a burden to the court as well as counsel.

The effect of the revisions is to place a burden on prevailing parties who desire certainty that the time for appeal is running. Such parties can take the initiative to assure that their adversaries receive effective notice. An appropriate procedure for such notice is provided in Rule 5.

The revised rule lightens the responsibility but not the workload of the clerk's offices, for the duty of that office to give notice of entry of judgment must be maintained.

2001 AMENDMENT

Rule 77(d) is amended to reflect changes in Rule 5(b). A few courts have experimented with serving Rule 77(d) notices by electronic means on parties who consent to this procedure. The success of these experiments warrants express authorization. Because service is made in the manner provided in Rule 5(b), party consent is required for service by electronic or other means described in Rule 5(b)(2)(D). The same provision is made for a party who wishes to ensure actual communication of the Rule 77(d) notice by also serving notice.

Changes Made After Publication and Comments

Rule 77(d) was amended to correct an oversight in the published version. The clerk is to note "service," not "mailing," on the docket.

2007 AMENDMENTS

The language of Rule 77 has been amended as part of the general restyling of the Civil Rules to make them more easily understood and to make style and terminology consistent throughout the rules. These changes are intended to be stylistic only.

Rule 78.   Motion Day

1937 ADOPTION

Compare former Equity Rule 6 (Motion Day) with the first paragraph of this rule. The second paragraph authorizes a procedure found helpful for the expedition of business in some of the federal and state courts. See Rule 43(e) of these rules dealing with evidence on motions. Compare Civil Practice Rules of the Municipal Court of Chicago (1935), Rules 269, 270, 271.

1987 AMENDMENT

The amendment is technical. No substantive change is intended.

2007 AMENDMENTS

The language of Rule 78 has been amended as part of the general restyling of the Civil Rules to make them more easily understood and to make style and terminology consistent throughout the rules. These changes are intended to be stylistic only.

Rule 16 has superseded any need for the provision in former Rule 78 for orders for the advancement, conduct, and hearing of actions.

Rule 79.   Books and Records Kept by the Clerk and Entries Therein

1937 ADOPTION

Compare Equity Rule 3 (Books Kept by Clerk and Entries Therein). In connection with this rule, see also the following statutes of the United States:

U.S.C., Title 5:

§ 301   (Officials for investigation of official acts, records and accounts of marshals, attorneys, clerks of courts, United States commissioners, referees and trustees)

§ 318   (Accounts of district attorneys)

U.S.C., Title 28, former:

§ 556   (Clerks of district courts; books open to inspection)

§ 567   (Same; accounts)

§ 568   (Same; reports and accounts of moneys received; dockets)

§ 813   (Indices of judgment debtors to be kept by clerks)

And see "Instructions to United States Attorneys, Marshals, Clerks and Commissioners" issued by the Attorney General of the United States.

1946 AMENDMENT

Note to Subdivision (a). The amendment substitutes the Director of the Administrative Office of the United States Courts, acting subject to the approval of the Judicial Conference of Senior Circuit Judges, in the place of the Attorney General as a consequence of and in accordance with the provisions of the act establishing the Administrative Office and transferring functions thereto. Act of August 7, 1939, ch. 501, §§ 1–7, 53 Stat. 1223, 28 U.S.C. formerly §§ 444–450 (now §§ 601–610).

Subdivision (b). The change in this subdivision does not alter the nature of the judgments and orders to be recorded in permanent form but it does away with the express requirement that they be recorded in a book. This merely gives latitude for the preservation of court records in other than book form, if that shall seem advisable, and permits with the approval of the Judicial Conference and adoption of such modern, space-saving methods as microphotography. See Proposed Improvements in the Administration of the Offices of Clerks of United States District Courts, prepared by the Bureau of the Budget, 1941, 38–42. See also Rule 55, Federal Rules of Criminal Procedure [following section 687 of Title 18 U.S.C.].

Subdivision (c). The words "Separate and" have been deleted as unduly rigid. There is no sufficient reason for requiring that the indices in all cases be separate; on the contrary, the requirement frequently increases the labor of persons searching the records as well as the labor of the clerk's force preparing them. The matter should be left to administrative discretion.

The other changes in the subdivision merely conform with those made in subdivision (b) of the rule.

Subdivision (d). Subdivision (d) is a new provision enabling the Administrative Office, with the approval of the Judicial Conference, to carry out any improvements in clerical procedure with respect to books and records which may be deemed advisable. See report cited in Note to subdivision (b), supra.

1948 AMENDMENT

The amendment effective October 1949 substituted the name, "Judicial Conference of the United States," for "Judicial Conference of Senior Circuit Judges," in the first sentence of subdivision (a), and in subdivisions (b) and (d).

1963 AMENDMENT

The terminology is clarified without any change of the prescribed practice. See amended Rule 58, and the Advisory Committee's Note thereto.

2007 AMENDMENTS

The language of Rule 79 has been amended as part of the general restyling of the Civil Rules to make them more easily understood and to make style and terminology consistent throughout the rules. These changes are intended to be stylistic only.

Rule 80.   Stenographer; Stenographic Report or Transcript as Evidence

1937 ADOPTION

Note to Subdivision (a). This follows substantially former Equity Rule 50 (Stenographer—Appointment—Fees). [This subdivision was abrogated. See amendment note of Advisory Committee below.]

Note to Subdivision (b). See Reports of Conferences of Senior Circuit Judges with the Chief Justice of the United States (1936), 22 A.B.A.J. 818, 819, (1937), 24 A.B.A.J. 75, 77. [This subdivision was abrogated. See amendment note of Advisory Committee below.]

Note to Subdivision (c). Compare Iowa Code (1935) § 11353.

1946 AMENDMENT

Note. Subdivisions (a) and (b) of rule 80 have been abrogated because of Public Law 222, 78th Cong., ch. 3, 2d Sess., approved Jan. 20, 1944, 28 U.S.C. formerly § 9a (now §§ 550, 604, 753, 1915, 1920), providing for the appointment of official stenographers for each district court, prescribing their duties, providing for the furnishing of transcripts, the taxation of the fees therefor as costs and other related matters. This statute has now been implemented by Congressional appropriation available for the fiscal year beginning July 1, 1945.

Subdivision (c) of Rule 80 (Stenographic Report or Transcript as Evidence) has been retained unchanged.

2007 AMENDMENTS

The language of Rule 80 has been amended as part of the general restyling of the Civil Rules to make them more easily understood and to make style and terminology consistent throughout the rules. These changes are intended to be stylistic only.

XI. GENERAL PROVISIONS

Rule 81. **Applicability in General**

1937 ADOPTION

Note to Subdivision (a). Paragraph (1): Compare the enabling act, act of June 19, 1934, U.S.C., Title 28, formerly § 723b (now § 2072)(Rules in actions at law; Supreme Court authorized to make) and formerly § 723c (now § 2072)(Union of equity and action at law rules; power of Supreme Court). For the application of these rules in bankruptcy and copyright proceedings, see Orders xxxvi and xxxvii in Bankruptcy and Rule 1 of Rules of Practice and Procedure under § 25 of the copyright act, act of March 4, 1909, U.S.C., Title 17, § 25 (now § 101)(Infringement and rules of procedure).

For examples of statutes which are preserved by paragraph (2) see: U.S.C., Title 8, ch. 9 (Naturalization); Title 28, former ch. 14 (Habeas corpus); Title 28, former §§ 377a–377c (Quo warranto); and such forfeiture statutes as U.S.C., Title 7, former § 116 (Misbranded seeds, confiscation), and Title 21, formerly § 14 (now § 334(b))(Pure Food and Drug Act— condemnation of adulterated or misbranded food; procedure). See also *Four Hundred and Forty–Three Cans of Frozen Egg Product* v. *U.S.*, 226 U.S. 172, 33 S.Ct. 50, 57 L.Ed. 174 (1912).

For examples of statutes which under paragraph (7) will continue to govern procedure in condemnation cases, see U.S.C., Title 40, § 258 (Condemnation of realty for sites for public building, etc., procedure); U.S.C., Title 16, § 831x (Condemnation by Tennessee Valley Authority); U.S.C., Title 40, § 120 (Acquisition of lands for public use in District of Columbia); Title 40, ch. 7 (Acquisition of lands in District of Columbia for use of United States; condemnation).

Note to Subdivision (b). Some statutes which will be affected by this subdivision are:

U.S.C., Title 7:

§ 222 (Federal Trade Commission powers adopted for enforcement of Stockyards Act)(By reference to Title 15, § 49)

U.S.C., Title 15:

§ 49 (Enforcement of Federal Trade Commission orders and antitrust laws)

§ 77t(c) (Enforcement of Securities and Exchange Commission orders and Securities Act of 1933)

§ 78u(f) (Same; Securities Exchange Act of 1934)

§ 79r(g) (Same; Public Utility Holding Company Act of 1935)

U.S.C., Title 16:

§ 820 (Proceedings in equity for revocation or to prevent violations of license of Federal Power Commission licensee)

§ 825m–b (Mandamus to compel compliance with Federal Water Power Act, etc.)

U.S.C., Title 19:

§ 1333(c) (Mandamus to compel compliance with orders of Tariff Commission, etc.)

U.S.C., Title 28, former:

§ 377   (Power to issue writs)

§ 572   (Fees, attorneys, solicitors and proctors)

§ 778   (Death of parties; substitution of executor or administrator).   Compare Rule 25(a)(Substitution of parties; death), and the note thereto.

U.S.C., Title 33:

§ 495   (Removal of bridges over navigable waters)

U.S.C., Title 45:

§ 88   (Mandamus against Union Pacific Railroad Company)

§ 153(p)   (Mandamus to enforce orders of Adjustment Board under Railway Labor Act)

§ 185   (Same; National Air Transport Adjustment Board)(By reference to § 153)

U.S.C., Title 47:

§ 11   (Powers of Federal Communications Commission)

§ 401(a)   (Enforcement of Federal Communications Act and orders of Commission)

§ 406   (Same; compelling furnishing of facilities; mandamus)

U.S.C., Title 49:

§ 19a(*l*)   (Mandamus to compel compliance with Interstate Commerce Act)

§ 20(9)   (Jurisdiction to compel compliance with interstate commerce laws by mandamus)

For comparable provisions in state practice see Ill. Rev. Stat. (1937), ch. 110, § 179; Calif. Code Civ. Proc. (Deering, 1937) § 802.

Note to Subdivision (c).   Such statutes as the following dealing with the removal of actions are substantially continued and made subject to these rules:

U.S.C., Title 28, former:

§ 71   (Removal of suits from state courts)

§ 72   (Same; procedure)

§ 73   (Same; suits under grants of land from different states)

§ 74   (Same; causes against persons denied civil rights)

§ 75   (Same; petitioner in actual custody of state court)

§ 76   (Same; suits and prosecutions against revenue officers)

§ 77   (Same; suits by aliens)

§ 78   (Same; copies of records refused by clerk of state court)

§ 79   (Same; previous attachment bonds or orders)

§ 80   (Same; dismissal or remand)

§ 81   (Same; proceedings in suits removed)

§ 82   (Same; record; filing and return)

§ 83   (Service of process after removal)

U.S.C., Title 28, formerly § 72 (now §§ 1446, 1447), *supra*, however, is modified by shortening the time for pleading in removed actions.

Note to Subdivision (e).   The last sentence of this subdivision modifies U.S.C., Title 28, formerly § 725 (now § 1652)(Laws of States as rules of decision) in so far as that statute has been construed to govern matters of procedure and to exclude state judicial decisions relative thereto.

1946 AMENDMENT

Note to Subdivision (a).   Despite certain dicta to the contrary, *Lynn v. United States,* C.C.A.5, 1940, 110 F.2d 586; *Mount Tivy Winery, Inc. v. Lewis,* Cal.1942, 42 F.Supp. 636, it is manifest that the rules apply to actions against the United States under the Tucker Act.   See *United States to Use of Foster Wheeler Corp. v. American Surety Co. of New York,* N.Y.1939, 25 F.Supp. 700; *Boerner v. United States,* N.Y.1939, 26 F.Supp. 769; *United States v. Gallagher,* C.C.A.9, 1945, 151 F.2d 556.   Rules 1 and 81 provides that the rules shall apply to all suits of a civil nature, whether cognizable as cases at law or in equity, except those specifically excepted; and the character of the various proceedings excepted by express statement in Rule 81, as well as the language of the rules generally, shows that the term "civil action" [Rule 2] includes actions against the United States. Moreover, the rules in many places expressly make provision for the situation wherein the United States is a party as either plaintiff or defendant. See Rules 4(d)(4), 12(a), 13(d), 25(d), 37(f), 39(c), 45(c), 54(d), 55(e), 62(e), and 65(c). In *United States v. Sherwood,* 1941, 312 U.S. 584, 61 S.Ct. 767, 85 L.Ed. 1058, the Solicitor General expressly conceded in his brief for the United States that the rules apply to Tucker Act cases. The Solicitor General stated: "The Government, of course, recognizes that the Federal Rules of Civil Procedure apply to cases brought under the Tucker Act." (Brief for the United States, p. 31). Regarding *Lynn v. United States, supra,* the Solicitor General stated: "The Government, of course, recognizes that the Federal Rules of Civil Procedure apply to cases brought under the Tucker Act." (Brief for the United States, p. 31). Regarding *Lynn* v. *United States, supra,* the Solicitor General said: "In *Lynn* v. *United States* ... the Circuit Court of Appeals for the Fifth Circuit went beyond the Government's contention there, and held that an action under the Tucker Act is neither an action at law nor a suit in equity and, seemingly, that the Federal Rules of Civil Procedure are, therefore, inapplicable. We think the suggestion is erroneous. Rules 4(d), 12(a), 39(c), and 55(e) expressly contemplate suits against the United States, and nothing in the Enabling Act (48 Stat. 1064, 28 U.S.C. § 2072, formerly §§ 723b, 723c) suggests that the Rules are inapplicable to Tucker Act proceedings, which in terms are to accord with court rules and their subsequent modifications (Sec. 4, Act of March 3, 1887, 24 Stat. 505, 28 U.S.C. §§ 2071, 2072, formerly § 761)." (Brief for the United States, p. 31, n. 17.)

United States v. *Sherwood, supra,* emphasizes, however, that the application of the rules in Tucker Act cases affects only matters of procedure and does not operate to extend jurisdiction. See also Rule 82. In the Sherwood case, the New York Supreme Court, acting under § 795 of the New York Civil Practice Act, made an order, authorizing Sherwood, as a judgment creditor, to maintain a suit under the Tucker Act to recover damages from the United States for breach of its contract with the judgment debtor, Kaiser, for construction of a post office building. Sherwood brought suit against the United States and Kaiser in the District Court for the Eastern District of New York. The question before the United States Supreme Court was whether a United States District Court had jurisdiction to entertain a suit against the United States wherein private parties were joined as parties defendant. It was contended that either the Federal Rules of Civil Procedure or the Tucker Act, or both, embodied the consent of the United States to be sued in litigations in which issues between the plaintiff and third persons were to be adjudicated. Regarding the effect of the Federal Rules, the Court declared that nothing in the rules, so far as they may be applicable in Tucker Act cases, authorized the maintenance of any suit against the United States to which it had not otherwise consented. The matter involved was not one of procedure but of jurisdiction, the limits of which were marked by the consent of the United States to be sued. The jurisdiction thus limited is unaffected by the Federal Rules of Civil Procedure.

Subdivision (a)(2). The added sentence makes it clear that the rules have not superseded the requirements of U.S.C., Title 28, § 2253, formerly § 466. *Schenk* v. *Plummer,* C.C.A.9, 1940, 113 F.2d 726.

For correct application of the rules in proceedings for forfeiture of property for violation of a statute of the United States, such as under U.S.C., Title 22, § 405 (seizure of war materials intended for unlawful export) or U.S.C., Title 21, § 334(b)(Federal Food, Drug, and Cosmetic Act; formerly Title 21, U.S.C., § 14, Pure Food and Drug Act), see *Reynal* v. *United States,* C.C.A.5, 1945, 153 F.2d 929; *United States* v. *108 Boxes of Cheddar Cheese,* D.Iowa 1943, 3 F.R.D. 40.

Subdivision (a)(3). The added sentence makes it clear that the rules apply to appeals from proceedings to enforce administrative subpoenas. See *Perkins* v. *Endicott Johnson Corp.,* C.C.A.2d, 1942, 128 F.2d 208, affirmed 317 U.S. 501, 63 S.Ct. 339, 87 L.Ed. 424; *Walling* v. *News Printing, Inc.,* C.C.A.3, 1945, 148 F.2d 57; *McCrone* v. *United States,* 1939, 307 U.S. 61, 59 S.Ct. 685, 83 L.Ed. 1108. And, although the provision allows full recognition of the fact that the rigid application of the rules in the proceedings themselves may conflict with the summary determination desired, *Goodyear Tire & Rubber Co.* v. *National Labor Relations Board,* C.C.A.6, 1941, 122 F.2d 450; *Cudahy Packing Co.* v. *National Labor Relations Board,* C.C.A.10, 1941, 117 F.2d 692, it is drawn so as to permit application of any of the rules in the proceedings whenever the district court deems them helpful. See, e.g., *Peoples Natural Gas Co.* v. *Federal Power Commission,* App.D.C.1942, 127 F.2d 153, certiorari denied 316 U.S. 700, 62 S.Ct. 1298, 86 L.Ed. 1769; *Martin* v. *Chandis Securities Co.,* C.C.A.9th, 1942, 128 F.2d 731. Compare the application of the rules in summary proceedings in bankruptcy under General Order 37. See 1 Collier on Bankruptcy, 14th ed. by Moore and Oglebay, 326–327; 2 Collier, op.cit.supra, 1401–1402; 3 Collier, op.cit.supra, 228–231; 4 Collier, op.cit.supra, 1199–1202.

Subdivision (a)(6). Section 405 of U.S.C., Title 8 originally referred to in the last sentence of paragraph (6), has been repealed and § 1451, formerly § 738, U.S.C.A., Title 8, has been enacted in its stead. The last sentence of paragraph (6) has, therefore, been amended in accordance with this change. The sentence has also been amended so as to refer directly to the statute regarding the provision of time for answer, thus avoiding any confusion attendant upon a change in the statute.

That portion of subdivision (a)(6) making the rules applicable to proceedings for enforcement or review of compensation orders under the Longshoremen's and Harbor Workers' Compensation Act [33 U.S.C. § 901 et seq.] was added by an amendment made pursuant to order of the Court, December 28, 1939, effective three months subsequent to the adjournment of the 76th Congress, January 3, 1941.

Subdivision (c). The change in subdivision (c) effects more speedy trials in removed actions. In some states many of the courts have only two terms a year. A case, if filed 20 days before a term, is returnable to that term, but if filed less than 20 days before a term, is returnable to the following term, which convenes six months later. Hence, under the original wording of Rule 81(c), where a case is filed less than 20 days before the term and is removed within a few days but before answer, it is possible for the defendant to delay interposing his answer or presenting his defenses by motion for six months or more. The rule as amended prevents this result.

Subdivision (f). The use of the phrase "the United States or an officer or agency thereof" in the rules (as e.g., in Rule 12(a) and amended Rule 73(a)) could raise the question of whether "officer" includes a collector of internal revenue, a former collector, or the personal representative of a deceased collector, against whom suits for tax refunds are frequently instituted. Difficulty might ensue for the reason that a suit against a collector or his representative has been held to be a personal action. *Sage* v. *United States,* 1919, 250 U.S. 33, 39 S.Ct. 415, 63 L.Ed. 828; *Smietanka* v. *Indiana Steel Co.,* 1921, 257 U.S. 1, 42 S.Ct. 1, 66 L.Ed. 99; *United States* v. *Nunnally Investment Co.,* 1942, 316 U.S. 258, 62 S.Ct. 1064, 86 L.Ed. 1455. The addition of subdivision (f) to Rule 81 dispels any doubts on the matter and avoids further litigation.

1948 AMENDMENT

The amendment effective October 1949, substituted the words "United States District Court" for the words "District Court of the United States" in the last sentence of subdivision (a)(1) and in the first and third sentences of subdivision (e). The amendment substituted the words "United States district courts" in lieu of "district courts of the United States" in subdivision (a)(4) and (5) and in the first sentence of subdivision (c).

The amendment effective October 20, 1949, also made the following changes:

In subdivision (a)(1), the reference to "Title 17, U.S.C." was substituted for the reference to "the Act of March 4, 1909, c. 320, § 25 (35 Stat. 1081), as amended, U.S.C., Title 17, § 25."

In subdivision (a)(2) the reference to "Title 28, U.S.C., § 2253" was substituted for "U.S.C., Title 28, § 466."

In subdivision (a)(3) the reference in the first sentence to "Title 9, U.S.C.," was substituted for "the Act of February 12, 1925, c. 213 (43 Stat. 883), U.S.C., Title 9".

In subdivision (a)(5), the words "as amended" were inserted after the parenthetical citation of "(49 Stat. 453)," and after the citations of "Title 29, §§ 159 and 160," former references to subdivisions "(e), (g), and (i)" were deleted.

In subdivision (a)(6) after the words "These rules" at the beginning of the first sentence, the following words were deleted: "do not apply to proceedings under the Act of September 13, 1888, c. 1015, § 13 (25 Stat. 479), as amended, U.S.C., Title 8, [former] § 282, relating to deportation of Chinese; they". Also in the first sentence, after the parenthetical citation of "(44 Stat. 1434, 1436)," the words "as amended" were added. In the last sentence, the words "October 14, 1940, c. 876, § 338 (54 Stat. 1158)" were inserted in lieu of the words "June 29, 1906, c. 3592, § 15 (34 Stat. 601), as amended."

In subdivision (c), the word "all" originally appearing in the first sentence between the words "govern" and "procedure" was deleted. In the third sentence, the portion beginning with the words "20 days after the receipt" and including all the remainder of that sentence was substituted for the following language: "the time allowed for answer by the law of the state or within 5 days after the filing of the transcript of the record in the district court of the United States, whichever period is longer, but in any event within 20 days after the filing of the transcript". In the fourth or last sentence, after the words at the beginning of the sentence, "If at the time of removal all necessary pleadings have been," the word "served" was inserted in lieu of the word "filed," and the concluding words of the sentence, "petition for removal is filed if he is the petitioner," together with the final clause immediately following, were substituted for the words "record of the action is filed in the district court of the United States."

1963 AMENDMENT

Subdivision (a)(4). This change reflects the transfer of functions from the Secretary of Commerce to the Secretary of the Interior made by 1939 Reorganization Plan No. II, § 4(e), 53 Stat. 1433.

Subdivision (a)(6). The proper current reference is to the 1952 statute superseding the 1940 statute.

Subdivision (c). Most of the cases have held that a party who has made a proper express demand for jury trial in the State court is not required to renew the demand after removal of the action. *Zakoscielny* v. *Waterman Steamship Corp.,* 16 F.R.D. 314 (D.Md. 1954); *Talley* v. *American Bakeries Co.,* 15 F.R.D. 391 (E.D.Tenn.1954); *Rehrer* v. *Service Trucking Co.,* 15 F.R.D. 113 (D.Del.1953); 5 Moore's Federal Practice ¶ 38.39[3] (2d ed. 1951); 1 Barron & Holtzoff, Federal Practice & Procedure § 132 (Wright ed. 1960). But there is some authority to the contrary. *Petsel* v. *Chicago, B. & Q. R. Co.,* 101 F.Supp. 1006 (S.D.Iowa 1951); *Nelson* v. *American Nat. Bank & Trust Co.,* 9 F.R.D. 680 (E.D.Tenn. 1950). The amendment adopts the preponderant view.

In order still further to avoid unintended waivers of jury trial, the amendment provides that where by State law applicable in the court from which the case is removed a party is entitled to jury trial without making an express demand, he need not make a demand after removal. However, the district court for calendar or other purposes may on its own motion direct the parties to state whether they demand a jury, and the court must make such a direction upon the request of any party. Under the amendment a district court may find it convenient to establish a routine practice of giving these directions to the parties in appropriate cases.

Subdivision (f). The amendment recognizes the change of nomenclature made by Treasury Dept. Order 150–26(2), 18 Fed.Reg. 3499 (1953).

As to a special problem arising under Rule 25 (Substitution of parties) in actions for refund of taxes, see the Advisory Committee's Note to the amendment of Rule 25(d), effective July 19, 1961; and 4 Moore's Federal Practice ¶ 25.09 at 531 (2d Ed. 1950).

1966 AMENDMENT

See Note to Rule 1, supra.

Statutory proceedings to forfeit property for violation of the laws of the United States, formerly governed by the admiralty rules, will be governed by the unified and supplemental rules. See Supplemental Rule A.

Upon the recommendation of the judges of the United States District Court for the District of Columbia, the Federal Rules of Civil Procedure are made applicable to probate proceedings in that court. The exception with regard to adoption proceedings is removed because the court no longer has jurisdiction of those matters; and the words "mental health" are substituted for "lunacy" to conform to the current characterization in the District.

The purpose of the amendment to paragraph (3) is to permit the deletion from Rule 73(a) of the clause "unless a shorter time is provided by law." The 10 day period fixed for an appeal under 45 U.S.C. § 159 is the only instance of a shorter time provided for appeals in civil cases. Apart from the unsettling effect of the clause, it is eliminated because its retention would preserve the 15 day period heretofore allowed by 28 U.S.C. § 2107 for appeals from interlocutory decrees in admiralty, it being one of the purposes of the amendment to make the time for appeals in civil and admiralty cases uniform under the unified rules. See Advisory Committee's Note to subdivision (a) of Rule 73.

1967 AMENDMENT

The amendments eliminate inappropriate references to appellate procedure.

1971 AMENDMENT

Title 28, U.S.C., § 2243 now requires that the custodian of a person detained must respond to an application for a writ of habeas corpus "within three days unless for good cause additional time, not exceeding twenty days, is allowed." The amendment increases to forty days the additional time that the district court may allow in habeas corpus proceedings involving persons in custody pursuant to a judgment of a state court. The substantial increase in the number of such proceedings in recent years has placed a considerable burden on state authorities. Twenty days has proved in practice too short a time in which to prepare and file the return in many such cases. Allowance of additional time should, of course, be granted only for good cause.

While the time allowed in such a case for the return of the writ may not exceed forty days, this does not mean that the state must necessarily be limited to that period of time to provide for the federal court the transcript of the proceedings of a state trial or plenary hearing if the transcript must be prepared after the habeas corpus proceeding has begun in the federal court.

1987 AMENDMENT

The amendments are technical. No substantive change is intended.

2001 AMENDMENT

Former Copyright Rule 1 made the Civil Rules applicable to copyright proceedings except to the extent the Civil Rules were inconsistent with Copyright Rules. Abrogation of the Copyright Rules leaves the Civil Rules fully applicable to copyright proceedings. Rule 81(a)(1) is amended to reflect this change.

The District of Columbia Court Reform and Criminal Procedure Act of 1970, Pub.L. 91–358, 84 Stat. 473, transferred mental health proceedings formerly held in the United States District Court for the District of Columbia to local District of Columbia courts. The provision that the Civil Rules do not apply to these proceedings is deleted as superfluous.

The reference to incorporation of the Civil Rules in the Federal Rules of Bankruptcy Procedure has been restyled.

Changes Made After Publication and Comments

The Committee Note was amended to correct the inadvertent omission of a negative. As revised, it correctly reflects the language that is stricken from the rule.

2002 AMENDMENT

This amendment brings Rule 81(a)(2) into accord with the Rules Governing § 2254 and § 2255 proceedings. In its present form, Rule 81(a)(2) includes return-time provisions that are inconsistent with the provisions in the Rules Governing §§ 2254 and 2255. The inconsistency should be eliminated, and it is better that the time provisions continue to be set out in the other rules without duplication in Rule 81. Rule 81 also directs that the writ be directed to the person having custody of the person detained. Similar directions exist in the § 2254 and § 2255 rules, providing additional detail for applicants subject to future custody. There is no need for partial duplication in Rule 81.

The provision that the civil rules apply to the extent that practice is not set forth in the § 2254 and § 2255 rules dovetails with the provisions in Rule 11 of the § 2254 rules and Rule 12 of the § 2255 rules.

2007 AMENDMENTS

The language of Rule 81 has been amended as part of the general restyling of the Civil Rules to make them more easily understood and to make style and terminology consistent throughout the rules. These changes are intended to be stylistic only.

Rule 81(c) has been revised to reflect the amendment of 28 U.S.C. § 1446(a) that changed the procedure for removal fiom a petition for removal to a notice of removal.

Former Rule 81(e), drafted before the decision in *Erie R.R. v. Tompkins*, 304 U.S. 64 (1938), defined state law to include "the statutes of that state and the state judicial decisions construing them." The *Erie* decision reinterpreted the Rules of Decision Act, now 28 U.S.C. § 1652, recognizing that the "laws" of the states include the common law established by judicial decisions. Long-established practice reflects this understanding, looking to state common law as well as statutes and court rules when a Civil Rule directs use of state law. Amended Rule 81(d)(1) adheres to this practice, including all state judicial decisions, not only those that construe state statutes.

Former Rule 81(f) is deleted. The office of district director of internal revenue was abolished by restructuring under the Internal Revenue Service Restructuring and Reform Act of 1998, Pub.L. 105–206, July 22, 1998, 26 U.S.C. § 1 Note.

Rule 82.   Jurisdiction and Venue Unaffected

1937 ADOPTION

These rules grant extensive power of joining claims and counterclaims in one action, but, as this rule states, such grant does not extend federal jurisdiction. The rule is declaratory of existing practice under the former Federal Equity Rules with regard to such provisions as former Equity Rule 26 on Joinder of Clauses of Action and former Equity Rule 30 on Counterclaims. Compare Shulman and Jaegerman, Some Jurisdictional Limitations on Federal Procedure, 45 Yale L.J. 393 (1936).

1948 AMENDMENT

The amendment effective October 1949, substituted the words "United States district courts" for "district courts of the United States."

1966 AMENDMENT

Title 28, U.S.C., § 1391(b) provides: "A civil action wherein jurisdiction is not founded solely on diversity of citizenship may be brought only in the judicial district where all defendants reside, except as otherwise provided by law." This provision cannot appropriately be applied to what were formerly suits in admiralty. The rationale of decisions holding it inapplicable rests largely on the use of the term "civil action": i.e., a suit in admiralty is not a "civil action" within the statute. By virtue of the amendment to Rule 1, the provisions of Rule 2 convert suits in admiralty into civil actions. The added sentence is necessary to avoid an undesirable change in existing law with respect to venue.

2001 AMENDMENT

The final sentence of Rule 82 is amended to delete the reference to 28 U.S.C. § 1393, which has been repealed.

Style Comment

The recommendation that the change be made without publication carries with it a recommendation that style changes not be made. Styling would carry considerable risks. The first sentence of Rule 82, for example, states that the Civil Rules do not "extend or limit the jurisdiction of the United States district courts." That sentence is a flat lie if "jurisdiction" includes personal or quasi-in rem jurisdiction. The styling project on this rule requires publication and comment.

2007 AMENDMENTS

The language of Rule 82 has been amended as part of the general restyling of the Civil Rules to make them more easily understood and to make style and terminology consistent throughout the rules. These changes are intended to be stylistic only.

Rule 83.   Rules By District Courts; Judge's Directives

1937 ADOPTION

This rule substantially continues U.S.C., Title 28, § 2071, formerly § 731 (Rules of practice in district courts) with the additional requirement that copies of such rules and amendments be furnished to the Supreme Court of the United States. See former Equity Rule 79 (Additional Rules by District Court). With the last sentence compare United States Supreme Court Admiralty Rules, 1920, Rule 44 (Right of Trial Courts to Make Rules of Practice)(originally promulgated in 1842).

1985 AMENDMENT

Rule 83, which has not been amended since the Federal Rules were promulgated in 1938, permits each district to adopt local rules not inconsistent with the Federal Rules by a majority of the judges. The only other requirement is that copies be furnished to the Supreme Court.

The widespread adoption of local rules and the modest procedural prerequisites for their promulgation have led many commentators to question the soundness of the process as well as the validity of some rules. See 12 C. Wright & A. Miller, *Federal Practice and Procedure: Civil* § 3152, at 217 (1973); Caballero, *Is There an Over-Exercise of Local Rule-Making Powers by the United States District Courts?*, 24 Fed. Bar News 325 (1977). Although the desirability of local rules for promoting uniform practice within a district is widely accepted, several commentators also have suggested reforms to increase the quality, simplicity, and uniformity of the local rules. See Note, *Rule 83 and the Local Federal Rules,* 67 Colum.L.Rev. 1251 (1967), and Comment, *The Local Rules of Civil Procedure in the Federal District Courts—A Survey,* 1966 Duke L.J. 1011.

The amended Rule attempts, without impairing the procedural validity of existing local rules, to enhance the local rulemaking process by requiring appropriate public notice of proposed rules and an opportunity to comment on them. Although some district courts apparently consult the local bar before promulgating rules, many do not, which has led to criticism of a process that has district judges consulting only with each other. See 12 C. Wright & A. Miller, *supra,* § 3152, at 217; Blair, *The New Local Rules for Federal Practice in Iowa,* 23 Drake L.Rev. 517 (1974). The new language subjects local rulemaking to scrutiny similar to that accompanying the Federal Rules, administrative rulemaking, and legislation. It attempts to assure that the expert advice of practitioners and scholars is made available to the district court before local rules are promulgated. See Weinstein, *Reform of Court Rule-Making Procedures* 84–87, 127–37, 151 (1977).

The amended Rule does not detail the procedure for giving notice and an opportunity to be heard since conditions vary from district to district. Thus, there is no explicit requirement for a public hearing, although a district may consider that procedure appropriate in all or some rulemaking situations. See generally, Weinstein, *supra,* at 117–37, 151. The new Rule does not foreclose any other form of consultation. For example, it can be accomplished through the mechanism of an "Advisory Committee" similar to that employed by the Supreme Court in connection with the Federal Rules themselves.

The amended Rule provides that a local rule will take effect upon the date specified by the district court and will remain in effect unless amended by the district court or abrogated by the judicial council. The effectiveness of a local rule should not be deferred until approved by the judicial council because that might unduly delay promulgation of a local rule that should become effective immediately, especially since some councils do not meet frequently. Similarly, it was thought that to delay a local rule's effectiveness for a fixed period of time would be arbitrary and that to require the judicial council to abrogate a local rule within a specified time would be inconsistent with its power under 28 U.S.C. § 332 (1976) to nullify a local rule at any time. The expectation is that the judicial council will examine all local rules, including those currently in effect, with an eye toward determining whether they are valid and consistent with the Federal Rules, promote inter-district uniformity and efficiency, and do not undermine the basic objectives of the Federal Rules.

The amended Rule requires copies of local rules to be sent upon their promulgation to the judicial council and the Administrative Office of the United States Courts rather than to the Supreme Court. The Supreme Court was the appropriate filing place in 1938, when Rule 83 originally was promulgated, but the establishment of the Administrative Office makes it a more logical place to develop a centralized file of local rules. This procedure is consistent with both the Criminal and the Appellate Rules. See Fed.R.Crim.P. 57(a); Fed.R.App.P. 47. The Administrative Office also will be able to provide improved utilization of the file because of its recent development of a Local Rules Index.

The practice pursued by some judges of issuing standing orders has been controversial, particularly among members of the practicing bar. The last sentence in Rule 83 has been amended to make certain that standing orders are not inconsistent with the Federal Rules or any local district court rules. Beyond that, it is hoped that each district will adopt procedures, perhaps by local rule, for promulgating and reviewing single-judge standing orders.

1995 AMENDMENT

Subdivision (a). This rule is amended to reflect the requirement that local rules be consistent not only with the national rules but also with Acts of Congress. The amendment also states that local rules should not repeat Acts of Congress or national rules.

The amendment also requires that the numbering of local rules conform with any uniform numbering system that may be prescribed by the Judicial Conference. Lack of uniform numbering might create unnecessary traps for counsel and litigants. A uniform numbering system would make it easier for an increasingly national bar and for litigants to locate a local rule that applies to a particular procedural issue.

Paragraph (2) is new. Its aim is to protect against loss of rights in the enforcement of local rules relating to matters of form. For example, a party should not be deprived of a right to a jury trial because its attorney, unaware of—or forgetting—a local rule directing that jury demands be noted in the caption of the case, includes a jury demand only in the body of the pleading. The proscription of paragraph (2) is narrowly drawn—covering only violations attributable to nonwillful failure to comply and only those involving local rules directed to matters of form. It does not limit the court's power to impose substantive penalties upon a party if it or its attorney contumaciously or willfully violates a local rule, even one involving merely a matter of form. Nor does it affect the court's power to enforce local rules that involve more than mere matters of form—for example, a local rule requiring parties to identify evidentiary matters relied upon to support or oppose motions for summary judgment.

Subdivision (b). This rule provides flexibility to the court in regulating practice when there is no controlling law. Specifically, it permits the court to regulate practice in any manner consistent with Acts of Congress, with rules adopted under 28 U.S.C. §§ 2072 and 2075, and with the district local rules.

This rule recognizes that courts rely on multiple directives to control practice. Some courts regulate practice through the published Federal Rules and the local rules of the court. Some courts also have used internal operating procedures, standing orders, and other internal directives. Although such directives continue to be authorized, they can lead to problems. Counsel or litigants may be unaware of various directives. In addition, the sheer volume of directives may impose an unreasonable barrier. For example, it may be difficult to obtain copies of the directives. Finally, counsel or litigants may be unfairly sanctioned for failing to comply with a directive. For these reasons, the amendment to this rule disapproves imposing any sanction or other disadvantage on a person for noncompliance with such an internal directive, unless the alleged violator has been furnished actual notice of the requirement in a particular case.

There should be no adverse consequence to a party or attorney for violating special requirements relating to practice before a particular court unless the party or attorney has actual notice of those requirements. Furnishing litigants with a copy outlining the judge's practices—or attaching instructions to a notice setting a case for conference or trial—would suffice to give actual notice, as would an order in a case specifically adopting by reference a judge's standing order and indicating how copies can be obtained.

2007 AMENDMENTS

The language of Rule 83 has been amended as part of the general restyling of the Civil Rules to make them more easily understood and to make style and terminology consistent throughout the rules. These changes are intended to be stylistic only.

Rule 84. Forms

1937 ADOPTION

In accordance with the practice found useful in many codes, provision is here made for a limited number of official forms which may serve as guides in pleading. Compare 2 Mass.Gen.Laws (Ter.Ed., 1932) ch. 231, § 147, Forms 1–47; English Annual Practice (1937) Appendix A to M, inclusive; Conn.Practice Book (1934) Rules, 47–68, pp. 123–427.

1946 AMENDMENT

Note. The amendment serves to emphasize that the forms contained in the Appendix of Forms are sufficient to withstand attack under the rules under which they are drawn, and that the practitioner using them may rely on them to that extent. The circuit courts of appeals generally have upheld the use of the forms as promoting desirable simplicity and brevity of statement. *Sierocinski* v. *E. I. DuPont DeNemours & Co.,* C.C.A.3, 1939, 103 F.2d 843; *Swift & Co.* v. *Young,* C.C.A.4, 1939, 107 F.2d 170; *Sparks* v. *England,* C.C.A.8, 1940, 113 F.2d 579; *Ramsouer* v. *Midland Valley R. Co.,* C.C.A.8, 1943, 135 F.2d 101. And the forms as a whole have met with widespread approval in the courts. See cases cited in 1 Moore's Federal Practice, 1938, Cum. Supplement § 8.07, under "Page 554"; see also Commentary, The Official Forms, 1941, 4 Fed.Rules Serv. 954. In Cook, "Facts" and "Statements of Fact", 1937, 4 U.Chi.L.Rev. 233, 245–246, it is said with reference to what is now Rule 84: "... pleaders in the federal courts are not to be left to guess as to the meaning of [the] language" in Rule 8(a) regarding the form of the complaint. "All of which is as it should be. In no other way can useless litigation be avoided." Ibid. The amended rule will operate to discourage isolated results such as those found in *Washburn* v. *Moorman Mfg. Co.,* Cal.1938, 25 F.Supp. 546; *Employers' Mutual Liability Ins. Co. of Wisconsin* v. *Blue Line Transfer Co.,* Mo.1941, 2 F.R.D. 121, 5 Fed.Rules Serv. 12e.235, Case 2.

The language of Rule 84 has been amended as part of the general restyling of the Civil Rules to make them more easily understood and to make style and terminology consistent throughout the rules. These changes are intended to be stylistic only.

Rule 85.   Title

2007 AMENDMENTS

The language of Rule 85 has been amended as part of the general restyling of the Civil Rules to make them more easily understood and to make style and terminology consistent throughout the rules. These changes are intended to be stylistic only.

Rule 86.   Effective Date

1937 ADOPTION

See former Equity Rule 81 (These Rules Effective February 1, 1913—Old Rules Abrogated).

1946 AMENDMENT

Effective Date of 1946 Amendment. The first regular session of the 80th Congress adjourned sine die on Friday, Dec. 19, 1947, therefore the amendments to Rules 6, 7, 12, 13, 14, 17, 24, 26, 27, 28, 33, 34, 36, 41, 45, 52, 54, 56, 58, 59, 60, 62, 65, 66, 68, 73, 75, 77, 79, 80, 81, 84, and 86, became effective Mar. 19, 1948 as provided for in subsection (b) of this rule.

1948 AMENDMENT

Effective Date of 1948 Amendment. The first regular session of the 81st Congress adjourned sine die on Oct. 19, 1949, therefore the amendments to Rules 1, 17, 22, 24, 25, 27, 37, 45, 57, 60, 65, 66, 67, 69, 72–76, 79, 81, 82, and 86 and to forms 1, 19, 22, 23, and 27 became effective on Oct. 20, 1949, following the adjournment as provided for in subsection (c) of this rule.

1966 AMENDMENT

Effective Date of 1966 Amendment; Transmission to Congress; Rescission. Sections 2–4 of the Order of the Supreme Court, dated Feb. 28, 1966, 383 U.S. 1031, provided:

"2. That the foregoing amendments and additions to the Rules of Civil Procedure shall take effect on July 1, 1966, and shall govern all proceedings in actions brought thereafter and also in all further proceedings in actions then pending, except to the extent that in the opinion of the court their application in a particular action then pending would not be feasible or would work injustice, in which event the former procedure applies.

"3. That the Chief Justice be, and he hereby is, authorized to transmit to the Congress the foregoing amendments and additions to the Rules of Civil Procedure in accordance with the provisions of Title 28, U.S.C., §§ 2072 and 2073.

"4. That: (a) subdivision (c) of Rule 6 of the Rules of Civil Procedure for the United States District Courts promulgated by this court on December 20, 1937, effective September 16, 1938; (b) Rule 2 of the Rules for Practice and Procedure under section 25 of An Act To amend and consolidate the Acts respecting copyright, approved March 4, 1909, promulgated by this court on June 1, 1909, effective July 1, 1909; and (c) the Rules of Practice in Admiralty and Maritime Cases, promulgated by this court on December 6, 1920, effective March 7, 1921, as revised, amended and supplemented, be, and they hereby are, rescinded, effective July 1, 1966."

1970 AMENDMENT

Effective Date of 1970 Amendments; Transmission to Congress. Sections 2 and 3 of the Order of the Supreme Court, dated Mar. 30, 1970, provided:

"2. That the foregoing amendments to the Rules of Civil Procedure shall take effect on July 1, 1970, and shall govern all proceedings in actions brought thereafter and also in all further proceedings in actions then pending, except to the extent that in the opinion of the court their application in a particular action then pending would not be feasible or would work injustice, in which event the former procedure applies.

"3. That the Chief Justice be, and he hereby is, authorized to transmit to the Congress the foregoing amendments to the Rules of Civil Procedure in accordance with the provisions of Title 28, U.S.C. § 2072.''

2007 AMENDMENTS

The language of Rule 86 has been amended as part of the general restyling of the Civil Rules to make them more easily understood and to make style and terminology consistent throughout the rules. These changes are intended to be stylistic only.

The subdivisions that provided a list of the effective dates of the original Civil Rules and amendments made up to 1963 are deleted as no longer useful.

Rule 86(b) is added to clarify the relationship of amendments taking effect on December 1, 2007, to other laws for the purpose of applying the "supersession" clause in 28 U.S.C. § 2072(b). Section 2072(b) provides that a law in conflict with an Enabling Act Rule "shall be of no further force or effect after such rule[] ha[s] taken effect." The amendments that take effect on December 1, 2007, result from the general restyling of the Civil Rules and from a small number of technical revisions adopted on a parallel track. None of these amendments is intended to affect resolution of any conflict that might arise between a rule and another law. Rule 86(b) makes this intent explicit. Any conflict that arises should be resolved by looking to the date the specific conflicting rule provision first became effective.

SUPPLEMENTAL RULES FOR CERTAIN ADMIRALTY AND MARITIME CLAIMS

Rule A.   Scope of Rules

1966 ADOPTION

Certain distinctively maritime remedies must be preserved in unified rules. The commencement of an action by attachment or garnishment has heretofore been practically unknown in federal jurisprudence except in admiralty, although the amendment of Rule 4(e) effective July 1, 1963, makes available that procedure in accordance with state law. The maritime Proceeding in rem is unique, except as it has been emulated by statute, and is closely related to the substantive maritime law relating to liens. Arrest of the vessel or other maritime property is an historic remedy in controversies over title or right to possession, and in disputes among co-owners over the vessel's employment. The statutory right to limit liability is limited to owners of vessels, and has its own complexities. While the unified federal rules are generally applicable to these distinctive proceedings, certain special rules dealing with them are needed.

Arrest of the person and imprisonment for debt are not included because there remedies are not peculiarly maritime. The practice is not uniform but conforms to state law. See 2 Benedict § 286 [Note: reference is to the 6th Edition of Benedict on Admiralty and not to the current 7th Edition]; 28 U.S.C., § 2007; FRCP 64, 69. The relevant provisions of Admiralty Rules 2, 3, and 4 are unnecessary or obsolete.

No attempt is here made to compile a complete and self-contained code governing these distinctively maritime remedies. The more limited objective is to carry forward the relevant provisions of the former Rules of Practice for Admiralty and Maritime Cases, modernized and revised to some extent but still in the context of history and precedent. Accordingly, these Rules are not to be construed as limiting or impairing the traditional power of a district court, exercising the admiralty and maritime jurisdiction, to adapt its Procedures and its remedies in the individual case, consistently with these rules, to secure the just, speedy, and inexpensive determination of every action. (*See Swift & Co. Packers v. Compania Columbiana Del Caribe, S/A* 339 U.S. 684, 70 S.Ct. 861, 94 L.Ed. 1206 (1950); Rule 1). In addition, of course, the district courts retain the power to make local rules not inconsistent with these rules. *See* Rule 83; cf. Admiralty Rule 44.

2006 AMENDMENT

Rule A is amended to reflect the adoption of Rule G to govern procedure in civil forfeiture actions. Rule G(1) contemplates application of other Supplemental Rules to the extent that Rule G does not address an issue. One example is the Rule E(4)(c) provision for arresting intangible property.

Rule B. In Personam Actions: Attachment and Garnishment
1966 ADOPTION

Subdivision (1).

This preserves the traditional maritime remedy of attachment and garnishment, and carries forward the relevant substance of Admiralty Rule 2. In addition, or in the alternative, provision is made for the use of similar state remedies made available by the amendment of Rule 4(e) effective July 1, 1963. On the effect of appearance to defend against attachment see Rule E(8).

The rule follows closely the language of Admiralty Rule 2. No change is made with respect to the property subject to attachment. No change is made in the condition that makes the remedy available. The rules have never defined the clause, "if the defendant shall not be found within the district," and no definition is attempted here. The subject seems one best left for the time being to development on a case-by-case basis. The proposal does shift from the marshal (on whom it now rests in theory) to the plaintiff the burden of establishing that the defendant cannot be found in the district.

A change in the context of the practice is brought about by Rule 4(f), which will enable summons to be served throughout the state instead of, as heretofore, only within the district. The Advisory Committee considered whether the rule on attachment and garnishment should be correspondingly changed to permit those remedies only when the defendant cannot be found within the state and concluded that the remedy should not be so limited.

The effect is to enlarge the class of cases in which the plaintiff may proceed by attachment or garnishment although jurisdiction of the person of the defendant may be independently obtained. This is possible at the present time where, for example, a corporate defendant has appointed an agent within the district to accept service of process but is not carrying on activities there sufficient to subject it to jurisdiction. (*Seawind Compania, S.A v. Crescent Line, Inc.*, 320 F.2d 580 (2d Cir.1963)), or where, though the foreign corporation's activities in the district are sufficient to subject it personally to the jurisdiction, there is in the district no officer on whom process can be served (*United States v. Cia. Naviera Continental, S.A.*, 178 F.Supp. 561, (S.D.N.Y.1959)).

Process of attachment or garnishment will be limited to the district. See Rule E(3)(a).

Subdivision (2).

The former Admiralty Rules did not provide for notice to the defendant in attachment and garnishment proceedings. None is required by the principles of due process, since it is assumed that the garnishee or custodian of the property attached will either notify the defendant or be deprived of the right to plead the judgment as a defense in an action against him by the defendant. *Harris v. Balk,* 198 U.S. 215, 25 S.Ct. 625, 49 L.Ed. 1023 (1905); *Pennoyer v. Neff,* 95 U.S. (5 Otto) 714, 24 L.Ed. 565 (1878). Modern conceptions of fairness, however, dictate that actual notice be given to persons known to claim an interest in the property that is the subject of the action where that is reasonably practicable. In attachment and garnishment proceedings the persons whose interests will be affected by the judgment are identified by the complaint. No substantial burden is imposed on the plaintiff by a simple requirement that he notify the defendant of the action by mail.

In the usual case the defendant is notified of the pendency of the proceedings by the garnishee or otherwise, and appears to claim the property and to make his answer. Hence notice by mail is not routinely required in all cases, but only in those in which the defendant has not appeared prior to the time when a default judgment is demanded. The rule therefore provides only that no default judgment shall be entered except upon proof of notice, or of inability to give notice despite diligent efforts to do so. Thus the burden of giving notice is further minimized.

In some cases the plaintiff may prefer to give notice by serving process in the usual way instead of simply by mail. (Rule 4(d).) In particular, if the defendant is in a foreign country the plaintiff may wish to utilize the modes of notice recently provided to facilitate compliance with foreign laws and procedures (Rule 4(i)). The rule provides for these alternatives.

The rule does not provide for notice by publication because there is no problem concerning unknown claimants, and publication has little utility in proportion to its expense where the identity of the defendant is known.

Subdivision (3).

Subdivision (a) incorporates the substance of Admiralty Rule 36.

The Admiralty Rules were silent as to when the garnishee and the defendant were to answer. See also 2 Benedict ch. XXIV [Reference is to the 6th Edition of Benedict on Admiralty and not to the current 7th Edition].

The rule proceeds on the assumption that uniform and definite Periods of time for responsive pleadings should be substituted for return days (see the discussion under Rule C(6), below). Twenty days seems sufficient time for the garnishee to answer (cf. FRCP 12(a)), and an additional 10 days should suffice for the defendant. When allowance is made for the time required for notice to reach the defendant this gives the defendant in attachment and garnishment approximately the same time that defendants have to answer when personally served.

1985 AMENDMENT

Rule B(1) has been amended to provide for judicial scrutiny before the issuance of any attachment or garnishment process. Its purpose is to eliminate doubts as to whether the Rule is consistent with the principles of procedural due process enunciated by the Supreme Court in *Sniadach v. Family Finance Corp.*, 395 U.S. 337, 89 S.Ct. 1820, 23 L.Ed.2d 349 (1969); and later developed in *Fuentes v. Shevin*, 407 U.S. 67, 92 S.Ct. 1983, 32 L.Ed.2d 556 (1972); *Mitchell v. W.T. Grant Co.*, 416 U.S. 600, 94 S.Ct. 1895, 40 L.Ed.2d 406 (1974); and *North Georgia Finishing, Inc. v. Di–Chem, Inc.*, 419 U.S. 601, 95 S.Ct. 719, 42 L.Ed.2d 751 (1975). Such doubts were raised in *Grand Bahama Petroleum Co. v. Canadian Transportation Agencies, Ltd.*, 450 F.Supp. 447 (W.D.Wash.1978); and *Schiffahartsgesellschaft Leonhardt & Co. v. A. Bottacchi S.A. de Navegacion*, 552 F.Supp. 771 (S.D.Ga.1982), which was reversed, 732 F.2d 1543 (11th Cir.1984). *But compare Polar Shipping Ltd. v. Oriental Shipping Corp.*, 680 F.2d 627 (9th Cir.1982), in which a majority of the panel upheld the constitutionality of Rule B because of the Unique commercial context in which it is invoked. practice described in Rule B(1) has been adopted in districts by local rule. E.g., N.D. Calif. Local Rule 603.3; W.D.Wash. Local Admiralty Rule 15(d).

The rule envisions that the order will issue when the plaintiff makes a prima facie showing that he has a maritime claim against the defendant in the amount sued for and the defendant is not present in the district. A simple order with conclusory findings is contemplated. The reference to review by the "court" is broad enough to embrace review by a magistrate as well as by a district judge.

The new provision recognizes that in some situations, such as when the judge is unavailable and the ship is about to depart from the jurisdiction, it will be impracticable, if not impossible, to secure the judicial review contemplated by Rule B(1). When "exigent circumstances" exist, the rule enables the plaintiff to secure the issuance of the summons and process of attachment and garnishment, subject to a later showing that the necessary circumstances actually existed. This provision is intended to provide a safety valve without undermining the requirement of preattachment scrutiny. Thus, every effort to secure judicial review, including conducting a hearing by telephone, should be pursued before resorting to the exigent-circumstances procedure.

Rule B(1) also has been amended so that the garnishee shall be named in the "process" rather than in the "complaint." This should solve the problem presented in *Filia Compania Naviera, S.A. v. Petroship, S.A.*, 1983 A.M.C. 1 (S.D.N.Y.1982), and eliminate any need for an additional judicial review of the complaint and affidavit when a garnishee is added.

1987 AMENDMENT

The amendments are technical No substantive change is intended.

2000 AMENDMENT

Rule B(1) is amended in two ways, and style changes have been made.

The service provisions of Rule C(3) are adopted in paragraph (d), providing alternatives to service by a marshal if the property to be seized is not a vessel or tangible property on board a vessel.

The provision that allows the plaintiff to invoke state attachment and garnishment remedies is amended to reflect the 1993 amendments of Civil Rule 4. Former Civil Rule 4(e), incorporated in Rule B(1), allowed general use of state quasi-in-rem jurisdiction if the defendant was not an inhabitant of, or found within, the state. Rule 4(e) was replaced in 1993 by Rule 4(n)(2), which permits use of state law to seize a defendant's assets only if personal jurisdiction over the defendant cannot be obtained in the district where the action is brought. Little purpose would be served by incorporating Rule 4(n)(2) in Rule B, since maritime attachment and garnishment are available whenever the defendant is not found within the district, a concept that allows attachment or garnishment even in some circumstances in which personal jurisdiction also can be asserted. In order to protect against any possibility that elimination of the reference to state quasi-in-rem jurisdiction remedies might seem to defeat continued use of state security devices, paragraph (e) expressly incorporates Civil Rule 64. Because Rule 64 looks only to security, not jurisdiction, the former reference to Rule E(8) is deleted as no longer relevant.

Rule B(2)(a) is amended to reflect the 1993 redistribution of the service provisions once found in Civil Rule 4(d) and (i). These provisions are now found in many different subdivisions of Rule 4. The new reference simply incorporates Rule 4, without designating the new subdivisions, because the function of Rule B(2) is simply to describe the methods of notice that suffice to support a default judgment. Style changes also have been made.

2005 AMENDMENT

Rule B(1) is amended to incorporate the decisions in *Heidmar, Inc. v. Anomina Ravennate Di Armamento Sp.A. of Ravenna*, 132 F.3d 264, 267–268 (5th Cir.1998), and *Navieros InterAmericanos, S.A. v. M/V Vasilia Express*, 120 F.3d 304, 314–315 (1st Cir.1997). The time for determining whether a defendant is "found" in the district is set at the time of filing the verified complaint that prays for attachment and the affidavit required by Rule B(1)(b). As provided by Rule B(1)(b), the affidavit must be filed with the complaint. A defendant cannot defeat the security purpose of attachment by appointing an agent for service of process after the complaint and affidavit are filed. The complaint praying for attachment need not be the initial complaint. So long as the defendant is not found in the district, the prayer for attachment may be made in an amended complaint; the affidavit that the defendant cannot be found must be filed with the amended complaint.

Rule C. In Rem Actions: Special Provisions
1966 ADOPTION

Subdivision (1).

This rule is designed not only to preserve the proceeding in rem as it now exists in admiralty cases, but to preserve the substance of Admiralty Rules 13–18. The general reference to enforcement of any maritime lien is believed to state the existing law, and is an improvement over the enumeration in the former Admiralty Rules, which is repetitious and incomplete (e.g., there was no reference to general average). The reference to any maritime lien is intended to include liens created by state law which are enforceable in admiralty.

The main concern of Admiralty Rules 13–18 was with the question whether certain actions might be brought in rem or also, or in the alternative, in personam. Essentially, therefore, these rules deal with questions of substantive law, for in general an action in rem may be brought to enforce any maritime lien, and no action in personam may be brought when the substantive law imposes no personal liability.

These rules may be summarized as follows:

1. Cases in which the plaintiff may proceed in rem and/or in personam:

a. Suits for seamen's wages;

b. Suits by materialmen for supplies, repairs, etc.;

c. Suits for pilotage;

d. Suits for collision damages;

e. Suits founded on mere maritime hypothecation;

f. Suits for salvage.

2. Cases in which the plaintiff may proceed only in personam:

a. Suits for assault and beating.

3. Cases in which the plaintiff may proceed only in rem:

a. Suits on bottomry bonds.

The coverage is incomplete, since the rules omit mention of many cases in which the plaintiff may proceed in rem or in personam. This revision proceeds on the principle that it is preferable to make a general statement as to the availability of the remedies, leaving out conclusions on matters of substantive law. Clearly it is not necessary to enumerate the cases listed under Item 1, above, nor to try to complete the list.

The rule eliminates the provision of Admiralty Rule 15 that actions for assault and beating may be brought only in personam. A preliminary study fails to disclose any reason for the rule. It is subject to so many exceptions that it is calculated to deceive rather than to inform. A seaman may sue in rem when he has been beaten by a fellow member of the crew so vicious as to render the vessel unseaworthy, *The Rolph*, 293 Fed. 269, aff'd 299 Fed. 52 (9th Cir.1923), or where the theory of the action is that a beating by the master is a breach of the obligation under the shipping articles to treat the seaman with proper kindness, *The David Evans*, 187 Fed. 775 (C.C.A. 9, 1911); and a passenger may sue in rem on the theory that the assault is a breach of the contract of passage, *The Western States*, 159 Fed. 354 (2d Cir.1908). To say that an action for money damages may be brought only in personam seems equivalent to saying that a maritime lien shall not exist; and that, in turn, seems equivalent to announcing a rule of substantive law rather than a rule of procedure. Dropping the rule will leave it to the courts to determine whether a lien exists as a matter of substantive law.

The specific reference to bottomry bonds is omitted because, as a matter of hornbook substantive law, there is no personal liability on such bonds.

Subdivision (2).

This incorporates the substance of Admiralty Rules 21 and 22.

Subdivision (3).

Derived from Admiralty Rules 10 and 37. The provision that the warrant is to be issued by the clerk is new, but is assumed to state existing law.

There is remarkably little authority bearing on Rule 37, although the subject would seem to be an important one. The rule appears on its face to have provided for a sort of ancillary process, and this may well be the case when tangible property, such as a vessel, is arrested, and intangible property such as freight is incidentally involved. It can easily happen, however, that the only property against which the action may be brought is intangible, as where the owner of a vessel under charter has a lien on subfreights. See 2 Benedict § 299 and cases cited. (Reference is to the 6th Edition of Benedict on Admiralty and not to the current 7th Edition). In such cases it would seem that the order to the person holding the fund is equivalent to original process, taking the place of the warrant for arrest. That being so, it would also seem that (1) there should be some provision for notice, comparable to that given when tangible property is arrested, and (2) it should not be necessary, as Rule 37 provided, to petition the court for issuance of the process, but that it should issue as of course. Accordingly the substance of Rule 37 is included in the rule covering ordinary process, and notice will be required by Rule C(4). Presumably the rules omit any requirement of notice in these cases because the holder of the funds (e.g., the cargo owner) would be required on general principles (*cf. Harris v. Balk*, 198 U.S. 215, 25 S.Ct. 625, 49 L.Ed. 1023 (1905)) to notify his obligee (*e.g.*, the charterer); but in actions in rem such notice seems plainly inadequate because there may be adverse claims to the fund (*e.g.*, there may be liens against the subfreights for seamen's wages, etc.). *Compare* Admiralty Rule 9.

Subdivision (4).

This carries forward the notice provision of Admiralty Rule 10, with one modification. Notice by publication is too expensive and ineffective a formality to be routinely required. When, as usually happens, the vessel or other property is released on bond or otherwise there is no point in publishing notice; the vessel is freed from the claim of the plaintiff and no other interest in the vessel can be affected by the proceedings. If, however, the vessel is not released, general notice is required in order that all persons, including unknown claimants, may appear and be heard, and in order that the judgment in rem shall be binding on all the world.

Subdivision (5).

This incorporates the substance of Admiralty Rule 9.

There are remarkably few cases dealing directly with the rule. In *The George Prescott*, 10 Fed.Cas. 222 (No. 5,339) (E.D.N.Y.1865), the master and crew of a vessel libeled her for wages, and other lienors also filed libels. One of the lienors suggested to the court that prior to the arrest of the vessel the master had removed the sails, and asked that he be ordered to produce them. He admitted removing the sails and selling them, justifying on the ground that he held a mortgage on the vessel. He was ordered to pay the proceeds into court. *Cf. United States v. The Zarco*, 187 F.Supp. 371 (S.D.Cal.1960), where an armature belonging to a vessel subject to a preferred ship mortgage was in possession of a repairman claiming a lien.

It is evident that, though the rule has had a limited career in the reported cases, it is a potentially important one. It is also evident that the rule is framed in terms narrower than the principle that supports it. There is no apparent reason for limiting it to ships and their appurtenances (2 Benedict § 299) [Reference is to the 6th Edition of Benedict on Admiralty and not to the current 7th Edition]. Also, the reference to "third parties" in the existing rule seems unfortunate. In *The George Prescott,* the person who removed and sold the sails was a plaintiff in the action, and relief against him was just as necessary as if he had been a stranger.

Another situation in which process of this kind would seem to be useful is that in which the principal property that is the subject of the action is a vessel, but her pending freight is incidentally involved. The warrant of arrest, and notice of its service, should be all that is required by way of original process and notice; ancillary process without notice should suffice as to the incidental intangibles.

The distinction between Admiralty Rules 9 and 37 is not at once apparent but seems to be this: Where the action was against Property that could not be seized by the marshal because it was intangible, the original process was required to be similar to that issued against a garnishee, and general notice was required (though not provided for by the present rule; *cf.* Advisory Committee's Note to Rule C(3)). Under Admiralty Rule 9 property had been arrested and general notice had been given, but some of the property had been removed or for some other reason could not be arrested. Here no further notice was necessary.

The rule also makes provision for this kind of situation: The proceeding is against a vessel's pending freight only; summons has been served on the person supposedly holding the funds, and general notice has been given; it develops that another person holds all or part of the funds. Ancillary process should be available here without further notice.

Subdivision (6).

Adherence to the practice of return days seems unsatisfactory. The practice varies significantly from district to district. A uniform rule should be provided so that any claimant or defendant can readily determine when he is required to file or serve a claim or answer.

A virtue of the return-day practice is that it requires claimants to come forward and identify themselves at an early stage of the proceedings—before they could fairly be required to answer. The draft is designed to preserve this feature of the present practice by requiring early filing of the claim. The time schedule contemplated in the draft is closely comparable to the present practice in the Southern District of New York, where the claimant has a minimum of 8 days to claim and three weeks thereafter to answer.

This rule also incorporates the substance of Admiralty Rule 25. The present rule's emphasis on "the true and bona fide owner" is omitted, since anyone having the right to possession can claim (2 Benedict § 324) [Reference is to the 6th Edition of Benedict on Admiralty and not to the current 7th Edition].

1985 AMENDMENT

Rule C(3) has been amended to provide for judicial scrutiny before the issuance of any warrant of arrest. Its purpose is to eliminate any doubt as to the rule's constitutionality under the *Sniadach* line of cases. *Sniadach v. Family Finance Corp.,* 395 U.S. 337, 89 S.Ct. 1820, 23 L.Ed.2d 349 (1969); *Fuentes v. Shevin,* 407 U.S. 67, 92 S.Ct. 1983, 32 L.Ed.2d 556 (1972); *Mitchell v. W. T. Grant Co.,* 416 U.S. 600, 94 S.Ct. 1895, 40 L.Ed.2d 406 (1974); and *North Georgia Finishing, Inc. v. Di–Chem, Inc.,* 419 U.S. 601, 95 S.Ct. 719, 42 L.Ed.2d 751 (1975). This was thought desirable even though both the Fourth and the Fifth Circuits have upheld the existing rule. *Amstar Corp. v. S/S Alexandros T.,* 664 F.2d 904 (4th Cir.1981); *Merchants National Bank of Mobile v. The Dredge General G.L. Gillespie,* 663 F.2d 1338 (5th Cir.1981), *cert. dismissed,* 456 U.S. 966, 102 S.Ct. 2263, 72 L.Ed.2d 865 (1982). A contrary view was taken by Judge Tate in the *Merchants National Bank* case and by the district court in *Alyeska Pipeline Service Co. v. The Vessel Bay Ridge,* 509 F.Supp. 1115 (D.Alaska 1981), *appeal dismissed,* 703 F.2d 381 (9th Cir.1983).

The rule envisions that the order will issue upon a prima facie showing that the plaintiff has an action in rem against the defendant in the amount sued for and that the property is within the district. A simple order with conclusory findings is contemplated. The reference to review by the "court" is broad enough to embrace a magistrate as well as a district judge.

The new provision recognizes that in some situations, such as when a judge is unavailable and the vessel is about to depart from the jurisdiction, it will be impracticable, if not impossible, to secure the judicial review contemplated by Rule C(3). When "exigent circumstances" exist, the rule enables the plaintiff to secure the issuance of the summons and warrant of arrest, subject to a later showing that the necessary circumstances actually existed. This provision is intended to provide a safety valve without undermining the requirement of pre-arrest scrutiny. Thus, every effort to secure judicial review, including conducting a hearing by telephone, should be pursued before invoking the exigent-circumstances procedure.

The foregoing requirements for prior court review or proof of exigent circumstances do not apply to actions by the United States for forfeitures for federal statutory violations. In such actions a prompt hearing is not constitutionally required, *United States v. Eight Thousand Eight Hundred and Fifty Dollars,* 461 U.S. 555, 103 S.Ct. 2005, 76 L.Ed.2d 143 (1983); *Calero-Toledo v. Pearson Yacht Leasing Co.,* 416 U.S. 663, 94 S.Ct. 2080, 40 L.Ed.2d 452 (1974), and could prejudice the government in its prosecution of the claimants as defendants in parallel criminal proceedings since the forfeiture hearing could be misused by the defendants to obtain by way of civil discovery information to which they would not otherwise be entitled and subject the government and the courts to the unnecessary burden and expense of two hearings rather than one.

1987 AMENDMENT

The amendments are technical. No substantive change is intended.

1991 AMENDMENT

These amendments are designed to conform the rule to Fed.R.Civ.P. 4, as amended. As with recent amendments to Rule 4, it is intended to relieve the Marshals Service of the burden of using its limited personnel and facilities for execution of process in routine circumstances. Doing so may involve a contractual arrangement with a person or organization retained by the government to perform these services, or the use of other government officers and employees, or the special appointment by the court of persons available to perform suitably.

The seizure of a vessel, with or without cargo, remains a task assigned to the Marshal. Successful arrest of a vessel frequently requires the enforcement presence of an armed government official and the cooperation of the United States Coast Guard and other governmental authorities. If the marshal is called upon to seize the vessel, it is expected that the same officer will also be responsible for the seizure of any property on board the vessel at the time of seizure that is to be the object of arrest or attachment.

2000 AMENDMENT

Style changes have been made throughout the revised portions of Rule C. Several changes of meaning have been made as well.

Subdivision 2. In rem jurisdiction originally extended only to property within the judicial district. Since 1986, Congress has enacted a number of jurisdictional and venue statutes for forfeiture and criminal matters that in some circumstances permit a court to exercise authority over property outside the district. 28 U.S.C. § 1355(b)(1) allows a forfeiture action in the district where an act or omission giving rise to forfeiture occurred, or in any other district where venue is established by § 1395 or by any other statute. Section 1355(b)(2) allows an action to be brought as provided in (b)(1) or in the United States District Court for the District of Columbia when the forfeiture property is located in a foreign country or has been seized by authority of a foreign government. Section 1355(d) allows a court with jurisdiction under § 1355(b) to cause service in any other district of process required to bring the forfeiture property before the court. Section 1395 establishes venue of a civil proceeding for forfeiture in the district where the forfeiture accrues or the defendant is found; in any district where the property is found; in any district in which the property is brought, if the property initially is outside any judicial district; or in any district where the vessel is arrested if the proceeding is an admiralty proceeding to forfeit a vessel. Section 1395(e) deals with a vessel or cargo entering a port of entry closed by the President, and transportation to or from a state or section declared to be in insurrection. 18 U.S.C. § 981(h) creates expanded jurisdiction and venue over property located elsewhere that is related to a criminal prosecution pending in the district. These amendments, and related amendments of Rule E(3), bring these Rules into step with the new statutes. No change is made as to admiralty and maritime proceedings that do not involve a forfeiture governed by one of the new statutes.

Subdivision (2) has been separated into lettered paragraphs to facilitate understanding.

Subdivision (3). Subdivision (3) has been rearranged and divided into lettered paragraphs to facilitate understanding.

Paragraph (b)(i) is amended to make it clear that any supplemental process addressed to a vessel or tangible property on board a vessel, as well as the original warrant, is to be served by the marshal.

Subdivision (4). Subdivision (4) has required that public notice state the time for filing an answer, but has not required that the notice set out the earlier time for filing a statement of interest or claim. The amendment requires that both times be stated.

A new provision is added, allowing termination of publication if the property is released more than 10 days after execution but before publication is completed. Termination will save money, and also will reduce the risk of confusion as to the status of the property.

Subdivision (6). Subdivision (6) has applied a single set of undifferentiated provisions to civil forfeiture proceedings and to in rem admiralty proceedings. Because some differences in procedure are desirable, these proceedings are separated by adopting a new paragraph (a) for civil forfeiture proceedings and recasting the present rule as paragraph (b) for in rem admiralty proceedings. The provision for interrogatories and answers is carried forward as paragraph (c). Although this established procedure for serving interrogatories with the complaint departs from the general provisions of Civil Rule 26(d), the special needs of expedition that often arise in admiralty justify continuing the practice.

Both paragraphs (a) and (b) require a statement of interest or right rather than the "claim" formerly required. The new wording permits parallel drafting, and facilitates cross-references in other rules. The substantive nature of the statement remains the same as the former claim. The requirements of (a) and (b) are, however, different in some respects.

In a forfeiture proceeding governed by paragraph (a), a statement must be filed by a person who asserts an interest in or a right against the property involved. This category includes every right against the property, such as a lien, whether or not it establishes ownership or a right to possession. In determining who has an interest in or a right against property, courts may continue to rely on precedents that have developed the meaning of "claims" or "claimants" for the purpose of civil forfeiture proceedings.

In an admiralty and maritime proceeding governed by paragraph (b), a statement is filed only by a person claiming a right of possession or ownership. Other claims against the property are advanced by intervention under Civil Rule 24, as it may be supplemented by local admiralty rules. The reference to ownership includes every interest that qualifies as ownership under domestic or foreign law. If an ownership interest is asserted, it makes no difference whether its character is legal, equitable, or something else.

Paragraph (a) provides more time than paragraph (b) for filing a statement. Admiralty and maritime in rem proceedings often present special needs for prompt action that do not commonly arise in forfeiture proceedings .

Paragraphs (a) and (b) do not limit the right to make a restricted appearance under Rule E(8).

2002 AMENDMENT

Rule C(3) is amended to reflect the provisions of 18 U.S.C. § 985, enacted by the Civil Asset Forfeiture Reform Act of 2000, 114 Stat. 202, 214–215. Section 985 provides, subject to enumerated exceptions, that real property that is the subject of a civil forfeiture action is not to be seized until an order of forfeiture is entered. A civil forfeiture action is initiated by filing a complaint, posting notice, and serving notice on the property owner. The summons and arrest procedure is no longer appropriate.

Rule C(6)(a)(i)(A) is amended to adopt the provision enacted by 18 U.S.C. § 983(a)(4)(A), shortly before Rule C(6)(a)(i)(A) took effect, that sets the time for filing a verified statement as 30 days rather than 20 days, and that sets the first alternative event for measuring the 30 days as the date of service of the Government's complaint.

Rule C(6)(a)(iii) is amended to give notice of the provision enacted by 18 U.S.C. § 983(a)(4)(B) that requires that the answer in a forfeiture proceeding be filed within 20 days. Without this notice, unwary litigants might rely on the provision of Rule 5(d) that allows a reasonable time for filing after service.

Rule C(6)(b)(iv) is amended to change the requirement that an answer be filed within 20 days to a requirement that it be served within 20 days. Service is the ordinary requirement, as in Rule 12(a). Rule 5(d) requires filing within a reasonable time after service.

2005 AMENDMENT

Rule C(6)(b)(i)(A) is amended to delete the reference to a time 10 days after completed publication under Rule C(4). This change corrects an oversight in the amendments made in 2000. Rule C(4) requires publication of notice only if the property that is the subject of the action is not released within 10 days after execution of process. Execution of process will always be earlier than publication.

2006 AMENDMENT

Rule C is amended to reflect the adoption of Rule G to govern procedure in civil forfeiture actions.

Rule D.   Possessory, Petitory, and Partition Actions
1966 ADOPTION

This carries forward the substance of Admiralty Rule 19.

Rule 19 provided the remedy of arrest in controversies involving title and possession in general. See *The Tilton*, 23 Fed.Cas.1277 (No. 14,054) (C.C.D.Mass.1830). In addition it provided that remedy in controversies between co-owners respecting the employment of a vessel. It did not deal comprehensively with controversies between co-owners, omitting the remedy of partition. Presumably the omission is traceable to the fact that, when the rules were originally promulgated, concepts of substantive law (sometimes stated as concepts of jurisdiction) denied the remedy of partition except where the parties in disagreement were the owners of equal shares. *See The Steamboat Orleans,* 36 U.S. (11 Pet.) 175, 9 L.Ed. 677 (1837). The Supreme Court has now removed any doubt as to the jurisdiction of the district courts to partition a vessel, and has held in addition that no fixed principle of federal admiralty law limits the remedy to the case of equal shares. *Madruga v. Superior Court*, 346 U.S. 556, 74 S.Ct. 298, 98 L.Ed. 290 (1954). It is therefore appropriate to include a reference to partition in the rule.

Rule E.   Actions in Rem and Quasi in Rem: General Provisions
1966 ADOPTION

Subdivisions (1), (2).

Adapted from Admiralty Rule 24. The rule is based on the assumption that there is no more need for security for costs in maritime personal actions than in civil cases generally, but that there is reason to retain the requirement for actions in which property is seized. As to proceedings for limitation of liability see Rule F(1).

Subdivision (3).

The Advisory Committee has concluded for practical reasons that process requiring seizure of property should continue to be served only within the geographical limits of the district. Compare Rule B(1), continuing the condition that process of attachment and garnishment may be served only if the defendant is not found within the district.

The provisions of Admiralty Rule 1 concerning the persons by whom process is to be served will be superseded by FRCP 4(c).

Subdivision (4).

This rule is intended to preserve the provisions of Admiralty Rules 10 and 36 relating to execution of process, custody of property seized by the marshal, and the marshal's return. It is also designed to make express provision for matters not heretofore covered.

The provision relating to clearance in subdivision (b) is suggested by Admiralty Rule 44 of the District of Maryland.

Subdivision (d) is suggested by English Rule 12, Order 75.

28 U.S.C., § 1921 as amended in 1962 contains detailed provisions relating to the expenses of seizing and preserving property attached or arrested.

Subdivision (5).

In addition to Admiralty Rule 11 (see Rule E(9)), the release of property seized on process of attachment or in rem was dealt with by Admiralty Rules 5, 6, 12, and 57, and 28

U.S.C., § 2464 (formerly Rev.Stat. § 941). The rule consolidates these provisions and makes them uniformly applicable to attachment and garnishment and actions in rem.

The rule restates the substance of Admiralty Rule 5. Admiralty Rule 12 dealt only with ships arrested on in rem process. Since the same ground appears to be covered more generally by 28 U.S.C., § 2464, the subject matter of Rule 12 is omitted. The substance of Admiralty Rule 57 is retained. 28 U.S.C., § 2464 is incorporated with changes of terminology, and with a substantial change as to the amount of the bond. See 2 Benedict 395 n. 1a [Reference is to the 6th Edition of Benedict on Admiralty and not to the current 7th Edition.] *The Lotosland*, 2 F.Supp. 42 (S.D.N.Y.1933). The provision for general bond is enlarged to include the contingency of attachment as well as arrest of the vessel.

Subdivision (6).

Adapted from Admiralty Rule 8.

Subdivision (7).

Derived from Admiralty Rule 50.

Title 46, U.S.C. § 783 extends the principle of Rule 50 to the Government when sued under the Public Vessels Act, presumably on the theory that the credit of the Government is the equivalent of the best security. The rule adopts this principle and extends it to all cases in which the Government is defendant although the Suits in Admiralty Act contains no parallel provisions.

Subdivision (8).

Under the liberal joinder provisions of unified rules the plaintiff will be enabled to join with maritime actions in rem, or maritime actions in personam with process of attachment and garnishment, claims with respect to which such process is not available, including nonmaritime claims. Unification should not, however, have the result that, in order to defend against an admiralty and maritime claim with respect to which process in rem or quasi in rem has been served, the claimant or defendant must subject himself personally to the jurisdiction of the court with reference to other claims with respect to which such process is not available or has not been served, especially when such other claims are nonmaritime. So far as attachment and garnishment are concerned this principle holds true whether process is issued according to admiralty tradition and the Supplemental Rules or according to Rule 4(e) as incorporated by Rule B(1).

A similar problem may arise with respect to civil actions other than admiralty and maritime claims within the meaning of Rule 9(h). That is to say, in an ordinary civil action, whether maritime or not, there may be joined in one action claims with respect to which process of attachment and garnishment is available under state law and Rule 4(e) and claims with respect to which such process is not available or has not been served. The general Rules of Civil Procedure do not specify whether an appearance in such cases to defend the claim with respect to which process of attachment and garnishment has issued is an appearance for the purposes of the other claims. In that context the question has been considered best left to case-by-case development. Where admiralty and maritime claims within the meaning of Rule 9(h) are concerned, however, it seems important to include a specific provision to avoid an unfortunate and unintended effect of unification. No inferences whatever as to the effect of such an appearance in an ordinary civil action should be drawn from the specific provision here and the absence of such a provision in the general Rules.

Subdivision (9).

Adapted from Admiralty Rules 11, 12, and 40. Subdivision (a) is necessary because of various provisions as to disposition of property in forfeiture proceedings. In addition to particular statutes, note the provisions of 28 U.S.C., §§ 2461–65.

The provision of Admiralty Rule 12 relating to unreasonable delay was limited to ships but should have broader application. See 2 Benedict 404 [Reference is to the 6th Edition of Benedict on Admiralty and not to the current 7th Edition]. Similarly, both Rules 11 and 12 were limited to actions, in rem, but should equally apply to attached property.

1985 AMENDMENT

Rule E(4)(f) makes available the type of prompt post-seizure hearing in proceedings under Supplemental Rules B and C that the Supreme Court has called for in a number of cases arising in other contexts. See *North Georgia Finishing, Inc. v. Di–Chem, Inc.*, 419 U.S. 601, 95 S.Ct. 719, 42 L.Ed.2d 751 (1975); *Mitchell v. W.T. Grant Co.*, 416 U.S. 600, 94 S.Ct. 1895, 40 L.Ed.2d 406 (1974). Although post-attachment and post-arrest hearings always have been available on motion, an explicit statement emphasizing promptness and elaborating the procedure has been lacking in the Supplemental Rules. Rule E(4)(f) is designed to satisfy the constitutional requirement of due process by guaranteeing to the shipowner a prompt post-seizure hearing at which he can attack the complaint, the arrest, the security demanded, or any other alleged deficiency in the proceedings. The amendment also is intended to eliminate the previously disparate treatment under local rules of defendants whose property has been seized pursuant to Supplemental Rules B and C.

The new Rule E(4)(f) is based on a proposal by the Maritime Law Association of the United States and on local admiralty rules in the Eastern, Northern, and Southern Districts of New York. E.D.N.Y. Local Rule 13; N.D.N.Y. Local Rule 13; S.D.N.Y. Local Rule 12. Similar provisions have been adopted by other maritime districts. E.g., N.D.Calif. Local Rule 603.4; W.D.La. Local Admiralty Rule 21. Rule E(4)(f) will provide uniformity in practice and reduce constitutional uncertainties.

Rule E(4)(f) is triggered by the defendant or any other person with an interest in the property seized. Upon an oral or written application similar to that used in seeking a temporary restraining order, see Rule 65(b), the court is required to hold a hearing as promptly as possible to determine whether to allow the arrest or attachment to stand. The plaintiff has the burden of showing why the seizure should not be vacated. The hearing also may determine the amount of security to be granted or the propriety of imposing counter-security to protect the defendant from an improper seizure.

The foregoing requirements for prior court review or proof of exigent circumstances do not apply to actions by the United States for forfeitures for federal statutory violations. In such actions a prompt hearing is not constitutionally required, *United States v. Eight Thousand Eight Hundred and Fifty Dollars*, 461 U.S. 555, 103 S.Ct. 2005, 76 L.Ed.2d 143 (1983); *Calero–Toledo v. Pearson Yacht Leasing Co.*, 416 U.S. 663, 94 S.Ct. 2080, 40 L.Ed.2d 452 (1974), and could prejudice the government in its prosecution of the claimants as defendants in parallel criminal proceedings since the forfeiture hearing could be misused by the defendants to obtain by way of civil discovery information to which they would not otherwise be entitled and subject the government and the courts to the unnecessary burden and expense of two hearings rather than one.

1987 AMENDMENT

The amendments are technical. No substantive change is intended.

1991 AMENDMENT

These amendments are designed to conform this rule to Fed.R.Civ.P. 4, as amended. They are intended to relieve the Marshals Service of the burden of using its limited personnel and facilities for execution of process in routine circumstances. Doing so may involve a contractual arrangement with a person or organization retained by the government to perform these services, or the use of other government officers and employees, or the special appointment by the court of persons available to perform suitably.

2000 AMENDMENT

Style changes have been made throughout the revised portions of Rule E. Several changes of meaning have been made as well.

Subdivision (3). Subdivision (3) is amended to reflect the distinction drawn in Rule C(2)(c) and (d). Service in an admiralty or maritime proceeding still must be made within the district, as reflected in Rule C(2)(c), while service in forfeiture proceedings may be made outside the district when authorized by statute, as reflected in Rule C(2)(d).

Subdivision (7). Subdivision (7)(a) is amended to make it clear that a plaintiff need give security to meet a counterclaim only when the counterclaim is asserted by a person who has given security to respond in damages in the original action.

Subdivision (8). Subdivision (8) is amended to reflect the change in Rule B(1)(e) that deletes the former provision incorporating state quasi-in-rem jurisdiction. A restricted appearance is not appropriate when state law is invoked only for security under Civil Rule 64, not as a basis of quasi-in-rem jurisdiction. But if state law allows a special, limited, or restricted appearance as an incident of the remedy adopted from state law, the state practice applies through Rule 64 "in the manner provided by" state law.

Subdivision (9). Subdivision 9(b)(ii) is amended to reflect the change in Rule C(6) that substitutes a statement of interest or right for a claim.

Subdivision (10). Subdivision 10 is new. It makes clear the authority of the court to preserve and to prevent removal of attached or arrested property that remains in the possession of the owner or other person under Rule E(4)(b).

Rule E is amended to reflect the adoption of Rule G to govern procedure in civil forfeiture actions.

Rule F.   Limitation of Liability
1966 ADOPTION

Subdivision (1).

The amendments of 1936 to the Limitation Act superseded to some extent the provisions of Admiralty Rule 51, especially with respect to the time of filing the complaint and with respect to security. The rule here incorporates in substance the 1936 amendment of the Act (46 U.S.C., § 185) with a slight modification to make it clear that the complaint may be filed at any time not later than six months after a claim has been lodged with the owner.

Subdivision (2).

Derived from Admiralty Rules 51 and 53.

Subdivision (3).

This is derived from the last sentence of 46 U.S.C. § 185 and the last paragraph of Admiralty Rule 51.

Subdivision (4).

Derived from Admiralty Rule 51.

Subdivision (5).

Derived from Admiralty Rules 52 and 53.

Subdivision (6).

Derived from Admiralty Rule 52.

Subdivision (7).

Derived from Admiralty Rule 52 and 46 U.S.C., § 185.

Subdivision (8).

Derived from Admiralty Rule 52.

Subdivision (9).

Derived from Admiralty Rule 54. The provision for transfer is revised to conform closely to the language of 28 U.S.C. §§ 1404(a) and 1406(a), though it retains the existing rule's provision for transfer to any district for convenience. The revision also makes clear what has been doubted: that the court may transfer if venue is wrongly laid.

1987 AMENDMENT

The amendments are technical. No substantive change is intended.

Rule G.   Forfeiture Actions In Rem
2006 ADOPTION

Rule G is added to bring together the central procedures that govern civil forfeiture actions. Civil forfeiture actions are in rem proceedings, as are many admiralty proceedings. As the number of civil forfeiture actions has increased, however, reasons have appeared to create sharper distinctions within the framework of the Supplemental Rules. Civil forfeiture practice will benefit from distinctive provisions that express and focus developments in statutory, constitutional, and decisional law. Admiralty practice will be freed from the pressures that arise when the needs of civil forfeiture proceedings counsel interpretations of common rules that may not be suitable for admiralty proceedings.

Rule G generally applies to actions governed by the Civil Asset Forfeiture Reform Act of 2000 (CAFRA) and also to actions excluded from it. The rule refers to some specific CAFRA provisions; if these statutes are amended, the rule should be adapted to the new provisions during the period required to amend the rule. Rule G is not completely self-contained. Subdivision (1) recognizes the need to rely at times on other Supplemental Rules and the place of the Supplemental Rules within the basic framework of the Civil Rules.

Supplemental Rules A, C, and E are amended to reflect the adoption of Rule G.

Subdivision (1). Rule G is designed to include the distinctive procedures that govern a civil forfeiture action. Some details, however, are better supplied by relying on Rules C and E. Subdivision (1) incorporates those rules for issues not addressed by Rule G. This general incorporation is at times made explicit—subdivision (7)(b)(v), for example, invokes the security provisions of Rule E. But Rules C and E are not to be invoked to create conflicts with Rule G. They are to be used only when Rule G, fairly construed, does not address the issue.

The Civil Rules continue to provide the procedural framework within which Rule G and the other Supplemental Rules operate. Both Rule G(1) and Rule A state this basic proposition. Rule G, for example, does not address pleadings amendments. Civil Rule 15 applies, in light of the circumstances of a forfeiture action.

Subdivision (2). Rule E(2)(a) requires that the complaint in an admiralty action "state the circumstances from which the claim arises with such particularity that the defendant or claimant will be able, without moving for a more definite statement, to commence an investigation of the facts and to frame a responsive pleading." Application of this standard to civil forfeiture actions has evolved to the standard stated in subdivision (2)(f). The complaint must state sufficiently detailed facts to support a reasonable belief that the government will be able to meet its burden of proof at trial. *See U.S. v. Mondragon*, 313 F.3d 862 (4th Cir. 2002). Subdivision (2)(f) carries this forfeiture case law forward without change.

Subdivision (3). Subdivision (3) governs in rem process in a civil forfeiture action.

Paragraph (a). Paragraph (a) reflects the provisions of 18 U.S.C. § 985.

Paragraph (b). Paragraph (b) addresses arrest warrants when the defendant is not real property. Subparagraph (i) directs the clerk to issue a warrant if the property is in the government's possession, custody, or control. If the property is not in the government's possession, custody, or control and is not subject to a restraining order, subparagraph (ii) provides that a warrant issues only if the court finds probable cause to arrest the property. This provision departs from former Rule C(3)(a)(i), which authorized issuance of summons and warrant by the clerk without a probable-cause finding. The probable-cause finding better protects the interests of persons interested in the property. Subparagraph (iii) recognizes that a warrant is not necessary if the property is subject to a judicial restraining order. The government remains free, however, to seek a warrant if it anticipates that the restraining order may be modified or vacated.

Paragraph (c). Subparagraph (ii) requires that the warrant and any supplemental process be served as soon as practicable unless the property is already in the government's possession, custody, or control. But it authorizes the court to order a different time. The authority to order a different time recognizes that the government may have secured orders sealing the complaint in a civil forfeiture action or have won a stay after filing. The seal or stay may be ordered for reasons, such as protection of an ongoing criminal investigation, that would be defeated by prompt service of the warrant. Subparagraph (ii) does not reflect any independent ground for ordering a seal or stay, but merely reflects the consequences for execution when sealing or a stay is ordered. A court also may order a different time for service if good cause is shown for reasons unrelated to a seal or stay. Subparagraph (iv) reflects the uncertainty surrounding service of an arrest warrant on property not in the United States. It is not possible to identify in the rule the appropriate authority for serving process in all other countries. Transmission of the warrant to an appropriate authority, moreover, does not ensure that the warrant will be executed. The rule requires only that the warrant be transmitted to an appropriate authority.

Subdivision (4). Paragraph (a). Paragraph (a) reflects the traditional practice of publishing notice of an in rem action.

Subparagraph (i) recognizes two exceptions to the general publication requirement. Publication is not required if the defendant property is worth less than $1,000 and direct notice is sent to all reasonably identifiable potential claimants as required by subdivision (4)(b). Publication also is not required if the cost would exceed the property's value and the court finds that other means of notice would satisfy due process. Publication on a government-established internet forfeiture site, as contemplated by subparagraph (iv), would be at a low marginal publication cost, which would likely be the cost to compare to the property value.

Subparagraph (iv) states the basic criterion for selecting the means and method of publication. The purpose is to adopt a means reasonably calculated to reach potential claimants. The government should choose from among these means a method that is reasonably likely to reach potential claimants at a cost reasonable in the circumstances.

If the property is in the United States and newspaper notice is chosen, publication may be where the action is filed, where the property was seized, or—if the property was not seized—where the property is located. Choice among these places is influenced by the probable location of potential claimants.

If the property is not in the United States, account must be taken of the sensitivities that surround publication of legal notices in other countries. A foreign country may forbid local publication. If potential claimants are likely to be in the United States, publication in the district where the action is filed may be the best choice. If potential claimants are likely to be located abroad, the better choice may be publication by means generally circulated in the country where the property is located.

Newspaper publication is not a particularly effective means of notice for most potential claimants. Its traditional use is best defended by want of affordable alternatives. Paragraph (iv)(C) contemplates a government-created internet forfeiture site that would provide a single easily identified means of notice. Such a site could allow much more direct access to notice as to any specific property than publication provides.

Paragraph (b). Paragraph (b) is entirely new. For the first time, Rule G expressly recognizes the due process obligation to send notice to any person who reasonably appears to be a potential claimant.

Subparagraph (i) states the obligation to send notice. Many potential claimants will be known to the government because they have filed claims during the administrative forfeiture stage. Notice must be sent, however, no matter what source of information makes it reasonably appear that a person is a potential claimant. The duty to send notice terminates when the time for filing a claim expires.

Notice of the action does not require formal service of summons in the manner required by Rule 4 to initiate a personal action. The process that begins an in rem forfeiture action is addressed by subdivision (3). This process commonly gives notice to potential claimants. Publication of notice is required in addition to this process. Due process requirements have moved beyond these traditional means of notice, but are satisfied by practical means that are reasonably calculated to accomplish actual notice.

Subparagraph (ii)(B) directs that the notice state a deadline for filing a claim that is at least 35 days after the notice is sent. This provision applies both in actions that fall within 18 U.S.C. § 983(a)(4)(A) and in other actions. Section 983(a)(4)(A) states that a claim should be filed no later than 30 days after service of the complaint. The variation introduced by subparagraph (ii)(B) reflects the procedure of § 983(a)(2)(B) for nonjudicial forfeiture proceedings. The nonjudicial procedure requires that a claim be filed "not later than the deadline set forth in a personal notice letter (which may be not earlier than 35 days after the date the letter is sent) * * *." This procedure is as suitable in a civil forfeiture action as in a nonjudicial forfeiture proceeding. Thirty-five days after notice is sent ordinarily will extend the claim time by no more than a brief period; a claimant anxious to expedite proceedings can file the claim before the deadline; and the government has flexibility to set a still longer period when circumstances make that desirable.

Subparagraph (iii) begins by stating the basic requirement that notice must be sent by means reasonably calculated to reach the potential claimant. No attempt is made to list the various means that may be reasonable in different circumstances. It may be reasonable, for example, to rely on means that have already been established for communication with a particular potential claimant. The government's interest in choosing a means likely to accomplish actual notice is bolstered by its desire to avoid post-forfeiture challenges based on arguments that a different method would have been more likely to accomplish actual notice. Flexible rule language accommodates the rapid evolution of communications technology.

Notice may be directed to a potential claimant through counsel, but only to counsel already representing the claimant with respect to the seizure of the property, or in a related investigation, administrative forfeiture proceeding, or criminal case.

Subparagraph (iii)(C) reflects the basic proposition that notice to a potential claimant who is incarcerated must be sent to the place of incarceration. Notice directed to some other place, such as a pre-incarceration residence, is less likely to reach the potential claimant. This provision does not address due process questions that may arise if a particular prison has deficient procedures for delivering notice to prisoners. See Dusenbery v. U.S., 534 U.S. 161 (2002).

Items (D) and (E) of subparagraph (iii) authorize the government to rely on an address given by a person who is not incarcerated. The address may have been given to the agency that arrested or released the person, or to the agency that seized the property. The government is not obliged to undertake an independent investigation to verify the address.

Subparagraph (iv) identifies the date on which notice is considered to be sent for some common means, without addressing the circumstances for choosing among the identified means or other means. The date of sending should be determined by analogy for means not listed. Facsimile transmission, for example, is sent upon transmission. Notice by personal delivery is sent on delivery.

Subparagraph (v), finally, reflects the purpose to effect actual notice by providing that a potential claimant who had actual notice of a forfeiture proceeding cannot oppose or seek relief from forfeiture because the government failed to comply with subdivision (4)(b).

Subdivision (5). Paragraph (a). Paragraph (a) establishes that the first step of contesting a civil forfeiture action is to file a claim. A claim is required by 18 U.S.C. § 983(a)(4)(A) for actions covered by § 983. Paragraph (a) applies this procedure as well to actions not covered by § 983. "Claim" is used to describe this first pleading because of the statutory references to claim and claimant. It functions in the same way as the statement of interest prescribed for an admiralty proceeding by Rule C(6), and is not related to the distinctive meaning of "claim" in admiralty practice.

If the claimant states its interest in the property to be as bailee, the bailor must be identified. A bailee who files a claim on behalf of a bailor must state the bailee's authority to do so.

The claim must be signed under penalty of perjury by the person making it. An artificial body that can act only through an agent may authorize an agent to sign for it. Excusable inability of counsel to obtain an appropriate signature may be grounds for an extension of time to file the claim.

Paragraph (a)(ii) sets the time for filing a claim. Item (C) applies in the relatively rare circumstance in which notice is not published and the government did not send direct notice to the claimant because it did not know of the claimant or did not have an address for the claimant.

Paragraph (b). Under 18 U.S.C. § 983(a)(4)(B), which governs many forfeiture proceedings, a person who asserts an interest by filing a claim "shall file an answer to the Government's complaint for forfeiture not later than 20 days after the date of the filing of the claim." Paragraph (b) recognizes that this statute works within the general procedures established by Civil Rule 12. Rule 12(a)(4) suspends the time to answer when a Rule 12 motion is served within the time allowed to answer. Continued application of this rule to proceedings governed by § 983(a)(4)(B) serves all of the purposes advanced by Rule 12(a)(4), *see U. S. v. $8,221,877.16, 330 F.3d 141 (3d Cir.2003)*; permits a uniform procedure for all civil forfeiture actions; and recognizes that a motion under Rule 12 can be made only after a claim is filed that provides background for the motion.

Failure to present an objection to in rem jurisdiction or to venue by timely motion or answer waives the objection. Waiver of such objections is familiar. An answer may be amended to assert an objection initially omitted. But Civil Rule 15 should be applied to an amendment that for the first time raises an objection to in rem jurisdiction by analogy to the personal jurisdiction objection provision in Civil Rule 12(h)(1)(B). The amendment should be permitted only if it is permitted as a matter of course under Rule 15(a).

A claimant's motion to dismiss the action is further governed by subdivisions (6)(c), (8)(b), and (8)(c).

Subdivision (6). Subdivision (6) illustrates the adaptation of an admiralty procedure to the different needs of civil forfeiture. Rule C(6) permits interrogatories to be served with the complaint in an in rem action without limiting the subjects of inquiry. Civil forfeiture practice does not require such an extensive departure from ordinary civil practice. It remains useful, however, to permit the government to file limited interrogatories at any time after a claim is filed to gather information that bears on the claimant's standing. Subdivisions (8)(b) and (c) allow a claimant to move to dismiss only if the claimant has standing, and recognize the government's right to move to dismiss a claim for lack of standing. Subdivision (6) interrogatories are integrated with these provisions in that the interrogatories are limited to the claimant's identity and relationship to the defendant property. If the claimant asserts a relationship to the property as bailee, the interrogatories can inquire into the bailor's interest in the property and the bailee's relationship to the bailor. The claimant can accelerate the time to serve subdivision (6) interrogatories by serving a motion to dismiss—the interrogatories must be served within 20 days after the motion is served. Integration is further accomplished by deferring the government's obligation to respond to a motion to dismiss until 20 days after the claimant moving to dismiss has answered the interrogatories.

Special interrogatories served under Rule G(6) do not count against the presumptive 25–interrogatory limit established by Rule 33(a). Rule 33 procedure otherwise applies to these interrogatories.

Subdivision (6) supersedes the discovery "moratorium" of Rule 26(d) and the broader interrogatories permitted for admiralty proceedings by Rule C(6).

Subdivision (7). Paragraph (a). Paragraph (a) is adapted from Rule E(9)(b). It provides for preservation orders when the government does not have actual possession of the defendant property. It also goes beyond Rule E(9) by recognizing the need to prevent use of the defendant property in ongoing criminal offenses.

Paragraph (b). Paragraph (b)(i)(C) recognizes the authority, already exercised in some cases, to order sale of property subject to a defaulted mortgage or to defaulted taxes. The authority is narrowly confined to mortgages and tax liens; other lien interests may be addressed, if at all, only through the general good-cause provision. The court must carefully weigh the competing interests in each case.

Paragraph (b)(i)(D) establishes authority to order sale for good cause. Good cause may be shown when the property is subject to diminution in value. Care should be taken before ordering sale to avoid diminished value.

Paragraph (b)(iii) recognizes that if the court approves, the interests of all parties may be served by their agreement to sale, aspects of the sale, or sale procedures that depart from governing statutory procedures.

Paragraph (c) draws from Rule E(9)(a), (b), and (c). Disposition of the proceeds as provided by law may require resolution of disputed issues. A mortgagee's claim to the property or sale proceeds, for example, may be disputed on the ground that the mortgage is not genuine. An undisputed lien claim, on the other hand, may be recognized by payment after an interlocutory sale.

Subdivision (8). Subdivision (8) addresses a number of issues that are unique to civil forfeiture actions.

Paragraph (a). Standing to suppress use of seized property as evidence is governed by principles distinct from the principles that govern claim standing. A claimant with standing to contest forfeiture may not have standing to seek suppression. Rule G does not of itself create a basis of suppression standing that does not otherwise exist.

Paragraph (b). Paragraph (b)(i) is one element of the system that integrates the procedures for determining a claimant's standing to claim and for deciding a claimant's motion to dismiss the action. Under paragraph (c)(ii), a motion to dismiss the action cannot be addressed until the court has decided any government motion to strike the claim or answer. This procedure is reflected in the (b)(i) reminder that a motion to dismiss the forfeiture action may be made only by a claimant who establishes claim standing. The government, moreover, need not respond to a claimant's motion to dismiss until 20 days after the claimant has answered any subdivision (6) interrogatories.

Paragraph (b)(ii) mirrors 18 U.S.C. § 983(a)(3)(D). It applies only to an action independently governed by § 983(a)(3)(D), implying nothing as to actions outside § 983(a)(3)(D). The adequacy of the complaint is measured against the pleading requirements of subdivision (2), not against the quality of the evidence available to the government when the complaint was filed.

Paragraph (c). As noted with paragraph (b), paragraph (c) governs the procedure for determining whether a claimant has standing. It does not address the principles that govern claim standing.

Paragraph (c)(i)(A) provides that the government may move to strike a claim or answer for failure to comply with the pleading requirements of subdivision (5) or to answer subdivision (6) interrogatories. As with other pleadings, the court should strike a claim or answer only if satisfied that an opportunity should not be afforded to cure the defects under Rule 15. Not every failure to respond to subdivision (6) interrogatories warrants an order striking the claim. But the special role that subdivision (6) plays in the scheme for determining claim standing may justify a somewhat more demanding approach than the general approach to discovery sanctions under Rule 37.

Paragraph (c)(ii) directs that a motion to strike a claim or answer be decided before any motion by the claimant to dismiss the action. A claimant who lacks standing is not entitled to challenge the forfeiture on the merits.

Paragraph (c)(ii) further identifies three procedures for addressing claim standing. If a claim fails on its face to show facts that support claim standing, the claim can be dismissed by judgment on the pleadings. If the claim shows facts that would support claim standing, those facts can be tested by a motion for summary judgment. If material facts are disputed, precluding a grant of summary judgment, the court may hold an evidentiary hearing. The evidentiary hearing is held by the court without a jury. The claimant has the burden to establish claim standing at a hearing; procedure on a government summary judgment motion reflects this allocation of the burden.

Paragraph (d). The hardship release provisions of 18 U.S.C. § 983(f) do not apply to a civil forfeiture action exempted from § 983 by § 983(i).

Paragraph (d)(ii) reflects the venue provisions of 18 U.S.C. § 983(f)(3)(A) as a guide to practitioners. In addition, it makes clear the status of a civil forfeiture action as a "civil action" eligible for transfer under 28 U.S.C. § 1404. A transfer decision must be made on the circumstances of the particular proceeding. The district where the forfeiture action is filed has the advantage of bringing all related proceedings together, avoiding the waste that flows from consideration of different parts of the same forfeiture proceeding in the court where the warrant issued or the court where the property was seized. Transfer to that court would serve consolidation, the purpose that underlies nationwide enforcement of a seizure warrant. But there may be offsetting advantages in retaining the petition where it was filed. The claimant may not be able to litigate, effectively or at all, in a distant court. Issues relevant to the petition may be better litigated where the property was seized or where the warrant issued. One element, for example, is whether the claimant has sufficient ties to the community to provide assurance that the property will be available at the time of trial. Another is whether continued government possession would prevent the claimant from working. Determining whether seizure of the claimant's automobile prevents work may turn on assessing the realities of local public transit facilities.

Paragraph (e). The Excessive Fines Clause of the Eighth Amendment forbids an excessive forfeiture. *U.S. v. Bajakajian*, 524 U.S. 321 (1998). 18 U.S.C. § 983(g) provides a "petition" "to determine whether the forfeiture was constitutionally excessive" based on finding "that the forfeiture is grossly disproportional to the offense." Paragraph (e) describes the procedure for § 983(g) mitigation petitions and adopts the same procedure for forfeiture actions that fall outside § 983(g). The procedure is by motion, either for summary judgment or for mitigation after a forfeiture judgment is entered. The claimant must give notice of this defense by pleading, but failure to raise the defense in the initial answer may be cured by amendment under Rule 15. The issues that bear on mitigation often are separate from the issues that determine forfeiture. For that reason it may be convenient to resolve the issue by summary judgment before trial on the forfeiture issues. Often, however, it will be more convenient to determine first whether the property is to be forfeited. Whichever time is chosen to address mitigation, the parties must have had the opportunity to conduct civil discovery on the defense. The extent and timing of discovery are governed by the ordinary rules.

Subdivision (9). Subdivision (9) serves as a reminder of the need to demand jury trial under Rule 38. It does not expand the right to jury trial. *See U.S. v. One Parcel of Property Located at 32 Medley Lane*, 2005 WL 465241 (D.Conn.2005), ruling that the court, not the jury, determines whether a forfeiture is constitutionally excessive.

PART VIII

TIMING FOR LAWYERS IN FEDERAL CASES

TIME TABLE FOR LAWYERS IN FEDERAL CIVIL CASES
By reference to the rules and statutes addressed in this Handbook.

This Time Table, prepared by the Publisher's editorial staff as a guide to the user, indicates the time for each of the steps of a civil action as provided by the Federal Rules of Civil Procedure and the Federal Rules of Appellate Procedure. Certain steps governed by statute and by the 1997 Revised Rules of the Supreme Court are also listed. *The user should always consult the actual text of the rule or statute.* Usually the periods permitted for each of these steps may be enlarged by the court in its discretion. In some cases no enlargement is permitted. Citations to supporting authority are in the form "Civ.R. _____" for the Rules of Civil Procedure; "App.R. _____" for the Rules of Appellate Procedure; "28 U.S.C.A. § _____" for statutes; and "Supreme Court Rule _____".

ADMISSIONS

Requests for admissions, service of — On any other party a written request, for purposes of the pending action only. Civ.R. 36(1).

Response to requested admissions — Written answers or objections must be served within 30 days after service of the request, or a shorter or longer time as may be stipulated to under Civ.R. 29 or be ordered by the court. Civ.R. 36(a).

ALTERNATE jurors — The institution of the alternate juror has been abolished. Civ.R. 47, 1991 Advisory Committee note, subd. (b).

ANSWER — See, also, "Responsive Pleadings", this table.

To complaint — Service within 20 days after being served with summons and complaint unless another time is specified by Civ.R. 12 or in a federal statute. Civ.R. 12(a)(1)(A)(i).
Service within 60 days after date request is sent for waiver of service of summons or within 90 days after that date if defendant was addressed outside

1633

any judicial district of the United States unless another time is specified by Civ.R. 12 or in a federal statute. Civ.R. 12(a)(1)(A)(ii).

Service within 60 days after service on the United States attorney, in action against the United States, a United States agency, or a United States officer or employee used only in an official capacity. Civ.R. 12(a)(2).

Service within 60 days after service on the officer or employee or service on the United States attorney, whichever is later, is an action against a United States officer or employee sued in an individual capacity in connection with duties performed in the United States' behalf. Civ.R. 12(a)(3).

The time for responsive pleading is altered by service of Civ.R. 12 motions. See "Responsive Pleadings", this table.

To counterclaim or cross-claim	Service within 20 days after being served with the pleading stating the counterclaim or cross-claim. Civ.R. 12(a)(1)(B).

60 days for United States, United States agency, or United States officer or employee. Civ.R. 12(a)(2), (3).

The time for responsive pleading is altered by service of Civ.R. 12(a) motions, see "Responsive Pleadings", this table.

To notice of condemnation	Service within 20 days after service of notice. Civ.R. 71A(e).
Removed actions	20 days after receipt of copy of initial pleading starting the claim for relief, or 20 days after service of summons for an initial pleading on file at time of service, or 5 days after filing notice of removal, whichever is longest. Civ.R. 81(c).
Proceedings to cancel certificates of citizenship under 8 U.S.C.A. § 1451	60 days after service of petition. Civ.R. 81(a)(3).
ANSWERS (or objections) to interrogatories to party	Service within 30 days after service of the interrogatories. A shorter or longer time may be stipulated to under Civ.R. 29 or be ordered by the court. Civ.R. 33(b)(2).

APPEAL

As of right	30 days from entry of judgment or order. App.R. 4(a)(1)(A).

APPEAL

60 days in cases in which the United States or its officers, agencies are parties. App.R. 4(a)(1)(B).

60 days in cases in which the United States or its officers, agencies are parties. App.R. 4(a)(1)(B).

Entry of a judgment or order in the civil docket under Civ.R. 79(a) is entry for purposes of App.R. 4, unless Civ.R. 58(a)(1) requires a separate document, in which case entry occurs when the judgment or order is entered under Civ.R. 79(a) and either the judgment or order is set forth on a separate document, or 150 days have run from entry of the judgment or order in the civil docket. App.R. 4(a)(7)(A).

If any party files a timely motion of a type specified below, time for appeal for all parties runs from entry of order disposing of last such motion outstanding. App.R. 4(a)(4).

(1) motion for judgment under Civ.R. 50(b);

(2) Motion under Civ.R. 52(b) to amend or make additional findings of fact, whether or not granting the motion would alter the judgement;

(3) motion under Civ.R. 59 to alter or amend judgment;

(4) Motion under Civ.R. 54 for attorney's fees if time to appeal extended under Civ.R. 58.

(5) Motion under Civ.R. 59 for new trial.

(6) Motion for relief under Civ.R. 60 if motion filed no later than 10 days after entry of judgement.

App.R. 4(a)(4).

District court may extend for excusable neglect or good cause upon motion filed not later than 30 days after expiration of time prescribed by App.R. 4(a); no extension to exceed 30 days past prescribed time or 10 days from entry of order granting motion, whichever occurs later. App.R. 4(a)(5).

By other parties, within 14 days of filing of first notice of appeal, or within the time otherwise prescribed by App.R. 4(a), whichever last expires. App.R. 4(a)(3).

APPEAL

By permission	Petition filed with circuit clerk with proof of service within time specified by statute or rule authorizing the appeal, or if no such time is specified, within the time provided by App.R. 4(a) for filing a notice of appeal. App.R. 5(a).
Bankruptcy	If a motion for rehearing under Bankruptcy Rule 8015 is filed in a district court or in a bankruptcy appellate panel, time for appeal to court of appeals runs from entry of order disposing of motion. App.R. 6(b)(2)(A).
Class actions	Within 10 days after entry of order of district court granting or denying class action certification. Civ.R. 23(f).
Inmates	A notice of appeal is timely filed if deposited in the institution's internal mail system on or before the last day for filing. App.R. 4(c), 25(a).
Representation statement	Within 10 days after filing notice of appeal unless court of appeals designates another time, attorney who filed notice shall file with the circuit clerk a statement naming each party represented on appeal by that attorney. App.R. 12(b).
Entry of judgment or order, notice of	Lack of notice of entry by clerk does not affect time to appeal or relieve or authorize court to relieve party for failure to appeal within time allowed, except as allowed by in App.R. 4(a). Civ.R. 77(d).
Record (Appellant)	Within 10 days after filing notice of appeal or entry of an order disposing of last timely remaining motion specified in App.R. 4(a)(4)(A), whichever is later: Appellant to place written order for transcript and file copy of order with clerk; if none to be ordered, file a certificate to that effect; unless entire transcript to be included, file a statement of issues and serve appellee a copy of order or certificate and of statement. App.R. 10(b).
Record (Appellee)	Within 10 days after service of appellant's order or certificate and statement, appellee to file and serve on appellant a designation of additional parts of transcript to be included. Unless within 10 days after designation appellant has ordered such parts and so notified appellee, appellee may within following 10 days either order the

	parts or move in district court for order requiring appellant to do so. App.R. 10(b).
Record (costs)	At time of ordering, party to make satisfactory arrangements with reporter for payment of cost of transcript. App.R. 10(b)(4).
Record (Reporter)	If transcript cannot be completed within 30 days of receipt of order, reporter shall request extension of time from circuit clerk. App.R. 11(b).
Stay of proceedings to enforce judgment	Effective when supersedeas bond is approved by court. Civ.R. 62(d).
	Supersedeas bond may be given upon or after filing notice of appeal or after obtaining the order allowing appeal. Civ.R. 62(d).
Briefs	Appellant must serve and file a brief within 40 days after the record is filed. Appellee must serve and file a brief within 30 days after service of the appellant's brief. A reply brief may be filed within 14 days after service of appellee's brief and, except for good cause shown, at least 3 days before argument. A court of appeals may shorten the times allowed for briefs either by local rule for all cases or by order for a particular case. App.R. 31(a).
Transcripts	See "RECORD", ante, this heading.
Tax Court decisions	Review must be obtained by filing a notice of appeal with the Tax Court clerk within 90 days after entry of decision. If a timely notice of appeal is filed by one party, any other party may take an appeal by filing a notice of appeal within 120 days after entry of decision by the Tax Court. If timely motion made to vacate or revise decision, time to file notice of appeal runs from entry of order disposing of motion or entry of new decision, whichever is later. App.R. 13(a).
APPEAL from magistrate judge to district judge under 28 U.S.C.A. § 636(c)(4) and Civ.R. 73(d)	
Notice of Appeal	[This Rule provided as follows, prior to its abrogation:] Filed with clerk of district court within 30 days of entry of judgment. Within 60 days if United

1637

**APPEAL from magistrate
judge to district judge
under 28 U.S.C.A.
§ 636(c)(4) and Civ.R.
73(d)**

States or officer or agency thereof is a party. Within 15 days after entry of an interlocutory decision or order. Civ.R. 74(a) [Civ.R. 74 abrogated eff. Dec. 1, 1997].

[This Rule provided as follows, prior to its abrogation:] When timely notice is filed by a party, any other party may file notice within 14 days thereafter or within time otherwise prescribed by Civ.R. 74(a), whichever period last expires. Civ.R. 74(a) [Civ.R. 74 abrogated eff. Dec. 1, 1997].

[This Rule provided as follows, prior to its abrogation:] Upon showing of excusable neglect, time for filing may be extended on motion filed not later than 20 days from expiration of time for filing. Civ.R. 74(a) [Civ.R. 74 abrogated eff. Dec. 1, 1997].

Running of time for filing terminated as to all parties by timely filing of any of the following motions with the magistrate judge by any party, and the full time for appeal from judgment entered commences to run anew from entry of any of the following orders:

(1) granting or denying motion for judgment under Civ.R. 50(b);

(2) granting or denying motion under Civ.R. 52(b) to amend or make additional findings of fact;

(3) granting or denying motion under Civ.R. 59 to alter or amend judgment;

(4) denying motion for new trial under Civ.R. 59. Civ.R. 74(a) [prior to its abrogation]
[Civ.R. 74 abrogated eff. Dec. 1, 1997.]

Joint statement of case

Parties could file in lieu of record within 10 days after filing of notice of appeal, under provisions of this rule prior to its abrogation. Civ.R. 75(b)(1) [Civ.R. 75 abrogated eff. Dec. 1, 1997].

Transcript

Within 10 days after filing notice of appeal appellant to make arrangements for production. Unless entire transcript is to be included, description of

1638

APPEAL from magistrate judge to district judge under 28 U.S.C.A. § 636(c)(4) and Civ.R. 73(d)

parts appellant intends to present must be served on the appellee and filed by the appellant within the 10 day period. If appellee deems transcript of other parts to be necessary, designation of additional parts to be included must be served on the appellant and filed within 10 days after service of appellant's statement. Civ.R. 75(b)(2) [Civ.R. 75 abrogated eff. Dec. 1, 1997].

Statement in lieu of transcript

If no record is available for transcription, parties must file a statement of evidence in lieu of transcript within 10 days after filing of notice of appeal. Civ.R. 75(b)(3) [Civ.R. 75 abrogated eff. Dec. 1, 1997].

Briefs

Appellant to serve and file within 20 days after the filing of transcript, statement of case, or statement of evidence. Civ.R. 75(c)(1) [Civ.R. 75 abrogated eff. Dec. 1, 1997].

Appellee to serve and file within 20 days after service of appellant's brief. Civ.R. 75(c)(2) [Civ.R. 75 abrogated eff. Dec. 1, 1997].

Appellant may serve and file reply brief within 10 days after service of appellee's brief. Civ.R. 75(c)(3) [Civ.R. 75 abrogated eff. Dec. 1, 1997].

If appellee files a cross-appeal, appellee may file a reply brief within 10 days after service of the reply brief of the appellant. Civ.R. 75(c)(4) [Civ.R. 75 abrogated eff. Dec. 1, 1997].

Stay of judgments

Decision of district judge stayed for 10 days during which term a party may petition for rehearing. Civ.R. 76(b) [Civ.R. 76 abrogated eff. Dec. 1, 1997].

APPEAL from magistrate judge under 28 U.S.C.A. § 636(c)(3)

Appeal to court of appeals in identical fashion as appeals from other judgments of district courts. App.R. 3.1. [App.R 3.1 abrogated eff. Dec. 1, 1998].

APPEAL from district court to court of appeals under 28 U.S.C.A. § 636(c)(5)

Petition for leave to appeal filed with clerk of the court of appeals within time provided by App.R. 4(a) for filing notice of appeal, with proof of service on all parties to action in district court. App.R. 5.1(a). [Rule 5.1 abrogated eff. Dec. 1, 1998].

Within 14 days after service of petition for leave to appeal, a party may file an answer or cross petition in opposition. App.R. 5.1(a). [Rule 5.1 abrogated eff. Dec. 1, 1998].

APPEAL to Supreme Court

Direct appeals

30 days after entry of interlocutory or final order, decree or judgment holding Act of Congress unconstitutional under circumstances provided by 28 U.S.C.A. §§ 1252, and 1253. 28 U.S.C.A. § 2101(a), as amended by Act May 24, 1949, c. 139, § 106, 63 Stat. 104. [28 U.S.C.A. § 1252 was repealed and 28 U.S.C.A. § 2101(a) was amended by Pub.L. 100–352, §§ 1, 5(b), June 27, 1988, 102 Stat. 662, 663, respectively. For effective date and applicability to cases, see section 7 of Pub.L. 100–352, set out as 28 U.S.C.A. § 1254 note.]

30 days from interlocutory judgment, order, or decree in any other direct appeal authorized by law from decision of district court. 28 U.S.C.A. § 2101(b).

60 days from final judgment, order, or decree in any other direct appeal authorized by law from decision of district court. 28 U.S.C.A. § 2101(b).

Other appeals and certiorari

90 days after entry of judgment or decree; justice of Supreme Court for good cause shown may extend time for applying for writ of certiorari for period not exceeding 60 days. 28 U.S.C.A. § 2101(c).

Briefs supporting certiorari

No separate brief supporting petition for certiorari shall be filed; See Supreme Court Rule 14.2.

Brief opposing certiorari

30 days after case is placed on the docket unless time is extended by Court or a Justice or by the Clerk; See Supreme Court Rule 15.3.

Brief on merits on appeal or certiorari

By appellant or petitioner, filed within 45 days of the order granting the writ of certiorari or the order noting probable jurisdiction or postponing consideration of jurisdiction; see Supreme Court Rule 25.1.

By appellee or respondent, filed within 35 days after the brief for the appellant or petitioner is filed; see Supreme Court Rule 25.2.

1640

Reply brief, if any, filed within 35 days after the brief for appellee or respondent is filed, but any reply brief must actually be received by Clerk not later than one week before the date of oral argument. See Supreme Court Rule 25.3.

Stay of mandate pending filing petition for certiorari

A stay of mandate pending filing a petition to the Supreme Court for certiorari must not exceed 90 days unless the period is extended for good cause or unless during the period of stay, the party who obtained the stay files a petition for the writ and so notifies the circuit clerk in writing in which case the stay will continue until final disposition by the Supreme Court. The court of appeals must issue the mandate immediately when a copy of the Supreme Court order denying the petition for writ of certiorari is filed. App.R. 41(d)(2).

ATTORNEY'S fees   See "Costs", this table.

BILL of particulars   Abolished. See Civ.R. 12(e), as amended in 1948. See, however, "More definite statement", this table.

CLASS actions
Certification

At an early practicable time after a person sues or is sued as a class representative, the court must determine by order whether to certify the action as a class action. Civ.R. 23(c)(1)(A).

Settlement, voluntary dismissal, or compromise

Approval by court of settlement, voluntary dismissal, or compromise that would bind class members only after hearing and on finding that it is fair, reasonable, and adequate. Civ.R. 23(e)(2).

Attorney's fees

Claim for award of attorney's fees and nontaxable costs must be made by motion under Civ.R. 54(d)(2) subject to Civ.R. 23(h) at a time the court sets. Notice of motion must be served on all parties and, for motions by class counsel, directed to class members in a reasonable manner. Civ.R. 23(h)(1).

CLERICAL mistakes in judgments, orders, or record

Whenever found, on motion or on court's own, with or without notice; but after appeal docketed and while pending, may be corrected only with appellate court's leave. Civ.R. 60(a).

COMPLAINT

Filing commences action—must be served with summons. Civ.R. 3, 4(c)(1).

Service of summons and complaint within 120 days after filing. Civ.R. 4(m).

COMPUTATION of time

Exclude day of the act, event, or default that begins the time period. Exclude intermediate Saturdays, Sundays, and legal holidays when the period is less than 11 days. Include last day of the period unless it is a Saturday, Sunday, legal holiday, or, if act to be done is filing a paper in court, a day on which weather or other conditions make the clerk's office inaccessible. When the last day is excluded, the period runs until the end of the next day that is not a Saturday, Sunday, or legal holiday, or day when the clerk's office is inaccessible. Civ.R. 6(a).

Intermediate Saturdays, Sundays, and legal holidays are excluded when the period is less than 11 days. Civ.R. 6(a).

Exclude day of the act, event, or default that begins the period. Exclude day of the act, event, or default that begins the time period. Exclude intermediate Saturdays, Sundays, and legal holidays when the period is less than 11 days, unless stated in calendar days. Include last day of the period unless it is a Saturday, Sunday, legal holiday, or, if the act to be done is filing a paper in court, a day on which weather or other conditions make the clerk's office inaccessible. App.R. 26(a).

Intermediate Saturdays, Sundays, and legal holidays are excluded when the period is less than 11 days, unless stated in calendar days. App.R. 26(a).

Service by mail is complete upon mailing. Civ.R. 5(b).

Service by mail or by commercial carrier is complete upon mailing or delivery to the carrier. App.R. 25(c).

Service under Civ.R. Rule 5(b)(2)(C), (D), (E), or (F) adds three days to the period. Civ.R. 6(d).

When a party is required or permitted to act within a prescribed period after service of a paper upon that party, three calendar days are added to the period unless the paper is delivered on the date of service stated in the proof

1642

of service. A paper served electronically is not treated as delivered on the date of service stated in the proof of service. App.R. 26(c).

Legal holidays are defined by Civ.R. 6(a)(4) and App.R. 26(a)(4).

Supreme Court matters—See Supreme Court Rule 30.

CONDEMNATION of property

Answer to notice of condemnation

20 days after service of notice. Civ.R. 71A(e).

CORPORATE DISCLOSURE

Nongovernmental corporate parties must file, with first appearance, pleading, motion, response, or other request addressed to the court, statement identifying any parent corporation and any publicly held corporation owning 10% or more of its stock or stating that there is no such corporation. Party must promptly file supplemental statement of any required information changes. Civ.R. 7.1.

COSTS

Taxation on 1 day's notice. Review taxation of costs on motion served within the next 5 days. Civ.R. 54(d)(1).

Failure, without good cause, to sign and return requested waiver of service of summons and to return waiver within a reasonable time which must be at least 30 days after request is sent or at least 60 days if sent to a defendant outside any judicial district of the United States. Civ.R. 4(d).

Attorney's fees and related nontaxable expenses

Motion filed no later than 14 days after entry of judgement. Civ.R. 54(d)(2)(B).

CROSS APPEAL

Optional appeal from magistrate judge to district judge

Appellee may file reply brief within 10 days after service of reply brief of appellant. Civ.R. 75(c)(4) [Civ.R. 75 abrogated eff. Dec. 1, 1997].

Appellate rules

Within 14 days of filing of first notice of appeal or within the time otherwise prescribed by App.R. 4(a), whichever period ends later. App.R. 4(a)(3).

Inmates

Within 14 days after date when first notice of appeal was filed, or within the time otherwise prescribed by App.R. 4(a) whichever period ends later. The

CROSS APPEAL

14 day period runs from date district court dockets first notice of appeal. App.R. 4(a)(3), (c).

DEFAULT

    Entry by clerk

No time stated. Civ.R. 55(b).

    Entry by court

If party against whom default judgment is sought has appeared personally or by representative that party or its representative must be served with written notice of application for default judgment at least 3 days before the hearing on such application. Civ.R. 55(b).

DEFENSES and objections, presentation of

    By pleading

See "Answer", this table.

    By motion

Motion must be made before pleading if responsive pleading is allowed. Civ.R. 12(b).

    At trial

Opposing party may assert at trial any defense to claim for relief to which such party is not required to serve responsive pleading. Civ.R. 12(b).

    Motion affects time for responsive pleading

Service of motion under Civ.R. 12 alters times for responsive pleading. See "Responsive Pleadings", this table.

DEMURRERS

Abolished. Civ.R. 7, 2007 Advisory Committee note relating to Civ.R 7(c).

DEPOSITIONS

See, also, "Interrogatories to parties", "Depositions on written questions", this table.

    Notice of filing

Promptly. Civ.R. 30(f)(4) and Civ.R. 31(c)(2).

    Notice of taking

Reasonable written notice to every other party. Civ.R. 30(b)(1).

    Objections

As to admissibility, objection may be made at hearing or trial, but subject to Civ.R. 28(b) and 32(d)(3). Civ.R. 32(b).

As to errors or irregularities in the notice, service promptly. Civ.R. 32(d)(1).

As to disqualification of officer, objection made before deposition begins or promptly after the basis for disqualification becomes known or could have been known with reasonable diligence. Civ.R. 32(d)(2).

As to competence of deponent or competence, relevance, or materiality of testimony—not waived by failure to make the objection before or during deposition, unless the ground might have been corrected at that time. Civ.R. 32(d)(3)(A).

As to errors and irregularities at oral examination in manner of taking deposition, in the form of questions or answers, in the oath or affirmation, or in conduct of parties, other errors that might have been corrected at that time—objection timely made during deposition. Civ.R. 32(d)(3)(B).

As to form of written questions under Civ.R. 31—service within time allowed for serving responsive questions or, if recross-question within 5 days after being served with it. Civ.R. 32(d)(3)(C).

As to completion and return (transcription, signing, certification, sealing, endorsing, sending, or otherwise)—motion to suppress made promptly after error or irregularity becomes known or, with reasonable diligence, could have been known. Civ.R. 32(d)(4).

Protective orders	Subsequent to certification that movant has in good faith conferred or attempted to confer with other affected parties to resolve dispute without court action. Civ.R. 26(c)(1).
Motion to terminate or limit examination	Any time during a deposition. Civ.R. 30(d)(3).
Perpetuate testimony pending appeal	Motion in court where judgment was rendered on same notice and service as if action was pending in district court. Civ.R. 27(b).
Perpetuate testimony before action	Service of notice and petition at least 20 days before date of hearing. Civ.R. 27(a)(2).
Taking	Time specified in the notice of taking. Civ. R. 30(b)(1).
	Prior notice by a party to deponent and other parties to designate another method for recording deponent's testimony in addition to method specified in original notice. Civ.R. 30(b)(3).
Review of transcript or recording	Request by a party or deponent before completion of deposition. Deponent has 30 days after notice of availability of transcript or recording to review and to sign statement listing changes and reasons for making them. Civ.R. 30(e).
When taken	After parties have conferred as required by Civ.R. 26(f), except in pro-

ceeding exempted from initial disclosure under Civ.R. 26(a)(1)(B), or when authorized by rules, stipulation, or court order. Civ.R. 26(d).

DEPOSITIONS on written questions

See, also, "Depositions", "Interrogatories to parties", this table.

When taken

After parties have conferred as required by Civ.R. 26(f). except in proceeding exempted from initial disclosure under Civ.R. 26(a)(1)(B), or when authorized by rules, stipulation, or court order. Civ.R. 26(d).

Cross questions

Service within 14 days after service of the notice and direct questions. Court may extend or shorten time. Civ.R. 31(a)(5).

Redirect questions

Service within 7 days after being served with cross questions. Court may extend or shorten time. Civ.R. 31(a)(5).

Recross questions

Service within 7 days after service with redirect questions. Court may extend or shorten time. Civ.R. 31(a)(5).

Notice of filing of deposition

Promptly. Civ.R. 31(c).

Objections to form

Service within the time for serving responsive questions or, if question is a recross-question, within 5 days after served with it. Civ.R. 32(d)(3)(C).

DISCOVERY

See, also, "Admissions", "Depositions", "Depositions on written questions", "Interrogatories to parties", "Production of documents", this Table.

Discovery Conference

Except in exempted proceedings or when otherwise ordered, as soon as practicable and at least 21 days before a scheduling conference is to be held or a scheduling order is due under Civ.R. 16(b), the parties must confer to consider the volume and basis of their claims, defenses, and possibility of settling or resolving the case, to make or arrange for disclosures required by Civ.R. 26(a)(1), to discuss any issues about preserving discoverable information, and to develop a proposed discovery plan. A written report outlining the plan is to be submitted to the court within 14 days after the conference. Civ.R. 26(f); See, also, Civ.R. 26(d). Without awaiting a discovery request and at or within 14 days after the parties' Civ.R. 26(f) conference, a party must provide information specified in Civ.R. 26(a)(1)(A). Disclosure of expert testimony under Civ.R. 26(a)(2), in absence of court order or stipulation, is to be made at least 90 days before trial date or date case is to be ready for trial or if evidence intended solely to contradict or rebut evidence on same subject matter identified by another party under Civ.R 26(a)(2)(B), within 30 days after the other party's disclosure. Civ.R. 26(a)(2)(C), Disclosures under Rule 26 (a)(1) or (2), depositions, interrogatories, requests for documents or tangible things or to permit entry onto land and requests for admission must not be filed until used in the proceeding or court orders filing. Civ.R. 26(d). Civ.R. 5(d).

Identification of witnesses, documents, exhibits, including summaries of other evidence, and designation of witnesses whose testimony is expected to be presented by deposition with a transcript of pertinent testimony if deposition is not taken stenographically to be provided to other parties at least 30 days before trial unless otherwise directed by court. Within 14 days thereafter, unless court sets different time, a party may serve and promptly file objections. Civ.R. 26(a)(3).

DISMISSAL for lack of subject-matter jurisdiction

Any time. Civ.R. 12(h)(3).

DISMISSAL by plaintiff voluntarily without court order

By filing notice of dismissal before service of answer or motion for summary judgment. Civ.R. 41(a)(1).

DISMISSAL of counterclaim, crossclaim or third-party claim, voluntary

Before service of responsive pleading, or if none, before introduction of evidence at trial or hearing. Civ.R. 41(c).

DISMISSAL without prejudice

Service of summons and complaint not made within 120 days after filing of complaint. Civ.R. 4(m).

DOCUMENTS, Production of

See "Production of documents", this Table.

ENLARGEMENT of time
generally

   Act may or must be done within specified time

Court for good cause may extend time (1) with or without motion or notice if court acts, or if request is made, before the original time or its extension expires, or (2) on motion made after the

ENLARGEMENT of time
generally

	time has expired if party failed to act because of excusable neglect; but court may not extend time for taking any action under Civ.R. 50(b) and (d), 52(b), 59(b), (d) and (e), and 60(b), except as those rules allow. Civ.R. 6(b).
Affidavits in opposition, service	At least 1 day before the hearing, unless court permits service at another time, except as Civ.R. 59(c) provides otherwise. Civ.R. 6(c)(2).
Hearing of motions and defenses	Heard and decided before trial unless court orders deferral until trial. Civ.R. 12(i).
Service under Rule 5(b)(2)(C), (D), (E) or (F)	Adds three days to a period that is computed from time of service. Civ.R. 6(d).
	When a party is required or permitted to act within a prescribed period after service of a paper upon that party, three calendar days are added to the period unless the paper is delivered on the date of service stated in the proof of service. A paper served electronically is not treated as delivered on the day of service stated in the proof of service. App.R. 26(c).
Injunction—temporary restraining order	May be extended 10 days by order of court or for a longer period by consent of party against whom order is directed. Civ.R. 65(b).
Response to request for admissions	Time may be lengthened or shortened by court or as the parties may stipulate to under Civ.R. 29. Civ.R. 36(a).
Optional appeal from magistrate judge to district judge	Upon showing of excusable neglect, time to file notice of appeal may be extended upon motion filed not later than 20 days form expiration of time for filing. [Civ.R. 74 abrogated eff. Dec.1, 1977].
Motion for judgment as a matter of law	No enlargement of the 10 day period except to the extent and under conditions stated in Civ.R. 50(b). Civ.R. 6(b).
Findings by the court, amendment of or make additional findings	No enlargement of the 10 day period except to the extent and under conditions stated in Civ.R. 52(b). Civ.R. 6(b).
Motion for new trial	No enlargement of the 10 day period except to the extent and under conditions stated in Civ.R. 50(d), 59(b), (d), and (e). Civ.R. 6(b).

ENLARGEMENT of time
generally

Motion for relief from judgment or order	No enlargement of the 1 year period except to the extent and under conditions stated in Civ.R. 60(b). Civ.R. 6(b).
Appellate rules	Court for good cause may extend time prescribed by App.Rules or by its order to perform any act or may permit act to be done after expiration of such time; but court may not extend time for filing notice of appeal, or petition for permission to appeal a notice of appeal from or a petition to enjoin, set aside, suspend, modify, enforce or otherwise review an order of an administrative agency, board, commission or officer of the United States, unless specifically authorized by law. App.R. 26(b).
Supreme Court matters, depositions	See Supreme Court Rule 30.

EXCEPTIONS for insufficiency of pleadings

Abolished. Civ.R. 7, 2007 Advisory Committee note, relating to Civ.R. 7(c).

EXECUTION

Stay

Automatically: No execution may issue, nor may proceedings be taken to enforce, until expiration of 10 days after entry of judgment; exceptions—injunctions, receiverships, and patent accountings. Civ.R. 62(a).

Stay according to state law. Civ.R. 62(f).

Motion for new trial or for judgment. Civ.R. 62(b).

Stay in favor of government. Civ.R. 62(e).

Supersedeas on appeal. Civ.R. 62(d).

Stay of judgment as to multiple claims or multiple parties. Civ.R. 62(h).

Stay of judgment pending appeal from magistrate judge to district judge. Civ.R. 74(c). Stay of decision of district judge for 10 days during which time a party may petition for rehearing. Civ.R. 76(b) [Civ.R. 74 and 76 abrogated eff. Dec. 1, 1997].

FILING papers

Filing complaint commences civil action. Civ.R. 3.

Service of summons and complaint within 120 days after filing of complaint. Civ.R. 4(m).

1649

FILING papers

Any paper required to be served, together with certificate of service, must be filed within reasonable time after service. Civ.R. 5(d).

Any papers after complaint that is required to be served, together with certificate of service, must be filed with clerk unless judge agrees to accept it for filing. Civ.R. 5(d).

Local court rules may allow papers to be filed, signed, or verified by electronic means if consistent with technical standards of Judicial Conference of the United States, and clerk must not refuse for filing any paper solely because it is not in the form prescribed by Rules of Civil Procedure or a local rule or practice. Civ.R. 5(d).

Any paper after the complaint required to be served, together with a certificate of service, must be filed with the court within a reasonable time after service. Civ.R. 5(d).

FINDINGS
    Motion to amend

10 days after entry of judgment. Civ.R. 52(b). Exception from general rule relating to enlargement. Civ.R. 6(b).

FOREIGN law

Notice by pleading or other writing required of party intending to raise an issue concerning the law of a foreign country. Civ.R. 44.1.

FORFEITURE

Civil forfeiture actions, procedures. Supp. Rule G.

HEARING of motions

A court may establish regular times and places for oral hearings on motions, by rule or order court may provide for submitting and determining motions on briefs, without oral hearings. Civ.R. 78.

Service of notice at least 5 days before time specified for hearing unless motion may be heard ex parte, otherwise at least these rules or a court order set a different time. Civ.R. 6(d).

Hearing of certain motions and defenses before trial on application of any party unless court orders deferral until trial. Civ.R. 12(i).

HOLIDAYS

New Year's Day, Birthday of Martin Luther King, Jr., Presidents' Day, Memorial Day, Independence Day, Labor

Day, Columbus Day, Veterans' Day, Thanksgiving Day, Christmas Day, and any other day declared a holiday by the President, Congress or the state in which is located either the district court that rendered the challenged judgment or order, or the circuit clerk's principal office. Civ.R. 6(a); App.R. 26(a).

Exclusion in computation of time. Civ.R. 6(a); App.R. 26(a).

INJUNCTION (Temporary restraining order granted without notice)

Order must state date and hour of issuance, promptly filed in clerk's office, and entered in the record. Civ.R. 65(b).

Expiration within the time after entry, not to exceed 10 days, that court sets, unless before that time the court for such cause extends the order for like period or, with consent of party against whom order is directed, for longer period. Civ.R. 65(b).

Motion for preliminary injunction must be set down for hearing at earliest possible time—takes precedence over all matters except older ones of same character. Civ.R. 65(b).

Motion for dissolution or modification on 2 days' notice or shorter notice set by the court; court must hear and decide motion as promptly as justice requires. Civ.R. 65(b).

INSTRUCTIONS

Requests

At close of evidence or at an earlier reasonable time that the court orders. After close of evidence for issues that could not reasonably have been anticipated at an earlier time for requests, and untimely requests for instructions on any issue with the court's permission. Civ.R. 51(a).

Proposed

Court must inform parties before instructing jury and before final argument, and give parties opportunity to object before instructions and arguments are delivered. Civ.R. 51(b)(1), (2).

Time of

Court may instruct jury at any time before jury is discharged. Civ.R. 51(b)(3).

Objections

For parties informed of instructions or actions on requests before the jury is instructed and before final jury argu-

1651

ments, at opportunity for objection provided under Civ.R. 51(b)(2). For parties not informed of instructions or actions on requests before time for objection under Civ.R. 51(b)(2), promptly after learning that instruction or request will be, or has been, given or refused. Civ.R. 51(c).

INTERROGATORIES to parties

See, also, "Depositions", "Depositions on written questions", this table.

Service after parties have conferred pursuant to Civ.R. 26(f). Civ.R. 26(d), 33(a).

Answers or objections

Service within 30 days after service of the interrogatories. A shorter or longer time may be stipulated to or ordered by the court. Civ.R. 33(b)(3).

INTERVENTION

Upon timely motion. Civ.R. 24(a), (b).

Person desiring to intervene shall serve a motion to intervene upon the parties as provided in Civ.R. 5. Civ.R. 24(c).

To challenge the constitutionality of a statute. Rule 5.1.

JUDGMENT or order

Alter or amend judgment, motion to

Shall be filed not later than 10 days after entry of judgment. Civ.R. 59(e). Exception to general rule, relating to enlargement. Civ.R. 6(b).

Clerical mistakes or from oversight or omission

May be corrected any time; but after an appeal has been docketed in appellate court and while appeal pending may be corrected only with leave of appellate court. Civ.R. 60(a).

Default

See "Default", this table.

Renewal of motion for judgment after trial

Not later than 10 days after entry of judgment. Exception from general rule relating to enlargement. Civ.R. 6(b).

Entry of judgment

Subject to Civ.R. 54(b), promptly by clerk without awaiting the court's direction, unless court orders otherwise, upon general verdict of jury or upon court decision that a party shall recover only a sum certain or costs or that all relief shall be denied. Promptly approved form of judgment by court, promptly entered by clerk, upon special verdict or general verdict with answers to written questions, or upon court decision granting other relief. Entry may not be delayed in order to tax costs or award fees. Civ.R. 58(b), (e).

1652

JUDGMENT or order

	Time of entry—Entry of a judgment if separate document is not required when judgment is entered in the civil docket under Civ.R. 79(a). If separate document is required, when the judgment is entered, in the civil docket under Civ.R. 79(a) and either the judgment is set forth in a separate document, or 150 days have run from entry of the judgment in the civil docket whichever is earlier. Civ.R. 58(c).
Entry, notice of	Immediately after entry, clerk must serve notice thereof as provided in Civ.R. 5(b) and record service on the docket. Any party may in addition serve a notice of such entry in manner provided in Civ.R. 5(b) for service of papers. Civ.R. 77(d).
	Lack of notice of entry by clerk does not affect time for appeal or relieve or authorize court to relieve party for failure to appeal within time allowed, except as allowed by App.R. 4(a). Civ.R. 77(d).
Offer of judgment	Service more than 10 days before trial begins. Civ.R. 68.
	Acceptance, written notice of—service within 10 days after service of offer. Civ.R. 68.
On pleadings, motion for judgment	After pleadings are closed but early enough not to delay the trial. Civ.R. 12(c).
Relief from, on grounds stated in Rule 60(b)	Motion within a reasonable time and not more than 1 year after entry of judgment or, order or the date of the proceeding, for following grounds: (1) mistake, inadvertence, surprise, or excusable neglect; (2) newly discovered evidence; (3) fraud, misrepresentation, or other misconduct. Civ.R. 60(b), (c). Exception from general rule relating to enlargement. Civ.R. 6(b).
	Motion within a reasonable time, for following grounds: (1) judgment void, (2) judgment satisfied, released, or discharged, (3) prior underlying judgment reversed or otherwise vacated, (4) no longer equitable that judgment have prospective application, (5) any other reason justifying relief. Civ.R. 60(b). Exception from general rule relating to enlargement. Civ.R. 6(b).
Stay	See "Execution", this table.

JUDGMENT or order

Summary judgment   See "Summary Judgment", this table.

JURORS   The institution of the alternate juror has been abolished. Civ.R. 47, 1991 Advisory Committee note, subd. (b).

JURY trial

Demand   Service any time after commencement of action and not later than 10 days after service of last pleading directed to the triable issue. Civ.R. 38(b).

Adverse party may serve demand for jury trial within 10 days after service of first demand or within a shorter time ordered by the court. Civ.R. 38(c).

Removed actions   If at the time of removal all necessary pleadings have been served, demand for jury trial may be served:

By petitioner, 10 days after the notice of removal is filed;

By another party, within 10 days after service on party of the notice of filing the petition. Civ.R. 81(c).

Demand after removal not necessary in either of two instances: (1) before removal, party has made express demand in accordance with state law; (2) state law does not require express demands and court does not order otherwise. Civ.R. 81(c).

LEGAL HOLIDAY   See "Holidays", this table.

MAGISTRATE JUDGES

Trial by consent   Consent of parties to magistrate judge's authority to be exercised by filing statement consenting to the referral. Civ.R. 73(b).

Pretrial matters   Objections of parties to order disposing of matter not dispositive of claim or defense to be served and filed within 10 days after being served with copy of order. Civ.R. 72(a).

Clerk to promptly mail copies to all parties of recommendation of magistrate judge for disposition of matter dispositive of claim or defense of a party or prisoner petition. Specific written objections to recommended disposition may be served and filed within 10 days after service. Response to objections may be made within 10 days after being served with copy. Civ.R. 72(b).

MAIL   Service under Rule 5(b)(2)(C), (D), (E) or (F) adds 3 days to a period computed from time of service. Civ.R. 6(d).

1654

When a party is required or permitted to act within a prescribed period after service of a paper upon that party, three calendar days are added to the period unless the paper is delivered on the date of service stated in the proof of service. A paper served electronically is not treated as delivered on the day of service stated in the proof of service. App.R. 26(c).

A brief or appendix is timely filed if on or before the last day for filing it is mailed First-Class or other class at least as expeditious, postage prepaid, or dispatched for delivery within three calendar days by a third-party commercial carrier. App.R. 25(a)(2)(B).

MASTERS

Order appointing master

Court may issue only after master has filed affidavit disclosing whether there is any ground for disqualification under 28 U.S.C. § 455 and, if ground is disclosed, after parties with court's approval waive the disqualification. Civ.R. 53(b)(3).

Amendment of order appointing

Order appointing master may be amended at any time after notice to parties, and opportunity to be heard. Civ.R. 53(b)(4).

Order of master

A master who issues an order must file the order and promptly serve a copy on each party. The clerk must enter the order on the docket. Civ.R. 53(d).

Report of master

Master must report to court as required by appointing order. The master must file the report and promptly serve a copy on each party unless the court orders otherwise. Civ.R. 53(e).

In acting on, the court must give parties notice and an opportunity to be heard. Civ.R. 53(f)(1).

A party may file objections or motion to adopt or modify no later than 20 days from the time the master's order, report, or recommendations are served, unless the court sets a different time. Civ.R. 53(f)(2).

Compensation of master

The court must fix the master's compensation before or after judgment on the basis and terms stated in the appointing order but the court may set a new basis and terms after notice and

1655

MASTERS

opportunity to be heard. Civ.R. 53(g)(1)

MORE DEFINITE STATEMENT

Furnished

Must be furnished within 10 days after notice of order or other time fixed by court or court may strike pleading or issue any other appropriate order. Civ.R. 12(e).

Motion for

Must be made before responsive pleading is filed. Civ.R. 12(e).

MOTIONS, notices, and affidavits

See, also, specific headings, this table.

In general

A written motion, supporting affidavits, and notice of hearing thereof— service at least 5 days before time specified for hearing unless motion may be heard ex parte, or a different time is fixed by rule or by order of court. Civ.R. 6(c).

Opposing affidavits must be served at least one day before hearing, unless court permits otherwise. Civ.R. 6(c).

Pleading, written motion, or other paper not signed by attorney or party shall be stricken unless omission of signature is corrected promptly after being called to attention of attorney or party. Civ.R. 11(a).

NEW TRIAL

Motion and affidavits

Motion shall be filed not later than 10 days after entry of judgment. Civ.R. 59(b). Exception from general rule relating to enlargement. Civ.R. 6(b). If motion based on affidavits, they must be filed with motion. Civ.R. 59(c).

Opposing affidavits

Shall be filed within 10 days of service of motion for new trial; period may be extended up to 20 days either by court for good cause shown or by parties by stipulation. Civ.R. 59(c).

Initiative of court

Not later than 10 days after entry of judgment, court may order new trial for any reason that would justify granting one on a party's motion. Civ.R. 59(d). Exception to general rule relating to enlargement. Civ.R. 6(b).

After giving parties notice and opportunity to be heard, court may grant a timely motion for new trial, for reason not stated in the motion. Civ.R. 59(d).

MORE DEFINITE STATEMENT

Exception to general rule relating to enlargement. Civ.R. 6(b).

Judgment as a matter of law

Party against whom judgment as a matter of law is rendered shall file a motion for a new trial under Civ.R. 59 no later than 10 days after entry of the judgment. Civ.R. 50(d).

OBJECTIONS to orders or rulings of court

At time ruling or order of court is requested or made; if party has no opportunity to object to ruling or order at time it is made, absence of objection does not prejudice the party. Civ.R. 46.

Pretrial matters referred to magistrate judge

Objections of parties to order disposing of matter not dispositive of claim or defense to be served and filed within 10 days after being served with copy of order. Civ.R. 72(a).

Specific written objections to recommended disposition of matter dispositive of claim or defense of a party may be served or filed within 10 days after service. Response to objections may be made within 10 days after being served with copy. Civ.R. 72(b).

OFFER of judgment

Must be served more than 10 days before trial. Civ.R. 68(a).

Acceptance must be served within 10 days after service of offer. Civ.R. 68(a).

ORDERS

See Judgment or order.

PARTICULARS, Bill of

Abolished. Civ.R. 12(e), as amended in 1948. See, however, "More definite statement", this table.

PLEADINGS
Amendment of

Once as matter of course before responsive pleading served or within 20 days after serving the pleading if no response is allowed and action is not yet on trial calendar. Civ.R. 15(a).

By leave of court or written consent of opposing parties, at any time. Civ.R. 15(a).

During trial or after judgment to conform to evidence or to raise an unpleaded issue, but tried by express or implied consent of parties. Civ.R. 15(b).

Supplemental

Upon motion of party—court may upon reasonable notice permit service of supplemental pleading setting out transactions, etc., that happened after the date

PLEADINGS

	of pleading sought to be supplemented. Civ.R. 15(d).
	Opposing party plead to supplemental pleading—court may so order within a specified time. Civ.R. 15(d)
Allegations of time	Such allegations are material when testing the sufficiency of a pleading. Civ.R. 9(f).
Judgment on, motion for	After pleadings are closed but early enough not to delay the trial. Civ.R. 12(c).
Striking of matter from	Motion made before responding to a pleading or, if no responsive pleading allowed, within 20 days after service of pleading. Civ.R. 12(f).
	On court's own initiative at any time. Civ.R. 12(f).
Signing of	Pleading, written motion, or other paper not signed by attorney or party must be stricken unless omission of signature is corrected promptly after being called to attention of attorney or party. Civ.R. 11(a).

PLEAS

Abolished. Civ.R. 7, 2007 Advisory Committee note, relating to Civ.R. 7(c).

PRETRIAL conferences

Scheduling order to issue as soon as practicable but in any event within the earlier of 120 days after complaint served on defendant or 90 days after appearance of any defendant. Civ.R. 16(b).

PROCESS

See "Summons", this Table.

PRODUCTION of documents

Request for, service of	Within the scope of Civ.R. 26(b). Civ.R. 34(a).
Response to request	Within 30 days after service of the request. A shorter or longer time may be ordered by court or stipulated to under Civ.R. 29. Civ.R. 34(b).
Time of inspection	The request must specify a reasonable time. Civ.R. 34(b).
Subpoena	See "Subpoena", this table.

REHEARING

Petition for panel rehearing	Petitions for panel rehearings may be filed within 14 days after entry of judgement unless the time is shortened or extended by order or local rule. In all civil cases in which the United States or its agency or officer thereof is a party, the time within which any

REHEARING

party may seek a rehearing shall be 45 days after entry of judgement unless the time is shortened or extended by order. App.R. 40(a).

Issuance of mandate

The mandate of the court must issue 7 calendar days after the time to file a petition for rehearing expires, or 7 calendar days after entry of an order denying a timely petition for panel rehearing, petition for rehearing en banc, or motion for stay of mandate, whichever is later. The court may shorten or extend the time. The timely filing of a petition for panel rehearing, petition for rehearing en banc, or motion for stay of mandate, stays the mandate until disposition of the petition or motion, unless the court orders otherwise. App.R. 41(b), (d)(1).

REMOVED actions

Answers and defenses

Within 20 days after the receipt through service or otherwise of a copy of the initial pleading setting forth the claim for relief upon which the action or proceeding is based, or within 20 days after the service of summons for an initial pleading on file at the time of service, or within 5 days after filing of the notice for removal, whichever period is longest. Civ.R. 81(c).

Demand for jury trial

Demand after removal not necessary in either of two instances: (1) before removal, party has made express demand in accordance with state law; (2) state law does not require express demands and court does not direct otherwise. Civ.R. 81(c).

Notice of removal

Within 30 days after receipt through service or otherwise of a copy of the initial pleading setting forth the claim for relief upon which the action or proceeding is based, or within 30 days after service of summons if such initial pleading has then been filed in court and is not required to be served on defendant, whichever period is shorter. 28 U.S.C.A. § 1446(b).

If the case stated by the initial pleading is not removable, a notice of removal may be filed within 30 days after receipt by the defendant, through service or otherwise, of a copy of an amended pleading, motion, order or other paper from which it may first be ascertained

1659

REMOVED actions

that the case is one which is or has become removable. 28 U.S.C.A. § 1446(b).

A case may not be removed on the basis of jurisdiction conferred by 28 U.S.C.A. § 1332 more than one year after action's commencement. 28 U.S.C.A. § 1446(b).

REPLY

See, also, "Responsive pleadings", this table.

To answer

If ordered by court. Civ.R. 7(a). Service within 20 days after service of order, unless order specifies a different time. Civ.R. 12(a).

To counterclaim or crossclaim

Service within 20 days after service of pleading that states the counterclaim or crossclaim. Civ.R. 12(a).

United States or agency or officer or employee thereof sued only in an official capacity shall serve reply within 60 days after service on U.S. attorney. Civ.R. 12(a).

United States officer or employee sued in an official capacity in connection with duties performed on the United States' behalf shall serve reply within 60 days after service on officer or employee or service on the United States attorney, whichever is later. Civ.R. 12(a).

Alteration of time by service of Civ.R. 12 motion

See "Responsive pleadings", this table.

RESPONSIVE PLEADINGS

See, also, "Answer", "Reply", this table.

To amend pleading

Within 10 days after service of amended pleading or within time remaining for response to original pleading, whichever is later, unless court otherwise orders. Civ.R. 15(a).

To supplemental pleading

As ordered by court. Civ.R. 15(d).

Alteration of time by service of Civ.R. 12 motion

Service of motion permitted under Civ.R. 12 alters times for responsive pleadings as follows unless different time fixed by court:

(1) if court denies motion or postpones its disposition until trial, service of responsive pleading within 10 days after notice of the court's action;

(2) if court grants motion for more definite statement, service of responsive pleading within 10 days after ser-

1660

	vice of the more definite statement. Civ.R. 12(a)(4).
RESTRAINING order, temporary, without notice	See "Injunction", this table.
RETURN	The court may allow a summons or proof of service to be amended. Civ.R. 4(a) & (*l*).
	Proof of service must be made to the court by server's affidavit, except for service by Untied States marshal or deputy marshal. Civ.R. 4(*l*).
SANCTIONS	Presentation to court of a pleading, written motion, or other paper is a certification under Civ.R. 11(b). If after notice and reasonable opportunity to respond, court determines that Civ.R. 11(b) was violated, sanctions may be imposed by a motion for sanctions which must not be filed or presented to court unless, within 21 days after service of the motion or another time period set by the court, the challenged matter is not withdrawn or corrected. Civ.R. 11(c). Sanctions are inapplicable to disclosure and discovery. Civ.R. 11(d).
SATURDAYS AND SUNDAYS, LEGAL HOLIDAYS	Exclusion in computation of time when period is less than 11 days. Civ.R. 6(a); App.R. 26(a).
STAY or supersedeas	See "Appeal", "Execution", this table.
SUBPOENA	
Objection	Before the earlier of 14 days after service of the subpoena or the time specified for compliance, on the party or attorney designated in the subpoena written objection to inspection or copying of any or all of the designated materials or of the premises. Civ.R. 45(c)(2)(B).
Motion to compel production	If objection has been made, the party serving the subpoena may, on notice to the person commanded to produce, move at any time for an order to compel the production or inspection. Civ.R. 45(c)(2)(B).
Motion to quash	The court by which a subpoena was issued must quash or modify the subpoena on timely motion under certain circumstances. Civ.R. 45(c)(3)(A).
Witnesses, documentary evidence, etc.	Subpoena specifies time for attendance and giving of testimony or to produce and permit inspection and copying of designated documents or tangible

things in the possession, custody or control of that person, or to permit inspection of premises. Civ.R. 45(a)(1)(A), (C).

SUBSTITUTION of parties

In cases of death, incompetency, or transfer of interest—motion to substitute, together with notice of hearing, served on parties as provided in Civ.R. 5 and on nonparties in manner provided in Civ.R. 4 for service of a summons. Civ.R. 25(a), (b), (c).

Dismissal as to deceased party unless motion for substitution is made within 90 days after service if a statement noting the death. Civ.R. 25(a).

Successor of public officer substituted automatically. Court may order substitution at any time, but absence of order does not affect substitution. Civ.R. 25(d).

SUMMARY JUDGMENT, motion for

    Claimant

May move at any time after 20 days have passed from commencement of action or after service of motion for summary judgment by opposing party. Civ.R. 56(a).

    Defending party

May move at any time. Civ.R. 56(b).

    Service

Service of motion at least 10 days before the day set for hearing. Civ.R. 56(c).

Service of opposing affidavits before the hearing day. Civ.R. 56(c).

SUMMONS

Served with a copy of complaint. Civ.R. 4(c)(1). If not served within 120 days after filing complaint, court must dismiss action without prejudice, order service be made within a specified time, or extend time for service. Civ.R. 4(m).

Proof of service must be made to the court by server's affidavit except for service by United States marshal or deputy marshal. Civ.R. 4(*l*).

Service by any nonparty at least 18, a U.S. marshal, deputy U.S. marshal, or other person specially appointed by the court. Civ.R. 4(c)(2), (3).

SUPPLEMENTAL pleadings

See "Pleadings", this table.

SUPERSEDEAS or stay

See "Appeal", "Execution", this table.

TERM

Every district court considered always open. Civ.R. 77(a).

Terms of court have been abolished. 28 U.S.C.A. §§ 138–141, as amended by Pub.L. 88–139, Oct. 16, 1963, 77 Stat. 248.

THIRD–PARTY practice

Third-party plaintiff need not obtain leave if third-party plaintiff files third-party complaint not later than 10 days after serving the original answer. Civ.R. 14(a).

VERDICT

Renewal of motion for judgment after trial

Movant may renew motion for judgment as a matter of law by filing a motion no later than 10 days after entry of judgment or — if the motion addresses a jury issue not decided by a verdict — no later than 10 days after the jury was discharged. Civ.R. 50(b).

Exception from general rule relating to enlargement. Civ.R. 6(b).

New trial where judgment as a matter of law rendered

Party against whom judgment as a matter of law is rendered must file a motion for a new trial under Civ.R. 59 no later than 10 days after entry of the judgment. Civ.R. 50(d).

PART IX

TITLE 28, JUDICIARY AND JUDICIAL PROCEDURE—SELECTED PROVISIONS

Including Amendments Received to October 1, 2007

Table of Sections

§ 41. Number and composition of circuits

The thirteen judicial circuits of the United States are constituted as follows:

Circuits and Composition

District of Columbia: District of Columbia

First: Maine, Massachusetts, New Hampshire, Puerto Rico, Rhode Island

Second: Connecticut, New York, Vermont

Third: Delaware, New Jersey, Pennsylvania, Virgin Islands

Fourth: Maryland, North Carolina, South Carolina, Virginia, West Virginia

Fifth: District of the Canal Zone, Louisiana, Mississippi, Texas

Sixth: Kentucky, Michigan, Ohio, Tennessee

Seventh: Illinois, Indiana, Wisconsin

Eighth: Arkansas, Iowa, Minnesota, Missouri, Nebraska, North Dakota, South Dakota

Ninth: Alaska, Arizona, California, Idaho, Montana, Nevada, Oregon, Washington, Guam, Hawaii

Tenth: Colorado, Kansas, New Mexico, Oklahoma, Utah, Wyoming

Eleventh: Alabama, Florida, Georgia

Federal: All Federal judicial districts

(June 25, 1948, c. 646, 62 Stat. 870; Oct. 31, 1951, c. 655, § 34, 65 Stat. 723; Oct. 14, 1980, Pub.L. 96–452, § 2, 94 Stat. 1994; Apr. 2,1982, Pub.L. 97–164, Title I, § 101, 96 Stat. 25.)

§ 144. Bias or prejudice of judge

Whenever a party to any proceeding in a district court makes and files a timely and sufficient affidavit that the judge before whom the matter is pending has a personal bias or prejudice either against him or in favor of any adverse party, such judge shall proceed no further therein, but another judge shall be assigned to hear such proceeding.

The affidavit shall state the facts and the reasons for the belief that bias or prejudice exists, and shall be filed not less than ten days before the beginning of the term at which the proceeding is to be heard, or good cause shall be shown for failure to file it within such time. A party may file only one such affidavit in any case. It shall be accompanied by a certificate of counsel of record stating that it is made in good faith.

(June 25, 1948, c. 646, 62 Stat. 898; May 24, 1949, c. 139, § 65, 63 Stat. 99.)

§ 451. Definitions

As used in this title:

The term "court of the United States" includes the Supreme Court of the United States, courts of appeals, district courts constituted by chapter 5 of this title, including the Court of International Trade and any court created by Act of Congress the judges of which are entitled to hold office during good behavior.

The terms "district court" and "district court of the United States" mean the courts constituted by chapter 5 of this title.

The term "judge of the United States" includes judges of the courts of appeals, district courts, Court of International Trade and any court created by Act of Congress, the judges of which are entitled to hold office during good behavior.

The term "justice of the United States" includes the Chief Justice of the United States and the associate justices of the Supreme Court.

The term "district" and "judicial district" mean the districts enumerated in Chapter 5 of this title.

The term "department" means one of the executive departments enumerated in section 1 of Title 5, unless the context shows that such term was intended to describe the executive, legislative, or judicial branches of the government.

The term "agency" includes any department, independent establishment, commission, administration, authority, board or bureau of the United States or any corporation in which the United States has a proprietary interest, unless the context shows that such term was intended to be used in a more limited sense.

(As amended Mar. 18, 1959, Pub.L. 86–3, § 10, 73 Stat. 9; Sept. 12, 1966, Pub.L. 89–571, § 3, 80 Stat. 764; Oct. 10, 1980, 96–417, Title V, § 501(10), 94 Stat. 1742; Apr. 2, 1982, Pub.L. 97–164, Title I, § 114, 96 Stat. 29.)

§ 452. Courts always open; powers unrestricted by expiration of sessions

All courts of the United States shall be deemed always open for the purpose of filing proper papers, issuing and returning process, and making motions and orders.

The continued existence or expiration of a session of court in no way affects the power of the court to do any act or take any proceeding.

(As amended Oct. 16, 1963, Pub.L. 88–139, § 2, 77 Stat. 248.)

§ 455. Disqualification of justice, judge, or magistrate

(a) Any justice, judge, or magistrate of the United States shall disqualify himself in any proceeding in which his impartiality might reasonably be questioned.

(b) He shall also disqualify himself in the following circumstances:

(1) Where he has a personal bias or prejudice concerning a party, or personal knowledge of disputed evidentiary facts concerning the proceeding;

(2) Where in private practice he served as lawyer in the matter in controversy, or a lawyer with whom he previously practiced law served during such association as a lawyer concerning the matter, or the judge or such lawyer has been a material witness concerning it;

(3) Where he has served in governmental employment and in such capacity participated as counsel, adviser or material witness concerning the proceeding or expressed an opinion concerning the merits of the particular case in controversy;

(4) He knows that he, individually or as a fiduciary, or his spouse or minor child residing in his household, has a financial interest in the subject matter in controversy or in a party to the proceeding, or any other interest that could be substantially affected by the outcome of the proceeding;

(5) He or his spouse, or a person within the third degree of relationship to either of them, or the spouse of such a person:

(i) Is a party to the proceeding, or an officer, director, or trustee of a party;

(ii) Is acting as a lawyer in the proceeding;

(iii) Is known by the judge to have an interest that could be substantially affected by the outcome of the proceeding;

(iv) Is to the judge's knowledge likely to be a material witness in the proceeding.

(c) A judge should inform himself about his personal and fiduciary financial interests, and make a reasonable effort to inform himself about the personal financial interests of his spouse and minor children residing in his household.

(d) For the purposes of this section the following words or phrases shall have the meaning indicated:

(1) "proceeding" includes pretrial, trial, appellate review, or other stages of litigation;

(2) the degree of relationship is calculated according to the civil law system;

(3) "fiduciary" includes such relationships as executor, administrator, trustee, and guardian;

(4) "financial interest" means ownership of a legal or equitable interest, however small, or a relationship as director, adviser, or other active participant in the affairs of a party, except that:

(i) Ownership in a mutual or common investment fund that holds securities is not a "financial interest" in such securities unless the judge participates in the management of the fund;

(ii) An office in an educational, religious, charitable, fraternal, or civic organization is not a "financial interest" in securities held by the organization;

(iii) The proprietary interest of a policyholder in a mutual insurance company, of a depositor in a mutual savings association, or a similar proprietary interest, is a "financial interest" in the organization only if the outcome of the proceeding could substantially affect the value of the interest;

(iv) Ownership of government securities is a "financial interest" in the issuer only if the outcome of the proceeding could substantially affect the value of the securities.

(e) No justice, judge, or magistrate shall accept from the parties to the proceeding a waiver of any ground for disqualification enumerated in subsection (b). Where the ground for disqualification arises only under subsection (a), waiver may be accepted provided it is preceded by a full disclosure on the record of the basis for disqualification.

(f) Notwithstanding the preceding provisions of this section, if any justice, judge, magistrate, or bankruptcy judge to whom a matter has been assigned would be disqualified, after substantial judicial time has been devoted to the matter, because of the appearance or discovery, after the matter was assigned to him or her, that he or she individually or as a fiduciary, or his or her spouse or minor child residing in his or her household, has a financial interest in a party (other than an interest that could be substantially affected by the outcome), disqualification is not required if the justice, judge, magistrate, bankruptcy judge, spouse or minor child, as the case may be, divests himself or herself of the interest that provides the grounds for the disqualification.

(June 25, 1948, c. 646, 62 Stat. 908; Dec. 5, 1974, Pub.L. 93–512, § 1, 88 Stat. 1609; Nov. 6, 1978, Pub.L. 95–598, Title II, § 214(a), (b), 92 Stat. 2661; Nov. 19, 1988, Pub.L. 100–702, Title X, § 1007, 102 Stat. 4667.)

§ 631. Appointment and Tenure

(a) The judges of each United States district court and the district courts of the Virgin Islands, Guam, and the Northern Mariana Islands shall appoint United States magistrate judges in such numbers and to serve at such locations within the judicial districts as the Judicial Conference may determine under this chapter. In the case of a magistrate judge appointed by the district court of the Virgin Islands, Guam, or the Northern Mariana Islands, this chapter shall apply as though the court appointing such a magistrate judge were a United States district court. Where there is more than one judge of a district court, the appointment, whether an original appointment or a reappointment, shall be by the concurrence of a majority of all the judges of such district court, and when there is no such concurrence, then by the chief judge. Where the conference deems it desirable, a magistrate may be designated to serve in one or more districts adjoining the district for which he is appointed. Such a designation shall be made by the concurrence of a majority of the judges of each of the district courts involved and shall specify the duties to be performed by the magistrate in the adjoining district or districts.

(b) No individual may be appointed or reappointed to serve as a magistrate under this chapter unless:

(1) He has been for at least five years a member in good standing of the bar of the highest court of a State, the District of Columbia, the Commonwealth of Puerto Rico, the Territory of Guam, the Commonwealth of the Northern Mariana Islands, or the Virgin Islands of the United States, except that an individual who does not meet the bar membership requirements of this paragraph may be appointed and serve as a part-time magistrate if the appointing court or courts and the conference find that no qualified individual who is a member of the bar is available to serve at a specific location;

(2) He is determined by the appointing district court or courts to be competent to perform the duties of the office;

(3) In the case of an individual appointed to serve in a national park, he resides within the exterior boundaries of that park, or at some place reasonably adjacent thereto;

(4) He is not related by blood or marriage to a judge of the appointing court or courts at the time of his initial appointment; and

(5) He is selected pursuant to standards and procedures promulgated by the Judicial Conference of the United States. Such standards and procedures shall contain provision for public notice of

all vacancies in magistrate positions and for the establishment by the district courts of merit selection panels, composed of residents of the individual judicial districts, to assist the courts in identifying and recommending persons who are best qualified to fill such positions.

(c) A magistrate may hold no other civil or military office or employment under the United States: Provided, however, That, with the approval of the conference, a part-time referee in bankruptcy or a clerk or deputy clerk of a court of the United States may be appointed and serve as a part-time United States magistrate, but the conference shall fix the aggregate amount of compensation to be received for performing the duties of part-time magistrate and part-time referee in bankruptcy, clerk or deputy clerk: And provided further, That retired officers and retired enlisted personnel of the Regular and Reserve components of the Army, Navy, Air Force, Marine Corps, and Coast Guard, members of the Reserve components of the Army, Navy, Air Force, Marine Corps, and Coast Guard, and members of the Army National Guard of the United States, the Air National Guard of the United States, and the Naval Militia and of the National Guard of a State, territory, or the District of Columbia, except the National Guard disbursing officers who are on a full-time salary basis, may be appointed and serve as United States magistrates.

(d) Except as otherwise provided in sections 375 and 636(h) of this title, no individual may serve under this chapter after having attained the age of seventy years: Provided, however, That upon a majority vote of all the judges of the appointing court or courts, which is taken upon the magistrate's attaining age seventy and upon each subsequent anniversary thereof, a magistrate who has attained the age of seventy years may continue to serve and may be reappointed under this chapter.

(e) The appointment of any individual as a full-time magistrate shall be for a term of eight years, and the appointment of any individuals as a part-time magistrate shall be for a term of four years, except that the term of a full-time or part-time magistrate appointed under subsection (k) shall expire upon—

    (1) the expiration of the absent magistrate's term,

    (2) the reinstatement of the absent magistrate in regular service in office as a magistrate,

    (3) the failure of the absent magistrate to make timely application under subsection (j) of this section for reinstatement in regular service in office as a magistrate after discharge or release from military service,

    (4) the death or resignation of the absent magistrate, or

    (5) the removal from office of the absent magistrate pursuant to subsection (i) of this section,

whichever may first occur.

(f) Upon the expiration of his term, a magistrate may, by a majority vote of the judges of the appointing district court or courts and with the approval of the judicial council of the circuit, continue to perform the duties of his office until his successor is appointed, or for 180 days after the date of the expiration of the magistrate's term, whichever is earlier.

(g) Each individual appointed as a magistrate under this section shall take the oath or affirmation prescribed by section 453 of this title before performing the duties of his office.

(h) Each appointment made by a judge or judges of a district court shall be entered of record in such court, and notice of such appointment shall be given at once by the clerk of that court to the Director.

(i) Removal of a magistrate during the term for which he is appointed shall be only for incompetency, misconduct, neglect of duty, or physical or mental disability, but a magistrate's office shall be terminated if the conference determines that the services performed by his office are no longer needed. Removal shall be by the judges of the district court for the judicial district in which the magistrate serves; where there is more than one judge of a district court, removal shall not occur unless a majority of all the judges of such court concur in the order of removal; and when there is a tie vote of the judges of the district court on the question of the removal or retention in office of a magistrate, then removal shall be only by a concurrence of a majority of all the judges of the council. In the case of a magistrate appointed under the third sentence of subsection (a) of this section, removal shall not occur unless a majority of all the judges of the appointing district courts concur in the order of removal; and where there is a tie vote on the question of the removal or retention in office of a magistrate, then removal shall be only by a concurrence of a majority of all the judges of the council or councils. Before any order or removal shall be entered, a full specification of the charges shall be furnished to the magistrate, and he shall be accorded by the judge or judges of the removing court, courts, council, or councils an opportunity to be heard on the charges.

(j) Upon the grant by the appropriate district court or courts of a leave of absence to a magistrate entitled to such relief under chapter 43 of title 38, such court or courts may proceed to appoint, in the manner specified in subsection (a) of this section, another magistrate, qualified for appointment and service under subsections (b), (c), and (d) of this section, who shall serve for the period specified in subsection (e) of this section.

(k) A United States magistrate appointed under this chapter shall be exempt from the provisions of subchapter I of chapter 63 of title 5.

[(**l**) Redesignated (k)]

(June 25, 1948, c. 646, 62 Stat. 915; May 24, 1949, c. 139, § 73, 63 Stat. 100; July 9, 1952, c. 609, § 1, 66 Stat. 509; July 25, 1956, c. 722, 70 Stat. 642; Oct. 17, 1968, Pub.L. 90–578, Title I, § 101, 82 Stat. 1108; Oct. 17, 1976, Pub.L. 94–520, § 2, 90 Stat. 2458; Nov. 6, 1978, Pub.L. 95–598, Title II, § 231, 92 Stat. 2665; Oct. 10, 1979, Pub.L. 96–82, § 3(a)-(d), 93 Stat. 644, 645; Aug. 6, 1982, Pub.L. 97–230, 96 Stat. 255; Nov. 14, 1986, Pub.L. 99–651, Title II, § 201(a)(1), 100 Stat. 3646; Nov. 15, 1988, Pub.L. 100–659, § 5, 102 Stat. 3918; Nov. 19, 1988, Pub.L. 100–702, Title X, § 1003(a)(2), 102 Stat. 4665; June 30, 1989, Pub.L. 101–45, Title II, § 104, 103 Stat. 122; Dec. 1, 1990, Pub.L. 101–650, Title III, § 308(b), 104 Stat. 5112; Oct. 13, 1994, Pub.L. 103–353, § 2(c), 108 Stat. 3169; Nov. 13, 2000, Pub.L. 106–518, Title II, § 201, 114 Stat. 2412.)

§ 632.   Character of Service

(a) Full-time United States magistrates may not engage in the practice of law, and may not engage in any other business, occupation, or employment inconsistent with the expeditious, proper, and impartial performance of their duties as judicial officers.

(b) Part-time United States magistrates shall render such service as judicial officers as is required by law. While so serving they may engage in the practice of law, but may not serve as counsel in any criminal action in any court of the United States, nor act in any capacity that is, under such regulations as the conference may establish, inconsistent with the proper discharge of their office. Within such restrictions, they may engage in any other business, occupation, or employment which is not inconsistent with the expeditious, proper, and impartial performance of their duties as judicial officers.

(June 25, 1948, c. 646, 62 Stat. 916; Oct. 17, 1968, Pub.L. 90–578, Title I, § 101, 82 Stat. 1110.)

§ 633.   Determination of Number, Locations, and Salaries of Magistrates

(a) Surveys by the Director.—

(1) The Director shall, within one year immediately following the date of the enactment of the Federal Magistrates Act, make a careful survey of conditions in judicial districts to determine (A) the number of appointments of full-time magistrates and part-time magistrates required to be made under this chapter to provide for the expeditious and effective administration of justice, (B) the locations at which such officers shall serve, and (C) their respective salaries under section 634 of this title. Thereafter, the Director shall, from time to time, make such surveys, general or local, as the conference shall deem expedient.

(2) In the course of any survey, the Director shall take into account local conditions in each judicial district, including the areas and the populations to be served, the transportation and communications facilities available, the amount and distribution of business of the type expected to arise before officers appointed under this chapter (including such matters as may be assigned under section 636(b) of this chapter), and any other material factors. The Director shall give consideration to suggestions from any interested parties, including district judges, United States commissioners or officers appointed under this chapter, United States attorneys, bar associations, and other parties having relevant experience or information.

(3) The surveys shall be made with a view toward creating and maintaining a system of full-time United States magistrates. However, should the Director find, as a result of any such surveys, areas in which the employment of a full-time magistrate would not be feasible or desirable, he shall recommend the appointment of part-time United States magistrates in such numbers and at such locations as may be required to permit prompt and efficient issuance of process and to permit individuals charged with criminal offenses against the United States to be brought before a judicial officer of the United States promptly after arrest.

(b) Determination by the conference.—Upon the completion of the initial surveys required by subsection (a) of this section, the Director shall report to the district courts, the councils, and the conference his recommendations concerning the number of full-time magistrates and part-time magistrates, their respective locations, and the amount of their respective salaries under section 634 of this title. The district courts shall advise their respective councils, stating their recommendations and the reasons therefor; the councils shall advise the conference, stating their recommendations and the reasons therefor, and shall also report to the conference the recommendations of the district courts. The conference shall determine, in the light of the recommendations of the Director, the district courts, and the councils, the number of full-time United States magistrates and part-time United States magistrates, the locations at which they shall serve, and their respective salaries. Such determinations shall take effect in each judicial district at such time as the district court for such judicial district shall determine, but in no event later than one year after they are promulgated.

(c) Changes in number, locations, and salaries.—Except as otherwise provided in this chapter, the conference may, from time to time, in the light of the recommendations of the Director, the district courts, and the councils, change the number, locations, and salaries of full-time and part-time magistrates, as the expeditious administration of justice may require.

(June 25, 1948, c. 646, 62 Stat. 916; Aug. 13, 1954, c. 728, § 1(a), (b), 68 Stat. 703, 704; Sept. 2, 1957, Pub.L. 85–276, §§ 1, 2, 71 Stat. 600; Oct. 17, 1968, Pub.L. 90–578, Title I, § 101, 82 Stat. 1111; Oct. 10, 1979, Pub.L. 96–82, § 4, 93 Stat. 645; Nov. 14, 1986, Pub.L. 99–651, Title II, § 202(d), 100 Stat. 3648.)

§ 636.   Jurisdiction, Powers, and Temporary Assignment

(a) Each United States magistrate judge serving under this chapter shall have within the district in which sessions are held by the court that appointed the magistrate judge, at other places where that court may function, and elsewhere as authorized by law—

(1) all powers and duties conferred or imposed upon United States commissioners by law or by the Rules of Criminal Procedure for the United States District Courts;

(2) the power to administer oaths and affirmations, issue orders pursuant to section 3142 of title 18 concerning release or detention of persons pending trial, and take acknowledgements, affidavits, and depositions;

(3) the power to conduct trials under section 3401, title 18, United States Code, in conformity with and subject to the limitations of that section;

(4) the power to enter a sentence for a petty offense; and

(5) the power to enter a sentence for a class A misdemeanor in a case in which the parties have consented.

(b)(1) Notwithstanding any provision of law to the contrary—

(A) a judge may designate a magistrate judge to hear and determine any pretrial matter pending before the court, except a motion for injunctive relief, for judgment on the pleadings, for summary judgment, to dismiss or quash an indictment or information made by the defendant, to suppress evidence in a criminal case, to dismiss or to permit maintenance of a class action, to dismiss for failure to state a claim upon which relief can be granted, and to involuntarily dismiss an action. A judge of the court may reconsider any pretrial matter under this subparagraph (A) where it has been shown that the magistrate judge's order is clearly erroneous or contrary to law.

(B) a judge may also designate a magistrate judge to conduct hearings, including evidentiary hearings, and to submit to a judge of the court proposed findings of fact and recommendations for the disposition, by a judge of the court, of any motion excepted in subparagraph (A), of applications for posttrial[1] relief made by individuals convicted of criminal offenses and of prisoner petitions challenging conditions of confinement.

(C) the magistrate judge shall file his proposed findings and recommendations under subparagraph (B) with the court and a copy shall forthwith be mailed to all parties.

Within ten days after being served with a copy, any party may serve and file written objections to such proposed findings and recommendations as provided by rules of court. A judge of the court shall make a de novo determination of those portions of the report or specified proposed findings or recommendations to which objection is made. A judge of the court may accept, reject, or modify, in whole or in part, the findings or recommendations made by the magistrate judge. The judge may also receive further evidence or recommit the matter to the magistrate judge with instructions.

(2) A judge may designate a magistrate judge to serve as a special master pursuant to the applicable provisions of this title and the Federal Rules of Civil Procedure for the United States district courts. A judge may designate a magistrate judge to serve as a special master in any civil case, upon consent of the parties, without regard to the provisions of rule 53(b) of the Federal Rules of Civil Procedure for the United States district courts.

(3) A magistrate judge may be assigned such additional duties as are not inconsistent with the Constitution and laws of the United States.

(4) Each district court shall establish rules pursuant to which the magistrate judges shall discharge their duties.

(c) Notwithstanding any provision of law to the contrary—

(1) Upon the consent of the parties, a full-time United States magistrate judge or a part-time United States magistrate judge who serves as a full-time judicial officer may conduct any or all proceed-

---

1.   So in original. Probably should be   "post-trial".

ings in a jury or nonjury civil matter and order the entry of judgment in the case, when specially designated to exercise such jurisdiction by the district court or courts he serves. Upon the consent of the parties, pursuant to their specific written request, any other part-time magistrate judge may exercise such jurisdiction, if such magistrate judge meets the bar membership requirements set forth in section 631(b)(1) and the chief judge of the district court certifies that a full-time magistrate judge is not reasonably available in accordance with guidelines established by the judicial council of the circuit. When there is more than one judge of a district court, designation under this paragraph shall be by the concurrence of a majority of all the judges of such district court, and when there is no such concurrence, then by the chief judge.

(2) If a magistrate judge is designated to exercise civil jurisdiction under paragraph (1) of this subsection, the clerk of court shall, at the time the action is filed, notify the parties of the availability of a magistrate judge to exercise such jurisdiction. The decision of the parties shall be communicated to the clerk of court. Thereafter, either the district court judge or the magistrate judge may again advise the parties of the availability of the magistrate judge, but in so doing, shall also advise the parties that they are free to withhold consent without adverse substantive consequences. Rules of court for the reference of civil matters to magistrate judges shall include procedures to protect the voluntariness of the parties' consent.

(3) Upon entry of judgment in any case referred under paragraph (1) of this subsection, an aggrieved party may appeal directly to the appropriate United States court of appeals from the judgment of the magistrate judge in the same manner as an appeal from any other judgment of a district court. The consent of the parties allows a magistrate judge designated to exercise civil jurisdiction under paragraph (1) of this subsection to direct the entry of a judgment of the district court in accordance with the Federal Rules of Civil Procedure. Nothing in this paragraph shall be construed as a limitation of any party's right to seek review by the Supreme Court of the United States.

(4) The court may, for good cause shown on its own motion, or under extraordinary circumstances shown by any party, vacate a reference of a civil matter to a magistrate judge under this subsection.

(5) The magistrate judge shall, subject to guidelines of the Judicial Conference, determine whether the record taken pursuant to this section shall be taken by electronic sound recording, by a court reporter, or by other means.

(d) The practice and procedure for the trial of cases before officers serving under this chapter shall conform to rules promulgated by the Supreme Court pursuant to section 2072 of this title.

(e) Contempt authority.—

(1) In general.—A United States magistrate judge serving under this chapter shall have within the territorial jurisdiction prescribed by the appointment of such magistrate judge the power to exercise contempt authority as set forth in this subsection.

(2) Summary criminal contempt authority.—A magistrate judge shall have the power to punish summarily by fine or imprisonment, or both, such contempt of the authority of such magistrate judge constituting misbehavior of any person in the magistrate judge's presence so as to obstruct the administration of justice. The order of contempt shall be issued under the Federal Rules of Criminal Procedure.

(3) Additional criminal contempt authority in civil consent and misdemeanor cases.—In any case in which a United States magistrate judge presides with the consent of the parties under subsection (c) of this section, and in any misdemeanor case proceeding before a magistrate judge under section 3401 of title 18, the magistrate judge shall have the power to punish, by fine or imprisonment, or both, criminal contempt constituting disobedience or resistance to the magistrate judge's lawful writ, process, order, rule, decree, or command. Disposition of such contempt shall be conducted upon notice and hearing under the Federal Rules of Criminal Procedure.

(4) Civil contempt authority in civil consent and misdemeanor cases.—In any case in which a United States magistrate judge presides with the consent of the parties under subsection (c) of this section, and in any misdemeanor case proceeding before a magistrate judge under section 3401 of title 18, the magistrate judge may exercise the civil contempt authority of the district court. This paragraph shall not be construed to limit the authority of a magistrate judge to order sanctions under any other statute, the Federal Rules of Civil Procedure, or the Federal Rules of Criminal Procedure.

(5) Criminal contempt penalties.—The sentence imposed by a magistrate judge for any criminal contempt provided for in paragraphs (2) and (3) shall not exceed the penalties for a Class C misdemeanor as set forth in sections 3581(b)(8) and 3571(b)(6) of title 18.

(6) Certification of other contempts to the district court.—Upon the commission of any such act—

> **(A)** in any case in which a United States magistrate judge presides with the consent of the parties under subsection (c) of this section, or in any misdemeanor case proceeding before a magistrate judge under section 3401 of title 18, that may, in the opinion of the magistrate judge, constitute a serious criminal contempt punishable by penalties exceeding those set forth in paragraph (5) of this subsection, or

> **(B)** in any other case or proceeding under subsection (a) or (b) of this section, or any other statute, where—

(**i**) the act committed in the magistrate judge's presence may, in the opinion of the magistrate judge, constitute a serious criminal contempt punishable by penalties exceeding those set forth in paragraph (5) of this subsection,

(**ii**) the act that constitutes a criminal contempt occurs outside the presence of the magistrate judge, or

(**iii**) the act constitutes a civil contempt,

the magistrate judge shall forthwith certify the facts to a district judge and may serve or cause to be served, upon any person whose behavior is brought into question under this paragraph, an order requiring such person to appear before a district judge upon a day certain to show cause why that person should not be adjudged in contempt by reason of the facts so certified. The district judge shall thereupon hear the evidence as to the act or conduct complained of and, if it is such as to warrant punishment, punish such person in the same manner and to the same extent as for a contempt committed before a district judge.

(**7**) Appeals of magistrate judge contempt orders.—The appeal of an order of contempt under this subsection shall be made to the court of appeals in cases proceeding under subsection (c) of this section. The appeal of any other order of contempt issued under this section shall be made to the district court.

(**f**) In an emergency and upon the concurrence of the chief judges of the districts involved, a United States magistrate judge may be temporarily assigned to perform any of the duties specified in subsection (a), (b), or (c) of this section in a judicial district other than the judicial district for which he has been appointed. No magistrate judge shall perform any of such duties in a district to which he has been temporarily assigned until an order has been issued by the chief judge of such district specifying (1) the emergency by reason of which he has been transferred, (2) the duration of his assignment, and (3) the duties which he is authorized to perform. A magistrate judge so assigned shall not be entitled to additional compensation but shall be reimbursed for actual and necessary expenses incurred in the performance of his duties in accordance with section 635.

(**g**) A United States magistrate judge may perform the verification function required by section 4107 of title 18, United States Code. A magistrate judge may be assigned by a judge of any United States district court to perform the verification required by section 4108 and the appointment of counsel authorized by section 4109 of title 18, United States Code, and may perform such functions beyond the territorial limits of the United States. A magistrate judge assigned such functions shall have no authority to perform any other function within the territory of a foreign country.

(**h**) A United States magistrate judge who has retired may, upon the consent of the chief judge of the district involved, be recalled to serve as a magistrate judge in any judicial district by the judicial council of the circuit within which such district is located. Upon recall, a magistrate judge may receive a salary for such service in accordance with regulations promulgated by the Judicial Conference, subject to the restrictions on the payment of an annuity set forth in section 377 of this title or in subchapter III of chapter 83, and chapter 84, of title 5 which are applicable to such magistrate judge. The requirements set forth in subsections (a), (b)(3), and (d) of section 631, and paragraph (1) of subsection (b) of such section to the extent such paragraph requires membership of the bar of the location in which an individual is to serve as a magistrate judge, shall not apply to the recall of a retired magistrate judge under this subsection or section 375 of this title. Any other requirement set forth in section 631(b) shall apply to the recall of a retired magistrate judge under this subsection or section 375 of this title unless such retired magistrate judge met such requirement upon appointment or reappointment as a magistrate judge under section 361.

(June 25, 1948, c. 646, 62 Stat. 917; Oct. 17, 1968, Pub.L. 90–578, Title I, § 101, 82 Stat. 1113; Mar. 1, 1972, Pub.L. 92–239, §§ 1, 2, 86 Stat. 47; Oct. 21, 1976, Pub.L. 94–577, § 1, 90 Stat. 2729; Oct. 28, 1977, Pub.L. 95–144, § 2, 91 Stat. 1220; Oct. 10, 1979, Pub.L. 96–82, § 2, 93 Stat. 643; Oct. 12, 1984, Pub.L. 98–473, Title II, § 208, 98 Stat. 1986; Nov. 8, 1984, Pub.L. 98–620, Title IV, § 402(29)(B), 98 Stat. 3359; Nov. 14, 1986, Pub.L. 99–651, Title II, § 201(a)(2), 100 Stat. 3647; Nov. 15, 1988, Pub.L. 100–659, § 4(c), 102 Stat. 3918; Nov. 18, 1988, Pub.L. 100–690, Title VII, § 7322, 102 Stat. 4467; Nov. 19, 1988, Pub.L. 100–702, Title IV, § 404(b)(1), Title X, § 1014, 102 Stat. 4651, 4669; Dec. 1, 1990, Pub.L. 101–650, Title III, §§ 308(a), 321, 104 Stat. 5112, 5117; Oct. 19, 1996, Pub.L. 104–317, Title II, §§ 201, 202(b), 207, 110 Stat. 3848, 3849, 3851; Nov. 13, 2000, Pub.L. 106–518, Title II, §§ 202, 203(b), 114 Stat. 2412, 2414; Nov. 2, 2002, Pub.L. 107–273, Div. B, Title III, § 3002(b), 116 Stat. 1805; Sept. 9, 2005, Pub.L. 109–63, § 2(d), 119 Stat. 1995.)

§ 639. Definitions

As used in this chapter—

(1) "Conference" shall mean the Judicial Conference of the United States;

(2) "Council" shall mean the Judicial Council of the Circuit;

(3) "Director" shall mean the Director of the Administrative Office of the United States Courts;

(4) "Full-time magistrate" shall mean a full-time United States magistrate;

(5) "Part-time magistrate" shall mean a part-time United States magistrate; and

(6) "United States magistrate" and "magistrate" shall mean both full-time and part-time United States magistrates.

(June 25, 1948, c. 646, 62 Stat. 917; Oct. 17, 1968, Pub.L. 90–578, Title I, § 101, 82 Stat. 1114.)

§ 1251. Original jurisdiction

(a) The Supreme Court shall have original and exclusive jurisdiction of all controversies between two or more States.

(b) The Supreme Court shall have original but not exclusive jurisdiction of:

(1) All actions or proceedings to which ambassadors, other public ministers, consuls, or vice consuls of foreign states are parties;

(2) All controversies between the United States and a State;

(3) All actions or proceedings by a State against the citizens of another State or against aliens.

(As amended Sept. 30, 1978, Pub.L. 95–393, § 8(b), 92 Stat. 810.)

§ 1253.   Direct appeals from decisions of three-judge courts

Except as otherwise provided by law, any party may appeal to the Supreme Court from an order granting or denying, after notice and hearing, an interlocutory or permanent injunction in any civil action, suit or proceeding required by any Act of Congress to be heard and determined by a district court of three judges.

§ 1254.   Courts of appeals; certiorari; certified questions

Cases in the courts of appeals may be reviewed by the Supreme Court by the following methods:

(1) By writ of certiorari granted upon the petition of any party to any civil or criminal case, before or after rendition of judgment or decree;

(2) By certification at any time by a court of appeals of any question of law in any civil or criminal case as to which instructions are desired, and upon such certification the Supreme Court may give binding instructions or require the entire record to be sent up for decision of the entire matter in controversy.

(As amended June 27, 1988, Pub.L. 100–352, § 2(a), (b), 102 Stat. 662.)

§ 1257.   State courts; certiorari

(a) Final judgments or decrees rendered by the highest court of a State in which a decision could be had, may be reviewed by the Supreme Court by writ of certiorari where the validity of a treaty or statute of the United States is drawn in question or where the validity of a statute of any State is drawn in question on the ground of its being repugnant to the Constitution, treaties, or laws of the United States, or where any title, right, privilege, or immunity is specially set up or claimed under the Constitution or the treaties or statutes of, or any commission held or authority exercised under, the United States.

(b) For the purposes of this section, the term "highest court of a State" includes the District of Columbia Court of Appeals.

(As amended July 29, 1970, Pub.L. 91–358, Title I, § 172(a)(1), 84 Stat. 590; June 27, 1988, Pub.L. 100–352, § 3, 102 Stat. 662.)

§ 1291.   Final decisions of district courts

The courts of appeals (other than the United States Court of Appeals for the Federal Circuit) shall have jurisdiction of appeals from all final decisions of the district courts of the United States, the United States District Court for the District of the Canal Zone, the District Court of Guam, and the District Court of the Virgin Islands, except where a direct review may be had in the Supreme Court. The jurisdiction of the United States Court of Appeals for the Federal Circuit shall be limited to the jurisdiction described in sections 1292(c) and (d) and 1295 of this title.

(As amended Oct. 31, 1951, c. 655, § 48, 65 Stat. 726; July 7, 1958, Pub.L. 85–508, § 12(e), 72 Stat. 348; Apr. 2, 1982, Pub.L. 97–164, Title I, § 124, 96 Stat. 36.)

§ 1292. **Interlocutory decisions**

(a) Except as provided in subsections (c) and (d) of this section, the courts of appeals shall have jurisdiction of appeals from:

(1) Interlocutory orders of the district courts of the United States, the United States District Court for the District of the Canal Zone, the District Court of Guam, and the District Court of the Virgin Islands, or of the judges thereof, granting, continuing, modifying, refusing or dissolving injunctions, or refusing to dissolve or modify injunctions, except where a direct review may be had in the Supreme Court;

(2) Interlocutory orders appointing receivers, or refusing orders to wind up receiverships or to take steps to accomplish the purposes thereof, such as directing sales or other disposals of property;

(3) Interlocutory decrees of such district courts or the judges thereof determining the rights and liabilities of the parties to admiralty cases in which appeals from final decrees are allowed.

(b) When a district judge, in making in a civil action an order not otherwise appealable under this section, shall be of the opinion that such order involves a controlling question of law as to which there is substantial ground for difference of opinion and that an immediate appeal from the order may materially advance the ultimate termination of the litigation, he shall so state in writing in such order. The Court of Appeals which would have jurisdiction of an appeal of such action may thereupon, in its discretion, permit an appeal to be taken from such order, if application is made to it within ten days after the entry of the order: *Provided, however,* that application for an appeal hereunder shall not stay proceedings in the district court unless the district judge or the Court of Appeals or a judge thereof shall so order.

(c) The United States Court of Appeals for the Federal Circuit shall have exclusive jurisdiction—

(1) of an appeal from an interlocutory order or decree described in subsection (a) or (b) of this section in any case over which the court would have jurisdiction of an appeal under section 1295 of this title; and

(2) of an appeal from a judgment in a civil action for patent infringement which would otherwise be appealable to the United States Court of Appeals for the Federal Circuit and is final except for an accounting.

(d)(1) When the chief judge of the Court of International Trade issues an order under the provisions of section 256(b) of this title, or when any judge of the Court of International Trade, in issuing any other interlocutory order, includes in the order a statement that a controlling question of law is involved with respect to which there is a substantial ground for difference of opinion and that an immediate appeal from that order may materially advance the ultimate termination of the litigation, the United States Court of Appeals for the Federal Circuit may, in its discretion, permit an appeal to be taken from such order, if application is made to that Court within ten days after the entry of such order.

(2) When the chief judge of the United States Court of Federal Claims issues an order under section 798(b) of this title, or when any judge of the United States Court of Federal Claims, in issuing an interlocutory order, includes in the order a statement that a controlling question of law is involved with respect to which there is a substantial ground for difference of opinion and that an immediate appeal from that order may materially advance the ultimate termination of the litigation, the United States Court of Appeals for the Federal Circuit may, in its discretion, permit an appeal to be taken from such order, if application is made to that Court within ten days after the entry of such order.

(3) Neither the application for nor the granting of an appeal under this subsection shall stay proceedings in the Court of International Trade or in the Court of Federal Claims, as the case may be, unless a stay is ordered by a judge of the Court of International Trade or of the Court of Federal Claims or by the United States Court of Appeals for the Federal Circuit or a judge of that court.

(4)(A) The United States Court of Appeals for the Federal Circuit shall have exclusive jurisdiction of an appeal from an interlocutory order of a district court of the United States, the District Court of Guam, the District Court of the Virgin Islands, or the District Court for the Northern Mariana Islands, granting or denying, in whole or in part, a motion to transfer an action to the United States Court of Federal Claims under section 1631 of this title.

(B) When a motion to transfer an action to the Court of Federal Claims is filed in a district court, no further proceedings shall be taken in the district court until 60 days after the court has ruled upon the motion. If an appeal is taken from the district court's grant or denial of the motion, proceedings shall be further stayed until the appeal has been decided by the Court of Appeals for the Federal Circuit. The stay of proceedings in the district court shall not bar the granting of preliminary or injunctive relief, where appropriate and where expedition is reasonably necessary. However, during the period in which proceedings are stayed as provided in this subparagraph, no transfer to the Court of Federal Claims pursuant to the motion shall be carried out.

(e) The Supreme Court may prescribe rules, in accordance with section 2072 of this title, to provide for an appeal of an interlocutory decision to the courts of appeals that is not otherwise provided for under subsection (a), (b), (c), or (d).

(As amended Oct. 31, 1951, c. 655, § 49, 65 Stat. 726; July 7, 1958, Pub.L. 85–508, § 12(e), 72 Stat. 348; Sept. 2, 1958, Pub.L. 85–919, 72 Stat. 1770; Apr. 2, 1982, Pub. L. 97–164, Title I, § 125, 96 Stat. 36; Nov. 8, 1984, Pub.L. 98–620, Title IV, § 412, 98 Stat. 3362; Nov. 19, 1988, Pub.L. 100–702, Title V, § 501, 102 Stat. 4652; Oct. 29, 1992, Pub.L. 102–572, Title I, § 101, Title IX, §§ 902(b), 906(c), 106 Stat. 4506, 4516, 4518.)

§ 1330.   Actions against foreign states

(a) The district courts shall have original jurisdiction without re-gard to amount in controversy of any nonjury civil action against a foreign state as defined in section 1603(a) of this title as to any claim for relief in personam with respect to which the foreign state is not entitled to immunity either under sections 1605–1607 of this title or under any applicable international agreement.

(b) Personal jurisdiction over a foreign state shall exist as to every claim for relief over which the district courts have jurisdiction under subsection (a) where service has been made under section 1608 of this title.

(c) For purposes of subsection (b), an appearance by a foreign state does not confer personal jurisdiction with respect to any claim for relief not arising out of any transaction or occurrence enumerated in sections 1605–1607 of this title.

(Added Pub.L. 94–583, § 2(a), Oct. 21, 1976, 90 Stat. 2891.)

§ 1331.   Federal question

The district courts shall have original jurisdiction of all civil actions arising under the Constitution, laws, or treaties of the United States.

(As amended July 25, 1958, Pub.L. 85–554, § 1, 72 Stat. 415; Oct. 21, 1976, Pub.L. 94–574, § 2, 90 Stat. 2721; Dec. 1, 1980, Pub. L. 96–486, § 2(a), 94 Stat. 2369.)

§ 1332.   Diversity of citizenship; amount in controversy; costs

(a) The district courts shall have original jurisdiction of all civil actions where the matter in controversy exceeds the sum or value of $75,000, exclusive of interest and costs, and is between—

(1) citizens of different States;

(2) citizens of a State and citizens or subjects of a foreign state;

(3) citizens of different States and in which citizens or subjects of a foreign state are additional parties; and

(4) a foreign state, defined in section 1603(a) of this title, as plaintiff and citizens of a State or of different States.

For the purposes of this section, section 1335, and section 1441, an alien admitted to the United States for permanent residence shall be deemed a citizen of the State in which such alien is domiciled.

(b) Except when express provision therefor is otherwise made in a statute of the United States, where the plaintiff who files the case originally in the Federal courts is finally adjudged to be entitled to recover less than the sum or value of $75,000, computed without regard to any setoff or counterclaim to which the defendant may be adjudged to be entitled, and exclusive of interest and costs, the district court may deny costs to the plaintiff and, in addition, may impose costs on the plaintiff.

(c) For the purposes of this section and section 1441 of this title—

(1) a corporation shall be deemed to be a citizen of any State by which it has been incorporated and of the State where it has its principal place of business, except that in any direct action against the insurer of a policy or contract of liability insurance, whether incorporated or unincorporated, to which action the insured is not joined as a party-defendant, such insurer shall be deemed a citizen of the State of which the insured is a citizen, as well as of any State by which the insurer has been incorporated and of the State where it has its principal place of business; and

(2) the legal representative of the estate of a decedent shall be deemed to be a citizen only of the same State as the decedent, and the legal representative of an infant or incompetent shall be deemed to be a citizen only of the same State as the infant or incompetent.

(d)(1) In this subsection—

(A) the term "class" means all of the class members in a class action;

(B) the term "class action" means any civil action filed under rule 23 of the Federal Rules of Civil Procedure or similar State statute or rule of judicial procedure authorizing an action to be brought by 1 or more representative persons as a class action;

(C) the term "class certification order" means an order issued by a court approving the treatment of some or all aspects of a civil action as a class action; and

(D) the term "class members" means the persons (named or unnamed) who fall within the definition of the proposed or certified class in a class action.

(2) The district courts shall have original jurisdiction of any civil action in which the matter in controversy exceeds the sum or value of $5,000,000, exclusive of interest and costs, and is a class action in which—

(A) any member of a class of plaintiffs is a citizen of a State different from any defendant;

(B) any member of a class of plaintiffs is a foreign state or a citizen or subject of a foreign state and any defendant is a citizen of a State; or

(C) any member of a class of plaintiffs is a citizen of a State and any defendant is a foreign state or a citizen or subject of a foreign state.

(3) A district court may, in the interests of justice and looking at the totality of the circumstances, decline to exercise jurisdiction under paragraph (2) over a class action in which greater than one-third but less than two-thirds of the members of all proposed plaintiff classes in the aggregate and the primary defendants are citizens of the State in which the action was originally filed based on consideration of—

(A) whether the claims asserted involve matters of national or interstate interest;

(B) whether the claims asserted will be governed by laws of the State in which the action was originally filed or by the laws of other States;

(C) whether the class action has been pleaded in a manner that seeks to avoid Federal jurisdiction;

(D) whether the action was brought in a forum with a distinct nexus with the class members, the alleged harm, or the defendants;

(E) whether the number of citizens of the State in which the action was originally filed in all proposed plaintiff classes in the aggregate is substantially larger than the number of citizens from any other State, and the citizenship of the other members of the proposed class is dispersed among a substantial number of States; and

(F) whether, during the 3–year period preceding the filing of that class action, 1 or more other class actions asserting the same or similar claims on behalf of the same or other persons have been filed.

(4) A district court shall decline to exercise jurisdiction under paragraph (2)—

(A)(i) over a class action in which—

(I) greater than two-thirds of the members of all proposed plaintiff classes in the aggregate are citizens of the State in which the action was originally filed;

(II) at least 1 defendant is a defendant—

(aa) from whom significant relief is sought by members of the plaintiff class;

(bb) whose alleged conduct forms a significant basis for the claims asserted by the proposed plaintiff class; and

(cc) who is a citizen of the State in which the action was originally filed; and

(III) principal injuries resulting from the alleged conduct or any related conduct of each defendant were incurred in the State in which the action was originally filed; and

(ii) during the 3–year period preceding the filing of that class action, no other class action has been filed asserting the same or similar factual allegations against any of the defendants on behalf of the same or other persons; or

(B) two-thirds or more of the members of all proposed plaintiff classes in the aggregate, and the primary defendants, are citizens of the State in which the action was originally filed.

(5) Paragraphs (2) through (4) shall not apply to any class action in which—

(A) the primary defendants are States, State officials, or other governmental entities against whom the district court may be foreclosed from ordering relief; or

(B) the number of members of all proposed plaintiff classes in the aggregate is less than 100.

(6) In any class action, the claims of the individual class members shall be aggregated to determine whether the matter in controversy exceeds the sum or value of $5,000,000, exclusive of interest and costs.

(7) Citizenship of the members of the proposed plaintiff classes shall be determined for purposes of paragraphs (2) through (6) as of the date of filing of the complaint or amended complaint, or, if the case stated by the initial pleading is not subject to Federal jurisdiction, as of the date of service by plaintiffs of an amended pleading, motion, or other paper, indicating the existence of Federal jurisdiction.

(8) This subsection shall apply to any class action before or after the entry of a class certification order by the court with respect to that action.

(9) Paragraph (2) shall not apply to any class action that solely involves a claim—

 (A) concerning a covered security as defined under 16(f)(3)[1] of the Securities Act of 1933 (15 U.S.C. 78p(f)(3)) and section 28(f)(5)(E) of the Securities Exchange Act of 1934 (15 U.S.C. 78bb(f)(5)(E));

 (B) that relates to the internal affairs or governance of a corporation or other form of business enterprise and that arises under or by virtue of the laws of the State in which such corporation or business enterprise is incorporated or organized; or

 (C) that relates to the rights, duties (including fiduciary duties), and obligations relating to or created by or pursuant to any security (as defined under section 2(a)(1) of the Securities Act of 1933 (15 U.S.C. 77b(a)(1)) and the regulations issued thereunder).

(10) For purposes of this subsection and section 1453, an unincorporated association shall be deemed to be a citizen of the State where it has its principal place of business and the State under whose laws it is organized.

(11)(A) For purposes of this subsection and section 1453, a mass action shall be deemed to be a class action removable under paragraphs (2) through (10) if it otherwise meets the provisions of those paragraphs.

 (B)(i) As used in subparagraph (A), the term "mass action" means any civil action (except a civil action within the scope of section 1711(2)) in which monetary relief claims of 100 or more persons are proposed to be tried jointly on the ground that the plaintiffs' claims involve common questions of law or fact, except that jurisdiction shall exist only over those plaintiffs whose claims in a mass action satisfy the jurisdictional amount requirements under subsection (a).

 (ii) As used in subparagraph (A), the term "mass action" shall not include any civil action in which—

  (I) all of the claims in the action arise from an event or occurrence in the State in which the action was filed, and that allegedly resulted in injuries in that State or in States contiguous to that State;

    (II) the claims are joined upon motion of a defendant;

    (III) all of the claims in the action are asserted on behalf of the general public (and not on behalf of individual claimants or members of a purported class) pursuant to a State statute specifically authorizing such action; or

    (IV) the claims have been consolidated or coordinated solely for pretrial proceedings.

    (C)(i) Any action(s) removed to Federal court pursuant to this subsection shall not thereafter be transferred to any other court pursuant to section 1407, or the rules promulgated thereunder, unless a majority of the plaintiffs in the action request transfer pursuant to section 1407.

    (ii) This subparagraph will not apply—

    (I) to cases certified pursuant to rule 23 of the Federal Rules of Civil Procedure; or

    (II) if plaintiffs propose that the action proceed as a class action pursuant to rule 23 of the Federal Rules of Civil Procedure.

    (D) The limitations periods on any claims asserted in a mass action that is removed to Federal court pursuant to this subsection shall be deemed tolled during the period that the action is pending in Federal court.

    (e) The word "States", as used in this section, includes the Territories, the District of Columbia, and the Commonwealth of Puerto Rico.

(June 25, 1948, c. 646, 62 Stat. 930; July 26, 1956, c. 740, 70 Stat. 658; July 25, 1958, Pub.L. 85–554, § 2, 72 Stat. 415; Aug. 14, 1964, Pub.L. 88–439, § 1, 78 Stat. 445; Oct. 21, 1976, Pub.L. 94–583, § 3, 90 Stat. 2891; Nov. 19, 1988, Pub.L. 100–702, Title II, §§ 201(a), 202(a), 203(a), 102 Stat. 4646; Oct. 19, 1996, Pub.L. 104–317, Title II, § 205(a), 110 Stat. 3850; Feb. 18, 2005, Pub.L. 109–2, § 4(a), 119 Stat. 9.)

    1.   So in original. Reference to "16(f)(3)" probably should be preceded by "section".

§ 1333.   Admiralty, maritime and prize cases

    The district courts shall have original jurisdiction, exclusive of the courts of the States, of:

    (1) Any civil case of admiralty or maritime jurisdiction, saving to suitors in all cases all other remedies to which they are otherwise entitled.

    (2) Any prize brought into the United States and all proceedings for the condemnation of property taken as prize.

(June 25, 1948, c. 646, 62 Stat. 931; May 24, 1949, c. 139, § 79, 63 Stat. 101.)

§ 1334.   Bankruptcy cases and proceedings

    (a) Except as provided in subsection (b) of this section, the district courts shall have original and exclusive jurisdiction of all cases under title 11.

(b) Except as provided in subsection (e)(2), and notwithstanding any Act of Congress that confers exclusive jurisdiction on a court or courts other than the district courts, the district courts shall have original but not exclusive jurisdiction of all civil proceedings arising under title 11, or arising in or related to cases under title 11.

(c)(1) Except with respect to a case under chapter 15 of title 11, nothing in this section prevents a district court in the interest of justice, or in the interest of comity with State courts or respect for State law, from abstaining from hearing a particular proceeding arising under title 11 or arising in or related to a case under title 11.

(2) Upon timely motion of a party in a proceeding based upon a State law claim or State law cause of action, related to a case under title 11 but not arising under title 11 or arising in a case under title 11, with respect to which an action could not have been commenced in a court of the United States absent jurisdiction under this section, the district court shall abstain from hearing such proceeding if an action is commenced, and can be timely adjudicated, in a State forum of appropriate jurisdiction.

(d) Any decision to abstain or not to abstain made under subsection (c) (other than a decision not to abstain in a proceeding described in subsection (c)(2)) is not reviewable by appeal or otherwise by the court of appeals under section 158(d), 1291, or 1292 of this title or by the Supreme Court of the United States under section 1254 of this title. Subsection (c) and this subsection shall not be construed to limit the applicability of the stay provided for by section 362 of title 11, United States Code, as such section applies to an action affecting the property of the estate in bankruptcy.

(e) The district court in which a case under title 11 is commenced or is pending shall have exclusive jurisdiction—

(1) of all the property, wherever located, of the debtor as of the commencement of such case, and of property of the estate; and

(2) over all claims or causes of action that involve construction of section 327 of title 11, United States Code, or rules relating to disclosure requirements under section 327.

(June 25, 1948, c. 646, 62 Stat. 931; Nov. 6, 1978, Pub.L. 95–598, Title II, § 238(a), 92 Stat. 2667; July 10, 1984, Pub.L. 98–353, Title I, § 101(a), 98 Stat. 333; Oct. 27, 1986, Pub.L. 99–554, Title I, § 144(e), 100 Stat. 3096; Dec. 1, 1990, Pub.L. 101–650, Title III, § 309(b), 104 Stat. 5113; Oct. 22, 1994, Pub.L. 103–394, Title I, § 104(b), 108 Stat. 4109; Apr. 20, 2005, Pub.L. 109–8, Title III, § 324(a), Title VIII, § 802(c)(2), Title XII, § 1219, 119 Stat. 98, 145, 195.)

§ 1335. Interpleader

(a) The district courts shall have original jurisdiction of any civil action of interpleader or in the nature of interpleader filed by any person, firm, or corporation, association, or society having in his or its custody or possession money or property of the value of $500 or more, or having issued a note, bond, certificate, policy of insurance, or other instrument of value or amount of $500 or more, or providing for the delivery or payment or the loan of money or property of such amount or value, or being under any obligation written or unwritten to the amount of $500 or more, if

(1) Two or more adverse claimants, of diverse citizenship as defined in subsection (a) or (d) of section 1332 of this title, are claiming or may claim to be entitled to such money or property, or to any one or more of the benefits arising by virtue of any note, bond, certificate, policy or other instrument, or arising by virtue of any such obligation; and if (2) the plaintiff has deposited such money or property or has paid the amount of or the loan or other value of such instrument or the amount due under such obligation into the registry of the court, there to abide the judgment of the court, or has given bond payable to the clerk of the court in such amount and with such surety as the court or judge may deem proper, conditioned upon the compliance by the plaintiff with the future order or judgment of the court with respect to the subject matter of the controversy.

(b) Such an action may be entertained although the titles or claims of the conflicting claimants do not have a common origin, or are not identical, but are adverse to and independent of one another.

§ 1337. Commerce and antitrust regulations; amount in controversy, costs

(a) The district courts shall have original jurisdiction of any civil action or proceeding arising under any Act of Congress regulating commerce or protecting trade and commerce against restraints and monopolies: Provided, however, That the district courts shall have original jurisdiction of an action brought under section 11706 or 14706 of title 49, only if the matter in controversy for each receipt or bill of lading exceeds $10,000, exclusive of interest and costs.

(b) Except when express provision therefor is otherwise made in a statute of the United States, where a plaintiff who files the case under section 11706 or 14706 of title 49, originally in the Federal courts is finally adjudged to be entitled to recover less than the sum or value of $10,000, computed without regard to any setoff or counterclaim to which the defendant may be adjudged to be entitled, and exclusive of any interest and costs, the district court may deny costs to the plaintiff and, in addition, may impose costs on the plaintiff.

(c) The district courts shall not have jurisdiction under this section of any matter within the exclusive jurisdiction of the Court of International Trade under chapter 95 of this title.

(June 25, 1948, c. 646, 62 Stat. 931; Oct. 20, 1978, Pub.L. 95–486, § 9(a), 92 Stat. 1633; Oct. 10, 1980, Pub.L. 96–417, Title V, § 505, 94 Stat. 1743; Jan. 12, 1983, Pub.L. 97–449, § 5(f), 96 Stat. 2442; Dec. 29, 1995, Pub.L. 104–88, Title III, § 305(a)(3), 109 Stat. 944.)

§ 1338. Patents, plant variety protection, copyrights, mask works, designs, trademarks, and unfair competition

(a) The district courts shall have original jurisdiction of any civil action arising under any Act of Congress relating to patents, plant variety protection, copyrights and trademarks. Such jurisdiction shall be exclusive of the courts of the states in patent, plant variety protection and copyright cases.

(b) The district courts shall have original jurisdiction of any civil action asserting a claim of unfair competition when joined with a substantial and related claim under the copyright, patent, plant variety protection or trademark laws.

(c) Subsections (a) and (b) apply to exclusive rights in mask works under chapter 9 of title 17, and to exclusive rights in designs under chapter 13 of title 17, to the same extent as such subsections apply to copyrights.

(June 25, 1948, c. 646, 62 Stat. 931; Dec. 24, 1970, Pub.L. 91–577, Title III, § 143(b), 84 Stat. 1559; Nov. 19, 1988, Pub.L. 100–702, Title X, § 1020(a)(4), 102 Stat. 4671; Oct. 28, 1998, Pub.L 105–304, Title V, § 503(b)(1), (2)(A), 112 Stat. 2917; Nov. 29, 1999, Pub.L. 106–113, Div. B, § 1000(a)(9) [S. 1948, Title III, § 3009(1)], 113 Stat. 1536, 1537-___.)

§ 1339.   Postal matters

The district courts shall have original jurisdiction of any civil action arising under any Act of Congress relating to the postal service.

(June 25, 1948, c. 646, 62 Stat. 932.)

§ 1340.   Internal revenue; customs duties

The district courts shall have original jurisdiction of any civil action arising under any Act of Congress providing for internal revenue, or revenue from imports or tonnage except matters within the jurisdiction of the Court of International Trade.

(June 25, 1948, c. 646, 62 Stat. 932; Oct. 10, 1980, Pub.L. 96–417, Title V, § 501(21), 94 Stat. 1742.)

§ 1343.   Civil rights and elective franchise

(a) The district courts shall have original jurisdiction of any civil action authorized by law to be commenced by any person:

    (1) To recover damages for injury to his person or property, or because of the deprivation of any right or privilege of a citizen of the United States, by any act done in furtherance of any conspiracy mentioned in section 1985 of Title 42;

    (2) To recover damages from any person who fails to prevent or to aid in preventing any wrongs mentioned in section 1985 of Title 42 which he had knowledge were about to occur and power to prevent;

    (3) To redress the deprivation, under color of any State law, statute, ordinance, regulation, custom or usage, of any right, privilege or immunity secured by the Constitution of the United States or by any Act of Congress providing for equal rights of citizens or of all persons within the jurisdiction of the United States;

    (4) To recover damages or to secure equitable or other relief under any Act of Congress providing for the protection of civil rights, including the right to vote.

(b) For purposes of this section—

(1) the District of Columbia shall be considered to be a State; and

(2) any Act of Congress applicable exclusively to the District of Columbia shall be considered to be a statute of the District of Columbia.

(As amended Sept. 3, 1954, c. 1263, § 42, 68 Stat. 1241; Sept. 9, 1957, Pub.L. 85–315, Part III, § 121, 71 Stat. 637; Dec. 29, 1979, Pub.L. 96–170, § 2, 93 Stat. 1284.)

§ 1345.   United States as plaintiff

Except as otherwise provided by Act of Congress, the district courts shall have original jurisdiction of all civil actions, suits or proceedings commenced by the United States, or by any agency or officer thereof expressly authorized to sue by Act of Congress.

§ 1346.   United States as defendant

(a) The district courts shall have original jurisdiction, concurrent with the United States Court of Federal Claims, of:

(1) Any civil action against the United States for the recovery of any internal-revenue tax alleged to have been erroneously or illegally assessed or collected, or any penalty claimed to have been collected without authority or any sum alleged to have been excessive or in any manner wrongfully collected under the internal-revenue laws;

(2) Any other civil action or claim against the United States, not exceeding $10,000 in amount, founded either upon the Constitution, or any Act of Congress, or any regulation of an executive department, or upon any express or implied contract with the United States, or for liquidated or unliquidated damages in cases not sounding in tort, except that the district courts shall not have jurisdiction of any civil action or claim against the United States founded upon any express or implied contract with the United States or for liquidated or unliquidated damages in cases not sounding in tort which are subject to sections 8(g)(1) and 10(a)(1) of the Contract Disputes Act of 1978. For the purpose of this paragraph, an express or implied contract with the Army and Air Force Exchange Service, Navy Exchanges, Marine Corps Exchanges, Coast Guard Exchanges, or Exchange Councils of the National Aeronautics and Space Administration shall be considered an express or implied contract with the United States.

(b)(1) Subject to the provisions of chapter 171 of this title, the district courts, together with the United States District Court for the District of the Canal Zone and the District Court of the Virgin Islands, shall have exclusive jurisdiction of civil actions on claims against the United States, for money damages, accruing on and after January 1, 1945, for injury or loss of property, or personal injury or death caused by the negligent or wrongful act or omission of any employee of the Government while acting within the scope of his office or employment, under circumstances where the United States, if a private person, would be liable to the claimant in accordance with the law of the place where the act or omission occurred.

(2) No person convicted of a felony who is incarcerated while awaiting sentencing or while serving a sentence may bring a civil action against the United States or an agency, officer, or employee of the Government, for mental or emotional injury suffered while in custody without a prior showing of physical injury.

(c) The jurisdiction conferred by this section includes jurisdiction of any set-off, counterclaim, or other claim or demand whatever on the part of the United States against any plaintiff commencing an action under this section.

(d) The district courts shall not have jurisdiction under this section of any civil action or claim for a pension.

(e) The district courts shall have original jurisdiction of any civil action against the United States provided in section 6226, 6228(a), 7426, or 7428 (in the case of the United States district court for the District of Columbia) or section 7429 of the Internal Revenue Code of 1986.

(f) The district courts shall have exclusive original jurisdiction of civil actions under section 2409a to quiet title to an estate or interest in real property in which an interest is claimed by the United States.

(g) Subject to the provisions of chapter 179, the district courts of the United States shall have exclusive jurisdiction over any civil action commenced under section 453(2) of title 3, by a covered employee under chapter 5 of such title.

(June 25, 1948, c. 646, 62 Stat. 933; Apr. 25, 1949, c. 92, § 2(a), 63 Stat. 62; May 24, 1949, c. 139, s 80(a), (b), 63 Stat. 101; Oct. 31, 1951, c. 655, § 50(b), 65 Stat. 727; July 30, 1954, c. 648, § 1, 68 Stat. 589; July 7, 1958, Pub.L. 85–508, § 12(e), 72 Stat. 348; Aug. 30, 1964, Pub.L. 88–519, 78 Stat. 699; Nov. 2, 1966, Pub.L. 89–719, Title II, § 202(a), 80 Stat. 1148; July 23, 1970, Pub.L. 91–350, § 1(a), 84 Stat. 449; Oct. 25, 1972, Pub.L. 92–562, s 1, 86 Stat. 1176; Oct. 4, 1976, Pub.L. 94–455, Title XII, § 1204(c)(1), Title XIII, § 1306(b)(7), 90 Stat. 1697, 1719; Nov. 1, 1978, Pub.L. 95–563, § 14(a), 92 Stat. 2389; Apr. 2, 1982, Pub.L. 97–164, Title I, § 129, 96 Stat. 39; Sept. 3, 1982, Pub.L. 97–248, Title IV, § 402(c)(17), 96 Stat. 669; Oct. 22, 1986, Pub.L. 99–514, § 2, 100 Stat. 2095; Oct. 29, 1992, Pub.L. 102–572, Title IX, § 902(b)(1), 106 Stat. 4516; Apr. 26, 1996, Pub.L. 104–134, Title I, § 101[(a)][Title VIII, § 806], 110 Stat. 1321–75; renumbered Title I May 2, 1996, Pub.L. 104–140, § 1(a), 110 Stat. 1327; Oct. 26, 1996, Pub.L 104–331, § 3(b)(1), 110 Stat. 4069.)

§ 1349.   Corporation organized under federal law as party

The district courts shall not have jurisdiction of any civil action by or against any corporation upon the ground that it was incorporated by or under an Act of Congress, unless the United States is the owner of more than one-half of its capital stock.

§ 1357.   Injuries under Federal laws

The district courts shall have original jurisdiction of any civil action commenced by any person to recover damages for any injury to his person or property on account of any act done by him, under any Act of Congress, for the protection or collection of any of the revenues, or to enforce the right of citizens of the United States to vote in any State.

§ 1359.   Parties collusively joined or made

A district court shall not have jurisdiction of a civil action in which any party, by assignment or otherwise, has been improperly or collusively made or joined to invoke the jurisdiction of such court.

§ 1361.   Action to compel an officer of the United States to perform his duty

The district courts shall have original jurisdiction of any action in the nature of mandamus to compel an officer or employee of the United States or any agency thereof to perform a duty owed to the plaintiff. (Added Pub.L. 87–748, § 1(a), Oct. 5, 1962, 76 Stat. 744.)

§ 1367.   Supplemental jurisdiction

(a) Except as provided in subsections (b) and (c) or as expressly provided otherwise by Federal statute, in any civil action of which the district courts have original jurisdiction, the district courts shall have supplemental jurisdiction over all other claims that are so related to claims in the action within such original jurisdiction that they form part of the same case or controversy under Article III of the United States Constitution. Such supplemental jurisdiction shall include claims that involve the joinder or intervention of additional parties.

(b) In any civil action of which the district courts have original jurisdiction founded solely on section 1332 of this title, the district courts shall not have supplemental jurisdiction under subsection (a) over claims by plaintiffs against persons made parties under Rule 14, 19, 20, or 24 of the Federal Rules of Civil Procedure, or over claims by persons proposed to be joined as plaintiffs under Rule 19 of such rules, or seeking to intervene as plaintiffs under Rule 24 of such rules, when exercising supplemental jurisdiction over such claims would be inconsistent with the jurisdictional requirements of section 1332.

(c) The district courts may decline to exercise supplemental jurisdiction over a claim under subsection (a) if—

    (1) the claim raises a novel or complex issue of State law,

    (2) the claim substantially predominates over the claim or claims over which the district court has original jurisdiction,

    (3) the district court has dismissed all claims over which it has original jurisdiction, or

    (4) in exceptional circumstances, there are other compelling reasons for declining jurisdiction.

(d) The period of limitations for any claim asserted under subsection (a), and for any other claim in the same action that is voluntarily dismissed at the same time as or after the dismissal of the claim under subsection (a), shall be tolled while the claim is pending and for a period of 30 days after it is dismissed unless State law provides for a longer tolling period.

(e) As used in this section, the term "State" includes the District of Columbia, the Commonwealth of Puerto Rico, and any territory or possession of the United States.

(Added Pub.L. 101–650, Title III, § 310(a), Dec. 1, 1990, 104 Stat. 5113.)

§ 1369.   Multiparty, multiforum jurisdiction

(a) In general.—The district courts shall have original jurisdiction of any civil action involving minimal diversity between adverse parties that arises from a single accident, where at least 75 natural persons have died in the accident at a discrete location, if—

(1) a defendant resides in a State and a substantial part of the accident took place in another State or other location, regardless of whether that defendant is also a resident of the State where a substantial part of the accident took place;

(2) any two defendants reside in different States, regardless of whether such defendants are also residents of the same State or States; or

(3) substantial parts of the accident took place in different States.

(b) Limitation of jurisdiction of district courts.—The district court shall abstain from hearing any civil action described in subsection (a) in which—

(1) the substantial majority of all plaintiffs are citizens of a single State of which the primary defendants are also citizens; and

(2) the claims asserted will be governed primarily by the laws of that State.

(c) Special rules and definitions.—For purposes of this section—

(1) minimal diversity exists between adverse parties if any party is a citizen of a State and any adverse party is a citizen of another State, a citizen or subject of a foreign state, or a foreign state as defined in section 1603(a) of this title;

(2) a corporation is deemed to be a citizen of any State, and a citizen or subject of any foreign state, in which it is incorporated or has its principal place of business, and is deemed to be a resident of any State in which it is incorporated or licensed to do business or is doing business;

(3) the term "injury" means—

(A) physical harm to a natural person; and

(B) physical damage to or destruction of tangible property, but only if physical harm described in subparagraph (A) exists;

(4) the term "accident" means a sudden accident, or a natural event culminating in an accident, that results in death incurred at a discrete location by at least 75 natural persons; and

(5) the term "State" includes the District of Columbia, the Commonwealth of Puerto Rico, and any territory or possession of the United States.

(d) Intervening parties.—In any action in a district court which is or could have been brought, in whole or in part, under this section, any person with a claim arising from the accident described in subsection (a) shall be permitted to intervene as a party plaintiff in the action, even if that person could not have brought an action in a district court as an original matter.

(e) Notification of judicial panel on multidistrict litigation.—A district court in which an action under this section is pending shall promptly notify the judicial panel on multidistrict litigation of the pendency of the action.

(Added Pub.L. 107–273, Div. C, Title I, § 11020(b)(1)(A), Nov. 2, 2002, 116 Stat. 1826.)

§ 1391.   Venue generally

(a) A civil action wherein jurisdiction is founded only on diversity of citizenship may, except as otherwise provided by law, be brought only in (1) a judicial district where any defendant resides, if all defendants reside in the same State, (2) a judicial district in which a substantial part of the events or omissions giving rise to the claim occurred, or a substantial part of property that is the subject of the action is situated, or (3) a judicial district in which any defendant is subject to personal jurisdiction at the time the action is commenced, if there is no district in which the action may otherwise be brought.

(b) A civil action wherein jurisdiction is not founded solely on diversity of citizenship may, except as otherwise provided by law, be brought only in (1) a judicial district where any defendant resides, if all defendants reside in the same State, (2) a judicial district in which a substantial part of the events or omissions giving rise to the claim occurred, or a substantial part of property that is the subject of the action is situated, or (3) a judicial district in which any defendant may be found, if there is no district in which the action may otherwise be brought.

(c) For purposes of venue under this chapter, a defendant that is a corporation shall be deemed to reside in any judicial district in which it is subject to personal jurisdiction at the time the action is commenced. In a State which has more than one judicial district and in which a defendant that is a corporation is subject to personal jurisdiction at the time an action is commenced, such corporation shall be deemed to reside in any district in that State within which its contacts would be sufficient to subject it to personal jurisdiction if that district were a separate State, and, if there is no such district, the corporation shall be deemed to reside in the district within which it has the most significant contacts.

(d) An alien may be sued in any district.

(e) A civil action in which a defendant is an officer or employee of the United States or any agency thereof acting in his official capacity or under color of legal authority, or an agency of the United States, or the United States, may, except as otherwise provided by law, be brought in any judicial district in which (1) a defendant in the action resides, (2) a substantial part of the events or omissions giving rise to the claim occurred, or a substantial part of property that is the subject of the action is situated, or (3) the plaintiff resides if no real property is involved in the action. Additional persons may be joined as parties to any such action in accordance with the Federal Rules of Civil Procedure and with such other venue requirements as would be applicable if the United States or one of its officers, employees, or agencies were not a party.

The summons and complaint in such an action shall be served as provided by the Federal Rules of Civil Procedure except that the delivery of the summons and complaint to the officer or agency as required by the rules may be made by certified mail beyond the territorial limits of the district in which the action is brought.

(f) A civil action against a foreign state as defined in section 1603(a) of this title may be brought—

　　(1) in any judicial district in which a substantial part of the events or omissions giving rise to the claim occurred, or a substantial part of property that is the subject of the action is situated;

　　(2) in any judicial district in which the vessel or cargo of a foreign state is situated, if the claim is asserted under section 1605(b) of this title;

　　(3) in any judicial district in which the agency or instrumentality is licensed to do business or is doing business, if the action is brought against an agency or instrumentality of a foreign state as defined in section 1603(b) of this title; or

　　(4) in the United States District Court for the District of Columbia if the action is brought against a foreign state or political subdivision thereof.

(g) A civil action in which jurisdiction of the district court is based upon section 1369 of this title may be brought in any district in which any defendant resides or in which a substantial part of the accident giving rise to the action took place.

(June 25, 1948, c. 646, 62 Stat. 935; Oct. 5, 1962, Pub.L. 87–748, § 2, 76 Stat. 744; Dec. 23, 1963, Pub.L. 88–234, 77 Stat. 473; Nov. 2, 1966, Pub.L. 89–714, § § 1, 2, 80 Stat. 1111; Oct. 21, 1976, Pub.L. 94–574, § 3, 90 Stat. 2721; Oct. 21, 1976, Pub.L. 94–583, § 5, 90 Stat. 2897; Nov. 19, 1988, Pub.L. 100–702, Title X, § 1013(a), 102 Stat. 4669; Dec. 1, 1990, Pub.L. 101–650, Title III, § 311, 104 Stat. 5114; Dec. 9, 1991, Pub.L. 102–198, § 3, 105 Stat. 1623; Oct. 29, 1992, Pub.L. 102–572, Title V, § 504, 106 Stat. 4513; Oct. 3, 1995, Pub.L. 104–34, § 1, 109 Stat. 293; Nov. 2, 2002, Pub.L. 107–273, Div. C, Title I, § 11020(b)(2), 116 Stat. 1827.)

§ 1392.   Defendants or property in different districts in same State

Any civil action, of a local nature, involving property located in different districts in the same State, may be brought in any of such districts.

(June 25, 1948, c. 646, 62 Stat. 935; Oct. 1, 1996, Pub.L. 104–220, § 1, 110 Stat. 3023.)

§ 1397.   Interpleader

Any civil action of interpleader or in the nature of interpleader under section 1335 of this title may be brought in the judicial district in which one or more of the claimants reside.

§ 1401.   Stockholder's derivative action

Any civil action by a stockholder on behalf of his corporation may be prosecuted in any judicial district where the corporation might have sued the same defendants.

§ 1402.   United States as defendant

(a) Any civil action in a district court against the United States under subsection (a) of section 1346 of this title may be prosecuted only:

(1) Except as provided in paragraph (2), in the judicial district where the plaintiff resides;

(2) In the case of a civil action in a district court by a corporation under paragraph (1) of subsection (a) of section 1346, in the judicial district in which is located the principal place of business or principal office or agency of the corporation; or if it has no principal place of business or principal office or agency in any judicial district (A) in the judicial district in which is located the office to which was made the return of the tax in respect of which the claim is made, or (B) if no return was made, in the judicial district in which lies the District of Columbia.   Notwithstanding the foregoing provisions of this paragraph a district court, for the convenience of the parties and witnesses, in the interest of justice, may transfer any such action to any other district or division.

(b) Any civil action on a tort claim against the United States under subsection (b) of section 1346 of this title may be prosecuted only in the judicial district where the plaintiff resides or wherein the act or omission complained of occurred.

(c) Any civil action against the United States under subsection (e) of section 1346 of this title may be prosecuted only in the judicial district where the property is situated at the time of levy, or if no levy is made, in the judicial district in which the event occurred which gave rise to the cause of action.

(d) Any civil action under section 2409a to quiet title to an estate or interest in real property in which an interest is claimed by the United States shall be brought in the district court of the district where the property is located or, if located in different districts, in any of such districts.

(As amended Sept. 2, 1958, Pub.L. 85–920, 72 Stat. 1770; Nov. 2, 1966, Pub.L. 89–719, Title II, § 202(b), 80 Stat. 1149; Oct. 25, 1972, Pub.L. 92–562, § 2, 86 Stat. 1176; Apr. 2, 1982, Pub.L. 97–164, Title I, § 131, 96 Stat. 39.)

§ 1404.   Change of venue

(a) For the convenience of parties and witnesses, in the interest of justice, a district court may transfer any civil action to any other district or division where it might have been brought.

(b) Upon motion, consent or stipulation of all parties, any action, suit or proceeding of a civil nature or any motion or hearing thereof, may be transferred, in the discretion of the court, from the division in which pending to any other division in the same district.   Transfer of proceedings in rem brought by or on behalf of the United States may be transferred under this section without the consent of the United States where all other parties request transfer.

(c) A district court may order any civil action to be tried at any place within the division in which it is pending.

(d) As used in this section, "district court" includes the District Court of Guam, the District Court for the Northern Mariana Islands, and the District Court of the Virgin Islands, and the term "district" includes the territorial jurisdiction of that court.

(As amended Oct. 18, 1962, Pub.L. 87–845, § 9, 76A Stat. 699; Oct. 19, 1996, Pub.L. 104–317, Title VI, § 610, 110 Stat. 3860.)

§ 1406. Cure or waiver of defects

(a) The district court of a district in which is filed a case laying venue in the wrong division or district shall dismiss, or if it be in the interest of justice, transfer such case to any district or division in which it could have been brought.

(b) Nothing in this chapter shall impair the jurisdiction of a district court of any matter involving a party who does not interpose timely and sufficient objection to the venue.

(c) As used in this section, "district court" includes the District Court of Guam, the District Court for the Northern Mariana Islands, and the District Court of the Virgin Islands, and the term "district" includes the territorial jurisdiction of that court.

(As amended May 24, 1949, c. 139, § 81, 63 Stat. 101; Sept. 13, 1960, Pub.L. 86–770, § 1, 74 Stat. 912; Oct. 18, 1962, Pub.L. 87–845, § 10, 76A Stat. 699; Apr. 2, 1982, Pub.L. 97–164, Title I, § 132, 96 Stat. 39; Oct. 19, 1996, Pub.L. 104–317, Title VI, § 610, 110 Stat. 3860.)

§ 1407. Multidistrict litigation

(a) When civil actions involving one or more common questions of fact are pending in different districts, such actions may be transferred to any district for coordinated or consolidated pretrial proceedings. Such transfers shall be made by the judicial panel on multidistrict litigation authorized by this section upon its determination that transfers for such proceedings will be for the convenience of parties and witnesses and will promote the just and efficient conduct of such actions. Each action so transferred shall be remanded by the panel at or before the conclusion of such pretrial proceedings to the district from which it was transferred unless it shall have been previously terminated: *Provided, however*, That the panel may separate any claim, cross-claim, counter-claim, or third-party claim and remand any of such claims before the remainder of the action is remanded.

(b) Such coordinated or consolidated pretrial proceedings shall be conducted by a judge or judges to whom such actions are assigned by the judicial panel on multidistrict litigation. For this purpose, upon request of the panel, a circuit judge or a district judge may be designated and assigned temporarily for service in the transferee district by the Chief Justice of the United States or the chief judge of the circuit, as may be required, in accordance with the provisions of chapter 13 of this title. With the consent of the transferee district court, such actions may be assigned by the panel to a judge or judges of such district. The judge or judges to whom such actions are assigned, the members of the judicial panel on multidistrict litigation, and other circuit and district judges designated when needed by the panel may exercise the powers of a district judge in any district for the purpose of conducting pretrial depositions in such coordinated or consolidated pretrial proceedings.

(c) Proceedings for the transfer of an action under this section may be initiated by—

(i) the judicial panel on multidistrict litigation upon its own initiative, or

(ii) motion filed with the panel by a party in any action in which transfer for coordinated or consolidated pretrial proceedings under this section may be appropriate. A copy of such motion shall be filed in the district court in which the moving party's action is pending.

The panel shall give notice to the parties in all actions in which transfers for coordinated or consolidated pretrial proceedings are contemplated, and such notice shall specify the time and place of any hearing to determine whether such transfer shall be made. Orders of the panel to set a hearing and other orders of the panel issued prior to the order either directing or denying transfer shall be filed in the office of the clerk of the district court in which a transfer hearing is to be or has been held. The panel's order of transfer shall be based upon a record of such hearing at which material evidence may be offered by any party to an action pending in any district that would be affected by the proceedings under this section, and shall be supported by findings of fact and conclusions of law based upon such record. Orders of transfer and such other orders as the panel may make thereafter shall be filed in the office of the clerk of the district court of the transferee district and shall be effective when thus filed. The clerk of the transferee district court shall forthwith transmit a certified copy of the panel's order to transfer to the clerk of the district court from which the action is being transferred. An order denying transfer shall be filed in each district wherein there is a case pending in which the motion for transfer has been made.

(d) The judicial panel on multidistrict litigation shall consist of seven circuit and district judges designated from time to time by the Chief Justice of the United States, no two of whom shall be from the same circuit. The concurrence of four members shall be necessary to any action by the panel.

(e) No proceedings for review of any order of the panel may be permitted except by extraordinary writ pursuant to the provisions of title 28, section 1651, United States Code. Petitions for an extraordinary writ to review an order of the panel to set a transfer hearing and other orders of the panel issued prior to the order either directing or denying transfer shall be filed only in the court of appeals having jurisdiction over the district in which a hearing is to be or has been held. Petitions for an extraordinary writ to review an order to transfer or orders subsequent to transfer shall be filed only in the court of appeals having jurisdiction over the transferee district. There shall be no appeal or review of an order of the panel denying a motion to transfer for consolidated or coordinated proceedings.

(f) The panel may prescribe rules for the conduct of its business not inconsistent with Acts of Congress and the Federal Rules of Civil Procedure.

(g) Nothing in this section shall apply to any action in which the United States is a complainant arising under the antitrust laws. "Antitrust laws" as used herein include those acts referred to in the Act of October 15, 1914, as amended (38 Stat. 730; 15 U.S.C. 12), and also include the Act of June 19, 1936 (49 Stat. 1526; 15 U.S.C. 13, 13a, and 13b) and the Act of September 26, 1914, as added March 21, 1938 (52 Stat. 116, 117; 15 U.S.C. 56); but shall not include section 4A of the Act of October 15, 1914, as added July 7, 1955 (69 Stat. 282; 15 U.S.C. 15a).

(h) Notwithstanding the provisions of section 1404 or subsection (f) of this section, the judicial panel on multidistrict litigation may consolidate and transfer with or without the consent of the parties, for both pretrial purposes and for trial, any action brought under section 4C of the Clayton Act.

(Added Pub.L. 90–296, § 1, Apr. 29, 1968, 82 Stat. 109, and amended Pub.L. 94–435, Title III, § 303, Sept. 30, 1976, 90 Stat. 1396.)

§ 1412.   Change of venue

A district court may transfer a case or proceeding under title 11 to a district court for another district, in the interest of justice or for the convenience of the parties.

(Added Pub.L. 98–353, Title I, § 102(a), July 10, 1984, 98 Stat. 335.)

§ 1441.   Actions removable generally

(a) Except as otherwise expressly provided by Act of Congress, any civil action brought in a State court of which the district courts of the United States have original jurisdiction, may be removed by the defendant or the defendants, to the district court of the United States for the district and division embracing the place where such action is pending. For purposes of removal under this chapter, the citizenship of defendants sued under fictitious names shall be disregarded.

(b) Any civil action of which the district courts have original jurisdiction founded on a claim or right arising under the Constitution, treaties or laws of the United States shall be removable without regard to the citizenship or residence of the parties. Any other such action shall be removable only if none of the parties in interest properly joined and served as defendants is a citizen of the State in which such action is brought.

(c) Whenever a separate and independent claim or cause of action within the jurisdiction conferred by section 1331 of this title is joined with one or more otherwise non-removable claims or causes of action, the entire case may be removed and the district court may determine all issues therein, or, in its discretion, may remand all matters in which State law predominates.

(d) Any civil action brought in a State court against a foreign state as defined in section 1603(a) of this title may be removed by the foreign state to the district court of the United States for the district and division embracing the place where such action is pending. Upon removal the action shall be tried by the court without jury. Where removal is based upon this subsection, the time limitations of section 1446(b) of this chapter may be enlarged at any time for cause shown.

(e)(1) Notwithstanding the provisions of subsection (b) of this section, a defendant in a civil action in a State court may remove the action to the district court of the United States for the district and division embracing the place where the action is pending if—

> **(A)** the action could have been brought in a United States district court under section 1369 of this title; or

> **(B)** the defendant is a party to an action which is or could have been brought, in whole or in part, under section 1369 in a United States district court and arises from the same accident as the action in State court, even if the action to be removed could not have been brought in a district court as an original matter.

The removal of an action under this subsection shall be made in accordance with section 1446 of this title, except that a notice of removal may also be filed before trial of the action in State court within 30 days after the date on which the defendant first becomes a party to an action under section 1369 in a United States district court that arises from the same accident as the action in State court, or at a later time with leave of the district court.

> **(2)** Whenever an action is removed under this subsection and the district court to which it is removed or transferred under section 1407(j) has made a liability determination requiring further proceedings as to damages, the district court shall remand the action to the State court from which it had been removed for the determination of damages, unless the court finds that, for the convenience of parties and witnesses and in the interest of justice, the action should be retained for the determination of damages.

> **(3)** Any remand under paragraph (2) shall not be effective until 60 days after the district court has issued an order determining liability and has certified its intention to remand the removed action for the determination of damages. An appeal with respect to the liability determination of the district court may be taken during that 60–day period to the court of appeals with appellate jurisdiction over the district court. In the event a party files such an appeal, the remand shall not be effective until the appeal has been finally disposed of. Once the remand has become effective, the liability determination shall not be subject to further review by appeal or otherwise.

> **(4)** Any decision under this subsection concerning remand for the determination of damages shall not be reviewable by appeal or otherwise.

> **(5)** An action removed under this subsection shall be deemed to be an action under section 1369 and an action in which jurisdiction is based on section 1369 of this title for purposes of this section and sections 1407, 1697, and 1785 of this title.

(6) Nothing in this subsection shall restrict the authority of the district court to transfer or dismiss an action on the ground of inconvenient forum.

(f) The court to which a civil action is removed under this section is not precluded from hearing and determining any claim in such civil action because the State court from which such civil action is removed did not have jurisdiction over that claim.

(June 25, 1948, c. 646, 62 Stat. 937; Oct. 21, 1976, Pub.L. 94–583, § 6, 90 Stat. 2898; June 19, 1986, Pub.L. 99–336, § 3(a), 100 Stat. 637; Nov. 19, 1988, Pub.L. 100–702, Title X, § 1016(a), 102 Stat. 4669; Dec. 1, 1990, Pub.L. 101–650, Title III, § 312, 104 Stat. 5114; Dec. 9, 1991, Pub.L. 102–198, § 4, 105 Stat. 1623; Nov. 2, 2002, Pub.L. 107–273, Div. C, Title I, § 11020(b)(3), 116 Stat. 1827.)

§ 1442.　Federal officers or agencies sued or prosecuted

(a) A civil action or criminal prosecution commenced in a State court against any of the following may be removed by them to the district court of the United States for the district and division embracing the place wherein it is pending:

(1) The United States or any agency thereof or any officer (or any person acting under that officer) of the United States or of any agency thereof, sued in an official or individual capacity for any act under color of such office or on account of any right, title or authority claimed under any Act of Congress for the apprehension or punishment of criminals or the collection of the revenue.

(2) A property holder whose title is derived from any such officer, where such action or prosecution affects the validity of any law of the United States.

(3) Any officer of the courts of the United States, for any act under color of office or in the performance of his duties;

(4) Any officer of either House of Congress, for any act in the discharge of his official duty under an order of such House.

(b) A personal action commenced in any State court by an alien against any citizen of a State who is, or at the time the alleged action accrued was, a civil officer of the United States and is a nonresident of such State, wherein jurisdiction is obtained by the State court by personal service of process, may be removed by the defendant to the district court of the United States for the district and division in which the defendant was served with process.

(As amended Oct. 19, 1996, Pub.L. 104–317, 110 Stat. 3847.)

§ 1442a.　Members of armed forces sued or prosecuted

A civil or criminal prosecution in a court of a State of the United States against a member of the armed forces of the United States on account of an act done under color of his office or status, or in respect to which he claims any right, title, or authority under a law of the United States respecting the armed forces thereof, or under the law of war, may at any time before the trial or final hearing thereof be removed for trial into the district court of the United States for the district where it is pending in the manner prescribed by law, and it shall thereupon be entered on the docket of the district court, which shall proceed as if the cause had been originally commenced therein and shall have full power to hear and determine the cause.

(Added Aug. 10, 1956, c. 1041, § 19(a), 70A Stat. 626.)

§ 1443.   Civil rights cases

Any of the following civil actions or criminal prosecutions, commenced in a State court may be removed by the defendant to the district court of the United States for the district and division embracing the place wherein it is pending:

(1) Against any person who is denied or cannot enforce in the courts of such State a right under any law providing for the equal civil rights of citizens of the United States, or of all persons within the jurisdiction thereof;

(2) For any act under color of authority derived from any law providing for equal rights, or for refusing to do any act on the ground that it would be inconsistent with such law.

§ 1445.   Nonremovable actions

(a) A civil action in any State court against a railroad or its receivers or trustees, arising under sections 1–4 and 5–10 of the Act of April 22, 1908 (45 U.S.C. 51–54, 55–60), may not be removed to any district court of the United States.

(b) A civil action in any State court against a carrier or its receivers or trustees to recover damages for delay, loss, or injury of shipments, arising under section 11706 or 14706 of title 49, may not be removed to any district court of the United States unless the matter in controversy exceeds $10,000, exclusive of interest and costs.

(c) A civil action in any State court arising under the workmen's compensation laws of such State may not be removed to any district court of the United States.

(d) A civil action in any State court arising under section 40302 of the Violence Against Women Act of 1994 may not be removed to any district court of the United States.

(June 25, 1948, c. 646, 62 Stat. 939; July 25, 1958, Pub.L. 85–554, § 5, 72 Stat. 415; Oct. 17, 1978, Pub.L. 95–473, § 2(a)(3)(A), 92 Stat. 1465; Oct. 20, 1978, Pub.L. 95–486, § 9(b), 92 Stat. 1634; Sept. 13, 1994, Pub.L. 103–322, Title IV, § 40302(e)(5), 108 Stat. 1942; Dec. 29, 1995, Pub.L. 104–88, Title III, § 305(b), 109 Stat. 944; Oct. 11, 1996, Pub.L. 104–287, § 3, 110 Stat. 3388.)

§ 1446.   Procedure for removal

(a) A defendant or defendants desiring to remove any civil action or criminal prosecution from a State court shall file in the district court of the United States for the district and division within which such action is pending a notice of removal signed pursuant to Rule 11 of the Federal Rules of Civil Procedure and containing a short and plain statement of the grounds for removal, together with a copy of all process, pleadings, and orders served upon such defendant or defendants in such action.

(b) The notice of removal of a civil action or proceeding shall be filed within thirty days after the receipt by the defendant, through service or otherwise, of a copy of the initial pleading setting forth the claim for relief upon which such action or proceeding is based, or within thirty days after the service of summons upon the defendant if such initial pleading has then been filed in court and is not required to be served on the defendant, whichever period is shorter.

If the case stated by the initial pleading is not removable, a notice of removal may be filed within thirty days after receipt by the defendant, through service or otherwise, of a copy of an amended pleading, motion, order or other paper from which it may first be ascertained that the case is one which is or has become removable, except that a case may not be removed on the basis of jurisdiction conferred by section 1332 of this title more than 1 year after commencement of the action.

(c)(1) A notice of removal of a criminal prosecution shall be filed not later than thirty days after the arraignment in the State court, or at any time before trial, whichever is earlier, except that for good cause shown the United States district court may enter an order granting the defendant or defendants leave to file the notice at a later time.

(2) A notice of removal of a criminal prosecution shall include all grounds for such removal. A failure to state grounds which exist at the time of the filing of the notice shall constitute a waiver of such grounds, and a second notice may be filed only on grounds not existing at the time of the original notice. For good cause shown, the United States district court may grant relief from the limitations of this paragraph.

(3) The filing of a notice of removal of a criminal prosecution shall not prevent the State court in which such prosecution is pending from proceeding further, except that a judgment of conviction shall not be entered unless the prosecution is first remanded.

(4) The United States district court in which such notice is filed shall examine the notice promptly. If it clearly appears on the face of the notice and any exhibits annexed thereto that removal should not be permitted, the court shall make an order for summary remand.

(5) If the United States district court does not order the summary remand of such prosecution, it shall order an evidentiary hearing to be held promptly and after such hearing shall make such disposition of the prosecution as justice shall require. If the United States district court determines that removal shall be permitted, it shall so notify the State court in which prosecution is pending, which shall proceed no further.

(d) Promptly after the filing of such notice of removal of a civil action the defendant or defendants shall give written notice thereof to all adverse parties and shall file a copy of the notice with the clerk of such State court, which shall effect the removal and the State court shall proceed no further unless and until the case is remanded.

(e) If the defendant or defendants are in actual custody on process issued by the State court, the district court shall issue its writ of habeas corpus, and the marshal shall thereupon take such defendant or defendants into his custody and deliver a copy of the writ to the clerk of such State court.

(f) With respect to any counterclaim removed to a district court pursuant to section 337(c) of the Tariff Act of 1930, the district court shall resolve such counterclaim in the same manner as an original complaint under the Federal Rules of Civil Procedure, except that the payment of a filing fee shall not be required in such cases and the counterclaim shall relate back to the date of the original complaint in the proceeding before the International Trade Commission under section 337 of that Act.

(As amended May 24, 1949, c. 139, § 83, 63 Stat. 101; Sept. 29, 1965, Pub.L. 89–215, 79 Stat. 887; July 30, 1977, Pub.L. 95–78, § 3, 91 Stat. 321; Nov. 19, 1988, Pub.L. 100–702, Title X, § 1016(b), 102 Stat. 4669; Dec. 9, 1991, Pub.L. 102–198, § 10(a), 105 Stat. 1626; Dec. 8, 1994, Pub.L. 103–465, Title III, § 321(b)(2), 108 Stat. 4946; Oct. 19, 1996, Pub.L. 104–317, 110 Stat. 3847.)

§ 1447. Procedure after removal generally

(a) In any case removed from a State court, the district court may issue all necessary orders and process to bring before it all proper parties whether served by process issued by the State court or otherwise.

(b) It may require the removing party to file with its clerk copies of all records and proceedings in such State court or may cause the same to be brought before it by writ of certiorari issued to such State court.

(c) A motion to remand the case on the basis of any defect other than lack of subject matter jurisdiction must be made within 30 days after the filing of the notice of removal under section 1446(a). If at any time before final judgment it appears that the district court lacks subject matter jurisdiction, the case shall be remanded. An order remanding the case may require payment of just costs and any actual expenses, including attorney fees, incurred as a result of the removal. A certified copy of the order of remand shall be mailed by the clerk to the clerk of the State court. The State court may thereupon proceed with such case.

(d) An order remanding a case to the State court from which it was removed is not reviewable on appeal or otherwise, except that an order remanding a case to the State court from which it was removed pursuant to section 1443 of this title shall be reviewable by appeal or otherwise.

(e) If after removal the plaintiff seeks to join additional defendants whose joinder would destroy subject matter jurisdiction, the court may deny joinder, or permit joinder and remand the action to the State court.

(As amended May 24, 1949, c. 139, § 84, 63 Stat. 102; July 2, 1964, Pub.L. 88–352, Title IX, § 901, 78 Stat. 266; Nov. 19, 1988, Pub.L. 100–702, Title X, § 1016(c), 102 Stat. 4670; Dec. 9, 1991, Pub.L. 102–198, § 10(b), 105 Stat. 1626; Oct. 1, 1996, Pub.L. 104–219, 110 Stat. 3022.)

§ 1448. Process after removal

In all cases removed from any State court to any district court of the United States in which any one or more of the defendants has not been served with process or in which the service has not been perfected prior to removal, or in which process served proves to be defective, such process or service may be completed or new process issued in the same manner as in cases originally filed in such district court.

This section shall not deprive any defendant upon whom process is served after removal of his right to move to remand the case.

§ 1449. State court record supplied

Where a party is entitled to copies of the records and proceedings in any suit or prosecution in a State court, to be used in any district court of the United States, and the clerk of such State court, upon demand, and the payment or tender of the legal fees, fails to deliver certified copies, the district court may, on affidavit reciting such facts, direct such record to be supplied by affidavit or otherwise. Thereupon such proceedings, trial, and judgment may be had in such district court, and all such process awarded, as if certified copies had been filed in the district court.

(As amended May 24, 1949, c. 139, § 85, 63 Stat. 102.)

§ 1451. Definitions

For purposes of this chapter—

(1) The term "State court" includes the Superior Court of the District of Columbia.

(2) The term "State" includes the District of Columbia.

(Added Pub.L. 91–358, Title I, § 172(d)(1), July 29, 1970, 84 Stat. 591.)

§ 1453. Removal of class actions

(a) **Definitions.**—In this section, the terms "class", "class action", "class certification order", and "class member" shall have the meanings given such terms under section 1332(d)(1).

(b) **In general.**—A class action may be removed to a district court of the United States in accordance with section 1446 (except that the 1–year limitation under section 1446(b) shall not apply), without regard to whether any defendant is a citizen of the State in which the action is brought, except that such action may be removed by any defendant without the consent of all defendants.

(c) **Review of remand orders.**—

(1) **In general.**—Section 1447 shall apply to any removal of a case under this section, except that notwithstanding section 1447(d), a court of appeals may accept an appeal from an order of a district court granting or denying a motion to remand a class action to the State court from which it was removed if application is made to the court of appeals not less than 7 days after entry of the order.

(2) **Time period for judgment.**—If the court of appeals accepts an appeal under paragraph (1), the court shall complete all action on such appeal, including rendering judgment, not later than 60 days after the date on which such appeal was filed, unless an extension is granted under paragraph (3).

(3) Extension of time period.—The court of appeals may grant an extension of the 60–day period described in paragraph (2) if—

    (A) all parties to the proceeding agree to such extension, for any period of time; or

    (B) such extension is for good cause shown and in the interests of justice, for a period not to exceed 10 days.

(4) Denial of appeal.—If a final judgment on the appeal under paragraph (1) is not issued before the end of the period described in paragraph (2), including any extension under paragraph (3), the appeal shall be denied.

(d) Exception.—This section shall not apply to any class action that solely involves—

    (1) a claim concerning a covered security as defined under section 16(f) (3) of the Securities Act of 1933 (15 U.S.C. 78p(f)(3)) and section 28(f)(5)(E) of the Securities Exchange Act of 1934 (15 U.S.C. 78bb(f)(5)(E));

    (2) a claim that relates to the internal affairs or governance of a corporation or other form of business enterprise and arises under or by virtue of the laws of the State in which such corporation or business enterprise is incorporated or organized; or

    (3) a claim that relates to the rights, duties (including fiduciary duties), and obligations relating to or created by or pursuant to any security (as defined under section 2(a)(1) of the Securities Act of 1933 (15 U.S.C. 77b(a)(1)) and the regulations issued thereunder).

(Added Pub.L. 109–2, § 5(a), Feb. 18, 2005, 119 Stat. 12.)

§ 1631.   Transfer to cure want of jurisdiction

Whenever a civil action is filed in a court as defined in section 610 of this title or an appeal, including a petition for review of administrative action, is noticed for or filed with such a court and that court finds that there is a want of jurisdiction, the court shall, if it is in the interest of justice, transfer such action or appeal to any other such court in which the action or appeal could have been brought at the time it was filed or noticed, and the action or appeal shall proceed as if it had been filed in or noticed for the court to which it is transferred on the date upon which it was actually filed in or noticed for the court from which it is transferred.

(Added Pub.L. 97–164, Title III, § 301(a), Apr. 2, 1982, 96 Stat. 55.)

§ 1651.   Writs

    (a) The Supreme Court and all courts established by Act of Congress may issue all writs necessary or appropriate in aid of their respective jurisdictions and agreeable to the usages and principles of law.

    (b) An alternative writ or rule nisi may be issued by a justice or judge of a court which has jurisdiction.

(As amended May 24, 1949, c. 139, § 90, 63 Stat. 102.)

§ 1652. State laws as rules of decision

The laws of the several states, except where the Constitution or treaties of the United States or Acts of Congress otherwise require or provide, shall be regarded as rules of decision in civil actions in the courts of the United States, in cases where they apply.

§ 1653. Amendment of pleadings to show jurisdiction

Defective allegations of jurisdiction may be amended, upon terms, in the trial or appellate courts.

§ 1654. Appearance personally or by counsel

In all courts of the United States the parties may plead and conduct their own cases personally or by counsel as, by the rules of such courts, respectively, are permitted to manage and conduct causes therein.

(As amended May 24, 1949, c. 139, § 91, 63 Stat. 103.)

§ 1657. Priority of civil actions

(a) Notwithstanding any other provision of law, each court of the United States shall determine the order in which civil actions are heard and determined, except that the court shall expedite the consideration of any action brought under chapter 153 or section 1826 of this title, any action for temporary or preliminary injunctive relief, or any other action if good cause therefor is shown. For purposes of this subsection, "good cause" is shown if a right under the Constitution of the United States or a Federal Statute (including rights under section 552 of title 5) would be maintained in a factual context that indicates that a request for expedited consideration has merit.

(b) The Judicial Conference of the United States may modify the rules adopted by the courts to determine the order in which civil actions are heard and determined, in order to establish consistency among the judicial circuits.

(Added Pub.L. 98–620, Title IV, § 401(a), Nov. 8, 1984, 98 Stat. 3356.)

§ 1658. Time limitations on the commencement of civil actions arising under Acts of Congress

(a) Except as otherwise provided by law, a civil action arising under an Act of Congress enacted after the date of the enactment of this section may not be commenced later than 4 years after the cause of action accrues.

(b) Notwithstanding subsection (a), a private right of action that involves a claim of fraud, deceit, manipulation, or contrivance in contravention of a regulatory requirement concerning the securities laws, as defined in section 3(a)(47) of the Securities Exchange Act of 1934 (*15 U.S.C. 78c(a)(47)*), may be brought not later than the earlier of—

 (1) 2 years after the discovery of the facts constituting the violation; or

 (2) 5 years after such violation.

(Added *Pub.L. 101–650, Title III, 313(a)*, Dec. 1, 1990, 104 Stat. 5114; as amended *Pub.L. 107–204, Title VIII, 804(a)*, July 30, 2002, 116 Stat. 801.)

§ 1691.   Seal and teste of process

All writs and process issuing from a court of the United States shall be under the seal of the court and signed by the clerk thereof.

§ 1692.   Process and orders affecting property in different districts

In proceedings in a district court where a receiver is appointed for property, real, personal, or mixed, situated in different districts, process may issue and be executed in any such district as if the property lay wholly within one district, but orders affecting the property shall be entered of record in each of such districts.

§ 1695.   Stockholder's derivative action

Process in a stockholder's action in behalf of his corporation may be served upon such corporation in any district where it is organized or licensed to do business or is doing business.

§ 1696.   Service in foreign and international litigation

(a) The district court of the district in which a person resides or is found may order service upon him of any document issued in connection with a proceeding in a foreign or international tribunal. The order may be made pursuant to a letter rogatory issued, or request made, by a foreign or international tribunal or upon application of any interested person and shall direct the manner of service. Service pursuant to this subsection does not, of itself, require the recognition or enforcement in the United States of a judgment, decree, or order rendered by a foreign or international tribunal.

(b) This section does not preclude service of such a document without an order of court.

(Added Oct. 3, 1964, Pub.L. 88–619, § 4(a), 78 Stat. 995.)

§ 1697.   Service in multiparty, multiforum actions

When the jurisdiction of the district court is based in whole or in part upon section 1369 of this title, process, other than subpoenas, may be served at any place within the United States, or anywhere outside the United States if otherwise permitted by law.

(Added Pub.L. 107–273, Div. C, Title I, § 11020(b)(4)(A)(i), Nov. 2, 2002, 116 Stat. 1828.)

§ 1712.   Coupon settlements

(a) **Contingent fees in coupon settlements.**—If a proposed settlement in a class action provides for a recovery of coupons to a class member, the portion of any attorney's fee award to class counsel that is attributable to the award of the coupons shall be based on the value to class members of the coupons that are redeemed.

(b) **Other attorney's fee awards in coupon settlements.**—

(1) **In general.**—If a proposed settlement in a class action provides for a recovery of coupons to class members, and a portion of the recovery of the coupons is not used to determine the attorney's fee to be paid to class counsel, any attorney's fee award shall be

based upon the amount of time class counsel reasonably expended working on the action.

(2) Court approval.—Any attorney's fee under this subsection shall be subject to approval by the court and shall include an appropriate attorney's fee, if any, for obtaining equitable relief, including an injunction, if applicable. Nothing in this subsection shall be construed to prohibit application of a lodestar with a multiplier method of determining attorney's fees.

(c) Attorney's fee awards calculated on a mixed basis in coupon settlements.—If a proposed settlement in a class action provides for an award of coupons to class members and also provides for equitable relief, including injunctive relief—

(1) that portion of the attorney's fee to be paid to class counsel that is based upon a portion of the recovery of the coupons shall be calculated in accordance with subsection (a); and

(2) that portion of the attorney's fee to be paid to class counsel that is not based upon a portion of the recovery of the coupons shall be calculated in accordance with subsection (b).

(d) Settlement valuation expertise.—In a class action involving the awarding of coupons, the court may, in its discretion upon the motion of a party, receive expert testimony from a witness qualified to provide information on the actual value to the class members of the coupons that are redeemed.

(e) Judicial scrutiny of coupon settlements.—In a proposed settlement under which class members would be awarded coupons, the court may approve the proposed settlement only after a hearing to determine whether, and making a written finding that, the settlement is fair, reasonable, and adequate for class members. The court, in its discretion, may also require that a proposed settlement agreement provide for the distribution of a portion of the value of unclaimed coupons to 1 or more charitable or governmental organizations, as agreed to by the parties. The distribution and redemption of any proceeds under this subsection shall not be used to calculate attorneys' fees under this section.

(Added Pub.L. 109–2, § 3(a), Feb. 18, 2005, 119 Stat. 6.)

§ 1713. Protection against loss by class members

The court may approve a proposed settlement under which any class member is obligated to pay sums to class counsel that would result in a net loss to the class member only if the court makes a written finding that nonmonetary benefits to the class member substantially outweigh the monetary loss.

(Added Pub.L. 109–2, § 3(a), Feb. 18, 2005, 119 Stat. 7.)

§ 1714. Protection against discrimination based on geographic location

The court may not approve a proposed settlement that provides for the payment of greater sums to some class members than to others solely on the basis that the class members to whom the greater sums are to be paid are located in closer geographic proximity to the court. (Added Pub.L. 109–2, § 3(a), Feb. 18, 2005, 119 Stat. 7.)

§ 1715.   Notifications to appropriate Federal and State officials

(a) Definitions.—

(1) Appropriate Federal official.—In this section, the term "appropriate Federal official" means—

(A) the Attorney General of the United States; or

(B) in any case in which the defendant is a Federal depository institution, a State depository institution, a depository institution holding company, a foreign bank, or a nondepository institution subsidiary of the foregoing (as such terms are defined in section 3 of the Federal Deposit Insurance Act (12 U.S.C. 1813)), the person who has the primary Federal regulatory or supervisory responsibility with respect to the defendant, if some or all of the matters alleged in the class action are subject to regulation or supervision by that person.

(2) Appropriate State official.—In this section, the term "appropriate State official" means the person in the State who has the primary regulatory or supervisory responsibility with respect to the defendant, or who licenses or otherwise authorizes the defendant to conduct business in the State, if some or all of the matters alleged in the class action are subject to regulation by that person. If there is no primary regulator, supervisor, or licensing authority, or the matters alleged in the class action are not subject to regulation or supervision by that person, then the appropriate State official shall be the State attorney general.

(b) In general.—Not later than 10 days after a proposed settlement of a class action is filed in court, each defendant that is participating in the proposed settlement shall serve upon the appropriate State official of each State in which a class member resides and the appropriate Federal official, a notice of the proposed settlement consisting of—

(1) a copy of the complaint and any materials filed with the complaint and any amended complaints (except such materials shall not be required to be served if such materials are made electronically available through the Internet and such service includes notice of how to electronically access such material);

(2) notice of any scheduled judicial hearing in the class action;

(3) any proposed or final notification to class members of—

(A)(i) the members' rights to request exclusion from the class action; or

(ii) if no right to request exclusion exists, a statement that no such right exists; and

(B) a proposed settlement of a class action;

(4) any proposed or final class action settlement;

(5) any settlement or other agreement contemporaneously made between class counsel and counsel for the defendants;

(6) any final judgment or notice of dismissal;

(7)(A) if feasible, the names of class members who reside in each State and the estimated proportionate share of the claims of such members to the entire settlement to that State's appropriate State official; or

(B) if the provision of information under subparagraph (A) is not feasible, a reasonable estimate of the number of class members residing in each State and the estimated proportionate share of the claims of such members to the entire settlement; and

(8) any written judicial opinion relating to the materials described under subparagraphs (3) through (6).

(c) Depository institutions notification.—

(1) Federal and other depository institutions.—In any case in which the defendant is a Federal depository institution, a depository institution holding company, a foreign bank, or a non-depository institution subsidiary of the foregoing, the notice requirements of this section are satisfied by serving the notice required under subsection (b) upon the person who has the primary Federal regulatory or supervisory responsibility with respect to the defendant, if some or all of the matters alleged in the class action are subject to regulation or supervision by that person.

(2) State depository institutions.—In any case in which the defendant is a State depository institution (as that term is defined in section 3 of the Federal Deposit Insurance Act (12 U.S.C. 1813)), the notice requirements of this section are satisfied by serving the notice required under subsection (b) upon the State bank supervisor (as that term is defined in section 3 of the Federal Deposit Insurance Act (12 U.S.C. 1813)) of the State in which the defendant is incorporated or chartered, if some or all of the matters alleged in the class action are subject to regulation or supervision by that person, and upon the appropriate Federal official.

(d) Final approval.—An order giving final approval of a proposed settlement may not be issued earlier than 90 days after the later of the dates on which the appropriate Federal official and the appropriate State official are served with the notice required under subsection (b).

(e) Noncompliance if notice not provided.—

(1) In general.—A class member may refuse to comply with and may choose not to be bound by a settlement agreement or consent decree in a class action if the class member demonstrates that the notice required under subsection (b) has not been provided.

(2) Limitation.—A class member may not refuse to comply with or to be bound by a settlement agreement or consent decree under paragraph (1) if the notice required under subsection (b) was directed to the appropriate Federal official and to either the State attorney general or the person that has primary regulatory, supervisory, or licensing authority over the defendant.

(3) Application of rights.—The rights created by this subsection shall apply only to class members or any person acting on a class member's behalf, and shall not be construed to limit any other rights affecting a class member's participation in the settlement.

(f) Rule of construction.—Nothing in this section shall be construed to expand the authority of, or impose any obligations, duties, or responsibilities upon, Federal or State officials.

(Added Pub.L. 109–2, § 3(a), Feb. 18, 2005, 119 Stat. 7.)

§ 1731.   Handwriting

The admitted or proved handwriting of any person shall be admissible, for purposes of comparison, to determine genuineness of other handwriting attributed to such person.

§ 1732.   Record made in regular course of business; photographic copies

If any business, institution, member of a profession or calling, or any department or agency of government, in the regular course of business or activity has kept or recorded any memorandum, writing, entry, print, representation or combination thereof, of any act, transaction, occurrence, or event, and in the regular course of business has caused any or all of the same to be recorded, copied, or reproduced by any photographic, photostatic, microfilm, micro-card, miniature photographic, or other process which accurately reproduces or forms a durable medium for so reproducing the original, the original may be destroyed in the regular course of business unless its preservation is required by law. Such reproduction, when satisfactorily identified, is as admissible in evidence as the original itself in any judicial or administrative proceeding whether the original is in existence or not and an enlargement or facsimile of such reproduction is likewise admissible in evidence if the original reproduction is in existence and available for inspection under direction of court. The introduction of a reproduced record, enlargement, or facsimile does not preclude admission of the original. This subsection shall not be construed to exclude from evidence any document or copy thereof which is otherwise admissible under the rules of evidence.

(As amended Aug. 28, 1951, c. 351, §§ 1, 3, 65 Stat. 206; Aug. 30, 1961, Pub.L. 87–183, 75 Stat. 413; Jan. 2, 1975, Pub.L. 93–595, § 2(b), 88 Stat. 1949.)

§ 1733.   Government records and papers; copies

(a) Books or records of account or minutes of proceedings of any department or agency of the United States shall be admissible to prove the act, transaction or occurrence as a memorandum of which the same were made or kept.

(b) Properly authenticated copies or transcripts of any books, records, papers or documents of any department or agency of the United States shall be admitted in evidence equally with the originals thereof.

(c) This section does not apply to cases, actions, and proceedings to which the Federal Rules of Evidence apply.

(As amended Jan. 2, 1975, Pub.L. 93–595, § 2(c), 88 Stat. 1949.)

§ 1734.   Court record lost or destroyed, generally

(a) A lost or destroyed record of any proceeding in any court of the United States may be supplied on application of any interested party not at fault, by substituting a copy certified by the clerk of any court in which an authentic copy is lodged.

(b) Where a certified copy is not available, any interested person not at fault may file in such court a verified application for an order establishing the lost or destroyed record.

Every other interested person shall be served personally with a copy of the application and with notice of hearing on a day stated, not less than sixty days after service. Service may be made on any nonresident of the district anywhere within the jurisdiction of the United States or in any foreign country.

Proof of service in a foreign country shall be certified by a minister or consul of the United States in such country, under his official seal.

If, after the hearing, the court is satisfied that the statements contained in the application are true, it shall enter an order reciting the substance and effect of the lost or destroyed record. Such order, subject to intervening rights of third persons, shall have the same effect as the original record.

§ 1735.   Court record lost or destroyed where United States interested

(a) When the record of any case or matter in any court of the United States to which the United States is a party, is lost or destroyed, a certified copy of any official paper of a United States attorney, United States marshal or clerk or other certifying or recording officer of any such court, made pursuant to law, on file in any department or agency of the United States and relating to such case or matter, shall, on being filed in the court to which it relates, have the same effect as an original paper filed in such court. If the copy so filed discloses the date and amount of a judgment or decree and the names of the parties thereto, the court may enforce the judgment or decree as though the original record had not been lost or destroyed.

(b) Whenever the United States is interested in any lost or destroyed records or files of a court of the United States, the clerk of such court and the United States attorney for the district shall take the steps necessary to restore such records or files, under the direction of the judges of such court.

§ 1736.   Congressional Journals

Extracts from the Journals of the Senate and the House of Representatives, and from the Executive Journal of the Senate when the injunction of secrecy is removed, certified by the Secretary of the Senate

1715

or the Clerk of the House of Representatives shall be received in evidence with the same effect as the originals would have.

§ 1737.   Copy of officer's bond

Any person to whose custody the bond of any officer of the United States has been committed shall, on proper request and payment of the fee allowed by any Act of Congress, furnish certified copies thereof, which shall be prima facie evidence in any court of the execution, filing and contents of the bond.

§ 1738.   State and Territorial statutes and judicial proceedings; full faith and credit

The Acts of the legislature of any State, Territory, or Possession of the United States, or copies thereof, shall be authenticated by affixing the seal of such State, Territory or Possession thereto.

The records and judicial proceedings of any court of any such State, Territory or Possession, or copies thereof, shall be proved or admitted in other courts within the United States and its Territories and Possessions by the attestation of the clerk and seal of the court annexed, if a seal exists, together with a certificate of a judge of the court that the said attestation is in proper form.

Such Acts, records and judicial proceedings or copies thereof, so authenticated, shall have the same full faith and credit in every court within the United States and its Territories and Possessions as they have by law or usage in the courts of such State, Territory or Possession from which they are taken.

§ 1739.   State and Territorial nonjudicial records; full faith and credit

All nonjudicial records or books kept in any public office of any State, Territory, or Possession of the United States, or copies thereof, shall be proved or admitted in any court or office in any other State, Territory, or Possession by the attestation of the custodian of such records or books, and the seal of his office annexed, if there be a seal, together with a certificate of a judge of a court of record of the county, parish, or district in which such office may be kept, or of the Governor, or secretary of state, the chancellor or keeper of the great seal, of the State, Territory, or Possession that the said attestation is in due form and by the proper officers.

If the certificate is given by a judge, it shall be further authenticated by the clerk or prothonotary of the court, who shall certify, under his hand and the seal of his office, that such judge is duly commissioned and qualified; or, if given by such Governor, secretary, chancellor, or keeper of the great seal, it shall be under the great seal of the State, Territory, or Possession in which it is made.

Such records or books, or copies thereof, so authenticated, shall have the same full faith and credit in every court and office within the United States and its Territories and Possessions as they have by law or usage in the courts or offices of the State, Territory, or Possession from which they are taken.

§ 1740.   Copies of consular papers

Copies of all official documents and papers in the office of any consul or vice consul of the United States, and of all official entries in the books or records of any such office, authenticated by the consul or vice consul, shall be admissible equally with the originals.

§ 1741.   Foreign official documents

An official record or document of a foreign country may be evidenced by a copy, summary, or excerpt authenticated as provided in the Federal Rules of Civil Procedure.

(As amended Oct. 3, 1964, Pub.L. 88–619, § 5(a), 78 Stat. 996.)

§ 1743.   Demand on postmaster

The certificate of the Postmaster General or the Government Accountability Office of the mailing to a postmaster of a statement of his account and that payment of the balance stated has not been received shall be sufficient evidence of a demand notwithstanding any allowances or credits subsequently made. A copy of such statement shall be attached to the certificate.

(June 25, 1948, c. 646, 62 Stat. 948; July 7, 2004, Pub.L. 108–271, § 8(b), 118 Stat. 814.)

§ 1744.   Copies of United States Patent and Trademark Office documents, generally

Copies of letters patent or of any records, books, papers, or drawings belonging to the United States Patent and Trademark Office and relating to patents, authenticated under the seal of the United States Patent and Trademark Office and certified by the Under Secretary of Commerce for Intellectual Property and Director of the United States Patent and Trademark Office, or by another officer of the United States Patent and Trademark Office authorized to do so by the Director, shall be admissible in evidence with the same effect as the originals.

Any person making application and paying the required fee may obtain such certified copies.

(As amended May 24, 1949, c. 139, § 92(c), 63 Stat. 103; Pub.L. 106–113, Div. B, § 1000(a)(9) [S. 1948, Title IV, § 4732(b)(15)(B), (C)], Nov. 29, 1999, 113 Stat. 1536–___.)

§ 1745.   Copies of foreign patent documents

Copies of the specifications and drawings of foreign letters patent, or applications for foreign letters patent, and copies of excerpts of the official journals and other official publications of foreign patent offices belonging to the United States Patent and Trademark Office, certified in the manner provided by section 1744 of this title are prima facie evidence of their contents and of the dates indicated on their face.

(Formerly § 1746. Renumbered § 1745, May 24, 1949, c. 139, § 92(e), 63 Stat. 103, amended Oct. 3, 1964, Pub.L. 88–619, § 7(a), 78 Stat. 996; Pub.L. 106–113, Div. B, § 1000(a)(9) [S. 1948, Title IV, § 4732(b)(16)], Nov. 29, 1999, 113 Stat. 1537–___.)

§ 1746. Unsworn declarations under penalty of perjury

Wherever, under any law of the United States or under any rule, regulation, order, or requirement made pursuant to law, any matter is required or permitted to be supported, evidenced, established, or proved by the sworn declaration, verification, certificate, statement, oath, or affidavit, in writing of the person making the same (other than a deposition, or an oath of office, or an oath required to be taken before a specified official other than a notary public), such matter may, with like force and effect, be supported, evidenced, established, or proved by the unsworn declaration, certificate, verification, or statement, in writing of such person which is subscribed by him, as true under penalty of perjury, and dated, in substantially the following form:

(1) If executed without the United States: "I declare (or certify, verify, or state) under penalty of perjury under the laws of the United States of America that the foregoing is true and correct. Executed on (date).

(Signature)".

(2) If executed within the United States, its territories, possessions, or commonwealths: "I declare (or certify, verify, or state) under penalty of perjury that the foregoing is true and correct. Executed on (date).

(Signature)".

(Added Pub.L. 94–550, § 1(a), Oct. 18, 1976, 90 Stat. 2534.)

§ 1781. Transmittal of letter rogatory or request

(a) The Department of State has power, directly, or through suitable channels—

(1) to receive a letter rogatory issued, or request made, by a foreign or international tribunal, to transmit it to the tribunal, officer, or agency in the United States to whom it is addressed, and to receive and return it after execution; and

(2) to receive a letter rogatory issued, or request made, by a tribunal in the United States, to transmit it to the foreign or international tribunal, officer, or agency to whom it is addressed, and to receive and return it after execution.

(b) This section does not preclude—

(1) the transmittal of a letter rogatory or request directly from a foreign or international tribunal to the tribunal, officer, or agency in the United States to whom it is addressed and its return in the same manner; or

(2) the transmittal of a letter rogatory or request directly from a tribunal in the United States to the foreign or international tribunal, officer, or agency to whom it is addressed and its return in the same manner.

(As amended Oct. 3, 1964, Pub.L. 88–619, § 8(a), 78 Stat. 996.)

§ 1782.   Assistance to foreign and international tribunals and to litigants before such tribunals

(a) The district court of the district in which a person resides or is found may order him to give his testimony or statement or to produce a document or other thing for use in a proceeding in a foreign or international tribunal, including criminal investigations conducted before formal accusation.   The order may be made pursuant to a letter rogatory issued, or request made, by a foreign or international tribunal or upon the application of any interested person and may direct that the testimony or statement be given, or the document or other thing be produced, before a person appointed by the court.   By virtue of his appointment, the person appointed has power to administer any necessary oath and take the testimony or statement.   The order may prescribe the practice and procedure, which may be in whole or part the practice and procedure of the foreign country or the international tribunal, for taking the testimony or statement or producing the document or other thing.   To the extent that the order does not prescribe otherwise, the testimony or statement shall be taken, and the document or other thing produced, in accordance with the Federal Rules of Civil Procedure.

A person may not be compelled to give his testimony or statement or to produce a document or other thing in violation of any legally applicable privilege.

(b) This chapter does not preclude a person within the United States from voluntarily giving his testimony or statement, or producing a document or other thing, for use in a proceeding in a foreign or international tribunal before any person and in any manner acceptable to him.

(June 25, 1948, c. 646, 62 Stat. 949; May 24, 1949, c. 139, § 93, 63 Stat. 103; Oct. 3, 1964, Pub.L. 88–619, § 9(a), 78 Stat. 997; Feb. 10, 1996, Pub.L. 104–106, Div. A, Title XIII, § 1342(b), 110 Stat. 486.)

§ 1783.   Subpoena of person in foreign country

(a) A court of the United States may order the issuance of a subpoena requiring the appearance as a witness before it, or before a person or body designated by it, of a national or resident of the United States who is in a foreign country, or requiring the production of a specified document or other thing by him, if the court finds that particular testimony or the production of the document or other thing by him is necessary in the interest of justice, and, in other than a criminal action or proceeding, if the court finds, in addition, that it is not possible to obtain his testimony in admissible form without his personal appearance or to obtain the production of the document or other thing in any other manner.

(b) The subpoena shall designate the time and place for the appearance or for the production of the document or other thing.   Service of the subpoena and any order to show cause, rule, judgment, or decree authorized by this section or by section 1784 of this title shall be effected in accordance with the provisions of the Federal Rules of Civil Procedure relating to service of process on a person in a foreign country.   The person serving the subpoena shall tender to the person to whom the subpoena is addressed his estimated necessary travel and attendance expenses, the amount of which shall be determined by the court and stated in the order directing the issuance of the subpoena.

(As amended Oct. 3, 1964, Pub.L. 88–619, § 10(a), 78 Stat. 997.)

§ 1784.   Contempt

(a) The court of the United States which has issued a subpoena served in a foreign country may order the person who has failed to appear or who has failed to produce a document or other thing as directed therein to show cause before it at a designated time why he should not be punished for contempt.

(b) The court, in the order to show cause, may direct that any of the person's property within the United States be levied upon or seized, in the manner provided by law or court rules governing levy or seizure under execution, and held to satisfy any judgment that may be rendered against him pursuant to subsection (d) of this section if adequate security, in such amount as the court may direct in the order, be given for any damage that he might suffer should he not be found in contempt. Security under this subsection may not be required of the United States.

(c) A copy of the order to show cause shall be served on the person in accordance with section 1783(b) of this title.

(d) On the return day of the order to show cause or any later day to which the hearing may be continued, proof shall be taken. If the person is found in contempt, the court, notwithstanding any limitation upon its power generally to punish for contempt, may fine him not more than $100,000 and direct that the fine and costs of the proceedings be satisfied by a sale of the property levied upon or seized, conducted upon the notice required and in the manner provided for sales upon execution.

(As amended Oct. 3, 1964, Pub.L. 88–619, § 11, 78 Stat. 998.)

§ 1785.   Subpoenas in multiparty, multiforum actions

When the jurisdiction of the district court is based in whole or in part upon section 1369 of this title, a subpoena for attendance at a hearing or trial may, if authorized by the court upon motion for good cause shown, and upon such terms and conditions as the court may impose, be served at any place within the United States, or anywhere outside the United States if otherwise permitted by law.

(Added Pub.L. 107–273, Div. C, Title I, § 11020(b)(4)(B)(i), Nov. 2, 2002, 116 Stat. 1828.)

§ 1821.   Per diem and mileage generally; subsistence

(a)(1) Except as otherwise provided by law, a witness in attendance at any court of the United States, or before a United States Magistrate, or before any person authorized to take his deposition pursuant to any rule or order of a court of the United States, shall be paid the fees and allowances provided by this section.

(2) As used in this section, the term "court of the United States" includes, in addition to the courts listed in section 451 of this title, any court created by Act of Congress in a territory which is invested with any jurisdiction of a district court of the United States.

(b) A witness shall be paid an attendance fee of $40 per day for each day's attendance. A witness shall also be paid the attendance fee for the time necessarily occupied in going to and returning from the place of attendance at the beginning and end of such attendance or at any time during such attendance.

(c)(1) A witness who travels by common carrier shall be paid for the actual expenses of travel on the basis of the means of transportation reasonably utilized and the distance necessarily traveled to and from such witness's residence by the shortest practical route in going to and returning from the place of attendance. Such a witness shall utilize a common carrier at the most economical rate reasonably available. A receipt or other evidence of actual cost shall be furnished.

(2) A travel allowance equal to the mileage allowance which the Administrator of General Services has prescribed, pursuant to section 5704 of title 5, for official travel of employees of the Federal Government shall be paid to each witness who travels by privately owned vehicle. Computation of mileage under this paragraph shall be made on the basis of a uniformed table of distances adopted by the Administrator of General Services.

(3) Toll charges for toll roads, bridges, tunnels, and ferries, taxicab fares between places of lodging and carrier terminals, and parking fees (upon presentation of a valid parking receipt), shall be paid in full to a witness incurring such expenses.

(4) All normal travel expenses within and outside the judicial district shall be taxable as costs pursuant to section 1920 of this title.

(d)(1) A subsistence allowance shall be paid to a witness when an overnight stay is required at the place of attendance because such place is so far removed from the residence of such witness as to prohibit return thereto from day to day.

(2) A subsistence allowance for a witness shall be paid in an amount not to exceed the maximum per diem allowance prescribed by the Administrator of General Services, pursuant to section 5702(a) of title 5, for official travel in the area of attendance by employees of the Federal Government.

(3) A subsistence allowance for a witness attending in an area designated by the Administrator of General Services as a high-cost area shall be paid in an amount not to exceed the maximum actual subsistence allowance prescribed by the Administrator, pursuant to section 5702(c)(B) of title 5, for official travel in such area by employees of the Federal Government.

(4) When a witness is detained pursuant to section 3144 of title 18 for want of security for his appearance, he shall be entitled for each day of detention when not in attendance at court, in addition to his subsistence, to the daily attendance fee provided by subsection (b) of this section.

(e) An alien who has been paroled into the United States for prosecution, pursuant to section 212(d)(5) of the Immigration and Nationality Act (8 U.S.C. 1182(d)(5)), or an alien who either has admitted belonging to a class of aliens who are deportable or has been determined pursuant to section 240 of such Act (8 U.S.C. 1252(b)) to be deportable, shall be ineligible to receive the fees or allowances provided by this section.

(f) Any witness who is incarcerated at the time that his or her testimony is given (except for a witness to whom the provisions of section 3144 of title 18 apply) may not receive fees or allowances under this section, regardless of whether such a witness is incarcerated at the time he or she makes a claim for fees or allowances under this section.

(As amended May 10, 1949, c. 96, 63 Stat. 65; May 24, 1949, c. 139, § 94, 63 Stat. 103; Oct. 31, 1951, c. 655, § 51(a), 65 Stat. 727; Sept. 3, 1954, c. 1263, § 45, 68 Stat. 1242; Aug. 1, 1956, c. 826, 70 Stat. 798; Mar. 27, 1968, Pub.L. 90–274, § 102(b), 82 Stat. 62; Oct. 27, 1978, Pub.L. 95–535, § 1, 92 Stat. 2033; Dec. 1, 1990, Pub.L. 101–650, Title III, § 314(a), 104 Stat. 5115; Oct. 14, 1992, Pub.L. 102–417, § 2(a)–(c), 106 Stat. 2138.)

Amendment of Subsec. (e)

Pub.L. 104–208, Div. C, Title III, §§ 308(g)(5)(E), 309, Sept. 30, 1996, 110 Stat. 3009–623, 3009–625, provided that, to take effect, with certain exceptions and subject to certain transitional rules, on the first day of the first month beginning more than 180 days after Sept. 30, 1996, subsec. (e) of this section is amended by striking "242(b)" and inserting "240".

§ 1826. Recalcitrant witnesses

(a) Whenever a witness in any proceeding before or ancillary to any court or grand jury of the United States refuses without just cause shown to comply with an order of the court to testify or provide other information, including any book, paper, document, record, recording or other material, the court, upon such refusal, or when such refusal is duly brought to its attention, may summarily order his confinement at a suitable place until such time as the witness is willing to give such testimony or provide such information. No period of such confinement shall exceed the life of—

(1) the court proceeding, or

(2) the term of the grand jury, including extensions,

before which such refusal to comply with the court order occurred, but in no event shall such confinement exceed eighteen months.

(b) No person confined pursuant to subsection (a) of this section shall be admitted to bail pending the determination of an appeal taken by him from the order for his confinement if it appears that the appeal is frivolous or taken for delay. Any appeal from an order of confinement under this section shall be disposed of as soon as practicable, but not later than thirty days from the filing of such appeal.

(c) Whoever escapes or attempts to escape from the custody of any facility or from any place in which or to which he is confined pursuant to this section or section 4243 of title 18, or whoever rescues or attempts to rescue or instigates, aids, or assists the escape or attempt to escape of such a person, shall be subject to imprisonment for not more than three years, or a fine of not more than $10,000, or both.

(Added Pub.L. 91–452, Title III, § 301(a), Oct. 15, 1970, 84 Stat. 932, and amended Pub.L. 98–473, Title II, § 1013, Oct. 12, 1984, 98 Stat. 2142.)

§ 1914.   District court; filing and miscellaneous fees; rules of court

(a) The clerk of each district court shall require the parties instituting any civil action, suit or proceeding in such court, whether by original process, removal or otherwise, to pay a filing fee of $350, except that on application for a writ of habeas corpus the filing fee shall be $5.

(b) The clerk shall collect from the parties such additional fees only as are prescribed by the Judicial Conference of the United States.

(c) Each district court by rule or standing order may require advance payment of fees.

(June 25, 1948, c. 646, 62 Stat. 954; Nov. 6, 1978, Pub.L. 95–598, Title II, § 244, 92 Stat. 2671; June 19, 1986, Pub.L. 99–336, § 4(a), 100 Stat. 637; Oct. 18, 1986, Pub.L. 99–500, Title I, § 101(b) [Title IV, § 407(a)], 100 Stat. 1783–39, 1783–64, and Oct. 30, 1986, Pub.L. 99–591, Title I, § 101(b) [Title IV, § 407(a)], 100 Stat. 3341–39, 3341–64; Oct. 19, 1996, Pub.L. 104–317, Title IV, § 401(a), 110 Stat. 3853; Pub.L. 108–447, Div. B, Title III, § 307(a), Dec. 8, 2004, 118 Stat. 2895; Feb. 8, 2006, Pub.L. 109–171, Title X, § 10001(a), 120 Stat. 183.)

§ 1915.   Proceedings in forma pauperis

(a)(1) Subject to subsection (b), any court of the United States may authorize the commencement, prosecution or defense of any suit, action or proceeding, civil or criminal, or appeal therein, without prepayment of fees or security therefor, by a person who submits an affidavit that includes a statement of all assets such prisoner possesses that the person is unable to pay such fees or give security therefor. Such affidavit shall state the nature of the action, defense or appeal and affiant's belief that the person is entitled to redress.

(2) A prisoner seeking to bring a civil action or appeal a judgment in a civil action or proceeding without prepayment of fees or security therefor, in addition to filing the affidavit filed under paragraph (1), shall submit a certified copy of the trust fund account statement (or institutional equivalent) for the prisoner for the 6-month period immediately preceding the filing of the complaint or notice of appeal, obtained from the appropriate official of each prison at which the prisoner is or was confined.

(3) An appeal may not be taken in forma pauperis if the trial court certifies in writing that it is not taken in good faith.

(b)(1) Notwithstanding subsection (a), if a prisoner brings a civil action or files an appeal in forma pauperis, the prisoner shall be required to pay the full amount of a filing fee. The court shall assess and, when funds exist, collect, as a partial payment of any court fees required by law, an initial partial filing fee of 20 percent of the greater of—

(A) the average monthly deposits to the prisoner's account; or

(B) the average monthly balance in the prisoner's account for the 6-month period immediately preceding the filing of the complaint or notice of appeal.

(2) After payment of the initial partial filing fee, the prisoner shall be required to make monthly payments of 20 percent of the preceding month's income credited to the prisoner's account. The agency having custody of the prisoner shall forward payments from the prisoner's account to the clerk of the court each time the amount in the account exceeds $10 until the filing fees are paid.

(3) In no event shall the filing fee collected exceed the amount of fees permitted by statute for the commencement of a civil action or an appeal of a civil action or criminal judgment.

(4) In no event shall a prisoner be prohibited from bringing a civil action or appealing a civil or criminal judgment for the reason that the prisoner has no assets and no means by which to pay the initial partial filing fee.

(c) Upon the filing of an affidavit in accordance with subsections (a) and (b) and the prepayment of any partial filing fee as may be required under subsection (b), the court may direct payment by the United States of the expenses of (1) printing the record on appeal in any civil or criminal case, if such printing is required by the appellate court; (2) preparing a transcript of proceedings before a United States magistrate in any civil or criminal case, if such transcript is required by the district court, in the case of proceedings conducted under section 636(b) of this title or under section 3401(b) of title 18, United States Code; and (3) printing the record on appeal if such printing is required by the appellate court, in the case of proceedings conducted pursuant to section 636(c) of this title. Such expenses shall be paid when authorized by the Director of the Administrative Office of the United States Courts.

(d) The officers of the court shall issue and serve all process, and perform all duties in such cases. Witnesses shall attend as in other cases, and the same remedies shall be available as are provided for by law in other cases.

(e)(1) The court may request an attorney to represent any person unable to afford counsel.

(2) Notwithstanding any filing fee, or any portion thereof, that may have been paid, the court shall dismiss the case at any time if the court determines that—

    (A) the allegation of poverty is untrue; or

    (B) the action or appeal—

        (i) is frivolous or malicious;

        (ii) fails to state a claim on which relief may be granted; or

        (iii) seeks monetary relief against a defendant who is immune from such relief.

(f)(1) Judgment may be rendered for costs at the conclusion of the suit or action as in other proceedings, but the United States shall not be liable for any of the costs thus incurred. If the United States has paid the cost of a stenographic transcript or printed record for the prevailing party, the same shall be taxed in favor of the United States.

(2)(A) If the judgment against a prisoner includes the payment of costs under this subsection, the prisoner shall be required to pay the full amount of the costs ordered.

(B) The prisoner shall be required to make payments for costs under this subsection in the same manner as is provided for filing fees under subsection (a)(2).

(C) In no event shall the costs collected exceed the amount of the costs ordered by the court.

(g) In no event shall a prisoner bring a civil action or appeal a judgment in a civil action or proceeding under this section if the prisoner has, on 3 or more prior occasions, while incarcerated or detained in any facility, brought an action or appeal in a court of the United States that was dismissed on the grounds that it is frivolous, malicious, or fails to state a claim upon which relief may be granted, unless the prisoner is under imminent danger of serious physical injury.

(h) As used in this section, the term 'prisoner' means any person incarcerated or detained in any facility who is accused of, convicted of, sentenced for, or adjudicated delinquent for, violations of criminal law or the terms and conditions of parole, probation, pretrial release, or diversionary program.

(June 25, 1948, c. 646, 62 Stat. 954; May 24, 1949, c. 139, § 98, 63 Stat. 104; Oct. 31, 1951, c. 655, § 51(b), (c), 65 Stat. 727; Sept. 21, 1959, Pub.L. 86–320, 73 Stat. 590; Oct. 10, 1979, Pub.L. 96–82, § 6, 93 Stat. 645; Apr. 26, 1996, Pub.L. 104–134, Title I, § 101[(a)][Title VIII, § 804(a), (c) to (e)], 110 Stat. 1321–73, 1321–74; renumbered Title I May 2, 1996, Pub.L. 104–140, § 1(a), 110 Stat. 1327.)

§ 1917.　District courts; fee on filing notice of or petition for appeal

Upon the filing of any separate or joint notice of appeal or application for appeal or upon the receipt of any order allowing, or notice of the allowance of, an appeal or of a writ of certiorari $5 shall be paid to the clerk of the district court, by the appellant or petitioner.

§ 1920.　Taxation of costs

A judge or clerk of any court of the United States may tax as costs the following:

(1) Fees of the clerk and marshal;

(2) Fees of the court reporter for all or any part of the stenographic transcript necessarily obtained for use in the case;

(3) Fees and disbursements for printing and witnesses;

(4) Fees for exemplification and copies of papers necessarily obtained for use in the case;

(5) Docket fees under section 1923 of this title;

(6) Compensation of court appointed experts, compensation of interpreters, and salaries, fees, expenses, and costs of special interpretation services under section 1828 of this title.

A bill of costs shall be filed in the case and, upon allowance, included in the judgment or decree.

(As amended Oct. 28, 1978, Pub.L. 95–539, § 7, 92 Stat. 2044.)

§ 1921. United States marshal's fees

(a)(1) The United States marshals or deputy marshals shall routinely collect, and a court may tax as costs, fees for the following:

(A) Serving a writ of possession, partition, execution, attachment in rem, or libel in admiralty, warrant, attachment, summons, complaints, or any other writ, order or process in any case or proceeding.

(B) Serving a subpoena or summons for a witness or appraiser.

(C) Forwarding any writ, order, or process to another judicial district for service.

(D) The preparation of any notice of sale, proclamation in admiralty, or other public notice or bill of sale.

(E) The keeping of attached property (including boats, vessels, or other property attached or libeled), actual expenses incurred, such as storage, moving, boat hire, or other special transportation, watchmen's or keepers' fees, insurance, and an hourly rate, including overtime, for each deputy marshal required for special services, such as guarding, inventorying, and moving.

(F) Copies of writs or other papers furnished at the request of any party.

(G) Necessary travel in serving or endeavoring to serve any process, writ, or order, except in the District of Columbia, with mileage to be computed from the place where service is returnable to the place of service or endeavor.

(H) Overtime expenses incurred by deputy marshals in the course of serving or executing civil process.

(2) The marshals shall collect, in advance, a deposit to cover the initial expenses for special services required under paragraph (1)(E), and periodically thereafter such amounts as may be necessary to pay such expenses until the litigation is concluded. This paragraph applies to all private litigants, including seamen proceeding pursuant to section 1916 of this title.

(3) For purposes of paragraph (1)(G), if two or more services or endeavors, or if an endeavor and a service, are made in behalf of the same party in the same case on the same trip, mileage shall be computed to the place of service or endeavor which is most remote from the place where service is returnable, adding thereto any additional mileage traveled in serving or endeavoring to serve in behalf of the party. If two or more writs of any kind, required to be served in behalf of the same party on the same person in the same case or proceeding, may be served at the same time, mileage on only one such writ shall be collected.

(b) The Attorney General shall from time to time prescribe by regulation the fees to be taxed and collected under subsection (a). Such fees shall, to the extent practicable, reflect the actual and reasonable cost of the service provided.

(c)(1) The United States Marshals Service shall collect a commission of 3 percent of the first $1,000 collected and 1½ percent on the excess of any sum over $1,000, for seizing or levying on property (including seizures in admiralty), disposing of such property by sale, setoff, or otherwise, and receiving and paying over money, except that the amount of commission shall be within the range set by the Attorney General. if [1] the property is not disposed of by marshal's sale, commission shall be in such amount, within the range set by the Attorney General, as may be allowed by the court. In any case in which the vessel or other property is sold by a public auctioneer, or by some party other than a marshal or deputy marshal, the commission authorized under this subsection shall be reduced by the amount paid to such auctioneer or other party. This subsection applies to any judicially ordered sale or execution sale, without regard to whether the judicial order of sale constitutes a seizure or levy within the meaning of State law. This subsection shall not apply to any seizure, forfeiture, sale, or other disposition of property pursuant to the applicable provisions of law amended by the Comprehensive Forfeiture Act of 1984 (98 Stat. 2040).

(2) The Attorney General shall prescribe from time to time regulations which establish a minimum and maximum amount for the commission collected under paragraph (1).

(d) The United States marshals may require a deposit to cover the fees and expenses prescribed under this section.

(e) Notwithstanding section 3302 of title 31, the United States Marshals Service is authorized, to the extent provided in advance in appropriations Acts—

   (1) to credit to such Service's appropriation all fees, commissions, and expenses collected by such Service for—

      (A) the service of civil process, including complaints, summonses, subpoenas, and similar process; and

      (B) seizures, levies, and sales associated with judicial orders of execution; and

   (2) to use such credited amounts for the purpose of carrying out such activities.

(As amended Sept. 9, 1950, c. 937, 64 Stat. 824; Aug. 31, 1962, Pub.L. 87–621, § 1, 76 Stat. 417; Nov. 10, 1986, Pub.L. 99–646, § 39(a), 100 Stat. 3600; Nov. 18, 1988, Pub.L. 100–690, Title VII, § 7608(c), 102 Stat. 4515; Nov. 29, 1990, Pub.L. 101–647, Title XII, § 1212, 104 Stat. 4833.)

§ 1924.   Verification of bill of costs

Before any bill of costs is taxed, the party claiming any item of cost or disbursement shall attach thereto an affidavit, made by himself or by his duly authorized attorney or agent having knowledge of the facts, that such item is correct and has been necessarily incurred in the case and that the services for which fees have been charged were actually and necessarily performed.

   1. So in original. Probably should be   "If".

§ 1927.   Counsel's liability for excessive costs

Any attorney or other person admitted to conduct cases in any court of the United States or any Territory thereof who so multiplies the proceedings in any case unreasonably and vexatiously may be required by the court to satisfy personally the excess costs, expenses, and attorneys' fees reasonably incurred because of such conduct.

(As amended Sept. 12, 1980, Pub.L. 96–349, § 3, 94 Stat. 1156.)

§ 1961.   Interest

(a) Interest shall be allowed on any money judgment in a civil case recovered in a district court. Execution therefor may be levied by the marshal, in any case where, by the law of the State in which such court is held, execution may be levied for interest on judgments recovered in the courts of the State. Such interest shall be calculated from the date of the entry of the judgment, at a rate equal to the weekly average 1–year constant maturity Treasury yield, as published by the Board of Governors of the Federal Reserve System, for the calendar week preceding the date of the judgment. The Director of the Administrative Office of the United States Courts shall distribute notice of that rate and any changes in it to all Federal judges.

(b) Interest shall be computed daily to the date of payment except as provided in section 2516(b) of this title and section 1304(b) of title 31, and shall be compounded annually.

(c)(1) This section shall not apply in any judgment of any court with respect to any internal revenue tax case. Interest shall be allowed in such cases at the underpayment rate or overpayment rate (whichever is appropriate) established under section 6621 of the Internal Revenue Code of 1986.

(2) Except as otherwise provided in paragraph (1) of this subsection, interest shall be allowed on all final judgments against the United States in the United States Court of Appeals for the Federal circuit,[1] at the rate provided in subsection (a) and as provided in subsection (b).

(3) Interest shall be allowed, computed, and paid on judgments of the United States Court of Federal Claims only as provided in paragraph (1) of this subsection or in any other provision of law.

(4) This section shall not be construed to affect the interest on any judgment of any court not specified in this section.

(June 25, 1948, c. 646, 62 Stat. 957; Apr. 2, 1982, Pub.L. 97–164, Title III, § 302(a), 96 Stat. 55; Sept. 13, 1982, Pub.L. 97–258, § 2(m) (1), 96 Stat. 1062; Jan. 12, 1983, Pub.L. 97–452, § 2(d)(1), 96 Stat. 2478; Oct. 22, 1986, Pub.L. 99–514, § 2, Title XV, § 1511(c)(17), 100 Stat. 2095, 2745; Oct. 29, 1992, Pub.L. 102–572, Title IX, § 902(b)(1), 106 Stat. 4516; Dec. 21, 2000, Pub.L. 106–554, § 1(a)(7) [Title III, § 307(d)(1)], 114 Stat. 2763, 2763A–636.)

[Interest on any money judgment in a civil case recovered in a district court is calculated from the date of entry of the judgment at a rate equal to the equivalent coupon issue yield of the average accepted auction price for the last auction of fifty-two week United States Treasury bills settled immediately prior to the date of the judgment. 28 U.S.C.A.

---

1. So in original. Probably should be   "Circuit,".

§ 1961(a). For a listing of historical and current interest rates, consult West's annually revised **Federal Civil Judicial Procedure and Rules** (and supplements).]

§ 1963. Registration of judgments for enforcement in other districts

A judgment in an action for the recovery of money or property entered in any court of appeals, district court, bankruptcy court, or in the Court of International Trade may be registered by filing a certified copy of the judgment in any other district or, with respect to the Court of International Trade, in any judicial district, when the judgment has become final by appeal or expiration of the time for appeal or when ordered by the court that entered the judgment for good cause shown. Such a judgment entered in favor of the United States may be so registered any time after judgment is entered. A judgment so registered shall have the same effect as a judgment of the district court of the district where registered and may be enforced in like manner.

A certified copy of the satisfaction of any judgment in whole or in part may be registered in like manner in any district in which the judgment is a lien.

The procedure prescribed under this section is in addition to other procedures provided by law for the enforcement of judgments.

(As amended Aug. 23, 1954, c. 837, 68 Stat. 772; July 7, 1958, Pub.L. 85–508, § 12(o), 72 Stat. 349; Nov. 19, 1988, Pub.L. 100–702, Title X, § 1002(a), (b)(1), 102 Stat. 4664; Nov. 29, 1990, Pub.L. 101–647, Title XXXVI, § 3628, 104 Stat. 4965; Oct. 19, 1996, Pub.L. 104–317, 110 Stat. 3847.)

§ 1964. Constructive notice of pending actions

Where the law of a State requires a notice of an action concerning real property pending in a court of the State to be registered, recorded, docketed, or indexed in a particular manner, or in a certain office or county or parish in order to give constructive notice of the action as it relates to the real property, and such law authorizes a notice of an action concerning real property pending in a United States district court to be registered, recorded, docketed, or indexed in the same manner, or in the same place, those requirements of the State law must be complied with in order to give constructive notice of such an action pending in a United States district court as it relates to real property in such State.

(Added Aug. 20, 1958, Pub.L. 85–689, § 1(a), 72 Stat. 683.)

§ 2071. Rule-making power generally

(a) The Supreme Court and all courts established by Act of Congress may from time to time prescribe rules for the conduct of their business. Such rules shall be consistent with Acts of Congress and rules of practice and procedure prescribed under section 2072 of this title.

(b) Any rule prescribed by a court, other than the Supreme Court, under subsection (a) shall be prescribed only after giving appropriate public notice and an opportunity for comment. Such rule shall take effect upon the date specified by the prescribing court and shall have such effect on pending proceedings as the prescribing court may order.

(c)(1) A rule of a district court prescribed under subsection (a) shall remain in effect unless modified or abrogated by the judicial council of the relevant circuit.

(2) Any other rule prescribed by a court other than the Supreme Court under subsection (a) shall remain in effect unless modified or abrogated by the Judicial Conference.

(d) Copies of rules prescribed under subsection (a) by a district court shall be furnished to the judicial council, and copies of all rules prescribed by a court other than the Supreme Court under subsection (a) shall be furnished to the Director of the Administrative Office of the United States Courts and made available to the public.

(e) If the prescribing court determines that there is an immediate need for a rule, such court may proceed under this section without public notice and opportunity for comment, but such court shall promptly thereafter afford such notice and opportunity for comment.

(f) No rule may be prescribed by a district court other than under this section.

(As amended May 24, 1949, c. 139, § 102, 63 Stat. 104; Nov. 19, 1988, Pub.L. 100–702, Title IV, § 403(a)(1), 102 Stat. 4650.)

§ 2072.   Rules of procedure and evidence; power to prescribe

(a) The Supreme Court shall have the power to prescribe general rules of practice and procedure and rules of evidence for cases in the United States district courts (including proceedings before magistrates thereof) and courts of appeals.

(b) Such rules shall not abridge, enlarge or modify any substantive right. All laws in conflict with such rules shall be of no further force or effect after such rules have taken effect.

(c) Such rules may define when a ruling of a district court is final for the purposes of appeal under section 1291 of this title.

(As amended Pub.L. 101–650, Title III, § 315, Dec. 1, 1990, 104 Stat. 5115.)

§ 2073.   Rules of procedure and evidence; method of prescribing

(a)(1) The Judicial Conference shall prescribe and publish the procedures for the consideration of proposed rules under this section.

(2) The Judicial Conference may authorize the appointment of committees to assist the Conference by recommending rules to be prescribed under sections 2072 and 2075 of this title. Each such committee shall consist of members of the bench and the professional bar, and trial and appellate judges.

(b) The Judicial Conference shall authorize the appointment of a standing committee on rules of practice, procedure, and evidence under subsection (a) of this section. Such standing committee shall review each recommendation of any other committees so appointed and recommend to the Judicial Conference rules of practice, procedure, and evidence and such changes in rules proposed by a committee appointed under subsection (a)(2) of this section as may be necessary to maintain consistency and otherwise promote the interest of justice.

(c)(1) Each meeting for the transaction of business under this chapter by any committee appointed under this section shall be open to the public, except when the committee so meeting, in open session and with a majority present, determines that it is in the public interest that all or part of the remainder of the meeting on that day shall be closed to the public, and states the reason for so closing the meeting. Minutes of each meeting for the transaction of business under this chapter shall be maintained by the committee and made available to the public, except that any portion of such minutes, relating to a closed meeting and made available to the public, may contain such deletions as may be necessary to avoid frustrating the purposes of closing the meeting.

(2) Any meeting for the transaction of business under this chapter, by a committee appointed under this section, shall be preceded by sufficient notice to enable all interested persons to attend.

(d) In making a recommendation under this section or under section 2072 or 2075, the body making that recommendation shall provide a proposed rule, an explanatory note on the rule, and a written report explaining the body's action, including any minority or other separate views.

(e) Failure to comply with this section does not invalidate a rule prescribed under section 2072 or 2075 of this title.

(Added Pub.L. 100–702, Title IV, § 401(a), Nov. 19, 1988, 102 Stat. 4649, and amended Pub.L. 103–394, Title I, § 104(e), Oct. 22, 1994, 108 Stat. 4110.)

§ 2074.   Rules of procedure and evidence;   submission to Congress;   effective date

(a) The Supreme Court shall transmit to the Congress not later than May 1 of the year in which a rule prescribed under section 2072 is to become effective a copy of the proposed rule.   Such rule shall take effect no earlier than December 1 of the year in which such rule is so transmitted unless otherwise provided by law.   The Supreme Court may fix the extent such rule shall apply to proceedings then pending, except that the Supreme Court shall not require the application of such rule to further proceedings then pending to the extent that, in the opinion of the court in which such proceedings are pending, the application of such rule in such proceedings would not be feasible or would work injustice, in which event the former rule applies.

(b) Any such rule creating, abolishing, or modifying an evidentiary privilege shall have no force or effect unless approved by Act of Congress.

§ 2075.   Bankruptcy rules

The Supreme Court shall have the power to prescribe by general rules, the forms of process, writs, pleadings, and motions, and the practice and procedure in cases under title 11.

Such rules shall not abridge, enlarge, or modify any substantive right.

The Supreme Court shall transmit to Congress not later than May 1 of the year in which a rule prescribed under this section is to become effective a copy of the proposed rule. The rule shall take effect no earlier than December 1 of the year in which it is transmitted to Congress unless otherwise provided by law.

The bankruptcy rules promulgated under this section shall prescribe a form for the statement required under section 707(b)(2)(C) of title 11 and may provide general rules on the content of such statement.

(Added Pub.L. 88–623, § 1, Oct. 3, 1964, 78 Stat. 1001, and amended Pub.L. 95–598, Title II, § 247, Nov. 6, 1978, 92 Stat. 2672; Pub.L. 103–394, Title I, § 104(f), Oct. 22, 1994, 108 Stat. 4110; Pub.L. 109–8, Title XII, § 1232, Apr. 20, 2005, 119 Stat. 202.)

§ 2077.   Publication of rules; advisory committees

(a) The rules for the conduct of the business of each court of appeals, including the operating procedures of such court, shall be published.   Each court of appeals shall print or cause to be printed necessary copies of the rules.   The Judicial Conference shall prescribe the fees for sales of copies under section 1913 of this title, but the Judicial Conference may provide for free distribution of copies to members of the bar of each court and to other interested persons.

(b) Each court, except the Supreme Court, that is authorized to prescribe rules of the conduct of such court's business under section 2071 of this title shall appoint an advisory committee for the study of the rules of practice and internal operating procedures of such court and, in the case of an advisory committee appointed by a court of appeals, of the rules of the judicial council of the circuit.   The advisory committee shall make recommendations to the court concerning such rules and procedures.   Members of the committee shall serve without compensation, but the Director may pay travel and transportation expenses in accordance with section 5703 of title 5.

(As amended Pub.L. 100–702, Title IV, § 401(b), Nov. 19, 1988, 102 Stat. 4650; Pub.L. 101–650, Title IV, § 406, Dec. 1, 1990, 104 Stat. 5124.)

§ 2101.   Supreme Court; time for appeal or certiorari; docketing; stay

(a) A direct appeal to the Supreme Court from any decision under section 1253 of this title, holding unconstitutional in whole or in part, any Act of Congress, shall be taken within thirty days after the entry of the interlocutory or final order, judgment or decree.   The record shall be made up and the case docketed within sixty days from the time such appeal is taken under rules prescribed by the Supreme Court.

(b) Any other direct appeal to the Supreme Court which is authorized by law, from a decision of a district court in any civil action, suit or proceeding, shall be taken within thirty days from the judgment, order or decree, appealed from, if interlocutory, and within sixty days if final.

(c) Any other appeal or any writ of certiorari intended to bring any judgment or decree in a civil action, suit or proceeding before the Supreme Court for review shall be taken or applied for within ninety days after the entry of such judgment or decree.   A justice of the Supreme Court, for good cause shown, may extend the time for applying for a writ of certiorari for a period not exceeding sixty days.

(d) The time for appeal or application for a writ of certiorari to review the judgment of a State court in a criminal case shall be as prescribed by rules of the Supreme Court.

(e) An application to the Supreme Court for a writ of certiorari to review a case before judgment has been rendered in the court of appeals may be made at any time before judgment.

(f) In any case in which the final judgment or decree of any court is subject to review by the Supreme Court on writ of certiorari, the execution and enforcement of such judgment or decree may be stayed for a reasonable time to enable the party aggrieved to obtain a writ of certiorari from the Supreme Court. The stay may be granted by a judge of the court rendering the judgment or decree or by a justice of the Supreme Court, and may be conditioned on the giving of security, approved by such judge or justice, that if the aggrieved party fails to make application for such writ within the period allotted therefor, or fails to obtain an order granting his application, or fails to make his plea good in the Supreme Court, he shall answer for all damages and costs which the other party may sustain by reason of the stay.

(g) The time for application for a writ of certiorari to review a decision of the United States Court of Appeals for the Armed Forces shall be as prescribed by rules of the Supreme Court.

(As amended May 24, 1949, c. 139, § 106, 63 Stat. 104; Dec. 6, 1983, Pub.L. 98–209, § 10(b), 97 Stat. 1406; June 27, 1988, Pub.L. 100–352, § 5(b), 102 Stat. 663; Oct. 5, 1994, Pub.L. 103–337, Div. A, Title IX, § 924(d)(1)(C), 108 Stat. 2832.)

§ 2104.   Reviews of State court decisions

A review by the Supreme Court of a judgment or decree of a State court shall be conducted in the same manner and under the same regulations, and shall have the same effect, as if the judgment or decree reviewed had been rendered in a court of the United States.

(As amended June 27, 1988, Pub.L. 100–352, § 5(d)(1), 102 Stat. 663.)

§ 2105.   Scope of review; abatement

There shall be no reversal in the Supreme Court or a court of appeals for error in ruling upon matters in abatement which do not involve jurisdiction.

§ 2106.   Determination

The Supreme Court or any other court of appellate jurisdiction may affirm, modify, vacate, set aside or reverse any judgment, decree, or order of a court lawfully brought before it for review, and may remand the cause and direct the entry of such appropriate judgment, decree, or order, or require such further proceedings to be had as may be just under the circumstances.

§ 2107.   Time for appeal to court of appeals

(a) Except as otherwise provided in this section, no appeal shall bring any judgment, order or decree in an action, suit or proceeding of a civil nature before a court of appeals for review unless notice of appeal is filed, within thirty days after the entry of such judgment, order or decree.

(b) In any such action, suit or proceeding in which the United States or an officer or agency thereof is a party, the time as to all parties shall be sixty days from such entry.

(c) The district court may, upon motion filed not later than 30 days after the expiration of the time otherwise set for bringing appeal, extend the time for appeal upon a showing of excusable neglect or good cause. In addition, if the district court finds—

> **(1)** that a party entitled to notice of the entry of a judgment or order did not receive such notice from the clerk or any party within 21 days of its entry, and

> **(2)** that no party would be prejudiced,

the district court may, upon motion filed within 180 days after entry of the judgment or order or within 7 days after receipt of such notice, whichever is earlier, reopen the time for appeal for a period of 14 days from the date of entry of the order reopening the time for appeal.

(d) This section shall not apply to bankruptcy matters or other proceedings under Title 11.

(As amended May 24, 1949, c. 139, §§ 107, 108, 63 Stat. 104; Dec. 9, 1991, Pub.L. 102–198, § 12, 105 Stat. 1627.)

§ 2111.   Harmless error

On the hearing of any appeal or writ of certiorari in any case, the court shall give judgment after an examination of the record without regard to errors or defects which do not affect the substantial rights of the parties.

(Added May 24, 1949, c. 139, § 110, 63 Stat. 105.)

§ 2201.   Creation of remedy

(a) In a case of actual controversy within its jurisdiction, except with respect to Federal taxes other than actions brought under section 7428 of the Internal Revenue Code of 1986, a proceeding under section 505 or 1146 of title 11, or in any civil action involving an antidumping or countervailing duty proceeding regarding a class or kind of merchandise of a free trade area country (as defined in section 516A(f)(10) of the Tariff Act of 1930), as determined by the administering authority, any court of the United States, upon the filing of an appropriate pleading, may declare the rights and other legal relations of any interested party seeking such declaration, whether or not further relief is or could be sought. Any such declaration shall have the force and effect of a final judgment or decree and shall be reviewable as such.

(b) For limitations on actions brought with respect to drug patents see section 505 or 512 of the Federal Food, Drug, and Cosmetic Act.

(As amended May 24, 1949, c. 139, § 111, 63 Stat. 105; Aug. 28, 1954, c. 1033, 68 Stat. 890; July 7, 1958, Pub.L. 85–508, § 12(p), 72 Stat. 349; Oct. 4, 1976, Pub.L. 94–455, Title XIII, § 1306(b)(8), 90 Stat. 1719; Nov. 6, 1978, Pub.L. 95–598, Title II, § 249, 92 Stat. 2672; Sept. 24, 1984, Pub.L. 98–417, Title I, § 106, 98 Stat. 1597; Sept. 28, 1988, Pub.L.

100–449, Title IV, § 402(c), 102 Stat. 1584; Nov. 16, 1988, Pub.L. 100–670, Title I, § 107(b), 102 Stat. 3984; Dec. 8, 1993, Pub.L. 103–182, Title IV, § 414(b), 107 Stat. 2147.)

§ 2202.   Further relief

Further necessary or proper relief based on a declaratory judgment or decree may be granted, after reasonable notice and hearing, against any adverse party whose rights have been determined by such judgment.

§ 2283.   Stay of State court proceedings

A court of the United States may not grant an injunction to stay proceedings in a State court except as expressly authorized by Act of Congress, or where necessary in aid of its jurisdiction, or to protect or effectuate its judgments.

§ 2284.   Three-judge court; when required; composition; procedure

(a) A district court of three judges shall be convened when otherwise required by Act of Congress, or when an action is filed challenging the constitutionality of the apportionment of congressional districts or the apportionment of any statewide legislative body.

(b) In any action required to be heard and determined by a district court of three judges under subsection (a) of this section, the composition and procedure of the court shall be as follows:

(1) Upon the filing of a request for three judges, the judge to whom the request is presented shall, unless he determines that three judges are not required, immediately notify the chief judge of the circuit, who shall designate two other judges, at least one of whom shall be a circuit judge. The judges so designated, and the judge to whom the request was presented, shall serve as members of the court to hear and determine the action or proceeding.

(2) If the action is against a State, or officer or agency thereof, at least five days' notice of hearing of the action shall be given by registered or certified mail to the Governor and attorney general of the State.

(3) A single judge may conduct all proceedings except the trial, and enter all orders permitted by the rules of civil procedure except as provided in this subsection. He may grant a temporary restraining order on a specific finding, based on evidence submitted, that specified irreparable damage will result if the order is not granted, which order, unless previously revoked by the district judge, shall remain in force only until the hearing and determination by the district court of three judges of an application for a preliminary injunction. A single judge shall not appoint a master, or order a reference, or hear and determine any application for a preliminary or permanent injunction or motion to vacate such an injunction, or enter judgment on the merits. Any action of a single judge may be reviewed by the full court at any time before final judgment.

(As amended June 11, 1960, Pub.L. 86–507, § 1(19), 74 Stat. 201; Aug. 12, 1976, Pub.L. 94–381, § 3, 90 Stat. 1119; Nov. 8, 1984, Pub.L. 98–620, Title IV, § 402(29)(E), 98 Stat. 3359.)

§ 2361. Process and procedure

In any civil action of interpleader or in the nature of interpleader under section 1335 of this title, a district court may issue its process for all claimants and enter its order restraining them from instituting or prosecuting any proceeding in any State or United States court affecting the property, instrument or obligation involved in the interpleader action until further order of the court. Such process and order shall be returnable at such time as the court or judge thereof directs, and shall be addressed to and served by the United States marshals for the respective districts where the claimants reside or may be found.

Such district court shall hear and determine the case, and may discharge the plaintiff from further liability, make the injunction permanent, and make all appropriate orders to enforce its judgment.

(As amended May 24, 1949, c. 139, § 117, 63 Stat. 105.)

§ 2401. Time for commencing action against United States

(a) Except as provided by the Contract Disputes Act of 1978, every civil action commenced against the United States shall be barred unless the complaint is filed within six years after the right of action first accrues. The action of any person under legal disability or beyond the seas at the time the claim accrues may be commenced within three years after the disability ceases.

(b) A tort claim against the United States shall be forever barred unless it is presented in writing to the appropriate Federal agency within two years after such claim accrues or unless action is begun within six months after the date of mailing, by certified or registered mail, of notice of final denial of the claim by the agency to which it was presented.

(As amended Apr. 25, 1949, c. 92, § 1, 63 Stat. 62; Sept. 8, 1959, Pub.L. 86–238, § 1(3), 73 Stat. 472; July 18, 1966, Pub.L. 89–506, § 7, 80 Stat. 307; Nov. 1, 1978, Pub.L. 95–563, § 14(b), 92 Stat. 2389.)

§ 2402. Jury trial in actions against United States

Subject to chapter 179 of this title, any action against the United States under section 1346 shall be tried by the court without a jury, except that any action against the United States under section 1346(a)(1) shall, at the request of either party to such action, be tried by the court with a jury.

(As amended July 30, 1954, c. 648, § 2(a), 68 Stat. 589; Oct. 26, 1996, Pub.L. 104–331, § 3(b)(3), 110 Stat. 4069.)

§ 2403. Intervention by United States or a State; constitutional question

(a) In any action, suit or proceeding in a court of the United States to which the United States or any agency, officer or employee thereof is not a party, wherein the constitutionality of any Act of Congress affecting the public interest is drawn in question, the court shall certify such fact to the Attorney General, and shall permit the United States to intervene for presentation of evidence, if evidence is otherwise admissible in the case, and for argument on the question of constitutionality. The United States shall, subject to the applicable provisions of law, have all the rights of a party and be subject to all liabilities of a party as to court costs to the extent necessary for a proper presentation of the facts and law relating to the question of constitutionality.

(b) In any action, suit, or proceeding in a court of the United States to which a State or any agency, officer, or employee thereof is not a party, wherein the constitutionality of any statute of that State affecting the public interest is drawn in question, the court shall certify such fact to the attorney general of the State, and shall permit the State to intervene for presentation of evidence, if evidence is otherwise admissible in the case, and for argument on the question of constitutionality. The State shall, subject to the applicable provisions of law, have all the rights of a party and be subject to all liabilities of a party as to court costs to the extent necessary for a proper presentation of the facts and law relating to the question of constitutionality.

(As amended Aug. 12, 1976, Pub.L. 94–381, § 5, 90 Stat. 1120.)

§ 2404.   Death of defendant in damage action

A civil action for damages commenced by or on behalf of the United States or in which it is interested shall not abate on the death of a defendant but shall survive and be enforceable against his estate as well as against surviving defendants.

§ 2408.   Security not required of United States

Security for damages or costs shall not be required of the United States, any department or agency thereof or any party acting under the direction of any such department or agency on the issuance of process or the institution or prosecution of any proceeding.

Costs taxable, under other Acts of Congress, against the United States or any such department, agency or party shall be paid out of the contingent fund of the department or agency which directed the proceedings to be instituted.

§ 2411.   Interest

In any judgment of any court rendered (whether against the United States, a collector or deputy collector of internal revenue, a former collector or deputy collector, or the personal representative in case of death) for any overpayment in respect of any internal-revenue tax, interest shall be allowed at the overpayment rate established under section 6621 of the Internal Revenue Code of 1986 upon the amount of the overpayment, from the date of the payment or collection thereof to a date preceding the date of the refund check by not more than thirty days, such date to be determined by the Commissioner of Internal Revenue. The Commissioner is authorized to tender by check payment of any such judgment, with interest as herein provided, at any time after such judgment becomes final, whether or not a claim for such payment has been duly filed, and such tender shall stop the running of interest, whether or not such refund check is accepted by the judgment creditor.

(As amended May 24, 1949, c. 139, § 120, 63 Stat. 106; Jan. 3, 1975, Pub.L. 93–625, § 7(a)(2), 88 Stat. 2115; Apr. 2, 1982, Pub.L. 97–164, Title III, § 302(b), 96 Stat. 56; Oct. 22, 1986, Pub.L. 99–514, § 2, Title XV, § 1511(c)(18), 100 Stat. 2095, 2746.)

§ 2412. Costs and fees

(a)(1) Except as otherwise specifically provided by statute, a judgment for costs, as enumerated in section 1920 of this title, but not including the fees and expenses of attorneys, may be awarded to the prevailing party in any civil action brought by or against the United States or any agency or any official of the United States acting in his or her official capacity in any court having jurisdiction of such action. A judgment for costs when taxed against the United States shall, in an amount established by statute, court rule, or order, be limited to reimbursing in whole or in part the prevailing party for the costs incurred by such party in the litigation.

(2) A judgment for costs, when awarded in favor of the United States in an action brought by the United States, may include an amount equal to the filing fee prescribed under section 1914(a) of this title. The preceding sentence shall not be construed as requiring the United States to pay any filing fee.

(b) Unless expressly prohibited by statute, a court may award reasonable fees and expenses of attorneys, in addition to the costs which may be awarded pursuant to subsection (a), to the prevailing party in any civil action brought by or against the United States or any agency or any official of the United States acting in his or her official capacity in any court having jurisdiction of such action. The United States shall be liable for such fees and expenses to the same extent that any other party would be liable under the common law or under the terms of any statute which specifically provides for such an award.

(c)(1) Any judgment against the United States or any agency and any official of the United States acting in his or her official capacity for costs pursuant to subsection (a) shall be paid as provided in sections 2414 and 2517 of this title and shall be in addition to any relief provided in the judgment.

(2) Any judgment against the United States or any agency and any official of the United States acting in his or her official capacity for fees and expenses of attorneys pursuant to subsection (b) shall be paid as provided in sections 2414 and 2517 of this title, except that if the basis for the award is a finding that the United States acted in bad faith, then the award shall be paid by any agency found to have acted in bad faith and shall be in addition to any relief provided in the judgment.

(d)(1)(A) Except as otherwise specifically provided by statute, a court shall award to a prevailing party other than the United States fees and other expenses, in addition to any costs awarded pursuant to subsection (a), incurred by that party in any civil action (other than cases sounding in tort), including proceedings for judicial review of agency action, brought by or against the United States in any court having jurisdiction of that action, unless the court finds that the position of the United States was substantially justified or that special circumstances make an award unjust.

(B) A party seeking an award of fees and other expenses shall, within thirty days of final judgment in the action, submit to the court an application for fees and other expenses which shows that the party is a prevailing party and is eligible to receive an award under this subsection, and the amount sought, including an itemized statement from any attorney or expert witness representing or appearing in behalf of the party stating the actual time expended and the rate at which fees and other expenses were computed. The party shall also allege that the position of the United States was not substantially justified. Whether or not the position of the United States was substantially justified shall be determined on the basis of the record (including the record with respect to the action or failure to act by the agency upon which the civil action is based) which is made in the civil action for which fees and other expenses are sought.

(C) The court, in its discretion, may reduce the amount to be awarded pursuant to this subsection, or deny an award, to the extent that the prevailing party during the course of the proceedings engaged in conduct which unduly and unreasonably protracted the final resolution of the matter in controversy.

(D) If, in a civil action brought by the United States or a proceeding for judicial review of an adversary adjudication described in section 504(a)(4) of title 5, the demand by the United States is substantially in excess of the judgment finally obtained by the United States and is unreasonable when compared with such judgment, under the facts and circumstances of the case, the court shall award to the party the fees and other expenses related to defending against the excessive demand, unless the party has committed a willful violation of law or otherwise acted in bad faith, or special circumstances make an award unjust. Fees and expenses awarded under this subparagraph shall be paid only as a consequence of appropriations provided in advance.

(2) For the purposes of this subsection—

(A) "fees and other expenses" includes the reasonable expenses of expert witnesses, the reasonable cost of any study, analysis, engineering report, test, or project which is found by the court to be necessary for the preparation of the party's case, and reasonable attorney fees (The amount of fees awarded under this subsection shall be based upon prevailing market rates for the kind and quality of the services furnished, except that (i) no expert witness shall be compensated at a rate in excess of the highest rate of compensation for expert witnesses paid by the United States; and (ii) attorney fees shall not be awarded in excess of $125 per hour unless the court determines that an increase in the cost of living or a special factor, such as the limited availability of qualified attorneys for the proceedings involved, justifies a higher fee.);

(B) "party" means (i) an individual whose net worth did not exceed $2,000,000 at the time the civil action was filed, or (ii) any owner of an unincorporated business, or any partnership, corporation, association, unit of local government, or organization, the net worth of which did not exceed $7,000,000 at the time the civil action was filed, and which had not more than 500 employees at the time the civil action was filed; except that an organization described in section 501(c)(3) of the Internal Revenue Code of 1986 (26 U.S.C. 501(c)(3)) exempt from taxation under section 501(a) of such Code, or a cooperative association as defined in section 15(a) of the Agricultural Marketing Act (12 U.S.C. 1141j(a)), may be a party regardless of the net worth of such organization or cooperative association or for purposes of subsection (d)(1)(D), a small entity as defined in section 601 of Title 5;

(C) "United States" includes any agency and any official of the United States acting in his or her official capacity;

(D) "position of the United States" means, in addition to the position taken by the United States in the civil action, the action or failure to act by the agency upon which the civil action is based; except that fees and expenses may not be awarded to a party for any portion of the litigation in which the party has unreasonably protracted the proceedings;

(E) "civil action brought by or against the United States" includes an appeal by a party, other than the United States, from a decision of a contracting officer rendered pursuant to a disputes clause in a contract with the Government or pursuant to the Contract Disputes Act of 1978;

(F) "court" includes the United States Court of Federal Claims and the United States Court of Appeals for Veterans Claims;

(G) "final judgment" means a judgment that is final and not appealable, and includes an order of settlement;

(H) "prevailing party", in the case of eminent domain proceedings, means a party who obtains a final judgment (other than by settlement), exclusive of interest, the amount of which is at least as close to the highest valuation of the property involved that is attested to at trial on behalf of the property owner as it is to the highest valuation of the property involved that is attested to at trial on behalf of the Government; and

(I) "demand" means the express demand of the United States which led to the adversary adjudication, but shall not include a recitation of the maximum statutory penalty (i) in the complaint, or (ii) elsewhere when accompanied by an express demand for a lesser amount.

(3) In awarding fees and other expenses under this subsection to a prevailing party in any action for judicial review of an adversary adjudication, as defined in subsection (b)(1)(C) of section 504 of title

5, United States Code, or an adversary adjudication subject to the Contract Disputes Act of 1978, the court shall include in that award fees and other expenses to the same extent authorized in subsection (a) of such section, unless the court finds that during such adversary adjudication the position of the United States was substantially justified, or that special circumstances make an award unjust.

(4) Fees and other expenses awarded under this subsection to a party shall be paid by any agency over which the party prevails from any funds made available to the agency by appropriation or otherwise.

[**(5)** Repealed. Pub.L. 104–66, Title I, § 1091(b), Dec. 21, 1995, 109 Stat. 722]

(e) The provisions of this section shall not apply to any costs, fees, and other expenses in connection with any proceeding to which section 7430 of the Internal Revenue Code of 1986 applies (determined without regard to subsections (b) and (f) of such section). Nothing in the preceding sentence shall prevent the awarding under subsection (a) of section 2412 of title 28, United States Code, of costs enumerated in section 1920 of such title (as in effect on October 1, 1981).

(f) If the United States appeals an award of costs or fees and other expenses made against the United States under this section and the award is affirmed in whole or in part, interest shall be paid on the amount of the award as affirmed. Such interest shall be computed at the rate determined under section 1961(a) of this title, and shall run from the date of the award through the day before the date of the mandate of affirmance.

(June 25, 1948, c. 646, 62 Stat. 973; July 18, 1966, Pub.L. 89–507, § 1, 80 Stat. 308; Oct. 21, 1980, Pub. L. 96–481, Title II, § 204(a), (c), 94 Stat. 2327, 2329; Sept. 3, 1982, Pub. L. 97–248, Title II, § 292(c), 96 Stat. 574; Aug. 5, 1985, Pub. L. 99–80, §§ 2, 6(a), (b)(2), 99 Stat. 184, 186; Oct. 22, 1986, Pub.L. 99–514, § 2, 100 Stat. 2095; Oct. 29, 1992, Pub.L. 102–572, Title III, § 301(a), Title V, §§ 502(b), 506(a), Title IX, § 902(b)(1), 106 Stat. 4511–4513, 4516; Dec. 21, 1995, Pub.L. 104–66, Title I, § 1091(b), 109 Stat. 722; Mar. 29, 1996, Pub.L. 104–121, Title II, § 232, 110 Stat. 863; Pub.L 105–368, Title V, § 521(b)(1)(B), Nov. 10, 1998, 112 Stat. 3342.)

§ 2413. Executions in favor of United States

A writ of execution on a judgment obtained for the use of the United States in any court thereof shall be issued from and made returnable to the court which rendered the judgment, but may be executed in any other State, in any Territory, or in the District of Columbia.

§ 2414. Payment of judgments and compromise settlements

Except as provided by the Contract Disputes Act of 1978, payment of final judgments rendered by a district court or the Court of International Trade against the United States shall be made on settlements by the Secretary of the Treasury. Payment of final judgments rendered by a State or foreign court or tribunal against the United States, or against its agencies or officials upon obligations or liabilities of the United States, shall be made on settlements by the Secretary of the Treasury after certification by the Attorney General that it is in the interest of the United States to pay the same.

Whenever the Attorney General determines that no appeal shall be taken from a judgment or that no further review will be sought from a decision affirming the same, he shall so certify and the judgment shall be deemed final.

Except as otherwise provided by law, compromise settlements of claims referred to the Attorney General for defense of imminent litigation or suits against the United States, or against its agencies or officials upon obligations or liabilities of the United States, made by the Attorney General or any person authorized by him, shall be settled and paid in a manner similar to judgments in like causes and appropriations or funds available for the payment of such judgments are hereby made available for the payment of such compromise settlements.

(As amended Aug. 30, 1961, Pub.L. 87–187, § 1, 75 Stat. 415; Nov. 1, 1978, Pub.L. 95–563, § 14(d), 92 Stat. 2390; Oct. 10, 1980, Pub.L. 96–417, Title V, § 512, 94 Stat. 1744; Oct. 19, 1996, Pub.L. 104–316, Title II, § 202(k), 110 Stat. 3843.)

§ 2415.   Time for commencing actions brought by the United States

(a) Subject to the provisions of section 2416 of this title, and except as otherwise provided by Congress, every action for money damages brought by the United States or an officer or agency thereof which is founded upon any contract express or implied in law or fact, shall be barred unless the complaint is filed within six years after the right of action accrues or within one year after final decisions have been rendered in applicable administrative proceedings required by contract or by law, whichever is later: *Provided,* That in the event of later partial payment or written acknowledgment of debt, the right of action shall be deemed to accrue again at the time of each such payment or acknowledgment: *Provided further,* That an action for money damages brought by the United States for or on behalf of a recognized tribe, band or group of American Indians shall not be barred unless the complaint is filed more than six years and ninety days after the right of action accrued: *Provided further,* That an action for money damages which accrued on the date of enactment of this Act in accordance with subsection (g) brought by the United States for or on behalf of a recognized tribe, band, or group of American Indians, or on behalf of an individual Indian whose land is held in trust or restricted status, shall not be barred unless the complaint is filed sixty days after the date of publication of the list required by section 4(c) of the Indian Claims Limitation Act of 1982: *Provided,* That, for those claims that are on either of the two lists published pursuant to the Indian Claims Limitation Act of 1982, any right of action shall be barred unless the complaint is filed within (1) one year after the Secretary of the Interior has published in the Federal Register a notice rejecting such claim or (2) three years after the date the Secretary of the Interior has submitted legislation or legislative report to Congress to resolve such claim or more than two years after a final decision has been rendered in applicable administrative proceedings required by contract or by law, whichever is later.

(b) Subject to the provisions of section 2416 of this title, and except as otherwise provided by Congress, every action for money damages brought by the United States or an officer or agency thereof which is founded upon a tort shall be barred unless the complaint is filed within three years after the right of action first accrues: *Provided,* That an action to recover damages resulting from a trespass on lands of the United States; an action to recover damages resulting from fire to such lands; an action to recover for diversion of money paid under a grant program; and an action for conversion of property of the United States may be brought within six years after the right of action accrues, except that such actions for or on behalf of a recognized tribe, band or group of American Indians, including actions relating to allotted trust or restricted Indian lands, may be brought within six years and ninety days after the right of action accrues, except that such actions for or on behalf of a recognized tribe, band or group of American Indians, including actions relating to allotted trust or restricted Indian lands, or on behalf of an individual Indian whose land is held in trust or restricted status which accrued on the date of enactment of this Act in accordance with subsection (g) may be brought on or before sixty days after the date of the publication of the list required by section 4(c) of the Indian Claims Limitation Act of 1982: *Provided,* That, for those claims that are on either of the two lists published pursuant to the Indian Claims Limitation Act of 1982, any right of action shall be barred unless the complaint is filed within (1) one year after the Secretary of the Interior has published in the Federal Register a notice rejecting such claim or (2) three years after the Secretary of the Interior has submitted legislation or legislative report to Congress to resolve such claim.

(c) Nothing herein shall be deemed to limit the time for bringing an action to establish the title to, or right of possession of, real or personal property.

(d) Subject to the provisions of section 2416 of this title and except as otherwise provided by Congress, every action for the recovery of money erroneously paid to or on behalf of any civilian employee of any agency of the United States or to or on behalf of any member or dependent of any member of the uniformed services of the United States, incident to the employment or services of such employee or member, shall be barred unless the complaint is filed within six years after the right of action accrues: *Provided,* That in the event of later partial payment or written acknowledgment of debt, the right of action shall be deemed to accrue again at the time of each such payment or acknowledgment.

(e) In the event that any action to which this section applies is timely brought and is thereafter dismissed without prejudice, the action may be recommenced within one year after such dismissal, regardless of whether the action would otherwise then be barred by this section. In any action so recommenced the defendant shall not be barred from interposing any claim which would not have been barred in the original action.

(f) The provisions of this section shall not prevent the assertion, in an action against the United States or an officer or agency thereof, of any claim of the United States or an officer or agency thereof against an opposing party, a co-party, or a third party that arises out of the transaction or occurrence that is the subject matter of the opposing party's claim. A claim of the United States or an officer or agency thereof that does not arise out of the transaction or occurrence that is the subject matter of the opposing party's claim may, if time-barred, be asserted only by way of offset and may be allowed in an amount not to exceed the amount of the opposing party's recovery.

(g) Any right of action subject to the provisions of this section which accrued prior to the date of enactment of this Act shall, for purposes of this section, be deemed to have accrued on the date of enactment of this Act.

(h) Nothing in this Act shall apply to actions brought under the Internal Revenue Code or incidental to the collection of taxes imposed by the United States.

(i) The provisions of this section shall not prevent the United States or an officer or agency thereof from collecting any claim of the United States by means of administrative offset, in accordance with section 3716 of title 31.

(Added Pub.L. 89–505, § 1, July 18, 1966, 80 Stat. 304, and amended Pub.L. 92–353, July 18, 1972, 86 Stat. 499; Pub.L. 92–485, Oct. 13, 1972, 86 Stat. 803; Pub.L. 95–64, July 11, 1977, 91 Stat. 268; Pub.L. 95–103, Aug. 15, 1977, 91 Stat. 842; Pub.L. 96–217, § 1, Mar. 27, 1980, 94 Stat. 126; Pub.L. 97–365, § 9, Oct. 25, 1982, 96 Stat. 1754; Pub.L. 97–394, Title I, § 2, Dec. 30, 1982, 96 Stat. 1976; Pub.L. 97–452, § 2(d)(2), Jan. 12, 1983, 96 Stat. 2478; Pub.L. 98–250, § 4(a), Apr. 3, 1984, 98 Stat. 118.)

§ 2416. Time for commencing actions brought by the United States—Exclusions

For the purpose of computing the limitations periods established in section 2415, there shall be excluded all periods during which—

(a) the defendant or the res is outside the United States, its territories and possessions, the District of Columbia, or the Commonwealth of Puerto Rico; or

(b) the defendant is exempt from legal process because of infancy, mental incompetence, diplomatic immunity, or for any other reason; or

(c) facts material to the right of action are not known and reasonably could not be known by an official of the United States charged with the responsibility to act in the circumstances; or

(d) the United States is in a state of war declared pursuant to article I, section 8, of the Constitution of the United States.

(Added Pub.L. 89–505, § 1, July 18, 1966, 80 Stat. 305.)

PART X

FEDERAL RULES OF EVIDENCE FOR UNITED STATES COURTS

Effective July 1, 1975

Latest Amendments Effective December 1, 2006

Table of Rules

ARTICLE I. GENERAL PROVISIONS

ARTICLE II. JUDICIAL NOTICE

ARTICLE III. PRESUMPTIONS IN CIVIL ACTIONS AND PROCEEDINGS

ARTICLE IV. RELEVANCY AND ITS LIMITS

ARTICLE I. GENERAL PROVISIONS

RULE 101. SCOPE

These rules govern proceedings in the courts of the United States and before the United States bankruptcy judges and United States magistrate judges, to the extent and with the exceptions stated in rule 1101.

[Amended March 2, 1987, effective October 1, 1987; April 25, 1988, effective November 1, 1988; April 22, 1993, effective December 1, 1993.]

RULE 102. PURPOSE AND CONSTRUCTION

These rules shall be construed to secure fairness in administration, elimination of unjustifiable expense and delay, and promotion of growth and development of the law of evidence to the end that the truth may be ascertained and proceedings justly determined.

RULE 103. RULINGS ON EVIDENCE

(a) Effect of Erroneous Ruling.—Error may not be predicated upon a ruling which admits or excludes evidence unless a substantial right of the party is affected, and

(1) *Objection.*—In case the ruling is one admitting evidence, a timely objection or motion to strike appears of record, stating the specific ground of objection, if the specific ground was not apparent from the context; or

(2) *Offer of Proof.*—In case the ruling is one excluding evidence, the substance of the evidence was made known to the court by offer or was apparent from the context within which questions were asked.

Once the court makes a definitive ruling on the record admitting or excluding evidence, either at or before trial, a party need not renew an objection or offer of proof to preserve a claim of error for appeal.

(b) Record of Offer and Ruling.—The court may add any other or further statement which shows the character of the evidence, the form in which it was offered, the objection made, and the ruling thereon. It may direct the making of an offer in question and answer form.

(c) Hearing of Jury.—In jury cases, proceedings shall be conducted, to the extent practicable, so as to prevent inadmissible evidence from being suggested to the jury by any means, such as making statements or offers of proof or asking questions in the hearing of the jury.

(d) Plain Error.—Nothing in this rule precludes taking notice of plain errors affecting substantial rights although they were not brought to the attention of the court.

[Amended April 17, 2000, effective December 1, 2000.]

RULE 104. PRELIMINARY QUESTIONS

(a) Questions of Admissibility Generally. Preliminary questions concerning the qualification of a person to be a witness, the existence of a privilege, or the admissibility of evidence shall be determined by the court, subject to the provisions of subdivision (b). In making its determination it is not bound by the rules of evidence except those with respect to privileges.

(b) Relevancy Conditioned on Fact. When the relevancy of evidence depends upon the fulfillment of a condition of fact, the court shall admit it upon, or subject to, the introduction of evidence sufficient to support a finding of the fulfillment of the condition.

(c) Hearing of Jury. Hearings on the admissibility of confessions shall in all cases be conducted out of the hearing of the jury. Hearings on other preliminary matters shall be so conducted when the interests of justice require, or when an accused is a witness and so requests.

(d) Testimony by Accused. The accused does not, by testifying upon a preliminary matter, become subject to cross-examination as to other issues in the case.

(e) Weight and Credibility. This rule does not limit the right of a party to introduce before the jury evidence relevant to weight or credibility.

[Amended March 2, 1987, effective October 1, 1987.]

RULE 105. LIMITED ADMISSIBILITY

When evidence which is admissible as to one party or for one purpose but not admissible as to another party or for another purpose is admitted, the court, upon request, shall restrict the evidence to its proper scope and instruct the jury accordingly.

RULE 106. REMAINDER OF OR RELATED WRITINGS OR RECORDED STATEMENTS

When a writing or recorded statement or part thereof is introduced by a party, an adverse party may require the introduction at that time of any other part or any other writing or recorded statement which ought in fairness to be considered contemporaneously with it.

[Amended March 2, 1987, effective October 1, 1987.]

ARTICLE II. JUDICIAL NOTICE

RULE 201. JUDICIAL NOTICE OF ADJUDICATIVE FACTS

(a) **Scope of Rule.** This rule governs only judicial notice of adjudicative facts.

(b) **Kinds of Facts.** A judicially noticed fact must be one not subject to reasonable dispute in that it is either (1) generally known within the territorial jurisdiction of the trial court or (2) capable of accurate and ready determination by resort to sources whose accuracy cannot reasonably be questioned.

(c) **When Discretionary.** A court may take judicial notice, whether requested or not.

(d) **When Mandatory.** A court shall take judicial notice if requested by a party and supplied with the necessary information.

(e) **Opportunity to Be Heard.** A party is entitled upon timely request to an opportunity to be heard as to the propriety of taking judicial notice and the tenor of the matter noticed. In the absence of prior notification, the request may be made after judicial notice has been taken.

(f) **Time of Taking Notice.** Judicial notice may be taken at any stage of the proceeding.

(g) **Instructing Jury.** In a civil action or proceeding, the court shall instruct the jury to accept as conclusive any fact judicially noticed. In a criminal case, the court shall instruct the jury that it may, but is not required to, accept as conclusive any fact judicially noticed.

ARTICLE III. PRESUMPTIONS IN CIVIL ACTIONS AND PROCEEDINGS

RULE 301. PRESUMPTIONS IN GENERAL IN CIVIL ACTIONS AND PROCEEDINGS

In all civil actions and proceedings not otherwise provided for by Act of Congress or by these rules, a presumption imposes on the party against whom it is directed the burden of going forward with evidence to rebut or meet the presumption, but does not shift to such party the burden of proof in the sense of the risk of nonpersuasion, which remains throughout the trial upon the party on whom it was originally cast.

RULE 302. APPLICABILITY OF STATE LAW IN CIVIL ACTIONS AND PROCEEDINGS

In civil actions and proceedings, the effect of a presumption respecting a fact which is an element of a claim or defense as to which State law supplies the rule of decision is determined in accordance with State law.

ARTICLE IV. RELEVANCY AND ITS LIMITS

RULE 401. DEFINITION OF "RELEVANT EVIDENCE"

"Relevant evidence" means evidence having any tendency to make the existence of any fact that is of consequence to the determination of the action more probable or less probable than it would be without the evidence.

RULE 402. RELEVANT EVIDENCE GENERALLY ADMISSIBLE; IRRELEVANT EVIDENCE INADMISSIBLE

All relevant evidence is admissible, except as otherwise provided by the Constitution of the United States, by Act of Congress, by these rules, or by other rules prescribed by the Supreme Court pursuant to statutory authority. Evidence which is not relevant is not admissible.

RULE 403. EXCLUSION OF RELEVANT EVIDENCE ON GROUNDS OF PREJUDICE, CONFUSION, OR WASTE OF TIME

Although relevant, evidence may be excluded if its probative value is substantially outweighed by the danger of unfair prejudice, confusion of the issues, or misleading the jury, or by considerations of undue delay, waste of time, or needless presentation of cumulative evidence.

RULE 404. CHARACTER EVIDENCE NOT ADMISSIBLE TO PROVE CONDUCT; EXCEPTIONS; OTHER CRIMES

(a) Character Evidence Generally.—Evidence of a person's character or a trait of character is not admissible for the purpose of proving action in conformity therewith on a particular occasion, except:

(1) *Character of Accused.*—In a criminal case, evidence of a pertinent trait of character offered by an accused, or by the prosecution to rebut the same, or if evidence of a trait of character of the alleged victim of the crime is offered by an accused and admitted under Rule 404(a)(2), evidence of the same trait of character of the accused offered by the prosecution;

(2) *Character of Alleged Victim.*—In a criminal case, and subject to the limitations imposed by Rule 412, evidence of a pertinent trait of character of the alleged victim of the crime offered by an accused, or by the prosecution to rebut the same, or evidence of a character trait of peacefulness of the alleged victim offered by the prosecution in a homicide case to rebut evidence that the alleged victim was the first aggressor;

(3) *Character of Witness.*—Evidence of the character of a witness, as provided in rules 607, 608, and 609.

(b) Other Crimes, Wrongs, or Acts.—Evidence of other crimes, wrongs, or acts is not admissible to prove the character of a person in order to show action in conformity therewith. It may, however, be admissible for other purposes, such as proof of motive, opportunity, intent, preparation, plan, knowledge, identity, or absence of mistake or accident, provided that upon request by the accused, the prosecution in a criminal case shall provide reasonable notice in advance of trial, or during trial if the court excuses pretrial notice on good cause shown, of the general nature of any such evidence it intends to introduce at trial.

[Amended March 2, 1987, effective October 1, 1987; April 30, 1991, effective December 1, 1991; April 17, 2000, effective December 1, 2000; April 12, 2006, effective December 1, 2006.]

RULE 405. METHODS OF PROVING CHARACTER

(a) Reputation or Opinion. In all cases in which evidence of character or a trait of character of a person is admissible, proof may be made by testimony as to reputation or by testimony in the form of an opinion. On cross-examination, inquiry is allowable into relevant specific instances of conduct.

(b) Specific Instances of Conduct. In cases in which character or a trait of character of a person is an essential element of a charge, claim, or defense, proof may also be made of specific instances of that person's conduct.

[Amended March 2, 1987, effective October 1, 1987.]

RULE 406.   HABIT;   ROUTINE PRACTICE

Evidence of the habit of a person or of the routine practice of an organization, whether corroborated or not and regardless of the presence of eyewitnesses, is relevant to prove that the conduct of the person or organization on a particular occasion was in conformity with the habit or routine practice.

RULE 407.   SUBSEQUENT REMEDIAL MEASURES

When, after an injury or harm allegedly caused by an event, measures are taken that, if taken previously, would have made the injury or harm less likely to occur, evidence of the subsequent measures is not admissible to prove negligence, culpable conduct, a defect in a product, a defect in a product's design, or a need for a warning or instruction.   This rule does not require the exclusion of evidence of subsequent measures when offered for another purpose, such as proving ownership, control, or feasibility of precautionary measures, if controverted, or impeachment.

[Amended April 11, 1997, effective December 1, 1997.]

RULE 408.   COMPROMISE AND OFFERS TO COMPROMISE

(a) Prohibited uses.—Evidence of the following is not admissible on behalf of any party, when offered to prove liability for, invalidity of, or amount of a claim that was disputed as to validity or amount, or to impeach through a prior inconsistent statement or contradiction:

(1) furnishing or offering or promising to furnish—or accepting or offering or promising to accept—a valuable consideration in compromising or attempting to compromise the claim; and

(2) conduct or statements made in compromise negotiations regarding the claim, except when offered in a criminal case and the negotiations related to a claim by a public office or agency in the exercise of regulatory, investigative, or enforcement authority.

(b) Permitted uses.—This rule does not require exclusion if the evidence is offered for purposes not prohibited by subdivision (a). Examples of permissible purposes include proving a witness's bias or prejudice; negating a contention of undue delay; and proving an effort to obstruct a criminal investigation or prosecution.

[Amended April 12, 2006, effective December 1, 2006.]

RULE 409.   PAYMENT OF MEDICAL
AND SIMILAR EXPENSES

Evidence of furnishing or offering or promising to pay medical, hospital, or similar expenses occasioned by an injury is not admissible to prove liability for the injury.

RULE 410. INADMISSIBILITY OF PLEAS, PLEA DISCUSSIONS, AND RELATED STATEMENTS

Except as otherwise provided in this rule, evidence of the following is not, in any civil or criminal proceeding, admissible against the defendant who made the plea or was a participant in the plea discussions:

(1) a plea of guilty which was later withdrawn;

(2) a plea of nolo contendere;

(3) any statement made in the course of any proceedings under Rule 11 of the Federal Rules of Criminal Procedure or comparable state procedure regarding either of the foregoing pleas; or

(4) any statement made in the course of plea discussions with an attorney for the prosecuting authority which do not result in a plea of guilty or which result in a plea of guilty later withdrawn.

However, such a statement is admissible (i) in any proceeding wherein another statement made in the course of the same plea or plea discussions has been introduced and the statement ought in fairness be considered contemporaneously with it, or (ii) in a criminal proceeding for perjury or false statement if the statement was made by the defendant under oath, on the record and in the presence of counsel.

[Amended by Pub.L. 94–149, § 1(9), December 12, 1975, 89 Stat. 805; amended April 30, 1979, effective December 1, 1980 (effective date pursuant to Pub.L. 96–42, July 31, 1979, 93 Stat. 326).]

RULE 411. LIABILITY INSURANCE

Evidence that a person was or was not insured against liability is not admissible upon the issue whether the person acted negligently or otherwise wrongfully. This rule does not require the exclusion of evidence of insurance against liability when offered for another purpose, such as proof of agency, ownership, or control, or bias or prejudice of a witness.

[Amended March 2, 1987, effective October 1, 1987.]

RULE 412. SEX OFFENSE CASES; RELEVANCE OF ALLEGED VICTIM'S PAST SEXUAL BEHAVIOR OR ALLEGED SEXUAL PREDISPOSITION

(a) Evidence Generally Inadmissible. The following evidence is not admissible in any civil or criminal proceeding involving alleged sexual misconduct except as provided in subdivisions (b) and (c):

(1) Evidence offered to prove that any alleged victim engaged in other sexual behavior.

(2) Evidence offered to prove any alleged victim's sexual predisposition.

(b) Exceptions.

(1) In a criminal case, the following evidence is admissible, if otherwise admissible under these rules:

(A) evidence of specific instances of sexual behavior by the alleged victim offered to prove that a person other than the accused was the source of semen, injury or other physical evidence;

(B) evidence of specific instances of sexual behavior by the alleged victim with respect to the person accused of the sexual misconduct offered by the accused to prove consent or by the prosecution; and

(C) evidence the exclusion of which would violate the constitutional rights of the defendant.

(2) In a civil case, evidence offered to prove the sexual behavior or sexual predisposition of any alleged victim is admissible if it is otherwise admissible under these rules and its probative value substantially outweighs the danger of harm to any victim and of unfair prejudice to any party. Evidence of an alleged victim's reputation is admissible only if it has been placed in controversy by the alleged victim.

(c) Procedure to Determine Admissibility.

(1) A party intending to offer evidence under subdivision (b) must—

(A) file a written motion at least 14 days before trial specifically describing the evidence and stating the purpose for which it is offered unless the court, for good cause, requires a different time for filing or permits filing during trial; and

(B) serve the motion on all parties and notify the alleged victim or, when appropriate, the alleged victim's guardian or representative.

(2) Before admitting evidence under this rule the court must conduct a hearing in camera and afford the victim and parties a right to attend and be heard. The motion, related papers, and the record of the hearing must be sealed and remain under seal unless the court orders otherwise.

[Adopted by Pub.L. 95–540, § 2(a), October 28, 1978, 92 Stat. 2046, applicable to trials that begin more than 30 days after October 28, 1978; amended by Pub.L. 100–690, Title VII, § 7046(a), November 18, 1988, 102 Stat. 4400; amended April 29, 1994, effective December 1, 1994; amended by Pub.L. 103–322, Title IV, § 40141(b), September 13, 1994, 108 Stat. 1919, effective December 1, 1994.]

RULE 413. EVIDENCE OF SIMILAR CRIMES IN SEXUAL ASSAULT CASES

(a) In a criminal case in which the defendant is accused of an offense of sexual assault, evidence of the defendant's commission of another offense or offenses of sexual assault is admissible, and may be considered for its bearing on any matter to which it is relevant.

(b) In a case in which the Government intends to offer evidence under this rule, the attorney for the Government shall disclose the evidence to the defendant, including statements of witnesses or a summary of the substance of any testimony that is expected to be offered, at least fifteen days before the scheduled date of trial or at such later time as the court may allow for good cause.

(c) This rule shall not be construed to limit the admission or consideration of evidence under any other rule.

(d) For purposes of this rule and Rule 415, "offense of sexual assault" means a crime under Federal law or the law of a State (as defined in section 513 of title 18, United States Code) that involved—

(1) any conduct proscribed by chapter 109A of title 18, United States Code;

(2) contact, without consent, between any part of the defendant's body or an object and the genitals or anus of another person;

(3) contact, without consent, between the genitals or anus of the defendant and any part of another person's body;

(4) deriving sexual pleasure or gratification from the infliction of death, bodily injury, or physical pain on another person; or

(5) an attempt or conspiracy to engage in conduct described in paragraphs (1)–(4).

[Added Sept. 13, 1994, Pub.L. 103–322, Title XXXII, § 320935(a), 108 Stat. 2135; amended by Pub.L. 103–322, Title XXXII, § 320935, Sept. 13, 1994, 108 Stat. 2135, effective July 9, 1995.]

RULE 414. EVIDENCE OF SIMILAR CRIMES IN CHILD MOLESTATION CASES

(a) In a criminal case in which the defendant is accused of an offense of child molestation, evidence of the defendant's commission of another offense or offenses of child molestation is admissible, and may be considered for its bearing on any matter to which it is relevant.

(b) In a case in which the Government intends to offer evidence under this rule, the attorney for the Government shall disclose the evidence to the defendant, including statements of witnesses or a summary of the substance of any testimony that is expected to be offered, at least fifteen days before the scheduled date of trial or at such later time as the court may allow for good cause.

(c) This rule shall not be construed to limit the admission or consideration of evidence under any other rule.

(d) For purposes of this rule and Rule 415, "child" means a person below the age of fourteen, and "offense of child molestation" means a crime under Federal law or the law of a State (as defined in section 513 of title 18, United States Code) that involved—

(1) any conduct proscribed by chapter 109A of title 18, United States Code, that was committed in relation to a child;

(2) any conduct proscribed by chapter 110 of title 18, United States Code;

(3) contact between any part of the defendant's body or an object and the genitals or anus of a child;

(4) contact between the genitals or anus of the defendant and any part of the body of a child;

(5) deriving sexual pleasure or gratification from the infliction of death, bodily injury, or physical pain on a child; or

(6) an attempt or conspiracy to engage in conduct described in paragraphs (1)–(5).

[Added Sept. 13, 1994, Pub.L. 103–322, Title XXXII, § 320935(a), 108 Stat. 2135; amended by Pub.L. 103–322, Title XXXII, § 320935, Sept. 13, 1994, 108 Stat. 2135, effective July 9, 1995.]

RULE 415. EVIDENCE OF SIMILAR ACTS IN CIVIL CASES CONCERNING SEXUAL ASSAULT OR CHILD MOLESTATION

(a) In a civil case in which a claim for damages or other relief is predicated on a party's alleged commission of conduct constituting an offense of sexual assault or child molestation, evidence of that party's commission of another offense or offenses of sexual assault or child molestation is admissible and may be considered as provided in Rule 413 and Rule 414 of these rules.

(b) A party who intends to offer evidence under this rule shall disclose the evidence to the party against whom it will be offered, including statements of witnesses or a summary of the substance of any testimony that is expected to be offered, at least fifteen days before the scheduled date of trial or at such later time as the court may allow for good cause.

(c) This rule shall not be construed to limit the admission or consideration of evidence under any other rule.

[Added Sept. 13, 1994, Pub.L. 103–322, Title XXXII, § 320935(a), 108 Stat. 2135; amended by Pub.L. 103–322, Title XXXII, § 320935, Sept. 13, 1994, 108 Stat. 2135, effective July 9, 1995.]

ARTICLE V. PRIVILEGES

RULE 501. GENERAL RULE

Except as otherwise required by the Constitution of the United States or provided by Act of Congress or in rules prescribed by the Supreme Court pursuant to statutory authority, the privilege of a witness, person, government, State, or political subdivision thereof shall be governed by the principles of the common law as they may be interpreted by the courts of the United States in the light of reason and experience. However, in civil actions and proceedings, with respect to an element of a claim or defense as to which State law supplies the rule of decision, the privilege of a witness, person, government, State, or political subdivision thereof shall be determined in accordance with State law.

ARTICLE VI. WITNESSES

RULE 601. GENERAL RULE OF COMPETENCY

Every person is competent to be a witness except as otherwise provided in these rules. However, in civil actions and proceedings, with respect to an element of a claim or defense as to which State law supplies the rule of decision, the competency of a witness shall be determined in accordance with State law.

RULE 602. LACK OF PERSONAL KNOWLEDGE

A witness may not testify to a matter unless evidence is introduced sufficient to support a finding that the witness has personal knowledge of the matter. Evidence to prove personal knowledge may, but need not, consist of the witness' own testimony. This rule is subject to the provisions of rule 703, relating to opinion testimony by expert witnesses.

[Amended March 2, 1987, effective October 1, 1987; April 25, 1988, effective November 1, 1988.]

RULE 603. OATH OR AFFIRMATION

Before testifying, every witness shall be required to declare that the witness will testify truthfully, by oath or affirmation administered in a form calculated to awaken the witness' conscience and impress the witness' mind with the duty to do so.

[Amended March 2, 1987, effective October 1, 1987.]

RULE 604. INTERPRETERS

An interpreter is subject to the provisions of these rules relating to qualification as an expert and the administration of an oath or affirmation to make a true translation.

[Amended March 2, 1987, effective October 1, 1987.]

RULE 605. COMPETENCY OF JUDGE AS WITNESS

The judge presiding at the trial may not testify in that trial as a witness. No objection need be made in order to preserve the point.

RULE 606. COMPETENCY OF JUROR AS WITNESS

(a) At the Trial. A member of the jury may not testify as a witness before that jury in the trial of the case in which the juror is sitting. If the juror is called so to testify, the opposing party shall be afforded an opportunity to object out of the presence of the jury.

(b) Inquiry Into Validity of Verdict or Indictment. Upon an inquiry into the validity of a verdict or indictment, a juror may not testify as to any matter or statement occurring during the course of the jury's deliberations or to the effect of anything upon that or any other juror's mind or emotions as influencing the juror to assent to or dissent from the verdict or indictment or concerning the juror's mental processes in connection therewith. But a juror may testify about (1) whether extraneous prejudicial information was improperly brought to the jury's attention, (2) whether any outside influence was improperly brought to bear upon any juror, or (3) whether there was a mistake in entering the verdict onto the verdict form. A juror's affidavit or evidence of any statement by the juror may not be received on a matter about which the juror would be precluded from testifying.

[Amended by Pub.L. 94–149, § 1(10), December 12, 1975, 89 Stat. 805; March 2, 1987, effective October 1, 1987; April 12, 2006, effective December 1, 2006.]

RULE 607. WHO MAY IMPEACH

The credibility of a witness may be attacked by any party, including the party calling the witness.

[Amended March 2, 1987, effective October 1, 1987.]

RULE 608. EVIDENCE OF CHARACTER AND CONDUCT OF WITNESS

(a) Opinion and Reputation Evidence of Character. The credibility of a witness may be attacked or supported by evidence in the form of opinion or reputation, but subject to these limitations: (1) the evidence may refer only to character for truthfulness or untruthfulness, and (2) evidence of truthful character is admissible only after the character of the witness for truthfulness has been attacked by opinion or reputation evidence or otherwise.

(b) Specific Instances of Conduct. Specific instances of the conduct of a witness, for the purpose of attacking or supporting the witness' character for truthfulness other than conviction of crime as provided in rule 609, may not be proved by extrinsic evidence. They may, however, in the discretion of the court, if probative of truthfulness or untruthfulness, be inquired into on cross-examination of the witness (1) concerning the witness' character for truthfulness or untruthfulness, or (2) concerning the character for truthfulness or untruthfulness of another witness as to which character the witness being cross-examined has testified.

The giving of testimony, whether by an accused or by any other witness, does not operate as a waiver of the accused's or the witness' privilege against self-incrimination when examined with respect to matters that relate only to character for truthfulness.

[Amended March 2, 1987, effective October 1, 1987; April 25, 1988, effective November 1, 1988; March 27, 2003, effective December 1, 2003.]

RULE 609. IMPEACHMENT BY EVIDENCE OF CONVICTION OF CRIME

(a) General Rule. For the purpose of attacking the character for truthfulness of a witness,

(1) evidence that a witness other than an accused has been convicted of a crime shall be admitted, subject to Rule 403, if the crime was punishable by death or imprisonment in excess of one year under the law under which the witness was convicted, and evidence that an accused has been convicted of such a crime shall be admitted if the court determines that the probative value of admitting this evidence outweighs its prejudicial effect to the accused; and

(2) evidence that any witness has been convicted of a crime shall be admitted regardless of the punishment, if it readily can be determined that establishing the elements of the crime required proof or admission of an act of dishonesty or false statement by the witness.

(b) Time Limit. Evidence of a conviction under this rule is not admissible if a period of more than ten years has elapsed since the date of the conviction or of the release of the witness from the confinement imposed for that conviction, whichever is the later date, unless the court determines, in the interests of justice, that the probative value of the conviction supported by specific facts and circumstances substantially outweighs its prejudicial effect. However, evidence of a conviction more than 10 years old as calculated herein, is not admissible unless the proponent gives to the adverse party sufficient advance written notice of intent to use such evidence to provide the adverse party with a fair opportunity to contest the use of such evidence.

(c) Effect of Pardon, Annulment, or Certificate of Rehabilitation. Evidence of a conviction is not admissible under this rule if (1) the conviction has been the subject of a pardon, annulment, certificate of rehabilitation, or other equivalent procedure based on a finding of the rehabilitation of the person convicted, and that person has not been convicted of a subsequent crime that was punishable by death or imprisonment in excess of one year, or (2) the conviction has been the subject of a pardon, annulment, or other equivalent procedure based on a finding of innocence.

(d) Juvenile Adjudications. Evidence of juvenile adjudications is generally not admissible under this rule. The court may, however, in a criminal case allow evidence of a juvenile adjudication of a witness other than the accused if conviction of the offense would be admissible to attack the credibility of an adult and the court is satisfied that admission in evidence is necessary for a fair determination of the issue of guilt or innocence.

(e) Pendency of Appeal. The pendency of an appeal therefrom does not render evidence of a conviction inadmissible. Evidence of the pendency of an appeal is admissible.

[Amended March 2, 1987, effective October 1, 1987; January 26, 1990, effective December 1, 1990; April 12, 2006, effective December 1, 2006.]

RULE 610. RELIGIOUS BELIEFS OR OPINIONS

Evidence of the beliefs or opinions of a witness on matters of religion is not admissible for the purpose of showing that by reason of their nature the witness' credibility is impaired or enhanced.

[Amended March 2, 1987, effective October 1, 1987.]

RULE 611. MODE AND ORDER OF INTERROGATION AND PRESENTATION

(a) Control by Court. The court shall exercise reasonable control over the mode and order of interrogating witnesses and presenting evidence so as to (1) make the interrogation and presentation effective for the ascertainment of the truth, (2) avoid needless consumption of time, and (3) protect witnesses from harassment or undue embarrassment.

(b) Scope of Cross-Examination. Cross-examination should be limited to the subject matter of the direct examination and matters affecting the credibility of the witness. The court may, in the exercise of discretion, permit inquiry into additional matters as if on direct examination.

(c) Leading Questions. Leading questions should not be used on the direct examination of a witness except as may be necessary to develop the witness' testimony. Ordinarily leading questions should be permitted on cross-examination. When a party calls a hostile witness, an adverse party, or a witness identified with an adverse party, interrogation may be by leading questions.

[Amended March 2, 1987, effective October 1, 1987.]

RULE 612. WRITING USED TO REFRESH MEMORY

Except as otherwise provided in criminal proceedings by section 3500 of title 18, United States Code, if a witness uses a writing to refresh memory for the purpose of testifying, either—

(1) while testifying, or

(2) before testifying, if the court in its discretion determines it is necessary in the interests of justice,

an adverse party is entitled to have the writing produced at the hearing, to inspect it, to cross-examine the witness thereon, and to introduce in evidence those portions which relate to the testimony of the witness. If it is claimed that the writing contains matters not related to the subject matter of the testimony the court shall examine the writing in camera, excise any portions not so related, and order delivery of the remainder to the party entitled thereto. Any portion withheld over objections shall be preserved and made available to the appellate court in the event of an appeal. If a writing is not produced or delivered pursuant to order under this rule, the court shall make any order justice requires, except that in criminal cases when the prosecution elects not to comply, the order shall be one striking the testimony or, if the court in its discretion determines that the interests of justice so require, declaring a mistrial.

[Amended March 2, 1987, effective October 1, 1987.]

RULE 613. PRIOR STATEMENTS OF WITNESSES

(a) Examining Witness Concerning Prior Statement. In examining a witness concerning a prior statement made by the witness, whether written or not, the statement need not be shown nor its contents disclosed to the witness at that time, but on request the same shall be shown or disclosed to opposing counsel.

(b) Extrinsic Evidence of Prior Inconsistent Statement of Witness. Extrinsic evidence of a prior inconsistent statement by a witness is not admissible unless the witness is afforded an opportunity to explain or deny the same and the opposite party is afforded an opportunity to interrogate the witness thereon, or the interests of justice otherwise require. This provision does not apply to admissions of a party-opponent as defined in rule 801(d)(2).

[Amended March 2, 1987, effective October 1, 1987; April 25, 1988, effective November 1, 1988.]

RULE 614. CALLING AND INTERROGATION OF WITNESSES BY COURT

(a) Calling by Court. The court may, on its own motion or at the suggestion of a party, call witnesses, and all parties are entitled to cross-examine witnesses thus called.

(b) Interrogation by Court. The court may interrogate witnesses, whether called by itself or by a party.

(c) Objections. Objections to the calling of witnesses by the court or to interrogation by it may be made at the time or at the next available opportunity when the jury is not present.

RULE 615. EXCLUSION OF WITNESSES

At the request of a party the court shall order witnesses excluded so that they cannot hear the testimony of other witnesses, and it may make the order of its own motion. This rule does not authorize exclusion of (1) a party who is a natural person, or (2) an officer or employee of a party which is not a natural person designated as its representative by its attorney, or (3) a person whose presence is shown by a party to be essential to the presentation of the party's cause, or (4) a person authorized by statute to be present.

[Amended March 2, 1987, effective October 1, 1987; April 25, 1988, effective November 1, 1988; amended by Pub.L. 100–690, Title VII, § 7075(a), November 18, 1988, 102 Stat. 4405 (although amendment by Pub.L. 100–690 could not be executed due to prior amendment by Court order which made the same change effective November 1, 1988); April 24, 1998, effective December 1, 1998.]

ARTICLE VII.   OPINIONS AND EXPERT TESTIMONY

RULE 701.   OPINION TESTIMONY BY LAY WITNESSES

If the witness is not testifying as an expert, the witness' testimony in the form of opinions or inferences is limited to those opinions or inferences which are (a) rationally based on the perception of the witness, (b) helpful to a clear understanding of the witness' testimony or the determination of a fact in issue, and (c) not based on scientific, technical, or other specialized knowledge within the scope of Rule 702.

[Amended March 2, 1987, effective October 1, 1987; April 17, 2000, effective December 1, 2000.]

RULE 702.   TESTIMONY BY EXPERTS

If scientific, technical, or other specialized knowledge will assist the trier of fact to understand the evidence or to determine a fact in issue, a witness qualified as an expert by knowledge, skill, experience, training, or education, may testify thereto in the form of an opinion or otherwise, if (1) the testimony is based upon sufficient facts or data, (2) the testimony is the product of reliable principles and methods, and (3) the witness has applied the principles and methods reliably to the facts of the case.

[Amended April 17, 2000, effective December 1, 2000.]

RULE 703.   BASES OF OPINION TESTIMONY BY EXPERTS

The facts or data in the particular case upon which an expert bases an opinion or inference may be those perceived by or made known to the expert at or before the hearing. If of a type reasonably relied upon by experts in the particular field in forming opinions or inferences upon the subject, the facts or data need not be admissible in evidence in order for the opinion or inference to be admitted. Facts or data that are otherwise inadmissible shall not be disclosed to the jury by the proponent of the opinion or inference unless the court determines that their probative value in assisting the jury to evaluate the expert's opinion substantially outweighs their prejudicial effect.

[Amended March 2, 1987, effective October 1, 1987; April 17, 2000, effective December 1, 2000.]

RULE 704.   OPINION ON ULTIMATE ISSUE

(a) Except as provided in subdivision (b), testimony in the form of an opinion or inference otherwise admissible is not objectionable because it embraces an ultimate issue to be decided by the trier of fact.

(b) No expert witness testifying with respect to the mental state or condition of a defendant in a criminal case may state an opinion or inference as to whether the defendant did or did not have the mental state or condition constituting an element of the crime charged or of a defense thereto.   Such ultimate issues are matters for the trier of fact alone.

[Amended by Pub.L. 98–473, Title II, § 406, October 12, 1984, 98 Stat. 2067.]

RULE 705.   DISCLOSURE OF FACTS OR DATA UNDERLYING EXPERT OPINION

The expert may testify in terms of opinion or inference and give reasons therefor without first testifying to the underlying facts or data, unless the court requires otherwise.   The expert may in any event be required to disclose the underlying facts or data on cross-examination.

[Amended March 2, 1987, effective October 1, 1987; April 22, 1993, effective December 1, 1993.]

RULE 706.   COURT APPOINTED EXPERTS

(a) Appointment.   The court may on its own motion or on the motion of any party enter an order to show cause why expert witnesses should not be appointed, and may request the parties to submit nominations.   The court may appoint any expert witnesses agreed upon by the parties, and may appoint expert witnesses of its own selection.   An expert witness shall not be appointed by the court unless the witness consents to act.   A witness so appointed shall be informed of the witness' duties by the court in writing, a copy of which shall be filed with the clerk, or at a conference in which the parties shall have opportunity to participate.   A witness so appointed shall advise the parties of the witness' findings, if any; the witness' deposition may be taken by any party; and the witness may be called to testify by the court or any party. The witness shall be subject to cross-examination by each party, including a party calling the witness.

(b) Compensation.   Expert witnesses so appointed are entitled to reasonable compensation in whatever sum the court may allow.   The compensation thus fixed is payable from funds which may be provided by law in criminal cases and civil actions and proceedings involving just compensation under the fifth amendment.   In other civil actions and proceedings the compensation shall be paid by the parties in such proportion and at such time as the court directs, and thereafter charged in like manner as other costs.

(c) Disclosure of Appointment.   In the exercise of its discretion, the court may authorize disclosure to the jury of the fact that the court appointed the expert witness.

(d) Parties' Experts of Own Selection.   Nothing in this rule limits the parties in calling expert witnesses of their own selection.

[Amended March 2, 1987, effective October 1, 1987.]

ARTICLE VIII.   HEARSAY

RULE 801.   DEFINITIONS

The following definitions apply under this article:

(a) Statement. A "statement" is (1) an oral or written assertion or (2) nonverbal conduct of a person, if it is intended by the person as an assertion.

(b) Declarant. A "declarant" is a person who makes a statement.

(c) Hearsay. "Hearsay" is a statement, other than one made by the declarant while testifying at the trial or hearing, offered in evidence to prove the truth of the matter asserted.

(d) Statements Which Are Not Hearsay. A statement is not hearsay if—

(1) *Prior Statement by Witness.* The declarant testifies at the trial or hearing and is subject to cross-examination concerning the statement, and the statement is (A) inconsistent with the declarant's testimony, and was given under oath subject to the penalty of perjury at a trial, hearing, or other proceeding, or in a deposition, or (B) consistent with the declarant's testimony and is offered to rebut an express or implied charge against the declarant of recent fabrication or improper influence or motive, or (C) one of identification of a person made after perceiving the person; or

(2) *Admission by Party-Opponent.* The statement is offered against a party and is (A) the party's own statement, in either an individual or a representative capacity or (B) a statement of which the party has manifested an adoption or belief in its truth, or (C) a statement by a person authorized by the party to make a statement concerning the subject, or (D) a statement by the party's agent or servant concerning a matter within the scope of the agency or employment, made during the existence of the relationship, or (E) a statement by a coconspirator of a party during the course and in furtherance of the conspiracy. The contents of the statement shall be considered but are not alone sufficient to establish the declarant's authority under subdivision (C), the agency or employment relationship and scope thereof under subdivision (D), or the existence of the conspiracy and the participation therein of the declarant and the party against whom the statement is offered under subdivision (E).

[Amended by Pub.L. 94–113, § 1, October 16, 1975, 89 Stat. 576; amended March 2, 1987, effective October 1, 1987; amended April 11, 1997, effective December 1, 1997.]

RULE 802.   HEARSAY RULE

Hearsay is not admissible except as provided by these rules or by other rules prescribed by the Supreme Court pursuant to statutory authority or by Act of Congress.

RULE 803. HEARSAY EXCEPTIONS; AVAILABILITY OF DECLARANT IMMATERIAL

The following are not excluded by the hearsay rule, even though the declarant is available as a witness:

(1) Present Sense Impression. A statement describing or explaining an event or condition made while the declarant was perceiving the event or condition, or immediately thereafter.

(2) Excited Utterance. A statement relating to a startling event or condition made while the declarant was under the stress of excitement caused by the event or condition.

(3) Then Existing Mental, Emotional, or Physical Condition. A statement of the declarant's then existing state of mind, emotion, sensation, or physical condition (such as intent, plan, motive, design, mental feeling, pain, and bodily health), but not including a statement of memory or belief to prove the fact remembered or believed unless it relates to the execution, revocation, identification, or terms of declarant's will.

(4) Statements for Purposes of Medical Diagnosis or Treatment. Statements made for purposes of medical diagnosis or treatment and describing medical history, or past or present symptoms, pain, or sensations, or the inception or general character of the cause or external source thereof insofar as reasonably pertinent to diagnosis or treatment.

(5) Recorded Recollection. A memorandum or record concerning a matter about which a witness once had knowledge but now has insufficient recollection to enable the witness to testify fully and accurately, shown to have been made or adopted by the witness when the matter was fresh in the witness' memory and to reflect that knowledge correctly. If admitted, the memorandum or record may be read into evidence but may not itself be received as an exhibit unless offered by an adverse party.

(6) Records of Regularly Conducted Activity.—A memorandum, report, record, or data compilation, in any form, of acts, events, conditions, opinions, or diagnoses, made at or near the time by, or from information transmitted by, a person with knowledge, if kept in the course of a regularly conducted business activity, and if it was the regular practice of that business activity to make the memorandum, report, record or data compilation, all as shown by the testimony of the custodian or other qualified witness, or by certification that complies with Rule 902(11), Rule 902(12), or a statute permitting certification, unless the source of information or the method or circumstances of preparation indicate lack of trustworthiness. The term "business" as used in this paragraph includes business, institution, association, profession, occupation, and calling of every kind, whether or not conducted for profit.

(7) Absence of Entry in Records Kept in Accordance With the Provisions of Paragraph (6). Evidence that a matter is not included in the memoranda reports, records, or data compilations, in any form, kept in accordance with the provisions of paragraph (6), to prove the nonoccurrence or nonexistence of the matter, if the matter was of a kind of which a memorandum, report, record, or data compilation was regularly made and preserved, unless the sources of information or other circumstances indicate lack of trustworthiness.

(8) Public Records and Reports. Records, reports, statements, or data compilations, in any form, of public offices or agencies, setting forth (A) the activities of the office or agency, or (B) matters observed pursuant to duty imposed by law as to which matters there was a duty to report, excluding, however, in criminal cases matters observed by police officers and other law enforcement personnel, or (C) in civil actions and proceedings and against the Government in criminal cases, factual findings resulting from an investigation made pursuant to authority granted by law, unless the sources of information or other circumstances indicate lack of trustworthiness.

(9) Records of Vital Statistics. Records or data compilations, in any form, of births, fetal deaths, deaths, or marriages, if the report thereof was made to a public office pursuant to requirements of law.

(10) Absence of Public Record or Entry. To prove the absence of a record, report, statement, or data compilation, in any form, or the nonoccurrence or nonexistence of a matter of which a record, report, statement, or data compilation, in any form, was regularly made and preserved by a public office or agency, evidence in the form of a certification in accordance with rule 902, or testimony, that diligent search failed to disclose the record, report, statement, or data compilation, or entry.

(11) Records of Religious Organizations. Statements of births, marriages, divorces, deaths, legitimacy, ancestry, relationship by blood or marriage, or other similar facts of personal or family history, contained in a regularly kept record of a religious organization.

(12) Marriage, Baptismal, and Similar Certificates. Statements of fact contained in a certificate that the maker performed a marriage or other ceremony or administered a sacrament, made by a clergyman, public official, or other person authorized by the rules or practices of a religious organization or by law to perform the act certified, and purporting to have been issued at the time of the act or within a reasonable time thereafter.

(13) Family Records. Statements of fact concerning personal or family history contained in family Bibles, genealogies, charts, engravings on rings, inscriptions on family portraits, engravings on urns, crypts, or tombstones, or the like.

(14) Records of Documents Affecting an Interest in Property. The record of a document purporting to establish or affect an interest in property, as proof of the content of the original recorded document and its execution and delivery by each person by whom it purports to have been executed, if the record is a record of a public office

and an applicable statute authorizes the recording of documents of that
kind in that office.

(15) Statements in Documents Affecting an Interest in Property. A statement contained in a document purporting to establish or
affect an interest in property if the matter stated was relevant to the
purpose of the document, unless dealings with the property since the
document was made have been inconsistent with the truth of the
statement or the purport of the document.

(16) Statements in Ancient Documents. Statements in a document in existence twenty years or more the authenticity of which is
established.

(17) Market Reports, Commercial Publications. Market quotations, tabulations, lists, directories, or other published compilations,
generally used and relied upon by the public or by persons in particular
occupations.

(18) Learned Treatises. To the extent called to the attention of
an expert witness upon cross-examination or relied upon by the expert
witness in direct examination, statements contained in published treatises, periodicals, or pamphlets on a subject of history, medicine, or other
science or art, established as a reliable authority by the testimony or
admission of the witness or by other expert testimony or by judicial
notice. If admitted, the statements may be read into evidence but may
not be received as exhibits.

(19) Reputation Concerning Personal or Family History.
Reputation among members of a person's family by blood, adoption, or
marriage, or among a person's associates, or in the community, concerning a person's birth, adoption, marriage, divorce, death, legitimacy,
relationship by blood, adoption, or marriage, ancestry, or other similar
fact of personal or family history.

(20) Reputation Concerning Boundaries or General History.
Reputation in a community, arising before the controversy, as to boundaries of or customs affecting lands in the community, and reputation as
to events of general history important to the community or State or
nation in which located.

(21) Reputation as to Character. Reputation of a person's
character among associates or in the community.

(22) Judgment of Previous Conviction. Evidence of a final
judgment, entered after a trial or upon a plea of guilty (but not upon a
plea of nolo contendere), adjudging a person guilty of a crime punishable
by death or imprisonment in excess of one year, to prove any fact
essential to sustain the judgment, but not including, when offered by the
Government in a criminal prosecution for purposes other than impeachment, judgments against persons other than the accused. The pendency
of an appeal may be shown but does not affect admissibility.

**(23) Judgment as to Personal, Family, or General History, or
Boundaries.** Judgments as proof of matters of personal, family or
general history, or boundaries, essential to the judgment, if the same
would be provable by evidence of reputation.

(24)   [Transferred to Rule 807]

[Amended by Pub.L. 94–149, § 1(11), December 12, 1975, 89 Stat. 805; amended March 2, 1987, effective October 1, 1987; amended April 11, 1997, effective December 1, 1997; April 17, 2000, effective December 1, 2000.]

RULE 804.   HEARSAY EXCEPTIONS; DECLARANT UNAVAILABLE

(a) Definition of Unavailability. "Unavailability as a witness" includes situations in which the declarant—

(1) is exempted by ruling of the court on the ground of privilege from testifying concerning the subject matter of the declarant's statement; or

(2) persists in refusing to testify concerning the subject matter of the declarant's statement despite an order of the court to do so; or

(3) testifies to a lack of memory of the subject matter of the declarant's statement; or

(4) is unable to be present or to testify at the hearing because of death or then existing physical or mental illness or infirmity; or

(5) is absent from the hearing and the proponent of a statement has been unable to procure the declarant's attendance (or in the case of a hearsay exception under subdivision (b)(2), (3), or (4), the declarant's attendance or testimony) by process or other reasonable means.

A declarant is not unavailable as a witness if exemption, refusal, claim of lack of memory, inability, or absence is due to the procurement or wrongdoing of the proponent of a statement for the purpose of preventing the witness from attending or testifying.

(b) Hearsay Exceptions. The following are not excluded by the hearsay rule if the declarant is unavailable as a witness:

(1) *Former Testimony.* Testimony given as a witness at another hearing of the same or a different proceeding, or in a deposition taken in compliance with law in the course of the same or another proceeding, if the party against whom the testimony is now offered, or, in a civil action or proceeding, a predecessor in interest, had an opportunity and similar motive to develop the testimony by direct, cross, or redirect examination.

(2) *Statement Under Belief of Impending Death.* In a prosecution for homicide or in a civil action or proceeding, a statement made by a declarant while believing that the declarant's death was imminent, concerning the cause or circumstances of what the declarant believed to be impending death.

(3) *Statement Against Interest.* A statement which was at the time of its making so far contrary to the declarant's pecuniary or proprietary interest, or so far tended to subject the declarant to civil or criminal liability, or to render invalid a claim by the declarant against another, that a reasonable person in the declarant's position would not have made the statement unless believing it to be true. A statement tending to expose the declarant to criminal liability and offered to exculpate the

accused is not admissible unless corroborating circumstances clearly indicate the trustworthiness of the statement.

(4) *Statement of Personal or Family History.*

(A) A statement concerning the declarant's own birth, adoption, marriage, divorce, legitimacy, relationship by blood, adoption, or marriage, ancestry, or other similar fact of personal or family history, even though declarant had no means of acquiring personal knowledge of the matter stated; or

(B) a statement concerning the foregoing matters, and death also, of another person, if the declarant was related to the other by blood, adoption, or marriage or was so intimately associated with the other's family as to be likely to have accurate information concerning the matter declared.

(5) [Transferred to Rule 807]

(6) *Forfeiture by Wrongdoing.* A statement offered against a party that has engaged or acquiesced in wrongdoing that was intended to, and did, procure the unavailability of the declarant as a witness.

[Amended by Pub.L. 94–149, § 1(12) and (13), December 12, 1975, 89 Stat. 806; amended March 2, 1987, effective October 1, 1987; amended by Pub.L. 100–690, Title VII, § 7075(b), November 18, 1988, 102 Stat. 4405; amended April 11, 1997, effective December 1, 1997.]

RULE 805. HEARSAY WITHIN HEARSAY

Hearsay included within hearsay is not excluded under the hearsay rule if each part of the combined statements conforms with an exception to the hearsay rule provided in these rules.

RULE 806. ATTACKING AND SUPPORTING CREDIBILITY OF DECLARANT

When a hearsay statement, or a statement defined in Rule 801(d)(2), (C), (D), or (E), has been admitted in evidence, the credibility of the declarant may be attacked, and if attacked may be supported, by any evidence which would be admissible for those purposes if declarant had testified as a witness. Evidence of a statement or conduct by the declarant at any time, inconsistent with the declarant's hearsay statement, is not subject to any requirement that the declarant may have been afforded an opportunity to deny or explain. If the party against whom a hearsay statement has been admitted calls the declarant as a witness, the party is entitled to examine the declarant on the statement as if under cross-examination.

[Amended March 2, 1987, effective October 1, 1987.]

RULE 807. RESIDUAL EXCEPTION

A statement not specifically covered by Rule 803 or 804 but having equivalent circumstantial guarantees of trustworthiness, is not excluded by the hearsay rule, if the court determines that (A) the statement is offered as evidence of a material fact; (B) the statement is more probative on the point for which it is offered than any other evidence which the proponent can procure through reasonable efforts; and (C) the general purposes of these rules and the interests of justice will best be served by admission of the statement into evidence. However, a statement may not be admitted under this exception unless the proponent of it makes known to the adverse party sufficiently in advance of the trial or hearing to provide the adverse party with a fair opportunity to prepare to meet it, the proponent's intention to offer the statement and the particulars of it, including the name and address of the declarant.

[Transferred from Rules 803(24) and 804(b)(5) April 11, 1997, effective December 1, 1997.]

ARTICLE IX. AUTHENTICATION AND IDENTIFICATION

RULE 901. REQUIREMENT OF AUTHENTICATION OR IDENTIFICATION

(a) General Provision. The requirement of authentication or identification as a condition precedent to admissibility is satisfied by evidence sufficient to support a finding that the matter in question is what its proponent claims.

(b) Illustrations. By way of illustration only, and not by way of limitation, the following are examples of authentication or identification conforming with the requirements of this rule:

(1) *Testimony of Witness With Knowledge.* Testimony that a matter is what it is claimed to be.

(2) *Nonexpert Opinion on Handwriting.* Nonexpert opinion as to the genuineness of handwriting, based upon familiarity not acquired for purposes of the litigation.

(3) *Comparison by Trier or Expert Witness.* Comparison by the trier of fact or by expert witnesses with specimens which have been authenticated.

(4) *Distinctive Characteristics and the Like.* Appearance, contents, substance, internal patterns, or other distinctive characteristics, taken in conjunction with circumstances.

(5) *Voice Identification.* Identification of a voice, whether heard firsthand or through mechanical or electronic transmission or recording, by opinion based upon hearing the voice at any time under circumstances connecting it with the alleged speaker.

(6) *Telephone Conversations.* Telephone conversations, by evidence that a call was made to the number assigned at the time by the telephone company to a particular person or business, if (A) in the case of a person, circumstances, including self-identification, show the person answering to be the one called, or (B) in the case of a business, the call was made to a place of business and the conversation related to business reasonably transacted over the telephone.

(7) *Public Records or Reports.* Evidence that a writing authorized by law to be recorded or filed and in fact recorded or filed in a public office, or a purported public record, report, statement, or data compilation, in any form, is from the public office where items of this nature are kept.

(8) *Ancient Documents or Data Compilation.* Evidence that a document or data compilation, in any form, (A) is in such condition as to create no suspicion concerning its authenticity, (B) was in a place where it, if authentic, would likely be, and (C) has been in existence 20 years or more at the time it is offered.

(9) *Process or System.* Evidence describing a process or system used to produce a result and showing that the process or system produces an accurate result.

(10) *Methods Provided by Statute or Rule.* Any method of authentication or identification provided by Act of Congress or by other rules prescribed by the Supreme Court pursuant to statutory authority.

RULE 902.   SELF–AUTHENTICATION

Extrinsic evidence of authenticity as a condition precedent to admissibility is not required with respect to the following:

(1) Domestic Public Documents Under Seal. A document bearing a seal purporting to be that of the United States, or of any State, district, Commonwealth, territory, or insular possession thereof, or the Panama Canal Zone, or the Trust Territory of the Pacific Islands, or of a political subdivision, department, officer, or agency thereof, and a signature purporting to be an attestation or execution.

(2) Domestic Public Documents Not Under Seal. A document purporting to bear the signature in the official capacity of an officer or employee of any entity included in paragraph (1) hereof, having no seal, if a public officer having a seal and having official duties in the district or political subdivision of the officer or employee certifies under seal that the signer has the official capacity and that the signature is genuine.

(3) Foreign Public Documents. A document purporting to be executed or attested in an official capacity by a person authorized by the laws of a foreign country to make the execution or attestation, and accompanied by a final certification as to the genuineness of the signature and official position (A) of the executing or attesting person, or (B) of any foreign official whose certificate of genuineness of signature and official position relates to the execution or attestation or is in a chain of certificates of genuineness of signature and official position relating to the execution or attestation. A final certification may be made by a secretary of an embassy or legation, consul general, consul, vice consul, or consular agent of the United States, or a diplomatic or consular official of the foreign country assigned or accredited to the United States. If reasonable opportunity has been given to all parties to investigate the authenticity and accuracy of official documents, the court may, for good cause shown, order that they be treated as presumptively authentic without final certification or permit them to be evidenced by an attested summary with or without final certification.

(4) Certified Copies of Public Records. A copy of an official record or report or entry therein, or of a document authorized by law to be recorded or filed and actually recorded or filed in a public office, including data compilations in any form, certified as correct by the custodian or other person authorized to make the certification, by certificate complying with paragraph (1), (2), or (3) of this rule or complying with any Act of Congress or rule prescribed by the Supreme Court pursuant to statutory authority.

(5) Official Publications. Books, pamphlets, or other publications purporting to be issued by public authority.

(6) Newspapers and Periodicals. Printed materials purporting to be newspapers or periodicals.

(7) Trade Inscriptions and the Like. Inscriptions, signs, tags, or labels purporting to have been affixed in the course of business and indicating ownership, control, or origin.

(8) Acknowledged Documents. Documents accompanied by a certificate of acknowledgment executed in the manner provided by law by a notary public or other officer authorized by law to take acknowledgments.

(9) Commercial Paper and Related Documents. Commercial paper, signatures thereon, and documents relating thereto to the extent provided by general commercial law.

(10) Presumptions Under Acts of Congress. Any signature, document, or other matter declared by Act of Congress to be presumptively or prima facie genuine or authentic.

(11) Certified Domestic Records of Regularly Conducted Activity.—The original or a duplicate of a domestic record of regularly conducted activity that would be admissible under Rule 803(6) if accompanied by a written declaration of its custodian or other qualified person, in a manner complying with any Act of Congress or rule prescribed by the Supreme Court pursuant to statutory authority, certifying that the record—

   (A) was made at or near the time of the occurrence of the matters set forth by, or from information transmitted by, a person with knowledge of those matters;

   (B) was kept in the course of the regularly conducted activity; and

   (C) was made by the regularly conducted activity as a regular practice.

A party intending to offer a record into evidence under this paragraph must provide written notice of that intention to all adverse parties, and must make the record and declaration available for inspection sufficiently in advance of their offer into evidence to provide an adverse party with a fair opportunity to challenge them.

(12) Certified Foreign Records of Regularly Conducted Activity.—In a civil case, the original or a duplicate of a foreign record of regularly conducted activity that would be admissible under Rule 803(6) if accompanied by a written declaration by its custodian or other qualified person certifying that the record—

    (A) was made at or near the time of the occurrence of the matters set forth by, or from information transmitted by, a person with knowledge of those matters;

    (B) was kept in the course of the regularly conducted activity; and

    (C) was made by the regularly conducted activity as a regular practice.

The declaration must be signed in a manner that, if falsely made, would subject the maker to criminal penalty under the laws of the country where the declaration is signed. A party intending to offer a record into evidence under this paragraph must provide written notice of that intention to all adverse parties, and must make the record and declaration available for inspection sufficiently in advance of their offer into evidence to provide an adverse party with a fair opportunity to challenge them.

[Amended March 2, 1987, effective October 1, 1987; April 25, 1988, effective November 1, 1988; April 17, 2000, effective December 1, 2000.]

RULE 903. SUBSCRIBING WITNESS' TESTIMONY UNNECESSARY

    The testimony of a subscribing witness is not necessary to authenticate a writing unless required by the laws of the jurisdiction whose laws govern the validity of the writing.

ARTICLE X. CONTENTS OF WRITINGS, RECORDINGS, AND PHOTOGRAPHS

RULE 1001. DEFINITIONS

    For purposes of this article the following definitions are applicable:

    (1) Writings and Recordings. "Writings" and "recordings" consist of letters, words, or numbers, or their equivalent, set down by handwriting, typewriting, printing, photostating, photographing, magnetic impulse, mechanical or electronic recording, or other form of data compilation.

    (2) Photographs. "Photographs" include still photographs, X-ray films, video tapes, and motion pictures.

    (3) Original. An "original" of a writing or recording is the writing or recording itself or any counterpart intended to have the same effect by a person executing or issuing it. An "original" of a photograph includes the negative or any print therefrom. If data are stored in a computer or similar device, any printout or other output readable by sight, shown to reflect the data accurately, is an "original".

(4) Duplicate. A "duplicate" is a counterpart produced by the same impression as the original, or from the same matrix, or by means of photography, including enlargements and miniatures, or by mechanical or electronic re-recording, or by chemical reproduction, or by other equivalent techniques which accurately reproduces the original.

RULE 1002.   REQUIREMENT OF ORIGINAL

To prove the content of a writing, recording, or photograph, the original writing, recording, or photograph is required, except as otherwise provided in these rules or by Act of Congress.

RULE 1003.   ADMISSIBILITY OF DUPLICATES

A duplicate is admissible to the same extent as an original unless (1) a genuine question is raised as to the authenticity of the original or (2) in the circumstances it would be unfair to admit the duplicate in lieu of the original.

RULE 1004.   ADMISSIBILITY OF OTHER EVIDENCE OF CONTENTS

The original is not required, and other evidence of the contents of a writing, recording, or photograph is admissible if—

(1) Originals Lost or Destroyed. All originals are lost or have been destroyed, unless the proponent lost or destroyed them in bad faith; or

(2) Original Not Obtainable. No original can be obtained by any available judicial process or procedure; or

(3) Original in Possession of Opponent. At a time when an original was under the control of the party against whom offered, that party was put on notice, by the pleadings or otherwise, that the contents would be a subject of proof at the hearing, and that party does not produce the original at the hearing; or

(4) Collateral Matters. The writing, recording, or photograph is not closely related to a controlling issue.

[Amended March 2, 1987, effective October 1, 1987.]

RULE 1005.   PUBLIC RECORDS

The contents of an official record, or of a document authorized to be recorded or filed and actually recorded or filed, including data compilations in any form, if otherwise admissible, may be proved by copy, certified as correct in accordance with rule 902 or testified to be correct by a witness who has compared it with the original. If a copy which complies with the foregoing cannot be obtained by the exercise of reasonable diligence, then other evidence of the contents may be given.

RULE 1006. SUMMARIES

The contents of voluminous writings, recordings, or photographs which cannot conveniently be examined in court may be presented in the form of a chart, summary, or calculation. The originals, or duplicates, shall be made available for examination or copying, or both, by other parties at reasonable time and place. The court may order that they be produced in court.

RULE 1007. TESTIMONY OR WRITTEN ADMISSION OF PARTY

Contents of writings, recordings, or photographs may be proved by the testimony or deposition of the party against whom offered or by that party's written admission, without accounting for the nonproduction of the original.

[Amended March 2, 1987, effective October 1, 1987.]

RULE 1008. FUNCTIONS OF COURT AND JURY

When the admissibility of other evidence of contents of writings, recordings, or photographs under these rules depends upon the fulfillment of a condition of fact, the question whether the condition has been fulfilled is ordinarily for the court to determine in accordance with the provisions of rule 104. However, when an issue is raised (a) whether the asserted writing ever existed, or (b) whether another writing, recording, or photograph produced at the trial is the original, or (c) whether other evidence of contents correctly reflects the contents, the issue is for the trier of fact to determine as in the case of other issues of fact.

ARTICLE XI. MISCELLANEOUS RULES

RULE 1101. APPLICABILITY OF RULES

(a) **Courts and Judges.** These rules apply to the United States district courts, the District Court of Guam, the District Court of the Virgin Islands, the District Court for the Northern Mariana Islands, the United States courts of appeals, the United States Claims Court, and to United States bankruptcy judges and United States magistrate judges, in the actions, cases, and proceedings and to the extent hereinafter set forth. The terms "judge" and "court" in these rules include United States bankruptcy judges and United States magistrate judges.

(b) **Proceedings Generally.** These rules apply generally to civil actions and proceedings, including admiralty and maritime cases, to criminal cases and proceedings, to contempt proceedings except those in which the court may act summarily, and to proceedings and cases under title 11, United States Code.

(c) **Rule of Privilege.** The rule with respect to privileges applies at all stages of all actions, cases, and proceedings.

(d) **Rules Inapplicable.** The rules (other than with respect to privileges) do not apply in the following situations:

(1) *Preliminary Questions of Fact.* The determination of questions of fact preliminary to admissibility of evidence when the issue is to be determined by the court under rule 104.

(2) *Grand Jury.* Proceedings before grand juries.

(3) *Miscellaneous Proceedings.* Proceedings for extradition or rendition; preliminary examinations in criminal cases; sentencing, or granting or revoking probation; issuance of warrants for arrest, criminal summonses, and search warrants; and proceedings with respect to release on bail or otherwise.

(e) Rules Applicable in Part. In the following proceedings these rules apply to the extent that matters of evidence are not provided for in the statutes which govern procedure therein or in other rules prescribed by the Supreme Court pursuant to statutory authority: the trial of misdemeanors and other petty offenses before United States magistrate judges; review of agency actions when the facts are subject to trial de novo under section 706(2)(F) of title 5, United States Code; review of orders of the Secretary of Agriculture under section 2 of the Act entitled "An Act to authorize association of producers of agricultural products" approved February 18, 1922 (7 U.S.C. 292), and under sections 6 and 7(c) of the Perishable Agricultural Commodities Act, 1930 (7 U.S.C. 499f, 499g(c)); naturalization and revocation of naturalization under sections 310–318 of the Immigration and Nationality Act (8 U.S.C. 1421–1429); prize proceedings in admiralty under sections 7651–7681 of title 10, United States Code; review of orders of the Secretary of the Interior under section 2 of the Act entitled "An Act authorizing associations of producers of aquatic products" approved June 25, 1934 (15 U.S.C. 522); review of orders of petroleum control boards under section 5 of the Act entitled "An Act to regulate interstate and foreign commerce in petroleum and its products by prohibiting the shipment in such commerce of petroleum and its products produced in violation of State law, and for other purposes", approved February 22, 1935 (15 U.S.C. 715d); actions for fines, penalties, or forfeitures under part V of title IV of the Tariff Act of 1930 (19 U.S.C. 1581–1624), or under the Anti-Smuggling Act (19 U.S.C. 1701–1711); criminal libel for condemnation, exclusion of imports, or other proceedings under the Federal Food, Drug, and Cosmetic Act (21 U.S.C. 301–392); disputes between seamen under sections 4079, 4080, and 4081 of the Revised Statutes (22 U.S.C. 256–258); habeas corpus under sections 2241–2254 of title 28, United States Code; motions to vacate, set aside or correct sentence under section 2255 of title 28, United States Code; actions for penalties for refusal to transport destitute seamen under section 4578 of the Revised Statutes (46 U.S.C. 679);* actions against the United States under the Act entitled "An Act authorizing suits against the United States in admiralty for damage caused by and salvage service rendered to public vessels belonging to the United States, and for other purposes", approved March 3, 1925 (46 U.S.C. 781–790), as implemented by section 7730 of title 10, United States Code.

[Amended by Pub.L. 94–149, § 1(14), December 12, 1975, 89 Stat. 806; Pub.L. 95–598, Title II, § 251, November 6, 1978, 92 Stat. 2673, effective October 1, 1979; Pub.L. 97–164, Title I, § 142, April 2, 1982, 96 Stat. 45, effective October 1, 1982; amended March 2, 1987, effective October 1, 1987; April 25, 1988, effective November 1, 1988; amended by Pub.L. 100–690, Title VII, § 7075(c)(1), November 18, 1988, 102 Stat. 4405 (although amendment by Pub.L. 100-690 could not be executed due to prior amendment by Court order which made the same change effective November 1, 1988); amended April 22, 1993, effective December 1, 1993.]

RULE 1102.   AMENDMENTS

Amendments to the Federal Rules of Evidence may be made as provided in section 2072 of title 28 of the United States Code.

[Amended April 30, 1991, effective December 1, 1991.]

RULE 1103.   TITLE

These rules may be known and cited as the Federal Rules of Evidence.

* Law Revision Counsel Note: Repealed and reenacted as 46 U.S.C. 11104(b)-(d) by Pub.L. 98–89, §§ 1, 2(a), 4(b), August 26, 1983, 97 Stat. 500.

PART XI
DIRECTORY

Summary of Contents

UNITED STATES FEDERAL COURTS DIRECTORY

(Current July 2007)

SUPREME COURT OF THE UNITED STATES

U.S. Supreme Court Building
1 First Street, N.E.
Washington, DC 20543
202–479–3000

UNITED STATES COURT OF APPEALS

DC CIRCUIT	E. Barrett Prettyman U.S. Courthouse 333 Constitution Avenue, N.W. Washington, DC 20001 202–216–7000		Cincinnati, OH 45202 513–564–7000
		SEVENTH CIRCUIT	219 South Dearborn Street, Room 2722 Chicago, IL 60604 312–435–5850
FIRST CIRCUIT	John Joseph Moakley U.S. Courthouse 1 Courthouse Way, Suite 2500 Boston, MA 02210 617–748–9057	EIGHTH CIRCUIT	Thomas F. Eagleton U.S. Courthouse, Room 24.329 111 S. 10th Street St. Louis, MO 63102 314–244–2400
SECOND CIRCUIT	Thurgood Marshall U.S. Courthouse 40 Foley Square, Room 1802 New York, NY 10007 212–857–8500	NINTH CIRCUIT	95 Seventh Street San Francisco, CA 94103 415–556–8000
THIRD CIRCUIT	21400 U.S. Courthouse 601 Market Street Philadelphia, PA 19106 215–597–2995	TENTH CIRCUIT	Byron White U.S. Courthouse 1823 Stout Street Denver, CO 80257 303–844–3157
FOURTH CIRCUIT	1100 East Main Street, Suite 501 Richmond, VA 23219–3517 804–916–2700	ELEVENTH CIRCUIT	Elbert P. Tuttle U.S. Court of Appeals Building 56 Forsyth Street, N.W. Atlanta, GA 30303 404–335–6100
FIFTH CIRCUIT	600 S. Maestri Place New Orleans, LA 70130–3408 504–310–7700	FEDERAL CIRCUIT	717 Madison Place, N.W. Washington, DC 20439 202–633–6550
SIXTH CIRCUIT	540 Potter Stewart U.S. Courthouse 100 East Fifth Street	COURT OF FEDERAL	717 Madison Place, N.W. Washington, DC 20005

CLAIMS   202–357–6400

COURT OF   One Federal Plaza
INTERNA-   New York, NY 10278–0001
TIONAL TRADE   212–264–2800

ARMED FORCES   450 E Street, N.W.
                         Washington, DC 20442–0001
                         202–761–1448

COURT OF   625 Indiana Avenue,
APPEALS FOR   Suite 900
VETERANS   Washington, DC 20004–2950
CLAIMS   202–501–5970

JUDICIAL   Thurgood Marshall Federal
PANEL ON   Judiciary Building
MULTIDISTRICT   One Columbus Circle, N.E.
LITIGATION   Room G–255, North Lobby
                         Washington, DC 20002–8004
                         202–502–2800

TAX COURT   400 Second Street, N.W.
                         Washington, DC 20217
                         202–521–0700

UNITED STATES DISTRICT COURTS

ALABAMA

Northern District   Hugo L. Black U.S. Court-
                         house
                         1729 Fifth Avenue North
                         Birmingham, AL 35203
                         205–278–1700

Middle District   One Church Street
                         Montgomery, AL 36104
                         334–954–3600

Southern District   113 St. Joseph Street
                         Mobile, AL 36602
                         251–690–2371

ALASKA

                         Federal Building and U.S.
                         Courthouse
                         222 West 7th Avenue, #4
                         Anchorage, AK 99513
                         907–677–6100

ARIZONA

                         Sandra Day O'Connor U.S.
                         Courthouse
                         401 W. Washington Street
                         Suite 130, SPC 1
                         Phoenix, AZ 85003–2118
                         602–322–7200

ARKANSAS

Eastern District   U.S. Courthouse
                         600 W. Capitol Avenue,
                         Suite 402
                         Little Rock, AR 72201–3325
                         501–604–5351

Western District   Federal Building, Room
                         1038
                         South 6th Street and Rogers
                         Avenue
                         Fort Smith, AR 72901
                         479–783–6833

CALIFORNIA

Northern District   U.S. Courthouse
                         450 Golden Gate Avenue
                         San Francisco, CA 94102
                         415–522–2000

Eastern District   501 I Street, suite 4–200
                         Sacramento, CA 95814
                         916–930–4000

Central District   U.S. Courthouse
                         312 N. Spring Street
                         Los Angeles, CA 90012
                         213–894–1565

Southern District   Edward J. Schwartz U.S.
                         Courthouse
                         940 Front Street
                         San Diego, CA 92101–8900
                         619–557–5600

COLORADO

                         Alfred A. Arraj U.S. Court-
                         house, room A105
                         901 19th Street
                         Denver, CO 80294–3589
                         303–844–3433

CONNECTICUT

                         Richard C. Lee U.S. Court-
                         house
                         141 Church Street
                         New Haven, CT 06510
                         203–773–2140

DELAWARE

                         J. Caleb Boggs Federal
                         Building
                         844 N. King Street
                         Wilmington, DE 19801
                         302–573–6170

DISTRICT OF COLUMBIA

                         333 Constitution Avenue,
                         N.W.
                         Washington, DC 20001
                         202–354–3000

FLORIDA

Northern District   U.S. Courthouse
                         111 N. Adams Street
                         Tallahassee, FL 32301–7730
                         850–521–3501

Middle District   George C. Young U.S. Court-
                         house and Federal Build-
                         ing
                         80 North Hughey Avenue
                         Orlando, FL 32801
                         407–835–4200

Southern District   301 N. Miami Avenue, room
                         150
                         Miami, FL 33128
                         305–523–5100

GEORGIA

Northern District	75 Spring Street, S.W.. Room 2211 Atlanta, GA 30303–3361 404–215–1600
Middle District	475 Mulberry Street Macon, GA 31202 478–752–3497
Southern District	125 Bull Street, Room 304 Savannah, GA 31401 912–650–4020

GUAM

U.S. Courthouse, 4th Floor
520 West Soledad Avenue
Hagatña, Guam 96910
671–473–9100

HAWAII

U.S. Courthouse
300 Ala Moana Boulevard,
Room C 338
Honolulu, HI 96813
808–522–8100

IDAHO

550 West Fort Street
Boise, ID 83724
208–334–1361

ILLINOIS

Northern District	Everett McKinley Dirksen Building 219 South Dearborn Street Chicago, IL 60604 312–435–5670
Central District	151 U.S. Courthouse 600 E. Monroe Street Springfield, IL 62701 217–492–4020
Southern District	750 Missouri Avenue East St. Louis, IL 62201 618–482–9371

INDIANA

Northern District	Robert A. Grant Courthouse 204 South Main Street South Bend, IN 46601 574–246–8000
Southern District	46 East Ohio Street, room 105 Indianapolis, IN 46204 317–229–3700

IOWA

Northern District	Federal Building and U.S. Courthouse 101 First Street, S.E. Cedar Rapids, IA 52401 319–286–2300
Southern District	123 E. Walnut Street, Room 300 Des Moines, IA 50306–9344 515–284–6248

KANSAS

259 U.S. Courthouse
500 State Avenue
Kansas City, KS 66101
913–551–6719

KENTUCKY

Eastern District	101 Barr Street, Room 206 Lexington, KY 40588–3074 859–233–2503
Western District	U.S. Courthouse 601 West Broadway, Room 106 Louisville, KY 40202 502–625–3500

LOUISIANA

Eastern District	500 Poydras Street, Room C–151 New Orleans, LA 70130 504–589–7650
Middle District	777 Florida Street, Room 139 Baton Rouge, LA 70801 225–389–3500
Western District	1167 U.S. Courthouse 300 Fannin Street Shreveport, LA 71101 318–676–4273

MAINE

156 Federal Street
Portland, ME 04101
207–780–3356

MARYLAND

101 W. Lombard Street
Baltimore, MD 21201
410–962–2600

MASSACHUSETTS

1 Courthouse Way
Boston, MA 02210
617–748–9152

MICHIGAN

Eastern District	Theodore Levin U.S. Court- house 231 W. Lafayette Boulevard Detroit, MI 48226 313–234–5055
Western District	399 Federal Building 110 Michigan Street, N.W. Grand Rapids, MI 49503 616–456–2381

MINNESOTA

Federal Building, Room 708
316 N. Robert Street
St. Paul, MN 55101
651–848–1100

MISSISSIPPI

Northern District   U.S. Courthouse, Room 369
911 Jackson Avenue
Oxford, MS 38655
662–234–1971

Southern District   James O. Eastland U.S.
Courthouse
245 East Capitol Street,
Suite 316
Jackson, MS 39201
601–965–4439

MISSOURI

Eastern District   Thomas F. Eagleton U.S.
Courthouse
111 South 10th Street,
Third Floor
St. Louis, MO 63102
314–244–7900

Western District   Charles Evans Whittaker
Courthouse
400 E. 9th Street
Kansas City, MO 64106
816–512–5000

MONTANA

Russell Smith Courthouse
201 East Broadway
Missoula, MT 59801
406–542–7260

NEBRASKA

111 S. 18th Plaza, Suite
1152
Omaha, NE 68102
402–661–7350

NEVADA

333 Las Vegas Boulevard
South
Las Vegas, NV 89101
702–464–5400

NEW HAMPSHIRE

55 Pleasant Street, Room
110
Concord, NH 03301
603–225–1423

NEW JERSEY

Martin Luther King, Jr.
Federal Building and U.S.
Courthouse
50 Walnut Street, Room 405
Newark, NJ 07102
973–645–3730

NEW MEXICO

333 Lomas Boulevard, N.W.
Albuquerque, NM 87102
505–348–2000

NEW YORK

Northern District   100 S. Clinton Street
Syracuse, NY 13261–7367
315–234–8500

Southern District   U.S. Courthouse
500 Pearl Street
New York, NY 10007–1312
212–805–0136

Eastern District   225 Cadman Plaza East
Brooklyn, NY 11201
718–613–2600

Western District   304 U.S. Courthouse
68 Court Street
Buffalo, NY 14202
716–551–4211

NORTH CAROLINA

Eastern District   Terry Sanford Federal
Building & Courthouse
310 New Bern Avenue
Raleigh, NC 27601
919–645–1700

Middle District   324 West Market Street,
Suite 401
Greensboro, NC 27401
336–332–6000

Western District   401 W. Trade Street, Room
212
Charlotte, NC 28202
704–350–7400

NORTH DAKOTA

220 East Rosser Avenue
Bismarck, ND 58502
701–530–2300

NORTHERN MARIANA ISLANDS

P.O. Box 500687
Saipan, MP 96950
670–236–2902

OHIO

Northern District   Carl B. Stokes United States
Court House
801 West Superior Avenue
Cleveland, OH 44113–1830
216–357–7000

Southern District   Joseph P. Kinneary U.S.
Courthouse
85 Marconi Boulevard,
Room 260
Columbus, OH 43215
614–719–3000

OKLAHOMA

Northern District   224 S.Boulder Avenue
Tulsa, OK 74103
918–699–4000

Eastern District   101 N. 4th Street
Okmulgee, OK 74402–0607
918–684–7920

Western District   215 Dean A. McGee Avenue
Oklahoma City, OK 73102
405–609–5700

OREGON

Mark O. Hatfield U.S.
Courthouse
1000 S.W. Third Street
Portland, OR 97204–2902
503–326–8000

PENNSYLVANIA

Eastern District

U.S. Courthouse
601 Market Street, Room
2609
Philadelphia, PA 19106–
1797
215–597–7704

Middle District

William J. Nealon Federal
Building and U.S. Court-
house
235 N. Washington Avenue
Scranton, PA 18501
570–207–5600

Western District

3110 U.S. Courthouse
700 Grant Street
Pittsburgh, PA 15219
412–208–7500

PUERTO RICO

Federico Degetau Federal
Building
150 Carlos Chardon Street
San Juan, PR 00918
787–772–3000

RHODE ISLAND

Federal Building and Courthouse
One Exchange Terrace
Providence, RI 02903
401–752–7200

SOUTH CAROLINA

Matthew J. Perry Jr. U.S.
Courthouse
901 Richland Street
Columbia, SC 29201
803–765–5816

SOUTH DAKOTA

U.S. Courthouse, Room 128
400 S. Phillips Avenue
Sioux Falls, SD 57104
605–330–6600

TENNESSEE

Eastern District

800 Market Street, Suite 130
Knoxville, TN 37902
865–545–4228

Middle District

801 Broadway
Nashville, TN 37203
615–736–5498

Western District

Federal Building, Room 242
167 N. Main Street
Memphis, TN 38103
901–495–1200

TEXAS

Northern District

1100 Commerce Street,
Room 1452
Dallas, TX 75242
214–753–2200

Southern District

1217 U.S. Courthouse
515 Rusk Avenue
Houston, TX 77002
713–250–5500

Eastern District

211 W. Ferguson Street,
Room 106
Tyler, TX 75702
903–590–1000

Western District

655 E. Durango Boulevard,
Room G–65
San Antonio, TX 78206
210–472–6550

UTAH

Frank E.Moss U.S. Court-
house
350 South Main Street, 301
Salt Lake City, UT 84101
801–524–6687

VERMONT

11 Elmwood Avenue, Room
506
Burlington, VT 05401
802–951–6301

VIRGIN ISLANDS

5500 Veteran's Drive, room
310
St. Thomas, VI 00802
340–774–0640

VIRGINIA

Eastern District

Albert V. Bryan U.S. Courthouse
401 Courthouse Square
Alexandria, VA 22314
703–299–2100

Western District

210 Franklin Road, Room
308
Roanoke, VA 24011
540–857–5100

WASHINGTON

Eastern District

Thomas S. Foley U.S. Courthouse
920 West Riverside Avenue
Spokane, WA 99210
509–458–3400

Western District

U.S Courthouse
700 Stewart Street
Seattle, WA 98101
206–370–5598

WEST VIRGINIA

Northern District

300 Third Street
Elkins, WV 26241
304–636–1445

Southern District	Robert C. Byrd U.S. Court- house 300 Virginia Street, E., Room 320 Charleston, WV 25301 304–347–3000		414–297–3372
		Western District	120 N. Henry Street, Room 320 Madison, WI 53703 608–264–5156

WISCONSIN

Eastern District	362 U.S. Courthouse 517 E. Wisconsin Avenue Milwaukee, WI 53202

WYOMING

2120 Capitol, Room 2141
Cheyenne, WY 82001
307–433–2120

Federal Judges Directory

(Current as of May 2007)

THE SUPREME COURT OF THE UNITED STATES

John G. Roberts, Jr.,
  Chief Justice . . . . **Washington, DC**
John Paul Stevens,
  Associate Justice .Washington, DC
Antonin Scalia,
  Associate Justice .Washington, DC
Anthony M. Kennedy,
  Associate Justice .Washington, DC
David H. Souter,
  Associate Justice .Washington, DC
Clarence Thomas,
  Associate Justice .Washington, DC
Ruth Bader Ginsburg,
  Associate Justice .Washington, DC
Stephen G. Breyer,
  Associate Justice .Washington, DC
Samuel A. Alito, Jr.,
  Associate Justice .Washington, DC

DISTRICT OF COLUMBIA CIRCUIT
John G. Roberts, Jr., Circuit Justice

CIRCUIT JUDGES

Douglas H. Ginsburg,
  Chief Justice . . . . **Washington, DC**
David B. Sentelle . . . . .Washington, DC
Karen LeCraft Henderson . . . . .Washington, DC
A. Raymond Randolph . . . . .Washington, DC
Judith W. Rogers . . . . .Washington, DC
David S. Tatel . . . . .Washington, DC
Merrick B. Garland . . . . .Washington, DC
Janice Rogers Brown . . . . .Washington, DC
Thomas B. Griffith . . . . .Washington, DC
Brett M. Kavanaugh . . . . .Washington, DC

SENIOR CIRCUIT JUDGES

Harry Thomas Edwards . . . . .Washington, DC
Laurence H. Silberman . . . . .Washington, DC
Stephen F. Williams . . . . .Washington, DC

DISTRICT JUDGES

Thomas F. Hogan,
  Chief Judge . . . . **Washington, DC**
Royce C. Lamberth . . . . .Washington, DC
Paul L. Friedman . . . . .Washington, DC
Ricardo M. Urbina .Washington, DC
Emmet G. Sullivan . . . . .Washington, DC
James Robertson . . . . .Washington, DC
Colleen M. Kollar–Kotelly . . . . .Washington, DC
Henry H. Kennedy, Jr. . . . . .Washington, DC
Richard W. Roberts . . . . .Washington, DC
Ellen Segal Huvelle . . . . .Washington, DC
Reggie B. Walton . . . . .Washington, DC
John D. Bates . . . . .Washington, DC
Richard J. Leon . . . . .Washington, DC
Rosemary M. Collyer . . . . .Washington, DC

SENIOR DISTRICT JUDGES

Louis F. Oberdorfer . . . . .Washington, DC
John Garrett Penn .Washington, DC
Gladys Kessler . . . . .Washington, DC

MAGISTRATE JUDGES

Alan Kay . . . . .Washington, DC
Deborah Ann Robinson . . . . .Washington, DC
John M. Facciola . . . . .Washington, DC

BANKRUPTCY JUDGE

S. Martin Teel, Jr. . . . . .Washington, DC

FIRST CIRCUIT
Districts of Maine; Massachusetts; New Hampshire;
Puerto Rico and Rhode Island
David H. Souter, Circuit Justice

CIRCUIT JUDGES

Michael Boudin,
  Chief Judge . . . . **Boston, MA**
Juan R. Torruella . . . . San Juan, PR
Sandra L. Lynch . . . . Boston, MA
Kermit Lipez . . . . Portland, ME
Jeffrey R. Howard . . . . Concord, NH

SENIOR CIRCUIT JUDGES

Levin H. Campbell . . . . Boston, MA
Bruce M. Selya . . . . Providence, RI
Conrad K. Cyr . . . . Bangor, ME
Norman H. Stahl . . . . Boston, MA

DISTRICT JUDGES

George Z. Singal,
  Chief Judge . . . . .ME . . . . **Portland**
D. Brock Hornby . . . . .ME . . . . Portland
John A. Woodcock, Jr. . . . . . . .ME . . . . .Bangor
Mark L. Wolf,
  Chief Judge . . . . .MA . . . . **Boston**
Joseph L. Tauro . . . . .MA . . . . Boston
Rya W. Zobel . . . . .MA . . . . Boston
William G. Young . . . . .MA . . . . Boston
Douglas P. Woodlock . . . . . . .MA . . . . Boston
Nathaniel M. Gorton . . . . . . .MA . . . . Boston
Reginald C. Lindsay . . . . .MA . . . . Boston
Patti B. Saris . . . . .MA . . . . Boston
Richard G. Stearns . . . . .MA . . . . Boston
Nancy Gertner . . . . .MA . . . . Boston
Michael A. Ponsor . . . . .MA . . . . Springfield
George A. O'Toole . . . . .MA . . . . Boston
F. Dennis Saylor, IV . . . . .MA . . . . Worcester
Steven J. McAuliffe,
  Chief Judge . . . . .NH . . . . **Concord**
Paul J. Barbadoro . . . . .NH . . . . .Concord
Jose A. Fuste,
  Chief Judge . . . . .PR . . . . **Hato Rey**
Carmen Consuelo Cerezo . . .PR . . . . .Hato Rey
Daniel R. Dominguez . . . . . . .PR . . . . .Hato Rey
Jay A. Garcia–Gregory . . . . . .PR . . . . .Hato Rey
Aida Delgado–Colon . . . . .PR . . . . .Hato Rey
Gustavo Antonio Gelpi . . . . .PR . . . . .Hato Rey
Francisco Augusto Besosa . .PR . . . . .Hato Rey
Mary M. Lisi,
  Chief Judge . . . . .RI . . . . **Providence**
William E. Smith . . . . .RI . . . . Providence

SENIOR DISTRICT JUDGES

Gene Carter . . . . .ME . . . . Portland
Morris E. Lasker . . . . .MA . . . . Boston
Edward F. Harrington . . . . . . .MA . . . . Boston
Joseph A. Di Clerico, Jr. . . . . .NH . . . . .Concord
Juan M. Perez-Gimenez . . . .PR . . . . .Hato Rey
Jaime Pieras, Jr. . . . . .PR . . . . .San Juan
Raymond L. Acosta . . . . .PR . . . . .San Juan
Salvador E. Casellas . . . . .PR . . . . .San Juan
Ronald R. Lagueux . . . . .RI . . . . Providence
Ernest C. Torres . . . . .RI . . . . Providence

MAGISTRATE JUDGES

David M. Cohen . . . . .ME . . . . Portland
Margaret J. Kravchuk . . . . . .ME . . . . Bangor
Joyce London Alexander . . . .MA . . . . Boston
Robert B. Collings . . . . .MA . . . . Boston
Marianne B. Bowler . . . . .MA . . . . Boston

Kenneth P. Neiman	MA	Springfield
Judith Gail Dein	MA	Boston
Leo T. Sorokin	MA	Boston
Timothy S. Hillman	MA	Worcester
James R. Muirhead	NH	Concord
Justo Arenas	PR	Hato Rey
Camille Velez–Rive	PR	Hato Rey
Bruce J. McGiverin	PR	Hato Rey
Marcos E. Lopez–Gonzalez	PR	Hato Rey
David L. Martin	RI	Providence
Jacob Hagopian	RI	Providence
Robert W. Lovegreen	RI	Providence
Lincoln D. Almond	RI	Providence

BANKRUPTCY JUDGES

Louis H. Kornreich,
Chief Judge ... **ME** ... **Bangor**
James B. Haines, Jr. ... ME ... Portland
Henry J. Boroff,
Chief Judge ... **MA** ... **Worcester**
Joan N. Feeney ... MA ... Boston
William C. Hillman ... MA ... Boston
Joel B. Rosenthal ... MA ... Worcester
Robert Somma ... MA ... Boston
Mark W. Vaughn,
Chief Judge ... **NH** ... **Manchester**
J. Michael Deasy ... NH ... Manchester
Gerardo Carlo,
Chief Judge ... **PR** ... **Old San Juan**
Sara E. de Jesus ... PR ... Old San Juan
Enrique S. Lamoutte ... PR ... Old San Juan
Brian K. Tester ... PR ... San Juan
Arthur N. Votolato ... RI ... Providence

SECOND CIRCUIT

**Districts of Connecticut; Northern, Eastern,
Western and Southern New York; and Vermont**
Ruth Bader Ginsburg, Circuit Justice

CIRCUIT JUDGES

Dennis Jacobs,
Chief Judge ... **New York, NY**
Guido Calabresi ... New Haven, CT
José A. Cabranes ... New Haven, CT
Chester J. Straub ... New York, NY
Rosemary S. Pooler ... Syracuse, NY
Robert D. Sack ... New York, NY
Sonia Sotomayor ... New York, NY
Robert A. Katzmann ... New York, NY
Barrington D. Parker, Jr. ... New York, NY
Reena Raggi ... Brooklyn, NY
Richard C. Wesley ... Geneseo, NY
Peter W. Hall ... Rutland, CT

SENIOR CIRCUIT JUDGES

Wilfred Feinberg ... New York, NY
James L. Oakes ... Brattleboro, VT
Thomas J. Meskill ... New Britain, CT
Jon O. Newman ... Hartford, CT
Amalya L. Kearse ... New York, NY
Richard J. Cardamone ... Utica, NY
Ralph K. Winter ... New Haven, CT
Roger J. Miner ... Albany, NY
John M. Walker ... New York, NY
Joseph M. McLaughlin ... New York, NY
Pierre N. Leval ... New York, NY

DISTRICT JUDGES

Robert N. Chatigny,
Chief Judge ... **CT** ... **Hartford**
Alvin W. Thompson ... CT ... Hartford
Janet Bond Arterton ... CT ... New Haven
Christopher F. Droney ... CT ... Hartford
Janet C. Hall ... CT ... Bridgeport
Stefan R. Underhill ... CT ... Bridgeport
Mark R. Kravitz ... CT ... New Haven
Vanessa Lynne Bryant ... CT ... Hartford
Norman A. Mordue,
Chief Judge ... **NY**
       Northern ... **Syracuse**

Lawrence E. Kahn ... NY
       Northern ... Albany
David N. Hurd ... NY
       Northern ... Utica
Gary L. Sharpe ... NY
       Northern ... Albany
Raymond J. Dearie,
Chief Judge ... **NY**
       Eastern ... **Brooklyn**
Edward R. Korman ... NY
       Eastern ... Brooklyn
Carol Bagley Amon ... NY
       Eastern ... Brooklyn
Joanna Seybert ... NY
       Eastern ... Central Islip
John Gleeson ... NY
       Eastern ... Brooklyn
Allyne R. Ross ... NY
       Eastern ... Brooklyn
Nina Gershon ... NY
       Eastern ... Brooklyn
Nicholas Garaufis ... NY
       Eastern ... Brooklyn
Sandra J. Feuerstein ... NY
       Eastern ... Central Islip
Dora L. Irizarry ... NY
       Eastern ... Brooklyn
Sandra L. Townes ... NY
       Eastern ... Brooklyn
Joseph Frank Bianco ... NY
       Eastern ... Brooklyn
Eric Nicholas Vitaliano ... NY
       Eastern ... Brooklyn
Brian M. Cogan ... NY
       Eastern ... Central Islip
Richard J. Arcara,
Chief Judge ... **NY**
       Western ... **Buffalo**
David G. Larimer ... NY
       Western ... Rochester
William M. Skretny ... NY
       Western ... Buffalo
Charles J. Siragusa ... NY
       Western ... Rochester
Kimba M. Wood, Chief
Judge ... **NY**
       Southern ... **New York**
Charles L. Brieant ... NY
       Southern ... White Plains
Loretta A. Preska ... NY
       Southern ... New York
Deborah A. Batts ... NY
       Southern ... New York
Denny Chin ... NY
       Southern ... New York
Lewis A. Kaplan ... NY
       Southern ... New York
Denise Cote ... NY
       Southern ... New York
John G. Koeltl ... NY
       Southern ... New York
Shira A. Scheindlin ... NY
       Southern ... New York
Sidney H. Stein ... NY
       Southern ... New York
Barbara S. Jones ... NY
       Southern ... New York
Jed S. Rakoff ... NY
       Southern ... New York
Colleen McMahon ... NY
       Southern ... New York
William H. Pauley, III ... NY
       Southern ... New York
Richard M. Berman ... NY
       Southern ... New York
Alvin K. Hellerstein ... NY
       Southern ... New York
Naomi Reice Buchwald ... NY
       Southern ... New York
Victor Marrero ... NY
       Southern ... New York
George B. Daniels ... NY
       Southern ... New York
Gerard E. Lynch ... NY
       Southern ... New York

Laura Taylor Swain ....NY
    Southern ....New York
Stephen C. Robinson ....NY
    Southern ......White Plains
Richard J. Holwell ....NY
    Southern ....New York
P. Kevin Castel ....NY
    Southern ....New York
Kenneth M. Karas ....NY
    Southern ....New York
Paul A. Crotty ....NY
    Southern ....New York
William K. Sessions,
    Chief Judge ....**VT** ....**Burlington**
J. Garvan Murtha..........VT .... Burlington

SENIOR DISTRICT JUDGES

Ellen Bree Burns ....CT .... New Haven
Warren W. Eginton ....CT .... Bridgeport
Peter C. Dorsey ....CT .... New Haven
Alan N. Nevas ....CT .... Bridgeport
Alfred V. Covello...........CT .... Hartford
Dominic J. Squatrito ....CT .... Hartford
Howard G. Munson ....NY
    Northern .... Syracuse
Neal P. McCurn ....NY
    Northern .... Syracuse
Thomas J. McAvoy ....NY
    Northern .... Binghamton
Frederick J. Scullin, Jr......NY
    Northern .... Syracuse
Jack B. Weinstein ....NY
    Eastern .... Brooklyn
Thomas C. Platt, Jr.........NY
    Eastern .... Central Islip
Charles P. Sifton...........NY
    Eastern .... Brooklyn
Israel Leo Glasser ....NY
    Eastern .... Brooklyn
Leonard D. Wexler ....NY
    Eastern .... Central Islip
Arthur D. Spatt............NY
    Eastern .... Central Islip
Sterling Johnson, Jr. ....NY
    Eastern .... Brooklyn
Denis R. Hurley ....NY
    Eastern .... Central Islip
David G. Trager ....NY
    Eastern .... Brooklyn
Frederic Block ....NY
    Eastern .... Brooklyn
John T. Curtin ....NY
    Western.............Buffalo
John T. Elfvin ....NY
    Western.............Buffalo
Michael A. Telesca ....NY
    Western.......... Rochester
Thomas P. Griesa ....NY
    Southern .... New York
Robert L. Carter ....NY
    Southern .... New York
Kevin Thomas Duffy ....NY
    Southern .... New York
Richard Owen ....NY
    Southern .... New York
William C. Conner ....NY
    Southern ...... White Plains
Charles S. Haight, Jr. ......NY
    Southern .... New York
Robert W. Sweet ....NY
    Southern .... New York
Leonard B. Sand ....NY
    Southern .... New York
John E. Sprizzo............NY
    Southern .... New York
Shirley Wohl Kram ....NY
    Southern .... New York
John F. Keenan.............NY
    Southern .... New York
Peter K. Leisure ....NY
    Southern .... New York
Louis L. Stanton ....NY
    Southern .... New York

Miriam Goldman
    Cedarbaum..............NY
    Southern .... New York
Robert P. Patterson, Jr. ....NY
    Southern .... New York
Lawrence M. McKenna .....NY
    Southern .... New York
Harold Baer, Jr. ....NY
    Southern .... New York

MAGISTRATE JUDGES

Thomas P. Smith ....CT .... Hartford
Joan G. Margolis...........CT .... New Haven
Holly B. Fitzsimmons ......CT .... Bridgeport
Donna F. Martinez ....CT .... Hartford
William I. Garfinkel ....CT .... Bridgeport
Gustave J. DiBianco........NY
    Northern.......... Syracuse
David R. Homer ....NY
    Northern.............Albany
David E. Peebles ....NY
    Northern.......... Syracuse
Randolph F. Treece ....NY
    Northern.............Albany
George H. Lowe ....NY
    Northern.......... Syracuse
Steven M. Gold ....NY
    Eastern .... Brooklyn
Joan M. Azrack ....NY
    Eastern .... Brooklyn
Marilyn Dolan Go ....NY
    Eastern .... Brooklyn
Arlene R. Lindsay ....NY
    Eastern .... Central Islip
Roanne L. Mann ....NY
    Eastern .... Brooklyn
Viktor V. Pohorelsky ....NY
    Eastern .... Brooklyn
Robert M. Levy ....NY
    Eastern .... Brooklyn
E. Thomas Boyle...........NY
    Eastern .... Central Islip
Cheryl Pollak ....NY
    Eastern .... Brooklyn
William D. Wall ....NY
    Eastern .... Central Islip
Lois S. Bloom..............NY
    Eastern .... Brooklyn
James Orenstein ....NY
    Eastern .... Brooklyn
Kiyo A. Matsumoto ....NY
    Eastern .... Brooklyn
Ramon E. Reyes, Jr.........NY
    Eastern .... Brooklyn
A. Kathleen Tomlinson .....NY
    Eastern .... Central Islip
Michael L. Orenstein ....NY
    Eastern .... Central Islip
Leslie G. Foschio...........NY
    Western.............Buffalo
Hugh B. Scott ....NY
    Western.............Buffalo
Jonathan W. Feldman ....NY
    Western.......... Rochester
H. Kenneth Schroeder, Jr. ..NY
    Western.............Buffalo
Marian W. Payson ....NY
    Western.......... Rochester
Victor E. Bianchini.........NY
    Western.............Buffalo
Jeremiah L. McCarthy......NY
    Western.............Buffalo
Theodore H. Katz ....NY
    Southern .... New York
Michael H. Dolinger ....NY
    Southern .... New York
James C. Francis, IV ....NY
    Southern .... New York
Mark D. Fox...............NY
    Southern ...... White Plains
Martin R. Goldberg ....NY
    Southern .... Middletown
Ronald L. Ellis.............NY
    Southern .... New York

Andrew J. Peck . . . . .NY
    Southern . . . . New York
Lisa Margaret Smith . . . . . . .NY
    Southern . . . . . . White Plains
Douglas F. Eaton . . . . .NY
    Southern . . . . New York
Henry B. Pitman . . . . .NY
    Southern . . . . New York
George A. Yanthis . . . . .NY
    Southern . . . . . . White Plains
Kevin N. Fox . . . . .NY
    Southern . . . . New York
Frank Maas . . . . .NY
    Southern . . . . New York
Gabriel W. Gorenstein . . . . . .NY
    Southern . . . . New York
Debra C. Freeman . . . . .NY
    Southern . . . . New York
Jerome J. Niedermeier . . . . .VT . . . . Burlington

BANKRUPTCY JUDGES

Albert S. Dabrowski,
  Chief Judge . . . .**CT** . . . . **New Haven**
Robert L. Krechevsky . . . . . .CT . . . . Hartford
Alan H. W. Shiff . . . . .CT . . . . Bridgeport
Lorraine M. Weil . . . . .CT . . . . New Haven
Stephen D. Gerling,
  Chief Judge . . . .**NY**
    Northern . . . .**Utica**
Robert E. Littlefield, Jr. . . . . .NY
    Northern . . . . .Albany
Margaret Cangilos–Ruiz . . . .NY
    Northern . . . . Syracuse
Carla E. Craig,
  Chief Judge . . . .**NY**
    Eastern . . . .**Brooklyn**
Jerome Feller . . . . .NY
    Eastern . . . . Brooklyn
Dennis E. Milton . . . . .NY
    Eastern . . . . Brooklyn
Elizabeth S. Stong . . . . .NY
    Eastern . . . . Brooklyn
Stan Bernstein . . . . .NY
    Eastern . . . . Central Islip
Dorothy T. Eisenberg . . . . . .NY
    Eastern . . . . Central Islip
Joel B. Rosenthal . . . . .NY
    Eastern . . . . Central Islip
Carl L. Bucki,
  Chief Judge . . . .**NY**
    Western . . . .**Buffalo**
Michael J. Kaplan . . . . .NY
    Western . . . . .Buffalo
John C. Ninfo, II . . . . .NY
    Western . . . . Rochester
Stuart M. Bernstein,
  Chief Judge . . . .**NY**
    Southern . . . . . . **New York**
Prudence Carter Beatty . . . .NY
    Southern . . . . New York
Burton R. Lifland . . . . .NY
    Southern . . . . New York
Adlai S. Hardin, Jr. . . . . .NY
    Southern . . . . . . White Plains
Arthur J. Gonzalez . . . . .NY
    Southern . . . . New York
Cecelia G. Morris . . . . .NY
    Southern . . . . . . Poughkeepsie
Robert E. Gerber . . . . .NY
    Southern . . . . New York
Allan L. Gropper . . . . .NY
    Southern . . . . New York
Robert D. Drain . . . . .NY
    Southern . . . . New York
James M. Peck . . . . .NY
    Southern . . . . New York
Martin Glenn . . . . .NY
    Southern . . . . New York
Colleen A. Brown . . . . .VT . . . . Rutland

THIRD CIRCUIT

**Districts of Delaware; New Jersey; Eastern, Middle
and Western Pennsylvania; and the Virgin Islands**
David H. Souter, Circuit Justice

CIRCUIT JUDGES

Anthony J. Scirica,
  Chief Judge . . . . **Philadelphia, PA**
Dolores K. Sloviter . . . . Philadelphia, PA
Theodore Alexander McKee . . . . Philadelphia, PA
Marjorie O. Rendell . . . . Philadelphia, PA
Maryanne Trump Barry . . . . Newark, NJ
Thomas L. Ambro . . . . .Wilmington, DE
Julio M. Fuentes . . . . Newark, NJ
D. Brooks Smith . . . . Duncansville, PA
D. Michael Fisher . . . . Pittsburgh, PA
Michael A. Chagares . . . . Newark, NJ
Kent A. Jordan . . . . .Wilmington, DE
Thomas M. Hardiman . . . . Pittsburgh, PA

SENIOR CIRCUIT JUDGES

Ruggero J. Aldisert . . . . Santa Barbara, CA
Joseph F. Weis, Jr. . . . . Pittsburgh, PA
Leonard I. Garth . . . . Newark, NJ
Walter K. Stapleton . . . . Wilmington, DE
Morton I. Greenberg . . . . Trenton, NJ
Robert E. Cowen . . . . Trenton, NJ
Richard Lowell Nygaard . . . . Erie, PA
Jane R. Roth . . . . .Wilmington, DE
Franklin S. Van Antwerpen . . . . Easton, PA

DISTRICT JUDGES

Sue L. Robinson,
  Chief Judge . . . . .DE . . . . **Wilmington**
Joseph J. Farnan, Jr. . . . . . . .DE . . . . Wilmington
Gregory M. Sleet . . . . .DE . . . . Wilmington
Garrett E. Brown, Jr.,
  Chief Judge . . . .**NJ** . . . . **Trenton**
Mary Little Cooper . . . . .NJ . . . . .Trenton
Jerome B. Simandle . . . . .NJ . . . . Camden
Joseph A. Greenaway, Jr. . . .NJ . . . . Newark
Katharine S. Hayden . . . . . . .NJ . . . . Newark
Faith S. Hochberg . . . . .NJ . . . . Newark
Joel A. Pisano . . . . .NJ . . . . .Trenton
Dennis M. Cavanaugh . . . . . .NJ . . . . Newark
William J. Martini . . . . .NJ . . . . Newark
Jose L. Linares . . . . .NJ . . . . Newark
Stanley R. Chesler . . . . .NJ . . . . Newark
Robert B. Kugler . . . . .NJ . . . . Camden
Freda L. Wolfson . . . . .NJ . . . . .Trenton
Peter G. Sheridan . . . . .NJ . . . . Newark
Susan D. Wigenton . . . . .NJ . . . . Newark
Noel Lawrence Hillman . . . . .NJ . . . . Newark
Renee Marie Bumb . . . . .NJ . . . . Camden
Harvey Bartle, III,
  Chief Judge . . . .**PA**
    Eastern . . . . . **Philadelphia**
James T. Giles . . . . .PA Eastern . . . . . Philadelphia
Stewart Dalzell . . . . .PA Eastern . . . . . Philadelphia
John R. Padova . . . . .PA Eastern . . . . . Philadelphia
J. Curtis Joyner . . . . .PA Eastern . . . . . Philadelphia
Eduardo C. Robreno . . . . .PA Eastern . . . . . Philadelphia
Anita B. Brody . . . . .PA Eastern . . . . . Philadelphia
Bruce W. Kauffman . . . . .PA Eastern . . . . . Philadelphia
Mary A. McLaughlin . . . . . . .PA Eastern . . . . . Philadelphia
Petrese B. Tucker . . . . .PA Eastern . . . . . Philadelphia
Berle M. Schiller . . . . .PA Eastern . . . . . Philadelphia
R. Barclay Surrick . . . . .PA Eastern . . . . . Philadelphia
Legrome D. Davis . . . . .PA Eastern . . . . . Philadelphia
Cynthia M. Rufe . . . . .PA Eastern . . . . . Philadelphia
Michael M. Baylson . . . . .PA Eastern . . . . . Philadelphia
Timothy J. Savage . . . . .PA Eastern . . . . . Philadelphia
James Knoll Gardner . . . . . . .PA Eastern . . . . Allentown
Gene E. K. Pratter . . . . .PA Eastern . . . . . Philadelphia
Lawrence F. Stengel . . . . . . .PA Eastern . . . . Reading
Paul S. Diamond . . . . .PA Eastern . . . . . Philadelphia
Juan R. Sanchez . . . . .PA Eastern . . . . . Philadelphia
Thomas M. Golden . . . . .PA Eastern . . . . Reading
Yvette Kane,
  Chief Judge . . . .**PA**
    Middle . . . .**Harrisburg**
Thomas I. Vanaskie . . . . .PA Middle . . . . Scranton
A. Richard Caputo . . . . .PA Middle . . . . Scranton
James M. Munley . . . . .PA Middle . . . . Scranton
Christopher C. Conner . . . . .PA Middle . . . . . . Harrisburg
John E. Jones, III . . . . .PA Middle . . . . Williamsport

Donetta W. Ambrose,
  Chief Judge . . . . PA
                    Western . . . . Pittsburgh
Gary L. Lancaster . . . . PA
                    Western . . . . Pittsburgh
Sean J. McLaughlin . . . . PA
                    Western . . . . Erie
Joy Flowers Conti . . . . PA
                    Western . . . . Pittsburgh
David Stewart Cercone . . . PA
                    Western . . . . Pittsburgh
Terrence F. McVerry . . . . PA
                    Western . . . . Pittsburgh
Arthur J. Schwab . . . . PA
                    Western . . . . Pittsburgh
Kim R. Gibson . . . . PA
                    Western . . . . Johnstown
Nora Barry Fischer . . . . PA
                    Western . . . . Pittsburgh
Curtis V. Gomez,
  Chief Judge . . . . VI . . . . **St. Thomas**
Raymond L. Finch . . . . VI . . . . St. Croix

SENIOR DISTRICT JUDGES

Murray M. Schwartz . . . . DE . . . . Wilmington
Joseph J. Longobardi . . . . . DE . . . . Wilmington
Harold A. Ackerman . . . . NJ . . . . Newark
Dickinson R. Debevoise . . . . . NJ . . . . Newark
Anne E. Thompson . . . . NJ . . . . Trenton
Joseph H. Rodriguez . . . . NJ . . . . Camden
John C. Lifland . . . . NJ . . . . Newark
Joseph E. Irenas . . . . NJ . . . . Camden
William H. Walls . . . . NJ . . . . Newark
John P. Fullam . . . . PA Eastern . . . . . Philadelphia
J. William Ditter, Jr. . . . . PA Eastern . . . . . Philadelphia
Donald W. VanArtsdalen . . . PA Eastern . . . . . Philadelphia
Clifford Scott Green . . . . PA Eastern . . . . . Philadelphia
Louis H. Pollak . . . . PA Eastern . . . . . Philadelphia
Norma L. Shapiro . . . . PA Eastern . . . . . Philadelphia
Thomas N. O'Neill, Jr. . . . . . . PA Eastern . . . . . Philadelphia
Marvin Katz . . . . PA Eastern . . . . . Philadelphia
Edmund V. Ludwig . . . . PA Eastern . . . . . Philadelphia
Robert F. Kelly . . . . PA Eastern . . . . . Philadelphia
Lowell A. Reed, Jr. . . . . PA Eastern . . . . . Philadelphia
Jan E. DuBois . . . . PA Eastern . . . . . Philadelphia
Ronald L. Buckwalter . . . . . . PA Eastern . . . . . Philadelphia
William H. Yohn, Jr. . . . . PA Eastern . . . . . Philadelphia
William J. Nealon, Jr. . . . . . . PA Middle . . . . Scranton
Malcolm Muir . . . . PA Middle . . . . Williamsport
Richard P. Conaboy . . . . PA Middle . . . . Scranton
Sylvia H. Rambo . . . . PA Middle . . . . . Harrisburg
William W. Caldwell . . . . PA Middle . . . . . Harrisburg
Edwin M. Kosik . . . . PA Middle . . . . Scranton
James F. McClure, Jr. . . . . . . PA
                    Middle . . . . Williamsport
Maurice B. Cohill, Jr. . . . . . . PA
                    Western . . . . Pittsburgh
Gustave Diamond . . . . PA
                    Western . . . . Pittsburgh
Alan E. Bloch . . . . PA
                    Western . . . . Pittsburgh
William L. Standish . . . . PA
                    Western . . . . Pittsburgh

MAGISTRATE JUDGES

Mary Pat Thynge . . . . DE . . . . Wilmington
John J. Hughes . . . . NJ . . . . Trenton
Madeline Cox Arleo . . . . NJ . . . . Newark
Mark Falk . . . . NJ . . . . Newark
Patty Shwartz . . . . NJ . . . . Newark
Ann Marie Donio . . . . NJ . . . . Camden
Tonianne J. Bongiovanni . . . NJ . . . . Trenton
Claire C. Cecchi . . . . NJ . . . . Newark
Joel Schneider . . . . NJ . . . . Camden
Esther Salas . . . . NJ . . . . Newark
Charles B. Smith . . . . PA Eastern . . . . . Philadelphia
Thomas J. Rueter . . . . PA Eastern . . . . . Philadelphia
Carol Sandra Wells . . . . PA Eastern . . . . . Philadelphia
Jacob P. Hart . . . . PA Eastern . . . . . Philadelphia
Linda K. Caracappa . . . . PA Eastern . . . . . Philadelphia
Timothy R. Rice . . . . PA Eastern . . . . . Philadelphia
David R. Strawbridge . . . . . . PA Eastern . . . . . Philadelphia
Luis Felipe Restrepo . . . . . . PA Eastern . . . . . Philadelphia
Henry S. Perkin . . . . PA Eastern . . . . . Philadelphia

Elizabeth T. Hey . . . . PA Eastern . . . . . Philadelphia
Peter B. Scuderi . . . . PA Eastern . . . . . Philadelphia
Arnold C. Rapoport . . . . PA Eastern . . . . . . Allentown
M. Faith Angell . . . . PA Eastern . . . . . Philadelphia
J. Andrew Smyser . . . . PA
                    Middle . . . . Harrisburg
Thomas M. Blewitt . . . . PA
                    Middle . . . . Scranton
Malachy E. Mannion . . . . PA
                    Middle . . . . . Wilkes–Barre
Ila Jeanne Sensenich . . . . . . PA
                    Western . . . . Pittsburgh
Robert C. Mitchell . . . . PA
                    Western . . . . Pittsburgh
Frances X. Caiazza . . . . PA
                    Western . . . . Pittsburgh
Susan Paradise Baxter . . . . . PA
                    Western . . . . Erie
Amy R. Hay . . . . PA
                    Western . . . . Pittsburgh
Lisa P. Lenihan . . . . PA
                    Western . . . . Pittsburgh
Geoffrey W. Barnard . . . . VI . . . . St. Thomas
George W. Cannon . . . . VI . . . . St. Croix

BANKRUPTCY JUDGES

Mary F. Walrath,
  Chief Judge . . . . DE . . . . **Wilmington**
Peter J. Walsh . . . . DE . . . . Wilmington
Kevin J. Carey . . . . DE . . . . Wilmington
Christopher S. Sontchi . . . . . DE . . . . Wilmington
Kevin Gross . . . . DE . . . . Wilmington
Brendan L. Shannon . . . . DE . . . . Wilmington
Judith H. Wizmur,
  Chief Judge . . . . NJ . . . . **Camden**
Gloria M. Burns . . . . NJ . . . . Camden
Rosemary Gambardella . . . . . NJ . . . . Newark
Novalyn L. Winfield . . . . NJ . . . . Newark
Kathryn C. Ferguson . . . . NJ . . . . Trenton
Raymond T. Lyons . . . . NJ . . . . Trenton
Donald H. Steckroth . . . . NJ . . . . Newark
Morris Stern . . . . NJ . . . . Newark
Michael B. Kaplan . . . . NJ . . . . Trenton
Diane Weiss Sigmund,
  Chief Judge . . . . PA
                    Eastern . . . . . **Philadelphia**
Bruce I. Fox . . . . PA Eastern . . . . . Philadelphia
Stephen Raslavich . . . . PA Eastern . . . . . Philadelphia
Richard E. Fehling . . . . PA Eastern . . . . . Reading
Eric L. Frank . . . . PA Eastern . . . . . Philadelphia
Jean K. FitzSimon . . . . PA Eastern . . . . . Philadelphia
John J. Thomas,
  Chief Judge . . . . PA
                    Middle . . . . . Wilkes–Barre
Mary D. France . . . . PA Middle . . . . . . Harrisburg
Robert N. Opel . . . . PA Middle . . . . Wilkes–Barre
M. Bruce McCullough,
  Chief Judge . . . . PA
                    Western . . . . **Pittsburgh**
Judith K. Fitzgerald . . . . PA
                    Western . . . . Pittsburgh
Thomas P. Agresti . . . . PA
                    Western . . . . Erie
Jeffery A. Deller . . . . PA
                    Western . . . . Pittsburgh
Warren W. Bentz . . . . PA
                    Western . . . . Erie
Bernard Markovitz . . . . PA
                    Western . . . . Pittsburgh

FOURTH CIRCUIT

**Districts of Maryland; Eastern, Middle and Western
North Carolina; South Carolina; Eastern and
Western Virginia; and Northern and Southern West
Virginia**
John G. Roberts, Jr., Chief Justice

CIRCUIT JUDGES

William W. Wilkins,
  Chief Judge . . . . **Greenville, SC**
H. Emory Widener, Jr. . . . . Abingdon, VA
J. Harvie Wilkinson III . . . . Charlottesville, VA
Paul V. Niemeyer . . . . Baltimore, MD

Karen J. Williams .... Orangeburg, SC
M. Blane Michael....................... Charleston, WV
Diana Gribbon Motz..................... Baltimore, MD
William B. Traxler, Jr................... Greenville, SC
Robert B. King.......................... Charleston, WV
Roger L. Gregory........................ Richmond, VA
Dennis W. Shedd .... Columbia, SC
Allyson K. Duncan .... Raleigh, NC

SENIOR CIRCUIT JUDGE

Clyde H. Hamilton ....7–22–91 .... Columbia, SC

DISTRICT JUDGES

Benson Everett Legg,
  Chief Judge ....**MD** .... **Baltimore**
J. Frederick Motz ....MD .... Baltimore
Peter J. Messitte ....MD .... Greenbelt
Deborah K. Chasanow ......MD .... Greenbelt
Alexander Williams, Jr......MD .... Greenbelt
Catherine C. Blake ....MD .... Baltimore
Andre M. Davis ....MD .... Baltimore
William D. Quarles.........MD .... Baltimore
Richard D. Bennett ....MD .... Baltimore
Roger W. Titus ....MD .... Greenbelt
Louise W. Flanagan,
  Chief Judge ....**NC**
    Eastern .... **New Bern**
Terrence William Boyle.....NC
    Eastern ...... Elizabeth City
James C. Dever, III ....NC
    Eastern .... Raleigh
James A. Beaty, Jr.,
  Chief Judge ....**NC**
    Middle ... **Winston–Salem**
N. Carlton Tilley, Jr. ....NC
    Middle .... Greensboro
Robert J. Conrad, Jr.,
  Chief Judge ....**NC**
    Western .... **Charlotte**
Richard L. Voorhees........NC
    Western.......... Charlotte
Lacy H. Thornburg ....NC
    Western.......... Asheville
Frank D. Whitney..........NC
    Western.......... Charlotte
Joseph F. Anderson,
  Chief Judge ....**SC** .... **Columbia**
G. Ross Anderson, Jr. ......SC............... Anderson
David C. Norton ....SC............... Charleston
Henry M. Herlong, Jr.......SC............... Greenville
Cameron McGowan Currie..SC............... Columbia
Patrick Michael Duffy ......SC............... Charleston
Margaret B. Seymour ......SC............... Columbia
Terry L. Wooten ....SC............... Florence
Henry F. Floyd ....SC...............Spartanburg
R. Bryan Harwell ....SC............... Florence
James R. Spencer,
  Chief Judge ....**VA**
    Eastern .... **Richmond**
Rebecca Beach Smith.......VA Eastern...... Norfolk
Leonie M. Brinkema ....VA Eastern...... Alexandria
Raymond Alvin Jackson ....VA Eastern...... Norfolk
Jerome B. Friedman ....VA Eastern...... Norfolk
Gerald Bruce Lee ....VA Eastern...... Alexandria
Henry E. Hudson ....VA Eastern...... Richmond
Walter D. Kelley, Jr. ....VA Eastern...... Norfolk
James P. Jones,
  Chief Judge ....**VA**
    Western .... **Abingdon**
Samuel Grayson Wilson ....VA
    Western.......... Roanoke
Norman K. Moon ....VA
    Western.......... Lynchburg
Glen E. Conrad ....VA
    Western.......... Roanoke
Irene M. Keeley,
  Chief Judge ....**WV**
    Northern .....**Clarksburg**
John Preston Bailey........WV
    Northern.......... Wheeling
David A. Faber,
  Chief Judge ....**WV**
    Southern ...... **Bluefield/**
    Charleston

John T. Copenhaver, Jr. .....WV
    Southern........ Charleston
Joseph R. Goodwin.........WV
    Southern........ Charleston
Robert C. Chambers........WV
    Southern....... Huntington
Thomas E. Johnston ....WV
    Southern.......... Beckley

SENIOR DISTRICT JUDGES

Marvin J. Garbis...........MD .... Baltimore
William M. Nickerson ......MD .... Baltimore
W. Earl Britt ....NC
    Eastern .... Raleigh
James C. Fox ....NC
    Eastern .... Wilmington
Malcolm J. Howard ....NC
    Eastern .... Greenville
William L. Osteen, Sr. ......NC
    Middle .... Greensboro
Graham C. Mullen ....NC
    Western.......... Charlotte
Solomon Blatt, Jr. ....SC............... Charleston
Matthew J. Perry, Jr. ......SC............... Columbia
C. Weston Houck ....SC............... Charleston
Richard L. Williams ....VA
    Eastern .... Richmond
James C. Cacheris ....VA
    Eastern .... Alexandria
Robert G. Doumar ....VA
    Eastern .... Norfolk
Claude M. Hilton ....VA
    Eastern .... Alexandria
T. S. Ellis, III..............VA
    Eastern .... Alexandria
Henry Coke Morgan, Jr.....VA
    Eastern .... Norfolk
Robert E. Payne ....VA
    Eastern .... Richmond
James C. Turk.............VA
    Western.......... Roanoke
Glen M. Williams ....VA
    Western.......... Abingdon
Jackson L. Kiser ....VA
    Western..........Danville
Robert Earl Maxwell ....WV
    Northern........... Elkins
Frederick P. Stamp, Jr......WV
    Northern.......... Wheeling

MAGISTRATE JUDGES

Paul W. Grimm ....MD .... Baltimore
Jillyn K. Schulze ....MD .... Greenbelt
William Connelly ....MD .... Greenbelt
Susan K. Gauvey ....MD .... Baltimore
Charles B. Day ....MD .... Greenbelt
James K. Bredar ....MD .... Baltimore
Beth P. Gesner ....MD .... Baltimore
Thomas M. Digirolamo .....MD .... Greenbelt
William A. Webb ....NC
    Eastern .... Raleigh
David W. Daniel ....NC
    Eastern .... Greenville
James E. Gates ....NC
    Eastern .... Raleigh
Paul Trevor Sharp ....NC
    Middle .... Greensboro
Russell A. Eliason ....NC
    Middle ...... Winston–Salem
Wallace W. Dixon ....NC
    Middle ....Durham
Carl Horn, III ....NC
    Western.......... Charlotte
David C. Keesler ....NC
    Western.......... Charlotte
Dennis L. Howell ....NC
    Western.......... Asheville
Robert S. Carr ....SC............... Charleston
William M. Catoe, Jr........SC............... Greenville
Joseph R. McCrorey ....SC............... Columbia
Bristow Marchant..........SC............... Columbia
George C. Kosko...........SC............... Charleston
Bruce H. Hendricks ....SC............... Greenville
Thomas E. Rogers, III ......SC............... Florence

Barry R. Poretz . . . . VA Eastern . . . . . . Alexandria
Tommy E. Miller . . . . VA Eastern . . . . Norfolk
James E. Bradberry . . . . VA Eastern . . . . Norfolk
Thomas Rawles Jones, Jr. . . VA Eastern . . . . . . Alexandria
Theresa Carroll Buchanan . . VA Eastern . . . . . . Alexandria
Dennis W. Dohnal . . . . VA Eastern . . . . . . Richmond
F. Bradford Stillman . . . . VA Eastern . . . . Norfolk
Liam O'Grady . . . . VA Eastern . . . . . . Alexandria
M. Hannah Lauck . . . . VA Eastern . . . . . . Richmond
B. Waugh Crigler . . . . VA
     Western . . . . . . Charlottesville
Pamela M. Sargent . . . . VA
     Western . . . . Abingdon
Michael F. Urbanski . . . . VA
     Western . . . . Roanoke
James E. Seibert . . . . WV
     Northern . . . . Wheeling
John S. Kaull . . . . WV
     Northern . . . . Clarksburg
Maurice G. Taylor, Jr. . . . . . . WV
     Southern . . . . . . Huntington/
                      Parkersburg
Mary E. Stanley . . . . WV
     Southern . . . . Charleston
R. Clarke Vandervort . . . . WV
     Southern . . Bluefield/Beckley

BANKRUPTCY JUDGES

Duncan W. Keir,
     Chief Judge . . . . **MD** . . . . **Baltimore**
Paul Mannes . . . . MD . . . . Greenbelt
James F. Schneider . . . . MD . . . . Baltimore
E. Stephen Derby . . . . MD . . . . Baltimore
Nancy V. Alquist . . . . MD . . . . Baltimore
Thomas J. Catliota . . . . MD . . . . Greenbelt
Wendelin I. Lipp . . . . MD . . . . Greenbelt
Robert A. Gordon . . . . MD . . . . Baltimore
A. Thomas Small,
     Chief Judge . . . . **NC**
     Eastern . . . . **Raleigh**
J. Rich Leonard . . . . NC
     Eastern . . . . Raleigh
Randy Davis Doub . . . . NC
     Eastern . . . . Wilson
William L. Stocks,
     Chief Judge . . . . **NC**
     Middle . . . . **Greensboro**
Catharine R. Carruthers . . . . NC
     Middle . . . . . . Winston–Salem
Thomas W. Waldrep, Jr. . . . . NC
     Middle . . . . Greensboro
J. Craig Whitley,
     Chief Judge . . . . **NC**
     Western . . . . **Charlotte**
Marvin R. Wooten . . . . NC
     Western . . . . Charlotte
George R. Hodges . . . . NC
     Western . . . . Charlotte
John E. Waites,
     Chief Judge . . . . **SC** . . . . **Columbia**
Helen E. Burris . . . . SC . . . . Spartanburg
David R. Duncan . . . . SC . . . . Columbia
Douglas O. Tice,
     Chief Judge . . . . **VA**
     Eastern . . . . **Richmond**
David H. Adams . . . . VA
     Eastern . . . . Norfolk
Stephen S. Mitchell . . . . VA
     Eastern . . . . Alexandria
Stephen C. St. John . . . . VA
     Eastern . . . . Norfolk
Robert G. Mayer . . . . VA
     Eastern . . . . Alexandria
Kevin R. Huennekens . . . . . . VA
     Eastern . . . . Richmond
Ross W. Krumm,
     Chief Judge . . . . **VA**
     Western . . . . **Harrisonburg**
William E. Anderson . . . . VA
     Western . . . . Lynchburg
William F. Stone, Jr. . . . . VA
     Western . . . . Roanoke
Patrick M. Flatley,
     Chief Judge . . . . **WV**
     Northern . . . . **Wheeling**

Ronald G. Pearson . . . . WV
     Southern . . . . Charleston

FIFTH CIRCUIT

**Districts of Eastern, Middle and Western Louisiana;
Northern and Southern Mississippi; and Northern,
Eastern, Western and Southern Texas**
Antonin Scalia, Circuit Justice

CIRCUIT JUDGES

Edith H. Jones, Chief Judge . . . . **Houston, TX**
Carolyn Dineen King . . . . Houston, TX
E. Grady Jolly . . . . Jackson, MS
W. Eugene Davis . . . . Lafayette, LA
Jerry E. Smith . . . . Houston, TX
Jacques L. Wiener, Jr. . . . . New Orleans, LA
Rhesa H. Barksdale . . . . Jackson, MS
Emilio M. Garza . . . . San Antonio, TX
Harold R. DeMoss, Jr. . . . . Houston, TX
Fortunato P. Benavides . . . . Austin, TX
Carl E. Stewart . . . . Shreveport, LA
James L. Dennis . . . . New Orleans, LA
Edith Brown Clement . . . . New Orleans, LA
Edward C. Prado . . . . San Antonio, TX
Priscilla R. Owen . . . . Austin, TX

SENIOR CIRCUIT JUDGES

Thomas M. Reavley . . . . Houston, TX
Will Garwood . . . . Austin, TX
Patrick E. Higginbotham . . . . Austin, TX
John M. Duhé . . . . Lafayette, LA

DISTRICT JUDGES

Helen G. Berrigan,
     Chief Judge . . . . **LA**
     Eastern . . . . . **New Orleans**
Martin L. C. Feldman . . . . . . LA Eastern . . . . New Orleans
Stanwood R. Duval, Jr. . . . . . LA Eastern . . . . New Orleans
Sarah S. Vance . . . . LA Eastern . . . . New Orleans
G. Thomas Porteous, Jr. . . . . LA Eastern . . . . New Orleans
Eldon E. Fallon . . . . LA Eastern . . . . New Orleans
Mary Ann Vial Lemmon . . . . LA Eastern . . . . New Orleans
Ivan L. R. Lemelle . . . . LA Eastern . . . . New Orleans
Carl J. Barbier . . . . LA Eastern . . . . New Orleans
Kurt D. Engelhardt . . . . LA Eastern . . . . New Orleans
Jay C. Zainey . . . . LA Eastern . . . . New Orleans
Lance M. Africk . . . . LA Eastern . . . . New Orleans
Ralph E. Tyson,
     Chief Judge . . . . **LA**
     Middle . . . . . . **Baton Rouge**
James J. Brady . . . . LA Middle . . . . Baton Rouge
Richard T. Haik,
     Chief Judge . . . . **LA**
     Western . . . . **Lafayette**
Rebecca F. Doherty . . . . LA
     Western . . . . Lafayette
Tucker L. Melancon . . . . LA
     Western . . . . Lafayette
Robert G. James . . . . LA
     Western . . . . Monroe
Dee D. Drell . . . . LA
     Western . . . . Alexandria
S. Maurice Hicks, Jr. . . . . LA
     Western . . . . Shreveport
Patricia H. Minaldi . . . . LA
     Western . . . . Lake Charles
Glen H. Davidson,
     Chief Judge . . . . **MS**
     Northern . . . . . . **Aberdeen**
W. Allen Pepper, Jr. . . . . MS
     Northern . . . . Greenville
Michael P. Mills . . . . MS
     Northern . . . . Oxford
Henry T. Wingate,
     Chief Judge . . . . **MS**
     Southern . . . . **Jackson**
Louis Guirola, Jr. . . . . MS
     Southern . . . . Gulfport
Keith Starrett . . . . MS
     Southern . . . . Hattiesburg
Daniel P. Jordan, III . . . . MS
     Southern . . . . Jackson

Sul Ozerden	MS	
	Southern	Gulfport
A. Joe Fish,		
Chief Judge	**TX**	
	Northern	**Dallas**
Mary Lou Robinson	TX	
	Northern	Amarillo
Sidney A. Fitzwater	TX	
	Northern	Dallas
Samuel Ray Cummings	TX	
	Northern	Lubbock
John H. McBryde	TX	
	Northern	Fort Worth
Jorge A. Solis	TX	
	Northern	Dallas
Terry R. Means	TX	
	Northern	Fort Worth
Sam A. Lindsay	TX	
	Northern	Dallas
Barbara M. G. Lynn	TX	
	Northern	Dallas
David C. Godbey	TX	
	Northern	Dallas
James Edgar Kinkeade	TX	
	Northern	Dallas
Jane J. Boyle	TX	
	Northern	Dallas
Thad Heartfield, Sr.,		
Chief Judge	**TX**	
	Eastern	**Tyler**
Richard A. Schell	TX Eastern	Sherman
David J. Folsom	TX Eastern	Texarkana
T. John Ward	TX Eastern	Marshall
Leonard E. Davis	TX Eastern	Tyler
Ron Clark	TX Eastern	Beaumont
Marcia A. Crone	TX Eastern	Beaumont
Michael Schneider	TX Eastern	Tyler
Walter S. Smith, Jr.,		
Chief Judge	**TX**	
	Western	**Waco**
Sam Sparks	TX	
	Western	Austin
W. Royal Furgeson, Jr.	TX	
	Western	San Antonio
Orlando L. Garcia	TX	
	Western	San Antonio
Fred Biery	TX	
	Western	San Antonio
David Briones	TX	
	Western	El Paso
Philip R. Martinez	TX	
	Western	El Paso
Alia Moses Ludlum	TX	
	Western	Del Rio
Robert A. Junell	TX	
	Western	Midland
Lee Yeakel	TX	
	Western	Austin
Kathleen Cardone	TX	
	Western	El Paso
Frank Montalvo	TX	
	Western	El Paso
Xavier Rodriguez	TX	
	Western	San Antonio
Hayden W. Head, Jr.,		
Chief Judge	**TX**	
	Southern	**Corpus Christi**
George P. Kazen	TX	
	Southern	Laredo
Ricardo H. Hinojosa	TX	
	Southern	McAllen
Lynn N. Hughes	TX	
	Southern	Houston
Kenneth M. Hoyt	TX	
	Southern	Houston
Sim Lake	TX	
	Southern	Houston
Melinda Harmon	TX	
	Southern	Houston
John D. Rainey	TX	
	Southern	Houston
Samuel B. Kent	TX	
	Southern	Houston
Lee H. Rosenthal	TX	
	Southern	Houston

Janis Graham Jack	TX	
	Southern	Corpus Christi
Vanessa D. Gilmore	TX	
	Southern	Houston
Nancy F. Atlas	TX	
	Southern	Houston
Hilda G. Tagle	TX	
	Southern	Brownsville
Keith P. Ellison	TX	
	Southern	Houston
Randy Crane	TX	
	Southern	McAllen
Andrew S. Hanen	TX	
	Southern	Brownsville
Micaela Alvarez	TX	
	Southern	Laredo
Gray Hampton Miller	TX	
	Southern	Houston

SENIOR DISTRICT JUDGES

Frederick J. R. Heebe	LA Eastern	New Orleans
Charles Schwartz, Jr.	LA Eastern	New Orleans
Adrian G. Duplantier	LA Eastern	New Orleans
Peter Beer	LA Eastern	New Orleans
A. J. McNamara	LA Eastern	New Orleans
Marcel Livaudais, Jr.	LA Eastern	New Orleans
John V. Parker	LA Middle	Baton Rouge
Frank J. Polozola	LA Middle	Baton Rouge
Tom Stagg	LA	
	Western	Shreveport
Donald E. Walter	LA	
	Western	Shreveport
James T. Trimble, Jr.	LA	
	Western	Lake Charles
Neal B. Biggers, Jr.	MS	
	Northern	Oxford
Dan M. Russell, Jr.	MS	
	Southern	Gulfport
L. T. Senter, Jr.	MS	
	Southern	Gulfport
William Henry Barbour, Jr.	MS	
	Southern	Jackson
Tom S. Lee	MS	
	Southern	Jackson
Walter J. Gex, III	MS	
	Southern	Gulfport
David Bramlette	MS	
	Southern	Natchez
Barefoot Sanders	TX	
	Northern	Dallas
Jerry Buchmeyer	TX	
	Northern	Dallas
Robert B. Maloney	TX	
	Northern	Dallas
William Wayne Justice	TX	
	Western	Austin
Harry Lee Hudspeth	TX	
	Western	Austin
James R. Nowlin	TX	
	Western	Austin
David Hittner	TX	
	Southern	Houston
Ewing Werlein, Jr.	TX	
	Southern	Houston

MAGISTRATE JUDGES

Alma L. Chasez	LA Eastern	New Orleans
Louis Moore, Jr.	LA Eastern	New Orleans
Joseph C. Wilkinson, Jr.	LA Eastern	New Orleans
Sally A. Shushan	LA Eastern	New Orleans
Karen Wells Roby	LA Eastern	New Orleans
Daniel E. Knowles, III	LA Eastern	New Orleans
Stephen C. Riedlinger	LA Middle	Baton Rouge
Christine A. Noland	LA Middle	Baton Rouge
Docia L. Dalby	LA Middle	Baton Rouge
Mildred E. Methvin	LA	
	Western	Lafayette
Alonzo P. Wilson	LA	
	Western	Lake Charles
James D. Kirk	LA	
	Western	Alexandria
C. Michael Hill	LA	
	Western	Lafayette

Mark L. Hornsby . . . . .LA
    Western . . . . Shreveport
Karen L. Hayes . . . . .LA
    Western . . . . Monroe
Jerry A. Davis . . . . .MS
    Northern . . . . Aberdeen
S. Allan Alexander . . . . .MS
    Northern . . . . Oxford
Eugene M. Bogen . . . . .MS
    Northern . . . . Greenville
John M. Roper . . . . .MS
    Southern . . . . Gulfport
James S. Sumner . . . . .MS
    Southern . . . . Jackson
Robert H. Walker . . . . .MS
    Southern . . . . Gulfport
Michael T. Parker . . . . .MS
    Southern . . . . Hattiesburg
Linda R. Anderson . . . . .MS
    Southern . . . . Jackson
Clinton E. Averitte . . . . .TX
    Northern . . . . Amarillo
William F. Sanderson, Jr. . . . .TX
    Northern . . . . Dallas
Jeff Kaplan . . . . .TX
    Northern . . . . Dallas
Charles M. Bleil . . . . .TX
    Northern . . . . Fort Worth
Paul D. Stickney . . . . .TX
    Northern . . . . Dallas
Nancy M. Koenig . . . . .TX
    Northern . . . . Lubbock
Irma C. Ramirez . . . . .TX
    Northern . . . . Dallas
Philip R. Lane . . . . .TX
    Northern . . . . Abilene
Earl S. Hines . . . . .TX Eastern . . . . . . Beaumont
Judith K. Guthrie . . . . .TX Eastern . . . . Tyler
Caroline M. Carven . . . . .TX Eastern . . . . . . Texarkana
Donald D. Bush . . . . .TX Eastern . . . . . . Sherman
Keith Giblin . . . . .TX Eastern . . . . . . Beaumont
John D. Love . . . . .TX Eastern . . . . Tyler
Chad Everingham . . . . .TX Eastern . . . . Marshall
Durwood Edwards . . . . .TX
    Western . . . . Alpine/Pecos
Dennis G. Green . . . . .TX
    Western . . . . Del Rio
Nancy Stein Nowak . . . . .TX
    Western . . . . San Antonio
Richard P. Mesa . . . . .TX
    Western . . . . El Paso
Michael S. McDonald . . . . . . .TX
    Western . . . . El Paso
L. Stuart Platt . . . . .TX
    Western . . . . Midland
Pamela Ann Mathy . . . . .TX
    Western . . . . San Antonio
John W. Primomo . . . . .TX
    Western . . . . San Antonio
Andrew W. Austin . . . . .TX
    Western . . . . Austin
Norbert J. Garney . . . . .TX
    Western . . . . El Paso
Jeffrey C. Manske . . . . .TX
    Western . . . . Waco
Victor Roberto Garcia . . . . . .TX
    Western . . . . Del Rio
Robert L. Pitman . . . . .TX
    Western . . . . Austin
Maryrose Milloy . . . . .TX
    Southern . . . . Houston
John R. Froeschner . . . . .TX
    Southern . . . . Galveston
John Wm. Black . . . . .TX
    Southern . . . . Brownsville
Calvin Botley . . . . .TX
    Southern . . . . Houston
Frances H. Stacy . . . . .TX
    Southern . . . . Houston
Nancy K. Johnson . . . . .TX
    Southern . . . . Houston
Dorina Ramos . . . . .TX
    Southern . . . . McAllen
B. Janice Ellington . . . . .TX
    Southern . . . . . Corpus Christi

Felix Recio, Jr. . . . . .TX
    Southern . . . . Brownsville
Adriana Arces–Flores . . . . . . .TX
    Southern . . . . Laredo
Stephen W. Smith . . . . .TX
    Southern . . . . Houston
Peter E. Ormsby . . . . .TX
    Southern . . . . McAllen
Brian L. Owsley . . . . .TX
    Southern . . . . . Corpus Christi
Diana Saldaña . . . . .TX
    Southern . . . . Laredo

BANKRUPTCY JUDGES

Jerry A. Brown,
    Chief Judge . . . .**LA**
        Eastern . . . . . New Orleans
Elizabeth W. Magner . . . . . . .LA
    Eastern . . . . New Orleans
Douglas D. Dodd . . . . .LA
    Middle . . . . Baton Rouge
Stephen V. Callaway,
    Chief Judge . . . .**LA**
        Western . . . . . . .Shreveport
Henley A. Hunter . . . . .LA
    Western . . . . Alexandria
Robert R. Summerhays . . . .LA
    Western . . . . .Lafayette
David W. Houston, III . . . . . .MS
    Northern . . . . Aberdeen
Edward Ellington,
    Chief Judge . . . .**MS**
        Southern . . . . Jackson
Edward R. Gaines . . . . .MS
    Southern . . . . Gulfport
Neil P. Olack . . . . .MS
    Southern . . . . Jackson
Barbara J. Houser,
    Chief Judge . . . .**TX**
        Northern . . . . Dallas
Robert L. Jones . . . . .TX
    Northern . . . . Lubbock
D. Michael Lynn . . . . .TX
    Northern . . . . Fort Worth
Harlin D. Hale . . . . .TX
    Northern . . . . Dallas
Russell F. Nelms . . . . .TX
    Northern . . . . Fort Worth
Stacey G. C. Jernigan . . . . . .TX
    Northern . . . . Dallas
Bill G. Parker,
    Chief Judge . . . .**TX**
        Eastern . . . . .Tyler
Brenda T. Rhoades . . . . .TX
    Eastern . . . . Plano
Ronald B. King,
    Chief Judge . . . .**TX**
        Western . . . . . San Antonio
Leif M. Clark . . . . .TX
    Western . . . . San Antonio
Frank R. Monroe . . . . .TX
    Western . . . . Austin
Karen K. Brown,
    Chief Judge . . . .**TX**
        Southern . . . . Houston
Letitia Z. Clark . . . . .TX
    Southern . . . . Houston
Richard S. Schmidt . . . . .TX
    Southern . . . . . Corpus Christi
Wesley W. Steen . . . . .TX
    Southern . . . . Houston
Marvin P. Isgur . . . . .TX
    Southern . . . . Houston
Jeffrey E. T. Bohm . . . . .TX
    Southern . . . . Houston

SIXTH CIRCUIT

**Districts of Eastern and Western Kentucky; Eastern
and Western Michigan; Northern and Southern
Ohio; and Eastern, Middle and Western Tennessee**
John Paul Stevens, Circuit Justice

CIRCUIT JUDGES

Danny J. Boggs, Chief Judge .... Louisville, KY
Boyce F. Martin, Jr. .... Louisville, KY
Alice M. Batchelder........................ Medina, OH
Martha Craig Daughtrey .... Nashville, TN
Karen Nelson Moore..................... Cleveland, OH
R. Guy Cole, Jr. .... Columbus, OH
Eric L. Clay............................... Detroit, MI
Ronald Lee Gilman .... Memphis, TN
Julia S. Gibbons.......................... Memphis, TN
John M. Rogers .... Lexington, KY
Jeffrey S. Sutton .... Columbus, OH
Deborah L. Cook .... Akron, OH
David W. McKeague .... Lansing, MI
Richard Allen Griffin .... Traverse City, MI

SENIOR CIRCUIT JUDGES

Damon J. Keith .... Detroit, MI
Gilbert S. Merritt .... Nashville, TN
Cornelia G. Kennedy .... Detroit, MI
Ralph B. Guy, Jr. .... Ann Arbor, MI
James L. Ryan .... Detroit, MI
Alan E. Norris .... Columbus, OH
Richard F. Suhrheinrich .... Lansing, MI
Eugene E. Siler, Jr......................... London, KY

DISTRICT JUDGES

Joseph M. Hood,
  Chief Judge .... KY
    Eastern .... Lexington
Jennifer B. Coffman .... KY
    Eastern .... Lexington
Karen K. Caldwell .... KY
    Eastern .... Frankfort
Danny C. Reeves .... KY
    Eastern .... London
David L. Bunning .... KY
    Eastern .... Covington
Gregory F. Van Tatenhove .. KY
    Eastern .... Pikeville
John G. Heyburn, II,
  Chief Judge .... KY
    Western .... Louisville
Charles R. Simpson, III ..... KY
    Western.......... Louisville
Jennifer B. Coffman .... KY
    Eastern/
    Western.......... Lexington
Thomas B. Russell .... KY
    Western .... Paducah
Joseph H. McKinley, Jr. .... KY
    Western.......... Owensboro
Bernard A. Friedman,
  Chief Judge .... MI
    Eastern .... Detroit
Gerald E. Rosen .... MI Eastern .... Detroit
Robert H. Cleland.......... MI Eastern .... Detroit
Nancy G. Edmunds .... MI Eastern .... Detroit
Denise Page Hood.......... MI Eastern .... Detroit
Paul D. Borman .... MI Eastern .... Detroit
Arthur J. Tarnow .... MI Eastern .... Detroit
George C. Steeh .... MI Eastern .... Detroit
Victoria S. Roberts .... MI Eastern .... Detroit
Marianne O. Battani .... MI Eastern .... Detroit
David M. Lawson .... MI Eastern .... Bay City
Sean F. Cox .... MI Eastern .... Detroit
Thomas Lamson Ludington MI Eastern .... Bay City
Robert Holmes Bell,
  Chief Judge .... MI
    Western .... Grand Rapids
James G. Carr,
  Chief Judge .... OH
    Northern .... Toledo
Solomon Oliver, Jr. .... OH
    Northern......... Cleveland
Kathleen M. O'Malley ...... OH
    Northern......... Cleveland
Donald C. Nugent .... OH
    Northern......... Cleveland
Peter C. Economus .... OH
    Northern....... Youngstown
Patricia A. Gaughan .... OH
    Northern......... Cleveland
James S. Gwin .... OH
    Northern......... Cleveland

Dan A. Polster .... OH
    Northern......... Cleveland
John R. Adams .... OH
    Northern........... Akron
Christopher A. Boyko ...... OH
    Northern......... Cleveland
Jack Zouhary .... OH
    Northern........... Toledo
Sara Lioi .... OH
    Northern........... Akron
Sandra S. Beckwith,
  Chief Judge .... OH
    Southern ..... Cincinnati
Susan J. Dlott .... OH
    Southern ....Cincinnati
Edmund A. Sargus, Jr. ..... OH
    Southern .... Columbus
Algenon L. Marbley .... OH
    Southern .... Columbus
Thomas M. Rose .... OH
    Southern ....Dayton
Gregory L. Frost .... OH
    Southern .... Columbus
Michael H. Watson .... OH
    Southern .... Columbus
Michael R. Barrett .... OH
    Southern ....Cincinnati
Curtis L. Collier,
  Chief Judge .... TN
    Eastern ..... Chattanooga
Thomas W. Phillips .... TN
    Eastern ....Knoxville
Thomas A. Varlan .... TN
    Eastern ....Knoxville
J. Ronnie Greer............ TN
    Eastern .... Greeneville
H. Sandy Mattice, Jr........ TN
    Eastern .... Chattanooga
Todd J. Campbell,
  Chief Judge .... TN
    Middle .... Nashville
Aleta A. Trauger .... TN Middle ...... Nashville
William J. Haynes .... TN Middle ..... Nashville
James D. Todd,
  Chief Judge .... TN
    Western .... Jackson
Jon P. McCalla .... TN
    Western .... Memphis
Bernice B. Donald........... TN
    Western .... Memphis
Samuel H. Mays, Jr........ TN
    Western .... Memphis
J. Daniel Breen .... TN
    Western .... Memphis

SENIOR DISTRICT JUDGES

William O. Bertelsman ..... KY
    Eastern .... Covington
G. Wix Unthank .... KY
    Eastern .... London
Henry R. Wilhoit, Jr. .... KY
    Eastern ....Ashland
Karl S. Forester .... KY
    Eastern .... Lexington
Edward H. Johnstone ...... KY
    Western........... Paducah
John Feikens .... MI Eastern ...... Detroit
Charles W. Joiner .... MI Eastern ... Ann Arbor
James P. Churchill .... MI Eastern ...... Bay City
Julian Abele Cook, Jr....... MI Eastern ....Detroit
Stewart A. Newblatt .... MI Eastern ..... Glen Arbor
Avern Cohn .... MI Eastern ....Detroit
Anna Diggs Taylor .... MI Eastern .... Detroit
Lawrence P. Zatkoff....... MI Eastern ....Port Huron
Patrick J. Duggan.......... MI Eastern ....Detroit
Paul V. Gadola .... MI Eastern ....Flint
John C. O'Meara........... MI Eastern ...... Ann Arbor
Wendell A. Miles........... MI
    Western.......Grand Rapids
Richard A. Enslen.......... MI
    Western......... Kalamazoo
Gordon J. Quist............ MI
    Western.......Grand Rapids
Ann Aldrich .... OH
    Northern......... Cleveland

David D. Dowd, Jr. . . . . .OH
Northern . . . . Akron
Sam H. Bell . . . . .OH
Northern . . . . Akron
Lesley Wells . . . . .OH
Northern . . . . Cleveland
David A. Katz . . . . .OH
Northern . . . . Toledo
S. Arthur Spiegel . . . . .OH
Southern . . . . Cincinnati
John D. Holschuh . . . . .OH
Southern . . . . Columbus
Walter Herbert Rice . . . . .OH
Southern . . . . .Dayton
Herman J. Weber . . . . .OH
Southern . . . . Cincinnati
James L. Graham . . . . .OH
Southern . . . . Columbus
George C. Smith . . . . .OH
Southern . . . . Columbus
Thomas Gray Hull . . . . .TN
Eastern . . . . Greeneville
James H. Jarvis. . . . . .TN
Eastern . . . . Knoxville
R. Allan Edgar. . . . . .TN
Eastern . . . . Chattanooga
Robert Leon Jordan . . . . .TN
Eastern . . . . Knoxville
Thomas A. Wiseman, Jr. . . . . .TN Middle . . . . .Nashville
John T. Nixon . . . . .TN Middle . . . . .Nashville
Robert L. Echols . . . . .TN Middle . . . . .Nashville

MAGISTRATE JUDGES

James Black Todd . . . . .KY
Eastern . . . . Lexington
J. Gregory Wehrman . . . . . . .KY
Eastern . . . . Covington
Edward B. Atkins . . . . .KY
Eastern . . . . Ashland
Robert E. Wier . . . . .KY
Eastern . . . . London
W. David King . . . . .KY
Western . . . . Paducah
James D. Moyer . . . . .KY
Western . . . . Louisville
E. Robert Goebel. . . . . .KY
Western . . . . Owensboro
Dave Whalin . . . . .KY
Western . . . . Louisville
Charles E. Binder . . . . .MI Eastern . . . . Bay City
Paul J. Komives . . . . .MI Eastern . . . . .Detroit
Steven D. Pepe . . . . .MI Eastern . . . . Ann Arbor
Virginia M. Morgan . . . . .MI Eastern . . . . .Detroit
Donald A. Scheer . . . . .MI Eastern . . . . .Detroit
R. Steven Whalen . . . . .MI Eastern . . . . .Detroit
Mona K. Majzoub . . . . .MI Eastern . . . . .Detroit
Hugh W. Brenneman, Jr. . . .MI
Western . . . . . . .Grand Rapids
Timothy P. Greeley . . . . .MI
Western . . . . .Marquette
Joseph G. Scoville . . . . .MI
Western . . . . . . .Grand Rapids
Ellen S. Carmody . . . . .MI
Western . . . . . . .Grand Rapids
James S. Gallas . . . . .OH
Northern . . . . Akron
Patricia A. Hemann . . . . .OH
Northern . . . . Cleveland
Vernelis K. Armstrong . . . . .OH
Northern . . . . Toledo
Nancy A. Vecchiarelli. . . . . . .OH
Northern . . . . Cleveland
George J. Limbert . . . . .OH
Northern . . . . . . .Youngstown
William H. Baughman, Jr. . .OH
Northern . . . . Cleveland
Kenneth S. McHargh . . . . . . .OH
Northern . . . . Cleveland
Mark R. Abel . . . . .OH
Southern . . . . Columbus
Norah McCann King . . . . . . .OH
Southern . . . . Columbus
Michael R. Merz . . . . .OH
Southern . . . . .Dayton

Terence P. Kemp . . . . .OH
Southern . . . . Columbus
Timothy S. Hogan . . . . .OH
Southern . . . . .Cincinnati
Sharon L. Ovington . . . . .OH
Southern . . . . .Dayton
Timothy S. Black . . . . .OH
Southern . . . . .Cincinnati
H. Bruce Guyton. . . . . .TN
Eastern . . . . Knoxville
Dennis H. Inman . . . . .TN
Eastern . . . . Greeneville
William B. Mitchell Carter . .TN
Eastern . . . . Chattanooga
C. Clifford Shirley, Jr. . . . . . .TN
Eastern . . . . Knoxville
Susan K. Lee . . . . .TN
Eastern . . . . Chattanooga
Juliet Griffin . . . . .TN Middle . . . . .Nashville
E. Clifton Knowles . . . . .TN Middle . . . . .Nashville
John S. Bryant . . . . .TN Middle . . . . .Nashville
Joe B. Brown . . . . .TN Middle . . . . .Nashville
Diane K. Vescovo . . . . .TN
Western . . . . Memphis
Tu M. Pham. . . . . .TN
Western . . . . Memphis
S. Thomas Anderson . . . . . . .TN
Western . . . . Jackson
James H. Allen . . . . .TN
Western . . . . Memphis

BANKRUPTCY JUDGES

Joseph M. Scott, Jr.,
  Chief Judge . . . .**KY**
                Eastern . . . .**Lexington**
Joe Lee . . . . .KY
Eastern . . . . Lexington
William S. Howard . . . . .KY
Eastern . . . . Lexington
Joan A. Lloyd,
  Chief Judge . . . .**KY**
                Western . . . .**Louisville**
David T. Stosberg . . . . .KY
Western . . . . Louisville
Thomas H. Fulton . . . . .KY
Western . . . . Louisville
Steven W. Rhodes,
  Chief Judge . . . .**MI**
                Eastern . . . .**Detroit**
Walter Shapero . . . . .MI Eastern . . . . .Detroit
Marci B. McIvor . . . . .MI Eastern . . . . .Detroit
Phillip J. Shefferly . . . . .MI Eastern . . . . .Detroit
Thomas J. Tucker . . . . .MI Eastern . . . . .Detroit
Daniel S. Opperman. . . . . . . .MI Eastern . . . Bay City/Flint
Jo Ann C. Stevenson,
  Chief Judge . . . .**MI**
                Western . . . . **Grand Rapids**
James D. Gregg. . . . . .MI
Western . . . . . . .Grand Rapids
Jeffrey R. Hughes . . . . .MI
Western . . . . . . .Grand Rapids
Randolph Baxter,
  Chief Judge . . . .**OH**
                Northern . . . . . .**Cleveland**
Richard L. Speer . . . . .OH
Northern . . . . Toledo
Marilyn Shea–Stonum . . . . .OH
Northern . . . . Akron
Pat E. Morgenstern–Clarren OH
Northern . . . . Cleveland
Russ Kendig. . . . . .OH
Northern . . . . Canton
Mary Ann Whipple . . . . .OH
Northern . . . . Toledo
Arthur I. Harris . . . . .OH
Northern . . . . Cleveland
Kay Woods . . . . .OH
Northern . . . . . . .Youngstown
J. Vincent Aug, Jr.,
  Chief Judge . . . .**OH**
                Southern . . . .**Dayton**
Thomas F. Waldron . . . . .OH
Southern . . . . .Dayton
Charles M. Caldwell . . . . .OH
Southern . . . . Columbus

Jeffrey P. Hopkins ....OH
Southern ....Columbus
John E. Hoffman, Jr. ....OH
Southern ....Cincinnati
Lawrence S. Walter ....OH
Southern ....Columbus
C. Kathryn Preston ....OH
Southern ....Columbus
Burton Perlman ....OH
Southern ....Cincinnati
Donald E. Calhoun ....OH
Southern ....Columbus

John C. Cook,
Chief Judge ....**TN**
Eastern ..... **Chattanooga**
Richard S. Stair, Jr. ....TN
Eastern ....Knoxville
Marcia Phillips Parsons ....TN
Eastern ....Greeneville
R. Thomas Stinnett ....TN
Eastern ....Chattanooga

George C. Paine, II,
Chief Judge ....**TN**
Middle .... **Nashville**
Keith M. Lundin ....TN
Middle ....Nashville
Marian F. Harrison ....TN
Middle ....Nashville

David S. Kennedy,
Chief Judge ....**TN**
Western .... **Memphis**
G. Harvey Boswell ....TN
Western ....Jackson
Jennie D. Latta ....TN
Western ....Memphis
Paulette J. Delk ....TN
Western ....Memphis
George W. Emerson, Jr. ....TN
Western ....Memphis

SEVENTH CIRCUIT

Districts of Northern, Central and Southern
Illinois; Northern and Southern Indiana; and
Eastern and Western Wisconsin
John Paul Stevens, Circuit Justice

CIRCUIT JUDGES

Frank H. Easterbrook,
Chief Judge ....**Chicago, IL**
Richard A. Posner ....Chicago, IL
Joel M. Flaum ....Chicago, IL
Kenneth F. Ripple.......................South Bend, IN
Daniel A. Manion ....South Bend, IN
Michael S. Kanne ....Lafayette, IN
Ilana Diamond Rovner ....Chicago, IL
Diane P. Wood ....Chicago, IL
Terence T. Evans ....Milwaukee, WI
Ann Claire Williams ....Chicago, IL
Diane S. Sykes ....Milwaukee, WI

SENIOR CIRCUIT JUDGES

William J. Bauer ....Chicago, IL
Richard D. Cudahy ....Chicago, IL
John L. Coffey ....Milwaukee, WI

DISTRICT JUDGES

James F. Holderman,
Chief Judge ....**IL**
Northern ....**Chicago**
Charles R. Norgle, Sr. IL
Northern..........Chicago
James B. Zagel IL
Northern..........Chicago
Wayne R. Andersen IL
Northern..........Chicago
Ruben Castillo IL
Northern..........Chicago
Blanche M. Manning IL
Northern..........Chicago
David H. Coar IL
Northern..........Chicago

Robert W. Gettleman IL
Northern..........Chicago
Elaine E. Bucklo IL
Northern..........Chicago
Joan B. Gottschall IL
Northern..........Chicago
Rebecca R. Pallmeyer IL
Northern..........Chicago
William H. Hibbler IL
Northern..........Chicago
Matthew F. Kennelly IL
Northern..........Chicago
Ronald A. Guzman IL
Northern..........Chicago
Joan Humphrey Lefkow IL
Northern..........Chicago
John W. Darrah IL
Northern..........Chicago
Amy J. St. Eve.............IL
Northern..........Chicago
Samuel Der–Yeghiayan IL
Northern..........Chicago
Mark R. Filip IL
Northern..........Chicago
Virginia Mary Kendall......IL
Northern..........Chicago

Michael P. McCuskey,
Chief Judge ....**IL**
Central .... **Urbana**
Michael M. Mihm ....IL Central ....Peoria
Joe Billy McDade ....IL Central ....Peoria
Jeanne E. Scott ....IL Central ......Springfield

G. Patrick Murphy,
Chief Judge ....**IL**
Southern .. **East St. Louis**
J. Phil Gilbert IL
Southern............Benton
David R. Herndon..........IL
Southern..... East St. Louis
Michael J. Reagan IL
Southern..... East St. Louis

Robert L. Miller, Jr.,
Chief Judge ....**IN**
Northern .... **South Bend**
Allen Sharp ....IN
Northern....... South Bend
Rudy Lozano ....IN
Northern.........Hammond
Philip P. Simon ....IN
Northern.........Hammond
Theresa L. Springmann ....IN
Northern....... Fort Wayne

Larry J. McKinney,
Chief Judge ....**IN**
Southern ... **Indianapolis**
Sarah Evans Barker........IN
Southern...... Indianapolis
John Daniel Tinder ....IN
Southern...... Indianapolis
David F. Hamilton ....IN
Southern...... Indianapolis
Richard L. Young ....IN
Southern...... Evansville

Rudolph T. Randa,
Chief Judge ....**WI**
Eastern .... **Milwaukee**
J. P. Stadtmueller..........WI Eastern...... Milwaukee
Charles N. Clevert, Jr......WI Eastern...... Milwaukee
Lynn S. Adelman ....WI Eastern...... Milwaukee
William C. Griesbach ....WI Eastern...... Green Bay

Barbara B. Crabb,
Chief Judge ....**WI**
Western .... **Madison**
John C. Shabaz ....WI
Western..........Madison

SENIOR DISTRICT JUDGES

John F. Grady IL
Northern..........Chicago
Marvin E. Aspen IL
Northern..........Chicago
James B. Moran IL
Northern..........Chicago
Milton I. Shadur IL
Northern..........Chicago

Charles P. Kocoras IL
    Northern . . . . Chicago
John A. Nordberg IL
    Northern . . . . Chicago
William T. Hart IL
    Northern . . . . Chicago
Paul E. Plunkett IL
    Northern . . . . Chicago
Harry D. Leinenweber IL
    Northern . . . . Chicago
Suzanne B. Conlon IL
    Northern . . . . Chicago
George M. Marovich IL
    Northern . . . . Chicago
George W. Lindberg IL
    Northern . . . . Chicago
Philip G. Reinhard IL
    Northern . . . . Rockford
Harold Albert Baker . . . . IL Central . . . . Urbana
Richard Mills . . . . IL Central . . . . . . Springfield
James L. Foreman IL
    Southern . . . . Benton
William D. Stiehl IL
    Southern . . . . . East St. Louis
William C. Lee . . . . IN
    Northern . . . . Fort Wayne
James T. Moody . . . . IN
    Northern . . . . Hammond
Thomas J. Curran . . . . WI
    Eastern . . . . Milwaukee

MAGISTRATE JUDGES

Morton Denlow IL
    Northern . . . . Chicago
P. Michael Mahoney IL
    Northern . . . . Rockford
Martin C. Ashman IL
    Northern . . . . Chicago
Arlander Keys IL
    Northern . . . . Chicago
Nan R. Nolan IL
    Northern . . . . Chicago
Sidney I. Schenkier IL
    Northern . . . . Chicago
Geraldine Soat Brown IL
    Northern . . . . Chicago
Michael T. Mason IL
    Northern . . . . Chicago
Jeffrey N. Cole IL
    Northern . . . . Chicago
Maria G. Valdez IL
    Northern . . . . Chicago
Charles H. Evans IL
    Central . . . . Springfield
David G. Bernthal IL
    Central . . . . Urbana
Byron G. Cudmore IL
    Central . . . . Springfield
John A. Gorman IL
    Central . . . . Peoria
Philip M. Frazier IL
    Southern . . . . Benton
Clifford J. Proud IL
    Southern . . . . . East St. Louis
Donald G. Wilkerson IL
    Southern . . . . . East St. Louis
Andrew P. Rodovich . . . . IN
    Northern . . . . Hammond
Roger B. Cosbey . . . . IN
    Northern . . . . Fort Wayne
Christopher A. Nuechterlein IN
    Northern . . . . South Bend
Paul R. Cherry . . . . IN
    Northern . . . . Hammond
William G. Hussmann, Jr. . . IN
    Southern . . . . Evansville
Tim A. Baker . . . . IN
    Southern . . . . Indianapolis
William T. Lawrence . . . . IN
    Southern . . . . Indianapolis
Jane Magnus–Stinson . . . . . . IN
    Southern . . . . Indianapolis
John Paul Godich . . . . IN
    Southern . . . . Indianapolis

Kennard P. Foster . . . . IN
    Southern . . . . Indianapolis
Aaron E. Goodstein . . . . WI Eastern . . . . . Milwaukee
Patricia J. Gorence . . . . WI Eastern . . . . . Milwaukee
William E. Callahan, Jr. . . . . WI Eastern . . . . . Milwaukee
Stephen L. Crocker . . . . WI
    Western . . . . Madison

BANKRUPTCY JUDGES

Eugene R. Wedoff,
  Chief Judge . . . . **IL**
    Northern . . . . **Chicago**
Jack B. Schmetterer IL
    Northern . . . . Chicago
Susan Pierson Sonderby IL
    Northern . . . . Chicago
John H. Squires IL
    Northern . . . . Chicago
Manuel Barbosa IL
    Northern . . . . Rockford
Carol A. Doyle IL
    Northern . . . . Chicago
John D. Schwartz IL
    Northern . . . . Chicago
Bruce W. Black IL
    Northern . . . . Chicago
Pamela S. Hollis IL
    Northern . . . . Chicago
A. Benjamin Goldgar IL
    Northern . . . . Chicago
Jacqueline P. Cox IL
    Northern . . . . Chicago
Thomas L. Perkins,
  Chief Judge . . . . **IL**
    Central . . . . **Peoria**
Gerald D. Fines . . . . IL Central . . . . Danville
Mary Patricia Gorman . . . . . IL Central . . . . . Springfield
William V. Altenberger . . . . . IL Central . . . . Peoria
Kenneth J. Meyers,
  Chief Judge . . . . **IL**
    Southern . . **East St. Louis**
Harry C. Dees, Jr.,
  Chief Judge . . . . **IN**
    Northern . . . . **South Bend**
Robert E. Grant . . . . IN
    Northern . . . . Fort Wayne
J. Philip Klingeberger . . . . . . IN
    Northern . . . . Hammond
Kent Lindquist . . . . IN
    Northern . . . . Hammond
Basil H. Lorch, III,
  Chief Judge . . . . **IN**
    Southern . . . . **New Albany**
Frank J. Otte . . . . IN
    Southern . . . . Indianapolis
Anthony Metz, III . . . . IN
    Southern . . . . Indianapolis
James K. Coachys . . . . IN
    Southern . . . . Indianapolis
Margaret Dee McGarity,
  Chief Judge . . . . **WI**
    Eastern . . . . **Milwaukee**
James E. Shapiro . . . . WI Eastern . . . . . Milwaukee
Susan V. Kelley . . . . WI Eastern . . . . . Milwaukee
Pamela Pepper . . . . WI Eastern . . . . . Milwaukee
Robert D. Martin,
  Chief Judge . . . . **WI**
    Western . . . . **Madison**
Thomas S. Utschig . . . . WI
    Western . . . . Eau Claire

EIGHTH CIRCUIT

**Districts of Eastern and Western Arkansas;
Northern and Southern Iowa; Minnesota; Eastern
and Western Missouri; Nebraska; North
Dakota and South Dakota**
Samuel A. Alito, Jr., Circuit Justice

CIRCUIT JUDGES

James B. Loken, Chief Judge . . . . . . **Minneapolis, MN**
Roger L. Wollman . . . . Sioux Falls, SD
Diana E. Murphy . . . . Minneapolis, MN
Kermit Bye . . . . Fargo, ND

William Jay Riley .... Omaha, NE
Michael J. Melloy .... Cedar Rapids, IA
Lavenski R. Smith .... Little Rock, AR
Steven M. Colloton .... Des Moines, IA
Raymond W. Gruender .... St. Louis, MO
Duane Benton .... Kansas City, MO
Bobby E. Shepherd .... El Dorado, AR

SENIOR CIRCUIT JUDGES

Myron H. Bright .... Fargo, ND
John R. Gibson .... Kansas City, MO
Pasco M. Bowman .... Kansas City, MO
Frank J. Magill .... Fargo, ND
C. Arlen Beam .... Lincoln, NE
David R. Hansen .... Cedar Rapids, IA
Morris S. Arnold .... Little Rock, AR

DISTRICT JUDGES

J. Leon Holmes,
    Chief Judge ....**AR**
                    Eastern ...... **Little Rock**
Susan Webber Wright ......AR Eastern..... Little Rock
William R. Wilson, Jr. ......AR Eastern..... Little Rock
James M. Moody ....AR Eastern..... Little Rock
Jimm Larry Hendren,
    Chief Judge ....**AR**
                    Western ...... **Fayetteville**
Harry F. Barnes ....AR
                    Western.......... El Dorado
Robert T. Dawson..........AR
                    Western......... Fort Smith
Linda R. Reade,
    Chief Judge ....**IA**
                    Northern .. **Cedar Rapids**
Mark W. Bennett ....IA
                    Northern......... Sioux City
Robert W. Pratt,
    Chief Judge ....**IA**
                    Southern .... **Des Moines**
James E. Gritzner ....IA
                    Southern .... Des Moines
John A. Jarvey ....IA
                    Northern......... Davenport
James M. Rosenbaum,
    Chief Judge ....**MN**.......... **Minneapolis**
Michael J. Davis ....MN.......... Minneapolis
John R. Tunheim ....MN.......... Minneapolis
Ann D. Montgomery ....MN.......... Minneapolis
Donovan W. Frank.........MN............ St. Paul
Joan N. Ericksen ....MN.......... Minneapolis
Patrick J. Schiltz ....MN............ St. Paul
Carol E. Jackson,
    Chief Judge ....**MO**
                    Eastern .... **St. Louis**
Jean C. Hamilton ....MO
                    Eastern .... St. Louis
Charles A. Shaw ....MO
                    Eastern .... St. Louis
Catherine D. Perry.........MO
                    Eastern .... St. Louis
E. Richard Webber ....MO
                    Eastern .... St. Louis
Rodney W. Sippel ....MO
                    Eastern .... St. Louis
Henry Edward Autrey ......MO
                    Eastern .... St. Louis
Fernando J. Gaitan, Jr.,
    Chief Judge ....**MO**
                    Western ...... **Kansas City**
Ortrie D. Smith............MO
                    Western....... Kansas City
Gary A. Fenner ....MO
                    Western....... Kansas City
Nanette K. Laughrey ....MO
                    Western....... Kansas City
Richard E. Dorr ....MO
                    Western......... Springfield
Joseph F. Bataillon,
    Chief Judge ....**NE** .... **Omaha**
Richard G. Kopf ....NE .... Lincoln
Laurie Smith Camp ....NE .... Omaha
Daniel Hovland,
    Chief Judge ....**ND** .... **Bismarck**
Ralph R. Erickson..........ND .... Fargo

Karen Schreier,
    Chief Judge ....**SD** .... **Rapid City**
Lawrence L. Piersol ....SD .... Sioux Falls
Charles B. Kornmann ......SD .... Aberdeen

SENIOR DISTRICT JUDGES

Garnett Thomas Eisele .....AR Eastern...... Little Rock
Edward J. McManus ....IA
                    Northern...... Cedar Rapids
Donald E. O'Brien ....IA
                    Northern......... Sioux City
Harold D. Vietor ....IA
                    Southern........ Des Moines
Charles R. Wolle ....IA
                    Southern........ Des Moines
Ronald E. Longstaff ....IA
                    Southern........ Des Moines
Donald D. Alsop ....MN .... St. Paul
Paul A. Magnuson ....MN .... St. Paul
David S. Doty.............MN .... Minneapolis
Richard H. Kyle ....MN .... St. Paul
John F. Nangle ....MO
                    Eastern .... Savannah
Edward L. Filippine ....MO
                    Eastern .... St. Louis
Stephen N. Limbaugh ......MO
                    Eastern .... St. Louis
Donald J. Stohr ....MO
                    Eastern .... St. Louis
Scott O. Wright ....MO
                    Western........ Kansas City
Howard F. Sachs...........MO
                    Western........ Kansas City
Dean Whipple ....MO
                    Western........ Kansas City
Warren K. Urbom...........NE .... Lincoln
Lyle E. Strom ....NE ....Omaha
Patrick A. Conmy ....ND ....Bismarck
Rodney S. Webb ....ND .... Fargo
Andrew W. Bogue ....SD .... Rapid City
John B. Jones ....SD .... Sioux Falls
Richard H. Battey.........SD .... Rapid City

MAGISTRATE JUDGES

Henry L. Jones, Jr..........AR Eastern...... Little Rock
H. David Young...........AR Eastern...... Little Rock
John F. Forster, Jr. ....AR Eastern...... Little Rock
Jerry W. Cavaneau.........AR Eastern...... Little Rock
J. Thomas Ray.............AR Eastern...... Little Rock
Beth M. Deere ....AR Eastern...... Little Rock
James R. Marschewski .....AR
                    Western......... Fort Smith
Barry A. Bryant ....AR
                    Western......... Texarkana
Paul A. Zoss ....IA
                    Northern......... Sioux City
Jon S. Scoles ....IA
                    Northern...... Cedar Rapids
Celeste F. Bremer..........IA
                    Southern........ Des Moines
Ross A. Walters............IA
                    Southern........ Des Moines
Thomas J. Shields ....IA .... Davenport
Raymond L. Erickson ......MN .... Duluth
Franklin L. Noel ....MN .... Minneapolis
Arthur J. Boylan..........MN .... St. Paul
Susan R. Nelson ....MN .... Minneapolis
Janie S. Mayeron ....MN .... St. Paul
Jeanne J. Graham ....MN .... St. Paul
David D. Noce ....MO
                    Eastern .... St. Louis
Frederick R. Buckles ....MO
                    Eastern .... St. Louis
Lewis M. Blanton ....MO
                    Eastern ..... Cape Girardeau
Terry I. Adelman ....MO
                    Eastern .... St. Louis
Mary Ann Medler ....MO
                    Eastern .... St. Louis
Thomas C. Mummert, III ...MO
                    Eastern .... St. Louis
Audrey G. Flessig ....MO
                    Eastern .... St. Louis

James C. England	MO	
	Western	Springfield
Sarah Hays	MO	
	Western	Kansas City
William A. Knox	MO	
	Western	Jefferson City
John T. Maughmer	MO	
	Western	Kansas City
Robert E. Larsen	MO	
	Western	Kansas City
David L. Piester	NE	Lincoln
Thomas D. Thalken	NE	Omaha
F. A. Gossett, III	NE	Omaha
Karen K. Klein	ND	Fargo
Charles S. Miller, Jr.	ND	Bismarck
Marshall P. Young	SD	Rapid City
John E. Simko	SD	Sioux Falls

BANKRUPTCY JUDGES

Audrey R. Evans,
  Chief Judge .... **AR**
  Eastern/
  Western ...... **Little Rock**
Richard Taylor .... AR
  Eastern/
  Western .... Little Rock
James G. Mixon .... AR
  Eastern/
  Western .... Little Rock
William L. Edmonds,
  Chief Judge .... **IA**
  Northern ..... **Sioux City**
Paul J. Kilburg .... IA
  Northern ...... Cedar Rapids
Lee M. Jackwig,
  Chief Judge .... **IA**
  Southern .... **Des Moines**
Gregory F. Kishel,
  Chief Judge .... **MN** .... **Minneapolis**
Robert J. Kressel .... MN .... Minneapolis
Dennis D. O'Brien .... MN .... Minneapolis
Nancy C. Dreher .... MN .... Minneapolis
Barry S. Schermer,
  Chief Judge .... **MO**
  Eastern .... **St. Louis**
David P. McDonald .... MO
  Eastern .... St. Louis
Kathy A. Surratt–States .... MO
  Eastern .... St. Louis
Charles E. Rendlen, III ..... MO
  Eastern .... St. Louis
Jerry Venters,
  Chief Judge .... **MO**
  Western ..... **Kansas City**
Arthur B. Federman .... MO
  Western .... Kansas City
Dennis R. Dow .... MO
  Western .... Kansas City
Timothy J. Mahoney,
  Chief Judge .... **NE** .... **Omaha**
Thomas L. Saladino .... NE .... Lincoln
William A. Hill .... ND .... Fargo
Charles L. Nail, Jr. .... SD .... Pierre

NINTH CIRCUIT

Districts of Alaska; Arizona; Northern, Eastern,
Central and Southern California; Hawaii; Idaho;
Montana; Nevada; Oregon; Eastern and Western
Washington; Guam and Northern Mariana Islands
Anthony M. Kennedy, Circuit Justice

CIRCUIT JUDGES

Mary M. Schroeder,
  Chief Judge .... **Phoenix, AZ**
Harry Pregerson .... Woodland Hills, CA
Stephen Reinhardt .... Los Angeles, CA
Alex Kozinski .... Pasadena, CA
Diarmuid F. O'Scannlain .... Portland, OR
Pamela Ann Rymer .... Pasadena, CA
Andrew J. Kleinfeld .... Fairbanks, AK
Michael Daly Hawkins .... Phoenix, AZ
Sidney R. Thomas .... Billings, MT
Barry G. Silverman .... Phoenix, AZ

Susan P. Graber	Portland, OR
M. Margaret McKeown	San Diego, CA
Kim McLane Wardlaw	Los Angeles, CA
William A. Fletcher	San Francisco, CA
Raymond C. Fisher	Pasadena, CA
Ronald M. Gould	Seattle, WA
Richard A. Paez	Los Angeles, CA
Marsha S. Berzon	San Francisco, CA
Richard C. Tallman	Seattle, WA
Johnnie B. Rawlinson	Las Vegas, NV
Richard R. Clifton	Honolulu, HI
Jay S. Bybee	Las Vegas, NV
Consuelo M. Callahan	Sacramento, CA
Carlos T. Bea	San Francisco, CA
Milan D. Smith, Jr.	Pasadena, CA
Sandra Segal Ikuta	Pasadena, CA
Norman Randy Smith	Boise, ID

SENIOR CIRCUIT JUDGES

James R. Browning	San Francisco, CA
Alfred T. Goodwin	Pasadena, CA
J. Clifford Wallace	San Diego, CA
Joseph T. Sneed	San Francisco, CA
Proctor Hug, Jr.	Reno, NV
Otto R. Skopil, Jr.	Portland, OR
Betty B. Fletcher	Seattle, WA
Jerome Farris	Seattle, WA
Arthur L. Alarcon	Los Angeles, CA
Warren J. Ferguson	Santa Ana, CA
Dorothy W. Nelson	Pasadena, CA
William C. Canby, Jr.	Phoenix, AZ
Robert Boochever	Pasadena, CA
Robert R. Beezer	Seattle, WA
Cynthia Holcomb Hall	Pasadena, CA
Melvin Brunetti	Reno, NV
John T. Noonan, Jr.	San Francisco, CA
David R. Thompson	San Diego, CA
Edward Leavy	Portland, OR
Stephen S. Trott	Boise, ID
Ferdinand F. Fernandez	Pasadena, CA
Thomas G. Nelson	Boise, ID
A. Wallace Tashima	Pasadena, CA

DISTRICT JUDGES

John W. Sedwick,
  Chief Judge .... **AK** .... **Anchorage**
Ralph R. Beistline .... AK .... Anchorage
Timothy Mark Burgess ..... AK .... Anchorage
John M. Roll,
  Chief Judge .... **AZ** .... **Tucson**
Stephen M. McNamee ...... AZ .... Phoenix
Roselyn O. Silver .... AZ .... Phoenix
Frank R. Zapata .... AZ .... Tucson
Raner C. Collins .... AZ .... Tucson
James A. Teilborg .... AZ .... Phoenix
Susan R. Bolton .... AZ .... Phoenix
Mary H. Murguia .... AZ .... Phoenix
Frederick J. Martone ...... AZ .... Phoenix
Cindy K. Jorgenson .... AZ .... Tucson
David C. Bury .... AZ .... Tucson
David G. Campbell .... AZ .... Phoenix
Neil Vincent Wake .... AZ .... Phoenix
Vaughn R. Walker,
  Chief Judge .... **CA**
  Northern .... **San**
  Francisco
Marilyn H. Patel .... CA
  Northern ..... San Francisco
James Ware .... CA
  Northern .... San Jose
Saundra Brown Armstrong CA
  Northern .... Oakland
Ronald M. Whyte .... CA
  Northern .... San Jose
Claudia Wilken .... CA
  Northern .... Oakland
Maxine M. Chesney .... CA
  Northern ..... San Francisco
Susan Y. Illston .... CA
  Northern ..... San Francisco
Martin J. Jenkins .... CA
  Northern ..... San Francisco
Charles R. Breyer .... CA
  Northern ..... San Francisco

Jeremy D. Fogel	CA	
	Northern	San Jose
William H. Alsup	CA	
	Northern	San Francisco
Phyllis J. Hamilton	CA	
	Northern	San Francisco
Jeffrey S. White	CA	
	Northern	San Francisco
David F. Levi,		
Chief Judge	**CA**	
	Eastern	**Sacramento**
Garland E. Burrell, Jr.	CA Eastern	Sacramento
Anthony W. Ishii	CA Eastern	Fresno
Frank C. Damrell, Jr.	CA Eastern	Sacramento
Lawrence J. O'Neill	CA Eastern	Fresno
Morrison C. England, Jr.	CA Eastern	Sacramento
Alicemarie H. Stotler,		
Chief Judge	**CA**	
	Central	**Santa Ana**
Manuel L. Real	CA Central	Los Angeles
Stephen V. Wilson	CA Central	Los Angeles
Audrey B. Collins	CA Central	Los Angeles
George H. King	CA Central	Los Angeles
Dean D. Pregerson	CA Central	Los Angeles
Christina A. Snyder	CA Central	Los Angeles
Margaret M. Morrow	CA Central	Los Angeles
A. Howard Matz	CA Central	Los Angeles
David O. Carter	CA Central	Santa Ana
Gary Feess	CA Central	Los Angeles
Florence–Marie Cooper	CA Central	Los Angeles
Virginia Anne Phillips	CA Central	Riverside
John F. Walter	CA Central	Los Angeles
Percy Anderson	CA Central	Los Angeles
R. Gary Klausner	CA Central	Los Angeles
S. James Otero	CA Central	Los Angeles
James V. Selna	CA Central	Los Angeles
Cormac J. Carney	CA Central	Santa Ana
Dale S. Fischer	CA Central	Los Angeles
George F. Schiavelli	CA Central	Los Angeles
Stephen G. Larson	CA Central	Riverside
Andrew J. Guilford	CA Central	Santa Ana
Valerie Baker Fairbank	CA Central	Los Angeles
Philip S. Gutierrez	CA Central	Los Angeles
Otis D. Wright, II	CA Central	Los Angeles
George H. Wu	CA Central	Los Angeles
Irma E. Gonzalez,		
Chief Judge	**CA**	
	Southern	**San Diego**
Marilyn L. Huff	CA	
	Southern	San Diego
Napoleon A. Jones, Jr.	CA	
	Southern	San Diego
Barry Ted Moskowitz	CA	
	Southern	San Diego
Jeffrey T. Miller	CA	
	Southern	San Diego
Thomas J. Whelan	CA	
	Southern	San Diego
M. James Lorenz	CA	
	Southern	San Diego
Larry Alan Burns	CA	
	Southern	San Diego
Dana M. Sabraw	CA	
	Southern	San Diego
William Q. Hayes	CA	
	Southern	San Diego
John A. Houston	CA	
	Southern	San Diego
Roger T. Benitez	CA	
	Southern	El Centro
Vacant, Chief Judge	**Guam**	**Hagatna**
Helen Gillmor,		
Chief Judge	**HI**	**Honolulu**
David Alan Ezra	HI	Honolulu
Susan Oki Mollway	HI	Honolulu
J. Michael Seabright	HI	Honolulu
B. Lynn Winmill,		
Chief Judge	**ID**	**Boise**
Edward J. Lodge	ID	Boise
Donald W. Molloy,		
Chief Judge	**MT**	**Missoula**
Richard F. Cebull	MT	Billings
Sam E. Haddon	MT	Great Falls
Roger L. Hunt,		
Chief Judge	**NV**	**Las Vegas**

Philip M. Pro,		
Chief Judge	NV	Las Vegas
Kent J. Dawson	NV	Las Vegas
Larry R. Hicks	NV	Reno
James C. Mahan	NV	Las Vegas
Robert Clive Jones	NV	Las Vegas
Brian E. Sandoval	NV	Reno
Alex R. Munson,		
Chief Judge	**NMI**	**Saipan**
Ancer L. Haggerty,		
Chief Judge	**OR**	**Portland**
Michael R. Hogan	OR	Eugene
Ann Aiken	OR	Eugene
Garr M. King	OR	Portland
Anna J. Brown	OR	Portland
Michael W. Mosman	OR	Portland
Robert H. Whaley,		
Chief Judge	**WA**	
	Eastern	**Spokane**
Fred L. Van Sickle	WA	
	Eastern	Spokane
Edward F. Shea	WA	
	Eastern	Richland
Lonny R. Suko	WA	
	Eastern	Yakima
Robert S. Lasnik,		
Chief Judge	**WA**	
	Western	**Seattle**
Marsha J. Pechman	WA	
	Western	Seattle
Ronald B. Leighton	WA	
	Western	Tacoma
Ricardo S. Martinez	WA	
	Western	Seattle
James L. Robart	WA	
	Western	Seattle

SENIOR DISTRICT JUDGES

James A. von der Heydt	AK	Anchorage
James M. Fitzgerald	AK	Anchorage
H. Russel Holland	AK	Anchorage
James K. Singleton, Jr.	AK	Anchorage
Charles L. Hardy	AZ	Phoenix
Earl H. Carroll	AZ	Phoenix
Alfredo C. Marquez	AZ	Tucson
William D. Browning	AZ	Tucson
Paul G. Rosenblatt	AZ	Phoenix
Roger G. Strand	AZ	Phoenix
Robert C. Broomfield	AZ	Phoenix
Samuel Conti	CA	
	Northern	San Francisco
William W Schwarzer	CA	
	Northern	San Francisco
Thelton E. Henderson	CA	
	Northern	San Francisco
D. Lowell Jensen	CA	
	Northern	Oakland
Lawrence K. Karlton	CA Eastern	Sacramento
Robert E. Coyle	CA Eastern	Fresno
Edward J. Garcia	CA Eastern	Sacramento
William B. Shubb	CA Eastern	Sacramento
Oliver W. Wanger	CA Eastern	Fresno
Robert J. Kelleher	CA Central	Los Angeles
Robert M. Takasugi	CA Central	Los Angeles
Marianna R. Pfaelzer	CA Central	Los Angeles
Terry J. Hatter, Jr.	CA Central	Los Angeles
Consuelo Bland Marshall	CA Central	Los Angeles
Edward Rafeedie	CA Central	Los Angeles
William Duffy Keller	CA Central	Los Angeles
J. Spencer Letts	CA Central	Los Angeles
Ronald S. W. Lew	CA Central	Los Angeles
Robert J. Timlin	CA Central	Los Angeles
Howard B. Turrentine	CA	
	Southern	San Diego
Gordon Thompson, Jr.	CA	
	Southern	San Diego
William B. Enright	CA	
	Southern	San Diego
Rudi M. Brewster	CA	
	Southern	San Diego
John S. Rhoades	CA	
	Southern	San Diego
Samuel P. King	HI	Honolulu
Alan Cooke Kay	HI	Honolulu
Charles C. Lovell	MT	Helena

Jack D. Shanstrom	MT	Billings
Edward C. Reed, Jr.	NV	Reno
Lloyd D. George	NV	Las Vegas
Howard D. McKibben	NV	Reno
James A. Redden	OR	Portland
Owen M. Panner	OR	Medford
Malcolm F. Marsh	OR	Portland
Robert E. Jones	OR	Portland
Justin L. Quackenbush	WA Eastern	Spokane
Alan A. McDonald	WA Eastern	Yakima
Wm. Fremming Nielsen	WA Eastern	Spokane
Walter T. McGovern	WA Western	Seattle
John C. Coughenour	WA Western	Seattle
Carolyn R. Dimmick	WA Western	Seattle
Robert J. Bryan	WA Western	Tacoma
Thomas S. Zilly	WA Western	Seattle
Franklin D. Burgess	WA Western	Tacoma

MAGISTRATE JUDGES

John D. Roberts	AK	Anchorage
Deborah M. Smith	AK	Anchorage
Glenda E. Edmonds	AZ	Tucson
Lawrence O. Anderson	AZ	Phoenix
Jay R. Irwin	AZ	Yuma
Bernardo P. Velasco	AZ	Tucson
David K. Duncan	AZ	Phoenix
Charles R. Pyle	AZ	Tucson
Jacqueline Marshall	AZ	Tucson
Edward C. Voss, III	AZ	Phoenix
Mark E. Aspey	AZ	Flagstaff
Jennifer C. Guerin	AZ	Tucson
Hector C. Estrada	AZ	Tucson
Michelle H. Burns	AZ	Phoenix
Morton Sitver	AZ	Phoenix
James L. Larson	CA Northern	San Francisco
Wayne D. Brazil	CA Northern	Oakland
Patricia V. Trumbull	CA Northern	San Jose
Maria–Elena James	CA Northern	San Francisco
Bernard Zimmerman	CA Northern	San Francisco
Elizabeth D. Laporte	CA Northern	San Francisco
Joseph C. Spero	CA Northern	San Francisco
Richard G. Seeborg	CA Northern	San Jose
Edward M. Chen	CA Northern	San Francisco
Howard R. Lloyd	CA Northern	San Jose
John F. Moulds	CA Eastern	Sacramento
Gregory G. Hollows	CA Eastern	Sacramento
Dennis L. Beck	CA Eastern	Fresno
Sandra Snyder	CA Eastern	Fresno
Dale A. Drozd	CA Eastern	Sacramento
Kimberly J. Mueller	CA Eastern	Sacramento
Theresa A. Goldner	CA Eastern	Bakersfield
William Wunderlich	CA Eastern	Yosemite National Park
Craig M. Kellison	CA Eastern	Redding
Edmund F. Brennan	CA Eastern	Sacramento
Ralph Zarefsky	CA Central	Los Angeles
Charles F. Eick	CA Central	Los Angeles
Carolyn Turchin	CA Central	Los Angeles
Stephen J. Hillman	CA Central	Los Angeles
Andrew J. Wistrich	CA Central	Los Angeles
Robert N. Block	CA Central	Santa Ana
Rosalyn M. Chapman	CA Central	Los Angeles
Carla M. Woehrle	CA Central	Los Angeles
Arthur Nakazato	CA Central	Santa Ana
Margaret A. Nagle	CA Central	Los Angeles
Jeffrey W. Johnson	CA Central	Los Angeles

Marc L. Goldman	CA Central	Santa Ana
Victor B. Kenton	CA Central	Los Angeles
Patrick J. Walsh	CA Central	Los Angeles
Jennifer T. Lum	CA Central	Los Angeles
Fernando M. Olguin	CA Central	Los Angeles
Paul L. Abrams	CA Central	Los Angeles
Suzanne H. Segal	CA Central	Los Angeles
Jacqueline Chooljian	CA Central	Los Angeles
Oswald Parada	CA Central	Riverside
Frederick M. Mumm	CA Central	Los Angeles
John C. Rayburn, Jr.	CA Central	Riverside
Alicia G. Rosenberg	CA Central	Los Angeles
Ruben Brooks	CA Southern	San Diego
Louisa S Porter	CA Southern	San Diego
Leo S. Papas	CA Southern	San Diego
Anthony J. Battaglia	CA Southern	San Diego
Nita L. Stormes	CA Southern	San Diego
Jan M. Adler	CA Southern	San Diego
Barbara L. Major	CA Southern	San Diego
William McCurine, Jr.	CA Southern	San Diego
Peter C. Lewis	CA Southern	El Centro
Cathy Ann Bencivengo	CA Southern	San Diego
Joaquin V. E. Manibusan, Jr.	Guam	Hagatna
Barry M. Kurren	HI	Honolulu
Leslie E. Kobayaski	HI	Honolulu
Kevin S. C. Chang	HI	Honolulu
Mikel H. Williams	ID	Boise
Larry M. Boyle	ID	Boise
Richard W. Anderson	MT	Billings
Carolyn S. Ostby	MT	Billings
Jeremiah C. Lynch	MT	Missoula
Keith Strong	MT	Great Falls
Robert J. Johnston	NV	Las Vegas
Lawrence R. Leavitt	NV	Las Vegas
Robert A. McQuaid, Jr.	NV	Reno
Valerie P. Cooke	NV	Reno
Peggy A. Leen	NV	Las Vegas
George W. Foley, Jr.	NV	Las Vegas
Thomas M. Coffin	OR	Eugene
Donald C. Ashmanskas	OR	Portland
Janice M. Stewart	OR	Portland
Dennis J. Hubel	OR	Portland
Paul J. Papak	OR	Portland
Mark D. Clarke	OR	Medford
Cynthia Imbrogno	WA Eastern	Spokane
Michael W. Leavitt	WA Eastern	Yakima
J. Kelley Arnold	WA Western	Tacoma
Monica J. Benton	WA Western	Seattle
Karen L. Strombom	WA Western	Tacoma
Mary Alice Theiler	WA Western	Seattle
James P. Donohue	WA Western	Seattle

BANKRUPTCY JUDGES

Donald MacDonald, IV, Chief Judge	AK	Anchorage
Herbert A. Ross, Recalled	AK	Anchorage
Redfield T. Baum, Sr., Chief Judge	AZ	Phoenix
George B. Nielsen, Jr.	AZ	Phoenix
Sarah Sharer Curley	AZ	Phoenix
James M. Marlar	AZ	Tucson
Charles G. Case II	AZ	Phoenix
Randolph J. Haines	AZ	Phoenix
Eileen W. Hollowell	AZ	Tucson
Randall J. Newsome, Chief Judge	CA Northern	Oakland

Edward D. Jellen .... CA
    Northern .... Oakland
Arthur S. Weissbrodt .... CA
    Northern ..... San Jose
Thomas E. Carlson .... CA
    Northern ..... San Francisco
Alan Jaroslovsky .... CA
    Northern .... Santa Rose
Leslie Tchaikovsky .... CA
    Northern .... Oakland
Marilyn Morgan .... CA
    Northern ..... San Jose
Dennis Montali .... CA
    Northern ..... San Francisco
Roger L. Efremsky .... CA
    Northern ..... San Jose
Michael S. McManus,
  Chief Judge .... **CA**
    Eastern ..... **Sacramento/**
        Modesto
Christopher M. Klein .... CA Eastern ..... Sacramento
Whitney Rimel .... CA Eastern .... Fresno
Thomas C. Holman .... CA Eastern ..... Sacramento
W. Richard Lee .... CA Eastern .... Fresno
Robert S. Bardwil .... CA Eastern ..... Sacramento/
        Modesto
Richard T. Ford .... CA Eastern ..... Fresno
David E. Russell .... CA Eastern ..... Sacramento
Brett Dorian .... CA Eastern ..... Fresno
Vincent P. Zurzolo,
  Chief Judge .... **CA**
    Central ..... **Los Angeles**
Barry Russell .... CA Central .... Los Angeles
David N. Naugle .... CA Central .... Riverside
Geraldine Mund .... CA Central .. Woodland Hills
Samuel L. Bufford .... CA Central ... Los Angeles
Robin L. Riblet .... CA Central ... Santa Barbara
Alan M. Ahart .... CA Central ... Los Angeles
Kathleen Thompson .... CA Central .. Woodland Hills
Mitchel R. Goldberg .... CA Central .... Riverside
Ernest M. Robles .... CA Central ... Los Angeles
Thomas B. Donovan .... CA Central ... Los Angeles
Erithe A. Smith .... CA Central ..... Santa Ana
Meredith A. Jury .... CA Central .... Riverside
Ellen Carroll .... CA Central ... Los Angeles
Sheri Bluebond .... CA Central ... Los Angeles
Peter H. Carroll .... CA Central .... Riverside
Maureen A. Tighe .... CA Central .. Woodland Hills
Theodor C. Albert .... CA Central ..... Santa Ana
Richard M. Neiter .... CA Central ... Los Angeles
Victoria S. Kaufman ...... CA Central ... Los Angeles
Robert N. Kwan .... CA Central ..... Santa Ana
Peter W. Bowie,
  Chief Judge .... **CA**
    Southern ...... **San Diego**
James W. Meyers .... CA
    Southern .... San Diego
Louise DeCarl Adler .... CA
    Southern .... San Diego
John J. Hargrove .... CA
    Southern .... San Diego
Robert J. Faris,
  Chief Judge .... **HI** .... **Honolulu**
Lloyd King .... HI .... Honolulu
Terry Myers,
  Chief Judge .... **ID** .... **Boise**
Jim D. Pappas .... ID .... Boise
Ralph Kirscher,
  Chief Judge .... **MT** .... **Butte**
John L. Peterson .... MT .... Butte
Gregg W. Zive, Chief
  Judge .... **NV** .... **Reno**
Linda B. Riegle .... NV .... Las Vegas
Bruce Markell .... NV .... Las Vegas
Mike K. Nakagawa .... NV .... Las Vegas
Elizabeth L. Perris,
  Chief Judge .... **OR** .... **Portland**
Albert E. Radcliffe .... OR .... Eugene
Frank R. Alley, III .... OR .... Eugene
Randall L. Dunn .... OR .... Portland
Patricia M. Brown .... OR .... Portland
Frank Kurtz,
  Chief Judge .... **WA**
    Eastern .... **Yakima**
Patricia C. Williams .... WA
    Eastern .... Spokane

John A. Rossmeissl .... WA
    Eastern .... Yakima
Karen A. Overstreet,
  Chief Judge .... **WA**
    Western .... **Seattle**
Samuel J. Steiner .... WA
    Western .... Seattle
Thomas T. Glover .... WA
    Western .... Seattle
Philip H. Brandt .... WA
    Western ..... Tacoma/Seattle
Paul B. Snyder .... WA
    Western .... Tacoma

TENTH CIRCUIT
Districts of Colorado; Kansas; New Mexico;
Northern, Eastern and Western Oklahoma;
Utah and Wyoming
Stephen G. Breyer, Circuit Justice

CIRCUIT JUDGES

Deanell Reece Tacha,
  Chief Judge .... **Lawrence, KS**
Paul J. Kelly, Jr. .... Santa Fe, NM
Robert H. Henry .... Oklahoma City, OK
Mary Beck Briscoe .... Lawrence, KS
Carlos F. Lucero .... Denver, CO
Michael R. Murphy .... Salt Lake City, UT
Harris L. Hartz .... Albuquerque, NM
Terrence L. O'Brien .... Cheyenne, WY
Michael W. McConnell .... Salt Lake City, UT
Timothy M. Tymkovich .... Denver, CO
Neil M. Gorsuch .... Denver, CO
Jerome A. Holmes .... Oklahoma City, OK

SENIOR CIRCUIT JUDGES

William J. Holloway, Jr. .... Oklahoma City, OK
Robert H. McWilliams .... Denver, CO
Monroe G. McKay .... Salt Lake City, UT
Stephanie K. Seymour .... Tulsa, OK
John C. Porfilio .... Denver, CO
Stephen H. Anderson .... Salt Lake City, UT
Bobby R. Baldock .... Roswell, NM
Wade Brorby .... Cheyenne, WY
David M. Ebel .... Denver, CO

DISTRICT JUDGES

Lewis T. Babcock,
  Chief Judge .... **CO** .... **Denver**
Edward W. Nottingham .... CO .... Denver
Wiley Y. Daniel .... CO .... Denver
Walker D. Miller .... CO .... Denver
Marcia S. Krieger .... CO .... Denver
Robert E. Blackburn .... CO .... Denver
Philip S. Figa .... CO .... Denver
John W. Lungstrum,
  Chief Judge .... **KS** .... **Kansas City**
Monti L. Belot .... KS .... Wichita
Kathryn H. Vratil .... KS .... Kansas City
John Thomas Marten ...... KS .... Wichita
Carlos Murguia .... KS .... Kansas City
Julie A. Robinson .... KS .... Topeka
Martha Vázquez,
  Chief Judge .... **NM** .... **Santa Fe**
Bruce D. Black .... NM .... Santa Fe
M. Christina Armijo .... NM .... Albuquerque
William P. Johnson .... NM .... Albuquerque
Robert C. Brack .... NM .... Las Cruces
James O. Browning .... NM .... Albuquerque
Judith C. Herrera .... NM .... Albuquerque
Claire V. Eagan,
  Chief Judge .... **OK**
    Northern .... **Tulsa**
Terence C. Kern .... OK
    Northern .... Tulsa
Gregory Kent Frizzell ...... OK
    Northern .... Tulsa
James H. Payne,
  Chief Judge .... **OK**
    Eastern .... **Muskogee**
Ronald A. White .... OK
    Eastern .... Muskogee

Robin J. Cauthron,
   Chief Judge . . . . OK
                   Western . . Oklahoma City
David L. Russell . . . . OK
                   Western . . . . . Oklahoma City
Vicki Miles–LaGrange . . . . . . OK
                   Western . . . . . Oklahoma City
Stephen P. Friot . . . . OK
                   Western . . . . . Oklahoma City
Joe Heaton . . . . OK
                   Western . . . . . Oklahoma City
Tena Campbell,
   Chief Judge . . . . UT . . . . Salt Lake City
Dee Benson . . . . UT . . . . Salt Lake City
Dale A. Kimball . . . . UT . . . . Salt Lake City
Ted Stewart . . . . UT . . . . Salt Lake City
Paul G. Cassell . . . . UT . . . . Salt Lake City
William F. Downes,
   Chief Judge . . . . WY . . . . Casper
Alan B. Johnson . . . . WY . . . . Cheyenne

SENIOR DISTRICT JUDGES

Richard P. Matsch . . . . CO . . . . Denver
John L. Kane . . . . CO . . . . Denver
Zita L. Weinshienk . . . . CO . . . . Denver
Wesley E. Brown . . . . KS . . . . Wichita
Richard Dean Rogers . . . . . . KS . . . . Topeka
Sam A. Crow . . . . KS . . . . Topeka
John E. Conway . . . . NM . . . . Albuquerque
James A. Parker . . . . NM . . . . Albuquerque
C. Leroy Hansen . . . . NM . . . . Albuquerque
H. Dale Cook . . . . OK
                   Northern . . . . Tulsa
Frank Howell Seay . . . . OK
                   Eastern . . . . Muskogee
Ralph G. Thompson . . . . OK
                   Western . . . . . Oklahoma City
Lee R. West . . . . OK
                   Western . . . . . Oklahoma City
Tim Leonard . . . . OK
                   Western . . . . . Oklahoma City
Bruce S. Jenkins . . . . UT . . . . Salt Lake City
David K. Winder . . . . UT . . . . Salt Lake City
J. Thomas Greene . . . . UT . . . . Salt Lake City
David Sam . . . . UT . . . . Salt Lake City
Clarence A. Brimmer, Jr. . . . WY . . . . Cheyenne

MAGISTRATE JUDGES

Michael J. Watanabe . . . . CO . . . . Denver
Boyd N. Boland . . . . CO . . . . Denver
Craig B. Shaffer . . . . CO . . . . Denver
Michael E. Hegarty . . . . CO . . . . Denver
Karen M. Humphreys . . . . . . KS . . . . Wichita
Donald W. Bostwick . . . . KS . . . . Wichita
David J. Waxse . . . . KS . . . . Kansas City
James P. O'Hara . . . . KS . . . . Kansas City
K. Gary Sebelius . . . . KS . . . . Topeka
Gerald L. Rushfelt . . . . KS . . . . Kansas City
John Thomas Reid . . . . KS . . . . Wichita
Lorenzo F. Garcia . . . . NM . . . . Albuquerque
Don J. Svet . . . . NM . . . . Albuquerque
Leslie C. Smith . . . . NM . . . . Las Cruces
Richard L. Puglisi . . . . NM . . . . Albuquerque
Karen Ballard Molzen . . . . . . NM . . . . Las Cruces
Alan C. Torgerson . . . . NM . . . . Albuquerque
W. Daniel Schneider . . . . NM . . . . Albuquerque
Lourdes A. Martinez . . . . NM . . . . Las Cruces
Robert Hayes Scott . . . . NM . . . . Albuquerque
William P. Lynch . . . . NM . . . . Las Cruces
Carmen E. Garza . . . . NM . . . . Las Cruces
Frank H. McCarthy . . . . OK
                   Northern . . . . Tulsa
Sam A. Joyner . . . . OK
                   Northern . . . . Tulsa
Paul J. Cleary . . . . OK
                   Northern . . . . Tulsa
Kimberly E. West . . . . OK
                   Eastern . . . . Muskogee
Steven Shreder . . . . OK
                   Eastern . . . . Muskogee
Doyle W. Argo . . . . OK
                   Western . . . . . Oklahoma City
Bana Roberts . . . . OK
                   Western . . . . . Oklahoma City

Gary M. Purcell . . . . OK
                   Western . . . . . Oklahoma City
Valerie K. Couch . . . . OK
                   Western . . . . . Oklahoma City
Robert E. Bacharach . . . . OK
                   Western . . . . . Oklahoma City
Ronald L. Howland . . . . OK
                   Western . . . . . Oklahoma City
Samuel Alba . . . . UT . . . . Salt Lake City
David O. Nuffer . . . . UT . . . . Salt Lake City
Brooke C. Wells . . . . UT . . . . Salt Lake City
Paul M. Warner . . . . UT . . . . Salt Lake City
William C. Beaman . . . . WY . . . . Cheyenne
Stephen E. Cole . . . . WY . . . . Yellowstone
                                National Park

BANKRUPTCY JUDGES

Howard R. Tallman,
   Chief Judge . . . . CO . . . . Denver
A. Bruce Campbell . . . . CO . . . . Denver
Sidney B. Brooks . . . . CO . . . . Denver
Elizabeth E. Brown . . . . CO . . . . Denver
Michael E. Romero . . . . CO . . . . Denver
Robert E. Nugent,
   Chief Judge . . . . KS . . . . Wichita
Janice Karlin . . . . KS . . . . Topeka
Dale L. Somers . . . . KS . . . . Wichita
Robert D. Berger . . . . KS . . . . Kansas City
Mark B. McFeeley,
   Chief Judge . . . . NM . . . . Albuquerque
James S. Starzynski . . . . NM . . . . Albuquerque
Dana L. Rasure,
   Chief Judge . . . . OK
                   Northern . . . . Tulsa
Terrence L. Michael . . . . OK
                   Northern . . . . Tulsa
Tom R. Cornish . . . . OK
                   Eastern . . . . Okmulgee
T. M. Weaver,
   Chief Judge . . . . OK
                   Western . . Oklahoma City
Richard L. Bohanon . . . . OK
                   Western . . . . . Oklahoma City
Niles Jackson . . . . OK
                   Western . . . . . Oklahoma City
Glen E. Clark,
   Chief Judge . . . . UT . . . . Salt Lake City
Judith A. Boulden . . . . UT . . . . Salt Lake City
William T. Thurman . . . . UT . . . . Salt Lake City
Peter J. McNiff . . . . WY . . . . Cheyenne

ELEVENTH CIRCUIT
Districts of Northern, Middle and Southern Alabama; Northern, Middle and Southern Florida; and Northern, Middle and Southern Georgia
Clarence Thomas, Circuit Justice

CIRCUIT JUDGES

J. L. Edmondson, Chief Judge . . . . **Atlanta, GA**
Gerald Bard Tjoflat . . . . Jacksonville, FL
R. Lanier Anderson . . . . Macon, GA
Stanley F. Birch, Jr. . . . . Atlanta, GA
Joel F. Dubina . . . . Montgomery, AL
Susan H. Black . . . . Jacksonville, FL
Edward E. Carnes . . . . Montgomery, AL
Rosemary Barkett . . . . Miami, FL
Frank M. Hull . . . . Atlanta, GA
Stanley Marcus . . . . Miami, FL
Charles R. Wilson . . . . Tampa, FL
William H. Pryor, Jr. . . . . Birmingham, AL

SENIOR CIRCUIT JUDGES

John C. Godbold . . . . Montgomery, AL
James C. Hill . . . . Jacksonville, FL
Peter T. Fay . . . . Miami, FL
Phyllis A. Kravitch . . . . Atlanta, GA
Emmett Ripley Cox . . . . Mobile, AL

DISTRICT JUDGES

Sharon Lovelace
   Blackburn,

Chief Judge . . . . **AL**		
	Northern . . . **Birmingham**	
U. W. Clemon . . . . AL		
	Northern . . . . Birmingham	
C. Lynwood Smith . . . . AL		
	Northern . . . . Huntsville	
Inge Prytz Johnson . . . . AL		
	Northern . . . . Birmingham	
Karon O. Bowdre . . . . AL		
	Northern . . . . Birmingham	
L. Scott Coogler . . . . AL		
	Northern . . . . Birmingham	
R. David Proctor . . . . AL		
	Northern . . . . Birmingham	
Virginia E. Hopkins . . . . AL		
	Northern . . . . Birmingham	
Mark E. Fuller,		
Chief Judge . . . . **AL**		
	Middle . . . . . . **Montgomery**	
Myron H. Thompson . . . . AL		
	Middle . . . . Montgomery	
William Keith Watkins . . . . . AL		
	Middle . . . . Montgomery	
Callie V. S. Granade,		
Chief Judge . . . . **AL**		
	Southern . . . . **Mobile**	
William H. Steele . . . . AL		
	Southern . . . . Mobile	
Kristi K. DuBose . . . . AL		
	Southern . . . . Southern	
Robert L. Hinkle,		
Chief Judge . . . . **FL**		
	Northern . . . . **Tallahassee**	
Stephen P. Mickle . . . . FL		
	Northern . . . . Gainesville	
Margaret C. Rodgers . . . . FL		
	Northern . . . . Pensacola	
John Richard Smoak, Jr. . . . FL		
	Northern . . . . . . Panama City	
Patricia C. Fawsett,		
Chief Judge . . . . **FL Middle** . . . . **Orlando**		
Elizabeth A. Kovachevich . . . FL Middle . . . . Tampa		
Anne C. Conway . . . . FL Middle . . . . Orlando		
Steven D. Merryday . . . . FL Middle . . . . Tampa		
Henry L. Adams, Jr. . . . . FL Middle . . . . . Jacksonville		
Susan C. Bucklew . . . . FL Middle . . . . Tampa		
Richard A. Lazzara . . . . FL Middle . . . . Tampa		
James D. Whittemore . . . . . . FL Middle . . . . Tampa		
John Antoon, II . . . . FL Middle . . . . Orlando		
John E. Steele . . . . FL Middle . . . . . . Ft. Myers		
James S. Moody, Jr. . . . . FL Middle . . . . Tampa		
Gregory A. Presnell . . . . FL Middle . . . . Orlando		
Timothy J. Corrigan . . . . FL Middle . . . . Jacksonville		
Virginia Maria Hernandez		
Covington . . . . FL Middle . . . . Jacksonville		
Marcia Morales Howard . . . . FL Middle . . . . . . Ft. Myers		
William J. Zloch,		
Chief Judge . . . . **FL**		
	Southern . . . . **Fort**	
	Lauderdale	
Federico A. Moreno . . . . FL		
	Southern . . . . Miami	
Donald L. Graham . . . . FL		
	Southern . . . . Miami	
K. Michael Moore . . . . FL		
	Southern . . . . Miami	
Ursula Ungaro . . . . FL		
	Southern . . . . Miami	
Daniel T. K. Hurley . . . . FL		
	Southern . . . . West Palm	
	Beach	
Joan A. Lenard . . . . FL		
	Southern . . . . Miami	
Donald M. Middlebrooks . . . . FL		
	Southern . . . . West Palm	
	Beach	
Alan Stephen Gold . . . . FL		
	Southern . . . . Miami	
William P. Dimitrouleas . . . . FL		
	Southern . . . . Fort	
	Lauderdale	
Patricia A. Seitz . . . . FL		
	Southern . . . . Miami	
Adalberto Jordan . . . . FL		
	Southern . . . . Miami	

Paul C. Huck . . . . FL		
	Southern . . . . Miami	
Kenneth A. Marra . . . . FL		
	Southern . . . . Fortt	
	Lauderdale	
Jose E. Martinez . . . . FL		
	Southern . . . . Miami	
Cecilia M. Altonaga . . . . FL		
	Southern . . . . Miami	
James I. Cohn . . . . FL		
	Southern . . . . Fortt	
	Lauderdale	
Marcia G. Cooke . . . . FL		
	Southern . . . . Miami	
Jack T. Camp,		
Chief Judge . . . . **GA**		
	Northern . . . . **Atlanta/**	
	Newnan	
Harold L. Murphy . . . . GA		
	Northern . . . . Rome	
Orinda D. Evans . . . . GA		
	Northern . . . . Atlanta	
Julie E. Carnes . . . . GA		
	Northern . . . . Atlanta	
Clarence Cooper . . . . GA		
	Northern . . . . Atlanta	
Thomas W. Thrash, Jr. . . . . . GA		
	Northern . . . . Atlanta	
Richard W. Story . . . . GA		
	Northern . . . . Atlanta	
Charles A, Pannell, Jr. . . . . . GA		
	Northern . . . . Atlanta	
Beverly B. Martin . . . . GA		
	Northern . . . . Atlanta	
William S. Duffey . . . . GA		
	Northern . . . . Atlanta	
Timothy C. Batten, Sr. . . . . . GA		
	Northern . . . . Atlanta	
Hugh Lawson,		
Chief Judge . . . . **GA**		
	Middle . . . . **Macon**	
W. Louis Sands . . . . GA Middle . . . . Albany		
C. Ashley Royal . . . . GA Middle . . . . Macon		
Clay D. Land . . . . GA Middle . . . . Columbus		
William T. Moore, Jr.,		
Chief Judge . . . . **GA**		
	Southern . . . . . . **Savannah**	
Lisa Godbey Wood . . . . GA		
	Southern . . . . Augusta	

SENIOR DISTRICT JUDGES

James Hughes Hancock . . . . AL		
	Northern . . . . Birmingham	
J. Foy Guin, Jr. . . . . AL		
	Northern . . . . Birmingham	
Robert B. Propst . . . . AL		
	Northern . . . . Anniston	
William M. Acker, Jr. . . . . AL		
	Northern . . . . Birmingham	
Truman M. Hobbs . . . . AL Middle . . . . . Montgomery		
W. Harold Albritton, III . . . . AL Middle . . . . . Montgomery		
Ire De Ment . . . . AL Middle . . . . . Montgomery		
W. Brevard Hand . . . . AL		
	Southern . . . . Mobile	
Charles R. Butler, Jr. . . . . . . AL		
	Southern . . . . Mobile	
William Stafford . . . . FL		
	Northern . . . . Tallahassee	
Maurice Mitchell Paul . . . . . . FL		
	Northern . . . . Gainesville	
Roger Vinson . . . . FL		
	Northern . . . . Pensacola	
Lacey A. Collier . . . . FL		
	Northern . . . . Pensacola	
George C. Young . . . . FL Middle . . . . Orlando		
Wm. Terrell Hodges . . . . FL Middle . . . . Ocala		
Howell W. Melton . . . . FL Middle . . . . . Jacksonville		
William J. Castagna . . . . FL Middle . . . . Tampa		
John H. Moore, II . . . . FL Middle . . . . . Jacksonville		
G. Kendall Sharp . . . . FL Middle . . . . Orlando		
Harvey E. Schlesinger . . . . . . FL Middle . . . . . Jacksonville		
Charles M. Metzner . . . . FL		
	Southern . . . . Sarasota	
James Lawrence King . . . . . FL		
	Southern . . . . Miami	

William M. Hoeveler ....FL
    Southern .... Miami
Jose A. Gonzalez, Jr. ....FL
    Southern .... Fortt
               Lauderdale
James C. Paine ....FL
    Southern .... West Palm
               Beach
Kenneth L. Ryskamp ....FL
    Southern .... West Palm
               Beach
Shelby Highsmith ....FL
    Southern .... Miami
Charles A. Moye, Jr........GA
    Northern........... Atlanta
William C. O'Kelley ....GA
    Northern........ Gainesville
G. Ernest Tidwell ....GA
    Northern........... Atlanta
Marvin H. Shoob...........GA
    Northern........... Atlanta
Robert L. Vining, Jr. ....GA
    Northern............ Rome
Horace T. Ward............GA
    Northern........... Atlanta
J. Owen Forrester ....GA
    Northern........... Atlanta
Willis B. Hunt, Jr. ....GA
    Northern........... Atlanta
Wilbur D. Owens, Jr........GA Middle .... Macon
Duross Fitzpatrick ....GA Middle .... Macon
Anthony A. Alaimo.........GA
    Southern........ Brunswick
B. Avant Edenfield ....GA
    Southern .... Savannah
Dudley H. Bowen, Jr........GA
    Southern ....Augusta

MAGISTRATE JUDGES

Paul W. Greene ....AL
    Northern...... Birmingham
Terry Michael Putnam .....AL
    Northern...... Birmingham
Robert R. Armstrong, Jr. ...AL
    Northern...... Birmingham
Harwell G. Davis, III ....AL
    Northern.........Huntsville
John E. Ott ....AL
    Northern...... Birmingham
Charles S. Coody...........AL Middle .....Montgomery
Susan Russ Walker ....AL Middle .....Montgomery
Wallace Capel, Jr...........AL Middle .....Montgomery
Terry Moorer ....AL Middle .....Montgomery
William E. Cassady.........AL
    Southern .... Mobile
Bert W. Milling, Jr. ....AL
    Southern .... Mobile
Sonja F. Bivins ....AL
    Southern .... Mobile
William C. Sherrill, Jr. .....FL
    Northern........Tallahassee
G. Miles Davis ....FL
    Northern......... Pensacola
Allan Kornblum ....FL
    Northern........ Gainesville
Elizabeth M. Timothy ......FL
    Northern......... Pensacola
Thomas G. Wilson ....FL Middle .... Tampa
Howard T. Snyder ....FL Middle .... Jacksonville
Elizabeth A. Jenkins ....FL Middle .... Tampa
David A. Baker ....FL Middle .... Orlando
Thomas B. McCoun, III .....FL Middle .... Tampa
Mark A. Pizzo ....FL Middle .... Tampa
Mary S. Scriven ....FL Middle .... Tampa
Karla R. Spaulding.........FL Middle .... Orlando
Douglas N. Frazier ....FL Middle .... Ft. Myers
Gary R. Jones ....FL Middle .... Ocala
Thomas E. Morris..........FL Middle .... Jacksonville
Sheri P. Chappell ....FL Middle .... Ft. Myers
Monte C. Richardson ....FL Middle ..... Jacksonville
Linnea Ruth Johnson ......FL
    Southern .... West Palm
               Beach

Lurana S. Snow............FL
    Southern .... Fortt
               Lauderdale
Barry L. Garber ....FL
    Southern .... Miami
Ann E. Vitunac ....FL
    Southern .... West Palm
               Beach
William C. Turnoff ....FL
    Southern .... Miami
Ted Eugene Bandstra ......FL
    Southern .... Miami
Stephen T. Brown ....FL
    Southern .... Miami
Barry S. Seltzer............FL
    Southern .... Fortt
               Lauderdale
Frank J. Lynch, Jr. ....FL
    Southern .... Ft. Pierce
Robert L. Dubé ....FL
    Southern .... Miami
Andrea M. Simonton ....FL
    Southern .... Miami
John J. O'Sullivan ....FL
    Southern .... Miami
Patrick A. White ....FL
    Southern .... Miami
James M. Hopkins ....FL
    Southern .... West Palm
               Beach
Edwin G. Torres ....FL
    Southern .... Miami
Chris M. McAliley..........FL
    Southern .... Miami
Gerrilyn G. Brill ....GA
    Northern .... Atlanta
E. Clayton Scofield, III .....GA
    Northern .... Atlanta
C. Christopher Hagy ....GA
    Northern .... Atlanta
Janet F. King..............GA
    Northern .... Atlanta
Linda T. Walker ....GA
    Northern .... Atlanta
Alan J. Baverman ....GA
    Northern .... Atlanta
Susan S. Cole..............GA
    Northern .... Gainesville
Walter E. Johnson ....GA
    Northern............ Rome
Russell G. Vineyard ....GA
    Northern .... Atlanta
Claude W. Hicks, Jr. ....GA Middle .... Macon
Richard L. Hodge ....GA Middle ....Albany
G. Mallon Faircloth ....GA Middle .... Columbus
James E. Graham ....GA
    Southern .... Brunswick
G. R. Smith ....GA
    Southern .... Savannah
W. Leon Barfield ....GA
    Southern ....Augusta

BANKRUPTCY JUDGES

Benjamin Cohen,
  Chief Judge ....**AL**
    Northern ... Birmingham
Jack Caddell................AL
    Northern........... Decatur
Tamara O. Mitchell ....AL
    Northern...... Birmingham
Thomas B. Bennett ....AL
    Northern...... Birmingham
C. Michael Stilson..........AL
    Northern....... Tuscaloosa
James Jack Robinson.......AL
    Northern....... Anniston
Dwight H. Williams,
  Chief Judge ....**AL**
    Middle ...... Montgomery
William R. Sawyer ....AL
    Middle ....Montgomery
William S. Shulman,
  Chief Judge ....**AL**
    Southern .... Mobile

Margaret A. Mahoney ......AL
    Southern .... Mobile
Lewis M. Killian, Jr. ....FL
    Northern........Tallahassee

Paul M. Glenn,
  Chief Judge ....**FL**
    Middle .... **Tampa**
Arthur B. Briskman ....FL Middle .... Orlando
George L. Proctor ....FL Middle ..... Jacksonville
Jerry A. Funk ....FL Middle ..... Jacksonville
Karen S. Jennemann ....FL Middle .... Orlando
Michael G. Williamson .....FL Middle .... Tampa
K. Rodney May ....FL Middle .... Tampa
Catherine McEwen ....FL Middle .... Tampa
Alexander L. Paskay ....FL Middle .... Tampa

Paul Hyman, Jr.,
  Chief Judge ....**FL**
    Southern ..... **West Palm**
                Beach
Robert A. Mark ....FL
    Southern .... Miami
A. Jay Cristol ....FL
    Southern .... Miami
Steven H. Friedman ....FL
    Southern .... West Palm
                Beach
Raymond B. Ray ....FL
    Southern .... Fortt
              Lauderdale
John Karl Olson ....FL
    Southern .... Fortt
              Lauderdale
Laurel M. Isicoff ....FL
    Southern .... Miami

Joyce Bihary,
  Chief Judge ....**GA**
    Northern .... **Atlanta**
W. Homer Drake, Jr. ....GA
    Northern...........Newnan
Margaret H. Murphy ....GA
    Northern........... Atlanta
Robert E. Brizendine ....GA
    Northern........... Atlanta
James E. Massey...........GA
    Northern........... Atlanta
C. Ray Mullins.............GA
    Northern........... Atlanta
Paul W. Bonapfel ....GA
    Northern........... Atlanta
Mary Grace Diehl ....GA
    Northern........... Atlanta

Robert F. Hershner, Jr.,
  Chief Judge ....**GA**
    Middle .... **Macon**
John T. Laney, III ....GA Middle .... Columbus
James D. Walker, Jr. ....GA Middle .... Macon

Lamar W. Davis, Jr.,
  Chief Judge ....**GA**
    Southern ..... **Savannah**
John S. Dalis ....GA
    Southern .... Brunswick
Susan D. Barrett...........GA
    Southern .... Augusta

FEDERAL CIRCUIT

John G. Roberts, Jr., Circuit Justice

CIRCUIT JUDGES

Paul R. Michel, Chief Judge .... **Washington, DC**
Pauline Newman...................Washington, DC
H. Robert Mayer ....Washington, DC
Alan D. Lourie ....Washington, DC
Randall R. Rader ....Washington, DC
Alvin A. Schall ....Washington, DC
William C. Bryson ....Washington, DC
Arthur J. Gajarsa ....Washington, DC
Richard Linn ....Washington, DC
Timothy Belcher Dyk ....Washington, DC
Sharon Prost ....Washington, DC
Kimberly A. Moore ....Washington, DC

SENIOR CIRCUIT JUDGES

Daniel M. Friedman ....Washington, DC

Glenn L. Archer, Jr. ....Washington, DC
S. Jay Plager ....Washington, DC
Raymond C. Clevenger, III ....Washington, DC

UNITED STATES COURT OF INTERNATIONAL TRADE JUDGES

Jane A. Restani, Chief Judge .... **New York, NY**
Gregory W. Carman .... New York, NY
Donald C. Pogue .... New York, NY
Evan J. Wallach .... New York, NY
Judith M. Barzilay .... New York, NY
Delissa A. Ridgway .... New York, NY
Richard K. Eaton....................... New York, NY
Timothy C. Stanceu .... New York, NY
Leo M. Gordon .... New York, NY

SENIOR JUDGES

Thomas J. Aquilino, Jr. .... New York, NY
Nicholas Tsoucalas .... New York, NY
R. Kenton Musgrave..................... New York, NY
Richard W. Goldberg .... New York, NY

UNITED STATES COURT OF FEDERAL CLAIMS JUDGES

Edward J. Damich, Chief Judge ... **Washington, DC**
Christine Odell Cook Miller ....Washington, DC
Marian Blank Horn ....Washington, DC
Francis M. Allegra.....................Washington, DC
Lawrence M. Baskir ....Washington, DC
Lynn J. Bush ....Washington, DC
Nancy B. Firestone ....Washington, DC
Emily C. Hewitt.......................Washington, DC
Lawrence J. Block ....Washington, DC
Mary Ellen Coster Williams ....Washington, DC
Charles F. Lettow ....Washington, DC
Susan G. Braden ....Washington, DC
Victor J. Wolski ....Washington, DC
George W. Miller ....Washington, DC
Margaret M. Sweeney ....Washington, DC
Thomas C. Wheeler.....................Washington, DC

SENIOR JUDGES

Thomas J. Lydon......................Washington, DC
John P. Wiese.........................Washington, DC
Robert J. Yock ....Washington, DC
James F. Merow ....Washington, DC
Lawrence S. Margolis ....Washington, DC
Loren A. Smith ....Washington, DC
Eric G. Bruggink ....Washington, DC
Bohdan A. Futey ....Washington, DC
Robert H. Hodges, Jr..................Washington, DC

UNITED STATES TAX COURT JUDGES

John O. Colvin, Chief Judge ....Washington, DC
Mary Ann Cohen ....Washington, DC
Thomas B. Wells ....Washington, DC
James S. Halpern ....Washington, DC
Carolyn P. Chiechi ....Washington, DC
David Laro ....Washington, DC
Maurice B. Foley ....Washington, DC
Juan F. Vasquez ....Washington, DC
Joseph H. Gale........................Washington, DC
Michael B. Thornton ....Washington, DC
L. Paige Marvel ....Washington, DC
Stephen J. Swift ....Washington, DC
Harry Allen Haines.....................Washington, DC
Joseph Robert Goeke ....Washington, DC
Robert A. Wherry, Jr...................Washington, DC
Diane L. Kroupa ....Washington, DC
Mark V. Holmes ....Washington, DC

SENIOR JUDGES

Howard A. Dawson, Jr. ....Washington, DC
Julian L. Jacobs.......................Washington, DC
Joel Gerber ....Washington, DC
Robert P. Ruwe ....Washington, DC
Arthur L. Nims, III....................Washington, DC
Laurence J. Whalen ....Washington, DC
Renato Beghe ....Washington, DC
Herbert L. Chabot.....................Washington, DC

SPECIAL TRIAL JUDGES

Peter J. Panuthos, Chief Judge ... **Washington, DC**
D. Irvin Couvillion .... Washington, DC
Stanley J. Goldberg..................... Washington, DC
Carleton D. Powell .... Washington, DC
Robert N. Armen........................ Washington, DC
Lewis R. Carluzzo .... Washington, DC
John F. Dean .... Washington, DC

UNITED STATES COURT OF APPEALS FOR THE ARMED FORCES JUDGES

Andrew S. Effron, Chief Judge ..... **Washington, DC**
James E. Baker .... Washington, DC
Charles E. Erdmann..................... Washington, DC
Scott W. Stucky .... Washington, DC
Margaret A. Ryan .... Washington, DC

SENIOR JUDGES

William H. Darden .... Washington, DC
Robinson O. Everett .... Washington, DC
Walter T. Cox, III .... Washington, DC
Eugene R. Sullivan .... Washington, DC

Susan J. Crawford...................... Washington, DC
H. F. "Sparky" Gierke................. Washington, DC

UNITED STATES COURT OF APPEALS FOR VETERANS CLAIMS JUDGES

William P. Greene, Jr., Chief Judge .... **Washington, DC**
Bruce E. Kasold .... Washington, DC
Lawrence B. Hagel .... Washington, DC
William A. Moorman .... Washington, DC
Alan G. Lance, Sr...................... Washington, DC
Robert N. Davis .... Washington, DC
Mary J. Schoelen .... Washington, DC

JUDICIAL PANEL ON MULTIDISTRICT LITIGATION JUDGES

Wm. Terrell Hodges, Chairman........... **Ocala, FL**
D. Lowell Jensen .... Oakland, CA
J. Frederick Motz .... Baltimore, MD
Robert L. Miller, Jr. .... South Bend, IN
Kathryn H. Vratil .... Kansas City, KS
David R. Hansen .... Cedar Rapids, IA
Anthony J. Scirica.................... Philadelphia, PA

Perpetual Calendar

The number accompanying each year indicates the calendar to use.

1821 . .2	1847 . . 6	1873 . . 4	1899 . . 1	1925 . . 5	1951 . . 2	1977 . . 7	2003 . . 4	2029 . . 2	2055 . . 6
1822 . . 3	1848 . 14	1874 . . 5	1900 . . 2	1926 . . 6	1952 . 10	1978 . . 1	2004 . 12	2030 . . 3	2056 . 14
1823 . . 4	1849 . . 2	1875 . . 6	1901 . . 3	1927 . . 7	1953 . . 5	1979 . . 2	2005 . . 7	2031 . . 4	2057 . . 2
1824 . 12	1850 . . 3	1876 . 14	1902 . . 4	1928 . . 8	1954 . . 6	1980 . 10	2006 . . 1	2032 . 12	2058 . . 3
1825 . . 7	1851 . . 4	1877 . . 2	1903 . . 5	1929 . . 3	1955 . . 7	1981 . . 5	2007 . . 2	2033 . . 7	2059 . . 4
1826 . . 1	1852 . 12	1878 . . 3	1904 . 13	1930 . . 4	1956 . . 8	1982 . . 6	2008 . 10	2034 . . 1	2060 . 12
1827 . . 2	1853 . . 7	1879 . . 4	1905 . . 1	1931 . . 5	1957 . . 3	1983 . . 7	2009 . . 5	2035 . . 2	2061 . . 7
1828 . 10	1854 . . 1	1880 . 12	1906 . . 2	1932 . 13	1958 . . 4	1984 . . 8	2010 . . 6	2036 . 10	2062 . . 1
1829 . . 5	1855 . . 2	1881 . . 7	1907 . . 3	1933 . . 1	1959 . . 5	1985 . . 3	2011 . . 7	2037 . . 5	2063 . . 2
1830 . . 6	1856 . 10	1882 . . 1	1908 . 11	1934 . . 2	1960 . 13	1986 . . 4	2012 . . 8	2038 . . 6	2064 . 10
1831 . . 7	1857 . . 5	1883 . . 2	1909 . . 8	1935 . . 3	1961 . . 1	1987 . . 5	2013 . . 3	2039 . . 7	2065 . . 5
1832 . . 8	1858 . . 6	1884 . 10	1910 . . 7	1936 . 11	1962 . . 2	1988 . 13	2014 . . 4	2040 . . 8	2066 . . 6
1833 . . 3	1859 . . 7	1885 . . 5	1911 . . 1	1937 . . 6	1963 . . 3	1989 . . 1	2015 . . 5	2041 . . 3	2067 . . 7
1834 . . 4	1860 . . 8	1886 . . 6	1912 . . 9	1938 . . 7	1964 . 11	1990 . . 2	2016 . 13	2042 . . 4	2068 . . 8
1835 . . 5	1861 . . 3	1887 . . 7	1913 . . 4	1939 . . 1	1965 . . 6	1991 . . 3	2017 . . 1	2043 . . 5	2069 . . 3
1836 . 13	1862 . . 4	1888 . . 8	1914 . . 5	1940 . . 9	1966 . . 7	1992 . 11	2018 . . 2	2044 . 13	2070 . . 4
1837 . . 1	1863 . . 5	1889 . . 3	1915 . . 6	1941 . . 4	1967 . . 1	1993 . . 6	2019 . . 3	2045 . . 1	2071 . . 5
1838 . . 2	1864 . 13	1890 . . 4	1916 . 14	1942 . . 5	1968 . . 9	1994 . . 7	2020 . 11	2046 . . 2	2072 . 13
1839 . . 3	1865 . . 1	1891 . . 5	1917 . . 2	1943 . . 6	1969 . . 4	1995 . . 1	2021 . . 6	2047 . . 3	2073 . . 1
1840 . 11	1866 . . 2	1892 . 13	1918 . . 3	1944 . 14	1970 . . 5	1996 . . 9	2022 . . 7	2048 . 11	2074 . . 2
1841 . . 6	1867 . . 3	1893 . . 1	1919 . . 4	1945 . . 2	1971 . . 6	1997 . . 4	2023 . . 1	2049 . . 6	2075 . . 3
1842 . . 7	1868 . 11	1894 . . 2	1920 . 12	1946 . . 3	1972 . 14	1998 . . 5	2024 . . 9	2050 . . 7	2076 . 11
1843 . . 1	1869 . . 6	1895 . . 3	1921 . . 7	1947 . . 4	1973 . . 2	1999 . . 6	2025 . . 4	2051 . . 1	2077 . . 6
1844 . . 9	1870 . . 7	1896 . 11	1922 . . 1	1948 . 12	1974 . . 3	2000 . 14	2026 . . 5	2052 . . 9	2078 . . 7
1845 . . 4	1871 . . 1	1897 . . 6	1923 . . 2	1949 . . 7	1975 . . 4	2001 . . 2	2027 . . 6	2053 . . 4	2079 . . 1
1846 . . 5	1872 . . 9	1898 . . 7	1924 . 10	1950 . . 1	1976 . 12	2002 . . 3	2028 . 14	2054 . . 5	2080 . . 9

2006 — 1 — 2017

JANUARY

S	M	T	W	T	F	S
1	2	3	4	5	6	7
8	9	10	11	12	13	14
15	16	17	18	19	20	21
22	23	24	25	26	27	28
29	30	31				

FEBRUARY

S	M	T	W	T	F	S
			1	2	3	4
5	6	7	8	9	10	11
12	13	14	15	16	17	18
19	20	21	22	23	24	25
26	27	28				

MARCH

S	M	T	W	T	F	S
			1	2	3	4
5	6	7	8	9	10	11
12	13	14	15	16	17	18
19	20	21	22	23	24	25
26	27	28	29	30	31	

APRIL

S	M	T	W	T	F	S
						1
2	3	4	5	6	7	8
9	10	11	12	13	14	15
16	17	18	19	20	21	22
23	24	25	26	27	28	29
30						

MAY

S	M	T	W	T	F	S
	1	2	3	4	5	6
7	8	9	10	11	12	13
14	15	16	17	18	19	20
21	22	23	24	25	26	27
28	29	30	31			

JUNE

S	M	T	W	T	F	S
				1	2	3
4	5	6	7	8	9	10
11	12	13	14	15	16	17
18	19	20	21	22	23	24
25	26	27	28	29	30	

JULY

S	M	T	W	T	F	S
						1
2	3	4	5	6	7	8
9	10	11	12	13	14	15
16	17	18	19	20	21	22
23	24	25	26	27	28	29
30	31					

AUGUST

S	M	T	W	T	F	S
		1	2	3	4	5
6	7	8	9	10	11	12
13	14	15	16	17	18	19
20	21	22	23	24	25	26
27	28	29	30	31		

SEPTEMBER

S	M	T	W	T	F	S
					1	2
3	4	5	6	7	8	9
10	11	12	13	14	15	16
17	18	19	20	21	22	23
24	25	26	27	28	29	30

OCTOBER

S	M	T	W	T	F	S
1	2	3	4	5	6	7
8	9	10	11	12	13	14
15	16	17	18	19	20	21
22	23	24	25	26	27	28
29	30	31				

NOVEMBER

S	M	T	W	T	F	S
			1	2	3	4
5	6	7	8	9	10	11
12	13	14	15	16	17	18
19	20	21	22	23	24	25
26	27	28	29	30		

DECEMBER

S	M	T	W	T	F	S
					1	2
3	4	5	6	7	8	9
10	11	12	13	14	15	16
17	18	19	20	21	22	23
24	25	26	27	28	29	30
31						

2007 — 2 — 2018

JANUARY

S	M	T	W	T	F	S
	1	2	3	4	5	6
7	8	9	10	11	12	13
14	15	16	17	18	19	20
21	22	23	24	25	26	27
28	29	30	31			

FEBRUARY

S	M	T	W	T	F	S
				1	2	3
4	5	6	7	8	9	10
11	12	13	14	15	16	17
18	19	20	21	22	23	24
25	26	27	28			

MARCH

S	M	T	W	T	F	S
				1	2	3
4	5	6	7	8	9	10
11	12	13	14	15	16	17
18	19	20	21	22	23	24
25	26	27	28	29	30	31

APRIL

S	M	T	W	T	F	S
1	2	3	4	5	6	7
8	9	10	11	12	13	14
15	16	17	18	19	20	21
22	23	24	25	26	27	28
29	30					

MAY

S	M	T	W	T	F	S
		1	2	3	4	5
6	7	8	9	10	11	12
13	14	15	16	17	18	19
20	21	22	23	24	25	26
27	28	29	30	31		

JUNE

S	M	T	W	T	F	S
					1	2
3	4	5	6	7	8	9
10	11	12	13	14	15	16
17	18	19	20	21	22	23
24	25	26	27	28	29	30

JULY

S	M	T	W	T	F	S
1	2	3	4	5	6	7
8	9	10	11	12	13	14
15	16	17	18	19	20	21
22	23	24	25	26	27	28
29	30	31				

AUGUST

S	M	T	W	T	F	S
			1	2	3	4
5	6	7	8	9	10	11
12	13	14	15	16	17	18
19	20	21	22	23	24	25
26	27	28	29	30	31	

SEPTEMBER

S	M	T	W	T	F	S
						1
2	3	4	5	6	7	8
9	10	11	12	13	14	15
16	17	18	19	20	21	22
23	24	25	26	27	28	29
30						

OCTOBER

S	M	T	W	T	F	S
	1	2	3	4	5	6
7	8	9	10	11	12	13
14	15	16	17	18	19	20
21	22	23	24	25	26	27
28	29	30	31			

NOVEMBER

S	M	T	W	T	F	S
				1	2	3
4	5	6	7	8	9	10
11	12	13	14	15	16	17
18	19	20	21	22	23	24
25	26	27	28	29	30	

DECEMBER

S	M	T	W	T	F	S
						1
2	3	4	5	6	7	8
9	10	11	12	13	14	15
16	17	18	19	20	21	22
23	24	25	26	27	28	29
30	31					

2013   **3**   2019

JANUARY
```
S  M TW T F S
       1  2  3  4  5
 6  7  8  9 10 11 12
13 14 15 16 17 18 19
20 21 22 23 24 25 26
27 28 29 30 31
```
FEBRUARY
```
S  M TW T F S
                1  2
 3  4  5  6  7  8  9
10 11 12 13 14 15 16
17 18 19 20 21 22 23
24 25 26 27 28
```
MARCH
```
S  M TW T F S
                1  2
 3  4  5  6  7  8  9
10 11 12 13 14 15 16
17 18 19 20 21 22 23
24 25 26 27 28 29 30
31
```
APRIL
```
S  M TW T F S
    1  2  3  4  5  6
 7  8  9 10 11 12 13
14 15 16 17 18 19 20
21 22 23 24 25 26 27
28 29 30
```
MAY
```
S  M TW T F S
          1  2  3  4
 5  6  7  8  9 10 11
12 13 14 15 16 17 18
19 20 21 22 23 24 25
26 27 28 29 30 31
```
JUNE
```
S  M TW T F S
                   1
 2  3  4  5  6  7  8
 9 10 11 12 13 14 15
16 17 18 19 20 21 22
23 24 25 26 27 28 29
30
```
JULY
```
S  M TW T F S
    1  2  3  4  5  6
 7  8  9 10 11 12 13
14 15 16 17 18 19 20
21 22 23 24 25 26 27
28 29 30 31
```
AUGUST
```
S  M TW T F S
          1  2  3
 4  5  6  7  8  9 10
11 12 13 14 15 16 17
18 19 20 21 22 23 24
25 26 27 28 29 30 31
```
SEPTEMBER
```
S  M TW T F S
 1  2  3  4  5  6  7
 8  9 10 11 12 13 14
15 16 17 18 19 20 21
22 23 24 25 26 27 28
29 30
```
OCTOBER
```
S  M TW T F S
    1  2  3  4  5
 6  7  8  9 10 11 12
13 14 15 16 17 18 19
20 21 22 23 24 25 26
27 28 29 30 31
```
NOVEMBER
```
S  M TW T F S
             1  2
 3  4  5  6  7  8  9
10 11 12 13 14 15 16
17 18 19 20 21 22 23
24 25 26 27 28 29 30
```
DECEMBER
```
S  M TW T F S
 1  2  3  4  5  6  7
 8  9 10 11 12 13 14
15 16 17 18 19 20 21
22 23 24 25 26 27 28
29 30 31
```

4   2014

JANUARY
```
S  M TW T F S
          1  2  3  4
 5  6  7  8  9 10 11
12 13 14 15 16 17 18
19 20 21 22 23 24 25
26 27 28 29 30 31
```
FEBRUARY
```
S  M TW T F S
                   1
 2  3  4  5  6  7  8
 9 10 11 12 13 14 15
16 17 18 19 20 21 22
23 24 25 26 27 28
```
MARCH
```
S  M TW T F S
                   1
 2  3  4  5  6  7  8
 9 10 11 12 13 14 15
16 17 18 19 20 21 22
23 24 25 26 27 28 29
30 31
```
APRIL
```
S  M TW T F S
       1  2  3  4  5
 6  7  8  9 10 11 12
13 14 15 16 17 18 19
20 21 22 23 24 25 26
27 28 29 30
```
MAY
```
S  M TW T F S
             1  2  3
 4  5  6  7  8  9 10
11 12 13 14 15 16 17
18 19 20 21 22 23 24
25 26 27 28 29 30 31
```
JUNE
```
S  M TW T F S
 1  2  3  4  5  6  7
 8  9 10 11 12 13 14
15 16 17 18 19 20 21
22 23 24 25 26 27 28
29 30
```
JULY
```
S  M TW T F S
       1  2  3  4  5
 6  7  8  9 10 11 12
13 14 15 16 17 18 19
20 21 22 23 24 25 26
27 28 29 30 31
```
AUGUST
```
S  M TW T F S
                1  2
 3  4  5  6  7  8  9
10 11 12 13 14 15 16
17 18 19 20 21 22 23
24 25 26 27 28 29 30
31
```
SEPTEMBER
```
S  M TW T F S
    1  2  3  4  5  6
 7  8  9 10 11 12 13
14 15 16 17 18 19 20
21 22 23 24 25 26 27
28 29 30
```
OCTOBER
```
S  M TW T F S
          1  2  3  4
 5  6  7  8  9 10 11
12 13 14 15 16 17 18
19 20 21 22 23 24 25
26 27 28 29 30 31
```
NOVEMBER
```
S  M TW T F S
                   1
 2  3  4  5  6  7  8
 9 10 11 12 13 14 15
16 17 18 19 20 21 22
23 24 25 26 27 28 29
30
```
DECEMBER
```
S  M TW T F S
    1  2  3  4  5  6
 7  8  9 10 11 12 13
14 15 16 17 18 19 20
21 22 23 24 25 26 27
28 29 30 31
```

2009   **5**   2015

JANUARY
```
S  M TW T F S
             1  2  3
 4  5  6  7  8  9 10
11 12 13 14 15 16 17
18 19 20 21 22 23 24
25 26 27 28 29 30 31
```
FEBRUARY
```
S  M TW T F S
 1  2  3  4  5  6  7
 8  9 10 11 12 13 14
15 16 17 18 19 20 21
22 23 24 25 26 27 28
```
MARCH
```
S  M TW T F S
 1  2  3  4  5  6  7
 8  9 10 11 12 13 14
15 16 17 18 19 20 21
22 23 24 25 26 27 28
29 30 31
```
APRIL
```
S  M TW T F S
          1  2  3  4
 5  6  7  8  9 10 11
12 13 14 15 16 17 18
19 20 21 22 23 24 25
26 27 28 29 30
```
MAY
```
S  M TW T F S
                1  2
 3  4  5  6  7  8  9
10 11 12 13 14 15 16
17 18 19 20 21 22 23
24 25 26 27 28 29 30
31
```
JUNE
```
S  M TW T F S
    1  2  3  4  5  6
 7  8  9 10 11 12 13
14 15 16 17 18 19 20
21 22 23 24 25 26 27
28 29 30
```
JULY
```
S  M TW T F S
          1  2  3  4
 5  6  7  8  9 10 11
12 13 14 15 16 17 18
19 20 21 22 23 24 25
26 27 28 29 30 31
```
AUGUST
```
S  M TW T F S
                   1
 2  3  4  5  6  7  8
 9 10 11 12 13 14 15
16 17 18 19 20 21 22
23 24 25 26 27 28 29
30 31
```
SEPTEMBER
```
S  M TW T F S
       1  2  3  4  5
 6  7  8  9 10 11 12
13 14 15 16 17 18 19
20 21 22 23 24 25 26
27 28 29 30
```
OCTOBER
```
S  M TW T F S
             1  2  3
 4  5  6  7  8  9 10
11 12 13 14 15 16 17
18 19 20 21 22 23 24
25 26 27 28 29 30 31
```
NOVEMBER
```
S  M TW T F S
 1  2  3  4  5  6  7
 8  9 10 11 12 13 14
15 16 17 18 19 20 21
22 23 24 25 26 27 28
29 30
```
DECEMBER
```
S  M TW T F S
       1  2  3  4  5
 6  7  8  9 10 11 12
13 14 15 16 17 18 19
20 21 22 23 24 25 26
27 28 29 30 31
```

2010   **6**   2021

JANUARY
```
S  M TW T F S
                1  2
 3  4  5  6  7  8  9
10 11 12 13 14 15 16
17 18 19 20 21 22 23
24 25 26 27 28 29 30
31
```
FEBRUARY
```
S  M TW T F S
    1  2  3  4  5  6
 7  8  9 10 11 12 13
14 15 16 17 18 19 20
21 22 23 24 25 26 27
28
```
MARCH
```
S  M TW T F S
    1  2  3  4  5  6
 7  8  9 10 11 12 13
14 15 16 17 18 19 20
21 22 23 24 25 26 27
28 29 30 31
```
APRIL
```
S  M TW T F S
          1  2  3
 4  5  6  7  8  9 10
11 12 13 14 15 16 17
18 19 20 21 22 23 24
25 26 27 28 29 30
```
MAY
```
S  M TW T F S
                   1
 2  3  4  5  6  7  8
 9 10 11 12 13 14 15
16 17 18 19 20 21 22
23 24 25 26 27 28 29
30 31
```
JUNE
```
S  M TW T F S
       1  2  3  4  5
 6  7  8  9 10 11 12
13 14 15 16 17 18 19
20 21 22 23 24 25 26
27 28 29 30
```
JULY
```
S  M TW T F S
             1  2  3
 4  5  6  7  8  9 10
11 12 13 14 15 16 17
18 19 20 21 22 23 24
25 26 27 28 29 30 31
```
AUGUST
```
S  M TW T F S
 1  2  3  4  5  6  7
 8  9 10 11 12 13 14
15 16 17 18 19 20 21
22 23 24 25 26 27 28
29 30 31
```
SEPTEMBER
```
S  M TW T F S
          1  2  3  4
 5  6  7  8  9 10 11
12 13 14 15 16 17 18
19 20 21 22 23 24 25
26 27 28 29 30
```
OCTOBER
```
S  M TW T F S
                1  2
 3  4  5  6  7  8  9
10 11 12 13 14 15 16
17 18 19 20 21 22 23
24 25 26 27 28 29 30
31
```
NOVEMBER
```
S  M TW T F S
    1  2  3  4  5  6
 7  8  9 10 11 12 13
14 15 16 17 18 19 20
21 22 23 24 25 26 27
28 29 30
```
DECEMBER
```
S  M TW T F S
          1  2  3  4
 5  6  7  8  9 10 11
12 13 14 15 16 17 18
19 20 21 22 23 24 25
26 27 28 29 30 31
```

7 — 2005, 2011

JANUARY
S	M	T	W	T	F	S
						1
2	3	4	5	6	7	8
9	10	11	12	13	14	15
16	17	18	19	20	21	22
23	24	25	26	27	28	29
30	31					

FEBRUARY
S	M	T	W	T	F	S
		1	2	3	4	5
6	7	8	9	10	11	12
13	14	15	16	17	18	19
20	21	22	23	24	25	26
27	28					

MARCH
S	M	T	W	T	F	S
		1	2	3	4	5
6	7	8	9	10	11	12
13	14	15	16	17	18	19
20	21	22	23	24	25	26
27	28	29	30	31		

APRIL
S	M	T	W	T	F	S
					1	2
3	4	5	6	7	8	9
10	11	12	13	14	15	16
17	18	19	20	21	22	23
24	25	26	27	28	29	30

MAY
S	M	T	W	T	F	S
1	2	3	4	5	6	7
8	9	10	11	12	13	14
15	16	17	18	19	20	21
22	23	24	25	26	27	28
29	30	31				

JUNE
S	M	T	W	T	F	S
			1	2	3	4
5	6	7	8	9	10	11
12	13	14	15	16	17	18
19	20	21	22	23	24	25
26	27	28	29	30		

JULY
S	M	T	W	T	F	S
					1	2
3	4	5	6	7	8	9
10	11	12	13	14	15	16
17	18	19	20	21	22	23
24	25	26	27	28	29	30
31						

AUGUST
S	M	T	W	T	F	S
	1	2	3	4	5	6
7	8	9	10	11	12	13
14	15	16	17	18	19	20
21	22	23	24	25	26	27
28	29	30	31			

SEPTEMBER
S	M	T	W	T	F	S
				1	2	3
4	5	6	7	8	9	10
11	12	13	14	15	16	17
18	19	20	21	22	23	24
25	26	27	28	29	30	

OCTOBER
S	M	T	W	T	F	S
						1
2	3	4	5	6	7	8
9	10	11	12	13	14	15
16	17	18	19	20	21	22
23	24	25	26	27	28	29
30	31					

NOVEMBER
S	M	T	W	T	F	S
		1	2	3	4	5
6	7	8	9	10	11	12
13	14	15	16	17	18	19
20	21	22	23	24	25	26
27	28	29	30			

DECEMBER
S	M	T	W	T	F	S
				1	2	3
4	5	6	7	8	9	10
11	12	13	14	15	16	17
18	19	20	21	22	23	24
25	26	27	28	29	30	31

8 — 2012

JANUARY
S	M	T	W	T	F	S
1	2	3	4	5	6	7
8	9	10	11	12	13	14
15	16	17	18	19	20	21
22	23	24	25	26	27	28
29	30	31				

FEBRUARY
S	M	T	W	T	F	S
			1	2	3	4
5	6	7	8	9	10	11
12	13	14	15	16	17	18
19	20	21	22	23	24	25
26	27	28	29			

MARCH
S	M	T	W	T	F	S
				1	2	3
4	5	6	7	8	9	10
11	12	13	14	15	16	17
18	19	20	21	22	23	24
25	26	27	28	29	30	31

APRIL
S	M	T	W	T	F	S
1	2	3	4	5	6	7
8	9	10	11	12	13	14
15	16	17	18	19	20	21
22	23	24	25	26	27	28
29	30					

MAY
S	M	T	W	T	F	S
		1	2	3	4	5
6	7	8	9	10	11	12
13	14	15	16	17	18	19
20	21	22	23	24	25	26
27	28	29	30	31		

JUNE
S	M	T	W	T	F	S
					1	2
3	4	5	6	7	8	9
10	11	12	13	14	15	16
17	18	19	20	21	22	23
24	25	26	27	28	29	30

JULY
S	M	T	W	T	F	S
1	2	3	4	5	6	7
8	9	10	11	12	13	14
15	16	17	18	19	20	21
22	23	24	25	26	27	28
29	30	31				

AUGUST
S	M	T	W	T	F	S
			1	2	3	4
5	6	7	8	9	10	11
12	13	14	15	16	17	18
19	20	21	22	23	24	25
26	27	28	29	30	31	

SEPTEMBER
S	M	T	W	T	F	S
						1
2	3	4	5	6	7	8
9	10	11	12	13	14	15
16	17	18	19	20	21	22
23	24	25	26	27	28	29
30						

OCTOBER
S	M	T	W	T	F	S
	1	2	3	4	5	6
7	8	9	10	11	12	13
14	15	16	17	18	19	20
21	22	23	24	25	26	27
28	29	30	31			

NOVEMBER
S	M	T	W	T	F	S
				1	2	3
4	5	6	7	8	9	10
11	12	13	14	15	16	17
18	19	20	21	22	23	24
25	26	27	28	29	30	

DECEMBER
S	M	T	W	T	F	S
						1
2	3	4	5	6	7	8
9	10	11	12	13	14	15
16	17	18	19	20	21	22
23	24	25	26	27	28	29
30	31					

9 — 2024

JANUARY
S	M	T	W	T	F	S
	1	2	3	4	5	6
7	8	9	10	11	12	13
14	15	16	17	18	19	20
21	22	23	24	25	26	27
28	29	30	31			

FEBRUARY
S	M	T	W	T	F	S
				1	2	3
4	5	6	7	8	9	10
11	12	13	14	15	16	17
18	19	20	21	22	23	24
25	26	27	28	29		

MARCH
S	M	T	W	T	F	S
					1	2
3	4	5	6	7	8	9
10	11	12	13	14	15	16
17	18	19	20	21	22	23
24	25	26	27	28	29	30
31						

APRIL
S	M	T	W	T	F	S
	1	2	3	4	5	6
7	8	9	10	11	12	13
14	15	16	17	18	19	20
21	22	23	24	25	26	27
28	29	30				

MAY
S	M	T	W	T	F	S
			1	2	3	4
5	6	7	8	9	10	11
12	13	14	15	16	17	18
19	20	21	22	23	24	25
26	27	28	29	30	31	

JUNE
S	M	T	W	T	F	S
						1
2	3	4	5	6	7	8
9	10	11	12	13	14	15
16	17	18	19	20	21	22
23	24	25	26	27	28	29
30						

JULY
S	M	T	W	T	F	S
	1	2	3	4	5	6
7	8	9	10	11	12	13
14	15	16	17	18	19	20
21	22	23	24	25	26	27
28	29	30	31			

AUGUST
S	M	T	W	T	F	S
				1	2	3
4	5	6	7	8	9	10
11	12	13	14	15	16	17
18	19	20	21	22	23	24
25	26	27	28	29	30	31

SEPTEMBER
S	M	T	W	T	F	S
1	2	3	4	5	6	7
8	9	10	11	12	13	14
15	16	17	18	19	20	21
22	23	24	25	26	27	28
29	30					

OCTOBER
S	M	T	W	T	F	S
		1	2	3	4	5
6	7	8	9	10	11	12
13	14	15	16	17	18	19
20	21	22	23	24	25	26
27	28	29	30	31		

NOVEMBER
S	M	T	W	T	F	S
					1	2
3	4	5	6	7	8	9
10	11	12	13	14	15	16
17	18	19	20	21	22	23
24	25	26	27	28	29	30

DECEMBER
S	M	T	W	T	F	S
1	2	3	4	5	6	7
8	9	10	11	12	13	14
15	16	17	18	19	20	21
22	23	24	25	26	27	28
29	30	31				

10 — 2008

JANUARY
S	M	T	W	T	F	S
		1	2	3	4	5
6	7	8	9	10	11	12
13	14	15	16	17	18	19
20	21	22	23	24	25	26
27	28	29	30	31		

FEBRUARY
S	M	T	W	T	F	S
					1	2
3	4	5	6	7	8	9
10	11	12	13	14	15	16
17	18	19	20	21	22	23
24	25	26	27	28	29	

MARCH
S	M	T	W	T	F	S
						1
2	3	4	5	6	7	8
9	10	11	12	13	14	15
16	17	18	19	20	21	22
23	24	25	26	27	28	29
30	31					

APRIL
S	M	T	W	T	F	S
		1	2	3	4	5
6	7	8	9	10	11	12
13	14	15	16	17	18	19
20	21	22	23	24	25	26
27	28	29	30			

MAY
S	M	T	W	T	F	S
				1	2	3
4	5	6	7	8	9	10
11	12	13	14	15	16	17
18	19	20	21	22	23	24
25	26	27	28	29	30	31

JUNE
S	M	T	W	T	F	S
1	2	3	4	5	6	7
8	9	10	11	12	13	14
15	16	17	18	19	20	21
22	23	24	25	26	27	28
29	30					

JULY
S	M	T	W	T	F	S
		1	2	3	4	5
6	7	8	9	10	11	12
13	14	15	16	17	18	19
20	21	22	23	24	25	26
27	28	29	30	31		

AUGUST
S	M	T	W	T	F	S
					1	2
3	4	5	6	7	8	9
10	11	12	13	14	15	16
17	18	19	20	21	22	23
24	25	26	27	28	29	30
31						

SEPTEMBER
S	M	T	W	T	F	S
	1	2	3	4	5	6
7	8	9	10	11	12	13
14	15	16	17	18	19	20
21	22	23	24	25	26	27
28	29	30				

OCTOBER
S	M	T	W	T	F	S
			1	2	3	4
5	6	7	8	9	10	11
12	13	14	15	16	17	18
19	20	21	22	23	24	25
26	27	28	29	30	31	

NOVEMBER
S	M	T	W	T	F	S
						1
2	3	4	5	6	7	8
9	10	11	12	13	14	15
16	17	18	19	20	21	22
23	24	25	26	27	28	29
30						

DECEMBER
S	M	T	W	T	F	S
	1	2	3	4	5	6
7	8	9	10	11	12	13
14	15	16	17	18	19	20
21	22	23	24	25	26	27
28	29	30	31			

2020 — 11 | 12 — 2004

JANUARY	FEBRUARY	MARCH		JANUARY	FEBRUARY	MARCH
S M T W T F S	S M T W T F S	S M T W T F S		S M T W T F S	S M T W T F S	S M T W T F S
1 2 3 4	1	1 2 3 4 5 6 7		1 2 3	1 2 3 4 5 6 7	1 2 3 4 5 6
5 6 7 8 9 10 11	2 3 4 5 6 7 8	8 9 10 11 12 13 14		4 5 6 7 8 9 10	8 9 10 11 12 13 14	7 8 9 10 11 12 13
12 13 14 15 16 17 18	9 10 11 12 13 14 15	15 16 17 18 19 20 21		11 12 13 14 15 16 17	15 16 17 18 19 20 21	14 15 16 17 18 19 20
19 20 21 22 23 24 25	16 17 18 19 20 21 22	22 23 24 25 26 27 28		18 19 20 21 22 23 24	22 23 24 25 26 27 28	21 22 23 24 25 26 27
26 27 28 29 30 31	23 24 25 26 27 28 29	29 30 31		25 26 27 28 29 30 31	29	28 29 30 31

APRIL	MAY	JUNE		APRIL	MAY	JUNE
S M T W T F S	S M T W T F S	S M T W T F S		S M T W T F S	S M T W T F S	S M T W T F S
1 2 3 4	1 2	1 2 3 4 5 6		1 2 3	1	1 2 3 4 5
5 6 7 8 9 10 11	3 4 5 6 7 8 9	7 8 9 10 11 12 13		4 5 6 7 8 9 10	2 3 4 5 6 7 8	6 7 8 9 10 11 12
12 13 14 15 16 17 18	10 11 12 13 14 15 16	14 15 16 17 18 19 20		11 12 13 14 15 16 17	9 10 11 12 13 14 15	13 14 15 16 17 18 19
19 20 21 22 23 24 25	17 18 19 20 21 22 23	21 22 23 24 25 26 27		18 19 20 21 22 23 24	16 17 18 19 20 21 22	20 21 22 23 24 25 26
26 27 28 29 30	24 25 26 27 28 29 30 / 31	28 29 30		25 26 27 28 29 30	23 24 25 26 27 28 29 / 30 31	27 28 29 30

JULY	AUGUST	SEPTEMBER		JULY	AUGUST	SEPTEMBER
S M T W T F S	S M T W T F S	S M T W T F S		S M T W T F S	S M T W T F S	S M T W T F S
1 2 3	1	1 2 3 4 5		1 2 3	1 2 3 4 5 6 7	1 2 3 4
5 6 7 8 9 10 11	2 3 4 5 6 7 8	6 7 8 9 10 11 12		4 5 6 7 8 9 10	8 9 10 11 12 13 14	5 6 7 8 9 10 11
12 13 14 15 16 17 18	9 10 11 12 13 14 15	13 14 15 16 17 18 19		11 12 13 14 15 16 17	15 16 17 18 19 20 21	12 13 14 15 16 17 18
19 20 21 22 23 24 25	16 17 18 19 20 21 22	20 21 22 23 24 25 26		18 19 20 21 22 23 24	22 23 24 25 26 27 28	19 20 21 22 23 24 25
26 27 28 29 30 31	23 24 25 26 27 28 29 / 30 31	27 28 29 30		25 26 27 28 29 30 31	29 30 31	26 27 28 29 30

OCTOBER	NOVEMBER	DECEMBER		OCTOBER	NOVEMBER	DECEMBER
S M T W T F S	S M T W T F S	S M T W T F S		S M T W T F S	S M T W T F S	S M T W T F S
1 2 3	1 2 3 4 5 6 7	1 2 3 4 5		1 2	1 2 3 4 5 6	1 2 3 4
4 5 6 7 8 9 10	8 9 10 11 12 13 14	6 7 8 9 10 11 12		3 4 5 6 7 8 9	7 8 9 10 11 12 13	5 6 7 8 9 10 11
11 12 13 14 15 16 17	15 16 17 18 19 20 21	13 14 15 16 17 18 19		10 11 12 13 14 15 16	14 15 16 17 18 19 20	12 13 14 15 16 17 18
18 19 20 21 22 23 24	22 23 24 25 26 27 28	20 21 22 23 24 25 26		17 18 19 20 21 22 23	21 22 23 24 25 26 27	19 20 21 22 23 24 25
25 26 27 28 29 30 31	29 30	27 28 29 30 31		24 25 26 27 28 29 30 / 31	28 29 30	26 27 28 29 30 31

13 — 2016 | 14 — 2028

JANUARY	FEBRUARY	MARCH		JANUARY	FEBRUARY	MARCH
S M T W T F S	S M T W T F S	S M T W T F S		S M T W T F S	S M T W T F S	S M T W T F S
1 2	1 2 3 4 5 6	1 2 3 4 5		1	1 2 3 4 5	1 2 3 4
3 4 5 6 7 8 9	7 8 9 10 11 12 13	6 7 8 9 10 11 12		2 3 4 5 6 7 8	6 7 8 9 10 11 12	5 6 7 8 9 10 11
10 11 12 13 14 15 16	14 15 16 17 18 19 20	13 14 15 16 17 18 19		9 10 11 12 13 14 15	13 14 15 16 17 18 19	12 13 14 15 16 17 18
17 18 19 20 21 22 23	21 22 23 24 25 26 27	20 21 22 23 24 25 26		16 17 18 19 20 21 22	20 21 22 23 24 25 26	19 20 21 22 23 24 25
24 25 26 27 28 29 30 / 31	28 29	27 28 29 30 31		23 24 25 26 27 28 29 / 30 31	27 28 29	26 27 28 29 30 31

APRIL	MAY	JUNE		APRIL	MAY	JUNE
S M T W T F S	S M T W T F S	S M T W T F S		S M T W T F S	S M T W T F S	S M T W T F S
1 2	1 2 3 4 5 6 7	1 2 3 4		1	1 2 3 4 5 6	1 2 3
3 4 5 6 7 8 9	8 9 10 11 12 13 14	5 6 7 8 9 10 11		2 3 4 5 6 7 8	7 8 9 10 11 12 13	4 5 6 7 8 9 10
10 11 12 13 14 15 16	15 16 17 18 19 20 21	12 13 14 15 16 17 18		9 10 11 12 13 14 15	14 15 16 17 18 19 20	11 12 13 14 15 16 17
17 18 19 20 21 22 23	22 23 24 25 26 27 28	19 20 21 22 23 24 25		16 17 18 19 20 21 22	21 22 23 24 25 26 27	18 19 20 21 22 23 24
24 25 26 27 28 29 30	29 30 31	26 27 28 29 30		23 24 25 26 27 28 29 / 30	28 29 30 31	25 26 27 28 29 30

JULY	AUGUST	SEPTEMBER		JULY	AUGUST	SEPTEMBER
S M T W T F S	S M T W T F S	S M T W T F S		S M T W T F S	S M T W T F S	S M T W T F S
1 2	1 2 3 4 5 6	1 2 3		1	1 2 3 4 5	1 2
3 4 5 6 7 8 9	7 8 9 10 11 12 13	4 5 6 7 8 9 10		2 3 4 5 6 7 8	6 7 8 9 10 11 12	3 4 5 6 7 8 9
10 11 12 13 14 15 16	14 15 16 17 18 19 20	11 12 13 14 15 16 17		9 10 11 12 13 14 15	13 14 15 16 17 18 19	10 11 12 13 14 15 16
17 18 19 20 21 22 23	21 22 23 24 25 26 27	18 19 20 21 22 23 24		16 17 18 19 20 21 22	20 21 22 23 24 25 26	17 18 19 20 21 22 23
24 25 26 27 28 29 30 / 31	28 29 30 31	25 26 27 28 29 30		23 24 25 26 27 28 29 / 30 31	27 28 29 30 31	24 25 26 27 28 29 30

OCTOBER	NOVEMBER	DECEMBER		OCTOBER	NOVEMBER	DECEMBER
S M T W T F S	S M T W T F S	S M T W T F S		S M T W T F S	S M T W T F S	S M T W T F S
1	1 2 3 4 5	1 2 3		1 2 3 4 5 6 7	1 2 3 4	1 2
2 3 4 5 6 7 8	6 7 8 9 10 11 12	4 5 6 7 8 9 10		8 9 10 11 12 13 14	5 6 7 8 9 10 11	3 4 5 6 7 8 9
9 10 11 12 13 14 15	13 14 15 16 17 18 19	11 12 13 14 15 16 17		15 16 17 18 19 20 21	12 13 14 15 16 17 18	10 11 12 13 14 15 16
16 17 18 19 20 21 22	20 21 22 23 24 25 26	18 19 20 21 22 23 24		22 23 24 25 26 27 28	19 20 21 22 23 24 25	17 18 19 20 21 22 23
23 24 25 26 27 28 29 / 30 31	27 28 29 30	25 26 27 28 29 30 31		29 30 31	26 27 28 29 30	24 25 26 27 28 29 30 / 31

INDEX

Abbreviations

Rule . . . . Federal Rules of Civil Procedure (Part III)
Evid. Rule . . . . Federal Rules of Evidence (Part X)
Form . . . . Forms Appendix to Federal Rules of Civil Procedure (Part IV)
Auth. Comm. [ ] . . . Authors' Commentary to [ ] (Part III)
Juris. [ ] . . . . Federal Jurisdiction and Venue [ ] (Part II)

ABATEMENT OF ACTIONS
Substitution of parties where public officer was party, Rule 25(d).

ABSENCE
Hearsay exception,
    Declarant from hearing and proponent of statement unable to procure his attendance, "unavailability as witness" as including, Evid. Rule 804.
    Entry in records of regularly conducted activity, Evid. Rule 803.
    Public record or entry, Evid. Rule 803.
Joinder, persons needed for just adjudication, Rule 19(a).
Witness, waiver, signing, depositions upon oral examination, Rule 30(e).

ABSTRACTS
Business records, interrogatories, Rule 33(c).

ACCEPTANCE
Offer of Judgment, Auth. Comm. Rule 68.

ACCIDENT
Absence of, admissibility of evidence of other wrongs or acts to prove, Evid. Rule 404.

ACCORD AND SATISFACTION
Affirmative defense, Rule 8(c).

ACCOUNTS AND ACCOUNTING
Complaint in action on, form of, Form 4.
Default judgment, necessity of taking account, Rule 55(b)(2).
Masters, statement of accounts, Rule 53(d)(3); Auth. Comm. Rule 53(d)(3).
Reference to master, Rule 53(b).
Stay of judgment for accounting for infringement, Rule 62(a); Auth. Comm. Rule 62(a).

ACCUSED
Character evidence, Evid. Rule 404.
Juvenile adjudication of witness other than, evidence of, impeachment of witness, Evid. Rule 609.
Self-incrimination privilege not waived when examined respecting matters relating only to credibility, Evid. Rule 608.
Testimony on preliminary matter, cross-examination as to other issues, Evid. Rule 104.

ACTIONS AND PROCEEDINGS
Appeal and Review, generally, this index.
Applicability of rules, Rule 81(a); Evid. Rule 1101; Auth. Comm. Rules 2 and 81(a).
Capacity to Sue or Be Sued, Rule 17(b).
Civil action, one form of action, Rule 2; Auth. Comm. Rule 2.
Class Actions, generally, this index.
Commencement, Rule 3; Auth. Comm. Rule 3.
Consolidation for trial or hearing, Rule 42(a); Auth. Comm. Rule 42(a).
Costs, generally, this index.
Counterclaims, generally, this index.
Criminal Actions and Procedure, generally, this index.
Cross–Claims, generally, this index.
Default Judgments, generally, this index.
Dismissal, generally, this index.

INDEX

ADOPTION
Hearsay exception,
> Reputation concerning, Evid. Rule 803.
> Statement of declarant concerning, Evid. Rule 804.

Written statement as prior statement concerning action or subject matter made by party or person, obtaining of discovery, Rule 26(b); Auth. Comm. Rule 26(b)(3).

ADOPTION BY REFERENCE, Auth. Comm. Rules 10(b) and (c).

ADVANCEMENT
Causes on docket, Rule 78.

ADVERSE PARTIES
Parties, this index.

ADVISORY COMMITTEE NOTES
> Generally, Part VII (text of original Notes and Notes to amendments)

Effect, Auth. Comm. Rule 1.

ADVISORY JURY
Trial by court with advisory jury, Rules 39(c) and 52(a); Auth. Comm. Rule 39(c).

AFFIDAVITS
Contempt for filing affidavit for summary judgment in bad faith, Rule 56(g); Auth. Comm. Rule 56(g).

Default judgment, Rule 55; Auth. Comm. Rule 55.

Motion based on facts appearing of record, hearing on affidavits, Rule 43(e); Auth. Comm. Rule 7(b).

New trial, time for serving no motion for, Rule 59(c).

Opposing affidavits,
> Made in bad faith, Rule 56(g).
> Time for service, Rule 6(d).

Rule 11, effect on, Auth. Comm. Rule 11.

Service of Process, this index.

Summary judgment, Rule 56.

Temporary restraining order, notice, Rule 65(b).

AFFIRMATIONS
Oaths and Affirmations, generally, this index.

AFFIRMATIVE DEFENSES
Pleading, Rule 8(c); Auth. Comm. Rule 8(c).

Reply to, Auth. Comm. Rule 7(a)

Service of pleadings, numerous defendants, Rule 5(c).

Sua Sponte assertion, Auth. Comm. Rule 8.

AGE
Witness, inability to attend or testify, depositions, use in court proceedings, Rule 32(a); Auth. Comm. Rule 32(a).

AGENCIES OF UNITED STATES
Actions of, set aside by reviewing authority, facts subject to trial de novo, rules applicable in part, Evid. Rule 1101.

Amended pleadings against the United States, Rule 15(c)(3).

Answer or reply, time for service, Rule 12(a).

Appeal, stay without bond or security, Rule 62(e).

Definition of, 28 U.S.C.A. § 451.

Depositions,
> Introduction in evidence as making deponent witness of introducing party, nonapplicability, Rule 32(c).
> Oral examination, Rule 30(b).
>> Failure of officer, etc., to attend at own deposition, sanctions, Rule 37(d).
>> Failure to comply with order compelling designation, sanctions, Rule 37(b).
>> Motion for order compelling designation, Rule 37(a).
> Use in court proceedings, Rule 32(a).
> Written questions, Rule 31(a).
>> Failure of officer, etc., to attend at own deposition, sanctions, Rule 37(d).
>> Failure to comply with order compelling answer, sanctions, Rule 37(b).
>> Motion for order compelling answer, Rule 37(a).

Documents of under or not under seal, self-authentication, Evid. Rule 902.

INDEX

BAPTISMAL RECORDS
Hearsay exception, Evid. Rule 803.

BIAS OR PREJUDICE
Compromise and offers to compromise claims, admissibility of evidence to prove, Evid. Rule 408.
Exclusion of relevant evidence on grounds of unfair prejudice, Evid. Rule 403.
Extraneous prejudicial information improperly brought to jury's attention, testimony of juror respecting, Evid. Rule 606.
Insurance against liability, evidence of, admissibility to prove, Evid. Rule 411.

BIBLES
Hearsay exception, statements in bible concerning personal or family history, Evid. Rule 803.

BILLS OF REVIEW
Abolished, Rule 60(b).

BIRTHS
Hearsay, this index.

BIVENS ACTIONS
Service issues in, Auth. Comm. Rule 4.

BOARDS AND COMMISSIONS
Pleading decision, Rule 9(e).

BONDS (OFFICERS AND FIDUCIARIES)
General bond, admiralty or maritime claims, actions in rem and quasi in rem, release, property, Supp. Rules E(5)(b), (c).
Injunction pending appeal, Rule 62(c).
Interpleader, Auth. Comm. Rule 22 and Statutory Interpleader.
Preliminary injunction, Rule 65(c); Auth. Comm. Rule 65(c).
Proceedings against sureties, Rule 65.1.
Removal, abolition of requirement for bond, Removal, Juris. § 2.17.
Shareholder derivative suits, Auth. Comm. Rule 23.1.
Special bond, admiralty or maritime claims, actions in rem and quasi in rem, release, property, Supp.Rules E(5)(a) to (c).
Stay pending appeal, Rule 62.
Surety, Rule 65.1.
Temporary restraining order, Rule 65(c); Auth. Comm. Rule 65(c).

BOOKS AND PAPERS
Clerk to keep, Rule 79(d).
Discovery, scope of, Rule 26(b).
Documents, generally, this index.
Master, compelling production, Rule 53(c).
Official, self-authentication, Evid. Rule 902.
Subpoena for production, Rule 45(a); Auth. Comm. Rule 45(a).

BOUNDARIES
Reputation concerning or judgment as to, hearsay exception, Evid. Rule 803.

BRIEFS
Appeal from magistrate to district judge, Rule 75(c), (d); Auth. Comm. Rule 75(c), (d).
Appeal to courts of appeal, Auth. Comm. Appeals.
Supporting or opposing Motions, Auth. Comm. Rule 7(b).

BURDEN OF PROOF
Class Certification, Auth. Comm. Rule 23.
Presumption as not shifting, Evid. Rule 301.

BUSINESS RECORDS
Admissibility, 28 U.S.C.A. § 1732.
Interrogatories, option to produce, Rule 33(c); Auth. Comm. Rule 33(c).

CALENDARS
Assignment of cases for trial, Rule 40; Auth. Comm. Rule 40.
Clerk to prepare, Rule 79(c).
Declaratory judgment case advanced on calendar, Rule 57.
Pre-trial calendar, establishment by rule, Rule 16.

CONSENT—Continued
Parties—Continued
Order for trial by jury, Rule 39(c); Auth. Comm. Rule 39(c).
Trial by court, Rule 39(a); Auth. Comm. Rule 39(a).
Withdrawal of demand for jury trial, Rule 38(d); Auth. Comm. Rule 38(d).
Personal jurisdiction, Jurisdiction, Juris. § 2.4.
Release, property, admiralty or maritime claims, actions in rem and quasi in rem, Supp. Rule E(5)(c).
Unanimity and removal, Removal.
Venue, generally, this index.

CONSERVATOR
Infant or incompetent, action or defense, Rule 17(c).

CONSIDERATION
Pleading failure of consideration as defense, Rule 8(c).

CONSOLIDATION
Actions for trial or hearing, Rule 42(a); Auth. Comm. Rule 42(a).
Defenses in motion, Rule 12(g); Auth. Comm. Rule 12(g).
Multidistrict Litigation Rules (Part V).
Pleadings to do justice, Rule 8(f).
Preliminary injunction hearing with trial on merits, Rule 65(a)(2).

CONSPIRACY
Statement by co-conspirator of party during course and in furtherance of, not hearsay, Evid. Rule 801.

CONSTITUTION OF UNITED STATES
Certifying constitutional questions, 28 U.S.C.A. § 2403.
Privilege of witnesses, etc., law governing, exception, Evid. Rule 501.
Relevant evidence admissible except as otherwise provided by, Evid. Rule 402.

CONSTRUCTION OF RULES
Generally, Auth. Comm. Rule 1; Evid. Rule 102.

CONSUL GENERAL
Foreign public documents, final certification, genuineness of signature, etc., Evid. Rule 902.

CONSULS AND CONSULAR AGENTS
Authentication of official record, Rule 44(a).
Depositions, taking, Rule 28(b).

CONSULTANTS
Discovery, trial and litigation, preparation, need of material, Rule 26(b); Auth. Comm. Rule 26(b)(4).

CONTEMPT
Applicability of rules to proceedings respecting, Evid. Rule 1101.
Depositions, refusal to answer, etc., Rule 37(b); Auth. Comm. Rule 37(b).
Discovery, sanction for failure to comply with order compelling, Rule 37(b); Auth. Comm. Rule 37(b).
Foreign country subpoenas, 28 U.S.C.A. § 1784.
Judgment directing performance of specific acts, disobedience, Rule 7.
Service, persons required to respond to order of commitment, places outside state but within United States, Rule 4(f).
Subpoena, disobedience, Rule 45(e); Auth. Comm. Rule 45(e).
Summary judgment, filing affidavit in bad faith, Rule 56(g).
Witnesses, failure to appear before master, Rule 53(d); Auth. Comm. Rule 53(d)(2).

CONTENTS, DEPOSITIONS UPON
Oral examination, notice of taking, Rule 30(b).
Written questions, notice, Rule 31(a).

CONTINUANCES
Summary judgment, continuance to procure opposing affidavit, Rule 56(f); Auth. Comm. Rule 56(f).

CONTRADICTING
Testimony of deponent, use of deposition in court proceedings, Rule 32(a); Auth. Comm. Rule 32(a).

DISCOVERY

Generally, Rule 26; Auth. Comm. Rule 26.

Attorney's Fees, generally, this index.

Delay prohibited, Rule 26(d).

Depositions, generally, this index.

Disclosures, generally, this index.

Discovery plan; Rule 26(f); Auth. Comm. Rule 26(f).

Entry upon Land, generally, this index.

Expenses and Expenditures, this index.

Expert witnesses, Rule 26(a)(2); Rule 26(b)(4); Auth. Comm. Rule 26(a)(2); Auth. Comm. Rule 26(b)(4).

Failure to make, sanctions, Rule 37; Auth. Comm. Rule 37.

Fees, etc., expert witnesses, trial or litigation preparation, Rule 26(b); Auth. Comm. Rule 26(b)(4).

Foreign country, subpoena of person in, Rule 37(e).

Frequency, use of methods, limitation prohibited, Rule 26(a).

Initial disclosures, Rule 26(a)(1); Auth. Comm. Rule 26(a)(1).

Insurance agreements, existence and contents, Rule 26(b); Auth. Comm. Rule 26(b)(2).

Interrogatories, generally, this index.

Judgment or execution, obtaining in aid of, Rule 69(a).

Jurisdictional discovery, Auth. Comm. Rule 72(b)(2).

Meeting, Rule 26(f); Auth. Comm. Rule 26(f).

Methods,

Of obtaining, Rule 26(a); Auth. Comm. Rule 26(a).

Use, timing and sequence for, Rule 26(d); Auth. Comm. Rule 26(d).

Modification of procedures, stipulations, Rule 29; Auth. Comm. Rule 29.

Motions, this index.

Objections, Rule 26(b); Auth. Comm. Rules 33, 34.

Signature, Rule 26(g); Auth. Comm. Rule 26(g).

Orders, this index.

Physical and Mental Examinations, generally, this index.

Pretrial disclosures, Rule 26(a)(3); Auth. Comm. Rule 26(a)(3).

Privileges, Rule 26(b); Auth. Comm. Rule 26(6).

Production of Documents or Things, generally, this index.

Protective Orders, this index.

Request for, responses to,

Extension of time, stipulations, approval of court, Rule 29; Auth. Comm. Rule 29.

Signature, Rule 26(g); Auth. Comm. Rule 26(g).

Supplementation of, Rule 26(e); Auth. Comm. Rule 26(e).

Requests for admissions. Admissions, this index.

Sanctions, Auth. Comm. Rule 37.

Scope, Rule 26(b); Auth. Comm. Rule 26(b).

Sequence, use of methods, Rule 26(d); Auth. Comm. Rule 26 (d).

Service, papers relating to, Rule 5(a).

Signature of discovery documents, Rule 26(g); Auth. Comm. Rule 26(g).

State practice, applicability, proceedings in aid of judgment or execution, Rule 69(a); Auth. Comm. Rule 69(a).

Statements previously made by parties or persons, of action or subject matter, obtaining of, Rule 26(b); Auth. Comm. Rule 26(b)(3).

Stipulations regarding procedure, Rule 29; Auth. Comm. Rule 29.

Summary judgment, continuance to procure discovery opposing, Rule 56(f).

Supplementation of responses, Rule 26(e); Auth. Comm. Rule 26(e).

Time, methods, use of, Rule 26(d); Auth. Comm. Rule 26(d).

Trial or litigation preparation,

Expert witnesses, Rule 26(b).

Substantial need of materials, Rule 26(b); Auth. Comm. Rule 26(b)(3).

Witnesses, Rule 26 et seq.

DISCRETION OF COURT

Bond for injunctions or temporary restraining orders, Rule 65(c); Auth. Comm. Rule 65(c).

Class actions,

Additional notice, Rule 23(d).

Certification, Rule 23(c).

Dismissal or compromise, Rule 23(e).

Counterclaims and crossclaims,

After-acquired or late maturing counterclaims, Rule 13(e).

Omitted counterclaims, Rule 13(f).

INDEX

DOCUMENTS
Admission of genuineness. Admissions, generally, this index.
Ancient Documents, generally, this index.
Authentication, generally, this index.
Discovery,
> Need requirement, litigation or trial, preparation, Rule 26(b); Auth. Comm. Rule 26(b)(2).
> Scope of, Rule 26(b); Auth. Comm. Rule 26(b).
Disobedience to judgment directing delivery, Rule 70.
Foreign official documents, 28 U.S.C.A. § 1741.
Masters, compelling production, Rule 53(c).
Order for production, Rule 27(a), (b).
Patent documents, 28 U.S.C.A. §§ 1744–1745.
Pleading official document, Rule 9(d).
Postmaster demand, 28 U.S.C.A. § 1743.
Production of documents or things, generally, this index.
Subpoenas, response, Rule 45(d).

DOMESTIC OFFICIAL RECORDS
Authentication, Rule 44(a)(1); Auth. Comm. Rule 44(a)(1).

DOMICILE
Parties, capacity to sue or be sued, Rule 17(b).
Subject matter jurisdiction and citizenship, Jurisdiction, Juris. § 2.12.

DRAWINGS
Production of documents or things, generally, this index.

DRUGS
Criminal libel for condemnation, exclusion of imports or other proceedings, applicability of rules in part, Evid. Rule 1101.

DUE PROCESS
Personal jurisdiction, quasi in rem jurisdiction, in rem jurisdiction, Jurisdiction.

DURESS
Pleading as affirmative defense, Rule 8(c).

DWELLING HOUSE
Service of pleading, etc., Rule 5(b).

E-MAIL
Substituted service by, Auth. Comm. Rule 4(f).

EFFECTIVE DATE
Offer to plead guilty, nolo contendere, etc., provisions concerning, Evid. Rule 410.
Original rules and amendments, Rule 86; Auth. Comm. Rule 86.

ELECTRICAL RECORDING
Obtaining prior statement concerning action or subject matter by party or person, Rule 26(b).

EMBARRASSMENT
Depositions upon oral examination, motion to terminate or limit, Rule 30(d); Auth. Comm. Rule 30(d).
Protective orders relating to depositions, grounds for, Rule 26(c); Auth. Comm. Rule 26(c).

EMINENT DOMAIN
Condemnation of Property, generally, this index.

EMOTION
Hearsay exceptions, statement respecting, Evid. Rule 803.

EMPLOYEES
Officers and Employees, generally, this index.
Employer and Employee,
> Preliminary injunctions and temporary restraining orders, Rule 65(e).

ENGRAVINGS
Rings, urns, crypts or tombstones, statements concerning, hearsay exception, Evid. Rule 803.

INDEX

FILING—Continued

Complaint, admiralty or maritime claims, limitation of liability, Supp. Rule F(1).

Depositions upon,

> Oral examination, officer taking, Rule 30(f); Auth. Comm. Rule 30(f).
>
> Written questions, Rule 31(b); Auth. Comm. Rule 31(c).

Discovery papers, Auth. Comm. Rule 5(d).

Electronic means, filing by, Auth. Comm. Rule 5(e).

Facsimile transmission, Rule 5(e); Auth. Comm. Rule 5(e).

Fees, Auth. Comm. Rule 3 & Rule 5(e).

Judge, filing with, Auth. Comm. Rule 5(e).

Master's reports, Rule 53(e); Auth. Comm. Rule 53(e)(1).

Papers after complaint, Rule 5(d).

Pleading,

> Complaint,
>
> > Commencement of civil action, Rule 3.
> >
> > Issuance of summons, Rule 4(a)(b).
>
> Numerous defendants, Rule 5(c).

Prisoners, filing by, Auth. Comm. Rule 5(e).

Reasonable time for filing, Auth. Comm. Rule 5(d).

Seizure actions, Auth. Comm. Rule 5(a).

Temporary restraining order, Rule 65(b).

Time for, Rule 5(d); Auth. Comm. 5(d).

With the court, defined, Rule 5(e); Auth. Comm. Rule 5(e).

FINDINGS

Amendment of findings, Rule 52(b); Auth. Comm. Rule 52(b).

> Extension of time, Rule 6(b).
>
> Motion for new trial, Rule 59(a).
>
> Stay of proceedings to enforce judgment pending disposition of motion to amend, Rule 62(b).

Class actions maintainable, Rule 23(b).

Court, findings by, Rule 52; Auth. Comm. Rule 52.

Master, findings of, Rule 53(e); Auth. Comm. Rule 53(e)(1).

> Findings by court, Rule 52(a); Auth. Comm. Rule 52(a).

Motion for amendment of findings by court, Rule 52(b); Auth. Comm. Rule 52(b).

Partial findings, judgment on, Rule 52; Auth. Comm. Rule 52(c).

Special verdict, Rule 49(a).

Stay of proceedings to enforce judgment pending disposition of motion to amend, Rule 62(b).

Unanimity of jurors, Rule 48.

FINES AND PENALTIES

Customs duties, actions for, application of rules in part, Evid. Rule 1101.

Death Penalty, generally, this index.

Sentence and Punishment, generally, this index.

Witnesses, failure to appear before master, Rule 53(d); Auth. Comm. Rule 53(d)(2).

FOOD

Criminal libel for condemnation, exclusion of imports or other proceedings, applicability of rules in part, Evid. Rule 1101.

FOREIGN CORPORATIONS

Service, Rule 4(d).

FOREIGN COUNTRIES

Depositions, persons before whom taken, Rule 28(b); Auth. Comm. Rule 28(b).

Discovery, subpoena of person in, Rule 37(e).

Foreign and international tribunals, assistance to, 28 U.S.C.A. § 1782.

Removal in suits against, Removal.

Service in, alternative provisions for, Rule 4(i).

Subpoena directed to witness in foreign country, Rule 45(b); Auth. Comm. Rule 45(b); 28 U.S.C.A. § 1783.

Venue and, Venue, Juris. § 2.14.

FOREIGN DIPLOMATIC AND CONSULAR OFFICERS

Certification, genuineness of signature and official position of executing or attesting person, etc., foreign public documents, Evid. Rule 902.

Foreign and international tribunals, assistance to, 28 U.S.C.A. § 1782.

FOREIGN DOCUMENTS
Certification, genuineness of signature and official position of executing or attesting person, etc., Evid. Rule 902.

FOREIGN GOVERNMENTS AND AGENCIES
Service on, Auth. Comm. Rule 4(d).

FOREIGN JUDGMENTS
Pleading, Rule 9(e).

FOREIGN LAW
Determination, Rule 44.1; Auth. Comm. Rule 44.1.

FOREIGN OFFICIAL RECORDS
Authentication, Rule 44(a)(2); Auth. Comm. Rule 44(a)(2).

FOREIGN SERVICE
Certification, signatures, etc., foreign public documents, authority of consular agents, vice consul, etc., Evid. Rule 902.

FORFEITURES
Deposition, property, admiralty or maritime claims, actions in rem and quasi in rem, Supp. Rule, E(9)(a).

FORM OF ACTION
One form of action, civil action, Rule 2; Auth. Comm. Rule 2.

FORMER DISTRICT DIRECTOR OR COLLECTOR OF INTERNAL REVENUE
"Officer" as including, Rule 81(f).

FORMS
Answer, Form 21.
    Intervener, Form 23.
    Presenting defenses, Form 20.
Appendix Forms, intent to indicate simplicity and brevity of statement contemplated, Rule 84.
Complaint. Pleadings, generally, this index.
Counterclaim, Form 20.
    Interpleader, Form 21.
Cross-claim, Form 20.
Evidence, Rule 43(a).
Exhibit accompanying motion, bringing in third-party defendant, Form 22–B.
Judgment on,
    Decision by the court, Form 32.
    Jury verdict, Form 31.
Jurisdiction, allegation of, Form 2.
Motions,
    Bringing in third-party defendant, Form 22–B.
    Dismissal of complaint, Form 19.
    Intervention as defendant, Form 23.
    Production of documents, form of, Form 24.
    Technical forms not required, Rule 8(e)(1).
Notice,
    Appeal to court of appeals, Form 27.
    Bringing in third-party defendant, Form 22–B.
    Condemnation of property, Form 28.
    Intervention as defendant, Form 23.
    Lawsuit, Form 1A.
    Motion,
        Dismiss complaint, Form 19.
        Production of documents, Form 24.
Pleadings, this index.
Purpose of, Rule 84.
Request,
    For admission, Form 25.
    Production of documents or things, Form 24.
Statement of accounts before master, Rule 53(d); Auth. Comm. Rule 53(d)(3).
Subpoenas, Rule 45(a); Auth. Comm. Rule 45(a).

INDEX

FORMS—Continued

Suggestion of death upon the record under rule concerning substitution of parties, Form 30.

Summons, Rule 4(b), Form 1.

Third-party defendant, summons against, Forms 22–a, 22–A.

Third-party practice, Forms 22, 22–A.

Waiver of service, Form 1B.

Request for, Form 1A.

FORUM NON CONVENIENS

Deference to plaintiff and, Forum non Conveniens, Juris. § 2.15.

Remedy for inappropriate forum,

Dismissal of action, Forum non Conveniens, Juris. § 2.15 & Auth. Comm. Rule 12(b)(3).

Transfer of action, Forum non Conveniens, Juris. § 2.15.

FRAUD

Pleading, Rule 9(b); Auth. Comm. Rule 9(b).

Relief from judgment, Rule 60(b).

FRAUDULENT CONVEYANCES

Complaint in action to set aside, form of, Form 13.

Joinder of remedy, Rule 18(b).

GARNISHMENT

Availability of, Rule 64.

GENEALOGIES

Statement of personal or family history contained in, hearsay exception, Evid. Rule 803.

GOOD CAUSE

Failure to timely serve process, Auth. Comm. Rule 4(m).

Motion for protective orders relating to depositions, Rule 26(c); Auth. Comm. Rule 26(c).

Physical and mental examinations, order for, Rule 35(a); Auth. Comm. Rule 35(a).

GOODS SOLD AND DELIVERED

Complaint, Form 5.

GOVERNMENTAL AGENCIES

Agencies of United States, generally, this index.

GOVERNMENTAL ORGANIZATION

Service of summons and complaint, Rule 4(d); Auth. Comm. Rule 4(d).

GOVERNMENTS

Privilege of, general rule, Evid. Rule 501.

GRAND JURY

Proceedings before, inapplicability, Evid. Rule 1101.

GRAPHS

Production of documents or things, generally, post.

GROUNDS

Class actions maintainable, Rule 23(b).

New trial, Rule 59(d).

GROUP PLEADING

Limitations upon, Auth. Comm. Rule 9(b) & Rule 10(b).

GUAM

District court, applicability of rules, Evid. Rule 1101.

Subject matter jurisdiction, Jurisdiction, Juris. §§ 2.12–2.13.

GUARDIANS

Action or defense by representative, Rule 17(a), (c).

GUILTY

Plea of Guilty, generally, this index.

HABEAS CORPUS

Applicability of rules in part, Evid. Rule 1101.

Application of rules to, Rule 81(a); Auth. Comm. Rule 81(a).

HABEAS CORPUS—Continued
Direction of writ or show cause order to person having custody, Rule 81(a); Auth. Comm. Rule 81(a).
Return of writ or show cause order, time, Rule 81(a); Auth. Comm. Rule 81(a).

HABIT
Relevant evidence, Evid. Rule 406.

HANDWRITING
Admissibility, 28 U.S.C.A. § 1731.
Writings, generally, this index.

HARASSMENT
Witnesses, control of mode and order of interrogation and presentation of evidence to protect from, Evid. Rule 611.

HARMLESS ERROR
Disregard of error not affecting substantial rights, Rule 61; Auth. Comm. Rule 61; 28 U.S.C.A. § 2111.

HEALTH
Hearsay exceptions, statements respecting, Evid. Rule 803.

HEARINGS
Conducted outside district, Rule 77(b).
Consolidation of actions for hearing, Rule 42(a); Auth. Comm. Rule 42(a).
Discovery, order to compel, award of expenses, Rule 37(a); Auth. Comm. Rule 37(a).
Inability of judge to proceed, Rule 63.
Judicial notice, adjudicative facts, opportunity to be heard as to propriety of taking, Evid. Rule 201.
Jury, this index.
Motions,
    Depositions, use of, Rule 32(a).
    Without oral hearing, determination of, Rule 78; Auth. Comm. Rule 78.
New trial, Rule 59(d).
Preliminary hearing on defenses in pleading, etc., Rule 12(d); Auth. Comm. Rule 12(d).
Preliminary injunction, consolidation with trial on merits, Rule 65(a)(2).
Service of notice, Rule 6(d).
Subpoena for attendance at, Rule 45(a).
Successor judges, Rule 63.
Temporary restraining order, Rule 65(b).
Voluntary dismissal before introduction of evidence, Rule 41(c).

HEARSAY
    Generally, Evid. Rule 802.
Absence of,
    Declarant from hearing and proponent of statement unable to procure attendance of, "unavailability as witness" as including, exception, Evid. Rule 804.
    Entry in records of regularly conducted activity, exception, Evid. Rule 803.
    Public record or entry, exception, Evid. Rule 803.
Admission by party-opponent, statements which are not hearsay, Evid. Rule 801.
Adoption,
    Reputation concerning, exception, Evid. Rule 803.
    Statement of declarant concerning, exception, Evid. Rule 804.
Agent or servant, statements by not hearsay, Evid. Rule 801.
Ancestry, records of religious organizations, exception, Evid. Rule 803.
Attacking and supporting credibility of declarant, Evid. Rule 806.
Availability of declarant immaterial, Evid. Rule 803.
Baptismal certificates, exception, Evid. Rule 803.
Births,
    Records of, exception, Evid. Rule 803.
    Statement of declarant concerning, exception, Evid. Rule 804.
Bodily health, statements respecting, exception, Evid. Rule 803.
Boundaries, reputation concerning or judgment as to, exception, Evid. Rule 803.
Certificates, marriage, baptismal, etc., exception, Evid. Rule 803.
Commercial publications, exception, Evid. Rule 803.
Criminal liability, statement tending to expose declarant to and offered to exculpate accused, admissibility, exception, Evid. Rule 804.
Cross-examination by party against whom statement of declarant admitted, Evid. Rule 806.

HEARSAY—Continued
Regularly conducted activity, records of, exception, Evid. Rule 803.
Relationship by blood or marriage, records of religious organizations, exception, Evid. Rule 803.
Religious organizations, records of, exception, Evid. Rule 803.
Reputation,
 As to character, exception, Evid. Rule 803.
 Concerning boundaries or general history, exception, Evid. Rule 803.
Ruling of court, declarant exempted by on ground of privilege from testifying concerning subject matter of his statement, "unavailability as witness" as including, exception, Evid. Rule 804.
Statements,
 Defined, Evid. Rule 801.
 Not specifically covered in enumerated exceptions, exception of, Evid. Rules 803, 804.
 Which are not hearsay, Evid. Rule 801.
Unavailability as a witness, defined, Evid. Rule 804.
Urns, crypts or tombstones, statement concerning engravings on, exception, Evid. Rule 803.
Vital statistics, records of, exception, Evid. Rule 803.
Within hearsay, exclusion, Evid. Rule 805.

HISTORY
Hearsay, generally, this index.

HOLIDAYS
Excluded in computing time, Auth. Comm. Rule 6.

HOMICIDE
Statement under belief of impending death, criminal prosecution, hearsay exception, Evid. Rule 804.
Victim, character of, as peaceful or aggressive, Evid. Rule 404.

HOSPITALS
Expenses, payment, admissibility to prove liability for injury, Evid. Rule 409.

HOSTILE WITNESSES
Leading questions, interrogation by, Evid. Rule 611.

HYPOTHETICAL STATEMENT
Claim or defense, Rule 8(e)(2).

IDENTIFICATION
Documents and things produced for inspection, depositions upon oral examination, Rule 30(f).
Expert witnesses, trial preparation, interrogatories, Rule 26(b); Auth. Comm. Rule 26(b)(4).
Persons with knowledge of discoverable matter,
 Discovery, scope of, Rule 26(b).
 Supplementation of responses to request for discovery, Rule 26(e); Auth. Comm. Rule 26(e).

ILLEGALITY
Pleading as affirmative defense, Rule 8(c).

ILLEGITIMACY
Legitimacy and Illegitimacy, generally, this index.

ILLNESS OF WITNESS
Inability to attend or testify, depositions, use in court proceedings, Rule 32(a); Auth. Comm. Rule 32(a).
Waiver, signing depositions upon oral examination, Rule 30(e).

IMMUNITY
From service, Auth. Comm. Rule 4.

IMPAIRMENT OF SECURITY
Admiralty or maritime claims, actions in rem and quasi in rem, Supp. Rule E(6).

IMPEACHMENT OF WITNESSES
 Generally, Rule 43 (b).
Conviction of crime, evidence of, Evid. Rule 609.

INDEX

INSURANCE COMPANIES
Subject matter jurisdiction, Jurisdiction.

INSURER
Discovery, trial and litigation preparation, need of materials, Rule 26(b); Auth. Comm. Rule 26(b)(2).

INTANGIBLE PROPERTY
Admiralty or maritime claims, actions in rem, ancillary process, Supp. Rule C(5).
Custody, etc., admiralty or maritime claims, action in rem and quasi in rem, Supp. Rule E(4)(c).

INTENT
Pleading, Rule 9(b).
Proof of, admissibility of other crimes, wrongs or acts, Evid. Rule 404.

INTEREST
Civil cases, 28 U.S.C.A. § 1961.
Class actions, protection, Rule 23(a).
Depositions, disqualification for taking, Rule 28(c); Auth. Comm. Rule 28(c).
In,
> Property, etc., inability to protect, right to intervene, Rule 24(a).
> Subject of action, joinder, persons needed for just adjudication, Rule 19(a).

Prejudgment interest, motions for, Auth. Comm. Rule 59(e).
Statement against, hearsay exception, Evid. Rule 804.
Transfer of, substitution of new party, Rule 25(c); Auth. Comm. Rule 25(c).

INTERLOCUTORY
Injunction, findings of facts and conclusions of law, Rule 52(a); Auth. Comm. Rule 52(a).
Order, admiralty or maritime claims, actions in rem and quasi in rem, security, Supp. Rule E(9)(b).
Proceeding, depositions, use of, Rule 32(a).
Sales, admiralty or maritime claims, actions in rem and quasi in rem, Supp. Rule E(9)(b).

INTERNAL PATTERNS
Authentication and identification, conformity with requirements, Evid. Rule 901.

INTERNAL REVENUE OFFICER
Execution against, Rule 69(b); Auth. Comm. Rule 69(b).

INTERPLEADER
> Generally, Rule 22 and 28 U.S.C.A. § 1335.

Competency of witnesses, determination, Evid. Rule 601.
Complaint for interpleader and declaratory relief, form of, Form 18.
Counterclaim for interpleader, form of, Form 21; Auth. Comm. Rule 22 and Statutory Interpleader.
Injunction in action of, Rule 65(e).
Process and procedure, 28 U.S.C.A. § 2361.
Venue, 28 U.S.C.A. § 1397.

INTERPRETERS
Appointment and compensation, Rule 43(f).
Subject to rules relating to qualification as expert, Evid. Rule 604.

INTERROGATION
Witnesses, by court, Evid. Rule 614.

INTERROGATORIES
> See, also, Discovery, generally, this index.
> Generally, Rule 33(a) et seq.; Auth. Comm. Rule 33.

Adverse parties, Rule 43(b).
Answer, Rule 33(a); Auth. Comm. Rule 33(a).
Business records, option to produce, Rule 33(c); Auth. Comm. Rule 33(c).
Copies of answers and objections, service, time, Rule 33(a); Auth. Comm. Rule 33(a).
Evasive or incomplete answer, defined, motion for order to compel, Rule 37(a).
Examination of accounting parties before master, Rule 53(d)(3).
Expert witnesses, Rule 26(b); Auth. Comm. Rule § 26(b)(4) and 33(b).
Failure of party to serve answers or objections, to, sanctions, Rule 37(b).
Failure to comply with order compelling answer, sanction, Rule 37(d); Auth. Comm. Rule 37(d).

INTERROGATORIES—Continued
General verdict accompanied by answer to interrogatories, Rule 49(b); Auth. Comm. Rule 49(b).
Method of obtaining discovery, Rule 26(a).
Motion for order to compel answer, Rule 37(a); Auth. Comm. Rule 37(a).
Number of interrogatories, Rule 33(a); Auth. Comm. Rule 33(a).
Objections to, Rule 33(b); Auth. Comm. Rule 33(b).
Orders, this index.
Privileged information, Auth. Comm. Rule 33(b).
Scope of, Rule 33(b); Auth. Comm. Rule 33(b).
Service, Rule 33(a); Auth. Comm. Rule 33(a).
Special interrogatories to jury, Rule 49; Auth. Comm. Rule 49.
Stipulations, extension of time, responses to, approval of court, Rule 29; Auth. Comm. Rule 29.
Submission to jury with forms for a general verdict, Rule 49(b); Auth. Comm. Rule 49(b).
Summary judgment,
    Affidavits for, supplemented or opposed by answers to, Rule 56(e).
    Rendered where answers show no genuine issue, etc., Rule 56(c).
Supplement, duty to, Rule 26(e); Auth. Comm. Rules 26(e) and 33(a).
Time of service, Rule 33(a); Auth. Comm. Rule 33(a).
Trial, use at, Rule 33(b); Auth. Comm. Rule 33(b).

INTERVENTION
    Generally, Rule 24.
Form, Form 23.
Subject matter jurisdiction, jurisdiction, Juris. § 2.13; Auth. Comm. Rule 24(a).
United States, intervention by, 28 U.S.C.A. § 2403.

INTRODUCTION OF DESIGNATED MATTERS IN EVIDENCE
Prohibition, sanction for failure to comply with order compelling discovery, Rule 37(b); Auth. Comm. Rule 37(b).

INVESTIGATION
Criminal Investigations, generally, this index.
Factual findings resulting from, hearsay exception, Evid. Rule 803.
Foreign official records, Rule 44(a)(2).
Foreign public documents, authenticity and accuracy, Evid. Rule 902.

INVOLUNTARY DISMISSAL
Procedure, Rule 41(b); Auth. Comm. Rule 41(b).

INVOLUNTARY PLAINTIFF
Refusal to join, Rule 19(a).

IRREPARABLE INJURY
Preliminary injunctions and temporary restraining orders, Auth. Comm. Rule 65.

ISSUANCE OF PROCESS
Admiralty or maritime claims, actions in rem and quasi in rem, Supp. Rule E(3)(b).

ISSUES
Capacity of party, pleading, Rule 9(a).
Confusion of, exclusion of relevant evidence on grounds of, Evid. Rule 403.
Fact in issue,
    Expert testimony, Evid. Rule 702.
    Opinion testimony by lay witnesses, Evid. Rule 701.
Jury trial,
    Specification of issues in demand for, Rule 38(c); Auth. Comm. Rule 38(c).
    Trial of issues, Rule 39(a); Auth. Comm. Rule 39(a).
Pre-trial procedure, Rule 16.
Separate trial, Rule 42(b).
Trial by court, Rule 39(b).
Ultimate issue, opinion on, Evid. Rule 704.

JOINDER
Claims, Rule 18(a); Auth. Comm. Rule 2.
Dismissal for failure to join, Rules 12(b)(7), 19(b); Auth. Comm. Rules 12(b)(7), 19(b).
Parties, this index.
Property in condemnation proceeding, Rule 71A(b); Auth. Comm. Rule 71A(b).

MARRIAGE
Hearsay exception,
    Records of, Evid. Rule 803.
    Statement of declarant concerning, Evid. Rule 804.

MARSHALS
Fees of, 28 U.S.C.A. § 1921.
Process, service, Rule 4(c).

MASTER AND SERVANT
Complaint for negligence under Federal Employer's Liability Act, form of, Form 14.
Injunctions in proceedings affecting, Rule 65(e).

MASTERS
    Generally, Rule 53; Auth. Comm. Rule 53.
Costs, Recovery of, Auth. Comm. Rule 54(d)
Defined, Rule 53(a).
Findings,
    Acceptance by court in action tried without jury or with advisory jury, Rules 52(a), 53(e).
    Court, Rule 52(a); Auth. Comm. Rule 52(a).
Magistrate subject to rule governing masters, when, Rule 53(f); Auth. Comm. Rule 53(f).
Powers, Rule 53(c).
Report, Rule 53; Auth. Comm. Rule 53(e).
    Judgment not required to recite, Rule 54(a).

MATTER OF LAW
Judgment as a matter of law, Rule 50; Auth. Comm. Rule 50(a).

MEASURING OF PROPERTY OR OBJECTS
Entry upon land, etc., for inspection and other purposes, generally, ante.

MECHANICAL OR ELECTRONIC RECORDING
Obtaining prior statement concerning action or subject matter by party or person, Rule 26(b); Auth. Comm. Rule 26(b)(3).
"Writings" and "recordings" as including, contents of writings, etc., Evid. Rule 1001.

MEDICAL AND SURGICAL CARE AND ASSISTANCE
Expenses, payment, admissibility to prove liability for injury, Evid. Rule 409.
Hearsay exceptions, statements concerning medical diagnosis or treatment, Evid. Rule 803.

MEDICINE
Learned treatises, statements in, hearsay exception, Evid. Rule 803.

MEMORANDUM
Hearsay exceptions, Evid. Rule 803.

MEMORIAL DAY
Clerks of court, business hours for office, exceptions concerning opening, Rule 77(c).
"Legal holiday" as including for purposes of computing time, Rule 6(a).

MEMORY
Lack of, declarant testifying to, concerning subject matter of his statement, "unavailability as witness" as including, hearsay exception, Evid. Rule 804.
Writing used to refresh, Evid. Rule 612.

MENTAL CAPACITY OR CONDITION
Hearsay exceptions, statements respecting, Evid. Rule 803.

MENTAL EXAMINATIONS
Physical and mental examinations, generally, this index.

MENTAL HEALTH PROCEEDINGS
Nonapplicability of rules in U.S. District Court for District of Columbia, Rule 81(a).

MENTAL ILLNESS OR INFIRMITY
Declarant unable to be present or to testify at hearing because of, "unavailability as witness" as including, hearsay exception, Evid. Rule 804.

MERCHANT MARINE ACT
Complaint for damages under, form of, Form 15.

INDEX

NATURALIZATION

Applicability of rules to proceedings, Rule 81(a).

Review, action respecting naturalization and revocation thereof, rules applicable in part, Evid. Rule 1101.

NEGLIGENCE

Pleadings, this index.

Subsequent remedial measures, admissibility to prove, Evid. Rule 407.

NEGOTIATIONS

Compromise, claims, conduct or statements made, admissibility, Evid. Rule 408.

NEW TRIALS

Generally, Rule 59; Auth. Comm. Rule 59.

Additur, Auth. Comm. Rule 59(a).

Against weight of evidence, Auth. Comm. Rule 59(a).

Alternative motion, judgment as a matter of law, Rule 50; Auth. Comm. Rule 50(b).

Answers to written interrogatories inconsistent with general verdict, Rule 49(b); Auth. Comm. Rule 49(b).

Discretion in granting, Auth. Comm. Rule 59(a).

Grounds for new trial, Rule 59(a); Auth. Comm. Rule 59(a).

Harmless error not ground for, Rule 61.

Improper conduct by Counsel, Court, or Jury, Auth. Comm. Rule 59(a).

Judgment as a matter of law, alternative motion with, Rule 50; Auth. Comm. Rule 50(b).

Motions, Rule 59(d).

    Affidavits, in support of motion, Rule 59(c); Auth. Comm. Rule 59(c).

    Appealability, Auth. Comm. 59(a).

    Extension of time, Rule 6(b).

    Judgment as a matter of law motion, alternative, Rule 50; Auth. Comm. Rule 50(b).

    Time for moving, Rule 59(b); Auth. Comm. Rule 59(b).

Newly discovered evidence, Auth. Comm. Rule 59(a).

Order for, Rule 59(d); Auth. Comm. Rule 59(d).

    Extension of time, Rule 6(b).

Partial new trial, Auth. Comm. 59(a).

Remittitur, Auth. Comm. Rule 59(a).

Stay of execution or proceedings to enforce judgment on motion for, Rule 62(b); Auth. Comm. Rule 62(b).

Time for making, Auth. Comm. Rule 59(b).

Waiver of right to seek, Auth. Comm. 59(a).

NEW YEAR'S DAY

Clerks of court, business hours for office, exceptions concerning opening, Rule 77(c).

"Legal holiday" as including for purposes of computing time, Rule 6(a).

NEWLY DISCOVERED EVIDENCE

Relief from judgment, order or proceeding, Rule 60(b).

NEWSPAPERS

Notice, admiralty or maritime claims,

    Actions in rem, Supp. Rule C(4).

    Limitation of liability, Supp.Rule F(4).

Printed material purporting to be, self-authentication, Evid. Rule 902.

NEXT FRIEND

Action by infant or incompetent person, Rule 17(c).

NOLO CONTENDERE

Plea of Nolo Contendere, generally, this index.

NONJOINDER

Persons needed for just adjudication, pleading, reasons, Rule 19(c).

NONRESIDENTS

Form of summons, etc., to correspond to requirement of statute or rule of state court pursuant to which service was made, Rule 4(b).

Service on, Rule 4(e).

Subpoena requiring attendance for taking deposition, Rule 45(b).

INDEX

INDEX

INDEX

INDEX

INDEX

SECURITY

Injunctions, Rule 65(c).
    Pending appeal, Rule 62(c); Auth. Comm. Rule 62(c).
Master not to retain report as security for compensation, Rule 53(a).
Proceedings against sureties, Rule 65.1.
Stay of proceedings to enforce judgment, Rule 62(b).
Surety, Rule 65.1.

SEIZURE

Searches and Seizures, generally, this index.

SELF–INCRIMINATION

Not waived by accused or other witness when examined respecting matters relating only to
    credibility, Evid. Rule 608.

SENSATION

Hearsay exceptions, statement respecting, Evid. Rule 803.

SENTENCE AND PUNISHMENT

    See, also, Fines and Penalties, generally, this index.
Death Penalty, generally, this index.
Impeaching credibility of witness, conviction of crime punishable by imprisonment exceed-
    ing one year, court determination, probative value, Evid. Rule 609.
Judgment of previous conviction, crime punishable by imprisonment exceeding one year,
    evidence of, hearsay exception, Evid. Rule 803.
Motions to vacate, set aside or correct, applicability of rules in part, Evid. Rule 1101.
Proceedings, inapplicability, Evid. Rule 1101.

SEPARATE

Actions, risk created, class actions maintainable, Rule 23(b).
Judgment as to one or more but fewer than all claims, staying enforcement, Rule 62(h);
    Auth. Comm. Rule 62(h).
Summons, issuance against defendants, Rule 4(a).
Trials, Rule 42(b); Auth. Comm. Rule 42(b).
    Generally, this index.

SEPARATE DOCUMENT RULE

Requirement of, Rule 58; Auth. Comm. Rule 58.

SEQUESTRATION

Property of person disobeying judgment directing performance of specific acts, Rule 70;
    Auth. Comm. Rule 70.

SERVICE OF PROCESS

    Generally, Rule 4, 4.1.
Adults, service on, Auth. Comm. Rule 4(e)–(f).
Affidavits, Rule 4.1.
    New trial, Rule 59(c).
    Supporting motion, Rule 6(d).
Agents and Agency, this index.
Amended complaints, Auth. Comm. Rule 4.
Answer, time, Rule 12(a).
Answers or objections to requests for admission, Rule 36(a).
Appearance, Rule 5(a); Auth. Comm. Rule 5(a).
Associations, service on, Rule 4(h); Auth. Comm. Rule 4(h).
Attorney, original service or, Auth. Comm. Rule 4(e).
Attorney, pleading and other papers, Rule 5(b); Auth. Comm. Rule 5(b).
Attorney General of United States, Rule 4(h).
Burden of proving proper service, Auth. Comm. Rule 4.
Business, service at, Auth. Comm. Rule 4(e).
Certificate of service, filing, Rule 5(d).
Certified mail, summons and complaint against United States or officers or agencies
    thereof, Rule 4(h).
Clerk of court, agent, proceeding against sureties, Rule 65.1.
Corporations, service on, Rule 4(h); Auth. Comm. Rule 4(h).
Cross, redirect and recross questions, depositions upon written questions, Rule 31(a).
Defense, insufficiency, Rules 12(b), (h).
Demand, Rule 5(a).
    Jury trial, failure to serve as waiver, Rule 38(d).

SHIPPING
Prize, applicability of rules in part, Evid. Rule 1101.
Seamen, generally, this index.

SHORT TITLE
Generally, Evid. Rule 1103.

SHORTENING OF TIME
Extension of time, generally, ante.

SHOW CAUSE ORDERS
Habeas corpus, generally, ante.

SIGNATURE
Answer or objection to requests for admission, Rule 36(a).
Depositions upon oral examination, Rule 30(e); Auth. Comm. Rule 30(e).
 Notice of, attorneys, constituting certification, Rule 30(b).
Discovery requests, responses and objections, Rule 26(g); Auth. Comm. Rule 26(g).
Duty to sign pleadings and other documents, Rule 11.
Foreign official records, authentication, Rule 44(a)(2); Auth. Comm. Rule 44(a)(2).
Foreign public documents, certification, genuineness and official position of executing or attesting person, etc., Evid. Rule 902.
Interrogatories, answers to, Rule 33(a); Auth. Comm. Rule 33(a).
Motions, this index.
Objections to answers to interrogatories, Rule 33(a).
Pleadings, this index.
Self-authentication,
 Commercial paper and related documents, Evid. Rule 902.
 Domestic public documents under or not under seal, Evid. Rule 902.
Summons by clerk, Rule 4(b).
Written statement as prior statement concerning action or subject matter made by party or person, obtaining of discovery, Rule 26(b).

SIGNS
Purporting to be affixed in course of business and indicating ownership, control or origin, self-authentication, Evid. Rule 902.

SPECIAL
Appearances, Auth. Comm. Rule 12(b)(2).
Appointments, service of process, Rule 4(c).
Damages, pleading, Rule 9(g); Auth. Comm. Rule 9(g).
Master, appointment, Rule 53(a), (b).
Matters, pleading, Rule 9; Auth. Comm. Rule 9.
Verdict,
 Entry of judgment on, Rule 58.
 Requirement of return, Rule 49(a); Auth. Comm. Rule 49(a).

SPECIFIC PERFORMANCE, CONTRACT TO CONVEY LAND
Complaint in action for, form of, Form 12.
Disobedience to judgment directing execution of conveyance, Rule 70; Auth. Comm. Rule 70.

SPECIMENS
Comparison by trier or expert witness, authentication and identification, conformity with requirements, Evid. Rule 901.

"SPIRIT" OF RULES
Influence in interpreting Rules, Auth. Comm. Rule 1.

STAKEHOLDER
Generally, Auth. Comm. Rule 22 and Statutory Interpleader.

STANDING
Shareholder derivative actions, Rule 23.1; Auth. Comm. Rule 23.1.

STATE
Documents of under or not under seal, self-authentication, Evid. Rule 902.
"Legal holiday" as including day appointed as holiday by state in which district court is held, computation of time, Rule 6(a).
Official record, authentication, Rule 44(a)(1); Auth. Comm. Rule 44(a)(1).

INDEX

STATUTES

Authentication or identification, methods provided by, Evid. Rule 901.

Computation, time, Rule 6(a).

Maritime action in rem, Supp.Rule C(1).

Question arising under, jurisdiction, form of allegation, Form 2.

Right to intervene, conferring, Rule 24(a).

Service, application, Rule 4(d).

    Party not inhabitant of or found within state, Rule 4(e).

        Foreign countries, alternative provisions for service in, Rule 4(i).

        Form to correspond to that required by, Rule 4(b).

    Territorial limits of effective service, Rule 4(f).

State Laws, generally, this index.

STAY

Accounting in action for infringement of patent, Rule 62(a); Auth. Comm. Rule 62(a).

Appeal without bond, United States or officer or agency thereof, Rule 62(e); Auth. Comm. Rule 62(e).

Appellate court's powers, Rule 62(g); Auth. Comm. Rule 62(g).

Approval of supersedeas bond by court, Rule 62(d); Auth. Comm. Rule 62(d).

Bond for stay in favor of United States, Rule 62(e); Auth. Comm. Rule 62(e).

Discovery, sanction for failure to comply with order compelling, Rule 37(b).

District judge decision on consent appeal from magistrate, Rule 76(b); Auth. Comm. Rule 76(b).

Execution, Rules 62, 62(b).

Injunction judgment, Rule 62(a); Auth. Comm. Rule 62(a).

Judgments and Decrees, this index.

Payment of costs of previously dismissed action, Rule 41(d).

Receivership judgment, Rule 62(a); Auth. Comm. Rule 62(a).

State law, stay according to, Rule 62(f); Auth. Comm. Rule 62(f).

Supersedeas bond for stay on appeal, Rule 62(d); Auth. Comm. Rule 62(d).

United States or agency thereof, stay in favor of, Rule 62(e); Auth. Comm. Rule 62(e).

STENOGRAPHERS

Report or transcript as evidence, Rule 80(c); Auth. Comm. Rule 80(c).

STENOGRAPHIC

Recording, obtaining prior statement concerning action or subject matter by party or person, Rule 26(b).

Transcription, depositions upon oral examination, Rule 30(b), (c); Auth. Comm. Rule 30(c).

STIPULATIONS

Depositions,

    Taking, Rule 29; Auth. Comm. Rule 29.

    Upon oral examination, waiver of signing, Rule 30(e).

Discovery procedure, Rule 29; Auth. Comm. Rule 29.

Dismissal, Rule 41(a); Auth. Comm. Rule 41(a).

    Action for condemnation of property, Rule 71A(i); Auth. Comm. Rule 71A(i).

Findings of master, Rule 53(e); Auth. Comm. Rule 53(e)(4).

Jury verdict, unanimity and size of jury, Rule 48; Auth. Comm. Rule 48.

New trial, stipulations extending time for filing, Rule 59(c).

Proceedings against sureties, Rule 65.1.

Trial by court, Rule 39(a); Auth. Comm. Rule 39(a).

STRIKING OF PLEADING

    Generally, Rule 12(f); Auth. Comm. Rule 12(f).

Discovery, sanction for failure to comply with order compelling, Rule 37(b); Auth. Comm. Rule 37(b).

Failure to make more definite statement, Rule 12(e).

Third-party claim, Rule 14(a).

SUBCLASSES

Treatment, class actions, Rule 23(c).

SUBJECT MATTER

Expert witnesses, trial preparation interrogatories, Rule 26(b).

Lack of jurisdiction, defense, Rule 12(b)(1), (h); Jurisdiction; Auth. Comm. Rule 12(b)(1).

Requirements, subject matter jurisdiction, Jurisdiction, Juris. §§ 2.10–2.13.

INDEX

SUBPOENA DUCES TECUM
Designation of materials in notice to take deposition upon oral examination, Rules 30(b), 45(a); Auth. Comm. Rules 30(b)(5), 45(a).

SUBPOENAS
Generally, Rule 45; Auth. Comm. Rule 45.
Depositions, this index.
Discovery, person in foreign country, Rule 37(e).
Failure to obey, contempt, Rule 45(e); Auth. Comm. Rule 45(e).
Foreign countries, persons in, 28 U.S.C.A. § 1783.
Contempt, 28 U.S.C.A. § 1784.
Form, Rule 45(a); Auth. Comm. Rule 45(a).
Master, procuring attendance of witnesses, Rule 53(d).
Objections, Rule 45(c); Auth. Comm. Rule 45(c).
Production of documents, application of rules, Rule 81(a).
Protection of persons subject to, Rule 45; Auth. Comm. Rule 45(c).
Service, Rule 45(b); Auth. Comm. Rule 45(b).

SUBSTANCE
Authentication and identification, conformity with requirements, Evid. Rule 901.

SUBSTANTIAL RIGHTS
Disregard of error not affecting, Rule 61.

SUBSTITUTION
Copies, documents and things produced for inspection, depositions, upon oral examination, Rule 30(f).
Parties, Rule 25.
Condemnation proceedings, Rule 71A(g); Auth. Comm. Rule 71A(g).
Depositions, effect on use of, Rule 32(a); Auth. Comm. Rule 32(a).
Suggestion of death upon the record under rule concerning, form of, Form 30.

SUCCESSORS OF DECEASED PARTY
Motion for substitution made by, Rule 25(a).
Suggestion of death, Rule 25(a); Auth. Comm. Rule 25(a).

SUM CERTAIN
Defined, Auth. Comm. Rule 55.

SUMMARIES
Business records, interrogatories, Rule 33(c).
Foreign official records, evidence, Rule 44(a)(2).
Voluminous writings, recordings or photographs, contents of, Evid. Rule 1006.

SUMMARY JUDGMENT
Generally, Rule 56; Auth. Comm. Rule 56.
Affidavits, Rule 56(e); Auth. Comm. Rule 56(e).
Bad faith affidavits, Rule 56(g).
Pro se drafters, Auth. Comm. Rule 56(g).
Unavailable affidavits, Rule 56(f); Auth. Comm. Rule 56(f).
Verified complaints and statements in place of, Auth. Comm. Rule 56(e).
Appealability of rulings on motions for, Auth. Comm. Rule 56(c).
Authenticating exhibits, Auth. Comm. Rule 56(e).
Burden of proving, Auth. Comm. Rule 56(c).
Credibility questions, Auth. Comm. Rule 56(c).
Cross motions for, Auth. Comm. Rule 56(c).
Discovery while summary judgment pending, Rule 56(f).
Distinct from dismissal or judgment on pleadings or judgment as a matter of law, Auth. Comm. Rule 56.
Findings of fact and conclusions of law, Rule 52(a).
Form of, Auth. Comm. Rule 56(c).
Hearings on motions for, Auth. Comm. Rule 56(c).
Law of the case on, Auth. Comm. Rule 56(c) & 54(d).
Motions, Rules 12(b), (c), 56.
Multiple motions for, Auth. Comm. Rule 56(c).
Non-moving party, Auth. Comm. Rule 56(c).
Oral argument, Auth. Comm. Rule 56(c).
Oral testimony, Auth. Comm. Rule 56(c).
Partial summary judgment, Rule 56(c)-(d); Auth. Comm. Rule 56(c)-(d).

INDEX